THE KOVELS' COMPLETE ANTIQUES PRICE LIST

BOOKS BY RALPH AND TERRY KOVEL

Dictionary of Marks—Pottery and Porcelain

Directory of American Silver, Pewter and Silver Plate

American Country Furniture, 1780–1875

Know Your Antiques,® Revised

The Kovels' Complete Antiques Price List

The Kovels' Complete Bottle Price List

The Kovels' Collector's Guide to Limited Editions

The Kovels' Collector's Guide to American Art Pottery

TENTH EDITION

THE KOVELS' COMPLETE ANTIQUES PRICE LIST

A guide to the 1977–1978 market
for professionals, dealers, and collectors

by Ralph and Terry Kovel

ILLUSTRATED

Crown Publishers, Inc., New York

Inquiries should be addressed to Crown Publishers, Inc.,
One Park Avenue, New York, N.Y. 10016

Printed in the United States of America

Published simultaneously in Canada by General Publishing Company Limited
Library of Congress Catalog Card Number: 72-84290

ISBN: 0-517-531437

GUIDE TO USE

There are just a few simple rules to follow in using this book. Each listing is arranged in the following manner: CATEGORY (such as pressed glass, silver, or furniture); OBJECT (such as vase, spoon, table); DESCRIPTION (which includes as much information as possible about size, age, color, and pattern). All items are presumed perfect unless otherwise noted. Leaf through the book and examine the various category headings. Most of them are exactly as one would expect.

Several special categories were formed to make a more sensible listing of items possible. "Fire" includes andirons, firefighting equipment, fireplace equipment, and related pieces. "Kitchen" and "tool" include special equipment. It seems impossible to expect the casual collector to know the proper name for each variety of tool, such as an "adze" or a "trephine," so we have lumped them in the special categories.

This book has several idiosyncrasies of style that must be noted before it can be used properly. The prices are compiled by computer, and the machine has dictated several strange rules. Everything in the book is listed alphabetically according to the IBM alphabetic system. This means that words such as "mt." are alphabetized as "M-T," not as "M-O-U-N-T." Another peculiarity of the machine alphabetizing is that all numerals come after all letters, thus 2 comes after z. A quick glance at a listing will make this clear, as the alphabetizing is consistent throughout the book. No price over $9,999 can be listed.

We have made several editorial decisions that affect the use of the book. A bowl is a bowl and not a dish unless it is a special type of dish such as a sauce dish. A butter dish is a "butter" and a celery dish is a "celery." A salt dish is called a "salt" to differentiate it from a saltshaker. A toothpick holder is called a "toothpick." It is always a "sugar and creamer," never a "creamer and sugar." Where one dimension is given, it is the height of the antique, or, if the object is round, the dimension is the diameter. Height of a picture is listed before width.

This book does not include price listings of fine art paintings, books, comic books, coins, stamps, and a few other categories that are already fully priced in specialized books. Prices for collector's editions and bottles are included, although both are more completely reported in *The Kovels' Collector's Guide to Limited Editions* and *The Kovels' Complete Bottle Price List.*

Beer cans and baskets are now listed as categories instead of as part of the store listing as before. Autumn Leaf, Boch Freres, brownware, Mosier, Kemple, Phoenix bird dishes, Rowland and Marsellus, and Verona are a few of the new pottery, porcelain, and glass categories. Nautical and airplane items are under their own headings.

Several categories such as "milk glass" and "bottles" include special reference numbers. These numbers refer the reader to the most widely known books about the category. When these numbers appear, the name of the special book is given in the paragraph heading. All these numbers take the form "B-22, C-103," and so forth. The letter is the author's initial; the number refers to a picture in the author's book.

All black-and-white pictures in THE KOVELS' COMPLETE ANTIQUES PRICE LIST are of antiques sold during the past year. The prices are as reported by the seller. Each piece pictured is listed with the word *illus* as part of the description. Pictures are placed as close to the price listing as is possible. Color pictures are all from the collections of the William Penn Memorial Museum and no prices are given for these antiques.

All prices listed in this book were recorded from antique shows, sales, flea markets, and auctions between June 1976 and June 1977. The prices have been taken from sales in all parts of the country, and variations are sometimes due to the geographic differences in pricing. Antiques of top quality tend to be most expensive near the town where they originated because the local collectors are informed about them. We have tried to be accurate in all of the prices reported, but we cannot be responsible for any errors that may have occurred. We welcome any suggestions for future editions of this book, but cannot answer letters asking for advice or appraisals.

INTRODUCTION

The antique market for June 1976 to June 1977 has been filled with rising prices, surprise sales, and good news for most collectors. The highest selling items worldwide were top-quality jade, fine, signed French furniture, and Russian enamels. American collectors paid highest prices ever for quilts, wallpaper, cloisonné, and top-quality American eighteenth-century furniture.

Many types of antiques continued on an upward trend. These included English and American Victorian art pottery, corkscrews, Victorian furniture, oak furniture, baskets, Heisey glass, dolls, Canton ware, fairings, spongeware, Gallé glass, Victorian Chinese furniture, and gemstone Victorian jewelry.

Prices on a few types of antiques were lower than in previous years: English eighteenth-century porcelains (unless extremely rare types), English delft, Victorian art glass, Prattware, average quality, English early nineteenth-century furniture, Carnival glass, Centennial items, Civil War items, and English Georgian silver. Bronzes started the year at an all-time high but dropped a little by June.

Record prices were paid for a large number of antiques. A Louis XVI Boulle cabinet sold for $57,300, a record for Boulle. The Edward Curtis twenty-volume set of books *The North American Indian* brought $60,000. The John James Audubon set *Birds of America* set the record at $352,-000. A Tiffany laburnum floor lamp set a new high for a floor lamp at $47,400. The top price ever paid for a Pairpoint lamp was $4,750 for a lilac Puffy style.

An antique microscope brought $73,624 and a sword brought $145,-000. A Dutch silver-gilt ewer set the astounding record price of $262,000. A stamp brought $90,000, a record price for an American stamp, even more amazing because the same stamp sold two years ago for $42,400.

American furniture set records in early 1977. A Duncan Phyfe record price was set by a $22,000 chair. A Chippendale mahogany bombé chest of drawers from Massachusetts brought $135,000, the highest price ever for a piece of American furniture. A pair of Queen Anne shell-carved, cherry side chairs from Philadelphia set a record at $140,000. The record $85,000 was paid for a Queen Anne shell-carved, walnut, wing armchair from Philadelphia. A 12- by 9-foot Heriz Oriental rug in almost perfect condition brought a record $200,000.

Even some of the minor antiques were setting records. A daguerreotype sold for $9,860; a twentieth-century photograph for $8,750; a set of eight lead soldiers in a box brought $668; a Coca-Cola bottle (gold) for $11,500; a leather fire bucket for $1,650; a fireman's parade hat for $2,200; a "West of Scotland Insurance" firemark sold at a record $1,050; and a corkscrew for $1,795. The record price for a fruit jar was $3,100 paid for a cobalt Mason jar, "CFJCO, Improved, Clyde, New York."

The Mentmore Towers sale in England in May set a record for the total of any furniture auction at $2,990,825. It set the record for a house sale at $10,926,785. Top-priced pieces were sold at the sale; an automaton dated 1757 for $153,900; an Augsburg clock for $119,700; a piece of Victorian silver for $22,230; a piece of Sèvres porcelain for $102,600; a piece of amber for $88,920; and an ivory figure for $51,300.

Special exhibitions, new books, and the women's movement have caused a rise in prices in any works by female artists. This includes the arts, sewing, crafts, and art pottery made by women.

Twentieth-century oak furniture and the less formal types of pottery and glass are still rising in price. This is because of the twenty- to thirty-five-year-old buyers that are rapidly entering the antiques market. The nostalgia craze continues as advertising items, political pieces, comic book and radio-related mementos, and even TV-personality collectibles are going up in price. Twentieth-century glasswares continue to be in demand, and as the special publications, new books, and clubs devoted to Heisey glass, Fenton, Cambridge, McKee, Depression glass, and the others sort out the histories of the firms and identify the glasswares, the prices go up.

All the prices included in this book are reports, not estimates. This means that at some sale in the United States, the antique described was offered for sale at the price we have listed. A few of the prices are from auctions but most are from shops and shows. We feel this is as accurate a method of reporting as is possible although there are many regional variations in pricing. We have tried to avoid prices from auctions where it is apparent that "auction fever" has taken hold and the prices paid include the buyer's interest in the fame of the original owner.

Ralph M. Kovel, American Society of Appraisers, Senior Member

Terry H. Kovel, American Society of Appraisers, Senior Member

AN IMPORTANT ANNOUNCEMENT TO COLLECTORS AND DEALERS

Each year *The Kovels' Complete Antiques Price List* is completely rewritten. Every entry is new because of the rapidly changing antiques market. The only way so complete a revision can be accomplished is by using a computer, making it possible to publish the bound book two months after the last price is received.

Yet many price changes occur between editions of *The Kovels' Complete Antiques Price List.* Important sales produce new record prices each day. Inflation, the changing price of silver and gold, and the international demand for some types of antiques influence sales in the United States.

The collector will want to keep up with developments from month to month. Therefore, we call your attention to a new service to provide price information almost instantaneously: *Kovels on Antiques and Collectables,* a nationally distributed illustrated newsletter, published monthly.

This new monthly newsletter covers prices, special interest antiques, what to buy, how to buy or sell antiques, forums and classes to attend, refinishing and first aid for your possessions, marks, book reviews, and other pertinent antiques news.

A complimentary copy and additional information about the newsletter are available from the authors at P.O. Box 22200, Beachwood, Ohio 44122.

PICTURE ACKNOWLEDGMENTS

Bruce Abell, Jack Adamson, Gloria Albrecht, Robert and Cynthia Baker, Barbara Bako, Virginia Bare, Max Beals, Richard A. Bourne Co., Inc., Child's Play, George Consolo, Jim Cook, Joan Coulter, H. C. Dedrick, Harris & Gladys Diamant, George Dietrich, Douglas Galleries, Early's Antiques & Auction Co., Robert C. Eldred Co., Inc., Bernard Ellinghaus, Sam Forsythe, Garth's Auctions, Inc., O. Rundle Gilbert, Gene Harris Antique Center, Mary Anne Harsh, Haskell House, Sally Heffner, Betty Herriman, Hillsway House, Ellie Hoover, Kent House, Evelyn Kidman, Kinzle Auction Center, McCullough's, James Matthews, Larry Melvin, Miscellaneous Man, Ray Mongenas, Morton's Auction Exchange, Jackie Olson, Ox Yoke Antiques, Lowell Peltier, Pennypacker Auction Centre, Portfolio Press Corporation, Poster America, Frank Roan, III, Auctioneer, Bill Robinson, H. Jane Scott, Sotheby Parke Bernet—Los Angeles, Sotheby Parke Bernet—New York, Dee Sunderland, Christopher Sykes Antiques (England), Sally Thomas & Co., Tinker's Dam, Valley View Antiques, Ethel Vallos, Claude Walter, Weiss Americana, Wilhelms Antiques, Wood & Stone, The Wooden Bridge.

A special thanks to Jack and Jean Frost and Ed Grauberger for allowing us to photograph at their shows.

WILLIAM PENN MEMORIAL MUSEUM COLOR PICTURES

The state of Pennsylvania is filled with museums of interest to all antique collectors. The color pictures in this book are from the William Penn Memorial Museum in Harrisburg, Pennsylvania. The decorative arts gallery of the museum has a series of period rooms dating from the 1600s through the Victorian parlor pictured on the cover. Early shops and commercial buildings are in another section of the museum. The museum has special exhibits throughout the year that feature tools, glassware, pottery, pewter, silver, copper, brass, tin, iron, textiles, furniture, and other decorative arts. The main exhibition for 1978 is the Pennsylvania German show and a new exhibition, the "Furniture of Chester County."

Another section of the museum includes a Hall of Industry and Technology, which is devoted to the study of power in Pennsylvania. Examples range from a horse-drawn vehicle to a 1910 electrically powered truck. The Hall of Anthropology shows the early history of Pennsylvania, the Indian artifacts discovered throughout the state, the excavation of an Indian site, the major happenings in the life of a Delaware Indian, and how man-made useful objects are all portrayed. The museum also has a Gallery of Military History, a planetarium, exhibits of natural science and ecology, Pennsylvania mammals, and of geology.

The color picture on the cover is a view of the Rococo Revival parlor at the William Penn Museum. The marble-top table at the left of the picture was made in Philadelphia in 1855. The tea set is Wedgwood ware dated 1878. On the mantel is an amethyst-glass French box, and a pair of Bennington figures. The small marble-topped stand at the right of the picture next to the fireplace was made by Regester, Bell, and Company of Philadelphia. The table is labeled Alexander Roux, and the lamp on top was made by Cornelius and Company of Philadelphia.

Our special thanks to Jim Mitchell, Director of the William Penn Memorial Museum, and Cathryn J. McElroy, Curator of Decorative Arts.

ABC plates, or children's alphabet plates, were popular from 1780 to 1860. The letters on the plate were meant as teaching aids for the children who were learning to read. The plates were made of pottery, porcelain, metal, or glass.

ABC, Book, Saalfield, 1921 .... 8.50
ABC, Bowl, Red Riding Hood, K.T.K. 35.00
ABC, Breakfast Set, Child's, Animal Between Letters, German 35.00
ABC, Cup & Saucer, Farmyard Animals, Germany 34.50
ABC, Cup, Child's Milk, Letters In Squares & Sign Language 150.00
ABC, Cup, Tin, Embossed Floral 10.00
ABC, Dish, Child's, Baby Bunting & Bunch 29.50
ABC, Dish, Child's, Baby Bunting, 6 1/2 In. 18.00
ABC, Plate, Aesop's Fables, The Fox And Grapes 55.00
ABC, Plate, Apple Green, Thousand Eye, Glass Clock Center 40.00
ABC, Plate, Baby's, Porcelain, Germany 30.00
ABC, Plate, Baby's, Ring-Around-The-Rosy, Porcelain 35.00
ABC, Plate, Boys At Marbles Play, 6 In.Diameter .... *Illus* 29.00
ABC, Plate, Bulldog Center, 6 1/2 In. 25.00
ABC, Plate, Chick's First Day 16.00
ABC, Plate, Children At Breakfast, Cow Looking Through Window 32.50
ABC, Plate, Clockface Center, Calendar, Chas.Allerton, 8 In. 50.00
ABC, Plate, Dog Wearing Glasses, J.Meir & Son, 8 1/2 In. 32.50
ABC, Plate, First Nibble, Children Fishing, Black Transfer, Soft Paste, 8 In. 35.00
ABC, Plate, Franklin Maxim, Meakin, 5 1/2 In. 35.00
ABC, Plate, Frosted Center, Sancho Panza And Dapples, 6 In. 30.00
ABC, Plate, Girl & Boy Reading Book Titled Liberty, Tin, 5 1/2 In. 43.00
ABC, Plate, Glass, Scalloped & Beaded Border, 6 In. 25.00
ABC, Plate, He That By The Plough Would Thrive, Meakin, 5 1/4 In. 48.00
ABC, Plate, Hen & Chickens Center, Clear, 6 In. 29.50
ABC, Plate, Hey Diddle Diddle, Wm.Rogers 35.00
ABC, Plate, Ice Cream, Glass, Miniature 35.00
ABC, Plate, Indian Chief On Horse, Sioux, Blue On White, 7 1/2 In. 20.00
ABC, Plate, Jumbo, Tin, 6 1/4 In. 25.00
ABC, Plate, Kittens With Yarn, Tin, 4 In. 35.00
ABC, Plate, Liberty, Boy & Girl Reading, Raised Border, Tin, 5 1/2 In. 43.00
ABC, Plate, Miss Muffet, England, 6 1/2 In.Diameter .... *Illus* 32.00
ABC, Plate, Mother, Daughter, & Verse, Elsmore & Son, England, 7 In. 36.00
ABC, Plate, Potters Art Printing, 6 3/4 In. 30.00
ABC, Plate, Raised Letters, Scalloped, Glass, 6 In. 20.00
ABC, Plate, Robinson Crusoe At Work, Brown, Blue, Cream 30.00
ABC, Plate, Rosaline, Florals, 8 1/2 In. 75.00
ABC, Plate, Staffordshire, Hurdy-Gurdy Man & Children, C.A.& Sons, English 38.00
ABC, Spoon, Sterling Silver, Loop Handle 20.00

Adams china was made by William Adams and Sons of Staffordshire, England. The firm was founded in 1769 and is still working.

Adams, see also Flow Blue

ABC Plate, Boys At Marbles Play, 6 In.Diameter

Adams, Barrel, Biscuit, Jasperware, Dark Blue, 5 1/2 In. 75.00
Adams, Berry Set, Chinese Ching, Blue, Pink, Green, Polychrome, 13 Piece 78.50
Adams, Bowl, Fairy Villa, Rampant Lions In Trademark, 10 3/8 In. 68.00
Adams, Creamer, Dickensware, 4 In. 22.00
Adams, Cup & Saucer, Beehive, Pink 29.00
Adams, Cup & Saucer, English Country Seat & Church, Deep Blue 83.00
Adams, Cup & Saucer, Palestine, Pink 25.00
Adams, Cup Plate, Blue, 14 Sided 21.00
Adams, Cup Plate, Regents Park 75.00
Adams, Dish, Child's, Rooster, Save Your Breath To Cool Your Porridge 18.50
Adams, Gravy Pitcher, Blue On White, Mobetta, 8 1/4 In. 22.00
Adams, Humidor, Shakespeare Series, Play On Each Side 45.00
Adams, Jar, Cookie, Dark Blue Jasper, England, 5 1/2 In. 45.00
Adams, Jar, Cookie, Dark Blue, 1891-1930 Mark, 3 X 2 In. 30.00
Adams, Jardiniere, Blue & White Jasperware, 10 In. 70.00
Adams, Pepper Pot, 5 In. *Illus* 50.00
Adams, Pitcher, American Eagle, Blue, 6 In. 500.00
Adams, Pitcher, Mr.Bumble & Mrs.Corney Taking Tea & Mrs.Gummidge, 7 In. 55.00
Adams, Plate, Audubon Birds Of America, Florida Jay, 10 1/2 In. 25.00
Adams, Plate, Black & White, Home Of President Coolidge, Plymouth, Vermont 18.00
Adams, Plate, Caledonia, Purple, 9 1/2 In. 35.00
Adams, Plate, Castle Scene, Blue & White, Octagonal, Pierced, 12 In. 60.00
Adams, Plate, Chinese Ching, Polychrome, 9 In. 15.00
Adams, Plate, Columbia, Medium Blue, 7 1/2 In. 18.00
Adams, Plate, Cries Of London, Coach, Woman, Children, & Dog, 3 1/4 In. 25.00
Adams, Plate, Dickensware, Mr.Micawber Delivers Some Remarks, 9 1/2 In. 45.00
Adams, Plate, Do You Want Any Matches, Cries Of London Series, 9 3/4 In. 25.00
Adams, Plate, Fenimore House, Cooperstown, N.Y., Floral Border, 1914-40 15.00
Adams, Plate, Florida, America's Playground, Purple, 7 1/2 In. 5.00
Adams, Plate, Gaudy Red Rose, Scalloped Rim, C.1830, 8 1/2 In. 95.00

ABC, Plate, Miss Muffet, England, 6 1/2 In.Diameter

(See Page 1)

Adams, Pepper Pot, 5 In.

Adams, Plate, Lorna Doone, Octagonal, Lorna Doone Farm, 8 In. 30.00
Adams, Plate, Lorna Doone, Round, Annie Learns To Charm The Cream, 6 1/2 In. 20.00
Adams, Plate, My Old Kentucky Home, Rose Color, 6 1/2 In. 5.00
Adams, Plate, Palestine, Brown, 7 1/2 In. 10.00
Adams, Plate, Palestine, Green & Carmine, C.1830, 7 1/2 In. 22.00
Adams, Plate, Rose, Scalloped Rim, C.1830, 8 1/2 In. 95.00
Adams, Plate, Scaleby Castle, Cumberland, Blue, Bluebell Border, 7 3/4 In. 45.00
Adams, Plate, Shanghai, 8 In. 15.00
Adams, Plate, Venetian Scenery, 9 In. 28.00
Adams, Plate, Villa In Regents Park, London, Cobalt, C.1810, 9 In. 85.00
Adams, Plate, Wistow Hall, Leicestershire, Cobalt, 9 In. 80.00
Adams, Plate, Yellowstone Falls, 4 Pictures, Geyser Center, 10 In. 30.00
Adams, Plate, 1000 Islands, Bridge Center, Blue & White, 9 3/4 In. 30.00
Adams, Platter, Columbia, Blue & White, Cut Corners, 18 X 13 3/4 In. 85.00
Adams, Saucer, Venetian Scenery 6.50
Adams, Sugar, Jasperware, Silver Plate Tongs In Lid 95.00
Adams, Sugar, Tongs Lid, Blue, White Figures 59.00
Adams, Teapot, Jeddo, Mulberry, Stoneware, C.1845, 9 In. 125.00
Adams, Tray, Pin, Pickwick Papers 12.00

Adams, Vegetable Bowl, Covered, Bow 16.00
Adams, Vegetable Bowl, Covered, Jeddo, Mulberry 65.00
Adams, Waste Bowl, Beehive, Black Transfer, Soft Paste 22.00
Advertising, see Store

Agata glass was made by Joseph Locke of the New England Glass Company of Cambridge, Massachusetts, after 1885. A metallic stain was applied to New England Peachblow and the mottled design characteristic of agata appeared.

Agata, Celery, 4 1/2 In. 1650.00
Agata, Decanter, Enameled Decorations, Handled, 12 In. 48.00
Agata, Tumbler, Deep Raspberry, Blue Black Oil Spots, Gold Tracery 695.00
Agata, Tumbler, Mottled ..... 650.00 To 795.00
Agata, Tumbler, Wild Rose, 3 3/4 In. 650.00
Agata, Vase, Stick, 11 1/8 In. 995.00
Agate, Figurine, Horse, Lying On Back With Feet Raised, 4 1/2 In. 85.00
Agate, Tray, Pin, Polished, 5 3/4 X 3 1/4 In. 40.00
Airplane, Creamer, T.W.A., International Silver, 4 In. 12.50
Airplane, Propeller, Wooden, Brass Edges, 5 1/2 Ft. 135.00

AKRO AGATES

Akro agate glass was made in Clarksburg, West Virginia, from 1932 to 1951. Before that time the firm made children's glass marbles. Most of the glass is marked with a crow flying through the letter A.

Akro Agate, Box, Dark Green, Lady Design On Lid 16.50
Akro Agate, Cereal Bowl, Child's, Ivory, Octagonal 6.50
Akro Agate, Cereal Bowl, Child's, Oxblood, Octagonal 24.90
Akro Agate, Cereal Bowl, Child's, Pink, Octagonal 7.50
Akro Agate, Creamer, Blue, Rose Point Band 5.50
Akro Agate, Creamer, Child's, Oxblood, Octagonal 19.90
Akro Agate, Creamer, Green, 1 3/8 In. 6.50
Akro Agate, Cup & Saucer, Child's, Green, Concentric Rings 7.90
Akro Agate, Cup & Saucer, Child's, Orange & Gold, Little Hostess 3.90
Akro Agate, Cup & Saucer, Yellow 7.50
Akro Agate, Cup, Child's Demitasse, Orange & White, Concentric Rings 6.50
Akro Agate, Cup, Child's, Cobalt, Chiquita 6.00
Akro Agate, Cup, Child's, Gray, Little Hostess 2.80
Akro Agate, Cup, Child's, Green 2.00
Akro Agate, Cup, Child's, Green, Interior Panel 5.50
Akro Agate, Cup, Child's, Green, Raised Daisy 17.50
Akro Agate, Cup, Child's, Orange 6.00
Akro Agate, Cup, Child's, Pink Opaque, Interior Panel, 1 1/4 In. 9.90
Akro Agate, Cup, Pumpkin Color, Octagon, Open Handle 6.00
Akro Agate, Dish, Scottie Dog Cover 45.00
Akro Agate, Jar, Powder, Blue Opaque, Pair 38.00
Akro Agate, Jar, Powder, Blue, Scottie Dogs 50.00
Akro Agate, Jar, Powder, Green With White, Concentric Ring 9.50
Akro Agate, Jar, Powder, Scottie Dog Cover, Milk Glass, Pink 30.00
Akro Agate, Match Holder, Blue & White, Cornucopia Shape 10.00
Akro Agate, Match Holder, Orange & White, Horn Of Plenty 10.00
Akro Agate, Match Holder, White & Green, Cornucopia Shape, 3 In. 7.00
Akro Agate, Plate, Child's, Amber, Interior Panel ..... 4.50 To 5.50
Akro Agate, Plate, Child's, Aqua, Octagonal 3.00
Akro Agate, Plate, Child's, Blue 3.25
Akro Agate, Plate, Child's, Blue, Octagonal 2.50
Akro Agate, Plate, Child's, Green, Interior Panel ..... 4.50 To 5.50
Akro Agate, Plate, Child's, Green, Octagonal 1.50
Akro Agate, Plate, Child's, Green, Stippled Band 4.25
Akro Agate, Plate, Green, Octagonal, 4 1/2 In. 4.00
Akro Agate, Pot, Flower, Blue 4.00
Akro Agate, Pot, Flower, Opal Slag 4.50
Akro Agate, Saucer, Child's, Green, Stippled Band 4.00
Akro Agate, Saucer, Child's, Oxblood, Octagonal 10.50
Akro Agate, Saucer, Child's, White 1.50
Akro Agate, Saucer, Child's, Yellow, Chiquita 12.50
Akro Agate, Saucer, Demitasse, Blue & White, Stippled Band 3.00

Akro Agate, Set Of Dishes, Child's, Blue, Gray, & White, C.1910, 30 Piece 160.00
Akro Agate, Set Of Dishes, Child's, Cobalt, 16 Piece 65.00
Akro Agate, Set Of Dishes, Child's, Green Opaque, Chiquita, 22 Piece 75.00
Akro Agate, Set Of Dishes, Child's, Green, Chiquita, 16 Piece 25.00
Akro Agate, Set Of Dishes, Child's, Green, 13 Piece 16.00
Akro Agate, Soup, Children's, Octagon, Custard Color 4.75
Akro Agate, Sugar & Creamer, Blue, Concentric Rings 9.00
Akro Agate, Sugar & Creamer, Child's, Cover, Green, Interior Panel 18.95
Akro Agate, Sugar & Creamer, Child's, Orange, Little Hostess 6.25
Akro Agate, Sugar, Child's, Aqua, Octagonal 6.00
Akro Agate, Sugar, Child's, Green, Interior Panel 9.00
Akro Agate, Sugar, Child's, Orange, Little Hostess 3.20
Akro Agate, Tea Set, Child's, Green & White, Boxed, 16 Piece 28.00
Akro Agate, Tea Set, Child's, Green, 12 Piece 32.00
Akro Agate, Tea Set, Child's, Yellow, 22 Piece 120.00
Akro Agate, Tea Set, Doll's, Transparent Green, 3 Piece 14.00
Akro Agate, Tea Set, 16 Piece 45.00
Akro Agate, Teapot, Child's, Amber, Stippled Band .... 7.00 To 9.75
Akro Agate, Teapot, Child's, Green, Interior Panel 12.90
Akro Agate, Teapot, Child's, Green, Octagonal 3.50
Akro Agate, Teapot, Child's, Oxblood, Octagonal 41.90
Akro Agate, Teapot, Navy, Stacked Disc & Panel, 2 3/8 In. 14.50
Akro Agate, Toothpick, Brown & White 12.00
Akro Agate, Tumbler, Navy 14.90
Akro Agate, Vase, Orange & Blue, Sculptured Lily, 4 In., Pair 50.00
Akro Agate, Vase, Orange, White Streaks, Lily, 4 1/2 In. 15.00
Akro Agate, Water Set, Child's, Green Pitcher, , 6 Tumblers, Box 40.00
Akro Agate, Water Set, Child's, Green Pitcher, 6 White Tumblers 18.00
Alabaster, Pedestal, 4 Ft. 190.00

Albums were popular in Victorian times to hold the myriad pictures and cutouts favored by the collectors. All sorts of scrapbooks and albums can still be found.

Album, Photograph, see Photography, Album

Alexandrite glass was first made by Thomas Webb & Sons at the beginning of the 20th century. It is a transparent glass shading from pale yellow to rose to blue. Stevens & Williams later produced alexandrite glassware by plating a transparent yellow body with rose and blue glass.

Alexandrite, Vase, Bud, Citron, Transparent, Applied Base, 3 1/2 In. 695.00
Aluminum, Cocktail Set, Continental, Chrysanthemums, 3 Piece 20.00
Aluminum, Tray, Rodney Kent, Roses & Tulips, 2 Ornate Handles, 16 1/2 In. 35.00

Amber glass is the name of any glassware with the proper yellow-brown shade. It was a popular color after the Civil War.

Amber Glass, Basket, Rope Handle, 9 Feet, Colors 225.00
Amber Glass, Bottle, Perfume, Clown's Head, Art Deco, 3 1/4 In. 38.00
Amber Glass, Box, Hinged, Enamel Floral, Footed, Brass Side Rings, 3 In. 65.00
Amber Glass, Box, Hinged, Enamel Floral, Footed, 4 In. 75.00
Amber Glass, Cake Stand, Dahlia 85.00
Amber Glass, Candlestick, Floral Etched, Marked Sinclaire, 3 1/4 In., Pair 25.00
Amber Glass, Coaster, Furniture, Set Of 8 .... 3.50
Amber Glass, Compote, Bohemian Type, Amber Overlay, Deer, Forest, 6 1/2 In. 150.00
Amber Glass, Compote, Covered, Open Latticework, Lion Cover, 7 1/2 X 6 In. 55.00
Amber Glass, Compote, Covered, Sawtooth, 8 1/4 X 7 1/4 In. 65.00
Amber Glass, Cradle, Hush Baby, Victorian, 4 In. 22.00
Amber Glass, Creamer, Bulbous, Applied Reeded Handle 65.00
Amber Glass, Cruet, Coin Spot 35.00
Amber Glass, Cruet, Hobnail 75.00
Amber Glass, Cruet, Threaded Sandwich, Ornate Metal Neck, Handle & Stopper 85.00
Amber Glass, Decanter, English, Handpainted Hunting Scene, 11 In. 75.00
Amber Glass, Dish, Hen Cover, Basket Base, 5 In. 35.00
Amber Glass, Dish, Lion Cover, Lacy Base, 1879 .... 87.50
Amber Glass, Dish, Powder, Soldier's Cap 12.50
Amber Glass, Finger Bowl, Melon Ribbed 32.50

Amber Glass, Match Holder, Monkey 16.00
Amber Glass, Match Holder, Saddle, Victorian 17.00
Amber Glass, Perfume, Czech Cut, Tall Stopper 15.00
Amber Glass, Pitcher, Frosted, Swirl, Gonterman 100.00
Amber Glass, Pitcher, Half Gallon, Daisy & Button With Cross Bars 50.00
Amber Glass, Pitcher, Inverted Thumbprint, Reeded Crystal Handle, 8 1/2 In. 85.00
Amber Glass, Pitcher, Ribbed Pin Handle, 7 1/2 In. 40.00
Amber Glass, Pitcher, Water, Ribbed Pink Handle, 7 1/2 In. 40.00
Amber Glass, Plate, Intaglio Rose Center, Overlay Sterling Border, 9 In. 40.00
Amber Glass, Plate, Open Forget-Me-Not Border, 7 1/4 In. 22.00
Amber Glass, Platter, Knights Of Labor, 11 3/4 X 8 3/4 In. 245.00
Amber Glass, Salt, Christmas, Agitator 4800 .... 60.00
Amber Glass, Salt, Pewter Top, Diagonal Diamond 28.00
Amber Glass, Salt, Pressed Diamond, Pewter Top 12.00
Amber Glass, Salt, Stepped Sides, Serrated Rim, Waffle Base, Rectangular 55.00
Amber Glass, Salt, Swan 9.50
Amber Glass, Saltshaker, Daisy & Button 26.00
Amber Glass, Saltshaker, Squatty, Ribbed 16.50
Amber Glass, Shoe On Roller Skate 27.00
Amber Glass, Shoe, Daisy & Button, Dated 1887, 5 In. 28.00
Amber Glass, Stein, Thumbprint, Pewter Lid, 15 In. 225.00
Amber Glass, Sugar & Creamer, Copper Wheel Engraving, Floral 30.00
Amber Glass, Sugar & Creamer, Four Petal 160.00
Amber Glass, Syrup, Leaf & Flower, Not Frosted 125.00
Amber Glass, Toothpick, Boot 28.00
Amber Glass, Toothpick, Boot, Satin Finish 30.00
Amber Glass, Toothpick, Bundle Of Sticks 22.00
Amber Glass, Toothpick, Cherub 30.00
Amber Glass, Toothpick, Elephant 25.00
Amber Glass, Toothpick, Hobnail 16.00
Amber Glass, Toothpick, Three Dolphins 55.00
Amber Glass, Tray, Large Oval, Wildflower 45.00
Amber Glass, Tumbler, Whiskey, 6 Panels, 2 7/8 In. 90.00
Amber Glass, Vase, Art Deco, Boat Shape, Fan Handles, 14 1/4 X 5 1/2 In. 10.00
Amber Glass, Vase, Engraved Frosted To Clear Flowers & Scrolls, 11 1/4 In. 60.00
Amber Glass, Vase, Supported By 2 Nudes, 9 1/2 X 8 In. 60.00
Amber Glass, Whiskey Taster, 6 Panels, 2 1/4 In. 85.00
Amber Glass, Wine Set, Intaglio Of Monkeys, Birds, Butterflies, Bohemian 190.00

Amberette, see Pressed Glass, Klondike

Amberina is a two-toned glassware made from 1883 to about 1900. It was patented by Joseph Locke of the New England Glass Company. The glass shades from red to amber.

Amberina, Basket, Decorated Swirl, Cranberry To Amber, Enameled, 6 1/4 In. 265.00
Amberina, Basket, Diamond Speldor, Applied Amber Handle, Scalloped, 11 In. 125.00
Amberina, Basket, Red & Green, 11 1/2 In. 45.00
Amberina, Bowl, Inverted Thumbprint, 4 1/2 In. 50.00
Amberina, Bowl, Tri-Cornered Form, 4 1/2 In. 115.00
Amberina, Bowl, 3 Legged, Thumbprint, 7 In. 45.00
Amberina, Butter, Covered, Inverted Baby Thumbprint 375.00
Amberina, Carafe, Amber Floral Garland At Neck, Scalloped Mouth, 6 In. 550.00
Amberina, Carafe, Inverted Thumbprint, Deep Fuschia, Colors Reversed 225.00
Amberina, Carafe, Inverted Thumbprint, 7 In. 175.00
Amberina, Castor, Pickle, Enameled, Bull's Eyes Inside, Ornate Frame 285.00
Amberina, Celery, Deep Fuchsia, Double Quilt 295.00
Amberina, Celery, Diamond Quilted & Ribbed, Square Top, 6 1/2 In. 265.00
Amberina, Celery, Diamond Quilted, Square Mouth 225.00
Amberina, Celery, Inverted Fuchsia To Amber, Scalloped Top, 7 In. 65.00
Amberina, Compote, Fuchsia Base, Cambridge, Ohio, 7 X 6 1/2 In. 125.00
Amberina, Compote, Libbey, Ribbed, 12 Scalloped Top, 7 1/2 In. 585.00
Amberina, Compote, 4 3/4 X 9 3/8 In. 75.00
Amberina, Creamer, Diamond Quilted, Reversed Color, Amber Applied Handle 165.00
Amberina, Creamer, Wheeling, Floral & Leaf Sprays, Crimped Rim, 5 In. 145.00
Amberina, Cruet, Clear Handled, Stopper 250.00
Amberina, Cruet, Faceted Amber Stopper, Inverted Thumbprint, 5 1/2 In. 275.00

Amberina, Cruet, Inverted Thumbprint 165.00
Amberina, Cruet, Inverted Thumbprint, Deep Fuchsia, Applied Amber Handle 225.00
Amberina, Cruet, Opalescent Coin Spot, Clear Applied Handle 250.00
Amberina, Cruet, Sandwich 250.00
Amberina, Cruet, Satin, Tricorner Lip, Applied Handle, 3 Knob Stopper 250.00
Amberina, Cruet, Vinegar, Inverted Panel, Applied Handle, 7 In. 250.00
Amberina, Cup, Punch, Diamond Quilted, Reeded Amber Handle 120.00
Amberina, Cup, Punch, Fuchsia, New England 95.00
Amberina, Cup, Punch, Inverted Thumbprint, Applied Reeded Amber Handle 125.00
Amberina, Cup, Punch, Mt.Washington, Corset Shape 95.00
Amberina, Cup, Punch, New England 59.00
Amberina, Decanter, Thumbprint, Reversed Coloring, Faceted Stopper 225.00
Amberina, Dish, Butter, Covered 265.00
Amberina, Dish, Candy, Inverted Thumbprint, Ball Feet 185.00
Amberina, Dish, Canoe Shape, Daisy & Button, 6 1/2 In. 50.00
Amberina, Dish, Sauce, Square, Daisy & Button, 5 In. 95.00
Amberina, Goblet, Amber Stem & Foot, 4 7/8 In. 45.00
Amberina, Jug, Thumbprint, Tricorner Top, 8 3/4 In. 210.00
Amberina, Lightshade, Quilted, Flared Top, 9 X 5 In. 75.00
Amberina, Pitcher, Inverted Thumbprint, Applied Amber Handle, 7 In. 210.00
Amberina, Pitcher, Inverted Thumbprint, Applied Amber Reeded Handle, 8 In. 225.00
Amberina, Pitcher, Inverted Thumbprint, Applied Clear Reeded Handle, 8 In. 185.00
Amberina, Pitcher, Libbey, Inverted Thumbprint, Clear Reeded Handle, 8 In. 275.00
Amberina, Pitcher, Thumbprint, Applied Handle, Fluted Top, 8 1/2 In. 250.00
Amberina, Rose Bowl, Knobby Diamond Quilted, World's Fair, 1893, 3 1/2 In. 150.00
Amberina, Sauce, Daisy & Button, Square 60.00
Amberina, Shade, Daisy & Button 350.00
Amberina, Shade, Gas, Daisy & Button, Ruffled Rim, 8 In. 150.00
Amberina, Sugar & Creamer, Individual, Cambridge, Ruby To Amber Base & Foot 40.00
Amberina, Toothpick, Fishscale 215.00
Amberina, Toothpick, Inverted Thumbprint, Square Top 185.00
Amberina, Toothpick, Reverse, Inverted Thumbprint, Libbey 165.00
Amberina, Toothpick, Sandwich Glass, Daisy & Button 145.00
Amberina, Toothpick, Tricorner .... 125.00 To 275.00
Amberina, Tumbler 50.00
Amberina, Tumbler, Baby Inverted Thumbprint, 4 X 2 1/2 In. 65.00
Amberina, Tumbler, Baby Thumbprint 45.00
Amberina, Tumbler, Cut Floral & Leaves At Center 450.00
Amberina, Tumbler, Elongated Diamond 85.00
Amberina, Tumbler, Expanded Diamond 150.00
Amberina, Tumbler, Fuchsia, Diamond-Quilted Body 95.00
Amberina, Tumbler, Ground Pontil, Quilted 85.00
Amberina, Tumbler, Inverted Diamond, Ground Pontil 90.00
Amberina, Tumbler, Inverted Thumbprint .... 38.00 To 125.00
Amberina, Tumbler, Inverted Thumbprint, Fuschia 95.00
Amberina, Tumbler, New England Glass Co.Fuchsia, Venetian Diamond 110.00
Amberina, Tumbler, Thumbprint 45.00
Amberina, Tumbler, 16 Ribs, Amber To Fuchsia, 3 3/4 In. 85.00
Amberina, Vase, Applied Ruffled Amber Edge, Enamel Floral, 9 1/4 In. 165.00
Amberina, Vase, Art Nouveau, Gold Fleur De Lis, Bronze Base 165.00
Amberina, Vase, Cranberry Edge, Bird & Flowers, Multicolor Enamel, 6 1/2 In. 275.00
Amberina, Vase, Fluted Top, 10 Panels, 7 1/4 In. 65.00
Amberina, Vase, Inverted Thumbprint, Fuschia, 6 1/2 In. 250.00
Amberina, Vase, Libbey, Folded Down Top At Front, Long Stem, 15 In. 450.00
Amberina, Vase, Libbey, Ribbed, Scalloped, 6 1/2 In. 175.00
Amberina, Vase, Lily, Ribbed, 3-Petal Top, 9 In. 225.00
Amberina, Vase, Lily, Tricornered, Turns Down, 9 In. 245.00
Amberina, Vase, Scalloped Square Top, Round Base, 6 In. 275.00
Amberina, Vase, Trumpet, Ruffled Top, 7 1/2 In. 185.00

American Encaustic Tiling Co. of Zanesville, Ohio, worked from 1879 to 1935. Decorative glazed, embossed, and faience tiles were made.

American Encaustic Tiling Co., Inkwell, Double, Pen Tray, Blue, Green 175.00
American Encaustic Tiling Co., Paperweight, Pen Tray, Goat Handle, 5 In. 65.00
American Encaustic Tiling Co., Tile, Snail & Leaf, Light Blue, 6 In. 22.00

American Encaustic Tiling Co., Tile, Wm.Jennings Bryan, Blue & White, 3 In. 55.00
American Encaustic Tiling Co., 6 Tiles, Depicting Troubadour 210.00

Amethyst glass is any of the many glasswares made in the proper dark purple shade. It was a color popular after the Civil War.

Amethyst Glass, Basket, Crimped, Clear Handle, 8 In. 15.00
Amethyst Glass, Bottle, Barber, Enameled, Thistles, Porcelain Stopper 75.00
Amethyst Glass, Bottle, Cologne, 12 Sided, 7 1/4 In. 70.00
Amethyst Glass, Bowl, Applied Amber Rigaree, Prunts, Ormolu Mounting, 7 In. 198.00
Amethyst Glass, Bowl, Hobnail, Opalescent Ruffled Top, Fluted, 8 In. 65.00
Amethyst Glass, Candlestick, 10 Clear Prisms, Twist Stick, 10 In. 48.00
Amethyst Glass, Creamer, Inverted Thumbprint, Applied Clear Handle 30.00
Amethyst Glass, Cruet, Applied Handle And Stopper 12.00
Amethyst Glass, Cruet, Thumbprint 50.00
Amethyst Glass, Decanter, Silver Deposit Stopper, Bulbous, Elaborate, 9 In. 55.00
Amethyst Glass, Decanter, 11 X 7 In. 35.00
Amethyst Glass, Jar, Biscuit, Silver Plate Fittings, 6 In. 85.00
Amethyst Glass, Plate, Blown Glass 24.00
Amethyst Glass, Shoe, Scrolls, 3 1/2 In. 45.00
Amethyst Glass, Slipper, Flat Bow 17.50
Amethyst Glass, Sugar Shaker, Panelled Thumbprint, Brass Lid 48.00
Amethyst Glass, Toothpick, Block Decoration 15.00
Amethyst Glass, Tumbler, Classical Figures, Gold Around Base 45.00
Amethyst Glass, Tumbler, 10 Concave Panels, 5 1/8 In. 60.00
Amethyst Glass, Vase, Jack-In-The-Pulpit 95.00
Amethyst Glass, Vase, Trumpet, Wheelcut, 11 X 7 In. 50.00
Amethyst Glass, Vase, Wide Gold On Gold Band, 6 1/2 In., Pair 55.00
Amethyst Glass, Water Set, White & Gold Enamel Flowers, 7 Piece 145.00
Amethyst Glass, Wine Set, Blown Decanter Stopper, Nickel Plated Silver Tray 50.00
Amos & Andy, Ashtray, Chalkware 18.00
Amos & Andy, Map, Weber City With Envelope & Letter 65.00
Amos & Andy, Music Sheet, Pepsodent 10.00
Amos & Andy, Music Sheet, Three Little Words 7.00

Amphora, see Teplitz
Andiron, many related fireplace items, see, Fire
Apothecary jar, see Bottle, Apothecary
Apple Peeler, see Kitchen, Peeler, Apple
Argy-Rousseau, see G. Argy-Rousseau

Arita, Bowl, Polychrome, Gilt Phoenix Birds & Floral Panels, C.1690, 4 In. 45.00
Arita, Chocolate Pot, Brick Red & Cobalt, Decoration In Vertical Panels 50.00
Arita, Vase, Diamond Shape, Flying Squirrel On Browns, Green, Black, 12 In. 130.00
Arita, Vase, Warriors & Servants, Double Gourd Shape, 9 1/2 In. 165.00

Art Deco, or Art Moderne, is a style started at the Paris Exposition of 1925, characterized by linear, geometric designs.All types of furniture and decorative arts, jewelry, bookbindings, and even games, were designed in this style.

Art Deco, Ashtray, Arched Stag, Signed Frankart 7.50
Art Deco, Ashtray, Cubist, Signed Higgins, 10 X 7 In. 25.00
Art Deco, Ashtray, Flapper In Bathing Suit On Inner Tube 45.00
Art Deco, Ashtray, Green Onyx, Enameled Bronze Arab Boy On One Side 175.00
Art Deco, Ashtray, Queen Nefertiti, Bronzed, 6 X 5 In. 11.00
Art Deco, Base, Blue Glass, Supported By 2 Satin Blue Females, 9 1/2 In. 60.00
Art Deco, Bookend, Dancing Girls With Scarves, Cast Metal, Pair 17.00
Art Deco, Bottle, Dice Bottle, Porcelain, French, Card Theme, 9 1/2 In., Pair 160.00
Art Deco, Bottle, Perfume, Blue, Engraved Flowers, 6 1/2 In. 40.00
Art Deco, Box, Cigarette, Sterling On Bronze, Cedar Lined 25.00
Art Deco, Box, Powder, Alabaster, Black Handle 20.00
Art Deco, Buckle, Glass Belt, Czechoslovakia, Ornate, Pair 22.00
Art Deco, Candelabra, Brass, 5 Branch, Square Base, 12 In., Pair 145.00
Art Deco, Candlestick, Dancing Girl, Satin And Clear Glass 35.00
Art Deco, Candlestick, Square Base, Flowers, Pastel, 8 3/4 In., Pair 40.00
Art Deco, Cocktail, Opalescent, Bottoms Up, Molded Nude Draped On Base 23.00
Art Deco, Compact, Silver Plate 12.50
Art Deco, Console Set, Orange Painted Glass, Gold & Black Bands, 3 Piece 24.50

Art Deco, Stools, Bauhaus School, 17 In.High, Pair

Art Deco, Cup & Saucer, Blue, Enameled Grape Design	20.00
Art Deco, Cup & Saucers, Carlton Ware, Red, Enameled Grape Design	20.00
Art Deco, Doll, Dresser, Black Flapper Hairdo, Marked Nancy Pert, Erphilla	22.50
Art Deco, Dresser Set, Webster, Silver & Black Enamel, 5 Piece	75.00
Art Deco, Figurine, Female Figure, Harlow Type Gown, Porcelain, 8 In.	22.00
Art Deco, Figurine, Girl Holding Tray, Pewter, 8 5/8 In.	49.00
Art Deco, Figurine, Kneeling Nude Girl, Flesh Toned Plaster, 12 1/4 In.	45.00
Art Deco, Figurine, Naked Woman, Baby, Artist, Lena Torino, 1936, 16 In.	125.00
Art Deco, Figurine, Nude, Hands Over Eyes In Shame, Chrome, 5 1/2 In.	15.00
Art Deco, Figurine, Statue Of Liberty, Bronzed, 10 In.	9.00
Art Deco, Figurine, The Long Skirt, Bronze & Ivory, Signed D.H.Chiparus	1650.00
Art Deco, Flower Frog, Figural, Nude Girl Holding Towel, Amber, 12 1/2 In.	55.00
Art Deco, Flower Frog, Nude Lady, Germany	15.00
Art Deco, Glass, Stemmed, Dancing Girls, Garlands, Gold Rimmed, Set Of 12	150.00
Art Deco, Incense Burner, Oriental Woman, Multicolored, Signed ROBJ	125.00
Art Deco, Jigger, Nude Lady, 3 1/2 In.	25.00
Art Deco, Jug, Golds & Blacks, Hummingbird Motif, 7 1/2 In.	32.00
Art Deco, Lamp, Amber Glass Base, Tall Amber Shade 10 In.	18.00
Art Deco, Lighter, Electric, Custard Type Glass, Nude Draped Over Top	45.00
Art Deco, Plaque, Green, 5 Dancing Girls, Scarves, Foliage, Oval, 8 X 12 In.	85.00
Art Deco, Shade, Electric, Impressed Scottie	40.00
Art Deco, Stools, Bauhaus School, 17 In.High, Pair ... *Illus*	150.00
Art Deco, Tray, Brass, Signed Loys, Paris, France	37.50
Art Deco, Tumbler, Juice, Crystal, Gold Band	5.00
Art Deco, Vase, Deer, Turquoise, Blue, Black, Crackled Ground, Signed Boch	190.00
Art Deco, Vase, Encrusted Bronze, Signed Pomone, Silver Geometric, 11 1/2 In.	550.00
Art Deco, Vase, French, Free Design On Pale Green Ground	30.00
Art Deco, Vase, Hand-Painted, Green Ground, Stylized Floral, Czechoslovakia	12.00
Art Deco, Vase, Multi-Colored Flowers, Boch Freres, Signed Lison, 9 In.	75.00
Art Deco, Vase, Pottery, Bock Belgium, Yellow, Black, & Blue Stripes, 12 In.	90.00
Art Deco, Vase, Red, Cobalt Handles, Czechoslovakia	12.00
Art Deco, Vase, Silvercrest Sterling On Bronze, 7 In.	35.00

Art glass means any of the many forms of glassware made during the late nineteenth century or early twentieth century. These wares were expensive and made in limited production. Art glass is not the typical commercial glass that was made in large quantities, and most of the art glass was produced by hand methods.

Art Glass, see also separate headings such as Burmese, Nash, Schneider, etc.

Art Glass, Ashtray, Red, Violet Iridescent, Molded Design	28.00
Art Glass, Basket, Amberina Swirl, Applied Amber Handle & Bee, 12 1/2 In.	335.00
Art Glass, Basket, Apple Green, White Spatter, Raindrop Inside, 5 1/4 In.	58.00
Art Glass, Basket, Blue To White, Clear Handle, 5 In.	19.00
Art Glass, Basket, Blue To White, Clear Handle, 10 In.	25.00
Art Glass, Basket, Bride's, Blue To White, Opalescent, 7 1/4 In.	50.00
Art Glass, Basket, Bride's, Cranberry To White, Silver Plate Frame, 12 In.	100.00

Art Glass, Basket, Bride's, Cranberry, Green Rim, Brass Stand, 9 1/2 In. 65.00
Art Glass, Basket, Bride's, Pink, Silver Plate, Frame, Warren, 13 In. 115.00
Art Glass, Basket, Bride's, Yellow Overlay, Rogers Silver Plate Frame, 5 In. 60.00
Art Glass, Basket, Cranberry To Opalescent Spatter, Clear Handle, 8 In. 90.00
Art Glass, Basket, Dark Green, Swirled, Applied Handles, 10 X 7 In. 22.00
Art Glass, Basket, Embossed Fruit Around Rim & Base, 8 3/4 X 6 In. 18.00
Art Glass, Basket, Green, Blue & Gold, Polished Pontil, 20 In. 350.00
Art Glass, Basket, Green, Opalescent, 7 Applied Green Feet, Ruffled, 5 In. 48.00
Art Glass, Basket, Mint Green, Concave Diamond Optic, 9 1/4 X 9 In. 50.00
Art Glass, Basket, Purple, Applied Green Around Ruffled Top, 8 In. 100.00
Art Glass, Basket, Red, Bronze, Gray Cased, Applied Handle, Czechoslovakia 85.00
Art Glass, Basket, Ruffled Yellow, Cased, Crystal Applied Handle 50.00
Art Glass, Basket, Swan, Acid Finish 75.00
Art Glass, Basket, Thorn Handle, Cased Glass, Lemon, Raspberry, 9 1/2 In. 150.00
Art Glass, Basket, Yellow Ruffled Top, Clear Twisted Thorn Handle, 6 In. 60.00
Art Glass, Bottle, Gentleman's Vanity, Military Cap, Cobalt & Frosted, 5 In. 15.00
Art Glass, Bottle, Perfume, Graja, Blown, Pink Rose, Brass Stand, 4 1/2 In. 79.00
Art Glass, Bottle, Scent, Swirled Real Gold In Glass 50.00
Art Glass, Bowl Vase, Citrine, Gold Enameling, 7 1/2 X 5 1/2 In. 145.00
Art Glass, Bowl, Blue, Opalescent, Reverse Drapery, Fluted, 9 In. 42.00
Art Glass, Bowl, Blue, Pearl Flowers, Opalescent Edge, 3 Footed, 9 1/2 In. 29.00
Art Glass, Bowl, Console, Imperial Freehand, Gold Luminescence 95.00
Art Glass, Bowl, Flower, Green Etching, Gold Iridescence, Crimped Top, 7 In. 52.00
Art Glass, Bowl, Green To White, Overlay, Cobalt Floral, Ruffled, 7 In. 28.00
Art Glass, Bowl, Jade Green, Lotus Shape, 9 In. 7.00
Art Glass, Bowl, Shaded Greens, Crimped Edge, Low, Signed Higgins, 7 In. 35.00
Art Glass, Box, Cream Ground, Enameled Flowers, Marked, 3 1/2 In. 95.00
Art Glass, Box, Dresser, Hinged Cover, Cobalt, White Enamel, Ormolu Feet, 5 In. 80.00
Art Glass, Box, Hinged, Cobalt & White Enamel, 3 Ormolu Feet, 5 1/2 In. 78.00
Art Glass, Box, Trinket, Green, Gold & White Enamel, Footed 35.00
Art Glass, Bride's Bowl, Green To Red, Ruffled, Pairpoint Holder, 9 In. 185.00
Art Glass, Candlestick, Frosted Draped Cherub, 10 In., Pair 55.00
Art Glass, Candlestick, Light Blue, Curved Stem, Prism Drop, 7 In., Pair 20.00
Art Glass, Casket, Jewel, Lime Green, Beveled, Enamel Cupids, Brass Mounted 225.00
Art Glass, Centerpiece Bowl, Sapphire Blue, Clear Feet & Edge, 7 1/4 In. 185.00
Art Glass, Chandelier, White Lustreless, 4 Shades, Urns & Swags, 26 In. 87.50
Art Glass, Compote, Blue Jade, Swirled, Dolphin Stem, 8 1/2 In. 150.00
Art Glass, Cordial Set, Turquoise, Steeple Stoppers, Handled Cups, 6 Piece 30.00
Art Glass, Creamer, Blown Opaline, Turquoise Spatter, Miniature, 2 1/4 In. 22.50
Art Glass, Creamer, Green To Amber, Overshot, Tankard Shape, Applied Handle 90.00
Art Glass, Decanter, Enamel Floral, Bulbous, Applied Handles, 12 In. 32.00
Art Glass, Decanter, Wine, Josephinenhutte, Faceted Stopper, Enamel Floral 75.00
Art Glass, Decanter, Wine, Lime Green, Clear Bubble Stopper, Handle, 10 In. 78.00
Art Glass, Dish, Pair Of Open Hands Shape, White, Opalescent, 1875, 6 1/4 In. 35.00
Art Glass, Dish, Powder, Art Deco Finial, Green Frosted, 2 Nudes 20.00
Art Glass, Dish, Sweetmeat, Blue Overlay, Ruffled, Silver Plate Frame, 7 In. 65.00
Art Glass, Epergne, Cased, Pink & Opalescent White, Enamel Floral, 16 In. 195.00
Art Glass, Epergne, Cased, 4 Flower, Pewter Base, Richardson, Stourbridge 145.00
Art Glass, Epergne, Green Overlay, 3 Trumpet Holders, Marked Silver Holder 90.00
Art Glass, Epergne, Opalescent Chartreuse, 3-Lily, Hanging Baskets, 20 In. 265.00
Art Glass, Epergne, Opalescent, Ruffled Purple Edges, 2 Piece, 12 In. 90.00
Art Glass, Epergne, Tulip, Green To Clear, Metal Pedestal Base, 15 In. 125.00
Art Glass, Epergne, 1 Lily, Clear To Cranberry, Repousse Silver Holder 260.00
Art Glass, Ewer, Pearl Herringbone, Crystal Threading, 11 3/4 In. 525.00
Art Glass, Ewer, White Canes, Handled, Applied Crimped Foot, 8 In. 45.00
Art Glass, Finger Bowl, Amber, Threaded, White Enamel Berry & Leaf, Gold 12.50
Art Glass, Flower Holder, Crystal Elephant, Applied Legs & Ears, C.1910 .... 65.00
Art Glass, Frame, Picture, Easel, Red, White, & Blue, Ribbon Glass, 13 In. 95.00
Art Glass, Goblet, Crystal, Opaque Black Foot, Engraved Medallions, 6 1/2 In. 25.00
Art Glass, Goblet, Emerald Green Cut To Clear, Window Panels, 7 In. 25.00
Art Glass, Humidor, Tobacco, Amethyst, Metal Lid & Pipe Finial 150.00
Art Glass, Jar, Cracker, White Frosted, Barrel Shape, Silver Fittings 35.00
Art Glass, Jar, Powder, Iridescent, Enamel Violets, Hinged Lid, 6 In. 165.00
Art Glass, Lampshade, Opalescent, 8 Panels, 8 In. 40.00
Art Glass, Lampshade, Reverse Painting Of Landscape, 8 In. 25.00
Art Glass, Lemonade Set, Acid-Etched Roses & Friendship, 7 Piece 50.00

Art Glass, Muffineer, Blue Opaque, Cone 65.00
Art Glass, Muffineer, Rose, Opaque 95.00
Art Glass, Pitcher, Acid Finish, Black, Red, Yellow, La Verre Francais, 9 In. 195.00
Art Glass, Pitcher, French, Opalescent, Enamel In Panels, Melon Ribbed, 7 In. 125.00
Art Glass, Pitcher, Lemonade, Apple Green, Melon Ribbed, Enamel Floral 60.00
Art Glass, Pitcher, Lemonade, Blown, Daisies, Ruffled Top, Floral Panels 55.00
Art Glass, Pitcher, Milk, Light Blue Overshot, Applied Amber Reeded Handle 88.00
Art Glass, Pitcher, Opalescent, Crown Milano Type Decoration, 8 1/2 In. 375.00
Art Glass, Rose Bowl, Brass Flower Holder, Pearlized, Iridescent, 5 1/2 In. 50.00
Art Glass, Rose Bowl, Pastel Green, Shadow Stripe, White Lined, Floral, 6 In. 135.00
Art Glass, Rose Bowl, Silver Iridescent, Rough Pontil, 4 X 3 In. 30.00
Art Glass, Salt, Emerald Green, 6 Applied Clear Feet, White Enamel, Gold 28.00
Art Glass, Shade, Chandelier, Frosted White & Tan, Pink Roses, Ribbon, 6 In. 10.00
Art Glass, Shade, German, Frosted, Band Of Pink & Green Floral, 3 3/8 In. 8.00
Art Glass, Shade, Gold Iridescent, 5 1/2 In., Pair 170.00
Art Glass, Shade, Gold Iridescent, 6 1/4 In. 67.50
Art Glass, Shade, Gold Luster, Tiffany Type, Bell Shape, 5 1/2 X 5 In. 50.00
Art Glass, Shade, Green, Blue Iridescent, Tiffany Look, Probably Aurene 175.00
Art Glass, Shade, Ribbed Calcite, Gold Iridescent, Not Signed 70.00
Art Glass, Shade, Yellow, Milky With Fiery Opalescence, Set Of 4 95.00
Art Glass, Sugar & Creamer, Amber Applied Petal Feet & Handle, Pink 90.00
Art Glass, Tankard, Sapphire Blue, Enamel, Floral, Reeded Claw Handle, 10 In. 65.00
Art Glass, Tankard, White Frosted Gold & Enamel Bands, 11 1/2 In. 85.00
Art Glass, Toilet Set, Gold Finish Ornate Metal Frames, 3 Piece 38.00
Art Glass, Tumbler, Green Opaque, Color Border 60.00
Art Glass, Tumbler, Green, Enamel Floral, Gold Trim, C.1850 16.00
Art Glass, Tumbler, Green, Ribbed, Enameled, Beaded 20.00
Art Glass, Tumbler, Pink, Opaque, Reverse Swirl 75.00
Art Glass, Vase, Aqua, Overlay, Portrait Medallion, Blonde Lady, 10 In. 125.00
Art Glass, Vase, Baluster Shape, Satinized, Silver Applied Grapes, 10 1/2 In. 85.00
Art Glass, Vase, Blue Green Iridescent, Floriform, 12 Rib Mold, 10 In. 35.00
Art Glass, Vase, Blue Green Swirled Crystal, Enameled Butterflies, Pair 125.00
Art Glass, Vase, Blue White To Royal Blue, Enamel Bird & Floral, 7 In. 52.50
Art Glass, Vase, Blue, Flapper Girl On 3 Sides, 6 Sided, 8 1/2 In. 19.50
Art Glass, Vase, Blue, Orange, Gold, Oyster, Scailmont, Crimped Rim, 6 1/2 In. 125.00
Art Glass, Vase, Bud, Amber, Beige Stripes, Pink Feet & Decoration, 8 1/2 In. 22.00
Art Glass, Vase, Dark Blue, White Overlay, Applied Clear Handles, 9 In., Pair 22.50
Art Glass, Vase, Deep Blue, Dragonfly & Flowers, Stevens Williams, 8 In. 1250.00
Art Glass, Vase, Enamel, Lady In 1890 Dress, Mottled Red, Tan, Roger, French 100.00
Art Glass, Vase, Fluted & Ribbed, Applied Rigaree, Butterscotch, 8 In. 89.00
Art Glass, Vase, Gourd Shape, Mottled, Iridescent, 4 Pinches, 7 X 7 1/4 In. 70.00
Art Glass, Vase, Green Frosted, Enamel Floral, Folded Tricorner Top, 9 In. 30.00
Art Glass, Vase, Green, Engraved Foliate, Gold Washed, Trumpet, 14 In. 35.00
Art Glass, Vase, Green, Lavender & White Floral, Gold Trim, 10 In. 68.00
Art Glass, Vase, Light Blue, Paneled, Silver Overlay, 3 1/2 In. 42.50
Art Glass, Vase, Lorraine, Mauve, Swirled Spatter, Acid Finish, 12 X 5 In. 135.00
Art Glass, Vase, Lorraine, Orange, Mottled Blue & Brown, 9 X 7 1/2 In. 85.00
Art Glass, Vase, Overlay, Tortoiseshell & White Spatter, Gourd Shape, 5 In. 55.00
Art Glass, Vase, Pink, Sepia Girl, Boy, & Flowers, 10 In. 35.00
Art Glass, Vase, Raspberry Red, Floral, Signed Thos Webb & Sons, 7 3/4 In. 3250.00
Art Glass, Vase, Robin's-Egg Blue, Enamel Butterfly & Floral, Footed, 8 In. 125.00
Art Glass, Vase, Roger, Mottled Red & Tan, Enamel Lady In Hoop Skirt, 11 In. 100.00
Art Glass, Vase, Round, Short Chimney Neck, Orange, Blue, Lorraine, 9 In. 85.00
Art Glass, Vase, Scenic, Leune, 16 In. 175.00
Art Glass, Vase, Stylized Butterflies, Mold Blown, Etling, France, 12 In. 150.00
Art Glass, Vase, Translucent Green Glass, Silver Metal Encased, 8 X 5 In. 75.00
Art Glass, Vase, White Cased, Reds, Yellows, Aventurine, Pinched Base, Pair 145.00
Art Glass, Water Set, Emerald Green, Enamel Floral, Ruffled Rim, 7 Piece 185.00
Art Glass, Wine, Stemmed, 2 Shades Of Green, Lucca, Hamburg, Paris, 1933, 8 In. 37.50

Art Nouveau, a style characterized by free-flowing organic design, reached its zenith between 1895 and 1905. The style encompassed all decorative and functional arts from architecture to furniture and posters.

Art Nouveau, see also Furniture, Various Glass Categories, etc.

Art Nouveau, Ashtray, Aluminum, Girl's Face, Cincinnati Casting Co. 25.00
Art Nouveau, Book End, Toy Soldier, Pair 15.00

Art Nouveau, Bowl, Sterling Silver, Applied Repousse Floral, 12 In. 145.00
Art Nouveau, Box, Hairpin, A Friend Of The Fair Sex, Rockford Silver Co. 22.50
Art Nouveau, Box, Hinged, Silver, Footed, 4 1/2 X 3 In. 38.00
Art Nouveau, Box, Jewel, Footed, Blue Lining, Flowers Embossed 12.00
Art Nouveau, Box, Jewel, Footed, Pink Lining, Flowers & Vines, 4 In. 12.00
Art Nouveau, Brush, Baby's Clothes, Cherub 10.00
Art Nouveau, Brush, Hair, Poppies, Girl Along Side, Unger Bros. 95.00
Art Nouveau, Buttonhook, Sterling Silver, Female Figure 35.00
Art Nouveau, Buttonhook, Sterling Silver, Seminude Woman 25.00
Art Nouveau, Candelabra, Egyptian Influence, 3 Cups, 16 3/4 In. 85.00
Art Nouveau, Candleholder, Yellow Streaked, Blue, Franz Mehlen, 14 1/2 In. 65.00
Art Nouveau, Candlestick, Double, Maiden, Bronzed, 12 1/2 In., Pair 75.00
Art Nouveau, Case, Pencil, Sterling Silver 7.00
Art Nouveau, Chatelaine, Sterling Silver, 3 Discs 12.00
Art Nouveau, Decanter, Austrian, E.W.Turn Wien, Semi Nude Forms Handle 175.00
Art Nouveau, Dish, Copper Alloy, Butterfly Girl, 8 In. 45.00
Art Nouveau, Doll's Bench, Oak, Lady's Head Tile, 13 In. 64.00
Art Nouveau, Dresser Set, Cleopatra Head On Mirror & Brush, Tortoise Comb 105.00
Art Nouveau, Dresser Set, Gold, Women With Harp & Lilacs, 3 Piece 125.00
Art Nouveau, Dresser Set, Silver Plate, Beveled Mirror, Cherubs And Fish 60.00
Art Nouveau, Dresser Set, Sterling Silver, Mirror, Brush, & Comb, 3 Piece 65.00
Art Nouveau, Dresser Set, 3 Brushes And Comb, Unger Bros., Women's Faces 125.00
Art Nouveau, Figurine, Bronze, Nude, Arms Outstretched, 13 1/2 In. 35.00
Art Nouveau, Figurine, Woman, Metal, Signed L & F Moreau, 9 In. 100.00
Art Nouveau, Figurine, Woman, Porcelain, 10 1/4 In. 125.00
Art Nouveau, Frame For Beaded Bag 20.00
Art Nouveau, Frame, Picture, Sterling Silver, Heart-Shaped Opening, 7 In. 40.00
Art Nouveau, Hairbrush, Cupid Handle, Victor Silver Co., May 16, 1905 25.00
Art Nouveau, Hairbrush, Sterling Silver 12.00
Art Nouveau, Jar, Dresser, Silver Plated Lid, Paneled Glass, 3 In. 10.00
Art Nouveau, Jar, Tobacco, Octagon, Silverplated Top, Hibiscus Pattern 60.00
Art Nouveau, Lamp, Baker Putting Loaf In Oven, Paris Foundry, 13 1/4 In. 225.00
Art Nouveau, Lamp, Gent Glass, Table, Ribbed, Cream, Amber, E Miller & Co. 190.00
Art Nouveau, Lorgnette, 14k Gold, Case With Raised Motif 125.00
Art Nouveau, Manicure Set, Silver Plate, 5 Piece 11.00
Art Nouveau, Match Safe, Pocket, Sterling, Ornate 20.00
Art Nouveau, Match Safe, Sterling Silver, Lady With Flowing Hair 35.00
Art Nouveau, Match Safe, Sterling, Floral 35.00
Art Nouveau, Mirror, Hand, Burnt Wood, Girl, Jeweled Headband, Bevel Glass 15.00
Art Nouveau, Mirror, Hand, Lady, Leather Back, Quadruple Plate 20.00
Art Nouveau, Mirror, Hand, Silver Plate, Floral, Beveled Glass, Curved Handle 35.00
Art Nouveau, Pitcher, Flower Handle, Tulips, Austria, 9 1/4 In. 90.00
Art Nouveau, Plate, Door, Brass Plated, 9 In. 4.75
Art Nouveau, Shade, Gas, Green Opaque Stained, Brass Overlay, Pair 87.50
Art Nouveau, Spoon, Marrow, Sterling Silver 45.00
Art Nouveau, Vase, Bronze, Angels Signed, Dore Girls, 17 1/2 In. 375.00
Art Nouveau, Vase, Copper With Sterling Silver Overlay, Signed, 10 In. 75.00
Art Nouveau, Vase, Enamel On Oyster Ground, French, Scailmont, Artist Signed 125.00
Art Nouveau, Vase, Iris Pattern, 8 1/4 In. 15.00
Art Nouveau, Vase, Lake Scene, French, Signed Leune, 16 In. 175.00
Art Nouveau, Vase, Signed Barolac, 9 1/2 In. 95.00
Art Nouveau, Vase, Sterling Silver Rim, 8 In. 16.00
Art Nouveau, Vase, 3 Dimensional Woman Holding Periwinkles, 7 In. 18.00
Arthur Osborne, see Ivorex

AURENE

Aurene glass was made by Frederick Carder of New York about 1904. It is an iridescent gold glass, usually marked Aurene or Steuben.

Aurene, see also Tiffany Glass
Aurene, Atomizer, F.Carder, Blue Iridescent 200.00
Aurene, Bottle, Perfume, Blue 175.00
Aurene, Bowl & Flower Block, Steuben, Blue, Stretch Edge, 10 In. 325.00
Aurene, Bowl, Gold, Signed, 6 X 2 In. 110.00
Aurene, Bowl, Steuben, Gold, Blue & Red Highlights, 10 X 3 In. 350.00
Aurene, Candlestick, Blue, 8 In. 310.00
Aurene, Candlestick, Steuben, Blue, 10 In., Pair 850.00
Aurene, Candlestick, Steuben, Gold, Twisted, 8 In., Pair 435.00

Aurene, Goblet, Gold Iridescent, Twisted Stem, 6 In. 165.00
Aurene, Goblet, Oriental Poppy, Green Stem, Pink Opalescent Top, Carder 225.00
Aurene, Lamp, Brown, Gold Leaf & Vine, 20 In., Shade 12 In. 550.00
Aurene, Plate, Gold, Signed And Numbered, 6 In. 115.00
Aurene, Shade, Green Iridescent, Applied Zigzag Band, 10 In. 1250.00
Aurene, Shade, Steuben, Gold, Bellflower Shape, 9 1/2 X 5 1/2 In., Pair 260.00
Aurene, Shade, Steuben, Gold, Ribbed, Flared, 6 In. 55.00
Aurene, Toothpick, Steuben, Gold 175.00
Aurene, Tumbler, Juice, Steuben, Gold Iridescent 175.00
Aurene, Tumbler, Steuben, Gold, 4 In. 125.00
Aurene, Vase, Blue Iridescent, Ovington Sticker, Signed, Numbered, 10 1/2 In. 325.00
Aurene, Vase, Blue, Signed 400.00
Aurene, Vase, Gold Iridescent, Reddish Highlights, Signed, 5 1/4 In. 135.00
Aurene, Vase, Gold Over White, Hooked Feathers, Numbered, 2 1/2 In. 475.00
Aurene, Vase, Gold, Rainbow Highlights, Pedestal, Rose Bowl Shape, 4 1/2 In. 310.00
Aurene, Vase, Ivory, Signed, 5 1/2 In. 75.00
Aurene, Vase, Platinum, Green Drape, Floriform, 10 1/2 In. 975.00
Aurene, Vase, Steuben, Amber, Tulip Shape, Footed, 6 1/2 In. 390.00
Aurene, Vase, Steuben, Blue, Ribbed, 5 1/2 In. 350.00
Aurene, Vase, Steuben, Blue, Stick, No.2556, 8 In. 245.00
Aurene, Vase, Steuben, Blue, Stick, Signed, 6 In. 190.00
Aurene, Vase, Steuben, Blue, Thorn, 6 1/2 In. 275.00
Aurene, Vase, Steuben, Blue, Urn Shape, 6 In. 395.00
Aurene, Vase, Steuben, Blue, 2 Earred Handles, 13 In. 2500.00
Aurene, Vase, Steuben, Gold Iridescent, 3 Applied Handles, Footed, 7 1/2 In. 750.00
Aurene, Vase, Steuben, Gold Iridescent, 7 In. 237.00
Aurene, Vase, Steuben, Gold, Decorated, 2 1/2 In. 650.00
Aurene, Vase, Steuben, Gold, Red & Blue Iridescence, Ruffled Top, 3 1/2 In. 250.00
Aurene, Vase, Stick, Blue, Signed 8 1/4 In. 135.00
Aurene, Wine, Dimpled 105.00
Aurene, Wine, Gold Iridescent, Twisted Stem, 6 1/4 In. 175.00
Aurene, Wine, Gold, Twisted Stem And Colors 125.00

Austria, see Royal Dux, Kauffmann, Porcelain
Auto, Ornament, Hood, see also Lalique

Auto parts and accessories are collectors' items today.

Auto, Ameter, Wooden Case 15.00
Auto, Button, Ford Motor Co., 1932, Pinback 5.00
Auto, Cap, Gas, Model A Ford 2.00
Auto, Cap, Radiator, Chevrolet, Brass 3.50
Auto, Cap, Radiator, Model T Ford, Brass 3.50
Auto, Cap, Radiator, Ram, Dodge, 1935 15.00
Auto, Cap, Radiator, Tee Bone, Brass, Moto Meter 18.00
Auto, Cap, Radiator, 1915 Maxwell, Brass, Symbol 7.00
Auto, Charger, Battery, Model T Ford, Wooden Case 18.00
Auto, Clock, Oval, 8 Day, Stem Wind 25.00
Auto, Curtains, Side, Maxwell, 1914 65.00
Auto, Emblem, Figural, Flying Lady Mounted On Walnut Base 40.00
Auto, Emblem, Radiator, Chevrolet, Blue & White Enamel 7.00
Auto, Gauge, Balloon Tire, Brass, 1916 8.00
Auto, Gauge, Tire, Schrader, Balloon Tires, Cloth Bag 14.00
Auto, Gauge, Tire, Schrader, 1923, Brass, Round 5.00
Auto, Goggles, Driving, C.1900 22.00
Auto, Gong, Brass Nickel Plated, Floor Operated, 5 1/2 In. 85.00
Auto, Headlight, Model A Ford, Double, '31 15.00
Auto, Headlight, Model A Ford, Stainless Steel 10.00
Auto, Horn, Electric Auto-Lite, 12 In. 28.50
Auto, Hubcap, Hudson, Brass, Set Of 4 12.00
Auto, Hubcap, 1937 Ford 4.00
Auto, Keycase, Dodge, Leather 4.00
Auto, Knob, Gearshift, Blue & White Swirl Ball 50.00
Auto, Knob, Gearshift, Carole Lombard Picture 15.00
Auto, Lamp, Brass And Black Painted, Yankee Type 40.00
Auto, Lamp, Kerosene, Nickel Plate, Neverout Insulated Safety Lamp 28.00
Auto, License Plate, Alabama, 1971 1.00

Auto, License Plate, California, 1951, Pair 15.00
Auto, License Plate, Illinois, 1929, Tin 6.00
Auto, License Plate, Illinois, 1937 2.00
Auto, License Plate, Iowa, 1962 1.00
Auto, License Plate, Kansas, 1932 3.00
Auto, License Plate, Kansas, 1968 & 1969, Each 1.00
Auto, License Plate, Louisiana, 1966 To 1973, Each 1.00
Auto, License Plate, Michigan, 1916 30.00
Auto, License Plate, Mississippi, 1968, 1969, & 1970, Each 1.00
Auto, License Plate, Missouri, 1924, 1926, Each 6.00
Auto, License Plate, Missouri, 1973 & 1974, Each 1.00
Auto, License Plate, Nebraska, 1927 3.00
Auto, License Plate, New Hampshire, 1915, Porcelain 12.00 To 15.00
Auto, License Plate, New Jersey, 1916 5.00
Auto, License Plate, New York, 1917 3.00
Auto, License Plate, Ohio, 1919 15.00
Auto, License Plate, Ohio, 1926 3.00
Auto, License Plate, Ohio, 1932 4.00
Auto, License Plate, Ontario, 1921 5.00
Auto, License Plate, Pennsylvania, 1908, Yellow Enamel 31.00
Auto, License Plate, Rhode Island, 1933, 1935, Each 3.00
Auto, License Plate, South Dakota, 1933 4.00
Auto, License Plate, Texas, 1962 To 1968, Each 1.00
Auto, License Plate, Virginia, 1925 5.00
Auto, License Plate, Virginia, 1930 3.00
Auto, License Plate, Virginia, 1937 3.00
Auto, License Plate, Wisconsin, 1930 3.00
Auto, Light, Car Trouble, Unity Mfg.6 Volts, Stand, 6 1/2 In. 18.50
Auto, Light, Carbide, With Yoke 20.00
Auto, Mascot, Rolls-Royce, Gold Plated, 2 In. 10.00
Auto, Meter Cover, Keystone, 1901-1910, Brass 10.00
Auto, Mirror, Rear View, Model A Ford 5.00
Auto, Moto Meter, Brass 12.00
Auto, Oilcan, Pierce Arrow, Dash Mounting Bracket 45.00
Auto, Ornament, Radiator, Franklin Lion, C.Derujinsky, 1924 95.00
Auto, Ornament, Radiator, Indian, Pontiac 15.00
Auto, Ornament, Radiator, Lion, Franklin 25.00
Auto, Ornament, Radiator, Pontiac Indian Chief, 1929 55.00
Auto, Ornament, Radiator, Pontiac Indian Chief, 1933 35.00
Auto, Radiator & Shell, Chevrolet, 1917 75.00
Auto, Radiator & Shell, Willys Knight 75.00
Auto, Radiator, 1925 Dodge 20.00
Auto, Refacer, Valve, Model T Ford 18.00
Auto, Sparkplug, Firestone, 1938, Original Box .95
Auto, Sparkplug, Model T Ford, 1911, Priming Valve 17.50
Auto, Taillight, Model T, Red Glass, Set Of 4 26.50
Auto, Toolbox, Fordson 8.00
Auto, Vase, Clear Glass, From Packard Hearse, Bird & Grapes In Relief 25.00
Auto, Vase, Glass Flower, Metal Holder Attachment, Benser 18.00
Auto, Wheel, Model A Ford, Pair 17.50
Auto, Windshield Wiper, Hand-Held Brass Reservoir, Cork Capped, Felt Blade 40.00
Auto, Wrench, Crescent, Fordson, S Shape 5.00
Auto, Wrench, Ford, Script 5.00

Autumn Leaf pattern china was made by the Hall China Co., from 1936.

Autumn Leaf, Creamer, Jewel Tea, Hall 3.50
Autumn Leaf, Cup & Saucer, Jewel Tea, Hall 3.50
Autumn Leaf, Cup, Jewel Tea 1.75
Autumn Leaf, Plate, Cake, Jewel Tea, Hall, 9 1/2 In. 4.00
Autumn Leaf, Plate, Jewel Tea, Hall, 10 In. 3.50
Autumn Leaf, Plate, Jewel Tea, Hall, 8 In. 1.50
Autumn Leaf, Plate, Jewel Tea, Hall, 9 In. 2.25
Autumn Leaf, Platter, Jewel Tea, Hall, 11 1/2 In. 4.50
Autumn Leaf, Salt & Pepper, Range, Jewel Tea, Hall 6.00

Autumn Leaf, Saucer, Jewel Tea, Hall 1.00
Autumn Leaf, Sugar, Covered, Jewel Tea, Hall 4.50
Autumn Leaf, Teapot, Jewel Tea, Aladdin, Hall 15.00
Autumn Leaf, Teapot, Jewel Tea, Long Spout, Hall 18.00
Autumn Leaf, Tumbler, Jewel Tea, Frosted, Hall 6.50
Autumn Leaf, Tumbler, Jewel Tea, 5 3/4 In. 6.00
Aventurine, Tumbler, Scattered Pulled Paperweight Canes, 3 1/2 In. 30.00
Avon, see Bottle, Avon

Baccarat glass was made in France by La Compagnie des Cristalleries de Baccarat, located about 150 miles from Paris. The factory was started in 1765. The firm went bankrupt and began operating again about 1822. Famous cane and millefiori paperweights were made there during the 1860-1880 period. The firm is still working near Paris making paperweights and glasswares.

Baccarat, Bottle, Blue & White Enamel, Signed, G.Chevalier, 5 In., Set Of 3 .... 165.00
Baccarat, Bottle, Cologne, Cane Cutting, Cranberry To Clear, 4 In. 285.00
Baccarat, Bottle, Cologne, Cane Cutting, Cranberry To Clear, 6 3/8 In., Pair 450.00
Baccarat, Bottle, Cologne, Shalimar, Purple Velvet Box 15.00
Baccarat, Bottle, Perfume, Amberina Swirl, Stopper, Unsigned 25.00
Baccarat, Bottle, Perfume, Clear Swirl, Blue Decoration, 6 In., Pair 35.00
Baccarat, Bottle, Perfume, Clear Swirl, Enameled Leaves, Unsigned, 7 In. 25.00
Baccarat, Bottle, Perfume, Cobalt, Butterfly Shape, 3 1/2 X 5 In. 38.00
Baccarat, Bottle, Perfume, Figural, Sitting Buddha, Houbigant Case 65.00
Baccarat, Bottle, Perfume, Frosted Sphinx Stopper, Pyramid Shape 45.00
Baccarat, Bottle, Perfume, Gold Designs, Art Deco, Pair 70.00
Baccarat, Bottle, Perfume, Ovoid, Gold Lion's Head, Flank Neck 37.00
Baccarat, Bottle, Perfume, Red With Gold, Melon Shape, Pinched Panels 65.00
Baccarat, Bottle, Red Medallions On Stopper & Body, Cut Floral, 7 In. 185.00
Baccarat, Claret, Petallike Cutting, 5 1/2 In. 15.00
Baccarat, Compote, Bronze Base, 12 In. 125.00
Baccarat, Cruet, Blue Satin Finish, Pansies 170.00
Baccarat, Cruet, Electric Blue, Iridescent, Floral 160.00
Baccarat, Decanter, Block Cut Stopper, Paneled, 9 In. 60.00
Baccarat, Decanter, Cut Glass, Mushroom Stopper, Signed 45.00
Baccarat, Decanter, Wine, Flute Cut, Signed, 9 1/4 In 45.00
Baccarat, Dish, Butter, Cow Pressed On Lid, Pressed Blue Glass, Signed 38.00
Baccarat, Dish, Long Oval With Swirls, Amber, Signed 48.00
Baccarat, Dish, Soap, Amberina Color, Swirled, Rooled Edge, 3 1/2 In. 30.00
Baccarat, Epergne, Marble & Brass Base & Fittings, 16 1/2 In. 200.00
Baccarat, Goblet, Cranberry To Clear, Signed 35.00
Baccarat, Inkstand, Circular Swirl With Sterling Top, 4 1/2 In. 150.00
Baccarat, Jar, Powder, Covered, Diamond Point, Signed 35.00
Baccarat, Jar, Smelling Salts, Covered, Silver Collar, Edwardian Period 75.00
Baccarat, Knife Rest, Baby's Head At Each End, Camphor Satin, 4 In., Pair 55.00
Baccarat, Paperweight, Blue Cornflower, Latticinio Base 235.00
Baccarat, Paperweight, Bonaparte, Napoleon 60.00
Baccarat, Paperweight, Bonaparte, Napoleon, Overlay 200.00
Baccarat, Paperweight, Cane Flower Group, Latticinio Base 100.00
Baccarat, Paperweight, Church, Zodiac Silhouettes, 1967 .... 150.00
Baccarat, Paperweight, Concentric Circles, Geometrics, Millefiori Canes 175.00
Baccarat, Paperweight, Eisenhower, Dwight D., Overlay 1200.00
Baccarat, Paperweight, Eisenhower, Dwight D., Sulfide 750.00
Baccarat, Paperweight, Elephant, Gridel Silhouette 150.00
Baccarat, Paperweight, Flower With Swirl, Red & White 235.00
Baccarat, Paperweight, Hoover, Herbert, Overlay 300.00
Baccarat, Paperweight, Hoover, Herbert, Sulfide .... 60.00 To 100.00
Baccarat, Paperweight, Horse, Gridel Silhouette 150.00
Baccarat, Paperweight, Hunter, Gridel Silhouette 150.00
Baccarat, Paperweight, Intertwined Chains, Pink, Millefiori Canes 120.00
Baccarat, Paperweight, Jackson, Andrew, Overlay 250.00
Baccarat, Paperweight, Jackson, Andrew, Sulfide .... 60.00 To 100.00
Baccarat, Paperweight, Jefferson, Thomas, Overlay 1000.00
Baccarat, Paperweight, Jefferson, Thomas, Sulfide 500.00
Baccarat, Paperweight, Kennedy, John F., Overlay 750.00

Baccarat, Paperweight, Kennedy, John F., Sulfide .... 225.00 To 300.00
Baccarat, Paperweight, Lincoln, Abraham, Overlay 1050.00
Baccarat, Paperweight, Lincoln, Abraham, Sulfide 675.00
Baccarat, Paperweight, Millefiori Concentric Rings 175.00
Baccarat, Paperweight, Millefiori Flower 175.00
Baccarat, Paperweight, Millefiori On White Muslin, 1847 .... 1275.00
Baccarat, Paperweight, Monkey, Gridel Silhouette 175.00
Baccarat, Paperweight, Monroe, James, Overlay 225.00
Baccarat, Paperweight, Monroe, James, Sulfide .... 75.00 To 100.00
Baccarat, Paperweight, Mushroom Swirl, Star Cut Base, Millefiori Canes 250.00
Baccarat, Paperweight, Our Lady Of Lourdes, Millefiori Canes 60.00
Baccarat, Paperweight, Paine, Thomas, Sulfide 75.00
Baccarat, Paperweight, Pansy, Signed, Numbered, 1973 .... 199.00
Baccarat, Paperweight, Pelican, Gridel Silhouette 150.00
Baccarat, Paperweight, Pheasant, Gridel Silhouette 175.00
Baccarat, Paperweight, Pope John XXIII, Overlay 650.00
Baccarat, Paperweight, Pope Pious XII, Overlay 650.00
Baccarat, Paperweight, Rogers, Will, Overlay 450.00
Baccarat, Paperweight, Rogers, Will, Sulfide 200.00
Baccarat, Paperweight, Roosevelt, Eleanor, Sulfide 100.00
Baccarat, Paperweight, Roosevelt, Theodore, Overlay 425.00
Baccarat, Paperweight, Roosevelt, Theodore, Sulfide .... 150.00 To 200.00
Baccarat, Paperweight, Rooster, Gridel Silhouette 150.00
Baccarat, Paperweight, Squirrel, Gridel Silhouette 150.00
Baccarat, Paperweight, Stevenson, Adlai, Sulfide .... 80.00 To 85.00
Baccarat, Paperweight, Swan, Gridel Silhouette 150.00
Baccarat, Paperweight, Truman, Harry S., Sulfide 85.00
Baccarat, Paperweight, Washington, George, Sulfide 550.00
Baccarat, Paperweight, Wilson, Woodrow, Overlay 225.00
Baccarat, Paperweight, Wilson, Woodrow, Sulfide .... 55.00 To 85.00
Baccarat, Plate, Doughnut Server, Amber, Swirl Stem, Round Foot, 5 In. 75.00
Baccarat, Tumbler, Prism Cut 6.50
Baccarat, Vase, Chartreuse Yellow To Frosted, Bronze Base, 10 In., Pair 525.00
Baccarat, Vase, Etched In Louis XVI Style, Ovoid, Signed, 9 In. 62.50
Baccarat, Vase, Kate Greenaway Child & Rabbits, Signed 95.00
Baccarat, Wine, Cranberry Overlay, Clear Bowl, 3 1/2 .... 22.50

Bag, Beaded, see Beaded Bag

Metal banks have been made since 1868. There are still banks, mechanical banks, and registering banks (those which total money deposited on the face of the bank). Many old banks have been reproduced since the 1950s in iron or plastic. The Whiting numbers refer to the book "Old Iron Still Banks" by Hubert B. Whiting.

Bank, A & P Eight O'clock Coffee, Tin 5.00
Bank, Acorn, Brown Glazed Pottery, 2 1/2 In. 13.75
Bank, American Can Co., Century Of Progress, 1934 .... 12.00
Bank, Aunt Jemima, Iron, 5 1/2 In. 48.00
Bank, Aunt Jemima, Porcelain 8.00
Bank, Baby's Shoe, Metal, Bronze Finish 6.00
Bank, Bank Building, Iron, 3 1/2 X 2 In., Wh-423 .... 19.75
Bank, Bank Building, Iron, 4 3/4 In., Wh-421 .... 24.75
Bank, Bank Of Industry, Labor Picture, Iron 45.00
Bank, Barrel, Dodge 6.50
Bank, Barrel, Happy Days, Tin 6.00
Bank, Barrel, Rush To Rockies, Ceramic, Tivoli, 8 1/2 In. 27.00
Bank, Barrel, Thompson Whiskey 10.00
Bank, Baseball Batter, Iron 63.00
Bank, Baseball, Clear Glass 29.00
Bank, Battleship Oregon, 5 In., Wh-144 .... 92.00
Bank, Bear, Harper's, Cast Iron 55.00
Bank, Bear, Snowcrest 5.00
Bank, Bear, 5 1/4 In., Wh-330 .... 35.00
Bank, Bell, Wh-281 .... 40.00
Bank, Ben Franklin, Suffolk Franklin Savings Bank, Boston, Metal 6.95
Bank, Betsy Ross Tea, Tin & Cardboard 2.00

Bank, Billiken, Cast Iron, Wh-50 2900 ..... 38.00
Bank, Billy Goat, Combination Doorstop, Cast Iron 50.00
Bank, Bokar Coffee, Tin 3.00
Bank, Book, Monumental, Key 10.00
Bank, Boy Scout, Wh-14 ..... 40.00
Bank, Buffalo, Wh-208 ..... 34.75
Bank, Building, Iron, 3 1/2 X 2 3/4 In. 25.00
Bank, Building, New York World's Fair, 1940, Glass 20.00
Bank, Building, 3 1/4 In., Wh-409 ..... 75.00
Bank, Building, 6 Sided, Wh-320 ..... 45.00
Bank, Bulbous, Brown Glaze, Pottery, 6 1/4 In. 170.00
Bank, Bulldog, Seated, Wh-105 3500 ..... 45.00
Bank, Bust Of Ben Franklin, Metal, Wh-313 ..... 7.00
Bank, Camel, Wh-201 ..... 125.00
Bank, Camel, Wh-202 ..... 45.00
Bank, Campbell Kids, Painted, Iron 195.00
Bank, Can, Dodge Dart 5.00
Bank, Candy Jar, Independence Hall 28.00
Bank, Cannon Ball, Iron 85.00
Bank, Cash Box, Green, Tin, Chein 4.00
Bank, Cash Register, Bell Rings, Patented 1913 ..... 12.50
Bank, Castle, 4 Turrets, Iron 22.00
Bank, Cat Sitting, White, Pink Ribbon, Cast Iron 15.00
Bank, Cat With Bow Tie, Blue, 4 1/2 In. 35.00
Bank, Cat, Chalk 5.00
Bank, Cat, Seated, Wh-248 ..... 55.00
Bank, Cat, Sitting, Chalkware, Green Eyes, Cork Stopper, 9 In. 25.00
Bank, Charlie McCarthy, Composition, 9 1/2 In. 48.00
Bank, Clown, Chein 15.00
Bank, Clown, Grapette 2.50
Bank, Clown, Wh-29 ..... 40.00
Bank, Coffee Grinder, Daisy 45.00
Bank, Columbian Exposition, 1892, Magic Savings, Iron 75.00
Bank, Cow, Brass, Penny 12.00
Bank, Cow, Wh-200 ..... 75.00
Bank, Crown, Wh-321 ..... 24.00
Bank, Decker's Pig, Still 90.00
Bank, Deer, Iron, Wh-195 ..... 24.00 To 55.00
Bank, Deer, Wh-194 ..... 25.00
Bank, Dime Register, Astronaut 5.00
Bank, Dime Register, Lucky 9.00
Bank, Dime, Calibrations, Tin, Pocket 16.00
Bank, Dime, Christmas, 1923, Nativity, Color On Metal 4.50
Bank, Dog On Turntable 140.00
Bank, Dog Pack, Wh-106 ..... 35.00
Bank, Dog With Bee On His Back, Cast Iron, 5 In. 16.00
Bank, Dog With Pack, I Hear A Call 75.00
Bank, Dog With Pack, Iron, 8 In. 45.00
Bank, Dog With Pack, painted, Wh-113 ..... 41.00 To 75.00
Bank, Dog With Pack, Still, Large 25.00
Bank, Dog With Pack, Wh-106 ..... 30.00 To 37.50
Bank, Dog With Pack, Wh-136 ..... 50.00
Bank, Dog, Wh-109 ..... 100.00
Bank, Donkey With Saddle, Iron, Presidential Election, 4 In. 27.50
Bank, Donkey, Iron 45.00
Bank, Donkey, Wh-198 ..... 25.00
Bank, Drum, Centennial, 1876, Tin 20.00
Bank, Drum, Chein 12.00
Bank, Drum, Fern Bisel Peat, Lithographed, Tin, Ohio Art 9.50
Bank, Drum, God Bless America, Tin, Chein 6.50
Bank, Drum, Tin, Chein 5.00
Bank, Duck, Wh-215 ..... 100.00
Bank, Egg, Cream Glaze, 4 In. 10.50
Bank, Eggs In Nest, Redware, Painted, 3 1/4 In. 55.00
Bank, Electrolux, Still Bank 13.00

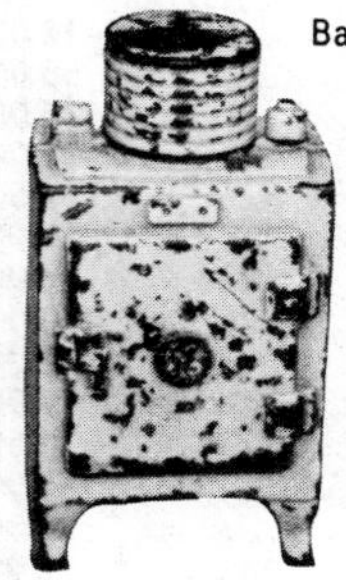
Bank, G.E.Refrigerator, Iron, 3 In.

Bank, Golliwog, Iron, 6 In.

Bank, Elephant On Bench On Tub, Wh-55 .... 55.00
Bank, Elephant With Howdah, Movable Trunk, 3 1/2 In. 30.00
Bank, Elephant, Grapette 2.50
Bank, Elephant, Howdah On Top, Penny, Iron, Gilt Finish, 4 In. 25.00
Bank, Elephant, Reversible Trunk 30.00
Bank, Elephant, Wh-63 .... 40.00
Bank, Elephant, Wh-73 .... 65.00
Bank, Embossed Man's Face, Clear Glass, Square, 4 In. 55.00
Bank, Empire State, Still Bank, Heavy Metal, 6 In. 12.00
Bank, Excelsior, Hall 125.00
Bank, Ferry Boat, W-148 .... 110.00
Bank, Figural, Boy Scout 65.00
Bank, Flatiron Building, Cast Iron 18.00
Bank, Football, Wh-12 .... 200.00
Bank, Footed, Square, Security Safe Deposit, Dated 1888-1887, 4 In. 55.00
Bank, G.E.Refrigerator, Iron, 3 In. .... *Illus* 10.00
Bank, Gas Pump 425.00
Bank, General Pershing, Painted, 8 In., Wh-312 .... 50.00 To 85.00
Bank, General Pershing, 1917 .... 38.50
Bank, George Washington, Still 40.00
Bank, Glass, Lincoln 20.00
Bank, Golliwog, Iron, 6 In. .... *Illus* 45.00
Bank, Golliwog, Metal Alloy 70.00
Bank, Goose, Red Goose Shoes, Iron 50.00
Bank, Horse Beauty, Wh-82 .... 30.00
Bank, Horse, Bronze Metal, 5 In. 7.50
Bank, Horse, Bronze, Metal Closure 6.50
Bank, Horse, Prancing, Iron, Wh-77 .... 45.00
Bank, House, Iron, Wh-356 .... 29.50
Bank, House, Pittsburgh Paints, Glass 20.00
Bank, House, Wh-375 .... 75.00
Bank, Humpty Dumpty, Tin, Chein 32.00
Bank, Independence Hall, Glass 100.00
Bank, Independence Hall, Iron 35.00
Bank, Iron, Bank Building, Cupola Top, 5 1/2 X 4 1/4 In. 35.00
Bank, Iron, Buffalo, Wh-208 .... 34.75
Bank, Iron, 9 Story Turreted Building, 4 1/2 In. 23.00
Bank, Jack & Jill, Copper 6.00
Bank, Jack Benny, Wood Composition Safe 25.00
Bank, Jackie Robinson, Dime 17.00
Bank, Kettle, Registering 70.00
Bank, Kewpie Type Doll, Carnival 9.50
Bank, Leprechaun, Cast Iron, 12 In. 135.00
Bank, Liberty Bell, Carnival Glass, Marigold 11.00
Bank, Liberty Bell, Glass 3.00
Bank, Liberty Bell, Iowa Bank 30.00
Bank, Liberty Bell, Wh-279 .... 30.00 To 35.00
Bank, Lincoln Bottle 10.00
Bank, Lincoln Pass Around The Hat, Small 125.00

Bank, Lincoln's Head, Bronze Color 12.00
Bank, Lion On A Tub, Iron, 5 1/4 In. 65.00
Bank, Lion On Wheels, Wh-95 125.00
Bank, Lion With Open Mouth On Wheels 85.00
Bank, Lion, Iron, Wh-91 39.50
Bank, Lion, Iron, 3 In. 25.00
Bank, Lion, Wh-90 35.00
Bank, Lion, Wh-913 25.00
Bank, Lion, Wh-92 20.00 To 55.00
Bank, Loaf Of Bread, Papier-Mache, 5 In.Long *Illus* 35.00
Bank, Lucky Joe, Donald Duck Face 1.50
Bank, Lucky Joe, Nash 2.00
Bank, Mahogany Wooden Box With Post Office Dial 20.00
Bank, Mailbox, Black & Gold 18.00
Bank, Mailbox, Cast Iron 20.00
Bank, Mailbox, Hanging, Wh-382 35.00
Bank, Mailbox, Movable Slot, Letters, 4 In. 28.00
Bank, Mailbox, Rural, Sheet Metal, 10 In. 10.00
Bank, Mailbox, Tin, 9 In. 10.00
Bank, Mailbox, Wh-122 20.00 To 40.00
Bank, Mailbox, 4 1/4 X 3 1/4 In., Wh-126 30.00
Bank, Mammy, Wh-17 40.00
Bank, Mary Had A Little Lamb, 4 X 5 In. *Illus* 200.00

Mechanical banks were first made about 1870. Any bank with moving parts is considered mechanical, although those most collected are the metal banks made before World War I. Reproductions are being made.

Bank, Mechanical, Always Did 'Spise A Mule, Boy On Bench 250.00
Bank, Mechanical, Boys Stealing Watermelons, 6 In. *Illus* 5000.00
Bank, Mechanical, Cabin 190.00
Bank, Mechanical, Chief Big Moon, Iron, Painted 475.00
Bank, Mechanical, Church, Tin, Chein 80.00
Bank, Mechanical, Clown, Tin, Chein 28.00
Bank, Mechanical, Dinah 350.00
Bank, Mechanical, Dinah, Long Sleeve 195.00
Bank, Mechanical, Dinah, Short Sleeve, Cast Aluminum 180.00
Bank, Mechanical, Dog On Turntable 160.00
Bank, Mechanical, Eagle & Eaglettes 225.00 To 275.00
Bank, Mechanical, Elephant, Chein 25.00
Bank, Mechanical, Elephant, Swings Trunk 75.00
Bank, Mechanical, Football Kicker, Painted 1150.00
Bank, Mechanical, Globe On Arc 125.00
Bank, Mechanical, Globe On Stand 95.00 To 125.00
Bank, Mechanical, Hall's Excelsior 130.00
Bank, Mechanical, Humpty Dumpty, Chein 20.00
Bank, Mechanical, Independence Hall Tower, Centennial 180.00
Bank, Mechanical, Jolly Nigger, 1882 190.00
Bank, Mechanical, Lucky Negro, Starkie Patent 45.00
Bank, Mechanical, Monkey Holding Windup Organ, J.Chein & Co., 5 In. 25.00

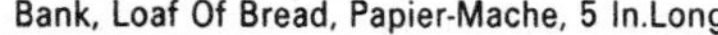

Bank, Loaf Of Bread, Papier-Mache, 5 In.Long

Bank, Mary Had A Little Lamb, 4 X 5 In.

Bank, Mechanical, Boys Stealing Watermelons, 6 In.

Bank, Mechanical, Professor Pug Frog's Great Bicycle Feat

Bank, Mechanical, Zoo, 4 In.

Bank, Mechanical, Owl, Turns Head .... 175.00 To 200.00
Bank, Mechanical, Paddy & Pig, Cast Iron 385.00
Bank, Mechanical, Presto 45.00
Bank, Mechanical, Professor Pug Frog's Great Bicycle Feat .... *Illus* 1500.00
Bank, Mechanical, Punch & Judy 325.00
Bank, Mechanical, Rocket, Metal 6.00
Bank, Mechanical, Saro Bank, Tin 250.00
Bank, Mechanical, Southern Comfort, Soldier Shoots Coin Into Bottle 50.00
Bank, Mechanical, Tammany Hall 100.00
Bank, Mechanical, Trapper Cabin, Cast Iron 135.00
Bank, Mechanical, Trick Dog, Solid Base 180.00
Bank, Mechanical, Trick Dog, 6-Part Base 245.00
Bank, Mechanical, Trunk, Registers Dimes To 10 Dollars, Iron, 1888 .... 48.00
Bank, Mechanical, Two Frogs 385.00
Bank, Mechanical, Uncle Wiggley, Tin, Chein 16.00
Bank, Mechanical, William Tell, Dated 1870 .... 285.00 To 275.00
Bank, Mechanical, Windmill, Tin 125.00
Bank, Mechanical, World's Fair 325.00
Bank, Mechanical, Woven Basket Shape, Iron, Copper Finish 5.00
Bank, Mechanical, Zoo, 4 In. .... *Illus* 500.00
Bank, Meter, Key, 25 Cent Slot, 8 X 5 In. 15.00
Bank, Middy Bank, Wh-26 .... 20.00 To 85.00
Bank, Monarch Paint Can 4.00
Bank, Money Box, Save N' Smile, Cast Iron 125.00

Bank, Negro Mammy, Glazed 8.50
Bank, Negro, Iron 75.00
Bank, Penguin, Papier-Mache, Crown Toy Co. 10.50
Bank, Penny, Cast Iron 2.95
Bank, Pershing, Iron 65.00
Bank, Peter Rabbit, Tin 30.00
Bank, Peters Weatherbird Shoes, Tin, 2 1/4 X 2 In. 75.00
Bank, Pig Sitting On Haunches, Brass 35.00
Bank, Pig Wearing Tuxedo, Bank On Republic 50.00
Bank, Pig, Chalk 16.50
Bank, Pig, Cream With Brown Splotch Glaze, 3 1/2 In. 16.00
Bank, Pig, Milk Glass 3.00
Bank, Pig, Seated, Wh-179 .... 20.00 To 35.00
Bank, Pig, Sitting, Rockingham Type, Mottled Brown & Yellow, 6 1/4 In. 30.00
Bank, Pig, Sitting, Wh-179 .... 24.00
Bank, Pig, Standing, Brass, W-176 .... 55.00
Bank, Pig, Wh-175 .... 35.00
Bank, Pig, Wh-182 .... 75.00
Bank, Pittsburgh Corning Glass 10.00
Bank, Plymouth County Trust Co., Brockton, Ma., Oval, Nickel Over Brass 8.00
Bank, Popeye, Daily Quarter, Tin 45.00
Bank, Porcelain, Girl Poking Head From Basket, German, 3 X 2 1/2 In. 20.00
Bank, Porky Pig & Barrel, Painted, Metal 35.00
Bank, Possum, Wh-205 .... 250.00
Bank, Prancing Horse 25.00
Bank, Puppy With Bee On Pillow 65.00
Bank, Rabbit, Iron 50.00
Bank, Rabbit, Red Egg In Red Basket, Slot In Egg, 11 1/2 In. 25.00
Bank, Radio, Marx, Red, With Key, 4 1/4 In. 12.00
Bank, Red Globe, Cast Iron, 5 In. 58.00
Bank, Red Goose School Shoes, Wh-215 .... 95.00
Bank, Redware, 1831, 7 In. 600.00
Bank, Register, Tin, Chein 5.00
Bank, Registering, Prudential, Cast Iron 55.00
Bank, Reindeer, Iron, White Paint 28.00
Bank, Rhinoceros, Wh-252 .... 325.00
Bank, Rooster, Wh-187 .... 35.00 To 45.00
Bank, Safe, Cast Iron, Patent 1891 .... 10.00
Bank, Safe, Coin Deposit On Door, Cast Iron, 7 In. 45.00
Bank, Safe, Figure Of Blacksmith In Relief, Cast Iron, Kenton 52.50
Bank, Safe, Iron, 5 In. .... *Illus* 30.00
Bank, Safe, Japanese, Iron, Wh-349 .... 33.00
Bank, Safe, Kenton's The Bank Of Industry, Nickel Plated, Raised Designed 75.00
Bank, Safe, Man & Dog Front, Angel Top, Combination Lock, Iron, 4 In. 18.75
Bank, Safe, Mosler Combination, Tin 7.00
Bank, Safe, National Safe 19.00
Bank, Safe, Royal Safe Deposits, Combination Lock, Iron, Decorated, 6 1/4 In. 47.50

Bank, Safe, Iron, 5 In.

Bank, Stove, Radiation, Tin, 6 In.

Bank, Safe, Star, Combination Door, Iron 25.00
Bank, Safe, Tiney Mite, Black Iron, Combination 18.00
Bank, Safe, Wh-347 ..... 40.00
Bank, Sailor, Seamen's Savings, Tin 5.00
Bank, Santa Claus, Wh-32 ..... 55.00
Bank, Schoolhouse, Iron 25.00
Bank, Scottie Dog, Metal 16.00
Bank, Scotties In Basket 34.00
Bank, Seated Pig On Iron Bank, Wh-179 ..... 37.50
Bank, Security Safe Deposit, Combination, 3 Floral Panels, 1870, 4 In. 40.00
Bank, Security Safe Deposit, Iron 125.00
Bank, Share Cropper, W-18 ..... 65.00
Bank, Sheep, Brass, Penny 12.00
Bank, Six-Sided Building, Wh-320 ..... 50.00
Bank, Skyscraper, 6 Towers, Wh-41 ..... 36.00
Bank, Spaniel, Staffordshire 50.00
Bank, Sports Safe, W-374 ..... 46.00
Bank, Square, Gold Trim, Security Safe Deposit, Movable Dial 55.00
Bank, Squirrel With Nut 425.00
Bank, State Bank, Iron 40.00
Bank, Statue Of Liberty, Iron, Painted ..... 29.00 To 65.00
Bank, Still, Iron, Square, Gold Trim, Security Safe Deposit, Movable Dial 55.00
Bank, Stove, Radiation, Tin, 6 In. ..... *Illus* 150.00
Bank, Tally Ho, Wh-168 ..... 95.00
Bank, Tank, Tin 25.00
Bank, Teddy Roosevelt, W-309 ..... 69.00
Bank, Texaco, Glass Baseball & Flying Red Horse 4.50
Bank, Three Little Pigs, Copper 6.00
Bank, Thrifty Dwarf 10.00
Bank, Tiny Building, Dome, Wh-424 ..... 16.00
Bank, Tootsie Roll, Cardboard & Tin 2.00
Bank, Topo The Mouse, Composition 4.00
Bank, Treasure Chest, 2 3/4 In. 25.00
Bank, Treasure Safe, Combination, Iron, 1897, 5 X 4 In. 25.00
Bank, Trolley, Wh-265 ..... 250.00
Bank, Trunk, Wh-232 ..... 33.00
Bank, Turkey, Wh-193 ..... 45.00
Bank, Uncle Wiggily, Chein 30.00
Bank, Underwood Typewriter, Metal, World's Fair, 1939 ..... 12.00
Bank, Watch Me Grow, Tin, 6 In. ..... *Illus* 35.00

Bank, Watch Me Grow, Tin, 6 In.

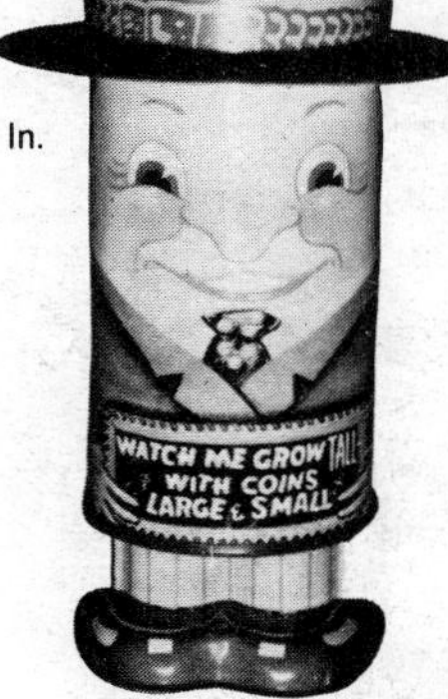

Bank, Witch's Pot, Red, 1 Nickel Register 55.00
Bank, Woolworth Building, Wh-387 ..... 30.00
Bank, World Globe, New York World's Fair, 1964-65, Pottery, Brown 4.50
Bank, World War I Hat, W-167 ..... 64.00
Bank, World War I Shell, Lb., ... 95.00
Bank, Zeppelin, W-171 ..... 55.00

Item		Price
Banko, Jar, Covered, Dogs And Figures, 6 In.		140.00
Banko, Match Holder & Receptacle, Elephants, 4 3/4 In.		58.00
Banko, Urn, Red, Birds & Bamboo, Multicolor Drip Glaze Top, 17 1/2 In.		895.00
Barbed Wire, T.V. Allis Buckhorn, 150 Ft.		100.00
Barometer, French, Pocket, Case		39.00
Barometer, German, 1930		8.50
Barz, Ewer, Cameo, Blue, Lavender, & Purple, Country & Windmill Scene, 17 In.		1350.00

Basalt is a black stoneware made by mixing iron and oxides into a basic clay. It is very hard and can be finished on a lathe. Wedgwood developed his famous black basalt in 1769, which was an improvement on a similar ware made in Staffordshire, England, as early as 1740. Basalt is still being made in England and on the Continent.

Item		Price
Basalt, Creamer, Ribbed Molded Body, C.1800, 4 In.		40.00
Basalt, Figurine, English Bulldog, Amber Eyes, 4 1/2 In.		95.00
Basalt, Figurine, Halloween Cat, 4 1/2 In.		95.00
Basalt, Sugar, Relief Of Woman & Children, Sheep, Impressed, Turner, C.1780		185.00
Basalt, Sugar, Widow Knop, Engine Turned, Lion Handles, C.1800, 6 In.		55.00
Basalt, Teapot & Stopper, Ovoid, Fluting, Case Mark, C.1780, 5 1/2 In.		475.00
Basalt, Teapot, Stand, Patrician Pattern, C.1790, 9 In.		475.00
Basket, Berry, Wood Slatted, Round, Impressed 1859 Union Mfg.Co., Set Of 4		56.00
Basket, Cheese Curd, Splint, Round		155.00
Basket, Deep, Rounded Shape, Hand-Painted, 17 In.		40.00
Basket, Double Check With Handle, 5 In. At Opening	*Illus*	75.00
Basket, Interlaced Rim, Twisted Handle, 5 X 6 1/4 In.	*Illus*	10.00
Basket, Japanese, C.1880, Woven Reeds, Multicolors, Round, 8 In.		95.00
Basket, Mission, Large, C.1800		350.00
Basket, Nootka, Rectangular, Checkerboard Cedar Bark, 10 X 4 In.		110.00
Basket, Peking Handles & Beads, Sewing, Footed		55.00
Basket, Pima, Large, C.1880		275.00
Basket, Round With Handle, 6 In.	*Illus*	27.50
Basket, Rye Straw, 2 Handles, 11 X 5 In.		28.00
Basket, Sewing, Wicker And Bentwood		62.50
Basket, Shaker, 35 X 19 1/2 In.		140.00
Basket, Straw, Covered, Handled, 12 X 9 X 8 In.		22.00
Basket, Swinging Lids, 2 X 3 1/4 In.	*Illus*	37.50
Basket, 7 In.Length	*Illus*	36.00
Batchelder, Tile, Peacock		35.00
Batman, Bank, Figural		6.00
Batman, Book, Coloring, 1966, 128 Pages		4.00
Batman, Mug, White Glass		3.00

Basket, Double Check With Handle, 5 In. At Opening

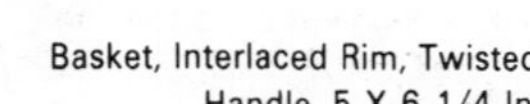

Basket, Interlaced Rim, Twisted Handle, 5 X 6 1/4 In.

Basket, Round With Handle, 6 In.

Basket, Swinging Lids, 2 X 3 1/4 In.

Battersea enamels are enamels painted on copper and made in the Battersea District of London from about 1750 to 1756. Many similar enamels are mistakenly called Battersea.

Battersea Type, Figurine, Buddha, 6 In. 100.00
Battersea, Box, Oval, Jade Green Body, I Present This To You, Etc., 1 In. 275.00
Battersea, Box, Stamp, Hinged Lid, Cobalt, Raised Enamel, 2 Bronze Inkwells 190.00
Bauer, Cup & Saucer, Lime 3.50

Bavaria was a district where many types of pottery and porcelain were made for centuries. The words Bavaria, Germany, appeared after 1871.

Bavarian, see also Rosenthal

Bavarian, Berry Set, Gold Rim, Yellow Roses, 6 Piece 45.00
Bavarian, Berry Set, Painted Wild Roses, Gold Trim, 5 Piece 42.00
Bavarian, Bottle, Perfume, Figure Of Ballerina, 1920s 25.00
Bavarian, Bowl, Cavalier Playing To Lady, Etzlich-Schutz, 9 In. 20.50
Bavarian, Bowl, Courting Scene, Pierced Gold Edge, 5 In. 4.50
Bavarian, Bowl, Grapes, Openwork, Oval, 9 1/2 In. 18.00
Bavarian, Bowl, Green Shaded, Red Orange Poppies, Handled, Oval, 8 1/4 In. 6.50
Bavarian, Bowl, Green Shaded, Strawberries & Floral, Gold Edge, 9 In. 34.00

Basket, 7 In.Length

Bavarian, Bowl, Orchid Flowers & Gold, Footed, 10 1/2 In. 15.00
Bavarian, Bowl, Portrait, Dark-Haired Lady, Cobalt & Gold, 10 1/4 In. 69.00
Bavarian, Bowl, Yellow Roses, Pierced Edge, 5 3/4 In. 6.00
Bavarian, Box, Dresser, Covered, Lavender & White Floral, Gold Trim 20.00
Bavarian, Box, Jewel, Apricot Roses, Art Nouveau Designs, Favorite Bavaria 98.00
Bavarian, Cachepot, White, Applied Leaf & Scroll Handles, 5 In. 8.00
Bavarian, Cachepot, White, Applied Scroll & Leaf Handles, 5 In. 6.00
Bavarian, Celery, Pink & White Roses, Gold Rim, Ragouse 25.00
Bavarian, Celery, Poppies & Gold, 12 X 5 1/2 In. 15.00
Bavarian, Chocolate Pot, White With Florals & Gold, C.S. With Crown 55.00
Bavarian, Chocolate Pot, White, Raised Pink Floral 65.00
Bavarian, Chocolate Set, Gold, Orange, & Green Floral, 13 Piece 48.00
Bavarian, Chocolate Set, White & Gold, Empire, Z.S.& Co., 12 Piece 135.00
Bavarian, Chocolate Set, Z.S. & Co., 3 Piece 55.00
Bavarian, Coffeepot, Bulbous, Pink & Lavender Flowers, Gold Trim, 9 In. 35.00
Bavarian, Coffeepot, White, Band Of Pink Roses, Gold Trim, 9 In. 14.00
Bavarian, Creamer, Floral Panels, Gold Trim, Octagonal 5.00
Bavarian, Creamer, Sevres Type, Hand-Painted 32.00
Bavarian, Cup & Saucer, Green, Pink & Red Roses, Gold Handle, Footed 12.50
Bavarian, Cup, Demitasse, Cobalt, Gold Tracery, Black Knight, Bavaria 38.50
Bavarian, Dish, Cheese, White, Pink & White Roses, Gold Trim 43.00
Bavarian, Eggcup, White, Gold Trim, Double 4.00
Bavarian, Figurine, Russian Wolfhound, 9 In. 29.00
Bavarian, Gravy Boat On Plate, Pink Roses, Lion Mark 10.00
Bavarian, Gravy Boat, Attached Tray, Crown Lion Ivory, Selb 26.00
Bavarian, Group, Madonna & Child, Blue & White, 13 In. 45.00
Bavarian, Hatpin Holder, Hand-Painted, R.C.Royal 30.00
Bavarian, Hatpin Holder, Yellow, Pink Roses, Gold Rim, Handles, Ruffled Top 30.00
Bavarian, Inkwell, Portrait, Martha & George Washington, White 30.00
Bavarian, Invalid Feeder, White 5.00

Bavarian, Muffineer, Hand-Painted Forget-Me-Nots 38.00
Bavarian, Pitcher, Lemonade, Heavy Gold With Purple Grapes, Z.S.Bavaria 55.00
Bavarian, Pitcher, Pint, Iridescent Finish, Two Peacocks 20.00
Bavarian, Plaque, White Roses On Shaded Pastels, Artist Signed, 12 1/2 In. 35.00
Bavarian, Plate, Bird, Duck Center, Green, Gold, Pierced, RM Bavaria 22.00
Bavarian, Plate, Bird, Gold Rim, Marked Wurtemburg 27.50
Bavarian, Plate, Blue & Gold Border, Hand-Painted, Signed, 7 1/2 In. 10.00
Bavarian, Plate, Cake, Green To Ivory, Roses, Gold Trim, Scalloped, 11 In. 45.00
Bavarian, Plate, Cake, Pink & Yellow Floral, Green Leaves, Z.S.& Co., 11 In. 30.00
Bavarian, Plate, Cake, Red Roses, Gold Trim, Pierced Handles, Z.S.Co., 11 In. 18.00
Bavarian, Plate, Favorite, Maroon & Green Designs, Green Border, 7 1/2 In. 9.00
Bavarian, Plate, Game, Pheasant, Roses & Gold Swags Border, 12 1/2 In. 85.00
Bavarian, Plate, Give Us This Day 30.00
Bavarian, Plate, Gray-Striped Cat, Gold Border, F.S.Holbrook, 1922, 10 In. 30.00
Bavarian, Plate, Green Shaded, Red Orange Poppies, 6 In. 4.50
Bavarian, Plate, Green Shaded, Red Orange Poppies, 8 In. 12.50
Bavarian, Plate, Green, Cream, & Gold, C.1859 .... 20.50
Bavarian, Plate, Green, Yellow Roses, Gold Trim, R C Versailles, 7 3/4 In. 6.50
Bavarian, Plate, Hand-Painted Floral, 7 1/2 In. 9.00
Bavarian, Plate, Hand-Painted Forget-Me-Nots, J & C, 7 3/4 In. 25.00
Bavarian, Plate, Peacocks And Floral Branches, 10 In. 27.50
Bavarian, Plate, Pink Roses, Lion Mark, 8 In. 3.00
Bavarian, Plate, Pink Roses, Shaded Ground, Gold Trim, 6 In. 4.00
Bavarian, Plate, Portrait, Queen Louise, Z.S.& Co., 7 1/2 In. 15.00
Bavarian, Plate, Thomas, Hand-Painted, Pink Flowers, Signed, 10 3/4 In. 25.00
Bavarian, Plate, Wedding Band, White & Gold, 7 3/4 In. 2.50
Bavarian, Platter, Pink Roses, Lion Mark, 13 In. 7.50
Bavarian, Platter, Scalloped Edge, Pink Rose, 15 In. 15.00
Bavarian, Relish, Roses, Handled, Blue Crown Mark, 10 In. 19.00
Bavarian, Relish, Violets, Leaf-Shaped Bowl, 10 In. 15.00
Bavarian, Sauce, Pink Roses, Shaded Ground, Gold Trim 4.00
Bavarian, Saucer, Pink Roses, Lion Mark 2.00
Bavarian, Sugar & Creamer, Cover, Orange Trumpet Flowers, Gold Trim 14.00
Bavarian, Sugar & Creamer, Covered, Gray Green Ground, Pink & Ivory Poppies 25.00
Bavarian, Sugar, Covered, Pink Roses, Lion Mark 10.00
Bavarian, Tankard, Left-Handed, Helmet Spout, Hand-Painted Grapes, 14 In. 195.00
Bavarian, Tea Set, Cobalt, Gold Floral & Leaf Swags, 3 Piece 38.00
Bavarian, Tea Set, Embossed, Purple Violets, 15 Piece 69.00
Bavarian, Teacup & Saucer, Gold 20.00
Bavarian, Teacup, Child's, Red Riding Hood & Wolf 5.00
Bavarian, Teapot, Berry Finial, Tan, White Roses, Green Trim, Thomas, 5 In. 55.00
Bavarian, Tray, Celery, Gold Rim, Pink, Yellow Roses, ZS Bavaria, 12 1/4 In. 24.00
Bavarian, Urn, Pink & Lavender Chrysanthemums, Covered, Marked, 11 In. 118.00
Bavarian, Vase, Embossed Gold Enamel Cover, 7 1/2 In. 29.00
Bavarian, Vase, Roses On Pastel Blue, H & Co., Artist Signed, 7 In. 175.00

Bayonet, see Weapon, Bayonet

Beach Babies, Cachepot, Ring Around The Rosie, Gold Handles, Royal Bayreuth 90.00
Beach Babies, Figurine, Ring Around The Rosie, Signed, Royal Bayreuth 90.00
Beaded Bag, Art Nouveau, Brown Suede & Marcasite, Silver Plate Frame, Chain 18.00
Beaded Bag, Black Velvet, Art Nouveau Metal Closure 8.50
Beaded Bag, Blue Ground, Silver Frame And Chain, 7 In. 37.00
Beaded Bag, Blue Iridescent, 9 In. 30.00
Beaded Bag, Blue, Green, Yellow, & Red, 9 In. 18.00
Beaded Bag, Change Purse, Mother-Of-Pearl Hinged Top, Gold Rim 18.00
Beaded Bag, Evening, Beige, 6 In. 7.00
Beaded Bag, French, Jewels, Blues & Roses, Silk Lining 45.00
Beaded Bag, German Silver Mesh, Flapper 14.00
Beaded Bag, Gorham Sterling Silver Mesh, 7 Pear-Shaped Drops, 5 3/8 In. 48.00
Beaded Bag, Jet Beads, Black Satin, Black Strap 5.00
Beaded Bag, Jet Beads, Drawstring 15.00
Beaded Bag, Mesh, Silver, Whiting & Davis 20.00
Beaded Bag, Multicolors, Goldtone Clasp 60.00
Beaded Bag, Silver Beads, Floral, German Silver Clasp 70.00
Beaded Bag, Silver Mesh, Chain Handle 15.00
Beaded Bag, Silver Mesh, Jeweled Clasp, Art Nouveau 20.00

Beaded Bag, Steel Mesh ... 12.00 To 15.00
Beaded Bag, Sterling Silver Mesh, 7 X 6 1/2 In. ... 35.00
Beaded Bag, Vicuna Hide, Polychrome Jewels, Chased Golden Frame, 9 In. ... 115.00
Beatles, Album, Record, A Hard Day's Night ... 15.00
Beatles, Album, Record, Rubber Soul ... 15.00
Beatles, Album, Record, Something New, Jacket ... 12.00
Beatles, Bank, Figural, Ringo, Marked England ... 15.00
Beatles, Bracelet, Figural Charm ... 10.00
Beatles, Bracelet, Pictures & Yeh, Yeh, Yeh, Marked Nems ... 10.00
Beatles, Button, I Love The Beatles, Round, 3 1/2 In. ... 3.00
Beatles, Button, Official Fan Club, 2 1/4 In. ... .50
Beatles, Cards, Deck, Marked England ... 10.00
Beatles, Decals, Set On Card ... 15.00
Beatles, Diary, 1965, Over 30 Pictures ... 5.00
Beatles, Doll, Four With Hair ... 45.00
Beatles, Doll, Paul McCartney, Plastic, 4 1/2 In. ... 8.00
Beatles, Figurine, John Lennon With Guitar, Bisque ... 7.50
Beatles, Game, Flip Your Wig, Boxed ... 20.00
Beatles, Key Chain, All Four Beatles ... 9.00
Beatles, Key Chain, Pictures & Yeh, Yeh, Yeh ... 10.00
Beatles, Lunch Box, Yellow Submarine ... 10.00
Beatles, Nodder, 4 Composition, 7 1/2 In. ... 95.00
Beatles, Pin, Picture, 3 1/2 In., Set Of 4 ... 15.00
Beatles, Record, Beatles VI, Capitol, No.T2358 ... 12.00
Beatles, Record, Meet The Beatles, Capitol, No.T2047 ... 12.00
Beatles, Record, Sgt.Pepper's Lonely Heart Club Band, Capitol ... 12.00
Beatles, Sharpener, Pencil ... 7.00
Beatles, Tie Tac, Beatle Heads, Gold, On Original Card ... 8.50
Beatles, Tie Tac, Ringo, Marked Nems, 1964 ... 7.00
Beatles, Toy, Yellow Submarine, Metal, Corgi Toys ... 15.00
Beatles, Tray, Pictures With Names, C.1964, 13 X 13 In. ... 12.00
Beatles, Tumbler, Figural, Glass ... 8.00
Beatles, Tumbler, Figural, Hard Plastic ... 8.00
Beatles, Wallet, Dated 1964 ... 20.00
Beatles, Wig ... 25.00

Beck, see also Buffalo Pottery

Beck, Game Set, Deer, Buffalo Pottery, 7 Piece ... 250.00
Beck, Gravy Boat & Underplate, Wall-Eyed Pike, Woodwin Pottery Co. ... 20.00
Beck, Plate, Calendar, 1914, Two Guinea, Signed R.C.Beck, 9 1/4 In. ... 38.00
Beck, Plate, Game, Water Spaniels Flushing Bird, Signed, 10 1/8 In. ... 35.00
Beck, Plate, Hanging, Large Turkeys, 12 In. ... 40.00
Beck, Plate, Retriever With Mallard & Bird Dog With Pheasant, 10 In., Pair ... 55.00
Beck, Plate, Swimming Fish, Green & Gold Border, Goodwin Co., 9 1/4 In. ... 10.00
Beck, Plate, Wall-Eyed Pike, Green & Gold Border, Goodwin Co., 9 1/4 In. ... 8.00
Beck, Platter, Fish And Lure, Signed, 14 In. ... 25.00
Beck, Platter, Game, Bass Caught On Lure, Signed, 14 In. ... 35.00
Beck, Stein, Lidded, Ornate, 1 Liter ... 52.50
Beck, Stein, Lidded, 2 Liter, Ornate & Colorful ... 52.50

Beehive, Austria, or Beehive, Vienna, china includes all the many types of decorated porcelain marked with the famous beehive mark. The mark has been used since the eighteenth century.

Beehive, see also Royal Vienna

Beehive, Bowl, Transfer Print, Amorous Scenes, Gold Trim, Oval, 10 X 4 In. ... 30.00
Beehive, Plate, Hand-Painted Roses, Signed Ullrich ... 25.00
Beehive, Plate, Oyster, Pink With Gold ... 35.00
Beehive, Syrup & Underplate, Green & White, Dancing Cherubs, Gold Trim ... 125.00
Beehive, Tray, Dresser, Green, Inset Of Lady & Man, Boucher, 9 X 6 1/2 In. ... 25.00
Beer Can, Abbot, English, 9 Oz. ... 1.00
Beer Can, Alta, 16 Oz. ... .75 To 1.00
Beer Can, Anheuser Busch Silver Light, 12 Oz. ... 1.00
Beer Can, Ballentine Ale, 1950, Copper, Quart ... 10.00
Beer Can, Ballentine Export Light, 1939 World's Fair, Copper, Quart ... 15.00
Beer Can, Beckers, 11 Oz. ... 7.00
Beer Can, Berghoff, 1887, Cone Top, 12 Oz. ... 20.00

Beer Can, Big Cat Malt, 12 Oz. .40
Beer Can, Big Cat, 12 Oz. 1.00
Beer Can, Black Label, Grey, 12 Oz. 3.00
Beer Can, Black Label, 12 Oz. .65
Beer Can, Bohemian, 12 Oz. .50
Beer Can, Boston Stock Ale, Cone, Quart 35.00
Beer Can, Breunigs, 12 Oz. .75
Beer Can, Brewers Best, Flat Top, 12 Oz. 8.00
Beer Can, Brewers Best, 16 Oz. 10.00
Beer Can, Brown Derby, Flat Top, 12 Oz. 6.00
Beer Can, Brown Derby, 12 Oz. .50
Beer Can, Brown Derby, 16 Oz. .75
Beer Can, Buckhorn No.73, 12 Oz. 1.00
Beer Can, Buckhorn, 12 Oz. .35
Beer Can, Budweiser Lager, All Over Label Gold, 12 Oz. 24.00
Beer Can, Budweiser, Quart, Flat Top 3.00
Beer Can, Burgemeister, Man Holding Glass Of Beer, Punchtop, 15 Oz. 6.25
Beer Can, Burgemeister, 12 Oz. .50
Beer Can, Burgemeister, 16 Oz. .75
Beer Can, Bush Bavarian, Flat Top, 12 Oz. 4.00
Beer Can, Canadian Ace, Chicago, Cone Top, 12 Oz. 20.00
Beer Can, Carling's Red Cap Ale, 12 Oz. .50
Beer Can, Champagne Velvet, Cone Top, 12 Oz. 18.00
Beer Can, Colt 45, Phoenix Suns, 1975-76 Bank, 12 Oz. 2.50
Beer Can, Colt, 45, 9 2/3 Oz. 1.00
Beer Can, Colt 45, 12 Oz. .50
Beer Can, Columbia, 12 Oz. .50
Beer Can, Coors, 7 Oz., 1964 3.00
Beer Can, Country Club, Red, Cone Top, 12 Oz. 14.00
Beer Can, Country Tavern, 12 Oz. .50
Beer Can, Courage Light, 9 2/3 Oz. 1.00
Beer Can, Courage, English, 9 Oz. 1.00
Beer Can, Das Enzig Whare, 1 Gallon 8.50
Beer Can, Draft Beer By Iroquois, 12 Oz. 2.00
Beer Can, Drewrys, 12 Oz. .25
Beer Can, Drummond Bros., 16 Oz. 1.00
Beer Can, Dunks, 12 Oz. 1.50 To 2.00
Beer Can, Dutch Club, Cone, 1 Gallon 45.00
Beer Can, Eastside, 16 Oz. .75
Beer Can, English, Tankard, 94 Oz. 10.00
Beer Can, Falls City, 12 Oz. .25 To .65
Beer Can, Falstaff Bicentennial, 12 Oz. .50
Beer Can, Falstaff Light, 12 Oz. .65
Beer Can, Falstaff President Series, Washington, 12 Oz. .50
Beer Can, Fischer, 16 Oz. .75
Beer Can, Fox Head Bock, 12 Oz. 10.00
Beer Can, Fuller's Pale Ale, 9 2/3 Oz. 1.00
Beer Can, Gablinger's Extra Light, 12 Oz. .75
Beer Can, Gablinger's, 12 Oz. .50
Beer Can, Gainsbury, English, 9 Oz. 1.00
Beer Can, Gainsbury's Bitter, English, 4 Pint 10.00
Beer Can, German Moninger Export, Barrel Shape, 5 Liter 15.00
Beer Can, Gibbons, George Washington, 12 Oz. .60
Beer Can, Goetz, 12 Oz. .50
Beer Can, Grain Belt Bock, 12 Oz. 1.25
Beer Can, Grain Belt, Heieman, 12 Oz. .50
Beer Can, Grain Belt, 16 Oz. 1.25
Beer Can, Grolsch Tall Ships, White, 12 Oz. 1.00 To 10.00
Beer Can, Hals, 12 Oz. 33.00
Beer Can, Hamms, Flat Top, 12 Oz. 6.00
Beer Can, Hanley, 12 Oz. .50
Beer Can, Harp Guinness, 9 2/3 Oz. 1.00
Beer Can, Harvard 25th Reunion Class Of '41, 12 Oz. 15.00
Beer Can, Heidel Brau, 12 Oz. .50
Beer Can, Heineken, 9 2/3 Oz. 1.00

Beer Can, Henninger Export, 1 Gallon 10.00
Beer Can, Horlacher Hex, 12 Oz. .... .75 To 1.00
Beer Can, Huber Bock, 12 Oz. .... .50 To .65
Beer Can, Hudepohl Draft, 1 Gallon 35.00
Beer Can, India Coope, English, 9 Oz. 1.00
Beer Can, Ivy League, 12 Oz. 1.00
Beer Can, Jax, 12 Oz. .... .35
Beer Can, King Kullen, Quart 5.00
Beer Can, King Snedleys, 12 Oz. .... .75
Beer Can, Kingsbury Brew, 12 Oz. .... .50
Beer Can, Kingsbury Malt Tonic, Punch Top, 12 Oz. 2.50
Beer Can, Lammers, 12 Oz. 1.00
Beer Can, Light Olympia, 16 Oz. 10.00
Beer Can, Lone Star, 12 Oz. .... .50
Beer Can, Longlife, English, 9 Oz. 1.00
Beer Can, Longlife, English, 15 1/2 Oz. 1.00
Beer Can, Longlife, 9 2/3 Oz. 1.00
Beer Can, Lucky Bock, 12 Oz. .... .50
Beer Can, Lucky Lager, 12 Oz. .... .50
Beer Can, Lucky Lager, 16 Oz. .... .75
Beer Can, Lucky Malt Liquor, 16 Oz. 15.00
Beer Can, Lucky, President Adams, 12 Oz. .... .75
Beer Can, Lucky, President Washington, 12 Oz. .... .75
Beer Can, Manheim, Flat Top, Quart 4.00
Beer Can, Mark V, 12 Oz. .... .50
Beer Can, Matterhorn, 16 Oz. 4.25
Beer Can, McEwan's, English, 15 1/2 Oz. 1.50
Beer Can, McEwan's, English, 9 Oz. 1.00
Beer Can, Metz, Flat Top, Quart 8.00
Beer Can, Michelob, Bowling Pin Shape, 12 Oz. 10.00
Beer Can, Miller Lite, 16 Oz. .... .75
Beer Can, Millers, White, Flat Top, Quart 5.00
Beer Can, Milwaukee, Cone Top, 12 Oz. 2.00
Beer Can, Mule, 16 Oz. 9.00
Beer Can, National Bohemian, Flat Top, Quart 6.00
Beer Can, National Bohemian, Quart 80.00
Beer Can, National Bohemian, 12 Oz. 48.00
Beer Can, Neuweiler's Cream Ale, Cone Top, 12 Oz. 30.00
Beer Can, Neuweiler's Pilsener Beer, Cone Top, 12 Oz. 35.00
Beer Can, Neuweiler's Pilsener, Multicolor, 1947, Quart 235.00
Beer Can, New Castle Amber Ale, 1 Gallon 7.00
Beer Can, New Falstaff, 12 Oz. .... .50
Beer Can, Newcastle, English, 15 1/2 Oz. 1.50
Beer Can, Nine O'five, 12 Oz. .... .65
Beer Can, Octoberfest, 1 Gallon 25.00
Beer Can, Ohio State Rose Bowl Record, 1974, 12 Oz. 3.00
Beer Can, Oktoberfest, 1 Gallon 4.00
Beer Can, Old Bohemian, 1 Gallon .... 15.00 To 35.00
Beer Can, Old Crown Beer, 12 Oz. .... .50
Beer Can, Old Dutch, 12 Oz. .... .40
Beer Can, Old Frothingslosh, 12 Oz. .... .75
Beer Can, Old German Brand, Cone Top, 12 Oz. 13.00
Beer Can, Old Milwaukee, 16 Oz. .... .75
Beer Can, Old Peculiar, 9 203 Oz. 1.00
Beer Can, Old Topper Snappy Ale, Cone Top, 12 Oz. 15.00
Beer Can, Old Tyme, Flat Top, Quart 7.00
Beer Can, Olde English 800, 16 Oz. .... .75
Beer Can, Olympia Gold, 12 Oz. .... .50
Beer Can, Olympia, Flat Top, Quart 5.00
Beer Can, Ortels, 92, Cone Top, 12 Oz. 17.00
Beer Can, Ortlieb Mummers Parade, 12 Oz. 1.00
Beer Can, Ortlieb, Tea Party, 12 Oz. .... .60
Beer Can, Oyster House, 12 Oz. .... .75
Beer Can, Paulaner, 1 Gallon .... 8.50 To 20.00
Beer Can, Pearl Light, 8 Oz. .... .45

Beer Can, Pearl Light, 12 Oz. .45
Beer Can, Phoenix Suns, 1973-74, 12 Oz. 3.00
Beer Can, Point Bicentennial, 12 Oz. 1.00
Beer Can, Polaski Pivo, 12 Oz. 1.00
Beer Can, Premium Light, 12 Oz. .65
Beer Can, Primo, 12 Oz. 1.00
Beer Can, Rainier Ale, 12 Oz. .50
Beer Can, Rainier Ale, 16 Oz. .75
Beer Can, Rainier Beer, 16 Oz. .75
Beer Can, Reading Light, 16 Oz. .75
Beer Can, Reading, Misprint, 16 Oz. 3.00
Beer Can, Reading, 16 Oz. 1.00
Beer Can, Red Cap Ale, 12 Oz. .40
Beer Can, Rheingold Scotch Ale, Flat Top, Quart 10.00
Beer Can, Rheinlander, Huber, 12 Oz. .50
Beer Can, Rheinlander, Seattle, 12 Oz. .50
Beer Can, Robin Hood, 16 Oz. 1.00
Beer Can, Rolling Rock, 7 Oz. .25 To .45
Beer Can, San Manguel, 12 Oz. 2.00
Beer Can, Schlitz Light, 12 Oz. .50
Beer Can, Schlitz Tall Boy, 1960, Flat Top, Quart 9.00
Beer Can, Schlitz, Cone Top, 12 Oz. 18.00
Beer Can, Schlitz, 1949, Flat Top, Quart 8.00
Beer Can, Schmidt, Cornwallis, 16 Oz. 1.00
Beer Can, Schmidt, Signers Of The Declaration, 12 Oz. 1.00
Beer Can, Schmidt, Valley Forge, 12 Oz. .60
Beer Can, Schmidt, 16 Oz. 1.00
Beer Can, Schmidt's Tiger Ale, Flat Top, 12 Oz. 12.00
Beer Can, Skol, English, 9 Oz. 1.00
Beer Can, Skol, 9 2/3 Oz. 1.00
Beer Can, Spring Beer, 12 Oz. .50
Beer Can, Stauder Pilsener, 1 Gallon 12.00
Beer Can, Steelers, 1975, 12 Oz. 1.00
Beer Can, Steelers, 1976, 12 Oz. .50
Beer Can, Stegmaier Bible, No.2738, 12 Oz. 12.00
Beer Can, Steinbrau, Flat Top, 12 Oz. 5.00
Beer Can, Sterling, 12 Oz. .35
Beer Can, Stortz, Flat Top, 12 Oz. 5.00
Beer Can, Storz Triumph, 12 Oz. 1.25
Beer Can, Stout Malt Liquor, 16 Oz. 5.00
Beer Can, Tartan, English, 15 1/2 Oz. 1.00
Beer Can, Tecate, 16 Oz. .75
Beer Can, Tennents Lager, Yellow, Red, Flat Top, Quart 9.00
Beer Can, Theakston, 9 2/3 Oz. 1.00
Beer Can, Tivoli Bible, 12 Oz. 4.00
Beer Can, Toby, English, 9 Oz. 1.00
Beer Can, Truman, English, 9 Oz. 1.00
Beer Can, Unser Feldschlobschen, 1 Gallon 9.50
Beer Can, Valley Forge Birch Beer, 12 Oz. 1.50
Beer Can, Walters Bicentennial, 12 Oz. 1.00
Beer Can, Watney's Pale, English, 15 1/2 Oz. 1.00
Beer Can, Watney's Pale, 9 2/3 Oz. 1.00
Beer Can, Watney's Party Four, English, 4 Pint 10.00
Beer Can, Watney's Party Seven, English, 8 Pint 12.00
Beer Can, Wellington, 12 Oz. 6.00
Beer Can, West Virginia, 12 Oz. 3.00
Beer Can, Whitbread Ale, English, 9 Oz. 100 1.50
Beer Can, Whitbread Pale Ale, 9 2/3 Oz. 1.00
Beer Can, White Schells, 12 Oz. 3.00
Beer Can, Wisconsin Club, 12 Oz. .50
Beer Can, Worthington Special Bitter, 1 Gallon 9.50
Beer Can, Wunderbar, 12 Oz. 20.00
Beer Can, Yuengling, 12 Oz. .50
Beer Can, Zodiak By Peter Hand, 12 Oz. 1.00
Beer Can, 102 Stout, 16 Oz. 8.00
Beer Can, 905 Light, 12 Oz. .50

Bells have been made of china, glass, or metal. All types are collected.

Bell, see also Bohemian Glass, Bell; Custard Glass, Bell

Bell, Art Glass, Violet Color, Applied Blue Threading, Colored Canes, 11 In. 245.00
Bell, Brass, C.1650, 4 In. 20.00
Bell, Brass, Chinese, Dinner, Brass Mallet, Teak Stand, 3 1/2 In. 25.00
Bell, Brass, Chinese, 7 In. 58.00
Bell, Brass, Dinner, Chinese, Pagoda Shape, 3 3/4 In. 5.00
Bell, Brass, Door, Hussel & Erwin, Conn., 1893, Iron Frame 38.00
Bell, Brass, Figural, Lucy Locket, 6 In. 110.00
Bell, Brass, Lady With Hoop Skirt, 4 In. 15.00
Bell, Brass, Made In Peking, 1926 .... 24.00
Bell, Brass, Old Woman, Legs Are Clappers 22.00
Bell, Brass, Saucer, Eagle Center, Children & Cupids Handle, 6 In. 45.00
Bell, Brass, School, Wooden Handle, 6 1/2 In. 16.00
Bell, Brass, School, Wooden Handle, 7 In. 20.00
Bell, Brass, School, Wooden Handle, 8 In. 22.00
Bell, Brass, School, 5 1/2 In. 12.00
Bell, Brass, School, 7 In. 16.00
Bell, Brass, Sleigh, 26 On Strap 80.00
Bell, Brass, Sleigh, 44 On Strap 185.00
Bell, Brass, Streetcar, Foot Operated, 13 In. 45.00
Bell, Brass, String Of 5 Half Bells, Conestoga Wagon, Iron Frame 85.00
Bell, Brass, Teacher's, Brass Handle, 5 In. 30.00
Bell, Brass, Wooden Handle, 4 In. 8.00
Bell, Brass, Wooden Handle, 6 1/4 In. 14.00
Bell, Brass, 1878 Saignelegier, Chaintel Fondeur, Cast, 4 In. 24.00
Bell, Bronze, Amberlike Handle, 4 In. 12.00
Bell, Bronze, Angel Holder And Embossed Cupids 85.00
Bell, Bronze, Coal & Wood, Arizona, 1925 .... 6.00
Bell, Camel's, Bronze, Diamond Figures Around Outside, 5 X 9 In. 50.00
Bell, Cast Iron, Mechanical, Owl's Head, Glass Eyes, German, 4 3/4 In. 125.00
Bell, China, German, Flapper In Yellow Dress, 4 1/2 In. 22.50
Bell, Cow, Leather Collar 6.00
Bell, Cow, New England, 5 1/2 In. 5.95
Bell, Cow, Sargent, Kentucky, No.2, New Haven, Conn. 35.00
Bell, Dinner, Ornate Sterling Handle 8.50
Bell, Door, Hand Cranked, Solid Brass, Through The Door 45.00
Bell, Dutch Girl, Brass, 6 In. 15.00
Bell, Figural, Lady, Curved Skirt, Heavy Brass, 3 1/4 In. 32.00
Bell, Fire Alarm, From Horse-Drawn Fire Engine, Bracket, 7 In. 30.00
Bell, French Crystal, Dinner, Ruffled Edge, 3-Ball Finial, 8 In. 35.00
Bell, Glass, Blue 45.00
Bell, Glass, Ruby Stained, Wide Band At Base With Gold, Clapper 75.00
Bell, Gold Metal, On Footed Stand Decorated With Pearls 7.00
Bell, Horse's Hoof, Tap, Stars III, 1927-1939 .... 145.00
Bell, Iron, Cow, Hand Forged, Wooden Clapper 15.00
Bell, Iron, Dinner, Hanger, 14 In. 100.00
Bell, Iron, Farm, Yoke, 18 In. 225.00
Bell, Iron, Sheep 2.50
Bell, Iron, Sleigh, String Of 39 .... 40.00
Bell, Iron, Trolley Car, C.1900, Wall Type, Pull Rope, 9 In. 55.00
Bell, Majolica, Cat Shape 27.50
Bell, Nailsea, Cranberry & Opaque Loops, Clear Handle, Colored Canes, 9 In. 275.00
Bell, Nickel Plate Over Iron & Brass, Tap, Leaf Design, 3 Footed 7.95
Bell, Nickel, Dinner, Ornate 8.00
Bell, Occupied Japan, Little Girl Figural, 3 In. 8.00
Bell, Pewter, Sterling Silver Handle 20.00
Bell, Pressed Glass, Smokey 2.50
Bell, School With Wooden Handle, Brass, 8 1/2 In. 39.00
Bell, School, Brass, 6 X 10 1/2 In. 50.00
Bell, School, Wooden Handle, Brass, 10 1/2 In. 48.00
Bell, School, Wooden Handle, 6 1/2 In. 65.00
Bell, School, Wooden Handle, 8 1/4 In. 75.00
Bell, School, Wooden Handle, 9 1/2 In. 85.00
Bell, School, 5 In. 43.00
Bell, Schoolmaster's Handbell, Nickel Silver, 6 1/2 In. 25.00

Bell, Schoolmaster's, Hand, 5 1/2 In. 25.00
Bell, Sleigh, String Of 39, Iron 40.00
Bell, Sleigh, 24 Graduated On Leather Strap 95.00
Bell, Sleigh, 26 On Strap .... 52.00 To 80.00
Bell, Sleigh, 29, Unstrung, Each Dated 1876 .... 79.00
Bell, Sleigh, 44 On Strap 185.00
Bell, St.Claire Glass, Bicentennial 5.00
Bell, Sterling Silver, Birth Record, Sterling Chain 22.50
Bell, Sterling Silver, Colonial Woman, Vermeil, 3 1/2 In. 115.00
Bell, Tumbler, Hand-Blown, Lead Crystal, Diamond Pattern, Signed, Set Of 6 .... 125.00

Belle Ware was made in 1903 by Carl V. Helmschmied. In 1904 he started a corporation known as the Helschmied Manufacturing Company. His factory closed in 1908 and he worked on his own until his death in 1934.

Belle Ware, Box, Blue & White, Blue Floral, Brass Collar, Round, 5 1/2 In. 60.00
Belle Ware, Dish, Pin, Opalescent, Violet Decoration, Silk Lined, 3 1/2 In. 55.00
Belle Ware, Saltshaker, Blue With White, Sanded Finish 125.00
Belle Ware, Sugar & Creamer, Yellow To White, Enamel Floral, Twisted Handle 145.00
Belle Ware, Syrup, Egg Base, Lid, Pink Flowers, Decorated 55.00
Belle Ware, Syrup, Opaline, Egg Base 95.00

Belleek china is made in Ireland, other European countries, and the United States. The glaze is creamy yellow and appears wet. The first Belleek was made in 1857.

Belleek, see also Ceramic Art Co., Haviland, Lenox, Matt Morgan, Ott & Brewer

Belleek, Basket, Henshall's, Black Mark, 11 In. 575.00
Belleek, Basket, Purse, 1st Black Mark, 6 In. 220.00
Belleek, Basket, Purse, 2nd Black Mark, 6 In. 190.00
Belleek, Basket, 1st Period, Round, 3 Strand, 8 In. 350.00
Belleek, Basket, 3 Strand, 1st Period, Woven, 12 X 2 In. 450.00
Belleek, Bowl, Cardium On Coral Shell, Pink Edged, 2nd Black Mark, 4 1/2 In. 185.00
Belleek, Bowl, Mask, Yellow Lining, 3rd Black Mark, 4 1/2 X 2 7/8 In. 40.00
Belleek, Bowl, Slop, Enamel Ware, Roses, 2nd Black Mark, 5 In. 40.00
Belleek, Bowl, White, Gray Marbling, 1st Black Mark, 8 In. 75.00
Belleek, Bowl, Willet, Browns, Yellow Roses Top, May Peisen, 1905, 8 1/4 In. 50.00
Belleek, Bust, Clyte, 2nd Black Mark, 9 In. 890.00
Belleek, Centerpiece, 1st Black Mark, 3 Holder, 7 X 10 In. 550.00
Belleek, Chalice, Willet, Portrait Medallion, Lady, 3 Handles, 1906, 7 1/2 In. 350.00
Belleek, Cheese House, Doors, Windows, & Chimney, Green Mark, 6 3/4 In. 72.50
Belleek, Coffeepot, Harp Shamrock, Gold Trim, 3rd Black Mark 95.00
Belleek, Coffeepot, Yellow Limpet, 3rd Black Mark 95.00
Belleek, Compote, Dolphin Pedestal, 1st Black Mark, 10 X 3 1/4 In. 325.00
Belleek, Compote, Hand Holding Shell, White, 4 1/2 X 3 In. 35.00
Belleek, Compote, Shell, Dolphin Base, 1st Black Mark 165.00
Belleek, Creamer, Figural, Swan, Black Mark, 3 1/4 In. 77.50
Belleek, Creamer, Purple & Green Shamrocks On Basketweave, 1st Mark 75.00
Belleek, Creamer, Shamrock Pattern, Twig Handle, 2nd Black Mark 25.00
Belleek, Creamer, Shamrock, 3rd Black Mark, 3 Feet, Twig Handle 38.00
Belleek, Creamer, Shell, Hound, Harp, & Castle Mark 15.00
Belleek, Creamer, Shell, Miniature, Pink Trim, 2nd Black Mark 75.00
Belleek, Creamer, Shell, 2nd Black Mark, 4 In. 58.00
Belleek, Creamer, Toy, Cleary, Twisted Pink Handle, 2nd Black Mark 60.00
Belleek, Cup & Saucer, Demitasse, Willet, Floral & Molded Arches, Twig Handle 90.00
Belleek, Cup & Saucer, Demitasse, Yellow Limpet, 3rd Black Mark 30.00
Belleek, Cup & Saucer, Demitasse, 3rd Black Mark 40.25
Belleek, Cup & Saucer, Erne, White, Pink Trim, 2nd Black Mark 40.00
Belleek, Cup & Saucer, Harp Shamrock, 3rd Black Mark 37.50
Belleek, Cup & Saucer, Neptune, 1st Green Mark 32.50
Belleek, Cup & Saucer, Neptune, 2nd Black Mark .... 40.00 To 46.00
Belleek, Cup & Saucer, Pink Nautilus, Shell Feet, Black Mark 45.00
Belleek, Cup & Saucer, Pink Trim, Gold Outline, Hexagonal, 2nd Black Mark 45.00
Belleek, Cup & Saucer, Shamrock, Basket Weave, 3rd Black Mark 40.00
Belleek, Cup & Saucer, Shamrock, Harp & 2nd Black Mark 32.00
Belleek, Cup & Saucer, Shell, Pink Rims & Handle, Black Mark 35.00
Belleek, Cup & Saucer, Tridacna, Pink Trim, 2nd Black Mark 35.00

Belleek, Cup & Saucer, Willets, White, Heavy Gold And Blue Enamel 65.00
Belleek, Cup & Saucer, Yellow Limpet, 3rd Black Mark 30.00
Belleek, Cup, Demitasse, 2 1/4 In. 20.00
Belleek, Cup, Loving, Palette Mark, Violets, Gold Handles, Pedestal, 1905 ..... 158.00
Belleek, Cup, Tridacna, Pink 20.00
Belleek, Dish, Candy, Covered, Commemorative, Belleek Anniversary 375.00
Belleek, Dish, Heart Shape, 2nd Black Mark, 5 In. 33.00
Belleek, Dish, Leaf Shape, 2nd Green Mark, 5 In. 12.00
Belleek, Dish, Sauce, Willets, White Enamel Floral On Square Rim 20.00
Belleek, Figurine, Affection, 1st Black Mark, 14 1/2 In. 1050.00
Belleek, Figurine, Cardium On Coral, 3rd Black Mark, Irish 135.00
Belleek, Figurine, Leprechaun, Green Mark, 4 1/2 In. 35.00
Belleek, Figurine, Meditation, Polychrome Glaze, 1st Black Mark, 14 1/2 In. 105.00
Belleek, Figurine, Sea Horse With Shell, 1st Black Mark Impressed, 4 In. 195.00
Belleek, Figurine, Seated Pig, Irish, Green Mark, 3 1/2 In. 30.00
Belleek, Figurine, Swan, First Black Mark 84.00
Belleek, Figurine, Woman & Man With Baskets, Black Mark, 7 1/2 In., Pair 150.00
Belleek, Frame, Oval, 1st Black Mark, Green Coral, Pink Conch Shells, 9 In. 690.00
Belleek, Honey Pot, Shamrock, 2nd Black Mark 145.00
Belleek, Jar, Biscuit, Diamond, 2nd Black Mark 225.00
Belleek, Kettle, Water, Shamrock, Handle, 2nd Black Mark 125.00
Belleek, Match Holder, Figural, Little Red Riding Hood, 3 1/2 In. 85.00
Belleek, Muffineer, Lenox, 7 In. 45.00
Belleek, Mug, American, Pallet Mark, Monk Drinking Wine, Brown, Colors 75.00
Belleek, Mug, Brown & Green Pinecones, Palette Mark, 5 In. 35.00
Belleek, Mug, Grasses, White, Yellow Luster, Green Mark, 1956 ..... 10.00
Belleek, Mug, Stork Decoration, American 110.00
Belleek, Mug, Two-Handled, Sons Of St. Patrick, March 17, 1898, Wreath Mark 135.00
Belleek, Mug, Willet, Art Nouveau, Red Lines On Tan, 12 Birds, 4 1/2 In. 95.00
Belleek, Mug, Willet, Dark Brown, Indian's Head With Feather 40.00
Belleek, Mug, Willet, Hand-Painted Grapes, 4 1/2 In. 45.00
Belleek, Mug, Willet, Left Handed, Man Sipping Wine, H.A.Tunseh, 1909, Red 135.00
Belleek, Mug, Willet, Portrait, Man Drinking 95.00
Belleek, Mug, Yellow Corn And Husks On Brown, Palette Mark, 5 In. 55.00
Belleek, Pitcher, Bacchus & Grape, Blown-Out, Green Mark, 6 In. 40.00
Belleek, Pitcher, Pear Shape, 4 1/2 In. 65.00
Belleek, Pitcher, White, Classical Style, 2nd Black Mark, 8 In. 85.00
Belleek, Pitcher, Willet, Hand-Painted Floral, Dragon Handle, 11 In. 105.00
Belleek, Plate, Bread, Neptune, Green Trim, 2nd Black Mark 37.00
Belleek, Plate, Cake, Basket Weave, Black Mark, 9 1/3 In. 55.00
Belleek, Plate, Cake, Handles, Grass, 1st Black Mark 55.00
Belleek, Plate, Cake, Rose & Morning Glory, 1st Black Mark, 9 1/2 In. 165.00
Belleek, Plate, Cake, Seashell, Black Mark 65.00
Belleek, Plate, Cake, 2nd Black Mark, 7 In. 15.00
Belleek, Plate, Hawthorne Pattern, Blue, Gold, 1st Black Mark, C.1878 ..... 125.00
Belleek, Plate, Neptune, Pink Trim, 6 In. 15.00
Belleek, Plate, Sandwich, Shamrock, Basket Weave, Black Mark, 7 1/4 In. 18.00
Belleek, Plate, Shamrock, Basket Weave, 3rd Black Mark, 6 1/2 In. 20.00
Belleek, Plate, Sunray, Hand-Reticulated Edge, Fermanagh, 9 1/2 In. 60.00
Belleek, Salt & Scoop, Fermanagh, Black Mark, Oval, 3 In. 32.00
Belleek, Salt, Pink Trim, 1st Mark 35.00
Belleek, Salt, Shamrock, Black Mark, Oval, 3 In. 20.00
Belleek, Salt, Shell, Handled, Green Mark, 4 X 3 In. 10.00
Belleek, Salt, Tridacna, 1st Green Mark 10.00
Belleek, Salt, White, Gold Trim, Footed, Pallet With L In Circle, M In Gold, 6 ..... 65.00
Belleek, Salt, Willet, Footed, Set Of 6 ..... 55.00
Belleek, Saucer, Morning Glory & Monogram, 5 1/4 In. 20.00
Belleek, Spill, Floral, Black Mark, 3 1/4 In. 65.00
Belleek, Sugar & Creamer, Echinus, Gilt Trim, 2nd Black Mark 85.00
Belleek, Sugar & Creamer, Hexagon, Green Trim, 2nd Black Mark 70.00
Belleek, Sugar & Creamer, Ivory, Embossed Berries & Leaves, Green Mark 28.00
Belleek, Sugar & Creamer, Ivy, 3rd Black Mark ..... 40.00 To 61.50
Belleek, Sugar & Creamer, Lily, Green Trim, 3rd Black Mark 56.00
Belleek, Sugar & Creamer, Lotus, Yellow Handle, 3rd Black Mark 60.00
Belleek, Sugar & Creamer, Mask, Bacchus, 3rd Black Mark 58.00
Belleek, Sugar & Creamer, New Shell, 3rd Black Mark 75.00

Belleek, Sugar & Creamer, Ribbon, 3rd Black Mark 48.00
Belleek, Sugar & Creamer, Shamrock, Green Mark 40.00
Belleek, Sugar & Creamer, Shamrock, 3rd Black Mark 75.00
Belleek, Sugar & Creamer, Shell Feet, Black Mark 95.00
Belleek, Sugar & Creamer, Tangerine Trim, Black Mark 55.00
Belleek, Sugar & Creamer, Toy, Shell, 3rd Green Mark 26.00
Belleek, Sugar & Creamer, Twig Finial, Shamrock, 3rd Black Mark 85.00
Belleek, Sugar & Creamer, White, Yellow Interior 55.00
Belleek, Sugar, Covered, Grass, 1st Black Mark 55.00
Belleek, Sugar, Shamrock Pattern, 3rd Black Mark 25.00
Belleek, Sugar, Shamrock, Basket Weave, 1st Green Mark 22.00
Belleek, Sugar, Yellow Limpet, 3rd Black Mark 25.00
Belleek, Swan, Green Mark, 4 1/2 In. 45.00
Belleek, Swan, Trumpet Flower Vase, 1st Black Mark, 4 In. 165.00
Belleek, Swan, 3rd Green Mark, 4 1/2 In. 12.00
Belleek, Tankard, Grapes, Gold Handle, Signed KR, April, 1904, 14 In. 175.00
Belleek, Tea Set, Limpet, Black Mark, 80 Piece 850.00
Belleek, Tea Set, Neptune, Pink Trim, 2nd Black Mark, 8 Piece 900.00
Belleek, Tea Set, Shamrock, Twig Handles, 3rd Black Mark, 3 Piece 165.00
Belleek, Tea Set, Shamrock, 2nd Black Mark 275.00
Belleek, Tea Set, Tridacna, Green Trim, 2nd Black Mark, 7 Piece 300.00
Belleek, Tea Set, Willet, Cream Color, Sterling Overlay, Scenic, 3 Piece 275.00
Belleek, Tea Set, Willet, Pink Floral, Green And Gold Lines, Chains Of Gilt 125.00
Belleek, Teakettle, Grass, Overhead Handle & Stand, 1st Black Mark 450.00
Belleek, Teakettle, White, 3rd Black Mark 98.00
Belleek, Teapot, Grass, Large, 1st Black Mark 225.00
Belleek, Teapot, Neptune, Green Trim, 2nd Black Mark 125.00
Belleek, Teapot, Shamrock, 3rd Black Mark 100.00
Belleek, Teapot, Tea Making Instructions In Lid, 1st Mark, Grass Pattern 235.00
Belleek, Teapot, Tridacna, Green Trim, 2nd Black Mark 125.00
Belleek, Teapot, Willet, Cream Color, Silver Deposit Dutch Scene 80.00
Belleek, Teapot, Yellow Limpet, 3rd Black Mark 95.00
Belleek, Tray, Swirled, Pink Scalloped Edge, 2nd Black Mark, 17 In. 165.00
Belleek, Tub, Butter, Shamrock, 2nd Black Mark 22.00
Belleek, Vase, Aberdeen, Applique Floral, 2nd Black Mark, 9 In. 245.00
Belleek, Vase, Bud, Lenox, Enamel Florals, Artist M.W.Roberts 85.00
Belleek, Vase, Flying Fish, 1st Black Mark 125.00
Belleek, Vase, Green Shamrocks, Embossed Daisies, 3rd Green Mark, 5 1/2 In. 22.00
Belleek, Vase, Lenox, Palette Mark, Art Nouveau, Red, Gold, Black, 6 In. 80.00
Belleek, Vase, Metallic Crackle, Early Art Nouveau, Artist Signed 75.00
Belleek, Vase, Nile, Large, Irish 223.00
Belleek, Vase, Portrait, Woman Wearing Long Dress, White Lilies, 14 In. 210.00
Belleek, Vase, Scenic, Boats, Water, Land, Willets, 15 3/4 In. 95.00
Belleek, Vase, Shell, White, Pink Trim, 2nd Black Mark, 9 In. 165.00
Belleek, Vase, Spill, 2nd Black Mark 325.00
Belleek, Vase, Tree, Shamrocks, 2nd Mark 49.00
Belleek, Vase, Tulip, Purple Luster Blooms, 1st Black Mark, 9 In. 435.00
Belleek, Vase, Willet, Art Deco, Artist Signed, Dated 1905, 10 In. 145.00
Belleek, Vase, Willet, Blue, Green, Yellow, & Orange, Nasturtiums, 1903, 8 In. 185.00
Belleek, Vase, Willet, Hand-Painted Poppies, 11 In. 85.00
Belleek, Vase, Willet, Hand-Painted Roses, Gold Trim, 15 In. 230.00
Belleek, Vase, Willet, Hand-Painted Roses, 13 In. 125.00
Belleek, Vase, Willet, Landscape At Twilight, 16 In. 150.00
Belleek, Vase, Willet, Pink Flowers, Green Leaves On Gray, Signed, 19 In. 175.00
Belleek, Vase, Willet, Poppies, Ivory, Green, Blue, Brown Mark, 16 In. 145.00
Belleek, Vase, Willet, Purple Peacocks, Gold Band In Black, 12 In. 125.00

Bennington, see also Rockingham

Bennington ware was the product of two factories working in Bennington, Vermont. Both firms were out of business by 1896. The wares include brown and yellow mottled pottery, Parian, scroddled ware, stoneware, graniteware, yellowware, and Staffordshire-like vases.

Bennington Type, Head, Black Boy, Brown Glaze, 4 In. .... *Illus* 75.00
Bennington Type, Mug, Parrots In Relief 35.00
Bennington Type, Pitcher, Brown, 10 1/4 X 8 In. 65.00

Bennington Type, Head, Black Boy, Brown Glaze, 4 In.

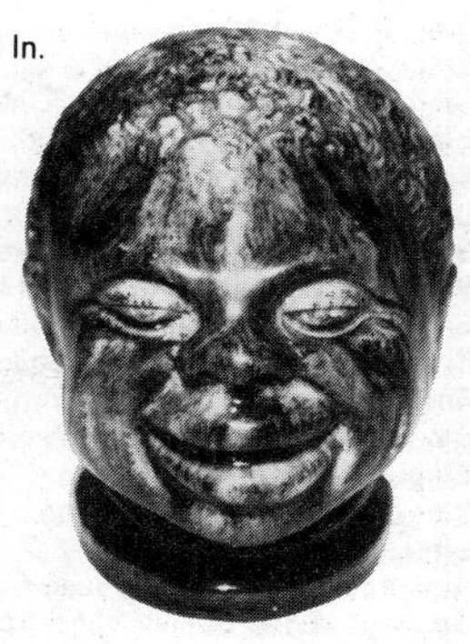

Bennington Type, Plate, Pie, Dark Mottled Brown, 8 1/4 In. 40.00
Bennington Type, Spittoon, Mottled, Medallion With Bust On Side, 8 1/4 In. 17.50
Bennington Type, Tankard, Rockingham Mottled Glaze, Bird & Foliage, 19 In. 95.00
Bennington Type, Washboard Insert, 11 X 10 1/2 In. 20.00
Bennington, Bedpan, Flint Enamel 115.00
Bennington, Box, Trinket, Parian 30.00
Bennington, Cuspidor, Lyman Fenton, 1849-58, 4 X 9 In. 97.00
Bennington, Dish, Vegetable, Oval, 9 1/2 In. 95.00
Bennington, Doorknob, Brown, Pair 6.50
Bennington, Figurine, Spaniel, Brown & Yellow, 11 1/2 X 10 X 6 In. 375.00
Bennington, Foot Warmer 60.00
Bennington, Knob, Door, Pair 10.00
Bennington, Mug, Acanthus Scrolls, Glass Handle, Rockingham 12.00
Bennington, Pitcher, Anchor, 6 1/4 In. 40.00
Bennington, Pitcher, Brown Glaze, 10 1/4 In. 45.00
Bennington, Pitcher, Embossed Busts Of A Man, 8 In. 118.00
Bennington, Pitcher, Parian, Love & War Pattern, E Mark, C.1845 .... 250.00
Bennington, Pitcher, Parian, Tiger & Elephant On Sides, 2 1/8 In. 28.00
Bennington, Pitcher, Rockingham Glaze, Hunter & Game Birds, 8 In. 110.00
Bennington, Pitcher, Rockingham Glaze, 5 3/4 In. 25.00
Bennington, Pitcher, Toby, Ben Franklin, Grape Vine Handle, 5 3/4 In. 300.00
Bennington, Spittoon .... 30.00 To 35.00
Bennington, Spittoon, Brown Flint Enamel, Lyman Fenton & Co., 9 1/2 In. 150.00
Bennington, Spittoon, Brown Flint Enamel, Signed Lyman Fenton, Patent 1849 .... 135.00
Bennington, Spittoon, Brown Flint, Enamel, Lyman Fenton & Co., 1849, 10 In. 135.00
Bennington, Spittoon, Rockingham, Martha & George Washington Medallions 50.00
Bennington, Syrup, Palm Tree, Ribbon Mark, C.1852, 7 3/8 In. 125.00
Bennington, Vase, Blue & White, Two Children, 8 In. 60.00
Bennington, Vase, Parian, Grapes & Tendrils, 9 In. 55.00
Bennington, Vase, Parian, Sparrow & Crocus 26.00
Bennington, Vase, Parian, White, 8 1/2 In. 50.00
Beswick, Figurine, Cairn Dog, 3 In. 8.50
Beswick, Figurine, Imperial, Horse Ridden By The Queen, 8 1/4 In. 22.00
Beswick, Figurine, Lakeland Terrier, 3 In. 11.50
Beswick, Figurine, Little Nell's Grandfather, 5 1/2 In. 55.00
Beswick, Figurine, Owl, 4 1/2 In. 14.00
Beswick, Figurine, Shetland Sheepdog, 3 In. 8.50
Bicycle, Columbia, 1885, High Wheel, 56 In. 900.00
Bicycle, Springfield, High Wheel 1400.00
Bicycle, Star, C.1890, High Wheel, Star Gun Company, Ratchet-Powered Wheel 2350.00

Bing and Grondahl is a famous Danish factory making fine porcelains from 1853 to the present. Their Christmas plates are especially well known.

Bing & Grondahl, see also Collector, Plate

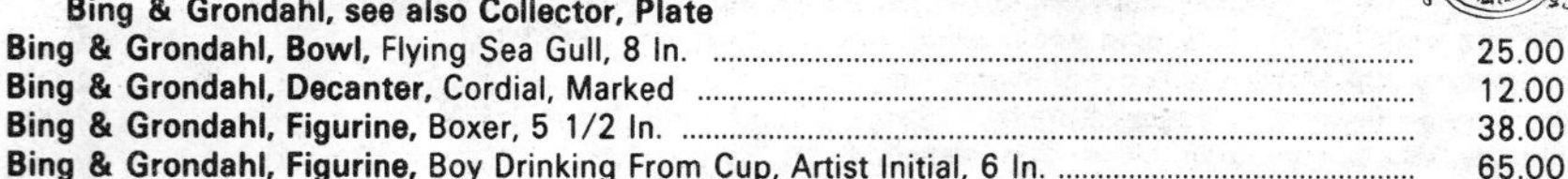

Bing & Grondahl, Bowl, Flying Sea Gull, 8 In. 25.00
Bing & Grondahl, Decanter, Cordial, Marked 12.00
Bing & Grondahl, Figurine, Boxer, 5 1/2 In. 38.00
Bing & Grondahl, Figurine, Boy Drinking From Cup, Artist Initial, 6 In. 65.00

Bing & Grondahl, Figurine, Cat, Sitting, Gray & White, 5 In. 42.00
Bing & Grondahl, Figurine, Dog, Springer Spaniel, Brown & White, 8 X 6 In. 68.00
Bing & Grondahl, Figurine, Fisherman In Fishing Gear, Signed F.B., 8 1/2 In. 115.00
Bing & Grondahl, Figurine, Girl Feeding Chicks, Axel Locher, Blue & White 125.00
Bing & Grondahl, Figurine, Hans Christian Andersen, Gray & Blue, 9 In. 125.00
Bing & Grondahl, Figurine, Merry Sailor, Tan & White, 8 1/4 In. 95.00
Bing & Grondahl, Figurine, Naked Boy, White Porcelain, Earache, Lindhart 25.00
Bing & Grondahl, Figurine, Old Fisherman, 8 1/4 In. 150.00
Bing & Grondahl, Figurine, Scotch Terrier, 7 X 5 1/2 In. 55.00
Bing & Grondahl, Figurine, Young Girl On Floor With Pet, No.1526, 4 1/2 In. 60.00
Bing & Grondahl, Plaque, Morning Angel & Evening Angel, 5 1/2 In., Pair 68.00
Bing & Grondahl, Vase, Scenic On Light Blue, Gloss Glaze, 3 1/2 In., Pair 62.00
Bing & Grondahl, Vase, Water & Trees, Blue, Green, Gray, White, 8 1/2 In. 95.00
Bing & Grondahl, Vase, Winter Scene, Narrow, Rectangular, 3 1/2 In. 22.00
Birdcage, Red Paint, 9 X 8 X 7 In. 65.00
Birdcage, Tin & Wire, Ribbed Glass, Painted, 1879, 17 1/2 In. 95.00
Birdcage, Wire, Dome Shape, 15 X 13 In. 6.00

Bisque is an unglazed baked porcelain. Finished bisque has a slightly sandy texture with a dull finish. Some of it may be decorated with various colors. Bisque gained favor during the late Victorian era when thousands of bisque figurines were made.

Bisque, see also Disneyana

Bisque, Boot, Girl Standing By Side, Cream, Gold Trim, German, 4 3/8 In. 38.00
Bisque, Box, Dresser, Covered, Gold Trim, Hand-Painted Violets, Signed NLS 45.00
Bisque, Box, Girl-Shaped Lid, Egg Base, White, Easter Candy, 6 1/4 In. 89.00
Bisque, Box, Trinket, Baby In Wicker Basket, Pink Trim, 4 1/2 X 3 In. 35.00
Bisque, Bust, Beatrice, Woman, 6 In. 12.50
Bisque, Eggcup, Molded Pond Lilies, Gold Stripe 12.50
Bisque, Figurine, A Froggy Would A' Travelin' Go, German, 5 1/2 In. 45.00
Bisque, Figurine, Bathing Beauty, On Beach Ball, German, Souvenir, N.Y., 3 In. 10.00
Bisque, Figurine, Bathing Beauty, 3 1/2 In. 40.00
Bisque, Figurine, Boy Holding Bouquet, German, 6 1/4 In. 40.00
Bisque, Figurine, C.D.Kenny Boy With Golden Bee 27.50
Bisque, Figurine, Cat, Pink Blanket, Blue Ribbon, German, C.1900, 4 In. 20.00
Bisque, Figurine, Child's Face Peeking Out Of Bear's Mouth, German, 6 In. 37.50
Bisque, Figurine, Colonial Man, Green Coat, German, 15 In. 125.00
Bisque, Figurine, Duck, Number & Clover Incised 35.00
Bisque, Figurine, English Boy Scout, German, 7 1/8 In. 50.00
Bisque, Figurine, Floating Duck, German 35.00
Bisque, Figurine, French Dandy, Signed And Numbered, 8 In. 22.00
Bisque, Figurine, Girl In Blue Dress, 8 In. 20.00
Bisque, Figurine, Girl In Gold & White, German, 9 In. 45.00
Bisque, Figurine, Girl In Pink & Blue With Fan, Signed & Numbered, 11 In. 65.00
Bisque, Figurine, Girl Putting Flowers In Her Hair, German, 14 In. 45.00
Bisque, Figurine, Girl With Music Box, Light Blue Costume, 9 /4 In. 26.00
Bisque, Figurine, Hanging, Young Man On Branches, 18th Century Dress, 6 In. 50.00
Bisque, Figurine, Hanging, Young Woman, 18th Century Dress, 6 In. 50.00
Bisque, Figurine, Kneeling Negro Eating Watermelon, 5 1/2 In. 15.00
Bisque, Figurine, Lady & Man Playing Mandolin, 9 1/2 In., Pair 55.00
Bisque, Figurine, Lady Holding Umbrella, German, 7 1/2 In. 65.00
Bisque, Figurine, Lady In Boat Pulled By Swan, 4 1/2 In. 22.50
Bisque, Figurine, Lady Wearing Large Hat, German, 6 1/4 In. 125.00
Bisque, Figurine, Lady, Roses In Skirt, Japan Fern Mark, 8 1/4 In. 16.00
Bisque, Figurine, Mermaid, Bathing Beauty, 3 3/4 In. 35.00
Bisque, Figurine, Mermaid, Molded Flower Wreath On Head 55.00
Bisque, Figurine, Negro Boy Sitting On Potty, 4 1/2 In. 15.00
Bisque, Figurine, Oriental Boy, Glass Eyes, German 400.00
Bisque, Figurine, Sitting Boy, Heubach, 8 1/2 In. 125.00
Bisque, Figurine, Troubador With Guitar, White, 13 In. 95.00
Bisque, Figurine, Victorian Lady, Hand-Painted, 14 In. 85.00
Bisque, Figurine, Wall Hanging Angel, Holy Water Font, German, Pre-1891 .... 25.00
Bisque, Group, Dutch Girl & Boy Dancing, German, 6 In. 45.00
Bisque, Group, Four Children At Breakfast Table, German, 8 X 7 In. 125.00
Bisque, Group, Lady & Little Girl With Baskets, 6 1/2 In. 55.00
Bisque, Group, Teepee, Campfire, & 5 Indians, 3 1/2 In., 7 Piece 75.00

Bisque, Group, 2 Babes On Tub, Applied Hair Wigs, German 125.00
Bisque, Group, 4 Children At Breakfast Table, German, 8 In. 110.00
Bisque, Jar, Tobacco, Figural, Seafaring Frog Holding Stein, Austria, Signed 68.00
Bisque, Jar, Tobacco, Negro Boy, 4 1/2 In. 75.00
Bisque, Lamp, Owl Head, Night Light, White, Pink Trim, Glass Eyes, 4 In. 145.00
Bisque, Match Holder, Collie Dog's Face, Pewter Rim 32.00
Bisque, Match Holder, Devil, Striker On Back 27.50
Bisque, Match Holder, Girl & Boy Holding Baskets, Hand Painted, Wall 50.00
Bisque, Match Holder, Girl Sitting Beside Open Cabbage Rose, 4 1/2 In. 20.00
Bisque, Match Strike, Bear Wearing Top Hat, Tree Stump, 4 1/2 X 3 In. 55.00
Bisque, Mermaid, Boy On Fish, Girl On Seahorse, Pink, German, Pair 125.00
Bisque, Piano Babies, Heubach, 10 In., Pair 250.00
Bisque, Piano Baby, Lying On Back, Marked 82/68, 6 In. 50.00
Bisque, Pitcher, Cream Color, Raised Birds, Rope Handle, 2 1/2 In. 7.00
Bisque, Shoe, Pink Pigs, Green Shamrocks, Germany 22.00
Bisque, Sugar & Creamer, Greens & Lavender, Gold Beading, Japan 16.00
Bisque, Tea Set, Doll's, Japan, Blown-Out Child's Face, 7 Piece 65.00
Bisque, Tobacco Jar, Figural, Boy With Turban, 5 1/4 In. Tall 45.00
Bisque, Toby Mug, Dour Looking Person's Face, Hanging, 3 In. 35.00
Bisque, Toothbrush Holder, Moon Mullins P Kayo Figural, F.A.S. 42.00
Bisque, Toothpick, Black Boy's Head 27.50
Bisque, Toothpick, Girl Standing By Open Sack, Victorian, 6 In. 45.00
Bisque, Toothpick, Wee Willie Winkie, Top Hat, Ladder By Chimney, 6 In. 55.00
Bisque, Toothpick, White Owl On Tree Trunk 14.00
Bisque, Toothpick, White, Brown Cat's Face At Side 15.00
Bisque, Trinket Box In Wicker Basket, 4 1/2 X 3 In. 45.00
Bisque, Vase, Boy Holding Book, Flower Forms Vase, , French, 5 1/4 In. 46.00
Bisque, Vase, Bud, Boy On Pedestal, White, 9 1/2 In. 50.00
Bisque, Vase, Bud, Boy Standing At Tree, 1 1/2 In. 20.00
Bisque, Vase, Bud, Dog Sitting At Tree, 1 1/2 In. 20.00
Bisque, Vase, Bud, Girl Standing At Tree, 1 1/2 In. 20.00

Black amethyst glass appears black until it is held to the light, then a dark purple can be seen. It was made in many factories from 1860 to the present time.

Black Amethyst, Ashtray, South Tahoe Nugget, Round, 3 1/2 In. 6.00
Black Amethyst, Basket, Basket Weave, Handle, 6 In. 14.00
Black Amethyst, Bowl, Embossed Florals, Footed, 11 1/4 In. 27.00
Black Amethyst, Bowl, Gray Floral, Footed, Triangular, 5 1/2 X 5 In. 15.00
Black Amethyst, Candleholder, Greensburg, Pair 12.00
Black Amethyst, Centerpiece Set, 12 In.Scalloped Footed Bowl, Candleholders 57.00
Black Amethyst, Compote, Enameled Flowers 25.00
Black Amethyst, Console Set, Mary Gregory Type, Birds & Foliage, 3 Piece 95.00
Black Amethyst, Console Set, Sterling Floral, Flared Bowl, 3 Piece 55.00
Black Amethyst, Console Set, White Enamel Bird & Foliage, Gold, 3 Piece 85.00
Black Amethyst, Cup & Saucer, Saucer Is Square 12.50
Black Amethyst, Dish, Candy, Center Handle, 7 In. 15.00
Black Amethyst, Dish, Candy, Covered 22.00
Black Amethyst, Dish, Open Swan 25.00
Black Amethyst, Jar, Covered, Gold Bird In Tree, 11 In. 15.00
Black Amethyst, Jar, Figural, Muzzled Standing Bear, Flint 147.50
Black Amethyst, Muffineer, Acorn, Gold Enamel Flowers 85.00
Black Amethyst, Muffineer, Black, Star & Frost Silver Top 225.00
Black Amethyst, Plate, Silver Overlay, 11 In. 18.00
Black Amethyst, Rose Bowl, 4 1/2 In. 15.00
Black Amethyst, Table Set, Inverted Shell, 3 Piece 55.00
Black Amethyst, Vase, Art Nouveau Dancing Girls, Inside Heart, 2 Handles 35.00
Black Amethyst, Vase, Bud, Enamel Floral, Gold Trim, 10 In., Pair 25.00
Black Amethyst, Vase, France, C.1925, Wheel Cut, Diana & Gazelles, 8 In. 325.00
Black Amethyst, Vase, Greek Key, 6 In. 6.00
Black Amethyst, Vase, Hand-Painted, Open Pontil, Ruffle Top, 9 In. 18.50
Black Amethyst, Vase, Handles, 12 In. 15.00
Black Amethyst, Vase, Hobnail, Scalloped Top, 8 In. 12.00
Black Amethyst, Vase, Silver Flowers, 6 In. 20.00
Black Amethyst, Vase, Silver Overlay, English Tavern Scene, 12 In. 75.00
Blanc De Chine, Burner, Incense, Squatty, 4 Footed, 4 1/2 X 3 In. 35.00

Blanc De Chine, Figurine, Foo Dog, Lying, 3 In., Pair 25.00
Bloor Derby, Bowl, View In North Wales, Cobalt & Gilt Border, C.1820, 12 In. 150.00
Bloor Derby, Dish, Shell Shape, Floral & Gold, C.1820, 9 3/4 In., Pair 65.00
Bloor Derby, Inkwell, C.1820, Round 165.00

Blown glass was formed by forcing air through a rod into molten glass. Early glass and some forms of art glass were hand blown. Other types of glass were molded or pressed. The McKearin numbers refer to the book "American Glass" by George and Helen McKearin.

Blown Glass, Amphora, Amethyst, Applied Ribbed Strap Handle, C.1890, 15 In. 400.00
Blown Glass, Bookend, WPA, Swirled, Amber, Pair 60.00
Blown Glass, Bottle, Bar, Pittsburgh, Flint, Pillar Mold, Neck Ring, 11 1/4 In 52.00
Blown Glass, Bottle, Case, Ball Stopper, Gilt Decoration, 8 1/2 In. 40.00
Blown Glass, Bottle, Case, Flint, Amelung Type, Soda Lime, 7 1/4 In. 35.00
Blown Glass, Bottle, Case, Flint, Stiegel Type, Gilt Decoration, 8 1/2 In. 40.00
Blown Glass, Bottle, Castor, Three Mold, McK G I-10 24.00
Blown Glass, Bottle, Castor, Three Mold, McK G I-15 22.00
Blown Glass, Bottle, Dutch Slipper, 6 In. 32.50
Blown Glass, Bottle, Ink, Olive Amber, Three Mold, McK G II-18 140.00
Blown Glass, Bottle, Scent, Emerald Green, Stiegel Type 125.00
Blown Glass, Bottle, Scent, Flint, Stiegel Type, Swirled 35.00
Blown Glass, Bottle, Scent, Flint, Swirled Ribs 35.00
Blown Glass, Bottle, Scent, Purple Blue 125.00
Blown Glass, Bottle, Scent, South Jersey, Seahorse 75.00
Blown Glass, Bottle, Smelling, Clear, Pewter Cap 45.00
Blown Glass, Bottle, Snuff, Olive Green, Free Blown 70.00
Blown Glass, Bottle, Toilet, Three Mold, 1/2 Pint, McK G I-7 45.00
Blown Glass, Bottle, Toilet, 3 Mold, Blue, McK GI-17 180.00
Blown Glass, Bowl, Bedside, Zanesville, Witch Ball Cover 225.00
Blown Glass, Bowl, Electric Blue, Flared, Fluted, 6 1/2 In. 45.00
Blown Glass, Bowl, Flint, Fluted, Infolded Rim, 5 In. 45.00
Blown Glass, Bowl, McK G III-24, 6 In. 180.00
Blown Glass, Bowl, Midwestern, Light Green, Swirled Ribs, 5 1/2 In. 550.00
Blown Glass, Bowl, New England Glass Co., 7 1/8 In. 175.00
Blown Glass, Bowl, Three Mold, Concave Dots, Diamond Base, 6 1/2 In. 75.00
Blown Glass, Bowl, Three Mold, Geometrics, McK G III-5 65.00
Blown Glass, Bowl, Three Mold, Geometrics, McK G III-7 75.00
Blown Glass, Candlestick, Corning, Gold & Amber, Blue Iridescent Rim, 12 In. 50.00
Blown Glass, Cane, Light Green, Amber Center, Twisted At Knob & Tip, 43 In. 45.00
Blown Glass, Carafe, Flint, Mold Blown, Quart, McK G II-27 155.00
Blown Glass, Carafe, Flint, Teardrop, Applied Lip, 6 1/4 In. 30.00
Blown Glass, Carafe, Ribbed Stopper, Three Mold, McK G I-20 90.00
Blown Glass, Carafe, Riverboat, Flint, Pillar Molded, 8 Ribs 50.00
Blown Glass, Carafe, Variant Quart, McK GI-20 90.00
Blown Glass, Castor Shaker, Three Mold, McK GI-15 22.00
Blown Glass, Celery, Pittsburgh, Flint, Pillar Mold, 8 Ribs, Knob Stem, 10 In. 85.00
Blown Glass, Compote, Flint, C.1900, Panel-Cut Stem, Polychrome Floral, 7 In. 65.00
Blown Glass, Compote, Flint, Loop, Scalloped Rim, 4 In. 10.00
Blown Glass, Compote, Pittsburgh, Flint, C.1800, Folded Rim, 7 In. 100.00
Blown Glass, Cordial, Flint, Conical Bowl 15.00
Blown Glass, Creamer, Mantua, Yellow 900.00
Blown Glass, Creamer, New York State, Aqua, Lily Pad 700.00
Blown Glass, Creamer, South Jersey, Cobalt 200.00
Blown Glass, Creamer, Three Mold 350.00
Blown Glass, Crocus Bowl, Germany, Lacy Top, 5 X 4 1/4 In. 18.50
Blown Glass, Cruet, Castor, Three Mold, McK G I-28 20.00
Blown Glass, Cruet, Castor, Three Mold, McK G II-11 24.00
Blown Glass, Cruet, Castor, Three Mold, McK G II-31 28.00
Blown Glass, Cruet, Cut Flowers, Ground Bottom, Cut Stopper, 7 1/2 In. 20.00
Blown Glass, Cruet, Pattern, With Stopper 15.00
Blown Glass, Cruet, 24 Ribs, Hollow Stopper, Applied Handle, 10 In. 40.00
Blown Glass, Cup, Bleeding, Cobalt, Expanded Flared Mouth, 3 3/4 In. 140.00
Blown Glass, Decanter, Amelung Type, C.1750, Faceted Stopper, Engraved, Quart 125.00
Blown Glass, Decanter, Amethyst, 8 3/4 In. 20.00
Blown Glass, Decanter, Flint, Amelung Type, Tapered, Quart 40.00
Blown Glass, Decanter, Flint, C.1750, 1/2 Pint 35.00

Blown Glass, Decanter, Flint, C.1750, 11 Panels, 1/2 Pint 40.00
Blown Glass, Decanter, Flint, C.1800, Neck Ring, Bar Lip, Quart 30.00
Blown Glass, Decanter, Flint, C.1800, Neck Ring, Flange Lip, Quart 35.00
Blown Glass, Decanter, Flint, C.1800, Neck Ring, Pint 35.00
Blown Glass, Decanter, Flint, Eight Pillar Molded Ribs, Quart 100.00
Blown Glass, Decanter, Flint, McK G I-29 .... 95.00 To 100.00
Blown Glass, Decanter, Ground Stopper, Crimped, 9 3/4 In. 25.00
Blown Glass, Decanter, Hexagonal, Pint 100.00
Blown Glass, Decanter, Quart, McK GI-20 .... 100.00
Blown Glass, Decanter, Riverboat, Pittsburgh, Flint, 8 Ribs, Bar Lip, Quart 80.00
Blown Glass, Decanter, Three Mold, McK G II-18 .... 95.00
Blown Glass, Decanter, Three Mold, Quart, McK G II-18 .... 70.00 To 95.00
Blown Glass, Decanter, Three Mold, Quart, McK G II-29 .... 95.00
Blown Glass, Decanter, Three Mold, Quart, McK G III-15 .... 95.00
Blown Glass, Decanter, Three Mold, Quart, McK G III-24 .... 95.00
Blown Glass, Decanter, Three Mold, Rigaree Neck, Quart, McK G II-18 .... 95.00
Blown Glass, Decanter, Three Mold, Triple Neck Rings, Quart, McK G I-29 .... 45.00
Blown Glass, Decanter, 3-Mold, Clear Glass, Quart, Rigaree Neck, Stopper 88.00
Blown Glass, Dispenser, Beverage, Blue, Diamond-Quilted, Metal Spigot, 7 In. 55.00
Blown Glass, Egg, French, Hinged Lid, Cream Color, Enamel, Ormolu Base, 11 In. 365.00
Blown Glass, Epergne, Blue Bristol, 2 Piece, Ruffle Tops 52.00
Blown Glass, Ewer, Cobalt, Applied Crystal Handle, Enamel Floral, 7 1/2 In. 72.00
Blown Glass, Fish Bowl, South Boston Glass Co., C.1812, 15 In. 145.00
Blown Glass, Flask, Midwestern, Hip, Sapphire Blue, 1/2 Pint 700.00
Blown Glass, Flip, Flint, Enameled Windmill Scene, 5 1/2 In. 50.00
Blown Glass, Flip, Flint, McK G I-6, 6 In. .... 90.00 To 120.00
Blown Glass, Flip, Flint, McK G Ii-18, 6 In. 225.00
Blown Glass, Flip, Flint, McK G Ii2-22, 5 In. 150.00
Blown Glass, Flip, Three Mold, McK G II-33, 5 1/2 In. 220.00
Blown Glass, Flip, Three Mold, 6 In., McK G I-6 .... 90.00
Blown Glass, Flip, Three Mold, 6 In., McK G II-18 .... 135.00
Blown Glass, Float, Black, 5 In. 20.00
Blown Glass, Float, Blue Green, 4 3/4 In. 10.00
Blown Glass, Float, Deep Aqua, 14 1/2 In. 25.00
Blown Glass, Float, Green, Elongated, 6 In. 5.00
Blown Glass, Float, Green, 9 1/2 In. 30.00
Blown Glass, Float, Topaz, Expanded Thumbprint, 6 1/2 In. 20.00
Blown Glass, Float, Yellow Green, Swirled To Right, 6 In. 30.00
Blown Glass, Goblet, Amethyst, Applied Stem & Foot, 6 In., Pair 25.00
Blown Glass, Goblet, Flint, Soda Lime, Cone Bowl 24.00
Blown Glass, Goblet, Olive Amber, Free-Blown 55.00
Blown Glass, Hat, Flint, McK G III-4 .... 110.00
Blown Glass, Hat, Green, Applied Opalescent Stripes, Victorian, 5 1/2 In. 38.00
Blown Glass, Hat, Three Mold, McK G III-3 .... 110.00
Blown Glass, Hat, Three Mold, McK G III-4 .... 110.00
Blown Glass, Inkwell, Charles Yockel, 1876, Memorial Hall Shape 85.00
Blown Glass, Inkwell, Coventry, Three Mold, Olive Amber, McK G II-2 .... 95.00
Blown Glass, Jar, Figural, Owl, Emerald Green, Mold Blown, 10 In. 37.50
Blown Glass, Jug, Cream, French, Cobalt, Baroque, Applied Collared Base 100.00
Blown Glass, Jug, Flint, Applied Handle, Tooled Neck, Pontil 22.00
Blown Glass, Jug, Neck Ring, Applied Handle, Painted, Pewter Top, Quart 38.00
Blown Glass, Lemonade Set, Victorian, Aquamarine, Hand-Painted, Flowers, Gold 75.00
Blown Glass, Liqueur, Flint, Pair 30.00
Blown Glass, Mug, Flint, Opalescent, Applied Handle, Flared Lip, Enameled 40.00
Blown Glass, Mug, Friendship, Fine Ribbing, Painted Flowers, Applied Handle 48.00
Blown Glass, Mug, Friendship, Painted Flowers, "Remember Me" In Gold 48.00
Blown Glass, Mug, Maryland 250.00
Blown Glass, Mug, Ruby, Applied Clear Handle 15.00
Blown Glass, Pitcher, Amethyst, Swirled Ribs, Crimped Spout, 5 In. 10.00
Blown Glass, Pitcher, Applied Handle, Gray Green With Blue Circles, 9 In. 57.00
Blown Glass, Pitcher, Aqua, Swirled Ribs, Hourglass Shape, Crimped, 8 1/2 In. 18.00
Blown Glass, Pitcher, Cranberry On Clear, Graduated Thumbprints, 7 In. 85.00
Blown Glass, Pitcher, Frosted Pink, Hand-Painted Roses, 8 Glasses, Set 270.00
Blown Glass, Pitcher, Imperial Eagle Engraved Under Spout, 4 In. 77.50
Blown Glass, Pitcher, Pittsburgh Type, Vertical Ribs, 9 3/4 In. 50.00
Blown Glass, Pitcher, Saratoga, Emerald Green, Applied Foot, Handle, Ring 260.00

Blown Glass, Pitcher, Water, Blue, Opalescent, Swirl 110.00
Blown Glass, Pitcher, Water, Green, Opalescent, Daffodil 135.00
Blown Glass, Rinsing Bowl, Amethyst, 4 1/2 In., Pair 120.00
Blown Glass, Salt & Pepper, Pewter Tops 19.00
Blown Glass, Salt, Jacony, McK G V-24 .... 30.00
Blown Glass, Salt, Master, Manuta, Yellow, Footed 750.00
Blown Glass, Salt, Serrated Top Edge 150.00
Blown Glass, Salt, Three Mold, Pinched-Waist, McK G I-6 .... 65.00
Blown Glass, Shaker, Castor, Three Mold, McK G I-12 .... 20.00
Blown Glass, Shaker, Castor, Three Mold, McK G I-13 .... 20.00
Blown Glass, Swan, Red, Yellow Enamel Beak & Eyes, 3 1/4 In. 25.00
Blown Glass, Syllabub, Flint, 4 1/4 In. 18.00
Blown Glass, Syrup, Flint, Soda Lime, Crimped Handle, Tin & Pewter Top 40.00
Blown Glass, Tumbler, Flint, 3 Mold, 3 7/8 In. 60.00
Blown Glass, Tumbler, Silver German Coin Inside Hollow Base, 1864, 6 In. 200.00
Blown Glass, Tumbler, White Enamel Flowers, Gold Trim 8.00
Blown Glass, Vase, Blue With Amber Applique, Enameled Flowers, 7 3/4 In. 35.00
Blown Glass, Vase, Blue, Applied Coil Threading, 6 1/2 In. 39.00
Blown Glass, Vase, Cobalt Cased Center Section, Clear Foot & Top, 10 In. 255.00
Blown Glass, Vase, Engraved Grapes, Applied Base, 9 1/2 In. 45.00
Blown Glass, Vase, European, Ruby Flashed, Frosted, Flowers, 7 In., Pair 65.00
Blown Glass, Vase, Hyacinth, Opaque, White, 8 In. 22.50
Blown Glass, Vase, Jack-In-The-Pulpit, Opalescent Frill, 7 In. 30.00
Blown Glass, Vase, Tapered, Large Teardrop In Stem, Folded Foot Base 75.00
Blown Glass, Vase, Trumpet, Emerald Green, Sommerville, 5 3/4 X 11 3/4 In. 32.00
Blown Glass, Vigil Light, Flint, Stiegel Type, Green, 16 Diamond 55.00
Blown Glass, Vigil Light, Flint, Stiegel Type, 13 Diamonds, Folded Rim 55.00
Blown Glass, Wine, Cut Panels, Sheared Rim, Ground Pontil, 4 1/8 In. 10.00
Blown Glass, Wine, Flint, Cone Bowl 15.00
Blown Glass, Wine, Flint, Tulip Bowl, 12 Pattern Molded Flutes 22.00
Blown Glass, Wine, Green, Sheared Rim, Hollow Stem, 5 In. 15.00
Blown Glass, Wine, Hand Painted 17.50
Blown Glass, Wine, Hoch, Russian, Etched Ruby & Gold, 7 1/4 In., Pair 98.00
Blown Glass, Wine, Rhine, German, Pale Green, Gold Baroque Designs 45.00
Blown Glass, Witch's Ball, Amethyst, 3 1/2 In. 15.00
Blown Glass, Witch's Ball, Dark Amber, 4 1/2 In. 50.00
Blown Glass, Witch's Ball, Golden Amber, 5 3/4 In. 55.00
Blown Glass, Witch's Ball, Green, Expanded Diamond, 4 In. 40.00
Blown Glass, Witch's Ball, Green, Swirled To Right, 7 In. 55.00
Blown Glass, Witch's Ball, Green, White Loopings, 2 1/4 In. 50.00
Blown Glass, Witch's Ball, Milk Glass, Blue & Red Splotches, 3 3/4 In. 85.00
Blown Glass, Witch's Ball, Multicolor Splotches, 5 1/2 In. 100.00
Blown Glass, Witch's Ball, Olive Amber Ball Inside, 3 1/2 In. 250.00
Blown Glass, Witch's Ball, Olive Amber, 4 1/4 In. 70.00
Blown Glass, Witch's Ball, Red Splotches, 3 1/4 In. 25.00
Blown Glass, Witch's Ball, Ruby, 4 In. 65.00
Blown Glass, Witch's Ball, Sapphire Blue, 6 In. 80.00
Blown Glass, Witch's Ball, Seedy Copper, 5 1/2 In. 100.00
Blown Glass, Witch's Ball, Seedy Green, 5 In. 50.00
Blown Glass, Witch's Ball, Smoky Aqua, Red, White, Blue, & Green Specks, 7 In. 60.00
Blown Glass, Witch's Ball, Violet, 3 1/4 In. 75.00
Blown Glass, Witch's Ball, White & Ruby Swirls, 3 1/2 In. 120.00
Blown Glass, Witch's Ball, White Loopings, 4 1/2 In. .... 30.00 To 50.00
Blown Glass, Witch's Ball, White Loopings, 6 1/4 In. 50.00

Blue Amberina, see Bluerina

Blue Daisy, Zimmerman 7.00

Blue Glass, see Cobalt Blue

Blue Onion, see Onion

Blue Satin, Vase, Pineapple Bottom, 6 1/4 In. 150.00

Blue Willow pattern has been made in England since 1780. The pattern has been copied by factories in many countries, including Germany, Japan, and the United States. It is still being made. Willow was named for a pattern that pictures a bridge, birds, willow trees, and a Chinese landscape.

Blue Willow, Bowl, Square Vegetable, Ridgway, 8 X 9 1/2 In. 18.00
Blue Willow, Bowl, White Interior, Doulton, 7 X 3 1/2 In. 85.00

Blue Willow, Butter Pat, England 6.00
Blue Willow, Butter, Covered, Nippon 30.00
Blue Willow, Butter, England, Set Of 5 ..... 20.00
Blue Willow, Coffee Set, Japan, 11 Piece 25.00
Blue Willow, Creamer, Buffalo Pottery, 4 1/4 In. 10.00
Blue Willow, Creamer, English 5.50
Blue Willow, Cup & Saucer, Japan 9.50
Blue Willow, Cup Plate, Soft Paste, C.1820, 4 5/8 In. 18.00
Blue Willow, Eggcup, Newhall, C.1831 ..... 35.00
Blue Willow, Jardiniere, Brown Interior, Fluted Top, Doulton, 8 In. 150.00
Blue Willow, Jug, Chicago, Buffalo Pottery, 7 In. 85.00
Blue Willow, Jug, Serpent Handle, Mason's, C.1850, Octagonal, 4 In. 48.00
Blue Willow, Mustard Pot, Covered, Buffalo Pottery 10.00
Blue Willow, Pitcher, Buffalo Pottery, 7 In. 75.00
Blue Willow, Pitcher, Bulbous, Buffalo Pottery, 1911, 5 In. 15.00
Blue Willow, Plate, Adams, 7 3/4 In. 10.00
Blue Willow, Plate, Allerton, 9 In. 12.00
Blue Willow, Plate, Britannia Pottery, 6 1/2 In. 4.00
Blue Willow, Plate, Buffalo Pottery, 10 In. 13.50
Blue Willow, Plate, J.Stevenson, 5 1/2 In. 3.00
Blue Willow, Plate, Occupied Japan, 9 In. 2.50
Blue Willow, Platter, Iron Stone China, R.H. & Co., 17 1/2 X 14 In. 55.00
Blue Willow, Platter, Miniature 7.00
Blue Willow, Platter, Oregon, 10 X 7 3/4 In. 45.00
Blue Willow, Platter, Wedgwood & Co., C.1801, 11 X 8 3/4 In. 12.00
Blue Willow, Relish, Yorkshire 28.00
Blue Willow, Sauce Boat, Barker Bros., England 7.00
Blue Willow, Set Of Dishes, Child's, 10 Piece 45.00
Blue Willow, Sugar & Creamer, Buffalo Pottery, 1905 ..... 40.00
Blue Willow, Sugar & Creamer, Cover, Allerton 45.00
Blue Willow, Sugar, Buffalo Pottery, 1911 ..... 15.00
Blue Willow, Sugar, Ridgeway, 5 In. 18.00
Blue Willow, Tea Set, Miniature, 18 Pieces 40.00
Blue Willow, Vegetable Bowl, Soft Paste, 12 In. 45.00
Blue Willow, Washstand Set, Emancu, C.1900, 2 Piece 75.00

Bluerina is a type of art glass which shades from light blue to ruby. It is often called blue amberina.

Bluerina, Bowl, 5 In. 82.00
Bluerina, Bowl, 6 In. 70.00
Bluerina, Saltshaker, Bulbous 75.00
Bluerina, Saltshaker, Inverted Thumbprint, Bulbous 75.00
Boch Freres, Pitcher, Glossy Pink, White Mythological Animal, Art Deco 50.00
Boch Freres, Vase, Citron To Cobalt, Drip Technique, Ormolu Rims, 8 1/4 In. 65.00
Boch Freres, Vase, Cream Crackle, Blue & Brown Antelopes, Pottery, 10 1/4 In 150.00
Boch Freres, Vase, Flying Geese, Blue Green & Yellow, Art Deco, 8 1/2 In. 115.00
Boch Freres, Vase, Yellow, Black, & Green Design, Art Deco, 11 1/2 In. 135.00
Boch, Vase, Belgium, Art Deco, Multicolored, 11 1/2 In. 95.00

Bohemian glass is an ornate, overlay, or flashed glass made during the Victorian era. It has been reproduced in Bohemia, which is now a part of Czechoslovakia. Glass made from 1875 to 1900 is preferred by collectors.

Bohemian Glass, Berry Bowl, Ruby, Vintage, 8 1/2 X 3 5/8 In. 40.00
Bohemian Glass, Bowl, Amber, Deer, Tree, & Pavillion, 3 Legged, 9 In. 35.00
Bohemian Glass, Butter, Covered, Ruby, Etched 65.00
Bohemian Glass, Butter, Ruby, Cut & Engraved 55.00
Bohemian Glass, Centerpiece, White Grape & Leaf Decoration, 11 X 9 X 5 In. 150.00
Bohemian Glass, Cordial Set, Green To Clear, Thumbprints, 6 Piece 165.00
Bohemian Glass, Cruet, Etched Ruby 100.00
Bohemian Glass, Decanter, Blown Molded, Early, 12 In. 150.00
Bohemian Glass, Decanter, Claret, Ruby, Enamel Floral, Rigaree Foot, 9 In. 110.00
Bohemian Glass, Decanter, Faceted Stopper, Amber, Castle, Deer, & Dog, 13 In. 150.00
Bohemian Glass, Decanter, Ruby, Cut & Engraved, 15 In., Pair 90.00
Bohemian Glass, Dresser Set, Intaglio Animals & Forests, 2 Jars, 3 Bowls 750.00
Bohemian Glass, Dresser Set, Leaf Pattern, 3 Piece 40.00
Bohemian Glass, Goblet, Intaglio Cut, Floral, Amber Feet & Knob Stem 50.00

Bohemian Glass, Goblet, Purple, Blue, Yellow Flashing, Birds, 6 In. 40.00
Bohemian Glass, Jar, Boudoir, Covered, Amethyst To Clear, Thumbprint, Fan 25.00
Bohemian Glass, Liqueur Set, Ruby, Cut Floral Medallions & Scrolls, 7 Piece 85.00
Bohemian Glass, Liqueur Set, Ruby, Deer & Castle, 7 Piece 95.00
Bohemian Glass, Lustre, Ruby With Enamel Floral Decoration, Cut Prisms, Pair 95.00
Bohemian Glass, Mug, Etched Flowers, Polished Base, Gold Inscription, 4 In. 45.00
Bohemian Glass, Pokal & Cover, Faceted Finial, Etched Deer & Castle, Ruby 125.00
Bohemian Glass, Table Set, Intaglio Cut Animals, Faceted Knobs, 2 Jars, Bowl 750.00
Bohemian Glass, Tankard, Applied Clear Handle, Deep Cut Panels, 5 5/8 In. 75.00
Bohemian Glass, Toothpick, Blue, Etched 15.00
Bohemian Glass, Tray, Etched Gold & Crystal, Large 48.50
Bohemian Glass, Tumbler, Red, Deer & Castle, Cut & Engraved 10.50
Bohemian Glass, Tumbler, Red, Etched Vintage, Footed 16.00
Bohemian Glass, Tumbler, Ruby, Castle In Leaf & Scroll Medallion, Footed 45.00
Bohemian Glass, Urn, Covered, Ruby, Intaglio Deer & Trees, 14 In. 135.00
Bohemian Glass, Vase, Amber, Bird & Castle, 6 1/2 In. 85.00
Bohemian Glass, Vase, Amber, Deer & Castle, Blown Pontil, 8 In. 85.00
Bohemian Glass, Vase, Amber, Engraved Floral, Flared Rim, 11 1/4 In. 65.00
Bohemian Glass, Vase, Amber, Top Curves Down, Out, Back Into Base, 12 In. 125.00
Bohemian Glass, Vase, Butterflies & Flowers Medallion, 14 In. 85.00
Bohemian Glass, Vase, Hand-Painted Bird & Floral, 7 In. 35.00
Bohemian Glass, Vase, Hand-Painted Enameled Flowers, 6 1/2 In. 28.00
Bohemian Glass, Vase, Red Rim, Deer Leaves On Clover Decoration, 8 1/2 In. 50.00
Bohemian Glass, Vase, Red, Etched Cut Stag, 5 In. 45.00
Bohemian Glass, Vase, Red, Frosted White Hand-Painted Pontil, 8 In. 35.00
Bohemian Glass, Vase, Ruby, Castle & Bird, Conical, 10 1/4 In. 115.00
Bohemian Glass, Vase, Ruby, Castle & Deer, Gourd Shape, 9 1/2 In. 125.00
Bohemian Glass, Vase, Ruby, Etched, 12 1/2 In. 80.00
Bohemian Glass, Vase, Ruby, Grape Leaf & Bud On White, 10 In. 70.00
Bohemian Glass, Vase, Ruby, Tree, Forest, & Hound, Pedestal, 6 3/4 In. 50.00
Bohemian Glass, Vase, White Cut To Cranberry, Gold Gilt Trim, 12 1/2 In. 185.00
Bohemian Glass, Vase, White To Emerald Green, Overlay, Lacy Gold, 13 In. 160.00
Bohemian Glass, Wine Set, Milk Glass, Cranberry Overlay, Floral, 5 Piece 225.00
Bohemian Glass, Wine Set, Red, Deer & Castle, 7 Piece 85.00
Bohemian Glass, Wine, Cranberry, Etched Cherries & Leaves 16.00
Bohemian Glass, Wine, Rhine, Ruby, Cut & Engraved 25.00
Bonn, Dish, Wedge-Shape Cheese, German, Rose Decoration 25.00

Book, see Hopalong Cassidy, Book; Paper, Book Shirley Temple; Book, and others.
Boston & Sandwich Co., see Sandwich, Fireglow, Lutz

Bottle collecting has become a major American hobby. There are several general categories of bottles such as historic flasks, bitters, household, figural, and others. The McK numbers refer to the book "American Glass" by George and Helen McKearin.

Bottle, see also Hopalong Cassidy, Bottle

Bottle, Apothecary, Walton On Base, 1862, Glass Label, 9 3/4 In. 25.00
Bottle, Apothecary, Walton On Base, 1862, 9 3/4 In. 20.00

Avon started in 1886 as the California Perfume Company. It was not until 1929 that the name Avon was used. In 1939 it became Avon Products, Inc. Each year Avon sells many figural bottles filled with cosmetic products. Ceramic, plastic, and glass bottles are made in limited editions.

Bottle, Avon, After Shave Caddy, 1968, Full & Boxed 9.95
Bottle, Avon, Attention Cologne, 1943 30.00
Bottle, Avon, Car, Touring T Test, 1969, Amber 35.00
Bottle, Avon, Charisma Jewelry Set, 1968 20.00
Bottle, Avon, Christmas, Ornament, 1967, Silver 6.00
Bottle, Avon, Cologne Trilogy, 1969, Full & Boxed 9.95
Bottle, Avon, Commemorative, 1973 35.00
Bottle, Avon, Cream Hair Lotion, 1948 12.00
Bottle, Avon, Daisies Won't Tell Set, 1957, Full & Boxed 39.50
Bottle, Avon, Factory, 1974 35.00
Bottle, Avon, First Lady, 1972 100.00

Bottle, Avon, Flowertime Toilet Water, 1949, Full & Boxed 13.00
Bottle, Avon, Fragrance Belle Cologne, 1965, Full 10.00
Bottle, Avon, Gold Coast, 1974 .... 50.00
Bottle, Avon, Golden Promise Cologne, 1947, Full 11.00
Bottle, Avon, Here's My Heart Cologne Mist, 1958 .... 5.00
Bottle, Avon, McConnell, 1973 .... 50.00
Bottle, Avon, Pine Bath Salts, 1940, Full 20.00
Bottle, Avon, Rose Cold Cream, 1936 .... 2.00
Bottle, Avon, Splash & Spray Set, 1968 .... 20.00
Bottle, Avon, Three Bears Baby Shampoo, 1966-67 .... 9.00
Bottle, Avon, To A Wild Rose Toilet Water, 1950, Full & Boxed 12.00
Bottle, Avon, Twenty Paces, 1967, Red-Lined Box 35.00
Bottle, Avon, Twenty Paces, 1974, Black-Lined Box 35.00
Bottle, Avon, Twenty Paces, 1974, Blue-Lined Box 35.00
Bottle, Avon, Twenty Paces, 1974, Red-Lined Box 35.00
Bottle, Avon, Viking Horn, 1972 .... 50.00
Bottle, Avon, Wishing Toilet Water, 1947, 61st Anniversary, Gold, Boxed 20.00
Bottle, Bar, Pittsburgh, 6 Panels, Cobalt 200.00
Bottle, Bar, Pittsburgh, 8 Panels, Amethyst 180.00
Bottle, Bar, Pittsburgh, 8 Panels, Emerald Green 310.00
Bottle, Barber, Apple Green, Enameled Flowers & Decoration 52.00
Bottle, Barber, Camphor White With Witch Hazel Across 69.00
Bottle, Barber, Clambroth, Opaque, 8 In., Stopper 45.00
Bottle, Barber, Clear With Heavy Enamel Flowers 24.00
Bottle, Barber, Cobalt, Enameled Daisies 65.00
Bottle, Barber, Cranberry Opalescent, Hobnail 75.00
Bottle, Barber, Cranberry Thumbprints Inside, Enameled, Green 40.00
Bottle, Barber, Honey Amber, Floral Decoration, Bulged Neck, Pewter Spout 68.00
Bottle, Barber, Opalescent Swirl, Ground Pontil, 9 In. 75.00
Bottle, Barber, Spout, Green, Checkered 63.00
Bottle, Barber, Vaseline, Spanish Lace 58.00
Bottle, Barber, White Satin With Flowers 75.00

Beam bottles are made to hold Kentucky Straight Bourbon made by the James B.Beam Distilling Company. The Beam series of ceramic bottles began in 1953.

Bottle, Beam, , Blue Cherub, Executive, 1960 .... 75.00 To 135.00
Bottle, Beam, B.P.O., Does, 1971 .... 7.00 To 9.00
Bottle, Beam, Bing Crosby, 33rd Pro-Am, 1974 .... 14.00 To 25.00
Bottle, Beam, Black Katz Cat, 1968 .... 8.00 To 12.95
Bottle, Beam, Blue Cherub, Executive, 1960 .... 75.00 To 135.00
Bottle, Beam, Blue Fox, 1967, Club 120.00 To 125.00
Bottle, Beam, Bob Hope Desert Classic, 1973 .... 14.50 To 15.00
Bottle, Beam, Bohemian Girl, 1974 .... 20.00
Bottle, Beam, Churchill Downs, 95th, Red Roses, 1969, 1970 .... 7.00 To 10.00
Bottle, Beam, Civil War, North, Centennial, 1961 .... 35.00 To 40.00
Bottle, Beam, Dancing Couple, 1964 .... 70.00 To 75.00
Bottle, Beam, Doe, English Foremost Pink Speckled, 1956, Customer Specialty 650.00
Bottle, Beam, Doe, English Fox, Gold, 1969, Club .... 65.00 To 75.00
Bottle, Beam, Doe, English Setter, 1959, Trophy .... 59.00 To 70.00
Bottle, Beam, Franklin Mint, 1970 .... 7.00
Bottle, Beam, Grand Canyon, 1969, Regal China Specialty 15.00
Bottle, Beam, Great Dane, 1976 .... 16.00 To 17.00
Bottle, Beam, Grecian, 1956, Glass Specialty 3.95
Bottle, Beam, Hannah Duston, 1973, Regal China Specialty 17.00
Bottle, Beam, Hansel & Gretel, 1971, Fantasy Series 5.00
Bottle, Beam, Harold's Club, Gray Slot Machine, 1967 .... 4.00 To 9.00
Bottle, Beam, Harold's Club, V.I.P., 1967, Customer Special .... 59.00 To 70.00
Bottle, Beam, Harvey's Wagonwheel, 1969, Glass Specialty 6.00
Bottle, Beam, Jackalope, 1972, Gold .... 22.00 To 30.00
Bottle, Beam, Jewel Tea Wagon, 1974, Customer Specialty 25.00
Bottle, Beam, Jug, Oatmeal, 1966 .... 35.00 To 42.00
Bottle, Beam, Kentucky Colonel, 1970 .... 6.00
Bottle, Beam, Kiwi, 1973, Trophy 7.00
Bottle, Beam, Las Vegas, 1969, Regal China 5.00

Bottle, Beam, London Bridge, 1971, Medallion, Regal China 25.00
Bottle, Beam, Mark Antony, 1962 20.00 To 24.00
Bottle, Beam, Nixon Bottle & Plate Set 1700.00 To 1900.00
Bottle, Beam, Political, Agnew Elephant, 1970 1600.00 To 2000.00
Bottle, Beam, Political, 1960, Elephant & Donkey, Pair 25.00
Bottle, Beam, Presidential, Executive, 1968 110.00
Bottle, Beam, Royal Gold, Executive, 1956 100.00 To 125.00
Bottle, Beam, State, Hawaii, 1967, Reissue 50.00 To 55.00
Bottle, Beam, Trophy, 1957, Duck 32.00 To 35.00
Bottle, Beam, Trophy, 1968, Cardinal, Male 44.00
Bottle, Beam, Trophy, 1971, Texas Rabbit 9.00
Bottle, Beam, Uncle Sam Fox, 1971, Club 10.00 To 15.00
Bottle, Beer, Denver Brand, Pint 1.50
Bottle, Beer, Muth, Miniature 10.00
Bottle, Beer, Ruby Red, Quart 7.00
Bottle, Beer, Rupert, Paper Label, Miniature 15.00
Bottle, Beer, Sterling, Paper Label, Quart 3.50
Bottle, Beer, Tivoli, Pint 1.50
Bottle, Beer, William Simon Brewery, Buffalo, N.Y., 1934, Amber, 12 Ozs. 5.00
Bottle, Bellows, Nailsea, White On Clear, 12 In. 225.00
Bottle, Bitters, Atwood's Jaundice, Georgetown, Ma., 12 Sided, Aqua, 6 In. 4.95
Bottle, Bitters, Caroni, Dug, Olive Green, 8 1/2 In. 20.00
Bottle, Bitters, Clarke's Vegetable Sherry Wine, Aqua, 1/2 Gallon 100.00
Bottle, Bitters, Doyle's Hop, 1872, Deep Amber, 10 In. 35.00
Bottle, Bitters, Dr.C.W.Roback's Stomach Bitters, Cincinnati, Ohio, Amber 100.00
Bottle, Bitters, Drake's Plantation, 1860, 6 Log, Amber 60.00
Bottle, Bitters, Drake's Plantation, 4 Log 55.00
Bottle, Bitters, Drake's Plantation, 4 Log, Yellow 125.00
Bottle, Bitters, Drake's Plantation, 6 Log, Amber 45.00 To 46.00
Bottle, Bitters, Drake's Plantation, 6 Log, Copper Puce 85.00
Bottle, Bitters, Greeley's, Bourbon Bitters, Dark Amber 100.00
Bottle, Bitters, Green, Bruise, 9 1/2 In. *Illus* 110.00
Bottle, Bitters, Hentz's Curative, Sample 25.00
Bottle, Bitters, National Bitters, Red Amber Ear Of Corn 100.00
Bottle, Bitters, Olive Figural In Shape Of Bear 35.00
Bottle, Carter, Cathedral, Cobalt With Cap And Label 50.00
Bottle, Carter, Figural, Ma & Pa Carter, Dated, 1 Pair 70.00
Bottle, Case Gin, Applied Seal, Bubbles, Dark Olive, 8 1/2 In. 30.00
Bottle, Case Gin, Applied Seal, Embossed, Olive, 10 3/4 In. 47.50
Bottle, Case Gin, Applied Seal, 10 1/4 In. 22.50
Bottle, Case Gin, Applied Seal, 11 In. 25.00
Bottle, Case Gin, Applied Top, Whittled, Air Bubbles, Olive Green, 10 1/2 In. 18.00
Bottle, Case Gin, Flared Lip, Open Pontil, Deep Olive Amber, 8 3/4 In. 45.00
Bottle, Coca-Cola, see Coca-Cola, Bottle
Bottle, Cologne, Beaded Rib, 8 In. 200.00
Bottle, Cosmetic, Cremex Shampooing Vase, Blue, 8 1/2 In. *Illus* 55.00
Bottle, Cosmetic, Roger's Nursery Hair Lotion, Aqua, 6 1/2 In. *Illus* 22.00
Bottle, Cream, Big Mac Penitentiary, McAlester, Oklahoma, 1/2 Pint .20
Bottle, Decanter, Bulbous, White Enamel, Gold Trim, Green, C.1800, 8 3/4 In. 60.00
Bottle, Decanter, Ship's, Blown Stopper, 9 7/8 In. 35.00
Bottle, Demijohn, Wicker-Covered, Aqua, Quart 12.00
Bottle, Drug, Day's Pharmacy, San Rafael, Cal., 5 In. 4.00
Bottle, Drug, Syr. Vanilla, Cut Glass, Flutes, Vines, & Fruits, 11 In. 65.00
Bottle, Figural, Bunch Of Grapes, Cap Marked Bologna, Purple, 5 In. 27.50
Bottle, Figural, Bust Of Columbus, Milk Glass, Clear Pedestal, 1892, 6 In. 125.00
Bottle, Figural, Bust Of Old Soldier, 12 In. 25.00
Bottle, Figural, Cigar, Amber, 5 1/2 In. 10.00
Bottle, Figural, Dagger, 8 1/2 In. 15.00
Bottle, Figural, Duck, Beak Pours, Ceramic, 12 In. *Illus* 20.00
Bottle, Figural, Duck, Swimming, 5 In. 30.00
Bottle, Figural, Fish, Amber, 9 3/4 In. 15.00
Bottle, Figural, George Washington, 9 1/2 In. 6.95
Bottle, Figural, Hand, Palm Down, 5 1/8 In. 26.50
Bottle, Figural, Hot Tamale, Austria, Patent Applied For, 8 In. 30.00
Bottle, Figural, Hot Tamale, Porcelain, Patent Applied For, 6 In. 30.00
Bottle, Figural, Log Cabin, 10 1/2 In. *Illus* 85.00

Bottle, Bitters, Green, Bruise, 9 1/2 In.

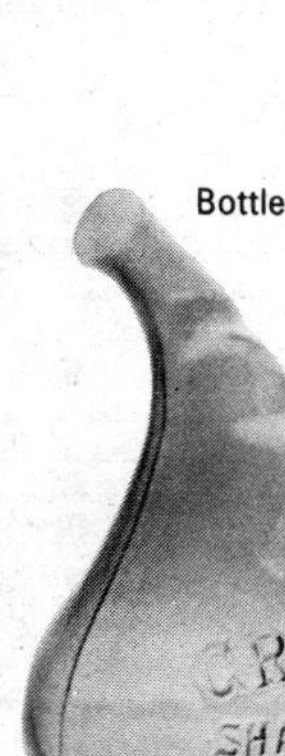

Bottle, Cosmetic, Cremex Shampooing Vase, Blue, 8 1/2 In.

Bottle, Figural, Duck, Beak Pours, Ceramic, 12 In.

Bottle, Cosmetic, Roger's Nursery Hair Lotion, Aqua, 6 1/2 In.

Bottle, Figural, Log Cabin, 10 1/2 In.

Bottle, Figural, Man Sitting On Barrel, "What We Want, " Blue, 6 In. 75.00
Bottle, Figural, Man With Mirror In Stomach, Giggle Soup, 5 1/4 In. 45.00
Bottle, Figural, Pig, Female, Pottery, 6 In. 200.00
Bottle, Figural, Pistol, Victorian, Cork, 9 In. 25.00
Bottle, Figural, Pretzel, Porcelain, 6 In. 30.00
Bottle, Figural, Shampoodle, Blue, 8 In. 14.00
Bottle, Figural, Slipper, Bow, 5 3/4 In. 22.75
Bottle, Figural, Three Cupids Supporting Globe, Depose, 11 3/4 In. 300.00
Bottle, Flask, Albany Glass Works, Aqua, Pint, McK G I-28 .... 45.00
Bottle, Flask, Amber, McK G VIII-18 .... 275.00
Bottle, Flask, Aqua, McK G II-24 .... 150.00
Bottle, Flask, Aqua, McK G II-52 .... 115.00
Bottle, Flask, Aqua, McK G IX-34 .... 100.00
Bottle, Flask, Aqua, McK G V-4 .... 675.00
Bottle, Flask, Blue Green, McK G III-14 .... 265.00
Bottle, Flask, Byron & Scott, Amber, 1/2 Pint, McK G I-114 .... 140.00
Bottle, Flask, Calabash, Jenny Lind, Aquamarine, McK G I-103 .... 95.00
Bottle, Flask, Ceramic, Happiness, Comic Couple, 1/2 Pint 12.00
Bottle, Flask, Chestnut, Handled, Red Amber, Pint 37.00
Bottle, Flask, Clasped Hands & Eagle With Banner, Aqua, 1/2 Pint 60.00
Bottle, Flask, Coffin, A.Weinberg, Tacoma, W.T. In Slug Plate, 1/2 Pint 200.00
Bottle, Flask, Cognac, San Francisco, Aqua, Pint 9.00

Bottle, Flask, Cornucopia & Basket, Olive Green, Pint 65.00
Bottle, Flask, Cornucopia & Urn, Green, 1/2 Pint, McK G III-8 .... 130.00
Bottle, Flask, Dog & Grapes, Cobalt, 1/2 Pint 60.00
Bottle, Flask, Double Eagle & Pittsburgh, Aqua, Pint 60.00
Bottle, Flask, Double Eagle Over Oval, Aqua, 1/2 Pint 34.00
Bottle, Flask, Double Eagle, Amber, 1/2 Pint 50.00
Bottle, Flask, Double Eagle, Olive Green, Pint 50.00
Bottle, Flask, Double Eagle, Open Pontil, Deep Olive, Pint 85.00
Bottle, Flask, Eagle & Cornucopia, Aqua, Pint, McK G II-72 .... 70.00
Bottle, Flask, Eagle & Cornucopia, Olive Green, Pint, McK G II-73 .... 50.00
Bottle, Flask, Eagle & Willington Glass Co., Amber, Quart, McK G II-61 .... 145.00
Bottle, Flask, Edwardian, Glass & Leather, Silver Cap, 1904, 2 Ozs., 4 1/2 In. 25.00
Bottle, Flask, Emerald, McK G I-54 .... 375.00
Bottle, Flask, Flag & Eagle, Medium Green, McK G II-48 .... 775.00
Bottle, Flask, For Pike's Peak & Eagle, Aqua, Pint, McK G II-21 .... 50.00
Bottle, Flask, Franklin & Dyott, Amber, McK G I-94 .... 1650.00
Bottle, Flask, German Silver Top, Leather Around Top, 21 Ozs. 23.50
Bottle, Flask, Granite Glass Works, Amber, Pint 85.00
Bottle, Flask, Green, McK G II-62 .... 225.00
Bottle, Flask, Horse & Cart & Eagle & Stars, McK G V-8 .... 150.00
Bottle, Flask, Jenny Lind & Lyre, Pint, McK G I-108 .... 800.00
Bottle, Flask, Jenny Lind, Blue, McK G I-104 .... 1900.00
Bottle, Flask, Keene & Masonic, Olive Amber, Pint, McK G IV-17 .... 130.00
Bottle, Flask, Kent, Ohio, Yellow Green, Pint 775.00
Bottle, Flask, Kossuth & Frigate Mississippi, Blue Green, McK G I-112 .... 800.00
Bottle, Flask, Kossuth & Sloop, Aqua, McK G I-2 .... 290.00
Bottle, Flask, Louisville, Ky., Glassworks, Strap Sided, Aqua, Quart 44.50
Bottle, Flask, Manuta, Hip, Amethyst, 1/2 Pint 350.00
Bottle, Flask, McK G I-11, Bust Of Washington & Eagle, C.1850, Aqua, Pint 700.00
Bottle, Flask, McK G I-12, Washington & Eagle, C.1850, Green, Pint 3250.00
Bottle, Flask, McK G I-39, Washington & Taylor, Emerald, Quart 450.00
Bottle, Flask, McK G I-68, General Jackson, Facing Left, Green, Pint 3100.00
Bottle, Flask, McK G I-77, Taylor & Eagle & Masterson, Aqua, Quart 2100.00
Bottle, Flask, McK G II-14, Eagle & Cornucopia, C.1850, Aqua, 1/2 Pint 450.00
Bottle, Flask, McK G II-17, Eagle & Cornucopia, C.1850, Aqua, 1/2 Pint 200.00
Bottle, Flask, McK G II-26, Double Eagle, C.1850, Emerald Green, Quart 750.00
Bottle, Flask, McK G X-30, Trapper & Buck, C.1850, Aquamarine, Pint 375.00
Bottle, Flask, New London & Eagle, Aqua, Pint, McK G II-66 .... 270.00
Bottle, Flask, Olive Amber, McK G II-72 .... 95.00
Bottle, Flask, Olive Amber, McK G VIII-16 .... 270.00
Bottle, Flask, Pewter & Glass, C.1866, 1/4 Pint 18.00
Bottle, Flask, Pewter & Glass, 1886, Pint 25.00
Bottle, Flask, Pewter & Leather Encased, C.1865, 1/2 Pint 9.95
Bottle, Flask, Pewter Screw Cap, 3 1/4 In. 5.00
Bottle, Flask, Picnic, Clock & Cobweb, 1/2 Pint 9.00
Bottle, Flask, Pitkin, Kent, Light Green, 1/2 Pint 365.00
Bottle, Flask, Pitkin, Mantua, Blue Green, Pint 350.00
Bottle, Flask, Pitkin, Mantua, Dark Green, Pint 250.00
Bottle, Flask, Sapphire Blue, McK G IX-1 .... 1300.00
Bottle, Flask, Scroll, Open Pontil, Lime Green, Pint, McK G IX-17 .... 125.00
Bottle, Flask, Smooth Base, Amber, McK G II-63 .... 185.00
Bottle, Flask, Soldier On Horseback, Yellow, Quart 310.00
Bottle, Flask, Star, Single Seam, Pewter Lid, Amber, Pint 20.00
Bottle, Flask, Success To The Railroad, Aqua, Pint, McK G V-1 .... 350.00
Bottle, Flask, Union & Clasped Hands & A & Co., Quart 100.00
Bottle, Flask, Union & Clasped Hands & Cannon & F A & Co., Aqua, 1/2 Pint 85.00
Bottle, Flask, Union & Clasped Hands, Aqua, Quart 65.00
Bottle, Flask, Washington & Taylor, Blue Green, McK G I-41 .... 150.00
Bottle, Flask, Washington & Taylor, Deep Blue, McK G I-54 .... 2150.00
Bottle, Flask, Washington & Taylor, Lavender, Quart 2000.00
Bottle, Flask, Westford & Sheaf Of Wheat, Light Amber, Pint 95.00
Bottle, Flask, Yellow Green, McK G III-15 .... 375.00
Bottle, Flask, Yellow, McK G X-15 .... 675.00
Bottle, Flask, Zanesville, Dark Amber, 1/2 Pint 700.00
Bottle, Flask, Zanesville, Flat, Golden Amber, Pint 1300.00
Bottle, Flask, Zanesville, Hip, Deep Amber, 1/2 Pint 700.00

Bottle, Food, Catsup, Three Mold, Whittled, Aqua, 10 In. 13.00

Bottle, Food, Genuine Sanford's Ginger, Patent 1876, Aqua, 6 3/4 In. 3.95

Bottle, Food, Penguin Syrup, Tin Screw Cap, 8 In. 4.50

Bottle, Fruit Jar, A.G.Smalley, Tin Top & Handle, Quart 32.00

Bottle, Fruit Jar, Acme, Embossed, Pint 5.00

Bottle, Fruit Jar, Acme, In Shield, Pint 5.00

Bottle, Fruit Jar, Ball Mason, Amber Swirls, Emerald Green, Pint 69.00

Bottle, Fruit Jar, Ball Perfect Mason, Amber, 1/2 Gallon 20.00 To 22.00

Bottle, Fruit Jar, Ball Standard, 1/2 Gallon 15.00

Bottle, Fruit Jar, Ball, Zinc Lid, Light Olive Green, Quart 11.00

Bottle, Fruit Jar, Bernardin, Latchford Marble Glass Co., Embossed, Quart 3.50

Bottle, Fruit Jar, C F J Co., Mason's Improved, Whittled, Zinc Lid, Midget 8.00

Bottle, Fruit Jar, C.F.Spencer, Lift Top, Quart 80.00

Bottle, Fruit Jar, Clarke, Aqua, Pint 75.00

Bottle, Fruit Jar, Cohansey, Aqua, Quart 17.00

Bottle, Fruit Jar, Cohansey, Quart 17.00

Bottle, Fruit Jar, Crown Imperial, Midget 7.00

Bottle, Fruit Jar, Crown, Ground Mouth, Midget 8.00

Bottle, Fruit Jar, Crystal Jar, 1/2 Gallon 30.00

Bottle, Fruit Jar, Dandy, 1/2 Gallon 81.00

Bottle, Fruit Jar, Eagle, Whittled, Quart 65.00

Bottle, Fruit Jar, Empire, Quart 17.00

Bottle, Fruit Jar, Federal, Quart 85.00

Bottle, Fruit Jar, Flaccus Bros., E.C., Steer's Head, Pint 40.00

Bottle, Fruit Jar, Flaccus, Steer's Head, Simplex Lid, Pint 37.00

Bottle, Fruit Jar, Flaccus, Steer's Head, Threaded Glass Lid, Amber, Pint 250.00

Bottle, Fruit Jar, Flaccus, Steer's Head, Threaded Glass Lid, Square, Pint 75.00

Bottle, Fruit Jar, Fruit-Keeper, Aqua, Quart 25.00

Bottle, Fruit Jar, Globe, Amber, Quart 31.00

Bottle, Fruit Jar, Globe, Pint 17.00

Bottle, Fruit Jar, Hazel, Embossed On Milk Glass Lid, Zinc Band, Amber, Quart 75.00

Bottle, Fruit Jar, Hemingray, Patent June, 1861, Metal Lid, 1/2 Gallon 79.00

Bottle, Fruit Jar, Kerr Mason, 1/2 Pint 4.00

Bottle, Fruit Jar, Kerr 65th Anniversary, Applied Gold, Quart 22.00

Bottle, Fruit Jar, Kerr 65th Anniversary, Blue Streaked, Quart 14.00

Bottle, Fruit Jar, Kerr, Amber, Quart 7.50

Bottle, Fruit Jar, Kerr, Square, 1/2 Pint 1.00

Bottle, Fruit Jar, Lightning Trademark, Glass Lid, Aqua, Quart 2.75

Bottle, Fruit Jar, Lightning, Amber, Pint 43.00

Bottle, Fruit Jar, Lyman, W.W., Crimped Tin Lid, Pint 75.00

Bottle, Fruit Jar, Lynchburg Standard Mason, Quart 11.50

Bottle, Fruit Jar, Mason's CFJ Co., Improved, Clyde, N.Y., Midget 12.75

Bottle, Fruit Jar, Mason's Patent Nov.30th, 1858, C.G.Co., Quart 6.50

Bottle, Fruit Jar, Mason's Patent Nov.30th, 1858, Snowflake, Zinc Lid, Quart 17.00

Bottle, Fruit Jar, Mason's Patent Nov.30th, 1858, Whittled, Vaseline, Pint 150.00

Bottle, Fruit Jar, Mason's Patent Nov.30th, 1858, Whittled, Zinc Lid, Midget 8.00

Bottle, Fruit Jar, Mason's 7, 1858, Aqua, Quart 5.00

Bottle, Fruit Jar, Millville Atmospheric, High Relief, 1/2 Gallon 30.00

Bottle, Fruit Jar, Millville Improved, C.W.T.Co. Monogram, Quart 45.00

Bottle, Fruit Jar, Millville, Quart 22.00

Bottle, Fruit Jar, Millville, 1/2 Gallon 27.00

Bottle, Fruit Jar, Moore's Patent Dec.3rd, 1861, Aqua, Quart 60.00

Bottle, Fruit Jar, Palace Home Jar, Hansee's, Quart 40.00

Bottle, Fruit Jar, Patent June 9, 1860, Cincinatti, Ohio, Aqua, 1/2 Gallon 75.00

Bottle, Fruit Jar, Protector, Paneled, Aqua, Quart 25.00

Bottle, Fruit Jar, Protector, Quart 40.00

Bottle, Fruit Jar, Protector, 7 In. *Illus* 30.00

Bottle, Fruit Jar, Putnam, Amber, Pint 41.00

Bottle, Fruit Jar, Queen, The, CFJ Co., 1869, Embossed, Aqua, Quart 12.00

Bottle, Fruit Jar, Queen, The, Light Green, 1/2 Gallon 40.00

Bottle, Fruit Jar, Root Mason, Aqua, Quart 4.00

Bottle, Fruit Jar, Safety, Amber, Quart 68.00

Bottle, Fruit Jar, Schaefer, The, Aqua, Quart 160.00

Bottle, Fruit Jar, Tillyer Winslow, Ghost Letters, Quart 80.00

Bottle, Fruit Jar, Winslow, Wire Clamp, Quart 50.00

Bottle, Fruit Jar, Woodbury, Quart 25.00

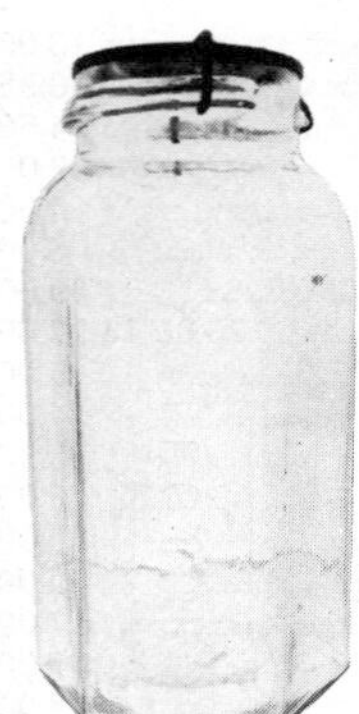

Bottle, Fruit Jar, Protector, 7 In.
(See Page 45)

Bottle, Milk, National Dairy Show, 6 In.

Bottle, Medicine, Mal-A-Bar Tiffin, Ohio, Amber, 9 1/2 In.

Bottle, Nursing, Happy Baby, 7 In.

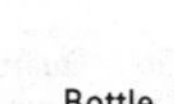

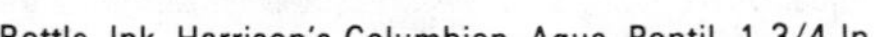

Bottle, Ink, Harrison's Columbian, Aqua, Pontil, 1 3/4 In.

Bottle, Fruit Jar, 1858, Hourglass Monogram Reverse, Midget 29.00
Bottle, Fruit Jar, 1858, Maltese Cross Reverse, Midget 11.00
Bottle, Gemel, Emerald Green, Engraved Gold Metal Lids, 5 1/2 In. 35.00
Bottle, Gin, Taper, Olive Green, Pint 12.50
Bottle, Ink, Bixby, Aqua, Truncated Cone, 2 1/2 In. 25.00
Bottle, Ink, Carter's, Cathedral, Quart 45.00
Bottle, Ink, Carter's, Master, Stain, Amber, 6 Ozs. 12.50
Bottle, Ink, Carter's, Washington, D.C., Embossed, Quart 12.00
Bottle, Ink, Figural, Carter's, Crosslegged Man 35.00
Bottle, Ink, Fostoria Safety, No.486, 2 1/2 In. 6.50
Bottle, Ink, Geometric, Dark Green, McK G II-16a 95.00
Bottle, Ink, Harrison's Columbian, Aqua, Pontil, 1 3/4 In. .... *Illus* 85.00
Bottle, Ink, J.Bourne & Son, Pottery, Pint 15.00
Bottle, Ink, Ma & Pa Carter, Pair 70.00
Bottle, Ink, P.J.Arnold, Pour Lip, Pottery, Quart 11.00
Bottle, Ink, Pair In Leather Book Box Titled Rollin's Ancient History 59.00
Bottle, Ink, Stafford's, Pouring Lip, Blue, 16 Ozs. 9.00
Bottle, Liqueur, Sloe Gin, M.J.Weisskopf, Brown, 25/32 Quart 3.50
Bottle, Medicine, American Eagle Liniment, Hexagonal, 5 In. 20.00
Bottle, Medicine, Ayer's Cherry Pectoral, 7 In. 20.00
Bottle, Medicine, Chamberlain's Liver Pills, Oval, Pocket Size 6.50
Bottle, Medicine, Dr.Cumming's Vegetine, Oval, Aqua, 9 1/2 In. 3.95
Bottle, Medicine, Dr.Hubbard's Vegetable Disinfectant, Aqua, Oval, 6 1/2 In. 3.95
Bottle, Medicine, Dr.Jaugo's Spanish Ague Remedy, Label, Iron Pontil, 8 In. 30.00

Bottle, Medicine, Dr.Lunt's Ague Killer, 7 In. 50.00
Bottle, Medicine, Dr.Tobia's Venetian Liniment, Oval, 4 In. 20.00
Bottle, Medicine, J.Russell Spaulding, Genvine, Boston, Paneled, Aqua, 8 In. 65.00
Bottle, Medicine, Louden's Indian Expectorant, Oval, 7 1/2 In. 60.00
Bottle, Medicine, Mal-A-Bar Tiffin, Ohio, Amber, 9 1/2 In. *Illus* 45.00
Bottle, Medicine, McEelree's Cardui, Aqua, 8 1/2 In. 2.50
Bottle, Medicine, Mexican Mustang Liniment, Open Pontil, Aqua, 4 In. 125.00
Bottle, Medicine, Mrs.Winslow's Soothing Syrup, Blown, Embossed, Aqua, 5 In. 10.00
Bottle, Medicine, Preston's Vegetable Purifying Catholicon, Aqua, 9 1/2 In. 60.00
Bottle, Medicine, S.A.Richmond, Md., Samaritan Nervine, C.1882, Flint, 8 In. 3.00
Bottle, Medicine, W.T.Co., Acorn Stopper, Rectangular, Milk Glass, 7 1/2 In. 27.50
Bottle, Medicine, Warner's Safe Cure, D.C., Pint 45.00
Bottle, Medicine, Warner's Safe Cure, London, Green, 1/2 Pint 160.00
Bottle, Medicine, Warner's Safe Cure, London, 1/2 Pint 85.00
Bottle, Medicine, Warner's Safe Cure, Melbourne, Pint 45.00
Bottle, Medicine, Wheatley's Compound Syrup, 6 In. 40.00
Bottle, Milk, Alpine Milk Co., Quart 2.00
Bottle, Milk, Big Mac Penitentiary, McAlester, Oklahoma, Quart .20
Bottle, Milk, Borden's, 2 In. 2.00
Bottle, Milk, Broughton's Dairy, Quart 2.00
Bottle, Milk, Deer Foot Farm, Turnip Shape, Tin Screw Lid, 1/2 Pint 7.00
Bottle, Milk, Golden State Store, 1/2 Gallon 6.00
Bottle, Milk, Graber Dairy, Golden Guernsey, Quart 2.00
Bottle, Milk, Hampden, Embossed Cow, 1/2 Pint 6.00
Bottle, Milk, Horlick's, Embossed, Pint 9.50
Bottle, Milk, Montpelier, Vt., Pint 3.00
Bottle, Milk, National Dairy Show, 6 In. *Illus* 12.50
Bottle, Milk, Northfield, Vt., Tin Top, 1/4 Pint 15.00
Bottle, Milk, Old Forge Farm, Spring Grove, Pa., Embossed, Quart 25.00
Bottle, Milk, One Pint B.B., Embossed, 2 1/4 In. 5.00
Bottle, Milk, Washington, D.C., Embossed Cow, House, & Tree, Tin Top, Pint 12.00
Bottle, Milk, World War II, V For Victory, Buy War Bonds & Stamps, Quart 25.00
Bottle, Mineral Water, Artesian Spring, Ballston Spa, N.Y., Dug, Green, Pint 35.00
Bottle, Mineral Water, Buffalo Water, Lithia Springs, Aqua, 10 1/2 In. 14.75
Bottle, Mineral Water, Congress & Empire Spring Co., Olive Green, 9 3/4 In. 22.00
Bottle, Mineral Water, D.A.Knowlton, Saratoga, N.Y., Emerald Green, Quart 45.00
Bottle, Mineral Water, Empire Spring Co., Saratoga, N.Y., Green, Quart 22.00
Bottle, Mineral Water, Excelsior Springs, Green, Quart 25.00
Bottle, Mineral Water, Hanbury Smith Vichy, Teal Blue, 1/2 Pint 30.00
Bottle, Mineral Water, Queen City Pure, Buffalo, N.Y., Porcelain Top, 64 Ozs. 15.00
Bottle, Nursing, Happy Baby, 7 In. *Illus* 5.00
Bottle, Nursing, The Little Papoose, 8 In. *Illus* 125.00
Bottle, Oil, Shell, Embossed, Quart, 14 1/2 In. 22.00
Bottle, Pepsi Cola, 1940s 20.00
Bottle, Perfume, Czechoslovakia, Acid Cut Portrait, Black Amethyst 95.00
Bottle, Perfume, Czechoslovakia, C.1920, Lalique Style, Honey Color, 3 In. 15.00
Bottle, Perfume, Czechoslovakia, Stones In Brass Base, Black Amethyst 95.00
Bottle, Perfume, Figural, Clown, Head Stopper, Porcelain, 3 In. 15.00
Bottle, Perfume, Fish Stopper, Relief Vases & Bubbles, 6 1/2 In. 15.00
Bottle, Perfume, Flint, Floral Gilt In Panels, Loops On Base 65.00
Bottle, Perfume, French, Crystal, Copper Wheel, Mythical Figures, 6 In. 60.00
Bottle, Perfume, Golliwogg, Afro Face & Hair, 2 1/2 In. 35.00
Bottle, Perfume, Golliwogg, Afro Face & Hair, 3 In. 35.00
Bottle, Perfume, Le Chic Chic De Vigny, France, Figural, 3 1/2 In. 25.00
Bottle, Perfume, Long Stopper, Crystal, Square, 5 1/4 In. 15.00
Bottle, Perfume, Moon Mullins, Black Removable Hat Cap 13.00
Bottle, Perfume, Pink, Enamel Floral, Ormolu Screw Cap, 4 Lobed, C.1900, 3 In. 30.00
Bottle, Perfume, Red, Swirled Feather Stopper, 3 3/4 In. 38.00
Bottle, Perfume, Sterling Overlay, Minneapolis In Design, 3 1/2 In. 25.00
Bottle, Perfume, Taylor's Dummy, Schiaparelli, Figural, Woman, 4 1/2 In. 30.00
Bottle, Sarsaparilla, Ayer's, Open Pontil, Aqua, 7 3/4 In. 50.00
Bottle, Sarsaparilla, Hood's, Lowell, Ma., Rectangular, Aqua, 9 In. 3.95
Bottle, Sarsaparilla, John Bull Extract Of, Louisville, Aqua, 8 3/4 In. 100.00
Bottle, Scent, Ruby & Clear Cut Crystal, Block Pattern, Silver Top, Hallmarks 225.00
Bottle, Scent, Seahorse, White Stripes 45.00

Bottle, Nursing, The Little Papoose, 8 In.

(See Page 47)

Bottle, Whiskey, Extra Superior, Black, 10 In.

Bottle, Scent, Shoe 12.00
Bottle, Scent, Wistarberg 450.00
Bottle, Shoe Polish, Gilt Edge Dressing, Patent 1890, Aqua, 4 In. 4.95
Bottle, Smelling Salts, Sterling Filigree Casing & Ball Top, 6 1/4 In. 40.00
Bottle, Smelling Salts, Sterling Top, Zipper, Pierced, Inside Stopper, 4 In. 25.00
Bottle, Snuff, Amethyst, Pewter Screw Top 60.00
Bottle, Snuff, Blown, Olive Amber 80.00
Bottle, Snuff, Carved Amber With Animal 125.00
Bottle, Snuff, Fighting Warriors, Oriental 100.00
Bottle, Snuff, German Woman In Blue Gown Holding Fan 26.00
Bottle, Snuff, Hand-Painted Porcelain, Jade Stopper, 2 1/2 In. 30.00
Bottle, Snuff, Malachite, Banded, Carved Bonsai Tree, 2 1/4 In. 140.00
Bottle, Snuff, Malachite, Bosanji Growing Into Side, 2 1/4 In. 125.00
Bottle, Snuff, Opalescent, Pewter Screw Top 60.00
Bottle, Snuff, Tortoise Color, Genre Scene, Oriental 80.00
Bottle, Soda, A.F.Dietz, Altamont, N.Y., Hutchinson, Dug, Quart 15.00
Bottle, Soda, Blue Ridge, St.Louis, Mo., 24 Fluid Ozs., Quart 8.00
Bottle, Soda, Fanta, Filled & Capped, 3 1/2 In. 1.00
Bottle, Soda, Grapette, 1947, 6 Ozs., 7 In. 1.00
Bottle, Soda, Hippo, Nov.2, 1926, 13 Ozs. 5.00
Bottle, Soda, Lemonette, 1947, 6 Ozs., 7 In. 1.00
Bottle, Soda, Mayer & Bernstein, Albany, N.Y., Hutchinson, Dug, Aqua, Quart 17.00
Bottle, Soda, Moxie, Aqua, Quart 1.50
Bottle, Soda, National Bottling Co., St.Louis, Mo., 23 Fluid Ozs. 3.00
Bottle, Soda, Nu Icy, March 9, 1920, 1/2 Pint 7.50
Bottle, Soda, Orangette, 1947, 6 Ozs., 7 In. 1.00
Bottle, Soda, Royal, St.Louis, Mo., 22 Fluid Ozs. 2.00
Bottle, Soda, Silver Seal, American Soda Water Co., St.Louis, Mo., Quart 9.00
Bottle, Soda, St.Louis, Mo., 7 Circular Ribs, Pint, 7 Fluid Ozs. 12.00
Bottle, Soda, Tip-Top Bottling Co., St.Louis, Mo., Quart 8.00
Bottle, Soda, Vess Cola, 5 1/2 In. 2.75
Bottle, Soda, VP Valley Park, Mo., 24 Ozs. 3.00
Bottle, Stoneware, Chivas Regal, Brass Corked Stopper, Doulton 40.00
Bottle, Toilet, Pittsburgh, Amethyst 300.00
Bottle, Whiskey, Altschul, Springfield, Ohio, Square, Quart 12.00
Bottle, Whiskey, Ambassador Scotch, Figural, Fish, 8 In. 27.50
Bottle, Whiskey, Arak Of Lebanon, Red Felt Covering, 13 In. 5.00
Bottle, Whiskey, D.Pariser, Brooklyn, 8 Panels, Amber, 1/2 Gallon 60.00
Bottle, Whiskey, Extra Superior, Black, 10 In. .... *Illus* 45.00
Bottle, Whiskey, Farmville, Va., Dispensary, Pint 27.00
Bottle, Whiskey, Four Roses, Louisville, Embossed, Amber, Quart 5.00
Bottle, Whiskey, Golden Wedding, Screw Top, Carnival, 1/10 Pint 16.00
Bottle, Whiskey, Good Old Bourbon In A Hog's–, Pig, 6 3/4 In. 50.00
Bottle, Whiskey, Good Old Rye In A Hog's–, Pig, Embossed, Pottery, 7 In. 350.00
Bottle, Whiskey, Hanlen Brothers, Harrisburg, Pa., Handled, Crockery, Pint 35.00
Bottle, Whiskey, Hayner Distilling Co., Springfield, O., Stoneware, 2 Gallon 38.00
Bottle, Whiskey, Heather Dew Scotch, 2 Handles, 4/5 Quart 6.00
Bottle, Whiskey, J.C.Schnell's Sour Mash Kiln Dried Grain, Pottery, Quart 34.50

Bottle, Whiskey, Jackman, Embossed, Carnival Glass, Pint 9.50
Bottle, Whiskey, Meredith, East Liverpool, Ohio, Quart 12.00
Bottle, Whiskey, Meredith's Diamond Club Pure Rye, Porcelain, White, Quart 75.00
Bottle, Whiskey, O'Donnel's Brand Irish, Pottery, Handled, Quart 24.50
Bottle, Whiskey, O'Keffe's, Oswego, N.Y., Pottery, Quart 45.00
Bottle, Whiskey, Oak Valley Distilling Co., San Francisco, 9 1/2 In. 30.00
Bottle, Whiskey, Old Overholt Straight Rye, Flat, Miniature 30.00
Bottle, Whiskey, P.Claudius & Co., San Francisco, Inside Screw, Amber, Fifth 28.00
Bottle, Whiskey, Paul Jones Rye, Seal, Turn Mold, Red Amber, Quart 22.00
Bottle, Whiskey, Raleigh, N.C., Dispensary, 1/2 Pint 40.00
Bottle, Whiskey, S.Rosenthal, N.Y., 6 Panels, Amber, 1/2 Gallon 60.00
Bottle, Whiskey, Sherman Rye, Hildebrandt, Posner & Co., C.1900, Amber, Quart 20.00
Bottle, Whiskey, Shoteau House, Ft.Benton, Montana, Sterling Overlay, Pint 75.00
Bottle, Whiskey, South Carolina Dispensary & Tree, Monogrammed, Pint 30.00
Bottle, Whiskey, South Carolina Dispensary & Tree, Strap Sided, Pint 75.00
Bottle, Whiskey, South Carolina Dispensary, Monogrammed, 1/2 Pint 9.00
Bottle, Whiskey, Taylor, Strap Sided, Label, Amber, Pint 10.00
Bottle, Whiskey, Teddy's Pet, Turtle Shape, Sample 18.00
Bottle, Whiskey, Thos. Moore Possom Hollow, Pinch, Aluminum Top, Miniature 6.00
Bottle, Wine, Porcelain, Gold-Trimmed Lid, Cream Color, Enamel Floral, 12 In. 30.00
Bottle, Zanesville, Globular, Green 500.00
Bottle, Zanesville, Swirled Globular, Golden Amber 405.00
Bottle, Zanesville, Swirled Globular, Green 825.00
Bottle, Zanesville, Swirled Globular, Red Amber 25.00
Bow, Basket, Quail Pattern, Circular, Kakiemon Flowers, 9 3/4 In. 550.00

Boxes of all kinds are collected. They were made of thin strips of inlaid wood, metal, tortoiseshell, embroidery, or other material.

Box, see also Ivory, Box; Porcelain, Box; Shaker, Box; Store Box; Tin, Box; and various porcelain categories.
Box, Tea Caddy, see also Furniture, Tea Caddy, Silver, Sterling, Tea Caddy, and various porcelain categories.
Box, Battersea, see Battersea, Box

Box, Candle, Molded Sliding Ring, 12 3/4 X 8 3/4 In. *Illus* 45.00

Box, Candle, Molded Sliding Ring, 12 3/4 X 8 3/4 In.

Box, Trinket, Decorated, 7 3/4 X 5 1/4 In.

(See Page 50)

Box, Collar & Button, Oriental, Black & Gold, Round, 6 1/2 In. 9.00
Box, Glove, Hinged Glass Lid, Leather-Covered Sides, Victorian, 12 In. 28.00
Box, Jewel, Spanish Import, Tortoise, Silver Mounted, C 1825, 7 X 5 In. 225.00
Box, Jewelry Chest, Cabinet Shape, Brass Trim, 5 Drawers, Jade Inserts 150.00
Box, Jewelry, French, Music Box, Mirrored, Clown On Top 125.00
Box, Jewelry, French, Musical, Mirrored, China Head Clown Doll 125.00
Box, Jewelry, Silver Plate, Art Nouveau, Lined 22.00
Box, Jewelry, Sterling Silver, Ornate Lift-Off Lid, Round, 4 In. 75.00
Box, Love Letters, Leather & Brass, C.1870 55.00
Box, Opaque Glass, European, Cupids On Hinged Lid, Brass Fittings, 3 3/4 In. 65.00
Box, Oriental, Camphorwood, Brass Lock, Hand-Carved, Nest Of 3 125.00
Box, Overlay, Covered, Deep Pink, White Lining, Enamel Jewels, 4 In. 105.00
Box, Patch, Glass, Lady's, Green, Enameled Pansies, 4 1/4 X 3 In. 44.00
Box, Portrait, Pola Negri, Canco Beautebox, 1920s, Round, 10 In. 35.00
Box, Powder, Glass, Japan, Covered, Engraved, Round, 4 In. 7.00
Box, Sailor's, Covered, Ebony, Baleen & Quill Inlay, 2 3/4 In. 125.00

Box, Trinket, Ivory Trim

Box, Trinket, Snap Lock, 4 In.

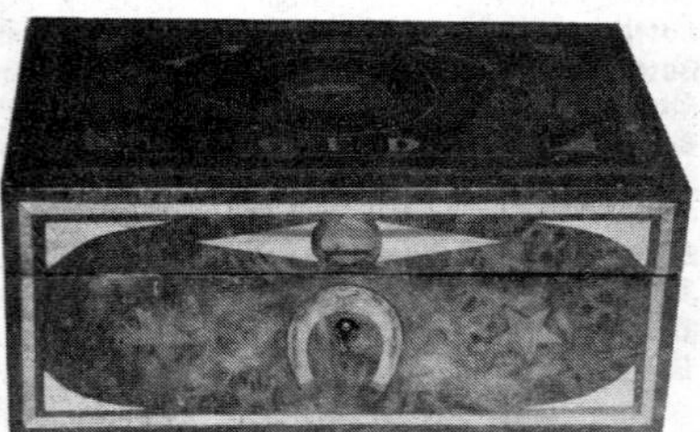

Box, Wood, Inlaid, 6 In.

Box, Snuffbox, Birchbark & Leather, C.1850, Oval, 3 In. 47.00
Box, Snuffbox, English, C.1850, Black Lacquer, Scottish Scene On Lid, 4 In. 145.00
Box, Snuffbox, Leather Flip Top, Oval 24.00
Box, Tea Caddy, Coffin Type, Bun Feet, Ivory Compartment Buttons 125.00
Box, Tin, Portrait, Bebe Daniels, Canco Beautebox, 1920's, Round, 4 In. 15.00
Box, Tin, Portrait, Gloria Swanson, Canco Beautebox, 1920's, Round, 5 In. 20.00
Box, Trinket, Beaded, Handmade, 1902 10.00
Box, Trinket, Decorated, 7 3/4 X 5 1/4 In. *Illus* 55.00
Box, Trinket, Ivory Trim *Illus* 28.00
Box, Trinket, Snap Lock, 4 In. *Illus* 36.00
Box, Wood, Inlaid, 6 In. *Illus* 45.00
Boy Scout, Ax, Winchester 35.00
Boy Scout, Book, Boy Scouts Book Of Stories, N.Y., 1919 10.00
Boy Scout, Book, Boy Scouts In Mexico, 1911 3.00
Boy Scout, Book, Handbook For Scoutmasters, 1937 6.00
Boy Scout, Book, Hitting The Trail, Mathews, 1924 5.50
Boy Scout, Book, Linen Cover, 1924 10.00
Boy Scout, Book, Lord Braden, Powell, 1941 4.50
Boy Scout, Book, Scouting Encyclopedia, 1952, McNally 5.50
Boy Scout, Book, Scouting On Two Continents, Major Burnham, 1926 3.50
Boy Scout, Book, 1938, Norman Rockwell Cover, 1st Edition 5.50
Boy Scout, Box, Pencil, Tin, Colorful 15.00
Boy Scout, Box, Trinket, Pottery, A Scout Is Trustworthy On Lid, 4 1/4 In. 10.00
Boy Scout, Bugle, Brass, Emblem 21.00
Boy Scout, Bugle, Official Boy Scouts Of America, Case 25.00
Boy Scout, Card, Picture, 1921, 10 X 7 In. 8.50
Boy Scout, Diary, 1920 7.50
Boy Scout, Diary, 1924 10.00
Boy Scout, Doll, Holding Flag, Bisque, Japan, 5 1/2 In. 25.00
Boy Scout, Emblem, Hand-Carved Wood, 13 X 9 1/2 In. 42.50
Boy Scout, Figurine, Bronze Patina Plaster, Signed, Dated 1915, 17 In. 68.00
Boy Scout, Handbook, 1918 10.00
Boy Scout, Kit, First Aid, 1940 12.00
Boy Scout, Knapsack, Camping Utensils, C.1950 7.00
Boy Scout, Knife, Remington, Metal Handle, 2 Blades, Bottle Opener 22.00

Boy Scout, Knife, Remington, No. R3333 .... 12.00
Boy Scout, Magazine, 1932 .... 4.50
Boy Scout, Medal, July 1910, The Boy Scout Shoe For Boys 10.00
Boy Scout, Paperweight, Be Prepared Motto 10.00
Boy Scout, Plaque, 1923 .... 25.00
Boy Scout, Token, Oath, Silver Dollar Size 6.00
Boy Scout, Whistle, Nickel Over Brass, Insignia On Front 2.50
Boy Scout, Yearbook, 1932 .... 5.50
Bradley & Hubbard, Candleholder, Metal, Ornate, 9 1/2 In. 65.00
Bradley & Hubbard, Desk Set, 4 Piece 48.00
Bradley & Hubbard, Frame, Picture, Brass-Plated Iron, Dutch Lass, 14 1/2 In. 37.50
Bradley & Hubbard, Humidor, Brass 25.00
Bradley & Hubbard, Inkwell, Brass, Hinged Lid, Square Base, 5 In. 44.00
Bradley & Hubbard, Inkwell, Solid Brass 22.50
Bradley & Hubbard, Lamp, Dome Shape Shade, Red Roses & Leaves, 20 X 12 In. 650.00
Bradley & Hubbard, Lamp, Oil, Brass, 7 In.Chimney 68.00
Bradley & Hubbard, Lamp, Student, Brass Double Burner, 20 X 20 In., Signed 375.00
Bradley & Hubbard, Lamp, Student, Brass, Single, Signed, 21 In. 275.00
Bradley & Hubbard, Lamp, Table, Signed Shade & Base, Chocolate Glass, 24 In. 300.00
Bradley & Hubbard, Lamp, Table, 8 Panel Chocolate Glass, Reverse Painted 300.00
Bradley & Hubbard, Letter Holder, Gold Dore Over White Metal 22.00
Bradley & Hubbard, Opener, Letter, Brass 17.00
Bradley & Hubbard, Pen Rest, Desk, Brass 5.00
Bradley & Hubbard, Tray, Pen, Brass 10.00
Bradley & Hubbard, Vase, Brass, Enamel Floral On Olive Green, Flared, 4 In. 22.00
Bradley Hubbard, Bookend, Adjustable, Urn Design, Brass 30.00

Brass has been used for decorative pieces and useful tablewares since ancient times. It is an alloy of copper, zinc, and other metals.

Brass, see also Bell, Tool, Trivet, etc.

Brass, Ashtray, Arab Wheeling Shell, 6 X 6 In. 50.00
Brass, Ashtray, Art Nouveau Maiden, Arms Outstretched, Canada, 7 X 3 1/2 In. 25.00
Brass, Ashtray, Bulldog's Head Shape, 4 1/2 In. 15.00
Brass, Ashtray, Chinese, Pair Of Attached Slippers, Enameled, 4 In. 15.00
Brass, Ashtray, Chinese, Raised Frogs On Leaf 6.00
Brass, Ashtray, Cone-Shaped Match Holder Center, Striker, 3 Footed 8.00
Brass, Ashtray, Green Marble Base, 28 X 11 In. 75.00
Brass, Ashtray, Matchbox Holder In Center 5.00
Brass, Ashtray, Nude Girl, Art Nouveau, 7 1/2 In. 20.00
Brass, Ashtray, Slipper Shape, 3 1/2 In. 15.00
Brass, Ashtray, Tilt Top, Enameled, Chinese 10.00
Brass, Bell, Brass Gong Shaped Alarm, Attached Trip Hammer, 14 In., 25 Lbs. 75.00
Brass, Bell, Farm, Bracket, Clapper 50.00
Brass, Bell, Figural, Double Clapper, Mary Queen Of Scots 25.00
Brass, Birdcage, Polished & Lacquered, Hendrix 65.00
Brass, Birdcage, Singing Bird, C.1920, 11 In. 175.00
Brass, Birdcage, 3 Singing Birds, Heads Move, 18 In. 650.00
Brass, Book Holder, Owl On Ends, Telescopic, Holds 12-15 Books 25.00
Brass, Book Rack, Lady & Flowers On Ends, Expandable, Art Nouveau 25.00
Brass, Bookend, Sailing Ships, 4 In., Pair 15.00
Brass, Bowl, Chinese, Dragons, Teak Stand, 10 In. 15.00
Brass, Bowl, Etched Cow, Men, Trees, Signed Wurttemberg 7.50
Brass, Bowl, Hand Hammered, C.1750, 14 In. 78.00
Brass, Bowl, Rice, Hand Wrought, Figures, 5 In. 45.00
Brass, Box, Card, Chinese, Enameled, Double 30.00
Brass, Box, Chinese, Dragon On Hinged Lid, Wooden Liner, 4 X 3 1/4 In. 9.75
Brass, Box, Cigarette, Chinese, Enameled 30.00
Brass, Box, Jacoby-Benz, Shape Of Lincoln Memorial, 5 X 3 In. 45.00
Brass, Box, Jewel, French, C.1850, Blue Agate Lid, Repousse, Footed, 1 3/4 In. 125.00
Brass, Box, Oriental, Engraved, Carved Jade Trim, 2 1/2 X 4 In. 22.00
Brass, Box, Patch, Cobalt & Aqua Enamel 26.00
Brass, Box, Peguy, France, Inlaid Butterfly On Dome Lid, 2 3/4 In. 35.00
Brass, Box, Powder, Art Nouveau, Pozzonis 6.00
Brass, Box, Stamp, Austrian, 3 Compartments 25.00
Brass, Box, Stamp, Double, Peking Glass Decoration, China 22.00
Brass, Box, Stamp, Fly Shape, 3 X 2 X 1 1/2 In. 6.00

Brass, Box, Stamp, Holly Sprigs On Lid, 3 1/2 X 2 1/2 In. 12.50
Brass, Brazier, Polished 70.00
Brass, Brush Holder, Japanese, Mischievous Monkeys, 10 1/8 In. 175.00
Brass, Bucket, Bail, American Brass Kettle Co., 15 1/2 X 13 1/2 In. 85.00
Brass, Bucket, Hayden's Ansonia Brass Co., 1851, Wrought-Iron Bail, 14 In. 55.00
Brass, Burner, Incense, Chinese, Beveled Crystal Dome, Openwork, Footed, 4 In. 32.50
Brass, Button, Doorbell, Electric 38.00
Brass, Buttonhook, Glove, Ivory Handle, 2 1/2 In. 7.00
Brass, Cage, Cardinal & Blue Bird Inside, Birds Tweet, French, 20 1/2 In. 650.00
Brass, Candelabra, Ornate Cast Brass, 3 Cup, Pair 85.00
Brass, Candelabra, 3-Arm, Ormolu & Porcelain On Base, 14 In., Pair 135.00
Brass, Candelabrum, Chinese, 5-Arm, 9 X 8 In. 11.75
Brass, Candelabrum, Dragons, Openwork, 7-Arm, 10 1/2 In. 27.00
Brass, Candelabrum, Five Light, Miniature 25.00
Brass, Candelabrum, Four Removable Arms, Detailed, 5 3/4 X 6 1/2 In. 40.00
Brass, Candelabrum, K Arm, Very Ornate 145.00
Brass, Candelabrum, 3-Arm, Champleve Enamel, 12 X 9 In. 95.00
Brass, Candelabrum, 3-Arm, Held By 2 Lions, 11 1/2 In. 30.00
Brass, Candelabrum, 3-Arm, Scrolls, Chinese 6 3/4 In. 6.95
Brass, Candelabrum, 4-Arm, Square, 14 X 13 In. 60.00
Brass, Candelabrum, 5-Arm, 15 In. 79.00
Brass, Candelabrum, 7-Arm, Chinese, 12 X 11 3/4 In. 19.75
Brass, Candelabrum, 7-Arm, 8 5/8 In. 25.00
Brass, Candelstick, Push-Up, Beehive, English, Register 1896 55.00
Brass, Candlestick & Incense Burner, French, Griffins On Base, 10 In., Pair 280.00
Brass, Candlestick With Bell, 13 In. 65.00
Brass, Candlestick, Beehive & Diamond Pattern, 12 In., Pair 135.00
Brass, Candlestick, C.1750, 12 In., Pair 625.00
Brass, Candlestick, C.1875, 4 In., Pair 35.00
Brass, Candlestick, Chinese, Floral, 4 3/4 In., Pair 10.00
Brass, Candlestick, Chinese, Medallions & Flowers, 8 1/4 In. 10.00
Brass, Candlestick, Classical Revival, Square Base, C.1780 165.00
Brass, Candlestick, Dragon, Parts Unscrew, 8 In. 21.00
Brass, Candlestick, English, Beehive, Push-Up, 10 In., Pair 79.00
Brass, Candlestick, Figural, Cossacks Holding Socket In Each Hand, Pair 65.00
Brass, Candlestick, Floral Engraved Bases Marked China, 7 1/2 In., Pair 35.00
Brass, Candlestick, Louis XVI, C.1790, 10 1/2 In., Pair 150.00
Brass, Candlestick, Octagonal Stem, Round Base, C.1915, 11 In., Pair 50.00
Brass, Candlestick, Push-Up, Molded Bobeche, C.1830, 12 1/4 In., Pair 125.00
Brass, Candlestick, Push-Up, 5 3/4 In., Pair 42.50
Brass, Candlestick, Push-Up, 6 In., Pair 75.00
Brass, Candlestick, Push-Up, 9 1/4 In., Pair 78.00
Brass, Candlestick, Rectangular Base, 9 1/2 In., Pair 75.00
Brass, Candlestick, Russian, 18th Century, Footed, 10 In. 35.00
Brass, Candlestick, Saucer Base, 6 3/4 In., Pair 35.00
Brass, Candlestick, Square Footed Base, 9 In., Weigh 2 1/2 Lbs.Each, Pair 45.00
Brass, Candlestick, Storrar's Chester, English, Push-Up, Faceted, 10 In., Pair 60.00
Brass, Candlestick, Stretch Double, Used On Organs, Pair 75.00
Brass, Candlestick, Turned, C.1850, 3 In., Pair 28.00
Brass, Candlestick, Turtle, Holder Unscrews From Turtle's Back, 3 In., Pair 12.00
Brass, Candlestick, Twisted Stick, C.1850, 11 3/4 In., Pair 150.00
Brass, Case, Shaving Brush, Cylindrical, Brush 5.95
Brass, Chamberstick, China 5.50
Brass, Chamberstick, English, 4 1/2 In. 35.00
Brass, Chamberstick, 8 1/4 X 4 1/2 In. 35.00
Brass, Cigar Cutter, Large Embossed Dog 25.00
Brass, Clip, Paper, Chinese, Turtle, 4 In. 35.00
Brass, Clip, Paper, Clam 65.00
Brass, Clip, Paper, Englishman Wearing Knee Pants Reading Book, 3 3/4 In. 12.50
Brass, Clip, Paper, Engraved, Set With Stone 16.00
Brass, Clip, Paper, Figural, Owl, 4 In. 35.00
Brass, Coaster, Chinese, Set Of 4 10.00
Brass, Coffeepot On Stand, Burner 62.00
Brass, Coffeepot, Hot Coal Compartment 75.00
Brass, Coffeepot, Russian, Double Eagle Mark, Long Spout, Covered, 9 In. 69.00
Brass, Compote, Arab Holding Shell, 3-Footed Base, 6 X 4 In. 55.00

Brass, Container, With Scissors & Letter Opener, Figured, 11 In. 45.00
Brass, Corkscrew, Eagle Mark, Enameled 28.00
Brass, Cup, Collapsible, Nickel Plated, Marked Vest Pocket, 1 1/2 In. 5.95
Brass, Cup, Grease, 1 1/2 In. 5.00
Brass, Cuspidor 15.00
Brass, Cutter, Cigar, Vest Pocket, Wild Boar's Head, Spring Release 30.00
Brass, Desk Set, Chinese, Engraved Flowers & Vines, 4 Piece 65.00
Brass, Door Knocker, Anchor, C.1920 10.00
Brass, Door Knocker, Cat 8.00
Brass, Door Knocker, Cat, 3 In. 21.00
Brass, Door Knocker, Eagle, Spread Wings, 8 3/4 In. 100.00
Brass, Door Knocker, England, Bust Of William Wordsworth, Floral, 2 1/2 In. 35.00
Brass, Door Knocker, Grapes, 7 X 5 In. 24.50
Brass, Door Knocker, Lady's Hand 18.50
Brass, Door Knocker, Oriental, Deer, 4 1/4 In. 15.00
Brass, Door Knocker, Woman's Hand Holding Ball 16.75
Brass, Doorbell, Fire Gong, Latchstring, 7 In. 45.00
Brass, Ewer, Hammered, Copper Seams, Hand Done, Russian, 17 In. 72.00
Brass, Ewer, Russian, Hand Done, Lip Turned, Hammered, 17 In. 70.00
Brass, Ewer, Russian, Marked, Hand Done, 17 In. 50.00
Brass, Figurine, Camel, Holder On Back For Pack Of Cigarettes, 4 1/2 In. 6.00
Brass, Footscraper, Iron Crossbar, 15 X 13 X 11 In. 95.00
Brass, Fork, Toasting, Cat Handle, 20 In. 14.00
Brass, Frame, Easel, 6 1/2 X 5 In. 6.00
Brass, Frame, Picture, Blue Enamel, Heart Shape, 2 1/8 In. 22.00
Brass, Frame, Picture, Easel Type, Rococo, Victorian, 12 X 8 In. 20.00
Brass, Frame, Picture, Filigree Bows & Tassels, 1 3/4 In. 10.00
Brass, Frypan, Chinese, 2 1/2 In. Diameter 3.00
Brass, Garniture, Mantel, Champleve Enamels, Blue Celeste, C.1850, 3 Piece 725.00
Brass, Gong, Engraved Animals And Florals, China 35.00
Brass, Gong, With Striker, In English Oak Frame, 9 X 9 In. 28.00
Brass, Hatpin, Bust Of Indian 16.00
Brass, Hook, Ceiling, Dolphin End, 9 In. 5.00
Brass, Hook, Wall, England, Cutout Figure Of St.George Slaying Dragon 12.00
Brass, Horn, Ear, Bakelite Ear Tip, 3 3/4 In. 25.00
Brass, Humidor, Enameled Bands, Porcelain Painted Lid, China 85.00
Brass, Incense Burner, Marked In Chinese, Small 12.00
Brass, Inkstand, Rococo, Floral Scrolls & Butterflies, Crystal Well, Signed 115.00
Brass, Inkwell & Pair Of 6 In. Candlesticks, Diamond Mark 135.00
Brass, Inkwell, Crab Shape, Pewter-Lined Well, 6 X 5 In. 45.00
Brass, Inkwell, Double, Cut Glass Inserts, Harvard Cutting, Pen Rest 100.00
Brass, Inkwell, Double, Drawer 75.00
Brass, Inkwell, Floral & Country Scene, Openwork, Pen Holder, 10 In. 50.00
Brass, Inkwell, French, Empire, Heart Shape, Crystal Insert, 3 1/2 In. 165.00
Brass, Inkwell, German, Mephistopheles 58.50
Brass, Inkwell, Glass Insert, Ornate 75.00
Brass, Inkwell, Inland Turquoise Medallion On Cover 23.00
Brass, Inkwell, Ornate, Porcelain Liner, 6 1/4 In. 45.00
Brass, Inkwell, Owl's Head Lid, Art Nouveau, 11 In. 175.00
Brass, Inkwell, Two Well, Mephistopheles 62.00
Brass, Jardiniere On Stand, Russian, C.1880, 26 1/2 In. Stand 495.00
Brass, Jardiniere, Lion Heads 45.00
Brass, Kettle On Stand, Finial, Burner, 10 In. 55.00
Brass, Kettle, Jelly, Burnished, 12 In. 78.00
Brass, Kettle, Jelly, 12 In. 68.00
Brass, Kettle, Original Iron Handle, 21 1/2 In. 100.00
Brass, Kettle, Rattail Bail, 1868, 12 In. 55.00
Brass, Kettle, Toddy, Black Handle, Button Feet 75.00
Brass, Key, Hollow, 12 In. 12.00
Brass, Knocker, William Wordsworth 12.00
Brass, Ladle, C.1750, 16 3/4 In. 80.00
Brass, Lamp & Heater, Ship's Cabin 95.00
Brass, Lamp Fount For Gone With Wind Lamp, Unelectrified 225.00
Brass, Lamp, Candlestick, 19 In., Pair 40.00
Brass, Lantern, Fireman's, Dietz King Fire Dept., Nickel Plated, 16 In. 75.00
Brass, Letter Opener, Heads Of 3 Dogs, 10 1/4 In. 10.00

Brass, Letter Seal, Dutch Gold Holding Cat, 5 In. 50.00
Brass, Light Fixture, Fishbowl Globe In Center, 4 Shades 95.00
Brass, Light, Auto, Solar, Patented 1909, 13 1/2 In. 85.00
Brass, Lighter, Cigarette, Cannon Shape, 9 In. 35.00
Brass, Lighter, Cigarette, Germany, Candlestick Type 12.00
Brass, Lighter, Tinder, English, C.1880, Flintlock, Candleholder, & Container 495.00
Brass, Lock, Champion, Round, 6 Lever With Key 12.00
Brass, Lock, G.W.Co., 1829-1929, Hardened Shackle 25.00
Brass, Lock, Yale, 4 In. 5.00
Brass, Mailbox, Combination Lock 4.00
Brass, Mailbox, Polished, 13 X 7 X 3 In. 18.00
Brass, Match Holder, Sideboard Shape, Hinged Lid, Fruit & Leaves, 1871 30.00
Brass, Match Holder, Ugly Man's Face For Holder, Bent Brass For Wall 39.00
Brass, Match Safe, England, C.1850, Fist Shape, 2 1/2 In. 65.00
Brass, Match Safe, England, C.1850, Hoof Shape, 3 In. 65.00
Brass, Match Safe, Man On Horseback, Pocket 20.00
Brass, Mirror, Folding, Beveled Glass 75.00
Brass, Mold, Spoon, C.1790 300.00
Brass, Mold, Spoon, Rattail, Wavy End, 8 In. 265.00
Brass, Mortar & Pestle, 8 1/2 In. Pestle 75.00
Brass, Mulling Pot, Ireland, C.1800, 12 1/2 In. 75.00
Brass, Nut Cracker, Parrot, 5 1/2 In. 30.00
Brass, Nut Cracker, Shakespeare Embossed 12.00
Brass, Nut Set, Betel, 19th Century, 5 Containers With Lids, Footed Tray 48.00
Brass, Nutcracker, Alligator 12.00
Brass, Nutcracker, Figural, Rooster, 5 1/2 In. 25.00
Brass, Nutcracker, Parrot 19.00
Brass, Nutcracker, Rooster 12.50
Brass, Opener, Bottle, Elephant 5.95
Brass, Opener, Letter, Devil's Head 2.00
Brass, Opener, Letter, England, C.1840, Horn Insert, 20 In. 135.00
Brass, Opener, Letter, Stork Handle 5.00
Brass, Padlock, Bulldog, Embossed 6.50
Brass, Padlock, Internal Revenue, Prohibition Days, Key 25.00
Brass, Pan, Iron Handle, Pouring Lip, 6 X 3 X 7 In. 75.00
Brass, Pan, Iron Handle, 8 X 4 X 9 In. 95.00
Brass, Pan, Russian, Shallow, Round, 15 In. 75.00
Brass, Paperweight, Raised Oak Leaves & Acorns, Clenched Fish, 4 In. 12.75
Brass, Pen Tray, Lion In Center, Ornate Border, 8 1/2 In. 18.00
Brass, Pillbox, Watch Shape 31.00
Brass, Pipe, Opium, Water, Flat Bottom, Chinese Marks 45.00
Brass, Pitcher, Italian, 23 In. 225.00
Brass, Plaque, Bronze Finish, Raised Bust, Washington, 10 X 14 In., Signed 75.00
Brass, Pot, Hammered Finish, 3 Legged, 8 1/2 X 7 In. 38.00
Brass, Powder Box, Porcelain Painted Scene, 2 1/2 In. 85.00
Brass, Pump, Hardwood Plunger, 32 In. 48.00
Brass, Quill Holder, 5 Holes 14.00
Brass, Rack, Necktie, Running Figure On Openwork Ground, 9 In. 14.75
Brass, Scissors, Art Nouveau, Brass Case 75.00
Brass, Sconce, Hanging Wall Candle, 2 Cup, Pair 75.00
Brass, Sconce, Wall, For 2 Lamps, Rope Design, White Ball Shades, 5 1/2 In. 70.00
Brass, Sconce, Wall, French, 19 1/2 X 9 1/2 In., Pair 125.00
Brass, Sconce, Wall, Queen Anne, 2 Scrolled Arms, Pierced, 8 1/4 In., Pair 275.00
Brass, Sconce, Wall, 2 Arm, C.1700, Pair 800.00
Brass, Sconce, Wall, 2 Arm, English, Victorian, Pair 95.00
Brass, Sconce, Wall, 3 Arm, Scroll, Drip Pans, 15 1/2 In., Pair 300.00
Brass, Scoop, Curl Finger Ring For Handle, 6 In. 15.00
Brass, Screen, Fireplace, Hand Hammered, Town Scene, 24 X 26 In. 145.00
Brass, Seal, Dutch Girl, 5 In. 75.00
Brass, Shade, Glass Beads, 4 1/2 X 4 In. 5.00
Brass, Shelf, Book, Owls On Ends, Pull-Out, 14 1/2 In. 15.50
Brass, Shoe Rest, 15 In., Pair 25.00
Brass, Silent Butler, Chinese, Enamel Handle & Trim, 4 3/4 In. 20.00
Brass, Silent Butler, Enamel Chicken, China, 4 1/2 X 6 1/2 In. 22.00
Brass, Silent Butler, Raised Flower Top 15.00
Brass, Snuff Bottle, Silver Plated, Ivory Panels, Studding Of Corals & Jade 125.00

Brass, Spittoon, Agates, Coral, & Turquoise Stones 20.00
Brass, Spittoon, Weighted Bottom, 9 1/2 X 8 In. 22.00
Brass, Spittoon, 11 In. 100.00
Brass, Spoon, Tea Caddy, Art Nouveau Handle 12.00
Brass, Stand, Book, Jeweled Stones & Cloisonne Crosses, 14 X 7 X 13 1/2 In. 275.00
Brass, Strainer, Tea, Footed Stand, Cupid Handle, Cutout Flowers, Victorian 15.00
Brass, Strainer, Tea, Woven 6.00
Brass, Syrup, Nickel Plated, Scroll Handle, Hinged Lid, 5 In. 8.95
Brass, Tape Measure, Figural, Lamp, Colored Enamel 45.00
Brass, Tea Caddy, Embossed, Tin Lined, Square, 5 1/4 X 4 1/4 In. 50.00
Brass, Tea Caddy, Embossed, 5 1/4 X 4 In. 45.00
Brass, Tea Caddy, Octagonal, 5 1/2 In. 22.00
Brass, Tea Set, Miniature 15.00
Brass, Teakettle On Stand, Alcohol Burner 60.00
Brass, Teakettle On Stand, S & Co., Patent 1892, Alcohol Burner, Tips 30.00
Brass, Teakettle, Bail Handle, 2 3/4 In. 10.00
Brass, Teakettle, Chinese, Green & Red Peking Glass Insets, Wooden Handle 35.00
Brass, Teakettle, Stand With Burner, Dated Jan.12, 1892, 4-Cup 60.00
Brass, Teapot On Stand, Tilting, Gooseneck Spout, Copper & Wood Handle, 1750 .... 240.00
Brass, Teapot, Ornate, 8 In. 25.00
Brass, Teaspoon, Chinese, Chrysanthemums 6.00
Brass, Teaspoon, Chinese, Dragon 6.00
Brass, Telescope, Extends 23 In. 45.00
Brass, Telescope, With Case, Extends To 23 1/2 In. 85.00
Brass, Telescope, 3 Pull, Pocket Size, 7 In.Extended, 3 In.Closed 25.00
Brass, Telescope, 4 Section 35.00
Brass, Tieback, Drapery, Ornate, Victorian, Pair 5.00
Brass, Tinder Lighter, English, Flintlock, Tinder Compartment, C 1800 .... 495.00
Brass, Tray, Etched Indian Scene, Scalloped Edge, 18 In. 45.00
Brass, Tray, Manning Bowman, Engraved Floral & Leaf, 10 1/2 In. 26.00
Brass, Tray, P.Berndorf, Embossed Elk, 6 X 5 In. 45.00
Brass, Tray, St.Petersburg, Russia, Hammered, Handled, Oval, 15 X 9 1/2 In. 115.00
Brass, Tumbler, Russian, 3 3/4 In. 28.00
Brass, Umbrella Stand, Lion Head Handles, 27 In. 125.00
Brass, Urn, Russian, Pitcher Type, Applied Rivetted Brass Handle, 11 1/2 In. 50.00
Brass, Vaporizer, Lamp In Bottom, Long Spout, Bowl For Breathing 55.00
Brass, Vase, Champleve Bands, Cobalt, Red And Green Enamel, Japan, 6 In. 18.00
Brass, Vase, Feet Become Supports, Etched, Art Nouveau, 10 3/4 In. 285.00
Brass, Vase, Incised Symbols, Stand, 8 In. 14.00
Brass, Vase, Jack-In-The-Pulpit, Polished, 8 In. 17.00
Brass, Vase, Spill, Russian, 4 1/2 In. 8.00
Brass, Warmer, Bed, Wooden Handle, 15 In. 145.00
Brass, Whistle, Factory, Steam, 8 In. 35.00
Brass, Whistle, Steam, Powell's Improved 60.00
Brass, Whistle, Steam, 13 1/2 In. .... 45.00 To 52.00
Brass, Whistle, Train Conductor's, 2 Tubed 12.00
Brass, Whistle, Used For Small River Boats, Attached To 15 In.Pump 125.00

Bread Plate, see various Pressed Glass patterns.

Bread Plate, Porcelain, Flying Turkey 5.00
Bretby, Potpourri, Mr.Micawber & Mr.Pickwick, Polychrome, 7 1/2 In. 85.00

Brides' baskets of glass were usually one-of-a-kind novelties made in American and European glass factories. They were especially popular about 1880 when the decorated basket was often given as a wedding gift. Cut-glass baskets were popular after 1890. All brides' baskets lost favor about 1905.

Bride's Basket, Amber Glass, Vaseline Opalescent, Plated Frame, 7 1/2 In. 65.00
Bride's Basket, Apricot Yellow, White Cased, Cohannet Silver Frame, 11 In. 80.00
Bride's Basket, Art Glass Threaded Pink With Cranberry Rim, 5 1/2 In. 150.00
Bride's Basket, Art Glass, Cased, White To Pink, Flared, Scalloped, 8 In. 48.00
Bride's Basket, Blue, Shell & Tassel, Silver Plate, Rogers Smith, 10 In. 155.00
Bride's Basket, Cased, Shaded Peach, Pleated, Ruffled Rim, Enameled 145.00
Bride's Basket, Insert, 8 Pointed Star, Ribbed Sides, Pink & Opalescent 50.00
Bride's Basket, Pastel Blue, Ruffled, 10 In. 27.50
Bride's Basket, Peachblow, White Shades To Deep Rose 175.00
Bride's Basket, Pigeon Blood Ruffled Top, Blown, 11 1/2 In. 29.50
Bride's Basket, Pink To Rose, Cased White, Squarish, Ornate Footed Frame 145.00

Bride's Basket, Pink, Pleated And Scalloped Rim, Overhead Bail 89.00
Bride's Basket, Pink, White Exterior, Silver Footed Holder, 8 Sided 135.00
Bride's Basket, Plated Glass, Custard Center, Amberina Ruffle Edges, 12 In. 325.00
Bride's Basket, Rose Overlay, Ruffled & Crimped, Quadruple Plate Stand 145.00
Bride's Basket, Silver Plate Holder, Scrolled, Embossed, Art Glass Overlay 120.00
Bride's Basket, White, Blue Stripes, Applied Glass, Pontil, Metal Frame 65.00
Bride's Bowl, Blue Opalescent Swirl, Cranberry On Crimped Edge, 9 In. 90.00
Bride's Bowl, Bristol Blown, Green To Red, Cased White, Pairpoint Holder 175.00
Bride's Bowl, Cased, Crimped Rim, Hobnails, Pontil, Green Over White, 6 In. 35.00

Bristol glass was made in Bristol, England, after the 1700s. The Bristol glass most often seen today is a Victorian, lightweight opaque glass that is often blue. Some of the glass was decorated with enamels.

Bristol Type, Vase, Blue, Florals, 7 In. 8.00
Bristol, Birde's Bowl, Pink & White, Hand Painted, 8 1/2 In. 40.00
Bristol, Bottle, Cologne, Blue Frosted, Teardrop Stopper, 7 3/4 In. 50.00
Bristol, Bottle, Dresser, Blownout Lion Head, White, 9 In., Pair 60.00
Bristol, Bottle, Dresser, Blue With Gold Enamel, 10 1/2 In. 42.00
Bristol, Candleholder, Duck, Mouth Open, Enameled, 12 3/4 In., Pair 95.00
Bristol, Decanter, Enameled Flowering, Stopper, 9 In., Pair 70.00
Bristol, Decanter, Taper, Green, Marked Rum In Gold Circle, Pint 45.00
Bristol, Ewer, White, Applied Clear Handle, Enamel Floral, 7 In. 22.50
Bristol, Jar, Biscuit, Cream Color, Berries & Floral, Silver Fittings 85.00
Bristol, Jar, Cookie, Aqua, Hand-Painted Floral, Silver Fittings 85.00
Bristol, Jar, Rose, Ball Shape, Roses, Creamy Ground, 7 In., Pair 85.00
Bristol, Jar, Rose, Roses, Green Leaves, 6 X 21 In., Pair 85.00
Bristol, Rolling Pin 18.00
Bristol, Sugar, White, Painted Scene 22.50
Bristol, Vase, Applied Tapestry In Relief, 13 In., Pair 90.00
Bristol, Vase, Birds & Leaves, Pair 30.00
Bristol, Vase, Blue & White, Child With Basket, Trellis Of Flowers 45.00
Bristol, Vase, Blue, Glossy, 6 1/2 In. 60.00
Bristol, Vase, Blue, Hand Blown, 6 1/2 In. 65.00
Bristol, Vase, Brown, Newly Hatched Chick, Shell, 12 In. 68.00
Bristol, Vase, Bud, Enamel Winter Farm Scene, Hand-Blown, 7 In. 32.50
Bristol, Vase, Bud, Pink, Blue Floral, Quadruple-Plated Holder, 12 In. 40.00
Bristol, Vase, Cafe Au Lait, White Floral, 14 In. 60.00
Bristol, Vase, Cased, Pink, Birds On Branch, 12 In., Pair 125.00
Bristol, Vase, Cobalt With Hand Enameled Florals, Slender Neck, 10 In. 27.00
Bristol, Vase, Cream Color, Yellow, Rust, & Green Floral, Bulbous, 8 1/2 In. 18.50
Bristol, Vase, Deep Blue, Enamel Floral, Pedestal Foot, 9 1/2 In. 35.00
Bristol, Vase, Enamel Branches, Flowers, & Scenic Medallion, 9 In. 35.00
Bristol, Vase, Enameled Branches, Flowers, Scenic Medallion, 9 In. 30.00
Bristol, Vase, Figures, White, 9 In., Pair 75.00
Bristol, Vase, Fireglow, Hand-Painted Flowers, Footed, Long Neck, 11 1/4 In. 65.00
Bristol, Vase, Girl On Fence, Pedestal, 15 In. 60.00
Bristol, Vase, Green To White, Hand-Painted Flowers, 10 In. 28.00
Bristol, Vase, Green, Gold & White Floral & Dots, 8 In. 20.00
Bristol, Vase, Hand-Painted Multicolor Apple Blossoms, 8 1/2 In. 32.50
Bristol, Vase, Hand-Painted, Bulbous, Heinrich, 9 1/2 In. 55.00
Bristol, Vase, Hand-Painted, Signed Heinrich, Bulbous, 10 In. 45.00
Bristol, Vase, Hand-Painted, 10 1/2 In. 15.00
Bristol, Vase, Light Blue, Flowers, 10 In., Pair 60.00
Bristol, Vase, Melon Shape, Pink, Fluted Top, Pair 37.50
Bristol, Vase, Milky Blue, Slender Neck, Fluted, 8 1/2 In. 38.00
Bristol, Vase, Mint Green, Brown & White Butterflies & Bees, 9 3/4 In. 55.00
Bristol, Vase, Opaque White, Gold Butterfly, Enamel Leaf Spray, 12 In., Pair 29.50
Bristol, Vase, Pedestal & Urn Shape, Cream & Brown Floral, 10 In., Pair 70.00
Bristol, Vase, Pink Cased, Hand-Painted, Ruffled Top, 8 In. 47.50
Bristol, Vase, Pink Overlay On White Enameled Ground, 7 1/2 In., Pair 58.00
Bristol, Vase, Pink With Enamel Butterflies & Flowers, 14 In., Pair 120.00
Bristol, Vase, Pink, Birds & Flowers, 11 In., Pair 180.00
Bristol, Vase, Pink, Hand-Painted Flowers & Leaves, 9 In. 60.00
Bristol, Vase, Pink, Hand-Painted Flowers, 12 In., Pair 60.00
Bristol, Vase, Pink, White Casing, Enamel Floral, 7 In. 22.50

Bristol, Vase, Rose, Brown, & White, 6 1/2 In. 25.00
Bristol, Vase, Smoky Tan, White Birds & Floral, 13 In., Pair 195.00
Bristol, Vase, Smoky, Hand-Painted, 12 In. 40.00
Bristol, Vase, Tan, Hand-Painted Floral, 12 In. 45.00
Bristol, Vase, White Ground, Dark Flowers, 10 In. 45.00
Britannia, see Pewter
Broadmoor, Vase, Fan Shape, 1930s 8.00
Broadmoor, Vase, Fan Shaped Copper Luster, Artist Signed, Pair 12.50
Bronze Figurine, Barye, Lion Stalking, 16 X 8 In. 495.00
Bronze Figurine, Barye, Lioness Stalking, 16 X 8 In. 495.00
Bronze, Ashtray, Brewmeister With Tankard 20.00
Bronze, Ashtray, Egyptian Princess & Ra Symbols, C.1920, Keystone Shape 40.00
Bronze, Ashtray, Elephant 22.00
Bronze, Ashtray, Erotica, Maiden & Soldier 18.50
Bronze, Ashtray, Soldier Holding Stein 22.00
Bronze, Basket, French, Hand Woven, 2 Handles, 8 1/2 X 3 In. 35.00
Bronze, Bell, Civil War Cavalry, Embossed Eagles, Stars, 3 3/4 In. 45.00
Bronze, Bell, Figural Handle, Asian, 7 1/2 In. 37.50
Bronze, Bell, Signed Meneely & Kimberely, Troy, N.Y., 1876, 17 In. 700.00
Bronze, Bell, Temple With Striker, Large 425.00
Bronze, Bell, Trolley 120.00
Bronze, Bookend, Dancers, Art Deco, Painted, Pompeiian, 8 In., Pair 75.00
Bronze, Bookend, Eagle Head, Pair 42.00
Bronze, Bookend, Elephant, 6 In., Pair 15.00
Bronze, Bookend, Indian, Armour Bronze Co., Signed Ruhl, 10 In., Pair 150.00
Bronze, Bookend, Liberty Bell 25.00
Bronze, Bookend, Recumbent Lion, Pair 48.00
Bronze, Bookend, Scotties On Books, C.1920, Pair 26.50
Bronze, Bookend, Trojan Horses, Enameled Riders, Large, Pair 250.00
Bronze, Bowl, Raised Designs, Footed, 7 In. 27.00
Bronze, Bowl, Teamster's Union Commemorative, Art Deco.5 1/4 In. 12.00
Bronze, Box, Dog On Top, McClelland Barclay, 5 1/2 X 3 1/2 In. 45.00
Bronze, Box, Mechanical, Red Devil Pops Out, Square, 2 In. 250.00
Bronze, Box, Silver Crest, Footed, Wood Lined, 8 X 5 3/4 In. 22.50
Bronze, Box, Vienna, Mechanical, Red Devil Pops Out, Press Button, 1 3/4 In. 195.00
Bronze, Burner, Incense, Chinese, C.1850, Filigree Top, Floral, 4 In. 110.00
Bronze, Burner, Incense, Dragon Handles, Frogs, Fish, Unicorns, 11 In. 450.00
Bronze, Burner, Incense, Embossed Fish & Floral On Lid, Dore, 5 X 3 In. 59.00
Bronze, Burner, Incense, Foo Dog On Lid, Footed, 7 X 4 In. 55.00
Bronze, Bust, A.Failguere, Diana, Thiebaut Freres, Fondeurs, Paris, 23 1/2 In. 1250.00
Bronze, Bust, A.Lesieux, Frenchman On Marble Base, 18 In. 500.00
Bronze, Bust, Carrier, Young Woman On Marble Plinth, Ormulu, Signed, 8 1/2 In. 450.00
Bronze, Bust, Frederic Remington, Sergeant, Green Patina, 11 In. 1050.00
Bronze, Bust, Geo.E.Bissell, C.1887, Gorham Foundries, 26 In. 7500.00
Bronze, Bust, Milton, 11 In. 175.00
Bronze, Bust, Pushkin, Marble Base, 5 In. 225.00
Bronze, Bust, Roman Warrior On Black Marble Plinth, Wooden Base, 13 In. 165.00
Bronze, Bust, Viennese, C.1880, Woman & Man, 3 In., Pair 250.00
Bronze, Candelabra, 3-Arm, 1880, 7 3/4 In., Pair 295.00
Bronze, Candelabrum, Mercury Figure, 2-Arm, Gray Marble Footed Base, 12 In. 100.00
Bronze, Candleholder, H.C.T.Ferrat, Figural, Woman Holding 6 Candles, 24 In. 950.00
Bronze, Candlestick, Bell In Middle Of Stem 65.00
Bronze, Candlestick, Chelsea Clock Co., Boston, Tuscan Column, 10 In., Pair 375.00
Bronze, Candlestick, Enamel Floral, Tricorner, Art Deco, 12 In. 40.00
Bronze, Candlestick, French, Ornate Design, 9 1/2 In. 75.00
Bronze, Candlestick, Greek Key, 8 In. 18.00
Bronze, Candlestick, Push-Up, Beaded Trim, 6 In. 5.00
Bronze, Candlestick, Water Fowl Standing On Turtle, 13 In., Pair 135.00
Bronze, Corkscrew, Baller, Austria, Figural, Dachshund 25.00
Bronze, Cutter, Cigar, Rooster 59.00
Bronze, Desk Set, French, Empire, Marble Bases, 4 Piece 248.00
Bronze, Desk Set, Viking, Art Nouveau, Marshall Field, 8 Piece 165.00
Bronze, Door Knocker, Art Nouveau, 13 3/4 In. 300.00
Bronze, Door Knocker, Lady's Hand Holding Ball 45.00
Bronze, Ewer, L.Lerolle, Embossed Wheat Sprays, 8 X 5 1/2 In. 125.00

Bronze Figurines

Bronze, Figurine, A.Deva, Russian Wolfhound, Signed, 2 1/2 In. 150.00
Bronze, Figurine, Alonzo, Milkmaid, Ivory Face & Hands, Polychrome, Signed 765.00
Bronze, Figurine, Art Deco, Huntress And Fawn 1000.00
Bronze, Figurine, Art Nouveau, Nude With Flowers, Gerschutz Mark, 5 1/4 In. 375.00
Bronze, Figurine, Art Nouveau, Zodiac Girl, Marble Base, 22 X 20 1/2 In. 1600.00
Bronze, Figurine, Austria, Dancing Pig, Shiny, 2 In. 35.00
Bronze, Figurine, Austria, Fox, Seated On Haunches, Crystal Base, 2 3/4 In. 75.00
Bronze, Figurine, Austria, Monkey, Signed, 2 In. 58.00
Bronze, Figurine, Austrian, Dog, Polychrome Finish, 2 In. 20.00
Bronze, Figurine, Barileer, 1889, Lion With Spear Through Body, 27 In. 1250.00
Bronze, Figurine, Barye, C.1840, Wolf, Front Leg In Bear Trap, 10 In. 850.00
Bronze, Figurine, Barye, Elephant, Running, 13 X 9 In. 950.00
Bronze, Figurine, Barye, Lion Stalking, 15 In. 575.00
Bronze, Figurine, Barye, Lion, 15 X 9 X 4 In. 75.00
Bronze, Figurine, Barye, Lion, 16 1/2 In. 550.00
Bronze, Figurine, Barye, Lioness Stalking, 15 In. 575.00
Bronze, Figurine, Barye, Lioness, 15 X 9 X 4 In. 750.00
Bronze, Figurine, Barye, Lioness, 16 1/2 In. 550.00
Bronze, Figurine, Barye, Ostrich, 7 X 8 In. 375.00
Bronze, Figurine, Barye, Panther Of Tunisia, Signed, 7 3/4 In. 160.00
Bronze, Figurine, Barye, Panther Of Tunisia, 10 In.Long 525.00
Bronze, Figurine, Barye, Rabbit, 3 In. 100.00
Bronze, Figurine, Barye, Seated Hare 275.00
Bronze, Figurine, Bear Dressed As Organ Grinder, Hinged Organ Lid, 5 In. 225.00
Bronze, Figurine, Bear Reclining, Gold Dore Finish, Russian, C.1880, 7 In. 195.00
Bronze, Figurine, Bear Walking, 4 1/2 In. 59.00
Bronze, Figurine, Boogar, Man Hoeing, 2 In. 38.00
Bronze, Figurine, Border Boss, Castleberry
Bronze, Figurine, Boyer, Dante, Ivory Face & Hands, 14 In. 750.00
Bronze, Figurine, Boyer, Dante, Ivory Hands & Face, Onyx Base, 15 In. 595.00
Bronze, Figurine, Bulldog, Vienna, Signed, 2 1/4 X 1 1/4 In. 65.00
Bronze, Figurine, C.H.Heizler, Leopard On Marble Base, 12 1/2 In. 895.00
Bronze, Figurine, C.Kauba, Chief Smoking Peace Pipe, Shot In The Eye 550.00
Bronze, Figurine, C.Kauba, Indian Holding Rifle, Standing Bear 550.00
Bronze, Figurine, C.Kauba, Indian, Holding Shield & Tomahawk, Swift Dog 500.00
Bronze, Figurine, C.S.Samson, Schnauzer, 4 In. 125.00
Bronze, Figurine, Camille, Boy Chasing Geese, Signed, 12 X 10 In. 550.00
Bronze, Figurine, Charles Bissel, Abe Lincoln, Henry Bonnard Bronze Co. 3500.00
Bronze, Figurine, Charles Knight, 1922, Moose, Standing, Kuntz Foundry, 14 In. 1500.00
Bronze, Figurine, Chinese, Taoist Patriarch, Mahogany Base, 14 X 7 In. 350.00
Bronze, Figurine, Ching Dynasty, Warrior On Horse, Bejeweled, Dore, 9 1/2 In. 450.00
Bronze, Figurine, Cleopatra, Signed &-Vis, Dated 1895, 6 X 5 X 3 In. 225.00
Bronze, Figurine, Commille, Lad Chasing Two Geese, Onyx Base, 9 1/2 In. 495.00
Bronze, Figurine, Coustou, Rearing Horse & Trainer, 14 X 15 1/2 In. 375.00
Bronze, Figurine, Demiere, Cumberwolf In Script, 17 In. 750.00
Bronze, Figurine, Dilorenzo, Girl, Basket Of Flowers, Ivory Features, 10 In. 975.00
Bronze, Figurine, Dubut, Arab Carrying Buckets, Signed, C.1880, 13 In. 395.00
Bronze, Figurine, E.Fremiet, C.1824, Knight Holding Credo Banner, 15 In. 1250.00
Bronze, Figurine, E.Furst, EKL, Signed, 24 X 24 1/2 In. 675.00
Bronze, Figurine, Eagle, Oval Marble Base, 6 1/2 X 10 1/2 X 5 3/4 In. 500.00
Bronze, Figurine, Eagle, Wings Spread, 8 X 6 1/2 In. 135.00
Bronze, Figurine, Elk, Signed Stolzer, 17 1/2 X 16 In. 850.00
Bronze, Figurine, Emanuel Villanes, C.1880, Woman Playing Mandolin, 28 In. 995.00
Bronze, Figurine, F.Barbedienne Fondeur, Jason, 25 In. 575.00
Bronze, Figurine, Flamond, Lady Reading Book, Signed, Art Nouveau, 5 X 5 In. 225.00
Bronze, Figurine, Frederic Remington, Sergeant, Onyx Base, 11 In. 1250.00
Bronze, Figurine, Frederic Remington, Sergeant, Restrike, Patina, 11 In. 1250.00
Bronze, Figurine, Frederick James Halnon, C.1881, Vintage, 14 In. 750.00
Bronze, Figurine, Frederick MacMonnies, Boy, Marble Base, 1890, 18 1/2 In. 1950.00
Bronze, Figurine, French, C.1880, Spaniel, Lying Down, Tiffany & Co., 9 In. 525.00
Bronze, Figurine, Frog, C1900, 4 X 2 1/8 In. 75.00
Bronze, Figurine, G.Luchoni, Nudes, Marble Base, , 1926, 9 1/2 In., Pair 650.00
Bronze, Figurine, G.Parente, Boy In Swim Suit, Hat, Oar In Hand, 15 In. 425.00
Bronze, Figurine, Garnier, Ivory Face, Blue, Rose & Gold, Onyx Base, 9 1/2 In. 425.00

Bronze, Figurine, German, Dog, Sitting, Dressed In Cap & Tie, 4 In. 80.00
Bronze, Figurine, Geucaley, Wrestler, Signed, 22 1/2 X 18 1/2 In. 700.00
Bronze, Figurine, Gorham, Scottish Terrier, M.Kirmse, 3 In. 145.00
Bronze, Figurine, Gorham, Standing Spaniel, Tyson, 3 1/2 In. 150.00
Bronze, Figurine, Gotham Art, Juggling Girl, Copper Base, Signed, 10 In., Pair 75.00
Bronze, Figurine, H.Pie, Child Carrying Basket, 7 1/2 In. 295.00
Bronze, Figurine, Harriet Frishmuth, Crest Of The Wave, 20 3/4 In. 1750.00
Bronze, Figurine, Harvester, Signed J. Oust, 20 1/4 X 14 1/2 In. 700.00
Bronze, Figurine, Head Of Soldier, Signed Coul DuGols, 24 X 17 In. 750.00
Bronze, Figurine, Heck, Nude Woman, Marble Base, Art Deco, 12 In. 140.00
Bronze, Figurine, Henri Bouillon, Porteuse Aux Champs, 6 1/4 In. 92.50
Bronze, Figurine, I.Bonheur, Bull, 15 1/2 X 12 1/2 In. 975.00
Bronze, Figurine, I.Bonheur, C.1850, Man Wrestling Bull, 16 In. 1450.00
Bronze, Figurine, I.Bonheur, Hound, Rockefeller Dodge Estate, 12 1/4 In. 850.00
Bronze, Figurine, I.Bonheur, Hound, 12 1/4 In. 875.00
Bronze, Figurine, I.Epreve, Lady Holding Bouquet, For Cartier, 20 In. 495.00
Bronze, Figurine, Ivory Faces, Onyx Base, Art Deco, Dore, 7 In. 260.00
Bronze, Figurine, J.De Roncourt, C.1930, Kneeling Archer, Drawn Bow, 20 In. 695.00
Bronze, Figurine, J.Moigniez, C.1835, Hound Flushing Quail, 7 1/2 In. 550.00
Bronze, Figurine, J.Moigniez, Mountain Sheep, C.1870, 8 1/2 X 8 1/2 In. 595.00
Bronze, Figurine, Japanese, C.1880, Samurai Warrior, Sword & Spear, 12 In. 650.00
Bronze, Figurine, Japanese, Falcon, Wooden Base, 12 In. 795.00
Bronze, Figurine, Japanese, Okina Actor, Silver & Gold Finish, 12 In. 140.00
Bronze, Figurine, Japanese, Okina Dancer, Embossed Floral Kimono, 12 In. 195.00
Bronze, Figurine, Japanese, Okina Dancer, Silver Finish, 12 In. 165.00
Bronze, Figurine, Jean Alexandre Falquiere, 1872, Egyptian Dancer, Signed 5000.00
Bronze, Figurine, Jules Moigniez, Mountain Sheep, French, C.1870 .... 595.00
Bronze, Figurine, Jules Moigniez, Partridge On Foliate Base, Dore, 9 In. 595.00
Bronze, Figurine, Kauba, Crouched Indian With Rifle, Marble Base, 4 In. 175.00
Bronze, Figurine, Kauba, Indian In Canoe, Polychrome, 9 7/8 In. 350.00
Bronze, Figurine, Kauba, Indian With Rifle, Polychrome, 4 3/4 In. 275.00
Bronze, Figurine, L.Pilet, Mozart With Don Juan Score, 13 In. 475.00
Bronze, Figurine, La Porte, Peasant Mother Tenderly Nursing Baby, 32 In. 3200.00
Bronze, Figurine, Lanceray, Cossack On Horse, C.1874, Russian, 9 X 9 In. 1950.00
Bronze, Figurine, Lanceray, Cossack On Horseback, C.1847, 3 1/2 In. 1950.00
Bronze, Figurine, Lanceray, Cossack On Horseback, 9 In. 2200.00
Bronze, Figurine, Lavergne, Boy Fishing On Dock, French, 17 In. 595.00
Bronze, Figurine, Lavergne, C.1880, Boy With Fishing Pole, 17 In. 595.00
Bronze, Figurine, Lecourtier, Spaniel, 9 X 5 In. 325.00
Bronze, Figurine, Louis Moreau, Seminude Female, 16 1/2 In. 95.00
Bronze, Figurine, Luce, Jester, Signed, 10 1/2 In. 795.00
Bronze, Figurine, M.Bouval, Gold Dore, Draped Female Figure, Signed, 10 In. 750.00
Bronze, Figurine, Man Digging Coal, Signed R. Zisseniss, 34 In. 2500.00
Bronze, Figurine, Martell, Collie Dog, Marble Base, 14 In., Signed 425.00
Bronze, Figurine, Moos, Sailor, German, Signed, 11 1/2 In. 850.00
Bronze, Figurine, Ouvet, Woman, Ivory Face, Arms & Hands, Signed, 10 1/2 In. 775.00
Bronze, Figurine, P.J.Mene, Bull, Brown Patina, 14 In. 1250.00
Bronze, Figurine, P.J.Mene, Pointer On Rectangular Base, 5 X 2 1/2 In. 295.00
Bronze, Figurine, P.J.Mene, Pointer, Recast, 7 1/2 X 5 1/2 In. 325.00
Bronze, Figurine, P.J.Mene, Retriever, Dark Patina, 12 X 6 1/2 In. 695.00
Bronze, Figurine, P.Tourgueneff, Shepherd Dog, French, 15 1/2 X 7 1/2 In. 695.00
Bronze, Figurine, Partridge, Thomas Jefferson, Standing, 22 In. 1950.00
Bronze, Figurine, Pautrout, C.1860, Setter Dog In Point, 13 In. 795.00
Bronze, Figurine, Pautrout, C.1860, Setter In Point, 13 In. 795.00
Bronze, Figurine, Peasant Lady With Infant, Wooden Base, 8 In. 90.00
Bronze, Figurine, Phillippe, Nude Dancing, Signed, 20 In. 495.00
Bronze, Figurine, Picault, C.1870, 17th Century Soldier, Weapons, 10 In. 695.00
Bronze, Figurine, Roman Centurion, Greek Temple Clock, Marble Base, 27 In. 1800.00
Bronze, Figurine, Rosa B.Bonheur, Grazing Ewe, 8 1/2 X 6 In. 850.00
Bronze, Figurine, Russian, Bear, Reclining, 12 In. 595.00
Bronze, Figurine, Russian, C.1880, Bear, Reclining, Gold Dore, 7 In. 195.00
Bronze, Figurine, Russian, Cossack On Rock Crystal Ice, Rifle, 6 In. 600.00
Bronze, Figurine, Rusty Phelps, Cowboy Resting With Utensils, 12 In. 800.00
Bronze, Figurine, Scalvarfenberg, Man Sawing, Signed, 20 1/2 In. 750.00
Bronze, Figurine, Schmidt-Cassel, Girl, Castanets, Ivory Face, 12 In. 475.00

Bronze, Figurine, Scottish Terrier, 3 X 4 1/2 In. 150.00
Bronze, Figurine, Segar, Dancing Lady, Onyx Base, 8 1/2 In. 295.00
Bronze, Figurine, Squirrel Holding Nut, 2 In. 47.00
Bronze, Figurine, Tezeszizuk, Lady, Ivory Face, Dore, 8 3/4 In. 425.00
Bronze, Figurine, Tiger Attacked By Bear, 7 In. 136.00
Bronze, Figurine, Ulrich, Clown Astride Ostrich, Ivory Face, Signed, 9 In. 795.00
Bronze, Figurine, Ulrich, Clown Playing Banjo, Sitting On Bird, Ivory, 9 In. 350.00
Bronze, Figurine, Verrocchio, Man On Horse, Marble Base, 11 1/2 In. 1500.00
Bronze, Figurine, Vienna, Antlered Stag, 2 1/4 X 1 3/4 In. 75.00
Bronze, Figurine, Vienna, Arched Back Cat, 3 In. 58.00
Bronze, Figurine, Vienna, Bird, Sitting, 1 1/2 In. 50.00
Bronze, Figurine, Vienna, Bull Mastiff, 5 X 4 In. 135.00
Bronze, Figurine, Vienna, Bulldog, 4 1/4 X 2 1/4 In. 128.00
Bronze, Figurine, Vienna, Carpet Seller, Long Beard, 8 1/2 In. 275.00
Bronze, Figurine, Vienna, Cleopatra With Snake, Red, Yellow, Blue, 8 1/2 In. 125.00
Bronze, Figurine, Vienna, Devil With Top Hat & Cane, Miniature 55.00
Bronze, Figurine, Vienna, Erotic, Woman In Chair, Removable Dress, 2 1/2 In. 125.00
Bronze, Figurine, Vienna, Frog, Hand-Painted, 3/4 In. 35.00
Bronze, Figurine, Vienna, Hand-Painted Bull, Ivory Horns, 1 3/4 In. 50.00
Bronze, Figurine, Vienna, Irish Setter, Tracking Position, 4 1/2 X 8 In. 90.00
Bronze, Figurine, Vienna, Irish Setter, 2 1/2 In. 45.00
Bronze, Figurine, Vienna, Lion Standing Over Lioness, 4 3/4 X 3 In. 135.00
Bronze, Figurine, Vienna, Little Devil Thumbing Nose 28.00
Bronze, Figurine, Vienna, Miniature Magpie, 1 1/2 In. 29.00
Bronze, Figurine, Vienna, Monkey Holding Half Walnut Shell, 4 1/4 In. 155.00
Bronze, Figurine, Vienna, Monkey, Artist Signed, 4 X 5 In. 95.00
Bronze, Figurine, Vienna, Owl, 1 3/4 In. 50.00
Bronze, Figurine, Vienna, Parrot, Green & Red, Signed Geschutz, 5 1/2 In. 125.00
Bronze, Figurine, Vienna, Pig, Polychrome, 2 1/2 In. 32.00
Bronze, Figurine, Vienna, Polychrome, Cobra, 5 In. 145.00
Bronze, Figurine, Vienna, Polychrome, Dog, 1 3/4 In. 40.00
Bronze, Figurine, Vienna, Polychromed, 1 1/2 X 3 1/4 In. 75.00
Bronze, Figurine, Vienna, Red Devil On Yellow Stilts, Sack Of Devils, 9 In. 600.00
Bronze, Figurine, Vienna, Terrier, 8 X 6 1/2 In. 240.00
Bronze, Figurine, Vienna, Tiger Rug, Polychrome, 6 1/2 X 4 1/2 In. 150.00
Bronze, Figurine, Vienna, Tiny Pug 22.00
Bronze, Figurine, Vienna, Wild Boar, 5 X 9 In., Bristle Back Penwipe 250.00
Bronze, Figurine, Viennese, Mother Bear Playing With Cub, 1 3/4 In. 90.00
Bronze, Figurine, Western, The Border Boss, 9 1/2 X 7 In. 1200.00
Bronze, Figurine, Wetzstein, Dancer, Pink & Green Marble Base, 16 1/4 In. 450.00
Bronze, Figurine, Whippet Dog Looking At Ball 150.00
Bronze, Figurine, Zach, Diana, The Huntress & Dog, Marble Base, 18 In. 725.00
Bronze, Figurine, Zach, Diana, The Huntress, Viennese, Art Deco, 18 In. 725.00
Bronze, Figurine, Zumel, Dachshund, Marble Base, Separated In Center, 8 In. 75.00
Bronze, Frame, Ornate Gilded, Self-Standing, 11 1/2 X 8 1/2 In. 45.00
Bronze, Frame, Picture, Louis XV Style, Standing, C.1860, 12 X 7 In., Pair 185.00

Bronze Group

Bronze, Group, B In Urn & Geschutzt, Cow With Calf, 9 1/2 In. 350.00
Bronze, Group, Carvin, 2 German Shepherds, Mutton Fat Alabaster Base 2200.00
Bronze, Group, Coustou, Man Restraining Rearing Horse, 15 1/2 X 13 In. 395.00
Bronze, Group, Dubucand, Stag & Doe, 6 1/2 X 5 1/2 In. 375.00
Bronze, Group, E.Fremiet, C.1860, Cat, Kitten, & Ball Of Yarn, 6 1/4 In. 200.00
Bronze, Group, Geschutz, 2 Bunnies On Cabbage Leaf, Depose, 7 X 6 In. 265.00
Bronze, Group, Heinz Warneke, Running Colts, Signed, Dated 1930, 14 In. 1100.00
Bronze, Group, Jean Baptiste Germain, Summer Chasing Spring, 31 1/2 In. 3250.00
Bronze, Group, P.J.Mene, Animaliere, 15 X 9 X 7 In. 1275.00
Bronze, Group, P.J.Mene, Pointer & Setter, 5 X 2 In. 450.00
Bronze, Group, P.J.Mene, Three Terriers Chasing Prey Into Cave, 15 In. 1250.00
Bronze, Group, P.J.Mene, 2 Lurches & 1 Bouveir De Flanders & Prey, 15 In. 1175.00
Bronze, Group, Pautrout, C.1860, Frency, 2 Pheasants, 31 In. 5500.00
Bronze, Group, Pautrout, C.1860, 2 European Pheasants, Male & Female, 31 In. 5500.00
Bronze, Group, Rochard, Art Deco, Deer At Pool, Pewter Finish, Marble Base 350.00
Bronze, Group, Vienna, Bear Playing With Her Cub, 1 3/4 In. 90.00
Bronze, Group, Vienna, Cat Orchestra, 6 Piece, 2 In. 250.00
Bronze, Group, Vienna, Three Parrots, 1 1/2 In. 48.00

Bronze, Group, Vienna, 2 Cats Saying Goodbye, 2 In. 90.00
Bronze, Incense Burner, Chinese, Signed, Floral Designed, 4 In., C 1850 110.00
Bronze, Inkstand, Dolphins, Hinged Lid, 3 Footed, Dore, White Insert, 6 In. 95.00
Bronze, Inkstand, Signed Douval, Frogs 108.00
Bronze, Inkwell, Crab Form, Movable Claws, K.Nissell Glass Well, 1903, 7 In. 35.00
Bronze, Inkwell, Sterling Silver Bird & Branch On Lid, Aug 27, 1912 35.00
Bronze, Inkwell, Viennese, C.1880, Skull & Crossbones, Hinged, Gold Dore 245.00
Bronze, Inkwell, Viennese, Gold Dore, Skull & Crossbones, Hinged, C.1880 245.00
Bronze, Jardiniere, Panels Of Griffins & Fruit, Signed F.C., 10 1/2 In. 270.00
Bronze, Lamp Base, Champleve, Bulbous, 28 In. 250.00
Bronze, Lamp, Whale, Sherman Fearing, Rochester, Mass., 1 1/2 X 3 3/4 In. 65.00
Bronze, Lantern, Japanese, C.1850, Garden, 6 Ft. 2900.00
Bronze, Letter Opener, Bust Of Mozart On Top, 7 3/4 In. 35.00
Bronze, Letter Opener, Head Of Setter, Signed F.O.Klar, 11 1/2 In. 78.00
Bronze, Letter Opener, Large, Embossed 29.00
Bronze, Letter Opener, Migneau, Art Nouveau 35.00
Bronze, Letter Opener, Turkey Claw, C.1880 18.00
Bronze, Letter Opener, Yellowstone National Park 6.00
Bronze, Lighter, Art Deco, Figural, Nude With Rhinestones, 8 In. 75.00
Bronze, Match Holder And Striker, Gold Dore, Bacchanalian Figures, 3 In. 225.00
Bronze, Medallion, French Commemorative, Armistice Day, Morlon, 2 3/4 In. 85.00
Bronze, Mirror, Hand, Japanese, Herons & Calligraphy, 9 1/2 In. 85.00
Bronze, Mirror, Japanese, 3 1/4 In. 50.00
Bronze, Paper Clip, Figural, Bronzed Black Boy 44.00
Bronze, Paper Clip, With Hand 55.00
Bronze, Paperweight, Dog & Pups, 3 1/2 X 3 1/2 In. 50.00
Bronze, Paperweight, Figural, Tiger, 4 1/2 X 2 1/2 In. 30.00
Bronze, Pen Holder, Deck, C.Remberger, Chicago, 1929, Nude Woman, Onyx Base 450.00
Bronze, Plaque, Abraham Lincoln, 6 X 4 1/4 In. 25.00
Bronze, Plaque, Brenner, Lincoln, Marble Easel, 7 X 9 1/2 In. 350.00
Bronze, Plaque, Carron, Paris, 1900-10, Neptune, Mermaids, Sea Horses, 7 1/2 In. 20.00
Bronze, Plaque, Carron, 1900-10, Neptune, Mermaids, Sea Horses, 7 1/2 In. 20.00
Bronze, Plaque, John Hassenfort, Philadelphia Safe Makers, 6 X 4 In. 38.00
Bronze, Plaque, P.Lenoir, Chein De Beauceron, 5 X 4 In. 80.00
Bronze, Plaque, Thorvaldsen, Flight Of The Cupids, Mahogany Frame 250.00
Bronze, Plaquette, Barye, Eck Et Durand, Pointer Dog, 5 3/4 X 4 1/8 In. 450.00
Bronze, Plaquette, Bayre, Pointer, Eck Et Durand, Signed, 4 1/8 In. 450.00
Bronze, Plate, Carron, Cutout Neptune, Mermaids, Paris, 1900-10, 7 1/2 In. 20.00
Bronze, Relief, John Mossman, Dated 1868, Man & Woman Profiles 200.00
Bronze, Rowboat, Vienna, Oarlocks, Signed Haganenauer Wien, 4 X 2 1/2 In. 55.00
Bronze, Sconce, 3-Arm, Openwork, Oval Mirror & Round Mirror, 19 1/2 In. 125.00
Bronze, Seal, Foo Dog, C.1820, 2 In. 165.00
Bronze, Sun Dial, Let Others Tell Of Storms, Etc., 9 In. 165.00
Bronze, Tea Caddy, Embossed On Lid & Oval Sides, 5 In. 35.00
Bronze, Tray, Art Nouveau, Handled, 4 Ball Feet, Gesch, 12 X 7 In. 35.00
Bronze, Tray, Card, Raised Grapes 45.00
Bronze, Tray, Pen, Vienna, Spaniel Dog, Onyx Inserts, Quill Holder 85.00
Bronze, Umbrella Stand, Champleve Cutout Work At Top, 6 Sided, 24 In. 475.00
Bronze, Umbrella Stand, Champleve, 15 In. 300.00
Bronze, Urn, Funeral, Vienna, Portrait Front Signed Gratner 145.00
Bronze, Urn, Two Satyr Heads, Art Nouveau Florals, Signed Levellain, 6 In. 175.00
Bronze, Vase, C. H. Korschann, Louchet Foundry, Paris, Dore, Bronze Patina 760.00
Bronze, Vase, C.H.Korschann, Louchet Foundry, Paris, Gilt, Art Nouveau, 7 In. 695.00
Bronze, Vase, Carl Sorenson, Art Deco, 10 3/4 In. 40.00
Bronze, Vase, Chinese, C.1700, Champleve Enamel, 6 Sided, 12 X 9 In. 375.00
Bronze, Vase, France, Oak Leaf Design, 10 In., Pair 250.00
Bronze, Vase, Kauba, Girl, Art Nouveau, 5 1/4 In. 350.00
Bronze, Vase, Leda And The Swan, Art Nouveau, C.1900 525.00
Bronze, Vase, Ormolu-Mounted Ring Handles, Marble Base, 7 In. 59.00
Bronze, Vase, Silver Overlay Of A Peacock, 9 X 3 In. 90.00
Bronze, Vessel, Drinking, Roman Orgy, C.1880, 7 In. 95.00
Brown Ware, Jar, Cookie, 12 1/2 In.High *Illus* 80.00
Brown Ware, Pitcher, Raised Figure Of Baby Crying, 9 3/4 In. *Illus* 40.00
Brown Ware, Pitcher, Raised Figure Of Hunter And Dog *Illus* 35.00
Brown Ware, Spittoon, 13 In.Dia., 6 1/2 In.High *Illus* 170.00
Brownie, Book, Adventures Of A Brownie, Miss Mulock 15.00

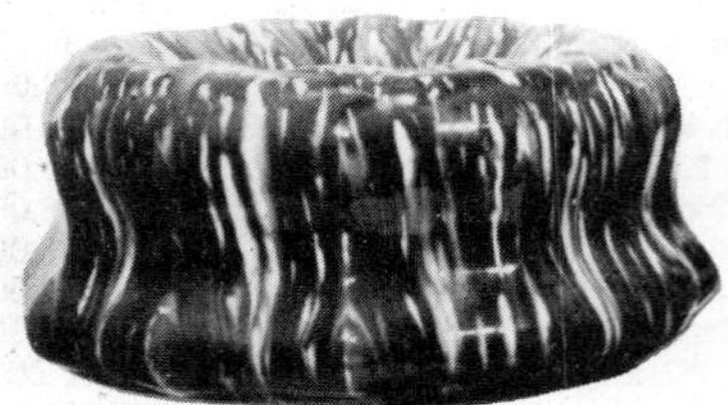

Brown Ware, Jar, Cookie, 12 1/2 In.High

Brown Ware, Pitcher, Raised Figure Of Baby Crying, 9 3/4 In.

Brown Ware, Pitcher, Raised Figure Of Hunter And Dog
(See Page 61)

Brown Ware, Spittoon, 13 In.Dia., 6 1/2 In.High

Brownie, Book, Brownies In Switzerland, Carine Cadby, N.Y., 1924, 1st Issue 6.00
Brownie, Book, Palmer Cox Brownies & Other Stories, M.A.Donahue & Co. 25.00
Brownie, Box, Pin, 6 Brownies On Lid, Brass & Metal 15.00
Brownie, Clip, Brass, Face With Handlebar Mustache, 2 1/4 In. 30.00
Brownie, Cup & Saucer, Brownies 12.00
Brownie, Cup, Child's, Engraved Brownies, Silver Plate 54.00
Brownie, Cup, Palmer Cox, Porcelain 22.50
Brownie, Figurine, Brownie, Bisque, 3 1/2 In. 12.00
Brownie, Game, Horseshoe 4.00
Brownie, Knife, Palmer Cox 15.00
Brownie, Mug, Brown & White 18.00
Brownie, Mug, Palmer Cox, 7 Brownies, Limoges Blank, 6 In. 75.00
Brownie, Plate, Brownies, 4 In., Pair 12.00
Brownie, Plate, Brownies, 6 1/2 In. 10.00
Brownie, Plate, Brownies, 7 1/2 In. 12.00
Brownie, Puzzle, McLoughlin, 1891, Blind Man's Bluff & The Dance, Mounted 100.00
Brownie, Salt & Pepper, White Opaque 60.00
Brownie, Saucer, Palmer Cox 12.00
Brownie, Spoon, Brass, Brownie Wearing Green Overcoat, Cutout, 4 1/2 In. 14.00
Brownie, Tea Set, Doll's, Brownies At Dancing School, Cox, Service For 4 ..... 150.00
Brownie, Tiepin, Palmer Cox, Brownie As Keystone Cop, Silver 35.00
Brownie, Toy, Brownie In Horse-Drawn Cart, Palmer Cox, Iron, Wilkins, 5 In. 275.00
Brush, Jar, Cookie, Clown, Brush Co. 25.00
Brush, Vase, Yellow, White Mottled Decoration, 16 1/2 In. 16.00
Buck Rogers, Book, Dangerous Mission, Pop Up 42.00
Buck Rogers, Book, 25th Century A.D., Big Little Book 5.00
Buck Rogers, Gun, Atomic Disintegrator, Red Handle With Holster 50.00
Buck Rogers, Gun, Atomic Pistol, 9 1/2 In. 75.00
Buck Rogers, Gun, Disintegrator, 9 1/2 In. 75.00
Buck Rogers, Gun, Ray, 25th Century, Daisy Mfg.Co. ..... 79.00 To 90.00
Buck Rogers, Gun, Supersonic Ray, Boxed 35.00

Buck Rogers, Gun, 1238 Atomic Pistol, Holster, Box, & Booklet 75.00
Buck Rogers, Gun, 25th Century Pistol, 9 1/2 In. 75.00
Buck Rogers, Kite, Star 18.00
Buck Rogers, Pistol, Atomic, 9 1/2 In. 50.00
Buck Rogers, Pistol, Rocket, Small Size 85.00
Buck Rogers, Pistol, Water, Liquid Helium 75.00
Buck Rogers, Skates, Roller, Pair 230.00
Buck Rogers, Space Ranger Kit, Sylvania, Uncut 90.00
Buck Rogers, Toy, Buck Rogers Patrol 150.00
Buck Rogers, Toy, Rocket Police Patrol Space Ship 65.00
Buck Rogers, Toy, Space Ship, Marx 45.00

Buffalo pottery was made in Buffalo, New York, after 1902. The company was established by the Larkin Company, famous manufacturers of soap. The wares are marked with a picture of a buffalo and the date of manufacture. Deldare ware is the most famous pottery made at the factory. It is a khaki-colored transfer-decorated ware.

Buffalo Pottery, Ashtray, Cowboy, Tan 18.00
Buffalo Pottery, Ashtray, Cowboy, White 18.00
Buffalo Pottery, Butter Pat, Princess 2.50
Buffalo Pottery, Butter, Covered, Floral, Insert, 5 In. 20.00
Buffalo Pottery, Candlestick, Village Scene, Deldare, Pair, 9 In. 465.00
Buffalo Pottery, Canister, Citron, Blue Floral, 1906 45.00
Buffalo Pottery, Canister, Covered, Citron, Blue & White, 7 1/2 X 5 In. 45.00
Buffalo Pottery, Canister, Covered, Tapioca, Blue & White, 7 1/2 X 5 In. 45.00
Buffalo Pottery, Canister, Tapioca, Blue Floral, 1906 45.00
Buffalo Pottery, Creamer, Princess 7.50
Buffalo Pottery, Cup & Saucer, Multifleur 10.00
Buffalo Pottery, Cup Plate, Wanamaker's, Phila., Jubilee, 1911 50.00
Buffalo Pottery, Deldare, Bowl, Fern, Ye Village Street, Artist Signed 245.00
Buffalo Pottery, Deldare, Bowl, Ye Village Street, Artist Signed 2450.00
Buffalo Pottery, Deldare, Candlestick, 1909, 9 1/2 In., Pair 475.00
Buffalo Pottery, Deldare, Creamer, Dr.Syntax, Dairy Maid, Emerald 225.00
Buffalo Pottery, Deldare, Creamer, Fallowfield Hunt, Breaking Cover 85.00
Buffalo Pottery, Deldare, Cup & Saucer, Ye Olden Days, JG & L.Newman 135.00
Buffalo Pottery, Deldare, Hair Receiver, Ye Village Streets, A.Newman 195.00
Buffalo Pottery, Deldare, Mug, At Ye Lion Inn, 4 1/2 In. 165.00
Buffalo Pottery, Deldare, Mug, Breaking Chase, 4 In. 175.00
Buffalo Pottery, Deldare, Mug, Fallowfield Hunt, 1908, 4 1/2 In. 16.00
Buffalo Pottery, Deldare, Pitcher, Breaking Cover, I.Gerhardt, 7 In. 300.00
Buffalo Pottery, Deldare, Pitcher, Fallowfield Breaking Cover, 7 In. 285.00
Buffalo Pottery, Deldare, Pitcher, Their Manner Of Telling-, 1908, 6 In. 175.00
Buffalo Pottery, Deldare, Plate, Art Nouveau, Emerald, 8 In. 245.00
Buffalo Pottery, Deldare, Plate, At Ye Lion Inn, 6 1/2 In. 75.00
Buffalo Pottery, Deldare, Plate, Calendar, 1910, 9 1/2 In. 650.00
Buffalo Pottery, Deldare, Plate, Dr.Syntax Soliloquizing, Emerald, 7 3/8 In. 265.00
Buffalo Pottery, Deldare, Plate, Dr.Syntax, Emerald, 7 1/4 In. 235.00
Buffalo Pottery, Deldare, Plate, Fallowfield Hunt, Death, 8 1/2 In. 95.00
Buffalo Pottery, Deldare, Plate, Fallowfield Hunt, Finish, 1908, 8 1/4 In. 125.00
Buffalo Pottery, Deldare, Plate, Fallowfield Hunt, Newman, 6 1/4 In. 70.00
Buffalo Pottery, Deldare, Plate, Garden Trio, J.Gerhardt, Emerald, 9 1/4 In. 350.00
Buffalo Pottery, Deldare, Plate, Village Scenes, 8 1/2 In. 135.00
Buffalo Pottery, Deldare, Plate, Ye Olden Times, Signed, 1909, 9 1/4 In. 90.00
Buffalo Pottery, Deldare, Plate, Ye Town Crier, B.Pattison, 1908, 8 1/2 In. 90.00
Buffalo Pottery, Deldare, Sugar, Covered, Village Life Scenes 110.00
Buffalo Pottery, Deldare, Tankard, Fallowfield Hunt, 12 1/4 In., 6 Mugs 450.00
Buffalo Pottery, Deldare, Teapot, Village Life In Ye Olden Days 285.00
Buffalo Pottery, Deldare, Teapot, Village Scenes 350.00
Buffalo Pottery, Deldare, Tray, Card, Ye Olden Days, J.Gerhardt, 6 1/2 In. 195.00
Buffalo Pottery, Dish, Child's Feeding, Boy Presenting Flowers, Drayton 26.00
Buffalo Pottery, Dish, Child's, Campbell Kids 38.00
Buffalo Pottery, Gravy Boat, Blue Willow 22.00
Buffalo Pottery, Gravy Boat, Princess 7.50
Buffalo Pottery, Gravy Pitcher, Blue Willow 20.00
Buffalo Pottery, Jug, George Washington & Mt.Vernon, Blue & Gold, 7 1/2 In. 225.00
Buffalo Pottery, Jug, George Washington, Blue With Gold Handle, Scenic 200.00

Buffalo Pottery, Main Street, Blue Green, 7 1/2 In. 50.00
Buffalo Pottery, Pitcher, Bluebird 6.00
Buffalo Pottery, Pitcher, Bulbous Pink And Yellow Roses, 7 1/2 In. 25.00
Buffalo Pottery, Pitcher, Pink Chrysanthemum, 7 In. 45.00
Buffalo Pottery, Pitcher, Sailor, Dated 1906 275.00
Buffalo Pottery, Plate, Advance, Blue Green, 7 1/2 In. 50.00
Buffalo Pottery, Plate, Capitol, Blue Green, 10 In. 40.00
Buffalo Pottery, Plate, Chop, Vienna 30.00
Buffalo Pottery, Plate, Dinner, Multifleur, 9 In. 12.00
Buffalo Pottery, Plate, Dinner, Willow, Pink 10.00
Buffalo Pottery, Plate, Faneuil Hall, Blue Green, 10 In. 40.00
Buffalo Pottery, Plate, Faneuil Hall, Boston, Green, 10 1/4 In. 29.00
Buffalo Pottery, Plate, Faneuil Hall, Floral Border, 10 In. 45.00
Buffalo Pottery, Plate, Game, American Woodcock, Dated 1908, Green, 9 In. 40.00
Buffalo Pottery, Plate, Game, Grouse, Teal Green Transfer 85.00
Buffalo Pottery, Plate, Game, Pheasant, Teal Green Transfer 85.00
Buffalo Pottery, Plate, General Wolfe, 1908, 7 1/2 In. 65.00
Buffalo Pottery, Plate, Gunner, Green, 1907 45.00
Buffalo Pottery, Plate, Mallard Duck 45.00
Buffalo Pottery, Plate, Modern Woodmen Of America, 7 1/2 In. 40.00
Buffalo Pottery, Plate, Mt.Vernon 20.00
Buffalo Pottery, Plate, New Haven R.R. 32.50
Buffalo Pottery, Plate, Niagara Falls 20.00
Buffalo Pottery, Plate, Niagara Falls, Blue & White, 10 In. 22.00
Buffalo Pottery, Plate, Niagara Falls, Blue Green, 7 1/2 In. 40.00
Buffalo Pottery, Plate, Niagara Falls, Green, 10 In. 40.00
Buffalo Pottery, Plate, U.S.Capitol, Blue Green, 10 In. 45.00
Buffalo Pottery, Plate, U.S.Capitol, Washington, D.C., Blue Green, 7 1/2 In. 60.00
Buffalo Pottery, Plate, Wanamaker's, Phila., 60th Anniversary, 1911, 4 In. 30.00
Buffalo Pottery, Plate, White House 20.00
Buffalo Pottery, Plate, Wild Ducks, Green 45.00
Buffalo Pottery, Plate, Ye Olde Ivory, Grecian Garden, 11 In. 20.00
Buffalo Pottery, Platter, Blue Willow, Dated 1909, 14 X 11 1/4 In. 25.00
Buffalo Pottery, Platter, Princess, 11 1/4 In. 6.00
Buffalo Pottery, Platter, Remington, Buffalo Hunt Scene, 14 In. 155.00
Buffalo Pottery, Tub, Butter, Insert, 1910 15.00
Buffalo Pottery, Vase, American Beauty 375.00
Buffalo Pottery, Vegetable Bowl, Covered, Princess, Oval 12.50
Buggy, Baby, Quebec, C.1880, Wicker 650.00
Buggy, Baby's, Wicker, Parasol Top 225.00
Bugs Bunny, Clock, Animated 225.00
Bugs Bunny, Watch 20.00
Burgess Ware, Jar, Jelly, Chinoiserie, Rose & Tan, Black Metal Lid, 4 3/8 In. 6.00
Burgun & Schverer, Rose Bowl, Silver Collar At Base, Floral, 4 In. 1650.00

Burmese glass was developed by Frederick Shirley at the Mt.Washington Glass Works in New Bedford, Massachusetts, in 1885. It is a two-toned glass, shading from peach to yellow. Some have a pattern mold design. A few Burmese pieces were decorated with pictures or applied glass flowers of colored Burmese glass.

Burmese, see also Gunderson

Burmese, Bell, Smoke, Rings 49.50
Burmese, Creamer, Applied Pink Handle, Ruffled Top, 5 1/4 In. 180.00
Burmese, Jar, Biscuit, Mt.Washington, Enamel Flowers, Signed Lid 300.00
Burmese, Jar, Cracker, Mt.Washington, Floral & Leaves, Pairpoint Lid, 9 In. 650.00
Burmese, Jar, Ginger, Mt.Washington, Bulbous, Handles 750.00
Burmese, Lamp, Base, Scenic Arab 5200.00
Burmese, Lamp, Fairy, Clarke Base, 3 1/2 In. 195.00
Burmese, Lamp, Fairy, Clear Clarke Base, Hand-Painted Floral, 4 In. 255.00
Burmese, Lamp, Fairy, Deep Rose To Yellow, Crimped Bottom 650.00
Burmese, Lamp, Fairy, Signed Clark Base, 5 In. 300.00
Burmese, Pitcher, Applied Yellow Handle, 3 3/4 In. 350.00
Burmese, Pitcher, Crimped Top, Yellow Handle, 8 1/2 X 5 In. 225.00
Burmese, Pitcher, Mt.Washington, Lemon Yellow Handle, 7 1/2 In. 475.00
Burmese, Pitcher, Shell Handle, Inverted Thumbprint, Flesh To Yellow, 10 In. 695.00

Burmese, Rose Bowl, Maple Leaf 25.00
Burmese, Rose Bowl, Queen's, Decorated, 10 1/2 In. 340.00
Burmese, Rose Bowl, Shiny, Decorated, 10 1/2 In. 300.00
Burmese, Rose Bowl, Turned-In Scalloped Yellow Edge, 2 1/2 In. 250.00
Burmese, Salt & Pepper, Shrimp, Enameled, Unfired 145.00
Burmese, Saltshaker, Mt.Washington, Tomato, Blue & White Forget-Me-Nots 50.00
Burmese, Saltshaker, Ribbed, Acid Finish, Pewter Top 145.00
Burmese, Tankard, Water, Polished Handle, Acid Finish, 9 In. 500.00
Burmese, Toothpick, Diamond-Quilted, 2 1/2 In. 210.00
Burmese, Toothpick, Hand-Painted White, Green, & Brown Floral, Fluted Rim 200.00
Burmese, Toothpick, Mt.Washington, Diamond-Quilted, Tricorner Top 275.00
Burmese, Toothpick, Mt.Washington, Glossy, Venetian Diamond 325.00
Burmese, Toothpick, Mt.Washington, Melon Ribbed, Enamel, Unfired 145.00
Burmese, Toothpick, Mt.Washington, Square Mouth, Bulbous Bottom 195.00
Burmese, Toothpick, Mt.Washington, Tricorn, Venetian Diamond, Pink 300.00
Burmese, Toothpick, Mt.Washington, Tricorner, Acid Finish, Yellow Rim 250.00
Burmese, Tumbler, Mt.Washington, Satin Finish, Fired 3 Times 275.00
Burmese, Tumbler, Whiskey, Mt.Washington, Diamond-Quilted, Glossy 185.00
Burmese, Vase, Berries & Leaves, Crimped Ruffled Top, 4 In. 250.00
Burmese, Vase, Jack-In-The-Pulpit, Crimped Edge, 7 1/2 In. 395.00
Burmese, Vase, Jack-In-The-Pulpit, Ruffled Top, Footed, 7 1/2 In. 495.00
Burmese, Vase, Mt.Washington, Acid Finish, Fluted Rim, 4 1/4 In., Pair 650.00
Burmese, Vase, Scenic, Flying Ducks 1800.00
Burmese, Vase, 6-Petal Top, 3 1/4 In. 166.00
Burmese, Water Set, Mt.Washington, Squat Pitcher, 6 Tumblers 1350.00

Burmese, Webb, see Webb Burmese

Buster Brown, Book, Buster Brown's Latest, BB Hosiery Mills, 1909 .... 16.50
Buster Brown, Button, Buster Brown & Tige By Outcault, Jolly Pair 7.00
Buster Brown, Button, Squeeky, Buster Brown Gang Member 7.00
Buster Brown, Camera, Box, No.8a, 6 1/4 X 5 1/4 In. 12.00
Buster Brown, Clicker, Round 12.00
Buster Brown, Cup, Buster, Tige With Teapot On His Nose 22.00
Buster Brown, Doll, Composition Head & Arms, Cloth Body, 16 1/2 In. 125.00
Buster Brown, Figurine, Buster Brown & Tige, Plaster Paris, 1903, Denivelle 25.00
Buster Brown, Figurine, In Sailor Suit 21.00
Buster Brown, Hobby Horse, Picture Of Buster & Tige On Each Side 85.00
Buster Brown, Hook, Bill, Buster Brown Shoes, Tin & Wire, C.1940 .... 3.00
Buster Brown, Magazine, Buster Brown Shoes, Buster & Tige, 1907 .... 7.00
Buster Brown, Mug, Buster & Tige With Teakettle 22.00
Buster Brown, Mug, Embossed & Scalloped Bottom, German, 3 Crown 37.50
Buster Brown, Notebook, Buster & Tige 4.00
Buster Brown, Pencil, Mechanical 3.50
Buster Brown, Pitcher, Milk, Buster & Tige Balancing Pot On Nose, German 25.00
Buster Brown, Plate, Serving Dog Tige, 5 1/2 In. 29.50
Buster Brown, Postcard, Valentine, Buster & Tige, R.F.Outcalt, 1904 .... 10.00
Buster Brown, Print, Buster In Grove City, Pa., C.1910, 18 X 14 In. 2.50
Buster Brown, Ring, Buster & Tige, Gold Plated 10.00
Buster Brown, Stickpin, Round Oak Stoves 12.00
Buster Brown, Stove, Cook, Child's 35.00
Buster Brown, Top, Spinning 8.00
Buster Brown, Toy, Tiger, Sitting, Metal, 3 In. 20.00

Buttermilk Glass, see Custard Glass

Buttons have been known throughout the centuries, and there are millions of styles. Only a few of the most common types are listed for comparison.

Button, Brass, Elizabeth II, 1 In., Set Of 3 .... 25.00
Button, Brass, Teddy Bear, 7/8 In. 3.50
Button, French, Portrait, Lady, Gold & White Filigree, 1 In., 3 In Case 45.00
Button, Gold-Colored Art Nouveau Bust Of Girl, Wood Frame, 1 3/4 In. 4.00
Button, Stanley In Africa, Silver Figure On Camel, Brass Finish, 1 1/2 In. 5.00
Button, Tortoiseshell, Inlaid Silver & Mother-Of-Pearl Florals, 1 1/4 In. 4.50

Buttonhook, see Silver, Sterling; Buttonhook, Store; Buttonhook

Bybee, Vase, Handled, Matte Green, 8 1/2 In. 25.00
C.Pardee Works, Tile, New Orleans Scene, M.Hardwick, 6 1/4 X 3 1/2 In. 75.00

Calcite, see also Steuben

Calcite, Compote, Blue, Colored, 4 X 6 1/2 In. 600.00
Calcite, Compote, Gold, 6 X 4 In. 90.00

Calendar plates were very popular in the United States from 1906 to 1929. Since then plates have been made every year. A calendar, the name of a store, a picture of flowers, a girl, or a scene was featured on the plate.

Calendar, Plate, 1906, Four Seasons 75.00
Calendar, Plate, 1906, Pennsylvania, 9 In. 40.00
Calendar, Plate, 1908, Bulldog, 7 1/4 In. 27.00
Calendar, Plate, 1908, Violets 25.00
Calendar, Plate, 1909, Floral Center, 8 In. 16.50
Calendar, Plate, 1909, Gibson Girl Bust Center, 9 1/4 In. 30.00
Calendar, Plate, 1909, Portrait 37.50
Calendar, Plate, 1909, Rose Center, 9 1/4 In. 22.00
Calendar, Plate, 1909, T.Ed.Carter, 8 1/2 In. 18.50
Calendar, Plate, 1909, Wagner, S.D. 20.00
Calendar, Plate, 1910, Cupids Ringing New Year Bell 18.00
Calendar, Plate, 1910, Dog Center, West Virginia, 7 3/8 In. 22.00
Calendar, Plate, 1910, Dog Holding Calendar In Mouth, Fischer's Bakery 22.00
Calendar, Plate, 1910, Forest City, Ia. 22.00
Calendar, Plate, 1910, Fruit Center, Rose Garlands 22.00
Calendar, Plate, 1910, Fruit Center, 8 In. 23.00
Calendar, Plate, 1910, Gibson Girl 25.00
Calendar, Plate, 1910, Girl In Large Veiled Automobile Hat 25.00
Calendar, Plate, 1910, Girl With Horse, 10 1/2 In. 15.00
Calendar, Plate, 1910, Indian Brave, Souvenir, Royal Iowa, 7 In. 25.00
Calendar, Plate, 1910, Lighthouse Scene, Waverly, Ohio 20.00
Calendar, Plate, 1910, Lighthouse, Water, Birds, & Ships, 8 In. 40.00
Calendar, Plate, 1910, Mulberry, Kansas, 7 3/4 In. 17.50
Calendar, Plate, 1910, Peacock In Center, Months On Spread Wings 15.00
Calendar, Plate, 1910, Portrait 37.50
Calendar, Plate, 1910, Water Lily Center 22.00
Calendar, Plate, 1911-12, Pink Flowers, Green Leaves, Gold Rim, 8 In. 18.00
Calendar, Plate, 1911, Cupid, Ryan Clothier, San Francisco, Calif. 22.00
Calendar, Plate, 1911, Old Car With 1911 License Plate 30.00
Calendar, Plate, 1911, Panama Canal 24.00
Calendar, Plate, 1912, Austin Grocery, Woodburn, Ore., 8 1/2 In. 24.50
Calendar, Plate, 1912, God Bless This Home, Brown, Flower Border, 10 In. 20.00
Calendar, Plate, 1912, Portrait 37.50
Calendar, Plate, 1913, Dan Patch, Famous Racehorse, 9 3/4 In. 25.00
Calendar, Plate, 1913, Floral Center, 7 3/8 In. 30.00
Calendar, Plate, 1913, House, Bridge And Water 28.00
Calendar, Plate, 1913, Old Fashioned Couple, Christy 30.00
Calendar, Plate, 1915, Cherry Center, 8 1/4 In. 30.00
Calendar, Plate, 1915, Panama Canal 15.00
Calendar, Plate, 1915, Panama Canal, 8 1/4 In. 22.00
Calendar, Plate, 1918, Pheasants 25.00
Calendar, Plate, 1921, Game Bird Center 22.00
Calendar, Plate, 1929, Boy With Dog, 9 In. 65.00
Calendar, Plate, 1930, Bird Design 12.50
Calendar, Plate, 1937, Carnations 75.00
Calendar, Plate, 1938, Pansies 25.00
Calendar, Plate, 1954, Fiesta Ware, Ivory, 10 In. 18.50
Calendar, Plate, 1955, Fiesta Ware, Light Green, 10 In. 18.50
Calendar, Plate, 1956, Gold On White Dutch Harbor Scene, Taylor, Smith, Taylor 15.00
California Faience, Planter, Dark Blue, Round, 9 In. 37.00
Camark, Teapot & Warmer, Maroon 15.00

C

The Cambridge Glass Company made pressed glass in Cambridge, Ohio. The words "near-cut"were used after 1906. it was marked with a C in a triangle about 1916.

Cambridge, Ashtray, Crown Tuscan, Seashell, Footed, 4 In. 13.00
Cambridge, Ashtray, 4 Stacked On A Stick, Different Colors, Unsigned 35.00
Cambridge, Banana Boat, Open Handles, 10 Panels, 11 X 4 1/2 In. 15.00
Cambridge, Basket, Crystal, Near Cut, 13 In. 65.00
Cambridge, Basket, Emerald Green, Georgian, Applied Crystal Handle, 7 In. 65.00

Cambridge, Basket, Gold Basket Frame, 3 1/2 In. 32.50
Cambridge, Basket, May, Ebony, Pink Roses, 8 1/2 In. 85.00
Cambridge, Bell, Rosepoint, 6 In. 67.50
Cambridge, Bonbon, Black Amethyst, Etched, Gold Trim, Octagonal 25.00
Cambridge, Bookend, Powder Pigeon, Crystal, Pair 160.00
Cambridge, Bowl & Stand, Azurite, Paper Label, 10 1/4 X 4 3/4 In. 48.00
Cambridge, Bowl, Amethyst, Honeycomb, 10 In. 18.00
Cambridge, Bowl, Azurite 35.00
Cambridge, Bowl, Blue Milk Glass, Shell, 8 3/4 In. 85.00
Cambridge, Bowl, Blue, Alpine, 4 1/2 X 2 In. 20.00
Cambridge, Bowl, Blue, Caprice, Footed, 10 In. 20.00
Cambridge, Bowl, Blue, Caprice, Footed, 11 In. 28.00
Cambridge, Bowl, Blue, Caprice, Handled, 10 In. 12.50
Cambridge, Bowl, Blue, Caprice, 13 In. 30.00
Cambridge, Bowl, Blue, White Swirl, 8 1/4 In. 25.00
Cambridge, Bowl, Caprice, Sterling Floral & Rims, 3 Sections, 7 1/2 In. 25.00
Cambridge, Bowl, Caprice, 4 Footed, 12 In. 44.00
Cambridge, Bowl, Console, Tally-Ho, Carmine Color, Signed 55.00
Cambridge, Bowl, Crown Tuscan, Crimped, Pedestal, Handled, 7 X 3 In. 25.00
Cambridge, Bowl, Crown Tuscan, Shell, 4-Toed, Oval, 8 In. 65.00
Cambridge, Bowl, Crystal, Rosepoint, Gold Encrusted, Flated, 4 Feet, 12 In. 50.00
Cambridge, Bowl, Deep Scalloped, 4-Footed, 12 X 10 In. 40.00
Cambridge, Bowl, Ebony, Silver Encrusted, Large And Heavy 45.00
Cambridge, Bowl, Flying Nude Lady, Moonstone Finish 125.00
Cambridge, Bowl, Frosted Everglade Pattern, Large 16.00
Cambridge, Bowl, Ivy, Cobalt 35.00
Cambridge, Bowl, Milk Glass, Ruffled, Footed, 10 1/2 In. 22.00
Cambridge, Bowl, Pink, Caprice, Flared, Footed, 11 In. 14.90
Cambridge, Bowl, Ram's Head 75.00
Cambridge, Bowl, Royal Blue, Ruffled, 10 3/4 X 9 1/2 In. 35.00
Cambridge, Bowl, Shell, Flying Nude Lady, Crown Tuscan, 12 X 9 In. 145.00
Cambridge, Bowl, Wreaths, Urns, 10 Panels, C In Triangle, 11 X 4 1/2 In. 15.00
Cambridge, Box & Ashtray, Cigarette, Crystal, Caprice 12.50
Cambridge, Box, Cigarette, Blue, Opaque, Shell 30.00
Cambridge, Box, Cigarette, Covered, Crown Tuscan, Seashell, 4 1/2 In. 39.00
Cambridge, Box, Cigarette, Crown Tuscan, Dolphin Feet, Hand Painted 40.00
Cambridge, Box, Cigarette, Crown Tuscan, Dolphin Feet, 4 1/2 In. 18.00
Cambridge, Brandy, Nude Stem, Amber Top 45.00
Cambridge, Bucket, Alpine, Caprice, Chrome Handle, 5 1/2 In. 12.00
Cambridge, Bucket, Ice, Cleo, Pink, Handled, Marked 24.00
Cambridge, Bucket, Ice, Pink, Etched 18.00
Cambridge, Bucket, Ice, Rosepoint, Chrome Handle 35.00
Cambridge, Butter, Covered, Beaded Elipse, C.1900 33.00
Cambridge, Butter, Rosepoint, Oblong, 1/4 Lb. 55.00
Cambridge, Cake Plate, Octagonal With Handle, Black Amethyst 18.00
Cambridge, Candelabra, Crystal Prisms, 13 In., Pair 115.00
Cambridge, Candleholder, Crown Tuscan, Etched Gold Rosepoint, Double 55.00
Cambridge, Candleholder, Crown Tuscan, Nudes, 9 In., Pair 150.00
Cambridge, Candleholder, Green, Rosepoint, Silver Etching, 5 1/2 In., Pair 25.00
Cambridge, Candleholder, Moonlight Blue, Caprice, 7 In., Pair 18.00
Cambridge, Candlestick, Custard, Column, Square Base, Gold Trim, 7 1/2 In. 15.00
Cambridge, Candlestick, Everglades, Satin Finish, 5 In., Pair 40.00
Cambridge, Candlestick, Rosepoint, 2-Arm, 6 In., Pair 40.00
Cambridge, Candlestick, Yellow Calla Lily, Pair 25.00
Cambridge, Card Holder, Carmen, Crystal Stem Base 15.00
Cambridge, Celery & Relish, Rosepoint, Etched, 12 In. 23.00
Cambridge, Celery, Oval, Amber, 12 In. 12.00
Cambridge, Centerpiece Bowl, Jade 20.00
Cambridge, Champagne, Caprice 10.00
Cambridge, Champagne, Green, Blown 3.00
Cambridge, Cigarette & Placecard Holder, Royal Blue 20.00
Cambridge, Claret, Crystal Nude Figure Stem, 4 1/2 Ozs. 50.00
Cambridge, Claret, Green, Crystal Nude Figure Stem, 4 1/2 Ozs. 50.00
Cambridge, Claret, Mt.Vernon, 4 1/2 Ozs. 9.50
Cambridge, Claret, Royal Blue, Crystal Nude Figure Stem, 4 1/2 Ozs. 55.00
Cambridge, Cocktail Shaker, Dianne, Glass Top, 12 In. 67.50

Cambridge, Compote, Amber, Applied Crystal Scrolls & Shells, 2 3/4 In. 12.50
Cambridge, Compote, Amber, Farber Holder, 6 In. 8.00
Cambridge, Compote, Amethyst, Crystal Nude Figure Stem, Flared, 8 In. 85.00
Cambridge, Compote, Apple Green, Nude, Farber Stem & Frame, 5 1/2 In. 32.50
Cambridge, Compote, Barber Holder, Amber 18.00
Cambridge, Compote, Carmen, Crystal Nude Figure Stem, 8 In. 95.00
Cambridge, Compote, Covered, Crown Tuscan, Shell, Roses & Gold, 6 In. 68.00
Cambridge, Compote, Crown Tuscan, Nude Stem, 8 In. 155.00
Cambridge, Compote, Crown Tuscan, Nude, Gold Border, 5 In. 65.00
Cambridge, Compote, Crown Tuscan, Nude, Red Roses, 5 In. 110.00
Cambridge, Compote, Crown Tuscan, Nude, Red Roses, 7 In. 140.00
Cambridge, Compote, Crown Tuscan, Seashell, Decorated, 7 In. 45.00
Cambridge, Compote, Crown Tuscan, Seashell, Flared, Footed, 9 In. 55.00
Cambridge, Compote, Etched Peacocks, 7 In. 14.00
Cambridge, Compote, Farberware Nude Stem, Purple, 5 In. 55.00
Cambridge, Compote, Nude Stem, Amethyst Bowl 70.00
Cambridge, Compote, Nude Stem, Carmen Top 78.00
Cambridge, Compote, Nude Stem, Emerald Green Plate, 8 1/2 In. 75.00
Cambridge, Compote, Rosepoint, Gold Encrusted, 4 Toed, 6 In. 24.00
Cambridge, Compote, Royal Blue, Crystal Nude Figure Stem, 8 In. 95.00
Cambridge, Compote, Shell, Crown Tuscan, 7 X 4 1/2 In. 30.00
Cambridge, Compote, Stretch Glass, Yellow Ribbed, 6 In. 15.00
Cambridge, Compote, Tomato Glass, 7 X 6 In. 55.00
Cambridge, Console Bowl, Caprice, Footed 12.50
Cambridge, Console Bowl, Etched Peacocks, 11 1/2 In. 18.00
Cambridge, Console Bowl, Green, Etched 16.00
Cambridge, Console Bowl, Pink, Etched Flowers, Rolled Edge, 10 Sided 13.50
Cambridge, Console Bowl, Pink, Gold Overlay 35.00
Cambridge, Console Set, Amber, Apple Blossom, 3 Piece 45.00
Cambridge, Console Set, Amber, Gold Encrusted Floral, 6 Piece 100.00
Cambridge, Console Set, Crown Tuscan, Flying Lady, 3 Piece 300.00
Cambridge, Console Set, Moonlight Blue, Caprice, Prisms, 3 Piece 55.00
Cambridge, Console Set, Moonlight Blue, Rings, 10 In. Bowl, 3 Piece 70.00
Cambridge, Cordial Set, Amber, Blue, Green, Farber Bros.Chrome Holder 125.00
Cambridge, Cordial Set, Gadroon, Amethyst Wines, Handled Tray, 7 Piece 28.00
Cambridge, Cordial Set, Honey Amber, 6 Piece 25.00
Cambridge, Cordial, Amber, Farber Holder 8.50
Cambridge, Cordial, Cadet Cut 20.00
Cambridge, Cordial, Green, Blown 3.00
Cambridge, Cordial, Wildflower, 6 In. 18.00
Cambridge, Cornucopia, Crown Tuscan, Miniature 15.00
Cambridge, Cornucopia, Crown Tuscan, Seashell, 9 1/2 In. 70.00
Cambridge, Cornucopia, Shell, Crown Tuscan, 5 In. 26.00
Cambridge, Cruet Set, Amethyst, Farber Holders, 5 Piece 65.00
Cambridge, Cruet, Amber, Farber Holder, Small 18.00
Cambridge, Cruet, Buzz Saw, Iridescent, Green, Signed Near Cut, 4 In. 350.00
Cambridge, Cruet, Buzz Saw, Marigold, Stopper 350.00
Cambridge, Cup & Saucer, Pink, Cleo 12.00
Cambridge, Cup, Nut, Pink, Cleo, Ribbed, Stemmed 7.00
Cambridge, Decanter, Amethyst 30.00
Cambridge, Dish & Underplate, Mayonnaise, Rosepoint, Handled, Footed 28.00
Cambridge, Dish, Candy, Amethyst, Swirl Cover, 5 1/2 In. 22.00
Cambridge, Dish, Candy, Covered, Crown Tuscan, Roses & Gold, 3 Sections 68.00
Cambridge, Dish, Candy, Covered, Crown Tuscan, Shell, Decorated 55.00
Cambridge, Dish, Candy, Covered, Rosepoint 25.00
Cambridge, Dish, Candy, Mandarin Gold, Chrome Holder & Lid 15.00
Cambridge, Dish, Candy, Rosepoint 18.00
Cambridge, Dish, Candy, Yellow, Etched Peacocks, 6 In. 11.00
Cambridge, Dish, Covered Oval Soap, Helio 27.00
Cambridge, Dish, Nut, Crown Tuscan, Pink, Covered, 3 Sections 36.00
Cambridge, Dish, Red, 3 Sections, Farber Holder & Lid, 7 In. 18.00
Cambridge, Dish, Sea Food, Crown Tuscan, Dolphin 45.00
Cambridge, Dish, Seashell Shape, Crown Tuscan, 3 Toed, 4 In. 15.00
Cambridge, Dish, Turkey Cover, 8 In. 27.00
Cambridge, Dish, Underplate, & Ladle, Mayonnaise, Blossom Time 30.00
Cambridge, Figurine, Cow, Miniature 12.50

Cambridge, Figurine, Nude Lady, 6 1/2 In. 40.00
Cambridge, Figurine, Pouter Pigeon, 6 In. 25.00
Cambridge, Flower Block, Nude Boy Hugging Baby Lamb, 9 X 4 In. 37.00
Cambridge, Flower Frog, Bashful Charlotte, 13 In. 75.00
Cambridge, Flower Frog, Dove 25.00
Cambridge, Flower Frog, Girl 30.00
Cambridge, Flower Frog, Green, Bashful Charlotte, 8 In. 50.00
Cambridge, Flower Frog, Green, September Morn Girl 135.00
Cambridge, Flower Frog, Moonlight Blue, 9 In. 48.00
Cambridge, Flower Frog, Pink, September Morn Girl 135.00
Cambridge, Flower Frog, Sea Gull, 8 In. 26.00
Cambridge, Flower Holder, Amber, Draped Lady 60.00
Cambridge, Flower Holder, Bashful Charlotte, 8 1/2 In. 32.00
Cambridge, Flower Holder, Crystal, Sea Gull, 10 In. .... 35.00 To 45.00
Cambridge, Flower Holder, Draped Lady 28.00
Cambridge, Flower Holder, Nude Figure, Emerald Green, 12 3/4 In. 85.00
Cambridge, Flower Holder, Pink, Dianthus, 8 1/2 In. 55.00
Cambridge, Fruit Bowl, Caprice, 4 Footed, 12 1/2 X 8 In. 12.00
Cambridge, Fruit Bowl, Crown Tuscan, Flying Lady, Footed, 10 In. 165.00
Cambridge, Fruit Bowl, Crown Tuscan, Shell 75.00
Cambridge, Goblet, Caprice, 7 3/4 In. 10.00
Cambridge, Goblet, Carmen, 10 Ozs. 14.00
Cambridge, Goblet, Cascade Line 5.00
Cambridge, Goblet, Cobalt, Goldball Stem, 10 Ozs., 6 1/2 In. 14.50
Cambridge, Goblet, Cobalt, Tally-Ho 18.00
Cambridge, Goblet, Cobalt, 10 Ozs., 6 5/8 In. 16.00
Cambridge, Goblet, Cocktail, Amber, Farber Holder, 3 Ozs. 16.00
Cambridge, Goblet, Cocktail, Amber, Nude Crystal Stem 45.00
Cambridge, Goblet, Cocktail, Amber, Nude Stem, 6 1/2 In. 50.00
Cambridge, Goblet, Cocktail, Amethyst, Farber Bros. Chrome Holder 12.00
Cambridge, Goblet, Cocktail, Amethyst, Nude Stem, 6 1/2 In. 50.00
Cambridge, Goblet, Cocktail, Black, Nude Stem 30.00
Cambridge, Goblet, Cocktail, Green, Nude Stem, 6 1/2 In. 50.00
Cambridge, Goblet, Cocktail, Mandarin Red, Nude Stem, 6 1/2 In. 50.00
Cambridge, Goblet, Green, Banquet, Nude Stem 60.00
Cambridge, Goblet, Green, Blown 3.00
Cambridge, Goblet, Lavender, Alexandrite 10.00
Cambridge, Goblet, Mt.Vernon, 6 In. 7.50
Cambridge, Goblet, Oyster Cocktail, Pink, Caprice, 4 1/2 Ozs. 5.00
Cambridge, Goblet, Oyster Cocktail, Rosepoint, 4 1/2 In. 15.00
Cambridge, Goblet, Pink, Etched 7.50
Cambridge, Goblet, Red, Faceted Ball On Crystal Stem 9.00
Cambridge, Goblet, Rosepoint .... 15.00 To 17.00
Cambridge, Honey Pot, Bees On Lid, Crown Tuscan 35.00
Cambridge, Ivy Ball, Amber, Crystal Knob Stem, 7 In. 22.00
Cambridge, Ivy Ball, Amethyst, 7 In. 22.00
Cambridge, Ivy Ball, Cobalt, Ribbed Optic, Crystal Foot, 8 1/2 In. 27.50
Cambridge, Ivy Ball, Nude Stem, Amber 80.00
Cambridge, Ivy Ball, Royal Blue, Ribbed Optic, Crystal Foot, 8 In. 35.00
Cambridge, Ivy Ball, Royal Blue, 8 In. 35.00
Cambridge, Jar, Cracker, Wheat Sheaf, Cover 30.00
Cambridge, Jar, Powder, Green, Etched 704 .... 25.00
Cambridge, Jug, Amethyst, Crystal Handle, Ice Lip, No.3400, 80 Ozs. 45.00
Cambridge, Jug, Blue, Caprice, Ball, Crystal Handle, 80 Ozs. 52.00
Cambridge, Jug, Martini, Chantilly, Etched, Sterling Base, 32 Oz. 35.00
Cambridge, Jug, Rosepoint, Ball Shape, 80 Ozs. 80.00

Cambridge, Lamp, see Lamp, Cambridge

Cambridge, Luncheon Set, Apple Green, 14 Piece 55.00
Cambridge, Mug, Beer, Ruby, Tally Ho 16.50
Cambridge, Parfait, Red, Rock Crystal 25.00
Cambridge, Pitcher, Crystal, Caprice 35.00
Cambridge, Pitcher, Rosepoint, 7 In. 67.50
Cambridge, Pitcher, Round Jug, Amber 19.50
Cambridge, Pitcher, Water, Chantilly, Etched, Sterling Base, 9 1/2 In. 52.00
Cambridge, Pitcher, Water, Cobalt, Applied Clear Handle, Ice Lip 50.00
Cambridge, Pitcher, Water, Etched 25.00

Cambridge, Plate, Apple Green, Etched Floral, 8 In. 3.50
Cambridge, Plate, Apple Green, Ribbed, Key-Patterned Tab Handle, 8 1/2 In. 4.50
Cambridge, Plate, Blue, Caprice, Handled, Square, 6 In. 4.00
Cambridge, Plate, Bread & Butter, Mt.Vernon, 6 In. 5.00
Cambridge, Plate, Cake, Pink Handle, Similar To Candlelight, 10 In. 25.00
Cambridge, Plate, Cake, Square Pattern, 12 In. 35.00
Cambridge, Plate, Caprice, 8 1/2 In. 3.00
Cambridge, Plate, Chop, Rosepoint, Footed, 12 1/2 In. 37.50
Cambridge, Plate, Crown Tuscan, Shell, Hand-Painted Roses, Gold Trim, 7 In. 65.00
Cambridge, Plate, Crown Tuscan, 13 In. 44.00
Cambridge, Plate, Dinner, Amethyst, Scalloped, 10 In. 6.50
Cambridge, Plate, Dinner, Rosepoint 30.00
Cambridge, Plate, Luncheon, Mt.Vernon, 8 In. 7.50
Cambridge, Plate, Pink, Cleo, 5 3/4 In. 5.00
Cambridge, Plate, Pink, Cleo, 8 3/4 In. 6.00
Cambridge, Plate, Pink, 10 Sided, 7 In. 2.50
Cambridge, Plate, Salad, Cascade Line, 8 In. 4.00
Cambridge, Plate, Salad, Rosepoint, Etched, 8 In. 8.00
Cambridge, Plate, Salad, Wildflower 14.00
Cambridge, Plate, Serving, Cupid, Amber, Handled 100.00
Cambridge, Plate, Serving, Rosepoint, Handled, 12 1/4 In. 35.00
Cambridge, Plate, Serving, Rosepoint, Open Handled, 15 1/2 X 11 In.
Cambridge, Punch Bowl, Tally Ho, Footed, Frosted Base, Gold Stripes, 11 In. 37.50
Cambridge, Relish, Crown Tuscan, Shell, Divided, 3 Footed, 8 In. 37.50
Cambridge, Relish, Eagle, Center Handle, 3 Sections 48.00
Cambridge, Relish, Moonlight Blue, Caprice, 3 Sections, 8 1/2 In. 5.75
Cambridge, Relish, Portia, 3 Sections, 4 Footed, 9 In. 27.50
Cambridge, Relish, Rosepoint, Gold Encrusted, 3 Sections, 6 1/2 In. 20.00
Cambridge, Relish, Rosepoint, Handled, 3 Sections, 8 In. 25.00
Cambridge, Rose Bowl, Crystal, Caprice, 5 In. 29.50
Cambridge, Salad Bowl, Crown Tuscan, 13 In. 42.50
Cambridge, Salt & Pepper, Amethyst, Farber Holder 14.00
Cambridge, Salt & Pepper, Apple Green, Nautilus, 3 In. 8.50
Cambridge, Salt & Pepper, Chantilly, Handled, Sterling Silver Tops 18.00
Cambridge, Salt & Pepper, Mt.Vernon, Sterling Tops, Footed 18.50
Cambridge, Salt, Crown Tuscan 6.00
Cambridge, Salt, Swan, Signed, 3 1/2 In. 12.50
Cambridge, Salt, Swan, Twisted Neck, 3 In., Pair 18.00
Cambridge, Sherbet, Blue, Caprice, 8 1/2 In. 5.00
Cambridge, Sherbet, Cascade 4.00
Cambridge, Sherbet, Cobalt, 6 Ozs., 5 In. 12.00
Cambridge, Sherbet, Mt.Vernon, 4 1/4 In. 7.00
Cambridge, Sherbet, Red, Clear Stem & Foot 6.00
Cambridge, Sherbet, Rosepoint, Etched, 7 Ozs. 13.00
Cambridge, Sherbet, Rosepoint, High Stem 15.00
Cambridge, Sherbet, Rosepoint, Low Stem 15.50
Cambridge, Shot Glass, Amethyst, Farber Holder 3.50
Cambridge, Spooner, Blue Opalescent 28.00
Cambridge, Spooner, Child's, Colonial 9.00
Cambridge, Spooner, Child's, Green, Colonial 14.00
Cambridge, Sugar & Creamer, Gadroon 9.00
Cambridge, Sugar & Creamer, Individual, Blue, Caprice 8.95
Cambridge, Sugar & Creamer, Pink 5.00
Cambridge, Sugar & Creamer, Rosepoint, Etched .... 22.00 To 25.00
Cambridge, Sugar & Creamer, Virginian 22.50
Cambridge, Sugar, Creamer, & Stand, Pink, Zigzag Handles, Footed 15.00
Cambridge, Sugar, Creamer, & Tray, Amber, Thorn-Handled Tray, 3 Piece 29.00
Cambridge, Sugar, Creamer, & Tray, Peachblow, Decagon, Center Handle In Tray 23.00
Cambridge, Swan, Amber, 3 1/2 In. 32.00
Cambridge, Swan, Apple Green, 3 In. 21.50
Cambridge, Swan, Apple Green, 3 1/2 In. 18.00
Cambridge, Swan, Apple Green, 6 1/2 In. 35.00
Cambridge, Swan, Apple Green, 8 1/2 In. 55.00
Cambridge, Swan, Black, 10 In. 140.00
Cambridge, Swan, Crown Tuscan, Gold Trim, 3 1/2 In. 47.50

Cambridge, Swan, Crown Tuscan, 2 1/2 In. 22.00
Cambridge, Swan, Crown Tuscan, 3 In. 28.00
Cambridge, Swan, Crown Tuscan, 3 1/2 In. 25.00
Cambridge, Swan, Crown Tuscan, 8 1/2 In. 140.00
Cambridge, Swan, Crystal, 3 In. 15.00
Cambridge, Swan, Crystal, 8 1/2 In. 40.00
Cambridge, Swan, Ebony, 6 1/2 In. 95.00
Cambridge, Swan, Emerald Green, 6 1/2 In. 95.00
Cambridge, Swan, Frosted Crystal, 10 In. 80.00
Cambridge, Swan, Mandarin Gold, 3 1/2 In. 28.50
Cambridge, Swan, Mandarin Gold, 8 1/2 In. 85.00
Cambridge, Swan, Sterling Silver Overlay, 3 1/2 In. 75.00
Cambridge, Table Set, Child's, Colonial Green 125.00
Cambridge, Table Set, Child's, Colonial, 4 Piece 65.00
Cambridge, Toothpick, Blue, Marked 19.00
Cambridge, Toothpick, Ruby, 1901 .... 18.00
Cambridge, Tray, Sandwich, Amber, Decagon Ring, Handled, Etched Cleo 18.00
Cambridge, Tray, Tally Ho, Handled, Frosted Bottom, Gold Stripes, 11 3/4 In. 7.50
Cambridge, Tumbler, Amethyst, Newport 4.50
Cambridge, Tumbler, Blue, Caprice, Thin, 12 Ozs. 10.00
Cambridge, Tumbler, Blue, Caprice, 4 1/2 In. 5.00
Cambridge, Tumbler, Chanticleer, 3 In. 5.50
Cambridge, Tumbler, Feather, Near Cut 12.00
Cambridge, Tumbler, Iced Tea, Rosepoint 15.00
Cambridge, Tumbler, Iced Tea, Rosepoint, Footed 17.00
Cambridge, Tumbler, Juice, Dark Green 4.50
Cambridge, Tumbler, Juice, Emerald Green, Gyro Optic, 4 Oz. 6.25
Cambridge, Tumbler, Juice, Rosepoint, Footed, 5 Oz. 18.00
Cambridge, Tumbler, Lemonade, Frosted Apple Green, Gold Foot, Handle 12.00
Cambridge, Tumbler, Moonlight Blue, Georgian, 12 Oz. 10.00
Cambridge, Tumbler, Mount Vernon, 7 Ozs., 3 1/2 In. 5.50
Cambridge, Tumbler, Near Cut, No.2631 .... 12.00
Cambridge, Tumbler, Pink, Cleo, Footed 9.00
Cambridge, Tumbler, Red, 3 In. 1.50
Cambridge, Tumbler, Rosepoint, Etched, Footed, 10 Oz. 14.00
Cambridge, Vase, Amber, Ball Type, 6 In. 12.00
Cambridge, Vase, Amber, Caprice, Blown, 5 In. 15.00
Cambridge, Vase, Amber, Caprice, 8 In. 25.00
Cambridge, Vase, Bell Shape, Gold Etching, 10 In. 32.00
Cambridge, Vase, Blue, Caprice, Blown, 3 1/2 In. 12.00
Cambridge, Vase, Bud, Rosepoint, 10 In. 30.00
Cambridge, Vase, Bud, Rosepoint, 10 1/4 In. 37.50
Cambridge, Vase, Cobalt, Clear Foot, Flared, 12 In. 35.00
Cambridge, Vase, Crown Tuscan, Globe, Black Trim, 6 1/2 In. 200.00
Cambridge, Vase, Crown Tuscan, No.6004, 10 In. 35.00
Cambridge, Vase, Crown Tuscan, Ring Stem, 12 In. 50.00
Cambridge, Vase, Crown Tuscan, 5 In. 35.00
Cambridge, Vase, Rosepoint, Keyhole, 12 In. 35.00
Cambridge, Vase, Rosepoint, 10 3/4 In. 32.00
Cambridge, Vase, Rubena, Basket Weave, 8 In. 85.00
Cambridge, Vase, Tomato Glass, Trumpet, 10 In. 95.00
Cambridge, Wine, Amber, Nude Stem 45.00
Cambridge, Wine, Green, Blown 3.00
Cambridge, Wine, Mt.Vernon, 4 1/4 In. 9.00
Cambridge, Wine, Nude Girl Holding Bunch Of Grapes Stem, 6 1/4 In. 25.00
Cambridge, Wine, Red, Faceted Ball On Crystal Stem 9.00
Cambridge, Wine, Sauterne, Royal Blue, Crystal Nude Figure Stem, 4 1/2 Ozs. 55.00
Cambridge, Wine, Tally Ho, Tulip Shape, Frosted Base, Gold Stripes 5.50

Cameo glass was made in layers in much the same manner as a cameo in jewelry. Part of the top layer of glass was cut away to reveal a different colored glass beneath. The most famous cameo glass was made during the nineteenth century.

Cameo, see also Daum Nancy, De Vez, G. Raspillier, Galle, Le Verre Francais, Richard, Webb, Weis

Cameo, Bottle, Perfume, Bamboo Trees, Red, English, 5 In. 895.00
Cameo, Bottle, Perfume, English, Silver Top, Blue, Butterflies & Floral, 7 In. 550.00
Cameo, Centerpiece, LaVerre, Candy Cane Signature, Huge 595.00
Cameo, Compote, Low Stand, 8 In. 25.00
Cameo, Figurine, Seagull Over Waves, Lobmeyer, White, Gold Flecked, 5 In. 495.00
Cameo, Inkwell, Vaseline Open Roses, Frosted Ground, Gold Lined Cover 150.00
Cameo, Jar, Biscuit, V & S, French, Dandelions, Gilt Lid, Scroll Handle, 6 In. 195.00
Cameo, Pitcher, Red To Orange, Amethyst Handle, Signed Francais & Charder 375.00
Cameo, Rose Bowl, English, Frosted & Clear, Butterflies & Floral, 3 3/4 In. 350.00
Cameo, Salt, Fluted Top, Ruby Cutting On Striped Base 60.00
Cameo, Vase, Blue Acid Cut Hunt Scene, 10 1/2 In. 150.00
Cameo, Vase, Bud, Bulbous, Carved Dragon, Translucent Frosted Body, Signed, 4 I 595.00
Cameo, Vase, English, Matte Red, White Butterfly & Floral, 6 In. 1350.00
Cameo, Vase, English, Morning Glories On Lime Ground, 9 1/2 In. 650.00
Cameo, Vase, English, Tricolor, Pink & White On Citron, 4 In. 600.00
Cameo, Vase, English, White Leaves On Citron, Dated, 1905, 9 1/2 In. 900.00
Cameo, Vase, English, White On Citron, Blossoms, Etched Cameo On Bottom 900.00
Cameo, Vase, English, White On Citron, Floral, 6 3/4 In. 1050.00
Cameo, Vase, English, White On Cranberry, Bird, Butterfly, 7 1/2 In. 2100.00
Cameo, Vase, English, White On Cranberry, Butterfly On Back, 6 In. 1650.00
Cameo, Vase, English, White On Raisin, Deeply Carved, 4 1/2 In. 960.00
Cameo, Vase, Es.De Crystal Paris, Crackle, Hounds Chasing Stag, 8 In. 200.00
Cameo, Vase, Etling, France, Gray, Butterflies, Mold Blown, 12 In. 160.00
Cameo, Vase, French, Apricot, Teal & Frost, Signed Barr, 15 In. 795.00
Cameo, Vase, French, Tortoiseshell & Citrine, Footed, 10 In. 85.00
Cameo, Vase, Green Background, Pink & White Flowers, Burgun & Schverer, Pair 5500.00
Cameo, Vase, Miniature, Weis 65.00
Cameo, Vase, Pink, Brown Lilies, Semifooted, Art Deco.7 In. 155.00
Cameo, Vase, Pink, Red Brown Tulips, 7 In. 165.00
Cameo, Vase, Spider & Web, Plum On Frosted, Signed VSL, 10 In. 595.00

Campaign, see Political Campaign

Campbell Kid, Book, Menu & Cook, 1910 9.00
Campbell Kid, Cup, Silver Plate 8.00
Campbell Kid, Dish, Child's, Buffalo Pottery, 8 In. 45.00
Campbell Kid, Doll, Horsman, 1948, 12 In. 75.00
Campbell Kid, Doll, Ideal Co., Vinyl, Dressed, 8 In. 16.00
Campbell Kid, Hairbrush, Child's, C.1920 7.00
Campbell Kid, Jar, Cookie, Bennington Type 26.00
Campbell Kid, Knife, Fork, & Spoon Set, Wm.Rogers 20.00
Campbell Kid, Soup Bowl, Alphabet 4.00
Campbell Kid, Soup Bowl, Thermo, Figural Handle 6.00
Campbell Kid, Spoon, Silver Plate 5.00

Camphor glass is a cloudy white glass that has been blown or pressed. It was made by many factories in the Midwest during the mid-nineteenth century.

Camphor Glass, Bottle, Perfume, Embossed Sitting Nude, Semioval, 4 3/4 In. 30.00
Camphor Glass, Bowl, Blown Out Pink & Yellow Leaves, Pedestal, 12 In. 33.00
Camphor Glass, Bowl, Scalloped Top, Gold Trim, 10 In. 12.00
Camphor Glass, Box, Powder, Lady On Lid, Green 17.50
Camphor Glass, Decanter, Hand-Painted, Can Can Dancers, Stopper 17.50
Camphor Glass, Decanter, Hand-Painted, Gin & Bourbon, Stopper 17.50
Camphor Glass, Dish, Candy, Fan Finial, Peach Color, 6 1/4 X 5 1/4 In. 23.00
Camphor Glass, Flower Frog, Draped Nude, Art Deco, 10 In. 80.00
Camphor Glass, Jar, Powder, German Shepherd On Top, Green, 6 1/2 X 6 In. 28.00
Camphor Glass, Jar, Powder, Nude With Crossed Legs, Pink, 5 X 6 In. 20.00
Camphor Glass, Mug, Tennessee 35.00
Camphor Glass, Paperweight, Dog In Base, Oval, 7 1/2 In. 36.00
Camphor Glass, Pitcher, Hobnail, Bulbous, Triangular Spout, Applied Handle 115.00
Camphor Glass, Plate, The Easter Opening 22.00
Camphor Glass, Salt, Blue, Hen On Nest Base 14.00
Camphor Glass, Salt, 3 Face 25.00
Camphor Glass, Tray, Bureau, Versailles Shape 17.50
Camphor Glass, Vase, Hand Holding Torch, Centennial, 1876, 6 1/2 In. 28.00
Camphor Glass, Vase, Overlapping Leaves Form Handles, Pedestal, 8 In. 14.50

Candlestick, Brass, 18th Century, 6 In.

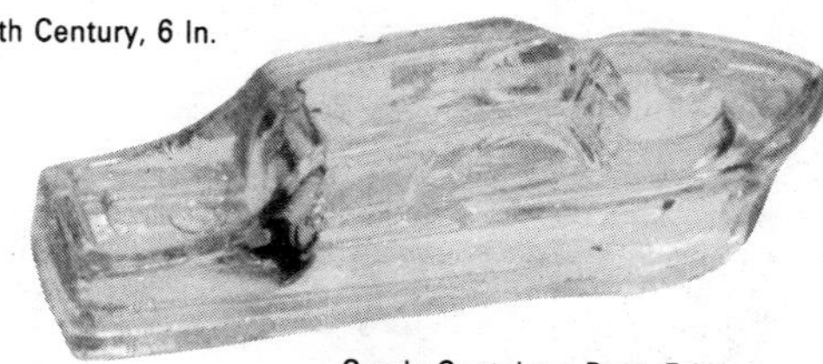
Candy Container, Boat, 5 In.

Canary Glass, see Vaseline Glass
Candleholder, see also Wooden, Candleholder, and various porcelain categories
Candleholder, Diamond-Quilted Center, Scalloped Rim, 8 In., Pair 58.00
Candleholder, Glass Rooster, 5 1/2 In., Pair 65.00
Candleholder, Hogscraper, 4 In. 34.00
Candleholder, Rushlight, Wooden Base, 18th Century, 15 In. 150.00
Candleholder, Sterling Silver, Removable Bobeche, 10 In., Pair 45.00
Candlestick, see also Brass, Candlestick; Pewter, Candlestick; Vaseline Glass, Candlestick; and various porcelain categories
Candlestick, Brass, 18th Century, 6 In. .... *Illus* 135.00
Candlestick, Farber, Chrome, Nude, Art Deco, 8 1/2 In., Pair 22.00
Candlestick, Fluted Stem, Petal Top, 8 7/8 In. 45.00
Candlestick, Hogscraper, Chair Hook, Push-Up, Patent 1855, 4 In. 40.00
Candlestick, Opaque Blue, Hexagonal, Sanded Finish, 6 7/8 In. 150.00
Candlestick, Pewter, Camphor Glass Top, 4 1/2 In., Pair 65.00
Candlestick, Pewter, Pricket, C.1750, 39 In., Pair 398.00
Candlestick, Stepped Cascade Base, Lacy, 5 In. 85.00

Candy containers, especially those made of glass, were popular during the late Victorian era.

Candy Container, see also Kewpie, Candy Container
Candy Container, Airplane 12.50
Candy Container, Airplane, Spirit Of St.Louis, Green Glass 125.00
Candy Container, Auto 15.00
Candy Container, Barney Google 68.00
Candy Container, Barrel Keg 14.00
Candy Container, Baseball 15.00
Candy Container, Basket .... 15.00 To 16.00
Candy Container, Basket Hanging, Glass 14.00
Candy Container, Battleship .... 6.00 To 20.00
Candy Container, Bear Reading Book 35.00
Candy Container, Beau Brummel 29.00
Candy Container, Betty Boop Perfume 12.00
Candy Container, Boat .... 12.50 To 14.00
Candy Container, Boat, 5 In. .... *Illus* 3.00
Candy Container, Bond Mono Cell 20.00
Candy Container, Bottle 8.50
Candy Container, Building, Milk Glass 45.00
Candy Container, Bulldog .... 6.00 To 25.00
Candy Container, Candleholder 15.00
Candy Container, Car 10.00
Candy Container, Car, Electric Coupe 40.00
Candy Container, Charlie Chaplin .... 50.00 To 65.00
Candy Container, Chicken 9.00
Candy Container, Chicken On Oblong Basket 18.00
Candy Container, Child, Naked 35.00

Candy Container, Jumbo, Green, 3 1/4 In.

Candy Container, Egg, Paper, 5 In.

Candy Container, Clear Kewpie, Barrel, Marked & Numbered 40.00
Candy Container, Clock, Mantel 45.00
Candy Container, Clock, Octagon 65.00
Candy Container, Coupe With Long Hood, USA 70.00
Candy Container, Cruiser Boat 12.50
Candy Container, Dirigible, Los Angeles 65.00
Candy Container, Dog 10.00
Candy Container, Dog, Cork Top With Bail 11.00
Candy Container, Dog, Sitting, 3 In. 6.50
Candy Container, Doll With Bonnet 32.00
Candy Container, Duck 22.50
Candy Container, Duck, Tin Bottom 20.00
Candy Container, Dutch Windmill 28.00
Candy Container, Easter Egg, Papier-Mache, Red, Rabbit's Head, Germany 17.50
Candy Container, Egg, Paper, 5 In. .... *Illus* 10.00
Candy Container, Engine 20.00
Candy Container, Engine, Musical 25.00
Candy Container, Fat Boy 22.00
Candy Container, Fire Engine .... 6.00 To 45.00
Candy Container, Fire Engine, Candy Inside 20.00
Candy Container, Fire Engine, Victory Glass Co. 5.00
Candy Container, Fire Truck, Driver, Boiler 15.00
Candy Container, Fox, Learned 45.00
Candy Container, French Telephone 7.50
Candy Container, Goose Girl 16.00
Candy Container, Gun 22.50
Candy Container, Gun, VG Co. 10.00
Candy Container, Happifats On Drum 65.00
Candy Container, Hat 22.00
Candy Container, Hatching Rabbit 22.50
Candy Container, Helicopter 25.00
Candy Container, Hen On Nest 6.00
Candy Container, Hen, Tin Closure, Colored, 3 1/2 In. 15.00
Candy Container, High Suitcase, Metal Closure 15.00
Candy Container, Horse & Cart 7.00
Candy Container, Hound Dog Pup 3.00
Candy Container, Independence Hall, 1876 .... 65.00
Candy Container, Iron 16.00
Candy Container, Jack-O-Lantern 25.00
Candy Container, Jumbo, Green, 3 1/4 In. .... *Illus* 65.00
Candy Container, Kiddie Car 60.00
Candy Container, Lamp, Tin Top 12.50
Candy Container, Lantern 10.00
Candy Container, Lantern Barn Type 18.00

Candy Container, Lantern, Barn, Dark Red 30.00
Candy Container, Lantern, Candy 10.00
Candy Container, Lantern, Dec.2, 1904 .... 15.00
Candy Container, Lantern, Flint Globe 20.00
Candy Container, Lantern, Glass & Tin, Metal Handle 15.00
Candy Container, Lantern, Green Globe 10.00
Candy Container, Lantern, Tin Top & Bottom, 4 1/2 In., Jeanette 10.00
Candy Container, Lantern, Tin Top And Bail, Victory 12.00
Candy Container, Liberty Bell, Amber .... 18.00 To 26.00
Candy Container, Liberty Bell, 1776-1876, Cork Top 32.00
Candy Container, Lighthouse, 5 In. 21.00
Candy Container, Limousine With Rear Trunk & Tire 65.00
Candy Container, Locomotive 14.00
Candy Container, Los Angeles Dirigible 40.00
Candy Container, Man's Boot 16.00
Candy Container, Military Hat 8.50
Candy Container, Moon Mullins 22.00
Candy Container, Mug 20.00
Candy Container, Nesting Hen 8.50
Candy Container, Nurser 5.00
Candy Container, Opera Glasses .... 30.00 To 35.00
Candy Container, Opera Glasses, Milk Glass 65.00
Candy Container, Opera Glasses, Red, Plain Panels 45.00
Candy Container, Owl 12.00
Candy Container, Papier-Mache, 13 In. .... *Illus* 85.00
Candy Container, Peter Rabbit .... 8.00 To 12.50
Candy Container, Phone .... 10.00 To 20.00
Candy Container, Pistol, Screw Cap, 7 In. 25.00
Candy Container, Pistol, Tin Screw Top, 4 1/2 In. 12.00
Candy Container, Pistol, 3 3/4 In. 13.00
Candy Container, Powder Horn .... 25.00 To 32.50
Candy Container, Puppy, Metal Lid 5.00
Candy Container, Rabbit .... 22.00 To 65.00
Candy Container, Rabbit Eating Carrot 13.00
Candy Container, Rabbit With Basket On Arm, 4 1/2 In. 35.00
Candy Container, Rabbit, By Stough 12.00
Candy Container, Rabbit, Sitting 9.00
Candy Container, Rabbit, Sitting, Jeanette Glass Co., 6 1/2 In. 12.00
Candy Container, Rabbit, Sitting, 6 1/4 In. 18.00
Candy Container, Rabbit, Standing, Tin Screw Bottom 30.00

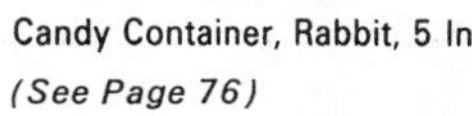

Candy Container, Rabbit, 5 In.

(See Page 76)

Candy Container, Tank, 5 In.

(See Page 76)

Candy Container, Papier-Mache, 13 In.

Candy Container, Rabbit, 5 In. .... *Illus* 12.00
Candy Container, Rabbits, Eating Carrot 12.00
Candy Container, Railroad Lantern 7.50
Candy Container, Rocking Horse With Clown Rider 65.00
Candy Container, Rooster Crowing .... 50.00 To 70.00
Candy Container, Santa Claus .... 18.00 To 65.00
Candy Container, Santa Claus, Paneled Coat 45.00
Candy Container, Santa Emerging From Chimney 20.00
Candy Container, Santa With Plastic Head 25.00
Candy Container, Santa's Boot, Paper Label 8.00
Candy Container, Scottie Dog .... 4.00 To 10.00
Candy Container, Ship 20.00
Candy Container, Sitting Cat, 8 In. 25.00
Candy Container, Sitting Duck, Clear Glass, Pink Eyes, Yellow Beak 22.50
Candy Container, Small Telephone 14.00
Candy Container, Soda Mug, Design In Panels, 2 1/2 In. 10.00
Candy Container, Spark Plug 85.00
Candy Container, Spark Plug, Closure 70.00
Candy Container, Spinning Top, Wooden Winder 25.00
Candy Container, Station Wagon .... 10.00 To 15.00
Candy Container, Storks, German 18.00
Candy Container, Suitcase 17.00
Candy Container, Tank .... 9.00 To 16.00
Candy Container, Tank, Khaki Paint, Victory Glass, 4 In. 16.50
Candy Container, Tank, 2 Cannons, Victory, U.S.A. & Star 28.00
Candy Container, Tank, 5 In. .... *Illus* 19.00
Candy Container, Teddy Bear 12.00
Candy Container, Telephone 15.00
Candy Container, Telephone, Millsteins 20.00
Candy Container, Train .... 15.00 To 49.50
Candy Container, Train Engine 14.00
Candy Container, Trunk, Milk Glass, Butler Bros., C.1907 .... 60.00
Candy Container, Turkey Gobbler 35.00
Candy Container, Turkey, 2 Part, 7 In. 52.00
Candy Container, U.S.Military Hat, Small 30.00
Candy Container, Washboard .... 16.00 To 22.50
Candy Container, Wheelbarrow 30.00
Candy Container, Willys Jeep 6.00
Candy Container, Windmill .... 25.00 To 26.00
Cane, Bamboo, Curved Handle 6.00
Cane, Bamboo, Great Lakes Exposition, Cleveland, 1937 .... 10.00
Cane, Blackthorn, Natural Shape 6.00
Cane, Chinese, 4 Monkeys, Silver, Copper, & Brass 150.00
Cane, Hand-Carved Bearded Animal 30.00
Cane, Handle, Gold, Mother-Of-Pearl Panels 15.00
Cane, Ivory Walrus's Head, Gold Ring 25.00
Cane, Ivory, Carved Hound's Head, 2 1/2 In. 25.00
Cane, Lyons, Sterling Silver, Woman's Head, Gold Stars & Bands 25.00
Cane, Metal, Chicago, 1933 .... 10.00
Cane, Walking Stick, Birth, Life, & Death Of Thomas Jefferson, Carved 210.00
Cane, 13 Ivory Inlays, Gold Ring 25.00

Canton china is a blue-and-white ware made near Canton, China, from about 1785 to 1895. It is hand-decorated with Chinese scenes.

Canton, Bowl, Chinese Mandarin, 18 In. 475.00
Canton, Bowl, Goldfish, C.1800 .... 1200.00
Canton, Bowl, Oblong, 14 X 10 1/2 In. 85.00
Canton, Cup, Berry Finial On Lid, Twisted Handle, 3 1/2 In. 115.00
Canton, Dish, Leaf Shape, 8 X 6 In. 85.00
Canton, Dish, Shrimp, Orange Peel, 10 X 10 1/2 In. 225.00
Canton, Jar, Covered, Blue Ducks, Water, Lily Pads, & Flowers, 5 1/2 In. 75.00
Canton, Jar, Ginger, Dark Blue Flowers & Leaves, 5 X 2 3/4 In. 58.00
Canton, Pitcher, 7 In. .... *Illus* 75.00
Canton, Plate, Reticulated, Blue & White, 6 In. 120.00
Canton, Plate, Round, Hot Water 175.00

Canton, Pitcher, 7 In.

Canton, Platter, Blue & White, 13 1/2 In. 140.00

Canton, Platter, C.1820, 10 In. 170.00

Canton, Platter, C.1820, 20 In. 450.00

Canton, Platter, Orange Peel Bottom, Clipped Corners, 19 X 16 In. 235.00

Canton, Pot, Brush, C.1900, Marked China, 5 1/2 In. 32.00

Canton, Pot, Punch, Double Twisted Branch Handle, Blue, White, C.1833, 9 In. 395.00

Canton, Rice Bowl, Covered, Blue & White, 4 In. 20.00

Canton, Sugar Pot, Strawberry Finial, Blue & White, Scenic, Celery Handles 80.00

Canton, Syllabub, C.1820 .... 75.00

Canton, Teapot, Blue & White, Gold Rim, 6 1/4 In. 150.00

Canton, Teapot, Blue & White, 6 In. 140.00

N

Capo-Di-Monte porcelain was first made in Naples, Italy, from 1743 to 1759. The factory moved near Madrid, Spain, and reopened in 1771 and worked to 1834. Since that time the Doccia factory of Italy acquired the molds and style, even using the N and crown mark, which was made famous by the factory.

Capo-Di-Monte.Kardomere.Porcelain Men Hunting, Women In Garden, Blue N 175.00

Capo-Di-Monte, Ashtray, Children Playing, Flowers, Signed, Numbered 30.00

Capo-Di-Monte, Basket Of Flowers, Miniature, Signed 48.00

Capo-Di-Monte, Bell, Blue Crown Mark 25.00

Capo-Di-Monte, Box, Covered, Women In Landscape, Scalloped, 5 X 4 In. 100.00

Capo-Di-Monte, Box, Jewel Casket, Relief, Ad Majorem Dei Gloria On Cover 350.00

Capo-Di-Monte, Box, Patch, Angel & Floral Garlands, Kidney Shape, 4 In. 105.00

Capo-Di-Monte, Cup & Saucer, Chocolate, Marechal Le Febvre, Signed 90.00

Capo-Di-Monte, Cup & Saucer, Farm Scene, Soft Paste, Blue Crown Mark 55.00

Capo-Di-Monte, Dish, Covered, Footed, High Relief Figures On Cover 45.00

Capo-Di-Monte, Figurine, Man In Fancy Dress, Blue Mark Crown & N 190.00

Capo-Di-Monte, Figurine, Monkey On Bell Pull, 22 In. 375.00

Capo-Di-Monte, Figurine, 19th Century Man, Blue Crown Mark, 8 In. 65.00

Capo-Di-Monte, Group, Barmaid, Man, & 2 Musicians, 11 In. 525.00

Capo-Di-Monte, Group, Dancing Baby Cherubs, Seven 200.00

Capo-Di-Monte, Group, Pastoral Figures, 18 X 8 X 5 In., Pair 550.00

Capo-Di-Monte, Jardiniere, The Hunt, Women of Pleasure, 6 X 8 1/2 In. 165.00

Capo-Di-Monte, Lamp, Figural, 9 In. 120.00

Capo-Di-Monte, Plaque, Five Children Playing In A Field, Brass Frame, 4 In. 75.00

Capo-Di-Monte, Plaque, 5 Children Playing, Crowned Blue & Saxony 85.00

Capo-Di-Monte, Plate, Portrait, Marechal Le Febvre, Signed C.D. 95.00

Capo-Di-Monte, Urn, Champleve Lid, Cupids, Ormolu Handles & Foot, 10 In. 175.00

Capo-Di-Monte, Urn, Classical, Ram Head Handles, Battle Scene, N Mark, Pair 325.00

Capo-Di-Monte, Urn, Covered, Crown N Mark, 6 In. 35.00

Capo-Di-Monte, Urn, Covered, Polychrome, Haut Relief Figures, 21 In., Pair 1700.00

Captain Midnight, Booklet, Trick & Riddle, Skelly Oil, 1939 .... 5.00

Captain Midnight, Code-O-Graph, 1942, Picture 45.00

Captain Midnight, Coin, Brass, 3 Embossed Figures, Dollar Size 8.00

Captain Midnight, Decoder Badge, 1945 .... 20.00

Captain Midnight, Decoder, Secret, 1948 .... 30.00

Captain Midnight, Decoder, 1942 .... 35.00

Captain Midnight, Decoder, 1949 .... 30.00

Captain Midnight, Ring, Secret Compartment 25.00

Captain Video, Space Port, Litho Tin, Plastic Rangers, Space Men, Vehicles 35.00

Caramel Slag, see Chocolate Glass

Card, Birthday, Prang, Seashell, 5 1/4 X 3 1/4 In. 7.50
Card, Calling, U.S.Grant, Floral, 1883 50.00 To 75.00
Card, Christmas, 1947 Ford, Man Holding 1923 Master Peanut Machine 1.00
Card, Easter, Flower Girls 5.00
Card, Easter, H.B.G., Easter In The Future, Girl Flying, Propeller Hat 5.00
Card, Easter, Tuck 4.50
Card, Greeting, Valentine, Mechanical, Felix The Cat, German, 5 1/2 In. 8.00
Card, Halloween, Brundage 5.00
Card, Playing, American Airlines, Deck 1.00
Card, Playing, Betty Boop 45.00
Card, Playing, Chicago, A Century Of Progress, Sky Ride, Deck, Boxed 15.00
Card, Playing, Chicago, 1934, Century Of Progress, Deck 8.50
Card, Playing, Flinch Card Co., 1913, Boxed 5.00
Card, Playing, Little Lord, Fauntleroy, 2 1/2 X 1 3/4 In., Deck 2.75
Card, Playing, Maxfield Parrish, Mazda Lamps 45.00
Card, Playing, New York City Scenes, C.1905, Deck 23.00
Card, Playing, Niagara Falls, 1901, Deck 15.00
Card, Playing, Norry, Deck 5.00
Card, Playing, Old Maid, Deck Of 39 10.00
Card, Playing, Pan American Exposition, Deck 14.00
Card, Playing, Panama Canal, Gilt Edge, Deck 15.00
Card, Playing, Panama, Deck 14.00
Card, Playing, Pinochle, 2 Decks In Leather-Bound Folder 20.00
Card, Playing, Rio De Janerio, Deck 15.00
Card, Playing, U.S.Playing Cards, Miniature, 2 Decks In Box 15.00
Card, Playing, Vermont, Green Mountain State, Deck 12.00
Card, Playing, Yellowstone National Park Souvenir, C.1918, Deck 5.00
Card, Playing, Yosemite National Park, C.1920, Deck 15.00
Card, Store, Crystal Coffee, Our Nation's Politics, 1864-1896, 6 X 3 In. 15.00
Card, Store, Nabisco, Flying Circus .50
Card, Store, Nabisco, Straight Arrow .50
Card, Store, Playing, Old Reliable Coffee & Tea, Pinochle 6.00
Card, Store, Playing, Old Scotch Whiskey, George IV On Back, Deck 15.00
Card, Valentine, Comic, 9 X 6 In. 1.00
Card, Valentine, German, Lace, Set Of 10 10.00
Card, Valentine, Germany, C.1910, Girl, Dog, & Flowers, Lattice, Set Of 4 20.00
Card, Valentine, Germany, C.1929, House, Boy, & Dog 3.50
Card, Valentine, Germany, C.1929, Lion In Cage, Mouth Opens 3.50
Card, Valentine, Gold & White Paper Lace, Moss Roses, 7 X 5 In. 18.50
Card, Valentine, Lacy, 3 Dimensional, 6 In. 3.00
Card, Valentine, Lounsberry 4.00
Card, Valentine, Mechanical, Indian 4.00
Card, Valentine, Negro 10.00
Card, Valentine, Negro Boy, 3 1/2 X 3 In. 3.50
Card, Valentine, Raphael Tuck, Mechanical, 8 In. 10.00
Card, Valentine, Red Tissue, Fold-Out, 3 Dimensional 5.00
Card, Valentine, Sailor's, Round, 7 In. 25.00
Card, Valentine, Ship, Angel, & Roses, Transparent Red Sails, Fold-Out 10.00
Card, Valentine, Streetcar With Girl & Boy, Foldout 10.00
Card, Valentine, Tuck, Movable Parts, Easel Type 7.50
Card, Valentine, Whitney, C.1925, 4 X 4 In., Set Of 5 9.00
Card, Valentine, 5 Dimensional, Standup, Die-cut, 11 X 7 In. 8.00

Carder, see Steuben, Aurene

Carlsbad, Germany, is a mark found on china made by several factories in Germany. Most of the pieces available today were made after 1891.

Carlsbad, Basket, Cream With Hand-Painted Floral Design, 5 In. 20.00
Carlsbad, Butter Pat, Festoon Of Roses & Broken Band Of Circles, Set Of 10 25.00
Carlsbad, Celery, Gold Trim, Scalloped, Yellow & Blue Flowers, 11 1/2 In. 22.00
Carlsbad, Chamberstick, Ornate, Floral, Austria 15.00
Carlsbad, Cup & Saucer, Much Design, Man & Woman In Middle 40.00
Carlsbad, Cup, Demitasse, Shell Shape, Footed 6.00
Carlsbad, Hair Receiver, Small Roses, Gilt 12.00
Carlsbad, Humidor, Tobacco, Kauffmann Portrait On Front, Silver Plate Lid 95.00
Carlsbad, Jar, Cookie, Flower Finial, Embossed, Pink, Blue Flowers 39.00

Carlsbad, Pitcher, Milk, Purple Violets, Embossed, 4 3/4 In. 12.50
Carlsbad, Plate, Flowers, Pond, Mallard Duck, 6 1/4 In. 18.00
Carlsbad, Plate, Ladies & Angels, Gold & Green, 8 In. 18.50
Carlsbad, Plate, Oyster, White, Floral Border, Pink & Gold Center 27.00
Carlsbad, Plate, Souvenir, BPOE, York, Pa., 1905, 8 In. 12.00
Carlsbad, Ring Tree, Porcelain With Pale Blue Flowers 19.00
Carlsbad, Syrup & Underplate, White, Pink Floral, Green & Gold Rims 23.50
Carlsbad, Tile, Tea, Colonial Children, 5 3/4 In. 9.00
Carlsbad, Toothpick, Souvenir, Old Man Of The Mountain 8.00
Carlsbad, Vase, Floral Decorations, Signed 28.00
Carlton Ware, Jar, Cracker, Green, Dance Of The Hours, Metal Fittings 65.00
Carlton Ware, Jar, Tobacco, Cobalt, Red, White, Blue Crest, Fribourg & Treyer 40.00
Carlton Ware, Plate, Baby's, Jack & Jill 35.00
Carlton Ware, Plate, Hand-Painted & Enameled, Petunia, Reg.1896, 8 1/2 In. 22.00
Carlton Ware, Plate, Hand-Painted, Enamel, Peony, Registered 1896, 8 1/2 In. 22.00
Carlton Ware, Vase, Covered, Green, Black, & Gold, Red & Gold Dragons, 7 In. 50.00
Carlton Ware, Vase, Gold Outlined Trees & Clouds, Art Deco, 8 In. 50.00
Carlton, Bowl, Chinoiserie, Blue, Gold & Polychrome, C.1790, 9 1/4 In. 120.00
Carnelian, Figurine, Dog, Sitting, Long Ears, 2 1/4 In. 100.00

Carnival, or taffeta, glass was an inexpensive, pressed, iridescent glass made from about 1900 to 1920. Over 200 different patterns are known. Carnival glass is currently being reproduced.

Carnival Glass, see also Northwood

Carnival Glass, , Lamp, Gone With The Wind, Roses & Ruffles, Marigold 475.00
Carnival Glass, , Pitcher, Multi Fruits, Marigold 6000.00
Carnival Glass, Banana Boat, Grape & Cable, Blue 185.00
Carnival Glass, Banana Boat, Grape & Cable, Green 160.00
Carnival Glass, Banana Boat, Grape & Cable, Ice Blue 390.00
Carnival Glass, Banana Boat, Grape & Cable, Ice Green 285.00
Carnival Glass, Banana Boat, Grape & Cable, Marigold 95.00
Carnival Glass, Banana Boat, Grape & Cable, Purple 200.00
Carnival Glass, Banana Boat, Grape & Cable, Purple, Northwood, 12 In. 175.00
Carnival Glass, Banana Boat, Grape & Cable, Purple, 4 Footed, 12 1/4 In. 250.00
Carnival Glass, Banana Boat, Grape & Cable, White 250.00
Carnival Glass, Banana Boat, Kittens, Marigold .... 49.00 To 65.00
Carnival Glass, Banana Boat, Peach & Pear, Marigold 58.00
Carnival Glass, Banana Boat, Thistle, Cobalt, Footed, Fenton 275.00
Carnival Glass, Banana Boat, Wreathed Cherry, Marigold 55.00
Carnival Glass, Banana Boat, Wreathed Cherry, Purple 110.00
Carnival Glass, Banana Boat, Wreathed Cherry, White 145.00
Carnival Glass, Bell, Hammered, White 40.00
Carnival Glass, Berry Bowl, Acorn Burr, Purple, Northwood, 4 In. 28.00
Carnival Glass, Berry Bowl, Butterfly & Berry, Blue, Footed, 9 1/2 In. 50.00
Carnival Glass, Berry Bowl, Butterfly & Berry, Marigold, Claw Feet 15.00
Carnival Glass, Berry Bowl, Butterfly & Berry, Marigold, Footed .... 35.00 To 42.50
Carnival Glass, Berry Bowl, Circled Scroll, Purple 100.00
Carnival Glass, Berry Bowl, Fentonia, Cobalt 55.00
Carnival Glass, Berry Bowl, Gothic Arch, Marigold, 8 In. 25.00
Carnival Glass, Berry Bowl, Grape & Cable, Purple, Footed, 4 1/2 In. 25.00
Carnival Glass, Berry Bowl, Grape & Cable, Purple, Northwood 85.00
Carnival Glass, Berry Bowl, Grape & Thumbprint, Purple, Northwood, 5 In. 25.00
Carnival Glass, Berry Bowl, Grape, Cobalt 20.00
Carnival Glass, Berry Bowl, Kittens, Marigold, Miniature 85.00
Carnival Glass, Berry Bowl, Little Fishes, Marigold 59.00
Carnival Glass, Berry Bowl, Little Flowers, Amethyst, 5 In. 25.00
Carnival Glass, Berry Bowl, Master, Panther, Green 200.00
Carnival Glass, Berry Bowl, Orange Tree & Windmill, Marigold 15.00
Carnival Glass, Berry Bowl, Orange Tree, Blue, Footed, 4 1/2 In. 28.00
Carnival Glass, Berry Bowl, Panther, Blue, Claw Feet 39.00
Carnival Glass, Berry Bowl, Panther, Blue, Footed 139.00
Carnival Glass, Berry Bowl, Panther, Marigold 15.00
Carnival Glass, Berry Bowl, Vintage, Cobalt, 5 In. 20.00
Carnival Glass, Berry Bowl, Vintage, Green, 5 In. 15.00
Carnival Glass, Berry Bowl, Wreathed Cherry, Marigold, Oval 12.00

Carnival Glass, Berry Set, Acorn Burrs, Marigold, 7 Piece 135.00
Carnival Glass, Berry Set, Butterfly & Berry, Marigold, 7 Piece .... 85.00 To 125.00
Carnival Glass, Berry Set, Little Flowers, Blue, 7 Piece 161.50
Carnival Glass, Berry Set, Maple Leaf, Marigold 55.00
Carnival Glass, Berry Set, Maple Leaf, Purple 170.00
Carnival Glass, Berry Set, Millersburg Peacock, Amethyst 325.00
Carnival Glass, Berry Set, Open Rose, Marigold, 7 Piece 72.00
Carnival Glass, Berry Set, Peacock At Fountain, Blue, Northwood, 7 Piece 255.00
Carnival Glass, Berry Set, Peacock At Fountain, Ice Blue, 6 Piece 395.00
Carnival Glass, Berry Set, Peacock At Fountain, Purple, Northwood, 7 Piece 225.00
Carnival Glass, Berry Set, Wreathed Cherry, Marigold, Oval, 7 Piece 155.00
Carnival Glass, Bonbon, Basket Weave, Purple, Grape & Cable Interior 48.00
Carnival Glass, Bonbon, Butterflies, Amethyst 45.00
Carnival Glass, Bonbon, Butterflies, Green, Stippled Rays Interior, N 40.00
Carnival Glass, Bonbon, Butterflies, Marigold 40.00
Carnival Glass, Bonbon, Butterfly, Amethyst, Northwood 40.00
Carnival Glass, Bonbon, Fruits & Flowers, Blue, Stemmed 38.00
Carnival Glass, Bonbon, Fruits & Flowers, Marigold, Stippled, Stemmed 32.00
Carnival Glass, Bonbon, Grape & Cable, Marigold, 2 Handles 25.00
Carnival Glass, Bonbon, Grape, Amethyst, Northwood 40.00
Carnival Glass, Bonbon, Persian Medallion, Marigold 38.00
Carnival Glass, Bonbon, Question Mark, Marigold, 2 Handles, Pedestal 25.00
Carnival Glass, Bonbon, Stippled Rays, Amethyst 40.00
Carnival Glass, Bonbon, Three Fruits, Amethyst, Footed 40.00
Carnival Glass, Bonbon, Three Fruits, Cobalt, Pedestal 60.00
Carnival Glass, Bottle, Cologne, Grape & Cable, Amethyst 225.00
Carnival Glass, Bottle, Cologne, Grape & Cable, Marigold 129.00
Carnival Glass, Bottle, Cologne, Grape & Cable, Purple 150.00
Carnival Glass, Bottle, Perfume, Grape & Cable, Purple .... 345.00 To 375.00
Carnival Glass, Bottle, Whiskey, Golden Wedding, Marigold, Pint 15.00
Carnival Glass, Bottle, Whiskey, Golden Wedding, Marigold, 1/2 Pint 12.00
Carnival Glass, Bottle, Whiskey, Waffle Block, Marigold, Pair 18.00
Carnival Glass, Bowl, Acorns, Peach, Opalescent, 6 In. 27.50
Carnival Glass, Bowl, Apple Blossom Twig, Marigold 25.00
Carnival Glass, Bowl, Atlantic City Elk, Blue 80.00
Carnival Glass, Bowl, Atlantic City Elks, Round, 1911 .... 300.00
Carnival Glass, Bowl, Australian, Purple, 9 In. 95.00
Carnival Glass, Bowl, Autumn Acorn, Amethyst, Scalloped, 8 1/2 In. 40.00
Carnival Glass, Bowl, Autumn Acorns, Green, Ruffled, 7 1/2 In. 35.00
Carnival Glass, Bowl, Autumn Acorns, Marigold, 7 1/2 In. 15.00
Carnival Glass, Bowl, Banana, Peach & Pear, Purple 80.00
Carnival Glass, Bowl, Banana, Thistle, Fenton, Blue 95.00
Carnival Glass, Bowl, Basket Weave, Marigold, Openwork Edge, 6 In. 17.00
Carnival Glass, Bowl, Basket Weave, Marigold, Ruffled, 6 In. 18.00
Carnival Glass, Bowl, Bearded Berry, Blue, Persian Medallion Inside, 8 In. 55.00
Carnival Glass, Bowl, Bells & Beads, Purple, Crimped, 7 In. 30.00
Carnival Glass, Bowl, Berry, Beaded Shell, Marigold 60.00
Carnival Glass, Bowl, Berry, Blue, Leaf Chain Interior, 7 In. 35.00
Carnival Glass, Bowl, Berry, Green, Peacock & Grape Inside, 8 1/2 In. 55.00
Carnival Glass, Bowl, Bird On Bough, Blue 37.50
Carnival Glass, Bowl, Blackberry Wreath, Marigold, Millersburg, 10 In. 27.50
Carnival Glass, Bowl, Blackberry, Amethyst, Ruffled, Millersburg, 8 In. 50.00
Carnival Glass, Bowl, Blackberry, Green, Millersburg, 6 In. .... 14.00 To 18.00
Carnival Glass, Bowl, Brocaded Acorn, Aqua, 3 Footed, 11 1/2 In. 34.00
Carnival Glass, Bowl, Bunches Of Grapes, Purple, Footed, Oval, 12 1/2 In. 175.00
Carnival Glass, Bowl, Butterfly & Berry, Blue 70.00
Carnival Glass, Bowl, Captive Rose, Green, 9 In. 35.00
Carnival Glass, Bowl, Caroline, Peach, Opalescent, 9 In. 35.00
Carnival Glass, Bowl, Cherries, Amethyst, Millersburg, 7 1/2 In. 32.00
Carnival Glass, Bowl, Cherries, Cobalt, Orange Tree Back, 9 1/2 In. 48.00
Carnival Glass, Bowl, Cherry Chain, Peach, Opalescent, Ruffled, 9 In. 40.00
Carnival Glass, Bowl, Coin Dot, Amethyst, Ruffled, 8 In. 20.00
Carnival Glass, Bowl, Coin Dot, Amethyst, 7 In. 15.00
Carnival Glass, Bowl, Coin Spot, Blue, 7 In. 30.00
Carnival Glass, Bowl, Coin Spot, Purple, Footed, 8 1/2 In. 35.00

Carnival Glass, Bowl, Comet, Amethyst, 8 In. 40.00
Carnival Glass, Bowl, Comet, Marigold, Pinched-In, 8 In. 32.00
Carnival Glass, Bowl, Cosmos Variant, Marigold, 9 In. 18.00
Carnival Glass, Bowl, Dahlia, Marigold, Footed, 9 In. 40.00
Carnival Glass, Bowl, Detroit Elks, 1910, Green 275.00
Carnival Glass, Bowl, Dogwood Sprays, Marigold, Tricornered, 7 1/2 In. 27.00
Carnival Glass, Bowl, Double Stem Roses, Marigold, Collared Base, 7 1/2 In. 35.00
Carnival Glass, Bowl, Dragon & Lotus, Blue, Ruffled, Collared Base, 8 In. 45.00
Carnival Glass, Bowl, Dragon & Lotus, Blue, 9 In. 38.00
Carnival Glass, Bowl, Dragon & Lotus, Cobalt, Fluted Edge, 8 1/2 In. 47.00
Carnival Glass, Bowl, Dragon & Lotus, Cobalt, 8 1/2 In. 45.00
Carnival Glass, Bowl, Dragon & Lotus, Marigold, 9 In. 30.00
Carnival Glass, Bowl, Dragon & Lotus, Purple, 3 Footed, 8 In. 45.00
Carnival Glass, Bowl, Dragon & Lotus, Red, 9 In. 285.00
Carnival Glass, Bowl, Embroidered Mums, Blue, 8 In. 49.00
Carnival Glass, Bowl, Fantail, Blue, Footed, 9 In. 50.00
Carnival Glass, Bowl, Farmyard, Candy Ribbon Edge, Purple 725.00
Carnival Glass, Bowl, Farmyard, Green 7500.00
Carnival Glass, Bowl, Feathered Serpent, Amethyst, 10 In. 65.00
Carnival Glass, Bowl, Feathered Serpent, Marigold, 5 1/2 In. 16.00
Carnival Glass, Bowl, Fleur-De-Lis, Amethyst, Footed, Ruffled Edge, 9 In. 72.00
Carnival Glass, Bowl, Floral & Loops, Orange, Footed, 9 In. 20.00
Carnival Glass, Bowl, Fluted, Marigold, 6 In. 10.00
Carnival Glass, Bowl, Fluted, Marigold, 6 1/2 In. 8.00
Carnival Glass, Bowl, Fluted, Marigold, 9 In. 20.00
Carnival Glass, Bowl, Four Flowers, Peach, Opalescent, 8 In. 65.00
Carnival Glass, Bowl, Frosted Block, White, 5 In. 45.00
Carnival Glass, Bowl, Fruit, Horse's Head, Green, 9 In. 40.00
Carnival Glass, Bowl, Fruit, Orange Tree, Footed, Marigold 45.00
Carnival Glass, Bowl, Good Luck, Amethyst, 9 In. 69.00
Carnival Glass, Bowl, Good Luck, Cobalt, Ruffled, Scalloped, 8 7/8 In. 85.00
Carnival Glass, Bowl, Good Luck, Green, Basket Weave Outside, N, 8 1/2 In. 125.00
Carnival Glass, Bowl, Good Luck, Marigold, 9 In. 50.00
Carnival Glass, Bowl, Good Luck, Purple, 8 3/4 In. 110.00
Carnival Glass, Bowl, Grape & Cable, Amethyst, Fluted, 3 Spatula Feet, 9 In. 48.00
Carnival Glass, Bowl, Grape & Cable, Amethyst, 3 Spatula Feet, 8 3/4 In. 48.00
Carnival Glass, Bowl, Grape & Cable, Blue, 9 In. 35.00
Carnival Glass, Bowl, Grape & Cable, Green, Piecrust Edge, 8 1/2 In. 55.00
Carnival Glass, Bowl, Grape & Cable, Green, Scalloped, Ball Feet, 7 1/2 In. 42.00
Carnival Glass, Bowl, Grape & Cable, Green, 3 Footed, 7 1/2 In. 35.00
Carnival Glass, Bowl, Grape & Cable, Marigold, Footed, 7 In. 23.00
Carnival Glass, Bowl, Grape & Cable, Marigold, Meander Outside, Footed, 9 In. 50.00
Carnival Glass, Bowl, Grape & Cable, Marigold, Northwood, 7 1/2 In. 25.00
Carnival Glass, Bowl, Grape & Cable, Marigold, Northwood, 8 In. 45.00
Carnival Glass, Bowl, Grape & Cable, Marigold, Ruffled, Northwood, 8 1/2 In. 40.00
Carnival Glass, Bowl, Grape & Cable, Marigold, Spatula Feet, 7 In. 20.00
Carnival Glass, Bowl, Grape & Cable, Marigold, 7 1/2 In. 20.00
Carnival Glass, Bowl, Grape & Cable, Purple 40.00
Carnival Glass, Bowl, Grape & Cable, Purple, Ruffled, Footed, 7 In. 38.00
Carnival Glass, Bowl, Grape & Leaf, Red, Star Of David Inside, N, 7 1/2 In. 70.00
Carnival Glass, Bowl, Grape Leaves, Purple, Northwood, 8 1/2 In. 45.00
Carnival Glass, Bowl, Grape Wreath, Amethyst, Millersburg, 5 3/4 In. 20.00
Carnival Glass, Bowl, Grape, Marigold, Imperial, 7 In. 15.00
Carnival Glass, Bowl, Grape, Marigold, Ruffled Edge, 6 1/2 In. 21.00
Carnival Glass, Bowl, Grape, Purple, Imperial, 9 In. 35.00
Carnival Glass, Bowl, Grapes, Peach, Ruffled Edge, Northwood, 8 1/2 In. 40.00
Carnival Glass, Bowl, Greek Key, Green, Northwood, 9 In. 50.00
Carnival Glass, Bowl, Green Key, Green, Pedestal Base, Northwood, 8 In. 65.00
Carnival Glass, Bowl, Heart & Feather, Green, Ruffled Edge, 9 In. 40.00
Carnival Glass, Bowl, Heart & Vine, Amethyst, 9 In. 25.00
Carnival Glass, Bowl, Heart & Vine, Green, 8 In. 60.00
Carnival Glass, Bowl, Hearts & Vines, Blue, 9 In. 75.00
Carnival Glass, Bowl, Hearts & Vines, Emerald Green, 9 In. 45.00
Carnival Glass, Bowl, Holly, Blue, Ruffled, 8 1/2 In. 40.00
Carnival Glass, Bowl, Holly, Blue, 8 In. 35.00

Carnival Glass, Bowl, Holly, Blue, 9 In. .... 35.00 To 39.00
Carnival Glass, Bowl, Holly, Green, Scalloped, 8 In. 85.00
Carnival Glass, Bowl, Holly, Marigold, Ruffled Edge, 8 1/2 In. 45.00
Carnival Glass, Bowl, Holly, Orange, Fluted, 7 3/4 In. 20.00
Carnival Glass, Bowl, Holly, Purple Green, Ruffled, 9 In. 38.00
Carnival Glass, Bowl, Holly, Purple, Fluted, 8 In. 45.00
Carnival Glass, Bowl, Horse Medallion, Marigold 37.50
Carnival Glass, Bowl, Horse's Head Medallion, Marigold, Footed, 8 In. 75.00
Carnival Glass, Bowl, Horse's Head, Marigold, 8 1/2 In. 38.00
Carnival Glass, Bowl, Horse's Head, Marigold, 8 3/8 In. 40.00
Carnival Glass, Bowl, Horse's Head, Marigold, 9 In. 40.00
Carnival Glass, Bowl, Imperial Pansy, Purple 30.00
Carnival Glass, Bowl, Jewels, Gold, Imperial, 6 In. 14.00
Carnival Glass, Bowl, Jewels, Green, Imperial, 9 1/2 In. 16.00
Carnival Glass, Bowl, Kangaroo, Kookaburra, Australia, 1920 .... 70.00 To 125.00
Carnival Glass, Bowl, Kangaroo, Kookaburra, Marigold, Australia, 9 1/2 In. 70.00
Carnival Glass, Bowl, Kingfisher, Kookaburra, Marigold, Australia, 5 1/2 In. 22.00
Carnival Glass, Bowl, Kingfisher, Magpie, Thunderbird, Swan, Purple, 5 1/2 In. 40.00
Carnival Glass, Bowl, Kingfisher, Magpie, Thumderbird, Swan, Purple, 9 1/2 In. 85.00
Carnival Glass, Bowl, Kittens, Fluted Rim, Marigold, 4 1/2 X 1 1/2 In. 75.00
Carnival Glass, Bowl, Kittens, Marigold, 3 In. 42.00
Carnival Glass, Bowl, Kittens, Plain Rim, Marigold, 3 1/4 In. 75.00
Carnival Glass, Bowl, Kittens, Round, Marigold 30.00
Carnival Glass, Bowl, Lily & Poinsettia, Red, Footed, 6 In. 135.00
Carnival Glass, Bowl, Little Fishes, Marigold, Footed, 9 1/4 In. 100.00
Carnival Glass, Bowl, Little Fishes, Periwinkle Blue, Footed, 6 In. 75.00
Carnival Glass, Bowl, Little Flowers, Amethyst, Ruffled, 8 1/2 In. 35.00
Carnival Glass, Bowl, Little Flowers, Marigold, 9 In. 29.00
Carnival Glass, Bowl, Little Stars, Green 50.00
Carnival Glass, Bowl, Lotus & Grape, Blue, 8 In. 45.00
Carnival Glass, Bowl, Luster Rose, Marigold, Footed, 7 1/2 In. 32.50
Carnival Glass, Bowl, Magnolia & Poinsettia, Marigold, Footed, 9 In. 50.00
Carnival Glass, Bowl, Marigold, 15 In. 35.00
Carnival Glass, Bowl, Mayan, Green, Helio, 8 In. 30.00
Carnival Glass, Bowl, Millersburg Bernheimer, Blue 240.00
Carnival Glass, Bowl, Millersburg Courthouse, Amethyst 275.00
Carnival Glass, Bowl, Millersburg Holly, Purple 75.00
Carnival Glass, Bowl, Millersburg Peacock At Urn, Purple 130.00
Carnival Glass, Bowl, Nesting Swan, Millersburg, Green 185.00
Carnival Glass, Bowl, Nippon, Amethyst, 7 1/4 In. 20.00
Carnival Glass, Bowl, Nippon, Purple, Ruffled, 8 In. 38.00
Carnival Glass, Bowl, Nut, Vintage, Purple 45.00
Carnival Glass, Bowl, Open Rose, Amber, Fluted, 8 In. 55.00
Carnival Glass, Bowl, Open Rose, Marigold, 3 Footed, 10 In. 60.00
Carnival Glass, Bowl, Orange Tree, Cobalt, 8 In. 45.00
Carnival Glass, Bowl, Orange Tree, Marigold, Footed, 8 1/4 In. 28.50
Carnival Glass, Bowl, Orange Tree, Marigold, Wreathed Cherry Inside, 10 In. 35.00
Carnival Glass, Bowl, Pansy, Marigold, Fluted Edge, 9 In. 25.00
Carnival Glass, Bowl, Panther, Marigold, Ball Footed, 6 In. 24.00
Carnival Glass, Bowl, Peacock & Grape, Blue, 9 In. 40.00
Carnival Glass, Bowl, Peacock & Grape, Marigold 25.00
Carnival Glass, Bowl, Peacock & Grape, Marigold, Ruffled, 8 In. 35.00
Carnival Glass, Bowl, Peacock & Grape, Purple, 8 In. 38.00
Carnival Glass, Bowl, Peacock At Urn, Green, 8 1/2 In. 62.50
Carnival Glass, Bowl, Peacock At Urn, Marigold, Ruffled, 8 7/8 In. 45.00
Carnival Glass, Bowl, Peacock At Urn, Purple, Bearded Berry Back, 8 7/8 In. 55.00
Carnival Glass, Bowl, Peacock On Fence, Blue, Ruffled Fluted Edge, 8 In. 95.00
Carnival Glass, Bowl, Peacock On Fence, Marigold, Scalloped Rim, 8 3/4 In. 40.00
Carnival Glass, Bowl, Peacock's-Eye & File, Purple, 6 In. 20.00
Carnival Glass, Bowl, Peacock's-Eye & File, Purple, 10 In. 35.00
Carnival Glass, Bowl, Peacock Tail, Amethyst, Fluted, Collared, 7 In. 40.00
Carnival Glass, Bowl, Peacock Tail, Marigold, 7 1/4 In. 15.00
Carnival Glass, Bowl, Persian Garden, White, 11 In. 175.00
Carnival Glass, Bowl, Petals & Cane, Marigold, Australia, C.1923, 9 1/2 In. 40.00
Carnival Glass, Bowl, Pinwheel, Amethyst, 8 1/2 In. 28.00

Carnival Glass, Bowl, Poinsettia & Lattice, Purple, Footed, Millersburg, 8 In 70.00
Carnival Glass, Bowl, Pony Head, Amethyst 100.00
Carnival Glass, Bowl, Pony Head, Marigold 45.00
Carnival Glass, Bowl, Pony, Marigold, Greek Key Border, Ruffled, 8 In. 48.00
Carnival Glass, Bowl, Punch, Millersburg Thistle, Amethyst 5800.00
Carnival Glass, Bowl, Punch, Wreath Of Roses, Amethyst 155.00
Carnival Glass, Bowl, Raindrops, Peach, Opalescent, 9 In. 37.50
Carnival Glass, Bowl, Raindrops, Purple, Ruffled, Pedestal, 9 In. 44.00
Carnival Glass, Bowl, Rays, Purple 40.00
Carnival Glass, Bowl, Ribbed, Green, Northwood, 8 In. 25.00
Carnival Glass, Bowl, Ribbon Tie, Green, 9 In. 35.00
Carnival Glass, Bowl, Rosalind, Marigold, Fluted, Millersburg, 10 In. 30.00
Carnival Glass, Bowl, Rose Garden, Marigold, 10 In. 49.00
Carnival Glass, Bowl, Sailboat, Marigold, Fluted Edge, 6 In. 30.00
Carnival Glass, Bowl, Sailing Ships, Marigold, 5 1/2 In. 35.00
Carnival Glass, Bowl, Sailing Ships, Marigold, 6 In. 35.00
Carnival Glass, Bowl, Scales, Purple, 4 1/2 In. 15.00
Carnival Glass, Bowl, Show, Poppy, Marigold 85.00
Carnival Glass, Bowl, Show, Rose, Ice Blue 125.00
Carnival Glass, Bowl, Show, Rose, Purple 175.00
Carnival Glass, Bowl, Singing Birds, Purple, 8 In. 60.00
Carnival Glass, Bowl, Ski Star, Peach, Opalescent, Near Cut, 10 I .... 55.00 To 65.00
Carnival Glass, Bowl, Soutache, Marigold, 9 1/2 In. 34.00
Carnival Glass, Bowl, Stag & Holly 45.00
Carnival Glass, Bowl, Stag & Holly, Amethyst, Footed, 8 In. 62.50
Carnival Glass, Bowl, Stag & Holly, Blue, Footed, 10 In. 85.00
Carnival Glass, Bowl, Stag & Holly, Emerald Green, 3 Spatula Feet, 7 7/8 In. 55.00
Carnival Glass, Bowl, Stag & Holly, Green, Footed, 8 In. 62.50
Carnival Glass, Bowl, Stag & Holly, Marigold, Footed, 10 In. 58.00
Carnival Glass, Bowl, Stag & Holly, Marigold, Footed, 11 In. 55.00
Carnival Glass, Bowl, Star Of David & Bows, Amethyst, Grape Back, N, 7 1/4 In. 55.00
Carnival Glass, Bowl, Star Of David, Green, Fluted Edge, 9 In. 46.00
Carnival Glass, Bowl, Star Of David, Purple, Collared Footed Base, 8 In. 38.00
Carnival Glass, Bowl, Stippled Rays, Amberina, 6 In. 85.00
Carnival Glass, Bowl, Stippled Rays, Amethyst, 7 1/2 In. 25.00
Carnival Glass, Bowl, Stippled Rays, Green, Ruffled, Button Feet, N, 10 In. 50.00
Carnival Glass, Bowl, Stippled Rays, Green, 7 1/2 In. 25.00
Carnival Glass, Bowl, Stippled Rays, Purple, Ruffled, Northwood, 9 In. 32.00
Carnival Glass, Bowl, Stippled Rays, Red, 6 In. 125.00
Carnival Glass, Bowl, Strawberry & Dragon, Blue, 8 In. .... 300.00 To 310.00
Carnival Glass, Bowl, Strawberry, Green, Northwood, 8 In. 55.00
Carnival Glass, Bowl, Strawberry, Purple, 9 In. 35.00
Carnival Glass, Bowl, Sunflower, Green 60.00
Carnival Glass, Bowl, Sunflower, Marigold, Northwood, 8 In. 29.00
Carnival Glass, Bowl, Thistle, Amethyst, Ribbon Candy Edge, 8 In. 30.00
Carnival Glass, Bowl, Thistle, Green, Marked Near Cut, 6 1/2 In. 36.00
Carnival Glass, Bowl, Thistle, Green, Ruffled, 7 In. 35.00
Carnival Glass, Bowl, Thistle, Green, 8 3/4 In. 35.00
Carnival Glass, Bowl, Thistle, Marigold, 7 1/2 In. 20.00
Carnival Glass, Bowl, Thistle, Purple, Near Cut, 8 In. 40.00
Carnival Glass, Bowl, Thorn & Thistle, Marigold, 4 Footed, 8 1/2 In. 24.00
Carnival Glass, Bowl, Three Fruits, Aqua, Footed, Northwood, 9 In. 225.00
Carnival Glass, Bowl, Three Fruits, Green, Collared Base, 8 In. 55.00
Carnival Glass, Bowl, Trout & Fly, Amethyst, Scalloped, Millersburg, 8 In. 135.00
Carnival Glass, Bowl, Twins, Marigold, 6 In. 15.00
Carnival Glass, Bowl, Two Flowers, Cobalt, Footed, 6 In. 22.00
Carnival Glass, Bowl, Vintage Grape, Purple, 8 1/2 In. 40.00
Carnival Glass, Bowl, Vintage, Amethyst, Ruffled, 8 In. 45.00
Carnival Glass, Bowl, Vintage, Amethyst, Ruffled, 9 In. 42.00
Carnival Glass, Bowl, Vintage, Blue, Ruffled, 8 1/2 In. 45.00
Carnival Glass, Bowl, Vintage, Blue, 6 In. 20.00
Carnival Glass, Bowl, Vintage, Cobalt, 10 In. 65.00
Carnival Glass, Bowl, Vintage, Marigold, 8 1/2 In. 35.00
Carnival Glass, Bowl, Vintage, Red, Ruffled, 9 In. 150.00
Carnival Glass, Bowl, Water Lily, Blue, Spatula Feet, Ruffled Rim, 6 In. 24.00

Carnival Glass, Bowl, Wildrose & Fan, Marigold, Northwood, 9 In. 30.00
Carnival Glass, Bowl, Windflower, Blue, Ruffled, 8 In. 40.00
Carnival Glass, Bowl, Windflower, Marigold, Ruffled, 8 In. 40.00
Carnival Glass, Bowl, Wishbone, Green, Fluted, Footed, Northwood, 8 1/2 In. 55.00
Carnival Glass, Bowl, Zigzag, Amethyst, Piecrust Edge, Tricornered, 9 In. 58.00
Carnival Glass, Bowl, Zigzag, Marigold, Millersburg, 8 3/4 In. 49.00
Carnival Glass, Box, Powder, Orange Tree, Marigold, Covered 65.00
Carnival Glass, Brandy Snifter, Four Feathers, Marigold 29.00
Carnival Glass, Bucket, Ice, Brocaded Acorns, Ice Blue, Miniature 65.00
Carnival Glass, Butter, Cherry Circle, Green 65.00
Carnival Glass, Butter, Chicken On Nest, Blue 120.00
Carnival Glass, Butter, Chicken, Marigold 65.00
Carnival Glass, Butter, Dahlia, Marigold 90.00
Carnival Glass, Butter, Diamond & Fan, Ruby Trim, Covered 35.00
Carnival Glass, Butter, Gothic Arch, Marigold 25.00
Carnival Glass, Butter, Late Thistle, Marigold 80.00
Carnival Glass, Butter, Leaf Tiers, Marigold 30.00
Carnival Glass, Butter, Luster Rose, Teal Green 75.00
Carnival Glass, Candle Lamp, Grape, Marigold, N. 775.00
Carnival Glass, Candleholder, Flowers, Marigold, 2 1/4 In., Pair 20.00
Carnival Glass, Carafe, Imperial Grape, Purple 75.00
Carnival Glass, Carafe, Water, Fashion, Marigold .... 25.00 To 40.00
Carnival Glass, Carafe, Water, Grape, Amethyst, Imperial 135.00
Carnival Glass, Carafe, Water, Grape, Blue, Imperial 115.00
Carnival Glass, Carafe, Water, Grape, Marigold, Imperial 60.00
Carnival Glass, Cereal Bowl, Kittens, Marigold, Ruffled 49.00
Carnival Glass, Champagne, Shrine, Aqua 49.00
Carnival Glass, Champagne, Tobacco Leaf, Aqua 44.00
Carnival Glass, Champagne, Tobacco Leaf, Ice Crystal 45.00
Carnival Glass, Compote, Blackberry, Marigold 10.00
Carnival Glass, Compote, Blackberry, Purple, Daisy & Plume Outside, N, 8 In. 60.00
Carnival Glass, Compote, Butterfly & Bells, Marigold, Australia, 7 1/2 In. 48.00
Carnival Glass, Compote, Butterfly & Bells, Purple, Australia, C.1920, 8 In. 85.00
Carnival Glass, Compote, Butterfly & Bush, Purple, Australia, C.1923, 8 In. 85.00
Carnival Glass, Compote, Candy, Peacock's Tail, Green, Fluted, 6 In. 20.00
Carnival Glass, Compote, Fruit, Mikado, Marigold 125.00
Carnival Glass, Compote, Hearts & Flowers, Aqua Opalescent 250.00
Carnival Glass, Compote, Holly, Marigold, 5 In. 15.00
Carnival Glass, Compote, Jewels, Gold, Imperial, 5 In. 12.00
Carnival Glass, Compote, Little Flowers, Green, Miniature 51.50
Carnival Glass, Compote, Mikado, Blue, 10 X 8 In. 125.00
Carnival Glass, Compote, Mikado, Marigold 85.00
Carnival Glass, Compote, Mikado, Marigold, 10 X 8 In. 75.00
Carnival Glass, Compote, Miniature Blackberry, Blue 55.00
Carnival Glass, Compote, Peacock At Urn, Blue, 5 1/2 In. 55.00
Carnival Glass, Compote, Peacock At Urn, Marigold, 5 1/2 In. 55.00
Carnival Glass, Compote, Pineapple, Marigold, 5 In. 14.00
Carnival Glass, Compote, Wreath Of Roses, Green, 6 1/4 In. 23.00
Carnival Glass, Creamer, Apple Wreath, Marigold 20.00
Carnival Glass, Creamer, Breakfast, Cherry Circle, Amethyst 65.00
Carnival Glass, Creamer, Breakfast, Grape, Purple, Northwood 55.00
Carnival Glass, Creamer, Breakfast, Luster Flute, Marigold 15.00
Carnival Glass, Creamer, Gothic Arch, Blue 30.00
Carnival Glass, Creamer, Grape & Cable, Marigold 25.00
Carnival Glass, Creamer, Grape & Cable, Purple .... 65.00 To 135.00
Carnival Glass, Creamer, Grape & Cable, Purple, Northwood 135.00
Carnival Glass, Creamer, Luster Fruit, Purple, Northwood 29.00
Carnival Glass, Creamer, Luster Rose, Marigold 22.00
Carnival Glass, Creamer, Luster, Flute, Green, Gold Iridescence 27.00
Carnival Glass, Creamer, Maple Leaf, Marigold 25.00
Carnival Glass, Creamer, Pineapple, Marigold 20.00
Carnival Glass, Creamer, Snow Fancy, Marigold 14.00
Carnival Glass, Creamer, Star & File, Marigold 20.00
Carnival Glass, Creamer, Stork In Rushes, Marigold 35.00
Carnival Glass, Creamer, Wreathed Cherry, Marigold 25.00

Carnival Glass, Creamer, Wreathed Cherry, Purple 60.00
Carnival Glass, Cruet, Buzz Saw, Large, Green 125.00
Carnival Glass, Cup & Saucer, Grape, Green, Imperial .... 55.00 To 75.00
Carnival Glass, Cup, Coffee, Grape & Cable, Purple, Northwood 55.00
Carnival Glass, Cup, Fashion, Marigold 12.75
Carnival Glass, Cup, Grape & Cable, Blue 20.00
Carnival Glass, Cup, Kittens, Marigold 60.00
Carnival Glass, Cup, Loving, Mary Ann, Blue 70.00
Carnival Glass, Cup, Loving, Orange Tree, Marigold .... 50.00 To 85.00
Carnival Glass, Cup, Punch, Acorn Burrs, Aqua, Northwood 38.00
Carnival Glass, Cup, Punch, Acorn Burrs, Green 25.00
Carnival Glass, Cup, Punch, Acorn Burrs, Marigold 18.00
Carnival Glass, Cup, Punch, Acorn Burrs, Purple, Northwood 28.50
Carnival Glass, Cup, Punch, Acorn Burrs, White, Northwood 40.00
Carnival Glass, Cup, Punch, Fashion, Marigold 12.00
Carnival Glass, Cup, Punch, Flute, Marigold, Millersburg 14.00
Carnival Glass, Cup, Punch, Grape & Cable, Aqua 285.00
Carnival Glass, Cup, Punch, Grape & Cable, Green, Stippled 19.00
Carnival Glass, Cup, Punch, Grape & Cable, Marigold, Stippled 17.50
Carnival Glass, Cup, Punch, Grape & Cable, Purple 20.00
Carnival Glass, Cup, Punch, Grape, Green, Northwood 15.00
Carnival Glass, Cup, Punch, Grape, Marigold, Imperial 12.00
Carnival Glass, Cup, Punch, Luster Flute, Green, Northwood .... 1200 To 12.50
Carnival Glass, Cup, Punch, Memphis, Green 17.00
Carnival Glass, Cup, Punch, Memphis, Green, Northwood 23.00
Carnival Glass, Cup, Punch, Memphis, Marigold, Northwood 15.00
Carnival Glass, Cup, Punch, Memphis, Purple, Northwood 23.00
Carnival Glass, Cup, Punch, Orange Tree, Marigold 6.50
Carnival Glass, Cuspidor, Grape, Purple, N. 7000.00
Carnival Glass, Cuspidor, Hobnail Swirl, Marigold 225.00
Carnival Glass, Decanter, Whiskey, Grape & Cable, Marigold, Solid Stopper 550.00
Carnival Glass, Decanter, Wine, Diamond & Sunburst, Purple 125.00
Carnival Glass, Decanter, Wine, Imperial Grape, Marigold 20.00
Carnival Glass, Dish, Candy, Apple & Pear, Marigold, Covered, Pair 24.00
Carnival Glass, Dish, Candy, Drape, White, Northwood, 6 In. 40.00
Carnival Glass, Dish, Candy, Grape, Blue, Covered, Pedestal, 10 X 7 In. 25.00
Carnival Glass, Dish, Candy, Leaf & Beads, Green, Northwood 40.00
Carnival Glass, Dish, Candy, Paneled Holly, Emerald Green, 2 Handles, N 45.00
Carnival Glass, Dish, Candy, Peacock Tail, Green, Pedestal, Fluted, 6 In. 25.00
Carnival Glass, Dish, Candy, Persian Medallion, Marigold, 2 Handles, 8 In. 23.00
Carnival Glass, Dish, Candy, Shell, Amethyst, Footed 25.00
Carnival Glass, Dish, Nut, Grape Delight, Purnle, Footed, Set Of 6 .... 150.00
Carnival Glass, Dish, Pickle, Pansy, Amber, Imperial 29.00
Carnival Glass, Dish, Pickle, Poppy, Ice Blue, Northwood 75.00
Carnival Glass, Dish, Powder, Doe, Marigold, Deer On Lid 7.50
Carnival Glass, Dresser Set, Concave Diamond, Marigold, 6 Piece 350.00
Carnival Glass, Epergne, Colonial, Marigold 160.00
Carnival Glass, Epergne, Fine Rib, 5 Lily, Sterling Holder 265.00
Carnival Glass, Epergne, Fishnet, Peach 140.00
Carnival Glass, Epergne, Grape & Cable, Green, 1 Lily 55.00
Carnival Glass, Epergne, Vintage, Cobalt, 4 1/2 In. 100.00
Carnival Glass, Fernery, Grape, Cobalt, Little Fern Dish, Footed, 5 3/4 In. 75.00
Carnival Glass, Fruit Bowl, Double Stem Rose, White, Footed 60.00
Carnival Glass, Fruit Bowl, Grape & Cable, Amethyst, Northwood 250.00
Carnival Glass, Fruit Bowl, Peacock At Fountain, Amethyst, Northwood 275.00
Carnival Glass, Fruit Bowl, Peacock At Fountain, Blue, Footed, 10 1/2 In. 180.00
Carnival Glass, Goblet, Banded Flute, Red 125.00
Carnival Glass, Goblet, Buttermilk, Wide Panel, Marigold 78.00
Carnival Glass, Goblet, Flute, Marigold 20.00
Carnival Glass, Goblet, Octagon, Marigold 45.00
Carnival Glass, Goblet, Peacock At Urn, Marigold 55.00
Carnival Glass, Goblet, Soda Gold, Marigold, 4 3/4 X 3 1/2 In. 18.00
Carnival Glass, Gravy Boat, Holly Sprig, Purple 38.00
Carnival Glass, Gravy Boat, Holly Whirl, Purple 35.00

Carnival Glass, Gravy Boat, Nautilus, Purple, Northwood 129.00
Carnival Glass, Hairpin Holder, Grape & Cable, Green, Handle, Northwood 85.00
Carnival Glass, Hairpin Holder, Grape & Cable, Purple 85.00
Carnival Glass, Hat, Blackberry Spray, Marigold 10.00
Carnival Glass, Hatpin Holder, Grape & Cable, Amethyst, Northwood 135.00
Carnival Glass, Hatpin Holder, Grape & Cable, Marigold .... 85.00 To 100.00
Carnival Glass, Hatpin Holder, Grape & Cable, Purple 105.00
Carnival Glass, Hatpin Holder, Grape, Purple, Northwood 125.00
Carnival Glass, Hatpin Holder, Orange Tree, Blue 115.00
Carnival Glass, Hatpin Holder, Orange Tree, Marigold .... 65.00 To 89.50
Carnival Glass, Humidor, Pipe, Marigold 1650.00
Carnival Glass, Ice Cream Bowl, Grape & Cable, Purple, Footed, Northwood 40.00
Carnival Glass, Ice Cream Bowl, Grape & Thumbprint, Amethyst, Footed, N 45.00
Carnival Glass, Ice Cream Bowl, Grape, Purple, Footed, Northwood 38.50
Carnival Glass, Ice Cream Bowl, Hanging Cherries, Amethyst, Millersburg 75.00
Carnival Glass, Ice Cream Bowl, Maple Leaf, Purple, Stemmed 25.00
Carnival Glass, Ice Cream Bowl, Peacock At Urn, Amethyst, N, 9 1/2 In. 125.00
Carnival Glass, Ice Cream Bowl, Peacock At Urn, Blue, 5 In. 40.00
Carnival Glass, Ice Cream Bowl, Peacock At Urn, Marigold, Millersburg, 6 In. 29.00
Carnival Glass, Ice Cream Bowl, Peacock At Urn, White, 10 In. 140.00
Carnival Glass, Ice Cream Bowl, Persian Garden, White .... 100.00 To 110.00
Carnival Glass, Ice Cream Bowl, Persian Garden, White, 10 In. 130.00
Carnival Glass, Ice Cream Bowl, Persian Garden, White, 11 In. 140.00
Carnival Glass, Ice Cream Set, Peacock At Urn, White, N. 550.00
Carnival Glass, Jar, Cookie, Grape & Cable, Marigold, Northwood 185.00
Carnival Glass, Jar, Cracker, Grape & Cable, Marigold, Northwood 185.00
Carnival Glass, Jar, Cracker, Illinois Dairy, Marigold 40.00
Carnival Glass, Jar, Powder, Bambi, Marigold 7.50
Carnival Glass, Jar, Powder, Beaded Panels, Marigold, Powder Puff 29.00
Carnival Glass, Jar, Powder, Covered, Grape & Cable, Marigold, Northwood 65.00
Carnival Glass, Jar, Powder, Grape & Cable, Green, Northwood 25.00
Carnival Glass, Jar, Powder, Grape & Cable, Ice Blue 49.00
Carnival Glass, Jar, Powder, Grape & Cable, Purple .... 38.00 To 125.00
Carnival Glass, Jar, Powder, Grape & Cable, White, Northwood 175.00
Carnival Glass, Jar, Powder, Grape, Amethyst 30.00
Carnival Glass, Jar, Powder, Inverted Strawberry, Green 125.00
Carnival Glass, Jar, Powder, Inverted Strawberry, Green, Gold Trim 100.00
Carnival Glass, Jar, Powder, Orange Tree, Blue 59.00
Carnival Glass, Jar, Powder, Orange Tree, Blue, Covered 59.00
Carnival Glass, Jar, Powder, Orange Tree, Cobalt, Covered, Round 100.00
Carnival Glass, Jar, Powder, Orange Tree, Green 69.00
Carnival Glass, Jar, Powder, Orange Tree, Green, Covered 69.00
Carnival Glass, Jar, Powder, Orange Tree, Marigold, Covered 40.00
Carnival Glass, Jar, Powder, Poodle, Marigold 10.00
Carnival Glass, Jar, Powder, Vintage Grape, Marigold, Covered 32.50
Carnival Glass, Jar, Powder, Vintage Grape, Marigold, Covered, 3 1/2 In. 37.00
Carnival Glass, Jar, Powder, Vintage, Marigold 25.00
Carnival Glass, Lamp, Cologne Base, Grape Top, Marigold, N., Pair 300.00
Carnival Glass, Lamp, Gone With The Wind, Hollyhock, Marigold 900.00
Carnival Glass, Lamp, Gone With The Wind, Hyacinth, Marigold 475.00
Carnival Glass, Lamp, Gone With The Wind, Red Satin, Gold Decoration 475.00
Carnival Glass, Lamp, Miller, Metal 75.00
Carnival Glass, Lamp, Turkey Foot 1500.00
Carnival Glass, Lamp, Zippered Loop, Marigold 200.00
Carnival Glass, Mug, Banded Vintage, Marigold .... 22.00 To 27.50
Carnival Glass, Mug, Beaded Shell, Marigold 160.00
Carnival Glass, Mug, Beaded Shell, Purple .... 55.00 To 85.00
Carnival Glass, Mug, Bo Peep, Marigold 75.00
Carnival Glass, Mug, Fisherman's, Marigold 105.00
Carnival Glass, Mug, Fisherman's, Purple .... 17.50 To 80.00
Carnival Glass, Mug, Fisherman's, Purple, Signed Ruth, 1910 .... 65.00
Carnival Glass, Mug, Fisherman's, Purple, Silver Iridescent 85.00
Carnival Glass, Mug, Grape, Marigold .... 17.50 To 19.00
Carnival Glass, Mug, Heron, Amethyst 170.00
Carnival Glass, Mug, Orange Tree, Amber 75.00

Carnival Glass, Mug, Orange Tree, Blue 37.50
Carnival Glass, Mug, Orange Tree, Marigold .... 14.00 To 30.00
Carnival Glass, Mug, Robin 40.00
Carnival Glass, Mug, Robin, Marigold 30.00
Carnival Glass, Mug, Singing Birds, Blue 70.00
Carnival Glass, Mug, Singing Birds, Blue, Northwood 85.00
Carnival Glass, Mug, Singing Birds, Green 75.00
Carnival Glass, Mug, Singing Birds, Marigold .... 33.00 To 50.00
Carnival Glass, Mug, Singing Birds, Purple 55.00
Carnival Glass, Mug, Singing Birds, Purple, Northwood .... 32.00 To 42.50
Carnival Glass, Mug, Stork & Rushes, Amethyst, Not Iridized 40.00
Carnival Glass, Mug, Stork & Rushes, Purple 90.00
Carnival Glass, Mug, Stork In Rushes, Marigold 25.00
Carnival Glass, Nappy, Butterfly, Green 45.00
Carnival Glass, Nappy, Grape & Cable, Marigold 22.50
Carnival Glass, Nappy, Grape & Cable, Purple, Handle 85.00
Carnival Glass, Nappy, Holly, Emerald Green, Northwood 39.00
Carnival Glass, Nappy, Holly, Green, Northwood 35.00
Carnival Glass, Nappy, Leaf Ray, Marigold, Handled 12.00
Carnival Glass, Nappy, Ribbed, Marigold, Handle 15.00
Carnival Glass, Nappy, Water Lily, Amethyst 35.00
Carnival Glass, Orange Bowl, Grape & Cable, Purple, Footed, Northwood, 11 In. 175.00
Carnival Glass, Orange Bowl, Grape & Cable, Purple, Northwood, 11 In. 225.00
Carnival Glass, Orange Bowl, Grape, Purple, Persian Medallion Inside, Fenton 100.00
Carnival Glass, Orange Bowl, Orange Tree, Marigold, Footed, Fenton 48.00
Carnival Glass, Orange Bowl, Peacock At Fountain, Marigold, 3 Footed, 10 In. 95.00
Carnival Glass, Orange Bowl, Persian Medallion, Cobalt, Grape & Cable Back 150.00
Carnival Glass, Orange Bowl, Stag & Holly, Marigold 45.00
Carnival Glass, Orange Bowl, Stag & Holly, Marigold, 3 Legs, 11 In. 65.00
Carnival Glass, Orange Bowl, Stretch, Ice Blue, 3 Footed 90.00
Carnival Glass, Pitcher, Fieldflower, Clambroth 60.00
Carnival Glass, Pitcher, Frolicking Bears, Green 3100.00
Carnival Glass, Pitcher, Milk, Fans, Marigold 59.00
Carnival Glass, Pitcher, Milk, Poinsettia, Marigold .... 30.00 To 45.00
Carnival Glass, Pitcher, Milk, Poinsettia, Orange .... 27.50 To 30.00
Carnival Glass, Pitcher, Milk, Raspberry, Green, Northwood 100.00
Carnival Glass, Pitcher, Milk, Raspberry, Marigold 80.00
Carnival Glass, Pitcher, Milk, Star Medallion, Marigold 34.00
Carnival Glass, Pitcher, Milk, Windmill, Marigold 40.00
Carnival Glass, Pitcher, Raspberry, Marigold, 9 In. 75.00
Carnival Glass, Pitcher, Water, Fieldflower, Purple 225.00
Carnival Glass, Pitcher, Water, Grape, Purple, Imperial 120.00
Carnival Glass, Pitcher, Water, Inverted Coin Dot, Marigold 99.00
Carnival Glass, Pitcher, Water, Singing Bird, Purple, Northwood 375.00
Carnival Glass, Plate, Advertising, Morris N.Smith, Amethyst 100.00
Carnival Glass, Plate, Apple Twig, Blue, Basket Weave Back, 8 1/2 In. 58.00
Carnival Glass, Plate, Captive Rose, Blue 120.00
Carnival Glass, Plate, Captive Rose, Marigold, 9 In. 35.00
Carnival Glass, Plate, Chop, Garden Path, Purple 4000.00
Carnival Glass, Plate, Chop, Grape, Amber, Fenton, 11 In. 150.00
Carnival Glass, Plate, Chop, Heavy Grape, Purple 195.00
Carnival Glass, Plate, Concord Grape, Amethyst, 9 In. 385.00
Carnival Glass, Plate, Concord, Amethyst, 9 In. 425.00
Carnival Glass, Plate, Daisy Pinwheel & Cable, Cobalt, 9 In. 85.00
Carnival Glass, Plate, Egg, Dots, Purple, 11 In. 35.00
Carnival Glass, Plate, Embossed Scroll, Green, 9 1/4 In. 69.50
Carnival Glass, Plate, Garden Mums, Amethyst, Hand Grip, 6 In. 40.00
Carnival Glass, Plate, Good Luck, Green, 9 In. .... 195.00 To 200.00
Carnival Glass, Plate, Good Luck, Purple, Northwood, 9 In. 185.00
Carnival Glass, Plate, Good Luck, Purple, 9 In. 185.00
Carnival Glass, Plate, Grape & Cable, Bronze, Basket Weave Back, N, 8 1/2 In. 95.00
Carnival Glass, Plate, Grape & Cable, Cobalt, 3 Spatula Feet, 9 1/4 In. 55.00
Carnival Glass, Plate, Grape & Cable, Green, Ribbed Back, 8 1/2 In. 60.00
Carnival Glass, Plate, Grape & Cable, Green, Rose Distillery, 9 In. 115.00
Carnival Glass, Plate, Grape & Cable, Marigold, Footed, 9 In. 35.00

Carnival Glass, Plate, Grape & Cable, Marigold, Ribbed Back, 8 1/2 In. 45.00
Carnival Glass, Plate, Grape & Cable, Marigold, 9 In. 40.00
Carnival Glass, Plate, Grape & Cable, Purple, Footed, 9 In. 95.00
Carnival Glass, Plate, Greek Key, Marigold, Northwood, 9 In. 185.00
Carnival Glass, Plate, Grill, Normandie, Marigold 4.00
Carnival Glass, Plate, Holly, Blue, 9 In. 78.00
Carnival Glass, Plate, Horse Medallion, Blue 200.00
Carnival Glass, Plate, Horse Medallion, Marigold 40.00
Carnival Glass, Plate, Illinois Soldiers & Sailors, Blue 400.00
Carnival Glass, Plate, Illinois Soldiers & Sailors, Marigold 450.00
Carnival Glass, Plate, Jewels, Yellow, Imperial, 8 In. 4.00
Carnival Glass, Plate, Leaf Chain, Marigold, 9 1/2 In. 40.00
Carnival Glass, Plate, Leaf Chain, White, 9 1/2 In. 75.00
Carnival Glass, Plate, Open Rose, Marigold, 9 In. 59.00
Carnival Glass, Plate, Orange Tree, Clambroth 75.00
Carnival Glass, Plate, Orange Tree, White, 9 In. .... 90.00 To 100.00
Carnival Glass, Plate, Parkersburg Elks, 1914, Blue 500.00
Carnival Glass, Plate, Peacock At Urn, Marigold, 9 In. 135.00
Carnival Glass, Plate, Peacock On Fence, Marigold, Northwood, 9 In. 100.00
Carnival Glass, Plate, Peacock On Fence, Purple, 9 In. 55.00
Carnival Glass, Plate, Peacocks, Pastel Blue, Northwood, 9 In. 225.00
Carnival Glass, Plate, Persian Medallion, Marigold, 6 In. 25.00
Carnival Glass, Plate, Peter Rabbit, Marigold 1000.00
Carnival Glass, Plate, Pinecone, Green, 6 In. 48.00
Carnival Glass, Plate, Pinecone, Marigold, 6 In. 30.00
Carnival Glass, Plate, Poppy Show, White, 9 1/2 In. 210.00
Carnival Glass, Plate, Rose Show Variant, Marigold, 9 In. 195.00
Carnival Glass, Plate, Rose Show, Purple, 9 1/2 In. 210.00
Carnival Glass, Plate, Rose Show, White, 9 1/2 In. 210.00
Carnival Glass, Plate, Round Up, White, Ruffled, 9 In. 98.00
Carnival Glass, Plate, Roundup, Flat, Amethyst 160.00
Carnival Glass, Plate, Scales, Green, 7 In. 30.00
Carnival Glass, Plate, Show, Poppy, Green 275.00
Carnival Glass, Plate, Show, Rose, Green 400.00
Carnival Glass, Plate, Star Medallion, Marigold, 9 1/2 In. 24.00
Carnival Glass, Plate, Stippled Three Fruits, Marigold, Northwood, 9 In. 75.00
Carnival Glass, Plate, Strawberry, Marigold, Northwood, 9 In. 70.00
Carnival Glass, Plate, Strawberry, Purple, Basket Weave Back, Fluted, N, 8 In. 75.00
Carnival Glass, Plate, Strawberry, Purple, Basket Weave Back, N, 6 In. 36.00
Carnival Glass, Plate, Strawberry, Purple, Northwood, 9 In. .... 62.00 To 85.00
Carnival Glass, Plate, Strawberry, Purple, 9 In. 62.00
Carnival Glass, Plate, Three Fruits, Amethyst, 9 In. 75.00
Carnival Glass, Plate, Three Fruits, Green, 8 In. 60.00
Carnival Glass, Plate, Three Fruits, Green, 9 In. 65.00
Carnival Glass, Plate, Three Fruits, Marigold, Basket Weave Back, 9 In. 40.00
Carnival Glass, Plate, Three Fruits, Marigold, 9 In. .... 40.00 To 60.00
Carnival Glass, Plate, Three Fruits, Purple 70.00
Carnival Glass, Plate, Three Fruits, Purple, 9 In. 65.00
Carnival Glass, Plate, Vintage, Green, 7 In. 55.00
Carnival Glass, Plate, Vintage, Green, 7 1/2 In. 40.00
Carnival Glass, Plate, Vintage, Marigold, 9 In. 22.00
Carnival Glass, Plate, Windflower, Blue 100.00
Carnival Glass, Plate, Wishbone, Purple, Footed, 9 In. 225.00
Carnival Glass, Punch Bowl & Base, Grape & Cable, Purple, Tiffany Blue 500.00
Carnival Glass, Punch Bowl & Base, Orange Tree, Cobalt, 10 In. 95.00
Carnival Glass, Punch Bowl & Base, Wreath Of Roses, Marigold 125.00
Carnival Glass, Punch Set, Fashion, Marigold, 6 Piece 85.00
Carnival Glass, Punch Set, Fashion, Marigold, 8 Piece 150.00
Carnival Glass, Punch Set, Fashion, Marigold, 9 Piece 95.00
Carnival Glass, Punch Set, Fruit Salad, Marigold, 8 Piece 395.00
Carnival Glass, Punch Set, Fruit Salad, Peach, Opalescent, 7 Piece 900.00
Carnival Glass, Punch Set, Grape & Cable, Marigold, Northwood, 6 Piece 150.00
Carnival Glass, Punch Set, Grape & Cable, Purple, Northwood, 8 Piece 380.00
Carnival Glass, Punch Set, Grape, Purple, N. 4100.00
Carnival Glass, Punch Set, Hobstar & Feather, Marigold, 14 Piece 1195.00

Carnival Glass, Punch Set, Many Fruits, Purple, 8 Piece .... 375.00 To 600.00
Carnival Glass, Punch Set, Memphis, Green & Purple, 7 Piece 325.00
Carnival Glass, Punch Set, Orange Tree, Blue 170.00
Carnival Glass, Punch Set, Orange Tree, Marigold 100.00
Carnival Glass, Punch Set, Orange Tree, White 165.00
Carnival Glass, Punch Set, Peacock At Fountain, Blue, 7 Piece 429.00
Carnival Glass, Relish, Quilted, Marigold, Pansies Inside, Scalloped 25.00
Carnival Glass, Rose Bowl, Captive Rose, Bronze, Ruffled, 9 In. 45.00
Carnival Glass, Rose Bowl, Leaf & Beads, Purple, Footed, 5 1/8 In. 50.00
Carnival Glass, Rose Bowl, Louisa, Amethyst 30.00
Carnival Glass, Salt, Master, Swan, Purple 64.00
Carnival Glass, Salt, Master, Swan, Purple, 5 In. 48.00
Carnival Glass, Salt, Swan, Amethyst 130.00
Carnival Glass, Salt, Swan, Blue 18.00
Carnival Glass, Salt, Swan, Green 18.00
Carnival Glass, Salt, Swan, Ice Green 16.50
Carnival Glass, Salt, Swan, Pastel Green 15.00
Carnival Glass, Salt, Swan, Turquoise, 4 In. 20.00
Carnival Glass, Sauce Set, Singing Birds, Green, Northwood, 7 Piece 235.00
Carnival Glass, Sauce, Beaded Shell, Marigold, Footed 25.00
Carnival Glass, Sauce, Dahlia, Amethyst 25.00
Carnival Glass, Sauce, Grape & Cable, Blue 25.00
Carnival Glass, Sauce, Grape & Cable, Green 20.00
Carnival Glass, Sauce, Panther, Marigold 25.00
Carnival Glass, Sauce, Pinecone, Marigold 15.00
Carnival Glass, Sauce, Pinecone, Marigold, Orange Tree Exterior 18.00
Carnival Glass, Sauce, Sailboat, Amberina 35.00
Carnival Glass, Sauce, Springtime, Green, Northwood 25.00
Carnival Glass, Sauce, Strawberry, Marigold 15.00
Carnival Glass, Sauce, Windflower, Marigold, Boat Shape, Handle 20.00
Carnival Glass, Sauce, Windmill, Purple, 5 In. 17.00
Carnival Glass, Saucer, Kittens, Blue 100.00
Carnival Glass, Saucer, Kittens, Marigold 65.00
Carnival Glass, Saucer, Kittens, Marigold, Pinched Edges 85.00
Carnival Glass, Server, Jelly, Nippon, Marigold, 2 Sided, Metal Stand & Spoon 42.00
Carnival Glass, Shade, Gas, Bleeding Hearts, Marigold, 2 1/4 In. At Top 26.00
Carnival Glass, Shade, Light, Ribbed, Orange, Lightolier Co., 5 1/2 In. 27.50
Carnival Glass, Sherbet, Orange Tree, Marigold, Stemmed 12.00
Carnival Glass, Shot Glass, Grape & Cable, Marigold 115.00
Carnival Glass, Shot Glass, Grape, Purple, Northwood 185.00
Carnival Glass, Spittoon, Lady's, Swirled Hobnail, Marigold 319.00
Carnival Glass, Spittoon, Rolled Top, Marigold, 8 X 5 In. 38.00
Carnival Glass, Spooner, Acorn Burrs, Marigold 69.00
Carnival Glass, Spooner, Acorn Burrs, Purple 99.00
Carnival Glass, Spooner, Acorn Burrs, Purple, Northwood .... 95.00 To 135.00
Carnival Glass, Spooner, Butterfly & Berry, Marigold, Claw Footed 39.00
Carnival Glass, Spooner, Cherry Circle, Green 65.00
Carnival Glass, Spooner, Grape & Cable, Marigold 20.00
Carnival Glass, Spooner, Grape & Cable, Purple .... 110.00 To 135.00
Carnival Glass, Spooner, Grape & Cable, Purple, Northwood 135.00
Carnival Glass, Spooner, Kittens, Marigold, Miniature 85.00
Carnival Glass, Spooner, Luster Rose, Marigold 18.00
Carnival Glass, Spooner, Maple Leaf, Marigold 25.00
Carnival Glass, Spooner, Orange Tree, Blue 65.00
Carnival Glass, Spooner, Orange Tree, Ice Blue 80.00
Carnival Glass, Spooner, Springtime, Marigold, Northwood 40.00
Carnival Glass, Spooner, Wreathed Cherry, Marigold 25.00
Carnival Glass, Sugar & Creamer, Anniversary, Marigold 5.00
Carnival Glass, Sugar & Creamer, Fashion, Smoky 45.00
Carnival Glass, Sugar & Creamer, Flute, Purple 65.00
Carnival Glass, Sugar & Creamer, Grape & Gothic Arches, Marigold 50.00
Carnival Glass, Sugar & Creamer, Shell & Jewel, Green 60.00
Carnival Glass, Sugar & Creamer, Shell & Jewel, Green, Covered 65.00
Carnival Glass, Sugar, Breakfast, Grape & Cable, Green 30.00
Carnival Glass, Sugar, Cherry Circle, Green, Handled 65.00

Carnival Glass, Sugar, Fluffy Peacock, Purple 38.00
Carnival Glass, Sugar, Flute, Purple, Northwood 48.00
Carnival Glass, Sugar, Grape & Cable, Marigold, Northwood 35.00
Carnival Glass, Sugar, Grape & Cable, Purple, Northwood 48.00
Carnival Glass, Sugar, Hobnail, Marigold 80.00
Carnival Glass, Sugar, Luster Rose, Marigold 18.00
Carnival Glass, Sugar, Maple Leaf, Purple 20.00
Carnival Glass, Sugar, Peacock At Fountain, Marigold, Covered 20.00
Carnival Glass, Sugar, Peacock At Fountain, Pastel Blue, Cover, Northwood 235.00
Carnival Glass, Sugar, Star & File, Marigold, Handled 20.00
Carnival Glass, Sugar, Strutting Peacock, Purple, Covered 40.00
Carnival Glass, Sundae Glass, Birds & Boughs, Marigold, Stemmed, 5 1/2 In. 43.00
Carnival Glass, Table Set, Country Kitchen, Purple 625.00
Carnival Glass, Table Set, Grape & Gothic Arches, Marigold, 4 Piece 315.00
Carnival Glass, Table Set, Luster Rose, Marigold 120.00
Carnival Glass, Table Set, Millersburg Cherry 475.00
Carnival Glass, Toothpick, Kittens, Marigold .... 65.00 To 100.00
Carnival Glass, Toothpick, S Repeat, Purple 135.00
Carnival Glass, Toothpick, Swan, Green 12.50
Carnival Glass, Toothpick, Wreathed Cherry, Purple 175.00
Carnival Glass, Tray, Card, Fruits & Flowers, Amethyst, Northwood 45.00
Carnival Glass, Tray, Card, Pansy, Plum 30.00
Carnival Glass, Tray, Dresser, Grape & Cable, Green .... 120.00 To 210.00
Carnival Glass, Tray, Dresser, Grape & Cable, Marigold 95.00
Carnival Glass, Tray, Dresser, Grape & Cable, Purple 150.00
Carnival Glass, Tray, Dresser, Grape, Purple, Northwood 165.00
Carnival Glass, Tray, Pin, Grape & Cable, Purple 150.00
Carnival Glass, Tray, Pin, Sunflower, Purple 150.00
Carnival Glass, Tumbler, Acorn Burr, Green .... 30.00 To 42.50
Carnival Glass, Tumbler, Acorn Burr, Green, Northwood 45.00
Carnival Glass, Tumbler, Acorn Burr, Marigold 37.50
Carnival Glass, Tumbler, Acorn Burr, Purple .... 29.00 To 39.00
Carnival Glass, Tumbler, Acorn Burr, Purple, Northwood 40.00
Carnival Glass, Tumbler, Beaded Shell, Amethyst 40.00
Carnival Glass, Tumbler, Beaded Shell, Purple .... 39.00 To 42.50
Carnival Glass, Tumbler, Bird & Strawberry, Blue 20.00
Carnival Glass, Tumbler, Blackberry & Checkerboard, Green, Northwood 28.00
Carnival Glass, Tumbler, Blackberry Block, Amethyst 45.00
Carnival Glass, Tumbler, Blackberry Block, Marigold 22.50
Carnival Glass, Tumbler, Blueberry, Marigold .... 29.00 To 40.00
Carnival Glass, Tumbler, Butterfly & Berry, Amethyst 25.00
Carnival Glass, Tumbler, Butterfly & Berry, Blue .... 30.00 To 32.50
Carnival Glass, Tumbler, Butterfly & Berry, Marigold 12.00
Carnival Glass, Tumbler, Butterfly & Fern, Amethyst 35.00
Carnival Glass, Tumbler, Butterfly & Fern, Marigold 25.00
Carnival Glass, Tumbler, Butterfly & Plume, Amethyst 30.00
Carnival Glass, Tumbler, Butterfly & Plume, Blue 35.00
Carnival Glass, Tumbler, Butterfly, Amethyst 30.00
Carnival Glass, Tumbler, Cattail & Water Lily, Marigold 14.00
Carnival Glass, Tumbler, Concave Diamond, Ice Blue $ 22.00 To 30.00
Carnival Glass, Tumbler, Crab Claw, Marigold 20.00
Carnival Glass, Tumbler, Dahlia, Marigold 160.00
Carnival Glass, Tumbler, Dahlia, White 95.00
Carnival Glass, Tumbler, Daisy & Lattice Bouquet, Marigold 15.00
Carnival Glass, Tumbler, Daisy & Lattice, Blue 40.00
Carnival Glass, Tumbler, Daisy & Lattice, Marigold .... 8.00 To 15.00
Carnival Glass, Tumbler, Dandelion, Marigold, Northwood 24.00
Carnival Glass, Tumbler, Dandelion, Purple 40.00
Carnival Glass, Tumbler, Dandelion, Purple, Northwood 45.00
Carnival Glass, Tumbler, Diamond Lace, Purple 42.50
Carnival Glass, Tumbler, Diamond, Green 28.00
Carnival Glass, Tumbler, Diamond, Purple, Millersburg 45.00
Carnival Glass, Tumbler, Double Star, Green 34.00
Carnival Glass, Tumbler, Fashion, Marigold 210.00
Carnival Glass, Tumbler, Fentonia, Blue 40.00

Carnival Glass, Tumbler, Fentonia, Marigold 34.00
Carnival Glass, Tumbler, Fieldflower, Purple 45.00
Carnival Glass, Tumbler, Floral & Grape, Amethyst .... 19.00 To 36.00
Carnival Glass, Tumbler, Floral & Grape, Blue 29.00
Carnival Glass, Tumbler, Floral & Grape, Green .... 55.00 To 85.00
Carnival Glass, Tumbler, Fluffy Peacock, Purple 40.00
Carnival Glass, Tumbler, Gothic Arches, Marigold 18.00
Carnival Glass, Tumbler, Grape & Cable With Thumbprint, Amethyst 30.00
Carnival Glass, Tumbler, Grape & Cable, Amber & Green 25.00
Carnival Glass, Tumbler, Grape & Cable, Amethyst 25.00
Carnival Glass, Tumbler, Grape & Cable, Green 25.00
Carnival Glass, Tumbler, Grape & Cable, Marigold 15.00
Carnival Glass, Tumbler, Grape & Cable, Purple .... 25.00 To 27.00
Carnival Glass, Tumbler, Grape & Cable, Purple, Northwood .... 27.50 To 30.00
Carnival Glass, Tumbler, Grape & Gothic Arches, Blue .... 18.00 To 35.00
Carnival Glass, Tumbler, Grape & Gothic Arches, Cobalt 35.00
Carnival Glass, Tumbler, Grape & Lattice, Blue 29.00
Carnival Glass, Tumbler, Grape Arbor, Marigold 27.50
Carnival Glass, Tumbler, Grape Arbor, Purple .... 35.00 To 45.00
Carnival Glass, Tumbler, Grape Arbor, White 68.00
Carnival Glass, Tumbler, Grape, Green, Imperial .... 20.00 To 30.00
Carnival Glass, Tumbler, Grape, Marigold 14.00
Carnival Glass, Tumbler, Grape, Marigold, Imperial 14.50
Carnival Glass, Tumbler, Grape, Purple, Imperial 32.50
Carnival Glass, Tumbler, Grape, Purple, Northwood 26.00
Carnival Glass, Tumbler, Grapevine Lattice, Purple 40.00
Carnival Glass, Tumbler, Greek Key, Purple .... 65.00 To 69.00
Carnival Glass, Tumbler, Greek Key, 1914, Purple 75.00
Carnival Glass, Tumbler, Harvest Flower, Marigold 49.00
Carnival Glass, Tumbler, Heavy Iris, Amethyst 40.00
Carnival Glass, Tumbler, Heavy Iris, Purple 45.00
Carnival Glass, Tumbler, Imperial Grape, Marigold 15.00
Carnival Glass, Tumbler, Inverted Strawberry, Amethyst, Signed Near Cut 150.00
Carnival Glass, Tumbler, Jeweled Heart, Marigold 40.00
Carnival Glass, Tumbler, Juice, Minuet, Marigold 60.00
Carnival Glass, Tumbler, Lattice & Daisy, Marigold 18.00
Carnival Glass, Tumbler, Lattice & Grape, Blue .... 27.00 To 29.00
Carnival Glass, Tumbler, Luster Fruit, Marigold 12.75
Carnival Glass, Tumbler, Luster Rose, Marigold 15.00
Carnival Glass, Tumbler, Luster Rose, Purple 45.00
Carnival Glass, Tumbler, Maple Leaf, Blue, Northwood 35.00
Carnival Glass, Tumbler, Maple Leaf, Purple .... 20.00 To 30.00
Carnival Glass, Tumbler, Milady, Marigold 34.00
Carnival Glass, Tumbler, Orange Tree Variant, Blue 40.00
Carnival Glass, Tumbler, Orange Tree, Marigold, Footed 35.00
Carnival Glass, Tumbler, Oriental Poppy Variant, Marigold 23.00
Carnival Glass, Tumbler, Oriental Poppy, Marigold 22.00
Carnival Glass, Tumbler, Oriental Poppy, Purple .... 32.00 To 35.00
Carnival Glass, Tumbler, Oriental Poppy, Purple, Northwood 45.00
Carnival Glass, Tumbler, Paneled Dandelion, Blue 45.00
Carnival Glass, Tumbler, Paneled Dandelion, Green .... 35.00 To 37.50
Carnival Glass, Tumbler, Pastel Panels, Ice Blue 24.50
Carnival Glass, Tumbler, Peach, Blue, Northwood .... 39.00 To 42.50
Carnival Glass, Tumbler, Peacock At Fountain, Black, Purple Interior 35.00
Carnival Glass, Tumbler, Peacock At Fountain, Blue 30.00
Carnival Glass, Tumbler, Peacock At Fountain, Electric Blue 35.00
Carnival Glass, Tumbler, Peacock At Fountain, Marigold 32.00
Carnival Glass, Tumbler, Rambler Rose, Blue 25.00
Carnival Glass, Tumbler, Raspberry, Amber To Green 25.00
Carnival Glass, Tumbler, Raspberry, Green & Amber 22.00
Carnival Glass, Tumbler, Raspberry, Green, Northwood 45.00
Carnival Glass, Tumbler, Raspberry, Marigold, Northwood 20.00
Carnival Glass, Tumbler, Raspberry, Purple 22.00
Carnival Glass, Tumbler, Roses, Purple, I.C. 25.00
Carnival Glass, Tumbler, Singing Birds, Green .... 30.00 To 45.00

Carnival Glass, Tumbler, Singing Birds, Green, Northwood 22.00 To 35.00
Carnival Glass, Tumbler, Singing Birds, Marigold 30.00 To 32.00
Carnival Glass, Tumbler, Singing Birds, Purple 30.00
Carnival Glass, Tumbler, Singing Birds, Purple, Northwood 35.00
Carnival Glass, Tumbler, Soda Gold, Marigold 22.00 To 29.00
Carnival Glass, Tumbler, Springtime, Purple 69.00 To 75.00
Carnival Glass, Tumbler, Star Medallion, Marigold 15.00
Carnival Glass, Tumbler, Stork In Rushes With Beading, Blue 25.00
Carnival Glass, Tumbler, Stork In Rushes With Lattice Band, Blue 27.50
Carnival Glass, Tumbler, Stork In Rushes, Blue 25.00 To 28.00
Carnival Glass, Tumbler, Stork In Rushes, Marigold 16.00 To 18.50
Carnival Glass, Tumbler, Swirl, Marigold, Northwood 15.00
Carnival Glass, Tumbler, Ten Mums, Blue 50.00
Carnival Glass, Tumbler, Tiger Lily, Purple 65.00
Carnival Glass, Tumbler, Vineyard, Purple 40.00 To 50.00
Carnival Glass, Tumbler, Water Lily & Cattail, Marigold 17.00
Carnival Glass, Tumbler, Windmill, Purple 45.00
Carnival Glass, Tumbler, Wreathed Cherry, Amethyst 50.00
Carnival Glass, Tumbler, Wreathed Cherry, Marigold 30.00
Carnival Glass, Tumbler, Wreathed Cherry, Purple 37.50 To 50.00
Carnival Glass, Tumbler, 474, Purple 65.00
Carnival Glass, Vase, Bark, Blue, 9 3/4 In. 38.00
Carnival Glass, Vase, Basket Weave, White, 10 In. 50.00
Carnival Glass, Vase, Beaded Medallion, Marigold, 12 In. 22.00
Carnival Glass, Vase, Bud, Twig, Amethyst, 9 In. 20.00
Carnival Glass, Vase, Corn, Green 225.00
Carnival Glass, Vase, Corn, Ice Green 30.00
Carnival Glass, Vase, Corn, Purple 300.00
Carnival Glass, Vase, Diamond & Ribbed, Purple, 16 1/4 In. 35.00
Carnival Glass, Vase, Jack-In-The-Pulpit, Marigold, 10 In. 20.00
Carnival Glass, Vase, Jack-In-The-Pulpit, Marigold, 9 In. 33.00
Carnival Glass, Vase, Lattice & Points, White, 9 In. 25.00
Carnival Glass, Vase, Mary Ann, Marigold 45.00
Carnival Glass, Vase, Maryland, Green, 10 In., Pair 25.00
Carnival Glass, Vase, Millersburg Peoples, Ruffled Top, Amethyst 5900.00
Carnival Glass, Vase, Ribbed, Green, 8 In. 20.00
Carnival Glass, Vase, Ribbed, Marigold, Fluted Top, 9 1/2 In. 18.00
Carnival Glass, Vase, Ribbed, Orange, 11 In. 25.00
Carnival Glass, Vase, Ribbed, Purple, Points On Top, Northwood, 9 1/2 In. 25.00
Carnival Glass, Vase, Ribbed, Red, 10 In. 110.00
Carnival Glass, Vase, Rippled, Purple, Fluted Top, 10 1/2 In. 25.00
Carnival Glass, Vase, Tornado, Marigold 160.00
Carnival Glass, Vase, Tornado, Marigold With Applied Green 310.00
Carnival Glass, Vase, Tornado, Rayed Purple 170.00
Carnival Glass, Vase, Tree Of Life, Marigold, 7 In. 20.00
Carnival Glass, Vase, Tree Trunk, Green, 9 3/4 In. 28.00
Carnival Glass, Vase, Tree Trunk, Marigold, 14 In. 38.00
Carnival Glass, Vase, Tree Trunk, Purple, 14 In. 38.00
Carnival Glass, Vase, Vertical Ribbed, Blue, 13 In. 14.00
Carnival Glass, Water Set, Acorn Burr, Amethyst, Northwood, 7 Piece 650.00
Carnival Glass, Water Set, Acorn Burr, Purple, Northwood, 7 Piece 670.00
Carnival Glass, Water Set, Acorn Burr, Purple, 7 Piece 679.00 To 695.00
Carnival Glass, Water Set, Bark, Marigold, 9 Piece 50.00
Carnival Glass, Water Set, Butterfly & Berry, Marigold, 7 Piece 300.00
Carnival Glass, Water Set, Cathedral, Marigold 120.00
Carnival Glass, Water Set, Cherry & Blossoms, Blue, Enameled, 7 Piece 150.00
Carnival Glass, Water Set, Dandelion, Ice Blue, N. 2000.00
Carnival Glass, Water Set, Dandelion, Purple, 7 Piece 1040.00
Carnival Glass, Water Set, Diamond Lace, Purple 225.00
Carnival Glass, Water Set, Fashion, Marigold, 5 Piece 132.00
Carnival Glass, Water Set, Floral & Grape Variant, Marigold, 7 Piece 130.00
Carnival Glass, Water Set, Floral & Grape, Amethyst, 7 Piece 325.00
Carnival Glass, Water Set, Floral & Grape, Blue, 7 Piece 295.00 To 300.00
Carnival Glass, Water Set, Grape & Cable With Thumbprint, Purple, N, 7 Piece 450.00
Carnival Glass, Water Set, Grape & Cable, Marigold, Northwood, 7 Piece 290.00

Carnival Glass, Water Set, Grape & Cable, Purple, Northwood, 7 Piece ... 395.00
Carnival Glass, Water Set, Grape & Gothic Arches, Emerald Green, 7 Piece ... 460.00
Carnival Glass, Water Set, Grape & Lattice, Marigold, 7 Piece ... 185.00
Carnival Glass, Water Set, Grape Arbor, Marigold, 7 Piece ... 310.00
Carnival Glass, Water Set, Grape Arbor, Pastel Blue, 7 Piece ... 1200.00
Carnival Glass, Water Set, Grape Arbor, Purple ... 500.00
Carnival Glass, Water Set, Grape, Dark Marigold, Imperial, 7 Piece ... 150.00
Carnival Glass, Water Set, Grape, Marigold, Imperial, 7 Piece ... 139.00 To 150.00
Carnival Glass, Water Set, Heavy Iris, Purple ... 1200.00
Carnival Glass, Water Set, Imperial Grape, Green ... 175.00
Carnival Glass, Water Set, Imperial Grape, Marigold ... 95.00 To 125.00
Carnival Glass, Water Set, Imperial Grape, Purple ... 180.00 To 275.00
Carnival Glass, Water Set, Iris, Marigold ... 165.00
Carnival Glass, Water Set, Irish Lace, Marigold, Footed, 7 Piece ... 44.00
Carnival Glass, Water Set, Lattice & Daisy, Marigold, 6 Piece ... 210.00
Carnival Glass, Water Set, Maple Leaf, Purple ... 310.00
Carnival Glass, Water Set, Melon Rib, Aqua, 5 Piece ... 34.00
Carnival Glass, Water Set, Multicolored Mums, Dark Green, 4 Piece ... 145.00
Carnival Glass, Water Set, Octagon, Marigold, 6 Piece ... 125.00
Carnival Glass, Water Set, Orange Tree, Blue ... 400.00
Carnival Glass, Water Set, Orange Tree, Marigold ... 200.00
Carnival Glass, Water Set, Orange Tree, White With Gold ... 310.00
Carnival Glass, Water Set, Oriental Poppy, Green, 7 Piece ... 825.00
Carnival Glass, Water Set, Oriental Poppy, Ice Green, N. ... 3000.00
Carnival Glass, Water Set, Peach, White, Gold Trim, Northwood, 7 Piece ... 600.00
Carnival Glass, Water Set, Peacock At Fountain, Blue, Northwood, 7 Piece ... 420.00
Carnival Glass, Water Set, Peacock At Fountain, Marigold, 6 Piece ... 275.00
Carnival Glass, Water Set, Peacock At Fountain, Marigold, 7 Piece ... 339.00
Carnival Glass, Water Set, Raspberry, Green, Northwood, 5 Piece ... 199.00
Carnival Glass, Water Set, Raspberry, Marigold, 7 Piece ... 135.00
Carnival Glass, Water Set, Robin, White, Imperial, 9 Piece ... 65.00
Carnival Glass, Water Set, Roll, Marigold, 4 Piece ... 38.00
Carnival Glass, Water Set, Singing Birds, Purple ... 300.00
Carnival Glass, Water Set, Star Medallion, Marigold ... 85.00
Carnival Glass, Water Set, Stork & Rushes, Marigold ... 140.00
Carnival Glass, Water Set, Ten Mums, White ... 2100.00
Carnival Glass, Water Set, Tiger Lily, Marigold ... 90.00
Carnival Glass, Water Set, Tiger Lily, Purple ... 400.00
Carnival Glass, Water Set, Vineyard, Marigold ... 120.00
Carnival Glass, Water Set, Windmill, Marigold, 5 Piece ... 75.00
Carnival Glass, Water Set, Wine & Roses, Marigold ... 130.00
Carnival Glass, Water Set, Wishbone, Green ... 975.00
Carnival Glass, Water Set, Wishbone, Marigold ... 875.00
Carnival Glass, Water Set, Wishbone, Purple ... 1050.00
Carnival Glass, Wine Set, Golden Harvest, Marigold, 7 Piece ... 200.00
Carnival Glass, Wine Set, Grape, Helois Green, Imperial, 7 Piece ... 285.00
Carnival Glass, Wine Set, Grape, Marigold, Imperial, 5 Piece ... 129.00 To 149.00
Carnival Glass, Wine Set, Imperial Grape, Marigold ... 95.00
Carnival Glass, Wine, Diamond & Sunburst, Marigold ... 15.00
Carnival Glass, Wine, Grape, Marigold ... 10.00
Carnival Glass, Wine, Imperial Grape, Marigold ... 20.00
Carnival Glass, Wine, Imperial, Grape, Green ... 35.00
Carnival Glass, Wine, Orange Tree, Marigold ... 32.50
Carnival Glass, Wine, Sailboats, Blue, Twisted Stem ... 40.00
Carnival Glass, Wine, Wine & Roses, Marigold ... 35.00
Carousel, Chariot Sides, Plain Carvings ... 150.00
Carousel, Chariot, Carved Designs & Undercuts, 6 1/2 X 4 X 7 In. ... 1350.00
Carousel, Dog, Spillman ... 650.00
Carousel, Horse, Aluminum ... 595.00
Carousel, Horse, Armitage Herschell, Wood, Metal ... 300.00
Carousel, Horse, John Zalar, Philadelphia Toboggan Company ... 1250.00
Carousel, Horse, Jumper, Parker ... 500.00
Carousel, Horse, Jumper, Spillman, 53 X 33 In. ... 400.00
Carousel, Mule, Kicking ... 500.00
Carousel, Roman Soldier, Wooden, Painted, Carved, C.1890, 42 In. ... 325.00
Carousel, Rooster, Spillman ... 1200.00

Cased glass is made with one thin layer of glass over another layer or layers of colored glass. Many types of art glass were cased. Cased glass is usually a well-made piece by a reputable factory.

Cased Glass, Bottle, Blue To Clear, Rippled Design, Stopper, 10 In. 50.00
Cased Glass, Bottle, Perfume, Cobalt To Clear, Arched Medallions, Gold Cap 30.00
Cased Glass, Condiment Set, Pink, Florette, 4 Piece 145.00
Cased Glass, Creamer, Pink, Bulging Loops 95.00
Cased Glass, Decanter, Grape And Flower Cutting, Blue To Clear, 12 In. 100.00
Cased Glass, Jar, Pink Powder & Lid, Swirls, 6 In. 55.00
Cased Glass, Muffineer, Deep Rose Color, Cone, Pewter Top, 5 1/4 In. 75.00
Cased Glass, Muffineer, Green, Quilted Phlox 75.00
Cased Glass, Muffineer, Pink, Quilted Phlox 95.00
Cased Glass, Pitcher, Water, Pink, Swirl, Mica Flakes 145.00
Cased Glass, Rose Bowl, Aqua, Quilted Phlox, 4 1/2 In. 36.00
Cased Glass, Rose Bowl, Pink Inside, White Outside, Ruffled Clear Trim 55.00
Cased Glass, Saltshaker, Pink, Beaded Dahlia 30.00
Cased Glass, Saltshaker, Pink, Cone 22.50
Cased Glass, Saltshaker, Pink, Flower Band 29.00
Cased Glass, Saltshaker, Pink, Scroll, Footed 20.00
Cased Glass, Sugar & Creamer, Cobalt, Gold Enamel, Silver Plate Holder 95.00
Cased Glass, Toothpick, Frosted Cranberry Over Crystal, Ribbed Pillar 22.00
Cased Glass, Tumbler, Blue & White, Guttate 58.00
Cased Glass, Tumbler, Juice, Yellow 15.00
Cased Glass, Tumbler, Pink, Half Cone 35.00
Cased Glass, Vase, Amber To Clear, Contemporary Design, 1940s, Czechoslovakia 26.00
Cased Glass, Vase, Pink & White, Applied Amber Bellflowers & Leaves, 10 In. 215.00
Cased Glass, Vase, Pink With White, Fluted Top, 6 In. 15.00

Castor sets have been known as early as 1705. Most of those that have been found today date from Victorian times. A castor set usually consists of a silver-plated frame that holds three to seven condiment bottles. The pickle castor was a single glass jar about six inches high and held in a silver frame. A cover and tongs were kept with the jar. They were popular from 1890 to 1900. The McK numbers refer to the book "American Glass" by George and Helen McKearin.

Castor Set, see also various porcelain and glass categories

Castor Set, 3 Bottle, Purple Croesus, Gold Trim 295.00
Castor Set, 3 Bottle, X-Ray, Gold Decorated, Green 260.00
Castor Set, 3 Bottles, Amber Stars & Bars, Raised Tray 135.00
Castor Set, 3 Bottles, Blue Milk Glass, Tree Of Life Cruet 165.00
Castor Set, 3 Bottles, Cut & Etched, Oil, Vinegar, & Mustard 95.00
Castor Set, 3 Bottles, Leaf & Lattice, Miniature 58.00
Castor Set, 3 Bottles, Owls, Brown, Gold & White, 3 3/4 In. 85.00
Castor Set, 3 Bottles, Pink Challinor, Opaque Handle On Cruet 190.00
Castor Set, 3 Bottles, Plated Holder, Cased Glass 37.00
Castor Set, 3 Bottles, Ruby-Stained Paneled Finecut, Pewter Holder 85.00
Castor Set, 4 Bottles, Child's, Metal Stand With Handle 45.00
Castor Set, 4 Bottles, Cut Glass, Oil & Vinegar, & 2 Saucers 120.00
Castor Set, 4 Bottles, Dunham Pewter Stand, McK G I-14 .... 170.00
Castor Set, 4 Bottles, Flint, Excelsior, Pewter Holder 75.00
Castor Set, 4 Bottles, New England Pineapple, Holder 80.00
Castor Set, 4 Bottles, Pewter Frame, Eben Smith, McK G I-14 .... 160.00
Castor Set, 4 Bottles, Pewter Stand, 6 1/2 In. 45.00
Castor Set, 4 Bottles, Wheat, Pewter Frame 55.00
Castor Set, 5 Bottle, Pewter, Revolving 75.00
Castor Set, 5 Bottles, Etched & Engraved, Revolving Silver Plate Stand 75.00
Castor Set, 5 Bottles, Etched, Revolving Silver Plate Frame 65.00
Castor Set, 5 Bottles, Flint Gothic Arch, Pewter Stand, C.1860 .... 60.00
Castor Set, 5 Bottles, Flint, Cut Engraved, Ornate Stand 60.00
Castor Set, 5 Bottles, Trask Pewter Stand, McK G I-13 .... 250.00
Castor Set, 6 Bottles, Cranberry Inverted Thumbprint, Silver Holder 145.00
Castor Set, 6 Bottles, Cut Glass, Square, Silver Plate Holder 165.00
Castor Set, 6 Bottles, Daisy & Button, Blue & Amber, Clear Glass Frame 47.50
Castor Set, 6 Bottles, Etched & Cut, Silver Plate Frame 100.00
Castor Set, 7 Bottles, Ornate, Clear Glass 200.00

Castor, Pickle, see also various glass categories

Castor, Pickle, Amber 175.00
Castor, Pickle, Amber, Silver Holder, Lid, & Tongs 195.00
Castor, Pickle, Block Insert, Silver Claw-Footed Frame, Dragon Top, Tongs 71.00
Castor, Pickle, Blue Daisy & Button, Silver Plate Holder & Tongs 135.00
Castor, Pickle, Blue Frosted Satin Glass, Decorated 200.00
Castor, Pickle, Blue Opalescent Hobnail In Square, Silver Frame & Lid 88.00
Castor, Pickle, Blue Opalescent Swirl 175.00
Castor, Pickle, Blue Satin Glass, Swirled, Lined 275.00
Castor, Pickle, Bulbous Insert Flashed In Blue, Enameled, Gold Washed Frame 125.00
Castor, Pickle, Cane & Rosette, Footed Meriden Frame, 11 In. 72.50
Castor, Pickle, Cane & Rosette, Meriden 65.00
Castor, Pickle, Cane & Rosette, Meriden Frame 62.00
Castor, Pickle, Cherry Red, High Looped, 4 Legs 120.00
Castor, Pickle, Colonial, Ornate Tongs, Silver Lid, Enameled Floral, Crystal 75.00
Castor, Pickle, Cranberry Glass, Decorated 250.00
Castor, Pickle, Cranberry Liner, Enamel Decoration, Meriden Silver 225.00
Castor, Pickle, Cream-Colored Satin Glass, Decorated 200.00
Castor, Pickle, Crystal Insert, Silver Plate Frame & Lid 35.00
Castor, Pickle, Cupid & Venus 45.00
Castor, Pickle, Daisy & Button With V Ornament, Pairpoint Frame & Fork 85.00
Castor, Pickle, Double, Acid Etched Jars, Silver Plate, Tongs 85.00
Castor, Pickle, Enamel Floral 250.00
Castor, Pickle, Findlay Artichoke, Red Orange, Resilvered, Britannia Metal 185.00
Castor, Pickle, Green Zipper Insert 125.00
Castor, Pickle, Octagonal Insert, Tongs 65.00
Castor, Pickle, Pairpoint, Silver Plate, Clear Glass Insert, Tongs, 14 In. 92.50
Castor, Pickle, Paneled Flower, Tongs, Frame 75.00
Castor, Pickle, Peach To Cream Stain Glass, Decorated 250.00
Castor, Pickle, Pressed Diamond, Vaseline, Silver Plate Frame & Fork 125.00
Castor, Pickle, Pressed Glass, Bamboo, Canary, Forbes Silver Plate Frame 165.00
Castor, Pickle, Pressed Glass, Block 75.00
Castor, Pickle, Pressed Glass, Blue Cane 95.00
Castor, Pickle, Pressed Glass, Buttons & Bars, Reed & Barton Footed Frame 65.00
Castor, Pickle, Pressed Glass, Crystal, Silver Plate Frame & Lid 35.00
Castor, Pickle, Pressed Glass, Oriental, Vaseline, Silver Frame & Fork 75.00
Castor, Pickle, Psyche & Cupid 58.00
Castor, Pickle, Raised Birds, Flowers, Signed Reed & Barton 225.00
Castor, Pickle, Red Block, Metal Frame 115.00
Castor, Pickle, Reed & Barton Tongs & Footed Frame 90.00
Castor, Pickle, Rubena, Decorated 250.00
Castor, Pickle, Sapphire Blue Daisy & Button, Ornate Frame 110.00
Castor, Pickle, Square Flower & Quill Insert, Footed Silver Frame 47.50
Castor, Pickle, Waffle, Double, Fire-Glazed Inserts 95.00

Catalogue, see Paper, Catalogue

Caughley, see also Salopian

Caughley, Bowl, Sauce, Molded, Diaper Enclosed Flower & Scroll, Chinoiserie 250.00
Caughley, Dish, Junket, Blue & White, Scalloped, Flowers, Fruits, C Mark, 10 In. 125.00
Caughley, Plate, Dessert, Salopian, Blue Geometrics, C.1785 .... 100.00

Cauldon is an English pottery factory working after 1905.

Cauldon, see also Indian Tree

Cauldon, Chocolate Pot, White, Gold Trim & Twisted Rope Handle, 8 In. 30.00
Cauldon, Cup & Saucer, Blue Floral, Silver Luster Bands 16.00
Cauldon, Cup & Saucer, Demitasse, Cobalt & Engraved Bands, Gold Handles 20.00
Cauldon, Cup & Saucer, Sylvan, Blue & White, Miniature 8.00
Cauldon, Cup & Saucer, White, Heavy Gold Decoration 45.00
Cauldon, Fish Set, Seashell & Seaweed Borders, Blue & White, 7 Piece 95.00
Cauldon, Plate, Dickens, Bill Sikes 15.00
Cauldon, Plate, Dickens, Little Nell 15.00
Cauldon, Plate, Dickens, Mr.Micawber 15.00
Cauldon, Plate, Dickens, Mr.Pickwick 15.00
Cauldon, Plate, Orange And Cobalt, Numbered, 9 In., Pair 62.00

Celadon is a Chinese porcelain having a velvet-textured green-gray glaze. Japanese and Korean factories also made a celadon-colored glaze.

Celadon, Bowl, C.1850, Oblong, 8 X 6 1/2 In. 225.00
Celadon, Bowl, C.1850, Oval, 10 1/2 X 8 3/4 In. 275.00
Celadon, Bowl, C.1850, Square, 9 In. 225.00
Celadon, Bowl, Molded Fish, 9 1/2 In. 125.00
Celadon, Box, Covered Bamboo Finial, Raised Flowers, 5 X 3 3/4 X 3 1/2 In. 28.00
Celadon, Box, Enamel Scene On Lid, 4 3/4 In. 18.00
Celadon, Charger, Thousand Butterflies, C.1850, 16 In. 550.00
Celadon, Dish, Shrimp, C.1850 325.00
Celadon, Figurine, Buddha, 15 In. 100.00
Celadon, Figurine, Chinese Charger, Butterflies, Chien Lung Mark, 10 In. 65.00
Celadon, Humidor, Decorated, 9 In. 135.00
Celadon, Planter, Japanese, C.1920 6.00
Celadon, Plate, C.1850, 9 3/4 In. 225.00
Celadon, Plate, Foo Dog, Peony, & Leaves, 6 1/4 In. 12.00
Celadon, Tea Set, Thousand Butterflies, C.1850, 3 Piece 650.00
Celadon, Vase, Leaves & Flowers, 6 In., Pair 68.00
Celadon, Vase, 3 Lizards Around Neck, C.1830, 5 1/2 X 5 1/4 In. 105.00
Celluloid, Box, Dresser, Victorian Childrens' Heads, 10 1/2 X 5 X 3 In. 37.00
Celluloid, Box, Neckties On Top, White, Floral, Silk Lining, 13 3/4 In. 15.00
Celluloid, Buttonhook 2.50
Celluloid, Dresser Set, Green, Stones, 8 Piece 16.00
Celluloid, Dresser Set, Peach Color, 5 Piece 6.00
Celluloid, Letter Opener, Art Nouveau Lady 7.50
Celluloid, Tape Measure, Patent 1919, Shell 6.00
Celluloid, Tape Measure, Victorian Chair Shape, 2 1/4 In. 25.00
Centennial, Banner, Memorial Hall Art Gallery, 1876, Red & White, Framed 62.00
Centennial, Book, Philadelphia, Red, 4 3/4 In. 7.95
Centennial, Bookmark, Washington, 1876, B.B.Tilt & Son, Silk, Eagle 75.00
Centennial, Match Holder, Miss Liberty, Dated 46.00
Centennial, Mug, Constitution Hall, 1876, Etched Bessie 25.00
Centennial, Silk, Memorial Hall, 1776-1876, Woven, Black & Gray, 6 In. 25.00

The Ceramic Art Company of Trenton, N.J., was established in 1889 by J. Coxon and W. Lenox, and was an early producer of American Belleek porcelain.

Ceramic Art Co., Basket, Bough Handles, Gold Pine Cones, Purple Mark 125.00
Ceramic Art Co., Bowl, Belleek, Enamel & Gold Trim, 5 In. 60.00
Ceramic Art Co., Condiment Set, Belleek, Yellow Basketweave, 3 Pieces 95.00
Ceramic Art Co., Cup & Saucer, Demitasse, Belleek, Roses, Peters 35.00
Ceramic Art Co., Cup & Saucer, Demitasse, Belleek, Violets, Gilt Handle 45.00
Ceramic Art Co., Cup & Saucer, Demitasse, Lenox, Brown With Silver Overlay 40.00
Ceramic Art Co., Dish, Belleek, Heart Shape, Yellow Rose Decoration, Signed 60.00
Ceramic Art Co., Dish, Heart Shape, Purple Mark, Signed & Dated, Roses 60.00
Ceramic Art Co., Dish, Souvenir, Knight's Templar, Philadelphia, 1903, Lenox 50.00
Ceramic Art Co., Ewer, Belleek, Floral Branches, Fanny Snyder, 9 In. 85.00
Ceramic Art Co., Figurine, Toad, Belleek 35.00
Ceramic Art Co., Jar, Tobacco, Lenox, Monk, Artist E.A.Delan, 1899 75.00

Chalkware, Figurine, Cat, 6 1/2 In.

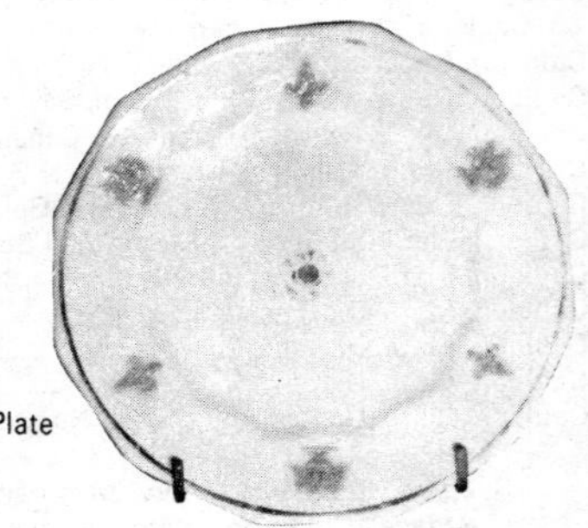

Chelsea Sprig, Plate

(See Page 98)

Ceramic Art Co., Jug, Belleek, Currants & Leaves, C.1898, 5 3/4 In. 105.00
Ceramic Art Co., Jug, Silver Overlay, Brown, Green Wreath, 4 3/4 In. 58.00
Ceramic Art Co., Mug, Belleek, Corn 48.00
Ceramic Art Co., Mug, Belleek, Floral, C.1895 .... 85.00
Ceramic Art Co., Mug, Belleek, Hand-Painted Cherries 45.00
Ceramic Art Co., Mug, Belleek, Monk With Stein, C.1895 .... 85.00
Ceramic Art Co., Mug, Belleek, Portrait, Indian Chief, Palette Mark 79.00
Ceramic Art Co., Mug, Cherries, Palette Mark 40.00
Ceramic Art Co., Mug, Elk, Palette Mark 45.00
Ceramic Art Co., Mug, German Beer Taster, Tankard Type, Palette Mark, 1898 .... 75.00
Ceramic Art Co., Mug, Grapes, Tankard Type, Palette Mark 75.00
Ceramic Art Co., Mug, Hops, Tankard Type, Palette Mark 75.00
Ceramic Art Co., Mug, Portrait Of Negro Woman 125.00
Ceramic Art Co., Pitcher, Cider, Belleek, Apples & Leaves, Studded Handle 95.00
Ceramic Art Co., Pitcher, Cider, Belleek, Deep Blue Fruit 75.00
Ceramic Art Co., Salt, Belleek, Pale Green, Gold Trim, Pearl Luster Interior 8.25
Ceramic Art Co., Sherbet, Belleek, Gold Floral, Rim, & Handles, 6 1/4 In. 60.00
Ceramic Art Co., Sugar & Creamer, Cover, Belleek, Footed, Helen Wild, 1905 .... 75.00
Ceramic Art Co., Tankard, Belleek, Hand-Painted Grapes, 7 In. 45.00
Ceramic Art Co., Tankard, Belleek, Indian Portrait, N.Easton, 1901, 5 1/2 In. 165.00
Ceramic Art Co., Tankard, Belleek, Tan To Brown, Indian Corn, 13 In. 225.00
Ceramic Art Co., Tankard, Green, Monk With Stein, Sterling Rim, 5 3/4 In. 135.00
Ceramic Art Co., Vase, Belleek, Black, Magpies, Gold Foot & Insert, 1897, 8 In. 115.00
Ceramic Art Co., Vase, Belleek, Daffodils Against Blue, Green Mark 85.00
Ceramic Art Co., Vase, Belleek, Metallic Crackle, Art Nouveau, 9 1/2 In. 75.00
Ceramic Art Co., Vase, Belleek, Orange To Brown, Negro Boy, Signed M.B.P. 225.00
Ceramic Art Co., Vase, Belleek, Pink & Yellow Roses, Signed, 14 1/2 In. 140.00
Ceramic Art Co., Vase, Belleek, White Cockatoo On Branch, Carlisle, 16 In. 285.00
Ceramic Art Co., Vase, Belleek, White Enamel, Purple Florals, Purple Mark 125.00
Ceramic Art Co., Vase, Pink & Yellow Roses, Artist Signed, 14 1/2 In. 140.00

Chalkware is really plaster of Paris decorated with watercolors. The pieces were molded from known Staffordshire and other porcelain models and painted and sold as inexpensive decorations. Most of this type of chalkware was made from about 1820 to 1870.

Chalkware, Figurine, see also Kewpie

Chalkware, Bust, Brown-Skinned Woman, C.1890, 18 In. 100.00
Chalkware, Bust, George Washington, 19 In. 35.00
Chalkware, Bust, Indian Chief, 5 1/2 In. 12.00
Chalkware, Bust, Shakespeare, 24 In. 30.00
Chalkware, Bust, Signed Layer, St.Louis, 1886, 13 In. 25.00
Chalkware, Cigar Store Indian, Reclining, C.1890, 23 In. 185.00
Chalkware, Figurine Atala, Bronze Color, 18 In. 200.00
Chalkware, Figurine, Boy Carrying Basket Of Fruit, 10 In. 55.00
Chalkware, Figurine, Cat, 6 1/2 In. .... *Illus* 115.00
Chalkware, Figurine, Dancing Lady, 14 In. 8.00
Chalkware, Figurine, Dog, Pennsylvania Dutch, 7 In., Pair 100.00
Chalkware, Figurine, Indian, Headdress, Crossed Arms, C.1850, 25 In. 65.00
Chalkware, Figurine, Lady With 2 Baskets, Gold Trim, 22 1/2 In. 65.00
Chalkware, Figurine, Lass Reading 2 Books, Pastels, 10 1/2 In. 65.00
Chalkware, Figurine, Man Holding Tricorner Hat & Rose, Pennsylvania, 15 In. 35.00
Chalkware, Figurine, Tomb Figure, Musical, Green & Brown, Chinese, 12 1/2 In. 75.00
Chalkware, Figurine, Trojan Horse 7.50
Chalkware, Figurine, Woman, Clock On Head, 24 In. 75.00
Chalkware, Holder, Twine, Black Boy 12.00
Chalkware, Plaque, Horn Of Plenty, 14 In. 4.00
Challinor, Tumbler, Green Opaque Scroll, Taylor, Pittsburgh 28.00
Chantilly, Pot, Rouge, Cover, Signed, 4 X 3 In. 95.00
Chantilly, Pot, Rouge, Decorated, Signed, 3 X 2 1/2 In. 65.00
Chantilly, Rouge Pot, Covered, Floral, 3 X 2 1/2 In. 75.00
Charlie Chaplin, Box, Pencil, Rectangular 17.50
Charlie Chaplin, Box, Tin, Pencil, 2 X 8 In. 12.00
Charlie Chaplin, Candy Container 65.00
Charlie Chaplin, Doll, Cadeaux, 1972, 19 1/2 In. 15.00
Charlie Chaplin, Doll, Louis Amberg & Son, 1915, Composition, 16 1/2 In. 250.00

Charlie Chaplin, Film, For Mutoscope, Charlie Playing Cop On Skid Row 75.00
Charlie Chaplin, Music Sheet, With You Dear In Bombay 8.00
Charlie Chaplin, Puppet, Wooden, 23 In. 24.00
Charlie Chaplin, Toy, Air Operated, Plastic, Squeeze 15.00
Charlie Chaplin, Toy, Windup, Plastic, Made In Spain 9.00
Charlie McCarthy, Book, 1938 .... 20.00
Charlie McCarthy, Bottle, Perfume, Figural 16.00
Charlie McCarthy, Doll, Composition, Dressed, 30 In. 65.00
Charlie McCarthy, Doll, Dressed, 24 In. 58.00
Charlie McCarthy, Doll, Working Dummy, 1940, 32 In. 50.00
Charlie McCarthy, Figurine, Chalkware, 11 In. 15.00
Charlie McCarthy, Fork & Spoon, Figural 9.00
Charlie McCarthy, Game, Question & Answer, 1938 .... 20.00
Charlie McCarthy, Pot Holder, Figural 4.00
Charlie McCarthy, Spoon 7.00
Charlie McCarthy, Spoon, Silver Plate 6.00
Charlie McCarthy, Teaspoon, Duchess Silver Plate 8.00
Charlie McCarthy, Teaspoon, Figural Head 4.00
Charlie McCarthy, Toy, Charlie In His Benzine Buggy 135.00
Charlie McCarthy, Toy, Crazy Car 75.00

Chelsea grape pattern was made before 1840. A small bunch of grapes in a raised design, colored with purple or blue luster, is on the border of the white plate. Most of the pieces are unmarked. The pattern is sometimes called Aynsley or Grandmother.

Chelsea Grape, Luncheon Set, Purple Luster, 28 Piece 235.00
Chelsea Grape, Plate, Cup, Purple Luster 14.00
Chelsea Grape, Plate, Porcelaine A La Perle, J.E., Lavender, 8 In. 15.00
Chelsea Keramic Art Works, see Dedham

Chelsea porcelain was made in the Chelsea area of London from about 1745 to 1784. Recent copies of this work have been made from the original molds.

Chelsea Sprig, Plate .... *Illus* 5.00
Chelsea, Creamer, Sprig, Miniature 11.00
Chelsea, Cup & Saucer, Raised Blue Thistle 30.00
Chelsea, Figurine, Boy Sitting With Basket Of Flowers, Anchor Mark, 6 In. 150.00
Chelsea, Figurine, Girl Sitting With Hat & Flower, Anchor Mark, 6 In. 150.00
Chelsea, Figurine, Reclining Lamb On White, Gold Trim, Anchor Mark, Pair 250.00
Chelsea, Group, Lady, Gentleman, & Lamb, Gold Anchor Mark, 6 1/2 In. 375.00
Chelsea, Group, Woman & Man, Bocage, 4 3/4 In. 195.00
Chelsea, Plate, Raised Blue Thistle, 6 3/4 In. 11.00
Chelsea, Plate, Sprig, Square, 9 In. 14.00
Chelsea, Vase, Rectangle Sides Like Embossed Tile, Frogs Applied As Handles 275.00
Chesapeake, Ice Cream Set, Ivory Color, Raspberry Maple Leaves, 9 Piece 65.00

Chinese export porcelain is all the many kinds of porcelain made in China for export to America and Europe in the eighteenth and nineteenth centuries. Included in the category are Nanking, Canton, Chinese Lowestoft, Armorial, Jesuit, and other types of the ware.

Chinese Export, see also Canton, Celadon, Nanking
Chinese Export, Belt, Woman's, Beaded, Sterling Buckle, Chased With Dragons 295.00
Chinese Export, Berry Bowl, Armorial, Wilkinson, C.1780, 6 1/8 In., Pair 250.00
Chinese Export, Bisque Face & Hands, Holding Scroll, 11 In. 110.00
Chinese Export, Bough Pot, Pierced Lid, Famille Verte, C.1820, 9 In., Pair 1600.00
Chinese Export, Bowl, Blue & White, Floral, C.1780, 4 In. 55.00
Chinese Export, Bowl, Branches & Floral, Birds On Magenta Inside, 8 1/4 In. 115.00
Chinese Export, Bowl, Famille Rose, Flowers, Scalework Panels, C.1780, 11 In. 375.00
Chinese Export, Bowl, Famille Rose, Peony Trees, Gray Rockwork, C.1755, 8 In. 350.00
Chinese Export, Bowl, Female Goat Herder, Reticulated, C.1780, 11 1/8 In. 375.00
Chinese Export, Bowl, Hawthorne, 14 1/4 In. 268.00
Chinese Export, Bowl, Mandarin Palette, Figures & Birds, C.1780, 10 1/4 In. 475.00
Chinese Export, Bowl, Polychrome Figures Out, Flowers In, 9 In. 328.00
Chinese Export, Bowl, River Scene, Blue & Polychrome, C.1780, 4 In. 55.00
Chinese Export, Bowl, Scalloped Handle, Cobalt Bouquet, Gold, Oriental Sign 32.00
Chinese Export, Box, Brush, Covered, Rose Mandarin, C.1850 .... 465.00

Chinese Export, Tureen, Soup, Matching Platter

(See Page 100)

Chocolate Glass, Candleholder, Griffin

(See Page 101)

Chinese Export, Box, Famille Rose, Pierced Lid, Oval, 5 In. 45.00
Chinese Export, Charger, Floral, C.1790, 11 In. 235.00
Chinese Export, Chocolate Pot, Famille Rose, Chair & Vases, C.1750, 9 In. 400.00
Chinese Export, Chocolate Set, Stenciled Birds, Iris, Chinese Mark, 11 Piece 60.00
Chinese Export, Creamer, Helmet 175.00
Chinese Export, Cricket Cage, Rose & Pink Floral, C.1870 .... 85.00
Chinese Export, Cup & Saucer, Coffee, Bats 55.00
Chinese Export, Cup & Saucer, Coffee, En Grisaille, Armorial, Vaughan, C.1755 .... 162.50
Chinese Export, Cup & Saucer, Coffee, Famille Rose, Armorial, C.1750, Pair 700.00
Chinese Export, Cup, Burnt Orange & Green Flying Birds & Peonies 35.00
Chinese Export, Cup, Peonies & Birds, Burnt Orange & Green 32.00
Chinese Export, Dish, Kidney Shape, Sepia Mountain Medallions, C.1775, 11 In. 337.50
Chinese Export, Dish, Lotus Shape, Turquoise, Cockerel, C.1750, 5 1/2 In. 450.00
Chinese Export, Dish, Lozenge Shape, Famille Rose, Armorial .... 250.00 To 400.00
Chinese Export, Dish, Shield Design, Greek Emblem, 10 1/2 X 5 1/2 In. 145.00
Chinese Export, Dish, Sweetmeat, Famille Rose, Scallop Shape, C.1770, Pair 325.00
Chinese Export, Ecuelle, Covered, Famille Rose, Bouquets, C.1760, Pair 560.00
Chinese Export, Figurine, Chinese Holy Man, Tan Luster Robes, 9 In. 25.00
Chinese Export, Figurine, Cockerels, Famille Rose, 15 1/2 In., Pair 1000.00
Chinese Export, Figurine, Foo Dog, Porcelain, Teak Base, Blue Glaze, Impressed 35.00
Chinese Export, Jar, Ginger, Blue & White, Peacock, Butterflies, & Floral 275.00
Chinese Export, Jar, Ginger, Dragons, Brick Red, Black, & Gold, 5 1/2 In. 20.00
Chinese Export, Jar, Ginger, Oriental Figures, 6 In. 65.00
Chinese Export, Jardiniere, Hawthorne, 15 In. 378.00
Chinese Export, Jug, Milk, Covered, Famille Rose, Peonies, C.1765, 5 In. 150.00
Chinese Export, Jug, Milk, Covered, Meissen Style, Quay Scenes, C.1760 .... 275.00
Chinese Export, Lantern, Marriage, Famille Rose, C.1760 .... 700.00
Chinese Export, Mug, Famille Rose, Peony Trees, Salmon Rockwork, C.1755, Pair 325.00
Chinese Export, Plaque, Geisha Girl, Bats, Shou Lau & Deer, Ch'ing, 21 In. 600.00
Chinese Export, Plaque, Woman, Bats, Shou Lau, Spotted Deer, 21 X 13 1/2 In. 600.00
Chinese Export, Plaque, Women Preparing Sword, Cherry Stand, Ivory, 16 In. 590.00
Chinese Export, Plate, Armorial, Hanbury With Comyn, C.1735, 9 In. 450.00
Chinese Export, Plate, Butterflies, Black, 10 In. 40.00
Chinese Export, Plate, Dessert, Birds, Squirrels, & Butterflies, C.1850, 9 In. 35.00
Chinese Export, Plate, Dessert, Famille Rose, Birds & Landscape, C.1850 .... 37.50
Chinese Export, Plate, Dessert, Famille Rose, Figures In Rickshaws, C.1850 .... 39.50
Chinese Export, Plate, Dessert, Famille Verte, Figures In Garden, C.1850 .... 70.00
Chinese Export, Plate, Dessert, Oriental Ladies & Mums, C.1850, 8 1/2 In. 55.00
Chinese Export, Plate, Famille Rose, Crowned Figure, C.1760, 9 In., Pair 1100.00
Chinese Export, Plate, Famille Rose, En Grisaille, Armorial, 1765, 8 5/8 In. 300.00
Chinese Export, Plate, Famille Rose, Floral, Barbed Scrolls, 1770, 9 1/8 In. 50.00
Chinese Export, Platter, Armorial, Viscount De Mirandella, 1780, 12 5/8 In. 850.00
Chinese Export, Platter, En Grisaille, Armorial, Vaughan, C.1755 .... 325.00 To 600.00
Chinese Export, Platter, Famille Rose, Armorial, Garfoote, C.1765, 11 3/8 In. 500.00
Chinese Export, Platter, Famille Rose, Birds & Peonies, C.1745, 13 1/4 In. 475.00

Chinese Export, Platter, Famille Rose, Peacock, C.1765, 11 3/8 In. 400.00
Chinese Export, Platter, Pseudo Tobacco Leaf, C.1750, 11 7/8 In., Pair 1200.00
Chinese Export, Platter, Swan Medallion, Coral Edge, C.1806, 17 3/8 In. 300.00
Chinese Export, Platter, Swan Medallion, Coral Rim, C.1806, 15 7/8 In., Pair 950.00
Chinese Export, Pot, Puzzle, Wine Pot, Green & Purple Tones, 5 In. 135.00
Chinese Export, Punch Bowl, Famille Rose, Bacchus & Putti, C.1750, 16 In. 4400.00
Chinese Export, Punch Bowl, Famille Verte, Peafowl & Figure, Persian Market 975.00
Chinese Export, Punch Pot, Kylin Knop, Famille Rose, Mandarin Palette, 1775 650.00
Chinese Export, Sauce, Fruit Shape, Enamel Coloring, 5 X 5 In. 38.00
Chinese Export, Sauceboat & Stand, Famille Rose, Cornucopias, C.1780, Pair 325.00
Chinese Export, Sauceboat, En Grisaille, Armorial, Vaughan, C.1755, Pair 350.00
Chinese Export, Sauceboat, Pseudo Tobacco Leaf, C.1750, 8 3/8 In. 375.00
Chinese Export, Saucer, Libation, Enamel Floral, Red Border, C.1885, 6 1/2 In. 75.00
Chinese Export, Saucer, Libation, Floral, Red Border, C.1885, 6 1/2 In. 75.00
Chinese Export, Seat, Garden, Famille Rose, Peafowl & Peonies, C.1850, 18 In. 1100.00
Chinese Export, Seat, Garden, Fitzhugh, Green, Hexagonal, C.1850, 18 1/2 In. 3300.00
Chinese Export, Serving Bowl, Swan Medallion, Coral Edge, C.1806, 13 1/2 In. 225.00
Chinese Export, Sewing Basket, Beads And Ring 9.50
Chinese Export, Sugar, Covered, Meissen Style, Figures & Bridges, C.1760 250.00
Chinese Export, Sugar, Lotus Knop, Famille Rose, Marriage Cartouche, C.1760 425.00
Chinese Export, Tankard, Famille Rose, Bird On Peony Branch, C.1750, 6 In. 275.00
Chinese Export, Tankard, Famille Rose, Floral Medallion, C.1780, 5 1/2 In. 310.00
Chinese Export, Tankard, Famille Rose, Peony Trees, C.1755, 5 In. 175.00
Chinese Export, Tankard, Famille Rose, Quatrefoil Panels, C.1765, 4 1/2 In. 175.00
Chinese Export, Tea Caddy, Burnt Orange Bamboo Plants 45.00
Chinese Export, Tea Set, En Grisaille, Peonies, C.1750, 17 Piece 1600.00
Chinese Export, Tea Set, Mandarin Figures, Aqua & Blue, C.1820, 35 Piece 3250.00
Chinese Export, Teabowl & Saucer, Brown Eagle, Gilt Stars & Bands, C.1790 275.00
Chinese Export, Teabowl & Saucer, En Grisaille, Venus & Cupid, C.1745 183.30
Chinese Export, Teabowl & Saucer, Famille Rose, Lotus, Lotus Shape, C.1750 425.00
Chinese Export, Teapot, Bamboo Handle, 11 1/2 In. 98.00
Chinese Export, Tile, Famille Rose, Mandarin Ducks, C.1850, Square, 9 1/4 In. 75.00
Chinese Export, Tureen & Stand, Red Knop, En Grisaille, Arms, C.1755, 17 In. 600.00
Chinese Export, Tureen & Stand, Sauce, Covered, Pseudo Tobacco Leaf, C.1750 100.00
Chinese Export, Tureen & Stand, Soup, Pierced Knop, Bouquets, C.1765, 16 In. 2100.00
Chinese Export, Tureen, Covered, Famille Rose, En Grisaille, C.1750, 11 In. 1200.00
Chinese Export, Tureen, Sauce, Famille Rose, Floral, Covered, 1750, 6 3/4 In. 575.00
Chinese Export, Tureen, Soup, Crown Knob, Famille Rose, Floral, C.1750, 13 In. 2100.00
Chinese Export, Tureen, Soup, Matching Platter *Illus* 4800.00
Chinese Export, Vase, Bird Of Paradise & Floral, Gold Trim, 6 1/2 In. 57.50
Chinese Export, Vase, Famille Rose, Dragons & Dogs, C.1850, 17 3/4 In., Pair 900.00
Chinese Export, Vase, Famille Rose, Tobacco, Bird & Squirrel, C.1750, 5 In. 350.00
Chinese Export, Vase, Garden, Water Scene, Proverb In Calligraphy 85.00
Chinese Export, Vase, Green Gray Ground, Figural, Decorated, 23 In., C.1890 175.00
Chinese Export, Vase, Hawthorn, 19 In. 425.00
Chinese Export, Vase, Sang De Boeuf, 6 3/4 In. 75.00
Chinese Export, Vase, Square, Tapered, Multicolored Flowers On Black, 20 In. 250.00
Chinese Export, Vase, Temple, Sang De Boeuf, K'ang Hsi, 11 1/4 In. 200.00
Chinese Export, Vase, Temple, Wide Men In Garden, C'hing, 25 In., Pair 600.00
Chinese Export, Vase, Turquoise, Red, Blue, & Green Floral, 9 In. 45.00
Chinese Export, Vegetable Bowl, Covered, Swan Medallion, C.1806, 9 1/8 In. 500.00
Chinese Export, Water Holder, Figure Of Child On Top, Brush Paintings, 1800 65.00

Chocolate glass, sometimes mistakenly called caramel slag, was made by the Indiana Tumbler and Goblet Company of Greentown, Indiana, from 1900 to 1903.

Chocolate Glass, Berry Bowl, Rose & Bowknot, 8 In. 110.00
Chocolate Glass, Bowl, Cactus, Scalloped Top & Base, Greentown, 7 1/4 In. 80.00
Chocolate Glass, Bowl, Cactus, 8 In. 90.00
Chocolate Glass, Butter, Covered, Cactus 172.50
Chocolate Glass, Butter, Covered, Leaf Bracket, Greentown 85.00 To 165.00
Chocolate Glass, Butter, On Standard *Illus.* 225.00
Chocolate Glass, Butter, Swan Cover & Finial, Handled 125.00
Chocolate Glass, Cactus, Sugar, Greentown, 5 In. 50.00

Chocolate Glass, Collar & Cuff Set

Chocolate Glass, Butter, On Standard

Chocolate Glass, Chalice, Chrysanthemum, Leaf, Pair

Chocolate Glass, Candleholder, Griffin .... *Illus* 600.00
Chocolate Glass, Chalice, Chrysanthemum, Leaf, Pair .... *Illus* 475.00
Chocolate Glass, Collar & Cuff Set .... *Illus* 350.00
Chocolate Glass, Compote, Cactus 85.00
Chocolate Glass, Compote, Footed, Cactus 110.00
Chocolate Glass, Compote, Melrose .... *Illus* 325.00
Chocolate Glass, Creamer, Cactus 45.00
Chocolate Glass, Creamer, Shuttle, Greentown, 6 In. 75.00
Chocolate Glass, Dish, Berry, Cactus, 4 In. 30.00
Chocolate Glass, Dish, Candy, Hand Mold .... *Illus* 550.00
Chocolate Glass, Dish, Lamb Cover, Greentown 1000.00
Chocolate Glass, Dish, Oval, Footed, 8 In. 35.00
Chocolate Glass, Dish, Relish, Thistle .... *Illus* 425.00
Chocolate Glass, Dish, Swan Covered Butter, Challinor, Taylor 100.00
Chocolate Glass, Dish, Sweetmeat, On Standard .... *Illus* 200.00
Chocolate Glass, Match Holder, Dog Head .... *Illus* 250.00
Chocolate Glass, Match Holder, Footed, 4 In.High 27.00
Chocolate Glass, Mug, Buttress Herringbone 50.00
Chocolate Glass, Mug, Old Cactus 55.00
Chocolate Glass, Nappy, Leaf Bracket, Handled, Tricorner 39.50
Chocolate Glass, Nappy, Leaf Bracket, Ring Handle, Triangular, Greentown 39.50

Chocolate Glass, Compote, Melrose

(See Page 101)

Chocolate Glass, Dish, Relish, Thistle

(See Page 101)

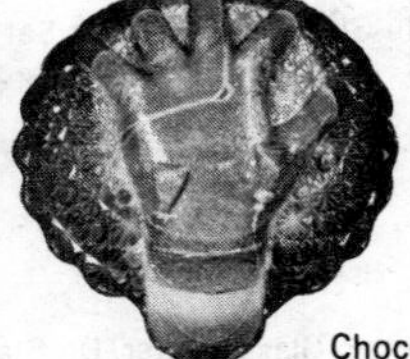

Chocolate Glass, Dish, Candy, Hand Mold

(See Page 101)

Chocolate Glass, Nappy, Star & Rays, Handled, Tricorner, Greentown, 6 1/2 In. 40.00
Chocolate Glass, Pitcher, Heron .... *Illus* 225.00
Chocolate Glass, Pitcher, Heron, Greentown 265.00
Chocolate Glass, Pitcher, Rose Garland, Greentown 1500.00
Chocolate Glass, Pitcher, Strigil, 6 1/4 In. 40.00
Chocolate Glass, Pitcher, Water, Cattail & Water Lily .... *Illus* 1000.00
Chocolate Glass, Pitcher, Water, Chrysanthemum Leaf, Greentown 1800.00
Chocolate Glass, Pitcher, Water, File, Greentown 450.00
Chocolate Glass, Pitcher, Water, Fleur-De-Lis, Greentown 750.00
Chocolate Glass, Plate, Cactus, Greentown, 7 1/2 In. 47.00
Chocolate Glass, Relish, Leaf Bracket, Greentown, 7 1/4 X 4 3/4 In. 37.50
Chocolate Glass, Relish, Leaf Bracket, Greentown, 8 1/4 X 5 1/4 In. 39.50
Chocolate Glass, Saltshaker, Cactus 60.00
Chocolate Glass, Sauce, Cactus 45.00
Chocolate Glass, Sauce, Leaf Bracket, Footed 32.00
Chocolate Glass, Saucer, Dewey, Footed 50.00
Chocolate Glass, Shade, Hanging Dome, Leaded, Urn, Panels, 20 In. 485.00
Chocolate Glass, Spooner, Leaf Bracket, Greentown 35.00
Chocolate Glass, Sugar, Covered, Leaf Bracket, Greentown 75.00
Chocolate Glass, Syrup, Cactus 32.50
Chocolate Glass, Syrup, Shuttle, Greentown 110.00
Chocolate Glass, Toothpick, Cactus 47.50
Chocolate Glass, Toothpick, Just A Thimble Full 48.00
Chocolate Glass, Tray, Pin, Brush .... *Illus* 150.00
Chocolate Glass, Tumbler, Cactus, Greentown, 4 In. 40.00
Chocolate Glass, Tumbler, Uneeda Biscuit .... 65.00 To 75.00
Chocolate Glass, Tumbler, Uneeda Biscuit, Greentown 45.00
Chocolate Pot, Blue & White, Flowers, Vines, & Leaves, Ribbed, 9 1/2 In. 45.00
Chocolate Pot, Dark Green To Cream, Pink & White Roses, Gold Trim, 6 In. 38.00
Chocolate Pot, Dark Pink To Lilac Floral 55.00
Christmas Plate, see Collector, Plate
Christmas Tree Light, 1, 000-Eye, Blue, 3 3/4 In. 35.00
Christmas Tree, Holder, Cast Iron, Cutout Work 14.00
Christmas Tree, Light Bulb Set, Noma, Bubble Lights 12.00
Christmas Tree, Light Bulb, Dick Tracy 12.00
Christmas Tree, Light Bulb, Rose 4.00
Christmas Tree, Light Bulb, Santa 9.00
Christmas Tree, Light, Aqua, 3 In. .... *Illus* 11.00
Christmas Tree, Light, Diamond Quilted, Blown, Amethyst, 3 In. 75.00
Christmas Tree, Light, Diamond Quilted, Blown, Cobalt, 4 In. 75.00
Christmas Tree, Light, Stiegel Type, Opalescent 500.00
Christmas Tree, Light, 1, 000-Eye, Green, 3 3/4 In. 35.00

Christmas Tree, Light, 1, 000-Eye, Ruby Stained, 3 3/8 In. 47.50

Christmas Tree, Ornament, Angel, Copper, Russia, 3 1/2 In. 5.00

Christmas Tree, Ornament, Child, White Milk Glass 5.00

Christmas Tree, Ornament, Football Player, Milk Glass 10.00

Christmas Tree, Ornament, Heat From Candles Gives Revolving Action, C.1910 35.00

Christmas Tree, Ornament, Icicle, Glass, Set Of 11 12.00

Christmas Tree, Ornament, Indian Chief Head, Iridescent, Clip On, Early 1920 55.00

Christmas Tree, Ornament, Milk Glass, Figural 2.50

Christmas Tree, Ornament, Santa Claus, Glass 14.50

Christmas Tree, Ornament, Santa Claus, Milk Glass 10.00

Christmas Tree, Ornament, Santa Claus, Occupied Japan, Chenille, Composition 1.50

Christmas Tree, Ornament, Santa On Sled, Metal, Yellow & Red, 2 1/2 In. 10.00

Christmas Tree, Ornament, Snowman, Milk Glass 10.00

Christmas Tree, Ornament, Spun Glass, Boxed 4.00

Christmas Tree, Stand, Musical, 2 Tunes, Hand Wind, Lador, Swiss, 13 1/2 In. 125.00

Cigar Cutter, see Brass, Cutter, Cigar; Store, Cutter, Cigar

Cinnabar is a vermilion or red lacquer. Some pieces are made with hundreds of thicknesses of the lacquer that is later carved.

Cinnabar, Bookend, Hand Carved With Birds, Marked China, Pair 60.00

Cinnabar, Bottle, Snuff, Lacquer, Chinese 20.00

Cinnabar, Bottle, Snuff, Red 67.50

Cinnabar, Bottle, Snuff, Scenic Carving 90.00

Cinnabar, Bottle, Snuff, Scenic Carving, Dark Red, Signed 85.00

Cinnabar, Box, Carved Ivory Figure On Lid, 4 X 3 In. 70.00

Cinnabar, Box, Characters In Garden Scene, 5 1/2 X 3 3/4 In. 40.00

Cinnabar, Box, Stamp, China, 3 X 1 1/2 X 1 1/2 In. 30.00

Cinnabar, Box, White, 5 X 3 1/2 In. 50.00

Cinnabar, Figurine, Buddha, Red, Black Designs 75.00

Cinnabar, Vase, Floral, 4 In., Pair 50.00

Civil War mementos are important collectors' items. Most of the pieces are military items used from 1861 to 1865.

Civil War, Baton, Drum Major's, Wooden Shaft, Brass 80.00

Civil War, Bayonet, Union 15.00

Civil War, Box, Cartridge, Union, For .58 Caliber Musket 95.00

Civil War, Buckle, Belt, Marked Boys & Son, Yankee Officers 125.00

Civil War, Buckle, Belt, Yankee, Eagle On Front, Brass 22.00

Civil War, Canteen, Stopper, Silk Embroidered Cover, Company A, Illinois 200.00

Civil War, Coat, Confederate Officer's, Black & Gray 40.00

Civil War, Cup, Collapsible, Pewter, Issued To Union Soldier 21.00

Civil War, Gun & Saber 125.00

Civil War, Hat, Confederate Officer's, Black & Gray 10.00

Civil War, Kit, Surgical, Captain, J.H.Morrison, 8 Tools, Wooden Box 230.00

Civil War, Knapsack, Union 12.50

Chocolate Glass, Dish, Sweetmeat, On Standard

(See Page 101)

Chocolate Glass, Match Holder, Dog Head

(See Page 101)

Civil War, Knife, Boot, Confederate, Flat Wooden Grip, 16 1/8 In. 100.00
Civil War, Lantern, Double Wick Burner, Signal 20.00
Civil War, Lithograph, Mountain Rangers, Battle Scenics, 19 X 23 In. 200.00
Civil War, Poster, Union War Meeting, New York Town, 1862, 12 3/4 X 10 In. 39.50
Civil War, Revolver, Sharp's 4 Barrel With Patent Jan.25, 1859 .... 160.00
Civil War, Spoon & Fork, Folding 18.00
Civil War, Sword, Confederate 70.00
Civil War, Sword, Union 60.00
Civil War, Sword, Union Dress Parade, 1862 .... 100.00
Civil War, Sword, Union Navy 15.00
Civil War, Sword, 1860 Staff & Field, Wm.Read & Sons, Boston, Mass.Etched 175.00

Clambroth glass, popular in the Victorian era, is a grayish color and is semiopaque like clambroth

Clambroth, Bottle, Barber, Porcelain Stopper 27.50
Clambroth, Bottle, Barber, Witch Hazel, Porcelain Stopper 45.00
Clambroth, Bowl, Enameled Florals 9.00
Clambroth, Candlestick, Hexagonal, 3 Small Snowflakes 150.00
Clambroth, Cream, Swan, Greenery 700.00
Clambroth, Creamer, Button Arches 16.00
Clambroth, Goblet, Worthington, Minnesota 22.00
Clambroth, Mug, Souvenir, Cadillac, Michigan 18.00
Clambroth, Mug, Souvenir, Fennimore, Wisc. 20.00
Clambroth, Mug, Souvenir, Spencer, Iowa 8.50
Clambroth, Pipe, Souvenir, Liberal, Kansas, Painted Flower, 6 In. 12.00
Clambroth, Whiskey Taster, 9 Panels, 1 5/8 In. 60.00

Clewell ware was made in limited quantities by Charles Walter Clewell of Canton, Ohio, from 1902 to 1955.

Clewell, Pitcher, Riveted Copper Decoration, 10 In. 88.00
Clewell, Vase, 8 In. .... *Illus* 125.00

Clews pottery was made by George Clews & Co.of Brownhill Pottery, Tunstall, England, from 1806 to 1861.

Clews, see also Flow Blue

Clews, Cup Plate, Near Sandy Hill, Pink, 3 7/8 In. 65.00
Clews, Cup Plate, River Scene, Double Print 70.00
Clews, Cup Plate, St.Catherine Hill, Guilford, Double Print 70.00
Clews, Pitcher, Near Ft.Miller Hudson River, Black, 8 In. 180.00

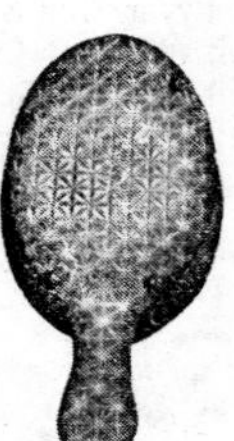

Chocolate Glass, Tray, Pin, Brush

(See Page 102)

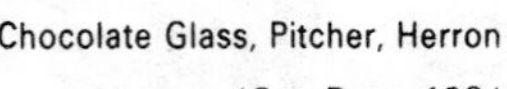

Chocolate Glass, Pitcher, Herron

(See Page 102)

Chocolate Glass, Pitcher, Water, Cattail & Water Lily

(See Page 102)

Christmas Tree, Light, Aqua, 3 In.

(See Page 102)

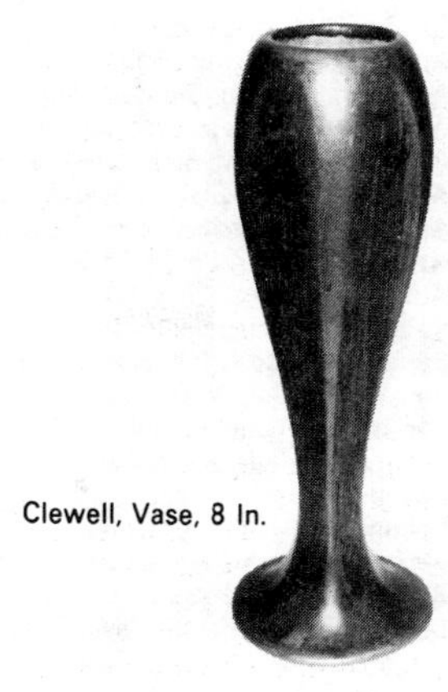

Clewell, Vase, 8 In.

Clews, Plate, Blue On White, Flowers, Fruit, Bird, Stamped Coronation, 10 In. 52.00
Clews, Plate, Christmas Eve, Wilkie Series, Blue, 9 In. 125.00
Clews, Plate, Dr.Syntax Painting Portrait, C.1818, 10 1/4 In. 135.00
Clews, Plate, Landing Of Lafayette 87.00
Clews, Plate, Near Hudson, Black & White, 9 In. 55.00
Clews, Plate, Near Sandy Hill, Sepia, 8 In. 58.00
Clews, Plate, Sancho Meets Dapple, Don Quixote, Deep Blue, 8 3/4 In. 125.00
Clews, Plate, Soup, Wilkie Series, Playing At Draughts, Blue, C.1818, 9 In. 95.00
Clews, Plate, States, Dark Blue, 7 5/8 In. 155.00
Clews, Plate, West Point, Hudson River, Black & White, 7 In. 60.00
Clews, Plate, Wilkie Series, The Valentine, C.1818, 10 1/4 In. 345.00
Clews, Platter, Landing Of Lafayette, Blue, 15 1/2 In. 575.00
Clews, Saltshaker, Fort & River Scene, Deep Blue, 4 5/8 In. 125.00
Clews, Tray, Game Bird, Dark Blue, 6 3/4 X 5 1/2 In. 75.00
Clews, Vegetable Bowl, Zoological Gardens, Pink, 9 5/8 In. 48.00

The Clifton Pottery was founded by William Long in Clifton, New Jersey, in 1905. He worked there until 1908 making a line called Crystal Patina.

Clifton, Mug, Little Colorado, Arizona 35.00
Clifton, Teapot, Crystal Patina, 11 X 4 In. 72.00
Clifton, Vase, Arkansas Tribe Pattern, 5 3/4 In. 55.00
Clifton, Vase, Green Glaze, Flowers In Relief, 1906, W.A.Long, 8 1/2 In. 150.00
Clifton, Vase, Green Shades, 1905, 5 1/2 In. 65.00

Clock, see also Coca-Cola, Clock; Disneyana, Clock; Store, Clock

Clock, A.Twiss, Montreal, C.1825, Grandfather 1000.00
Clock, Admiral Dewey, Mantel, Gingerbread, Oak 375.00
Clock, American, C.1830, Mahogany Veneer, Brass Works, 7 Ft.9 In. 2500.00
Clock, American, Gingerbread, Walnut Case, Roman Numerals 95.00
Clock, Amerika, Western Clock Co., Alarm 5.00
Clock, Anniversary, Brass, Porcelain Face, Rose Garlands 65.00
Clock, Ansonia, Cabinet, Oak Case, 8 Day, Strikes, 14 5/8 In. 70.00
Clock, Ansonia, China, Porcelain Dial, Blue Flowers, 11 X 11 In. 250.00
Clock, Ansonia, Female Figure, Bird On Branch, Strikes, 24 In. 350.00
Clock, Ansonia, Gas Jet 160.00
Clock, Ansonia, Hall, Oak, Brass Trimmings, 7 Ft.10 In. 4000.00
Clock, Ansonia, Iron Case, Brass Dial, Ram's Head Ends, 8 Day, 16 1/2 In. 90.00
Clock, Ansonia, Iron, Parthenon Top, Visible Escapement, Porcelain Dial 85.00
Clock, Ansonia, King, Walnut 295.00
Clock, Ansonia, Long Drop Regulator, Case 320.00
Clock, Ansonia, Mercury Pendulum 295.00
Clock, Ansonia, Royal Bonn China Case, Floral & Gold, 12 In. 275.00

Clock, Ansonia, Steeple, Dated June, 1882, 1/2 Hour Strike 125.00
Clock, Ansonia, Steeple, 30 Hour 175.00
Clock, Ansonia, Suringer, Tin Can Movement 750.00
Clock, Ansonia, Wall, Regulator, Calendar, 32 X 17 1/2 In. 450.00
Clock, Ansonia, 1881, Mantel, Iron, Black, Receded Porcelain Face, 6 Pillars 110.00
Clock, Art Deco, Green Glass, Silver Stylized Birds, Sommer, Germany 100.00
Clock, Art Nouveau, German, Swirls & Lilies, Copper And Brass 45.00
Clock, Atkins & Porter, Banjo, Seth Thomas Works, Reverse Painting On Glass 95.00
Clock, Austrian, Musical, Grande Sonnerie 490.00
Clock, Baby Ben, Alarm, Electric 10.00
Clock, Baird Clock Co., Wall, Figure 8, 30 1/2 X 18 1/2 In. 450.00
Clock, Ball Watch Co., Cleveland, Oak Schoolhouse, Short Drop 200.00
Clock, Banjo, Mahogany, Pendulum Picture Of Washington & Mt.Vernon, C.1925 .... 150.00
Clock, Bayard, Carriage, Brass Case 140.00
Clock, Beacon, Alarm 2.00
Clock, Belgium, Oak Case, Calendar, Porcelain Dial, 7 1/2 Ft. 1400.00
Clock, Berceuse Bleue, Par Garapon, Bronze Nymph, Marble Base, 27 In. 600.00
Clock, Big Ben, Alarm, Brass 6.50
Clock, Birge & Fuller, Empire Case, 8 Day, 32 1/4 X 20 1/4 In. 550.00
Clock, Birge & Gilbert, Empire Case, Reverse Painting, 8 Day, 36 X 20 In. 650.00
Clock, Birge & Peck, Empire Case, Reverse Paintings, 8 Day, 32 1/2 In. 650.00
Clock, Birge & Peck, Triple Decker, 8 Day, 34 X 15 1/2 In. 650.00
Clock, Boston Clock Co., 14 In. Dial, Weight Movement 700.00
Clock, Brass Paper Clip, Made In Germany, 4 1/2 X 3 In. 20.00
Clock, Brass, French, 5 Ivory Dice Inside Glass Dome, Andre Wyler, 4 In. 225.00
Clock, Bronze, Elephant Base 275.00
Clock, Bronze, Ornament Poet Laureate, 8 In. 45.00
Clock, Carriage, Embossed With Figures & Flowers, Porcelain Face, 8 Day 210.00
Clock, Carriage, French Bronze, Alarm 295.00
Clock, Carriage, French, H & H Incised, 3 1/2 X 4 1/2 In. 160.00
Clock, Carriage, French, Hourly Repeater, Drocourt, Pierre & Alfred, 5 In. 550.00
Clock, Carriage, French, Porcelain Fancy Face, Brass Front, 3 1/4 X 5 In. 300.00
Clock, Carriage, French, Quarter Hour Repeater, Brass Case, Ovington Brs., N.Y 850.00
Clock, Carriage, Hourly Repeater, Brass Case, Beveled Glass, Brass Face 600.00
Clock, Case, Tall, Cherry Case .... *Illus* 1900.00
Clock, Case, Tall, Cherry Case, 86 In.High .... *Illus* 1800.00
Clock, Case, Tall, 30 Hour Works, Jacob Hendel, Carlisle, Pa. 3000.00
Clock, Cetts & Stroud, Oak, Wall Regulator, 8 Day, Strikes, German 80.00
Clock, Charles Stratton, Transition, Wooden Works, 33 X 15 1/2 In. 595.00
Clock, Chauncey Boardman, Transition, Shelf, Wooden Works, 34 1/2 In. 525.00
Clock, Chauncey Jerome, Schoolhouse, Ripple Front, 8 Day, Strikes 350.00
Clock, Chauncey Jerome, Shelf, 4 Columns, 30 Hour, 26 X 15 1/2 In. 425.00
Clock, Chauncey Jerome, 1838, Ogee, Brass Works 175.00
Clock, Chelsea, World War II Message Center, U.S.Navy, Melamine Case 95.00
Clock, China, French, Painted Scene, 12 1/2 X 7 In. 275.00
Clock, City Of London, Canadian Clock Co., Hamilton, Gingerbread 95.00
Clock, Columbus, C.1892, Wooden Works, 14 X 6 In. 350.00
Clock, Continental, Baroque, Oak, Long Case, Brass Dial, Carved, 7 Ft. 475.00
Clock, Cosmos, Wall, Beveled Glass In Lower 1/2 Door, Time And Strike 110.00
Clock, Daniel Pratt & Sons, Beehive, Mahogany Case, 8 Day, Strikes, 19 In. 140.00
Clock, Daniel Pratt, Weight Banjo 850.00
Clock, Deeme, 1735, Grandfather, Oak Case, Brass Face, 30 Hour 1200.00
Clock, Drocourt, Pierre & Alfred, Carriage, Brass Case, Beveled Glass, 5 In. 650.00
Clock, Dubuc, Paris, C.1805, Mantel, Figure Of Washington, Gilt Bronze, 20 In. 6500.00
Clock, Duverdrey & Bloqul, Carriage, Brass Case, Beveled Glass, 4 1/2 In. 250.00
Clock, E.Butler, Chippendale Style, Tall Case, Round Painted Dial, 1791 .... 1100.00
Clock, E.Howard & Co., Bank, Regulator, 65 X 21 In. 950.00
Clock, E.Howard, C.1850, Keyhole, Model 11, Pendulum Type 800.00
Clock, E.I & Samuel Terry, Conn., C.1824, Shelf, Pillar & Scroll, Mahogany 900.00
Clock, E.Ingraham, C.1870, School, Short Drop 225.00
Clock, E.N.Welch, C.1884, Calendar, Octagonal, Long Drop 325.00
Clock, E.N.Welch, Lucca, Shelf, Walnut Case, Side Windows, Pendulum, 8 Day 425.00
Clock, E.N.Welch, School, Golden Oak, Calendar & Time 450.00
Clock, Elgin, Advertising, Electric, Large 150.00

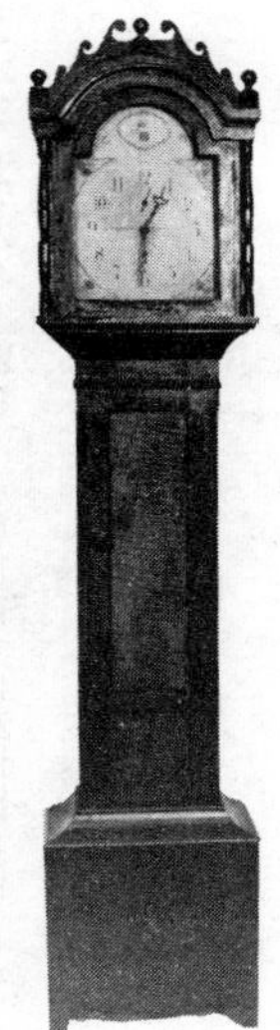

Clock, Case, Tall, Cherry Case

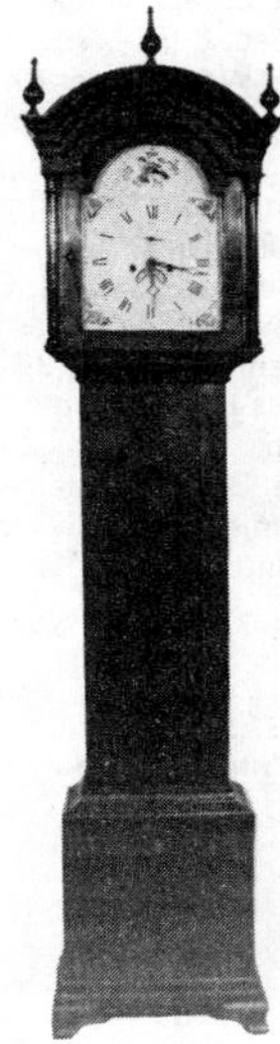

Clock, Case, Tall, Cherry Case, 86 In.High

Clock, Empire, Birge & Peck 375.00
Clock, English, C.1690, Grandfather Movement, Brass Dial, 30 Hour 225.00
Clock, English, C.1750, Grandfather, Mahogany Case 598.00
Clock, English, C.1750, Musical, Corinthian Columns, 3 Weights, 7 Ft. 2400.00
Clock, English, Fusee, Round, 11 In. 165.00
Clock, English, Fussee, Round Gallery 150.00
Clock, English, Grandfather, Wall, Regulator, Strikes 850.00
Clock, English, Station, Single Fusee, Round, 14 1/2 In. 375.00
Clock, English, Station, Single Fusee, Round, 15 In. 375.00
Clock, English, Wall, Regulator, Walnut Case, Grandfather Type Movement 875.00
Clock, F.Pasteur, Amsterdam, White Enamel Dial, Directoire Style, 17 In. 400.00
Clock, Flemish, Oak, Long Case, Mid 18th Century, Carved & Strapwork, 8 Ft. 600.00
Clock, Forestville Mfg.Co., Empire Case, Reverse Painting, 8 Day, 36 1/4 In. 650.00
Clock, Forestville, Triple Decker, Reverse Painting, Weight, 8 Day 325.00
Clock, French Bronze, Dore, Hanging, Tine & Strike, Hanging Pendulum, C 1830 .... 450.00
Clock, French Crystal Regulator, Porcelain Dial, 11 In. 245.00
Clock, French, Alarm & Calendar, Porcelain Face, Beveled Glass, 5 1/4 In. 1950.00
Clock, French, Biscuit, Boy With Puppy, Ormolu Band, 19th Century, 9 In. 125.00
Clock, French, Bombay, Bronze Diana & Cherub, Sevres Type Plaques, 20 In. 1500.00
Clock, French, Brass, Empire, Gold-Plated Front & Columns 425.00
Clock, French, Carriage, Alarm 135.00
Clock, French, Carriage, Brass, Beveled Glass, Porcelain Dial, 5 1/4 In. 225.00
Clock, French, Carriage, Brass, Beveled Glass, Porcelain Face .... 160.00 To 175.00
Clock, French, Carriage, English Bowling Trophy, 1900 .... 375.00
Clock, French, Carriage, Repeater 950.00
Clock, French, Carriage, 11 Jewel 165.00
Clock, French, Cherubs, Bacchus On Top, Ornate 100.00
Clock, French, Mantel, Porcelain Case, Cathedral, Brass, Cupids, 21 In. 965.00
Clock, French, Marble & Bronze, Maidens Reading & Writing On Sides, 27 In. 875.00

Clock, French, Onyx, Bronze Ormolu, 9 X 4 1/2 In. 325.00
Clock, French, Regulator, Brass Case, Beveled Glass, Porcelain Face, 7 3/4 In. 225.00
Clock, French, Regulator, Brass Case, Porcelain Face, 7 3/4 In. 225.00
Clock, French, Shelf, Calendar 850.00
Clock, French, Swinging Doll 550.00
Clock, French, Walnut, Minute Repeater, 22 In. 200.00
Clock, George III, Bracket, Satinwood, Verge Escapement, 16 1/2 In. 425.00
Clock, German, Boudoir, Matte Gold Scalloped, 8 In. 95.00
Clock, German, Bracket, Carved Ebony Case, Westminster Chimes, 30 X 15 In. 2200.00
Clock, German, C.1840, Picture Frame, Free Swinger, Weight Driven, Alarm 100.00
Clock, German, Desk, Brass 7.00
Clock, German, Grandfather, Mahogany, Canterbury & Westminster Tunes, C.1915 .... 750.00
Clock, German, Wall, Beveled Glass In Bottom Half Of Door, 13 X 28 In. 150.00
Clock, Germany, HECO, Black Forest, Cuckoo, Carved Birds, Chain Winder 125.00
Clock, Gilbert Mfg.Co., 1868, Steeple, Rosewood Case, Brass On Dial, 18 In. 130.00
Clock, Gilbert, Banjo, Balance Wheel Escapement, 8 Day, 23 1/2 In. 95.00
Clock, Gilbert, Banjo, Wood Side Arms, Brass Eagle, Country Scene, 36 In. 175.00
Clock, Gilbert, Coca-Cola, Oak Top & Bottom 275.00
Clock, Gilbert, Crystal Regulator, Brass Case, Open Escapement, 9 1/2 In. 175.00
Clock, Gilbert, European Porcelain Case, Chimes Hour, Lavender Iris, 12 In. 175.00
Clock, Gilbert, Gamboling Symbols Carved Into Case 275.00
Clock, Gilbert, Gingerbread, Lion's Head 125.00
Clock, Gilbert, Mantel, Black 40.00
Clock, Gilbert, Mantel, Double Strike 45.00
Clock, Gilbert, Mantel, Lions On Ends 62.50
Clock, Gilbert, Porcelain Case, Lavender, Painted Panel, Brass Dial, 12 In. 145.00

Clock, Hour Glass, 2 In.

Clock, Gilbert, Regulator, Brass Case, Beveled Glass, Porcelain Face, 10 In. 175.00
Clock, Gilbert, Schoolhouse, Calendar, Long Drop, Coronet 75.00
Clock, Gilbert, Shelf, Walnut, Patented Flywheel 100.00
Clock, Gilbert, Store Regulator With Calendar 225.00
Clock, Gingerbread, New Haven Clock, 8 Day Time & Strike, Oak, 20 1/2 In. 120.00
Clock, Gingerbread, Walnut Case 45.00
Clock, Grandfather, Tho. Muddle, Rotherfield, England, 1700 .... 3500.00
Clock, Grandfather, Westminster, Canterbury, Whittington Chimes, Herschede 2300.00
Clock, Gustave Becker, Vienna, Porcelain Face, 2 Weights 495.00
Clock, Henry A.Miller, 1830, Split Column, Wooden Works 195.00
Clock, Holtzer Magneto, Boston, 2 Seth Thomas Movements, Oak Case, 3 1/2 Ft. 1000.00
Clock, Hour Glass, 2 In. .... *Illus* 24.00
Clock, Howard & Davis, No.4, Banjo, Rosewood Case, 32 X 13 1/2 In. 2900.00
Clock, Howard, Banjo 1175.00
Clock, Howard, No.70 Oak, Chelsea Movement 650.00
Clock, Howard, No.71, Walnut Case, Regulator, Dial Marked Ball Standard 4700.00
Clock, Howard, Weight And Pendulum, Marked No. 70 .... 450.00
Clock, Imperial Clock Co., 1903, Battery Wind Electric, 45 1/2 X 18 In. 850.00

Clock, Ingraham, Banjo, Doric, Rosewood Veneer Case, 8 Day 80.00
Clock, Ingraham, C.1880, Store, Oak Case, Calendar, Rectangular 295.00
Clock, Ingraham, Calendar Wall, Oak Case, 8 Day, 36 X 16 In. 285.00
Clock, Ingraham, Gingerbread, Alarm, Strikes, 8 Day 100.00
Clock, Ingraham, Gingerbread, 21 1/2 In. 85.00
Clock, Ingraham, Mantel, Adrian, Pillars & Lion Heads 65.00
Clock, Ingraham, Mantel, Black Wood, 8 Day, Strikes 35.00
Clock, Ingraham, Mantel, Inlaid Mahogany, Camel Back, Greek Key Border 75.00
Clock, Ingraham, Regulator, 11 In.Dial 225.00
Clock, Ingraham, Tambour 40.00
Clock, Ingraham, Treasure Isle, Banjo, Brass Rails, Eagle, Pirates, 39 In. 335.00
Clock, Ingraham, Wall, Double Dial, Lewis Calendar, C.1879 .... 925.00
Clock, Ingraham, Wall, Octagon Short Drop, Oak, Time And Calendar 225.00
Clock, Ingraham, Wall, 11 In. 65.00
Clock, Ingraham, Walnut, Mantel, 8 Day, Time & Strike 160.00
Clock, Ingraham, 30 Hour Mantel 55.00
Clock, International, Alarm & Bell On Top, Cream Color, 6 In. 14.50
Clock, Ithaca, Band, Double Dial, Calendar, Regulator, 38 1/2 X 18 1/2 In. 1900.00
Clock, Ithaca, Calendar, 2 Dials 450.00
Clock, Ithaca, Parlor, Double Dial, Calendar, 20 X 10 In. 3000.00
Clock, Ithaca, Shelf, Library Case, Walnut, Refinished 150.00
Clock, Jansen Clock Co., Nitelight 25.00
Clock, Japanese, School, Scroll 55.00
Clock, Japy Freres, Med D'Honneur, C.1890, Crystal Regulator, Bronze Case 650.00
Clock, Jerome & Co., Gothic Steeple 110.00
Clock, Jerome & Co., New Haven, Rosewood Case, Painting On Door, 30 In. 168.00
Clock, Jerome, Walnut, 30 Hour Mantel 135.00
Clock, Jeunet Freres, C.1830, Cherry Country Style Case, 7 Ft. 11 In. 6500.00
Clock, John Lumsden, Montreal, 1810, Tall Case 2650.00
Clock, John Newson, Split Arch, Tall Case, Painted Dial, 1760 .... 1250.00
Clock, Jung Hans, Clock, Walnut Back & Base, Nickel Tulip Overlays, Alarm 50.00
Clock, Kelly, Springfield Tire, Electric, 6 In. 25.00
Clock, Keno, Alarm 2.00
Clock, L. & F. Andrews, Ogee, Wooden Works 145.00
Clock, Leavenworth, C.1829, Pillar & Scroll, Wooden Works, Brass Finials 1600.00
Clock, Leavenworth, C.1829, Pillar & Scroll, Wooden Works, 30 Hour, 31 In. 1200.00
Clock, Leavenworth, C.1830, Transition, Wooden Works, 30 Hour, 33 In. 495.00
Clock, Leroy Parin, 1900, Bronze & Marble, Ivory Figure Of Huntress 1100.00
Clock, Lincolnshire, Split Arch, Tall Case, C.1770 .... 1250.00
Clock, Longines, Deck Clock, Gimbaled 600.00
Clock, Louis XV, Ormolu & Bronze, Elephant Base, Chinaman Top, 15 In. 800.00
Clock, Louis XVI, Carved Oak, Carved Base, Enamel Dial, 7 Ft. 700.00
Clock, M.Welton, Shelf, 4 Columns, 30 Hour, 26 X 16 In. 390.00
Clock, Macedonia, Shelf, Carved Frame 100.00
Clock, Mantel, Barometer & Clock, Lever Movement, Black Wood, French 475.00
Clock, Mantel, Marble, White With Black, Leopard On Top 125.00
Clock, Mantel, Pressed Oak, 19th Century 148.00
Clock, Matthew Eggerton, Jr., New Brunswick, N.J., C.1810, Mahogany, Tall Case 3000.00
Clock, Mauthe, Delft, Porcelain On Tin, Open Pendulum, 10 X 10 In. 85.00
Clock, Moncrieff, South Shields, Wall Double, Fusee, Striking, 23 X 16 1/2 In. 65.00
Clock, Moncrieff, South Shields, Wall, Striking, 23 X 16 1/2 In. 65.00
Clock, National, Double Dial 450.00
Clock, New Haven Co., Banjo, Federal Style, American Eagle Crest, 42 In. 250.00
Clock, New Haven, Banjo, Bim Ban Strike, 29 In. 125.00
Clock, New Haven, Banjo, Brass Side Rails, Eagle & Ships Pictures, 29 In. 130.00
Clock, New Haven, Banjo, Reversed Painting, Ships, Time & Strike, 37 In. 225.00
Clock, New Haven, Banjo, Strikes, 31 In. 175.00
Clock, New Haven, Banjo, Wood Side Rails, Cows Painting On Glass, 40 In. 315.00
Clock, New Haven, Banjo, Wood Side Rails, War Ships Painting, 40 In. 315.00
Clock, New Haven, Boudoir, Brass 28.00
Clock, New Haven, Bronze, Pedestal, Art Nouveau 22.50
Clock, New Haven, Carriage, Repeater 295.00
Clock, New Haven, Gloriana Regulator, Golden Oak, 30 Day, 42 In. 450.00
Clock, New Haven, Golden Oak, Weight Regulator, Brass Bob, 65 In. 900.00

Clock, New Haven, Kitchen, Walnut, 8 Day & Alarm, Refinished, Original Dial 80.00
Clock, New Haven, Mantel, Mahogany Finish, 8 Day 55.00
Clock, New Haven, Porcelain, White, Blue Floral, 7 1/2 In. 60.00
Clock, New Haven, School, Golden Oak, Short Drop 150.00
Clock, New Haven, School, Rosewood Case, T.S. & C., Refinished, Original Dial 225.00
Clock, New Haven, School, 10 In.Dial 160.00
Clock, New Haven, Shelf, Rosewood Case, 30 Hour 115.00
Clock, New Haven, Split Column, Reverse Painting, Weight, 24 1/2 In. 200.00
Clock, New Haven, Tambour 45.00
Clock, New Haven, Wall, 30 Day, Spring Driven, 48 In. 325.00
Clock, New Haven, 8 Day, Strike & Alarm, Rosewood, 16 1/2 In., Octagon Top 65.00
Clock, Plymouth, Banjo, Brass Side Rails, Jefferson Painting On Case, 29 In. 140.00
Clock, Pomeroy, Shelf, Oak 75.00
Clock, Poole, C.1931, Battery, Pendulum, Domed 150.00
Clock, Preece, 1780, Oak Case, Broken Arch, Painted Face 950.00
Clock, Riley Whiting, Transition, Wooden Works, 29 X 16 1/2 In. 475.00
Clock, Riley Whiting, Winchester, Conn., C.1820, Tall Case, Pine, 7 Ft.1 In. 1200.00
Clock, Royal Bonn, Shelf, Delft 250.00
Clock, Samuel Terry, Transition, Wooden Works, 31 1/2 X 16 1/4 In. 650.00
Clock, School, Oak & Rosewood 195.00
Clock, Self Winding Clock Company, Western Union, Brass Works, Battery 69.95
Clock, Sessions, Banjo, Eagle Finial, George Washington Picture 150.00
Clock, Sessions, Banjo, Spring Driven, Lever Escapement, 22 In. 90.00
Clock, Sessions, Calendar, Regulator 250.00
Clock, Sessions, Kitchen, Oak 110.00
Clock, Sessions, Mantel, Oak Case 45.00
Clock, Sessions, Mantle, Westminster Chimes 85.00
Clock, Sessions, School, Long Drop, 9 1/2 In. Dial .... 140.00 To 155.00
Clock, Sessions, School, 11 In.Dial 155.00
Clock, Sessions, Schoolhouse, 27 In. 155.00
Clock, Sessions, Tambour 40.00
Clock, Sessions, Wall, Round, 8 Day 95.00
Clock, Sessions, Walnut Finish, 8 Day, Strikes 55.00
Clock, Seth Thomas, Adamantine, Banjo, Lions, Porcelain Dial, 8 Day 60.00
Clock, Seth Thomas, American Protection Co., 24 Hour Dial To Open Safe 75.00
Clock, Seth Thomas, Banjo, Steeple, Reverse Painting, 8 Day, 14 1/2 In. 145.00
Clock, Seth Thomas, Beehive, 8 Day, Strikes, 19 In. 135.00
Clock, Seth Thomas, Brass Case, 7 1/4 In. 115.00
Clock, Seth Thomas, C.1895, 24K Gold Over Bronze, Woman & Cherub 475.00
Clock, Seth Thomas, Cathedral Style, Westminster 1/4 Hour Strike 275.00
Clock, Seth Thomas, Column Weight, Plymouth Hollow Paper 150.00
Clock, Seth Thomas, Cottage, Round Movement, 30 Hour 85.00
Clock, Seth Thomas, Crystal Regulator, Beveled Glass, Porcelain Face, 16 In. 300.00
Clock, Seth Thomas, Empire Case, Reverse Paintings, 8 Day, 32 1/4 In. 650.00
Clock, Seth Thomas, Gallery, Square, 15 In. 75.00
Clock, Seth Thomas, Hudson, Gallery, Inlaid Mahogany Case, Square, 18 In. 250.00
Clock, Seth Thomas, Kitchen, Walnut, Gingerbread, Carved 140.00
Clock, Seth Thomas, Kitchen, Wooden Case, Key Wind, Blue On White, Square 25.00
Clock, Seth Thomas, Long Drop, C 1875, World Model, 32 In. 475.00
Clock, Seth Thomas, Mahogany Case, Shell Carvings, Balance Wheel Escapement 95.00
Clock, Seth Thomas, Mantel, Brass Case, Beveled Glass 130.00
Clock, Seth Thomas, Mantel, Pendulum & Weights 130.00
Clock, Seth Thomas, Mantel, Pillars And Lion Heads 65.00
Clock, Seth Thomas, Mantel, 5 Towers, Chimes On Half Hour, 3 1/2 Ft. 1500.00
Clock, Seth Thomas, Mantel, 6 Pillars, Fancy Feet, Lion-Head Holders 60.00
Clock, Seth Thomas, No.2, Regulator, Oak Case, Weight Driven 650.00
Clock, Seth Thomas, Oak Case, Regulator, Ball Watch Co., Cleveland, 12 Sided 895.00
Clock, Seth Thomas, Pillar & Scroll 1050.00
Clock, Seth Thomas, Rosewood Case, Column, Reverse Painting On Glass, 25 In. 225.00
Clock, Seth Thomas, Schoolhouse, Oak Octagon Case, Short Drop 195.00
Clock, Seth Thomas, Schoolhouse, Signet, 15 Day 250.00
Clock, Seth Thomas, Scroll, Ornate Inlaid Mercury Pendulum, Signed, C.1880 .... 425.00
Clock, Seth Thomas, Shelf, Mahogany, Tambour Style, 8 Day, Strikes, 20 In. 35.00
Clock, Seth Thomas, Shelf, Mirror Tablet, C.1885 .... 215.00

Clock, Seth Thomas, Ship 110.00
Clock, Seth Thomas, Walnut Case, Weight Driven 550.00
Clock, Seymour, Williams & Porter-Terry Patent, Transition, Wooden Works 550.00
Clock, Smith, 2-Train Skeleton, Flower Dial, Gilt Gothic Frame 2600.00
Clock, Solomon Parke, Phila., C.1800, Walnut, Inlaid, Tall Case, 5 1/2 Ft. 2300.00
Clock, Standard Electric Time Co., Gallery 25.00
Clock, Stowell, C.1845, Banjo, Weight Driven, 33 X 10 In. 1900.00
Clock, Stromberg Electric Co., Master, Golden Oak, Beveled Glass 500.00
Clock, Strutt, Epicyclic Skeleton 2550.00
Clock, Tall Case, Mahogany, Painted Dial, English, 18th Century 798.00
Clock, Tambour, Ship's Bell Strike, 110 Volt 48.00
Clock, Telechron, Banjo, Electric 200.00
Clock, Terry & Sons, Pillar & Scroll 825.00
Clock, Thos.Parker, Phila., C.1815, Bracket, Mahogany, Inlaid, 15 In. 750.00
Clock, Thwaites & Reed, Bracket, 8 Bell Chimes, Ebonized, 1860 .... 2200.00
Clock, Tiffany, see Tiffany, Clock
Clock, Travel, Elgin, Sterling, Compact Shape, Enamel Top, C.1930 .... 65.00
Clock, Treasure Island, Banjo, 8 Day, Strikes 325.00
Clock, True Time Teller Alarms, Store, Golden Oak, Regulator 225.00
Clock, Vadette, French, Wall 70.00
Clock, Vienna, I Weights 325.00
Clock, Vienna, Spring Driven, Porcelain Face, Time & Strike, 8 Day 200.00
Clock, Vienna, Wall, Oak Case, Weight Driven, 5 Ft. 625.00
Clock, Waltham, Boudoir, Chrome, 8 Day, 7 Jewel, 4 In.Square Face 37.50
Clock, Waltham, Mantel, Gold-Plated Brass, Double Lion Base, 8 Day, 8 In. 300.00
Clock, Waterbury, Carriage, Nickel & Brass, Embossed Front, Alarm, 30 Hour 125.00
Clock, Waterbury, Carriage, Repeater 750.00
Clock, Waterbury, Carriage, 5 In. 125.00
Clock, Waterbury, Double Dial Calendar, No.43 .... 675.00
Clock, Waterbury, Iron Front, 8 Day, Strikes, 13 In. 90.00
Clock, Waterbury, Kitchen, Gingerbread, Strike, 8 Day 100.00
Clock, Waterbury, Kitchen, Oak Case, Calendar, Pendulum, 21 In. 138.00
Clock, Waterbury, May 6, 1859, Shelf, Cast Iron Front, 8 Day 195.00
Clock, Waterbury, Ogee Style, Weight Driven 185.00
Clock, Waterbury, Orange Velvet Case, Beveled Mirrors, 1878, 7 1/2 In. 45.00
Clock, Waterbury, Parlor, No.97, Porcelain, Green, Pink & Yellow Floral, 8 Day 135.00
Clock, Waterbury, Walton, Wall, Regulator 275.00
Clock, Welch, Kitchen, Wall, Oak 175.00
Clock, Welch, Mahogany, 30 Hour 195.00
Clock, Welch, Schoolhouse, Pearl Inlay 155.00
Clock, Westclox, Alarm, Metal 36.00
Clock, Westclox, Bantam 9.00
Clock, Western Clock Mfg.Co., Lasalle, Ill., Art Nouveau, Lady's, Ornate 95.00
Clock, Western Union, Gallery, Self-Winding, Large 59.50
Clock, Will Rogers 50.00
Clock, William Cummens, Mass., C.1800, Banjo, Mahogany, Acorn Finial, 33 In. 2300.00
Clock, Wm.Hargraves, Chippendale, Tall Case, Silver Dial, 1720 .... 3200.00
Clock, Wurttemberg, Tin Case, Gilt & Glass Sides, Second Hand, Alarm, 7 In. 85.00

Cloisonne Enamel was developed during the nineteenth century. A glass enamel was applied between small ribbonlike pieces of metal on a metal base. Most Cloisonne is Chinese or Japanese.

Cloisonne, Ashtray, Black Base, White Flowers, Copper Rim, China, 3 1/2 In. 22.50
Cloisonne, Ashtray, Green 22.50
Cloisonne, Ashtray, Royal Blue, Peach Blossoms, 3 1/2 In. 17.50
Cloisonne, Beads, 50 Floral On Blue 85.00
Cloisonne, Bottle, Snuff, Chinese, Pandas In Bamboo, 3 1/4 In. 145.00
Cloisonne, Bottle, Snuff, Floral 195.00
Cloisonne, Bowl, Blue, Floral, 3 Footed, 1 1/2 X 1 1/4 In. 18.00
Cloisonne, Bowl, Blue, Gold Designs, Teak Stand, 8 X 5 In. 185.00
Cloisonne, Bowl, Chinese, Bronze, White, Light & Dark Blue Designs, 8 In. 200.00
Cloisonne, Bowl, Dragon, Flaming Pearl, Cloud Scrolls On Black, 5 3/4 In. 95.00
Cloisonne, Bowl, Green & Yellow Plum Blossom, 6 X 3 1/4 In. 475.00
Cloisonne, Bowl, Multicolored Rose Pattern, 3 5/8 X 1 7/8 In. 200.00

Cloisonne, Bowl, Tall, Multicolored Rose Pattern, 3 5/8 X 1 7/8 In. 200.00
Cloisonne, Bowl, Tall, White Blossom On Rose, 4 1/4 X 2 1/8 In. 275.00
Cloisonne, Bowl, Yellow Dragon, Black Ground, 4 1/4 In. 30.00
Cloisonne, Bowl, Yellow Plum Blossom On Green, 6 X 3 1/4 In. 475.00
Cloisonne, Box, Black, Fishscale, 5 X 3 1/4 In. 55.00
Cloisonne, Box, Chinese, Hinged, Brass Bound, 4 1/4 X 3 1/4 X 2 In. 58.00
Cloisonne, Box, Chinese, Hinged, Brass Serpents, Blue, Green, & Red, 3 1/2 In. 38.00
Cloisonne, Box, Chinese, Hinged, Jade Mount, Cobalt, Yellow Floral, 4 1/4 In. 65.00
Cloisonne, Box, Chinese, Jade Mount, Cobalt, Yellow Floral, 2 In. 30.00
Cloisonne, Box, Chinese, White, Dragon, Round, 4 In. 125.00
Cloisonne, Box, Cigarette, Carving Inset On Hinged Lid, Floral, 4 Footed 55.00
Cloisonne, Box, Cigarette, Hinged, Apple Blossoms 45.00
Cloisonne, Box, Domed Lid, Black, Cobalt Floral, Applied Scrolls, 4 In. 55.00
Cloisonne, Box, Flowered Design On White, 5 1/2 X 4 In. 125.00
Cloisonne, Box, French, Goldstone, 2 1/2 In. 125.00
Cloisonne, Box, Hinged, 4 Feet, Magenta Flowers, Double T Fret, 4 X 3 In. 60.00
Cloisonne, Box, Japanese, Figural, Black, Greens, & Reds, 2 5/8 In. 110.00
Cloisonne, Box, Red Background, Chest Type, Marked China 35.00
Cloisonne, Box, Round, Azure Blue, Florals, 4 X 3 1/2 In. 35.00
Cloisonne, Box, Round, Dragon On Blue, 1 X 2 1/2 In. 60.00
Cloisonne, Box, Round, Gray Elephant, Scenic Ground, 3 5/8 In.Deep 150.00
Cloisonne, Box, Royal Blue, Spring Scroll Cloisons, Floral, 3 3/4 In. 58.00
Cloisonne, Box, Snuff, Lidded With 4 Snuff Spoons 300.00
Cloisonne, Box, Stamp, China 27.50
Cloisonne, Brush Pot, Japanese, On Porcelain, Floral & Butterfly, Footed 150.00
Cloisonne, Burner, Incense, Cachepot Shape, Geometric Designs, Signed, 5 In. 350.00
Cloisonne, Burner, Incense, Foo Dog Finial, Powder Blue, Demon's Mask, 5 In. 330.00
Cloisonne, Burner, Incense, Foo Dog Temple, Cobalt, Pierced Gilded Top, 9 In. 635.00
Cloisonne, Camels, Chinese, 16 In.High, Pair .... *Illus* 6000.00
Cloisonne, Candleholder, Holds 3 Sizes, Royal Dragon, Flaming Pearl 375.00
Cloisonne, Candlestick, Blue, Mythological Turtle Shape, Pricket, 7 In., Pair 900.00
Cloisonne, Candlestick, Mythological Turtle, Pricket, Pastel, 6 3/4 In., Pair 850.00
Cloisonne, Case, Cigarette, Chinese, White, Blue & Green Floral, Black Edge 175.00
Cloisonne, Case, Cigarette, French, Black & Gold, Scrolls, 4 In. 125.00
Cloisonne, Case, Cigarette, Pocket, Black, Dragons, 3 1/2 X 2 1/2 In. 30.00
Cloisonne, Chalice Cover, Dragon, Black Ground, Multicolor, Chinese, 8 In. 165.00
Cloisonne, Charger, Blue, Multicolor Bird & Floral, C.1850, 12 In. 375.00
Cloisonne, Charger, Floral, Goldstone, 12 In. 295.00
Cloisonne, Charger, Phoenix Bird Center, Scalloped, 14 1/2 In. 475.00
Cloisonne, Coffeepot, Purple, Florals, Butterflies, 7 In. 240.00
Cloisonne, Crane, Teak Base, Chinese, 26 1/2 In.Pair .... *Illus* 5000.00
Cloisonne, Cranes, Teak Bases, 18th Century, 29 1/2 In.High .... *Illus* 6000.00
Cloisonne, Cup & Saucer, Multicolored, Two Sets, C 1820 .... 375.00
Cloisonne, Desk Set, Chinese, Brass, 3 Piece 100.00
Cloisonne, Dish, Candy, Aqua, Floral, Covered, Large 85.00
Cloisonne, Figurine, Bird, Round Urn In Center Of Back, Floral & Scroll, Pair 900.00

Cloisonne, Camels, Chinese, 16 In.High, Pair

Cloisonne, Crane, Teak Base, Chinese, 26 1/2 In.Pair

Cloisonne, Cranes, Teak Bases, 18th Century, 29 1/2 In.High

Cloisonne, Goblet, Chinese, 18th Century, 7 In.High

Cloisonne, Horses, Chinese, 18th Century, 10 1/2 In., Pair

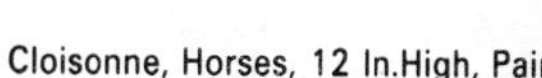

Cloisonne, Horses, 12 In.High, Pair

Cloisonne, Ox Carts, Chinese, 18th Century, 12 In., Pair

(See Page 114)

Cloisonne, Goblet, Chinese, 18th Century, 7 In.High .... *Illus* 260.00
Cloisonne, Group, Rooster & Hen, Blue With Green, Pink, With Gilt, 9 3/4 In. 985.00
Cloisonne, Horses, Chinese, 18th Century, 10 1/2 In., Pair .... *Illus* 6000.00
Cloisonne, Horses, 12 In.High, Pair .... *Illus* 2200.00
Cloisonne, Inkwell 150.00
Cloisonne, Jar, Ginger, Black, Apple Blossoms, 7 In. 125.00
Cloisonne, Jar, Ginger, Blue & Yellow, 11 In. 150.00
Cloisonne, Jar, Ginger, Mustard Yellow, Blossoms, Wirework 110.00
Cloisonne, Jar, Japanese, Goldstone, Butterfly & Floral, Covered, 3 1/2 In. 235.00
Cloisonne, Jar, Rose, Japanese, Green, Turquoise Butterflies, Goldstone, 4 In. 385.00
Cloisonne, Jar, Tea, Cobalt With Dragons, 4 1/2 In. 95.00
Cloisonne, Jardiniere & Stand, Chien Lung, Turquoise, Polychrome Lotus, Pair 4050.00
Cloisonne, Lamp Base, Gold Dust, Paneling, 24 In. 115.00
Cloisonne, Lamp, Table 350.00
Cloisonne, Match Holder, Scholar's Tools, Scrolls, Books, Vases, 2 X 2 In. 60.00
Cloisonne, Match Safe, Carved Mutton Fat Jade Insert 20.00

Cloisonne, Peacock, Turquoise & Coral, Chinese, 21 In., Pair

Cloisonne, Picture Frame, 7 In.

Cloisonne, Matchbox Holder, Blue, Floral	25.00
Cloisonne, Napkin Ring, Blue, China	12.00
Cloisonne, Napkin Ring, Floral	18.00
Cloisonne, Napkin Ring, Flowers	17.00
Cloisonne, Necklace, Jade & Cloisonne, 29 In., Pendant	130.00
Cloisonne, Oxcarts, Chinese, 18th Century, 12 In., Pair ... *Illus*	6000.00
Cloisonne, Peacock, Turquoise & Coral, Chinese, 21 In., Pair ... *Illus*	6000.00
Cloisonne, Picture Frame, 7 In. ... *Illus*	35.00
Cloisonne, Pitcher, Unfinished Type, C.1920, Miniature	24.95
Cloisonne, Plaque, Scenic, 18 In., Pair	900.00
Cloisonne, Plate, Blue, Multicolor Patterns, 4 3/8 In.	37.00
Cloisonne, Plate, Deep Blue Ground, Birds, Flowers, Unmarked	175.00
Cloisonne, Plate, Gray Goose On Blue Ground, 12 In.	325.00
Cloisonne, Plate, Heart Panel On Square, Flowers, Dragonfly, 10 In.	250.00
Cloisonne, Plate, Iridescent Green, Apple Blossoms, Silver Wire, 6 1/2 In.	110.00
Cloisonne, Plate, Japanese, C.1720, 12 In.	485.00
Cloisonne, Plate, On Porcelain, 7 In.	120.00
Cloisonne, Plate, Pottery, Blue, Butterflies & Clouds, Black Edge, 7 In.	165.00
Cloisonne, Plate, Turquoise, Butterfly & Orange & Pink Tiger Lilies, 12 In.	265.00
Cloisonne, Rice Bowl, Red, Flowers, 4 1/2 In.	15.00
Cloisonne, Rose Bowl, Floral, Miniature, 3 In.	175.00
Cloisonne, Salt & Pepper, Blue, Fish Scale Of Copper Wire, Brass Trim	36.00
Cloisonne, Salt & Pepper, Chinese, Gold Wires, White Enamel, Miniature	35.00
Cloisonne, Salt, Individual, Chinese, Tan, Fishscale, Brass, Sterling Spoon	24.00
Cloisonne, Saltshaker, Blue, Floral, Metal Screw Cap, 2 1/4 In.	25.00
Cloisonne, Smoking Set, Blue & Green, Red, Pink, & Yellow Floral, 3 Piece	75.00
Cloisonne, Smoking Set, Chinese, Brick Red, White Lotus & Scrolls, 3 Piece	75.00
Cloisonne, Smoking Set, Chinese, Rust, White Floral, 3 Piece	125.00
Cloisonne, Snuff Bottle, Double Gourd On Seto Pottery, Kidney Diaper	185.00
Cloisonne, Snuff Bottle, Double Leaf	175.00
Cloisonne, Spittoon, 8 In.	485.00
Cloisonne, Spoon, Rice	135.00
Cloisonne, Stirrup, Royal Blue, Multicolor Floral, Pair	185.00
Cloisonne, Teapot, Bird & Butterfly, Blue, Rust, Gold Sprinkles, 4 In.	135.00
Cloisonne, Teapot, Blue Ground, Goldstone, Butterflies, Bird, 4 1/8 In.	175.00
Cloisonne, Teapot, Blue, Green, Brown, Black, & White, 5 X 4 In.	325.00
Cloisonne, Teapot, Butterfly And Flower, 4 In.	145.00
Cloisonne, Teapot, Floral & Butterflies, Foil Backing, 4 1/2 In.	225.00

Cloisonne, Teapot, Goldstone, Flowers, Birds, Miniature, Unusual Handle 155.00
Cloisonne, Teapot, Miniature 95.00
Cloisonne, Teapot, Royal Dragon, Yellow With Background Of Yellow, Small 250.00
Cloisonne, Toothpick, Blue Floral 17.00
Cloisonne, Toothpick, Blue, Green, Goldstone, Flowers, 2 In. 48.00
Cloisonne, Toothpick, Chinese, C.1920, 2 In. 22.50
Cloisonne, Tray, Chinese, Black, White Floral, Green Back, 3 1/2 In. 22.50
Cloisonne, Urn, Chinese, Bronze, 13 1/2 In.High, Pair ..... *Illus* 3800.00
Cloisonne, Urn, Covered, Rust, Flowers, Bluebirds, Made In China, 7 In. 85.00
Cloisonne, Urn, Phoenix Bird Stem, Powder Blue, Pastels, 9 1/2 In., Pair 1000.00
Cloisonne, Vase, Barkware, Lacquer, 6 X 5 1/2 In. 195.00
Cloisonne, Vase, Bird And Bamboo, Large Roses, Pair, 6 In. 245.00
Cloisonne, Vase, Black Monochrome, Pink Peonies, Daffodils & Mums, 7 In. 110.00
Cloisonne, Vase, Black, Blue, Green, & White Floral, 4 1/4 In. 55.00
Cloisonne, Vase, Black, Multicolor Floral & Scrolls, C.1840, 5 In., Pair 325.00
Cloisonne, Vase, Black, White & Gray Flying Herons, C.1850, 7 1/4 In. 185.00
Cloisonne, Vase, Blue Panels, Flowers, Butterflies, 4 In. 65.00
Cloisonne, Vase, Blue, Cherry Blossoms In Garden Urn, Geometrics, 7 1/4 In. 75.00
Cloisonne, Vase, Blue, White & Lavender Wisteria, Silver Rim, 14 In. 300.00
Cloisonne, Vase, Bud, Japanese, Blue & Silver Ground, Raised Fishes, 9 3/4 In. 195.00
Cloisonne, Vase, Butterflies, Goldstone, Multicolored, 6 In. 90.00
Cloisonne, Vase, Chinese, Black, White Design, On Copper, 5 1/2 In. 45.00
Cloisonne, Vase, Chinese, Maroon, Pink & White Floral, Green Leaves, 4 In. 35.00
Cloisonne, Vase, Chinese, Rust, Turquoise & Green Landscape, 9 In. 195.00
Cloisonne, Vase, Cobalt, Apple Blossoms, 8 In. 80.00
Cloisonne, Vase, Dragons, Green Ground, Gold Speckled, 5 1/8 In. 125.00
Cloisonne, Vase, Fishscale, Turquoise, Dragon On Foil, 6 1/4 In. 78.00
Cloisonne, Vase, Flying Phoenix, Flowers, Insects, Butterfiles, 6 In., Pair 135.00
Cloisonne, Vase, Globular, Multicolored Rose Pattern, 3 1/2 In. 175.00
Cloisonne, Vase, Inverted Cathedral Panels, Flowers, Butterflies, 7 In. 75.00
Cloisonne, Vase, Japanese, Ando, Yellow, Bird On Prunus Branch, 4 In. 135.00
Cloisonne, Vase, Japanese, Butterflies, 5 In. 62.00
Cloisonne, Vase, Japanese, C.1880, Scale Ground, Floral, Silver Mounted, 7 In. 165.00
Cloisonne, Vase, Japanese, Cobalt, Multicolor Iris & Butterflies, 5 1/2 In. 225.00
Cloisonne, Vase, Japanese, Fishscale, Dragon & Waves, Wire On Foil, 6 In. 150.00
Cloisonne, Vase, Japanese, Gray, Cranes, Silver Wire, 6 In., Pair 345.00
Cloisonne, Vase, Japanese, On Silver, Light Blue, White Floral, 4 In. 85.00
Cloisonne, Vase, Japanese, Silver Mounted, Signed, Floral Design, 6 1/2 In. 165.00
Cloisonne, Vase, Kyoto, Mirror Black, Prunus, Bird, Silver Wires, 4 3/4 In. 140.00
Cloisonne, Vase, Lavender, Blue Leaves & Blackberries, 6 1/4 In. 235.00
Cloisonne, Vase, Lavender, Fishscale, 5 3/4 In. 180.00
Cloisonne, Vase, Light Blue, Fishscale, 3 1/2 In. 95.00
Cloisonne, Vase, Moss Green, Butterflies & Floral, C.1835, 12 1/4 In., Pair 428.00
Cloisonne, Vase, Mottled Yellow, Blossom Spray, Chrome, 3 1/2 In. 25.00
Cloisonne, Vase, Multicolors, Hexagonal, 7 In. 220.00
Cloisonne, Vase, On Stand, Large, 29 In.High ..... *Illus* 2750.00

Cloisonne, Urn, Chinese, Bronze, 13 1/2 In.High, Pair

Cloisonne, Vase, Palace Size, 36 In. 1750.00
Cloisonne, Vase, Peach Dragon, Goldstone Stars, Orange Flames, 7 In. 185.00
Cloisonne, Vase, Phoenix Bird, Medallions, White, Goldstone, 7 In .... 95.00 To 185.00
Cloisonne, Vase, Robin's Egg Blue, Lilies, Leaves, Silver Base, Japan, 8 In. 82.50
Cloisonne, Vase, Rust Red, Hibiscus, Mums, & Butterfly, 10 In. 225.00
Cloisonne, Vase, Shaded Pigeon's Blood, Pink Rose, Foil, Silver Rim, 4 In. 85.00
Cloisonne, Vase, Silver, Blood Red, Girds & Bamboo, 9 In. 145.00
Cloisonne, Vase, Sterling Silver, Blue Green, Fishscale, Iris, 3 1/4 In. 100.00
Cloisonne, Vase, Tall, Globular Shape, Rose Pattern, 3 1/2 In. 185.00
Cloisonne, Vase, White To Orchid, Floral, Foil Type, 2 1/2 In. 135.00
Cloisonne, Vase, Yellow Royal Dragon, Black Ground, 7 In., Pair 265.00
Cloisonne, Vase, 48 1/2 In.High, Pair .... *Illus* 7250.00
Cloisonne, Wine Pot, Standing Bird Shape, Blue, Gold Gilding, 6 1/2 In. 575.00

Clothing, see Textile

Cluthra glass is a two-layered glass with small air pockets that form white spots. The Steuben Glass Works of Corning, New York, made it after 1903. Kimball Glass Company of Vineland, New Jersey, made Cluthra from about 1925.

Cluthra, see also Steuben

Cluthra, Rose Bowl, Purple, White Ovals, Clear Bubbles, 4 1/2 In. 165.00

Cloisonne, Vase, On Stand, Large, 29 In.High

(See Page 115)

Cloisonne, Vase, 48 1/2 In.High, Pair

Coalport ware has been made by the Coalport Porcelain Works of England from 1795 to the present time.

Coalport, see also Indian Tree

Coalport, Box, Jeweled, Round, Pink, Gold, 4 X 2 1/2 In. 225.00
Coalport, Cottage 55.00
Coalport, Cup & Saucer, Demitasse, Completely Jeweled 75.00
Coalport, Cup & Saucer, Demitasse, Gold, Blue Floral, Cloverleaf Shape, 1891 .... 125.00
Coalport, Cup & Saucer, Demitasse, Gold, Blue Floral, Scalloped, 1891 .... 125.00
Coalport, Cup & Saucer, Pemrose Pattern 12.50
Coalport, Plate, Dark Blue Country Scene, 10 1/2 In. 21.00
Coalport, Plate, Dewey Commemorative, Portrait & Ship Names 52.00
Coalport, Plate, Dinner, Brookdale 20.50
Coalport, Plate, Engraved Gold Edge, Tiffany & Co., N.Y., 5 1/2 In. 7.50
Coalport, Plate, View Of Bonneville Savoy, Light Blue, Gold, 8 7/8 In. 150.00
Coalport, Vase, Blue De Roi, Reserves, Gold Handles, C.1894, 6 In., Pair 178.00
Coalport, Vase, Oyster Color, Shell Shape, 8 In., Pair 75.00
Coalport, Vase, Oyster Color, Shell Shape, 8 X 4 1/2 In., Pair 85.00

Cobalt blue glass was made using oxide of cobalt. The characteristic bright dark blue identifies it for the collector. Most cobalt glass found today was made after the Civil War.

Cobalt Blue Glass, Ashtray, Hat 12.00
Cobalt Blue Glass, Compote, Silver Designs, Slender Footed Stem, 6 In. 35.00
Cobalt Blue Glass, Cruet, Optic Swirl In Glass, Crystal Applied Handle 70.00
Cobalt Blue Glass, Match Holder, Jumbo 12.00
Cobalt Blue Glass, Mug, Thumbprint, Heavy 25.00
Cobalt Blue Glass, Slipper 6.00
Cobalt Blue, see also Shirley Temple
Cobalt Blue, Bottle, Cologne, Intaglio Cut Flowers To Clear, 6 1/2 In. 60.00
Cobalt Blue, Bottle, Cordial, Cut To Clear, Matching Stopper, Teardrop 95.00
Cobalt Blue, Bottle, Eyecup Stopper, Square, 5 In. 9.95
Cobalt Blue, Bottle, Figural, Violin, Hinging Holder, 12 1/2 In. 10.00
Cobalt Blue, Bottle, Powder, Sterling Silver Filigree, 2 1/2 In. 25.00
Cobalt Blue, Bowl, Footed, Cased In White, Flared Rim, Applied Foot 35.00
Cobalt Blue, Box, Enamel Floral On Hinged Lid, Brass Feet & Collar, 4 In. 125.00
Cobalt Blue, Box, Floral On Hinged Lid, Brass Mounted, 4 X 3 3/8 In. 85.00
Cobalt Blue, Box, Frosted Intaglio Lid, Grecian Lady, Cupid, & Doves, 6 In. 25.00
Cobalt Blue, Box, Hinged, White Enamel Floral, Gold Trim, Round, 4 1/4 In. 88.00
Cobalt Blue, Box, Patch, Hinged, Enamel Daisies, Gold Leaves, Round, 2 In. 55.00
Cobalt Blue, Candleholder, Stars & Stripes, Brooklyn, N.Y., 2 In. 25.00
Cobalt Blue, Candlestick, Iridescent, Blue Stretch, 4 In., Pair 60.00
Cobalt Blue, Condiment Set, Nickel Silver Frame, 3 Piece 45.00
Cobalt Blue, Cruet, Swirl 50.00
Cobalt Blue, Cup, Punch, Broken Column 75.00
Cobalt Blue, Dresser Set, Gold Enameled, Victorian, 4 Piece 150.00
Cobalt Blue, Eyecup, Royal, Original Box 9.00
Cobalt Blue, Eyecup, Wyeth, Embossed 7.00
Cobalt Blue, Finger Bowl, Ground Pontil 90.00
Cobalt Blue, Jar, Candy, Silver Plate Lid & Holder 47.50
Cobalt Blue, Jar, Mustard, Metal Lid 15.00
Cobalt Blue, Knife Rest, Bar, Beveled Edges, 3 1/8 In. 12.50
Cobalt Blue, Lamp Base, Oil, Coolidge Drape 75.00
Cobalt Blue, Match Holder, Hat Shape 22.00
Cobalt Blue, Pitcher, Applied Clear Ribbed Handle, 7 1/2 In. 15.00
Cobalt Blue, Pitcher, Tankard, B.P.O.E., Clock & Elk, 12 In. 135.00
Cobalt Blue, Salt & Pepper, St John's Church And Washington's Headquarters 25.00
Cobalt Blue, Salt, F.B.Rogers Silver Co. Holder & Spoon, Set Of 4 .... 75.00
Cobalt Blue, Shot Glass, Nine Panels, 2 In. 85.00
Cobalt Blue, Toothpick, High Hat 15.00
Cobalt Blue, Toothpick, Silver Enamel 15.00
Cobalt Blue, Toothpick, St.Clair, 1971 .... 3.50
Cobalt Blue, Toothpick, Tiny Optic 22.00
Cobalt Blue, Tray, Diana The Huntress, 12 X 9 In. 15.00
Cobalt Blue, Tumbler, 8 Panels, 3 1/2 In. 40.00
Cobalt Blue, Urn, Double Handles, Raised Gold Enamel, 6 In. 85.00
Cobalt Blue, Vase, Hand Holding Vase, C.1940, 9 In. 6.00
Cobalt Blue, Vase, Ruffled Edge, 4 1/4 In., Pair 7.50
Cobalt Blue, Whiskey Taster, 6 Panels, 2 7/8 In. 35.00
Cobalt Blue, Whiskey Taster, 8 Panels, 2 1/4 In. 30.00

Coca-Cola advertising items have become a special field for collectors.

Coca-Cola, Ashtray, 1963, Metal 2.00
Coca-Cola, Blotter, Ink, 1956, Friendliest Drink On Earth 3.75
Coca-Cola, Blotter, 1942 .... 3.00 To 5.00
Coca-Cola, Book Mark, Celluloid, 1899 .... 75.00
Coca-Cola, Bookmark, Victorian Lady 7.00
Coca-Cola, Bottle Holder, 1933, For 6 Bottles 35.00
Coca-Cola, Bottle Protector, 1932, Envelope Type, No Drip, Paper 5.00
Coca-Cola, Bottle, A.C.L., 3 In. .... .50
Coca-Cola, Bottle, Best By A Damsite 35.00
Coca-Cola, Bottle, Dec.25, 1923, 20 In. 100.00

Coca-Cola, Bottle, Donald Duck, Painted, 7 Ozs. 3.50
Coca-Cola, Bottle, Israel Exposition, 1975, 6 1/2 Ozs. 6.00
Coca-Cola, Bottle, Verner Springs 20.00
Coca-Cola, Bottle, Water, 1920s 60.00
Coca-Cola, Bottle, 1923, Display, 20 In. 95.00
Coca-Cola, Box, C.1923, Wooden, 13 X 10 X 8 In. 15.00
Coca-Cola, Calendar, 1917, Girl With Parasol 50.00
Coca-Cola, Calendar, 1918, Distributor's 60.00
Coca-Cola, Calendar, 1923, Girl Wearing Stole 135.00
Coca-Cola, Calendar, 1931, Dog & Boy Fishing, No Months, Framed 65.00
Coca-Cola, Calendar, 1937, Dog & Boy With Fishing Rod Running 35.00
Coca-Cola, Calendar, 1938, Girl With Venetian Blind Background 150.00
Coca-Cola, Calendar, 1941 45.00
Coca-Cola, Calendar, 1943 20.00
Coca-Cola, Calendar, 1949 20.00
Coca-Cola, Calendar, 1951 35.00
Coca-Cola, Calendar, 1956 14.00
Coca-Cola, Calendar, 1961 10.00
Coca-Cola, Calendar, 1965 14.00
Coca-Cola, Calendar, 1966 10.00
Coca-Cola, Calendar, 1968 10.00
Coca-Cola, Cards, 1940, Plane Spotter 17.50
Coca-Cola, Carrier, Bottle, C.1930, Cardboard 20.00
Coca-Cola, Carrier, 1933, Cardboard, 6 Pack 20.00
Coca-Cola, Carton, 1923, Wooden, 6 Pack 8.00
Coca-Cola, Carton, 1923, Wooden, 6-Pack 15.00
Coca-Cola, Cigarette Lighter, 1950 2.50
Coca-Cola, Clock, Drink Coca-Cola, Electric, Red & Brown, 18 In. 15.00
Coca-Cola, Clock, Square, 1950 35.00
Coca-Cola, Clock, Store Regulator, Gilbert 275.00
Coca-Cola, Clock, 1915 350.00
Coca-Cola, Coupon, 1924, Worth 1/4 Cent, Goldsboro, N.C., 4 1/2 In. 3.00
Coca-Cola, Coupon, 1924, Worth 1/4 Cent, Harrisburg, Pa., 4 1/2 In. 3.00
Coca-Cola, Cuff Links, 1923 50.00
Coca-Cola, Dart Board, 1935 25.00
Coca-Cola, Declaration Of Independence, 1942, 32 X 26 In. 8.00
Coca-Cola, Dish, Pretzel, 1935 30.00
Coca-Cola, Dispenser, Fountain, Hand Pump, Marked On Handle 12.50
Coca-Cola, Door Pull, Bottle Shape 45.00
Coca-Cola, Flashlight, C.1950, Bottle Shape, 3 1/2 In. 2.50
Coca-Cola, Gun, 1954 3.00
Coca-Cola, Ice Pick & Bottle Opener, 1936, Bristol, Tenn. 3.50
Coca-Cola, Ice Pick, Wood Handle, Marked Drink Coca-Cola 10.00
Coca-Cola, Knife 50.00
Coca-Cola, Knife, Child's, 1960 2.50
Coca-Cola, Knife, Fork, & Spoon, C.1920, Silver 75.00
Coca-Cola, Knife, 1908, Metal, Embossed Bottle 55.00
Coca-Cola, Knife, 1933, Chicago World's Fair 2.00
Coca-Cola, Knife, 2-Blade 2.25
Coca-Cola, Lighter, Cigarette, C.1950, Bottle Shape 2.50
Coca-Cola, Lighter, Cigarette, 1950, Bottle Shape 2.50
Coca-Cola, Machine, C.1950, Plastic, Top Opens, 2 3/4 In. 15.00
Coca-Cola, Map, U.S., 1940, Census On Back, 36 X 29 In. 20.00
Coca-Cola, Marker, Street, 1933, Brass 55.00
Coca-Cola, Mirror, Pocket, 5 Cents, Girl With Train, Fan, Vase Of Roses, 3 In. 25.00
Coca-Cola, Mirror, Pocket, 5 Cents, Girls Head With Roses, 2 1/4 In. 12.00
Coca-Cola, Mirror, Pocket, 5 Cents, Oval, Girl In Bonnet, 2 3/4 In. 15.00
Coca-Cola, Napkin, C.1910, Rice Paper 10.00
Coca-Cola, Opener, Bottle, 1925, Cast Iron, Wall Type 6.00
Coca-Cola, Opener, Bottle, 1925, Wall Mounted 10.00
Coca-Cola, Pad, Bridge Score, C.1930, Royal Bottling Works, Ontario 10.00
Coca-Cola, Paperweight, C.1950, Coke Is Coca-Cola, Red 25.00
Coca-Cola, Paperweight, 1960 7.00
Coca-Cola, Plaque, Push & Pull Door Plaques 18.00

Mine lamp, iron, first half of 19th century.

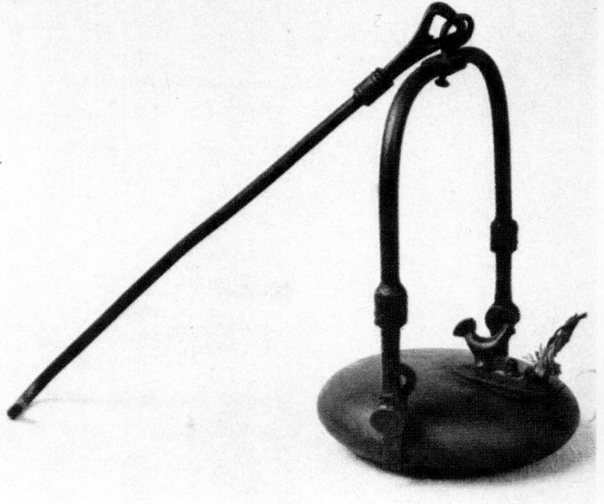

Pierced lanterns, tin, c. 1800.

Burning fluid lamps, pewter, first half of 19th century.

Candle molds, tin, 19th century.

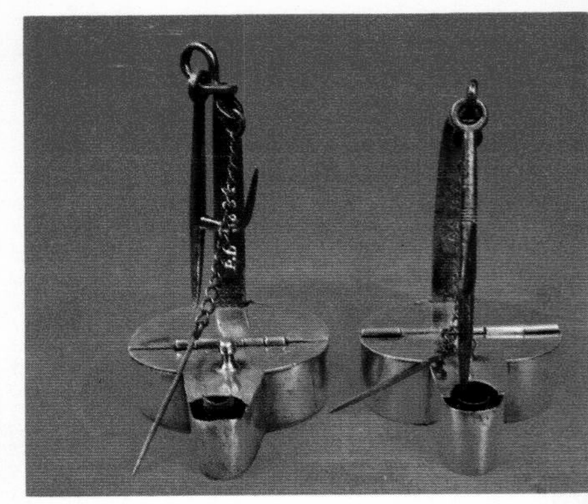

Peter Derr "betty" lamps, wrought iron and brass.

John Smith "betty" lamps, wrought iron.

Lard oil lamp, tin, c. 1850s.

Printed taufschein, Catharine Kobee, 1790, 13¼ in. × 16¼ in.

Diesen beyden Ehegatten,
als und seiner ehelichen Hausfrau eine gebohrne ist ein zur Welt gebohren, Namens
im Jahr unsers HErrn den Tag
um Uhr Morgens im Zeichen des Getauft von Pfarrer
den Tag Taufzeugen war
Gebohren in
Taunschip, County, in America, in dem Staate

Schuller, 1787, 7⅝ in. × 13 in.

Henrich, ist von Christ-
lich, und Ehrlichen, der evangelisch
Lutherischen Religion, zugethanen Eltern in Penn-
silvanien Gebohren, in Heidelberg Taunschip, in Nort-
hampton Caunty, im Jahr unsers herrn. 1804 den 17ten
September, und Getaufft worden von herrn Pfarrn
Fridrich Oberhaus, den 1ten Jenner 1805. Seine
Eltern waren, Jacob Geiger, und seine Ehfrau
Apollonia, eine Gebohrne Bärin,
die erbetene Taufzeugen damals waren,
die erbetene Henrich Hofmann, und die
Maria Rezin, beide ledig.

Hand-painted tauf-
schein, 1805, 8 in. × 13 in.

Pewter teapot, "Love," late 18th century.

Pewter pint and quart measure, Philadelphia mark "CP."

Pint measure, pewter, Philadelphia mark "CP."

Two Lehnware saffrons.

Glass tumbler, Europe, c. 1780, 4 in. high, 3 in. top diameter.

Vases, c. 1810 (Amelung?), engraved, 8¾ in. high.

Stemmed goblet, c. 1790 (English?), 6 in. high.

Amethyst glass duck, Atterbury, Pittsburgh, 11 in. long.

Stiegel-type glass, sugar, creamer.

Beehive basket, rye straw collection, 19th century, 13 in. high.

Doll house, c. 1900, 51 in. wide, 58 in. high.

Noah's Ark, c. 1900, 3 in. × 10 in. overall.

Belter armchair, rosewood, 1855–1865.

Blown glass biscuit jar, cased, 3 layers, cut knob, late 19th century, American, 8½ in. high, approx. 5 in. diameter.

Silver tea–coffee set, Harvey Lewis, 1811–1826, Philadelphia.

Day bed, Pa., c. 1700, 23 in. × 77 in.

Doll, "Anna," china bisque head & hands, kid body, 1893, 16 in. long.

Doll, "Clara," porcelain head, knit body, c. 1892, 23 in. long.

Earthenware, English Willow pattern, soft paste plate.

Carnival glass plate.

Doll, papier-mâché head, wood limbs, late 19th century, 23½ in. long.

Papier-mâché doll, rag body, c. 1890, 22 in. long.

Interior, general store, c. 1900.

Glass dome, white marble cross, braided hair flowers, wax fruit, mounted birds, U.S., 1900–1910, 20 in. high, 12 in. bottom diameter.

Horse, child's toy, 32 in. high, 39 in. long.

Gothic side chair, walnut, Gothic design gros point, 1840–1850, U.S.

Girandole mirror, U.S., 1790–1800, 28½ in. high.

Coca-Cola, Plate, China, 1920s 75.00
Coca-Cola, Ruler, 1937, Wooden 4.50
Coca-Cola, Ruler, 1940 .... 10.00
Coca-Cola, Shade, Celluloid 32.00
Coca-Cola, Sign, Betty, Tin 1200.00
Coca-Cola, Sign, C.1930, Cooler With Arrow Shape, Tin, 3 Ft. 85.00
Coca-Cola, Sign, C.1930, Girl Holding Glass, Cardboard, 30 X 18 In. 65.00
Coca-Cola, Sign, C.1940, Gals & Guy In Pool, Cardboard, Framed, 36 In. 45.00
Coca-Cola, Sign, Cardboard, Soda Jerk, Dated 1931 .... 25.00
Coca-Cola, Sign, School Policeman, 5 Ft. On Iron Coke Stand 200.00
Coca-Cola, Sign, Tin, Copyright Date 1926, 19 X 27 In. 85.00
Coca-Cola, Sign, White On Red, Dated 1938, Tin 22.00
Coca-Cola, Sign, 1923, Bottle Picture, Tin, 34 X 11 In. 50.00
Coca-Cola, Sign, 1923, Drink Coca-Cola, Bottle, Tin, 34 1/2 X 11 1/2 In. 65.00
Coca-Cola, Sign, 1934, Christmas Bottle, 36 X 12 In. 65.00
Coca-Cola, Sign, 1955, Santa Claus, Cardboard, Easel Back, 19 In. 10.00
Coca-Cola, Sign, 1957, M.G. Auto Picture, Cardboard, 24 X 9 In. 10.00
Coca-Cola, Sign, 1957, Volvo Picture, Cardboard, 24 X 9 In. 10.00
Coca-Cola, Sign, 1960, 4 X 3 Ft. 15.00
Coca-Cola, Sign, 5-Piece Fountain Backbar Display, 1932, N.M. 125.00
Coca-Cola, Spoon, 1957, Gold Plated, Seasons Greetings, Piqua, Oh. 5.00
Coca-Cola, Thermometer, 1939 .... 18.00
Coca-Cola, Thimble, C.1940, Plastic, Yellow With Red 1.00
Coca-Cola, Thimble, C.1940, Yellow, "Drink Coca-Cola," Plastic 1.00
Coca-Cola, Tray, Tip, 1904, Hilda Clark 245.00
Coca-Cola, Tray, Tip, 1904, St.Louis Fair, Oval .... 145.00 To 185.00
Coca-Cola, Tray, Tip, 1905, Juanita, Round, 4 In. 145.00
Coca-Cola, Tray, Tip, 1909, Coca-Cola Girl, Oval, 6 1/8 In. 100.00
Coca-Cola, Tray, Tip, 1912 .... 55.00
Coca-Cola, Tray, Tip, 1912, Betty 85.00
Coca-Cola, Tray, Tip, 1914, Betty, Oval .... 65.00 To 75.00
Coca-Cola, Tray, Tip, 1915 .... 45.00
Coca-Cola, Tray, Tip, 1917, Elaine, Oval, 6 1/8 X 4 3/8 In. .... 45.00 To 60.00
Coca-Cola, Tray, Tip, 1920, Garden Girl, Oval, 6 3/8 X 4 1/2 In. .... 85.00 To 110.00
Coca-Cola, Tray, 1905, Western Bottling Co. 90.00
Coca-Cola, Tray, 1917, Elaine 48.00
Coca-Cola, Tray, 1920, Garden Girl, Large Oval 30.00
Coca-Cola, Tray, 1921, Summer Girl .... 45.00 To 145.00
Coca-Cola, Tray, 1923, Flapper Girl .... 60.00 To 75.00
Coca-Cola, Tray, 1925, Girl At Party 60.00
Coca-Cola, Tray, 1925, Girl With Fox Fur 70.00
Coca-Cola, Tray, 1930, Bathing Beauty 95.00
Coca-Cola, Tray, 1931, Farm Boy With Dog 95.00
Coca-Cola, Tray, 1933, Frances Dee 17.50
Coca-Cola, Tray, 1934, Weissmuller 150.00
Coca-Cola, Tray, 1936, Hostess .... 50.00 To 75.00
Coca-Cola, Tray, 1938, Girl In The Afternoon 35.00
Coca-Cola, Tray, 1939, Springboard Girl .... 35.00 To 40.00
Coca-Cola, Tray, 1940, Sailor Girl .... 20.00 To 35.00
Coca-Cola, Tray, 1941, Girl Ice Skater .... 30.00 To 35.00
Coca-Cola, Tray, 1942, Two Girls At Car .... 30.00 To 38.00
Coca-Cola, Tray, 1971, 1909 Reproduction, 14 3/4 X 10 3/4 In. 5.00
Coca-Cola, Tray, 1973, Santa Claus, 15 X 11 In. 18.50
Coca-Cola, Tray, 1976, Olympic Games, 15 X 11 In. 9.50
Coca-Cola, Truck, C.1920, Metal, 2 Bottles 89.00
Coca-Cola, Truck, Metal, Five Bottles On Each Side, Toy 125.00
Coca-Cola, Truck, 1929 .... 95.00
Coca-Cola, Truck, 1945 .... 55.00
Coca-Cola, Truck, 1949, Boxed 60.00
Coca-Cola, Truck, 1950, Boxed 50.00
Coca-Cola, Wallet, 4 X 8 1/2 In. 60.00
Coca-Cola, Watch Fob, 1915-1916, Free Bottle 30.00
Coco-Cola, Knife, Round, 2 Bladed 2.50
Coffee Grinder, Iron, Wall Type 27.50

Coffee grinders, home size, were first made about 1894. They lost favor by the 1930s.

Coffee Grinder, Arcade, Cast Iron, Wall 20.00
Coffee Grinder, Arcade, Crystal, No.1, Glass Jar, Wall 35.00
Coffee Grinder, Arcade, Glass & Iron Wall Model 27.00
Coffee Grinder, Arcade, Wall Type 19.50
Coffee Grinder, Chas. Parker Co., Meriden, Conn., Red Paint, 2 Wheels, 12 In. 165.00
Coffee Grinder, China, Wall Hanging, Windmill Design 80.00
Coffee Grinder, China, White And Red 25.00
Coffee Grinder, Crystal, Glass Jar, Tin Top, Spring Holder, Wall 40.00
Coffee Grinder, Elgin, National, 5 1/2 Ft. 475.00
Coffee Grinder, Elma, Lap Type, Tin, Wooden Bowl 20.00
Coffee Grinder, Enterprise Manufacturing Co., Phila., Cast Iron, 5 Ft. 850.00
Coffee Grinder, Enterprise, Black Finish, 9 In. Wheels 80.00
Coffee Grinder, Imperial Mill, No.157, Arcade Mfg., Patent 1889, Dovetailed 65.00
Coffee Grinder, Landers Frary & Clark, New Britain 80.00
Coffee Grinder, Lap, Blue Paint 17.00
Coffee Grinder, Parker & White, Breadboard End, 9 X 6 In. 36.00
Coffee Grinder, Parker's Rapid Grinding 42.50
Coffee Grinder, Patent 1890, Iron Grinder & Cup, Tin Canister, Wall Type 65.00
Coffee Grinder, Queen, 3 In. 42.00
Coffee Grinder, Regal, Tin, Wall 30.00
Coffee Grinder, Swift Mill, Lane Bros., Poughkeepsie, N.Y., C.1870 ..... 850.00
Coffee Grinder, Tin & Iron, Lap 20.00
Coffee Grinder, Tin, Red Paint 35.00
Coffee Grinder, Wall, Cast Metal, S-Shaped Handle, Wooden Grip 30.00
Coffee Grinder, Wood & Iron, 1 Drawer, 13 X 7 1/2 In. 75.00
Coffee Grinder, 2-Wheel, Counter Model, Patented 1873, Flowers 250.00

Collector plates are any of the plates produced in limited editions. The most famous were made by the Bing & Grondahl Factory of Denmark, after 1895, and the Royal Copenhagen Factory, after 1908.

Collector, Plate, see also Buffalo Pottery, Plate, Christmas

Collector, Bell, Bing & Grondahl, Christmas, 1974, 1st Issue ..... 110.00 To 125.00
Collector, Bell, Noritake, Christmas, 1974 ..... 10.00
Collector, Calendar, Wedgwood, 1971 ..... 15.00
Collector, Dish, Condiment, Royal Bayreuth, Sunbonnet Babies, Sunday, 1974 ..... 10.00
Collector, Egg, Noritake, Easter, 1975, Ducks 15.00
Collector, Egg, Royal Bayreuth, Easter, 1974 ..... 19.00
Collector, Egg, Royal Bayreuth, Easter, 1975 ..... 15.00 To 17.50
Collector, Music Box, Hummel, Christmas, 1974 ..... 9.95
Collector, Ornament, Haviland, 1972 ..... 5.00
Collector, Ornament, Haviland, 1973 ..... 5.00
Collector, Paperweight, Gentile, Mother's Day, 1971, Spinning Woman 12.00
Collector, Plate, Bing & Grondahl, Christmas, 1895 ..... 1900.00 To 3000.00
Collector, Plate, Bing & Grondahl, Christmas, 1896 ..... 1185.00 To 1950.00
Collector, Plate, Bing & Grondahl, Christmas, 1897 ..... 600.00 To 1050.00
Collector, Plate, Bing & Grondahl, Christmas, 1898 ..... 300.00 To 750.00
Collector, Plate, Bing & Grondahl, Christmas, 1899 ..... 400.00 To 1050.00
Collector, Plate, Bing & Grondahl, Christmas, 1900 ..... 425.00 To 750.00
Collector, Plate, Bing & Grondahl, Christmas, 1901 ..... 200.00 To 327.00
Collector, Plate, Bing & Grondahl, Christmas, 1902 ..... 147.00 To 360.00
Collector, Plate, Bing & Grondahl, Christmas, 1903 ..... 119.00 To 270.00
Collector, Plate, Bing & Grondahl, Christmas, 1904 ..... 74.00 To 150.00
Collector, Plate, Bing & Grondahl, Christmas, 1905 ..... 74.00 To 120.00
Collector, Plate, Bing & Grondahl, Christmas, 1906 ..... 60.00 To 105.00
Collector, Plate, Bing & Grondahl, Christmas, 1907 ..... 100.00
Collector, Plate, Bing & Grondahl, Christmas, 1908 ..... 49.00 To 62.00
Collector, Plate, Bing & Grondahl, Christmas, 1909 ..... 55.00 To 96.00
Collector, Plate, Bing & Grondahl, Christmas, 1910 ..... 56.00 To 81.00
Collector, Plate, Bing & Grondahl, Christmas, 1911 ..... 56.00 To 81.00
Collector, Plate, Bing & Grondahl, Christmas, 1912 ..... 56.00 To 80.00
Collector, Plate, Bing & Grondahl, Christmas, 1913 ..... 56.00 To 80.00
Collector, Plate, Bing & Grondahl, Christmas, 1914 ..... 45.00 To 72.00
Collector, Plate, Bing & Grondahl, Christmas, 1915 ..... 68.00 To 108.00

Collector, Plate, Bing & Grondahl, Christmas, 1916 .... 50.00 To 75.00
Collector, Plate, Bing & Grondahl, Christmas, 1917 .... 46.00 To 75.00
Collector, Plate, Bing & Grondahl, Christmas, 1918 .... 45.00
Collector, Plate, Bing & Grondahl, Christmas, 1919 .... 45.00 To 84.00
Collector, Plate, Bing & Grondahl, Christmas, 1920 .... 44.00 To 75.00
Collector, Plate, Bing & Grondahl, Christmas, 1921 .... 43.00 To 60.00
Collector, Plate, Bing & Grondahl, Christmas, 1922 .... 45.00 To 75.00
Collector, Plate, Bing & Grondahl, Christmas, 1923 .... 45.00 To 75.00
Collector, Plate, Bing & Grondahl, Christmas, 1924 .... 45.00 To 67.50
Collector, Plate, Bing & Grondahl, Christmas, 1925 .... 45.00 To 67.50
Collector, Plate, Bing & Grondahl, Christmas, 1926 .... 52.00 To 60.00
Collector, Plate, Bing & Grondahl, Christmas, 1927 .... 47.00 To 84.00
Collector, Plate, Bing & Grondahl, Christmas, 1928 .... 45.00 To 60.00
Collector, Plate, Bing & Grondahl, Christmas, 1929 .... 48.00 To 75.00
Collector, Plate, Bing & Grondahl, Christmas, 1930 .... 57.00 To 96.00
Collector, Plate, Bing & Grondahl, Christmas, 1931 .... 49.00 To 84.00
Collector, Plate, Bing & Grondahl, Christmas, 1932 .... 50.00 To 78.00
Collector, Plate, Bing & Grondahl, Christmas, 1933 .... 45.00 To 66.00
Collector, Plate, Bing & Grondahl, Christmas, 1934 .... 45.00 To 75.00
Collector, Plate, Bing & Grondahl, Christmas, 1935 .... 40.00 To 85.00
Collector, Plate, Bing & Grondahl, Christmas, 1936 .... 46.00 To 75.00
Collector, Plate, Bing & Grondahl, Christmas, 1937 .... 46.00 To 75.00
Collector, Plate, Bing & Grondahl, Christmas, 1938 .... 42.00 To 108.00
Collector, Plate, Bing & Grondahl, Christmas, 1939 .... 60.00 To 143.00
Collector, Plate, Bing & Grondahl, Christmas, 1940 .... 87.00 To 139.00
Collector, Plate, Bing & Grondahl, Christmas, 1941 .... 151.00 To 300.00
Collector, Plate, Bing & Grondahl, Christmas, 1942 .... 89.00 To 165.00
Collector, Plate, Bing & Grondahl, Christmas, 1943 .... 89.00 To 150.00
Collector, Plate, Bing & Grondahl, Christmas, 1944 .... 59.00 To 110.00
Collector, Plate, Bing & Grondahl, Christmas, 1945 .... 71.00 To 135.00
Collector, Plate, Bing & Grondahl, Christmas, 1946 .... 45.00 To 75.00
Collector, Plate, Bing & Grondahl, Christmas, 1947 .... 45.00 To 81.00
Collector, Plate, Bing & Grondahl, Christmas, 1948 .... 45.00 To 75.00
Collector, Plate, Bing & Grondahl, Christmas, 1949 .... 59.00 To 135.00
Collector, Plate, Bing & Grondahl, Christmas, 1950 .... 50.00 To 90.00
Collector, Plate, Bing & Grondahl, Christmas, 1951 .... 50.00 To 90.00
Collector, Plate, Bing & Grondahl, Christmas, 1952 .... 43.00 To 60.00
Collector, Plate, Bing & Grondahl, Christmas, 1953 .... 45.00 To 81.00
Collector, Plate, Bing & Grondahl, Christmas, 1954 .... 58.00 To 96.00
Collector, Plate, Bing & Grondahl, Christmas, 1955 .... 56.00 To 75.00
Collector, Plate, Bing & Grondahl, Christmas, 1956 .... 67.00 To 135.00
Collector, Plate, Bing & Grondahl, Christmas, 1957 .... 67.00 To 137.50
Collector, Plate, Bing & Grondahl, Christmas, 1958 .... 63.00 To 112.50
Collector, Plate, Bing & Grondahl, Christmas, 1959 .... 75.00 To 149.00
Collector, Plate, Bing & Grondahl, Christmas, 1960 .... 87.00 To 240.00
Collector, Plate, Bing & Grondahl, Christmas, 1961 .... 60.00 To 135.00
Collector, Plate, Bing & Grondahl, Christmas, 1962 .... 37.00 To 90.00
Collector, Plate, Bing & Grondahl, Christmas, 1963 .... 38.00 To 139.00
Collector, Plate, Bing & Grondahl, Christmas, 1964 .... 42.00
Collector, Plate, Bing & Grondahl, Christmas, 1965 .... 42.00
Collector, Plate, Bing & Grondahl, Christmas, 1966 .... 30.00 To 34.00
Collector, Plate, Bing & Grondahl, Christmas, 1967 .... 30.00 To 34.00
Collector, Plate, Bing & Grondahl, Christmas, 1968 .... 30.00
Collector, Plate, Bing & Grondahl, Christmas, 1969 .... 18.75 To 25.00
Collector, Plate, Bing & Grondahl, Christmas, 1970 .... 15.00
Collector, Plate, Bing & Grondahl, Christmas, 1971 .... 11.90 To 20.00
Collector, Plate, Bing & Grondahl, Christmas, 1972 .... 20.00
Collector, Plate, Bing & Grondahl, Christmas, 1973 .... 18.75 To 27.00
Collector, Plate, Bing & Grondahl, Christmas, 1974 .... 20.00
Collector, Plate, Bing & Grondahl, Christmas, 1975 .... 11.00 To 32.00
Collector, Plate, Bing & Grondahl, Christmas, 1976 .... 27.50
Collector, Plate, Bing & Grondahl, Jubilee, 1970 .... 12.00
Collector, Plate, Bing & Grondahl, Mother's Day, 1969, 1st Issue 310.00
Collector, Plate, Bing & Grondahl, Mother's Day, 1970 .... 27.50
Collector, Plate, Bing & Grondahl, Mother's Day, 1971 .... 8.00 To 9.75

Collector, Plate, Bing & Grondahl, Mother's Day, 1972 .... 9.00
Collector, Plate, Bing & Grondahl, Mother's Day, 1973 .... 13.00
Collector, Plate, Bing & Grondahl, Olympic, 1972 .... 9.00 To 11.00
Collector, Plate, Delft, Father's Day, 1970 .... 4.00
Collector, Plate, Delft, Mother's Day, 1970 .... 4.00
Collector, Plate, Dresden, Christmas, 1972 .... 11.00
Collector, Plate, Dresden, Mother's Day, 1972 .... 11.00
Collector, Plate, Haviland, Bicentennial, 1972, 1st Issue 10.00
Collector, Plate, Haviland, Christmas, 1970, Partridge In A Pear Tree 115.00
Collector, Plate, Haviland, Christmas, 1971 .... 30.00 To 35.00
Collector, Plate, Haviland, Christmas, 1972 .... 18.50 To 25.00
Collector, Plate, Haviland, Christmas, 1973 .... 25.00
Collector, Plate, Haviland, Mother's Day, 1973 .... 15.00
Collector, Plate, Hummel, Annual, 1971 .... 365.00
Collector, Plate, K.P.M., Christmas, 1975 .... 35.00
Collector, Plate, Lenox, Boehm Bird, 1970, Woodthrush 198.00
Collector, Plate, Lenox, Boehm Bird, 1971 .... 80.00
Collector, Plate, Lenox, Boehm Bird, 1972 .... 45.00
Collector, Plate, Lenox, Boehm Bird, 1973 .... 45.00
Collector, Plate, Rosenthal, Mother's Day, 1976 .... 48.00 To 52.00
Collector, Plate, Royal Bayreuth, Christmas, 1972 .... 64.00
Collector, Plate, Royal Bayreuth, Mother's Day, 1975 .... 75.00
Collector, Plate, Royal Bayreuth, Mother's Day, 1976 .... 55.00
Collector, Plate, Royal Copenhagen, Christmas, 1908 .... 850.00 To 1000.00
Collector, Plate, Royal Copenhagen, Christmas, 1909 .... 65.00 To 100.00
Collector, Plate, Royal Copenhagen, Christmas, 1910 .... 60.00 To 95.00
Collector, Plate, Royal Copenhagen, Christmas, 1911 .... 65.00 To 110.00
Collector, Plate, Royal Copenhagen, Christmas, 1912 .... 81.00 To 110.00
Collector, Plate, Royal Copenhagen, Christmas, 1913 .... 80.00 To 105.00
Collector, Plate, Royal Copenhagen, Christmas, 1914 .... 73.00 To 90.00
Collector, Plate, Royal Copenhagen, Christmas, 1915 .... 63.00 To 90.00
Collector, Plate, Royal Copenhagen, Christmas, 1916 .... 48.00 To 65.00
Collector, Plate, Royal Copenhagen, Christmas, 1917 .... 48.00 To 65.00
Collector, Plate, Royal Copenhagen, Christmas, 1918 .... 48.00 To 65.00
Collector, Plate, Royal Copenhagen, Christmas, 1919 .... 48.00 To 65.00
Collector, Plate, Royal Copenhagen, Christmas, 1920 .... 40.00 To 60.00
Collector, Plate, Royal Copenhagen, Christmas, 1921 .... 42.50 To 52.50
Collector, Plate, Royal Copenhagen, Christmas, 1922 .... 36.50 To 52.50
Collector, Plate, Royal Copenhagen, Christmas, 1923 .... 50.00 To 65.00
Collector, Plate, Royal Copenhagen, Christmas, 1924 .... 50.00 To 60.00
Collector, Plate, Royal Copenhagen, Christmas, 1925 .... 50.00 To 60.00
Collector, Plate, Royal Copenhagen, Christmas, 1926 .... 5000 To 55.00
Collector, Plate, Royal Copenhagen, Christmas, 1927 .... 65.00 To 80.00
Collector, Plate, Royal Copenhagen, Christmas, 1928 .... 45.00 To 65.00
Collector, Plate, Royal Copenhagen, Christmas, 1929 .... 45.00 To 60.00
Collector, Plate, Royal Copenhagen, Christmas, 1930 .... 45.00 To 60.00
Collector, Plate, Royal Copenhagen, Christmas, 1931 .... 47.50 To 65.00
Collector, Plate, Royal Copenhagen, Christmas, 1932 .... 47.00 To 65.00
Collector, Plate, Royal Copenhagen, Christmas, 1933 .... 65.00 To 80.00
Collector, Plate, Royal Copenhagen, Christmas, 1934 .... 65.00 To 80.00
Collector, Plate, Royal Copenhagen, Christmas, 1935 .... 75.00 To 87.00
Collector, Plate, Royal Copenhagen, Christmas, 1936 .... 77.00 To 100.00
Collector, Plate, Royal Copenhagen, Christmas, 1937 .... 85.00 To 100.00
Collector, Plate, Royal Copenhagen, Christmas, 1938 .... 150.00 To 215.00
Collector, Plate, Royal Copenhagen, Christmas, 1939 .... 150.00 To 215.00
Collector, Plate, Royal Copenhagen, Christmas, 1940 .... 250.00 To 300.00
Collector, Plate, Royal Copenhagen, Christmas, 1941 .... 175.00 To 275.00
Collector, Plate, Royal Copenhagen, Christmas, 1942 .... 225.00 To 300.00
Collector, Plate, Royal Copenhagen, Christmas, 1943 .... 300.00 To 450.00
Collector, Plate, Royal Copenhagen, Christmas, 1944 .... 90.00 To 125.00
Collector, Plate, Royal Copenhagen, Christmas, 1945 .... 225.00 To 325.00
Collector, Plate, Royal Copenhagen, Christmas, 1946 .... 90.00 To 120.00
Collector, Plate, Royal Copenhagen, Christmas, 1947 .... 100.00 To 150.00
Collector, Plate, Royal Copenhagen, Christmas, 1948 .... 65.00 To 95.00

Collector, Plate, Royal Copenhagen, Christmas, 1949 .... 75.00 To 115.00
Collector, Plate, Royal Copenhagen, Christmas, 1950 .... 70.00 To 110.00
Collector, Plate, Royal Copenhagen, Christmas, 1951 .... 175.00 To 220.00
Collector, Plate, Royal Copenhagen, Christmas, 1952 .... 50.00 To 70.00
Collector, Plate, Royal Copenhagen, Christmas, 1953 .... 50.00 To 70.00
Collector, Plate, Royal Copenhagen, Christmas, 1954 .... 75.00 To 105.00
Collector, Plate, Royal Copenhagen, Christmas, 1955 .... 100.00 To 195.00
Collector, Plate, Royal Copenhagen, Christmas, 1956 .... 65.00 To 105.00
Collector, Plate, Royal Copenhagen, Christmas, 1957 .... 60.00 To 75.00
Collector, Plate, Royal Copenhagen, Christmas, 1958 .... 65.00 To 80.00
Collector, Plate, Royal Copenhagen, Christmas, 1959 .... 75.00 To 100.00
Collector, Plate, Royal Copenhagen, Christmas, 1960 .... 75.00 To 100.00
Collector, Plate, Royal Copenhagen, Christmas, 1961 .... 80.00 To 100.00
Collector, Plate, Royal Copenhagen, Christmas, 1962 .... 120.00 To 130.00
Collector, Plate, Royal Copenhagen, Christmas, 1963 .... 37.50 To 50.00
Collector, Plate, Royal Copenhagen, Christmas, 1964 .... 46.00
Collector, Plate, Royal Copenhagen, Christmas, 1965 .... 46.00
Collector, Plate, Royal Copenhagen, Christmas, 1966 .... 20.00 To 44.00
Collector, Plate, Royal Copenhagen, Christmas, 1967 .... 20.00 To 44.00
Collector, Plate, Royal Copenhagen, Christmas, 1968 .... 30.00
Collector, Plate, Royal Copenhagen, Christmas, 1969 .... 32.00
Collector, Plate, Royal Copenhagen, Christmas, 1970 .... 27.00
Collector, Plate, Royal Copenhagen, Christmas, 1971 .... 11.90 To 24.00
Collector, Plate, Royal Copenhagen, Christmas, 1972 .... 10.90 To 21.00
Collector, Plate, Royal Copenhagen, Christmas, 1973 .... 14.00 To 21.00
Collector, Plate, Royal Copenhagen, Christmas, 1974 .... 21.00
Collector, Plate, Royal Copenhagen, Christmas, 1975 .... 14.95 To 29.00
Collector, Plate, Royal Copenhagen, Christmas, 1976 .... 17.00 To 27.00
Collector, Plate, Royal Copenhagen, Mother's Day, 1971 .... 19.00
Collector, Plate, Royal Copenhagen, Mother's Day, 1972 .... 6.00
Collector, Plate, Royal Copenhagen, Olympics, 1972 .... 11.00
Collector, Plate, Royal Doulton, Valentine's Day, 1976 .... 22.50
Collector, Plate, Royal Worcester, Bicentennial, 1976 .... 150.00
Collector, Plate, Wedgwood, Christmas, 1970 .... 18.00 To 30.00
Collector, Plate, Wedgwood, Christmas, 1971 .... 30.00
Collector, Plate, Wedgwood, Christmas, 1972 .... 22.50
Collector, Tankard, Royal Doulton, Christmas, 1975 .... 27.50

Commemoration items have been made to honor members of royalty and those of great national fame. World's fairs and important historical events are also remembered with commemoration pieces.

Commemoration, see also Coronation, World's Fair

Commemoration, Bowl, Royal Jubilee, 1837-1888, Pattern Glass, 10 In. 25.00
Commemoration, Bowl, Soup, Prince Albert, Pale Green Transfer, 8 Medallions 90.00
Commemoration, Bowl, Victoria, Year Of Jubilee, Portrait Of Queen, 8 1/2 In. 45.00
Commemoration, Box, Tin, Queen Elizabeth, 1939 .... 9.50
Commemoration, Can, Tin, Picturing Royal Family 9.50
Commemoration, Compote, Queen Victoria, 1827-1887, Molded, Clear, 6 1/2 In. 65.00
Commemoration, Glass, Etched Building, Pan-Am Exposition, Buffalo, 1901 .... 10.00
Commemoration, Medal, Elizabeth II, 1953, Sterling 15.00
Commemoration, Medal, George VI, 1937, Sterling 15.00
Commemoration, Mug, Charles As Prince Of Wales, 1969, Wedgwood, 4 In. 45.00
Commemoration, Mug, Elizabeth VI & George, Visit To Canada, Burleigh 12.00
Commemoration, Mug, 1776-1786, Dates In Stars, 4 1/2 In. 50.00
Commemoration, Pitcher, Admiral Dewey, Pressed Glass, Naval Emblems & Face 65.00
Commemoration, Pitcher, Beef, Yale University, C.1905, Laughlin, 11 In. 135.00
Commemoration, Pitcher, Dewey, Eagle Spout, Cook Pottery, Trenton, N.J. 85.00
Commemoration, Pitcher, Queen Elizabeth Bust, 1953, 5 In. 12.75
Commemoration, Plate, Edward VII & Alexandra, Foley Co, England, White, Seal 18.00
Commemoration, Plate, Fall Of Montmorency, Quebec, Wood, 8 1/2 In. 210.00
Commemoration, Plate, Founding Fathers, Blue, Enoch Wood & Sons, 9 1/2 In. 125.00
Commemoration, Plate, King George VI & Queen Elizabeth In Canada, 1939 .... 15.00
Commemoration, Plate, Queen Elizabeth, Small, 1959 .... 5.00
Commemoration, Plate, Rear Admiral George Dewey, Flow Blue On White, 10 In. 25.00

Commemoration, Platter, Napoleon At Waterloo, Sepia, G.M. & C.J.Mason, C.1813 .... 145.00
Commemoration, Portrait, William IV, Steel Engraved, Autograph & Seal 95.00
Commeration, Box, Edward VIII, Prince Of Wales, 1924, Tin, Portrait 22.00
Coors, Cup, Custard 1.50
Coors, Jar, Cookie, Flowers On Plum, 8 1/4 In. 15.00
Coors, Pot, Honey, Rose Bud 15.00
Coors, Tureen, Matte, 8 1/2 In. 5.50
Coors, Vase, Pink, Handled, 5 In. 10.00
Coors, Vase, Rope Handles, Blue, 8 In. 12.00
Coors, Vase, Yellow, Handled, 5 In. 10.00
Coors, Vase, Yellow, 8 1/2 In. 12.00

COPELAND

W.T.Copeland & Sons, Ltd., ran the Spode Works in Staffordshire, England, from 1847 to the present. Copeland & Garrett was the firm name from 1833 to 1847.

Copeland Spode, see also Flow Blue

Copeland Spode, Bough Pot, Italian, Blue, Footed Ring Handles, 11 In. 42.00
Copeland Spode, Bowl, Bologna, Green & White, Garret, C.1840, 10 In. 69.00
Copeland Spode, Bowl, Fox Hunt, First Over, 6 1/4 In. 5.00
Copeland Spode, Bowl, Fox Hunt, Full Cry, 6 1/4 In. 5.00
Copeland Spode, Bowl, Fox Hunt, Huntsman, 6 1/4 In. 5.00
Copeland Spode, Coffee Set, Buttercup, 3 Piece 45.00
Copeland Spode, Constitution Hall, Light Blue, 10 In. 10.00
Copeland Spode, Creamer, Beige, Raised White Figures On Green Band 30.00
Copeland Spode, Creamer, Roses Transfer, Bulbous, 2 3/4 In. 9.00
Copeland Spode, Creamer, Tower, Royal Blue 15.00
Copeland Spode, Cup & Saucer, And 7 1/2 In. Cake Plate, First Over 35.00
Copeland Spode, Cup & Saucer, Buttercup 15.00
Copeland Spode, Mustard, Sterling Lid & Spoon, No. 629599, Chinese Rose 24.00
Copeland Spode, Pitcher, Blue, White Fox Hunt Scene, 3 1/2 In. 59.00
Copeland Spode, Pitcher, Green, White Hunt Scene, 4 1/2 In. 45.00
Copeland Spode, Pitcher, Tower, Royal Blue, Bulbous, 5 In. 20.00
Copeland Spode, Plate, Cake, Buttercup 15.00
Copeland Spode, Plate, Dinner, Buttercup 15.00
Copeland Spode, Plate, Fox Chase, Flower Border, Signed 16.00
Copeland Spode, Plate, Fruit, White On White Scalloped Rim, 9 1/2 In. 7.00
Copeland Spode, Plate, Independence Hall, Phila., Light Blue, 10 In. 10.00
Copeland Spode, Plate, Tower, Royal Blue, 8 In. 15.00
Copeland Spode, Platter, Tower, Royal Blue, 11 X 7 1/2 In. 30.00
Copeland Spode, Sugar & Creamer, Pink Luster, Countryside & Windmills 45.00
Copeland Spode, Sugar, Covered, Tower, Royal Blue 15.00
Copeland Spode, Tea Set, Fox Hunt Scene, White Figures On Blue 110.00
Copeland Spode, Toby Mug, Winston Churchill, Seated, 8 1/2 In. 70.00
Copeland Spode, Tray, White, Blue Floral & Trim, 11 In. 11.00
Copeland Spode, Washstand Set, Floral, Yellow Tops, 9 Piece 425.00

Copeland, see also Spode

Copeland, Butter, Brown Tranfer Castles, C.1850, Stoke On Trent 10.00
Copeland, Compote, Oriental, Initialed Huston, 1960s, 8 1/2 X 4 3/8 In. 25.00
Copeland, Dish, Pickle, Oriental, Brick Red, Blue, & Green 6.00
Copeland, Dish, Sauce, Cobalt & White, Oriental Scene, C.1881 .... 9.00
Copeland, Figurine, John Wilson As Christopher North, Parian, 17 3/4 In. 185.00
Copeland, Mug, Centennial, 1876, George Washington, Eagle, & Flags 76.00
Copeland, Pitcher Vase, Figural, Mandarin, Bamboo Handle, C.1851, 4 In. 52.00
Copeland, Pitcher Vase, Figural, White Mandarin, Seated, C.1885, 4 In. 55.00
Copeland, Pitcher, Blue, White Medallions Of Chicago History, C.1893, 8 In. 350.00
Copeland, Pitcher, Jasperware, Blue, White, Columbian Exposition, 21 In. 165.00
Copeland, Pitcher, Salt Glaze, Parian, Blue & White, C.1860, 7 In. 35.00
Copeland, Pitcher, Tan & Cream, Hunting Scene, C.1840, 4 1/2 In. 45.00
Copeland, Plate, Autumn Leaves, Incised, Fluted, 8 1/2 In. 19.00
Copeland, Plate, Robin Hood & Tinker, Blue & White, 10 1/2 In. 37.00
Copeland, Plate, Soup, Oriental, Brick Red, Blue, & Green 7.00
Copeland, Tray, Pin, Multicolor Floral, Blue Mark, C.1833, 5 In. 25.00
Copeland, Vase, Gold, Pink & Turquoise, Signed, English, 5 3/4 In. 75.00
Copeland, Vegetable Bowl, Covered, Gold Cranes & Bamboo 85.00

Copeland, Vegetable Bowl, Covered, Oriental, Brick Red, Blue, & Green 25.00
Copper Luster, see Luster, Copper
Copper Teakettle, Gooseneck, 10 In. 75.00
Copper, Ashtray, AYPE Official Seal, C.1909 .... 7.50
Copper, Ashtray, Mexican, Coin 8.00
Copper, Bottle, Hot Water, Brass Screw Top, Oval 35.00
Copper, Box, Horse's Head On Lid, Footed, Hand Wrought, 1928, 11 X 8 In. 45.00
Copper, Box, Jewelry, Art Nouveau 10.00
Copper, Bucket, Apple Butter, 16 In. 85.00
Copper, Candlesnuffer, Handmade 3.50
Copper, Coffeepot, Portugal 25.00
Copper, Coffeepot, Rome Mfg.Co., Rome, N.Y., Nickel Plated 20.00
Copper, Coffeepot, Wooden Knob & Handle, 10 In. 35.00
Copper, Container, Hammered, Loop Handles, 5 X 2 3/4 In. 5.00
Copper, Cup, Wedding, Russian, 2 Handles, 6 1/8 In. 85.00
Copper, Dish, Chafing, Brass Trim, Burner, Patent 1902 .... 45.00
Copper, Dish, Chafing, Wooden Knob & Handle, Manning Bowman, 1907, 9 1/2 In. 75.00
Copper, Figurine, Game Cock, Gilt Painted, Repousse, Metal Stand, 16 In. 175.00
Copper, Figurine, Seated Basset Hound, Painted Black, 6 In. 28.00
Copper, Funnel, Handmade 4.50
Copper, Humidor & Tray, Jos.Heinrichs, N.Y., Tin-Lined Humidor, Handmade 75.00
Copper, Humidor, Brown, Silver Inlay, 3 1/2 In. 295.00
Copper, Inkwell & Attached Base, Brass Trim, Crystal Insert, 6 1/2 In. 50.00
Copper, Kettle, Apple Butter, With Handles, 18 In. 148.00
Copper, Kettle, Covered, D.H.& M.Co., N.Y., 10 1/2 In. 110.00
Copper, Kettle, Gooseneck, Flange 45.00
Copper, Kettle, Gypsy, Hanging, 3 Legged, 2 In. 12.00
Copper, Kettle, Iron Bail Handle, Hammered, Dovetailed, 11 X 7 3/4 In. 150.00
Copper, Kettle, 5 Ft. X 32 In. 600.00
Copper, Lantern, Ship, Pair 328.00
Copper, Letter Opener, Spanish Galleon On Top, 9 In. 15.00
Copper, Lighter, Cigarette, Al Malakah, Los Angeles, 1925, Ship's Wheel 6.50
Copper, Match Safe, Lady & Man On Fence Under Umbrella 12.50
Copper, Mold, Flower, 6 1/4 In. 20.00
Copper, Mold, Fluted, 8 1/2 In. 30.00
Copper, Mold, Horse Head, Zinc Lined, 5 In. 45.00
Copper, Mold, Pear, 7 3/4 In. 25.00
Copper, Mold, Sunburst, 8 1/4 In. 25.00
Copper, Opener, Letter, Indian's Head Handle, Silver Feathers 75.00
Copper, Pan, Brass Handles, 13 X 4 In. 50.00
Copper, Pan, Covered, Du Parquet, Iron Handles, 8 1/2 In. 95.00
Copper, Pan, Covered, Du Parquet, N.Y., Iron Handles, 7 1/2 In. 95.00
Copper, Pan, Wrought Iron Handle, 21 X 12 X 2 In. 45.00
Copper, Pitcher, Scalloped, Rolled Rim, 7 X 7 In. 45.00
Copper, Plaque, Abraham Lincoln, 5 X 3 1/2 In. 75.00
Copper, Roaster, 2 Nested Open, Oval, Brass Handles, 14 1/2 X 10 1/4 In. 92.50
Copper, Spill, E W China, Fluted, Blue Enamel Lining, Oval, 3 1/2 In. 20.00
Copper, Stein, Art Nouveau With Brass, 14 In. 55.00
Copper, Stein, German, Art Nouveau, Brass Lid, Handle, & Base, 14 In. 85.00
Copper, Still 350.00
Copper, Syrup, Russian, Brass Rim, 7 1/2 In. 35.00
Copper, Tea Caddy, Brass Finial On Lid, 5 In. 35.00
Copper, Tea Caddy, Heart Decoration 27.50
Copper, Teakettle, Brass Knob, Spout, & Handle, Wooden Grip 26.00
Copper, Teakettle, Gooseneck Spout 48.00
Copper, Teakettle, Nickel Plated, 2 Quart 16.00
Copper, Teakettle, Round, 6 In. 25.00
Copper, Teakettle, Scandinavian, C.1850, Gooseneck Spout, Tin Lined, 6 In. 38.00
Copper, Teakettle, 1898 .... 10.00
Copper, Teapot, Brass Lid, Pewter Spout & Handle 25.00
Copper, Teapot, Gooseneck, Swing Handle, Hammered, Heart Shape Hinge Base 175.00
Copper, Teapot, Hammered Oriental Design, Brass Bottom 28.50
Copper, Teapot, With Brass, Glass Top, Burner, Strainer, Lamp 65.00
Copper, Tray, Frank Lee, Starfish, Crab & Bubbles On Blue Green, 4 3/4 In. 35.00

Copper, Tray, North African, Etched, Pewter Accents, Gadroon Edge, 24 In. 278.00
Copper, Vase, Chinese, Enamel Bands & 4 Oval Plaques, 10 In., Pair 275.00
Copper, Vase, Christofle, C.1925, Silver Overlay, Geometrics, 9 In. 395.00
Copper, Vase, Russian Hallmarks, 12 X 10 In. 75.00
Copper, Vase, Silver & Gold Against Dark Ground, Signed Durand 475.00
Copper, Warmer, Bed, Long Handle, C.1850 110.00

Coralene glass was made by firing many small colored beads on the outside of glassware. It was made in many patterns in the United States and Europe in the 1880s. Reproductions are made today.

Coralene, Japanese Pottery, see Japanese Coralene

Coralene, Sugar Shaker, Enameled, Cherries, Nickel Silver Top 75.00
Coralene, Vase, Amber To Pink, Snowflake Mother-Of-Pearl, 8 In. 595.00
Coralene, Vase, Blue To White, Quilted Mother-Of-Pearl, 5 In. 247.00
Coralene, Vase, Blue, Cased In White, Yellow Beads, Seaweed Pattern, 8 In. 250.00
Coralene, Vase, Blush Pink & Yellow, All Over Applications, 6 In. 485.00
Coralene, Vase, Camphor, Orange Beading, Black Enamel, 8 In. 115.00
Coralene, Vase, Dark Amber, Floral & Buds, Enamel Leaves, Patent, 7 In. 260.00
Coralene, Vase, Green And Floral, Gold Rim, Signed, Dated 1910, 8 1/2 In. 135.00
Coralene, Vase, Orchid & White Stripes, 17 1/2 In. 550.00
Coralene, Vase, Pink To Rose, White Cased, Seaweed, 7 1/2 In. 550.00
Coralene, Vase, Rainbow, Satin Glass, 7 1/2 In. 425.00
Coralene, Vase, Satin Shading From Pink To Rose, Yellow Coralene, 5 3/8 In. 500.00
Coralene, Vase, Scenic, Trees, Houses, Green, Beige, Rust, Signed, 8 3/4 X 5 In. 225.00
Coralene, Vase, Two Handled, Beading, Gold On Powder Blue, Flowers, 4 In. 85.00
Cordey, Bust, Lady, White Shawl On Head, 6 In. 75.00

Coronation cups have been made since the 1800s. Pieces of pottery or glass with a picture of the monarch and the date have been made as souvenirs for many coronations.

Coronation, see also Commemoration

Coronation, Ashtray, 1953, Wedgwood 20.00
Coronation, Bank, George V, 1911, Nickel-Plated Cast Iron 95.00
Coronation, Beaker, George V & Mary, Purple, Royal Doulton 27.50
Coronation, Bell, Elizabeth II, 1953, Brass, Head Is Handle, 6 In. 15.00
Coronation, Bell, 1953, Queen's Head Is Handle, Elizabeth II, Brass, 6 In. 15.00
Coronation, Bottle, Elizabeth II, Brass Crown Top, Royal Doulton, 19 In. 150.00
Coronation, Bowl, Edward VIII, 1937, Moorcroft, 8 1/4 In. 250.00
Coronation, Cup & Saucer, Elizabeth II, Floral, Gold 12.50
Coronation, Cup, Edward VIII, Porcelain, England 15.00
Coronation, Cup, Elizabeth II, 1953, Royal Doulton 45.00
Coronation, Cup, George V, 1911, Royal Doulton 35.00
Coronation, Cup, Tall Coffee, Edward VIII 15.00
Coronation, Mug, Edward VIII, Likeness, May 12, 1937 18.00
Coronation, Mug, Elizabeth II, Coat Of Arms, Staffordshire 10.00
Coronation, Mug, Elizabeth II, Royal Doulton, June 2, 1953 24.00
Coronation, Mug, George & Elizabeth, 1937 6.50
Coronation, Mug, George VI & Elizabeth, May, 1937 12.00
Coronation, Pin, Christian X, Denmark, 1912, Sterling, Red Enamel 15.00
Coronation, Pin, Coronation Crown, Enamel, 1937, Cutty Sark 20.00
Coronation, Pin, George VI, 1937, Sterling, Multicolor Enamel 10.00
Coronation, Pincushion, Edward, 1904, Beaded, Lion & Unicorn Insignia 24.00
Coronation, Pitcher, Elizabeth II, Clear, 5 3/4 In. 25.00
Coronation, Plate, Elizabeth II, 1953, Gold Trim, Bone China, 9 In. 9.95
Coronation, Plate, George V, 1911, 5 1/2 In. 12.00
Coronation, Plate, George VI & Elizabeth, 1937, Dewdrop, Glass, 8 1/2 In. 22.50
Coronation, Plate, George, 1937, Crystal, 10 In. 18.00
Coronation, Plate, Queen Elizabeth, Philip, Tin, Colorful, Pair 25.00
Coronation, Program, Racing, Elizabeth, June 2, 1953 5.00
Coronation, Spoon, Demitasse, Elizabeth II, 1950, 2 Ruby Stones In Crown 4.95
Coronation, Spoon, Demitasse, Elizabeth, 1953, Harrison Fisher, Sheffield, 3 35.00
Coronation, Tea Set, Doll's, George V And Mary, 8 Piece 50.00
Coronation, Tea Set, Edward VIII, Royal Blue, Medallions & Crest, 3 Piece 460.00
Coronation, Tea Set, Edward VIII, Wedgwood, Cobalt & Jasper, 3 Piece 550.00

Coronation, Tumbler, Edward VIII, 1937, 4 1/2 In. 14.00
Coronation, Tumbler, George VI, 1937, Glass 12.00
Coronet, Plate, Pierced Handles, Red Tulips, Signed Barbot, 10 3/4 In. 48.00

Cosmos pattern glass is a pressed milk glass pattern with colored flowers.

Cosmos, Creamer, Pink Band, 5 In. 85.00
Cosmos, Lamp, Ball-Shaped Base, Umbrella Shade, 8 In. 55.00
Cosmos, Lamp, Clear, Painted Decoration, Miniature 40.00
Cosmos, Lamp, Enameled Floral, Miniature 58.00
Cosmos, Lamp, Frosted, Polychrome Flowers, Miniature 134.00
Cosmos, Lamp, Hand-Painted Floral, Miniature 60.00
Cosmos, Lamp, Pink Band, Miniature 145.00
Cosmos, Lamp, Pink Top Band, Clear Burner, Miniature 60.00
Cosmos, Lamp, Table, Yellow Band, Wired, 15 In. 325.00
Cosmos, Lamp, Yellow Band, Miniature 265.00
Cosmos, Pitcher, Water, Pink Top 300.00

Country Store, see Store

Cowan pottery was made in Cleveland, Ohio, from 1913 to 1920. Most pieces of the art pottery were marked with the name of the firm in various ways.

Cowan, Ashtray, Stylized Bird, Marked 18.00
Cowan, Ashtray, With Cigarette Holder, Sea Horses, Hearts, Yellow Glaze 42.00
Cowan, Bowl, Purple Luster, 9 In. 15.00
Cowan, Candlestick, Eggshell, Pair 10.00
Cowan, Candlestick, Orange, Pair 12.50
Cowan, Compote, Cream Glaze Base, Sea Horse, Shells, Impressed, 3 1/2 In., Pair 20.00
Cowan, Figurine, Black Elephant, Signed 20.00
Cowan, Flower Frog, Dancing Nude, 6 In. 32.00
Cowan, Planter, Eggshell, Pink Interior, 3 Sea Horse Candlesticks 25.00
Cowan, Vase, Larkspur Luster, 3 1/4 In. 18.00
Cowan, Vase, Orange Luster, Dragonflies, 13 In. 99.00

Crackle glass was originally made by the Venetians, but most of the ware found today dates from the 1800s. The glass was heated, cooled, and refired so that many small lines appeared inside the glass. It was made in many factories in the United States and Europe.

Crackle Glass, see also Fry

Crackle Glass, Bowl, Punch, 6 Cups, Fruit Stem Finial & Ladle 500.00
Crackle Glass, Cup, Punch, Amber 5.00
Crackle Glass, Cup, Punch, Blue 5.00
Crackle Glass, Pitcher, Overshot, Sandwich Twisted Rope Handle, 13 In. 220.00
Crackle Glass, Pitcher, Water, Covered 25.00
Crackle Glass, Pitcher, Water, Cranberry & Opalescent 145.00
Crackle Glass, Pitcher, Water, Rubena, Applied Clear Reeded Handle, 8 In. 165.00
Crackle Glass, Vase, Amber, Applied Spiral On Neck, 5 1/2 In. 14.00
Crackle Glass, Vase, Cranberry, Mica Flakes, Clear Rigaree, 3 1/2 In. 52.00
Crackle Glass, Vase, Smoky Amber, Swirled, 5 In. 15.00

Cranberry glass is an almost transparent yellow red glass. It resembles the color of cranberry juice.

Cranberry Glass, Basket, Bride's, Pleated Rim, Silver Frame, 12 In. 175.00
Cranberry Glass, Basket, Diamond-Quilted, Crystal Handle, Ruffled, 4 7/8 In. 70.00
Cranberry Glass, Basket, Iris Shape, Crystal Handle & Petals, 6 1/2 In. 69.00
Cranberry Glass, Basket, Opalescent Hobnail, Clear Handle, 7 In. 24.50
Cranberry Glass, Basket, Ruffled, Clear Thorn Handle, 6 1/2 In. 85.00
Cranberry Glass, Basket, Spiked Feet, Boat Shape, Clear Looped Handle 90.00
Cranberry Glass, Bell, Gold Rose 35.00
Cranberry Glass, Bell, Swirl, English Wedding, Clear Handle 85.00
Cranberry Glass, Bobeche, Cut To Clear, 8-Pointed Stars, Square, 3 In., Pair 12.00
Cranberry Glass, Bobeche, Opalescent, Swirl, Ruffled Edge, 4 In. 10.00
Cranberry Glass, Bottle, Barber, White Opaline Stripe, Daisy & Fern 25.00
Cranberry Glass, Bottle, Finger Perfume, Teardrop, Enameled White Flowers 55.00
Cranberry Glass, Bottle, Oil, Swirled, Clear Stopper & Handle, 6 In. 28.00
Cranberry Glass, Bottle, Perfume, Blown, Victorian, 4 1/2 In. 58.00

Cranberry Glass, Bottle, Perfume, French, Paperweight Bottom 50.00
Cranberry Glass, Bottle, Perfume, Silver Overlay, 4 3/4 In. 85.00
Cranberry Glass, Bottle, Wine, Enamel Floral & Butterflies, Bulbous 125.00
Cranberry Glass, Bowl, Applied Clear Top Ruffle & Base Rim, 8 3/4 In. 85.00
Cranberry Glass, Bowl, Coin Dot, Ruffled, Flared, 9 1/2 In. 69.00
Cranberry Glass, Bowl, Enamel & Gold Decoration, 3 1/2 In., Pair 15.00
Cranberry Glass, Bowl, Enamel Geometrics On Hinged Lid, 3 1/2 X 3 In. 70.00
Cranberry Glass, Bowl, Finger, Inverted Thumbprint 23.00
Cranberry Glass, Bowl, Finger, Shell Filigree 28.00
Cranberry Glass, Bowl, Hobnail Square Ruffled, Opalescent, 3 1/2 In. 165.00
Cranberry Glass, Bowl, Outside White Milk Glass 75.00
Cranberry Glass, Bowl, Overlay, Threaded, 6 X 3 1/4 In. 85.00
Cranberry Glass, Bowl, Square, Fluted Top, Heavy Enamel Decoration, 3 1/2 In. 95.00
Cranberry Glass, Bowl, White Quilted Opalescent, Cranberry Lined, 7 In. 45.00
Cranberry Glass, Box, Bee On Hinged Lid, Brass Scroll Feet, Round, 5 In. 250.00
Cranberry Glass, Box, Covered, Gold Filigree, Round, 2 1/2 In. 50.00
Cranberry Glass, Box, Dresser, Hinged, Enamel Decoration, Metal Fittings 375.00
Cranberry Glass, Box, Hinged, Covered, Floral Enamel, 2 1/2 In. 45.00
Cranberry Glass, Butter, Crystal Ball Finial, 6 1/2 In. 105.00
Cranberry Glass, Castor Insert, Paneled Sprig, Silver Cover 88.00
Cranberry Glass, Castor, Pickle, Enameled, Ornate Frame 185.00
Cranberry Glass, Chatelaine, Perfume, Enamel Floral 45.00
Cranberry Glass, Creamer, Coin Spot, Opalescent Spots, 4 In. 45.00
Cranberry Glass, Creamer, Overshot, Gold Decoration 65.00
Cranberry Glass, Cruet, Blown, Encrusted With Enameling, Gold Stopper 170.00
Cranberry Glass, Cruet, Crystal Steeple Stopper & Handle, 10 In. 65.00
Cranberry Glass, Cruet, Fern Inverted, Clear Stopper 85.00
Cranberry Glass, Cruet, Hand-Painted Flowers 35.00
Cranberry Glass, Cruet, Hobnail 135.00
Cranberry Glass, Cruet, Plain, Watermelon Rib 125.00
Cranberry Glass, Cruet, White Swirls 20.00
Cranberry Glass, Cup, Loving, Gold & Enamel, 3 Applied Clear Handles 75.00
Cranberry Glass, Cup, Punch, Floradora, Gold Trim 29.00
Cranberry Glass, Cup, Punch, Inverted Thumbprint 7.00
Cranberry Glass, Decanter, Crystal Stopper, Cut To Clear, 15 In. 185.00
Cranberry Glass, Decanter, Thumbprint, Applied Handle, Stopper, 10 1/4 In. 82.00
Cranberry Glass, Dish, Sweetmeat, Vintage Silver Plate Holder, 6 1/2 In. 85.00
Cranberry Glass, Epergne, 3 Baskets, Twisted Crystal Arms, 21 In. 250.00
Cranberry Glass, Epergne, 3-Lily, Applied Clear Rigaree, 18 In. 275.00
Cranberry Glass, Finger Bowl & Underplate, Threaded, Ruffled Edges 120.00
Cranberry Glass, Goblet, Blackberry Julep 12.50
Cranberry Glass, Hat, Opalescent Swirl, 6 X 3 In. 29.00
Cranberry Glass, Inkwell, Ormolu Base & Lid With Chain, 2 1/2 In. 75.00
Cranberry Glass, Inset For Pickle Castor, Inverted Thumbprint, Enameled 125.00
Cranberry Glass, Jar, Biscuit, Silver Plate Fittings, 6 In. 85.00
Cranberry Glass, Jar, Biscuit, Swirled 135.00
Cranberry Glass, Jar, Pickle Castor, Inverted Thumbprint, Silver Lid, 4 In. 67.00
Cranberry Glass, Jardiniere, Overlay, Enameled 595.00
Cranberry Glass, Juice Set, Inverted Thumbprint, 2 Piece 50.00
Cranberry Glass, Lamp, Swirl, Miniature, 8 In. 150.00
Cranberry Glass, Muffineer, Acorn 275.00
Cranberry Glass, Muffineer, Blown, Silver Plate Dome Lid, 6 1/2 In. 45.00
Cranberry Glass, Muffineer, Coin Spot, Opalescent 115.00
Cranberry Glass, Muffineer, Daisy & Fern, Apple Blossom Mold 110.00
Cranberry Glass, Muffineer, Diamond Quilted, Ring Neck 78.00
Cranberry Glass, Muffineer, Diamond-Quilted, Shaker Top 69.50
Cranberry Glass, Muffineer, E.P.N.S. Top, Square, 5 In. 60.00
Cranberry Glass, Muffineer, Faceted Panels And Dome Cover 63.00
Cranberry Glass, Muffineer, Frosted, Enamel Decoration, 2-Piece Brass Top 85.00
Cranberry Glass, Muffineer, Inverted Thumbprint 65.00
Cranberry Glass, Muffineer, Opalescent Coin Spot .... 55.00 To 115.00
Cranberry Glass, Muffineer, Paneled, Shaker Top, 5 X 3 In. 90.00
Cranberry Glass, Muffineer, Paneled, Silver Plate Top 48.00
Cranberry Glass, Muffineer, Pewter Top, 5 X 2 3/4 In. 85.00

Cranberry Glass, Muffineer, Polished Panels, Dome Top 83.00
Cranberry Glass, Muffineer, Ribbed, Opalescent Swirl, Pewter Top 65.00
Cranberry Glass, Muffineer, Ring Neck, White Spatter 75.00
Cranberry Glass, Muffineer, Thumbprint 67.50
Cranberry Glass, Muffineer, Venetian Diamond 80.00
Cranberry Glass, Mug, Clear Applied Handle, 2 3/8 In., Set Of 4 .... 20.00
Cranberry Glass, Mug, Gold Trim, "Remember Me" 28.00
Cranberry Glass, Mug, Nine Flutes, Applied Handle, Grapes & Gilt, Pair 140.00
Cranberry Glass, Mustard Pot, Paneled, Silver Plate Lid & Handle, 4 In. 18.00
Cranberry Glass, Pickle Castor, Thumbprint, Silver Plated Frame, Tongs 165.00
Cranberry Glass, Pitcher & 6 Glasses, Opalescent, Swirls, Applied Handle 135.00
Cranberry Glass, Pitcher, Applied Clear Handle & Foot, 4 In. 88.00
Cranberry Glass, Pitcher, Clear Handle, Crimped Top, Ribbed Base, 7 In. 88.00
Cranberry Glass, Pitcher, Coin Spot, 6 Tumblers, Pitcher 9 1/2 In. 275.00
Cranberry Glass, Pitcher, Cream, Clear Twisted Handle, Enamel 150.00
Cranberry Glass, Pitcher, English, C.1850, Blown, Applied Clear Handle, 5 In. 45.00
Cranberry Glass, Pitcher, Gold, White Enamel Decoration .... *Illus* 95.00
Cranberry Glass, Pitcher, Handblown, 19th Century, Serpentine Handle, 4 In. 35.00
Cranberry Glass, Pitcher, Hobnail, Applied Clear Handle, Flared Top, 9 In. 82.00
Cranberry Glass, Pitcher, Paneled, Bulbous, Clear Reeded Handle, 6 1/4 In. 98.00
Cranberry Glass, Pitcher, Ribbed, Applied Clear Hollow Reeded Handle, 5 In. 65.00
Cranberry Glass, Pitcher, Ruffled Top, Clear Handle, 4 1/2 In. 10.00
Cranberry Glass, Pitcher, Tankard Shape, Clear Handle, 4 3/4 In. 60.00
Cranberry Glass, Pitcher, Water, Coin Spot 125.00

Cranberry Glass, Pitcher, Gold, White Enamel Decoration

Cranberry Glass, Pitcher, Water, Daisy & Fern, Opalescent 125.00
Cranberry Glass, Pitcher, Water, Diamond-Shaped Opalescent Thumbprints 145.00
Cranberry Glass, Pitcher, Water, Hobnail, Frosted Handle, Square Mouth 125.00
Cranberry Glass, Pitcher, Water, Inverted Thumbprint, Serpentine Rim 114.00
Cranberry Glass, Pitcher, Water, Opalescent Overlay, Cut, Cloverleaf Top 125.00
Cranberry Glass, Pitcher, Water, Spatter Leaf Umbrella 138.00
Cranberry Glass, Plate, Cake, Cut To Clear 12.00
Cranberry Glass, Plate, Overshot 55.00
Cranberry Glass, Ramekin & Saucer, Opalescent Hobnail, Ruffled Edge 42.00
Cranberry Glass, Rose Bowl, Blown And Ribbed, Ruffled Top, 4 In. 58.00
Cranberry Glass, Rose Bowl, Opalescent, Daisy & Fern, Ruffled Rim 68.00
Cranberry Glass, Rose Bowl, Paneled, Ruffled Top, Pedestal Base, 8 In. 60.00
Cranberry Glass, Rose Bowl, Paneled, 8 In. 15.00
Cranberry Glass, Rose Bowl, 8 Crimped Top, Miniature, 2 3/8 In. 37.00
Cranberry Glass, Salt & Pepper, Baby Thumbprint, Enameled Flowers 40.00
Cranberry Glass, Salt & Pepper, Fig, Decorated 100.00
Cranberry Glass, Salt, Cut, Pierced Silver Plate Holder, C.1895, 2 In. 18.00
Cranberry Glass, Salt, Metal Holder 85.00
Cranberry Glass, Saltshaker, Baby Thumbprint, Oval 35.00
Cranberry Glass, Saltshaker, Reverse Swirl, Ground Top 65.00
Cranberry Glass, Shade, Inverted Thumbprint, Bulbous, Ruffled Rim, Flowers 125.00
Cranberry Glass, Spooner, Swirled, Chrysanthemum Base 85.00
Cranberry Glass, Sugar Shaker, Bulbous, Inverted Thumbprint, Deep Color 60.00

Cranberry Glass, Sugar Shaker, Opalescent Swirl, 5 X 3 1/2 In. ... 75.00
Cranberry Glass, Sugar Shaker, Opalescent, 4 1/2 In. ... 55.00
Cranberry Glass, Syrup, Opalescent Coin Spot, Bird On Pewter Lid, 1872 ... 120.00
Cranberry Glass, Toothpick, Opalescent, Enameled Flowers ... 50.00
Cranberry Glass, Toothpick, Reverse Swirl, Opalescent ... 55.00
Cranberry Glass, Toothpick, Ribbed Lattice, Opalescent ... 55.00
Cranberry Glass, Top Hat, Opalescent Stripe, 4 In. ... 65.00
Cranberry Glass, Tumbler, Barrel Shape ... 25.00
Cranberry Glass, Tumbler, Enamel Floral ... 48.00
Cranberry Glass, Tumbler, Inverted Thumbprint, Pair ... 35.00
Cranberry Glass, Tumbler, Inverted Thumbprint, White Honeysuckle ... 65.00
Cranberry Glass, Tumbler, Opalescent Coin Spot ... 32.00 To 45.00
Cranberry Glass, Tumbler, Opalescent Hobnail ... 68.00
Cranberry Glass, Tumbler, Opalescent Swirl ... 25.00
Cranberry Glass, Tumbler, Opalescent With Camphor Glass Finish ... 45.00
Cranberry Glass, Vase, Applied Crystal Petals, Ribbed, 6 3/4 In. ... 69.00
Cranberry Glass, Vase, Coin Dot, Ruffled & Crimped Rim, 7 1/2 In. ... 165.00
Cranberry Glass, Vase, Coin Spot, Flared, Ruffled Top, 11 In ... 75.00
Cranberry Glass, Vase, Double Gourd Shape, 12 1/2 In. ... 40.00
Cranberry Glass, Vase, Gold Enamel, Ruffled, Gold-Plated Bronze Base, 15 In. ... 165.00
Cranberry Glass, Vase, Inverted Thumbprint, Fuchsia Pink, Pair ... 30.00
Cranberry Glass, Vase, Melon Shaped, 4 In., Pair ... 70.00
Cranberry Glass, Vase, Molded Plume Design, Enameled Florals, 3 In. ... 24.00
Cranberry Glass, Vase, Ruffled Top, Opalescent, 8 In., Pair ... 95.00
Cranberry Glass, Vase, Scalloped Edge, 12 In. ... 105.00
Cranberry Glass, Vase, White Opaque Stripes, Applied Ruffle, 9 3/8 In. ... 68.00
Cranberry Glass, Vinaigrette, Gold Decoration, Rectangular ... 50.00
Cranberry Glass, Washstand Set, Applied Crystal Handle, Blown, 2 Piece ... 115.00
Cranberry Glass, Water Set, Opalescent Coin Spot, Mold Blown, 7 Piece ... 250.00
Cranberry Glass, Wine, Clear Stem & Foot, 4 5/8 In. ... 20.00
Cranberry Glass, Wine, Clear Stem, 4 3/4 In. ... 28.00
Cranberry Glass, Wine, Cut Crystal Stem ... 27.50
Cranberry Glass, Wine, Stemmed, Cranberry Foot, 3 3/8 In., Set Of 4 ... 25.00

Creamware, or queensware, was developed by Josiah Wedgwood about 1765. It is a cream-colored earthenware that has been copied by many factories.

Creamware, see also Wedgwood

Creamware, Bowl, Black Transfer Of Birds & Castle Scene, 7 In. ... 125.00
Creamware, Plate, Octagonal, Center Enameled With Peafowl, C.1800, 7 5/8 In. ... 275.00
Creil, Plate, Le Quilles, C.1800, 8 In. ... 150.00
Creil, Plate, Le Voland, C.1800, 8 In. ... 150.00
Creil, Toby Mug, Man Wearing Monk's Robe & Tricornered Hat, 9 1/2 In. ... 48.00

Croesus, see Pressed Glass, Croesus

Crown Derby is the nickname given to the works of the Royal Crown Derby Factory which began working in England in 1859. An earlier and more famous English Derby factory existed from 1750 to 1848. The two factories were not related. Most of the porcelain found today with the Derby mark is the work of the later Derby factory.

Crown Derby, see also Royal Crown Derby

Crown Derby, Candlestick, Sapphire Blue, Floral, Gold, 10 In., Pair ... 425.00
Crown Derby, Figurine, Whippet, Purple S-H Mark, Pair ... 250.00
Crown Derby, Jar, Biscuit, Floral, Blue Underglaze, Crown, Reef Knot, W & W ... 215.00
Crown Derby, Plate, Turquoise, Autumn Colors Scene, Trowell, 8 5/8 In. ... 200.00
Crown Derby, Urn, Turquoise With Round Floral Medallions, Gold Handles, Pair ... 250.00

Crown Ducal is the name used on some pieces of porcelain made by the A. G. Richardson and Co., Ltd., England. The name has been used since 1916.

Crown Ducal, Plate, First Thanksgiving In America, Pink & White, 10 In. ... 25.00
Crown Ducal, Plate, First Thanksgiving, Mulberry, 10 In. ... 12.00
Crown Ducal, Plate, Landing Of Pilgrims, Mulberry, 10 In. ... 12.00
Crown Ducal, Plate, Mayflower In Plymouth Harbour, Mulberry, 10 In. ... 12.00
Crown Ducal, Plate, Mayflower In Plymouth Harbour, Pink & White, 10 In. ... 25.00

Crown Ducal, Plate, Monticello, Mulberry, 10 In. 12.00
Crown Ducal, Plate, Monticello, Pink & White, 10 In. 25.00
Crown Ducal, Plate, Mt.Vernon, Mulberry, 10 In. 12.00
Crown Ducal, Plate, Mt.Vernon, Pink & White, 10 In. 25.00
Crown Ducal, Plate, Signing Contract On Mayflower, Mulberry, 10 In. 12.00
Crown Ducal, Plate, Signing Contract On Mayflower, Pink & White, 10 In. 25.00
Crown Ducal, Saucer, Colonial Times, C.1925, 6 In. 5.00
Crown Ducal, Vase, Hummingbirds & Branches, 6 Sided, 8 1/4 In. 40.00

Crown Milano glass was made by Frederick Shirley about 1890. It had a plain biscuit color with a satin finish. It was decorated with flowers, and often had large gold scrolls.

Crown Milano, Box, Blue Swirl, Gold Chrysanthemums, Silver Collar, 5 In. 165.00
Crown Milano, Ewer, Glossy, Floral Decoration, 5 1/4 In. 750.00
Crown Milano, Jardiniere, Signed In Pontil, 8 X 7 In. 675.00
Crown Milano, Lamp Base, Gold Oakleaf Over Beige, Signed Crown & CM 375.00
Crown Milano, Lamp, Jewels & Floral On White Shade, 20 In. 995.00
Crown Milano, Muffineer, Ribbed, 6 In. 150.00
Crown Milano, Salt & Pepper, Egg 90.00
Crown Milano, Salt & Pepper, Tomato, Mt.Washington 70.00
Crown Milano, Sugar, 2 Ribbed Handles, 3 1/2 In. 110.00
Crown Milano, Vase, Cream Ground, Orange & Gold, Jeweled, 15 1/2 In. 1250.00
Crown Milano, Vase, Tan, Jeweled, Beige, Orange, & Gold Designs, 15 1/2 In. 1950.00
Crown Saxe, Plate, Cake, Green, Apples, Gold Leaves, Open Handles, 10 In. 22.00
Crown Tuscan, see Cambridge

Cruets of glass or porcelain were made to hold vinegar or oil. They were especially popular during Victorian times.

Cruet, see also Amber Glass, and other glass sections
Cruet Set, 4 Bottles, Handled Flat Stand 35.00
Cruet Set, 4 Bottles, Revolving Silver Plate Frame 125.00
Cruet, Blown Clear Glass, Pinched Top, Raised Enamel Decorations 19.00
Cruet, Blue To Clear, Heavily Enameled, Faceted Stopper, Miniature, 3 1/4 In. 85.00
Cruet, Blue Wicker 75.00
Cruet, Blue With Amber Applied Handled, Enameled Flowers, 7 3/4 In. 68.00
Cruet, Daisy & Fern, Faceted Stopper, White 38.00
Cruet, Diamond Quilted, Clear, Enameled Blue Forget-Me-Nots 35.00
Cruet, Emerald Green With White Enameled Daisies 100.00
Cruet, Emerald Green, The Prize, Green Faceted Stopper 75.00
Cruet, French Porcelain, Gold Scale Overlay 150.00
Cruet, Green Ivorina Verde 100.00
Cruet, Green, Beaded Grape, Green Stopper 90.00
Cruet, Light Amber, Etched Designed, Tall 50.00
Cruet, Medallion Sprig, Cobalt Blue To Clear, Clear Faceted Stopper 125.00
Cruet, Millefiori, Matching Stopper 175.00
Cruet, Nailsea Loop, Blue & White 50.00
CT Altwasser, Bowl, Eagle, Divided, Green Blue To White, Handle, 14 In. 35.00
CT Altwasser, Bowl, Fruit, Oval, Open Handles, With Eagle, 1800s 29.00
CT Altwasser, E.H.E., 1912, Cherries On Cream, 8 1/2 In. 30.00
CT Altwasser, Plate, Green, Floral, Germany, 1845, 11 In. 35.00
CT Germany, Coffee Set, Blue Floral, Gold Trim, 23 Piece 550.00

Cup plates are small glass or china plates that held the cup, while a gentleman of the mid-nineteenth century drank his coffee or tea from the saucer. The most famous cup plates were made of glass at the Boston and Sandwich Factory located in Massachusetts. The L numbers refer to the book "American Glass Cup Plates" by R. W. Lee and J. H. Rose.

Cup Plate, Blue, Henry Clay, Lacy, 3 5/8 In. 85.00
Cup Plate, Bunker Hill, Lacy, 3 1/2 In. 12.50
Cup Plate, Eagle & Fort Pitt, Lacy, 3 11/16 In. 40.00
Cup Plate, Eagle & Fort Pitt, Lacy, 3 3/4 In. 32.50
Cup Plate, Eagle, Lacy, 3 In. 15.00
Cup Plate, Flint, Blue With Violet Heart 145.00

Cup Plate, Henry Clay, Lacy, 3 5/8 In. 25.00
Cup Plate, Jacony, McK G V-24 24.00
Cup Plate, Maid Of The Mist, Lacy, 3 7/16 In. 20.00
Cup Plate, Midwestern, Lacy, 2 3/4 In. 27.50
Cup Plate, Ship, Lacy, Uneven Edge, 3 5/8 In. 20.00
Cup Plate, Ship, Lacy, 3 1/2 In. 30.00
Cup Plate, 13 Hearts, Lacy, 3 1/2 In. 12.50

Currier & Ives made the famous American lithographs marked with their name from 1857 to 1907.

Currier & Ives, Belle Of New York 35.00
Currier & Ives, General Andrew Jackson, Full Portrait 45.00
Currier & Ives, Joan Of Arc, Framed 48.00
Currier & Ives, Kittens 22.50
Currier & Ives, Lake Placid, Adirondacks, Small Folio, Matted 60.00
Currier & Ives, Little Brother, Walnut Shadowbox Frame, Medium Folio 45.00
Currier & Ives, Little Daisy, Oak Frame, Large Folio 30.00
Currier & Ives, Magic Lake, Medium Folio 50.00
Currier & Ives, Roses Of May, 1870, Hand Colored, Framed, Small Folio 48.00
Currier & Ives, Sacred Heart Of Mary 15.00
Currier & Ives, Sale Of The Pet Lamb, Framed, Medium Folio 60.00
Currier & Ives, Sunnyside On The Hudson, 15 3/4 X 11 3/4 In., Frame 95.00
Currier & Ives, Surrender Of Lee At Appomattox, Framed 125.00
Currier & Ives, Tomb Of Washington, Medium Folio 25.00
Currier & Ives, View From Fort Putnam, West Point, Hudson River, 12 3/4 In. 100.00
Currier & Ives, Who's Afraid Of You, Framed, 12 1/2 X 8 1/2 In. 40.00
Currier, Death Of Harrison, Lithograph, Color, Small Folio 10.00
Currier, Death Of Washington, Framed 48.00
Currier, Henry Clay Of Kentucky, 1844, Color, Framed, 18 1/4 X 14 1/4 In. 150.00

Custard glass is an opaque glass sometimes known as buttermilk glass. It was first made after 1886 at the La Belle Glass Works, Bridgeport, Ohio.

Custard Glass, see also Maize

Custard Glass, Banana Boat, Argonaut Shell, N In Circle, 11 X 6 1/2 In. 145.00
Custard Glass, Banana Boat, Chrysanthemum Sprig, Northwood 135.00
Custard Glass, Banana Boat, Geneva 160.00
Custard Glass, Banana Boat, Louis XV 135.00 To 160.00
Custard Glass, Banana Boat, Oval, Louis XV, 10 1/2 In. 170.00
Custard Glass, Banana Boat, Winged Scroll, B-309 165.00
Custard Glass, Bell, Smocking Pattern, 5 1/2 In. 135.00
Custard Glass, Berry Bowl, Diamond Peg, Roses 40.00
Custard Glass, Berry Bowl, Green, Georgia Gem 59.00
Custard Glass, Berry Bowl, Individual, Inverted Fan & Feather 75.00
Custard Glass, Berry Set, Blue, Chrysanthemum Sprig, 7 Piece 795.00
Custard Glass, Berry Set, Geneva, 6 Piece 265.00
Custard Glass, Berry Set, Honeycomb & Flower Rim, Painted Floral, 7 Piece 350.00
Custard Glass, Berry Set, Louis XV, Gold Trim, 7 Piece 550.00
Custard Glass, Berry Set, Ring Band, Red Rose, 5 Piece 360.00
Custard Glass, Berry Set, Winged Scroll, Gold Trim, 5 Piece 345.00
Custard Glass, Bonbon, Prayer Rug 14.00
Custard Glass, Bowl, Basket Weave, Grape & Cable Inside, Nutmeg, N, 7 In. 58.50
Custard Glass, Bowl, Beaded Circle, Painted Floral, Footed, 4 X 2 1/2 In. 45.00
Custard Glass, Bowl, Berry, Individual, Louis XV 55.00
Custard Glass, Bowl, Berry, Louis XV, Oval, Northwood 125.00
Custard Glass, Bowl, Berry, Louis XV, 11 1/4 In X 4 3/4 In. 155.00
Custard Glass, Bowl, Berry, Master, Louis XV 175.00
Custard Glass, Bowl, Berry, Ring Band, Red Roses, 8 1/2 In. 42.50
Custard Glass, Bowl, Berry, Winged Scroll, Gold Trim 795.00
Custard Glass, Bowl, Bluebirds, 8 In. 145.00
Custard Glass, Bowl, Chrysanthemum With Grapes, 2 Handles, Brown, 7 In. 50.00
Custard Glass, Bowl, Peacock At Urn, Northwood, 10 In. 195.00
Custard Glass, Butter Base, Blue Chrysanthemum Sprig, Louis XV 185.00
Custard Glass, Butter Bowl, Louis XV, Gold Trim 225.00

Custard Glass, **Butter**, Chrysanthemum Sprig, Northwood 185.00
Custard Glass, **Butter**, Covered, Chrysanthemum Sprig 225.00
Custard Glass, **Butter**, Covered, Geneva 120.00
Custard Glass, **Butter**, Covered, Intaglio, Blue & Gold Trim, Footed 165.00
Custard Glass, **Butter**, Covered, Inverted Fern, Heisey 250.00
Custard Glass, **Butter**, Louis XV, Gold Trim 145.00
Custard Glass, **Butter**, Maple Leaf, Gold Feet, Heisey 35.00
Custard Glass, **Compote**, Footed, Intaglio, Bright Blue And Gold Decoration 195.00
Custard Glass, **Compote**, Jelly, Argonaut Shell, Gold Trim 95.00
Custard Glass, **Compote**, Jelly, Intaglio, Green & Gold Trim, Northwood 72.00
Custard Glass, **Compote**, Jelly, Ring Band, Heisey 135.00
Custard Glass, **Console Bowl**, Green, Autumn, McKee, 10 In. 28.00
Custard Glass, **Console Bowl**, Yellow, McKee, 7 In. 18.00
Custard Glass, **Cracker Barrel**, Staves & Hoops, Silver Plate Fittings 85.00
Custard Glass, **Creamer**, Argonaut Shell .... 75.00 To 80.00
Custard Glass, **Creamer**, Blue, Chrysanthemum Sprig, Gold Trim, Northwood 225.00
Custard Glass, **Creamer**, Child's, Laurel, McKee 12.00
Custard Glass, **Creamer**, Chrysanthemum Sprig 95.00
Custard Glass, **Creamer**, Diamond Peg, Souvenir, Rockaway Beach, L.I., 5 In. 48.00
Custard Glass, **Creamer**, Grape & Cable, Nutmeg 12.00
Custard Glass, **Creamer**, Indiana 12.00
Custard Glass, **Creamer**, Intaglio, Green Trim 95.00
Custard Glass, **Creamer**, Little Gem, Floral Decoration, 3 Footed 48.00
Custard Glass, **Creamer**, Louis XV .... 75.00 To 80.00
Custard Glass, **Creamer**, Maple Leaf 125.00
Custard Glass, **Creamer**, Pineapple & Fan, Roses, Heisey 52.00
Custard Glass, **Creamer**, Pineapple & Fan, Tankard Shape, Heisey 75.00
Custard Glass, **Creamer**, Punty Band, St.Joseph, Mich., Miniature 45.00
Custard Glass, **Creamer**, Souvenir, Court House, Beloit, Kansas 24.00
Custard Glass, **Creamer**, Souvenir, Lake Forest College, Ill., North Hall 45.00
Custard Glass, **Creamer**, Souvenir, New Sharon, Maine 20.00
Custard Glass, **Creamer**, Souvenir, Scenic, Northwood Center 22.00
Custard Glass, **Creamer**, Winged Scroll 75.00
Custard Glass, **Cruet**, Blue Chrysanthemum Sprigs 700.00
Custard Glass, **Cruet**, Intaglio, Gold 150.00
Custard Glass, **Cruet**, Louis XV 175.00
Custard Glass, **Cup**, Punch, Diamond Peg 50.00
Custard Glass, **Eggcup**, Green, Double, McKee 5.00
Custard Glass, **Glass**, Shot, Souvenir, Akron, Ohio 22.00
Custard Glass, **Globe**, For Banquet Lamp, 25 In. 45.00
Custard Glass, **Goblet**, Beaded Loop, Rose Spray, Dennison, Minn., 6 In. 95.00
Custard Glass, **Goblet**, Beaded Swag 85.00
Custard Glass, **Goblet**, Grape & Gothic Arches 32.00
Custard Glass, **Hair Receiver**, Roses, Heisey 60.00
Custard Glass, **Ice Cream Set**, Maple, Gold & Green Leaves, Northwood, 7 Piece 350.00
Custard Glass, **Jar**, Biscuit, Green Cast, Enameled Florals, Silver Rim, Small 85.00
Custard Glass, **Jar**, Powder, Georgia Gem, Covered 75.00
Custard Glass, **Juicer**, Sunkist 18.00
Custard Glass, **Lamp**, Table 400.00
Custard Glass, **Muffineer**, Green Opaque, Paneled Teardrop .... 60.00 To 135.00
Custard Glass, **Muffineer**, Little Shrimp 65.00
Custard Glass, **Muffineer**, Many Lobes 65.00
Custard Glass, **Mug**, Band Of Stars & Punties Around Base, 3 1/4 In. 22.00
Custard Glass, **Mug**, Beaded Shell, Northwood 40.00
Custard Glass, **Mug**, Chrysanthemum Sprig, Souvenir, Stratford, Tex, 3 In. 27.50
Custard Glass, **Mug**, Geneva 55.00
Custard Glass, **Mug**, Serenade 35.00
Custard Glass, **Mug**, Shield 18.00
Custard Glass, **Mug**, Souvenir, Canajoharie, N.Y., 2 1/2 In. 19.00
Custard Glass, **Mug**, Souvenir, Exeter, Maine 20.00
Custard Glass, **Mug**, Souvenir, Punty & Star Band, North Leeds, Maine 28.00
Custard Glass, **Pitcher**, Diamond & Peg, Red Rose Decoration 35.00
Custard Glass, **Pitcher**, Large, Maple Leaf 145.00
Custard Glass, **Pitcher**, Ring Band, Gold Chrysanthemum, Signed 210.00

Custard Glass, Pitcher, Water, Argonaut Shell, Northwood 325.00
Custard Glass, Pitcher, Water, Jackson 145.00
Custard Glass, Plate, Grape & Cable, Northwood, 7 1/2 In. 38.00
Custard Glass, Plate, Prayer Rug, 7 3/4 In. 18.00
Custard Glass, Plate, Stalking Lion, Green Staining, Fruit Underside, 7 In. 100.00
Custard Glass, Rose Bowl, Blown, Applied Flowers 75.00
Custard Glass, Rose Bowl, Cased With Pink Lining, Bent-Down Petals 75.00
Custard Glass, Salt & Pepper, Argonaut Shell 600.00
Custard Glass, Salt & Pepper, Geneva, Decorated 115.00
Custard Glass, Salt & Pepper, Intaglio 125.00
Custard Glass, Salt & Pepper, Punty Band 25.00
Custard Glass, Salt & Pepper, Ring Band, Heisey 78.00
Custard Glass, Salt, Souvenir, Court House, Cresco, Ia. 35.00
Custard Glass, Saltshaker, Chrysanthemum Sprig 45.00
Custard Glass, Saltshaker, Intaglio, Melon Ribbed, No Enamel 40.00
Custard Glass, Saltshaker, Louis XV 120.00
Custard Glass, Saltshaker, Souvenir, Dickinson County H.S., Chapman, Kans. 25.00
Custard Glass, Saltshaker, Souvenir, Mendota, Ill., Red & Green Floral 30.00
Custard Glass, Saltshaker, Spider Web 19.00
Custard Glass, Sauce, Argonaut Shell 50.00
Custard Glass, Sauce, Louis XV, Footed, 5 In. 50.00
Custard Glass, Sauce, Louis XV, Oval, 4 Footed, 3 1/2 X 5 In. 45.00
Custard Glass, Sauce, Master, Argonaut Shell, Northwood, Oval 300.00
Custard Glass, Shade, Stalacite Shape, Teardrop Point, 11 In. 38.00
Custard Glass, Sherbet, Indiana 25.00
Custard Glass, Shot Glass, Souvenir, Popham Beach, Maine 30.00
Custard Glass, Spooner, Argonaut Shell, Signed, Gold 80.00
Custard Glass, Spooner, Chrysanthemum Sprig .... 90.00 To 95.00
Custard Glass, Spooner, Chrysanthemum Sprig, Gold Trim, Footed 85.00
Custard Glass, Spooner, Chrysanthemum, Blue, Signed Northwood 225.00
Custard Glass, Spooner, Diamond Peg , Roses, Paynesville, Minnesota, Krystal 65.00
Custard Glass, Spooner, Fan, Gold Trim, Northwood 75.00
Custard Glass, Spooner, Fluted At Top, 5 In. 55.00
Custard Glass, Spooner, Geneva .... 60.00 To 90.00
Custard Glass, Spooner, Honeycomb With Flower Band 55.00
Custard Glass, Spooner, Iris 75.00
Custard Glass, Spooner, Louis XV .... 65.00 To 80.00
Custard Glass, Spooner, Maple Leaf .... 100.00 To 110.00
Custard Glass, Spooner, Ruffled Edge, 5 In. 35.00
Custard Glass, Spooner, Trailing Vine, 4 In. 25.00
Custard Glass, Sugar & Creamer, Laurel, Footed, McKee 30.00
Custard Glass, Sugar & Creamer, Winged Scroll, Gold Trim 170.00
Custard Glass, Sugar Bowl, Covered, Winged Scroll 95.00
Custard Glass, Sugar, Argonaut Shell 100.00
Custard Glass, Sugar, Breakfast, Heart With Thumbprint 55.00
Custard Glass, Sugar, Covered, Chrysanthemum Sprig, Gold Trim, Footed 105.00
Custard Glass, Sugar, Covered, Louis XV .... 85.00 To 90.00
Custard Glass, Sugar, Grape 60.00
Custard Glass, Sugar, Individual, Souvenir, Petoskey, Heisey 35.00
Custard Glass, Sugar, Jackson 25.00
Custard Glass, Sugar, Louis XV 60.00
Custard Glass, Sugar, Souvenir, Green, Little Gem, Warner, N.H. 30.00
Custard Glass, Sugar, Souvenir, Orrs Island, Maine, 3 X 2 1/2 In. 22.00
Custard Glass, Sugar, Yellow, Souvenir, Coleman, S.D. 47.50
Custard Glass, Syrup, Ring Band, Roses, Gold Trim, Heisey 235.00
Custard Glass, Table Set, Argonaut Shell, Gold Trim, Northwood, 3 Piece 285.00
Custard Glass, Table Set, Chrysanthemum Sprig, Northwood, 4 Piece 395.00
Custard Glass, Table Set, Geneva, 4 Piece 425.00
Custard Glass, Table Set, Intaglio, 4 Piece 390.00
Custard Glass, Table Set, Louis XV, 4 Piece 300.00
Custard Glass, Table Set, Maple Leaf, 3 Piece 275.00
Custard Glass, Table Set, Maple Leaf, 4 Piece 650.00
Custard Glass, Table Set, Winged Scroll, 3 Piece 425.00
Custard Glass, Teacup, Jackson 25.00

Custard Glass, Toothpick, Chrysanthemum Sprig, Gold Trim 175.00
Custard Glass, Toothpick, Diamond Peg 55.00
Custard Glass, Toothpick, Diamond Peg, Souvenir, Elgin, Ia. 55.00
Custard Glass, Toothpick, Diamond Peg, Souvenir, Gettysburg, 1863 .... 45.00
Custard Glass, Toothpick, Green, Georgia Gem 45.00
Custard Glass, Toothpick, Green, Harvard, Souvenir 23.50
Custard Glass, Toothpick, Inverted Fan & Feather .... 400.00 To 425.00
Custard Glass, Toothpick, Memorial Bridge, Milford, Conn. 24.00
Custard Glass, Toothpick, Pitcher Shape, Souvenir, Bellevue, Ohio, 1904 .... 27.00
Custard Glass, Toothpick, Ring Band .... 60.00 To 65.00
Custard Glass, Toothpick, Ring Band, Souvenir 55.00
Custard Glass, Toothpick, Ring Band, Souvenir, Geneva, N.Y., Heisey 40.00
Custard Glass, Toothpick, Souvenir, Green, Little Gem, West Townshend, Vt. 24.00
Custard Glass, Toothpick, Souvenir, Haverhill, Mass. 12.00
Custard Glass, Toothpick, Souvenir, Ottumwa, Iowa 55.00
Custard Glass, Toothpick, Souvenir, Scenic, Orrs Island Bridge 22.00
Custard Glass, Toothpick, Sunapee Lake, N.H. 22.00
Custard Glass, Tray, Condiment, Ring Band, Gold Trim, Heisey 210.00
Custard Glass, Tray, Pin, Delaware, Blue Trim 38.00
Custard Glass, Tray, Pin, Delaware, Green Trim 40.00
Custard Glass, Tumbler, Argonaut Shell 110.00
Custard Glass, Tumbler, Beaded Circle 78.00
Custard Glass, Tumbler, Casino, Hampton Beach, N.H. 95.00
Custard Glass, Tumbler, Delaware, Green Trim 58.00
Custard Glass, Tumbler, Diamond Peg, Signed Souvenir Of Cleveland 40.00
Custard Glass, Tumbler, Intaglio, Gold & Green Trim 46.00
Custard Glass, Tumbler, Little Gem, Hand-Painted Cosmos, Heisey 45.00
Custard Glass, Tumbler, Maple Leaf 78.00
Custard Glass, Tumbler, Pearlized Grape & Gothic Arches, Gold Trim 45.00
Custard Glass, Tumbler, Punty Band, Roses 35.00
Custard Glass, Tumbler, Ribbed Thumbprint, Souvenir, State Fair, 1912, Roses 45.00
Custard Glass, Tumbler, Souvenir, Casino, Hampton Beach, N.H., Trolley 55.00
Custard Glass, Tumbler, Souvenir, Pipestone, Minn.4 In. 50.00
Custard Glass, Tumbler, Souvenir, Scenic, Northwood Narrows, N.H. 30.00
Custard Glass, Tumbler, Winged Scroll, Gold Trim .... 55.00 To 75.00
Custard Glass, Vase, Blue, Scroll & Arabesque, Collared Base & Rim, 9 In. 75.00
Custard Glass, Vase, Diamond Peg, Souvenir Coney Island 25.00
Custard Glass, Vase, Drapery With Nutmeg Stain, 9 In., Pair 55.00
Custard Glass, Vase, Gold Paint, Scalloped Top, Souvenir, Alamo, 6 In. 22.00
Custard Glass, Vase, Green, Ribbed, Very Heavy, 12 In. 30.00
Custard Glass, Vase, Green, Ribbed, 12 In. 30.00
Custard Glass, Vase, High School, Marble Rock, Iowa, 6 In. 22.50
Custard Glass, Vase, Northwood, 8 In. 32.00
Custard Glass, Vase, Northwood, 9 1/2 In., Drapery Pattern, Marked N 45.00
Custard Glass, Vase, Pisgah, Iowa, 6 In., Pair 25.00
Custard Glass, Vase, Souvenir, Trumpet Shape, Beading, 6 In. 27.50
Custard Glass, Water Set, Chrysanthemum Sprig, Northwood, 7 Piece 495.00
Custard Glass, Water Set, Geneva, 7 Piece 585.00
Custard Glass, Water Set, Intaglio, 7 Piece 635.00
Custard Glass, Water Set, Inverted Fan & Feather, 7 Piece .... 775.00 To 800.00
Custard Glass, Water Set, Maple Leaf, 7 Piece 600.00
Custard Glass, Water Set, Owl Decoration 850.00
Custard Glass, Wine, Diamond Peg, Gilded, 4 In. 35.00
Custard Glass, Wine, Sailboat & Mountain Medallions, Twisted Stem 85.00
Custard, Dish, Prayer Rug, 3-Handled, 6 1/4 In. 25.00

Cut glass has been made since ancient times, but the large majority of the pieces now for sale date from the brilliant period of glass design, 1880 to 1905. These pieces had elaborate geometric designs with a deep miter cut.

Cut Glass, see also Vaupel

Cut Glass, Apple Bowl, Fan & Star, Pedestal, 8 In. 87.00
Cut Glass, Atomizer, Aurene Intaglio, Colors 198.00
Cut Glass, Banana Boat, Hobstar & Diamond, 11 1/2 X 8 X 4 1/2 In. 185.00
Cut Glass, Banana Boat, Hobstar & Vesica, 11 In. 125.00

Cut Glass, Banana Boat, Pinwheel, Flashed Fan, & Crosscut Diamond, 9 In. 150.00
Cut Glass, Banana Boat, Pinwheel, 11 X 7 1/2 In. 85.00
Cut Glass, Banana Boat, Pinwheels, Cut Pears, Sawtooth Rim, 12 X 6 In. 65.00
Cut Glass, Basket, Candy, Stars, Grooved Handle & Rim, Rayed Base, 5 1/2 In. 40.00
Cut Glass, Basket, Cane, Straw Button Floral, Notched Handle, 14 In. 310.00
Cut Glass, Basket, Cut Handle, Signed Tuthill, 18 In. 1500.00
Cut Glass, Basket, Fan, Block, & Crosshatching, 9 X 8 In. 95.00
Cut Glass, Basket, Fan, Buzz, & Strawberry Diamond, Notched Handle, 8 In. 175.00
Cut Glass, Basket, Flowers, Leaves, Harvard Border, Double-Notch Cut Handle 300.00
Cut Glass, Basket, Harvard & Cornflowers, Thumbprint Handle, 12 In. 275.00
Cut Glass, Basket, Harvard, Brilliant, 15 In. 375.00
Cut Glass, Basket, Hobstar & Cane, Flower At Ends, Notched Handle, 12 In. 325.00
Cut Glass, Basket, Rope Handle, Rayed Flowers, Diamond Cut Centers, 5 In. 55.00
Cut Glass, Basket, Thumbprint & Cut Rim, Intaglio Cut, Strawberry & Hobnail 275.00
Cut Glass, Basket, 2 Butterflies & Leaves, Mark Patented, 8 In. 28.00
Cut Glass, Bell, Hobstars, Fans, Notched, Faceted Handle, 5 In. 135.00
Cut Glass, Bell, Stawberry Diamond & Fan, Handle Cut, 6 In. 180.00
Cut Glass, Berry Bowl, Hobstars, Brilliant Period, 8 X 3 In. 55.00
Cut Glass, Berry Bowl, Louis XIV, Hawkes, Pair 110.00
Cut Glass, Berry Set, Diamond Points, 9 Piece 275.00
Cut Glass, Bonbon, Covered, Allover European Cut, Star, Cut Knob On Lid, 7 In. 60.00
Cut Glass, Bonbon, Pinwheels, Sawtooth Edge, Signed Clock, 5 In. 40.00
Cut Glass, Bottle, Catsup 27.00
Cut Glass, Bottle, Cologne, Dido 100.00
Cut Glass, Bottle, Cologne, Engraved Flowers, Rayed Base, Sterling Top, Enamel 40.00
Cut Glass, Bottle, Cologne, Leaves, Acid-Etched Blossoms, Black Enamel, 5 In. 20.00
Cut Glass, Bottle, Cologne, Paneled, Engraved Lizzie, 1876, 9 1/2 In. 35.00
Cut Glass, Bottle, Cordial, Diamond Stopper, Hobstar & Strawberry Diamond 115.00
Cut Glass, Bottle, Cordial, Fern 150.00
Cut Glass, Bottle, Liqueur, Strawberry Diamond 75.00
Cut Glass, Bottle, Perfume & Smelling Salts, Emerald, Muff, Sterling Cap 65.00
Cut Glass, Bottle, Perfume, Amber & Clear Stopper, Amber Blocks, 5 In. 58.00
Cut Glass, Bottle, Perfume, Bulbous, Clarke 47.00
Cut Glass, Bottle, Perfume, Canes, English, 7 In. 42.50
Cut Glass, Bottle, Perfume, Diamond Cut Stopper, Hobstar, Strawberry, Clark 75.00
Cut Glass, Bottle, Perfume, Emerald Green, Clear Stopper, Cut Base, 9 In. 95.00
Cut Glass, Bottle, Perfume, Enameled Silver Top, 6 In., Pair 175.00
Cut Glass, Bottle, Perfume, Faceted Stopper, Spade Shape 95.00
Cut Glass, Bottle, Perfume, French Sterling Stopper, Intaglio, 4 In. 39.00
Cut Glass, Bottle, Perfume, Gold Band, Black Enamel Blue Beads, Hawkes, 7 In. 45.00
Cut Glass, Bottle, Perfume, Hinged Crown With Stones Lid, Faceted, 9 In. 135.00
Cut Glass, Bottle, Perfume, Hingéd Sterling Top, English, C.1890 35.00
Cut Glass, Bottle, Perfume, Lying Down, Russian, Sterling Top 45.00
Cut Glass, Bottle, Perfume, Pointed Stopper, Crisscross & Slash, Ball Shape 12.00
Cut Glass, Bottle, Perfume, Russian Sterling Repousse Hinged Top, English 65.00
Cut Glass, Bottle, Perfume, Russian, Starred Buttons, Sterling Lid, 5 In. 175.00
Cut Glass, Bottle, Perfume, Sapphire Blue, Faceted Stopper, Enamel, 4 In. 65.00
Cut Glass, Bottle, Perfume, Silver Top, Lay-Down, Diamonds, 7 In. 45.00
Cut Glass, Bottle, Perfume, Sterling Lid, Etched, Hawkes 22.00
Cut Glass, Bottle, Perfume, Sterling Stopper, Brilliant Period 20.00
Cut Glass, Bottle, Sachet, Hinged, Embossed Sterling Cover, Hobstars, 3 In. 22.00
Cut Glass, Bottle, Salts, Hinged Sterling Top & Chain, Paneled, 4 1/2 In. 45.00
Cut Glass, Bottle, Smelling Salts, Amber, Ovoid Shape, No Stopper 18.00
Cut Glass, Bottle, Smelling Salts, Sterling Cap, Diamonds, Birmingham, 1921 15.00
Cut Glass, Bottle, Smelling Salts, Sterling Cap, Paneled, London, 1920 20.00
Cut Glass, Bottle, Water, Strawberries, 8 X 5 1/2 In. 125.00
Cut Glass, Bottle, Whiskey, Hobstar, Diamond, & Fan, 11 In. 110.00
Cut Glass, Bottle, Wine, Hindoo, J.Hoare 195.00
Cut Glass, Bowl & Base, Punch, Cane & Medallion 75.00
Cut Glass, Bowl & Underplate, Mayonnaise, Hobstar, Strawberry Diamond, & Fan 115.00
Cut Glass, Bowl, Amber, Sinclaire, 6 3/4 X 6 In. 75.00
Cut Glass, Bowl, Blue Overlay Cut To Clear, Faceted Pedestal, C.1900, 8 In. 275.00
Cut Glass, Bowl, Brunswick, Signed Hawkes, 2 X 8 In. 175.00
Cut Glass, Bowl, Bull's-Eye Column & Vertical Miter, Fluted Rim, 7 X 3 In. 30.00

Cut Glass, Bowl, Cane & Hobstar, Scalloped Sawtooth Edge, 11 In. 150.00
Cut Glass, Bowl, Crosscut Diamond & Fan, Hobstar Base, 10 X 4 1/4 In. 110.00
Cut Glass, Bowl, Crosscut Diamond Band, 32-Point Star Base, Footed, 8 In. 50.00
Cut Glass, Bowl, Diamond Point & Crosshatching, Star Base, Hawkes, 8 1/2 In. 135.00
Cut Glass, Bowl, Expanding Stars, Hawkes, 8 X 2 In. 85.00
Cut Glass, Bowl, Fan, Hobstar, & Crosshatching, 7 In. 47.50
Cut Glass, Bowl, Fern, Chain Of Hobs, Hobnail, Brilliant, 3 Feet, 7 1/4 In. 95.00
Cut Glass, Bowl, Finger, Cranberry Bands, Relief Diamond, Monogram 40.00
Cut Glass, Bowl, Finger, Underplate, Intaglio Flower Sprays, Hawkes 35.00
Cut Glass, Bowl, Fortuna, Scalloped Rim, Maple Leaf Signed, 9 1/2 In. 195.00
Cut Glass, Bowl, Fruit, Heavy Notched Top, Star Bottom, 11 1/2 X 5 In. 150.00
Cut Glass, Bowl, Fruit, Pedestal, Pinwheels, Hobstars, Fans, Cut Prisms 225.00
Cut Glass, Bowl, Geometric Cut, Egginton's Trellis, 8 X 4 In. 270.00
Cut Glass, Bowl, Gorham Sterling Openwork Rim, Hobstars, 10 3/4 In. 275.00
Cut Glass, Bowl, Gravic, Iris, Hawkes, 8 1/4 In. 215.00
Cut Glass, Bowl, Grecian, Flashed Hobstars, 8 In. 87.75
Cut Glass, Bowl, Harvard, 5 3/4 X 9 1/2 In. 250.00
Cut Glass, Bowl, Hawkes, 8 X 3 1/2 In. 110.00
Cut Glass, Bowl, Hoare, 7 1/2 In. 49.00
Cut Glass, Bowl, Hobstar Center & Ends, Oval, 10 3/4 X 5 In. 55.00
Cut Glass, Bowl, Hobstar Chain & Crosscut Diamond, Star Base, 8 In. 55.00
Cut Glass, Bowl, Hobstar Vesica & Fan, 9 X 2 In. 135.00
Cut Glass, Bowl, Hobstar, Cane, Fan, & Star, Sawtooth Rim, 6 3/4 In. 45.00
Cut Glass, Bowl, Hobstar, Fan, Horizontal Step, & Strawberry Diamond, 8 In. 64.00
Cut Glass, Bowl, Hobstar, Hobnail, Strawberry Diamond, & Fan, Clarke, 9 In. 140.00
Cut Glass, Bowl, Hobstar, Miter, & Notched Prism Radial, Libbey, 8 In. 80.00
Cut Glass, Bowl, Hobstar, Parallel Lines, Fans, Straus, 3 1/4 X 7 In. 105.00
Cut Glass, Bowl, Hobstar, 7 X 3 In. 85.00
Cut Glass, Bowl, Intaglio Cut Flowers & Leaves, Fluted, 11 X 3 1/2 In. 65.00
Cut Glass, Bowl, Intaglio Cut, Floral Sprays & Leaf, Hawkes, 8 In. 100.00
Cut Glass, Bowl, Iris, 9 X 4 In. 145.00
Cut Glass, Bowl, Kimberly, Libbey, 7 In. 120.00
Cut Glass, Bowl, Octagonal, Royal, Signed Hunt, 9 In. 340.00
Cut Glass, Bowl, Oval Hobstar Center, Hobstar Chain & Cane, Oval, 7 In. 50.00
Cut Glass, Bowl, Pedestal, Crosses, Signed Stewart, 8 X 5 In. 85.00
Cut Glass, Bowl, Pinwheel & Cane, Shallow, 7 In. 60.00
Cut Glass, Bowl, Pinwheel & Hobstar, 8 X 3 3/4 In. 95.00
Cut Glass, Bowl, Pinwheel, Diamond, Scalloped Rim, 8 In. 125.00
Cut Glass, Bowl, Rolled Scalloped Rim, Intaglio Cut, Rayed Cut Base, 10 In. 80.00
Cut Glass, Bowl, Rosette, Cane, & Fan, Honesdale, 8 In. 50.00
Cut Glass, Bowl, Rosette, Cane, Floral, & Feathered Leaf, 8 3/4 In. 85.00
Cut Glass, Bowl, Royal, Hunt, 9 In. 235.00
Cut Glass, Bowl, Russian Cutting, Hobstars, 6 In. 50.00
Cut Glass, Bowl, Russian, Plain Button, Kidney Shape, 8 X 7 X 3 1/2 In. 325.00
Cut Glass, Bowl, Shallow, Signed Egginton, 7 1/2 In. 70.00
Cut Glass, Bowl, Sinclaire, 8 In. 58.00
Cut Glass, Bowl, Small, Signed Tuthill 45.00
Cut Glass, Bowl, Spinning Wheel, Fan, & Hobstar, 8 In. 145.00
Cut Glass, Bowl, Square, Trellis Pattern, Unsigned Sinclaire, 9 X 6 1/2 In. 85.00
Cut Glass, Bowl, Star Of David, Flared, 6 Hobstars, 10 In. 125.00
Cut Glass, Bowl, Star, Libbey, 1906, 9 X 2 In. 75.00
Cut Glass, Bowl, Starred Hobnails, Sawtooth Rim, 7 3/4 In. 80.00
Cut Glass, Bowl, Stars, 6 1/2 In. 25.00
Cut Glass, Bowl, Straight Sided, Star In Diamonds, Hawkes, 5 1/2 In. 65.00
Cut Glass, Bowl, Straus, 8 X 2 In. 95.00
Cut Glass, Bowl, Strawberry Diamond, Canoe Shape, 13 1/2 In. 76.00
Cut Glass, Bowl, Strawberry Diamond, Fan & Hobstar, Hobstar Ends, Oval, 11 In. 70.00
Cut Glass, Bowl, Strawberry Diamond, Fan, & Star, Star Base, 9 1/2 In. 225.00
Cut Glass, Bowl, Strawberry Diamond, Hobstar, & Floral, Hawkes, 6 In. 75.00
Cut Glass, Bowl, Strawberry, Diamond And Fan, 8 1/2 In. 45.00
Cut Glass, Bowl, Swirl, White Blank, Cane Outline, Hobstars, Rayed Sawtooth 350.00
Cut Glass, Bowl, Triple Square, Clarke, 9 In. 200.00
Cut Glass, Bowl, Vintage, Tuthill, Oval, 8 In. 210.00
Cut Glass, Bowl, Wheel Cutting, Stepped Edge, 7 X 2 In. 97.50

Cut Glass, Bowl, Whipped Cream, With Tray, Stars, Leaves, Brilliant, 5 In. 69.00
Cut Glass, Bowl, 12 Panels, Hobstars, Diamond Point, Brilliant, 9 X 4 In. 150.00
Cut Glass, Bowl, 3 Footed, Nickel Rim, Star & Cross, Shallow Cut, 7 In. 55.00
Cut Glass, Bowl, 8-Pointed Star Base, Libbey, 8 1/2 X 4 In. 250.00
Cut Glass, Box, Candy, Pinwheels, Footed, 7 X 6 In. 35.00
Cut Glass, Box, Covered, Oval Harvard Border, Cornflowers 55.00
Cut Glass, Box, Dresser, Hinged, Underplate, Button & Fan, English, 5 In.Round 65.00
Cut Glass, Box, Dresser, Russian, Strawberry, Buttons, 3 1/2 X 5 1/2 In. 175.00
Cut Glass, Box, Dresser, Square, Hinged Lid, Daisy & Cornflower, 5 X 4 In. 95.00
Cut Glass, Box, Flower On Hinged Lid, Strawberry Diamond & Cane, 6 In. 175.00
Cut Glass, Box, Heart Shape, Covered, Cane & Intaglio, Hobnail, 3 X 6 In. 165.00
Cut Glass, Box, Hinged, Round, 5 In. 125.00
Cut Glass, Box, Hinged, Silver Rims, Florence, Rayed Base, 7 1/2 X 3 1/2 In. 550.00
Cut Glass, Box, Hinged, Silver Rims, Hobstars, Rayed Base, 5 In. 200.00
Cut Glass, Box, Jewel, Oval Hinged, Hobstar, Strawberry Diamond, 5 1/2 X 3 In. 250.00
Cut Glass, Box, Jewel, Round, Hobstar On Top, Brilliant, 5 1/4 In. 150.00
Cut Glass, Box, Pill, Strawberry Diamond, Fans, Star Base, Sterling Lid 15.00
Cut Glass, Box, Powder, Covered, Pinwheels, 16-Pointed Star Base 55.00
Cut Glass, Box, Powder, Love's Dream, Silver Top, Unger Brothers, 3 1/2 In. 85.00
Cut Glass, Box, Powder, Ruby, Cut To Clear Floral, 5 X 3 In. 24.00
Cut Glass, Box, Powder, Russian, Strawberry Buttons, 3 1/2 In. 225.00
Cut Glass, Box, Powder, Unger Bros. Sterling Lid, Love's Dream 65.00
Cut Glass, Box, Silver Fittings, Handle, & Hinged Lid, Footed, Oval, 8 In. 90.00
Cut Glass, Bucket, Ice, Brazilian, Hawkes, Silver Handle, 9 In. 300.00
Cut Glass, Bucket, Ice, Crosshatching, Nailhead, & Fan, Tab Handled, 7 In. 165.00
Cut Glass, Bucket, Ice, Diamonds, Tab Handles, 2 X 1 1/4 In. 40.00
Cut Glass, Bucket, Ice, Harvard Cut, 5 3/4 X 7 In. 275.00
Cut Glass, Bucket, Ice, Strawberry Diamond & Fan, Handled, 5 1/2 In. 115.00
Cut Glass, Bucket, Ice, Vesica, Hobstar, & Strawberry Diamond, Tab Handles 300.00
Cut Glass, Butter Pat, Russian Cut, Buttons, Square, 2 3/4 In. 20.00
Cut Glass, Butter, Covered, Brilliant, Hobstars, Hobnail, Fan, Diamond 165.00
Cut Glass, Butter, Covered, Pinwheel, Vesica, & Comet 193.00
Cut Glass, Butter, Diamond & Star 175.00
Cut Glass, Butter, Dome Lid, Harvard, Geometric, Hobstar & Nailhead, 8 In. 350.00
Cut Glass, Butter, Domed Lid, Underplate, Flashed Fan, Scalloped Rim 225.00
Cut Glass, Butter, Hobstars, White Brilliant Blank, Hawkes 375.00
Cut Glass, Butter, Princess 6.00
Cut Glass, Candelabra, 3-Arm, Button & Prism, 7 1/2 In., Pair 250.00
Cut Glass, Candelabrum, 3-Arm, Screws Apart, 60 Prisms, 23 In. 1200.00
Cut Glass, Candleholder, Intaglio Cut, Floral Stem & Base, Libbey, 10 In. 95.00
Cut Glass, Candlestick, Blue To Clear, 8 In. 195.00
Cut Glass, Candlestick, Colonial, 10 In. 60.00
Cut Glass, Candlestick, Engraved Floral & Leaf, Libbey, 10 In., Pair 265.00
Cut Glass, Candlestick, Engraved Leaf & Berry, Crosshatching, 5 In. Base 50.00
Cut Glass, Candlestick, Flowers & Leaves, Signed Libbey, 10 In., Pair 265.00
Cut Glass, Candlestick, Flute, Rayed Bottom, Hawkes, 9 In., Pair 325.00
Cut Glass, Candlestick, Hobstars, , 1/4 In. 65.00
Cut Glass, Candlestick, Intaglio Flowers, Teardrop Stem, 9 In., Pair 300.00
Cut Glass, Candlestick, Turquoise Blue, Bobeche Step, 12 X 5 3/4 In., Pair 225.00
Cut Glass, Canoe, Harvard Cut, 11 1/2 In. 175.00
Cut Glass, Canoe, Hobstar, Notched Prism, Fan, & Strawberry Diamond, 9 In. 25.00
Cut Glass, Canoe, Sterling Mounts, Strawberry Diamond, 9 3/4 X 4 1/4 In. 235.00
Cut Glass, Carafe, Block And Fan 25.00
Cut Glass, Carafe, Brilliant Period, Signed 134.00
Cut Glass, Carafe, Diamond & Strawberry, Notched Neck, 8 In., Pair 165.00
Cut Glass, Carafe, Hawkes, Quart 100.00
Cut Glass, Carafe, Hobstar & Clover 40.00
Cut Glass, Carafe, Hobstar And Rayed Star, 8 1/2 In. 55.00
Cut Glass, Carafe, Notched Prism, Vesica, & Star, Star Base, 8 1/4 In. 60.00
Cut Glass, Carafe, Prism & Fan, Quart 75.00
Cut Glass, Carafe, Russian, Starred Button, 8 In. 285.00
Cut Glass, Carafe, Russian, Starred Buttons, 7 1/2 X 5 1/4 In. 275.00
Cut Glass, Carafe, Split Vesica & Bead, 8 1/4 In. 110.00
Cut Glass, Carafe, Water, Harvard Cutting, Prism Stem, 24-Point Star Base 89.00

Cut Glass, Carafe, Water, Hobstar & Notched Prism, Paneled Notched Neck 62.00
Cut Glass, Carafe, Water, Notched & Fluted Neck, 8 In. 40.00
Cut Glass, Carafe, Water, Pinwheel, Flashed Fan, & Crosscut Diamond, 7 In. 65.00
Cut Glass, Carafe, Wide Bottom, Deep Notched Prisms And Stars, 8 In. 60.00
Cut Glass, Carafe, Wine, Galt & Bro. Sterling Collar, Hobstar & Fan 95.00
Cut Glass, Casket, Jewelry, Etched Morning Glory & Leaf, Footed Brass Holder 50.00
Cut Glass, Castor, Pickle, Tongs, Lid, Finecut 40.00
Cut Glass, Celery, Caprice, J.D.Bergen, 12 X 5 1/2 In. ..... 110.00 To 125.00
Cut Glass, Celery, Diamond Thumbprint 100.00
Cut Glass, Celery, Flashed Pinwheel, & Fan, Boat Shape 56.50
Cut Glass, Celery, Greek Key Chain Top, Flute Stem, 16-Point Star Base 30.00
Cut Glass, Celery, Hobstar & Fan, Violet Bowl, Hawkes, 10 3/4 In. 145.00
Cut Glass, Celery, Leaf, Hobstar, & Diamond Point, Copper Wheel Floral, 8 In. 24.00
Cut Glass, Celery, Pinwheel, Hobstar, Fan, & Checkered Diamond, 4 1/2 In. 70.00
Cut Glass, Celery, Rectangular, Hobnail, 11 1/2 X 4 1/2 In. 65.00
Cut Glass, Celery, Scalloped Edge, 11 X 5 In. 50.00
Cut Glass, Celery, Strawberry Diamond, Hobstars, Signed Hoare, 12 1/2 X 5 In. 145.00
Cut Glass, Champagne, Cranberry Stem, Almond & Circle, Libbey 27.50
Cut Glass, Champagne, Crosscut Diamond & Fan, Cut Stems, Rayed Base, 2 ..... 45.00
Cut Glass, Champagne, Double Wafer Stem, Hawkes 22.50
Cut Glass, Champagne, Strawberry Diamond & Split, Hawkes 16.00
Cut Glass, Cheese & Cracker Set, Intaglio Underplate, Strawberry Cut Bowl 150.00
Cut Glass, Cocktail Shaker, Hawkes, 12 In. 95.00
Cut Glass, Compote, American Brilliant, Pedestal, Pinwheel & Hobstar, 8 In. 85.00
Cut Glass, Compote, Broadway, G.W.Huntley Co., 6 1/2 X 4 1/2 In. 65.00
Cut Glass, Compote, Brunswick, Paneled Stem With Teardrop, 8 In. 175.00
Cut Glass, Compote, Candy, Gold Filled Designs, Intaglio, 7 X 8 In. 32.00
Cut Glass, Compote, Canoe Shape, Brilliant, Hobstar, 7 X 7 X 4 In. 175.00
Cut Glass, Compote, Deep Cut Ferns, 24 Point Star On 4 In Diameter, 5 In. 85.00
Cut Glass, Compote, Dorflinger Kalana Pansy, Hollow Stem, 8 X 5 1/2 In. 275.00
Cut Glass, Compote, Fan Shape, Pinwheel & Hobs, 8 3/4 In. 175.00
Cut Glass, Compote, Fry, 10 In. 285.00
Cut Glass, Compote, Gravic, Intaglid Iris, Star Cut, Funnel Shape, Hawkes 195.00
Cut Glass, Compote, Harvard Type, Bulbous Base, Scalloped Rim, 6 In. 75.00
Cut Glass, Compote, Hobstar & Cane, St.Louis Diamond, 7 1/2 In. ..... 125.00 To 150.00
Cut Glass, Compote, Hobstar & Cane, 9 1/2 In. 110.00
Cut Glass, Compote, Hobstar Chain, Strawberry Diamond, Prism Stem, 8 In. 140.00
Cut Glass, Compote, Hobstar, Strawberry Diamond, & Star, Star Base, 6 1/4 In. 75.00
Cut Glass, Compote, Hobstar, Strawberry Diamond, Hobnail, & Star, 9 1/4 In. 325.00
Cut Glass, Compote, Intaglio Cut, Berry & Leaf, Paneled Stem, 11 In. 175.00
Cut Glass, Compote, Intaglio Cut, Berry & Leaf, Pinched Top, 5 In. 40.00
Cut Glass, Compote, Intaglio Cut, Libbey, 6 1/4 In. 95.00
Cut Glass, Compote, Intaglio, Cosmos, Teardrop Stem, Rolled Rim, 10 In. 95.00
Cut Glass, Compote, Jelly, Hobstar & Diamond Point, 6 1/2 In. 110.00
Cut Glass, Compote, Jelly, Paperweight Base, Hobstar, Fan, Flute, 5 X 3 In. 56.00
Cut Glass, Compote, Roses, 9 1/2 X 8 1/2 In. 85.00
Cut Glass, Compote, Russian, Square, 10 X 7 In. 650.00
Cut Glass, Compote, Serrated Edge, Teardrop Stem, 8 In. 85.00
Cut Glass, Compote, Teardrop Stem, Hobstar, Strawberry Diamond, & Fan, 8 In. 135.00
Cut Glass, Compote, Teardrop Stem, 4 Sections, Wilcox Sterling Band, 7 In. 425.00
Cut Glass, Compote, Teardrop Stem, 8 1/2 X 6 In. 235.00
Cut Glass, Console Set, Amber, Engraved Raspberries, Hollow Stems, 3 Piece 225.00
Cut Glass, Cordial Set, Punties, Teardrop Stopper, 6 Piece 125.00
Cut Glass, Cordial, Cubes, 7 In. 5.00
Cut Glass, Cordial, Fern & Buzz, Thin, Tall Stem 2.50
Cut Glass, Cordial, Harvard 24.00
Cut Glass, Cordial, Magnet & Grape, Frosted Leaf, 4 In. 145.00
Cut Glass, Cordial, Signed Maple City, Harvard, Hobstar, Fan, Zipper 24.00
Cut Glass, Cordial, Teardrop Stem 30.00
Cut Glass, Creamer, Pinwheel, Pedestal 62.00
Cut Glass, Creamer, Pinwheel, Strawberry Diamond & Hobstar, Footed, 4 3/4 In. 75.00
Cut Glass, Cruet, Dated Oct.6, 1914, Signed Hawkes, 7 3/4 In. 55.00
Cut Glass, Cruet, Deep Cut, Signed Hawkes, Matching Stopper 65.00
Cut Glass, Cruet, Faceted Stopper & Handle, Hobstar & Fan, 6 In., Pair 85.00

Cut Glass, Cruet, Faceted Stopper, Fan, Star, & Diamond, Applied Handle, 6 In. 22.00
Cut Glass, Cruet, Faceted Stopper, Prisms, 7 1/2 In. 22.00
Cut Glass, Cruet, Pinwheel, Hobstars, 3 Lipped 38.00
Cut Glass, Cruet, Sterling Stopper, Hawkes 35.00
Cut Glass, Cruet, Strawberry Diamond & Fan, Small, Squatty 85.00
Cut Glass, Cruet, Triple Lip, Notched Handle, Signed Sinclaire 80.00
Cut Glass, Cruet, Vinegar, Ladder-Cut Neck, 6 In. 95.00
Cut Glass, Cruet, Wine, Amber, Faceted Stopper, Applied Handle, 14 1/2 In. 68.00
Cut Glass, Cup, Custard, Waterford 6.00
Cut Glass, Cup, Punch, Feathered Star, Hobstar, & Fan 21.50
Cut Glass, Cup, Punch, Hobstar, Fan, & Crosshatching 18.00
Cut Glass, Cup, Punch, Hobstars, Hawkes 30.00
Cut Glass, Cup, Punch, Monarch, J.Hoare 75.00
Cut Glass, Cup, Punch, Strawberry Diamond, Crosscut Diamond & Fan, Pair 25.00
Cut Glass, Cup, Punch, Sunburst Pineapple & Feathered Leaf 25.00
Cut Glass, Cup, Punch, Triple Notched Handle, Footed 75.00
Cut Glass, Cup, Punch, Tusk & Hobstar, Hawkes 25.00
Cut Glass, Decanter, Amber, Faceted Stopper, Castle & Animals, 12 1/2 In. 138.00
Cut Glass, Decanter, Applied Clear Handle, Sterling Cover, Signed Hawkes 75.00
Cut Glass, Decanter, Captain's, Hobstars, Diamond Point, Brilliant, Hawkes 385.00
Cut Glass, Decanter, Diamond Stopper, Handle, Hobstar & Diamond, 15 In. 165.00
Cut Glass, Decanter, Faceted Neck Ring, Loop Cut Base, 16 1/4 In. 35.00
Cut Glass, Decanter, Flat Flared, Fan & Diamond, 8 X 9 In. 75.00
Cut Glass, Decanter, Gorham Sterling Handle & Lid, Convex Cut, 10 In. 250.00
Cut Glass, Decanter, Hobstar, Strawberry Diamond, Fan, Stopper, 11 1/2 In. 225.00
Cut Glass, Decanter, Lapidary Stopper, Crosscut Diamond & Fan, 11 In. 110.00
Cut Glass, Decanter, Lapidary Stopper, Crosscut, Strawberry Diamond, 11 In. 110.00
Cut Glass, Decanter, Lapidary Stopper, Fan & Crosscut Diamond, 11 1/2 In. 165.00
Cut Glass, Decanter, Original Stopper, 15 In., Heavy 95.00
Cut Glass, Decanter, Ruby To Clear, Faceted Stopper, Diamond & Fan, 13 In. 45.00
Cut Glass, Decanter, Square, Double Cross, Panelled Neck 50.00
Cut Glass, Decanter, Sterling Stopper, Hobstar & Cane, 10 In. 110.00
Cut Glass, Decanter, Sterling Top, Etched Hunting Scene, Hawkes, 12 In. 95.00
Cut Glass, Decanter, Teardrop Stopper, Creswick, Neck Ring, 13 In. 150.00
Cut Glass, Decanter, Topaz To Clear, Bull's-Eyes, 12 In. 100.00
Cut Glass, Decanter, Wine, Bulbous 135.00
Cut Glass, Decanter, Wine, Crosscut Diamond, Strawberry, English Sterling 85.00
Cut Glass, Decanter, Winona, Clark, Stopper, 15 In. 185.00
Cut Glass, Dish & Underplate, Cheese, Dome Lid, Russian Cut, Hobstars 400.00
Cut Glass, Dish, Bonbon, Hunt Royal Pattern, 5 In. 40.00
Cut Glass, Dish, Brunswick, Signed Hawkes, 6 1/2 In. 65.00
Cut Glass, Dish, Candy, Floral, Hawkes, 5 1/4 X 5 1/4 In. 48.00
Cut Glass, Dish, Candy, Strawberry Diamond & Fan, Russian Cut Base, 8 X 4 In. 80.00
Cut Glass, Dish, Candy, 2 Part, Intaglio Cut, Sterling Center, Handle, Hawkes 32.50
Cut Glass, Dish, Candy, 8-Pointed Stars, 3 Turned-In Edges 10.00
Cut Glass, Dish, Cheese & Cracker, Dome With Teardrop Handle, Signed Hoare 295.00
Cut Glass, Dish, Cheese & Cracker, Hobstar & Strawberry Diamond, P & B 90.00
Cut Glass, Dish, Cheese, Covered, Blown Blank, Hobstars, Cane, Diamond, Fan 350.00
Cut Glass, Dish, Cheese, Covered, Cane, Diamond, & Fan 375.00
Cut Glass, Dish, Cheese, Covered, Hobstar, Fan, & Diamond, Blown Blank 325.00
Cut Glass, Dish, Cheese, Cut Knob On Dome Top, Strawberry Diamond & Hobstars 375.00
Cut Glass, Dish, Cheese, Pinwheels 275.00
Cut Glass, Dish, Heart Shape, Hobstars, Notch Cutting & Fan, 5 In. 85.00
Cut Glass, Dish, Hobs, Cane, Diamond, Cut Handle Applied, 7 3/4 In. 65.00
Cut Glass, Dish, Ice Cream, Hobstar, Cane, 17 1/4 X 9 3/4 In. 395.00
Cut Glass, Dish, Large Fruit In Center, Smaller On Edges, Heavy, 10 In. 29.00
Cut Glass, Dish, Lemon, Sterling Rim & Handle, Signed Hawkes 28.00
Cut Glass, Dish, Nut, Hobstar, Fan, & Notched Prism, Pitkin & Brooks, 8 In. 125.00
Cut Glass, Dish, Nut, Hobstars, Fans, Pitkins & Brooks, 4 1/2 X 8 In. 125.00
Cut Glass, Dish, Olive, Hobstar & Comet 34.00
Cut Glass, Dish, Pin, Harvard, Handles At Each End, 8 1/2 In. 65.00
Cut Glass, Dish, Shell Type, Signed Hoare, 7 X 1 In. 85.00
Cut Glass, Dish, Signed Omega 40.00
Cut Glass, Dish, Square, Brilliant, Sunburst Surrounding Hobstar, 7 In. 85.00

Cut Glass, Dish, Square, Imperial, Signed Libbey, Saber Mark, 6 In. 165.00
Cut Glass, Dish, Sweetmeat, Melon Pattern, Red, Plated Collar, 1 1/2 In. 375.00
Cut Glass, Dish, Trefoil Shape, Strawberry Diamond Base, Hobstar & Fan, 6 In. 65.00
Cut Glass, Dish, 4 Sections, Strawberry Diamond Points, Star & Fan Rim 135.00
Cut Glass, Dresser Set, Brilliant, Clock, Powder Jar, Hair Receiver, Cologne 325.00
Cut Glass, Dresser Set, Cane, Lift-Off Lids, 3 Piece 165.00
Cut Glass, Dresser Set, Harvard Cut, Floral & Leaf, Rayed Bases, 3 Piece 225.00
Cut Glass, Dresser Set, Harvard Cut, Pinwheels, Rayed Bases, 3 Piece 90.00
Cut Glass, Dresser Set, Intaglio Cut Flowers, Hobnail Centers, 3 Piece 300.00
Cut Glass, Ferner, Faceted Hobstar, 24-Point Star Base, 3 Clear Feet, 8 In. 145.00
Cut Glass, Ferner, Footed, Signed Clark, Triple Square Pattern, 9 In. 195.00
Cut Glass, Fernery, Hobstars, 3 Footed, 7 3/4 In. 60.00
Cut Glass, Fernery, Napoleon, 3 Footed, 8 X 4 1/2 In. 65.00
Cut Glass, Finger Bowl, Brunswick, Hawkes 50.00
Cut Glass, Finger Bowl, Cobalt Cut To Clear, Diamonds 12.50
Cut Glass, Finger Bowl, Fruit, Gravic Cutting, Almond Base, Hawkes 50.00
Cut Glass, Finger Bowl, Intaglio Cut, Grape & Leaf, Libbey, 5 In. 55.00
Cut Glass, Finger Bowl, Iris, Gravic Cutting, Hawkes 50.00
Cut Glass, Finger Bowl, Serrated, Fan Top 17.00
Cut Glass, Finger Bowl, Stars, Rayed Base 17.00
Cut Glass, Flask, Cane, Round, Sterling Cup Over Bottom, Hinged Top, 6 1/2 In. 50.00
Cut Glass, Flask, Lady's, Sterling Lid, Russian, Starred Buttons, 6 In. 165.00
Cut Glass, Flask, Perfume, Cabochon Stone In Sterling Top, Prism & Diamond 35.00
Cut Glass, Flower Center, Hobstars, 25 In. 295.00
Cut Glass, Flower Center, Russian, Diamond Buttons, 10 In. 450.00
Cut Glass, Flower Center, Strawberry Diamond Bands, Star, & Cane, 9 In. 425.00
Cut Glass, Fruit Bowl & Base, Hobstar, Diamond, Fan, & Notched Prism, 11 In. 175.00
Cut Glass, Fruit Bowl & Base, Pinwheel, Hobstar, Fan, & Notched Prism, 9 In. 225.00
Cut Glass, Fruit Bowl, Cut & Etched Flowers, Leaves, & Vines 70.00
Cut Glass, Fruit Bowl, Feathered Fan, Hobnail, Star, & Waffle, 9 1/2 In. 110.00
Cut Glass, Globe, Lamp, Frosted, Signed Gillinder, 7 X 4 X 4 In., Pair 25.00
Cut Glass, Glue Pot, Sterling Lid, Cherub & Roses 35.00
Cut Glass, Goblet, Cobalt Cut To Clear, Thumbprint In Diamond 20.00
Cut Glass, Goblet, Crosscut Diamond & Fan, Cut Stem, Signed Hawkes, 6 In. 30.00
Cut Glass, Goblet, Double Lozenge 55.00
Cut Glass, Goblet, Etched Floral, Rayed Base, Blown 7.50
Cut Glass, Goblet, Hawkes 50.00
Cut Glass, Goblet, Hobstar & Fan, Notched Stem, Clarke 65.00
Cut Glass, Goblet, Russian Cut, Teardrop 85.00
Cut Glass, Hair Receiver & Powder Jar, Tortoiseshell & Sterling Lids 42.00
Cut Glass, Hair Receiver, Engraved Birds, Harvard Bottom 50.00
Cut Glass, Hair Receiver, Sterling Lid, 16-Pointed Star Base 27.00
Cut Glass, Hatpin Holder, Heavy Cut 22.50
Cut Glass, Humidor, Sterling Top, Zipper, Cross Hatch, Fan Vesicas 350.00
Cut Glass, Ice Bucket, Hobstar Chain, Flashed Fans, 7 In. 250.00
Cut Glass, Inkwell, Cane Cut, Cover Grass, 2 1/2 In. 40.00
Cut Glass, Inkwell, Faceted Hinged Lid, Beveled Sides, Diamond Shape, 3 In. 38.00
Cut Glass, Inkwell, Harvard, Sterling Rims & Covers 65.00
Cut Glass, Inkwell, Hinged Brass Lids, Harvard Cutting, Pen Rest, 4 1/2 In. 100.00
Cut Glass, Inkwell, Hinged Silver Plate Lid, Horizontal Ribs, 3 In. 50.00
Cut Glass, Inkwell, Hobstars, Fans, Silver Floral Repousse Cover, 3 1/2 In. 80.00
Cut Glass, Inkwell, Silver Hinged Cover, Silver Underplate, Cane, Hobnail 165.00
Cut Glass, Inkwell, Sterling Lid, Flutes, English 50.00
Cut Glass, Inkwell, Sterling Top, Hobstar, Vesicas, Marked Wilcox, 3 1/2 In. 150.00
Cut Glass, Inkwell, Triangle Shape, Solid Brass Hinged Lid, 2 1/4 X 3 In. 40.00
Cut Glass, Jar, Apothecary, Knob Finial, Bull's-Eye & Diamond, Pairpoint 300.00
Cut Glass, Jar, Art Nouveau Sterling Lid, Notched Prisms, 2 1/4 X 2 In. 35.00
Cut Glass, Jar, Candy, Sterling Finial & Foot, Millicent, Hawkes, 11 In. 185.00
Cut Glass, Jar, Cracker, Harvard & Pillar, Silver Handle And Top, 9 1/2 In. 225.00
Cut Glass, Jar, Dresser, Alvin Sterling Lid, Checkered Diamond & Fan 32.00
Cut Glass, Jar, Dresser, Intaglio Cut, Flower & Leaf, Wallace Sterling Lid 37.50
Cut Glass, Jar, Dresser, Silver Lid, Checkered Diamond & Fan, Rayed Base 20.00
Cut Glass, Jar, Mustard, Silvered Lid & Handle 23.00
Cut Glass, Jar, Paste, Sterling Lid, Punty & Prism, Barrel Shape, 4 1/2 In. 45.00

Cut Glass, Jar, Powder, Art Nouveau Sterling Lid, Hobstar & Fan 58.00
Cut Glass, Jar, Powder, Floral & Feather On Sterling Lid, 3 X 3 In. 35.00
Cut Glass, Jar, Powder, Frosted Intaglio Floral & Leav Lid, Paneled, 5 In. 29.00
Cut Glass, Jar, Powder, Reine Des Fleurs 65.00
Cut Glass, Jar, Powder, Turquoise Stones In Sterling Lid 48.00
Cut Glass, Jar, Preserve, Sterling Lid, Engraved Berries, 5 3/4 In. 75.00
Cut Glass, Jar, Puff, Engraved Sterling Lid, Teardrop & Notched Prism, 5 In. 58.00
Cut Glass, Jar, Rose Petal, Bull's-Eye & Flute, Mushrose Lid 140.00
Cut Glass, Jar, Sterling Lid, Bull's-Eye, Strawberry Diamond, & Prism, 6 In. 70.00
Cut Glass, Jar, Tobacco, Incised & Frosted Floral, Cherub On Sterling Lid 88.00
Cut Glass, Jar, Tobacco, Sterling Lid, Dorflinger, 1896 .... 190.00
Cut Glass, Jar, Tobacco, Sterling Top, Thatch & Fan, 7 In. 125.00
Cut Glass, Jug, Diamond-Cut Stopper, Hobstar Rosette, Prism, & Star, 9 In. 145.00
Cut Glass, Jug, Whiskey, Clarke 275.00
Cut Glass, Jug, Whiskey, Signed Hawkes, 13 1/4 In. 195.00
Cut Glass, Jug, Whiskey, Thistle, Hawkes, Unsigned 225.00
Cut Glass, Knife Rest, Child's Head At Each End, 3 1/2 In., Pair 50.00
Cut Glass, Knife Rest, Daisy 24.50
Cut Glass, Knife Rest, Diamonds, Ball Ends 35.00
Cut Glass, Knife Rest, Faceted Ends, Dumbbell Type, 3 1/2 In. 19.00
Cut Glass, Knife Rest, Hobstar Ends, Ovals Around Side, 3 1/2 In. 40.00
Cut Glass, Knife Rest, Knob Ends, 4 In. 10.00
Cut Glass, Knife Rest, Star Ends, 4 1/4 In. 26.00
Cut Glass, Lamp, see Lamp
Cut Glass, Lamp, Boudoir, Flowers, Leaves, Diamond Point Prisms, 12 In. 400.00
Cut Glass, Match Striker, Amber, Silver Rim, Edinborough, Victorian, 2 In. 50.00
Cut Glass, Match Striker, Silver Rim, Birmingham, C.1872, 3 5/8 In. 50.00
Cut Glass, Match Striker, Silver Rim, Birmingham, Victorian, 1 5/8 In. 30.00
Cut Glass, Match Striker, Silver Rim, Birmingham, 1894, 2 1/8 In. 40.00
Cut Glass, Match Striker, Silver Rim, Birmingham, 1899, 2 1/8 In. 40.00
Cut Glass, Match Striker, Silver Rim, Chester, Edinborough, Victorian, 2 In. 40.00
Cut Glass, Match Striker, Silver Rim, Edinborough, Victorian, 1 5/8 In. 30.00
Cut Glass, Match Striker, Silver Rim, London, Victorian, 1 5/8 In. 30.00
Cut Glass, Match Striker, Silver Rim, London, Victorian, 2 1/8 In. 40.00
Cut Glass, Mayonnaise Bowl & Underplate, Hobstar, Strawberry Diamond, & Fan 175.00
Cut Glass, Mayonnaise Bowl & Underplate, Hobstars, Sawtooth Rim, 5 1/2 In. 145.00
Cut Glass, Mayonnaise Bowl & Underplate, Hobstars, Vesicas, Brilliant 95.00
Cut Glass, Mayonnaise Bowl, Hobstars 35.00
Cut Glass, Muffineer, Pewter Top 25.00
Cut Glass, Muffineer, Silver Lid, Red Cut To Clear 170.00
Cut Glass, Muffineer, Silver Plated Top, 4 3/4 In. 90.00
Cut Glass, Napkin Ring, see Napkin Ring
Cut Glass, Nappy, American, Brilliant, Geometric, Hobstars, Fans, 6 In. 29.00
Cut Glass, Nappy, Blackmere Columbia, 7 In. 100.00
Cut Glass, Nappy, Chain Of Hobstars, Ring Handle 57.00
Cut Glass, Nappy, Cross Ovals, Handled, 5 In. 45.00
Cut Glass, Nappy, Harvard Cutting, Handled, 6 In. 45.00
Cut Glass, Nappy, Hobstar & Chain Of 8 Hobstars, 2 Handles, 8 1/2 In. 55.00
Cut Glass, Nappy, Hobstars, Faceted Handle & Rim, Hawkes 45.00
Cut Glass, Nappy, Hobstars, Hawkes, 5 In. 46.00
Cut Glass, Nappy, Hobstars, Notched Handle, 6 In. 24.00
Cut Glass, Nappy, Intaglio Cutting, Raspberries & Thorns, Heart Shape 20.00
Cut Glass, Nappy, Intaglio Cutting, Roses, Sawtooth Edge, Oval, 7 1/2 In. 35.00
Cut Glass, Nappy, Loop Handle, Facet Cut, Hobstars, American Brilliant Period 40.00
Cut Glass, Nappy, Open Cut With Large Center Hob, Notched Prism, 6 In. 55.00
Cut Glass, Nappy, Royal, 2 Handles, Hunt 250.00
Cut Glass, Nappy, Sawtooth Edge, 6 In. 35.00
Cut Glass, Nappy, Spinning Wheel & Hobstar, 6 In. 45.00
Cut Glass, Nappy, Stars, Double Handles, 6 In. 45.00
Cut Glass, Nappy, Strawberry Diamond & Fan, Rayed Base 28.00
Cut Glass, Orange Bowl, Desdemona, Clarke, 9 X 9 In. 175.00
Cut Glass, Orange Bowl, Pinwheel, Flashed Fan, & Crosscut Diamond, 12 In. 175.00
Cut Glass, Pitcher, Bulbous, Hawkes, 8 In. 145.00
Cut Glass, Pitcher, Butterfly, Floral, & Feathered Leaf, Star Base, 11 In. 175.00

Cut Glass, Pitcher, Buttermilk, Pinwheels 135.00
Cut Glass, Pitcher, Cider, Hobnail, Hobstars, Fans, Notched Handle, 8 In. 175.00
Cut Glass, Pitcher, Floral With Hobnail Centers, 24-Point Star Base, 11 In. 110.00
Cut Glass, Pitcher, Harvard & Intaglio Cut, 12 In. 90.00
Cut Glass, Pitcher, Harvard Cut, Floral, Hobnail, & Leaf, 10 1/2 In. 125.00
Cut Glass, Pitcher, Hobstar & Fan, Notched Handle & Under Lip, 7 In. 48.00
Cut Glass, Pitcher, Hobstar, Fan, & Strawberry Diamond, Scalloped, 7 1/2 In. 140.00
Cut Glass, Pitcher, Hobstar, Fan, & Strawberry, 24-Pointed Star Base, 8 In. 85.00
Cut Glass, Pitcher, Hobstar, 8 In. 125.00
Cut Glass, Pitcher, Hobstars & Fine Diamond, Hand Polished, Straus 175.00
Cut Glass, Pitcher, Hobstars In 3 Panels, Thumbprints, Crescents, Hawkes 155.00
Cut Glass, Pitcher, Intaglio, Quart 125.00
Cut Glass, Pitcher, Intaglio, Tiger Lilies, Cut Handle, Sterling Overlay Base 275.00
Cut Glass, Pitcher, Milk, Hobstar & Strawberry Diamond Bands, Star Base 85.00
Cut Glass, Pitcher, Milk, Strawberry Diamond & Fan, Hobstar Base, 4 1/4 In. 90.00
Cut Glass, Pitcher, Milk, Strawberry Diamond, Cross Cut Diamond, 4 1/2 In. 80.00
Cut Glass, Pitcher, Millicent, Hawkes Signed, 8 1/2 X 6 In. 195.00
Cut Glass, Pitcher, Pinwheel, Strawberry Diamond, & Fan, 10 1/2 In. 125.00
Cut Glass, Pitcher, Plaza, 9 3/4 In. 110.00
Cut Glass, Pitcher, Premier, Bulbous, Bergen, 5 1/2 X 5 1/2 In. 225.00
Cut Glass, Pitcher, Prism & Diamond, Hawkes, 9 In. 225.00
Cut Glass, Pitcher, Water, Dorflinger Pattern No. 40, 9 In. 175.00
Cut Glass, Pitcher, Water, Harvard And Floral, Brilliant 85.00
Cut Glass, Pitcher, Water, Harvard, Cosmos 85.00
Cut Glass, Pitcher, Water, Intaglio Cut, Primrose, Hobstar, Diamond, & Fan 135.00
Cut Glass, Pitcher, Water, Jacob's Ladder & Suns, Thistles, Helmet Spout 150.00
Cut Glass, Pitcher, Water, Jeweled Moon & Star 45.00
Cut Glass, Pitcher, 24-Pointed Star Base, 10 1/2 In. 100.00
Cut Glass, Planter, Intaglio Cut, Fan, Vine, Floral, & Hobstar, Footed, 8 In. 32.00
Cut Glass, Plate, Bread, Cane, Strawberry Diamond, Star, & Fan, Libbey, 13 In. 175.00
Cut Glass, Plate, Bread, Hobstars, Hawkes, 14 X 8 In. 275.00
Cut Glass, Plate, Hobstar, Fan, & Crosshatching, 7 In. 35.00
Cut Glass, Plate, Hobstar, Flashed Fan, & Crosscut Diamond, 12 In. 225.00
Cut Glass, Plate, Ice Cream, Hobstar, Star, Strawberry Diamond, & Fan, 6 In. 31.50
Cut Glass, Plate, Round, Diamond Point & Strawberry, Intaglio Birds, Hawkes 550.00
Cut Glass, Plate, Sprays Of Copper Wheel Floral & Leaf, 10 In. 58.00
Cut Glass, Plate, Strawberry & Fan, 6 1/2 In. 35.00
Cut Glass, Plate, 12 Radiating Frosted & Clear Panels, 10 In. 195.00
Cut Glass, Platter, Ice Cream, Fan, Notched Ribbon, Star & Medallion, 15 In. 168.00
Cut Glass, Platter, Ice Cream, Vesicas, Bulged-Out Center, 14 In. 173.00
Cut Glass, Pot, Wassail, Round, Silver Plated Foot, Stand, Top, Ladle, 18 In. 2500.00
Cut Glass, Punch Bowl & Base, Crosscut Diamond & Flute 300.00
Cut Glass, Punch Bowl & Base, Flashed Hobstars, 10 In. 240.00
Cut Glass, Punch Bowl & Base, Hawkes 750.00
Cut Glass, Punch Bowl & Base, Hobstar, Fan, & Strawberry Diamond, 10 1/2 In. 325.00
Cut Glass, Punch Bowl, Birds & Trees 1500.00
Cut Glass, Punch Bowl, Corinthian, 24 In.Around, Original Standard 370.00
Cut Glass, Punch Set, Star, Cane, & Diamond Point, Pairpoint, 13 Piece 1400.00
Cut Glass, Relish, Double, Pineapple & Fan, Sterling Fittings, Hawkes 85.00
Cut Glass, Relish, Oval, Strawberry, Diamond & Fan, 9 1/2 In. 110.00
Cut Glass, Relish, Scalloped Fluted Edge, 7 7/8 X 3 3/4 In. 45.00
Cut Glass, Rose Bowl, Block Pattern, Hand Polished, 8 X 8 In. 250.00
Cut Glass, Rose Bowl, Buzz, Cut Leaves, Rayed Base, Large 78.00
Cut Glass, Rose Bowl, Clear Liner, Checkered Diamond & Fan, 4 In. 95.00
Cut Glass, Rose Bowl, Crosscut Diamond, Strawberry Diamond & Fans, 7 In. 110.00
Cut Glass, Rose Bowl, Green, Engraved, Hawkes, Signed, 4 3/4 In. 125.00
Cut Glass, Rose Bowl, Hobstar Rosette & Cane, 7 In., Pair 750.00
Cut Glass, Rose Bowl, Hobstars, Tusks, Vesicas & Fans, 5 3/4 In. 165.00
Cut Glass, Rose Bowl, Pedestal, Hobstar, Strawberry Diamond, Fan, 6 In. 150.00
Cut Glass, Rose Bowl, Pinwheel, Crossed Vesicas, Stars, 6 1/2 X 4 1/2 In. 115.00
Cut Glass, Rose Bowl, Russian Cut, 3 Applied Shell Feet, Notched Rim, 8 In. 265.00
Cut Glass, Rose Bowl, Stemmed, Clarke, 10 In. 150.00
Cut Glass, Rose Bowl, Thumbprint, Miniature, 1 3/4 In. 10.00
Cut Glass, Rose Bowl, Vertical Notched Prisms, 32-Pointed Star Base, 4 In. 55.00

Cut Glass, Salad Bowl, Hobstar, Cane, & Fan, Birks, 8 X 3 1/2 In. 150.00
Cut Glass, Salesman Sample, Canoe, Hobstars, Diamond, Fan, 3 1/4 In. 69.00
Cut Glass, Salt & Pepper, Diamonds, Sterling Tops 18.00
Cut Glass, Salt & Pepper, Floral Pointed Sterling Tops, 4 In. 35.00
Cut Glass, Salt & Pepper, Lay-Down Eggs, Columbian Exposition, 1893, Libbey 225.00
Cut Glass, Salt & Pepper, Master, Green To Clear 95.00
Cut Glass, Salt & Pepper, Silver & Mother-Of-Pearl Tops 19.00
Cut Glass, Salt & Pepper, Sterling Floral Top, Notched Vesicas 22.00
Cut Glass, Salt & Pepper, Sterling Tops, Panel & Notch, Pedestal Base, 3 In. 30.00
Cut Glass, Salt, Blue, Winded Nude Figure Blowing Bubbles, 2 3/4 In., Pair 15.00
Cut Glass, Salt, Diamonds, English Sterling Spoon 25.00
Cut Glass, Salt, English, Sterling Rims, Pair 20.00
Cut Glass, Salt, Ferns 10.50
Cut Glass, Salt, Floral, Set Of 6 .... 15.00
Cut Glass, Salt, Heart Shape, Crosscut Diamond & Fan 12.50
Cut Glass, Salt, Individual, Hobstars, Star Base, Set Of 9 .... 45.00
Cut Glass, Salt, Master, Diamonds, 24-Point Star Base, 2 1/2 In. 25.00
Cut Glass, Salt, Master, Geometrics, Pedestal, Tudor, 3 1/2 In. 32.00
Cut Glass, Salt, Master, Rectangular, Sapphire Blue, 1 3/4 X 3 1/4 In. 25.00
Cut Glass, Salt, Pedestal, Libbey, 3 X 2 In., Set Of 6 .... 150.00
Cut Glass, Salt, Round, Large Diamonds, American, 3 In., Pair 39.00
Cut Glass, Salt, Scalloped Top 9.25
Cut Glass, Salt, Sterling Silver Rim, English, Pair 25.00
Cut Glass, Saucer, Ice Cream, 5 Point Star, Flower, 6 In. 40.00
Cut Glass, Sherbet & Tray, Louis XIV, Monogrammed, Hawkes 60.00
Cut Glass, Sherbet & Underplate, Vertical & Horizontal Lines, Webb Corbett 16.00
Cut Glass, Sherbet, Cobalt Cut To Clear, Thumbprint In Diamond, Stemmed 15.50
Cut Glass, Soup Bowl, Intaglio Flower & Leaves, Tuthill, 8 In. 35.00
Cut Glass, Spooner, Hobnail, Cane & Strawberry Diamond & Fan, 4 3/4 In. 95.00
Cut Glass, Spooner, Hobstars, Strawberry & Fan, 3 1/2 X 4 1/2 In. 110.00
Cut Glass, Spooner, Large Pinwheel And Strawberry Diamond Sides, 4 1/2 In. 50.00
Cut Glass, Spooner, Prism With Thumbprint Band, Cobalt, Iridescent, Flint 350.00
Cut Glass, Spooner, 2 Handled, Pinwheel Pattern, 4 1/2 In. 125.00
Cut Glass, Sugar & Creamer, Beverly 85.00
Cut Glass, Sugar & Creamer, Buzz Star, Cross Hatching, Applied Handles 85.00
Cut Glass, Sugar & Creamer, Copper Wheel Flowers, Harvard Border 75.00
Cut Glass, Sugar & Creamer, Cut Chain Of Hobstars, Hobnail & Hobs, Rims 75.00
Cut Glass, Sugar & Creamer, Feathered Floral, Butterfly Base, Miniature 60.00
Cut Glass, Sugar & Creamer, Floral, Leaf, Star, & Crosshatching 50.00
Cut Glass, Sugar & Creamer, Footed, Heisey 65.00
Cut Glass, Sugar & Creamer, Geometrics 65.00
Cut Glass, Sugar & Creamer, Harvard Cutting, Floral, Notched Handles 50.00
Cut Glass, Sugar & Creamer, Hobstar & Pinwheel 45.00
Cut Glass, Sugar & Creamer, Hobstar, Diamond Point, & Fan, Faceted Handles 72.00
Cut Glass, Sugar & Creamer, Hobstar, Fan, & Cane, Serrated Rims 95.00
Cut Glass, Sugar & Creamer, Hobstar, Strawberry Diamond, & Fan, Footed 160.00
Cut Glass, Sugar & Creamer, Hobstars, Heavy 65.00
Cut Glass, Sugar & Creamer, Hunts Royal, Signed 275.00
Cut Glass, Sugar & Creamer, Pedestal, Hobstar Chain, Strawberry Diamond 380.00
Cut Glass, Sugar & Creamer, Pinwheels .... 60.00 To 95.00
Cut Glass, Sugar & Creamer, Sterling Rims, Rockwell 28.00
Cut Glass, Sugar & Creamer, Strawberry Cut, Small Size 65.00
Cut Glass, Sugar & Creamer, Vesicas, Hobstars, Intaglio, Signed Tuthill 325.00
Cut Glass, Sugar & Creamer, White Rose, Irving, Oblong 90.00
Cut Glass, Sugar, Hobstar, Strawberry Diamond & X, Libbey 45.00
Cut Glass, Sugar, Pinwheels, Footed 50.00
Cut Glass, Syrup, Ball Body, Silver Handle, Lid, Collar, & Lift 40.00
Cut Glass, Syrup, Brass Top, Wheeler 46.00
Cut Glass, Syrup, Bull's-Eye & Geometric, Silver Fittings 20.00
Cut Glass, Syrup, Cross Cut Diamond & Fan, Silver Handle & Cover, 3 1/2 In. 40.00
Cut Glass, Syrup, Green Overlay 175.00
Cut Glass, Syrup, Harvard, Silver Plate Top & Handle 125.00
Cut Glass, Syrup, Pineapple & Fan, Silver Plate Top With Thumb Lift, 5 In. 45.00
Cut Glass, Syrup, Silver Lid, Strawberry Diamonds, Prism Neck 60.00

Cut Glass, Syrup, Silver Plate Handle & Hinged Lid, Diamond & Fan 48.00
Cut Glass, Syrup, Silver Plate Top & Rim, Rosette, Notched Handle, 6 3/4 In. 110.00
Cut Glass, Syrup, Strawberry & Diamond, Polished Base, Hinged Lid 78.00
Cut Glass, Tankard, American Brilliant Period, 9 In., Hobstar 77.00
Cut Glass, Tankard, Bevel Cut Prisms Under Spout, 9 3/4 In. 90.00
Cut Glass, Tankard, Brilliant, American, Heavy, 10 In. 165.00
Cut Glass, Tankard, Floral & Leaf, Step-Cut Spout, 10 1/2 In. 75.00
Cut Glass, Tankard, Florence, Double Notched Handle, Star Base, 10 3/4 In. 185.00
Cut Glass, Tankard, Hobstar & Pinwheel, Beveled Under Spout, 10 In. 90.00
Cut Glass, Tankard, Hobstar, Star In Diamond, & Fan, Star Base, 7 1/4 In. 127.50
Cut Glass, Tankard, Hobstar, Strawberry Diamond Rayed Base, 11 1/2 In. 190.00
Cut Glass, Tankard, Hobstars, Brilliant Period, 9 In. 90.00
Cut Glass, Tankard, Pinwheel, Strawberry Diamond, & Fan, Double Handle, 9 In. 135.00
Cut Glass, Tankard, Thumpbrint Edge, Prism Under Spout, 7 1/4 In. 85.00
Cut Glass, Tankard, Water, Buzz Stars, Clarke 165.00
Cut Glass, Tankard, Water, Diamond Point & Poinsettia 195.00
Cut Glass, Tankard, Water, Diamond Point & Poinsettia, Bows Near Base 135.00
Cut Glass, Tantalus Set, Rye & Scotch, Silver Stand, Lock, & Key, Hawkes 185.00
Cut Glass, Tazza, Intaglio Cut, Hobstar, Split Vesica & Floral, 6 1/4 In. 70.00
Cut Glass, Toothpick, American Brilliant, 3 Handled 15.00
Cut Glass, Toothpick, Hobstar & Fan, Fry 55.00
Cut Glass, Toothpick, Icicle 30.00
Cut Glass, Toothpick, Separate Underplate, Prism, Star, Thumbprint Cut 30.00
Cut Glass, Toothpick, Step Notched With Rings 25.00
Cut Glass, Toothpick, 3 Stepped Notched Prism, 2 3/8 In. 25.00
Cut Glass, Tray, Bread, Hobstar, Diamond, Fan, Signed Fry, 11 1/2 X 8 In. 145.00
Cut Glass, Tray, Daisy & Button Border, Floral & Leaf, Turtle Shape, 14 In. 85.00
Cut Glass, Tray, Dresser, Harvard Cut, Floral & Leaf, Sawtooth Edge, 11 In. 75.00
Cut Glass, Tray, Dresser, Harvard, Tooth Cut Rim, 11 X 6 1/4 In. 75.00
Cut Glass, Tray, Handled, Sharp Hobnail, 8 X 1 3/4 In X 14 3/4 In. 225.00
Cut Glass, Tray, Hoare, 18 In. 450.00
Cut Glass, Tray, Hobstar, Fan, & Cane, Hoare, 18 X 10 1/4 In. 475.00
Cut Glass, Tray, Ice Cream, Brazian, Hawkes, 12 1/2 X 8 1/2 In. 175.00
Cut Glass, Tray, Ice Cream, Brilliant, Signed Hoare, 14 X 8 In. 425.00
Cut Glass, Tray, Ice Cream, Cane, Prism, & Vesica, Star Base, Hoare, 9 In. 175.00
Cut Glass, Tray, Ice Cream, Corinthian, Scalloped Tooth Rim, 14 X 8 1/2 In. 225.00
Cut Glass, Tray, Ice Cream, Fortuna By Maple City Glass, 15 X 8 In. 235.00
Cut Glass, Tray, Ice Cream, Hobstar, Fan, Crosshatching, & Nailhead Diamond 175.00
Cut Glass, Tray, Ice Cream, Miter & Notched Prism In Panels, 12 X 7 In. 125.00
Cut Glass, Tray, Ice Cream, Russian Pattern, Starred Buttons, 12 X 8 In. 450.00
Cut Glass, Tray, Mt.Washington, 10 X 6 1/2 In. 135.00
Cut Glass, Tray, Pin, Cane, Fan, & Lines, 7 In. 30.00
Cut Glass, Tub, Butter, Hobstar, Fan, & Crosshatching, Tab Handles, 7 In. 92.00
Cut Glass, Tub, Hobstars, Notched Prism, Signed Fry, Miniature, 1 1/2 X 2 In. 25.00
Cut Glass, Tub, Ice, Harvard, Cane, Tulip, Cornflower, & Hobnail, Tab Handles 150.00
Cut Glass, Tub, Ice, Intaglio Cut, Floral On Tab Handles 94.00
Cut Glass, Tub, Sietz Bath, Blue, Daisy & Button 115.00
Cut Glass, Tumbler, Cane, Strawberry Diamond, Star, & Fan, Libbey 30.00
Cut Glass, Tumbler, Chain Of Hobstars 18.00
Cut Glass, Tumbler, Engraved Floral, Long Stems, Leaves 22.00
Cut Glass, Tumbler, Etched Star, Libbey 3.50
Cut Glass, Tumbler, Grape, Leaf, & Vine, Paperweight Base, 3 1/2 In. 12.00
Cut Glass, Tumbler, Hobstar, Fan, Cross Cut Diamond, Hoare & Corning, Signed 30.00
Cut Glass, Tumbler, Iced Tea, Pinwheel & Crosscutting, Flared Top 15.00
Cut Glass, Tumbler, Juice, Diamond & Fan 12.50
Cut Glass, Tumbler, Juice, Engraved Diagonal Bands Of Flower & Leaf 12.50
Cut Glass, Tumbler, Juice, Russian Cut, Clear Buttons 33.50
Cut Glass, Tumbler, Juice, Russian Pattern 27.00
Cut Glass, Tumbler, Juice, Strawberry Diamond 10.00
Cut Glass, Tumbler, Leaf & Stem, Star Base 15.00
Cut Glass, Tumbler, Pineapple, Fan, Hobstar & Pinwheel, 3 3/4 In. 30.00
Cut Glass, Tumbler, Pinwheels 12.50
Cut Glass, Tumbler, Russian Cut 75.00
Cut Glass, Tumbler, Russian, Starred Buttons, 3 3/4 In. 45.00

Cut Glass, Wine Glass Cooler, 4 1/2 In.

Cut Glass, Tumbler, Strawberry Diamond, Fan, & Star, Hobstar Base 25.00
Cut Glass, Tumbler, Wheel Cut Floral & Pointed Leaf, Star Base 15.00
Cut Glass, Vase, Basket Shape Fan, Strawberry Diamond Cutting, 6 3/4 In. 170.00
Cut Glass, Vase, Brilliant, Full Star Cutting, 11 1/2 In. 110.00
Cut Glass, Vase, Bud, Bethlehem Star, 7 1/4 In. 35.00
Cut Glass, Vase, Bud, Crosscut Diamonds, Fans At Top, Pedestal, 7 In., Pair 95.00
Cut Glass, Vase, Bud, Sinclaire, 11 In. 68.00
Cut Glass, Vase, Bull's-Eye, Fan, & Hobstar, Footed, Hawkes, 10 1/4 In. 262.00
Cut Glass, Vase, Butterflies & Floral, 12 In. 95.00
Cut Glass, Vase, Cobalt Cut To Clear, Floral & Crosshatching, 8 In. 35.00
Cut Glass, Vase, Cobalt Cut To Clear, Floral, Off-Center, 9 In. 22.00
Cut Glass, Vase, Corset Shape, Floral, 12 In. 45.00
Cut Glass, Vase, Corset Shape, 10 In. 80.00
Cut Glass, Vase, Dahlias & Leaves, Thumbprints, Corset Shape, Fry, 8 In. 110.00
Cut Glass, Vase, Deep Ruby, Square Holder, 4 Brass Paws 150.00
Cut Glass, Vase, Floral & Leaf, Corset Shape, 14 In. 65.00
Cut Glass, Vase, Flowers & Leaves, 10 In. 28.00
Cut Glass, Vase, Flowers, Square, 12 In. 75.00
Cut Glass, Vase, Grapes & Leaves, Pedestal, Libbey, 12 In. 150.00
Cut Glass, Vase, Green To Clear, Gravic Sunflower & Diamond Point, 12 In. 185.00
Cut Glass, Vase, Green To Clear, Strawberry Diamond, Trumpet, 8 In. 285.00
Cut Glass, Vase, Harvard Cutting, Fans, 21 In. 500.00
Cut Glass, Vase, Harvard Cutting, 8-Petaled Flower, 11 1/2 X 8 In. 200.00
Cut Glass, Vase, Hawkes, 18 In. 145.00
Cut Glass, Vase, Hobnail In Diamond, 32-Pointed Star Base, 3 1/4 In. 35.00
Cut Glass, Vase, Hobstar, Bull's-Eye, & Notched Prism, Scalloped, 14 In. 250.00
Cut Glass, Vase, Hobstar, Strawberry Diamond, Fan, & Hobnail, 10 In. 275.00
Cut Glass, Vase, Intaglio Cut, Floral & Leaf, Amethyst Trim, Pedestal, 9 In. 30.00
Cut Glass, Vase, Intaglio Cut, Floral & Leaf, Trumpet, Libbey, 11 1/2 In. 150.00
Cut Glass, Vase, Intaglio Cut, Floral, Etched Bands, Hawkes, 7 1/2 X 3 In. 40.00
Cut Glass, Vase, Intaglio Cut, Fry, 12 In. 150.00
Cut Glass, Vase, Intaglio Cut, Rose, Franz Grosz, 7 1/2 In. 94.00
Cut Glass, Vase, Intaglio Cutting, Paneled, Corset Shape, 10 In. 48.00
Cut Glass, Vase, Intaglio Cutting, Sterling Pedestal Holder, 9 1/2 In. 15.00
Cut Glass, Vase, Intaglio, Cut Rose, Tuthill, 12 In. 325.00
Cut Glass, Vase, Lateral Block, Double Miter, & Grapes, Footed, 6 3/4 In. 75.00
Cut Glass, Vase, Oriole, 24-Point Star Base, 11 In. 110.00
Cut Glass, Vase, Pedestal, Buzz, Notched & Cross Cut, Sawtooth Edge, 16 In. 115.00
Cut Glass, Vase, Pedestal, 10 1/8 In. 200.00
Cut Glass, Vase, Pinwheel, Star, Strawberry Diamond, & Fan, 11 3/4 In. 120.00
Cut Glass, Vase, Pinwheel, Strawberry Diamond, & Fan, Teardrop Stem, 8 In. 50.00
Cut Glass, Vase, Ruby, Roses & Leaves Cut To Clear, 6 1/4 In. 30.00
Cut Glass, Vase, Silsbee, 12 1/2 X 5 1/2 In. 185.00
Cut Glass, Vase, Spinning Wheel & Diamond, Fluted Edge, Corset Shape, 8 In. 75.00
Cut Glass, Vase, Sterling Base, Vertical Cuts, Almond Top & Base, 8 1/2 In. 35.00
Cut Glass, Vase, Strawberry, Diamond, Mary Hassal, Bedford, 1887, 8 3/4 In. 65.00
Cut Glass, Vase, Sunburst Pattern, Brilliant 700.00
Cut Glass, Vase, Trumpet Shape, Queens Pattern, 7 1/2 In. 385.00
Cut Glass, Vase, Trumpet, Brilliant Cuttings, 16 In. 295.00

Cut Glass, Vase, Trumpet, Notched Stem, Rayed Base, 6 1/2 X 6 In. 60.00
Cut Glass, Vase, Verre De Soie, Copper Wheel Decoration, Signed Hawkes 125.00
Cut Glass, Vase, Vertical Notched Prisms, Sawtooth Edge, 3 1/4 In. 60.00
Cut Glass, Water Set, Floral & Meter, Heavy, 7 Piece 185.00
Cut Glass, Water Set, Panel, Prism, & Comet, Star Bases, 6 Piece 62.50
Cut Glass, Wine Glass Cooler, 4 1/2 In. .... *Illus* 59.50
Cut Glass, Wine Rinser, Giant Flutes, 2 Lips 32.00
Cut Glass, Wine, Centauri, Hawkes 55.00
Cut Glass, Wine, Cross Cut Diamond & Fan, 4 3/4 In., Set Of 8 .... 165.00
Cut Glass, Wine, Diagonal Band, Star Case 8.00
Cut Glass, Wine, Engraved Border, Parallel Cuttings, 5 1/4 In. 5.00
Cut Glass, Wine, Green To Clear, St.Louis Diamond & Vesica, 7 1/2 In. 22.50
Cut Glass, Wine, Hawkes 25.00
Cut Glass, Wine, Hollow Stem, 5 In. 28.00
Cut Glass, Wine, Intaglio Cut, Rose Bud & Leaf, Trumpet Shape 45.50
Cut Glass, Wine, Parisian, Teardrop, Strauss 55.00
Cut Glass, Wine, Ritchie & Wheat, Wheeling, West Va., 1840 .... 23.50
Cut Glass, Wine, Rose, Libbey, 5 1/2 In. 37.50
Cut Glass, Wine, Russian Cut, Starred Buttons 75.00
Cut Glass, Wine, Strawberry Diamond & Fan, 3-Flute Bowl, C.1830 .... 15.00

Cut velvet is a special type of art glass made with two layers of blown glass, which shows a raised pattern. It usually had an acid finish or velvetlike texture. It was made by many glass factories during the late Victorian years.

Cut Velvet, Rose Bowl, Deep Rose Color, Diamond-Quilted, White Lining, 4 In. 165.00
Cut Velvet, Tumbler, Blue Overlay, Diamond-Quilted, White Lining, 4 3/4 In. 89.00
Cut Velvet, Vase, Blue Satin, Diamond-Quilted, Stick, 8 1/2 In. 195.00
Cut Velvet, Vase, Chartreuse, Ovoid, 8 In. 225.00

D'Albret, Paperweight, see Paperweight, D'Albret

D'Argental was a French cameo glassmaker of the late Victorian period. The D'Argental factory made multilayered, acid-cut cameo glass in France in the late nineteenth century. The glass is decorated with floral or scenic designs.

D'Argental, Box, Powder, Cameo, Red Roses 475.00
D'Argental, Jar, Dresser, Cameo Cover, Deep Rose, Signed In Cameo, 4 In. 385.00
D'Argental, Jar, Dresser, Rose Color, Maroon Leaves & Vines, 4 In. 385.00
D'Argental, Jar, Dresser, Rose Ground, Maroon Leaves, Signed, 4 In. 385.00
D'Argental, Vase, Brown Cherries & Branches, Tapering Neck, 4 1/2 In. 235.00
D'Argental, Vase, Brown Cherries, Tapering Neck, 4 1/2 In. 235.00
D'Argental, Vase, Cameo, Deep Blue Lilies, 5 In. 275.00
D'Argental, Vase, Floral & Scenic, Miniature, Pair 350.00
D'Argental, Vase, Frosted Pink, Navy Woodland & Island Scene, 3 7/8 In. 295.00
D'Argental, Vase, Green With Brown Iris, Signed, 4 3/4 In. 230.00
D'Argental, Vase, Green, Dark Brown Flowers & Buds, 4 1/2 In. 230.00
D'Argental, Vase, Lime Green, Magenta Colored Tulips & Leaves, 8 In. 275.00
D'Argental, Vase, Red Poppies On Golden Amber, 8 In. 425.00
D'Argental, Vase, Scenic, Carnelian, Gold, Brown, Lake, Hills, Sailboats, 5 In. 320.00
D'Argyl, Dish, Candy, Amethyst Glass, Silver Flashed Florals, Signed 125.00

Daguerreotype, see Photography, Daguerreotype
Danish Christmas Plate, see Collector, Plate, Bing & Grondahl, Collector, Plate, Royal Copenhagen

DAUM NANCY

Daum Nancy is the mark used by Auguste and Antonin Daum on pieces of French cameo glass made after 1875.

Daum Nancy, Bottle, Man's Cologne, White & Lavender, Dolce Relieno Method 290.00
Daum Nancy, Bottle, Perfume, Cameo & Enamel, Blue Cornflowers, 3 In. 250.00
Daum Nancy, Bottle, Perfume, Green, Pink, & Frosted, Enamel Cornflowers, 3 In. 275.00
Daum Nancy, Bottle, Spirit, Sterling Top, Purple Floral, Green Leaves, 5 In. 325.00
Daum Nancy, Bowl, Acid Cut, Leaves And Thistles, Red Enameling, Signed 130.00
Daum Nancy, Bowl, Footed, Green Mottled, 5 1/2 In. 100.00
Daum Nancy, Bowl, Frosted, Black Forest Rain Scene, 7 3/4 In. 850.00

Daum Nancy, Bowl, Frosted, Rain Scene, Black Forest, 7 3/4 In. 950.00
Daum Nancy, Bowl, Moss Green, Bark & Blue Base, 6 1/2 X 3 In. 385.00
Daum Nancy, Bowl, Mottled Gold & Orange, Sailboats, Lake, Oblong, 9 1/4 In. 650.00
Daum Nancy, Bowl, Silveria, Gold Foil Spatterings, Orange Glass, Signed, 4 In. 225.00
Daum Nancy, Bowl, Silveria, Red Foil Spatter, Blue Gray Lining, 4 1/4 In. 95.00
Daum Nancy, Bowl, Splotched Green & Royal Blue, 6 X 3 In. 125.00
Daum Nancy, Cruet, Blue Violets, Signed Cameo 700.00
Daum Nancy, Cruet, French Cameo, Miniature, Carved Flowers, Apricot 495.00
Daum Nancy, Cruet, Gold Decorated, Small 190.00
Daum Nancy, Cup & Saucer, Lavender Floral & Dragon, Enamel Farm Scene 250.00
Daum Nancy, Figurine, Crystal Donkey, Signed, 12 1/2 In. 100.00
Daum Nancy, Figurine, Penguin, Signed Daum, France, 5 In. 95.00
Daum Nancy, Jar, Covered, Pink Sunset, Pasture, Tree, & Floral, Enamel, 3 In. 300.00
Daum Nancy, Lamp Base, Baluster Vessel, C.1900, Signed, 8 1/2 In. 475.00
Daum Nancy, Lamp, Boats, Island, & Trees Scene, Orange & Brown, 16 In. 1450.00
Daum Nancy, Lamp, Gold Ground, Blue Flowers, Metal Mount, 9 1/4 In. 1200.00
Daum Nancy, Lamp, Lavender Base, Purple & Green Vines On White, 23 1/2 In. 550.00
Daum Nancy, Lamp, Scenic, Yellows, Oranges, Browns, Water Trees, Buildings 2950.00
Daum Nancy, Paperweight, Pate De Verre, Signed, Beetle On Green, 4 In. 975.00
Daum Nancy, Salt, Gold Frosted To Brown, Yellow Floral, Tub Shape 160.00
Daum Nancy, Salt, Winter Scene, Tub Shape, 1 7/8 In. 185.00
Daum Nancy, Shot Glass, Enameled, 2 In. 75.00
Daum Nancy, Tumbler, Green Frosted, Gold Leaves, White Enamel Berries, 5 In. 135.00
Daum Nancy, Tumbler, Juice, Chipped Ice, Cranberry Mistletoe & Berries 175.00
Daum Nancy, Tumbler, Winter Scene, Signed 650.00
Daum Nancy, Vase, Acid Etched, Dark To Pinkish Orange, 14 1/2 In. 200.00
Daum Nancy, Vase, Amber & Amethyst Bisque Crackle, Bottle Of Floral, 11 In. 490.00
Daum Nancy, Vase, Art Glass, Mottled Coloring, Bulbous Base, Stemmed, 20 In. 175.00
Daum Nancy, Vase, Art Glass, Mottled Purple To Pink, Horn Shape, 14 1/2 In. 150.00
Daum Nancy, Vase, Art Glass, Mottled Yellow, 11 3/4 In. 150.00
Daum Nancy, Vase, Autumn Scene, 8 1/2 In. 598.00
Daum Nancy, Vase, Blue, Etched Random Dots & Lines, Barrel Shape, 10 In. 125.00
Daum Nancy, Vase, Brown Matte, Pale Green Leaves, Amber Foot, 17 1/2 In. 800.00
Daum Nancy, Vase, Browns & Tans, Like Tree Bark Signed, 6 In. 95.00
Daum Nancy, Vase, Bud, Winter Scene, Miniature 225.00
Daum Nancy, Vase, Cameo Trees, Lake & Swan 225.00
Daum Nancy, Vase, Clear Glass Shading To Blue, Enamel Flowers, Signed, 13 In. 140.00
Daum Nancy, Vase, Coralene Style, Daisy Leaf Pattern, Green & Lilac, 12 In. 290.00
Daum Nancy, Vase, Daisy & Leaf, Coralene, Signed, 12 1/2 In. 290.00
Daum Nancy, Vase, Enamel And Cameo, Miniature, Birds, Blue & Gold, 3 1/2 In. 295.00
Daum Nancy, Vase, Frosted Deep Red Floral, 9 3/4 In. 495.00
Daum Nancy, Vase, Frosted Purple, Deep Purple Floral, Gold Trim, 11 1/2 In. 275.00
Daum Nancy, Vase, Gold & Peach, Mauve Sailboats In Sunset, 12 In. 450.00
Daum Nancy, Vase, Gold Outlined Green Flowers, Lily Pods Base, 8 1/2 In. 225.00
Daum Nancy, Vase, Green & Orange, Brown Sailboats & Figures, 21 In. 1150.00
Daum Nancy, Vase, Lake, Green, Purple, & Blue, Inverted Bell Shape, 5 In. 345.00
Daum Nancy, Vase, Lily Pond Scene, Dragonfly, Enameled Lilies, Signed, 5 In. 475.00
Daum Nancy, Vase, Lion In Hammered Gold, Green, Chiseled Ground, 11 1/2 In. 390.00
Daum Nancy, Vase, Matte Amber, Dark Green May Apple Leaves, 9 In. 895.00
Daum Nancy, Vase, Orange & Green, Purple Grapes, 4 3/4 In. 50.00
Daum Nancy, Vase, Orange, Green Scene, Flared Mouth, 20 1/2 In. 750.00
Daum Nancy, Vase, Ovoid, Blue, Transparents Etched On Milky Field, 10 1/4 In. 150.00
Daum Nancy, Vase, Pale Ground, Apricots & Green Leaves, 6 1/2 In. 450.00
Daum Nancy, Vase, Pink & Orange, Green Lake & Mountains, Brown Trees, 15 In. 525.00
Daum Nancy, Vase, Round, Domed Base, Purple, White, Cluthra, Signed, 16 In. 145.00
Daum Nancy, Vase, Summer Scene, Chartreuse Ground, Seasons Piece, 6 3/4 In. 425.00
Daum Nancy, Vase, Summer Scenic, Gold & Yellow, Trees, Island, 11 1/2 In. 480.00
Daum Nancy, Vase, Swan Scene, Cameo, Miniature, 2 In. 250.00
Daum Nancy, Vase, Textured, Blue Crystal Dancing Ladies, 12 In., Pair 495.00
Daum Nancy, Vase, Wheel Carved, Green Flowers, Pink Ground, 9 3/4 In. 1650.00
Daum Nancy, Vase, Winter Scene, Rose & Brown, White Enamel, 9 3/4 In. 775.00
Daum Nancy, Vase, Yellow And Orange, 6 X 3 1/2 In. 135.00
Daum Nancy, Vase, 2 Tab Handles, Scenic, Cameo, 1 1/4 In. 250.00
Daum Nancy, Wine, Green To Crystal Base, Coin Gold Iris, Crystal Stem 95.00

Davenport pottery and porcelain were made at the Davenport Factory in Longport, Staffordshire, England, from 1793 to 1887. Earthenwares, creamwares, porcelains, ironstone wares, and other products were made. Most of the pieces are marked with a form of the word Davenport.

Davenport, Bowl, Rimmed, Stoneware, C.1825, 9 3/4 In. 60.00
Davenport, Breakfast Set, Blue & Gold, Bowl & Pitcher, Longport 115.00
Davenport, Candlestick, Japan, Blue, Orange, Gold, & White, C.1870, 7 In., Pair 160.00
Davenport, Compote, Hand-Painted Floral, Longport, 5 In. 125.00
Davenport, Cup & Saucer, Hand Colored Ivy, Butterfly On Saucer, 1805 Mark 45.00
Davenport, Cup & Saucer, Ivy, Hand Colored, Butterfly, C.1825 .... 35.00
Davenport, Pitcher, Muleteer, Light Blue On White, C.1820, 4 Quart, 9 In. 75.00
Davenport, Plate, Child's, Daisies, Enameled Scene, Anchor Mark, C.1815, 7 In. 35.00
Davenport, Plate, Chinese, Blue Transfer, C.1805, 9 1/2 In. 35.00
Davenport, Plate, Grape, 8 1/2 In. 85.00
Davenport, Plate, Montreal, Lavender, C.1830, 10 1/4 In. 275.00
Davenport, Plate, Muleteer Pattern, Blue, Anchor Mark, 10 1/4 In. 45.00
Davenport, Plate, Stoneware, C.1810, 9 1/2 In. 50.00
Davenport, Plate, White, Ironstone, 12 Sided, C.1852, 9 In. 6.00
Davenport, Platter, Athena, Blue & Black, C.1830, 21 X 16 In. 125.00
Davenport, Platter, Blue Underglaze, Bird & Floral, C.1805, 12 X 9 1/2 In. 125.00
Davenport, Platter, Chinoiserie Floral & Bird, C.1805, 10 X 8 In. 45.00
Davenport, Platter, Leeds, White, Blue Stroke Border, Signed, 1852, 11 In. 120.00
Davenport, Platter, Nankin, Mulberry, 16 In. 110.00
Davenport, Saucer, Deep Cup, Blue Scene 8.00
Davy Crocket, Clock, Wall, Face & Pendulum Picture Davy, Weight Driven 35.00
Davy Crockett, Jar, Cookie, McCoy 8.00
Davy Crockett, Mug 5.00
Davy Crockett, Mug, White Glass 3.00
Davy Crockett, Ring, Plastic 7.50
Davy Crockett, Scarf, Neck, Yellow, Metal Rifles & Coonskin Cap 3.00
Davy Crockett, Tumbler, Figural 7.50
De Morgan, Tile, Hispano-Moresque Trees, Blue & Green, Square, 6 In. 100.00

De Vez is a name found on special pieces of French cameo glass made by the Cristallerie de Pantin about 1890. Monsieur de Varreux was the art director of the glassworks and he signed pieces "De Vez."

De Vez, Atomizer, Yellow, Brown Floral & Butterflies, Metal Fittings, 9 In. 265.00
De Vez, Bowl, Frosted Yellow, Navy Scene, Church & Trees, 4 1/4 In. 345.00
De Vez, Vase, Blue, White, & Pink, Island, Mountains, & Trees, 4 In. 299.00
De Vez, Vase, Bud, Floral & Leaf, Miniature 200.00
De Vez, Vase, Egg Shape, Amethyst, Art Nouveau, Signed, 3 1/2 In. 235.00
De Vez, Vase, Frosted Gold, Navy To Rose Palm Trees & Island, 4 1/4 In. 275.00
De Vez, Vase, Frosted Pink, Navy Mountains & Pines, 5 3/4 In. 295.00
De Vez, Vase, Green Shading, Lake, Birds, & Mountains Scene, 6 In. 375.00
De Vez, Vase, Palm Trees, Pyramids, Pink Ground, Navy To Yellow, 6 3/4 In. 375.00
De Vez, Vase, Turquoise, Black Water Lilies, Pyriform, 4 1/2 In. 225.00
De Vez, Vase, Yellow, Brown Birds, Branches & Leaves, 5 3/8 In. 325.00

Decoys are carved or turned wooden copies of birds. The decoy was placed in the water to lure flying birds to the pond for hunters.

Decoy, Black Duck, Dan English 450.00
Decoy, Black Duck, New Jersey Area, Green Bill 80.00
Decoy, Black Duck, Thomas Gelston, Quogue, Long Island, N.Y. 275.00
Decoy, Black Head & Back, Gray Breast, Wooden, Glass Eyes, 11 In. 25.00
Decoy, Bluebill Hen, Keyes Chadwick 225.00
Decoy, Crow, Papier Mache 17.50
Decoy, Curlew, 2 Feet 95.00
Decoy, Drake Scaup, Mason, Painted 85.00
Decoy, Drake, Mason 80.00
Decoy, Duck, Gray, White, Green, Folk Art Hand-Carved, 17 In. 45.00
Decoy, Duck, Maine, Hand-Carved Feathers In Relief, 13 In. 45.00
Decoy, Fish, For Spear Fishing, Trelot House Sutton West, C.1860, Pine 25.00
Decoy, Fish, Wood, Tin, 4 1/2 In.Long .... *Illus* 28.00
Decoy, Mallard Drake, Cork, Glass Eyes 15.00

Decoy, Fish, Wood, Tin, 4 1/2 In.Long
(See Page 149)

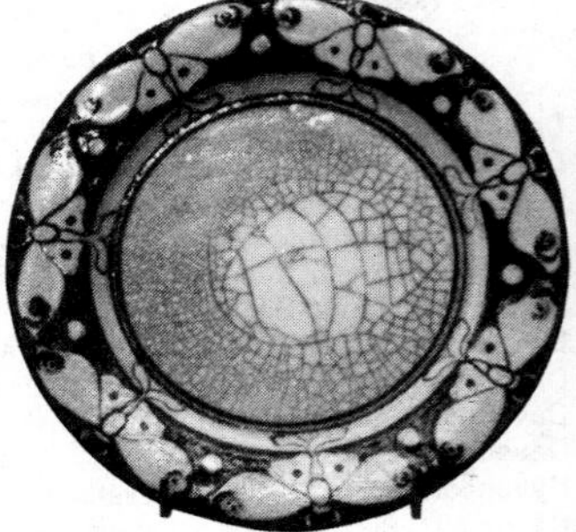

Dedham, Plate, Moth, 8 In.

Decoy, Mallard Drake, Johnson's, Folding Fiberboard 5.00
Decoy, Mallard Hen, Johnson's, Folding Fiberboard 5.00
Decoy, Mallard, Papier-Mache 11.00
Decoy, Merganser, Painted, Pratt Factory 75.00
Decoy, Red-Breasted Merganser Hen, Islip, Long Island, C.1880 .... 175.00

The Dedham Pottery Company of Dedham, Massachusetts, started making pottery in 1866. It was reorganized as the Chelsea Pottery Company in 1891, and became the Dedham Pottery Company in 1895. The factory was famous for its crackleware dishes, which picture blue outlines of animals, flowers, and other natural motifs.

Dedham, Bowl, Grape Border, 9 In. 225.00
Dedham, Bowl, Rabbit, 4 1/2 In. .... 49.50 To 55.00
Dedham, Bowl, Rabbit, 4 5/8 In. 65.00
Dedham, Bowl, Rabbit, 6 X 1 1/2 In. 59.50
Dedham, Bowl, Rabbit, 10 1/2 X 2 1/2 In. .... 138.00 To 245.00
Dedham, Charger, One Ear Rabbit, 12 In. 225.00
Dedham, Cup & Saucer, Rabbit 85.00
Dedham, Cup & Saucer, Rabbit, Oversize 115.00
Dedham, Cup, Rabbit, Oversize 85.00
Dedham, Mug, Rabbits Base, Fruit Band Top, 1896-1929 Mark, 4 1/2 In. 87.50
Dedham, Pitcher, Greek Key, Gloss Streaked Green, Chelsea, Keramic, 8 In. 350.00
Dedham, Plate, Azalea Border, 8 In. 58.00
Dedham, Plate, Bread, Magnolia, 6 In. 45.00
Dedham, Plate, Double-Eared Rabbit, 6 In. 65.00
Dedham, Plate, Duck, 8 1/2 In. 70.00
Dedham, Plate, Elephants, 7 1/2 In. 165.00
Dedham, Plate, Five Pairs Of Turtles Border, 6 In. 125.00
Dedham, Plate, Grape Border, 10 In. 85.00
Dedham, Plate, Iris, 10 In. 115.00
Dedham, Plate, Iris, 6 In. 43.50
Dedham, Plate, Grape, 10 In. 120.00
Dedham, Plate, Magnolia, Crackle, Dated 1915 .... 75.00
Dedham, Plate, Magnolia, 6 In. 55.00
Dedham, Plate, Moth, 8 In. .... *Illus* 85.00
Dedham, Plate, Mushroom, 8 1/2 In. 65.00
Dedham, Plate, Mushroom, 10 In. 110.00
Dedham, Plate, Pond Lily, 8 1/2 In. 135.00
Dedham, Plate, Pond Lily, 10 In. 135.00
Dedham, Plate, Poppy, Floral Center, Pods Border, 8 1/2 In. 125.00
Dedham, Plate, Rabbit, 7 3/4 In. 50.00
Dedham, Plate, Rabbit, 8 In. 75.00
Dedham, Plate, Rabbit, 8 1/2 In. 50.00
Dedham, Plate, Rabbit, 8 5/8 In. 75.00
Dedham, Plate, Rabbit, 10 In. 55.00
Dedham, Plate, Rabbits, Marked, 6 1/2 In. 32.00
Dedham, Plate, Tufted-Duck, 10 In. 135.00

Dedham, Platter, Bacon, Rabbit, 9 7/8 X 6 1/4 In. 95.00
Dedham, Platter, Rabbit, 9 7/8 X 6 1/4 In. 95.00
Dedham, Rasher, Bacon, Swan Border 150.00
Dedham, Salt & Pepper, Rabbit 125.00
Dedham, Sugar & Creamer, Azalea 100.00
Dedham, Sugar & Creamer, Rabbit 200.00
Dedham, Sugar, Covered, Rabbit Border, Incised Rabbit Ears, Blue Mark 89.00
Dedham, Tile, Tea, Rabbit, Crackle, 5 1/2 In.Square 125.00
Dedham, Vase, Full Bodied, High Gloss Streaked, Ivory To Brown, 8 1/4 In. 350.00
Dedham, Vase, Volcanic, Green Glossy Glaze Drips Over Olive, Signed B.W. 400.00
DeGue, Shade, Gray, Mottled, Pink, Purple, Yellow At Base, Signed 150.00
DeGue, Vase, Green, Stylized Flowers, White To Orange, Cameo 265.00
DeGue, Vase, Pale Green, Orange Stylized Floral, Cameo, 14 In. 295.00

Delatte glass is a French cameo glass made by Andre Delatte. It was first made in Nancy, France, in 1921. Lighting fixtures and opaque glassware in imitation of Bohemian opaline were made.

Delatte, Vase, Brown Berries On Camphor Center, Signed, 8 In. 325.00
Delatte, Vase, Burnt Umber On Orange Ground, Signed, 4 In. 185.00
Delatte, Vase, Lavender, 2-Toned Purple Floral Vines, 8 In. 200.00
Delatte, Vase, Owl, Lavender On Frosted Ground, Signed, 9 In. 550.00
Delatte, Vase, 2 Handled, Pink, Venetian Scene, French Cameo, 3 Cuttings 630.00
Delaware, see Pressed Glass, Custard Glass
Deldare, see Buffalo Pottery, Deldare

Delft is a tin-glazed pottery that has been made since the seventeenth century. It is decorated with blue on white or with colored decorations. Most of the pieces sold today were made after 1891, and the name Holland appears with the Delft factory marks.

Delft, Ashtray, Blue, Sombrero 8.00
Delft, Bowl, Bird Center, MA, 12 In. 40.00
Delft, Bowl, German, Windmills, Handled, 7 In. 12.00
Delft, Bowl, Pagodas In Landscape, Shallow, English, C.1720 .... 300.00
Delft, Charger, Farm Couple, Horse & Buggy, Blue, Royal Sphinx, 12 In. 72.00
Delft, Condiment Set, Windmill Decoration, 15 Pieces 85.00
Delft, Creamer, Reclining Cow 47.00
Delft, Cup & Saucer, Demitasse, Green 18.50
Delft, Dish, Crossed Pipes, Germany, Slipper, Windmill Scene, 5 1/2 In. 18.50
Delft, Flacon, Ring Neck, Dutch Landscape, C.1860, Pair 150.00
Delft, Holder, Kitchen Utensil, 14 In. 78.00
Delft, Inkwell, Mulberry, Scene Of Man In 16th Century Dress On Tree Limb 70.00
Delft, Inkwell, Mulberry, Scene Of Man In 16th Century Dress, Cartouche 75.00
Delft, Mug, Scene Of Minute, Crossed Pipes, Germany 22.50
Delft, Plaque, Landscape With Figures, Grays, Green, & Brown, 12 1/2 In. 125.00
Delft, Plaque, Serenity & Composure, Blues, ARTZ, C.1840, 12 X 8 In. 130.00
Delft, Plaque, Windmill Decoration, 8 In. 80.00
Delft, Plate, Fighting Cocks, Chinese Borders, English, C.1760, 13 3/4 In. 175.00
Delft, Plate, Floral Bouquet Center, Dutch, 18th Century, 13 1/2 In. 150.00
Delft, Plate, Port Amsterdam, Norelco, 1969 .... 10.00
Delft, Plate, Red, Green, Yellow, Blue, Lambeth, C.1740, 8 7/8 In. 325.00
Delft, Plate, Windmill & Trees, Scalloped Edge, 8 In. 22.00
Delft, Plate, Windmill Scene, Petallike Border, 9 In. 25.00
Delft, Shoe, Hand-Painted, 6 1/2 In. 10.00
Delft, Tazza, Strolling Man, Blue & White, C.1700, 9 In. 275.00
Delft, Vase, Baluster Shape, Polychrome Decorations, Flowers, Insects, Pair 475.00
Delft, Vase, Foo Dog Finial, Germany, Church, People, & Seascape, 10 In. 65.00
Dentist, see Doctor

Depression glass was an inexpensive glass manufactured in large quantities during the 1920s and early 1930s. It was made in many colors and patterns by dozens of factories in the United States. The name depression glass is a modern one.

Depression Glass, Ashtray, Cloverleaf, Black 46.90
Depression Glass, Ashtray, Princess, Green 35.00

Depression Glass, Berry Bowl, American Sweetheart, Pink, 3 1/2 In. 4.50
Depression Glass, Berry Bowl, Cherry Blossom, Pink, 4 3/4 In. 4.00
Depression Glass, Berry Bowl, Georgian, Green 2.00
Depression Glass, Berry Bowl, Gold, Anchor Hocking 2.50
Depression Glass, Berry Bowl, Iris & Herringbone, Beaded Edge, 8 In. 11.90
Depression Glass, Berry Bowl, Iris & Herringbone, Fluted 1.50
Depression Glass, Berry Bowl, Monax, Petalware, 9 In. 9.00
Depression Glass, Berry Bowl, Patrician, Amber 2.95
Depression Glass, Berry Bowl, Rosemary, Amber 1.90
Depression Glass, Berry Bowl, Rosemary, Green 2.50
Depression Glass, Berry Bowl, Sandwich, Amber, 5 In. 2.75
Depression Glass, Berry Bowl, Sylvan, Green 4.25
Depression Glass, Berry Set, Doric, Pink, 9 Piece 28.00
Depression Glass, Berry Set, Iris, 5 Piece 12.00
Depression Glass, Bonbon, Moonstone, Heart Shape 5.00
Depression Glass, Bowl, Adam, Pink, 9 In. 8.00
Depression Glass, Bowl, American Sweetheart, Monax, 9 In. 20.00
Depression Glass, Bowl, Berry, Madrid, Green 4.75
Depression Glass, Bowl, Berry, Rosemary, Pink, Small 4.25
Depression Glass, Bowl, Berry, Sharon, Amber 5.00
Depression Glass, Bowl, Berry, Sharon, Amber, Small 4.00
Depression Glass, Bowl, Cameo, Green, 5 1/2 In. 5.90
Depression Glass, Bowl, Cameo, Green, 8 1/2 In. 8.00
Depression Glass, Bowl, Cereal, American Sweetheart, Pink, 5 In. 3.00
Depression Glass, Bowl, Cherry Blossom, Green, Handled, 9 In. 10.00
Depression Glass, Bowl, Cherry Blossom, 3 Legged, 10 1/2 In. 17.00
Depression Glass, Bowl, Cherry, Pink, 3 Legged, 10 1/2 In. 15.00
Depression Glass, Bowl, Cherry, Pink, 9 In. 8.00
Depression Glass, Bowl, Console, Cameo, 3 Legged, Pink 25.00
Depression Glass, Bowl, Console, Floragold, Iridescent, 12 In. Ruff 6.00
Depression Glass, Bowl, Diamond Quilted, Pink, 7 In. 3.50
Depression Glass, Bowl, Dogwood, Green, 8 1/2 In. 25.00
Depression Glass, Bowl, Floragold, Amber, Ruffled, 8 1/2 In. 3.50
Depression Glass, Bowl, Floragold, Amber, 4 1/2 In. 3.00
Depression Glass, Bowl, Floragold, 9 1/2 In. 2.50
Depression Glass, Bowl, Florentine, Green, 4 1/2 In. 2.50
Depression Glass, Bowl, Iris & Herringbone, 11 In. 9.50
Depression Glass, Bowl, Iris, Carnival, Ruffled, 9 In. 4.00
Depression Glass, Bowl, Lace Edge, Crystal, 6 1/2 In. 2.50
Depression Glass, Bowl, Laurel, Jade Green, Flanged, McKee, 6 In. 4.00
Depression Glass, Bowl, Laurel, Jade Green, McKee, 5 In. 2.75
Depression Glass, Bowl, Lovebird, Green, 7 1/2 In. 6.00
Depression Glass, Bowl, Manhattan, 7 1/2 In. 3.00
Depression Glass, Bowl, Mayfair, Blue, 11 3/4 In. 35.00
Depression Glass, Bowl, Moderntone, Blue, 9 In. 8.00
Depression Glass, Bowl, Moonstone, Scalloped, 10 In. 7.00
Depression Glass, Bowl, Moonstone, 9 1/2 In. 3.00
Depression Glass, Bowl, Mt.Pleasant, Blue, Handled, Scalloped, 8 In. 9.00
Depression Glass, Bowl, Parrot, Amber, 7 In. 7.50
Depression Glass, Bowl, Patrician, Green, 5 In. 3.50
Depression Glass, Bowl, Patrician, Green, 8 1/2 In. 9.00
Depression Glass, Bowl, Sandwich, Anchor Hocking, Oval, 5 3/4 In. 3.50
Depression Glass, Bowl, Sandwich, Anchor Hocking, 6 1/2 In. 1.50
Depression Glass, Bowl, Sandwich, Anchor Hocking, 8 In. 2.00
Depression Glass, Bowl, Sandwich, Forest Green, Anchor Hocking, 6 In. 7.00
Depression Glass, Bowl, Sandwich, Forest Green, Anchor Hocking, 7 In. 10.00
Depression Glass, Bowl, Sandwich, Forest Green, Anchor Hocking, 8 In. 12.00
Depression Glass, Bowl, Sharon, Amber, 8 In. 2.50
Depression Glass, Bowl, Sharon, Amber, 8 1/2 In. 3.00
Depression Glass, Bowl, Sharon, Yellow, 8 1/2 In. 7.00
Depression Glass, Bowl, Soup, Cream, Rosemary, Amber, With Arches 6.00
Depression Glass, Bowl, Soup, Madrid, Amber, 7 In. 7.50
Depression Glass, Bowl, Soup, Royal Ruby, Flat 4.50
Depression Glass, Bowl, Stacked Tire, Cobalt, Fluted, Flared, 10 In. 30.00

Depression Glass, Bowl, Stag & Holly, Green, 10 In. 18.50
Depression Glass, Bowl, Strawberry, Green, 7 1/2 In. 7.90
Depression Glass, Bowl, Swirl, Delphite, 9 In. 12.00 To 15.00
Depression Glass, Bowl, Swirl, Ultramarine, Petalware, 5 1/2 In. 4.00
Depression Glass, Bowl, Ultramarine, 9 In. 10.00
Depression Glass, Bowl, Vegetable, Madrid, Oval, Amber 8.50
Depression Glass, Bowl, Windsor, Pink, 4 3/4 In. 2.00
Depression Glass, Box, Cigarette, Moonstone, Covered 6.00
Depression Glass, Box, Puff, Sandwich, Covered, Indiana 8.50
Depression Glass, Butter, Adam, Pink 45.00
Depression Glass, Butter, Baltimore Pear, Crystal 7.00
Depression Glass, Butter, Block, Green 22.00
Depression Glass, Butter, Cameo, Green 65.00
Depression Glass, Butter, Cherry Blossom, Pink 45.00
Depression Glass, Butter, Colonial, Green, Covered 35.00
Depression Glass, Butter, Columbia 12.00
Depression Glass, Butter, Cubist, Pink 25.00
Depression Glass, Butter, Doric, Pink 35.00
Depression Glass, Butter, Floragold, Amber 8.00
Depression Glass, Butter, Floragold, Covered, Round 20.00
Depression Glass, Butter, Florentine, Amber 25.00
Depression Glass, Butter, Lace Edge, Pink 25.00
Depression Glass, Butter, Louisa 22.00
Depression Glass, Butter, Lovebird 40.00
Depression Glass, Butter, Mayfair, Pink 26.00 To 45.00
Depression Glass, Butter, Miss America, Metal Cover 18.50
Depression Glass, Butter, Parrot, Green 200.00
Depression Glass, Butter, Patrician, Amber 40.00
Depression Glass, Butter, Patrician, Pink 125.00
Depression Glass, Butter, Princess, Green 45.00
Depression Glass, Butter, Royal Lace 35.00
Depression Glass, Butter, Royal Lace, Blue, Covered 250.00
Depression Glass, Butter, Sandwich 12.00
Depression Glass, Butter, Sandwich, Covered, Anchor Hocking 12.00
Depression Glass, Butter, Sharon, Amber 32.00 To 47.50
Depression Glass, Butter, Sharon, Pink 27.00 To 55.00
Depression Glass, Butter, Sierra, Green 15.00
Depression Glass, Butter, Sierra, Pink, Covered 45.00
Depression Glass, Candleholder, Madrid, Pink 9.95
Depression Glass, Candleholder, Madrid, Sunburst 9.00
Depression Glass, Candleholder, Viking, Swan, 6 In. 15.00
Depression Glass, Candlestick, Diamond Quilted, Pink 4.95
Depression Glass, Celery, Miss America, Oblong, 10 1/2 In. 4.50
Depression Glass, Celery, Miss America, Pink, 10 1/4 In. 9.00
Depression Glass, Celery, Sandwich, Indiana 6.00
Depression Glass, Cereal Bowl, American Sweetheart, Monax 5.90 To 6.00
Depression Glass, Cereal Bowl, American Sweetheart, Pink 4.00
Depression Glass, Cereal Bowl, Gold, Anchor Hocking 3.50
Depression Glass, Cereal Bowl, Miss America 2.75
Depression Glass, Cereal Bowl, Petalware, Cremax 2.50
Depression Glass, Child's Set, Doric & Pansy, Pink, Plate, Cup & Saucer 25.00
Depression Glass, Coaster, Adam, Green 4.00
Depression Glass, Coaster, Iris & Herringbone 12.90
Depression Glass, Coaster, Miss America 10.00
Depression Glass, Cocktail Shaker, Plymouth, Cobalt 42.50
Depression Glass, Compote, Florentine No.2, Blue, Ruffled, 3 1/2 In. 22.50
Depression Glass, Console Bowl, American Sweetheart, Gold Trim, 18 In. 225.00
Depression Glass, Console Bowl, Cameo, Yellow 37.90
Depression Glass, Console Bowl, Holiday, Pink, 10 1/2 In. 20.00
Depression Glass, Console Bowl, Moondrops, Amethyst, Handled 45.00
Depression Glass, Console Bowl, Moonstone, 9 1/2 In. 8.50
Depression Glass, Console Bowl, Ultramarine 15.00
Depression Glass, Console Set, Sandwich, Apple Green, 3 Piece 45.00
Depression Glass, Cordial, Colonial, Green 10.00

Depression Glass, Cordial, Knife & Fork, Pink 10.00
Depression Glass, Cream & Sugar, Block, Topaz 12.00
Depression Glass, Cream & Sugar, Madrid, Green 10.50
Depression Glass, Cream & Sugar, Princess, Pink 12.50
Depression Glass, Cream & Sugar, Tea Room, Pink 12.00
Depression Glass, Creamer, American Sweetheart, Pink 8.90
Depression Glass, Creamer, Cherry Blossom, Pink .... 3.00 To 4.50
Depression Glass, Creamer, Child's, Cherry Blossom, Pink 20.00
Depression Glass, Creamer, Child's, Cherry, Delphite 24.25
Depression Glass, Creamer, Child's, Cherry, Pink 22.50
Depression Glass, Creamer, Child's, Doric & Pansy, Ultramarine 24.95
Depression Glass, Creamer, Cloverleaf, Black .... 5.75 To 7.50
Depression Glass, Creamer, Doric & Pansy, Pink 21.00
Depression Glass, Creamer, Doric & Pansy, Ultramarine 110.00
Depression Glass, Creamer, Florentine, Green 4.00
Depression Glass, Creamer, Iris .... 2.00 To 2.50
Depression Glass, Creamer, Iris, Carnival 4.00
Depression Glass, Creamer, Madrid, Amber 1.50
Depression Glass, Creamer, Miss America 5.00
Depression Glass, Creamer, Moonstone 3.50
Depression Glass, Creamer, Mt.Pleasant, Cobalt 6.00
Depression Glass, Creamer, Newport Hairpin, Purple 2.50
Depression Glass, Creamer, Newport, Cobalt 3.00
Depression Glass, Creamer, Royal Ruby 1.75
Depression Glass, Creamer, Sandwich, Anchor Hocking 1.50
Depression Glass, Creamer, Sandwich, Forest Green, Anchor Hocking 7.00
Depression Glass, Creamer, Sharon, Pink 6.75
Depression Glass, Creamer, Sierra, Pink 4.00
Depression Glass, Cup & Saucer, American Sweetheart, Monax .... 5.50 To 9.75
Depression Glass, Cup & Saucer, American Sweetheart, Pink 5.65
Depression Glass, Cup & Saucer, American Sweetheart, Red .... 110.00 To 125.00
Depression Glass, Cup & Saucer, Cabbage Rose, Amber 3.25
Depression Glass, Cup & Saucer, Cameo Ballerina, Topaz 4.00
Depression Glass, Cup & Saucer, Cameo, Yellow 3.50
Depression Glass, Cup & Saucer, Cherry, Pink 5.00
Depression Glass, Cup & Saucer, Child's, Cherry Delphite 18.00
Depression Glass, Cup & Saucer, Chinex, Ivory 5.00
Depression Glass, Cup & Saucer, Cloverleaf, Black 6.25
Depression Glass, Cup & Saucer, Columbia 2.25
Depression Glass, Cup & Saucer, Demitasse, Iris & Herringbone 18.90
Depression Glass, Cup & Saucer, Dogwood, Pink, Thin .... 4.25 To 5.00
Depression Glass, Cup & Saucer, Doric, Pink .... 4.00 To 4.50
Depression Glass, Cup & Saucer, Frosted Block, Green 2.75
Depression Glass, Cup & Saucer, Homespun, Pink 9.50
Depression Glass, Cup & Saucer, Iris & Herringbone 5.95
Depression Glass, Cup & Saucer, Madrid, Amber .... 5.25 To 5.50
Depression Glass, Cup & Saucer, Mayfair, Pink 6.50
Depression Glass, Cup & Saucer, Miss America 6.50
Depression Glass, Cup & Saucer, Miss America, Pink 7.00
Depression Glass, Cup & Saucer, Mt.Pleasant, Blue 5.50
Depression Glass, Cup & Saucer, Normandie, Pink 4.00
Depression Glass, Cup & Saucer, Old Florentine, Pink 4.00
Depression Glass, Cup & Saucer, Patrician, Pink 6.00
Depression Glass, Cup & Saucer, Roulette, Green 3.00
Depression Glass, Cup & Saucer, Royal Ruby 4.50
Depression Glass, Cup & Saucer, Sandwich, Amber, Anchor Hocking 4.00
Depression Glass, Cup & Saucer, Sandwich, Dark Green, Anchor Hocking 1.00
Depression Glass, Cup & Saucer, Sandwich, Forest Green, Anchor Hocking 10.00
Depression Glass, Cup & Saucer, Sharon, Amber 3.25
Depression Glass, Cup & Saucer, Sharon, Green 11.00
Depression Glass, Cup & Saucer, Sharon, Pink 5.50
Depression Glass, Cup & Saucer, Swirl, Pink 3.50
Depression Glass, Cup & Saucer, Swirl, Ultramarine 5.50
Depression Glass, Cup & Saucer, Waffle, Pink 3.00

Depression Glass, Cup, Adam, Pink 5.00
Depression Glass, Cup, Cameo, Green 5.00
Depression Glass, Cup, Cameo, Topaz, Curly Handle 6.50
Depression Glass, Cup, Child's, Cherry, Delphite 19.75
Depression Glass, Cup, Child's, Doric, Pink 15.00
Depression Glass, Cup, Cloverleaf, Black 4.25
Depression Glass, Cup, Custard, Sandwich, Green, Anchor Hocking 1.50
Depression Glass, Cup, Diamond Quilted, Pink 3.50
Depression Glass, Cup, Dogwood, Pink, Gold Trim 3.50
Depression Glass, Cup, Doric & Pansy, Teal 20.00
Depression Glass, Cup, Floral, Pink 11.00
Depression Glass, Cup, Florentine No.1, Pink 2.75
Depression Glass, Cup, Florentine No.1, Yellow 2.75
Depression Glass, Cup, Horseshoe, Green 6.50
Depression Glass, Cup, Iris, Carnival 3.00
Depression Glass, Cup, Madrid, Amber 3.50
Depression Glass, Cup, Madrid, Blue .... 7.50 To 9.00
Depression Glass, Cup, Miss America 4.50
Depression Glass, Cup, Miss America, Green 8.00
Depression Glass, Cup, Moderntone, Blue 2.25
Depression Glass, Cup, Moonstone 3.50
Depression Glass, Cup, Open Lace, Pink 5.00
Depression Glass, Cup, Parrot, Green 10.00
Depression Glass, Cup, Patrician, Green 3.00
Depression Glass, Cup, Pear Optic, Green 1.50
Depression Glass, Cup, Punch, Colonial 1.75
Depression Glass, Cup, Punch, Royal Ruby .... 1.00 To 1.50
Depression Glass, Cup, Ring, Green 1.50
Depression Glass, Cup, Rosemary, Green 4.25
Depression Glass, Cup, Roulette, Green .... 1.50 To 2.50
Depression Glass, Cup, Royal Ruby 1.25
Depression Glass, Cup, Sharon, Pink 3.50
Depression Glass, Cup, Sierra, Pink 7.00
Depression Glass, Decanter, Wine, Waterford 23.00
Depression Glass, Dish, Banana Split, Pineapple & Floral 3.00
Depression Glass, Dish, Candy, Cameo, Covered, Low 25.00
Depression Glass, Dish, Candy, Crackle, Green, Covered 9.50
Depression Glass, Dish, Candy, No.612, Pink, Covered 300.00
Depression Glass, Dish, Candy, Sharon, Amber, Covered 22.00
Depression Glass, Dish, Candy, Sharon, Pink, Covered 20.00
Depression Glass, Dish, Cheese, Floragold, Covered 17.50
Depression Glass, Dish, Cheese, Laurel, French Ivory, Covered 40.00
Depression Glass, Dish, Dessert, Madrid, Amber, Cone, Footed 3.50
Depression Glass, Dish, Hot, Madrid, Green, 5 In. 25.00
Depression Glass, Dish, Kraft Cheese, Dark Green Bottom 10.50
Depression Glass, Dish, Pickle, Aunt Polly, Blue 7.00
Depression Glass, Dripolator, Poppy 12.50
Depression Glass, Flower Bowl, Lace Edge, Pink 3.00
Depression Glass, Fruit Bowl, Cherry Blossom, Green, 3 Legged, 10 1/2 In. 22.50
Depression Glass, Fruit Bowl, Mayfair, Blue 28.00
Depression Glass, Fruit Bowl, Miss America, Pink 16.50
Depression Glass, Fruit Bowl, Sharon, Pink 8.00
Depression Glass, Goblet, Iris & Herringbone, 8 Ozs., 5 3/4 In. .... 7.00 To 10.00
Depression Glass, Goblet, Iris, 8 Ozs., 5 3/4 In. 8.00
Depression Glass, Goblet, Mayfair, Pink, 4 1/2 In. 30.00
Depression Glass, Goblet, Miss America, Pink, 5 1/2 In. 18.00
Depression Glass, Goblet, Moonstone 5.25
Depression Glass, Goblet, Royal Ruby, Ball Stem 5.50
Depression Glass, Goblet, Royal Ruby, 3 Knob Stem, 5 1/4 In. 3.00
Depression Glass, Insert, Lazy Susan, Windsor, Crystal 5.00
Depression Glass, Jar, Candy, Cabbage Rose, Amber 15.00
Depression Glass, Jar, Candy, Doric, Green, Covered 25.00
Depression Glass, Jar, Candy, Iris, Covered 30.00
Depression Glass, Jar, Candy, Mayfair, Pink, Covered 10.00

Depression Glass, Jar, Candy, Miss America, Pink 65.00
Depression Glass, Jar, Candy, Sharon, Amber 15.00
Depression Glass, Jar, Candy, Sharon, Amber, Covered 18.00
Depression Glass, Jar, Candy, Sharon, Pink, Covered 22.50
Depression Glass, Jar, Cookie, Lace Edge, Pink 13.75
Depression Glass, Jar, Cookie, Madrid, Covered 16.00
Depression Glass, Jar, Cookie, Mayfair, Pink 18.00
Depression Glass, Jar, Cookie, Patrician, Amber, Covered 20.00
Depression Glass, Jar, Cookie, Poppy 17.50
Depression Glass, Jar, Cookie, Royal Lace, Blue 85.00
Depression Glass, Jar, Cookie, Royal Lace, Blue, Covered 50.00
Depression Glass, Jar, Cookie, Royal Lace, Green, Covered 35.00
Depression Glass, Jar, Cookie, Royal Lace, Pink, Covered 14.50
Depression Glass, Jar, Cracker, Madrid, Pink 37.50
Depression Glass, Jug, Water, Manhattan, Covered 5.00
Depression Glass, Juice Set, Floragold, 7 Piece 20.00
Depression Glass, Luncheon Set, Heritage, 16 Piece 35.00
Depression Glass, Mold, Jello, Little Princess 1.25
Depression Glass, Mold, Pudding, Betty Jane 4.50
Depression Glass, Mug, Tom & Jerry, Jade, McKee 2.50
Depression Glass, Nappy, Cabbage Rose, Amber, 8 1/2 In. 2.00
Depression Glass, Nappy, Columbia, 5 In. 1.00
Depression Glass, Nappy, Coronation, Pink, Handles 1.50
Depression Glass, Nappy, Madrid, Amber, Square 2.25
Depression Glass, Nappy, Royal Ruby, 4 1/2 In. 3.00
Depression Glass, Nappy, Royal Ruby, 8 1/2 In. 7.50
Depression Glass, Nappy, Sharon, Amber, 8 1/2 In. 2.00
Depression Glass, Nut Bowl, Iris 15.00
Depression Glass, Pitcher, Adam, Pink, Square Base 15.00
Depression Glass, Pitcher, Adam, Pink, 8 In. 11.50
Depression Glass, Pitcher, Cameo Ballerina, Green, Rope Top, 39 Ozs., 6 In. 23.00
Depression Glass, Pitcher, Cameo, Green, 8 In. 18.50
Depression Glass, Pitcher, Cherry Blossom, Green, 44 Ozs. 12.00
Depression Glass, Pitcher, Cherry Blossom, Pink, Scalloped Bottom, 36 Ozs. 14.00
Depression Glass, Pitcher, Doric, Pink, 5 In. 12.00
Depression Glass, Pitcher, Floral, Pink, Cone, 32 Ozs. 9.50
Depression Glass, Pitcher, Floral, Pink, 8 In. .... 8.00 To 9.00
Depression Glass, Pitcher, Florentine No.1, Green, 36 Ozs., 6 1/2 In. 12.50
Depression Glass, Pitcher, Florentine No.2, Topaz, 8 In. 10.00
Depression Glass, Pitcher, Iris & Herringbone, Footed, 9 1/2 In. 8.00
Depression Glass, Pitcher, Iris & Herringbone, 8 In. 11.00
Depression Glass, Pitcher, Iris, 9 1/2 In. 10.00
Depression Glass, Pitcher, Juice, Manhattan 4.75
Depression Glass, Pitcher, Lydia Ray, Pink, 80 Ozs. 20.00
Depression Glass, Pitcher, Madrid, Amber, Square, 8 In. 17.50
Depression Glass, Pitcher, Madrid, Amber, 8 In. 15.00
Depression Glass, Pitcher, Mayfair, Blue, 83 Ozs. 75.00
Depression Glass, Pitcher, Mayfair, Pink, 8 1/2 In. 15.00
Depression Glass, Pitcher, Mayfair, 6 In. 12.50
Depression Glass, Pitcher, Milk, Cameo 90.00
Depression Glass, Pitcher, Patrician, Amber, 60 Ozs., 8 In. .... 23.00 To 28.00
Depression Glass, Pitcher, Patrician, Green, 8 In. 55.00
Depression Glass, Pitcher, Poinsettia, Pink, 8 In. 10.00
Depression Glass, Pitcher, Princess, Green, 8 In. 29.50
Depression Glass, Pitcher, Princess, Yellow, 8 In. 42.00
Depression Glass, Pitcher, Royal Lace, Blue, Ice Lip, 96 Ozs., 8 1/2 In. 97.50
Depression Glass, Pitcher, Royal Lace, Pink, 68 Ozs., 8 In. 24.75
Depression Glass, Pitcher, Royal Ruby, 3 Quart .... 11.00 To 12.00
Depression Glass, Pitcher, Royal Ruby, 32 Ozs. 8.00
Depression Glass, Pitcher, Sierra, Pink, 32 Ozs., 6 1/2 In. 22.00
Depression Glass, Pitcher, Spiral, Large Bulbous 15.00
Depression Glass, Pitcher, Water, Miss America, Pink, Ice Lip 50.00
Depression Glass, Pitcher, Water, Poppy, Yellow 10.00
Depression Glass, Pitcher, Water, Princess, Green, 8 In. 18.00

Depression Glass, Pitcher, Water, Sailboat, Blue, 8 1/2 In. 14.00
Depression Glass, Pitcher, Water, Tearoom, Green 53.00
Depression Glass, Pitcher, Water, Windsor, Pink 9.00
Depression Glass, Pitcher, Windsor, Pink, 48 Ozs. 10.00
Depression Glass, Pitcher, Windsor, Pink, 6 1/2 In. 17.50
Depression Glass, Plate, Adam, Pink, 10 In. 4.50
Depression Glass, Plate, Adam, 6 In. 1.85
Depression Glass, Plate, American Sweetheart, Monax, 6 In. 3.00
Depression Glass, Plate, American Sweetheart, Monax, 8 In. .... 3.00 To 4.00
Depression Glass, Plate, American Sweetheart, Monax, 9 In. 6.00
Depression, Glass, Plate, American Sweetheart, Monax, 11 3/4 In. 20.00
Depression Glass, Plate, American Sweetheart, Pink, 10 In. 4.50
Depression Glass, Plate, American Sweetheart, Pink, 12 In. .... 5.00 To 6.00
Depression Glass, Plate, Banded Fine Rib, Pink, 6 In. 1.25
Depression Glass, Plate, Block, Topaz, 8 In. 4.75
Depression Glass, Plate, Bread & Butter, American Sweetheart, M .... 1.50 To 6.50
Depression Glass, Plate, Bread & Butter, American Sweetheart, Pink 2.00
Depression Glass, Plate, Bread & Butter, Cabbage Rose, Amber, 6 In. 1.50
Depression Glass, Plate, Bread & Butter, Cameo, Yellow 1.50
Depression Glass, Plate, Bread & Butter, Columbia, 6 In. .... .75
Depression Glass, Plate, Bread & Butter, Sharon, Amber, 6 In. 1.50
Depression Glass, Plate, Bread & Butter, Sharon, Green 1.50
Depression Glass, Plate, Bread & Butter, Sharon, Green, 6 In. 1.25
Depression Glass, Plate, Bubble, Blue, 6 3/4 In. .... .75
Depression Glass, Plate, Cake, Adam, Footed 5.50
Depression Glass, Plate, Cake, Adam, Pink 5.00
Depression Glass, Plate, Cake, American Sweetheart, Pink 6.50
Depression Glass, Plate, Cake, Cameo, Green 8.75
Depression Glass, Plate, Cake, Cherry, Pink, Handled, 10 In. 7.00
Depression Glass, Plate, Cake, Mayfair, Blue, Handled 25.00
Depression Glass, Plate, Cake, Miss America, Pink, Footed, 12 In. 15.00
Depression Glass, Plate, Cake, Mt.Pleasant, Blue, 10 1/2 In. 9.00
Depression Glass, Plate, Cake, Princess, Pink, Square, 10 In. 4.00
Depression Glass, Plate, Cake, Waterford Waffle, Pink, Handled 3.50
Depression Glass, Plate, Cake, Waterford, Pink, Handled 4.25
Depression Glass, Plate, Cameo Ballerina, Green, 6 1/8 In. 1.50
Depression Glass, Plate, Cameo Ballerina, Topaz, 9 1/2 In. 3.50
Depression Glass, Plate, Cameo, Yellow, 6 In. 1.25
Depression Glass, Plate, Cherry Blossom, Pink, 7 In. 5.50
Depression Glass, Plate, Cherry Blossom, Pink, 9 In. 5.00
Depression Glass, Plate, Child's, Homespun, Pink 8.50
Depression Glass, Plate, Children's, Homespun, Pink 8.50
Depression Glass, Plate, Chinex Classic, Floral Decal, 9 3/4 In. 3.00
Depression Glass, Plate, Cloverleaf, Black, 8 In. 6.00
Depression Glass, Plate, Colonial, Pink, 6 In. 1.50
Depression Glass, Plate, Dinner, Adam, Green 4.50
Depression Glass, Plate, Dinner, Cameo, Topaz 6.50
Depression Glass, Plate, Dinner, Cherry Blossom, Green, 9 In. 7.50
Depression Glass, Plate, Dinner, Cherry, Pink, 9 In. 4.00
Depression Glass, Plate, Dinner, Daisy, Amber 2.00
Depression Glass, Plate, Dinner, Dogwood, Pink 5.50
Depression Glass, Plate, Dinner, Doric, Pink 2.50
Depression Glass, Plate, Dinner, Floral, Green 4.50
Depression Glass, Plate, Dinner, Miss America, Pink 7.50
Depression Glass, Plate, Dinner, Moderntone, Blue 2.00
Depression Glass, Plate, Dinner, Patrician Spoke, Amber, 10 1/2 In. 3.00
Depression Glass, Plate, Dinner, Patrician, Amber 3.00
Depression Glass, Plate, Dinner, Patrician, Crystal 2.00
Depression Glass, Plate, Dinner, Petalware, Monax, 9 In. 4.00
Depression Glass, Plate, Dinner, Royal Lace, Blue, 10 In. 15.00
Depression Glass, Plate, Dinner, Royal Ruby .... 3.50 To 3.75
Depression Glass, Plate, Dinner, Sandwich, Indiana, 10 1/2 In. 5.50
Depression Glass, Plate, Dinner, Sharon, Amber 2.50
Depression Glass, Plate, Dinner, Sharon, Pink 3.50

Depression Glass, Plate, Dinner, Waterford, Pink 5.00
Depression Glass, Plate, Dogwood, Pink, 6 In. 1.50
Depression Glass, Plate, Dogwood, Pink, 8 In. .... 1.50 To 2.00
Depression Glass, Plate, Doric & Pansy, Teal, 9 In. .... 8.50 To 12.00
Depression Glass, Plate, Doric, Pink, 9 In. 2.50
Depression Glass, Plate, Floral & Foliage Border, Custard, 8 In. 8.50
Depression Glass, Plate, Floral, Pink, 8 In. 2.00
Depression Glass, Plate, Florentine No.1, Green, 10 In. 3.50
Depression Glass, Plate, Florentine No.2, Yellow, 10 In. 4.00
Depression Glass, Plate, Florentine, Green, 6 In. 2.00
Depression Glass, Plate, Flower Garden & Butterflies, Pink, 8 In. 7.50
Depression Glass, Plate, Grill, Cameo, Green 2.50
Depression Glass, Plate, Grill, Cameo, Yellow 2.50
Depression Glass, Plate, Grill, Cherry Blossom, Green 4.00
Depression Glass, Plate, Grill, Mayfair, Pink 6.00
Depression Glass, Plate, Grill, Miss America, Pink .... 5.00 To 7.25
Depression Glass, Plate, Grill, Normandie, Iridescent, 10 1/2 In. 3.00
Depression Glass, Plate, Grill, Parrot, Green 10.00
Depression Glass, Plate, Grill, Patrician, Amber 3.00
Depression Glass, Plate, Grill, Sylvan, Green 5.75
Depression Glass, Plate, Horseshoe, Green, 11 1/2 In. 12.00
Depression Glass, Plate, Iris, 12 In. 5.00
Depression Glass, Plate, Lorain, Yellow, 7 1/2 In. 2.50
Depression Glass, Plate, Luncheon, Cameo, Green .... 3.50 To 4.50
Depression Glass, Plate, Luncheon, Cameo, Green, Original Label 5.25
Depression Glass, Plate, Luncheon, Cameo, Yellow 2.90
Depression Glass, Plate, Luncheon, Cloverleaf, Black .... 6.00 To 6.78
Depression Glass, Plate, Luncheon, Colonial, Pink 2.50
Depression Glass, Plate, Luncheon, Columbia, 9 1/2 In. 1.50
Depression Glass, Plate, Luncheon, Cubist, Green, 8 In. 3.00
Depression Glass, Plate, Luncheon, Dogwood, Pink 3.00
Depression Glass, Plate, Luncheon, Hobnail, Pink, Anchor Hocking, 8 1/2 In. 2.00
Depression Glass, Plate, Luncheon, Iris & Herringbone, 8 In. 8.90
Depression Glass, Plate, Luncheon, Mayfair, Pink 5.00
Depression Glass, Plate, Luncheon, Moderntone, Cobalt 2.50
Depression Glass, Plate, Madrid, Amber, 10 1/2 In. 8.00
Depression Glass, Plate, Madrid, Amber, 11 In. 2.00
Depression Glass, Plate, Madrid, Amber, 11 1/2 In. 4.50
Depression Glass, Plate, Madrid, Green, 9 In. 6.50
Depression Glass, Plate, Manhattan, 6 In. 1.25
Depression Glass, Plate, Miss America, Pink, 10 In. 8.50
Depression Glass, Plate, Miss America, 10 In. 2.00
Depression Glass, Plate, Moonstone, 6 In. 2.00
Depression Glass, Plate, Mt.Pleasant, Ebony, Fluted, 8 In. 5.00
Depression Glass, Plate, Newport, Cobalt, 8 1/2 In. 3.00
Depression Glass, Plate, Normandie, Iridescent, 6 In. 1.25
Depression Glass, Plate, Patrician Spoke, Amber, 11 In. 6.00
Depression Glass, Plate, Patrick, Yellow, Lancaster Glass, 9 In. 1.50
Depression Glass, Plate, Queen Mary, Pink, 6 In. 1.50
Depression Glass, Plate, Royal Lace, Blue, 10 In. 8.00
Depression Glass, Plate, Royal Lace, Cobalt, 6 In. 3.00
Depression Glass, Plate, Royal Ruby, Handled, 8 In. 3.00
Depression Glass, Plate, Royal Ruby, Square, 8 1/2 In. 2.00
Depression Glass, Plate, Royal Ruby, 6 In. 1.50
Depression Glass, Plate, Royal Ruby, 7 In. 2.50
Depression Glass, Plate, Royal Ruby, 7 1/2 In. 2.00
Depression Glass, Plate, Salad, Miss America, Pink, 8 1/2 In. 5.00
Depression Glass, Plate, Salad, Petalware, Monax, 6 In. 1.25
Depression Glass, Plate, Salad, Rosemary, Amber 2.25
Depression Glass, Plate, Sandwich, Forest Green, Anchor Hocking, 9 In. 10.00
Depression Glass, Plate, Sandwich, Green, Anchor Hocking, 9 In. 7.00
Depression Glass, Plate, Sandwich, Horseshoe, Green .... 5.50 To 6.00
Depression Glass, Plate, Sandwich, Indiana, 8 3/8 In. 3.00
Depression Glass, Plate, Sandwich, Iris, 11 3/4 In. 10.00

Depression Glass, Plate, Sandwich, Oyster & Pearl, Ruby, 13 1/2 In. 12.00
Depression Glass, Plate, Sherbet, Mayfair, Pink, 6 1/2 In. 2.50
Depression Glass, Plate, Sherbet, Moderntone, Blue 1.00
Depression Glass, Plate, Sierra, Green, 9 In. 3.50
Depression Glass, Plate, Thistle, Green, 8 In. 2.00
Depression Glass, Platter, Adam, Pink .... 6.00 To 12.50
Depression Glass, Platter, American Sweetheart, Pink, 13 In. 6.50
Depression Glass, Platter, Cherry Blossom, Pink, 13 In. 14.00
Depression Glass, Platter, Madrid, Amber 9.50
Depression Glass, Platter, Miss America, Oval, 12 In. 8.50
Depression Glass, Platter, Miss America, 12 In. 5.50
Depression Glass, Platter, Royal Lace, Blue, 13 In. 17.00
Depression Glass, Relish, Adam, Pink 4.00
Depression Glass, Relish, Madrid, Pink 3.50
Depression Glass, Relish, Moonstone 5.00
Depression Glass, Relish, Moonstone, Divided, 7 In. 5.00
Depression Glass, Relish, No.612, Green, 3 Sections 3.50
Depression Glass, Salt & Pepper, Cloverleaf, Black 40.00
Depression Glass, Salt & Pepper, Cloverleaf, Green 17.50
Depression Glass, Salt & Pepper, Cubist, Green 17.50
Depression Glass, Salt & Pepper, Doric, Pink 16.00
Depression Glass, Salt & Pepper, Floragold 15.00
Depression Glass, Salt & Pepper, Floral, Pink 12.50
Depression Glass, Salt & Pepper, Florentine No.1, Pink 30.00
Depression Glass, Salt & Pepper, Florentine No.2, Green 18.00
Depression Glass, Salt & Pepper, Madrid, Amber, Footed 35.00
Depression Glass, Salt & Pepper, Madrid, Blue, Footed 98.00
Depression Glass, Salt & Pepper, Mayfair, Pink 20.00
Depression Glass, Salt & Pepper, Moderntone, Blue 10.00
Depression Glass, Salt & Pepper, Moonstone 18.75
Depression Glass, Salt & Pepper, Parrot, Green 125.00
Depression Glass, Salt & Pepper, Royal Lace 20.00
Depression Glass, Salt & Pepper, Royal Lace, Blue .... 100.00 To 195.00
Depression Glass, Salt & Pepper, Royal Lace, Green 60.00
Depression Glass, Salt & Pepper, Sharon, Amber 35.00
Depression Glass, Salt & Pepper, Sharon, Pink 20.00
Depression Glass, Salt & Pepper, Sierra, Pink 13.75
Depression Glass, Salt & Pepper, Swirl, Ultramarine 11.50
Depression Glass, Salt & Pepper, Tearoom, Pink 19.50
Depression Glass, Salt & Pepper, Wedding Band, Cobalt 15.00
Depression Glass, Salt & Pepper, Windsor, Pink 9.00
Depression Glass, Salt, Ribbon, Green 5.00
Depression Glass, Saltshaker, Cubist, Pink 7.50
Depression Glass, Saltshaker, Floral, Green 8.50
Depression Glass, Saltshaker, Miss America, Pink 9.50
Depression Glass, Saltshaker, Patrician, Amber 8.00
Depression Glass, Saltshaker, Poppy, Green 7.00
Depression Glass, Saltshaker, Princess, Green 7.00
Depression Glass, Saltshaker, Sharon, Amber 8.00
Depression Glass, Saltshaker, Swirl, Ultramarine 6.75
Depression Glass, Saltshaker, Windsor, Pink 16.00
Depression Glass, Salver, Cake, Petalware, Monax, Red Flower, 11 In. 7.50
Depression Glass, Sauce, Madrid, Green 2.50
Depression Glass, Saucer, Adam, Green 1.50
Depression Glass, Saucer, Cabbage Rose, Amber 1.25
Depression Glass, Saucer, Cherry Bosssom, Pink 1.25
Depression Glass, Saucer, Child's, Cherry, Delphite 8.00
Depression Glass, Saucer, Child's, Doric & Pansy, Pink 4.00
Depression Glass, Saucer, Child's, Doric & Pansy, Ultramarine 5.50
Depression Glass, Saucer, Dogwood, Pink 1.75
Depression Glass, Saucer, Florentine, Pink 2.00
Depression Glass, Saucer, Homespun 3.00
Depression Glass, Saucer, Miss America 2.00
Depression Glass, Saucer, Normandie, Iridescent 1.00

Depression Glass, Saucer, Patrick, Yellow, Lancaster Glass 1.25
Depression Glass, Saucer, Petalware, Monax 1.00
Depression Glass, Saucer, Royal Lace, Black 4.00
Depression Glass, Saucer, Sharon, Amber 1.25
Depression Glass, Saucer, Swirl, Pink 1.25
Depression Glass, Server, Open Lace, Pink, Etched, Center Handle 20.00
Depression Glass, Server, Sandwich, Center Handle, Indiana 8.00
Depression Glass, Server, Sandwich, Sierra, Green 5.50
Depression Glass, Set Of Dishes, Child's, Cherry Blossom, Delphite, 24 Piece 250.00
Depression Glass, Shade, Ceiling Light, Petalware, 11 In. 6.00
Depression Glass, Sherbet, American Sweetheart 4.25
Depression Glass, Sherbet, American Sweetheart, Monax 9.75
Depression Glass, Sherbet, American Sweetheart, Pink, Footed 3.25
Depression Glass, Sherbet, American Sweetheart, Pink, 4 In. .... 4.00 To 4.90
Depression Glass, Sherbet, American Sweetheart, Pink, 4 1/2 In. 3.00
Depression Glass, Sherbet, Cabbage Rose, Amber 2.50
Depression Glass, Sherbet, Cameo, Green, 5 In. .... 10.90 To 14.00
Depression Glass, Sherbet, Cherry Blossom, Pink 4.50
Depression Glass, Sherbet, Cloverleaf, Black 6.00
Depression Glass, Sherbet, Colonial, Green 3.00
Depression Glass, Sherbet, Doric, Pink 2.00
Depression Glass, Sherbet, Duchess, Metal Stand 4.00
Depression Glass, Sherbet, Florentine No.1, Pink 2.50
Depression Glass, Sherbet, Hobnail, Pink, Anchor Hocking 1.75
Depression Glass, Sherbet, Madrid, Amber 2.50
Depression Glass, Sherbet, Mayfair, Pink 4.00
Depression Glass, Sherbet, Mayfair, Pink, Thin, 4 3/4 In. 20.00
Depression Glass, Sherbet, Moderntone, Cobalt 3.00
Depression Glass, Sherbet, Moonstone .... 2.75 To 3.00
Depression Glass, Sherbet, Normandie, Iridescent 2.00
Depression Glass, Sherbet, Patrician Spoke, Amber, Low 2.50
Depression Glass, Sherbet, Patrician, Amber 2.50
Depression Glass, Sherbet, Petalware, Monax, Footed 2.50
Depression Glass, Sherbet, Queen Mary, Pink, Footed 1.50
Depression Glass, Sherbet, Royal Lace, Amethyst, Metal Holder 12.00
Depression Glass, Sherbet, Royal Lace, Cobalt 7.50
Depression Glass, Sherbet, Royal Lace, Green 8.00
Depression Glass, Sherbet, Royal Ruby, Collared Base 3.50
Depression Glass, Sherbet, Royal Ruby, Low Stem 1.75
Depression Glass, Sherbet, Royal Ruby, 2 Knob Stem, 3 In. 2.00
Depression Glass, Sherbet, Sharon, Amber 3.25
Depression Glass, Sherbet, Sharon, Green 2.50
Depression Glass, Sherbet, Sylvan, Green 5.50
Depression Glass, Sherbet, Waterford 1.50
Depression Glass, Shot Glass, Royal Ruby, 6 In Holder 10.00
Depression Glass, Soup Bowl, Madrid, Amber, 7 In. 5.00
Depression Glass, Soup Bowl, Sharon, Pink, 7 1/2 In. 5.25
Depression Glass, Sugar & Creamer, American Sweetheart, Monax .... 9.00 To 17.50
Depression Glass, Sugar & Creamer, Block Optic, Pink, Cone 4.00
Depression Glass, Sugar & Creamer, Cameo, Green 8.95
Depression Glass, Sugar & Creamer, Cherry, Pink, Cover 10.00
Depression Glass, Sugar & Creamer, Child's, Doric & Pansy, Pink 38.00
Depression Glass, Sugar & Creamer, Cubist, Pink, Cover, 3 In. 4.50
Depression Glass, Sugar & Creamer, Dogwood, Pink, Thin 6.90
Depression Glass, Sugar & Creamer, Doric & Pansy, Pink 38.00
Depression Glass, Sugar & Creamer, Florentine No.1, Pink 7.50
Depression Glass, Sugar & Creamer, Florentine No.1, Pink, Cover 10.00
Depression Glass, Sugar & Creamer, Indiana Custard 15.00
Depression Glass, Sugar & Creamer, Lovebird, Green 5.00
Depression Glass, Sugar & Creamer, Madrid, Amber 8.00
Depression Glass, Sugar & Creamer, Mayfair, Pink 8.50
Depression Glass, Sugar & Creamer, Mayfair, Pink, Footed 8.00
Depression Glass, Sugar & Creamer, Miss America, Pink 11.00
Depression Glass, Sugar & Creamer, Moonstone 5.00

Depression Glass, Sugar & Creamer, Patrician, Amber 4.50
Depression Glass, Sugar & Creamer, Petalware, Cremax 7.00
Depression Glass, Sugar & Creamer, Royal Ruby 8.00
Depression Glass, Sugar & Creamer, Royal Ruby, Footed 6.00
Depression Glass, Sugar & Creamer, Sandwich, Anchor Hocking 3.50
Depression Glass, Sugar & Creamer, Sandwich, Red, Footed, Indiana Glass Co. 47.50
Depression Glass, Sugar & Creamer, Swirl, Delphite .... 12.00 To 13.00
Depression Glass, Sugar & Creamer, Tearoom, Green 6.00
Depression Glass, Sugar, American Sweetheart, Monax 2.75
Depression Glass, Sugar, Cherry Blossom, Green, Covered .... 8.00 To 10.00
Depression Glass, Sugar, Cherry Blossom, Pink, Covered 7.50
Depression Glass, Sugar, Cherry, Delphite 20.00
Depression Glass, Sugar, Child's, Cherry, Delphite 24.25
Depression Glass, Sugar, Child's, Cherry, Pink 22.50
Depression Glass, Sugar, Doric & Pansy, Pink 21.00
Depression Glass, Sugar, Floragold, Iridescent 5.00
Depression Glass, Sugar, Florentine No.1, Green, Covered 5.50
Depression Glass, Sugar, Florentine No.1, Pink 3.00
Depression Glass, Sugar, Forest, Green, Paper Label 1.25
Depression Glass, Sugar, Indiana Custard 7.50
Depression Glass, Sugar, Lovebird, Green, 3 In. 3.00
Depression Glass, Sugar, Madrid, Blue 10.00
Depression Glass, Sugar, Miss America 5.00
Depression Glass, Sugar, Moderntone, Cobalt 3.00
Depression Glass, Sugar, Moonstone 3.50
Depression Glass, Sugar, Patrician Spoke 4.00
Depression Glass, Sugar, Patrician, Pedestal 15.00
Depression Glass, Sugar, Patrician, Pink 9.00
Depression Glass, Sugar, Rosemary, Pink, Footed 6.50
Depression Glass, Sugar, Royal Lace, Cobalt 10.00
Depression Glass, Sugar, Royal Lace, Crystal 3.00
Depression Glass, Sugar, Royal Ruby 1.75
Depression Glass, Sugar, Royal Ruby, Covered, Footed 7.50
Depression Glass, Sugar, Sandwich, Covered, Anchor Hocking 5.00
Depression Glass, Sugar, Sharon, Amber 3.00
Depression Glass, Sugar, Swirl, Ultramarine 4.00
Depression Glass, Sugar, Windsor, Pink, Covered 6.00
Depression Glass, Swan, Viking, Emerald Green, 6 In. 18.00
Depression Glass, Tray, Condiment, Florentine No.2, Topaz 20.00
Depression Glass, Tray, Mayfair, Blue, Center Handle 24.00
Depression Glass, Tray, Old Cafe, Pink 2.25
Depression Glass, Tray, Sandwich, Doric, Pink, Handled 5.00
Depression Glass, Tumbler, Adam, Green 7.00
Depression Glass, Tumbler, Adam, Green, 5 1/2 In. 11.00
Depression Glass, Tumbler, American Sweetheart, Pink 16.75
Depression Glass, Tumbler, Block, Pink, Footed, 5 3/4 In. 4.00
Depression Glass, Tumbler, Cabbage Rose, Amber, 9 Ozs., 4 In. 7.00
Depression Glass, Tumbler, Cameo Ballerina, Topaz, 9 Ozs., 5 In. 6.00
Depression Glass, Tumbler, Cameo, Green, 5 In. 7.90
Depression Glass, Tumbler, Cameo, Topaz, Footed, 5 In. 15.00
Depression Glass, Tumbler, Cameo, Yellow, 5 In. 5.00
Depression Glass, Tumbler, Cherry, Delphite, 4 1/2 In. 10.00
Depression Glass, Tumbler, Cherry, Green 6.00
Depression Glass, Tumbler, Cherry, 4 In. 3.00
Depression Glass, Tumbler, Corded Optic, Cobalt, 5 1/2 In. 5.00
Depression Glass, Tumbler, Dogwood, Pink, Decorated, 13 Ozs. 12.50
Depression Glass, Tumbler, Floral, Green, Footed, 4 3/4 In. 4.50
Depression Glass, Tumbler, Floral, Pink, Footed, 7 Ozs. 4.50
Depression Glass, Tumbler, Florentine No.2, Green 5.00
Depression Glass, Tumbler, Florentine, Yellow, Footed, 3 1/4 In. 5.00
Depression Glass, Tumbler, Georgian, Cobalt, Footed, 12 Ozs. 6.00
Depression Glass, Tumbler, Hobnail, Ruby 5.00
Depression Glass, Tumbler, Holiday, Pink, 4 In. 8.00
Depression Glass, Tumbler, Horseshoe, Green, Footed, 9 Ozs. 6.00

Depression Glass, Tumbler, Iced Tea, Grapes, Green, Etched, Footed 2.00
Depression Glass, Tumbler, Iced Tea, Lincoln Inn, Ruby, Fenton 22.50
Depression Glass, Tumbler, Iced Tea, Old Cape Cod, Footed, Imperial 6.00
Depression Glass, Tumbler, Iris & Herringbone, 4 In. .... 8.00 To 12.90
Depression Glass, Tumbler, Iris, Footed, 6 In. 5.00
Depression Glass, Tumbler, Iris, Footed, 7 In. 7.00
Depression Glass, Tumbler, Iris, 6 In. 5.00
Depression Glass, Tumbler, Juice, American Sweetheart, Pink 12.00
Depression Glass, Tumbler, Juice, Cherry Blossom, Delphite 16.00
Depression Glass, Tumbler, Juice, Cherry, Pink 4.50
Depression Glass, Tumbler, Juice, Cherry, Pink, Footed 3.00
Depression Glass, Tumbler, Juice, Grapes, Green, Etched 1.50
Depression Glass, Tumbler, Juice, Holiday, Pink, Footed 8.50
Depression Glass, Tumbler, Juice, Royal Lace, Pink, 3 In. 5.00
Depression Glass, Tumbler, Juice, Royal Ruby 1.80
Depression Glass, Tumbler, Juice, Royal Ruby, Collared Base, 5 Ozs. 4.00
Depression Glass, Tumbler, Juice, Royal Ruby, 5 Ozs. 3.00
Depression Glass, Tumbler, Lace Edge, Pink, 3 3/4 In. 6.00
Depression Glass, Tumbler, Lydia Ray, Pink, 9 Ozs., 4 1/8 In. 4.50
Depression Glass, Tumbler, Lydia Ray, Purple, 5 Ozs. 2.50
Depression Glass, Tumbler, Madrid, Amber, 4 1/2 In. 8.00
Depression Glass, Tumbler, Manhattan 3.00
Depression Glass, Tumbler, Mayfair, Pink, Footed, 6 1/2 In. 8.00
Depression Glass, Tumbler, Mayfair, Pink, 5 1/4 In. 10.00
Depression Glass, Tumbler, Miss America, Pink, 4 In. 10.00
Depression Glass, Tumbler, Miss America, 10 Ozs., 4 1/2 In. 7.50
Depression Glass, Tumbler, Newport Hairpin, Purple 5.00
Depression Glass, Tumbler, Patrician, Amber, 4 1/2 In. 6.00
Depression Glass, Tumbler, Ring, Green, 5 In. 1.75
Depression Glass, Tumbler, Rose Cameo, Green, Footed, 5 In. 5.00
Depression Glass, Tumbler, Rosemary, Amber 6.75
Depression Glass, Tumbler, Royal Lace, Pink, 9 Ozs. 4.50
Depression Glass, Tumbler, Royal Lace, 3 1/2 In. 12.50
Depression Glass, Tumbler, Royal Ruby, 9 Ozs. .... 2.50 To 3.00
Depression Glass, Tumbler, Royal Ruby, 10 Ozs. 3.00
Depression Glass, Tumbler, Royal Ruby, 13 Ozs. 2.50
Depression Glass, Tumbler, Sailboat, Blue, 5 Ozs. 3.50
Depression Glass, Tumbler, Sailboat, Blue, 9 Ozs. 3.50
Depression Glass, Tumbler, Sandwich, Forest Green, Anchor Hocking, 9 Ozs. 3.00
Depression Glass, Tumbler, Sandwich, Green, Anchor Hocking, 2 1/2 In. 2.00
Depression Glass, Tumbler, Sandwich, Green, Anchor Hocking, 4 In. 2.00
Depression Glass, Tumbler, Sharon, Amber, 9 Ozs., 4 In. 7.00
Depression Glass, Tumbler, Sharon, Pink, Footed, 6 1/2 In. 16.00
Depression Glass, Tumbler, Sharon, Pink, Thick, 4 In. 10.00
Depression Glass, Tumbler, Sharon, Pink, Thin, 4 In. 8.00
Depression Glass, Tumbler, Sharon, Pink, 5 1/4 In. 10.00
Depression Glass, Tumbler, Spun, Amber, 5 In. 7.00
Depression Glass, Tumbler, Stacked Tire, Cobalt, 2 Oz. 2.00
Depression Glass, Tumbler, Stacked Tire, Cobalt, 6 Oz. 2.00
Depression Glass, Tumbler, Stacked Tire, Cobalt, 10 Ozs. 2.50
Depression Glass, Tumbler, Stacked Tire, Cobalt, 14 Ozs. 3.00
Depression Glass, Tumbler, Whiskey, Colonial, Green 3.75
Depression Glass, Vase, Royal Ruby, 6 1/2 In. 1.80
Depression Glass, Vase, Spiral, 9 In. 8.00
Depression Glass, Vase, Swirl, Ultramarine, 8 1/2 In. 8.00
Depression Glass, Vegetable Bowl, American Sweetheart, Pink, Oval 7.90
Depression Glass, Vegetable Bowl, Cherry Blossom, Green, Oval, 9 In. 10.00
Depression Glass, Vegetable Bowl, Cherry, Green, Oval 8.75
Depression Glass, Vegetable Bowl, Doric, Pink, Oval 7.25
Depression Glass, Vegetable Bowl, Jadite, Oval 15.00
Depression Glass, Vegetable Bowl, Laurel, Ivory, Oval 9.75
Depression Glass, Vegetable Bowl, Lorain, Green, Oval 8.75
Depression Glass, Vegetable Bowl, Madrid, Amber, Oval .... 6.50 To 7.50
Depression Glass, Vegetable Bowl, Madrid, Green, Oval 10.00

Depression Glass, Vegetable Bowl, Mayfair, Pink, Oval ... 5.25
Depression Glass, Vegetable Bowl, Miss America, Pink, Oval ... 6.50 To 8.75
Depression Glass, Vegetable Bowl, Princess, Green, Oval ... 7.50
Depression Glass, Vegetable Bowl, Royal Lace, Blue, Oval, 11 In. ... 16.00
Depression Glass, Vegetable Bowl, Royal Ruby ... 4.00
Depression Glass, Vegetable Bowl, Sandwich, Oval ... 5.25
Depression Glass, Vegetable Bowl, Sharon, Pink ... 5.00
Depression Glass, Vegetable Bowl, Sharon, Pink, Oval ... 7.50
Depression Glass, Vegetable Bowl, Windsor, Green, Boat Shape ... 14.75
Depression Glass, Vegetable Bowl, Windsor, Green, Oval ... 6.75
Depression Glass, Water Set, Cameo, Green, Rope Top, 7 Piece ... 80.00
Depression Glass, Water Set, Crackle, Blue Floral, 6 Piece ... 48.00
Depression Glass, Water Set, Florentine, Green, 6 Piece ... 40.00
Depression Glass, Wine, Gold, Indiana ... 6.90
Depression Glass, Wine, Iris ... 4.50
Depression Glass, Wine, Iris & Herringbone ... 3.50
Depression Glass, Wine, Iris & Herringbone, 4 Ozs., 5 3/4 In. ... 8.50
Depression Glass, Wine, Iris, Iridescent ... 8.00
Depression Glass, Wine, Iris, 4 1/2 In. ... 8.00
Depression Glass, Wine, Royal Ruby ... 5.00
Depression Glass, Wine, Royal Ruby, Footed ... 5.00

Derby porcelain was made in Derby, England, from 1756 to the present. The factory changed names and marks several times. Chelsea Derby (1770-1784), Crown Derby (1784-1811), and the modern Royal Crown Derby are some of the most famous periods of the factory.

Derby, see also Chelsea, Crown Derby, Royal Crown Derby

Derby, Cup, Rouge De Fer, Gilding, Fluted, No.569, C.1820 ... 25.00
Derby, Jug, Floral Festoons, Crossed Batons & D Mark, Late 1700s, Pair ... 250.00
Derby, Plate, Blue & Gold Floral, Gilt Edge, C.1820, 7 In. ... 25.00
Derby, Plate, Gold Leaf, Blue Gilded Rim, C.1820, 6 In. ... 25.00
Derby, Plate, Orange & Blue Floral & Geometrics, C.1800, 8 In. ... 50.00
Desert Sands, Cup & Saucer, Blue & Green Swirled ... 10.00
DeVilbiss, Atomizer, Bulb, 1916, Boxed ... 15.00
DeVilbiss, Atomizer, Mottled Gold Enamel & Floral On Foot, C.1930 ... 35.00
DeVilbiss, Atomizer, Nose & Throat, Amber ... 15.00
DeVilbiss, Atomizer, Nose & Throat, Atlas Pattern Glass ... 8.00
DeVilbiss, Atomizer, Perfume, Blue, Opalescent ... 18.00
Dick Tracy, Book, Ace Detective, 1940 ... 5.00
Dick Tracy, Book, Dick Tracy & Hotel Murders, Big Little Book ... 6.00
Dick Tracy, Book, Hotel Murders, Big Little Book ... 8.00
Dick Tracy, Book, Spider Gang, Big Little Book ... 12.00
Dick Tracy, Book, Whitman ... 6.00
Dick Tracy, Camera, Plastic ... 15.00
Dick Tracy, Doll, Cardboard, 1944 ... 6.00
Dick Tracy, Doll, Honeymoon, Dressed, 16 In. ... 12.00
Dick Tracy, Doll, Sparkle Plenty, Paper ... 5.50
Dick Tracy, Game, Card, 1937 ... 15.00
Dick Tracy, Gun, Cap, Metal ... 7.50
Dick Tracy, Gun, Siren Pistol ... 10.00 To 25.00
Dick Tracy, Jackknife, Whistle, & Clue Detector, Crime Stopper ... 15.00
Dick Tracy, Postcard, 1935 ... .35
Dick Tracy, Toy, Squad Car Runs Out Of Police Station, Windup, Marx ... 75.00
Dick Tracy, Wristwatch, New Haven ... 140.00
Dick Tracy, Wristwatch, 1930s ... 75.00
Dionne Quintuplet, Album, Picture, First Two Years ... 5.50
Dionne Quintuplet, Album, 1936, Picture ... 12.00
Dionne Quintuplet, Book, Dionne Quintuplets, 1936 ... 8.50
Dionne Quintuplet, Book, Soon We'll Be Three Years Old, 32 Pages ... 11.00
Dionne Quintuplet, Book, Story Of The Dionne Quints, 1934-40 ... 25.00
Dionne Quintuplet, Book, Story Of The Dionne Quintuplets, 1934, 40 Pages ... 12.50
Dionne Quintuplet, Book, We Are 2 Years Old ... 11.00
Dionne Quintuplet, Book, We're Three Years Old ... 3.00
Dionne Quintuplet, Book, We're Two Years Old ... 3.00

Dionne Quintuplet, Book, 1935 .... 12.00
Dionne Quintuplet, Booklet, Three Years Old 11.00
Dionne Quintuplet, Booklet, Two Years Old 11.00
Dionne Quintuplet, Bowl, Chrome Cereal, 6 In. 10.00
Dionne Quintuplet, Calendar, 1935-36, Color Photograph 12.00
Dionne Quintuplet, Calendar, 1937 .... 9.00
Dionne Quintuplet, Dish, Feeding, Embossed Babies, Silver Metal 8.00
Dionne Quintuplet, Doll, Alexander, Sunsuit, Pink Merry-Go-Round, 8 In., 5 .... 300.00
Dionne Quintuplet, Doll, Baby, Dressed, 24 In. 275.00
Dionne Quintuplet, Doll, Quints And Nurse, Bisque, Jointed, 3 1/2 In., Set 75.00
Dionne Quintuplet, Doll, Toddler, Closed Mouth, Brown Wig, 14 1/2 In. 135.00
Dionne Quintuplet, Doll, Toddler, Molded Hair, Painted Features, 7 1/2 In., 5 .... 195.00
Dionne Quintuplet, Doll, Toddler, 14 In. 125.00
Dionne Quintuplet, Fan, Morius Funeral Home, Spencer, Mass. 6.50
Dionne Quintuplet, Game, The Baby Game, Glass Front, Tin Sides, Instructions 6.00
Dionne Quintuplet, Plate, Pictures And Names, Metal 10.00
Dionne Quintuplet, Scrapbook, 200 Pictures 20.00
Dionne Quintuplet, Spoon, Annette 8.00
Dionne Quintuplet, Spoon, Cecile 7.00
Dionne Quintuplet, Spoon, Emilie 9.50
Dionne Quintuplet, Spoon, Marie .... 7.00 To 8.00
Dionne Quintuplet, Spoon, Yvonne .... 7.00 To 9.50
Disneyana, Album, Picture, Mickey Mouse, Volume 1, 28 Cards 65.00
Disneyana, Bank, Donald Duck, Made In U.S.A. 24.00
Disneyana, Bank, Mickey Mouse, Head Turns, Papier-Mache 18.00
Disneyana, Bank, Mickey Mouse, Post Office, Red, Tin 30.00
Disneyana, Bank, Mickey Mouse, Tin Post Office 30.00
Disneyana, Basket, Waste Paper, Minnie Mouse, Tin 8.00
Disneyana, Book, Adventures Of Mickey Mouse, 1931 .... 35.00
Disneyana, Book, Art Of Walt Disney, 763 Illustrations 45.00
Disneyana, Book, Bambi, 1949 .... 4.50
Disneyana, Book, Better Little Book, Mickey Mouse, Caveman Island 10.00
Disneyana, Book, Comic, Donald Duck, 1955 .... 2.00
Disneyana, Book, Mickey Mouse & The Pirate Submarine 5.00
Disneyana, Book, Mickey Mouse & The Sacred Jewels, 1936, Big Little Book 5.00
Disneyana, Book, Mickey Mouse & The 7 Ghosts, Big Little Book 12.00
Disneyana, Book, Mickey Mouse In The Foreign Legion, Big Little Book 12.00
Disneyana, Book, Mickey Mouse Library Of Games 28.00
Disneyana, Book, Mickey Mouse Recipe, 1930s 20.00
Disneyana, Book, Mickey Mouse The Mail Pilot, Big Little Book 8.50
Disneyana, Book, Mickey Mouse, Big Little Book 8.50
Disneyana, Book, Mickey Mouse, Silly Symphonies 5.00
Disneyana, Book, Mickey Mouse, 1934, 48 Pages 20.00
Disneyana, Book, Pinocchio Store & Coloring, 1939 .... 20.00
Disneyana, Book, Walt Disney's Storyland, 1964 .... 16.50
Disneyana, Book, 1939 Disneyville, Mickey & Friends, 102 Pages 9.00
Disneyana, Bowl, Mickey Mouse, Red Beetleware 13.00
Disneyana, Box, Pencil, Mickey Mouse 15.00
Disneyana, Box, Straws, Mickey Mouse, C.1940, 9 X 4 In. 3.00
Disneyana, Bracelet, Gold Color, 12 Characters 10.50
Disneyana, Bracelet, Seven Dwarfs, Silver Plate 10.50
Disneyana, Brochure, Opening Day Disneyland, July 18, 1955 .... 18.00
Disneyana, Buckle, Mickey Mouse, Hand-Painted Mickey In Silver .... *Color* 7.00
Disneyana, Camera, Donald Duck 25.00
Disneyana, Car, Mickey Mouse Roadster, Windup, Tin 35.00
Disneyana, Case, Pencil, Mickey Mouse & Donald Duck, Contents 18.00
Disneyana, Celluloid, The Practical Pig Cartoon, 1938, 7 3/4 X 6 1/2 In. 350.00
Disneyana, Chair, Mickey Mouse Canvas Beach, Walt Disney Enterprises 95.00
Disneyana, Christmas Tree Ornament, Light Bulb, String Of 7 .... 55.00
Disneyana, Clock, Animated Mickey Mouse, Made In West Germany 10.00
Disneyana, Clock, Mickey Mouse, Elgin, Electric 35.00
Disneyana, Container, Candy, Mickey Mouse, 3 1/2 In. 46.00
Disneyana, Cup, Baby's, Mickey Mouse, International Silver Co., 1934 .... 45.00
Disneyana, Cup, Mickey Mouse, International Silver Co., 1934 .... 25.00

Disneyana, Doll, Bashful, Dwarf, Bisque, 5 In. 20.00
Disneyana, Doll, Bashful, Dwarf, Mask Face, C.1930, 13 1/2 In. 28.00
Disneyana, Doll, Doc, Dwarf, Hard Rubber, 5 1/2 In. 15.00
Disneyana, Doll, Donald Duck, Semimechanical, 1st National Bank 45.50
Disneyana, Doll, Donald Duck, Walt Disney, Bisque 18.00
Disneyana, Doll, Dopey, Buckram Painted Face, 1938 35.00
Disneyana, Doll, Dopey, Dwarf, Stuffed, 12 In. 18.00
Disneyana, Doll, Dwarf, Happy, Rubber, 8 In. 6.50
Disneyana, Doll, Ginger, Mouseketeer Outfit, 8 In. 20.00
Disneyana, Doll, Grumpy, Dwarf, Composition, Effanbee, 14 In. 75.00
Disneyana, Doll, Happy, Dwarf, Soft Rubber, 8 In. 12.00
Disneyana, Doll, Happy, Dwarf, Stuffed, 12 In. 18.00
Disneyana, Doll, Mickey Mouse Clown, Celluloid, Cloth Body, Wood Legs, 7 In. 75.00
Disneyana, Doll, Mickey Mouse, Bisque, Marked Walt E.Disney, Japan, 4 In. 22.50
Disneyana, Doll, Mickey Mouse, Hair, 3 In. 7.50
Disneyana, Doll, Mickey Mouse, Hard Rubber, Seiberling, 3 1/2 In. 25.00
Disneyana, Doll, Mickey Mouse, Rubber, 8 3/4 In. 2.00
Disneyana, Doll, Mickey Mouse, Sun Rubber, C.1950, 10 In. 10.00
Disneyana, Doll, Minnie Mouse, Bisque, Marked Walt E.Disney, Japan, 4 In. 22.50
Disneyana, Doll, Minnie Mouse, Sun Rubber, C.1950, 10 In. 8.00
Disneyana, Doll, Pinocchio, Composition, 9 In. 49.00
Disneyana, Doll, Pinocchio, Vinyl Head, Plush Body, 12 In. 12.00
Disneyana, Doll, Pluto, Rubber, 7 In. 2.00
Disneyana, Doll, Set Of 3, Mickey, Minnie, Pluto, Walt Disney 1933, Metal 20.00
Disneyana, Doll, Snow White, Cloth, Seven Dwarfs On Dress, 16 In. 35.00
Disneyana, Doll, Snow White, Composition, Dressed, 14 In. 95.00
Disneyana, Doll, Snow White, Composition, W.D.P., 13 In. 65.00
Disneyana, Doll, Snow White, Molded Dress, 2 1/2 In. 25.00
Disneyana, Dopey, Marx 100.00
Disneyana, Figurine, Dopey, Walt Disney, Seiberling Latex, 5 1/2 In. 11.00
Disneyana, Figurine, Fantasia Hippo, 6 In. 5.00
Disneyana, Figurine, Fox, Bisque, 3 In. 12.50
Disneyana, Figurine, Jiminey Cricket, Bisque, 3 In. 12.50
Disneyana, Figurine, Joe Carioca, 6 In. 5.00
Disneyana, Figurine, Mickey Mouse, Black Rubber, Sieberling, 1930s 20.00
Disneyana, Figurine, Minnie Mouse With Mandolin, Bisque 15.00
Disneyana, Figurine, Pinocchio, Bisque, 3 In. 12.50
Disneyana, Figurine, Seven Dwarfs, 2 3/4 In., Each 12.50
Disneyana, Figurine, Sleeping Beauty & Animals, Rubber 10.00
Disneyana, Figurine, Snow White, Bisque, 3 1/4 In. 12.50
Disneyana, Figurine, Snow White, 7 Dwarfs, Bisque, German, 1 1/2 To 2 1/2 In. 125.00
Disneyana, Figurine, Wicked Cat, Bisque, 3 In. 12.50
Disneyana, Figurine, 3 Little Pigs, Bisque, 3 1/2 In., Set 28.00
Disneyana, Fork, Donald Duck, Stainless Steel 1.50
Disneyana, Fork, Mickey Mouse, Stainless Steel 1.50
Disneyana, Game, Donald Duck, Board, Parker Bros., 1938 15.00
Disneyana, Gloves, Spin & Marty, Gauntlet 2.00
Disneyana, Gravy Boat, Mickey & Minnie Mouse, Japan 20.00
Disneyana, Guitar, Mousegetar Jr., Mattel, 14 In. 22.50
Disneyana, Handcar, Lionel, Mickey & Minnie Mouse 225.00
Disneyana, Handcar, Mickey Mouse, Lionel Corp., Keywind 245.00
Disneyana, Ironing Board, Snow White & Seven Dwarfs, Tin, 27 In. 35.00
Disneyana, Jar, Cookie, Donald Duck 10.00 To 18.00
Disneyana, Jar, Cookie, Mickey & Minnie Mouse 37.50 To 52.00
Disneyana, Jar, Cookie, Mickey Mouse & Minnie, Reversible 31.00
Disneyana, Jar, Cookie, Turn About, White, McCoy, Round 8.00
Disneyana, Kit, Minnie Mouse Nurse, C.1940 15.00
Disneyana, Lamp, Donald Duck, Soren, Manegold Co., Chicago, 16 In. 60.00
Disneyana, Machine, Bubble Gum, Mickey Mouse, Plastic 10.00
Disneyana, Mask, Face, Minnie Mouse, C.1933, Paper 10.00
Disneyana, Mickey & Minnie, Tin, Windup, 9 X 5 1/2 In. *Illus* 385.00
Disneyana, Mickey Mouse Choo Choo Pull Toy, Fisher Price, 1938 32.00
Disneyana, Mickey Mouse Club Set, 8 Pieces On Card 12.00
Disneyana, Mickey Mouse, Rubber Fire Engine, Sun Rubber 12.00

Disneyana, Mirror, Mickey Mouse, Handbag, Case 3.50
Disneyana, Mug, Mickey Mouse & Pluto, Patriot, Porcelain 15.00
Disneyana, Ornament, Snow White 7.50
Disneyana, Pail, Candy, 3 Pigs, Tin 15.00
Disneyana, Paper Doll, Snow White & 7 Dwarfs, Cardboard, Clothes, 15 In. 35.00
Disneyana, Paperweight, Mickey Mouse, 1969, American Flag, Iron 9.00
Disneyana, Pinocchio, Doll, Wooden 60.00
Disneyana, Pitcher, Tweetie Bird, Figural 5.00
Disneyana, Planter, Bambi 8.00
Disneyana, Plate, Mickey Mouse Club, Plastic 13.00
Disneyana, Platter, Mickey & Minnie Mouse, Japan 20.00
Disneyana, Projector, Movie, Mickey Mouse Club, 3 Films, Original Box 25.00
Disneyana, Pull Toy, Ferdinand The Bull, Disney 1938, Tin & Wood, 9 1/2 In. 50.00
Disneyana, Puppet, Donald Duck Astronaut, Plastic, Wheat Cereal 5.00
Disneyana, Puppet, Mickey Mouse, Hand 5.00
Disneyana, Puzzle, Donald Duck, 300 Pieces 12.50
Disneyana, Salt & Pepper, Dumbo 5.00
Disneyana, Salt & Pepper, Mickey & Minnie Mouse, Made In Japan 17.00

Disneyana, Mickey & Minnie, Tin, Windup, 9 X 5 1/2 In.

(See Page 165)

Disneyana, Salt & Pepper, Mickey & Minnie On Bench 20.00
Disneyana, Salt & Pepper, Mickey Mouse 25.00
Disneyana, Scrapbook, Recipe, Mickey Mouse, 2 Cards 48.00
Disneyana, Serving Bowl, Covered, Mickey & Minnie Mouse, Japan 20.00
Disneyana, Sharpener, Pencil, Casey 6.00
Disneyana, Snow White & Seven Dwarfs, Bisque, Marked Walt, Disney, Japan 110.00
Disneyana, Spoon, Mickey Mouse 14.00
Disneyana, Spoon, Mickey Mouse, Silver Plate .... 6.50 To 7.50
Disneyana, Spoon, Minnie Mouse 5.00
Disneyana, Stage, T.V., 38 Hard Rubber Figures & Props, Tin 29.00
Disneyana, Stove, Snow White, Tin, Wolverine Co. 12.50
Disneyana, Sugar & Creamer, Cover, Mickey Mouse 9.75
Disneyana, Sugar & Creamer, Cover, Snow White & The Seven Dwarfs, 1937 .... 9.90
Disneyana, Tambourine, Mickey Mouse, U.S.A. 20.00
Disneyana, Tea Set, Cup, Saucer, Plate, Chein, Tin 15.00
Disneyana, Tea Set, Mickey & Minnie Mouse, Pie Eye, Japan, 15 Piece 85.00
Disneyana, Teapot, Mickey Mouse 5.50
Disneyana, Toothbrush Holder, Mickey Mouse Blowing Pluto's Nose, Bisque 40.00
Disneyana, Toothbrush Holder, 3 Pigs, Bisque 28.00
Disneyana, Toy, Acrobatic Pinocchio, Original Box 135.00
Disneyana, Toy, Black Lamb Called Daisy, Daisies For Eyes, 10 In. 20.00
Disneyana, Toy, Donald Duck Crazy Shoe, Windup, Plastic 4.00
Disneyana, Toy, Donald Duck Duet, Original Box 150.00
Disneyana, Toy, Donald Duck Playing Xylophone, Sitting, Pull Toy, Wooden 40.00
Disneyana, Toy, Donald Duck Robot, Windup, Plastic 5.00
Disneyana, Toy, Donald Duck, Cast Iron 8.00
Disneyana, Toy, Donald Duck, Pull 10.00
Disneyana, Toy, Donald Duck, Windup, Celluloid, 3 In. 14.00
Disneyana, Toy, Donald Duck, Windup, Chein 25.00
Disneyana, Toy, Ferdinand The Bull, Windup, Tin, Marx, 1938, 6 In. 18.00
Disneyana, Toy, Mickey Mouse Crazy Shoe, Windup, Plastic 4.00

Disneyana, Truck, Fire, Mickey Mouse, Rubber, 5 In.

Doctor, Hypnotist's Device, C.1900, 8 1/2 In.High

Disneyana, Toy, Mickey Mouse Dipsy Car, Windup, Tin, Marx, C.1947 .... 15.00 To 35.00
Disneyana, Toy, Mickey Mouse In Fire Truck, Rubber, 6 1/2 In. 18.00
Disneyana, Toy, Mickey Mouse Robot, Windup, Plastic 5.00
Disneyana, Toy, Mickey Mouse, Windup, Linemar 20.00
Disneyana, Toy, Mickey's Air Mail, Rubber, 7 In. 10.00
Disneyana, Toy, Mickey's Tractor, Rubber, 5 In. 10.00
Disneyana, Toy, Parade Roadster, Windup, Tin, Marx, 10 In. 35.00
Disneyana, Toy, Parade Roadster, Windup, Tin, Plastic Windshield, 4 Figures 48.00
Disneyana, Toy, Pinocchio & Water Pails, Windup, Tin 50.00
Disneyana, Toy, Pinocchio, Acrobatic 125.00
Disneyana, Toy, Pluto Acrobat, Battery Operated, Celluloid & Metal 78.00
Disneyana, Toy, Pluto Pop-Up Kritter, String Operated, Wooden 17.00
Disneyana, Toy, Pluto, Roll Over, Windup, Tin, 1939 .... 14.50
Disneyana, Toy, Pluto, Stuffed 5.50
Disneyana, Toy, Pluto, Windup, Slinky Body, Tin, Linemar 20.00
Disneyana, Toy, Pop-Up Kritter, Pluto 12.00
Disneyana, Toy, Snow White, Pull, 1939 .... 12.00
Disneyana, Toy, Train, Windup, Engine & 3 Cars, Marx, Japan, 12 In. 19.50
Disneyana, Toy, Walt Disney's Playhouse, Lithographed, 38 Characters 30.00
Disneyana, Toy, Walt Disney's T.V. Playhouse, Metal, Plastic Props 30.00
Disneyana, Train, Windup, Lithographed Figures, Tin & Rubber, 4 Piece 18.00
Disneyana, Tray, T.V., Mickey Mouse Club 11.00
Disneyana, Truck, Fire, Mickey Mouse, Rubber, 5 In. .... *Illus* 22.00
Disneyana, Wallet, Donald Duck 6.00
Disneyana, Wallet, Mickey Mouse Mouseketeers 6.00
Disneyana, Watch Fob, Mickey Mouse, Metal 7.00
Disneyana, Watch, Cinderella, U.S.Time, 1950 .... 35.00
Disneyana, Watch, Mickey Mouse, Ingersoll .... 75.00 To 200.00
Disneyana, Watch, Mickey Mouse, 1936 .... 75.00
Disneyana, Watch, Minnie Mouse 15.00
Disneyana, Watch, Wrist, Mickey Mouse, Ingersoll, Silver Figures On Band 123.00
Disneyana, Watch, Wrist, Mickey Mouse, Red Strap, 1940s 75.00
Doctor, Bag, Alligator 35.00
Doctor, Box, Dr.T.W.Graydon, Diseases Of Nose, Throat, & Lungs, Ohio, 9 In. 20.00
Doctor, Box, Veterinarian, Bottles & Equipment, Scales, Pestle, Leather 190.00
Doctor, Cabinet, Dental Implements, Bone Mallets, Walnut 175.00
Doctor, Cabinet, Dental, Oak, Victorian 650.00
Doctor, Cabinet, Dentist's, Gas, Drill, Walnut, Foot Operated 350.00
Doctor, Case, Instrument With 5 Instruments, Dated 1885 .... 25.00
Doctor, Chair, Dentist's, Mahogany, Milk Glass, 5 Drawers 95.00
Doctor, Chair, Dentist's, Peerless, Harvard, 1909, Holders & Bowls 500.00
Doctor, Clamp, Veterinarian's, For Castrating Bulls 7.50
Doctor, Cutter, Suture, Steel, Flat Heart Shaped Blades, C.1810 .... 20.00
Doctor, Drill, Dental, Electric 60.00
Doctor, Drill, Dentist's, Foot Treadle Powered 267.50
Doctor, Fleam, Surgeon's, Brass Case, 3 Steel Blades 35.00
Doctor, Hypnotist's Device, C.1900, 8 1/2 In.High .... *Illus* 250.00
Doctor, Inhaler, Steam, Brass & Iron, S.Mawson & Thompson, London, 8 1/2 In. 120.00

Doctor, Kit, Box With Implements & Instruments, Dated 1879, 7 In. 175.00
Doctor, Kit, Ear Inspection, Royal Flash Light, Leatherette Case 9.00
Doctor, Knife, Bleeding, C.1870, 2 Blades 35.00
Doctor, Machine, Apollo, Medical, Electrical, Quack 55.00
Doctor, Machine, Baloptican, Bausch-Lomb, Case, 300 Slides, Spare Bulb 375.00
Doctor, Machine, Cure, Chloride Of Silver, Dry Cell, Patent 1890 32.00
Doctor, Machine, Heart Testing 125.00
Doctor, Machine, Inhaler, Boots Hygenic, Ceramic, Blue, White, 7 In. 40.00
Doctor, Machine, Quack, Chloride Of Silver, Patent 1896, Dry Cell Battery 68.00
Doctor, Machine, Shock Treatment, Quack, Original Box, 1919, Instructions 28.50
Doctor, Machine, Shocking, Frank S.Betz Co., Battery Operated 9.00
Doctor, Machine, Ultra Violet, Electric, Quack 20.00
Doctor, Machine, Violet Ray, Instruction Book 15.00
Doctor, Optical Testing Glasses, 224 Lenses In Case 97.50
Doctor, Pliers, Dentist's, Iron 12.00
Doctor, Saw, Surgeons Amputating, Bone Handle, 11 1/2 In. 35.00
Doctor, Syringe, Dr.Robert's Veterinary, Patent 1903 4.50
Doctor, Syringe, Pewter, 19th Century, 10 In. 30.00
Doctor, Syringe, Veterinarian's, Brass 5.00
Doctor, Tester, Eye, Brass Angle Stand, Patent 1896, Lenses 85.00
Doctor, Tool, Bellows, Dentist's 95.00

Doll entries are listed by marks printed or incised on doll, if possible. If there are no marks, the doll is listed by name of subject or country.

Doll, see also Campbell Kid, Doll; Charlie Chaplin, Doll; Dionne Quintuplet, Doll; Disneyana, Doll; Kewpie, Doll; Political Campaign, Doll; Popeye, Doll; Shirley Temple Doll
Doll, Alexander, see Doll, Madame Alexander
Doll, A.B.G., Toddler, Bisque Head, Breather, Composition Body, 23 In. 315.00
Doll, A.M., see also Doll, Armand Marseille
Doll, A.M. 210, Baby, Googlie Intaglio Eyes, 6 1/2 In. 225.00
Doll, A.M. 323, Blue Glass, Googlie Sleep Eyes, 11 In. 650.00
Doll, A.M. 323, Girl, Googlie Eyes, 7 1/2 In. 425.00
Doll, A.M. 370, Bisque Head, Kid Body, Brown Sleep Eyes, 23 In. 125.00
Doll, A.M. 370, Jointed Kid Body, Composition Arms, Human Hair Wig, 16 In. 95.00
Doll, A.M. 370, Kid Body, 18 In. 150.00
Doll, A.M. 390 Germany, Bisque, Ursuline Nun, 10 In. 125.00
Doll, A.M. 390, Bisque Head, Ball-Jointed Body, 24 In. 155.00
Doll, A.M. 390, Bisque, French Canadian Costume, 12 In. 65.00
Doll, A.M. 390, Bye-Lo Baby, Bisque Head, Jointed Body, 12 1/2 In. 160.00
Doll, A.M. 390, Girl, Brown Sleep Eyes, Wig, 21 In. 135.00
Doll, A.M. 560, Character Face, Green Satin Outfit, 24 In. 275.00
Doll, A.M. 977, Baby Girl, Brown Sleep Eyes, 15 In. 225.00
Doll, A.M. 985, Baby, Bent Limbs, 16 In. 240.00
Doll, A.M. 992, Toddler, Bisque Head, Composition Body, 19 1/2 In. 225.00
Doll, A.M., Baby, Character Face, 2 Teeth, Composition Body, 15 In. Head 310.00
Doll, A.M., Ball-Jointed Body, Blue Sleep Eyes, 24 In. 110.00
Doll, A.M., Ball-Jointed Body, Blue Sleep Eyes, 37 In. 550.00
Doll, A.M., Ball-Jointed Composition Body, Blue Eyes, 18 In. 125.00
Doll, A.M., Bisque Head, Stick Body, 13 In. 85.00
Doll, A.M., Blue Sleep Eyes, 22 In. 120.00
Doll, A.M., Dream Baby, Bisque Head, Cloth Body, Christening Gown, 13 In. 165.00
Doll, A.M., Dream Baby, Pat-A-Cake, Mechanical, 12 In. 375.00
Doll, A.M., Dutch Child, Bisque Head, Jointed Composition Body, 9 In., Pair 40.00
Doll, A.M., Floradora, Bisque, Jointed, 24 In. 165.00
Doll, A.M., Girl, Bisque, Open Mouth, 4 Teeth, Blue Paperweight Eyes, 15 In. 250.00
Doll, A.M., Googlie Eyes, 9 In. 525.00
Doll, A.M., Oriental Lady, Bisque Head, Jointed Composition Body, 8 1/2 In. 395.00
Doll, A.M., Rock-A-Bye Baby, Bisque Head, Papier-Mache Body, 18 In. 170.00
Doll, A.M., Rock-A-Bye Baby, Blue Sleep Eyes, 6 In. Head 125.00
Doll, A.M., Shoulder Head, Brown Paperweight Eyes, 13 In. 80.00
Doll, A.17 M., Blue Sleep Eyes, 17 1/2 In. 550.00
Doll, A-13, Paris, La Parisien, Steiner, Molded Teeth, 19 In. 800.00
Doll, Alexander, see Doll, Madame Alexander

Doll, Alsatian, Girl, Bisque Head

Doll, Canadian, Boy, H.M.S.Uniform, 11 1/2 In.
Doll, Canadian, Girl, H.M.S.Uniform, 11 In.

Doll, Alsatian, Girl, Bisque Head .... *Illus* 150.00
Doll, Amberg, Baby, Composition Body, Blue Glass Sleep Eyes, 8 In. 160.00
Doll, American, Boy, Celluloid Head, Cloth Body, Painted Features, 10 In. 75.00
Doll, American, Little Rickey Type Face, Rooted Curly Hair, 13 In. 6.00
Doll, American, Sweet Sue, Bride, Walker, Hard Plastic, 18 In. 30.00
Doll, American, Toddles, Flirty Eyes, Rooted Hair, 20 In. 13.00
Doll, American, Toni, Tea Time Outfit, 10 1/2 In. 25.00
Doll, Animated Watchmaker, Longines Never Wind Watch 300.00
Doll, Armand Marseille, see also Doll, A.M.
Doll, Armand Marseille, Bisque Shoulder Head, Kid Body, Blonde Hair, 22 In. 145.00
Doll, Armand Marseille, Googlie Eyes, Bisque Head, Composition Body, 12 In. 475.00
Doll, Arranbee, Brikette, Orange Hair, Freckles, Grinning, 22 In. 50.00
Doll, Arthur Gerling, Negro Baby, Closed Mouth, Pierced Nostrils, 20 In. 995.00
Doll, B J & Co. 101, My Sweetheart, Composition Body, Brown Eyes, 20 In. 185.00
Doll, B.S.W. & Heart, Walker, 23 In. 400.00
Doll, Bavaria, Boy, Open Mouth, Blue Sleep Eyes, 20 In. 150.00
Doll, Belton 204, Bisque, Closed Mouth, Brown Stationary Eyes, 15 In. 465.00
Doll, Belton, Girl, Brown Paperweight Eyes, 13 1/2 In. 395.00
Doll, Bergmann Simon & Halbig, Girl, Jointed Composition Body, 30 In. 250.00
Doll, Betty Boop, 9 1/2 In., Jointed 15.00
Doll, Bill Price, 1972, Negro Girl, Ceramic Head & Limbs, Cloth Body, 15 In. 45.00
Doll, Bonnie Braids, Dick Tracy 35.00
Doll, Borgfeldt, Composition, 24 In. 175.00
Doll, Borgfeldt, Milly, Kid Body, 24 In. 270.00
Doll, Boudoir, Blond Hair, Ruffled Dress, French WW I 45.00
Doll, Brevette, Brown Hair, 10 1/2 In. 2300.00
Doll, C.M.Bergmann, see also Doll, S.&H., Doll, Simon & Halbig
Doll, C.M.Bergmann, Baby, Bisque, Brown Eyes & Hair, 23 In. 175.00
Doll, C.M.Bergmann, Ball-Jointed Body, Brown Sleep Eyes, 24 In. 165.00
Doll, C.M.Bergmann, Girl, Blue Sleep Eyes, Blonde Wig, 22 In. 165.00
Doll, C.M.Bergmann, Molded Brows, Ball-Jointed Body, 22 In. 165.00
Doll, Campbell Kid, 1940s 48.00
Doll, Canadian, Boy, H.M.S.Uniform, 11 1/2 In. .... *Illus* 20.00
Doll, Canadian, Girl, H.M.S.Uniform, 11 In. .... *Illus* 20.00
Doll, Carl P.Anderson, Henry, CR, 1934, Bisque, Movable Arms, 6 3/4 In. 60.00
Doll, Century Baby, Bisque Head, Cloth Body, Composition Hands, 12 In. 375.00
Doll, Century, Composition Head & Arms, Cloth Body, 13 In. 55.00
Doll, Chad Valley, Dutch Girl & Boy, Felt Head, Stuffed Velvet, 11 In., Pair 105.00
Doll, Chad Valley, Princess Elizabeth, 15 In. 165.00
Doll, Chase, Hospital Baby, Stamp Under Arm, 29 In. 120.00
Doll, Chris Allen, Rock-A-Bye Baby, 15 1/2 In. Head 249.00
Doll, Clarmaid 1959, Gibson Girl, 20 In. 90.00
Doll, Clothespin, Hand-Hewn Pine, 15 In. 120.00
Doll, Crazy Ignatz Mouse, Jaymar, Wooden, Jointed 20.00
Doll, Cuno & Otto Dressel, Open Mouth, Ball-Jointed Body, Human Hair, 24 In. 280.00

Doll, D.R.G.M., Baby, Bisque, Kid Body, 15 In. 250.00
Doll, Dewees Cochran, Ice Queen, 15 In. 150.00
Doll, Dotter, Porcelain Head, Corset Body, Black Hair, 16 In. 95.00
Doll, Dressel 1912, Jointed Body, Blue Sleep Eyes, 24 In. 175.00
Doll, E.B., French, Fashion, Bisque Arms, Brown Eyes, 14 In. 1195.00
Doll, E.C.Spirin, London, 1862, Jenny Lind, Autoperipatetikos, 10 In. 925.00
Doll, E.D., Boy, Open Mouth, Blue Paperweight Eyes, 25 In. 650.00
Doll, E.S.T.P. Germany, Baby, 2 Teeth, Character Face, Blonde, 15 In. 175.00
Doll, Edmund Steiner, Girl, Bisque Head & Hands, Kid Body, Brown Eyes, 24 In. 215.00
Doll, Effanbee, Bride, Composition, 9 1/2 In. 15.00
Doll, Effanbee, C.1925, Composition, Open & Closed Mouth, 24 In. 65.00
Doll, Effanbee, C.1950, Honey Walker, Hard Plastic, 14 In. 18.00
Doll, Effanbee, Dy-Dee Baby, Nurser, Vinyl Body, Blue Sleep Eyes, 20 In. 30.00
Doll, Effanbee, Fleishman & Bodell, Boy Toddler, Dome Head, 22 In. 1100.00
Doll, Effanbee, Girl, Dress & Parasol, 27 In. 60.00
Doll, Effanbee, Patsyette, Composition, 9 1/2 In. 45.00
Doll, Emma Clear, China With Snood, 18 In. 225.00
Doll, Emma Clear, Lady, Pierced Ears, Blue Eyes, Blonde Hair, 17 In. 155.00
Doll, Emma Clear, Martha Washington, 19 In. 325.00
Doll, Emma Clear, 1946, George Washington, Cloth Body, China Limbs, 20 In. 225.00
Doll, Eric James, Rock-A-Bye Baby, 16 In. Head 255.00
Doll, Ernst Heubach, Baby, Bisque Head & Arms, Kid Body, 4 Teeth, 15 In. 80.00
Doll, F.G. In Scroll, 2 Rows Of Teeth, Solid Wrists, Blue Eyes, 29 In. 1295.00
Doll, F.G., Fashion, Bisque Face, Cork Pate, Cloth Body, Leather Arms, 15 In. 450.00
Doll, F.G., Fashion, Lady, Swivel Neck, Kid Body, Closed Mouth, 12 1/2 In. 750.00
Doll, F.G., French, Fashion, Lady, Kid Body, Pierced Ears, 17 In. 875.00
Doll, F.G., Lady, Swivel Neck, Pierced Ears, Closed Mouth, Blue Eyes, 12 In. 750.00
Doll, F.S.& Co., Baby, Breather, Blue Sleep Eyes, 15 In. 250.00
Doll, Fanny Brice, Baby Snooks, Intaglio Eyes, Doll Of 1000 Poses 150.00
Doll, Farnell's Alpha Toys, England, Felt Face, Velvet Limbs, 15 In. 110.00
Doll, Flapper Bed Doll Smoking, 1920 Giveaway By Cigarette Co. 42.00
Doll, Flapper, Pink Ribbon Dress & Hat, Gold Hair, Painted Features, 1939 27.50
Doll, France 35, Lady, Celluloid, Painted Features, Dressed, 15 In. 85.00
Doll, France, Peasant Woman & Man, Raca Type, Cloth Body, 23 In., Pair 45.00
Doll, Franz Schmidt, Boy Toddler, Breather, Velvet Suit, 15 1/2 In. 375.00
Doll, French, Bisque Face, Jointed Composition Body, Blue Glass Eyes, 18 In. 245.00
Doll, French, Cancan Girl, Celluloid, 7 In. 10.00
Doll, French, DEP, Girl, Molded Brown, Blue Eyes, 24 In. 350.00
Doll, French, Fashion, Closed Mouth, Painted Eyes, 10 In. 325.00
Doll, French, Fashion, Girl, Bisque Head & Hands, Wooden Body, 19 In. 1595.00
Doll, French, Fashion, Lady, Bisque, Cork Pate, Kid Body, Blue Eyes, 10 In. 475.00
Doll, French, Fashion, Lady, Cobalt Eyes, 17 In. 650.00
Doll, French, Fashion, Lady, Dressed, 15 In. 650.00
Doll, French, Girl Badminton Player, Mechanical, 10 In. 695.00
Doll, French, Girl, Bisque, Closed Mouth, Blue Paperweight Eyes, 9 1/2 In. 500.00
Doll, French, Incised 224, Girl, 15 In. 250.00
Doll, French, Lady, Celluloid, Jointed, Painted Features, 3 1/2 In. 14.00
Doll, Frozen Charlotte, Hard Rubber, Victorian, 2 In. 25.00
Doll, Frozen Charlotte, 1 In. 18.00

Doll, Fulper, see also Doll, Horsman

Doll, Fulper, Baby, 2 Teeth, Brown Stationary Eyes, Mohair Wig, 14 In. 195.00
Doll, Fulper, Girl, Ball-Jointed Body, Dressed, 20 In. 155.00
Doll, Fulper, Shoulder Head, Kid Body, Blue Sleep Eyes, 23 In. 250.00
Doll, Fulper, Toddler, Open Mouth, Blue Glass Eyes, 24 In. 350.00
Doll, Furga, Bisque, Open Mouth, Brown Glass Eyes, Mohair Wig, 7 In. 95.00
Doll, G & F III, 24 In. 275.00
Doll, G.K.Belton, Girl, Solid Wrists, Blue Paperweight Eyes, 11 1/2 In. 350.00
Doll, Garbet, Patendo, Made In Spain, Bullfighter, Bandilleras, 9 In. 20.00
Doll, Gebruder Heubach 10532, Baby, Open Mouth, Glass Eyes, 8 In. 195.00
Doll, Gebruder Heubach, Boy Toddler, 7 1/2 In. 285.00
Doll, Gebruder Heubach, Boy, Bisque Hands, Intaglio Eyes, Velvet Suit, 15 In. 500.00
Doll, Gebruder Heubach, Boy, Bisque Head & Hands, Intaglio Eyes, 15 In. 500.00
Doll, Gebruder Kraus, Girl, Composition Body, Painted Shoes & Sox, 8 1/2 In. 65.00
Doll, Geisha, With Samisen On Lacquered Wood Stand, Silk Dress, 17 In. 50.00

Doll, General Electric Cameo, Bandi, 19 In. 125.00
Doll, Georgene Averill, Baby Yawn, 19 In. 175.00
Doll, Georgene Averill, Baby, Blue Sleep Eyes, 22 In. 975.00
Doll, Georgene Averill, Baby, Composition Head, Cloth Body, 23 In. 85.00
Doll, Georgene Averill, Cherie, 24 In. 175.00
Doll, Georgene Averill, Yawn Baby, Composition Head & Arms, 19 In. 250.00
Doll, German Sp. 1275, Bathing Beauty, Bisque, Molded Hair Ribbon, 5 1/4 In. 45.00
Doll, German, Admiral Dewey Type, Bisque Head, 5-Piece Body, 10 In. 500.00
Doll, German, Bisque Head, Pink Kid Body, Closed Mouth, Blue Eyes, 11 1/2 In. 245.00
Doll, German, Bisque, Open Mouth, Jointed Body, Sleep Eyes, 7 1/2 In. 70.00
Doll, German, Boy, Bisque, Movable Arms, Molded Hair, 2 In. 20.00
Doll, German, Boy, Dollhouse, Bisque, Jointed, Molded Curls, 3 1/4 In. 40.00
Doll, German, Dollhouse, Bisque Head & Limbs, Cloth Body, 4 In. 28.00
Doll, German, Fashion, Bisque, Painted Eyes, Dressed, 11 1/2 In. 200.00
Doll, German, Fashion, Closed Mouth, 18 In. 300.00
Doll, German, Flapper, Bisque, Dressed, 3 In. 25.00
Doll, German, Frozen Charlotte, China, Black Hair, 5 In. 45.00
Doll, German, Girl & Boy, Bisque, Painted Features, 3 1/2 In., Pair 20.00
Doll, German, Girl, Bisque Head, Papier-Mache Body, Brown Eyes, 7 In. 50.00
Doll, German, Girl, Bisque, Movable Arms, Painted Eyes, Molded Hair, 2 In. 17.50
Doll, German, Girl, Bisque, Movable Limbs, Glass Eyes, 4 1/2 In. 150.00
Doll, German, Girl, Bisque, Open Mouth, Brown Sleep Eyes, 32 In. 325.00
Doll, German, Girl, Bisque, Swivel Head, Jointed, Crocheted Outfit, 4 In. 80.00
Doll, German, Girl, Closed Mouth, Blue Paperweight Eyes, 18 In. 450.00
Doll, German, Little Imp, Bisque, 7 In. 295.00
Doll, German, Mlle Detroit, Bisque Head & Hands, 18 In. 95.00
Doll, German, Twins, Bisque, 4 In., Pair 60.00
Doll, German, 6248, Boy, Bisque, Painted Blue Eyes, Jointed, 6 In. 78.00
Doll, Germany 7, Twins, Bisque Heads, Ball-Jointed Bodies, 22 In., Pair 450.00
Doll, Germany, Baby Boy, Bisque, Jointed Arms & Legs, Intaglio Eyes, 4 In. 70.00
Doll, Germany, Baby Boy, Bisque, Jointed Arms & Legs, 3 In. 35.00
Doll, Germany, Baby, Bisque Head, Blonde Hair, Brown Eyes, 19 In. 115.00
Doll, Germany, Baby, Bisque, Jointed, Painted Features, 5 In. 35.00
Doll, Germany, Bisque, Jointed Arms & Legs, Molded Hair, 4 1/2 In. 35.00
Doll, Germany, Bisque, Jointed Arms & Legs, Molded Hair, 5 1/2 In. 35.00
Doll, Germany, Bisque, Jointed Shoulders & Hips, Painted Shoes, 4 1/2 In. 37.00
Doll, Germany, Bisque, Jointed, Molded Hair, Painted Features, 3 1/4 In. 27.50
Doll, Germany, Bisque, Open Dome, Jointed Arms & Legs, 3 1/4 In. 28.00
Doll, Germany, Boy, Bisque, Jointed Arms & Legs, Painted Shoes, 3 1/2 In. 65.00
Doll, Germany, China, Black Hair, Dressed, 9 In. 45.00
Doll, Germany, China, Black Hair, 6 1/2 In. 35.00
Doll, Germany, Dolly Dingle, Composition, Movable Arms, 5 In. 20.00
Doll, Germany, Girl, Bisque, Jointed Arms & Legs, Molded Hair, 6 1/2 In. 45.00
Doll, Germany, Girl, Bisque, Jointed Body, Brown Sleep Eyes, 5 1/2 In. 75.00
Doll, Germany, Kate Greenaway Type, Bisque Head, Papier-Mache, 5 1/4 In. 65.00
Doll, Germany, Toddler, Bisque, Jointed Arms & Legs, Googlie Eyes, 4 1/2 In. 95.00
Doll, Germany, Viola, Bisque, Brown Sleep Eyes, Human Hair Wig, 25 In. 225.00
Doll, Germany, 30/B5, American Schoolboy, Cloth Body, 15 In. 325.00
Doll, Goebel, Laughter, Toddler, Blue Sleep Eyes, 13 In. 795.00
Doll, Grace S.Putnam, Bye-Lo Baby, Bisque, Solid Dome Head, 4 1/2 In. 125.00
Doll, Grace S.Putnam, Bye-Lo Baby, Brown Sleep Eyes, Dressed, 13 In. 335.00
Doll, Grace S.Putnam, Bye-Lo Baby, Celluloid Head, 12 1/2 In.Head 350.00
Doll, Grace S.Putnam, Bye-Lo Baby, Christening Gown, 11 1/2 In. Head 395.00
Doll, Grace S.Putnam, Bye-Lo Baby, Rubber & Cloth, Voice Box, 14 In. 235.00
Doll, H & H & S & H, Composition Body, 24 In. 275.00
Doll, H.W.Company, Swivel Head, Composition Body, 23 In. 250.00
Doll, Handwerck Halbig, Pull String, Voice Box, 19 In. 145.00
Doll, Handwerck S & H, Girl, Blue Threaded Eyes, Human Hair, 30 In. 275.00
Doll, Handwerck 109, Blue Sleep Eyes, 31 In. 285.00
Doll, Handwerck 119-13, Girl, Pierced Ears, Sleep Eyes, Umbrella, 28 In. 265.00
Doll, Handwerck, Boy, Brown Eyes, Blond Hair, Green Velvet Suit, 17 In. 140.00
Doll, Handwerck, DEP 99, Girl, Blue Eyes, Blonde Human Hair Wig, 27 In. 275.00
Doll, Handwerck, DEP, Girl, Molded Brown, Blue Eyes, Human Hair Wig, 22 In. 225.00
Doll, Handwerck, Girl, Bisque Head, Open Mouth, Brown Eyes, Mohair Wig, 18 In. 185.00

Doll, Handwerck, Girl, Norwegian Dress, Pierced Ears, Human Hair Wig, 21 In. 165.00
Doll, Hasbro, Little Miss No Name, 15 In. 15.00
Doll, Hasbro, 1965, Friday, Dolly Darling, 4 1/2 In. 3.00
Doll, Hasbro, 1965, John, Dolly Darling, 4 1/2 In. 3.00
Doll, Hasbro, 1965, Sunday, Dolly Darling, 4 1/2 In. 3.00
Doll, Heinrich Handwerck S & H, Oriental Girl, Bisque Head, 17 In. 495.00
Doll, Heinrich Handwerck Simon & Halbig, Baby, Composition Body, 26 In. 240.00
Doll, Heinrich Handwerck Simon & Halbig, Girl, Ball-Jointed Body, 18 1/2 In. 155.00
Doll, Heinrich Handwerck, Brown Sleep Eyes, 33 In. 325.00
Doll, Heinrich Handwerck, Negro Girl, 17 In. 495.00
Doll, Hermann Steiner, Boy, Jointed, Blue Sleep Eyes, 10 In. 95.00
Doll, Hermann Steiner, Girl, Bisque Head, Composition Body, 9 In. 125.00
Doll, Hermann Steiner, 7 In. 60.00
Doll, Heubach Kopplesdorf 250, Girl, Composition Body, Brown Eyes, 21 In. 110.00
Doll, Heubach Kopplesdorf 275 9/0, Girl, Kid Body, Composition Arms, 17 In. 118.00
Doll, Heubach Kopplesdorf 312, Ball-Jointed Body, Brown Hair, 23 In. 185.00
Doll, Heubach Kopplesdorf 342, Toddler, 26 In. 295.00
Doll, Heubach Kopplesdorf, Baby, Blue Sleep Eyes, 21 In. 195.00
Doll, Heubach Kopplesdorf, Baby, Breather, Brown Sleep Eyes, 12 In. 200.00
Doll, Heubach Kopplesdorf, Baby, Breather, Upper Teeth, 14 In. 165.00
Doll, Heubach Kopplesdorf, Girl, Bisque, Brown Sleep Eyes, 21 In. 135.00
Doll, Heubach Kopplesdorf, Girl, Composition Arms, Kid Body, 15 In. 110.00
Doll, Heubach Kopplesodrf 444, Red Indian Baby, Black Mohair Wig, 12 In. 295.00
Doll, Heubach, Baby Stewart, Bisque Head, Molded Bonnet, Intaglio Eyes, 8 In. 645.00
Doll, Heubach, Baby, Bisque Head, Papier-Mache Body, Flocked Hair, 6 In. 200.00
Doll, Heubach, Baby, Bisque, Bent Legs, 5 In. 200.00
Doll, Heubach, Baby, Character Face, Closed Mouth, Molded Curls, 8 In. 195.00
Doll, Heubach, Baby, Molded Tongue & 4 Teeth, Blue Painted Eyes, 7 In. 185.00
Doll, Heubach, Baby, Pouty Face, Jointed Kid Body, Intaglio Eyes, 13 In. 210.00
Doll, Heubach, Boy, Bisque, Whistling, Squeeze Box, Cloth Body, 10 1/2 In. 745.00
Doll, Heubach, Boy, Bisque, 5-Piece Body, Intaglio Eyes, 9 1/2 In. 185.00
Doll, Heubach, Boy, Laughing Face, 2 Teeth, Intaglio Eyes, Blond Hair, 15 In. 365.00
Doll, Heubach, Closed Mouth, Molded Hair, Blue Intaglio Eyes, 18 1/2 In. 695.00
Doll, Holz-Masse, C.1884, Man, Papier-Mache Head, Kid Body, 23 1/2 In. 375.00
Doll, Horsman 210, Cindy, Hard Plastic, 19 In. 22.50
Doll, Horsman, Brickette, Eyes To Side, 22 In. 25.00
Doll, Horsman, Bye-Lo, 14 In. 18.00
Doll, Horsman, Ginny, Walker, Hard Plastic, 7 In. 15.00
Doll, Horsman, Jill, Hard Plastic, 10 In. 15.00
Doll, Horsman, Laurel & Hardy, Talking & Singing, 13 In., Pair 15.00
Doll, Horsman, Lullabye Baby, Plays Lullabye, 12 In. 5.00
Doll, Horsman, Mary Poppins, Dressed, 12 In. 12.00
Doll, Horsman, Pippi, Long Stockings, Boxed, 18 In. 10.00
Doll, Horsman, Pollyanna, Dressed, 31 In. 25.00
Doll, Horsman, 1961, Jackie Kennedy, 24 1/2 In. 45.00
Doll, Horsman, 1963, Pitiful Pearl, 17 In. 20.00
Doll, Horsman, 1968, Thirstee Baby, 6 1/2 In. 2.50
Doll, Horsman, 1968, Zodiac Baby, 6 1/2 In. 3.50
Doll, Hummel, Baker, Rubber, 12 In. 95.00
Doll, Hummel, Boy, Rubber, Marked Wm.Goebel, Original Clothes 55.00
Doll, Hummel, Max, Rubber, 11 1/2 In. 60.00
Doll, Hummel, Postman, Rubber, 12 In. 95.00
Doll, Ideal Toy Corp., 1914, Uneeda Biscuit Kid, Composition, 15 In. 75.00
Doll, Ideal, Baby Crissy, Negro, Hard Plastic, Boxed, 24 In. 12.50
Doll, Ideal, Emerald The Witch, Hard Plastic, 3 Outfits, Boxed, 7 In. 10.00
Doll, Ideal, Fashion Crissy, Negro, Hard Plastic, Boxed, 18 In. 12.00
Doll, Ideal, Giggles, Baby, Hard Plastic, 16 In. 15.00
Doll, Ideal, Giggles, Toddler, Hard Plastic, 18 In. 15.00
Doll, Ideal, Girl, Blue Sleep Eyes, Blonde Hair, 16 In. 45.00
Doll, Ideal, Miss Curity, Hard Plastic, 14 In. 28.50
Doll, Ideal, Monkees Singing Group, Vinyl, 4 1/2 In., Set Of 3 In Box 3.50
Doll, Ideal, Pebbles, Flintstones, Cloth Body, 15 In. 7.00
Doll, Ideal, Pepper, 9 In. 4.00
Doll, Ideal, Tammy, 12 In. 4.00

Doll, Ideal, Thumbelina, Hard Plastic, 1962, 20 In. 10.00
Doll, Ideal, Toni, 14 In. 20.00
Doll, Ideal, Walker, 21 In. 24.00
Doll, Indian, see Indian, Doll
Doll, Italian, Composition, Dressed, 20 In. 35.00
Doll, J.D.B., 22 In. 270.00
Doll, J.D.K., see also Doll, Kestner
Doll, J.D.K. 200-0-1/2 & Turtle, Celluloid Head, Jointed, 16 In. 150.00
Doll, J.D.K. 211, Baby Sammy, Lamb's Wool Wig, Blue Eyes, 11 In. Head 285.00
Doll, J.D.K. 211, Baby, Character Face, Jointed Composition Body, 22 In. 250.00
Doll, J.D.K. 211, Bisque Head, Composition Body, Bent Legs, 16 In. Head 400.00
Doll, J.D.K. 211, Open & Closed Mouth, Blue Eyes, 14 In. 375.00
Doll, J.D.K. 211, Toddler, Curved Limbs, Blue Eyes, 12 In. 350.00
Doll, J.D.K. 214, Blue Sleep Eyes, 33 In. 295.00
Doll, J.D.K. 214, Girl, Bisque Head, Jointed Body, 27 In. 350.00
Doll, J.D.K. 214, Open Mouth, Ball-Jointed Body, Human Hair Wig, 27 In. 345.00
Doll, J.D.K. 257, Baby, Flirty Eyes, Blonde Mohair Wig, 14 In. 275.00
Doll, J.D.K. 257, Baby, Gray Sleep Eyes, Wobbly Tongue, 13 1/2 In. 225.00
Doll, J.D.K. 257, Kestner Baby, Composition Body, Blue Sleep Eyes, 16 In. 285.00
Doll, J.D.K., Baby, Closed Mouth, Molded Head, Blue Sleep Eyes, 11 In. 165.00
Doll, J.D.K., Baby, Open & Closed Mouth, Curved Limbs, Brown Eyes, 16 In. 275.00
Doll, J.I.O., C.1926, Baby Kiddiejoy, Celluloid Hands, Cloth Body, 19 In. 650.00
Doll, J.Steiner, Applied Ears, Blue Paperweight Eyes, 19 In. 1695.00
Doll, Jane Furbee, Alvert White, Clown, 17 In. 35.00
Doll, Jane Furbee, Emmet Kelly, Carved Wood, Dressed, 22 In. 45.00
Doll, Japan, Baby Boy, Bisque Head, Jointed Body, Sleep Eyes, Wig, 14 In. 100.00
Doll, Japan, Baby, Jointed Body, Sleep Eyes, Wig, 9 In. 100.00
Doll, Japan, Bathing Beauty, 5 In. 10.00
Doll, Japan, Bisque, Jointed Arms & Legs, Molded Hair, Painted Shoes, 5 In. 18.00
Doll, Japan, Bisque, Movable Arms, Painted Features, 7 1/2 In. 20.00
Doll, Japan, Chinese Twins, Girl & Boy, Bisque, Jointed, 3 1/2 In., Pair 15.00
Doll, Japan, Dolly Sisters, Black, Celluloid, 2 In., Set Of 5 .... 10.00
Doll, Japan, Frozen, Stone Bisque, Holding Rabbit, Molded Hair, 6 1/2 In. 15.00
Doll, Japan, Girl, Bisque, Jointed Shoulders & Hips, Molded Hair, 7 In. 37.00
Doll, Japan, Mother, Dollhouse, Painted Features, 4 1/2 In. 25.00
Doll, Japanese, Friendship, 13 In. 45.00
Doll, Japanese, Katsuraningyo, 3 Wigs, Boxed, 7 In. 10.00
Doll, Joel Ellis, Johnson, Wooden, Jointed, Pewter Hands, 11 1/2 In. 375.00
Doll, Jumeau 12, Girl, Blue Paperweight Eyes, 27 In. 495.00
Doll, Jumeau 1907, Negro, Open Mouth, 11 In. 495.00
Doll, Jumeau, Bisque Head, Ball-Jointed Composition Body, Dressed, 15 In. 395.00
Doll, Jumeau, Bisque Head, Jointed Composition Body, Blue Eyes, 14 1/2 In. 375.00
Doll, Jumeau, Closed Mouth, Brown Paperweight Eyes, 25 In. 1395.00
Doll, Jumeau, Closed Mouth, Solid Wrists, Blue Paperweight Eyes, 16 1/4 In. 1495.00
Doll, Jumeau, Depolma D'honneur, Pull String, Says Mamma & Pappa, 27 In. 700.00
Doll, Jumeau, Depose, Girl, Applied Ears, Brown Paperweight Eyes, 20 In. 1350.00
Doll, Jumeau, Girl, Bisque, Closed Mouth, Paperweight Eyes, 22 In. 950.00
Doll, Jumeau, Medaille D'or, Original Clothes, 24 In. .... *Illus* 1500.00

Doll, Jumeau, Medaille D'Or, Original Clothes, 24 In.

Doll, Jumeau, Open Mouth, Blue Paperweight Eyes, 28 In. 695.00
Doll, Jumeau, Portrait, Closed Mouth, Applied Ears, Brown Eyes, 20 In. 1395.00
Doll, Jumeau, 1907, Walker, 23 In. 500.00
Doll, Jutta 1912, Girl Toddler, Blue Sleep Eyes, 24 In. 395.00
Doll, Jutta 1914, Toddler, Brown Eyes, 24 In. 325.00
Doll, K & H 150 10, Girl, Open & Closed Mouth, Blue Eyes, 18 In. 425.00
Doll, K & H 250, Composition Body, 22 In. 250.00
Doll, K * R Simon & Halbig, Toddler, Bisque & Composition, 25 In. 375.00
Doll, K * R 101, Pouty Face, 8 In. 650.00
Doll, K * R 114, Boy, Character Face, Brown Sleep Eyes, 16 In. 3500.00
Doll, K * R 114, Brown Glass Sleep Eyes, 19 In. 2300.00
Doll, K * R 115/a, Baby, Brown Sleep Eyes, 17 In. 1395.00
Doll, K * R 116/a, Baby, Closed Mouth, Blue Sleep Eyes, 13 In. 795.00
Doll, K * R 117/n, Girl, Blue Flirty Eyes, 29 In. 595.00
Doll, K * R 117, Blue Flirty Eyes, 29 In. 565.00
Doll, K * R 122, Baby, Blue Sleep Eyes, 15 In. 335.00
Doll, K * R 122, Baby, Wiggle Tongue, Blue Sleep Eyes, 15 In. 375.00
Doll, K * R, Girl, Jointed Body, 11 In. 160.00
Doll, K * R, Santa Claus, Bisque Head, Composition Body, 9 In. 125.00
Doll, K.W., Toddler, Blue Sleep Eyes, 26 In. 350.00
Doll, Kaiser, Baby, Blue Eyes, 19 In. 650.00
Doll, Kaiser, Negro Baby, 11 In. 695.00
Doll, Kathy Kruse, No.384, Boy, 17 In. 165.00
Doll, Keatner, Girl, Closed Mouth, Brown Sleep Eyes, Human Hair Wig, 32 In. 1150.00
Doll, Kenner, Crumpet, 18 In. 8.00

Doll, Kestner, see also Doll, J.D.K.

Doll, Kestner 146, Girl, Jointed Body, Blue Sleep Eyes, 23 In. 225.00
Doll, Kestner 146, Nun, Ball-Jointed Body, Blue Sleep Eyes, 24 In. 175.00
Doll, Kestner 148, Bisque Head, Kid Body, Open Mouth, Brown Eyes, 17 In. 185.00
Doll, Kestner 150, Baby, Bisque, Swivel Neck, Blue Sleep Eyes, 9 In. 325.00
Doll, Kestner 150, Baby, Character Face, Christening Dress, 21 In. 350.00
Doll, Kestner 150, Our Darling, Open Mouth, Jointed Body, 7 1/2 In. 160.00
Doll, Kestner 151, Baby, Bisque Head & Arms, Kid Body, Blue Eyes, 17 In. 125.00
Doll, Kestner 151, Baby, Solid Dome, Character Face, 13 In. 175.00
Doll, Kestner 151, Girl, Bisque Head & Arms, Teeth, Kid Body, 15 In. 119.00
Doll, Kestner 152, Baby, Brown Sleep Eyes, 22 In. 225.00
Doll, Kestner 152, Boy, Bisque, Gray Eyes, 13 In. 225.00
Doll, Kestner 152, Girl, Bent Limbs, Gray Sleep Eyes, 15 In. 295.00
Doll, Kestner 154, Bisque Head, Kid Body, Blue Sleep Eyes, 20 In. 125.00
Doll, Kestner 154, Girl, Bisque Head & Arms, Kid Body, Brown Eyes, 18 In. 140.00
Doll, Kestner 171, Ball-Jointed Body, Blue Sleep Eyes, 26 In. 175.00
Doll, Kestner 171, Molded Eyebrows, Brown Sleep Eyes, Dressed, 31 In. 320.00
Doll, Kestner 192, Girl, Open Mouth, Jointed Composition Body, 12 In. 250.00
Doll, Kestner 211, Baby, Character Face, 11 In. 225.00
Doll, Kestner 309-7, Baby, Bisque Shoulder Head, Cloth Body, Teeth, 17 In. 118.00
Doll, Kestner 5274/3, Bisque, Jointed Body, Painted Features, 3 In. 40.00
Doll, Kestner, Alice, Kid Body, 12 In. 95.00
Doll, Kestner, Bisque Head & Limbs, Kid Body, Human Hair Wig, 17 In. 225.00
Doll, Kestner, Bisque Head, Jointed Wooden & Composition Body, Teeth, 21 In. 185.00
Doll, Kestner, Bisque Head, Teeth, Kidette Body, Brown Sleep Eyes, 15 In. 115.00
Doll, Kestner, Bisque, Closed Mouth, Jointed Body, Cobalt Eyes, 4 In. 85.00
Doll, Kestner, Boy, Closed Mouth, Jointed Body, Painted Eyes, 7 3/4 In. 95.00
Doll, Kestner, Boy, Velvet Suit, 20 In. 225.00
Doll, Kestner, Girl, Bisque Head & Hands, Kid Body, Dressed, 18 In. 190.00
Doll, Kestner, Girl, Bisque Turned Head & Hands, Kid Body, 27 In. 235.00
Doll, Kestner, Girl, Teeth, Ball-Jointed Body, Human Hair, 19 In. 155.00
Doll, Kestner, Turned Bisque Head, Brown Sleep Eyes, 30 In. 290.00

Doll, Kewpie, see Kewpie, Doll

Doll, Knickerbocker, Raggedy Ann & Andy, 18 In., Pair 35.00
Doll, L W & Co., Bisque Shoulder Head & Arms, Kid Body, 19 In. 75.00
Doll, Lenci, Boy, Felt, 8 In. .... *Illus* 22.50
Doll, Lenci, Child, Plaid Sweater, 19 In. 85.00
Doll, Lenci, Girl & Boy, Felt, Ski Outfits, 8 1/2 In., Pair 38.00
Doll, Lenci, Girl, Felt Clothes, 22 In. 125.00

Doll, Lenci, Girl, Felt, 8 1/2 In. .... *Illus* 22.50
Doll, Lenci, Girl, Felt, 9 In. .... *Illus* 22.50
Doll, Lenci, Lady, Tiara In Hair, Dressed, 16 1/2 In. 135.00
Doll, Lettie Lane, Daisy, Blue Sleep Eyes, Blonde Mohair Wig, 18 In. 235.00
Doll, Limoges, Blue Paperweight Eyes, 22 In. 485.00
Doll, Limoges, Caprice, Child, Smiling, Tearducts, Teeth, 27 In. 875.00
Doll, Limoges, Caprice, Toddler, Blue Eyes, 23 In. 595.00
Doll, Limoges, Cherie, Brown Sleep Eyes, 15 In. 165.00
Doll, Little Annie Rooney, Bisque, Tam & Jacket 125.00
Doll, Little Lulu, Cloth 5.00
Doll, Lori, Baby, Solid Dome, Jointed Composition Body, 2 Teeth, 21 In. 550.00
Doll, M.B., Baby, Bisque Head, Composition Body, Blue Eyes, 15 In.Head 325.00
Doll, M.M., Lady, Kid Body, 16 1/2 In. 270.00

Doll, Lenci, Girl, Felt, 8 1/2 In. Doll, Lenci, Boy, Felt, 8 In. Doll, Lenci, Girl, Felt, 9 In.

Doll, Madame Alexander, Agatha, Aqua Blue Gown, 21 In. 75.00
Doll, Madame Alexander, Alice In Wonderland, 21 In. 100.00
Doll, Madame Alexander, Alice, 14 In. 16.95
Doll, Madame Alexander, Amy, Little Women, 12 In. 17.95
Doll, Madame Alexander, Amy, Little Women, 14 In. 17.95
Doll, Madame Alexander, Babs The Ice Skating Queen, 18 In. 85.00
Doll, Madame Alexander, Ballerina, 15 In. 35.00
Doll, Madame Alexander, Beth, Little Women, 8 In. 11.95
Doll, Madame Alexander, Binnie Walker, Boxed, 19 In. 50.00
Doll, Madame Alexander, Black Pussy Cat, 14 In. 16.95
Doll, Madame Alexander, Blueboy, 12 In. 20.00
Doll, Madame Alexander, Bride, Composition, 15 In. 95.00
Doll, Madame Alexander, Bride, 14 In. 23.95
Doll, Madame Alexander, Brigetta, 7 In. 35.00
Doll, Madame Alexander, Cinderella, Ball Gown, 14 In. 22.95
Doll, Madame Alexander, Cissy, 20 In. 25.00
Doll, Madame Alexander, Cornelia, 21 In. 75.00
Doll, Madame Alexander, Elise, 16 In. 15.00
Doll, Madame Alexander, Elsie, Ballerina, Hard Plastic, Jointed, 17 In. 45.00
Doll, Madame Alexander, Elsie, Ballerina, 21 In. 24.00
Doll, Madame Alexander, Elsie, Bride, Hard Plastic, Jointed Body, 15 In. 25.00
Doll, Madame Alexander, Elsie, Bride, 21 In. 33.00
Doll, Madame Alexander, Heidi, 14 In. 19.95
Doll, Madame Alexander, Jo, Little Women, 8 In. 11.95
Doll, Madame Alexander, Lissy, Dressed, 11 1/2 In. 45.00
Doll, Madame Alexander, Lucinda, 14 In. 20.95
Doll, Madame Alexander, Marmee, Little Women, 14 In. 17.95
Doll, Madame Alexander, Mary Ellen, Jointed, 33 In. 135.00

Doll, Madame Alexander, Mary, Mary, Bent Knee, 8 In. 45.00
Doll, Madame Alexander, Marybelle, Suitcase, 15 In. 15.00
Doll, Madame Alexander, Meg, Little Women, 8 In. 12.00
Doll, Madame Alexander, Miss Brazil, Sleep Eyes, Gold Sandals, 8 In. 19.50
Doll, Madame Alexander, Nina, Ballerina, Red Hair, 18 In. 65.00
Doll, Madame Alexander, Peasant Boy, Composition, Collie Dog, 9 In. 60.00
Doll, Madame Alexander, Pegos Girl, 21 In. 20.00
Doll, Madame Alexander, Princess Elizabeth, Composition, 12 In. 65.00
Doll, Madame Alexander, Princess Elizabeth, 16 In. 55.00
Doll, Madame Alexander, Rebecca, 14 In. 18.95
Doll, Madame Alexander, Renoir Girl, 21 In. 21.00
Doll, Madame Alexander, Scarlet O'Hara, Composition, 11 In. 95.00
Doll, Madame Alexander, Scarlett O'Hara, Green Gown, 21 In. 75.00
Doll, Madame Alexander, Scarlett O'Hara, 14 In. 25.95
Doll, Madame Alexander, Sleeping Beauty, 14 In. 22.95
Doll, Madame Alexander, Snow White, 14 In. 22.95
Doll, Madame Alexander, Wendy Ann, Composition, Dressed, 9 In. 32.00
Doll, Madame Alexander, Wendy, Bride, 18 In. 70.00
Doll, Madame, Alexander, Tyrolean Boy, Bent Knee, 8 In. 45.00
Doll, Mattel, Aimee, Boxed, 18 In. 10.00
Doll, Mattel, Charmin Chatty, Talks, Records, 25 In. 20.00
Doll, Mattel, Chatty Cathy, Dressed, 20 In. 7.50
Doll, Mattel, Cheerful Tearful, 13 In. 5.00
Doll, Mattel, Honey West, Boxed, 11 1/2 In. 10.00
Doll, Mattel, Julia, Dianne Carrol, Nurse Uniform, 11 1/2 In. 9.00
Doll, Mattel, Little Miss No Name, 15 In. 12.50
Doll, Mattel, Mattie & Sister Belle, Talking, 17 In., Pair 15.00
Doll, Mattel, Poor Pitiful Pearl, Boxed, 17 In. 15.00
Doll, Mattel, Randy Reader, 19 In. 10.00
Doll, Max Handwerck, Girl, Ball-Jointed Body, Sleep Eyes, 25 In. 185.00
Doll, Max Handwerck, Girl, Brown Sleep Eyes, Blonde Wig, 22 In. 175.00
Doll, Mechanical, Crawls And Turns Head, Celluloid, Signed Irwin, 7 In. 42.00
Doll, Minerva, Metal Head, 14 In. 38.00
Doll, Nippon, Baby, Bisque, Jointed Arms & Legs, 4 1/2 In. 30.00
Doll, Nippon, Baby, Stone Bisque Shoulder Head, 6 In. 15.00
Doll, Nippon, Baby, Wearing Swimming Suit, Bisque, Arms Move, 6 In. 69.00
Doll, Nippon, Baby, 5-Piece Composition Body, Brown Glass Eyes, 10 In. Head 75.00
Doll, Nippon, Bisque, Molded Hair, Painted Features, Movable Arms, 5 1/2 In. 20.00
Doll, Nippon, Boy, Bisque, Jointed Arms & Legs, Painted Hair, 3 1/2 In. 25.00
Doll, Nippon, Boy, Bisque, Jointed Shoulders, 4 3/4 In. 45.00
Doll, Nobbi Kid, Googlie Eyes, Original Box, 7 In. 450.00
Doll, Norah Wellings, Gypsy Girl, 15 In. 80.00
Doll, Occupied Japan, Betty Boop, Celluloid, 6 1/2 In. 4.50
Doll, Otto & Cuno Dressel 1912, Bisque Head, Ball-Jointed Body, 24 In. 155.00
Doll, Paris Bebe Tete Depose, Girl, Cork Pate, Jointed Body, 18 In. 975.00
Doll, Paris Bebe, Blue Paperweight Eyes, 17 In. 1195.00
Doll, Pincushion, see Pincushion Doll
Doll, Planters Peanuts, Rag, 18 In. 12.00
Doll, Poupard, Musical Twirler On Stick, 6 Teeth, Blue Glass Eyes, 8 In. 175.00
Doll, Puppet, Hand, Man, Painted Wood Head, Embroidered Costume, 1 Ft. 110.00
Doll, R & A Googley, Smiling, Intaglio Eyes, 5-Piece Body, 6 1/2 In. 175.00
Doll, R & B, Girl, Pigtails, 20 In. 25.00
Doll, R & B, Swivel Head, Composition Body, Blue Sleep Eyes, 20 In. 45.00
Doll, R.A. 1920, Girl, Bisque, Brown Sleep Eyes, Human Hair Wig, 29 In. 250.00
Doll, R-IV-12, Baby, Solid Dome, Composition Body, Closed Mouth, 8 In. 65.00
Doll, Rag, Mr.Peanut, 18 In. 8.00
Doll, Ravca, C.1930, Paris, Normandy Peasant Woman, 8 In. 58.00
Doll, Ravca, Elderly Peasant, Woman & Man, 7 1/2 In., Pair 65.00
Doll, Reliable, Canada, Eskimo Boy, Composition Body, Painted Eyes, 14 In. 45.00
Doll, Revalo, Blue Sleep Eyes, 23 In. 225.00
Doll, Rex Harrison As Dr.Doolittle, Talking, 22 In. 15.00
Doll, Richard Jason, Rock-A-Bye Baby, 14 1/2 In. Head 245.00
Doll, S & H C.M.Bergmann, Brown Sleep Eyes, 16 In. 120.00
Doll, S & H H.H., Girl, Ball-Jointed Composition Body, Brown Eyes, 25 In. 265.00

Doll, S & H Handwerck, Girl, Bisque Head, Composition Body, 28 In. 295.00
Doll, S & H K * R, Composition, 24 In. 285.00
Doll, S & H 1079, Brown Sleep Eyes, Molded Brows, Pierced Ears, 34 In. 350.00
Doll, S & H 1079, Girl, Ball-Jointed Composition Body, Blue Eyes, 24 In. 235.00
Doll, S & H 1079, Jointed Body, Brown Sleep Eyes, Human Hair Wig, 28 In. 295.00
Doll, S & H 1079, Negro Girl, Ball-Jointed Body, 8 In. 595.00
Doll, S & H 1080, Kid Body, Open Mouth, Pierced Ears, Blue Eyes, 24 In. 350.00
Doll, S & H 1159, Gibson Girl, Composition Body, Paperweight Eyes, 19 In. 739.00
Doll, S & H 1160, Bisque Shoulder Head, 7 In. 100.00
Doll, S & H 1249, Ruby, Pierced Ears, 21 In. 300.00
Doll, S & H 939, Girl, Open Mouth, Jointed Composition Body, 13 In. 250.00
Doll, S & H, Ball-Jointed Body, Blue Eyes, Human Hair, 22 In. 150.00
Doll, S.F.B.J. 236, Boy Toddler, Blue Sleep Eyes, Navy Suit, 28 In. 675.00
Doll, S.F.B.J. 236, Girl Toddler, Bisque, Dressed, 28 In. 1500.00
Doll, S.F.B.J. 236, Girl Toddler, Brown Sleep Eyes, 15 In. 595.00
Doll, S.F.B.J. 236, Girl Toddler, 2 Teeth, Blue Paperweight Eyes, 27 In. 775.00
Doll, S.F.B.J. 236, Toddler, Hazel Sleep Eyes, 20 In. 475.00
Doll, S.F.B.J. 238, Girl, Mechanical Legs, Blue Paperweight Eyes, 20 In. 895.00
Doll, S.F.B.J. 247, Twerp Toddler, Brown Sleep Eyes, 16 1/2 In. 1395.00
Doll, S.F.B.J. 251, Boy Toddler, Bisque, Dressed, 28 In. 1500.00
Doll, S.F.B.J. 257, Boy, Holding Rabbit, Jewel Eyes, Velvet Suit, 22 In. 1500.00
Doll, S.F.B.J. 60 Paris, Girl, Cork Pate, Brown Eyes, Dressed, 21 In. 250.00
Doll, S.F.B.J. 60, Girl, Open Mouth, Brown Sleep Eyes, 16 1/2 In. 225.00
Doll, S.F.B.J., Girl, Jumeau Body, Blue Sleep Eyes, Silk Dress, 29 In. 550.00
Doll, S.F.B.J., Paris, Walker, 4 Teeth, Pierced Ears, 18 In. 365.00
Doll S & H, see Doll, C. M. Bergmann, Doll, Simon & Halbig
Doll, S.P.B.H. Hanna, Baby, Blue Sleep Eyes, 19 In. 225.00
Doll, S.P.B.H., Oriental, Brown Sleep Eyes, 15 In. 895.00
Doll, Sasha, Baby, Playsuit, 12 In. 17.95
Doll, Sasha, Baby, White Bird, 12 In. 17.95
Doll, Sasha, Caleb, , Negro, 16 In. 22.95
Doll, Sasha, Cora, Negro Girl, 16 In. 25.50 To 26.50
Doll, Sasha, Girl, Blonde Hair, Long Dress, 16 In. 22.95
Doll, Sasha, Girl, Brunette Hair, Red Dress, 16 In. 22.95
Doll, Sasha, Gregor Baby, Blond Hair, 12 In. 17.95
Doll, Sasha, Gregor, Blond, Blue Suit, 16 In. 22.95
Doll, Sasha, Gregor, Dark Denims, 16 In. 22.95
Doll, Sasha, Gregor, Dark Sports Outfit, 16 In. 22.95
Doll, Sasha, Negro Baby, 12 In. 17.95
Doll, Sayco, Snow White & 7 Dwarfs, Vinyl, Boxed, 21 In. 165.00
Doll, Schoenau & Hoffmeister, Bisque Head, Kid Body, 16 In. 100.00
Doll, Schoenau & Hoffmeister, Scotch Boy, Jointed Composition Body, 14 In. 140.00
Doll, Schoenhut, Boy Toddler, Blue Eyes, Blond Mohair Wig, 13 In. 325.00
Doll, Schoenhut, Boy, Walker, Bisque Head, 16 In. 550.00
Doll, Schoenhut, Clown, Bisque, 8 1/2 In. 55.00
Doll, Schoenhut, Girl, Carved Head, Pink Bow In Hair, 16 In. 750.00
Doll, Schoenhut, Girl, Open Mouth, Painted Teeth, Blue Painted Eyes, 18 In. 350.00
Doll, Schoenhut, Girl, Pouty Face, Brown Eyes, 16 In. 425.00
Doll, Schoenhut, Girl, Pouty, Blue Painted Eyes, 18 In. 450.00
Doll, Schoenhut, Girl, Pouty, Closed Mouth, Brown Intaglio Eyes, 14 1/2 In. 300.00
Doll, Schoenhut, Patent 1911, Sailor Boy, Wooden, Spring Jointed, 17 In. 285.00
Doll, Schoenhut, Ringmaster, 4 1/2 In. 80.00
Doll, Schoenhut, 1911, Girl, Wooden, Teeth, Spring Jointed, Blue Eyes, 19 In. 295.00
Doll, Schoenhut, 1913, Baby, Bisque, Curved Limbs, 15 In. 450.00
Doll, Shindanna, 1968, Negro, 13 In. 8.00
Doll, Shirley Temple, see Shirley Temple
Doll, Simon & Halbig, see also Doll, C.M.BErgmann; Doll, S.&H.
Doll, Simon & Halbig 1078, Girl, Molded Brow, Blonde Human Hair Wig, 32 In. 325.00
Doll, Simon & Halbig 1079, Brown Sleep Eyes, 30 In. 275.00
Doll, Simon & Halbig 1129, Oriental, 10 In. 550.00
Doll, Simon & Halbig 1295, Baby, Blue Sleep Eyes, 18 In. 295.00
Doll, Simon & Halbig 1329, Girl, 18 1/2 In. 895.00
Doll, Simon & Halbig, Flapper, Blue Sleep Eyes, 14 1/2 In. 550.00
Doll, Simon & Halbig, Jointed Composition Body, Pierced Ears, 19 In. 150.00

Doll, Swiss Alps, Girl, Stockinet, 10 1/2 In.

Doll, Unis, France, Bisque Head

Doll, Simon & Halbig, Pierced Ears, Ball-Jointed Body, 22 In. 150.00
Doll, Simon & Halbig, Toddler, Ball-Jointed Composition Body, Teeth, 22 In. 190.00
Doll, Steiner, Closed Mouth, Solid Wrists, Blue Paperweight Eyes, 25 In. 1395.00
Doll, Steiner, Girl, Bisque, Pierced Ears, Closed Mouth, 11 In. 945.00
Doll, Steiner, La Parisienne, Open Mouth, 5 Teeth, 19 In. 800.00
Doll, Strobel & Wilken, American Beauty, Turned Bisque Head, 23 In. 180.00
Doll, Sun Rubber Co., Ruth E.Newton, 10 In. 18.00
Doll, Sun Rubber, 1956, 13 In. 10.00
Doll, Swiss Alps, Girl, Stockinet, 10 1/2 In. .... *Illus* 20.00
Doll, Tete Jumeau, Bisque Head, Pierced Ears, Brown Paperweight Eyes, 18 In. 1500.00
Doll, Tete Jumeau, Closed Mouth, Pierced Ears, Brown Paperweight Eyes, 21 In 1050.00
Doll, Tete Jumeau, Girl, Cork Pate, Pierced Ears, Closed Mouth, 14 1/2 In. 995.00
Doll, Tete Jumeau, Open Mouth, Talk String, Dressed, 22 In. 495.00
Doll, Topper, Penny Bright, 8 In. 4.50
Doll, Topper, 1958, Sweet Rosemary, 29 In. 10.00
Doll, Toto, French, Bisque, Says Mama & Papa, Red Curls, 24 In. 950.00
Doll, Turtle, Girl, Celluloid, Blue Glass Eyes, 19 In. 50.00
Doll, Uneeda, Tinyteens, Coatdress, 5 In. 4.50
Doll, Unis, France, Bisque Head .... *Illus* 130.00
Doll, Unis, France, Boy, Bisque Head, Jointed Composition Body, 5 In. 70.00
Doll, Unis, France, Girl, Bisque Head, Jointed Composition Body, 5 In. 70.00
Doll, Unis, France, Girl, Blue Eyes, Brown Hair, 20 In. 560.00
Doll, Verlingue Laine, Girl, Open Mouth, Wig, 16 In. 255.00
Doll, Wm.Goebel, Bavaria, Girl, Ball-Jointed Composition Body, 15 In. 135.00

Donald Duck, see Disneyana

Doorstop, see Iron, Doorstop

Dorchester, Warmer, Foot, Henderson, Stoneware, 11 In. 45.00

Doulton pottery and porcelain were made by Doulton and Co.of Burslem, England, after 1882. The name Royal Doulton appeared on their wares after 1902.

Doulton, see also Royal Doulton

Doulton, Barrel, Biscuit, Blue & Gold Tapestry, Silver Plate Fittings, 1882 .... 88.00
Doulton, Barrel, Biscuit, Chineware, Copper Birds, Silver Fittings, C.1883 .... 235.00
Doulton, Barrel, Biscuit, Gray White, Running Horses, Silver Fittings, HBB 350.00
Doulton, Base, Globular, Cobwebs, Florals Under Glaze, Holbeinware, 18 In. 275.00
Doulton, Base, Sung, Handled, Red & Blue, Signed Noke, Initialed Fred Allan 275.00
Doulton, Beaker, Leatherware, Sterling Rim, C.1891, 4 3/4 In. 50.00
Doulton, Beaker, Toby Ware, Sterling Rim, A.Partridge, Lambeth, 4 1/2 In. 65.00
Doulton, Box, Flambe, Hexagonal, C.1920, 5 In. 185.00
Doulton, Bucket, Silver Plate Rim, Handle, Lambeth, Edith D.Lupton, 4 1/2 In. 135.00
Doulton, Candlestick, Lambeth Stoneware, Lionheads, Signed George Tinworth 485.00
Doulton, Castor Set, 3 Bottles, Plated Tops, Leaf Pattern, C.1876, Youatt 175.00

Doulton, Cup & Saucer, Nankin, Burslem, England 8.50
Doulton, Cup, Loving, Basalt, Mayflower 100.00
Doulton, Cup, Loving, 3 Handled, The Smaller The Drink, Lambeth, 6 In. 115.00
Doulton, Dish, Candy, Clover Shape, Floral, Burslem, 1886 65.00
Doulton, Dish, Cheese, Domed Lid, White, Cobalt Butterflies & Floral, 10 In. 120.00
Doulton, Eggcup, Floral, Large 12.00
Doulton, Ewer, Blue, Applied Florals, E.Kemp, Lambeth, C.1891, 6 1/2 In. 45.00
Doulton, Ewer, Chineware, Silicon, Lambeth, C.1882, 9 1/2 In., Pair 265.00
Doulton, Ewer, Silicon, Gold Honeycomb, C.1882, Miniature, 3 1/2 In. 52.00
Doulton, Humidor, Tan & Brown, White Raised Monks, Lambeth, Artist Signed 65.00
Doulton, Inkwell, Brown, Blue Decoration, Lambeth, 3 1/2 In. 55.00
Doulton, Jam Pot, Gray, Blue Horses, Silver Plate Fittings, H.Barlow, 1885 225.00
Doulton, Jar, Biscuit, Cream Color, Arundel, Blue & Gold, Burslem, 6 1/2 In. 48.00
Doulton, Jar, Biscuit, Ivory Tapestry, Cobalt, Gold, Doulton & Slaters Patent 175.00
Doulton, Jar, Biscuit, Tree Bark, Floral, Eliz Atkins, Lambeth 115.00
Doulton, Jar, Covered, White & Blue Leaf & Floral Applied, 4 3/4 In. 52.50
Doulton, Jar, Sweetmeat, Silver Plate Lid, Fittings, Brown, Blue, White, 5 In. 69.00
Doulton, Jar, Tobacco, Cobalt Top, Sanded Lighter, Blue Bottom, 5 1/2 In. 45.00
Doulton, Jar, Tobacco, Verse By Kingsley, Lambeth, E.Beard 90.00
Doulton, Jardiniere, Hannah Barlow, Lambeth 305.00
Doulton, Jardiniere, Tapestry, Ruffled Cobalt Rim, Slater's, 6 3/4 In. 80.00
Doulton, Jug, Buff, Rugby Scrimmage, 2 Handles, E.M., Lambeth, 1883, 6 In. 165.00
Doulton, Jug, Hannah Barlow, Incised Scene, Horse Running, Lambeth, 8 1/2 In. 295.00
Doulton, Jug, Highland Whiskey, Beige, White Viking Ship, Lambeth, 7 In. 78.00
Doulton, Jug, Hunt, Irish Silver Cover, Dublin, 1832, Edward Power, 9 1/2 In. 188.00
Doulton, Jug, Lambeth Stoneware, Applied Work, A.H., Dated 1877, 4 1/2 In. 85.00
Doulton, Jug, Lambeth Stoneware, Mountain Goat, Signed Hannah B.Barlow 565.00
Doulton, Jug, Leatherware, Dark Brown, Wax Stitching, Silver Plate Rim, 8 In. 95.00
Doulton, Jug, Salt Glaze, Emily J.Edwards, C.1874 150.00
Doulton, Jug, Sea Shanty, Polychrome Sailors And Songs 95.00
Doulton, Jug, Whiskey, Dewar, Etched Country Scenes, Scotch Thistles, Lambeth 105.00
Doulton, Lamp, Oil, Lambeth Stoneware, Incised Foliage, Edith D.Lupton, 9 In. 345.00
Doulton, Mug, Beige, Horses, Hannah Barlow, Lambeth, 1879, 4 1/8 In. 235.00
Doulton, Mug, Copperware, Lambeth 125.00
Doulton, Mug, Friendship, Raised Figures, 3 Handles, 6 In. 145.00
Doulton, Mug, Lambeth Stoneware, Sporting, Man Running, Putting Shot, C.1900 245.00
Doulton, Mug, Leatherware, Sterling Rim, C.1894, 6 In. 95.00
Doulton, Mug, Sporting, Lambeth, C.1900, 5 1/4 In. 250.00
Doulton, Mug, Sporting, Stoneware, Lambeth, 6 In. 200.00
Doulton, Mug, Sporting, 2 Vignettes, Lambeth, C.1900, 5 1/4 In. 250.00
Doulton, Mug, Stoneware, Lambeth, Hannah Barlow, Dated, 1873, Cobalt On Blue 300.00
Doulton, Pitcher Vase, Gilded Tan Chine, Floral, Blue Handle, Slater's, 5 In. 65.00
Doulton, Pitcher, Allsop's Ales, Long Life To Prince Of Wales, C.1872, 7 In. 95.00
Doulton, Pitcher, Bayeux Tapestry, Battle Of Hastings, C.1870, 8 In. 210.00
Doulton, Pitcher, Brown To Tan, Relief Toby, Lambeth, 4 1/2 In. 80.00
Doulton, Pitcher, Buff, Cobalt & Gold Floral, Sterling Rim, C.B., 7 1/2 In. 90.00
Doulton, Pitcher, Burslem, C.1891, George Moreland Hunt Scene 89.00
Doulton, Pitcher, Busts Of Columbus & Washington, Eagles, Flags, Lambeth 250.00
Doulton, Pitcher, Lambeth, Brown & Tan Stoneware, Hunt & Tavern Scene, 6 In. 45.00
Doulton, Pitcher, Lambeth, Salt Glaze, Miniature, 1 3/4 In. 18.00
Doulton, Pitcher, Leather, Floral, Snakeskin Band, John Broad, 11 1/2 In. 140.00
Doulton, Pitcher, Milk, Burslem, Florals, Raised Border, C.1885, 6 1/2 In. 95.00
Doulton, Pitcher, Queen Victoria, 1837-97, Cameo Busts, Lambeth, 6 1/2 In. 95.00
Doulton, Pitcher, Scuttle, Old Sea Dogs, Jack's The Boy For Play, C.1900 65.00
Doulton, Pitcher, Watchman, What Of The Night, Leaf & Scroll, 7 In. 65.00
Doulton, Plate, Burslem Luster, Pink & Copper, Griffin, C.1895, 8 In. 75.00
Doulton, Plate, Dessert, Enamel Flower, Burslem, C.1895, 8 In., Pair 65.00
Doulton, Plate, Eglington Tournament, Jousting Scene, Dated 1902, 10 1/2 In. 52.50
Doulton, Pot, Chocolate, Lacy Blue & White Applied Decoration, Silicon, 4 In. 52.50
Doulton, Salt, Salt Glaze, Sterling Rim, Lambeth, C.1897 30.00
Doulton, Stein, World's Columbian Exposition, 1893, Cobalt Base, Burslem 150.00
Doulton, Tankard, Buff Orange Peel, White Cats, HBB, Lambeth, 9 1/4 In. 345.00
Doulton, Tankard, Cavalier, Street & Tavern Scene, C.1920, 6 In. 68.50
Doulton, Tankard, Three Musketeers, Lion & Shield Rim, 6 In. 42.00

Doulton, Teacup & Saucer, Nankin, Burslem, England 8.50
Doulton, Teapot, Flow Blue, Persian Spray, 1882-91 Mark, Burslem 89.95
Doulton, Tray, Bread, Dickensware, Cap'n Cuttle, C.1907, 10 1/2 In. 110.00
Doulton, Trivet, Bayeux Tapestry, Soldiers In Crude Vassel, C.1907, 5 In. 72.50
Doulton, Tumbler, Hannah Barlow, Signed, 1875 .... 145.00
Doulton, Tumbler, Horses, Hannah Barlow, 1875 .... 145.00
Doulton, Tumbler, Incised Deer, Hannah Barlow, Dated 1875 .... 225.00
Doulton, Vase, Art Nouveau Handles, Portrait Of Woman, Leslie Johnson 225.00
Doulton, Vase, Blue & Purple Leaves, Arthur Barlow, Lambeth, 1874, 7 1/4 In. 175.00
Doulton, Vase, Bone China, Colors Deep Orange To Yellow, Signed Harry Nixon 215.00
Doulton, Vase, Brown And Green Ground, Signed Aida, Don Quixote, 8 3/4 In. 95.00
Doulton, Vase, Brown, Green Ground, Signed Aida, Dancing Maiden, 11 1/4 In. 95.00
Doulton, Vase, Brown, Tan, Slatters, Lambeth, C.1880, 5 1/4 In. 75.00
Doulton, Vase, Buff, Pigs & Foxes In Meadow, F.C.Roberts, HBB, 11 In., Pair 550.00
Doulton, Vase, Burslem, Lactolianware, Pate-Sur-Pate Bell Flowers, W.Slater 350.00
Doulton, Vase, Carrara Ware, Geometric Design, Bulbous, Artist Signed, Pair 220.00
Doulton, Vase, Chine Gilt, Art Nouveau Shape, Artist Signed, 3 3/4 In. 65.00
Doulton, Vase, Chine, Cream Color, Roses, Gilt Trim, Slater's, C.1900, 12 In. 75.00
Doulton, Vase, Chocolate, Light Blue, White, Cobalt Applied, Silicon, 6 In. 45.00
Doulton, Vase, Covered, Faience, Floral, Mary Arding, Lambeth, 1877, 10 1/2 In. 150.00
Doulton, Vase, Cows Grazing, Hannah Barlow, 10 In. 325.00
Doulton, Vase, Crown Lambeth, Pixies, Margaret E. Thompson, C.1900, 7 In. 165.00
Doulton, Vase, Dancing Maiden At Seaside, Signed Aida On Face, 44 1/4 In. 100.00
Doulton, Vase, Dancing Maiden, Signed On Face Aida, 11 3/4 In. 100.00
Doulton, Vase, Don Quixote Tilting At Windmills, Signed Aida On Face 100.00
Doulton, Vase, Don Quixote Tilting At Windmills, 8 3/4 In. 100.00
Doulton, Vase, Don Quixote, Signed, Marked, 8 1/2 In. 125.00
Doulton, Vase, Eight Horses, Hannah Barlow, 12 In. 275.00
Doulton, Vase, Frieze Of Stags, Blue On Ivory 195.00
Doulton, Vase, High Glaze, Blue, Green, Florals, Artist Signed, 6 In. 52.00
Doulton, Vase, Impasto, Autumn Foliage, Rosa Keen 300.00
Doulton, Vase, Incised Cattle, Gray Ground, Signed H B, Lambeth, 11 In., Pair 500.00
Doulton, Vase, Lambeth Faience, Morning Glories, Artist Mark, C1895, 7 1/2 In. 145.00
Doulton, Vase, Lambeth, Blue & Gray With Leaves In Relief, 9 In., Dated 1884 .... 58.00
Doulton, Vase, Lambeth, Tapestry Look, Blue, Light Brown, Long Neck 60.00
Doulton, Vase, Raised & Carved Foliage, Florence C.Roberts, 9 In., Lambeth 135.00
Doulton, Vase, Silicon Body, Floral Chineware, C1882, 9 1/2 In., Pair 265.00
Doulton, Vase, Silicon, Blue & White Geometrics, C.1902, 2 1/2 In. 25.00
Doulton, Vase, Silicon, Chocolate, Cobalt, C.1880, 6 In. 60.00
Doulton, Vase, Sung Flambe, F.Moore & Noke, 6 In. 195.00
Doulton, Vase, Titanian Ware, Long-Tailed Bird, Dated 1926, 6 3/4 In. 265.00
Doulton, Vase, Trumpet, Japanese Style, Pate Sur Pate, Lambeth, Signed 175.00
Doulton, Vase, White, Cows & Donkey, HBB, Lambeth, 9 3/4 In., Pair 595.00

Dr.Syntax, see Adams, Staffordshire

Dresden china is any china made in the town of Dresden, Germany. The most famous factory in Dresden is the Meissen Factory.

Dresden, see also Meissen

Dresden, Basket, Open Pierce Work, Painted Flowers, 1 1/2 X 4 In. 40.00
Dresden, Bell, Dinner, Swags Of Purple Floral, Gilding, 4 1/2 In. 38.00
Dresden, Bell, Dinner, White, Purple Floral Swags, Gilding, 4 1/2 In. 38.00
Dresden, Bowl, Covered, Reticulated Latticework Top, Applied Flowers, 5 In. 65.00
Dresden, Bowl, Cutout Floral, Floral Inside, Upright Handles, 8 1/2 In. 115.00
Dresden, Bowl, Floral, Reticulated Border, Gold Trim, C.1869, 7 1/2 In. 75.00
Dresden, Bowl, Romantic Couple Painting On Scalloped Lid, Gold Feet, 9 In. 245.00
Dresden, Box, Covered, Floral, Gold Trim, Heart Shape, 5 In. 57.50
Dresden, Butter Pat, Floral, Set Of 4 .... 22.50
Dresden, Casserole & Plate, Flowers, Gold Scroll, Gold Edge 55.00
Dresden, Celery, Floral, Gold Trim 30.00
Dresden, Chocolate Pot, Pink Ground, Sampler Pattern, Blue, Pink, Gold 150.00
Dresden, Compote, Cutout & Color Floral, Gold Trim, Thieme, C.1890, 8 3/4 In. 95.00
Dresden, Compote, Underglaze Blue Mark, 7 In. 225.00
Dresden, Cup & Saucer, Demitasse, Panels Of Portraits & Floral, Gold Trim 17.00
Dresden, Cup & Saucer, Floral, C.1905 .... 22.00

Dresden, Dish, Center Handle, 4 Sections, Aqua, Pink, & Gold, 12 3/4 In. 165.00
Dresden, Figurine, Bacchus Cherub Holding Wine Goblet Riding Goat, 8 In. 125.00
Dresden, Figurine, Ballerina, White & Pink Lace Dress, 5 In. 50.00
Dresden, Figurine, Ballerina, 13 In. 250.00
Dresden, Figurine, Ballet Dancer, Girl, Pink Lace Skirt, Gold Floral, 5 In. 50.00
Dresden, Figurine, Bird, Impressed Hanfling And Marked, 5 X 4 In. 69.00
Dresden, Figurine, Cat, Life-Size, Ginger, White, Green Eyes, 14 In. 285.00
Dresden, Figurine, Cat, Sitting, Long Haired, Green Eyes, 14 In. 235.00
Dresden, Figurine, Dancing Couple, Underglaze Blue Mark 375.00
Dresden, Figurine, Dog, Seated, Burnt Orange, Purple Collar, 12 1/2 In. 280.00
Dresden, Figurine, Female & Male Pug Dogs, Gold Collars, 8 In., Pair 325.00
Dresden, Figurine, Little Girl, Yellow & White Lace Dress, 3 In. 30.00
Dresden, Figurine, Macaw On Stump, Red, Yellow, Green, & Blue, 14 1/2 In., Pair 395.00
Dresden, Figurine, Sealyham Terrier, Sitting, 4 1/2 X 3 1/2 In. 55.00
Dresden, Figurine, Thrush Among Dogwoods, Brown, Orange Breast, 8 1/4 In. 100.00
Dresden, Group, Mother Dog & Puppy, 9 1/2 In. 260.00
Dresden, Group, Pug Dog & Puppy, 9 1/2 In. 275.00
Dresden, Group, Two Nymphs Riding & Playing With Goat, Grapes, 11 In. 165.00
Dresden, Inkstand, 2 Bottles, Garlands Of Flowers, Gold Banding, Potschapel 35.00
Dresden, Inkwell, Covered, Multicolor Floral, 2 1/4 In. 25.00
Dresden, Lamp, Miniature, Floral, Milk Glass Shade, Cross Swords, Signed H 110.00
Dresden, Pitcher, Floral, Swirled, C.1890, 7 In. 38.00
Dresden, Pitcher, Yellow, Cobalt Imperial Eagles, Floral, 4 3/4 In. 85.00
Dresden, Pitcher, Yellow, Imperial Eagles & Florals In Cobalt, Red Enamel 85.00
Dresden, Plate, Floral & Scenic Panels, Lattice Rim, 8 In. 30.00
Dresden, Plate, Floral, Reticulated Border, Schumann, C.1881, 8 1/4 In. 35.00
Dresden, Plate, Service, Pastel Floral, Pierced Border, Scalloped, 11 In. 100.00
Dresden, Platter, Dropped Rose, Marked, 11 In. 30.00
Dresden, Ramekin & Saucer, Nosegays & Floral Clusters, Gold Scalloped Edge 18.00
Dresden, Shoe, Applied Red, Blue, Pink, & Green Floral, 5 In. 20.00
Dresden, Slipper, Applied Red, Blue, & Pink Floral, High Heel, 4 In., Pair 40.00
Dresden, Swan, Applied Red, Blue, Pink, & Green Floral, 3 3/8 In., Pair 40.00
Dresden, Teapot, Snowball, Applied Canaries, Floral, & Roses 375.00
Dresden, Tray, Pin, Scrolling, Gold, White, Lavender Orchids, German, 11 In. 22.00
Dresden, Vase, Cobalt, Stippled Gold Floral, 4 Footed, C.1900, 5 3/4 In. 88.00
Dresden, Vase, Gold, Ladies & Gentlemen, Jeweled, Scalloped, Handled, 7 In. 110.00

Duncan & Miller glass was made at the George A. Duncan and Sons Company in Washington, Pennsylvania. The company was started in 1894, with James E. Duncan, president, and Edwin C. Miller, secretary.

Duncan & Miller, Ashtray, Blue, 3-Footed, 1 1/2 X 2 1/2 In. 16.00
Duncan & Miller, Ashtray, Duck 18.00
Duncan & Miller, Basket, Blue, Opalescent, Canterbury, 9 In. 70.00
Duncan & Miller, Basket, Canterbury, 11 X 11 In. 37.00
Duncan & Miller, Basket, Cut Flower, C.1900, 6 1/4 In. 20.00
Duncan & Miller, Basket, Hobnail, 6 X 5 In. 17.00
Duncan & Miller, Basket, Hobnail, 7 1/2 X 7 In. 20.00
Duncan & Miller, Basket, Pink, Opalescent, Canterbury, 8 1/2 In. 40.00
Duncan & Miller, Basket, Pink, Opalescent, Canterbury, 9 In. 65.00
Duncan & Miller, Berry Bowl, Sandwich 10.00
Duncan & Miller, Blue, Opalescent, Hobnail, Sides Turn Up, 10 In. 38.00
Duncan & Miller, Bottle, Barber, No.42 .... 22.00
Duncan & Miller, Bowl, Blue, Opalescent, Canterbury, Scalloped, 10 1/2 In. 37.50
Duncan & Miller, Bowl, Blue, Opalescent, Hobnail, Turned-Up Sides, 10 1/2 In. 35.00
Duncan & Miller, Bowl, Canterbury, 11 In. 45.00
Duncan & Miller, Bowl, Chartreuse, Canterbury, 10 In. 40.00
Duncan & Miller, Bowl, Chartreuse, Morano, 10 In. 40.00
Duncan & Miller, Bowl, Fruit, Pink, Opalescent, Sanibel, Oval, 13 In. 85.00
Duncan & Miller, Bowl, Gardian, 8 In. 28.00
Duncan & Miller, Bowl, Hobnail, Pink Opal, 11 In. 48.00
Duncan & Miller, Bowl, Hobnail, 12 In. .... 20.00 To 45.00
Duncan & Miller, Bowl, Magnolia, Gold Trim, 10 1/2 In. 35.00
Duncan & Miller, Bowl, Murano, Crimped, 10 In. 22.00
Duncan & Miller, Bowl, No.42, 9 In. 28.50

Duncan & Miller, Bowl, Pink, Opalescent, Canterbury, Oval, 10 In. 38.00
Duncan & Miller, Bowl, Pink, Opalescent, Canterbury, 10 1/2 X 4 1/2 In. 39.00
Duncan & Miller, Bowl, Pink, Opalescent, Chartreuse On 2 Sides, Murano, 10 In. 47.50
Duncan & Miller, Bowl, Pink, Opalescent, Hobnail, Crimped, 10 In. 32.00
Duncan & Miller, Bowl, Pink, Opalescent, Hobnail, Ruffled, 6 3/4 In. 12.00
Duncan & Miller, Bowl, Pink, Opalescent, Hobnail, Scalloped, Flared, 7 1/2 In. 45.00
Duncan & Miller, Bowl, Pink, Opalescent, Incurved Edge, 6 In. 12.00
Duncan & Miller, Bowl, Pink, Opalescent, Ivy, Crimped, 7 In. 45.00
Duncan & Miller, Bowl, Ruby, Canterbury, 10 In. 50.00
Duncan & Miller, Bowl, Sanibel, 8 In. 4.00
Duncan & Miller, Bowl, Sapphire Blue, Canterbury, 9 1/2 In. 32.00
Duncan & Miller, Box, Cigarette, Covered, Canterbury 15.00
Duncan & Miller, Box, Cigarette, Covered, Patio 20.00
Duncan & Miller, Box, Cigarette, 4-Footed Rogers Plate Cover 22.50
Duncan & Miller, Butter, Silver Lid, Teardrop, Stick 26.00
Duncan & Miller, Candelabrum, Prisms, Sandwich, 1 Light, 10 In. 85.00
Duncan & Miller, Candleholder, Pink, Opalescent, American Way, 2 In., Pair 28.00
Duncan & Miller, Candlestick, Pink Opalescent, Single, Canterbury, Pair 32.00
Duncan & Miller, Candlestick, Pink, Opalescent, 4 In., Pair 25.00
Duncan & Miller, Candlestick, Teardrop, 2 Light With Prisms, 5 In. 85.00
Duncan & Miller, Carafe, Water, No.42 39.50
Duncan & Miller, Celery & Relish, No.41, 3 Sections, Oblong, 10 1/2 In. 20.00
Duncan & Miller, Celery, Blue, Nautical 28.00
Duncan & Miller, Celery, Heavy Paneled Finecut, Pedestal, C.1880 25.00
Duncan & Miller, Champagne, First Love 12.00
Duncan & Miller, Champagne, Rose 6.00
Duncan & Miller, Cocktail Shaker, Frosted Crystal, Chanticleer, 32 Ozs. 35.00
Duncan & Miller, Cocktail, Lily Of The Valley 6.00
Duncan & Miller, Compote, Covered, Block, Amber Stained, Engraved, 9 In. 55.00
Duncan & Miller, Compote, No.41, Crimped, 5 1/2 In. 8.00
Duncan & Miller, Compote, Pink, Opalescent, Hobnail, Crimped, 5 In. 22.00
Duncan & Miller, Compote, Sapphire Blue, 5 In. 25.00
Duncan & Miller, Compote, Tree Of Life, Hand Base, 9 1/4 X 9 In. 100.00
Duncan & Miller, Condiment Set, Teardrop, 5 Piece 22.00
Duncan & Miller, Console Set, Discoveries Dawn, Set 125.00
Duncan & Miller, Console Set, Pink, Opalescent, Canterbury, 3 Piece 65.00
Duncan & Miller, Console Set, Rose Color, Swirl, 12 1/2 In. Bowl, 3 Piece 70.00
Duncan & Miller, Cordial, No.42 23.00
Duncan & Miller, Cordial, No.48 19.50
Duncan & Miller, Cornucopia, Blue, Lay Down, 14 In. 85.00
Duncan & Miller, Cornucopia, Crystal, 12 1/2 In. 20.00
Duncan & Miller, Cornucopia, Pink Opal, Lay Down 75.00
Duncan & Miller, Cornucopia, Pink Opalescent, 16 In. 85.00
Duncan & Miller, Cornucopia, 11 In. 95.00
Duncan & Miller, Creamer, Diamond Ridge 10.00
Duncan & Miller, Creamer, No.42 12.00
Duncan & Miller, Creamer, No.42, Miniature 35.00
Duncan & Miller, Creamer, Yellow, Lacy, Footed, 4 In. 8.00
Duncan & Miller, Cruet Set, 2 Bottle, Salt, Pepper & Tray, Teardrop 32.00
Duncan & Miller, Cup & Saucer, Bouillon, Swirl, Handled 8.00
Duncan & Miller, Cup, Punch, No.42 6.50
Duncan & Miller, Dish, Candy, Black, Footed 40.00
Duncan & Miller, Dish, Candy, Canterbury, 3 Sections 25.00
Duncan & Miller, Dish, Candy, Covered, Silver Overlay, 3 Sections 25.00
Duncan & Miller, Dish, Mint, Blue, Scalloped Rim, 3 Sections 35.00
Duncan & Miller, Dish, Nut, Teardrop, 2 Sections, 6 In. 8.00
Duncan & Miller, Dish, Relish, Divided, Teardrop 7.00
Duncan & Miller, Epergne, Murano, 12 In. 45.00
Duncan & Miller, Figurine, Dolphin, Solid, 8 1/2 In. 50.00
Duncan & Miller, Figurine, Swan, Chartreuse, 10 1/2 In. 65.00
Duncan & Miller, Figurine, Swan, Ruby, 10 1/2 In. 55.00
Duncan & Miller, Flower Arranger, Blue, Opalescent, Canterbury, 7 1/2 In. 30.00
Duncan & Miller, Flower Arranger, Murano, Oval, 10 1/2 In. 20.00
Duncan & Miller, Flower Arranger, Pink, Opalescent, Murano, Oval, 12 1/2 In. 78.00

Duncan & Miller, Fruit Bowl, Blue, Opalescent, Sanibel, 13 In. 65.00
Duncan & Miller, Goblet, Carmen, 5 3/4 In. 15.00
Duncan & Miller, Goblet, Cocktail, First Love 12.00
Duncan & Miller, Goblet, Cocktail, Sandwich 5.50
Duncan & Miller, Goblet, Cocktail, Sandwich, 3 Ozs. 5.00
Duncan & Miller, Goblet, Etched Floral 5.00
Duncan & Miller, Goblet, Green, Lacy, 6 In. 8.00
Duncan & Miller, Goblet, Hobnail, Opalescent 11.00
Duncan & Miller, Goblet, No.42, Gold Trim 20.00
Duncan & Miller, Goblet, Sandwich, 9 Ozs. 7.00
Duncan & Miller, Goblet, Teepee 12.00
Duncan & Miller, Hat, Blue, Opalescent, Hobnail, 4 In. 18.50
Duncan & Miller, Hat, Hobnail, 3 1/2 In. 12.00
Duncan & Miller, Hat, Hobnail, 9 In. 37.50
Duncan & Miller, Hat, Pink, Opalescent, Hobnail, 3 3/4 In. 18.50
Duncan & Miller, Ice Cream Bowl & Underplate, Amber, Sandwich 10.00
Duncan & Miller, Ivy Ball, Carmen, Hobnail, Footed, 6 1/2 In. 37.50
Duncan & Miller, Ivy Ball, Red, Hobnail, Footed, 6 1/2 In. 45.00
Duncan & Miller, Ivyball, Carmen, Hobnail, Footed, 6 1/2 In. 37.50
Duncan & Miller, Jar, Candy, Pink, Opalescent, Covered, 9 In. 110.00
Duncan & Miller, Jar, Cracker, No.42 .... 30.00
Duncan & Miller, Muddler, Crystal, 5 In. 8.50
Duncan & Miller, Nappy, Canterbury, 6 In. 7.00
Duncan & Miller, Nappy, Crimped Handle, 6 In. 23.00
Duncan & Miller, Nappy, Pink, Opalescent 25.00
Duncan & Miller, Parfait, Indian Tree 12.00
Duncan & Miller, Parfait, Sandwich, 5 1/4 In. 4.00
Duncan & Miller, Pitcher, Ruby Flashed Button & Arches 48.00
Duncan & Miller, Pitcher, Sandwich, Ice Lip, 8 In. 49.50
Duncan & Miller, Pitcher, Water, First Love, Etched, Sterling Base 85.00
Duncan & Miller, Plate, Bread & Butter, First Love, Etched, 6 In. 5.00
Duncan & Miller, Plate, Chantilly, 8 1/2 In. 6.00
Duncan & Miller, Plate, Lily Of The Valley, 8 1/2 In. 6.00
Duncan & Miller, Plate, No.41, 6 In. 5.00
Duncan & Miller, Plate, No.41, 7 In. 7.00
Duncan & Miller, Plate, No.41, 8 In. 15.00
Duncan & Miller, Plate, Salad, Pink, Opalescent, Sanibel, 8 1/2 In. 28.00
Duncan & Miller, Plate, Sandwich, 6 In. 5.00
Duncan & Miller, Plate, Sandwich, 7 In. 2.90
Duncan & Miller, Punch Bowl & Base, No.42 .... 87.50
Duncan & Miller, Punch Set, Caribbean, Amber Handled Cups, 13 Piece 98.00
Duncan & Miller, Punch Set, Caribbean, Cobalt Handles, 11 Piece 45.00
Duncan & Miller, Relish, Caribbean, 5 Sections 18.00
Duncan & Miller, Relish, Etched Indian Tree, 3 Sections, 8 In. 10.00
Duncan & Miller, Relish, Gondola, Pink Opalescent, 14 X 6 1/2 In. 45.00
Duncan & Miller, Relish, Indian Tree On Canterbury Blank, 8 1/2 X 4 In. 10.00
Duncan & Miller, Relish, No.41, Handle, 2 Sections, 5 1/2 In. 8.00
Duncan & Miller, Relish, Pink, Opalescent, Shell, 2 Sections, 2 Handles 20.00
Duncan & Miller, Relish, Pink, Opalescent, Shell, 3 Sections, 3 Handles, 7 In. 25.00
Duncan & Miller, Relish, Teardrop, 3 Sections, 3 Handles, 8 In. 15.00
Duncan & Miller, Salad Bowl, Blue, Opalescent, Sanibel, 12 1/2 In. 88.00
Duncan & Miller, Salt, Mardi Gras 8.00
Duncan & Miller, Salt, Master, No.42 .... 10.00
Duncan & Miller, Salt, No.42 .... 3.50
Duncan & Miller, Salt, No.42, Oval 3.50
Duncan & Miller, Saltshaker, No.42 .... 8.50
Duncan & Miller, Saucer, No.41, 6 In. 4.00
Duncan & Miller, Sherbet, Hobnail 12.00
Duncan & Miller, Sherbet, June, Footed 8.00
Duncan & Miller, Sherbet, Sandwich, 5 Ozs. 4.50
Duncan & Miller, Spooner, Child's, No.42 .... 18.50
Duncan & Miller, Spooner, Diamond Ridge 10.00
Duncan & Miller, Sugar & Creamer, Canterbury 6.00
Duncan & Miller, Sugar & Creamer, Green, Canterbury 35.00

Duncan & Miller, Sugar & Creamer, Pink, Versailles 22.50
Duncan & Miller, Sugar, Covered, No.42, Miniature 35.00
Duncan & Miller, Sugar, Creamer, & Tray, Canterbury 15.00
Duncan & Miller, Sugar, Creamer, & Tray, No.41, Footed, Oval Tray 20.00
Duncan & Miller, Sugar, First Love, Etched 10.00
Duncan & Miller, Sugar, Individual, No.42 .... 9.00
Duncan & Miller, Sugar, Teardrop 4.50
Duncan & Miller, Swan, Amberina, 7 1/2 In. 65.00
Duncan & Miller, Swan, Blue, Opalescent, Sylvan, 8 In. 50.00
Duncan & Miller, Swan, Chartreuse, 10 1/2 In. 70.00
Duncan & Miller, Swan, Clear Neck, Ruby, 7 In. 22.50
Duncan & Miller, Swan, Clear, Heavy Sterling Floral Overlay, 5 In. 22.00
Duncan & Miller, Swan, Crystal, Applied Neck, 7 In. 20.00
Duncan & Miller, Swan, Etched, 7 In. 35.00
Duncan & Miller, Swan, Gold Head & Trim At Top, 6 In. 42.50
Duncan & Miller, Swan, Green, Clear Neck, Open Back 55.00
Duncan & Miller, Swan, Green, 10 In. 48.00
Duncan & Miller, Swan, Green, 10 1/2 In. 50.00
Duncan & Miller, Swan, Lavender Neck, 4 In. 20.00
Duncan & Miller, Swan, Open Back, 3 1/2 In. 20.00
Duncan & Miller, Swan, Red, 7 1/2 In. 35.00
Duncan & Miller, Swan, Ruby, Clear Neck, 14 1/2 In. 85.00
Duncan & Miller, Swan, Ruby, 7 In. 20.00
Duncan & Miller, Swan, Ruby, 8 In. 28.00
Duncan & Miller, Swan, Ruby, 10 In. 50.00
Duncan & Miller, Swan, Sapphire Blue, Sylvan, 7 1/2 X 5 1/2 In. 69.00
Duncan & Miller, Swan, Silver Trim Top, Silver Floral Inside, 7 In. 57.50
Duncan & Miller, Swan, Smoky Topaz 48.00
Duncan & Miller, Swan, Solid Crystal, 3 X 2 1/4 In. 24.00
Duncan & Miller, Swan, Solid, 3 In. .... 20.00 To 30.00
Duncan & Miller, Swan, Solid, 5 In. 29.00
Duncan & Miller, Swan, Solid, 7 In. 90.00
Duncan & Miller, Swan, Sterling Overlay, 7 In. 48.00
Duncan & Miller, Swan, Sylvan, 5 In. 20.00
Duncan & Miller, Swan, Sylvan, 6 In. 17.00
Duncan & Miller, Table Set, Prism Ring, Etched, No.415, 4 Piece 123.00
Duncan & Miller, Tankard, Water, No.42, Applied Handle 37.50
Duncan & Miller, Toothpick, No.42, Gold Rim 18.00
Duncan & Miller, Tray, Pink, Opalescent, Sanibel, 15 In. 68.00
Duncan & Miller, Tray, Sanibel, Divided, 13 In. 45.00
Duncan & Miller, Tumbler, Green, Swirl, Footed 15.00
Duncan & Miller, Tumbler, Iced Tea, Sandwich, Footed, 12 Ozs. 8.00
Duncan & Miller, Tumbler, Sandwich, 9 Ozs. 8.00
Duncan & Miller, Vase, Blue, Caribbean, 2 Handles, 8 1/2 X 5 1/2 In. 22.00
Duncan & Miller, Vase, Blue, Opalescent, Canterbury, 6 X 5 In. 37.00
Duncan & Miller, Vase, Blue, Opalescent, Hobnail, Crimped, 4 1/2 In. 14.00
Duncan & Miller, Vase, Blue, Opalescent, Hobnail, 8 In. 65.00
Duncan & Miller, Vase, Bud, First Love, 9 In. 17.00
Duncan & Miller, Vase, Canterbury, Blue, Opalescent, 6 In. 47.00

Durand, Vase, Gold Aurene, Amphora Shape, 11 7/8 In.High

Durand, Vase, 8 In.High

Duncan & Miller, Vase, Canterbury, Crimped, 3 1/2 In. 10.00
Duncan & Miller, Vase, Canterbury, Sterling Overlay, Flowers, 8 1/2 In. 35.00
Duncan & Miller, Vase, Flip, Pink, Opalescent, Hobnail Crimped Top, 8 In. 45.00
Duncan & Miller, Vase, Frosted, Silver Overlay, Roses, 11 In. 35.00
Duncan & Miller, Vase, Pink, Opalescent, Canterbury, Flared, 4 In. 18.50
Duncan & Miller, Vase, Pink, Opalescent, Canterbury, 8 1/2 In. 37.00
Duncan & Miller, Vase, Pink, Opalescent, Hobnail, Flared, 4 1/4 In. 18.50
Duncan & Miller, Vase, Pink, Opalescent, Murano, 9 X 5 1/2 In. 48.00
Duncan & Miller, Vase, Pink, Opalescent, 5 3/4 In. 50.00
Duncan & Miller, Vase, Teardrop, Fan, 8 1/2 In. 9.00
Duncan & Miller, Vase, Violet, Blue, Opalescent, Cape Cod, 3 1/2 In. 15.00
Duncan & Miller, Wine, First Love, Etched 8.00
Duncan & Miller, Wine, No.42 .... 18.00
Duncan & Miller, Wine, Sandwich .... 5.50 To 12.00

Durand glass was made by Victor Durand from 1879 to 1935 at several factories. Most of the iridescent Durand glass was made by Victor Durand, Jr., from 1912 to 1924 at the Durand Art Glass Works in Vineland, New Jersey.

Durand, Atomizer, Yellow, Engraved Flower & Leaf, Bulb, Pedestal Base, 9 In. 60.00
Durand, Basket, Amber, Paperweight Design Of Leaves, 4 3/4 X 5 1/2 In. 125.00
Durand, Champagne, Azure, 8 1/2 In. 50.00
Durand, Console Set, Ruby Tops, Pink & White Feather, Amber Bases, 3 Piece 695.00
Durand, Finger Bowl & Underplate, Blue Cut To Clear Bull's-Eyes 65.00
Durand, Jar, Cracker, Purple Iridescent, Blue & Green Veined 165.00
Durand, Lamp Base, Threading, Gold, Iridescent, 14 In. 225.00
Durand, Lamp, Blue Hearts & Vines, Silk Shade, 14 In. 325.00
Durand, Lamp, Buffet, Trumpet, Gold & Green Iridescent, Crackle Glass, Pair 500.00
Durand, Liquor, Blue & White Feathers, Canary Stem, 4 1/2 In. 195.00
Durand, Plate, Gold Luster, Blue Highlights, 8 1/8 In. 25.00
Durand, Rose Bowl, Blue, Applied Iridescent Threading, 4 In. 400.00
Durand, Rose Bowl, Iridescent, Blue, Signed & Numbered, 4 In. 395.00
Durand, Vase, Blue Iridescent, Opalescent Hearts & Clinging Vines, 8 In. 650.00
Durand, Vase, Blue Iridescent, Short Neck, Flared Mouth 200.00
Durand, Vase, Emerald Iridescent, Signed, 5 In., Pair 140.00
Durand, Vase, Gold Aurene, Amphora Shape, 11 7/8 In.High .... *Illus* 425.00
Durand, Vase, Gold Intaglio, Signed 600.00
Durand, Vase, Green & Gold, King Tut, Gold Interior, 6 1/4 In. 575.00
Durand, Vase, Green, Gold King Tut Design, Gold Interior, 9 1/4 In. 575.00
Durand, Vase, Hat Shape, Blue Iridescent, Small 95.00
Durand, Vase, Orange Iridescent, Blue Pull Ups, 8 In. 185.00
Durand, Vase, Orange, Threaded, Blue Trim, 9 In. 450.00
Durand, Vase, 8 In.High .... *Illus* 900.00
Elvis Presley, Locket, 24 In. Chain 9.50
Elvis Presley, Pillow, Dated 1950 .... 15.00
Elvis Presley, Pillow, Elvis Playing Guitar, Signed Pierotti, 10 X 10 In. 7.00
Elvis Presley, Tumbler, Figural 18.00

Enamel Ware, see Graniteware

Enamel, Austrian, Case, Cigarette, Silver, Mother & Child In Woods, Gold 140.00
Enamel, Chinese, Bottle, Snuff, Silver, Blue 52.00
Enamel, Chinese, Box, Brass Hinge & Rim, Green, Floral, Camelback, 3 In. 27.50
Enamel, Chinese, Kettle, Brass, Dragon & Floral, Square, 6 X 5 In. 35.00
Enamel, Chinese, Tray, Copper With Brass, People, Outdoor Scene, 4 X 3 In. 25.00

Enamel, French, Frame, Picture, Blue, Gold-Colored Metal, Oval, 3 1/2 In. 17.50
Enamel, French, Vase, Avocado Green, Butterflies & Foliage, 12 In. 115.00
Enamel, French, Vase, On Copper, Limoges, Lady, Signed Ganert, 5 In. 350.00
Enamel, French, Vase, On Copper, Limoges, Man, Signed Vibert, Pedestal, 6 In. 350.00
Enamel, French, Vase, Sarlandie, Limoges, Copper, Art Nouveau, Floral, 4 In. 325.00
Enamel, Peking, Box, Green Swirled Glass Knob On Lid, 4 Panels, 3 1/2 In. 40.00

Enamel, Russian, see also Faberge

Enamel, Russian, Box, Paper 195.00
Enamel, Russian, Box, Patch, G.K., 1 3/4 In. 285.00
Enamel, Russian, Box, Pill, Red On Eglomise Roses, Bottom Sunburst, 1 3/4 In. 100.00
Enamel, Russian, Case, Cigarette, Silver Base, Frogs, Nikolai Alekseyev 1675.00
Enamel, Russian, Cup, Vodka, Multicolored, Hallmarked, 2 In. 325.00
Enamel, Russian, Egg, Gold Over Brass, Red, Dots & Circles, 2 3/4 In. 35.00
Enamel, Russian, Eggcup, Cockerel Handle, Faberge Workmaster Saltykov 450.00
Enamel, Russian, Matchbox Cover, Queen Of Diamonds 250.00
Enamel, Russian, Napkin Ring, Multicolors, S.W. 250.00
Enamel, Russian, Pin, Bowknot, St.George & Dragon, Silver-Gilt 150.00
Enamel, Russian, Salt, Ball Feet, Moscow, 1889, Set Of 6 .... 345.00
Enamel, Russian, Salt, Gold Wash, Red, White, & Blue, 3 Ball Feet, G.K. 285.00
Enamel, Russian, Salt, Hallmarked, Six Colors, 1 In. 250.00
Enamel, Russian, Salt, 3 Ball Feet, Moscow, 1889, Set Of 6 .... 345.00
Enamel, Russian, Salt, 3 Feet, Gold On Silver, Worker's Mark 175.00
Enamel, Russian, Scoop, Sugar, Gold On Silver, Signed N.C.Red, Blues, White 350.00
Enamel, Russian, Spoon, Champleve, Moscow In Gold-Washed Bowl 65.00
Enamel, Russian, Spoon, Dessert, Kuznichev, C.1888, Silver 160.00
Enamel, Russian, Spoon, Pastel Floral, Khlebnikov, Kokoshnik, 6 3/4 In. 200.00
Enamel, Russian, Spoon, Pastel Shading, C.1896 .... 180.00
Enamel, Russian, Spoon, Red & White 300.00
Enamel, Russian, Tea Strainer, Silver Gilt, Postwar Mark, Ermine Tails 250.00
Enamel, Russian, Tongs, Sugar, Multicolor, Maker's Mark 250.00
Enamel, Russian, Tumbler, Crowned Double-Headed Eagle, 1896, 4 1/2 In. 50.00
Enamel, Viennese, Plaque, Dancing Women, Boy Musicians, 9 1/2 X 5 3/4 In. 1100.00
Enamel, Viennese, Urn, Covered, Scenic, Gilt Bronze Mounts, 6 1/2 In., Pair 650.00
Enamel, Vinaigrette, Egg, Pendant, Hallmark A & LP 235.00

End-of-day glass is now an out-of-fashion name for spattered glass. The glass was made of many bits and pieces of colored glass. Traditionally, the glass was made by workmen from the odds and ends left from the glass used during the day. Actually it was a deliberately manufactured product popular about 1880 to 1900, and some of it is still being made.

End-Of-Day, Basket, Brown & Yellow, Twisted Thorn Handle, 7 In. 85.00
End-Of-Day, Basket, Brown & Yellow, White Lining, Twisted Thorn Handle, 7 In 85.00
End-Of-Day, Bowl, Orange, Gold, Brown, Gold Mica Flecks 42.50
End-Of-Day, Candleholder, Red, Green, Blue, & White, 9 1/2 In., Pair 68.00
End-Of-Day, Candlestick, Spatter .... *Illus* 125.00
End-Of-Day, Candlestick, Yellow Lining, Brown & White Spatter, 9 1/4 In. 48.00

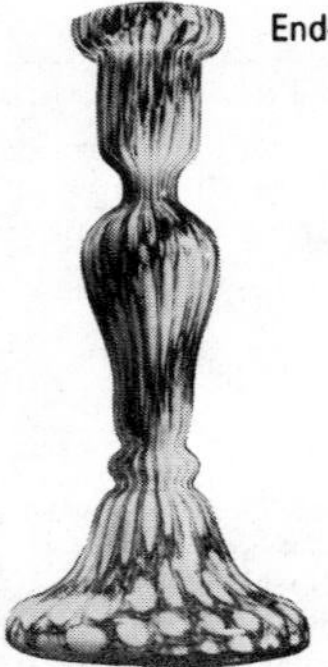

End-Of-Day, Candlestick, Spatter

End-Of-Day, Cruet, Yellow 125.00
End-OF-Day, Dish, Candy, Glass Swans, Mauve, Brown, Clear Blue & White 25.00
End-Of-Day, Muffineer, Pink & White, Bulbous 28.00
End-Of-Day, Paperweight, Steeple Shape, 2 X 6 1/4 In. 69.00
End-Of-Day, Pitcher, Cranberry & Opalescent On Clear, Ribbed 95.00
End-Of-Day, Slipper, Raised Work, 3 3/4 In. 57.50
End-Of-Day, Vase, Bowl, Sunny Colors, 6 X 4 In. 65.00
End-Of-Day, Vase, Cased Glass, Applied Clear Footed Base, 6 1/4 In. 88.00
End-Of-Day, Vase, Jack-In-The-Pulpit, Maroon & Light Blue, 7 1/2 In. 30.00
End-Of-Day, Vase, Mottled Yellow & White, Enamel Floral, Piecrust Rim, 7 In. 65.00
End-Of-Day, Vase, Mottled Yellow & White, Enamel Floral, 7 In. 65.00
End-Of-Day, Vase, Oranges, Reds, Yellows 78.50
End-Of-Day, Voot, Triple Cased, Dark, White Lining, Applied Rigaree, Pair 175.00
ES Germany, Bowl, Yellow Roses, Gold Trim, 9 1/4 In. 21.00
ES Germany, Butter Pat, Pair 18.00
ES Germany, Cake Set, Poppies, Gold Open Handles, 7 Piece 47.50
ES Germany, Dish, Candy, Classical Scene, Saxe 35.00
ES Germany, Hair Receiver, Fancy Decoration 30.00
ES Germany, Hair Receiver, Pink Floral, Gold Trim, Crown Mark 22.00
ES Germany, Plate, Cake, Lavender Florals, Hand-Painted, Gold Trim, 10 In. 19.00
ES Germany, Plate, Hand-Painted Rose, F.Earneck, 6 1/2 In. 5.00
ES Germany, Plate, Portrait, Flowers, 11 3/4 In. 90.00
ES Germany, Vase, Double Handled, Gold, Portrait Of Lady & Birds, 6 In. 87.50
ES Germany, Vase, Portrait, 3 Gold Handles, Lady Draped In White, 7 1/2 In. 350.00
Eskimo, Carving, Mating Polar Bears, Ivory, 4 In. 175.00
Eskimo, Cribbage Board, C.1915 350.00
Eskimo, Letter Opener, Caribou Etchings, Set Of 5 7.50
Eskimo, Woodmask, Nunivak, C.1925 700.00
Etruscan Majolica, see Majolica

Faberge was a firm of jewelers and goldsmiths founded in St. Petersburg, Russia, in 1842, by Gustav Faberge. Peter Carl Faberge, his son, was jeweler to the Russian Imperial Court from about 1870 to 1914.

Faberge, Bowl, Silver, Gilt & Enamel, 6 Coasters, Lion Masks On Side, C.1910 1200.00
Faberge, Box, Cigarette, Gold Mounted Nephrite, Red Enamel, 4 1/2 In. 6500.00
Faberge, Box, Silver, Gold, Enamel, Strawberry Red, Sunray Cover, 2 5/8 In. 2750.00
Faberge, Buckle, Silver, Gilt, Gold, Translucent Enamel, Seed Pearls, 2 3/4 In. 800.00
Faberge, Carving, Georg Wild, Obsidian Panther, Signed, Numbered, 12 X 11 In. 3000.00
Faberge, Case, Cigarette, Silver, Enamel, Boyar & Wife On Bridge, 4 In. 2500.00
Faberge, Cup, Vodka, Silver, Gilt, Shaded Enamel, Flowers On Apricot, 2 3/4 In. 1500.00
Faberge, Dish, Silver Gilt, Translucent Enamel, Triangular, Case, 3 3/4 In. 3500.00
Faberge, Dressing Table Set, Silver Gilt, Shaded Enamel, Holly, Iris, 3 Piece 3000.00
Faberge, Falcon, Gray Agate And Gold, Brilliant Eyes, Wood Box, 1 1/8 In. 2000.00
Faberge, Figurine, Georg Wild, Mineral Carving, Obsidian Horse, Signed 1200.00
Faberge, Frame, Silver, Enamel, Swags Of Leafage, Silver Gilt Easel, 8 3/8 In. 5250.00
Faberge, Frog, Bowenite, Brilliant Eyes, C.1900, 1 3/8 X 2 5/8 In. 3250.00
Faberge, Jug, Silver, Etched Red Glass, Bulbous Body, 6 1/4 In. 1500.00
Faberge, Knife, Paper, Nephrite, Mounted In Silver Gilt And Enamel, 11 In. 900.00
Faberge, Letter Opener, Gold, Enamel, Bowenite, Cabochon Red Stones, 8 3/8 In. 3200.00
Faberge, Pencil, Gold & Enamel, C.1870, Crests, 4 Enameled Plaques, 2 1/2 In. 750.00
Faberge, Pencil, Gold, Reeded And Chased Case, Vladimir Soloviev, 2 1/2 In. 400.00
Faberge, Pitcher, Silver Mounted Cut Glass, 11 In. 1600.00
Faberge, Salt & Spoon, Silver Gilt & Enamel, Fitted Case, Set Of 4, 1 1/2 In. 3000.00
Faberge, Sugar, Silver, Art Nouveau Water Plants, 8 1/4 In. 1100.00
Faberge, Tongs, Sugar, Hallmarked, 5 In. 165.00 To 475.00
Faberge, Trophy, Silver, 2nd Imperial Racing, C.1903, 26 In. 4000.00
Faience, Candlestick, Gaudy Decoration, Hand-Painted, Blue, Orange, Green, Pair 110.00
Faience, Charger, Cupid & Piper Medallion, Blue & White, Early 1700s 600.00
Faience, Dish, Hen Cover, Yellow Basketweave Base, Egersung, 7 1/2 In. 100.00
Faience, Figurine, Elephant, German, White, Yellow Tusks, JH Mark, 10 7/8 In. 1400.00
Faience, Figurine, Man In Sunday Best Walking, Copenhagen, 1903, 6 1/2 In. 38.00
Faience, Figurine, Woman, Basket Of Eggs On Head, Copenhagen, 1903, 6 1/2 In. 38.00
Faience, Flask, Book, Green, Ochre, Lion Rampant Cover, Talavera, 18th Century 500.00

Faience, Inkstand, Octagonal, Flowers, 4 Holes, Ship Crest, St.Jean De Luz 225.00
Faience, Inkwell, Octagon Shape, Royal Blue, Rust, Red, Artist Signed 60.00
Faience, Inkwell, Red, Rust, Blue, Enameled, Rouen, Marked, Dated 1780, No Insets 85.00
Faience, Inkwell, Rounded Curves, Dome Cover, Marked Chantilly Bugle & C.L. 200.00
Faience, Jug, Blue & White, Pewter Mounted, Ludwigsburg, 10 In. 700.00
Faience, Planter, Hanging Hat, 5 1/2 X 7 3/4 In. 88.00
Faience, Pot, Cache, Gaudy Decoration, Hand-Painted, Blue, Orange, Green 60.00
Faience, Stein, Peasants Observing Castle, Blue, White, & Green, 1769, 8 In. 650.00

Fairings are small souvenir china boxes sold at country fairs during the nineteenth century.

Fairing Box, Trinket, Draped Table, Tea Set On Lid, Green, 6 1/4 In. 95.00
Fairing, Box, Trinket, Bible, Crucifix, Chalice On Lid 45.00
Fairing, Box, Trinket, Boy With Boat & Mirror 40.00
Fairing, Box, Trinket, Child In Front Of Mirror, 1 1/2 X 1 1/4 X 2 1/2 In. 45.00
Fairing, Broken Chamber Pot, Girl Sitting On Top Hat, Staffordshire Type 85.00
Fairing, Happy Father, What, Two?yes Sir, Two Little Beauties, 4 In. 95.00
Fairing, Matchbox, Reclining Dog, Trumpet & Ball On Lid, Staffordshire 38.00
Fairing, Toddler In Tub, Paddling His Own Canoe, Goss & Crest, 4 In. 85.00
Fairing, Toddler Piggyback On Little Girl 45.00
Fairing, Tug O' War, Child & Dog Pulling On Doll 98.00
Fairing, Twelve Months After Marriage 65.00
Famille Rose, see Chinese Export
Fan, see also Store, Fan
Fan, Ceiling, Iron And Wood Blades, Fancy 100.00
Fan, Cellophane, Ivory Color, Silk Ribbon, Roses On Edges 20.00
Fan, Cotton Satin, Hand-Painted Flowers & Birds 27.50
Fan, Feather, Hand-Painted, Florals, Gold Sticks, 18 In. 25.00
Fan, French, Colonial Scene, Carved & Painted Spokes, Artist Signed 45.00
Fan, Geisha Girl, Silk 5.00
Fan, Hand-Painted On Silk, Dog & Books 25.00
Fan, Hand-Painted Peacock, Spread Plumage, Sequins, Mother-Of-Pearl Ribs 47.50
Fan, Hand-Painted Sweet Peas, Sequins, Ivory Ribs, Enamel Flowers 45.00
Fan, Ivory And Lace, C.1900 ..... 39.00
Fan, Ivory Posts, Black Net Decorated With Sequins 15.00
Fan, Ivory, Oriental Scene, Punchwork, Mother-Of-Pearl Inlay 20.00
Fan, Ivory, Ribbon Laced, 19 Carved Stays, Oriental, 10 1/2 In. 45.00
Fan, Long Black Net 7.50
Fan, Maribou Feathers, Satin, Hand Painted 85.00
Fan, Oriental, Woven Straw, Gold Trim, Black Lacquer Handle 7.50
Fan, Ostrich Plume, Blue, Tortoise Shell Bracelet Mounting 11.00
Fan, Pearl Ends & Spokes, Beige Fabric, Silver Sequin Design, 8 X 15 In. 30.00
Fan, Pheasant's Feathers, Tortoiseshell Sticks 35.00
Fan, Satin, Flowers & Butterflies In Gold, Brown Birch Stick 25.00
Fan, Silk, Black, Yellow, Green Flowers, Wood Stick With Silver Lacy Design 25.00
Fan, Silk, Cream With White Flowers, Ivory Sticks, Large 27.50
Fan, Souvenir Of 1876 Centennial, Scenes Of Buildings 50.00
Fan, Victorian Bride's, Ivory Slats, Lace, Paillettes, Hand-Painted 19.00
Fan, White Ostrich Feathers, Ivory Sticks 14.00
Fan, White Ostrich, Celluloid Handle, Opens To 16 1/2 X 27 In. 55.00
Fan, Wood & Cloth, Hand-Painted Floral, Folding 12.00

Fenton Art Glass Company, founded in Martins Ferry, Ohio, by Frank L.Fenton, is now located in Williamstown, West Virginia. It is noted for early carnival glass produced between 1907 and 1920. Many other types of glass were also made.

Fenton, Basket, Burmese, Maple Leaf 35.00
Fenton, Bowl, Flame, Opaque Scarlet & Orange, Shallow Cupped 35.00
Fenton, Creamer, White Opalescent 10.00
Fenton, Cruet, Burmese, Hand-Painted Flowers 75.00
Fenton, Dish, Amberina Basketweave, 1930s 95.00
Fenton, Dish, Water Lily & Cattails, Handled 25.00
Fenton, Jar, Biscuit, Red Slag, Wicker Handle, 1930s 95.00
Fenton, Jar, Cracker, Vaseline, Opalescent, Hobnail, Reeded Handle 85.00

Fenton, Punch Set, Satin Type, Holly & Berries, Marked F In Shield, 13 Piece 50.00
Fenton, Rose Bowl, Amberina Hobnail 30.00
Fenton, Vase, Art Deco, Green, Dancing Females As Harem Ladies, 9 In. 85.00
Fenton, Vase, Fan, Red Slag, 1930s 35.00
Fenton, Vase, Hat Shape, Opalescent, Swirl, Royal Blue, Crimped Edge 35.00
Fenton, Vase, Murrhina Cased, Green And Pink, 1964 .... 75.00
Fenton, Vase, Pink & White, Ruffled Edge 14.00
Fenton, Vase, Pink Hobnail In Brass Mount 65.00

Fiesta dinnerware was introduced in 1936 by the Homer Laughlin China Co., redesigned in 1969, and withdrawn in 1973. The simple design was characterized by a band of concentric circles, beginning at the rim. Cups had full-circle handles until 1969, when partial-circle handles were made. Harlequin and Riviera were related wares.

Fiesta Ware, Ashtray, Gray .... 10.00 To 12.00
Fiesta Ware, Ashtray, Red .... 15.00 To 20.00
Fiesta Ware, Ashtray, Turquoise 12.50
Fiesta Ware, Ashtray, White 12.00
Fiesta Ware, Ashtray, Yellow 8.00
Fiesta Ware, Bowl, Aqua, 8 1/2 In. 6.50
Fiesta Ware, Bowl, Blue, 9 1/2 In. 7.50
Fiesta Ware, Bowl, Green, Kitchen Kraft, 6 In. 10.00
Fiesta Ware, Bowl, Green, 5 1/2 In. 4.00
Fiesta Ware, Bowl, Green, 8 1/2 In. 4.75
Fiesta Ware, Bowl, Green, 9 1/2 In. 7.50
Fiesta Ware, Bowl, Ivory, 5 1/2 In. 4.00
Fiesta Ware, Bowl, Medium Green, 8 1/2 In. 7.00
Fiesta Ware, Bowl, Rose Color, 4 1/2 In. 4.00
Fiesta Ware, Bowl, Yellow, 9 1/2 In. 8.00
Fiesta Ware, Cake Set, Ivory, Floral, Gold Trim, 7 Piece 85.00
Fiesta Ware, Carafe, Cobalt 22.00
Fiesta Ware, Casserole, Covered, Aqua 25.00
Fiesta Ware, Coffeepot, After Dinner, Light Green 42.50
Fiesta Ware, Coffeepot, Demitasse, Green 65.00
Fiesta Ware, Coffeepot, Gold, Casualstone 15.00
Fiesta Ware, Coffeepot, Green 40.00
Fiesta Ware, Coffeepot, Ivory 15.00
Fiesta Ware, Coffeepot, Red .... 23.00 To 27.00
Fiesta Ware, Compote, Fruit, Ivory 35.00
Fiesta Ware, Compote, Fruit, White, 12 In. 18.00
Fiesta Ware, Compote, Fruit, Yellow 22.00
Fiesta Ware, Compote, Sweetmeat, Ivory 12.00
Fiesta Ware, Compote, Yellow, 12 In. 18.00
Fiesta Ware, Creamer, Green, Stick Handle 4.00
Fiesta Ware, Creamer, Orange, Stick 7.00
Fiesta Ware, Creamer, Red 5.00
Fiesta Ware, Cup & Saucer, After Dinner Coffee, Navy 17.50
Fiesta Ware, Cup & Saucer, After Dinner, Blue 15.00
Fiesta Ware, Cup & Saucer, After Dinner, Green 15.00
Fiesta Ware, Cup & Saucer, Blue 22.50
Fiesta Ware, Cup & Saucer, Demitasse, Orange 16.00
Fiesta Ware, Cup & Saucer, Green 6.00
Fiesta Ware, Cup & Saucer, Light Green 6.50
Fiesta Ware, Cup & Saucer, Navy 6.50
Fiesta Ware, Cup & Saucer, Turquoise .... 5.25 To 6.50
Fiesta Ware, Cup & Saucer, White 5.75
Fiesta Ware, Cup, Red 6.00
Fiesta Ware, Egg Cooker Set, Hankscraft, Oval Metal Tray 42.50
Fiesta Ware, Eggcup, Gray 9.90
Fiesta Ware, Eggcup, Navy 11.00
Fiesta Ware, Fruit Bowl, Navy, 4 3/4 In. 3.50
Fiesta Ware, Gravy Boat, Cobalt 7.00
Fiesta Ware, Gravy Boat, Light Green 6.00
Fiesta Ware, Gravy Boat, Orange 15.00

Fiesta Ware, Gravy Boat, Turquoise 6.00
Fiesta Ware, Jar, Covered, Green, Kitchen Kraft 65.00
Fiesta Ware, Jar, Marmalade, Gold, Casualstone 15.00
Fiesta Ware, Jug, Medium Green, 2 Pint 11.50
Fiesta Ware, Mug, Medium Green 30.00
Fiesta Ware, Mug, Red 35.00
Fiesta Ware, Mug, Turquoise 14.50
Fiesta Ware, Mug, Yellow 12.00
Fiesta Ware, Nappy, Dark Blue, Metal Holder, 9 1/2 In. 16.00
Fiesta Ware, Nappy, Light Green, 9 1/2 In. 8.00
Fiesta Ware, Nappy, Red, Metal Holder, 9 1/2 In. .... 20.00 To 50.00
Fiesta Ware, Pitcher, Juice, Gray 28.00
Fiesta Ware, Pitcher, Juice, Gray With 6 Tumblers 47.50
Fiesta Ware, Pitcher, Juice, Yellow 7.50
Fiesta Ware, Pitcher, Water, Blue, Disk 10.00
Fiesta Ware, Pitcher, Water, Red 20.00
Fiesta Ware, Pitcher, Water, Turquoise 10.00
Fiesta Ware, Pitcher, Water, Yellow, Disc 9.00
Fiesta Ware, Pitcher, Yellow, Quart 12.00
Fiesta Ware, Plate, Blue, 6 In. 2.00
Fiesta Ware, Plate, Blue, 7 In. 3.00
Fiesta Ware, Plate, Blue, 9 In. 4.00
Fiesta Ware, Plate, Chartreuse, 7 In. 1.25
Fiesta Ware, Plate, Chop, Green, 15 In. 12.00
Fiesta Ware, Plate, Chop, Red, 12 In. 15.00
Fiesta Ware, Plate, Chop, Red, 14 In. 15.00
Fiesta Ware, Plate, Chop, White, 13 In. 3.00
Fiesta Ware, Plate, Chop, Yellow, 13 In. 7.00
Fiesta Ware, Plate, Cobalt, 7 In. 1.25
Fiesta Ware, Plate, Dinner, Yellow 1.50
Fiesta Ware, Plate, Gray, 7 In. 1.25
Fiesta Ware, Plate, Green, Compartments, 11 5/8 In. 8.90
Fiesta Ware, Plate, Green, 6 In. .... 1.50 To 2.00
Fiesta Ware, Plate, Green, 7 In. .... 1.25 To 3.00
Fiesta Ware, Plate, Green, 9 In. 2.50
Fiesta Ware, Plate, Ivory, 7 In. 1.25
Fiesta Ware, Plate, Ivory, 9 In. 1.50
Fiesta Ware, Plate, Light Green, 6 In. 1.00
Fiesta Ware, Plate, Light Green, 7 In. 1.25
Fiesta Ware, Plate, Light Green, 9 In. .... 1.50 To 1.75
Fiesta Ware, Plate, Navy, 7 In. 1.30
Fiesta Ware, Plate, Navy, 9 In. 1.50
Fiesta Ware, Plate, Orange, 6 In. 2.00
Fiesta Ware, Plate, Orange, 7 In. 3.00
Fiesta Ware, Plate, Orange, 9 In. .... 2.50 To 4.00
Fiesta Ware, Plate, Pie, Yellow 25.00
Fiesta Ware, Plate, Red, 11 In. 2.50
Fiesta Ware, Plate, Turquoise, 7 In. 1.25
Fiesta Ware, Plate, Turquoise, 8 In. 4.25
Fiesta Ware, Plate, Turquoise, 9 In. 1.50
Fiesta Ware, Plate, Yellow, Metal & Raffia Handle, 12 In. 5.00
Fiesta Ware, Plate, Yellow, Sectioned, 10 1/2 In. 3.00
Fiesta Ware, Plate, Yellow, 6 In. 1.00
Fiesta Ware, Plate, Yellow, 7 In. 3.00
Fiesta Ware, Plate, Yellow, 9 In. 1.75
Fiesta Ware, Platter, Gravyboat, Gold, Casualstone 4.00
Fiesta Ware, Platter, Turquoise, 12 1/2 In. 3.50
Fiesta Ware, Relish Set, Aqua, 6 Piece 25.00
Fiesta Ware, Relish, Turquoise 40.00
Fiesta Ware, Salad Bowl, Turquoise, Footed 50.00
Fiesta Ware, Salt & Pepper, Green 4.00
Fiesta Ware, Salt & Pepper, Turquoise, Ball Shape 6.00
Fiesta Ware, Saltshaker, Cobalt 3.00
Fiesta Ware, Saucer, Green 1.00

Fiesta Ware, Saucer, Ivory 1.00
Fiesta Ware, Saucer, Red 1.50
Fiesta Ware, Server, Tidbit, Medium Green, 2 Tiers 45.00
Fiesta Ware, Sugar & Creamer, Cobalt 7.00
Fiesta Ware, Sugar & Creamer, Cover, Yellow 7.00
Fiesta Ware, Sugar & Creamer, Light Green 6.50
Fiesta Ware, Sugar, Covered, Ivory 3.75
Fiesta Ware, Syrup, Green 49.90
Fiesta Ware, Teapot, Cobalt 15.00
Fiesta Ware, Teapot, Green 18.00
Fiesta Ware, Teapot, Turquoise .... 18.00 To 23.00
Fiesta Ware, Tray, Relish, Multicolor Inserts, Red 30.00
Fiesta Ware, Tumbler, Ivory, 10 Ozs. 8.95
Fiesta Ware, Tumbler, Turquoise 9.00
Fiesta Ware, Tumbler, Yellow, 10 Ozs. 8.95
Fiesta Ware, Vase, Bud, Red 20.00
Fiesta Ware, Vase, Cobalt, 8 In. 60.00
Fiesta Ware, Vase, Green, 6 1/4 In. 85.00
Fiesta Ware, Vase, Green, 8 In. 90.00

Findlay, or onyx, glass was made using three layers of glass. It was manufactured by the Dalzell Gilmore Leighton Company about 1889 in Findlay, Ohio. The silver, ruby, or black pattern was molded into the glass. The glass came in several colors, but was usually white or ruby.

Findlay Onyx, Butter, Raspberry Tint With Platinum 700.00
Findlay Onyx, Sugar Shaker 285.00

Findlay Onyx, Sugar, Covered, Platinum, 5 3/4 In.High

Findlay Onyx, Sugar, Covered, Platinum, 5 3/4 In.High .... *Illus* 500.00
Findlay Onyx, Tumbler, Barrel Shape, Ivory With Silver Florals 300.00
Fire, Andiron, Brass & Wrought Iron, Scrolled Base, C.1700, 29 1/2 In., Pair 1700.00
Fire, Andiron, Brass, Ball Top, Pair 27.00
Fire, Andiron, Brass, C.1820, 18 In., Pair 250.00
Fire, Andiron, Brass, C.1850, Pair 195.00
Fire, Andiron, Brass, Pineapple, 26 In., Pair 450.00
Fire, Andiron, C.1789 .... 450.00
Fire, Andiron, Hessian, Cast Iron, 19 1/2 In., Pair 150.00
Fire, Andiron, Iron, Gooseneck, C.1750, 24 X 13 In., Pair 128.00
Fire, Andiron, Long Gooseneck, 23 In., Pair 88.00
Fire, Andiron, New York, C.1780, Brass, Urn Finial, 26 In., Pair 2100.00
Fire, Andiron, Regency, Iron, Black, 14 X 13 1/2 In., Pair 55.00
Fire, Andiron, Wrought & Cast Iron, Curled Feet, 16 1/2 In., Pair 100.00
Fire, Andiron, Wrought Iron, Northwind, 38 In., Pair 450.00
Fire, Ax Head, Spike 10.00
Fire, Bellows & Tender, Blacksmith's 90.00
Fire, Bellows, Fireplace, Copper & Leather, Embossed Man Smoking Pipe 35.00
Fire, Bellows, Yellow Paint, Decorated, C.1835 .... 125.00
Fire, Bin, Coal, Tole, Stenciled, Claw Feet, Victorian 42.00
Fire, Box, Coal, Wooden, Brass Handle & Trim 110.00
Fire, Box, Firewood, Copper Clad, Sailing Ship Scene 35.00
Fire, Brass, Andirons, Adam Shape, 18 In. 68.00

Fire, Bucket, Leather, Painted Red .... *Illus* 160.00
Fire, Bucket, Leather, 1804 .... *Illus* 180.00
Fire, Bucket, Lechlade Manor Fire, Iron, Red, Black, & Yellow 85.00
Fire, Chenet, French, Bronze & Onyx, Reticulated Crossbar, 18 In., Pair 1200.00
Fire, Coal Hod, Helmet Shape, White Paint 40.00
Fire, Dowser, Bulbous, Three Lion Faces, Mason, Clyde, N.Y.Glass Works, 1880's 25.00
Fire, Engine, Horse Cart, Gleason & Bailey Mfg. Co., Seneca Falls, N.Y.1845 .... 3850.00
Fire, Extinguisher, Copper & Brass 27.50
Fire, Fender, Fireplace, Brass & Cast Iron, Ornate, 32 In. 35.00
Fire, Fender, Fireplace, Brass, 54 X 14 In. 188.00
Fire, Fireplace Front, Bird's-Eye Maple, Mirror, Pillared, C.1860, 7 Ft. 5000.00
Fire, Fireplace Set, Brass & Iron, Shovel, Poker, & 22 In. Stand, 3 Piece 35.00
Fire, Grate, Empire Brass, Steel And Iron, Lion's Mask Ring Handle, 31 In. 425.00

Fire, Salvage Bag, Linen, 1803

Fire, Bucket, Leather, Painted Red

Fire, Bucket, Leather, 1804

Fire, Hat, Painted Beaver's Skin, Washington, 1796

Fire, Hat, Painted Beaver's Skin, Washington, 1796 .... *Illus* 700.00
Fire, Hook, Fireplace, Iron, 16 In. 22.00
Fire, Hook, Snaffle, Fireplace, Iron Chain 170.00
Fire, Horn, Fireman's Speaking, Ellicott Hose Co., Batavia, Silver Plate 80.00
Fire, Ladle, Hearth, Iron, Long Handle 125.00
Fire, Lantern, Dietz, King, Copper Bottom, Brass Handle 65.00
Fire, Nozzle, Brass, 2 Handles On Connecting End, 2 1/2 Ft. 45.00
Fire, Nozzle, Hose, Brass, 10 In. 12.50
Fire, Pot, Ring For Hanging On Crane, Copper, 8 X 6 1/2 In. 65.00
Fire, Pump, Fire Fighter's Hand, Brass, Hanging Chain, 32 In. 27.50
Fire, Raker, Ash, For Wood Stove 2.00
Fire, Roaster, Chestnut, Fireplace, Brass, Openwork Handle, Copper Studs 65.00
Fire, Roaster, Chestnut, Perrage, England, C.1900, Brass 40.00
Fire, Salvage Bag, Linen, 1803 .... *Illus* 260.00
Fire, Screen, Chippendale, Still Life & Landscape Paintings 1675.00
Fire, Screen, Fireplace, English, Oak 52.00
Fire, Screen, Fireplace, Walnut, Reversible Oil Painting, Ornate 150.00
Fire, Screen, Leather, Hand-Painted Florals, 3 Panels, European, 39 X 48 In. 800.00
Fire, Scuttle, Coal, Brass, American Shields, 15 In. 268.00
Fire, Scuttle, Coal, Copper, Iron Bail Top Handle & End Grip, 18 In. 175.00
Fire, Scuttle, Coal, Copper, 3 In. 6.00
Fire, Shovel, Never Break, Iron 5.00
Fire, Siren, Midway, Ga., Fire Truck, 1937, Copper, 6 Volts 95.00
Fire, Stove, Cast Iron, Acme, Pans, Lifter 125.00
Fire, Stove, Child's Eagle Coal Range, 7 Cooking Units, Iron, 23 In. 75.00
Fire, Stove, Cook, Model No.P881, Copper Clad, Warming Shelf, 4 Ft. 200.00
Fire, Stove, Eager Beaver, Japan, Cast Iron, Filigree, Grate Top, 5 In. 12.00

Fire, Stove, Florence, No.153, Hot Blast, C.1920 .... 85.00
Fire, Stove, Old Comfort Range, Reversible Reservoir 125.00
Fire, Stove, Perfection Stove Co., Cleveland, O., Kerosene, 2 Burners, 30 In. 185.00
Fire, Stove, Potbelly, Cast Iron, Montgomery Ward, 4 Lids At Top 300.00
Fire, Stove, Potbelly, Four Eyes 175.00
Fire, Stove, Railroad, Cabin, Cast Iron Spears 450.00
Fire, Stove, Royal Princess, Porcelain Medallion 350.00
Fire, Stove, Wood, Pink 150.00
Fire, Tile, Stove, Superior, Cherubs In Grape Arbor, 7 X 4 In. 25.00
Fire, Trivet, Fireplace Cooking, Hand-Forged Iron, 3 Legs, Handle, 22 In. 38.00
Fire, Trivet, Fireplace, Footman, Home Sweet Home, Queen Anne Legs, C.1830 .... 268.00
Fire, Trivet, Fireplace, Hand-Forged Iron, 3 Legs, 17 In. 90.00

Fireglow glass resembles English Bristol glass. But a reddish-brown color can be seen when the piece is held to the light. It is a form of art glass made by the Boston and Sandwich Glass Co.of Massachusetts, and other companies.

Fireglow, Vase, Ruffled, Dotted Enamel Flower, Sandwich, 3 3/4 In. 50.00
Fireglow, Vase, Sepia & Brown Shells, Ruffled, Sandwich, 7 1/2 In. 1375.00

Fireplace Tools, see Fire, Tongs, etc.

Fischer porcelain was made in Herend, Hungary. The factory was founded in 1839, and has continued working into the twentieth century. The wares are sometimes referred to as Herend porcelain.

Fischer, Bowl, Punch, Tray, 8 Cups, Clematis, Gold, Signed K.Franz 600.00
Fischer, Box, Insect, Covered, 6-Legged Insect Shape, Meig, 4 1/2 In. 85.00
Fischer, Candlestick, Applied Roses On Base, Green Leaves, Gold, 5 In. 35.00
Fischer, Dish, Openwork, Gold Touches, Birds, 7 X 7 In. 37.50
Fischer, Egg, Easter, Polychrome & Gilt, Reticulated, Blue Mark, 4 1/2 In. 85.00
Fischer, Egg, Hand-Painted, Stamped Blue Trademark, 5 In. 75.00
Fischer, Ewer, Pastel Colors 135.00
Fischer, Ewer, Snake Handle, Hand Painted, C.1850, 17 In. 148.00
Fischer, Figurine, Bird, Colors, Signed, 8 1/2 In. 75.00
Fischer, Figurine, Bird, Long Tail, 8 1/2 In. 75.00
Fischer, Figurine, Cat, Sitting, White, 5 1/2 In. 36.00
Fischer, Figurine, Cat, White Except For Eyes, Sitting, 4 1/4 In. 36.00
Fischer, Inkstand, Pierced Railing, Porcelain Bouquet Center, Blue Mark 150.00
Fischer, Pitcher, Royal Blue With Gold, 1895, 16 X 13 In. 625.00
Fischer, Vase, Blue, Gold Openwork, Fish Scale, 14 X 10 In. 175.00
Fischer, Vase, Pottery, Openwork, Florals, Cameo Areas, 19 1/2 In. 275.00
Fischer, Vase, Reticulated, Blue Florals, Green & Brown Foliage, Gold Handles 115.00
Fischer, Vase, Signed Budapest, Pair 195.00
Flaconware, Toby Mug, Dick Turpin, Caramel Glaze, 4 1/2 In. 20.00

Flag, see Textile, Flag

Flash Gordon, Book, Power Men Of Mongo 16.00
Flash Gordon, Book, Tournaments Of Mongo, Big Little Book 20.00
Flash Gordon, Compass, Wrist Strap 22.00
Flash Gordon, Ring, Cereal Premium 6.50
Flash Gordon, Toy, Space Ship 65.00

Flatiron, see Kitchen, Flatiron

Flow blue, or flo blue, was made in England about 1830 to 1900. The plates were printed with designs using a cobalt blue coloring. The color flowed from the design to the white plate so the finished plate had a smeared blue design. The plates were usually made of ironstone china.

Flow Blue, Bowl, Alaska, Scalloped Rim, 9 3/4 In. 25.00
Flow Blue, Bowl, Argyle, Oval, 9 1/4 X 7 1/2 In. 30.00
Flow Blue, Bowl, Berry, Large, Lois 20.00
Flow Blue, Bowl, Blue Floral, Gilt Tracery, Luneville, K & G, France, 5 1/2 In. 15.00
Flow Blue, Bowl, Brushstroke Painted, C.1900, 10 In. 35.00
Flow Blue, Bowl, Covered Vegetable, Shanghai, J.F.& Co., 1860, 11 1/2 In. 285.00
Flow Blue, Bowl, Floral, Grindley, 7 1/2 In. 14.50
Flow Blue, Bowl, Jeddo, 10 In. 35.00
Flow Blue, Bowl, La Belle, Leaf Shape, 11 In. 45.00

Flow Blue, Bowl, Lid & Ladle, Eric, 7 In.Across 45.00
Flow Blue, Bowl, Madras, Royal Doulton, 10 3/4 X 8 1/4 In. 30.00
Flow Blue, Bowl, Mattean, Hancock, 9 1/4 In. 35.00
Flow Blue, Bowl, Octagonal, Open, Scinde, Alcock, C.1840, 8 1/2 X 6 1/2 In. 75.00
Flow Blue, Bowl, Oval Vegetable, Argyle, 7 X 10 In. 25.00
Flow Blue, Bowl, Oval Vegetable, Ridgway, Dundee, 10 X 7 1/2 In. 35.00
Flow Blue, Bowl, Raised Scrolls, Flowered Band, Oval, 9 1/2 X 6 1/2 In. 12.00
Flow Blue, Bowl, Soup, Cashmere, 10 In. 55.00
Flow Blue, Bowl, Soup, Flora, K & Co., 10 In. 7.50
Flow Blue, Bowl, Soup, Indian Urn 29.00
Flow Blue, Bowl, Soup, Kyber, 9 In. 25.00
Flow Blue, Bowl, Soup, Osborne, Grindley 25.00
Flow Blue, Bowl, Soup, Portman, Grindley, 7 1/2 In. 15.00
Flow Blue, Bowl, Soup, Shanghai, Globe Mark 12.50
Flow Blue, Bowl, Vegetable, Alaska, Grindley, 10 In. 38.00
Flow Blue, Bowl, Vegetable, Conway, 9 In. .... 22.50 To 30.00
Flow Blue, Bowl, Vegetable, Covered Le Pavot, Grindley, 11 1/2 X 8 In. 65.00
Flow Blue, Bowl, Vegetable, Covered, Fairy Villas, 12 X 9 X 5 1/2 In. 125.00
Flow Blue, Bowl, Vegetable, Covered, Jeddo, Adams 240.00
Flow Blue, Bowl, Vegetable, Covered, Kiji, 2 Handles, Ashworth, 12 In. 150.00
Flow Blue, Bowl, Vegetable, Covered, Temple, P.W.& Co., C.1850, Octagonal 175.00
Flow Blue, Bowl, Vegetable, Covered, Togo, Oval, F.Winkle 75.00
Flow Blue, Bowl, Vegetable, Fairy Villas, 12 X 9 In. 75.00
Flow Blue, Bowl, Vegetable, Floral Garland, Johnson Bros., Oval 30.00
Flow Blue, Bowl, Vegetable, Individual, Fairy Villas, Wm.Adams & Co. 24.00
Flow Blue, Bowl, Vegetable, Keswick 25.00
Flow Blue, Bowl, Vegetable, Lorne, Grindley, Oval, 10 In. 40.00
Flow Blue, Bowl, Vegetable, Melbourne, Grindley, Oval, 9 1/2 In. 25.00
Flow Blue, Bowl, Vegetable, Normandy, Gold Trim, Johnson Bros., 8 1/2 In. 45.00
Flow Blue, Bowl, Vegetable, Pekin 30.00
Flow Blue, Bowl, Vegetable, Roseville, Oval, 8 1/2 In. 17.50
Flow Blue, Bowl, Vegetable, Togo, 9 X 7 In. 85.00
Flow Blue, Bowl, Waste, Amoy, Davenport, C.1845, 7 In. 100.00
Flow Blue, Bowl, Waste, Chen Si, Meir 95.00
Flow Blue, Bowl, Waste, Normandy, Gold Trim, Johnson Bros 55.00
Flow Blue, Bowl, Waste, Versailles, Furnival, 1894 .... 18.00
Flow Blue, Bowl, Watteau, Francis Morley & Co., C.1845, 10 1/4 In. 48.00
Flow Blue, Bowl, Willow Pattern, Doulton, C.1891, 9 In. 45.00
Flow Blue, Butter Pat, Brussels .... 7.00 To 8.00
Flow Blue, Butter Pat, Celtic, Grindley 12.00
Flow Blue, Butter Pat, Delph 8.00
Flow Blue, Butter Pat, Marie Grindley 7.00
Flow Blue, Butter Pat, Montana, Johnson 10.00
Flow Blue, Butter Pat, Normandy, Gold Trim, Johnson Bros. 13.00
Flow Blue, Butter Pat, Versailles, Furnival, 1894 .... 8.00
Flow Blue, Butter, Blue Manilla 38.00
Flow Blue, Butter, Covered, Drain, Round Chip Cover, Montana, Johnson 65.00
Flow Blue, Butter, Covered, Melbourne, Insert, Grindley 95.00
Flow Blue, Butter, Covered, Normandy, Gold Trim, Johnson Bros. 75.00
Flow Blue, Celery, Versailles, Furnival, 1894, 10 X 5 1/4 In. 18.00
Flow Blue, Cereal Bowl, Lorne, Grindley, 6 1/2 In. 14.00
Flow Blue, Chamber Pot, Doulton, Burslem 95.00
Flow Blue, Chamber Pot, Tulip, 8 In. 53.00
Flow Blue, Coffeepot, Amoy, Davenport, C.1845, 10 In. 275.00
Flow Blue, Coffeepot, Scinde, Alcock, C.1840 .... 350.00
Flow Blue, Creamer, Amoy, Davenport, C.1845 .... 125.00
Flow Blue, Creamer, Dundee, Ridgway 75.00
Flow Blue, Creamer, Holland, Alfred Meakin 45.00
Flow Blue, Creamer, Lorne, Grindley 65.00
Flow Blue, Creamer, Nonpareil, Burgess & Leigh 75.00
Flow Blue, Creamer, Normandy, Gold Trim, Johnson Bros. 75.00
Flow Blue, Creamer, Peking, C.1845 .... 98.00
Flow Blue, Creamer, Touraine, Stanley 55.00
Flow Blue, Creamer, Versailles, Furnival, 1894 .... 30.00

Flow Blue, Creamer, Virginia, Maddock 75.00
Flow Blue, Cup & Saucer, Amoy, Davenport 55.00
Flow Blue, Cup & Saucer, Argyle, Grindley 45.00
Flow Blue, Cup & Saucer, Argyle, 1896 .... 40.00
Flow Blue, Cup & Saucer, Bouillon, Shanghai, 2 Handled 35.00
Flow Blue, Cup & Saucer, Demitasse, Idris, Grindley 15.00
Flow Blue, Cup & Saucer, Fairy Villas, Adams 35.00
Flow Blue, Cup & Saucer, Handleless, Coburg, J.Edwards, C.1860 .... 55.00
Flow Blue, Cup & Saucer, Handleless, Farmer Size, Scinde, Alcock, C.1840 .... 70.00
Flow Blue, Cup & Saucer, Handleless, Lustre Band, Elsmore & Forster, C.1860 .... 40.00
Flow Blue, Cup & Saucer, Handleless, Strawberry, T.Walker, C.1856 .... 55.00
Flow Blue, Cup & Saucer, Hofburg 25.00
Flow Blue, Cup & Saucer, Indian 60.00
Flow Blue, Cup & Saucer, Kyber, Adams 35.00
Flow Blue, Cup & Saucer, Lorne, Grindley 25.00
Flow Blue, Cup & Saucer, Martha Washington 50.00
Flow Blue, Cup & Saucer, Martha Washington, States, Shawmut Co., Boston 75.00
Flow Blue, Cup & Saucer, Melbourne, Grindley 32.50
Flow Blue, Cup & Saucer, Normandy, Gold Trim, Johnson Bros. 35.00
Flow Blue, Cup & Saucer, Oriental, Alcock 50.00
Flow Blue, Cup & Saucer, Oriental, Ridgway 50.00
Flow Blue, Cup & Saucer, Osborne, Grindley 26.50
Flow Blue, Cup & Saucer, Scinde, Alcock, C.1840 .... 65.00
Flow Blue, Cup & Saucer, Touraine .... 29.00 To 33.50
Flow Blue, Cup & Saucer, Versailles, Furnival, 1894 .... 30.00
Flow Blue, Cup & Saucer, Virginia, Maddock 28.00
Flow Blue, Cup & Saucer, Waldorf 38.00
Flow Blue, Cup & Saucer, Wheel 45.00
Flow Blue, Cup, Bouillon, Shanghai, 2 Handles 20.00
Flow Blue, Cup, Handleless, Kin Shan 38.00
Flow Blue, Cup, Handleless, Sabroa Pattern 18.00
Flow Blue, Cup, Normandy, Gold Trim, Johnson Bros. 27.00
Flow Blue, Dish, Bone, Alton 20.00
Flow Blue, Dish, Bone, Argyle 15.00
Flow Blue, Dish, Bone, Clarence, Grindley 15.00
Flow Blue, Dish, Bone, Gironde, Grindley 13.50
Flow Blue, Dish, Bone, Nonpareil, Burgess & Leigh 25.00
Flow Blue, Dish, Candy, LaBelle, Round, Ring Handle, Fluted 50.00
Flow Blue, Dish, Celery, Gironde, Grindley 22.00
Flow Blue, Dish, Covered Vegetable, Versailles, Furnival, 1894 .... 25.00
Flow Blue, Dish, Covered, Baroque, Scinde 450.00
Flow Blue, Dish, Oval Vegetable, Individual, Dundee, Ridgway 18.00
Flow Blue, Dish, Pickle, Raised Scrolls, Flowered Band, 9 In. 8.00
Flow Blue, Dish, Pickle, Rose, Ridgway 45.00
Flow Blue, Dish, Sauce, Scinde, Alcock, C.1840, 5 1/4 In. 25.00
Flow Blue, Dish, Serving, Clyde, Florals & Acanthus, F & Sons, Burslem, 12 In. 27.00
Flow Blue, Dish, Vegetable, Oval, Covered, Madras, Doulton 75.00
Flow Blue, Dresser Set, Roses & Gold, Tray, Candlesticks, Ring Tree, Hat Pin 140.00
Flow Blue, Ewer, Chinoiserie, Tin Glaze, Flemish Boch Bros., 12 3/4 In. 175.00
Flow Blue, Gravy Boat & Underplate, Belmont 32.50
Flow Blue, Gravy Boat & Underplate, Gironde, W.H.Grindley 55.00
Flow Blue, Gravy Boat & Underplate, Lonsdale, Red, Green, & Gold, S.A.& Co. 125.00
Flow Blue, Gravy Boat & Underplate, Normandy, Gold Trim, Johnson Bros. 70.00
Flow Blue, Gravy Boat, Atlantic, W.H.Grindley 25.00
Flow Blue, Gravy Boat, Coburg, J.Edwards, C.1860 .... 65.00
Flow Blue, Gravy Boat, Denton, Grindley 25.00
Flow Blue, Gravy Boat, Gironde, Grindley 35.00
Flow Blue, Gravy Boat, Marguerite 35.00
Flow Blue, Gravy Boat, Melbourne, Grindley 25.00
Flow Blue, Gravy Boat, Paisley 35.00
Flow Blue, Gravy Boat, Portman, Grindley 35.00
Flow Blue, Gravy Boat, Scinde, Alcock, C.1840 .... 110.00
Flow Blue, Gravy Boat, With Underplate, Eclipse, Johnson 45.00
Flow Blue, Gravy, Blue Scenic, Alhambra, Late Victorian 22.00

Flow Blue, Hair Receiver, Heart Shape, Ironstone, Staffordshire 10.00
Flow Blue, Jar, Cookie, Metal Bale, Burleigh Pattern, C.1903, 5 1/2 In. 75.00
Flow Blue, Jardiniere, Gold-Outlined Floral, Haddon & K Co., 8 In. 155.00
Flow Blue, Libertas, Prussia, 9 In. 20.00
Flow Blue, Pitcher, Allerton, Mark On Bottom 58.00
Flow Blue, Pitcher, Crawford Cooking Ranges, Hanley Pottery Co., 5 In. 45.00
Flow Blue, Pitcher, Deers Around In Relief, 7 1/2 In. 55.00
Flow Blue, Pitcher, Ewer Shape, 1893 Floral Type, 11 In. 50.00
Flow Blue, Pitcher, Floral & Scroll, Gold Trim, C.1916, 7 In. 35.00
Flow Blue, Pitcher, Floral, C.1860, Quart, 7 1/2 In. 75.00
Flow Blue, Pitcher, Gravy, Fairy Villas 35.00
Flow Blue, Pitcher, Madras, Royal Doulton, 5 1/2 In. 45.00
Flow Blue, Pitcher, Milk, Gothic, Bulbous, J.Furnival, Quart, 7 In. 165.00
Flow Blue, Pitcher, Milk, Trent, 7 1/2 In. 68.00
Flow Blue, Pitcher, Nonpareil, 7 In. 150.00
Flow Blue, Pitcher, Nonpareil, 7 In.High 185.00
Flow Blue, Pitcher, Triangle, Don Quixote, 1935, 8 In. 93.00
Flow Blue, Pitcher, Virginia, 8 1/2 In. 60.00
Flow Blue, Pitcher, Wash, Helmet Shape, Floral, Cauldon .1900 .... 95.00
Flow Blue, Pitcher, Water, Labelle, Bulbous, Wheeling, 3 Quart, 8 In. 100.00
Flow Blue, Pitcher, Water, Pansy, Gold Trim, 8 3/4 In. 77.00
Flow Blue, Pitcher, Watteau, Doulton, C.1900, 5 1/2 In. 42.00
Flow Blue, Plate, Acadia, 8 1/2 In. 35.00
Flow Blue, Plate, Amoy, Davenport, C.1845, 9 1/4 In. 50.00
Flow Blue, Plate, Amoy, Davenport, C.1845, 10 In. 60.00
Flow Blue, Plate, Amoy, 8 In. 35.00
Flow Blue, Plate, Amoy, 9 In. 40.00
Flow Blue, Plate, Arabesque, Mayer, 6 In. 30.00
Flow Blue, Plate, Arabesque, T.J.& J.Mayer, 9 1/2 In. 48.50
Flow Blue, Plate, Argyle, 8 In. 18.00
Flow Blue, Plate, Bell, C.1910, 9 In. 15.00
Flow Blue, Plate, Bell, C.1910, 10 In. 18.00
Flow Blue, Plate, Belmont, 7 3/4 In. 6.95
Flow Blue, Plate, Belmont, 10 1/2 In. 9.95
Flow Blue, Plate, Blue Rose, Grindley, 6 In. 15.00
Flow Blue, Plate, Blue Rose, Grindley, 9 In. 17.00
Flow Blue, Plate, Bread & Butter, Nonpareil, 6 In. 15.00
Flow Blue, Plate, Cambridge, Meakin, 10 In. 30.00
Flow Blue, Plate, Canton, J.Edwards, C.1845, 10 1/2 In. 50.00
Flow Blue, Plate, Canton, James Edwards, C.1845, 10 1/2 In. 55.00
Flow Blue, Plate, Carlton, S.Alcock, C.1850, 9 1/2 In. 36.00
Flow Blue, Plate, Cashmere, 9 In. 50.00
Flow Blue, Plate, Castle & Lake Scene, 9 1/4 In. 35.00
Flow Blue, Plate, Cattle Scenery, Wm.Adams, 10 In. 27.00
Flow Blue, Plate, Chen-Si, 8 In. 27.00
Flow Blue, Plate, Chop, La Belle, Wheeling 18.00
Flow Blue, Plate, Conway, Newport, 10 In. 30.00
Flow Blue, Plate, Corean, Ironstone, 9 3/4 In. 28.00
Flow Blue, Plate, Damascus, Maastricht, 8 1/2 In. 25.00
Flow Blue, Plate, Darby, Wm.Grindley, 8 3/4 In. 22.50
Flow Blue, Plate, Dundee, Ridgway, 10 In. 22.00
Flow Blue, Plate, Edgewater, Gold Rim, Ridgway, 9 In. 12.00
Flow Blue, Plate, F & Sons, Douglas, Burslem, 10 1/2 In. 27.50
Flow Blue, Plate, Fairy Villas, 10 In. 35.00
Flow Blue, Plate, Fish, Flower Border, Fish Center, Dated 1886, 10 1/2 In. 25.00
Flow Blue, Plate, Formosa, Mayer, 7 1/2 In. 23.00
Flow Blue, Plate, Genevese, 9 In. 30.00
Flow Blue, Plate, George V & Mary, Commemoration, Trent, 8 1/2 In. 14.00
Flow Blue, Plate, Gironde, Grindley, 9 1/2 In. 22.00
Flow Blue, Plate, Gothic, Jacob Furnival, C.1850, 12 Sided, 10 1/4 In. 45.00
Flow Blue, Plate, Hindustan, J.Maddock, C.1855, 9 1/2 In. 38.00
Flow Blue, Plate, Hong Kong, 8 In. 25.00
Flow Blue, Plate, Hong Kong, 10 1/2 In. 45.00
Flow Blue, Plate, Indian, Pratt, 8 1/2 In. 18.00

Flow Blue, Plate, Ironstone, Excelsior, Livesley Powell & Hanley, 10 In. 65.00
Flow Blue, Plate, Ivanhoe, Friar Tuck, 10 In. 50.00
Flow Blue, Plate, Ivanhoe, Rebecca, 10 In. 50.00
Flow Blue, Plate, Japanese, W & B, 7 In. 30.00
Flow Blue, Plate, Jewel, Johnson Bros., 10 In. 22.00
Flow Blue, Plate, Knox, New Wharf Pottery, 10 In. 16.00
Flow Blue, Plate, Kyber, 7 1/2 In. 18.00
Flow Blue, Plate, Kyber, 8 In. 12.00
Flow Blue, Plate, Lakewood, Wood & Sons, 9 In. 21.00
Flow Blue, Plate, Le Parot, 8 3/4 In. 18.00
Flow Blue, Plate, Lorne, Grindley, 10 In. .... 16.95 To 20.00
Flow Blue, Plate, Lorne, Grindley, 6 In. 11.00
Flow Blue, Plate, Lorne, Grindley, 7 In. 12.50
Flow Blue, Plate, Lorne, Grindley, 8 In. 15.00
Flow Blue, Plate, Lusitania, Colley & Co., Ltd., 8 In. 10.00
Flow Blue, Plate, Lusitania, Colley & Co., Ltd., 9 In. 12.00
Flow Blue, Plate, Madras, Doulton, Burslem, 9 1/2 In. 19.00
Flow Blue, Plate, Madras, Doulton, 10 In. 25.00
Flow Blue, Plate, Manilla, 8 1/2 In. 38.00
Flow Blue, Plate, Marie, Grindley, 10 In. 18.00
Flow Blue, Plate, Marie, 8 In., Pair 32.50
Flow Blue, Plate, Martha Washington, 8 In. 40.00
Flow Blue, Plate, Melbourne, Grindley, 6 3/4 In. 10.00
Flow Blue, Plate, Melbourne, Grindley, 8 In. 14.00
Flow Blue, Plate, Melbourne, Grindley, 8 3/4 In. 16.00
Flow Blue, Plate, Montana, Johnson, 10 In. 22.00
Flow Blue, Plate, Newstone, Spode, 7 In. 35.00
Flow Blue, Plate, Nonpareil, Burgess & Leigh, 10 In. 32.00
Flow Blue, Plate, Nonpariel, 9 In. 30.00
Flow Blue, Plate, Normandy, Gold Trim, Johnson Bros., 7 In. 14.00
Flow Blue, Plate, Normandy, Gold Trim, Johnson Bros., 8 In. 16.00
Flow Blue, Plate, Normandy, Gold Trim, Johnson Bros., 9 In. 20.00
Flow Blue, Plate, Oregon, Mayer, 10 In. 60.00
Flow Blue, Plate, Oriental, New Wharf Pottery, 7 In. 24.00
Flow Blue, Plate, Oriental, New Wharf Pottery, 8 3/4 In. 18.00
Flow Blue, Plate, Oriental, Newport, 9 In. 27.50
Flow Blue, Plate, Osborne, Grindley, 6 3/4 In. 10.00
Flow Blue, Plate, Pekin, Davenport, C.1844, 10 1/4 In. .... 18.00 To 30.00
Flow Blue, Plate, Pekin, Dimmock, 10 In. 45.00
Flow Blue, Plate, Persian Moss, Sarreguemines, 9 In. 15.00
Flow Blue, Plate, Pie, Blue Rose, W.H.Grindley, 6 In. 15.00
Flow Blue, Plate, Pie, Nonpareil, Burgess & Leigh, 6 In. 22.00
Flow Blue, Plate, Poppy, Imperial Porcelain, Wedgwood, 9 In. 30.00
Flow Blue, Plate, Portman, Grindley, 8 1/2 In. 20.00
Flow Blue, Plate, Rangoon, M & Co., 1875, 9 In. 17.00
Flow Blue, Plate, Rebecca, 8 In. 35.00
Flow Blue, Plate, Ridgway, Dundee, 10 In. 24.00
Flow Blue, Plate, Scenic, Lake & Bridge, 9 1/4 In. 35.00
Flow Blue, Plate, Scinde, Alcock, C.1840, 7 1/2 In. 32.50
Flow Blue, Plate, Scinde, Alcock, C.1840, 8 1/2 In. 42.50
Flow Blue, Plate, Scinde, Alcock, C.1840, 9 1/2 In. 50.00
Flow Blue, Plate, Scinde, Alcock, 10 1/2 In. 55.00
Flow Blue, Plate, Shanghai, Furnival, 8 1/4 In. 24.50
Flow Blue, Plate, Shapoo, Boote, 8 1/4 In. 42.50
Flow Blue, Plate, Shell, 10 1/4 In. 45.00
Flow Blue, Plate, Soup, Amoy, Flange Rim, Davenport, C.1845, 10 1/2 In. 50.00
Flow Blue, Plate, Soup, Asiatic Pheasants, Huges & Son, 8 1/2 In. 19.75
Flow Blue, Plate, Soup, Celtic, 9 In. 20.00
Flow Blue, Plate, Soup, Fairy Villas, Flange Rim, Adams 20.00
Flow Blue, Plate, Soup, Flanged, Stanley 18.00
Flow Blue, Plate, Soup, Floral, Scrollwork Rim, 9 In. 20.00
Flow Blue, Plate, Soup, Scinde, Flange Rim, Alcock, C.1845, 9 1/2 In. 35.00
Flow Blue, Plate, Soup, Versailles, Furnival, 1894, 9 In. 12.00
Flow Blue, Plate, St.Louis, Flower Edge, 8 3/4 In. 15.00

Flow Blue, Plate, Staffordshire, The Narrows, The Dells, Wis., 9 3/4 In. 27.50
Flow Blue, Plate, Stanley, 8 3/4 In. 20.00
Flow Blue, Plate, Strawberry, Podmore Walker, C.1856, 7 In. 20.00
Flow Blue, Plate, Tonquin, J.Heath, 7 1/2 In. 32.00
Flow Blue, Plate, Touraine, Stanley Pottery Co., Gold Trim, 8 3/4 In. 13.00
Flow Blue, Plate, Touraine, Stanley, 10 In. 28.00
Flow Blue, Plate, Touraine, 7 1/2 In. 13.50
Flow Blue, Plate, Touraine, 7 3/4 In. 15.00
Flow Blue, Plate, Touraine, 8 1/2 In. 17.50
Flow Blue, Plate, Venus, P.S. & Co, C.1855, 10 In. 18.00
Flow Blue, Plate, Versailles, Furnival, 1894, 7 In. 8.00
Flow Blue, Plate, Versailles, Furnival, 1894, 8 In. 10.00
Flow Blue, Plate, Versailles, Furnival, 1894, 9 In. 12.00
Flow Blue, Plate, Virginia, Gold Trim, Maddock, 8 In. 21.00
Flow Blue, Plate, Virginia, Maddock, 10 In. 22.00
Flow Blue, Plate, Waldorf, New Wharf, 10 In. 20.00
Flow Blue, Plate, Waldorf, 9 In. 18.00
Flow Blue, Plate, Watteau, Doulton, 9 1/2 In. 25.00
Flow Blue, Plate, Watteau, New Wharf Pottery Co., Burslem, 1848-94 .... 22.00
Flow Blue, Plate, 9 In., Matching Dessert, Mongolia, Johnson Bros. 49.00
Flow Blue, Platter, Alaska, Grindley, 12 X 9 In. 22.00
Flow Blue, Platter, Albany, Johnson Bros., 16 1/2 X 12 1/2 In. 45.00
Flow Blue, Platter, Amoy, Davenport, C.1845, 13 1/2 X 10 In. 125.00
Flow Blue, Platter, Bacon, Amoy, Davenport, C.1845, 13 1/2 X 10 In. 125.00
Flow Blue, Platter, Belmont, 11 1/2 In. 28.50
Flow Blue, Platter, Berne Pattern 65.00
Flow Blue, Platter, Blue Onion Pattern, 16 X 11 In. 60.00
Flow Blue, Platter, Cambridge, Wood & Son, C.1891, 18 1/2 X 13 In. 75.00
Flow Blue, Platter, Chinese Dimmock, 15 5/8 In. 100.00
Flow Blue, Platter, Clairemont, Johnson Bros., 15 In. 70.00
Flow Blue, Platter, Clarissa, Johnson Bros., Oval, 12 1/2 X 9 In. 25.00
Flow Blue, Platter, Clifton, Grindley, 16 1/4 X 12 1/2 In. 25.00
Flow Blue, Platter, Coburg, J.Edwards, C.1860, 20 1/2 X 16 In. 200.00
Flow Blue, Platter, Coral, Johnson Bros., Oval, 14 In. 34.00
Flow Blue, Platter, Corona, 16 In. 40.00
Flow Blue, Platter, Delamere, 11 In. 32.00
Flow Blue, Platter, Devon, Ford & Sons, 10 X 13 In. 55.00
Flow Blue, Platter, Devon, 15 1/2 X 11 1/2 In. 55.00
Flow Blue, Platter, Diamond Shape, Bird & Floral, Pinder Bourne, 8 1/2 In. 32.50
Flow Blue, Platter, Dudley, Ford & Sons, 12 X 9 In. 45.00
Flow Blue, Platter, Dudley, Ford & Sons, 15 X 12 In. 55.00
Flow Blue, Platter, Dudley, Ford & Sons, 17 X 12 In. 65.00
Flow Blue, Platter, Dundee, Ridgway, 16 X 11 In. 55.00
Flow Blue, Platter, Dundee, 10 1/4 In. 20.00
Flow Blue, Platter, Fairy Villas, 11 3/4 X 9 3/4 In. 48.00
Flow Blue, Platter, Gironde, Grindley, 15 X 10 In. 55.00
Flow Blue, Platter, Hindustan, 12 X 16 In. 135.00
Flow Blue, Platter, Indian Jar, J & T Furnival, C.1843, 16 X 12 1/2 In. 135.00
Flow Blue, Platter, Jenny Lind, 11 X 8 1/2 In. 65.00
Flow Blue, Platter, Kaolin, 15 1/4 In. 95.00
Flow Blue, Platter, Kyber, 10 In. 35.00
Flow Blue, Platter, Lorne, Grindley, Oval, 14 In. 45.00
Flow Blue, Platter, Lorne, 14 X 10 3/4 In. 50.00
Flow Blue, Platter, Lyric, Grindley, 16 X 12 In. 45.00
Flow Blue, Platter, Manilla, P.W.& Co., C.1845, 16 X 12 In. 175.00
Flow Blue, Platter, Melbourne, Grindley, 11 1/2 In. 22.00
Flow Blue, Platter, Melbourne, Grindley, 14 In. 30.00
Flow Blue, Platter, Melbourne, 16 In. 75.00
Flow Blue, Platter, Melrose, Doulton, Burslem, 15 X 20 1/2 In. 52.50
Flow Blue, Platter, Milan, Grindley 45.00
Flow Blue, Platter, Nankin, Doulton, Burslem, 1901, 12 1/2 X 15 In. 36.00
Flow Blue, Platter, Nankin, Doulton, Burslem, 1901, 14 X 17 1/2 In. 52.50
Flow Blue, Platter, Nonpareil, Burgess & Leigh, 12 X 9 In. 70.00
Flow Blue, Platter, Nonpareil, Scalloped, 13 1/2 In. 115.00

Flow Blue, Platter, Normandy, Gold Trim, Johnson Bros., 12 1/2 In. 40.00
Flow Blue, Platter, Normandy, Gold Trim, Johnson Bros., 14 In. 45.00
Flow Blue, Platter, Normandy, 9 3/4 In. 32.00
Flow Blue, Platter, Oval, Scalloped, 12 X 15, Lonsdale 50.00
Flow Blue, Platter, Pagodas, Ashworth Bros., 19 X 14 In. 85.00
Flow Blue, Platter, Raised Scrolls, Flowered Band, 13 X 9 In. 21.00
Flow Blue, Platter, Ruins, Copeland, C.1848, 18 1/2 X 12 1/2 In. 90.00
Flow Blue, Platter, Scinde, Alcock, C.1840, 10 X 7 In. 125.00
Flow Blue, Platter, Scinde, Alcock, C.1840, 13 X 10 In. 125.00
Flow Blue, Platter, Scinde, Alcock, C.1845, 13 1/2 X 10 In. 120.00
Flow Blue, Platter, Scinde, Alcock, 16 X 12 1/2 In. 200.00
Flow Blue, Platter, Scinde, Alcock, 7 1/2 X 5 3/4 In. 65.00
Flow Blue, Platter, Tonquin, 12 1/2 X 9 1/2 In. 37.00
Flow Blue, Platter, Versailles, Furnival, 1894, 11 3/4 X 9 In. 20.00
Flow Blue, Platter, Versailles, Furnival, 1894, 14 1/2 X 11 In. 30.00
Flow Blue, Platter, Virginia, Maddock, 12 X 9 1/2 In. 35.00
Flow Blue, Platter, Waldorf, New Wharf Pottery, 11 X 9 In. .... 28.50 To 35.00
Flow Blue, Platter, Waldorf, 10 1/2 X 9 In. 25.00
Flow Blue, Platter, Well & Tree, Flanged Base, Orchid, John Maddock & Sons 55.00
Flow Blue, Punch Bowl, Coburg, Edwards, Stoneware, C.1845, 13 1/2 In. 350.00
Flow Blue, Sauce, Amoy, Davenport 25.00
Flow Blue, Sauce, Celtic, Grindley, Oval 15.00
Flow Blue, Sauce, Dundee, Ridgway 12.00
Flow Blue, Sauce, Lugano, Ridgway 6.00
Flow Blue, Sauce, Marie, 4 3/4 In. 9.00
Flow Blue, Sauce, Melbourne, Grindley 10.00
Flow Blue, Sauce, Nonpareil, Burgess & Leigh, 6 In. 18.00
Flow Blue, Sauce, Normandy, Gold Trim, Johnson Bros., 4 3/4 In. 13.00
Flow Blue, Sauce, Osborne, Grindley, 5 1/4 In. 7.00
Flow Blue, Sauce, Portman, Grindley 12.00
Flow Blue, Sauce, Scinde, Alcock 28.50
Flow Blue, Sauce, Shanghai, Globe Mark 8.50
Flow Blue, Saucer, Amoy 25.00
Flow Blue, Saucer, Hofburg 6.00
Flow Blue, Saucer, Lorne, Grindley 7.00
Flow Blue, Saucer, Madras, Royal Doulton 7.50
Flow Blue, Saucer, Shanghai, Grindley 8.00
Flow Blue, Saucer, Stanley, Johnson Bros. 6.50
Flow Blue, Saucer, Touraine, Alcock 3.00
Flow Blue, Saucer, Touraine, Clayton 6.50
Flow Blue, Serving Bowl, Nonpariel 50.00
Flow Blue, Soup, Madras Pattern, 10 In. 25.00
Flow Blue, Stand, Doughnut, Floral, Doulton, Burslem, England 42.50
Flow Blue, Sucrier, Floral, W.Ridgway, C.1840 .... 90.00
Flow Blue, Sugar & Creamer, Shanghai, Grindley 125.00
Flow Blue, Sugar, Covered, Amoy, Davenport, C.1845 .... 125.00
Flow Blue, Sugar, Covered, Dundee, Ridgway 85.00
Flow Blue, Sugar, Covered, Normandy, Gold Trim, Johnson Bros. 85.00
Flow Blue, Sugar, Gironde 32.00
Flow Blue, Sugar, Scinde, J & S Alcock Jr, Marked Oriental Stone 95.00
Flow Blue, Tankard, Fraternal Emblem, Thos.Maddocks 125.00
Flow Blue, Teapot, Manilla, P.W.& Co., C.1845 .... 198.00
Flow Blue, Teapot, Scinde, Alcock, C.1840 .... 350.00
Flow Blue, Teapot, Self Pouring, For J.F.Royale, 1886 .... 120.00
Flow Blue, Teapot, Touraine 135.00
Flow Blue, Teapot, Vinranka 75.00
Flow Blue, Tray, Bread, Flowers With Luster 47.50
Flow Blue, Tureen & Attached Underplate, Sauce, Watteau, Doulton 55.00
Flow Blue, Tureen & Ladle, Gravy, Covered, Cambridge, Hollingshead & Kirkham 80.00
Flow Blue, Tureen & Underplate, Gravy, Kiji, Ashworth Bros. 163.00
Flow Blue, Tureen, Covered Sauce, Oregon 165.00
Flow Blue, Tureen, Covered Vegetable, Gironde, Grindley 65.00
Flow Blue, Tureen, Covered, Dundee, Ridgway, 11 1/2 In. 65.00
Flow Blue, Tureen, Covered, Normandy, 2 Handles, Johnson Bros., 8 In. 90.00

Flow Blue, Tureen, Covered, Normandy, 2 Handles, Johnson Bros., 9 1/2 In. 95.00
Flow Blue, Tureen, Grindley, Milan, 12 In., Lid And Matching Ladle 90.00
Flow Blue, Tureen, Lorne, Grindley 70.00
Flow Blue, Tureen, Oval Octagonal, Covered, Footed, Scinde, Alcock, C.1840 .... 265.00
Flow Blue, Tureen, Soup, Nonpareil, Burgess & Leigh, Octagonal 220.00
Flow Blue, Tureen, Underplate, Covered, Gloucester, K & G, France, 8 In. 12.00
Flow Blue, Tureen, Vegetable, Oval, Covered, Haddon 50.00
Flow Blue, Tureen, Vegetable, Oval, Covered, Lorne 50.00
Flow Blue, Tureen, Vegetable, Round, Covered, Ring Handle, Watteau 85.00
Flow Blue, Vase, Arcadian, Scenic, 6 1/2 In. 42.00
Flow Blue, Vase, Babes In Woods, Blind Man's Bluff, Doulton, C.1900, 9 In. 110.00
Flow Blue, Vase, Foresters, C.1800, 16 In. 225.00
Flow Blue, Washstand Bowl, Petunia, 15 1/2 In. 85.00
Flow Blue, Washstand Set & Chamber Pot, Athena, Cover, Grindley, 3 Piece 285.00
Flow Blue, Washstand Set, Easter Vines, Meigh 300.00

Foo dogs are mythical Chinese figures, part dog and part lion. They were made of pottery, porcelain, carved stone, and wood.

Foo Dog, Figurine, Porcelain, Teak Base, Blue Glaze, Impressed 35.00

FOSTORIA *Fostoria glass was made in Fostoria, Ohio, from 1887 to 1891. The factory was moved to Moundsville, West Virginia, and most of the glass seen in shops today is a twentieth-century product.*

Fostoria, see also Milk Glass

Fostoria, Berry Bowl, Saint Bernard 15.00
Fostoria, Bonbon, June 9.00
Fostoria, Bookend, Horse, 7 3/8 In. 12.00
Fostoria, Bowl, Baroque, 11 In. 14.00
Fostoria, Bowl, Handkerchief, Green, Opalescent, 6 3/8 In. 23.50
Fostoria, Bowl, Heirloom, Pink, Opalescent, 8 1/2 In. 14.50
Fostoria, Bowl, Punch, Stand, American, 5 Gallon, 13 In. 125.00
Fostoria, Bowl, Versailles, Blue, Footed, 12 In. 19.50
Fostoria, Bucket, Ice, American 10.00
Fostoria, Can, Molasses 30.00
Fostoria, Candleholder, Colony, Double, Pair 32.00
Fostoria, Celery, Notched Flute 25.00
Fostoria, Celery, Paneled Diamond & Finecut 17.50
Fostoria, Champagne, Blue, Versailles 10.00
Fostoria, Champagne, Corsage, Saucer Base 9.50
Fostoria, Compote, Baroque, Yellow, 5 1/2 In. 6.75
Fostoria, Compote, Etched Grape, Green, 6 In. 24.00
Fostoria, Console Bowl, Baroque, Blue, Footed 14.50
Fostoria, Console Bowl, June, Handled, 10 In. 23.50
Fostoria, Cream Soup Bowl & Underplate, June, Footed Bowl, 7 1/2 In. Plate 5.00
Fostoria, Creamer, Priscilla, Green 35.00
Fostoria, Cup, Fairfax, Green, Footed 3.00
Fostoria, Dish, Pickle, Royal 5.00
Fostoria, Figurine, Baby Duck, Green 10.00
Fostoria, Figurine, Horse, Standing, 4 In. 40.00
Fostoria, Figurine, Mama Duck, Green 15.00
Fostoria, Goblet, American Lady, Burgundy, Clear Base 5.00
Fostoria, Goblet, Cocktail, Spartan, Green 5.00
Fostoria, Goblet, Colony 2.95
Fostoria, Goblet, Corsage 10.00
Fostoria, Goblet, Hermitage 3.50
Fostoria, Goblet, Orchid, C.1927 .... 8.25
Fostoria, Goblet, Oyster Cocktail, Spartan, Green 4.00
Fostoria, Goblet, Spartan, Green, 9 Ozs. 7.00
Fostoria, Goblet, Versailles, Blue 12.00
Fostoria, Ice Cream Bowl, Hermitage 3.50
Fostoria, Jar, Powder, Sterling Lid, Brazilian 15.00
Fostoria, Nappy, Baroque, Handled, 5 In. 4.50
Fostoria, Nappy, Meadow Rose, Handled, 3 Footed, Triangular 8.00
Fostoria, Nappy, Victoria, Handled, Triangular, Patented 11.50

Fostoria, Pitcher, Block, Amber 12.50
Fostoria, Pitcher, Water, Florette, Pink Satin 225.00
Fostoria, Plate, Cake, June, 10 In. 14.50
Fostoria, Plate, Etched Royal, Amber, 8 1/2 In. 5.75
Fostoria, Plate, Luncheon, Royal 3.50
Fostoria, Plate, Optic, Amber, 7 1/4 In. 10.00
Fostoria, Plate, Royal, Green, Etched, 8 1/2 In. 3.50
Fostoria, Plate, Salad, Baroque, Amber 3.50
Fostoria, Plate, Spiral Optic, Amber, 8 1/2 In. 15.00
Fostoria, Platter, Serving, Topaz, Double Open Handles, 12 In. 25.00
Fostoria, Sherbet, Spartan, Green, High Stem 6.00
Fostoria, Sugar & Creamer, Baroque, Yellow 12.00
Fostoria, Sugar & Creamer, Colony 12.00
Fostoria, Sugar & Creamer, Corsage 18.00
Fostoria, Sugar, Amber, Hermitage 2.50
Fostoria, Sugar, Amber, Priscilla 2.50
Fostoria, Sugar, Creamer, & Tray, Individual, American 18.00
Fostoria, Sugar, Versailles, Green 8.50
Fostoria, Syrup, Milk Glass, Blue & Pink Pearly Panels, Metal Lid 62.00
Fostoria, Teacup & Saucer, Vesper, Amber, Footed Cup 4.00
Fostoria, Toothpick, Carmen 16.00
Fostoria, Toothpick, Carmen, Lacy, Footed 16.00
Fostoria, Tray, Cake, Fleur-De-Lis, Handled 6.00
Fostoria, Tumbler, Garland 3.75
Fostoria, Tumbler, Navarre, Footed, 12 Ozs. 10.00
Fostoria, Tumbler, Vesper, Amber, Footed, 9 Ozs. 5.00
Fostoria, Vase, Tut, Amber 25.00
Fostoria, Vase, Tut, Black, Milk Glass 22.00
Fostoria, Vase, Tut, Green 25.00
Fostoria, Wine, Spartan, Green 5.00

Foval, see Fry Foval
Fry, see also Cut Glass
Frame, see Furniture, Frame

Francisware is an amber hobnail glassware made by Hobbs Brockunier and Company, Wheeling, West Virginia, in the 1880s.

Francisware, Butter, Covered 80.00
Francisware, Celery, Frosted, Sharp Hobs 65.00
Francisware, Creamer, Frosted Hobnail With Amber Band, Applied Handle 50.00
Francisware, Dish, Covered Butter, Swirl 85.00
Francisware, Fruit Bowl, Frosted Hobs 85.00
Francisware, Pitcher, Frosted, Square Spout, 8 In. 175.00
Francisware, Salt & Pepper 62.00
Francisware, Sauce, Frosted Hobs, Square 32.00
Francisware, Spooner .... 50.00 To 58.00
Francisware, Sugar Shaker, Swirl 125.00
Francisware, Sugar, Covered .... 60.00 To 65.00
Francisware, Syrup, Pewter Top 125.00
Francisware, Toothpick, Clear Hobs 50.00
Francisware, Tumbler 55.00
Frankoma, Canteen, Brown & Green, Aztec Design, 6 1/2 In. 15.00
Frankoma, Celery, Black & Blue Glaze 8.00
Frankoma, Figurine, Hanging Wall, Heads Of Indian Brave & Squaw, Pair 25.00
Frankoma, Vase, Bud, Brown Glaze, Upright Snail Shape, 6 In. 29.00

Fry glass was made by the famous H.C.Fry Glass Company of Rochester, Pennsylvania. It includes cut glass, but the famous Fry glass today is the foval, or pearl, art glass. This is an opal ware decorated with colored trim. It was made from 1926 to 1927

Fry Foval, Bowl & Underplate, Yellow, White, & Light Blue, 7 In. Plate 95.00
Fry Foval, Bowl, Opalescent, Green Edge, Heart Shape, 5 1/4 In. 100.00
Fry Foval, Bowl, Pink, 10 1/2 X 3 1/2 In. 48.00
Fry Foval, Butter, Cobalt Finial, Opalescent To Clear 30.00
Fry Foval, Candleholder, Blue, Threaded Wafer Trim, Opalescent, Tall, Pair 125.00

Fry Foval, Candlestick, Blue & Opalescent, Applied Threading, 10 In. 95.00
Fry Foval, Candlestick, Blue Spiral Decoration, Blue Collar, Pair 295.00
Fry Foval, Candlestick, Diagonal Threading, Blue Wafer, 10 1/2 In., Pair 310.00
Fry Foval, Candlestick, Opalescent Glass, Applied Blue Rigaree, Hand Blown 85.00
Fry Foval, Candlestick, Opalescent, Blue Threading, 10 1/2 In., Pair 190.00
Fry Foval, Chocolate Pot, Green Jade Handle And Cover Knob 95.00
Fry Foval, Creamer, Pearl Art Glass, Applied Delft Blue Handle, 2 1/2 In. 48.00
Fry Foval, Cruet, Opalescent, Blue Handle And Stopper, Signed 250.00
Fry Foval, Cup & Saucer, Blue Handle 45.00
Fry Foval, Cup & Saucer, Pink With Black Applied Handle, Large 60.00
Fry Foval, Fruit Bowl, Pale Green To Rose, Ribbed Crystal Feet, 11 1/2 In. 95.00
Fry Foval, Jar, Jam, Saucer, Purple With Black Handles, Foot & Finial 150.00
Fry Foval, Lemonade Set, Applied Cobalt Handles, Cover, 7 Piece 650.00
Fry Foval, Pitcher, Aqua, Applied Clear Handle, 1908, 20 X 5 1/2 In. 95.00
Fry Foval, Pitcher, Water, Blue Edge 125.00
Fry Foval, Pitcher, Water, Tankard, Opalescent Stripes 160.00
Fry Foval, Sugar & Creamer, Opalescent, Applied Jade Green Handles, 3 In. 70.00
Fry Foval, Water Set, Blue, Opalescent, Cobalt Handles, 7 Piece 185.00
Fry, Candlestick, Band Of Colored Fruit, 13 In., Pair 270.00
Fry, Candlestick, Blue, Shimmering Gold, Multicolored Fruit, 10 In., Pair 245.00
Fry, Casserole, Opalescent, Farber Holder, 8 X 6 1/2 In. 20.00
Fry, Casserole, Round, Knobbed Cover, Opalescent, Marked 1938, 8 1/4 In. 10.00
Fry, Compote, Blue With Gold Shimmer, Band Of Colored Fruit, 6 X 9 In. 225.00
Fry, Compote, Blue With Gold Shimmering, Multicolored Fruit, 11 1/2 X 9 In. 195.00
Fry, Compote, Blue, Gold Shimmering Effect, Band Of Multicolor Fruit, 12 In. 225.00
Fry, Cruet, Cut Glass 79.50
Fry, Cup, Custard, Opalescent, Ovenware, 1927, Set Of 6 .... 35.00
Fry, Dish, Baking, Milky Opalescent Finial On Dome Lid, 5 1/2 In. 16.50
Fry, Dish, Custard 3.50
Fry, Dish, Cut Glass Center Handle, 10 In. 325.00
Fry, Juicer, Hand-Painted 12.00
Fry, Lemonade Set, Crackle, Covered Jug, 5 Piece 30.00
Fry, Mug, Cobalt Handle, Striped, 5 In. 38.00
Fry, Pitcher, Crackle Glass, With Lid, 9 In. 22.00
Fry, Pitcher, Crackle With Sapphire Handle & Base, Ground Pontil 65.00
Fry, Reamer 20.00
Fry, Teapot, Light Green, Applied Handle, Knob On Top, 6 1/2 In. 125.00
Fry, Toothpick, 2 Cobalt Handles 60.00
Fry, Tray, Opalescent, Fry Cooking Glass, 1859, Footed, 8 In. 10.00
Fry, Trivet, Opalescent, 3 Footed, Signed 20.00
Fry, Tumbler, Lemonade, Green Stripes 25.00
Fry, Tumbler, Lemonade, Vaseline & Cobalt, Handled 25.00
Fulham, Jug, Bellarmine, Tigerware, Mottled Brown, PVA & 1661, 8 1/4 In. 1350.00

FULPER

Fulper is the mark used by the American Pottery Company of Flemington, New Jersey. The art pottery was made from 1910 to 1929. The firm had been making bottles, jugs, and housewares from 1805. Doll heads were made about 1928. The firm became Stangl Pottery in 1929.

Fulper, see also Doll

Fulper, Base, Mirror Black, Full-Bodied, 10 In. 50.00
Fulper, Bell, Orange To Cream, Green Leaves, Paneled, Lily Shape, 4 1/2 In. 65.00
Fulper, Bookend, Open, Marked, 5 In., Pair 30.00
Fulper, Bowl & Flower Frog, Mottled Blue, Duck Frog, Vertical Mark 55.00
Fulper, Bowl, Blue, Coral & Brown Glaze, Signed, 5 1/2 X 7 In. 22.50
Fulper, Bowl, Copper Glaze, Blue Interior, 2 Handles, 6 X 5 In. 45.00
Fulper, Bowl, Flaring, Ruffled, Crystalline Blue On Blue Glaze, 6 1/2 In. 33.00
Fulper, Bowl, Flower, Effigy Feet, Blue Matte, 10 1/2 In. 69.00
Fulper, Bowl, Hexagon, Yellow Brown Drips, 3 X 5 In. 22.00
Fulper, Bowl, High Glaze, Brown, Cream Flambe, 8 In. 32.00
Fulper, Bowl, Purple With Yellow, C.1915, Signed, 8 1/2 In. 95.00
Fulper, Bowl, Shades Of Green To Royal Blue Base, 5 1/2 In. 14.00
Fulper, Bowl, With Frog, Mottled Blue To Olive, Duck On Frog, 8 X 4 In. 75.00
Fulper, Box, Half Figure Cover, Arms Akimbo, Art Deco, 6 1/2 In. 45.00
Fulper, Box, Powder, Figural Lady Lid, Yellow 60.00

Fulper, Box, Powder, Lady Wearing Hoop Skirt On Lid, Blue, Floral, 7 In. 72.00
Fulper, Box, Powder, Musical, Lady With Billowing Skirt, Bisque, 8 In. 150.00
Fulper, Crock, Coiled, Green, Brown, & Gunmetal Metallic, Pulled Handles, 9 In. 95.00
Fulper, Jar, Powder, Art Deco 55.00
Fulper, Lamp, Mottled Green, Bulbous, 18 In. 75.00
Fulper, Lamp, Perfume, Deco Ballerina, Pink To White Tutu, Signed 95.00
Fulper, Mug, Green Crystalline 38.00
Fulper, Night-Light, Perfume, Art Deco Lady, Blue Dress, 5 1/2 In. 110.00
Fulper, Sconce, Art Deco, Green, Vertical Marks 25.00
Fulper, Shield, Candle, Stained Glass Insets, Blue Glaze, Signed, 10 1/2 In. 325.00
Fulper, Vase, Black, 2 Handled 45.00
Fulper, Vase, Blue Flame With Divided Collar 35.00
Fulper, Vase, Boat Shape, Blue Mottled Glaze, Art Deco, 6 In. 22.00
Fulper, Vase, Bulbous, Green Matte, Handles, 8 In. 27.00
Fulper, Vase, Flambe, Blues & Greens, 2 Handled 22.50
Fulper, Vase, Flambe, Green & Rose, Fan Shape, 6 In. 18.00
Fulper, Vase, Gold With Brown Flambe, Iridescent, 5 In., Marked 38.00
Fulper, Vase, Green Drip On Brown, 8 In. 22.00
Fulper, Vase, Green Glaze, 2 Handles, 6 1/2 In. 25.00
Fulper, Vase, Green, Flambe, Ovoid, Small Neck, 13 In. 65.00
Fulper, Vase, High Gloss Blue Flame 45.00
Fulper, Vase, Moss To Violet, 3 Handles, 6 1/2 In. 42.00
Fulper, Vase, Purple 22.50
Fulper, Vase, Purple Flambe, Oriental Style, 7 1/2 In. 32.00
Fulper, Vase, S Crossed Handles, Olive Green, 8 In. 50.00
Fulper, Vase, Streaked Powder Blue Over Crystalline Green, 7 In. 32.00
Furniture, Armchair, Federal, Martha Washington, Mahogany, Floral Damask 2000.00
Furniture, Armchair, Federal, Martha Washington, Mahogany, White Muslin 850.00
Furniture, Armchair, Italian, Rococo, Walnut, Mid 1700s, Petit Point, Pair 2000.00
Furniture, Armchair, Ladderback, Red Paint, Decorated, C.1780 .... 775.00
Furniture, Armchair, Library, George II, Walnut, Emerald Silk, Damask 1600.00
Furniture, Armchair, Louis XV, Gilt, Tapestry Covered 625.00
Furniture, Armchair, Mahogany, Chippendale, Slip Seat .... *Illus* 400.00
Furniture, Armchair, Mahogany, Open, Serpentine Crest, Square Seat, C.1780 .... 1000.00
Furniture, Armchair, New England, C.1750, Birch, Painted, Rush Seat 250.00
Furniture, Armchair, Painted, Decorated, Rush Seat, Early 18th Century 350.00
Furniture, Armchair, Queen Anne, High Back 500.00
Furniture, Armchair, Queen Anne, Turned Cherry, 1720-40, New England 450.00
Furniture, Armchair, Queen Anne, Turned Maple & Pine, New England, 1700s 1000.00
Furniture, Armchair, Queen Anne, Turned Maple, Crush Seat, C.1740 .... 900.00
Furniture, Armchair, Queen Anne, Walnut, Carved, Cupid's-Bow Crest 1300.00
Furniture, Armchair, South German, Walnut, X-Frame, C.1680 .... 1000.00
Furniture, Armchair, Thonet, Bentwood, Cane Seat, Pair .... *Illus* 450.00

Furniture, Armchair, Mahogany, Chippendale, Slip Seat

Furniture, Armchair, Thonet, Bentwood, Cane Seat, Pair

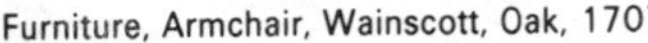
Furniture, Armchair, Wainscott, Oak, 1707

Furniture, Armchair, Windsor, Brace Back, Saddle Seat

Furniture, Armchair, Windsor, Bow Back

Furniture, Armchair, Windsor, Shaped Saddle Seat

Furniture, Armchair, Windsor, Curved Arms, Comb Back

Furniture, Armchair, Turned & Painted Maple Ladderback, New England, C.1700 .... 550.00
Furniture, Armchair, Wainscott, Oak, 1707 .... *Illus* 425.00
Furniture, Armchair, William & Mary, Painted Maple, Banister Back, C.1700 .... 300.00
Furniture, Armchair, Windsor, Bamboo Turned, Sack Back, C.1800 .... 375.00
Furniture, Armchair, Windsor, Bow Back .... *Illus* 270.00
Furniture, Armchair, Windsor, Brace Back, Connecticut, C.1790 .... 1400.00
Furniture, Armchair, Windsor, Brace Back, Saddle Seat .... *Illus* 700.00
Furniture, Armchair, Windsor, Comb Back, Saddle Seat, C.1780 .... 550.00
Furniture, Armchair, Windsor, Curved Arms, Comb Back .... *Illus* 375.00
Furniture, Armchair, Windsor, Hoop Back, C.1800 .... 600.00
Furniture, Armchair, Windsor, Lancaster, Ohio, Step Down 350.00
Furniture, Armchair, Windsor, Sack Back, Pennsylvania, 1790-1800 .... 700.00
Furniture, Armchair, Windsor, Shaped Saddle Seat .... *Illus* 500.00
Furniture, Armchair, Windsor, 9 Spindles, Continuous Arms, C.1770 .... 1175.00
Furniture, Armchair, Wing, Chippendale, Carved Mahogany, New York, C.1760 .... 3250.00
Furniture, Armchair, Wing, Federal, Carved Mahogany, Massachusetts, C.1790 .... 2750.00

Furniture, Armoire, French Country, C.1750, Dark Oak, 2 Sections, 84 In. 2300.00
Furniture, Armoire, French Provincial, Carved Oak, 6 X 4 Ft. 2200.00
Furniture, Armoire, Louis XV, Provincial, Fielded Doors, C.1780, 5 Ft. 800.00
Furniture, Armoire, Quebec, C.1775, Diamond Point Doors 5500.00
Furniture, Armoire, Tyrolean, C.1806, Painted Bouquets On Panels 2200.00
Furniture, Bagatelle, English, Mahogany, Table Top 375.00
Furniture, Bar & Back Bar, Oak, Brass Fittings, Icebox, Sinks, C.1920, 8 Ft. 125.00
Furniture, Bar & Back Bar, Onyx, 10 Ft X 20 Ft. 5000.00
Furniture, Bed, Brass, Double Tuba Scroll, Massive 2800.00
Furniture, Bed, Brass, Queen Mountain Top 2200.00
Furniture, Bed, Brass, Round Posts, Large 250.00
Furniture, Bed, Federal, Maple, Four Post Tester, New England, 1800-15, 5 Ft. 725.00
Furniture, Bed, Federal, Turned Maple, Four Post Tester, New England, 54 In. 200.00
Furniture, Bed, Federal, Turned Maple, Four Post, Tester, C.1800, 7 Ft. 550.00
Furniture, Bed, Four Post, Federal, Carved Mahogany & Maple, C.1820, 7 Ft. 400.00
Furniture, Bed, Hired Hand's, Victorian, Cast Iron & Steel, Portable 125.00
Furniture, Bed, Jenny Lind, Walnut Spool 198.00
Furniture, Bed, Murphy, Oak, Mirror & Crown, 7 Ft.High 350.00
Furniture, Bed, Pennsylvania, C.1800, Cherry & Pine, Turned, Tester, 6 1/2 Ft. 600.00
Furniture, Bed, Pine & Ash, Turned, Red Paint, C.1810, 16 X 14 In. 175.00
Furniture, Bed, Rope, Turned Posters & Stretchers, C.1850, 72 In. Long 325.00
Furniture, Bed, Solid Pine, 3/4, Rope 105.00
Furniture, Bed, Walnut, C.1800, Full Size, 71 In. High 600.00
Furniture, Bedroom Set, Country, Pine, C.1840, 5 Piece 1200.00
Furniture, Bedroom Set, Walnut, Marble Topped Dresser & Washstand, Wardrobe 7000.00
Furniture, Bedroom Set, 3 Piece, Golden Oak 500.00
Furniture, Bench, Cobbler's, Walnut 300.00
Furniture, Bench, Deacon's, Half Spindle Back, 8 Legs, 6 Ft. 750.00
Furniture, Bench, Mammy, New England, C.1830, Arrow Back, Green Paint 575.00
Furniture, Bench, Waiting Room, Long With Arms, Oak 100.00
Furniture, Bench, Windsor, Bamboo Turnings, 9 In.Long *Illus* 375.00
Furniture, Bergere, Fruitwood, En Cabriolet, Louis XV-XVI, I.Lebas 1400.00
Furniture, Bonheur Du Jour, Italian, Rococo, Walnut And Elmwood, 37 In. 650.00
Furniture, Bonheur Du Jour, Ormolu, Porcelain Mounted, Napoleon III, 4 Ft. 650.00
Furniture, Book Stand, Sheraton, Mahogany, Revolving 498.00
Furniture, Bookcase Desk, Oak 225.00
Furniture, Bookcase, Burl Walnut, Brass Lion Head Lock, Key 350.00
Furniture, Bookcase, George III, Revolving, Pair 1100.00
Furniture, Bookcase, New York, C.1790, Mahogany, Inlaid, 2 Parts, Eagle Crest 2100.00
Furniture, Bookcase, Oak, 4 Glass Doors, Drawer, 2 Pull-Out Shelves 110.00
Furniture, Bookcase, Oak, 5 Shelves, Glass Door, 4 Ft.7 In. 175.00
Furniture, Bookholder, Rosewood, Inlaid Ivory, Adjustable, Opens To 24 In. 45.00
Furniture, Bookshelf, Open Shelves, Cupboard, English, C.1800 1200.00
Furniture, Box, Blanket, Ile D'Orleans, Quebec, C.1790, Painted, V Molding 550.00
Furniture, Box, Blanket, Ohio, Yellow & Amber Graining, 3 Bos Panels, 36 In. 125.00
Furniture, Box, Blanket, Red Brown Graining, Gold Floral Medallion, 28 In. 120.00
Furniture, Box, Desk, Victorian, Walnut, Black & Bronze Banding, 13 In. 28.00
Furniture, Box, Ditty, Panbone, Wood, Tortoise Shell, 1868, 7 In. *Illus* 3250.00

Furniture, Bench, Windsor, Bamboo Turnings, 9 In.Long

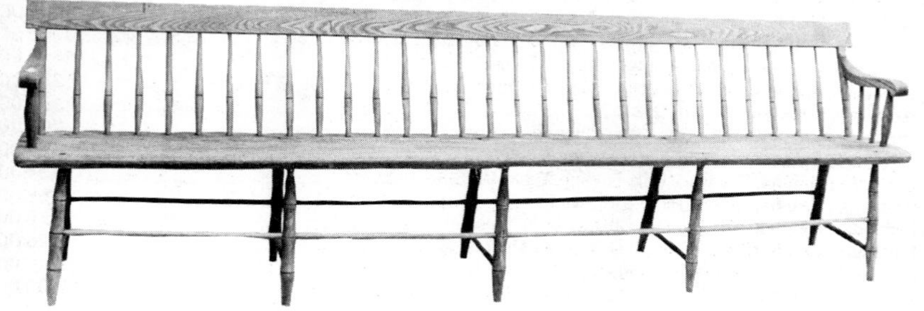

Furniture, Cabinet, George III, 14 1/2 X 8 X 15 In.High

Furniture, Box, Ditty, Panbone, Wood, Tortoise Shell, 1868, 7 In.

(See Page 205)

Furniture, Box, Knife & Fork, Mahogany, Center Handle, 15 1/2 In. 65.00
Furniture, Box, Knife, Mahogany, Inlaid, Serpentine Front, C.1790, 14 In., Pair 850.00
Furniture, Box, Knife, Pressed Wood 19.00
Furniture, Bucket Bench, Cherry And Ash 185.00
Furniture, Buffet-Bas, Hotel Dieu, P.Q., C.1750, Pine, Brass Hardware 6250.00
Furniture, Buffet, Dutch, Marquetry, Serpentine Hinged Top, 35 In. 800.00
Furniture, Buffet, Empire, Manitoulin Island, Canada 85.00
Furniture, Bureau Plat, Carel, Louis XV, King & Tulip Woods, Ormolu Mounts 9000.00
Furniture, Bureau, Child's, Mirror, Ivory, Sprays Of Pink Flowers, Brass Pulls 45.00
Furniture, Bureau, Dutch, Rococo Marquetry, Mid-18th Century, 44 In. 325.00
Furniture, Bureau, Louis XV, Provincial Fruitwood, Mid-1700s, 40 In. 240.00
Furniture, Bureau, Pine, 4 Drawer, C.1830 .... 150.00
Furniture, Butcher's Block, Maple, 4 Round Legs, 40 X 30 In. 150.00
Furniture, Butcher's Block, Oak 100.00
Furniture, Cabinet, China, Oak 400.00
Furniture, Cabinet, Curio, Hand Decorated, Bronze Trim, French, 5 Ft. 2500.00
Furniture, Cabinet, Display, Japanese, C.1850, Carved, Gessoed, 8 Ft.4 In. 2600.00
Furniture, Cabinet, Dutch Rococo, Walnut, Marquetry, Glazed Doors, 7 Ft. 4750.00
Furniture, Cabinet, Dutch, Marquetry & Lacquer, 18th Century, 36 In. X 4 Ft. 5200.00
Furniture, Cabinet, Dutch, Marquetry, Tambour Fronted, Hanging, 14 In. 150.00
Furniture, Cabinet, Flemish, Baroque, Bone & Mother-Of-Pearl, Inlaid Oak 2000.00
Furniture, Cabinet, George III, 14 1/2 X 8 X 15 In.High .... *Illus* 575.00
Furniture, Cabinet, German, Baroque Walnut Marquetry, Late 1600s, 5 Ft. 3000.00
Furniture, Cabinet, Italian, Painted, Marble Top, Shelf Door, 31 In. 3500.00
Furniture, Cabinet, Italian, Rococo, Brass Mounted Walnut, Mid-1700s, 7 Ft. 5250.00
Furniture, Cabinet, Kitchen, Oak 150.00
Furniture, Cabinet, Red Lacquered, Chinese 200.00
Furniture, Cabinet, Section, Chippendale, English, 18th Century 3750.00
Furniture, Cabinet, Sewing, Oak, Folding Table On Side, Drawers 35.00
Furniture, Cabinet, Spice, Pine, 8 Drawer 58.00
Furniture, Cabinet, Thread, Oak, 3 Drawer, Refinished 65.00
Furniture, Cabinet, Wall, Oak, Oval Beveled Mirror 28.00
Furniture, Candlestand Pole Screen, Mahogany, Tripod Base, C.1760, 53 In. 2500.00
Furniture, Candlestand, Chippendale, Carved Mahogany, C.1760, 28 In. 4500.00

Furniture, Candlestand, Chippendale, Mahogany, Tilt Top, Round Top, 28 In. 225.00
Furniture, Candlestand, Chippendale, Mahogany, Tilt Top, Salem, C.1780, 28 In. 6500.00
Furniture, Candlestand, Chippendale, Maple, Turned Cherry, C.1780, 28 In. 300.00
Furniture, Candlestand, Chippendale, Walnut, Dish Top, Philadelphia, 1760-80 .... 2100.00
Furniture, Candlestand, Federal, Mahogany, Tilt Top, Massachusetts, 1790 .... 500.00
Furniture, Candlestand, Massachusetts, C.1760, Maple, Tilt Top, Scalloped Top 1300.00
Furniture, Candlestand, New England, C.1750, Birch, Oblong Top, Vase Standard 425.00
Furniture, Candlestand, New England, C.1750, Maple, Square Top, Vase Standard 450.00
Furniture, Candlestand, New England, C.1750, Red Paint, 24 In. 395.00
Furniture, Candlestand, Pennsylvania, C.1770, Mahogany, Birdcage Support 1700.00
Furniture, Candlestand, Philadelphia, C.1760, Mahogany, Birdcage, 27 In. 2300.00
Furniture, Candlestand, Ratchet 1900.00
Furniture, Candlestand, Walnut, Desk Top, C.1760 .... 875.00
Furniture, Carriage, Baby, Wicker 350.00
Furniture, Carriage, Baby's, Oak, Parasol 170.00
Furniture, Cart, Tea, Oak, 3 Shelf, Separate Tray 155.00
Furniture, Cellarette On Stand, Chippendale, Walnut, Hinged, Drawer, 36 In. 650.00
Furniture, Cellarette, Inlaid Mahogany, Hinged Top, Fan Paterae, C.1790 .... 850.00
Furniture, Cellarette, Mahogany, Inlaid Medallion On Hinged Top, C.1790 .... 1400.00
Furniture, Chair & Stool, Western Shaker, Refinished Rush Seats 185.00
Furniture, Chair, American, C.1810, Black Lacquer, Cane Seat, Sawtooth Inlay 425.00
Furniture, Chair, American, C.1810, Regency Style, Black Lacquer, Pair 150.00
Furniture, Chair, Burgomaster, Continental Oak, Late 17th Century 700.00
Furniture, Chair, Butter, Walnut, Black 135.00
Furniture, Chair, Canadian, C.1840, Pillowback, Set Of 4 .... 700.00
Furniture, Chair, Carved Curly Maple, Classical, Caned Seat, New York, Pair 1000.00
Furniture, Chair, Child's, Carpeted 65.00
Furniture, Chair, Child's, Dutch Elm, Pierced Backrest, 17th Century 850.00
Furniture, Chair, Child's, Red & White, Lacy Seat Pad 65.00
Furniture, Chair, Child's, Sheraton, 21 3/4 In., Pair 350.00
Furniture, Chair, Chippendale, Carved Walnut, Cupid Bow Crestrail, C.1760 .... 3100.00
Furniture, Chair, Corner, Country, Dark Paint 250.00
Furniture, Chair, Corner, Queen Anne, Turned Maple & Ash, Connecticut, C.1750 .... 325.00
Furniture, Chair, Dining, Grand Rapids, Oak 12.50
Furniture, Chair, Directoire Painted, C.1780, Molded Frame, Tapered Legs 650.00
Furniture, Chair, Directoire, C.1800, Set Of 4 .... 800.00
Furniture, Chair, Federal, Painted & Decorated Arrow Back, C.1820, Set Of 6 .... 2900.00
Furniture, Chair, Gentleman's, Rose Carved, Needlepoint Floral, C.1860 .... 375.00
Furniture, Chair, Hitchcock, Curly Maple, C.1830, Set Of 4 .... 650.00
Furniture, Chair, Hitchcock, Rush Seat, Original Decoration, Set Of Four 350.00
Furniture, Chair, Hudson River, Queen Anne, Rush Seat .... 375.00 To 475.00
Furniture, Chair, Hutch, Pine & Maple, C.1790 .... 850.00
Furniture, Chair, Ile D'Orleans, Quebec, Set Of 4 .... 825.00
Furniture, Chair, J.Pratt, Lunenburg, C.1835, Painted, Pair 590.00
Furniture, Chair, Lady's & Gentleman's, Victorian, Pair 400.00
Furniture, Chair, Louis XVI, Bergere, Late 18th Century 650.00
Furniture, Chair, Louis XVI, Painted Fauteuil, Late 1700s, L.M.Pluvinet 700.00
Furniture, Chair, Mahogany, Vase Back, Cabriole Legs, C.1880, Set Of 4 .... 350.00
Furniture, Chair, Oak, Pattern Back, Caned, Set Of Six 600.00
Furniture, Chair, Oak, T Back 35.00
Furniture, Chair, Office, Swivel, For Roll Top Desk, C.1920 .... 45.00
Furniture, Chair, Parlor, Walnut, Needlepoint Seat & Back, Pair 650.00
Furniture, Chair, Pennsylvania, Arrowback, Green Paint, Set Of 6 .... 630.00
Furniture, Chair, Pressed Back, Oak, Scroll Design 35.00
Furniture, Chair, Pressed Back, Oak, Solid Seat 50.00
Furniture, Chair, Quebec, Fish Back, Woven Seat, Pair 50.00
Furniture, Chair, Queen Anne, Country, Rush Seat 175.00
Furniture, Chair, Reading, Victorian, Carved, Upholstered 225.00
Furniture, Chair, Regency, Caned, Set Of 4 .... 385.00
Furniture, Chair, Rocking, Cane Bottom, Child's 15.00
Furniture, Chair, Shaker, Ladder Back, Rush Seat, Slides Under Table 280.00
Furniture, Chair, Shaker, Straight 80.00
Furniture, Chair, Sheraton, 2 Arm & 4 Side, Set Of 6 .... 850.00
Furniture, Chair, Shield Back, Leather Upholstered, Hepplewhite, American, 6 .... 6250.00

Furniture, Chair, Side, Banister Back ... *Illus* 275.00
Furniture, Chair, Side, Cage Back, Bamboo Turnings ... *Illus* 300.00
Furniture, Chair, Side, Chippendale, Carved Mahogany, Massachusetts, 1760-80 ... 900.00
Furniture, Chair, Side, Chippendale, Carved Mahogany, New England, C.1760 ... 150.00
Furniture, Chair, Side, Chippendale, Carved Mahogany, New York, C.1760, Pair ... 3200.00
Furniture, Chair, Side, Chippendale, Carved Mahogany, 1770-80, Philadelphia ... 600.00
Furniture, Chair, Side, Chippendale, Carved Walnut, C.1770 ... 1700.00
Furniture, Chair, Side, Chippendale, Cherry, New England, C.1750 ... 1000.00
Furniture, Chair, Side, Chippendale, Cherry, New England, 1770-90 ... 150.00
Furniture, Chair, Side, Chippendale, Mahogany, Slip Seat ... *Illus* 3000.00
Furniture, Chair, Side, Chippendale, Pierced Ribbon Slats, Pair ... 600.00
Furniture, Chair, Side, Chippendale, Walnut, Slip Seat ... *Illus* 3600.00
Furniture, Chair, Side, Connecticut, C.1740, Banister Back, Rush Seat, Pair ... 1000.00
Furniture, Chair, Side, Dutch, Walnut Marquetry, Mid-18th Century, Pair ... 600.00
Furniture, Chair, Side, Empire, Inlaid Mahogany, C.1830, Pair ... 125.00
Furniture, Chair, Side, Federal Mahogany, Concave Crestrail, Set Of 10 ... 1000.00
Furniture, Chair, Side, Federal, Carved Mahogany, Racquet Back, C.1790, Pair ... 800.00
Furniture, Chair, Side, Federal, Carved Mahogany, Rhode Island, C.1790 ... 425.00
Furniture, Chair, Side, Federal, Cherry, Shield Back, New England, C.1790 ... 100.00
Furniture, Chair, Side, Hudson River Valley, C.1720, Maple, Painted, Rush Seat ... 475.00
Furniture, Chair, Side, Italian, Painted, Rush Seat, C.1725, Pair ... 225.00
Furniture, Chair, Side, Joseph Hasner, C.1750, Country, Maple ... 350.00
Furniture, Chair, Side, Louis XVI, Fruitwood, Late 1700s, Pair ... 175.00
Furniture, Chair, Side, Mahogany, Chippendale, Damask Seat, English, Pair ... 250.00
Furniture, Chair, Side, Mahogany, Chippendale, Red Plush Seat, Old Finish ... 350.00
Furniture, Chair, Side, Maple, Turned, Banister Back, Rush Seat, C.1750 ... 375.00

Furniture, Chair, Side, Bannister Back

Furniture, Chair, Side, Chippendale, Mahogany, Slip Seat

Furniture, Chair, Side, Cage Back, Bamboo Turnings

Furniture, Chair, Side, Chippendale, Walnut, Slip Seat

Furniture, Chair, Side, Massachusetts, C.1760, Mahogany, Carved, Cupid's-Bow 1400.00
Furniture, Chair, Side, Massachusetts, C.1790, Mahogany, Carved, Set Of 3 ..... 2700.00
Furniture, Chair, Side, New England, C.1750, Maple, Banister Back, Rush Seat 200.00
Furniture, Chair, Side, New England, C.1820, Painted, Decorated, Rush Seat 325.00
Furniture, Chair, Side, New York, C.1760, Mahogany, Carved, Cupid's-Bow Crest 1800.00
Furniture, Chair, Side, New York, C.1760, Mahogany, Carved, Pierced Vase Splat 665.00
Furniture, Chair, Side, New York, C.1790, Mahogany, Carved, Shield Back, Pair 3250.00
Furniture, Chair, Side, North Italian, Carved, Painted, Parcel Gilt, C.1750 ..... 325.00
Furniture, Chair, Side, Painted, Open Back, Napoleon III, Set Of 4 ..... 900.00
Furniture, Chair, Side, Philadelphia, C.1760, Mahogany, Carved, Cupid's-Bow 1100.00
Furniture, Chair, Side, Philadelphia, C.1790, Mahogany, Carved, Racquet Back 425.00
Furniture, Chair, Side, Queen Anne, Carved Walnut, Balloon Seat, C.1740 ..... 3000.00
Furniture, Chair, Side, Queen Anne, Inlaid Walnut, Baroque Marquetry, Pair 3500.00
Furniture, Chair, Side, Queen Anne, Mahogany, White Paint, Oxbow Crest 600.00
Furniture, Chair, Side, Queen Anne, Maple, Rush Seat, New England, C.1740, Pair 5750.00
Furniture, Chair, Side, Queen Anne, Oak, Spanish Feet ..... *Illus* 200.00
Furniture, Chair, Side, Queen Anne, Turned Maple, Hudson River, C.1790, Pair 1600.00
Furniture, Chair, Side, Sheraton ..... *Illus* 90.00
Furniture, Chair, Side, Tassel Back, Chippendale, Carved Mahogany, C.1760, Pair 7000.00
Furniture, Chair, Side, Turned Yoke-Backed Banister, Mahogany Stain 200.00
Furniture, Chair, Side, Victorian, Finger Carved 150.00
Furniture, Chair, Side, Walnut, Carved, Horsehair Cushions, Porcelain Caster, 2 ..... 155.00
Furniture, Chair, Side, Wicker, Ornate ..... 65.00 To 135.00
Furniture, Chair, Side, Windsor, Bow Back, 7 Spindle Back, Shaped Seat 240.00
Furniture, Chair, Side, Windsor, Bow Back, 9 Spindle Back, Dark Finish 220.00
Furniture, Chair, Side, Windsor, Brace Back, New England, 1780-90 ..... 325.00
Furniture, Chair, Side, Windsor, Pennsylvania, C.1780, Hoop Back, Set Of 6 ..... 2300.00
Furniture, Chair, Side, Yellow Paint, Decorated, Plank Seat, C.1800, Set Of 6 ..... 650.00
Furniture, Chair, Spanish, C.1650, Sultana, Painted, Rush Seat, Pair 750.00
Furniture, Chair, Spinning, Scandinavian, Birchwood & Pine, Late 1700s 850.00
Furniture, Chair, Tiger Maple, Cane Seat 95.00
Furniture, Chair, Victorian Balloon Back, Upholstered, C.1840, Set Of 6 ..... 1200.00
Furniture, Chair, Victorian, Walnut, Carved Back, Spindles, Set Of 4 ..... 150.00
Furniture, Chair, Wedgwood Regency, Black Lacquer, Enamel Designs, 1830, Pair 600.00
Furniture, Chair, Windsor, Fanback 190.00
Furniture, Chair, Windsor, Lancaster, Ohio, Step Down 350.00
Furniture, Chair, Windsor, Nova Scotia 235.00
Furniture, Chair, Windsor, Wishbone, Painted, Set Of 4 ..... 1295.00
Furniture, Chaise, Gilt Wood, Cartouche Shape, Upholstered Back, Pair 1600.00
Furniture, Chest On Frame, William & Mary, Oyster Burl 3500.00

Furniture, Chair, Side, Queen Anne, Oak, Spanish Feet

Furniture, Chair, Side, Sheraton

Furniture, Chest On Stand, William & Mary, Walnut, Inlaid, Marquetry	4200.00
Furniture, Chest-On-Chest, Connecticut, C.1780, Cherry, 74 1/2 In.	4200.00
Furniture, Chest, A.Snow, New England, 1831, Yellow Paint, 3 Drawer, Miniature	800.00
Furniture, Chest, American, C.1790, Mahogany, Ebony Inlay	495.00
Furniture, Chest, Apothecary, Gray Paint, 16 Dovetailed Drawers	280.00
Furniture, Chest, Apothecary, Walnut, 20 Drawer, 61 X 35 X 13 In.	500.00
Furniture, Chest, Black Graining On Red, 4 Drawer, High Feet, Shaped Apron	1200.00
Furniture, Chest, Blanket, Chippendale, Walnut, Lift Top, Pennsylvania, 28 In.	900.00
Furniture, Chest, Blanket, Country, Lift Top, C.1820, 43 X 42 X 19 In.	525.00
Furniture, Chest, Blanket, Curly Maple, C.1810	975.00
Furniture, Chest, Blanket, Curly Maple, Sheraton, C.1820	900.00
Furniture, Chest, Blanket, Lift Top, Oak, Paneled, Late 17th Century, 29 In.	450.00
Furniture, Chest, Blanket, Painted, H Hinges, Black Banding, 2 Drawer	425.00
Furniture, Chest, Blanket, Pennsylvania, C.1840, Red Paint	145.00
Furniture, Chest, Blanket, Red, Brasses, C.1750	750.00
Furniture, Chest, Blanket, Tiger Maple, C.1820	1050.00
Furniture, Chest, Bow Front, Federal, Inlaid Mahogany & Birch, C.1790, 37 In.	1100.00
Furniture, Chest, Bow Front, Painted In Old Graining, 4 Drawers	400.00
Furniture, Chest, Butler's, Maple, Rosewood Front, 4 Drawer, C.1820	1200.00
Furniture, Chest, Campaign, English, Desk, Brass Bound	2000.00
Furniture, Chest, Campaign, 2-Part, 42 1/2 X 36 X 18 In. *Illus*	1100.00
Furniture, Chest, Canadian, C.1840, Butternut, French Feet, 5 Drawer	550.00
Furniture, Chest, Canadian, Empire, Mahogany, Painted, Stenciled, 7 Drawer	450.00
Furniture, Chest, Cherry, Scalloped Base	1300.00
Furniture, Chest, Chester County, Pa., C.1760, Walnut, 9 Graduated Drawers	3300.00
Furniture, Chest, Chippendale, Birch, Serpentine Front, C.1770, 38 In.	1800.00
Furniture, Chest, Chippendale, Cherry, New England, 1770-90, 35 In.	1300.00
Furniture, Chest, Chippendale, Curly Maple, 4 Thumb-Molded Drawers, 39 In.	400.00
Furniture, Chest, Chippendale, Inlaid Cherrywood, C.1780, 5 Ft.	2600.00
Furniture, Chest, Chippendale, Mahogany, Reverse Serpentine, C.1760, 32 In.	4250.00
Furniture, Chest, Chippendale, Walnut, Pennsylvania, C.1760, 33 In.	2000.00
Furniture, Chest, Dower, Pennsylvania Dutch, C.1810, Decorated, Signed	1600.00
Furniture, Chest, Dower, Pennsylvania Dutch, Decorated, Early 1800s	1250.00
Furniture, Chest, Dower, Pennsylvania, C.1770, Walnut, Hinged, Drawer, 31 In.	450.00
Furniture, Chest, Dowry, Inside Drawers, Pine, Refinished	125.00
Furniture, Chest, English, C.1805, Mahogany, Bowfront	935.00
Furniture, Chest, English, C.1820, Mahogany, 5 Drawer, 26 In.	295.00
Furniture, Chest, English, C.1820, Yew Wood, Satinwood Banding, 4 Drawer	950.00
Furniture, Chest, Federal, Curly Maple & Mahogany, Massachusetts, C.1800	1000.00
Furniture, Chest, Federal, Curly Maple, Bow Front, New York, 1810, 43 In.	750.00

Furniture, Chest, Campaign, 2-Part, 42 1/2 X 36 X 18 In.

Furniture, Chest, Sea, Pine, Decorated, 54 1/4 In.Long

Furniture, Cupboard, Corner, Cherry
(See Page 212)

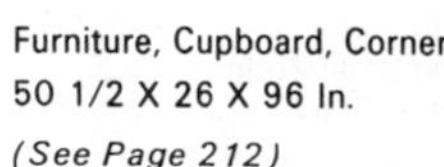

Furniture, Cupboard, Corner,
50 1/2 X 26 X 96 In.
(See Page 212)

Furniture, Chest, Federal, Inlaid Cherry, C.1790, 37 In. 1300.00
Furniture, Chest, Federal, Inlaid Cherry, Holden, C.1810, 37 1/2 In. 800.00
Furniture, Chest, Federal, Inlaid Mahogany, Bow Front, C.1790, 38 In. 650.00
Furniture, Chest, Federal, Mahogany And Cherry, C.1810, 44 In. 500.00
Furniture, Chest, Federal, Mahogany And Maple, Massachusetts, 1800-10, 41 In. 350.00
Furniture, Chest, Federal, Maple, New England, C.1800, 38 In. 400.00
Furniture, Chest, Hotel Dieu, Quebec, C.1790, Red Finish, 3 Drawer 785.00
Furniture, Chest, Levis County, Canada, C.1870, Chestnut & Pine, Bonnet 550.00
Furniture, Chest, Liquor, 12 Bottles, 2 Tumblers, & 3 Wines, Gold Leaf 950.00
Furniture, Chest, Mahantango Valley, Grain Decoration, 4 Drawer 850.00
Furniture, Chest, Mahogany, Bow Front, 4 Graduated Drawers, C.1800, 42 In. 375.00
Furniture, Chest, Mahogany, 5 Drawer, C.1830, 4 1/4 In. 50.00
Furniture, Chest, Massachusetts, C.1800, Mahogany, Inlaid, Carved, 4 Drawer 400.00
Furniture, Chest, Military Field, Painted Pine, 19th Century, 24 In. 200.00
Furniture, Chest, North Italian, Baroque, Walnut, Late 1600s, 35 In. 1800.00
Furniture, Chest, Nova Scotia, Childproof, Drawers Push Open From Back 750.00
Furniture, Chest, Oak, Burl Walnut Panel Insets, Marble Top 395.00
Furniture, Chest, Oak, 3 Drawer 55.00
Furniture, Chest, Painted Blanket, Pennsylvania, 18th Century, Blue Ground 850.00
Furniture, Chest, Pennsylvania Dutch Dower, Decorated, Signed 1295.00
Furniture, Chest, Pennsylvania, C.1760, Walnut, 4 Thumb-Molded Drawers 2400.00
Furniture, Chest, Quebec, C.1840, Painted, Carved Gallery, 4 Drawer 495.00
Furniture, Chest, Quebec, Empire, Pine & Butternut, Linenfold Inlays 425.00
Furniture, Chest, Quebec, Painted Graining, Stenciled, 4 Drawer 135.00
Furniture, Chest, Salem, C.1810, Bow Front, 4 Drawer, Carved Corner Posts 1200.00
Furniture, Chest, Sea, Pine, Decorated, 54 1/4 In.Long .... *Illus* 700.00
Furniture, Chest, Sherry & Mahogany, Bow Front, 4-Drawer, Satinwood, C.1780 .... 1650.00
Furniture, Chest, Silverware, Holds Service For 36, Maple, 20 X 4 X 10 In. 75.00
Furniture, Chest, Spanish, C.1650, Walnut, Carved, 10 Fitted Drawers 1800.00
Furniture, Chest, Spice, Brown Paint, 12 Drawer 250.00
Furniture, Chest, Storage, Curly Maple, C.1890 .... 350.00
Furniture, Chest, Tea, Rosewood, Casket Shape, 1830s 70.00
Furniture, Chest, Tyrolean Parquetry Cassone, 16th Century, 23 In. 4000.00
Furniture, Chest, Walnut, C.1778, 5 1/2 Ft. 3300.00
Furniture, Chest, William & Mary On Frame, Oyster Burl, 1690 Period 2900.00

Furniture, Coffer, Oak, Elizabethan, C.1560 .... 850.00
Furniture, Commode, Italian, Rococo Parquetry, Serpentine Front, 38 In. 2100.00
Furniture, Commode, Louis XV, Walnut, Serpentine Front, Mid 17 .... 600.00 To 1500.00
Furniture, Commode, Oak, Carving, Towel Bar 145.00
Furniture, Commode, Oak, Serpentine Front, Louis XV, L. Leroy, 32 In. 2300.00
Furniture, Commode, Provincial, Fruitwood, Louis XV, 32 In. 4500.00
Furniture, Commode, Purplewood Parquetry, Bow Front, Marble Top, 34 In. 4750.00
Furniture, Commode, Tulip, Kingwood Parquetry, Marble Top, Louis XV, 33 In. 3100.00
Furniture, Commode, Tulipwood Parquetry, Marble Top, Louis XV, 35 In. 7000.00
Furniture, Commode, Walnut, Side Towel Bar 95.00
Furniture, Connecticut Chippendale, Cherry, Slant Top, 4 Drawer, 38 In. 2500.00
Furniture, Console, Dutch Marquetry, Rectangular Marble Top, Early 1800s 350.00
Furniture, Cradle, Bentwood, Maple, Rockers, Burl 95.00
Furniture, Cradle, Lunenburg County, Nova Scotia, C.1860, Cutouts 185.00
Furniture, Cradle, Mahogany, Shaped Hood, Pierced Hearts In Side, 26 In. 200.00
Furniture, Cradle, Maplewood, Nova Scotia, C.1860, Cutouts At Top 185.00
Furniture, Cradle, Pine, Painted, 19th Century 150.00
Furniture, Cradle, Swinging, Bentwood Frame, Wheels On One End, 1876 .... 150.00
Furniture, Cradle, Wicker, Doll's, 8 In., Trimmed With Chalkware Flowers 27.50
Furniture, Cradle, Windsor Style, Maple, 100 Years Old, 40 X 38 In. 250.00
Furniture, Credenza, Italian, Walnut Baroque, Late 1600s, 36 In. 1300.00
Furniture, Credenza, Italian, Walnut, Baroque, Late 1600s, 40 In. 1300.00
Furniture, Cupboard, American, 1808, Corner, Pine & Poplar, 2 Piece, 80 In. 1425.00
Furniture, Cupboard, California, C.1830, Redwood, 1 Piece, 84 In. 725.00
Furniture, Cupboard, Corner, Cherry .... *Illus* 2000.00
Furniture, Cupboard, Corner, Chippendale, Pine, New England, C.1800 .... 700.00
Furniture, Cupboard, Corner, Federal, Inlaid Mahogany, New York, C.1810, 6 Ft. 500.00
Furniture, Cupboard, Corner, Pine & Poplar, Pennsylvania, 7 Ft. 1500.00
Furniture, Cupboard, Corner, 50 1/2 X 26 X 96 In. .... *Illus* 900.00
Furniture, Cupboard, English, Victorian, Corner, Oak, Carved 900.00
Furniture, Cupboard, Federal, Curly Maple, 2 Parts, New York, C.1800 .... 2400.00
Furniture, Cupboard, Ireland, 2 Piece, 2 Glass Doors, Drawers In Base 225.00
Furniture, Cupboard, Jelly, Chamfered Corners, Molded Edges On Drawers 1500.00
Furniture, Cupboard, Jelly, Fluted Band Top, Chamfered Corners 1500.00
Furniture, Cupboard, Kitchen, Oak & Pine, Handmade 135.00
Furniture, Cupboard, Mennonite, R.Kuger, Berlin, Ontario, Pine, Corner, Painted 1150.00
Furniture, Cupboard, Oak, Glass Door .... 195.00 To 285.00
Furniture, Cupboard, Pennsylvania Dutch, Soft Wood 1400.00
Furniture, Cupboard, Pennsylvania, C.1790, Cherry, Carved, Corner, 2 Parts 1700.00
Furniture, Cupboard, Pennsylvania, Pine, Corner, 2 Piece, Bracket Feet, 7 Ft. 895.00
Furniture, Cupboard, Pewter, Gray Paint, 81 X 45 In. 460.00
Furniture, Cupboard, Pie, Punched Tin .... *Illus* 700.00
Furniture, Cupboard, Pine, Corner, Raised Door Panels, C.1750, 6 Ft.8 In. 1500.00

Furniture, Cupboard, Pie, Punched Tin

Furniture, Cupboard, Soft Wood, 52 1/2 In.High, Red Paint

Furniture, Cupboard, Pine, Hanging Corner, Refinished 225.00
Furniture, Cupboard, Poplar, Red, Blue Pie Shelf, 2 Glass Doors Top, 84 In. 585.00
Furniture, Cupboard, Primitive, Walnut, Pegged, 3 Glass Doors, 2 Without 300.00
Furniture, Cupboard, Quebec, Shell Carvings, Blue, Step Back, Fluted Columns 750.00
Furniture, Cupboard, Quebec, 1878, Blue Paint, 2 Doors 190.00
Furniture, Cupboard, Renfrew County, Ont., C.1850, Red Paint, Open Top 950.00
Furniture, Cupboard, Soft Wood, 52 1/2 In.High, Red Paint .... *Illus* 850.00
Furniture, Daybed, Empire, Grained Rosewood, New York, C.1835, Pair 3000.00
Furniture, Daybed, Italian, Rococo, Painted, Upholstered Ends, 1880s, 5 Ft. 275.00
Furniture, Daybed, Oak Head & Footboard, C.1860, 72 In. Long 225.00
Furniture, Daybed, Ontario Provenance, C.1840, Curly Maple 170.00
Furniture, Daybed, Philadelphia, C.1690, Walnut, Turned, Rush Seat 4200.00
Furniture, Daybed, Queen Anne, Turned Cherry, C.1735, 6 Ft. 950.00
Furniture, Desk & Bookcase, Lady's, Federal, Inlaid Mahogany, C.1790 .... 2000.00
Furniture, Desk & Bookcase, Lady's, Federal, Inlaid Mahogany, Satinwood 1300.00
Furniture, Desk, Art Deco, Walnut, Stained, 38 X 42 In. .... *Illus* 2000.00
Furniture, Desk, Back Desk, Jens Marie Hotel, Oak 200.00
Furniture, Desk, Bowmanville, Ontario, Bird's-Eye Maple 3000.00
Furniture, Desk, Butler's, Cherry, C.1840 .... 500.00
Furniture, Desk, Butler's, Federal, Inlaid Mahogany, C.1800, 40 In. 375.00
Furniture, Desk, Butler's, Federal, Inlaid Mahogany, New York, C.1800, 43 In. 650.00
Furniture, Desk, Butler's, Ontario, C.1820, Figured Maple 1750.00
Furniture, Desk, Campaign, Mahogany, Mid-1900s, 24 In. 150.00
Furniture, Desk, Captain's, Light Fruitwood, 32 X 21 1/2 X 20 In. 800.00
Furniture, Desk, Cherry, Original Brasses, C.1800, 43 X 41 X 19 In. 1500.00
Furniture, Desk, Child's, Oak, Kneehole, Claw Feet, Bow Front 95.00
Furniture, Desk, Connecticut, C.1760, Cherry, Slant Front, 4 Drawer, 43 In. 2400.00
Furniture, Desk, Country Schoolhouse 12.50
Furniture, Desk, Country, Birch & Pine, 2 Drawer, C.1890 .... 450.00
Furniture, Desk, Curly Maple, Slant Front, High Bracket Feet, 36 In. 4500.00
Furniture, Desk, English, C.1690, Walnut, Marquetry, Slant Front 8500.00
Furniture, Desk, English, C.1790, Tambour, Mahogany & Satinwood, 39 In. 2200.00
Furniture, Desk, English, C.1860, Magistrate's, Mahogany, Tambour Roll Top 6500.00
Furniture, Desk, English, Queen Anne, Georgian Base 2000.00
Furniture, Desk, French, Boule, Fall Front, 3 Fitted Drawers 900.00
Furniture, Desk, French, Oak, Bombe, Drawers On 4 Sides, 52 X 32 In. 1500.00
Furniture, Desk, George II, Mahogany, C.1780, 21 1/2 X 30 1/2 In. 4500.00
Furniture, Desk, Golden Oak, Roll Top, 65 In. 600.00
Furniture, Desk, Lady's, New England, C.1825, Painted & Grained, 49 3/4 In. 275.00
Furniture, Desk, Lady's, Oak, Roll Top, 1898, 42 In. 450.00
Furniture, Desk, Lady's, Oak, Slant Top 135.00

Furniture, Desk, Art Deco, Walnut, Stained, 38 X 42 In.

Furniture, Desk, Queen Anne, Birch, 20 3/4 X 44 X 32 1/2 In.

Furniture, Desk, Lady's, Pennsylvania Dutch, C.1860, Oak 95.00
Furniture, Desk, Lap, Blue Velvet Lining, Secret Compartment, 19th Century 75.00
Furniture, Desk, Lap, Inlaid Wood, Purple Velvet Lined, Ink Bottle 98.00
Furniture, Desk, Lap, Ivory Nameplate, 12 In. 45.00
Furniture, Desk, Lap, Mahogany, Hinged, Lid, 6-Compartment, 1850s 55.00
Furniture, Desk, Lap, Oak, With Inkwell, 9 X 11 3/4 In. 65.00
Furniture, Desk, Lap, Walnut 72.00
Furniture, Desk, Massachusetts, C.1760, Curly Maple, Slant Front, 41 In. 5000.00
Furniture, Desk, Oak, Drop Front 100.00
Furniture, Desk, Oak, Roll Top .... 200.00 To 350.00
Furniture, Desk, Oak, Roll Top, Brass Fittings 925.00
Furniture, Desk, Oak, Roll Top, Refinished 500.00
Furniture, Desk, Oak, Roll Top, S Design, 49 1/2 X 34 In. 75.00
Furniture, Desk, Oak, Roll Top, With Chair, Refinished, 60 X 30 X 43 1/4 In. 120.00
Furniture, Desk, Oak, Roll Top, 60 In. 750.00
Furniture, Desk, Oak, Shelves At One Side, Curved Glass Door 180.00
Furniture, Desk, Partners, Georgian, 2 Pedestal, Leather Top 1800.00
Furniture, Desk, Partners, Mahogany, Carved, Ball & Claw Feet, C.1890, 53 In. 850.00
Furniture, Desk, Plantation, Oak, Marble Change Section 500.00
Furniture, Desk, Queen Anne, Birch, 20 3/4 X 44 X 32 1/2 In. .... *Illus* 4000.00
Furniture, Desk, Queen Anne, Slant Top, Walnut, Pine Sides, English, C.1720 .... 2800.00
Furniture, Desk, Schoolmaster, Cherry, 18th Century 585.00
Furniture, Desk, Schoolmaster's, Pine & Tiger Maple, 34 X 28 X 20 In. 275.00
Furniture, Desk, Seymour, Boston, C.1800, Mahogany & Curly Maple, Tambour 1900.00
Furniture, Desk, Slant Front, American Walnut, Shell Carving, C.1785 .... 0300.00
Furniture, Desk, Slant Front, Chippendale, Mahogany, Massachusetts, 42 In. 9000.00
Furniture, Desk, Slant Top, Child's, Fancy Brass Pulls 65.00
Furniture, Desk, Walnut, Carved, Lady's With Cabriole Legs, 40 X 46 In. 600.00
Furniture, Desk, Wellington, English, C.1850, Mahogany, 6 Ft.5 In X 17 In. 1500.00
Furniture, Desk, Wooton, American, Walnut, 72 X 41 X 28 In. .... *Illus* 3000.00
Furniture, Dining Room Set, Hoosier, 8 Piece 900.00
Furniture, Dining Set, Saginaw, Mich., C.1926, Walnut, Carved, 9 Piece 5500.00
Furniture, Dining Set, Spanish, Oak, Carved, 8 Piece 1000.00
Furniture, Dining Set, Trestle Table, C.1930, 8 Piece 375.00
Furniture, Doll, Bureau And Mirror, Ivory Finish, Pink Flowers, Brass Pulls 45.00
Furniture, Doll, Settee, 2 Chairs, Table, C 1914 .... 65.00
Furniture, Door, Mother-Of-Pearl Inlay, Carved, 6 X 3 Ft. 6500.00

Furniture, Dresser, Child's, Oak, Mirror 125.00
Furniture, Dresser, Doll's, Victorian, Oak, Mirror 125.00
Furniture, Dresser, Oak, Long Mirror .... 325.00 To 365.00
Furniture, Dresser, Victorian, Walnut, Salesman's Sample, 27 X 14 In. 95.00
Furniture, Dresser, Welsh, C.1750, Oak 2400.00
Furniture, Dresser, Welsh, C.1830, Oak, 6 1/2 X 5 1/2 Ft. 1650.00
Furniture, Dressing Glass, Pennsylvania, C.1780, Curly Maple, Bow Front 475.00
Furniture, Dry Sink, Pine, Dark Red Paint 350.00
Furniture, Dry Sink, Pine, Tin Top, Primitive 395.00
Furniture, Dry Sink, Quebec, Colored Finish, Door In Base 235.00
Furniture, Etagere, Federal, Turned Mahogany, J.Ellis, Early 1900s, 50 In. 850.00
Furniture, Etagere, Walnut, Marble Base, Mirrors 1000.00
Furniture, Fauteuil, Carved Walnut, En Cabriolet, Late 18th Century, Pair 1200.00
Furniture, Fern Stand, Oak, 35 In. 25.00
Furniture, Fire Screen, Victorian, Hand-Carved Walnut, Needlepoint 750.00
Furniture, Fireplace & Mantel, Carved Black Walnut, 80 X 52 In. 100.00
Furniture, Flowerpot Stand, Markham, Ontario, C.1850, Pine, Gray Paint, 3 Step 225.00
Furniture, Footstool, Horn Legs, Red Velvet Cover, 10 X 6 1/2 In. 40.00
Furniture, Footstool, Needlepoint, Ornate Carving 85.00
Furniture, Footstool, Shaker, Mt.Lebanon Decal 140.00
Furniture, Frame, Beaded, Heart Shape, Two Tintypes Of Children, 1888 .... 55.00
Furniture, Frame, FAD, Italy, Mosaic, Brass Trim & Feet, 4 X 3 In. 12.00
Furniture, Frame, Fireplace, Oak, Mirror, 92 X 60 In. 125.00
Furniture, Frame, Made Of Twigs, 13 In. .... *Illus* 20.00
Furniture, Frame, Oval, Deep, Walnut, 10 X 12 In. 25.00
Furniture, Frame, Picture, Etched Glass, Easel, 4 1/2 X 3 1/2 In. 5.00
Furniture, Frame, Shadowbox, Walnut, Gold Liner, 10 X 8 In. 45.00
Furniture, Frame, Victorian, Wooden, Art Nouveau, 12 In., Pair 35.00
Furniture, Frame, Walnut, Black, Victorian, Oval, 14 X 12 In., Pair 90.00
Furniture, Frame, Walnut, Crisscross, 7 X 5 In. 12.00
Furniture, Frame, Walnut, Gold Leaf Inner Edge, Oval, 13 X 11 In. 35.00
Furniture, Frame, Walnut, Gold Liner, Oval, 13 1/2 X 11 In. 47.50
Furniture, Frame, Walnut, Oval, 12 X 10 In., Pair 75.00
Furniture, Frame, Walnut, Oval, 22 1/2 X 19 1/2 In. 35.00
Furniture, Hall Rack, Rosewood, Triangle With 3 Brass Hooks & Plate Mirror 42.00
Furniture, Hall Stand, Mirror & Hocks 50.00
Furniture, Hall Tree, Oak, Seat 62.50

Furniture, Desk, Wooton, American, Walnut, 72 X 41 X 28 In.

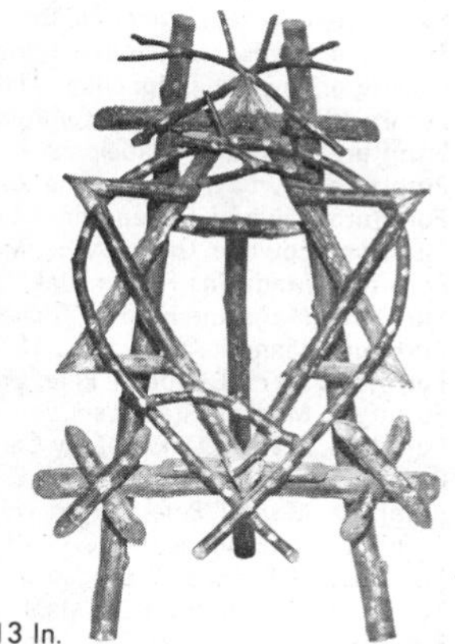
Furniture, Frame, Made Of Twigs, 13 In.

Furniture, Highchair, Child's, Victorian, Stained Wood

Furniture, Hamper, Clothes, Wicker, 23 X 22 In. 30.00
Furniture, Hat Rack, Brass, 6 Ft. 95.00
Furniture, Hat Rack, Rosewood, Plate Mirror, 3 Hooks, Triangular, 27 In. 45.00
Furniture, Headboard, Spanish Provincial, C.1835, Green Scene, 40 1/2 In. 375.00
Furniture, High Chair, Windsor, Bamboo Turned, C.1800 175.00
Furniture, Highboy, Chippendale, Mahogany, Bonnet Top, Swanneck Crest, 7 Ft. 2550.00
Furniture, Highboy, Golden Oak 85.00
Furniture, Highboy, Massachusetts, C.1730, Crotch Walnut, 6 Ft.4 In. 9750.00
Furniture, Highboy, New England, C.1735, Walnut, William & Mary Style 4500.00
Furniture, Highboy, Philadelphia, C.1790, Mahogany, Carved, Bonnet Top, 8 Ft. 4500.00
Furniture, Highboy, Queen Anne, Carved Maple, Flat Top, 2 Part, C.1750, 6 Ft. 6250.00
Furniture, Highboy, Queen Anne, Maple, Bonnet Top, Swanneck Crest, 7 Ft. 2500.00
Furniture, Highboy, Queen Anne, Massachusetts, Mahogany, Veneered Front 6000.00
Furniture, Highboy, Walnut And Maple, Massachusetts, Small Proportions 8500.00
Furniture, Highchair, Child's, Victorian, Stained Wood *Illus* 200.00
Furniture, Highchair, Oak 65.00
Furniture, Highchair, Stenciled Decorations 19.00
Furniture, Ice Cream Set, Oak Table Top, Wooden Seats, 5 Piece 325.00
Furniture, Ice Cream Set, White Paint, Heart-Shaped Chairs, 5 Piece 225.00
Furniture, Icebox, Oak 175.00
Furniture, Kitchenette, Napanee, Dutch, Oak, Enamel Top, Rolltop, Condiment Set 350.00
Furniture, Lectern, Mahogany, Carved American Eagle, C.1850, 56 In. 850.00
Furniture, Looking Glass, Chippendale, Protruded Golden Bits At Top, 21 In. 330.00
Furniture, Loveseat, Eastlake, Victorian, Walnut & Walnut Burl, 5 Ft. 650.00
Furniture, Loveseat, Victorian, Double Harp Inlaid Back, Needlepoint 175.00
Furniture, Loveseat, Victorian, Hand-Carved Mahogany, Upholstered 1500.00
Furniture, Lowboy, Chippendale, Philadelphia, 18th Century 3750.00
Furniture, Lowboy, English, Georgian, Oak, 3 Drawer 1500.00
Furniture, Lowboy, Philadelphia, C.1850, Mahogany, Carved, Frieze Drawer 2000.00
Furniture, Lowboy, Queen Anne, Carved Walnut, New England, C.1730, 30 In. 4500.00
Furniture, Lowboy, Queen Anne, Carved Walnut, Pennsylvania, 1740-50 7750.00
Furniture, Lowboy, Queen Anne, Mahogany, English, Mid-1800s 950.00
Furniture, Magazine Holder, Oak, Carrying Handle, Turned Wood Ends 28.00
Furniture, Magazine Holder, Wicker, White, Carrying Handle 34.00
Furniture, Mantel, American, C.1810, White Paint, Carved, 6 Ft.1 In. 195.00
Furniture, Mantel, Federal, Pine, Gray Paint, Fluted Pilasters, Side Panels 120.00
Furniture, Mantel, Fireplace, Cypress, New Orleans, C.1850 200.00 To 300.00
Furniture, Mantel, Oak, Heavily Carved 150.00
Furniture, Mantel, Pennsylvania, C.1800, Pine, Chip Carved Reserves, 7 Ft. 650.00
Furniture, Mantel, Pine, Carved Trailing Leafage, C.1800, 6 Ft.7 In. 400.00
Furniture, Massachusetts, C.1790, Mahogany, Carved, Barrel Back, 5 Ft.10 In. 4500.00
Furniture, Milk Stool, 3-Legged 12.00
Furniture, Mirror, Bird's-Eye Maple, Beveled, Metal Stand, 6 In. 15.00
Furniture, Mirror, Brass Over Iron, Bacchus Head Top, Beveled, 15 In. 45.00

Furniture, Mirror, Carved Gilt Borders, Beveled, Rectangular, 43 X 20 In. 200.00
Furniture, Mirror, Chippendale, Carved, Mahogany, Philadelphia, C.1760, 46 In. 1300.00
Furniture, Mirror, Chippendale, Mahogany & Parcel Gilt, Basket Crest, 48 In. 950.00
Furniture, Mirror, Chippendale, Mahogany & Parcel Gilt, Eagle Crest, 36 In. 375.00
Furniture, Mirror, Concave, Georgian, Reeded Mahogany Frame, 14 1/2 In. 140.00
Furniture, Mirror, Dressing Table, Iron, Gold Finish, Cupid & Gargoyles 65.00
Furniture, Mirror, Dressing, Empire, Mahogany Burl, Glove Box Below, 36 In. 135.00
Furniture, Mirror, Empire, Ormolu Mounted, Mahogany, Cheval, 5 Ft. 600.00
Furniture, Mirror, Empire, 1810, 50 X 24 1/2 In. 150.00
Furniture, Mirror, Federal Gilt Wood And Gesso, American Eagle Panel, 39 In. 1800.00
Furniture, Mirror, Federal Gilt Wood, Convex Girandole, C.1810, 46 In. 2100.00
Furniture, Mirror, Federal, Gilt Wood & Gesso, Eglomise 15, 30 In. 1500.00
Furniture, Mirror, Gilt Wood & Gesso, Broken Cornice, C.1820, 47 In. 200.00
Furniture, Mirror, Gilt Wood & Gesso, Eagle Crest, Convex, C.1810, 49 In. 650.00
Furniture, Mirror, Italian Baroque, Carved & Painted, 40 In. 225.00
Furniture, Mirror, Italian Rococo Gilt Wood, Urn And Swag Top, 5 Ft. 950.00
Furniture, Mirror, Italian Rococo, Carved Gilt Wood, 43 In., Pair 1000.00
Furniture, Mirror, Louis XV, Carved Gilt Wood, 5 Ft. 850.00
Furniture, Mirror, Louis XV, Gilt Wood, Rope-Twist Pierced Borders, 42 In. 400.00
Furniture, Mirror, Louis XVI, Carved, Painted, Acanthus Columns, 4 Ft. 225.00
Furniture, Mirror, Louis XVI, Carved, Painted, Flower-Filled Urn Top, 4 Ft. 400.00
Furniture, Mirror, Louis XVI, Carved, Painted, 23 1/2 In. 200.00
Furniture, Mirror, Mahogany & Parcel Gilt, Phoenix Crest, C.1760, 31 In. 750.00
Furniture, Mirror, Mahogany Veneer, 1840, 24 X 17 In. 25.00
Furniture, Mirror, Mahogany, Scrolled Crest & Pendant, C.1760, 41 1/2 In. 400.00
Furniture, Mirror, Mantel, Mid-1800, Painted Frame, Porcelain Brackets, 6 Ft. 1300.00
Furniture, Mirror, New York, C.1825, Gilt Wood & Gesso, Molded Slip, 50 In. 250.00
Furniture, Mirror, Oak Frame, Beveled Glass, 36 X 10 In. 60.00
Furniture, Mirror, Oak Frame, Beveled Glass, 38 1/2 X 10 1/2 In. 75.00
Furniture, Mirror, Pier, Gold Leaf Rope & Shell, Marble Top 400.00
Furniture, Mirror, Plateau, Scrolled Border, Fancy Feet .... 25.00 To 35.00
Furniture, Mirror, Queen Anne, Walnut & Parcel Gilded, C.1740 .... 250.00
Furniture, Mirror, Reverse Painted, Girl, Gold Frame, Brass Rosettes 65.00
Furniture, Mirror, Shaving, Georgian, Reeded Mahogany, Concave, 14 1/2 In. 140.00
Furniture, Mirror, Shaving, Mahogany & Pine, Jan.8, 1813 .... *Illus* 525.00
Furniture, Mirror, Shaving, Mahogany Frame, Oval Beveled Glass, 7 X 5 In. 45.00
Furniture, Mirror, Shaving, Victorian, Carved Leaf, Mug & Razor, 14 In. 42.50
Furniture, Mirror, South German, Rococo Carved Gilt Wood, 4 Ft. 275.00
Furniture, Mirror, Traveling, Inlaid Medallion, Hinged, C.1850, 6 1/2 In. 32.00
Furniture, Mirror, Traveling, Inlaid Wood, Hinged, Carved Scene, C.1850, Oval 22.00
Furniture, Mirror, Venetian Rococo Carved Gilt Wood, 2 Candleholders, 44 In. 500.00
Furniture, Mirror, Venetian, Painted, Parcel Gilt, Oval, 25 In. 300.00
Furniture, Mirror, Victorian Carved Gilt Wood, Oval, 43 1/2 In. 200.00
Furniture, Mirror, Walnut & Parcel Gilt, Swanneck Crest, C.1760, 5 Ft.9 In. 4500.00
Furniture, Mirror, Walnut, Beveled Glass, C.1850, 54 X 40 In., Pair 1000.00
Furniture, Mixing Stand, Mahogany, Marble Top, Chamfered Legs, C.1760, 30 In. 550.00

Furniture, Mirror, Shaving, Mahogany & Pine, Jan.8, 1813

Furniture, Music Stand, English, Brass & Iron, Adjustable 250.00
Furniture, Nightstand, Inlaid, Carriole Legs, 22 X 16 X 31 In. 425.00
Furniture, Pew, Church, Oak, 8 Ft. 140.00
Furniture, Piano, Grand, Steinway, With Aeolian Player, 145 Rolls, Mahogany 5500.00
Furniture, Pie Safe, C.1860 .... 187.50
Furniture, Pie Safe, Maple, Pierced Tin Doors, Drawer In Bottom 72.50
Furniture, Pie Safe, Oak 161.00
Furniture, Pie Safe, Painted 35.00
Furniture, Press, Linen, Chippendale, Carved Mahogany, New York, C.1760, 6 Ft. 1900.00
Furniture, Press, Linen, New York, C.1790, Mahogany, Inlaid, 2 Parts, 2 Doors 750.00
Furniture, Press, Linen, Pennsylvania, C.1760, Cherry, Carved, 2 Parts, 7 Ft. 2300.00
Furniture, Press, Linen, Pine, C.1850 .... 425.00
Furniture, Press, Walnut, 24 Blown Glass Panes In Doors, C.1750 .... 965.00
Furniture, Pulpit, Oak, Hand-Carved, Ornate 5500.00
Furniture, Rack, Boot, American, Mahogany, 19th Century, Trestle Feet, 48 In. 200.00
Furniture, Rack, Magazine, Victorian, Wall, Walnut 50.00
Furniture, Rack, Walnut Hat, Projecting Arms Tipped With White Porcelain 35.00
Furniture, Rocker, Arrow Back, Scrolled Seat & Arms, Stenciled 60.00
Furniture, Rocker, Child's, Oak, Cane Seat 65.00
Furniture, Rocker, Child's, Quebec, Red Paint 16.00
Furniture, Rocker, Child's, Wicker, Rolled Arms, Upholstered 125.00
Furniture, Rocker, Eastlake, Walnut, Platform 80.00
Furniture, Rocker, Frontenac County, Ontario, C.1820, Arrow Back, Combed 275.00
Furniture, Rocker, Japanese Revival, Wicker, Platform 125.00
Furniture, Rocker, Lincoln Style, Fruitwood, Arms, Carved Fruit, Velvet 365.00
Furniture, Rocker, Oak .... 30.00 To 75.00
Furniture, Rocker, Press Back, Oak 200.00
Furniture, Rocker, Sewing, Golden Oak, Cane Seat 75.00
Furniture, Rocker, Spindle Back, Scrolled Seat, Floral Design On Crest 95.00
Furniture, Rocker, Victorian, Walnut, Upholstered 240.00
Furniture, Rocker, Windsor, Signed 450.00
Furniture, Schrank, Pennsylvania, C.1770, Walnut, 2 Parts, Paneled Doors, 7 Ft 3500.00
Furniture, Screen, Baroque Painted Canvas, Palace, Fountain, Figures, 6 Ft. 3000.00
Furniture, Screen, Leather, 3 Fold, Foliage Design, Rectangular Panels, 6 Ft. 375.00
Furniture, Screen, Leather, 4 Fold, Courting Scenes, Flowers, 6 Ft.Panels 500.00
Furniture, Screen, Mahogany, Inlaid, Pole, Oval, Needlework, C.1800, 5 Ft. 275.00
Furniture, Screen, Table, Chinese, C.1870, 4-Fold, Carved Wood, Lacquer, 24 In. 195.00
Furniture, Seat, German Baroque, Walnut X-Frame, Late 1600s, Upholstered Seat 1600.00
Furniture, Seat, Hall, Oak, Carved, Lion Mask, Mirror, Hooks, Lift Top, 82 In. 400.00
Furniture, Secretary & Bookcase, Gentleman's, Federal, Mahogany Inlay, 8 Ft. 4000.00
Furniture, Secretary Bookcase, Carved Mahogany, Chippendale, New York, C.1760 .... 2000.00
Furniture, Secretary Bookcase, Chippendale, Carved, Cherry Inlay, 1770, 6 Ft. 6500.00
Furniture, Secretary Bookcase, Rhode Island, C.1750, Curly Maple & Pine 2800.00
Furniture, Secretary, Blockfront, American Queen Anne 5000.00
Furniture, Secretary, German Baroque, Walnut, C.1700, Slant Front, 7 Ft. 3250.00
Furniture, Secretary, Hepplewhite, Cherry & Tiger Maple, Secret Drawer 160.00
Furniture, Secretary, Tulipwood & Purplewood, Marquetry, Louis XV, 4 Ft. 5500.00
Furniture, Secretary, Victorian, Barrel, Rolltop .... 900.00 To 1400.00
Furniture, Secretary, Victorian, Rosewood, 100 X 45 X 21 In. 2500.00
Furniture, Secretary, Walnut, Burl Front 2000.00
Furniture, Server, Hepplewhite, Long Bow Front 2500.00
Furniture, Settee, Biedermeier, Fruitwood, Curved Ends, 60 In. 550.00
Furniture, Settee, Chippendale, 3 Chair Back, Mahogany, Claw & Ball Foot 1500.00
Furniture, Settee, French, 1st Empire, Mahogany, Carved Egyptian Heads 1200.00
Furniture, Settee, George II, Mahogany, C.1780, Upholstered In Needlepoint 1300.00
Furniture, Settee, Queen Anne, C.1875, 2 Matching Wingback Chairs 750.00
Furniture, Settee, Steerhorn, Upholstered, 45 In. 1200.00
Furniture, Settle, Child's, Pine, Red Stain, Shoe Feet, 32 In. 1250.00
Furniture, Shelf, Corner, Papier-Mache, Black, Daisies & Butterfly, 11 In. 25.00
Furniture, Shelf, Oak, Carved Wood And Under Shelf, Mirror Between 55.00
Furniture, Shelf, Oak, Towel Rack At Bottom, Grooved For Plates, 34 In. 43.00
Furniture, Shelf, Wall Hanging, Pine, Painted Orange & Black, C.1850, 26 In. 220.00
Furniture, Shelf, What-Not, Corner, Carved Walnut, 15 In. 22.50
Furniture, Sideboard, Bake, Leeds County, Canada, C.1860, 2 Doors 650.00

Furniture, Sideboard, English, C.1840, Mahogany, Bowfront, 3 Drawer ... 850.00
Furniture, Sideboard, European, C.1750, Walnut, Hand Carved, 8 Ft.10 In. ... 9500.00
Furniture, Sideboard, Federal, Inlaid Cherry, Serpentine Front, C.1790, 39 In. ... 8750.00
Furniture, Sideboard, Federal, Inlaid Mahogany, Bow Front, New York, C.1815 ... 800.00
Furniture, Sideboard, Federal, Inlaid Mahogany, Serpentine Front, New York ... 3250.00
Furniture, Sideboard, Federal, Inlaid Mahogany, Serpentine, 1790-1810, 39 In. ... 2100.00
Furniture, Sideboard, Golden Oak, Bevel Mirror ... 500.00
Furniture, Sideboard, Inlaid Mahogany, Hepplewhite, Serpentine Front, C.1795 ... 4600.00
Furniture, Sideboard, Mahogany, Inlaid, Bow Front, C.1790, 6 Ft. ... 2100.00
Furniture, Sideboard, Marble Top, Hand-Painted Medallions In Bronze, French ... 650.00
Furniture, Sideboard, Massachusetts, C.1790, Mahogany & Curly Maple, 6 Ft. ... 1600.00
Furniture, Sideboard, Mission Oak, Stained Glass, Locks & Keys ... 325.00
Furniture, Sideboard, New York, C.1800, Mahogany, Inlaid, Bow Front, 6 Ft. ... 600.00
Furniture, Sideboard, Oak, Hand-Carved, Ornate, 9 X 7 Ft. ... 5500.00
Furniture, Sideboard, Oak, Round Glass ... 265.00
Furniture, Sideboard, Philadelphia, C.1790, Mahogany, Inlaid, 6 Ft.1 In. ... 3000.00
Furniture, Sideboard, Pine, 3 Dovetailed Drawers In Base, Gallery Top ... 210.00
Furniture, Sideboard, Sheraton, 18th Century ... 3750.00
Furniture, Sideboard, Victorian, Oak, Carved Lion, Dolphin, & Neptune, Mirror ... 700.00
Furniture, Sideboard, Victorian, Oak, Ornate ... 250.00
Furniture, Sideboard, Viennese, C.1840, Oak, Carved, 2-Piece, 8 Ft.1 In. ... 2200.00
Furniture, Sideboard, Walnut, Carved, C.1840 ... 3200.00
Furniture, Sofa, American, Carved Walnut, Mid-19th Century, One Armrest ... 2100.00
Furniture, Sofa, Chippendale, Ecru Damask, 79 In.Long ... *Illus* 700.00
Furniture, Sofa, Empire, Carved Mahogany, 5 Ft. ... 160.00
Furniture, Sofa, Ephraim Haines, Phila., C.1800, Mahogany, Carved, Square Back ... 1900.00
Furniture, Sofa, Federal, Carved Mahogany, C.1820 ... 650.00
Furniture, Sofa, Federal, Carved Mahogany, New York, C.1810, 6 Ft.Long ... 1500.00
Furniture, Sofa, Federal, Carved, Mahogany, Massachusetts, 1790-1800, 17 In. ... 1800.00
Furniture, Sofa, New York, C.1810, Mahogany, Carved, Crest Rail, 6 Ft.9 In. ... 350.00
Furniture, Sofa, Rococo, Walnut, Pierced Carved ... 2500.00
Furniture, Sofa, Samuel McIntire, Salem, Federal, Mahogany, Scrolled Rail ... 2100.00
Furniture, Sofa, Victorian, Cameo Back, Red Velvet Upholstery ... 450.00
Furniture, Sofa, Victorian, Recamier, Mahogany Veneer, Navy Velvet ... 375.00
Furniture, Spinning Wheel, Wool, Wheel Is 49 1/2 In. ... 135.00
Furniture, Stand, Basin, Federal, Inlaid Mahogany, New England, C.1815, 40 In. ... 150.00
Furniture, Stand, Bedside, Cherry, Country Hepplewhite, One Drawer ... 165.00
Furniture, Stand, Bedside, 2 Dovetailed Drawers, Cherry, 19 1/2 X 20 In. ... 155.00
Furniture, Stand, Candlemaker, Pine, C.1840, Refinished ... 500.00
Furniture, Stand, Music, Bamboo ... 79.00
Furniture, Stand, Sheraton, Walnut, Bird's-Eye Maple Drawer ... 85.00
Furniture, Stool, Gout, On Rockers, Victorian, Upholstered ... 68.00
Furniture, Stool, Milking, Handmade, Handle, 3 Legs, 12 In. ... 44.00

Furniture, Sofa, Chippendale, Ecru Damask, 79 In.Long

Furniture, Stool, Oak, Bootjack Legs, Oblong, 16 X 10 In. 32.00
Furniture, Stool, Piano, Wooden, Cast Iron Feet, Needlepoint Top, 1873 .... 50.00
Furniture, Stove, Franklin Type, Dated 1885, Fancy 450.00
Furniture, Stove, Lifter, Shovel, 6 Round & 1 Oblong Cover 150.00
Furniture, Table, American Hepplewhite, Walnut Drop-Leaf Dining, C.1790 .... 850.00
Furniture, Table, Bird Cage Title Top, 29 X 20 3/4 In. .... *Illus* 675.00
Furniture, Table, Breakfast, English, C.1830, Mahogany, Inlaid Band At Top 435.00
Furniture, Table, Breakfast, New England, C.1750, Cherry 1600.00
Furniture, Table, Canadian, Victorian, Figured Maple Oval Top 325.00
Furniture, Table, Card, Cherry & Maple, Inlaid, Carved, Bow Front, C.1800 .... 700.00
Furniture, Table, Card, Federal, Inlaid Mahogany, Duncan Phyfe, New York, 30 In. 850.00
Furniture, Table, Card, Federal, Inlaid Mahogany, George Shipley, New York 2500.00
Furniture, Table, Card, Federal, Inlaid Mahogany, Maryland, C.1790, 35 In. 3000.00
Furniture, Table, Card, Federal, Inlaid Mahogany, Serpentine, C.1790, 29 In. 1700.00
Furniture, Table, Card, Federal, Inlaid Maple, Serpentine Front, C.1800, 29 In. 750.00
Furniture, Table, Card, Mahogany, Inlaid, Lyre Base, C.1820, 36 3/4 In. 550.00
Furniture, Table, Card, Mahogany, Inlaid, Oblong Top, C.1790, 39 In. 450.00
Furniture, Table, Card, Mahogany, Inlaid, Oblong Top, Ovolo Corners, C.1790 .... 850.00
Furniture, Table, Card, Massachusetts, C.1790, Mahogany & Bird's-Eye Maple 1100.00
Furniture, Table, Card, New York, C.1760, Mahogany, Carved, Serpentine, 34 In. 8500.00
Furniture, Table, Card, Philadelphia, C.1770, Mahogany, Hinged Top, 36 In. 1700.00
Furniture, Table, Center, Brentwood, 29 X 41 In. .... *Illus* 325.00
Furniture, Table, Cherry, Queen Anne, Drop Leaf, Swing Leg .... *Illus* 3150.00

Furniture, Table, Bird Cage Title Top, 29 X 20 3/4 In.

Furniture, Table, Center, Brentwood, 29 X 41 In.

Furniture, Table, Cherry, Queen Anne, Drop Leaf, Swing Leg

Furniture, Table, Chinese Temple, Gilded Figures In Relief 450.00
Furniture, Table, Chippendale, Mahogany, Carved, Tripod Base, 21 In. 250.00
Furniture, Table, Clerk's, Pine, Turned Legs, Dovetailed Drawer, 20 X 28 In. 115.00
Furniture, Table, Coffee, Chinese, Carved, Cloisonne Floral & Fish Inserts 550.00
Furniture, Table, Console, Inlaid Mahogany, Demilune Top, C.1790, 47 3/4 In. 500.00
Furniture, Table, Console, Mahogany, Inlaid, D-Shaped Top, C.1790, 36 In. 350.00
Furniture, Table, Console, Pennsylvania, C.1780, Mahogany, Demilune Top, 46 In 200.00
Furniture, Table, Console, Regency, Black Lacquer, Chinoiserie, Demilune, Pair 3000.00
Furniture, Table, Convent Of Grey Sisters, Montreal, Pine, 9 Drawer, 10 Ft. 795.00
Furniture, Table, Dining, Drop Leaf, Chippendale, Carved Mahogan .... 4000.00 To 6750.00
Furniture, Table, Dining, Drop Leaf, Federal, Carved Mahogany, Allison, N.Y. 700.00
Furniture, Table, Dining, Mahogany, Queen Anne Legs, Civil War Period 775.00
Furniture, Table, Dining, Marquetry On Legs, Fiddleback Mahogany Banding 1500.00
Furniture, Table, Dining, Massachusetts, C.1760, Mahogany, Drop Leaf, 42 In. 4500.00
Furniture, Table, Dining, Oak, Extension, 2 Leaves, Square 150.00
Furniture, Table, Dining, Oak, Marble Top, Carved-Leaf Legs, 72 X 44 In. 850.00
Furniture, Table, Dining, Square Oak, Clawfoot Pedestal, 3 Leaves, 42 In. 165.00
Furniture, Table, Dining, Walnut, Carved Legs 585.00
Furniture, Table, Dressing, Country Hepplewhite, Pine & Poplar, 1 Drawer 110.00
Furniture, Table, Dressing, Federal, Cherry & Curly Maple, New England, 36 In. 250.00
Furniture, Table, Dressing, Federal, Turned Cherry, New England, C.1810, 37 In. 300.00
Furniture, Table, Dressing, Nova Scotia, C.1870, Painted 195.00
Furniture, Table, Dressing, Sheraton, Pine, Yellow Paint, Black Striping 475.00
Furniture, Table, Dressing, Yellow Paint, Decorated, Brasses, C.1835 .... 825.00
Furniture, Table, Drop Leaf Pembroke, Mahogany, Hepplewhite, New Eng., C.1790 .... 750.00
Furniture, Table, Drop Leaf, Birch, Turned Legs, 19 X 42 In., 11 In.Leaves 110.00
Furniture, Table, Drop Leaf, Chippendale, Walnut, 8 Leg, 16 X 48, 17 In. Leaves 425.00
Furniture, Table, Drop Leaf, Dining, Queen Anne, Carved Walnut, C.1750, 29 In. 1900.00
Furniture, Table, Drop Leaf, Federal, Carved Mahogany, New York, C.1810, 29 In. 500.00
Furniture, Table, Drop Leaf, Federal, Cherry, Noyes, Connecticut, C.1810, 41 In. 1500.00
Furniture, Table, Drop Leaf, Flame Birch, Rope-Turned Legs, 39 X 29 In. 275.00
Furniture, Table, Drop Leaf, Mahogany, Louis XVI, 29 In. 1300.00
Furniture, Table, Drop Leaf, Mahogany, Two-Drawer, 29 In. 135.00
Furniture, Table, Drop Leaf, Queen Anne, Carved Walnut, Philadelphia, C.1740 .... 3000.00
Furniture, Table, Drop Leaf, Wide Boards, Pine, Refinished 100.00
Furniture, Table, Drop Leaf, Work, Federal, Inlaid Mahogany, C.1810, 29 In. 225.00
Furniture, Table, Drum, Walnut Top, 2 Drawers, Tripod Base, 32 X 27 In. 100.00
Furniture, Table, Dutch, Marquetry Center, Circular, Early 1800s, 30 In. 600.00
Furniture, Table, Eastlake, Walnut, Porcelain Castors, Oval, 29 In. 175.00
Furniture, Table, English, C.1780, Tulipwood & Walnut, Tilt Top, 51 In. 2400.00
Furniture, Table, English, Chinese Chippendale, Walnut, C.1760 .... 1500.00
Furniture, Table, Federal, Inlaid Mahogany, Pembroke, New York, C.1790, 28 In. 2700.00
Furniture, Table, Gaming, Felt Top, Walnut Trim, Claw Feet, Drawer 900.00
Furniture, Table, Gateleg, Turned Maple, Massachusetts, 1680-1710, 26 In. 3750.00
Furniture, Table, Harvest, Ontario, 2 Drawers, 6 Ft. 200.00
Furniture, Table, Hutch, Pine & Birch, Drawer & Shelf Under Seat, 28 1/2 In. 510.00
Furniture, Table, Hutch, Pine, C.1850 .... 600.00
Furniture, Table, Italian, Walnut, Painted Marble, Bacchus, 29 In., Pair 1200.00
Furniture, Table, Kitchen, Oak, Drop Leaf 150.00
Furniture, Table, Library, Drop Leaf, Federal, Carved Mahogany, C.1810 .... 2300.00
Furniture, Table, Library, Oak 60.00
Furniture, Table, Lily-Form, Bronze-Mounted Brass, 36 X 22 In. .... *Illus* 550.00
Furniture, Table, Madison County, N.Y., C.1820, Maple, Drop Leaf, 62 1/2 In. 2500.00
Furniture, Table, Mahogany, English, Sheraton, Pembroke, 19 1/2 X 38 1/2 In. 120.00
Furniture, Table, Mixing, Curly Maple, Marble Top, Turned Legs 350.00
Furniture, Table, Mixing, New York, C.1790, Red Paint 285.00
Furniture, Table, New England, C.1700, Maple, Gateleg, Turned Legs, 42 In. 3500.00
Furniture, Table, Oak, Claw Feet, 3 Leaves, Round, 42 In. 375.00
Furniture, Table, Oak, Claw Foot 285.00
Furniture, Table, Oak, Round .... 180.00 To 260.00
Furniture, Table, Pembroke, Chippendale, Carved Mahogany, C.1780, 28 In. 450.00
Furniture, Table, Pembroke, Chippendale, Philadelphia, C.1770, 28 1/4 In. 4000.00
Furniture, Table, Pembroke, Federal Inlaid Mahogany, New England, C.1790 .... 1600.00
Furniture, Table, Pembroke, Federal, Carved Mahogany, New York, C.1820, 28 In. 200.00

Furniture, Table, , Lily-Form, Bronze-Mounted Brass, 36 X 22 In.
(See Page 221)

Furniture, Table, Pembroke, Federal, Curly Maple, New England, C.1790 .... 475.00
Furniture, Table, Pembroke, Federal, Inlaid Mahogany, 28 In. 700.00
Furniture, Table, Pembroke, Mahogany, Leaves, 35 1/2 In. 395.00
Furniture, Table, Pembroke, New York, C.1810, Mahogany, Oblong Top, 33 In. 325.00
Furniture, Table, Pennsylvania, C.1770, Walnut Top, Beaded Edge, 30 In. 775.00
Furniture, Table, Pier, Brass Mounted Rosewood, New York, C.1815, 37 In. 700.00
Furniture, Table, Pier, Marble Top, Classical Painted & Stenciled, C.1820 .... 1600.00
Furniture, Table, Pool, Brunswick, Amaranth, Inlaid Woods 5000.00
Furniture, Table, Pool, Brunswick, Dragonhead, Patent 1875, Iron Base 7000.00
Furniture, Table, Pool, Brunswick, Dragons' Heads, Patent 1875, Iron Base 7000.00
Furniture, Table, Quebec, C.1790, Gateleg, 1 Drop Leaf, Stretcher Base 1250.00
Furniture, Table, Quebec, Maple, Oval Top 47.00
Furniture, Table, Queen Anne, Mahogany, Drop Leaf, Swing Legs 625.00
Furniture, Table, Roulette, Claw Feet, 8 Ft.X 44 In. 2700.00
Furniture, Table, Round Oak, Carved Foxheads Pedestal, One Leaf, Refinished 750.00
Furniture, Table, Round Tilt, English, Mahogany, 1757, 47 In. 1500.00
Furniture, Table, Sawbuck, Pennsylvania, Pink & Oak 925.00
Furniture, Table, Serving, Empire 200.00
Furniture, Table, Sewing, Fruitwood, Charles X, 28 1/2 In. 200.00
Furniture, Table, Side, Federal, Inlaid Mahogany & Birch, C.1810, 28 In. 275.00
Furniture, Table, Side, Mahogany, Fretted Gallery, C.1750 .... 1600.00
Furniture, Table, Side, Pine, Painted, Stenciled, Demilune Top, C.1815, 35 In. 425.00
Furniture, Table, Small Drop Leaf, Federal, Mahogany, C.1800, 27 In. 325.00
Furniture, Table, Snooker, Professional, Pool Sticks & Rack, C.1940 .... 225.00
Furniture, Table, Tavern, One Board Scrubbed Top, Drawer, C.1790 .... 1800.00
Furniture, Table, Tavern, Queen Anne, Maple & Cherry, Turned, Oval Top, 34 In. 800.00
Furniture, Table, Tavern, Queen Anne, Turned Maple & Pine, C.1730, 24 In. 2500.00
Furniture, Table, Tavern, Splay Leg, Queen Anne, Turned Maple & Pine, C.1730 .... 1900.00
Furniture, Table, Tea, Dish Top, Chippendale, Mahogany, Pennsylvania, 28 In. 2000.00
Furniture, Table, Tea, Louis XV, Mahogany 425.00
Furniture, Table, Tea, Mahogany, Carved, Tray Top, Beaded Apron, C.1750, 30 In. 1600.00
Furniture, Table, Tea, Mahogany, 1 Board Top, Desk Top, C.1769 .... 1500.00
Furniture, Table, Tea, Octagon, Marble Top, Black Walnut Base 250.00
Furniture, Table, Tea, Philadelphia, C.1760, Mahogany, Carved, Birdcage, Tripod 2600.00
Furniture, Table, Tea, Philadelphia, C.1760, Mahogany, Carved, Dish Top, 33 In. 1700.00
Furniture, Table, Tea, Pine, Cabriole Legs, Dutch Feet, 30 X 20 In.Top, 29 In. 795.00
Furniture, Table, Tea, Queen Anne, Maple, Scalloped Top, Valance Apron, 31 In. 450.00
Furniture, Table, Tea, Queen Anne, Walnut, Tray Top, Arcaded Apron, 32 In. 1100.00
Furniture, Table, Tilt Top Square With Bird Cage 650.00
Furniture, Table, Tilt Top, A.Stephen & Son, Halifax, N.S., C.1860 .... 395.00
Furniture, Table, Tilt Top, Birdcage, Maple & Bird's-Eye Maple, 28 In. 380.00
Furniture, Table, Tilt Top, Nova Scotia, C.1840, Pine, Maple Undercarriage 395.00
Furniture, Table, Tilt Top, Queen Anne, Cherry 600.00
Furniture, Table, Tilt Top, Round, English, Mahogany, C.1760 .... 1500.00

Furniture, Table, Tilt Top, Walnut, Birdcage Pedestal Base, C.1820, 35 In. 600.00
Furniture, Table, Tripod, Chippendale, Mahogany, Carving, 21 In. 295.00
Furniture, Table, Tyrolean Baroque, Pine And Oak, C.1680, 28 In. 2500.00
Furniture, Table, Victorian, Walnut, Drop Leaf 165.00
Furniture, Table, Wagon Wheel, Oak Pedestal & Base, Glass Surface, 48 In. 500.00
Furniture, Table, Walnut & Chestnut, Trestle, C.1720, 8 Ft.2 1/2 In. 1750.00
Furniture, Table, Work, Federal, Carved Mahogany, New York, C.1810, 33 In. 8500.00
Furniture, Table, Work, Federal, Carved Mahogany, Salem, C.1820, 29 In. 900.00
Furniture, Table, Work, Federal, Inlaid Curly Maple, C.1810, 27 1/2 In. 400.00
Furniture, Table, Work, Federal, Inlaid Mahogany, Massachusetts, C.1790, 27 In. 225.00
Furniture, Table, Work, Federal, Inlaid Mahogany, New York, C.1800, 30 In. 375.00
Furniture, Table, Work, Federal, Inland And Carved Maple, New England, C.1800 .... 300.00
Furniture, Table, Work, Federal, Mahogany, New England, C.1800, 30 In. 275.00
Furniture, Table, Work, Inlaid Mahogany, Lyre Base, C.1815, 31 In. 1300.00
Furniture, Table, Work, New York, C.1815, Mahogany, Inlaid, 2 Beaded Drawers 650.00
Furniture, Table, Writing, Louis XV, Provincial, Fruitwood, C.1750, 28 In. 400.00
Furniture, Table, Writing, Mahogany, Leather Top, 3 Drawer, C.1815, 53 In. 2500.00
Furniture, Tea Caddy, Mahogany, Inlaid Stellates, Hinged, C.1790, 12 3/4 In. 325.00
Furniture, Tea Caddy, Mahogany, Ivory Escutcheon, Bristol Bowl, 12 In. 268.00
Furniture, Teapoy, Federal, Inlaid Mahogany, Early 19th Century, 13 In. 300.00
Furniture, Towel Rack, Pennsylvania Dutch, Walnut, Hex Signs, Roller 50.00
Furniture, Tray, Cheese, English, Mahogany, 2 Sections, Shaped Ends 185.00
Furniture, Tray, Galle, Wooden, Inlaid Butterfly, 12 In. 225.00
Furniture, Trunk, Wooden, Norwegian, Rope Handles 95.00
Furniture, Wall Pocket, Walnut, Carved Leaf & Branch, Victorian, 24 X 13 In. 18.00
Furniture, Wardrobe, Cherry, Large, Refinished 600.00
Furniture, Wardrobe, Crown Top, 3 Sections, Beveled Mirror Doors, Claw Feet 300.00
Furniture, Washstand, American, Oak, Drawer, 2 Drawers & Shelf Inside 248.00
Furniture, Washstand, Child's, Oak, Red Paint, 2 Shelves Inside, 18 In. 35.00
Furniture, Washstand, Oak 100.00
Furniture, Washstand, Stencil Decoration, Drawer In Base 105.00
Furniture, Washstand, Tambour, Federal, Inlaid Mahogany, New York, C.1815 .... 750.00
Furniture, Water, Bench, Square Nails, Pine, Refinished 45.00
Furniture, Whatnot, Victorian, Walnut, Corner, 5 Shelves, Square Nails 90.00
Furniture, Yarn Winder, Turned Legs, Chip Carved Base, 40 In. 75.00
Furstenburg, Jar, Covered, Roses, Multicolors, C.1750, 5 In. 90.00

Gabriel Argy-Rousseau, born in 1885, was a French glass artist who produced a variety of objects in Art Deco style. His mark, G. Argy-Rousseau, was usually impressed.

G.Argy-Rousseau, Ewer, Turquoise & Purple, 3 1/2 In. 1500.00
G.Argy-Rousseau, Lamp Base, Pate De Verre, Gray & Lilac, C.1920, 21 In. 725.00
G.Argy-Rousseau, Lamp Base, Pate De Verre, Pink, Gray, Lilac, 21 In. 490.00
G.Argy-Rousseau, Vase, Pate De Verre, Gray, Purple & Blue Zinnias, 6 In. 735.00
G.Argy-Rousseau, Vase, Pate De Verre, Purple To Green Blue, Rosettes, 8 In. 1350.00
G.Raspillier, Jar, Frosted Gray, Red Brown Leaves, Metal Rim, 6 1/2 In. 240.00

Galle glass was made by the Galle Factory founded in 1874 by Emile Galle of France. The firm made cameo glass, furniture, and other Art Nouveau items, including some pottery. After Galle's death in 1904, the firm continued in production until 1935.

Galle Pottery, Vase, Floral, Dimpled Sides, 2 Eared, 5 In. 375.00
Galle Pottery, Vase, Yellow To Brown, Floral, Dimpled Sides, 2 Eared, 5 In. 375.00
Galle, Atomizer, Honey Tones, Sable-Colored Designs, 5 3/4 In. 240.00
Galle, Bottle, Perfume, Frosted Gold, Purple To Blue Violets, 4 1/8 In. 325.00
Galle, Bowl, Blue White Frosted, Polished Purple Flowers & Leaves, 4 In. 185.00
Galle, Bowl, Boat-Shape, Green On Blue On Frosted, 9 1/2 In. 275.00
Galle, Bowl, Purple & Yellow Pansies, Rope Handle, Nancy, Signed, 3 3/4 In. 185.00
Galle, Bowl, Red Leaves, & Acorns On Yellow Ground, 3 X 4 1/2 In. 350.00
Galle, Bowl, Red Leaves, Acorns, Yellow Ground, 3 X 4 1/4 In. 350.00
Galle, Box, Cameo, Covered, Gold With Purple Irises, 4 1/4 In. 415.00
Galle, Box, Cameo, Covered, Pansies & Foliage, Pansies Under Lid, 6 X 3 In. 345.00
Galle, Box, Frosted, Green Floral, Diamond Shape, 8 1/2 X 5 1/2 In. 475.00
Galle, Box, Raised Leaves, Green Ground, Purple Flower, 6 1/2 In. 1150.00

Galle, Cruet, Amber, Dragon, Beetle, Butterfly, Signed Nancy 325.00
Galle, Cruet, Cameo, Signed 325.00
Galle, Cup & Saucer, Floral, Enameled 105.00
Galle, Cup & Underplate, Blue & White Floral Enamel, Signed 150.00
Galle, Egg, Yellows & Greens, Brown Trees & Butterflies, Pedestal, 12 In. 1750.00
Galle, Lamp Base, Amber, Wheel Cut, Deep Maroon Leaves, 13 1/2 In. 500.00
Galle, Lamp Base, Light Amber, Maroon Leaves, Wheel Cut, 13 1/4 In. 500.00
Galle, Lamp Base, 3-Color, Cameo, Metal Neck, Signed, 5 3/4 In. 225.00
Galle, Lamp, Blue Amber, Wine & Blue Veined Leaves, Cloth Shade, 7 3/4 In. 425.00
Galle, Lamp, Night Light, Fuchsias, Lemon Ground, Brass Fitting 495.00
Galle, Lamp, Perfume, Satin Beige, Rust Berries, Leaves, Metal Top, 5 1/4 In. 210.00
Galle, Pitcher, Raised Dots, Bird In Flight, Autumn Colors, 3 In. 145.00
Galle, Shot Glass, Green Thistle Cameos, 2 1/4 In. 175.00
Galle, Tumbler, Whiskey, Frosted, Orange Flower & Leaves, 2 1/2 In. 145.00
Galle, Vase, Acid Cut, Frosted Gold, Flowers, Burgundy, Signed, 17 In. 1200.00
Galle, Vase, Acid Cut, 3 Colors, Signed, 5 1/2 In. 390.00
Galle, Vase, Amber Crackle, Enamel Fish & Seaweed, 4 In. 65.00
Galle, Vase, Amber, Enameled Yellow, Green, Gold, Signed 595.00
Galle, Vase, Amber, Yellow, Green & Gold Enamel Floral, 12 In. 975.00
Galle, Vase, Atomizer Top, Honey Toned, Sable Color Design, 5 3/4 In. 240.00
Galle, Vase, Autumn Colors, Gold, Oranges, Brown, Acid & Wheel Carved, 6 In. 425.00
Galle, Vase, Beige, Amber Blossoms, 13 In. 1200.00
Galle, Vase, Blue, Amethyst Floral, Green Leaves, 11 1/4 In. 390.00
Galle, Vase, Blue, Maroon Cuttings, 6 In. 650.00
Galle, Vase, Blues, Green, & Gold, Intaglio Water Lilies, 12 1/2 In. 1450.00
Galle, Vase, Brown To Amber, Signed, 5 1/2 X 5 In. 495.00
Galle, Vase, Browns, Gold & Tan, Blownout, 6 In. 1650.00
Galle, Vase, Bud, Blue, Signed, 7 In. 365.00
Galle, Vase, Bud, Floral, Miniature .... 175.00 To 225.00
Galle, Vase, Bud, Thistle, Miniature 250.00
Galle, Vase, Bud, 5 Colors, 4 1/2 In. .... 238.00 To 268.00
Galle, Vase, Butterscotch & Umber, Cut Foliage, 6 X 5 In. 495.00
Galle, Vase, Cameo & Enamel, Pink, Burgundy, Black, Gilt, E.Galle, 7 1/4 In. 775.00
Galle, Vase, Cameo, Crocus Blossoms, Magenta, Pink, Early Signature, 8 1/2 In. 775.00
Galle, Vase, Cameo, Narrow Stick Stem, Bulbous Base, Maroon, Signed, 6 3/4 In. 525.00
Galle, Vase, Cameo, 5 In. .... *Illus* 375.00
Galle, Vase, Clear, Enameled, 4 In. .... *Illus* 125.00
Galle, Vase, Crocus On Pink To White, Fire Polished, 8 3/4 In. 950.00
Galle, Vase, Cut Foliage, 5 1/2 X 3 In. 395.00
Galle, Vase, Deep Cameo, Sable-Colored Cameo On Honey Tones, Atomizer 180.00
Galle, Vase, Dimpled, 4-Sided, Sculpted Art Nouveau, Marked, 5 In. 375.00
Galle, Vase, Dragonfly, 4 Colors, 17 1/4 In. 1250.00

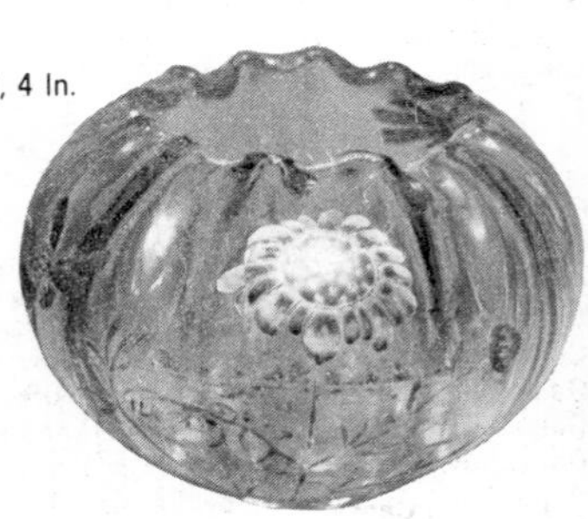

Galle, Vase, Clear, Enameled, 4 In.

Galle, Vase, Cameo, 5 In.

Galle, Vase, Figs, Gold Background, Leaves, Flowers, Fruit Pink & Red, 10 In. 795.00
Galle, Vase, Forest On Pink, Ferns, Tri-Petal Top, 11 1/2 In. 975.00
Galle, Vase, Frosted Gray & Pale Green, Blue Floral, 15 In. 600.00
Galle, Vase, Frosted Yellow, Red Floral & Leaves, Slim Stem, 4 1/4 In. 200.00
Galle, Vase, Frosted, Wine Grapes, Lilies, & Leaves, 3 In. 195.00
Galle, Vase, Globular, Fern Designs In Green, Signed, 2 1/2 In. 245.00
Galle, Vase, Gold Acid Ground, Brown Purple Floral, 6 In. 565.00
Galle, Vase, Gold To White, Ruby To Magenta Roses & Leaves, 17 1/2 In. 1250.00
Galle, Vase, Gold, Red Blossoms & Red To Purple Leaves, 15 1/2 In. 1950.00
Galle, Vase, Gray & Amber Floral, Green Foot, Frosted, Signed, 4 1/2 In. 485.00
Galle, Vase, Gray Green, Brown Tulips & Vines, Baluster Shape, 7 1/2 In. 345.00
Galle, Vase, Green & Blue, Wheel Cut Berries, Leaves, & Vines, 14 In. 1050.00
Galle, Vase, Green & Brown, Scenic, Wheel Polished, 6 In. 650.00
Galle, Vase, Green, Amber Floral, 7 1/2 X 5 In. 298.00
Galle, Vase, Green, White & Mauve Dandelions, 12 In. 400.00
Galle, Vase, Horseman Decoration, Simulated Leather Straps, Enamel, 10 In. 975.00
Galle, Vase, Lavender Satin, Purple Tulip & Leaves, 3 1/4 In. 155.00
Galle, Vase, Light Green River, Trees, & Pink Sky, 6 1/2 In. 530.00
Galle, Vase, Light Purple, Deep Purple Wisteria, Banjo Shape, 6 3/4 In. 260.00
Galle, Vase, Orange, Pale Brown, Berry-Laden Branches, 5 3/8 In. 250.00
Galle, Vase, Pale Green, Green & Brown Daisies & Leaves, 11 1/2 In. 480.00
Galle, Vase, Pale Yellow, Mauve Freesias, 8 1/2 In. 310.00
Galle, Vase, Pink & Mauve, Sunflowers, Frosted Ground, Chinese Style, Signed 475.00
Galle, Vase, Pink Pebbly Matte Finish, Enamel Floral, 10 1/2 In. 1650.00
Galle, Vase, Praying Mantis In High Relief, Crystal & Enamel, 5 1/2 In. 575.00
Galle, Vase, Purple Base, Brown Crocuses On Matte Yellow, Signed, 5 In. 475.00
Galle, Vase, Purple, Leaves, 9 1/2 In. 250.00
Galle, Vase, Red Nasturtiums & Foliage On Yellow Satin, 15 1/2 In. 525.00
Galle, Vase, Rose To Burgundy, Hyacinth, Mold Blown, 12 In. 2500.00
Galle, Vase, Ruby, Pale Blue Morning Glories, Cased Interior, Square, 6 In. 650.00
Galle, Vase, Rust & Green Underwater Plants, 6 3/4 In. 200.00
Galle, Vase, Scenic, Purple, Blue, Yellow, Layers, Trees, Mountains, Lake, 12 In. 625.00
Galle, Vase, Scenic, Purples, Blues, & Greens, Gold Top, 5 1/2 In. 695.00
Galle, Vase, Scenic, Trees, River, Picket Fence, Salmon Pink, Signed, 5 In. 425.00
Galle, Vase, Smoke & Pink, Wine Red Fruits & Leaves, 7 In. 340.00
Galle, Vase, Smoky Color, Rust & Coral Spider Berries, 9 In. 300.00
Galle, Vase, Spider Berries On Rust And Coral, Smoke Ground, Signed, 9 In. 250.00
Galle, Vase, Swirled Crystal, Red & Gold Enamel Floral, Ruffled Base, 6 In. 105.00
Galle, Vase, Three Color, Green, Pink, White, 9 3/4 In. 375.00
Galle, Vase, Three Colors, Inverted Bell Shape, 4 3/8 In. 198.00
Galle, Vase, White To Yellow, Etched Red Floral, Wheel Cut, 9 1/4 In. 585.00
Galle, Vase, White, Green Wisteria, Pink Orange Base & Top, 17 1/2 In. 395.00
Galle, Vase, 3 Color Ground, Pink To Cranberry Flowers, Paperweight, 13 In. 525.00
Galle, Vase, 3 Color, Floral Cutting, Signed, 9 3/4 In. 310.00
Galle, Vase, 3 Color, 5 In. 465.00
Galle, Vase, 3 Shades Of Amethyst, Wheel & Acid Cut Floral, 6 In. 692.00

Game plates are any type of plate decorated with pictures of birds, animals, or fish. The game plates usually came in sets consisting of twelve dishes and a serving platter. These game plates were most popular during the 1880s.

Game Plate, J.K.W., 1930, West Germany, Green Border, 10 1/2 In. 50.00
Game Plate, Pheasant, Gold Edge, 10 In. 32.50

Game, see also Disneyana; Game; Lone Ranger, Game; Popeye, Game

Game, Around The World With Nellie Bly, McLoughlin, 1890 55.00
Game, Authors, 1896 8.50
Game, Baron Munchausen 6.50
Game, Baseball, Pinch Hitter, Marble, Marked JS 20.00
Game, Ben Casey, 1962, Boxed 5.00
Game, Blondie, Westinghouse, 1933, Original Envelope 10.00
Game, Board, Elsie The Borden Cow 20.00
Game, Board, Little Black Sambo, 1940 15.00
Game, Camelot, 1930, Board 5.50
Game, Checkerboard, Inlaid Walnut & Oak, Dated 1896 19.00
Game, Checkerboard, Inlaid, C.1900 85.00

Game, Checkers, French, World War I, YMCA Package 5.00
Game, Checkers, Stagecoach, Pegged Checkers, Folding Wooden Board 35.00
Game, Checkers, Wooden, Occupied Japan, Boxed 1.50
Game, Chess Set, Jade Men, Carved, Marble Board 90.00
Game, Cribbage Board, Ivory, 7 In. 125.00
Game, Cribbage Board, Lash's Bitters, Wooden 24.50
Game, Crisscross Mystery Puzzle, Zulu Toy Co., 1927, Boxed 5.00
Game, District Messenger Boy, McLoughlin, 1890s 68.00
Game, Domino Set, Crown Beer, Syracuse, Wooden 10.00
Game, Domino Set, Ivory On Black Wood, Miniature, 28 Piece 30.00
Game, Dominoes, Embossed Airplanes, Boxed Set Of 52 25.00
Game, Dominoes, Germany, Boxed 5.00
Game, Dominoes, Ivory & Ebony, Riveted, Set 45.00
Game, Dominoes, Railroad Engine On Dominoes, 1900, 72 In Box 10.00
Game, Fibber McGee And Molly 7.50
Game, Fibber McGee, Wistful Vista Mystery, Milton Bradley 15.00
Game, Flinch, Card, Parker Bros. 5.00
Game, Fortune's Wheel, Parker Bros., 1903 45.00
Game, Game Of Snaps, West & Lee, 1873 8.50
Game, Hey Culligan Man, Boxed 4.00
Game, Hood's War Game, U.S.Vs.Spain, 1900, Boxed 10.00
Game, Jake & Lena Jigsaw Puzzle, Sohio 18.00
Game, Jigsaw Puzzle, Currier & Ives, 1935 5.00
Game, Jolly Game Of The Alabama Coon, Spear's, C.1900, Boxed 55.00
Game, Lotto, Lithographed Birds On Cover 7.00
Game, Mah-Jong Set, C.1920, Ivory & Bamboo Tiles, Leatherette Case 42.00
Game, Mah-Jong Set, Ivory & Bamboo Counters, Brass Bound Wood Case 85.00
Game, Mah-Jong Set, Ivory & Bamboo Tiles 74.00
Game, Mah-Jong Set, Wooden Tiles 10.00
Game, Mah-Jong, Bone & Bamboo 40.00
Game, Mah-Jong, Bone & Bamboo Tiles, Black Lacquer Box, C.1923 38.00
Game, Newsboy, Parker Bros., 1895 4.00
Game, Pick-Up Sticks, Wooden, Original Box, 1937 2.00
Game, Pit, C.1919 28.00
Game, Pit, Cards, Grain Exchange, 1919 28.00
Game, Pit, Parker Bros., Bull & Boar, Boxed, Instructions, 1904 10.00
Game, Puzzle Parties, Gilbert 4.00
Game, Puzzle Peg Lubbers, Bell Mfg.Co., 1924 5.00
Game, Puzzle, Fire Engine, Parker Bros., 1890s 55.00
Game, Puzzle, Goldberg Family, Radio Program, 1932 14.50
Game, Puzzle, Jigsaw, Captain Marvel Rides The Engine Of Doom, 1941, 18 In. 60.00
Game, Puzzle, Spanish American War, Get Spain Out Of Cuba & U.S.Boxed 8.00
Game, Puzzle, U.S.Map, Die Cut On State Lines, Selchow & Righter 12.00
Game, Radio Questionnarie, Battery Operated, 1928, Boxed 20.00
Game, Radio Tube, A.C.Gilbert, Boxed 4.50
Game, Shari Lewis, 1962, Boxed 5.00
Game, Sherlock Holmes, Parker, 1904 12.00
Game, Stage, 1904, Boxed 15.00
Game, Tell It To The Judge, Eddie Cantor, 1936, Board 17.00
Game, The Wizard, Fulton Specialty Co., 1915, Answers Questions With Arrow 15.00
Game, Tiddlywinks, J.W.& S.Bavaria China Cup 16.00
Game, Tiddlywinks, Machine-Turned Wooden Cup, Boxed 12.00
Game, Twiggy, Movie Star, Boxed 9.00
Game, U.S.Map Puzzle, Parker Bros., 1915 18.00
Game, What's My Line, C.1950, T.V.Board Game 5.00
Game, Wings, 1928, Parker Bros. 5.00
Game, Young Folks Historical, McLoughlin Bros. 20.00

The Gardner porcelain works was founded in Verbilki, outside Moscow, by the English-born Francis Gardner in 1766. Gardner made porcelain tablewares, figurines, and faience.

Gardner, Bowl, White, Blue Edge, Eagle & St.George, C.1758, 8 In. 110.00

Gaudy Dutch pottery was made in England for America from about 1810 to 1820. It is a white earthenware with Imari style decorations of red, blue, green, yellow, and black. Only sixteen patterns of Gaudy Dutch were made: Butterfly, Carnation, Dahlia, Double Rose, Dove, Grape, Leaf, Oyster, Primrose, Single Rose, Strawflower, Sunflower, Urn, War Bonnet, Zinnia, and No Name. Other similar wares are called Soft Paste, Gaudy Ironstone, or Gaudy Welsh.

Gaudy Dutch, Coffeepot, Single Rose 1400.00
Gaudy Dutch, Cup & Saucer, Butterfly 500.00
Gaudy Dutch, Cup & Saucer, War Bonnet .... 210.00 To 240.00
Gaudy Dutch, Cup Plate, Butterfly 1100.00
Gaudy Dutch, Plate, Soup, War Bonnet, 8 In. 190.00
Gaudy Dutch, Plate, Strawflower, Riley, 10 In. 680.00
Gaudy Dutch, Plate, Urn, 7 1/2 In. 275.00
Gaudy Dutch, Washstand Set, Sunflower Pattern, Burslem Mark On Bowl 550.00
Gaudy Ironstone, Bowl, Amherst, Japan, 6 3/4 In. 68.00
Gaudy Ironstone, Bowl, Japan, Amherst, Pedestal Base, 8 1/2 X 5 In. 115.00
Gaudy Ironstone, Cup & Saucer, Imari Style 35.00
Gaudy Ironstone, Cup & Saucer, Seeing Eye, Niagara, Handleless 125.00
Gaudy Ironstone, Jar, Cookie, Cane Handle 50.00
Gaudy Ironstone, Jar, Cookie, Cane Handle, Bright Colors 48.00
Gaudy Ironstone, Pitcher, Serpent Handle, Mason's Patent, 5 In. 65.00
Gaudy Ironstone, Plate, Ashworth, 9 1/2 In. 13.50
Gaudy Ironstone, Plate, Cake 28.00
Gaudy Ironstone, Plate, Double Handled, 10 7/8 X 9 3/4 In. 58.00
Gaudy Ironstone, Plate, Double Handled, 11 1/2 X 9 In. 58.00
Gaudy Ironstone, Plate, Morning Glory 50.00
Gaudy Ironstone, Plate, Urn, Pagodas, & Blossoms, Monfort, 10 1/2 In. 38.00
Gaudy Ironstone, Platter, Oriental, Mason's, 17 X 13 3/4 In. 68.00
Gaudy Ironstone, Sugar, Covered, Brick Red Floral, Pink Luster Trim, Handled 58.00
Gaudy Ironstone, Washstand Set, Blue & Burnt Orange, Octagonal, 2 Piece 85.00

Gaudy Welsh is an Imari decorated earthenware with red, blue, green, and gold decorations. It was made after 1820.

Gaudy Welsh, Biscuit Barrel 58.00
Gaudy Welsh, Bowl, Footed Fruit, Oyster Pattern, Scalloped Rim, C.1850 .... 125.00
Gaudy Welsh, Creamer, Doll's, Mask Spout, 2 1/4 In. 43.00
Gaudy Welsh, Cup & Saucer, Dahlia 38.00
Gaudy Welsh, Cup & Saucer, Oyster .... 58.00 To 68.00
Gaudy Welsh, Cup & Saucer, Tulip .... 30.00 To 37.00
Gaudy Welsh, Jar, Biscuit, Ivory Color, Cobalt Orange, & Copper, Brass Handle 125.00
Gaudy Welsh, Mug, Oyster, 3 In. 28.50
Gaudy Welsh, Pitcher, C.1830, 8 In. 65.00
Gaudy Welsh, Pitcher, Enamel Flowers, Cobalt On Gray, 7 In. 65.00
Gaudy Welsh, Pitcher, Milk, Tulip 52.00
Gaudy Welsh, Plate, Cake, Tulip 40.00
Gaudy Welsh, Plate, Oyster Pattern, 7 1/2 In. 19.00
Gaudy Welsh, Plate, Oyster, 7 1/8 In. 58.00
Gaudy Welsh, Plate, Tulip, 7 In. 25.00
Gaudy Welsh, Plate, Urn Pattern, 7 1/2 In. 55.00
Gaudy Welsh, Sugar, Covered, Flower Basket 75.00
Gaudy Welsh, Tea Set, Service For 8, Cake Plate 600.00
Gaudy Welsh, Teapot, Tulip Pattern 85.00
Gaudy Welsh, Teapot, 8 1/2 X 10 1/2 In. 130.00
Gene Autry, Book, Public Cowboy No.1, 1938, Big Little Book 4.00
Gene Autry, Film, Silent, Indian Uprising 15.00
Gene Autry, Horseshoe Ring On Card 6.00
Gene Autry, Lunch Box And Thermos 9.50
Gene Autry, Wallet 6.00

Gibson Girl plates were made in the early 1900s by the Royal Doulton Pottery at Lambeth, England. There are twenty-four different plates featuring a picture of the Gibson Girl by the artist Charles Dana Gibson.

Gibson Girl, Calendar, 1917, 6 Signed Girls, Fischer 15.00
Gibson Girl, Plate, A Quiet Dinner With Dr.Bottles, Royal Doulton 48.00

Gibson Girl, Plate, Among The Old Ones, 1900, 10 1/2 In. 55.00
Gibson Girl, Plate, Dinner With Dr.Bottles, 1900, 10 1/2 In. 55.00
Gibson Girl, Plate, Disturbed By A Vision, 1900, 10 1/2 In. 55.00
Gibson Girl, Plate, Hostile Criticism, Life, 1900, 10 1/2 In. 55.00
Gibson Girl, Plate, Message From Outside World, 10 1/2 In. 55.00
Gibson Girl, Plate, Miss Babbles Brings Copy 55.00
Gibson Girl, Plate, Miss Babbles The Authoress 60.00
Gibson Girl, Plate, Miss Diggs Is Alarmed 45.00
Gibson Girl, Plate, Mr.Waddles Arrives 55.00
Gibson Girl, Plate, She Becomes A Trained Nurse, 10 1/2 In. 55.00
Gibson Girl, Plate, She Is Subject Of More 40.00
Gibson Girl, Vase, Portraits, Royal Bayreuth, 4 3/4 In. 70.00
Gien, Flask, Pilgrim's, French Faience, White, Birds & Floral, 7 1/4 In. 75.00

GILLINDER *Gillinder pressed glass was first made by William T. Gillinder of Philadelphia in 1863. Many pressed glass items were made for the Centennial.*

Gillinder, Bust, Abraham Lincoln, Opaque White Satin Glass, 1876, 6 In. 375.00
Gillinder, Bust, Lincoln, Opaque White, Centennial, 1876, 6 In. 395.00
Gillinder, Bust, Washington, Centennial Exhibition, Frosted & Clear, 6 In. 75.00
Gillinder, Dish, Muffineer, Satin Finish, Melon, Floral Decoration 75.00
Gillinder, Dish, Pickle, Duck Cover, Amber 40.00
Gillinder, Figure, Buddha, Red, Clambroth Or Amber, Signed 38.00
Gillinder, Figurine, Goddess Of Fortune, Amberina 125.00
Gillinder, Muffineer, Melon Ribbed, Satin Finish, Enamel Decoration, 5 In. 67.00
Gillinder, Muffineer, Pale Blue, Melon Ribbed, Floral 79.00
Gillinder, Paperweight, British Lion, Frosted, Centennial Exhibition 85.00
Gillinder, Paperweight, Buddha, Honey Color, 6 In. 55.00
Gillinder, Paperweight, George Washington, Frosted & Clear, Oval 75.00
Gillinder, Paperweight, Independence Hall, Frosted & Clear, Oval 75.00
Gillinder, Paperweight, Memorial, Frosted & Clear, Oval 75.00
Gillinder, Shade, Frosted, Dated 1909, Signed, Set Of 4 .... 60.00
Gillinder, Shoe, Centennial, 1876, Bow On Front, 5 1/2 In. 17.00
Gillinder, Toothpick, Lady's Slipper, Bow, Centennial Exposition 40.00
Ginori, Dish, Hand-Painted, Floral And Gold, One Handle, Signed 35.00
Ginori, Plate, Hand-Painted, Corn, Signed L.Conti, & Crown, 13 In. 125.00
Ginori, Plate, Ivory, Cobalt, Open Work, Footed, Sea Creature, Cupid 30.00
Girl Scout, Handbook, 1923 .... 6.50
Girl Scout, Knife, Kutmaster, Green, 4 Blades, Attached Bell, 3 1/2 In. 8.00
Girandole, Marble Base, Bronze Lady, Child, Prisms, Set Of 3, 14 In. 100.00
Girandole, Marble Base, Shakespearean Figure, 30 Prisms, Set Of 3, 15 In. 90.00
Glasses, Granny, Tin Case, 1864 .... 12.50
Glasses, Ladies, Rimless, Gold Filled Chain & Hairpin Attached 6.00
Glasses, Pince-Nez, Leather Case 12.00
Glasses, Salesman's Set, 152 Lenses & Holders, Wooden Case, Velvet Lining 350.00
Gold, Lorgnette, Engraved Gold Case, Chain, Spring Button Release 75.00
Gold, Penknife, 2 Blade, Etched Design, 14K, Empire Winsted, 2 1/4 In. 54.00
Gold, Penknife, 2 Blade, 14K White Gold, George Wostenmold, Sheffield 50.00
Goldscheider, Figurine, Lady Poinsettia, Artist Signed, 7 1/4 In. 15.00
Goldscheider, Figurine, Marie Antoinette, Music Box Base, Anniversary Song 15.00
Golf Club, see Toy, Golf Club
Gonder, Pitcher, Skirted, Mottled Pink & Blue Lustrous Glaze, Pink Inside 15.00
Gonder, Vase, Mottled Pink And Blue 7.50
Gonder, Vase, Swan, Green, Brown Glaze, Marked, 10 X 6 X 4 In. 12.00

Goofus glass was made from about 1900 to 1920 by many American factories. It was originally painted gold, red, green, bronze, pink, purple, and other bright colors.

Goofus Glass, Bowl, Big Red Roses 12.50
Goofus Glass, Bowl, Carnation, Gilt & Red, 10 In. 15.00
Goofus Glass, Bowl, Gold Butterflies, Red Roses, Gold Stems, 7 In. 40.00
Goofus Glass, Bowl, Iris, Gilt & Red, 8 3/4 In. 15.00
Goofus Glass, Bowl, Rose, Gilt & Red, 9 In. 15.00
Goofus Glass, Bowl, Silver On Red, Iris, 12 In. 15.00

Goofus Glass, Bowl, Small Red Flowers, 10 In. 12.50
Goofus Glass, Bowl, Strawberry Design, Scallop Edge, 10 1/2 X 2 1/2 In. 24.00
Goofus Glass, Bowl, 9 In. 15.00
Goofus Glass, Coaster 4.00
Goofus Glass, Dish, Jam, Opalescent With Goofus Center 22.50
Goofus Glass, Jar, Powder, Covered, Painted 7.00
Goofus Glass, Jar, Powder, Covered, Puffy Roses 16.50
Goofus Glass, Jar, Powder, La Belle Rose 12.00
Goofus Glass, Jar, Powder, Molded Roses, Lady's Profile, Covered 14.00
Goofus Glass, Plate, Roses 9.50
Goofus Glass, Plate, 1904 World's Fair, St.Louis, Festival Hall 10.00
Goofus Glass, Saucer, Gold, Gold Oak Leaves, Red Acorns 1.50
Goofus Glass, Tray, Bureau, Chrysanthemum Pattern, Red Roses, 8 X 11 In. 27.50
Goofus Glass, Tray, Lord's Supper, Grapes On Vine Border, 11 X 7 In. 21.00
Goofus Glass, Vase, Blown-Out Roses & Scrolls, Ball Top, 14 In. 8.00

W.H.COSS

Goss china has been made since 1858. English potter William Henry Goss first made it at the Falcon Pottery in Stoke-on-Trent. In 1934 the factory name was changed to Goss China Company when it was taken over by Cauldon Potteries. Goss china resembles Irish Belleek in both body and glaze. The company also made popular souvenir china.

Goss, Beaker, High St., Oxford, 3 1/8 In. 22.50
Goss, Bowl, Magdalen College, Oxford, Fluted, 3 1/2 In. 20.00
Goss, Box, Miniature, Crest, Liverpool 10.00
Goss, Bust, Sir Walter Scott, Falcon Mark 45.00
Goss, Bust, Sir Walter Scott, Parian, 5 In. 40.00
Goss, Cigarette Holder, Crest, Lord MacDonald, Ball Type 25.00
Goss, Creamer, Man, July 2, 1894 On Front, Story Of Scarlett On Back, 4 In. 37.00
Goss, Cup & Saucer, Lord Armstrong 18.00
Goss, Cup & Saucer, Manchester Crest, Enameled, Miniature 15.00
Goss, Mug, Netley Abbey, 3 In. 22.00
Goss, Pitcher, Chagford Crest, 2 1/8 In. 18.00
Goss, Pitcher, Kington Crest.4 1/2 In. 22.50
Goss, Pitcher, Shield & Crown, Model Of Romano Salopian Ewer, 2 3/4 In. 15.00
Goss, Pot, Model Of Ancient Cook Pot, Eastbourne Crest 10.00
Goss, Teacup & Saucer, Ivory Color, Arms Of Blackpool, Progress Motto 16.50
Goss, Urn, Seal Of Dorothy Vernon, 2 In. 14.00
Goss, Vase, Bud, Seal Of Tothes, 4 1/2 In. 18.00
Goss, Vase, Terra-Cotta, 4 1/2 In. 75.00
Goss, Washstand Set, Seal Of Brechin 25.00

Gouda is a district in Holland famous for tin-glazed pottery and tiles. Gouda pottery has been made by many factories in the district since the seventeenth century and is still being made. Most of the pieces found today are from the nineteenth and twentieth centuries.

Gouda, Ashtray, Match Holder, High Glaze, Zuid Mark, 5 1/2 In. 65.00
Gouda, Bowl, Areo, Strap Handle, 7 In. 24.00
Gouda, Bowl, Art Deco, Zenith, Artist Signed 39.50
Gouda, Bowl, Blue, Brown Art Nouveau Design, C.1895, 8 In. 95.00
Gouda, Bowl, Flowers On High Glaze, Marked Areo & Royal Gouda 35.00
Gouda, Bowl, Ivory Color, Floral On Green Brown, 7 X 4 In. 45.00
Gouda, Box, High Glaze, Gray, White Ground, Anjer, Covered, 3 3/4 X 3 1/4 In. 40.00
Gouda, Candlestick With Handle, Candia, 7 1/2 In. 70.00
Gouda, Candlestick, Blue, Dark Green, Grays, & White, Handle, 10 In., Pair 125.00
Gouda, Candlestick, Dark Green, Blue & Yellow, 12 In. 75.00
Gouda, Candlestick, Drip Pan, Handle, 7 Colors, Plazuid & House Mark, 4 In. 55.00
Gouda, Candlestick, Green, Blue, Yellow, 12 In., Pair 75.00
Gouda, Candlestick, Green, Orange, Yellow, Rondo Mark, Holland, 15 In., Pair 175.00
Gouda, Candlestick, Stylized Floral & Scrolls, Zoner & House Mark, 8 In. 45.00
Gouda, Case, Corona, 7 1/2 In. 60.00
Gouda, Chamberstick, 8 In. 85.00
Gouda, Charger, Jaska, Green On Beige, Royal Plazuid, 1935, 14 1/2 In. 140.00
Gouda, Compote, Art Nouveau, Black, Blue, Orange, & Gold, Plazuid, 7 3/4 In. 97.00
Gouda, Compote, Cobalt, Yellow Lavender, House Mark, Clareth, Signed, 5 In. 45.00

Gouda, Compote, Peacock Feather, 9 Panel, Rim Marked In Blue, 4 X 3 3/4 In. 65.00
Gouda, Cup & Saucer, Lindes, Arnhem 25.00
Gouda, Ewer, Metz Royal, 6 In. 35.00
Gouda, Inkwell, Covered, Removable Well, Dark Blue, Green, Ivora Pattern 100.00
Gouda, Inkwell, Crocus, Covered, 4 In. 125.00
Gouda, Inkwell, Glazed, Dark Colors, House Mark, 3 X 3 1/2 In. 65.00
Gouda, Inkwell, Milk Glass Insert, Floral, E.S.Norwich, Plazuid 75.00
Gouda, Jar, Covered, Ships, Church, Windmills, 4 1/2 In. 45.00
Gouda, Jardiniere, Olive Background, Blue, Green, Orange, 2-Handled, 12 In. 160.00
Gouda, Lantern, Ring Handle, Signed Candia, 20 In. 475.00
Gouda, Lantern, Signed Candia, 20 X 10 1/2 In. 475.00
Gouda, Mug, Fishermen, No.1236 30.00
Gouda, Mug, Regina Osiris Gouda Holland, 4 1/2 In. 75.00
Gouda, Pitcher, Art Nouveau Style Floral, House Mark, 6 1/2 In. 115.00
Gouda, Pitcher, Bulbous, Light Ground, Yellow, Orange Flowers, 6 1/2 In. 45.00
Gouda, Pitcher, Floral, Art Nouveau Style, House Mark, 6 1/2 In. 115.00
Gouda, Pitcher, Irene, Miniature, House Mark, Vivid Colors 30.00
Gouda, Pitcher, Marked Plazuid, R.Gromus, 4 In. 45.00
Gouda, Pitcher, Regina, Miniature, House Mark, Vivid Color, 3 In. 30.00
Gouda, Pitcher, Zenith With Manily Mark, Blue, Wine, Yellow, 3 1/8 In. 30.00
Gouda, Plate, Brown, Blue, Gold, Green, & Red, Zenith, HH, 9 In. 65.00
Gouda, Plate, Lindes, Arnhem, 8 In. 30.00
Gouda, Plate, Regina, 6 1/2 In. 30.00
Gouda, Pot, House Mark, Vivid Color, Rodian, 2 1/8 In. 30.00
Gouda, Pot, Rodian, House Mark, 2 1/8 In. 30.00
Gouda, Shoe, House & Tree Sumac, 4 1/2 In. 28.00
Gouda, Sugar & Creamer, Cover, Ispahan, Arnhem 65.00
Gouda, Sugar & Creamer, Regina Osiris 32.00
Gouda, Tile, Dutch Girl & Farm Scene, Zeeland, PUG, 11 X 8 In. 70.00
Gouda, Tile, Dutch Woman, Dutch Man, Hanging, Pair 35.00
Gouda, Tile, Dutch Woman, Holland Scene, Hanging 20.00
Gouda, Tray, Heart-Shaped Leaf & Stem, Lavender, Orange, Purple, 7 1/2 In. 30.00
Gouda, Tray, Princess 2016 Ivora, Signed, 11 In. 65.00
Gouda, Urn, Signed Verona, Gouda, Holland, 9 In. 95.00

Gouda, Vase, Betty, 4 In.

Gouda, Vase, Art Nouveau, Green, Orange, Blue, Brown, & Black, C.1900, 7 In. 63.00
Gouda, Vase, Betty, 4 In. *Illus* 50.00
Gouda, Vase, Black & Beige, Abstract Designs, 2 Handles, 6 1/2 In. 60.00
Gouda, Vase, Bulb, Ivora, White, Orange & Violet Daisies, Green Bands, 13 In. 195.00
Gouda, Vase, Cobalt High Glaze, 2 Yellow Birds With Split Tails, 11 1/2 In. 50.00
Gouda, Vase, Dark High Glaze, Floral, Squat, 3 1/2 X 2 In. 55.00
Gouda, Vase, Floral On Green & Black, Turquoise Interior, House Mark, 5 In. 55.00
Gouda, Vase, High Glaze, Art Nouveau, 12 In. 225.00
Gouda, Vase, High Glaze, Purple, Blue, Orange Floral, Dark Ground, Signed 50.00
Gouda, Vase, Kiro, Goedewaagen, 6 3/4 In. 55.00
Gouda, Vase, Lavender With Orange And Purple Florals 28.00
Gouda, Vase, Many Colors, Signed Berea, 7 1/2 In. 90.00
Gouda, Vase, Mushroom, Art Nouveau Pansies On White, 2 1/2 In. 42.00
Gouda, Vase, Pastel On Black, 5 1/2 In. 75.00
Gouda, Vase, Pitcher, Pensee, Matte Finish, 5 In. 38.00
Gouda, Vase, Portland Shape, 6 1/2 In. 135.00
Gouda, Vase, Quid High Glaze, Art Nouveau 85.00

Gouda, Vase, Ramid, Miniature, House Mark, Vivid Colors, 3 In. 30.00
Gouda, Vase, Regina, Art Nouveau Red & Black, 6 1/4 In. 38.00
Gouda, Vase, Regina, Red & Black Designs, White Ground, 6 1/4 In. 38.00
Gouda, Vase, Rust Black Green, High Glaze, Signed Rolf, Numbered, 4 3/4 In. 65.00
Gouda, Vase, Shiny Black, Art Nouveau Floral, 12 In. 75.00
Gouda, Vase, Turquoise, Vea, 6 1/4 In. 65.00
Gouda, Vase, White, Pastel Colors, Double-Handled, Zuid, 10 In. 165.00

Graniteware is an enameled tinware that has been used in the kitchen from the late nineteenth century to the present. Earlier graniteware was green or turquoise blue, with white spatters. The later ware was gray with white spatters. Reproductions are being made in all colors.

Graniteware, Bedpan, Blue 9.50
Graniteware, Bedpan, Gray 5.00
Graniteware, Boiler, Double, Gray 5.00
Graniteware, Box, Hinged, White, Profile Of Lady On Front, 14 1/2 In. 23.00
Graniteware, Coffeepot, Blue & White, 20 In. 20.00
Graniteware, Coffeepot, Cobalt Marbleized 20.00
Graniteware, Coffeepot, Gray, Gooseneck Spout, 3 Cup Size 15.50
Graniteware, Coffeepot, Gray, Porcelain Knob On Tin Lid, 6 Cup Size 14.00
Graniteware, Coffeepot, Gray, Tin Lid, 2 Handles 10.00
Graniteware, Coffeepot, White, Black Trim, 9 In. 12.00
Graniteware, Kraut Pot, German, Blue, Latch Lock, Air Holes On Top, 3 Gal. 30.00
Graniteware, Mold, Brown Bread, Blue 15.00
Graniteware, Pan, Gray, 12 In. 10.00
Graniteware, Pan, Muffin, Blue, Gray, & White 11.00
Graniteware, Pan, Vegetable, Green & White, 10 1/2 In. 18.00
Graniteware, Spittoon, Gray 17.50
Graniteware, Teakettle, Gray 15.00

Greentown glass was made by the Indiana Tumbler and Goblet Company of Greentown, Indiana, from 1894 to 1903. In 1899, the factory name was changed to National Glass Company. A variety of pressed, milk, and chocolate glass was made.

Greentown, see also Chocolate Glass, Custard Glass, Holly Amber, Milk Glass, Pressed Glass

Greentown, Bowl, Leaf Bracket, Chocolate Glass 25.00
Greentown, Bowl, Leaf Bracket, Footed 25.00
Greentown, Cruet, Chocolate Glass, Cactus 110.00
Greentown, Cruet, Green, Stopper 65.00
Greentown, Cruet, Wild Rose & Bowknot Frosted, Frosted Faceted Stopper 60.00
Greentown, Cup, Punch, Shuttle, Clear 12.00
Greentown, Dish, Butter, Covered, Wild Rose & Bowknot, Chocolate Glass 165.00
Greentown, Dish, Pickle, Handled, Holly, Clear 45.00
Greentown, Dish, Rabbit Cover, Translucent Blue 225.00
Greentown, Dustpan, Canary 45.00
Greentown, Figurine, Mitted Hand 30.00
Greentown, Jar, Ginger, Bisque, Yellow Floral 32.00
Greentown, Mug, Aqua And Blue 25.00
Greentown, Mug, Aqua And White 20.00
Greentown, Mug, Elf Scene, Nile Green 60.00
Greentown, Mug, Green Milk Glass, Serenade 33.00
Greentown, Mug, Opaque Blue, Elves Playing Games 35.00
Greentown, Mug, Serenade, Transparent Green 52.00
Greentown, Mug, Troubador Scene, Milk Glass With Gold 50.00
Greentown, Mug, White, Elves 18.00
Greentown, Pitcher, Blue, Teardrop & Tassel 125.00
Greentown, Pitcher, Squirrel, Clear 85.00
Greentown, Pitcher, Vaseline, Austrian 45.00
Greentown, Plate, Amber Sandwich, 4 1/2 In. 22.50
Greentown, Sugar & Creamer, White, Teardrop & Tassel 50.00
Greentown, Syrup, Hearts Of Lock Laven, 6 In. 75.00
Greentown, Syrup, Open, Hearts Of Loch Laven, Chocolate Glass, 6 In. 75.00
Greentown, Toothpick, Holly, Clear 30.00

Greentown, Tumbler, Lemonade, Cactus, Chocolate Glass, 4 3/4 In. 35.00
Greentown, Tumbler, Lemonade, Cactus, 4 3/4 In. 35.00
Greentown, Wine, No.11 22.50

Grueby Faience Company of Boston, Massachusetts, was incorporated in 1897 by William H. Grueby. Garden statuary, art pottery, and architectural tiles were made until 1920.

Grueby, Tile, Pirate Ship & English Cottage, Square, 4 In., Pair 155.00
Grueby, Tile, Ship In Full Sail, Blue, Ivory, Brown, Signed MS, 6 In. 350.00
Grueby, Vase, Blue, 4 1/2 In. 400.00
Grueby, Vase, Matte Green, Yellow Lotus Buds, 5 In. 255.00
Grueby, Vase, Pumpkin Shape, Green Glaze, 3 In. 105.00
Gum Ball Machine, see Store, Machine
Gun, see Weapon, Handgun; Weapon, Rifle; Weapon, Shotgun; etc.

Gunderson glass was made at the Gunderson Pairpoint Works of New Bedford, Massachusetts, from 1952 to 1957. Gunderson Peachblow is especially famous.

Gunderson, Cruet, Burmese 350.00
Gunderson, Cruet, Burmese, Pedestal, Rose To Creamy Yellow, Trefoil Top 230.00
Gunderson, Cruet, Glossy 275.00
Gunderson, Cruet, Satin 275.00
Gunderson, Peachblow, Tumbler, Satin Finish, Pink To White 175.00
Gunderson, Peachblow, Vase, Flared Top, Bulbous, 3 3/4 In. 135.00
Gutta-Percha, see also Photography, Daguerreotype Case
Gutta-Percha, Box, Lid Depicts Patriotic Scene, C.1875, 5 X 5 In. 32.00
Gutta-Percha, Match Safe, Horseshoe Shape, Striker 28.00
Gutta-Percha, Match Safe, Slipper 25.00
Gutta-Percha, Mirror, Hand, Black, Berries & Leaves, Patent 1868 & 1878 15.75
Gutta-Percha, Mirror, Hand, Black, Raised Leaves & Berries, C.1868 15.75
Gutta-Percha, Mirror, Hand, Cream With Cherub, Venus & Garlands Raised, 9 In. 16.00
Gutta-Percha, Mirror, Lady's Hand, Black, Berries & Leaves, 1868 & 1878 14.95
Gutta-Percha, Pencil, Automatic, Checkered Design, Dated 1854 25.00
Gutta-Percha, Plate, Gypsy Fortune Teller 90.00
Gutta-Percha, Tray, Medallion Profile, Scroll & Floral, Wood Stem, 12 In. 145.00
Hall, see also Autumn Leaf
Hall, Jar, Cracker, Opalescent, Pansies & Violets, Silver Fittings, 6 1/2 In. 120.00
Hall, Pitcher, Water, Tan, Orange, & Brown 9.00
Hamilton, Tile, Green High Glaze, Greek Woman With Jug, 12 X 6 In. 85.00
Hammersley, Cup & Saucer, Blue, Green Flowers 10.00

Hampshire pottery was made in Keene, New Hampshire, between 1871 and 1923. Hampshire developed a popular line of colored glazed works as early as 1883, which included a Royal Worcester-type pink, olive green, blue, and mahogany.

Hampshire, Bowl, Flower, Green, 7 In. 30.00
Hampshire, Candleholder, Cape Cod, Shield Back, Green Matte 90.00
Hampshire, Dish, Nut, Ring Handle, Thayer Memorial Building, Uxbridge, Mass. 28.00
Hampshire, Jardiniere, Shaded Green Matte, 6 X 3 In. 25.00
Hampshire, Mug, Cream Color, Black Transfer Of Indian's Head, Richmond, Va. 50.00
Hampshire, Mug, Matte Glace, Green, Line Pattern, 9 In. 40.00
Hampshire, Mug, Plain Green, Tankard, Impressed, 8 1/2 In. 35.00
Hampshire, Tankard, Green Matte, Decorated, Open Handle, 12 In. 43.00
Hampshire, Vase, Bowl In Shape Of Cabbage 24.00
Hampshire, Vase, High Glaze, Cobalt, 7 In. 58.00
Hampshire, Vase, Lava Design, Green And Blue 40.00
Hampshire, Vase, Matte Green, Marked, Impressed M In Circle 45.00
Hampshire, Vase, Matte Green, Twisted Vines, 6 In. 48.00
Hampshire, Vase, Parsley Design, Green 30.00

Philip Handel worked in Meriden, Connecticut, about 1885 and in New York City from about 1900 to the 1930s. His firm made art glass and other types of lamps.

Handel, Box, Open, 2 Handles, Indian In Bottom, Red & Blue Ground, Marked 90.00

Handel, Holder, Cigar, Opalescent, Portrait Of Indian, Signed, 5 In. 150.00
Handel, Humidor, Running Rabbit, Acid Cut Back 175.00
Handel, Humidor, Tobacco, Hinged Lid, Indian Shief 175.00
Handel, Jar, Sweetmeat, Brown, Green, & White, Moose's Head In Front 125.00
Handel, Jar, Tobacco, Tan, Geometrics 235.00
Handel, Lamp, Basket Of Flowers, Teroma Finish, Red, Orange, Black, 16 In. 745.00
Handel, Lamp, Boudoir, Blue Shade Scenic And Signed 275.00
Handel, Lamp, Boudoir, Chipped Ice, Pastoral Scene, 7 In. 450.00
Handel, Lamp, Boudoir, Leaded, Copper Foil, Amber & Green Shade, 13 3/4 In. 615.00
Handel, Lamp, Brown Mosserine Square 7 In.Shade, Basketweave Base 345.00
Handel, Lamp, Chipped Ice, Scenic Butterflies & Floral 7 In. Dome Shade 495.00
Handel, Lamp, Dogwood, Green, Pink & White Floral, Green Leaves, 26 In. 1850.00
Handel, Lamp, Floor, Bent Glass Domical Shade, Browns & Beige, 61 In. 2200.00
Handel, Lamp, Floor, 8 Sections, Intricate Design, Seated Lions On Standard 1300.00
Handel, Lamp, Floral Geometric, Leaded, Red, Yellow, Green, Blue, 18 In. 1500.00
Handel, Lamp, Forest Scene On Shade, Bronze Base Signed, 12 In. 500.00
Handel, Lamp, Hanging, Brass Palm Trees On Glass Shade, 24 In. 750.00
Handel, Lamp, Indian Scenes On 16 In. Shade 1100.00
Handel, Lamp, Leaded, Dark Pink Floral, Scalloped Edges, 19 In. Shade 2500.00
Handel, Lamp, Leaded, Table, Pink Dogwood Shade, Bronze Base, Signed, 27 In. 2750.00
Handel, Lamp, Reverse Painted Landscape, Chipped Ice, 16 In. 985.00
Handel, Lamp, Reverse Painted Shade, Overlay, 23 In. 1200.00
Handel, Lamp, Reverse Painted, Acid Cut Scene, Conical Shape, 18 In. Shade 1600.00
Handel, Lamp, Scenic, Signed Shade & Base, 14 X 7 1/2 In., Pair 425.00
Handel, Lamp, Scenic, Trees, Water, Orange Ground, Signed, 18 In. 975.00
Handel, Lamp, Table, Tropical Sunset, Reticulated, 16 In. 1000.00
Handel, Night-Light, Turquoise Crackle Egg-Shaped Top, Metal Base, 8 In. 585.00
Handel, Shade, Bronze, Tan Marbleized, Palm Trees, 6 Panels, Signed, 6 X 7 In. 200.00
Handel, Shade, Cased, Orange With Green Leaves, Signed, 12 In. 350.00
Handel, Table Lamp, Green Shade, Salmon Batwing Design, Signed, 18 In.Shade 785.00

Harlequin dinnerware was produced by the Homer Laughlin Company from 1938 to 1964, and sold without trademark by the F. W. Woolworth Co. It had a concentric ring design like Fiesta, but the rings were separated from the rim by a plain margin and cup handles were angular in shape

Harlequin Ware, Ashtray, Turquoise 28.00
Harlequin Ware, Butter, Rose Color 35.00
Harlequin Ware, Cereal Bowl, Green 1.75
Harlequin Ware, Cereal Bowl, Yellow 1.75
Harlequin Ware, Cup & Saucer, Demitasse, Rose Color 15.00
Harlequin Ware, Cup & Saucer, Demitasse, Turquoise 15.00
Harlequin Ware, Cup & Saucer, Gold 3.50
Harlequin Ware, Cup, Turquoise 2.50
Harlequin Ware, Cup, Yellow 2.25
Harlequin Ware, Dish, Mint, Maroon 6.00
Harlequin Ware, Dish, Nut, Gold, 3 In. 7.00
Harlequin Ware, Dish, Nut, Orange 10.00
Harlequin Ware, Dish, Nut, Turquoise, 3 In. 7.00
Harlequin Ware, Eggcup, Spruce Green 15.00
Harlequin Ware, Eggcup, Yellow 15.00
Harlequin Ware, Plate, Chartreuse, 6 In. 1.00
Harlequin Ware, Plate, Chartreuse, 9 In. 1.50
Harlequin Ware, Plate, Gold, 7 In. 1.50
Harlequin Ware, Plate, Gold, 9 1/4 In. 2.00
Harlequin Ware, Plate, Rose Color, 6 In. 1.00
Harlequin Ware, Plate, Turquoise, 7 In. 1.50
Harlequin Ware, Plate, Yellow, 6 In. 1.00
Harlequin Ware, Plate, Yellow, 9 In. 1.50
Harlequin Ware, Sugar, Turquoise 1.75
Harlequin Ware, Syrup, Yellow 35.00
Harlequin Ware, Tumbler, Mauve 12.00
Harlequin Ware, Tumbler, Turquoise 12.00

Hatpin Holder, see also Porcelain and various porcelain categories

Hatpin Holder, Austrian, Gold, Steel Luster Flowers 30.00
Hatpin Holder, Carnival Glass, Orange Tree, Iridescent 125.00
Hatpin Holder, Face With Open Mouth, Porcelain, 1900, 3 1/2 In. 24.00
Hatpin Holder, Floral All Around 30.00
Hatpin Holder, France, Pastel Background, Apple Blossoms, Signed Miller 32.00
Hatpin Holder, Hand-Painted Floral, Bavarian 18.00
Hatpin Holder, Hand-Painted, Austria 16.00
Hatpin Holder, Nippon, Green Mark, Gold Bands, Flowers 18.00
Hatpin Holder, Nippon, Pink & Cerise Roses, Beading, Square, Open Top 19.00
Hatpin Holder, Oriental Decoration, Bulbous Center, Japan, 4 1/4 In. 15.00
Hatpin Holder, Porcelain, Roses, 5 1/4 In. 12.00
Hatpin Holder, Red Carnations & Lily Of The Valley, 5 In. 12.00
Hatpin Holder, Tan, Floral 15.00
Hatpin, Faceted, Clear 7.50
Hatpin, Rhinestone Studded 8.00
Hatpin, Sterling Overlay, Pink Opaque 15.00
Hatpin, Sterling, Enameled Swastika 9.00

Haviland & Co. Limoges

Haviland china has been made in Limoges, France, since 1846. The factory was started by the Haviland Brothers of New York City. Other factories worked in the town of Limoges making a similar chinaware.

H&Co DEPOSE

Haviland, Bowl, Covered, Bretagne, 9 1/4 X 7 1/2 In. 32.00
Haviland, Bowl, Vegetable, Covered, Miami, Octagonal 29.50
Haviland, Bowl, Vegetable, Covered, No.320 35.00
Haviland, Bowl, Vegetable, Covered, St.Lazarre 29.50
Haviland, Bowl, Vegetable, No.320, Square 30.00
Haviland, Bowl, Vegetable, Pink Floral, Covered, Hand-Painted, 8 1/4 In. 28.00
Haviland, Butter Pat, Floral 5.00
Haviland, Butter Pat, White 4.00
Haviland, Butter, Covered, Rajah 32.00
Haviland, Butter, Covered, Sprays Of Pink Roses & Floral, Insert, C.1886 35.00
Haviland, Cake Set, White, Blue Pansies, Gold Enamel, 9 Piece 195.00
Haviland, Chocolate Pot, Limoges, White, Gold Trim 45.00
Haviland, Chocolate Pot, Pontarlier 45.00
Haviland, Chocolate Set, Limoges, Pink Rosebud Garlands, Gold Trim, 13 Piece 140.00
Haviland, Chocolate Set, No.597, 9 Piece 65.00
Haviland, Coffeepot, Moss Rose, 8 In. 45.00
Haviland, Creamer, Green & Ivory, Ribbon Handle 10.00
Haviland, Cup & Saucer, Bouillon, Limoges, White, Pink Roses, Gold Border 6.00
Haviland, Cup & Saucer, Bouillon, Miami 6.50
Haviland, Cup & Saucer, Bouillon, Vassar 12.50
Haviland, Cup & Saucer, Coffee, Baltimore Rose 15.00
Haviland, Cup & Saucer, Demitasse, Apple Blossoms 12.00
Haviland, Cup & Saucer, Demitasse, Buff, Yellow Floral, Gold Rim 18.00
Haviland, Cup & Saucer, Demitasse, Ganga 14.25
Haviland, Cup & Saucer, Demitasse, Marked C.F.H., GDA Limoges 8.00
Haviland, Cup & Saucer, Demitasse, White, Gold Band & Handle 10.00
Haviland, Cup & Saucer, Lavender Violets & Leaves, Pedestaled Cup 15.00
Haviland, Cup & Saucer, Limoges, Pink Roses, Sheer Porcelain 10.00
Haviland, Cup & Saucer, Miami 10.00
Haviland, Cup & Saucer, No.330/133 21.50
Haviland, Cup & Saucer, Pink Roses & Blue Ribbons 13.00
Haviland, Cup & Saucer, Red Cherries, Green Leaves, Artist Signed, Dated 1901 22.00
Haviland, Cup & Saucer, St.Lazarre 11.00
Haviland, Cup & Saucer, White & Gold, Leeds Pattern 12.50
Haviland, Cup, Bouillon, No.481e, Pink Roses, Blue Ribbon, 2 Handles 12.50
Haviland, Cup, Limoges 5.00
Haviland, Cup, No.562 7.50
Haviland, Cup, No.656d 8.00
Haviland, Demitasse Set, White, Gold Trim, 8 Piece 110.00
Haviland, Dish & Tray, Sauce, Covered, Multicolor Floral, Gold Trim 45.00
Haviland, Dish, Bone, White, Scalloped Edges 4.50
Haviland, Dish, Leaf Shape, Baltimore Rose, 10 In. 35.00
Haviland, Dish, Oval, Gold Handles And Rim, France Green Mark, 12 In. 32.50

Haviland, Dish, Pancake, Covered, White, Roses, Blue Floral, 9 In. 70.00
Haviland, Dish, Vegetable, Covered, Frontenac 25.00
Haviland, Dish, Vegetable, Covered, No. 86 40.00
Haviland, Gravy Boat & Attached Underplate, Pink Roses & Blue Ribbons 25.00
Haviland, Gravy Boat, Covered, No.221z 30.00
Haviland, Gravy Boat, Underplate, Miramar, Limoges, France 22.50
Haviland, Hatpin Holder, Hand-Painted, Blue Flowers, Signed By Artist 26.50
Haviland, Ice Cream Set, Violets, 7 Piece 65.00
Haviland, Jar, Biscuit, Covered, Handled, Hand-Painted Pansies, Artist Signed 38.00
Haviland, Luncheon Set, Limoges, Red Roses, C.1900, 23 Piece 200.00
Haviland, Oyster Set, Pink & Green Shell Scenes, C.1893, 7 Piece 135.00
Haviland, Pitcher, Hand-Painted, Violets On White, 1893, 10 In. 70.00
Haviland, Plate, Bacon, Pink Roses & Blue Ribbons, 11 In. 15.00
Haviland, Plate, Bread & Butter, Chambord 3.50
Haviland, Plate, Bread & Butter, Frontenac 6.50
Haviland, Plate, Bread & Butter, No.100a 4.00
Haviland, Plate, Bread & Butter, No.320 6.50
Haviland, Plate, Bread & Butter, No.330/133 8.00
Haviland, Plate, Bread & Butter, No.432 5.00
Haviland, Plate, Bread & Butter, No.513 3.00
Haviland, Plate, Bread & Butter, Pink Roses & Blue Ribbons 5.00
Haviland, Plate, Bread & Butter, St.Lazarre 3.50
Haviland, Plate, Bread & Butter, Wedding Ring 6.00
Haviland, Plate, Bread & Butter, 1/8 In. Gold Band 6.00
Haviland, Plate, Cake, Limoges, Floral Sprays, Square, 10 In. 8.50
Haviland, Plate, Cake, St.Lazarre 5.50
Haviland, Plate, Chop, Oak Leaves & Daisies 25.00
Haviland, Plate, Chop, White, Floral Bouquets, 12 In. 48.00
Haviland, Plate, Cobalt, White, & Green, Pink & Blue Floral, Gold, 9 In. 17.50
Haviland, Plate, Cookie, Baltimore Rose, Handled, Square 32.00
Haviland, Plate, Coupe Dessert, White Ransom, 7 1/2 In. 6.50
Haviland, Plate, Dessert, Limoges, Roses, Gold & Green Scalloped, 8 1/2 In. 9.25
Haviland, Plate, Dessert, Pink & Yellow Roses, Gold Rim, Red Mark, 8 1/4 In. 7.50
Haviland, Plate, Dinner, Chambord 6.00
Haviland, Plate, Dinner, No.100a 6.00
Haviland, Plate, Dinner, No.320 6.75
Haviland, Plate, Dinner, No.330/133 12.00
Haviland, Plate, Dinner, No.432 8.00
Haviland, Plate, Dinner, No.481e, Pink Roses, Blue Ribbon 8.00
Haviland, Plate, Dinner, White, No. 5 Star 7.00
Haviland, Plate, Fish, Limoges, Cobalt & Gold Maple Leaf Border, Set Of 4 130.00
Haviland, Plate, Fish, Mont Mery, 1892, St.Cloud Set, Artist B.Albert 35.00
Haviland, Plate, Floral, Gold Scalloped Edge, 10 In. 10.00
Haviland, Plate, Game, Mont Mery Mark, Artist B.Albert, Marine Underwater 35.00
Haviland, Plate, Goldfish Among Plants, 1913, 9 1/2 In. 19.00
Haviland, Plate, Luncheon, Frontenac, 8 1/2 In. 7.50
Haviland, Plate, Luncheon, No.320 6.00
Haviland, Plate, Luncheon, No.330/133 8.00
Haviland, Plate, Luncheon, Pink Roses & Blue Ribbons 8.00
Haviland, Plate, Luncheon, White, Green Border, 8 1/2 In. 5.00
Haviland, Plate, No.46, 8 1/2 In. 8.00
Haviland, Plate, No.142, 7 1/2 In. 6.00
Haviland, Plate, No.142, 8 3/4 In. 5.00
Haviland, Plate, No.142, 9 3/4 In. 7.00
Haviland, Plate, No.144, 8 In. 5.00
Haviland, Plate, Oyster, Blue Mums, Gold Trim, Six Wells 47.50
Haviland, Plate, Oyster, Gold Trim, 5 Wells 35.00
Haviland, Plate, Oyster, Gold-Edged Rose-Sprigged Indentations, 8 1/2 In. 35.00
Haviland, Plate, Pale Green, White & Gold Design, Crimped Edge, 8 3/4 In. 9.50
Haviland, Plate, Pink & Yellow Roses, Gold Scroll Handles, 13 In. 35.00
Haviland, Plate, Salad, Pink Roses & Blue Ribbons 6.00
Haviland, Plate, Salad, 1/8 In. Gold Band 6.00
Haviland, Plate, Swags Of Roses, 6 1/4 In. 5.00
Haviland, Plate, Two Musical Cherubs, Gold Basketweave 33.00

Haviland, Platter, Baltimore Rose, 14 In. 28.00
Haviland, Platter, Deer, Artist Signed, C 1915, 15 1/2 X 12 In. 145.00
Haviland, Platter, Fish, Limoges, Oyster & Clams, Gold Rococo Border, 24 In. 145.00
Haviland, Platter, Limoges, Pink Floral, Blue Scrolls, Green Edge, 14 In. 15.00
Haviland, Platter, Limoges, Pink Rosebuds, Gold Scalloped Edge, 16 In. 16.00
Haviland, Platter, No.330/133, 12 In. 25.00
Haviland, Platter, No.330/133, 14 In. 35.00
Haviland, Platter, No.481e, Pink Roses, Blue Ribbon, 20 In. 35.00
Haviland, Platter, White, Pink Roses, Gold On Handles, 14 X 9 3/4 In. 22.50
Haviland, Punch Bowl, Baltimore Rose, Scalloped, Footed, 14 1/2 In. 350.00
Haviland, Ramekin & Saucer, No.320 .... 15.00
Haviland, Ramekin & Underplate, Gold & Black Line Border, Smooth Blank 8.00
Haviland, Ramekin, Blue Floral, Gold Edging 10.00
Haviland, Ramekin, Limoges, Pink Carnations, Gold Trim & Handle 4.75
Haviland, Relish, Frontenac 11.00
Haviland, Sauce, No.144, 6 1/4 In. 4.00
Haviland, Sauce, No.330/133 .... 8.50
Haviland, Sauce, No.432 .... 4.00
Haviland, Sauce, 1/8 In. Gold Band .... 6.00 To 6.50
Haviland, Soup Bowl, Pink Roses & Blue Ribbons 6.50
Haviland, Sugar & Creamer, Cover, Autumn Leaves, Gold Handles 60.00
Haviland, Sugar & Creamer, Cover, Limoges, Autumn Leaves, Gold Handles 52.00
Haviland, Sugar & Creamer, Cover, No.46, Gold Trim 32.00
Haviland, Sugar & Creamer, Floral, Pink & Green 25.00
Haviland, Sugar & Creamer, Petite Tankard, Pink Flowers, Gold, 3 1/2 In. 40.00
Haviland, Sugar, Cover, Lambelle, France 21.00
Haviland, Tea Set, Limoges, Oriental, C.1876, 2 Piece 40.00
Haviland, Tea Set, Pale Brown & Blue, Gray Leaves, G.D.M., 4 Piece 97.50
Haviland, Tea Set, White, Floral Festoons, Gold & Black Edges, 3 Piece 75.00
Haviland, Teacup & Saucer, Coin Gold, 3 Ball Feet 25.00
Haviland, Teacup & Saucer, No.279, Smooth Blank 15.50
Haviland, Teacup & Saucer, 5 O'Clock Tea, No.621 .... 8.00
Haviland, Teapot, Yellow Duck Form, Signed Sandoz 45.00
Haviland, Teapot, Yellow Roses, Gold Scrolled Handle, C.F.H. 50.00
Haviland, Tray, Dessert, Limoges, Trumpet Vines & Green Leaves, 11 X 8 In. 25.00
Haviland, Tureen, Covered, Limoges, 9 In. 14.00
Haviland, Tureen, Covered, Pink & Yellow Rose Garlands, Gold Trim, 13 In. 95.00
Haviland, Tureen, Oval, Covered, Miramar, Limoges, France, 13 In. 45.00
Haviland, Tureen, Tray, Miniature, Leaves & Flowers, Gold Trim, 5 In. 25.00
Haviland, Tureen, White With Gold, H & C, L., 10 In. 95.00
Haviland, Vegetable Bowl, Covered, Limoges, Floral, Gold Handles, 11 In. 27.50
Haviland, Vegetable Bowl, Covered, Limoges, Pink Roses, Gold Trim 28.50
Haviland, Vegetable Bowl, Covered, No.330/133 .... 25.00
Haviland, Vegetable Bowl, Covered, Pink Floral, G.D.A., Oval 25.00
Haviland, Vegetable Bowl, Covered, Pink Roses & Blue Ribbons, Oval 18.00
Haviland, Vegetable Bowl, Gold Finial & Handles, Gray Shadow Foliage 50.00
Haviland, Vegetable Bowl, No.330/133 .... 20.00

T.G.Hawkes & Company of Corning, New York, was founded in 1880. The firm cut glass made at other firms until 1962. Many pieces are marked with the trademark, a trefoil ring enclosing a fleur-de-lis and two hawks.

Hawkes, see also Cut Glass

Hawkes, Bottle, Oil & Vinegar, Copper Wheel Engraved, Double Lip, 8 In. 45.00
Hawkes, Compote, Candy, Engraved Floral & Ribbons, Silver Floral, Rim, 5 In. 28.00
Hawkes, Compote, Covered, Green, Copper Wheel Engraving, 4 1/2 In. 60.00
Hawkes, Compote, Engraved Lattice, Poppy Sprays & Oval Thumbprints, 10 In. 85.00
Hawkes, Compote, Verre De Soie, Engraved Garlands, Turned-Up Top, 7 X 5 In. 125.00
Hawkes, Hair Receiver & Powder Jar, Sterling Silver Lids, Pair 200.00
Hawkes, Sugar & Creamer, Clear, Green Handles And Pedestals, Signed 65.00
Hawkes, Vase, Amethyst, Sterling Collar, Engraved Panels, 9 In. 125.00
Hawkes, Vase, Black Enameled Crystal, Copper Wheel Engraved, Coiled Dragon 140.00
Hawkes, Vase, Fan, Green, Copper Wheel Engraved Leaves, 10 3/4 In. 87.00
Hawkes, Vase, Sapphire Blue, Silver Overlay Band, Acid Cut Back, 8 1/2 In. 135.00

H

Heisey glass was made from 1895 to 1958 in Newark, Ohio, by A.H. Heisey and Co., Inc.

Heisey, see also Custard Glass

Heisey, Ashtray, Crystolite 2.00
Heisey, Ashtray, Duck 12.00
Heisey, Basket, Cut Flowers On 8 Scallops, 14 In. 125.00
Heisey, Basket, Cut Flowers, Double Notched Handle, 15 1/2 In. 150.00
Heisey, Basket, Etched Butterfly, 16 In. 85.00
Heisey, Basket, Etched Flowers, No.461, 9 1/2 In. 35.00
Heisey, Basket, Etched, 14 In. 85.00
Heisey, Basket, Intaglio Cutting, Handled, 10 1/2 X 8 In. 155.00
Heisey, Basket, Lariat, Handle 45.00
Heisey, Basket, Recessed Panel, 11 X 8 X 5 1/2 In. 60.00
Heisey, Berry Bowl, Provincial 8.00
Heisey, Berry Bowl, Sawtooth Bands, Etched, Cranberry Stain, 8 1/2 In. 27.00
Heisey, Berry Set, Colonial, 7 Piece 40.00
Heisey, Berry Set, Paneled, 13 Piece 85.00
Heisey, Bobeche, Flower, Waverly, 6 In., Pair 15.00
Heisey, Bobeche, Ridgeleigh, 6 In. 7.50
Heisey, Bonbon, Flamingo, Red & Panel 18.00
Heisey, Bonbon, Moongleam, Twist 18.50
Heisey, Bonbon, No.1540 .... 7.00
Heisey, Bonbon, Oceanic, 2 Handles 18.75
Heisey, Bonbon, Pink, No.1252 .... 8.00
Heisey, Bookend, Fish 95.00
Heisey, Bottle, Perfume, Etched, Translucent Blue Enameled Sterling Stopper 48.00
Heisey, Bottle, Perfume, Intaglio Engraved Aqua Enameled Lid, Sterling Rim 40.00
Heisey, Bowl, Alexandrite, 10 1/2 X 5 In. 100.00
Heisey, Bowl, Colonial, Scalloped, 11 In. 27.00
Heisey, Bowl, Console, Clear With Rays In Bottom, 10 In. 17.50
Heisey, Bowl, Crystolite, Oval, 12 In. 17.00
Heisey, Bowl, Crystolite, 4 1/2 In. 5.00
Heisey, Bowl, Crystolite, 10 In. 12.00
Heisey, Bowl, Dessert, Orchid, Etched, Stemmed 10.00
Heisey, Bowl, Dessert, Pied Piper, Stemmed 14.50
Heisey, Bowl, Etched Orchid, No.1510, Footed, 6 1/2 In. 15.00
Heisey, Bowl, Fandango, Fluted, 9 1/2 In. 25.00
Heisey, Bowl, Fandango, Ruffled Edge 32.00
Heisey, Bowl, Finger, Fancy Loop 26.00
Heisey, Bowl, Greek Key, 8 In. 60.00
Heisey, Bowl, Green, Whirlpool, Scalloped, 4 In. 11.00
Heisey, Bowl, Locket On Chain, Footed, 8 In. 85.00
Heisey, Bowl, Moongleam, Octagon, 8 In. 45.00
Heisey, Bowl, Orchid, Pedestal, 11 In. 65.00
Heisey, Bowl, Pink, Queen Anne, Square, 6 1/4 In. 9.50
Heisey, Bowl, Pleat & Panel, Silver Overlay Of Grapes, 8 1/2 In. 35.00
Heisey, Bowl, Prince Of Wales Plumes, 8 1/2 X 4 In. 45.00
Heisey, Bowl, Prince Of Wales, 8 In. 10.00
Heisey, Bowl, Punch, Fancy Loop, Footed, Crimped & Flared, 11 In. 375.00
Heisey, Bowl, Punch, Marked, 2 Piece, 12 X 9 In. 175.00
Heisey, Bowl, Punch, Prince Of Wales Plumes, Marked 250.00
Heisey, Bowl, Sahara, Empress, Dolphin Footed, 10 3/4 In. 30.00
Heisey, Bowl, Sahara, Old Sandwich, Floral, Footed, 12 X 6 1/2 X 4 1/2 In. 45.00
Heisey, Bowl, Sahara, Ridgeleigh, Oval, 11 3/4 In. 42.00
Heisey, Bowl, Satellite, Cupped, 8 In. 12.00
Heisey, Bowl, Seahorse, Footed, 11 1/4 In. 37.00
Heisey, Bowl, Sunflower, 12 In. 25.00
Heisey, Bowl, Yeoman, Painted Flower Band, 11 In. 45.00
Heisey, Box, Cigarette, Covered, Crystolite, 4 X 3 In. 15.00
Heisey, Box, Cigarette, Covered, Lariat 30.00
Heisey, Box, Cigarette, Horse's Head Cover 39.00
Heisey, Box, Powder, Crystolite 30.00
Heisey, Box, Trinket, Opalescent, Winged Scroll, Decorated 65.00
Heisey, Bride's Basket, Signed 33.00

Heisey, Bucket, Ice, Crystolite, Hammered-Plated Bail Handle, 6 In. 48.00
Heisey, Bucket, Ice, Flamingo, Octagon 45.00
Heisey, Bucket, Ice, Moongleam, Twist, 8 3/4 X 5 1/2 X 5 1/4 In. 35.00
Heisey, Bucket, Ice, Rose 67.50
Heisey, Bucket, Ice, Twist 35.00
Heisey, Butter Pat, Silver Overlay, Pedestal 20.00
Heisey, Butter, Child's, Sawtooth Band, Lillian, 1900 60.00
Heisey, Butter, Covered, No.1225, Miniature 45.00
Heisey, Butter, Rose 65.00
Heisey, Cake Stand, Flute, 11 In. 16.00
Heisey, Candleholder, Crystolite, 3 In. 6.00
Heisey, Candleholder, Orchid, Etched, 3 1/2 In., Pair 28.00
Heisey, Candleholder, Warwick, Horn Of Plenty, 2 3/4 In., Pair 28.00
Heisey, Candlestick, Baluster Shape, 7 1/2 In., Pair 55.00
Heisey, Candlestick, Baluster, 4 1/2 In., Pair 35.00
Heisey, Candlestick, Blown, 9 In., Pair 85.00
Heisey, Candlestick, Bobeche & 8 Prisms, 8 In., Pair 80.00
Heisey, Candlestick, Clear, Six Sided, Intricate Shape, 7 1/2 In., Pair 48.00
Heisey, Candlestick, Empress Sahara 36.50
Heisey, Candlestick, Figural, Fish 165.00
Heisey, Candlestick, Intaglio Cutting, Oval, 10 1/2 In., Pair 60.00
Heisey, Candlestick, Orchid, Etched, 2 Handled 25.00
Heisey, Candlestick, Ridgeleigh, Prisms, 10 1/2 In., Pair 75.00
Heisey, Candlestick, Sahara, Old Sandwich, Pair, 6 1/2 In. 65.00
Heisey, Candlesticks, Pair, Square Base, Clear, 9 1/4 X 4 1/2 In. 48.00
Heisey, Celery, Empress, Lafayette Etching 20.00
Heisey, Celery, Fancy Loop, Flat Large Roll Edge 32.00
Heisey, Celery, Flamingo, 12 In. 20.00
Heisey, Celery, Fluted, Scalloped Edge, 12 In. 55.00
Heisey, Celery, Orchid, Needle Etched, 12 In. 28.00
Heisey, Centerpiece Bowl, Flamingo, Pattern No.1401, Dolphin Feet 40.00
Heisey, Centerpiece Bowl, Orchid 35.00
Heisey, Chamberstick, Iridescent, Deco Orange Painted Base, 4 1/2 In., Pair 35.00
Heisey, Champagne, Carolina, Etched 22.00
Heisey, Champagne, Carolina, Etched Stem 25.00
Heisey, Champagne, Marigold, Empress Etched 42.00
Heisey, Champagne, Orchid, Etched 10.00
Heisey, Champagne, Pied Piper 14.50
Heisey, Champagne, Sahara, Diamond Optic, Yeoman 18.00
Heisey, Cigarette Holder, Ridgeleigh 15.00
Heisey, Claret, Cobalt, Spanish Stem, 4 Ozs. 42.00
Heisey, Cocktail Shaker, Rooster Stopper, Strainer 65.00
Heisey, Cocktail Shaker, Rooster's Head 95.00
Heisey, Compote, Colonial, 9 1/2 X 8 1/2 In. 37.50
Heisey, Compote, Crystolite, 3 In. 14.00
Heisey, Compote, Jelly, Colonial, No.341, 4 1/2 In. 12.00
Heisey, Compote, Jelly, Rib & Panel, Etched 14.00
Heisey, Compote, Lobster Lid, Lariat, 6 In. 25.00
Heisey, Compote, Oval, Rose Etch, Waverly 42.00
Heisey, Compote, Plantation, 6 1/2 X 3 1/2 In. 17.00
Heisey, Compote, Williamsburg, 6 X 4 1/2 In. 15.00
Heisey, Console Bowl, Ipswich, Footed 35.00
Heisey, Console Bowl, Ipswich, Pedestal 37.50
Heisey, Console Bowl, Queen Anne 45.00
Heisey, Console Set, Diamond Crystal, Floral, 3 Piece 45.00
Heisey, Console Set, Dolphin Footed Bowl, 2 Light Candlesticks, Cuttings 40.00
Heisey, Console Set, Sandwich, 3 Piece 75.00
Heisey, Cornucopia, Leaves & Flowers, Gold Paint, 5 1/2 In. 25.00
Heisey, Creamer On Sugar Cube Tray, Lavender Tinted, 4 In. 45.00
Heisey, Creamer, Child's, Colonial 9.00
Heisey, Creamer, Etched Basket Of Flowers & Butterflies 10.00
Heisey, Creamer, Flamingo, Hotel 15.00
Heisey, Creamer, Individual, Fancy Loop 18.50
Heisey, Creamer, Lavender Sugar Cube Tray, Signed & Dated, 4 In. 50.00

Heisey, Creamer, Waverly 12.00
Heisey, Cup & Saucer, Demitasse, Flamingo, Diamond Optic 20.00
Heisey, Cup & Saucer, Moongleam, Diamond Optic 20.00
Heisey, Cup & Saucer, Orchid, Etched 12.50
Heisey, Cup & Saucer, Pink 8.00
Heisey, Cup & Saucer, Queen Anne 12.50
Heisey, Cup & Saucer, Sahara, Empress 21.50
Heisey, Cup, Custard, Greek Key 9.00
Heisey, Cup, Custard, Whirlpool, No.1506 .... 6.50
Heisey, Cup, Ivorina Verde, Winged Scroll 150.00
Heisey, Cup, Punch, Colonial .... 3.00 To 6.00
Heisey, Cup, Punch, Continental 8.50
Heisey, Cup, Punch, Crystolite 5.50
Heisey, Cup, Punch, Diamond Optic 4.50
Heisey, Cup, Punch, Fancy Loop, 4 1/4 In. 25.00
Heisey, Cup, Punch, Flamingo 29.50
Heisey, Cup, Punch, Lariat 7.50
Heisey, Cup, Punch, No.1833 .... 4.00
Heisey, Cup, Punch, Rib & Panel 5.50
Heisey, Cup, Punch, Williamsberg 5.50
Heisey, Cup, Sherbet, Rib & Panel 5.25
Heisey, Decanter, Sahara Old Sandwich, Original Stopper, 8 1/4 In. 65.00
Heisey, Dish, Baked Apple, Moongleam, Swirl 9.00
Heisey, Dish, Candy, Covered, Divided, Round 22.00
Heisey, Dish, Candy, Covered, Gold Trim, Footed 22.00
Heisey, Dish, Candy, Covered, Swirls, Pedestal Foot, 10 In. 49.00
Heisey, Dish, Candy, Crystal Rose On Brass Lid, Crystolite, Divided 35.00
Heisey, Dish, Candy, Crystolite, Scalloped, Applied Handle, 6 In. 7.00
Heisey, Dish, Candy, Dolphin Finial, Shell Handles, Swirled Ribs 30.00
Heisey, Dish, Candy, Glass Flower On Metal Lid, 7 In. 28.00
Heisey, Dish, Candy, Glass Flower On Metal Top 50.00
Heisey, Dish, Candy, Hammered Silver Edges & Handle, Footed, 7 In. 23.00
Heisey, Dish, Candy, Yellow, Royal Rochester Container, 6 In. 25.00
Heisey, Dish, Cheese & Cracker, Saturn 32.00
Heisey, Dish, Colonial, Connected Plate, Cut Flowers And Leaves 35.00
Heisey, Dish, Dolphin Finial 30.00
Heisey, Dish, Jelly, Waverly 10.00
Heisey, Dish, Lemon, Ridgeleigh, Handled 15.00
Heisey, Dish, Nut, Pink, 6 Sided, Open Handles, Pair 18.00
Heisey, Dish, Pickle, Crystolite, Enamel Floral, Shell Shape 42.50
Heisey, Dish, Round Dessert, Lodestar Dawn, Signed, 4 1/2 In. 17.50
Heisey, Dish, Sundae, Colonial, Flared, 5 1/2 In. 12.00
Heisey, Dish, Swan 15.00
Heisey, Figurine, Cygnet 125.00
Heisey, Figurine, Donkey, Signed 225.00
Heisey, Figurine, Duck Sitting 110.00
Heisey, Figurine, Elephant, Frosted, Large 140.00
Heisey, Figurine, Geese, Wings Half Way 50.00
Heisey, Figurine, Geese, Wings Up 60.00
Heisey, Figurine, Giraffe, 11 In. 75.00
Heisey, Figurine, Goose, Wings Half Way 65.00
Heisey, Figurine, Goose, Wings Up 75.00
Heisey, Figurine, Horse, Head Forward, 8 In. 900.00
Heisey, Figurine, Horse, 5 In. 75.00
Heisey, Figurine, Imperial Airedale 48.00
Heisey, Figurine, Mallard, Wing Half Up 125.00
Heisey, Figurine, Parlor Pup, 4/5 In. 12.00
Heisey, Figurine, Plug Horse 75.00
Heisey, Figurine, Pony, Standing, 5 In. 62.00
Heisey, Figurine, Pouter Pigeon, Signed 625.00
Heisey, Figurine, Pup, 4/5 In. 12.00
Heisey, Figurine, Ringneck Pheasant .... 90.00 To 110.00
Heisey, Figurine, Rooster, 8 In. 42.00
Heisey, Figurine, Scotty 75.00
Heisey, Figurine, Small Bunny, Head Down 95.00

Heisey, Figurine, Sparrow 65.00
Heisey, Figurine, Standing Colt 55.00
Heisey, Finger Bowl, Carolina 18.00
Heisey, Finger Bowl, Carolina, Etched 18.00
Heisey, Glass, Juice, Footed, Continental 14.00
Heisey, Glass, Shot, Fox Chase, Deep Plate Etching 35.00
Heisey, Glass, Soda, Tall Sailboat Etching 100.00
Heisey, Goblet, Ambassador, Etched 32.50
Heisey, Goblet, Cabochon 16.00
Heisey, Goblet, Carolina, Etched 25.00
Heisey, Goblet, Carolina, Etched Stem 25.00
Heisey, Goblet, Cocktail, Marigold, Twist, Sparkle 30.00
Heisey, Goblet, Cocktail, Rooster, No.5038 .... 30.00
Heisey, Goblet, Colonial 15.00
Heisey, Goblet, Colonial, 8 Ozs. 9.00
Heisey, Goblet, Comet Leaf, Marked 85.00
Heisey, Goblet, Creme De Menthe, Colonial, 4 In. 9.00
Heisey, Goblet, Etched Minuet On Stem, 9 Ozs. 15.50
Heisey, Goblet, Marigold, Empress Etched 48.00
Heisey, Goblet, Minuet, Etched, 9 Ozs. 16.50
Heisey, Goblet, Parklane Stem, 10 Ozs. 12.50
Heisey, Goblet, Pied Piper 19.50
Heisey, Goblet, Plantation Ivy 22.50
Heisey, Goblet, Sahara, Diamond Optic 20.00
Heisey, Goblet, Sahara, Empress 25.00
Heisey, Goblet, Snowflake, 6 1/4 In. 70.00
Heisey, Holder, Fountain Straw, Purple, Open Side 30.00
Heisey, Humidor, Very Large 55.00
Heisey, Ice Bucket, Ribbed 22.00
Heisey, Ice Cream Bowl, Colonial, Flared, 3 1/2 In. 9.50
Heisey, Jar, Candy, Gold Decoration On Finial, Foot, & Bowl, 10 In. 45.00
Heisey, Jar, Candy, Greek Key, Covered, 10 1/2 In. 25.00
Heisey, Jar, Candy, Recessed Panels, Gold Trim 35.00
Heisey, Jar, Candy, Recessed Panels, Gold Trim, Covered 20.00
Heisey, Jar, Candy, Trimmed With Gold 25.00
Heisey, Jar, Covered, Sterling Lid, Fisherman Finial, Tall, Etched 60.00
Heisey, Jar, Fisherman Finial On Sterling Lid, Engraved, 9 3/4 In. 58.00
Heisey, Jar, Marmalade, Crystolite 17.50
Heisey, Jar, Powder, Covered, Colonial, 5 1/4 In. 35.00
Heisey, Jar, Powder, Silver Plate Lid 25.00
Heisey, Julep Tumbler, Colonial, 7 Ozs. 3.00
Heisey, Match Holder, Figural, Fish 125.00
Heisey, Mayonnaise Bowl & Underplate, Queen Anne, Dolphin Foot, Etched 25.00
Heisey, Mayonnaise Set, 3 Piece 25.00
Heisey, Mug, Punty Band, Red Stained, Souvenir 25.00
Heisey, Mug, Punty Band, Ruby Flashed, Ida Weimer, 1902 .... 35.00
Heisey, Mustard Pot, Colonial 18.00
Heisey, Nappy, Narrow Flute, Oval, 6 In. 7.00
Heisey, Nappy, No.352 .... 4.00
Heisey, Nappy, No.355, 4 In. 4.00
Heisey, Nappy, Orchid, Ribbed, Handled, Heart Shape 15.00
Heisey, Parfait, Plantation Ivy 19.75
Heisey, Pitcher, Colonial, Quart 25.00
Heisey, Pitcher, Colonial, Signed, 5 1/2 X 7 In. 55.00
Heisey, Pitcher, Colonial, Squat Type, 1/2 Gallon 37.50
Heisey, Pitcher, Colonial, 16 Ozs., 4 In. 15.00
Heisey, Pitcher, Colonial, 48 Ozs., 7 In. 42.50
Heisey, Pitcher, Milk, Wedding Band 45.00
Heisey, Pitcher, Narrow Flute, Quart 33.00
Heisey, Pitcher, No.393, Quart 35.00
Heisey, Pitcher, Silver Overlay, Colonial, 7 1/2 In. 80.00
Heisey, Pitcher, Tankard, Lavender, Floral Decoration, Opalescent White 92.00
Heisey, Pitcher, Water, Applied Handle, Enameled Flowers 25.00
Heisey, Pitcher, Water, Emerald Green, Winged Scroll 150.00
Heisey, Pitcher, Water, Greek Key 100.00

Heisey, Pitcher, Water, Medium Flat Panel, No.353, 2 Quart, 6 1/2 In. 30.00
Heisey, Pitcher, Water, Narrow Flute, No.173, 3 Pint, 6 1/2 In. 33.00
Heisey, Pitcher, Water, Sunburst, No.343, 3 Pint, 6 In. 77.00
Heisey, Plate, Cake, Orchid, Etched, 14 In. 35.00
Heisey, Plate, Cake, Silver Overlay, 14 1/2 In. 55.00
Heisey, Plate, Cracker & Cheese, Greek Key, Star Base, Marked 65.00
Heisey, Plate, Design On Border, Square, 8 1/2 In., Pair 12.00
Heisey, Plate, Dinner, Queen Anne, Square 15.75
Heisey, Plate, Emerald Green, Ridgeleigh, 7 1/2 In. .... 7.00 To 7.50
Heisey, Plate, Flamingo, Empress, Etched, 8 In. 12.00
Heisey, Plate, Flamingo, Narrow Flute, 7 In. 8.00
Heisey, Plate, Flamingo, 6 In. 5.50
Heisey, Plate, Hawthorne, 6 In. 10.00
Heisey, Plate, Ipswich, 8 In. .... 12.00 To 12.50
Heisey, Plate, Luncheon, Oceanic 6.00
Heisey, Plate, Luncheon, Sahara, Empress, 8 1/2 In. 12.75
Heisey, Plate, Moongleam, Queen Anne, 7 In. 27.00
Heisey, Plate, No.1183, 5 1/2 In. 3.00
Heisey, Plate, No.353, 7 In. 4.00
Heisey, Plate, Orchid, Etched, 8 1/2 In. 10.00
Heisey, Plate, Party, Satellite, 14 In. 25.00
Heisey, Plate, Pied Piper, 8 1/2 In. 8.00
Heisey, Plate, Pink, No.1235, 6 In. 5.00
Heisey, Plate, Pink, No.1243, 7 1/2 In. 4.50
Heisey, Plate, Pink, Queen Anne, Square, 7 1/4 In. 7.50
Heisey, Plate, Plantation, 8 1/2 In. 8.00
Heisey, Plate, Queen Anne, Alexandrite, Marked, 7 In.Square 65.00
Heisey, Plate, Rayed, 13 1/4 In. 52.00
Heisey, Plate, Ridgeleigh, Square, 8 In. 10.00
Heisey, Plate, Sahara Yellow, Pattern No.1401, 7 In. 5.00
Heisey, Plate, Salad, Queen Anne 9.75
Heisey, Plate, Sandwich, Cut & Etched, Ring Handle 50.00
Heisey, Plate, Soup, No.416 .... 6.00
Heisey, Plate, Star Cut Base, Signed H In Diamond, 5 3/4 In. 5.00
Heisey, Plate, Tangerine, Empress, Square, 8 1/4 In. 110.00
Heisey, Plate, Torte, Crystolite, 14 In. 15.00
Heisey, Punch Bowl & Base, Greek Key, 15 In. 255.00
Heisey, Punch Bowl, Greek Key, 15 In. 95.00
Heisey, Punch Set, Colonial, 14 In. Bowl, 14 Piece 235.00
Heisey, Punch Set, Pinwheel & Fan, 15 Piece 600.00
Heisey, Relish, Amber, Ridgeleigh, Nickel Holder, 12 1/2 In. 36.00
Heisey, Relish, Crystolite, 3 Sections, 13 X 8 In. 26.00
Heisey, Relish, Divided 45.00
Heisey, Relish, Etched, Divided, Sterling Silver Base 28.00
Heisey, Relish, Flamingo, Narrow Flute, 9 In. 18.00
Heisey, Relish, Flamingo, 12 In. 18.00
Heisey, Relish, Pink Twist, 7 In. 10.00
Heisey, Relish, Ridgeleigh, Star, Divided 30.00
Heisey, Relish, 3 Part, Lariat, 10 In. 27.50
Heisey, Salad Bowl, Crystolite, 12 In. 17.00
Heisey, Salt & Pepper, Fancy Loop 50.00
Heisey, Salt, Fancy Loop 16.50
Heisey, Salt, Fluted, 2 1/2 In. 6.00
Heisey, Salt, Pedestal, Colonial 7.50
Heisey, Salt, Sawtooth Band 16.50
Heisey, Salt, Vaseline, Paneled Sides, Square, 2 1/4 In. 12.50
Heisey, Saltshaker, Basketweave, Pewter & Glass Top 12.00
Heisey, Saucer, Pink, Queen Anne, Square, 6 1/4 In. 3.50
Heisey, Set Of 3 Saltshakers On Stand, Waffle, Metal Tops 22.00
Heisey, Shaker, Cocktail, 2 Quart, Special Cuttings 55.00
Heisey, Sherbet, Banded Flute, 4 In. 7.00
Heisey, Sherbet, Colonial 48.00
Heisey, Sherbet, Etched Minuet On Stem 15.00
Heisey, Sherbet, Flamingo, Pleat & Panel 15.00

Heisey, Sherbet, Greek Key, Cupped, 6 Ozs. 10.00
Heisey, Sherbet, Greek Key, Flared, 4 1/2 Ozs. 10.00
Heisey, Sherbet, Greek Key, Low Foot, 4 1/2 Ozs. 9.00
Heisey, Sherbet, Greek Key, 4 1/2 Ozs. 10.00
Heisey, Sherbet, Greek Key, 6 Ozs. 10.00
Heisey, Sherbet, Ipswich .... 9.50 To 15.00
Heisey, Sherbet, Minuet, Etched 15.00
Heisey, Sherbet, No.150 .... 5.50
Heisey, Sherbet, Plantation 7.00
Heisey, Sherbet, Plantation Ivy 19.75
Heisey, Sherbet, Plantation, Etched Ivy 9.00
Heisey, Sherbet, Sahara, Diamond Optic 15.00
Heisey, Sherbet, Snowflake, 2 3/4 In. 40.00
Heisey, Sherbet, Tangerine, Duquesne, Stemmed 150.00
Heisey, Sherbet, Victorian, 5 Ozs. 10.00
Heisey, Sherbet, Yellow Carnival, 6 In. 55.00
Heisey, Slat, Pedestal, Greek Key, 2 3/4 In., Set Of 8 .... 64.00
Heisey, Spooner, Greek Key 25.00
Heisey, Stopper, Figural, Girl's Head 225.00
Heisey, Stopper, Figural, Rooster Head 65.00
Heisey, Sugar & Creamer, Amber, No.1401 .... 30.00
Heisey, Sugar & Creamer, Child's, Colonial 2.00
Heisey, Sugar & Creamer, Colonial 25.00
Heisey, Sugar & Creamer, Colonial, Miniature 23.00
Heisey, Sugar & Creamer, Colonial, Squat 22.00
Heisey, Sugar & Creamer, Crystolite 40.00
Heisey, Sugar & Creamer, Embossed Vertical Ribbing, Oval 12.50
Heisey, Sugar & Creamer, Flamingo, Hotel, Etched, Oval 35.00
Heisey, Sugar & Creamer, Greek Key, Oval 50.00
Heisey, Sugar & Creamer, Individual, Sahara, Queen Anne 28.50
Heisey, Sugar & Creamer, Pink 9.50
Heisey, Sugar & Creamer, Pink, No.479 .... 25.00
Heisey, Sugar & Creamer, Ridgeleigh .... 15.00 To 27.50
Heisey, Sugar & Creamer, Ridgeleigh, Miniature 28.00
Heisey, Sugar & Creamer, Sahara, Queen Anne 52.00
Heisey, Sugar & Creamer, Silver Overlay, Etched Floral 35.00
Heisey, Sugar, Covered, Lariat 18.50
Heisey, Sugar, Creamer, & Tray, Individual, Crystolite .... 24.00 To 30.00
Heisey, Sugar, Creamer, & Underplate, Crystolite, Miniature 28.00
Heisey, Sugar, Flute, Miniature 10.00
Heisey, Sugar, Hotel, Ground Bottom 18.50
Heisey, Sugar, Hotel, Oval 25.00
Heisey, Sugar, Individual, Hotel, Oval 26.50
Heisey, Sugar, Lump Carrier, Colonial, Raised Foot, Exaggerated Handle Back 22.00
Heisey, Sugar, Pink, No.355 .... 6.00
Heisey, Sugar, Pink, No.7023 .... 7.00
Heisey, Sugar, Pink, 2 Open Handles, Pedestal Base, 2 3/4 In. 20.00
Heisey, Sugar, Purplish, Prescut 5.00
Heisey, Swan, Crystolite, 6 In. 35.00
Heisey, Syrup, Applied Clear Handle, 1909 .... 36.00
Heisey, Syrup, Etched 30.00
Heisey, Syrup, Opalescent, Beaded Swag 125.00
Heisey, Toothpick, Beaded Swag, Red Flashed 45.00
Heisey, Toothpick, Beaded Swag, Red Stained 58.00
Heisey, Toothpick, Cobalt, Star Pattern 26.00
Heisey, Toothpick, Crystolite, Footed 20.00
Heisey, Toothpick, Fancy Loop 45.00
Heisey, Toothpick, Priscilla, Silver Overlay 18.50
Heisey, Toothpick, Ruby Stained, Engraved John, 1908 .... 35.00
Heisey, Tray, Fluted Sides, 12 1/2 In. 13.00
Heisey, Tray, Spice, Pleat & Panel 30.00
Heisey, Tub, Ice, Greek Key, 3 1/2 In. 25.00
Heisey, Tumbler, Coarse Rib .... 9.00 To 12.00
Heisey, Tumbler, Coleport, 4 Ozs. 4.00

Heisey, Tumbler, Colonial 9.00
Heisey, Tumbler, Emerald Green, Fancy Loop 48.00
Heisey, Tumbler, Fancy Loop 28.00
Heisey, Tumbler, Golfer, Deep Plate, Etched 85.00
Heisey, Tumbler, Ipswich, Footed 10.00 To 18.00
Heisey, Tumbler, Juice, Ipswich 9.00
Heisey, Tumbler, Juice, Victorian 15.00
Heisey, Tumbler, Pineapple & Fan, Gilt Trim 14.50
Heisey, Tumbler, Rib & Panel, 4 1/2 Ozs. 4.50
Heisey, Tumbler, Sahara, Empress 16.75
Heisey, Tumbler, Sahara, Old Colony, Etched, Footed 22.50
Heisey, Tumbler, Sahara, Thumbprint, Footed, 14 Ozs., 5 1/2 In. 15.00
Heisey, Tumbler, Sandwich, Footed 15.00
Heisey, Tumbler, Souvenir, Cedar Point, 1911, Custard, Band & Roses 50.00
Heisey, Tumbler, Victorian, 8 Oz. 5.00
Heisey, Vase, Crystal, 21 In. 40.00
Heisey, Vase, Orchid, Etched, Fan, 6 1/2 In. 29.00
Heisey, Vase, Orchid, Lariat, Etched, 7 1/2 X 4 1/2 In., Pair 45.00
Heisey, Vase, Orchid, Sunburst, 6 In. 40.00
Heisey, Vase, Ridgeleigh, 6 In. 15.00
Heisey, Vase, Ridgeleigh, 8 In. 28.00 To 30.00
Heisey, Vase, Rooster 55.00
Heisey, Vase, Scalloped Top, Footed, Double Handled, 7 1/2 In. 10.00
Heisey, Vase, Scalloped Top, 21 In. 30.00
Heisey, Vase, Warwick, 5 In., Pair 35.00
Heisey, Wine, Carolina, Etched 25.00
Heisey, Wine, Cut Stars, Hollow Stem, 5 In. 12.00
Heisey, Wine, Emerald Green, Fancy Loop 55.00
Heisey, Wine, Ipswich 8.50
Heisey, Wine, Orchid, Etched 12.50
Heisey, Wine, Pink, Acorn Stem, 4 1/4 In. 20.00
Heisey, Wine, Plantation Ivy 25.00
Heisey, Wine, Tally Ho 37.50
Heisey, Wine, Whirlpool 14.00
Heisey, Wine, Yorktown 10.00

Herend, see Fischer

Heubach, Cup & Saucer, Fruit 18.50
Heubach, Figurine, Bagpiper, Bisque, 12 3/4 In. 145.00
Heubach, Figurine, Country Miss, Bisque, 15 1/2 In. 95.00
Heubach, Figurine, Dancing Girl, Green Dress & Slippers, 6 3/4 In. 77.50
Heubach, Figurine, Dutch Boy Leaning Against Basket, 6 1/2 In. 50.00
Heubach, Figurine, Peasant Girl With Mandolin, Bisque, 14 1/4 In. 125.00
Heubach, Figurine, Woman Wearing Blue Skirt, Bronze Dore, 6 X 5 In. 135.00
Heubach, Group, Girl Kissing Boy, Egg-Shaped Vase Behind, 6 1/4 In. 28.00
Heubach, Jar, Indian's Head On Lid, Jasperware, Green, 5 1/2 In. 150.00
Heubach, Lamp Base, Couple, Standing, Elegant 18th Century Dress, 5 1/4 In. 55.00
Heubach, Lamp, Woman & Man In 18th Century Dress & Fluted Column, 9 In. 55.00
Heubach, Vase, Center Medallion Of Victorian Lady On Burnt Umber, Signed 65.00
Heubach, Vase, Gray, 6 Rooks, Klotzer, Sunburst Mark, 6 1/4 In. 37.50
Heubach, Vase, High Glaze, 3 White Swans On Green Water 35.00

Higbee glass was made by the J.B.Higbee Company of Bridgeville, Pennsylvania, about 1900.

Higbee, see also Pressed Glass

Higbee, Rose Bowl, Wide Flutes, Rayed Base, 4 1/2 In. 14.50
Higbee, Sugar, Covered, Handled 14.00

Historic Blue, see Adams, Clews, Ridgway, Staffordshire

Hobbs Brockunier, Bowl, Citron, Applied Rose Edge, Heart-Shaped Rim, 10 In. 350.00
Hobbs Brockunier, Syrup, Leaf & Flower, Amber & Frosted, Pewter Top, C.1885 150.00

Hobnail, see also Francisware

Hobnail glass is a pattern of pressed glass with bumps in an allover pattern. Dozens of hobnail patterns and variants have been made. Reproductions of many types of hobnail glass can be found.

Hobnail, Bowl, White Ruffled Edge, 6 In. 5.00
Hobnail, Dish, Bone, Blue 22.50
Hobnail, Epergne, Pink, 3 Lilies, 7 In. 34.00
Hobnail, Fruit Bowl, Ruffled Edge, Pedestal, Three Mold 18.00
Hobnail, Hat, Ice Blue Opalescent, 3 In. 20.00
Hobnail, Lampshade, Red, Ruffled Top, 9 X 6 In. 75.00
Hobnail, Pitcher, Milk, Pointed Thumbprint Base, Blue 72.00
Hobnail, Rose Bowl, Ruffled & Crimped Top, 5 1/4 X 4 3/4 In. 20.00
Hobnail, Vase, Pink & White, Ruffled Top, 4 3/4 In. 25.00

Holly amber, or golden agate, glass was made by the Indiana Tumbler and Goblet Company from January 1, 1903, to June 13, 1903. It is a pressed glass pattern featuring holly leaves in the amber shaded glass.

Holly Amber, Bowl, Berry, 8 1/4 In. 395.00
Holly Amber, Butter 600.00
Holly Amber, Cake Stand 1500.00
Holly Amber, Compote, Jelly 550.00
Holly Amber, Compote, Jelly, Covered, 6 In. 700.00
Holly Amber, Plate, Cake 550.00
Holly Amber, Plate, Square, 7 1/2 In. 475.00
Holly Amber, Salt & Pepper 450.00
Holly Amber, Sauce 145.00 To 350.00
Holly Amber, Sauce, Set Of 3 240.00
Holly Amber, Toothpick 210.00
Holly Amber, Vase, 6 In. 395.00
Honesdale, Vase, Etched Crystal, Topaz & Green Tulips, Gold Trim, 12 In. 450.00
Hopalong Cassidy, Banner, Felt 3.00
Hopalong Cassidy, Banner, Portrait, Felt 3.00
Hopalong Cassidy, Camera, Box 35.00
Hopalong Cassidy, Chinese Checkers 12.00
Hopalong Cassidy, Clock, Alarm 40.00
Hopalong Cassidy, Cowboy Outfit, Girl's, 1950 20.00
Hopalong Cassidy, Cup, Milk 10.00
Hopalong Cassidy, Dental Kit 15.00
Hopalong Cassidy, Gun, Zoomerang 6.00
Hopalong Cassidy, Lunch Pail With Thermos, William Boyd, 1954 25.00
Hopalong Cassidy, Mug, Milk Glass 4.00
Hopalong Cassidy, Placemat, Celluloid 3.00
Hopalong Cassidy, Plate, Hopalong On Horseback, Colored 9.00
Hopalong Cassidy, Puzzle, Milton Bradley, 1950 5.00
Hopalong Cassidy, Puzzle, T.V., Dated 1950 10.00
Hopalong Cassidy, Revolving Lamp 35.00
Hopalong Cassidy, Ring, Compass, Black Cowboy Hat Fits On Top 25.00
Hopalong Cassidy, Ring, Metal 7.50
Hopalong Cassidy, Ring, Radio Premium 20.00
Hopalong Cassidy, Shooting Gallery 17.50
Hopalong Cassidy, Watch, Wrist, Good Luck, Hoppy 50.00
Horn, Box, Hanging Wall, Slant Front, Arch Back, 7 1/4 X 3 1/2 X 2 In. 32.00
Horn, Snuffbox, Light & Dark Coloring, 3 X 1 1/2 In. 21.00
Horn, Snuffbox, Norwegian, Engraved Hinged Silver Lid, 1902, 3 1/2 In. 45.00
Horn, Snuffbox, Wooden Top, Leather Thong, Oval 35.00
Howdy Doody, Bag, Shoulder, Cloth 20.00
Howdy Doody, Camera, Developers 14.00
Howdy Doody, Chart, Behavior, Clarabell & Flub-A-Dub, 1949, 18 1/2 In. 11.00
Howdy Doody, Doll, Marionette, Wood & Composition, Peter Puppet, 1951, 12 In. 22.50
Howdy Doody, Doll, Movable Mouth, 29 In. 55.00
Howdy Doody, Doll, Vinyl Head, Cloth Body, String Moves Mouth, 12 In. 20.00
Howdy Doody, Game, Bean Bag 10.00
Howdy Doody, Lamp 25.00
Howdy Doody, Pendant, National Broadcasting Co. On Back, Enameled 15.00
Howdy Doody, Polisher, Shoe, In Box With Contents 5.00
Howdy Doody, Salt & Pepper, Plastic 6.00

Hull pottery is made in Crooksville, Ohio. The factory started in 1903 as the Acme Pottery Company. Art pottery was first made in 1917.

Hull, Basket, Aqua & White Spatter, Gray To White Top, 9 In. 16.00
Hull, Basket, Aqua Spatter, 8 3/4 In. 9.50
Hull, Basket, Glossy, S-Shaped Handle, No.51, 12 In. 22.00
Hull, Basket, Woodland, Glossy, 13 In. 25.00
Hull, Bowl, Seashell, 2 Snails At Top 12.50
Hull, Compote, Blue, Bird Decorations, 5 In. 15.00
Hull, Console Set, Bowknot, Handled Candlesticks, 3 Piece 12.00
Hull, Console Set, Bowknot, 3 Piece 35.00
Hull, Console Set, Parchment & Pine, Brown And Green, 3 Pieces 35.00
Hull, Cornucopia 14.00
Hull, Cornucopia, Bowknot, Pink To Blue, 7 1/2 In., Pair 20.00
Hull, Cornucopia, Green Shading, Shell Bowl, Ribbed, Pink Interior, 11 In. 24.00
Hull, Cornucopia, Pink & Blue Matte Glaze, W 10, 8 1/2 In. 18.00
Hull, Cornucopia, Pink & Blue, W-7, 7 1/2 In. 12.00
Hull, Cornucopia, Water Lily, Beige To Brown, 6 1/2 In. 18.00
Hull, Cornucopia, Water Lily, Tan, 9 1/4 In. 24.00
Hull, Cornucopia, Woodland, Glazed Finish, W 10, 11 In. 13.50
Hull, Cornucopia, Woodland, Matte Finish, 11 In. 13.50
Hull, Dish, Candy, Ivory, Blue & Gold Butterflies & Floral, Pedestal 15.00
Hull, Ewer, Bowknot, Blue To Green, 5 1/2 In. 15.00
Hull, Ewer, Pink, 7 In. 4.00
Hull, Ewer, Tulip, Yellow To Blue, 13 In. 50.00
Hull, Flower Holder, White Swan On Turquoise Leaf Base, 6 In. 17.00
Hull, Jar, Cookie, Little Red Riding Hood 19.50
Hull, Jar, Cookie, Mottled Light To Medium Green, 9 In. 12.00
Hull, Jar, Cookie, Red Riding Hood .... 15.00 To 55.00
Hull, Jar, Mustard, Red Riding Hood 15.00
Hull, Pitcher & Underplate, Brown Glaze, Eagle & Stars, 2 Cup Size 10.00
Hull, Pitcher Vase, Marked 14, 4 3/4 In. 6.00
Hull, Pitcher, Lemonade, Ice Guard, 2 Quart 8.00
Hull, Pitcher, Magnolia, Pink, No.5, 7 In. 12.00
Hull, Pitcher, Matte, 5 1/2 In. 12.00
Hull, Pitcher, Open Rose, Matte Finish, 4 3/4 In. 6.00
Hull, Pitcher, Wild Flower, Pink & Blue, 7 In. 12.00
Hull, Pitcher, Woodland, White, W-3, 5 1/4 In. 12.00
Hull, Planter & Underplate, Water Lilies, 6 In. 9.00
Hull, Planter, Dancing Girl 15.00
Hull, Planter, Duck, Green, 10 1/2 In. 12.50
Hull, Planter, Figural, Pig 10.00
Hull, Planter, Figural, Pig's Head, Pink, 6 In. 6.00
Hull, Planter, Girl With Basket, C.1940, 8 1/2 In. 12.00
Hull, Planter, Green, Duck, 8 In. 7.50
Hull, Planter, Pink To Blue, Round, 5 3/4 In. 14.00
Hull, Planter, Swan, White Matte, 9 In. 15.00
Hull, Planter, Swan, White, Double, 10 1/2 X 8 1/2 In. 18.00
Hull, Plaque, Wall, Speckled, 13 X 7 1/2 In. 8.00
Hull, Saltbox, Green, Ribbed, Wooden Lid 15.00
Hull, Sugar & Creamer, Medium Green, Shaded At Top 6.50
Hull, Swan, Open Top, 11 In. 21.00
Hull, Tea Set, Ebb Tide, Chartreuse To Burgundy, Shell Shape, 3 Piece 65.00
Hull, Tea Set, Red Riding Hood, 6 Piece 85.00
Hull, Teapot And Lid, Red Riding Hood 25.00
Hull, Teapot, Rose, Full Size 20.00
Hull, Teapot, Woodland, Chartreuse With Pink 25.00
Hull, Teapot, Woodland, Glossy Pink With Chartreuse 20.00
Hull, Vase, Blossomflite, Pink, 10 1/4 In. 20.00
Hull, Vase, Blossomflite, T-7, 10 1/4 In. 25.00
Hull, Vase, Bowknot, B11, 10 1/2 In. 25.00
Hull, Vase, Bowknot, Pink, Blue, & Pale Green, B-10, 10 1/2 In. 25.00
Hull, Vase, Bowknot, 10 1/2 In. 18.50
Hull, Vase, Bowknot, 11 In. 20.00
Hull, Vase, Bud, Double, Woodland, 8 1/2 In. 18.00
Hull, Vase, Cornucopia, Brown & Tan, Wheat, 13 In. 18.00
Hull, Vase, Cream To Dark Pink Base, Pink Crocus, 5 In. 12.00

Hull, Vase, Deer In Forest, 9 In. 17.50
Hull, Vase, Deer, 10 In. 22.00
Hull, Vase, Double, Wh15, 8 1/2 In., Pair 20.00
Hull, Vase, Figural, Peacock, 10 In. 18.00
Hull, Vase, Fish With Seashell, E 9, 12 1/2 In. 25.00
Hull, Vase, Glazed, Stem Handles, Pink Base And Flower, 11 In. 25.00
Hull, Vase, Green Glaze, 7 1/2 In. 17.00
Hull, Vase, Magnolia, Beige To Brown, 15 In. 65.00
Hull, Vase, Magnolia, Matte Finish, 8 1/2 In. 12.00
Hull, Vase, Magnolia, Matte Finish, 10 1/2 In. 20.00
Hull, Vase, Magnolia, Matte Glaze, 6 1/4 In. 15.00
Hull, Vase, Magnolia, Pink & Blue, 6 1/2 In. 12.00
Hull, Vase, Magnolia, Pink To Blue, 15 In. 65.00
Hull, Vase, Magnolia, Yellow To Tan, No.4, 6 1/4 In. 12.00
Hull, Vase, Magnolia, Yellow To Tan, No.13, 4 3/4 In. 8.00
Hull, Vase, Magnolia, Yellow To Tan, No.15, 6 1/4 In. 12.00
Hull, Vase, Open Rose, Pink To Blue, Cornucopia Shape, 8 1/2 In. 18.00
Hull, Vase, Open Rose, White, No.131, 4 3/4 In. 8.00
Hull, Vase, Pink & Blue, Bowknot, 10 1/2 In. 28.00
Hull, Vase, Pink & Blue, W-6, 7 1/2 In. 13.00
Hull, Vase, Pink Base, Blue Top, 2 Wing Shaped Handles, 6 1/2 In. 12.00
Hull, Vase, Pink Magnolia, Matte, 8 1/2 In. 10.00
Hull, Vase, Rosella, Pink & Blue, Closed Handles, C.1940, 6 1/2 In. 10.00
Hull, Vase, Rosella, R-15, 8 1/2 In. 14.00
Hull, Vase, Wildflower, Pink, W-5, 6 1/2 In. 8.50
Hull, Vase, Wildflower, Pink, W-15, 10 1/2 In. 15.00
Hull, Vase, Wildflower, 10 1/2 In. 12.00
Hull, Vase, Wildflower, 4 Handles, W-5, 6 1/2 In. 18.00
Hull, Vase, Woodland, Trumpet Shape, W 5, 6 1/2 In. 12.00
Hull, Vase, Woodland, W-4, 6 1/2 In. 10.00
Hull, Vase, Woodland, 8 1/2 In. 12.00
Hull, Wall Pocket, Turquoise High Glaze, W-13, 7 1/2 In. 22.00
Humidor, Rhinoceros's Foot, C.1876 475.00

Hummel figurines, based on the drawings of Berta Hummel, are made by the W.Goebel Porzellanfabrik of Oeslau, Germany. They were first made in 1934.

Hummel, Ashtray, Bird Boy, Crown Mark 90.00
Hummel, Ashtray, Happy Pastime, 1938 75.00
Hummel, Ashtray, Singing Lesson, V & Bee, West Germany Mark, 6 3/4 In. 40.00
Hummel, Bookend, Bookworm, 5 1/2 In., Pair 90.00
Hummel, Bottle, Monk, V-Bee Mark, 10 1/2 In. 47.50
Hummel, Box, Candy, Playmates 42.00
Hummel, Candleholder, Angelic Sleep, 5 X 3 1/2 In. 31.00
Hummel, Candleholder, Boy With Rocking Horse, 1938, 3 1/2 In. 24.00
Hummel, Candleholder, Christ Child & Singing Angel, U.S.Zone, Germany, 5 In. 45.00
Hummel, Candleholder, Flower Girl, 1938, 3 1/2 In. 24.00
Hummel, Candleholder, Girl With Christmas Tree, V & Bee Mark, 3 1/2 In. 18.75
Hummel, Candleholder, Silent Night, 5 1/2 X 4 3/4 In. 41.50
Hummel, Dish, Covered, Joyful 85.00
Hummel, Feeding Time, 5 3/4 In. 190.00
Hummel, Figurine, Accordion Boy, Crown Germany Mark, 5 1/2 In. 115.00
Hummel, Figurine, Accordion Boy, Goebel, Bee & Black Germany Mark, 5 1/4 In. 135.00
Hummel, Figurine, Accordion Boy, Stylized Bee Mark, 5 1/4 In. 31.00
Hummel, Figurine, Adoration, Bee & Germany Mark, 7 In. 125.00
Hummel, Figurine, Adoration, Blue Bee Mark, 6 7/8 In. 175.00
Hummel, Figurine, Adoration, Stylized Bee Mark, 1960, 6 1/4 In. 60.00
Hummel, Figurine, Adoration, Stylized Bee Mark, 6 1/4 In. 68.00
Hummel, Figurine, Adoration, 9 In. 95.00
Hummel, Figurine, Angel Serenade, With Lamb, Full Bee 500.00
Hummel, Figurine, Angel With Banjo, V & Bee, West Germany Mark, 2 1/2 In. 16.50
Hummel, Figurine, Angel With Lamb & Mandolin, U.S.Zone, Germany, 6 In. 50.00
Hummel, Figurine, Apple Tree Boy, Bee & Black Germany Mark, 4 In. 90.00
Hummel, Figurine, Apple Tree Boy, Bee & West Germany Mark, 6 In. 80.00

Hummel, Figurine, Apple Tree Boy, Black Bee & Germany Mark, 6 3/4 In. 110.00
Hummel, Figurine, Apple Tree Boy, 1959, 4 In. 28.00
Hummel, Figurine, Apple Tree Boy, 4 In. 21.50
Hummel, Figurine, Apple Tree Boy, 6 In. 100.00
Hummel, Figurine, Apple Tree Boy, 10 In. 275.00
Hummel, Figurine, Apple Tree Boy, 10 1/4 In. 250.00
Hummel, Figurine, Apple Tree Girl, Bee & Black Germany Mark, 4 In. 90.00
Hummel, Figurine, Apple Tree Girl, 4 In. 21.50
Hummel, Figurine, Apple Tree Girl, 6 In. .... 38.50 To 41.50
Hummel, Figurine, Apple Tree Girl, 10 In. .... 250.00 To 275.00
Hummel, Figurine, Auf Wiedersehen, 5 1/2 In. .... 35.50 To 39.00
Hummel, Figurine, Autumn Harvest, 4 3/4 In. 40.00
Hummel, Figurine, Baker, 1938, 5 1/4 In. 65.00
Hummel, Figurine, Baker, 4 3/4 In. 25.50
Hummel, Figurine, Baker, 5 In. 28.00
Hummel, Figurine, Band Leader, V & Bee, West Germany Mark, 5 In. 37.50
Hummel, Figurine, Band Leader, 5 1/4 In. .... 30.50 To 31.00
Hummel, Figurine, Barnyard Hero, Bee & Germany Mark, 4 In. 46.00
Hummel, Figurine, Barnyard Hero, Three Line Mark, 5 1/2 In. 53.50
Hummel, Figurine, Barnyard Hero, 4 In. .... 24.50 To 26.50
Hummel, Figurine, Barnyard Hero, 5 1/2 In. 43.00
Hummel, Figurine, Bashful, 4 3/4 In. 32.00
Hummel, Figurine, Be Patient, Bee Mark, 4 3/4 In. 45.00
Hummel, Figurine, Be Patient, Black Bee & Germany Mark, 4 5/8 In. 70.00
Hummel, Figurine, Be Patient, Three Line Mark, 4 1/4 In. 31.00
Hummel, Figurine, Be Patient, 4 1/4 In. .... 25.50 To 29.00
Hummel, Figurine, Be Patient, 6 1/4 In. .... 35.00 To 40.00
Hummel, Figurine, Big House Cleaning, 4 In. .... 46.50 To 50.00
Hummel, Figurine, Birthday Serenade, Black West Germany & Circle, 5 1/4 In. 125.00
Hummel, Figurine, Birthday Serenade, Reverse Mold, Full Bee, 5 3/8 In. 600.00
Hummel, Figurine, Birthday Serenade, 1971, 4 1/2 In. 29.00
Hummel, Figurine, Blessed Event, 5 1/4 In. 75.00
Hummel, Figurine, Bookworm, Black West Germany & B & B Mark, 4 1/2 In. 45.00
Hummel, Figurine, Bookworm, Girl, Bee Mark, 5 1/2 In. 148.00
Hummel, Figurine, Bookworm, Stylized Bee Mark, 5 1/2 In. 91.00
Hummel, Figurine, Bookworm, West Germany Mark, 5 1/2 In. 90.00
Hummel, Figurine, Bookworm, 4 In. 29.50
Hummel, Figurine, Bookworm, 5 1/2 In. .... 53.00 To 70.00
Hummel, Figurine, Bookworm, 8 1/2 In. 330.00
Hummel, Figurine, Boots, Bee Mark, 5 1/2 In. 95.00
Hummel, Figurine, Boots, Incised Crown & Black Bee Mark, 6 3/4 In. 500.00
Hummel, Figurine, Boots, V & Bee, West Germany Mark, 5 1/4 In. 33.00
Hummel, Figurine, Boy With Horn, 4 1/2 In. 55.00
Hummel, Figurine, Boy With Toothache, 5 1/2 In. 28.50
Hummel, Figurine, Brother, Bee & Black Germany Mark, 5 1/2 In. 95.00
Hummel, Figurine, Brother, Black Bee & Germany Mark, 5 7/8 In. 65.00
Hummel, Figurine, Brother, V & Bee, West Germany Mark, 5 3/4 In. 28.50
Hummel, Figurine, Brother, 5 3/4 In. 25.50
Hummel, Figurine, Candlelight, 6 3/4 In. 54.00
Hummel, Figurine, Celestial Musician, Black Bee & Germany Mark, 7 1/4 In. 130.00
Hummel, Figurine, Chick Girl, Bee Mark, 4 1/4 In. 95.00
Hummel, Figurine, Chick Girl, Black Bee & Germany Mark, 4 In. 70.00
Hummel, Figurine, Chick Girl, Goebel, 3 1/2 In. 25.00
Hummel, Figurine, Chick Girl, Stylized Bee Mark, 3 1/2 In. 31.00
Hummel, Figurine, Chick Girl, 3 1/2 In. 24.50
Hummel, Figurine, Chick Girl, 4 1/4 In. 36.00
Hummel, Figurine, Chicken Licken, 4 3/4 In. 48.50
Hummel, Figurine, Chimney Sweep, Bee & West Germany Mark, 4 In. 18.00
Hummel, Figurine, Chimney Sweep, Bee Mark, 5 1/2 In. 110.00
Hummel, Figurine, Chimney Sweep, Black Bee & V Mark, 4 In. 40.00
Hummel, Figurine, Chimney Sweep, West Germany, 5 In. 35.00
Hummel, Figurine, Chimney Sweep, 5 1/2 In. .... 24.50 To 26.50
Hummel, Figurine, Christ Child, U.S.Zone, Germany, 6 In. 45.00

Hummel, Figurine, Christ Child, V & Bee, West Germany Mark, 5 1/2 In. 25.00
Hummel, Figurine, Cinderella, No.337, 5 In. 48.00
Hummel, Figurine, Cinderella, 4 1/2 In. 48.00
Hummel, Figurine, Cinderella, 4 9/16 In. 45.00
Hummel, Figurine, Confidentially, 5 1/4 In. 40.00
Hummel, Figurine, Confidentially, 5 1/2 In. 37.00
Hummel, Figurine, Congratulations, Bee & Germany Mark, 6 In. 150.00
Hummel, Figurine, Congratulations, With Sox, 5 1/2 In. 22.50
Hummel, Figurine, Congratulations, 6 In. 24.00
Hummel, Figurine, Crossroads, 6 11/16 In. 78.50
Hummel, Figurine, Culprits, Black Bee & Germany Mark, 7 In. 120.00
Hummel, Figurine, Doctor, Bee Mark, 5 1/4 In. 122.00
Hummel, Figurine, Doctor, V & Bee, West Germany Mark, 4 1/2 In. 32.50
Hummel, Figurine, Doctor, 4 3/4 In. 27.50
Hummel, Figurine, Doll Mother, 4 3/4 In. 38.00
Hummel, Figurine, Duet, Black Bee & Germany Mark, 5 1/2 In. 135.00
Hummel, Figurine, Easter Greetings, 5 In. 40.00
Hummel, Figurine, Easter Playmates, 3 15/16 In. 42.50
Hummel, Figurine, Easter Playmates, 4 In. 47.00
Hummel, Figurine, Eventide, Bee & Germany Mark, 5 1/4 In. 160.00
Hummel, Figurine, Fair Measure, 5 1/2 In. 47.00
Hummel, Figurine, Farewell, Black West Germany & V & B Mark, 4 3/4 In. 47.50
Hummel, Figurine, Farewell, Goebel, Crown, Stamped, & Incised, 4 3/4 In. 135.00
Hummel, Figurine, Farewell, Stylized Bee Mark, 4 1/2 In. 90.00
Hummel, Figurine, Farewell, 4 3/4 In. ..... 38.00 To 42.50
Hummel, Figurine, Farm Boy, Bee & Black Germany Mark, 5 In. 95.00
Hummel, Figurine, Farm Boy, 1938, 5 3/4 In. 57.00
Hummel, Figurine, Feeding Time, Black Bee & Germany Mark, 4 1/4 In. 75.00
Hummel, Figurine, Feeding Time, Goebel, Bee & West Germany Mark, 5 1/2 In. 80.00
Hummel, Figurine, Feeding Time, 5 1/2 In. 37.50
Hummel, Figurine, Festival Harmony, No.173/11, 10 1/4 In. 80.00
Hummel, Figurine, Festival Harmony, With Horn, 10 1/4 In. 85.00
Hummel, Figurine, Festival Harmony, With Horn, 3 Line Mark, 7 3/4 In. 55.00
Hummel, Figurine, Flower Madonna, Black West Germany & Circle, 11 1/2 In. 295.00
Hummel, Figurine, Flower Madonna, Color, 11 1/2 In. 150.00
Hummel, Figurine, Flower Madonna, Color, 8 1/2 In. 57.00
Hummel, Figurine, Flower Madonna, Full Impressed Bee, 12 In. 400.00
Hummel, Figurine, Flower Madonna, V & Bee, West Germany Mark, 8 1/4 In. 70.00
Hummel, Figurine, Flower Madonna, White, 11 1/2 In. 74.00
Hummel, Figurine, Flower Madonna, 11 1/2 In. 125.00
Hummel, Figurine, Flower Vendor, 5 1/2 In. 40.00
Hummel, Figurine, For Father, Black Bee & Germany Mark, 5 1/2 In. 80.00
Hummel, Figurine, For Father, Black Bee & Germany Mark, 5 3/4 In. 95.00
Hummel, Figurine, For Mother, 5 1/4 In. 24.00
Hummel, Figurine, Friends, Stylized Bee Mark, 5 In. 41.00
Hummel, Figurine, Friends, 3 Line Mark, 4 1/4 In. 37.50
Hummel, Figurine, Friends, 5 In. 28.50
Hummel, Figurine, Girl Serving Chocolate, Bochman, Goebel, 7 1/2 In. 35.00
Hummel, Figurine, Globe Trotter, 5 1/4 In. 36.00
Hummel, Figurine, Good Friends, Full Bee, Black Germany, 4 1/2 In. 65.00
Hummel, Figurine, Good Friends, V & Bee, West Germany Mark, 3 3/4 In. 34.75
Hummel, Figurine, Good Hunting, 3 Line Mark, 5 1/4 In. 43.00
Hummel, Figurine, Good Hunting, 5 1/4 In. 37.00
Hummel, Figurine, Good Shepherd, Blue Bee Mark, Germany In Black, 6 1/2 In. 90.00
Hummel, Figurine, Goose Girl, Bee & Germany Mark, 4 3/4 In. 65.00
Hummel, Figurine, Goose Girl, No.47/0, 4 3/4 In. 35.00
Hummel, Figurine, Goose Girl, Stylized Bee Mark, 1960, 7 1/2 In. 115.00
Hummel, Figurine, Goose Girl, West Germany, Mark, 4 In. 40.00
Hummel, Figurine, Goose Girl, 4 In. 30.00
Hummel, Figurine, Goose Girl, 4 1/2 In. 32.00
Hummel, Figurine, Goose Girl, 4 3/4 In. ..... 31.50 To 33.50
Hummel, Figurine, Goose Girl, 5 In. 36.00
Hummel, Figurine, Goose Girl, 7 1/2 In. 100.00
Hummel, Figurine, Goose Girl, 8 In. 100.00

Hummel, Figurine, Happiness, Crown Mark, 4 3/4 In. 118.00
Hummel, Figurine, Happiness, 4 1/2 In. 37.00
Hummel, Figurine, Happy Birthday, Full Bee, Black Germany, 5 1/2 In. 125.00
Hummel, Figurine, Happy Birthday, 5 1/2 In. 37.00
Hummel, Figurine, Happy Pastime, V & Bee, West Germany Mark, 3 1/2 In. 32.75
Hummel, Figurine, Happy Pastime, 3 1/2 In. 30.00
Hummel, Figurine, Happy Traveler, Bee & West Germany Mark, 5 In .... 32.00 To 40.00
Hummel, Figurine, Happy Traveler, V & Bee, West Germany Mark, 5 In. 27.50
Hummel, Figurine, Happy Traveler, 5 In. .... 20.00 To 23.00
Hummel, Figurine, Hear Ye, Hear Ye, Bee Mark, 5 3/4 In. 146.00
Hummel, Figurine, Hear Ye, Hear Ye, Bee, Germany & R Mark, 5 5/8 In. 95.00
Hummel, Figurine, Hear Ye, Hear Ye, No.15/1, 6 In. 47.00
Hummel, Figurine, Hear Ye, Hear Ye, 5 In. .... 29.00 To 30.00
Hummel, Figurine, Hear Ye, Hear Ye, 5 1/4 In. .... 33.00 To 39.00
Hummel, Figurine, Hear Ye, Hear Ye, 6 In. 50.00
Hummel, Figurine, Hear Ye, Hear Ye, 6 3/4 In. 49.00
Hummel, Figurine, Hear Ye, Hear Ye, 7 In. .... 75.50 To 81.50
Hummel, Figurine, Hear Ye, Hear Ye, 7 1/2 In. 90.00
Hummel, Figurine, Heavenly Angel, Crown Mark, 4 1/2 In. 65.00
Hummel, Figurine, Heavenly Angel, Goebel, 6 In. 31.00
Hummel, Figurine, Heavenly Angel, No.21/0, 4 1/4 In. 20.00
Hummel, Figurine, Heavenly Angel, No.21/01/2, 6 In. 28.50
Hummel, Figurine, Heavenly Angel, V & Bee, West Germany Mark, 8 3/4 In. 80.00
Hummel, Figurine, Heavenly Angel, 4 1/4 In. .... 22.00 To 23.00
Hummel, Figurine, Heavenly Angel, 6 In. .... 27.00 To 34.50
Hummel, Figurine, Heavenly Angel, 6 1/2 In. 32.00
Hummel, Figurine, Heavenly Angel, 7 3/4 In. 40.00
Hummel, Figurine, Heavenly Angel, 8 3/4 In. 65.00
Hummel, Figurine, Heavenly Protection, Bee Mark, 12 In. 145.00
Hummel, Figurine, Hello, Black U.S.Zone, Germany Mark, 6 3/4 In. 85.00
Hummel, Figurine, Hello, V & Bee, West Germany Mark, 5 3/4 In. 32.50
Hummel, Figurine, Home From Market, Baby Bee, 1958 Mark, 6 In. 65.00
Hummel, Figurine, Home From Market, West Germany Mark, 5 1/2 In. 45.00
Hummel, Figurine, Home From Market, 1938, 4 3/4 In. 55.00
Hummel, Figurine, Home From Market, 4 3/4 In. 22.50
Hummel, Figurine, Home From Market, 5 1/2 In. 31.00
Hummel, Figurine, Homeward Bound, 5 In. .... 70.00 To 75.00
Hummel, Figurine, Infant Of Krumbad, Bisque, No.78VI, 10 In. 75.00
Hummel, Figurine, Infant Of Krumbad, Bisque, No.78VIII, 14 In. 115.00
Hummel, Figurine, Infant Of Krumbad, 7 3/4 In. 45.00
Hummel, Figurine, Infant Of Krumbad, 10 In. .... 85.00 To 125.00
Hummel, Figurine, Joyful, Stylized Bee Mark, 3 3/4 In. 19.00
Hummel, Figurine, Joyful, V & Bee, West Germany Mark, 3 1/2 In. 23.50
Hummel, Figurine, Joyful, 3 1/2 In. 18.00
Hummel, Figurine, Just Resting, Bee & West Germany, 4 In. 40.00
Hummel, Figurine, Just Resting, Bee Mark, 4 1/4 In. 39.00
Hummel, Figurine, Just Resting, Bee Mark, 5 1/2 In. 55.00
Hummel, Figurine, Just Resting, Three Line Mark, 5 1/2 In. 40.00
Hummel, Figurine, Just Resting, 3 3/4 In. 22.50
Hummel, Figurine, Just Resting, 4 In. 22.50
Hummel, Figurine, Just Resting, 5 In. .... 34.00 To 36.00
Hummel, Figurine, Knitting Lesson, 7 1/2 In. .... 87.50 To 95.00
Hummel, Figurine, Latest News, Bee & West Germany Mark, 5 In. 55.00
Hummel, Figurine, Latest News, 5 1/4 In. 43.00
Hummel, Figurine, Let's Sing, Three Line Mark, 3 In. 25.50
Hummel, Figurine, Let's Sing, West Germany Mark, 3 1/4 In. 35.00
Hummel, Figurine, Let's Sing, 3 In. 23.50
Hummel, Figurine, Let's Sing, 4 In. .... 26.50 To 40.00
Hummel, Figurine, Letter To Santa Claus, 7 In. 60.00
Hummel, Figurine, Little Bookkeeper, 4 3/4 In. 50.00
Hummel, Figurine, Little Cellist, 6 In. 31.50
Hummel, Figurine, Little Fiddler, Black West Germany & Circle, 4 1/2 In. 30.00
Hummel, Figurine, Little Fiddler, Crown Germany Mark, 5 1/4 In. 120.00
Hummel, Figurine, Little Fiddler, 6 In. 34.50

Hummel, Figurine, Little Fiddler, 8 In.

Hummel, Figurine, Little Fiddler, 6 1/2 In. 34.00
Hummel, Figurine, Little Fiddler, 8 In. .... *Illus* 93.50
Hummel, Figurine, Little Goat Herder, Bee & Germany Mark, 5 1/2 In. 70.00
Hummel, Figurine, Little Goat Herder, Bee & West Germany, 4 3/4 In. 45.00
Hummel, Figurine, Little Goat Herder, Three Line Mark, 4 1/2 In. 30.50
Hummel, Figurine, Little Goat Herder, Three Line Mark, 5 1/2 In. 44.00
Hummel, Figurine, Little Goat Herder, 5 1/2 In. .... 37.50 To 40.00
Hummel, Figurine, Little Helper, Black Bee & Germany Mark, 4 1/2 In. 62.50
Hummel, Figurine, Little Helper, V & Bee, West Germany Mark, 4 1/4 In. 25.00
Hummel, Figurine, Little Helper, 4 In. 21.50
Hummel, Figurine, Little Helper, 4 1/4 In. 20.00
Hummel, Figurine, Little Hiker, Bee & Germany Mark, 6 In. 65.00
Hummel, Figurine, Little Hiker, Bee Mark, 4 1/4 In. 65.00
Hummel, Figurine, Little Hiker, Black Bee & Germany Mark, 4 1/4 In. 55.50
Hummel, Figurine, Little Hiker, V & Bee, West Germany Mark, 4 1/4 In. 25.00
Hummel, Figurine, Little Hiker, V & West Germany Mark, 6 1/2 In. 55.00
Hummel, Figurine, Little Hiker, 4 1/4 In. 18.50
Hummel, Figurine, Little Hiker, 6 In. 27.50
Hummel, Figurine, Little Pharmacist, 6 In. 37.00
Hummel, Figurine, Little Shopper, Bee & West Germany Mark, 4 3/4 In. 25.00
Hummel, Figurine, Little Shopper, Bee Mark, 5 In. 110.00
Hummel, Figurine, Little Shopper, Black Bee & Germany Mark, 5 In. 55.00
Hummel, Figurine, Little Tailor, 5 1/2 In. 42.00
Hummel, Figurine, Little Thrifty, No.118, 5 In. .... 30.00 To 30.50
Hummel, Figurine, Lost Sheep, Bee & Germany Mark, 6 In. 55.00
Hummel, Figurine, Lost Sheep, Bee & Germany Mark, 6 1/4 In. .... 125.00 To 250.00
Hummel, Figurine, Lost Sheep, Goebel, 4 1/5 In. 24.00
Hummel, Figurine, Lost Sheep, Three Line Mark, 4 1/4 In. 23.50
Hummel, Figurine, Lost Sheep, Three Line Mark, 4 1/2 In. 28.50
Hummel, Figurine, Lost Sheep, West Germany Mark, 4 1/4 In. 35.00
Hummel, Figurine, Lost Sheep, West Germany Mark, 5 In. 40.00
Hummel, Figurine, Lost Sheep, 1971, 4 1/2 In. 20.00
Hummel, Figurine, Lost Sheep, 5 1/2 In. 27.50
Hummel, Figurine, Lost Stocking, 4 1/2 In. 32.00
Hummel, Figurine, Madonna & Child, C.1930, 13 In. 125.00
Hummel, Figurine, Madonna, Blue, Halo, 12 In. 25.00
Hummel, Figurine, Madonna, Blue, 16 In. 150.00
Hummel, Figurine, Madonna, Green Gown, Goebel, Crown Germany, 13 1/2 In. 150.00
Hummel, Figurine, Madonna, Halo, White, V & Bee, West Germany Mark, 10 1/2 In. 17.50
Hummel, Figurine, Madonna, Halo, White, 12 In. 20.00
Hummel, Figurine, Madonna, Orange, 12 In. 25.00
Hummel, Figurine, Madonna, Praying, Bee & West Germany Mark, 11 1/2 In. 24.00
Hummel, Figurine, Madonna, White, Bee & Green West Germany, 11 In. 22.00
Hummel, Figurine, Madonna, White, Stylized Bee In Circle, 10 1/2 In. 15.00
Hummel, Figurine, Madonna, White, W.Goebel, C.1930, 10 In. 23.00
Hummel, Figurine, Madonna, White, 12 In. 20.00
Hummel, Figurine, March Winds, 5 In. 21.00
Hummel, Figurine, Meditation, Stylized Bee Mark, 5 1/4 In. 36.00
Hummel, Figurine, Meditation, Three Line Mark, 4 1/4 In. 28.50
Hummel, Figurine, Meditation, West Germany Mark, 4 1/4 In. 35.00
Hummel, Figurine, Meditation, 4 1/4 In. 21.50

Hummel, Figurine, Meditation, 5 1/2 In. 28.50
Hummel, Figurine, Merry Wanderer, Bee & Black Germany Mark, 4 1/2 In. 65.00
Hummel, Figurine, Merry Wanderer, Crown Mark, 4 1/4 In. 124.00
Hummel, Figurine, Merry Wanderer, Stylized Bee Mark, 4 3/4 In. 34.00
Hummel, Figurine, Merry Wanderer, V & Bee, West Germany Mark, 4 1/4 In. 25.00
Hummel, Figurine, Merry Wanderer, V & Bee, West Germany Mark, 4 3/4 In. 33.00
Hummel, Figurine, Merry Wanderer, V & Bee, West Germany Mark, 6 In. 52.50
Hummel, Figurine, Merry Wanderer, V & Bee, West Germany Mark, 7 1/4 In. 93.00
Hummel, Figurine, Merry Wanderer, West Germany Mark, 4 3/4 In. 40.00
Hummel, Figurine, Merry Wanderer, 4 1/2 In. 21.50
Hummel, Figurine, Merry Wanderer, 4 3/4 In. 26.50
Hummel, Figurine, Merry Wanderer, 6 1/4 In. .... 41.50 To 45.00
Hummel, Figurine, Merry Wanderer, 10 1/4 In. 250.00
Hummel, Figurine, Mischief Maker, 4 3/4 In. 45.00
Hummel, Figurine, Mother's Darling, V & Bee, West Germany Mark, 5 1/2 In. 37.50
Hummel, Figurine, Mother's Darling, 5 1/2 In. 32.00
Hummel, Figurine, Mother's Helper, Bee Mark, 5 In. 120.00
Hummel, Figurine, Mother's Helper, 5 In. 33.00
Hummel, Figurine, Mountaineer, Three Line Mark, 5 1/4 In. 40.00
Hummel, Figurine, Mountaineer, 5 In. 40.00
Hummel, Figurine, On Secret Path, 5 1/4 In. 45.00
Hummel, Figurine, Photographer, 4 3/4 In. 40.00
Hummel, Figurine, Playmates, Black Bee & Germany Mark, 4 1/2 In. 110.00
Hummel, Figurine, Playmates, Crown Mark, 5 1/4 In. 175.00
Hummel, Figurine, Playmates, Stylized Bee Mark, 4 In. 31.00
Hummel, Figurine, Playmates, West Germany Mark, 4 In. 40.00
Hummel, Figurine, Playmates, 1959, 4 In. 32.00
Hummel, Figurine, Playmates, 4 In. 25.00
Hummel, Figurine, Pointer, 8 In. 39.00
Hummel, Figurine, Postman, 5 1/4 In. 30.00
Hummel, Figurine, Retreat To Safety, Goebel, 5 1/2 In. 42.00
Hummel, Figurine, Retreat To Safety, Three Line Mark, 5 1/2 In. 52.00
Hummel, Figurine, Retreat To Safety, West Germany Mark, 4 In. 40.00
Hummel, Figurine, Retreat To Safety, 4 In. 28.00
Hummel, Figurine, Retreat To Safety, 5 1/2 In. 47.00
Hummel, Figurine, Ride Into Christmas, No.396, 5 3/4 In. .... 100.00 To 135.00
Hummel, Figurine, Run-A-Way, 5 3/8 In. 49.00
Hummel, Figurine, School Boy, Bee & West Germany, 4 In. 40.00
Hummel, Figurine, School Boy, Stylized Bee Mark, 5 1/4 In. 34.00
Hummel, Figurine, School Boy, Three Line Mark, 7 1/2 In. 275.00
Hummel, Figurine, School Boy, West Germany Mark, 5 1/4 In. 40.00
Hummel, Figurine, School Boy, 4 In. 21.50
Hummel, Figurine, School Boy, 4 3/4 In. 28.00
Hummel, Figurine, School Boy, 5 1/4 In. 28.00
Hummel, Figurine, School Boy, 7 1/2 In. 210.00
Hummel, Figurine, School Boy, 9 3/4 In. 550.00
Hummel, Figurine, School Girl, Three Line Mark, 7 1/2 In. 275.00
Hummel, Figurine, School Girl, V & Bee, West Germany Mark, 4 1/2 In. 26.00
Hummel, Figurine, School Girl, West Germany Mark, K 1/4 In. 40.00
Hummel, Figurine, School Girl, 3 Line Mark, 7 1/4 In. 265.00
Hummel, Figurine, School Girl, 4 1/2 In. 21.50
Hummel, Figurine, School Girl, 5 1/4 In. 28.00
Hummel, Figurine, School Girl, 7 1/2 In. .... 210.00 To 225.00
Hummel, Figurine, School Girl, 9 1/4 In. 550.00
Hummel, Figurine, Sensitive Hunter, Black Bee & Germany Mark, 5 In. 70.00
Hummel, Figurine, Sensitive Hunter, V & Bee, West Germany Mark, 4 3/4 In. 32.00
Hummel, Figurine, Sensitive Hunter, West Germany Mark, 4 3/4 In. 40.00
Hummel, Figurine, Sensitive Hunter, 1938, 4 3/4 In. 65.00
Hummel, Figurine, Sensitive Hunter, 4 3/4 In. .... 22.00 To 26.00
Hummel, Figurine, Serenade, Goebel, 4 3/4 In. 20.00
Hummel, Figurine, Serenade, Stylized Bee Mark, 4 3/4 In. 25.50
Hummel, Figurine, Serenade, Stylized Bee Mark, 7 1/2 In. 102.00
Hummel, Figurine, Serenade, 7 1/2 In. 68.00
Hummel, Figurine, She Loves Me Not, 4 1/4 In. 30.00

Hummel, Figurine, She Loves Me, V & Bee Mark, 1959, 4 3/8 In. 65.00
Hummel, Figurine, Shepherd Boy, Bee, Germany & R Mark, 5 3/4 In. 225.00
Hummel, Figurine, Signs Of Spring, 3 Line Mark, 4 In. 32.50
Hummel, Figurine, Signs Of Spring, 4 In. 28.50
Hummel, Figurine, Signs Of Spring, 5 In. 39.00
Hummel, Figurine, Singing Lesson, V & Bee, West Germany Mark, 3 In. 26.50
Hummel, Figurine, Singing Lesson, 3 In. 22.50
Hummel, Figurine, Sister, Bee & Germany Mark, 5 3/4 In. 125.00
Hummel, Figurine, Sister, Bee & West Germany Mark, 5 3/4 In. 35.00
Hummel, Figurine, Sister, 4 3/4 In. 21.50 To 22.50
Hummel, Figurine, Skier, V & Bee, West Germany Mark, 5 1/4 In. 37.50
Hummel, Figurine, Skier, 5 1/2 In. 90.00
Hummel, Figurine, Smart Little Sister, 1971, 4 1/2 In. 39.00
Hummel, Figurine, Smart Little Sister, 4 3/4 In. 39.00 To 40.00
Hummel, Figurine, Soldier Boy, 3 Line Mark, 5 3/4 In. 31.00
Hummel, Figurine, Soldier Boy, 6 In. 24.00
Hummel, Figurine, Spring Cheer, Black Bee & Germany Mark, 5 3/8 In. 65.00
Hummel, Figurine, Spring Dance, 6 3/4 In. 110.00
Hummel, Figurine, Star Gazer, 4 3/4 In. 32.00
Hummel, Figurine, Stitch In Time, 6 3/4 In. 34.00
Hummel, Figurine, Stormy Weather, Bee & Crown Mark, 6 1/4 In. 275.00
Hummel, Figurine, Stormy Weather, No.71, 6 In. 100.00
Hummel, Figurine, Stormy Weather, Stylized Bee Mark, 1960, 6 1/4 In. 115.00
Hummel, Figurine, Stormy Weather, 6 1/4 In. 100.00
Hummel, Figurine, Street Singer, 1938, 5 1/4 In. 85.00
Hummel, Figurine, Strolling Along, 4 3/4 In. 28.00
Hummel, Figurine, Surprise, Stylized Bee Mark, 5 1/2 In. 47.00
Hummel, Figurine, Surprise, V & Bee, West Germany Mark, 4 1/4 In. 28.00
Hummel, Figurine, Surprise, West Germany Mark, 5 1/2 In. 55.00
Hummel, Figurine, Surprise, 4 In. 20.00 To 22.50
Hummel, Figurine, Surprise, 5 1/2 In. 33.00 To 39.00
Hummel, Figurine, Sweet Music, Black Bee & Germany Mark, 5 1/2 n. 75.00
Hummel, Figurine, Sweet Music, V & Bee, West Germany Mark, 5 1/4 In. 37.50
Hummel, Figurine, Sweet Music, 4 1/2 In. 65.00
Hummel, Figurine, Sweet Music, 5 1/4 In. 31.50
Hummel, Figurine, Telling Her Secret, V & West Germany Mark, 6 3/4 In. 350.00
Hummel, Figurine, Telling Her Secret, 3 Line Mark, 5 1/4 In. 52.00
Hummel, Figurine, Telling Her Secret, 5 1/4 In. 47.00
Hummel, Figurine, To Market, Bee & West Germany, 4 1/2 In. 50.00
Hummel, Figurine, To Market, Black Bee & Germany Mark, 4 1/4 In. 75.00
Hummel, Figurine, To Market, Stylized Bee Mark, 4 1/2 In. 37.50
Hummel, Figurine, To Market, 1938, 4 1/4 In. 75.00
Hummel, Figurine, To Market, 4 In. 40.00
Hummel, Figurine, To Market, 4 1/2 In. 31.00 To 33.00
Hummel, Figurine, To Market, 5 1/2 In. 47.00
Hummel, Figurine, Trumpet Boy, Bee Mark, 5 1/4 In. 95.00
Hummel, Figurine, Trumpet Boy, Black Bee & Germany Mark, 5 1/8 In. 65.00
Hummel, Figurine, Trumpet Boy, Goebel, Bee & Black Germany Mark, 4 3/4 In. 135.00
Hummel, Figurine, Trumpet Boy, V & Bee, West Germany Mark, 4 1/2 In. 25.00
Hummel, Figurine, Umbrella Boy, Black Bee & Germany Mark, 8 In. 500.00
Hummel, Figurine, Umbrella Boy, Black West Germany Mark, 8 In. 450.00
Hummel, Figurine, Umbrella Boy, Stylized Bee Mark, 8 In. 425.00
Hummel, Figurine, Umbrella Boy, V & Bee, West Germany Mark, 8 In. 450.00
Hummel, Figurine, Umbrella Boy, West Germany Mark, 8 In. 475.00
Hummel, Figurine, Umbrella Boy, 4 3/4 In. 110.00 To 120.00
Hummel, Figurine, Umbrella Girl & Boy, Bee & Germany Mark, 8 In., Pair 675.00
Hummel, Figurine, Umbrella Girl & Boy, 1938, 8 In., Pair 1000.00
Hummel, Figurine, Umbrella Girl, Black Bee & Germany Mark, 8 In. 500.00
Hummel, Figurine, Umbrella Girl, Stylized Bee Mark, 8 In. 450.00
Hummel, Figurine, Umbrella Girl, Three Line Mark, 8 In. 425.00
Hummel, Figurine, Umbrella Girl, West Germany Mark, 8 In. 475.00
Hummel, Figurine, Umbrella Girl, 4 In. 120.00
Hummel, Figurine, Umbrella Girl, 4 1/2 In. 115.00
Hummel, Figurine, Umbrella Girl, 4 3/4 In. 110.00 To 120.00

Hummel, Figurine, Umbrella Girl, 5 In.

Hummel, Figurine, Umbrella Girl, 5 In. .... *Illus* 120.00
Hummel, Figurine, Village Boy, Stylized Bee Mark, 4 In. 22.00
Hummel, Figurine, Village Boy, V & Bee, West Germany Mark, 3 3/4 In. 25.00
Hummel, Figurine, Village Boy, West Germany Mark, 6 In. 45.00
Hummel, Figurine, Village Boy, 3 3/4 In. 17.00
Hummel, Figurine, Village Boy, 4 In. 17.00
Hummel, Figurine, Village Boy, 5 1/4 In. 22.50
Hummel, Figurine, Visiting An Invalid, 5 In. .... 44.00 To 45.00
Hummel, Figurine, Waiter, 6 In. 32.00
Hummel, Figurine, Wash Day, 3 Line Mark, 6 In. 43.00
Hummel, Figurine, Wash Day, 6 In. 37.00
Hummel, Figurine, Wayside Devotion, Stylized Bee Mark, 7 1/2 In. 72.00
Hummel, Figurine, Wayside Devotion, West Germany Mark, 8 1/2 In. 150.00
Hummel, Figurine, Wayside Devotion, 7 1/2 In. .... 60.00 To 62.00
Hummel, Figurine, Wayside Harmony, Bee & Germany Mark, 5 3/4 In. 125.00
Hummel, Figurine, Wayside Harmony, Bee Mark, 6 In. 58.00
Hummel, Figurine, Wayside Harmony, Black Bee & Germany Mark, 5 1/2 In. 105.00
Hummel, Figurine, Wayside Harmony, 3 Line Mark, 3 3/4 In. 28.00
Hummel, Figurine, Wayside Harmony, 5 In. 36.00
Hummel, Figurine, We Congratulate, Black Bee & Germany Mark, 4 1/4 In. 85.00
Hummel, Figurine, Whitsuntide, 6 3/4 In. 1500.00
Hummel, Figurine, Worship, No.84/5, 13 1/2 In. 675.00
Hummel, Figurine, Worship, 5 1/4 In. 24.50
Hummel, Font, Holy Water, Angel With Bird, Full Bee Mark, 4 1/4 In. 75.00
Hummel, Font, Holy Water, Child Jesus, Full Bee Mark, 5 3/8 In. 55.00
Hummel, Font, Holy Water, Musicians, Late 40's Mark 30.00
Hummel, Group, Bird Duet, Bee & Black Germany Mark, Incised, 4 In. 97.50
Hummel, Lamp, Culprits, Black Bee & Germany Mark, 9 1/2 In. 250.00
Hummel, Plaque, Angel At Prayer, Crown Mark, Germany, 3 1/2 X 2 102 In., Pair 135.00
Hummel, Plaque, Dealer's, Full Bee 400.00
Hummel, Plaque, Retreat To Safety, 4 In. 26.50
Hummel, Plaque, School Boy, 5 In. 26.00
Hummel, Plaque, School Boys, 7 1/2 In. 220.00
Hummel, Plaque, School Girl, 5 In. 26.00
Hummel, Plaque, Sensitive Hunter, 5 1/2 In. 34.00
Hummel, Plaque, Serenade, 4 3/4 In. 22.50
Hummel, Plaque, Signs Of Spring, 5 1/2 In. 36.50
Hummel, Plaque, Sister, 4 3/4 In. 19.50
Hummel, Plaque, Surprise, 5 1/2 In. 36.50
Hummel, Plaque, Swaying Lullaby, Full Bee 1200.00
Hummel, Plaque, To Market, 5 1/2 In. 44.50
Hummel, Plaque, Umbrella Boy, 5 In. 109.00
Hummel, Plaque, Umbrella Girl & Boy, 8 In., Pair 775.00
Hummel, Plaque, Umbrella Girl, 5 In. 109.00
Hummel, Plaque, Wayside Harmony, 5 In. 34.00
Hutschenreuther, Bowl, Vegetable, Double Handle, Floral Design 65.00
Hutschenreuther, Cat, Siamese, Sitting, Artist Signed, 8 In. 65.00
Hutschenreuther, Cup & Saucer, Birds & Floral, Pale Blue Rims 12.00

Hutschenreuther, Figurine, Barn Swallow, In Flight, 9 3/4 X 8 1/4 In. 155.00
Hutschenreuther, Figurine, Beagle Dog, Standing, 5 1/2 X 4 1/4 In. 38.00
Hutschenreuther, Figurine, Borzoi, Running, 12 X 11 In., Pair 300.00
Hutschenreuther, Figurine, Boston Terrier, Standing, 5 X 4 In. 42.00
Hutschenreuther, Figurine, Boy Playing Flute, Gilded, 18th Century, 5 1/2 In. 25.00
Hutschenreuther, Figurine, Canary, Singing, 5 1/2 X 3 1/4 In. 50.00
Hutschenreuther, Figurine, Chihuahua Dog, Standing, 4 In. 42.00
Hutschenreuther, Figurine, Collie Dog, Standing, 6 1/4 X 4 1/2 In. 50.00
Hutschenreuther, Figurine, Dachshund Dog, Sitting, 5 X 2 1/4 In. 30.00
Hutschenreuther, Figurine, Dachshund Dog, Standing, 5 1/4 X 3 1/4 In. 35.00
Hutschenreuther, Figurine, Dolphin, Signed Granget, 4 X 4 1/2 In. 78.00
Hutschenreuther, Figurine, Donkey, Lying Down, 4 X 3 1/4 In. 35.00
Hutschenreuther, Figurine, Donkey, Standing, 5 X 4 1/4 In. 41.00
Hutschenreuther, Figurine, Elephant, Standing, Trunk Raised, 9 X 8 In. 100.00
Hutschenreuther, Figurine, Figure Skater, White 60.00
Hutschenreuther, Figurine, Finch, Leaves & Blueberries, Granget, 4 In. 80.00
Hutschenreuther, Figurine, Flying Seagull Over Waves, Artist Signed, 7 1/2 In. 110.00
Hutschenreuther, Figurine, Hummingbird, Blooming Flower, 4 In. 55.00
Hutschenreuther, Figurine, Laying Fawn, Artist Signed, 4 X 4 3/4 In. 65.00
Hutschenreuther, Figurine, Leaping Colt, 6 1/4 In. 40.00
Hutschenreuther, Figurine, Leopard, Stalking, 6 1/4 X 1 1/2 In. 70.00
Hutschenreuther, Figurine, Lizard, On Rock, 3 1/2 X 1 3/4 In. 32.00
Hutschenreuther, Figurine, Mother & Child, White, H.P.Chiziger, 8 1/2 In. 75.00
Hutschenreuther, Figurine, Mouse, Porcelain, Brown, 2 In. 30.00
Hutschenreuther, Figurine, Pekinese Standing, 4 X 5 In. 35.00
Hutschenreuther, Figurine, Rabbit, Sitting, 5 1/4 X 4 1/4 In. 26.00
Hutschenreuther, Figurine, Red Start, On Branch, 6 1/2 X 4 1/4 In. 75.00
Hutschenreuther, Figurine, Sailfish Leaping From Waves, 4 1/2 In. 55.00
Hutschenreuther, Figurine, Schnauzer Dog, Standing, 7 X 6 In. 60.00
Hutschenreuther, Figurine, Sea Gull, In Flight, 7 1/4 X 4 1/4 In. 100.00
Hutschenreuther, Figurine, Seahorse Swimming In Green Fernery, 5 1/4 In. 68.00
Hutschenreuther, Figurine, Siamese Cat, Sitting, 8 X 4 1/2 In. 64.00
Hutschenreuther, Figurine, Singing Canary On Branch, 5 1/4 In. 50.00
Hutschenreuther, Figurine, Squirrel With Acorn, 3 1/4 In. 28.00
Hutschenreuther, Figurine, Standing Fawn, Artist Signed, 5 1/2 X 4 3/4 In. 90.00
Hutschenreuther, Figurine, White Skater, Signed, 7 X 5 1/2 In. 55.00
Hutschenreuther, Figurine, Yellow Perch, Swimming, 4 1/2 X 3 1/4 In. 50.00
Hutschenreuther, Goldfinch On Tree Stump, K.Tutter, Green Mark, 6 In. 55.00
Hutschenreuther, Gravy Boat & Attached Tray, Birds & Floral, Pale Blue Rim 16.00
Hutschenreuther, Group, Parakeet, Artist Signed, 8 3/4 X 11 3/4 In. 190.00
Hutschenreuther, Group, Two Donkeys, One Standing & One Lying, 5 X 4 In. 75.00
Hutschenreuther, Group, 2 Parakeets On Branch, Yellow & Blue, 8 3/4 In. 175.00
Hutschenreuther, Plate, Calla Lilies, Artist Signed, 9 In. 8.00
Hutschenreuther, Plate, Dinner, Birds & Floral, Pale Blue Rim 8.00
Hutschenreuther, Plate, Service, Classical Figures & Floral, 10 In. 19.50
Hutschenreuther, Plate, Service, For Ovington Bros., N.Y., 10 1/2 In. 25.00
Hutschenreuther, Plate, Vegetable, Birds & Floral, Pale Blue Rim, Oval 10.00
Icebox, see Kitchen, Icebox
Icon, Russian, St.Nicholas, C.1880, Tin On Wood, 12 X 10 1/4 In. 88.50

Imari patterns are named for the Japanese ware decorated with orange and blue stylized flowers. The design on the Japanese ware became so characteristic that the name Imari has come to mean any pattern of this type. It was copied by the European factories of the eighteenth and early nineteenth centuries.

Imari, Bowl, Blue, Decorated On Underside, Teak Base, 9 In. 75.00
Imari, Bowl, C.1700, 9 1/2 In. 200.00
Imari, Bowl, Collared Base, Multicolored Panels, People & Florals, 4 5/8 In. 65.00
Imari, Bowl, Japanese, C.1790, Pine, Plum & Bamboo, Oblong, 8 1/4 X 4 1/2 In. 95.00
Imari, Bowl, Kirin Center, Plum Blossoms On Blue , C.1920, 16 1/4 In. 795.00
Imari, Charger, Alternating Panels Of Hut & Floral, 12 In. 70.00
Imari, Charger, Cobalt Outlined Red Butterfly, Floral Panels, 12 1/4 In. 225.00
Imari, Charger, Cobalt Vase Of Flowers, Scenic & Floral Panels, 13 In. 85.00
Imari, Charger, Cobalts & Rusts, Birds & Foliage, C.1840-50, 18 In. 425.00

Imari, Charger, Crab In Bottom, Signed, 10 X 4 In. 65.00
Imari, Charger, Cranes, Gold Brocade Ground, C.1860, 15 In. 175.00
Imari, Charger, Figures In Scene, Butterflies & Floral, 16 In. 385.00
Imari, Charger, Floral, Leaf, & Vine, Blue, White, & Gold Border, C.1820, 19 In. 795.00
Imari, Charger, Orange And Gold With Cobalt, 15 3/4 In. 248.00
Imari, Charger, Scalloped Edge, 6 Panels With Basket Of Flowers, Blue 95.00
Imari, Dessert Bowl, Chrysanthemum & Pomegranate, Scalloped 22.50
Imari, Dish, Candy, White, Inside Decoration, Character On Bottom, 6 3/8 In. 24.00
Imari, Figurine, Standing Jurojin, Blue & White, Bisque Face, 18 In. 180.00
Imari, Figurine, Temple Dog, Gilded Flaming Pearls, 5 X 8 In. 95.00
Imari, Inkwell, Birds & Floral, Blue, Rust, & Gilt, Scalloped Base 58.00
Imari, Jar, Ginger, Foo Dog Finial, Clobbered, 6 In., Pair 148.00
Imari, Plaque, Birds, Butterflies, & Floral, 1850, 14 1/2 In. 275.00
Imari, Plate, Basket Center, Panels Of Orange & Blue, Scalloped, 8 3/8 In. 25.00
Imari, Plate, Blue & White, Pierced, Oval, 11 In. 75.00
Imari, Plate, Blue Floral Center, Polychrome Fish Reserves, 8 1/2 In. 38.00
Imari, Plate, Chop, Bowl Of Flowers 50.00
Imari, Plate, Chop, Cobalt, Red, Green, Plum Blossoms, Tree Of Life, 13 In. 95.00
Imari, Plate, Flower Basket Center, Bird Panels, Floral, 8 In. 39.00
Imari, Plate, Flower Basket Decoration, Unmarked, 8 1/2 In. 40.00
Imari, Plate, Rust & Cobalt Decoration, 8 1/2 In. 38.00
Imari, Plate, Scalloped Edge, 8 In. 55.00
Imari, Plate, Six Panels, 3 With Figure Of Juggler, 7 1/4 In. 45.00
Imari, Plate, Terra-Cotta, Cobalt & Green, Floral, Square, 8 In. 28.00
Imari, Plate, 6 Floral Panels, Terra-Cotta & Blue, Scalloped Edge, 8 1/2 In. 36.00
Imari, Platter, Cobalt, Pale Blue, & White, C.1850, 15 1/2 X 11 In. 50.00
Imari, Vase, Green Birds, Flowers & Foliage, 12 In. 45.00

Imperial Glass Corporation was founded in Bellaire, Ohio, in 1902. Stretch glass and art glass are two of the many kinds of glass made.

Imperial, Bowl, Purple Iridescent, Jewels, 9 In. 70.00
Imperial, Candlesticks, Green, Paneled, 6 1/2 In., Pair 26.00
Imperial, Centerpiece Bowl, Vaseline, Black Base, Stretch, Rolled Edge, 11 In 37.50
Imperial, Creamer, No.526 8.50
Imperial, Figurine, Airedale 65.00
Imperial, Figurine, Pup With Floppy Ear 30.00
Imperial, Figurine, Sitting Pup 30.00
Imperial, Goblet, No.3 10.00
Imperial, Plate, Turquoise, Colonial, Stretch, 8 1/2 In. 6.50
Imperial, Sugar & Creamer, Light Amethyst, Beaded Band & Panel, Cross Mark 23.00
Imperial, Swan, Chocolate Glass, 8 1/2 In. 28.00
Imperial, Swan, Marigold Over Milk Glass, 10 In. 55.00
Imperial, Vase, Blue Pulled Swirls On Cream, Peach Lined, 8 In. 200.00
Imperial, Vase, Brown Iridescent, Random Threading, Free Hand, 12 In. 200.00
Imperial, Vase, Bulb, Amethyst With Pearl Green Luster, Jewel, 5 5/8 In. 80.00
Imperial, Vase, Cobalt Blue To Deep Orange, 10 1/2 In. 165.00
Imperial, Vase, Cobalt, Opalescent Vines, Crimped Top, Free Form, 8 1/2 In. 75.00
Imperial, Vase, Corset Shape, Cobalt With Orange, Freehand, 8 In. 85.00
Imperial, Vase, Dark Blue Iridescent Lining, 10 In. 145.00
Imperial, Vase, Dark Gold To Dark Blue Iridescent, 5 3/4 X 4 3/4 In. 95.00
Imperial, Vase, Free-Blown, Blue, 8 1/2 In. 50.00
Imperial, Vase, Free-Blown, Orange, 8 1/2 In. 50.00
Imperial, Vase, Gold & Blue Decoration, Gold Foot & Handles, 14 In. 395.00
Imperial, Vase, Green, Blue-White Vines, Orange Luster Lined, 10 1/4 In. 235.00
Imperial, Vase, Jade Green, Heart-Shaped Leaves & Twigs, 9 In. 315.00
Imperial, Vase, Orange Mirror Finish, Pedestal, 10 1/2 In. 125.00
Imperial, Vase, Swirled Blue & White Satin, 9 1/2 In. 125.00

Indian art from North America has attracted the collector for many years. Each tribe has its own distinctive designs and techniques. Baskets, jewelry, and leatherwork are of greatest collector interest.

Indian Tree is a china pattern that was popular during the last half of the nineteenth century. It was copied from earlier patterns of English china that were very similar. The pattern includes the crooked branch of a tree and a partial landscape with exotic flowers and leaves. It is colored green, blue, pink, and orange.

Indian Tree, Berry Set, John Maddock & Son, 13 Piece 75.00
Indian Tree, Bowl, Browns, Woods & Sons, For Imperial Hotel, London, 8 In. 7.50
Indian Tree, Bowl, Salad, Deep, Coalport, 12 In. 98.00
Indian Tree, Butter Pat, Buffalo China 5.50
Indian Tree, Creamer, Mark 1891-1920, Coalport, 4 In. 20.00
Indian Tree, Dish, Sauce, Coalport, C.1891 .... 6.00
Indian Tree, Eggcup, Footed, 5 1/2 In. 16.50
Indian Tree, Mayonnaise Set, Coalport 25.00
Indian Tree, Pitcher, Coalport, 7 In. 35.00
Indian Tree, Plate, Burgess & Leigh, 9 In. 7.50
Indian Tree, Plate, Green & Pink, Minton, 1897, 9 In. 15.00
Indian Tree, Plate, Johnson Bros., 10 In. 15.00
Indian Tree, Plate, O.P.Co., Syracuse, For N.Y.N.H. & H.R.R.Co., 8 In. 525.00
Indian Tree, Platter, Burgess & Leigh, Oblong, 13 1/2 X 11 In. 17.50
Indian Tree, Saucer, Demitasse, Pinks & Green, Copeland Spode, 4 3/4 In. 4.00
Indian Tree, Teapot, Gold Trim 25.00
Indian Tree, Washstand Set, Woods, Burslem, Miniature, 2 Piece 25.00
Indian, Bag, Carrying, Beaded, Sioux Origin, C.1910, 12 X 12 In. 195.00
Indian, Bag, Carrying, Sioux, C.1910, Beaded, Geometrics, 12 In. 195.00
Indian, Bag, Nez Perce, Beaded Geometric Designs, 16 X 13 In. 90.00
Indian, Bag, Nez Perce, Corn Husk, 15 X 12 In. 50.00
Indian, Bag, Nez Perce, Twine, Designs, 15 X 12 In. 25.00
Indian, Bag, Parfleche, Canton Beaded Fringe, 11 X 10 In. 45.00
Indian, Bag, Parfleche, Crow & Nez Perce Designs, Painting, 30 X 18 In. 80.00
Indian, Bag, Parfleche, Designs, Rawhide Ties, 18 1/2 X 14 1/2 In. 125.00
Indian, Bag, Pipe, Cheyenne, Yellow Paint, Geometric Beading, Quilwork, 5 In. 750.00
Indian, Bag, Sioux, Beaded Horse Motif, C.1890 .... 500.00
Indian, Bag, Sioux, Beaded, Green & White Geometrics, Sinew Sewn, 8 X 7 In. 125.00
Indian, Bag, Sioux, Strikealite, Beaded, Sinew Sewn, 5 X 3 In. 75.00
Indian, Bag, Woodlands Bandolier, C.1870 .... 425.00
Indian, Basket, Acoma, Pottery, Bird's Heads & Black Stylized Designs, 3 In. 10.00
Indian, Basket, Alaskan, Woven Reeds & Deerhide With Fur, 1/2 Bushel 35.00
Indian, Basket, Chitamacha, Caned, Twilled, 5 In. 48.00
Indian, Basket, Covered, 2 1/2 In.Diameter .... *Illus* 86.00
Indian, Basket, Hopi, Polychrome Kachina Faces, Rectangular, 7 X 6 In. 300.00
Indian, Basket, Hupa, Geometrics, Light & Dark Brown, 7 In. 85.00
Indian, Basket, Makah, 6 X 6 In. 20.00
Indian, Basket, Passamaquoddy, 8 In. 45.00
Indian, Basket, Penobscot Tribe In Old Town , Maine, 50 Years Old, 8 1/2 In. 8.00
Indian, Basket, Pima, Covered
Indian, Belt, Crow, Beaded, Brass Studding 75.00
Indian, Belt, Man's, Blackfoot, C.1880, Beaded, Leather, Geometrics 195.00
Indian, Belt, Men's, Blackfoot, Geometric Design, Leather, C1880 .... 195.00
Indian, Belt, Plains, Harness Leather, Beaded, Geometrics 100.00
Indian, Blanket, Navajo Saddle, 29 X 34 In. 135.00
Indian, Blanket, Shimayo, Southwestern, C.1935 .... 35.00
Indian, Bow, Sioux, C.1880, Steel-Tipped Arrow In Beaded Quiver 150.00
Indian, Box, Quills & Birchbark, 2 1/2 In.Diameter .... *Illus* 28.00
Indian, Bustle, Dance, Plains, C.1870, Wild Turkey Feathers, Mirrors, Bells 150.00
Indian, Case, Awl, Crow, Beaded, Blue, Reds, & Yellows, 10 In. 50.00
Indian, Case, Gun, Woodlands, C.1950, Moosehide, Beaded 100.00
Indian, Cradle Board, Yakima, C.1950, Corduroy, Buckskin Fringe, 40 In. 50.00
Indian, Doll, Nez Perce, C.1900, Beaded, Cradle Board, 27 X 15 In. 300.00
Indian, Gauntlet, Nez Perce, Seed Beads, Pair 85.00
Indian, Hat, Hupa Maiden's, Woven, Design 85.00
Indian, Knife, Leather Sheath, Cord-Wrapped Grip, Cross Impressed On Back 80.00
Indian, Leggings, Nez Perce, Beaded, Cloth Fringe 150.00
Indian, Leggings, Sioux, C.1880, Loom, Beaded, Painted Yellow 100.00
Indian, Letter Opener, Sterling With Turquoise, Handmade, 7 In. 40.00
Indian, Mask, Hand-Carved, Cherokee, Twisted Mouth, C.1920 .... 125.00
Indian, Moccasin, Man's, Cheyenne, Beaded, Sinew Sewn, Pair 90.00

Indian, Basket, Covered, 2 1/2 In.Diameter

Indian, Box, Quills & Birchbark, 2 1/2 In.Diameter

Indian, Moccasin, Man's, Nez Perce, Beaded, Geometrics, Pair 55.00
Indian, Moccasin, Nez Perce, Lady's, Floral Beading, Beaded Fringe, Pair 30.00
Indian, Necklace, Navajo, Silver Beads, 10 Mercury Dimes, & Turquoise, 24 In. 125.00
Indian, Necklace, Navajo, Silver Dollar & Dimes, Turquoise Naja 500.00
Indian, Necklace, Zuni, Shell Pendant, Turquoise, Silver, & Pearl 150.00
Indian, Pipe, Ceremonial, Plains, Catlinite Bowl, 6 In. 50.00
Indian, Pipe, Peace, Cherokee, Clay Bowl, Wooden Stem, Wrapped 22.00
Indian, Pipe, Sioux, 3 Figure Carved Stem, Quill, C.1880 .... 575.00
Indian, Pouch, Envelope, Apache, Beaded, Swastikas On Red, Sinew Sewn, 9 In. 125.00
Indian, Pouch, Sioux, Beaded, Painted, Sinew Sewn, 5 X 4 In. 45.00
Indian, Robe, Buffalo, Ojibwa, Geometric, C.1900 .... 750.00
Indian, Rug, Chimayo, Gray, Tan, Black, 48 X 72 In. 175.00
Indian, Rug, Navajo, C.1920, Multicolors On Cream, 6 X 4 Ft. 175.00
Indian, Rug, Navajo, Natural Colors, Small Zigzags, 38 X 56 In. 175.00
Indian, Rug, Navajo, Two Gray Hills, 4 Ft.X 32 In. 425.00
Indian, Rug, Navajo, Weaver Mae Yazzie, 22 X 34 1/2 In. 240.00
Indian, Sheath, Knife, Parfleche, Canton Beaded Fringe 45.00
Indian, Sheath, Knife, Sioux, Beaded, Sinew Sewn, 10 In. 75.00
Indian, Sheath, Lady's Knife, Sioux, Beaded, Tin Dangles, Sinew Sewn 75.00
Indian, Shirt, Man's, Sauk-Fox, C.1870, Beaded 150.00
Indian, Sifter, Meal 20.00
Indian, Spear, Plains, Feathers & Horsehair Decorations 175.00
Indian, Vase, Acoma, Effigy, 6 X 8 In. 150.00
Indian, Vase, Black On Black Geometrics, Sa Ildefonso, Pueblo, Tonita Roybal 250.00
Indian, Vest, Man's, Nez Perce, Beaded Floral, Size 40 .... 275.00
Indian, Vest, Woman's, Hopi, C.1900, Geometrics On Cream 575.00
Indian, Vest, Woman's, Hopi, C.1900, Hand Woven, Geometrics 575.00
Inkstand, China, 2 Bottles, Hand-Decorated Roses, Blue Flowers, Gold Trim 47.50
Inkstand, Chinese Lacquer, Mother-Of-Pearl Inlay & Drawer, 2 Wells 95.00
Inkstand, French, C.1850, Bronzed Stalking Lion, 2 Glass Bottles, 17 In. 185.00
Inkstand, Gold-Washed Metal, 2 Pressed-Glass Bottles, 6 1/2 X 4 1/2 In. 25.00
Inkstand, Green Design, Silver, 2 Frosted Bottles, Stag On Top, 13 In. 185.00
Inkstand, Metal, Hinged Lid, China Insert, 7 1/2 In. 18.00
Inkstand, Oak, Center Handle, 2-Hinged Cover, Crystal Well, 11 X 6 In. 55.00
Inkstand, Silver Plate, Mother-Of-Pearl Tip, Cut Glass Insert, 10 In. 75.00
Inkstand, W.Houghton, London, C.1840, Mahogany Box, Drawer 375.00
Inkstand, Wooden, Hinged Lids, 2 Cut-Glass Inserts, Handle 29.50

Inkwell, see also Brass, Inkwell,Pewter, Inkwell; and various porcelain categories

Inkwell & Stand, Dresden Type Porcelain, Cupid & Lovenote, 5 In. 125.00
Inkwell, Bears, Standing, Double Wells 28.50
Inkwell, Bicentennial, 1876, Cast Iron 100.00
Inkwell, Brass & Copper, Cubed Crystal Insert, From Old Ship 55.00
Inkwell, Brass, Art Nouveau Design Glass Insert 20.00

Inkwell, Camel Shape, Pot Metal, Painted, Insert, 6 In. 36.00
Inkwell, Capstan, Pewter, 2 Lids 45.00
Inkwell, Crystal, Boat Shape, Bronze Top, Ormolu Base, 7 X 3 In. 87.00
Inkwell, Cut Glass Harvard Base, Sterling Rims & Covers 65.00
Inkwell, Delft, Mulberry, Shell Shape, Embossed, Scene Of Man On Tree Limb 70.00
Inkwell, Figural, Girl, Art Nouveau, Silver Plate 115.00
Inkwell, Figural, Joan Of Arc, Double, Footed Openwork Base, 11 In., A.Bossu 225.00
Inkwell, Figural, Little Girl Behind Dog, Silver Plate 65.00
Inkwell, Figural, Metal German Helmet, 3 In. 19.50
Inkwell, Figural, Puppy Bonzo, Glass, Hinged, Czechoslovakia, C.1930, 4 In. 18.00
Inkwell, French Faience, Octagon, Blue, Rust, Red, Yellow, Artist Signed 60.00
Inkwell, Glass, Pewter Collar & Lid, Pat.1869, Done Style, 5 1/2 In. 30.00
Inkwell, Glass, Sengbusch, Black Top, 3 X 3 In. 6.00
Inkwell, Glass, 1885, Revolving Metal Top Over 3 Wells 28.00
Inkwell, Iron, Apple On Branch With Leaves, Black Finish, Apple Opens 95.00
Inkwell, Lady's Desk, Nickel-Plated Steel, Penholder, Clear Insert 6.95
Inkwell, Lochman's Locomotive 550.00
Inkwell, Ma Carter, Carter's Ink, Porcelain, Dated 1914 35.00
Inkwell, Mandolin On Music Roll, Hinged Head, Brass Well, 10 In. 78.00
Inkwell, Octagon, Four Quill Holes, French Pottery, Floral Center Holder 65.00
Inkwell, Pewter, C.1800, Porcelain Insert, 5 Quill Holes 90.00
Inkwell, Porcelain, Bronze Shell Base, Signed Roquet Brevete, Rue Richelieu 125.00
Inkwell, Porcelain, English, C.1850, White, Blue & Orange Decoration 135.00
Inkwell, Porcelain, French, C.1850, Boy Wearing Tricorner Hat, Ormolu, 11 In. 275.00
Inkwell, Porcelain, German, Hand-Painted, Six Sides, Crown Mark, 3 X 1 3/4 In. 30.00
Inkwell, Porcelain, Hand-Painted 30.00
Inkwell, Pressed Glass, Silver Plate Tops, Triple Wells, Marked TY 30.00
Inkwell, Ram's Head, Blown-Glass Insert 25.00
Inkwell, Rouen, French Faience, Florals, Enamel, Blue, Rust, Red, Dated 1780 85.00
Inkwell, Running Stag, Brass Plated 85.00
Inkwell, School Desk, Marble Inside, Bakelite Top 5.00
Inkwell, Slipper, Glass, 3 1/2 In. 18.50
Inkwell, Soapstone, C.1830, Quill Holder, 8 1/8 X 3 In. 45.00
Inkwell, Soapstone, Dated 1827, 2 In. 55.00
Inkwell, Sterling Silver, Pen Nib Shape, Glass Insert, 5 1/2 In. 255.00
Inkwell, Sterling Silver, Resist, Clear Glass, Shreve Crump & Low, 3 1/2 In. 45.00
Inkwell, Swirl Glass, White Metal Neck & Hinge, Ball Top, 2 1/2 In. 45.00
Inkwell, Tiffany, see Tiffany, Inkwell
Inkwell, Traveling, Figural, Brass Suitcase 39.00
Inkwell, Traveling, Figural, Man's Shoe, Brown Leather Over Metal 60.00
Inkwell, Traveling, Tin Box, Brass Handle, 1 1/2 X 1 1/4 In. 15.00
Inkwell, Tupelo Wood Dinghy, Beveled Glass Well, Sterling Top, 7 3/4 In. 22.50

Insulators of glass or pottery have been made for use on telegraph or telephone poles since 1844.

Insulator, A.G.M., Australian, Light Green 10.00
Insulator, A.G.M., Australian, Squat, Amber 30.00
Insulator, Agee, CD 121, Purple 7.00
Insulator, Agee, CD 124.6, Purple 6.00
Insulator, Agee, CD 152.9, Purple 7.00
Insulator, AGM, CD 124.7, Amber 3.50
Insulator, AM Insulator Co., Patent, Embossed Base, Aqua 2.00
Insulator, American Insulator Co., CD 156, Aqua 30.00
Insulator, American Telephone & Telegraph, Green 10.00
Insulator, Armstrong, No.10, CD 214 2.25
Insulator, B & O, 136, Aqua 5.00
Insulator, Brookfield, Aqua 1.75 To 3.00
Insulator, Brookfield, New York, 1883 & 1884 5.00
Insulator, Brookfield, No.6, 55 Fulton St. 10.00
Insulator, Brookfield, 38, CD 164, Green 8.00
Insulator, Brookfield, 38, CD 164, Olive 12.00
Insulator, C.C.G., Australian, Light Green 10.00
Insulator, C.E.W., CD 120, Deep Sun-Colored Amethyst 40.00
Insulator, C.P.R., 1875-1900, Blue 1.50

Item	Price
Insulator, C.T.N.E., 154, Light Green	10.00
Insulator, Cable, CD 261, Aqua	35.00
Insulator, Cable, No.3, CD 254, Aqua	15.00
Insulator, California, CD 260, Sage Green	30.00
Insulator, California, Signal, Purple	6.00
Insulator, Carnival Glass, 3 In.	12.00
Insulator, Castle, CD 206	85.00
Insulator, CD 145, Olive	5.00
Insulator, CD 234, Carnival Glass	5.00
Insulator, CD 728, Threadless, Aqua	72.00
Insulator, CD 731, Aqua	100.00
Insulator, CD 740, Threadless, Olive Green	130.00
Insulator, CD 742, Threadless, Aqua	110.00
Insulator, Chicago Ins.Co., Diamond Groove, Embossed, Date At Top	45.00
Insulator, Columbia, No.2, CD 262, Dark Aqua	45.00
Insulator, Corkscrew, CD 110.5	100.00
Insulator, Diamond, CD 102, Olive	2.75
Insulator, E.S.B.Co., Bird Feeder, Aqua	25.00
Insulator, Egg, CD 700, Extended Lower Skirt, Aqua Blue	100.00
Insulator, Gayner 38-20, CD 164, Aqua	5.00
Insulator, H.G.Co., Aqua	.47
Insulator, H.G.Co., CD 145, Petticoat, Steel Blue	12.00
Insulator, H.G.Co., CD 145, Yellow	60.00
Insulator, H.G.Co., CD 162, Cobalt	50.00
Insulator, H.G.Co., Petticoat, Aqua	1.75
Insulator, H.G.Co., Petticoat, Ice Blue	3.75
Insulator, H.G.Co., Standard, Patent, Drips, CD 133, Aqua	2.00
Insulator, H.G.Co., Transformer, CD 201, Aqua	35.00
Insulator, Half Diamond	3.75
Insulator, Hemingray, Lowex 660, CD 219, Amber	5.00
Insulator, Hemingray, No.16, CD 122	1.00
Insulator, Hemingray, No.16, Chocolate Swirls	6.00
Insulator, Hemingray, No.16, Green	5.00
Insulator, Hemingray, No.40, CD 152, Olive	3.50
Insulator, Hemingray, 43, CD 214	2.00
Insulator, Hemingray, 514, CD 238	3.00
Insulator, Hemingray, 660, CD 218	2.00
Insulator, Johnny Ball	14.00
Insulator, Kimble, 820, CD 231	2.00
Insulator, Label, No.4, CD 267, Aqua	100.00
Insulator, Lynchburg, No.10	4.50
Insulator, Lynchburg, 36, CD 162, Green	4.00
Insulator, Manhattan, CD 256, Green	35.00
Insulator, Mickey Mouse, Porcelain, Dark Brown Glaze	40.00
Insulator, N.A.T.Co., CD 151, Cobalt	100.00
Insulator, National, CD 110.5, Segmented	45.00
Insulator, Patent, CD 147, Aqua	2.00
Insulator, Patent, Conical, Paneled Sides, Olive Amber, 5 3/4 In.	70.00
Insulator, Pleated Skirt	8.00
Insulator, Prism, CD 252, Lime Green	35.00
Insulator, Pyrex, Sombrero, Dark Rainbow-Colored Carnival, 10 In.	12.00
Insulator, Pyrex, Sombrero, Light Rainbow-Colored Carnival, 10 In.	8.00
Insulator, Pyrex, Sombrero, Medium Rainbow-Colored Carnival, 10 In.	10.00
Insulator, San Francisco, Pony, Blue	4.00
Insulator, San Francisco, Pony, Green	4.00
Insulator, Spratt, Patent 1850, Lightning Rod, Emerald Green	10.00
Insulator, Square D, Peru, Indiana On Top, Porcelain, Brown	4.50
Insulator, Square D, Peru, Indiana On Top, Porcelain, White	7.00
Insulator, Thomas, White	5.00
Insulator, U300, Green	4.50
Insulator, U365, White	7.00
Insulator, U399 A, White	5.00
Insulator, U399 B, Brown Black	5.00
Insulator, U399, Brown	5.00

Iron, Band, Hound, For Conestoga Wagon, 1846

Iron, Bootjack, Cast, American, C.1850, 11 In.High

Insulator, U521, Brown ... 5.00
Insulator, W.Brookfield, Patent, 55 Fulton St., CD 126, Aqua ... 2.75
Insulator, W.G.M.Co., Beehive, Sun-Colored Amethyst, 4 In. ... 10.00
Insulator, W.U. Tel., Rubber ... 4.00
Insulator, Whitall Tatum, Signal, Purple ... 5.00
Insulator, Wooden, Threadless, Similar To E.C. & M. In Shape & Size ... 5.00
Insulator, WT, No.10, CD 214 ... 2.00
Insulator, WU, No.5, Patent 1893, CD 125, Aqua ... 5.00
Insulator, 132, Aqua ... 7.00

Iron, see also Kitchen, Tool, Store

Iron, Ashtray & Pipe Rest, Austria, Scottie Dog, Hinged Head, Black & White ... 16.00
Iron, Ashtray, Bowling Design, Ball And Pins ... 20.00
Iron, Band, Hound, For Conestoga Wagon, 1846 ... *Illus* 55.00
Iron, Bathtub, Salesman's Sample, 5 1/2 In. ... 42.00
Iron, Bookend, Bronze Finish, Bust Of A.Lincoln, 6 In., Pair ... 12.75
Iron, Bookend, Bust Of Abraham Lincoln, Bronze Finish, 6 In., Pair ... 12.75
Iron, Bookend, Dancing Nude Girl, Art Deco, 5 1/2 In., Pair ... 27.00
Iron, Bookend, Fisherman, Pair ... 18.00
Iron, Bookend, Galleon Shape, 4 1/2 X 4 1/2 In., Pair ... 7.95
Iron, Bookend, Indian's Head In Relief, 4 1/2 In., Pair ... 14.50
Iron, Bookend, Lions, 4 In., Pair ... 15.00
Iron, Boot Scraper, Scroll Ends, For Doorstep ... 12.75
Iron, Bootjack, Bug ... 4.00
Iron, Bootjack, Cast, American, C.1850, 11 In.High ... *Illus* 300.00
Iron, Bootjack, Cricket ... 23.00
Iron, Bootjack, His & Hers, Double-Ended ... 12.00
Iron, Bootjack, Naughty Nellie ... 22.75
Iron, Box, Frog, Top Lifts On Back Hinge, 3 3/4 X 3 In. ... 9.00
Iron, Box, Letter, Treasure Chest Shape, Brass Finish, 3 Sections Inside ... 20.00
Iron, Bracket, Shelf, Ornate, 17 X 13 1/2 In., Pair ... 18.00
Iron, Bracket, Shelf, Ornate, 19 X 18 In., Pair ... 25.00
Iron, Brazier, Table, Ceremonial, Pierced Chrysanthemums Lid, 5 In. ... 15.00
Iron, Broiler, Wrought, Straight & Serpentine Bars, Three Feet, 11 1/2 In. ... 165.00
Iron, Bucket, Fire, Lechlade Manor Fire, Red With Black & Yellow ... 85.00
Iron, Burner, Incense, Vantine's ... 6.50
Iron, Candelabra, Arch Shaped, Painted Hold, Holds 5 Candles ... 50.00
Iron, Candlestick, Milk-Glass Ball In Center, Enamel Floral, C.1900, 5 In. ... 40.00
Iron, Christmas Tree Holder, North Bros. Mfg.Co., 3 Legs, 2 Piece, 11 In. ... 18.00

Iron, Coffee Grinder, see Coffee Grinder

Iron, Cutter, Tobacco, Embossed Peace & Good Will, 12 In. ... 20.00
Iron, Door Knocker, Flower Basket ... 12.00 To 15.00
Iron, Door Knocker, Lady's Hand Holding Ball, 4 In. ... 19.50
Iron, Door Knocker, Parrot ... 14.00
Iron, Door Knocker, Rose ... 8.00

Iron, Door Knocker, Woodpecker On Tree, 3 3/4 In. 7.00
Iron, Door Latch, Maple Leaf Shape, 9 1/2 In.Long .... *Illus* 70.00
Iron, Door Latch, Suffolk, 10 3/8 In. .... *Illus* 120.00
Iron, Door Latch, Suffolk, 12 In. .... *Illus* 80.00

Iron doorstops have been made in all types of designs. The vast majority of the doorstops sold today are cast iron and were made from about 1890 to 1930. Most of them are shaped like people, animals, flowers, or ships.

Iron, Doorstop, Aunt Jemima 25.00
Iron, Doorstop, Basket Of Flowers, Green & Gold 20.00
Iron, Doorstop, Bird, Flatback 23.00
Iron, Doorstop, Black Cat, Green Eyes, Heavy 30.00
Iron, Doorstop, Boston Terrier, Painted 26.00
Iron, Doorstop, Bulldog, Gold Painted 30.00
Iron, Doorstop, Bulldog, 9 X 9 In. 25.00
Iron, Doorstop, Cat, Half Back, White With Blue Ribbon, 7 In. 45.00
Iron, Doorstop, Cat, Sitting, Black Paint, 7 In. 22.00
Iron, Doorstop, Cockatoo Standing On Tree Stump 15.00
Iron, Doorstop, Dog, 10 1/2 In. 20.00
Iron, Doorstop, Elephant 25.00
Iron, Doorstop, Elephant, Trunk Up 25.00
Iron, Doorstop, Flower Basket 25.00
Iron, Doorstop, Galleon Ship, Painted, 1930, 11 1/2 In. 14.75
Iron, Doorstop, Kitten 25.00
Iron, Doorstop, Kittens 30.00
Iron, Doorstop, Lady, 11 In. 22.00
Iron, Doorstop, Mail Coach With Horses & Driver, Pair 55.00
Iron, Doorstop, Man With Long Nose & Pot Belly 21.00
Iron, Doorstop, Monkey, Curved Tail Base, 9 1/4 In. 90.00
Iron, Doorstop, Nude Woman, 7 In. .... *Illus* 15.00

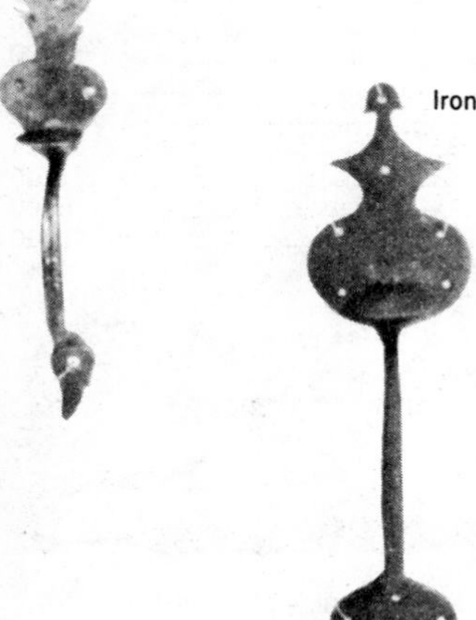

Iron, Door Latch, Maple Leaf Shape, 9 1/2 In.Long

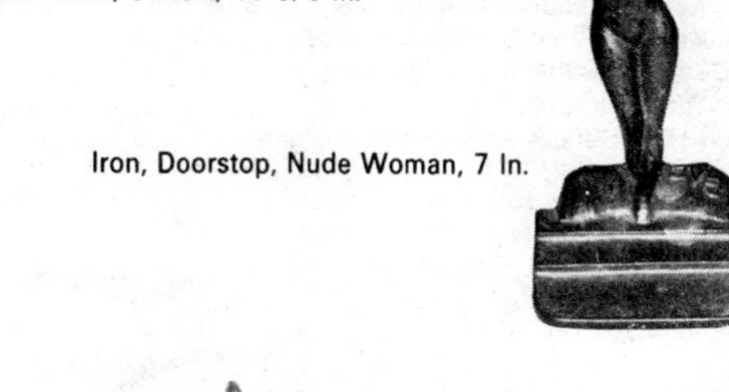

Iron, Door Latch, Suffolk, 10 3/8 In.

Iron, Doorstop, Nude Woman, 7 In.

Iron, Door Latch, Suffolk, 12 In.

Iron, Doorstop, Oriental Lady Holding Decorated Fan, 11 X 4 In. 25.00
Iron, Doorstop, Oriental Lady, Painted 19.00
Iron, Doorstop, Parrot, 12 In. 38.00
Iron, Doorstop, Penguin 30.00
Iron, Doorstop, Pot Of Flowers, Painted, 8 In. 28.50
Iron, Doorstop, Rabbit, Signed B & H 35.00
Iron, Doorstop, Scotty, Red Paint 27.50
Iron, Doorstop, Setter Dog, Black & White, 15 1/4 In. 40.00
Iron, Doorstop, Ship, Painted, 11 1/2 In. 14.00
Iron, Doorstop, Spanish Galleon In Full Sail, 11 In. 26.00
Iron, Doorstop, Squirrel, Signed B & H 35.00
Iron, Doorstop, Standing Bird, 4 1/2 X 6 1/4 In. 11.00
Iron, Doorstop, Standing Fox Terrier, 8 1/2 In. 25.00
Iron, Doorstop, Windmill 25.00
Iron, Doorstop, Wolf, Seated 8.50
Iron, Eagle On Spherical Base, Schoolhouse, Black Paint, C.1800, 5 1/2 Ft. 1000.00
Iron, Figure, Bootjack, Naughty Nellie 22.75
Iron, Figurine, Bison, 9 In. 29.00
Iron, Figurine, Dog, Miniature, 1 In., Pair 25.00
Iron, Figurine, Monkey, 3 1/2 In. 19.75
Iron, Figurine, Zep Dirigible, 5 In. 30.00
Iron, Fork, Rounded Handle, 22 1/2 In. .... *Illus* 95.00
Iron, Grand Piano, Filigree Design, Paper Keyboard, Miniature, 2 1/2 In. 20.00
Iron, Griddle, 2 Handled, 24 In. 10.00
Iron, Hanger, Coat, Hall, Embossed Man's Head 8.50
Iron, Hinge, Door, Barn, 42 In.Long, Pair .... *Illus* 175.00
Iron, Hinges, Spider-Leg, 15 X 17 In. .... *Illus* 130.00
Iron, Holder, Burning Splints Inside Whiskey Barrels, 16 In. .... *Illus* 50.00
Iron, Holder, Rush, Spring, 20 In.High .... *Illus* 160.00
Iron, Holder, Rush, Wood Base, 18th Century 145.00
Iron, Hook, Boot, U.S.Cavalry, Cast Iron 3.50
Iron, Hook, Coat, Patent Dec.21, 1869, Set Of 6 .... 6.00
Iron, Hook, Meat, 8 1/4 In.Long .... *Illus* 37.50
Iron, Hook, Wall Bracket, Screw-In Type, 8 In. 4.95
Iron, Juicer, Landers, Frary & Clark, New Britain, Conn. 22.00
Iron, Kettle, Belly Shape, On Legs, Dated 1813, Initialed LT, 11 In. 100.00
Iron, Kettle, Swing Cover, Flanged 32.00
Iron, Kettle, 3 Legged, Bail Handle, Pale Blue Enamel, 10 Quart 25.00
Iron, Key, 3 1/2 In. 2.95
Iron, Ladle, For Pouring Molten Lead 4.00
Iron, Latch, Norfolk, 8 1/2 In. .... *Illus* 15.00
Iron, Latch, Suffolk, Arrow Head Designs .... *Illus* 35.00

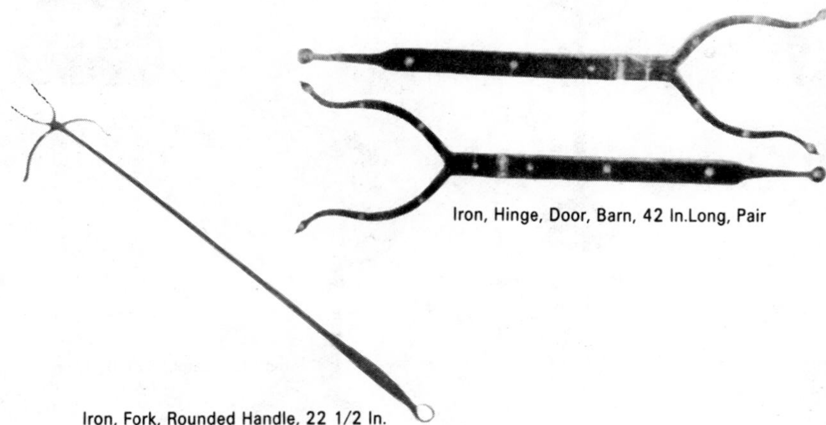

Iron, Hinge, Door, Barn, 42 In.Long, Pair

Iron, Fork, Rounded Handle, 22 1/2 In.

Iron, Match Holder, see also Match Holder
Iron, Match Holder, Basket Of Flowers, Wall 18.00
Iron, Match Holder, Bird Decoration 35.00
Iron, Match Holder, Chest With Lift Lid, Openwork Back, 4 Footed, 4 In. 16.75
Iron, Match Holder, Gargoyle Face & Church, Wall, C.1800 .... 15.00
Iron, Match Holder, Lift-Up Lid, Wall, 4 1/4 In. 14.75
Iron, Match Holder, Openwork 25.00
Iron, Match Holder, Rabbit & Bird, Horn Center, Double Pockets 25.00
Iron, Match Holder, Wall, 2 Part 18.00
Iron, Match Holder, Wellington's Red-Topped Boots 15.00
Iron, Match Holder, 2 Pockets, Openwork Back, Wall, 6 5/8 In. 12.75
Iron, Matchbox, Hanging, Self-Closing, Pat.Dec.20, 1864, DM & Co., New Haven 18.00
Iron, Mold, 12 Cake, Maple Sugar Candy 15.00
Iron, Nutcracker, Alligator 18.00
Iron, Nutcracker, Harold Lloyd Type Figure, Marked Nestorm, England 22.00
Iron, Nutcracker, St.Bernard Dog, Mounted On Board 30.00
Iron, Opener, Bottle, Old Snifter, Man Wearing Top Hat & Tails, 7 In. 25.00
Iron, Opener, Bottle, Seated Billy Goat 12.00
Iron, Paperweight, Figural, Lady In Red Ruffled Skirt, 5 In. 40.00
Iron, Paperweight, Steam Engine, Marked Fairbanks Morse 19.75
Iron, Peeler, Apple 16.50
Iron, Porringer, Cut-Out Sunray Handle, Back Impressed Little Traveller 35.00
Iron, Porringer, Leaf Handle, 6 In. 35.00
Iron, Pot, Pitch, Civil War Period, Hinged Cover, Bail Handle, 3 1/2 In. 14.95
Iron, Press, Meat Juice, Columbia, Cast 12.00
Iron, Pulley, Well, John A.Fletcher, Dayton, Ohio, Apr.5, 1887, 6 3/4 In. 22.00

Iron, Holder, Burning Splints Inside Whiskey Barrels, 16 In.

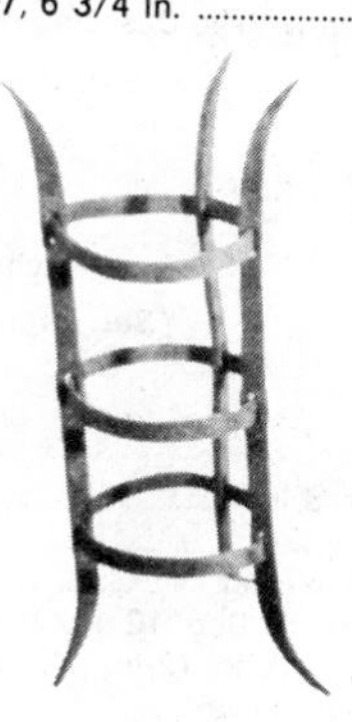

Iron, Hinges, Spider-Leg, 15 X 17 In.

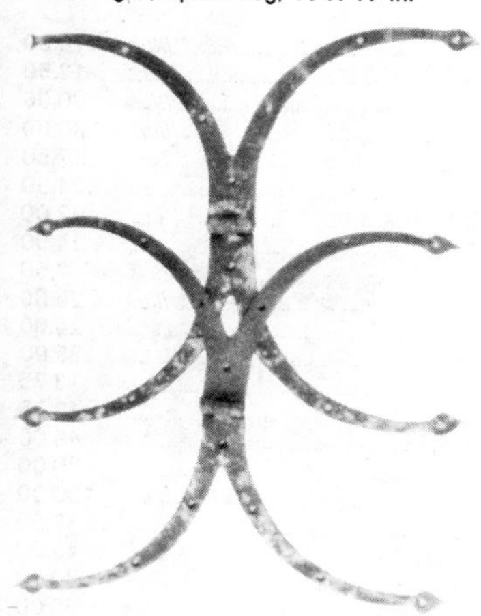

Iron, Holder, Rush, Spring, 20 In.High

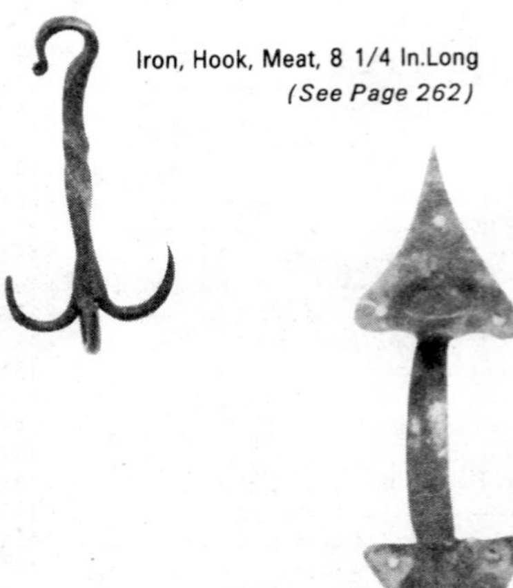

Iron, Hook, Meat, 8 1/4 In.Long
(See Page 262)

Iron, Rushlight Holder, 8 In.

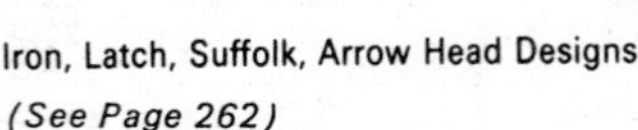

Iron, Latch, Suffolk, Arrow Head Designs
(See Page 262)

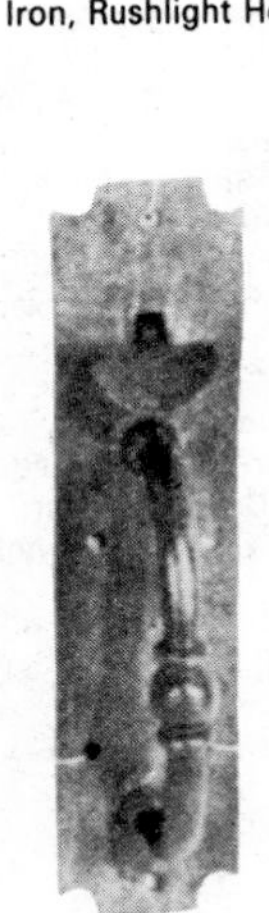

Iron, Latch, Norfolk, 8 1/2 In.
(See Page 262)

Iron, Rushlight Holder, 8 In. .... *Illus* 110.00
Iron, Scissors, Candlewick 12.50
Iron, Scissors, 14 1/2 In.Long .... *Illus* 30.00
Iron, Scraper, Shoe, Scottie Dog, 12 1/2 In.Long .... *Illus* 80.00
Iron, Seat, Implement, Jenkins, 12 In. 17.50
Iron, Seat, Machinery, Buckeye 24.50
Iron, Shelf, Ornate, Victorian, Diamond Shape, Curlicue Top, 12 X 10 X 6 In. 32.00
Iron, Shoe, Oxen, Patent Aug.10, 1880, Pair 14.00
Iron, Snow Eagle, Shield On Breast, 1897 .... 7.50
Iron, Snow Eagle, 5 In. .... *Illus* 25.00
Iron, Snuffer, Wick, Scissors Type 24.00
Iron, Spittoon, Figural, Turtle, Colden Novelty Co.Pat.1897, 14 In. 95.00
Iron, Steps, Buggy, Openwork 13.75
Iron, Steps, Buggy, Pair 12.75
Iron, Taper Holder, Spiral Base, Handwrought, Primitive, Pair 45.00
Iron, Teakettle, Sliding Lid 30.00
Iron, Teapot, Japanese, Lotus Bud Finial, Signed Brass Lid 100.00
Iron, Tobacco Cutter, Spearhead 37.50
Iron, Traveler, Wheel With Sawtooth Rim, Hole For Hanging, 13 1/2 In. 45.00
Iron, Trivet, Good Luck Horseshoe, Clasped Hands, Eagle On Top, 6 In. 30.00
Iron, Trivet, Triangular, 26 X 12 In. .... *Illus* 65.00
Iron, Trivet, Wooden Handle, Horseshoe Shape, Design 1881 .... 28.50
Iron, Warmer, Bed, Cutouts In Hinged Lid, Wooden Handle, 35 In. 56.00
Iron, Warmer, Bed, Vermont, C.1840, Cutout Tin Lid, Brown Paint On Handle 125.00
Iron, Warmer, Bed, Wooden Handle, 36 In. 95.00
Iron, Warmer, Plate, 12 In.Wide .... *Illus* 75.00
Iron, Winder, Yarn. Clamp On, Adjustable Wire Arms 35.00

Ironstone china was first made in 1813. It gained its greatest popularity during the mid-nineteenth century. The heavy, durable, off-white pottery was made in white or was colored with any of hundreds of patterns. Much flow blue pottery was made of ironstone. Some of the pieces had raised decorations.

Ironstone, Basin, Etruria Works, Lion & Unicorn Mark, 14 In. 30.00
Ironstone, Bowl, Black Matte, Dragons, White Interior, Mason's, 8 In. 75.00
Ironstone, Bowl, Covered, White, Oval, 14 In. 35.00
Ironstone, Bowl, Covered, White, Square, 14 In. 35.00
Ironstone, Bowl, Floral Band, Lord & Ladies, Mason's, 9 1/2 In. 22.00
Ironstone, Bowl, Imari-Like Color, Floral, Ashworth, C.1862, 10 In. 25.00
Ironstone, Bowl, Marked Genuine Ironstone With Crown, 10 In. 10.00
Ironstone, Bowl, Oval, Wheat 23.00
Ironstone, Bowl, Vista, Castle Scene, Rose Transfer, Mason's, 4 In. 4.00
Ironstone, Bowl, White, Wheat, Meakin, 9 1/4 X 5 3/4 In. 7.50
Ironstone, Chamber Pot, Cover, John Edwards, Oak Leaf Decoration 25.00
Ironstone, Chamber Pot, Wheat, Johnson Bros. 35.00
Ironstone, Child's Dishes, Blue, Yellow On Ground, 16 Pieces 65.00
Ironstone, Coffeepot, Clarke 35.00
Ironstone, Coffeepot, White 12.50
Ironstone, Creamer, Mason, Floral, C.1891 .... 15.00
Ironstone, Creamer, Meakin 20.00
Ironstone, Cup & Saucer, Handleless, Wheat 15.00
Ironstone, Cup & Saucer, Lily Of The Valley 55.00
Ironstone, Cup & Saucer, Roses, Ring Handle 22.50
Ironstone, Cup Plate, Lilies Of The Valley 3.50
Ironstone, Cup Plate, Vine & Scrolls 3.50
Ironstone, Dish, Covered Soap, Drainer, Meakin 25.00
Ironstone, Dish, Pickle, Wheat 18.00
Ironstone, Dish, Square, Covered, Oriental Decoration, Mason's, 9 X 9 In. 125.00
Ironstone, Dish, Sweetmeat, Gold Oriental Bird, Blue & White, Mason's, C.1820 .... 65.00
Ironstone, Eggcup, White, Double 4.00
Ironstone, Fruit Bowl, Mandarin, 2 Handles, Mason's, 9 1/2 In. 82.50
Ironstone, Gravy Boat, Wheat Pattern, Double Rope Border 15.00

Iron, Scraper, Shoe, Scottie Dog, 12 1/2 In.Long

Iron, Snow Eagle, 5 In.

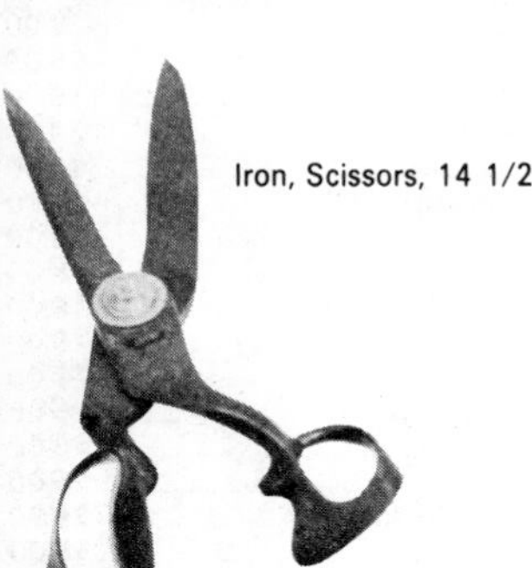

Iron, Scissors, 14 1/2 In.Long

Iron, Trivet, Triangular, 26 X 12 In.

(See Page 264)

Iron, Warmer, Plate, 12 In.Wide

(See Page 264)

Ironstone, Jar, Fruit Baskets On Sides, Bulbous, Mason's, 4 5/8 In. 11.00
Ironstone, Mortar, Herb, Covered, Wooden Pestle 7.00
Ironstone, Mug, Black-Faced Man, Blue Hat, 5 X 4 3/4 In. 37.00
Ironstone, Mug, Child's, Yellow Chicks 10.00
Ironstone, Mug, Indian Head In Relief, Handled 35.00
Ironstone, Pitcher Set, Oriental, Snake Handles, C.1850, 7 To 4 In., 5 Piece 426.00
Ironstone, Pitcher, Chinese Design, Blue, Gold, & Rust, 8 1/4 In. 90.00
Ironstone, Pitcher, Gaudy, 10 1/2 In. 125.00
Ironstone, Pitcher, Grape Design, Blue, Large 40.00
Ironstone, Pitcher, Ivory Color, Raised Boar Attacking Dogs, Mason's, 7 In. 85.00
Ironstone, Pitcher, Milk, Pastoral Scenes In Relief 32.00
Ironstone, Pitcher, Opaque, Scenic, Imari Colors, Meyer & Newbold, 5 1/2 In. 75.00
Ironstone, Pitcher, Oriental Decoration, Green Snake Handle, Mason's, 7 In. 100.00
Ironstone, Pitcher, Oriental Scene, Crown Mark, Mason's Patent, 7 In. 125.00
Ironstone, Pitcher, Oriental, Green Snake Handle, Mason's, 7 In. 100.00
Ironstone, Pitcher, Pink & Brown, Gold Trim, Maddock Works, 7 1/2 In. 21.00
Ironstone, Pitcher, St.Louis Shape, J.E.Edward, 6 1/2 In. 22.00
Ironstone, Pitcher, White With Acanthus Leaves In Relief, Davenport, 1861 .... 73.00
Ironstone, Pitcher, White, Johnson Bros., 5 1/2 In. 13.50
Ironstone, Pitcher, White, Marked Stone China, J.W. Parkhurst & Co., 8 In. 12.50
Ironstone, Pitcher, White, Meakin, 10 1/2 In. 20.00
Ironstone, Pitcher, White, Ornate Design, J & G Meakin, Pearl Ware, 11 In. 22.50
Ironstone, Pitcher, White, Ornate Design, Marked 4 & G Meakin, Pearl Ware, 11 .... 22.50
Ironstone, Plate, American Marine, Pink, Mason's, 10 In. 14.50
Ironstone, Plate, Bird & Floral, Imari Coloring, Mason's, C.1849, 9 1/2 In. 30.00
Ironstone, Plate, Bird, Flowers, & Leaves, Mason's, C.1820, 10 1/2 In. 26.00
Ironstone, Plate, Black, Pink Floral, Mason's, 9 1/2 In. 22.00
Ironstone, Plate, Blue & White, 1st Impressed Masons Patent Ironstone China 25.00
Ironstone, Plate, Corn 18.00
Ironstone, Plate, Dessert, Cobalt, Orange Floral, Gilt Trim, Mason's, C.1813 .... 30.00
Ironstone, Plate, Dinner, White, Pattern On Edge, Alfred Meakin 10.00
Ironstone, Plate, Flowers, Parrot, Oranges, Yellows, Blues, Mason, 8 In. 28.00
Ironstone, Plate, Mandarin, Mason's, Square, 8 3/4 In. 25.00
Ironstone, Plate, Mason, Blue, Dark Blue Serpent, 9 1/4 In. 78.00
Ironstone, Plate, Mr.Micawber Leaving Pawn Shop, Stanmore, Meakin, 8 In. 18.00
Ironstone, Plate, Orange Brown & Dark Blue Flowers, Mason, 10 In. 19.00
Ironstone, Plate, Pagoda Scene, P.W. & C.P., Pearlstone, Corean 17.00
Ironstone, Plate, Pie, Stilt Marks, 10 In. 25.00
Ironstone, Plate, White, Meakin, 9 In. 6.00
Ironstone, Plate, World's Fair, New York, 1939, Mason's, 10 1/2 In. 25.00
Ironstone, Platter, Huge, R.K.Beck 29.50
Ironstone, Platter, Meakin, 8 3/4 X 12 In. 18.00
Ironstone, Platter, Meakin, 10 X 14 In. 20.00
Ironstone, Salad Bowl, White, Footed, Alfred Meakin, 9 X 6 In. 35.00

Ironstone, Salad Bowl, White, Footed, Extra Quality, Lions, 10 In. 45.00
Ironstone, Soup Bowl, American Marine, Blue Transfer, Mason's, 8 1/4 In. 12.00
Ironstone, Soup Bowl, White, Meakin, 8 1/4 In. 3.50
Ironstone, Sugar, Child's, Covered, Girl & Dog, Malkin Co., C.1873 .... 40.00
Ironstone, Sugar, Covered, Meakin 20.00
Ironstone, Sugar, Crossed Bars On Lid, Gold Bands 15.00
Ironstone, Syrup, Floral 25.00
Ironstone, Syrup, Light Blue, Serpent Handle, Pewter Top, 6 Sided, Mason's 55.00
Ironstone, Tea Leaf, Butter Pat, Marked H.Burgess, Burslem, Set Of 10 .... 50.00
Ironstone, Tea Leaf, Butter Pat, Meakin 9.50
Ironstone, Tea Leaf, Butter Pat, Shaw, Square 8.50
Ironstone, Tea Leaf, Butter Pat, Square, Pair 15.00
Ironstone, Tea Leaf, Chamber Pot, Covered, Shaw 25.00
Ironstone, Tea Leaf, Coffeepot, Gray, Green Transfer Satsuma Pattern, C.1870 .... 25.00
Ironstone, Tea Leaf, Creamer, Edwards 52.00
Ironstone, Tea Leaf, Cup & Saucer, Anthony Shaw 30.00
Ironstone, Tea Leaf, Cup & Saucer, Edwards .... 35.00 To 40.00
Ironstone, Tea Leaf, Cup & Saucer, Handleless, Shaw 30.00
Ironstone, Tea Leaf, Cup & Saucer, Meakin 22.00
Ironstone, Tea Leaf, Dish, Square, Covered, Mellor, Taylor & Co. 35.00
Ironstone, Tea Leaf, Gravy Boat, Mellor, Taylor Co. 25.00
Ironstone, Tea Leaf, Pitcher, Milk, Burgess, Burslem, 6 1/2 In. 55.00
Ironstone, Tea Leaf, Pitcher, White, Blue Pattern, 7 In. 18.00
Ironstone, Tea Leaf, Plate, Alfred Meakin, 8 3/4 In. 10.00
Ironstone, Tea Leaf, Plate, Cake, Shaw 26.00
Ironstone, Tea Leaf, Plate, Edwards, 9 In. 6.50
Ironstone, Tea Leaf, Plate, Gilt Luster Band & Sprig, Shaw, 1883, 9 In. 8.50
Ironstone, Tea Leaf, Plate, Meakin, 8 1/2 In. 43.50
Ironstone, Tea Leaf, Platter, Alfred Meakin, 10 X 14 In. 32.50
Ironstone, Tea Leaf, Platter, Copper Luster, Thos.Funival & Sons, 17 X 12 In 35.00
Ironstone, Tea Leaf, Platter, Grindley, 12 X 9 In. 16.00
Ironstone, Tea Leaf, Platter, Meakin, 13 1/2 X 10 In. 25.00
Ironstone, Tea Leaf, Platter, Meakin, 14 X 10 In. 17.50
Ironstone, Tea Leaf, Soup, Shaw 15.00
Ironstone, Tea Leaf, Sugar, Cable, Shaw 28.00
Ironstone, Tea Leaf, Sugar, Dolphin Handles, Edwards 40.00
Ironstone, Tea Leaf, Teapot, Cable, Bulbous, Shaw 75.00
Ironstone, Tea Leaf, Teapot, Wedgwood 45.00
Ironstone, Tea Set, White & Gold, Acorn Finial, John Voght, 3 Piece 67.00
Ironstone, Teapot, Lily Of The Valley 80.00
Ironstone, Toothbrush Holder, Leaf Design Around Knob, 8 In. 12.00
Ironstone, Toothbrush Safe, Nut Finial, Salmon Pink, Blue Floral 16.00
Ironstone, Tray, Bread, Where Reason Rules, Etc., Wheat Pattern, Lattice Shell 85.00
Ironstone, Tray, Bread, Where Reason Rules, Wheat Pattern, Lattice Shell 85.00
Ironstone, Tray, Green Border, Center Maids & Cherubs, Empire Works, 1896 .... 20.00
Ironstone, Tureen & Attached Underplate, Covered, Embossed, Miniature 26.00
Ironstone, Tureen, Ladle Hole In Lid, White & Gray, Meakin, C.1875, 11 In. 55.00
Ironstone, Tureen, Leaf And Pear Finial, Marked 4 Wedgwood Ironstone, 1856 .... 100.00
Ironstone, Tureen, Soup, Gold Trim, Oval 29.00
Ironstone, Tureen, Soup, Meakin 50.00
Ironstone, Tureen, Tray, & Ladle, Soup, Covered, Morley 150.00
Ironstone, Vase, Chartreuse, Mason's, 4 1/2 In. 16.00
Ironstone, Vase, Oriental Birds & Flowers, Mason, Black Mark, 5 1/2 In. 35.00
Ironstone, Vegetable Bowl, Covered, White, Blue & Gold Floral, Meakin, 9 In. 35.00
Ironstone, Washstand Set, Birds, Snake Handle, Mason's, C.1845, 2 Piece 295.00
Ironstone, Washstand Set, D.E.McNP Co. 32.00
Ironstone, Washstand Set, Marked Charles Meakin, Hanley, England 125.00
Ironstone, Washstand Set, Mason, Mulberry, 7 In. 42.00
Ironstone, Washstand Set, White With Blue 65.00
Ironstone, Washstand Set, White, Maddock & Gater, Staffordshire, 2 Piece 125.00
Ironstone, Washstand Set, White, Thos.Hughes & John Maddock & Son, 2 Piece 34.00
Ironstone, Washstand Set, White, Wheat Pattern, Johnson Bros. 125.00
Ivorex, Plaque, Anne Hathaway's Cottage, 9 3/4 X 6 1/2 In. 42.00
Ivorex, Plaque, Shakespeare's House, Stratford On Avon, 9 3/4 X 6 1/2 In. 42.00

Ivory, see also **Napkin Ring, Netsuke**

Ivory, Binoculars, Show Pictures, 7/8 In. 22.50
Ivory, Bottle, Snuff, Carved Figures 50.00
Ivory, Bottle, Snuff, Carved Figures & Trees, 3 In. 200.00
Ivory, Bottle, Snuff, Carvings On Both Sides 85.00
Ivory, Bottle, Snuff, Double Gourd Shape, Etched Mountain Scene 50.00
Ivory, Bottle, Snuff, Woman & Man Under Tree, Carved 60.00
Ivory, Box, Covered, Carved Flowers, Round, 8 In. 350.00
Ivory, Box, European, Hand-Painted Scene On Lid, 4 1/4 X 3 3/8 In. 335.00
Ivory, Box, Stamp, 3 Blue Silk Compartments, Oval, 2 1/2 In. 95.00
Ivory, Button Hook, 3 In. 6.00
Ivory, Cage, Cricket, Hand-Carved, Latticing, Barrel Shape, 2 3/4 In. 45.00
Ivory, Cane Handle, Carved, 4 1/4 In. 225.00
Ivory, Cane Handle, Walnut Emerging From Leaves 45.00
Ivory, Cane, Carved Foo Dog Handle, Glass Eyes, Signed 45.00
Ivory, Carved Eagle Head, 5 In. 225.00
Ivory, Carving Set, Landers, Frary, & Clark, Sterling Ferrules, 1886, 3 Piece 100.00
Ivory, Cigarette Holder, Leather Case, 4 In. 20.00
Ivory, Cuttle Holder, For Birdcage, Carved Horse, Colt, & Man, 1 3/4 In. 45.00
Ivory, Elephant Bridge, 7 Elephants With Raised Trunks, 17 In., Wood Stand 125.00
Ivory, Figurine, African Drummer, Kenya, 8 In. 135.00
Ivory, Figurine, Ball, 10 Layers, Pedestal, China, 8 In. 68.00
Ivory, Figurine, Camel, Carved, 1 1/4 In. 25.00
Ivory, Figurine, Camel, China, 2 1/2 In. 14.00
Ivory, Figurine, Carved Bridge, 7 Elephants, Wood Stand, 17 In. 170.00
Ivory, Figurine, Doctor's Lady, Carved, Movable Bracelet, 9 In. 125.00
Ivory, Figurine, Doctor's Lady, Figure Reclining, Movable Bracelet, 6 In. 75.00
Ivory, Figurine, Doctor's Lady, Movable Bracelets 115.00
Ivory, Figurine, Elephant, Wooden Base, 4 In. 150.00
Ivory, Figurine, Eskimo In Kayak, C.1900 350.00
Ivory, Figurine, Fisherman Holding Carp & Net, Chinese, Carved, 6 1/2 In. 185.00
Ivory, Figurine, Fisherman On Teak Base, 4 1/2 In. 85.00
Ivory, Figurine, Goddess Of Thousand Hands, Koon Yum, Carved, 8 1/2 In. 175.00
Ivory, Figurine, Hoeti With Arms Raised Over Head, 4 1/4 In. 42.00
Ivory, Figurine, Hoeti, Seated, Carved, 2 1/2 In. 38.00 To 40.00
Ivory, Figurine, Lady Of The Court, Carved, Wooden Base, 10 In., Pair 300.00
Ivory, Figurine, Man Holding Fish And Net, 6 3/4 In. 175.00
Ivory, Figurine, Man With Mallet In Hand Opening Barrel, 2 1/2 In. 80.00
Ivory, Figurine, Man With Scroll & Horse, 5 In. 125.00
Ivory, Figurine, Man With Staff, Signed, 6 3/4 In. 175.00
Ivory, Figurine, Nude Oriental Woman In Clamshell With Sea Life, 8 In. 215.00
Ivory, Figurine, Oriental Man, Flatback, 3 In. 15.00
Ivory, Figurine, Rabbi, Carved, 4 1/2 In., Set Of 6 510.00
Ivory, Figurine, Red Jacket, 3-Masted Schooner, Carved, 9 In. 85.00
Ivory, Figurine, Voltaire, French, C.1780, 7 In. 325.00
Ivory, Figurine, Winged Cupid Playing Harp, Swan & Roses, Carved, 3 1/4 In. 90.00
Ivory, Figurine, Woman Holding Bird, Carved, Ivory Plinth, 9 In. 350.00
Ivory, Figurine, Woman Holding Bowl, Chinese, C.1870, 9 In. 250.00
Ivory, Fish Set, J F & S S E P Sterling Blades & Bands, 11 Piece 90.00
Ivory, Group, Elephant Bridge, 7 Elephants, Wooden Stand, 17 In. 135.00
Ivory, Group, Fisherman & Boy With Fish, Wood Base, 10 In. 235.00
Ivory, Group, 2 Sumo Wrestlers, Black Belts & Heads, 2 In. 190.00
Ivory, Knife, Fruit, Landers, Frary, & Clark, Silver Plate Blade, Set Of 6 45.00
Ivory, Letter Opener, Ivory Bone Elephant Finial, 13 Walking Elephants 12.50
Ivory, Miniature, Carved, Scissors, 6 In. 10.00
Ivory, Napkin Ring, Ornate Carving 25.00
Ivory, Needle Holder 6.50
Ivory, Panel, Carved House Interiors And Garden Scenes, 4 1/8 X 8 In., Pair 200.00
Ivory, Portrait, Wood Frame, Lady Hamilton, Signed Joliry, 6 1/2 X 5 1/2 In. 49.50
Ivory, Snuff Bottle, Carved In Relief, Underside In Black Carving 95.00
Ivory, Spill, Carved Dragons, Pierced, C.1850, 4 1/2 In. 150.00
Ivory, Spoon, Child's, Carved, C.1850, Pair 38.00
Ivory, Teething Ring, Bell, 1912 35.00
Ivory, Umbrella Handle, Carved Oriental Man's Head, C.1850 115.00

Ivory, Writing Set, Carved, 4 Pieces In Satin-Lined Box ... 35.00
Jack Armstrong, Flashlight ... 20.00
Jack Armstrong, Flashlight, Bullet, 4 1/2 In. ... 7.50
Jack Armstrong, Flashlight, C.1930 ... 10.00
Jack Armstrong, Pedometer ... 10.00 To 23.00

Jack-In-The-Pulpit vases were named for their odd trumpetlike shape that resembles the wild plant called jack-in-the-pulpit. The design originated in the late Victorian years.

Jack-In-The-Pulpit, Vase, Amber To Vaseline, Blown, C.1850, 6 In. ... 85.00
Jack-In-The-Pulpit, Vase, Amethyst To Clear, Blown In The Mold, 7 3/8 In. ... 98.00
Jack-In-The-Pulpit, Vase, Blue, Opalescent, Silver Overlay, 5 In. ... 33.00
Jack-In-The-Pulpit, Vase, Cranberry & White, Mica Flecks, 8 1/2 In., Pair ... 112.00
Jack-In-The-Pulpit, Vase, Crystal To Milk White, Cranberry Edge, 9 In. ... 49.00
Jack-In-The-Pulpit, Vase, Pale To Deep Green, Swirled Ribbed Stem, 8 In. ... 55.00
Jack-In-The-Pulpit, Vase, Peach Cased, White Opalescent, Leaf Feet, 10 In. ... 154.00
Jack-In-The-Pulpit, Vase, White To Clear, Diamond-Quilted, Green Rim, 8 In. ... 75.00

Jackfield ware was originally a black glazed pottery made in Jackfield, England, from 1750 to 1775. A yellow glazed ware has also been called Jackfield ware. Most of the pieces referred to as Jackfield are black pieces made during the Victorian era.

Jackfield, Pitcher, Black, 6 1/2 In. ... 30.00
Jackfield, Syrup, Black Glaze, Gold Trim, 4 1/2 In. ... 55.00
Jackfield, Teapot, Black, Enameled ... 30.00
Jacob Petit, Vase, Ormolu Mounted Snowball, Grape Vines, C.1835, Pair ... 1800.00
Jade, Bottle, Cologne, S. & W.England, Square, Diamond Cutting Around Body ... 62.50
Jade, Buckle, Chinese, Dragon's Head, Green, 4 In. ... 30.00
Jade, Buckle, Chinese, Dragon's Head, White, 3 1/4 In. ... 25.00
Jade, Figurine, Buddha, Apple Green, Wood Base, Heavily Carved, 4 1/2 X 5 In. ... 200.00
Jade, Figurine, Elephant, Green, Trunk Up, 4 In. ... 185.00
Jade, Figurine, Goldfish Swimming, Plum, 2 1/2 X 1 1/2 In. ... 155.00
Jade, Needle, Hair, Chinese, C.1850, Silver Pin, Stone ... 20.00
Jade, Ornament, Hair, Carved, 6 In. ... 85.00
Jade, Seal, Turtle Top, Square Base, 1 1/4 In. ... 210.00

Japanese Coralene is a pottery decorated with small raised beads and dots. It was first made in the nineteenth century. Later wares made to imitate coralene had dots of enamel.

Japanese Coralene, Plate, 2 Lilies, Beading, 10 In. ... 30.00
Japanese Coralene, Vase, Beaded Orchid Spray, 6 In. ... 85.00
Japanese Coralene, Vase, Blue To Yellow, White Jonquils, 2 Handles, 11 In. ... 235.00
Japanese Coralene, Vase, Lavender & Green Matte, Floral, Nippon, 1909, 4 In. ... 85.00
Japanese Coralene, Vase, Pink, Blue, & Beige, Roses, 2 Handles, 1909, 4 In. ... 97.50

Jasperware is a fine-grained pottery developed by Josiah Wedgwood in 1755. The jasper was made in many colors including the most famous, a light blue. It is still being made.

Jasperware, see also Various Art Potteries, Wedgwood

Jasperware, Box, Light Green, Cherubs On Cover, 3 X 4 1/2 X 2 1/4 In. ... 35.00
Jasperware, Box, Trinket, Pink Cherubs On Lid, Green, 5 X 3 1/2 In. ... 35.00
Jasperware, Creamer, Blue & White, 1953, 2 1/2 In. ... 30.00
Jasperware, Dish, Cheese, Lavender, Domed Top, 10 3/4 X 9 1/2 In. ... 295.00
Jasperware, Flower Bowl, Greens & White ... 18.00
Jasperware, Hatpin Holder, Cameo Inside Gilded Frame, Crown & Shield Mark ... 75.00
Jasperware, Knife, Fruit, Green, Bronze Blade, K & F, France, Set Of 12 ... 95.00
Jasperware, Pitcher, Blue & White, Marked Germany, 3 In. ... 20.00
Jasperware, Plaque, Boy's Head, White On Green, No.732, 4 1/2 X 3 In. ... 50.00
Jasperware, Plaque, Full Headdress Indian Bust, Green, 4 X 5 In. ... 60.00
Jasperware, Plaque, German, 4 Colors, 5 3/4 X 4 3/4 In. ... 75.00
Jasperware, Plaque, Girl's Head, White On Green, No.732, 4 1/2 X 3 In. ... 50.00
Jasperware, Plaque, Grant's Tomb, Pale Green, 4 X 5 In. ... 22.00
Jasperware, Plaque, Portrait Bust, George Washington, Green & White, 5 In. ... 30.00
Jasperware, Plaque, Portrait, Franklin, Green & White, 5 X 4 1/4 In. ... 30.00

Jewelry, Brooch, Circular Diamond, C.1910, 1 1/8 In.

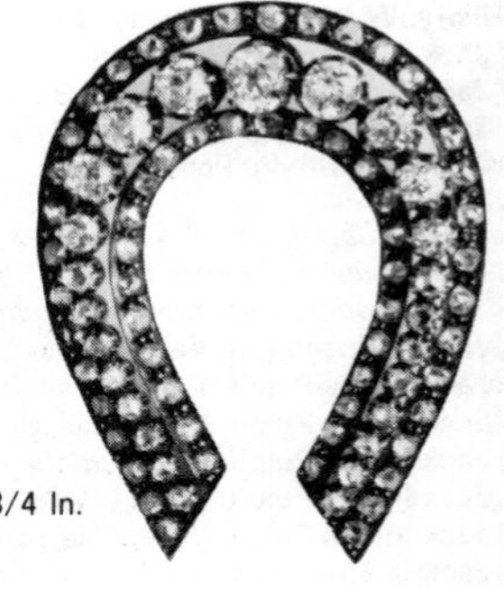

Jewelry, Brooch, Gold & Diamond Horseshoe, C.1880, 1 3/4 In.

Jewelry, Brooch, Gold & Diamond Star, C.1890, 1 1/8 In.

Jewelry, Brooch, Gold, Enamel, Hardstone Cameo, C.1900, 2 1/8 In.

Jasperware, Plaque, Raised Bust Of Longfellow, Acorn Border, 5 X 4 In. 28.00
Jasperware, Plaque, Three Dimensional, 9 X 6 In. 135.00
Jasperware, Sugar Shaker, Cupid 25.00
Jasperware, Tray, Heart Shape, Raised White Roses, Star & Crown, 3 1/2 In. 9.00
Jasperware, Vase, Black, Footed, Rams Heads, Classical Scenes, Handles, 6 1/2 I 345.00
Jasperware, Vase, Green, Profile Of Indian, 6 In. 110.00

Jewel Tea, see Autumn Leaf
Jewelery, Bracelet, see also Orphan Annie, Bracelet
Jewelery, Ring, see also Disneyana, Ring; Hopalong Cassidy, Ring
Jewelry, see also Coronation, Faberge, Gutta-Percha

Jewelry, Bangle, 14K Gold, Rose Diamonds In Discs, Victorian 110.00
Jewelry, Beads, Amber Glass, Long Strand 12.50
Jewelry, Bracelet, Bangle, Oval And Round Amethysts, 14K Gold 59.00
Jewelry, Bracelet, Cinnabar, China 50.00
Jewelry, Bracelet, Cuff, Kirk & Son, Sterling, 1 1/4 In. 35.00
Jewelry, Bracelet, Figures Of Women, Garnets, Sterling, Art Nouveau 35.00
Jewelry, Bracelet, Gold-Filled, 48 Garnets, Victorian, Safety Chain 85.00
Jewelry, Bracelet, Sodalite, 6 Stones, Victoria 85.00
Jewelry, Bracelet, Sterling Silver, Art Nouveau 14.00
Jewelry, Bracelet, Sterling, Signed Peruzzi, 4 Links, Dancing Figures 35.00
Jewelry, Bracelet, Wristwatch, 16 Rubies, 6 Diamonds, Pink Gold, Art Deco 150.00
Jewelry, Bracelet, 22K Pink Gold Serpent, Ruby Eyes, Victorian 245.00
Jewelry, Bracelet, 5 Carved Octagonal Ivories, Sterling Frame, C.1890 .... 125.00
Jewelry, Brooch, Art Nouveau, Sterling, Lady, Long Hair, Violin, 3 X 2 1/4 In. 25.00
Jewelry, Brooch, Circular Diamond, C.1910, 1 1/8 In. .... *Illus* 350.00
Jewelry, Brooch, Diamond Tremblant Floral, French 18th Century 1500.00
Jewelry, Brooch, Gold & Diamond Horseshoe, C.1880, 1 3/4 In. .... *Illus* 850.00
Jewelry, Brooch, Gold & Diamond Star, C.1890, 1 1/8 In. .... *Illus* 475.00
Jewelry, Brooch, Gold, Enamel, Hardstone Cameo, C.1900, 2 1/8 In. .... *Illus* 700.00
Jewelry, Brooch, Gold, Pearl, Hardstone Cameo, 1 3/4 In., C.1860 .... *Illus* 400.00

Jewelry, Brooch, Sterling, Gold Wash, 3 Rose Diamonds, Gorham, 1869 .... 65.00
Jewelry, Brooch, Swirled, 7 Rubies, 14K Gold, Art Deco 48.00
Jewelry, Brooch, 6 Rubies, 14K Gold, Art Deco 45.00
Jewelry, Buckle, Belt, 14K Gold, Engraved, Victorian, 1 1/2 In. 29.00
Jewelry, Chain & Slide, Watch, Gold-Filled, Turquoise & Pearls, Victorian 45.00
Jewelry, Chain, Rope Slide, 14K Gold, Art Nouveau 185.00
Jewelry, Chain, Slide, Mesh, Sterling Silver, Art Nouveau, 60 In. 50.00
Jewelry, Chain, Tubular, 14K Gold, Slide, Art Nouveau, 60 In. 225.00
Jewelry, Chatelaine, 10K Gold, Fleur-De-Lis, Art Nouveau 28.00
Jewelry, Cross, Gold, Russian, C.1870, 2 1/2 In. 210.00
Jewelry, Cuff Links, Diamond & Sapphire, Platinum, C.1920 .... 165.00
Jewelry, Earrings, Angel Figure, Sterling, Pierced, Art Nouveau, Pair 16.00
Jewelry, Earrings, Angel Type Figure & Floral, Sterling, Art Nouveau, Pair 16.00
Jewelry, Earrings, Bohemian Garnet Set In Sterling, Screwback, 3/4 X 1/2 In. 65.00
Jewelry, Earrings, Butterfly Dangle, Turquoise Flower, 14K Gold, Victorian 125.00
Jewelry, Earrings, Carnelian Marcasite, Sterling Silver, Art Deco, Pair 29.00
Jewelry, Earrings, Carved-Out Scene, Sterling Silver, Art Nouveau, Pair 19.00
Jewelry, Earrings, Drop, Garnets, Gold On Sterling, European Earwires 24.00
Jewelry, Earrings, Gold, Silver, & Rock Crystal, Ball, Art Deco, Pair 50.00
Jewelry, Earrings, Hair, Gold Grape & Leaves, Victorian, Pair 165.00
Jewelry, Earrings, Wedgwood, Blue Jasper In Sterling 85.00
Jewelry, Earrings, Woman With Garnets In Hair, Sterling Silver, Art Nouveau 15.00
Jewelry, Earrings, Woman's Head, Garnet In Hair, Sterling, Art Nouveau, Pair 19.00
Jewelry, Earrings, 2 Profiles & Garnet, Sterling Silver, Art Nouveau, Pair 19.00
Jewelry, Hatpin, White Porcelain, Butterfly 18.00
Jewelry, Indian, see Indian
Jewelry, Lavalier, Gold, Sapphire, Teardrop Loop Of Seed Pearls, Victorian 48.00
Jewelry, Locket, Enamel, 12 Pearls, Engraved, 14K Gold, Victorian, 1 3/4 In. 295.00
Jewelry, Locket, Gold, Engraved, C.1890, 1 1/4 In. 39.00
Jewelry, Locket, Lady, Rose Diamonds In Hair, 14K Yellow Gold, Art Nouveau 75.00
Jewelry, Lorgnette, Flowers, Unger Bros. Sterling Silver, Art Nouveau 170.00
Jewelry, Lorgnette, Tortoise & Gilt Sterling, 132 Gold Stars, C.1900 .... 195.00
Jewelry, Necklace, Jeweled, Enameled, St.George, Hungarian, 19th Century 5000.00
Jewelry, Necklace, Silver Plate, Lalique Type Pendant, Amazonite, Art Deco 12.00
Jewelry, Pendant, Bird With Wings Spread, Chain, Sterling 15.00
Jewelry, Pendant, Bracelet, & Ring, Gold, Enamel, C.1850 .... *Illus* 850.00
Jewelry, Pendant, Chain, Rose Quartz, Fluted Pendant, Art Deco 225.00
Jewelry, Pendant, Cherub, Opal, 14K Gold, Art Nouveau, Chain 38.00
Jewelry, Pendant, Cherub's Head With Opal, 14K Gold, Chain, Art Nouveau 39.00
Jewelry, Pendant, Greek Design, Carved, Large, Round, 18K Gold 56.00
Jewelry, Pendant, Moonstone, Sterling Chain, Victorian 50.00
Jewelry, Pendant, Sterling Silver, Heart Shape, Repousse, Art Nouveau 70.00
Jewelry, Pendant, Sterling Woman's Head, 2 Garnets, Art Nouveau, Chain 12.00
Jewelry, Pendant, Whistle, Devil's Head, Garnet Eyes, Sterling, Art Nouveau 19.00
Jewelry, Pendant, Whistle, Woman, Garnet At Neck, Sterling, Art Nouveau 19.00

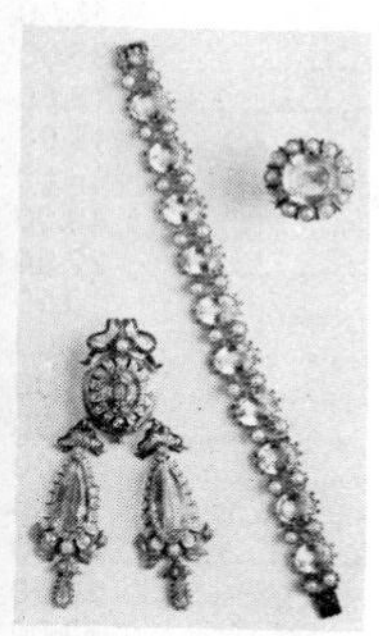

Jewelry, Pendant, Bracelet, & Ring, Gold, Enamel, C.1850

Jewelry, Brooch, Gold, Pearl, Hard Stone Cameo, 1 3/4 In.C.1860

Jewelry, Pendant, Woman Holding Wand, Sterling Silver, Chain, Art Nouveau 15.00
Jewelry, Pendant, Woman, 2 Opals In Her Hair, 14K Gold, Art Nouveau, Chain 38.00
Jewelry, Pendant, Woman's Head, 14K Gold, Chain, Art Nouveau 69.00
Jewelry, Pendant, Woman's Profile, Whistle, Sterling Silver, Art Nouveau 19.00
Jewelry, Pendant, 14K White Gold Triangle, 12 Sapphires, Art Deco 13.00
Jewelry, Pendant, 2 Emeralds & 4 Diamonds, 14K Gold, Art Deco, Chain 50.00
Jewelry, Pendant, 2 Profiles With Garnet & Opal, 14K Gold, Art Nouveau 38.00
Jewelry, Pendant, 3 Faces, 3 Diamonds, 14K Gold, Art Nouveau 92.00
Jewelry, Pin & Earrings, French Paste Moon & Star, 14K Gold, Victorian 125.00
Jewelry, Pin, Bar, Bohemian Garnet, Cluster, Low Karat Gold Setting, 21 In. 45.00
Jewelry, Pin, Bar, Onyx & 3 Pearls, 14K Gold Frame, Victorian, 2 1/2 In. 65.00
Jewelry, Pin, Bar, 14K White Gold Filigree, Sapphire Center, Art Deco 22.50
Jewelry, Pin, Bohemian Garnet, 8-Pointed Star, 2 Gold Chains, 1 3/4 In. 85.00
Jewelry, Pin, Brooch, 1877 American 1/2 Dollar, Initialed 12.00
Jewelry, Pin, Brooch, 1877 Quarter 10.00
Jewelry, Pin, Cat, 14K Gold, Jewellers To Her Majesty, Victorian 155.00
Jewelry, Pin, Gold, Enamel 4-Leaf Clover, Pearl, Art Nouveau, 1 1/4 In. 25.00
Jewelry, Pin, Pietra Dura, Marble Inlaid, Floral, Victorian, 2 In. 75.00
Jewelry, Pin, Swordfish, Sterling, Pierced, Beau, Art Nouveau, 2 5/8 In. 18.00
Jewelry, Pin, Topaz, Etched 14K Gold Frame, Victorian 125.00
Jewelry, Pin, Victorian, Whalebone, Dove With Letter On Flowers & Leaves 15.00
Jewelry, Pin, Winged Dragon, Pearl-Studded Crown, Gold, Art Nouveau, 1 1/8 In. 150.00
Jewelry, Ring, Amethyst & 2 Pearls, 14K Gold Setting, Art Deco 13.00
Jewelry, Ring, Angel With Flowers, Sterling Silver, Art Nouveau 14.00
Jewelry, Ring, Aquamarine & Ruby On Sides, 14K Gold, Art Deco 15.00
Jewelry, Ring, Aquamarine, 14K Gold 6-Prong Setting, Victorian 28.00
Jewelry, Ring, Aquamarine, 18K Gold Setting, Art Deco 32.00
Jewelry, Ring, Black Stone & Pearl, 14K Gold, Art Deco 35.00
Jewelry, Ring, Cameo Of Standing Lady, 14K Yellow Gold, Victorian 58.00
Jewelry, Ring, Cherub's Face In Heart Setting, Sterling, Art Nouveau 11.00
Jewelry, Ring, Child's, Madiera Topaz, 14K Gold, Victorian 38.00
Jewelry, Ring, Child's, 14K Gold, Opal In Prong Setting, Victorian 19.00
Jewelry, Ring, Deep Blue Stone, Pear Shape, Art Deco, 10K Gold 17.00
Jewelry, Ring, Deep Green Oval Stone, 14K Gold, Art Deco 30.00
Jewelry, Ring, Diamond In Swirl, 14K White Gold, Art Deco 16.00
Jewelry, Ring, Diamond In 14K White Gold Swirl Setting, Art Deco 19.00
Jewelry, Ring, Garnet & Opal, 2 Profiles, 14K Gold, Art Nouveau 52.00
Jewelry, Ring, Garnet, 14K Gold 19.00
Jewelry, Ring, Gibson Girl, Garnet, Sterling, Art Nouveau 14.00
Jewelry, Ring, Gold & Oriental Bronze, Bird & Leaf Motif 200.00
Jewelry, Ring, Gold Wash, Washington & Lee Basketball, Dated 1951 .... 14.00
Jewelry, Ring, Green Stone & 6 Pink Sapphires, 14K Gold, Art Deco 26.00
Jewelry, Ring, Hair, Goldwork, Victorian, Size 9 1/2 In. 85.00
Jewelry, Ring, Hand-Painted Porcelain Lady's Head, Yellow Gold, Victorian 22.00
Jewelry, Ring, Lady's, Gold, World's Fair, 1904, Dangling Heart, Lord's Prayer 25.00
Jewelry, Ring, Lapis Lazuli, Woman's Faces, 14K Gold, Art Nouveau 39.00
Jewelry, Ring, Lapis Lazuli, 10K Yellow Gold, Art Deco 35.00
Jewelry, Ring, Leslie Steinmetz, 7 Diamonds, Sterling & Gold, Art Deco 45.00
Jewelry, Ring, Man's, Onyx, Gold, Initial, 1885 .... 35.00
Jewelry, Ring, Man's, Rectangular Pink Sapphire, Art Deco, 10K Gold 19.00
Jewelry, Ring, Man's, Red Stone, 14K White Gold, Art Deco 18.00
Jewelry, Ring, Marcasite, Green Onyx, Sterling Silver, Art Deco 65.00
Jewelry, Ring, Opal & Garnet, Carved Profiles, 14K Gold, Art Nouveau 49.00
Jewelry, Ring, Oval Red Stone, 14K Gold, Openwork, Art Deco 22.00
Jewelry, Ring, Pearl, 14K Gold, Art Deco 10.00
Jewelry, Ring, Peridot & 2 Rubies, 14K Gold, Art Deco 18.00
Jewelry, Ring, Pink Coral, Elongated, Fancy Gold Work, 14K Gold 31.00
Jewelry, Ring, Pink Sapphire & Gold Flowers, 15K Gold, Art Deco 38.00
Jewelry, Ring, Pink Sapphire & 3 Rubies, 14K Gold, Art Deco 35.00
Jewelry, Ring, Pink Sapphire, 14K Gold, Art Deco 25.00
Jewelry, Ring, Profile Of Indian Woman, Garnet, 14K Gold, Art Nouveau 44.00
Jewelry, Ring, Rectangular Red Stone, 10K Gold Mounting, Art Deco 13.00
Jewelry, Ring, Rectangular Tourmaline & 4 Rubies, 14K Gold, Art Deco 62.00
Jewelry, Ring, Red Stone With 2 Rubies, 14K Gold, Art Deco 35.00

Jewelry, Ring, Red Stone, Ruby On Each Side, 14K Gold, Art Deco 17.00
Jewelry, Ring, Rose-Cut Green Onyx, Yellow Gold Claw Setting, Victorian 20.00
Jewelry, Ring, Ruby & 2 Diamonds, 14K Pink Gold, Art Deco 39.00
Jewelry, Ring, Sapphire & 16 Diamonds, 14K Gold, Victorian 595.00
Jewelry, Ring, Sapphire, 14K White Gold Setting, Art Deco 38.00
Jewelry, Ring, Seed Pearl, 14K Gold, 3 Joined By Loop, C.1850 .... 185.00
Jewelry, Ring, Sterling Silver, Carved Angel & Floral, Art Nouveau 15.00
Jewelry, Ring, Sterling Silver, Cherub's Face, Art Nouveau 12.00
Jewelry, Ring, Swirled Leaf, 14K Gold, Art Nouveau 45.00
Jewelry, Ring, Topaz & 6 Cabochon Red Stones, 14K Gold, Art Deco 24.00
Jewelry, Ring, Wedding Band, 14K Gold, 1909, Size 8 1/4 In. 16.00
Jewelry, Ring, Woman & Leafy Ground, 14K Gold, Art Nouveau 48.00
Jewelry, Ring, Woman With Diamond Necklace, 14K Gold, Art Nouveau 92.00
Jewelry, Ring, Woman With Garnets In Hair, Sterling Silver, Art Nouveau 13.00
Jewelry, Ring, Woman With Marcasites Necklace, Sterling, Art Nouveau 19.00
Jewelry, Ring, Woman's Face, Garnet In Hair, Sterling Silver, Art Nouveau 14.00
Jewelry, Ring, Woman's Head With Garnet, Sterling, Art Nouveau 14.00
Jewelry, Ring, Woman's Head, 14K Gold, Art Nouveau 54.00
Jewelry, Ring, Woman's Profile, Garnet In Forehead, Sterling, Art Nouveau 13.00
Jewelry, Ring, Woman's Profile, Marcasite Necklace, Sterling, Art Nouveau 19.00
Jewelry, Ring, Woman's Profile, Opal On Curl, 14K Gold, Art Nouveau 37.00
Jewelry, Ring, Woman's Profile, 4 Diamonds In Hair, 14K Gold, Art Nouveau 48.00
Jewelry, Ring, Yellow Gold, Engraved Initial D, Art Deco 95.00
Jewelry, Ring, 2 Hands Holding Garnet Cluster, 14K Gold, Victorian 40.00
Jewelry, Ring, 2 Profiles With Garnet & Opal, 14K Gold, Art Nouveau 49.00
Jewelry, Ring, 22 Diamonds In 3 Rows, 18K Gold & Platinum, Victorian 94.00
Jewelry, Ring, 3 Diamonds, Woman & Flowers, Openwork, 14K Gold, Art Nouveau 62.00
Jewelry, Ring, 3-Dimensional Cherub's Face, Sterling, Art Nouveau 12.00
Jewelry, Ring, 4 Rose Diamonds, 14K Gold Setting, Victorian 85.00
Jewelry, Ring, 4 Rubies, 3 Diamonds, Pink Gold, Art Deco 65.00
Jewelry, Ring, 5 Fire Opals, 14K Gold Band, Victorian 38.00
Jewelry, Ring, 5 Rubies, 14K Pink Gold, Art Deco, Size 6 1/2 In. 29.00
Jewelry, Ring, 6 Rubies & 3 Diamonds, Pink Gold, Fan Setting, Art Deco 75.00
Jewelry, Spectacles, 5 In. .... *Illus* 18.00
Jewelry, Stickpin Holder With Attached Gold Saucer, Hand-Painted, Signed 32.50
Jewelry, Stickpin, Gold And Onyx, Diamond Center, Octagonal, Engraved Gold 30.00
Jewelry, Stickpin, Tie, Gold, Indian On Face, 1854 .... 45.00
Jewelry, Watch, see Watch

John Rogers statues were made from 1859 to 1892. The originals were bronze, but the thousands of copies made by the Rogers Factory were of painted plaster. Eighty different figures were made.

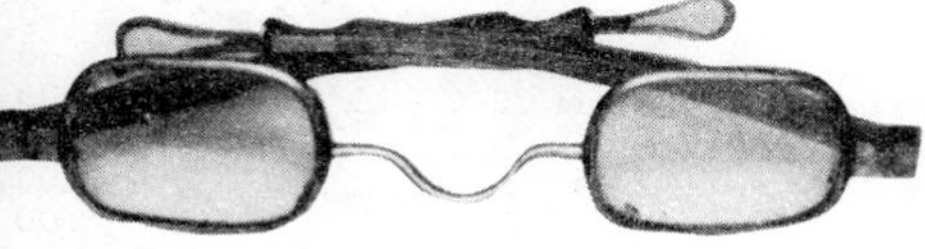

Jewelry, Spectacles, 5 In.

John Rogers, Group, Checkers Up At The Farm, 1875, 20 In.High

(See Page 274)

John Rogers, Group, Coming To The Parson, 1870, 22 In.High

John Rogers, Group, The Tap On The Window, 1874, 19 1/2 In.High

John Rogers, Group, Uncle Ned's School, 1866, 20 In.High

John Rogers, Group, Wounded To The Rear/One More Shot, 23 In.

John Rogers, Group, Checkers Up At The Farm, 1875, 20 In.High .... *Illus* 425.00
John Rogers, Group, Coming To The Parson, 1870, 22 In.High .... *Illus* 350.00
John Rogers, Group, Fugitive Story, Repainted White 535.00
John Rogers, Group, The Tap On The Window, 1874, 19 1/2 In.High .... *Illus* 375.00
John Rogers, Group, Uncle Ned's School, 1866, 20 In.High .... *Illus* 575.00
John Rogers, Group, Weighing The Baby, Repainted 435.00
John Rogers, Group, Wounded To The Rear/One More Shot, 23 In. .... *Illus* 325.00
Jones, McDuffie, Tile, Calendar, 1881 .... 95.00
Judaica, Box, Spice, Tower Shape, Filigree Hinged Door, 5 Flags Mark, Sterling 165.00
Judaica, Cup, Kiddush, Russian, Silver, 1 3/4 In., Pair 60.00
Judaica, Holder, Spice, Castle With Round Turrets, Chasing, 7 In. 135.00
Judaica, Spice Holder, Round Turret, Sterling, 7 In. 130.00
Judaica, Spice Holder, Six-Sided Turret, Sterling, 8 1/2 In. 180.00

Jugtown pottery refers to pottery made in North Carolina as far back as the 1750s. In 1915 Juliana and Jacques Busbee set up a training and sales organization for what they named Jugtown Pottery. In 1921 they built a shop at Jugtown, North Carolina, and hired Ben Owen as a potter in 1923. The Busbees moved the Village Store where the pottery was sold and promoted to 37 East Sixtieth Street in New York City. Juliana Busbee sold the New York store in 1926 and moved into a log cabin near the Jugtown Pottery. The pottery ended production in 1958.

Jugtown, Creamer, Blue, C.1925 .... 9.75
Jugtown, Tea Set, Salt Glaze, Gray, Cobalt Decoration, 3 Piece 75.00
Karlsbad, Coffee Maker, Drip, 2 Cup Coffeepot 14.00

Kate Greenaway, who was a famous illustrator of children's books, drew pictures of children in high-waisted Empire dresses. She lived from about 1846 to 1901. Her designs appear on china, glass, and other pieces.

Kate Greenaway Type, Figurine, Girl & Boy In Sunday Best, 5 1/2 In., Pair 70.00
Kate Greenaway Type, Figurine, Girl With Toy Sailboat, 7 In. 35.00
Kate Greenaway, Almanac, 1884, Leather Bound 55.00
Kate Greenaway, Almanac, 1887, Language Of Flowers 35.00
Kate Greenaway, Almanac, 1925 .... 22.00
Kate Greenaway, Autograph Album, 6 Color Plates, Leather Bound, 1882 .... 45.00
Kate Greenaway, Book, Almanac For 1888 .... 60.00
Kate Greenaway, Book, April Baby's Book On Tunes, Nov., 1900 .... 50.00
Kate Greenaway, Book, Babies, Cloth, 1907 .... 18.00
Kate Greenaway, Book, Birthday Book, Warne 25.00
Kate Greenaway, Book, Language Of Flowers, Routledge & Sons, London, 80 Page 55.00
Kate Greenaway, Book, Little Ann 45.00
Kate Greenaway, Book, Marigold Gardens 50.00
Kate Greenaway, Book, Speilmann & Layard, 300 Page, 53 Color Plates 99.00
Kate Greenaway, Bowl, Limoges, 4 In. 20.00
Kate Greenaway, Box, Jewel, Wood, Lacquered, 4 Children Running 50.00
Kate Greenaway, Butter Pat, Silver Plate, Boy Figural 55.00
Kate Greenaway, Button, Boy & Girl Sitting On Fence, Brass On Blue Steel 28.00
Kate Greenaway, Card, Christmas, Girl With Racquet 15.00
Kate Greenaway, Card, Greeting, Boy Wearing Pink Coat, Hat & Cane 15.00
Kate Greenaway, Card, Greeting, Head & Shoulders Of Little Boy 15.00
Kate Greenaway, Card, Greeting, Head & Shoulders Of Little Girl 15.00
Kate Greenaway, Cup, Sterling Silver 65.00
Kate Greenaway, Doll, Floradora, Bisque Head, Composition Body, 13 In. 125.00
Kate Greenaway, Figurine, Bisque, Full Figure, 7 In. 65.00
Kate Greenaway, Figurine, Girl & Boy, 5 3/4 In., Pair 85.00
Kate Greenaway, Figurine, Girl & Puppy & Boy & Sack, Bisque, 14 In., Pair 225.00
Kate Greenaway, Fork, Child's, Helen On Back, Sterling Silver 25.00
Kate Greenaway, Inkwell, Figural, Metal Holder, Dog In Relief, 5 X 3 1/4 In. 42.50
Kate Greenaway, Match Holder, Bisque, Girl & Boy, Blue & White 52.00
Kate Greenaway, Match Holder, Boy In Pink Trousers, Bisque, Striker 50.00
Kate Greenaway, Match Holder, Girl With Orange Satchel At Side, Striker 32.00
Kate Greenaway, Match Safe, Silver Plate 40.00
Kate Greenaway, Napkin Ring, Figural, Boy Offers Cracker To Dog 75.00
Kate Greenaway, Napkin Ring, Figural, Boy With Baseball Bat 95.00
Kate Greenaway, Salt & Pepper, Boy In Striped Pants, Girl, Long Dress, Pair 95.00
Kate Greenaway, Salt & Pepper, Girl Wearing Bonnet & Boy Wearing Top Hat 50.00
Kate Greenaway, Salt, Girl In Blue Coat With Muff, 4 In. 25.00
Kate Greenaway, Salt, Girl In White & Gold Dress, 4 In. 20.00
Kate Greenaway, Saltshaker, Bonnet Girl 30.00
Kate Greenaway, Saltshaker, Porcelain, Pink Hat, Green Feather, 3 1/2 In. 18.00
Kate Greenaway, Spill, Double Figural, Aqua, Gilt, 4 X 6 In. 25.00
Kate Greenaway, Spoon, Demitasse, Silver, Girl, Pair 30.00
Kate Greenaway, Tea Set, Child's, Figures, 18 Piece 125.00
Kate Greenaway, Tile, Autumn, Brown To Sepia To Cream, 1881, Square, 6 In. 27.50
Kate Greenaway, Toothpick, Boy, Meriden 75.00
Kate Greenaway, Vase, Bud, Girl In Mint Green Dress, Bisque, 4 1/2 In. 50.00
Kate Greenaway, Vase, French Ceramic, Children, 4 In. 35.00
Kate Greenaway, Whistle, Figural 7.50

Kauffmann refers to the type work done by Angelica Kauffmann, a painter and decorative artist for Adam Brothers in England between 1766 and 1781. She designed small-scale pictorial subjects in the neoclassic manner. Most porcelains signed Kauffmann were made in the nineteenth century.

Kauffmann, Box, Trinket, Hand-Painted, Royal Vienna, 816, 3 In. 55.00
Kauffmann, Coffee Set, Fuchsia, Gold Florettes, Scenic, 7 Piece 325.00
Kauffmann, Creamer, Cobalt Ground, Scene In Oval Panel, Signed 37.50
Kauffmann, Creamer, Scenic, Golds & Reds, Blue Beehive Mark, Royal Vienna 75.00
Kauffmann, Cup & Saucer, Demitasse, Scenic 28.50
Kauffmann, Cup, Turquoise & Gold, Classic Panel, Gilt Handle, 2 1/2 In. 24.00
Kauffmann, Jar, Cracker, Signed 65.00
Kauffmann, Plate, Classic Scene, Royal Vienna, Austria, Beehive 95.00
Kauffmann, Plate, Cupids And Maidens, 8 5/8 In. 18.00
Kauffmann, Plate, Dancing Girls, 6 In., Pair 40.00
Kauffmann, Plate, Dancing Ladies, Blue & Gilt Edge, 8 1/2 In. 35.00
Kauffmann, Plate, Maiden & Sleeping Warrior, Blue & Gilt Edge, 8 1/2 In. 35.00
Kauffmann, Platter, Beehive Mark, 14 1/2 In. 75.00
Kauffmann, Vase, Classical Scene In Oval, Cobalt & Gilt, 4 In. 27.50
Kauffmann, Vase, Portrait, 3 Ladies, Gold Open Handles, 7 In. 158.00

Kayserzinn, see Pewter
Kaziun, see Paperweight, Kaziun

KELVA

Kelva glassware was made by the C.F.Monroe Company of Meriden, Connecticut, about 1904. It is a pale pastel painted glass decorated with flowers, designs, or scenes.

Kelva, Basket, White Shasta Daisies, Brass Color, Pink, 4 1/2 In. 88.00
Kelva, Box, Blue, Pink Floral, Paneled, 6 In. 175.00
Kelva, Box, 6-Sided, Blown-Out Rose, Signed, 3 X 2 1/2 In. 300.00
Kelva, Salt & Pepper, Silver Tops, 4 In. 125.00
Kelva, Vase, Apricot Color, Red Poppies, Green Foliage, Silver Rim, 8 In. 200.00
Kelva, Vase, Apricot, Flower Spray, Red Mark, Signed, 13 In. 260.00
Kelva, Vase, Green Ground, Beading On Rim, Floral, Signed, 13 In. 260.00

Kemple glass was made by John Kemple of East Palestine, Ohio, and Kenova, West Virginia, from 1945 to 1970. The glass was made from old molds. Many designs and colors were made. Kemple pieces are usually marked with a K on the bottom.

Kemple Glass, Milk Glass, Plate 10.00
Kemple, Box, Lions, Milk Glass, Oblong, 4 X 2 1/2 In. 19.50
Kemple, Box, Milk Glass, Round 3 1/2 In. 12.50
Kemple, Candlestick, Beaded Jewel, Milk Glass, 5 In., Pair 15.00
Kemple, Figurine, Hen, Amethyst, 7 1/2 In. 50.00
Kemple, Plate, Openwork Border, Applied, Berries, & Walnuts, 7 In. 17.50
Kenton Hills, Figurine, Dove, Oxblood, Adventurine Glaze, David Seylar, 7 In. 295.00

Kew Blas is the name used by the Union Glass Company of Somerville, Massachusetts. The name refers to an iridescent golden glass made from the 1890s to 1924.

Kew Blas, Candlestick, Bulbous Twisted Stem, Gold, Blue Green Sheen, 8 In. 250.00
Kew Blas, Goblet, Gold Iridescent, Twisted Stem, Blue, Green, & Purple Lights 505.00
Kew Blas, Rose Bowl, Green & Gold Chains, Gold Speckles, 4 In. 775.00
Kew Blas, Salt, Master, Signed, 4 X 1 In. 150.00
Kew Blas, Tumbler, Gold Luster, Pinched Effect, 4 3/4 In. .... 230.00 To 325.00
Kew Blas, Vase, Gold Iridescent, 10 In. 575.00
Kew Blas, Vase, Gold With Green Loopings, 10 In. 1750.00
Kew Blas, Vase, Green, Gold Fish Scale, Signed, 8 In. 475.00
Kew Blas, Vase, Peach Color, Orange King Tut, 4 1/4 In. 825.00
Kew Blas, Vase, Pulled Feather, 6 In. 825.00

Kewpies were first pictured in the 'Ladies' Home Journal' by Rose O'Neill. The pixielike figures became an immediate success, and Kewpie dolls started appearing in 1911. Kewpie pictures and other items soon followed.

Kewpie Doll, Plate, Signed Rose O'Neill 10.00

Kewpie, Bell, Blue, Figural Handle, Wedgwood 25.00
Kewpie, Bell, Brass Kewpie Handle 35.00
Kewpie, Bell, Figural, Brass 25.00
Kewpie, Bell, Figural, Wedgwood, Green 25.00
Kewpie, Book, Cordially, Rose O'Neill 7.50
Kewpie, Book, I Wanna Be Loved By You, Cameo 5.00
Kewpie, Bowl, Baby's, 2 Kewpies Inside, Made In U.S.A. 57.50
Kewpie, Box, Tin With Action Kewpies 25.00
Kewpie, Bride & Groom, Celluloid 20.00
Kewpie, Butter Pat, Kewpie In Center, Haviland & Co., Limoges 45.00
Kewpie, Camera, Conley, Box 14.00
Kewpie, Camera, Large 20.00
Kewpie, Candy Container, Clear Glass 48.00
Kewpie, Candy Container, Doll Standing By Barrel 65.00
Kewpie, Card, Advertising, Framed, Kewpie Soap 12.50
Kewpie, Card, Christmas, O'Neill 10.00
Kewpie, Card, Plate, Rose O'Neill, Kewpie With Book, Germany 125.00
Kewpie, Card, Plate, Rose O'Neill, Kewpie With Pen, Germany 125.00
Kewpie, Creamer, Green Jasperware, 7 Kewpies & Flowers, 2 1/2 X 3 In. 110.00
Kewpie, Creamer, Rose O'Neill, Jasperware, Blue & White, Germany 95.00
Kewpie, Creamer, Rose O'Neill, Wilson, Miniature 70.00
Kewpie, Cup & Saucer, Signed 70.00
Kewpie, Dish, Child's, Milk Glass, Signed Rose O'Neill Wilson, 1920 .... 75.00
Kewpie, Dish, Divided, Action Kewpies, Rose O'Neill 48.00
Kewpie, Dish, Feeding, Five Kewpies Scene 48.00
Kewpie, Dish, Royal Rudolstadt, Signed Rose O'Neill, Miniature, 3 Pieces, Set 35.00
Kewpie, Doll, Bisque, Blue Wings, Marked Germany, C.1915, 5 In. 65.00
Kewpie, Doll, Bisque, 5 1/4 In. 63.50
Kewpie, Doll, Bisque, 5 3/4 In. 75.00
Kewpie, Doll, Bisque, 9 In. 15.00
Kewpie, Doll, Brass, Standing, 5 In. 45.00
Kewpie, Doll, Bride, Rose O'Neill Incised, Satin & Lace, 6 1/2 In. 525.00
Kewpie, Doll, Cameo, Jointed, Blue Dress, Lace Trim, 14 In. 9.00
Kewpie, Doll, Cameo, 17 In. 35.00
Kewpie, Doll, Carnival, 13 In. 10.00
Kewpie, Doll, Celluloid, Wiggly Eyes, 5 In. 4.00
Kewpie, Doll, Celluloid, With Hats, Beads, Feathers, Marked Occupied Japan 9.00
Kewpie, Doll, Chalk, Movable Arms, C.1930, 13 In. 28.50
Kewpie, Doll, Composition, 13 In. 35.00
Kewpie, Doll, Crown Tuscan, 3 In. 12.00
Kewpie, Doll, Glass, Pink, Trade Kewpie Mark, 1 In. 35.00
Kewpie, Doll, Hot 'n Tot, Negro, Bisque, 4 1/2 In. 10.00
Kewpie, Doll, Huggers, Bisque, Japan, 2 3/8 In. 32.50
Kewpie, Doll, Incised O'Neill Feet, Germany 60.00
Kewpie, Doll, Japan, Celluloid, 3 In. 1.50
Kewpie, Doll, Jointed, 1966, 27 In. 29.50
Kewpie, Doll, Kewpie In Wicker Chair, Bisque, Marked Boston, 4 1/2 In. 32.00
Kewpie, Doll, Marked Kewpie, 6 In. 6.00
Kewpie, Doll, Negro, Bisque, 9 In. 27.50
Kewpie, Doll, O'Neill, Bisque, Movable Arms, 8 In. 125.00
Kewpie, Doll, Rose O'Neill Heart On Chest, Composition, Blue Wings, 12 In. 85.00
Kewpie, Doll, Rose O'Neill, Bisque, Blue Wings, Brown Eyes, 4 1/2 In. 60.00
Kewpie, Doll, Rose O'Neill, Bisque, Movable Arms, 5 1/4 n. 62.00
Kewpie, Doll, Rose O'Neill, Cameo, Jointed, Dressed, 27 In. 29.50
Kewpie, Doll, Rose O'Neill, Heart On Chest, Bisque, 7 1/4 In. 245.00
Kewpie, Doll, Rose O'Neill, Ho Ho, Vinyl, Cameo Label, 4 In. 4.50
Kewpie, Doll, Rose O'Neill, Japanese, Celluloid, 1 1/2 In. 4.00
Kewpie, Doll, Rose O'Neill, Rubber, Squeeze, 11 In. 55.00
Kewpie, Doll, Rose O'Neill, Vinyl, Cameo, 1971, 4 In. 4.50
Kewpie, Doll, Rose O'Neill, Vinyl, Cameo, 1976, 11 In. 10.00
Kewpie, Doll, Rose O'Neill, Vinyl, Jointed, Cameo Label, 27 In. 29.50
Kewpie, Doll, Seiberling Latex, Baldy, 7 In. 12.00
Kewpie, Dresser, Child's, 6 Kewpies, Tilting Mirror, Ivory Color, 16 1/2 In. 135.00
Kewpie, Flannel, Rose O'Neill, Holding Bottle, 1914 .... 15.00

Kewpie, Flannel, Rose O'Neill, Smelling Rose, 1914 .... 15.00
Kewpie, Hair Receiver, Rose O'Neill, High Relief Action Kewpies, Blue, White 175.00
Kewpie, Lamp, A.M.Weber, Patent 1918, Iron, Ivory Enamel, 8 In. 65.00
Kewpie, Letter Opener, Figural, Marked 27.50
Kewpie, Match Holder, Pewter 27.50
Kewpie, Mold, Chocolate, Double, Clips, 8 In. 35.00
Kewpie, Mold, Ice Cream, Four Kewpies Standing In A Row, Pewter, American 95.00
Kewpie, Mug, Milk Glass 25.00
Kewpie, Mug, Rose O'Neill, Germany 110.00
Kewpie, Napkin Ring, Figural 27.50
Kewpie, Opener, Letter, Figural Handle 25.00
Kewpie, Opener, Letter, Kewpie Handle 18.50
Kewpie, Paperweight, Doll Inside, Sulfide Type 27.50
Kewpie, Paperweight, Rose O'Neill, Star Shape 15.00
Kewpie, Paperweight, Rose O'Neill, Sulfide Type 27.50
Kewpie, Paperweight, Star Shape, Signed Rose O'Neill 15.00
Kewpie, Plate, Happy Days Are Here Again, Rose O'Neill, Japan, 1923, 8 In. 25.00
Kewpie, Plate, Rose O'Neill, 5 1/4 In. 45.00
Kewpie, Plate, 2 Kewpies, White, Green, & Beige, 5 1/4 In. 87.50
Kewpie, Plate, 6 Kewpies, Haviland, France, 7 1/4 In. 65.00
Kewpie, Postcard, C.1900 .... 7.50
Kewpie, Postcard, Valentine, 1925 .... 6.00
Kewpie, Poster, Showing Doll Given As Flour Coupon Premium, 22 X 17 In. 1.50
Kewpie, Shaker, Talcum Powder, Paper Labels, Rose O'Neill, 1913, 6 1/2 In. 55.00
Kewpie, Tea Set, Rose O'Neill 275.00
Kewpie, Teapot, Rose O'Neill Wilson, Rudolstadt 75.00
Kewpie, Thimble 6.00
Kewpie, Tie Tack, Warrior 25.00
Kewpie, Toothpick, Basket Holder 27.50
Kewpie, Toothpick, Kewpie With Basket, Pewter 27.50
Kewpie, Tray, Ice Cream, Rose O'Neill, Purity Ice Cream 85.00
Kewpie, Vase, Kewpie Attached To Vase, Bisque, 5 In. 395.00
Key, Dungeon, Flat, Deep Slotted 12.00
Key, Dungeon, Tubular Type, 3 In. 3.00
Key, Dungeon, Tubular Type, 4 In. 4.00
Key, Excelsior Hotel, Rome, Italy, Brass, Tag 16.00

Kimball, see also Cluthra

Kimball, Vase, Cluthra, Green, 7 X 7 In. 275.00
Kimball, Vase, Cluthra, White, Ovoid, 7 In. 130.00

Kitchen, see also Iron, Store, Tool, Wooden

Kitchen, Match Safe, see Match Safe

Kitchen, Baked Potato Holder, Holds 6 Spuds, 1909 .... 7.00
Kitchen, Beater, Rug, Wire 12.00
Kitchen, Board, Cabbage, Pine, 1 Blade, Scalloped Top, 22 X 8 1/2 In. 16.00
Kitchen, Board, Carved Springerle, 12 Designed, Signed Hoeflein 55.00
Kitchen, Board, Chopping, Wooden 2.50
Kitchen, Bottle, Sprinkler, Celluloid Lady 10.00
Kitchen, Bowl, Bird's-Eye Maple, Munsing, 11 1/4 In. 35.00
Kitchen, Bowl, Chopping, Hand-Hewn, Notched Handles, 21 1/2 In. 68.00
Kitchen, Bowl, Chopping, Wooden, Pierced For Hanging, 15 In. 22.00
Kitchen, Bowl, Maple Butter, 15 1/2 In. 30.00
Kitchen, Bowl, Maple, Impressed Munsing, 13 X 4 In. 30.00
Kitchen, Bowl, Mixing, Jadite, 9 1/2 In. 12.00
Kitchen, Bowl, Wood, 24 In. 65.00
Kitchen, Box Set, Salt, Pewter, Hinged Lids, Graduated, 3 Piece 325.00
Kitchen, Box, Candle, Sliding Lift Lid, Black Oak, Dovetailed, 17 In. 270.00
Kitchen, Box, Knife, Hand-Forged Nails, Rectangular 12.00
Kitchen, Box, Recipe, Oak, Dovetailed 5.00
Kitchen, Box, Refrigerator, Covered, Pink, Crisscross, 4 In. 5.00
Kitchen, Box, Salt, Blue & White, Indian, Good Luck Emblem, Wooden Lid 25.00
Kitchen, Box, Salt, Wooden, Slant Lid, Salt In Black Letters, Hanging 22.50
Kitchen, Breadboard, Carved Bread, Round 45.00
Kitchen, Breadboard, Carved Wood, German Writing, 1936, Round, 11 In. 35.00
Kitchen, Breadboard, Carved, Take Freely And Thankfully 75.00

Kitchen, Breadboard, From Hoosier Cabinet, 19 X 19 In. 7.00
Kitchen, Breadboard, Pennsylvania Dutch, Handle, Hanging Type, Round 40.00
Kitchen, Breadboard, Round, Give Us This Day Our Daily Bread 60.00
Kitchen, Breadboard, Wooden, Carved Bread & Design 45.00
Kitchen, Breadbox, Granite, Domed Lid, White, Bread In Black Letters, 14 In. 37.00
Kitchen, Butter Bowl & Paddle, 16 In. Paddle 45.00
Kitchen, Cabinet, Oak, Flour Bin, Varnished 110.00
Kitchen, Cabinet, Spice, Oak, 8 Drawer 60.00
Kitchen, Cabinet, Wooden Counter Top, 2 Glass Doors 450.00
Kitchen, Cabinet, 4 Doors & Drawers, 68 In. 100.00
Kitchen, Can, Cream, Gray Granite, Wire Bail Handle, Tin Lid, 11 X 6 In. 27.00
Kitchen, Candy Pot, Copper, Pouring Spout, Tilt Handle, Dovetailed 185.00
Kitchen, Canister Set, Pewter, Domed Lids, 11 3/4 To 7 1/2 In., 4 Piece 650.00
Kitchen, Canister Set, Tin, Oriental Scenes, 5 Piece 35.00
Kitchen, Carving Set, E.H.Tryon, Phila., Stag Handles, Sterling Tips, 3 Piece 65.00
Kitchen, Castor, Coiled Wire, Hard-Boiled Egg, Holds 5, Carrying Ring, 7 In. 23.00
Kitchen, Chopper, Food, Hand-Forged Iron Blade, Wooden Handle 6.95
Kitchen, Chopper, Food, Single Blade, Hand-Forged Iron, Wooden Handle 6.95
Kitchen, Chopper, Food, Universal, Patent 1897-1900 .... 5.00
Kitchen, Chopper, Raisin, The Everett, Wood & Wire, 3 In. 40.00
Kitchen, Churn, Butter, Glass 15.00
Kitchen, Churn, Butter, Glass, Wooden Paddles, 6 Quart 25.00
Kitchen, Churn, Butter, Quebec, Wooden, Red Finish, Stretcher Base 75.00
Kitchen, Churn, Butter, Ureka, 12 Gallon 70.00
Kitchen, Churn, Butter, Wooden, Tan Paint, Dasher, Lapped Hoops, 18 1/2 In. 165.00
Kitchen, Churn, Butter, Wooden, 14 In. 40.00
Kitchen, Churn, Dazey, April, 1907, Tin, 23 In. 28.00
Kitchen, Churn, Dazey, December, 1917, Tin, 21 In. 28.00
Kitchen, Churn, Dazey, Glass, 15 In. 20.00
Kitchen, Churn, Dazey, Glass, 8 Quart, 15 In. 22.00
Kitchen, Churn, Dazey, 1/2 Gallon 25.00
Kitchen, Churn, Dog Treadle, 2 Sections, Arm Connector 360.00
Kitchen, Churn, Drum With Iron Crank & Wooden Paddles, Tin 43.00
Kitchen, Churn, F.P.Goold & Co., Brantford, Stoneware, C.1850 .... 275.00
Kitchen, Churn, Glazed, Brown, Carrying Handle, Lid & Dasher, 12 X 8 In. 52.00
Kitchen, Churn, Stoneware, Dash Type 42.50
Kitchen, Churn, Tin 140.00
Kitchen, Churn, Tin, Square, 28 In. 55.00
Kitchen, Churn, White Cedar, Wooden, Table Model, 16 In. 65.00
Kitchen, Churn, 6 Gallon, Tone Ware 90.00
Kitchen, Clock Jack, Fireplace, Rotates Spit, Weight Driven 450.00
Kitchen, Coffee Grinder, see Coffee Grinder
Kitchen, Coffeepot, Blue Granite, 3 Quart 25.00
Kitchen, Coffeepot, Brass & Copper, Ceramic Lining, Wooden Handle, 10 1/2 In. 45.00
Kitchen, Coffeepot, Child's, Drip, Aluminum, Wooden Handle 7.50
Kitchen, Coffeepot, Tin, Copper Bottom, 1 1/2 Gallon 50.00
Kitchen, Coffeepot, Tin, Copper Bottom, 3 Quart 30.00
Kitchen, Coffeepot, Tin, 3 Quart 35.00
Kitchen, Colander, Cottage Cheese, C.1920, Metal, Covered, 3 Legs, 4 In. 50.00
Kitchen, Colander, Graniteware, Gray, Handled 6.00
Kitchen, Colander, Green With White 8.00
Kitchen, Container, Milk & Cream, Pottery, Yellow, 10 In. 35.00
Kitchen, Corer, Apple, Folk Art, Hand Carved, 4 In., Bone 25.00
Kitchen, Corkscrew, Walnut Handle, 6 In. 5.00
Kitchen, Crimper, Pie, Wheel, Brass, Victorian, 4 1/2 In. 12.00
Kitchen, Crimper, Pie, Wooden Handle .... *Illus* 35.00
Kitchen, Crock, Butter, Blue & Gray, Cover, Corn Flower & Lattice, 7 X 5 In. 42.00
Kitchen, Crock, Butter, Blue, Butterfly Designs, Bail, 5 1/2 In. 28.00
Kitchen, Crock, Gray, Shepley Written On Banner In Cobalt Blue 145.00
Kitchen, Cup, Measuring, Creamy Yellow Glass 8.00
Kitchen, Cutter, Apple, Round, Iron, Rollman Mfg.Mt Joy, Pa. 12.00
Kitchen, Cutter, Biscuit, Knob Handle, Wood, Colonial Type 35.00
Kitchen, Cutter, Cabbage, Wooden 7.50
Kitchen, Cutter, Cookie, Bunny 9.00

Kitchen, Crimper, Pie, Wooden Handle

(See Page 279)

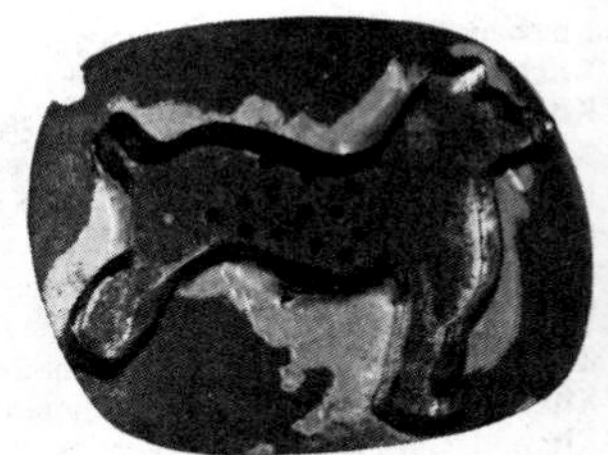

Kitchen, Cutter, Cookie, Lamb, Tin, 4 In.

Kitchen, Cutter, Cookie, Lamb, Tin, 4 In. .... *Illus* 10.00
Kitchen, Cutter, Cookie, Songbird, Tin, Small 14.00
Kitchen, Cutter, Cookie, 1/2 Moon, Tulip On Stem Handle, 5 In. 10.00
Kitchen, Cutter, Kraut, Wood, 23 In. 10.00
Kitchen, Cutter, Kraut, Wooden With Sliding Box 15.00
Kitchen, Cutter, Kraut, 18 In. 10.00
Kitchen, Cutter, Slaw, Wooden, 6 In. Blade 9.00
Kitchen, Deep Frier, French-Fried Potatoes, Cast Iron, Table Model 15.00
Kitchen, Dipper, Copper, 4 3/4 X 11 1/2 In. 12.00
Kitchen, Dipper, Egg, Wire 2.00
Kitchen, Dipper, Ice Cream, Tin, Primitive, Cone Shape 12.50
Kitchen, Dipper, U.S.Kreamer, 1944, Embossed, Tin, Quart 8.00
Kitchen, Dish, Ice Box, Covered, Custard Glass, Green 15.00
Kitchen, Dish, Pie, Medinger, Glazed Inside, 10 In. 60.00
Kitchen, Dish, Refrigerator, Bartlett Collins, Covered, Green, Oval, 6 In. 3.50
Kitchen, Dough Board, Handle, 2 Ft. 48.00
Kitchen, Dough Box, Turned Legs, Breadboard Top, 20 1/2 X 36 In. 115.00
Kitchen, Drainer, Dish, Wire 3.50
Kitchen, Drier, Clothes, Wooden, Folding, Wall Type 16.00
Kitchen, Drying Rack, Wooden, 8 Arm, Wall Type 8.00
Kitchen, Dustpan, Child's, Tin, Painted Design 14.00
Kitchen, Dustpan, Child's, Tin, Red Paint 18.00
Kitchen, Egg Timer, Metal, Hanging, Picture Of Negro Lady 5.50
Kitchen, Eggbeater, Brass Plaque, 1874 .... 22.00
Kitchen, Eggbeater, Dover, Cast Iron 5.00
Kitchen, Eggbeater, Patented 1903, Small 12.00
Kitchen, Flatiron, Brass, 1 In. 10.00
Kitchen, Flatiron, Child's, Duck Shape, Trivet 29.00
Kitchen, Flatiron, Geneva, Embossed 4.00
Kitchen, Flatiron, Stewart, Patent 1923, Gas 25.00
Kitchen, Flatiron, Tailor's, Cast Iron, Twisted Handle 17.50
Kitchen, Flatiron, Theober, Sharp Nose 12.00
Kitchen, Flatiron, 1 Piece 12.50
Kitchen, Fluting Iron, Crown, 1875, Brass Rollers 40.00
Kitchen, Fork, Roasting, Hand-Forged, 2 Tines, Hole To Hang, C.1830, 19 In. 25.00
Kitchen, Fork, 3 Tines, Wooden Handle, 11 In. 7.00
Kitchen, Frypan, Acme, Patent Nov.1876, Steel, 6 In. 7.95
Kitchen, Frypan, Open Hearth, Cast Iron, Hand-Forged Handle, C.1850, 12 In. 89.00
Kitchen, Funnel, Canning, Glass 5.00
Kitchen, Funnel, Canning, Metal 1.00
Kitchen, Grater, Crescent Shape, Tin 4.00
Kitchen, Grater, Horseradish, Enterprize, Sears, Patent 1893 .... 35.00
Kitchen, Grater, Nutmeg, Hand-Punched Tin 25.00
Kitchen, Grater, Nutmeg, Mechanical, Little Rhody 28.00
Kitchen, Grater, Nutmeg, Mechanical, The Edgar 22.00
Kitchen, Grater, Nutmeg, Tin 2.50

Kitchen, Grater, Nutmeg, Tin, 5 In. .... *Illus* 10.00
Kitchen, Grater, Pierced Tin On Hickory Board, 32 1/2 X 7 1/4 In. 38.00
Kitchen, Grater, Slaw, Wooden, Footed, 10 1/4 X 3 1/4 In. 28.00
Kitchen, Grater, Wood & Tin, Hand-Pierced, 11 1/2 X 2 1/4 In. 46.00
Kitchen, Griddle, Cast Iron, Bail Handle, Round, 17 1/4 In. 15.00
Kitchen, Grill, Rotary, Wrought Iron .... 300.00 To 400.00
Kitchen, Grinder, Coffee, Elna, Metal 22.50
Kitchen, Grinder, Coffee, Lap Type, Taller Than Usual 37.00
Kitchen, Grinder, Coffee, Tin, Lift Lid, Drawer, Decoration 55.00
Kitchen, Grinder, Coffee, Wall Mounted, Dated 1935, With Cup, Universal 45.00
Kitchen, Grinder, Food, Keen Kutter 9.00
Kitchen, Grinder, Nutmeat, Hazel Atlas 4.50
Kitchen, Grinder, Poppy Seed 35.00
Kitchen, Grinder, Poppy Seed, Antique White & Brass, Kosmos 18.00
Kitchen, Hammer, Meat Tenderizer, Hatchet Type, 1911 .... 6.00
Kitchen, Hotplate, For Wood Stove, Never Burn, Metal 5.00
Kitchen, Icebox Set, Depression Glass, Green, 14 Piece 45.00
Kitchen, Icebox, Cherry Wood, Brass Hinges & Knobs, 6 Doors, 6 Ft. 125.00
Kitchen, Icebox, Pine 95.00
Kitchen, Icebox, Porcelain Lined 195.00
Kitchen, Icebox, Walnut, Victorian 725.00
Kitchen, Ice Cream Maker, Wooden Bucket 25.00
Kitchen, Iron, Colt, Gas 27.50
Kitchen, Iron, Fluting, Brass Rollers, Dated Aug.1879 .... 40.00
Kitchen, Iron, Fluting, Crown, Brass Rollers, Stencilled 42.00
Kitchen, Iron, Fluting, Eclipse, Brass Rollers, Table Clamps 40.00
Kitchen, Iron, Fluting, Marked M.Mahoney, Troy, N.Y., Pat.1877 .... 7.95
Kitchen, Iron, Gas, Coleman 8.00
Kitchen, Iron, Gas, Coleman, Blue Enamel, Trivet, Pump, Filler Can 19.00
Kitchen, Iron, Gas, Ideal Co., Springfield, Ohio, 1911 .... 12.50
Kitchen, Iron, Gas, Laundry Maid 7.50
Kitchen, Iron, Gas, Montgomery Ward, Accessories, Original Box 12.00
Kitchen, Iron, Gas, Montgomery Ward, Quick Light, 1936, Fuel Can & Wrench 15.00
Kitchen, Iron, Kerosene, Diamond 15.00
Kitchen, Iron, Pennsylvania Dutch Heart Trivet With Handle, 2 1/2 In. 16.00
Kitchen, Iron, Waffle, Wrought Iron, Heart Design, Signed Klafrestrom 45.00
Kitchen, Juicer, Aluminum 4.00
Kitchen, Juicer, Fry, Opalescent 18.00
Kitchen, Juicer, Lemon, Sunkist, Blue Milk Glass 12.00
Kitchen, Juicer, Milk Glass 6.50
Kitchen, Juicer, Sunkist, Pink 15.00
Kitchen, Juicer, Wearever Aluminum 8.00
Kitchen, Kettle, Jelly, Brass, 12 1/4 In. 48.00
Kitchen, Kettle, Jelly, Iron Handle 55.00
Kitchen, Kettle, Rome Stove Works, Iron 17.00
Kitchen, Knife, Food Chopping, Double Bladed 5.00

Kitchen, Grater, Nutmeg, Tin, 5 In.

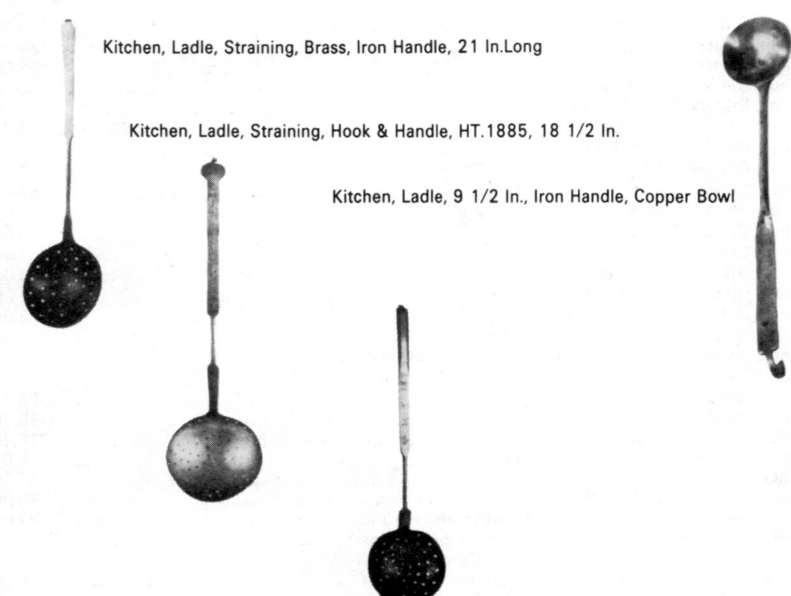
Kitchen, Ladle, Straining, Brass, Iron Handle, 21 In.Long

Kitchen, Ladle, Straining, Hook & Handle, HT.1885, 18 1/2 In.

Kitchen, Ladle, 9 1/2 In., Iron Handle, Copper Bowl

Kitchen, Ladle, Straining, Iron, 18 1/2 In.Long

Kitchen, Knife, Food Chopping, Double Bladed, Wooden Handle 5.00
Kitchen, Ladle, Hand-Carved Wood 65.00
Kitchen, Ladle, Hand-Forged Iron, 8 In. 18.00
Kitchen, Ladle, Straining, Brass, Iron Handle, 21 In.Long .... *Illus* 210.00
Kitchen, Ladle, Straining, Hook & Handle, "H.T.1885," 18 1/2 In. .... *Illus* 90.00
Kitchen, Ladle, Straining, Iron, 18 1/2 In.Long .... *Illus* 45.00
Kitchen, Ladle, 9 1/2 In., Iron Handle, Copper Bowl .... *Illus* 120.00
Kitchen, Lifter, Patented Five Way 22.00
Kitchen, Masher, Potato, Maple 7.50
Kitchen, Masher, Potato, Universal, Metal 8.00
Kitchen, Masher, Potato, Wooden .... 5.00 To 6.50
Kitchen, Masher, Wood, Knob Top, 7 1/4 In. 18.00
Kitchen, Measure, Gill, Pewter 45.00
Kitchen, Measure, Pint, Pewter, Tapered, Waisted, Tulip 95.00
Kitchen, Measure, Quart, Pewter, Tapered, Waisted, Tulip 125.00
Kitchen, Measure, Wooden, Peck & 1/2 Peck 32.50
Kitchen, Measure, 1/2 Gill, Pewter 35.00
Kitchen, Measure, 1/2 Pint, Pewter 25.00
Kitchen, Measure, 1/2 Pint, Pewter, Tapered, Waisted, Tulip 65.00
Kitchen, Measure, 1/4 Gill, Pewter 30.00
Kitchen, Mill, Sausage, Cast Iron, Dated 1873 .... 15.00
Kitchen, Mill, Sausage, Enterprise, 1886 .... 8.00
Kitchen, Mill, Sausage, Interior Knives, Cast Iron 12.00
Kitchen, Mill, Sausage, Keen Kutter 10.00
Kitchen, Mill, Sorghum, 8 In. Pulley, 24 X 10 In. 28.00
Kitchen, Mixing Bowl, Blue Spongeware, 10 In. 65.00
Kitchen, Mixing Bowl, Stoneware, Green, Embossed Waves & Shells, 8 1/2 In. 22.00

Kitchen, Mold, see also Pewter, Mold, Tin, Mold

Kitchen, Mold, Ice Cream, see Pewter, Mold, Ice Cream

Kitchen, Mold, Biscuit, Oval, Cast Iron 8.50
Kitchen, Mold, Butter Pat, Wooden 24.00
Kitchen, Mold, Butter, Acorn & Leaf, Brass Hook, 6 X 5 1/2 In. 20.00

Kitchen, Mold, Butter, Sheep Design, 3 Pat

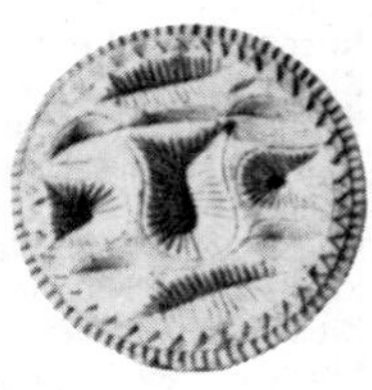
Kitchen, Mold, Butter, Wood Carving, 4 In.Diameter

Kitchen, Mold, Butter, Wood Carving, 5 In.Diameter

Kitchen, Mold, Butter, Wood Carved Eagle, 3 3/4 In.Diameter

Kitchen, Mold, Butter, Acorn, Wooden, Carved, Plunger Type, Round, 1 1/2 In. 12.00
Kitchen, Mold, Butter, Carved, Walnut, Round, 3 1/2 In. 12.50
Kitchen, Mold, Butter, Cow, Glass 50.00
Kitchen, Mold, Butter, Dovetailed, Wooden 6.50
Kitchen, Mold, Butter, Five-Petal Flower 25.00
Kitchen, Mold, Butter, Five-Petal Flower, Round 30.00
Kitchen, Mold, Butter, Flower, Wooden, Carved, Plunger Type, Round, 1 1/2 In. 12.00
Kitchen, Mold, Butter, Glass 45.00
Kitchen, Mold, Butter, Maple, Iron Ring Around Center 25.00
Kitchen, Mold, Butter, Maple, 2 Piece, Rectangular, 2 Flowers 40.00
Kitchen, Mold, Butter, Pine, 5 X 3 X 2 3/4 In. 9.50
Kitchen, Mold, Butter, Pineapple, Maple Wood, Round, 4 3/4 In. 50.00
Kitchen, Mold, Butter, Pineapple, Patented April 17, 1866 .... 12.00
Kitchen, Mold, Butter, Pineapple, Redware 140.00
Kitchen, Mold, Butter, Rectangular, Double Strawberry 60.00
Kitchen, Mold, Butter, Sheep Design, 3 Pat .... *Illus* 185.00
Kitchen, Mold, Butter, Star Print 30.00
Kitchen, Mold, Butter, Star, Rectangular, Lb. 22.50
Kitchen, Mold, Butter, Star, Wooden 22.00
Kitchen, Mold, Butter, Swan 60.00
Kitchen, Mold, Butter, Swan, Wooden, Lb. 25.00
Kitchen, Mold, Butter, Wheat, Wooden, 1/2 Lb. 45.00
Kitchen, Mold, Butter, Wood Carved Eagle, 3 3/4 In.Diameter .... *Illus* 185.00
Kitchen, Mold, Butter, Wood Carving, 4 In.Diameter .... *Illus* 130.00
Kitchen, Mold, Butter, Wood Carving, 5 In.Diameter .... *Illus* 120.00
Kitchen, Mold, Butter, Wood, Round, Pound Size, 8-Petal Cosmos Stamp 45.00
Kitchen, Mold, Butter, Wood, 5 1/2 X 3 1/4 In., Nickel-Plated Brass 18.00
Kitchen, Mold, Butter, Wooden, Dovetailed 6.50
Kitchen, Mold, Butter, 2 Lb., Brown Glass Cow On Plunger, Wooden Handle 45.00

Kitchen, Mold, Candle, see also Tin, Mold, Candle

Kitchen, Mold, Candle, 12 Tube, Tin 42.00
Kitchen, Mold, Candle, 12 Tube, Tin, Handmade 38.00
Kitchen, Mold, Candle, 12 Tube, 2 Handles, Loop For Hanging 13.00
Kitchen, Mold, Candle, 24 Tube, Pewter, Signed W.Webb 1150.00
Kitchen, Mold, Candle, 6 Tube, Tin 45.00
Kitchen, Mold, Candy, Christmas Bell, Metal, 10 X 13 In. 35.00
Kitchen, Mold, Candy, Circus Wagon, Metal, 10 X 13 In. 35.00

Kitchen, Mold, Candy, Clover, Metal, 10 X 13 In. 20.00
Kitchen, Mold, Candy, Iris, Metal, 10 X 13 In. 20.00
Kitchen, Mold, Cheese, Heart Shape, Tin 67.50
Kitchen, Mold, Chocolate, Hinged, Chicken In A Basket, 9 1/2 X 8 X 2 In. 32.50
Kitchen, Mold, Chocolate, Hinged, Double Bugs Bunny, 9 1/2 X 8 X 2 In. 32.50
Kitchen, Mold, Chocolate, Holland, Silver-Colored Metal, 21 Wafer, 10 X 16 In. 15.00
Kitchen, Mold, Cookie, Pineapple, Cast Iron 12.00
Kitchen, Mold, Cookie, 5 In. .... *Illus* 110.00
Kitchen, Mold, For Scotch Bread, Fluted Sides, Wooden, Cow Design 65.00
Kitchen, Mold, Hexagon Barrel Butter, Pewter Bands, Cow Print 125.00
Kitchen, Mold, Jello, Corn Cob, Pottery 22.50
Kitchen, Mold, Jello, Grape, Glass, Oval, 1897, 4 In. 24.00
Kitchen, Mold, Lobster, Copper, Tin Lined, Ring To Hang, 11 In. 22.00
Kitchen, Mold, Pudding, Center Tube, Tin, 7 In. 12.00
Kitchen, Mold, Pudding, Copper & Tin 38.00
Kitchen, Mold, Pudding, Figural, Lion, Tin Bottom, Tin Over Copper Lion 48.00
Kitchen, Mold, Pudding, Flower Bottom, Fluted, Tin, Hanging Ring, Quart 20.00
Kitchen, Mold, Pudding, Melon Ribbed, Covered, Gray Agate, 9 X 6 1/2 In. 26.00
Kitchen, Mold, Pudding, Melon, Tin, 2 Quart 14.00
Kitchen, Mold, Pudding, Melon, Tole 10.00
Kitchen, Mold, Pudding, Turk's Head, Redware, Glazed Outside 50.00
Kitchen, Mold, Pudding, Wear Ever Aluminum, No.110 .... 8.50
Kitchen, Mold, Sheaf Of Wheat, Tapered, Pottery, 6 1/2 X 5 In. 25.00
Kitchen, Muffin Pan, Iron, 13 In. .... *Illus* 95.00
Kitchen, Nutcracker, Alligator 39.95
Kitchen, Nutcracker, Hand-Carved Dog 22.00
Kitchen, Nutcracker, Lever Type, Wooden Base 5.00
Kitchen, Nutcracker, Sterling Silver Handles 25.00
Kitchen, Opener, Can, Sure Cut, C.1904 .... 3.50
Kitchen, Oven, Reflector, Tin, Spit 110.00
Kitchen, Oven, Stove Top, Tin, Portable 5.00
Kitchen, Paddle, Butter, Wooden, 5 X 4 In. 6.50
Kitchen, Pail, Milk, White Granite, Covered, 2 Quart 15.00
Kitchen, Pan, Bread Stick, Iron, 11 Sections 8.00
Kitchen, Pan, Bread, Tin, Oval 14.00
Kitchen, Pan, Copper And Iron, 18th Century, 19 In. 65.00
Kitchen, Pan, Corn Stick, Griswold, Cast Iron, 2 Piece 15.00
Kitchen, Pan, Muffin, Graniteware 6.00
Kitchen, Pan, Muffin, Graniteware, Gray, 6 Holes 14.00
Kitchen, Pan, Corn Stick, Iron 6.00
Kitchen, Pan, Muffin, Graniteware, Gray, 12 Holes 20.00
Kitchen, Pan, Muffin, 12 Holes 8.50
Kitchen, Pan, Muffin, 6 Holes, Fluted 6.50
Kitchen, Pan, Torte, Tin 1.50
Kitchen, Parer, Apple, Reading '78, First Patent 1873 .... 25.00
Kitchen, Pastry Crimper & Wheel, Wrought Iron 27.00
Kitchen, Peeler, Apple, Dated 1882 .... 25.00

Kitchen, Mold, Cookie, 5 In.

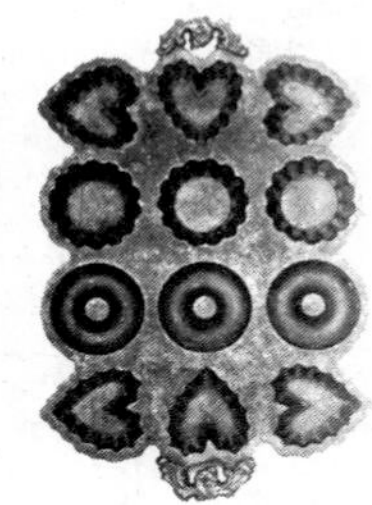
Kitchen, Muffin Pan, Iron, 13 In.

Kitchen, Peeler, Apple, Little Star 22.00
Kitchen, Peeler, Apple, Patent Jan.24, '82, Double Gear 32.50
Kitchen, Peeler, Apple, R.H.Co., Reading, Pa., Patent May 5, 1868, 4 Gears 28.00
Kitchen, Peeler, Apple, Sargent & Foster, Iron, Wooden Base, 10 X 4 1/4 In. 40.00
Kitchen, Peeler, Apple, Sinclair Scott Co., Baltimore, Iron 65.00
Kitchen, Peeler, Apple, Tiger Maple 175.00
Kitchen, Peeler, Apple, Turntable, Patent June 17, 1856 .... 30.00
Kitchen, Peeler, Apple, Walnut, Wheel Type, Turned Posts, Spear Made Of Fork 70.00
Kitchen, Peeler, Apple, White Mounting 16.00
Kitchen, Peeler, Corer, & Slicer, Apple, Wooden, Red Paint 200.00
Kitchen, Peeler, Potato, Hamlinite, Elliptical, Tin, 4 1/2 In. 20.00
Kitchen, Peeler, Potato, Nu Way 16.00
Kitchen, Picker, Blueberry 22.00
Kitchen, Piebird, Baby Chick, 5 In. 15.00
Kitchen, Piebird, Bird, 5 In. 12.00
Kitchen, Pitter, Cherry, Cast Iron, 13 In. 35.00
Kitchen, Pitter, Cherry, Enterprise 18.00
Kitchen, Plaiter, For Cloth Pleats, Wood & Metal, C.1850, 11 X 8 1/2 In. 12.00
Kitchen, Plate, Pie, Bake King, Tin 1.50
Kitchen, Poacher, Egg, Cast Iron, Fits Into Wood Stove, 7 Sections 15.00
Kitchen, Potholder, Bennett, Stove Warming, Cast Iron 6.00
Kitchen, Press, Garlic, Silver, Figural Bird 12.00
Kitchen, Press, Garlic, Wood 30.00
Kitchen, Press, Lard, Ash With Galvanized Pan With Handle, 44 In. 50.00
Kitchen, Press, Lard, Cast Iron, National, 1897 .... 20.00
Kitchen, Rack, Spoon, 11 Spoon Openings, Open Box At Base, Trefoil Carved 15.00
Kitchen, Rack, Towel, Wooden, 8 Arms, Folds Down 8.00
Kitchen, Reamer, Fry, Opalescent, Scalloped 30.00
Kitchen, Reamer, Jadite, Green 6.00
Kitchen, Reamer, Juice, McKee, Jade Green 15.00
Kitchen, Reamer, Lemon, Man's Head, Japan, 2 Piece 7.50
Kitchen, Reamer, McKee, Jade Green 14.50
Kitchen, Reamer, Orange Juicer, Opaque Green Glass 30.00
Kitchen, Reamer, Orange, Depression Glass, Green 5.00
Kitchen, Reamer, Orange, Green, Depression Glass 5.00
Kitchen, Reamer, Sunkist, Green Milk Glass 8.00
Kitchen, Reamer, Sunkist, Jadite 14.00
Kitchen, Reamer, Sunkist, Milk Glass 7.00
Kitchen, Reamer, Sunkist, White 17.50
Kitchen, Reamer, Sunkist, Yellow 40.00
Kitchen, Riser, Bread, Tin 25.00
Kitchen, Roaster, Chestnut, Tin 17.00
Kitchen, Roaster, Chestnut, Tin, Opens To Make 2 Pans, Handle, 16 In. 19.00
Kitchen, Roaster, Chestnut, Tin, Opens To Make 2 Pans, Handled, 20 In. 28.00
Kitchen, Roaster, Pigeon, Tripod With Adjustable Shield, Wrought Iron 300.00
Kitchen, Rolling Pin, Amber-Tinted Glass, Cork Closure 9.00
Kitchen, Rolling Pin, Aunt Jemima, Figural, Glass, 14 In. 30.00
Kitchen, Rolling Pin, Blue Glass, Painting Of Boat & Poem, 15 In. 85.00
Kitchen, Rolling Pin, Free Blown, Amethyst, 14 1/2 In. 210.00
Kitchen, Rolling Pin, Free Blown, Fiery Opalescent, 15 In. 70.00
Kitchen, Rolling Pin, Free Blown, Olive Green, 14 1/2 In. 75.00
Kitchen, Rolling Pin, Free Blown, Sapphire Blue, 16 In. 110.00
Kitchen, Rolling Pin, Free Blown, White Specks, Olive Green, 18 1/4 In. 130.00

Kitchen, Rolling Pin, Noodle, 13 In.

(See Page 286)

Kitchen, Spatula, Iron, 14 3/4 In.Long

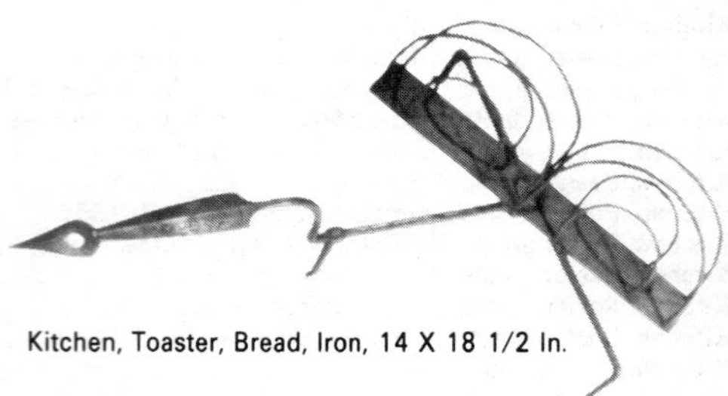

Kitchen, Toaster, Bread, Iron, 14 X 18 1/2 In.

Kitchen, Rolling Pin, Free Blown, 16 In. 20.00
Kitchen, Rolling Pin, Glass 10.00
Kitchen, Rolling Pin, Glass, Cork 7.00
Kitchen, Rolling Pin, Maple, Solid Handles 20.00
Kitchen, Rolling Pin, Milk Glass, Turned Maple Handles, 17 1/2 In. 32.50
Kitchen, Rolling Pin, Nailsea, Cobalt & White, C.1890, 14 In. 100.00
Kitchen, Rolling Pin, Nailsea, Cobalt, 1890, 14 In. 100.00
Kitchen, Rolling Pin, Nailsea, Cranberry & White Loopings, Blown, 9 1/2 In. 55.00
Kitchen, Rolling Pin, Nailsea, Green Tinged, Red & Blue Streaks 85.00
Kitchen, Rolling Pin, Noodle, 13 In. .... *Illus* 18.00
Kitchen, Rolling Pin, Pine, One Piece 4.00
Kitchen, Rolling Pin, Roll-Rite, Glass, Stopper 10.00
Kitchen, Rolling Pin, Screw Cap 8.00
Kitchen, Rolling Pin, White Glass 40.00
Kitchen, Rolling Pin, Wooden 2.75
Kitchen, Rolling Pin, Wooden, Child's, 10 1/2 In. 11.00
Kitchen, Rug Beater, Wire 4.00
Kitchen, Sadiron & Trivet, Brass, Miniature 5.00
Kitchen, Sadiron, Charcoal 12.50
Kitchen, Sadiron, Dover, U.S.A., 602, 3 1/2 In. 14.00
Kitchen, Sadiron, Miniature Swan 37.50
Kitchen, Sadiron, Sleeve, Wooden Handle 15.00
Kitchen, Sadiron, Wooden Handle .... 6.50 To 15.00
Kitchen, Salt & Pepper, Custard Glass 15.00
Kitchen, Salt Holder, Maple, Hole In Handle For Hanging, 10 In. 35.00
Kitchen, Saucepan, Copper, Dovetailed, Short Copper Handle, 5 X 3 In. 85.00
Kitchen, Saucepan, Copper, Dovetailed, 12 In. Copper Handle, 9 1/4 In. 145.00
Kitchen, Scale, Rev-O-Nec 4.00
Kitchen, Scoop, Cranberry 75.00
Kitchen, Scoop, Double Ended, Pewter, For Marrow 20.00
Kitchen, Scoop, Tin, 6 1/4 In. 6.00
Kitchen, Seeder, Raisin, Patent Dec.24, '88 .... 15.00
Kitchen, Sharpener, Knife, Steel Disc 3.50
Kitchen, Shaver, Ice, Hand Crank 26.00
Kitchen, Sheller, Corn, Cast Iron 12.50
Kitchen, Shredder, Peeler, Corer, & Scraper, Dandy, 1913, Tin, Wooden Handle 8.50
Kitchen, Sieve, Conical Splint, Stitched With Wire, 8 In. 28.00
Kitchen, Sieve, Horsehair, Iron Nails, Bound Edge, 8 In. 52.00
Kitchen, Sifter, Flour, Bromwell, Tin 2.50
Kitchen, Sifter, Flour, Dated May 17, 1887, Tin, Wooden-Handled Crank, 17 In. 65.00
Kitchen, Skillet, Bacon & Egg, Divided, Cast Iron 5.00
Kitchen, Skillet, Fireplace, Covered, Footed, Cast Iron, 14 In. 55.00
Kitchen, Skillet, Fireplace, Footed, Rattail Handle, Cast Iron, 11 In. 27.00
Kitchen, Smoke Jack, Fireplace, Spit Turns By Fan Activated By Hot Air 400.00
Kitchen, Spade, Butter, Wooden 6.00

Kitchen, Spade, Wooden 6.00
Kitchen, Spatula, Hand-Forged Iron .... 8.00 To 12.00
Kitchen, Spatula, Iron, 14 3/4 In.Long .... *Illus* 35.00
Kitchen, Spice Set, Tin, 6 Cans In Box, 8 In., 7 Piece 15.00
Kitchen, Spinning Wheel, see Tool, Spinning Wheel
Kitchen, Spoon Rack, Pine, Handmade, Drawer, Holds 15 Spoons, 26 In. 25.00
Kitchen, Sprinkler, Laundry, Lady, Celluloid 10.00
Kitchen, Squeezer, Lemon, Cast Iron & Porcelain 18.00
Kitchen, Squeezer, Lemon, Hand, Metal 3.50
Kitchen, Squeezer, Lemon, Porcelain 1.50
Kitchen, Squeezer, Lemon, T & D Mfg.Co., U.S.A., Wooden, Swan Mark 18.00
Kitchen, Squeezer, Lemon, White Depression Glass 4.00
Kitchen, Squeezer, Lemon, Wooden .... 10.00 To 29.00
Kitchen, Squeezer, Lemon, Wooden, Brass Hinges, 13 In. 40.00
Kitchen, Squeezer, Orange & Lemon, Hardwood, Silver Fittings, 1877, 13 In. 65.00
Kitchen, Squeezer, Orange Juice, Green Glass 8.50
Kitchen, Squeezer, Sunkist, Creamy Yellow Glass 15.00
Kitchen, Squeezer, Wooden, Hinged 25.00
Kitchen, Stamp, Butter, Cow 35.00
Kitchen, Stamp, Butter, Fruit & Leaf, Maple 40.00
Kitchen, Stamp, Butter, Hand-Hewn Birch, Carved, 9 1/2 In. 230.00
Kitchen, Stamp, Butter, Hearts & Diamonds 12.00
Kitchen, Stamp, Butter, Pineapple 22.00
Kitchen, Stamp, Butter, Wheat, Hand-Carved Wood 55.00
Kitchen, Stamp, Maple Butter, Fruit & Leaf 40.00
Kitchen, Strainer, Milk, Tin 2.00
Kitchen, Stuffer, Sausage, Enterprise Mfg. Co., C.1885, Painted, 20 In. 145.00
Kitchen, Stuffer, Sausage, Silver & Deming, Salem, O., Patent 1877, 2 Quart 85.00
Kitchen, Teakettle On Stand, Burner, 1892 .... 48.00
Kitchen, Teakettle, Copper 15.00
Kitchen, Teakettle, Copper & Brass, Gooseneck Spout, 8 1/2 Quart, 14 In. 325.00
Kitchen, Teakettle, Copper, 7 1/2 In. 45.00
Kitchen, Teakettle, White Porcelain Exterior, Cast-Iron Interior 62.50
Kitchen, Teapot On Stand, Nickel Plated, Burner Dated 1892, Black Handle 38.00
Kitchen, Thermometer, Butter Churn, Wooden Encased, B.Morse, Ithaca, N.Y. 25.00
Kitchen, Tin, Muffin, Granite, Gray, Dozen Muffins 12.00
Kitchen, Tin, Muffin, Graniteware, Gray, 12 Muffins 10.00
Kitchen, Toaster, Bread, Iron, 14 X 18 1/2 In. .... *Illus* 180.00
Kitchen, Toaster, Iron .... *Illus* 170.00
Kitchen, Tongs, Egg, France, Silver Metal 5.00
Kitchen, Tool, Iron, Fluting, Crown, Brass Rollers, Table Clamps 35.00
Kitchen, Tray, Cutlery, 11 3/4 X 9 In. .... *Illus* 90.00

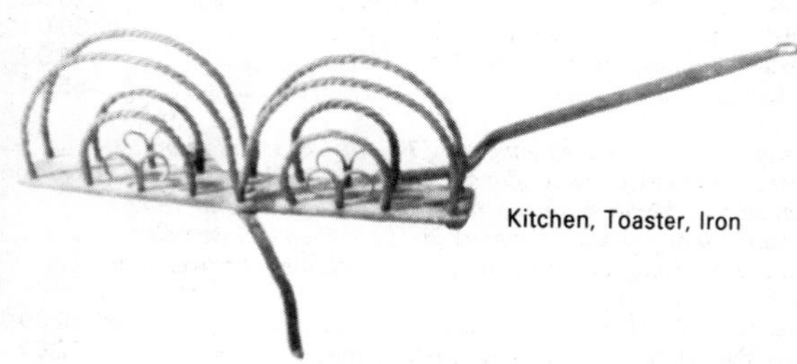
Kitchen, Toaster, Iron

Kitchen, Tray, Cutlery, 11 3/4 X 9 In.

Kitchen, Trencher, Wooden, Handles 55.00
Kitchen, Trivet, Broiler, Rotation, Wrought Iron, American, C.1800 ..... 475.00
Kitchen, Trough, Dough, Handmade, Wooden, 25 X 11 In. 58.00
Kitchen, Trough, Dough, Hole For Hanging, Oblong, 18 X 10 In. 34.00
Kitchen, Trough, Dough, Rectangular, 20 In. 42.00
Kitchen, Trough, Dough, Wooden, Rectangular, 20 In. 42.00
Kitchen, Turner, Flapjack, Hand-Forged Iron, 11 In. 29.95
Kitchen, Wafer Iron, Patent 1880, Fancy Design, 10 In. Handle, Round, 5 In. 65.00
Kitchen, Waffle Iron & Stand, Fireplace, Cast Iron 12.50
Kitchen, Waffle Iron, Arcade 18.00
Kitchen, Waffle Iron, B & W, Flowers & Stars, Range Top Type 48.00
Kitchen, Waffle Iron, Child's, Cast Iron, Wooden Handles 22.00
Kitchen, Waffle Iron, Favorite, No.8, Wooden Handle, Flip Over, Round 17.50
Kitchen, Waffle Iron, Griswold, Cast Iron, Ptd.1920 ..... 45.00
Kitchen, Waffle Iron, Heart Shape, Long Handle 140.00
Kitchen, Waffle Iron, 6 Panels With Different Designs 175.00
Kitchen, Waffle-Maker, Buster Brown, Cast Iron, Dated 1906 ..... 45.00
Kitchen, Washboard, Mother Hubbard, Wooden, Round Rollers 25.00
Kitchen, Washer, Clothes, Bell, Muncie, Ind., Wooden, 4 Legs 95.00
Kitchen, Whipper, Cream, Whippett, Original Box 2.50
Kitchen, Wrench, Jar, Liberty, Spirit Of 1776, Phila., 1926, Bell Center 18.00

Knowles, Taylor & Knowles, see KTK, Lotus Ware

Koch, Bowl, Apple, Louise, 9 1/4 In. 35.00
Koch, Bowl, Apples, Signed, 9 In. 35.00
Koch, Bowl, Berry, 3 Sauce Dishes, Green Cream Ground, Grapes, Set 75.00
Koch, Bowl, Grapes, Louise, 9 1/4 In. 35.00
Koch, Muffineer, Grapes, Signed 135.00
Koch, Plate, Apple, Louise, 8 1/2 In. 30.00
Koch, Plate, Apple, Uneven Rim, 8 In. 27.00
Koch, Plate, Apple, 7 1/2 In. 22.50
Koch, Plate, Apple, 8 1/2 In. 25.00
Koch, Plate, Apples, Leaves, Blossoms, Signed, 8 1/2 In. 40.00
Koch, Plate, Chop, Apple, Louise, 12 In. 110.00
Koch, Plate, Chop, Grapes, Louise, 12 In. 110.00
Koch, Plate, Grapes, Louise, 7 1/2 In. 25.00
Koch, Plate, Grapes, Louise, 8 1/2 In. 30.00
Koch, Plate, Green & Purple Grapes, Gold Scalloped Edge, Signed 20.00
Koch, Plate, Purple & Green Grapes, Gold Edge, Louise, Bavaria, 8 1/2 In. 22.50
Koch, Plate, Strawberries, Signed, 7 1/2 In. 35.00
Koch, Sauce, Apples & Cherries, Scalloped Gold Border 15.00
Korean Pottery, Vase, Green To Blue To Black Base, Tiger, C.1850, 12 In. 245.00
Korean Pottery, Vase, Multicolor Glaze, Tiger In Relief, C.1850, 12 In. 245.00
Korean Ware, Ashtray, Drip Glaze, Man Climbing Over Edge, 3 1/4 In. 20.00
Korean Ware, Jar, Chinese Dog Finial, Drip Glaze, Raised Figures, 6 1/4 In. 130.00
Korean Ware, Vase, Gray Crackle, Enamel Scene, Brown Center Band, 11 In. 48.00
Korean, Mug, Monkey 55.00

K.P.M

KPM is part of one of the marks used about 1723 by the Meissen Factory Konigliche Porzellan Manufaktur. Other firms using the letters include the Royal Manufactory of Berlin, Germany, that worked from 1832 to 1847. A factory in Scheibe, Germany, used the mark in 1928. The mark was also used in Waldenburg, Germany, and other German cities during the twentieth century.

KPM, Bowl, Apples & Leaves, R.Hershey, |916, 10 In. 30.00
KPM, Bowl, Faience, Pierced Handles, Pink Floral & Vines, Gold, Oval, 12 In. 22.50
KPM, Bowl, Fruit Center, 8 In. 6.00
KPM, Celery, Crown, White With Flowers, 12 1/2 X 5 In. 16.00
KPM, Charger, Bug, Flowers, & Scrolls, C.1870, 12 1/2 In. 35.00
KPM, Chocolate Pot, Roses, Ornate 35.00
KPM, Cup & Saucer, Hot Chocolate, Yellow & White, Signed 20.00
KPM, Figurine, Parrot, Green, Blue, White, Brown Filigree Base, Signed, 5 In. 75.00
KPM, Lithophane, Wine Taster & 2 Barrels In Cellar, 7 1/2 X 6 5/8 In. 185.00
KPM, Painting, Lady, Wagner, Framed, 7 X 5 In. 950.00
KPM, Painting, Psyche Am Wasserspiegel, L.Knohler, 13 X 11 In. 1250.00

KPM, Plaque, Blonde With Head Scarf, Smelling Roses, 5 X 7, Unframed 750.00
KPM, Plaque, Brunette, Cloaked, 5 X 7 In., Unframed 750.00
KPM, Plaque, Shakespeare Scene, Brass Frame, C.1835, Oval, 7 X 5 In. 750.00
KPM, Plate, Apples And Cherries, Lemon And Cherries, 6 3/4 In., Pair, Scepter 25.00
KPM, Plate, Floral Arrangement, Gold Border, 8 3/4 In. 125.00
KPM, Plate, Fruit, Lavender Shadow Foliage, Blue Mark 16.00
KPM, Plate, Fruit, White, 22K Gold Scalloped Rim, 8 1/2 In. 55.00
KPM, Plate, Green, Orange Floral, Silesia, 6 In., Pair 15.00
KPM, Plate, Hot, White, Pink & Blue Floral, Gold Filigree Border, 7 In. 9.00
KPM, Plate, Scenic, Man & Woman, Lattice Border, C.1763-70 .... 95.00
KPM, Plate, Sceptre Mark, Cherries & Apples 10.00
KPM, Plate, Sceptre Mark, Cherries & Lemons 10.00
KPM, Vase, Cherub On Each Side, Lilacs, 10 1/2 In. 325.00

K.T.&K. CHINA

KTK are the initials of the Knowles, Taylor and Knowles Company of East Liverpool, Ohio, founded by Isaac W.Knowles in 1853. They made Lotus Ware.

WARRANTED K.T.&K.

KTK Lotus Ware, see Lotus Ware

Ktk, Bouillon, Underplate, 2-Handled, Blue Florals 37.50
Ktk, Dish, Shell Shape, Ivory To White, Gold Trim, Footed, Joshua Poole, 9 In. 195.00
Ktk, Pitcher, Blue & Cream, 8 In. 75.00
Ktk, Pitcher, Hinged Pewter Lid, Floral, 12 In. 37.50
Ktk, Pitcher, Strawberry Transfer, Bulbous, 7 In. 15.00
Ktk, Plate, J.S.Kann, Washington, D.C., 9 In. 18.00
Ktk, Shaving Mug & Toothbrush Holder, White, Gold Trim, Pair 20.00
Ktk, Syrup, Decorated, Silver Plate Lid & Spout 65.00
Ktk, Vase, Gold Fishnet, Beaded Ruffled Top Over Blue, 5 X 3 3/4 In. 125.00
Ktk, Vase, 2-Handled, Hand-Painted Floral Sprays 85.00
Ktk, Vegetable Bowl, Covered, Bluebird 18.00
Ku Klux Klan, Book, Conspiracy, Senate Report, 1872 .... 8.50
Ku Klux Klan, Book, In Prophecy 8.50
Ku Klux Klan, Book, The Kloran, C.1920 .... 25.00
Ku Klux Klan, Magazine, The Kourier, 1933 .... 4.00
Ku Klux Klan, Music Sheet, Ku Klux Kismet, 1924 .... 18.00
Ku Klux Klan, Music Sheet, The Face Behind The Mask 9.00
Ku Klux Klan, Paperweight, Glass 6.00
Ku Klux Klan, Robe And Hood 35.00
Ku Klux Klan, Token, Atlanta, Ga., 1866-1966 .... 3.50
Ku Klux Klan, Uniform, C.1890 .... 95.00

Kutani ware is a Japanese porcelain made after the mid-seventeenth century. Most of the pieces found today are nineteenth century.

Kutani, Figurine, Jurojin Holding Staff Of Life, Coral & White, 18 In. 180.00
Kutani, Figurine, Porcelain, Standing Sage Holding Peach & Scroll, 11 In. 110.00
Kutani, Nut Set, Black, Silver Design, 5 Piece 30.00
Kutani, Plate, Red, Orange With Silver Overlay, C.1860, 8 In. 25.00
Kutani, Rose Jar 45.00
Kutani, Sugar & Creamer, Scenic, Pedestal Bases 35.00
Kutani, Vase, Bud, Bulbous, Florals On Gray, Signed In Japanese, 3 1/2 In. 22.00
Kutani, Vase, Panels Of Floral, Birds, House, & Figures, 9 1/2 In. 95.00
Kutani, Vase, Winding Path & Flowering Tree, Gold Outlines, Crackled, 7 In. 75.00
Lacquer, Box, Patch, Red & Gold, 3 Parts 45.00
Lacquer, Box, Red & Gold, Chinese Character On Top, 5 In. 25.00
Lacquer, Box, Red & Gold, Eagle In Pine Tree, 10 In. 95.00
Lacquer, Candlestick, Red, 4 In., Pair 5.95
Lacquer, Japanese, Box, Containing Sweetmeat Set, Black, Chikamamachie, 11 In. 15.00
Lacquer, Japanese, Box, Wooden, Gold, Quail On Lid, C.1900, 3 1/2 X 2 In. 125.00
Lacquer, Rice Bowl, Covered, Red 4.50

LALIQUE
LALIQUE

Lalique glass was made by Rene Lalique in Paris, France, between the 1890s and his death in 1945. The glass was molded, pressed, and engraved in Art Nouveau and Art Deco styles. Pieces were marked with the signature, "R. Lalique." Lalique glass is still being made. Pieces made after 1945 bear the mark "Lalique."

Lalique, Ashtray, Lovebirds, Frosted & Clear, 4 X 2 In. 37.50
Lalique, Atomizer, Frosted, 6 Nudes, Gold Metal Top, 3 1/2 In. 55.00
Lalique, Bottle, Perfume, Blask Stain, Beaded Curlicue, Pedestal, 5 1/2 In. 75.00
Lalique, Bottle, Perfume, Double Flower Shape 35.00
Lalique, Bottle, Perfume, Frosted & Clear, Tulip Pattern, Coty, 4 In., Pair 100.00
Lalique, Bottle, Perfume, Frosted Raised Design 68.00
Lalique, Bottle, Perfume, Hanging Blue Stopper, Art Nouveau, 4 1/2 In. 350.00
Lalique, Bottle, Perfume, Heart Shape 20.00
Lalique, Bottle, Perfume, Two Frosted Doves, 4 In. 30.00
Lalique, Bowl, Bird & Leaf, 9 1/4 X 4 In. 175.00
Lalique, Bowl, Detailed Dotted Circles & Scallops, 10 In. 110.00
Lalique, Bowl, Frosted, Ribbed, Carnations & Panels, 14 X 2 1/2 In. 100.00
Lalique, Bowl, Powder, Dragonfly On Lid, 3 X 2 In. 38.00
Lalique, Bowl, Ribbed Panels & Carnations, 14 X 2 1/2 In. 125.00
Lalique, Bowl, Roses & Cupids, 9 In. 65.00
Lalique, Bowl, White Frosted Iridescent, Art Deco Design, Signed, 4 In. 250.00
Lalique, Box, Powder, 3 Dancing Nudes On Cover, Signed 50.00
Lalique, Box, Round, Covered, Grecian Woman, Frosted, Beige, Signed, 4 1/4 In. 195.00
Lalique, Candlestick, Art Deco, Flower & Leaf Effect, 8 1/4 In., Pair 195.00
Lalique, Clock, Birds In Flight, Black Enamel Numerals, Omega, 8 In. 950.00
Lalique, Cordial, Band Of Frosted Fish Near Base, Pair 85.00
Lalique, Decanter, Gold, Molded Stopper, Signed 165.00
Lalique, Decanter, Square, Clear, Molded Bubbles, Signed R.Lalique, 8 X 6 In. 135.00
Lalique, Figurine, Bear, Iridescent Ice Color, Standing, Signed, 4 In. 150.00
Lalique, Figurine, Bird, White Frosted, Clear Base, Signed, 7 In. 150.00
Lalique, Figurine, Fish, Teal Blue, Art Deco, 2 X 2 In. 97.50
Lalique, Figurine, Lion, White Frosted, Reclining Position, Signed, 4 In. 150.00
Lalique, Figurine, Mourning Dove, Frosted, Turned Head, 2 1/2 In. 35.00
Lalique, Figurine, Nude Lady, 9 In. 175.00
Lalique, Figurine, Nude Male, White Frosted, Clear Base, Signed, 8 In. 250.00
Lalique, Figurine, Nude Woman, Bending Backward, Opalescent, 6 1/2 In. 170.00
Lalique, Figurine, Owl, Signed Lalique, France, 3 In. 55.00
Lalique, Figurine, White Frosted, 18th Century Garb, Signed, 6 In. 100.00
Lalique, Figurine, Woman In 18th Century Garb, White Frosted, 6 In. 100.00
Lalique, Finger Bowl & Underplate, Opalescent, Shells, Pair 225.00
Lalique, Finger Bowl, Enamel Medallion Of Black Cherries 29.50
Lalique, Glass, Frolicking Nudes In Relief 45.00
Lalique, Glass, Juice, Footed, Raised Fish Lower Third, Signed R.Lalique 55.00
Lalique, Glass, Raised Band Of 8 Roosters, Coq Et Plumes, 3 In. 20.00
Lalique, Globe, Opalescent, Swirled, Notch Cut, Bell Shape, 10 X 7 In. 190.00
Lalique, Globe, Swirl Cut & Notched, Bell Shape, 9 X 5 In. 195.00
Lalique, Inkwell, Art Nouveau Girls, Blue Opalescent, Signed, 5 In. 295.00
Lalique, Knife Rest, Baby's Head At Each End, Camphor Satin, 4 In., Pair 55.00
Lalique, Knife Rest, Frosted Ends, Script Signature, 3 3/4 In. 17.50
Lalique, Lamp, Base, Frosted Design, Clear Glass, No. 651, 4 X 3 In., Signed 95.00
Lalique, Lamp, Dancing Maidens, 10 1/2 In. 750.00
Lalique, Lamp, Nudes & Garlands Of Roses, 2 Parts, 10 1/2 In. 750.00
Lalique, Mascot Head, Eagle, 4 1/4 In. 250.00
Lalique, Ornament, Hood, Cock, Opalescent Glass 350.00
Lalique, Ornament, Hood, Female Head, Flowing Hair, Marble Base 425.00
Lalique, Plaque, Colored Nude Girl Bending, Old Mark, 9 X 9 In. 595.00
Lalique, Plaque, Green, Lovebirds & Flowers, Signed R.Lalique, 7 X 10 In. 475.00
Lalique, Plaque, Ice Green, 7 X 10 In. 650.00
Lalique, Plate, Cobalt, Embossed Tree, 8 In. 45.00
Lalique, Plate, Frosted Pansies Around Edge, 4 In. 35.00
Lalique, Plate, Nude Center, Flower Garlands, Signed R. Lalique, Frosted 150.00
Lalique, Sugar Shaker, Orange Egyptians, Frosted Ground, Signed, 5 1/4 In. 165.00
Lalique, Tray, Clear, Large Bird Center, Signed, 3 1/2 X 3 In. 45.00
Lalique, Tumbler, Crystal, Frosted Rickrack Band At Base, Flared 32.00
Lalique, Vase, Art Nouveau, Blue Frosted, 2 Cranes, Signed 7 1/4 In. 350.00
Lalique, Vase, Beaded Scallops, Signed In Mold And On Base, 4 3/4 In. 147.50
Lalique, Vase, Black Enamel Wavelike Designs, Mold Blown, C.1925, 8 In. 385.00
Lalique, Vase, Bowl, Embossed Birds, Footed, Signed 79.00
Lalique, Vase, Brown Stain, Wild Rose Handles With Thorns, 7 1/2 In. 225.00

Lalique, Vase, Charcoal Gray, Leaf Pattern, 6 1/2 In. 500.00
Lalique, Vase, Etched Crystal Nudes & Waves, 9 1/2 In. 350.00
Lalique, Vase, Frosted Cherries & Leaves, Bulbous, 7 In. 75.00
Lalique, Vase, Frosted Floral, Black Enamel Centers, Bowl Shape, 7 X 5 In. 165.00
Lalique, Vase, Frosted Nudes & Grapes, 12 Sides Base, 5 In. 55.00
Lalique, Vase, Frosted White To Clear, Vertical Bands Of Floral, 6 1/4 In. 65.00
Lalique, Vase, Frosted, Floral & Branch, Art Deco, 6 1/4 In. 95.00
Lalique, Vase, Frosted, Opalescent Snails, Blue Wash, 6 1/2 In. 265.00
Lalique, Vase, Frosted, 12 Molded Birds, Signed In Script, 6 3/4 In. 160.00
Lalique, Vase, Gray Stain On Frosted, Molded Thistles, 23 X 8 1/2 In. 125.00
Lalique, Vase, Holly, 8 In. 265.00
Lalique, Vase, Horses, R.Lalique, Paris, France, Signed, 6 X 8 In. 140.00
Lalique, Vase, Mold Blown, Swirling Fish, Opalescent, Signed, 6 1/2 In. 375.00
Lalique, Vase, Opalescent, Holly, Signed 7 In. 250.00
Lalique, Vase, Opaline Iridescent, Swimming Goldfish, Formosa, 6 3/4 In. 300.00
Lalique, Vase, Owl, 3 1/4 In. 39.00
Lalique, Vase, Roosters, Smoky, Signed R.Lalique, France, 6 X 4 In. 95.00
Lalique, Vase, Sculptured Dandelion Fernery In 4 Panels, 8 In. 235.00
Lalique, Vase, Smoke Gray, Rosebud Handles, Signed R.Lalique, 7 1/2 In. 325.00
Lalique, Vase, Three Nudes In Circle, 7 1/2 In. 135.00
Lalique, Vase, Turquoise, Roosters, Art Deco, Bulbous, 4 1/4 In. 315.00
Lalique, Vase, 5 Concentric Bands Decorated With Flowers, Beige, Signed 325.00
Lamartine, Vase, White, Rainbow Streaks, Scenic, House, Trees, 6 5/8 In. 265.00

Lamp, see also Bradley & Hubbard, Lamp; Burmese, Lamp
Handel, Lamp; Pairpoint, Lamp; Tiffany, Lamp

Lamp, A.Le Rainie, Bronzed Boy Holding Light, Sickle & Wheat, 13 In. 195.00
Lamp, Acme, Reflector, Miniature 49.00
Lamp, Aladdin, Alacite, Black Ground, Pale Pink Leaves, Marked, 17 In. 35.00
Lamp, Aladdin, Alacite, Ivory, No.B75 .... 85.00
Lamp, Aladdin, Alacite, Lincoln Drape 60.00
Lamp, Aladdin, Aluminum, Model C 20.00
Lamp, Aladdin, Bronze, Oil, Treasure 45.00
Lamp, Aladdin, Dark Background With Alacite Leaves & Finial 26.00
Lamp, Aladdin, Electric, Natural Alacite Glove, Blue Seas 165.00
Lamp, Aladdin, Figural Alacite Globe, Electric, Blue Oceans, Continents 180.00
Lamp, Aladdin, Green Alacite With Paper Shade 60.00
Lamp, Aladdin, Green Washington Drape 65.00
Lamp, Aladdin, Hanging, Brass & Brass Plated Frame, Electrified, 30 In. 145.00
Lamp, Aladdin, Nickel Plated Brass Lamp, Burner, Table 40.00
Lamp, Aladdin, No.B-85 .... 75.00
Lamp, Aladdin, No.B-92 .... 80.00
Lamp, Aladdin, No.9, With No.11 Flame Spreader 40.00
Lamp, Aladdin, No.11 .... 28.50
Lamp, Aladdin, Oil, Washington Drape, Burner & Chimney 55.00
Lamp, Aladdin, Pink Quilted, Opalescent Handles, 11 In. 25.00
Lamp, Aladdin, Red Beehive, Electrified 150.00
Lamp, Aladdin, Yellow Vertique Model B88 .... 195.00
Lamp, All Night, Brass, Nickel Reflector, Brass Hanger, 7 3/4 In. 32.00
Lamp, American, Sparking, Pewter, Saucer Base, 5 In. 225.00
Lamp, Art Deco, Dancing Couple, Alabaster & Marble, 24 In. 265.00
Lamp, Art Deco, Dancing Couple, Camphor Glass, 7 1/2 In., Pair 35.00
Lamp, Art Deco, Draped Lady Leaning On Apple Tree, Green Shade, 12 In. 46.00
Lamp, Art Deco, Frosted Glass Nude Holding Globe, 18 In. 95.00
Lamp, Art Deco, Girl Holding Hand-Painted Fan, Onyx Base, Italian Marble 250.00
Lamp, Art Deco, Gold Nudes, Camphor Glass Panel Behind, Signed, Dated, Pair 185.00
Lamp, Art Deco, Nude, Green With Amber Pyramid Shade, 10 X 7 1/2 In. 75.00
Lamp, Art Deco, Reverse Painted, Butterflies, Blue Skies, Marked LeMu 95.00
Lamp, Art Nouveau, Bent Glass, Table, Signed E.M. & Co. 165.00
Lamp, Art Nouveau, Bent Green Slag, 8 Panel Leaded Umbrella Shade 250.00
Lamp, Art Nouveau, Black Wrought Iron, Iridescent Shade, 15 1/2 In. 175.00
Lamp, Art Nouveau, Blue Teardrop Prisms, Metal Shade 500.00
Lamp, Art Nouveau, Bronze Patina On Metal, Aug.Moreau, Wall Hung, 26 In. 750.00
Lamp, Art Nouveau, Bronzed Standing Girl, Mother-Of-Pearl Sea Shell, 15 In. 150.00

Lamp, Art Nouveau, Girl With Ewer, Bronze & Ivory, P.Tereszczuk, 13 1/2 In. 750.00
Lamp, Asphaltum, Liquid Fuel, Tin, Crimped Saucer Base, Brass Burner, 5 In. 115.00
Lamp, Atterbury, Oil, Milk Glass, Goddess Of Liberty, Plume Font, 1881, 10 In. 150.00
Lamp, Banquet, Brass & Marble, 21 In. 85.00
Lamp, Banquet, Brass, C.1850, Electrified, 30 In. 128.00
Lamp, Banquet, Embossed Brass Base & Font, Blue Flowers, Electric 145.00
Lamp, Base, Milk Glass, Hand-Painted Florals, With Clear Chimney 75.00
Lamp, Beaded Glass, Basket Of Fruit Shape, 10 1/2 X 7 In. 95.00
Lamp, Beaded Heart, Clear Glass, Acorn Burner, Miniature 50.00
Lamp, Betty, Double, Complete 56.00
Lamp, Betty, Tin, 9 In. 65.00
Lamp, Betty, Wrought Iron, Double 32.00
Lamp, Bisque, Boar At Tree Trunk, Miniature 400.00
Lamp, Blown Glass, Crimped Handle, Pewter Collar, 2 1/4 In. 38.00
Lamp, Blown Glass, Three Mold, Green Pressed Base, McK G II-18 500.00
Lamp, Blown Glass, Whale Oil, Wafer Base, 8 1/4 In. 80.00
Lamp, Blown, New York State, Whale Oil, Aqua, Applied Handle, 5 In. 175.00
Lamp, Blown, Sparking, Applied Handle, 1 1/2 In. 30.00
Lamp, Blown, Sparking, Applied Handle, 2 In. 75.00
Lamp, Blown, Sparking, Conical Font, Applied Foot With Knob, 3 3/4 In. 75.00
Lamp, Blown, Sparking, Conical Font, Knob Stem, Applied Foot, 3 1/2 In. 70.00
Lamp, Blown, Sparking, Yellow-Tinted Spherical Font, Pressed Base, 3 In. 75.00
Lamp, Blown, Three Mold, Sparking, Applied Handle, Decanter Mold, 1 3/4 In. 200.00
Lamp, Blown, Three Mold, Whale Oil, Blue Pleated Font, Pressed Base, 7 In. 275.00
Lamp, Blown, Three Mold, Whale Oil, Green Base, McK G II-18 500.00
Lamp, Blown, Whale Oil, Amethyst Tint, Long Stem, Applied Foot, 6 1/2 In. 25.00
Lamp, Blown, Whale Oil, Cut Font, Pressed Flint Star Base, 9 1/2 In. 65.00
Lamp, Blown, Whale Oil, Etched Font, Waterfall Base, 7 In. 40.00
Lamp, Blown, Whale Oil, Knop Stem On Pressed Cup Plate Base, 6 1/2 In. 170.00
Lamp, Blown, Whale Oil, Light Bulb-Shaped Font, Quatrefoil Base, 9 In. 70.00
Lamp, Blown, Whale Oil, Long Stem, Applied Foot, 6 1/4 In. 20.00
Lamp, Blown, Whale Oil, Short Stem, Applied Foot, 4 3/4 In. 35.00
Lamp, Bohemian Glass Bowl, Frosted Vine Decoration, Milk Glass Base, 11 In. 115.00
Lamp, Bohemian Glass Font, Gilt Figural Stem, Child Seated, Waving 48.00
Lamp, Boudoir, C.1920, Iron Base, Hand-Painted Glass Shade, 12 In. 35.00
Lamp, Bouillotte, Brass, Crystal Trim, 14 In. Shade 350.00
Lamp, Bracket, Pattern Glass Font, Mercury Glass Reflector, 8 In. 48.00
Lamp, Bradley & Hubbard, see Bradley & Hubbard, Lamp
Lamp, Brass Carbide Miner's Forman, 6 In. 25.00
Lamp, Brass, Danish, C.1825, 14 In. 55.00
Lamp, Brass, Frosted & Green Shades, Art Deco, 19 1/2 In. 75.00
Lamp, Brass, Whale Oil, 3 Burners, Brass Chain, 22 In. 129.00
Lamp, Brevete Patent, Dresden China, Bouquets, Milk Glass Shade, 11 In. 150.00
Lamp, Bronze, Base, Mother-Of-Pearl Swirl, Clear Font, 30 In., Pair 1250.00
Lamp, Bronze, Black Enamel, Relief Painted Pagodas In Landscape, 23 In. 125.00
Lamp, Bronze, Lady & Russian Wolfhound, Ivory Face & Hands, 19 In. 125.00
Lamp, Bronze, Pierced Brass Dragon Design Shade, 11 1/2 In. 65.00
Lamp, Bronze, Rainbow Mother-Of-Pearl Swirl Shades, Marble Base, 30 In., Pair 1250.00
Lamp, Bull's-Eye, Emerald Green, Miniature 45.00
Lamp, Bull's-Eye, Finger Ring Handle, 3 3/4 In. 35.00
Lamp, Camphene, Pewter Fittings, Tiny 52.00
Lamp, Camphor Glass, Shepherd Dog Atop 5 In.Base 35.00
Lamp, Candle, Pottery Owl, Hanging, Ring At Top, 6 In. 8.50
Lamp, Capo-Di-Monte, Figural, 9 In. 120.00
Lamp, Cargo, Brass, Round, 14 In. 38.00
Lamp, Cargo, Brass, Square, 15 In. 48.00
Lamp, Carriage, Black Painted 30.00
Lamp, Champleve And Enamel, Green Font, C.1865 125.00
Lamp, Chandelier, Brass, Oriental, Leaf, Hinged Doors On 6 Shades, 18 In. 210.00
Lamp, Chandelier, French, C.1800, Iron Frame, Topaz & Amethyst Prisms, 42 In. 2800.00
Lamp, Chandelier, Louis XV, 6 Cut Glass Lights, Gilt Metal, 36 In., Pair 1700.00
Lamp, Chinese Champleve, Color Inserts Of People, Brass Design, 13 X 23 In. 225.00
Lamp, Chinese Tea Canister, Pair 150.00
Lamp, Chinese, Coal Oil, Bronze, Perforated Shade, Birds On Base, 26 In. 450.00

Lamp, Clambroth, Whale Oil, Clear Overlay Font, Brass Stem, Marble Base, 8 In. 90.00
Lamp, Clark's Crick Light, Fairy Pyramid, Clear Diamond Point Shade, 5 In. 65.00
Lamp, Classique 7001, Mantel, Frosted Cobalt & Red Trees, 14 In., Pair 200.00
Lamp, Clear Glass, Handled, Brass Collar, 1876, 3 1/4 In. 35.00
Lamp, Cobalt Blue, Oil, Ribbed On Font, 10 1/2 In. 85.00
Lamp, Copper, Tank & Burner, Amber Puffed-Out Chimney, Loop Handle, 4 1/2 In. 14.50
Lamp, Cosmos, see Cosmos, Lamp
Lamp, Cranberry Glass, Hanging, Electrified 185.00
Lamp, Cranberry Glass, Swirled, 10 1/8 In. 95.00
Lamp, Cranberry Thumbprint Pear-Shaped Font, Milk Glass Base, 26 In. 340.00
Lamp, Cranberry, Milk Glass Base, Daisy & Fern, Brass Fitting 110.00
Lamp, Crown Milano, Metal Canister Base, Floral, Jeweled Top, 20 In. 595.00
Lamp, Curling Iron Heater, Cut Star In Base, 5 1/2 In. 20.00
Lamp, Custard Glass, Jefferson Glass Co., 1906, Green, Embossed Daisies 75.00
Lamp, Custard Glass, Oil, Hearts, Pansies, 8 1/2 In. 125.00
Lamp, Cut Glass, Mushroom Hobstar, Strawberry Diamond Shade, 2 Light, 16 In. 1250.00
Lamp, Cut Glass, Oil, Diamond & Flute, Frosted Chimney, 13 1/2 In., Pair 250.00
Lamp, Cut Glass, Whale Oil, White & Sandhurst, C.1800, Thumbprint Cut, Pair 195.00
Lamp, Cut Glass, 2-Arm, Harvard Cutting, Hobstar & Prism, 23 In. 1200.00
Lamp, Cut Glass, 20 In., Shade 10 In. 1075.00
Lamp, Cut Velvet, Oil, Lavender, 10 In. 350.00
Lamp, Deitz, Eureka, Buggy, Kerosene, 7 In. 17.00
Lamp, Delft, Whale Oil, Blue & White, Boat Scenes, Chimney 75.00
Lamp, Depression Glass, English Hobnail, 6 1/4 In. 25.00
Lamp, Depression Glass, Lady Wearing Hoop Skirt, Pink, 8 In., Pair 12.00
Lamp, Depression Glass, Pink & White, 18 In. 35.00
Lamp, Desk, Abalone, Fabrique Amber Shade, Patent Pending, 1928, 17 In. 1495.00
Lamp, Desk, Small, Brass, Art Deco Female, Signed Rigual 75.00
Lamp, Dodge City, Wall, 18 In. Reflector, 25 In. 85.00
Lamp, Duffner Kimberly Style, C.1910, Leaded, Floral, Bronze Base, 24 In. 2350.00
Lamp, Dutch, Oil, Ceiling, Pull Down, White Porcelain Font & 12 In. Shade 175.00
Lamp, E.M.& Co., Kerosene, Nude Boy Holding Bowl, Floral Milk Shade, 30 In. 235.00
Lamp, Edward Miller, Brass Table, Hunting Scenes, 10 In.Dome 185.00
Lamp, Electrolier, Rose Quartz, Carved, Brass Base, 3 Sided, 19 In. 2500.00
Lamp, English, Parlor, Hanging, Brass, Glass Shade, Prisms, 36 X 14 In. 118.50
Lamp, Fairy, Amber Top, Diamond Point, Crystal Bottom, Marked Eden Lite 13.00
Lamp, Fairy, Blue Hobnail, Ruffled Insert, 3 Piece 65.00
Lamp, Fairy, Burmese Shade, Base Marked S.Clarke's Trade Fairy Mark 175.00
Lamp, Fairy, Burmese, Rose To Yellow, Crimped Bottom, Decorated, Large Size 650.00
Lamp, Fairy, Cameo Glass, Beehive Shape, Rose, Signed Degue, Frosted 85.00
Lamp, Fairy, Clark Base, Frosted Cranberry Dome Shade, 4 5/8 In. 395.00
Lamp, Fairy, Clarke Base, Overshot Opalescent Crown Shade, 4 3/8 In. 395.00
Lamp, Fairy, Clarke Base, Verre Moire Shade, Burglar's Horror Candle, 6 In. 475.00
Lamp, Fairy, Clarke Base, Yellow Satin Glass, Dome Shade, 3 3/8 In. 89.00
Lamp, Fairy, Clarke Cricklite Holder, Sapphire Blue Verre Moire, 7 In. 575.00
Lamp, Fairy, Clarke Pressed Glass Base, Ruffled Top Dome Shade, 4 5/8 In. 225.00
Lamp, Fairy, Clarke, Frosted Blue Verre Moire, White Loopings, 5 1/2 In. 395.00
Lamp, Fairy, Clarke, Pressed Base, Red Swirled Top, 5 In. 90.00
Lamp, Fairy, Miniature, Butterscotch Satin Glass, Ribbed Swirl 155.00
Lamp, Fairy, Miniature, Openwork Filigree Top, Jeweled Brass Base 160.00
Lamp, Fairy, S.Clark, Pyramid, Cobalt Blue, Diamond Quilted 35.00
Lamp, Fairy, Tin, Blue 7 In. 10.00
Lamp, Fairy, Votive, Cobweb Shade Of Filigree Brass, Jeweled, 6 1/4 In. 35.00
Lamp, Fairy, 3-Piece, One 8 In., One Shorter, One Cranberry Hobnail, Signed 180.00
Lamp, Finger, Blue Opalescent Windows, 2 1/2 In. 145.00
Lamp, Finger, Brass, 1 Hole Burner, 4 In. 32.00
Lamp, Finger, Green & Amber, Miniature 59.00
Lamp, Finger, Paneled, Amber, Miniature 65.00
Lamp, Flint, Blown, Green Ribbed Stem, McK G II-18 500.00
Lamp, Flint, Blown, Inverted Pear-Shaped Font, Pewter Collar, 9 In. 70.00
Lamp, Flint, Blown, Whale Oil, Pewter Burner, McK G I-6 80.00
Lamp, Flint, Oil, Blaze, Marble Base, Brass Connector, 8 1/2 In. 24.00
Lamp, Flint, Three Printie Block, Hexagonal, Pewter Collar, 9 1/2 In. 85.00
Lamp, Flint, Whale Oil, Armorial, Hexagon Pestle Base, Pewter 125.00

Lamp, Flint, Whale Oil, Blown, Pewter Burner, McK G I-6 .... 80.00
Lamp, Flint, Whale Oil, Ellipse, 8 1/2 In. 75.00
Lamp, Flint, Whale Oil, Pewter Top, 9 1/2 In., Pair 195.00
Lamp, Floor, Mahogany, Carved, Rams' Heads, Hoof Base, 6 Ft. 500.00
Lamp, Free Blown, Sparking, Knob Stem, 3 In. 70.00
Lamp, Free Blown, Sparking, Pressed Circular Stepped Base, 4 1/4 In. 80.00
Lamp, French Cameo, 3 Colors, Floral, Shade & Base Match, Signed Le Maitre 1500.00
Lamp, Geo.Anton, Monongehela City, Wash., Co., Pa., Miner"S, 2 1/2 In. 25.00
Lamp, German Porcelain, Owl, Yellow Glass Eyes, 5 In. 135.00
Lamp, Glass, Cable, Loop Handle, Hand Lamp 42.00
Lamp, Glass, Daisy Pattern, Apple Green Stem, 8 In. 42.50
Lamp, Glass, Fishscale Base, Loop Handle, 5 1/2 In. 21.00
Lamp, Glass, Whale Oil, Footed, 6 1/4 X 3 1/2 In. 75.00
Lamp, Goddess Of Liberty, Metal & Glass, Dated Metal Base, 11 1/2 In. 150.00
Lamp, Gone With The Wind, C.1879, Yellow, Pink Roses, Electrified, 21 In. 175.00
Lamp, Gone With The Wind, Desert Scenes, Kerosene, Ornate Slip In Fount 495.00
Lamp, Gone With The Wind, Grape Pattern, Puffed Out, Pink To Rose, 22 In. 425.00
Lamp, Gone With The Wind, Green & Rose Ground, Tiger Lilies, 30 In. 185.00
Lamp, Gone With The Wind, Jumbo Base, Yellow, Red Roses, Brass Tank 75.00
Lamp, Gone With The Wind, Pale Rose, Purple Iris, 20 In. 185.00
Lamp, Gone With The Wind, Pink Bottom, Metal Bottom 75.00
Lamp, Gone With The Wind, Pink Roses, Brass Font, Lacy Base, 21 1/2 In. 165.00
Lamp, Gone With The Wind, Red Satin, Embossed Roses On Metal Base, 26 In. 200.00
Lamp, Gone With The Wind, Red Satin, Poppies, Brass Pedestal, Ovoid Base 325.00
Lamp, Gone With The Wind, Red Satin, Round Embossed Oil Font, 31 In. 500.00
Lamp, Gone With The Wind, Tea Roses, 26 In. 285.00
Lamp, Gone With The Wind, White Satin, Grape & Leaf, 11 In. Globe 495.00
Lamp, Gone With The Wind, Yellow, Green Scrolls, 17 In. 145.00
Lamp, Greentown, Chocolate Glass, Wild Rose, 10 In. 435.00
Lamp, Hand, Applied Crimped Handle, Brass Collar, 4 In. 48.00
Lamp, Hand, Drum Shape, Strap Handle, Tin, 2 1/2 X 1 3/4 In. 55.00
Lamp, Hand, Pressed Glass, Drape, Bull's-Eye Chimney, 9 In. 30.00
Lamp, Handel, see Handel, Lamp
Lamp, Hanging Gas, Wellsbach, Brass, Opal Slant Shade, 4 Burner, 36 In. 595.00
Lamp, Hanging, Brass With Chocolate Glass Panels, 14 In. 40.00
Lamp, Hanging, Brass, 3 Fonts, Ball Shades, 30 X 24 In. 162.50
Lamp, Hanging, Cranberry With Prisms 625.00
Lamp, Hanging, Green Font With Roses, 14 In.White Shade, 42 Prisms, 38 In. 280.00
Lamp, Hanging, Hand-Painted Roses On Shade, Brass Frame, Dated 1895 .... 250.00
Lamp, Hanging, Opalescent Striped, Ornate Frame, Pull-Down Canopy, 13 In. 125.00
Lamp, Hitchcock, Mechanical 195.00
Lamp, Hurricane, Free Blown, 11 In., Pair 30.00
Lamp, Jefferson, Boudoir, Green Trees 195.00
Lamp, Jefferson, House & Trees Reflected In Water Scene, 19 In. 625.00
Lamp, Jiggs, Comic Character, Wooden, Electric, 20 In. 18.50
Lamp, Kerosene, Cabbage Rose Pattern 50.00
Lamp, Kerosene, Green Bowl, Milk Glass Bottom, C 1890, 10 In. 69.00
Lamp, Kerosene, Green Pattern Glass Bowl, Milk Glass Base, Medium Size 65.00
Lamp, Kerosene, Heart & Waffle Pattern 58.00
Lamp, Kerosene, Hobnail Pattern 22.50
Lamp, Kerosene, Openwork Shade, Jeweled, 11 1/2 In. 175.00
Lamp, Kerosene, With Iron 1881 Lacy Wall Bracket 34.00
Lamp, Kiss Bros., Windmill Scene 325.00
Lamp, Komax, Made In U.S.A., Brass, Conical, 3 1/2 In. 9.00
Lamp, Lady's Desk, Art Nouveau, Bronze, Brass, Deco Shade, 14 In. 145.00
Lamp, Lantern, Bicycle, Signed, 6 In. 48.00
Lamp, Leaded, Blue, 16-Petaled Daisies, 23 In. 450.00
Lamp, Leaded, Chocolate Glass Pieces, Red & Green Sets, Brass Base, Lamb Lamp 375.00
Lamp, Leaded, Dome Shade, Sculptured Leaf Base, 20 In. 1285.00
Lamp, Leaded, Pale Green, Pink & Green Floral Border, 23 In. 750.00
Lamp, Leaded, 6 Panel, Miniature 190.00
Lamp, Loetz Style, Blue Iridescent, Bronze Base, Paneled Shade, C.1890, 11 In. 350.00
Lamp, Log Cabin, Blown Handle Dated 1875 .... 225.00
Lamp, Louis Moreau, Charmeuse Girl, Bronze, Torch Light, Flame Shade, 28 In. 285.00

Lamp, Louis Moreau, Le Rythme De La Vaque, Bronze, Torch Light, 28 In. 285.00
Lamp, Mac-Beth, Nite Glow, Milk Glass Shade 28.00
Lamp, Mac-Beth, Nite Glow, Ruby Shade 28.00
Lamp, Madelon, Bronze Base, Floral & Jewels On Dome Shade, Tassels, 10 In. 115.00
Lamp, Metal Figurine, Signed Ruchot, Frosted Globe, Cut Stars, 32 1/2 In. 500.00
Lamp, Milk Glass Base, Cranberry Bowl, 10 In. 75.00
Lamp, Milk Glass, Atterbury, Clear Font With Spiral Brass Connector, 1873 .... 48.00
Lamp, Milk Glass, Blackberry Font, Milk Glass Base 48.00
Lamp, Milk Glass, Block & Dot Ball Shade, Acorn Burner, Miniature 95.00
Lamp, Milk Glass, Cosmos, Large 250.00
Lamp, Milk Glass, Double Step Base, Clear Font, 25 In., Gold & White Shade 150.00
Lamp, Milk Glass, Gaudy Rose, Blown Out Chimney 60.00
Lamp, Milk Glass, Glow, Dated 1895 .... 80.00
Lamp, Milk Glass, Hand-Painted, Rose Design, Brass Base, 20 In. 65.00
Lamp, Milk Glass, Hornet Burner, Embossed Base & Chimney, 9 1/2 In. 95.00
Lamp, Milk Glass, Kerosene, Brass Collar & Connector, 11 In. 85.00
Lamp, Milk Glass, Mantle Lamp Base, Florals, Berries, Light In Vase, 17 In. 60.00
Lamp, Milk Glass, Oil With Chimney 65.00
Lamp, Milk Glass, Oil, Embossed 1873, Clear Octagonal Font, Brass, 10 In. 48.00
Lamp, Milk Glass, Openwork Metal Base, White Umbrella Shade, 21 1/2 In. 160.00
Lamp, Milk Glass, Paneled Cosmos, Acorn Burner, Clear Chimney, S-241 .... 47.50
Lamp, Milk Glass, Raised Flower Design, Clear Chimney 45.00
Lamp, Milk Glass, Sulvan, Opalescent Shade, 1890 .... 195.00
Lamp, Milk Glass, Whale Oil, Loop & Petal Font, 9 In. 45.00
Lamp, Millefiori, Pink & White Canes On Mushroom Shade, Iron Base, 15 In. 295.00
Lamp, Millefiori, Shade, 15 In. 300.00
Lamp, Miner's Safety, Brass, Wolk 30.00
Lamp, Miner's, Brass, Justrite, 6 In. 24.00
Lamp, Miner's, 3 In. 14.00

The S numbers refer to the book "Miniature Lamps" by Frank R. and Ruth E. Smith

Lamp, Miniature, Bull's-Eye, Red, S-110 .... 45.00
Lamp, Miniature, Carlsbad, Austria, Flowers, Embossed, Burner, Chimney 35.00
Lamp, Miniature, Clear Cosmos, Complete With Shade 50.00
Lamp, Miniature, Cosmos, Pink Banded, Shade & Chimney, 8 1/4 In. 185.00
Lamp, Miniature, Cranberry Bull's-Eye & Base Trim 45.00
Lamp, Miniature, Cranberry Glass, Enameled Apple Blossom Base, 9 3/4 In. 275.00
Lamp, Miniature, Cranberry Glass, Enameled Flowers On Shade 375.00
Lamp, Miniature, Cresolene, Iron Holder, Milk Glass Chimney 22.00
Lamp, Miniature, Delft 150.00
Lamp, Miniature, Fairmount Glass Co., Indiana, C.1933, Camphor Base, Flutes 18.00
Lamp, Miniature, Frosted Font, S-114 .... 58.00
Lamp, Miniature, Glo Lamp, Milk Glass Shade, Ribbed Base, Marked 50.00
Lamp, Miniature, Gone With The Wind, Kerosene, Milk Glass, Acanthus 150.00
Lamp, Miniature, Goofus, Chimney 30.00
Lamp, Miniature, Grecian Key Shade And Base, Clear Glass, Acorn Burner 50.00
Lamp, Miniature, Handy, Cobalt 27.00
Lamp, Miniature, Hanging, Brass 39.50
Lamp, Miniature, Hobnail, Light Green 90.00
Lamp, Miniature, Kerosene, Bull's-Eye 35.00
Lamp, Miniature, Lincoln Drape, Clear Base 45.00
Lamp, Miniature, Little Buttercup 45.00
Lamp, Miniature, Little Buttercup, Clear Glass, Acorn Burner 35.00
Lamp, Miniature, Milk Glass, Blue Shading, Embossed Flowers 185.00
Lamp, Miniature, Milk Glass, Embossed Chimney, Blue & Gilt Trim, S-55 .... 64.00
Lamp, Miniature, Milk Glass, Majestic Embossed Plumes & Scrolls 195.00
Lamp, Miniature, Milk Glass, Maltese Cross, Embossed 60.00
Lamp, Miniature, Milk Glass, Reclining Elephant 250.00
Lamp, Miniature, Milk Glass, Virginia, Embossed 45.00
Lamp, Miniature, Milk Glass, Virginia, S-53 .... 38.00
Lamp, Miniature, Milk Glass, Yellow Iris On Shade, S-205 .... 210.00
Lamp, Miniature, Mt.Washington, Floral Design 195.00
Lamp, Miniature, Nutmeg, Cobalt Blue, S-29 .... 65.00
Lamp, Miniature, Nutmeg, Finger, Milk Glass Base, Patent Feb.27, 1877 .... 48.00

Lamp, Miniature, Pewter Font, Hornet Burner 25.00
Lamp, Miniature, Pink Cased, Melon Ribbed 85.00
Lamp, Miniature, Pressed Glass, Cosmos, Pink Band 225.00
Lamp, Miniature, Pressed Glass, Daisy & Button, Amber 47.50
Lamp, Miniature, Pressed Glass, Daisy With Bull's-Eye, Emerald Green, S-112 ..... 46.00
Lamp, Miniature, Pressed Glass, Emerald Green, Bull's-Eye, S-110 ..... 85.00
Lamp, Miniature, Pressed Glass, Kerosene, Daisy 25.00
Lamp, Miniature, Pressed Glass, Lincoln Drape 27.50
Lamp, Miniature, Pressed Glass, Lincoln Drape, Frosted & Clear 55.00
Lamp, Miniature, Pressed Glass, Lincoln Drape, Stippled 30.00
Lamp, Miniature, Pressed Glass, Paneled Star, Amber 225.00
Lamp, Miniature, Pressed Glass, Pineapple In Basket 295.00
Lamp, Miniature, Queens Burner, Kerosene, Embossed Pattern, Handle 35.00
Lamp, Miniature, Spanish Lace, Blue 250.00
Lamp, Miniature, Twinkle, Embossed Stars & Twinkle, Sapphire Blue 36.00
Lamp, Moe Bridges, Island, Trees, & Moon Scene, Blues, Handle Style, 12 1/2 In. 295.00
Lamp, Nellie Bly, Blue With White Flowers, S-219 ..... 125.00
Lamp, Night-Light, Conta & Boehne, Bisque, White, Red, Blue, & Green, 5 1/2 In. 195.00
Lamp, Night-Light, Frosted Glass Madonna, Black Amethyst Base, 8 1/2 In. 100.00
Lamp, Night-Light, Milk Glass, Round Metal Tank, Long Neck 32.00
Lamp, Night-Light, Porcelain Owl, Glass Eyes, 5 7/8 In. 168.00
Lamp, Night-Light, Pressed Hobstar Base, Ribbed English Shade, 9 In. 48.00
Lamp, Night, Art Nouveau, Black Glass Base, Blown Out Roses, Glass Shade 48.00
Lamp, NuArt, Art Deco, Squirrel & Bird, Yellow Crackle Shade, Signed 80.00
Lamp, Oil, Blue Leaf And Hobnail Design, Applied Handle 48.00
Lamp, Oil, Crystal, Bull's Eye, Holdspot 70.00
Lamp, Oil, Eye Winker Pattern, Wick & Chimney, 18 In. 80.00
Lamp, Oil, Swinging Iron, Mercury Reflector 75.00
Lamp, Oil, Zigzag & Diamond Font, Brass Stem, Square Iron Base 25.00
Lamp, Overlay, Flint, Blue & Clear, Gilt Decoration, Burner, Chimney, Globe 480.00
Lamp, Overlay, Rose, White, Clear, Flint, 11 1/2 In. 700.00
Lamp, Pairpoint, see Pairpoint, Lamp
Lamp, Paperweight, Cut Base, Orange & Yellow Lilies, Spatter Leaves, 12 In. 18.00
Lamp, Parlor, Hanging, Floral Champagne Satin Glass, Prisms, Victorian, 36 In. 195.00
Lamp, Parrot, Red With Green Head, Black Base, 13 1/2 In. 100.00
Lamp, Pate De Verre, Nude In White Against Red, A.Walter, 11 In. 1250.00
Lamp, Patent, Sep.20, 1870, On Base, Handled, 4 In. 25.00
Lamp, Pear-Shaped Font, Metal Openwork Base, Umbrella Shade, 21 1/2 In. 150.00
Lamp, Peg, Brass Burner & 2 Wick Tubes, 6 In. 50.00
Lamp, Peg, Glass, Spherical Font, 6 In. 30.00
Lamp, Perfume, Art Deco Ballerina, Salmon To White, Fulper Mark 75.00
Lamp, Petticoat, Star & Harp, Applied Handle, Double Brass Burner, 5 3/4 In. 160.00
Lamp, Piano, Embossed Baby Faces, Elaborate Base, Frosted Enameled Globe 650.00
Lamp, Pink Leaded Glass Shade, White Painted Metal Base, 15 In. 60.00
Lamp, Plume & Atwood, Hanging, Brass Font With Burner 47.50
Lamp, Porcelain, Lady With Mandolin, Germany 35.00
Lamp, Pressed Glass, Aladdin, Pink 75.00
Lamp, Pressed Glass, Atterbury Icicle, Marked 1868 ..... 37.00
Lamp, Pressed Glass, Bigler Font, Hexagonal Base, Brass Collar, 8 1/2 In. 40.00
Lamp, Pressed Glass, Boudoir, Etched Frosted Globe, Prisms, 14 In., Pair 75.00
Lamp, Pressed Glass, Bull's Eye, Clear Font, Brass Connection, Marble, 12 In. 65.00
Lamp, Pressed Glass, Bull's-Eye, Finger Handle, Miniature 40.00
Lamp, Pressed Glass, Centennial, Red, Blue Milk Glass Base, Oil, 17 1/2 In. 14.95
Lamp, Pressed Glass, Cobalt, Featherlike Design, Brass Collar, 8 1/4 In. 60.00
Lamp, Pressed Glass, Colored Flowers, Miniature 60.00
Lamp, Pressed Glass, Columbian Coin, Kerosene, Frosted, Half Dollars, 10 In. 85.00
Lamp, Pressed Glass, Coolidge Drape, Flint 70.00
Lamp, Pressed Glass, Corn, Corn Leaves, Wheat, 1880's, 7 1/2 In. 30.00
Lamp, Pressed Glass, Cranberry, Fern & Daisy, New Martinsville, Font Oil 95.00
Lamp, Pressed Glass, Diamond Sunburst, Applied Handle, Hand Lamp 24.00
Lamp, Pressed Glass, Drapery, Ornate Brass Foot, 23 In. 185.00
Lamp, Pressed Glass, English Hobnail, Applied Handle, Footed, 5 1/2 In. 30.00
Lamp, Pressed Glass, Fleur-De-Lis & Bull's Eye, Oil, Flint, Green Base 100.00
Lamp, Pressed Glass, Fleur-De-Lis, Clear 37.50

Lamp, Pressed Glass, Flint, Waffle & Thumbprint, 11 In. 35.00
Lamp, Pressed Glass, Harp, Flint, Finger, Applied Handle, 4 1/4 In. 98.00
Lamp, Pressed Glass, Lincoln Drape, Clear Font, Blue Shade 55.00
Lamp, Pressed Glass, Loop Font, Pewter Collar, 7 1/4 In. 65.00
Lamp, Pressed Glass, N.E.Glass Co., Washington, Brass Stem, Marble Base 90.00
Lamp, Pressed Glass, Oil, Bull's Eye And Peanut, Wick & Chimney 85.00
Lamp, Pressed Glass, Oil, Centennial, Amberina Color, Milk Glass Base, 18 In. 14.95
Lamp, Pressed Glass, Oil, Reverse Swirl, Blue, Opalescent, Clear Base, 8 In. 90.00
Lamp, Pressed Glass, Oil, 1, 000-Eye, Amber, 14 In. 95.00
Lamp, Pressed Glass, Peacock Feather, Oil, 10 In. 45.00
Lamp, Pressed Glass, Peanut, No.1, 8 1/2 In. 42.00
Lamp, Pressed Glass, Peanut, No.2, 8 1/2 In. 45.00
Lamp, Pressed Glass, Sawtooth, Bull's Eye Column, Pewter Whale Oil Burner 110.00
Lamp, Pressed Glass, Tree Of Life, Hand, Kerosene, 10 In. 75.00
Lamp, Pressed Glass, Waterfall Base, Blown Font, Cork Burner, 8 3/4 In. 55.00
Lamp, Pressed Glass, Whale Oil, Loop Font, 8 1/2 In. 30.00
Lamp, Pressed Glass, Yuma Loop Pattern, Handle And Foot 35.00
Lamp, Pull Down, Ornate Frame, Green Shade With Pink & White Roses, 14 In. 350.00
Lamp, Rayo, Nickel Plated Over Brass, Holder And 10 In. Opal Shade 88.00
Lamp, Reverse Painting Base, Indians, Ships, Sunset, Art Nouveau, 22 In. 800.00
Lamp, Reverse Painting Of Floral, Leaded, 8 Sections, 20 In. 285.00
Lamp, Reverse Painting Of Floral, Ornate Metalwork, 18 In. 375.00
Lamp, Reverse Painting Of Windmills, Sailboats, & Houses, 23 In. 395.00
Lamp, Reverse Painting, Sky With Apple Blossom And Blue Birds, 24 In. 500.00
Lamp, Roseville, Jonquil, 21 In. 60.00
Lamp, Sandwich Glass, Blue, Pressed Leaf & Flower Fonts, Opaque Base, Pair 250.00
Lamp, Sandwich Glass, Bull's Eye, Brass Stem, Marble Base 80.00
Lamp, Sandwich Glass, Flint, Thumbprint Font, Opalescent Baroque Base, 20 In. 110.00
Lamp, Sandwich Glass, Flint, Whale Oil, Heart & Thumbprint 135.00
Lamp, Sandwich Glass, Flint, Whale Oil, Sawtooth 110.00
Lamp, Sandwich Glass, Oil, Amethyst Overlay To Clear, Marble Base, 11 In. 500.00
Lamp, Sandwich Glass, Whale Oil, Amethyst, 10 In. 300.00
Lamp, Sandwich Glass, Whale Oil, Blue Frosted, Acanthus Leaf, Brass, 12 In. 275.00
Lamp, Sandwich Glass, Whale Oil, Overlay, Rose, White Clear, Burner, 1 1/2 In. 700.00
Lamp, Sandwich, Flint, Whale Oil, Inverted Sawtooth & Thumbprint, 9 1/2 In. 100.00
Lamp, Sapphire Blue, Arch Font, Hexagonal Cascade Base, Ring Shank, 10 In. 785.00

Lamp, Satin Glass, see Satin Glass, Lamp

Lamp, Sechrist Leaded Glass, Handel Gilt Bronze Lotus Leaf Base 3000.00
Lamp, Sevres, Brass Base, Hand-Painted 425.00
Lamp, Sevres, Silk Shade, Bisque Figure On Onyx Base 775.00
Lamp, Shade, Gas, Etched, Bell Tone, 5 X 8 X 7 In. 60.00
Lamp, Shanklin Brass Carbide 8.00
Lamp, Ship's, Round Lenses In Angular Brass Frame, 15 1/2 X 10 In. 85.00
Lamp, Simplex Lamp Co., N.Y., Alcohol, Tole, Pierced, 7 1/2 In. 35.00
Lamp, Sparking, Glass, Light Bulb-Shaped Font, Knob Stem, Applied Foot, 3 In. 80.00
Lamp, Sterling On Bronze, Urn Pattern, 16 X 8 In. 125.00
Lamp, Store Type, Hanging, Brass Font, Tin Shade, 31 In. 37.00
Lamp, Student, Brass, 2 Fonts, Electrified, 21 1/2 In. 150.00
Lamp, Student, Wall Hung, Welsbach Light Co., Nickel Brass, Cased Shade 210.00
Lamp, Student, 1875, Kerosene, Brass, Double Burner, 10 In. Green Shade 295.00
Lamp, Student, 2 Arms, Dark Aquamarine Shades, Adjustable, 28 In. 145.00
Lamp, Swirl, Matching Chimney, 8 In. 22.50
Lamp, T.G.Well, Astral, Marble Base, Etched Shade, Prisms, 1851, 18 1/2 In. 225.00
Lamp, Table, Brass, Ball Shade, 18 In. 27.50
Lamp, Table, Brass, Ball Shade, 23 In. 33.50
Lamp, Table, Brass, Embossed, Cased White Shade, 24 In. 55.00
Lamp, Table, Brass, Gooseneck, Frosted Shades, Electrified, 13 1/2 In. 25.00
Lamp, Table, Brass, Marble Column, Glass Shade & Prisms, 28 In. 125.00
Lamp, Table, Puffed Out, Red Grapes, Green Leaves, Brown Lattice, 21 In. 650.00
Lamp, The Kid, Jackie Coogan Productions, Marked Copyright 1925, Porcelain 35.00
Lamp, Three Metal Cherubs Holding Camphor Glass Shade, 13 1/2 In. 110.00

Lamp, Tiffany, see Tiffany, Lamp

Lamp, Tin, Drum Shape, Strap Handle, Old Wick 55.00
Lamp, Umbrella Shade, Pear Shape Metal Base, Glass Chimney, Floral Shade 145.00

Lamp, Vapo-Cresolene, Milk Glass Chimney, Patent 1888 .... 19.75
Lamp, Vapo-Cresolene, Milk Glass Chimney, With Stand 18.00
Lamp, Wall, Brass, Ball Shade, Ornate Font, 17 1/2 In. 90.00
Lamp, Washington, Brass Stem, Marble Base, New England Glass Co. 90.00
Lamp, Weller, Dickensware, Loving Cup, 3 Feet, 3 Handles, Iris & Leaves 395.00

The McK numbers refer to the book "American Glass" by George and Helen McKearin.

Lamp, Whale Oil, Amethyst Paneled Font, Marble Base, 10 In. 275.00
Lamp, Whale Oil, Blown, Green Flint Base, McK GIII-18 .... 500.00
Lamp, Whale Oil, Double Loop, 8 3/4 In. 60.00
Lamp, Whale Oil, Giant Sawtooth, 9 In. 90.00
Lamp, Whale Oil, Handled, 4 1/2 In. 15.00
Lamp, Whale Oil, Heart And Waffle Pattern, 9 1/2 In., 1850s 95.00
Lamp, Whale Oil, Opaque White, Pear-Shaped Font, Double Square Base, 11 In. 30.00
Lamp, Whale Oil, Paneled Font, Violet Blue, Marble Base, 10 In. 275.00
Lamp, Whale Oil, Petals Font, Waterfall Stem & Base, 11 1/2 In. 90.00
Lamp, Whale Oil, Punty & Loop, Pewter Burner 140.00
Lamp, Whale Oil, Sandwich Type, Blown And Cut Font, Brass Collar, 8 1/2 In. 85.00
Lamp, Whale Oil, Sandwich, Sweetheart, Pair, 11 In. 300.00
Lamp, Whale Oil, Star & Shield Font, Brass Stem, Marble Base, 9 1/4 In. 45.00
Lamp, Whale Oil, Star & Shield Pattern Font, Brass Stem, Marble Base, 7 In. 50.00
Lamp, Whale Oil, Tapered Blown Font, Gadrooned Base, Brass Burner 125.00
Lamp, Whale Oil, Tin, 7 In. .... *Illus* 55.00
Lamp, White Opaque, Opalescent Base, Lion & Basket Of Flowers Base, 8 In. 50.00
Lamp, White Slag Glass Shade, Triangle Shape, Daffodil Design, 17 In. 130.00
Lamp, Wicker, Table, Wicker Shade, 1917, 19 In. 45.00
Lamp, Wine Glass, Blown Font, Knop Stem, Round Base, 3 1/4 In. 70.00
Lantern, Barn, New England Glass Company Type, 1850 .... 95.00
Lantern, British Military, Oil 7.95
Lantern, Buggy Dashboard, Liberty, Kerosene 17.00
Lantern, Candle, Pierced Tin, Cone Top 90.00
Lantern, Child's, Patent 1918, Brass, Battery Operated, Wire Handle, 8 In. 20.00
Lantern, Chinese Junk, Brass, Oil, 15 In. 35.00
Lantern, Hall, American, C.1830, Brass & Frosted Glass, Smoke Bell, 36 In. 350.00
Lantern, Kerosene, Buggy Dashboard, Liberty 17.00
Lantern, Paul Revere Type, Tin, Punched, Modified Swirls 150.00
Lantern, Paul Revere, Tin, Tole Top & Bottom, Cutout Stars, 12 In. 65.00
Lantern, Railroad, see, Railroad, Lantern
Lantern, Rayo, Cold Blast, Farm 10.00
Lantern, Skater's, Kerosene, Brass, Amethyst Globe, Miniature 95.00
Lantern, Tin, Painted Red, 7 In. .... *Illus* 24.00
Lantern, Victor, Farm 7.50
Lapis Lazuli, Box, Hinged, Gold-Colored Metal Frame, 3 X 2 In. 85.00
Lapis Lazuli, Figurine, Duck, Ruby Eyes, Gold Legs, Feet, Russian, 2 1/4 In. 310.00
Lapis Lazuli, Figurine, Hoeti, Seated, Carved, 2 1/2 In. 375.00

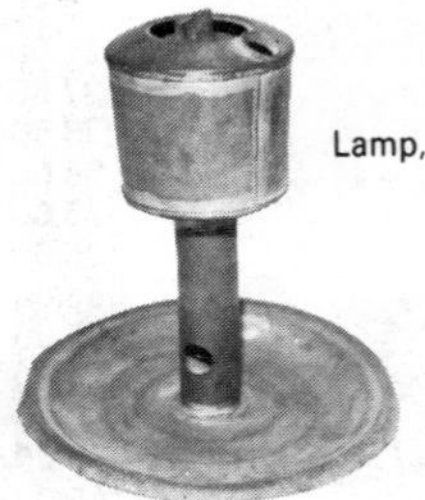

Lamp, Whale Oil, Tin, 7 In.

Lantern, Tin, Painted Red, 7 In.

Le Gras, Vase, Blue & White Enamel Leaves On Gray Ground, Signed, 8 In. 125.00
Le Gras, Vase, Raspberry Cameo Leaf On Smoked Gray, Signed, 6 In. 160.00

Le Verre Francais cameo glass was made in France between 1920 and 1933 by the C. Schneider Factory. It is mottled and usually decorated with floral designs, and bears the incised signature Le Verre Francais.

Le Verre Francais, Centerpiece, Cameo, Large 475.00
Le Verre Francais, Lamp Dome, Hanging, Orange To Yellow, Cobalt Edge, 18 In. 650.00
Le Verre Francais, Vase, Amber, Oriental Design Tortoiseshell, Footed, 8 In. 325.00
Le Verre Francais, Vase, Blue, Orange, & Red Cut To Frosted, 15 In. 695.00
Le Verre Francais, Vase, Bright Coloring, Deep Cuttings, Cameo, 8 X 4 In. 275.00
Le Verre Francais, Vase, Cameo, 3-Color, Signed, 8 X 5 In. 265.00
Le Verre Francais, Vase, Citrus, Tortoise, Orange, Deep Cut, Signed 6 1/4 In. 255.00
Le Verre Francais, Vase, Maroon & Citrine, Footed, 7 In. 295.00
Le Verre Francais, Vase, Orange Tortoiseshell & Citrine, Art Nouveau, 8 In. 325.00
Le Verre Francais, Vase, Orange, Citrine, & Deep Blue, Art Nouveau, 8 In. 350.00
Le Verre Francais, Vase, Pink Ground, Mushroom Flowers, Signed, 12 In. 320.00
Le Verre Francais, Vase, Wheel Cut, Footed, 7 In. 295.00
Leather, Box, Handkerchief, Indian Chief On Front 7.00
Leather, Case, Glove, 2 Pair Of Lady's White Kid Gloves, 5 3/4 In. 15.00
Leather, Game Brace, Rawhide Strips 8.50
Leather, Gloves, Lady's, White Kid, Long, Pearl Buttons, Pair 10.00

Leeds pottery was made at Leeds, Yorkshire, England, from 1774 to 1878. Most Leeds ware was not marked. Early Leeds pieces had distinctive twisted handles with a greenish glaze on part of the creamy ware. Later ware often had blue borders on the creamy pottery.

Leeds, Basket, Fruit, Creamware, Openwork 375.00
Leeds, Checkers Set, Majolica, Leeds Fireday Ltd., Worthy Leeds, 26 Piece 210.00
Leeds, Cup & Saucer, Handleless, White, Shamrocks 30.00
Leeds, Gravy Boat, Creamware, Green Trim 65.00
Leeds, Muffineer, Creamware, Green Trim 95.00
Leeds, Platter, Blue Edge, 16 1/2 In. 40.00
Leeds, Punch Pot, Polychrome, Esther Armytage, 1790 .... 575.00
Leeds, Saltshaker, Creamware, Green Trim 50.00

LEGRAS

Legras glass was made by August J. F. Legras in Saint-Denis, France, between 1864 and 1914. Cameo, acid cut, and enameled glass were made.

Legras, Bowl, Acid Etched Bleeding Hearts, Bulbous, 6 1/2 In. 120.00
Legras, Centerpiece Bowl, Mottled Orange & Brown, Enamel Floral, 9 In. 160.00
Legras, Centerpiece, Morning Glories In Lavender Shades, Signed 14 In. 265.00
Legras, Flower Bowl, Orange, Winter Scene, 4 1/2 In. 137.50
Legras, Lamp Base, Cameo, Enameling, Rose Ground, Butterflies, Signed 425.00
Legras, Rose Bowl, Cameo, Pair 460.00
Legras, Tray, Deep, 4 3/4 X 2 3/4 X 2 In. 50.00
Legras, Tray, Frosted, Orange Red Cameo Cuttings, 4 3/4 X 2 3/4 In. 80.00
Legras, Tray, Gray Frosted, Raspberry Design, 4 3/4 X 2 3/4 In. 80.00
Legras, Vase, Amethyst Cameo Leaf Pattern, 6 In. 125.00
Legras, Vase, Autumn Leaf, Green & Brown, Enamelware 135.00
Legras, Vase, Bowl Shape, Blue & White Enamel Leaves On Gray, 8 In. 90.00
Legras, Vase, Butterscotch, Colored Florals, Miniature, Cameo, 3 1/2 In. 250.00
Legras, Vase, Cream Color, Cameo & Enamel Seed Pods & Branches, 6 1/4 In. 326.00
Legras, Vase, Enamel Trees, Lake, Sailboats, Hexagonal Top, 11 In. 225.00
Legras, Vase, Enamel, Autumn Leaf In Dark Green & Rust, 5 In. 175.00
Legras, Vase, Forest And Landscape, Rust, Brown, Green, Red, Signed, 14 In. 125.00
Legras, Vase, Frosted Gray Crackle, Maroon Plants, 15 In. 350.00
Legras, Vase, Green, Art Deco, 6 X 2 3/4 In. 155.00
Legras, Vase, Green, Orange, Brown, Countryside Scene, Paneled, 8 1/2 In. 175.00
Legras, Vase, Green, Scenic, 8 1/4 In. 200.00
Legras, Vase, Greens, Browns, & Orange, Island Scene, Enameled, 9 In. 195.00
Legras, Vase, Lakes, Mountains, Trees, & Countryside, 8 1/2 In. 175.00
Legras, Vase, Orange, Green, & Brown, Lake, Mountains, & Trees, 8 1/2 In. 175.00

Legras, Vase, Raspberry Cameo Leaf On Smoked Gray, Signed, 6 In. 160.00
Legras, Vase, Red, Smoky Deer & Doe In Forest Scene, 6 In. 650.00
Legras, Vase, Scenic Tree & Landscape, Square, Rounded, 15 3/4 In. 140.00
Legras, Vase, Scenic Tree & Landscape, 14 In. 90.00
Legras, Vase, Scenic, Lake, Tall Trees, Rust, Brown & Green, 15 3/4 In. 185.00
Legras, Vase, Scenic, Tall Trees, Mountains, Brown & Green, 8 In. 285.00
Legras, Vase, Scenic, Tapered Stem, Squarish, 15 3/4 In. 185.00
Legras, Vase, Stick, Orange & Green, Brown Trees, 6 1/2 In. 95.00
Legras, Vase, Tangerine, Yellow, & Brown, Sailboats, 7 In. 495.00
Legras, Vase, White Mottled Ground, Geometrics In Blue, Black, Signed 145.00
Legras, Vase, Winter Figures, House, & Trees Scene, Enameled, 11 In. 125.00

LENOX

Lenox china was made in Trenton, New Jersey, after 1906. The firm also makes a porcelain similar to Belleek.

Lenox, Bottle, Made For Hattie Carnegie, Figural Stopper, Green Wreath 95.00
Lenox, Bottle, Perfume, DeVilbiss, Barrel Shape, Turkey Handle, 1 1/2 In. 65.00
Lenox, Bottle, Perfume, Ribbed Base, Gold Feather Finial, Green Wreath Mark 45.00
Lenox, Bowl, Centerpiece, Green Wreath And L Mark, Blue, 11 In. 15.00
Lenox, Bowl, Gold Edge, Green Mark, 9 In. 35.00
Lenox, Bowl, Picture Of Telephone In Center, 4 1/2 In. 4.00
Lenox, Bowl, Sterling Overlay, Reed & Barton, 6 In. 65.00
Lenox, Bowl, Twig Handles, Green Wreath 15.00
Lenox, Bowl, Verlys Type, Sculptured Opalescent Shell, 13 3/4 In. 57.50
Lenox, Bowl, White, Silver Overlay, Green Mark, 9 In. 62.00
Lenox, Bowl, White, Silver Overlay, Green Mark, 10 In. 48.00
Lenox, Box, Covered, Green, Pate-Sur-Pate, White Birds, Green Wreath, 5 X 2 In. 45.00
Lenox, Box, Covered, Pate-Sur-Pate, Green, White Birds, Green Mark, 5 In. 50.00
Lenox, Box, Floral On Lid, Green Mark, 4 X 3 In. 28.00
Lenox, Box, Hand-Painted Floral On Lid, Green Mark, 5 X 4 In. 28.00
Lenox, Bust, Woman's Head, White, Open Back, Art Deco, Green Mark, 8 3/4 In. 85.00
Lenox, Candlestick, Hexagonal, Gold Trim, Wreath Mark, Hutzler, 8 In., Pair 60.00
Lenox, Chocolate Pot, Brown Glaze, Silver Deposit, Wreath & L Mark, 11 In. 58.00
Lenox, Chocolate Set, Vodrel, Ivory, Gold Band, 7 Piece 69.50
Lenox; Coffee Set, Demitasse, Cobalt, Silver Overlay, Monogram, 3 Piece 175.00
Lenox, Coffee Set, Silver Deposit 95.00
Lenox, Compote, Art Deco, Round Pedestal, Leaf Embossed, Green Wreath, 4 In. 30.00
Lenox, Compote, Multicolor Geometric Decoration, Enamel & Gilt, 8 1/2 In. 45.00
Lenox, Compote, Mystic, Black Wreath Mark, 9 In. 30.00
Lenox, Cornucopia, Gold, Handle, 4 3/4 In. 22.50
Lenox, Cup & Saucer, Belefonte 13.50
Lenox, Cup & Saucer, Belleek, Silver Overlay 35.00
Lenox, Cup & Saucer, Bouillon, Gold With Cobalt, Gold Mark 12.00
Lenox, Cup & Saucer, Demitasse, Chocolate Brown, Green Wreath 30.00
Lenox, Cup & Saucer, Demitasse, Floralia 15.00
Lenox, Cup & Saucer, Demitasse, For Tiffany, Green Mark 18.50
Lenox, Cup & Saucer, Demitasse, Ivory Color, Coin Gold Handle & Band, Footed 15.50
Lenox, Cup & Saucer, Demitasse, Ming 8.35
Lenox, Cup & Saucer, Demitasse, 1/2 In. Gold Band, Made For Keeler 9.50
Lenox, Cup & Saucer, Demitasse, 6 Sided, Green Mark, Heavy Gold Decoration 15.00
Lenox, Cup & Saucer, Green Mark, Gorham Sterling Holder & Saucer 20.00
Lenox, Cup, Bouillon, Sterling Holder 20.00
Lenox, Dish, Handle In Center Of 2 Leaves, Gold Edges, Green Mark, 10 In. 35.00
Lenox, Dish, Leaf Shape, Pink, White Handle, Green Wreath Mark, 6 1/4 In. 25.00
Lenox, Dish, Relish, 3 Section, Handled, Pink & Cream, 10 In. 30.00
Lenox, Dish, Scallop Shell Shape, Crimped Edges, Green Wreath, 7 3/4 In. 22.00
Lenox, Dish, Shell Shape, Gold Edge, 5 3/4 X 3 3/4 In. 17.50
Lenox, Feeder, Invalid, Belleek, White, Green Palette Mark 30.00
Lenox, Figurine, Art Deco, Girl Dancing, Signed, Dated 1937, White, 14 In. 250.00
Lenox, Figurine, Bird, Pink, Green Mark, 4 In. 21.00
Lenox, Figurine, Bird, White 12.00
Lenox, Hatpin Holder, Silver Overlay 65.00
Lenox, Jug, Hot Milk, Covered, Mystic 25.00
Lenox, Jug, Toby, William Penn, Cream White, Green Wreath, 7 In. 110.00
Lenox, Lamp, Cream To Salmon, Metal Base, Porcelain Finial, 1931, 23 In. 75.00

Lenox, Mug, Belleek, Huckleberries, Gold Handle, Tankard Shape, Palette Mark 45.00
Lenox, Pitcher, Cider, Apples On Bough, Palette Mark, 8 1/2 In. 95.00
Lenox, Pitcher, Cider, Belleek, Mum Decoration, Green, Gold Rim & Handle 65.00
Lenox, Pitcher, Ribbed, Gold Rim, 5 1/2 In. 15.00
Lenox, Plate, Belleek, Sepia Scenes, Gold Edge, 10 1/2 In., Pair 30.00
Lenox, Plate, Blue Tree, Black Mark, 6 In. 12.50
Lenox, Plate, Chop, Mystic, 10 1/2 In. 28.00
Lenox, Plate, Dessert, Ming, 7 1/4 In. 15.00
Lenox, Plate, Florida, 7 1/2 In. 12.00
Lenox, Plate, Luncheon, White, Engraved Gold Bands, 9 In. 7.25
Lenox, Plate, Ming, 9 In. 20.00
Lenox, Plate, Mystic, 10 1/2 In. 11.00
Lenox, Plate, Service, Maroon & Cream, 22K Gold, Purple Mark, For Tiffany 20.00
Lenox, Plate, Soup, Mystic 7.50
Lenox, Plate, Soup, Tree Of Life, 9 In. 15.00
Lenox, Plate, Tea, Cream Color, Crimped Edge, 6 In. 5.50
Lenox, Plate, Tree Of Life, 7 1/2 In. 10.00
Lenox, Plate, Tree Of Life, 9 1/2 In. 15.00
Lenox, Ramekin & Underplate, Engraved Border, Green Mark, Ovington Bros. 35.00
Lenox, Ramekin Set, Brown Glazed, Silver Overlay, Green Mark, 3 1/4 In., 3 ..... 60.00
Lenox, Ramekin, Green Wreath Mark, 3 1/2 In., Set Of 6 ..... 35.00
Lenox, Salt & Pepper, Ming, Pair 15.00
Lenox, Salt, Belleek, Hand-Painted Roses, Gold Rim, Palette, Set Of 5 ..... 19.50
Lenox, Salt, Belleek, Swan, Pearl, Salmon Lining, Gold Trim, Palette Mark 9.50
Lenox, Salt, Sterling Silver Holder, Green Wreath Mark 12.00
Lenox, Salt, Swan, Green Wreath, Set Of 4 ..... 32.00
Lenox, Salt, Swan, Pink, Green Wreath Mark 20.00
Lenox, Salt, Swan, White, Green Wreath Mark 20.00
Lenox, Salt, Tub-Shaped 10.00
Lenox, Shoe, Green Wreath 12.00
Lenox, Soup, Bowl, Salmon & Gold Edging, Ruffled, Green Mark, 8 In. 7.50
Lenox, Stand, Cake, Ming Pattern, Green Wreath Mark, 9 In. 32.00
Lenox, Sugar & Creamer, Belleek, White, Sterling Overlay, Palette Mark 42.00
Lenox, Tea Set, Beige, Silver Overlay, 3 Piece 65.00
Lenox, Tea Set, Cobalt, Silver Overlay, Pedestaled, Lenox Wreath On Silver 250.00
Lenox, Tea Set, Gold Trim & Handles, For Tiffany & Co., 3 Piece 200.00
Lenox, Tea Set, Silver Overlay, Hand-Painted, Art Nouveau Design 225.00
Lenox, Teapot, Aladdin Lid, Sterling Overlay On Cobalt, Green Wreath Mark 180.00
Lenox, Teapot, Cobalt, Silver Overlay, Silver Mark 60.00
Lenox, Teapot, Mystic 25.00
Lenox, Toby Mug, Wm.Penn, White 95.00
Lenox, Vase, Belleek, Brown & Green, Daisies, Palette Mark, 12 In. 75.00
Lenox, Vase, Belleek, Green Shading, White Hydrangeas, 25 X 14 7/8 In. 195.00
Lenox, Vase, Belleek, Palette Mark, Art Nouveau, Golden Grapes, 6 In. 80.00
Lenox, Vase, Belleek, Pink & Yellow Roses, 12 1/4 In. 135.00
Lenox, Vase, Belleek, Pink, Red, White Roses, Gold Butterflies, Artist Signed 125.00
Lenox, Vase, Belleek, White, Sterling Overlay, Palette Mark, 10 1/4 In. 95.00
Lenox, Vase, Bud, White, Embossed, 10 3/4 In. 15.00
Lenox, Vase, Bulbous, Fluted Stem, 7 In. 20.00
Lenox, Vase, Classic Bottle Shape, Green Wreath, 12 In., Pair 42.00
Lenox, Vase, Fuchsia, Floral Bands, Gold Trim, Cream Lining, Flared, 8 1/4 In. 38.00
Lenox, Vase, Green, Flared, Green Mark, 7 In. 28.00
Lenox, Vase, Pink, Fluted Sides, White Interior, Green Wreath Mark, 7 In. 20.00
Lenox, Vase, Rose, Fluted Neck, 8 In., Pair 35.00
Lenox, Vase, Tubular, Black Line Decoration On White, 9 1/2 In. 25.00
Lenox, Vase, White, Swan Handles, Urn Shape, Green Mark, 8 1/2 In., Pair 40.00
Libbey, Basket, Allover Cut, Saber Mark, 8 X 9 In. 395.00
Libbey, Basket, Intaglio Cut, Signed 450.00
Libbey, Bowl, Centerpiece, Black Overlay, Diamond Point, Signed 325.00
Libbey, Bowl, Cut Glass, Signed, 8 X 3 1/2 In. 125.00
Libbey, Bowl, Hobstars, Miter Cuts & Prism Radials, Signed Libbey, 8 In. 75.00
Libbey, Bowl, Punch, Ladle, Hobstars, Thatching, Sunbursts, 9 3/4 In., Signed 2200.00
Libbey, Bowl, Punch, Miniature, Etched Flowers & Leaves 35.00
Libbey, Bowl, 6 Hobstars, Large Six Point Strawberry Diamond Star, 6 3/4 In. 125.00

Libbey, Candleholder, Intaglio Cut, Stylized Floral, 10 In. 95.00
Libbey, Candlestick, Nash, Camel Stems, Signed, 5 1/4 In., Pair 295.00
Libbey, Carafe, Five Overall Cut Patterns, Signed 115.00
Libbey, Celery, Signed 63.00
Libbey, Champagne, Malmaison 15.00
Libbey, Champagne, Opalescent, Squirrel Stem 65.50
Libbey, Compote, Intaglio Flowers & Leaves, Teardrop Stem, Signed, 8 X 7 In. 95.00
Libbey, Cordial, Vesta, Green, Platinum Band, Clear Stem, Nash Series 12.00
Libbey, Cornucopia, Blue Optic Swirl, 2 Footed, 14 In. 65.00
Libbey, Cup, Punch, Peachblow, World's Fair, 1893, Name Forest, Applied Handle 300.00
Libbey, Dish, Hobstars, 6 In. 45.00
Libbey, Dish, Pin, Covered, Signed 30.00
Libbey, Goblet, Cut And Etched, Stemmed, 7 1/2 In. 19.00
Libbey, Goblet, Diana, Nash Series 22.00
Libbey, Goblet, Menagerie, Opalescent Cat Stem 88.00
Libbey, Goblet, Menagerie, Silhouette, Bear Stem, 5 1/2 In. 65.00
Libbey, Goblet, Rabbit Silhouette, Opalescent Stem, Signed 49.50
Libbey, Goblet, Squirrel Silhouette, Opalescent Stem, Signed 49.50
Libbey, Goblet, Vesta, Green, Platinum Band, Clear Stem, Nash Series 15.00
Libbey, Hatchet, Bust Of George Washington, World's Fair, 1893, 8 In. 40.00
Libbey, Pitcher, 14 Tumblers, All Signed 1000.00
Libbey, Plate, Moonstone, Blue Opalescent, Signed, 8 In. 50.00
Libbey, Plate, Santa Maria, White, Lusterless, Gold Rim, Signed 300.00
Libbey, Sugar & Creamer, Hobstar Cut All Over, Signed 150.00
Libbey, Tumbler, Pink & Black Enamel Pagodas, Figures, & Trees 14.00
Libbey, Wine, Diana, Nash Series 16.00
Libbey, Wine, Menagerie, Opalescent Monkey Stem 88.00
Libbey, Wine, Silhouette Bear Stem 58.00
Libbey, Wine, Silhouette, Squirrel, Opalescent Stem, Signed 49.50

Lighting Devices, see Candleholder, Candlestick, Lamp, etc.

Lightning rod balls are collected for their variety of shape and color. These glass balls were at the center of the rod that was attached to the roof of a house or barn to avoid lightning damage.

Lightning Rod, Ball, Black Amethyst 45.00
Lightning Rod, Ball, Chestnut, Amber 20.00
Lightning Rod, Ball, Chestnut, Green 75.00
Lightning Rod, Ball, Chestnut, Milk Glass, Blue 10.00
Lightning Rod, Ball, Chestnut, Red 27.50 To 40.00
Lightning Rod, Ball, Cobalt, 4 1/4 In. 25.00
Lightning Rod, Ball, D & S, Cobalt 30.00
Lightning Rod, Ball, D & S, Milk Glass 4.00
Lightning Rod, Ball, D & S, Milk Glass, Green 10.00
Lightning Rod, Ball, Diamond Pleats, Sun-Colored Amethyst, 5 In. 15.00
Lightning Rod, Ball, Diddie 15.00
Lightning Rod, Ball, Diddie Blitzen, Sun-Colored Amethyst 20.00
Lightning Rod, Ball, Diddie, Red 65.00
Lightning Rod, Ball, Electra, Amber 15.00
Lightning Rod, Ball, Electra, Cobalt 20.00
Lightning Rod, Ball, Electra, Cone, Silver 100.00
Lightning Rod, Ball, Electra, Cone, Sun-Colored Amethyst 15.00
Lightning Rod, Ball, Electra, Red 65.00
Lightning Rod, Ball, Grape, Amber 18.00 To 20.00
Lightning Rod, Ball, Grape, Red 100.00
Lightning Rod, Ball, Grape, Sun-Colored Amethyst 10.00
Lightning Rod, Ball, Hawkeye, Milk Glass 8.00
Lightning Rod, Ball, K, Amber 25.00
Lightning Rod, Ball, K, Sun-Colored Amethyst 10.00
Lightning Rod, Ball, Maker, Red 80.00
Lightning Rod, Ball, Milk Glass, Blue 4.00
Lightning Rod, Ball, Milk Glass, Blue, 4 3/4 In. 10.00
Lightning Rod, Ball, Milk Glass, Purple 8.00
Lightning Rod, Ball, Milk Glass, 4 In. 25.00
Lightning Rod, Ball, National L.P.Co., St.Louis, Rib & Grape, Milk Glass 25.00

Lightning Rod, Ball, National, Amber 25.00
Lightning Rod, Ball, National, Belted, Amber 80.00
Lightning Rod, Ball, National, Double Belted, Amber 50.00
Lightning Rod, Ball, National, Double Belted, Sun-Colored Amethyst 45.00
Lightning Rod, Ball, National, Milk Glass, Blue 15.00
Lightning Rod, Ball, National, Sun-Colored Amethyst 16.00
Lightning Rod, Ball, Pee Wee, Red 100.00
Lightning Rod, Ball, Pink 85.00
Lightning Rod, Ball, Pleated, Amber, 5 1/2 In. 125.00
Lightning Rod, Ball, Quilted, Cobalt 125.00
Lightning Rod, Ball, Quilted, Flat, Amber 15.00
Lightning Rod, Ball, Quilted, Flat, Red 65.00
Lightning Rod, Ball, Red, 3 1/2 In. 25.00
Lightning Rod, Ball, RHF, Milk Glass 25.00
Lightning Rod, Ball, Ruby 10.00
Lightning Rod, Ball, S Company, Amber 25.00
Lightning Rod, Ball, S Company, Cobalt 30.00
Lightning Rod, Ball, S Company, Sun-Colored Amethyst 20.00
Lightning Rod, Ball, S L R, Cobalt 25.00
Lightning Rod, Ball, Star & Slag, Milk Glass, 4 1/2 In. 10.00
Lightning Rod, Ball, Sun-Colored Amethyst 40.00

Limoges, see also Haviland

Limoges porcelain has been made in Limoges, France, since the mid-nineteenth century. Fine porcelains were made by many factories, including Haviland, Ahrenfeldt, Guerin, Pouyat, Elite, and others.

CH. FIELD HAVILAND LIMOGES

Limoges, Basket, Lavender To White, Violets, Thorn Handle, Gold Trim, 5 In. 25.00
Limoges, Berry Bowl, Blueberries, Irregular Edge, J.P.L., 1906, 3 1/2 In. 13.50
Limoges, Berry Bowl, Strawberries, Irregular Edge, J.P.L., 1906, 3 1/2 In. 13.50
Limoges, Bowl, Beige, Gold Floral, Green Interior, Martin Freres, 11 In. 40.00
Limoges, Bowl, Berry, Blueberry, Gold Trim, 3 Footed, T & V, 9 1/4 In. 55.00
Limoges, Bowl, Carnations, Gold Scallop Border, T & V, 9 1/2 In. 18.00
Limoges, Bowl, Ears Of Corn & Floral, Browns, Yellows, & Gold, Handled, 12 In. 65.00
Limoges, Bowl, Multicolor Floral, Gold Leaf, L.S.S., France, 8 1/2 In. 13.00
Limoges, Bowl, Punch, Hand-Painted Roses, Artist Signed, Coronet, 15 In. 250.00
Limoges, Bowl, Roses & Foliage, Aqua & Gold Rim, 9 In. 125.00
Limoges, Bowl, Seashell, White, Primevera, France, 11 X 8 1/2 In. 75.00
Limoges, Box, Covered, Cupids, Heart Shape, 4 1/2 In. 30.00
Limoges, Box, Holly Decoration, Jeweled Effect, 7 X 3 1/2 In. 82.00
Limoges, Box, Powder, Hand-Painted, Enameled, Dated & Signed 27.50
Limoges, Box, Trinket, Oval, Green With Gold, French Lady On Top 32.50
Limoges, Bucket, Ice, With Liner, Blueberry Decoration, Gold, 6 3/4 X 3 In. 75.00
Limoges, Butter Pat, Figures In Scene, Gold Scalloped Border 16.00
Limoges, Butter Pat, Violets 7.00
Limoges, Butter, White, Green & Gold, Insert, C.Ahrenfeldt 30.00
Limoges, Cachepot, Aqua, Hand-Painted Floral, Pair 50.00
Limoges, Cake Stand, Portrait Scene, Gold Edge, 9 1/2 X 4 In. 42.00
Limoges, Candlestick, A.Lanternier, Orchids, 5 In. 20.00
Limoges, Candlestick, Rococo Edges, 2 1/2 In. 20.00
Limoges, Celery, Pastel Flower, Scroll Border, C.Ahrenfeldt 22.50
Limoges, Celery, Yellow Roses 16.00
Limoges, Charger, Pink & Yellow Roses, Gold Rococo Border, 15 1/4 In. 225.00
Limoges, Chocolate Pot, Floral Decoration, GDA Mark 48.00
Limoges, Chocolate Pot, Floral Decoration, Gold Trim, Hand-Painted 35.00
Limoges, Chocolate Pot, Green & White, Gold Trim 39.00
Limoges, Chocolate Pot, Green Leaves & Ribbon, Double Gold Handle 60.00
Limoges, Chocolate Pot, White To Green Top, Gold Handle & Lip 35.00
Limoges, Chocolate Pot, White, Pink Floral, Gold Trim, 11 In. 72.50
Limoges, Cider Set, White, Purple Floral, Gold Trim, B & C, 7 Piece 195.00
Limoges, Coffeepot, White, Pink Floral & Gold Deco, C.Ahrenfeldt, 9 In. 65.00
Limoges, Compote, Blueberry Decoration, Gold, T & V, 4 In. 45.00
Limoges, Creamer, Hand-Painted Prunus Blossoms, Gold Handle 10.00
Limoges, Creamer, Wild Roses, 8 In. 40.00
Limoges, Cup & Saucer, Beige, Orchid, Luc, A.Lanternier & Co., Limoges 15.00

Limoges, Cup & Saucer, Bouillon, Cobalt, Gold Handles & Trim, Redon 25.00
Limoges, Cup & Saucer, Bouillon, Floral, Gold Handles, L.Bernardoud & Co. 10.00
Limoges, Cup & Saucer, Bouillon, Green Laurel, Gold Band Edges 7.00
Limoges, Cup & Saucer, Chocolate, Pink Roses, Gilt Handle & Rim, Elite 20.00
Limoges, Cup & Saucer, Demitasse, Melon Section, Dull Gold, Footed Cup 30.00
Limoges, Cup & Saucer, Demitasse, Pink Floral, Green Leaves, G.D.A. 11.75
Limoges, Cup & Saucer, Demitasse, White, Gold Design, C.1800 ..... 18.50
Limoges, Cup & Saucer, Gold Trim, Fluted, Scalloped, Elite, Miniature 28.00
Limoges, Cup, Bouillon, Wreath & Flower Band, Gold Trim, 2 Handles 5.00
Limoges, Dish, Butter, Green & Yellow Ground, Pink Flowers, GDA 45.00
Limoges, Dish, Child's, Felix The Cat 35.00
Limoges, Dish, Pickle, Gold Greek Key 13.00
Limoges, Dish, Pin, Leaf Design, Yellow & Pink Roses 8.00
Limoges, Dish, Powder, Hand-Painted Violets, 7 In. 30.00
Limoges, Dresser Set, Cream Color, Pink Roses, Gold, Imperial, 4 Piece 150.00
Limoges, Dresser Set, Gold Tops & Trim On Cream, 9 Piece, Signed R.Perkins 85.00
Limoges, Dresser Set, Ivory Color, Pastel Floral, 3 Piece 85.00
Limoges, Fish Set, Coronet, Artist Signed, 14 In. Platter, 13 Pieces 750.00
Limoges, Fish Set, Fish & Shell Fish, White, Scalloped, 11 Piece 150.00
Limoges, Fish Set, Signed Lu Yut, 5 Piece 135.00
Limoges, Frame, Picture, Blue To Cream, Floral, Gold Trim, M.C.V., 1897, 9 In. 40.00
Limoges, Frame, Picture, Blue, Pink, & Cream, Floral, M.C.V., 1898, 8 3/4 In. 40.00
Limoges, Gravy Boat & Attached Underplate, White, Blue Floral, Gold Trim 18.00
Limoges, Gravy Boat, Game, Hunting Dogs, Poutous, Cobalt Border, Underplate 60.00
Limoges, Gravy Boat, Gold Relief, Jesse Dean, 1865 ..... 25.00
Limoges, Gravy Boat, Pink Roses, Green Leaves, Scalloped, J.Pouyat 5.50
Limoges, Gravy, Underplate, Game, Dogs Stalking, Wm.Guerin, Poutous 60.00
Limoges, Gravy, Underplate, Rose Decoration, Gold Beading, Elite 35.00
Limoges, Humidor, Tan, Floral, Footed, B & C, Square, 7 X 4 In. 60.00
Limoges, Ice Cream Set, Clover Edge, Gold Handles, Oval Tray, 7 Piece 27.50
Limoges, Ice Cream Set, Miniature, Table, 2 Chairs, Victorian Courting Scene 125.00
Limoges, Jar, Cracker, Green, Red & White Poppies, Gold Border, 16 In. 80.00
Limoges, Jar, Cracker, Hand-Painted, Shell Design Gold Lid, T & V, France 95.00
Limoges, Jar, Cracker, Swirl, Violets, Gold, Signed 70.00
Limoges, Jar, Dresser, Blue, Pink Rose Sprays, Gold Scrolls & Beading 35.00
Limoges, Jar, Dresser, Pink & Cream, Portrait, Gold Scrolls & Beading 35.00
Limoges, Jar, Jam, Pink Floral With Blue Ribbon, Ornate Handles, 5 1/2 In. 27.50
Limoges, Jar, Powder, Cherubs On Cover, Doves, Flowers 48.00
Limoges, Jar, Powder, Ormolu Mounted, 5 X 4 1/2 In. 75.00
Limoges, Jar, Powder, Roses & Gold, Pink Tint, Covered, Elite 55.00
Limoges, Jug, Cider, American Beauty Roses, Beaded Handle 37.50
Limoges, Jug, Cider, Blackberries & Leaves 35.00
Limoges, Mug, Child's, Pink & White, Hand-Painted 20.00
Limoges, Mug, Left-Handed, Portrait Of Owl, Artist Signed, 6 In. 65.00
Limoges, Mug, Man With Stein, Brown & White, 5 In. 45.00
Limoges, Mug, Monk, Hand-Painted, Signed J.M. Hockenhill 130.00
Limoges, Mug, Portrait, Indian Brave, Rust Ground, J.P.L., 5 In. 65.00
Limoges, Mug, Portrait, Indian Girl, Green Ground, T & V, 5 1/4 In. 65.00
Limoges, Mug, Portrait, Man, Mustache & Goatee, Green Ground, J.P.L., 51 In. 65.00
Limoges, Mug, Portrait, Monk, Brown Ground, 5 In. 65.00
Limoges, Pate, Coronet, 10 In., Two Grazing Buffalo, Artist Signed 45.00
Limoges, Pintray, Orchid Floral, Gold, 9 1/2 In. 15.00
Limoges, Pitcher, Cream Wild Roses, Slender, 8 In. 40.00
Limoges, Pitcher, Milk, Mottled, Pastel Plums, Matte Finish, 7 1/2 In. 45.00
Limoges, Plaque, Fruit, Rococo, Gold Edge, Albert, 11 In. 85.00
Limoges, Plaque, Grapes, Gold Spider Web & Border, 12 3/4 In. 90.00
Limoges, Plaque, Lady In Ornate Frame, 6 1/2 X 9 In. 300.00
Limoges, Plaque, Red Poppies, Blue Centers, Green Leaves, Elite, 7 1/2 X 5 In. 67.50
Limoges, Plate, Beige & Blue, Pink & White Floral, Le Fort, J.P.L., 8 1/2 In. 25.00
Limoges, Plate, Berry & Fruit, Hand-Painted, 7 1/2 In. 20.50
Limoges, Plate, Bird, Coronet, 9 3/4 In. 55.00
Limoges, Plate, Bird, Gold Rococo Border, Duboy, Flambeau, 8 1/2 In. 75.00
Limoges, Plate, Bird, Rococo Gold Border, Cornet, Artist Signed Barin 48.00
Limoges, Plate, Blue Jay, 14 In. 145.00

Limoges, Plate, Cake, Gold Band, Open Handles, B & Co., L.Bernardaud, 11 In. 25.00
Limoges, Plate, Cake, Hand-Painted Violets, 8 3/4 In. 16.50
Limoges, Plate, Cake, Open Handles, Hand-Painted, 10 1/2 In. 35.00
Limoges, Plate, Cake, Pastel Coloring, Roses, Set Of 6 .... 66.00
Limoges, Plate, Cavalier, Cornet, Signed Luc, 10 In. 70.00
Limoges, Plate, Chop, Corsair Souvenir, East & West, Home Is Best, 1894, 11 In. 45.00
Limoges, Plate, Chop, Roses, Gold 29.00
Limoges, Plate, Cornet, Game, 10 In. 65.00
Limoges, Plate, Coronet, Duck Landing On Water, 10 1/4 In. 145.00
Limoges, Plate, Cream Color, 3 Color Roses, A.Ruimilley, Coronet, 7 3/4 In. 30.00
Limoges, Plate, Dessert, White, Violets & Leaves, Lavender Ribbons, 7 1/2 In. 16.50
Limoges, Plate, Dinner, Old Abbey 10.00
Limoges, Plate, Exotic Bird On Apple Blossom Branch, Artist Signed 75.00
Limoges, Plate, Fish, Gold Border, Imperial Limoges, 9 1/2 In. 20.00
Limoges, Plate, Fish, Species Of Fish, Worrell, 9 3/8 In., Set Of 6 .... 150.00
Limoges, Plate, Fish, Swimming Fish, Irregular Edge, T & V, 9 In., Pair 28.00
Limoges, Plate, Fish, Underwater Scene, T & V, 9 In. 30.00
Limoges, Plate, Floral Center, Magenta Border, D & C, 8 1/2 In. 8.50
Limoges, Plate, Floral Center, Turquoise Border, D & C, 8 1/2 In. 8.50
Limoges, Plate, Fruit, Gold Rococo Border, Coronet, 10 1/2 In. 65.00
Limoges, Plate, Fruit, Heavy Gold Border, Pierced, 12 1/4 In. 95.00
Limoges, Plate, Fruits, Gold Rococo Border, 13 1/4 In. 150.00
Limoges, Plate, Game, Artist Signed, 9 1/2 In. 55.00
Limoges, Plate, Game, Birds, Hand-Painted, Signed DuBois 150.00
Limoges, Plate, Game, Chinese Pheasant, Comte De Artois, Limoges, 9 In. 35.00
Limoges, Plate, Game, Chinese Pheasant, Coronet, Signed Max, 9 1/2 In. 50.00
Limoges, Plate, Game, Coronet, Artist Signed, 10 In. 97.00
Limoges, Plate, Game, Dogs, Retrieving, Wm.Guerin, Poutous, 9 3/4 In. 40.00
Limoges, Plate, Game, Dubois, 10 1/2 In. 125.00
Limoges, Plate, Game, Ducks, Fence & Vines, Gold Edge, Coronet, 10 In. 47.00
Limoges, Plate, Game, Fish In Rushing Stream, Artist Signed, 8 1/2 In. 35.00
Limoges, Plate, Game, Fish, Valentin, 10 1/2 In. 125.00
Limoges, Plate, Game, Flower Ground, Standing Bird, 9 3/4 In. 65.00
Limoges, Plate, Game, Gold Ormolu Band, Dog With Bird In Mouth, Artist Signed 225.00
Limoges, Plate, Game, Gold Rococo Border, Artist Signed, Sena, Pair 95.00
Limoges, Plate, Game, Grouse, Comte De Artois, 9 In. 35.00
Limoges, Plate, Game, Grouse, Pierced, Gold Border, 12 1/4 In. 95.00
Limoges, Plate, Game, Hunting Dogs, Poutous, Cobalt Border, 9 3/4 In. 40.00
Limoges, Plate, Game, Mother Bird And 3 Babies, 9 In. 60.00
Limoges, Plate, Game, Pair Of Quail, 2 Handled, T & V, France, 16 In., Signed 125.00
Limoges, Plate, Game, Pheasant, Nasturtiums Border, J.P.L., 8 1/2 In., Pair 28.00
Limoges, Plate, Game, Pheasant, Signed Luc, La Seyrie Limoges P & P, France 85.00
Limoges, Plate, Game, Pheasant, Signed Max, 10 In. 85.00
Limoges, Plate, Game, Rabbit, Coudert, Coronet, 10 In. 165.00
Limoges, Plate, Game, Rococo Border, Signed Dubois, 12 1/2 In. 225.00
Limoges, Plate, Game, 2 Red Breasted Birds, Signed Du Bois, 12 1/2 In. 225.00
Limoges, Plate, Game, 3 Birds, Dubois, Gold Rococo Border, 15 1/2 In. 375.00
Limoges, Plate, Gold & Green Design, Gold Rim, A.Lanternier & Co., 9 3/4 In. 15.00
Limoges, Plate, Gold Border & Band, G.D.M., 1870, 8 1/2 In. 12.00
Limoges, Plate, Hand-Painted Floral, Gilt Edge, 7 1/4 In. 8.50
Limoges, Plate, Hand-Painted, Flowers, Artist Signed, Gold Border, 8 3/4 In. 28.50
Limoges, Plate, Hanging, Dictante Une Lettre, Bazanan, Gold Edge, 13 In. 125.00
Limoges, Plate, Luncheon, Lavender Floral, Gold Scalloped Edge, 9 In. 11.25
Limoges, Plate, Monk Sipping Coffee, Coronet, Signed Le Pic, 10 In. 70.00
Limoges, Plate, Monk Smoking, Signed Le Pic, 10 In. 70.00
Limoges, Plate, Old Abbey, Game, 10 In., Rooster 65.00
Limoges, Plate, Oriental Poppies, Gold Border, 7 1/2 In. 16.25
Limoges, Plate, Oyster, Pink Flowers, Elite, Set Of 6 .... 125.00
Limoges, Plate, Oyster, White, Roses, Gold Scalloped Rim, Elite, 8 1/2 In. 20.00
Limoges, Plate, Pheasant, Bauny, Gold Edge, Blakeman & Henderson, 12 In. 175.00
Limoges, Plate, Portrait, Girl, Budois, Rococo Border, 10 1/4 In. 125.00
Limoges, Plate, Purple Cactus, Gold & Beading, Hand-Painted, 9 In. 60.00
Limoges, Plate, Roses & Gold, Hand-Painted, Signed T & V, 9 1/2 In. 40.00
Limoges, Plate, Roses, Coronet, 12 In. 125.00

Limoges, Plate, Scalloped Blue Rim, Rose Design, Artist Signed, 9 1/2 In. 22.50
Limoges, Plate, Springtime, B & G, 6 1/2 In. 1.50
Limoges, Plate, Underwater Fish & Seaweed, Gold Rim, T & V, 9 In. 30.00
Limoges, Plate, Violets & Lilies Of The Valley, 8 1/2 In. 16.50
Limoges, Plate, Violets & Lilies Of The Valley, 9 In. 17.50
Limoges, Plate, Yellow & Blue, Pink Floral, R.Andersen, W.G.& Co., 7 1/4 In. 45.00
Limoges, Platter, Bass, Waterlilies, Embossed, Signed Max, 16 1/4 X 11 1/2 In. 75.00
Limoges, Platter, Fruits, Balzanar, 12 1/2 In. 125.00
Limoges, Platter, Game, Bass, Waterlilies, Signed Max, 16 1/4 In. 75.00
Limoges, Platter, Game, De Nerval, 15 1/2 In. 400.00
Limoges, Platter, Game, Dubois, 10 1/2 In. 125.00
Limoges, Platter, Game, Muville, 10 1/2 In. 125.00
Limoges, Platter, Grapes, Green & Brown Leaves, Gold, J.P.L., 11 1/2 In. 30.00
Limoges, Platter, Marked Elite, Heavy Gold Scalloped Edge, 12 In. 45.00
Limoges, Platter, Morning Glory, Gold Trim, T & V, 12 In. 75.00
Limoges, Platter, Turkey, Blue & Pink Floral, Scalloped, 17 X 12 1/2 In. 42.00
Limoges, Platter, White & Gold, 16 X 13 In. 15.00
Limoges, Punch Bowl, Fruit, Footed, T & V 225.00
Limoges, Punch Set, Blackberries, Gold Rococo Trim, Pedestals, T & V, 6 Piece 275.00
Limoges, Ramekin & Underplate, Floral 14.50
Limoges, Ramekin & Underplate, J.Pouyat 15.00
Limoges, Ramekin & Underplate, Pink Roses 9.00
Limoges, Ring Tree, Green & Gilt Ivy, C.1890 .... 17.50
Limoges, Ring Tree, Saucer Base, Violets, Gold Handle 18.50
Limoges, Spittoon, Lady's, Rococo Edge 30.00
Limoges, Sugar & Creamer, Cover, Blue Band, Pink Floral, Gold Handles, G.D.A. 48.00
Limoges, Sugar & Creamer, Cupids, Gold Handle & Trim 30.00
Limoges, Sugar & Creamer, Green & Cream, Multicolor Leaves, Gold, Roby 65.00
Limoges, Sugar & Creamer, Pink & Green, Pink & White Roses, Gold Handles 35.00
Limoges, Sugar & Creamer, Pink Roses, White Sprays, Gold Trim, J.P.L. 32.00
Limoges, Sugar & Creamer, Violets, Gold Handles & Rims, G.D.A. 34.00
Limoges, Sugar, Covered, Aqua & Gold, J.P.L. 15.00
Limoges, Tankard, Blue, Green, Yellow, & Pink, Blackberries, T & V, 15 1/4 In. 150.00
Limoges, Tankard, Ears Of Corn, T & V, Signed 42.00
Limoges, Tankard, Grapes, Leaves, & Vines, Dragon Handle, J.P.L., 15 In. 265.00
Limoges, Tankard, Green, Blackberries, T & V, 1899, 11 In. 120.00
Limoges, Tankard, Pink Brown, Grapes, Gold Band & Handle, W.G.& Co., 14 In. 145.00
Limoges, Tea Set, C.Ahrenfeldt, 27 Pieces, Pink & White Roses, Gold Border 85.00
Limoges, Tea Set, Gold Relief, Jesse Dean, 1865, 3 Piece 85.00
Limoges, Teapot, Green & Cream, Multicolor Leaves, Gold, Roby 65.00
Limoges, Tray, Bureau, Oval, Violets, 12 X 9 In. 60.00
Limoges, Tray, Cream Color, Plums, Gold Handle & Scalloped Edge, 1896, 10 In. 15.00
Limoges, Tray, Dresser, Floral, Gold Irregular Edge, Kidney Shape, W.G.& Co. 40.00
Limoges, Tray, Dresser, Pink & Cream Hand-Painted Roses, Signed Duval 45.00
Limoges, Tray, Dresser, Red & Green Holly, T & V, 13 X 8 1/2 In. 17.50
Limoges, Tray, Gold Floral & Irregular Rim, Green Anchor Mark, 11 X 6 In. 55.00
Limoges, Tray, Hand-Painted Poppies, Scallop Gold Edge, B & H Limoges, France 35.00
Limoges, Tray, Oval, Open Handles, Lily-Of-The-Valley & Rose 45.00
Limoges, Tray, Perfume, Floral, Pink & Gold Irregular Border, Elite, 11 In. 18.00
Limoges, Tray, Pierced Handles, B & Co., France, 16 X 6 In. 42.00
Limoges, Tray, Pin, Butterfly Shape, Forget-Me-Not Decoration 12.00
Limoges, Tray, Pin, Forget-Me-Nots, Gold-Winged Butterfly Shape 12.00
Limoges, Tray, Pin, Light Green, Yellow Daisies, 10 1/2 X 8 1/2 In. 35.00
Limoges, Tray, Portrait, Victorian Lady, Gold Border, J.M.Cain, 18 In. 390.00
Limoges, Tray, Yellow Floral, Gold Edge, 18 X 14 In. 135.00
Limoges, Tureen, Oval, 4 X 8 X 4 In. 45.00
Limoges, Vase, Amphora, Cherries & Grapes, Gold Leaves, Handled, Elite, 11 In. 75.00
Limoges, Vase, Cylinder, Owls, Gold Outline, Handle & Feet, 6 3/4 In. 78.00
Limoges, Vase, Envelope Type, Hand-Painted, Cupids, Footed, Signed 45.00
Limoges, Vase, Gold Bands, Hand-Painted, J.P.L., 13 In. 145.00
Limoges, Vase, Gold Ornate Handles, Bulbous Base, LEW, 13 In. 65.00
Limoges, Vase, Hand-Painted Floral, Gold Handles & Foot, M.R., 10 1/2 In. 50.00
Limoges, Vase, Hand-Painted Roses On Blue To Brown, JPL France, 6 In. 45.00
Limoges, Vase, Hand-Painted Roses, J.P.L., 7 X 5 In. 55.00

Limoges, Vase, Lady In Garden, Gamet, Bronze Mounts, 5 1/2 In. 500.00
Limoges, Vase, Lady Slipper, Gold Handles, Trim, & Foot, 10 1/2 In. 65.00
Limoges, Vase, Pink Roses On Green, Scroll Handles, J.P.L., France, Dated 150.00
Limoges, Vase, Violets, Elite, 7 1/2 In. 35.00
Limoges, Vase, White & Green Floral, Dragon Handles, Duvap, J.P.L., 10 1/2 In. 200.00
Limoges, Vegetable Bowl, Steam Holes In Lid, White, Blue Floral, G.D.A. 28.00
Limoges, Warmer, Egg, Stack Of Gilt-Rimmed Plates Shape, Bird & Plant, 8 In. 43.50
Lindbergh, Book, Lone Eagle, 1928 .... 20.00
Lindbergh, Book, Lone Scout Of The Sky, 1928 .... 4.50
Lindbergh, Booklet, 1941 .... 5.00
Lindbergh, Medal, 1928, Congressional, Bronze, 3 In. 25.00
Lindbergh, Music Sheet, Triumphant Lindbergh, 1928 .... 6.00
Lindbergh, Poker Chip, Spirit Of St.Louis 3.00
Lindbergh, Postcard, Lindbergh Riding With King Of Italy 7.00
Lindbergh, Postcard, Photograph 5.00

Locke, Goblet, 6 1/2 In.

(See Page 308)

Lindbergh, Postcard, Photograph Of Lindbergh & Airplane 3.00
Lindbergh, Textile, Commemorative Design, Lindbergh, Plane, Paris, Red, 1 Yard 75.00

Lithophanes are porcelain pictures made by casting clay in layers of various thicknesses. When a piece is held to the light, a picture of light and shadow is seen through it. Most lithophanes date from the 1825 to 1875 period. A few are still being made.

Lithophane, Austrian Scene, Staubbach, No.814, 7 3/4 X 6 In. 90.00
Lithophane, Berchtesgaden Scene, No.1050, 7 3/4 X 6 In. 96.00
Lithophane, Candle Shield, Lady At Well, Lover, P.R. Sickle Mark, 4 X 5 In. 75.00
Lithophane, Cup & Saucer, Lady's Head, Oriental Porcelain, Gold Palms 35.00
Lithophane, Cup, Sake, Peep-I, Japanese, 2 In. 25.00
Lithophane, German Lady Holding Prayerbook, GME-1-83, 7 3/4 In. 185.00
Lithophane, Little Girl In Garden With Boy, Pewter Stand, 4 3/4 In. 60.00
Lithophane, Panel, German Lady With Prayer Book, GME, 7 3/4 X 6 3/16 In. 185.00
Lithophane, Salzburg Scene, Vom Monchsberce Aub, No.1043, 7 3/4 X 6 In. 96.00
Lithophane, Scenic, PPM, No.783, 7 3/4 X 6 In. 88.00
Lithophane, Stein, Blue & White, Delph, Red Devil Faust Inlaid Porcelain Lid 105.00
Lithophane, Stein, Blue Onion, Rustic Scene Of Couple In Leiderhosen, 9 In. 225.00
Lithophane, Stein, German, Monk & Woman, Porcelain, Pewter, Early 19th Century 98.00
Lithophane, Stein, Heidelbert Picnic Scene, Pewter Lid, 1 Liter, German, 9 In. 235.00
Lithophane, Teacup & Saucer, Oriental Lady, White, Gold Palm Trees 22.50
Lithophane, Village Scene, French, No.758, 7 1/2 X 6 In. 93.00
Lithophane, Warmer, Colored Panels Of Castle Scenes With Titles 175.00
Lithophane, Warmer, Scenic Panels, Brass Frame, Burner, 5 In. 140.00
Lithophane, Warmer, Tea, Scenic, Nickel-Plated Stand 185.00
Lithophane, Warmer, Tea, 4 Scenic Panels, Brass Mounts, PPM & Drachenfels 150.00
Lithophane, Warmer, Tea, 4 Scenic Panels, Nickel-Plated Holder, 5 In. 85.00
Lithophane, Warmer, Tea, 4 Scenic Panels, Silver Plate Frame, 5 In. 110.00

Liverpool, England, has been the site of several pottery and porcelain factories from 1716 to 1785. Some earthenware was made with transfer decorations. Sadler and Green made print-decorated wares from 1756. Many of the pieces were made for the American market and featured patriotic emblems such as eagles, flags, and other special-interest motifs.

Liverpool, Jug, Transfer Printed Creamware, Farmers Arms, C.1790, 11 7/8 In. 450.00
Liverpool, Plate, Creamware, Ship, Green, Red, Yellow, & Black, 9 1/2 In. 125.00
Liverpool, Plate, Delft Blue & White, 2 Fighting Cocks, C.1760, 13 3/4 In. 175.00
Lobmeyr, Tumbler, Fluted With Enameled Colonial Man In Cartouche, 4 In. 125.00
Locke Art, Champagne, Vintage, Signed 85.00
Locke Art, Cordial, Vintage, Signed 75.00
Locke Art, Sugar Sifter, Pineapple, Peach To Yellow 95.00
Locke Art, Tumbler, Vintage, Signed 65.00
Locke Art, Wine, Clear Floral Motif 250.00
Locke, Goblet, 6 1/2 In. .... *Illus* 65.00
Loebmeyer, Tumbler, Colonial Gentleman Center, Enamel Floral, Fluted 125.00

Loetz glass was made in Austria in the late nineteenth century. Many pieces are signed Loetz, Loetz-Austria, or Austria, and a pair of crossed arrows in a circle. Some unsigned pieces are confused with Tiffany glass.

Loetz, Basket, Iridescent Blue, Oil Spot Technique, Looped Handle, 7 In. 185.00
Loetz, Bowl, Aqua, Lavender, & Gold Iridescent, Scalloped, 6 1/4 In. 280.00
Loetz, Bowl, Aqua, Lavender, Iridescent Gold, Signed Loetz, Austria, 3 In. 280.00
Loetz, Bowl, Green Iridescent, Ruffled, 8 In. 65.00
Loetz, Bowl, Green Iridescent, Threaded, 5 In. 50.00
Loetz, Bowl, Mounted On Deer Horns, German, Iridescent Amethyst 195.00
Loetz, Bowl, Ruffled Top, Cuspidor Shape, Iridescent Blue, 5 X 6 1/2 In. 168.00
Loetz, Candlestick, Green & Gold, Ribbed, 5 1/2 In. 72.00
Loetz, Centerpiece Bowl, Red Iridescent 150.00
Loetz, Cruet, Multicolor, Threaded Glass 150.00
Loetz, Epergne, 3 Lilies, 2 Nut Cups, Pink Tones, Bronze Base 345.00
Loetz, Inkwell, Green Iridescent, Hinged Brass Lid, Art Nouveau, 5 In. 110.00
Loetz, Inkwell, Green Iridescent, Hinged Floriform Metal Lid, Web Design 125.00
Loetz, Inkwell, Hinged Cover, Dark Blue Iridescent, Textured 135.00
Loetz, Inkwell, 4 Handled, Bronze Lid, Signed DRGM, 4 X 3 1/2 In. 145.00
Loetz, Jar, Biscuit, Applied Decoration, Handled 40.00
Loetz, Rose Bowl, Blue & Gold Swirls, Applied Lily Pads, 3 3/4 In. 275.00
Loetz, Shade, Gold Iridescent, Raindrop Pattern, Brass Connector 75.00
Loetz, Syrup, Blue & Green Iridescent, Random Threading 185.00
Loetz, Tumbler, Green, Ornate 55.00
Loetz, Vase, Applied Snake Handle, Green Iridescent, Lavender Highlights 175.00
Loetz, Vase, Blue Feather On Green Ground, 4 In. 65.00
Loetz, Vase, Blue Green Iridescent, Green Crackle Inner Layer, 12 1/2 In. 325.00
Loetz, Vase, Blue, Amber Pulled Honeycomb Decoration, Lozenge Shape, 5 In. 512.00
Loetz, Vase, Bulbous, Tree Trunk, Iridescent Green, 10 In. 400.00
Loetz, Vase, Burgundy, Random Threading, Square Ruffled Top, Pinches, 5 In. 85.00
Loetz, Vase, Cobalt, Sterling Overlay, Flower Design, Signed, 7 In. 150.00
Loetz, Vase, Crackle Glass, Green And Gold Iridescent, 8 In. 165.00
Loetz, Vase, Frosted, Iridescent, Gold Enamel Floral, 8 1/2 In. 295.00
Loetz, Vase, Gold & Orange Iridescent, 5 In. 95.00
Loetz, Vase, Goose Neck Jack-In-The-Pulpit, Iridescent, 10 1/2 In. 225.00
Loetz, Vase, Green & Blue, Drapery, Scalloped, Signed, 11 In. 350.00
Loetz, Vase, Green Ground With Feathering, Iridescent, 4 1/4 In. 125.00
Loetz, Vase, Green Iridescent, Swirled, Gold Iris, 6 1/2 In. 225.00
Loetz, Vase, Green Trim, 6 In. 150.00
Loetz, Vase, Ice Blue, Silver Overlay 250.00
Loetz, Vase, Iridescent Green, Blue Highlights, 6 1/2 X 4 In. 135.00
Loetz, Vase, Iridescent Pale Cranberry, Gold Highlights, 10 X 5 1/4 In. 250.00
Loetz, Vase, Iridescent Peacock Blue, Green Highlights, Dimple, 5 1/2 In. 185.00
Loetz, Vase, Iridescent Spatter, Ruffled Top, Signed, Austria, 8 3/4 In. 195.00
Loetz, Vase, Iridescent, Applied Random Threading, 4 1/2 X 4 1/2 In. 110.00
Loetz, Vase, Iridescent, Dimpled, 5 X 7 In. 110.00
Loetz, Vase, Iridescent, Pinched, 6 In. 55.00
Loetz, Vase, Iridescent, Spittoon Shape, Pinched Sides, Red, Blue & Gold, 8 In. 75.00

Loetz, Vase, Light Green, Dark Green Coin Dots, Spun Gold, Crimped, 7 In. 300.00
Loetz, Vase, Midnight Blue, Silver Loopings, Double Gourd Shape, 4 In. 575.00
Loetz, Vase, Pink, Green Iridescence, Mottled, 3 Handles, 5 In. 130.00
Loetz, Vase, Red With Silvery Blue Pull Feathers, Crossed Arrows, 6 1/2 In. 395.00
Loetz, Vase, Silvery Blue, Silver Overlay, Unsigned 350.00
Loetz, Vase, Slim Footed, Green Iridescent, Signed, 13 1/4 In. 250.00
Loetz, Vase, Sterling Overlay, Blue Iridescent, Crimped Neck, 6 X 4 In. 195.00
Loetz, Vase, Sterling Overlay, Crimped Rim, Bulbous Body, 5 X 3 In. 335.00
Loetz, Vase, 3 Flared Lips, Blue Veined, Ground Pontil, 5 3/4 In. 185.00
Lone Ranger, Badge, Town Talk 4.00
Lone Ranger, Belt, Premium, Glows In Dark, Secret Safety Phrases, 8 1/2 In. 60.00
Lone Ranger, Book, Black Shirt, Highwayman, Big Little Book 5.00
Lone Ranger, Book, Feature Book, No.31, 1938, Comic Strip, Black & White 25.00
Lone Ranger, Book, Feature No.21 .... 35.00
Lone Ranger, Book, Silver Bullet, Big Little Book 8.00
Lone Ranger, Bullet, Silver, Metal 7.50
Lone Ranger, Card, Gum, 1940, 1 To 24 .... 12.00
Lone Ranger, Doll, Cowboy Outfit & Guns, 16 In. 150.00
Lone Ranger, Figurine, Lone Ranger, Chalkware, 16 In. 13.00
Lone Ranger, Flashlight, Signal Siren, Booklet, Boxed 9.00
Lone Ranger, Game, Metal Men, Parker Bros. 24.00
Lone Ranger, Game, Target, Dated 1938 .... 25.00
Lone Ranger, Gun, Cap Pistol, 7 In. 10.00
Lone Ranger, Horseshoe, Silver's, Lucky 14.00
Lone Ranger, Pin, Sunday Herald Examiner, 1 In. 6.00
Lone Ranger, Puzzle, No.3 .... 4.00
Lone Ranger, Puzzle, No.6 .... 4.00
Lone Ranger, Ring, Pistol Mounted On Top 25.00
Lone Ranger, Ring, Six Gun 35.00
Lone Ranger, Spoon, Lone Ranger & Tonto On Handle 5.00
Lone Ranger, Token, Brass, Picture Of Lone Ranger On Horse 8.00
Lone Ranger, Vest & Mark Set 10.00
Lone Ranger, Viewer, 1948, 4 Rolls Of Film, Boxed 12.00
Lone Ranger, Watch, Lapel, New Haven, Art Deco, Picture On Back 180.00
Lone Ranger, Watch, New Haven, Lone Ranger & Silver Picture 200.00
Longwy, Candelabra, 3 Branch, Enamel On Brass, 11 In. 150.00
Longwy, Tray, Raised Edges, Square, 10 1/4 In. 235.00
Longwy, Vase, Cobalt Top, Blue Body, Black Geometric Designs, 8 X 14 In., Pair 100.00

Lonhuda Pottery Company of Steubenville, Ohio, was organized in 1892 by William Long, W. H. Hunter, and Alfred Day. Brown underglaze slip decorated pottery was made. The firm closed in 1896.

Lonhuda, Sugar & Creamer, Square, Decorated With Blossoms, Signed L.D.D. 275.00
Lonhuda, Vase, Dark Brown, Yellow Poppies, 8 In. 65.00

Lotus ware was made by the Knowles, Taylor & Knowles Company of East Liverpool, Ohio, from 1890 to 1900.

Lotus Ware, Creamer, K.T.K., Violets, Gold Handle, 4 3/4 In. 110.00
Lotus Ware, Cup, K.T.K., Pink And Gold 55.00
Lotus Ware, Pitcher, K.T.K., Pale Green To Cream Base, Florals, 6 In. 165.00
Lotus Ware, Rose Bowl, Florals, Marked Lotus Ware, K.T.K., 1895 .... 495.00
Lotus Ware, Saucer, Demitasse, K.T.K. 20.00
Lotus Ware, Sugar & Creamer, Cover, White, Violets, Gold Fishnet & Handles 280.00
Lotus Ware, Syrup, C.1895, K.T.K., 3 1/2 In. 100.00
Lotus Ware, Syrup, K.T.K., Cream Color, Floral, Gold Lacing, C.1895 .... 100.00
Lotus, Teapot, Fish Net Pattern, Squat Shape 275.00

Low art tiles were made by the J. and J.G. Low Art Tile Works of Chelsea, Massachusetts, from 1877 to 1902. A variety of art and other tiles were made.

Low, Tile, Ben Franklin, Marked F.S.A., Signed, A.O., Olive Brown 75.00
Low, Tile, Green, Child Reading Book, Chelsea, Mass., 6 X 6 In. 37.00
Low, Tile, Urn Picture, Keys Trademark 20.00
Lowestoft, Basket, Blue, White, Oval, Pine Cone Pattern, 9 1/8 In. 200.00

Loy-Nel-Art, see McCoy
Ludwigsburg, Tea Caddy, Floral & Gilding, Sevres Style, C.1790, 4 1/2 In. 150.00
Lundberg, Vase, Blue, Signed And Dated, 7 In. 95.00
Luneville, Umbrella Stand, White, Blue & White Floral 185.00

Lusterware was meant to resemble copper, silver, or gold. It has been used since the sixteenth century. Most of the luster found today was made during the nineteenth century.

Luster, Copper, Blue & Luster Bands, Gold Thorny Handle, 5 1/2 In. 100.00
Luster, Copper, Bowl, Blue Band With Roses, 3 X 4 1/4 In. 65.00
Luster, Copper, Bowl, Copper Leaf On Blue Band, Ye Old Gold Luster, 6 In. 35.00
Luster, Copper, Creamer, Blue Bands, Beaded, 3 1/4 In. 35.00
Luster, Copper, Creamer, Copper Luster Sprigs On Tan Center, 3 1/2 In. 20.00
Luster, Copper, Creamer, Pink Band, Flowers And Leaves, 3 1/2 In. 45.00
Luster, Copper, Cup & Saucer, Blue Band, Raised Pink Flowers 45.00
Luster, Copper, Cup & Saucer, Staffordshire 30.00
Luster, Copper, Cup, Pink Handles 28.50
Luster, Copper, Dish, Sponge, Covered, Pierced, Hand-Painted, 9 X 3 In. 35.00
Luster, Copper, Goblet, Ocher Band Of Green & White Floral & Copper Leaves 49.00
Luster, Copper, Jug, Pink Luster Roses On Blue Band, 3 In. 28.00
Luster, Copper, Jug, Pink Luster Roses On Cream Band, 4 In. 42.00
Luster, Copper, Mug, Blue Band In Middle, 3 1/2 In. 40.00
Luster, Copper, Mug, Tan Band, White & Blue Roses In Relief, Scroll Handle 45.00
Luster, Copper, Mug, Wide Band, Raised Floral Pastel Designs 35.00
Luster, Copper, Mustard Pot, Pink Luster Band, Specks Of Copper, 2 In. 38.00
Luster, Copper, Pitcher, Allerton-Longton 22.50
Luster, Copper, Pitcher, Blue Band & Baskets Of Flowers, 5 In. 60.00
Luster, Copper, Pitcher, Blue Band, 3 1/4 In. 38.00
Luster, Copper, Pitcher, Decal, Oliver Twist Asks For More, England, 4 In. 28.50
Luster, Copper, Pitcher, Diamond Base, Painted Flowers & Leaves, 5 1/2 In. 45.00
Luster, Copper, Pitcher, Embossed Scenes On Blue Band, 3 1/2 In. 25.00
Luster, Copper, Pitcher, Hand-Painted Cobalt Blue Center, 5 In. 50.00
Luster, Copper, Pitcher, Pink & White Bands, Green Leaf Decoration 50.00
Luster, Copper, Pitcher, Wide Blue Band Near Top 45.00
Luster, Copper, Pitcher, 2 Ivory Bands, 5 In. 75.00
Luster, Copper, Pitcher, 2 Yellow Bands, 4 3/4 In. 75.00
Luster, Copper, Pitcher, 4 1/2 In. *Illus* 85.00
Luster, Copper, Pitcher, 9 Panels, Blue Enamel & Flowers, Late 1800s, 8 In. 65.00
Luster, Copper, Salt, Pedestal, Pink Band, 2 1/4 X 2 1/2 In. 38.00
Luster, Copper, Tea Leaf, see Ironstone, Tea Leaf
Luster, Fairyland, see Wedgwood, Fairyland Luster
Luster, Gold, Ewer, Earthenware Lined, 7 1/2 In. 7.00
Luster, Green, Dish, Pancake, White Flowers, Embossed Border, German 32.00
Luster, Lamp, Boudoir, German, Applied Florals, Silk Shades, Pair 50.00
Luster, Mother-Of-Pearl, Bowl, Green Tint, Blue Dragon Center, 10 1/2 In. 495.00
Luster, Mother-Of-Pearl, Bowl, Ochre, Chinese Motif, Floral Medallion, 6 In. 325.00
Luster, Mother-Of-Pearl, Bowl, Octagonal, Orange, Butterflies, 8 In. 475.00
Luster, Orange, Tea Set, Child's, Hand-Painted Bluebirds, 9 Piece 12.50

Luster, Copper, Pitcher, 4 1/2 In.

Luster, Pin, Teapot, 4 X 6 In. 98.00
Luster, Pink, Box, Rock Pile With Dove On Top, 3 1/2 X 2 1/4 In. 85.00
Luster, Pink, Box, White Dove On Lid, 5 3/4 X 4 1/2 In. 85.00
Luster, Pink, Chocolate Pot, Raised Tree Trunk, Blossoms, Marked, 8 1/2 In. 125.00
Luster, Pink, Coffee Set, Child's, Christmas Scenes, Leuctenberg, 15 Piece 185.00
Luster, Pink, Cup & Saucer, Carnation 20.00
Luster, Pink, Cup & Saucer, Cherry 45.00
Luster, Pink, Cup & Saucer, Colored Transfer Of Milkmaid 45.00
Luster, Pink, Cup & Saucer, Enamel Flowers, Wishbone Handle 22.50
Luster, Pink, Cup & Saucer, Faith, Hope, & Charity 150.00
Luster, Pink, Cup & Saucer, Floral, Wishbone Handle 22.00
Luster, Pink, Cup & Saucer, Gold Cord & Tassel, Wishbone Handle, German 16.50
Luster, Pink, Cup & Saucer, Hand-Painted Florals, English, Pair 85.00
Luster, Pink, Cup & Saucer, Handleless Cut, Urn With Flowers, Enamels 31.00
Luster, Pink, Cup & Saucer, House .... 22.00 To 58.00
Luster, Pink, Cup & Saucer, Poppy 20.00
Luster, Pink, Cup & Saucer, Robert Burns, C.1850 .... 47.50
Luster, Pink, Cup Handleless, Floral, 2 1/2 In. 10.00
Luster, Pink, Cup, Lady's Spit, Footed 45.00
Luster, Pink, Eggcup, Inscribed A Present From Belfast 4.00
Luster, Pink, Gravy Boat, Strawberry 98.00
Luster, Pink, Hair Receiver, Silesia 24.00
Luster, Pink, House, Pratt Type, 6 In. 18.50
Luster, Pink, Mug, Floral, Pouring Lip 10.00
Luster, Pink, Mug, Frog, Outdoor Scenes, Hand-Colored Transfer, 4 1/2 In. 135.00
Luster, Pink, Mug, Shaving, Raised Decoration 12.50
Luster, Pink, Mug, Soldier's & Sailor's Home, Erie, Pa., Gold Trim, 3 1/2 In. 18.00
Luster, Pink, Pitcher, Black Transfer Cathedral Scene, Davenport, 8 In., 1805 .... 175.00
Luster, Pink, Pitcher, Sairey Gamp Entertains Betsy Prig, Lancaster, 4 In. 12.00
Luster, Pink, Plate, Cake, House Pattern, Handles 37.50
Luster, Pink, Plate, Cup, Davenport, Teaberry, 4 In. 22.50
Luster, Pink, Plate, Cup, Floral & Leaf Decoration 25.00
Luster, Pink, Plate, Scalloped Edge, 7 1/2 In. 8.00
Luster, Pink, Plate, Staffordshire, England, 7 In. 22.50
Luster, Pink, Sugar, Cover, 5 X 6 In. 28.00
Luster, Pink, Tea Set, Old Castle England, Flower Decoration 98.00
Luster, Pink, Toothpick, Gold Trim 36.00
Luster, Pink, Tumbler, West Baden, Ind. 11.00
Luster, Pink, Vase, Soldier's & Sailor's Home, Erie, Pa., Violets, 5 In. 18.00
Luster, Purple, Cup & Saucer, Handleless, English Temperance Movement, 1800s 40.00
Luster, Silver, Chalice, Copper Luster Lining, C.1840 .... 58.00
Luster, Silver, Creamer, Allover Diamond And Ribbed 55.00
Luster, Silver, Cup & Saucer, Blue And Gold 22.00
Luster, Silver, Goblet, Copper Luster Lining, C.1840, 4 1/4 In. 58.00
Luster, Silver, Pitcher, G & S Ltd., Albany & Harvey Potteries, Burslem 60.00
Luster, Silver, Pitcher, Milk, Roses, Bavaria, Blue 37.50
Luster, Silver, Pitcher, Squatty, Grape Design, J.P., France 75.00
Luster, Silver, Tea Set, 11 Piece, MZ Czechoslovakia 135.00
Luster, Silver, Teapot, Acorn Finial, 7 In. 125.00
Luster, Vase, Pink, Bird In Relief, 2 Handles, 6 1/2 In. 12.50

Lustre Art Glass Company was founded in Long Island, New York, in 1920 by Conrad Vahlsing and Paul Frank. The company made lampshades and globes that are almost indistinguishable from those made by Quezal.

Lustre Art, Shade, Gold Hooked Design On White Ground, Signed Set Of 4 .... 400.00
Lustre Art, Shade, Gold Ribbed Iridescent, Signed 75.00
Lustre Art, Shade, Gold Spider Webbing, Signed, 5 1/2 In. 85.00
Lustre Art, Shade, Green Iridescent, White Gold Interior 117.00
Lustre Art, Shade, Random Threading Over Green & Gold Hearts, Signed 130.00
Lustre Art, Shade, Ribbed, Iridescent, Signed 125.00

Lustres are mantel decorations, or pedestal vases, with many hanging glass prisms. The name really refers to the prisms, and it is proper to refer to a single glass prism as a lustre. Either spelling, luster or lustre, is correct.

Maize, Vase, Libbey

Majolica, Pitcher, 4 1/2 In.

Lustres, Cranberry, Opalescent Snake On Stem, Crystal Prisms, 14 In., Pair ... 400.00

Lustres, Opalescent, Hand-Painted, Notched Prisms, 13 1/2 In., Pair ... 225.00

Lustres, Silver, Sugar, Covered, Rib Design ... 110.00

Lutz glass was made in the 1870s by Nicholas Lutz at the Boston and Sandwich Company. He made a delicate and intricate threaded glass of several colors. Other similar wares are referred to as Lutz.

Lutz, Basket, Candy Cane Stripes, 6 In. ... 62.00

Lutz, Bottle, Perfume, Green, Blue, & Red, White Stripes, 5 In. ... 42.50

Lutz, Bowl, Finger And Underplate, White, Aqua, Yellow, Gold Twisted Thread ... 275.00

Lutz, Cup & Saucer, Latticinio ... 45.00

Lutz, Finger Bowl, Ribbed, Rose-Colored Threading, 5 In. ... 45.00

Lutz, Lamp, Pink & White Ribbon, Blown, 31 In. ... 135.00

Lutz, Tumbler, Lavender Stripes, Green & Gold Twisted Thread ... 275.00

Lutz, Vase, Filigree, Pink & Blue Spirals, Goldstone, Stick, 8 1/2 In. ... 195.00

Maastricht, Bowl, Pajong, Sphinx Mark, Cream & Black On White, 8 In. ... 65.00

Maastricht, Bowl, Waste, Flow Blue, Oriental Decoration, Hong, 6 In. ... 27.50

Maastricht, Cup & Saucer, Handleless, Small, Orange Band, P.Regout ... 10.00

Maastricht, Plate, Game Bird, Brown To Cream, Petrus Ragout & Co., 9 1/2 In. ... 8.50

Maastricht, Plate, Game, Pierced To Hang, Pair ... 35.00

Maastricht, Plate, Stick Spatter, 9 1/2 In. ... 20.00

Maize glass, sold by the W.L.libbey & Son Company of Toledo, Ohio, was made by Joseph Locke in 1889. It is pressed glass formed like an ear of corn. Most pieces were made for household use.

Maize, Celery, Ivory, 6 1/2 In. ... 150.00

Maize, Celery, Libbey, Joseph Locke, White, Green Shucks, 6 1/2 In. ... 175.00

Maize, Condiment Set, White, Green Husks, Stand, 4 Piece ... 95.00

Maize, Muffineer, Libbey ... 195.00

Maize, Tumbler, Blue, Opalescent, Swirled ... 48.00

Maize, Vase, Libbey ... *Illus* 87.50

Majolica, see also Wedgwood

Majolica is any pottery glazed with a tin enamel. Most of the majolica found today is decorated with leaves, shells, branches, and other natural shapes and in natural colors. It was a popular nineteenth-century product.

Majolica, Basket, Double Handled, Seaweed & Shell, 9 In. ... 55.00

Majolica, Bowl, Lily & Fern, Signed Hollcroft, 15 In. ... 150.00

Majolica, Bowl, 6 Plates, Green Lettuce Leaf ... 75.00

Majolica, Box & Attached Underplate, Sardine, Fish On Lily Pad Handle ... 70.00

Majolica, Butter Pat, Green & Cranberry, Leaf Shape ... 12.00

Majolica, Cake Stand, Etruscan, Tree Base And Leaf Effect Top, Footed ... 49.00

Majolica, Candlestick, Palmer Cox Uncle Sam, 9 In. ... 150.00

Majolica, Centerpiece Bowl, Ships & Anchors, Footed, Scalloped ... 375.00

Majolica, Compote, Decorated, Pierced Rim, Wedgwood ... 125.00

Majolica, Compote, Shell On 3 Dolphin Legs, Triangular Base, C.1850, 9 In. ... 62.00

Majolica, Compote, Wedgwood, Greenleaf, Orange, Cobalt Center, 11 In. ... 125.00

Majolica, Cup & Saucer, Green Leaf & Tan Shells, Pink Lining, Cane Handle ... 90.00

Majolica, Dish, Candy, Leaf Shape, Green, Wedgwood, C.1960 ... 8.00

Majolica, Dish, Cheese, House Shape ... 20.00

Majolica, Dish, Cheese, Multicolor ... 125.00

Majolica, Dish, Etruscan, Leaf Shape, Signed 18.00
Majolica, Dish, Leaf, Green, Brown, White, Lavender, 9 In. 20.00
Majolica, Dish, Shell Shape, GHS, Shell Feet, 6 In. 74.00
Majolica, Figurine, Negro Boy With Basket, 8 Colors, 8 1/2 In. 27.50
Majolica, Group, 2 Drunk Monks With Empty Tankards, 7 X 5 1/2 In. 75.00
Majolica, Humidor, American, Frog 42.00
Majolica, Jar, Tobacco, Alligator, Green, Pink Cape, Pipe In Hand 55.00
Majolica, Jar, Tobacco, Elephant, Gray With Pink Jacket, Pipe In Mouth 65.00
Majolica, Jar, Tobacco, Figure Of Pipe, Pink Floral Decoration On Jade 35.00
Majolica, Jar, Tobacco, Owl, 7 In. 45.00
Majolica, Jardiniere, Incised Flowers, Lear's Patent, Wine Color, 10 In. 60.00
Majolica, Match Holder, Boy Beside Barrel, Hohenstein, C.1850 .... 55.00
Majolica, Match Holder, Puppy Dog On Leaf 18.00
Majolica, Mug, Frog, 2 Handles, Dark Green, Raised Vines, 2 Frogs, 1860 .... 100.00
Majolica, Pitcher, Blue, Lavender, Calla Lilies, 7 1/2 In. 30.00
Majolica, Pitcher, Brown Ground, Sculptured Bird, Bamboo Handle, 6 3/4 In. 67.50
Majolica, Pitcher, England, 5 In., Yellow, Blackberries, Pink Interior 32.00
Majolica, Pitcher, Etruscan, Greek Temple Scene, Tin Glaze, 9 1/2 In. 45.00
Majolica, Pitcher, Etruscan, Light Blue, Scenic, Greek Key Design, 9 1/2 In. 65.00
Majolica, Pitcher, Etruscan, Tin Glaze, C.1865, Greek Temple, Greek Key Rim 45.00
Majolica, Pitcher, Figural, Fish, 9 In. .... 26.00 To 47.50
Majolica, Pitcher, Figural, Owl, Gray, Green, 9 In. 80.00
Majolica, Pitcher, France, Rooster, 9 X 6 In. 47.50
Majolica, Pitcher, Medallions, Swan Neck & Handle, Victorian, 3 In. 18.50
Majolica, Pitcher, Rooster, French, 9 In. 37.50
Majolica, Pitcher, Shorter & Son, Ltd., Corn Shape, Pink Lining, 6 1/2 In. 40.00
Majolica, Pitcher, Water, Griffin, Smith & Hill, C.1880, Begonia Leaves 65.00
Majolica, Pitcher, Wild Rose, Lavender Inside, 6 1/2 In. 35.00
Majolica, Pitcher, 4 Fish, Lined In Pink, Applied Handle 38.00
Majolica, Pitcher, 4 1/2 In. .... *Illus* 26.00
Majolica, Planter, Wall, Bird's Nest 35.00
Majolica, Plaque, E.Bingham Castle Hedingham, 10 In. 90.00
Majolica, Plate, Blackberries, Cream Basketweave Ground, 13 1/2 In. 24.00
Majolica, Plate, Etruscan, Shell & Seaweed, 7 In. 28.00
Majolica, Plate, Fish & Flower, J.Holdcroft, 8 1/2 In. 40.00
Majolica, Plate, Green, Cabbage Leaf, Chick On Side, 8 1/2 X 3 1/2 In. 42.00
Majolica, Plate, Green, Water Lilies, C.1865, 9 In. 18.00
Majolica, Plate, Hand-Painted Bull, Openwork, Wedgwood, 9 In. 125.00
Majolica, Plate, Raised Leaves, Green, Tan, & White, C.1850, 8 In., Pair 48.00
Majolica, Plate, Raised Leaves, Multicolors, C.1860, 8 1/4 In., Pair 45.00
Majolica, Plate, Shaggy Dog, 11 In. 20.00
Majolica, Plate, Shell And Seaweed, 8 In., Marked Etruscan 36.00
Majolica, Platter, Dog In Center, 12 In. 50.00
Majolica, Platter, Pineapple, Cobalt Center, Green Foliage, 10 In. 36.00
Majolica, Platter, Wedgwood, Butterfly And Basketweave Design 53.00
Majolica, Shoe, Bootie, Flowers, 4 In. 15.00
Majolica, Shoe, Jester's, Green, Floral & Leaf, Victorian, 9 In. 42.00
Majolica, Slipper, Applied Leaves And Large Flower 37.50
Majolica, Smoking Set, Negro Man Playing Banjo, 3 Piece 20.00
Majolica, Spittoon, Bamboo, C.1860 .... 39.50
Majolica, Spittoon, Floral Decoration, Green To Brown 16.00
Majolica, Spittoon, Shield & Rib, 7 In. 50.00
Majolica, Sugar, Covered, Ear Of Corn 12.00
Majolica, Syrup, Blue And Green Fern Pattern, Metal Hinged Cover, 4 In. 28.00
Majolica, Syrup, Etruscan, Signed GHS, Sunflower 87.00
Majolica, Syrup, Etruscan, Sunflower In High Relief 48.00
Majolica, Syrup, Lavender Lining, Pewter Lid 45.00
Majolica, Teapot, Etruscan, Cauliflower .... 65.00 To 85.00
Majolica, Teapot, Etruscan, Shell & Seaweed, Albino, Blue, Red & Gold 175.00
Majolica, Umbrella Stand, Brown & Orange Variegated Glaze 65.00
Majolica, Vase, Cobalt, Blues, & Aquas, Serpent Forms Handles, 12 In. 38.50
Majolica, Vase, Green & Turquoise, Pink Floral Top, 5 In. 12.50
Majolica, Vase, Green Bird On Tree Stump, 5 1/2 In. 40.00
Majolica, Vase, Pink & Lavender Floral, Leaf & Vine, P.D.V. & Acorn, 8 In. 37.50

Majolica, Vase, Protruding Grape, Leaves 22.00
Mantel, see Furniture, Mantel

Marbles of glass were made during the nineteenth century. Venetian swirl, clear glass, sulfides, and marbles with frosted white animal figures embedded in the glass were popular. Handmade clay marbles were made in many places, but most of them came from the pottery factories of Ohio and Pennsylvania. Occasionally, real stone marbles of onyx, carnelian, or jasper can be found.

Marble, Akro Agate, Cardinal Red, 1/2 In., Box Of 25 .... 17.00
Marble, Bennington, Blue, 3/4 In. 3.00
Marble, Bennington, Brown, 3/4 In. 2.00
Marble, Bennington, Light To Dark Brown, 1 1/2 In. 8.00
Marble, Candle Swirl, 2 Moons, 2 1/2 In. 40.00
Marble, Candy Swirl, 1 1/2 In. 40.00
Marble, Carving , C.1860, 6 In.High .... *Illus* 250.00
Marble, Latticinio, White Core, Red, Blue, & Orange Stripes, 1 3/4 In. 60.00
Marble, Mica Fleck, Clear, 7/8 In. 8.00
Marble, Sulfide, Elephant, 2 In. 110.00
Marble, Sulfide, Fish, 1 In. 45.00
Marble, Sulfide, Greyhound, 1 3/4 In. 49.00
Marble, Sulfide, Lion, Sitting, 6 In. 65.00
Marble, Sulfide, Long-Haired Dog 40.00
Marble, Sulfide, Prancing Horse, 1 1/4 In. 55.00
Marble, Sulfide, Rabbit, Running 55.00
Marble, Sulfide, Reclining Lion, 6 In. 75.00
Marble, Sulfide, Sitting Child, 6 In. 125.00
Marble, Sulfide, Squirrel, 1 1/2 In. 46.00
Marble, Swirl, Red With Yellow, 3/4 In. 4.00
Marble, Swirl, Solid Core Swirls, 3/4 In. 7.00
Marble, Swirl, Split Core Swirls, 1 In. 10.00
Marble, Swirl, Split Core Swirls, 3/4 In. 7.00
Marble, Swirl, 1 In. 5.00
Marble, Swirl, 1 1/8 In. 8.00
Marble, Swirl, 1 1/4 In. 12.00
Marble, Swirl, 1 3/8 In. 20.00
Marble, Swirl, 1 1/2 In. 22.00
Marble, Swirl, 1 5/8 In. 20.00
Marble Swirl, 1 11/16 In. 35.00
Marble, Swirl, 4 Moons, 1 3/4 In. 35.00
Marble, Swirl, 5 Moons, 1 3/4 In. 32.50

The Marblehead Pottery was founded in 1905 as a rehabilitative program for the patients of a Marblehead, Mass., sanitarium by Dr. J. Hall. Two years later it was separated from the sanitarium, and it continued operations until 1936. Many of the pieces were decorated with marine motifs.

Marblehead, Bowl, Blue Semimatte, Green, Blue, & Red Floral, 5 3/4 In. 350.00
Marblehead, Bowl, Cobalt, Miniature 18.00
Marblehead, Bowl, Cobalt, 10 In. 32.00
Marblehead, Bowl, Flat, Cobalt 32.00

Marble, Carving, C.1860, 6 In.High

Marblehead, Bowl, Stippled Blue Glaze, 8 In. 34.00
Marblehead, Planter, Light Green, 6 1/2 In. 37.00
Marblehead, Planter, Tobacco Brown, 5 1/2 In. 34.00
Marblehead, Plate, Border Of Dogs And Tree, 3 Colors 245.00
Marblehead, Vase, Blue Semimatte, Green Butterflies & Floral, 4 1/2 In. 375.00
Marblehead, Vase, Blue, 8 In. 55.00
Marblehead, Vase, Gray, Flying Geese, Ship Mark, 9 1/2 In. 65.00
Marblehead, Vase, Green, Speckled, 5 In. 40.00
Marblehead, Vase, Green, 4 1/2 In. 25.00
Marblehead, Vase, Rose, White Scenic Top Band, 4 1/2 In. 63.00
Marblehead, Vase, Stippled Blue Glaze, 4 1/4 In. 38.00
Marblehead, Vase, Stippled Gray Glaze, 4 In. 38.00
Marblehead, Wall Pocket, Blue, 5 In. 50.00
Marilyn Monroe, Calendar, 1954, Nude 6.00
Marilyn Monroe, Thermometer, 1949, Mirror, 6 X 8 In. 35.00
Marilyn Monroe, Tray, Tip, Nude 20.00
Marine, see Nautical
Marple, Sulfide, Cougar, 6 1/2 In. 65.00

Martinware is a salt-glazed stoneware made by the Martin Brothers of Middlesex, England, between 1873 and 1915. Many figural jugs and vases were made.

Martinware, Vase, Gourd Shape, 3 In. 110.00
Martinware, Vase, Imaginative Bird, 6 In. 1400.00

Mary Gregory glass is identified by a characteristic white figure painted on dark glass. It was made from 1870 to 1910. The name refers to any glass decorated with a white silhouette figure and not just the Sandwich glass originally painted by Miss Mary Gregory.

Mary Gregory, Ale Glass, Amber, Boy & Foliage, Gold Edge, Paneled 45.00
Mary Gregory, Ale Glass, Amber, Boy, Tinted Face, Ringed Pedestal Base 40.00
Mary Gregory, Ale Glass, Amber, Girl & Foliage, Gold Edge, Paneled 45.00
Mary Gregory, Ale Glass, Amber, Girl, Tinted Face, Ringed Pedestal Base 40.00
Mary Gregory, Ale Set, Amber, 13 In. Tankard, 4 Mugs 343.00
Mary Gregory, Bottle, Barber, Blue, Boy In White Enamel 80.00
Mary Gregory, Bottle, Barber, Cobalt, Tennis Girl 100.00
Mary Gregory, Bottle, Barber, Cobalt, White Enameled Girl With Tennis Racket 125.00
Mary Gregory, Bottle, Barber, Sandwich, Amethyst 125.00
Mary Gregory, Bottle, Barber's, Clear, 6 1/2 In. 55.00
Mary Gregory, Bottle, Dresser, White Enamel Boy, Faceted Stopper, 8 In. 115.00
Mary Gregory, Bottle, Dresser, White Enamel Girl, Faceted Stopper, 8 In. 115.00
Mary Gregory, Box, Jewel, Amber, Girl & Foliage, Hinged Lid, Brass Base, 4 In. 150.00
Mary Gregory, Box, Jewelry, Purple, Silver Plate Fittings, Square, 4 In. 145.00
Mary Gregory, Box, Opaline, Blue, White Enameled Girl, Enameled Flowers 50.00
Mary Gregory, Box, Patch, Hinged, Amethyst With White Enameled Boy 98.00
Mary Gregory, Box, Sandwich, Round, Covered, 3 Feet, 3 X 3 1/2 In. 95.00
Mary Gregory, Creamer, All White Girl, 6 In. 110.00
Mary Gregory, Creamer, Clear, Boy, Tinted Face, 3 In. 65.00
Mary Gregory, Creamer, Ground Pontil, Clear Handle, Blue, 4 In. 69.00
Mary Gregory, Cruet, All White Figure 90.00
Mary Gregory, Cruet, Amethyst With White, Angel & Flowers 175.00
Mary Gregory, Cruet, Boy, Pink Cheeks, Inverted Rib 95.00
Mary Gregory, Cruet, Cranberry Glass, 8 In. 110.00
Mary Gregory, Cruet, Emerald Green, White Scene Of Boy On Tree Stump 110.00
Mary Gregory, Cruet, Girl, Pink Face, Inverted Rib 110.00
Mary Gregory, Cruet, Green Ground 100.00
Mary Gregory, Decanter, Sapphire Blue, Girl, Crystal Steeple Stopper, 11 In. 105.00
Mary Gregory, Decanter, Wine, Boy & Dog Taking His Ship To Sail, Handled 60.00
Mary Gregory, Decanter, Wine, Steeple Stopper, Lime Green, Girl, 10 1/4 In. 110.00
Mary Gregory, Ewer, Pale Green, Applied Striated Handle, Blown, 12 In. 195.00
Mary Gregory, Finger Bowl, Cranberry, Girl Blowing Bubbles, 5 In. 60.00
Mary Gregory, Flask, Pocket, Blue, Silver-Plated Mounts, 5 1/2 In. 123.00
Mary Gregory, Glass, Ale, Olive Green, Enameled Girl & Boy, 6 In. 45.00
Mary Gregory, Glass, Cranberry, White Enameled Girl, 4 In. 55.00

Mary Gregory, Lamp, Black, Boy Fishing, Kerosene, Etched Shade, 21 In. 450.00
Mary Gregory, Lamp, Cranberry With White Enameled Girl, 11 1/2 In., Pair 300.00
Mary Gregory, Lamp, Cranberry, Miniature 225.00
Mary Gregory, Mug, Cranberry, White Boy, Engraved World's Fair, 1893 .... 50.00
Mary Gregory, Mug, Cranberry, 3 In. 76.00
Mary Gregory, Mug, Sapphire Blue, Boy, Applied Handle, 4 In. 48.00
Mary Gregory, Pitcher, Cranberry, Clear Handle, White Boy, 4 In. 110.00
Mary Gregory, Pitcher, Cranberry, White Dutch Colonial Men, Windmill, 8 In. 185.00
Mary Gregory, Pitcher, Emerald Green, Boy, Applied Handle, 5 In. 65.00
Mary Gregory, Pitcher, Emerald Green, Girl Standing In Tree, 6 In. 155.00
Mary Gregory, Pitcher, Emerald Green, White Woman On Bench 135.00
Mary Gregory, Pitcher, Girl Picking Flowers, Crystal Handle, 11 1/2 In. 145.00
Mary Gregory, Pitcher, Green, Boy, Paneled Sides, 5 In. 75.00
Mary Gregory, Pitcher, Honey Amber, Girl With Jump Rope In White, 13 In. 265.00
Mary Gregory, Pitcher, Olive Amber, Boy, Blue Handle & Foot, Flint, 12 In. 195.00
Mary Gregory, Pitcher, Water, Boy & Birds, Fluted Rim, Bulbous, 9 In. 100.00
Mary Gregory, Pitcher, Water, Girl, Floral, & Fauna 75.00
Mary Gregory, Pitcher, Water, Green, White Children, Applied Ribbed Handle 165.00
Mary Gregory, Plate, Amber, Girl Picking Flowers In White, 6 3/4 In. 88.00
Mary Gregory, Plate, Courting Couple, White Enamel On Amber, 10 1/2 In. 85.00
Mary Gregory, Plate, Man Leaning On Railing, White Enamel, Amber, 10 1/2 In. 85.00
Mary Gregory, Ring Stand, Ruby, 3 In. 80.00
Mary Gregory, Stein, Amber, Gilt In Garden, Thumb Lift, 3 In. 135.00
Mary Gregory, Sugar Shaker, Cranberry, 8-Piece Tin Top, 4 1/3 In. 125.00
Mary Gregory, Tray, Pin, Cranberry, 4 1/2 In. 84.00
Mary Gregory, Tumbler, Amber To Clear, White Girl 60.00
Mary Gregory, Tumbler, Amber, Boy 28.00
Mary Gregory, Tumbler, Amber, Girl 28.00
Mary Gregory, Tumbler, Apricot To Clear, White Decoration, 3 3/4 In. 50.00
Mary Gregory, Tumbler, Blue, Boy In Garden 54.00
Mary Gregory, Tumbler, Blue, Girl In Garden 54.00
Mary Gregory, Tumbler, Green, Boy 28.00
Mary Gregory, Tumbler, Green, Figure Of Oliver 95.00
Mary Gregory, Tumbler, Green, Girl 28.00
Mary Gregory, Tumbler, Pedestal, Blue With White Boy, Gold Trim 42.00
Mary Gregory, Tumbler, Sapphire Blue, Girl & Boy, 5 1/8 In., Pair 95.00
Mary Gregory, Tumbler, Sapphire Blue, Girl Holding Flowers 20.00
Mary Gregory, Vase, Apple Green, White Boy & Foliage, Paneled, 5 3/4 In. 40.00
Mary Gregory, Vase, Black Amethyst, Barefoot Children Blowing Bubbles, Pair 145.00
Mary Gregory, Vase, Black Amethyst, Boy Blowing Horn, Girl With Flower, Pair 265.00
Mary Gregory, Vase, Black Amethyst, Girl In Garden, Sandwich, 15 In. 165.00
Mary Gregory, Vase, Blue, Ruffled Top, 8 In. 65.00
Mary Gregory, Vase, Bud, Cranberry On Clear Pedestal, Boy In White, 6 In. 75.00
Mary Gregory, Vase, Cranberry, Boy Walking Midst Trees, Bulbous, 8 3/4 In. 114.00
Mary Gregory, Vase, Cranberry, Boy Wearing Hat, Bulbous, 5 3/4 In. 79.00
Mary Gregory, Vase, Cranberry, Boy With Hoop & Foliage, 7 In. 125.00
Mary Gregory, Vase, Emerald Green, Girl & Boy, Ruffled, 10 In., Pair 235.00
Mary Gregory, Vase, Green, Girl Among Ferns, 6 In. 45.00
Mary Gregory, Vase, Light Blue With White Boy, 7 1/4 In. 25.00
Mary Gregory, Vase, Light Blue, Girl With Flowers, Ribbed, 3 1/2 In. 60.00
Mary Gregory, Vase, Red, Girl & Floral, Clear Overlay, Footed, 8 1/4 In. 225.00
Mary Gregory, Vase, Royal Blue, Cherubs, Sharon Springs Souvenir, Pair 95.00
Mary Gregory, Vase, Sapphire Blue, Girl & Foliage, 9 5/8 In. 70.00
Mary Gregory, Veilleuse, Silver, Cranberry Insert, 3 White Scenes 185.00

Masonic Shrine glassware was made from 1893 to 1917. It is occasionally called Syrian Temple Shrine glassware. Most pieces are dated.

Masonic, Bag, Old Whiting Metal Mesh Cigarette, Shrine & Star Emblem 15.00
Masonic, Bracelet, 14K Gold, With 14K Masonic Charms, C.1920 .... 80.00
Masonic, Butter Pat, Eastern Star, Bone China 10.00
Masonic, Case, Cigarette, Sterling, Gold Stripes, Jeweled Button, W & H C 50.00
Masonic, Chalice, Louisville, 1909, Tobacco Leaf, Iridescent 60.00
Masonic, Chalice, Pittsburgh, Pa., 1899 .... 60.00
Masonic, Chalice, San Francisco, 1902, Bear 60.00

Masonic, Chalice, St.Paul, 1908, Red Bowl, Black Foot 65.00
Masonic, Chalice, Washington, D.C., 1900 .... 60.00
Masonic, Champagne, Alligators, Iridescent 50.00
Masonic, Champagne, Louisville, Kentucky, 1909 .... 45.00
Masonic, Champagne, New Orleans, 1910 .... 75.00
Masonic, Champagne, 1909, Louisville, Ky., Gold Swords, Iridescent 75.00
Masonic, Champagne, 1910, Syria Shrine, Alligators, Carnival Glass 45.00
Masonic, Champaign, Pittsburgh, New Orleans, 1910, Temple 30.00
Masonic, Chocolate Pot, Silver Luster Trim 95.00
Masonic, Clip, Paper, Figural, Heavy 35.00
Masonic, Cuff Links & Tie Clasp, Yellow Gold Filled, Sterling Emblems 10.00
Masonic, Cuff Links, Emblems, Pair 12.00
Masonic, Cuff Links, Enameled On Sterling, Pair 7.50
Masonic, Cuff Links, Gold Plated, Pair 10.00
Masonic, Cup & Saucer, Los Angeles, 1906 .... 48.00
Masonic, Cup, Punch, Orange Petal, Twig Handle 45.00
Masonic, Fez Glass, Chicago, 89th Session, Red 20.00
Masonic, Flask, Aquamarine, Union, Clasped Hands, Masonic Emblem, 7 3/4 In. 63.00
Masonic, Flask, Silver Plate, Almalaikah Engraved Scene 20.00
Masonic, Glass, Shot, Clear And Cranberry Flash, Fez, Louisville, 1911 .... 85.00
Masonic, Goblet, Los Angeles, 1907, Footed, Etched 65.00
Masonic, Goblet, Louisville, 1909 .... 48.00
Masonic, Goblet, New Orleans, 1910 .... 48.00
Masonic, Goblet, Rochester, N.Y., 1911 .... 48.00
Masonic, Goblet, Washington, D.C., 1900 .... 48.00
Masonic, Match Safe, Double-Sided Emblem, Patented, 1904 .... 9.00
Masonic, Match Safe, Sterling, Masonic Emblem 35.00
Masonic, Mug, Atlantic City, 1904, Fish Handle And Girl 55.00
Masonic, Mug, Atlantic City, 1904, ZaGaZig, Porcelain, 4 1/4 In. 30.00
Masonic, Mug, Emblem, Monk Eating, Brown Tones, Germany 45.00
Masonic, Mug, Louisville, 1909, Porcelain, 4 1/2 In. 25.00
Masonic, Mug, Niagara Falls, 1905, 3 Handled 55.00
Masonic, Mug, Osman, St.Paul, 1916, Porcelain, 4 1/2 In. 25.00
Masonic, Mug, Saratoga, 1903, Indian In Regalia 60.00
Masonic, Mug, Shaving, Pearlized, Marked 3 Crowns 23.00
Masonic, Paperweight, Metal, Compliments Of Frazier & Jones 14.00
Masonic, Paperweight, Open Bible, Potmetal, Bronze Finish 9.00
Masonic, Pin, Amethyst Pharaoh's Head On Gold Sword, 2 Diamonds, 4 Rubies 110.00
Masonic, Pin, Eastern Star, Enamel, Gold Plated 10.00
Masonic, Pin, Lapel, Platinum, 5 Diamonds 80.00
Masonic, Pin, Lapel, Rose Diamond 15.00
Masonic, Pin, Shriner, Gold, 11 Pearls & 1 Ruby 25.00
Masonic, Plate, Ironstone, 1939, 10 1/2 In. 20.00
Masonic, Plate, Los Angeles, 1906, Tulip 60.00
Masonic, Plate, Shrine Emblem In Gold, Medinah Athletic Club, 1929 .... 7.50
Masonic, Plate, Toledo, 1906, Lady Herding Sheep, Porcelain, 8 In. 30.00
Masonic, Plate, 51st Annual Conclave, York, Pa., 1904, Blue & White, 9 In. 47.00
Masonic, Ring, Black Onyx, 10K Gold 20.00
Masonic, Ring, Diamond, 10K Yellow Gold 75.00
Masonic, Ring, Eastern Star, 14K Gold, Diamond 80.00
Masonic, Ring, Eastern Star, 14K White Gold, Enameled 19.00
Masonic, Ring, Eastern Star, 5 Colored Stones In Points, 10K Yellow Gold 14.00
Masonic, Ring, Rectangular Red Stone, 14K Gold 22.00
Masonic, Ring, Sapphire, 10K Yellow Gold 45.00
Masonic, Ring, 32nd Degree, Diamond, 15K Gold Setting 88.00
Masonic, Shot Glass, St.Paul, Minn., 1908, Syria Shrine, Cranberry & Gold 75.00
Masonic, Spoon, Eastern Star, Silver Plate 5.00
Masonic, Spoon, Eastern Star, Sterling Silver 15.00
Masonic, Spoon, George Washington Handle, Sterling Silver 9.00
Masonic, Spoon, Sterling With Plain Gold Wash Bowl, Masonic Symbols Handle 20.00
Masonic, Spoon, Susquehanna 167, Bright Cut, Gold-Washed Bowl 14.00
Masonic, Spoon, Temple, Chicago In Bowl, Sterling 20.00
Masonic, Tankard, Egyptian Scene & Emblems, Willet's Belleek, 4 1/2 In. 60.00
Masonic, Tankard, Newark, N.J., 1853-1913, Blues, Silver Luster Trim, 12 In. 85.00

Masonic, Teaspoon, Chicago Temple, Sterling Silver 10.00
Masonic, Teaspoon, Emblems On Handle, Gold Wash Bowl, Sterling Silver 16.00
Masonic, Teaspoon, Pittsburgh In Bowl, Sterling Silver 16.00
Masonic, Tiepin, Blue Enamel Trowel With Gold Insignia, Gold 18.00
Masonic, Trivet, Brass, 7 In. 27.00
Masonic, Tumbler, Atlantic City, 1904, Fish Handle 35.00
Masonic, Tumbler, Fort Pitt., Child Riding Camel, 1896, 3 In. 75.00
Masonic, Tumbler, Pittsburgh, Pa., June 4, 1918, Al & Bill, Beige & White 22.00
Masonic, Watch Fob, Kansas City Commandery, Crossback Temple 20.00
Masonic, Watch Fob, Mother-Of-Pearl & Enamel In Gold, Square 25.00
Masonic, Wine, Rochester, 1900, Knights Of Pythias, Green & Gold 25.00
Masonic, Wine, San Francisco, June 10, 1902, Syria Shrine, Gold Trim 55.00

Massier pottery is iridescent French art pottery made by Clement Massier in Golfe-Juane, France, in the late nineteenth and early twentieth centuries. It is characterized by a metallic luster glaze.

Massier, Vase, Pale Violets On Green, Signed, French, 12 In. 150.00
Massier, Vase, Pink, Enamel Bees, Gold, & Raspberry Trim, Clement, 5 1/2 In. 125.00

Match Holder, see also Iron, Match Holder; Staffordshire, Match Holder; Store, Match Holder

Match Holder, A Match For Any Man, Beehive Shape, Floral, 3 In. 15.00
Match Holder, Atlanta Exposition, 1895, Metal Cotton Bale 19.00
Match Holder, Beaded Double Pocket, Dated 1906 .... 30.00
Match Holder, Beaded, 1899 .... 3.50
Match Holder, Bisque, Hanging With Two Cupid Holders 46.00
Match Holder, Blue Glass Boot, Wall 35.00
Match Holder, Book Shape, Glass 15.00
Match Holder, Bulldog, 1 Cent 8.00
Match Holder, Celluloid, Nude, Advertising 35.00
Match Holder, Double Pocket, Negro Lady's Head In Center 40.00
Match Holder, Elephant's Head, Glass, Hanging 16.00
Match Holder, Figural, Burnt Wood Hanging Indian Head, Matches Go In Pipe 16.00
Match Holder, Figural, Pair Of Boots, Porcelain, Pink & Green On White, 4 In. 28.00
Match Holder, Figural, Standing Pyrographic Wishing Well 11.00
Match Holder, Iron, Fireplace .... *Illus* 30.00
Match Holder, Iron, Wall, 4 1/2 In. .... *Illus* 15.00
Match Holder, Knights Of Columbus, 1919, Metal, Book Shape 12.00

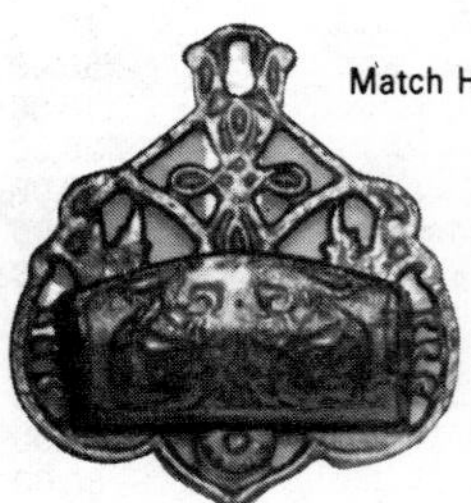

Match Holder, Iron, Wall, 4 1/2 In.

Matchbox, Tin, 4 In.

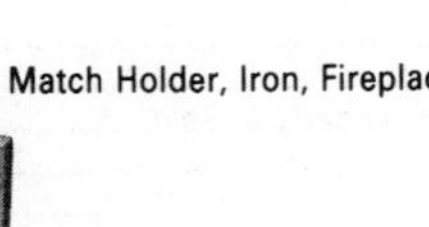

Match Holder, Iron, Fireplace

Match Holder, One Cent Box, Jade Enamel, Marked China 65.00
Match Holder, Peabody Hotel, Memphis, Tennessee, Union Porcelain 15.00
Match Holder, Pottery Base, Striker On Central Pedestal, 5 In. 20.00
Match Holder, Striker, German Boy As Chimney Sweep With Ladder 35.00
Match Holder, Tin, Victoria, Tin Cupids 13.00
Match Holder, Turtle With Lady's Head, Shell Lifts, Nude Body Inside 8.00
Match Holder, White Skull, Nodder Jar, Pottery, 3 In. 15.00
Match Safe, see also Silver, Sterling, Match Safe
Match Safe, Acorns, Sterling, Art Nouveau 42.00
Match Safe, Applied Thistle And Silver, Coin 20.00
Match Safe, B.P.O.E., Embossed Elk & Clock 25.00
Match Safe, Barrel, Silver Over Brass 29.00
Match Safe, Elephant, Ivory Tusks 75.00
Match Safe, Filigree, Sterling Silver, Round, 3 In. 22.50
Match Safe, Geisha Girl, Brass 14.00
Match Safe, Gold & Sterling, Cabochon Ruby, Cartier, 2 1/4 X 1 3/4 In. 50.00
Match Safe, Jeans With Suspenders Shape, 1886 .... 45.00
Match Safe, Louisiana Purchase 22.00
Match Safe, Mt.Washington, N.H., Leather Covered, Cigar Cutter, Pocket 9.95
Match Safe, Orchids, Sterling, Art Nouveau 42.00
Match Safe, Pig Holding Bag Marked One Dollar, Gold Washed 55.00
Match Safe, Pocket, Nickel-Plated Steel, 2 Rows Of Beading 7.50
Match Safe, Roaming Lions, Sterling Silver 52.50
Match Safe, Setters At Point In Relief, Silver, Pocket 24.00
Match Safe, Silver Plate, American Flag & Lady Liberty Medallions 15.00
Match Safe, Silver Plate, Columbian Exposition, Chicago, 1892, Uncle Sam 65.00
Match Safe, Silver Plate, Cord-Tied Bundle With Gift Card Under Cord 125.00
Match Safe, Silver, Hallmark Birmingham, 1908, St.Andrews Coat Of Arms 20.00
Match Safe, Souvenir, Atlantic City, Leather Covered Cigar Cutter Bottom 18.00
Match Safe, St.Louis, 1904 .... 25.00
Match Safe, Sterling Silver, Acanthus, Fleur-De-Lis, & Scroll, Unger Bros. 85.00
Match Safe, Sterling Silver, Chased & Engraved Floral, Pocket, 2 1/4 In. 25.00
Match Safe, Sterling Silver, Dancing Jester & 4 Women Scene 55.00
Match Safe, Sterling Silver, Engraved Lee 18.50
Match Safe, Sterling Silver, Floral 14.00
Match Safe, Sterling Silver, Fraternal Emblem 16.00
Match Safe, Sterling Silver, Golf Clubs 22.50
Match Safe, Sterling Silver, Griffin Supports Name Scroll, Floral 22.00
Match Safe, Sterling Silver, Raised Flowers & Leaves 18.00
Match Safe, Sterling Silver, Repousse Mythological Figures 52.50
Match Safe, Sterling Silver, Rococo Style, Relief Decoration, 2 5/8 In. 35.00
Match Safe, Sterling Silver, Rounded Corners, 2 1/2 In. 30.00
Match Safe, Sterling, Art Nouveau, Man, Girl, Fish Amid Waves 40.00
Match Safe, Tin 3.50
Matchbox Cover, Brass, San Fernando Mission 4.00
Matchbox Holder, Dog On Top, For 1 Cent Matches, Brass Type Finish 5.00
Matchbox, Tin, 4 In. .... *Illus* 18.00

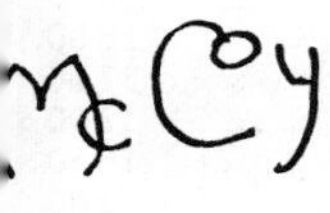

McCoy pottery is made in Roseville, Ohio. The J.W.McCoy Pottery was founded in 1899. It became the Brush McCoy Pottery Company in 1911. The name changed to the Brush Pottery in 1925. The Nelson McCoy Sanitary and Stoneware Company was founded in Roseville, Ohio, in 1910. This firm made art pottery after 1926. In 1933 it became the Nelson McCoy Pottery. Pieces marked McCoy were made by the Nelson McCoy Company.

McCoy, Basket, Green & Brown, Red Berries, 9 In. 14.00
McCoy, Basket, Pineapple, 9 In. 15.00
McCoy, Bean Pot, Brown 15.00
McCoy, Bulb Bowl, White, 8 1/2 In. 6.00
McCoy, Creamer, Pinecone 5.00
McCoy, Cup, Coffee, Brown With Cream, High Glaze 1.50
McCoy, Flowerpot, Green, Leaf & Lily, 6 In. 8.00
McCoy, Jar, Cookie, Apple 8.00
McCoy, Jar, Cookie, Bean Pot, Signed 18.00

McCoy, Jar, Cookie, Bear, Dark Brown, Fat Belly 25.00
McCoy, Jar, Cookie, Big Apple 8.00
McCoy, Jar, Cookie, Black Mammy 8.00
McCoy, Jar, Cookie, Black Potbellied Stove 10.00
McCoy, Jar, Cookie, Cabbage 8.00
McCoy, Jar, Cookie, Clown 25.00
McCoy, Jar, Cookie, Cookie Bank 20.00
McCoy, Jar, Cookie, Covered Wagon, Signed 25.00
McCoy, Jar, Cookie, Cow, Signed Brush 18.00
McCoy, Jar, Cookie, Duck 17.00
McCoy, Jar, Cookie, Hobby Rocking Horse 18.00
McCoy, Jar, Cookie, Indian Teepee 18.00
McCoy, Jar, Cookie, Kitten 8.00
McCoy, Jar, Cookie, Kittens, Ball Of Yarn, Signed 18.00
McCoy, Jar, Cookie, Kookie Kettle 18.00
McCoy, Jar, Cookie, Kookie Kettle, Black 8.00
McCoy, Jar, Cookie, Lantern Fortune Cookie 8.00
McCoy, Jar, Cookie, Little Red Riding Hood 8.00
McCoy, Jar, Cookie, Lollipops 18.00
McCoy, Jar, Cookie, Mammy .... 20.00 To 25.00
McCoy, Jar, Cookie, Man With Mug, Green 25.00
McCoy, Jar, Cookie, Mr. & Mrs. Owl 20.00
McCoy, Jar, Cookie, Oaken Bucket 15.00
McCoy, Jar, Cookie, Pear, Signed 18.00
McCoy, Jar, Cookie, Teakettle, Black 10.00
McCoy, Jar, Cookie, Teakettle, Black, Painted Flowers 10.00
McCoy, Jar, Cookie, Teakettle, Copper Luster 14.00
McCoy, Jar, Cookie, Touring Car 20.00
McCoy, Jar, Cookie, White, Hand-Painted Apple & Leaves 12.00
McCoy, Jar, Cookie, White, Painted Flowers, 9 In. 12.00
McCoy, Jar, Cookie, Wishing Well .... 4.00 To 16.00
McCoy, Jar, Cookie, Wren House, 2 Birds 20.00
McCoy, Jardiniere, Pinecone Feet, 7 X 7 In. 17.50
McCoy, Jardiniere, Pink Butterfly 15.00
McCoy, Mug, Green, Barrel Shape, Shield Mark, 4 1/2 In. 12.50
McCoy, Pitcher, Blue Glaze, 9 1/2 In. 10.00
McCoy, Pitcher, Maroon, 2 Quart 8.50
McCoy, Planter, Aqua, 7 1/2 X 4 In. 6.00
McCoy, Planter, Flying Ducks, 11 In. 18.00
McCoy, Planter, Hunting Dog 18.00
McCoy, Planter, Spinning Wheel 10.00
McCoy, Planter, Stand, Green, Quilt Pattern 35.00
McCoy, Planter, Turtle, 8 1/2 In. 6.00
McCoy, Planter, White, Scoop Type, Handle, 7 1/2 X 5 1/2 In. 5.00
McCoy, Sugar & Creamer, Green, Brown Floral 10.00
McCoy, Sugar & Creamer, Pinecone .... 12.50 To 14.00
McCoy, Tea Set, Gold Brocade, 3 Piece 20.00
McCoy, Tea Set, Green Leaf, 3 Piece 18.00
McCoy, Tea Set, Green With Brown, 3 Piece 30.00
McCoy, Tea Set, Pinecone, 3 Piece 25.00
McCoy, Teapot, Blue, Openwork Base With Candle, 8 In. 37.00
McCoy, Teapot, Green & Pink, Flowers 12.00
McCoy, Teapot, Ivy Leaf 16.50
McCoy, Teapot, Yellow 12.00
McCoy, Vase, Bird, 8 In. 12.00
McCoy, Vase, Green, 2 Handled, 8 In. 6.25
McCoy, Vase, Green, 9 In. 10.00
McCoy, Vase, Loy-Nel-Art, Brown, High Glaze With Irises, 9 In. 70.00
McCoy, Vase, Swan, Pink, 9 1/2 In. 7.95
McCoy, Vase, White Tulips, 8 In. 10.00
McCoy, Vase, White, Embossed Leaves, Ornate Handles, 10 In. 12.00
McCoy, Wall Pocket, Green Leaves 11.00
McCoy, Wishing Well 6.00

The McKee name has been associated with various glass enterprises in the U.S. since 1836, including J. & F. McKee (1850), Bryce, McKee & Co. (1850-1854), McKee and Brothers (1865), and National Glass Co. (1899). In 1903 the McKee Glass Company was formed in Jeanette, Pennsylvania; it became McKee Division of the Thatcher Glass Co. in 1951, and was bought out by the Jeanette Corporation in 1961.

McKee Candlestick, Rock Crystal, Oval Base 17.50
McKee, Bowl, Coach, Canary 110.00
McKee, Bowl, Custard 2.50
McKee, Bowl, Green, Laurel, Oval, 9 In. 9.00
McKee, Creamer, No.139, Marigold Top, 1/2 Pint 6.00
McKee, Creamer, Toltec 7.50
McKee, Dish, Dove Cover, Round, Milk Glass, Basketweave, 4 X 4 1/4 In. 235.00
McKee, Dish, Squirrel Cover, Split Ribbed Base 100.00
McKee, Goblet, Green, Rock Crystal 18.00
McKee, Goblet, Jadite 10.00
McKee, Goblet, Rock Crystal, Flower, 7 1/2 Ozs. 7.00
McKee, Plate, A Good Mother, 1875 .... 18.00
McKee, Salt & Pepper, Jade Green 8.00
McKee, Shot Glass, Rainbow 8.00
McKee, Sugar & Creamer, Custard, Signed 50.00
McKee, Sugar, Covered, Amber, Rock Crystal 22.50
McKee, Syrup, Sunbeam, C.1800 .... 27.50
McKee, Tom & Jerry Set, White, Red Letters, 12 In. Bowl, 13 Piece 55.00
McKee, Tumbler, Bottoms Up, Translucent Green 29.00
McKee, Tumbler, Clico, Jade Green, Black Footed 6.50
McKee, Tumbler, Juice, Rainbow 9.50
McKee, Tumbler, Majestic 6.50
McKee, Wine, Champion 9.50

Mechanical Bank, see Bank, Mechanical
Medicine, see Doctor

Meerschaum pipes and other carved pieces of meerschaum date from the nineteenth century to the present time.

Meerschaum, Cigar Holder, Amber, Case 12.50
Meerschaum, Cigar Holder, Lady, Case 20.00
Meerschaum, Holder, Cigar, Horse, Case 15.00
Meerschaum, Pipe, Bearded Man's Face, Carved, Leather-Covered Case 12.50
Meerschaum, Pipe, Carved Hand Holding Bowl, 5 1/2 In. 95.00
Meerschaum, Pipe, Carved Running Deer, Amber Stem 125.00
Meerschaum, Pipe, Cover, Carved Victorian Lady, Floral Hat, Ruffled Blouse 95.00
Meerschaum, Pipe, Fisherman With Net, 4 1/2 In. 95.00
Meerschaum, Pipe, Knight And Shield, 14 In. 175.00
Meerschaum, Pipe, Lincoln's Head 30.00
Meerschaum, Pipe, Lion's Head, Carved, Leather-Covered Case 12.50
Meerschaum, Pipe, Nude Girl, Carved, Leather-Covered Case 14.50
Meerschaum, Pipe, Nude Woman Holding Flowers On Head, 7 3/4 In. 95.00
Meerschaum, Pipe, Skull & Crossbones, Leather Case, 6 In. 55.00
Meerschaum, Pipe, Stags, Amber Stem, Case 100.00
Meerschaum, Pipe, Sultan's Head, 8 In. 35.00
Meerschaum, Pope, China Bowl, Partridge & Pine Trees, Bark Stem 75.00

Meissen, see also Dresden, Onion

Meissen is a town in Germany where porcelain has been made since 1710. Any china made in that town can be called Meissen, although the famous Meissen Factory made the finest porcelains of the area.

Meissen, Bowl, Deuche Blumen, , Gold Branch & Leaf Handle, C.1850, 11 1/2 In. 250.00
Meissen, Bowl, Fruit, Cobalt, Flower Overlay, 19th Century 250.00
Meissen, Box, Hinged, 1890s 65.00
Meissen, Candelabra, 3-Arm, Maiden & Man, C.1740, 19 In., Pair 1800.00
Meissen, Candleholder, 2 Figures On Sides, 13 1/2 In. 325.00
Meissen, Candlestick, Baluster, Painted Birds, Crossed Sword, 7 7/8 In., Pair 1000.00
Meissen, Chocolate Pot, Cobalt & White, Gold Trim, Crossed Swords Mark 150.00

Meissen, Chocolate Pot, Crossed Swords Mark, 8 X 8 In. 175.00
Meissen, Cornucopia, Gold Base, Floral, C.1900, Sword S Mark, 5 In. 65.00
Meissen, Cup & Saucer, Burgundy Ground, Pastoral Scene, Crossed Sword Mark 70.00
Meissen, Cup & Saucer, Demitasse, Floral, Gilt Rims, Vines, & Handle 50.00
Meissen, Cup & Saucer, Pastoral Scene, Crossed Swords 82.00
Meissen, Cup & Saucer, Portrait, Crossed Swords 72.00
Meissen, Cup & Saucer, Rose Molded, Crossed Swords, C.1750, Pair 1300.00
Meissen, Cup & Saucer, Scalloped Border, Vivid Roses 75.00
Meissen, Cup & Saucer, Wavy Gilt Lines, Molded, Blue Swords 85.00
Meissen, Cup & Saucer, 2 Handled, Marcolini, Fruits, Flowers, & Birds 396.00
Meissen, Desk Set, Bird Of Paradise, Blue, Red, & Gold, Tray & 2 Pots 375.00
Meissen, Dish, Bird Decorated, Crossed Swords, C.1750, 8 3/4 In., Pair 400.00
Meissen, Dish, Bone, Gold-Outlined Red & Blue Floral, Beehive Mark 10.00
Meissen, Ewer, Four Elements, 26 In., Pair 1900.00
Meissen, Figurine, American Indian Warrior On White Pony, C.1898 .... 600.00
Meissen, Figurine, Boston Terrier, Crossed Sword Mark, 6 In. 320.00
Meissen, Figurine, Boy Playing Fife, Tricorner Hat, 4 1/2 In. 200.00
Meissen, Figurine, Boy With Sheaf Of Wheat, Caduceus Period, 4 In. 195.00
Meissen, Figurine, Brown Collie Dog, White Markings, 6 X 4 In. 80.00
Meissen, Figurine, Bust, Madame DuBarry, 5 3/4 X 3 3/4 In. 175.00
Meissen, Figurine, Cat, Washing Paw, Gray, Crossed Swords Mark, 1 1/2 In. 80.00
Meissen, Figurine, Cavalier, Walking Stick & Tricorner Hat, 4 1/2 In. 150.00
Meissen, Figurine, Dog, Hunting, 2 X 4 1/4 In. 125.00
Meissen, Figurine, Gentleman Wearing Tricorner Hat & Sword, 6 1/2 In. 375.00
Meissen, Figurine, Girl With Chicken, Eggs In Basket, 4 1/4 In. 115.00
Meissen, Figurine, Green Parrot, C.1750, 2 In. 300.00
Meissen, Figurine, Little Girl Feeding Terrier, Green Dress, 5 1/2 In. 340.00
Meissen, Figurine, Little Girl Holding Cat, Crossed Swords Mark, 5 1/4 In. 345.00
Meissen, Figurine, Little Girl, Pink Lace Skirt, Gold Flowers, 5 In. 75.00
Meissen, Figurine, Little Girl, White Lace Skirt, Pink Flowers, 3 In. 40.00
Meissen, Figurine, Minerva, C.1750, Crossed Swords, 5 5/8 In. 750.00
Meissen, Figurine, Penguin On Snow, Head Bent, Wings Spread, Crossed Swords 95.00
Meissen, Figurine, Pug Dog, Green Collar With Gold Buckle, 6 In. 365.00
Meissen, Figurine, Seated On Stump, Crossed Swords, C.1760, 3 1/2 In., Pair 500.00
Meissen, Figurine, Sheep Dog, Sitting, Crossed Swords Mark, 5 In. 160.00
Meissen, Figurine, Sight On Vanity, C.1850, 6 X 4 In. 545.00
Meissen, Figurine, Street Vendor, Man, 5 1/2 In. 135.00
Meissen, Figurine, Street Vendor, Woman, 6 In. 150.00
Meissen, Figurine, Woman & Man, Standing, Marcolini, C.1880, 16 In., Pair 2350.00
Meissen, Group, Beggar Woman, Instrument, Child, Crossed Sword, 4 3/4 In. 400.00
Meissen, Group, Cupid Performing Wedding, C.1860, 9 X 8 In. 825.00
Meissen, Group, Drunken Silinus, C.1860, 8 1/2 X 8 In. 825.00
Meissen, Group, Lovers & Lamb Under Tree, Crossed Swords Mark, 9 1/2 In. 650.00
Meissen, Group, Pug Dog & 2 Long-Haired Dogs, Crossed Swords Mark, 7 In. 875.00
Meissen, Jar & Underplate, Jam, Lavender & White Floral, Push-Up Hole Base 17.50
Meissen, Knife & Fork, Pistol-Handled 100.00
Meissen, Lamp, Pink Raised Flowers 175.00
Meissen, Match Holder, Bluebird & Eggshell 28.00
Meissen, Mustard Pot, Blue Underglaze On White Flowers, Bird, Bamboo Handle 45.00
Meissen, Plate, Bread & Butter, Millefiori, Bugs, Bees, & Butterflies 18.50
Meissen, Plate, Cake, Blue & White, Double Handles, 10 1/4 In. 25.00
Meissen, Plate, Cobalt & Gold, Embossed Floral, Crossed Swords, 10 3/4 In. 135.00
Meissen, Plate, Dessert, White, Rose Center, Leaf Border, Crossed Swords Mark 16.50
Meissen, Plate, Green & Gold Leaves, Gold Trim, Crossed Swords Mark, 10 In. 135.00
Meissen, Plate, Horse & Rider, Gold & Floral Vine Border, 8 3/4 In. 95.00
Meissen, Plate, Imari, Kretschmar, C.1740, 8 1/2 In., Pair 850.00
Meissen, Plate, Yellow, Blue, Rose, & Orange Floral, Ruffled Edge, 11 1/2 In. 235.00
Meissen, Platter, White, Floral Center, Floral Cartouches Border, 14 1/2 In. 225.00
Meissen, Sauceboat, Schmetterling Pattern, C.1740, Crossed Swords, 9 In. 1500.00
Meissen, Shoe, High Heel, Crossed Swords, Cherub Decoration 195.00
Meissen, Snuffbox, Gold Mounted, Lovers, Children, Painted Ground, C.1750 .... 4000.00
Meissen, Stand, Cake, Tiered, Brass Handle, Scrolls, Birds, Roses, 11 In. 185.00
Meissen, Sugar Castor, Rococo Scrollwork, Birds, Crossed Swords, 6 In., Pair 600.00
Meissen, Tea Set, White, Green Grape Leaf Bands, Griffin Spout, 4 Piece 500.00

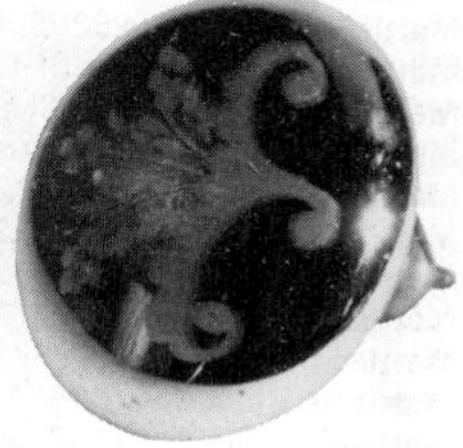
Mercury Glass, Tie Back, 3 1/2 In.Diameter

Meissen, Teacaddy And Cover, Green Ground, Chinoiserie, C.1730, 4 1/8 In. 8500.00
Meissen, Teapot, Melon Shape, Floral, Gold Gilt On Spout & Handle 125.00
Meissen, Teapot, Serpentine Spout, C. Kakimon, 19th Century 400.00
Meissen, Teapot, White, Serpent Handle, Band Of Ivy, C.1818, 13 1/2 In. 125.00
Meissen, Tureen & Cover, Oval, Painted Birds, Crossed Swords, 12 3/4 In. 1200.00
Meissen, Tureen And Cover, Painted Birds, Crossed Swords, 6 5/8 In., Pair 850.00
Meissen, Tureen, Covered, Handled, C.1820, 13 1/4 In. 248.00
Meissen, Tureen, Covered, Handled, 13 X 7 In. 228.00
Meissen, Vase, Cobalt & Gold, Bulbous, Pedestal Base, 11 1/2 In. 175.00
Meissen, Vase, Urn Shape, Double Handle, Cobalt, Floral, 12 X 6 In. 420.00

Mercury, or silvered, glass was first made in the 1850s. It lost favor for a while but became popular again about 1910. It looks like a piece of silver.

Mercury Glass, Candleholder 10.00
Mercury Glass, Pitcher, Applied Clear Handle, 6 In. 75.00
Mercury Glass, Rose Bowl, Pink, Melon Ribbed, 5 1/2 In. 28.50
Mercury Glass, Tieback, Pewter Post, 2 1/2 In. 6.00
Mercury Glass, Tieback, Pewter Post, 3 In. 8.00
Mercury Glass, Tieback, 3 1/2 In.Diameter .... *Illus* 8.50
Mercury Glass, Vase, Floral Decoration, 8 1/2 In. 9.00
Mercury Glass, Vase, Floral Decoration, 10 1/4 In. 11.00
Mercury Glass, Vase, Victorian, Painted, Large, Pair 40.00

Mettlach, Germany, is a city where the Villeroy and Boch factories worked. Steins from the firm are known as Mettlach steins. They date from about 1842. PUG means painted under glaze.

Mettlach, Beaker, Beer Importer, Deer Trademark, V & B, 5 In. 45.00
Mettlach, Beaker, No.2327/1091 .... 85.00
Mettlach, Beaker, No.2327/1200, Missouri State Seal, Kansas City, PUG 47.50
Mettlach, Beaker, No.2327/1214, Handled, Castle Mark 95.00
Mettlach, Beaker, No.2368/1032, 1/4 Liter, Dwarfs 48.00
Mettlach, Beaker, No.2368/1109, Musicians 95.00
Mettlach, Beaker, Stadt Stuttgart, 5 In. 40.00
Mettlach, Coaster, No.1032, Mercury Mark 40.00
Mettlach, Glass, No.2327, 1/4 Liter 85.00
Mettlach, Jug, No.2098 .... 325.00
Mettlach, Mug, Commemorative, Harvard College, 1898-1913 .... 30.00
Mettlach, Mug, No.1526, BPOE, Cream With Black Elk Head 60.00
Mettlach, Mug, No.1909, 4/10 Liter, If Drinking Interferes, Give Up Business 185.00
Mettlach, Pitcher, Serving, No.1920, 2 1/2 Liter 350.00
Mettlach, Pitcher, Serving, No.2098, 4 Liter 375.00
Mettlach, Plaque, Bowl Of Fruit, 12 In. 45.00
Mettlach, Plaque, Children Wading, Sailing Ships, 14 In. 185.00
Mettlach, Plaque, Mountain Climber, PUG, Villeroy & Boch, 16 In. 225.00
Mettlach, Plaque, No.1044/304, Children Wading Near Shore, 14 In. 185.00
Mettlach, Plaque, No.1044/306, Dutch Scene, PUG, 12 In. 150.00
Mettlach, Plaque, No.1384 .... 450.00
Mettlach, Plaque, No.1622, Blue Delft Type Ships Scene, PUG, 15 In. 200.00
Mettlach, Plaque, No.2199, & 2200, Grecian, Pair 1550.00
Mettlach, Plaque, No.2621 .... 250.00
Mettlach, Plaque, No.5037, PUG, 17 In. 175.00

Mettlach, Plaque, No.5208, Cherubs Playing, 22 X 17 In. 295.00
Mettlach, Plaque, No.5208, PUG, Large 250.00
Mettlach, Plaque, Pride Of The Rock, Blue & White, V & B, 17 In. 200.00
Mettlach, Plaque, Swiss Chalet, Marked Altes Stadtthar, Dec.94, 12 In. 225.00
Mettlach, Stein, No.24, Liter 425.00
Mettlach, Stein, No.171, 1/2 Liter 110.00
Mettlach, Stein, No.225, 1/2 Liter, Boot 400.00
Mettlach, Stein, No.228, 1/2 Liter, Relief With Conical Inlaid Top 205.00
Mettlach, Stein, No.812, 1/2 Liter, Cameo Type 275.00
Mettlach, Stein, No.932, 1/2 Liter, Etched, Inlaid Lid 550.00
Mettlach, Stein, No.1028, 1/2 Liter, Woodsman & Maiden, Winking Man Lid 225.00
Mettlach, Stein, No.1146, 1/2 Liter 450.00
Mettlach, Stein, No.1162, 1/2 Liter, Etched 350.00
Mettlach, Stein, No.1370, 1/2 Liter 125.00
Mettlach, Stein, No.1395, 1/2 Liter, Cards, Inlaid Lid 450.00
Mettlach, Stein, No.1403, 1/2 Liter, Etched .... 425.00 To 450.00
Mettlach, Stein, No.1452, 1/2 Liter 350.00
Mettlach, Stein, No.1467, 1/2 Liter 160.00
Mettlach, Stein, No.1526, 4/10 Liter 50.00
Mettlach, Stein, No.1526, 1/2 Liter, Drinking Scene, PUG 175.00
Mettlach, Stein, No.1526, 3 Liter, Falstaff 400.00
Mettlach, Stein, No.1527, 1/2 Liter, Etched .... 450.00 To 475.00
Mettlach, Stein, No.1562, 5 Liter, Etched 1550.00
Mettlach, Stein, No.1648, 1/2 Liter, Pewter Lid 275.00
Mettlach, Stein, No.1675, 1/2 Liter, Heidelberg, Etched 450.00
Mettlach, Stein, No.1740, 1/4 Liter, Relief 225.00
Mettlach, Stein, No.1741, 1/2 Liter, Engraved 500.00
Mettlach, Stein, No.1786, Liter 800.00
Mettlach, Stein, No.1786, 1/2 Liter, St.Florian, Dragon Handle, Glazed 550.00
Mettlach, Stein, No.1794, 1/2 Liter, Etched 395.00
Mettlach, Stein, No.1796, 1/2 Liter, Swashbuckler, Etched 425.00
Mettlach, Stein, No.1797, 1/2 Liter, Etched, Inlaid Lid 550.00
Mettlach, Stein, No.1909/727, 1/2 Liter, Elves Bowling, Schlitt, Pewter Lid 150.00
Mettlach, Stein, No.1909, 1/2 Liter, Man Playing Harp, Monkey, Cat, & Fish 325.00
Mettlach, Stein, No.1923, 1/4 Liter 135.00
Mettlach, Stein, No.1972, 1/2 Liter, Four Seasons, Etched 475.00
Mettlach, Stein, No.1986, 1/2 Liter, Etched With Fancy Pewter Lid 310.00
Mettlach, Stein, No.1997, 1/2 Liter 225.00
Mettlach, Stein, No.2001, Book, Lawyer 395.00
Mettlach, Stein, No.2001b, Book, Doctor 425.00
Mettlach, Stein, No.2001d, 1/2 Liter, Astronomer, Book, Inlaid Lid 475.00
Mettlach, Stein, No.2001f, 1/2 Liter, Architect, Book, Inlaid Lid 450.00
Mettlach, Stein, No.2002, 1 Liter, Pewter Lid 285.00
Mettlach, Stein, No.2002, 1/2 Liter, Munich, Etched 350.00
Mettlach, Stein, No.2005, 1/2 Liter, Etched 350.00
Mettlach, Stein, No.2012, 1/2 Liter, State Shields, Inlaid Lid, Castle Mark 475.00
Mettlach, Stein, No.2025, 1/2 Liter 350.00
Mettlach, Stein, No.2025, 1/2 Liter, Cherubs, Inlaid Lid 375.00
Mettlach, Stein, No.2028, 1/2 Liter, Etched, Inlaid Lid 395.00
Mettlach, Stein, No.2035, 1/2 Liter .... 325.00 To 350.00
Mettlach, Stein, No.2038, 4 Liter, Black Forest .... *Illus* 3600.00

Mettlach, Stein, No.2038, 4 Liter, Black Forest

Mettlach, Stein, No.2048, 3/10 Liter, Glazed 225.00
Mettlach, Stein, No.2057, 1/2 Liter 350.00
Mettlach, Stein, No.2065, Etched, Jewel Base, 15 In. 975.00
Mettlach, Stein, No.2077, 3/10 Liter, Geschutz 70.00
Mettlach, Stein, No.2086, 1/4 Liter, Relief 195.00
Mettlach, Stein, No.2089, 1/2 Liter, Etched, Inlaid Lid 500.00
Mettlach, Stein, No.2090, 1/2 Liter, Club, Inlaid Lid 450.00
Mettlach, Stein, No.2092 .... 390.00
Mettlach, Stein, No.2130, 1/2 Liter, Inlaid Lid, Castle Mark 525.00
Mettlach, Stein, No.2131, 1/2 Liter 250.00
Mettlach, Stein, No.2136, 1/2 Liter, Brewmaster, Anheuser Busch 295.00
Mettlach, Stein, No.2181, 1/2 Liter, PUG, Signed Schlitt 145.00
Mettlach, Stein, No.2182, 1/2 Liter, Relief 200.00
Mettlach, Stein, No.2204, Liter, Black German Eagle, Inlaid Lid 650.00
Mettlach, Stein, No.2210, Dated 1902, Bowling Scene, Pewter Thumbpiece 595.00
Mettlach, Stein, No.2231, 1/2 Liter, Etched, Inlaid Lid 395.00
Mettlach, Stein, No.2235, 1/2 Liter, Etched, Inlaid Lid 550.00
Mettlach, Stein, No.2235, 1/2 Liter, Target, Inlaid Lid 500.00
Mettlach, Stein, No.2241, 1/2 Liter, Etched, Inlaid Lid 550.00
Mettlach, Stein, No.2271/1020, 1/2 Liter 165.00
Mettlach, Stein, No.2271, 1/2 Liter, PUG 185.00
Mettlach, Stein, No.2271, 1/2 Liter, Signed C.K. 160.00
Mettlach, Stein, No.2285, 1/2 Liter 375.00
Mettlach, Stein, No.2364, Panolith, Stahl, 17 1/2 In. 850.00
Mettlach, Stein, No.2382, Liter 850.00
Mettlach, Stein, No.2382, 1/2 Liter, Etched, Inlaid Lid, Argentina 425.00
Mettlach, Stein, No.2382, 1/2 Liter, Thirsty Rider, Etched 750.00
Mettlach, Stein, No.2382, 1/2 Liter, VB Schultz 750.00
Mettlach, Stein, No.2388, 1/2 Liter, Pretzel, Pretzel Lid 400.00
Mettlach, Stein, No.2581, 1/2 Liter, Musical, Etched, Inlaid Lid 450.00
Mettlach, Stein, No.2582, 1/2 Liter, Signed 495.00
Mettlach, Stein, No.2716, Liter, Christmas, Etched 625.00
Mettlach, Stein, No.2776, 1/2 Liter 395.00
Mettlach, Stein, No.2833, 1/2 Liter, Etched A, Brick Base 375.00
Mettlach, Stein, No.2833a, 1/2 Liter, Etched 375.00
Mettlach, Stein, No.2893, 3 Liter 375.00
Mettlach, Stein, No.2903, 1/2 Liter, Etched, Inlaid Lid 275.00
Mettlach, Stein, No.2936, 1/2 Liter, Elk, Etched, Inlaid Lid 300.00
Mettlach, Stein, No.2939, 1/2 Liter, Etched 375.00
Mettlach, Stein, No.2951, 1/2 Liter, Cameo, Eagle On Front 450.00
Mettlach, Stein, No.2958, Bowling, 16 In. 650.00
Mettlach, Stein, No.2959, 1 Liter, Etched, Inlaid Lid 450.00
Mettlach, Stein, No.2989, Liter, Etched 500.00
Mettlach, Stein, No.3004, Professor Reimerschmidt 295.00
Mettlach, Stein, No.3241, Etched, Art Deco, Conical Inlay Lid, 1/2 Liter 295.00
Mettlach, Stein, No.3241, 1/2 Liter, Etched, Inlaid Dome Lid 325.00
Mettlach, Tea Set, Buff Gray, Raised Silver Luster, VB Seal, 3 Piece 125.00
Mettlach, Tea Set, Buff Gray, White Cameo Figures On Blue, 4 Piece 250.00
Mettlach, Tumbler, Stadt Frankfurt, 5 In. 55.00
Mettlach, Urn, No.862, Tangerine Ground, Blue Opal Gems, 2 Handles, 15 In. 350.00
Mettlach, Urn, No.2239, Etched Children Harvesting Scenes, 2 Handles, 16 In. 495.00
Mettlach, Vase, Elephant Trunk Handles, Castle Mark 2851, 14 In. 317.50
Mettlach, Vase, Marbleized, Platinum Overlay, 3 1/2 In. 50.00
Mettlach, Vase, No.2915, Blue & White Castle Marks, 14 In. 118.00
Michel, Vase, Chartreuse Matte, Lake & Sailboats In Browns, 10 In. 625.00
Michel, Vase, Peach Color, Dark Blue Castle Scene, Pedestal, 13 1/2 In. 375.00

Mickey Mouse, see Disneyana, Mickey Mouse

Milk glass was named for its milky white color. It was first made in England during the 1700s. The height of its popularity in the United States was from 1870 to 1880. It is now correct to refer to some colored glass as blue milk glass, black milk glass, etc. The letter B before the numbers xx refers to the book "Milk Glass" by E. Belknap.

Milk Glass, see also Cambridge, Cosmos

Milk Glass, Pressed Glass

Milk Glass, Basket Base, Black, 5 1/2 In. 20.00
Milk Glass, Basket, Basket Weave, Twisted Handle, Patent July 21, 1874, 4 In. 20.00
Milk Glass, Bell, Smoke, Fluted Rim, 6 In. 10.00
Milk Glass, Bell, Smoke, Pleated Rim, 7 In. 14.00
Milk Glass, Bonbon, Czar, C.1900 150.00
Milk Glass, Bottle, Belle Of Anderson, Pint 120.00
Milk Glass, Bottle, Belle Of Anderson, Quart 110.00
Milk Glass, Bottle, Black, Sitting Bear, B-259 36.00
Milk Glass, Bottle, Black, Sitting Bear, 11 In., B-242 175.00
Milk Glass, Bottle, Cologne, Actress 40.00 To 45.00
Milk Glass, Bottle, Cologne, Portrait Medallion Of Victorian Girl, 5 1/2 In. 55.00
Milk Glass, Bottle, Dresser, Actress, 11 In. 45.00
Milk Glass, Bottle, Dresser, Leaf, Parkville, 1874, 9 1/2 In. 21.00
Milk Glass, Bottle, Figural, Owl 38.00
Milk Glass, Bottle, Owl Drug Co., 5 In. 25.00
Milk Glass, Bottle, Perfume, Googlie Face Boy, Germany, C.1920, 1 3/4 In. 7.50
Milk Glass, Bottle, Perfume, Googlie Face Girl, Germany, C.1920, 1 3/4 In. 7.50
Milk Glass, Bottle, Perfume, Purse, Columbian Exposition, 1893, Mines Bldg. 75.00
Milk Glass, Bottle, World's Fair, 1939, 9 1/4 In., Pair 80.00
Milk Glass, Boudoir Set, Child's, Pitcher, Bowl, Slop Pot, Potty 85.00
Milk Glass, Boudoir Set, Pitcher, Bowl, Potty, Dutch 85.00
Milk Glass, Bowl, Acanthus Leaf, 10 In.Across, 5 In.Deep *Illus* 70.00
Milk Glass, Bowl, Acanthus, B-110c 36.00
Milk Glass, Bowl, Atterbury, Lacy Edge, Oval, Pedestal, 8 3/4 X 2 3/4 In. 25.00
Milk Glass, Bowl, Crinkled Lacy Edge, 3 1/2 In. 35.00
Milk Glass, Bowl, Embossed Roses Inside, 7 1/2 In. 21.00
Milk Glass, Bowl, Lacy Edge, Atterbury, Square, B-136 25.00
Milk Glass, Bowl, Lacy Edge, Basket Weave Interior, Oblong, B-153a 40.00
Milk Glass, Bowl, Lattice Edge, B-100c 57.00
Milk Glass, Bowl, Pink, 3 Molded Swans Holding Bowl, 8 In. 24.00
Milk Glass, Bowl, Ruffled Windmill Pattern, Imperial, C.1910 45.00
Milk Glass, Bowl, Scalloped Edge, 2 Handles, 11 In. 25.00
Milk Glass, Bowl, Slotted Ribs, Painted Autumn Leaves, Atterbury, B-113a 48.00
Milk Glass, Bowl, Sugar, Casque *Illus* 45.00
Milk Glass, Bowl, Thumbprint, 8 In.Across, 3 In.Deep *Illus* 30.00
Milk Glass, Bowl, Transparent Blue Ruffled Edge, 8 1/2 In. 15.00
Milk Glass, Bowl, Trumpet Vine, Lattice Edge, Sawtooth Base, B-100c 38.00
Milk Glass, Bowl, 3 Molded Swans Holding Bowl, 8 In. 24.00
Milk Glass, Box, Covered, Lion's Head & Scrolls, 5 1/2 X 5 X 2 1/2 In. 32.00
Milk Glass, Box, Dresser, Actress Cameo, Oval, 10 1/2 X 4 In. 65.00
Milk Glass, Box, Glove, Covered 35.00
Milk Glass, Box, Glove, Covered, Roses & Forget-Me-Nots, Gold Trim, 10 X 4 In. 28.50
Milk Glass, Box, Glove, Long 35.00
Milk Glass, Box, Hunt, Turquoise, Setter Dog Cover 48.00
Milk Glass, Box, Studs, Covered, 4 In. 15.00

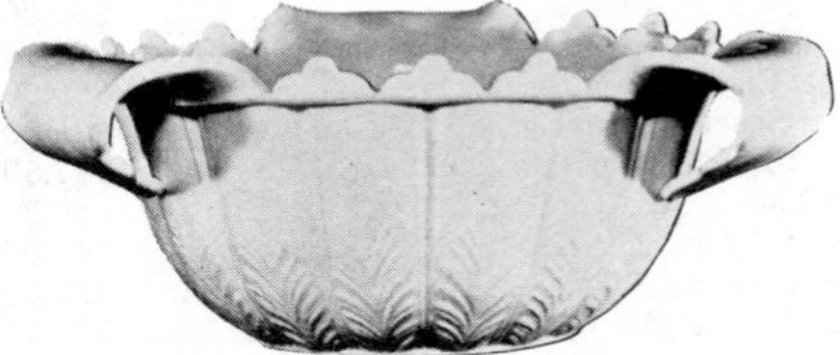

Milk Glass, Bowl, Acanthus Leaf, 10 In.Across, 5 In.Deep

Milk Glass, Bowl, Sugar, Casque

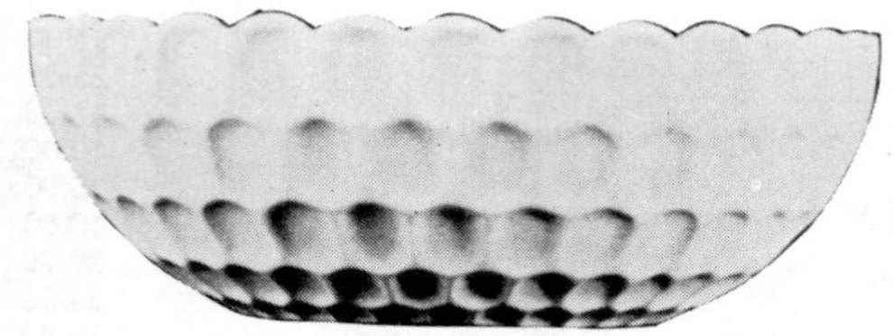

Milk Glass, Bowl, Thumbprint, 8 In.Across, 3 In.Deep

Milk Glass, Compote, Covered, Hamilton With Leaf, Pear Finial

Milk Glass, Butter, Apple Blossom 95.00
Milk Glass, Butter, Bent Twig Knob On Domed Lid, Footed, Red Medallions 25.00
Milk Glass, Butter, Covered Dome Lid, Diamond & Fan, Miniature 15.00
Milk Glass, Butter, Covered Dome Lid, Pink Floral 28.00
Milk Glass, Butter, Covered, Diamond Sunburst & Fan, Miniature 25.00
Milk Glass, Butter, Covered, Drapery, Opalescent, Gold Trim, Northwood 70.00
Milk Glass, Butter, Covered, Sawtooth, Opaque, B-197a 65.00
Milk Glass, Butter, Covered, Turquoise, Swirl, French, C.1880 .... 35.00
Milk Glass, Butter, Flattened Diamond & Sunburst 12.00
Milk Glass, Cake Stand, Blue, Orange Border & Base, Square, 10 1/2 In. 17.00
Milk Glass, Cake Stand, Open Hand, 11-Point Star Center, 11 X 6 In. 95.00
Milk Glass, Cake Stand, Openwork Twisted Rope Edge, Atterbury, 13 1/2 In. 45.00
Milk Glass, Cake Stand, Reticulated Edge, Hand-Painted 35.00
Milk Glass, Candlestick, Blue, Lions On Footed Base 25.00
Milk Glass, Candlestick, Crucifix, Round Base, 10 In. 22.00
Milk Glass, Candlestick, Dolphin, Westmoreland, 9 In., Pair 70.00
Milk Glass, Candlestick, Reeded Post & Base, 7 1/2 In., Pair 32.00
Milk Glass, Celery, Blackberry, Pair 300.00
Milk Glass, Celery, Maize 70.00
Milk Glass, Compote, Atlas, Scalloped, B-103 .... 45.00 To 88.00
Milk Glass, Compote, Atterbury, B-137 .... 35.00
Milk Glass, Compote, Banana, Ribbon Edge 25.00
Milk Glass, Compote, Blue, Conch Shell, Dolphin Stem, Hexagonal Foot, 8 In. 42.50
Milk Glass, Compote, Blue, Lattice Edge, Basket Weave Stem, 7 In. 75.00
Milk Glass, Compote, Covered, Dewdrop, 11 In. 45.00
Milk Glass, Compote, Covered, Hamilton With Leaf, Pear Finial .... *Illus* 90.00
Milk Glass, Compote, Cut Pattern Similar To Jewel Medallion, 5 In., B-115a 38.00
Milk Glass, Compote, Daisy & Button Stem & Base, Closed Lattice, 9 In.Pair 85.00
Milk Glass, Compote, Green, Gold Finial & Trim, 6 X 4 1/2 In. 24.50
Milk Glass, Compote, Lattice, Basket Weave Pedestal, Tall 45.00
Milk Glass, Compote, Lattice, Basket Weave Stem, 8 3/4 X 6 3/4 In. 43.00
Milk Glass, Compote, Open Edge, Appleblossom, Bell Tone 85.00
Milk Glass, Compote, Open Weave, Floral Decoration, Flint, 7 In. 55.00
Milk Glass, Compote, Raised Grapes, Pink, 6 In. 12.00
Milk Glass, Compote, Rose & Thistle, Flint, 5 In. 50.00
Milk Glass, Compote, Sandwich Loop & Hairpin, Flint, 6 In., B-136 .... 135.00
Milk Glass, Condiment Set, Child's, 4 Piece 37.50
Milk Glass, Condiment Set, Forget-Me-Not Pattern, 4 Piece 85.00
Milk Glass, Condiment Set, 3 Bottle, Fan Base, Decorated 38.00
Milk Glass, Creamer, Atterbury, Marbled Green & White, Open Lattice Border 50.00
Milk Glass, Creamer, Blackberry 25.00
Milk Glass, Creamer, Casque .... *Illus* 40.00
Milk Glass, Creamer, Covered, Forget-Me-Not Decoration 19.50
Milk Glass, Creamer, Crossed Ferns With Ball And Claw 35.00
Milk Glass, Creamer, Dutch Girl, Miniature 40.00
Milk Glass, Creamer, English, Thistle, Rose & Shamrock, White 45.00
Milk Glass, Creamer, Marquis & Marchioness .... *Illus* 50.00

Milk Glass, Creamer, Owl, B-91b 32.00
Milk Glass, Creamer, Owl, Blue, Small 95.00
Milk Glass, Creamer, Prism Arc 25.00
Milk Glass, Creamer, Relief Portrait, William Gladstone, Pedestal, 4 1/2 In. 47.50
Milk Glass, Creamer, Sawtooth, Flint 40.00
Milk Glass, Creamer, Sawtooth, Molded Handle 25.00
Milk Glass, Crucifix, Grayish White, 10 In. 10.00
Milk Glass, Cup, Child's Punch, Nursery Rhymes 20.00
Milk Glass, Decanter, 3 Mold, Quart Size 34.00
Milk Glass, Dish, American Hen Cover, Nest Base, 6 In. 39.00
Milk Glass, Dish, Baby Cover, Black Hat Base 450.00
Milk Glass, Dish, Battleship Cover, Marked Dewey, Tile Base, B-161b 30.00
Milk Glass, Dish, Battleship Cover, Marked Maine, 7 1/2 In., B-162b 30.00
Milk Glass, Dish, Battleship Cover, Marked Wheeling, 6 In. 39.00
Milk Glass, Dish, Bird-In-Hand Covered, Dated 1889 .... 75.00
Milk Glass, Dish, Blue Hen With White Head 45.00
Milk Glass, Dish, Cat Cover, B-174c 25.00
Milk Glass, Dish, Cat Cover, Blue And White Opalescent 95.00
Milk Glass, Dish, Cat Cover, Blue, White Head 40.00
Milk Glass, Dish, Cat Cover, Dark Blue, Basket Base, White Head, 5 In. 75.00
Milk Glass, Dish, Cat Cover, Drum Base, Portieux 35.00
Milk Glass, Dish, Cat Cover, Lacy Edge, Atterbury, B-164 .... 165.00
Milk Glass, Dish, Cattail & Swan Cover, Blue 50.00
Milk Glass, Dish, Chick In Egg Cover, Basket Base, C-294a 25.00
Milk Glass, Dish, Chick In Egg Cover, Sleigh Base, C-284b 30.00
Milk Glass, Dish, Chick In Egg Cover, 4 1/4 In. 38.50
Milk Glass, Dish, Chicken Cover, Basket Base, Red Comb, 2 1/2 In. 5.00
Milk Glass, Dish, Chicken Cover, Handled-Basket Base 35.00
Milk Glass, Dish, Chicken Cover, Nest Base, 6 X 4 1/2 In. 18.00
Milk Glass, Dish, Coach Cover 125.00
Milk Glass, Dish, Conestoga Wagon Cover 60.00
Milk Glass, Dish, Covered, Ribbed Sides, Lid, Finial, Pat.1888, 9 1/2 In. 45.00
Milk Glass, Dish, Cow Cover, Block Base, Frosted 50.00
Milk Glass, Dish, Cruiser Ship Cover .... 40.00 To 45.00
Milk Glass, Dish, Dog Cover, B-191b 25.00
Milk Glass, Dish, Dog Cover, Blue And White Opalescent 95.00
Milk Glass, Dish, Dog Cover, Ribbed Base, 5 1/2 In. 35.00
Milk Glass, Dish, Dog Cover, Wide Rib Base 25.00
Milk Glass, Dish, Dolphin Cover 40.00
Milk Glass, Dish, Dove Cover, Basket Weave Base, McKee, 4 1/4 In. 235.00
Milk Glass, Dish, Duck Cover, Amethyst Head, Atterbury 195.00
Milk Glass, Dish, Duck Cover, Glass Eyes, Atterbury 40.00
Milk Glass, Dish, Duck Cover, Wavy Base, Glass Eyes 75.00
Milk Glass, Dish, Emerging Chick Cover, Basket Base, Medallion Scene, B-205c 45.00
Milk Glass, Dish, Entwined Fish Cover, Atterbury, B-163a 165.00
Milk Glass, Dish, Fish Cover, Skiff Base 45.00
Milk Glass, Dish, Fox Cover, Glass Eyes 37.00

Milk Glass, Creamer, Casque

(See Page 327)

Milk Glass, Creamer, Marquis & Marchioness

(See Page 327)

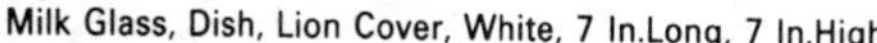
Milk Glass, Dish, Lion Cover, White, 7 In.Long, 7 In.High

Milk Glass, Dish, Fox Cover, Ribbed Base, Atterbury, B-169 .... 160.00
Milk Glass, Dish, Frog Cover, Basket Weave Base, Greentown 100.00
Milk Glass, Dish, Hand & Dove Cover, Atterbury, B-163b .... 60.00 To 145.00
Milk Glass, Dish, Hand & Dove Cover, Patent 1889 .... 75.00
Milk Glass, Dish, Hand And Dove Cover, Atterbury, Dated 145.00
Milk Glass, Dish, Hen Cover, Basket Base, B-323a 20.00
Milk Glass, Dish, Hen Cover, Basket Weave Base, B-149a 75.00
Milk Glass, Dish, Hen Cover, Basket Weave Base, Glass Eyes, 7 1/2 In. 48.00
Milk Glass, Dish, Hen Cover, Black With White Head 135.00
Milk Glass, Dish, Hen Cover, Blue, Basket Weave Base 35.00
Milk Glass, Dish, Hen Cover, Blue, Greentown 120.00
Milk Glass, Dish, Hen Cover, Blue, Nest Base, White Head, 5 1/2 In. 42.00
Milk Glass, Dish, Hen Cover, Blue, White Head, B-275b 28.00
Milk Glass, Dish, Hen Cover, Blue, White Head, 5 In. .... 30.00 To 37.50
Milk Glass, Dish, Hen Cover, Grassy Base 45.00
Milk Glass, Dish, Hen Cover, Hazel Atlas, 3 In. 12.50
Milk Glass, Dish, Hen Cover, Hen 25.00
Milk Glass, Dish, Hen Cover, Weed Base 38.00
Milk Glass, Dish, Kitten Cover, Blue 70.00
Milk Glass, Dish, Kitty Cover, 4 3/4 X 3 1/2 In. 22.50
Milk Glass, Dish, Lion Cover, Blue, Glass Eyes, WG, 7 1/2 In. 25.00
Milk Glass, Dish, Lion Cover, Lacy Base, Atterbury 95.00
Milk Glass, Dish, Lion Cover, Lacy Base, Atterbury, Dated 125.00
Milk Glass, Dish, Lion Cover, Scroll Base 40.00
Milk Glass, Dish, Lion Cover, Split Rib Octagonal Base 50.00
Milk Glass, Dish, Lion Cover, White, 7 In.Long, 7 In.High .... *Illus* 115.00
Milk Glass, Dish, Little Miss Muffet & Spider, Green On Brown 40.00
Milk Glass, Dish, Moses In Bulrushes Cover, Opalescent, B-160 .... 200.00
Milk Glass, Dish, Pen, Steeple Top Lid 8.00
Milk Glass, Dish, Pickle, Fish, Atterbury, June 4, 1872, B-210 .... 24.00
Milk Glass, Dish, Pig Cover, Drum Base, Portieux 25.00
Milk Glass, Dish, Pintail Duck Cover, B-183b 25.00
Milk Glass, Dish, Quail Cover 35.00
Milk Glass, Dish, Rabbit Cover, Atterbury, 9 1/4 In. 165.00
Milk Glass, Dish, Rabbit On Nest With Eggs Cover, Opalescent 40.00
Milk Glass, Dish, Reclining Camel Cover .... 55.00 To 115.00
Milk Glass, Dish, Robin Cover, Flowered Pedestal Base, Greentown, B-157 .... 108.00
Milk Glass, Dish, Rooster Cover, B-275a 22.00
Milk Glass, Dish, Rooster Cover, Nest Base, 8 In. 85.00
Milk Glass, Dish, Rooster Cover, 8 1/2 In. 45.00
Milk Glass, Dish, Santa Claus Cover, Sleigh Base 55.00
Milk Glass, Dish, Soap, Scroll Finial, Scrolls 20.00
Milk Glass, Dish, Spaniel Cover, Sandwich 125.00
Milk Glass, Dish, Squirrel Cover, Split Rib Base, McKee 125.00
Milk Glass, Dish, Steamship Cover, 2 Stacks 47.50
Milk Glass, Dish, Swan Cover, Lacy Base, Wings Up, Atterbury, 9 In., B-153b 135.00
Milk Glass, Dish, Swan Cover, Open Wing, 8 3/4 X 6 X 5 1/2 In. .... *Illus* 225.00
Milk Glass, Dish, Swimming Duck Cover 35.00
Milk Glass, Dish, Uncle Sam On Battleship Cover, Boat Base, B-185 .... 40.00

Milk Glass, Dish, Swan Cover, Open Wing, 8 3/4 X 6 X 5 1/2 In.

(See Page 329)

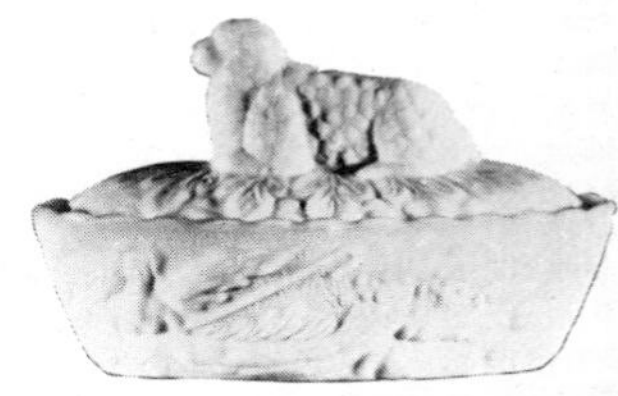

Milk Glass, Dish, Woolly Lamb Cover, Bo-Peep Base

Milk Glass, Dish, Woolly Lamb Cover, Bo-Peep Base .... *Illus* 150.00
Milk Glass, Dresser Set, Hobnail, 3 Piece 37.50
Milk Glass, Egg Set, Vallerystahl, 8 Pieces On Tray 175.00
Milk Glass, Eggcup, Basket Weave, Atterbury .... 22.00 To 25.00
Milk Glass, Eggcup, Beaded Swirl 13.00
Milk Glass, Eggcup, Birch Leaf .... 20.00 To 23.00
Milk Glass, Eggcup, Sandwich Loop, Rayed Base, Flint, 3 3/4 In. 85.00
Milk Glass, Eggcup, Strawberry 12.50
Milk Glass, Epergne, Blue Edge Ruffle 195.00
Milk Glass, Epergne, 3 Lilies, Hobnail, Pink, 3 X 8 In. 38.00
Milk Glass, Fan & Circle Square, 6 1/2 In. 35.00
Milk Glass, Figurine, Footed Rooster, Flint, 8 1/2 X 6 1/2 In. 32.00
Milk Glass, Figurine, Pin-Tail Duck, White 39.00
Milk Glass, Goblet, Blackberry .... 20.00 To 45.00
Milk Glass, Goblet, Blackberry, Flint 65.00
Milk Glass, Goblet, Cocktail, Rooster Body, French, 3 1/2 In. 19.50
Milk Glass, Goblet, Strawberry 35.00
Milk Glass, Hat, Blue, Cambridge, 1822-1922 On Rim 22.00
Milk Glass, Hat, Uncle Sam, 2 1/2 In. 25.00
Milk Glass, Jar, Button, Covered, Daisy & Button, 5 In. 50.00
Milk Glass, Jar, Dresser, Blue, Rococo Edge 5.00
Milk Glass, Jar, Owl, Atterbury, B-182 .... 140.00
Milk Glass, Jar, Queen Victoria, Covered 37.50
Milk Glass, Lamp, see Lamp, Milk Glass
Milk Glass, Lamp Base, Hand-Painted Flowers, Clark Bros., 6 1/2 In. 28.00
Milk Glass, Match Holder, Blue, Diamond & Swag, Seahorse Mark 22.00
Milk Glass, Match Holder, Blue, Oval Basket, Victorian 35.00
Milk Glass, Match Holder, Doghouse, Striker 18.00
Milk Glass, Match Holder, Hen & Rabbit, B-196b 12.00
Milk Glass, Match Holder, Indian Head, 5 In.X 4 3/4 In. .... *Illus* 65.00
Milk Glass, Match Holder, Lady's Hand With Fan, Flowers, Opalescent 15.00
Milk Glass, Match Holder, Pipe 21.00
Milk Glass, Match Safe, Raised Scrolls, Striker Inside Lid 15.00
Milk Glass, Muffineer, Beaded Swirl, 4 1/2 In. 32.00
Milk Glass, Muffineer, Blue & Yellow Enamel Floral, Tin Top 45.00
Milk Glass, Muffineer, Poppy 30.00
Milk Glass, Muffineer, Royal Oak, Gold Trim & Top, Northwood 85.00
Milk Glass, Mug, Brown Shaded, Elk's Head, Stag Horn-Shaped Handle, 5 In. 12.00
Milk Glass, Mug, Burred Hobnail 22.50
Milk Glass, Mug, Child's, Crawling Baby, Child & Dog 18.50
Milk Glass, Mug, Elves, Greentown 15.00
Milk Glass, Mug, Home Office Bldg., Security Mutual Life Ins. Co., 2 1/4 In. 4.95
Milk Glass, Nappy, Wistar, Handled 4.50
Milk Glass, Owl Creamer, Pin At Base 12.00
Milk Glass, Pitcher, Cream, Little Boy .... *Illus* 80.00
Milk Glass, Pitcher, Pink Flowers, Marked Rena, 7 1/4 In. 11.00

Milk Glass, Pitcher, Water, Guttate 95.00
Milk Glass, Pitcher, Water, Pink, Green Flower & Leaf, Square Mouth 50.00
Milk Glass, Plate, Anchor And Yacht 18.00
Milk Glass, Plate, Angel's Head Border, 9 In. 22.00
Milk Glass, Plate, Backward S, Square, 7 1/2 In. 9.00
Milk Glass, Plate, Battleship Maine 38.00
Milk Glass, Plate, Beaded Loop, Indian 25.00
Milk Glass, Plate, Black, Gothic, 9 In. 14.00
Milk Glass, Plate, Black, Square S Border, 9 In. 14.00
Milk Glass, Plate, Blue, Backward C, 8 In. 42.00
Milk Glass, Plate, Bread, B-54b 36.00
Milk Glass, Plate, Bread, Diamond Grill .... 35.00 To 48.00
Milk Glass, Plate, Bread, Retriever 100.00
Milk Glass, Plate, Bread, Rock Of Ages 145.00
Milk Glass, Plate, Canfield Gothic, 9 1/4 In. 10.00
Milk Glass, Plate, Chick & Eggs, Flint, 7 1/4 In. 20.00
Milk Glass, Plate, Chicks On Round Basket 27.00
Milk Glass, Plate, Child's, ABC's, Gilt On Letters, 8 1/4 In. 33.00
Milk Glass, Plate, Child's, Tree Owls .... *Illus* 40.00
Milk Glass, Plate, Club & Shell, 9 1/2 In. 11.00
Milk Glass, Plate, Columbus, 1492-1892 .... 25.00
Milk Glass, Plate, Cupid & Psyche 21.00
Milk Glass, Plate, Dogs & Squirrel, 7 In. 42.00
Milk Glass, Plate, Eagle, Flag And Star 20.00
Milk Glass, Plate, Eagle, Fleur-De-Lis, Flag, Wicket Edge, Patented 1903 .... 18.50
Milk Glass, Plate, Easter Chicks 20.00
Milk Glass, Plate, Easter Ducks, B-24d 30.00
Milk Glass, Plate, Easter Rabbit 25.00
Milk Glass, Plate, Forget-Me-Not Border, 8 1/2 In. 12.50
Milk Glass, Plate, Garfield Monument 25.00
Milk Glass, Plate, Gothic, 8 1/4 In., B-4b 8.00
Milk Glass, Plate, Indian Chief, Gilt Trim, 7 1/2 In. 19.00
Milk Glass, Plate, Lady Rabbit With Basket Of Eggs, "Easter Day," 6 1/4 In. 45.00
Milk Glass, Plate, Lattice Edge, Pink Floral Center, 10 1/2 In. 48.00
Milk Glass, Plate, No Easter Without Us, B-3e 30.00
Milk Glass, Plate, Open Lattice Edge, 10 1/2 In., B-25 .... 27.50
Milk Glass, Plate, Open Lattice Edge, 11 In. 24.00
Milk Glass, Plate, Paneled Peg 8.00
Milk Glass, Plate, Pinwheel, 8 1/2 In., B-15c 12.00
Milk Glass, Plate, Rabbit & Horseshoe, Hand-Painted 39.50

Milk Glass, Pitcher, Cream, Little Boy

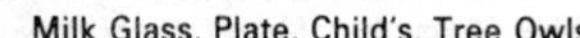

Milk Glass, Plate, Child's, Tree Owls

Milk Glass, Match Holder, Indian Head, 5 In.X 4 3/4 In.

Milk Glass, Plate, Remember The Maine, Ship's Picture, Open Edge 25.00
Milk Glass, Plate, Rooster Cover 40.00
Milk Glass, Plate, Scroll & Eye, 8 In., B-9a 11.00
Milk Glass, Plate, Serenade, Painted Trim, Greentown, 6 1/2 In. 36.00
Milk Glass, Plate, Serenade, 8 In. 45.00
Milk Glass, Plate, Shell And Grapes 18.00
Milk Glass, Plate, Ship Emblems With Seashells, Openwork Edge, 7 1/2 In. 24.00
Milk Glass, Plate, Single Forget-Me-Not 10.00
Milk Glass, Plate, Small Hen On Basket 20.00
Milk Glass, Plate, Stanchion Border 20.00
Milk Glass, Plate, Three Bears .... 25.00 To 37.50
Milk Glass, Plate, Three Kittens, Painted, B-10c 12.00
Milk Glass, Plate, Three Owls 25.00
Milk Glass, Plate, Triple Forget-Me-Not, Beaded Yoke 10.00
Milk Glass, Plate, Triple Forget-Me-Not, Plain Yoke 20.00
Milk Glass, Plate, Triple Forget-Me-Not, Westmoreland, 8 1/2 In. 5.00

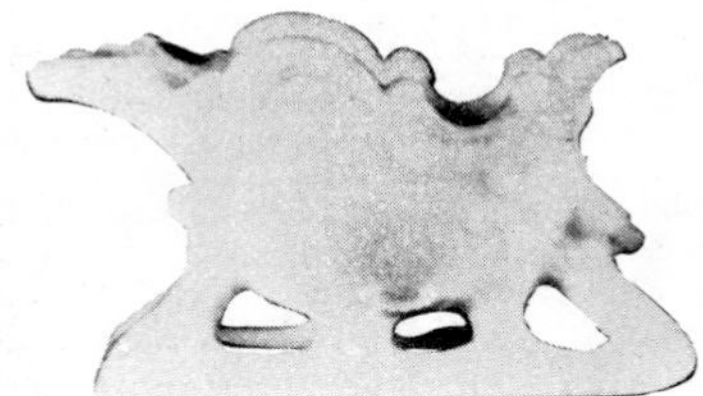
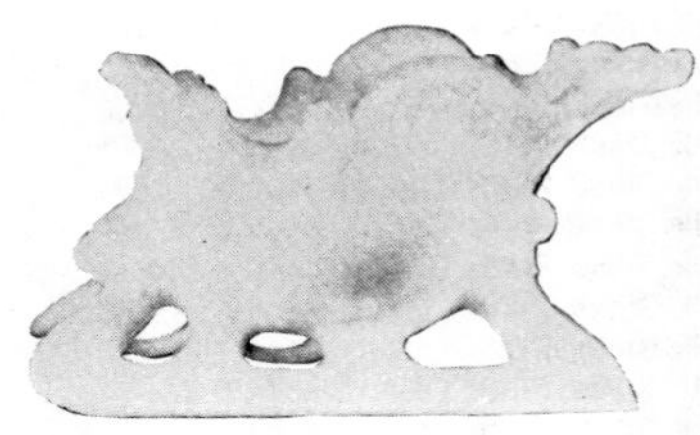

Milk Glass, Salt, Open, Sleigh, 4 X 2 1/2 In., Pair

Milk Glass, Plate, Wicket, 8 3/8 In. 11.00
Milk Glass, Plate, Woof Woof, B-13f 30.00
Milk Glass, Plate, Yacht With Anchor, 7 1/4 In., B-19 .... 20.00
Milk Glass, Platter, Blue, Fluted Edge, 13 In. 27.50
Milk Glass, Platter, John Hancock, Liberty Bell & Signature Center, 14 In. 250.00
Milk Glass, Platter, Liberty Bell, John Hancock, Twig Handles, 13 1/2 In. 175.00
Milk Glass, Platter, Liberty Bell, John Hancock, 11 X 7 In. 275.00
Milk Glass, Platter, Rock Of Ages, Clear & White, B-54a 145.00
Milk Glass, Punch Set, Pink, 14 Piece 25.00
Milk Glass, Relish, Fish, Dated 20.00
Milk Glass, Relish, Shell, B-60c 16.00
Milk Glass, Ring Tree, Hand-Painted, Ornate 25.00
Milk Glass, Rolling Pin, Wooden Handles 45.00
Milk Glass, Rose Bowl, Embossed Acanthus Leaves, Footed, Gilt Trim, 5 In. 10.00
Milk Glass, Salt & Pepper, Blue, Scroll Design, Tall 45.00
Milk Glass, Salt & Pepper, Enameled, Square 95.00
Milk Glass, Salt & Pepper, Grape 25.00
Milk Glass, Salt & Pepper, Green, Leaf & Palm 23.00
Milk Glass, Salt & Pepper, Square, Fine Decoration 75.00
Milk Glass, Salt & Pepper, Squatty, Embossed Flowers 15.00
Milk Glass, Salt & Pepper, Yellow, Basket Weave 30.00
Milk Glass, Salt, Master, Blackberry 25.00
Milk Glass, Salt, Open, Sleigh, 4 X 2 1/2 In., Pair .... *Illus* 75.00
Milk Glass, Salt, Swan 12.00
Milk Glass, Saltshaker, Beehive, Gold Paint On Bees 12.50
Milk Glass, Saltshaker, Blue Tree Stump With Brass Lid 35.00
Milk Glass, Saltshaker, Blue, Scrolls 12.00
Milk Glass, Saltshaker, Blue, Sunset 16.00
Milk Glass, Saltshaker, Christmas, Floral 60.00
Milk Glass, Saltshaker, Columbian Exposition, 1893 .... 40.00
Milk Glass, Saltshaker, Corn With Husk 18.00
Milk Glass, Saltshaker, Diagonal Swirled Ribs, Enamel Decoration 9.00

Milk Glass, Saltshaker, Egg Shape, Embossed Rabbits 28.00
Milk Glass, Saltshaker, Figural, Columbus 150.00
Milk Glass, Saltshaker, Green, Guttate 18.00
Milk Glass, Saltshaker, Heron & Lighthouse 17.00
Milk Glass, Saltshaker, Water Lily, Gold Trim 12.50
Milk Glass, Sauce, Cherry 10.00
Milk Glass, Sauce, Gooseberry 12.50
Milk Glass, Sauce, Strawberry 6.00
Milk Glass, Shade, Smoke Bell, Bell Shape, Ruffled Rim, 8 X 7 In. 30.00
Milk Glass, Sherbet, Rooster Stem 20.00
Milk Glass, Shoe, Child's, Shabby 22.00
Milk Glass, Shoe, Tramp 25.00
Milk Glass, Slipper, Blossom, 4 3/4 In. 25.00
Milk Glass, Smoke Bell 10.00
Milk Glass, Spooner, Blackberry .... 14.00 To 32.00
Milk Glass, Spooner, Footed, Red Medallions 15.00
Milk Glass, Spooner, Paneled, Scalloped Top 20.00
Milk Glass, Spooner, Pineapple 15.00
Milk Glass, Spooner, Swimming Swan, Scalloped Edge 30.00
Milk Glass, Spooner, Wheat, Milled Edge 18.00
Milk Glass, Stein, Monk, Miniature 25.00
Milk Glass, Sugar & Creamer, Blackberry 65.00
Milk Glass, Sugar & Creamer, Blue, Both Covered 50.00
Milk Glass, Sugar & Creamer, Covered, B-259a 25.00
Milk Glass, Sugar & Creamer, Covered, Forget-Me-Not 60.00
Milk Glass, Sugar & Creamer, Diamond & Fan, Miniature 35.00
Milk Glass, Sugar & Creamer, Footed 8.50
Milk Glass, Sugar & Creamer, Monax 10.00
Milk Glass, Sugar & Creamer, Ribbed, Open Lace Top 30.00
Milk Glass, Sugar & Creamer, Scroll & Shell, 3 1/2 In. 30.00
Milk Glass, Sugar & Creamer, Scrolled, Pair 35.00
Milk Glass, Sugar Shaker, Grape 20.00
Milk Glass, Sugar Shaker, Painted Flowers 3 Leaves, Tip Top 18.00
Milk Glass, Sugar, Basket Finial, Basket Weave, Loop Handles, Atterbury 100.00
Milk Glass, Sugar, Blue, Wild Rose, Miniature 35.00
Milk Glass, Sugar, Cat Cover, Hamper Base, Indiana Goblet & Tumbler Co. 365.00
Milk Glass, Sugar, Child's, Wild Rose 47.50
Milk Glass, Sugar, Covered, Signed Westmoreland 8.00
Milk Glass, Sugar, Diamond Shape, Cover 82.50
Milk Glass, Sugar, Wild Rose, Miniature 18.00
Milk Glass, Swan, Cambridge, 3 1/2 In. 65.00
Milk Glass, Swan, Closed Neck, B-155b 30.00
Milk Glass, Syrup, Applied Glass Handle, Metal Spout, Tree Of Life 25.00
Milk Glass, Syrup, Blue, Alba, Lavender Floral 38.00
Milk Glass, Syrup, Blue, Tree Of Life, Metal Top, B-74b 75.00
Milk Glass, Syrup, Pewter Top With Woman's Head Finial, Applied Handle 50.00
Milk Glass, Syrup, Scroll With Net 45.00
Milk Glass, Syrup, Stippled Dahlia, Original Top 40.00
Milk Glass, Table Set, Basket Weave, Atterbury, 4 Piece 150.00
Milk Glass, Table Set, Melon With Leaf, 3 Piece 150.00
Milk Glass, Tom & Jerry Set, Anchor Hocking, 11 Piece 25.00
Milk Glass, Toothpick, Blue, Fiber Bundle 30.00
Milk Glass, Toothpick, Cornucopia 15.00
Milk Glass, Toothpick, Daisy & Button, Hat Shape, 2 1/2 In. 12.50
Milk Glass, Toothpick, Light Blue, Basket With 3 Raised Bees 20.00
Milk Glass, Toothpick, Monkey & Stump .... 25.00 To 30.00
Milk Glass, Toothpick, Split Rib .... 22.00 To 25.00
Milk Glass, Toothpick, Square, Horseshoe, Clover 27.50
Milk Glass, Toothpick, Tree Trunk 18.00
Milk Glass, Tray, Actress, B-56a 35.00
Milk Glass, Tray, Bureau, Irregular Shape, Scroll & Scalloped Border 14.50
Milk Glass, Tray, Cake, Atterbury, Lacy Edge 30.00
Milk Glass, Tray, Cake, Lacy Edge .... *Illus* 20.00
Milk Glass, Tray, Cake, Lacy Edge, B-49 .... 42.00

Milk Glass, Tray, Card, Hands Emerging From Grape Cluster, 1876, 6 1/4 In. 45.00
Milk Glass, Tray, Currier & Ives, Balky Mule 35.00
Milk Glass, Tray, Dresser, Rose Garland 12.50
Milk Glass, Tray, Lady & Fan, 7 In.Across, 5 1/4 In.High .... *Illus* 85.00
Milk Glass, Tray, Pin, Artist's Palette & Brushes Shape 7.00
Milk Glass, Tray, Pin, Curlicue Edges, 9 In. 9.00
Milk Glass, Tray, Pin, Gold Scrolled Edge, 9 X 6 In. 8.00
Milk Glass, Tray, Pin, Heart Shape 3.50
Milk Glass, Tumbler, Black Trim 9.00
Milk Glass, Tumbler, Blue, Dart Bar, Footed 25.00

Milk Glass, Tray, Cake, Lacy Edge

(See Page 333)

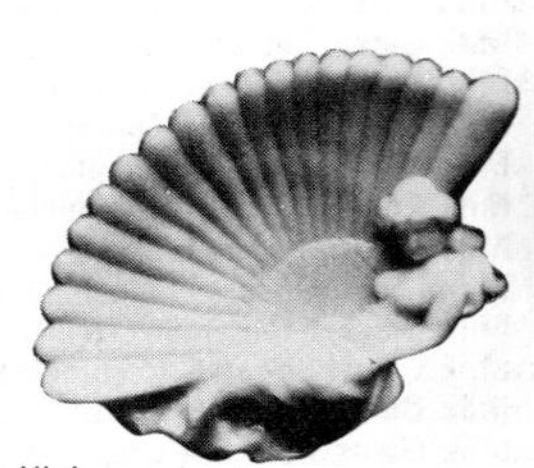

Milk Glass, Tray, Lady & Fan, 7 In.Across, 5 1/4 In.High

Milk Glass, Tumbler, Cuff With Button 25.00
Milk Glass, Tumbler, Guttate .... 25.00 To 28.00
Milk Glass, Tumbler, Lemonade, St.Louis Exposition 8.00
Milk Glass, Tumbler, Louisiana Purchase .... 12.00 To 14.00
Milk Glass, Tumbler, St. Louis Exposition 10.00
Milk Glass, Tumbler, View St.Louis World's Fair 16.50
Milk Glass, Tureen, Mustard, Slot In Lid, Footed, Loop Handles, Oval, 5 1/2 In. 12.00
Milk Glass, Vase, Blue, Jewel 65.00
Milk Glass, Vase, Gargoyle, 8 1/2 In. 22.00
Milk Glass, Vase, Green, Hand, 8 3/8 In. 22.00
Milk Glass, Vase, Opalescent, Ringed Hand With Ruffled Edge, 8 In. 60.00
Milk Glass, Vase, Pale Green, Molded Roses, Ruffled Top, France, 7 1/2 In. 16.00
Milk Glass, Vase, Swirled Rib, 9 In. 28.00
Milk Glass, Vase, Tan To Brown, Red & Yellow Tulip Spray, 11 In. 12.00
Milk Glass, Waste Bowl, Monkey 135.00
Milk Glass, Water Pitcher, Paneled Sprig 75.00

Millefiori means many flowers. It is a type of glasswork popular in paperweights. Many small flowerlike pieces of glass are grouped together to form a design.

Millefiori, see also Paperweight

Millefiori, Punch Set, Sample Size, 7 Piece 125.00
Millefiori, Rose Bowl, Ruffled, Blown, 6 In. 115.00
Millefiori, Vase, Green, 2 Handles, 7 1/4 In. 69.00
Millefiori, Vase, Stretched Multicolor Rods, Fluted Rim, 2 3/4 In. 35.00

Minton china has been made in the Staffordshire region of England from 1793 to the present. Many marks have been used; the one shown dates from c. 1873-1911.

Minton, Beaker, Flow Blue Underglaze Design Of Wine Taster, 1843, 5 In. 95.00
Minton, Bowl, Tree Of Life, Stoke-On-Trent, 6 X 6 In. 5.00
Minton, Bowl, Turquoise, Fruit Medallion, Red Inside, Footed, C.1912, 12 In. 125.00
Minton, Bread & Milk Set, Floral Garlands, For Plummer & Co., 4 Piece 27.50
Minton, Breakfast Set, Green & Yellow Floral On Cream, Black Mark, 18 Piece 36.00
Minton, Compote, Majolica, Two Cupids Holding Blue Shell, 1867, 11 1/4 In. 398.00
Minton, Cup & Saucer, Bouillon, Cobalt & Engraved Gold Band Border 20.00
Minton, Cup & Saucer, Demitasse, No.B1327 .... 7.50

Minton, Cup & Saucer, Demitasse, White, Gold Bands & Line Trim, C.1911 ..... 15.00
Minton, Cup & Saucer, Marked No.S-705 In Green 10.00
Minton, Cup & Saucer, Salt Glaze, White, Raised Leaves 15.00
Minton, Flask, Pate-Sur-Pate, Moon, Blue, Birds, Butterflies, 1875, 8 In., Pair 550.00
Minton, Mold, Food, White, Geometrics, C.1911, 9 1/2 X 5 1/4 In. 38.00
Minton, Plate, Bird, Essex Birds, C.1870, 10 In. 15.00
Minton, Plate, Blue & White, 1898, 15 In. 38.00
Minton, Plate, Cake, Salt Glaze, White, Raised Leaves 15.00
Minton, Plate, Cat Under Umbrella, Sepia 8.00
Minton, Plate, Dinner, Cobalt & Engraved Gold Band Border, 10 1/4 In. 20.00
Minton, Plate, Dinner, Salt Glaze, White, Raised Leaves 15.00
Minton, Plate, Floral & Fruit, Beaded Border, For Tiffany, C.1900, 10 1/4 In. 25.00
Minton, Plate, Floral With Bird, Pink, Green, Turquoise, 8 1/2 In. 12.00
Minton, Plate, Flower Center, Pink & White, Gold Rim, 9 In. 12.50
Minton, Plate, Luncheon, Cobalt & Engraved Gold Band Border, 8 3/4 In. 17.50
Minton, Plate, Off-White, Brown Decoration, 1881, 9 1/4 In. 22.00
Minton, Plate, Oriental Bouquet Center, Stone China, 9 In. 12.00
Minton, Plate, Oyster, Majolica, 9 X 7 1/2 In. ..... 38.00 To 58.00
Minton, Plate, Poonah, Florals, C.1862, 10 In. 25.00
Minton, Plate, Service, Ivory White, Gold Trim 25.00
Minton, Plate, Service, White, Maroon & Embossed Gold Scalloped Edge, 10 In. 130.00
Minton, Plate, Soup, Cobalt & Engraved Gold Band Border, Flange, 7 3/4 In. 15.00
Minton, Plate, Souvenir, State House, Black & White, 9 1/2 In. 23.00
Minton, Plate, Souvenir, Wm.Penn Cottage, Black & White, 9 1/2 In. 23.00
Minton, Platter, Cobalt & Engraved Gold Band Border, Round, 16 In. 65.00
Minton, Platter, Maroon, Blue, White, & Orange, Well, Footed, 19 1/2 In. 100.00
Minton, Relish, Fairyland Luster Type Fruit Decoration, 5 In. 50.00
Minton, Seat, Garden, Blue Black, Turquoise Medallions, Signed, 19 In. 340.00
Minton, Soup Bowl & Underplate, Salisbury, 2-Handled Bowl 24.50
Minton, Tea Set, C.1890, 6 Piece 50.00
Minton, Tea Set, Cheviot, 24 Piece 200.00
Minton, Teacup & Saucer, Cobalt & Engraved Gold Band Border 20.00
Minton, Tile, Biblical, Square, 6 In. 22.00
Minton, Tile, Blue & White, Mason 20.00
Minton, Tile, Blue & White, Potter 20.00
Minton, Tile, Blue & White, Smith 20.00
Minton, Tile, Boston State House, 1818, Blue, Macullar, Parker & Co. 40.00
Minton, Tile, Girl Picking Flowers, 6 In. 30.00
Minton, Tile, Tea, Mother & Child, Wrought Iron Footed Frame, 6 In. 22.50
Minton, Tile, Tea, Sheep Near Stable, Wrought Iron Footed Frame, 6 In. 22.50
Minton, Vase, Bottle Shape, Floral & Gold, C.1853, 10 In. 159.00
Minton, Vase, Brown Bulbous Body, Enamel Circles, Crown Mark, 10 3/4 In. 75.00
Minton, Vase, Chinese-Red Background, White Flowers, 7 1/4 In. 170.00
Minton, Vase, Cinnabar, Art Nouveau Decoration, Red Colors, 7 1/2 In. 145.00
Minton, Vase, Gold Leaf Floral With Silver Centers, C.1873, 10 In. 182.00
Minton, Vase, Lemon Yellow, Green Floral, Silver Centers, C.1853, 10 In. 149.00
Minton, Vase, Potpourri, Rose Pompadour, Birds, 19th Century, 11 In. 1600.00

Mirror, see Furniture, Mirror

Mocha ware is an English-made product that was sold in America during the early 1800s. It is a heavy pottery with pale coffee and cream coloring. Designs of blue, brown, green, orange, or black or white were added to the pottery.

Mocha, Bowl, Earthworm Design In Brown & Orange, 6 3/4 X 3 1/2 In. 175.00
Mocha, Chamber Pot, Blue Seaweed Decoration, Applied Handle 75.00
Mocha, Creamer, Seaweed, 5 In. 95.00
Mocha, Crock, Earthworm, One Quart 65.00
Mocha, Cup, Spit, White, Blue & Brown Stripes, Top Lifts Off, 2 3/4 In. 20.75
Mocha, Jug, Black Splotched Trees, Molded Circlets, Early 1800s, English 300.00
Mocha, Jug, Seaweed, Tan On White, Blue And Gray-Green Striping, 5 In. 105.00
Mocha, Jug, Seaweed, 7 1/4 In. 190.00
Mocha, Mug, Seaweed, Blue Band, 6 In. 65.00
Mocha, Mug, Seaweed, Strap Handle, 5 In. 75.00

Mold, Candle, see Kitchen, Mold, Candle; Tin, Mold, Candle

Mold, Bullet, see Weapon, Mold, Bullet
Mold, Ice Cream, see Pewter, Mold, Ice Cream

Monart, Vase, Cluthra Type, Blue & Rose, 6 3/4 X 6 1/2 In. 70.00
Monmouth, Vase, Green, Paper Label, 5 1/2 In., Pair 12.50
Monroe, Jar, Cookie, Oval Top, Lilac & Leaves, Paneled, Unsigned 145.00
Monroe, Jar, Cracker, White With Floral Decoration, Unsigned 95.00

Mont Joye, see Mt.Joye

Moorcroft Pottery was founded in Burslem, England, in 1914 by William Moorcroft. The earlier wares are similar to those made today, but color and marking will help indicate the age.

Moorcroft, Ashtray, White, Sterling Mounted, J.E.Caldwell, Burslem 65.00
Moorcroft, Base, Bulbous, Cobalt, Pansies, Signed, 5 1/2 In. 55.00
Moorcroft, Bowl, Dark To Light Green, Violet & Maroon Floral, 4 1/2 In. 18.00
Moorcroft, Bowl, Green, Pink & Blue Floral, 4 1/4 In. 20.00
Moorcroft, Bowl, Mushroom, Double Handles, Pedestal, Shreve & Co., 9 X 7 In. 375.00
Moorcroft, Bowl, Pomegranate, Pedestal Base, 9 X 4 In. 110.00
Moorcroft, Candlestick, Mushroom, Green Signature, No.42008, 8 In. 225.00
Moorcroft, Compote, Dark Blue, Purple Blossoms, Green Leaves, C.1921, 9 In. 80.00
Moorcroft, Cup & Saucer, Demitasse, Blue 12.00
Moorcroft, Cup & Saucer, Demitasse, Green Script Signature 22.50
Moorcroft, Dish, Cobalt With Bright Colored Flowers, Oval, 9 X 5 In. 15.00
Moorcroft, Humidor, Pomegranates, Green Burslem Signature, 8 X 5 In. 150.00
Moorcroft, Jar, Rose, Reticulated Screw Top, Green Signature, 1912, 4 In. 90.00
Moorcroft, Jar, Tobacco, Screw Top, Macintyre In Green 250.00
Moorcroft, Lighter, Cigarette, Floral, Paper Label 35.00
Moorcroft, Pitcher, Pewter Lid, Orange & Cobalt, Macintyre, C.1885, 6 In. 48.00
Moorcroft, Plate, Pomegranates, Blue Signature, 7 In., Pair 60.00
Moorcroft, Tea Set, Blue Green, Floral, 3 Piece 100.00
Moorcroft, Teapot, Blue, Plum & Lemons, Sheffield Silver Rim, 1898 125.00
Moorcroft, Teapot, Mushroom, Sterling Overlay, Art Nouveau, Shreve & Co. 750.00
Moorcroft, Vase, Aurelian Ware, Baluster, Macintyre, 10 3/4 In. 250.00
Moorcroft, Vase, Blooming Orchids, Script Signature, 12 In. 225.00
Moorcroft, Vase, Blue Ground, Purple, Blue, Green Flowers, Script Mark Wm. 60.00
Moorcroft, Vase, Cobalt, Fruit, Liberty & Co. Tudric Base, 7 1/4 In. 138.50
Moorcroft, Vase, Cobalt, Fruit, 4 In. 35.00
Moorcroft, Vase, Cobalt, Pansy, Blue Script Signature, 2 3/4 In. 55.00
Moorcroft, Vase, Cobalt, Pink & Rose Floral, 4 1/4 In. 45.00
Moorcroft, Vase, Cobalt, Rouge, Green, & Yellow Floral, 7 In. 54.00
Moorcroft, Vase, Fish Design, 12 3/4 In. 400.00
Moorcroft, Vase, Flambe, Blue Script, 7 3/4 In. 60.00
Moorcroft, Vase, Flambe, Fruit, Blue Script Signature, C.1930, 9 X 8 In. 250.00
Moorcroft, Vase, Flambe, Tapered Neck, 12 In. 175.00
Moorcroft, Vase, Flamminian, Bowl Shape, Green, Liberty & Co., 4 1/4 In. 85.00
Moorcroft, Vase, Floral Decoration, Blue Mark, 5 In. 38.00
Moorcroft, Vase, Floral Decoration, Green Mark, 11 In. 98.00
Moorcroft, Vase, Fruit Decoration, Blue Ground, 7 1/4 In. 65.00
Moorcroft, Vase, Green & Blue, Tree Design, 1930, 14 X 10 In. 350.00
Moorcroft, Vase, Green Signature, 1913, 7 In. 175.00
Moorcroft, Vase, Greens, 4 1/2 In. *Illus* 30.00

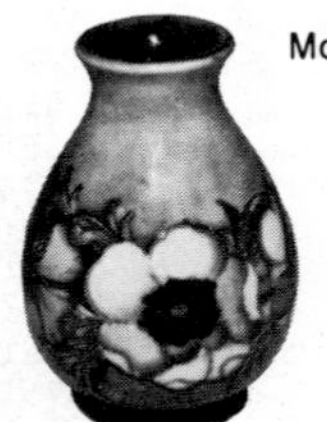

Moorcroft, Vase, Greens, 4 1/2 In.

Moorcroft, Vase, Macintyre, Green Signature, 5 In. 175.00
Moorcroft, Vase, Mushroom, Burslem, Green Signature, 9 In. 300.00
Moorcroft, Vase, Mushroom, 4 1/2 In. 195.00
Moorcroft, Vase, Orange Iridescent, Moorcroft, Burslem, 3 In. 20.00
Moorcroft, Vase, Roses & Foliage On Green, Macintyre, 2 Handled, 6 In. 275.00
Moorcroft, Vase, Roses On Green Ground, Macintyre, 4 In. 215.00
Moorcroft, Vase, Royal Blue, Enamel Fruit, Script Signature, 7 1/2 In. 70.00
Moorcroft, Vase, Spill, Dark Blue, Art Nouveau, C.1900, 3 1/2 In. 65.00
Moorcroft, Vase, White, Pansies, Macintyre, 5 3/4 In. 155.00
Moorcroft, Vase, White, Yellow Tulips, Macintyre, 7 In., Pair 425.00
Moorcroft, Vase, Yellow, Grapes, Green Leaves, Handled, Liberty & Co., 5 In. 150.00

Moriage is used to identify Japanese pottery to which a raised overglaze decoration has been added. This relief ornamentation may be elaborate. The term applies to the style or technique.

Moriage, Liqueur Set, Green, Orange, & Brown, Slip, Beading, Gold, 6 Piece 58.00
Moriage, Tea Set, Dragons, Green & Gray Matte, Ornate Interiors, 3 Piece 95.00
Moriage, Tea Set, Gray & Green, Dragons, Lima Mark, 15 Piece 65.00
Moriage, Vase, Cameo Florals, 3 Handled, Flared Neck, 4 In. 60.00
Moriage, Vase, Cobalt, Raised Dragons, Painted Red Roses, 13 In. 40.00
Moriage, Vase, Hand-Painted Flowers, Overglaze Decoration, 13 In. 45.00

Mosaic Tile Company of Zanesville, Ohio, was started by Karl Langenbeck and Herman Mueller in 1894. Many types of plain and ornamental tiles were made until 1959. The company closed in 1967.

Mosaic Tile Co., Paperweight, Globe 27.00
Mosaic Tile Co., Tile, Blue With White Pilgrim 25.00
Mosaic Tile Co., Tile, Fountain, Doves, Black, White, Frame, 7 1/2 In. 175.00
Mosaic Tile Co., Tile, Grizzly Bear 100.00
Mosaic Tile Co., Tile, Lincoln .... 20.00 To 38.00
Mosaic Tile Co., Tile, Woodrow Wilson 25.00
Mosaic, Frame, Blue, Inlaid With Flowers, 2 Ovals In Rectangle, 4 In. 35.00

Moser Karlsbad

Moser glass was made by Ludwig Moser and Sohne, a Bohemian glasshouse founded in 1857. Art Nouveau type glassware and iridescent glassware were made. The firm is still working.

Moser Type, Vase, Green To Clear, Enamel Floral, Gilt Trim, Stick, 12 In. 16.00
Moser, Ashray & Lighter, Glass Column, Marble Base, Prisms 30.00
Moser, Ashtray, Malachite, Rearing Horses 48.00
Moser, Bottle, Green Overlay, Clear Cut Warrior Band, 10 In.Stopper, 12 In. 250.00
Moser, Bottle, Perfume, Cranberry, Melon Ribbed, Gold Scrolls, Brass Cap, 4 In. 75.00
Moser, Bottle, Perfume, Crystal To Emerald Green Top, Crystal Stopper, 5 In. 65.00
Moser, Bottle, Scent, Amethyst, Gold Warrior Band, 4 In. 88.00
Moser, Bowl, Amethyst, Enamel Floral, 6 1/2 In. 65.00
Moser, Bowl, Malachite, Small, Signed 50.00
Moser, Box, Powder, Gold Cameo Frieze On Lid, Diamond Shape 195.00
Moser, Box, Powder, Hinged, Amber, Russian Decoration, Brass Fittings, 3 In. 195.00
Moser, Butter Pat, Green 15.00
Moser, Cordial Set, Cranberry, Gold Trim, Signed 350.00
Moser, Cruet, Gold Decoration, Raised Cobalt Panels, Gold Handle & Stopper 275.00
Moser, Cup & Saucer, Blue, Applied Acorns, Enameling 295.00
Moser, Decanter, Cobalt, Crystal Stopper, Signed, 19 In. 250.00
Moser, Decanter, Whiskey, Acid Cut, Gold Overlay, Moser Karlsbad, 10 In. 85.00
Moser, Ewer, Green, Applied Acorns & Insects, Enamel Oak Leaves, 12 In. 650.00
Moser, Goblet, Alexandrite, Signed, Pattern Like Argus 135.00
Moser, Goblet, Blue, Enameled In Gold, White, Blue & Red, Swirl Stem, Signed 140.00
Moser, Goblet, Cocktail, Aquamarine, St.Louis Diamond, Pyramid Stem 20.75
Moser, Goblet, Cranberry, Gold Design Of Birds, 5 1/2 In., Unsigned 135.00
Moser, Goblet, Emerald Green, Porcelain Portrait Plaque Of Woman, Gilding 85.00
Moser, Goblet, Green, Red, & Gold Enamel Medallions, Teardrop Stem 115.00
Moser, Lamp, Cranberry, Applied Amber Alligator, Enamel Floral, 16 1/2 In. 550.00
Moser, Match Holder, Amber, Signed, 3 1/2 In. 75.00
Moser, Mayonnaise Bowl, Underplate, & Ladle, Amber, Gold Rims 135.00
Moser, Pitcher, Water, Ruby Red, Decorated, 9 In. 350.00

Moser, Planter, Amethyst, Gold Band With Warriors, Oval, 12 X 6 In. 300.00
Moser, Rose Bowl, Intaglio Cut, Emerald Green To Clear, Unsigned, Pair 37.00
Moser, Sugar & Creamer, Cobalt Panels, Gold, Both Signed 140.00
Moser, Tray, Pin, Gold Cameo Frieze, Diamond Shape 65.00
Moser, Tumbler, Cranberry 40.00
Moser, Tumbler, Cranberry To Clear, Silver & Gold Grapes On Vines, 5 In. 95.00
Moser, Tumbler, Cranberry, Blue & White Enamel Floral, Gold Edge, 3 3/4 In. 75.00
Moser, Tumbler, Cranberry, Enameled 45.00
Moser, Tumbler, Cranberry, Gold Border Of Pink, Blue, & White Floral 60.00
Moser, Tumbler, Juice, Amber, Inverted Baby Thumbprint, Oak Leaves & Acorns 195.00
Moser, Vase, Amber With Amazon Gold Border, Signed, 6 In. 85.00
Moser, Vase, Amber, Butterflies & Floral, Brass Footed Satyr Base, 8 In. 225.00
Moser, Vase, Amber, Signed, 11 1/2 In. 245.00
Moser, Vase, Amber, Two Fish, Bulbous, 5 In. 65.00
Moser, Vase, Blue Crackle, 2 Applied Green & Brown Fish, Enamel, 8 In. 275.00
Moser, Vase, Blue, Enamel Fish & Seaweeds, 11 1/2 In. 200.00
Moser, Vase, Bulbous, Amber, Band Of Gold Engraved Trojan Scene, 13 In. 145.00
Moser, Vase, Cobalt Blue, Signed, 8 1/4 In. 225.00
Moser, Vase, Cobalt, Enamel Daffodils, 9 1/2 In. 225.00
Moser, Vase, Cranberry To Clear, Classic Figure Cameos, 12 1/2 In. 165.00
Moser, Vase, Cranberry To Clear, Enamel Chrysanthemums, 14 In. 195.00
Moser, Vase, Cranberry, Blue & White Enamel Floral, Gold Border, 15 In. 185.00
Moser, Vase, Cranberry, Enamel Floral, Gold Scrolls, Crystal Pedestal, 5 In. 120.00
Moser, Vase, Enamel, Hexagon Top, Lavender To Clear, Signed, 5 1/2 In. 300.00
Moser, Vase, Green, Gold, Blue, & Red Enamel Floral, Brass Collar, 16 In. 265.00
Moser, Vase, Light Green, Footed, 10 1/2 In. 60.00
Moser, Vase, Moss Green, Multicolor Enamel, 8 3/4 In. 650.00
Moser, Vase, Pastel Enamel, Green Ground, 8 3/4 In. 375.00
Moser, Vase, Pedestal, Amber Glass With Gold Warrior Band, Signed, 6 In. 125.00
Moser, Wine Set, Cranberry Panels, Gold Trim, Hexagonal Stems, 7 Piece 335.00
Moser, Wine Set, Royal Purple, Crystal, Gold Trim, Unsigned 650.00
Moser, Wine, Cranberry And Crystal, Signed, 8 In. 125.00
Moser, Wine, Cranberry, Enamel Acorns 185.00
Moser, Wine, Cranberry, Paperweight Stem 75.00
Moser, Wine, Cranberry, Trumpet Stem 75.00

Moss rose china was made by many firms from 1808 to 1900. It refers to any china decorated with the moss rose flower.

Moss Rose, Coffee Set, 3 Pieces 75.00
Moss Rose, Coffeepot, 9 In. 78.00
Moss Rose, Cup & Saucer, Edwards Bros. 11.50
Moss Rose, Plate, C.1850, 10 In. 32.00
Moss Rose, Plate, Cake, Handled, Edwards Bros., Square, 9 In. 15.50
Moss Rose, Plate, Dinner, Ironstone, Meakin 5.00
Moss Rose, Plate, Pink Roses On Green, Embossed Rim, Handled, 9 1/2 In. 7.50
Moss Rose, Plate, Pinks & Turquoise, Scalloped Open Lattice Edge, 7 1/2 In. 24.00
Moss Rose, Platter, Ironstone, Meakin, 14 In. 28.00
Moss Rose, Preserve Set, Royal Chelsea, 3 Piece 25.00
Moss Rose, Sugar & Creamer, Rope Handles, Raised Bow Knots, Haviland 75.00
Moss Rose, Tea Set, Child's, Japan, 19 Piece 22.00
Moss Rose, Tea Set, Japan, C.1930, Demitasse, 14 Piece 28.00

Mother-of -Pearl, see also Pearl

Mother-of-pearl glass, or pearl satin glass, was first made in the 1850s in England and in Massachusetts. It was a special type of mold-blown satin glass with air bubbles in the glass, giving it a pearlized color.

Mother-Of-Pearl, Ewer, Rose Petal Soft Satin Finish, 10 1/2 In. 265.00
Mother-Of-Pearl, Ewer, Rose To Pink, Cased, Footed, 8 1/2 In. 350.00
Mother-Of-Pearl, Ewer, Rose To White, Herringbone, Melon Ribbed, 8 3/4 In. 350.00
Mother-Of-Pearl, Lamp, Diamond Quilted, 10 In.Diameter Shade *Illus* 1400.00
Mother-Of-Pearl, Pitcher, Water, Butterscotch, Raindrop 185.00
Mother-Of-Pearl, Pitcher, Water, Rainbow, Coin Spot, Camphor Handle, 8 In. 675.00
Mother-Of-Pearl, Pitcher, Water, Rose Color, Peacock's-Eye, White Lining 350.00
Mother-Of-Pearl, Rose Bowl, Blue, Diamond-Quilted, Shell & Seaweed, 6 In. 250.00

Mother-Of-Pearl, Lamp, Diamond Quilted, 10 In.Diameter Shade

Mother-of-Pearl, Satin Glass, see also Satin Glass, Smith Brothers, Tiffany Glass, etc.

Mother-Of-Pearl, Tumbler, Blue, Diamond-Quilted 95.00
Mother-Of-Pearl, Tumbler, Diamond-Quilted, Raspberry 110.00
Mother-Of-Pearl, Tumbler, Raspberry, Diamond-Quilted 95.00
Mother-Of-Pearl, Tumbler, Shaded Satin, Enamel Florals 145.00
Mother-Of-Pearl, Tumbler, Yellow Diamond-Quilted, 3 7/8 In. 85.00
Mother-Of-Pearl, Vase, Blue, Herringbone, Applied Frosted Feet, 4 3/4 In. 94.00
Mother-Of-Pearl, Vase, Bud, Pink, Moire, 5 1/2 X 3 In. 95.00
Mother-Of-Pearl, Vase, Czechoslovakia, Pink & Violet, 12 1/2 In. 35.00
Mother-Of-Pearl, Vase, Deep Rose To Pink, Bulbous, Satin Finish, 5 In. 175.00
Mother-Of-Pearl, Vase, Lemon Yellow, Teardrop, 5 1/2 In. 55.00
Mother-Of-Pearl, Vase, Quilted, Gooseneck, 10 In. 150.00
Mother-Of-Pearl, Vase, Rainbow, Four Panel Sides, Round Neck, 7 In. 125.00
Mother-Of-Pearl, Vase, Satin Glass Swirled, Lemon To Ivory, Fluted Top 150.00

Moustache Cup, see Mustache Cup

Mt.Joye, Flower Bowl, Frosted, Lavender & Green Iris, 7 In. 195.00
Mt.Joye, Pitcher, Water, Green Shading, Enamel Iris 165.00
Mt.Joye, Vase, Dark Green, Applied Gold Decoration, 11 In. 290.00
Mt.Joye, Vase, Frosted Hammered Ground, Pink & White Floral, Gold, 14 In. 195.00
Mt.Joye, Vase, Iris & Butterflies, Enameled, 16 1/2 In. 195.00
Mt.Joye, Vase, Pigeon's Blood Red, Enamel Floral & Gold Lace, 11 In. 95.00

Mt. Washington Glass was made at the Mt. Washington Glass Co. located in New Bedford, Massachusetts. Many types of art glass were made there from 1850 to the 1890s.

Mt.Washington, see also Burmese, Crown Milano

Mt.Washington, Barrel, Biscuit, Ivory Color, Gold Mums, Silver Fittings 295.00
Mt.Washington, Berry Bowl, Red & Pink Floral, Metal Top Rim, 8 1/2 In. 85.00
Mt.Washington, Bowl, Blue To White, Diamond-Quilted, Satin Finish, 4 1/4 In. 200.00
Mt.Washington, Bowl, Diamond-Quilted, Pink To White, 2 1/2 In. 125.00
Mt.Washington, Bowl, Lusterless White, Enamel Floral, Hand Grip, 12 In. 35.00
Mt.Washington, Bowl, Melon Ribbed, Floral, Smith Bros., 4 In. 50.00
Mt.Washington, Box, Collar, Aqua, Gold Floral, Ornate Silver Collar, Numbers 165.00
Mt.Washington, Box, Puff, Covered, Melon Ribbed, Enameled Daisies, Libbey 225.00
Mt.Washington, Box, Sweetmeat, Ivory To Biscuit, Albertine Gold Poppies 300.00
Mt.Washington, Castor Set, Ribbed Cruets, Pairpoint Plate Salt Holder 1950.00
Mt.Washington, Creamer, Pink Floral, Silver Rim & Handle 45.00
Mt.Washington, Creamer, Pink, Silver Handle & Trim, Lavender Daisies 100.00
Mt.Washington, Cruet, Acid Cut Decorated, Mushroom Stopper, Caramel, Orange 600.00
Mt.Washington, Cruet, Burmese, Glossy 650.00
Mt.Washington, Cruet, Lusterless White 200.00
Mt.Washington, Cruet, Peachblow, Blue To Pink, Pink Throat And Stopper 2500.00
Mt.Washington, Dish, Sweetmeat, Pansies On White Luster 395.00
Mt.Washington, Flower Frog, Purple, Blue, Rust Flowers, Trailing Vines 165.00
Mt.Washington, Jar, Biscuit, White, Blue Floral, Silver Plate Lid 225.00
Mt.Washington, Jar, Cookie, Melon Sections, Gold Decoration 275.00
Mt.Washington, Muffineer, Acid Finish, Pink Clover, Egg Shape, 4 In. 125.00

Mt.Washington, Muffineer, Blue To White, Large Flowers, 4 3/4 In. 115.00
Mt.Washington, Muffineer, Burmese Color, Daisies, 4 1/2 In. 155.00
Mt.Washington, Muffineer, Melon Ribbed, Enamel Rose, Leaves, & Branches 85.00
Mt.Washington, Muffineer, Strawberry Decoration, Marked Patent 175.00
Mt.Washington, Muffineer, White, Ribbed, Pink Blossoms, Metal Top, 6 In. 150.00
Mt.Washington, Muffineer, White, Yellow Floral, Egg Shape, Pewter Top 155.00
Mt.Washington, Mustard Pot, Satin Finish, Flowers 40.00
Mt.Washington, Mustard Pot, Shiny, Lilies 30.00
Mt.Washington, Pitcher, Amberina, Fuchsia, Amber Reeded Handle, 7 3/4 In. 195.00
Mt.Washington, Pitcher, Milk, Peachblow, Blue To Raspberry 1850.00
Mt.Washington, Pitcher, Satin Glass, Pink Shell, Painted Flowers, Silver Top 225.00
Mt.Washington, Pitcher, Swirl Amberina, Square Top 225.00
Mt.Washington, Pitcher, Water, Burmese, Hobnail, Acid Finish, 10 In. 975.00
Mt.Washington, Plate, Lusterless White, 9 In. 18.00
Mt.Washington, Plate, Lusterless, Hand-Painted Flowers, 7 1/2 In. 35.00
Mt.Washington, Plate, White, Carnations & Lilies Of The Valley, 12 In. 55.00
Mt.Washington, Plate, White, Lusterless, Purple & Yellow Pansies, 7 1/2 In. 11.00
Mt.Washington, Plate, White, Lusterless, Roses, 12 In. 21.00
Mt.Washington, Plate, White, Lusterless, Snow Scene, Church, Holly, 6 1/4 In. 8.50
Mt.Washington, Rosebowl, Satin Finish, Blue, 4 1/2 In. 45.00
Mt.Washington, Salt & Pepper, Apple Shape, Flower Decoration 30.00
Mt.Washington, Salt & Pepper, Burmese Color, Tomatoes, Blue & White Trim 135.00
Mt.Washington, Salt & Pepper, Chicken's Head 315.00
Mt.Washington, Salt & Pepper, Chicks 350.00
Mt.Washington, Salt & Pepper, Chrysanthemums & Wild Roses, Egg Shape 95.00
Mt.Washington, Salt & Pepper, Egg, Pastel Flowers, Pair 95.00
Mt.Washington, Salt & Pepper, Opaque Satin, Shrimp, Enamel, Plated Holder 119.00
Mt.Washington, Salt & Pepper, Ribbed Pillar, Pansy Decoration 55.00
Mt.Washington, Salt & Pepper, Tomato 35.00
Mt.Washington, Salt & Pepper, Tomatoes With Burmese Coloring, Blue, White 120.00
Mt.Washington, Salt, Master, Off-White, Melon Ribbed, Pansies, Gold Dots 65.00
Mt.Washington, Salt, Master, Pink, Blue Violets, White Dots On Blue Top 60.00
Mt.Washington, Saltshaker, Cranberry, Frosted With Dotted Decoration 125.00
Mt.Washington, Saltshaker, Egg Shape, Floral 28.00
Mt.Washington, Saltshaker, Egg Shape, Pink To White, Blue & Yellow Floral 40.00
Mt.Washington, Saltshaker, Egg, Burmese Color, Daisies 40.00
Mt.Washington, Saltshaker, Egg, Shiny White, Pink & Yellow Roses 35.00
Mt.Washington, Saltshaker, Egg, White, Holly Berries & Leaves 40.00
Mt.Washington, Saltshaker, Egg, Yellow To White, Pink Floral, Green Leaves 40.00
Mt.Washington, Saltshaker, Fig 85.00
Mt.Washington, Saltshaker, Melon Ribbed Satin, Blue With Violet, Gold Top 55.00
Mt.Washington, Saltshaker, Pale Green, Orange Floral, Tomato Shape, Ribbed 70.00
Mt.Washington, Saltshaker, Pink, Egg Shape, Floral, Lusterless, Flat End 60.50
Mt.Washington, Saltshaker, Tomato, Cream To Pink, Decorated 65.00
Mt.Washington, Saltshaker, Tomato, White, Apple Blossoms 40.00
Mt.Washington, Saltshaker, Tomato, White, Yellow & Mauve Daisies 40.00
Mt.Washington, Saltshaker, Tomato, Yellow To White, Orange Pansies 40.00
Mt.Washington, Shade, Melon Shape, Smith Bros.Owls On Tree Branches, 5 In. 195.00
Mt.Washington, Sugar Shaker, Egg Shape, Plated Top, Fern Pattern 125.00
Mt.Washington, Sugar Shaker, Eggshell Satin, Blue To White, Blue Flowers 140.00
Mt.Washington, Sugar Shaker, Eggshell Satin, White, Green & Brown Fern 135.00
Mt.Washington, Sugar Shaker, Peachblow, Daisies, Brass Lid 155.00
Mt.Washington, Sugar Shaker, Ribbed Satin, White With Pink Blossom, Cover 150.00
Mt.Washington, Toothpick, Burmese, Square Top, Delicate Shading 135.00
Mt.Washington, Toothpick, Lusterless, Beaded Rim, Scroll & Floral Base 52.00
Mt.Washington, Toothpick, Opaque White, Melon Ribbed, Pink & Blue Pansies 75.00
Mt.Washington, Toothpick, Ribbed White Satin With Violet, Blue Dotted Top 75.00
Mt.Washington, Toothpick, Satin With Decorated Enamel 60.00
Mt.Washington, Tray, Pin, Sapphire Blue Satin, Star Shape 25.00
Mt.Washington, Tumbler, Acid Burmese Salmon Pink 165.00
Mt.Washington, Vase, Burmese, Double Gourd, 8 1/2 In. 475.00
Mt.Washington, Vase, Burmese, Gourd Shape, Lemon, Salmon Neck 200.00
Mt.Washington, Vase, Burmese, Jack-In-The-Pulpit, 7 In. 385.00
Mt.Washington, Vase, Burmese, Ruffled Rim, Ribbed Sides, Unsigned, 3 1/4 In. 225.00

Mt.Washington, Vase, Butterscotch Neck, White Melon Base, Cased, 10 In. 175.00
Mt.Washington, Vase, Diamond Quilt, Alice Blue, Flared, Crimped Top 145.00
Mt.Washington, Vase, Lava Glass, 4 3/4 In.High .... *Illus* 110.00
Mt.Washington, Vase, Lily, Amberina, 10 In. 195.00
Mt.Washington, Vase, Lusterless, White Satin, Pedestal Footed Stick, 6 In. 30.00
Mt.Washington, Vase, Mother-Of-Pearl, Diamond-Quilted, Cased, 3 In. 95.00
Mt.Washington, Vase, Smith Bros., Painted Heron, Scenic, 11 1/2 X 8 In. 145.00
Mt.Washington, Vase, Verona, Pansies, 5 1/4 X 2 5/8 In. 45.00
Mt.Washington, Vase, Verona, White Lilies, 9 1/2 X 4 In. 80.00
Mt.Washington, Vase, White Satin, Pink Blossom Decoration, 2 1/4 In. 35.00
Mt.Washington, Water Set, Burmese, Squat Bulbous Pitcher, 6 Tumblers 1350.00

Muffineer, see also Cranberry, Muffineer

Muffineer, English, Satin Finish, Gold & Pink Floral 40.00
Muffineer, Glass, Etched Flowers & Leaves, 6 1/2 In. 30.00
Muffineer, Hand-Painted, Green Shading, Maroon & White Floral, 4 In. 10.00
Muffineer, Opaline Diamond On Clear Ribbed, Metal Top, 5 In. 48.00
Muffineer, Porcelain, Hand-Painted Pink Tea Roses, Gold Leaf Top, 4 1/2 In. 24.00
Muffineer, Porcelain, Rose & Daisy Transfer, 4 1/4 In. 18.00
Muffineer, Sterling Silver, Queen Anne, 7 In. 70.00
Muffineer, White Glass, Hand-Painted Floral, Metal Lid, 6 In. 17.50

Muller Freres, French for Muller Brothers, made cameo and other art glass from the early 1900s to the late 1930s. Their factory was first located in Luneville and later moved to Croismaire, France.

Muller Freres, Bowl, Acid Finish, Orange, 4 3/4 X 1 3/8 In., Signed 95.00
Muller Freres, Lamp Base, Mottled Royal Blue, Footed, 6 In. 80.00
Muller Freres, Lamp Shade, Verre De Soie, Reddish Brown To Yellow, Signed 95.00
Muller Freres, Lamp, Cameo Base, Dark Blue On Frosted, Signed, 17 3/4 In. 475.00
Muller Freres, Lamp, Hanging, Dome & 3 Shades, Gray, Purple, And Orange, 14 In. 900.00
Muller Freres, Vase, Autumn Swirled Colors, 9 In. 45.00
Muller Freres, Vase, Cameo, Bottle Shape, Silhouette Of Woman, Blue, 12 In. 395.00
Muller Freres, Vase, Luneville, Satin, Dark Mottled On Pink, 5 1/2 In. 100.00
Muller Freres, Vase, Owl On Branch, Pink Ground, Croismare, 7 In. 495.00
Muller Freres, Vase, Pink, Black Owl On Branch, Urn Shape, Croismaire, 7 In. 875.00
Muller Freres, Vase, Purple, Butterflies, Gold Mica, Blue Enamel, 4 1/4 In. 495.00
Muller Freres, Vase, Scenic, Beige Ground, Pink Clouds, Acid Cut, 5 5/8 In. 525.00
Muncie, Vase, Dusty Rose, 6 In. 12.00
Muncie, Vase, Orange, 4 In. 10.00
Murano, Lamp, Stained Glass, Miniature 495.00
Music, Accordion, Electrified 695.00
Music, Accordion, 10 Melody Keys & 4 Bass Keys, C.1925, 10 1/4 In. Closed 38.00
Music, Autoharp, Finger Keyboard, Wood Box 75.00
Music, Banjo-Uke, 4 String, La Pacific 75.00
Music, Banjo, Paramount, Style B, Standard Neck Tenor, Mute 250.00
Music, Banjo, West Virginia Mountains, Hand Carved, 3 Strings 150.00
Music, Banjo, 4 String, Calvert Parker, Keene, N.H., Pat.1922 .... 125.00
Music, Baton, Conductor's, Ebony, Sterling 55.00
Music, Bird Singing In Round Cage, Brass 675.00

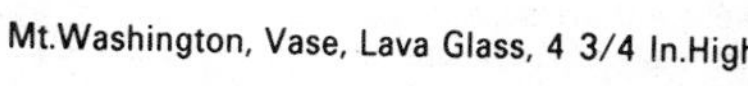
Mt.Washington, Vase, Lava Glass, 4 3/4 In.High

Music, Box, Albert Schild, Interlaken, Carved Wooden Compote Case, 9 1/2 In. 45.00
Music, Box, Automated Man With Mandolin, 17 In. 1750.00
Music, Box, Bird's-Eye, Cylinder, Dark Case, 6 Tune 485.00
Music, Box, Bremond, 10-Tune, 6 Bells 1675.00
Music, Box, Burled Walnut Veneer, Zither Mermod Freres, Two 6 Tune Cylinders 2500.00
Music, Box, Calliope, Upright, 38 1/2 In. 1595.00
Music, Box, Coin, Circus Box, 7 X 3 X 21 In., 8 Discs, 12 Bells, Hand Crank 1900.00
Music, Box, Criterion, Carved Oak Case, 15 Discs, 15 1/2 In. 1625.00
Music, Box, Criterion, Cherry, Double Comb, 15 In. 1500.00
Music, Box, Cylinder, Walnut With Flower Inlay, 10 Tune, 22 In. Cabinet 675.00
Music, Box, Disc, Music Box, Marked Kalliope, Perforated Metal, 13 1/4 In., 7 .... 55.00
Music, Box, Etouffoirs En Acier, No.5059, C.1865, Mahogany, 6 Tune, 12 1/2 In. 375.00
Music, Box, Euphonia, 34 15 1/2 In. Discs 995.00
Music, Box, Fortuna, 11 11 1/2 In. Discs 1500.00
Music, Box, French, Mandolin, Enamel, Cupids & Romantic Scene, 4 1/2 In. 525.00
Music, Box, Improved Celestina, Walnut 475.00
Music, Box, Inlaid Case, Swiss, 20 Tune 1475.00
Music, Box, Kalliope Disc, Plays 7 Inch Discs, C.1890 .... 475.00
Music, Box, Kreche, Wall Hanging, 2 Tune 275.00
Music, Box, Lucerne, Carved Wood, Opens To Hold Trinkets, 4 1/4 In. 18.00
Music, Box, Mermod Freres, Sublime Harmonie, Piccolo, Oak, Table, 7 Cylinders 6200.00
Music, Box, Mira, Double Comb, Disc, 12 In. 995.00
Music, Box, Mira, With Zither, Mahogany Case, 9 1/2 In. 595.00
Music, Box, Musik Automat, C.1880, Double Comb, Quarter Coin Slot 1500.00
Music, Box, Olympia, 24 Discs 2100.00
Music, Box, Orchestra, Bells, Drums, Castanets, & Reed Organ 3800.00
Music, Box, Orchestra, Cylinder, 4 Instruments 3800.00
Music, Box, Polyphon, Upright, Base Cabinet, 24 In. 3995.00
Music, Box, Polyphon, Upright, Cabinet With Storage Bin, 24 1/2 In. Disc 3900.00
Music, Box, Polyphon, Upright, 19 5/8 In. 2500.00
Music, Box, Polyphon, Walnut With Flower Inlay Case, 12 Disc, 11 1/4 In. 495.00
Music, Box, Regina Automatic Changer, Model No.35, 25 1/2 In.Discs 5000.00
Music, Box, Regina, Coin Operated, Restored, 15 1/2 In. 1650.00
Music, Box, Regina, Double Comb, Serpentine Case, 15 Discs, 15 1/2 In. 1250.00
Music, Box, Regina, Double Comb, 20 3/4 In. Disc 2750.00
Music, Box, Regina, Double, Oak, 15 1/2 In. 1595.00
Music, Box, Regina, Honduras Mahogany, 12 Tunes, 15 1/2 In. 975.00
Music, Box, Regina, Mahogany Case, Mother-Of-Pearl Inlay, 15 1/2 In. 1250.00
Music, Box, Regina, Oak, Double Comb, Coin Operated, 15 In. 1650.00
Music, Box, Regina, Solid Cherry, Rebuilt 2300.00
Music, Box, Regina, Table Model, Double Comb, Coin Operated, 15 1/2 In. 1500.00
Music, Box, Regina, Table Model, 15 1/2 In. 1395.00
Music, Box, Regina, Working Clock, 15 Music Box Discs .... *Illus* 1400.00
Music, Box, Regina, 17a, Table Top, Coin Operated, 24 Discs, 12 1/2 In. 1550.00
Music, Box, Rosewood Top, Inlaid Swans On Lid, 13 In.Brass Cylinder, 12 Tune 700.00
Music, Box, Stella, Table Model, 15 1/2 In. 600.00
Music, Box, Sublime Harmony, 13 1/2 In. Cylinder 930.00
Music, Box, Swiss Cylinder, Rosewood Case, 6 Tune Card, 16 X 8 X 5 1/4 In. 315.00
Music, Box, Swiss, Bombay Chest Case Of Rosewood, Mother-Of-Pearl Inlay, 1860 .... 6000.00
Music, Box, Swiss, Chalet With Gleaming Windows, Plays Two Tunes 95.00
Music, Box, Swiss, Cylinder, 8 Tune, 21 X 12 X 10 In. 1795.00
Music, Box, Swiss, Inlaid Cabinet, 7 1/2 In. Cylinder, 10 Tunes 375.00
Music, Box, Swiss, Thorens, Carved Fawn, Girl With Basket Of Chicks, 5 1/2 In. 45.00
Music, Box, Swiss, Thorens, 40 Discs 175.00
Music, Box, Swiss, 12 Tunes, 15 In. Cylinder 550.00
Music, Box, Swiss, 15 In. Cylinder, 12 Tunes, 25 In. 550.00
Music, Box, Swiss, 6 Tune, 5 In. Cylinder 265.00
Music, Box, Symphonium, Mahogany, Single Comb & Stand, Coin Operated, 15 In. 1700.00
Music, Box, Symphonium, 15 15 1/2 In. Discs 1500.00
Music, Bugle, Copper And Brass 50.00
Music, Bugle, U.S.Army Regulation, Brass, Nickel Silver, 17 1/2 In. 34.50
Music, Bugle, U.S.Army Regulation, Brass, 17 1/2 In. 34.50
Music, Calliope, Harrington, 43 Note, Air, Manual 3000.00
Music, Cutter, Wooden Needle, Victor Phonograph, Cast Iron & Steel 140.00

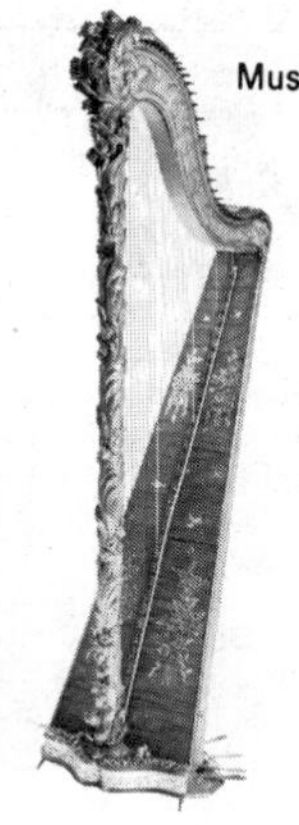

Music, Harp, French, Pedal, Cousineau, Paris, 1770

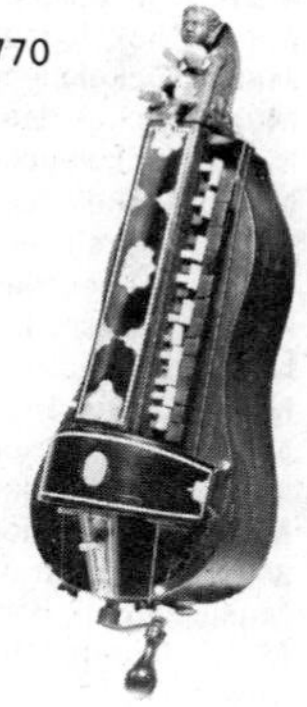

Music, Hurdy-Gurdy, French, C.1750, 14 1/4 In.

Music, Box, Regina, Working Clock, 15 Music Box Discs

Music, Drum, Boy's, Painted, Ropes, Leather Lugs, C.1750, 10 1/2 In. 200.00
Music, Dulcimer, B.Shelland, 172 Chrystie St., N.Y., Upright, Mechanical 1000.00
Music, Graphophone, Papier Mache Horn, Plays Cylinders 300.00
Music, Guitar, see also Disneyana, Guitar
Music, Guitar, Supertone 35.00
Music, Harmonica, FR Hotz, The Harmonica King, Lithographed Tin Box 15.00
Music, Harmonica, Hohner, Wooden Box 19.50
Music, Harmonica, Hohner, 1871, 4 In. 6.00
Music, Harmonophone, Windup Street Piano 1200.00
Music, Harp, Chickering, Patent 1894, Mahogany, Tuning Key, Hammer, 19 1/2 In. 30.00
Music, Harp, French, Pedal, Cousineau, Paris, 1770 .... *Illus* 2500.00
Music, Harp, Paramount, Concert 50.00
Music, Horn, French, Bundy, 25 In. 75.00
Music, Hurdy-Gurdy, French, C.1750, 14 1/4 In. .... *Illus* 1500.00
Music, Jew's Harp, Iron 10.00
Music, Jukebox, Mills, C.1920, Ferris Wheel 1500.00
Music, Jukebox, Mills, Vialano Virtuoso, Mahogany 5250.00
Music, Jukebox, Rokcola, Model 1468, Happy Days, 1959, 45 Rpm. 350.00
Music, Jukebox, Seeburg, 12 Records 400.00
Music, Jukebox, Williams, Counter Top 195.00
Music, Jukebox, Wurlitzer, Counter Top, Model 80 .... 650.00
Music, Jukebox, Wurlitzer, Model 600, 1938 .... 450.00
Music, Jukebox, Wurlitzer, Model 1080 .... 750.00
Music, Jukebox, Wurlitzer, Model 2700, 1963 .... 350.00
Music, Jukebox, Wurlitzer, No.1015, Arcade .... 495.00 To 725.00
Music, Mandolin Harp, Oscar Schmidt, Panama Canal Model, 1915, Original Box 35.00
Music, Mandolin, Lady Bug, Ivory Fittings, Ivory Disc Trademark, C.1890 .... 65.00
Music, Mandolin, 12 String, Gourd Type 150.00
Music, Melodeon, Dearborn & Bartlett, 1845, Rosewood & Tiger Maple Case 450.00
Music, Melodeon, Rosewood 2500.00
Music, Nickelodeon, Autopiano, 1908, 10 Rolls 3500.00
Music, Nickelodeon, Brewster Piano Co., 1910, 7 Instruments, Stained Glass 2995.00
Music, Nickelodeon, Coinola, Cupid, Cabinet Style 3995.00
Music, Nickelodeon, Cremona, Art Glass 3836.00
Music, Nickelodeon, Electrova, Keyboard, 7 Five-Tune Rolls 1500.00
Music, Nickelodeon, Englehart, Oak Case, Art Glass Front, Coin Operated 2950.00
Music, Nickelodeon, Italian, Barrel 800.00

Music, Nickelodeon, Khul & Klat, 4 Rolls 950.00
Music, Nickelodeon, Khul & Klat, 6 Rolls 950.00
Music, Nickelodeon, Nelson Wigger, Keyboard Type 2850.00
Music, Nickelodeon, O Roll, Keyboardless 4995.00
Music, Nickelodeon, Seeburgh, Oak Case, Stained Glass Front, Upright 3750.00
Music, Nickelodeon, Wurlitzer, A Roll, Art Glass 4520.00
Music, Nickelodeon, Wurlitzer, IX 2000.00
Music, Orchestrion, Barrel, Art Glass Doors, 5 Cent Slot, 7 Ft.4 In. 5500.00
Music, Orchestrion, C.1900, Art Glass Front, 8 Ft. 3000.00
Music, Orchestrion, Decap, Univox, Electronic, Double Accordion, Pipes, Etc. 4500.00
Music, Orchestrion, H.Peters & Co., Leipzig, 150 Rolls, 8 Ft., 4 In. 2000.00
Music, Orchestrion, Khul & Klat, Pneuma, 13 Rolls, Xylophone, Percussion 4000.00
Music, Orchestrion, Philipps, Pf2, Piano & Xylophone, 6 Rolls 1800.00
Music, Orchestrion, Popper's, Style X, Xylophone, 2 Rolls 2500.00
Music, Orchestrion, Weber, Grandeza, Xylophone, 6 Rolls 2900.00
Music, Organ, Band, Home Built, 13 Instruments, 10 Tune, Coin Operated 2500.00
Music, Organ, Band, North Tonawanda Style, 150 Rolls 9600.00
Music, Organ, Band, Wurlitzer No.125, Bass & Snare Head, 10 Rolls, Refinished 6000.00
Music, Organ, Beckwith, Concert Grand, Pump, Piano Case 300.00
Music, Organ, Bruder, Carousel, 44 Key 5250.00
Music, Organ, Burssens, Dance, Pipe 6750.00
Music, Organ, Burssens, Dance, Roll-Operated 4800.00
Music, Organ, Cecilian, Mechanical, Mahogany Cabinet, Farrand Organ Co., 1901 .... 475.00
Music, Organ, Celestina, Roller 400.00
Music, Organ, Chautauqua, Roller, Patent May 31, 1887, 6 Cobs 340.00
Music, Organ, Chicago, Cottage, Pump 400.00
Music, Organ, Concert Roller, 12 Cobs 650.00
Music, Organ, Decap, Dance, Electronic 3600.00
Music, Organ, Decap, Dance, 121 Key 4000.00
Music, Organ, Double Accordion, Book-Operated 2336.00
Music, Organ, Durwyn, Dance, 80 Key 6374.00
Music, Organ, Durwyn, Dance, 86 Key, Drums, Cymbal, Castanets, Accordion 1600.00
Music, Organ, Estey, Reed, Oak Case, 2 Manuals, Full Pedal Board 850.00
Music, Organ, European, Barrel, 8 Tunes 3522.00
Music, Organ, Hamilton, Pump, Walnut, Ornate 500.00
Music, Organ, Hammond Cecilian, 1901, Mahogany, 65 Keys, 13 1/4 In. Rolls 475.00
Music, Organ, Hershell Spillman, 2 Rolls 4500.00
Music, Organ, Imhoff, Monkey, Reed 1595.00
Music, Organ, Limonaire Freres, Band, With Books 1250.00
Music, Organ, Lowery, Player 500.00
Music, Organ, Mason & Hamlin, Church, Reed, Electric Bellows, 7 Stops, Bench 950.00
Music, Organ, Mason & Hamlin, Church, 2 Manual 2995.00
Music, Organ, Mason & Hamlin, Pump 225.00
Music, Organ, Monkey, German, Pipes, 8 Tune 1750.00
Music, Organ, Monkey, Pombia In Novara, Italia, Stenciled, Cart 1500.00
Music, Organ, Mortier, Dance, Book-Operated 1575.00
Music, Organ, Mortier, Univox, Electronic 3800.00
Music, Organ, Newman Bros., Pump, Piano Case 400.00
Music, Organ, Pump, Black Walnut, B.Shoninger, New Haven, Conn., 47 X 50 In. 700.00
Music, Organ, Pump, Sears & Roebuck, 1896 .... 425.00
Music, Organ, Reed, Estey, 2 Keyboard, Bench, Oak, Electric And Manual 950.00
Music, Organ, Reproduco Player Pipe, Chime Cabinet 4200.00
Music, Organ, Walley Gem, Walnut, Pump 200.00
Music, Organ, Weaver, Walnut, Pump, Carved 650.00
Music, Organ, Wicks, 2 Manual, 231 Pipes 3900.00
Music, Organ, Wurlitzer, 153 Band, Englehard, Flute Pipes, Krakhaur Welte 1095.00
Music, Organette, Concertina, 4 Paper Rolls 395.00
Music, Organette, Wurlitzer Organetter Double Tracker 4700.00

The Phonograph, invented by Thomas Edison in the 1880s, has been made by many firms.

Music, Phonograph, Cirola, Oak Case, Brass Hardware, Portable 185.00
Music, Phonograph, Columbia, Grafonola, Tabletop 80.00
Music, Phonograph, Columbia, Graphophone, Ribbed Wooden Horn 750.00

Music, Phonograph, Columbia, Jewel, Cylinder, 12 In. Bell Horn 265.00
Music, Phonograph, Columbia, Q, Wooden 195.00
Music, Phonograph, Columbia, 6 In. Cylinder 400.00
Music, Phonograph, Edison, Amberol, Cylinder, 201 Records 800.00
Music, Phonograph, Edison, Amberola No.50 .... 230.00
Music, Phonograph, Edison, Amberola, Built-In Horn 175.00
Music, Phonograph, Edison, Amberola, 30, Oak 225.00
Music, Phonograph, Edison, Cylinder, Big Horn 350.00
Music, Phonograph, Edison, Diamond Disc, Model C 150, Refinished 175.00
Music, Phonograph, Edison, Fireside, 2 Piece Horn & Crane 265.00
Music, Phonograph, Edison, Floor Models, Thick Record Player 175.00
Music, Phonograph, Edison, Gem, Crank Wind, 10 In. Horn 275.00
Music, Phonograph, Edison, Home Model, Brass Horn & Stand 365.00
Music, Phonograph, Edison, Home Model, Green Oak Case, 10 In. Horn 325.00
Music, Phonograph, Edison, Home Model, Suitcase, 14 In. Horn 325.00
Music, Phonograph, Edison, Home, Cylinder, 21 In. Bell Horn & Crane 255.00
Music, Phonograph, Edison, Home, H Reproducer 225.00
Music, Phonograph, Edison, Home, 244 Minute, C Reproducer 300.00
Music, Phonograph, Edison, Standard, C Reproducer 215.00
Music, Phonograph, Edison, Standard, Cylinder, 12 In. Bell Horn 245.00
Music, Phonograph, Edison, Standard, Serial No.3186544 .... 125.00
Music, Phonograph, Edison, Triumph, H Reproducer 650.00
Music, Phonograph, Pathe, Floor Model VII, Patent 1919 .... 150.00
Music, Phonograph, Victor II Talking Machine, Brass Bell Horn 315.00
Music, Phonograph, Victor, School Model 877.50
Music, Phonograph, Victor, Schoolhouse, Oak Horn 850.00
Music, Phonograph, Victor, Victrola, 13 1/2 In. 50.00
Music, Phonograph, Victrola, 300 Model, 1921, Floor Type 850.00
Music, Pianino, Wurlitzer 4250.00
Music, Piano, Ampico, Model A, Chickering, Grand, 5 Ft.4 In. 3750.00
Music, Piano, Ampico, Symphonique, Model B, Grand, 5 Ft.1 In. 3950.00

Music, Piano, French, Giraffe, C.1830

Music, Piano, Butler Bros., Player, Electrified 295.00
Music, Piano, Chickering, Concert Grand, Ebony, 9 Ft. 6500.00
Music, Piano, Cremona, Coin Operated 2000.00
Music, Piano, Duo Art, Upright, Reproducing 495.00
Music, Piano, Electrova Nickelodeon, Upright, Mission Oak, 5 Cent Slot 2250.00
Music, Piano, Empress, A, Roll, Art Glass 2995.00
Music, Piano, Fischer Square Grand, Rosewood, Bench 750.00
Music, Piano, French, Giraffe, C.1830 .... *Illus* 3250.00
Music, Piano, Geavert, Player, 88 Note, 50 Rolls 950.00
Music, Piano, Gebruder Weber, Grandezza 2695.00
Music, Piano, Gulbransen, Player, Registering 750.00
Music, Piano, Howard, Player, Manual 850.00
Music, Piano, John Broadwood & Sons, Inc., Grand, Rosewood Case, 7 1/2 Ft. 1400.00
Music, Piano, Large French Barrel, 7 Ft. 3500.00

Music, Piano, Losche Minerva, Pipes, 2 Rolls 2500.00
Music, Piano, M.Shulte, Grand, 5 Ft. 2500.00
Music, Piano, Mathushak Co., New Haven, Conn., C.1875, Square Grand, Rosewood 700.00
Music, Piano, Moldorf, Chicago, Player 650.00
Music, Piano, Player, Burmeister 300.00
Music, Piano, Player, Geavert, 50 Rolls, 88-Note 950.00
Music, Piano, Seeburg, Player, Oak Case, Leaded Glass Eagle, Coin Operated 7400.00
Music, Piano, Square Grand, Rosewood, Mathushak Piano Co., New Haven, Conn. 700.00
Music, Piano, Steger, 1914, Player, Upright, 100 Rolls 950.00
Music, Piano, Steinway & Sons, Grand, Rosewood Case, Restored, 1876 .... 1200.00
Music, Piano, Steinway & Sons, 1872, Square Grand 300.00
Music, Piano, Triumph Auto Player, London, England, 88-Note, Stool 2000.00
Music, Piano, W.M.Knabe, Ampico, Grand, Reproducer 3500.00
Music, Piano, Weber, Square Grand, Carved 1300.00
Music, Piano, Wurlitzer, Style 1, 65-Note, Coin Operated 3500.00
Music, Pianoforte, Rosewood, Square, Built Pre-Civil War 1000.00
Music, Pianolin, North Tonawanda, 2 Rolls, Restored 2900.00
Music, Record Shaver, Edison Crank Type, Pre-1900 .... 70.00
Music, Record, Edison, Thick 1.50
Music, Record, Night Before Christmas, Fibber McGee & Molly, 3 In Album 10.00
Music, Saxophone, Buescher, C Soprano 45.00
Music, Saxophone, Parisian Ambassador, French 85.00
Music, Scopitone, C.1940, Film & Music 475.00
Music, Sheet, America, First & Last, 1922 .... 10.00
Music, Sheet, Catalina, Lovely Isle Of The Sea, 1932, Art Deco Cover 12.50
Music, Sheet, Charlie Chaplin Walk, 1915 .... 24.00
Music, Sheet, Chicago March, 1921 .... 6.00
Music, Sheet, Come On Spark Plug, Shows Negro Riding Spark Plug 24.00
Music, Sheet, Daddy Longlegs, Pickford Cover 6.00
Music, Sheet, Dapper Dan, Eddie Cantor, Black Face 8.00
Music, Sheet, Down Souf In Alabama, Negro Doing Cake Walk 5.00
Music, Sheet, God Bless America, 1938, Kate Smith, Berlin, Armistice Day 3.50
Music, Sheet, I Love The U.S.A., 1915, Statue Of Liberty & Flag 4.50
Music, Sheet, It's A Long Way To Tipperary, 1912 .... 3.00
Music, Sheet, Little Ford Rambled Right Along 5.00
Music, Sheet, Little French Mother Good Bye, Norman Rockwell Cover 18.50
Music, Sheet, My Mother's Prayer, 1921 .... 5.00
Music, Sheet, Over The Rainbow, Judy Garland 5.00
Music, Sheet, Peaceful Evening, 1921 .... 5.00
Music, Sheet, Pistol Packin' Mama, Al Dexter 6.00
Music, Sheet, President Wilson, 1914, Take Our Hats Off 10.00
Music, Sheet, Return Franklin Roosevelt, 1936 .... 12.50
Music, Sheet, Swanee, Al Jolson 5.00
Music, Sheet, Theodore Roosevelt, 1912, Portrait 17.00
Music, Sheet, Trolley With Negro Motorman & Conductor, Negro Songs 22.00
Music, Sheet, Victory Polka, 1943, Girl & Boy In Red, White, & Blue 4.00
Music, Sheet, Westward Ho March, 1921 .... 10.00
Music, Sheet, When The Major Plays Those Minor Melodies 5.00
Music, Sheet, Whistling Rufus, 1899 .... 5.00
Music, Sheet, World War 1, Uncle Sam On Cover 4.00
Music, Symphonion, Double Comb, 15 Discs 1100.00
Music, Tape Playing Machine, Carnival, Wooden Case, Glass Doors, 49 In. 450.00
Music, Trumpet, Band Organ, Brass, Set Of 22 .... 995.00
Music, Trumpet, Brass, Mother-Of-Pearl On Taps, Case 20.00
Music, Trumpet, Carl Fischer Inc., Boston, School Model, Brass, Pearl 45.00
Music, Violano, Mill's, Virtuoso, Single, 2 Rolls 2500.00
Music, Violin, Copy Of Antonius Stradivarius, Conservatory, Wooden Case 100.00
Music, Violin, Label, Eduard Reichert, Dresden, 1911, Mother-Of-Pearl On Bow 100.00
Music, Violin, Paris, 1900 .... 100.00
Music, Zither, Eagle & Flag, 16 X 19 In. 35.00
Music, Zither, Oscar Schmidt, Jersey City 21.00

Mustache cups were popular from 1850 to 1900. A ledge of china or silver held the hair out of the liquid in the cup.

Mustache Cup & Attached Saucer, Worcester 80.00
Mustache Cup & Saucer, A Present, Gold Trim 27.50
Mustache Cup & Saucer, Bird With Floral, Gold Trim 27.50
Mustache Cup & Saucer, Colonial Couple & Floral 25.00
Mustache Cup & Saucer, German, Blue & Yellow Pansies, Blue Scrolls, Gold 45.00
Mustache Cup & Saucer, Germany, Love The Giver & Branches In Gold 32.50
Mustache Cup & Saucer, Hand-Painted Floral, French 45.00
Mustache Cup & Saucer, Pale Green, White Daisies 20.00
Mustache Cup & Saucer, Pink Floral Tapestry, Royal Worcester, C.1881 45.00
Mustache Cup & Saucer, Ribbed Pink Body, Watteau Picture On Cup 32.00
Mustache Cup & Saucer, Royal Bavaria, PMB, Roses, Cobalt & Gold Border 45.00
Mustache Cup & Saucer, Silver Plate, Pairpoint 75.00
Mustache Cup & Saucer, Victorian Porcelain, Pink Luster, Probably German 25.00
Mustache Cup & Saucer, White, Brown & Gold Birds, Nest, Eggs, & Butterflies 42.00
Mustache Cup & Saucer, 3 Crown, White, Violets & Lilies Of The Valley, Gold 30.00
Mustache Cup, Brandenburg, Portrait 12.50
Mustache Cup, Floral With 2 Horse Head Medallions 45.00
Mustache Cup, German, "Present" 25.00
Mustache Cup, Multicolor Floral, Gold Edge & Handle 12.50
Mustache Cup, Porcelain, White, Floral, Left-Handed 65.00
Mustache Cup, Raised Floral Design, 3 Crown Germany 20.00
Mustache Cup, Sailboats & Mountains, Pink & Gold Trim, 5 In. 45.00
Mustache Cup, Sailing Shop 6.00
Mustache Cup, Saucer, Birthplace Of Daniel Webster 65.00
MZ Austria, Berry Set, Pink, Yellow, & White Roses, Green Trim, 5 Piece 62.00
MZ Austria, Bowl, Green Luster, Pink Roses, 10 1/2 In. 18.50
MZ Austria, Chocolate Set, Decorated, 13 Piece 115.00
MZ Austria, Cup & Saucer, Pink Roses, Gold Trim 8.50
MZ Austria, Hair Receiver, Hand-Painted Raised Pink Roses, Footed 22.00
MZ Austria, Jar, Cracker, Pink Roses, Gold Trim, Bulbous Panels 42.00
MZ Austria, Jar, Jam, Underplate 16.00
MZ Austria, Plate, Fish, Beehive Underglaze, Cobalt, Raised Gold, Signed, 9 In. 45.00
MZ Austria, Plate, Fish, Cobalt Border, Beehive, Signed Kestler 35.00
MZ Aústria, Plate, Game, Carp, Beehive, Signed Kestler, 9 In. 25.00
MZ Austria, Plate, Game, Perch, Beehive, Signed Kestler, 9 In. 25.00
MZ Austria, Plate, Game, Red Eye, Beehive, Signed Kestler, 9 In. 25.00
MZ Austria, Plate, Game, Trout, Beehive, Signed Kestler, 9 In. 25.00
MZ Austria, Plate, Game, Whiting, Beehive, Signed Kestler, 9 In. 25.00
MZ Austria, Plate, Green Butterfly Border, 8 1/2 In. 8.50
MZ Austria, Plate, Luncheon, White, Gold Scalloped Edge, 8 In. 5.00
MZ Austria, Ramekin, Pink Roses, Gold Border 12.50
MZ Austria, Syrup & Underplate, White, Pink Roses, Gold Bands, 5 1/4 In. 23.50
MZ Austria, Tray, Calling Card, Forget-Me-Nots, Gold Handles, Haarer, 1916 15.00

Nailsea glass was made in the Bristol District in England from 1788 to 1873. Many pieces were made with loopings of colored glass as decorations.

Nailsea Type, Bottle, Perfume, Lay Down, Germany, Cobalt Stripes, 2 7/8 In. 22.00
Nailsea, Bell, 2 Color 275.00
Nailsea, Bowl Vase, Blue & White Stripes, 6 1/2 X 4 In. 95.00
Nailsea, Bowl, Blue & White Stripes, 6 1/2 X 3 1/2 In. 125.00
Nailsea, Flask, Double, Red & White Looping 275.00
Nailsea, Flask, Red & White, Double, 10 In. 220.00
Nailsea, Lamp, Fairy, Clarke Base, Pink, White, & Cranberry Loopings, 5 1/4 In. 95.00
Nailsea, Pitcher, Water, White Loopings, Threaded Top Band, Clear Handle 170.00
Nailsea, Vase, Blue & White Pull-Ups, Squatty, 5 In. 85.00
Nailsea, Vase, Cranberry, White Loops, Applied Rigaree, 6 1/2 In. 95.00

Nakara is a trade name for a white glassware made around 1900 that was decorated in pastel colors. It was made by the C. F. Monroe Company of Meriden, Connecticut.

Nakara, Basket, Robin's-Egg Blue, Enamel Floral, Brass Handle & Rim, 6 In. 250.00
Nakara, Basket, Sky Blue, Pink Dogwood, Brass Collar, Handle, 6 In. 165.00
Nakara, Box, Blue & Pink Satin, Elongated Swirls, 4 1/2 In. 60.00
Nakara, Box, Hinged, Paisley, Beading, 6 Sided, 5 X 5 In. 210.00

Nakara, Box, Jewel, Gray Ground, Pink Florals, Octagonal, Hinged, Signed, 7 In. 275.00
Nakara, Box, Patch, Lady On Lid, Apricot Color, 2 1/2 In.. .... 150.00
Nakara, Box, Ring, Covered, Blue, Pink Floral, 2 1/2 X 2 In. 85.00
Nakara, Box, Shaded Pink, Blue Flowers, Hinged, 5 In. 165.00
Nakara, Box, Sky Blue, Pink Blossoms, Open Pin Box, 3 1/2 In. 75.00
Nakara, Box, Trinket, Ormolu Handles, Burmese Colors, Signed 85.00
Nakara, Humidor, Elk Head, Souvenir, B.P.O.E., 7 In. 385.00
Nakara, Humidor, Face Of Indian On Front 350.00
Nakara, Tray, Pin, Apricot, Dots & Floral, Handled 100.00
Nakara, Vase, Indian Portrait, High Enamels, Avocado, Cream, Brass Rim, Signed 285.00

Nanking china is a blue-and-white porcelain made in China for export during the eighteenth century.

Nanking, Bowl, Clobbered, Riverscape Panels, Gilding, C.1790, 10 In. 575.00

Napkin rings were popular from 1869 to about 1900.

Napkin Ring, Art Deco, Figural, Squirrel, Sterling 22.00
Napkin Ring, Brass & Silver Plate, Embossed Dancing Peasants 6.00
Napkin Ring, China, Pink Roses 28.00
Napkin Ring, Cloisonne, Butterflies 20.00
Napkin Ring, Cloisonne, Chinese, Green, Red, Yellow, & Pink Floral 17.50
Napkin Ring, Cloisonne, Dragon 20.00
Napkin Ring, Coin Silver, Bright Cut, "Ella, " 7/8 In. Wide 10.00
Napkin Ring, Coin Silver, Bright Cut, Floral, C.1850, 1 1/4 In. Wide 11.00
Napkin Ring, Coin Silver, Dec.25, 1866, 1 1/2 In. 9.95
Napkin Ring, Cut Glass, Diamond Strawberry, Notched, 2 In. 25.00
Napkin Ring, Cut Glass, Pinwheel, Fan, & Strawberry Diamond, 2 1/4 In. 55.00
Napkin Ring, Doghouse Each Side, Rogers Smith 45.00
Napkin Ring, Embossed Birds And Flowers, Metal 30.00
Napkin Ring, Figural, Barking Dog At Base, Bird On Top, Silver Plate 45.00
Napkin Ring, Figural, Barrel Between Seated Cherubs, Meriden 75.00
Napkin Ring, Figural, Barrel On Tree Branch Chair 85.00
Napkin Ring, Figural, Barrel With Branch & Leaf On Sides, Silver Plate 38.00
Napkin Ring, Figural, Bird & Kneeling Boy, Eggs In Nest On Ring, Meriden 175.00
Napkin Ring, Figural, Bird On Square Base, Napier Silver Plate 32.00
Napkin Ring, Figural, Bird Perched On Ring, Porcelain, White 4.75

Napkin Ring, Figural, Bird, James Tufts, Silver Plate

Napkin Ring, Figural, Bird, James Tufts, Silver Plate .... *Illus* 75.00
Napkin Ring, Figural, Boy Lying On Stomach 60.00
Napkin Ring, Figural, Boy On Dolphin, Meriden 66.00
Napkin Ring, Figural, Boy Sitting On Wild Turtle With Whip In Hand 225.00
Napkin Ring, Figural, Boy Stealing Eggs 95.00
Napkin Ring, Figural, Bud Vase Atop Footed Ring, 5 In. 88.00
Napkin Ring, Figural, Bulldog Guards Elaborate Ring 100.00
Napkin Ring, Figural, Bulldog Leaping Into Ring, Cat, Meriden, Silver Plate 135.00
Napkin Ring, Figural, Bulldog, Openwork Top, James Tufts 48.00
Napkin Ring, Figural, Butterfly, Ring On Top, Fan At Sides, Silver 55.00
Napkin Ring, Figural, Cat, Glass Eyes 110.00
Napkin Ring, Figural, Chair With Bamboo Turnings, Silver Plate 45.00
Napkin Ring, Figural, Cherub In 3-Cornered Hat Riding Turtle, Silver Plate 165.00

Napkin Ring, Figural, Chicken Standing Alongside, Meriden Silver Co. 65.00
Napkin Ring, Figural, Clown Holding Hoop For Dog 76.00
Napkin Ring, Figural, Clown, Porcelain, Pair 8.50
Napkin Ring, Figural, Coat & Cart, Wheels Turn 95.00
Napkin Ring, Figural, Cockatoo On Branch, Rogers & Bros., Silver Plate 85.00
Napkin Ring, Figural, Crawling Infant With Ring On Back 90.00
Napkin Ring, Figural, Cupid With Flute, Simpson 125.00
Napkin Ring, Figural, Cupid With Mug In Hand And Ring On Back 225.00
Napkin Ring, Figural, Cupid With Ring On His Back, Octagonal Base, Miller 93.00
Napkin Ring, Figural, Dog Alongside, , J.M.Tufts, Boston, Mass. 65.00
Napkin Ring, Figural, Dog, Sitting 42.50
Napkin Ring, Figural, Eagle On Each Side, Inscribed Angelo, Meriden 50.00
Napkin Ring, Figural, Eagle, Rogers Bros. 49.50
Napkin Ring, Figural, Easter Nest & Rabbit 25.00
Napkin Ring, Figural, Fans On Side Hold Ring, Silver, Meriden 65.00
Napkin Ring, Figural, Fox, Rogers Silver 90.00
Napkin Ring, Figural, Furry Monkey Holding Out Pronged Ring 225.00
Napkin Ring, Figural, Girl With Pigtail Pushing Ring, William Rogers 150.00
Napkin Ring, Figural, Goat Pulls Ring Mounted On Wheeled Sulky 155.00
Napkin Ring, Figural, Goat, Scrolled Ring On Base, Meriden Silver Plate 75.00
Napkin Ring, Figural, Kangaroo On Leaf 50.00
Napkin Ring, Figural, Kate Greenaway Boy & Dog, Meriden Silver Plate 135.00
Napkin Ring, Figural, Kate Greenaway Boy, Meriden, Silver Plate 115.00
Napkin Ring, Figural, Kate Greenaway Girl With Hands In Muff, Meriden 175.00
Napkin Ring, Figural, Kate Greenaway, Girl & Dog, Engraved Flowers 60.00
Napkin Ring, Figural, Kitten Leans Against Beaded Ring 89.50
Napkin Ring, Figural, Kitten Pulling Cart, Wheels Go Round 125.00
Napkin Ring, Figural, Laughing Child In Nightgown 100.00
Napkin Ring, Figural, Leaf & Trumpet Flower, M B Co. 75.00
Napkin Ring, Figural, Long-Tailed Peacock Sitting On Top Of Ring 175.00
Napkin Ring, Figural, Old-Fashioned Sled, Wilcox, No.01532 .... 55.00
Napkin Ring, Figural, Ostrich On Leaf 50.00
Napkin Ring, Figural, Owl Family Tree, Ring On Fancy Footed Base 225.00
Napkin Ring, Figural, Pedestal Ring On Leaf Base, Acorn 50.00
Napkin Ring, Figural, Poles & Open Lattice Ring, Simpson Hall & Miller 30.00
Napkin Ring, Figural, Prancing Horse Pulling Ring On Sulky, Rogers 140.00
Napkin Ring, Figural, Rabbit Sitting At Side Of Ring 40.00
Napkin Ring, Figural, Reclining Lion, Meridan 45.00
Napkin Ring, Figural, Ring On Deer 125.00
Napkin Ring, Figural, Rosebud On Side Of Ring, Meriden 75.00
Napkin Ring, Figural, Sitting Dog, Tassel On Collar, West Silver Plate Co. 65.00
Napkin Ring, Figural, Spanish Comb 68.00
Napkin Ring, Figural, Squirrel Eating Nut, Oak Leaves & Acorn, Silver 65.00
Napkin Ring, Figural, Squirrel, Meriden 40.00
Napkin Ring, Figural, Stag, Ring On Back, Rogers, Smith & Co., Silver Plate 90.00
Napkin Ring, Figural, Sunflower Base, Leaves On Sides, Meriden 39.50
Napkin Ring, Figural, Swallon On Perch On Side Of Ring, Meriden 125.00
Napkin Ring, Figural, Two Butterflies Hold Ring, Fan Base, Roger & Bros. 65.00
Napkin Ring, Figural, Two Cherubs Holding Ring, Silver 60.00
Napkin Ring, Figural, Two Cherubs Playing, Meriden 35.00
Napkin Ring, Figural, Two Fans, Bee On Base, Rogers Smith 57.50
Napkin Ring, Figural, Two Kneeling Cherubs, Reed & Barton 75.00
Napkin Ring, Figural, Victorian Lady Standing Behind Ring, James W.Tufts 225.00
Napkin Ring, Figural, Victorian Sailor Boy, Rogers & Bros., Silver Plate 110.00
Napkin Ring, Figural, Violin 60.00
Napkin Ring, Figural, Water Lily, Rogers, Silver Plate .... *Illus* 35.00
Napkin Ring, Figural, Wine Barrel On Twigs & Leaves 35.00
Napkin Ring, Figural, Wishbone, Best Wishes, 4 Ball Feet, Wilcox 30.00
Napkin Ring, Hand-Painted, Royal Austria, China Footed 28.00
Napkin Ring, Ivory Bone, Openwork 7.50
Napkin Ring, Ivory, Carved Snake 25.00
Napkin Ring, Ivory, Cutout Designs 10.00
Napkin Ring, Ivory, Engraved Birds, China 14.00
Napkin Ring, Nippon, Oriental Teahouse Scene, 2 In.Wide 45.00

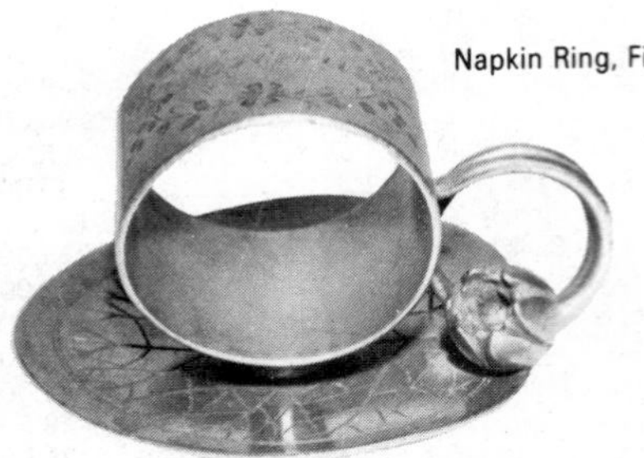

Napkin Ring, Figural, Water Lily, Rogers, Silver Plate

(See Page 349)

Napkin Ring, Nippon, Scenic, Autumn Colors, Green M Mark 35.00
Napkin Ring, Noritake, Portrait, Lady With Fur Around Neck 12.50
Napkin Ring, Oval, Beaded Design, Sterling 9.50
Napkin Ring, Pairpoint Silver, Cora & Dan, Engraved Ties, Pair 50.00
Napkin Ring, Pressed Glass, Etched Initial L 15.00
Napkin Ring, Ring With Scotty Dogs, Silver Plate 40.00
Napkin Ring, Shell, Souvenir, Brockton 16.00
Napkin Ring, Silver Plate, Openwork, Butterflies 15.00
Napkin Ring, Silver, Engraved Birds, Butterflies, & Foliage, Pair 18.00
Napkin Ring, Silver, Engraved Oak Leaves, Acorns, Eagle, & Nest, Set Of 6 .... 300.00
Napkin Ring, Steamship Princess Louise, Pierced Nickle 10.00
Napkin Ring, Sterling Silver, Bar Type, Monogram, 3/4 In. Wide 15.00
Napkin Ring, Sterling Silver, Betsy, Hammered, Art Silver Shop, 3 1/4 In. 9.50
Napkin Ring, Sterling Silver, Clara 12.00
Napkin Ring, Sterling Silver, Diana & Bow On Plaque, Shreve, Calif. 29.00
Napkin Ring, Sterling Silver, High Relief Floral Sprays & Scrolls, 2 In. 20.00
Napkin Ring, Sterling Silver, Louis, Hammered, Art Silver Shop, 3 1/4 In. 9.50
Napkin Ring, Sterling Silver, Openwork, Initials, 11 1/2 In. Wide 15.00
Napkin Ring, Sterling Silver, Repousse, Kirk, C.1900 .... 45.00
Napkin Ring, Wooden, Centennial, 1876, Philadelphia Fair 12.50

Nash glass was made in Corona, New York, by Arthur Nash and his sons after 1919. He worked at the Webb Factory in England and for the Tiffany Glassworks in the United States.

Nash, Bowl, Flared, Iridescent Gold, Abstract Baubles, Upper Chocolate Glass 190.00
Nash, Bowl, Glossy Chocolate Top Iridescent Gold Underside, Signed 205.00
Nash, Dish, Footed, Amber Iridescent, Signed Adna, Numbered, 4 X 1 1/4 In. 290.00
Nash, Goblet, Blue & Green, Chintz, 4 In. 65.00
Nash, Goblet, Blue & Green, Chintz, 5 In. 75.00
Nash, Vase, Bud, Iridescent, Signed, 8 In. 349.00
Nash, Wine, Chintz, Signed, 4 In. 55.00
Nash, Wine, Chintz, Signed, 5 In. 65.00

Nautical, see also Scrimshaw

Nautical, Anchor, Sailing Ship, 6 In., 500 Pounds 400.00
Nautical, Ax, Fire, S.S.Queen Elizabeth, 15 In. 60.00
Nautical, Bell, Bronze, Ship, Inscribed With Name & Date, 13 In. 95.00
Nautical, Bell, Ship, Brass 20.00
Nautical, Butter Pat, Rorstrand Clipper Line 5.00
Nautical, Canoe, Birchbark 225.00
Nautical, Chest, Sea, Canvas Top, Painting Of Old Ship 450.00
Nautical, Chronometer, Waltham, Brass Trim, 8 Day 225.00
Nautical, Clock Barometer Thermometer, Yacht Petrel, 1873, Oak Case, 22 In. 268.00
Nautical, Clock, Seth Thomas, Brass, 7 In. 135.00
Nautical, Clock, Ship's Wheel, RMS Carinthia, Mantel, Nickel Case, 4 1/2 In. 50.00
Nautical, Clock, U.S.Navy, Seth Thomas, Deck No.3, Walnut Stand 110.00
Nautical, Compass, Brass, For Bridge, 10 In., American 95.00
Nautical, Compass, Brass, For Bridge, 10 In., British 95.00
Nautical, Compass, Brass, For Bridge, 10 In., Germanan 95.00
Nautical, Compass, Brass, For Bridge, 10 In., Japanese 95.00

Nautical, Compass, Lifeboat, Binnacle Covered With Kerosene Lantern 150.00
Nautical, Compass, Lifeboat, English, C.1920, Sestrel, Brass 165.00
Nautical, Compass, Mariner's, Wilcox, Crittend Co., 1936, Wooden Case 48.00
Nautical, Compass, Sperry Gyroscope Compass Repeater, 1919, Brass, 9 1/2 In. 125.00
Nautical, Globe, Linen Covered, London, C.1875, 28 In.Long .... *Illus* 350.00
Nautical, Gong, For Engine Room, Brass, Mechanical 80.00
Nautical, Helmet, Deep Sea, Oriental, Brass & Copper, 17 In., Made In 30's 595.00
Nautical, Helmet, Diver's, Brass, Miniature 65.00
Nautical, Inclinometer, Mounted On Wood With Brass Gauge & Pointer, 11 In. 55.00
Nautical, Inkstand, Ship, Pewter, Insert, C.1830 .... 85.00
Nautical, Lamp, Ship, Cooper, Brass Fittings 45.00
Nautical, Lamp, Ship, Round Lenses In Angular Brass Frame, 14 X 10 In. 75.00
Nautical, Lamp, Ship, Signal, Navy, Aldis, Birmingham, England, Case 55.00
Nautical, Lamp, Ship, Whale Oil, Brass, 6 In. 45.00
Nautical, Lantern, Copper With Brass Fittings, 15 X 19 In. 195.00
Nautical, Lantern, Ship, Brass Top 35.00
Nautical, Lantern, Ship, Signal, 8 3/4 In. 60.00
Nautical, Light, Ship, Gimbal, Square Base, Brass Arm, Green Glass, 10 In. 65.00
Nautical, Menu, Normandie, 1936 .... 3.00
Nautical, Mother-Of-Pearl, Whaling Ship & Whale, 18K Gold Bezel 275.00
Nautical, Octant, Spencer & Co., London, Carrying Case, Late 18th Century 335.00
Nautical, Ostrich Egg, Sailing Ships, Lighthouse, Palms, Signed Jon 135.00
Nautical, Passenger List, Statendam, Turbine Steamer, 1935 .... 8.00
Nautical, Pencil, Island Queen, Paddlewheeler, Mechanical 3.50
Nautical, Porthole, Brass, 7 1/4 In. 19.00
Nautical, Propeller, Bronze, 12 Lbs. 19.00
Nautical, Ruler, Course Plotting, Parallel Pair, T.S.& J.D.Negus, Brass 45.00
Nautical, Sextant, Brass, 11 X 10 1/2 X 4 3/4 In.High, C.1840 .... *Illus* 350.00
Nautical, Sextant, Tilton, Pat.1856, Zogbaum & Fairchild, N.Y., Cherry Case 275.00
Nautical, Sextant, W.F.Cannon, London, England, C.1820 .... 395.00
Nautical, Ship Model, Whale, Joseph H.Starbudr, 32 In. .... *Illus* 225.00
Nautical, Spy Glass, Brass, C.1880 .... 50.00
Nautical, Telescope, Brass, Wooden Case, C.1690 .... 230.00
Nautical, Telescope, Jumelle Marine, Brass, 7 1/2 In. 18.50
Nautical, Valentine, Sailor's, Shell Display, 14 In.Diameter .... *Illus* 1000.00

Nautical, Sextant, Brass, 11 X 10 1/2 X 4 3/4 In.High, C.1840

Nautical, Ship Model, Whale, Joseph H. Starbudr, 32 In.

Nautical, Valentine, Sailor's, Shell Display, 14 In.Diameter

Nautical, Globe, Linen Covered, London, C.1875, 28 In.Long

Nautical, Valentine, Sailor's, Shell Work, Nautical Scene, Dome, 11 In. 40.00
Nautical, Valentine, Shell Work Frame, Nautical Scene Under Dome, 11 In. 40.00
Nautical, Watch, Elgin, Double Wood Case, Gimbaled, 21 Jewel 495.00
Nautical, Wheel, From Delaware Bay Coast Ship 225.00
Nautical, Wheel, Wooden, Brass Trim 35.00
Nautical, Whistle, Bosun's, Sterling Silver 6.50
Nautical, Whistle, Steam, Copper & Iron, Valve To Change Tone, 23 In. 275.00
Nautical, Whistle, Steamboat, Bronze, 12 In. .... 65.00 To 70.00

Needlework, see Textile, Picture; Textile, Sampler

Negro, Ashtray, Child Eating Watermelon, Metal 18.00
Negro, Book, Comic, Fat Clem Brown, The Laziest Coon In Town, 1901 .... 48.00
Negro, Jar, Cookie, Mammy 12.00
Negro, Salt & Pepper, Cook Holding Spoon 5.00
Negro, Salt & Pepper, Topsy, 5 In. 6.00
Negro, Sharpener, Pencil, Uncle Sam 18.00

Netsuke are small ivory, wood, metal, or porcelain pieces used as the button on the end of a cord holding a Japanese money pouch. The earliest date from the sixteenth century.

Netsuke, Carpenter Adjusting Plane, Kunimitsu 250.00
Netsuke, Catfish, Mitsuhide 46.00
Netsuke, Coiled Snake, Baisho 68.00
Netsuke, Coiled Snake, Signed Baisho 70.00
Netsuke, Colt, Ivory 500.00
Netsuke, Daruma, Pulling Cheeks, Yoshimatsu 72.00
Netsuke, Dog And Shellfish, Signed, Reddish Stone 32.00
Netsuke, Dutchman Holding Trumpet, Late 18th Century .... *Illus* 225.00
Netsuke, Enshi, Hinoki Figure, 19th Century .... *Illus* 275.00
Netsuke, European With Cape & Sword, Shosai, Ivory, C.1800, 2 In. 120.00
Netsuke, Fish By Masoyoshi, Mid-1800s 60.00
Netsuke, Fish With Tail On Back, Masayoshi, Ivory, C.1800, 2 In. 75.00
Netsuke, Frog, Early 19th Century .... *Illus* 225.00
Netsuke, Gentoku, The Warrior Riding Rearing Stallion 185.00
Netsuke, Ghost Of Oiwa Burning At The Door 110.00
Netsuke, Group Of Shells With Crab Peeping Out, Ivory, C.1840 .... 395.00
Netsuke, Human Skull With Coiled Snake On Top 100.00
Netsuke, Kappa Holding Basket 34.00
Netsuke, Lying Horse, Ihei, Ivory, C.1800, 2 In. 80.00
Netsuke, Lying Ox, Ivory, C.1800, 2 In. 55.00
Netsuke, Lying Ox, Not Signed, 1 1/8 In. 46.00
Netsuke, Man Holding Fan With Cabinet 37.00
Netsuke, Man Holding Tablet 26.00
Netsuke, Man Seated With Basket Of Food 28.00
Netsuke, Man Seated With Fan, Cabinet 36.00
Netsuke, Man Seated, Holding Opium Bag, Pipe 25.00
Netsuke, Man With Mask 37.00
Netsuke, Man With Okame Mask 35.00
Netsuke, Noh Mask, African, Ivory, Handcarved 35.00
Netsuke, Okimono Type, Dark Wood, Brad Eyes, By Nishimura 32.00
Netsuke, Old Lady With Knees Up, Signed, 1 1/2 In. 65.00
Netsuke, Old Man Holding Baby In Hands, 1 1/2 In. 60.00
Netsuke, Old Man With Monkey, 1 1/2 In. 60.00
Netsuke, Oriental Man Holding Carp On His Head, Ivory 65.00
Netsuke, Peasant, Dancing, 18th Century .... *Illus* 175.00
Netsuke, Revolving Face, Happy To Angry, Carved Ivory, 2 In. 28.00
Netsuke, Running Boar, Masaharu, Ivory, C.1800, 2 In. 75.00
Netsuke, Running Boar, Masaharu, Mid-1800s 75.00
Netsuke, Sennin With Leaf Cape, Signed, 2 3/8 In. 75.00
Netsuke, Shina-Fu-Dori By Hiroaki 130.00
Netsuke, Shoki Holding Oni By Foot 100.00
Netsuke, Sitting Baku, Youhei 60.00
Netsuke, Sitting Daruma Holding Leg, Saikaku 60.00
Netsuke, Sitting Dog, Shun, 2 In. 70.00
Netsuke, Sleeping Man, From Tusk Tip 23.00

Netsuke, Enshi, Hinoki Figure, 19th Century

Netsuke, Dutchman Holding Trumpet, Late 18th Century

Netsuke, Frog, Early 19th Century

Netsuke, Tiger, 19th Century

(See Page 354)

Netsuke, Peasant, Dancing, 18th Century

Netsuke, Two Rats On A Pail, 19th Century

(See Page 354)

Netsuke, Snake & Frog, Wooden, 2 In. 70.00
Netsuke, Standing Kappa Holding Gourd, Kouki 110.00
Netsuke, Tiger, 19th Century .... *Illus* 1400.00
Netsuke, Turtle 37.00
Netsuke, Twelve Zodiac Animals On Mountain, Mitsuyuki 80.00
Netsuke, Two Rats On A Pail, 19th Century .... *Illus* 350.00
New England Glass Co., Basket, Clear Thorn Handle, Ribbed, Pink Inside, 8 In. 95.00
New England Glass Co., Bottle, Cologne, Opalescent 37.50
New England Glass Co., Bowl, Brides, Lavender, Pleated & Scalloped 175.00
New England Glass Co., Cup Plate, Lacy, 3 1/4 In. 30.00
New England Glass Co., Cup Plate, Lacy, 3 3/8 In. 17.50
New England Glass Co., Darner, Peachblow, Glossy Finish 250.00
New England Glass Co., Pear, Peachblow, Open-End Stem, Glossy 300.00
New England Glass Co., Plate, Waffle With Fan, Lacy, 9 In. 80.00
New England Glass Co., Salt, Lacy, 2 7/8 In. 70.00
New England Glass Co., Toothpick, Amberina, Square Top 125.00
New England Glass Co., Vase, Peachblow, Square Scallop Top, Glossy 625.00

New Martinsville, see also Peachblow

New Martinsville, Ashtray, Cambridge Square, Ruby, 6 In. 35.00
New Martinsville, Basket, Crystal, Janice, 8 1/2 In. 13.50
New Martinsville, Basket, Janice, 9 In. 30.00
New Martinsville, Basket, Janice, 11 X 7 X 12 In. 45.00
New Martinsville, Bookend, Fish, Pair 55.00
New Martinsville, Bowl, Etched, 13 In. 17.50
New Martinsville, Bowl, Janice, Cobalt, Swan Handles 10 In. 30.00
New Martinsville, Bowl, White To Butterscotch, Ribbed, Pleated Rim, 9 In. 115.00
New Martinsville, Bride's Basket & Frame, Peachblow 450.00
New Martinsville, Candleholder, Emerald Swan, Clear Neck, 5 In., Pair 35.00
New Martinsville, Candleholder, Green, Swan, 5 In. 18.00
New Martinsville, Candleholder, Ruby, Moondrops, 2 In., Pair 45.00
New Martinsville, Candlestick, Green, Swan, 5 In., Pair 25.00
New Martinsville, Chicken 25.00
New Martinsville, Console Bowl, Green, Swan, 11 In. 38.00
New Martinsville, Creamer, Moondrops, Cobalt 15.00
New Martinsville, Creamer, Queen Anne, Ruby 18.00
New Martinsville, Cup, Ruby Radiance 10.00
New Martinsville, Dish, Blue Dolphin With Fish Lid 115.00
New Martinsville, Elephant 30.00
New Martinsville, Figurine, Baby Bear, 3 X 4 1/2 In. 45.00
New Martinsville, Figurine, Bear, 5 In. 65.00
New Martinsville, Figurine, Fish, 7 In. 35.00
New Martinsville, Figurine, Large Seal 55.00
New Martinsville, Figurine, Papa Bear 85.00
New Martinsville, Figurine, Police Dog 38.00
New Martinsville, Figurine, Seal, Crystal, 3 1/2 In. 37.50
New Martinsville, Figurine, Seal, Crystal, 7 In. 60.00
New Martinsville, Figurine, Seal, Frosted, 7 In. 65.00
New Martinsville, Figurine, Small Pig, 1 In. 27.50
New Martinsville, Figurine, Squirrel Sitting On Log 45.00
New Martinsville, Figurine, Squirrel, 5 1/2 In. 65.00
New Martinsville, Figurine, Wolfhound, 7 In. 40.00
New Martinsville, Jar, Cobalt, Covered, 8 1/2 In. 21.00
New Martinsville, Sugar And Creamer, With Tray, Blue Radiance 32.00
New Martinsville, Swan, Cobalt, 5 In. 25.00
New Martinsville, Swan, Crystal, Janice, Red Neck, 10 In. 35.00
New Martinsville, Swan, Crystal, Janice, 9 1/2 In. 30.00
New Martinsville, Swan, Green, 5 In. 18.00
New Martinsville, Swan, Janice, Blue Neck, 10 X 5 In. 28.00
New Martinsville, Swan, Janice, Cobalt Head & Neck, 5 1/2 In. 22.00
New Martinsville, Swan, Janice, Crystal Body, Cobalt Neck, 10 X 5 1/2 In. 29.50
New Martinsville, Swan, Janice, Crystal Body, Ruby Neck, 5 In. 18.50
New Martinsville, Tumbler, Leaf & Star, Clear, Signed 16.00
New Martinsville, Tumbler, Ruby, Georgian, 9 Ozs. 6.00
New Martinsville, Vase, Ruby, Flared Out, 3 Scallops, 3-Footed, 7 3/4 In. 57.00

Newhall, Cup & Saucer

New Martinsville, Wine Set, Ruby Moon Drops, 7 Piece 110.00
New Martinsville, Wine Set, Ruby, 7 Pieces 85.00

Newcomb Pottery was founded by Ellsworth and William Woodward at Sophie Newcomb College, New Orleans, Louisiana, in 1896. The work continued through the 1940s. Pieces of this art pottery are marked with the letter N inside the letter C.

Newcomb, Bowl, Blue, Pink Floral & Green Leaf, Henrietta Bailey, 8 In. 225.00
Newcomb, Bowl, Green, White Flowers, High Glaze, 3 X 8 In. 235.00
Newcomb, Bowl, 3 Handled, Marked 185.00
Newcomb, Vase, Floral Spray Around Base, High Glaze, Miniature, 2 In. 275.00
Newcomb, Vase, Pink With Blue, NC & JM, 6 3/4 X 3 In. 120.00

Newhall Porcelain Manufactory was started at Newhall, Shelton, Staffordshire, England, in 1782. Simple decorated wares were made. Between 1810 and 1825, the factory made a glassy bone porcelain marked with the factory name.

Newhall, Cup & Saucer .... *Illus* 35.00
Newhall, Cup & Saucer, Coffee, Willow Design, Gilding, C.1785 .... 95.00
Newhall, Cup & Saucer, Oriental Scene 65.00
Newhall, Tea Bowl & Saucer, Red Bomb, Oriental, Polychrome, C.1785 .... 110.00
Newhall, Tea Set, Roses, Swirled, Handleless Cups, C.1810, 30 Piece 575.00
Niagara Silver Plate Co., Napkin Ring, Figural, Grasshopper, Silver Plate 55.00
Niderville, Petit Four Stand, Floral, Pedestal, C.1770, 10 X 4 1/4 In. 50.00

NILOAK

Niloak Pottery (Kaolin spelled backwards) was made at the Hyten Brothers Pottery in Benton, Arkansas, between 1909 and 1946. Although the factory did make cast and molded wares, collectors are most interested in the marbleized art pottery line.

Niloak, Bowl, Browns, 12 X 4 In. 60.00
Niloak, Candlestick, Swirl, 8 In. 45.00
Niloak, Ewer, Blue, 3 In. 12.00
Niloak, Figurine, Elephant 18.00
Niloak, Figurine, Hen 25.00
Niloak, Figurine, Rooster 25.00
Niloak, Figurine, Squirrel, 6 In. 25.00
Niloak, Match Holder, Swirl, 2 1/2 In. 32.50
Niloak, Pitcher, Pink, 5 In. 7.50
Niloak, Planter, Brown, Rooster, 5 1/2 In. 8.00
Niloak, Planter, Brown, Squirrel, Paper Label, 6 1/2 In. 15.00
Niloak, Planter, Elephant, 6 In. 20.00
Niloak, Planter, Squirrel, Blue, 6 In. 12.00
Niloak, Vase, Aqua, Brown, & Rust Swirl, 10 1/2 In. 35.00
Niloak, Vase, Baby Blue, 7 In. 6.00
Niloak, Vase, Blue & Browns, Swirled, 5 3/4 In. 25.00
Niloak, Vase, Blue & Red Swirl, 8 In. 35.00
Niloak, Vase, Blue & Red Swirl, 9 In. 40.00
Niloak, Vase, Blue, Brown, Tan Swirls, 10 1/4 In. 65.00
Niloak, Vase, Marbleized Swirl, Impressed Sign, 3 1/4 In. 20.00
Niloak, Vase, Marbleized, Cylinder, 11 1/2 X 4 In. 25.00
Niloak, Vase, Marbleized, 9 1/2 In. 35.00

Niloak, Vase, Plum & Blue Matte With Molded Roses For Side Openings, 4 In. 20.00

Nippon-marked porcelain was made in Japan after 1891.

Nippon Type, Berry Set, Green, Roses, Gold Edges, 11 Piece 38.00
Nippon, Ashtray, Art Nouveau, Palm Scene, Triangular 28.00
Nippon, Ashtray, Bisque Finish, Moose Head, Leaves, Acorns, Green M Mark, 6 In. 70.00
Nippon, Ashtray, Comic, Soldier Driving General In Old Car, Green Wreath 45.00
Nippon, Ashtray, Floral, Cigarette Places On 4 Corners, 4 1/2 In. 35.00
Nippon, Ashtray, Moriye 29.00
Nippon, Ashtray, Red & Green Floral 30.00
Nippon, Ashtray, Sailing Ships, Square, 4 1/4 In. 24.00
Nippon, Ashtray, Scenic, 3 Rests, Blue Rising Sun Mark, 4 In. 28.00
Nippon, Ashtray, Tan, Horses' Heads, Green Mark, 6 Sided, 6 In. 55.00
Nippon, Ashtray, Warrior On Horseback 18.00
Nippon, Basket, Card, Black & Gold 25.00
Nippon, Basket, Flowers And Gold 40.00
Nippon, Basket, Scenic, Handled, 10 X 6 1/2 In. 20.00
Nippon, Berry Set, Blue Leaves, Gold Trim, 3 Footed, 5 Piece 27.50
Nippon, Berry Set, House Scenes, 5 Piece 45.00
Nippon, Berry Set, Pink Beige, Yellow Daisies, Black & Gold Scrolls, 7 Piece 65.00
Nippon, Berry Set, Roses, Rising Sun Mark 35.00
Nippon, Bonbon, Green, Yellow, White, & Gold Floral, Open Handles, 5 3/4 In. 18.00
Nippon, Bonbon, Scenic, Indians' Heads, 2 Self Handles, Green M Mark 75.00
Nippon, Bottle, Perfume, Cottage In Trees Scene, Jeweled Stopper, 4 1/2 In. 65.00
Nippon, Bottle, Perfume, Gold & White, Green Wreath Mark 30.00
Nippon, Bottle, Perfume, Landscape Scene, Jeweled Stopper, Satin Finish, 4 In. 65.00
Nippon, Bottle, Perfume, Pink Roses, Gold Trim 45.00
Nippon, Bowl & Underplate, Pink Roses, 3 Footed Bowl, 6 1/4 In. 11.95
Nippon, Bowl & Underplate, Violets, Gold Tracery, M In Wreath Mark, 5 1/4 In. 22.50
Nippon, Bowl, Acorns, Walnuts Interior, Jewels, Green Mark, 9 In. 60.00
Nippon, Bowl, Basket Of Corn & Acorn, Browns, Tab Handles, Octagonal, 8 In. 30.00
Nippon, Bowl, Blown-Out Acorns, Folded Rim, 7 In. 49.50
Nippon, Bowl, Blue & Pink Floral, Gold Greek Key, Pierced Handled, 13 In. 25.00
Nippon, Bowl, Browns, Blown-Out Blue & Yellow Grapes, Vine Handles, 11 In. 275.00
Nippon, Bowl, Country Scene, Handle 12.50
Nippon, Bowl, Covered, Yellow & Green Floral, Jeweled, Footed, 4 1/2 In. 16.50
Nippon, Bowl, Figures & Houses, Reds, Gold Trim, Royal Kaga, Square, 5 1/4 In. 10.00
Nippon, Bowl, Floral Medallions, 3 Footed, Maple Leaf Mark, 6 1/2 In. 49.00
Nippon, Bowl, Floral, Blue & Gold Border, Octagonal, 5 1/2 In. 12.50
Nippon, Bowl, Floral, Gold Beading, Footed, Green Mark, 4 1/4 In. 5.00
Nippon, Bowl, Flowers, Cobalt & Gold, Party Bisque, 11 In. 97.50
Nippon, Bowl, Fluted, Windmill Scene 18.00
Nippon, Bowl, Gold Square Handles, Four Section, Green Mark, 10 X 2 In. 25.00
Nippon, Bowl, Gold-Outlined Blue & Yellow Peonies, 3 Gold Handles, 8 In. 75.00
Nippon, Bowl, Green Matte, Pinecones, Gold Beading, Jeweled, Handled, 8 In. 48.00
Nippon, Bowl, Handled Fruit, Imari Decorated, Cobalt Blue, M In Wreath 55.00
Nippon, Bowl, Handled, Purple Mark, 7 In. 12.00
Nippon, Bowl, House & Lake Scene, 3 Scrolled Gold Feet, 11 In. 45.00
Nippon, Bowl, House On Lake At Sunset, Cutout Handles, Signed, 6 X 4 3/4 In. 22.00
Nippon, Bowl, Hunt Scene, Octagonal, 7 In. 40.00
Nippon, Bowl, Lake Scene, Gold, Hand-Painted, M In Green Wreath, 8 1/4 In. 50.00
Nippon, Bowl, Mayonnaise, Gilt Handles, Underplate, Iris, 7 Red Wreath 14.50
Nippon, Bowl, Molded Boy's Face, 5 1/2 In. 26.00
Nippon, Bowl, Moriye, Violets, Double Handles, Crimped, 4 1/2 In. 29.00
Nippon, Bowl, Nut, Blown-Out Nuts, Leaf Design Inside, Green Mark, 7 In. 85.00
Nippon, Bowl, Nut, Blown-Out Walnuts, 7 In. 28.00
Nippon, Bowl, Nut, Pedestal, 5 Small Nut Dishes, Pastel Florals, Set 22.00
Nippon, Bowl, Open Handles, Flowers On White, Gold Trim, 8 3/4 In. 22.50
Nippon, Bowl, Orange Floral, Black & Gold Outline, Pierced Handles, 8 1/2 In. 25.00
Nippon, Bowl, Palm Tree & Lake Scene, Turquoise Jewels, Pierced Ends, 10 In. 38.00
Nippon, Bowl, Pedestal, Floral & Birds, Gold Handles, 6 3/4 In. 35.00
Nippon, Bowl, Pink & Blue Floral, Heavy Gold, 11 1/2 X 9 In. 18.00
Nippon, Bowl, Pink Floral, Jeweled, Gold Trim, 8 1/2 In. 15.00
Nippon, Bowl, Pink Roses, Gold Trim, 2 Handles, 7 In. 8.00

Nippon, Bowl, Pinks, Greens, Yellows, & Gold, Green Jewels, 11 In. 65.00
Nippon, Bowl, Raised Chestnuts, Brown Beading, Ball Feet, Green Mark, 8 In. 75.00
Nippon, Bowl, Raised Gold Trim, Handled, Red Mark, 7 1/2 In. 20.00
Nippon, Bowl, River, Trees, & House Scene, Open Handles, 6 1/2 In. 28.00
Nippon, Bowl, Roses, Gold Edge, Tab Handles, Green M Mark, 6 1/2 In. 20.00
Nippon, Bowl, Roses, Green Wreath Mark, 7 In. 12.00
Nippon, Bowl, Scenic, Black & White, Pierced Gold Handles, 7 In. 30.00
Nippon, Bowl, Scenic, Browns & Lavender, Beaded, Square, 6 1/2 In. 36.00
Nippon, Bowl, Scenic, Dolphin Handles, 3 Footed, Brown Beading, 4 1/2 In. 75.00
Nippon, Bowl, Scenic, Pale Orange, Pierced Handles, Green Wreath Mark, 9 In. 55.00
Nippon, Bowl, Shallow, Blown-Out Oak Leaves & Strawberries, 8 In. 60.00
Nippon, Bowl, Strawberry, Removable Drain, Wild Roses, Gold, Green Wreath 82.00
Nippon, Bowl, Sunset Lake Scene, Jeweled, Pierced Handles, 10 In. 38.00
Nippon, Bowl, Violets, 9 1/2 In. 15.00
Nippon, Bowl, Wedgwood, Green M In Wreath Mark 85.00
Nippon, Bowl, White & Gold, Footed, Blue Mark, 5 1/2 In. 25.00
Nippon, Bowl, White, Black Inside, Silver Dragon, 7 1/4 X 3 In. 35.00
Nippon, Bowl, White, Carnations, Perforated, Footed, Gold Band & Beading, 7 In. 30.00
Nippon, Bowl, White, Floral, Gold Banding, Pedestal, 5 1/2 In. 48.00
Nippon, Bowl, Windmill Scene, Brown Beading, Handled, 5 In. 15.00
Nippon, Bowl, Women In Tea Garden, Red & Gold, 9 In. 49.00
Nippon, Box & Underplate, Sardine, Sardine Finial 48.00
Nippon, Box, Biscuit, Covered, Mosque Scene, Beaded, 3 Footed, Bisque Finish 125.00
Nippon, Box, Blooming Cherry Trees On Lid, Lake Scene, Green Mark, 3 In. 14.00
Nippon, Box, Collar Button, Gold Beading, Pedestaled, Pair 30.00
Nippon, Box, Covered, Cobalt & Gold, Satin Finish, 5 1/2 In. 65.00
Nippon, Box, Covered, Cobalt Blue Decoration, Round, 6 In. 23.00
Nippon, Box, Covered, Floral, Gold Trim, Round, 3 In. 9.00
Nippon, Box, Covered, Red Roses, Raised Dots, Green Mark, 5 In. 22.50
Nippon, Box, Covered, Sampans On Ocean Sunset Scene, Cobalt Trim, 5 1/2 In. 65.00
Nippon, Box, Patch, Ivory Color, Gold & Cobalt Rim, Jeweled 30.00
Nippon, Box, Sardine With Underplate, Sardine Finial 45.00
Nippon, Box, Stud, Butterfly On Lid, Ace Of Spades Shape, Green Mark 12.00
Nippon, Box, Trinket, Casket Shape, Gold Floral, Orange Leaves, 4 Footed 18.50
Nippon, Box, Trinket, Covered, House Scene, Heart Shape, Bulbous 22.00
Nippon, Box, Trinket, Crusted Gold, Floral On Base & Cover, Blue Mark 25.00
Nippon, Box, Trinket, Figural, Dog, 3 1/2 In. 12.50
Nippon, Box, Trinket, Geometrics & Floral, 6 Sided, Royal Crown Mark 15.00
Nippon, Bread & Butter Set, Roses, Gold Trim, Rising Sun Mark, 5 Piece 21.00
Nippon, Breakfast Set, Child's, Hand-Painted Blue Daisies, 3 Piece 30.00
Nippon, Butter Pat, Floral, Set Of 5 .... 15.00
Nippon, Butter Pat, Gold Handles, Roses 4.00
Nippon, Butter, Blue Maple Leaf Mark, 9 In. 35.00
Nippon, Butter, Covered, Gold Beading, RC Mark 27.50
Nippon, Butter, Covered, Gold, Red, & Blue, Round 38.00
Nippon, Butter, Covered, Gold, 7 1/2 In.Diameter .... *Illus* 40.00
Nippon, Cake Set, Brown, Gold-Outlined Floral, Pierced Handles, 7 Piece 48.00
Nippon, Cake Set, Child's, Gold Roses, Scrolls, & Loops, Spoke Mark, 7 Piece 65.00
Nippon, Cake Set, Dark Gray, Applied Silver Dragons, 19 Piece 67.00

Nippon, Butter, Covered, Gold, 7 1/2 In.Diameter

Nippon, Cake Set, Floral Border, Gold Tracery, 7 Piece 32.00
Nippon, Cake Set, Gold Beading, 7 Piece 29.00
Nippon, Cake Set, Gold Trim, Bright Flowers, Gold Tracery 22.50
Nippon, Cake Set, Orange, Gold Camels & Riders, Palm Trees, 50 Piece 52.00
Nippon, Cake Set, Pink Roses, Gold Scroll, 7 Piece 23.00
Nippon, Cake Set, White Flowers With Red Centers, Gold Trim, 5 Piece 24.00
Nippon, Cake Set, White, Border Of Apple Blossoms, 7 Piece 25.00
Nippon, Cake Set, Yellow, Shading Floral Design, Gold Outline, 7 Piece 20.00
Nippon, Cake Set, 6 Plates, Bisque Finish, Pink Roses, Temple Mark 75.00
Nippon, Can Holder & Underplate, Milk, Cobalt & Floral Decoration 30.00
Nippon, Can Holder & Underplate, Milk, Pink Floral, Green Leaves 45.00
Nippon, Candlestick, Chinese Scenes, Black & Gold, 9 In., Pair 120.00
Nippon, Candlestick, Ornate Beaded, Floral, Pair 60.00
Nippon, Candlestick, Tan, Roses & Trees, Blue Leaf Mark, 7 In. 38.00
Nippon, Celery Set, Azalea, Rising Sun Mark, 7 Piece 49.00
Nippon, Celery Set, Gold & Orange Trim, Open Handles, 5 Piece 25.00
Nippon, Celery Set, Green Laurel, Pink Roses, Gold Trim, 7 Piece 42.00
Nippon, Celery Set, Pink Roses & Gold Floral, Beaded, Green Mark, 7 Piece 26.00
Nippon, Celery Set, White, Gold Designs, 7 Piece 40.00
Nippon, Celery, Child's, Red & Pink Roses, Gold Medallions, Maple Leaf Mark 42.50
Nippon, Celery, Cottage & Lake Scene, Sunset Colors, Jeweled 22.00
Nippon, Celery, Tray & 4 Salts, Pink, Green, Gold, Set 23.00
Nippon, Charger, Red & Pink Roses, Gold & Beaded Scalloped Rim, 12 1/2 In. 95.00
Nippon, Chocolate Pot, Gold & Pink Roses 20.00
Nippon, Chocolate Pot, Gold, Roses, Rococo Handle & Finial, Superior Mark 45.00
Nippon, Chocolate Pot, Pink & Gold Roses, Blue Maple Leaf Mark, 9 3/4 In. 48.00
Nippon, Chocolate Pot, Pink Flowers 32.00
Nippon, Chocolate Pot, White, Yellow Roses, Tan & Gold Trim 34.00
Nippon, Chocolate Pot, 5 Cups & Saucers, Geisha Girl, Blue Trim 70.00
Nippon, Chocolate Set, Cobalt Trim, 10 Piece 95.00
Nippon, Chocolate Set, Floral & Green Leaf, Jeweled, 9 Piece 95.00
Nippon, Chocolate Set, Gold Decoration, 18 Piece 115.00
Nippon, Chocolate Set, Gold Floral, Spoke Mark, 16 Piece 125.00
Nippon, Chocolate Set, Hand-Painted Violets, 3 Cups & Saucers, Nippon Mark 60.00
Nippon, Chocolate Set, Imari, Orange, Blue, & Gold, Green Mark, 13 Piece 125.00
Nippon, Chocolate Set, Oriental Flower Sprays, Roman Key Border, 9 Piece 55.00
Nippon, Chocolate Set, Pink Floral, White Enamel Beading, 9 Piece 60.00
Nippon, Chocolate Set, Pink Wild Roses, Green Wreath, 8 Pieces 30.00
Nippon, Chocolate Set, Rising Sun, Flowered Border, 13 Piece 65.00
Nippon, Chocolate Set, White, Black With Gold Scene, 13 Piece 85.00
Nippon, Chocolate Set, White, Cream Bands, Gold Trim, Magenta Mark, 13 Piece 55.00
Nippon, Chocolate Set, White, Gold Lines, Rising Sun Mark, 13 Piece 72.00
Nippon, Chocolate Set, White, Gold Trim, 9 Piece 75.00
Nippon, Chocolate Set, White, Ivory Band Of Flowers, Gold Handles, 9 Piece 68.00
Nippon, Chocolate Set, White, Roses, Gold & Green Trim, Green Mark, 9 Piece 82.00
Nippon, Coaster, Azaleas 3.00
Nippon, Coaster, Roses, Rising Sun Mark 4.00
Nippon, Coffeepot, Demitasse, Geishas & Garden Scene, Red & Gold Trim 30.00
Nippon, Coffeepot, Floral & Leaf, Jeweled, Maple Leaf Mark, 7 1/4 In. 65.00
Nippon, Compote, Wild Flowers, 2 Handles, 9 In. 18.00
Nippon, Condiment Set, Moriye, Dragon, 5 Piece 35.00
Nippon, Condiment Set, Orange & Yellow, Orchids, Green Wreath Mark, 5 Piece 18.50
Nippon, Condiment Set, Pink Roses, Gold Trim, Wreath Mark, 4 Piece 38.00
Nippon, Condiment Set, White, Gold-Outlined Roses, R.C.Mark, 6 Piece 48.00
Nippon, Creamer, Blown-Out Child's Face 35.00
Nippon, Creamer, Flying Turkey, Blue & White 10.00
Nippon, Creamer, Sailboats In Sunset, M Mark 5.00
Nippon, Creamer, Tree In Meadow 8.00
Nippon, Cucumber Bowl & Underplate, Pink Shaded, Gold, Pierced, Footed 25.00
Nippon, Cup & Saucer, Capitol Building, Washington, D.C., Gold Beading 6.00
Nippon, Cup & Saucer, Chocolate, White, Gold Decoration 20.50
Nippon, Cup & Saucer, Chocolate, White, Ivory & Maroon Floral Bands 8.00
Nippon, Cup & Saucer, Cobalt, Gold Birds & Waves, Jeweled, S & K 20.00
Nippon, Cup & Saucer, Coffee, Gray Matte, Raised Dragon, Beaded & Jeweled 10.00

Nippon, Cup & Saucer, Demitasse, Black, Floral Medallions, Gold Trim 22.00
Nippon, Cup & Saucer, Demitasse, Peach, Raised Gold, Lima Mark 45.00
Nippon, Cup & Saucer, Green & Gold Inside Cup, 6 Sided 22.00
Nippon, Cup & Saucer, Green With Gold, Blue Crown Mark 4.25
Nippon, Cup & Saucer, Mustache, Pale Blue & White, Red & Yellow Roses, Gold 85.00
Nippon, Cup & Saucer, Pink Roses, Gold Scroll 10.00
Nippon, Cup & Saucer, White & Red Poppies, Rising Sun Mark 7.50
Nippon, Cup & Saucer, White, Blue Scenes, Royal Somet 9.00
Nippon, Cup & Saucer, White, Floral, Green Mark 6.00
Nippon, Cup, Nut, Raised Acorns, Bisque, 3 Ball Feet, Set Of 4 20.00
Nippon, Decanter, Scenic In Wicker, Maple Leaf, Handled, 1 1/2 Qt., 11 In. 125.00
Nippon, Dish, Bisque, Lake Scene, Beaded Rim, Enameled Handle, 7 3/4 In. 28.00
Nippon, Dish, Boat Shape, Gold Medallion, Gold Handles, Beaded, 9 1/2 In. 28.00
Nippon, Dish, Bonbon, Six Sided, Handled, White Florals On Wedgwood Bisque 75.00
Nippon, Dish, Butterflies, Gold Trim, Center Handle, Divided, 9 X 8 In. 14.00
Nippon, Dish, Candy, Beige, Yellow & Orange Floral, 2 Handles, Green Mark 14.00
Nippon, Dish, Candy, Lime Green, Pink Floral, Gold Trim, Leaf Shape, 7 In. 15.00
Nippon, Dish, Candy, Nuts Inside, Handled, 5 1/2 X 4 1/2 In. 14.00
Nippon, Dish, Candy, Scenic, Church, Green Wreath, 2 Handles, Beaded 15.00
Nippon, Dish, Candy, White, Pink & Blue Floral, Gold Handle & Border, 6 In. 14.00
Nippon, Dish, Canoe Shape, Bisque Interior, River With Indian, Green Wreath 75.00
Nippon, Dish, Canoe Shape, Yellow, Pink, & Green Floral, Gold Border, 7 In. 18.00
Nippon, Dish, Cheese & Cracker, Raised Center, Scroll Floral, 8 1/4 In. 28.00
Nippon, Dish, Cheese, Slant Top, Blue & Gold Bands, Gold Handle, Pink Floral 35.00
Nippon, Dish, Cheese, Slant Top, Floral, Gold Trim 35.00
Nippon, Dish, Cheese, Slant Top, Greek Key Border, Green & Floral Garlands 30.00
Nippon, Dish, Cracker, White, Bluebirds & Floral, Footed, Handled, 6 In. 28.00
Nippon, Dish, Cucumber, Floral, Insert, Pedestal, Green M Mark, 10 In. 24.00
Nippon, Dish, Cucumber, Flowers, Heavy Gold Trim 35.00
Nippon, Dish, Heart Shape, Floral, Handle, Marked M 18.00
Nippon, Dish, Jiggs With Crossed Eyes Face, Raised & Incised 35.00
Nippon, Dish, Master Nut With 12 Individuals, White, Gold Outline, Orange 25.00
Nippon, Dish, Mayonnaise, White Ground, Dainty Yellow & Gold Flowers, 3 Piece 20.00
Nippon, Dish, Pancake, Covered, White, Floral, Yellow Banding, 9 In. 45.00
Nippon, Dish, Pancake, White, Ivory Band Of Flowers, Gold Trim 45.00
Nippon, Dish, Powder, Covered, Cream With Gold, Marked 48.00
Nippon, Dish, Tidbit, Tiered, Cobalt & Gold Squares, Floral, Gold Trim 20.00
Nippon, Dish, Tidbit, Tiered, Green & Gold On Cream Band, Spoke Mark 22.00
Nippon, Dish, Vegetable, Oval Covered, Kiva, Green Wreath 23.00
Nippon, Dresser Set, Floral, Gold Beading, Pedestaled, 3 Piece 39.00
Nippon, Dresser Set, Floral, Gold Trim, 5 Piece 65.00
Nippon, Dresser Set, Green Wreath Mark, Violet Decoration, 4 Pieces 55.00
Nippon, Dresser Set, Heart-Shaped Tray, 4 Piece 55.00
Nippon, Dresser Set, Pink Floral Garlands, Black Urns, Gold, 5 Piece 75.00
Nippon, Dresser Set, Red & Gold, 3 Piece 135.00
Nippon, Dresser Set, White, Pink Roses, Blue Mark, 14 Piece 295.00
Nippon, Egg Warmer, Floral & Gold, Set Of 4 35.00
Nippon, Eggcup, White, Blue Grapes, Royal Sometuke 55.00
Nippon, Ewer, Bulbous, Roses, Green Ground, Blue Maple Leaf Mark, 6 In., Pair 125.00
Nippon, Ewer, Green, Red, Blue, & Black Geometrics, Gold Trim, 6 1/2 In. 110.00
Nippon, Ewer, Moriye, Roses, 7 In. 152.50
Nippon, Ewer, Moriye, 5 In. 45.00
Nippon, Ewer, Portrait, Woman With Blue Hair Ribbon, Leaf Mark, 6 1/2 In. 160.00
Nippon, Ferner, 4-Leaf Clover Shape, Floral, Footed, 9 In. 65.00
Nippon, Fernery, Coastal & Sailboat Scenes, Footed, 7 1/2 In. 78.00
Nippon, Fernery, Coastal Scene, Enamel Decoration, 7 1/2 In. 75.00
Nippon, Fernery, Enamel Lions, 3 Molded Pharaohs Feet, Green Mark, 7 In. 125.00
Nippon, Fernery, House Scene, Scrolls, Footed, Triangular 45.00
Nippon, Fernery, Pink Floral, Gold Beading, 4 Footed 32.00
Nippon, Fruit Bowl, Bird Perched On Cherry Tree Branch 42.00
Nippon, Hair Receiver & Powder Jar, Gold Beading, Footed, Pair 33.00
Nippon, Hair Receiver On Tray, House Scene, Souvenir, Springfield, Mass. 15.00
Nippon, Hair Receiver, Gold & Light Blue, Pastel Floral, Hexagonal 25.00
Nippon, Hair Receiver, Heavily Enameled Magenta Hibiscus, Green Ground 25.00

Nippon, Hair Receiver, Magenta, Gold Beading, R.C. Mark 28.00
Nippon, Hair Receiver, Magenta, Gold Overlay, Blue Maple Leaf Mark 60.00
Nippon, Hair Receiver, Moriye, Green Mark 70.00
Nippon, Hair Receiver, Pink Roses, White Beading, Gold Bands, Blue Mark 16.00
Nippon, Hair Receiver, Pink, Green & Gold Flowers, Green Wreath 18.00
Nippon, Hair Receiver, Roses, Gold, 3 Gold Feet, 2 1/4 In. 23.50
Nippon, Hatpin Holder, Aqua & Gold Trim 20.00
Nippon, Hatpin Holder, Blue Leaf Mark, Roses, Scalloped, Beading 29.00
Nippon, Hatpin Holder, Blue Ribbons On Forget-Me-Not Bouquets, Green Mark 15.00
Nippon, Hatpin Holder, Floral & Gold, White Ground, Black Leaf Mark 40.00
Nippon, Hatpin Holder, Orange & Brown On White 18.00
Nippon, Hatpin Holder, Pink Flowers, Gold Beading 22.00
Nippon, Hatpin Holder, Purple & Green Floral, Gold Trim 15.00
Nippon, Holder, Condensed Milk, Lovely Purple Grapes & Ornate Gold 35.00
Nippon, Humidor, American Indian With Eagles, Imperial Mark 155.00
Nippon, Humidor, Boat Scene, 3 Footed, Enamel Beading, 6 Sided, Blue Mark 68.00
Nippon, Humidor, Forest Scene, Sun Filtering Through Trees, Green Mark 135.00
Nippon, Humidor, Girl's Head Knob, Pipe On Side 75.00
Nippon, Humidor, Green, Gold Trim, Jeweled & Beaded 150.00
Nippon, Humidor, Man Walking Dog, Woman With Basket, Green Mark, 7 X 6 In. 95.00
Nippon, Humidor, Rectangular, Bisque Sunset, Water Scenes, Artist Symbol 140.00
Nippon, Humidor, Scenic, 4 Panels 149.50
Nippon, Humidor, 12 Men, 3 Animals, & Tree, Blown Out, Green, Mark, 6 1/2 In. 800.00
Nippon, Ice Cream Set, Gold, Pink, & Green Trim, 7 Piece 28.00
Nippon, Ice Cream Set, White With Pastel Flower Sprays, Green Mark, 5 Piece 50.00
Nippon, Inkwell, Brown To Gray, Egyptian Scenes On Lid & Sides, 2 1/2 In. 85.00
Nippon, Inkwell, Hand-Painted, Bisque Finish, 2 3/4 X 2 1/2 In. 19.00
Nippon, Inkwell, Moriye, 3 Piece 49.00
Nippon, Inkwell, Pink, Sailboat Scene, Beading, Square, 3 In. 95.00
Nippon, Jam Set, Pink Roses, 3 Piece 18.00
Nippon, Jar & Attached Saucer, Jelly, Scenic 25.00
Nippon, Jar & Ladle, Mustard, Rising Sun Mark 18.00
Nippon, Jar & Underplate, Jam, Covered, Rising Sun Mark 10.00
Nippon, Jar, Attached Underplate, & Ladle, Mustard, Pink & Red Roses, Gold 19.00
Nippon, Jar, Attached Underplate, & Spoon, Jam, Covered, Rosebuds, Gold Trim 12.00
Nippon, Jar, Biscuit, Light Blue, Gold & Purple Mums 75.00
Nippon, Jar, Biscuit, Red-Coated Riders 175.00
Nippon, Jar, Cookie, Blue, Pink, Purple Flowers And Gilt 16.50
Nippon, Jar, Cookie, Handled, Heavy Gold Fruit & Flower Decoration 32.50
Nippon, Jar, Cookie, White, Floral Banding, Gold Beading 55.00
Nippon, Jar, Covered, White, Gold & Orange Floral, 3 In. 19.00
Nippon, Jar, Cracker, Green Shading, Roses, 3 Footed, Covered, Blue Leaf Mark 145.00
Nippon, Jar, Cracker, House, Lake, & Trees Scene, Green Wreath Mark 40.00
Nippon, Jar, Cracker, White, Blue, Gold, & Pink Roses, Handled 32.00
Nippon, Jar, Cracker, White, Pink & Red Roses, Gold Vines, 3 Footed, Ribbed 75.00
Nippon, Jar, Ginger, Florals, Gold Tracery, 5 In. 65.00
Nippon, Jar, Ginger, Pink Roses, Moriye Enamel, Green Collar & Base, 5 In. 22.00
Nippon, Jar, Jam, Blue & Gold Decoration 8.00
Nippon, Jar, Jam, Pink Roses, Gold Beading 30.00
Nippon, Jar, Jam, Underplate, Gold Trim 40.00
Nippon, Jar, Mustard, Gold & Blue Floral, Spoon 18.00
Nippon, Jar, Rose, Green Wreath 18.00
Nippon, Jar, Underplate, & Ladle, Jam, Covered, Green Leaves, Gold Edges 15.00
Nippon, Jar, Underplate, & Ladle, Jam, Floral, Gold Handles & Beading 35.00
Nippon, Jar, Underplate, & Ladle, Jam, Gold Finial, Pink, Red, & White Roses 35.00
Nippon, Jardiniere, Square Footed Base, Round Bowl, Brown, Gray, Bisque, 6 In. 49.50
Nippon, Jug, Egyptian, Squat, 5 1/2 In. 132.50
Nippon, Jug, Stoppered, Brown, Black Scenes, Gold Trim, Square, 8 In. 250.00
Nippon, Jug, Whiskey, Seascape & Birds, Jeweled Handle & Stopper 165.00
Nippon, Jug, Wine, Scenic, 7 1/2 In. 135.00
Nippon, Keeper, Cheese, Slant Lid, Pink Roses, Blue Floral, Gold Handle, 8 In. 35.00
Nippon, Lamp Base, Boudoir, Yellow, Black & Gold, Hand-Painted, Green M, 15 In. 40.00
Nippon, Lazy Susan, Green, White Cherry Blossoms, Green Wreath, 7 Piece 125.00
Nippon, Lemonade Set, Red Roses, Gold Trim, 5 Piece 55.00

Nippon, Lemonade Set, 6 Cups, Violets 125.00
Nippon, Luncheon Set, Child's, Floral Design, Gold Edged, 18 Piece 95.00
Nippon, Match Holder & Ashtray, Fatima Turkish Cigarettes, Marked Nippon 64.00
Nippon, Match Holder & Attached Ashtray, Yellow & Blue Indian Type Design 35.00
Nippon, Match Holder, Green Dragon, Red Tongue, Hanging 48.00
Nippon, Match Holder, Hanging, Floral Decoration 29.00
Nippon, Match Holder, Lake & Trees Scene, Hanging, Green M Mark 30.00
Nippon, Mayonnaise Bowl, Blue & Gold Trim, 2 Part 15.00
Nippon, Mayonnaise Set, Floral & Leaf, Jeweled, Maple Leaf, 3 Piece 45.00
Nippon, Mayonnaise Set, Pink Azaleas, Rising Sun Mark, 3 Piece 15.00
Nippon, Mayonnaise Set, Red & Yellow Roses, Gold Medallions, 3 Piece 14.00
Nippon, Mayonnaise Set, Rising Sun Mark, 3 Piece 15.00
Nippon, Mayonnaise Set, Rosebuds, Gold Trim, 3 Piece 12.00
Nippon, Mayonnaise Set, White, Green & Apricot Floral, Footed, 2 Piece 18.00
Nippon, Muffineer & Creamer, Diamonds & Triangles, Art Deco 18.00
Nippon, Muffineer, Hand-Painted, Handled, Paneled, Floral, Gold, Wreath Mark 25.00
Nippon, Muffineer, Red Floral, Hexagonal, Handled, Spoke Mark, 5 In. 75.00
Nippon, Muffineer, Stork With Baby 47.50
Nippon, Mush Set, White, Green, Red Roses, 3 Piece 22.50
Nippon, Mustard Pot & Ladle, Scenic, 2 Handles 15.00
Nippon, Mustard Pot, Green, Pink, Blue, & Brown Floral, Pyramid Shape 19.00
Nippon, Napkin Ring, Scenic, Green Wreath 35.00
Nippon, Nappy, 3 Handled, Hand-Painted Acorns, Leaves On Brown, Green Wreath 74.00
Nippon, Nut Bowl, Blown-Out Leaves, Green Wreath Mark, 6 1/2 In. 65.00
Nippon, Nut Cup, Chestnut Pattern 8.00
Nippon, Nut Dish, Peanut Shape, Inside Painted Nuts And Leaves 45.00
Nippon, Nut Set, Blue, Black & White Borders, Footed, Superior Mark, 7 Piece 28.00
Nippon, Nut Set, Gold & Green Trim, Wreath Mark, 6 Piece 36.00
Nippon, Nut Set, Green Wreath, Footed Handled Dish, 5 Small Dishes 43.00
Nippon, Nut Set, Scenic, Footed Pieces, 7 Piece 65.00
Nippon, Nut Set, Scenic, Orange & Greens, Beaded Edges, 5 Piece 44.00
Nippon, Nut, Roses, Gold Trim, 7 Piece 75.00
Nippon, Pitcher & Lemon Squeezer, Band Of Floral & Leaves, Gold Trim 65.00
Nippon, Pitcher & Underplate, Sauce, Covered, Scenic 20.00
Nippon, Pitcher, Blue & White Phoenix Bird, Small 10.00
Nippon, Pitcher, Grape Pattern, Bulbous, 6 In. 50.00
Nippon, Pitcher, Lemonade, Roses, Red & Gold Border, Maple Leaf Mark, 7 In. 105.00
Nippon, Pitcher, Milk, Covered, Gold-Outlined Green Floral, 7 In. 40.00
Nippon, Pitcher, Pink & Rose Floral, Gold Base & Top, 13 In. 110.00
Nippon, Pitcher, Trees, House, Lake, & Mountains Scene, Beading, 10 1/2 In. 95.00
Nippon, Pitcher, Yellow & Red Roses, Raised Gold, Blue Mark, 7 1/2 In. 110.00
Nippon, Planter, Indian In Canoe, Green M Wreath 65.00
Nippon, Planter, Woods, Water & Canoe Scene, Jeweled Feet, Square, 6 In. 65.00
Nippon, Plaque, Arab On Camel, Tents, & Palm Trees, 10 In. 68.00
Nippon, Plaque, Beading & Enamel, Scenic, Green M In Wreath, 10 In. 65.00
Nippon, Plaque, Blown Out, 10 3/4 In., Deer 325.00
Nippon, Plaque, Blue Parrot On Branch, Pink Floral, Matte Finish, 10 In. 87.50
Nippon, Plaque, Castle & River Scene, 10 In. 55.00
Nippon, Plaque, Charger, Bisque, Fish On Table, 12 In. 135.00
Nippon, Plaque, Desert Scene, Green Wreath Mark, 10 1/2 In. 95.00
Nippon, Plaque, Egyptian Boat On Water & Palms, Bisque, Green Mark, 12 In. 135.00
Nippon, Plaque, Egyptian Warship In Sunset, Green Mark, 10 1/2 In. 125.00
Nippon, Plaque, Fox Hunt Scene, 9 1/2 In. 50.00
Nippon, Plaque, Game Birds, Signed, 11 In. 85.00
Nippon, Plaque, Hand-Painted, Green Wreath, Bisque Finish, Leaves And Nuts 22.50
Nippon, Plaque, House, Swans, & Pond Scene, Green Wreath Mark, 10 In. 52.00
Nippon, Plaque, Indian, Blown Out, 10 In. 275.00
Nippon, Plaque, Owl On Branch, Matte Finish, 10 In. 87.50
Nippon, Plaque, Pine Trees, Applied Red & Green Leaves, 8 1/4 In. 30.00
Nippon, Plaque, Portrait, Art Nouveau, Bisque Finish, 10 1/2 In., Blue Leaf 165.00
Nippon, Plaque, Scenic, Bisque Finish, Art Deco, 10 1/2 In. 38.00
Nippon, Plaque, Scenic, Blue Maple Leaf, 9 In. 53.00
Nippon, Plaque, Sheep At Water's Edge, Blue M Mark, 10 In. 125.00
Nippon, Plaque, Stag, Raised Enamel Leaves, Green M Mark, 10 In. 160.00

Nippon, Plaque, Wall, Glossy Sailing Ships, 10 In. 65.00
Nippon, Plaque, Windmill Scene, Bisque Finish, Floral, 11 1/4 In. 55.00
Nippon, Plaque, 3 Swans, Gold Enamel, Green Wreath, 10 In. 85.00
Nippon, Plate, Azalea, 7 3/4 In. 4.50
Nippon, Plate, Cake, Blue, Orchid, Pink Peonies, Green Leaves 38.00
Nippon, Plate, Cake, Gold Medallion, Cartouches, Roses, Pierced Handles, 11 In. 40.00
Nippon, Plate, Cake, Gray Matte, Raised Dragon, Beaded & Jeweled .... 8.25 To 55.00
Nippon, Plate, Cake, Hunt Scene, Green Bisque Ground, Black Mark, 10 In. 75.00
Nippon, Plate, Cake, Red Roses, Gold Trim, Pierced Handles, 11 1/4 In. 48.00
Nippon, Plate, Cake, White & Plum, Gold & Beading, Closed Handles, 10 1/2 In. 65.00
Nippon, Plate, Cake, White, Blue Floral & Green Leaves, Beige Border, 10 In. 22.00
Nippon, Plate, Floral & Gold Beading, Handled, Green Wreath Mark, 11 In. 60.00
Nippon, Plate, Floral, Gold Encrusted Decoration, Green Mark, 9 In. 12.00
Nippon, Plate, Forget-Me-Nots, 6 In. 3.00
Nippon, Plate, Green & Gold, Four Set In Yellow Jewels, 8 In. 22.50
Nippon, Plate, Green, 3 Roses Medallions, Gold, Blue Leaf Mark, 11 1/2 In. 160.00
Nippon, Plate, Lake & Boathouse Scene, Blue Border, 7 1/4 In., Pair 11.00
Nippon, Plate, Maroon Roses & Floral, Gold Trim, 8 1/2 In. 17.00
Nippon, Plate, Moriage Bird On Matte Finish, Blue Maple Leaf 45.00
Nippon, Plate, Oriental Impressed, White Floral Border, Bird, 8 1/2 In. 20.00
Nippon, Plate, Pastel, Roses, Blue Center Band, 6 1/2 In. 5.00
Nippon, Plate, Peacock & Floral, 8 In. 30.00
Nippon, Plate, Plums, Gold Trim, 9 In. 15.00
Nippon, Plate, Portrait, Juliet, Blue Leaf Mark, 10 1/2 In. 175.00
Nippon, Plate, Portrait, Lady, Head & Shoulders, White & Turquoise, 8 1/2 In. 35.00
Nippon, Plate, Portrait, Young Lady, Blue Ground, Gold Tracery 40.00
Nippon, Plate, Red & Yellow Roses, Gold, Oak Leaf Mark, , Fluted, 12 In. 87.00
Nippon, Plate, Roses, Gold-Outlined Leaves, Magenta M In Wreath Mark, 8 In. 150.00
Nippon, Plate, Scenic, Indian Type Border, Green M Mark 35.00
Nippon, Plate, Scenic, 2 Handled, Green Wreath Mark, 9 In. 16.00
Nippon, Plate, Scenic, 8 1/2 In. 20.00
Nippon, Plate, Spray Of Wild Roses, Crown Mark, 7 1/2 In. 2.75
Nippon, Plate, White, Gold & Green Floral, 6 In. 24.00
Nippon, Plate, Windmill By Water's Edge Scene, Hanging, 10 In. 55.00
Nippon, Platter, Kiva, Green Wreath, 16 In. 22.00
Nippon, Punch Bowl & Base, Peaches & Grapes Inside, Green M Mark, 12 In. 125.00
Nippon, Relish, Houses & Trees Scene 20.00
Nippon, Relish, Roses In Gold Scallops, Footed, 8 1/2 In. 65.00
Nippon, Relish, Water, Trees, & Swan Scene, 7 1/2 X 4 In. 7.00
Nippon, Ring Tree, Satin Finish, Roses And Gold Decoration 29.00
Nippon, Rose Bowl, Pink With White, Gold Decoration, 5 1/2 X 3 In. 35.00
Nippon, Rose Jar, Cover, Gold & Black Floral, Blue Leaf Mark, Ornate 90.00
Nippon, Salad Set, Yellow & Red Flowers, Gold Beading, Spoke Mark, 3 Piece 32.00
Nippon, Salt & Pepper, Arab Leading Camel 14.00
Nippon, Salt & Pepper, Beaded Animals 29.00
Nippon, Salt & Pepper, Blue, Floral & Gilt 12.50
Nippon, Salt & Pepper, Floral & Gold 10.00
Nippon, Salt & Pepper, House & Mountains Scene, Rising Sun Mark 15.00
Nippon, Salt & Pepper, Royal Satsuma, Much Beading, Gold 15.00
Nippon, Salt & Pepper, Scenic, Green Wreath Mark, 3 1/2 In. 21.50
Nippon, Salt & Pepper, Scenic, 4 Sided 12.00
Nippon, Salt & Pepper, Yellow Roses, Gold Tops, Green Wreath Mark 15.00
Nippon, Salt, Blue & Gold Decoration, Tab Handles, Set Of 5 .... 22.00
Nippon, Salt, Cream & Gold, Scalloped, 4 Gold Feet, Green Wreath Mark 7.50
Nippon, Salt, Pepper, & Tray, Windmills & Sunset Scene, Green Mark 67.00
Nippon, Salt, Tub Shape, 2 Handles, Scenic Decoration, Royal Satsuma 6.25
Nippon, Sauce Set, White, Green & Black Decoration, 3 Piece 45.00
Nippon, Server, Cake, Blue Flowers, Pierced Handle, Crown Mark, 9 1/2 In. 16.00
Nippon, Server, Center Handle, White, Ivory Band Of Flowers, 8 In. 22.50
Nippon, Server, Cheese & Cracker, White, Bands Of Pink Flowers, Gold Beading 20.00
Nippon, Server, Pancake, Covered, Gold Design 30.00
Nippon, Server, Pancake, White, Garlands Of Gold Floral 45.00
Nippon, Serving Bowl, Water Scene, Double Pierced Handles, Green Mark, 10 In. 65.00
Nippon, Spittoon, Lady's, Pink And Fuchsia Flowers, Gold, Maple Leaf 85.00

Nippon, Spoon, Rice, Cobalt, Grain Of Rice 28.00
Nippon, Spooner, Floral & Gold, Blue Birds, Green Wreath, Lay Down 37.50
Nippon, Stein, Desert Scene, Camel & Rider, Green, Brown, Rust, & Yellow, 6 In. 100.00
Nippon, Stickpin Holder, Orange & Black, Attached Underplate, Green Wreath 85.00
Nippon, Strainer, Tea, Gold Beading 22.50
Nippon, Strainer, Tea, Violets, Gold, 5 In. 12.50
Nippon, Sugar & Creamer, Blue & White, Royal Sometuke 15.00
Nippon, Sugar & Creamer, Capitol Building, Washington, D.C., Gold Beading 18.00
Nippon, Sugar & Creamer, Cover, Gold & Yellow Floral Border 20.00
Nippon, Sugar & Creamer, Cover, Moriye, Red Flower, White Beading 55.00
Nippon, Sugar & Creamer, Cover, Pink Roses, Gold Trim 20.00
Nippon, Sugar & Creamer, Cover, White, Gold Trim, Rising Sun Mark 15.00
Nippon, Sugar & Creamer, Dark Green, Camels & Floral, Wreath Mark 20.00
Nippon, Sugar & Creamer, Gold Maize, Green Trim 12.50
Nippon, Sugar & Creamer, Gray Matte, Raised Dragon, Beaded & Jeweled 40.00
Nippon, Sugar & Creamer, Jeweled Creamer, Palms, Lake Boats 27.00
Nippon, Sugar & Creamer, Lake, Swan, & House Scene, Blue & Gold Trim 18.00
Nippon, Sugar & Creamer, Ornate, Gold, Blue Enamel, Royal Hinode Mark 145.00
Nippon, Sugar & Creamer, Pink & Blue Floral, Gold Trim, Hexagonal 25.00
Nippon, Sugar & Creamer, Pink Blossoms, Gold Trim, Green M Mark 25.00
Nippon, Sugar & Creamer, Ribbed, Light Blue & White, Pink Floral, Jeweled 20.00
Nippon, Sugar & Creamer, Swans, Scenic 67.50
Nippon, Sugar & Creamer, Violet Medallions, Gold Trim 16.00
Nippon, Sugar, Covered, White, Blue Flowers 6.00
Nippon, Sugar, Creamer, Salt, & Pepper On Tray, Ivory, White, Pink, Red, & Green 55.00
Nippon, Sugar, Cube Holder, Green & White, Gold Floral & Trim, 2 Handles 35.00
Nippon, Sugar, Grapes & Floral, Gold Scrolls & Beads, Pedestal, 7 In. 22.00
Nippon, Sugar, White, Floral Bands, Gold Beading 42.00
Nippon, Sugar, White, Pink Floral, Miniature 15.00
Nippon, Sweetmeat Set, Blue, White Iris, Lacquered Box Holder, Set Of 8 .... 45.00
Nippon, Syrup & Underplate, Pink Floral, Gold Beading 22.00
Nippon, Syrup & Underplate, White & Gold, Green Mark 25.00
Nippon, Syrup & Underplate, Yellow Roses, Butterflies, Gold Handle & Trim 22.50
Nippon, Syrup With Plate, M Wreath Mark 22.00
Nippon, Syrup, Capitol Building, Washington, D.C., Gold Beading 18.00
Nippon, Table Set, Child's, Blown-Out Faces, Rising Sun Mark, 6 Piece 225.00
Nippon, Tankard, Antlered Deer In Forest, Blown Out, 11 In. 375.00
Nippon, Tea Set, Blue Bisque, Swans In Water, 17 Piece 225.00
Nippon, Tea Set, Blue Matte, Garlands Of White Roses, Green Wreath Mark 275.00
Nippon, Tea Set, Child's, Girl & Boy Clowns & Rabbit, Blue & White, 21 Piece 125.00
Nippon, Tea Set, Child's, Pink Floral, 7 Piece 35.00
Nippon, Tea Set, Fancy, Raised Gold, 3 Piece 60.00
Nippon, Tea Set, Gray, Raised Dragons, 11 Piece 125.00
Nippon, Tea Set, Japanese Warlords, Gold Decorated, 9 Piece 75.00
Nippon, Tea Set, Pagoda Scene, Cobalt, 11 Piece 105.00
Nippon, Tea Set, Pale Green, Flying Geese, Gold Trim, Green Jewels, 7 Piece 75.00
Nippon, Tea Set, Pink Roses, Gold Trim, Wreath Mark, 14 Piece 55.00
Nippon, Tea Set, Sailboat Scene, 3 Piece 88.00
Nippon, Tea Set, Scenic Medallions, Footed, Gold, Blue Leaf Mark, 13 Piece 300.00
Nippon, Tea Set, Warlords Scene, Slipware, Gold Trim, 15 Piece 75.00
Nippon, Tea Set, Washington, D.C., Capitol Medallion, Blue Slip, 5 Piece 58.00
Nippon, Tea Set, White, Raised Jeweled Decoration, 11 Piece 160.00
Nippon, Tea Set, Yellow With White Swans On Lake, Service For 6, 18 Pieces 100.00
Nippon, Tea Strainer, Pink, Blue, Gold Trim, Wreath Mark 24.00
Nippon, Tea Strainer, Two Piece, Blue, Purple Flowers, Gold, Hand-Painted 30.00
Nippon, Teacup & Saucer, Gold & Cobalt On White 22.50
Nippon, Teapot, Capitol Building, Washington, D.C., White, Gold Beading 22.00
Nippon, Teapot, Cherry Blossoms, Gold Trim, Blue Rising Sun Mark, 4 In. 18.00
Nippon, Teapot, Dragon, Tail Is Handle, Head Spout, Gray Bisque 50.00
Nippon, Teapot, Individual, Bird & Foliage 35.00
Nippon, Teapot, Mirrored Gold Floral, Red Berries, Green Leaves 30.00
Nippon, Teapot, Royal Satsuma, Much Beading, Gold 70.00
Nippon, Teapot, Thousand Faces, Signed, 8 1/2 X 5 In. 65.00
Nippon, Teapot, White & Cream, Heavy Gold 25.00

Nippon, Teapot, White, Azalea Type Flowers, Arched Gold Handle 40.00
Nippon, Teapot, White, Gold Finial & Handle, Pink Roses, Blue Mark, 9 In. 20.00
Nippon, Tile, Round, Tea, Azalea Type Pattern 15.00
Nippon, Toothpick & Attached Tray, Scenic, Green Wreath Mark 25.00
Nippon, Toothpick & Attached Underplate, White, Gold Trim 20.00
Nippon, Toothpick, Green Dragon, Red Tongue 25.00
Nippon, Toothpick, Heavy Gold Decoration 20.00
Nippon, Toothpick, Rising Sun Mark, 3 Handled, White With Bluebirds 15.00
Nippon, Toothpick, Sailboats & Windmill, Beading, 3 Ball Feet 38.00
Nippon, Toothpick, Scenic, Satin Finish, 3 Handles 39.00
Nippon, Toothpick, Scenic, 2 Handles 18.00
Nippon, Toothpick, White, Gold Trim, 3 Handles, Rising Sun Mark 25.00
Nippon, Toothpick, 3 Handles, Raised Gold, Roses, Signed Ho Nippon 18.00
Nippon, Tray, Beading, Pastel Enamel, Folded Edges, Keyhole Handles, 10 In. 38.00
Nippon, Tray, Bureau, Red Roses, 3/4 In. Gold Band, Beaded, Jeweled 35.00
Nippon, Tray, Card, Beading, Green & Gold, Maple Leaf Mark, 5 1/2 In. 22.00
Nippon, Tray, Desert Scene, 10 1/2 X 7 In. 38.00
Nippon, Tray, Double, Center Handle, Gold Beads, Pink Flowers, 7 3/4 In. 25.00
Nippon, Tray, Gold Vines, Leaves, Flowers, M Mark, 8 1/2 In. 15.00
Nippon, Tray, Greek Key, Stylized Oasis, Camel, Green M Mark, 9 3/4 In. 47.50
Nippon, Tray, Violets, 10 X 7 In. 18.50
Nippon, Tumbler, Hand-Painted, Scenic, Green M In Wreath 12.00
Nippon, Tureen, Gold Finial & Handles, Multicolor Floral, Scrolls, 9 1/2 In. 42.00
Nippon, Tureen, Moriye, Covered, 2 Handles, Floral On Gold, 11 In. 63.00
Nippon, Tureen, Vegetable, Covered, Floral, Gold Handles 11.00
Nippon, Urn, Gold & Ivory Trim, Azalea Type Floral, Handled, 5 In., Pair 58.00
Nippon, Urn, Moriye, 3 Handled, Enamel, Floral Medallions 155.00
Nippon, Vase, Aqua, Orange, Green, & Blues, Gouda Style, Blue Mark, 10 In. 95.00
Nippon, Vase, Arab, Camel, & Desert Scene, Bisque Finish, 3 Handles, 8 1/2 In. 85.00
Nippon, Vase, Autumn Country Scene, Ram's Head Handles, 9 1/4 In. 95.00
Nippon, Vase, Azalea Type Decoration, Gold Trim, Melon Shape, 7 1/2 In. 40.00
Nippon, Vase, Beaded & Jeweled, C.1800, 5 In. 125.00
Nippon, Vase, Black Silhouette Cowboy On Horse, Handles, 8 In. 35.00
Nippon, Vase, Blue & Green, Orange Poppies, Black Leaves, Handled, 8 In. 90.00
Nippon, Vase, Blue Satin, Easter Lilies, Blue Maple Leaf, 3 In.Collar, 8 In. 85.00
Nippon, Vase, Blue Satin, Yellow Daffodils, Black Beading, 6 In. 28.00
Nippon, Vase, Blue, Roses, Gold Top, Wreath Mark, 6 1/2 In. 40.00
Nippon, Vase, Boats, 3 1/2 In. 8.00
Nippon, Vase, Brown To Beige, Purple Irises, Marked Nismeki, 15 In. 45.00
Nippon, Vase, Bud, Moriye, Green, Roses, Gray Beading, 2 Handles, 4 In. 65.00
Nippon, Vase, Camel & Desert Scene, 4 Footed, Green M Mark, 8 1/2 In. 85.00
Nippon, Vase, Camel Scene, 6 Sided, 9 1/4 In. 86.00
Nippon, Vase, Charcoal To Gray, Dragon, Jewel Eyes, Moriaga, 12 In. 75.00
Nippon, Vase, Cobalt With Gold, Medallion And Scene, Blue Maple Leaf 65.00
Nippon, Vase, Cobalt, Gold Floral, 12 In. 85.00
Nippon, Vase, Cobalt, Gold Flowers, 12 In. 95.00
Nippon, Vase, Coralene, Green & Rust, Floral, Handled, Footed, 7 1/2 In. 175.00
Nippon, Vase, Coralene, 2 Handled, Floral On Green, Signed, 10 3/4 In. 145.00
Nippon, Vase, Country Scene, Ram's Head Handles, Enameled Slip, 9 1/4 In. 95.00
Nippon, Vase, Cylinder, Heavy Gold, 10 X 4 1/2 In. 60.00
Nippon, Vase, Dark Brown, Gold Trim, 4 Handles, 9 1/2 In. 45.00
Nippon, Vase, Desert Scene, Blue With Pink, Double Handled, Green Mark, 7 In. 55.00
Nippon, Vase, Dragon In Applied Slip 45.00
Nippon, Vase, Egyptian All Around Scenic, Green M Mark, , 9 1/2 In. 105.00
Nippon, Vase, Egyptian People & Animals, 9 In. 75.00
Nippon, Vase, Floral Banding, 4 Gold Legs, 2 Gold Handles, Tapered, 8 In. 95.00
Nippon, Vase, Floral Tapestry, Jeweled, Double Handles, 12 In. 60.00
Nippon, Vase, Floral, 2 Handles, Imperial Mark, 11 3/4 In. 85.00
Nippon, Vase, Gilded Symmetrical Body, Handled, 8 X 4 In. 36.00
Nippon, Vase, Gold & Brown, White, Lavender, & Blue Mums, Gilt, 9 In. 110.00
Nippon, Vase, Gold Handles, Pink Ground, Blue Flowers, Leaves, Green Mark 38.00
Nippon, Vase, Gold-Outlined Floral, 2-Handled, Jeweled, Superior, 11 1/2 In. 50.00
Nippon, Vase, Gray Blue Matte, Floral, Beaded & Jeweled, Gold Collar, 5 In. 45.00
Nippon, Vase, Green Shading, Moriye Type Poppies, 2 Handles, Blue Mark, 6 In. 55.00

Nippon, Vase, Imperial, Hand-Painted, Indian In Medallion, 11 In. 100.00
Nippon, Vase, Irises, Royal Kinran, 9 1/2 In. 98.00
Nippon, Vase, Lady & Water Scene, Double Handles, Gold Trim, 15 In. 70.00
Nippon, Vase, Lake Scene, Gold Flying Fish Handles, Maple Leaf Mark, 10 In. 195.00
Nippon, Vase, Lake Scene, Green Wreath Mark, 6 In. 32.00
Nippon, Vase, Lake Scene, Roses, Gold Beading, 14 1/2 In. 115.00
Nippon, Vase, Matte Finish, Floral, Gold Trim & Handles, 10 In. 32.00
Nippon, Vase, Moriye, Blue, Yellow, & Orchid, Floral, Handled, Footed, 19 1/2 In. 125.00
Nippon, Vase, Moriye, Dragon, Jewel Eyes, Aqua Slip, 2 Handles, 10 In. 90.00
Nippon, Vase, Moriye, Floral Medallions, 2 Handles, 8 In. 95.00
Nippon, Vase, Moriye, Scrolls & Beading, Turquoise Handles, 5 In. 65.00
Nippon, Vase, Moriye, Violets & Raised Green Slipwork, 6 1/2 In. 75.00
Nippon, Vase, Multicolor Roses, Gold Trim, Bulbous, 5 In. 12.00
Nippon, Vase, Owl On Branch Tapestry Panel, Handled, Royal Nishiki, 13 In. 300.00
Nippon, Vase, Panels Of Red Roses With Green & Gold Leaves, Handled, 3 In. 12.00
Nippon, Vase, Pastel Blue, Floral, Coin Gold Trim, 2 Handles, 10 1/2 In. 65.00
Nippon, Vase, Pastel, Wild Roses, Narrow Neck, 6 1/2 In. 15.00
Nippon, Vase, Peach, Yellow, & Greens, Gold Beading & Handles, 12 In. 95.00
Nippon, Vase, Pink & Blue Floral, Gold Handles, Blue Mark, 6 Sided, 6 In. 13.00
Nippon, Vase, Pink & Yellow Roses, Gold & Beading, 10 In. 60.00
Nippon, Vase, Portrait, Jeweled, 6 In. 135.00
Nippon, Vase, Red, Pansies, 2 Handles, Blue Leaf Mark, 8 In. 78.00
Nippon, Vase, Roses, White Beading, Gold Trim, Superior Mark, 9 In. 55.00
Nippon, Vase, Royal Imperial, Red, White, Black, Fox In Wilderness, 8 In. 49.00
Nippon, Vase, Rust & Green, Gold Floral & Leaf, Cherries, 18 In. 150.00
Nippon, Vase, Sampans On Ocean Sunset Scene, Jeweled, Satin Finish, 8 In. 75.00
Nippon, Vase, Satin Bisque, Hand-Painted Florals, Gold Handle, Green Mark 70.00
Nippon, Vase, Satin Finish, Scenic, Man In Rowboat, 12 1/4 In. 165.00
Nippon, Vase, Scenic, Green, Gold Handles, 4 Claw Feet, Corset Shape, 6 1/2 In. 75.00
Nippon, Vase, Scenic, House 16.50
Nippon, Vase, Stippled Finish, Floral, 2 Handles, 8 In. 175.00
Nippon, Vase, Stippled, Floral, 2 Handles, 8 In. 175.00
Nippon, Vase, Sunflowers, Gold Handles, 12 1/4 In. 95.00
Nippon, Vase, Swan Scene, Gold Decoration, Satin Finish, 8 1/4 In. 95.00
Nippon, Vase, Swan Scene, Handled, Gold Trim, 8 1/4 In. 110.00
Nippon, Vase, Tan, Gold-Outlined Red & White Roses, Gold Handles, 6 In. 65.00
Nippon, Vase, Tapestry, Fruits, 8 In. 395.00
Nippon, Vase, Tapestry, Fruits, 9 In. 325.00
Nippon, Vase, Tapestry, Winter & Spring Scenes, Woman & Child, 9 1/4 In. 95.00
Nippon, Vase, Trees, Lake, & Sunset Scene, Green Wreath Mark, 5 In. 40.00
Nippon, Vase, White To Pastel, Birds & Berries, Beaded, 2 Handles, 6 3/4 In. 135.00
Nippon, Vase, White, Pink Roses, Cobalt Top & Base, 3 Footed, 3 In. 12.00
Nippon, Vase, Windmill 16.50
Nippon, Vase, Yellow & White, Floral, Green Mark, 6 1/2 In. 14.00
Nippon, Vase, Yellow With Brown, White Roses, 11 1/2 In. 30.00
Nippon, Vase, Yellow, Green Trees, Pink Flowers, Gold Handles, 7 In. 25.00
Nippon, Vase, Yellow, Mountain Scenes, Blue Floral, Gold, 2 Handles, 9 In. 95.00
Nippon, Vase, Yellows & Blues, Wild Turkey & 4-Legged Rooster, 5 In. 40.00
Nippon, Wall Pocket, Pink Roses, Gold Beading & Trim, 7 In. 75.00
Nippon, Warmer, Egg, Sprays Of Blue Floral 70.00

Nodders or nodding figures, or pagods, are porcelain figures with heads and hands that are attached to wires. Any slight movement causes the parts to move up and down. They were made in many countries during the eighteenth and nineteenth centuries.

Nodder, Andy Gump, Bisque 45.00
Nodder, Auntie Blossom & Uncle Walt, 3 1/2 In. 38.00
Nodder, Bellboy And Bellgirl, German, 2 3/4 In., Pair 25.00
Nodder, Bisque, Oriental Woman Fanning Herself, Tree Trunk Vase, Marked TT 85.00
Nodder, Bisque, Rachel 45.00
Nodder, Boy Toddler, Bisque, Germany, 3 1/2 In. 55.00
Nodder, Boy With Teddy Bear, 3 In. 110.00
Nodder, Candelabra & Seesaw Holding 2 Brown Monkeys, Bisque, 8 1/4 In. 115.00
Nodder, Cartoon Character, 3 1/2 In., Little Girl In Red Bonnet, Jumper 20.00

Nodder, Chester Gump, Bisque, Germany 50.00
Nodder, Child Holding Porridge Pot, Blue Tam-O'-Shanter, 7 In. 75.00
Nodder, China Chow, German Bisque 40.00
Nodder, Ching Chow, Bisque 40.00
Nodder, Clown In Barrel, Script, I Never Feel Dry, German, Signed 95.00
Nodder, Donkey, Gray & White, Celluloid-Like 4.00
Nodder, Dutch Girl, Incised Germany, Painted, 3 In. 19.00
Nodder, Fat Sailor Holding Fan, Head & Fan Nods, Bisque, 5 3/4 In. 85.00
Nodder, Genie, German 20.00
Nodder, Girl & Boy, 4 In., Pair 95.00
Nodder, Girl In Red Coat, Bisque, Germany, 3 In. 32.00
Nodder, Girl Toddler, Bisque, Germany, 3 1/2 In. 55.00
Nodder, Girl Wearing Bonnet & Green Shawl, Bisque, Germany, 3 In. 35.00
Nodder, Happy Hooligan, 3 1/2 In. 20.00
Nodder, Lady Professor Holding Books & Quill, Blue, White, Staffordshire 49.00
Nodder, Lady, Holding Fan Behind Head, Costumed In Beige, Brown & Gold 125.00
Nodder, Lord Plushbottom, 3 1/2 In. 20.00
Nodder, Male Juggler, Female Drummer, Bisque, Signed Ardalt, Pair 150.00
Nodder, Mr.Bailey The Boss, German Bisque 30.00
Nodder, Mr.Peanut, Planters Peanuts, Made In Japan 9.00
Nodder, Negro Boy Wearing Strawhat On Ashtray, Austria, Metal, 4 In. 15.00
Nodder, Negro Man, Sitting, Hands Up In Air, Bisque, 4 In. 85.00
Nodder, Negro Woman, Sitting, Hands Up In Air, Bisque, 4 In. 85.00
Nodder, Old Lady & Man Sitting In Chair, Pair 92.00
Nodder, Oriental Man, Bisque, 4 In. 65.00
Nodder, Orphan Annie & Sandy, 3 1/2 In. 38.00
Nodder, Rachel, Bisque, Germany 65.00
Nodder, Rachel, Skeezix Strip Character, 4 In. 25.00
Nodder, Salt & Pepper, Fish On Floral Decorated Pedestal, Souvenir 22.00
Nodder, Santa Claus, Bisque, Germany, 3 1/2 In. 75.00
Nodder, Scotch Lass, Kilts & Head Nod, Bisque, 7 1/2 In. 135.00
Nodder, Seated Lady, 6 In. .... *Illus* 165.00
Nodder, Skeezix, German Bisque 30.00
Nodder, Standing Chinese Mandarin In Robes, German Porcelain, 7 In. 90.00
Nodder, Standing Girl Dressed As Clown, German Porcelain, 7 1/4 In. 115.00
Nodder, Woman Holding Book, Blue & White, Staffordshire, 7 In. 65.00

Noritake-marked porcelain was made in Japan after 1904 by Nippon Toki Kaisha.

Noritake, Bonbon, Azalea 20.00
Noritake, Bowl, Azalea, Oval, 10 1/2 In. 19.00
Noritake, Bowl, Azalea, 2 Handles, 10 1/2 In. 20.00
Noritake, Bowl, Black, Gold, & Floral, 2 Extended Inner Gold Handles, 8 In. 17.00
Noritake, Bowl, Blown-Out Chestnuts, Handled, Green M Mark, 8 3/4 In. 75.00
Noritake, Bowl, Covered, Bluebirds, Gold Flowers & Handles, 9 X 5 In. 20.00
Noritake, Bowl, Figural Flower Center, High Luster Blue, Yellow Interior 30.00
Noritake, Bowl, Fruit On Tables & Red Birds, Open Handles, 7 1/2 In. 7.25
Noritake, Bowl, Vegetable, Azalea 19.00
Noritake, Butter, Covered, Azalea 49.00
Noritake, Butter, Covered, Azalea, Liner 50.00
Noritake, Cake Set, Azalea, 7 Piece 38.00
Noritake, Cake Set, Cream Color, Peacocks & Flowers, Red Mark, 7 Piece 35.00
Noritake, Celery Set, Brown, Gold Trim, Green M In Wreath Mark, 7 Piece 25.00
Noritake, Celery, Azalea, 12 1/2 In. 22.00
Noritake, Cereal Bowl, Azalea 8.95
Noritake, Chamberstick, Aqua Stripes, Peach, Black Roses, 3 In. 7.00
Noritake, Child's Set Of Dishes, 24 Piece, Heavy Gold Band 95.00
Noritake, Chocolate Set, Hand Painted, Green Mark, 11 Piece 38.00
Noritake, Coffeepot, Azalea 325.00
Noritake, Condiment Set, Azalea, 4 Piece 25.00
Noritake, Condiment Set, Azalea, 5 Piece 22.00
Noritake, Condiment Set, Azalea, 6 Piece 18.00
Noritake, Cruet, Azalea 115.00
Noritake, Cup & Saucer, Azalea .... 8.00 To 12.00
Noritake, Cup & Saucer, Bouillon, Azalea .... 9.95 To 10.00

Nodder, Seated Lady, 6 In.

Noritake, Cup & Saucer, Demitasse, Apple Blossoms 15.00
Noritake, Cup & Saucer, Floragold, White With Gold Band 8.00
Noritake, Cup & Saucer, Lake, Swan, & House Scene, Cobalt & Gold Trim 6.00
Noritake, Cup & Saucer, White, Blue Scenes, Wreath Mark 9.00
Noritake, Cup & Underplate, Tea 'n Toast, Azalea, Green Mark 22.00
Noritake, Dish, Basket, Phoenix Birds, Pearlized 8.50
Noritake, Dish, 4 Divisions, Azalea, Handles 45.00
Noritake, Eggcup, Azalea 13.50
Noritake, Gravy Boat, Attached Tray & Ladle, Azalea 25.00
Noritake, Gravy Boat, Azalea .... 19.00 To 22.50
Noritake, Hatpin Holder, Forget-Me-Nots 6.00
Noritake, Hatpin Holder, Pink Rose, Blue Band, 5 In. 12.00
Noritake, Humidor, Brown & White Hunting Dog, Forest Scene, Enamel, 6 1/2 In. 70.00
Noritake, Humidor, Orange, Black Silhouettes Of Camels, Pyramids, & Palms 47.50
Noritake, Ice Cream Set, Roses, Gold Trim, Handled Tray, 7 Piece 38.00
Noritake, Jam Set, Azalea, 3 Piece 55.00
Noritake, Jar & Ladle, Jam, White, Purple Floral, Orange Leaves, Blue Edge 12.00
Noritake, Jar, Mustard, Cover, Spoon, Pink Roses & Gold, Green Mark, 3 In. 12.00
Noritake, Jar, Mustard, Hand-Painted Roses 6.00
Noritake, Jar, Tobacco, Gold Floral, Octagonal, 5 1/2 X 4 In. 20.00
Noritake, Jar, Tobacco, Pipe On Top 16.00
Noritake, Jar, Underplate, & Ladle, Jam, Covered, House On Shore Scene 18.00
Noritake, Jug, Milk, Azalea 80.00
Noritake, Luncheon Set, Floral, Orange Borders, 20 Piece 20.00
Noritake, Mayonnaise Set, Azalea 13.00
Noritake, Mayonnaise Set, White With Blue And Gold 18.00
Noritake, Muffineer & Creamer, Azalea 55.00
Noritake, Oatmeat Bowl, Azalea, 5 1/2 In. 8.50
Noritake, Plate, Azalea, 6 1/2 In. 2.95
Noritake, Plate, Azalea, 7 1/2 In. 2.95
Noritake, Plate, Azalea, 8 1/2 In. 7.95
Noritake, Plate, Bread & Butter, Brunswick 1.25
Noritake, Plate, Breakfast, Azalea, 8 1/2 In. 9.00
Noritake, Plate, Cake, Azalea .... 8.50 To 16.50
Noritake, Plate, Cake, Tree In The Meadow 16.00
Noritake, Plate, Child's, Little Jack Horner, 4 In. 7.00
Noritake, Plate, Dinner, Azalea 10.00
Noritake, Plate, Green Wreath, Lake, Swan, 7 1/2 In. 8.00
Noritake, Plate, Lemon, Azalea 10.00
Noritake, Plate, Soup, Azalea .... 8.00 To 9.00
Noritake, Plate, Soup, Azalea, Green Mark, 7 1/2 In. 9.50
Noritake, Platter, Azalea, 12 In. .... 19.00 To 22.00
Noritake, Platter, Azalea, 14 In. 22.50
Noritake, Platter, Bacon, Azalea, 10 In. 59.00
Noritake, Platter, Fleur Gold, No.77631, 13 1/2 In. 25.00
Noritake, Platter, Luster Finish, Flowers, 12 In. 10.00
Noritake, Platter, Modjeska, 12 In. 9.00

Noritake, Platter, Turkey, Azalea, 16 In. 210.00
Noritake, Refreshment Set, Azalea, 2 Piece 18.50
Noritake, Relish, Azalea, Double, Loop Handle 85.00
Noritake, Relish, Azalea, Oblong, 8 1/4 In. 6.95
Noritake, Relish, Azalea, Oval, 8 1/4 In. 8.00
Noritake, Relish, Azalea, Twin Loop 155.00
Noritake, Relish, Azalea, 2 Sections 23.00
Noritake, Relish, Tree In The Meadow, 2 Sections 22.00
Noritake, Ring Tree 22.50
Noritake, Salt & Pepper, Azalea, 3 In. 10.00
Noritake, Salt & Pepper, Modjeska, 3 In. 7.00
Noritake, Sauce, Azalea .... 2.95 To 3.00
Noritake, Sauce, Azalea, 5 1/4 In. 5.00
Noritake, Saucer, Azalea 4.00
Noritake, Soup Bowl, Azalea 8.95
Noritake, Soup Bowl, Modjeska 4.00
Noritake, Spooner, Azalea 39.00
Noritake, Spooner, Scenic, Open Handles, 8 In. 18.00
Noritake, Sugar & Creamer, Azalea 60.00
Noritake, Sugar & Creamer, Oriental Scene, Gold Trim 25.00
Noritake, Sugar & Creamer, Pink Floral, Gold & Pink Designs 15.00
Noritake, Sugar & Creamer, Sheraton 16.00
Noritake, Sugar Shaker, Heavy, Gold, 7 In. 22.00
Noritake, Sugar, Covered, Azalea 8.00
Noritake, Syrup & Underplate, White Roses, Gold Trim 32.50
Noritake, Syrup, Azalea 25.00
Noritake, Tea Set, , 7 Green Wreath, 12 In. Tray, 16 Pieces 97.50
Noritake, Tea Set, Azalea, 15 Piece 88.00
Noritake, Tea Set, Individual 18.00
Noritake, Tea Set, Off-White, Band Of Gold Floral & Leaves, 7 Piece 75.00
Noritake, Teapot, Azalea .... 37.50 To 39.00
Noritake, Teapot, Lake, Swan, & House Scene, Cobalt & Gold Trim 15.00
Noritake, Toothpick, Azalea 39.00
Noritake, Toothpick, 6-Sided, Pedestal 10.00
Noritake, Tray, Pin, Figural, Dog On Edge 8.50
Noritake, Tray, Roll, Azalea 19.00
Noritake, Trivet, Landscape, Jewels, Octagonal, 5 In. 15.00
Noritake, Tub, Butter, Azalea, Insert 22.50
Noritake, Tub, Butter, Azalea, Liner 35.00
Noritake, Tub, Butter, Modjeska, Drain 12.00
Noritake, Vase, Dresdina, 4 Feet, 9 1/2 In., Pair 125.00
Noritake, Vase, Hexagonal, Gold Rim, Sunset Lake Scene, Red 7 Wreath, 8 In. 25.00
Noritake, Vegetable Bowl, Azalea, Oval, 10 1/2 In. 22.00
Noritake, Vegetable Bowl, Covered, Azalea 29.00
Noritake, Vegetable Bowl, Covered, Azalea, Handled, Green Mark, 9 In. 29.50
Noritake, Vegetable Bowl, Covered, Azalea, 8 In. 24.00

The North Dakota School of Mines was established in 1892 at the University of North Dakota.

North Dakota School Of Mines, Ashtray, High-Gloss Amber, 3 In. 25.00

Northwood Glass Company worked in Martins Ferry, Ohio, in the 1880s. They marked some pieces with the letter N in a circle. Many pieces of carnival glass were made by this company.

N

Northwood, see also Carnival Glass; Custard Glass; Goofus Glass; Pressed Glass

Northwood, Berry Set, 7 Pieces, Signed, Clar With Pink And Gold 110.00
Northwood, Bowl, Blue, Opalescent, Alaska, 4 1/2 In., Ruffled 65.00
Northwood, Bowl, Mums, Fluted Rim, 8 1/2 In. 75.00
Northwood, Bowl, Opalescent, Ruffled Goofus, 8 In. 22.00
Northwood, Butter, Gold Rose 88.00
Northwood, Castor, Pickle, Frosted Royal Ivy 165.00
Northwood, Celery, Hobnail, White Opalescent 27.00
Northwood, Chalice, Blue, Leaf 55.00
Northwood, Compote, Blue Stretch, Signed, 9 1/2 X 4 1/2 In. 40.00

Occupied Japan, Toby Mug, Old Woman, Miniature 6.00
Occupied Japan, Toby Mug, Seated Lady & Man, 2 In., Pair 15.00
Occupied Japan, Toothpick, Figural, Pico, 3 In. 3.50
Occupied Japan, Vase, Figural, Nude, 3 In. 15.00
Occupied Japan, Vase, Rose Shape, 4 In. 4.50
Occupied Japan, Vase, Tulip Shape, 4 In. 4.50
Occupied Japan, Wall Pocket, Peacock On Limb & Floral, 8 In., Pair 26.00
Occupied Japan, Windup Celluloid Dog 5.50
Occupied Japan, Windup Celluloid Tumbler Doll 12.00

G. E. OHR,
BILOXI.

Ohr pottery was made by George E.Ohr in Biloxi, Mississippi, between 1883 and 1918. The pieces were made of very thin clay and were twisted, folded and dented into odd, graceful shapes.

Ohr, Bowl, Mottled Brown Glaze, 2 Sides Pushed Down & In, 4 1/2 In. 120.00
Ohr, Bowl, Mottled Orange Glaze, Greens & Browns, Free Form, 3 1/2 In. 135.00
Ohr, Candlestick, Black High Gloss, Gray Drippings, Finger Grip, 4 1/2 In. 275.00
Ohr, Chamberstick, Mottled Gunmetal Glaze, Handled, 4 1/2 In. 95.00
Ohr, Inkwell, Pottery Log Cabin, Impressed Mark, Yellow Glaze 115.00
Ohr, Mug, Brown, Script Signed, 4 1/2 In. 85.00
Ohr, Mug, Green To Brown Glaze At Top, 5 In. 150.00
Ohr, Mug, Puzzle, Rabbit On Handle, Signed 90.00
Ohr, Vase, Brown & Green Matte Glaze, Orange Interior, Pleated, 6 1/2 In. 250.00
Ohr, Vase, Brown High Gloss, Five Indents & Pleats, 4 1/4 In. 175.00
Ohr, Vase, Brown Marbleized Striated Clays, 4 1/2 In. 135.00
Ohr, Vase, Glossy Shaded Maroon To Cranberry, 3 In. 85.00
Ohr, Vase, Pink Volcanic Glaze Brushed With Green, 5 1/4 In. 175.00

Old ivory china was made in Silesia, Germany, at the end of the nineteenth century. It is often marked with a crown and the word Silesia. The pattern numbers appear on the base of each piece.

Old Ivory, Berry Bowl, Brown Magnolias, Gold Border, Silesia, 5 In. 12.75
Old Ivory, Berry Bowl, No.11, Silesia, 9 1/4 In. 95.00
Old Ivory, Berry Bowl, No.16, 5 In. 15.00
Old Ivory, Berry Set, No.16, Silesia, 7 Piece 195.00
Old Ivory, Biscuit Bowl, Covered, No.28, 2 Handles, Silesia 135.00
Old Ivory, Bowl, Berry, Tiny Blue Flowers, Germany 20.00
Old Ivory, Bowl, No.14, Silesia, 9 1/2 X 2 In. 52.00
Old Ivory, Bowl, No.16, Silesia, 9 1/2 X 2 1/2 In. 95.00
Old Ivory, Bowl, No.16, Silesia, 10 X 2 3/4 In. 95.00
Old Ivory, Bowl, No.33, Silesia, 9 1/2 In. 95.00
Old Ivory, Bowl, No.34, 6 In. 24.00
Old Ivory, Bowl, No.84, Silesia, 9 1/2 X 2 3/4 In. 95.00
Old Ivory, Bowl, No.204, Colored Flowers, Silesia, 9 X 2 1/2 In. 52.00
Old Ivory, Cake Set, No.16, Silesia, 7 Piece 195.00
Old Ivory, Cake Set, No.84, 5 Piece 145.00
Old Ivory, Celery, No.16, 11 1/4 X 5 3/4 In. 50.00
Old Ivory, Cereal Bowl, No.16, Silesia, 6 1/4 In. 32.50
Old Ivory, Cereal Bowl, No.84, 6 1/2 In. 15.00
Old Ivory, Chocolate Pot, No.32 .... 175.00
Old Ivory, Chocolate Pot, Thistle 75.00
Old Ivory, Chocolate Pot, Tiny Blue Flowers, Germany 30.00
Old Ivory, Chocolate Set, No.16, Silesia, 13 Piece 495.00
Old Ivory, Cream & Sugar, No.32 .... 60.00
Old Ivory, Creamer 48.00
Old Ivory, Creamer, No.33, Silesia 35.00
Old Ivory, Creamer, No.84, Silesia 52.00
Old Ivory, Cup & Saucer, Chocolate, No.15, Crown Mark, Silesia 35.00
Old Ivory, Cup & Saucer, Coffee, No.16, Round Bottom, Silesia 54.50
Old Ivory, Cup & Saucer, Coffee, No.75 .... 35.00
Old Ivory, Cup & Saucer, Demitasse, Floral & Birds, Syracuse 10.00
Old Ivory, Cup & Saucer, Demitasse, No.16, Silesia 25.00
Old Ivory, Cup & Saucer, Demitasse, No.75, Silesia 25.00
Old Ivory, Cup & Saucer, Grand Dad's, Ivory, Pink & Yellow Roses, Silesia 42.00
Old Ivory, Cup & Saucer, No.75, Silesia 42.50

Old Ivory, Cup & Saucer, No.200, Silesia 54.15
Old Ivory, Cup & Saucer, No.202, Silesia 35.00
Old Ivory, Cup & Saucer, Signed 30.00
Old Ivory, Dish, Relish 17.50
Old Ivory, Dish, Shell Shape, No.16, 6 In. 25.00
Old Ivory, Dish, Soap, No.11 .... 28.50
Old Ivory, Jar, Cracker, No.200 .... 135.00
Old Ivory, Pepper Shaker, No.84, Silesia 28.00
Old Ivory, Pitcher, Milk, No.84, Silesia, 5 In. 55.00
Old Ivory, Plate, Cake, No.16, Open Handles, 10 In. 40.00
Old Ivory, Plate, Cake, No.16, Silesia, 6 1/4 In. 23.75
Old Ivory, Plate, Cake, No.81, 12 In. 40.00
Old Ivory, Plate, Cake, Open Handles, Silesia, 9 1/2 In. 95.00
Old Ivory, Plate, Cake, Pierced Handles 65.00
Old Ivory, Plate, Cake, 2 Berry Dishes 65.00
Old Ivory, Plate, Dinner, No.123, Silesia 35.00
Old Ivory, Plate, Green Crown Mark, Silesia, 8 1/2 In. 32.50
Old Ivory, Plate, Green Roses, Brown Leaves, Gold Trim, Silesia, 6 In. 19.50
Old Ivory, Plate, Luncheon, Border Of Pink & Yellow Roses, Silesia, 7 1/2 In 9.50
Old Ivory, Plate, Luncheon, No.16, Silesia, 7 1/2 In. 35.00
Old Ivory, Plate, No.10, Silesia, 6 In. 15.00
Old Ivory, Plate, No.15, Open Ends, Silesia, 10 In. 65.00
Old Ivory, Plate, No.15, Sileisa, 6 In. 22.50
Old Ivory, Plate, No.16, Silesia, 6 3/4 In. 28.00
Old Ivory, Plate, No.16, Silesia, 7 1/2 In. 22.50
Old Ivory, Plate, No.16, 8 In. 22.00
Old Ivory, Plate, No.28, Silesia, 7 1/2 In. 22.00
Old Ivory, Plate, No.32, 6 1/2 In. 12.00
Old Ivory, Platter, No.10, 13 1/2 X 9 1/2 In. 75.00
Old Ivory, Platter, No.12, Silesia, 11 1/2 X 8 In. 95.00
Old Ivory, Platter, No.16, Silesia, 11 1/4 X 7 3/4 In. 95.00
Old Ivory, Relish, Extended Handle 40.00
Old Ivory, Relish, No.10, Silesia, 8 1/2 X 5 1/2 In. 35.00
Old Ivory, Relish, No.15, Silesia, Flowers, Leaves & Buds, 8 1/2 In. 35.00
Old Ivory, Relish, No.16 .... 35.00
Old Ivory, Relish, No.16, Silesia, 6 1/4 X 5 In. 35.00
Old Ivory, Relish, No.16, 6 3/4 X 4 3/4 In. 15.00
Old Ivory, Relish, No.16, 8 X 5 In. 25.00
Old Ivory, Relish, Thistle, 9 In. 20.00
Old Ivory, Salt & Pepper, No.16 .... 50.00
Old Ivory, Salt Cellar, No.16, Silesia 28.00
Old Ivory, Saltshaker, No.73 .... 18.00
Old Ivory, Sauce, No.11, Silesia, 5 In. 12.50
Old Ivory, Sauce, No.11, Silesia, 5 1/2 In. 13.50
Old Ivory, Sauce, No.16, 5 1/2 In. 20.00
Old Ivory, Sauce, No.32, 5 1/4 In. 15.00
Old Ivory, Saucer, Demitasse, No.16, Silesia 9.00
Old Ivory, Saucer, Demitasse, No.33, Silesia 9.00
Old Ivory, Serving Bowl, No.16, 9 1/2 In. 55.00
Old Ivory, Soup Bowl, No.16, 6 1/2 In. 20.00
Old Ivory, Sugar & Creamer, Cover, No.16, Silesia 95.00
Old Ivory, Sugar & Creamer, No.84, Silesia, Ohme 125.00
Old Ivory, Sugar Shaker, Silesia, Crown Mark, 4 In. 75.00
Old Ivory, Sugar, Covered, No.73, Silesia 48.00
Old Ivory, Teacup & Saucer, No.16, Sileisa 54.50
Old Ivory, Teacup & Saucer, No.22, Holly 38.50
Old Ivory, Toothpick, No.84, Silesia 30.00
Old Ivory, Tray, Bread 65.00
Old Ivory, Tray, No.81, 9 In. 35.00
Old Ivory, Trivet, No.16, Silesia 25.00

Onion, originally named "bulb pattern, " is a white ware decorated with cobalt blue. Although it is commonly associated with Meissen, other companies made the pattern in the latter part of the nineteenth century.

Onion, Coffeepot, Meissen 95.00
Onion, Dish, Butter, With Insert, Blue, Furnival 50.00
Onion, Dish, Cheese, Meissen, Germany 65.00
Onion, Invalid Feeder, Meissen Type, Incised Germany 18.00
Onion, Plate, Blue, Lattice Edge, Meissen, 6 In. 15.00
Onion, Platter, Blue, Meissen, Crossed Sword, 24 X 11 In. 125.00
Onion, Relish Set, Meissen, Saxony Mark, 7 Piece 70.00
Onion, Saucer, Blue, Johnson 8.00
Onion, Spooner, Blue, Marked Germany 25.00
Onion, Sugar & Creamer, Meissen 80.00

Opalescent glass is translucent glass that has the bluish-white tones of the opal gemstone. It is often found in pressed glassware made in Victorian times. Some dealers use the terms opaline and opalescent for any of the bluish-white translucent wares.

Opalescent Glass, Rose Bowl, Beaded Drapes, 4 X 4 1/2 In. 39.00
Opalescent, Basket, Blue, Applied Squared Handles, 4 Clear Petal Feet, 5 In. 50.00
Opalescent, Basket, Blue, Crimped Edging, Pressed Exterior, 5 1/2 In. 45.00
Opalescent, Basket, Blue, Pressed, Fan Shape, 5 1/2 In. 42.00
Opalescent, Basket, Green, Twisted Handle, Base Marked Pat.March 18, 1902 .... 25.00
Opalescent, Berry Set, Ribbed Spiral, Seven Piece 175.00
Opalescent, Bottle, Barber, Coin Spot, Sprinkle Top 50.00
Opalescent, Bottle, Cologne, White, Hobnail, C.1940, Pair 16.00
Opalescent, Bowl, Blue, Cashews, 9 In. 28.00
Opalescent, Bowl, Blue, Fluted, 9 In. 25.00
Opalescent, Bowl, Blue, Footed Flat, Pearl Flowers 50.00
Opalescent, Bowl, Blue, Tokyo, 8 1/2 In. 50.00
Opalescent, Bowl, Cranberry To White, Fluted, 10 In. 25.00
Opalescent, Bowl, Crystal, 3 Ruffles, Scroll Feet, 7 In. 25.00
Opalescent, Bowl, Fluted, Vintage Blue, 8 In. 24.00
Opalescent, Bowl, Footed, Green, Meander, 9 In. 32.00
Opalescent, Bowl, Hobnail, 8 Sided, 3 X 7 In. 40.00
Opalescent, Bowl, Jolly Bear, White 50.00
Opalescent, Bowl, Triangular, Spokes & Wheels, 8 X 2 In. 25.00
Opalescent, Bowl, White, Pearl Flower 27.50
Opalescent, Butter, Covered, Blue & White, Chrysanthemum Base Swirl, Satin 125.00
Opalescent, Candlestick, Cornucopia, Blue, Hobnail, 3 1/2 In., Pair 25.00
Opalescent, Compote, Blue, Button Panels 25.00
Opalescent, Compote, Blue, Ruffled, Argonaut Shell, 8 1/2 In. .... 25.00 To 65.00
Opalescent, Creamer, Alaska 40.00
Opalescent, Creamer, Blue, Jeweled Heart 55.00
Opalescent, Creamer, Green Flute Scrolls 12.00
Opalescent, Cruet, Blue, Miniature 50.00
Opalescent, Cruet, White, Gold Daisies 75.00
Opalescent, Cup & Saucer, Miniature 37.50
Opalescent, Cup Plate, Lacy, 3 5/8 In. 52.50
Opalescent, Dish, Blue, Argonaut Shell 22.50
Opalescent, Dish, Butter, Covered, Blue, Crown Jewels, 4 3/4 In. 69.00
Opalescent, Dish, Candy, Blue, Jewel & Fan, 7 In. 22.00
Opalescent, Dish, Candy, Heart Shape 3.75
Opalescent, Dish, Drapery-Covered Butter, White 65.00
Opalescent, Dish, Hen Cover, 5 1/2 In. 25.00
Opalescent, Dish, Hobnail, Blue, Handled, 5 In. 15.00
Opalescent, Dresser Set, 2 Bottle, Covered Jar, Hobnail, Blue 50.00
Opalescent, Epergne, Blue, Hobnail, 3 Removable Lilies, Ruffled Bowl, 9 In. 65.00
Opalescent, Epergne, Cranberry Fluted Edges, Silver Base, 14 3/4 In. 195.00
Opalescent, Epergne, Green, Fluted Bowl, 3 Lilies, C.1890, 23 1/2 In. 295.00
Opalescent, Epergne, Green, 1 Lily 68.00
Opalescent, Hat, Blue, 3 In. 18.00
Opalescent, Jar, Cracker, Pansies & Violets, Silver Veil, Signed H.A.Hall 120.00
Opalescent, Jar, White, Pewter Top, Raised Diamonds, Beaded Edge, 2 1/4 In. 50.00
Opalescent, Muffineer, Blown Twist 45.00
Opalescent, Mug, Applied Handle, Enamel Flora & Remember Me, 4 1/2 In. 37.50
Opalescent, Mug, Blue, Lacy, 2 3/8 In. 50.00

Opalescent, Mug, Brass Nailhead, White, Miniature, 1 1/2 In. 15.00
Opalescent, Mug, Friendship, Fiery, Remember Me In Gold Floral Medallion 38.00
Opalescent, Mug, Lavender, Swans With Bulrushes, 2 1/2 In. 45.00
Opalescent, Nappy, Blue 20.00
Opalescent, Nappy, Seaspray Blue, Handled, Triangular 28.50
Opalescent, Pitcher & 4 Tumblers, Coinspot 90.00
Opalescent, Pitcher & 6 Tumblers, Blue, Poinsettia 325.00
Opalescent, Pitcher, Blue Ribbon Stripe, Applied Handle 165.00
Opalescent, Pitcher, Blue, Coin Spot, Ruffled Top 100.00
Opalescent, Pitcher, Blue, Spanish Lace 145.00
Opalescent, Pitcher, Blue, Spanish Lace, Applied Clear Handle, 10 In. 150.00
Opalescent, Pitcher, Blue, Swirl 100.00
Opalescent, Pitcher, Pink, Hobnail, Fluted Rim, Clear Notch Handle 75.00
Opalescent, Pitcher, Water, Daisy & Fern, Vaseline Satinized, Ruffled Top 95.00
Opalescent, Pitcher, White Ribbed Lattice, 4 3/4 In. 36.00
Opalescent, Pitcher, White, Flora, Gold Trim 85.00
Opalescent, Pitcher, Wide Stripe, Fluted, Ruffled Edge, 8 1/2 In. 98.00
Opalescent, Plaque, Wall, Art Deco Lady's Head, Signed Verre Artistique 185.00
Opalescent, Plate, Blue, Iris Meander 45.00
Opalescent, Rose Bowl, Blue, Button Panels 25.00
Opalescent, Rose Bowl, Spanish Lace 20.00
Opalescent, Rose Bowl, White, Reverse Swirl 25.00
Opalescent, Rose Bowl, White, Shell & Wild Rose, Footed 30.00
Opalescent, Salt & Pepper, Alaska, Blue, Enamel, Pair 79.00
Opalescent, Salt, Blue, French 6.00
Opalescent, Salt, Eagles, Lacy, 3 1/8 In. 250.00
Opalescent, Sauce, Plume, 5 In. 72.50
Opalescent, Saucer, Blue, Intaglio 28.00
Opalescent, Spittoon, Lady's, Canary, Inverted Fan & Feather 45.00
Opalescent, Spooner, Blue, Fluted Scrolls 30.00
Opalescent, Spooner, Blue, Jewel And Flower 78.00
Opalescent, Spooner, Vertical Bars With Diamond Point, Scalloped Rim, 5 In. 70.00
Opalescent, Sugar & Creamer, Blue, Beatty's Rib 125.00
Opalescent, Sugar & Creamer, Blue, Petal Feet, 3 In. 60.00
Opalescent, Sugar & Creamer, Blue, Pressed Designed, Petal Feet 40.00
Opalescent, Sugar Shaker, Chrysanthemum Base, Cranberry, Satin Finish 100.00
Opalescent, Sugar, Blue, Jeweled Heart, Covered 110.00
Opalescent, Syrup, Block, Pewter Lid, Applied Handle, Crimped Base, 6 In. 130.00
Opalescent, Syrup, Reverse Swirl 25.00 To 75.00
Opalescent, Tie Back, Sandwich Glass, Blue, Pewter Shanks, Floral, 3 In., Pair 55.00
Opalescent, Toothpick, Blue, Hat, Hobnail 12.00
Opalescent, Toothpick, Green, Ruffled Top 15.00
Opalescent, Tumbler, Blue, Inverted Fan & Feather, Gold Trim 55.00
Opalescent, Tumbler, Blue, Ribbed, 4 1/2 In. 34.00
Opalescent, Tumbler, Blue, S Repeat 30.00
Opalescent, Tumbler, Green, Jefferson Drape 15.00
Opalescent, Tumbler, Lemonade, Blue Striped, Cobalt Handles 28.50
Opalescent, Tumbler, Northwood, Jewel & Flower 35.00
Opalescent, Tumbler, Polychrome Enamel Design, 4 In. 75.00
Opalescent, Vase, Blue, Ribbon Pattern 85.00
Opalescent, Vase, Blue, Ruffled Around Top, Crisscross Swirl 9 In. 40.00
Opalescent, Vase, Blue, Scalloped, 6 In. 25.00
Opalescent, Vase, Blue, Turned-Down Rim, 6 In., Pair 70.00
Opalescent, Vase, Jack-In-The-Pulpit, Green To Cranberry 27.00
Opalescent, Vase, Lavender, Jack-In-The-Pulpit, Squat 35.00
Opalescent, Vase, Spattered Blue, Ruffled Top, Pair, 11 In. 37.50
Opalescent, Vase, Striped, 11 In. 30.00
Opalescent, Vase, White & Clear, Squirrel, Acorns, & Leaves, Pedestal, 7 In. 42.00

Opaline glass, or opal glass, was made in white, apple green, and other colors. The glass had a matte surface and a lack of transparency. It was often gilded or painted. It was a popular mid-nineteenth-century European glassware.

Opaline, Bottle, Barber, White, Bay Rum 10.00
Opaline, Bottle, Barber, White, Toilet Water 10.00

Opaline, Bottle, Barber, White, Witch Hazel 10.00
Opaline, Bowl, Green, Dewdrop & Star, Ruffled, Draped, 8 In. 28.00
Opaline, Bowl, Green, 1 1/2 X 10 In. 45.00
Opaline, Box, Trinket, Hand-Painted Cherubs, Enamel & Gold, Hinged 75.00
Opaline, Dish, Candy, Gold Metal Frame, Marked Germany, 4 In. 22.00
Opaline, Dish, Cheese, French, Powder Blue, Jewels & Gilt, Scalloped 140.00
Opaline, Goblet, Light Blue, 7 In. 18.00
Opaline, Mug, Pink, Overlay, Enamel Butterfly & Floral, Black Handle 45.00
Opaline, Tazza, Shading, 5 X 5 In. 75.00
Opaline, Tumbler, Turquoise, Jeweled Heart 28.00
Opaline, Vase, English, C.1860, White, Portrait Of A Lady, Bulbous, 12 In. 85.00
Opaline, Vase, French, C.1840, Sea Green, Porcelain Insert Of Girl, 12 In. 80.00
Opaline, Vase, Jack-In-The-Pulpit, Cased, Green Inside, 9 In. 45.00
Opaline, Vase, Mauve, Thick, 6 1/2 In., Pair 125.00
Opera Glasses, Audemair, Paris, C.1900 .... 5.00
Opera Glasses, French, Ivory, Folding 15.00
Opera Glasses, Le Maire, Paris, Engraved Carrie B.Sheafer, Gold & Pearl 32.00
Opera Glasses, Le Maire, Paris, Mother-Of-Pearl 15.00
Opera Glasses, Loevre, Paris, Mother-Of-Pearl 15.00
Opera Glasses, Mother-Of-Pearl, Presentation Case Dated 1892 .... 35.00
Opera Glasses, Paris, Mother-Of-Pearl, Case Engraved Kitty Brady 45.00
Opera Glasses, Pearl And Gold Plated, Leather Case 30.00
Opera Glasses, Pearl, Chavance & Co., Paris 75.00
Organ, see Music, Organ
Ormolu, Sconce, Louis XVI, 3 Reeded Branches, 3 Light, Pair, 30 In. 650.00
Orphan Annie, Badge, Decoder, 1937 .... 10.00
Orphan Annie, Badge, Decoder, 1938 .... 10.00
Orphan Annie, Bank, Dime Register, Annie & Sandy, 1936, Tin 37.00
Orphan Annie, Book, Big Town Gunmen, 1937, Hard Cover 22.00
Orphan Annie, Book, Code, 1936 .... 8.25
Orphan Annie, Book, Coloring, 1933 .... 8.25 To 10.00
Orphan Annie, Book, Comic, Puffed Wheat 4.50
Orphan Annie, Book, Little Orphan Annie & Chizzler, Big Little Book 10.00
Orphan Annie, Book, Little Orphan Annie & The Bigtown Gunmen, 1937 .... 20.00
Orphan Annie, Book, Little Orphan Annie, Cuples & Leon, 1929-33, 9 Volumes 95.00
Orphan Annie, Book, Orphan Annie & Gila Monster Gang, Whitman, 1934 .... 7.50
Orphan Annie, Book, Secret Society Manual, 1935 .... 28.50
Orphan Annie, Decoder, 1935 .... 10.00
Orphan Annie, Decoder, 1936 .... 18.00
Orphan Annie, Decoder, 1937, Brass 18.00
Orphan Annie, Decoder, 1939 .... 20.00
Orphan Annie, Decoder, 1940 .... 20.00
Orphan Annie, Doll, Cardboard, 1944 .... 6.00
Orphan Annie, Doll, Composition, Marked Famous Artist 75.00
Orphan Annie, Figurine, Wooden 20.00
Orphan Annie, Manual, 1940 .... 25.00
Orphan Annie, Mug, Beetleware .... 12.00 To 14.00
Orphan Annie, Mug, Ovaltine, Annie & Sandy, 3 In. 30.00
Orphan Annie, Mug, Signed Harold Gray, Porcelain 30.00
Orphan Annie, Paper Doll, Jr.Commandos, 1943, Uncut 45.00
Orphan Annie, Pin, Silver Star, Original Card 12.00
Orphan Annie, Stove, Red, Tin, C.1930 .... 22.00
Orphan Annie, Stove, Toy Electric, Picture Of Annie & Sandy 22.50
Orphan Annie, Toy, Circus, Cardboard 45.00
Orphan Annie, Watch, Wrist, New Haven 140.00

Orrefors Glassworks, located in the Swedish Province of Smaaland, was established in 1916.

Orrefors, Bowl, Etched Birds, 6 X 3 In., Signed 46.00
Orrefors, Vase, Crystal, Intaglio Cut Satyr & Lady, Signed Or, 11 1/2 In. 295.00
Orrefors, Vase, Etched Sea Nymph Among Grass & Water, 6 1/2 In. 325.00
Orrefors, Vase, Fish, 4 In. 225.00
Orrefors, Vase, Intaglio-Cut Satyr & Dancing Nymph In Forest, 12 1/2 In. 750.00
Orrefors, Vase, Intaglio-Cut Satyr & Lady In Forest, Signed OR, 11 1/2 In. 295.00

Ott & Brewer Company operated the Etruria Pottery at Trenton, New Jersey, from 1863 to 1893. It was under the direction of William Bromley, Sr., from the Belleek factory at Belleek, Ireland, from 1883.

Ott & Brewer, Bowl, Egg Shape, Gold Trim, 5 In. 68.00
Ott & Brewer, Cup & Saucer, Belleek, Pink Nacreous Lining 110.00
Ott & Brewer, Cup & Saucer, Belleek, Tridacna, Gold Rim 50.00
Ott & Brewer, Cup & Saucer, Ribbed Basketweave, Orchid Interior 45.00
Ott & Brewer, Pitcher, Belleek, Tapioca Type, Gold Trim, 4 1/2 In. 225.00
Ott & Brewer, Plate, Bread, Graniteware, Turned-Down Edge, C.1863, 12 In. 60.00
Ott & Brewer, Washstand Set, White & Gold, Helmet Pitchers, 6 Piece 285.00

OWENS UTOPIAN

Owens Pottery was made in Zanesville, Ohio, from 1891 to 1928. The first art pottery was made after 1896. Utopian Ware, Cyrano, Navarre, Feroza, and Henri Deux were made. Pieces were usually marked with a form of the name Owens. About 1907 the firm began to make tile and gave up the art pottery wares.

Owens, Barber Bottle, Opalescent, Flower, Signed, 7 In. 235.00
Owens, Candlestick, Utopian, Brown To Rust, Leaves & Berries, 7 In. 46.00
Owens, Jardiniere, Cyrano 125.00
Owens, Jardiniere, Woman's Head, Brown Ground, Henri Deux, 6 1/2 In. 325.00
Owens, Jug, Cherries And Leaves 70.00
Owens, Jug, Left Handed, Standard Glaze, Cherries On Leaves 70.00
Owens, Mug, Utopian, High Glaze, Berries & Leaves, 4 1/2 In. 50.00
Owens, Tankard, Brown Glaze, 12 1/4 In. 145.00
Owens, Vase, Alpine, Bulbous, Slender Neck, Roses On Gray, Artist Signed 100.00
Owens, Vase, Brown Glaze, Floral, 7 In. 55.00
Owens, Vase, Double Neck, Matte Green, Owensart, 6 1/2 In. 135.00
Owens, Vase, Gourd Shape, Brown Luster Florals, Signed R.S.12 1/2 In. 195.00
Owens, Vase, High Glaze, Red & Green Leaf & Berries, 12 1/2 In. 80.00
Owens, Vase, Long Neck, Wide Green Leaf, Orange Flower, 13 In. 110.00
Owens, Vase, Matte Green, 8 1/2 X 3 1/2 In. 55.00
Owens, Vase, Opalescent, Utopian, White & Green Coralene On Gold Ground 350.00
Owens, Vase, Rose On Light To Dark Brown Ground, 6 1/2 In. 110.00
Owens, Vase, Utopian, Floral, Pinched Neck, V.A., 7 1/2 In. 135.00
Owens, Vase, Utopian, Matte Glaze, Raised Flower, Gourd Shape, 12 1/2 In. 140.00
Owens, Vase, Utopian, Orange Tulips, Artist Signed, Frank Ferrel 395.00
Owens, Vase, Utopian, Pillow, Blackberries & Leaves, M.T., 6 X 4 In. 70.00
Owens, Vase, Utopian, Swirl, Dark To Light Brown, Orange Floral, Signed Bell 80.00
Owens, Wall Pocket, Acorn Shape, 8 In. 45.00
Painting, Diorama, American Sailing Ship, Carved, Painted, 28 X 15 1/2 In. 325.00
Painting, Enamel On Copper, Scenic, J.J.Carmona, Limoges, 4 3/4 X 4 In. 49.00
Painting, Fraktur, Otto, 1875, Hand Colored 825.00
Painting, Fraktur, 1790, Birth, Baptismal & Wedding Records, Eagle 975.00
Painting, Fraktur, 1834, Wedding Record 575.00
Painting, Miniature, Boy Wearing Blue Jacket, American School, C.1820, 2 In. 175.00
Painting, Miniature, Gentleman, American School, C.1780, 2 3/8 In. 90.00
Painting, Miniature, Gentleman, Black Jacket, American School, C.1815, 2 In. 150.00
Painting, Miniature, Lady & Gentleman, American School, C.1815, 3 In., Pair 275.00
Painting, Miniature, Marcia Catherine Van De Vinder, American, C.1815, 4 In. 100.00
Painting, Miniature, On Ivory, Early-19th-Century American Man, Lock 125.00
Painting, Miniature, On Ivory, French, Early-19th-Century Woman 75.00
Painting, Miniature, Portrait, Lady Wearing Lace Cap, American, C.1810, 2 In. 175.00
Painting, Miniature, Young Gentleman, Robert Field School, 2 3/4 In. 175.00
Painting, Miniature, Young Lady, American School, C.1800, 2 7/8 In. 90.00
Painting, Miniature, Young Lady, Black Dress, American School, C.1820, 4 In. 260.00
Painting, Miniature, Young Man, American School, C.1795, 2 3/8 In. 50.00
Painting, Oil On Canvas, Allegorical Queen Holding Horn Of Plenty, 13 In. 65.00
Painting, Oil On Canvas, Custer's Last Stand, Framed, 42 1/2 X 29 1/2 In. 300.00
Painting, Oil On Porcelain, 17th-Century Boyar, Russian, C.1720, 8 1/2 In. 980.00
Painting, Oil, Portrait, Gentleman, 29 X 24 In. 510.00
Painting, On China, Platter, Gainsborough's Blue Boy, 12 1/2 X 16 In. 80.00
Painting, On Ivory, French Lady, Sterling Frame, Miniature 45.00
Painting, On Ivory, Hunters From Middle East, 4 3/4 X 4 In. 70.00
Painting, On Ivory, Marie Ferranda, Blond Woman, Plumed Hat, 2 1/2 X 3 In. 150.00

Painting, On Ivory, Mozart, 2 X 1 3/4 In. 35.00
Painting, On Ivory, Portrait, Woman, C.1800, Gold Oval Frame, 4 1/4 In. 95.00
Painting, On Ivory, Queen Louise, 2 X 1 3/4 In. 35.00
Painting, On Ivory, Reclining Nude Women & Cupid, Signed, Square Frame 100.00
Painting, On Ivory, Royal Family, Louis XVI, Signed Daisy 125.00
Painting, On Ivory, Royal Family, Marie Antoinette, Signed Daisy 125.00
Painting, On Ivory, Woman, Late 17th Century, Framed 160.00
Painting, On Ivory, Young Lady, C.1820, Signed N.Sheley, French, Frame 132.00
Painting, On Porcelain, Cavalier, Artist Signed, Paragon China, Pair 250.00
Painting, On Porcelain, Contessa Claudia Potocki, 1802-36, Miniature 275.00
Painting, On Porcelain, Crown Of Thorns, Brass Frame, 3 1/2 In. 125.00
Painting, On Porcelain, German, Baby With Apple, Early 20th Century, 3 In. 225.00
Painting, On Porcelain, Girl On Beach, 3 X 2 1/2 In., Gold Frame 100.00
Painting, On Porcelain, Gypsy Girl, Signed, 4 X 5 In. 250.00
Painting, On Porcelain, Lady & Gentleman, Oval, Marked KPM, 12 1/2 In. 295.00
Painting, On Porcelain, Lady, Signed Wagner, KPM, 5 X 7 In., Framed 825.00
Painting, On Porcelain, Little French Girl, Signed Charles Field Haviland 140.00
Painting, On Porcelain, Mademoiselle Lebrun, Florentine Frame, Sontag 375.00
Painting, On Porcelain, Madonna & Child, Hand-Carved Frame, C.1890, 11 In. 135.00
Painting, On Porcelain, Madonna Of The Chair, Wooden Frame, 18 In. 18.00
Painting, On Porcelain, Queen Louise, Gold Frame, Signed No.24 60.00
Painting, On Porcelain, Ruth With Sheaf Of Wheat, Framed, 13 In. 380.00
Painting, On Porcelain, Woman On Wooded Hill, Art Nouveau, 9 1/2 X 7 In. 340.00
Painting, On Porcelain, Young Lady, Drop Earrings, Oval Frame, 2 5/8 In. 95.00
Painting, On Silk, Lady Under Tree, Chinese, Framed, 12 X 10 In. 45.00
Painting, On Silk, Watercolor & Ink, Waterfall, Signed, Dated 1887 25.00
Painting, On Velvet, Pocahontas, Art Deco Frame, 34 X 24 In. 50.00
Painting, On Velvet, Theorem, Blue Comport Of Fruits, C.1850, 18 1/2 In. 1200.00
Painting, On Velvet, Theorem, Blue Vase Of Flowers, 28 1/2 In. 300.00
Painting, On Velvet, Theorem, Fruit-Filled Basket & Butterfly, 17 1/2 In. 275.00
Painting, On Velvet, Theorem, Women Picking Pears, C.1850, 20 In. 275.00
Painting, On Wood Panel, Atlanta Exposition, 1895, Men & Monk Playing Cards 225.00
Painting, Reverse On Glass, Castle, Landscape 20.00
Painting, Reverse On Glass, City Of Friedrichshafen, Framed, 12 X 10 1/4 In. 68.00
Painting, Reverse On Glass, Landscape With Figures, Framed, 3 In. 35.00
Painting, Reverse On Glass, Lighthouse & Sailboat, Gold Frame, 28 X 16 In. 65.00
Painting, Reverse On Glass, Oriental Scene, Mother-Of-Pearl, 10 X 7 3/4 In. 88.00
Painting, Reverse On Glass, President McKinley Cutting Ribbon, 1897, Framed 250.00
Painting, Reverse On Glass, River Scene, Mother-Of-Pearl 28.00
Painting, Reverse On Glass, St.Louis World's Fair, Framed, 11 3/4 X 10 In. 20.00
Painting, Reverse On Glass, Statue Of Liberty & City, Framed, Oval, 24 In. 65.00

Pairpoint Corporation was a silver and glass firm founded in New Bedford, Massachusetts, in 1880.

Pairpoint, Bottle, Perfume, Cathedral Stopper 27.00
Pairpoint, Bottle, Perfume, Paperweight 30.00
Pairpoint, Bowl, Amethyst, Folded Edges, 12 In. 85.00
Pairpoint, Bowl, Flared Wheel Cut, Pedestal, Bubbles In Knop, 6 3/4 In. 45.00
Pairpoint, Box, Amber Base, Black Amethyst Cover, 6 3/4 In. 75.00
Pairpoint, Box, Candy, Covered, Buckingham Pattern, 7 1/2 In. 145.00
Pairpoint, Box, Cigar, Green 135.00
Pairpoint, Box, Dresser, Covered, Rose Blossoms, Blue Dots, Shiny, 6 In. 190.00
Pairpoint, Bucket, Cut Diamonds, Frosted Band, Silver Plate Fittings 55.00
Pairpoint, Candlestick, Boy On Dolphin 85.00
Pairpoint, Candlestick, Honey Amber, Clear Bubble Connector, 12 In. 45.00
Pairpoint, Castor, Pickle, Egg-Shaped Cranberry Inverted Thumbprint, Holder 295.00
Pairpoint, Centerpiece, Canaria Green Cut Dish, Silver-Plate Holder, Signed 145.00
Pairpoint, Cigar Holder, Engraved, Bubble Ball Stem 49.00
Pairpoint, Compote, Ball Finial, Carmine, Bubble Ball Stem, 10 X 6 In. 98.00
Pairpoint, Compote, Covered, 9 1/2 In. 40.00
Pairpoint, Compote, Emerald Green, Paperweight Base 85.00
Pairpoint, Compote, Etched Fernery & Leaves, Blue Glass Threading, 7 In. 100.00
Pairpoint, Compote, Flambo, Black Foot, Clear Bubble Ball 295.00
Pairpoint, Console Set, Green, 13 In.Bowl, 12 In.Candlesticks 325.00
Pairpoint, Dish, Pudding, Silver Basket, Handles, Signed, 6 1/2 In. 70.00

Pairpoint, Figurine, Bryden, Swan, Peachblow, 7 1/4 X 6 1/2 In. 50.00
Pairpoint, Figurine, Swan, Peachblow, Bryden, 7 1/4 In. 45.00
Pairpoint, Goblet, Amethyst, Vintage 35.00
Pairpoint, Grape Juice Bowl, Cut Pattern, Sterling Rim, 8 1/2 In. 175.00
Pairpoint, Inkwell, Controlled Bubbles, Sterling Collar, Round, 4 X 3 In. 32.00
Pairpoint, Jar, Cracker, Shiny Green, Grape & Leaves, Gold, Shell Feet 175.00
Pairpoint, Jar, Cracker, Shiny White, Pink Roses, Gold, Silver Plate Fittings 165.00
Pairpoint, Jar, Cracker, Yellow, Enamel Apple Blossoms, Silver Fittings 195.00
Pairpoint, Lamp Base, Tree Trunk, Signed, 5 1/2 In. 65.00
Pairpoint, Lamp Base, Tree Trunk, 6 1/2 In. 34.00
Pairpoint, Lamp, Banquet, Blue Delft Globe, Brass & Marble, 29 In. 250.00
Pairpoint, Lamp, Blown-Out Red Floral, Wooden Base, 5 1/2 In. 395.00
Pairpoint, Lamp, Butterflies & Roses, Puffy, 10 In. 875.00
Pairpoint, Lamp, Coralene Flower Design, Signed, 13 In. 350.00
Pairpoint, Lamp, Exeter Shade, Painted Fall Scene, Windmill, Signed Fisher 950.00
Pairpoint, Lamp, Flower Garland, 6-Sided, 8 In. Shade, Urn Base 395.00
Pairpoint, Lamp, Helmet-Shape Shade, Signed Fisher, Pine Tree Scene, 24 In. 875.00
Pairpoint, Lamp, Hummingbirds & Roses, White Ground, Puffy, Signed, 16 In. 2950.00
Pairpoint, Lamp, Mountains & Trees On Shade, Signed Mahogany Base, 14 In. 675.00
Pairpoint, Lamp, Plymouth Shade, Reverse Painted Tulip Design, Closed Top 975.00
Pairpoint, Lamp, Puffed Flowers On Silver Base, Signed, 9 In. 875.00
Pairpoint, Lamp, Puffy Roses, Art Nouveau Base, Signed, 14 In. 2850.00
Pairpoint, Lamp, Puffy, Blown-Out Flowers, Signed S & B, 16 In. 2500.00
Pairpoint, Lamp, Puffy, Iris On Matching Base, Signed, 14 In. 2250.00
Pairpoint, Lamp, Puffy, Lilac, Green On Aqua *Illus* 4750.00
Pairpoint, Lamp, Puffy, Puffed Pansies, Wood Stand, Not Electrified 275.00
Pairpoint, Lamp, Puffy, 8 Papillon Shade, Flowers, Butterflies, Signed S & B 850.00
Pairpoint, Lamp, Reverse Painted, Blue, Butterflies, Silver Base, 10 In. 550.00
Pairpoint, Lamp, Reverse Painted, Figures In Landscape, Urn Base, 20 In. 950.00
Pairpoint, Lamp, Reverse Painting, Forest, Tepee, & Lake Scene, 20 In. 275.00
Pairpoint, Lamp, Reverse Painting, Mahogany Base, 16 In. 795.00
Pairpoint, Lamp, Roses & Butterflies, Wooden Candle Base, Miniature, Pair 750.00
Pairpoint, Lamp, Scenic, Cape Cod Sand Dunes, Signed Shade & Base, 18 In. 1450.00
Pairpoint, Lamp, Scenic, Old Boston Harbor, Candelabra Base, Signed, 16 In. 1900.00
Pairpoint, Lamp, Snow Scene, Sunset Colors 600.00
Pairpoint, Lamp, Table, Green & Red, Blown Out Flowers, Unsigned 500.00
Pairpoint, Napkin Ring, Figural, Bird In Flight, Silver Plate 57.00
Pairpoint, Paperweight, Cobalt & White Swirls, Bubbles, 3 In. 45.00
Pairpoint, Paperweight, Green Bubbly Ball, Snake Coiled Around 85.00
Pairpoint, Plate, Luncheon, Vines & Floral, Band Of Diamond Cuttings 15.50
Pairpoint, Salt & Pepper, Delft, Lay-Down Eggs, Blue Decoration 195.00
Pairpoint, Salt & Pepper, Eggs, Holly Decoration 135.00
Pairpoint, Salt & Pepper, Satin, Tulip 85.00

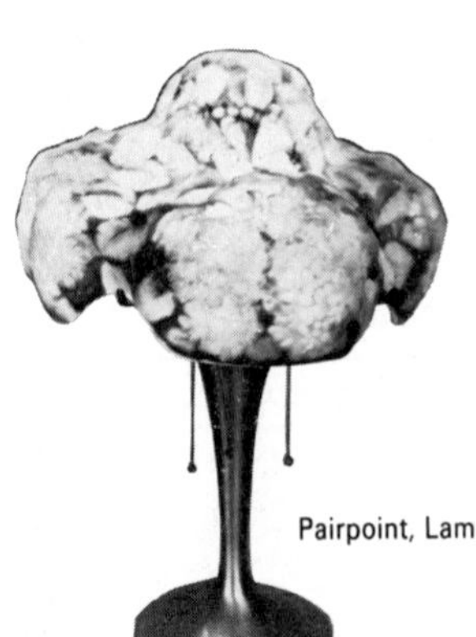

Pairpoint, Lamp, Puffy, Lilac, Green On Aqua

Pairpoint, Salt, Egg, Shiny With Enamel Decoration 27.00
Pairpoint, Shade, Reverse Painted, Jonquils, 18 In. 350.00
Pairpoint, Shade, Silver Base, Dogwood Border, Signed S & B, 8 In. 875.00
Pairpoint, Syrup, Figural, Lady's Head Thumb Rest And Handle, Resilvered 95.00
Pairpoint, Tazza, Intaglio Cutting, Daisy & Wheel, Amber Rim & Foot, 6 In. 68.00
Pairpoint, Tazza, Intaglio Daisy & Fan, Clear With Amber Rim & Knob, 8 In. 75.00
Pairpoint, Tazza, Intaglio Daisy, Fan, & Wheel, Amber Rim, 8 In. 75.00
Pairpoint, Tea Caddy, Delft, 3 1/2 In., Boat Scene And House, Trees 80.00
Pairpoint, Vase, Amethyst, Crystal Paperweight Base, 10 In. 165.00
Pairpoint, Vase, Amethyst, Scalloped Rim, Air Bubble Knob, 12 In. 70.00
Pairpoint, Vase, Bud, Paperweight Bubble Base, 7 5/8 In., Unsigned 15.00
Pairpoint, Vase, Delft, Melon Ribbed, Miniature 165.00
Pairpoint, Vase, Diamond & Thumprint, Knob Stem, 12 X 6 1/2 In. 185.00
Pairpoint, Vase, Gold-Plated Holder, Pink, Yellow Roses, Signed, 9 3/4 In. 160.00
Pairpoint, Vase, Jack-In-The-Pulpit, Cranberry, Cobalt, & White, 9 1/2 In. 60.00
Pairpoint, Vase, Ruby, Horn Of Plenty, Paperweight Base, 10 In., Pair 135.00
Pairpoint, Vase, Urn Shape, Bubble Base, Red Crystal 95.00
Pairpoint, Wine, Engraved Vintage, Bell-Shaped Bowl, 4 1/2 In. 15.50
Pairpoint, Wine, Flambo, Opaque Black Stem, C.1920, 5 In. 90.00
Paper Doll, Dolly Dingle's Little Friend Tottie, 1926 .... 15.00

Paper, Book, see also Dick Tracy, Book; Disneyana, Book; Lone Ranger, Book; Orphan Annie, Book; Store, Book; Gene Autry, Book; Kate Greenaway, Book; Kewpie, Book; Sunbonnet Babies, Book; World's Fair, Book

Paper, Almanac, Ayer's American, 1916 .... 2.25
Paper, Almanac, Ayer's, 1877 .... 5.00
Paper, Almanac, Delaware, Tercentenary, 1938 .... 4.00
Paper, Almanac, Farmer's, 1799 .... 20.00
Paper, Almanac, Lum & Abner's, 1936 .... 5.00
Paper, Almanac, Mutual Baseball, 1955 .... 8.50
Paper, Almanac, The World Almanac, 1893 .... 10.00
Paper, Almanac, Warner's, 1884 .... 5.00
Paper, Book, Alice In Wonderland, Paramount, 1934, Big Little Book 4.00
Paper, Book, Baby's Record, Maud Humphrey, 1898, 11 X 9 In. 135.00
Paper, Book, Bringing Up Father, 1931 .... 15.00
Paper, Book, Captain Easy, Soldier Of Fortune, Big Little Book 9.00
Paper, Book, Charles Dana Gibson, Everyday People, 1904 .... 14.00
Paper, Book, Charles Dana Gibson, Social Ladder, 1904 .... 14.00
Paper, Book, Clyde Beatty Lions & Tigers, Big Little Book 5.50
Paper, Book, David Copperfield, W.C.Fields On Cover, Big Little Book 15.00
Paper, Book, Dirigible-ZR90, 1941, Big Little Book 4.00
Paper, Book, Flash Gordon & The Red Sword Invaders, Big Little Book 20.00
Paper, Book, Flash Gordon In The Water World Of Mongo, Big Little Book 20.00
Paper, Book, Flip, Jean Harlow 6.00
Paper, Book, G-Man, Big Little Book 8.00
Paper, Book, Grimm's Fairy Tales, 2nd German Edition 2000.00
Paper, Book, Katharine Hepburn, Little Women, Big Little Book 4.50
Paper, Book, Little Women, RKO, 1934, Big Little Book 4.00
Paper, Book, Mac Of The Marines In Africa, Big Little Book 6.00
Paper, Book, Mandrake The Magician, Big Little Book 10.00
Paper, Book, My Life & Times, Big Little Book, 1936 .... 12.00
Paper, Book, Reg'lar Fellers, Gene Burnes, 1933, Big Little Book 4.00
Paper, Book, Sir Lancelot, Big Little Book 4.50
Paper, Book, Tailspin Tommy, Dirigible, North Pole, 1934, Big Little Book 4.00
Paper, Book, Ten Little Nigger Girls, E.P.Dutton, C.1905, 12 Pages 45.00
Paper, Book, Tom Beatty, Ace Of The Service, 1939, Big Little Book 4.00
Paper, Book, Tom Swift & His Giant Telescope, Big Little Book 15.00
Paper, Book, War Ration 1.00
Paper, Book, West Pointers On Gridiron, Big Little Book 4.50
Paper, Calendar, Maud Humphrey, 1905, 6 Prints 110.00
Paper, Catalogue, A Hirsch & Co., Jewelry, 1898, 256 Pages 48.00
Paper, Catalogue, Indian Motorcycle, 1918, 25 Pages 25.00
Paper, Catalogue, Ward Spring And Summer, 1929 .... 12.00
Paper, Catalogue, Will Thompson, East Liverpool, Musical Instrument, 1900 .... 35.00

Paper, Colored Comic Sheet, April 27, 1924 .... 20.00
Paper, Doll, Baby McCall Goes For A Ride, 1926, Book 8.00
Paper, Doll, Baby Sparkle Plenty 4.00
Paper, Doll, Baby, C.1930, Clothes 12.00
Paper, Doll, Betsy McCall .... .75
Paper, Doll, Betty Bonnet's New Year's Callers, 1918 .... 8.00
Paper, Doll, Bradley Tru-Life, Uncut, Patent 1919, 6 Dolls, Boxed 40.00
Paper, Doll, Cream Of Wheat Cook, Uncut 65.00
Paper, Doll, Dolly Dimple, Pictorial Review, 1927-32 .... 5.00
Paper, Doll, Dolly Dingle, World Flight In Sweden, Grace Drayton, 1933 .... 3.00
Paper, Doll, Dolly Dingle's Friend Sunny, 1926 .... 15.00
Paper, Doll, Dolly Dingle's Little Friend Tottie, 1926 .... 15.00
Paper, Doll, Elizabeth Taylor 15.00
Paper, Doll, Eloise, N.Y. Plaza 5.50
Paper, Doll, Fashion Book Of The Round About Dolls, McLoughlin, 1936 .... 14.00
Paper, Doll, Jill & Brother, McCalls, 1921, Uncut 7.00
Paper, Doll, Jolly Jane, 1923, Five Costumes 7.00
Paper, Doll, Katzenjammer Kids, Cardboard, 1944 .... 6.00
Paper, Doll, Kitty-Cutie, Uncut 8.00
Paper, Doll, Letty Lane, Clothes, Cut 5.00
Paper, Doll, Lucille Ball 25.00
Paper, Doll, Magic Mary Jane, Milton Bradley, 1962, Outfits 5.00
Paper, Doll, Negro, Remco, 1969, 41-Piece Wardrobe, 9 1/2 In. 2.50
Paper, Doll, Our Gang, Dated 1931, Uncut, 8 Dolls, 78 Outfits 45.00
Paper, Doll, Peter And Polly Perkins, Pictorial Review, 1927-32 .... 5.00
Paper, Doll, Pin-Up Girl, Saalfield, Uncut 12.00
Paper, Doll, Presidents' Wives, Maybelle Mercer, Book, Saalfield, 1937 .... 17.50
Paper, Doll, Princess Elizabeth, Coronation, Uncut 22.00
Paper, Doll, Quaker Crackle Girl, 1930, Uncut 60.00
Paper, Doll, Rabbit Family, McCalls, 1920 .... 7.00
Paper, Doll, Raggedy Ann, Uncut 17.00
Paper, Doll, Sonja Henie, 1931, Clothes, Cut 8.00
Paper, Doll, Sparkle Plenty, 10 1/2 In., Pair 5.00
Paper, Doll, Teddy Bear, C.1912, 5 Outfits 35.00
Paper, Doll, Tricia Nixon, Uncut 10.00
Paper, Doll, Wacs & Waves, 1942, Uncut Book 15.00
Paper, Doll, Winsome Winnie, Tuck, 1894 .... 40.00
Paper, Magazine, Playboy, Vol.1, No.6 .... 35.00
Paper, Magazine, Saturday Evening Post, Kennedy Memorial, Dec., 14, 1963 .... 6.50
Paper, Map, Ohio Railway, 1907 .... 22.00
Paper, Program, Gone With The Wind, Color 15.00
Paper, Scrapbook, Elbert Hubbard, 1923, 228 Pages 15.00
Paper, Silhouette, Regency Period, Signed J.Neville 125.00

Paperweight, see also Baccarat, Paperweight; Gillinder, Paperweight; Masonic, Paperweight; Political Campaign, Paperweight; Rookwood, Paperweight; Shirley Temple, Paperweight; Store, Paperweight

Paperweight, American Insurance Group, N.J., 1846-1946, Bronze 9.00
Paperweight, American Insurance Group, Newark, N.J., 1846-1946, Bronze 10.00
Paperweight, Anaconda, American Brass Co., Arrowhead On Base, Copper 9.00
Paperweight, B.H.Biscuits, Mouse Eating Biscuit Shape, Iron 13.75
Paperweight, Banford, Bumblebee Over White Flower & Buds, Blue Ground, 2 In. 175.00
Paperweight, Banford, Coiled Goldstone Snake, Blue Ground, 3 1/2 In. 95.00
Paperweight, Banford, Dragonfly Over 5-Petaled Pink Flower On Cobalt, 2 In. 145.00
Paperweight, Banford, Lavender Flower On White Trellis, Blue Ground 240.00
Paperweight, Banford, Red Rose On Green Vine, Cobalt Carpet, 1 3/4 In. 65.00
Paperweight, Banford, Red Rose, Cobalt Ground, Green Leaves, Signed, 1 3/4 In. 70.00
Paperweight, Banford, Stripped Snake Over Gray Pebbled, Goldstone 80.00
Paperweight, Barker, Crystal With Poinsettia, Signed & Faceted, 2 1/4 In. 110.00
Paperweight, Battleship, Maine, Sunk In Havana, 1898, 4 1/2 In. 10.00
Paperweight, Bear In Snow, Brown Pottery Base 9.50
Paperweight, Beveled Cut Glass, Insert For Cards, 4 Pen Traywells, 6 In. 25.00
Paperweight, Bird, Millefiori, Canes, Camphor Eye & Beak 55.00
Paperweight, Bird, Pewterlike Base, 4 In. 6.00

Paperweight, Bronze, Desk, Flying Horse, B.A.A. Clubhouse, Boston, 1902 .... 25.00
Paperweight, Bull's-Eye, Glass 2.00
Paperweight, Bust Of Dewey, Frosted 50.00
Paperweight, Cast-Iron Horseshoe & Horse's Head, Nails Hold Pens, 5 In. 7.50
Paperweight, Centennial, 1776-1876, Memorial Hall, Frosted 325.00
Paperweight, Centennial, 1876, Frosted Lion, Pressed Glass 115.00
Paperweight, Chevrolet Motor Co., 1932 .... 32.50
Paperweight, Chicago World's Fair, Sky Ride 17.00
Paperweight, Chinese, Rooster 10.00
Paperweight, Chinese, Scrambled Canes, 2 In. 22.50
Paperweight, Choko, Striped Salamander, Plants, Signed 155.00
Paperweight, Clichy, C.1846, 21 Canes, Roses On White Lace, 2 7/8 In. 600.00
Paperweight, Clichy, White Star & Rose & Green Millefiori Floral, 1851 .... 625.00
Paperweight, Clix Blades 7.50
Paperweight, Columbian Exposition, 1893, Fisheries Building 17.00
Paperweight, Cottage In Snow 8.00
Paperweight, Crystal, Intaglio Cut, Frosted Profile Of M. Fillmore, 1850 .... 225.00
Paperweight, Cut Glass, Strawberry & Blossom, 3 In. 39.50
Paperweight, D'Albret, Audubon, James John, Sulfide 68.00
Paperweight, D'Albret, Columbus, Christopher, Sulfide 100.00
Paperweight, D'Albret, DaVinci, Leonardo, Overlay 215.00
Paperweight, D'Albret, DaVinci, Leonardo, Sulfide 99.00
Paperweight, D'Albret, Hemingway, Ernest, Overlay 215.00
Paperweight, D'Albret, Hemingway, Ernest, Sulfide 87.00
Paperweight, D'Albret, Jones, John Paul, Overlay 170.00
Paperweight, D'Albret, Jones, John Paul, Sulfide 68.00
Paperweight, D'Albret, Kennedy, Jacqueline, Overlay 175.00
Paperweight, D'Albret, Kennedy, Jacqueline, Sulfide 68.00
Paperweight, D'Albret, Kennedy, John F., Overlay 175.00
Paperweight, D'Albret, Kennedy, John F., Sulfide 90.00
Paperweight, D'Albret, King Of Sweden, Sulfide 90.00
Paperweight, D'Albret, Lind, Jenny, Overlay 170.00
Paperweight, D'Albret, Lind, Jenny, Sulfide 68.00
Paperweight, D'Albret, Lindbergh, Charles, Sulfide 70.00
Paperweight, D'Albret, MacArthur, Douglas, Overlay 224.00
Paperweight, D'Albret, MacArthur, Douglas, Sulfide 90.00
Paperweight, D'Albret, Prince Charles, Overlay 225.00
Paperweight, D'Albret, Revere, Paul, Overlay 225.00
Paperweight, D'Albret, Revere, Paul, Sulfide 83.00
Paperweight, D'Albret, Roosevelt, Franklin D., Overlay 240.00
Paperweight, D'Albret, Roosevelt, Franklin D., Sulfide 100.00
Paperweight, D'Albret, Schweitzer, Albert, Overlay 224.00
Paperweight, D'Albret, Schweitzer, Albert, Sulfide 87.00
Paperweight, D'Albret, Twain, Mark, Sulfide .... 80.00 To 90.00
Paperweight, Denver University, Alabaster 3.50
Paperweight, Dewey Statuette, Frosted, Manilla 1898, P.S., 5 In. 60.00
Paperweight, Dog, Anta, Pressed Glass, 1874, 7 In. 32.00
Paperweight, Dog, Iron 15.00
Paperweight, Doorstop, Nailsea, Silvery Petal Teardrops, 4 In. 95.00
Paperweight, Dover Sadiron, 3 X 1 1/4 In. 10.00
Paperweight, Eads Bridge, Miss. River, St.Louis, Mo. 15.00
Paperweight, Elephant Figural, Iron, Independent Stove Co. 20.00
Paperweight, Elephant's Head, Hand-Carved Monkey Pod Wood 10.00
Paperweight, Employer's Reinsurance Corporation, 1914-1964 .... 12.50
Paperweight, Figural, Lion, LePere, Zanesville, O. 20.00
Paperweight, Five Clear-Cut Circles, 3 1/2 In. 65.00
Paperweight, Fort Dearborn World's Fair, Pot Metal 12.00
Paperweight, Fountain, Multicolored, Pontil, 1 3/4 In. 15.00
Paperweight, Franklin Fire Insurance Co., Phila., 1919, Bronze 15.00
Paperweight, French, C.1846, Millefiori, Multicolored, 1 3/4 In. 400.00
Paperweight, French, 1846, Millefiori, Multicolored, 2 7/8 In. 800.00
Paperweight, French, 1848, Millefiori, 4 Silhouettes, Multicolored, 2 1/2 In. 800.00
Paperweight, French, 1848, Millefiori, 5 Silhouettes, Multicolored, 2 1/2 In. 450.00
Paperweight, Frog, Green Glass 8.00

Paperweight, Greentown, Buffalo, Nile Green 300.00
Paperweight, Hammon, Pink Rose, 4 Green Leaves, Pedestal, 3 In. 60.00
Paperweight, Hand Blown, Millefiori, Cobalt And White, 2 1/2 In. 35.00
Paperweight, Indian Engraving Co., South Bend, Ind., Winged Indian, Metal 5.00
Paperweight, Indian In Snow, Round Glass Globe On Black Glass Base 22.00
Paperweight, Ivory, Carved Hand Clasping Ball, 4 1/8 In. 60.00
Paperweight, James & Sons, Importers, Crockery & Glass, Kansas City 15.00
Paperweight, James D. Mason Co.'s 5-O'clock Tea Biscuit, Glass 12.00

Kaziun glass has been made by Charles Kaziun since 1942. His paperweights have been gaining fame steadily. Most of his glass and all of the paperweights are signed with a K designed cane worked into the design. He makes buttons, earrings, perfume bottles, and paperweights.

Paperweight, Kaziun, Blue & White Pansy On White, Domed, 2 1/2 In. 485.00
Paperweight, Kaziun, Pink Lily On Turquoise & Goldstone, Pedestal, 2 In. 185.00
Paperweight, Kaziun, Red Lily On Jasper, Gold, Pedestal, 2 In. 190.00
Paperweight, Kossuth, Sulfide, 1851 .... 330.00
Paperweight, Lion, Milk Glass 10.00
Paperweight, Main St., Fox Lake, Ill. 12.00
Paperweight, Metal Hand, Life Lines 12.50
Paperweight, Missouri State Life Insurance Building, 1915, Glass 7.50
Paperweight, Monkey, Iron, 3 1/2 In. 19.75
Paperweight, National Lead Co., Figural, Dutch Boy 17.00
Paperweight, New England Glass Co., Millefiori, Latticinio Base, 1860 .... 875.00
Paperweight, New York Bell Telephone 48.00
Paperweight, Obear Nester Glass Co., Amber, Bottle Shape 30.00
Paperweight, Open Petal Rose, Green Leaves, Pedestal, 4 3/4 In. 65.00
Paperweight, Orange Crush, 1924, Glass, 4 1/2 In. 14.00
Paperweight, Pan-Am Exposition, 1901, Buffalo, N.Y., Round 30.00
Paperweight, Pear, Shaded Red & Green, Glass 25.00
Paperweight, Pears Soap, Glass, Rectangular 6.50
Paperweight, Pefection Stoves 10.00
Paperweight, Perfect-O-Lite, Peerless Air Brakes & Hose 10.00
Paperweight, Perthshire, Carpet Of Millefiore Canes On Amethyst, 1973 .... 99.00
Paperweight, Perthshire, Millefiori Canes On Amethyst, 1973 .... 99.00
Paperweight, Pittsburgh Glass Co., Octagonal 30.00
Paperweight, Planters Peanuts, 1938, Glass, 4 1/2 In. 14.00
Paperweight, Plymouth Rock, Base Inscription, 3 1/4 In. 37.00
Paperweight, Polar Bear, Snow 14.00
Paperweight, Quality CP Milk Cans 12.00
Paperweight, Reef Of Norman's Woe, Gloucester, Ma., Glass, Rectangular, 4 In. 6.95
Paperweight, Reindeer In Snow 8.00
Paperweight, Scrambled Candy, Sandwich Attribution, 2 1/2 In. 85.00
Paperweight, Sherwin Williams Paint Co. 10.00
Paperweight, Sinclair Dinosaur, Metal 6.50
Paperweight, Skier In Snow 8.00
Paperweight, Smith Brothers, Cough-Drop Shape, Cast Iron, Black 35.00
Paperweight, Sno-Globe, White Chicken 5.25
Paperweight, Snow, Bisque Clown On Pig 18.50
Paperweight, Snowman, Inside Glass 14.00
Paperweight, Souvenir, Soule College, New Orleans, Pat.Dated 1903, Tin Inset 12.00
Paperweight, St.Augustine, Florida, Fort Marion 8.50
Paperweight, St.Louis, Blue Dahlia, Faceted, 1970 .... 150.00
Paperweight, St.Louis, Churchill, Winston, Pinchbeck, Gold Finish 250.00
Paperweight, St.Louis, Churchill, Winston, Pinchbeck, Silver Finish 250.00
Paperweight, St.Louis, George Washington On Horseback, Overlay 450.00
Paperweight, St.Louis, George Washington On Horseback, Red & White, Overlay 450.00
Paperweight, St.Louis, George Washington On Horseback, 13 White Stars 310.00
Paperweight, St.Louis, Hawaiian Millefiori, 1975, Signed 175.00
Paperweight, St.Louis, King Of France Sulfide, 1967, Signed 199.00
Paperweight, St.Louis, Mushroom, Overlay, 1970 .... 225.00
Paperweight, St.Louis, Red Flower & Bud, Green Leaves, Faceted, 1970 .... 150.00
Paperweight, St.Louis, Washington On Horseback, Faceted 310.00
Paperweight, Steuben, Black Ribbon, Air Bubbles, 5 1/4 In. 350.00
Paperweight, Steuben, Pineapple, White Spiral Threading, 7 In. 165.00

Paperweight, Tiffany, Abalone, Dore 145.00
Paperweight, Tiffany, Art Deco Tower With 1919 Winged Mercury Dime 125.00
Paperweight, Tiffany, Fox 165.00
Paperweight, Tiffany, Grapevine Design, Signed And Numbered 85.00
Paperweight, Tiffany, Green, Pine Needle 115.00
Paperweight, Tiffany, Owl 125.00
Paperweight, Tokyo Bay, Sept., 1945, Embossed Ship & Anchor, Brass 15.50
Paperweight, Totem Pole Park, Calif., Glass Dome 8.00
Paperweight, Tulsa Court Jester Party, Bartlesville, Oklahoma, 1963 .... 8.50
Paperweight, Turtle, Cast Iron 3.50
Paperweight, Union Glass, Sommerville, Spattered Butterfly, Dated 1881, 3 In. 55.00
Paperweight, Val St. Lambert, Frosted Running Squirrel, Signed, 2 1/2 In. 95.00
Paperweight, Vassar Locks, Brass Raised Graduate, Iron, 2 1/2 In. 10.00
Paperweight, Victorian High School Building, Meridan Conn. 5.00
Paperweight, Western Electric 10.00
Paperweight, Wheeling, Virginia, Dated 1857, Transfers, Flowers, 3 3/8 In. 195.00
Paperweight, White Porcelain Hand On Cushion, Blue, Gold, 4 3/4 X 2 1/2 In. 27.50
Paperweight, Whitefriars, Blue Star, Concentric Rings, Sulfide 85.00
Paperweight, Whittemore, Blue Rose On Green Leaves, Pedestal, 2 1/2 In. 145.00
Paperweight, Whittemore, Butterfly & Flowers, 1972, Dome 350.00
Paperweight, Whittemore, Christmas Stocking, 1972, Dome 350.00
Paperweight, Whittemore, Hummingbird, Dome 350.00
Paperweight, Whittemore, Nosegay On White, Pedestal, 2 3/4 In. 199.00
Paperweight, Whittemore, Pink Rose, Pedestal 165.00
Paperweight, Whittemore, State Flower, Yellow Jasmine, South Carolina 350.00
Paperweight, Whittemore, Tilted White Rose On Green Leaves, Pedestal 165.00
Paperweight, Winchester Repeating Arms Co., 1910, Glass 39.00
Paperweight, Winchester, 1910, Glass, 4 1/2 In. 14.00
Paperweight, World's Fair, Ferris Wheel 10.00
Paperweight, World's Smallest Church, Festina, Ia. 12.00
Paperweight, Wyandotte Cement, Indian With Drawn Bow 12.50
Paperweight, Ysart, Bouquet, Goldstone Ribbon, Canes, Cobalt Ground 190.00
Paperweight, Ysart, Green & Red Aventurine Fish, Pebbled Sand, 3 In. 250.00
Paperweight, Ysart, Pastry Canes On Cobalt, 2 1/2 In. 100.00
Paperweight, Zimmerman, Three Lilies On Pebbled Orange, Magnum, 7 Lbs. 35.00

Papier-mache is a decorative form made from paper mixed with glue, chalk, and other ingredients, then molded and baked. It becomes very hard and can be decorated. Boxes, trays, and furniture were made of papier-mache. Some of the early-nineteenth-century pieces were decorated with mother-of-pearl.

Papier-Mache, Box, Hinged, Curved Bottom, 1 X 3 1/2 X 2 In. 14.00
Papier-Mache, Box, Hinged, Silver Inlay Top, 2 X 3 1/2 X 1 In. 14.00
Papier-Mache, Box, Pencil, Hinged Cover Scenic, 2 1/2 X 9 X 1 1/2 In. 20.00
Papier-Mache, Box, Snuff, People In Sled, Horses, Russia Mark, 3 5/8 In. 95.00
Papier-Mache, Case, Card, Black, Mother-Of-Pearl Inlay, Polychrome, Hinged 35.00
Papier-Mache, Cigar Store Indian, Chief On Wooden Platform, 40 In. 375.00
Papier-Mache, Decoy, Owl 15.00
Papier-Mache, Figurine, Cat, Sitting, Glass Eyes, Cream Color, 5 In. 25.00
Papier-Mache, Figurine, Santa Claus, 10 1/2 In. 10.00
Papier-Mache, Inkwell, Double, Inlaid Pearl, 1875 .... 79.00
Papier-Mache, Inkwell, Mother-Of-Pearl Inlay, Bottles, Stamp Holder On Lid 110.00
Papier-Mache, Plaque, Evening Winter Scene, Dated 1880, 5 1/2 In. 17.50
Papier-Mache, Snuffbox, Mother-Of-Pearl Border On Lid, 3 X 1 1/2 In. 22.00
Papier-Mache, Snuffbox, Spanish Lady, Round, 2 3/4 In. 30.00
Papier-Mache, Tea Caddy, Russian, Horses Pulling Sled With People, C 1890 .... 165.00
Papier-Mache, Tray, Handled, 12 X 10 X 1 1/2 In. 128.00
Papier-Mache, Watch Stand, Brass Feet, Gilded Decoration, 4 X 7 In. 48.00

Parian is a fine-grained, hard-paste porcelain named for the marble it resembles. It was first made in England in 1846 and gained in favor in the United States about 1860. Figures, tea sets, vases, and other items were made of Parian at many English and American factories.

Parian, Box, Powder, Round, Covered, Molded Floral, Gilt Finial, 4 In. 16.00
Parian, Box, Trinket, Oval, Embossed Colonial Figures 25.00
Parian, Bust, Beatrice, White, J.& T.B., 8 In. 85.00

Parian, Bust, Crestware, Queen Mary, Glazed Base, 5 In. 28.00
Parian, Bust, Garfield, 17 In. 160.00
Parian, Bust, Gentleman, Robinson & Leadbetter, J.A.Acton, 1878 48.00
Parian, Bust, Goethe, White, 6 In. 45.00
Parian, Bust, Laughing Boy, White, 4.& T.B., 6 1/2 In. 65.00
Parian, Bust, Mozart, Impressed Herco, 6 X 3 In. 25.00
Parian, Bust, President Garfield, 18 In. 150.00
Parian, Bust, Prince Albert, Robinson & Leadbetter, 1897, 7 1/2 In. 75.00
Parian, Bust, Shakespeare, Impressed H & L, 4 1/2 In. 35.00
Parian, Bust, Sir Walter Scott, Marked Germany, 6 In. 30.00
Parian, Bust, Thomas Sampson, Spanish American War Hero, 5 1/4 In. 30.00
Parian, Bust, Thorwaldsen, Danish Sculptor, White, 9 3/4 In. 55.00
Parian, Bust, William Penn, 8 In. 75.00
Parian, Dish, Pin, Heart Shape, Ball Finials, 4 In. 15.00
Parian, Figural, Anne Hathaway's Cottage, Marked Goss, 3 1/4 In. 12.00
Parian, Figurine, Boy And Girl, Mandolin, Early English Dress 90.00
Parian, Figurine, Crestware, Arms Of Burns, Scotsman Seated, 5 In. 32.00
Parian, Figurine, Crestware, Crest Of Ayr Castle, Man Drinking, 5 In. 22.00
Parian, Figurine, Red Riding Hood & Wolf, Sitting, 7 1/2 In. 68.00
Parian, Figurine, Seated Boy With Dog 47.50
Parian, Figurine, Young Girl Holding 2 Rabbits, Victorian, 9 In. 55.00
Parian, Matchbox, Bennington Type 15.00
Parian, Pitcher, Blue & White, Children Climbing Trees In Relief, C 1850 80.00
Parian, Pitcher, Delphinium & Canterbury Bells 25.00
Parian, Pitcher, Embossed Corn With Foliage, Ear-Of-Corn Handle, 11 In. 175.00
Parian, Pitcher, Melon Ribbed, Shell Design, Glazed, Twig Handle 30.00.To 38.00
Parian, Pitcher, Raised Bluebells, Porcelain Lined, Marked Harebell 135.00
Parian, Plate, Green Ground, White Leaves & Flowers, Meyers, C.1840, Pair 50.00
Parian, Shoe, Crestware, Cambridge Crest, Rufflied Top, 4 In. 22.00
Parian, Syrup, Spinning Wheel 55.00
Parian, Vase, Blue, White Relief Grapes & Vines, 2 Handles, 9 1/2 In. 55.00
Parian, Vase, White, Squirrel On Each Side, C.1870, 5 1/4 In. 19.50
Paris, Basket, Flat, Cobalt & Gold 65.00
Paris, Bowl, Pink & White, Gilt & Floral, Cherub Ormolu Stand, 25 In. 300.00
Paris, Box, Cherub & Urn On Lid, Pink & Ivory, Ormolu Mounted, Oval, 9 In. 300.00
Paris, Coffee Set, Gold Patina, 3 Piece 50.00
Paris, Figurine, Hummingbird On Stump, 5 In. 95.00
Paris, Plate, Cake, Floral Border, 9 X 6 X 3 In. 25.00
Paris, Plate, Gilt Ornaments, Medaille D'or, 1867, 4 3/8 In. 8.50
Paris, Pot De Creme Set, White With Gold, Pillivuyt, 6 Covered On Tray 35.00
Paris, Tea Set, Floral, Gilt Trim, 8 Piece 365.00
Paris, Vase, Portrait, Victorian Woman, Rigaree, Signed ECH, 11 In. 75.00

Pate de verre is an ancient technique in which glass is made by blending and refining powdered glass of different colors into molds. The process was revived by French glassmakers, especially Galle, around the end of the nineteenth century.

Pate De Verre, Atomizer, Turquoise, Brown Pinecones, Signed A.Walter 650.00
Pate De Verre, Compote, Berries & Green Leaf, Signed A.Walter & Berge 650.00
Pate De Verre, Coupe, Pedestal Base, Purple Grapes, Signed G.Argy-Rousseau 325.00
Pate De Verre, Figurine, Buddha, A.Walter, Green 450.00
Pate De Verre, Figurine, Buddha, A.Walter, Green, 4 In. 495.00
Pate De Verre, Figurine, Duck, A.Walter, Berge, Sitting, Blue & Green, 5 In. 950.00
Pate De Verre, Figurine, Sitting Duck, Signed A.Walter, Berge, 5 In. 695.00
Pate De Verre, Holder, Pen & Ink, Orange To Yellow, Raised, A.Walter 475.00
Pate De Verre, Inkwell, A.Walter, Locust Lid, Cobalt Well, 3 1/4 In. 675.00
Pate De Verre, Lamp, G.Argy-Rousseau, Signed, Lavender, Classic Scene 1125.00
Pate De Verre, Pendant, Pansy Decoration, Signed A.Walter, Nancy, 2 In. 185.00
Pate De Verre, Pendant, Pine Cones, Signed G.Argy-Rousseau, 2 1/4 In. 185.00
Pate De Verre, Pendant, Poppies, Signed G.Argy-Rousseau, 2 1/4 In. 185.00
Pate De Verre, Pendant, Signed Walter, Brown & Black Beetle, 2 In. 195.00
Pate De Verre, Plaque, A.Walter, Ferns, 3 Beetles, 7 In. 375.00
Pate De Verre, Plaque, A.Walter, Mercier, Artist's Palette, Apples, 4 1/2 In. 425.00
Pate De Verre, Tray, Walter, Iguana On Side, Boat Shape, 11 1/2 In. 1100.00

Pate De Verre, Vase, A.Walter, Deep Blue To Aqua, Yellow Pinecones, 4 1/2 In. 650.00
Pate De Verre, Vase, Aqua, Yellow Pinecones, A.Walter, Nancy 4 1/2 In. 650.00
Pate De Verre, Vase, Lavender, Spiderweb, G.Argy Rousseau, 5 In. 1450.00
Pate De Verre, Vase, Walter, Berge, Blue, Green, & Gold Pinecones, 4 In. 950.00

Pate-sur-pate means paste on paste. The design was made by painting layers of slip on the ceramic piece until a relief decoration was formed. The method was developed at the Sevres factory in France about 1850. It became even more famous at the English Minton factory about 1870.

Pate-Sur-Pate, Box, Portrait, Young Woman, Limoges, 6 X 4 In. 96.00
Pate-Sur-Pate, Sugar & Creamer, Pigeon Forge, Floral Garland On Gray 28.00
Pate-Sur-Pate, Vase, Bowl, Floral Spray On Top Of Red, Pigeon Forge 25.00
Pate-Sur-Pate, Vase, Butterflies And Leaves, Dragonflies 70.00
Patent Model, Jack, Shoemaker's Pegging, 1856, Wooden Base, 9 In. 85.00

Paul Revere pottery was made at several locations in and around Boston between 1906 and 1942. The pottery was operated as a settlement-house type of program for teen-aged girls. Many pieces were signed S.E.G. for Saturday Evening Girls. The firm concentrated on children's dishes and tiles. Decorations were outlined in black and filled in with color.

Paul Revere, Bowl, Matte White, Blue Band, 3 Yellow Chicks, Dated, 2 1/4 In. 65.00
Paul Revere, Mush Set, S.E.G., Rabbits, Calvin, His Bowl, His Pitcher, 1911 .... 45.00
Paul Revere, Pitcher, Blue High Glaze, Mottled Blue & Green, 7 1/4 In. 110.00
Paul Revere, Pitcher, Bulbous, Speckled Blue, Frothy White Top, 6 3/4 In. 55.00
Paul Revere, Pitcher, Matte Pink, 3 In. 40.00
Paul Revere, Plate, Gray Beige, Green Band On Rim, Black Line, 6 1/4 In. 7.00
Paul Revere, Vase, Blue Green With Incised Band Of White Tulips, Signed 225.00
Paul Revere, Vase, Blue Semimatte, Trees & Hills, F.L., 6-24, 4 In. 150.00

Peachblow glass originated about 1883 at Hobbs, Brockunier and Company of Wheeling, West Virginia. It is a glass that shades from yellow to peach. It was lined in white. New England peachblow is a one-layer glass with a lining shading from red to white. Mt.Washington peachblow shades from pink to blue. Reproductions of peachblow have been made, but they are of a poor quality and can be detected.

Peachblow, Bowl, Bride's, New Martinsville, Ribbed Center, 3 3/8 In. 170.00
Peachblow, Bowl, Finger, Gloss Finish, Wheeling, 2 5/8 X 4 5/8 In. 450.00
Peachblow, Bowl, Finger, New England, Ruffle Edge, Wild Rose Color 400.00
Peachblow, Bowl, New England, Deep Raspberry To Opaque White, Fluted, 5 In. 200.00
Peachblow, Carafe, Glossy Finish, Wheeling 685.00
Peachblow, Cruet, Shiny 200.00
Peachblow, Cruet, Wheeling, Amber Stopper & Applied Handle, 7 1/4 In. 1050.00
Peachblow, Cruet, Wheeling, Glossy, Ball Amber Trim 650.00
Peachblow, Cruet, Wheeling, Satin Ball, Amber Trim 700.00
Peachblow, Cup, Punch, Libbey, Applied White Handle, "World's Fair 1893" 300.00
Peachblow, Cup, Punch, Wheeling, Amber Camphor Handle, Satin Finish 450.00
Peachblow, Cup, Punch, Wheeling, Matte Finish 395.00
Peachblow, Decanter, Wheeling, Amber Applied Handle & Stopper, 9 1/2 In. 2800.00
Peachblow, Figurine, Bryden Pairpoint, Swimming Swan, 7 1/4 In. 45.00
Peachblow, Finger Bowl, New England, 5 X 2 1/2 In. 375.00
Peachblow, Gunderson, see Gunderson, Peachblow
Peachblow, Lamp Base, Yellow To Deep Cranberry, Wheeling, 9 In. 695.00
Peachblow, Muffineer 175.00
Peachblow, New Martinsville, Rose Bowl, 4 1/2 In. 75.00
Peachblow, Pairpoint, Hat, Bryden, Enamel Decoration, 3 1/2 In. 45.00
Peachblow, Pitcher, Water, Wheeling, Applied Frosted Reeded Handle, 9 In. 490.00
Peachblow, Rose Bowl, Burst Bubble On Side 25.00
Peachblow, Rose Bowl, Raspberry Fluted Top, White Lining 95.00
Peachblow, Toothpick, Wheeling, 2 1/2 In. 275.00
Peachblow, Tumbler, New England, Glossy 450.00
Peachblow, Tumbler, New England, Satin Finish 400.00
Peachblow, Tumbler, Wheeling, Acid Finish, 3 3/4 In., Pair 250.00
Peachblow, Tumbler, Wheeling, Glossy 450.00
Peachblow, Tumbler, Wheeling, Set Of 4 .... 1800.00

Peachblow, Tumbler, Whiskey, New England 195.00
Peachblow, Vase, Bud, 6 1/2 In. 125.00
Peachblow, Vase, Bulbous, Scalloped & Crimped, Sandwich, 4 3/4 In. 150.00
Peachblow, Vase, Cased, Blossoms & Dragonfly, Gold, 8 In., Pair 850.00
Peachblow, Vase, Cased, Stick, Gold Enameled, 6 In. 75.00
Peachblow, Vase, Crimped, Tricorner Top, Cream Lining, 7 1/2 In. 295.00
Peachblow, Vase, Mt.Washington, Pink To Blue Gray Base, 12 In. 950.00
Peachblow, Vase, New England, Jack-In-The-Pulpit, Glossy, 7 3/4 In. 365.00
Peachblow, Vase, Webb, Green, Blue, & Yellow Coralene, Stick, 8 3/4 In. 550.00
Peachblow, Vase, Wheeling, Large Bulbous, 22 In. 1250.00
Peachblow, Vase, Wheeling, Lemon Gold To Deep Red Mahogany, Large 975.00
Peachblow, Vase, Wheeling, Small Bulbous, 4 1/4 In. 450.00
Peachblow, Vase, Wheeling, White Interior, Long Neck, 13 In. 200.00
Pearl, Carving Set, Sterling Ferrules, 3 Piece 20.00
Pearl, Case, Card, Silver Initial Plate, Blue Satin Interior 38.00
Pearl, Fork, Pie, Sterling Silver Ferrules 3.00
Pearl, Fork, Sheffield, Embossed, 8 3/8 In. 10.00
Pearl, Knife & Fork, Abbey, Engraved, 24 Pieces In Case 85.00
Pearl, Knife, Buttonhook & Nail File, George Westenholm, 3 In. 22.50
Pearl, Knife, Dinner, Carved, Sterling Bands, Silver Plate Blade, Set Of 6 .... 55.00
Pearl, Knife, Fruit, Landers, Frary & Clark, Sterling Ferrules, Set Of 6 .... 42.00
Pearl, Knife, Luncheon, Sheffield Silver Blade & Band 7.00
Pearl, Knife, Sheffield, 8 In., Set Of 6 .... 21.00
Pearl, Knife, Sterling Ferrules, Ribbon Pattern, Set Of 6 .... 55.00
Pearl, Ladle, Gravy, Sterling Silver Ferrules 5.00

Pearl, Opera Glasses, see Opera Glasses

Pearl, Rattle & Teething Ring, Baby's, Bell Shape, Sterling Handle 20.00

Peking glass is a Chinese cameo glass of the eighteenth and nineteenth centuries.

Peking Glass, Bracelet

Peking Glass, Bottle, Scent, Light Blue Opalescent Cameo, 4 In. 75.00
Peking Glass, Bottle, Snuff, Blue 16.00
Peking Glass, Bowl, Cameo Peacock, Peony Plants, 6 In. 145.00
Peking Glass, Bowl, Cobalt, Carved Wood Base, 2 3/4 X 6 1/2 In. 150.00
Peking Glass, Bowl, Imperial Yellow, Octagonal, Underplate, 5 1/4 In. 365.00
Peking Glass, Bowl, Orange Cameo, Deep Cut, Birds, Foliage, 6 1/2 X 3 1/4 In. 425.00
Peking Glass, Bowl, White, Blue Casing, Warriors, Dragons, & Serpents, 6 In. 550.00
Peking Glass, Compote, Red Opaque, 9 X 3 1/2 In. 35.00
Peking Glass, Cup & Saucer, Blue, Silver Saucer, Dragons 95.00
Peking Glass, Jar, Covered, White, Royal Blue Geometrics, 5 3/4 In. 575.00
Peking Glass, Snuff Bottle, Hand-Painted Scene, Green, Legend Back, Signed 45.00
Peking Glass, Vase, Cadmium Yellow, Peonies & Butterflies, Monochrome, 8 In. 155.00
Peking Glass, Vase, Cobalt, Acidized Pattern, 9 X 4 1/2 In. 175.00
Peking, Glass, Jar, Covered, White, Royal Blue Geometrics, Urn Shape, 5 3/4 In. 168.00

Peloton glass is European glass with small threads of colored glass rolled onto the surface of clear or colored glass. It is sometimes called spaghetti, or shredded coconut glass

Peloton, Cruet, Clear Overshot 250.00
Peloton, Cruet, Thick Colored Straws 275.00
Peloton, Jar, Cracker, Blue Satin, Filaments, Ribbed, 6 1/2 In. 550.00
Peloton, Vase, Fan, Filaments On White Cased Body, Embossed Daisies, 4 In. 125.00
Peloton, Vase, Gold & Purple Iridescent, Threading, Green Handle, 8 In. 85.00
Peloton, Vase, White Satin, Ribbed, Multicolor Filaments, 6 1/4 In. 145.00

Pen, see Store, Pen

Pencil, see Store, Pencil

Pennsbury, Pitcher, Milk, Rooster, RB, 4 In. 12.00

Peters and Reed Pottery Company of Zanesville, Ohio, was founded by John D. Peters and Adam Reed in 1897. Chromal, Landsun, Montene, Pereco, and Persian are some of the art lines that were made until the company closed in 1920.

Peters & Reed, see also Zane

Peters & Reed, Bowl, Red, Dragonflies, Green Traces, 6 In. 12.00
Peters & Reed, Jug, Grapes, Handle, 6 1/2 In. 19.00
Peters & Reed, Spittoon, Lady's, Pinecone, Signed Ferrel, 5 X 6 In. 24.00
Peters & Reed, Umbrella Stand, Brown, Grapes, Leaves, & Vines, Ferrel, 18 In. 85.00
Peters & Reed, Vase, Chromal, Scenic, Bulbous, 8 1/2 In. 125.00
Peters & Reed, Vase, Corset Shape, Art Nouveau Floral, Moss Green 20.00
Peters & Reed, Vase, Dark Blue, Zane Mark, 4 1/2 In. 26.00
Peters & Reed, Vase, Landsun Glaze, Blue, Brown, & Tan, Zaneware, 5 In. 16.00
Peters & Reed, Vase, Moss Aztec, Raspberry, 7 1/2 In. 17.00
Peters & Reed, Vase, Sewer Tile, Pinecones, 10 1/2 In. 18.00
Peters & Reed, Vase, Sheen Ware, Herringbone, 4 Colors, Zaneware, 8 In. 28.00
Peters & Reed, Wall Pocket, Art Deco, 9 X 6 1/2 In. 45.00
Peters & Reed, Wall Pocket, Pereco, Matte Green, Phoenix Bird Rising, 8 In. 45.00
Pewabic, Box, Covered, Mottled Pink, Exotic Plumed Bird On Luster, 4 1/2 In. 195.00
Pewabic, Mug, Rooster, Early To Bed & Early To Rise, 3 1/2 In. 85.00
Pewabic, Plate, Crackleware, Apple, 9 In. 45.00
Pewabic, Plate, Crackleware, Rooster, 9 In. 45.00
Pewabic, Plate, Squeezebag Apple Border, 9 In. 85.00
Pewabic, Rose Bowl, Blue, 4 In. 35.00

Pewter is a metal alloy of tin and lead. Some of the pewter made after about 1840 has a slightly different composition and is called Britannia metal.

Pewter, Ashtray, Greyhound Dog Handle, Small 15.00
Pewter, Basin, Old English Touchmark, 6 1/2 In. 75.00
Pewter, Basin, Thomas Badger, Boston, C.1790, Shallow, 11 1/2 In. 400.00
Pewter, Bedpan, Boardman, Conn. 275.00
Pewter, Bowl, Fruit, Openwork, Cobalt Glass Liner, Poole, 9 1/2 X 5 In. 35.00
Pewter, Bowl, Kayserzinn, Scalloped Rim, Embossed Lobsters, 9 1/4 In. 65.00
Pewter, Bowl, Sauce, Underplate & Ladle, L.H.Vaughan, Taunton, Mass., 5 1/2 In. 55.00
Pewter, Bowl, Waste, Covered, Fruits, Kayserzinn, 7 In. 42.00
Pewter, Box, Chinese, Stone Finial On Dome Lid, Footed, 3 1/2 X 3 In. 25.00
Pewter, Box, Covered, Round, Fruits & Flowers, Kayserzinn, 7 In. 125.00
Pewter, Box, Stamp, Enameled 8.00
Pewter, Candle Snuffer, Bull Dog's Head 25.00
Pewter, Candlestick, American, 18th Century, No Marks, 8 In., Pair 72.00
Pewter, Candlestick, Art Nouveau, Kayserzinn, 9 3/4 X 6 1/4 In. 40.00
Pewter, Candlestick, Baluster Turned, 8 1/2 In., Pair 140.00
Pewter, Candlestick, Crescent Mark, 10 1/4 In., Pair 25.00
Pewter, Candlestick, Ohio, C.1820, Pair 190.00
Pewter, Castor Set, 4 Bottles, Miniature 48.50
Pewter, Celery, Orivit 34.00
Pewter, Chalice, Roswell Gleason, C.1830, 6 1/4 In. 225.00
Pewter, Chamberstick, Kayserzinn, Floral, Oval, 11 1/2 In. 85.00
Pewter, Cocktail Set, Kut Hing Pewter, Swaton, China, Dragons, 13 Piece 34.75
Pewter, Coffeepot, Ashbil Griswold, Meriden, Conn., C.1825, 11 1/4 In. 275.00
Pewter, Coffeepot, Banded And Engraved, I.Trask, Mass. 585.00
Pewter, Coffeepot, Bellied Shape, A.Porter, 12 In. 315.00
Pewter, Coffeepot, James Dixon, Wooden Handle, 11 In. 55.00
Pewter, Coffeepot, Pedestal Base, Flower Finial, Flagg & Homan, 10 In. 145.00
Pewter, Coffeepot, R.Dunham, Lighthouse, 12 In. 145.00
Pewter, Coffeepot, Westbrook, Conn. 450.00
Pewter, Cream & Sugar, Marked E.B.Smith, Boston 225.00
Pewter, Cup, Gasilell & Chambers 75.00
Pewter, Cup, Loving, Meriden, No.239, 3 Ornate Handles, Pinched Center, 6 In. 30.00
Pewter, Dish, Candy, Kayserzinn, Covered, 7 In. 48.00
Pewter, Dish, Deep, English, 12 1/4 In. 115.00
Pewter, Dish, Deep, 3 Eagles, Thomas Danforth 3rd, 2 Philadelphia Touches 485.00
Pewter, Dish, Leaf And Bud, Kayserzinn, 4 1/4 In. 18.00
Pewter, Dish, Liberty & Co., Hammered, Stylized Floral, 6 1/2 In. 65.00
Pewter, Dish, Nekrassoff, 3 Sections, Triangular, 11 X 10 In. 35.00
Pewter, Dish, Pancake, Domed Lid, Wallace 14.00
Pewter, Dish, Round, Footed, Fruit Relief Design, Kayserzinn, 6 In. 65.00
Pewter, Dish, Samuel Danforth, 106 Mark, 13 1/4 In. 500.00

Pewter, Dish, Shield In Center, G Gussisberg & Angel, 6 1/2 In. 35.00
Pewter, Dish, Small Oval, Rose Mark 25.00
Pewter, Ewer, Wine, Kayserzinn, Horned Satan, Orchids, Signed, 12 3/4 In. 180.00
Pewter, Flagon, H.H.Graves, Conn. 500.00
Pewter, Inkstand, Kayserzinn, Embossed Floral, Kidney Shape, 11 X 5 In. 125.00
Pewter, Inkwell, A.G.Whitcomb 68.00
Pewter, Inkwell, Dutch, C.1770, Louis XVI Type Feet 275.00

Pewter, Inkwell, 6 1/2 In.

Pewter, Inkwell, Fish On Leaf, Cherub Above, French 325.00
Pewter, Inkwell, 6 1/2 In. .... *Illus* 52.00
Pewter, Jardiniere, Orivit 27.50
Pewter, Jug, Charles Perron, Nymphs & Bearded Man Fountain, 7 1/2 In., Pair 335.00
Pewter, Ladle, Dixon, 13 1/2 In. 75.00
Pewter, Ladle, John Yates 35.00
Pewter, Lamp, Sparking, Double Wick, Saucer Base, Ringle Handle, Loop 125.00
Pewter, Measure, Pint, James Yates, C.1800, Fishtail Handle, Footed, Strainer 118.00
Pewter, Measure, 1 1/2 Pint, Dames Dixon, Music Box Base, Auld Lang Syne 36.00

Pewter, Mold, Ice Cream, see also Kewpie, Mold, Ice Cream

Pewter, Mold, Ice Cream, American Flag 20.00
Pewter, Mold, Ice Cream, Apple 22.50
Pewter, Mold, Ice Cream, Asparagus 12.00
Pewter, Mold, Ice Cream, Asparagus, E & Co. 29.50
Pewter, Mold, Ice Cream, Auto 25.00
Pewter, Mold, Ice Cream, Bell, Says Marriage On Interior 27.50
Pewter, Mold, Ice Cream, Boxer 25.00
Pewter, Mold, Ice Cream, Bride & Groom 32.50
Pewter, Mold, Ice Cream, Carrot 12.00
Pewter, Mold, Ice Cream, Child On Chicken 25.00
Pewter, Mold, Ice Cream, Chrysanthemum 30.00
Pewter, Mold, Ice Cream, Crouching Rabbit 17.50
Pewter, Mold, Ice Cream, Cupid On Rabbit 25.00
Pewter, Mold, Ice Cream, Daisy 30.00
Pewter, Mold, Ice Cream, Easter Lily, Hinged 10.00
Pewter, Mold, Ice Cream, Flower, No.395 .... 24.50
Pewter, Mold, Ice Cream, Hat, No.399 .... 24.00
Pewter, Mold, Ice Cream, Heart 15.00
Pewter, Mold, Ice Cream, Heart, Hinged, S & Co. 25.00
Pewter, Mold, Ice Cream, Lady's Shoe 17.50
Pewter, Mold, Ice Cream, Leaf, S & Co., No.268 .... 29.50
Pewter, Mold, Ice Cream, Lily 3 Sections, American 25.00
Pewter, Mold, Ice Cream, Monkey, E & Co. 35.00
Pewter, Mold, Ice Cream, Morning Glory 29.50
Pewter, Mold, Ice Cream, Mushroom 12.00
Pewter, Mold, Ice Cream, Mushroom, E & Co. 29.50
Pewter, Mold, Ice Cream, Open Lily 27.50
Pewter, Mold, Ice Cream, Open Rose 27.50
Pewter, Mold, Ice Cream, Orange, S & Co. 29.50
Pewter, Mold, Ice Cream, Pansy, S & Co. 29.50

Pewter, Mold, Ice Cream, Pear 25.00
Pewter, Mold, Ice Cream, Pineapple 20.00
Pewter, Mold, Ice Cream, Potato 12.00
Pewter, Mold, Ice Cream, Pumpkin 12.00
Pewter, Mold, Ice Cream, Pumpkin, E & Co. 29.50
Pewter, Mold, Ice Cream, Puss 'n Boots, American 25.00
Pewter, Mold, Ice Cream, Rose On Leaf, No.19 .... 29.50
Pewter, Mold, Ice Cream, Santa 40.00
Pewter, Mold, Ice Cream, Standing Turkey 17.50
Pewter, Mold, Ice Cream, Stork Carrying Baby 15.00
Pewter, Mold, Ice Cream, Swan, American 25.00
Pewter, Mold, Ice Cream, Turkey 30.00
Pewter, Mold, Ice Cream, Turkey, E & Co. 24.00
Pewter, Mold, Ice Cream, Two Love Birds, American 25.00
Pewter, Mold, Ice Cream, Two Santa Claus, Standing, American 95.00
Pewter, Mortar & Pestle, French, Brass Bail Handle, Indentations For Pills 75.00
Pewter, Mug, English, C.1890 .... 27.00
Pewter, Mug, English, Victorian, Pint, 5 In. 85.00
Pewter, Mug, Imperial, Pint, 5 In. 50.00
Pewter, Mug, Pint, Gaskell & Chambers, Birmingham 110.00
Pewter, Mug, Tudric, Golfer, 4 1/2 In. 28.00

Pewter, Napkin Ring, see Napkin Ring

Pewter, Noggin, Irish, Gill 50.00
Pewter, Pitcher & Drip Plate, Queen City, Ohio, C.1880, Hinged Lid, 5 1/2 In. 45.00
Pewter, Pitcher, Crown & Anchor, Marked Insico, 7 X 9 In. 85.00
Pewter, Pitcher, Freeman Porter, Westbrook, Me., C.1850, 2 Quart, 8 In. 295.00
Pewter, Pitcher, Kayserzinn, Horned Mythological Head, 12 In. 150.00
Pewter, Pitcher, Marked Pewter & Carriage On Bottom, 8 In. 22.50
Pewter, Pitcher, Milk, J.Dixon & Sons 75.00
Pewter, Plate, Edgar Curtis, London, C.1785, 8 In. 80.00
Pewter, Plate, Hot, J.C.Friggate Best Metal, 9 1/2 In. 52.00
Pewter, Plate, Joseph Danforth Lion, 4 Hallmark Touches, 8 In. 298.00
Pewter, Plate, Thomas D.Boardman, Conn., Eagle Touch, 8 3/8 In. 350.00
Pewter, Plate, Thomas S.Derby, Conn., Andrew Jackson Touch, 8 7/8 In. 850.00
Pewter, Platter, Kayserzinn, Floral, 11 X 14 In. 68.00
Pewter, Platter, Leaf Shape, Nekrassoff, 17 In. 25.00
Pewter, Porringer, CB, C.1800, Pierced Scroll Handle, 5 In. 325.00
Pewter, Porringer, Stede & Horse's Head, Openwork Handle, 3 3/4 In., Pair 25.00
Pewter, Pot, Warming, Acorn Cover, Fein English Zinn, Continental Pewter 125.00
Pewter, Pot, Warming, Double Handled, F.Reinhold, Continental Pewter 75.00
Pewter, Rice Bowl, Chinese, Twig Finial, Jade Trim, Side Handles 68.50
Pewter, Salt & Pepper, Acme Pewter, 4 1/2 In. 9.95
Pewter, Salt & Pepper, Wallace 15.00
Pewter, Salt, Viking Ship 10.00
Pewter, Spoon, Chinese, Carnelian In Jade Handle, Leaf-Shaped Bowl, 5 In. 72.00
Pewter, Spoon, Dutch, Cherubs 10.00
Pewter, Spoon, Round Bowl, Dutch, Rose & Crown, Set Of 6 .... 30.00
Pewter, Stein Holder, Wahlee Swatow, 5 1/2 In. 18.00
Pewter, Stein, Lidded, Glass Bottom, R & B, Pat.1898, American Whist Club 60.00
Pewter, Sugar & Creamer, Cover, Trumpet Flower, Kayserzinn 45.00
Pewter, Sugar & Creamer, Footed Tray, Windmill Mark 32.50
Pewter, Sugar & Creamer, Picture Of Quaker Lady, Marked Old Colony 45.00
Pewter, Syrup, American, C.1850, Covered, 5 In. 225.00
Pewter, Syrup, Hinged Lid, Engraving Of Dragon, Base Mark Of Blossom 48.00
Pewter, Tea Set, Leonard, Reed & Barton, C.1835, 4 Piece 325.00
Pewter, Teapot, Acorn Finial, Signed T.D. And S.Boardman, Hartford, C.1830 .... 200.00
Pewter, Teapot, Dixon & Son, Boat Shape, Black Wooden Handle 95.00
Pewter, Teapot, Federal Solid Pewter, 10 In. 19.75
Pewter, Teapot, H.B.Ward, S Scroll Handle 75.00
Pewter, Teapot, James Dixon & Sons, Sheffield, 1884, 5 1/2 In. 65.00
Pewter, Teapot, Jos.Bennet, Sheffield, England 45.00
Pewter, Teapot, Lid, Signed F.Pilgrim, No.2141, J.F., Crown, 6 1/2 In. 60.00
Pewter, Teapot, Melon Ribbed, Shaw & Fisher, Sheffield, 5 1/2 In. 110.00
Pewter, Teapot, Pear Shape, Continental, 7 In. .... *Illus* 185.00

Pewter, Teapot, Queen Anne, Curtis, London, Touchmark, 18th Century 385.00
Pewter, Teapot, R.B.& Rooster Mark, 2 Porcelain Inserts On Handle, 6 1/4 In. 47.50
Pewter, Teapot, Shaw & Fisher, Sheffield, 7 In. 105.00
Pewter, Teapot, Shaw & Fisher, Strawberry Finial, Footed, Paneled 62.00
Pewter, Teapot, Squat, Holdsworth & Sons, English, C.1850 .... 75.00
Pewter, Teapot, T.Otley, Sheffield, 6 In. 78.00
Pewter, Teaspoon, Hall & Elton 5.00
Pewter, Tray, Kayserzinn, Art Nouveau, Top Handled, 12 1/4 X 6 In. 75.00
Pewter, Tray, Kayserzinn, 16 3/4 X 12 In. 68.00
Pewter, Tray, Oblong, 2 Handled, Floral In Relief, Kayserzinn 85.00
Pewter, Tray, Potter Studio, Brass Dachshund Forms Center Handle, 5 1/2 In. 25.00
Pewter, Tureen, Covered, Kayserzinn, Poppies, 11 1/2 In. 87.00
Pewter, Tureen, Soup, Fruit Finial, German, Knuckle-Grip Handles, Footed 250.00

Pewter, Teapot, Pear Shape, Continental, 7 In.

(See Page 389)

Pewter, Vase, Art Nouveau, S Shaped, Hammered, Tudric, 11 In. 95.00
Pewter, Vase, Flower Vase For Limousine 65.00
Pewter, Vase, Hand Hammered, Liberty & Co., Tudric, 11 In. 95.00
Pewter, Vase, Kayserzinn, Art Nouveau, Floral, 8 In. 90.00
Pewter, Vase, Kayserzinn, Beaker Shape, Embossed Floral, Art Nouveau, 8 In. 90.00
Peynaud, Box, Lift Lid, Yellow, Crane, Mountains, & Grasses, 5 In. 175.00
Pfaultzcraft, Mug, York, Pa. 20.00

Phoenix Bird, or flying Phoenix, is the name given to a blue and white chinaware made between 1900 and World War II. A variant is known as the Flying Turkey.

Phoenix Bird, Eggcup, Double 8.50
Phoenix Bird, Salt & Pepper, Blue & White Porcelain, Flared Base 18.00
Phoenix Bird, Saucer 1.25
Phoenix Bird, Sugar, Covered 8.00

Phoenix Glass Company was founded in 1880 in Pennsylvania. The firm made commercial products such as lampshades, bottles, glassware. Collectors today are interested in the sculptured glassware made by the company from the 1930s until the mid-1950s.

Phoenix Glass, Vase, Oval, Italian Blue, Raised White Flying Geese, 10 In. 125.00
Phoenix, Bowl, Covered, Pink, Sculptured Floral & Leaves, 7 In. 62.50
Phoenix, Bowl, Fish, Amber & Clear, Sculptured Flowers 42.00
Phoenix, Bowl, Green, Opalescent, Flint Twist, 6 X 3 1/2 In. 30.00
Phoenix, Bowl, Lily, Clear On White, Polished Rim, 14 X 4 1/4 In. 45.00
Phoenix, Bowl, White Satin, Cockatoo Sculptured, 9 In. 45.00
Phoenix, Candleholder, Blue, Pair 45.00
Phoenix, Candlestick, Blue Bubble, Swirl, 3 1/4 In., Pair 20.00
Phoenix, Console Set, White Berry On Green, Center Frog 65.00
Phoenix, Dish, Candy, Basket Handle, Pink Dogwood, Leaf Handle, 4 3/4 In. 28.00
Phoenix, Jar, Powder, White Violets On Pink, Covered, 7 In. 85.00
Phoenix, Lamp, Coral Poppies On White Satin, Brass Trim, Large 95.00
Phoenix, Lamp, Reverse Painted Shade, Charles Parker Base, 20 In. 600.00

Phoenix, Plate, Amethyst, Bubble, Swirled, 7 1/4 In. 12.00
Phoenix, Plate, Dancing Nudes, 8 1/2 In. 30.00
Phoenix, Plate, Yellow, Blue Transfer Border, 8 1/2 In. 8.00
Phoenix, Shade, Gas, Opalescent, Flint Twist, 5 1/2 X 3 1/2 In. 10.00
Phoenix, Stand, Cake, White Satin With Blue & Yellow Floral, 13 X 1/2 In. 18.00
Phoenix, Vase, Amber, Dancing Girls, 12 In. 75.00
Phoenix, Vase, Aqua, Sculptured Clear Feather Design, 7 In. 67.50
Phoenix, Vase, Blue & White, Madonna, 10 1/4 In. 125.00
Phoenix, Vase, Blue Ground, Dancing White Nudes, 11 3/4 In. 85.00
Phoenix, Vase, Blue, Frosted Lilies, Tricorner, Footed, 8 1/2 In. 125.00
Phoenix, Vase, Blue, White Flying Ducks, 10 1/2 In. 95.00
Phoenix, Vase, Brown, Girl's Profile In White, Ribbed, 10 1/4 In., Pair 180.00
Phoenix, Vase, Cameo Satin, Pink Plumes On White 35.00
Phoenix, Vase, Cinnamon Color, Pearlized Geese, 12 1/4 In. 120.00
Phoenix, Vase, Cosmos, White Flowers On Green, 7 1/2 In. 40.00
Phoenix, Vase, Cream Color, Bluebirds & Cherries, 9 1/2 In. 165.00
Phoenix, Vase, Cream Opaque, Green Vines, Brown Leaves, Blueberries, 10 In. 64.00
Phoenix, Vase, Custard Color, Blue Owls On Brown Branches, Ovoid, 6 In. 55.00
Phoenix, Vase, Custard, Flying Geese, Pillow Shape, 10 X 7 In. 45.00
Phoenix, Vase, Custard, Seagulls, 11 In. 125.00
Phoenix, Vase, Fern, Heavy White Satin With Blue Ferns, 7 In. 40.00
Phoenix, Vase, Fern, White On Red, Original Label, 7 In. 65.00
Phoenix, Vase, Freesia, Blue, Flared, Original Label, 7 3/8 In. 65.00
Phoenix, Vase, Frosted Ferns On Aqua, 7 1/2 In. 55.00
Phoenix, Vase, Grasshopper, Clear On Frosted, Fan Shaped, 8 1/4 In. 45.00
Phoenix, Vase, Honey Amber, Owls, 6 In. 58.00
Phoenix, Vase, Ivory Color, Blue Foxgloves, 10 1/4 In. 95.00
Phoenix, Vase, Ivory, Sculptured Green & Tan Floral & Foliage, 11 In. 60.00
Phoenix, Vase, Lily, Heavy Sculptured, Frosted White, Clear Flowers, 9 In. 45.00
Phoenix, Vase, Lily, Heavy Sculptured, Pale Blue, Clear Flowers, 9 In. 45.00
Phoenix, Vase, Madonna, White On Blue, 10 In. 57.00
Phoenix, Vase, Madonna, White On Pink 10 In. 57.00
Phoenix, Vase, Philodendron, White Leaves On Blue, 11 1/2 In. 55.00
Phoenix, Vase, Pillow Shape, Green Frosted, Opalescent White Leaves, 7 In. 65.00
Phoenix, Vase, Pillow, White Pearlized Flying Birds, Blue Ground 90.00
Phoenix, Vase, Pink Dogwoods, Vines, Leaves, Molded, 11 1/2 In. 70.00
Phoenix, Vase, Powder Blue, Glossy White Freesias, Sculptured, 8 1/4 In. 65.00
Phoenix, Vase, Powder Blue, Glossy White Fresias, Sculptured, 8 1/4 In. 65.00
Phoenix, Vase, Praying Mantis, Amber, 7 1/4 In. 90.00
Phoenix, Vase, Ruby, Flowers, 6 1/4 In. 25.00
Phoenix, Vase, Sculptured Bittersweet 60.00
Phoenix, Vase, Sculptured Owls, Branches, Cream Ground 45.00
Phoenix, Vase, Soft Blue, White Freesias, Lafferty, 8 1/4 In. 35.00
Phoenix, Vase, Starflower, White Flowers On Rose, 7 In. 35.00
Phoenix, Vase, White Ground, Turquoise Vines, Blue Berries, 9 1/2 In. 85.00
Phoenix, Vase, White With Raised Lovebirds, 11 In. 150.00
Phoenix, Vase, White, Light Blue Relief Floral & Leaf, 7 1/2 In. 48.00
Phoenix, Vase, White, Pink Floral & Green Leaves, 6 1/2 In. 30.00
Phoenix, Vase, White, Pink Peonies, Green Stems & Leaves, 6 1/4 In. 80.00
Phoenix, Vase, Wild Geese, White On Green, 9 1/4 X 11 In., Pair 115.00
Phoenix, Vase, Wild Rose, White On White Satin, 10 1/2 In. 65.00
Phoenix, Vase, Yellow, Philodendron, 11 1/4 In. 80.00
Phoenix, Vase, Yellow, With Green Birds, 6 1/2 In. 47.00

Phonograph, see Music, Phonograph

Photography, Album, Blue Plush, Silver Frontpiece, Bird, Floral, 10 1/2 In. 40.00
Photography, Album, Brown Leather, Gold Leaf, Brass Fasteners, 9 X 6 In. 200.00
Photography, Album, Embossed Black Leather, Clasp 16.00
Photography, Album, Leather, Mild Glass Medallion, Brass Fittings, C.1870 14.00
Photography, Album, Music Box, Brass Clamps, Renaissance Picture On Cover 75.00
Photography, Album, Musical, 2 Tunes, Oak Cover, Red Plush Base, 10 1/2 In. 115.00
Photography, Album, Scenic Cover, Buildings, Waterwheel 55.00
Photography, Ambrotype, Boy, Gutta-Percha Labeled Union 1871, 3 X 2 1/2 In. 25.00
Photography, Ambrotype, Civil War Soldier With Revolver, Ninth Plate 50.00
Photography, Ambrotype, Little Girl Holding Doll, 2 1/2 X 3 In. 22.00

Photography, Ambrotype, Major Andre's Surrender, Signed, Rubber Case 135.00
Photography, Ambrotype, Man, Floral Cased, 3 X 3 1/2 In. 12.50
Photography, Ambrotype, Young Man, Gutta-Percha, The Apple Picker, 1858 .... 75.00
Photography, Ambrotype, 2 Young Girls, The Tangent Circle, 1852, 3 3/4 In. 20.00
Photography, Camera, Agfa Ansco, Shur-Shot, Box 12.00
Photography, Camera, Ansco, Viking, 120, Folding, Leather Case 9.50
Photography, Camera, Bausch & Lomb, Plastigmat, Patent 1900, Plate, 7 In. 50.00
Photography, Camera, Brownie, Automatic, Brass, Box 14.00
Photography, Camera, Brownie, No.24, Box 12.00
Photography, Camera, Century No. 2, Mahogany & Cherrywood, 10 X 12 X 4 In. 165.00
Photography, Camera, Cub, American Research Co. 6.00
Photography, Camera, Eastman Folding, 3a Autographic, 1913 .... 35.00
Photography, Camera, Eastman Kodak, Autographlex, Case, 9 X 10 X 9 In. 215.00
Photography, Camera, Eastman Kodak, No.5, Folding, Leather, Mahogany 65.00
Photography, Camera, Eastman, No.2, Bull's-Eye, Cherry Wood & Leather 22.00
Photography, Camera, IA Pocket II, Box 11.00
Photography, Camera, Jiffy Six, Box 9.00
Photography, Camera, Kodak, Enlarging, Vest Pocket, 14 In. 12.00
Photography, Camera, Kodak, Folding, Model B4, Mahogany 50.00
Photography, Camera, Kodak, No. 3 A, Model B J, Patent 1902, Folding, Pocket 35.00
Photography, Camera, Kodak, No.1a, Junior, Model A, Folding, Case 18.00
Photography, Camera, Kodak, No.2, Folding, Cartridge Premo 12.00
Photography, Camera, Kodak, No.2a, Brownie, Box 12.00
Photography, Camera, Kodak, No.3 A, Model C, Folding, Pocket, Case 30.00
Photography, Camera, Kodak, No.3a, Panoramic, Black Leather & Nickel Plate 125.00
Photography, Camera, Kodak, Patent 1902, Autographic, Vest Pocket 15.00
Photography, Camera, Kodak, Patent 1913, Autographic, Vest Pocket, Folding 19.00
Photography, Camera, Kodak, Rainbow, Hawkeye, No.2a, Model B, Box 10.00
Photography, Camera, Kodak, Vest Pocket, C.1915 .... 50.00
Photography, Camera, Movie, Bell & Howell, Filmo 75, Velvet Lined Case 30.00
Photography, Camera, Movie, Vitascope 68.00
Photography, Camera, Premier Detective 100.00
Photography, Camera, Premo, 1904, Case & Film Holder 100.00
Photography, Camera, Stirn, C.1880, John Conon, Ontario, Made In Germany 9000.00
Photography, Camera, Tom Thumb Radio Detective 85.00
Photography, Camera, Univex, Bellows, 4 1/2 In. 13.00
Photography, Camera, Univex, Miniature 13.00
Photography, Camera, Wollensak, Optimo No.1, Folding 10.00
Photography, Camera, Wollensak, Vest Pocket, 1925 .... 50.00
Photography, Camera, Wollensak, 1925, Vest Pocket 50.00
Photography, Carte De Visite, Barbara Frietchie, Great National Fair, 1876 .... 15.00
Photography, Carte De Visite, Civil War Soldier 10.00
Photography, Carte De Visite, General Grant 15.00
Photography, Carte De Visite, General McClellan 15.00
Photography, Carte De Visite, General Tom Thumb & Wife, Wedding 22.50
Photography, Carte De Visite, John Wilkes Booth 30.00
Photography, Carte De Visite, R.E.Lee 35.00
Photography, Carte De Visite, Stonewall Jackson 35.00
Photography, Carte De Visite, Tom Thumb, Wife & Child 10.00
Photography, Carte De Visite, 3 Midgets 10.00
Photography, Carte De Visite, 6 Midgets, Baron Littlefinger, Etc. 10.00
Photography, Case, Germany, Hand-Tooled Leather, Gold Engraving, 5 X 4 In. 10.00
Photography, Daguerreotype Case, Gutta-Percha, Abstract Rose 45.00
Photography, Daguerreotype Case, Gutta-Percha, Angel & Trumpet, 1857, 3 In. 35.00
Photography, Daguerreotype Case, Gutta-Percha, Civil War Officer 60.00
Photography, Daguerreotype Case, Gutta-Percha, Civil War Tintype, 7 X 9 In. 170.00
Photography, Daguerreotype Case, Gutta-Percha, Dark Brown, 3 1/8 In. 22.75
Photography, Daguerreotype Case, Gutta-Percha, Double Ornate Frame, 3 In. 25.00
Photography, Daguerreotype Case, Gutta-Percha, George Washington, 3 3/4 In. 90.00
Photography, Daguerreotype Case, Gutta-Percha, Gypsy Fortune Teller 90.00
Photography, Daguerreotype Case, Gutta-Percha, Indian Chief Profile, 2 In. 28.00
Photography, Daguerreotype Case, Gutta-Percha, La Follette, 5 X 4 In. 88.00
Photography, Daguerreotype Case, Gutta-Percha, Mary And Lamb 40.00
Photography, Daguerreotype Case, Gutta-Percha, Mother, Child, Dog, & Cat 55.00
Photography, Daguerreotype Case, Gutta-Percha, Nude Lady On Lion, 4 In. 65.00

Photography, Daguerreotype Case, Gutta-Percha, Rebecca At Well 110.00
Photography, Daguerreotype Case, Gutta-Percha, Scrolls, Medallions, Double 40.00
Photography, Daguerreotype Case, Gutta-Percha, Seahorses, Hinged, 3 In. 39.50
Photography, Daguerreotype Case, Gutta-Percha, Single Picture, J.H.Archibald 45.00
Photography, Daguerreotype Case, Gutta-Percha, Sir Henry Havelock 175.00
Photography, Daguerreotype Case, Gutta-Percha, The Flower Bier, 1859, Parsons 110.00
Photography, Daguerreotype Case, Gutta-Percha, Union Now & Forever, 3 In. 29.50
Photography, Daguerreotype Case, Gutta-Percha, Washington Monument, F.Goll 110.00
Photography, Daguerreotype, Case, Gutta-Percha, Union & Constitution 60.00
Photography, Daguerreotype, Delivery Man, 3 X 2 1/2 In. 45.00
Photography, Daguerreotype, Indian Chief, Paper By Heyn, 1900, 10 X 12 In. 56.00
Photography, Daguerreotype, Japanese Woman, Western Dress, Ninth Plate 42.00
Photography, Daguerreotype, Little Girl, Oval Cast-Iron Frame, 5 3/4 In. 12.00
Photography, Daguerreotype, Man, Red Shirt, Cowboy Hat, Ninth Plate 50.00
Photography, Daguerreotype, Two Children With Pet Birds, Sixth Plate 80.00
Photography, Daguerreotype, Woman In Elegant Furs, Fancy Hat, Sixth Plate 35.00
Photography, Magic Lantern, Around The World Cruise, 1926, 250 Slides 325.00
Photography, Magic Lantern, Bausch & Lomb, 1917, Wooden Slides 65.00
Photography, Magic Lantern, Germany, Tin, 10 Color Slides 65.00
Photography, Magic Lantern, MacIntosh, 126 Slides 1200.00
Photography, Magic Lantern, Tin & Wood, Kerosene Operated, 19 In. 180.00
Photography, Magic Lantern, Tin, Glass Lamp, Brass Burner, 10 Slides 75.00
Photography, Movie Film, Ken Maynard In Tombstone Canyon, C.1920, 35 Mm. 75.00
Photography, Photograph, Downtown Wooster, Ohio, 100 Years Old, 4 X 13, Frame 35.00
Photography, Photograph, General A Cardenas, Midget, Victorian, 3 1/2 In. 6.00
Photography, Photograph, General Grant, Last Photo, Mt.McGregor, N.Y. 45.00
Photography, Photograph, Gravure, Indian Policeman, Color, 1901, 10 X 8 In. 7.00
Photography, Photograph, Lincoln At Desk, Sepia, Brady, Round, 2 1/2 In. 35.00
Photography, Photograph, Medical School Autopsy, 10 X 8 In. 8.00
Photography, Photograph, Pike's Peak, Oct.11, 1891, Cable Car, 5 X 8 In. 35.00
Photography, Photograph, Union Soldier, Paper, 20 X 12 In. 25.00
Photography, Photograph, Woodrow Wilson, To Fredrick C.Howe, 14 X 10 In. 135.00
Photography, Photoscope, Exhibit Supply 275.00
Photography, Projector, Bausch & Lombe, 300 Glass Slides 275.00
Photography, Projector, Movie, Kodak, Model A, 16 Mm., Original Case 100.00
Photography, Projector, Movie, Pathescope, 1915, 32 Mm. 60.00
Photography, Projector, Slide, Thos.Mann, Dublin, C.1890, Kerosene, 50 Slides 275.00
Photography, Slide, Magic Lantern, T.H.McCallister, N.Y., Religious, 12 ..... 25.00
Photography, Slide, Movie, Simon The Jester, 1924, Color 6.95
Photography, Stereo, see Stereo
Photography, Stereopticon, Bausch & Lomb, Metal Case, 100 Slides 110.00
Photography, Tank, Film, Kodak, Patent 1907, Wooden 12.00
Photography, Timer, Kodak 7.00
Photography, Tintype, Black Woman In Fancy Dress, Tinted 22.00
Photography, Tintype, Boy On Tricycle, Victorian, 8 X 5 1/2 In. 18.00
Photography, Tintype, Family Portrait, Victorian, 8 X 5 1/2 In. 18.00
Photography, Tintype, Farmhouse Family By Fence, 5 X 7 In. 29.00
Photography, Tintype, Indian Child With White Child, Beaded Frame, 5 X 3 In. 56.00
Photography, Tintype, Man Holding Gun 20.00
Photography, Tintype, Matted, Two Civil War Soldiers 30.00
Photography, Tintype, Old-Timers With Tennis Racquets, 5 1/4 X 4 1/4 In. 40.00
Photography, Tintype, Pioneer Woman, White Bonnet, Tinted, 6 1/2 X 8 1/2 In. 11.00
Photography, Tintype, Three Men On Horseback 9.00
Photography, Tintype, Unmatted, Nine Swimmers In Bathing Suits 15.00
Photography, Tintype, Young Man In Trapper's Hat, 6 1/2 X 8 1/2 In. 11.00
Photography, Tintype, 2 Civil War Soldiers, Daguerreotype Case 60.00
Photography, Trimmer, Eastman Kodak Co., Metal & Wood, Square, 7 In. 17.50
Piano, see Music, Piano
Piano Baby, Bisque, Crawling, White Dress, Blue Cap, Bunny, Germany, 8 1/2 In. 150.00
Piano Baby, Bisque, Lying On Back, 6 In. 50.00
Piano Baby, Bisque, 7 1/2 In. 135.00
Piano Baby, Boy Removing Sock, Planter, Heubach 95.00
Piano Baby, Crawler, Heubach, 5 3/4 In. 195.00
Piano Baby, Girl & Boy, Sitting, 6 In., Pair 50.00
Piano Baby, Heubach, Bisque, Crawling, 4 1/2 In. 75.00

Piano Baby, Heubach, 6 In. 125.00

Piano Baby, On Stomach, Egg On Back, Heubach, 6 In. 195.00

Piano Baby, Sitting, Arms Crossed, Green Bonnet, Blonde, Bisque 125.00

Piano Baby, Sitting, Bisque, Walther 30.00

Pickard china was started in 1898 by Wilder Pickard. Hand-painted china was a featured product. The firm is still working in Antioch, Illinois.

Pickard, Bowl, Fruit, Deserted Garden, Faces On Handles, Signed Nessy 195.00

Pickard, Bowl, Fruit, Wine To Yellow, Pomegranates, Iridescent, Signed, 1905 200.00

Pickard, Bowl, Gold-Outlined Tulips, Open Handles, Gold Interior, 10 1/2 In. 75.00

Pickard, Bowl, Red Roses On Green And Ivory, Artist Signed, 1895-98 Mark 55.00

Pickard, Bowl, Yellow Ground, Violet Decoration, Signed Mark, 1898, 10 In. 75.00

Pickard, Bowl, 24K Gold Lotus, 8 1/2 In. 40.00

Pickard, Candlestick, White, Gold Cup, Base, & Designs, 5 7/8 In., Pair 50.00

Pickard, Celery, Black Lines & Red Roses, Gold Border, Open Handles, C.1912 12.50

Pickard, Celery, Etched China Gold Label, Pheasant Flowers, Signed E.Challin 125.00

Pickard, Chocolate Set, Gold Bands, Limoges Blank, 13 Piece 150.00

Pickard, Coffee Set, Demitasse, Gold Decoration, 3 Piece 55.00

Pickard, Compote, Gold With Etched Floral, Openwork Edge, 8 1/2 In. 45.00

Pickard, Compote, Violets, Gold Trim, 1912, 7 In. 60.00

Pickard, Compote, Violets, Leaf Mark, Signed Fisher, Low, 8 In.Wide 65.00

Pickard, Cream & Sugar, Bavaria, Gold Etched 40.00

Pickard, Creamer, Black No.1884, 5 In. 80.00

Pickard, Cup & Saucer, Clifford 25.00

Pickard, Cup & Saucer, Demitasse, Gold Decoration 6.00

Pickard, Cup & Saucer, Demitasse, Symphony, Ivory, Gold Leaves & Handle 6.00

Pickard, Dish, Cheese & Cracker, Gold, Stippled Top 65.00

Pickard, Dish, Nut, Leaf Shape, Acorns, Signed Nessy, 1898, 10 1/2 X 8 In. 139.50

Pickard, Jar, Jam, Underplate, Deserted Garden, Yeschek 250.00

Pickard, Muffineer, Floral 65.00

Pickard, Mug, Dutch Girl, 1908, 6 In. 95.00

Pickard, Pitcher, Gold & Blue Floral Panels, Hess, 8 X 7 In. 175.00

Pickard, Pitcher, Ivory Color, Silver & Gold Trim, Hessler, C.1905, 6 1/2 In. 265.00

Pickard, Pitcher, Lemonade, Gold Trim 70.00

Pickard, Pitcher, Rose Basket, Bavarian Blank, F.Vobor, C.1919, 8 3/4 In. 135.00

Pickard, Plate, Cake, Hills & Water Scene, Open Handles, Challinor, C.1912 135.00

Pickard, Plate, Cake, Open Handled, Floral, Gold Leaf Mark, 10 1/2 In. 28.00

Pickard, Plate, Cake, Pink Flowers, Gold Trim, Artist Signed, 10 1/4 In. 52.00

Pickard, Plate, Currants, Artist Signed, 8 3/4 In. 65.00

Pickard, Plate, Floral, Artist Signed 58.00

Pickard, Plate, Gooseberries, Foliage, Artist Signed, 1905-10 Mark, 8 1/2 In. 45.00

Pickard, Plate, Hand-Painted, Signed Challinor, Aqua & Gold Borders, 11 In. 30.00

Pickard, Plate, Moonlight Scene, Artist, Marker, 1905, 8 1/4 In. 65.00

Pickard, Plate, Peaches, Artist Signed, 1910-12 Mark, 8 3/4 In. 75.00

Pickard, Plate, Purple Violets On Greens, Artist Initialed, 1905-10, 6 In. 27.50

Pickard, Plate, Raspberries, Rean, Haviland Blank, 1905-10, 8 1/2 In. 40.00

Pickard, Plate, Rose Basket, Limoges Blank, Faladik, C.1922, 12 1/4 In. 110.00

Pickard, Plate, Violets, Gold Border, 8 1/4 In. 22.00

Pickard, Plate, Yellow, Violets In Orange Medallions, C.1905, 8 1/2 In. 35.00

Pickard, Rose Bowl, Poinsettias, Leaves, Stems, Iridescent, H.Tolley, 1905 250.00

Pickard, Salt & Pepper, Gold, Etched, 4 3/4 In. 12.50

Pickard, Salt & Pepper, Gold, Etched, 5 In. 25.00

Pickard, Salt & Pepper, Leaf Decoration, Green And Gold, 3 In. 22.50

Pickard, Salt & Pepper, Underplate, Stylized, Gold, 1905-10 Mark, 3 1/4 In. 65.00

Pickard, Sugar & Creamer, Cover, Gold 55.00

Pickard, Sugar & Creamer, Cream Color, Red Poppies, Gold Trim, Tolpin, 1905 125.00

Pickard, Sugar & Creamer, Cream Color, Violets, Gold Trim, R.H., C.1905 95.00

Pickard, Sugar & Creamer, Floral, Artist Signed 58.00

Pickard, Sugar & Creamer, Flowers, Ribbons, Gold, Signed 55.00

Pickard, Sugar & Creamer, Gold Finial & Handles 45.00

Pickard, Sugar & Creamer, Nippon Blank Rising Sun, Signed Tolpin 55.00

Pickard, Sugar & Creamer, Violets, Heavy Gold, 1895/98 Mark, Medium Size 70.00

Pickard, Tea Set, Birds On Royal Blue Band, Gold, C.1910, 3 Piece 195.00

Pickard, Tea Set, Landscape Scenes, Gold Trim, Marler, 3 Piece 350.00

Pickard, Teapot, White, Pink Floral, Gold Leaf Handle, Crown Finial, 6 In. 23.50

Pickard, Tray, Cookie, Flower Garden & Brick Wall, Gold Handles, Square, 8 In. 175.00
Pickard, Tray, Yellow To Orange, Violets Medallion, Michel, C.1898, 9 In. 45.00
Pickard, Vase, Blue, Cream, & Green, 2 Mallards Flying, Lily Shape, 1839, 7 In. 215.00
Pickard, Vase, Blue, Fall Harvest Scene, Gold Handles & Neck, 7 In. 85.00
Pickard, Vase, Cylinder, Poppies, Chalinor, 10 X 3 1/2 In. 95.00
Pickard, Vase, Gold Floral In Panels, Green Interior, Scalloped, 7 In. 22.00
Pickard, Vase, Gold Handles, Florals, Artist Signed, 1910-12 Mark, 8 1/2 In. 150.00
Pickard, Vase, Orchids, Butterfly, Signed Yeschek, 1898, 12 3/4 In. 195.00
Pickard, Vase, Pedestal, Oriental Birds, Gold Band, Samuelson, 7 3/4 In. 150.00
Pickard, Vase, Raised Floral, Gold Trim, Winged Lion Mark, 7 In. 25.00
Pickard, Vase, Scenic, Lake, Mountain, Gold Maple Leaf, 7 1/2 In. 150.00
Pickard, Vase, Scenic, Oriental, Artist Signed, 10 In. 255.00
Pickard, Vase, Wooded Scene, Volar, 10 In. 150.00

Picture, see also Painting, Print
Picture Frame, see Furniture, Frame

Picture, Cloth, American Eagle & Verse, 1904, Framed, 18 X 18 In. 45.00
Picture, Crewel On Silk, Birds Feeding Elijah, 22 1/2 X 19 1/2 In. 220.00
Picture, Embroidery On Silk, Chinese, Birds & Insects, 22 X 4 In. 12.00
Picture, Filigreework, Pearl Religious Scenes In Hearts, C.1750, 24 In. 150.00
Picture, Hair, Flowers & Leaves Wreath, Gilt Shadowbox Frame, 17 In. 74.00
Picture, Pastel Sandpaper Drawing, Castle & Mountains, 16 3/4 In. 65.00
Picture, Sandpaper, View Of New York City Hall, 1835, Black & White, 22 In. 175.00
Picture, Silhouette, Colonial Gentleman, Hollow Cutout Frame, 6 1/2 In. 55.00
Picture, Silhouette, George Washington's Profile, Peale's Museum, 6 In. 250.00
Picture, Silhouette, Man, White On Black, C.1850, Brass Frame, 7 In. 35.00
Picture, Silhouette, Sailing Ships, Brasch, Hand Cut, Framed, 10 X 8 1/2 In. 18.00
Picture, Silhouette, Woman, White On Black, C.1850, Brass Frame, 7 In. 35.00
Picture, Silk & Chenille Embroidery, Mourning, P.W.Simmons, C.1820, 18 In. 550.00
Picture, Silk, J.F.Kennedy, "Ask Not–, " 11 X 9 In. 6.50
Picture, Tinsel, Compote Of Flowers & Garland Of Flowers, 22 In., Pair 120.00
Picture, Tinsel, Floral & Butterflies, Signed Alice Knight, 8 X 10 In., Pair 65.00
Picture, Tinsel, Floral, 23 X 16 1/2 In. 85.00
Picture, Wax, Welsh Tea Party, Framed, 13 X 12 1/2 In. 250.00
Picture, Woolwork, C.1890, U.S.S.Charleston, 28 X 16 In. 125.00
Picture, Woolwork, Ship Flying British Flag, Vines & Roses, 18 X 15 In. 140.00
Picture, Woven Silk, Children At Play, C.1860, 8 X 6 In. 30.00
Picture, Woven Silk, French Street Scene, Signed NF, Framed, 9 X 8 In. 45.00

Pigeon Blood, see Cranberry Glass, Ruby Glass

Pilkington, Vase, Brown, Green, & Silver Vines & Leaf, Gladys Rodgers, 6 In. 325.00
Pincushion Doll, Blonde Curls, Rose In Hair, Blue Shawl, 3 In. 15.00
Pincushion Doll, Blonde Hair, Blue Band In Hair, 1 Hand On Breast, 3 In. 15.00
Pincushion Doll, Blonde Hair, 1 Hand On Breast, 1 Hand On Hip, 3 In. 15.00
Pincushion Doll, Child, Blonde Hair, Germany, 2 In. 35.00
Pincushion Doll, Flapper 10.00
Pincushion Doll, German Porcelain, Miniature 15.00
Pincushion Doll, German, Black-Painted Hair, Blue Comb, 3 In. 35.00
Pincushion Doll, German, Blonde Flapper, Hands On Waist, Hem Holds Puffs 40.00
Pincushion Doll, German, Blonde Lady, 3 In. 20.00
Pincushion Doll, German, Child, Blonde Hair, Arms Extended, 2 In. 35.00
Pincushion Doll, German, David Copperfield, 4 1/4 In. 22.50
Pincushion Doll, German, Dutch-Type Mother & Daughter, Pair 24.50
Pincushion Doll, German, Marie Antoinette, 2 1/2 In. 10.00
Pincushion Doll, German, Mr.Bumble, 4 In. 22.50
Pincushion Doll, German, Spanish Hairdo, Blue Comb, 3 In. 15.00
Pincushion Doll, Germany, Black Hair, Blue Bodice, 1 3/4 In. 9.00
Pincushion Doll, Germany, Brown Hair, White Bodice, 1 1/2 In. 9.00
Pincushion Doll, Germany, Child, Blonde Hair, Arms Extended, 2 In. 35.00
Pincushion Doll, Germany, Lady, Blue Velvet Bottom 18.00
Pincushion Doll, Germany, One Arm Behind Back, 2 In. 30.00
Pincushion Doll, Germany, White Hair, 1 3/4 In. 9.00
Pincushion Doll, Goebel, 4 In. 195.00
Pincushion Doll, Gray Hair, Marked Germany 15.00
Pincushion Doll, Heubach, Baby, Bisque, Painted Features, Jointed Arms, 2 In. 45.00
Pincushion Doll, Lady In Pink Dress, Germany 15.00
Pincushion Doll, Lady, Brown Hair, 4 In. 19.50

Pincushion Doll, Lady, Gray Hair, Blue Ribbon, Velvet Base, 8 In. 25.00
Pincushion Doll, Marie Antoinette, Dresser Lamp Type 45.00
Pincushion Doll, Nude Bald Head, Bisque Arms Outstretched, 1 3/4 In. 75.00
Pincushion Doll, Pink Hat, Hands Behind Head 22.00
Pincushion Doll, Porcelain, Dress, 9 In. 25.00
Pincushion Doll, Porcelain, Victorian, Full Length Pink Dress, 6 1/2 In. 16.00
Pincushion Doll, Spanish Dancer, Comb In Hair 25.00
Pincushion Doll, Spanish Hairdo, Pink Dress 15.00
Pincushion Doll, Superior Porcelain, Nude, 6 In. 125.00
Pincushion Doll, White Hair, Blue Band In Hair, 1 Hand On Head, 3 3/4 In. 15.00
Pincushion Doll, Wood & Papier-Mache, 6 1/2 In. 10.00
Pincushion Doll, Yellow Bonnet, Hands On Waist, Thread & Thimble, German 40.00
Pincushion Doll, Yellow Hat, Roses, German 11.00
Pincushion Doll, Yellow Ribbon In Brown Upsweep Hairdo, 3 1/2 In. 45.00
Pincushion, Doll, German Porcelain, Nude, Gray Bouffant Hair, Blue Band 16.00
Pincushion, Standing Pig, Glass Eyes, Stuffed Velvet, German Label 10.00

Pink Slag, see Slag, Pink
Pinocchio, see Disneyana
Pipe, see also Cloisonne, Pipe

Pipe, Bone, Pink, Figural, Man & Dog Lying On Stem 25.00
Pipe, Burl Wood, Silver & Ivory Inlaid, Ornate Designs 25.00
Pipe, Burl, Oblong Block, 2 1/4 In. 35.00
Pipe, Clambroth, Souvenir, Michigan 14.00
Pipe, Delft, Blue & White 12.00
Pipe, Findlay, Amber Mouthpiece 55.00
Pipe, German Porcelain, Hand Under Bowl, Hinged Lid, Cherry Stem 45.00
Pipe, Girl On Chamber Pot Bowl, Clay, German 15.00
Pipe, Gouda Bowl, Delft Decoration 22.00
Pipe, Holder, Porcelain, Pierrot Lying Down, Luster, Black Trim, 5 3/4 In. 12.50
Pipe, Ivory, 2 Pugs Standing On Stem 25.00

Pipe, Meerschaum, see Meerschaum, Pipe

Pipe, Nude Torso, Soapstone 7.50
Pipe, Opium, Brass, Chinese 50.00
Pipe, Opium, Chinese Silver 65.00
Pipe, Opium, Ivory, Carved Winged Female Suspended From Ivory Beads 65.00
Pipe, Opium, Water, Oriental Porcelain, Yellow Dragon, Gray Blue, 4 In. 45.00
Pipe, Porcelain, Hand-Painted Angel & German Soldiers, R.U.K., 1912 50.00
Pipe, Porcelain, Hand-Painted Winter Scene 25.00
Pipe, Porcelain, Hand-Painted, Lovers, Jetzt Passts On Back Of Bowl 90.00
Pipe, Regimental, 1912-1914 Infantry From Trier, No.29, 31 In. 200.00
Pipe, Victorian Lady, Cigar Holder Shape 42.00

Pirkenhammer is a porcelain manufactory started in 1802 by Friedrich Holke and J. G. List.

Pirkenhammer, Figurine, Boy With Ax Over Shoulder, Turnips, 5 1/2 In. 20.00
Pirkenhammer, Pitcher, Cream Satin Ground, 19th Century Date Mark, 3 In. 55.00
Pirkenhammer, Vase, Fish & Kingfishers 75.00

Pisgah pottery pieces that are marked Pisgah Forest Pottery were made in North Carolina from 1926 until the present. Vases, teapots, jugs, candlesticks, and many other items were made.

Pisgah Forest, Pitcher, Blue, 8 In. 15.00
Pisgah Forest, Saucer, One Signed By Stephen, Set Of 3 20.00
Pisgah Forest, Vase, Blue With Pink Interior, 1941 22.00
Pisgah Forest, Vase, Burgundy 32.00
Pisgah Forest, Vase, Cream Color, Turquoise Crystaline, 5 X 3 1/2 In. 45.00
Pisgah Forest, Vase, Crystallized Blue On Cream, 1941, Potters Wheel Mark 35.00
Pisgah Forest, Vase, Stippled Purple Pebbled Glaze, 6 1/2 In. 40.00
Pisgah Forest, Vase, Turquoise Crackle To Red Purple, 1950, 6 In. 22.00

Plate, see under special types such as ABC, Calendar, Christmas

Plated Amberina, Cruet, Maroon, Gold Flecks, Dark Ribs, Amber Handle 2800.00
Plated Amberina, Tumbler 2000.00

Plated Silver, see Silver Plate

Plique a jour is an enameling process. The enamel was laid between thin raised metal lines and heated. The finished piece has transparent enamel held between the thin metal wires.

Plique A Jour, Bowl, Green, Yellow Prunus Blossoms, 5 In. 230.00
Plique A Jour, Fork, Gold On Sterling Silver, 2 Prongs, 4 In. 200.00
Plique A Jour, Fork, Marked T, G, K. 115.00
Plique A Jour, Spoon, Coffee, Flared Handle 22.00
Plique A Jour, Spoon, Demitasse, Sterling Silver, Blues, Reds, & Greens 35.00
Plique A Jour, Vase, Green, Flowers, 4 In. 220.00
Plique A Jour, Wine Taster, Silver Gilt, Foliate Design, Sea Horse Handles 325.00
Political Campaign, Badge, Republican Delegate, Cleveland, 1936 .... 15.00
Political Campaign, Ballot, Sample, Fish & Brooks, 1888, Prohibition Ticket 15.00
Political Campaign, Ballot, Sample, Hoover, 1928 .... 2.00
Political Campaign, Ballot, Sample, Roosevelt, 1940 .... 4.00
Political Campaign, Bandana, Cleveland & Thurman, Red, White, & Black 80.00
Political Campaign, Bandana, Teddy Roosevelt, 1912, Battle Flag, Red, White 35.00
Political Campaign, Bank, Humphrey, 1968, Iron 15.00
Political Campaign, Bank, Nixon, 1968, Iron 15.00
Political Campaign, Bank, Peanut, Carter, Plastic, Button, 11 1/2 In. 4.50
Political Campaign, Bank, Wallace, 1968, Liberty Bell, Iron 14.00
Political Campaign, Banner, Harrison & Reid, Protection To Home, 24 X 24 In. 75.00
Political Campaign, Banner, J.F.K. 7.50
Political Campaign, Banner, L.B.J. 3.50
Political Campaign, Banner, Nixon's The One 4.00
Political Campaign, Belt, Nixon, Elephant Buckle, Link 8.50
Political Campaign, Bottle Opener, Jimmy Carter, Doll, 4 1/4 In. 12.50
Political Campaign, Bottle Opener, Jimmy Carter, Rubber Head, 7 In. 4.50
Political Campaign, Bottle Stopper, Charles DeGaulle 30.00
Political Campaign, Bottle Stopper, L.B.Johnson 30.00
Political Campaign, Bottle Stopper, Winston Churchill 30.00
Political Campaign, Box, Ballot, Sliding Top, White & Black Marbles 22.00
Political Campaign, Box, Ballot, Wooden 6.50
Political Campaign, Button, Al Smith, 1 1/2 In. 10.00
Political Campaign, Button, Alton B.Parker, Color, Pinback, 7/8 In. 15.00
Political Campaign, Button, Bryan, 1908 League, 7/8 In. 5.00
Political Campaign, Button, Carter & Mondale, Picture, 1 3/4 In. 1.00
Political Campaign, Button, Carter & Mondale, 2 1/2 In. .... .45
Political Campaign, Button, Carter For President, Picture, 3 1/2 In. 1.50
Political Campaign, Button, Carter, Flasher, 2 1/2 In. 1.00
Political Campaign, Button, Elect Ford, '76, Picture, 3 1/2 In. 1.00
Political Campaign, Button, F.D.R., Donkey, Ribbon, Pinback, 1 1/4 In. 8.00
Political Campaign, Button, Flasher, Nixon-Lodge 8.50
Political Campaign, Button, For President Harding, 7/8 In. 5.00
Political Campaign, Button, Ford & Dole, Picture, 1 3/4 In. 1.00
Political Campaign, Button, Ford, Flasher, 2 1/2 In. 1.00
Political Campaign, Button, Ford, 1976, Picture, 5 Colors, 1 3/4 In. 1.00
Political Campaign, Button, George Washington, Picture, Pinback, 1 1/4 In. 3.50
Political Campaign, Button, Goldwater, 1964, 3 1/2 In. 1.00
Political Campaign, Button, Honey Fitz For Mayor Of Boston 35.00
Political Campaign, Button, Hughes Bruce, Black And White, 1 1/4 In. 15.00
Political Campaign, Button, I Like Ike, Red, White, & Blue, 3 1/2 In. 2.00
Political Campaign, Button, J.F.K., 1964, Picture, Plastic, 3 1/2 In. 1.00
Political Campaign, Button, Jimmy Carter For President In 1976, 9 In. 8.50
Political Campaign, Button, Johnson & Goldwater, Ribbon, Donkey, 1 3/4 In. 1.50
Political Campaign, Button, Johnson & Humphrey, 1964, Picture, 3 In. 2.00
Political Campaign, Button, McGovern & Eagleton, 3 1/2 In. 1.50
Political Campaign, Button, McKinley & Roosevelt, 2 1/8 In. 30.00
Political Campaign, Button, My Name Is Jimmy Carter, Picture, 3 1/2 In. 1.00
Political Campaign, Button, President Ford In '76, Picture, 3 1/2 In. 1.00
Political Campaign, Button, The Grin Will Win, Carter, Peanut, 3 1/2 In. 1.00
Political Campaign, Button, The Nation Needs Nixon, 3 1/2 In. 7.50
Political Campaign, Button, Votes For Women, 1915, Rising Sun, 7/8 In. 15.00
Political Campaign, Button, Wallace For President, Picture, 1 3/4 In. 3.00
Political Campaign, Button, Willkie, 3 1/2 In. 10.00
Political Campaign, Button, Wilson, America First 20.00

Political Campaign, Candy Container, Gray Elephant, G.O.P. 68.00
Political Campaign, Cane, Franklin Roosevelt For President, 1932 55.00
Political Campaign, Cane, James G.Birney & Thos.Morris, Antislavery 185.00
Political Campaign, Cane, McKinley 60.00 To 67.50
Political Campaign, Card, Grant & Tilden, Metamorphic, Bull Durham Tobacco 25.00
Political Campaign, Card, Window, F.D.R., 1936 7.00
Political Campaign, Cards, Playing, L.B.J., Deck 2.75
Political Campaign, Carter, Inauguration Day, 4 In. 2.00
Political Campaign, Cigar, Woodrow Wilson 25.00
Political Campaign, Delegate Badge, Eisenhower, 1952 25.00
Political Campaign, Delegate, Hughes, 1916 40.00
Political Campaign, Delegate, Willkie, 1940 20.00
Political Campaign, Doll, Barry Goldwater, Jointed 20.00
Political Campaign, Doll, Nixon, Vinyl, Movable Head & Arms, 4 In. 6.00
Political Campaign, Doll, Nixon, 1972, Vinyl, 4 In. 15.00
Political Campaign, Elephant, I Like Ike, Battery Operated, Marline, 10 In. 45.00
Political Campaign, Eraser, Nixon & Agnew, 1968, Figural, 2 In., Pair 5.00
Political Campaign, Fan, Dewey 8.00
Political Campaign, Fan, Keep Coolidge President, Portrait, Paddle Shape 38.00
Political Campaign, Fan, McKinley & Roosevelt, 1900, Cardboard 45.00
Political Campaign, Figurine, Lincoln Bust, Annual Lincoln Dinner, 1904 15.00
Political Campaign, Flag Holder, Grand Army Of The Republic, 1924, Nickel 35.00
Political Campaign, Flag, Willkie For President, On 32 In. Stick 6.00
Political Campaign, Glass, Shot, FDR, Repeal Prohibition, Set Of 3 10.00
Political Campaign, Handbill, McKinley & Hobart, 1896, Dollar Not 53 Cent 12.00
Political Campaign, Handkerchief, Cleveland & Hendricks, White 60.00
Political Campaign, Hard Hat, J.F.K., Band 12.50
Political Campaign, Hat, L.B.J. 6.00
Political Campaign, Hat, Nixon & Lodge 6.00 To 7.00
Political Campaign, Hat, Richard Nixon 12.00 To 18.00
Political Campaign, Invitation, Agnew Inauguration, 1973 3.50
Political Campaign, Invitation, Nixon Inaugural, 1969 8.50
Political Campaign, Invitation, Nixon Inaugural, 1973 5.00
Political Campaign, Jugate, Carter & Mondale, Get America Moving, 2 1/4 In. 1.25
Political Campaign, Jugate, Cleveland & Stevenson, Red Celluloid, 5 In. 175.00
Political Campaign, Jugate, Debs & Seidel, 1912 95.00
Political Campaign, Jugate, Kennedy & Johnson, 1 3/8 In. 5.00
Political Campaign, Jugate, Landon & Knox, 1936 1.00
Political Campaign, Jugate, McGovern & Eagleton, 1972, 1 3/4 In. 2.50
Political Campaign, Jugate, McGovern & Eagleton, 1972, 3 1/2 In. 3.00
Political Campaign, Jugate, Nixon & Agnew, 3 1/2 In. 5.00
Political Campaign, Jugate, Parker & Davis, 1 1/4 In. 55.00
Political Campaign, Jugate, Truman & Barkley 7.00
Political Campaign, Knife, Pocket, Thurman & Wright, 1948, 2 Blades 5.00
Political Campaign, License Plate Attachment, Hoover For President 10.00
Political Campaign, License Plate, Wallace For President, Picture 5.00
Political Campaign, Medal, Calvin Coolidge, 1 1/4 In. 10.00
Political Campaign, Money, Bryan, 16 To 1 45.00
Political Campaign, Napkin, Cloth, James Blaine, John Logan, 19 X 18 In. 75.00
Political Campaign, Nodder, J.F.Kennedy Caricature Head, Football Helmet 50.00
Political Campaign, Paddle, Ping-Pong, Nixon & Mao, Pair 3.00
Political Campaign, Pamphlet, Taft & Sherman, 1908 12.50
Political Campaign, Pass, Inauguration Vehicle, 1965 6.00
Political Campaign, Pen, Harrison & Morton, 1888, Gold Plated 65.00
Political Campaign, Pencil, Figural Head, Smith For President, 1928 22.00
Political Campaign, Pencil, Hoover, Head On End 18.00
Political Campaign, Pennant, Socialist Party, Des Moines, C.1900, Felt 5.00
Political Campaign, Pennant, Thomas Dewey, Pictorial 6.00
Political Campaign, Photograph, Harrison & Morton, Cabinet Picture 10.00
Political Campaign, Pin, Al Smith, Bronze 6.00
Political Campaign, Pin, Charles E.Hughes For President, 1916, Whitehead Co. 10.00
Political Campaign, Pin, Coolidge & Dawes 5.00
Political Campaign, Pin, DFL, Carter, Mondale, Humphrey, Griffin, 3 In. 2.50
Political Campaign, Pin, Harrison & Morton, 1888, Gold Plated, Hanging Piece 45.00
Political Campaign, Pin, Impeach Nixon, 3 1/4 In. 10.00

Political Campaign, Pin, Landon And Knox 2.50
Political Campaign, Pin, McGovern, Picture, 3 In. 2.50
Political Campaign, Pin, McKinley Goldbug 15.00
Political Campaign, Pin, Stevenson & Sparkman, 2 1/4 In. 7.00
Political Campaign, Pin, Stevenson, Picture, 1 3/4 In. 6.00
Political Campaign, Pin, Truman, Barkley 9.00
Political Campaign, Plate, Eisenhower 5.00
Political Campaign, Plate, Garfield, China 20.00
Political Campaign, Plate, Mrs.Roosevelt, 5 1/2 In. 25.00
Political Campaign, Plate, Richard M.Nixon, 37th President, Ironstone, 10 In. 10.00
Political Campaign, Plate, Small Picture Of Mrs.Teddy Roosevelt 16.00
Political Campaign, Plate, Taft & Sherman, 1908, Tin, 9 1/2 In. 70.00
Political Campaign, Plate, William H. Taft, Portrait, 7 In. 28.00
Political Campaign, Postcard, Bryan For President 5.00
Political Campaign, Postcard, Calvin Coolidge 10.00
Political Campaign, Postcard, Carter & Mondale In '76 .... .50
Political Campaign, Postcard, Taft 4.00
Political Campaign, Postcard, Theodore Roosevelt For President, 7 In. 10.00
Political Campaign, Postcard, Wm.H.Taft, Bow Tie Flag 10.00
Political Campaign, Poster, Cleveland & Hendricks, Lithograph, 15 In. 16.00
Political Campaign, Poster, Franklin Roosevelt, 1936, Photo, 17 X 12 In. 10.50
Political Campaign, Poster, Nixon's The One, 1968, 28 X 20 In. 6.25
Political Campaign, Program, Official Cleveland's Inauguration, 1885 .... 42.00
Political Campaign, Puppet, Hand, Nixon & Agnew, Pair 25.00
Political Campaign, Record, The First Family, Kennedy Spoof, 33 1/3 Speed 10.00
Political Campaign, Ribbon, Cleveland & Hendricks, 2 1/4 X 6 In. 12.00
Political Campaign, Ribbon, Garfield & Arthur, 8 In. 18.00
Political Campaign, Ribbon, I Am For Wm.J.Bryan 3.00
Political Campaign, Ribbon, McKinley & Protection, Picture, 6 In. 22.00
Political Campaign, Ring, F.D.R., Copper 10.00
Political Campaign, Sash, HHH, 1968, Silk 10.00
Political Campaign, Scarf, I Like Ike 7.00
Political Campaign, Spoon, McKinley's Profile On Handle, Sterling 20.00
Political Campaign, Straw Hat, J.F.K. 21.00
Political Campaign, Stud, Lapel, Hoover, Elephant 4.00
Political Campaign, Thimble, Coolidge & Dawes, 1924, Aluminum 15.00
Political Campaign, Thimble, Nixon, Plastic 8.50
Political Campaign, Thimble, Willkie For President 12.00
Political Campaign, Tie Clip, Hoover, Elephant 7.50
Political Campaign, Tie Clip, J.F.K. 15.00
Political Campaign, Tiepin, McKinley, Shield, Eagle 18.00
Political Campaign, Tin, F.D.R. Is Good Enough For Me, 1936, 6 1/2 In. 22.00
Political Campaign, Token, Abraham Lincoln, 1860, White Metal, 1 1/4 In. 75.00
Political Campaign, Token, Lincoln, 1860, Not 1 Cent For Slavery 22.00
Political Campaign, Top Hat, Cleveland And Running Mate, Box 125.00
Political Campaign, Tray, Teddy Roosevelt On Horse, Oval, Tin, 1890-1900 .... 100.00
Political Campaign, Watch Fob, Wm.H.Taft, Our Next President, Leather Strap 20.00
Political Campaign, Watch, Pocket, Carter & Mondale 17.95
Political Campaign, Wm.Taft For President, Pictorial 12.00

Pomona glass is clear with a soft amber border decorated with pale blue or rose-colored flowers and leaves. The colors are very, very pale. The background of the glass is covered with a network of fine lines. It was made from 1885 to 1888 by the New England Glass Company.

Pomona, Bowl, Amber Stain On Crimped Top, 1st Grand, 10 In. 150.00
Pomona, Bowl, Amber, Ruffled Rims, 4 1/2 X 2 1/4 In., Pair 140.00
Pomona, Bowl, Blue Cornflowers, 4 3/8 In. 49.00
Pomona, Bowl, Ruffled Rim, 1st Grind, 5 X 2 1/4 In. 145.00
Pomona, Carafe, Raised Seaweed & Fish With Gold And Blue Backs 300.00
Pomona, Castor, Pickle, 2nd Grind Insert, Cornflower, Pairpoint Holder 295.00
Pomona, Cruet, Gold Sheen Top, Handle & Stopper, Decorated 190.00
Pomona, Cruet, Pansy & Butterfly, Gold Sheen Top, Handle And Stopper 350.00
Pomona, Cup, Punch, Thumbprint, 1st Grind 60.00
Pomona, Finger Bowl, Crimped Amber Rim, 2nd Grind, 5 In. 55.00
Pomona, Pitcher, Midwestern, Inverted Thumbprint, Amber Handle & Top, 5 In. 50.00

Pomona, Pitcher, Triangular Top, 1st Grind, 6 In. 175.00
Pomona, Plate, Ruffled Rim, 2nd Grind, 6 1/2 In. 155.00
Pomona, Rose Bowl, Midwestern, Crimped Top, Amber Legs & Top, 4 In. 90.00
Pomona, Tumbler, Baby Thumbprint, Western 45.00
Pomona, Tumbler, Cornflower, Blue & Amber 110.00
Pomona, Tumbler, Inverted Diamond, Amber Rim, Blue Cornflower, 2nd Grind 95.00
Pomona, Tumbler, Pansy & Butterfly, Gold Trim, 1st Grind, 4 1/2 In. 175.00
Pomona, Vase, Cornflower, Gold Trim, Crimped, Pedestal, 1st Grind, 6 1/2 In. 3250.00
Pomona, Vase, New England, Diamond Quilted, Cornflowers, 2nd Grind, 4 1/2 In. 325.00
Pomona, Vase, Pinched Top, 2nd Grind, 5 In. 125.00

Pontypool, see Tole

Popeye, Bag, Marble, Marked K.F.S., 1933 7.50
Popeye, Bank, Dime Register, Upside-Down Pipe, 1929 27.00
Popeye, Bank, Dome, 1956 10.00
Popeye, Book, Popeye In Puddleburg, Big Little Book 6.00
Popeye, Book, Popeye Sees The Sea, Big Little Book 13.00
Popeye, Book, Popeye The Spinach Eater, Big Little Book 11.00
Popeye, Book, Popeye, Saalfield, 1936, Soft Cover 16.00
Popeye, Box, Crayon, 1933 5.00
Popeye, Child's Set, Fork & Spoon, Blue & White Plastic 12.00
Popeye, Doll, Cardboard, 1944 6.00
Popeye, Doll, Olive Oyle, Rubber, 8 In. 15.00
Popeye, Doll, Rubber, 11 1/2 In. 20.00
Popeye, Figurine, Metal, Copyright 1929, E.F.S., Metal, 2 1/2 In. 17.00
Popeye, Figurine, Popeye & Wimpy, Chalkware 20.00
Popeye, Game, Card, King Features 5.00
Popeye, Glass, 1929-33, 6 In. 15.00
Popeye, Gun, Target, Roly Poly, 1958 12.00
Popeye, Paint Set, 1933 10.00
Popeye, Pin, Evening Journal 15.00
Popeye, Pipe, Wooden, On Card, 1958 14.00
Popeye, Plaque, Raised Bust Center, Round, 8 In. 25.00
Popeye, Popeye The Pilot, Marx 100.00
Popeye, Spinach Can, Pop-Up, Metal, Mattel, 1957 8.00
Popeye, Toy, Airplane, Eccentric 225.00
Popeye, Toy, Champ 450.00
Popeye, Toy, Pop-Up Spinach Can, Metal, Mattel, 1957 8.00
Popeye, Toy, Popeye & Olive Oyle Express 425.00
Popeye, Toy, Popeye & Olive Oyle On Roof 400.00
Popeye, Toy, Popeye & Parrot Cage, Windup, Tin 60.00
Popeye, Toy, Popeye Holding Can Of Spinach, Roller Skates, Key Wind, Tin 65.00
Popeye, Toy, Popeye, The Champ, Original Box 450.00
Popeye, Toy, Pull, Wooden, Lithographed, 1929 27.00

Porcelain, see also Copeland, Nippon, R.S.Prussia, etc.

Porcelain, Ashtray, Bathing Beauty, Lying On Stomach, Legs Hold Tray, German 10.00
Porcelain, Basket, Bride's, Keeling & Co., Decorated, 11 X 10 In. 150.00
Porcelain, Basket, Hand-Painted Floral, Gold Handle, England, 6 In. 22.50
Porcelain, Basket, Pierced Basketwork, Green, Furstenberg, 8 7/8 In., Pair 850.00
Porcelain, Bottle, Perfume, Japanese, Turquoise, Gold Tracery, Pair 15.00
Porcelain, Bowl, Czar Profile, Russian Mark, 19th Century, 7 In. 85.00
Porcelain, Bowl, Germany, Hand-Painted Floral, Gold Trim, Lacy Edge, 13 In. 65.00
Porcelain, Bowl, Germany, Satin Finish, Pastel Colors, Blown-Out Roses, 10 In. 85.00
Porcelain, Bowl, Girl In Flowered Hat, Signed Boileau, 1907 27.50
Porcelain, Bowl, Hand Decorated Red & Pink Roses, Signed, E.McCade, 7 In. 45.00
Porcelain, Bowl, Japan, Beaded Jewels & Floral, Footed, 6 1/4 In. 10.00
Porcelain, Bowl, JBT, Germany, White, Floral Bouquets, Gold Edge, 9 3/4 In. 28.00
Porcelain, Bowl, O.E.G., Austria, Green Shading, Pink Roses, Footed, 8 In. 22.00
Porcelain, Bowl, Punch, Rose To Shell Pink, Floral, Marked Fleur-De-Lis 175.00
Porcelain, Bowl, Three Crown, Germany, Hand-Painted Pears, 9 3/4 In. 28.00
Porcelain, Bowl, Three Crown, Germany, Hand-Painted Quince, 9 3/4 In. 28.00
Porcelain, Bowl, Toscana, Austria, Red Roses, Green Leaves, 10 1/4 In. 75.00
Porcelain, Box, Powder, Dresser Doll, Glass Dabber, Germany, 3 Pieces 55.00
Porcelain, Box, Powder, Figural, Girl Holding Flowers, German, 7 1/4 In. 68.00
Porcelain, Box, Ring, French, White, Egg Shape, Gold Velvet Lining 12.50

Porcelain, Box, Salt, Czechoslovakia, Pink Roses, Black Decorations 45.00
Porcelain, Box, Trinket, French, Picture On Lid 32.50
Porcelain, Box, White, Floral, Lavender & Gold Trim, France, 5 X 3 3/8 In. 55.00
Porcelain, Burner, Incense, French, Woman Kneeling, Art Deco, 7 1/4 In. 65.00
Porcelain, Butter Pat, R.F.Austria, White, Tulip, Coin Gold Border 15.00
Porcelain, Cachepot, Portugal, Pink, Gold Bands, Floral, 7 In., Pair 150.00
Porcelain, Cake Set, Germany, Green, Floral, 7 Piece 42.50
Porcelain, Can, Sprinkling, Hortense, Portrait, Lady, Blues & Greens, 3 1/4 In. 16.00
Porcelain, Celery Set, Japanese, Peonies & Parrot, Pink & Blue, 11 1/2 In. 10.00
Porcelain, Celery Set, Japanese, Scenic, 7 Piece 15.00
Porcelain, Celery, Germany, Purple Lilacs, Green Leaves, 12 X 4 1/2 In. 15.00
Porcelain, Celery, Imperial Austria & Crown, Portrait Bust, Green Rim, Gold 75.00
Porcelain, Celery, Leuchtenberg, Germany, Roses, Pastel Shading, 12 In. 20.00
Porcelain, Centerpiece Bowl, Carl Thieme, Mulberry Landscapes, 13 1/2 In. 350.00
Porcelain, Chamber Pot, England, Floral, Victorian 19.00
Porcelain, Chocolate Pot, Germany, Pink Carnations, Scrollwork 40.00
Porcelain, Chocolate Pot, Germany, White, Blue Design, Lilac Shading 50.00
Porcelain, Chocolate Pot, Japan, Oriental Scene, 10 In. 20.00
Porcelain, Chocolate Pot, Kugawa, Japan, Flying Birds, Jeweled, Gold Handle 45.00
Porcelain, Chocolate Pot, Von Henneberg, Tarzelian, Germany, Floral 35.00
Porcelain, Chocolate Pot, White Satin Finish, Roses, German, 9 1/4 In. 78.00
Porcelain, Chocolate Pot, White With Pink Floral & Leaf, B.R.C. & Crown 55.00
Porcelain, Chocolate Set, Geisha Girl Design, Cobalt Trim, Spider On Bottom 40.00
Porcelain, Chocolate Set, Germany, Pink & White Roses, 9 Piece 100.00
Porcelain, Chocolate Set, Germany, Pink & Yellow Roses, 7 1/2 In. 72.00
Porcelain, Chocolate Set, Japan, Blue Luster, Floral, Gold, 7 Piece 30.00
Porcelain, Compote, Hand-Painted Butterflies, Silver Band, O.& E.G., Austria 75.00
Porcelain, Condiment Set, Japan, Luster, Bird Shape, 4 Piece 10.00
Porcelain, Condiment Set, Mitoue-Boshi, Japan, Blue, Herons, 6 Piece 25.00
Porcelain, Creamer, Austria, Elk 30.00
Porcelain, Creamer, Austria, Moose's Head 12.00
Porcelain, Creamer, Baby And 4 Children, Czechoslovakia 14.00
Porcelain, Creamer, C.T.Altwasser, Germany, Roses, Green Leaves, Gold Trim 15.00
Porcelain, Creamer, Child's, Germany, Still Too Hot, Girl, & Animals 14.00
Porcelain, Creamer, Czechoslovakia, Chicken 10.00
Porcelain, Creamer, Czechoslovakia, Duck 5.95
Porcelain, Creamer, Czechoslovakia, Parrot 8.00
Porcelain, Creamer, Figural, Chicken, Germany 15.00
Porcelain, Creamer, German, Rat, Gray, Souvenir, Washington 12.00
Porcelain, Creamer, Germany, Cat, Pours Through Mouth, Necktie 12.00
Porcelain, Creamer, Germany, Cow, Rust & White, Black Hooves & Eyes, 7 1/4 In. 24.00
Porcelain, Creamer, Germany, Cow, White & Brown 15.00
Porcelain, Creamer, Germany, Crown & Star Mark, Oriental Woman & Baby 35.00
Porcelain, Creamer, Germany, Crown & Star Mark, Woman Holding Jug, Blue, White 35.00
Porcelain, Creamer, Germany, Eagle, 4 3/4 In. 22.50
Porcelain, Creamer, Germany, Figural, Doll 21.00
Porcelain, Creamer, Germany, Hand-Painted Floral, 3 3/4 In. 20.00
Porcelain, Creamer, Japan, Elephant, Luster Ware 6.00
Porcelain, Creamer, Japan, Green, Kitten 5.00
Porcelain, Creamer, Leonard, Vienna, Austria, 1842, Beige, 4 Footed 50.00
Porcelain, Creamer, Oval, Hand-Painted Sweet Peas, Signed T & V, France 25.00
Porcelain, Creamer, Standing Cow, Blue & White, Marked Germany, 7 X 4 1/2 In. 35.00
Porcelain, Cup & Saucer, Brazil, White 3.00
Porcelain, Cup & Saucer, Child's, Germany, Puss & Boots & Toys 18.00
Porcelain, Cup & Saucer, Chocolate, Austria, Pink Roses, Scroll Handle, Gold 8.00
Porcelain, Cup & Saucer, Chocolate, Japan, Oriental Scene 6.00
Porcelain, Cup & Saucer, Chocolate, Japan, Red Border 32.50
Porcelain, Cup & Saucer, Chocolate, RC, Crown, Madeleine, White, Pink Roses 11.00
Porcelain, Cup & Saucer, England, White, Hand-Painted Floral Band At Top 12.50
Porcelain, Cup & Saucer, German, Children Playing 10.00
Porcelain, Cup & Saucer, German, Father In Gold Letters, Pink Luster Edges 20.00
Porcelain, Cup & Saucer, Grandfather's, German, Roses, Green Luster Border 18.00
Porcelain, Cup & Saucer, Hilditch & Son, England, 1830, Chinoiserie, Lady 42.50
Porcelain, Cup & Saucer, Imari Pattern, England .... *Illus* 25.00

Porcelain, Cup & Saucer, Imari Pattern, England *(See Page 401)*

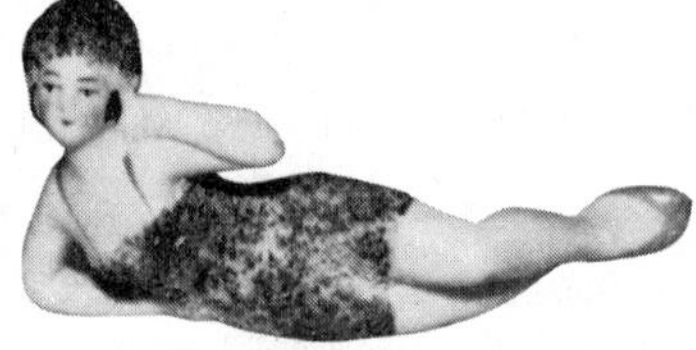

Porcelain, Figurine, Bathing Beauty, 3 In.

Porcelain, Cup & Saucer, Luneville, France, Violette, Dark Blue 12.50
Porcelain, Cup & Saucer, Moore & Co., England, 1869, White, Aqua Rope Handle 22.50
Porcelain, Cup & Saucer, Siedham-Weldman, Blue & White Floral 6.50
Porcelain, Cup & Saucer, Thomas, Ivory Color, Cobalt & Gold Trim 9.00
Porcelain, Decanter, Wade, England, Sauternes In Gold, Ivory Color, 11 1/4 In. 35.00
Porcelain, Demitasse Set, Germany, Luster, Green & Gold Decoration, 10 Piece 27.50
Porcelain, Dessert Set, R.Woodruff, Newport, 1870, Ivory & Gold, 22 Piece 250.00
Porcelain, Dish, Asparagus, Green Ivy On Pink Trellis, Crossed Sword Mark 32.50
Porcelain, Dish, Asparagus, Stalks, Purple Tips, Basket-Weave Border, G 85.00
Porcelain, Dish, Bone, Flower, Klosterle, Germany 15.00
Porcelain, Dish, Bone, Germany, Crescent Shape, Floral 5.00
Porcelain, Dish, Candy, Germany, Daisies, V Shape 8.00
Porcelain, Dish, Celery, Water Lilies, Germany, 11 1/2 In. 26.00
Porcelain, Dish, Child's Feeding, 3 Crown, Germany, Girl In Poppy Field 15.00
Porcelain, Dish, Feeding, Germany, Little Miss Muffet & Old King Cole 15.00
Porcelain, Dish, Pickle, Germany, Luster, Fox Hunt Scene, Handled 22.00
Porcelain, Dish, Sardine, Victoria, Austria, Sardine On Lid, White, Gold Trim 22.00
Porcelain, Dish, Sweetmeat, Germany, Onion Type Design, Pedestal, C.1850, 3 In. 20.00
Porcelain, Dish, Sweetmeat, Germany, Roses & Figures, Open Edge, Set Of 4 .... 18.00
Porcelain, Dish, Vegetable, Hand-Painted, Ribbon Handles, D & Co., 7 1/2 In. 85.00
Porcelain, Dog, Sealyham, Crown & Shield Mark, Germany, 2 1/4 In. 13.00
Porcelain, Dresser Set, German, Rose Stoppers, Signed, 3 Piece 42.00
Porcelain, Dresser Set, H & K, Tunstall, England, Pink Roses, Black, 6 Piece 45.00
Porcelain, Dresser Set, Pink Roses, Tray, Candlesticks, Jar, Hair Receiver 50.00
Porcelain, Dresser Set, White With Violets, Czechoslovakia, 4 Pieces 60.00
Porcelain, Egg Cup, Google-Eye Boy's Head, German 10.00
Porcelain, Egg Set, Salt And Four Egg Cups, Marked Austria, Crown, 6 In. 42.00
Porcelain, Ewer, Blue & Tan, Austria 25.00
Porcelain, Figurine, Angel On Pedestal, Flower Border, Lavender Bows, 6 In. 30.00
Porcelain, Figurine, Austria, Woman Skier, Yellow, Blue, Brown, C.1925, 13 In. 165.00
Porcelain, Figurine, Bathing Beauty, 3 In. .... *Illus* 45.00
Porcelain, Figurine, Carday, French Lady, Pompadour-Style Hat, 12 In. 55.00
Porcelain, Figurine, Cardinal Bird, Hungarian, Green Luster, Signed 25.00
Porcelain, Figurine, Cat, Amber Glass Eyes, Winstanton, 10 1/4 In. 55.00
Porcelain, Figurine, Cow, Tan & White, Lying, Legs Tucked Under, 3 1/2 X 7 In. 40.00
Porcelain, Figurine, Cupid Holding Bird, Metzler, Orloff, Germany, 5 In. 40.00
Porcelain, Figurine, France, Seated Girl, White Dress, Blue Scarf, 8 1/2 In. 175.00
Porcelain, Figurine, Germany, Pig Peeking Over Edge Of Chamberpot 28.00
Porcelain, Figurine, Germany, Pigs Peeking Over Inside Of Large Purse 35.00
Porcelain, Figurine, Germany, Pigs Sitting In Touring Car 45.00
Porcelain, Figurine, Germany, Reclining Boy Blowing Flute, 5 In. 25.00
Porcelain, Figurine, Marked Godey's Fashions For March, 1863 .... 130.00
Porcelain, Figurine, Pigs In Purse, Germany, 3 3/4 In. 49.50
Porcelain, Figurine, Queen Louise, Royal Rudolstadt, Ivory Color 95.00
Porcelain, Figurine, Russian, Enchantress With Malachite Box, 13 In. 65.00
Porcelain, Figurine, Swan, Gold Washed, Cross-Sword Mark, Set Of 3 .... 18.50
Porcelain, Figurine, U.S.A., Mallard Duck, Oval Base, 6 In., Pair 25.00
Porcelain, Figurine, Wagner, Seated, White And Gold, 5 X 3 In. 65.00

Porcelain, Figurine, Yellow Canary On White Branch, Germany, Signed, Pair 35.00
Porcelain, Flower Holder, Germany, Lady & Wave, Art Deco, 7 X 4 In. 22.00
Porcelain, Garniture, G.B.Brevete, Paris, Green, Pierced, Fruit, 3 Piece 1475.00
Porcelain, Gravy Boat & Underplate, D & Co., France, Pink & Blue Floral 22.00
Porcelain, Gravy Boat & Underplate, Germany, Aqua & Purples, Florals 22.00
Porcelain, Gravy Boat & Underplate, Germany, Floral, Aqua & Purple Tones 22.00
Porcelain, Group, Bathing Beauties, Germany 35.00
Porcelain, Group, German, Victorian Lady, Kneeling Gentleman, 5 1/2 In. 37.50
Porcelain, Group, Madonna & Child, Austria, 12 1/2 In. 45.00
Porcelain, Group, Russia, Traveling Woman & Man At Roadside, 8 3/4 In. 45.00
Porcelain, Group, Russia, Woman & Man Waiting At Roadside, Comic, 8 3/4 In. 42.00
Porcelain, Hair Receiver, Austria, Ivory Color, Red Floral On Lid, Gold 15.00
Porcelain, Hair Receiver, Austria, Princess Louise, Footed, Monogram 18.00
Porcelain, Hair Receiver, Germany, Diamond Shaped, Pink Blooms 15.00
Porcelain, Hatpin Holder & Attached Tray, TK, Hand-Painted 45.00
Porcelain, Hatpin Holder, C.Prussia, Floral, Corked Bottom 49.50
Porcelain, Hatpin Holder, Germany, Lilies 22.00
Porcelain, Hatpin Holder, Germany, Pastel Ground, Yellow Roses, White Floral 18.00
Porcelain, Holder, Shaving Mug, Marked Germany, Dog With Latticework Basket 15.00
Porcelain, Ice Cream Set, Austria, Print On Turquoise Rims, 7 Piece 65.00
Porcelain, Jar & Spoon, Jam, Japanese, Multicolors 8.00
Porcelain, Jar, Cookie, Germany, Red & Pink Roses 30.00
Porcelain, Jar, Cracker, C.S.Prussia, Charcoal Shading, Cream Roses, Gold 38.00
Porcelain, Jar, Cracker, O.S.St.Killian, Germany, Burgundy, Medallions 135.00
Porcelain, Jar, Figural, Covered, Dog, 6 In. 75.00
Porcelain, Jar, Jam, Lavender, White Satin, Silver Holder, Petal Top 73.00
Porcelain, Jar, Karlsbad Tischner, Gold Finial & Handles, Dogwoods, 7 1/2 In. 115.00
Porcelain, Jar, Rose, L.Strauss & Sons, C.1882, Covered, Beige, Gold, 8 1/2 In. 125.00
Porcelain, Jar, Rose, Pink & Red Roses, Gold Handles, 17 In., Pair 150.00
Porcelain, Jar, Tobacco, Austria, Monk's Head, Brown Cowl, 5 X 4 5/8 In. 69.50
Porcelain, Jar, Tobacco, Figural, Friar's Head, German, 8 In. 75.00
Porcelain, Jar, Tobacco, Figural, Sad Sack Dog, Blue Eyes, Covered 65.00
Porcelain, Jar, Tobacco, Germany, Fox Head Lid 24.00
Porcelain, Jar, Tobacco, Imperial Austria, Yellow, Pinecones, Brown Base 27.50
Porcelain, Jardiniere, Cyrano, Openwork Medallions, Black & Yellow, 9 In. 45.00
Porcelain, Living Room Furniture Set, Japan, White, 1 In., 6 Piece 9.00
Porcelain, Muffineer, Leonard, Star-Shaped Holes In Pewter Top 18.00
Porcelain, Mug, Child's, Germany, Gold Wolf Wearing Jacket & Cap, & Chicken 7.00
Porcelain, Mug, Child's, Three Children On Fence, German 15.00
Porcelain, Mug, Child's, Two Girls And Donkey 15.00
Porcelain, Mug, English, Brown Glaze, Big Ben With Tower Of London, Silver 12.50
Porcelain, Mug, German, Home Was Never Like This, 1 1/4 In. 4.00
Porcelain, Mug, Germany, Queens College, Belfast, 2 1/4 In. 10.00
Porcelain, Mug, Lancaster, Sundland, England, Shakespeare 17.00
Porcelain, Mug, Toby, Germany, 6 In. 95.00
Porcelain, Mush Set, Hand-Painted, Flowers And Leaves, German 40.00
Porcelain, Mustard Pot, Germany, Roses, Gold Trim 6.00

Porcelain, Napkin Ring, see Napkin Ring

Porcelain, Pitcher, C.B. & Crest, France, Blue, White Stars & Floral, 10 In. 42.00
Porcelain, Pitcher, Child's, Germany, Old-Fashioned Children In Color 8.00
Porcelain, Pitcher, Czechoslovakia, Tomato Shape, 6 In. 17.50
Porcelain, Pitcher, Germany, Pineapple Shape, 3 1/4 In. 6.50
Porcelain, Pitcher, Japanese, Ear Of Corn, 80 Ozs. 20.00
Porcelain, Pitcher, Milk, Figural, Monk's Head, DLV, 1902, Brown 25.00
Porcelain, Pitcher, Milk, Kahla, Germany, 4 1/2 In. 15.00
Porcelain, Pitcher, Octagonal, Yellow Glaze, Molded Flowers, C.1835, 6 1/2 In. 40.00
Porcelain, Plaque, English, C.1750, Scottish Harbor & Castle Scene, 8 In. 450.00
Porcelain, Plaque, Germany, Girl Picking Fruit, Lam, 7 X 4 In. 45.50
Porcelain, Plate, Austria, Hand-Painted Floral, Raised Gold Edge, 8 In. 9.00
Porcelain, Plate, Bread, German, Floral, Gold Trim, "Give Us This Day," 10 In. 14.00
Porcelain, Plate, Cake, England, Blue & Gold, Open Handles, 10 In. 21.00
Porcelain, Plate, Cake, Germany, Open Handles, Ornate Border, 11 3/4 In. 55.00
Porcelain, Plate, Cake, Germany, Roses, Silver Luster Edge, 6 In. 2.50
Porcelain, Plate, Card Decorated, 1843 W Thorley, 8 3/4 In. 400.00
Porcelain, Plate, Child's, Old King Cole, Wellsville, 7 1/2 In. 20.00

Porcelain, Plate, Molded Napkin

Porcelain, Plate, Empire China, Austria, Gold Center & Rim, Pink Roses, 9 In. 18.00
Porcelain, Plate, Empire China, Portrait, Bust Of Washington, 9 1/2 In. 25.00
Porcelain, Plate, English, Raised Floral, Victorian, 10 In. 6.00
Porcelain, Plate, Fish Scale, 7 In. 2.50
Porcelain, Plate, French, Hand-Painted Violets, 9 1/2 In. 25.00
Porcelain, Plate, German, Abstract Scene, Open Handles, Gold Trim, 10 In. 25.00
Porcelain, Plate, Germany, Hand-Painted Pink Roses, 9 1/4 In. 22.50
Porcelain, Plate, Germany, Roses, Ornate Edge, 10 1/2 In. 40.00
Porcelain, Plate, Germany, Saxe, Altenburg, Blown-Out Floral, 6 1/2 In. 25.00
Porcelain, Plate, Germany, White, Red Roses Border, Openwork Edge, 10 In. 27.50
Porcelain, Plate, Hand-Painted Rooster Center, Slam The Door On The Doctor 25.00
Porcelain, Plate, Hub, Austria, Game, Pheasant, Blue & Orchid Border, 9 1/2 In. 25.00
Porcelain, Plate, Molded Napkin *Illus* 25.00
Porcelain, Plate, Ovington Bros., Austria, Royal Blue, Yellow Dolphin, 9 In. 45.00
Porcelain, Plate, Oyster, Altrohla CA, Austrian, Floral & Gold 15.00
Porcelain, Plate, Oyster, Embossed, Rose Pink Floral, Weimar, German 10.00
Porcelain, Plate, Pink Roses, Pierced Roman Gold Edge, 12 In. 65.00
Porcelain, Plate, Portrait, Louis XV, Openwork Border, 9 In. 18.00
Porcelain, Plate, Portrait, Marie Antoinette, Gilded Bronze Holder, 6 1/2 In. 125.00
Porcelain, Plate, Prussia, Pink & Yellow Roses, 8 1/2 In. 38.00
Porcelain, Plate, S.Suzuki, Red Poppies, 6 1/2 In. 7.50
Porcelain, Plate, Victoria, Austria, Portrait, 9 In. 49.00
Porcelain, Platter, Allerton, C.1903, White, Blue Chinese Pagodas, 11 X 9 In. 25.00
Porcelain, Platter, RM & Crown, Germany, Copenhagen, 13 X 9 In. 22.00
Porcelain, Powder Box, Mirrored Cover, Pink, Signed, A.Kauffmann, 4 1/2 In. 55.00
Porcelain, Ramekin & Underplate, Germany, Pink Roses Border, Gold Trim 9.50
Porcelain, Relish, Crown, Germany, Violets & Leaves, 5 1/2 In. 15.00
Porcelain, Relish, Japan, Pale Green, Raised Pink Floral, Handled, 11 In. 7.00
Porcelain, Ring Tree, M R, France, Hand-Painted Pink Roses, Triangular 20.00
Porcelain, Rose Bowl, Austria, Cream & Pastel, Pink Wild Roses, 11 In. 30.00
Porcelain, Salt & Pepper In Center-Handled Holder, Germany, Birds 12.00
Porcelain, Salt & Pepper, France, Sitting Cats, White, 2 3/4 In. 7.50
Porcelain, Salt & Pepper, Germany, Browns, Full-Blown Pink Roses 10.50
Porcelain, Salt & Pepper, Germany, Pink Rose, Rust Tones 10.50
Porcelain, Salt & Pepper, Schlegel, Purple Violets, Coin Gold 26.00
Porcelain, Salt With Pepper Shaker On Top, JHR, White & Gold, Monogram 9.50
Porcelain, Server, Muffin, Schwartzburg, Covered, White, Pink Roses, Gold Trim 50.00
Porcelain, Server, Pancake, Austria, Flower Finial, White & Tan, Floral 40.00
Porcelain, Set Of Dishes, Doll's, Japan, Little Hostess, 11 Piece 22.00
Porcelain, Set Of Dishes, Doll's, Japan, Orange, Scenic, 19 Pieces 50.00
Porcelain, Shoe, Child's Flat Pump 12.50
Porcelain, Shoe, Germany, C.1920, Floral, Turned-Up Toe, 7 1/2 In. 9.00
Porcelain, Spooner, White With Gold Trim, Flat 12.00
Porcelain, Stein, Cavalier With Mandolin, White On Glossy Green, Germany 125.00
Porcelain, Stopper, Bottle, France, Lady With Exposed Breasts, C.1920, 4 In. 22.00
Porcelain, Strainer, Tea, Germany, Iridescent, 5 1/2 In. 9.50
Porcelain, Strainer, Tea, Germany, Roses, Gold Trim, Drip Cup 17.50

Porcelain, Sugar & Creamer, Beige To Green Luster, Germany 38.00
Porcelain, Sugar & Creamer, Germany, Stylized Peacocks, Gold Handles & Trim 20.00
Porcelain, Sugar & Creamer, Japan, Dragons 35.00
Porcelain, Sugar & Creamer, Prussia, Holly Berries & Floral, Gold Trim 40.00
Porcelain, Sugar, Covered, Painted, Mosaic Borders, Unmarked, C.1765, 4 1/4 In. 175.00
Porcelain, Syrup & Underplate, S E Prussia, Yellow Roses, Green & Gold Trim 32.50
Porcelain, Syrup & Underplate, Victoria, Austria, Roses, 5 1/2 In. 40.00
Porcelain, Syrup, Lavender Flower, Louise, Bavaria, 4 1/2 In. 22.50
Porcelain, Tazza, Berlin Buildings, Kaiser Frederick Cameo, C.1840, 13 In. 8000.00
Porcelain, Tea Bowl & Saucer, Liverpool, Pennington, Antlered Deer, C.1775 .... 125.00
Porcelain, Tea Caddy, Louis XIV, Reverse Marie Therese, Austria 62.00
Porcelain, Tea Set, Child's Germany, C.1920, Yellow, Black Luster, 9 Piece 36.00
Porcelain, Tea Set, Child's, Germany, Circus Scenes, 11 Piece 47.50
Porcelain, Tea Set, Child's, Germany, Floral, 14 Piece 17.00
Porcelain, Tea Set, Child's, Germany, Gold Flowers, C.1880, 13 Piece 65.00
Porcelain, Tea Set, Child's, Germany, White & Gold, 15 Piece 55.00
Porcelain, Tea Set, Child's, Japan, C.1920, Wild Roses, 15 Piece 30.00
Porcelain, Tea Set, Child's, Japan, House & Tree, 17 Piece 20.00
Porcelain, Tea Set, Child's, Japan, Little Hostess, White, Floral, 9 Piece 35.00
Porcelain, Tea Set, Child's, Lake Scene With Windmill, Gold Trim, 11 Piece 95.00
Porcelain, Tea Set, Florals, Artist Signed, M.Eggers, 1908, 3 Piece 50.00
Porcelain, Tea Set, France, Gold, Orchid, & Red, Miniature, 26 Piece 95.00
Porcelain, Tea Set, France, Victorian Women & Children, Miniature, 15 Piece 125.00
Porcelain, Tea Set, Germany, White, Pink Gray Center Band, Roses, 3 Piece 22.00
Porcelain, Tea Set, Germany, Yellow, Blue & White Decorations, 9 Piece 60.00
Porcelain, Tea Set, Japan, Boku-Haku, Figures In Scene, 13 Piece 160.00
Porcelain, Tea Set, Leonard, Vienna, White, Wild Roses, Gold Trim, 3 Piece 32.50
Porcelain, Tea Set, Miniature, Luster, Marked Germany 15.00
Porcelain, Tea Set, Oriental, Geisha Girl, Dragons, Raised, 17 Piece 65.00
Porcelain, Tea Strainer, Underpot, Blue And White Floral, Unmarked, Large 22.00
Porcelain, Teapot, Czechoslovakia, Multicolors 6.00
Porcelain, Teapot, Edon, Wicker Handle, Green & Pink Floral & Branches 28.00
Porcelain, Teapot, Windmill, Bonn, Germany, 7 In. 95.00
Porcelain, Toast Rack, M.V.Co., Germany, Roses, 6 Slices 22.50
Porcelain, Toby Mug, Germany, Monk, Full Figure, 6 In. 125.00
Porcelain, Toothbrush Holder, Black Man, Germany, 4 In. 8.50
Porcelain, Tray, Dresser, Pink & Rose, Victorian, Irregular Shape 32.00
Porcelain, Tray, Germany, Holly Decoration, Bisque Bottom, 12 X 8 1/2 In. 27.00
Porcelain, Tray, Pin, A L, France, Blue, Yellow, & Pink Floral, 4 In. 9.00
Porcelain, Tray, Pin, Austria, Hand-Painted Pink Roses, 6 In. 9.00
Porcelain, Tray, Pin, Figural, Bird On Edge, Germany 8.50
Porcelain, Tray, Pin, Figural, Pigs, Germany, 4 1/2 In. 48.50
Porcelain, Tray, Pin, France, Hand-Painted Pink Roses, 3 In. 8.00
Porcelain, Trinket Box, 4 In. .... *Illus* 75.00
Porcelain, Urn, Glass, Mid-Section, Burgundy, Cream Hand-Painted Roses, 18 In. 135.00
Porcelain, Vase, Austria, Columbian Exposition, Transfer, 2 Handles, 6 In. 12.00
Porcelain, Vase, Austria, Portrait, Lady, Yellow, Tan, & Gilt, 13 In., Pair 245.00
Porcelain, Vase, Austria, Tan, Floral, Gold Trim, 2 Handles, 17 In., Pair 100.00
Porcelain, Vase, Austria, White To Pink, Floral, Molded Leaves Handles, 8 In. 35.00

Porcelain, Trinket Box, 4 In.

Porcelain, Vase, Blown-Out Deer, Wild Boar, Forest Scene 75.00
Porcelain, Vase, Burgundy, Portrait, Hand-Painted, Signed, 7 In. 95.00
Porcelain, Vase, E.L.Wilkinson, Multicolor Floral, Grapevine Rim, 9 3/4 In. 55.00
Porcelain, Vase, Erphila, Czechoslovakia, Blue, 9 In. 6.00
Porcelain, Vase, Flowered, Wm.Adderley, England, C.1880 35.00
Porcelain, Vase, Japan K'ang Hsi, 19th Century, 24 In. 600.00
Porcelain, Vase, Japan, Tufted Herons, Reeds & Flowers, Edo Period 2750.00
Porcelain, Vase, K.B., U.S.A., Gold, Black Silhouette Scene, Cuttan, 15 In. 65.00
Porcelain, Vase, Portrait, Underglaze 1842, J.S. With Flower, 9 In. 235.00
Porcelain, Vase, Potpourri, Covered, German, Ovoid, Bouquets, 16 1/2 In. 550.00
Porcelain, Vase, Victoria, Austria, Pastoral Scene, H.Bradshaw, 14 In., Pair 195.00
Porcelain, Vase, ZS & Co., Portrait, Girl Holding Lamb, Purple, 9 3/4 In. 95.00
Porcelain, Washstand Set, Child's, White With Green & Gold Decoration 25.00
Porcelain, Washstand Set, E E C Co., White, Rose Clusters, 11 Piece 165.00
Porcelain, Washstand Set, Green And White, Deep Colors 95.00
Porcelain, Washstand Set, Norway, Blue Mark, 2 Piece 85.00
Porcelain, Washstand Set, Stoke-On-Trent, Red Orange, Black Ducks, 2 Piece 120.00
Porcelain, Washstand Set, Water Scene, Swan, Blue, Green, Brown 150.00

Postcards were first legally permitted in Austria on October 1, 1869.
The United States passed postal regulations allowing the card in 1873.
Most of the picture postcards collected today date from 1910.

Postcard, Admiral Perry 10.00
Postcard, Alabama Towns, C.1910, Set Of 8 1.25
Postcard, American Legion, Gold-Plated Auxiliary Emblem 2.00
Postcard, Amos & Andy 12.00
Postcard, Anheuser Busch, Wagon & Team 3.00
Postcard, April Fool, C.1900 7.50
Postcard, Arkansas, C.1900, Set Of 30 3.00
Postcard, Bamforth, Songs, Black & White, Set Of 15 10.00
Postcard, Bamforth, Songs, Color, Set Of 15 14.00
Postcard, Bamforth, World War I Songs, Set Of 22 15.00
Postcard, Bas Relief, Girls, Set Of 2 10.00
Postcard, Black Cat, Movable Head 3.00
Postcard, Buttonface, C.1900 8.00
Postcard, Cat, C.1900 .25
Postcard, Celluloid, Foldout 18.00
Postcard, Children 1.00
Postcard, Christmas & New Year, Holly, Beaded 5.00
Postcard, Christmas, Going Down Chimney, Beaded, Airbrushed 7.50
Postcard, Christmas, Hold To Light 18.00
Postcard, Christmas, Holly, Beaded 5.00
Postcard, Christmas, Poinsettias, Beaded 5.00
Postcard, Christmas, Santas, Toys, & Tree, Beaded, Airbrushed With Glitter 5.00
Postcard, Christmas, Trimming The Tree, Beaded, Airbrushed With Glitter 5.00
Postcard, Clapsaddle, Children, Set Of 2 7.00
Postcard, Clapsaddle, Christmas Greetings 2.00
Postcard, Clapsaddle, Washington's Birthday 8.00
Postcard, College Girls .50
Postcard, Colorado, C.1900, Set Of 450 36.00
Postcard, Columbian Exposition, Official Goldsmith, 1893 7.50
Postcard, Comic, Hold To Light 18.00
Postcard, Comic, Set Of 15 1.00
Postcard, Comical Soldier 1.00
Postcard, Detroit Publishing & Photographic Co., C.1900, Set Of 190 100.00
Postcard, Dewey Fleet 10.00
Postcard, Dirigible LZ 129, Berlin, 1931 8.50
Postcard, Dog, C.1900 .25
Postcard, Dolly Dingle, Color, 7 X 5 In., Set Of 3 1.25
Postcard, Donaldson, Captain John Smith 10.00
Postcard, Douglas, Lincoln, 1908 4.00
Postcard, Dr.Pepper, 1 Cent 2.00
Postcard, Dutch Boy, C.1900 .50
Postcard, Easter, Flowers On Cross, Beaded 5.00
Postcard, Embroidery On Silk 12.00

Postcard, Enrico Caruso 8.00
Postcard, Eugene Field, Blue Border, Set Of 12 6.00
Postcard, Eugene Field, Lover's Lane, Saint Jo, Gold Border, Set Of 12 6.00
Postcard, Falls, Seattle, Aluminum 15.00
Postcard, Farm Scene, C.1900 .25
Postcard, Flag Cancels, Set Of 70 7.00
Postcard, French, Art Nouveau 1.25
Postcard, Fringed Leather Pillow 3.50
Postcard, Grahame White & Airplane 5.00
Postcard, Greeting, Embossed 5.00
Postcard, Halloween, Francis Brundage, Germany 3.00
Postcard, Harvest Time, Clappsaddle 10.00
Postcard, Haynes, Yellowstone Park, C.1900, 50 In Original Box 14.50
Postcard, Hold To Light 5.00
Postcard, Hold To Light, Set Of 5 60.00
Postcard, House Of David Administration Building, C.1915 7.50
Postcard, Hugh C.Leighton, C.1900, Set Of 7 1.00
Postcard, Humphrey's Witch Hazel Oil, 1909, Biplane & 4 Children 18.00
Postcard, Illinios, Set Of 540 45.00
Postcard, Indiana, C.1900, Set Of 190 16.00
Postcard, International Art, Children, Set Of 5 5.00
Postcard, Jamestown Exposition, Egg-O-See 2.00
Postcard, Jessie Wilcox Smith, Children 3.50
Postcard, Jewish New Year, C.1900 2.00
Postcard, Jewish New Year, Set Of 8 18.00
Postcard, Joe Jefferson 5.00
Postcard, John D.Rockefeller & Old Car, 1911 2.00
Postcard, John Winsch, C.1900, Set Of 25 12.50
Postcard, Joseph Stalin 10.00
Postcard, Kingsport, Tenn., Brick Corp., 1937 1.00
Postcard, Labor Day Parade, El Reno, Okla. 10.00
Postcard, Larchmont Ship Disaster 6.00
Postcard, Lawrence Welk, Signed 3.50
Postcard, Leather, Comis Girls, Washington, D.C., Set Of 6 12.00
Postcard, Leather, Comis Message, Pillow Type, Square, 3 3/4 In., Set Of 3 6.00
Postcard, Leather, Teddy Bear, Verse, Unused 2.50
Postcard, Leather, 1907 1.50
Postcard, Lord's Prayer, Embossed, Gilt, Set Of 8 42.00
Postcard, Louisiana, C.1900, Set Of 150 14.00
Postcard, Madame Alexander Dolls, Color, Set Of 12 2.25
Postcard, Magee Art, 1906, Saturday 10.00
Postcard, Main Street, Set Of 4 1.00
Postcard, Maryland, C.1900, Set Of 246 23.00
Postcard, Massachusetts Mills & Bridges, Set Of 39 15.00
Postcard, McKinley, Roosevelt, & Taft, Past, Present, & Future 15.00
Postcard, Mechanical, Colors Change 5.00
Postcard, Mechanical, New Year, Purple & Pink Horseshoes, Set Of 2 16.00
Postcard, Melville, Language Of Flowers, C.1900 .50
Postcard, Metal Attached Bird 3.00
Postcard, Metropolitan Insurance .50
Postcard, Michigan, C.1900, Set Of 285 23.00
Postcard, Michigan, Horse-Drawn Trolley 5.00
Postcard, Mike Roberts, Set Of 20 4.00
Postcard, Mining Scene, C.1900 .25
Postcard, Missouri, C.1900, Set Of 300 25.00
Postcard, Nathan Collier, Comic Series, Set Of 15 5.50
Postcard, National Cupids 12.00
Postcard, Nebraska, C.1900, Set Of 94 9.00
Postcard, Nebraska, Set Of 38 3.50
Postcard, Negro 1.00
Postcard, New Hampshire, Set Of 120 10.00
Postcard, New Year, 1908, Tear-Off Calendar, Child & Basket Of Clover 12.00
Postcard, New York State, Set Of 40 4.00
Postcard, New York World's Fair, 1939, Set Of 10 2.50
Postcard, New York World's Fair, 1939, Set Of 50 25.00

Postcard, Nudes, C.1900, Set Of 9 .... 20.00
Postcard, Ocean Liner R.M.S. Saxonia, Woven Silk 25.00
Postcard, Oregon, C.1900, Set Of 220 .... 19.00
Postcard, Our Father 4.50
Postcard, Pan Pacific Exposition, 1915, Set Of 23 .... 10.00
Postcard, Patriotic, Signed Veenfliet 2.00
Postcard, Paul Revere's Ride 1.50
Postcard, Photograph Of Dirigible 10.00
Postcard, Pittsfield, Mass., Set Of 29 .... 6.00
Postcard, President Coolidge 10.00
Postcard, President Jackson 10.00
Postcard, President James Monroe 10.00
Postcard, President McKinley 10.00
Postcard, President Wilson, Victory Greeting 10.00
Postcard, Prince Charles Investiture, 1969, Color 2.00
Postcard, Prudential Insurance .... .50
Postcard, R.P.O. Postmarks, Set Of 4 .... 1.00
Postcard, Radio Quiz Kids 6.00
Postcard, Reiley, Lover's Lane, Saint Jo 1.50
Postcard, Rookwood Pottery, 1904 .... 10.00
Postcard, Roosevelt Family 3.00
Postcard, Rudolph Valentino 7.00
Postcard, Ruth Welch, Children, Silver, Set Of 6 .... 12.00
Postcard, San Francisco Earthquake 2.00
Postcard, Santa Claus & Dirigible, 1908 .... 5.00
Postcard, Santa Claus In Red Cloth Suit 3.50
Postcard, Santa Claus In Red Suit, 1911 .... 2.50
Postcard, Santa Claus, Gold Trim, Set Of 4 .... 7.00
Postcard, Santa With Christmas Seal, 1929 .... 1.25
Postcard, Schlesinger Bros., Ladies, Set Of 11 .... 10.00
Postcard, Sheffield, England, Fitzala Square, Hold To Light 15.00
Postcard, Sheffield, England, Parish Church, Hold To Light 15.00
Postcard, South Carolina, C.1900, Set Of 135 .... 13.00
Postcard, St.Louis World's Fair 4.00
Postcard, St.Patrick's Day, C.1900 .... .50
Postcard, State Of Maine Draft Board, World War I, Set Of 6 .... 7.00
Postcard, Stratton, Mexican War Of 1915, 15 .... 35.00
Postcard, Taft & Sherman 5.00
Postcard, Teddy Bear Holding Staff, Beaded, Air Brushed 8.00
Postcard, Teddy Bear, Roosevelt 12.50
Postcard, Tennessee, C.1900, Set Of 140 .... 12.00
Postcard, Thanksgiving, Pilgrim Kneeling Near Basket, Beaded 5.00
Postcard, Thanksgiving, Turkey & Scene, Beaded 5.00
Postcard, Thanksgiving, Turkey, American Flag, Germany, Set Of 6 .... 10.00
Postcard, Thiele, Cat, This Is So Sudden 3.50
Postcard, Thiele, Cat, You Ought To See The Other Fellow 3.50
Postcard, Three Teddy Bears Dancing, Beaded, Airbrushed 8.00
Postcard, Tom Thumb Wedding Party, 1863 .... 10.00
Postcard, Toronto, C.1900, 35 .... 9.00
Postcard, Tournament Of Roses, 1914 .... 3.00
Postcard, Transpolar Flight Expedition, 1924 .... 10.00
Postcard, Trommer's Beer & Ale, Set Of l/ 6.00
Postcard, Tuck, Breaking The Record 7.50
Postcard, Tuck, Decoration Day, G.A.R. 3.00
Postcard, Tuck, Hudson Fulton 4.00
Postcard, Tuck, Independence 3.00
Postcard, Tuck, Kept At School 7.50
Postcard, Tuck, Little Bears 7.50
Postcard, Tuck, New Year 2.50
Postcard, Tuck, State Capitol, Seal 3.00
Postcard, Tuck, Thanksgiving Day 2.50
Postcard, Tuck, Westminister Abbey, Oilette 4.00
Postcard, Tuck, Yuletide 2.00
Postcard, Turkey, Musical 3.00
Postcard, U.S. Domestic Ships, Set Of 15 .... 25.00

Postcard, U.S. Navy, Set Of 15 .... 30.00
Postcard, Valentine, Red Satin Pillow 4.00
Postcard, Virginia, C.1900, Set Of 483 .... 40.00
Postcard, Washington State, C.1900, Set Of 190 .... 16.00
Postcard, Washington, D.C., Hold To Light 18.00
Postcard, Weller Pottery, 1908 .... 10.00
Postcard, West Virginia, C.1900, Set Of 100 .... 8.00
Postcard, Windmill, Metal Glued On, 1907 .... 12.50
Postcard, Winsch, Santa, 1912 .... 1.00
Postcard, Wooden 5.00
Postcard, Worcester, Mass., Fire Department, Set Of 3 .... 16.00
Postcard, World War II, Comic, Set Of 21 .... 2.50
Postcard, World's Columbian Exposition 3.00
Postcard, World's Fair, 1939, 20 In Folder 4.50
Postcard, Wright Brothers Inspecting Airplane 8.00
Postcard, Wrong-Way Corrigan & Airplane 4.00
Postcard, 4th Of July 1.00

Potlid, see also Pratt

Potlid, Countie Of Boston 15.00
Potlid, Oriental Toothpaste .... 7.00 To 15.00

Pottery, see also Buffalo Pottery, Staffordshire, Wedgwood, etc.

Pottery, Butter, Blue & White, Cow 65.00
Pottery, Butter, Covered, Blue & White, Cow 100.00
Pottery, Charger, Flint Enamel, Streaky Brown, Yellow, & Green, C.1858, 17 In. 58.00
Pottery, Creamer, Mohume Banko, Japanese, Mottled Green, C.1750 .... 35.00
Pottery, Crock, Butter, White Glaze, 5 1/2 In. 10.00
Pottery, Crock, Butter, Yellow Glaze, 4 In. 10.00
Pottery, Crock, Flack & Van Arsdale, Cornwall, Ont., 3 In. 125.00
Pottery, Crock, John Mulholland & Co., Toronto, Ontario, 2 In. 85.00
Pottery, Crock, Orrin L.Ballard, St.Johns, C.E., 3 In. 125.00
Pottery, Crock, Weston & Gregg, Ellenville, N.Y., Blue Butterfly, 2 Gallon 60.00
Pottery, Deer, Walton Burslem, C.1815, 3 3/4 In. .... *Illus* 58.00
Pottery, Figurine, Little Red Riding Hood, 4 1/2 In. .... *Illus* 50.00
Pottery, Flowerpot & Attached Saucer, Hyssong, 6 In. 12.50
Pottery, Humidor, Austria, Figural, Seafaring Frog, Scar Face, 7 1/2 In. 115.00
Pottery, Jar, Covered, Brown Glaze, Ring Turnings, 9 In. 17.50
Pottery, Jar, Greenland, Brown Glaze, Sloping Shoulders, 9 1/2 In. 12.50
Pottery, Jug, Cobalt Flower, 2 Gallon 65.00
Pottery, Jug, Cobalt, Upside-Down Apple, Gallon 40.00
Pottery, Jug, F.R.Gould & Co., Brantford, C.W., 2 In. .... 165.00 To 175.00
Pottery, Jug, Ft.Edwards, N.Y., Gallon 25.00
Pottery, Jug, J.M, Hickerson, Strawsburg, Va., Gallon 850.00
Pottery, Jug, J.Swank, Johnstown, Pa., Brown Glaze, Wide Handle, 13 In. 30.00

Pottery, Figurine, Little Red Riding Hood, 4 1/2 In.

Pottery, Deer, Walton Burselm, C.1815, 3 3/4 In.

Pottery, Jug, West Ontario, Orange Red Glaze, 5 In. 85.00

Pottery, Mug, Beer, Cobalt Glaze, Embossed Decoration, .5 Liter 14.00

Pottery, Mug, English, Big Ben & Tower Of London, Brown Glaze, Silver Trim 12.50

Pottery, Pitcher, Blue Dutch Boy & Girl Kissing, Windmill, 7 In. 28.00

Pottery, Pitcher, Cider, Thomas Family, Brown Glaze, Strap Handle, 11 In. 30.00

Pottery, Pitcher, Milk, Blue & White, Embossed Fruit Medallions, 8 In. 30.00

Pottery, Plate, Chop, Italian, 16 X 14 In. 30.00

Pottery, Salt & Pepper, Floral, Jug Shape 3.00

Pottery, Saucer, Child's, Scottish, Little Girl & Lamb 7.00

Pottery, Shoe, Laguna, Dated 1940, 5 In. 22.00

Pottery, Shoe, Man's Oxford, Dull Black, 5 In. 15.00

Pottery, Spittoon, Cortland 22.00

Pottery, Stein, Mandarin Man, 1/2 Liter, Merkelbach & Wick 190.00

Pottery, Syrup, White Glaze, Raised Flower & Leaf, Pewter Top 25.00

Pottery, Vase, Aubergine Glaze, Bulbous, 5 1/2 In. 45.00

Pottery, Vase, Belgium, Cobalt Glaze, Tan Dripping, Art Nouveau, 7 3/4 In. 11.00

Pottery, Warmer, Foot, Brown Glaze, Nickel-Plated Stopper, 12 In. 15.00

Pottery, Warmer, Foot, English, 9 In. 12.00

Pottery, Weight, Horse, Dark Brown, 2 Holes For Tying, 13 In. 30.00

Pottery, Whistle, Pistol, Brown, 4 1/4 In. 15.00

Powder Horn, see Weapon, Powder Horn

PRATT
FENTON.

Pratt ware means two different things. It was an early Staffordshire pottery, cream colored with colored decorations, made by Felix Pratt during the late eighteenth century. There was also Pratt ware made with transfer designs during the mid-nineteenth century in Fenton, England.

Pratt, Jar, All The World's A Stage, Shakespeare, Yellow, Black Transfer 25.00

Pratt, Jar, Boar Hunt 25.00

Pratt, Jar, Light Blue, Hunting Scene, C.1856, 4 In. 45.00

Pratt, Jar, Ointment, Blue With Gold Hunt Scene, C 1856 .... 30.00

Pratt, Jar, Ointment, Hunt Scene, Blue, C.1856, 4 1/4 In. 32.00

Pratt, Jar, Pomade, Boar Hunt Scene, Blue 16.00

Pratt, Plate, Cake, Pedestal, Child At Brook, Dog, Fenton, 9 In. 145.00

Pratt, Plate, Cattle & Ruins Scene, Gold Border, Orange Trim, 7 1/4 In. 50.00

Pratt, Plate, Dinner, Boys Looking Into Schoolhouse, T.Webster, 1834 .... 75.00

Pratt, Plate, Hop Queen, Oak & Acorn Border, 10 In. 165.00

Pratt, Plate, Rustic Scene, Castle, Butterflies, Flowered Border 18.00

Pratt, Potlid, Children Crabbing On Nordic Beach, Ships, Jar 65.00

Pratt, Potlid, Cries Of London, Fine Black Cherries 20.00

Pratt, Potlid, Drayton Manor, Residence Of Sir Robert Peel, Kirkham, 1947 .... 35.00

Pratt, Potlid, Late Prince Consort 67.50

Pratt, Potlid, Lend A Bite 55.00

Pratt, Potlid, Melon Boys .... 20.00 To 50.00

Pratt, Potlid, Peace 50.00

Pratt, Potlid, Peace, I.Austin 35.00

Pratt, Potlid, Soldiers Dancing 65.00

Pratt, Potlid, Sportsman 48.50

Pratt, Potlid, Uncle Toby, Black Wooden Frame 58.00

Pratt, Potlid, Village Wedding 65.00

Pratt, Potlid, War 50.00

Pratt, Potlid, Wolf & The Lamb 60.00

Pratt, Saucer, Horses Medallion, Pink Border, 6 In. 48.00

Pratt, Snuff Jar, Blue, Tan And Black Transfer, Men, Animals 25.00

Pratt, Teapot, Bulbous With Pictures On Both Sides 88.00

Presidential China, Plate, Dessert, Andrew Jackson, Vieux Paris, C.1833 .... 1500.00

Presidential China, Plate, Dinner, Benjamin Harrison, Limoges .... 450.00 To 700.00

Presidential China, Plate, Oyster, Rutherford B.Hayes, Haviland, C.1885 .... 133.50

Pressed glass was first made in the United States in the 1820s after the invention of pressed-glass machines. Hundreds of patterns of pressed glass were made in complete table settings. Although the Boston and Sandwich Works was the most famous of the pressed glass factories, there were about sixteen other factories making pressed glass from 1830 to 1850, and still more from 1850 to 1900, when pressed glass reached its greatest popularity. It is now being widely reproduced.

Pressed Glass, see also Cosmos, Vaseline Glass
Pressed Glass, Aberdeen, Goblet 15.00
Acanthus, see Ribbed Palm
Pressed Glass, Acanthus Scroll, Sugar, Covered 18.00
Acme, see Butterfly & Spray
Pressed Glass, Acorn Band, Spooner 27.00
Pressed Glass, Acorn, Saltshaker, Pink, Opaque 40.00
Pressed Glass, Acorn, Syrup, Green 85.00
Pressed Glass, Actress, Bowl, Footed, 5 In. 18.00
Pressed Glass, Actress, Celery, H.M.S.Pinafore, Pedestal Foot 135.00
Pressed Glass, Actress, Compote, Covered, High Standard, 8 In. 75.00
Pressed Glass, Actress, Compote, Covered, 7 1/2 X 6 In. 55.00
Pressed Glass, Actress, Compote, Frosted & Clear, High Standard, 7 In. 89.50
Pressed Glass, Actress, Compote, High Standard, 8 In. 82.50
Pressed Glass, Actress, Compote, 8 In. 37.00
Pressed Glass, Actress, Pitcher, Water 145.00
Pressed Glass, Actress, Sauce, Footed, 5 In. 13.00
Pressed Glass, Actress, Sauce, 5 In. 25.00
Pressed Glass, Actress, Spooner 62.50
Pressed Glass, Admiral Dewey, Pitcher, Water 52.00
Pressed Glass, Admiral Dewey, Pitcher, Water, Naval Emblems & Face 65.00
Pressed Glass, Admiral Dewey, Tumbler, Embossed 44.00
Pressed Glass, Alabama, Bottle, Mustard, Castor 15.00
Pressed Glass, Alabama, Celery .... 15.50 To 16.50
Pressed Glass, Alabama, Sugar, Covered 17.50
Pressed Glass, Alaska, Berry Bowl, Dark Green, Square 25.00
Pressed Glass, Alaska, Creamer, Blue, Opalescent 50.00
Pressed Glass, Alaska, Creamer, Green 48.00
Pressed Glass, Alaska, Creamer, Green, Northwood 38.00
Pressed Glass, Alaska, Creamer, Opalescent 40.00
Pressed Glass, Alaska, Creamer, Vaseline, Opalescent .... 68.00 To 75.00
Pressed Glass, Alaska, Pitcher, Water, Decorated 215.00
Pressed Glass, Alaska, Sauce, Blue, Opalescent .... 32.00 To 35.00
Pressed Glass, Alaska, Sauce, Blue, Opalescent, Enamel Decoration 40.00
Pressed Glass, Alaska, Sauce, Opalescent 22.50
Pressed Glass, Alaska, Sauce, Vaseline, Opalescent 28.00
Pressed Glass, Alaska, Spooner, Blue, Opalescent 55.00
Pressed Glass, Alaska, Spooner, Green, Northwood 35.00
Pressed Glass, Alaska, Spooner, Vaseline, Opalescent .... 45.00 To 58.00
Pressed Glass, Alaska, Sugar, Blue, Opalescent, Covered 95.00
Pressed Glass, Almond Thumbprint, Compote, Jelly, Flint, 6 In. 35.00
Pressed Glass, Almond Thumbprint, Creamer, Applied Handle 45.00
Pressed Glass, Almond Thumbprint, Mug, Child's, Etched Emory, 3 1/2 In. 7.00
Pressed Glass, Amazon, Creamer, Child's 20.00
Pressed Glass, Amazon, Creamer, Tall 18.00
Pressed Glass, Amazon, Sugar, Child's, Covered 40.00
Pressed Glass, Amazon, Table Set, Child's, 4 Piece 95.00
Pressed Glass, Amazon, Tumbler 8.00
Pressed Glass, Amazon, Wine 18.00
Pressed Glass, Amberette, Berry Set, 7 Piece 185.00
Pressed Glass, Amberette, Bowl, 8 In. 65.00
Pressed Glass, Amberette, Bowl, 8 1/2 In. 45.00
Pressed Glass, Amberette, Celery 68.00
Pressed Glass, Amberette, Celery, Collared 85.00
Pressed Glass, Amberette, Creamer .... 45.00 To 85.00
Pressed Glass, Amberette, Fruit Bowl, 11 In. 75.00
Pressed Glass, Amberette, Fruit Set, 7 Piece 200.00
Pressed Glass, Amberette, Goblet 65.00
Pressed Glass, Amberette, Pitcher, Water 95.00
Pressed Glass, Amberette, Platter, Oval, 11 X 8 1/2 In. 65.00
Pressed Glass, Amberette, Spooner 65.00
Pressed Glass, Amberette, Sugar 32.50
Pressed Glass, American Beauty, Creamer, Green, Northwood 25.00
Pressed Glass, American Beauty, Spooner, Green, 2 Handles, Northwood 25.00
Pressed Glass, Angora, Pitcher, Water 20.00

Pressed Glass, Anthemion, Butter, Covered 25.00
Pressed Glass, Anthemion, Plate, 10 1/4 In. 22.50
Pressed Glass, Anthemion, Tumbler 12.75
Pressed Glass, Anvil, Toothpick 30.00
Pressed Glass, Apollo, Etched, Goblet 22.50
Pressed Glass, Apollo, Goblet, Frosted 22.50
Pressed Glass, Apollo, Muffineer, Etched 39.50
Pressed Glass, Apollo, Sauce, Footed 7.50
Pressed Glass, Apple Blossom, Spooner, Blue Band, Northwood 78.00
Pressed Glass, Apple Blossom, Tumbler, Blue Band 35.00
Pressed Glass, Arabesque, Creamer, Applied Handle 45.00
Pressed Glass, Arabesque, Goblet .... 17.50 To 20.00
Pressed Glass, Arch, Salt, Master, Flint 14.00
Pressed Glass, Arch, Salt, Master, Footed, Flint 14.00
Pressed Glass, Arched Grape, Goblet 20.00
Pressed Glass, Arched Grape, Spooner 21.00
Pressed Glass, Arched Grape, Sugar, Shell Knob 35.00
Pressed Glass, Arched Ovals, Celery 8.00
Pressed Glass, Arched Ovals, Tumbler, Gold Trim 7.00
Pressed Glass, Arched Ovals, Tumbler, Ruby Stained 30.00
Pressed Glass, Arched Ovals, Wine, Ruby Stained 24.00

Argonaut Shell, see Nautilus

Pressed Glass, Argus, Ale Glass, Bakewell Pears, 7 1/2 In. 110.00
Pressed Glass, Argus, Champagne, Flint 35.00
Pressed Glass, Argus, Decanter, Neck Rings, Flange Lip, Bakewell Pears, Quart 95.00
Pressed Glass, Argus, Eggcup 10.00
Pressed Glass, Argus, Eggcup, Flint 19.50
Pressed Glass, Argus, Goblet, Bulb Stem, Flint 35.00
Pressed Glass, Argus, Goblet, Flint 18.00
Pressed Glass, Argus, Goblet, Master, Flint 25.00
Pressed Glass, Argus, Jar, Mustard, Silver-Plated Lid, Handle, & Spoon Holder 30.00
Pressed Glass, Argus, Liqueur, Flint 12.00
Pressed Glass, Argus, Pitcher, Water, Applied Handle, 4 Rows, Bakewell Pears 185.00
Pressed Glass, Argus, Spooner, Flint 30.00
Pressed Glass, Argus, Tumbler, Footed, Bakewell Pears, 4 3/4 In. 35.00
Pressed Glass, Argus, Tumbler, Footed, Flint 38.00
Pressed Glass, Argus, Tumbler, Whiskey, Flint 34.00
Pressed Glass, Argus, Waste Bowl, Flint 30.00
Pressed Glass, Argus, Wine, Barrel, Flint 29.50
Pressed Glass, Argus, Wine, Flint .... 25.00 To 36.00
Pressed Glass, Argus, Wine, 4 1/4 In. 30.00
Pressed Glass, Arrowhead In Oval, Spooner, Child's 14.50

Art Novo, see Dogwood

Pressed Glass, Art, Berry Bowl, Square, 8 In. 18.00
Pressed Glass, Art, Cake Stand 38.00
Pressed Glass, Art, Celery 22.50
Pressed Glass, Art, Compote, Covered, High Standard, 7 In. 35.00
Pressed Glass, Art, Compote, 7 1/2 In. 35.00
Pressed Glass, Art, Compote, Flared, 8 In. 25.00
Pressed Glass, Art, Compote, 8 3/4 In. 25.00
Pressed Glass, Art, Compote, 10 X 9 In. 30.00
Pressed Glass, Art, Goblet .... 27.50 To 42.50
Pressed Glass, Art, Sauce, 4 In. 6.00
Pressed Glass, Art, Spooner 17.50
Pressed Glass, Art, Sugar, Covered .... 30.00 To 32.50
Pressed Glass, Art, Tumbler .... 36.00 To 45.00
Pressed Glass, Artichoke, Compote, High Standard, 8 1/2 In. 35.00
Pressed Glass, Artichoke, Spooner, Frosted, 2 Handles 30.00
Pressed Glass, Ashburton With Connected Ovals, Goblet, Flared, Flint 35.00
Pressed Glass, Ashburton With Connected Ovals, Goblet, Straight Top, Flint 35.00
Pressed Glass, Ashburton With Divided Ovals, Goblet, Straight Top, Flint 35.00
Pressed Glass, Ashburton With Sawtooth, Tumbler 115.00
Pressed Glass, Ashburton With Sawtooth, Tumbler, Footed 85.00
Pressed Glass, Ashburton With Sawtooth, Tumbler, Whiskey, Handled 115.00
Pressed Glass, Ashburton, Celery 95.00

Pressed Glass, Arched Grape, Goblet

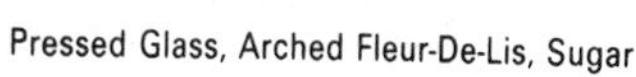

Pressed Glass, Arched Fleur-De-Lis, Sugar

Pressed Glass, Ashburton, Bottle, Amethyst, Tumbler Mold

Pressed Glass, Ashburton, Champagne, Presentation Piece

Pressed Glass, Ashburton, Celery, Flint .... 55.00 To 69.00
Pressed Glass, Ashburton, Celery, Scalloped 155.00
Pressed Glass, Ashburton, Champagne, 4 7/8 In. 55.00
Pressed Glass, Ashburton, Cordial 30.00
Pressed Glass, Ashburton, Decanter, Flint, Pint 55.00
Pressed Glass, Ashburton, Dish, Honey, Flint 10.00
Pressed Glass, Ashburton, Eggcup .... 19.00 To 22.50
Pressed Glass, Ashburton, Eggcup, Flint 16.00
Pressed Glass, Ashburton, Goblet 75.00
Pressed Glass, Ashburton, Goblet, Flint .... 28.00 To 35.00
Pressed Glass, Ashburton, Goblet, Slim, Flint 30.00
Pressed Glass, Ashburton, Sauce, Flint 7.00
Pressed Glass, Ashburton, Sauce, 4 In. 12.50
Pressed Glass, Ashburton, Sugar, Covered 60.00
Pressed Glass, Ashburton, Sugar, Covered, Flint .... 68.00 To 85.00
Pressed Glass, Ashburton, Tumbler 65.00
Pressed Glass, Ashburton, Tumbler, Footed, Flint 25.00
Pressed Glass, Ashburton, Tumbler, Vaseline, Footed, Flint 65.00
Pressed Glass, Ashburton, Tumbler, Whiskey, Handled 125.00
Pressed Glass, Ashburton, Wine, Flint .... 22.50 To 45.00
Pressed Glass, Ashburton, Wine, 4 1/2 In. 27.50
Pressed Glass, Ashland, Berry Bowl, 7 3/4 In. 8.50
Pressed Glass, Ashland, Tray, Ice Cream 14.50
Pressed Glass, Ashland, Waste Bowl 22.50
Pressed Glass, Ashman, Celery 25.00
Pressed Glass, Ashman, Celery, Engraved Leaf & Fern 23.50
Pressed Glass, Ashman, Goblet, Portland .... 6.00 To 10.00
Pressed Glass, Atlanta, Celery 35.00
Pressed Glass, Atlanta, Goblet 12.50
Pressed Glass, Atlanta, Wine 10.00
Pressed Glass, Atlantic Cable, Sauce, 4 1/2 In. 4.75

Pressed Glass, Atlas, Celery 10.00
Pressed Glass, Atlas, Creamer 14.00
Pressed Glass, Atlas, Goblet 22.00
Pressed Glass, Atlas, Jar, Jam, Acid Etched Flower 45.00
Pressed Glass, Atlas, Tankard, Applied Handle, 9 1/2 In. 22.00
Pressed Glass, Atlas, Tankard, Water 35.00
Pressed Glass, Atlas, Toothpick ..... 15.00 To 20.00
Pressed Glass, Atlas, Tumbler 9.50
Pressed Glass, Aurora, Decanter, Wine, Ruby Stained 85.00
Pressed Glass, Aurora, Tray, Ruby Stained, 10 In. 45.00
Pressed Glass, Aurora, Tray, Water 15.00
Pressed Glass, Aurora, Tray, Water, Ruby Stained 15.00
Pressed Glass, Aurora, Wine 18.50
Pressed Glass, Aurora, Wine, Ruby Stained ..... 38.50 To 45.00
Pressed Glass, Austrian, Creamer, Greentown 10.00
Pressed Glass, Austrian, Creamer, Vaseline, Miniature 75.00
Pressed Glass, Austrian, Goblet 22.00
Pressed Glass, Austrian, Nappy, Canary, Greentown 130.00
Pressed Glass, Austrian, Sauce 10.00
Pressed Glass, Austrian, Sugar, Canary, Miniature 25.00
Pressed Glass, Austrian, Wine 12.50
Pressed Glass, Aztec, Cup, Punch 4.00
Pressed Glass, Baby Face, Compote, Covered, 8 1/2 X 5 1/4 In. 95.00
Pressed Glass, Baby Face, Compote, Scalloped Rim, 8 In. 95.00
Pressed Glass, Baby Lion, Celery 38.00
Pressed Glass, Baby Lion, Celery, Cable Base 35.00
Pressed Glass, Baby Lion, Creamer, Etched 45.00
Pressed Glass, Baby Lion, Sugar 45.00

Balder, see also Pennsylvania Hand
Balder, see Pennsylvania

Pressed Glass, Balder, Berry Bowl, Gold Trim, 9 In. 29.50
Pressed Glass, Balder, Cordial 12.50
Pressed Glass, Balder, Creamer 8.50
Pressed Glass, Balder, Creamer, Individual, Gold Trim 10.00
Pressed Glass, Balder, Cup, Punch ..... 8.00 To 15.00
Pressed Glass, Balder, Goblet 10.00
Pressed Glass, Balder, Jar, Jam 21.50
Pressed Glass, Balder, Juice 6.50
Pressed Glass, Balder, Tumbler 12.50
Pressed Glass, Balder, Tumbler, Gold Trim 11.50
Pressed Glass, Balder, Tumbler, Juice 8.50
Pressed Glass, Balder, Tumbler, Whiskey 17.50
Pressed Glass, Balder, Tumbler, 3 Ozs. 5.00
Pressed Glass, Balder, Wine 18.50

Balky Mule, see Currier & Ives

Pressed Glass, Ball & Swirl, Cake Stand, 9 In. 18.00
Pressed Glass, Ball & Swirl, Celery, Etched 28.00
Pressed Glass, Ball & Swirl, Creamer ..... 18.00 To 24.50
Pressed Glass, Ball & Swirl, Goblet 21.00
Pressed Glass, Ball & Swirl, Sauce, 3 1/2 In. 12.50
Pressed Glass, Ball & Swirl, Syrup, Applied Handle, Spring Lid 35.00
Pressed Glass, Ball & Swirl, Tankard, Water 45.00
Pressed Glass, Ball & Swirl, Tankard, Wine, 12 In. 25.00
Pressed Glass, Baltimore Pear, Butter, Covered 32.00
Pressed Glass, Baltimore Pear, Butter, Round, 6 1/4 In. 10.00
Pressed Glass, Baltimore Pear, Plate, Serving, Handled, 12 In. 10.00
Pressed Glass, Baltimore Pear, Plate, 8 1/2 In. 5.00
Pressed Glass, Baltimore Pear, Sugar 20.00
Pressed Glass, Baltimore Pear, Sugar, Covered 15.00

Bamboo, see Broken Column
Banded Beaded Grape Medallion, see Beaded Grape Medallion,

Pressed Glass, Banded Buckle, Sauce, Flint 5.00
Pressed Glass, Banded Buckle, Sugar, Flint 25.00
Pressed Glass, Banded Crystal, Compote, Covered, 10 1/2 X 7 In. 22.50

Pressed Glass, **Banded Knife & Fork,** Wine 4.75
Pressed Glass, **Banded Paling,** Goblet 8.00

Banded Portland when flashed with pink is sometimes called Maiden Blush

Pressed Glass, **Banded Portland,** Creamer, Pink Flashed, Scalloped Opening 50.00
Pressed Glass, **Banded Portland,** Creamer, Pink Flashed, 4 In. 50.00
Pressed Glass, **Banded Portland,** Creamer, 4 1/2 In. 20.00
Pressed Glass, **Banded Portland,** Jar, Pomade 12.00
Pressed Glass, **Banded Portland,** Jar, Powder 9.50
Pressed Glass, **Banded Portland,** Muffineer 27.50
Pressed Glass, **Banded Portland,** Relish, Pink Flashed 30.00
Pressed Glass, **Banded Portland,** Relish, Pink Flashed, 5 1/2 X 2 1/2 In. 20.00
Pressed Glass, **Banded Portland,** Saltshaker 15.00
Pressed Glass, **Banded Portland,** Sauce, Gold Trim 6.50
Pressed Glass, **Banded Portland,** Sugar, Individual, Pink Flashed 15.00
Pressed Glass, **Banded Portland,** Syrup 46.00
Pressed Glass, **Banded Portland,** Taster, Whiskey, Flint 22.00
Pressed Glass, **Banded Portland,** Toothpick 15.00
Pressed Glass, **Banded Portland,** Toothpick, Pink Flashed 25.00
Pressed Glass, **Banded Portland,** Toothpick, Ruby Stained 40.00
Pressed Glass, **Banded Portland,** Tumbler .... 9.75 To 11.75
Pressed Glass, **Banded Portland,** Tumbler, Ruby Stained 45.00
Pressed Glass, **Banded Portland,** Vase, Fluted Rim, 6 In. 10.00
Pressed Glass, **Banded Portland,** Vase, Pink Flashed, Footed, 6 In. 45.00
Pressed Glass, **Banded Portland,** Vase, Pink Flashed, 6 In. 18.00
Pressed Glass, **Banded Portland,** Vase, 6 In. 12.50
Pressed Glass, **Banded Portland,** Vase, 9 5/8 In. 25.00
Pressed Glass, **Banded Portland,** Water Set, 7 Piece 175.00
Pressed Glass, **Banded Portland,** Wine .... 17.00 To 29.00
Pressed Glass, **Banded Portland,** Wine, Pink Flashed 38.00

Banded Raindrop, see Candlewick

Pressed Glass, **Banded Star,** Celery 20.00

Other "Banded" patterns, see under name of basic pattern. E.G.: Banded Honeycomb, see Honeycomb, Banded

Pressed Glass, **Bands Of Arches,** Punties, & Loops, Celery, Gothic Type, Flint 95.00

Bar & Diamond, see Kokomo

Pressed Glass, **Barberry,** Butter, Covered 38.00
Pressed Glass, **Barberry,** Celery 23.00
Pressed Glass, **Barberry,** Celery, Oval Berries 45.00
Pressed Glass, **Barberry,** Celery, Pedestal Base 22.50
Pressed Glass, **Barberry,** Compote, Covered, Low Standard, 8 In. 37.00
Pressed Glass, **Barberry,** Compote, Covered, 8 In. 37.00
Pressed Glass, **Barberry,** Creamer 20.00
Pressed Glass, **Barberry,** Dish, Honey 5.00
Pressed Glass, **Barberry,** Goblet 23.00
Pressed Glass, **Barberry,** Goblet, Oval Berries 17.00
Pressed Glass, **Barberry,** Pitcher, Water .... 58.00 To 58.50
Pressed Glass, **Barberry,** Pitcher, Water, Applied Handle 36.00
Pressed Glass, **Barberry,** Pitcher, Water, Oval Berries 65.00
Pressed Glass, **Barberry,** Plate, Oval Berries, 6 In. 35.00
Pressed Glass, **Barberry,** Plate, 6 In. .... 22.00 To 22.50
Pressed Glass, **Barberry,** Sauce, Footed, 4 In. 7.50
Pressed Glass, **Barberry,** Sauce, Oval Berries, Footed, 4 In. 7.50
Pressed Glass, **Barberry,** Wine, Oval Berries 15.00
Pressed Glass, **Barley,** Butter 17.00
Pressed Glass, **Barley,** Butter, Covered 36.00
Pressed Glass, **Barley,** Cake Stand 28.00
Pressed Glass, **Barley,** Cake Stand, 9 1/2 In. 22.50
Pressed Glass, **Barley,** Cake Stand, 9 3/4 In. 40.00
Pressed Glass, **Barley,** Celery 28.00
Pressed Glass, **Barley,** Compote, Covered, 7 In. 48.00
Pressed Glass, **Barley,** Goblet .... 20.00 To 22.50
Pressed Glass, **Barley,** Jar, Pickle Castor, Covered 45.00
Pressed Glass, **Barley,** Jar, Pickle, Covered 15.00
Pressed Glass, **Barley,** Pitcher, Water, Applied Handle 40.00

Pressed Glass, Barley, Plate, Bread 25.00
Pressed Glass, Barley, Relish, 8 1/2 In. 18.00
Pressed Glass, Barley, Sauce 6.50
Pressed Glass, Barley, Spooner 12.50
Pressed Glass, Barley, Vegetable Bowl, Oval, 9 1/2 X 6 3/4 In. 9.75
Pressed Glass, Barred Daisy, Spooner, Etched 15.00
Pressed Glass, Barred Forget-Me-Not, Celery 24.00
Pressed Glass, Barred Forget-Me-Not, Compote, Covered, High Standard, 8 In. 45.00
Pressed Glass, Barred Forget-Me-Not, Creamer 15.00
Pressed Glass, Barred Forget-Me-Not, Goblet 9.00
Pressed Glass, Barred Forget-Me-Not, Wine 9.00
Pressed Glass, Barred Hobnail, Creamer 12.00
Pressed Glass, Barred Hobnail, Goblet 15.00
Pressed Glass, Barred Hobnail, Mug, Amber 17.00
Pressed Glass, Barred Hobnail, Waste Bowl 12.50
Barred Ovals, see Banded Portland
Pressed Glass, Barred Star, Goblet 8.00
Barreled Block, see Red Block
Pressed Glass, Barreled Thumbprint, Turning Purple, 4 1/4 In. 17.50
Bartlett Pear, see Pear
Pressed Glass, Basket Weave, Basket, Reeded Handle, 4 Footed, 4 In. 6.50
Pressed Glass, Basket Weave, Goblet, Amber ..... 12.50 To 25.00
Pressed Glass, Basket Weave, Goblet, Blue 29.00
Pressed Glass, Basket Weave, Mug, Child's, Vaseline 18.00
Pressed Glass, Basket Weave, Pitcher, Milk, Blue ..... 25.00 To 34.00
Pressed Glass, Basket Weave, Pitcher, Vaseline, 7 In. 37.50
Pressed Glass, Basket Weave, Salt & Pepper, Tin Tops, In Basket Frame 25.00
Pressed Glass, Basket Weave, Tray, Water, Amber 27.50
Pressed Glass, Basket Weave, Wine 12.00
Pressed Glass, Basket, Saltshaker 9.00
Pressed Glass, Battleship Cover, Dish, Marked Wheeling 42.50
Pressed Glass, Bay State Campaign, Tumbler, Patent June 25th, 1861, 4 In. 110.00
Pressed Glass, Be Industrious, Platter, Frosted Beehive Center, Oval, 12 In. 45.00
Pressed Glass, Bead & Scroll, Table Set, Child's, 3 Piece 90.00
Pressed Glass, Beaded Acorn With Leaf Band, Spooner, Flint 45.00
Pressed Glass, Beaded Acorn, Butter, Covered 30.00
Pressed Glass, Beaded Acorn, Goblet ..... 18.00 To 19.00
Pressed Glass, Beaded Band, Butter 20.00
Pressed Glass, Beaded Band, Dish, Pickle 8.50
Pressed Glass, Beaded Band, Goblet 25.00
Beaded Bull"s-Eye & Drape, see also Alabama
Pressed Glass, Beaded Chain, Sugar, Covered 30.00
Pressed Glass, Beaded Chain, Sugar, Covered, C.1870 ..... 27.50
Pressed Glass, Beaded Circle, Compote, Jelly, Apple Green, Gold Trim, N. 45.00
Pressed Glass, Beaded Circle, Goblet, Sandwich 35.00
Pressed Glass, Beaded Coarse Bars, Cup 3.75
Pressed Glass, Beaded Dewdrop, Bowl, 5 In. 5.00
Pressed Glass, Beaded Dewdrop, Bowl, 7 1/2 In. 18.00
Pressed Glass, Beaded Dewdrop, Butter, Beaded Crown Finial, 7 1/2 In. 75.00
Pressed Glass, Beaded Dewdrop, Butter, Crown Finial, 8 X 5 In. 75.00
Pressed Glass, Beaded Dewdrop, Compote, Jelly ..... 11.00 To 22.50
Pressed Glass, Beaded Dewdrop, Compote, Triangular, 6 1/2 In. 18.50
Pressed Glass, Beaded Dewdrop, Nappy, Handled 15.00
Pressed Glass, Beaded Dewdrop, Pitcher, Water 65.00
Pressed Glass, Beaded Dewdrop, Plate, Cake, Stemmed, 8 1/2 In. 18.00
Pressed Glass, Beaded Dewdrop, Salt & Pepper 32.00
Pressed Glass, Beaded Dewdrop, Toothpick 10.00
Pressed Glass, Beaded Dewdrop, Wine ..... 24.00 To 45.00
Pressed Glass, Beaded Ellipse, Creamer 14.00
Pressed Glass, Beaded Finecut, Creamer 10.50
Pressed Glass, Beaded Frog's Eye, Goblet 15.00
Pressed Glass, Beaded Grape Medallion, Banded, Creamer 32.50
Pressed Glass, Beaded Grape Medallion, Banded, Goblet, Lady's ..... 18.00 To 23.00
Pressed Glass, Beaded Grape Medallion, Banded, Spooner 22.00
Pressed Glass, Beaded Grape Medallion, Butter, Covered 45.00

Pressed Glass, Beaded Grape Medallion, Butter, Flint 35.00
Pressed Glass, Beaded Grape Medallion, Eggcup 17.50
Pressed Glass, Beaded Grape Medallion, Goblet 14.50
Pressed Glass, Beaded Grape Medallion, Spooner ..... 12.00 To 18.00
Pressed Glass, Beaded Grape Medallion, Sugar 20.00
Pressed Glass, Beaded Grape, Berry Set, 7 Piece 45.00
Pressed Glass, Beaded Grape, Bowl, Covered, 8 1/2 In. 31.00
Pressed Glass, Beaded Grape, Bowl, 8 X 6 In. 10.00
Pressed Glass, Beaded Grape, Butter, Green, Covered 53.00
Pressed Glass, Beaded Grape, Cake Stand, Green, Square, 9 In. 35.00
Pressed Glass, Beaded Grape, Compote, Jelly, Green, Covered 65.00
Pressed Glass, Beaded Grape, Creamer 38.00
Pressed Glass, Beaded Grape, Creamer, 6 In. 36.50
Pressed Glass, Beaded Grape, Pitcher, Water, Green 85.00
Pressed Glass, Beaded Grape, Sauce, Square 7.50
Pressed Glass, Beaded Grape, Spooner 20.00
Pressed Glass, Beaded Grape, Sugar, Covered 50.00
Pressed Glass, Beaded Grape, Toothpick, Green, Gold Trim ..... 45.00 To 55.00
Pressed Glass, Beaded Grape, Tumbler 30.00
Pressed Glass, Beaded Loop, Butter 28.00
Pressed Glass, Beaded Loop, Creamer ..... 22.50 To 27.00
Pressed Glass, Beaded Loop, Doughnut Stand 12.50
Pressed Glass, Beaded Loop, Goblet 12.50
Pressed Glass, Beaded Loop, Toothpick 18.00

Beaded Medallion, see Beaded Mirror

Pressed Glass, Beaded Mirror, Spooner 20.00
Pressed Glass, Beaded Mirror, Spooner, Flint 20.00
Pressed Glass, Beaded Oval & Scroll, Goblet 9.00
Pressed Glass, Beaded Oval Window, Spooner, Amber 20.00
Pressed Glass, Beaded Ovals In Sand, Creamer, Green, Opalescent 75.00
Pressed Glass, Beaded Ovals In Sand, Saltshaker 16.00
Pressed Glass, Beaded Ovals, Pitcher, Milk 22.50
Pressed Glass, Beaded Panel, Bonbon, Blue, Opalescent 34.00
Pressed Glass, Beaded Raindrop, Creamer 18.50
Pressed Glass, Beaded Rosette, Goblet 16.50
Pressed Glass, Beaded Swag, Berry Bowl, Master, Ruby Stained 42.50
Pressed Glass, Beaded Swirl, Butter, Child's, Covered 35.00
Pressed Glass, Beaded Swirl, Creamer, Green 35.00
Pressed Glass, Beaded Swirl, Cruet, 7 In. 15.00
Pressed Glass, Beaded Swirl, Cup, Punch, Turning Purple 6.00
Pressed Glass, Beaded Swirl, Pitcher, Green, Gold Trim, 8 In. 48.00
Pressed Glass, Beaded Swirl, Tumbler 9.50
Pressed Glass, Beaded Swirl, Tumbler, Dark Green, Gold Beads 14.50
Pressed Glass, Beaded Tulip, Pitcher, Milk 45.00
Pressed Glass, Beaded Tulip, Pitcher, Water 42.50
Pressed Glass, Beaded, Plate, Bread, "Give Us This Day" 20.00

Bearded Man, see Viking

Pressed Glass, Bearded Man, Sugar 15.00
Pressed Glass, Beatrice, Goblet 10.00
Pressed Glass, Beatty Honeycomb, Mug, White, Opalescent 13.50
Pressed Glass, Beatty Honeycomb, Pitcher, White, Opalescent, 3 1/4 In. 22.50
Pressed Glass, Beatty Rib, Ashtray, Blue, Opalescent, Square, 4 In. 65.00
Pressed Glass, Beatty Rib, Berry Set, White, Opalescent, 5 Piece 45.00
Pressed Glass, Beatty Rib, Celery, Opalescent 26.00
Pressed Glass, Beatty Rib, Muffineer, Blue, Beatty Glass Co. 78.00
Pressed Glass, Beatty Rib, Mug 28.00
Pressed Glass, Beatty Rib, Mug, Opalescent 12.50
Pressed Glass, Beatty Rib, Pitcher, Blue, Opalescent, 5 In. 24.00
Pressed Glass, Beatty Rib, Salt, Blue, Opalescent 35.00
Pressed Glass, Beatty Rib, Spooner, Ruby Stained, Opalescent 22.00
Pressed Glass, Beatty Rib, Toothpick, Blue, Opalescent, 1 3/4 In. 25.00
Pressed Glass, Beatty Rib, Toothpick, Opalescent 30.00
Pressed Glass, Beatty Swirl, Butter, Opalescent, Covered 75.00
Pressed Glass, Beatty Swirl, Tray, Water, Vaseline, Opalescent 85.00
Pressed Glass, Beatty Swirl, Tumbler, Blue, Opalescent 45.00

Pressed Glass, Beatty Waffle, Salt & Pepper 35.00
Pressed Glass, Beautiful Lady, Celery 12.50
Pressed Glass, Beautiful Lady, Wine 14.50
Pressed Glass, Beauty, Saltshaker, Ruby Stained 35.00
Bellflower, see also Cut Bellflower
Pressed Glass, Bellflower, Banded, Creamer, Molded Handle, Flint 85.00
Pressed Glass, Bellflower, Banded, Tumbler 85.00
Pressed Glass, Bellflower, Barrel, Goblet, Flint 27.50
Pressed Glass, Bellflower, Bowl, Lacy, 7 1/2 In. 15.00
Pressed Glass, Bellflower, Butter, Flint 55.00
Pressed Glass, Bellflower, Celery 150.00
Pressed Glass, Bellflower, Champagne, Barrel, Knob Stem 95.00
Pressed Glass, Bellflower, Champagne, Knob Stem, Flint .... 95.00 To 108.00
Pressed Glass, Bellflower, Coarse Rib, Goblet, Barrel Shape 30.00
Pressed Glass, Bellflower, Compote, Flint, 8 1/4 In. 65.00
Pressed Glass, Bellflower, Compote, High Standard, 8 In. 50.00
Pressed Glass, Bellflower, Compote, Low Standard, 8 In. 45.00
Pressed Glass, Bellflower, Compote, Low Standard, 8 1/2 In. .... 45.00 To 55.00
Pressed Glass, Bellflower, Compote, Pedestal, Flint, 3 1/2 Pounds 475.00
Pressed Glass, Bellflower, Creamer 125.00
Pressed Glass, Bellflower, Creamer, Applied Handle, Pedestal, Flint 95.00
Pressed Glass, Bellflower, Decanter, Bar Lip, Cut Shoulders, Quart 135.00
Pressed Glass, Bellflower, Decanter, Pint 250.00
Pressed Glass, Bellflower, Double Vine, Fine Rib, Pitcher, Water .... 225.00 To 295.00
Pressed Glass, Bellflower, Double Vine, Pitcher, Water .... 220.00 To 275.00
Pressed Glass, Bellflower, Double Vine, Pitcher, Water, Applied Handle 225.00
Pressed Glass, Bellflower, Double Vine, Pitcher, Water, Flint 150.00
Pressed Glass, Bellflower, Double Vine, Spooner 40.00
Pressed Glass, Bellflower, Double Vine, Spooner, Flint 45.00
Pressed Glass, Bellflower, Double Vine, Sugar 30.00
Pressed Glass, Bellflower, Eggcup 25.00
Pressed Glass, Bellflower, Fine Rib, Barrel, Goblet, Knob Stem, Flint 39.50
Pressed Glass, Bellflower, Fine Rib, Barrel, Goblet, Rayed Base, Flint 32.50
Pressed Glass, Bellflower, Fine Rib, Goblet, Barrel Shape 32.00
Pressed Glass, Bellflower, Fine Rib, Goblet, Rayed Base, Flint 32.50
Pressed Glass, Bellflower, Goblet .... 22.50 To 30.00
Pressed Glass, Bellflower, Goblet, Barrel, Knob Stem 30.00
Pressed Glass, Bellflower, Goblet, Flint 30.00
Pressed Glass, Bellflower, Goblet, Knob Stem 65.00
Pressed Glass, Bellflower, Goblet, Knob Stem, Flint 35.00
Pressed Glass, Bellflower, Goblet, Knob Stem, Rayed Base 19.00
Pressed Glass, Bellflower, Goblet, Rayed Base, Flint 32.00
Pressed Glass, Bellflower, Mug 13.00

Pressed Glass, Beaded Grape Medallion, Dish, Covered

Pressed Glass, Beaded Grape, Toothpick, Green

Pressed Glass, Bellflower, Plate, 6 In. 75.00
Pressed Glass, Bellflower, Ribbed, Tumbler, Whiskey, Flint 65.00
Pressed Glass, Bellflower, Salt, Master 29.50
Pressed Glass, Bellflower, Salt, Master, Flint 29.50
Pressed Glass, Bellflower, Salt, Master, Footed, Flint 25.00
Pressed Glass, Bellflower, Salt, Scalloped Top, Footed 22.50
Pressed Glass, Bellflower, Sauce, 4 In. 7.00
Pressed Glass, Bellflower, Single Vine, Celery 30.00
Pressed Glass, Bellflower, Single Vine, Coarse Rib, Goblet, Flint 28.00
Pressed Glass, Bellflower, Single Vine, Compote, 8 1/2 X 8 In. 175.00
Pressed Glass, Bellflower, Single Vine, Decanter, Frosted, Bar Lip, Pint 125.00
Pressed Glass, Bellflower, Single Vine, Fine Rib, Barrel, Goblet 32.00
Pressed Glass, Bellflower, Single Vine, Fine Rib, Bottle, Bar, Flint, Quart 95.00
Pressed Glass, Bellflower, Single Vine, Fine Rib, Butter, Covered 125.00
Pressed Glass, Bellflower, Single Vine, Fine Rib, Eggcup 40.00
Pressed Glass, Bellflower, Single Vine, Fine Rib, Goblet 55.00
Pressed Glass, Bellflower, Single Vine, Fine Rib, Goblet, Flint 25.00
Pressed Glass, Bellflower, Single Vine, Fine Rib, Salt, Master 45.00
Pressed Glass, Bellflower, Single Vine, Fine Rib, Salt, Master, Footed, Flint 35.00
Pressed Glass, Bellflower, Single Vine, Fine Rib, Spill 55.00
Pressed Glass, Bellflower, Single Vine, Fine Rib, Tumbler, Flint, 3 1/2 In. 75.00
Pressed Glass, Bellflower, Single Vine, Goblet 25.00
Pressed Glass, Bellflower, Single Vine, Pitcher, Milk 60.00
Pressed Glass, Bellflower, Single Vine, Plate, 6 In. 35.00
Pressed Glass, Bellflower, Single Vine, Salt, Master 35.00
Pressed Glass, Bellflower, Single Vine, Spooner 29.50
Pressed Glass, Bellflower, Single Vine, Sugar, Covered 60.00
Pressed Glass, Bellflower, Spill, Flint 27.00
Pressed Glass, Bellflower, Spooner 29.50
Pressed Glass, Bellflower, Spooner, Flint .... 27.00 To 29.50
Pressed Glass, Bellflower, Sugar, Covered, Flint 68.00
Pressed Glass, Bellflower, Sugar, Flint 35.00
Pressed Glass, Bellflower, Sugar, Flint, 5 1/2 In. 29.50
Pressed Glass, Bellflower, Syrup, Applied Hollow Handle 225.00
Pressed Glass, Bellflower, Tumbler 85.00
Pressed Glass, Bellflower, Tumbler, Flint 85.00
Pressed Glass, Bellflower, Tumbler, 3 1/2 In. 75.00
Pressed Glass, Bellflower, Tumbler, 8 1/2 In. 75.00
Pressed Glass, Bellflower, Wine 75.00
Pressed Glass, Bellflower, Wine, Flint 95.00
Pressed Glass, Bellflower, Wine, Knob Stem, Rayed Base 85.00
Belted Worcester, see Worcester, Belted
Bent Buckle, see New Hampshire
Pressed Glass, Bethlehem Star, Goblet 18.50
Pressed Glass, Bethlehem Star, Sugar, Covered 20.00
Pressed Glass, Beveled Diamond & Star, Jar, Cracker 30.00
Pressed Glass, Beveled Diamond & Star, Tankard, Water 35.00
Pressed Glass, Beveled Star, Spooner, Amber 35.00
Pressed Glass, Bible, Plate, Bread .... 17.50 To 35.00
Big Block, see Henrietta
Pressed Glass, Big Daisy, Wine, Gold Trim 11.00
Pressed Glass, Big X, Celery, 11 In. 8.00
Pressed Glass, Bigler, Cordial, Flint 25.00
Pressed Glass, Bigler, Decanter, Bar, Flint, Quart 40.00
Pressed Glass, Bigler, Goblet, Flint .... 30.00 To 32.50
Pressed Glass, Bigler, Tumbler, Bar 25.00
Pressed Glass, Bigler, Tumbler, Whiskey, Applied Handle, Flint .... 55.00 To 85.00
Pressed Glass, Birch Leaf, Goblet 13.50
Pressed Glass, Birch Leaf, Sauce 4.75
Pressed Glass, Birch Leaf, Syrup, Applied Handle, Flint 20.00
Pressed Glass, Bird & Harp, Mug 20.00
Pressed Glass, Bird & Strawberry, Berry Bowl, 4 Footed, Oval 45.00
Pressed Glass, Bird & Strawberry, Bowl, Footed, 5 1/2 In. 20.00
Pressed Glass, Bird & Strawberry, Bowl, 9 X 3 3/4 In. 45.00
Pressed Glass, Bird & Strawberry, Cake Stand 42.50

Pressed Glass, Bird & Strawberry, Cake Stand, 9 1/2 In. 35.00
Pressed Glass, Bird & Strawberry, Compote, Grayish, Covered, 10 X 6 1/4 In. 71.00
Pressed Glass, Bird & Strawberry, Creamer 22.50
Pressed Glass, Bird & Strawberry, Cup, Punch .... 9.00 To 22.00
Pressed Glass, Bird & Strawberry, Sauce, Footed 15.00
Pressed Glass, Bird & Strawberry, Tumbler 22.50
Pressed Glass, Bird & Strawberry, Wine 35.00
Pressed Glass, Bird & Tree, Syrup, Applied Handle, Pewter Lid, Sept.4, 1867 .... 65.00
Bird in Ring, see Butterfly & Fan
Pressed Glass, Bird With Cherry, Salt, Canary, 3 In. 10.00

Pressed Glass, Bleeding Heart, Goblet

Pressed Glass, Bird, Relish, Sapphire Blue, Bird Shape, 1876, 10 1/2 In. 67.50
Pressed Glass, Birds At Fountain, Goblet 28.50
Pressed Glass, Blackberry Band, Goblet, Buttermilk 32.50
Pressed Glass, Blackberry Spray, Saucer, Blue, Opalescent 25.00
Pressed Glass, Blackberry, Butter, Covered 26.00
Pressed Glass, Blackberry, Creamer 35.00
Pressed Glass, Blackberry, Goblet, Naturalist 18.50
Pressed Glass, Blaine, Tumbler, Portrait Base 35.00
Pressed Glass, Blaze, Celery, Flint 45.00
Pressed Glass, Bleeding Heart, Butter, Covered .... 45.00 To 50.00
Pressed Glass, Bleeding Heart, Dish, Honey 12.50
Pressed Glass, Bleeding Heart, Dish, Pickle, Pear Shape, Scalloped, 8 3/4 In. 38.00
Pressed Glass, Bleeding Heart, Goblet .... 22.00 To 25.00
Pressed Glass, Bleeding Heart, Goblet, Knob Stem 22.00
Pressed Glass, Bleeding Heart, Mug .... 20.00 To 27.00
Pressed Glass, Bleeding Heart, Pitcher, Water 68.00
Pressed Glass, Bleeding Heart, Spooner .... 22.50 To 25.00
Pressed Glass, Bleeding Heart, Sugar .... 22.50 To 30.00
Pressed Glass, Bleeding Heart, Wine, Knob Stem 65.00
Pressed Glass, Block & Cube, Etched, Creamer, Miniature 12.50
Pressed Glass, Block & Fan, Bucket, Ice 26.00
Pressed Glass, Block & Fan, Cake Stand, Flint 35.00
Pressed Glass, Block & Fan, Cake Stand, 10 In. 35.00
Pressed Glass, Block & Fan, Celery .... 17.00 To 28.00
Pressed Glass, Block & Fan, Compote, High Standard, 8 In. 45.00
Pressed Glass, Block & Fan, Fruit Bowl 14.00
Pressed Glass, Block & Fan, Goblet 18.00
Pressed Glass, Block & Fan, Jar, Cracker, Covered 35.00
Pressed Glass, Block & Fan, Muffineer 24.00
Pressed Glass, Block & Fan, Muffineer, Brass Lid 27.00
Pressed Glass, Block & Fan, Pitcher, Milk 20.00
Pressed Glass, Block & Fan, Salt & Pepper, Flint 20.00
Pressed Glass, Block & Fan, Saltshaker 15.00
Pressed Glass, Block & Fan, Sauce 6.50
Pressed Glass, Block & Fan, Wine .... 25.00 To 32.00
Block & Finecut, see Finecut & Block
Pressed Glass, Block & Jewel, Goblet 12.00
Pressed Glass, Block & Lattice, Berry Bowl, Amber Stained, Scalloped 37.50

Pressed Glass, Block & Lattice, Jar, Cracker, Ruby Stained 85.00
Pressed Glass, Block & Lattice, Spooner, Ruby Stained 32.50
Pressed Glass, Block & Lattice, Tumbler, Ruby Stained, 3 1/2 In. 25.00
Pressed Glass, Block & Pleat, Celery 18.50
Pressed Glass, Block & Pleat, Sauce, Footed 5.00
Pressed Glass, Block & Pleat, Sauce, 3 Footed 4.75
Block & Star, see Valencia Waffle
Pressed Glass, Block & Sunburst, Creamer 10.00
Pressed Glass, Block & Thumbprint, Celery 22.50
Pressed Glass, Block & Thumbprint, Wine, Flint 18.00
Block with Stars, see Hanover
Pressed Glass, Block, Celery, Green, Opalescent, Northwood 28.00
Pressed Glass, Block, Creamer, Frosted, Footed 12.50
Pressed Glass, Block, Creamer, Ruby Stained, 3 In. 22.50
Pressed Glass, Block, Decanter, Bulbous, Pint 22.00
Pressed Glass, Block, Goblet 18.00
Pressed Glass, Block, Goblet, Amber Stained 24.00
Pressed Glass, Block, Wine, Amber 30.00
Blockade, see Diamond Block with Fan
Pressed Glass, Blocked Thumbprint & Beads, Saucer, White, Opalescent 12.00
Blockhouse, see Hanover
Pressed Glass, Blooming Flower, Salt & Pepper, Gold Trim 17.00
Pressed Glass, Blossom & Palm, Bowl, Green, Opalescent, Ruffled, N, 8 1/2 In. 25.00
Bluebird, see Bird & Strawberry
Pressed Glass, Bohemian, Bottle, Dresser, Green, Mushroom Stopper, Footed 125.00
Pressed Glass, Bohemian, Tumbler, Juice 14.00
Pressed Glass, Bosc Pear, Tumbler, Pink Pears, Gold Leaves 14.00
Pressed Glass, Bowtie, Compote, High Standard, 9 1/4 In. 45.00
Pressed Glass, Bowtie, Creamer 35.00
Pressed Glass, Bowtie, Fruit Bowl 47.50
Pressed Glass, Bowtie, Jar, Jam 13.00
Pressed Glass, Bowtie, Jar, Jam, Covered .... 38.00 To 39.50
Pressed Glass, Bowtie, Pitcher, 5 1/2 In. 35.00
Pressed Glass, Bowtie, Spooner, Scalloped Rim 28.50
Bradford Blackberry, see Bradford Grape
Pressed Glass, Bradford Grape, Goblet, Flint 50.00
Pressed Glass, Bradford Grape, Wine, Flint 50.00
Pressed Glass, Brand, Compote, High Standard, 9 In. 22.00
Pressed Glass, Brazen Shield, Sauce, Blue 18.00
Pressed Glass, Brazilian, Spooner 15.00
Pressed Glass, Brilliant, Goblet, Flint 57.50
Pressed Glass, Brilliant, Tumbler, Amber Stained 25.00
Pressed Glass, Broad Flute, Compote, Low Standard, Flint, 8 In. 10.00
Pressed Glass, Broken Column, Bowl, 9 In. 30.00
Pressed Glass, Broken Column, Celery .... 12.50 To 35.00
Pressed Glass, Broken Column, Compote, Covered, Square, 5 In. .... 29.00 To 32.00
Pressed Glass, Broken Column, Compote, Covered, 10 1/2 In. 28.00
Pressed Glass, Broken Column, Compote, Covered, 11 X 5 1/2 In. 27.50
Pressed Glass, Broken Column, Creamer .... 25.00 To 30.00
Pressed Glass, Broken Column, Creamer, Ruby Stained 85.00
Pressed Glass, Broken Column, Goblet, Lady's 22.00
Pressed Glass, Broken Column, Jar, Cookie 48.00
Pressed Glass, Broken Column, Jar, Cracker .... 45.00 To 75.00
Pressed Glass, Broken Column, Jar, Cracker, Covered .... 45.00 To 52.00
Pressed Glass, Broken Column, Spooner 22.00
Pressed Glass, Broken Column, Sugar, Covered, Red Dots 110.00
Pressed Glass, Broken Column, Tumbler, Red Dots .... 40.00 To 60.00
Pressed Glass, Broken Column, Tumbler, Ruby Stained 58.00
Pressed Glass, Broken Column, Water Set, Ruby Stained, 7 Piece 100.00
Pressed Glass, Broken Column, Wine 20.00
Pressed Glass, Brooklyn, Goblet 19.00
Pressed Glass, Brooklyn, Goblet, Flint 85.00
Pressed Glass, Broughton, Tumbler, Child's 7.00
Pressed Glass, Broughton, Water Set, Child's, 4 Piece 70.00
Pressed Glass, Bryan, Mug, Covered 30.00
Bryce, see Ribbon Candy

Pressed Glass, **Bubble Lattice,** Muffineer, Opalescent 30.00
Pressed Glass, **Bubble Lattice,** Muffineer, White, Opalescent 45.00
Pressed Glass, **Bubble Lattice,** Tumbler, Blue, Opalescent 29.00
Pressed Glass, **Buckle & Star,** Creamer .... 15.00 To 26.50
Pressed Glass, **Buckle & Star,** Jar, Jam 20.00
Pressed Glass, **Buckle & Star,** Wine .... 19.00 To 25.00
Pressed Glass, **Buckle,** Bowl, Rolled Rim, Flint, 10 In. 40.00
Pressed Glass, **Buckle,** Champagne, Flint 95.00
Pressed Glass, **Buckle,** Dish, Honey 6.50
Pressed Glass, **Buckle,** Eggcup 17.50
Pressed Glass, **Buckle,** Eggcup, Flint 32.00
Pressed Glass, **Buckle,** Goblet .... 14.50 To 22.00
Pressed Glass, **Buckle,** Goblet, Amber 18.00
Pressed Glass, **Buckle,** Goblet, Blue 22.50
Pressed Glass, **Buckle,** Goblet, Buttermilk, Flint 32.50
Pressed Glass, **Buckle,** Goblet, Flint 30.00
Pressed Glass, **Buckle,** Salt, Master 25.00
Pressed Glass, **Buckle,** Salt, Master, Footed 20.00
Pressed Glass, **Buckle,** Sauce 6.00
Pressed Glass, **Buckle,** Spooner .... 9.50 To 16.00
Pressed Glass, **Buckle,** Sugar 30.00
Pressed Glass, **Buckle,** Sugar, Covered 36.00
Pressed Glass, **Buckle,** Table Set, 3 Piece 55.00
Pressed Glass, **Buckle,** Tumbler, Bar 39.50
Pressed Glass, **Buckle,** Wine 25.00
Pressed Glass, **Budded Ivy,** Creamer 23.50
Pressed Glass, **Budded Ivy,** Spooner .... 18.00 To 20.00
Pressed Glass, **Bulging Petal,** Condiment Holder, Pink 37.00

Bull's-Eye & Fan, see Daisies in Oval Panels
Bull's-Eye Variant, see Texas Bull's-Eye

Pressed Glass, **Bull's Eye & Daisy,** Wine, Green Eyes 19.00
Pressed Glass, **Bull's Eye & Diamond Point,** Pitcher, Water, Amber, 9 In. 125.00
Pressed Glass, **Bull's-Eye & Bar,** Eggcup, Flint 80.00
Pressed Glass, **Bull's-Eye & Broken Column,** Goblet, Flint 55.00
Pressed Glass, **Bull's-Eye & Broken Column,** Tumbler, Footed, Flint 48.00
Pressed Glass, **Bull's-Eye & Cube,** Goblet, Flint 55.00
Pressed Glass, **Bull's-Eye & Daisy,** Berry Set, Ruby Eyes, 7 Piece 125.00
Pressed Glass, **Bull's-Eye & Daisy,** Goblet 15.00
Pressed Glass, **Bull's-Eye & Daisy,** Goblet, Amethyst Eyes, Gold Band 15.00
Pressed Glass, **Bull's-Eye & Daisy,** Goblet, Green Eyes, Gold Trim 20.00
Pressed Glass, **Bull's-Eye & Daisy,** Goblet, Pink Eyes 16.00
Pressed Glass, **Bull's-Eye & Daisy,** Goblet, Purple Eyes, Gold Trim 22.50
Pressed Glass, **Bull's-Eye & Daisy,** Pitcher, Blue, Gold Trim 95.00
Pressed Glass, **Bull's-Eye & Daisy,** Sugar & Creamer, Purple Eyes, Gold Trim 52.00
Pressed Glass, **Bull's-Eye & Daisy,** Table Set, Ruby Eyes, 4 Piece 145.00
Pressed Glass, **Bull's-Eye & Diamond Point,** Goblet, Flint .... 95.00 To 100.00
Pressed Glass, **Bull's-Eye & Diamond Point,** Tumbler, Whiskey, Flint 75.00
Pressed Glass, **Bull's-Eye & Loop,** Creamer, Flint 55.00
Pressed Glass, **Bull's-Eye & Prism,** Goblet, Flint 45.00
Pressed Glass, **Bull's-Eye & Rosette,** Tumbler, Whiskey, Flint 43.00

Bull's-Eye Band, see Reverse Torpedo

Pressed Glass, **Bull's-Eye With Fleur-De-Lis,** Celery, Gauffered Rim, Flint 135.00
Pressed Glass, **Bull's-Eye With Fleur-De-Lis,** Goblet 48.00
Pressed Glass, **Bull's-Eye With Fleur-De-Lis,** Goblet, Flint 72.50
Pressed Glass, **Bull's-Eye,** Celery .... 30.00 To 40.00
Pressed Glass, **Bull's-Eye,** Celery, Flint 75.00
Pressed Glass, **Bull's-Eye,** Decanter, 6 Sided, Pint 22.00
Pressed Glass, **Bull's-Eye,** Goblet, Flint .... 34.00 To 45.00
Pressed Glass, **Bull's-Eye,** Tumbler, Flint 58.00
Pressed Glass, **Bull's-Eye,** Tumbler, Flint, 3 3/4 In. 89.50
Pressed Glass, **Bull's-Eye,** Tumbler, Gold Eyes 18.00
Pressed Glass, **Bull's-Eye,** Wine, Flint .... 45.00 To 50.00
Pressed Glass, **Bullet Emblem,** Butter, Covered 195.00
Pressed Glass, **Bumper To The Flag,** Tumbler, Flint 80.00
Pressed Glass, **Bungalow,** Goblet 15.00
Pressed Glass, **Bunker Hill,** Plate, Bread 45.00

Pressed Glass, Broken Column, Goblet

Pressed Glass, Buckle, Goblet

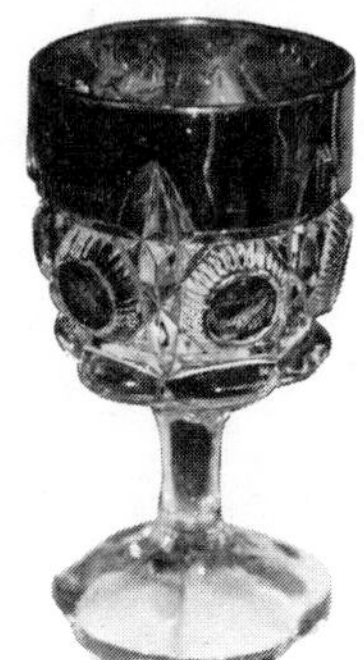

Pressed Glass, Bull's Eye & Daisy, Goblet

Pressed Glass, Bull's Eye & Diamond Point, Goblet, 7 In.

Pressed Glass, Butterfly & Fan, Celery 25.00
Pressed Glass, Butterfly & Fan, Creamer 14.50
Pressed Glass, Butterfly & Fan, Sugar, Covered 28.50
Pressed Glass, Butterfly With Spray, Mug, Amber 20.00
Pressed Glass, Butterfly, Mug, 3 1/4 In. 14.50
Pressed Glass, Butterfly, Saltshaker, Pewter Top 16.00
Pressed Glass, Butterfly, Sugar & Creamer, Etched 30.00
Pressed Glass, Butterfly, Sugar, Covered 30.00
Pressed Glass, Button & Star Panel, Toothpick 15.00
Pressed Glass, Button Arches, Butter, Ruby Stained, Grape Cuttings 69.00
Pressed Glass, Button Arches, Cup, Punch 4.50
Pressed Glass, Button Arches, Cup, Punch, Ruby Stained 15.00
Pressed Glass, Button Arches, Mug, Ruby Stained, Engraved Grapes 18.50
Pressed Glass, Button Arches, Pitcher, Milk 27.50
Pressed Glass, Button Arches, Salt & Pepper, Ruby Stained 20.00
Pressed Glass, Button Arches, Syrup, Ruby Stained 90.00
Pressed Glass, Button Arches, Tumbler, Frosted Band 24.00
Pressed Glass, Button Arches, Wine 15.50
Pressed Glass, Button Arches, Wine, Ruby Stained 24.50
Pressed Glass, Button Band, Butter, Covered 25.00
Pressed Glass, Button Band, Compote, Jelly 14.50
Pressed Glass, Button Band, Plate, Cake, Handled 24.00
Pressed Glass, Button Band, Spooner 15.00
Pressed Glass, Button Band, Sugar 10.00
Pressed Glass, Button Panel, Compote, Jelly, Yellow, Opalescent 35.00
Pressed Glass, Button Panel, Cup, Punch 6.00
Pressed Glass, Button, Sauce 7.50
Pressed Glass, Buttons & Braid, Water Set, Green, Opalescent, 7 Piece 275.00
Pressed Glass, Buttons & Braids, Pitcher, Water, Green, Opalescent 90.00
Pressed Glass, Buttons & Braids, Pitcher, Water, Opalescent 35.00
Pressed Glass, Buttons & Braids, Tumbler, Green, Opalescent 29.00
Pressed Glass, Buttress Sunburst, Creamer 14.00
Pressed Glass, Buttressed Loop, Salt, Master 13.50
Pressed Glass, C Scroll, Tumbler, White 28.00
Pressed Glass, Cabbage Rose, Bowl, 8 1/4 X 5 1/2 In. 21.50

Pressed Glass, Cabbage Rose, Mug

Pressed Glass, Cabbage Rose, Cake Stand 60.00
Pressed Glass, Cabbage Rose, Celery 35.00
Pressed Glass, Cabbage Rose, Goblet 29.00
Pressed Glass, Cabbage Rose, Salt, Master 17.00
Pressed Glass, Cabbage Rose, Spooner 19.50
Pressed Glass, Cabbage Rose, Tumbler 37.50
Pressed Glass, Cabbage Rose, Wine .... 28.50 To 45.00
Pressed Glass, Cabbage Rose, Wine, 4 1/2 In. 27.50
Pressed Glass, Cable With Ring, Sauce, Flint 8.00
Pressed Glass, Cable With Ring, Sugar & Creamer, Applied Handle, Flint 140.00
Pressed Glass, Cable With Ring, Sugar, Covered, Flint 68.00
Pressed Glass, Cable, Celery, Flint 60.00
Pressed Glass, Cable, Compote, Flint, 8 1/4 In. 50.00
Pressed Glass, Cable, Compote, Low Standard, Flint, 8 1/4 In. 50.00
Pressed Glass, Cable, Eggcup, Flint 32.00
Pressed Glass, Cable, Goblet, Flint 52.00
Pressed Glass, Cable, Goblet, Lady's, Flint 75.00
Pressed Glass, Cable, Sauce, Flint, 4 In. 8.00
Pressed Glass, Cable, Spooner 45.00
Pressed Glass, Cable, Spooner, Blue, Sandwich 155.00
Pressed Glass, Cable, Spooner, Flint 29.50
Pressed Glass, Cable, Spooner, Sandwich, Flint, C.1850 .... 18.00
Cameo, see Ceres
Canadian Drape, see Garfield Drape
Pressed Glass, Canadian, Celery 31.50
Pressed Glass, Canadian, Compote, 8 X 7 1/2 In. 28.00
Pressed Glass, Canadian, Goblet .... 27.00 To 29.00
Pressed Glass, Canadian, Plate, Bread, 9 1/2 In. 14.00
Pressed Glass, Canadian, Plate, Cake 20.00

Pressed Glass, Cable With Rings, Bowl, Footed

Pressed Glass, Cable, Spooner

Pressed Glass, Canadian, Compote, Covered

Pressed Glass, Cathedral, Compote

Pressed Glass, Canadian, Plate, 7 In. 23.50
Pressed Glass, Canadian, Plate, 8 In. 24.00
Pressed Glass, Canadian, Sugar, Covered 45.00
Pressed Glass, Canadian, Wine 47.50
Pressed Glass, Candlewick, Creamer 12.00
Pressed Glass, Candlewick, Cup & Saucer 4.50
Pressed Glass, Candlewick, Wine 22.50
Candy Ribbon, see Ribbon Candy
Pressed Glass, Cane & Column, Creamer, Covered 19.00
Pressed Glass, Cane & Shield, Saltshaker 6.50
Pressed Glass, Cane Column, Spooner 11.00
Pressed Glass, Cane, Creamer 12.00
Pressed Glass, Cane, Goblet 14.00
Pressed Glass, Cane, Goblet, Amber 18.00
Pressed Glass, Cane, Pitcher, Water, Green 45.00
Pressed Glass, Cannonball, Creamer, Applied Handle 10.00
Pressed Glass, Cannonball, Goblet .... 21.50 To 24.50

Pressed Glass, **Canterbury,** Sugar & Creamer, Individual, Cape Cod Blue 50.00
Pressed Glass, **Cape Cod,** Goblet .... 20.00 To 22.50
Pressed Glass, **Capitol Building,** Champagne 18.00
Pressed Glass, **Capitol Building,** Champagne, Saucer Base 25.00
Pressed Glass, **Capitol Building,** Goblet 25.00
Pressed Glass, **Capitol,** Goblet, Ribbed, Oak Leaves 17.50
Pressed Glass, **Cardinal Bird,** Goblet .... 22.50 To 25.50
Pressed Glass, **Cardinal,** Creamer .... 25.00 To 35.00
Pressed Glass, **Cardinal,** Goblet .... 28.00 To 30.00
Pressed Glass, **Cardinal,** Sauce 8.00
Pressed Glass, **Cardinal,** Spooner 25.00

Carmen, see Paneled Diamond & Finecut

Pressed Glass, **Carolina,** Plate, 7 1/2 In. 10.00
Pressed Glass, **Cat In Basket,** Mug, Child's 32.00
Pressed Glass, **Cathedral,** Butter, Canary 115.00
Pressed Glass, **Cathedral,** Compote, Blue, High Standard, Ruffled Top, 8 In. 65.00
Pressed Glass, **Cathedral,** Compote, Blue, Ruffled Top, 9 X 7 In. 85.00
Pressed Glass, **Cathedral,** Compote, Blue, Scalloped, 9 1/4 X 6 1/4 In. 63.00
Pressed Glass, **Cathedral,** Compote, 8 1/4 In. 28.50
Pressed Glass, **Cathedral,** Creamer 26.00
Pressed Glass, **Cathedral,** Creamer, Vaseline 42.00
Pressed Glass, **Cathedral,** Dish, Pickle, Amethyst, Fish Shape 27.50
Pressed Glass, **Cathedral,** Goblet 21.00
Pressed Glass, **Cathedral,** Goblet, Amber 48.00
Pressed Glass, **Cathedral,** Goblet, Vaseline 48.00
Pressed Glass, **Cathedral,** Sauce, Footed .... 9.75 To 11.50
Pressed Glass, **Cathedral,** Sauce, Footed, 4 1/4 X 3 In. 18.00
Pressed Glass, **Cathedral,** Sauce, Ruby Stained 7.50
Pressed Glass, **Cathedral,** Spooner 28.00
Pressed Glass, **Cathedral,** Sugar, Covered .... 29.00 To 45.00
Pressed Glass, **Cathedral,** Sugar, Vaseline, Covered .... 48.00 To 60.00
Pressed Glass, **Cathedral,** Tumbler 22.00
Pressed Glass, **Cathedral,** Tumbler, Amber 32.50
Pressed Glass, **Cathedral,** Wine, Amber 35.00
Pressed Glass, **Cattail & Water Lily,** Tumbler, Blue, Opalescent 18.00
Pressed Glass, **Celtic Cross,** Celery .... 18.00 To 20.00

Pressed Glass, Ceres, Bowl, Covered

Pressed Glass, Chain & Shield, Pitcher

Pressed Glass, Chicken, Jar, Mustard, Frosted, Covered

Pressed Glass, Circle & Ellipse, Vase, Canary, 7 1/4 In.

Pressed Glass, Classic, Compote, Covered

Centennial, see also Liberty Bell, Washington Centennial

Pressed Glass, Centennial Exhibition, Mug, Memorial 85.00
Pressed Glass, Centennial, Ale Glass, 1776-1876 .... 35.00 To 45.00
Pressed Glass, Centennial, Champagne, Independence Hall 32.50
Pressed Glass, Centennial, Goblet 32.50
Pressed Glass, Centennial, Goblet, Cord & Tassel 36.00
Pressed Glass, Centennial, Goblet, Emblem With Keystone 40.00
Pressed Glass, Centennial, Goblet, Shield & Keystone 45.00
Pressed Glass, Centennial, Goblet, 1876 .... 45.00
Pressed Glass, Centennial, Mug, Beer .... 50.00 To 115.00
Pressed Glass, Centennial, Plate, Bread, George Washington Center 70.00
Pressed Glass, Ceres, Spooner 20.00
Pressed Glass, Chain & Saw, Cake Stand 45.00
Pressed Glass, Chain & Shield, Creamer 21.50
Pressed Glass, Chain & Shield, Goblet 12.50
Pressed Glass, Chain & Shield, Pitcher, Water 20.00
Pressed Glass, Chain & Shield, Plate, Bread .... 24.00 To 30.00

Chain with Diamonds, see Washington Centennial

Pressed Glass, Chain With Star, Creamer 21.50
Pressed Glass, Chain With Star, Goblet .... 18.00 To 18.50
Pressed Glass, Chain With Star, Wine, Flint 9.50
Pressed Glass, Chain, Butter, Covered 20.00
Pressed Glass, Chain, Creamer 18.00
Pressed Glass, Chain, Goblet 14.00
Pressed Glass, Chain, Plate, Bread, Amber .... 18.00 To 22.50
Pressed Glass, Challinor, Cruet, Blue 150.00
Pressed Glass, Challinor, Spooner 21.00
Pressed Glass, Champion, Toothpick, Emerald Green 35.00
Pressed Glass, Champion, Toothpick, Gold Trim 15.00
Pressed Glass, Champion, Toothpick, Green 29.00
Pressed Glass, Champion, Water Set, 7 Piece 55.00

Chandelier, see also Crown Jewels

Pressed Glass, Chandelier, Celery 24.50
Pressed Glass, Chandelier, Celery, Etched Floral 25.00
Pressed Glass, Chandelier, Compote, 9 1/4 X 7 3/4 In. 115.00
Pressed Glass, Charleston Swirl, Tumbler, Vaseline, Footed 23.50

Pressed Glass, **Checkerboard,** Bowl, 9 In. 17.50
Pressed Glass, **Checkerboard,** Butter, Covered 22.00 To 30.00
Pressed Glass, **Checkerboard,** Creamer 17.00
Pressed Glass, **Checkerboard,** Goblet 10.00
Pressed Glass, **Checkerboard,** Pitcher, Milk 20.00
Pressed Glass, **Checkerboard,** Spooner 12.00 To 21.00
Pressed Glass, **Checkerboard,** Sugar, Covered 40.00
Pressed Glass, **Checkerboard,** Wine 8.50
Pressed Glass, **Cherry & Fan,** Butter, Pointed Paneled Finial, Scalloped 50.00
Pressed Glass, **Cherry & Plum,** Creamer, Gold Trim, Northwood 55.00
Pressed Glass, **Cherry Lattice,** Berry Bowl, Northwood, 4 1/2 In. 12.50
Pressed Glass, **Cherry Lattice,** Butter, Covered 18.50
Pressed Glass, **Cherry,** Butter, Covered 25.00
Pressed Glass, **Cherry,** Butter, Covered, Scalloped Edge, 7 1/2 In. 30.00
Pressed Glass, **Cherry,** Butter, Covered, 6 In. 27.50
Pressed Glass, **Cherry,** Goblet 18.00
Pressed Glass, **Cherry,** Goblet, Blue, Opaque, Bakewell Pears 100.00
Pressed Glass, **Cherry,** Pitcher, Water 20.00
Pressed Glass, **Cherry,** Toothpick 35.00
Pressed Glass, **Chicken,** Celery 28.50
Pressed Glass, **Chicken,** Jar, Jam, Frosted Chicken Finial, Handled, 6 1/2 In. 35.00
Pressed Glass, **Chilson,** Goblet, Flint 110.00
Pressed Glass, **Choked Ashburton,** Goblet, Flint 32.00
Pressed Glass, **Chrysanthemum Leaf,** Celery 18.00
Pressed Glass, **Chrysanthemum Leaf,** Compote, Jelly 20.00
Pressed Glass, **Chrysanthemum Leaf,** Jar, Cracker 75.00
Pressed Glass, **Chrysanthemum,** Lemonade Set, Etched, C.1925, 10 Piece 250.00
Pressed Glass, **Chrysanthemum,** Tumbler, Blue, Opalescent, Swirled Base 48.00
Pressed Glass, **Circled Scrolls,** Creamer, Opalescent 29.50
Pressed Glass, **Civil War,** Tumbler, Flint 85.00
Pressed Glass, **Civil War,** Tumbler, Flint, 4 3/4 In. 95.00
Pressed Glass, **Classic Medallion,** Spooner 15.00 To 18.00
Pressed Glass, **Classic Warrior,** Frosted Center, Jacobus, 11 1/2 In. 95.00
Pressed Glass, **Classic,** Butter, Covered 110.00
Pressed Glass, **Classic,** Butter, Covered, Open Log Feet 190.00
Pressed Glass, **Classic,** Celery, Collared Base 75.00
Pressed Glass, **Classic,** Celery, Open Log Feet 195.00
Pressed Glass, **Classic,** Compote, Covered, Open Feet, 6 1/2 In. 145.00 To 150.00
Pressed Glass, **Classic,** Compote, Covered, Open Feet, 7 1/2 In. 165.00
Pressed Glass, **Classic,** Compote, Covered, Open Log Feet, 7 1/2 In. 200.00
Pressed Glass, **Classic,** Compote, Covered, 7 1/2 In. 200.00
Pressed Glass, **Classic,** Compote, Low Standard, Footed, 7 3/8 In. 75.00
Pressed Glass, **Classic,** Compote, Open Log Feet, 6 1/2 In. 80.00
Pressed Glass, **Classic,** Creamer 120.00
Pressed Glass, **Classic,** Creamer, Open Log Feet 148.00
Pressed Glass, **Classic,** Goblet 165.00
Pressed Glass, **Classic,** Goblet, Open Log Feet 165.00
Pressed Glass, **Classic,** Pitcher, Open Feet, 10 In. 225.00
Pressed Glass, **Classic,** Pitcher, Water 165.00 To 310.00
Pressed Glass, **Classic,** Pitcher, Water, Open Log Feet 295.00
Pressed Glass, **Classic,** Pitcher, Water, Open Log Feet, Collared Base 275.00
Pressed Glass, **Classic,** Plate, Warrior 95.00
Pressed Glass, **Classic,** Sauce, Open Log Feet, 4 In. 32.50
Pressed Glass, **Classic,** Sauce, Twig Feet 20.00
Pressed Glass, **Classic,** Sauce, 3 3/4 In. 24.50
Pressed Glass, **Classic,** Sauce, 4 1/4 In. 32.50
Pressed Glass, **Classic,** Spooner 95.00
Pressed Glass, **Classic,** Spooner, Open Log Feet 95.00
Pressed Glass, **Classic,** Sugar 37.50 To 65.00
Pressed Glass, **Classic,** Sugar, Covered 125.00
Pressed Glass, **Classic,** Sugar, Covered, Open Log Feet 170.00
Pressed Glass, **Classic,** Sugar, Footed 55.00
Pressed Glass, **Clear & Diamond Panels,** Butter, Blue, Covered, Miniature 60.00
Pressed Glass, **Clear & Diamond Panels,** Creamer, Miniature 20.00
Pressed Glass, **Clear & Diamond Panels,** Spooner, Miniature 20.00
Pressed Glass, **Clear Band,** Goblet 3.00

Pressed Glass, Clear Circle, Tumbler, Juice 17.50
Pressed Glass, Clear Diagonal Band, Goblet 12.50
Pressed Glass, Clear Diagonal Band, Plate, Bread 20.00
Pressed Glass, Clear Diagonal Band, Wine 20.00
Pressed Glass, Clear Panels With Cord Band, Butter, Covered 20.00
Pressed Glass, Clear Panels With Cord Band, Plate, Bread 18.50
Pressed Glass, Clear Panels With Cord Band, Wine 20.00
Pressed Glass, Clear Ribbon, Celery 25.00
Pressed Glass, Clear Ribbon, Celery, Stemmed 28.00
Pressed Glass, Clear Ribbon, Creamer 22.00
Pressed Glass, Clear Ribbon, Jar, Jam, Covered, Squat 18.50
Pressed Glass, Clear Ribbon, Plate, Bread, "Give Us This Day-" 17.50
Pressed Glass, Cleat, Pitcher, Milk, Flint 125.00
Pressed Glass, Cleat, Pitcher, Water 125.00
Pressed Glass, Cleat, Pitcher, Water, Flint 85.00
Pressed Glass, Clematis, Sugar, Covered 25.00
Pressed Glass, Clio, Creamer 15.00
Pressed Glass, Clio, Goblet 12.50
Pressed Glass, Clio, Plate, 10 In. 11.50
Pressed Glass, Coarse Cut & Block, Creamer, Tankard Shape 8.00
Pressed Glass, Coarse Diamond Point, Goblet 10.00
Pressed Glass, Coarse Rib, Salt, Master, Footed 25.00
Pressed Glass, Coin & Dewdrop, Goblet 12.50
Pressed Glass, Coin Dot & Swirl, Tumbler, Opalescent 22.50
Pressed Glass, Coin Dot, Pitcher, Opalescent With Clear Dots, 8 In. 175.00
Pressed Glass, Coin Spot & Swirl, Syrup, Blue 85.00
Pressed Glass, Coin Spot, Compote, Vaseline, Opalescent, Fluted, 4 3/4 In. 20.00
Pressed Glass, Coin Spot, Muffineer, Blue, Opalescent 75.00
Pressed Glass, Coin Spot, Muffineer, Blue, Tapered 60.00
Pressed Glass, Coin Spot, Pitcher, Water, Blue, Ruffled Top 55.00
Pressed Glass, Coin Spot, Pitcher, Water, Opalescent, Applied Clear Handle 75.00

Pressed Glass, Clover, Creamer, 3 1/2 In.

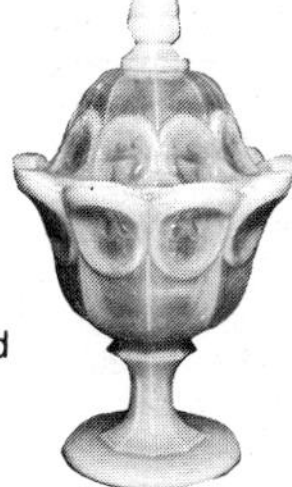

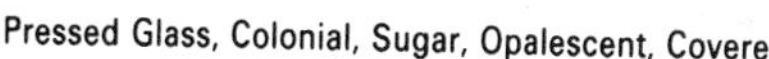

Pressed Glass, Colonial, Sugar, Opalescent, Covered

Pressed Glass, Clear Diagonal Band, Creamer

Pressed Glass, Columbian Coin, Salt & Pepper

Pressed Glass, Coin Spot, Syrup, Opalescent 50.00
Pressed Glass, Coin Spot, Syrup, Opalescent, 7 1/2 In. 55.00
Pressed Glass, Coin Spot, Syrup, Ruby To Opalescent 90.00
Pressed Glass, Coin Spot, Tumbler, Blue, Opalescent Rim 18.00
Pressed Glass, Coin Spot, Tumbler, Opalescent, 3 3/4 In. 20.00
Pressed Glass, Coin Spot, Vase, Blue, Opalescent, Ruffled Top, 7 1/2 In. 34.00
Pressed Glass, Coin Spot, Water Set, Blue, Opalescent, 7 Piece 225.00
Pressed Glass, Coin Spot, Water Set, Green, Opalescent, 7 Piece 195.00
Pressed Glass, Coin Spot, Water Set, Opalescent & Clear, 5 Piece 90.00
Pressed Glass, Colonial, Butter 18.50
Pressed Glass, Colonial, Goblet, Flint 40.00
Pressed Glass, Colonial, Goblet, Knob Stem, Flint .... 39.00 To 42.50
Pressed Glass, Colonial, Sugar, Covered, Flint 45.00
Pressed Glass, Colonial, Tumbler, Whiskey, Footed, Flint 34.00
Pressed Glass, Colonial, Wine Set, McKee, 7 Piece 35.00
Pressed Glass, Colonial, Wine, Flint 40.00
Pressed Glass, Colorado, Banana Bowl, Blue, Gold Trim .... 47.50 To 48.00
Pressed Glass, Colorado, Bowl, Beaded Edge, Square, 6 In. 8.50
Pressed Glass, Colorado, Bowl, 3 Flared Handles, 3 Footed, 8 In. 14.00
Pressed Glass, Colorado, Bowl, 6 In. 10.00
Pressed Glass, Colorado, Cup, Green, Gold Trim 33.00
Pressed Glass, Colorado, Finger Bowl, Amethyst 35.00
Pressed Glass, Colorado, Finger Bowl, Emerald Green 30.00
Pressed Glass, Colorado, Finger Bowl, Light Green, Enameled 30.00
Pressed Glass, Colorado, Finger Bowl, Ruby Stained 25.00
Pressed Glass, Colorado, Nappy, Rolled Edge, Tricorner, 4 In. 30.00
Pressed Glass, Colorado, Sauce, Blue, Footed, Miniature 30.00
Pressed Glass, Colorado, Sauce, Blue, Gold Trim, Beaded Top, 4 In. 30.00
Pressed Glass, Colorado, Sugar, Blue 72.50
Pressed Glass, Colorado, Sugar, Blue, Gold Trim 33.75
Pressed Glass, Colorado, Sugar, Green, Covered 55.00
Pressed Glass, Colorado, Toothpick, Blue .... 19.00 To 22.00
Pressed Glass, Colorado, Toothpick, Blue, Gold Trim .... 40.00 To 42.00
Pressed Glass, Colorado, Toothpick, Green 20.00
Pressed Glass, Colorado, Toothpick, Green, Gold Foot 30.00
Pressed Glass, Colorado, Toothpick, Green, Gold On Feet 30.00
Pressed Glass, Colorado, Tray, Card, Green, Gold Trim 22.50
Pressed Glass, Colorado, Tumbler, Green, Gold Trim .... 15.00 To 30.00
Pressed Glass, Columbia, Banana Stand, Fluted Rim, Findlay 35.00
Pressed Glass, Columbia, Cake Stand, Fluted Rim, Findlay 20.00
Pressed Glass, Columbia, Toothpick, Co-Op 17.00
Pressed Glass, Columbian Coin, Berry Bowl, Frosted, Dollars, 10 In. 85.00
Pressed Glass, Columbian Coin, Butter, Frosted, Covered, Dollars 85.00
Pressed Glass, Columbian Coin, Cake Stand, Frosted, Dollars 115.00
Pressed Glass, Columbian Coin, Celery, Frosted, Quarters 65.00
Pressed Glass, Columbian Coin, Champagne 30.00
Pressed Glass, Columbian Coin, Champagne, Frosted, Dimes 60.00
Pressed Glass, Columbian Coin, Compote, Covered, Quarters, 7 In. 110.00
Pressed Glass, Columbian Coin, Compote, Frosted, Covered, Quarters, 6 In. 100.00
Pressed Glass, Columbian Coin, Creamer, Frosted, Quarters 65.00
Pressed Glass, Columbian Coin, Creamer, Gilded, Quarters 60.00

Pressed Glass, Columbian Coin, Goblet, Frosted, Dimes 65.00
Pressed Glass, Columbian Coin, Mug, Beer, Gilded, Dollars 55.00
Pressed Glass, Columbian Coin, Sauce, Frosted, Pedestal Base, Quarters 25.00
Pressed Glass, Columbian Coin, Sauce, Frosted, Quarters 25.00
Pressed Glass, Columbian Coin, Spooner, Frosted, Quarters 50.00
Pressed Glass, Columbian Coin, Sugar, Covered, Gilded, Quarters & 1/2 Dollar 80.00
Pressed Glass, Columbian Coin, Sugar, Covered, Quarters & Half Dollars 85.00
Pressed Glass, Columbian Coin, Syrup, Frosted, Quarters 100.00
Pressed Glass, Columbian Coin, Toothpick 37.00
Pressed Glass, Columbian Coin, Toothpick, Frosted, Dollars 30.00
Pressed Glass, Columbian Coin, Tumbler, Gilded, Quarters 35.00
Pressed Glass, Columbian Coin, Wine, Gold Coins 55.00
Pressed Glass, Columbian Exposition, Goblet 12.00
Pressed Glass, Comet, Goblet 65.00
Pressed Glass, Comet, Goblet, Flint 65.00
Pressed Glass, Comet, Goblet, Flint, 6 1/4 In. 45.00
Compact, see Snail
Pressed Glass, Concave Almond, Toothpick 20.00
Pressed Glass, Concave Column, Vase, Blue, Opalescent, 7 In. 30.00
Pressed Glass, Connecticut, Compote, 8 X 5 In. 25.00
Pressed Glass, Coral, Bowl, Blue, Opalescent, 9 In. 22.00
Pressed Glass, Coral, Bowl, Green, Opalescent, 9 In. 18.00
Pressed Glass, Corcoran, Spooner 16.50
Pressed Glass, Cord & Tassel, Cake Stand, Flint 35.00
Pressed Glass, Cord & Tassel, Creamer 20.00
Pressed Glass, Cord Drapery, Compote, Jelly, Blue, Covered, Greentown 125.00
Pressed Glass, Cord Drapery, Compote, Jelly, Covered 28.00
Pressed Glass, Cord Drapery, Creamer 27.00
Pressed Glass, Cord Drapery, Sauce 6.50
Pressed Glass, Cordova, Bottle, Dresser 30.00
Pressed Glass, Cordova, Bottle, Perfume 15.00
Pressed Glass, Cordova, Celery 28.00
Pressed Glass, Cordova, Compote, 7 X 7 In. 15.00
Pressed Glass, Cordova, Mug 8.00
Pressed Glass, Cordova, Pitcher, Milk 27.50
Pressed Glass, Coreopsis, Creamer 58.00
Pressed Glass, Coreopsis, Pitcher, Water 125.00
Pressed Glass, Corn, Pitcher, 8 1/2 In. 45.00
Pressed Glass, Cornell, Wine, Green, Gold Trim 30.00
Pressed Glass, Cornucopia & Cherries, Pitcher, Water 85.00
Pressed Glass, Cornucopia, Pitcher, Water 35.00
Pressed Glass, Corrigan, Compote, High Standard, Ruffled, Findlay, 8 In. 45.00
Pressed Glass, Cottage, Bowl, Oval, 7 3/4 In. 11.50
Pressed Glass, Cottage, Butter 20.00
Pressed Glass, Cottage, Butter, Covered 27.50
Pressed Glass, Cottage, Creamer 14.00
Pressed Glass, Cottage, Cup & Saucer 38.00
Pressed Glass, Cottage, Goblet 15.00
Pressed Glass, Cottage, Plate, 7 In. 13.50
Pressed Glass, Cottage, Saltshaker .... 9.50 To 9.75
Pressed Glass, Cottage, Saucer 8.00

Pressed Glass, Compote, Bellflower

Pressed Glass, Cottage, Syrup 35.00
Pressed Glass, Cottage, Tumbler 12.00
Pressed Glass, Cow Cover, Dish, Amber, Split Rib Base, 6 In. 25.00
Crane, see Stork
Pressed Glass, Crane's-Bill, Table Set, 4 Piece 65.00
Pressed Glass, Creased Ashburton, Champagne, Flint 36.00
Crisscross, see Rexford
Pressed Glass, Croesus, Berry Bowl, Purple, Gold Trim 45.00
Pressed Glass, Croesus, Butter, Green 90.00
Pressed Glass, Croesus, Sauce, Amethyst, Gold Trim, Miniature 35.00
Pressed Glass, Croesus, Sauce, Emerald Green, Gold Trim, Footed 30.00
Pressed Glass, Croesus, Spooner, Green 55.00
Pressed Glass, Croesus, Sugar, Green, Covered .... 100.00 To 125.00
Pressed Glass, Croesus, Sugar, Green, Covered, Gold Trim 90.00
Pressed Glass, Croesus, Sugar, Purple 125.00
Pressed Glass, Croesus, Sugar, Purple, Covered 85.00
Pressed Glass, Croesus, Table Set, Green, 5 Piece 365.00
Pressed Glass, Croesus, Toothpick, Green .... 62.00 To 65.00
Pressed Glass, Croesus, Toothpick, Green, Gold Trim 75.00
Pressed Glass, Croesus, Toothpick, Purple 60.00
Pressed Glass, Croesus, Tumbler, Emerald Green, Gold Trim 55.00
Pressed Glass, Croesus, Tumbler, Green, Gold Trim 50.00
Pressed Glass, Croesus, Tumbler, Purple 35.00
Pressed Glass, Crosby, Toothpick, Gold Trim, 3 Handles 15.00
Pressed Glass, Cross Dart & Finecut, Pitcher, Water 45.00
Crossbar & Finecut, see Ashman
Pressed Glass, Crow's-Foot, Bowl, 8 1/2 In. 20.00
Pressed Glass, Crow's-Foot, Butter 30.00
Pressed Glass, Crow's-Foot, Cake Stand 30.00
Pressed Glass, Crow's-Foot, Compote, High Standard, 7 In. 28.00
Pressed Glass, Crow's-Foot, Creamer 22.50
Pressed Glass, Crow's-Foot, Dish, Pickle 9.50
Pressed Glass, Crow's-Foot, Goblet 25.00
Pressed Glass, Crow's-Foot, Pitcher, Water 32.00
Pressed Glass, Crow's-Foot, Relish, 8 In. 14.00
Pressed Glass, Crow's-Foot, Sauce, 5 1/2 In. 6.00
Pressed Glass, Crow's-Foot, Spooner 14.50
Pressed Glass, Crow's-Foot, Sugar 16.50
Pressed Glass, Crow's-Foot, Sugar, Covered .... 28.00 To 30.00
Pressed Glass, Crow's-Foot, Tumbler 12.00
Crown Jewels, see also Chandelier, Queen"s Necklace
Pressed Glass, Crown Jewels, Butter, Blue, Opalescent, Covered, 6 In. 69.00
Pressed Glass, Crystal Wedding, Compote, 6 In. 30.00
Pressed Glass, Crystal Wedding, Creamer .... 22.50 To 29.00
Pressed Glass, Crystal Wedding, Creamer, Frosted 40.00
Pressed Glass, Crystal Wedding, Dish, Honey, Covered, Square, 6 In. 55.00
Pressed Glass, Crystal Wedding, Goblet, Ruby Stained 47.50
Pressed Glass, Crystal Wedding, Spooner, Amber Flashed 25.00
Pressed Glass, Crystal Wedding, Spooner, Frosted 25.00
Pressed Glass, Crystal Wedding, Sugar, Frosted 50.00
Pressed Glass, Crystal, Celery, Flint 35.00
Pressed Glass, Crystal, Celery, Footed, Flint 38.00
Pressed Glass, Crystal, Celery, Stemmed 40.00

Pressed Glass, Cupid & Psyche, Creamer

Pressed Glass, Cupid & Venus, Plate, Bread

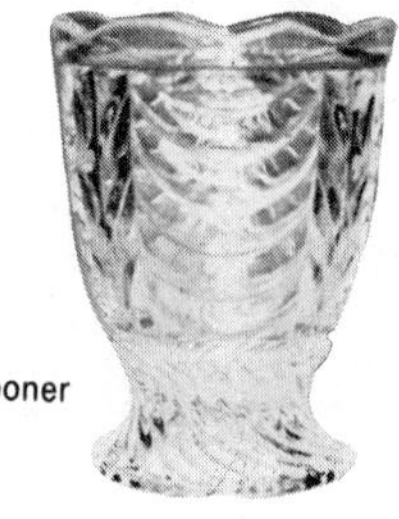

Pressed Glass, Curtain, Spooner

Pressed Glass, Crystal, Cordial, Flint 20.00

Pressed Glass, Crystal, Wine, Flint 18.00

Cube & Diamond, see Milton

Cube & Fan, see Pineapple & Fan

Pressed Glass, Cube, Mug 18.00

Pressed Glass, Cube, Tumbler 9.50

Pressed Glass, Cupid & Venus, Bowl, Covered, Footed, 8 In. 55.00

Pressed Glass, Cupid & Venus, Celery 40.00

Pressed Glass, Cupid & Venus, Champagne 50.00

Pressed Glass, Cupid & Venus, Compote, Covered, Low Standard, 8 In. 54.50

Pressed Glass, Cupid & Venus, Compote, 8 5/8 In. 32.50

Pressed Glass, Cupid & Venus, Creamer 28.00

Pressed Glass, Cupid & Venus, Goblet 50.00

Pressed Glass, Cupid & Venus, Jar, Marmalade 45.00

Pressed Glass, Cupid & Venus, Jar, Marmalade, Covered 41.00

Pressed Glass, Cupid & Venus, Mug 20.00

Pressed Glass, Cupid & Venus, Mug, 2 1/2 In. 18.00

Pressed Glass, Cupid & Venus, Pitcher, Milk 59.50

Pressed Glass, Cupid & Venus, Pitcher, Water 125.00

Pressed Glass, Cupid & Venus, Plate, 10 1/4 In. 27.00 To 29.00

Pressed Glass, Cupid & Venus, Plate, 10 1/2 In. 39.50

Pressed Glass, Cupid & Venus, Plate, 2 Handles, 10 In. 20.00

Pressed Glass, Cupid & Venus, Sauce, Footed, 3 3/4 In. 5.50

Pressed Glass, Cupid & Venus, Sauce, Footed, 4 1/2 In. 6.50 To 12.00

Pressed Glass, Cupid & Venus, Spooner 28.00

Pressed Glass, Cupid & Venus, Wine 50.00 To 55.00

Pressed Glass, Cupid Riding Lion, Plate, Bread 30.00

Pressed Glass, Cupid's Hunt, Relish, Oval, 9 In. 22.50

Pressed Glass, Currant, Celery 45.00

Pressed Glass, Currant, Dish, Honey 5.00

Pressed Glass, Currant, Goblet 13.50

Pressed Glass, Currant, Spooner 15.00 To 16.00

Pressed Glass, Currier & Ives, Cordial, 3 1/4 In. 28.00

Pressed Glass, Currier & Ives, Cup 9.75

Pressed Glass, Currier & Ives, Goblet 15.00 To 20.00

Pressed Glass, Currier & Ives, Pitcher, Clear 37.50

Pressed Glass, Currier & Ives, Pitcher, Water 35.00

Pressed Glass, Currier & Ives, Pitcher, Water, Sapphire Blue, 9 In. 175.00

Pressed Glass, Currier & Ives, Tray, Water, Balky Mule 27.00

Pressed Glass, Currier & Ives, Tray, Water, Blue, Balky Mule, 12 In. 87.50

Pressed Glass, Currier & Ives, Tray, Water, Blue, Basket Weave Rim, 12 1/2 In. 49.75

Pressed Glass, Currier & Ives, Wine 14.00

Pressed Glass, Curtain Tieback, Berry Bowl, Square, 7 In. 10.00

Pressed Glass, Curtain Tieback, Goblet 18.50

Pressed Glass, Curtain Tieback, Plate, Bread 35.00

Pressed Glass, Curtain Tieback, Sauce, Amber, 4 In. 6.00

Pressed Glass, Curtain Tieback, Sauce, Green 6.00

Pressed Glass, Cut Bellflower, Double Vine, Fine Rib, Champagne, 5 In. 250.00

Pressed Glass, Cut Bellflower, Double Vine, Fine Rib, Compote, Flint, 8 In. 475.00

Pressed Glass, Cut Bellflower, Double Vine, Fine Rib, Goblet, 6 1/4 In. 250.00

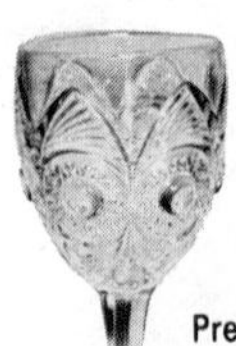
Pressed Glass, Daisies In Oval Panels, Goblet

Pressed Glass, Cut Bellflower, Double Vine, Fine Rib, Tumbler, Footed 250.00
Pressed Glass, Cut Bellflower, Double Vine, Fine Rib, Tumbler, 3 1/2 In. 250.00
Pressed Glass, Cut Bellflower, Double Vine, Fine Rib, Wine, 4 In. 250.00
Pressed Glass, Cut Bellflower, Double Vine, Goblet 225.00
Pressed Glass, Cut Bellflower, Single Vine, Fine Rib, Tumbler, 3 1/2 In. 250.00
Pressed Glass, Cut Diamond & Leaf, Plate, 7 3/8 In. 25.00
Pressed Glass, Cut Diamond Point, Tumbler, Whiskey, Flint 32.00
Pressed Glass, Cut Honeycomb, Wine 35.00
Pressed Glass, Cut Log, Cake Stand 55.00
Pressed Glass, Cut Log, Celery .... 24.00 To 26.00
Pressed Glass, Cut Log, Compote, 6 In. 24.50
Pressed Glass, Cut Log, Compote, 7 X 5 In. 19.00
Pressed Glass, Cut Log, Compote, 9 1/4 X 7 3/4 In. 50.00
Pressed Glass, Cut Log, Creamer 13.00
Pressed Glass, Cut Log, Creamer, Miniature 9.50
Pressed Glass, Cut Log, Dish, Honey, Handled 15.00
Pressed Glass, Cut Log, Goblet 21.50
Pressed Glass, Cut Log, Mug .... 10.00 To 12.00
Pressed Glass, Cut Log, Tumbler 20.00
Pressed Glass, Cut Log, Tumbler, Juice 35.00
Pressed Glass, Cut Log, Wine .... 19.00 To 22.00
Pressed Glass, Daffodil, Pitcher, Water, Green, Opalescent 225.00
Pressed Glass, Dahlia, Goblet 30.00
Pressed Glass, Dahlia, Goblet, Etched 10.00
Pressed Glass, Dahlia, Mug, Amber 40.00
Pressed Glass, Dahlia, Mug, Vaseline 55.00
Pressed Glass, Dahlia, Plate, Cake, Handled 11.50
Pressed Glass, Dahlia, Plate, Handles, 9 In. 21.50
Pressed Glass, Dahlia, Plate, 6 7/8 In. 30.00
Pressed Glass, Dahlia, Platter, Cake, Closed Handles 22.00
Pressed Glass, Dahlia, Spooner, Footed 12.00
Pressed Glass, Dahlia, Stippled, Spooner 15.00
Pressed Glass, Dahlia, Sugar, Covered 25.00
Pressed Glass, Dahlia, Wine .... 20.00 To 30.00
Pressed Glass, Daisies In Oval Panels, Creamer, Gold Trim 16.50
Pressed Glass, Daisies In Oval Panels, Goblet 12.00
Pressed Glass, Daisies In Oval Panels, Goblet, Gold Trim 14.50
Pressed Glass, Daisies In Oval Panels, Sugar & Creamer, Gold Trim 23.50
Pressed Glass, Daisies In Oval Panels, Toothpick .... 14.00 To 14.50
Pressed Glass, Daisies In Oval Panels, Water Set, Amethyst & Gold, 5 Piece 125.00
Pressed Glass, Daisy & Block, Goblet 14.00
Pressed Glass, Daisy & Block, Wine 13.00
Pressed Glass, Daisy & Bull's-Eye, Goblet 10.00

Daisy & Button, see also Paneled Daisy & Button

Pressed Glass, Daisy & Button With Amber Panels, Berry Bowl 85.00
Pressed Glass, Daisy & Button With Amber Panels, Bowl, Flared, 10 In. 70.00
Pressed Glass, Daisy & Button With Amber Panels, Dish Pickle 42.50
Pressed Glass, Daisy & Button With Amber Panels, Relish 42.50
Pressed Glass, Daisy & Button With Amber Panels, Sauce 32.50
Pressed Glass, Daisy & Button With Amber Panels, Spooner 69.00
Pressed Glass, Daisy & Button With Crossbar, Celery, Amber 35.00
Pressed Glass, Daisy & Button With Crossbar, Compote, Amber, Covered, 8 In. 47.50

Pressed Glass, Daisy & Button With Crossbar, Creamer, Amber ... 18.50 To 35.00
Pressed Glass, Daisy & Button With Crossbar, Pitcher, Water, Amber, 7 In. ... 40.00
Pressed Glass, Daisy & Button With Crossbar, Plate, Bread ... 14.00
Pressed Glass, Daisy & Button With Crossbar, Sauce, Vaseline, Footed ... 12.00
Pressed Glass, Daisy & Button With Crossbar, Spooner, Amber, 7 In. ... 65.00
Pressed Glass, Daisy & Button With Crossbar, Spooner, Vaseline ... 20.00 To 22.00
Pressed Glass, Daisy & Button With Crossbar, Tumbler, Amber ... 23.50
Pressed Glass, Daisy & Button With Crossbar, Wine, Vaseline ... 30.00
Pressed Glass, Daisy & Button With Finecut Panels, Pitcher, Water ... 27.50
Pressed Glass, Daisy & Button With Narcissus, Goblet ... 10.00 To 18.00
Pressed Glass, Daisy & Button With Narcissus, Wine ... 13.00 To 14.00
Daisy & Button with Oval Panels, see Hartley
Pressed Glass, Daisy & Button With Panel, Bowl, Amber Dots, Cloverleaf, 5 In. ... 14.00
Pressed Glass, Daisy & Button With Pointed Panels, Wine ... 14.50
Pressed Glass, Daisy & Button With Red Dots, Toothpick, Ruby Stained ... 35.00
Pressed Glass, Daisy & Button With Thumbprint Panel, Compote, Amber, 7 In. ... 47.50
Pressed Glass, Daisy & Button With Thumbprint, Goblet, Vaseline, 6 In. ... 35.00
Pressed Glass, Daisy & Button With Thumbprint, Pitcher, Amber, 1/2 Gallon ... 50.00
Pressed Glass, Daisy & Button With V Ornament, Berry Bowl, Amber, 9 In. ... 25.00
Pressed Glass, Daisy & Button With V Ornament, Bowl, Vaseline, 9 X 3 In. ... 30.00
Pressed Glass, Daisy & Button With V Ornament, Celery ... 19.50 To 30.00
Pressed Glass, Daisy & Button With V Ornament, Creamer, Amber ... 47.00
Pressed Glass, Daisy & Button With V Ornament, Pitcher, Water ... 32.00
Pressed Glass, Daisy & Button, Banana Bowl, Amberina ... 80.00
Pressed Glass, Daisy & Button, Basket, Amber, 6 1/4 X 4 In. ... 35.00
Pressed Glass, Daisy & Button, Bell, Blue ... 5.00
Pressed Glass, Daisy & Button, Berry Set, 6 Piece ... 45.00
Pressed Glass, Daisy & Button, Bowl, Amber, Oval, 12 X 7 In. ... 30.00
Pressed Glass, Daisy & Button, Bowl, Fan Shape, 10 1/2 In. ... 10.00
Pressed Glass, Daisy & Button, Butter Pat, Blue, Triangular ... 10.00
Pressed Glass, Daisy & Button, Butter Pat, Vaseline ... 10.00
Pressed Glass, Daisy & Button, Canoe, Vaseline, 11 In. ... 25.00
Pressed Glass, Daisy & Button, Canoe, 14 In. ... 32.50
Pressed Glass, Daisy & Button, Cornucopia, 13 X 3 In. ... 12.00
Pressed Glass, Daisy & Button, Cruet, Blue ... 75.00
Pressed Glass, Daisy & Button, Eggcup, Canary ... 13.00
Pressed Glass, Daisy & Button, Fruit Bowl, Reticulated Top, Pedestal, 9 In. ... 48.00
Pressed Glass, Daisy & Button, Goblet, Amber ... 20.00
Pressed Glass, Daisy & Button, Goblet, Flat Stem ... 14.00
Pressed Glass, Daisy & Button, Hat, Vaseline, 2 1/2 In. ... 12.00
Pressed Glass, Daisy & Button, Hat, 8 X 6 In. ... 65.00
Pressed Glass, Daisy & Button, Ice Bowl ... 45.00
Pressed Glass, Daisy & Button, Ice Cream Set, Vaseline, 11 Piece ... 125.00
Pressed Glass, Daisy & Button, Inkwell, Sapphire Blue, Throne Shape ... 35.00
Pressed Glass, Daisy & Button, Pitcher, Water, Etched, Petticoat ... 47.50
Pressed Glass, Daisy & Button, Punch Bowl, High Standard, 10 In. ... 75.00
Pressed Glass, Daisy & Button, Rack, Wall, Sapphire Blue, Hanging, 11 In. ... 245.00
Pressed Glass, Daisy & Button, Railroad Gondola, Golden Amber, 8 X 4 In. ... 125.00
Pressed Glass, Daisy & Button, Salt & Pepper, Blue, Metal Tops, 4 1/4 In. ... 55.00

Pressed Glass, Daisy Whorl With Diamond Band, Goblet

Pressed Glass, Daisy & Button With Thumbprint, Goblet

Pressed Glass, Daisy & Button, Salt, Dark Purple, Anvil Shape 7.50
Pressed Glass, Daisy & Button, Sauce, Honey Amber, Boat Shape 12.00
Pressed Glass, Daisy & Button, Sauce, Vaseline, Triangular 12.00
Pressed Glass, Daisy & Button, Shade, Smoke Bell, Amber 55.00
Pressed Glass, Daisy & Button, Shoe, Clear 15.00
Pressed Glass, Daisy & Button, Sleigh, Red, Large 89.50
Pressed Glass, Daisy & Button, Slipper, Vaseline, Oct.'86, 5 In. 18.00
Pressed Glass, Daisy & Button, Tankard, Water, Amber, Applied Amber Handle 77.50
Pressed Glass, Daisy & Button, Toothpick 12.50
Pressed Glass, Daisy & Button, Toothpick, Amber, Cube Shape 16.00
Pressed Glass, Daisy & Button, Toothpick, Amber, Metal Band 15.00
Pressed Glass, Daisy & Button, Toothpick, Blue 22.00
Pressed Glass, Daisy & Button, Toothpick, Blue, Anvil Shape 25.00
Pressed Glass, Daisy & Button, Toothpick, Footed 12.00
Pressed Glass, Daisy & Button, Toothpick, Ruby Stained, Scalloped Rim 45.00
Pressed Glass, Daisy & Button, Toothpick, Vaseline, Hat Shape 25.00
Pressed Glass, Daisy & Button, Toothpick, Vaseline, 3 Footed 28.00
Pressed Glass, Daisy & Button, Top Hat, 4 1/4 In. 20.00
Pressed Glass, Daisy & Button, Tray, Canary, 11 In. 42.00
Pressed Glass, Daisy & Button, Tumbler, Vaseline .... 15.00 To 22.00
Pressed Glass, Daisy & Button, Water Set, Ruby Stained Buttons, 7 Piece 275.00
Pressed Glass, Daisy & Cube, Saltshaker 6.50
Pressed Glass, Daisy & Fern, Pitcher, Water, Blue, Opalescent, Ruffled Top 75.00
Pressed Glass, Daisy & Fern, Pitcher, Water, White, Opalescent, Ruffled Top 50.00
Pressed Glass, Daisy & Fern, Tumbler, Canary 18.50
Pressed Glass, Daisy & Greek Key, Sauce, Blue, Opalescent .... 30.00 To 35.00
Pressed Glass, Daisy Fern, Spittoon, Lady's 59.00
Pressed Glass, Daisy In Oval, Butter, Gold Trim 17.00
Pressed Glass, Daisy With Bull's-Eye, Goblet, Green Eyes 15.00
Pressed Glass, Daisy, Salt & Pepper, Red, Long Petals 125.00
Pressed Glass, Dakota With Band, Wine 15.00
Pressed Glass, Dakota, Basket, Fruit, Etched, Ruffled, Handle, 10 In. 60.00
Pressed Glass, Dakota, Butter 28.00
Pressed Glass, Dakota, Butter, Covered 38.50
Pressed Glass, Dakota, Butter, Covered, Etched .... 37.50 To 45.00
Pressed Glass, Dakota, Butter, Flint 38.50
Pressed Glass, Dakota, Celery 28.00
Pressed Glass, Dakota, Celery, Etched .... 27.00 To 32.00
Pressed Glass, Dakota, Celery, Etched Bird & Flower 30.00
Pressed Glass, Dakota, Celery, Etched Fern & Berry .... 28.50 To 35.00
Pressed Glass, Dakota, Celery, Etched Fern & Berry, Footed 27.50
Pressed Glass, Dakota, Celery, Etched, Footed 29.50
Pressed Glass, Dakota, Celery, Etched, Pedestal 45.00
Pressed Glass, Dakota, Celery, Footed 17.00
Pressed Glass, Dakota, Compote, Covered, Etched, 9 In. 40.00
Pressed Glass, Dakota, Compote, Covered, Etched, 9 1/2 In. 21.00
Pressed Glass, Dakota, Compote, Etched Berry & Leaf, High Standard, 5 In. 30.00
Pressed Glass, Dakota, Compote, Etched Fern & Berry, 7 In. 22.50
Pressed Glass, Dakota, Compote, Etched, 8 In. 35.00
Pressed Glass, Dakota, Compote, Jelly, Etched 38.50
Pressed Glass, Dakota, Dessert Bowl, Footed 10.00
Pressed Glass, Dakota, Dish, Cheese, Covered, Etched, Ruffled 47.50
Pressed Glass, Dakota, Dish, Ice Cream, 4 1/2 In. 12.00
Pressed Glass, Dakota, Goblet 18.50
Pressed Glass, Dakota, Goblet, Etched .... 24.00 To 35.00
Pressed Glass, Dakota, Goblet, Etched Fern & Berry .... 19.75 To 25.00
Pressed Glass, Dakota, Goblet, Etched, 6 1/2 In. 24.00
Pressed Glass, Dakota, Jar, Marmalade, Covered 20.00
Pressed Glass, Dakota, Pitcher, Water, Etched 50.00
Pressed Glass, Dakota, Pitcher, Water, Etched Fern & Berry, Applied Handle 55.00
Pressed Glass, Dakota, Sauce, Etched, Footed 12.50
Pressed Glass, Dakota, Spooner 19.00
Pressed Glass, Dakota, Spooner, Etched 27.00
Pressed Glass, Dakota, Spooner, Etched, Footed 29.50
Pressed Glass, Dakota, Sugar, Covered, Etched 42.50

Pressed Glass, Dakota, Sugar, Covered, Etched Fern & Berry 55.00
Pressed Glass, Dakota, Sugar, Etched 25.00
Pressed Glass, Dakota, Tumbler, Etched 16.00
Pressed Glass, Dakota, Tumbler, Etched Berry & Leaf, 3 1/2 In. 35.00
Pressed Glass, Dakota, Tumbler, Ruby Top, Etched Mama, 1891 .... 30.00
Pressed Glass, Dakota, Wine .... 16.50 To 19.00
Pressed Glass, Dakota, Wine, Etched 32.50
Pressed Glass, Dancing Goat, Mug, Beer, Frosted, 7 In. 42.00
Pressed Glass, Dancing Goat, Mug, Frosted 50.00
Pressed Glass, Dart, Compote, Covered, 5 1/4 In. 25.00
Pressed Glass, Dart, Creamer 12.00
Pressed Glass, Dart, Table Set, 3 Piece 65.00
Pressed Glass, Deep Star, Spooner 12.50
Pressed Glass, Deer & Bull, Mug, Child's, 2 In. 20.00
Pressed Glass, Deer & Doe With Lily Of The Valley, Goblet 48.50
Pressed Glass, Deer & Doe, Plate, Bread, Frosted Center, "Be Industrious" 80.00
Pressed Glass, Deer & Dog, Butter, Frosted Dog Finial, Frosted & Etched 160.00
Pressed Glass, Deer & Dog, Celery, Scalloped Rim, Gillinder 67.50
Pressed Glass, Deer & Dog, Creamer, Frosted & Etched 65.00
Pressed Glass, Deer & Dog, Goblet, Frosted & Etched 75.00
Pressed Glass, Deer & Dog, Pitcher, Water, Applied Reeded Handle, Frosted 150.00
Pressed Glass, Deer & Dog, Spooner, Etched, Footed 32.00
Pressed Glass, Deer & Dog, Spooner, Frosted & Etched 52.50
Pressed Glass, Deer & Dog, Sugar, Frosted Dog Finial, Frosted & Etched 145.00
Pressed Glass, Deer & Oak Tree, Pitcher, Water 88.00
Pressed Glass, Deer & Oak Tree, Pitcher, Water, Greentown 125.00
Pressed Glass, Deer & Pine Tree, Butter, Covered 45.00
Pressed Glass, Deer & Pine Tree, Compote, Covered, High Standard, 9 X 7 In. 37.50
Pressed Glass, Deer & Pine Tree, Compote, High Standard, 8 X 6 In. 22.50
Pressed Glass, Deer & Pine Tree, Goblet .... 25.00 To 33.00
Pressed Glass, Deer & Pine Tree, Mug, Amber 28.00
Pressed Glass, Deer & Pine Tree, Plate, Bread 22.00
Pressed Glass, Deer & Pine Tree, Plate, Bread, Green 45.00
Pressed Glass, Deer & Pine Tree, Plate, Bread, 13 X 7 1/2 In. 36.00
Pressed Glass, Deer & Pine Tree, Plate, 13 X 7 3/4 In. 20.00
Pressed Glass, Deer & Pine Tree, Platter, 12 X 7 3/4 In. 35.00
Pressed Glass, Deer & Pine Tree, Relish, 7 1/4 X 4 1/4 In. 15.00
Pressed Glass, Deer & Pine Tree, Relish, 8 X 5 1/4 In. 12.50
Pressed Glass, Deer & Pine Tree, Sauce, Footed, 4 X 3 In. 10.00
Pressed Glass, Deer & Pine Tree, Sauce, Footed, 4 1/2 X 3 1/2 In. 14.50
Pressed Glass, Deer & Pine Tree, Sauce, 4 1/2 X 3 1/2 In. 7.50
Pressed Glass, Deer & Pine Tree, Tray, Handled, Raised Sides, Oval, 15 X 9 In. 52.50
Pressed Glass, Deer & Pine Tree, Tray, Water .... 50.00 To 85.00
Pressed Glass, Deer & Pine Tree, Tray, Water, Handled 85.00
Pressed Glass, Deer & Pine Tree, Tray, Water, 15 X 9 In. 75.00
Pressed Glass, Deer Alert, Pitcher, Water 88.00
Pressed Glass, Deer Alert, Pitcher, Water, Greentown 145.00

Pressed Glass, Deer & Dog, Goblet

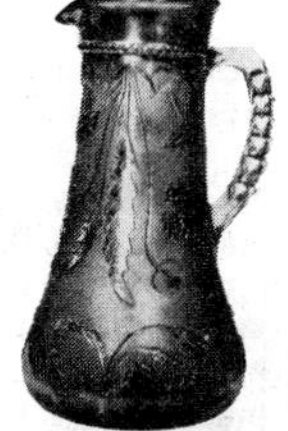
Pressed Glass, Delaware, Pitcher, Rose Color, 9 1/2 In.

Pressed Glass, Deer Racing, Pitcher, Water, Greentown 125.00
Pressed Glass, Deer, Dog, & Hunter, Goblet, Engraved 65.00
Pressed Glass, Deer, Dog, & Hunter, Pitcher, Etched, Applied Reeded Handle 135.00
Pressed Glass, Delaware, Banana Boat, Cranberry 85.00
Pressed Glass, Delaware, Banana Boat, Green .... 35.00 To 43.00
Pressed Glass, Delaware, Banana Boat, Green, Gold Trim .... 30.00 To 67.50
Pressed Glass, Delaware, Banana Boat, Ruby Stained, Gold Trim, Boat Shape 80.00
Pressed Glass, Delaware, Banana Bowl, Green 42.00
Pressed Glass, Delaware, Berry Bowl, Green 20.00
Pressed Glass, Delaware, Berry Bowl, Green, Gold Fluted Top 23.00
Pressed Glass, Delaware, Berry Bowl, Green, Gold Trim 20.00
Pressed Glass, Delaware, Berry Bowl, Green, Gold Trim, Boat Shape 65.00
Pressed Glass, Delaware, Berry Bowl, Rose Color, Gold Trim, Oval 24.00
Pressed Glass, Delaware, Bowl, Fruit, 11 X 7 In. 75.00
Pressed Glass, Delaware, Bowl, Green, 10 In. 22.50
Pressed Glass, Delaware, Butter, Green, Gold Trim 115.00
Pressed Glass, Delaware, Celery 25.00
Pressed Glass, Delaware, Celery, Green, Gold Trim 55.00
Pressed Glass, Delaware, Celery, Rose Color, Gold Trim 37.00
Pressed Glass, Delaware, Creamer, Green 38.00
Pressed Glass, Delaware, Creamer, Green, Gold Trim 85.00
Pressed Glass, Delaware, Creamer, Individual, Gold Trim 8.00
Pressed Glass, Delaware, Creamer, Rose Color, Gold 60.00
Pressed Glass, Delaware, Cup, Custard, Rose Color, Gold Trim 35.00
Pressed Glass, Delaware, Cup, Punch, Emerald Green, Gold Trim 18.00
Pressed Glass, Delaware, Fruit Bowl, Green, Gold Trim 25.00
Pressed Glass, Delaware, Pitcher, Claret, Gold Trim 65.00
Pressed Glass, Delaware, Pitcher, Claret, Green, Gold Trim 75.00
Pressed Glass, Delaware, Pitcher, Milk, Green, Gold Trim 77.50
Pressed Glass, Delaware, Pitcher, Water, Gold Trim, Bulbous 135.00
Pressed Glass, Delaware, Sauce, Cranberry, Gold Trim, Boat Shape 29.50
Pressed Glass, Delaware, Sauce, Gold Trim, Oval 20.00
Pressed Glass, Delaware, Spooner, Green, Gold Trim 40.00
Pressed Glass, Delaware, Sugar, Rose Color, Gold Trim, Footed 55.00
Pressed Glass, Delaware, Table Set, Pink & Gold Trim, 4 Piece 235.00
Pressed Glass, Delaware, Tray, Pin, Green Trim 40.00
Pressed Glass, Delaware, Tumbler, Green 38.00
Pressed Glass, Delaware, Tumbler, Green, Gold Trim 29.50
Pressed Glass, Delaware, Tumbler, Mottled Rose Stain, Gold Trim 22.00
Pressed Glass, Delaware, Vase, Amethyst Leaves & Flowers, Gold Trim, 8 In. 45.00
Pressed Glass, Delaware, Vase, Amethyst Stained Floral, Gold Trim, 8 In. 40.00
Pressed Glass, Delaware, Vase, Green, Gold Trim, 9 1/2 X 6 In. 60.00
Pressed Glass, Delaware, Vase, Rose Color, Gold Trim, Crimped Edge, 9 1/2 In. 110.00
Pressed Glass, Delaware, Water Set, Green, Gold Trim, 7 Piece 275.00
Pressed Glass, Della Robbia, Bowl, Raised Fruit, Footed; 12 3/4 In. 35.00
Pressed Glass, Despot, Goblet 7.50
Pressed Glass, Dew & Raindrop, Saltshaker, Square 6.50
Pressed Glass, Dew & Raindrop, Wine .... 7.50 To 12.50
Pressed Glass, Dewdrop Band, Goblet 12.00
Pressed Glass, Dewdrop With Sheaf Of Wheat, Plate, Bread, Motto .... 25.00 To 32.50
Pressed Glass, Dewdrop With Star, Cake Stand 30.00
Pressed Glass, Dewdrop With Star, Goblet 45.00
Pressed Glass, Dewdrop With Star, Sugar, Covered 50.00
Pressed Glass, Dewdrop, Goblet, Amber 24.00
Pressed Glass, Dewdrop, Saltshaker, Footed 6.00

Dewey, see also Admiral Dewey

Pressed Glass, Dewey, Butter 22.50
Pressed Glass, Dewey, Butter, Amber, Covered 55.00
Pressed Glass, Dewey, Butter, Amber, Greentown 65.00
Pressed Glass, Dewey, Creamer, Vaseline, Greentown 38.00
Pressed Glass, Dewey, Pitcher, Water .... 55.00 To 62.50
Pressed Glass, Dewey, Sauce Set, Vaseline, 7 Piece 250.00
Pressed Glass, Dewey, Tumbler 55.00
Pressed Glass, Dewey, Tumbler, Bust In Base, Icicle Pattern Sides 20.00
Pressed Glass, Diagonal Band & Fan, Champagne 20.00
Pressed Glass, Diagonal Band & Fan, Wine 15.00

Pressed Glass, Diagonal Band, Goblet 11.50
Pressed Glass, Diagonal Band, Jar, Pickle, Covered 25.00
Diamond, see Umbilicated Sawtooth
Pressed Glass, Diamond & Dewdrops, Goblet 15.00
Pressed Glass, Diamond & Fan, Goblet 12.50
Diamond & Sunburst, see also Flattened Diamond & Sunburst
Pressed Glass, Diamond & Sunburst, Creamer, Child's 7.00
Pressed Glass, Diamond & Sunburst, Goblet 12.00
Pressed Glass, Diamond Band, Goblet 15.00
Pressed Glass, Diamond Block With Fan, Creamer 20.00
Pressed Glass, Diamond Block With Fan, Spooner, Footed 14.00
Pressed Glass, Diamond Cut With Leaf, Goblet 22.50
Pressed Glass, Diamond Cut With Leaf, Plate, 7 1/4 In. 10.00
Pressed Glass, Diamond Flute, Creamer, Miniature .... 9.50 To 14.50
Diamond Horseshoe, see Aurora
Pressed Glass, Diamond Medallion, Butter 22.00
Pressed Glass, Diamond Medallion, Butter, Covered 15.00
Pressed Glass, Diamond Medallion, Cake Stand, 8 1/2 In. 15.00
Pressed Glass, Diamond Medallion, Celery 20.00
Pressed Glass, Diamond Medallion, Goblet 15.00
Pressed Glass, Diamond Medallion, Relish 7.00
Pressed Glass, Diamond Medallion, Sauce 6.00
Pressed Glass, Diamond Medallion, Sugar, Covered 10.00
Pressed Glass, Diamond Medallion, Wine .... 12.50 To 16.00
Pressed Glass, Diamond Peg, Toothpick, Ruby Stained 28.00
Pressed Glass, Diamond Point Band, Cake Stand 22.50
Diamond Point Discs, see Eyewinker
Pressed Glass, Diamond Point With Flute, Goblet 15.00
Diamond Point with Panels, see Hinoto
Pressed Glass, Diamond Point, Celery, Flint .... 40.00 To 54.00
Pressed Glass, Diamond Point, Champagne 75.00
Pressed Glass, Diamond Point, Claret, Flint 87.50
Pressed Glass, Diamond Point, Creamer, Applied Handle 145.00
Pressed Glass, Diamond Point, Decanter, Quart 135.00
Pressed Glass, Diamond Point, Eggcup, Clambroth 110.00
Pressed Glass, Diamond Point, Goblet 47.50
Pressed Glass, Diamond Point, Goblet, Flint .... 34.00 To 45.00
Pressed Glass, Diamond Point, Pitcher, Footed, 6 1/2 In. 32.00
Pressed Glass, Diamond Point, Sauce, Flint 6.00
Pressed Glass, Diamond Point, Sauce, 12-Pointed Star Base, Flint, 4 3/8 In. 8.00

Pressed Glass, Diamond Cut With Leaf, Plate

Pressed Glass, Diamond Point, Claret

Pressed Glass, Diamond Point, Spill, Flint 30.00
Pressed Glass, Diamond Point, Spooner 55.00
Pressed Glass, Diamond Point, Spooner, Flint, 5 3/8 In. 35.00
Pressed Glass, Diamond Point, Sugar, Covered, Flint 85.00
Pressed Glass, Diamond Point, Tumbler, Whiskey, Handled, Flint ..... 68.00 To 95.00
Pressed Glass, Diamond Point, Wine, Claret, 5 1/4 In. 65.00
Pressed Glass, Diamond Point, Wine, 6 Panels In Base, 4 1/2 In. 20.00
Pressed Glass, Diamond Spear, Sauce, Vaseline, Opalescent 20.00
Pressed Glass, Diamond Spear, Toothpick, Vaseline, Opalescent ..... 40.00 To 48.00
Pressed Glass, Diamond Sunburst, Butter, Covered 20.00
Pressed Glass, Diamond Sunburst, Syrup, Applied Handle, Tin Top 21.50
Pressed Glass, Diamond Sunburst, Wine 15.00
Pressed Glass, Diamond Thumbprint, Bottle, Bitters, Blob Top, Flint, 7 In. 95.00
Pressed Glass, Diamond Thumbprint, Celery, Scalloped Top, Flint, 9 1/4 In. 175.00
Pressed Glass, Diamond Thumbprint, Champagne, Flint 165.00
Pressed Glass, Diamond Thumbprint, Compote, Flint, 11 3/4 In., Pair 220.00
Pressed Glass, Diamond Thumbprint, Compote, Knob Stem, Flint, 11 1/4 In. 225.00
Pressed Glass, Diamond Thumbprint, Cordial, Flint, 4 1/4 In. 195.00
Pressed Glass, Diamond Thumbprint, Creamer, Applied Foot & Handle, Flint 42.50
Pressed Glass, Diamond Thumbprint, Decanter, Bar Lip, Flint, Quart, 10 1/2 In. 135.00
Pressed Glass, Diamond Thumbprint, Fruit Stand 175.00
Pressed Glass, Diamond Thumbprint, Goblet, Flint ..... 350.00 To 425.00
Pressed Glass, Diamond Thumbprint, Pitcher, Water 155.00
Pressed Glass, Diamond Thumbprint, Sauce 15.00
Pressed Glass, Diamond Thumbprint, Spooner, Flint ..... 22.50 To 65.00
Pressed Glass, Diamond Thumbprint, Spooner, Flint, 5 3/8 In. 80.00
Pressed Glass, Diamond Thumbprint, Spooner, Scalloped Rim, Flint 65.00
Pressed Glass, Diamond Thumbprint, Tumbler, Flint 95.00
Pressed Glass, Diamond Thumbprint, Tumbler, Flint, 3 1/2 In. 125.00
Pressed Glass, Diamond Thumbprint, Tumbler, Whiskey, Flint, 3 In. 125.00
Pressed Glass, Diamond Thumbprint, Vase, Flint, 9 In. 130.00
Pressed Glass, Diamond Thumbprint, Wine 60.00
Pressed Glass, Diamond Thumbprint, Wine, Flint 145.00
Pressed Glass, Diamond With Double Fan, Celery 18.00
Pressed Glass, Diamond With Double Fan, Spooner 15.00
Pressed Glass, Diamond-Quilted, Bowl, Blue, Opalescent, Pleated, Square, 8 In. 50.00
Pressed Glass, Diamond-Quilted, Compote, 6 1/2 In. 15.00
Pressed Glass, Diamond-Quilted, Goblet, Vaseline 29.00
Pressed Glass, Diamond-Quilted, Pitcher, Water, Amber 30.00
Pressed Glass, Diamond-Quilted, Sauce, Vaseline, Cut Base 8.00
Pressed Glass, Diamond-Quilted, Shot Glass, Tumbler, & Tray, Sapphire Blue 135.00
Pressed Glass, Diamond-Quilted, Vase, Blue, Opalescent, Fluted, 11 In., Pair 70.00
Pressed Glass, Dickinson, Creamer, Sandwich Flint 85.00
Pressed Glass, Dickinson, Goblet, Sandwich 38.00
Pressed Glass, Dickinson, Pitcher, Water, Applied Handle, Flint 78.00
Pressed Glass, Dirigo Pear, Sauce 9.00
Pressed Glass, Divided Diamonds, Goblet, Flint 40.00
Pressed Glass, Divided Hearts, Eggcup, Flint 55.00
Pressed Glass, Divided Hearts, Goblet, Flint ..... 50.00 To 57.50
Pressed Glass, Divided Square Panes, Goblet 23.00
Pressed Glass, Dodged Prisms, Cruet, Pedestal Foot, 9 1/2 In. 35.00
Pressed Glass, Dog & Cart, Plate, Bread 45.00
Pressed Glass, Dog & Deer, Plate, Rose & Thistle Border, 8 In. 29.00

Dog on Drum, see **Cat in Basket & Dog on Drum**

Pressed Glass, Dog's Head, Dish, Pet's, Findlay 30.00
Pressed Glass, Dolly Madison, Berry Bowl, Green, Opalescent 45.00
Pressed Glass, Dolly Madison, Bowl, Opalescent, 5 1/2 In. 8.00
Pressed Glass, Dolly Madison, Spooner, Blue, Opalescent 55.00
Pressed Glass, Dolphin, Compote, Amber, Square Bowl, 9 3/4 In., Pair 700.00
Pressed Glass, Dolphin, Nappy, Pink, Handled, 6 In. 11.50
Pressed Glass, Dolphin, Sugar 40.00
Pressed Glass, Dolphin, Toothpick 30.00
Pressed Glass, Dolphin, Vase, Blue To Opalescent, Fan, 7 In. 28.00

Doric, see **Feather**

Pressed Glass, Dot With Swirl, Syrup, Opalescent 62.00
Pressed Glass, Dots & Dashes, Spooner 12.00

Pressed Glass, Double Beaded Band, Tumbler 3.50
Pressed Glass, Double Beaded Band, Wine 9.00
Pressed Glass, Double Beetle Band, Goblet, Amber 18.00
Pressed Glass, Double Crossroads, Saltshaker, Amber 12.50
Pressed Glass, Double Crossroads, Saltshaker, Blue 12.50
Pressed Glass, Double Crossroads, Saltshaker, Vaseline 12.50
Pressed Glass, Double Dahlia & Lens, Sauce, Emerald Green, Gold Trim 18.00
Double Daisy, see Rosette Band
Pressed Glass, Double Disc Prism, Goblet, Flint 45.00
Pressed Glass, Double Eye Hobnail, Creamer 15.50
Pressed Glass, Double Greek Key, Butter, Blue, Opalescent 165.00
Pressed Glass, Double Greek Key, Spooner, Opalescent 48.00
Double Loop, see Double Loop & Dart
Pressed Glass, Double Loop & Dart, Goblet 14.00
Pressed Glass, Double Loop & Dart, Spooner 12.00
Pressed Glass, Double Ribbon, Creamer 20.00
Pressed Glass, Double Spear, Goblet 20.00
Pressed Glass, Double Spear, Sugar & Creamer 50.00
Double Vine, see Bellflower, Double Vine
Pressed Glass, Double Wedding Ring, Wine, Flint 45.00
Pressed Glass, Dove Cover, Dish, Amber, Split Rib Base, 6 In. 25.00
Pressed Glass, Doyle No.500, Spooner, Child's, Amber 40.00
Pressed Glass, Dragon, Compote, Amber, 9 1/2 X 7 In. 60.00
Pressed Glass, Draped Red Top, Compote, Jelly, Ruby Stained 47.50
Pressed Glass, Drapery, Bowl, Green, Opalescent, Fluted, 8 In. 22.00
Pressed Glass, Drapery, Butter, White, Opalescent, Covered, Gold Trim, N 90.00
Pressed Glass, Drapery, Eggcup 13.00
Pressed Glass, Drapery, Goblet .... 10.00 To 21.00
Pressed Glass, Drapery, Spooner 15.00
Pressed Glass, Drapery, Sugar 15.00
Pressed Glass, Drapery, Tumbler, Opalescent 25.00
Pressed Glass, Drum With Eagle, Mug, Gold Paint 20.00
Pressed Glass, Drum, Butter, Child's 75.00

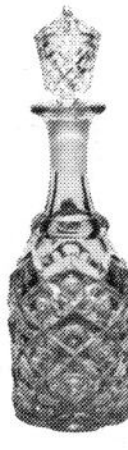
Pressed Glass, Diamond Thumbprint, Decanter

Pressed Glass, Dolphin, Pitcher, Frosted

Pressed Glass, Egg In Sand, Goblet

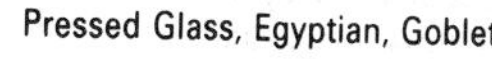
Pressed Glass, Egyptian, Goblet

Pressed Glass, Drum, Creamer, Child's ... 30.00 To 35.00
Pressed Glass, Drum, Mug, Gold Eagle ... 6.50
Pressed Glass, Drum, Spooner, Child's ... 40.00
Pressed Glass, Duchess Loop, Eggcup, Flint ... 16.00
Pressed Glass, Duchess, Water Set, Green, Gold Trim, 7 Piece ... 250.00
Pressed Glass, Duquesne, Goblet ... 12.50
Pressed Glass, Eagle With Drum, Mug, Child's, Gilt Trim ... 22.00
Pressed Glass, Eagle, Plate, 48 Stars, 8 1/2 In. ... 14.00
Earl, see Spirea Band
Pressed Glass, Eastern Star, Goblet ... 12.50
Pressed Glass, Effulgent Star, Goblet ... 32.50
Pressed Glass, Egg In Sand, Goblet ... 16.00
Pressed Glass, Egg In Sand, Pitcher, Milk ... 24.50
Pressed Glass, Egg In Sand, Tray, Water ... 32.50
Pressed Glass, Egyptian, Compote, Sphinx On Base, 6 In. ... 45.00
Pressed Glass, Egyptian, Creamer ... 24.00
Pressed Glass, Egyptian, Creamer, 5 1/2 In. ... 35.00
Pressed Glass, Egyptian, Pitcher, Water ... 95.00
Pressed Glass, Egyptian, Plate, Bread ... 39.00
Pressed Glass, Egyptian, Relish ... 12.00 To 14.50
Pressed Glass, Egyptian, Sauce, Footed ... 14.50
Pressed Glass, Egyptian, Spooner ... 24.50
Pressed Glass, Eight Flute, Goblet, Flint ... 19.50
Pressed Glass, Eight Panel, Wine, 4 1/4 In. ... 9.00
Pressed Glass, Elaine, Plate, Bread, Frosted, 101 Border ... 72.50
Pressed Glass, Elaine, Plate, 101 Border, Iowa City, 8 In. ... 48.00
Pressed Glass, Electric, Sugar, Covered ... 27.50
Pressed Glass, Electric, Syrup ... 32.50
Pressed Glass, Elk Medallion, Compote, High Standard, 8 1/2 In. ... 45.00
Pressed Glass, Ellipses, Celery ... 28.00
Pressed Glass, Elongated Thumbprint, Wine, 4 3/8 In. ... 25.00
Pressed Glass, Empress, Spooner, Emerald Green, Gold Trim ... 65.00
Pressed Glass, Empress, Syrup, Green, Gold Trim ... 85.00
Pressed Glass, English Herringbone, Creamer, Pedestal Base, Flint ... 20.00
English Hobnail Cross, see Klondike
Pressed Glass, English Hobnail, Castor Set, Child's, Shamrock Tray, 3 Piece ... 30.00
Pressed Glass, English Hobnail, Condiment Set, Child's, 4 Piece ... 39.00
Pressed Glass, English Hobnail, Cruet, Child's ... 12.50
Pressed Glass, English Hobnail, Goblet, 6 In. ... 10.00
Pressed Glass, English Hobnail, Pepper Shaker, Child's ... 6.50
Pressed Glass, Esther, Berry Bowl, Green ... 30.00
Pressed Glass, Esther, Berry Bowl, 3 Footed, Riverside, 4 1/2 In. ... 9.50
Pressed Glass, Esther, Butter, Knob Finial, 9 X 6 1/2 In. ... 35.00
Pressed Glass, Esther, Creamer ... 14.00
Pressed Glass, Esther, Cruet, 5 In. ... 22.50
Pressed Glass, Esther, Dish, Cheese, Dome Lid ... 35.00
Pressed Glass, Esther, Dish, Jelly, Green, Stemmed, Gold Trim ... 60.00
Pressed Glass, Esther, Goblet ... 17.50
Pressed Glass, Esther, Sugar, Emerald Green, Covered, Gold Trim ... 65.00
Pressed Glass, Esther, Toothpick, Green, Gold Trim ... 75.00 To 95.00
Etched Band, see Dakota
Etched Dakota, see Dakota
Etched Fern, see Ashman
Pressed Glass, Etched Flowers, Goblet ... 10.00
Pressed Glass, Etched Lily Of The Valley, Goblet ... 13.50
Pressed Glass, Etched Mascotte, Spooner ... 17.50
Etched patterns, see under main pattern, e.g.: Etched Dakota, see Dakota
Pressed Glass, Eugenie, Eggcup, Flint ... 32.00
Pressed Glass, Eureka, Butter, Flint ... 30.00
Pressed Glass, Eureka, Champagne ... 16.00
Pressed Glass, Eureka, Compote, Jelly, Ruby Stained, National ... 50.00
Pressed Glass, Eureka, Eggcup, Flint ... 25.00
Pressed Glass, Eureka, Goblet ... 27.50
Pressed Glass, Eureka, Goblet, Etched Acorn, Flint ... 30.00
Pressed Glass, Eureka, Goblet, Flint ... 18.00

Pressed Glass, Eureka, Goblet, Short Stem, Flint 18.00
Pressed Glass, Eureka, Wine, Flint 27.50
Pressed Glass, Everglades, Berry Bowl, Blue, Opalescent 18.00
Pressed Glass, Everglades, Pitcher, Water, Vaseline 275.00
Pressed Glass, Everglades, Sauce, Opalescent, Oval 26.00
Pressed Glass, Everglades, Sauce, Vaseline 40.00
Pressed Glass, Everglades, Table Set, Vaseline, 4 Piece 475.00
Pressed Glass, Excelsior With Diamond, Eggcup, Ring Stem, Flint 45.00
Pressed Glass, Excelsior, Barrel, Goblet, Flint 25.00
Pressed Glass, Excelsior, Carafe, Rayed Base, Flint, 1 1/2 Pint.6 1/4 In. 40.00
Pressed Glass, Excelsior, Champagne, Flint 55.00
Pressed Glass, Excelsior, Creamer, Molded Handle, Flint 12.00
Pressed Glass, Excelsior, Eggcup 21.50
Pressed Glass, Excelsior, Eggcup, Flint 25.00
Pressed Glass, Excelsior, Goblet 55.00
Pressed Glass, Excelsior, Goblet, Barrel, Flint 29.50
Pressed Glass, Excelsior, Goblet, Flint 32.00
Pressed Glass, Excelsior, Sugar, 5 1/2 In., Pair 45.00
Pressed Glass, Excelsior, Tumbler, Footed, Flint 35.00
Pressed Glass, Excelsior, Wine, Double Ring Stem, Flint 36.00
Pressed Glass, Eyewinker, Butter, Covered 48.00
Pressed Glass, Eyewinker, Butter, Covered, Findlay 55.00
Pressed Glass, Eyewinker, Cake Stand, 9 In. 65.00
Pressed Glass, Eyewinker, Compote, Jelly 25.00
Pressed Glass, Eyewinker, Compote, 5 1/4 In. 65.00
Pressed Glass, Eyewinker, Plate, Turned-Up Sides, 8 1/2 In. 28.00
Pressed Glass, Eyewinker, Syrup 60.00

Fagot, see Vera

Pressed Glass, Faith, Hope, & Charity, Plate, Bread .... 27.50 To 28.00
Pressed Glass, Faith, Hope, & Charity, Plate, Bread, Handled, Nov.23, 1875 .... 55.00

Fan, see also Butterfly & Fan

Pressed Glass, Fan & Acanthus Leaf, Celery 25.00
Pressed Glass, Fan & Feather, Sauce, Blue Opalescent, Gold Trim, Footed 55.00
Pressed Glass, Fan With Diamond, Goblet, Buttermilk 27.50
Pressed Glass, Fan, Tray, Card 15.00
Pressed Glass, Fancy Cut, Cup, Child's Punch 7.50
Pressed Glass, Fancy Cut, Pitcher, Water, Child's 21.00
Pressed Glass, Fancy Loop, Relish, Turned-Up Edges, 6 3/4 In. 27.50
Pressed Glass, Fancy Loop, Salt 9.50
Pressed Glass, Fans With Crossbars, Sugar, Breakfast, Ruby Stained 38.00
Pressed Glass, Feather & Fan With Crossbar, Wine 12.00
Pressed Glass, Feather & Finecut, Butter, Covered 32.50
Pressed Glass, Feather & Finecut, Creamer 12.50
Pressed Glass, Feather & Finecut, Spooner 10.00
Pressed Glass, Feather & Finecut, Sugar, Covered 17.50
Pressed Glass, Feather & Heart, Pitcher, Water, Millersburg 30.00
Pressed Glass, Feather Duster, Goblet 18.00
Pressed Glass, Feather, Butter 30.00
Pressed Glass, Feather, Butter, Covered .... 19.00 To 20.00
Pressed Glass, Feather, Cake Stand, 8 In. 19.50
Pressed Glass, Feather, Cake Stand, 8 1/2 In. 18.00

Pressed Glass, Excelsior, Bottle, Bitters

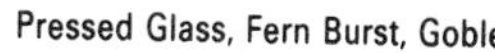

Pressed Glass, Fern Burst, Goblet

Pressed Glass, Fine Rib With Cut Ovals, Cordial

Pressed Glass, Feather, Cake Stand, 9 1/2 In. 25.00
Pressed Glass, Feather, Compote, High Standard, 6 3/4 In. 20.00
Pressed Glass, Feather, Compote, Jelly 15.00
Pressed Glass, Feather, Compote, Jelly, 4 1/2 In. 17.50
Pressed Glass, Feather, Compote, 7 In. 24.00
Pressed Glass, Feather, Creamer, Near Cut 14.00
Pressed Glass, Feather, Pitcher, Water 22.50
Pressed Glass, Feather, Pitcher, Water, Greentown 25.00
Pressed Glass, Feather, Relish 11.00 To 12.00
Pressed Glass, Feather, Relish, Oval 8.00
Pressed Glass, Feather, Saltshaker 30.00
Pressed Glass, Feather, Sauce, 4 In. 6.00
Pressed Glass, Feather, Spooner 12.00 To 25.00
Pressed Glass, Feather, Spooner, Scalloped Edge 12.50
Pressed Glass, Feather, Sugar, Covered 25.00
Pressed Glass, Feather, Tumbler 30.00
Pressed Glass, Feather, Vase, Blue, Opalescent, 10 In. 15.00
Pressed Glass, Feather, Vase, Green, Opalescent, Ruffled, 7 1/2 In. 12.50
Pressed Glass, Feather, Vase, Green, Opalescent, 8 In., Pair 32.00
Pressed Glass, Feather, Wine 20.00 To 35.00
Pressed Glass, Feather, Wine, Indiana 15.00
Pressed Glass, Fern & Waffle, Celery, Etched, 8 In. 18.50
Pressed Glass, Fern & Waffle, Compote, Covered, Etched, C.1880, 12 X 8 In. 65.00
Pressed Glass, Fern & Waffle, Goblet, Etched, C.1880 12.50
Pressed Glass, Fern & Waffle, Goblet, Etched, Flared Rim, C.1880 12.50
Pressed Glass, Fern & Waffle, Sugar, Covered, Etched, C.1880, 9 In. 22.50
Pressed Glass, Fern Garland, Sugar & Creamer 20.00
Pressed Glass, Fern Sprig, Saltshaker 7.50
Pressed Glass, Fern, Celery, Ruby Stained, Opalescent 32.00
Pressed Glass, Fernland, Creamer, Child's 14.50
Festoon & Grape, see Grape & Festoon
Pressed Glass, Festoon, Berry Bowl, 9 1/4 In. 25.00
Pressed Glass, Festoon, Bowl, Rectangular, 9 In. 15.00
Pressed Glass, Festoon, Bowl, 7 1/4 In. 15.00
Pressed Glass, Festoon, Bowl, 9 In. 19.00
Pressed Glass, Festoon, Cake Stand 37.50
Pressed Glass, Festoon, Compote, High Standard, 8 3/4 In. 45.00
Pressed Glass, Festoon, Creamer 12.50 To 16.00
Pressed Glass, Festoon, Pitcher, Water 29.50
Pressed Glass, Festoon, Plate, 7 3/8 In. 35.00
Pressed Glass, Festoon, Sauce 5.50
Pressed Glass, Festoon, Sauce, 4 1/2 In. 6.50
Pressed Glass, Festoon, Spooner 15.00 To 19.50
Pressed Glass, Festoon, Sugar, Covered 45.00
Pressed Glass, Festoon, Tumbler 12.50
Pressed Glass, Festoon, Waste Bowl 17.50
Pressed Glass, Fickle Block, Goblet 15.00
Pressed Glass, Fighting Cats, Mug 16.50 To 17.00
Pressed Glass, File, Creamer 4.50

Pressed Glass, File, Spooner 21.00
Pressed Glass, File, Sugar 4.50
Pressed Glass, Fine Diamond Point, Goblet, Flint 29.00
Pressed Glass, Fine Diamond Point, Plate, 7 In. 25.00
Pressed Glass, Fine Prism, Wine, Flint 34.50
Pressed Glass, Fine Rib With Cut Ovals, Celery, Flint 108.00
Pressed Glass, Fine Rib With Cut Ovals, Champagne, Flint 155.00
Pressed Glass, Fine Rib With Cut Ovals, Compote, 6 In. 115.00
Pressed Glass, Fine Rib With Cut Ovals, Eggcup, Flint 100.00
Pressed Glass, Fine Rib With Cut Ovals, Wine, Flint 110.00
Pressed Glass, Fine Rib With Cut Ovals, Wine, 3 Rows, Flint 65.00
Pressed Glass, Fine Rib With Plain Band, Champagne, Flint 34.00
Pressed Glass, Fine Rib With Plain Band, Compote, 7 X 4 In. 30.00
Pressed Glass, Fine Rib With Plain Band, Goblet 10.00
Pressed Glass, Fine Rib With Plain Band, Salt, Master 30.00
Pressed Glass, Fine Rib, Celery, Flint 40.00
Pressed Glass, Fine Rib, Eggcup, White Opaque, Acorn Finial 350.00
Pressed Glass, Fine Rib, Goblet, Flint 60.00
Pressed Glass, Fine Rib, Salt, Flint 10.50
Pressed Glass, Fine Rib, Tumbler, Whiskey, Handled, Flint 40.00
Pressed Glass, Fine Rib, Whiskey Taster, Applied Handle, Flint 58.00
Pressed Glass, Fine Rib, Whiskey Taster, Flint 15.00 To 28.00
Pressed Glass, Fine Rib, Wine, Flint 36.00 To 50.00
Pressed Glass, Fine Rib, Wine, 4 In. 30.50
Pressed Glass, Finecut & Block, Creamer 16.00
Pressed Glass, Finecut & Block, Creamer, Footed 18.00
Pressed Glass, Finecut & Block, Cup, Punch 8.50
Pressed Glass, Finecut & Block, Fruit Bowl, Blue, Collared Base, 9 In. 85.00
Pressed Glass, Finecut & Block, Sauce, Amber, Footed 16.00
Pressed Glass, Finecut & Block, Sauce, Amber, 4 In. 12.50
Pressed Glass, Finecut & Block, Sauce, Yellow Blocks 22.50
Pressed Glass, Finecut & Block, Wine 25.00
Pressed Glass, Finecut & Diamond, Celery 22.50
Pressed Glass, Finecut & Panel, Goblet 25.00 To 60.00
Pressed Glass, Finecut & Panel, Plate, Bread 10.00 To 29.50
Pressed Glass, Finecut & Panel, Plate, 6 In. 14.00
Pressed Glass, Finecut & Panel, Plate, 7 In. 9.50
Pressed Glass, Finecut & Panel, Sauce, Blue, Footed 6.00
Pressed Glass, Finecut & Panel, Sauce, Canary, Footed 6.00
Pressed Glass, Finecut & Panel, Tray, Water, Handled, 12 In. 65.00
Pressed Glass, Finecut & Panel, Tray, 13 X 9 In. 25.00
Pressed Glass, Finecut & Panel, Wine 11.50
Pressed Glass, Finecut & Panel, Wine, Amber 23.00 To 32.50
Pressed Glass, Finecut & Panel, Wine, Vaseline 32.50
Pressed Glass, Finecut Block, Celery, Amber Blocks, Boat Shape 60.00
Pressed Glass, Finecut Medallion, Creamer 20.00
Pressed Glass, Finecut Medallion, Goblet 22.00
Pressed Glass, Finecut With Amber Blocks, Relish, Handled 10.00
Pressed Glass, Finecut, Butter, Turning Purple 45.00
Pressed Glass, Finecut, Goblet 15.00
Pressed Glass, Finecut, Plate, Cake, Lions' Heads Handles, 12 X 7 1/2 In. 15.00
Pressed Glass, Finecut, Plate, Vaseline, 6 In. 18.50
Pressed Glass, Finecut, Salt, Master, Sled Shape 12.00
Pressed Glass, Finecut, Toothpick, Amber, Hat Shape 19.00 To 28.00
Pressed Glass, Finecut, Tray, Water 20.00
Pressed Glass, Finecut, Waste Bowl 15.00
Pressed Glass, Finecut, Waste Bowl, Footed 16.50
Pressed Glass, Fish, Spooner, Child's, Blue 50.00
Pressed Glass, Fishscale, Berry Set, 6 Piece 46.00
Pressed Glass, Fishscale, Bowl, 8 1/2 In. 18.00
Pressed Glass, Fishscale, Butter, Covered 31.50
Pressed Glass, Fishscale, Cake Stand, 8 In. 22.50
Pressed Glass, Fishscale, Cake Stand, 9 In. 19.00
Pressed Glass, Fishscale, Cake Stand, 10 In. 22.50
Pressed Glass, Fishscale, Celery 18.50 To 25.00

Pressed Glass, Fishscale, Compote, Jelly 14.50
Pressed Glass, Fishscale, Compote, Jelly, 4 1/2 In. 16.00
Pressed Glass, Fishscale, Compote, Jelly, 4 3/4 In. 12.50
Pressed Glass, Fishscale, Compote, Scalloped Rim, 7 In. 22.50
Pressed Glass, Fishscale, Creamer 18.50
Pressed Glass, Fishscale, Dish, Pickle, Pear Shape 14.00
Pressed Glass, Fishscale, Goblet .... 27.50 To 28.00
Pressed Glass, Fishscale, Mug 9.00
Pressed Glass, Fishscale, Pitcher, Milk .... 24.00 To 29.50
Pressed Glass, Fishscale, Plate, Square, 9 In. 26.00
Pressed Glass, Fishscale, Plate, 7 In. .... 14.00 To 17.50
Pressed Glass, Fishscale, Plate, 8 In. .... 20.00 To 28.50
Pressed Glass, Fishscale, Sauce .... 4.50 To 6.00
Pressed Glass, Fishscale, Sauce, Footed 12.50
Pressed Glass, Fishscale, Sauce, Square 6.50
Pressed Glass, Fishscale, Spooner 12.50
Pressed Glass, Fishscale, Tray, Water 32.00
Pressed Glass, Flag & Shield, Tumbler, Flint 87.00
Pressed Glass, Flamingo Habitat, Celery 28.00
Pressed Glass, Flamingo Habitat, Compote, 7 In. 25.00
Pressed Glass, Flamingo Habitat, Goblet, Etched 20.00
Pressed Glass, Flamingo Habitat, Wine 21.00

Flat Diamond & Panel, see Lattice & Oval Panels

Pressed Glass, Flat Diamond, Goblet 12.50
Pressed Glass, Flattened Diamond & Sunburst, Butter, Child's, Covered 15.00
Pressed Glass, Flattened Diamond & Sunburst, Cup, Punch, Child's 4.00
Pressed Glass, Flattened Sawtooth, Salt, Master, Flint 10.00
Pressed Glass, Flattened Sawtooth, Spill, Flint 24.00
Pressed Glass, Flattened Sawtooth, Spooner, Flint 24.00
Pressed Glass, Flattened Sawtooth, Tumbler, Juice, Footed, 4 1/4 In. 11.00
Pressed Glass, Fleur-De-Lis & Drape, Compote, Jelly, Emerald 24.00
Pressed Glass, Fleur-De-Lis & Drape, Creamer, Emerald 30.00
Pressed Glass, Fleur-De-Lis & Drape, Pitcher, Milk, Emerald 38.50
Pressed Glass, Fleur-De-Lis & Drape, Pitcher, Water, Emerald 45.00
Pressed Glass, Fleur-De-Lis & Drape, Plate, Emerald Green, 8 In. 15.00
Pressed Glass, Fleur-De-Lis & Drape, Plate, Emerald, 8 In. 25.00
Pressed Glass, Fleur-De-Lis & Drape, Sugar, Emerald, Covered 33.50
Pressed Glass, Fleur-De-Lis & Tassel, Pitcher, Milk 39.50
Pressed Glass, Fleur-De-Lis & Tassel, Pitcher, Milk, Emerald Green 45.00
Pressed Glass, Fleur-De-Lis & Tassel, Plate, 10 In. 17.25
Pressed Glass, Fleur-De-Lis, Banded, Saltshaker, Pewter Top 12.50
Pressed Glass, Fleur-De-Lis, Cake Stand 23.50
Pressed Glass, Fleur-De-Lis, Goblet 18.00
Pressed Glass, Fleur-De-Lis, Relish 6.00
Pressed Glass, Fleur-De-Lis, Spooner 15.00
Pressed Glass, Fleur-De-Lis, Toothpick .... 14.00 To 22.50
Pressed Glass, Flora, Goblet 15.00
Pressed Glass, Flora, Syrup, Gold Trim 58.00
Pressed Glass, Flora, Tumbler, Emerald Green, Gold Trim 18.00
Pressed Glass, Floradora, Straw Holder, Frosted, Covered, Red & Green Trim 42.00
Pressed Glass, Floral Oval, Bowl, 7 X 5 1/4 X 2 In. 18.50
Pressed Glass, Floral Oval, Cup, Punch, Footed 12.50

Florida, see Herringbone

Pressed Glass, Florida Palm, Compote, Covered, 7 In. 37.50
Pressed Glass, Florida Palm, Tumbler 10.00
Pressed Glass, Florida Palm, Wine 15.00
Pressed Glass, Flower & Quill, Spooner 21.00
Pressed Glass, Flower Band, Celery 34.00
Pressed Glass, Flower Band, Frosted, Butter, Lovebirds Finial 65.00
Pressed Glass, Flower Band, Frosted, Celery 35.00
Pressed Glass, Flower Band, Frosted, Creamer .... 35.00 To 45.00

Flower Flange, see Dewey

Pressed Glass, Flower Medallion, Goblet, Flint 30.00
Pressed Glass, Flower Pleat, Syrup, Frosted 39.00
Pressed Glass, Flowerpot, Cake Stand, 10 In. 35.00
Pressed Glass, Flowerpot, Cake Stand, 10 1/4 In. 45.00

Pressed Glass, **Flowerpot,** Pitcher, Milk 26.00
Pressed Glass, **Flowerpot,** Pitcher, Water 37.00
Pressed Glass, **Flowerpot,** Plate, Bread 22.50
Pressed Glass, **Flowers,** Etched, Goblet 10.00
Pressed Glass, **Flute & Cane,** Pitcher, Milk 18.00
Pressed Glass, **Flute,** Butter, Blue, Opalescent 75.00
Pressed Glass, **Flute,** Butter, Child's, Covered, Beaded Top Edges 25.00
Pressed Glass, **Flute,** Claret, Flint 27.00
Pressed Glass, **Flute,** Creamer, Child's 10.00
Pressed Glass, **Flute,** Eggcup, Double 14.00
Pressed Glass, **Flute,** Eggcup, Flint 16.00
Pressed Glass, **Flute,** Goblet, Flint .... 16.00 To 22.00
Pressed Glass, **Flute,** Mug, Applied Crimped Handle, Flint 40.00
Pressed Glass, **Flute,** Mug, Flint 40.00
Pressed Glass, **Flute,** Spooner, Child's 15.00
Pressed Glass, **Flute,** Sugar, Child's, Covered, Beaded Top Edge 15.00
Pressed Glass, **Flute,** Tumbler .... 8.50 To 9.00
Pressed Glass, **Flute,** Tumbler, Bar, Flint 16.00
Pressed Glass, **Flute,** Tumbler, Child's .... 3.00 To 7.00
Pressed Glass, **Flute,** Tumbler, Whiskey, Deep Blue, Flint 60.00
Pressed Glass, **Flute,** Tumbler, Whiskey, Flint 20.00
Pressed Glass, **Flute,** Tumbler, Whiskey, Handled, Flint 20.00
Pressed Glass, **Flute,** Water Set, Child's, 4 Piece 38.00
Pressed Glass, **Flute,** Whiskey Taster, Canary Yellow, Flint 85.00
Pressed Glass, **Flute,** Whiskey Taster, Flint 12.00
Pressed Glass, **Flute,** Whiskey Taster, Peacock Blue, Flint 85.00
Pressed Glass, **Flute,** Wine 6.00
Pressed Glass, **Flute,** Wine, Flint 15.00
Pressed Glass, **Flute,** Wine, Hexagonal Base & Stem 10.00
Pressed Glass, **Fluted Ribbon,** Sugar & Creamer 25.00
Pressed Glass, **Fluted Scrolls With Flower Band,** Creamer, Green, Jackson 45.00
Pressed Glass, **Fluted Scrolls,** Bowl, Opalescent, Footed, 8 In. 18.00
Pressed Glass, **Fluted Scrolls,** Bowl, Vaseline, Opalescent, Footed, 8 In. 20.00
Pressed Glass, **Fluted Scrolls,** Bowl, Vaseline, Opalescent, 7 1/2 In. 22.00
Pressed Glass, **Fluted Scrolls,** Creamer, Green, Opalescent 58.00
Pressed Glass, **Fluted Scrolls,** Creamer, Vaseline, Opalescent .... 55.00 To 65.00
Pressed Glass, **Fluted Scrolls,** Dish, Candy, Vaseline, Opalescent, Footed 25.00
Pressed Glass, **Fluted Scrolls,** Dish, Candy, White, Opalescent, Jackson 22.50
Pressed Glass, **Fluted Scrolls,** Jar, Powder, Vaseline, Opalescent 55.00
Pressed Glass, **Fluted Scrolls,** Jar, Powder, White, Opalescent, Covered 35.00
Pressed Glass, **Fluted Scrolls,** Jar, Puff, White, Opalescent 40.00
Pressed Glass, **Fluted Scrolls,** Spooner, Blue, Opalescent 55.00
Pressed Glass, **Fluted Scrolls,** Spooner, Blue, Opalescent, Northwood 50.00
Pressed Glass, **Fluted Scrolls,** Spooner, White, Opalescent 17.00
Pressed Glass, **Fluted Scrolls,** Sugar, Covered, Opalescent 45.00
Pressed Glass, **Fluted Scrolls,** Sugar, Vaseline, Opalescent, Covered 65.00
Pressed Glass, **Flying Birds,** Goblet 25.00

Flying Robin, see Hummingbird

Pressed Glass, **Flying Stork,** Goblet 35.00
Pressed Glass, **Flying Wild Geese,** Pitcher, Water 58.00
Pressed Glass, **For A Good Boy,** Mug 29.50
Pressed Glass, **For A Good Girl,** Mug 20.00
Pressed Glass, **Forest Fantasy,** Goblet 13.50
Pressed Glass, **Forget-Me-Not In Scroll,** Sugar 15.00

Forget-Me-Not in Snow, see Stippled Forget-Me-Not

Pressed Glass, **Forget-Me-Not,** Muffineer, Chartreuse, Opaque 88.00
Pressed Glass, **Forget-Me-Not,** Salt & Pepper, Pee Wee 32.75
Pressed Glass, **Forget-Me-Not,** Saltshaker, Green 23.00
Pressed Glass, **Forget-Me-Not,** Toothpick, Pink 38.00
Pressed Glass, **Four Fruits,** Bowl, Footed, 8 1/2 In. 22.50
Pressed Glass, **Four Petal,** Sugar & Creamer, Cover, Flint 90.00
Pressed Glass, **Four Petal,** Sugar & Creamer, Flint 150.00
Pressed Glass, **Four Petal,** Sugar, Covered 65.00
Pressed Glass, **Four Petal,** Sugar, Covered, Flint .... 28.50 To 45.00
Pressed Glass, **Fox & Crow,** Pitcher, Water 88.00
Pressed Glass, **Framed Circles,** Bowl, Miniature 35.00

Pressed Glass, Framed Circles, Vase, Miniature 75.00
Pressed Glass, Frog & Spider, Goblet 75.00
Pressed Glass, Frog Cover, Dish, Blue, Basket Weave Base, 6 In. 25.00
Pressed Glass, Frost Crystal, Tumbler, Ruby Stained, Gold Trim 22.00
Frosted patterns, see also under name of main pattern
Pressed Glass, Frosted Artichoke, Sauce, Footed 17.00
Pressed Glass, Frosted Circle, Cake Stand 27.50
Pressed Glass, Frosted Circle, Compote, Covered, 7 In. 40.00
Pressed Glass, Frosted Circle, Compote, Low Standard, Scalloped, 8 In. 25.00
Pressed Glass, Frosted Circle, Creamer .... 27.00 To 28.00
Pressed Glass, Frosted Circle, Plate, 9 In. 25.00
Pressed Glass, Frosted Circle, Relish 15.00
Pressed Glass, Frosted Circle, Sugar, Covered 42.50
Frosted Crane, see Frosted Stork
Pressed Glass, Frosted Dolphin, Butter, Covered, 8 X 6 In. 110.00
Pressed Glass, Frosted Dolphin, Compote, 8 1/2 In. 55.00
Pressed Glass, Frosted Dolphin, Creamer 67.50
Pressed Glass, Frosted Dolphin, Pitcher, Water, 10 In. 95.00
Pressed Glass, Frosted Eagle, Celery, Etched 34.00
Frosted Flower Band, see Flower Band, Frosted
Pressed Glass, Frosted Fruit, Pitcher, Water 75.00
Pressed Glass, Frosted Leaf, Bottle, Bar, Pint 125.00
Pressed Glass, Frosted Leaf, Celery 175.00
Pressed Glass, Frosted Leaf, Champagne 175.00
Pressed Glass, Frosted Leaf, Champagne, Flint 165.00
Pressed Glass, Frosted Leaf, Eggcup 85.00
Pressed Glass, Frosted Leaf, Goblet 85.00
Pressed Glass, Frosted Leaf, Goblet, Flint .... 60.00 To 75.00
Pressed Glass, Frosted Leaf, Goblet, Flint, 6 In. 80.00
Pressed Glass, Frosted Leaf, Goblet, Lady's, Flint 95.00
Pressed Glass, Frosted Leaf, Salt, Master 85.00
Pressed Glass, Frosted Leaf, Sauce, 4 In. 35.00
Pressed Glass, Frosted Leaf, Spooner, Flint 75.00
Pressed Glass, Frosted Leaf, Tumbler, Footed 125.00

Pressed Glass, Forget-Me-Not, Jar, Marmalade

Pressed Glass, Frosted Ribbon With Double Bands, Goblet

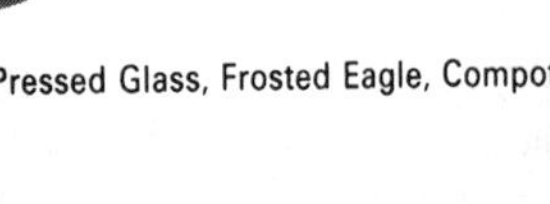

Pressed Glass, Frosted Eagle, Compote

Pressed Glass, Frosted Stork, Goblet

Pressed Glass, Fruit Panels, Goblet

Pressed Glass, Frosted Ribbon With Double Bar, Creamer 25.00

Pressed Glass, Frosted Ribbon, Butter, Covered, 6 1/4 X 6 In. 39.00

Pressed Glass, Frosted Ribbon, Compote, Frosted Dolphin Stem, 8 X 7 X 5 In. 155.00

Pressed Glass, Frosted Ribbon, Creamer 25.00

Pressed Glass, Frosted Square, Plate, Amber, 7 3/4 In. 12.50

Pressed Glass, Frosted Stork, Plate, Bread 45.00

Pressed Glass, Frosted Stork, Plate, Bread, Picture Border 65.00

Pressed Glass, Frosted Stork, Plate, Bread, 101 Border, Oval 30.00

Pressed Glass, Frosted Stork, Plate, 101 Border, Iowa City, 9 In. 62.00

Pressed Glass, Frosted Stork, Platter, Iowa City, 11 1/2 X 8 In. 55.00

Pressed Glass, Frosted Tennessee With Cherokee Rose, Mug 37.50

Frosted Waffle, see Hidalgo

Pressed Glass, Fuchsia, Creamer, Square 20.00

Pressed Glass, Fulton, Wine 10.00

Pressed Glass, G.A.R., Goblet 35.00

Pressed Glass, Gaelic, Goblet .... 10.00 To 12.00

Pressed Glass, Gaelic, Salt & Pepper 9.75

Pressed Glass, Gaelic, Sauce, Hand-Painted Pink Floral, 4 1/2 In. 28.00

Pressed Glass, Galloway, Berry Set, 5 Piece 48.50

Pressed Glass, Galloway, Bowl, 7 1/2 In. 17.50

Pressed Glass, Galloway, Celery 20.00

Pressed Glass, Galloway, Creamer 14.00

Pressed Glass, Galloway, Cup, Punch 7.00

Pressed Glass, Galloway, Dish, Fruit 2.50

Pressed Glass, Galloway, Dish, Fruit, Gold Trim 3.00

Pressed Glass, Galloway, Fruit Bowl 20.00

Pressed Glass, Galloway, Fruit Bowl, Scalloped Rim, Pedestal, 10 In. 30.00

Pressed Glass, Galloway, Salt & Pepper 11.00

Pressed Glass, Galloway, Sauce, Boat Shape 12.00

Pressed Glass, Galloway, Sugar 23.00

Pressed Glass, Galloway, Toothpick .... 17.00 To 20.00

Pressed Glass, Galloway, Toothpick, Amethyst, Gold Trim 65.00

Pressed Glass, Galloway, Toothpick, Gold Trim 18.00

Pressed Glass, Galloway, Tumbler, Gold Trim, Flared, 3 3/4 In. 12.50

Pressed Glass, Galloway, Tumbler, Tarentum 12.50

Pressed Glass, Galloway, Vase, 11 1/4 In. 23.50

Pressed Glass, Garden Fruits, Sugar & Creamer, Etched, High Stems, 6 In. 25.00

Garden of Eden, see Lotus & Serpent

Pressed Glass, Garden, Berry Set, Pink, Footed, 5 Piece 39.00

Pressed Glass, Garden, Tumbler, Pink 8.50

Pressed Glass, Garfield Drape, Cake Stand, Flint 42.00

Pressed Glass, Garfield Drape, Cake Stand, 9 1/4 In. 50.00

Pressed Glass, Garfield Drape, Celery .... 32.50 To 39.00

Pressed Glass, Garfield Drape, Compote, Covered, High Standard, 8 In. 68.00

Pressed Glass, Garfield Drape, Compote, 8 1/2 X 6 In. 30.00

Pressed Glass, Garfield Drape, Creamer .... 20.00 To 29.50

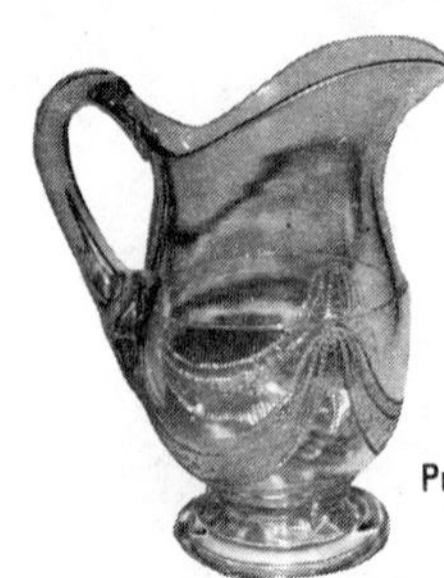

Pressed Glass, Garfield Drape, Pitcher, Water

Pressed Glass, Garfield Drape, Goblet .... 22.00 To 27.00
Pressed Glass, Garfield Drape, Goblet, Lady's 28.00
Pressed Glass, Garfield Drape, Pitcher, Footed, 6 In. 22.50
Pressed Glass, Garfield Drape, Pitcher, Milk .... 45.00 To 65.00
Pressed Glass, Garfield Drape, Pitcher, Water, Applied Handle 62.50
Pressed Glass, Garfield Drape, Sauce 8.50
Pressed Glass, Garfield Drape, Sauce, Footed 10.00
Pressed Glass, Garfield Drape, Spooner 20.00
Pressed Glass, Garfield Drape, Sugar .... 19.50 To 20.00
Pressed Glass, Garfield Drape, Sugar, Covered 42.50
Pressed Glass, Garfield Memorial, Mug, 2 1/4 In. 55.00
Pressed Glass, Garfield Memorial, Plate, 10 In. 25.00
Pressed Glass, Garfield, Plate, Bread, Frosted Center 55.00
Pressed Glass, Garfield, Plate, Bread, Washington, Lincoln 52.00
Pressed Glass, Garfield, Plate, Bread, 101 Border 52.00
Pressed Glass, Garfield, Plate, Frosted, 101 Border, 9 In. 40.00
Pressed Glass, Garfield, Tumbler 30.00
Pressed Glass, Gathered Knot, Goblet 8.00
Pressed Glass, Georgia Gem, Butter 28.00
Pressed Glass, Georgia Gem, Butter, Covered 27.00
Pressed Glass, Georgia Gem, Sugar, Emerald Green, Covered, Enamel Floral 35.00
Pressed Glass, Georgia, Compote, 7 1/2 X 6 3/4 In. 12.00
Pressed Glass, Giant Baby Thumbprint, Goblet, Bulbous Stem, Flint 42.00
Pressed Glass, Giant Bull's-Eye, Goblet, Flint 50.00
Pressed Glass, Giant Bull's-Eye, Tumbler, Findlay 12.50
Pressed Glass, Giant Prism With Thumbprint Band, Goblet, Flint 80.00
Pressed Glass, Giant Prism With Thumbprint Band, Tumbler, Flint 40.00
Pressed Glass, Giant Prism, Champagne, Flint 35.00
Pressed Glass, Giant Thumbprint, Tumbler, Flint 27.50
Pressed Glass, Girl With Fan, Goblet, Knob Stem 45.00
Pressed Glass, Girl With Fan, Goblet, Knob Stem, Findlay 42.00
Pressed Glass, Gloria, Butter, Ruby Stained 95.00
Pressed Glass, Goat's Head, Compote, 6 In. 45.00
Pressed Glass, Gonterman, Toothpick, Amber Top, Frosted Swirl 58.00
Good Luck, see Horseshoe
Pressed Glass, Gooseberry, Creamer .... 22.50 To 24.00
Pressed Glass, Gooseberry, Goblet 27.50
Pressed Glass, Gooseberry, Mug 10.00
Pressed Glass, Gooseberry, Mug, Lemonade 16.00
Pressed Glass, Gothic Windows, Creamer 18.00
Pressed Glass, Gothic, Eggcup, Flint 29.50
Pressed Glass, Gothic, Goblet, Flint 65.00
Grace, see Butterfly & Fan
Grand, see Diamond Medallion
Grand Army of the Republic, see G.A.R.
Pressed Glass, Grand Inverted Thumbprint, Waste Bowl, Vaseline 25.00
Pressed Glass, Grant, Plate, 9 1/2 In. 40.00
Grape, see also Beaded Grape, Beaded Grape Medallion, Magnet &

Grape, Magnet & Grape with Frosted Leaf, Paneled Grape, Paneled Grape Band

Pressed Glass, Grape & Festoon With Shield, Tumbler, Footed 24.50
Pressed Glass, Grape & Festoon With Stippled Leaf, Goblet 18.50
Pressed Glass, Grape & Festoon With Stippled Leaf, Pitcher, Milk 52.00
Pressed Glass, Grape & Festoon With Stippled Leaf, Spooner .... 17.50 To 24.50
Pressed Glass, Grape & Festoon With Stippled Leaf, Sugar, Covered 22.50
Pressed Glass, Grape & Festoon, Goblet .... 16.00 To 25.00
Pressed Glass, Grape & Festoon, Goblet, Acorn Finial 25.00
Pressed Glass, Grape & Festoon, Goblet, Stippled & Clear 16.00
Pressed Glass, Grape & Festoon, Sugar & Creamer 45.00
Pressed Glass, Grape & Leaf, Syrup, Green, Opaque, Metal Top 95.00
Pressed Glass, Grape & Shield, Goblet 19.00
Pressed Glass, Grape Band With Dot, Spooner 19.00
Pressed Glass, Grape Band, Creamer, Applied Handle 28.00
Pressed Glass, Grape Band, Eggcup 15.00
Pressed Glass, Grape Band, Goblet .... 15.00 To 18.00
Pressed Glass, Grape Band, Salt, Master 16.00
Pressed Glass, Grape Band, Spooner 16.00
Pressed Glass, Grape With Ovals, Creamer, Amber, Miniature 20.00
Pressed Glass, Grape, Cake Stand, 9 1/2 In. 35.00
Pressed Glass, Grape, Goblet 11.50
Pressed Glass, Grape, Mug 22.00
Pressed Glass, Grape, Plate, Bread, "Tis Pleasant To Labor" .... 29.00 To 30.00
Pressed Glass, Grape, Sugar, Blue, Opalescent, Covered 45.00
Pressed Glass, Grape, Toothpick 15.00
Pressed Glass, Grapevine With Ovals, Creamer, Child's, Blue 40.00
Pressed Glass, Grasshopper, Bowl, Covered, Etched, 7 In. 47.50
Pressed Glass, Grasshopper, Creamer 12.50
Pressed Glass, Grasshopper, Goblet, With Insects, Turning Purple 65.00
Pressed Glass, Grasshopper, Spooner, Insects 65.00

Pressed Glass, Grape & Festoon, Cup

Pressed Glass, Grape & Festoon With Shield, Goblet

Pressed Glass, Hairpin, Goblet, Rayed Base

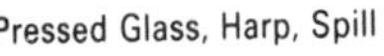

Pressed Glass, Hamilton, Compote

Pressed Glass, Greek Key, Compote, Emerald Green, Fluted, Northwood, 8 In. 35.00
Pressed Glass, Greek Key, Compote, Frosted Bowl, 7 X 6 In. 19.00
Pressed Glass, Gridley, Pitcher, Water 55.00
Pressed Glass, Hairpin, Champagne, Flint 23.00
Pressed Glass, Hairpin, Champagne, Rayed Base, Flint 32.00
Pressed Glass, Hairpin, Compote, Fiery Opalescent, 7 In. 91.00
Pressed Glass, Hairpin, Compote, Low Standard, Flint, 8 In. 46.00
Pressed Glass, Hairpin, Creamer, Applied Handle, Flint 32.00
Pressed Glass, Hairpin, Goblet, Flint 30.00
Pressed Glass, Hairpin, Goblet, Rayed Base, Flint 27.00
Pressed Glass, Hairpin, Tumbler, Whiskey, Rayed Base, Handled, Flint 40.00
Pressed Glass, Halley's Comet, Goblet 16.50
Pressed Glass, Halley's Comet, Tumbler 12.00
Pressed Glass, Halley's Comet, Tumbler, Etched 15.00
Pressed Glass, Halley's Comet, Wine 18.50
Hamilton with Clear Leaf, see Hamilton with Leaf
Pressed Glass, Hamilton With Leaf, Eggcup 30.00
Pressed Glass, Hamilton With Leaf, Goblet, Flint 44.50
Pressed Glass, Hamilton With Leaf, Goblet, Flint, 5 1/4 In. 30.00
Pressed Glass, Hamilton With Leaf, Sugar, Flint 20.00
Pressed Glass, Hamilton With Leaf, Tumbler, Bar, Flint 47.50
Pressed Glass, Hamilton With Leaf, Tumbler, Whiskey, Flint 55.00
Pressed Glass, Hamilton With Leaf, Tumbler, Whiskey, Handled, Flint 95.00
Pressed Glass, Hamilton, Eggcup, Flint 22.00
Pressed Glass, Hamilton, Goblet, Flint 35.00
Pressed Glass, Hamilton, Sauce, Flint, 4 In. 6.00
Pressed Glass, Hamilton, Spooner .... 15.00 To 26.50
Pressed Glass, Hamilton, Spooner, Flint 24.00
Pressed Glass, Hamilton, Sugar, Flint 20.00
Hand, see Pennsylvania
Pressed Glass, Hand & Fishscale, Salt & Pepper 95.00
Pressed Glass, Hand, Vase, Vaseline, 8 1/2 In. 45.00
Pressed Glass, Hanover, Celery .... 17.50 To 18.00
Pressed Glass, Harp, Plate, Cake, Stemmed, 9 In. 12.50
Pressed Glass, Harp, Server, Cake, Pedestal Foot, 10 In. 15.00
Pressed Glass, Hartley, Celery 15.00
Pressed Glass, Hartley, Creamer 18.50
Pressed Glass, Hartley, Sauce, Amber, Footed 8.00
Pressed Glass, Hartley, Wine 15.00

Pressed Glass, Hawaiian Lei, Cake Stand 14.00
Pressed Glass, Hawaiian Lei, Champagne 20.00
Pressed Glass, Hawaiian Lei, Creamer, Child's 16.50
Pressed Glass, Hawaiian Lei, Table Set, Miniature, 4 Piece 75.00
Pressed Glass, Hawaiian Lei, Wine, Bee Mark, 4 1/2 In. 9.50
Pressed Glass, Hawaiian Pineapple, Goblet, Flint .... 70.00 To 85.00
Pressed Glass, Hawaiian Pineapple, Tumbler, Bar, Flint 75.00
Pressed Glass, Heart With Thumbprint, Banana Bowl 17.50
Pressed Glass, Heart With Thumbprint, Berry Bowl 12.50
Pressed Glass, Heart With Thumbprint, Bucket, Ice 65.00
Pressed Glass, Heart With Thumbprint, Carafe, Water 25.00
Pressed Glass, Heart With Thumbprint, Celery .... 38.00 To 45.00
Pressed Glass, Heart With Thumbprint, Compote, High Standard, 8 1/2 In. 45.00
Pressed Glass, Heart With Thumbprint, Creamer 45.00
Pressed Glass, Heart With Thumbprint, Cruet, Oil 25.00
Pressed Glass, Heart With Thumbprint, Cup, Punch 9.00
Pressed Glass, Heart With Thumbprint, Goblet .... 29.00 To 29.50
Pressed Glass, Heart With Thumbprint, Goblet, Gold Trim 28.00
Pressed Glass, Heart With Thumbprint, Nappy 12.50
Pressed Glass, Heart With Thumbprint, Plate, Card, Folded Edge 13.50
Pressed Glass, Heart With Thumbprint, Plate, 10 In. 25.00
Pressed Glass, Heart With Thumbprint, Plate, 12 In. 35.00
Pressed Glass, Heart With Thumbprint, Rose Bowl, Miniature .... 19.50 To 28.00
Pressed Glass, Heart With Thumbprint, Sauce 5.50
Pressed Glass, Heart With Thumbprint, Sauce, Square 7.50
Pressed Glass, Heart With Thumbprint, Sauce, 4 1/2 In. 8.50
Pressed Glass, Heart With Thumbprint, Sugar, Covered 49.50
Pressed Glass, Heart With Thumbprint, Sugar, Individual 5.00
Pressed Glass, Heart With Thumbprint, Syrup 25.00
Pressed Glass, Heart With Thumbprint, Toothpick, 2 Handles 16.00
Pressed Glass, Heart With Thumbprint, Tray, Card 20.00
Pressed Glass, Heart With Thumbprint, Tumbler 25.00
Pressed Glass, Heart With Thumbprint, Tumbler, Ruby Stained 65.00
Pressed Glass, Heart With Thumbprint, Vase, 6 X 5 In. 17.50
Pressed Glass, Heart With Thumbprint, Wine 17.50
Pressed Glass, Heart, Cup Plate, Flint 12.00
Hearts of Loch Laven, see Shuttle
Pressed Glass, Heavy Diamond, Creamer, Individual 9.50
Pressed Glass, Heavy Drape, Cup, Punch 8.00
Heavy Paneled Finecut, see Paneled Diamond Cross
Pressed Glass, Hen Cover, Dish, Frosted, Vallerystahl, 7 1/2 In. 25.00
Pressed Glass, Hen Cover, Dish, Teal Blue, Nest Base, 7 1/2 X 6 1/2 In. 35.00
Pressed Glass, Hen Cover, Dish, Yellow, Nest Base, 7 X 5 1/4 In. 22.00
Pressed Glass, Henrietta, Rose Bowl, 6 In. 30.00
Pressed Glass, Hercules Pillar, Eggcup, Double, Flint 32.00
Pressed Glass, Hercules Pillar, Tumbler, Whiskey, Handled, Flint, 3 In. 22.50
Pressed Glass, Heron & Lighthouse, Salt & Pepper 25.00
Pressed Glass, Heron & Peacock, Mug 17.50
Pressed Glass, Heron, Creamer .... 25.00 To 26.00
Pressed Glass, Herringbone Band, Goblet .... 12.50 To 14.00
Pressed Glass, Herringbone Band, Spooner 14.50
Pressed Glass, Herringbone Buttress, Wine, Green, Greentown 50.00
Pressed Glass, Herringbone, Berry Bowl, Emerald Green, 9 In. 15.00
Pressed Glass, Herringbone, Berry Set, Green, 6 Piece 60.00
Pressed Glass, Herringbone, Butter, Emerald Green 48.00
Pressed Glass, Herringbone, Butter, Emerald Green, Covered 39.50
Pressed Glass, Herringbone, Compote, Jelly, Emerald Green 35.00
Pressed Glass, Herringbone, Creamer, Emerald Green 23.00
Pressed Glass, Herringbone, Goblet .... 10.00 To 15.00
Pressed Glass, Herringbone, Pitcher, Water, Emerald Green 65.00
Pressed Glass, Herringbone, Sauce, Emerald Green, 4 1/2 In. 7.00
Pressed Glass, Herringbone, Toothpick 60.00
Pressed Glass, Herringbone, Tumbler, Green 18.00
Pressed Glass, Herringbone, Water Set, Emerald Green, 7 Piece 135.00
Pressed Glass, Hexagon Block, Goblet 10.00

Pressed Glass, **Hexagon Block,** Tumbler, Ruby Stained 22.00
Pressed Glass, **Hexagonal Block Band,** Goblet 10.00
Pressed Glass, **Hickman,** Condiment Set, Child's, 4 Piece 28.00
Pressed Glass, **Hickman,** Cup, Punch 7.00
Pressed Glass, **Hickman,** Goblet .... 12.00 To 25.00
Pressed Glass, **Hickman,** Jar, Cracker 34.00
Pressed Glass, **Hickman,** Wine, Green 22.50
Pressed Glass, **Hidalgo,** Celery .... 12.00 To 12.50
Pressed Glass, **Hidalgo,** Celery, Etched Leaf 22.00
Pressed Glass, **Hidalgo,** Celery, Frosted 28.00
Pressed Glass, **Hidalgo,** Celery, Frosted, Pair 37.00
Pressed Glass, **Hidalgo,** Goblet, Enamel Floral Spray At Top 17.50
Pressed Glass, **Hidalgo,** Goblet, Frosted 18.00
Pressed Glass, **Hill & Dale,** Spooner 8.00
Pressed Glass, **Hinoto,** Goblet, Flint .... 35.00 To 45.00
Pressed Glass, **Hinoto,** Spooner, Flint 20.00
Pressed Glass, **Hinoto,** Sugar, Covered, Flint 75.00
Pressed Glass, **Hinoto,** Sugar, Flint 22.50
Pressed Glass, **Hinoto,** Tumbler, Footed, Flint 36.00
Pressed Glass, **Hinoto,** Tumbler, Whiskey, Flint 32.00
Pressed Glass, **Hinoto,** Tumbler, Whiskey, Handled, Flint 55.00
Pressed Glass, **Hob In Square,** Celery 30.00
Pressed Glass, **Hob In Square,** Sauce 8.00
Pressed Glass, **Hobbs Block,** Pitcher, Water, Frosted, Amber Rim 245.00

Hobnail & Bars, see Barred Hobnail

Pressed Glass, **Hobnail Band,** Pitcher, Water 30.00
Pressed Glass, **Hobnail In Square,** Mug 8.50
Pressed Glass, **Hobnail In Square,** Wine 10.00
Pressed Glass, **Hobnail With Decorated Band,** Spooner 25.00
Pressed Glass, **Hobnail With Paneled Thumbprint,** Butter, Vaseline, Covered 75.00
Pressed Glass, **Hobnail With Paneled Thumbprint,** Creamer, Vaseline 32.00
Pressed Glass, **Hobnail,** Berry Bowl, Opalescent, 7 3/4 In. 30.00
Pressed Glass, **Hobnail,** Bottle, Perfume, Blue, 7 In. 8.00
Pressed Glass, **Hobnail,** Bowl, Blue, Opalescent, 10 X 3 1/2 In. 35.00
Pressed Glass, **Hobnail,** Bowl, 8 X 5 1/4 In. 32.50
Pressed Glass, **Hobnail,** Creamer, Amber .... 20.00 To 30.00
Pressed Glass, **Hobnail,** Creamer, Bulbous 25.00
Pressed Glass, **Hobnail,** Creamer, Opalescent 30.00
Pressed Glass, **Hobnail,** Creamer, Opalescent & Clear, 4 1/2 In. 27.00
Pressed Glass, **Hobnail,** Creamer, Tankard Type 25.00
Pressed Glass, **Hobnail,** Creamer, Vaseline, Frosted 65.00
Pressed Glass, **Hobnail,** Cruet, Blue, Opalescent, Miniature 19.00
Pressed Glass, **Hobnail,** Cup 7.00
Pressed Glass, **Hobnail,** Dish, Bone, Opalescent 15.00
Pressed Glass, **Hobnail,** Epergne, Vaseline, 3 Lilies, Fluted Bowl, 9 In. 90.00
Pressed Glass, **Hobnail,** Goblet, Fan Top 16.50
Pressed Glass, **Hobnail,** Goblet, Hobnail Stem, 5 3/4 In. 15.00
Pressed Glass, **Hobnail,** Marmalade With Lid 35.00
Pressed Glass, **Hobnail,** Muffineer, Blue 50.00
Pressed Glass, **Hobnail,** Mug, Amber 12.00
Pressed Glass, **Hobnail,** Mug, Amber, Rope Handle 12.50
Pressed Glass, **Hobnail,** Mug, Child's, Dark Amber 17.00
Pressed Glass, **Hobnail,** Pitcher, Milk, Opalescent, Square Handle 52.00
Pressed Glass, **Hobnail,** Pitcher, Milk, Ruby Stained Rim Band 34.95
Pressed Glass, **Hobnail,** Pitcher, Water, Opalescent 75.00
Pressed Glass, **Hobnail,** Plate, Opalescent, 8 1/4 In. 4.00
Pressed Glass, **Hobnail,** Salt 6.50
Pressed Glass, **Hobnail,** Salt, Covered 45.00
Pressed Glass, **Hobnail,** Salt, Master, Opalescent, Swan 18.50
Pressed Glass, **Hobnail,** Salt, 3 X 2 In. 8.00
Pressed Glass, **Hobnail,** Sauce 8.00
Pressed Glass, **Hobnail,** Sauce, Amber, Findlay 17.50
Pressed Glass, **Hobnail,** Sauce, Opalescent 12.00
Pressed Glass, **Hobnail,** Shade, Gas, Blue, Opalescent, Flared, 8 1/2 In. 55.00
Pressed Glass, **Hobnail,** Spooner, Blue, Opalescent 45.00

Pressed Glass, Hobnail, Tumbler, 4 1/2 In.High

Pressed Glass, Hobnail, Pitcher, 8 1/2 In.High

Pressed Glass, Holly Band, Celery

Pressed Glass, Holly, Compote, Covered

Pressed Glass, Hobnail, Spooner, Blue, Opalescent, 3 Footed, 4 1/2 In. 35.00
Pressed Glass, Hobnail, Spooner, Opalescent, Northwood 25.00
Pressed Glass, Hobnail, Sugar & Creamer, Child's, Blue, Opalescent 25.00
Pressed Glass, Hobnail, Sugar & Creamer, White To Clear, Miniature 13.00
Pressed Glass, Hobnail, Sugar Shaker, Green 22.00
Pressed Glass, Hobnail, Sugar, Child's, Blue, Opalescent 9.50
Pressed Glass, Hobnail, Sugar, Covered 24.00
Pressed Glass, Hobnail, Syrup, Opalescent, Pewter Top 85.00
Pressed Glass, Hobnail, Toothpick 22.00
Pressed Glass, Hobnail, Toothpick, Blue 20.00
Pressed Glass, Hobnail, Toothpick, Blue Hobs 40.00
Pressed Glass, Hobnail, Toothpick, Blue Opalescent Hobs 28.00
Pressed Glass, Hobnail, Toothpick, Blue, Frosted 22.00
Pressed Glass, Hobnail, Toothpick, Blue, Opalescent, Footed 40.00
Pressed Glass, Hobnail, Toothpick, Frosted 15.00
Pressed Glass, Hobnail, Toothpick, Opalescent .... 18.00 To 20.00
Pressed Glass, Hobnail, Toothpick, Opalescent, Fluted Edge, 3 Footed 20.00
Pressed Glass, Hobnail, Toothpick, Opalescent, Footed 15.00
Pressed Glass, Hobnail, Toothpick, White Hobs 30.00
Pressed Glass, Hobnail, Tray, Ice Cream, Opalescent 62.00
Pressed Glass, Hobnail, Tray, Water 17.50
Pressed Glass, Hobnail, Tumbler, Opalescent 22.50
Pressed Glass, Hobnail, Tumbler, 4 1/2 In.High .... *Illus* 35.00
Pressed Glass, Hobnail, Vase, Vaseline, Opalescent, Fan Shape, 10 X 8 In. 60.00
Pressed Glass, Hobnail, Vase, Yellow, Signed J.G., 8 In., Pair 50.00
Pressed Glass, Hobnail, Waste Bowl, Thumbprint Base, Scalloped Top 14.00

Pressed Glass, Hobnail, Water Set, 7 Piece 55.00
Pressed Glass, Hobnail, Wine .... 9.50 To 12.00
Pressed Glass, Hobstar & Daisy, Cruet, Green 100.00
Pressed Glass, Hobstar & Feather, Celery 15.00
Holbrook, see Pineapple & Fan
Pressed Glass, Holland, Creamer 20.00
Pressed Glass, Holly Band, Pitcher, Water 85.00
Pressed Glass, Holly Leaves, Goblet 16.00
Pressed Glass, Holly With Cord & Tassel, Spooner 45.00
Pressed Glass, Holly, Eggcup 65.00
Pressed Glass, Holly, Pitcher, Water, Flint 65.00
Pressed Glass, Holly, Sauce, Gold & Red Trim, Northwood 32.50
Pressed Glass, Holly, Toothpick, Green Frosted 25.00
Pressed Glass, Homestead, Spooner 21.00
Honeycomb, see also Vernon Honeycomb
Pressed Glass, Honeycomb & Pillar, Wine 14.00
Pressed Glass, Honeycomb & Shield, Tumbler 8.00
Pressed Glass, Honeycomb With Diamond, Goblet 25.00
Pressed Glass, Honeycomb With Diamond, Goblet, Flint 25.00
Pressed Glass, Honeycomb With Ovals, Champagne, Flint 27.50
Pressed Glass, Honeycomb With Ovals, Goblet, Flint 20.00
Pressed Glass, Honeycomb With Strawberry, Bowl, Green, Opalescent, 8 3/4 In. 35.00
Pressed Glass, Honeycomb, Barrel, Goblet 12.50
Pressed Glass, Honeycomb, Celery, Barrel Shape 8.50
Pressed Glass, Honeycomb, Celery, Footed, Flint 35.00
Pressed Glass, Honeycomb, Champagne, Flint 22.00
Pressed Glass, Honeycomb, Compote, Flint, 9 3/4 In. 50.00
Pressed Glass, Honeycomb, Cordial 8.00
Pressed Glass, Honeycomb, Cordial, Flint 20.00
Pressed Glass, Honeycomb, Goblet 20.00
Pressed Glass, Honeycomb, Goblet, Flint 16.00
Pressed Glass, Honeycomb, Goblet, Flint, 6 1/2 In. 22.50
Pressed Glass, Honeycomb, Goblet, Two Mold 15.00
Pressed Glass, Honeycomb, Mug, Flint 35.00
Pressed Glass, Honeycomb, Mug, Whiskey, Flint 35.00
Pressed Glass, Honeycomb, Mug, Whiskey, Handled, Flint 35.00
Pressed Glass, Honeycomb, Pitcher, Applied Cobalt Handle, 7 3/4 In. 55.00
Pressed Glass, Honeycomb, Pitcher, Water, Bulbous 39.50
Pressed Glass, Honeycomb, Pitcher, Water, 1865 .... 125.00
Pressed Glass, Honeycomb, Pitcher, White, Opalescent, Beatty, 3 In. 22.00
Pressed Glass, Honeycomb, Salt 2.50
Pressed Glass, Honeycomb, Salt & Pepper, Ruby, Pewter Tops 35.00
Pressed Glass, Honeycomb, Salt, Pair 5.00
Pressed Glass, Honeycomb, Spooner 16.00
Pressed Glass, Honeycomb, Spooner, Footed, 5 5/8 In. 45.00
Pressed Glass, Honeycomb, Sugar, Flint 20.00
Pressed Glass, Honeycomb, Toothpick, Blue, Beatty 35.00
Pressed Glass, Honeycomb, Tumbler, Whiskey 10.00
Pressed Glass, Honeycomb, Wine, Flint 18.50
Pressed Glass, Honeycomb, Wine, Flint, 4 1/2 In. 20.00
Pressed Glass, Honeycomb, Wine, 4 In. 15.00
Pressed Glass, Honeycomb, Wine, 4 Rows 15.00
Pressed Glass, Hook, Creamer, Miniature 20.00
Pressed Glass, Hook, Mug, Miniature 20.00
Pressed Glass, Hoop, Celery, Hexagonal Base & Wafer, Flint 125.00
Pressed Glass, Hops Band, Eggcup 16.50
Pressed Glass, Hops Band, Goblet 15.00
Pressed Glass, Hops Band, Spooner 20.00
Pressed Glass, Horn Of Plenty, Celery .... 100.00 To 110.00
Pressed Glass, Horn Of Plenty, Champagne 125.00
Pressed Glass, Horn Of Plenty, Champagne, Flint 95.00
Pressed Glass, Horn Of Plenty, Compote, Flint, 8 In. 80.00
Pressed Glass, Horn Of Plenty, Compote, High Standard, Flint, 10 In. 135.00
Pressed Glass, Horn Of Plenty, Compote, High Standard, 7 1/2 In. 50.00
Pressed Glass, Horn Of Plenty, Compote, Low Standard, 7 In. 30.00

Pressed Glass, Horn Of Plenty, Bowl

Pressed Glass, Horseshoe, Bowl, Covered, Stemmed

Pressed Glass, Horn Of Plenty, Tumbler, Whiskey

Pressed Glass, Horn Of Plenty, Compote, Low Standard, 8 1/2 In. 75.00
Pressed Glass, Horn Of Plenty, Compote, Low Standard, 9 In. 55.00
Pressed Glass, Horn Of Plenty, Decanter, Quart 125.00
Pressed Glass, Horn Of Plenty, Decanter, 14 In., Pair 185.00
Pressed Glass, Horn Of Plenty, Dish, Honey 7.50
Pressed Glass, Horn Of Plenty, Dish, Honey, Flint 10.00
Pressed Glass, Horn Of Plenty, Eggcup 35.00
Pressed Glass, Horn Of Plenty, Eggcup, Flint .... 34.50 To 35.00
Pressed Glass, Horn Of Plenty, Goblet 57.50
Pressed Glass, Horn Of Plenty, Goblet, Flint 57.50
Pressed Glass, Horn Of Plenty, Plate, 6 In. 47.50
Pressed Glass, Horn Of Plenty, Relish, Beaded Edge, 7 1/2 X 5 In. 22.50
Pressed Glass, Horn Of Plenty, Sauce, Flint 10.00
Pressed Glass, Horn Of Plenty, Sauce, 4 1/2 In. 9.50
Pressed Glass, Horn Of Plenty, Sauce, 5 In. 25.00
Pressed Glass, Horn Of Plenty, Spill, Flint .... 34.50 To 55.00
Pressed Glass, Horn Of Plenty, Spooner 35.00
Pressed Glass, Horn Of Plenty, Sugar 30.00
Pressed Glass, Horn Of Plenty, Sugar, Covered .... 75.00 To 80.00
Pressed Glass, Horn Of Plenty, Sugar, Flint 52.00
Pressed Glass, Horn Of Plenty, Tumbler, Bar, Flint 69.50
Pressed Glass, Horn Of Plenty, Wine, Flint, 3 3/4 In. 27.50
Pressed Glass, Horsehead Medallion, Celery 20.00
Pressed Glass, Horsehead Medallion, Celery, Portland 61.00
Pressed Glass, Horsemint, Wine 12.00
Pressed Glass, Horseshoe, Bowl, Rectangular, 9 X 5 3/4 In. 25.00
Pressed Glass, Horseshoe, Bowl, 8 X 5 In. 12.50
Pressed Glass, Horseshoe, Bowl, 9 X 5 3/4 In. 12.50
Pressed Glass, Horseshoe, Cake Stand 45.00
Pressed Glass, Horseshoe, Cake Stand, 8 In. .... 20.00 To 29.50
Pressed Glass, Horseshoe, Celery, Footed 32.50
Pressed Glass, Horseshoe, Compote, High Standard, 7 X 7 In. 32.50
Pressed Glass, Horseshoe, Compote, 7 1/2 In. 30.00
Pressed Glass, Horseshoe, Creamer 20.00
Pressed Glass, Horseshoe, Creamer, Stemmed 24.00
Pressed Glass, Horseshoe, Creamer, 5 1/2 In. 22.00

Pressed Glass, Iconoclast, Goblet

Pressed Glass, Horseshoe, Dish, Cheese, Covered 165.00
Pressed Glass, Horseshoe, Dish, Pickle, Oval 16.00
Pressed Glass, Horseshoe, Goblet .... 22.50 To 26.00
Pressed Glass, Horseshoe, Goblet, Knob Stem 22.50
Pressed Glass, Horseshoe, Jar, Jam 22.00
Pressed Glass, Horseshoe, Muffineer, Amber 55.00
Pressed Glass, Horseshoe, Pitcher, 5 7/8 X 3 3/4 In. 67.50
Pressed Glass, Horseshoe, Plate, Bread 22.00
Pressed Glass, Horseshoe, Plate, Bread, 13 X 9 In. 19.50
Pressed Glass, Horseshoe, Plate, 8 In. .... 18.00 To 38.00
Pressed Glass, Horseshoe, Plate, 8 1/4 In. 45.00
Pressed Glass, Horseshoe, Plate, 10 In. 55.00
Pressed Glass, Horseshoe, Platter, Handled, Oval, 13 In. 38.00
Pressed Glass, Horseshoe, Platter, Single Horseshoe Handles, 11 X 9 In. 27.50
Pressed Glass, Horseshoe, Relish 28.00
Pressed Glass, Horseshoe, Salt 15.00
Pressed Glass, Horseshoe, Spooner .... 17.50 To 20.00
Pressed Glass, Horseshoe, Tray, Water, Double Horseshoe Handles 55.00
Pressed Glass, Horseshoe, Tumbler 2.00
Pressed Glass, Horseshoe, Wine 150.00
Pressed Glass, Hotel Argus, Wine 18.00
Pressed Glass, Hotel Thumbprint, Goblet 12.00
Pressed Glass, Huber, Champagne, Barrel, Flint 18.00
Pressed Glass, Huber, Compote, Flint, 6 1/2 X 6 In. 22.50
Pressed Glass, Huber, Cordial 17.00
Pressed Glass, Huber, Eggcup, Flint 22.50
Pressed Glass, Huber, Flip, Flint, 5 In. 20.00
Pressed Glass, Huber, Goblet, Etched, Flint 35.00
Pressed Glass, Huber, Mug, Flint, 3 In. 15.25
Pressed Glass, Huber, Mug, Molded Handle, Flint 18.00
Pressed Glass, Huber, Sugar, Covered, Flint 45.00
Pressed Glass, Huber, Wine, Flint 18.00
Huckle, see Feather Duster
Pressed Glass, Hummingbird, Creamer 29.00
Pressed Glass, Hummingbird, Pitcher, Milk 49.50
Pressed Glass, Hummingbird, Pitcher, Water, Blue .... 75.00 To 95.00
Hundred-Eye, see 100-Eye
Pressed Glass, Icicle & Loops, Goblet, Flint 29.50
Pressed Glass, Icicle With Diamond Quilted, Goblet, Flint 30.00
Pressed Glass, Icicle With Panels, Goblet, Flint 40.00
Pressed Glass, Icicle, Goblet, Flint 15.00
Ida, see Sheraton
Pressed Glass, Idyll, Berry Set, Gold Trim, 5 Piece 45.00
Pressed Glass, Idyll, Creamer, Gold Trim, Northwood 16.00
Pressed Glass, Illinois, Creamer 10.00

Pressed Glass, Illinois, Pitcher, Water, Square .... 35.00 To 97.50
Pressed Glass, Illinois, Salt, Individual 2.80
Pressed Glass, Illinois, Tankard, Water 45.00
Pressed Glass, Illinois, Toothpick 15.00
Pressed Glass, Imperial Jewels, Compte, White, Scalloped Edge, 5 In. 5.00
Pressed Glass, Independence Hall, Plate, Bread 60.00
Pressed Glass, Independence Hall, Plate, Bread, Dated Handles 90.00
Pressed Glass, Indian Feather, Butter, Deep 24.00
Indian Tree, see Sprig
Indiana Swirl, see Feather
Pressed Glass, Indiana, Bowl, 4 1/2 X 2 3/4 In. 7.00
Pressed Glass, Indiana, Spooner 8.00
Pressed Glass, Intaglio, Compote, Jelly, Opalescent 25.00
Pressed Glass, Intaglio, Compote, Jelly, Opalescent, Northwood .... 16.00 To 28.00
Pressed Glass, Intaglio, Compote, Jelly, Vaseline, Opalescent 25.00
Pressed Glass, Intaglio, Creamer, Blue, Opalescent 65.00
Pressed Glass, Intaglio, Creamer, Emerald Green, Gold Trim 35.00
Pressed Glass, Intaglio, Creamer, Ice Blue, Opalescent 40.00
Pressed Glass, Intaglio, Sauce, Blue, Opalescent 30.00
Pressed Glass, Intaglio, Sauce, Opalescent, Northwood 20.00
Pressed Glass, Intaglio, Sauce, Vaseline, Opalescent, Footed 22.00
Pressed Glass, Intaglio, Spooner, White To Clear, Opalescent 38.00
Pressed Glass, Intaglio, Table Set, Opalescent, Northwood, 4 Piece 285.00
Pressed Glass, Interlocked Hearts, Wine 15.00
Pressed Glass, Interlocking Crescents, Butter, Covered 45.00
Pressed Glass, Inverted Coin Spot, Tumbler, Green, Opalescent 15.00
Pressed Glass, Inverted Fan & Feather, Bonbon, Blue, Opalescent, Footed, 7 In. 25.00
Pressed Glass, Inverted Fan & Feather, Compote, Blue, Opalescent, N, 6 In. 65.00
Pressed Glass, Inverted Fan & Feather, Fruit Bowl, Pink, Gold Trim, N, 9 In. 210.00
Pressed Glass, Inverted Feather, Covered, Near Cut 30.00
Pressed Glass, Inverted Fern, Butter, Covered, Flint 47.50
Pressed Glass, Inverted Fern, Dish, Honey, Flint 6.00
Pressed Glass, Inverted Fern, Goblet, Flint 27.00
Pressed Glass, Inverted Fern, Sauce, Flint 10.00
Pressed Glass, Inverted Fern, Spooner, Flint 25.00
Pressed Glass, Inverted Fern, Sugar, Covered 42.00
Pressed Glass, Inverted Fern, Sugar, Covered, Flint 58.00
Pressed Glass, Inverted Fern, Sugar, Flint .... 20.00 To 45.00
Pressed Glass, Inverted Hearts, Dish, Honey, Flint .... 7.00 To 8.00
Pressed Glass, Inverted Hearts, Sauce, Flint .... 6.00 To 8.00
Pressed Glass, Inverted Strawberry, Punch Bowl, Child's .... 40.00 To 65.00
Pressed Glass, Inverted Strawberry, Punch Bowl, Miniature 40.00
Pressed Glass, Inverted Strawberry, Toothpick 30.00
Pressed Glass, Inverted Strawberry, Toothpick, Near Cut 7.50
Pressed Glass, Inverted Strawberry, Tumbler .... 18.50 To 19.50
Pressed Glass, Inverted Thistle, Sugar, 3 Footed, Near Cut 21.50
Pressed Glass, Inverted Thumbprint & Star, Goblet .... 12.50 To 13.00
Pressed Glass, Inverted Thumbprint, Mug, Amber 10.00
Pressed Glass, Inverted Thumbprint, Pitcher, Milk, Blue, Clear Handle, 8 In. 60.00
Pressed Glass, Inverted Thumbprint, Pitcher, Water, Ruby, Clear Handle 65.00
Pressed Glass, Inverted Thumbprint, Spooner, Turquoise Blue, 3 Shell Feet 28.00
Pressed Glass, Inverted Thumbprint, Syrup, Amber, Pewter Lid, 1884 .... 48.00
Pressed Glass, Inverted Thumbprint, Toothpick, Amberina To Amber 60.00
Pressed Glass, Inverted Thumbprint, Toothpick, Emerald Green 20.00
Pressed Glass, Inverted Thumbprint, Tumbler, Amethyst 20.00
Pressed Glass, Ionia, Goblet .... 12.50 To 15.00
Pressed Glass, Iowa City, Dish, Cheese 60.00
Pressed Glass, Iris & Herringbone, Wine 4.50
Pressed Glass, Iris With Meander, Berry Bowl, Green, Opalescent 65.00
Pressed Glass, Iris With Meander, Plate, Blue, Opalescent, 7 In. 20.00
Pressed Glass, Iris With Meander, Toothpick, Amethyst 45.00
Pressed Glass, Iris With Meander, Toothpick, Blue 70.00
Pressed Glass, Iris With Meander, Toothpick, Blue, Opalescent .... 50.00 To 68.00
Pressed Glass, Iris With Meander, Toothpick, White, Opalescent 30.00
Pressed Glass, Iris With Meander, Water Set, Blue, Gold Trim, 7 Piece 250.00

Pressed Glass, **Iron Kettle,** Spooner 10.00
Pressed Glass, **Ivanhoe,** Plate, Findlay, 8 In. 10.00
Pressed Glass, **Ivanhoe,** Relish 14.00
Pressed Glass, **Ivy In Snow,** Cake Stand 19.50
Pressed Glass, **Ivy In Snow,** Celery 20.00
Pressed Glass, **Ivy In Snow,** Celery, 8 In. 22.50
Pressed Glass, **Ivy In Snow,** Creamer 16.50
Pressed Glass, **Ivy In Snow,** Creamer, Frosted, Red Leaves 40.00
Pressed Glass, **Ivy In Snow,** Creamer, Gilt Leaves 17.50
Pressed Glass, **Ivy In Snow,** Pitcher, Water, Gold Leaf & Stem 35.00
Pressed Glass, **Ivy In Snow,** Relish 7.50
Pressed Glass, **Ivy In Snow,** Sauce, Gilt Trim, 4 1/4 In. 6.00
Pressed Glass, **Ivy In Snow,** Spooner, Frosted, Red Leaves 35.00
Pressed Glass, **Ivy In Snow,** Sugar, Frosted, Covered, Red Leaves 45.00
Pressed Glass, **Ivy In Snow,** Sugar, Gilt Trim 7.50
Pressed Glass, **Ivy In Snow,** Wine, Gilt Trim 6.50
Pressed Glass, **Ivy Leaves,** Cup & Saucer, Findlay 18.00
Pressed Glass, **Jackson,** Creamer, Green, Opalescent 55.00
Pressed Glass, **Jacob's Ladder,** Butter 40.00
Pressed Glass, **Jacob's Ladder,** Compote, Maltese Cross Finial, 13 X 7 1/2 In. 55.00
Pressed Glass, **Jacob's Ladder,** Creamer, Pedestal Base 24.50
Pressed Glass, **Jacob's Ladder,** Pitcher, Water .... 35.00 To 65.00
Pressed Glass, **Jacob's Ladder,** Relish, Cross Handles 12.50
Pressed Glass, **Jacob's Ladder,** Relish, Maltese Cross Handles 12.50
Pressed Glass, **Jacob's Ladder,** Salt, Master 14.00
Pressed Glass, **Jacob's Ladder,** Sauce, Footed 15.00
Pressed Glass, **Jacob's Ladder,** Wine 35.00
Pressed Glass, **Janssen,** Goblet 15.00
Pressed Glass, **Jenny Lind,** Plate, Bread 40.00
Pressed Glass, **Jersey Swirl,** Celery, Pedestal 29.50
Pressed Glass, **Jersey Swirl,** Plate, 6 In. .... 5.50 To 8.00
Pressed Glass, **Jersey Swirl,** Plate, 6 1/2 In. 8.50
Pressed Glass, **Jersey Swirl,** Salt 3.00
Pressed Glass, **Jersey Swirl,** Salt, Electric Blue 20.00
Pressed Glass, **Jersey Swirl,** Sauce, Footed 5.00
Pressed Glass, **Jersey Swirl,** Tumbler 15.00
Pressed Glass, **Jersey,** Butter, Covered 36.00
Pressed Glass, **Jewel & Dewdrop,** Pitcher, Water 37.50
Pressed Glass, **Jewel & Dewdrop,** Plate, Bread, "Our Daily Bread, " Oval 45.00
Pressed Glass, **Jewel & Dewdrop,** Toothpick 28.00

Pressed Glass, Jeweled Heart, Pitcher

Jewel & Festoon, see Loop & Jewel
Pressed Glass, **Jewel & Flower,** Sauce, Opalescent 38.00
Pressed Glass, **Jewel & Flower,** Tumbler, Vaseline, Opalescent 45.00
Jewel Band, see Scalloped Tape
Pressed Glass, **Jewel,** Berry Bowl, Frosted & Clear, Northwood, 3 1/2 In. 10.00
Pressed Glass, **Jeweled Drapery,** Goblet 17.50
Pressed Glass, **Jeweled Heart,** Berry Set, Green, Gold Trim, 7 Piece 145.00

Pressed Glass, Jumbo, Jar, Marmalade

Pressed Glass, Jeweled Heart, Berry Set, White, Opalescent, N.7 Piece 135.00
Pressed Glass, Jeweled Heart, Bowl, Apple Green, Opalescent, Ruffled, 6 In. 15.00
Pressed Glass, Jeweled Heart, Creamer, Blue, Gold Trim 32.00
Pressed Glass, Jeweled Heart, Creamer, Blue, Opalescent 55.00
Pressed Glass, Jeweled Heart, Creamer, Blue, Opalescent, Northwood 65.00
Pressed Glass, Jeweled Heart, Creamer, Green, Gold Trim 25.00
Pressed Glass, Jeweled Heart, Saltshaker 12.50
Pressed Glass, Jeweled Heart, Saltshaker, Blue, Northwood 35.00
Pressed Glass, Jeweled Heart, Tumbler 20.00
Pressed Glass, Jeweled Heart, Tumbler, Green, Gold Trim, Northwood 22.00
Pressed Glass, Jeweled Heart, Water Set, 6 Piece 90.00
Pressed Glass, Jeweled Moon & Star, Bowl, Frosted, Amber, & Blue, 7 3/4 In. 22.50
Pressed Glass, Jeweled Moon & Star, Cake Stand, 10 In. 36.00
Pressed Glass, Jeweled Moon & Star, Carafe, Water 35.00
Pressed Glass, Jeweled Moon & Star, Tumbler, Gold Top 17.50
Job's Tears, see Art
Pressed Glass, John Mitchell, Plate, Bread, Gilded Portrait Center 125.00
Jubilee, see Hickman
Pressed Glass, Jumbo, Butter, Head Under Handles 295.00
Kamoni, see Balder
Kansas, see Jewel & Dewdrop
Pressed Glass, Kansas, Pitcher, Water 42.00
Pressed Glass, Kansas, Sauce 7.50
Pressed Glass, Kansas, Spooner 10.00
Pressed Glass, Kentucky, Sauce, Cobalt, Footed, 4 1/4 In. 23.00
Pressed Glass, Keyhole, Bowl, Green, Opalescent, Footed, 9 In. 35.00
Pressed Glass, Keyhole, Bowl, Opalescent, Footed, 9 In. 32.00
Pressed Glass, King's Crown, Celery 44.00
Pressed Glass, King's Crown, Creamer, Individual .... 26.50 To 30.00
Pressed Glass, King's Crown, Creamer, Ruby Stained 22.00
Pressed Glass, King's Crown, Creamer, Ruby Stained, Tankard Shape 50.00
Pressed Glass, King's Crown, Cup & Saucer 47.00
Pressed Glass, King's Crown, Goblet .... 12.00 To 32.50
Pressed Glass, King's Crown, Goblet, Green Thumbprint, Gold Top 18.50
Pressed Glass, King's Crown, Goblet, Ruby Stained .... 18.50 To 32.00
Pressed Glass, King's Crown, Pitcher, Milk 40.00
Pressed Glass, King's Crown, Sauce, Boat Shape 25.00
Pressed Glass, King's Crown, Sherbet 12.00
Pressed Glass, King's Crown, Spooner .... 25.00 To 39.00
Pressed Glass, King's Crown, Tankard, Water, Etched Tulips, 13 In. 85.00
Pressed Glass, King's Crown, Tankard, 8 In. 55.00
Pressed Glass, King's Crown, Toothpick 20.00
Pressed Glass, King's Crown, Toothpick, Ruby Stained .... 20.00 To 28.50
Pressed Glass, King's Crown, Tumbler .... 25.00 To 28.50
Pressed Glass, King's Crown, Tumbler, Ruby Stained 28.50
Pressed Glass, King's Crown, Wine .... 13.50 To 24.50
Pressed Glass, King's Crown, Wine, Clear .... 5.00 To 13.50

Pressed Glass, King's Crown, Wine, Ruby Stained 26.00
Pressed Glass, Kitten, Plate, Bread 55.00
Pressed Glass, Klondike, Bowl, Amber Cross, Frosted, 6 In. 195.00
Pressed Glass, Klondike, Bowl, Amber Cross, Frosted, 7 In. 210.00
Pressed Glass, Klondike, Bowl, Frosted & Amber, Square, 6 1/4 In. 95.00
Pressed Glass, Klondike, Cup, Punch 150.00
Pressed Glass, Klondike, Salt & Pepper, Frosted 195.00
Pressed Glass, Klondike, Saltshaker, Amber & Frosted ..... 62.00 To 68.00
Pressed Glass, Klondike, Sauce, Amber Cross, Frosted 80.00
Pressed Glass, Klondike, Sugar, Covered 95.00
Pressed Glass, Klondike, Tray, Condiment, Amber Cross, Scalloped, 5 In. 135.00
Pressed Glass, Klondike, Tumbler 250.00
Pressed Glass, Knights Of Labor, Mug ..... 17.00 To 48.50
Pressed Glass, Knights Of Labor, Platter, Amber, 11 3/4 X 8 3/4 In. 245.00
Pressed Glass, Knights Of Pythias, Goblet, Green 14.50
Pressed Glass, Knobby Bull's-Eye, Berry Set, Amethyst, Gold Trim, 7 Piece 80.00
Pressed Glass, Knobby Bull's-Eye, Creamer 10.50
Pressed Glass, Knobby Bull's-Eye, Goblet, Amethyst Eyes, Gold Trim 25.00
Pressed Glass, Kokomo, Celery, Etched 22.50
Pressed Glass, Kokomo, Compote, Covered, 8 In. 25.00
Pressed Glass, Kokomo, Goblet 20.00
Pressed Glass, Kokomo, Wine ..... 16.00 To 17.50
Pressed Glass, Krom, Goblet, Flint 30.00
Pressed Glass, Krystol, Tumbler, 4 In. 5.00
Pressed Glass, La Belle Rose, Saltshaker, Rose Color 8.00

Lace, see Drapery

Pressed Glass, Lacy Daisy, Berry Set, Miniature, 5 Piece 40.00
Pressed Glass, Lacy Daisy, Berry Set, Miniature, 7 Piece ..... 65.00 To 75.00
Pressed Glass, Lacy Daisy, Bowl, 6 1/2 In. 5.00
Pressed Glass, Lacy Daisy, Sauce, Miniature 4.50
Pressed Glass, Lacy Floral, Relish 11.00
Pressed Glass, Lacy Medallion, Creamer, Emerald Green, Gold Trim, 2 1/4 In. 22.00
Pressed Glass, Lacy Medallion, Mug, Emerald Green, Gold Trim 25.00
Pressed Glass, Lacy Medallion, Mug, Green, 3 3/4 In. 25.00
Pressed Glass, Lacy Medallion, Toothpick, Emerald Green, Gold Trim 14.00
Pressed Glass, Lacy Medallion, Toothpick, Green, Gold Trim 18.00
Pressed Glass, Lacy Medallion, Toothpick, Green, Souvenir, Lisbon, N.H. 20.00
Pressed Glass, Lacy Medallion, Tumbler, Green 17.00
Pressed Glass, Ladder With Diamond, Water Set, 7 Piece 185.00
Pressed Glass, Lamb, Mug 20.00
Pressed Glass, Lamb, Table Set, Child's, 3 Piece 150.00
Pressed Glass, Laminated Petals, Champagne, Flint 58.00
Pressed Glass, Laminated Petals, Wine, Flint 40.00

Pressed Glass, Lamp, see Lamp, Pressed Glass

Pressed Glass, Laredo Honeycomb, Celery 12.50
Pressed Glass, Large Drop, Salt, Master, Flint ..... 23.00 To 30.00
Pressed Glass, Late Block, Cup, Ruby Stained 25.00
Pressed Glass, Late Block, Rose Bowl, Ruby Stained, 5 1/2 In. 65.00
Pressed Glass, Lattice & Oval Panels, Claret, Sandwich 120.00

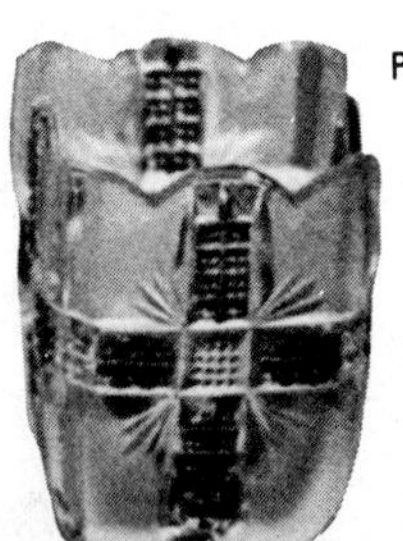

Pressed Glass, Klondike, Toothpick

Pressed Glass, Liberty Bell, Plate

Pressed Glass, Lattice & Oval Panels, Goblet, Flint 97.50
Pressed Glass, Lattice, Bowl, 9 1/2 X 5 1/4 In. 15.00
Pressed Glass, Lattice, Goblet 15.00
Pressed Glass, Lattice, Pitcher, Water, Pink, Opalescent 135.00
Pressed Glass, Lattice, Plate, 6 In. 12.00
Pressed Glass, Lattice, Wine 15.00
Pressed Glass, Leaf & Beads, Bowl, Blue, Opalescent, 8 1/4 X 3 In. 40.00
Pressed Glass, Leaf & Beads, Bowl, Opalescent, 6 In. 30.00
Pressed Glass, Leaf & Beads, Bowl, White, Opalescent, Footed, 9 In. 22.50
Pressed Glass, Leaf & Dart, Goblet .... 18.00 To 32.50
Pressed Glass, Leaf & Dart, Goblet, Flint 24.00
Pressed Glass, Leaf & Dart, Goblet, Low, Flint 24.00
Pressed Glass, Leaf & Dart, Pitcher, Water, Applied Handle 45.00
Pressed Glass, Leaf & Dart, Salt, Footed 22.50
Pressed Glass, Leaf & Dart, Sugar 15.00
Pressed Glass, Leaf & Dart, Tumbler, Footed .... 19.50 To 27.50
Pressed Glass, Leaf & Flower, Spooner, Frosted 18.50
Pressed Glass, Leaf & Flower, Tankard, Water, Frosted & Clear 65.00
Pressed Glass, Leaf & Flower, Water Set, Yellow & Frosted, 6 Piece 195.00
Pressed Glass, Leaf & Star, Jar, Tobacco 37.50
Pressed Glass, Leaf Umbrella, Muffineer, Cranberry, Northwood 95.00
Pressed Glass, Leaf, Compote, Opalescent To Clear, Tripod Stem, 4 5/8 In. 25.00
Pressed Glass, Lee, Wine, Flint 85.00
Lens & Star, see Star & Oval
Pressed Glass, Lens & Star With Frosted Band, Tumbler 12.50
Pressed Glass, Leopard, Tumbler, Etched, Thin 14.00
Pressed Glass, Liberty Bell, Bowl, Footed, 8 In. 75.00
Pressed Glass, Liberty Bell, Butter, Covered 95.00
Pressed Glass, Liberty Bell, Butter, Miniature 40.00
Pressed Glass, Liberty Bell, Compote, 1776-1876, Gillinder, 8 In. 65.00
Pressed Glass, Liberty Bell, Compote, 7 In. 65.00
Pressed Glass, Liberty Bell, Compote, 8 In. 75.00
Pressed Glass, Liberty Bell, Compote, 8 X 4 1/4 In. 85.00
Pressed Glass, Liberty Bell, Creamer, Applied Handle 95.00
Pressed Glass, Liberty Bell, Creamer, Applied Reeded Handle 95.00
Pressed Glass, Liberty Bell, Creamer, Miniature 95.00
Pressed Glass, Liberty Bell, Creamer, 1776-1876, Reeded Handle, Gillinder 115.00
Pressed Glass, Liberty Bell, Fruit Bowl, Collared Base, 8 X 4 1/2 In. 45.00
Pressed Glass, Liberty Bell, Goblet .... 37.00 To 37.50
Pressed Glass, Liberty Bell, Goblet, Knob Stem 45.00
Pressed Glass, Liberty Bell, Goblet, 1776-1876 .... 38.00
Pressed Glass, Liberty Bell, Goblet, 1776-1876, Knob Stem, Gillinder 40.00
Pressed Glass, Liberty Bell, Mug, Miniature 115.00
Pressed Glass, Liberty Bell, Mug, Snake Handle 250.00
Pressed Glass, Liberty Bell, Pitcher, Water, Applied Handle 500.00
Pressed Glass, Liberty Bell, Plate, Bread 85.00
Pressed Glass, Liberty Bell, Plate, Bread, Signers .... 60.00 To 88.00
Pressed Glass, Liberty Bell, Plate, Dated, 6 1/4 In. 55.00
Pressed Glass, Liberty Bell, Plate, Twig Handles, Gillinder, 1875, 8 In. 55.00
Pressed Glass, Liberty Bell, Plate, 10 In. 75.00

Pressed Glass, Lincoln Drape, Compote, 8 In.

Pressed Glass, Lily Of The Valley, Etched, Goblet

Pressed Glass, Loop With Fisheye, Goblet

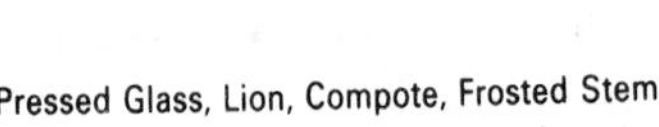

Pressed Glass, Lion, Compote, Frosted Stem

Pressed Glass, Liberty Bell, Platter, Shells, Oval, 11 X 7 In. 110.00
Pressed Glass, Liberty Bell, Platter, Signers, 1776-1876, 13 In. 55.00
Pressed Glass, Liberty Bell, Relish 30.00
Pressed Glass, Liberty Bell, Relish, States, 9 1/2 In. 45.00
Pressed Glass, Liberty Bell, Relish, 13 Colonies, Twig Handles, Gillinder 45.00
Pressed Glass, Liberty Bell, Relish, 1876 .... 25.00
Pressed Glass, Liberty Bell, Salt 35.00
Pressed Glass, Liberty Bell, Sauce, Collared Base 20.00
Pressed Glass, Liberty Bell, Sauce, Footed 22.50
Pressed Glass, Liberty Bell, Sauce, Footed, Collared, 4 5/8 In. 14.00
Pressed Glass, Liberty Bell, Sauce, Footed, 4 1/2 In. .... 28.50 To 35.00
Pressed Glass, Liberty Bell, Sauce, Scalloped Rim 23.50
Pressed Glass, Liberty Bell, Sauce, 1776-1875, Footed, Gillinder, 4 1/2 In. 27.50
Pressed Glass, Liberty Bell, Sauce, 1776-1876, Gillinder, 4 In. 20.00
Pressed Glass, Liberty Bell, Spooner 65.00
Pressed Glass, Liberty Bell, Spooner, Scalloped Rim 48.50
Pressed Glass, Liberty Bell, Spooner, 1776-1876, Gillinder 55.00
Pressed Glass, Liberty Bell, Sugar, Covered 110.00
Pressed Glass, Liberty Bell, Sugar, Miniature 55.00
Pressed Glass, Lily Of The Valley, Celery 38.50
Pressed Glass, Lily Of The Valley, Celery, Etched 25.00
Pressed Glass, Lily Of The Valley, Creamer, Applied Handle .... 34.00 To 45.00
Pressed Glass, Lily Of The Valley, Creamer, Footed 25.00
Pressed Glass, Lily Of The Valley, Creamer, 3 Footed 45.00
Pressed Glass, Lily Of The Valley, Creamer, 3 Legged 32.50

Pressed Glass, Lily Of The Valley, Etched, Goblet .... 11.00 To 13.50
Pressed Glass, Lily Of The Valley, Etched, Wine 15.00
Pressed Glass, Lily Of The Valley, Goblet 28.00
Pressed Glass, Lily Of The Valley, Pickle 13.50
Pressed Glass, Lily Of The Valley, Pitcher, Milk 67.50
Pressed Glass, Lily Of The Valley, Relish 18.00
Pressed Glass, Lily Of The Valley, Wine 45.00
Pressed Glass, Lincoln Drape With Tassel, Goblet, Flint 135.00
Pressed Glass, Lincoln Drape, Compote, Flint, 7 1/2 X 7 In. 65.00
Pressed Glass, Lincoln Drape, Compote, 8 1/2 In. 43.50
Pressed Glass, Lincoln Drape, Eggcup 37.50
Pressed Glass, Lincoln Drape, Eggcup, Flint 45.00
Pressed Glass, Lincoln Drape, Goblet 57.50
Pressed Glass, Lincoln Drape, Goblet, Flint .... 48.00 To 55.00
Pressed Glass, Lincoln Drape, Syrup, Metal Top 79.50
Pressed Glass, Lined Smocking, Goblet, Flint 47.50
Pressed Glass, Lion & Baboon, Creamer 60.00
Pressed Glass, Lion With Cable, Spooner 25.00
Pressed Glass, Lion, Compote, Covered, High Standard, Stump, 8 In. 145.00
Pressed Glass, Lion, Compote, Covered, 7 In. 63.00
Pressed Glass, Lion, Compote, Lion & Stump Finial, Lion Base, 8 In. 145.00
Pressed Glass, Lion, Compote, Lion's Head Finial, 12 In. 85.00
Pressed Glass, Lion, Creamer 42.50
Pressed Glass, Lion, Creamer, Etched 30.00
Pressed Glass, Lion, Goblet .... 45.00 To 55.00
Pressed Glass, Lion, Jar, Marmalade 50.00
Pressed Glass, Lion, Paperweight 85.00
Pressed Glass, Lion, Paperweight, Gillinder 85.00
Pressed Glass, Lion, Plate, Bread 45.00
Pressed Glass, Lion, Plate, Bread, "Give Us This Day" 85.00
Pressed Glass, Lion, Plate, Bread, Closed Handles, 12 In. 75.00
Pressed Glass, Lion, Plate, Bread, 10 In. 45.00
Pressed Glass, Lion, Sauce 20.00
Pressed Glass, Lion, Sauce, Footed 17.50
Pressed Glass, Lion, Sauce, Footed, 4 In. 15.00
Pressed Glass, Lion, Spooner 35.00
Pressed Glass, Lion, Spooner, Etched 20.00
Pressed Glass, Lion, Spooner, Miniature 37.50
Pressed Glass, Lion, Sugar, Covered .... 50.00 To 55.00
Pressed Glass, Lion, Sugar, Rampant Lion Finial 75.00
Pressed Glass, Lion, Toothpick, Square 18.00
Pressed Glass, Lion, Tray, Ice Cream, Apple, Lions' Heads Handles 52.00
Pressed Glass, Lion, Wine, 4 1/8 In. 85.00
Lion's Leg, see Alaska
Lippman, see Flat Diamond
Pressed Glass, Little Bullet, Tumbler 7.50
Pressed Glass, Little Jewel, Pitcher, Milk 18.50
Pressed Glass, Little Lamb, Creamer, Child's 37.50
Pressed Glass, Little Lamb, Mug, Child's, Lamb Finial On Lid 40.00
Pressed Glass, Little Lamb, Table Set, Child's, 3 Piece 125.00
Pressed Glass, Little River, Jar, Pickle Castor 20.00
Pressed Glass, Log & Star, Mug, Amber, 2 1/4 In. 12.50
Pressed Glass, Log Cabin, Pitcher, Water 150.00
Pressed Glass, Log Cabin, Table Set, 4 Piece 250.00
Pressed Glass, Long Spears, Bowl, Covered, Etched Ferns, Footed, 10 In. 45.00
Loop, see also Seneca Loop, Yuma Loop
Pressed Glass, Loop & Block, Celery, Ruby Stained 55.00
Pressed Glass, Loop & Block, Spooner, Ruby Stained 45.00
Pressed Glass, Loop & Block, Sugar, Covered, Ruby Stained 55.00
Pressed Glass, Loop & Block, Sugar, Ruby Stained 25.00
Pressed Glass, Loop & Crystal, Goblet, Flint 25.00
Pressed Glass, Loop & Dart With Diamond Ornament, Eggcup 13.00
Pressed Glass, Loop & Dart With Diamond Ornament, Sugar, Covered 22.00
Pressed Glass, Loop & Dart With Diamond Ornament, Tumbler, Footed 12.50
Pressed Glass, Loop & Dart With Round Ornament, Butter Pat 15.00

Pressed Glass, Loop & Dart With Round Ornament, Creamer, Applied Handle ... 27.50
Pressed Glass, Loop & Dart With Round Ornament, Cup Plate ... 14.00
Pressed Glass, Loop & Dart With Round Ornament, Plate, 6 In. ... 25.00
Pressed Glass, Loop & Dart With Round Ornament, Salt, Master ... 28.50
Pressed Glass, Loop & Dart With Round Ornament, Spooner ... 20.00
Pressed Glass, Loop & Dart, Celery, Flint ... 45.00
Pressed Glass, Loop & Dart, Eggcup ... 13.00
Pressed Glass, Loop & Dart, Eggcup, Flint ... 18.00
Pressed Glass, Loop & Dart, Goblet ... 15.00
Pressed Glass, Loop & Dart, Goblet, 9 Darts ... 16.50
Pressed Glass, Loop & Dart, Relish, Scoop ... 13.50
Pressed Glass, Loop & Dart, Serving Bowl, Oval, 7 1/2 In. ... 10.00
Pressed Glass, Loop & Dewdrop, Creamer ... 14.50 To 15.00
Pressed Glass, Loop & Diamond, Spooner ... 12.50
Pressed Glass, Loop & Fan, Celery ... 19.50
Pressed Glass, Loop & Fan, Pitcher, Milk ... 22.50
Pressed Glass, Loop & Jewel, Bowl, Rounded Corners, 5 1/2 In. ... 5.00
Pressed Glass, Loop & Jewel, Relish, Square, 5 In. ... 5.00
Pressed Glass, Loop & Jewel, Sugar ... 18.00
Pressed Glass, Loop & Long Petals, Tumbler, Jade Green, Footed, Flint ... 250.00
Pressed Glass, Loop & Moose Eye, Champagne, Flint ... 32.00
Pressed Glass, Loop & Moose Eye, Eggcup, Flint ... 18.00
Pressed Glass, Loop & Noose, Champagne ... 15.00
Pressed Glass, Loop & Ovals, Goblet, Flint ... 26.00
Pressed Glass, Loop With Dewdrop, Compote, Jelly ... 14.50
Pressed Glass, Loop With Dewdrop, Creamer ... 15.00
Pressed Glass, Loop With Garter Band, Goblet ... 12.50
Pressed Glass, Loop With Honeycomb Band, Goblet, Flint ... 24.00
Pressed Glass, Loop With Leaf, Bowl, Scalloped Rim, 7 In. ... 35.00

Loop with Stippled Panels, see Texas

Pressed Glass, Loop, Celery ... 28.00
Pressed Glass, Loop, Celery, Flint ... 25.00 To 40.00
Pressed Glass, Loop, Celery, Hexagonal Wafer & Base, Flint ... 125.00
Pressed Glass, Loop, Celery, 8 In., Pair ... 65.00
Pressed Glass, Loop, Compote, Flint, 7 1/2 In. ... 40.00
Pressed Glass, Loop, Compote, Scalloped, 10 In. ... 55.00
Pressed Glass, Loop, Compote, 10 1/2 X 8 1/4 In. ... 50.00
Pressed Glass, Loop, Eggcup, Flint ... 27.00
Pressed Glass, Loop, Goblet ... 22.00 To 30.00
Pressed Glass, Loop, Goblet, Flint ... 22.00
Pressed Glass, Loop, Salt, Master, Flint ... 18.00
Pressed Glass, Loop, Salt, Master, Footed, Flint ... 18.00
Pressed Glass, Loop, Sugar ... 28.00
Pressed Glass, Loop, Sugar, Covered, Flint ... 65.00
Pressed Glass, Loop, Tumbler, Applied Handle, Flint, 4 In. ... 22.50
Pressed Glass, Loop, Vase, Flint, 10 In. ... 25.00
Pressed Glass, Loop, Wine, Flint ... 22.00
Pressed Glass, Lorne, Butter, Covered ... 32.50
Pressed Glass, Lotus & Serpent, Mug ... 17.50
Pressed Glass, Lotus & Serpent, Plate, Bread ... 28.00
Pressed Glass, Lotus, Cake Stand, Scalloped Edge, 11 1/2 In. ... 40.00
Pressed Glass, Lotus, Plate, Bread, "Give Us This Day" ... 25.00
Pressed Glass, Lotus, Relish, Handled, Oval, 9 In. ... 14.50
Pressed Glass, Louis XV, Butter, Covered ... 145.00
Pressed Glass, Louis XV, Creamer ... 70.00
Pressed Glass, Louis XV, Spooner ... 55.00
Pressed Glass, Louisiana Purchase, Tumbler ... 6.50 To 10.00
Pressed Glass, Louisiana, Butter ... 21.00
Pressed Glass, Louisiana, Cake Stand ... 18.00
Pressed Glass, Lustre Rose, Pitcher, Water, Green, Gold Trim ... 55.00
Pressed Glass, Magnet & Grape With Frosted Leaf & Shield, Goblet, Flint ... 175.00
Pressed Glass, Magnet & Grape With Frosted Leaf, Celery, Flint ... 185.00
Pressed Glass, Magnet & Grape With Frosted Leaf, Champagne ... 85.00
Pressed Glass, Magnet & Grape With Frosted Leaf, Goblet ... 43.50 To 56.00
Pressed Glass, Magnet & Grape With Frosted Leaf, Spooner, Flint ... 28.00

Pressed Glass, Magnet & Grape With Stippled Leaf, Goblet

Pressed Glass, Maine, Syrup

Pressed Glass, Magnet & Grape With Stippled Leaf, Goblet 40.00
Pressed Glass, Magnet & Grape, Goblet .... 14.00 To 22.00
Pressed Glass, Magnet & Grape, Sugar, Frosted, Knob Stem, Flint 35.00
Pressed Glass, Magnet & Grape, Wine 20.00
Pressed Glass, Magnolia, Cake Stand, 9 1/2 In. 42.50
Pressed Glass, Magnolia, Tumbler, Frosted 28.00
Maiden Blush, see Banded Portland
Pressed Glass, Maine, Bowl, 8 X 6 In. 12.00
Pressed Glass, Maine, Cake Stand .... 57.50 To 65.00
Pressed Glass, Maine, Cake Stand, 8 1/2 In. 25.00
Pressed Glass, Maine, Celery 26.00
Pressed Glass, Maine, Compote, Green, 5 X 4 1/4 In. 20.00
Pressed Glass, Maine, Relish 6.00
Pressed Glass, Majestic, Sugar, Covered 15.00
Pressed Glass, Majestic, Wine, Ruby Stained 35.00
Pressed Glass, Maltese Cross In Circles, Plate, Bread 30.00
Pressed Glass, Man Of The Woods, Creamer 29.00
Pressed Glass, Man's Head, Creamer 15.00
Pressed Glass, Manhattan, Berry Bowl, Gold Trim 14.50
Pressed Glass, Manhattan, Cake Stand, 8 1/2 In. 30.00
Pressed Glass, Manhattan, Creamer 9.50
Pressed Glass, Manhattan, Goblet 10.00
Pressed Glass, Manhattan, Wine 12.00
Pressed Glass, Many Loops, Bowl, Blue, 8 In. 20.00
Pressed Glass, Many Loops, Bowl, Opalescent, 8 1/2 In. 22.00
Pressed Glass, Maple Leaf Band, Goblet 25.00
Pressed Glass, Maple Leaf Band, Goblet, Amber 65.00
Pressed Glass, Maple Leaf, Bowl, Blue, Footed, Oval, 10 In. 30.00
Pressed Glass, Maple Leaf, Bowl, Footed, Oval, 10 In. 27.50
Pressed Glass, Maple Leaf, Bowl, Green, Oval, 10 X 6 1/4 In. 37.50
Pressed Glass, Maple Leaf, Bowl, Vaseline, Dome Lid, Footed, Oval, 5 1/2 In. 40.00
Pressed Glass, Maple Leaf, Butter, Cobalt, Covered, Northwood 68.00
Pressed Glass, Maple Leaf, Creamer, Canary 35.00
Pressed Glass, Maple Leaf, Creamer, Vaseline 35.00
Pressed Glass, Maple Leaf, Pitcher, Water, Vaseline, Footed 70.00
Pressed Glass, Maple Leaf, Tumbler, Blue, Northwood 35.00
Pressed Glass, Marquisette, Goblet .... 15.00 To 17.50
Pressed Glass, Marsh Fern, Tankard, Water 40.00
Pressed Glass, Marsh Pink, Cake Stand, 9 X 6 3/4 In. 30.00
Pressed Glass, Marsh Pink, Goblet 28.50
Pressed Glass, Martha's Tears, Wine, Blue 23.00
Pressed Glass, Maryland, Celery 20.00
Pressed Glass, Maryland, Goblet 22.00
Pressed Glass, Maryland, Pitcher, Milk 25.00
Pressed Glass, Maryland, Plate, Bread 25.00
Pressed Glass, Maryland, Tumbler 15.00

Pressed Glass, Mascotte, Basket, Cake, Etched, Metal Handle 75.00
Pressed Glass, Mascotte, Butter, Covered, Etched Leaf 35.00
Pressed Glass, Mascotte, Celery, 8 In. 15.00
Pressed Glass, Mascotte, Etched, Spooner 17.50
Pressed Glass, Mascotte, Goblet 10.00
Pressed Glass, Mascotte, Spooner, Pedestal 22.00
Pressed Glass, Mascotte, Sugar, Covered, 9 In. 19.00
Pressed Glass, Mascotte, Tray, Water, 12 In. 30.00
Pressed Glass, Masonic, Celery, McKee 27.50
Pressed Glass, Massachusetts, Mug, Gold Trim 15.00
Pressed Glass, Massachusetts, Plate, 8 1/4 In. 32.50
Pressed Glass, Massachusetts, Sugar 12.00
Pressed Glass, Massachusetts, Vase, Gold Trim, 6 3/4 In. 9.00
Pressed Glass, Massachusetts, Wine .... 25.00 To 29.00
Pressed Glass, McCormick Reaper, Plate, Bread 70.00
Pressed Glass, McKinley Memorial, Plate, Bread 30.00
Pressed Glass, McKinley, Cup, Covered 30.00
Pressed Glass, McKinley, Mug .... 13.00 To 18.00
Pressed Glass, McKinley, Plate, Bread, "It Is God's Way" 35.00
Pressed Glass, McKinley, Tumbler, Bust In Base 25.00
Pressed Glass, Meander, Bowl, Green, Opalescent, 9 In. 24.00
Pressed Glass, Medallion Sprig, Muffineer, Amber 80.00
Pressed Glass, Medallion Sprig, Saltshaker, Blue To Clear 16.00
Pressed Glass, Medallion, Cake Stand, Vaseline, 12 In. 68.00
Pressed Glass, Medallion, Goblet 17.50
Pressed Glass, Medallion, Sauce, Blue, 4 1/4 In. 12.00
Pressed Glass, Mellor, Creamer, Bulbous 27.00
Pressed Glass, Melrose, Butter 32.00
Pressed Glass, Melrose, Wine 20.00
Pressed Glass, Memphis, Butter, Covered, Gold Trim, Northwood 35.00
Pressed Glass, Memphis, Creamer, Green, Gold Trim, Northwood 35.00
Pressed Glass, Memphis, Pitcher, Water, Gold Trim, Northwood 50.00
Pressed Glass, Memphis, Spooner, Gold Trim, Northwood 25.00
Pressed Glass, Memphis, Spooner, Green, Gold Trim, Northwood 35.00
Pressed Glass, Memphis, Tumbler, Gold Trim, Northwood 16.00
Pressed Glass, Memphis, Tumbler, Green, Northwood 14.00
Pressed Glass, Memphis, Water Set, Green, Gold Trim, Northwood, 7 Piece 225.00
Pressed Glass, Menagerie, Sugar, Child's, Bear Cover 50.00
Pressed Glass, Michigan, Celery 19.00
Pressed Glass, Michigan, Celery, Pink & Gold Trim 38.00
Pressed Glass, Michigan, Creamer, Child's, Yellow Eyes, Red Carnation 30.00
Pressed Glass, Michigan, Goblet 20.00
Pressed Glass, Michigan, Goblet, Gold Trim 25.00
Pressed Glass, Michigan, Mug, Lemonade, Yellow Flashed 12.50
Pressed Glass, Michigan, Sauce 5.50
Pressed Glass, Michigan, Table Set, Sugar, Creamer, Spooner, Miniature 50.00
Pressed Glass, Michigan, Toothpick 18.00
Pressed Glass, Millard, Celery, Ruby Stained 48.00
Pressed Glass, Millard, Saltshaker, Ruby Stained 15.00
Pressed Glass, Milton, Goblet 18.50
Pressed Glass, Minerva, Cake Stand, 9 In. 46.00
Pressed Glass, Minerva, Creamer 35.00
Pressed Glass, Minerva, Goblet 75.00
Pressed Glass, Minerva, Platter, 13 X 9 In. 47.50
Pressed Glass, Minerva, Sauce 6.50
Pressed Glass, Minerva, Sauce, Footed .... 10.00 To 12.00
Pressed Glass, Minerva, Spooner 26.00
Pressed Glass, Minnesota, Celery .... 12.50 To 25.00
Pressed Glass, Minnesota, Compote, 9 In. 23.50
Pressed Glass, Minnesota, Cup, Flint 22.50
Pressed Glass, Minnesota, Goblet 16.50
Pressed Glass, Minnesota, Relish 7.00
Pressed Glass, Minnesota, Tankard, Water 37.50
Pressed Glass, Minnesota, Toothpick 16.00
Pressed Glass, Minnesota, Toothpick, Gold Trim 35.00

Pressed Glass, Minnesota, Wine 17.00
Pressed Glass, Minnestoa, Goblet, Gold Trim 15.00
Pressed Glass, Mirror, Champagne, Flint 29.50
Pressed Glass, Mirror, Compote, Flint, 6 In. 50.00
Pressed Glass, Mirror, Cordial, Flint 24.00
Pressed Glass, Mirror, Goblet, Flint 30.00
Pressed Glass, Mirror, Goblet, Knob Stem, Flint 35.00
Pressed Glass, Mirror, Spooner 12.50
Pressed Glass, Mirror, Wine, Flint 36.00
Pressed Glass, Missouri, Creamer, Green 29.00
Pressed Glass, Missouri, Pitcher, Milk 24.00
Pressed Glass, Mitered Bars, Celery 18.00
Pressed Glass, Mitered Bars, Goblet 12.50

Mitered Diamond Point, see Mitered Bars

Pressed Glass, Mitered Prisms, Butter 20.00
Pressed Glass, Mitered Prisms, Cake Stand, 9 In. 29.50
Pressed Glass, Mitered Prisms, Celery 17.50
Pressed Glass, Mitered Prisms, Goblet 10.00
Pressed Glass, Model Peerless, Celery, Findlay 17.00
Pressed Glass, Monkey & Turtle, Mug 22.50
Pressed Glass, Monkey Under Tree, Mug 80.00
Pressed Glass, Monkey Under Tree, Tumbler 72.00
Pressed Glass, Monkey, Mug, Amethyst 70.00
Pressed Glass, Monkey, Spooner 55.00
Pressed Glass, Monkey, Sugar 25.00
Pressed Glass, Moon & Star, Banana Boat, Pedestal, 11 X 9 In. 95.00
Pressed Glass, Moon & Star, Bowl, Footed, 6 1/4 In. 18.00
Pressed Glass, Moon & Star, Bowl, 6 In. 12.00
Pressed Glass, Moon & Star, Celery .... 18.00 To 25.00
Pressed Glass, Moon & Star, Champagne 25.00
Pressed Glass, Moon & Star, Compote, 8 1/4 X 8 In. 30.00
Pressed Glass, Moon & Star, Compote, 8 1/2 X 8 In. 45.00
Pressed Glass, Moon & Star, Fruit Bowl, 7 In. 35.00
Pressed Glass, Moon & Star, Pitcher, Water, Applied Reeded Handle 135.00
Pressed Glass, Moon & Star, Pitcher, Water, Applied Rope Handle, 9 1/4 In. 165.00
Pressed Glass, Moon & Star, Pitcher, Water, Twisted Reeded Handle 100.00
Pressed Glass, Moon & Star, Spill, Flint 35.00
Pressed Glass, Moon & Star, Spooner 22.00
Pressed Glass, Moon & Star, Spooner, Frosted 42.00
Pressed Glass, Moon & Star, Sugar, Covered 40.00
Pressed Glass, Moon & Star, Toothpick, Amber 14.00
Pressed Glass, Moon & Star, Tumbler, Footed, Flint 165.00
Pressed Glass, Moon & Star, Tumbler, Footed, Flint, 4 1/2 In. 78.00
Pressed Glass, Moon & Star, Waste Bowl, 4 In. 20.00

Moon & Stork, see Ostrich Looking at the Moon

Pressed Glass, Morning Glory, Champagne, Flint 200.00
Pressed Glass, Morning Glory, Eggcup 140.00

Pressed Glass, Mitered Diamond, Goblet

Pressed Glass, Moon & Star, Bowl, Covered, Footed

Pressed Glass, **Morning Glory,** Etched, Goblet 10.00
Pressed Glass, **Morning Glory,** Salt, Individual 100.00
Pressed Glass, **Morning Glory,** Tumbler, Footed, Flint 135.00
Pressed Glass, **Morning Glory,** Wine, Flint 155.00
Pressed Glass, **Nail,** Berry Bowl, Master 23.00
Pressed Glass, **Nail,** Goblet 21.50
Pressed Glass, **Nail,** Saltshaker, Ruby Stained 25.00
Pressed Glass, **Nail,** Syrup, Etched 35.00
Pressed Glass, **Nail,** Syrup, Ruby Stained 135.00
Pressed Glass, **Nailhead,** Cake Stand 22.00
Pressed Glass, **Nailhead,** Cake Stand, 9 In. 15.00
Pressed Glass, **Nailhead,** Goblet 15.00
Pressed Glass, **Nailhead,** Goblet, Flint 12.50
Pressed Glass, **Nailhead,** Pitcher, Water 27.50
Pressed Glass, **Nailhead,** Plate, 9 1/4 In. 8.00
Pressed Glass, **Nailhead,** Sugar .... 10.00 To 20.00
Pressed Glass, **Nailhead,** Wine 17.00
Pressed Glass, **Naturalistic Blackberry,** Goblet .... 18.50 To 20.00
Pressed Glass, **Nautilus,** Bowl, Vaseline, Opalescent, Footed, 8 X 6 In. 45.00
Pressed Glass, **Nautilus,** Compote, Jelly, Blue, Opalescent 45.00
Pressed Glass, **Nautilus,** Sauce, Blue, Opalescent 20.00
Pressed Glass, **Nautilus,** Sauce, Blue, Opalescent, Boat Shape 22.00
Pressed Glass, **Nautilus,** Sugar, Blue, Opalescent 25.00
Pressed Glass, **Nautilus,** Tray, Card, Vaseline, Opalescent, Footed 40.00
Pressed Glass, **Nautilus,** Tray, Card, White To Clear, Opalescent, N 22.00
Pressed Glass, **Near Cut,** Punch Bowl, Child's 21.00
Pressed Glass, **Nestor,** Creamer, Amethyst 38.00
Pressed Glass, **Netted Oak,** Muffineer, Northwood 61.00
Pressed Glass, **Nevada,** Spooner 10.00
Pressed Glass, **New England Centennial,** Goblet 45.00
Pressed Glass, **New England Pineapple,** Butter, Flint 55.00
Pressed Glass, **New England Pineapple,** Compote, 8 X 5 In. 85.00
Pressed Glass, **New England Pineapple,** Eggcup 38.50
Pressed Glass, **New England Pineapple,** Eggcup, Flint .... 26.00 To 38.50
Pressed Glass, **New England Pineapple,** Goblet, Flint .... 45.00 To 52.50
Pressed Glass, **New England Pineapple,** Goblet, Lady's 35.00
Pressed Glass, **New England Pineapple,** Goblet, Lady's, Flint 45.00
Pressed Glass, **New England Pineapple,** Salt, Master, Flint 30.00
Pressed Glass, **New England Pineapple,** Spooner 27.50
Pressed Glass, **New England Pineapple,** Spooner, Flint 60.00
Pressed Glass, **New England Pineapple,** Sugar, Covered 75.00
Pressed Glass, **New England Pineapple,** Sugar, Covered, Flint .... 58.00 To 60.00
Pressed Glass, **New Hampshire,** Creamer 12.50
Pressed Glass, **New Hampshire,** Cup, Punch 3.75
Pressed Glass, **New Hampshire,** Goblet 12.00
Pressed Glass, **New Hampshire,** Relish 7.00
Pressed Glass, **New Hampshire,** Sugar & Creamer 15.00
Pressed Glass, **New Hampshire,** Sugar & Creamer, Individual .... 10.50 To 15.50

Pressed Glass, New England Flute, Goblet

Pressed Glass, New England Pineapple, Pitcher

Pressed Glass, New Hampshire, Syrup 45.00
Pressed Glass, New Hampshire, Table Set, Pink Stained, 4 Piece 165.00
Pressed Glass, New Hampshire, Toothpick, Ruby Stained 30.00
Pressed Glass, New Hampshire, Wine 11.00
Pressed Glass, New Hampshire, Wine, Flared 11.00
Pressed Glass, New Hampshire, Wine, Gold Trim 8.50
Pressed Glass, New Jersey, Bowl, 9 1/4 In. 9.50
Pressed Glass, New Jersey, Bowl, 10 In. 45.00
Pressed Glass, New Jersey, Celery 9.50
Pressed Glass, New Jersey, Fruit Bowl, 8 1/2 In. 13.00
Pressed Glass, New Jersey, Plate, Cake, 11 1/2 In. 24.75
Pressed Glass, New Jersey, Plate, Scalloped Edge, 8 In. 15.00
Pressed Glass, New Jersey, Spooner, Ruby Stained 40.00
Pressed Glass, New Jersey, Tumbler 10.00
Pressed Glass, New Jersey, Tumbler, Gold Trim 85.00
Pressed Glass, New Jersey, Wine, Gold Trim 10.00
Pressed Glass, New York Honeycomb, Goblet, Flint 20.00
Pressed Glass, New York Honeycomb, Sugar, Flint 20.00
Pressed Glass, Niagara Falls, Plate, Bread, Frosted 80.00
Pressed Glass, Niagara Falls, Plate, Bread, Frosted, Etched, 16 X 11 1/2 In. 85.00
Pressed Glass, Nine Panel, Sugar, Acorn Finial On 10 Panel Lid, Flint 55.00
Pressed Glass, Nine Panel, Taster, Whiskey, Pittsburgh, Flint 12.00
Pressed Glass, Nokomis Swirl, Goblet 22.00
Pressed Glass, Northwood, Sugar, Geneva, Green, Gold Trim 30.00
Pressed Glass, Notched Bars, Creamer 47.50
Pressed Glass, Nursery Rhymes, Creamer, Child's .... 45.00 To 50.00
Pressed Glass, Nursery Rhymes, Punch Bowl .... 55.00 To 75.00
Pressed Glass, Nursery Rhymes, Punch Set, Riding Hood, Miniature, 5 Piece 130.00
Pressed Glass, Nursery Rhymes, Spooner, Child's 50.00
Pressed Glass, Nursery Rhymes, Sugar, Child's, Covered 60.00
Pressed Glass, Nursery Rhymes, Table Set, Miniature, 4 Piece 225.00
Pressed Glass, Nursery Rhymes, Tumbler, Miniature 20.00
Pressed Glass, Nursery Rhymes, Water Set, Miniature, 7 Piece 175.00
Pressed Glass, O'Hara Diamond, Celery 25.00
Pressed Glass, O'Hara Diamond, Etched, Spooner, Ruby Stained 45.00
Pressed Glass, O'Hara, Compote, Oval, 8 1/2 X 5 1/2 In. 22.00
Pressed Glass, Oak Leaf Band, Goblet .... 11.50 To 21.00
Pressed Glass, Oak Leaf Band, Salt, Master 16.00
Pressed Glass, Oak Leaf, Sauce, Lacy, 4 1/2 In., Pair 10.00
Pressed Glass, Oak Wreath, Pitcher, Water, Applied Handle 55.00
Pressed Glass, Oaken Bucket, Butter, Covered, Handled 45.00
Pressed Glass, Oaken Bucket, Creamer, Miniature 30.00
Pressed Glass, Oaken Bucket, Match Holder, Amber, Wire Handle, 2 5/8 In. 12.00
Pressed Glass, Oaken Bucket, Spooner 10.00
Pressed Glass, Oasis, Creamer, Etched 25.50
Pressed Glass, Odd Fellows, Goblet 22.50
Pressed Glass, Old Abe, Compote, Frosted Eagle, 7 In. 165.00
Pressed Glass, Old Abe, Sugar, Covered, Frosted Eagle 135.00
Pressed Glass, Old State House, Philadelphia, Plate, Bread 90.00
Pressed Glass, Old State House, Philadelphia, Tray, Water, 12 In. 55.00

One Hundred, see 100
One Hundred One, see 101

Pressed Glass, Opalescent Swirl, Tumbler 20.00
Pressed Glass, Open Plaid, Creamer 15.00
Pressed Glass, Open Plaid, Goblet 10.00
Pressed Glass, Open Rose, Eggcup .... 17.50 To 18.50
Pressed Glass, Open Rose, Goblet 19.50
Pressed Glass, Open Rose, Relish 14.50
Pressed Glass, Open Rose, Spooner 18.50
Pressed Glass, Open Rose, Spooner, Flint 15.00
Pressed Glass, Open Rose, Tumbler 35.00
Pressed Glass, Opposing Pyramids, Saltshaker 7.50
Pressed Glass, Opposing Pyramids, Wine 9.50
Pressed Glass, Optic, Creamer, Green 22.50
Pressed Glass, Optic, Toothpick, Cobalt 38.00

Pressed Glass, Oval & Crossbar, Tumbler, Whiskey

Pressed Glass, Orange Peel, Goblet

Pressed Glass, Oval Miter, Salt, Footed

Pressed Glass, Optic, Water Set, Amethyst, Enamel Floral, 7 Piece 95.00
Pressed Glass, Orange Peel Band, Goblet 15.00
Oregon, see Beaded Loop, Skilton
Pressed Glass, Oriental Poppy, Tumbler, Blue, Northwood 22.00
Pressed Glass, Oriental Poppy, Tumbler, Green, Northwood 15.00
Pressed Glass, Oriental, Celery 37.50
Pressed Glass, Oriental, Tumbler 14.00
Orion, see Cathedral
Pressed Glass, Ostrich Looking At The Moon, Goblet 62.00
Pressed Glass, Oswego, Goblet 9.00
Oval Loop, see Question Mark
Pressed Glass, Oval Miter, Goblet 27.50
Pressed Glass, Oval Miter, Goblet, Flint 25.00
Pressed Glass, Oval Panels, Goblet, Amber 25.00
Pressed Glass, Oval Panels, Goblet, Flint 32.00
Pressed Glass, Oval Star, Butter, Child's 50.00
Pressed Glass, Oval Star, Butter, Child's, Covered 18.50
Pressed Glass, Oval Star, Creamer 9.50
Pressed Glass, Oval Star, Cup, Child's Punch 7.50
Pressed Glass, Oval Star, Pitcher, Child's Water .... 17.00 To 18.00
Pressed Glass, Oval Star, Punch Set, Child's, 5 Piece 50.00
Pressed Glass, Oval Star, Spooner, Child's 16.50
Pressed Glass, Oval Star, Sugar, Child's, Covered .... 11.50 To 18.50
Pressed Glass, Oval Star, Table Set, Child's, 3 Piece .... 26.00 To 40.00
Pressed Glass, Oval Star, Table Set, Child's, 4 Piece 50.00
Pressed Glass, Oval Star, Tumbler, Child's .... 7.50 To 9.00
Pressed Glass, Oval Star, Water Set, Child's, 7 Piece 75.00
Owl, see Bull's-eye & Diamond Point
Owl & Fan, see Parrot & Fan
Pressed Glass, Owl & Possum, Goblet 58.00
Pressed Glass, Owl & Pussy Cat, Dish, Cheese, Dome Cover 225.00
Pressed Glass, Paisley, Cup, Punch 7.50
Pressed Glass, Palm & Scroll, Bowl, Green, Opalescent, Ruffled Rim, 9 1/2 In. 35.00
Pressed Glass, Palm Beach, Pitcher, Water, Vaseline, Opalescent 165.00
Pressed Glass, Palm Beach, Spooner, Red Purple & Green Trim 85.00
Pressed Glass, Palm Beach, Sugar & Creamer, Cover, Red Purple & Green Trim 165.00
Pressed Glass, Palmette, Bottle, Castor, Shaker Top 10.50
Pressed Glass, Palmette, Celery 24.00
Pressed Glass, Palmette, Celery, Footed .... 18.75 To 28.00
Pressed Glass, Palmette, Creamer, Applied Handle 52.50
Pressed Glass, Palmette, Goblet 17.00
Pressed Glass, Palmette, Relish 7.50
Pressed Glass, Palmette, Salt, Master, Pedestal 15.00
Pressed Glass, Palmette, Sauce 6.50
Pressed Glass, Palmette, Tumbler, Footed 17.50

Pressed Glass, Palmette, Wine 20.00
Pressed Glass, Panel & Flute, Tumbler, Bar, Electric Blue 65.00
Pressed Glass, Panel & Rib, Sauce, Square, 3 3/4 In. 4.25
Pressed Glass, Panel & Star, Celery 16.50
Pressed Glass, Panel & Star, Celery, Electric Blue, C.1880, 7 In. 45.00
Pressed Glass, Paneled Acorn Band, Celery 55.00
Pressed Glass, Paneled Apple Blossom, Tumbler 13.50
Pressed Glass, Paneled Block, Compote, Blue, 6 X 6 In. 40.00
Pressed Glass, Paneled Cane & Rosette, Butter, Covered 32.50
Pressed Glass, Paneled Cane & Rosette, Creamer 21.50
Pressed Glass, Paneled Cane, Bowl, 8 1/2 In. 18.00
Pressed Glass, Paneled Cane, Butter, Covered 36.00
Pressed Glass, Paneled Cane, Goblet 18.00
Pressed Glass, Paneled Cane, Wine 13.50
Pressed Glass, Paneled Cherry, Butter & Thumbprint, Covered, Ruby Stained, N 65.00
Pressed Glass, Paneled Cherry, Butter, Green, Gold Trim, Northwood 72.00
Pressed Glass, Paneled Cherry, Creamer, Green, Gold Trim, Northwood 42.00
Pressed Glass, Paneled Cherry, Creamer, Northwood 25.00
Pressed Glass, Paneled Cherry, Fruit Bowl, Green, Gold Trim, Northwood 72.00
Pressed Glass, Paneled Cherry, Goblet 25.00
Pressed Glass, Paneled Cherry, Sugar, Green, Covered, Gold Trim, Northwood 45.00
Pressed Glass, Paneled Cherry, Tumbler, Northwood .... 10.00 To 12.50

Paneled Daisy & Button, see also Daisy & Button with Amber Panels

Pressed Glass, Paneled Daisy & Button, Celery 40.00
Pressed Glass, Paneled Daisy & Button, Goblet 12.50
Pressed Glass, Paneled Daisy & Button, Goblet, Flat Stem 23.50
Pressed Glass, Paneled Daisy & Button, Sauce, Octagonal 5.00
Pressed Glass, Paneled Daisy, Celery 24.00
Pressed Glass, Paneled Daisy, Mug 20.00
Pressed Glass, Paneled Daisy, Relish 18.00
Pressed Glass, Paneled Daisy, Relish, 7 X 5 In. 10.00
Pressed Glass, Paneled Daisy, Waste Bowl 20.00
Pressed Glass, Paneled Dewdrop, Celery 22.50
Pressed Glass, Paneled Dewdrop, Celery, Footed, Flint 36.00
Pressed Glass, Paneled Dewdrop, Cordial, 3 1/4 In. 21.50
Pressed Glass, Paneled Dewdrop, Goblet .... 12.50 To 15.00
Pressed Glass, Paneled Dewdrop, Pitcher, Milk 30.00
Pressed Glass, Paneled Dewdrop, Sugar & Creamer, Cover 35.00
Pressed Glass, Paneled Dewdrop, Wine .... 16.00 To 19.00
Pressed Glass, Paneled Diamond & Finecut, Butter, Covered 32.00
Pressed Glass, Paneled Diamond Cross, Celery 12.00
Pressed Glass, Paneled Diamond Cross, Creamer 9.50
Pressed Glass, Paneled Diamond Cross, Spooner 12.00
Pressed Glass, Paneled Diamond Cross, Sugar 5.50

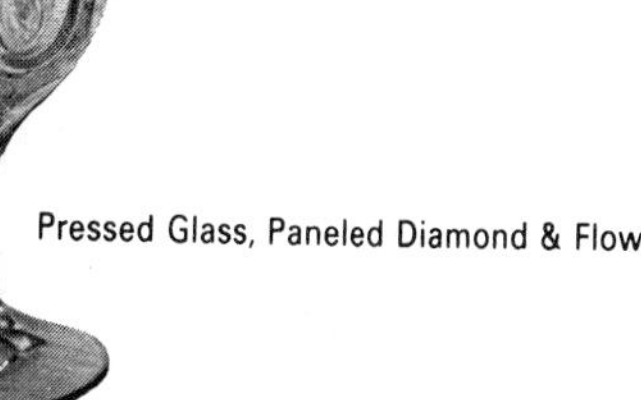

Pressed Glass, Paneled Diamond & Flowers, Goblet

Pressed Glass, Paneled Diamond Cross

Pressed Glass, Paneled Diamond Cut & Fan, Creamer 14.00
Pressed Glass, Paneled Diamond Point, Goblet 9.00
Pressed Glass, Paneled Diamond Point, Pitcher, Water 42.50
Pressed Glass, Paneled Diamond, Goblet .... 10.00 To 12.50
Pressed Glass, Paneled Fern, Goblet, Buttermilk, Flint 32.50
Pressed Glass, Paneled Forget-Me-Not, Block, Celery 18.00
Pressed Glass, Paneled Forget-Me-Not, Butter, Covered 27.00
Pressed Glass, Paneled Forget-Me-Not, Celery 34.00
Pressed Glass, Paneled Forget-Me-Not, Compote, Scalloped Rim, 7 In. 14.00
Pressed Glass, Paneled Forget-Me-Not, Compote, 8 3/4 In. 12.50
Pressed Glass, Paneled Forget-Me-Not, Compote, 10 In. 32.00
Pressed Glass, Paneled Forget-Me-Not, Creamer 21.50
Pressed Glass, Paneled Forget-Me-Not, Goblet 15.00
Pressed Glass, Paneled Forget-Me-Not, Jar, Jam, Covered 22.00
Pressed Glass, Paneled Forget-Me-Not, Pitcher, Footed, 8 In. 37.50
Pressed Glass, Paneled Forget-Me-Not, Pitcher, Milk 29.50
Pressed Glass, Paneled Forget-Me-Not, Pitcher, Water .... 24.00 To 38.00
Pressed Glass, Paneled Forget-Me-Not, Plate, Bread 22.00
Pressed Glass, Paneled Forget-Me-Not, Relish, Blue, Pear Shape 20.00
Pressed Glass, Paneled Forget-Me-Not, Sauce, Footed 10.00
Pressed Glass, Paneled Forget-Me-Not, Sauce, Footed, 4 In. 9.00
Pressed Glass, Paneled Forget-Me-Not, Sauce, Handled 4.50
Pressed Glass, Paneled Forget-Me-Not, Spooner, Blue, Opalescent, Northwood 58.00
Pressed Glass, Paneled Forget-Me-Not, Tumbler, Blue, Opalescent, Northwood 48.00
Pressed Glass, Paneled Forget-Me-Not, Tumbler, Green, Opalescent 25.00
Pressed Glass, Paneled Forget-Me-Not, Wine 49.00
Pressed Glass, Paneled Grape Band, Goblet, Flint 35.00
Pressed Glass, Paneled Grape With Thumbprint, Goblet 18.50
Pressed Glass, Paneled Grape, Butter, Red Tinted Grapes, Green Leaf, Gold 30.00
Pressed Glass, Paneled Grape, Compote, Covered, 11 X 8 In. 45.00
Pressed Glass, Paneled Grape, Cordial 22.00
Pressed Glass, Paneled Grape, Creamer .... 15.00 To 33.00
Pressed Glass, Paneled Grape, Goblet 15.00
Pressed Glass, Paneled Grape, Pitcher, Blue, 3 1/2 In. 18.00
Pressed Glass, Paneled Grape, Sugar, Covered 22.00
Pressed Glass, Paneled Grape, Water Set, 7 Piece 125.00
Pressed Glass, Paneled Grape, Wine .... 12.50 To 18.00
Pressed Glass, Paneled Heather, Goblet, Gold Trim 16.00
Pressed Glass, Paneled Heather, Wine 19.50
Pressed Glass, Paneled Herringbone, Butter, Footed, 1/2 Lb. 65.00
Pressed Glass, Paneled Hobnail, Plate, Toddy, Amber, 4 1/2 In. 13.75
Pressed Glass, Paneled Hobnail, Plate, Toddy, Blue, 4 1/2 In. 15.00
Pressed Glass, Paneled Holly, Berry Bowl, Gold Trim, Northwood 6.00
Pressed Glass, Paneled Holly, Berry Set, White, Opalescent, N, 3 Piece 150.00
Pressed Glass, Paneled Holly, Creamer, Blue, Opalescent 75.00
Pressed Glass, Paneled Holly, Tumbler, Green, Gold Trim, Greentown 42.00
Pressed Glass, Paneled Jewels, Celery 12.00
Pressed Glass, Paneled Jewels, Champagne 20.00
Pressed Glass, Paneled Jewels, Goblet .... 15.00 To 16.50
Pressed Glass, Paneled Jewels, Goblet, Sun Colored 16.00
Pressed Glass, Paneled Jewels, Wine, Vaseline 35.00
Pressed Glass, Paneled Long Jewels, Goblet 15.00
Pressed Glass, Paneled Nightshade, Celery .... 25.00 To 34.00
Pressed Glass, Paneled Ovals, Eggcup, Flint 30.00
Pressed Glass, Paneled Palm, Mug 10.00
Pressed Glass, Paneled Potted Flower, Goblet, C.1880 .... 18.00
Pressed Glass, Paneled Sage, Goblet 30.00
Pressed Glass, Paneled Sprig, Muffineer, Green & White Opaque, Metal Top 60.00

Paneled Star & Button, see Sedan
Paneled Stippled Bowl, see Stippled Band

Pressed Glass, Paneled Stippled Scroll, Creamer 8.50
Pressed Glass, Paneled Strawberry, Goblet 14.00
Pressed Glass, Paneled Sunflower, Goblet 15.00
Pressed Glass, Paneled Thistle, Berry Bowl 15.00
Pressed Glass, Paneled Thistle, Bowl, Bee Mark, 9 In. 24.50

Pressed Glass, Paneled Nightshade, Goblet

Pressed Glass, Paneled Wheat, Compote, Covered, 7 1/2 In.

Pressed Glass, Paneled Thistle, Bowl, Footed, 10 In. 18.00
Pressed Glass, Paneled Thistle, Bowl, 8 In. 15.75
Pressed Glass, Paneled Thistle, Bowl, 8 X 3 1/2 In. 15.75
Pressed Glass, Paneled Thistle, Butter, Covered 20.00
Pressed Glass, Paneled Thistle, Butter, Covered, Bee 30.00
Pressed Glass, Paneled Thistle, Cake Stand, Bee Mark, 9 3/4 In. 26.50
Pressed Glass, Paneled Thistle, Compote, Jelly, 6 In. 24.00
Pressed Glass, Paneled Thistle, Compote, 7 1/2 X 7 In. 32.50
Pressed Glass, Paneled Thistle, Nappy, Handled 15.00
Pressed Glass, Paneled Thistle, Plate, 8 In. 12.00
Pressed Glass, Paneled Thistle, Relish 15.00
Pressed Glass, Paneled Thistle, Relish, 8 1/4 In. 14.50
Pressed Glass, Paneled Thistle, Spooner .... 18.50 To 20.00
Pressed Glass, Paneled Thistle, Sugar & Creamer 15.00
Pressed Glass, Paneled Thistle, Vase, 6 1/2 In. 16.50
Pressed Glass, Paneled Thistle, Wine 15.00
Pressed Glass, Paneled Wee Blossoms, Pitcher, Milk 12.00
Pressed Glass, Paneled Wheat & Barley, Goblet 38.50
Pressed Glass, Paneled 44, Creamer, Silver Trim 16.50
Pressed Glass, Paneled 44, Spooner, Silver Trim 18.00
Pressed Glass, Paneled, Compote, Flint, 9 In. 29.00
Pressed Glass, Paneled, Dish, Candy, Molded Handle, 4 In. 4.00
Pressed Glass, Paneled, Forget-Me-Not, Toothpick, Emerald Green 17.00
Pressed Glass, Paneled, Tumbler, Green, Raised Poppy, Gold Trim 12.50
Pressed Glass, Pansy & Moss Rose, Creamer 17.50
Pressed Glass, Pansy & Moss Rose, Spooner 17.50
Pressed Glass, Pansy, Toothpick, Blue 40.00
Pressed Glass, Paris, Celery 18.00
Pressed Glass, Parrot & Fan, Wine 35.00
Pressed Glass, Parrot, Goblet .... 32.50 To 36.00
Pattee Cross, see Broughton
Pressed Glass, Pavonia, Celery .... 20.00 To 28.00
Pressed Glass, Pavonia, Cup Plate 12.50
Pressed Glass, Pavonia, Dish, Olive, Engraved Ivy & Berries 14.50
Pressed Glass, Pavonia, Dish, Olive, Engraved Leaves & Berries, Handle 14.50
Pressed Glass, Pavonia, Etched, Tumbler 12.50
Pressed Glass, Pavonia, Tumbler, Pineapple Stem 16.00
Pressed Glass, Pavonia, Tumbler, Ruby Stained Top 18.50
Pressed Glass, Peach, Creamer, Green, Northwood 45.00
Pressed Glass, Peach, Pitcher, Water, Emerald Green, Gold Trim, Northwood 75.00
Pressed Glass, Peach, Spooner, Green, Northwood 45.00
Pressed Glass, Peach, Sugar, Green, Covered, Northwood 65.00
Pressed Glass, Peach, Tumbler, Green, Northwood 35.00
Pressed Glass, Peach, Water Set, Green, Gold Trim, Northwood, 7 Piece 250.00
Pressed Glass, Peacock Feather, Butter 23.00
Pressed Glass, Peacock Feather, Fruit Set, 7 Piece 60.00

Pressed Glass, Parrot & Fan, Goblet

Pressed Glass, Pennsylvania, Goblet

Pressed Glass, Peacock Feather, Pitcher, Water .... 35.00 To 39.50
Pressed Glass, Peacock Feather, Relish 10.50
Pressed Glass, Peacock Feather, Sauce 6.50
Pressed Glass, Peacock Feather, Sauce, 6 1/2 In. 24.00
Peacock's Eye, see Peacock Feather
Pressed Glass, Pear, Butter, Covered .... 34.00 To 35.00
Pressed Glass, Pear, Sugar & Creamer, Green 35.00
Pressed Glass, Pearl & Flowers, Bowl, Blue, Opalescent, Footed, 9 1/2 In. 28.00
Pressed Glass, Pearl & Flowers, Bowl, Opalescent, Footed, 9 In. 24.00
Pressed Glass, Pearls & Scales, Compote, Blue, Opalescent, 7 In. 28.00
Peerless, see also Model Peerless
Pressed Glass, Peerless, Celery 27.00
Pressed Glass, Peerless, Pitcher, Water, Applied Handle, Flint 45.00
Pressed Glass, Peerless, Wine 9.50
Pressed Glass, Peerless, Wine, Model 10.50
Pennsylvania, see Balder, Pennsylvania Hand
Pennsylvania Hand, see also Balder
Pressed Glass, Pennsylvania Hand, Celery 35.00
Pressed Glass, Pennsylvania Hand, Jar, Jam, Covered 38.00
Pressed Glass, Pennsylvania Hand, Jar, Jam, Hand Cover 45.00
Pressed Glass, Pennsylvania Hand, Salt & Pepper, Frosted, 3 In. 55.00
Pressed Glass, Pennsylvania Hand, Saltshaker 10.00
Pressed Glass, Pennsylvania Hand, Sugar & Creamer, Child's, 2 1/2 In. 32.00
Pressed Glass, Pennsylvania Hand, Wine 12.00
Pressed Glass, Pequot, Compote, Scalloped, 7 1/2 In. 65.00
Pressed Glass, Pequot, Fruit Bowl, Scalloped, Footed, 4 In. 35.00
Pressed Glass, Pequot, Goblet 42.00
Pressed Glass, Pequot, Sauce 15.00
Pressed Glass, Petal & Loop, Bowl, Shallow, Flint, 7 1/2 In. 32.00
Pressed Glass, Petal & Loop, Bowl, 12 1/4 In. 125.00
Pressed Glass, Petticoat, Creamer, Ruby Stained, Etched 45.00
Pressed Glass, Picket Band, Goblet 20.00
Pressed Glass, Picket, Compote, High Standard, 8 In. 31.50
Pressed Glass, Picket, Compote, Jelly .... 19.50 To 24.50
Pressed Glass, Picket, Dish, Pickle, Covered 24.50
Pillar & Bull's-eye, see Thistle
Pressed Glass, Pillar, Bottle, Bar, 7 In. 23.00
Pressed Glass, Pillar, Goblet, Flint 38.00
Pressed Glass, Pillar, Goblet, Flint, C.1840 .... 50.00
Pressed Glass, Pillow & Sunburst, Sugar & Creamer 40.00
Pressed Glass, Pillow & Sunburst, Sugar & Creamer, Westmoreland 28.00
Pressed Glass, Pillow Encircled, Celery, Ruby Stained 40.00
Pressed Glass, Pillow Encircled, Spooner, Ruby Stained 25.00
Pressed Glass, Pillow Encircled, Sugar, Ruby Stained, Covered 65.00
Pressed Glass, Pillow Encircled, Sugar, Ruby Stained, Covered, 6 3/4 In. 35.00
Pressed Glass, Pillow Encircled, Tankard, Water, Ruby Stained 110.00

Pressed Glass, Pillow Encircled, Tankard, 11 1/2 In. 28.50
Pressed Glass, Pillow Encircled, Tumbler, Ruby Stained 18.50
Pinafore, see Actress
Pressed Glass, Pineapple & Fan, Compote, Jelly 25.00
Pressed Glass, Pineapple & Fan, Finger Bowl 8.00
Pressed Glass, Pineapple & Fan, Tankard, Milk, 7 1/2 In. 30.00
Pressed Glass, Pineapple & Fan, Tankard, Water, 9 In. 35.00
Pressed Glass, Pineapple & Fan, Toothpick 20.00
Pressed Glass, Pineapple & Fan, Waste Bowl .... 8.00 To 12.50
Pressed Glass, Pineapple, Creamer 15.00
Pressed Glass, Pinwheel, Cake Stand, Emerald Green, 9 In. 30.00
Pressed Glass, Pinwheel, Goblet 12.50
Pressed Glass, Pitcairn, Goblet 8.00
Pressed Glass, Pittsburgh Flute, Tumbler, Bar, Deep Purple, Flint 85.00
Pressed Glass, Pittsburgh, Goblet 75.00
Pressed Glass, Plaid, Plate, 6 In. 25.00
Plain Smocking, see Smocking
Pressed Glass, Pleat & Panel, Butter Pat .... 20.00 To 25.00
Pressed Glass, Pleat & Panel, Cake Stand, 8 In. 21.50
Pressed Glass, Pleat & Panel, Celery .... 25.00 To 27.00
Pressed Glass, Pleat & Panel, Creamer 22.50
Pressed Glass, Pleat & Panel, Plate, Bread 18.50
Pressed Glass, Pleat & Panel, Plate, 5 In. 20.00
Pressed Glass, Pleat & Panel, Plate, 6 In. 16.00
Pressed Glass, Pleat & Panel, Plate, 7 In. 10.00
Pressed Glass, Pleat & Panel, Spooner .... 12.00 To 18.00
Pressed Glass, Pleat & Panel, Sugar 22.50
Pressed Glass, Pleated Bands, Goblet 12.50
Pressed Glass, Plume, Berry Bowl 20.00
Pressed Glass, Plume, Butter, Covered 25.00
Pressed Glass, Plume, Cake Stand, 7 In. 27.50
Pressed Glass, Plume, Celery 22.50
Pressed Glass, Plume, Compote, 7 In. 22.00
Pressed Glass, Plume, Compote, 8 In. 18.00
Pressed Glass, Plume, Creamer 18.50
Pressed Glass, Plume, Sauce 6.00
Pressed Glass, Plume, Sauce, Flint 18.00
Pressed Glass, Plume, Sauce, Opalescent, Flint 75.00
Pressed Glass, Plume, Sauce, Ruby Stained 7.00
Pressed Glass, Plume, Spooner 16.00
Pressed Glass, Plume, Sugar 17.00
Pressed Glass, Plume, Tumbler 12.00
Pressed Glass, Plume, Tumbler, Etched 12.00
Pressed Glass, Plume, Waste Bowl 27.00
Pressed Glass, Pogo Stick, Bowl, Footed, 9 In. 20.00
Pressed Glass, Poinsettia, Tankard, Water, Blue, Opalescent 135.00
Pressed Glass, Pointed Cube, Tumbler 10.00
Pressed Glass, Pointed Hobnail, Berry Bowl, Electric Blue, Fan Top, 8 In. 35.00

Pressed Glass, Pleat & Panel, Bowl

Pressed Glass, Pleat Band, Compote, Covered

Pressed Glass, Pointed Hobnail, Creamer, Blue 40.00
Pressed Glass, Pointed Hobnail, Sugar, Blue 50.00
Pressed Glass, Pointed Hobnail, Tumbler, Amber, 7 Rows 18.00
Pressed Glass, Pointed Hobnail, Tumbler, 7 Rows 15.00
Pressed Glass, Pointed Hobnial, Salt & Pepper 15.00
Pointed Paneled Daisy & Button, see Queen
Pointed Thumbprint, see Almond Thumbprint
Pressed Glass, Polar Bear, Pitcher, Water 195.00
Pressed Glass, Polar Bear, Waste Bowl, Frosted 38.00
Pressed Glass, Popcorn With Ears, Creamer .... 26.50 To 42.00
Pressed Glass, Popcorn, Creamer 20.00
Pressed Glass, Pope Leo, Plate, Bread 20.00
Portland with Diamond Point Band, see Galloway, Virginia
Pressed Glass, Portland, Compote, Covered, 10 X 6 1/4 In. 28.00
Pressed Glass, Portland, Compote, 9 X 7 1/2 In. 30.00
Pressed Glass, Portland, Muffineer 25.00
Pressed Glass, Portland, Sauce, Gold Trim 6.50
Pressed Glass, Portland, Sugar 19.00
Pressed Glass, Portland, Sugar, Covered, Gold On Panels 23.50
Pressed Glass, Portland, Toothpick .... 12.00 To 13.50
Pressed Glass, Portland, Tumbler .... 10.00 To 12.50
Pressed Glass, Portland, Vase, 6 In. 10.50
Pressed Glass, Portland, Wine .... 15.00 To 18.00
Pressed Glass, Post, Goblet 18.50
Pressed Glass, Post, Goblet, Etched 30.00
Potted Plant, see Flowerpot
Pressed Glass, Powder & Shot, Creamer, Applied Handle 45.00
Pressed Glass, Powder & Shot, Goblet, Flint .... 45.00 To 48.00
Pressed Glass, Powder & Shot, Spooner 25.00
Pressed Glass, Powder & Shot, Spooner, Flint 35.00
Prayer Rug, see Horseshoe
Pressed Glass, Pres Cut, Punch Bowl & Base, 15 In. 62.50
Pressed Glass, Pres Cut, Relish, Oval, 8 In. 12.00
Pressed Glass, Pressed Block, Compote, Flint, 6 1/2 In. 65.00
Pressed Glass, Pressed Block, Compote, High Hexagonal Base, Flint, 10 In. 85.00
Pressed Glass, Pressed Block, Compote, 7 In. 100.00
Pressed Glass, Pressed Diamond, Bowl, Amber, Covered, 7 1/2 In. 39.50
Pressed Glass, Pressed Diamond, Cake Stand, Amber, 9 1/2 In. 30.00
Pressed Glass, Pressed Diamond, Celery 22.50
Pressed Glass, Pressed Diamond, Compote, Vaseline, 9 3/4 In. 125.00
Pressed Glass, Pressed Diamond, Condiment Set, Child's, 4 Piece 26.00
Pressed Glass, Pressed Diamond, Pitcher, Water, Blue 55.00
Pressed Glass, Pressed Diamond, Tumbler, Blue 18.50
Pressed Glass, Pressed Diamond, Waste Bowl 15.00
Pressed Glass, Pressed Leaf With Chain, Goblet 12.50
Pressed Glass, Pressed Leaf, Cordial 18.50
Pressed Glass, Pressed Leaf, Eggcup, Flint 16.00
Pressed Glass, Pressed Leaf, Goblet .... 16.00 To 18.50
Pressed Glass, Pressed Leaf, Goblet, Flint 24.00
Pressed Glass, Pressed Leaf, Salt, Master, Flint 16.50
Pressed Glass, Pressed Leaf, Spooner .... 18.00 To 20.00
Pressed Glass, Pressed Leaf, Spooner, Flint .... 18.50 To 20.00
Pressed Glass, Primrose, Pitcher, Milk 30.00
Pressed Glass, Primrose, Plate, Card, Blue, 4 1/2 In. 16.50
Pressed Glass, Primrose, Sugar 21.00
Pressed Glass, Primrose, Sugar, Covered 22.00
Pressed Glass, Primrose, Tray, Water, 11 In. 16.00
Pressed Glass, Primrose, Wine, Stippled 16.00
Princess Feather, see also Lacy Medallion
Pressed Glass, Princess Feather, Celery .... 27.00 To 39.50
Pressed Glass, Princess Feather, Goblet 15.00
Pressed Glass, Princess Feather, Relish 10.50
Pressed Glass, Princess Feather, Spooner, Flint .... 18.00 To 20.00
Pressed Glass, Printed Hobnail, Goblet 10.00
Pressed Glass, Printed Hobnail, Tumbler, Amber 17.00

Pressed Glass, Primrose, Pitcher, 7 In.

Pressed Glass, Princess Feather, Spooner

Pressed Glass, Princess Feather, Tazza

Pressed Glass, Prism With Diamond Point, Salt, Master

Pressed Glass, Printed Hobnail, Water Set, Amber, 5 Piece 95.00
Pressed Glass, Priscilla, Cake Stand, 10 In. 32.00
Pressed Glass, Priscilla, Compote, Jelly, Covered, 7 In., Pair 55.00
Pressed Glass, Priscilla, Compote, Scalloped Rim, 6 X 4 In. 22.00
Pressed Glass, Priscilla, Compote, 7 In. 47.50
Pressed Glass, Priscilla, Flower Bowl, Square, 8 X 3 1/2 In. 50.00
Pressed Glass, Priscilla, Fruit Bowl 15.00
Pressed Glass, Priscilla, Fruit Set, 7 Piece 150.00
Pressed Glass, Priscilla, Spooner 21.50
Pressed Glass, Priscilla, Sugar & Creamer, Individual, Cover 37.50
Pressed Glass, Priscilla, Wine 24.50
Pressed Glass, Prism & Clear Panels, Wine 7.50
Pressed Glass, Prism & Daisy Bar, Goblet 12.50
Pressed Glass, Prism & Flattened Sawtooth, Goblet, Flint 40.00
Pressed Glass, Prism & Flute, Wine 10.00
Pressed Glass, Prism & Sawtooth, Celery, Flint 40.00
Pressed Glass, Prism & Sawtooth, Goblet, Flint 24.00
Pressed Glass, Prism Arc, Pitcher, Milk 23.50
Pressed Glass, Prism With Diamond Point, Pitcher, 6 1/2 In. 55.00
Pressed Glass, Prism With Loops, Goblet 9.50
Pressed Glass, Prism, Champagne, Rayed Base, Flint 34.00
Pressed Glass, Prism, Goblet, Flint 35.00
Pressed Glass, Prism, Goblet, Rayed Base, Flint 22.00
Pressed Glass, Prism, Sugar 12.00
Pressed Glass, Prism, Tankard, Water 15.00
Pressed Glass, Prisms & Hexagons, Sauce 6.50
Pressed Glass, Prize, Cup 3.75
Pressed Glass, Prize, Toothpick, Gold Trim 18.00
Pressed Glass, Proxy Ashburton, Goblet, Flint 55.00

Pressed Glass, Punty, Syrup, Opalescent

Pressed Glass, Viking, Compote, Covered

Pressed Glass, Psyche & Cupid, Celery 30.00
Pressed Glass, Psyche & Cupid, Creamer 30.00
Pressed Glass, Psyche & Cupid, Goblet 32.50
Pressed Glass, Psyche & Cupid, Pitcher, Water 47.50
Pressed Glass, Psyche & Cupid, Spooner 17.50
Pressed Glass, Psyche & Cupid, Sugar ..... 25.00 To 35.00
Pressed Glass, Psyche & Cupid, Sugar, Covered 40.00
Pressed Glass, Punty Band, Goblet, Etched 10.00
Pressed Glass, Punty, Spill, Moss Green, 5 In. 650.00
Pressed Glass, Pyramid, Tumbler, Blue 22.00
Pressed Glass, Quaker Lady, Goblet, Findlay 35.00
Pressed Glass, Quaker Lady, Waste Bowl 20.00
Queen Anne, see Viking
Pressed Glass, Queen, Compote, Covered, 10 X 7 In. 30.00
Pressed Glass, Queen, Goblet 12.50
Pressed Glass, Queen, Goblet, Amber 24.00
Pressed Glass, Queen, Goblet, Green 25.00
Pressed Glass, Queen, Pitcher, Water, Amber 45.00
Pressed Glass, Queen, Spooner, Amber 20.00
Pressed Glass, Queen, Wine 14.00
Queen's Necklace, see also Crown Jewels
Pressed Glass, Queen's Necklace, Bottle, Dresser, 6 1/2 In. 37.50
Pressed Glass, Question Mark, Bonbon, Marigold, Opalescent Edge 20.00
Pressed Glass, Quilted Phlox, Saltshaker, Light Blue 25.00
Pressed Glass, Quixote, Creamer 8.50
Pressed Glass, Rabbit In Tree, Toothpick 20.00
Pressed Glass, Rabbit Tracks, Goblet 17.50
Pressed Glass, Rail Fence, Goblet 10.00
Pressed Glass, Railroad Train, Plate, Bread 75.00
Pressed Glass, Rain & Dewdrop, Cordial 35.00
Pressed Glass, Rainbow, Saltshaker 6.50
Pressed Glass, Rainbow, Tray, Water, McKee, 1894 ..... 18.00
Pressed Glass, Raindrop, Pitcher, Water, Opalescent 58.00
Pressed Glass, Raindrop, Plate, Amber, 11 In. 18.50
Pressed Glass, Ramsay Grape, Compote, Covered, High Standard, Skirted, 7 In. 45.00
Pressed Glass, Ramsay Grape, Goblet 15.00
Pressed Glass, Rayed Flower, Wine ..... 8.50 To 9.00
Pressed Glass, Rayed Pineapple, Punch Bowl & Base 40.00
Pressed Glass, Reaper, Platter, Handled, 13 X 8 In. 75.00
Pressed Glass, Red Block, Berry Bowl 15.00
Pressed Glass, Red Block, Cup, Punch 15.00
Pressed Glass, Red Block, Goblet 32.00
Pressed Glass, Red Block, Mug, Ruby Stained 35.00
Pressed Glass, Red Block, Spooner 32.00
Pressed Glass, Red Block, Sugar & Creamer 75.00

Pressed Glass, Red Block, Sugar, Covered .... 41.00 To 42.50
Pressed Glass, Red Block, Sugar, Ruby Stained 48.00
Pressed Glass, Red Block, Tumbler .... 25.00 To 27.00
Pressed Glass, Red Block, Tumbler, Ruby Stained, 3 3/4 In. 25.00
Pressed Glass, Red Block, Tumbler, 2 Rows Of Blocks 28.00
Pressed Glass, Red Riding Hood, Pitcher, Child's Water 58.00
Regal, see Paneled Forget-Me-Not
Pressed Glass, Reverse Swirl, Bottle, Water, Vaseline, Opalescent 95.00
Pressed Glass, Reverse Swirl, Bowl, Canary, 4 1/2 In. 18.00
Pressed Glass, Reverse Swirl, Pitcher, Vaseline, Opalescent, 5 1/2 In. 65.00
Pressed Glass, Reverse Swirl, Sugar, Opalescent, Covered 42.00
Pressed Glass, Reverse Swirl, Toothpick, Opalescent, Satin 35.00
Pressed Glass, Reverse Torpedo, Banana Stand, High Standard 95.00
Pressed Glass, Reverse Torpedo, Cake Stand 85.00
Pressed Glass, Reverse Torpedo, Compote, Turned-Over Rim, 8 3/4 In. 60.00
Pressed Glass, Reverse Torpedo, Sugar, Covered 50.00
Pressed Glass, Reverse 44, Berry Bowl 5.00
Pressed Glass, Reverse 44, Goblet, Pink & Gold Trim 18.00
Pressed Glass, Rexford, Creamer, Child's 12.00
Pressed Glass, Rexford, Muffineer, Blue, Opalescent 95.00
Pressed Glass, Rexford, Table Set, Miniature, 4 Piece 65.00
Pressed Glass, Rib Bands, Butter, Ruby Stained, Covered 52.00
Pressed Glass, Rib, Muffineer, Blue, Opalescent, Beatty 65.00
Pressed Glass, Ribbed Block, Goblet 7.50
Pressed Glass, Ribbed Forget-Me-Not, Creamer .... 14.00 To 14.50
Pressed Glass, Ribbed Grape, Creamer, Flint 85.00
Pressed Glass, Ribbed Grape, Goblet, Flint 45.00
Pressed Glass, Ribbed Grape, Plate, 6 In. 32.00
Pressed Glass, Ribbed Ivy With Bull's-Eye, Salt, Master, Footed, Flint 33.00
Pressed Glass, Ribbed Ivy, Butter, Covered, Flint .... 48.00 To 95.00
Pressed Glass, Ribbed Ivy, Compote, Flint, 6 In. 35.00
Pressed Glass, Ribbed Ivy, Compote, Inverted Bell-Shaped Bowl, Flint, 9 In. 195.00
Pressed Glass, Ribbed Ivy, Compote, Low Standard, Scalloped, Flint, 8 In. 57.00
Pressed Glass, Ribbed Ivy, Creamer, Applied Handle, Flint 165.00
Pressed Glass, Ribbed Ivy, Eggcup .... 25.00 To 35.00
Pressed Glass, Ribbed Ivy, Eggcup, Flint 25.00
Pressed Glass, Ribbed Ivy, Goblet, Flint 28.00
Pressed Glass, Ribbed Ivy, Salt, Master, Covered, Flint 115.00
Pressed Glass, Ribbed Ivy, Sauce, Flint 10.00
Pressed Glass, Ribbed Ivy, Spooner, Scalloped Rim, Flint 28.50
Pressed Glass, Ribbed Ivy, Sugar, Covered, Scalloped Flange, Flint 85.00
Pressed Glass, Ribbed Ivy, Sugar, Scalloped Top 25.00
Pressed Glass, Ribbed Ivy, Tumbler, Bar, Flint 70.00
Pressed Glass, Ribbed Ivy, Tumbler, Water, Flint 75.00
Pressed Glass, Ribbed Ivy, Tumbler, Whiskey 50.00
Pressed Glass, Ribbed Ivy, Tumbler, Whiskey, Flint 52.50
Pressed Glass, Ribbed Lattice, Celery, Blue, Opalescent 49.00

Pressed Glass, Rexford, Goblet

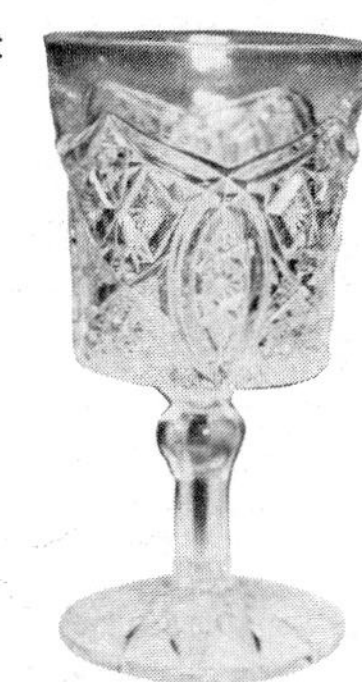

Pressed Glass, Ribbon, Etched, Goblet

Pressed Glass, Roman Cross, Goblet

Pressed Glass, Robin, Mug, Blue

Pressed Glass, Ribbed Lattice, Muffineer, Blue, Opalescent 65.00
Pressed Glass, Ribbed Lattice, Toothpick, Opalescent 35.00
Ribbed Leaf, see Bellflower
Pressed Glass, Ribbed Loop, Goblet, Flint 35.00
Ribbed Opal, see Beatty Rib
Pressed Glass, Ribbed Palm, Bottle, Castor, Mustard, Shaker 12.50
Pressed Glass, Ribbed Palm, Eggcup 26.50
Pressed Glass, Ribbed Palm, Eggcup, Flint 25.00
Pressed Glass, Ribbed Palm, Goblet 26.50
Pressed Glass, Ribbed Palm, Goblet, Flint 27.50
Pressed Glass, Ribbed Palm, Plate, 6 In. 48.50
Pressed Glass, Ribbed Palm, Salt, Master, Footed 25.00
Pressed Glass, Ribbed Palm, Spill, Flint 22.00
Pressed Glass, Ribbed Palm, Spooner, Flint .... 18.00 To 22.00
Pressed Glass, Ribbed Palm, Spooner, Flint, 6 In. 30.00
Pressed Glass, Ribbed Palm, Sugar, Flint 35.00
Pressed Glass, Ribbed Pillar, Toothpick, Pink & White 37.50
Ribbed Pineapple, see Prism & Flattened Sawtooth
Pressed Glass, Ribbed Scroll, Muffineer, Green, Gillinder 50.00
Pressed Glass, Ribbed Spiral, Berry Bowl, Vaseline, Opalescent 45.00
Pressed Glass, Ribbed Spiral, Bowl, Blue, 7 X 6 1/2 X 3 In. 34.00
Pressed Glass, Ribbed Spiral, Bowl, Vaseline, Opalescent, Ruffled, 8 1/2 In. 37.50
Pressed Glass, Ribbed Spiral, Bowl, Vaseline, Opalescent, 8 In. 25.00
Pressed Glass, Ribbed Spiral, Celery, Blue, Opalescent, Beatty 68.00
Pressed Glass, Ribbed Spiral, Cup & Saucer, Ruby Stained, Opalescent 60.00
Pressed Glass, Ribbed Spiral, Sauce, Blue, Opalescent 18.00
Pressed Glass, Ribbed Spiral, Spooner, Blue, Opalescent 60.00
Pressed Glass, Ribbed Spiral, Tumbler, Blue, Opalescent 25.00
Pressed Glass, Ribbed Spiral, Vase, Vaseline, Opalescent, 9 3/4 In. 32.50
Pressed Glass, Ribbed Stars, Compote, Frosted, 7 In. 14.50
Pressed Glass, Ribbed Swirl, Creamer, Opalescent, Beatty 25.00
Pressed Glass, Ribbed Swirl, Tumbler, Opalescent & Clear 26.50
Pressed Glass, Ribbed, Creamer 20.00
Pressed Glass, Ribbed, Creamer, Opalescent, Flint, 3 In. 25.00
Pressed Glass, Ribbed, Dish, Amber, Opalescent, Divided, 6 1/4 X 2 1/2 In. 7.00
Pressed Glass, Ribbed, Vase, Vaseline, Opalescent, Victorian, 7 In. 25.00
Pressed Glass, Ribbon Candy, Cake Stand, Flint 25.00

Pressed Glass, Roman Rosette, Sugar & Creamer

Pressed Glass, Rose In Snow, Goblet

Pressed Glass, Ribbon Candy, Cake Stand, 9 1/2 In. 25.00
Pressed Glass, Ribbon Candy, Creamer 14.00
Pressed Glass, Ribbon Candy, Dish, Honey, 3 In. 5.75
Pressed Glass, Ribbon Candy, Relish .... 7.00 To 10.00
Pressed Glass, Ribbon, Celery, Footed, Flint 28.00
Pressed Glass, Ribbon, Compote, Covered, Low Standard, 7 In. 27.50
Pressed Glass, Ribbon, Compote, Dolphin Stem, Frosted Base, 8 1/4 In. 125.00
Pressed Glass, Ribbon, Compote, Frosted Stem & Base, 10 1/2 In. 145.00
Pressed Glass, Ribbon, Jar, Jam, Frosted, Covered 35.00
Pressed Glass, Ribbon, Sugar 20.00
Pressed Glass, Ribbon, Table Set, 4 Piece 105.00
Pressed Glass, Ribbon, Waste Bowl 20.00
Pressed Glass, Ribs & Diamonds, Goblet 12.50
Ripple Band, see Ripple
Pressed Glass, Ripple, Eggcup 15.00
Pressed Glass, Ripple, Spooner 12.00
Pressed Glass, Rising Sun, Goblet, Purple & Clear 22.00
Pressed Glass, Rising Sun, Toothpick, Gold Sun 18.00
Pressed Glass, Roanoke Star, Goblet 12.50
Pressed Glass, Roanoke, Berry Bowl 4.00
Pressed Glass, Robin Hood, Spooner 18.50
Pressed Glass, Robin, Mug, Blue, Squared Handle 19.00
Rochelle, see Princess Feather
Pressed Glass, Rock Crystal, Bowl, 7 1/2 In. 10.00
Pressed Glass, Rock Crystal, Bowl, 9 In. 6.00
Pressed Glass, Rock Crystal, Creamer, Amber, McKee 22.50
Pressed Glass, Rock Of Ages, Plate, Bread 48.00
Pressed Glass, Roman Key, Celery, Flint 58.00
Pressed Glass, Roman Key, Creamer, U.S.Glass Co. 65.00
Pressed Glass, Roman Key, Eggcup, Flint 24.50
Pressed Glass, Roman Key, Goblet, Flint .... 30.00 To 42.00
Pressed Glass, Roman Key, Spooner, U.S.Glass Co. 65.00
Pressed Glass, Roman Key, Sugar, Covered, U.S.Glass Co. 85.00
Pressed Glass, Roman Rosette, Bowl, Lacy, 5 1/2 In. 10.00
Pressed Glass, Roman Rosette, Bowl, Lacy, 6 1/2 In. 48.00
Pressed Glass, Roman Rosette, Cake Stand 52.00
Pressed Glass, Roman Rosette, Compote, Covered, 6 In. 39.00
Pressed Glass, Roman Rosette, Creamer 18.00
Pressed Glass, Roman Rosette, Dish, Pickle, Oval 20.00
Pressed Glass, Roman Rosette, Goblet 16.00
Pressed Glass, Roman Rosette, Mug 15.00
Pressed Glass, Roman Rosette, Plate, Bread 24.00
Pressed Glass, Roman Rosette, Plate, 7 1/2 In. 35.00
Pressed Glass, Roman Rosette, Spooner 15.00
Pressed Glass, Roman Rosette, Sugar, Covered 32.00
Pressed Glass, Roman Rosette, Wine 25.00

Pressed Glass, Royal, Butter, Covered

Pressed Glass, Rose Sprig, Goblet

Pressed Glass, Romeo, Goblet 10.00
Rope Bands, see Clear Panels with Cord Band
Pressed Glass, Rope With Thumbprint, Syrup, Amber 65.00
Pressed Glass, Rose In Snow, Compote, Covered, 9 X 6 In. 110.00
Pressed Glass, Rose In Snow, Compote, Low Standard, 7 X 4 1/2 In. 55.00
Pressed Glass, Rose In Snow, Compote, 6 In. 17.50
Pressed Glass, Rose In Snow, Creamer 45.00
Pressed Glass, Rose In Snow, Creamer, Square 25.00
Pressed Glass, Rose In Snow, Dish, Pickle 18.50
Pressed Glass, Rose In Snow, Dish, Pickle, Blue, Oval, 8 1/4 In. 55.00
Pressed Glass, Rose In Snow, Dish, Pickle, Handles, Oval, 8 1/2 In. 36.00
Pressed Glass, Rose In Snow, Dish, Pickle, Oval, 8 1/4 In. 25.00
Pressed Glass, Rose In Snow, Goblet, Amber 30.00
Pressed Glass, Rose In Snow, Goblet, Vaseline 30.00
Pressed Glass, Rose In Snow, Jar, Jam, Covered 75.00
Pressed Glass, Rose In Snow, Pitcher, Water, Applied Handle 85.00
Pressed Glass, Rose In Snow, Plate, Bread 20.00
Pressed Glass, Rose In Snow, Plate, 7 In. .... 22.50 To 26.00
Pressed Glass, Rose In Snow, Plate, 7 1/4 In. 24.00
Pressed Glass, Rose In Snow, Sauce .... 6.00 To 7.50
Pressed Glass, Rose In Snow, Sauce, Footed, 4 In. .... 12.50 To 16.50
Pressed Glass, Rose In Snow, Sauce, 4 In. .... 7.00 To 14.00
Pressed Glass, Rose In Snow, Spooner 25.00
Pressed Glass, Rose In Snow, Spooner, Square 48.00
Pressed Glass, Rose In Snow, Sugar, Covered, Square 25.00
Pressed Glass, Rose In Snow, Sugar, Square 20.00
Pressed Glass, Rose Sprig, Cake Stand, 9 1/4 In. 29.50
Pressed Glass, Rose Sprig, Creamer, Vaseline 45.00
Pressed Glass, Rose Sprig, Nappy, Handled 7.00
Pressed Glass, Rose Sprig, Pitcher, Milk, Amber 32.50
Pressed Glass, Rose Sprig, Pitcher, Water 45.00
Pressed Glass, Rose Sprig, Relish, 6 X 4 In. 10.00
Pressed Glass, Rose Sprig, Sauce, Footed 7.50
Pressed Glass, Rose Sprig, Sleigh, Amber, 6 X 4 In. 45.00
Pressed Glass, Rose Sprig, Tumbler 29.50
Pressed Glass, Rose, Spooner 10.00
Pressed Glass, Rosette Band, Celery 24.50
Pressed Glass, Rosette Band, Compote, Jelly 15.00
Pressed Glass, Rosette Band, Compote, Twisted Finial & Stem, 12 1/2 In. 95.00
Rosette Medallion, see Feather Duster
Pressed Glass, Rosette Pinwheel, Berry Set, Footed, 7 Piece 45.00
Pressed Glass, Rosette Pinwheel, Creamer 14.50
Pressed Glass, Rosette Pinwheel, Sugar 14.50
Pressed Glass, Rosette With Palm, Compote, Jelly, Covered, 6 In. 28.00
Pressed Glass, Rosette With Palms, Celery 19.00
Pressed Glass, Rosette With Palms, Compote, Covered, 7 In. 48.00
Pressed Glass, Rosette, Cake Stand, 9 In. 15.00

Pressed Glass, Rosette, Compote, Jelly 13.50
Pressed Glass, Rosette, Compote, Jelly, Open Stem 15.00
Pressed Glass, Rosette, Pitcher, Milk 25.00
Pressed Glass, Rosette, Pitcher, Water .... 25.00 To 35.00
Pressed Glass, Rosette, Plate, Cake, Stemmed, 8 1/2 In. 18.00
Pressed Glass, Rosette, Plate, Handled, 9 1/4 In. 17.50
Pressed Glass, Round Thumbprint, Tumbler, Bar 45.00
Pressed Glass, Royal Crystal, Butter, Clear Knob Finial, Ruby Border 55.00
Pressed Glass, Royal Crystal, Butter, Covered 55.00
Pressed Glass, Royal Crystal, Butter, Ruby Stained 85.00
Pressed Glass, Royal Crystal, Cake Stand 22.50
Pressed Glass, Royal Crystal, Celery 19.00
Pressed Glass, Royal Crystal, Creamer 15.00
Pressed Glass, Royal Crystal, Creamer, 3 In. 16.50
Pressed Glass, Royal Crystal, Jar, Cracker 45.00
Pressed Glass, Royal Crystal, Pitcher, Water, Ruby Stained, Bulbous 125.00
Pressed Glass, Royal Crystal, Salt & Pepper, Ruby Stained 85.00
Pressed Glass, Royal Crystal, Spooner, Ruby Stained .... 30.00 To 32.50
Pressed Glass, Royal Crystal, Spooner, Ruby Stained Top, 4 1/2 In. 38.00
Pressed Glass, Royal Crystal, Spooner, Ruby Stained, 4 1/2 In. 30.00
Pressed Glass, Royal Crystal, Sugar, Covered, Ruby Stained .... 55.00 To 85.00
Pressed Glass, Royal Crystal, Syrup 30.00
Pressed Glass, Royal Crystal, Table Set, Ruby Stained, 4 Piece 250.00
Pressed Glass, Royal Lady, Sugar & Creamer, Cover, Belmont 50.00
Pressed Glass, Royal Oak, Berry Bowl, Frosted, Rubena, 4 In. 16.00
Pressed Glass, Royal Oak, Pitcher, Water, Frosted, Rubena 200.00
Pressed Glass, Royal Oak, Saltshaker, Cranberry To Clear 40.00
Pressed Glass, Royal Oak, Spooner, Cranberry & Frosted 110.00
Pressed Glass, Royal Oak, Sugar Sifter, Frosted Cranberry To Clear 135.00
Pressed Glass, Royal Oak, Sugar, Covered, Rubena 95.00
Pressed Glass, Royal, Sugar, 3 Footed 25.00

Ruby Rosette, see Pillow Encircled
Ruby Thumbprint, see King's Crown

Pressed Glass, Ruffles & Rings, Bowl, Opalescent, 3 Footed, 8 In. 20.00
Pressed Glass, S Repeat, Berry Set, Blue, Gold Trim, 7 Piece 165.00
Pressed Glass, S Repeat, Condiment Set, Apple Green, 5 Piece 195.00
Pressed Glass, S Repeat, Cruet, Wine, Sapphire Blue, Gold Trim 125.00
Pressed Glass, S Repeat, Tray, Condiment, Apple Green 35.00
Pressed Glass, S Repeat, Tumbler, Blue, Opalescent 35.00
Pressed Glass, S Repeat, Wine, Blue 25.00
Pressed Glass, Salt & Pepper 15.00
Pressed Glass, Sandwich Ivy, Sugar & Creamer, Lump Sugar Type Sugar 135.00
Pressed Glass, Sandwich Ivy, Toothpick 48.00

Sandwich Loop, see Hairpin

Pressed Glass, Sandwich Star, Goblet 290.00
Pressed Glass, Sandwich Star, Goblet, Flint 325.00
Pressed Glass, Sandwich Star, Spill, Flint .... 30.00 To 65.00
Pressed Glass, Sandwich Tulip, Celery, Flint 45.00
Pressed Glass, Sandwich Waffle, Celery, Flint, Pair 90.00
Pressed Glass, Sandwich Waffle, Creamer, Flint, 6 1/4 In. 85.00
Pressed Glass, Sawtooth & Star, Tumbler 10.00
Pressed Glass, Sawtooth With Fan, Cup, Punch 5.50

Sawtooth with Panels, see Hinoto

Pressed Glass, Sawtooth, Bottle, Perfume 25.00
Pressed Glass, Sawtooth, Butter, Covered, Flint .... 75.00 To 85.00
Pressed Glass, Sawtooth, Butter, Covered, Miniature 45.00
Pressed Glass, Sawtooth, Cake Stand, Wafer Connector, Flint, 9 In. 45.00
Pressed Glass, Sawtooth, Celery .... 20.00 To 35.00
Pressed Glass, Sawtooth, Celery, Footed 35.00
Pressed Glass, Sawtooth, Celery, Stemmed 28.00
Pressed Glass, Sawtooth, Champagne, Flint 25.00
Pressed Glass, Sawtooth, Compote, Covered, 12 In. 90.00
Pressed Glass, Sawtooth, Compote, Flint, 8 In. 40.00
Pressed Glass, Sawtooth, Compote, 7 1/2 X 6 In. 25.00
Pressed Glass, Sawtooth, Compote, 8 In. 25.00

Pressed Glass, Sawtooth, Jar, Pomade

Pressed Glass, Sawtooth, Compote, 9 X 8 1/2 In. 60.00
Pressed Glass, Sawtooth, Compote, 9 1/2 In. 45.00
Pressed Glass, Sawtooth, Creamer 24.00
Pressed Glass, Sawtooth, Creamer, Applied Handle, Flint .... 70.00 To 75.00
Pressed Glass, Sawtooth, Creamer, Applied Handle, Rayed Base, Flint, 6 In. 40.00
Pressed Glass, Sawtooth, Creamer, Flint 75.00
Pressed Glass, Sawtooth, Eggcup, Flint 32.00
Pressed Glass, Sawtooth, Goblet .... 12.50 To 25.00
Pressed Glass, Sawtooth, Goblet, Knob Stem 12.50
Pressed Glass, Sawtooth, Salt, Covered 40.00
Pressed Glass, Sawtooth, Salt, Master, Covered, Flint 60.00
Pressed Glass, Sawtooth, Salt, Master, Flint 20.00
Pressed Glass, Sawtooth, Salt, Master, Opalescent, Flint 40.00
Pressed Glass, Sawtooth, Spill, Flint .... 20.00 To 40.00
Pressed Glass, Sawtooth, Spill, Sandwich 33.00
Pressed Glass, Sawtooth, Spooner, Flint .... 22.00 To 24.50
Pressed Glass, Sawtooth, Spooner, Flint, 5 X 3 1/2 In. 22.50
Pressed Glass, Sawtooth, Spooner, Flint, 5 1/4 In. 52.50
Pressed Glass, Sawtooth, Spooner, Gold Rim & Base, Sandwich Flint 45.00
Pressed Glass, Sawtooth, Spooner, Opaque White, 5 1/8 In. 30.00
Pressed Glass, Sawtooth, Sugar & Creamer, Child's 14.00
Pressed Glass, Sawtooth, Sugar, Child's, Covered 40.00
Pressed Glass, Sawtooth, Sugar, Flint 30.00
Pressed Glass, Sawtooth, Tumbler, Footed, Flint 27.00
Pressed Glass, Sawtooth, Wine 30.00
Pressed Glass, Sawtooth, Wine, Flint .... 25.00 To 34.00
Pressed Glass, Sawtooth, Wine, Knob Stem 30.00
Pressed Glass, Sawtooth, Wine, Knob Stem, Flint 52.50
Pressed Glass, Scallop Shell, Wine 12.50
Pressed Glass, Scalloped Lines, Eggcup 13.00
Pressed Glass, Scalloped Lines, Salt, Master 15.00
Pressed Glass, Scalloped Panel, Toothpick, Emerald Green 15.00
Pressed Glass, Scalloped Six Point, Vase, Ruby Stained, 8 In. 15.00
Pressed Glass, Scalloped Swirl, Toothpick 35.00
Pressed Glass, Scalloped Tape, Celery, Footed 20.00
Pressed Glass, Scalloped Tape, Creamer 20.00
Pressed Glass, Scalloped Tape, Eggcup .... 12.00 To 16.00
Pressed Glass, Scalloped Tape, Goblet .... 20.00 To 22.50
Pressed Glass, Scalloped Tape, Plate, Bread, "Staff Of Life," 13 X 9 In. 26.00
Pressed Glass, Scalloped Tape, Sugar 20.00
Pressed Glass, Scalloped Yoke, Goblet, Ruby Stained 30.00
Pressed Glass, Scarab, Goblet 85.00
Pressed Glass, Scarab, Goblet, Flint 85.00
Pressed Glass, Scottish Rite, Goblet 22.50
Pressed Glass, Scroll With Acanthus, Compote, Jelly, Green, Opalescent 35.00
Pressed Glass, Scroll With Acanthus, Creamer, Green, Enamel 22.00
Pressed Glass, Scroll With Flowers, Creamer 17.50

Pressed Glass, Scroll With Flowers, Eggcup ..... 13.00 To 14.50
Pressed Glass, Scroll With Flowers, Plate, Bread 15.00
Pressed Glass, Scroll With Flowers, Relish 9.00
Pressed Glass, Scroll, Eggcup 14.00
Pressed Glass, Scroll, Goblet ..... 10.00 To 12.50
Pressed Glass, Scroll, Stippled, Goblet 10.00
Pressed Glass, Scrolled Rib, Muffineer, Blue, Opaque 53.00
Pressed Glass, Seaweed, Butter, Opalescent, Covered 58.00
Pressed Glass, Sedan, Mug 7.50
Pressed Glass, Sedan, Salt, Master ..... 12.50 To 15.00
Pressed Glass, Seed Pod, Compote, Jelly, Blue, Gold Trim 36.00
Pressed Glass, Seneca Loop, Celery, Tooled Rim, Flint, 9 3/4 In. 40.00
Pressed Glass, Seneca Loop, Celery, Tooled Tulip Rim, Pedestal Base, Flint 20.00
Pressed Glass, Seneca Loop, Celery, 10 In. 65.00
Pressed Glass, Seneca Loop, Goblet, Flint ..... 18.00 To 21.00
Pressed Glass, Seneca Loop, Pitcher, Water, Applied Handle 95.00
Pressed Glass, Seneca Loop, Salt, Master 15.00
Pressed Glass, Sequoia, Cake Stand, Vaseline, Square 44.50
Pressed Glass, Sequoia, Creamer 12.50
Pressed Glass, Sequoia, Spooner 14.50
Pressed Glass, Sequoia, Sugar, Covered, Square 22.50
Pressed Glass, Serenade, Plate, White Opaque, Greentown, 6 In. 35.00
Pressed Glass, Serrated Block, Sugar, Covered, Ruby Stained 65.00
Pressed Glass, Serrated Prisms, Cup, Punch, Gold Trim 5.00
Pressed Glass, Shamrock, Toothpick, Ruby Stained 29.00
Pressed Glass, Sheaf & Block, Celery 22.50
Sheaf & Diamond, see Fickle Block
Pressed Glass, Sheaf Of Wheat, Plate, Bread, "Give Us This Day" 32.00
Pressed Glass, Shelby, Goblet 14.00
Pressed Glass, Shell & Jewel, Bowl, 8 In. 10.50
Pressed Glass, Shell & Jewel, Pitcher, Water ..... 16.00 To 35.00
Pressed Glass, Shell & Jewel, Pitcher, Water, Green 65.00
Pressed Glass, Shell & Jewel, Sauce ..... 4.00 To 5.00
Pressed Glass, Shell & Jewel, Tumbler 14.50
Pressed Glass, Shell & Jewel, Tumbler, Blue ..... 18.00 To 20.00
Pressed Glass, Shell & Jewel, Tumbler, Emerald Green 25.00
Pressed Glass, Shell & Jewel, Water Set, 6 Piece 85.00
Pressed Glass, Shell & Tassel, Bowl, Oblong, No Frame 22.00
Pressed Glass, Shell & Tassel, Bowl, Silver Plate Frame, Portland, 12 In. 95.00
Pressed Glass, Shell & Tassel, Cake Stand 65.00
Pressed Glass, Shell & Tassel, Cake Stand, Square 27.00
Pressed Glass, Shell & Tassel, Celery 48.50
Pressed Glass, Shell & Tassel, Celery, 2 Handles 45.00
Pressed Glass, Shell & Tassel, Compote, High Standard, Square, 8 In. 37.50
Pressed Glass, Shell & Tassel, Compote, Jelly, Square 18.00
Pressed Glass, Shell & Tassel, Compote, 4 1/2 In. 37.50
Pressed Glass, Shell & Tassel, Compote, 6 3/4 X 6 3/4 X 6 1/2 In. 51.00
Pressed Glass, Shell & Tassel, Creamer, Square ..... 27.00 To 59.50
Pressed Glass, Shell & Tassel, Goblet 20.00
Pressed Glass, Shell & Tassel, Pitcher, Water 55.00
Pressed Glass, Shell & Tassel, Plate, Oyster 175.00
Pressed Glass, Shell & Tassel, Plate, Oyster, 9 3/4 In. 89.50
Pressed Glass, Shell & Tassel, Relish 12.00
Pressed Glass, Shell & Tassel, Relish, Etched, Square 45.00
Pressed Glass, Shell & Tassel, Sauce, Handled, 4 In. 6.00
Pressed Glass, Shell & Tassel, Sauce, Square 9.50
Pressed Glass, Shell & Tassel, Sugar, Footed 9.00
Pressed Glass, Shell, Bowl, Blue, Opalescent, Footed, 7 In. 35.00
Pressed Glass, Shell, Salt & Pepper, Blue & Green 35.00
Pressed Glass, Shell, Sauce, Green, Opalescent 25.00
Pressed Glass, Shell, Sauce, Green, Opalescent, Footed 25.00
Pressed Glass, Shell, Sugar & Creamer, Apple Green, Gold Trim, Jefferson 60.00
Pressed Glass, Sheraton, Celery 18.50
Pressed Glass, Sheraton, Goblet ..... 15.00 To 16.50
Pressed Glass, Sheraton, Pitcher, Milk 15.00

Pressed Glass, Sheraton, Plate, Bread 12.00
Pressed Glass, Sheraton, Spooner 15.00
Pressed Glass, Shield, Goblet 22.50
Pressed Glass, Shield, Toothpick, Ruby Stained 29.00
Pressed Glass, Shimmering Star, Sugar, Covered 35.00
Pressed Glass, Shoe, Blue, 4 In. 12.00
Pressed Glass, Short Flute, Tumbler, Juice, Stemmed 1.65
Pressed Glass, Short Loops, Goblet, Engraved Decoration, Flint 12.00
Short Teasel, see Teasel
Pressed Glass, Shoshone, Fruit Bowl, Footed, 9 X 3 In. 16.00
Pressed Glass, Shoshone, Toothpick 10.00
Pressed Glass, Shoshone, Tumbler, Gold Trim 16.50
Pressed Glass, Shoshone, Vase, Twisted Stem, Scalloped Top, 9 In., Pair 35.00
Pressed Glass, Shovel, Goblet 10.00
Pressed Glass, Shovel, Syrup, Glass Top 18.50
Pressed Glass, Shrimp, Muffineer, Blue 65.00
Pressed Glass, Shrine, Compote, Jelly 15.00
Pressed Glass, Shrine, Pitcher, Water 35.00
Pressed Glass, Shrine, Tumbler, Lemonade 21.50
Pressed Glass, Shuttle, Goblet, Greentown 35.00
Pressed Glass, Shuttle, Mug, Blue, Greentown 240.00
Pressed Glass, Shuttle, Wine .... 10.00 To 15.00
Pressed Glass, Siamese Twins, Saltshaker 25.00
Pressed Glass, Single Frosted Ribbon, Spooner 25.00
Pressed Glass, Single Rose, Creamer, Gold Trim 29.50
Pressed Glass, Single Rose, Syrup 25.00
Pressed Glass, Single Rose, Table Set, Green, Gold Trim, 4 Piece 225.00
Pressed Glass, Siskyou, Goblet 15.00
Pressed Glass, Six Panel Finecut With Amber Bars, Creamer 35.00
Pressed Glass, Six Panel Finecut With Amber Bars, Goblet 65.00
Pressed Glass, Six Panel Finecut, Pitcher, Water, Amber Stained, Findlay 65.00
Pressed Glass, Six Panel Finecut, Tumbler, Amber 27.50
Pressed Glass, Six Panel Finecut, Tumbler, Etched 12.50
Pressed Glass, Six Panel Pinecut With Amber Bars, Cake Stand 47.50
Pressed Glass, Six Panel, Wine, Flint, 3 1/2 In. 3.00
Pressed Glass, Skilton, Goblet 16.00
Pressed Glass, Slewed Horseshoe, Wine 13.50
Pressed Glass, Smocking, Creamer, Applied Handle, Scalloped Base, Flint 60.00
Pressed Glass, Smocking, Creamer, Flint 85.00
Pressed Glass, Smocking, Goblet, Flint 57.00
Pressed Glass, Smocking, Spill 32.00
Pressed Glass, Smocking, Spill, Flint 40.00
Pressed Glass, Smocking, Sugar & Creamer, Covered, Applied Handle, Flint 160.00
Pressed Glass, Smocking, Sugar, Covered, Flint 85.00
Pressed Glass, Smocking, Sugar, Covered, Flint, 6 3/4 In. 50.00
Pressed Glass, Snail, Berry Bowl, Master, 8 In. 28.00
Pressed Glass, Snail, Butter, Covered 21.00
Pressed Glass, Snail, Butter, Etched 60.00
Pressed Glass, Snail, Creamer 9.75
Pressed Glass, Snail, Spooner .... 23.00 To 24.50
Pressed Glass, Snail, Sugar, Covered 62.00

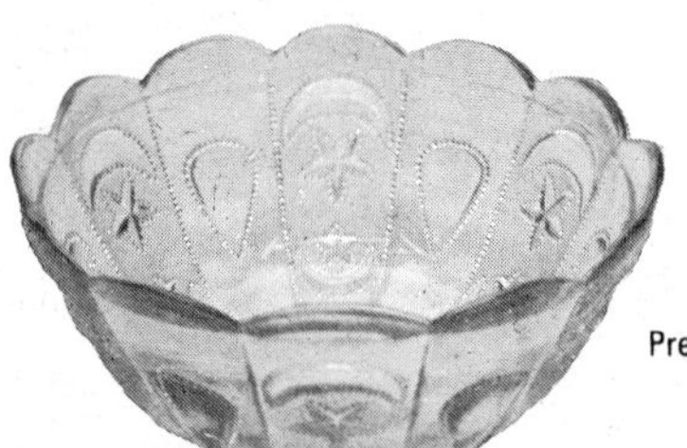

Pressed Glass, Shrine, Bowl

Pressed Glass, Squirrel, Creamer

Pressed Glass, Snail, Sugar, Covered, Etched ... 39.50
Pressed Glass, Snake Drape, Goblet ... 9.00
Pressed Glass, Snakeskin & Dot, Goblet ... 16.50
Pressed Glass, Snowflake, Butter, Miniature ... 25.00
Pressed Glass, Southern Ivy, Pitcher, Water ... 28.00
Spanish American, see Admiral Dewey
Spanish Coin, see Columbian Coin
Pressed Glass, Spear Point Band, Toothpick, Gold Trim ... 16.00
Pressed Glass, Spider Web, Shot Glass ... 16.00
Pressed Glass, Spirea Band, Compote, Blue, Covered, 6 In. ... 45.00
Pressed Glass, Spirea Band, Goblet ... 11.00
Pressed Glass, Spirea Band, Goblet, Amber ... 20.00 To 24.00
Pressed Glass, Spirea Band, Goblet, Blue ... 27.00
Pressed Glass, Spirea Band, Goblet, Yellow ... 22.00
Pressed Glass, Spool, Compote, Jelly, Blue, Opalescent ... 28.00
Pressed Glass, Sprig, Compote, Covered, High Standard, 6 In. ... 42.00
Pressed Glass, Sprig, Goblet ... 12.50
Pressed Glass, Sprig, Spooner ... 25.00
Pressed Glass, Sprig, Wine ... 15.00
Pressed Glass, Squirrel, Pitcher, Water ... 85.00
Pressed Glass, Squirrel, Pitcher, Water, Greentown ... 125.00
Pressed Glass, Squirrel, Pitcher, Water, 9 In. ... 85.00
Pressed Glass, Staff Of Life, Plate, Bread ... 25.00
Pressed Glass, Stag & Holly, Centerpiece Bowl, Ice Green, 10 In. ... 35.00
Pressed Glass, Stag, Goblet, Etched ... 23.00
Pressed Glass, Star & Bars, Sugar & Creamer ... 48.50
Pressed Glass, Star & Circle, Compote, Scalloped Edge, Flint, 6 In. ... 35.00
Pressed Glass, Star & Fan, Cake Stand, 10 X 5 In. ... 15.00
Pressed Glass, Star & Feather, Plate, Blue, Wire Basket, 7 In. ... 58.00
Pressed Glass, Star & Feather, Plate, 7 In. ... 15.00
Pressed Glass, Star & Oval, Syrup, Tin Top ... 32.50
Pressed Glass, Star & Palm, Goblet ... 15.00
Pressed Glass, Star & Pillar, Creamer, 1876 ... 39.50
Pressed Glass, Star & Pillar, Pitcher, Water, 1876 ... 65.00
Star & Punty, see Moon & Star
Pressed Glass, Star Arches, Berry Bowl, Miniature, Set Of 5 ... 11.00
Pressed Glass, Star Arches, Punch Set, Child's, 4 Piece ... 38.00
Pressed Glass, Star In Bull's-Eye, Tumbler ... 12.00
Pressed Glass, Star In Diamond, Creamer ... 10.00
Pressed Glass, Star In Honeycomb, Relish ... 7.00
Pressed Glass, Star Medallion, Spooner ... 15.50
Pressed Glass, Star Rosetted, Creamer ... 26.00
Pressed Glass, Star Rosetted, Spill, Flint ... 38.00
Pressed Glass, Star Whorl, Goblet ... 12.50 To 14.50
Pressed Glass, Star With File, Wine ... 7.50
Pressed Glass, Starred Cosmos, Pitcher, Water ... 27.50
Pressed Glass, Stars & Stripes, Creamer ... 16.50
Pressed Glass, Stars & Stripes, Wine ... 15.00
Pressed Glass, States, Goblet ... 22.00
Pressed Glass, States, Salt & Pepper ... 16.50
Pressed Glass, States, Tumbler ... 14.00 To 17.50
Pressed Glass, States, Wine ... 15.00
Stayman, see Tidy

Pressed Glass, Star & Dewdrop, Butter, Covered

Pressed Glass, Stedman, Champagne 27.50
Pressed Glass, Stedman, Champagne, Flint 27.00
Pressed Glass, Stedman, Eggcup 22.50
Pressed Glass, Stedman, Goblet 19.50
Pressed Glass, Stedman, Goblet, Flint 28.00
Pressed Glass, Stedman, Spooner, Flint 25.00
Pressed Glass, Stedman, Sugar 24.00
Pressed Glass, Stedman, Wine 29.50
Stippled Band, see also Stippled Bowl
Pressed Glass, Stippled Band, Banded, Salt, Master 12.50
Pressed Glass, Stippled Band, Creamer, Applied Handle 26.00
Pressed Glass, Stippled Band, Goblet, Flint 20.00
Pressed Glass, Stippled Bowl, Eggcup 13.00
Pressed Glass, Stippled Bowl, Spooner 20.00
Pressed Glass, Stippled Bowl, Spooner, 5 1/4 In. 15.00
Pressed Glass, Stippled Chain, Salt, Master 16.00
Pressed Glass, Stippled Chain, Salt, Master, Footed 17.00
Pressed Glass, Stippled Chain, Spooner 25.00
Pressed Glass, Stippled Cherry, Butter, Covered 25.00
Pressed Glass, Stippled Cherry, Pitcher, Water 40.00
Stippled Dahlia, see Dahlia
Pressed Glass, Stippled Double Loop, Goblet 15.00
Pressed Glass, Stippled Fleur-De-Lis, Goblet 18.50
Pressed Glass, Stippled Flower Band, Goblet 12.00
Pressed Glass, Stippled Forget-Me-Not, Mug 12.50
Pressed Glass, Stippled Forget-Me-Not, Pitcher, Milk 40.00
Pressed Glass, Stippled Forget-Me-Not, Plate, Kitten Center, 9 In. 75.00
Pressed Glass, Stippled Forget-Me-Not, Wine 32.50
Pressed Glass, Stippled Fuchsia, Goblet 18.50
Pressed Glass, Stippled Grape & Festoon With Clear Leaf, Celery 25.00
Pressed Glass, Stippled Grape & Festoon With Clear Leaf, Goblet 16.00
Pressed Glass, Stippled Grape & Festoon, Goblet 22.50
Pressed Glass, Stippled Grape & Festoon, Goblet, Buttermilk 23.00
Pressed Glass, Stippled Grape & Festoon, Pitcher, Water, Applied Handle 45.00
Pressed Glass, Stippled Grape & Festoon, Sauce, 4 In. 5.50
Pressed Glass, Stippled Ivy, Creamer, Applied Handle 45.00
Pressed Glass, Stippled Ivy, Eggcup 16.50
Pressed Glass, Stippled Ivy, Goblet 12.00
Pressed Glass, Stippled Ivy, Spooner 17.00
Pressed Glass, Stippled Ivy, Sugar, Covered 40.00
Pressed Glass, Stippled Lattice, Tumbler, Pink Cherries, Gold Leaves 8.50
Pressed Glass, Stippled Leaf, Sugar, Covered 30.00
Pressed Glass, Stippled Loop, Goblet 12.50
Pressed Glass, Stippled Magnet & Grape, Goblet 25.00
Pressed Glass, Stippled Medallion, Goblet, Flint 25.00
Pressed Glass, Stippled Panel & Band, Spooner 21.00
Stippled Paneled Flower, see Maine
Pressed Glass, Stippled Pepper, Goblet 19.00
Pressed Glass, Stippled Sandburr, Bowl, 8 In. 22.50

Stippled Scroll, see Scroll
Stippled Star Variant, see Stippled Sandburr
Pressed Glass, Stippled Star, Creamer 33.00
Pressed Glass, Stippled Woodflower, Creamer 25.00
Stork Looking at the Moon, see Ostrich Looking at the Moon
Pressed Glass, Stork, Creamer 20.00
Pressed Glass, Stork, Spooner .... 10.00 To 19.50
Pressed Glass, Stork, Spooner, Iowa City 39.00
Pressed Glass, Stork, Sugar .... 19.75 To 20.00
Pressed Glass, Stork, Toothpick 6.00
Pressed Glass, Stove, Butter, Vaseline 15.00
Pressed Glass, Strawberry & Loganberry, Spooner 28.00
Pressed Glass, Strawberry & Pear, Goblet 15.00
Pressed Glass, Strawberry, Berry Set, 7 Piece 45.00
Pressed Glass, Strawberry, Compote, Low Standard, 8 In. 15.00
Pressed Glass, Strawberry, Goblet 30.00
Pressed Glass, Strawberry, Sauce, 4 In. 4.50
Pressed Glass, Strigil, Plate, 8 In. 6.50
Pressed Glass, Stripe, Celery, Ruby Stained, Opalescent 30.00
Pressed Glass, Stump, Saltshaker 11.00
Pressed Glass, Sunbeam, Toothpick, Green 29.00
Pressed Glass, Sunburst & Block, Punch Set, Sawtooth Edge, 14 Piece 45.00
Pressed Glass, Sunburst Medallion, Compote, Covered, 10 1/2 In. 35.00
Pressed Glass, Sunburst Medallion, Mug, 3 1/4 In. 12.00
Pressed Glass, Sunburst Medallion, Sugar & Creamer, Cover 23.50
Pressed Glass, Sunburst Medallion, Wine 15.00
Pressed Glass, Sunburst On Shield, Sugar & Creamer, White & Opalescent 50.00
Pressed Glass, Sunburst, Celery 17.50
Pressed Glass, Sunburst, Creamer 7.50
Pressed Glass, Sunburst, Eggcup .... 13.00 To 15.00
Pressed Glass, Sunburst, Plate, Bread 25.00
Pressed Glass, Sunburst, Waste Bowl 12.50
Pressed Glass, Sunflower, Compote, Scalloped Edge, 7 In. 14.50
Pressed Glass, Sunk Daisy, Jar, Cracker 45.00
Pressed Glass, Sunk Daisy, Syrup, Tin Top 22.50
Pressed Glass, Sunk Honeycomb, Berry Set, Ruby Stained, 7 Piece 115.00
Pressed Glass, Sunk Honeycomb, Cup, Punch, Ruby Stained 15.00
Pressed Glass, Sunk Honeycomb, Jar, Cracker, Ruby Stained 85.00
Pressed Glass, Sunk Honeycomb, Pitcher, Water, Ruby Stained, Etched Floral 125.00
Pressed Glass, Sunk Honeycomb, Spooner, Ruby Stained 35.00
Pressed Glass, Sunk Honeycomb, Tankard, Water, Ruby Stained 95.00
Sunken Buttons, see Mitered Diamond
Pressed Glass, Sunken Primrose, Creamer, Gold Trim 55.00
Pressed Glass, Sunken Teardrop, Creamer 12.50
Pressed Glass, Sunken Teardrop, Sugar 20.00
Sunrise, see Rising Sun
Pressed Glass, Sunset, Syrup, Opalescent 59.00
Pressed Glass, Swag With Brackets, Compote, Jelly, Green, Opalescent 25.00
Pressed Glass, Swag With Brackets, Compote, Jelly, Vaseline, Opalescent 42.50

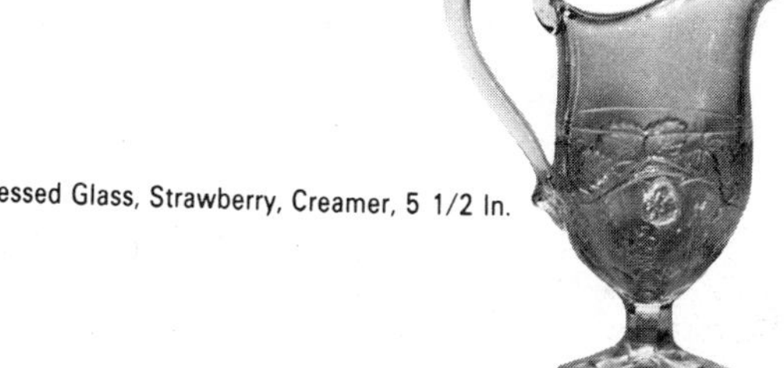
Pressed Glass, Strawberry, Creamer, 5 1/2 In.

Pressed Glass, Swag With Brackets, Creamer, Green, Opalescent 55.00
Pressed Glass, Swag With Brackets, Saltshaker, Amethyst, Gilt Trim 18.50
Pressed Glass, Swag With Brackets, Sauce, Blue, Opalescent 22.00
Pressed Glass, Swag With Brackets, Sauce, Vaseline, Opalescent 28.00
Pressed Glass, Swag With Brackets, Table Set, Green Opalescent, 4 Piece 210.00
Pressed Glass, Swan, Compote, Swan Finial, 12 X 8 1/2 In. 120.00
Pressed Glass, Sweet Pear, Sugar & Creamer, Pedestaled 15.00
Pressed Glass, Sweetheart, Creamer 25.00
Pressed Glass, Sweetheart, Spooner 25.00
Pressed Glass, Swimming Duck Cover, Dish, Frosted 75.00
Pressed Glass, Swirl, Celery, Amber Top, Frosted Bottom, Gonterman 65.00
Pressed Glass, Swirl, Celery, Chrysanthemum Base, Ruby Stained, Opalescent 40.00
Pressed Glass, Swirl, Creamer 20.00
Pressed Glass, Swirl, Creamer, Blue, Opalescent, Miniature 55.00
Pressed Glass, Swirl, Creamer, Child's 16.50
Pressed Glass, Swirl, Cup & Saucer, Child's, Gold Trim, Federal 7.00
Pressed Glass, Swirl, Mug 9.00
Pressed Glass, Swirl, Pitcher, Water, Blue, Opalescent, Square Mouth 50.00
Pressed Glass, Swirl, Pitcher, Water, Green, Opalescent, Fluted Top 65.00
Pressed Glass, Swirl, Pitcher, Water, Opalescent, Beatty 60.00
Pressed Glass, Swirl, Plate, 10 In. 22.50
Pressed Glass, Swirl, Sauce, Blue, Opalescent, Beatty 20.00
Pressed Glass, Swirl, Sauce, Opalescent, Blue Rim, Gonterman 40.00
Pressed Glass, Swirl, Spooner, Child's 14.50
Pressed Glass, Swirl, Spooner, Vaseline, Opalescent, Miniature 45.00
Pressed Glass, Swirl, Sugar 20.00
Pressed Glass, Swirl, Sugar, Child's, Covered 10.00
Pressed Glass, Swirl, Tumbler, Blue, Opalescent 30.00
Pressed Glass, Swirl, Tumbler, Blue, Opalescent, Chrysanthemum Base 40.00
Pressed Glass, Swirl, Tumbler, Ruby Stained, Opalescent 28.00
Pressed Glass, Swirl, Water Set, Green, Opalescent, 6 Piece 235.00
Pressed Glass, Swirled Feathers, Bottle, Perfume, Opalescent 10.00
Pressed Glass, Swirled Opal, Spooner 32.50
Pressed Glass, Syrup 32.50
Pressed Glass, Tackle Block, Celery, Double Knob Stem, Flint 90.00
Pressed Glass, Tackle Block, Goblet, Flint 40.00
Pressed Glass, Tacoma, Toothpick 10.00
Pressed Glass, Talisman Ashburton, Goblet, Flint 32.00
Pressed Glass, Tandem Bicycle, Goblet 24.00
Pressed Glass, Tappan, Sugar & Creamer, Child's, Amber, Cover 30.00
Pressed Glass, Tappan, Table Set, Child's, 4 Piece 75.00
Pressed Glass, Teardrop & Tassel, Butter 34.00
Pressed Glass, Teardrop & Tassel, Butter, Covered 75.00
Pressed Glass, Teardrop & Tassel, Compote, Covered, Greentown, 7 5/8 In. 47.50
Pressed Glass, Teardrop & Tassel, Creamer 26.00
Pressed Glass, Teardrop & Tassel, Pitcher, Water .... 50.00 To 87.50
Pressed Glass, Teardrop & Tassel, Pitcher, Water, Blue, Greentown 185.00
Pressed Glass, Teardrop & Tassel, Relish 15.00
Pressed Glass, Teardrop & Tassel, Salt & Pepper, Nile Green, Greentown 250.00

Pressed Glass, Tandem Diamonds And Thumbprint, Goblet

Pressed Glass, Thistle, Goblet

Pressed Glass, Teardrop & Tassel, Sauce, Blue, Greentown 80.00
Pressed Glass, Teardrop & Tassel, Sauce, 4 1/2 In. 12.00
Pressed Glass, Teardrop & Tassel, Tumbler ..... 28.00 To 32.00
Pressed Glass, Teardrop & Tassel, Tumbler, Blue 35.00
Teardrop & Thumbprint, see Teardrop
Pressed Glass, Teardrop, Goblet 15.00
Pressed Glass, Teardrop, Tumbler, Cobalt 28.50
Pressed Glass, Teardrop, Vase, Flint, 10 X 5 In. 16.00
Pressed Glass, Teardrop, Wine 15.00
Pressed Glass, Teardrop, Wine, Etched 9.50
Pressed Glass, Teasel, Toothpick 22.00
Pressed Glass, Teddy Roosevelt, Plate, Bread ..... 60.00 To 80.00
Pressed Glass, Teddy Roosevelt, Plate, Bread, Clear 80.00
Pressed Glass, Teddy Roosevelt, Plate, Bread, Frosted 90.00
Pressed Glass, Teddy Roosevelt, Plate, Bread, Frosted Center 85.00
Pressed Glass, Teddy Roosevelt, Plate, Bread, Frosted, Dancing Bear Border 95.00
Pressed Glass, Teddy Roosevelt, Platter, Frosted Bust, Oval, 10 1/4 In. 85.00
Pressed Glass, Teepee, Syrup 29.00
Pressed Glass, Ten Flute, Goblet, Flint 18.00
Pressed Glass, Tennessee, Compote, Jelly 18.00
Pressed Glass, Tennessee, Pitcher, 8 In. 38.00
Pressed Glass, Tennessee, Wine 20.00
Pressed Glass, Texas Bull's-Eye, Eggcup 13.00
Pressed Glass, Texas Bull's-Eye, Goblet 15.00
Pressed Glass, Texas Bull's-Eye, Tumbler, Footed 16.50
Pressed Glass, Texas Centennial, Goblet 21.50
Pressed Glass, Texas, Creamer 8.00
Pressed Glass, Texas, Mug, Blue, 4 In. 12.50
Pressed Glass, Texas, Pitcher, 8 1/2 In. 37.00
Pressed Glass, Texas, Sugar ..... 8.00 To 12.50
Pressed Glass, Texas, Sugar & Creamer, Individual, Gold Trim 15.00
Pressed Glass, Texas, Toothpick 30.00
Pressed Glass, Texas, Vase, Turned-In Top, 6 3/4 In. 10.00
Pressed Glass, Texas, Wine, Pink Blush Flashed 45.00
Pressed Glass, Texas, Wine, Pink Flashed 25.00
Pressed Glass, Thistle, Compote, 8 In. 15.00
Pressed Glass, Thistle, Goblet, Flint ..... 47.00 To 48.50
Pressed Glass, Thistle, Pitcher, Milk 24.50
Pressed Glass, Thistle, Salt Dip, Three-Footed, Paneled 7.50
Pressed Glass, Thistle, Wine, Bee 12.00
Thousand Eye, see 1, 000 eye
Pressed Glass, Threaded, Butter, Child's 42.00
Pressed Glass, Threaded, Creamer, Child's, Ruby Stained, Etched Leaves 35.00
Pressed Glass, Threaded, Sugar, Child's, Ruby Stain, Etched Leaves, 2 Handles 35.00
Pressed Glass, Three Face, Butter 25.00
Pressed Glass, Three Face, Cake Stand, 9 1/2 In. 82.50

Pressed Glass, Three Face, Bowl, Covered, Footed

Pressed Glass, Three Printie, Vase, 10 In.

Pressed Glass, Three Face, Cake Stand, 10 In. 110.00
Pressed Glass, Three Face, Champagne 85.00
Pressed Glass, Three Face, Compote, Engraved Border, 8 1/2 X 8 In. 75.00
Pressed Glass, Three Face, Compote, Etched, 7 3/4 X 7 1/4 In. 75.00
Pressed Glass, Three Face, Compote, Etched, 9 3/4 In. 75.00
Pressed Glass, Three Face, Compote, 6 In. 50.00
Pressed Glass, Three Face, Compote, 6 1/2 In. 50.00
Pressed Glass, Three Face, Creamer 74.00
Pressed Glass, Three Face, Creamer, Applied Handle, Etched 65.00
Pressed Glass, Three Face, Goblet 45.00 To 47.50
Pressed Glass, Three Face, Goblet, Etched 45.00
Pressed Glass, Three Face, Goblet, Frosted Stem & Base 37.50
Pressed Glass, Three Face, Plate, Cake 150.00
Pressed Glass, Three Face, Salt 28.50
Pressed Glass, Three Face, Salt & Pepper 55.00
Pressed Glass, Three Face, Saltshaker 19.00
Pressed Glass, Three Face, Saltshaker, Pewter Top 22.00
Pressed Glass, Three Face, Sauce, Pedestal 25.00
Pressed Glass, Three Flowers, Creamer 10.00
Three Graces, see also Three Face
Pressed Glass, Three Panel, Bowl, Flared, 10 In. 14.50
Pressed Glass, Three Panel, Bowl, Yellow, Scalloped, Footed, 7 In. 30.00
Pressed Glass, Three Panel, Celery 22.00
Pressed Glass, Three Panel, Celery, Amber, Flared Top 43.00
Pressed Glass, Three Panel, Celery, Vaseline 32.00
Pressed Glass, Three Panel, Creamer 12.50
Pressed Glass, Three Panel, Goblet 17.00
Pressed Glass, Three Panel, Goblet, Blue 32.00
Pressed Glass, Three Panel, Mug 13.00
Pressed Glass, Three Panel, Sauce, Blue, Footed 12.00
Pressed Glass, Three Panel, Sauce, Vaseline 13.50
Pressed Glass, Three Panel, Sauce, Vaseline, Footed 10.00
Pressed Glass, Three Panel, Sugar, Amber 20.00
Pressed Glass, Three Panel, Sugar, Vaseline 28.50
Pressed Glass, Three Panel, Tumbler, Blue 26.00
Pressed Glass, Three Presidents, Goblet 200.00
Pressed Glass, Three Presidents, Plate, Bread 33.00
Pressed Glass, Three Presidents, Plate, Bread, Frosted 60.00
Pressed Glass, Three Presidents, Plate, Bread, In Remembrance 28.50 To 49.50
Pressed Glass, Three Presidents, Plate, Bread, In Remembrance, Frosted 55.00
Pressed Glass, Three Shields, Butter, Amber, Shield Finial, Flange Base 135.00
Three Sisters, see Three Face
Pressed Glass, Three Stories, Mug 11.00
Pressed Glass, Three Stories, Sugar 18.50
Pressed Glass, Thumbprint, Cake Stand, Hexagonal Stem, Flint, 9 1/2 In. 70.00
Pressed Glass, Thumbprint, Celery, Flint 78.00
Pressed Glass, Thumbprint, Compote, Flint, 9 X 4 In. 20.00
Pressed Glass, Thumbprint, Compote, High Standard, Flint, 6 1/4 In. 55.00

Pressed Glass, Thumbprint, Creamer, Ruby Stained, Miniature 14.00
Pressed Glass, Thumbprint, Decanter, Bar Lip, Quart 85.00
Pressed Glass, Thumbprint, Dish, Honey 12.50
Pressed Glass, Thumbprint, Goblet, Barrel 16.00
Pressed Glass, Thumbprint, Goblet, Flint 35.00
Pressed Glass, Thumbprint, Goblet, Knob Stem, Flint 30.00
Pressed Glass, Thumbprint, Goblet, Knob Stem, Flint, 6 1/2 In. 55.00
Pressed Glass, Thumbprint, Jar, Sweetmeat, Covered, Flint, 8 1/4 In. 40.00
Pressed Glass, Thumbprint, Mug, Pressed Handle, Flint 28.00
Pressed Glass, Thumbprint, Mug, Ruby Stained 7.00
Pressed Glass, Thumbprint, Pitcher, Water, Flint, 9 In. 75.00
Pressed Glass, Thumbprint, Sugar, Covered, Flint 45.00
Pressed Glass, Thumbprint, Sugar, Covered, Stemmed, Flint 85.00
Pressed Glass, Thumbprint, Toothpick, Ruby Stained 30.00
Pressed Glass, Thumbprint, Tumbler, Bakewell Pears, Footed, 4 1/4 In. 38.00
Pressed Glass, Thumbprint, Tumbler, Bar 52.50
Pressed Glass, Thumbprint, Tumbler, Footed, Flint .... 30.00 To 32.00
Pressed Glass, Thumbprint, Tumbler, Whiskey, Footed, Flint 40.00
Pressed Glass, Thumbprint, Tumbler, Whiskey, Footed, Handled, Flint 155.00
Pressed Glass, Thumbprint, Wine 5.00
Pressed Glass, Thumbprint, Wine, Flint 18.00
Pressed Glass, Tidy, Eggcup 13.00
Pressed Glass, Tidy, Goblet 15.00
Pressed Glass, Tidy, Sugar, Covered 25.00
Pressed Glass, Tiny Finecut, Wine, Green 25.00
Pressed Glass, Tiny Lion, Creamer 22.50
Pressed Glass, Tiny Lion, Pitcher, Water 30.00
Pressed Glass, Tiny Optic, Toothpick, Amethyst 26.00
Pressed Glass, Tiny Optic, Toothpick, Green, Enameled 29.00
Pressed Glass, Tobacco Leaf, Champagne 65.00
Tobin, see Leaf & Star
Pressed Glass, Tokyo, Berry Bowl, Green, Opalescent 35.00
Pressed Glass, Tokyo, Bowl, Green, Opalescent, 8 In. 24.00
Pressed Glass, Tokyo, Creamer, Green, Opalescent 50.00
Pressed Glass, Tokyo, Creamer, Opalescent 20.00
Pressed Glass, Tokyo, Pitcher, Water, Green, Opalescent 150.00
Pressed Glass, Tokyo, Pitcher, Water, Ruby Stained, Opalescent 65.00
Pressed Glass, Tokyo, Sauce, Green, Opalescent 25.00
Pressed Glass, Tokyo, Table Set, Green, Opalescent, 3 Piece 195.00
Pressed Glass, Torpedo, Bowl, 9 1/2 In. 18.00
Pressed Glass, Torpedo, Celery 27.50
Pressed Glass, Torpedo, Celery, Scalloped Top 25.00
Pressed Glass, Torpedo, Compote, 8 In. 32.50
Pressed Glass, Torpedo, Creamer 29.50
Pressed Glass, Torpedo, Goblet 25.00
Pressed Glass, Torpedo, Salt 15.00
Pressed Glass, Torpedo, Syrup 35.00
Pressed Glass, Torpedo, Syrup, Metal Spring Top 25.00

Pressed Glass, Thumbprint, Pitcher

Item	Price
Pressed Glass, Transcontinental Railroad Train, Plate, Bread	45.00
Pressed Glass, Tree Bark, Pitcher, Water	22.50
Pressed Glass, Tree Bark, Vase, Blue, Opalescent, Northwood, 10 3/4 In.	29.50
Pressed Glass, Tree Of Life, Bowl, 4 1/2 X 2 1/2 In.	12.50
Pressed Glass, Tree Of Life, Cake Stand, P.G.Co.	65.00
Pressed Glass, Tree Of Life, Cake Stand, Samuel Standard, Davis, Portland	165.00
Pressed Glass, Tree Of Life, Celery, Flint	38.50
Pressed Glass, Tree Of Life, Compote, Covered, Scalloped, Pittsburgh, 9 In.	70.00
Pressed Glass, Tree Of Life, Compote, Etched, 9 1/4 X 7 1/2 In.	60.00
Pressed Glass, Tree Of Life, Compote, Frosted Hand & Ball Stem, 8 In.	68.00
Pressed Glass, Tree Of Life, Compote, Hand Finial & Stem, Pittsburgh, 9 In.	80.00
Pressed Glass, Tree Of Life, Compote, Hand Stem, Pittsburgh, 9 In.	57.50
Pressed Glass, Tree Of Life, Compote, Hand Stem, Scalloped, 10 In.	42.00
Pressed Glass, Tree Of Life, Compote, Hand Stem, 6 X 5 1/2 In.	35.00
Pressed Glass, Tree Of Life, Compote, Hand Stem, 9 X 9 In.	48.00
Pressed Glass, Tree Of Life, Compote, Jelly, Frosted Hand Base, 5 3/4 In.	75.00
Pressed Glass, Tree Of Life, Compote, Portland, 6 In.	75.00
Pressed Glass, Tree Of Life, Compote, Portland, 8 In.	40.00
Pressed Glass, Tree Of Life, Compote, Portland, 8 1/2 In.	57.50
Pressed Glass, Tree Of Life, Epergne, Child & Book Stem, Davis, C.1870, 11 In.	165.00
Pressed Glass, Tree Of Life, Finger Bowl, Blue	60.00
Pressed Glass, Tree Of Life, Finger Bowl, Portland	25.00
Pressed Glass, Tree Of Life, Goblet	60.00
Pressed Glass, Tree Of Life, Goblet, Portland, Flint	42.50
Pressed Glass, Tree Of Life, Ice Cream Set, Portland, 7 Piece	55.00
Pressed Glass, Tree Of Life, Pitcher, Applied Ribbed Handle, 5 In.	10.00
Pressed Glass, Tree Of Life, Sauce	6.00
Pressed Glass, Tree Of Life, Sauce, Amber, Leaf Shape	22.50
Pressed Glass, Tree Of Life, Sauce, Portland	10.00
Pressed Glass, Tree Of Life, Sugar, Ball Finial & Stem	45.00
Pressed Glass, Tree Of Life, Sugar, Portland	20.00
Pressed Glass, Tree Of Life, Tray, Ice Cream, Amber, Rectangular	37.50
Pressed Glass, Tree Of Life, Tumbler, Pittsburgh	19.50
Pressed Glass, Tree Of Life, Waste Bowl, Blue	30.00
Pressed Glass, Tree Of Life, Waste Bowl, Portland	15.00
Pressed Glass, Tree Stump, Toothpick, Amber	45.00
Pressed Glass, Triangular Prism, Celery, Flint	30.00
Pressed Glass, Triangular Prism, Goblet, Lady's, Flint	42.50
Pressed Glass, Triple Triangle, Goblet, Ruby Stained	30.00 To 35.00
Pressed Glass, Triple Triangle, Mug	38.00
Pressed Glass, Triple Triangle, Mug, Ruby Stained	15.00
Pressed Glass, Triple Triangle, Spooner, Ruby Stained	35.00
Pressed Glass, Triple Triangle, Wine, Ruby Stained	22.50
Pressed Glass, Triple Triangle, Wine, Ruby Stained, Diamond Cut Knob Stem	12.50
Pressed Glass, Truncated Cube, Saltshaker, Ruby Stained	12.50
Pressed Glass, Truncated Cube, Wine	14.50
Pressed Glass, Tulip & Diamond Point, Goblet, Flint	35.00
Pressed Glass, Tulip & Honeycomb, Butter, Child's, Covered	22.00

Pressed Glass, Tulip & Sawtooth, Decanter

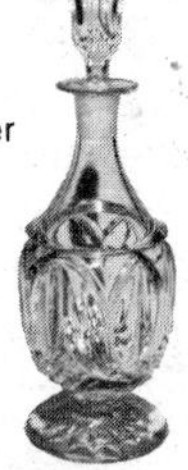

Pressed Glass, Tree Of Life, Compote

Pressed Glass, Tulip & Honeycomb, Creamer, Child's .... 15.00 To 20.00
Pressed Glass, Tulip & Honeycomb, Cup, Child's Punch 9.00
Pressed Glass, Tulip & Honeycomb, Punch Bowl, Child's 29.50
Pressed Glass, Tulip & Honeycomb, Punch Set, Miniature, 7 Piece .... 75.00 To 95.00
Pressed Glass, Tulip & Honeycomb, Spooner, Child's .... 10.00 To 20.00
Pressed Glass, Tulip & Honeycomb, Sugar, Covered, Miniature 18.00
Pressed Glass, Tulip & Honeycomb, Sugar, Miniature 9.50
Pressed Glass, Tulip & Honeycomb, Table Set, Child's, 4 Piece .... 65.00 To 75.00
Pressed Glass, Tulip With Ovals, Celery, Flint 58.00
Pressed Glass, Tulip With Ribs, Eggcup, Flint 32.00
Pressed Glass, Tulip With Ribs, Goblet, Flint 38.00
Pressed Glass, Tulip With Sawtooth With Petal Top, Salt 19.50
Pressed Glass, Tulip With Sawtooth, Celery, Flint 35.00
Pressed Glass, Tulip With Sawtooth, Compote, High Standard, Flint, 9 In. 85.00
Pressed Glass, Tulip With Sawtooth, Goblet, Flint 47.50
Pressed Glass, Tulip With Sawtooth, Salt, Master 16.00
Pressed Glass, Tulip With Sawtooth, Tumbler, Bar, Flint 48.50
Pressed Glass, Tulip With Sawtooth, Wine .... 13.00 To 17.00
Pressed Glass, Tulip With Sawtooth, Wine, Flint 25.00
Pressed Glass, Tulip, Compote, Covered, Low Standard, Flint, 10 X 7 In. 110.00
Pressed Glass, Tulip, Goblet, Flint 35.00
Pressed Glass, Tulip, Pitcher, Water, Applied Handle, Scalloped Base, Flint 275.00
Pressed Glass, Tulip, Salt, Master 15.00
Pressed Glass, Tulip, Salt, Master, 6 Panels, Footed, 3 5/8 In. 17.50
Pressed Glass, Tulip, Tumbler 8.50
Pressed Glass, Tulip, Vase, 8 In., Pair 20.00
Pressed Glass, Turkey Cover, Dish, Candy 35.00
Pressed Glass, Turkey Cover, Dish, Ruby Stained 30.00
Pressed Glass, Turtle Cover, Dish, Green, Basket Weave Base 25.00
Pressed Glass, Twelve Panel, Bottle, Vinegar, Pewter Top 10.00
Pressed Glass, Twist, Muffineer, Green, Opalescent 75.00
Pressed Glass, Two Band, Celery 20.00
Pressed Glass, Two Band, Plate, Bread 10.00
Pressed Glass, Two Panel, Bowl, Apple Green, Oval, 10 X 8 1/4 In. 37.50
Pressed Glass, Two Panel, Bowl, Blue, Oval, 10 X 8 1/4 In. 37.50
Pressed Glass, Two Panel, Bowl, Green, Oval, 9 X 7 1/4 In. 12.50
Pressed Glass, Two Panel, Bowl, Oval, 9 X 7 1/2 In. 17.50
Pressed Glass, Two Panel, Bowl, Waste, Amber 26.00
Pressed Glass, Two Panel, Celery, Blue 30.00
Pressed Glass, Two Panel, Creamer 32.50
Pressed Glass, Two Panel, Dessert Set, Apple Green, Cover, Footed, 7 Piece 175.00
Pressed Glass, Two Panel, Goblet 13.50
Pressed Glass, Two Panel, Goblet, Blue 30.00
Pressed Glass, Two Panel, Goblet, Canary 30.00
Pressed Glass, Two Panel, Goblet, Vaseline 32.50
Pressed Glass, Two Panel, Mug, Child's 23.00
Pressed Glass, Two Panel, Relish, Oval, 7 X 4 1/2 In. 5.00
Pressed Glass, Two Panel, Salt, Individual 2.00
Pressed Glass, Two Panel, Sauce, Vaseline 13.00
Pressed Glass, Two Panel, Tumbler, Amber 29.50
Pressed Glass, Two Panel, Waste Bowl, Amber 25.00
Pressed Glass, Two Panel, Wine 15.50
Pressed Glass, Two Panel, Wine, Canary, 4 In. 26.50
Pressed Glass, Two Panel, Wine, Vaseline 25.00
Pressed Glass, U.S.Coin, Compote, Covered, 6 In. 395.00
Pressed Glass, U.S.Coin, Compote, Frosted Quarters, Dimes On Stem, 8 In. 375.00
Pressed Glass, U.S.Coin, Mug, Frosted, 6 Dollars At Base, 4 3/4 In. 350.00
Pressed Glass, U.S.Coin, Toothpick, Frosted 50.00
Pressed Glass, U.S.Coin, Tumbler, Dollar In Base Dated 1879 .... 75.00
Pressed Glass, U.S.Rib, Table Set, Green, Gold Trim, 4 Piece 165.00
Pressed Glass, Umbilicated Sawtooth, Celery, Green, Footed 30.00
Pressed Glass, Umbilicated Sawtooth, Spill, Flint 24.00
Pressed Glass, Umbilicated Sawtooth, Tumbler, Whiskey, Flint 33.00
Pressed Glass, Valencia Waffle, Pitcher, Water, Amber 38.00
Pressed Glass, Valencia Waffle, Pitcher, Water, Square 25.00

Pressed Glass, Valencia Waffle, Sauce, Amber, Footed, Square, 4 In. 9.00
Pressed Glass, Valencia Waffle, Syrup, Flip Off Top 25.00
Pressed Glass, Vera, Berry Bowl, Frosted & Clear 14.50
Pressed Glass, Vera, Compote, Frosted Fagots, 11 X 9 In. 75.00
Pressed Glass, Vermont, Bowl, Oval, 11 1/2 In. 15.00
Pressed Glass, Vermont, Butter, Emerald Green, Gold Trim 45.00
Pressed Glass, Vernon Honeycomb, Celery 25.00
Pressed Glass, Vernon Honeycomb, Celery, Flint 55.00
Pressed Glass, Vernon Honeycomb, Celery, Footed, Flint 95.00
Pressed Glass, Vernon Honeycomb, Celery, Stemmed, 12 In. 90.00
Pressed Glass, Vernon Honeycomb, Compote, Covered, Flint, 8 1/4 In. 42.50
Pressed Glass, Vernon Honeycomb, Pitcher, Water, Flint, 2 1/2 Quart 65.00
Pressed Glass, Versailles, Claret, 4 Ozs. 5.00
Pressed Glass, Victoria, Compote, Covered, 15 X 10 In. 150.00
Pressed Glass, Victoria, Tumbler, Green, Gold Trim, Tarentum 12.50
Pressed Glass, Viking, Bowl, 7 X 4 In. 25.00
Pressed Glass, Viking, Butter 30.00
Pressed Glass, Viking, Butter, Covered .... 28.75 To 75.00
Pressed Glass, Viking, Candleholder, Swan, 6 In. 14.00
Pressed Glass, Viking, Celery .... 25.00 To 27.50
Pressed Glass, Viking, Compote, Covered, Handled, 10 In. 36.00
Pressed Glass, Viking, Jar, Spice, Ground Stopper 65.00
Pressed Glass, Viking, Pitcher, Water 45.00
Pressed Glass, Viking, Salt, Master 25.00
Pressed Glass, Viking, Spooner .... 30.00 To 35.00
Pressed Glass, Viking, Sugar 15.00
Pressed Glass, Viking, Sugar, Covered .... 30.00 To 45.00
Pressed Glass, Viking, Swan, Green, New Martinsville, 6 In. 16.50
Pressed Glass, Viking, Table Set, 4 Piece 175.00
Pressed Glass, Vincent's Valentine, Spooner, Ruby Stained 75.00
Pressed Glass, Vincent's Valentine, Sugar, Covered, Ruby Stained 75.00
Pressed Glass, Vine Panel, Saltshaker 7.50
Pressed Glass, Vine, Plate, Bread, Double 14.00
Pressed Glass, Vintage, Plate, Blue, Opalescent, Scalloped, Ruffled, 10 In. 35.00

Virginia, see also Galloway

Pressed Glass, Virginia, Tumbler 16.00
Pressed Glass, Virginia, Vase, 6 In. 8.00
Pressed Glass, Virginia, Wine 10.00
Pressed Glass, Wading Heron, Pitcher, Water 82.50
Pressed Glass, Waffle & Star Band, Goblet 10.00
Pressed Glass, Waffle & Thumbprint, Champagne, Flint 40.00
Pressed Glass, Waffle & Thumbprint, Decanter, Flint, 10 5/8 In. 20.00
Pressed Glass, Waffle & Thumbprint, Eggcup, Flint 37.00

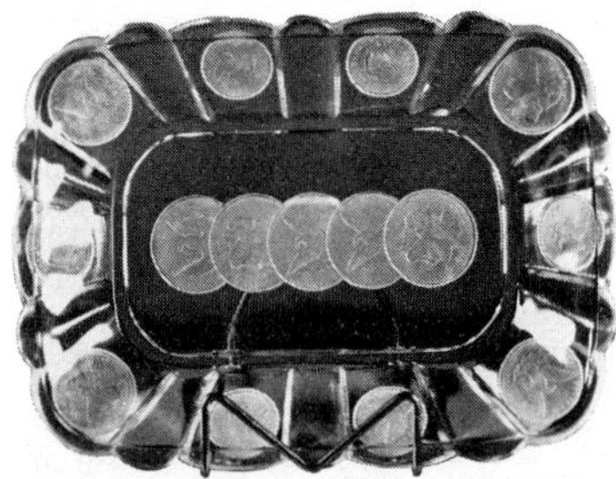

Pressed Glass, U.S.Coin, Plate, Bread

Pressed Glass, Washington Centennial, Relish Dish

Pressed Glass, Waffle & Thumbprint, Flip Glass

Pressed Glass, Waffle & Thumbprint, Goblet, Bulb Stem, Flint 70.00
Pressed Glass, Waffle & Thumbprint, Goblet, Flint 60.00
Pressed Glass, Waffle & Thumbprint, Spill, Flint 45.00
Pressed Glass, Waffle & Thumbprint, Spooner, Flint 38.00
Pressed Glass, Waffle & Thumbprint, Tumbler, Bar 95.00
Pressed Glass, Waffle & Thumbprint, Tumbler, Footed, Flint 43.00
Pressed Glass, Waffle & Thumbprint, Wine, Flint .... 40.00 To 45.00
Pressed Glass, Waffle With Spearpoints, Tumbler, 4 In. 14.00
Pressed Glass, Waffle, Basket, 10 In. 18.00
Pressed Glass, Waffle, Butter, Flint 55.00
Pressed Glass, Waffle, Celery, Flint 40.00
Pressed Glass, Waffle, Creamer, Applied Foot & Handle, Flint, 6 In. 55.00
Pressed Glass, Waffle, Eggcup, Flint 19.50
Pressed Glass, Waffle, Goblet, Flint 75.00
Pressed Glass, Waffle, Plate, 6 In. 24.00
Pressed Glass, Waffle, Tumbler, Frosted 7.00
Pressed Glass, Waffle, Wine 12.00
Pressed Glass, Washington & Lafayette, Mug 35.00
Pressed Glass, Washington & Lafayette, Mug, Purple 21.00
Pressed Glass, Washington Bicentenary, Blue, Square, Scenic, Mt.Vernon 22.00
Pressed Glass, Washington Centennial, Cake Stand 68.50
Pressed Glass, Washington Centennial, Celery 52.50
Pressed Glass, Washington Centennial, Celery, Footed 35.00
Pressed Glass, Washington Centennial, Pitcher, Water 85.00
Pressed Glass, Washington Centennial, Relish, Bear Paw Handles, 1876 .... 24.50
Pressed Glass, Washington Centennial, Salt, Master 30.00
Pressed Glass, Washington Centennial, Sauce 8.50
Pressed Glass, Washington, Celery, Flint 62.50
Pressed Glass, Washington, Celery, Footed, New England Glass Co., Flint 89.50
Pressed Glass, Washington, Creamer, Applied Handle, Flint, 5 3/4 In. 205.00
Pressed Glass, Washington, Eggcup, Flint 45.00
Pressed Glass, Water Lily & Cattails, Bowl, Blue, Opalescent, 8 1/2 In. 30.00
Pressed Glass, Water Lily & Cattails, Bowl, Opalescent, 2 Handles, 7 In. 28.00
Pressed Glass, Water Lily & Cattails, Spooner, Green, Opalescent 55.00
Pressed Glass, Water Lily & Cattails, Spooner, Ruby Stained, Opalescent 45.00
Pressed Glass, Water Lily & Cattails, Tumbler, Blue, Opalescent .... 22.50 To 45.00
Pressed Glass, Water Lily & Cattails, Tumbler, Ruby Stained, Opalescent 35.00
Pressed Glass, Waterfall, Saltshaker 25.00
Pressed Glass, Way Colonial, Goblet, Flint 38.00
Pressed Glass, Wedding Band, Goblet, Flint 28.00
Pressed Glass, Wedding Bells, Creamer, Amethyst Stained 28.00
Pressed Glass, Wedding Bells, Creamer, 4 Footed 15.75
Pressed Glass, Wee Branches, Table Set, Miniature, 4 Piece 285.00

Pressed Glass, Wedding Ring, Syrup, Flint

Pressed Glass, Westward Ho, Compote, Covered, 7 3/4 In.

Pressed Glass, Wellsburg, Berry Bowl, 8 In. 39.50
Pressed Glass, Westmoreland, Celery, Scalloped Top, 5 3/4 In. 10.00
Pressed Glass, Westmoreland, Rose Bowl, 2 1/2 In. 14.75
Pressed Glass, Westward Ho, Celery 95.00
Pressed Glass, Westward Ho, Compote, Covered, High Standard, 6 In. 165.00
Pressed Glass, Westward Ho, Compote, Covered, High Standard, 8 In. 175.00
Pressed Glass, Westward Ho, Compote, Covered, Low Standard, 5 In. 275.00
Pressed Glass, Westward Ho, Compote, Covered, Low Standard, 8 In. 125.00
Pressed Glass, Westward Ho, Compote, Covered, Oval, 10 X 7 3/4 In. 125.00
Pressed Glass, Westward Ho, Compote, Covered, Oval, 12 X 8 3/4 In. 165.00
Pressed Glass, Westward Ho, Compote, Covered, Oval, 7 3/4 X 4 3/4 In. 150.00
Pressed Glass, Westward Ho, Compote, Covered, 12 1/2 X 8 In. 180.00
Pressed Glass, Westward Ho, Compote, Covered, 15 In. 350.00
Pressed Glass, Westward Ho, Compote, High Standard, 5 In. 145.00
Pressed Glass, Westward Ho, Compote, High Standard, 7 In. 45.00
Pressed Glass, Westward Ho, Compote, High Standard, 8 In. 35.00
Pressed Glass, Westward Ho, Compote, Indian Finial, Low Standard, 5 In. 275.00
Pressed Glass, Westward Ho, Creamer 85.00
Pressed Glass, Westward Ho, Dish, Pickle, Frosted Deer Handles, Oval 68.00
Pressed Glass, Westward Ho, Goblet 75.00
Pressed Glass, Westward Ho, Goblet, Frosted & Clear 45.00
Pressed Glass, Westward Ho, Jar, Marmalade 20.00
Pressed Glass, Westward Ho, Jar, Marmalade, Covered 150.00
Pressed Glass, Westward Ho, Pitcher, Milk 225.00
Pressed Glass, Westward Ho, Pitcher, Water 165.00
Pressed Glass, Westward Ho, Platter, 13 X 9 In. 65.00
Pressed Glass, Westward Ho, Sauce 24.00
Pressed Glass, Westward Ho, Sauce, Footed 22.00
Pressed Glass, Westward Ho, Sauce, 3 1/2 In. 17.50
Pressed Glass, Westward Ho, Sauce, 4 In. 20.00
Pressed Glass, Westward Ho, Spooner 65.00
Pressed Glass, Wheat & Barley, Butter, Covered 15.00
Pressed Glass, Wheat & Barley, Compote, Amber, Covered, 7 1/4 In. 60.00
Pressed Glass, Wheat & Barley, Compote, Jelly 17.50
Pressed Glass, Wheat & Barley, Creamer .... 16.00 To 17.00
Pressed Glass, Wheat & Barley, Goblet 27.50
Pressed Glass, Wheat & Barley, Goblet, Blue 45.00
Pressed Glass, Wheat & Barley, Mug, Amber 20.00
Pressed Glass, Wheat & Barley, Mug, 3 1/8 In. 18.00
Pressed Glass, Wheat & Barley, Plate, Cake, Pedestal 22.00
Pressed Glass, Wheat & Barley, Spooner 16.00
Pressed Glass, Wheat & Barley, Sugar, Covered 35.00
Pressed Glass, Wheat & Barley, Tumbler 17.00
Pressed Glass, Wheat & Barley, Tumbler, Amber .... 22.50 To 24.00
Pressed Glass, Wheat Sheaf, Punch Set, Child's, 4 Piece 38.00
Pressed Glass, Wheel & Block, Bowl, Opalescent, Red & Gold Trim, 10 In. 24.00
Pressed Glass, Wheel & Block, Plate, Opalescent, Northwood, 9 3/4 In. 32.50
Pressed Glass, Wheel & Comma, Spooner 21.00

Pressed Glass, Whirligig, Creamer, Child's 20.00

Pressed Glass, Whirligig, Cup, Child's Punch 9.00

Pressed Glass, Whirligig, Punch Bowl, Child's 15.00

Pressed Glass, Whirligig, Punch Set, Child's, 7 Piece .... 60.00 To 75.00

Pressed Glass, Whirligig, Spooner, Child's 9.00

Pressed Glass, Wide Band Baby Thumbprint, Goblet 12.50

Pressed Glass, Wild Bouquet, Berry Bowl, Blue, Gold Trim, Northwood 22.00

Pressed Glass, Wild Bouquet, Creamer, Opalescent .... 32.00 To 55.00

Pressed Glass, Wild Bouquet, Sauce, Blue, Opalescent, 4 1/2 In. 32.00

Pressed Glass, Wild Bouquet, Spooner, Opalescent 55.00

Pressed Glass, Wild Rose With Bowknot, Sugar, Covered, Greentown 28.00

Pressed Glass, Wild Rose With Bowknot, Tumbler, Frosted, Painted 16.00

Pressed Glass, Wild Rose With Bowknot, Tumbler, White, Painted, Greentown 28.00

Pressed Glass, Wild Rose, Spooner, Opalescent, Northwood 45.00

Pressed Glass, Wild Rose, Table Set, Miniature, 4 Piece 275.00

Pressed Glass, Wildflower, Cake Stand, Vaseline, 9 1/2 In. 55.00

Pressed Glass, Wildflower, Celery, Blue, 9 3/8 X 4 3/8 In. 30.00

Pressed Glass, Wildflower, Champagne, Amber 30.00

Pressed Glass, Wildflower, Compote, Blue, 7 X 4 1/4 In. 43.50

Pressed Glass, Wildflower, Creamer 16.00

Pressed Glass, Wildflower, Creamer, Vaseline 29.50

Pressed Glass, Wildflower, Creamer, Yellow 35.00

Pressed Glass, Wildflower, Goblet, Apple Green 35.00

Pressed Glass, Wildflower, Pitcher, Milk, Vaseline, Sandwich 35.00

Pressed Glass, Wildflower, Pitcher, Water, Amber 47.50

Pressed Glass, Wildflower, Spooner .... 12.00 To 16.50

Pressed Glass, Wildflower, Spooner, Vaseline 21.50

Pressed Glass, Wildflower, Sugar & Creamer, Amber 75.00

Pressed Glass, Wildflower, Sugar, Green 25.00

Pressed Glass, Wildflower, Table Set, Blue, 4 Piece 175.00

Pressed Glass, Wildflower, Tray, Water, Amber 37.50

Pressed Glass, Wildflower, Tray, Water, Blue 33.00

Pressed Glass, Wildflower, Tumbler, Dark Amber 22.50

Pressed Glass, Wildflower, Wine, Apple Green 40.00

Pressed Glass, William & Mary, Cake Stand, Vaseline, Opalescent, 8 7/8 In. 69.00

Pressed Glass, Willow Oak, Butter, Blue, Covered 55.00

Pressed Glass, Willow Oak, Cake Stand, 8 1/4 In. 25.00

Pressed Glass, Willow Oak, Compote, Blue, 9 In. 50.00

Pressed Glass, Willow Oak, Compote, Covered, High Standard, 6 In. 6.00

Pressed Glass, Willow Oak, Creamer 22.00

Pressed Glass, Willow Oak, Creamer, Amber 30.00

Pressed Glass, Willow Oak, Creamer, Blue 38.00

Pressed Glass, Willow Oak, Goblet .... 15.00 To 20.00

Pressed Glass, Willow Oak, Goblet, Amber 30.00

Pressed Glass, Willow Oak, Pitcher, Milk .... 26.00 To 28.50

Pressed Glass, Willow Oak, Pitcher, Water, Amber, Footed, 9 1/2 In. 47.50

Pressed Glass, Willow Oak, Plate, 7 In. 12.00

Pressed Glass, Willow Oak, Sauce 6.00

Pressed Glass, Willow Oak, Tray, Water 25.00

Pressed Glass, Willow Oak, Tray, Water, Amber .... 32.00 To 34.00

Pressed Glass, Willow Oak, Tray, Wine, Amber 30.00

Pressed Glass, Willow Oak, Tumbler 20.00

Pressed Glass, Windflower, Creamer 32.50

Pressed Glass, Windflower, Eggcup 25.00

Pressed Glass, Windows, Pitcher, Opalescent 145.00

Winona, see Barred Hobnail

Wisconsin, see Beaded Dewdrop

Pressed Glass, Wooden Pail, Creamer 12.75

Pressed Glass, Wooden Pail, Pitcher, Water, Amethyst 75.00

Pressed Glass, Worcester, Belted, Champagne, Flint 25.00

Pressed Glass, Worcester, Belted, Tumbler, Footed, Flint 32.00

Pressed Glass, World, Saltshaker, Flint 6.50

Pressed Glass, Wreath & Shell, Berry Bowl, Vaseline, Opalescent 75.00

Pressed Glass, Wreath & Shell, Bowl, Blue, Opalescent, Footed, 7 1/2 In. 45.00

Pressed Glass, Wreath & Shell, Celery, Ruby Stained, Opalescent 95.00

Pressed Glass, Wreath & Shell, Celery, Vaseline, Opalescent 95.00
Pressed Glass, Wreath & Shell, Salt, Opalescent 55.00
Pressed Glass, Wreath & Shell, Sauce, Blue, Opalescent 28.50
Pressed Glass, Wreath & Shell, Sauce, Vaseline, Opalescent 23.00
Pressed Glass, Wreath & Shell, Tumbler, Yellow, Opalescent 45.00
Pressed Glass, Wyoming, Pitcher, Water 37.50
Pressed Glass, X-Ray, Berry Set, Green, Gold Trim, 7 Piece 95.00
Pressed Glass, X-Ray, Celery, Emerald Green, Gold Trim, Scalloped Rim 48.00
Pressed Glass, X-Ray, Sugar, Emerald Green, Covered, Gold Trim 28.50
Pressed Glass, X-Ray, Table Set, Green, Cover, Gold Trim, 3 Piece 145.00
Pressed Glass, X-Ray, Table Set, Green, Gold Trim, 4 Piece 155.00
Pressed Glass, X-Ray, Toothpick, Green, Gold Trim 40.00
Yale, see Crow's-Foot
Pressed Glass, Yoke & Circle, Cup, Punch 4.50
Pressed Glass, Yoked Loop, Bowl, Footed, Flint, 8 In. 45.00
Pressed Glass, Yoked Loop, Goblet, Flint 25.00
Pressed Glass, Yoked Loop, Sugar, Covered, Flint .... 50.00 To 70.00
Pressed Glass, Yoked Loop, Sugar, Flint 15.00
Pressed Glass, Yoked Loop, Tumbler, Whiskey, Flint 28.00
Pressed Glass, Yoked Loop, Tumbler, Whiskey, Footed 45.00
Pressed Glass, Yoked Loop, Tumbler, Whiskey, Handled, Flint 38.00
Pressed Glass, York Herringbone, Creamer, Ruby Stained, Miniature 25.00
Pressed Glass, York Herringbone, Creamer, Ruby Stained, Tankard Shape 45.00
Pressed Glass, Yuma Loop, Compote, 8 In. 27.50
Pressed Glass, Yuma Loop, Goblet 13.50
Pressed Glass, Zipper & Star, Bottle, Cologne 15.00
Pressed Glass, Zipper Slash, Wine 12.50
Pressed Glass, 100-Eye, Dish, Candy, Open Handles 18.00
Pressed Glass, 100-Eye, Goblet .... 8.00 To 12.50
Pressed Glass, 100-Eye, Sugar 15.00
Pressed Glass, 100-Eye, Toothpick, Hat Shape 12.50
Pressed Glass, 100-Eye, Tumbler 15.00
Pressed Glass, 101, Butter, Covered 22.50
Pressed Glass, 101, Creamer 28.00
Pressed Glass, 101, Plate, Bread 42.00
Pressed Glass, 101, Plate, 7 In. 11.50
Pressed Glass, 101, Plate, 8 In. 6.50
Pressed Glass, 101, Sauce, Footed 6.00
Pressed Glass, 101, Sauce, 4 In. 6.00
Pressed Glass, 101, Spooner 15.00
Pressed Glass, 101, Spooner, Flint 18.00
Pressed Glass, 101, Sugar, Covered 36.00
Pressed Glass, 1, 000-Eye, Bottle, Cologne 18.00
Pressed Glass, 1, 000-Eye, Bowl, Footed, 8 In. 28.50
Pressed Glass, 1, 000-Eye, Celery, Amber, 3 Knob Stem 32.50
Pressed Glass, 1, 000-Eye, Celery, Opalescent 55.00
Pressed Glass, 1, 000-Eye, Champagne 12.00
Pressed Glass, 1, 000-Eye, Compote, Apple Green, 3 Knob Stem, 8 In. 45.00
Pressed Glass, 1, 000-Eye, Compote, 8 In. 30.00
Pressed Glass, 1, 000-Eye, Creamer, Opalescent 55.00
Pressed Glass, 1, 000-Eye, Creamer, 3 Knob Stem 32.00
Pressed Glass, 1, 000-Eye, Dish, Trinket 6.00
Pressed Glass, 1, 000-Eye, Eggcup 15.00
Pressed Glass, 1, 000-Eye, Goblet, Amber 25.00
Pressed Glass, 1, 000-Eye, Goblet, Apple Green 35.00
Pressed Glass, 1, 000-Eye, Goblet, Green .... 29.50 To 35.00
Pressed Glass, 1, 000-Eye, Mug, Amber 18.00
Pressed Glass, 1, 000-Eye, Mug, Child's, Blue 16.50
Pressed Glass, 1, 000-Eye, Pitcher, Water, Opalescent 125.00
Pressed Glass, 1, 000-Eye, Plate, Blue, Beveled Corners, 7 3/4 In. 36.00
Pressed Glass, 1, 000-Eye, Plate, Bread 28.50
Pressed Glass, 1, 000-Eye, Plate, Bread, Green 35.00
Pressed Glass, 1, 000-Eye, Plate, Green, 10 In. 27.50
Pressed Glass, 1, 000-Eye, Plate, Green, 8 In. 22.50
Pressed Glass, 1, 000-Eye, Plate, Honey Amber, Square, 10 In. 16.00

Pressed Glass, 1, 000-Eye, Plate, Vaseline, Square, 10 In. 30.00
Pressed Glass, 1, 000-Eye, Plate, Yellow, 8 In. 18.00
Pressed Glass, 1, 000-Eye, Plate, 8 In. 12.00
Pressed Glass, 1, 000-Eye, Plate, 10 In. 22.50
Pressed Glass, 1, 000-Eye, Salt & Pepper 17.50
Pressed Glass, 1, 000-Eye, Sauce 6.00
Pressed Glass, 1, 000-Eye, Sauce, Footed 12.50
Pressed Glass, 1, 000-Eye, Spooner 58.00
Pressed Glass, 1, 000-Eye, Spooner, Blue, Knob Stem 38.00
Pressed Glass, 1, 000-Eye, Sugar, Covered, 3 Knob Stem 35.00
Pressed Glass, 1, 000-Eye, Sugar, Green, Covered, Knob Base 40.00
Pressed Glass, 1, 000-Eye, Syrup, Blue 85.00
Pressed Glass, 1, 000-Eye, Toothpick, Hat Shape 18.00
Pressed Glass, 1, 000-Eye, Tray, Dresser, Apple Green, 11 X 8 In. 22.50
Pressed Glass, 1, 000-Eye, Tray, Water, Amber, Oval, 14 X 12 In. 35.00
Pressed Glass, 1, 000-Eye, Tray, Water, Blue, Oval 47.50
Pressed Glass, 1, 000-Eye, Tumbler 17.50
Pressed Glass, 1, 000-Face, Relish, Triangular, 4 Made Into 1, 8 1/2 In. 125.00

The size of the print is given, not the overall size with frame.

Print, see also Store, Sign

Print, Aldin, Fallowfield Hunt, The Death, Framed, 15 X 13 In. 40.00
Print, Asti, Bust Of Victorian Girl, Framed, 16 X 22 In. 80.00
Print, Audubon, Carolina Pigeon, Hand-Colored Engraving & Aquatint, 25 In. 400.00
Print, Audubon, Ferruginous Thrush, Hand-Colored Engraving, Aquatint, 37 In. 950.00
Print, Bailey & Fowler, 1903, Aerial View Of Dover, N.J., 26 X 21 In. 150.00
Print, Benton, Frisky Day, Etching, 21 X 17 In. 125.00
Print, Bowyer, Ancient Bath, Palici, 1809, Aquatint, 13 X 9 1/2 In. 50.00
Print, Boydell, View On Twickenham Common, 1753, Engraving, Color, 17 1/2 In. 125.00
Print, Buttre, Abraham Lincoln, 1864, Engraving, Brady's Photograph, 14 In. 185.00
Print, Carson, Washington Headquarters, Etching, Black & White, 6 1/2 In. 8.00
Print, Christy, Marriage Of Priscilla & Miles Standish, 1903, Color, 10 In. 6.00
Print, Christy, Spinning Wheel, 1903, Color, 9 1/2 X 7 In. 6.00

Print, Currier, see Currier

Print, Currier & Ives, see Currier & Ives

Print, Dainty, Washington Family, Engraving, Oval Frame, 14 1/2 X 12 1/2 In. 20.00
Print, Fetherton, U.S.S. Maine, 1898, Lithograph, Color, Frame, 16 X 9 In. 43.00
Print, Fisher, Girl On Tree Limb, 18 X 24 .... 35.00
Print, Fisher, Here's Happiness To You, Frame & Mat, 9 X 13 In. 28.00
Print, Fisher, You Will Marry A Dark Man, Frame & Mat, 12 X 16 In. 28.00
Print, Frost, Ordered Off, 1903, Hunting Scene, Lithograph, Color, 16 X 11 In. 34.00
Print, Gerolimo, Children Of The Wood, C.1850, Engraving, Color, 6 In., 4 .... 165.00
Print, Godey, July, 1871 .... 12.00
Print, Godey, Petit Courier Des Dames, 1873, Mahogany Frame, 15 X 13 In. 80.00
Print, Guttman, Little Bit Of Heaven, Framed, 17 X 13 1/2 In. 18.00
Print, H.C.Christy, The Road To Heart's Desire, Dated 8/10, 1914, Framed 18.50
Print, Harrah's Pony Express, Siege Of Limerick, 1690, Lithograph, 30 In. 150.00
Print, Hendron, Blue Boy, Mezzotint, 17 3/4 X 12 1/2 In. 45.00
Print, Humphrey, Colonial Couple Beside Carriage, 1892, Framed, 18 X 15 In. 29.50
Print, Humphrey, Snow Balling, Winter, 1893, Lithograph, Color, 12 1/2 X 9 In. 37.50
Print, Humphrey, Woman & Man Beside Carriage, 1892, Framed, 18 X 15 In. 38.00
Print, Icart, Dame Aux Camelias, Framed 500.00
Print, Icart, Etching, Symphony In Blue 450.00
Print, Icart, Girl In The Rain, Framed 550.00
Print, Icart, Girl With Parrot 250.00
Print, Icart, Lady With Two Dogs, Framed, 21 1/2 X 26 1/2 In. 235.00
Print, Icart, Peonies 395.00
Print, Icart, Poem, Old Frame And Mat 550.00
Print, Icart, Spanish Dancer, Framed 400.00
Print, Icart, The Black Fan, Signed, Paris Seal, 22 X 28, Framed 300.00
Print, Karr, Robert E.Lee, Color, 24 X 20 In. 30.00
Print, Kellogg, Colonel Elmer Ellsworth, N.Y., Lithograph, Color, 17 X 14 In. 35.00
Print, Kellogg, John Marshall, Silhouette, Lithograph, 17 1/2 X 13 1/2 In. 75.00
Print, Kowalski, End Of The Trail, C.1920, 16 X 12 In. 155.00
Print, Kowalski, Indian Appeal, C.1920, 16 X 12 In. 145.00

Print, Lee, Comrades In Arms, 1918, Doughboys In Trench, Framed, 17 1/2 In. 18.50
Print, Map, Central Virginia, U.S.Grant, 1964, 29 1/2 X 18 1/2 In. 12.00
Print, Map, Kentucky, 1933, Karl Smith, Cardboard, Framed, 28 X 19 In. 15.00
Print, Map, New England States Of America, Russell, 1795, 18 X 14 In. 80.00
Print, Map, Petersburg, Va., 1864, 29 1/2 X 18 1/2 In. 15.00
Print, Map, Petersburg, 4th Army Corp., 1862, 29 1/2 X 18 1/2 In. 10.00
Print, Map, Siege Of Atlanta, Sherman, Civil War, 29 1/2 X 18 1/2 In. 12.00
Print, Map, Texas, Johnson, 1866, 23 X 17 In. 35.00
Print, Map, Texas, 1850, Cowper Thwait, Hand-Colored, 17 X 13 1/2 In. 17.50
Print, Maud Humphrey, Children In Field, 1890, 20 X 16 In. 65.00
Print, Nutting, All Sunshine, Framed, 21 In. 45.00
Print, Nutting, Almost Ready, 1908, Interior, Framed, 16 3/4 In. 50.00
Print, Nutting, Birch Grove, 17 X 13 In. 35.00
Print, Nutting, Bonnie May, Color, Framed, 16 X 14 In. 30.00
Print, Nutting, Brook & Blossom 16.00
Print, Nutting, Elm & Bridge, Framed 9 3/4 X 4 In. 24.00
Print, Nutting, Fall Foliage, Framed, 7 X 4 In. 18.00
Print, Nutting, Garden Entrance, Framed, 7 X 4 In. 18.00
Print, Nutting, Honeymoon Drive, Color, 15 In. 22.00
Print, Nutting, Interior, Lady At Fireplace, Signed, 5 3/4 In. 25.00
Print, Nutting, Ivy & Rose Cloisters, Matted, Framed, 18 In. 27.00
Print, Nutting, Ladies In Early American Room, Framed, 14 X 12 In. 35.00
Print, Nutting, Lady Knocking On Front Door, Framed, 19 In. 30.00
Print, Nutting, Mass.Beautiful, Autographed, 1935 .... 20.00
Print, Nutting, Mohawk Drive, Framed, 21 1/2 In. 25.00
Print, Nutting, Pastoral Brook, Framed, 16 1/2 X 10 1/2 In. 18.00
Print, Nutting, Pergola, Amalfi, Framed, 6 1/2 X 4 1/2 In. 16.00
Print, Nutting, Polishing The Sheffield, Rosewood Frame, 18 X 10 In. 42.50
Print, Nutting, Purity, Framed, 21 1/2 In. 26.00
Print, Nutting, River & Road Scene, Framed, 4 3/4 X 2 1/2 In. 14.50
Print, Nutting, Rug Maker, 1916, 12 1/2 X 9 3/4 In. 35.00
Print, Nutting, Rural Stream, Framed, 9 1/2 X 7 1/2 In. 22.50
Print, Nutting, Rural Sweetness, 25 X 21 In., Framed And Signed 35.00
Print, Nutting, Sea Ledges, 1916, 13 1/2 X 11 1/2 In. 25.00
Print, Nutting, Slack Water, Color Tinted Photograph, 9 1/4 X 3 1/4 In. 12.00
Print, Nutting, Summer Wind, Framed, 21 1/2 In. 27.00
Print, Nutting, Unbroken Flow, Framed, 21 X 12 In. 25.00
Print, Nutting, Water, Road, Sky, Flowering Trees, Long, 12 3/4 In. 17.00
Print, Ogden, 19th Century Soldiers, 1885, Color, Framed, 23 X 20 In. 38.00
Print, Parrish, Air Castles, Framed, 16 X 12 In. 25.00
Print, Parrish, Circe's Palace, Framed, 14 X 11 In. 30.00
Print, Parrish, Daybreak, Framed, 15 X 12 In. 30.00
Print, Parrish, Daybreak, Framed, 21 X 13 In. 80.00
Print, Parrish, Daybreak, Framed, 21 X 33 In. 80.00
Print, Parrish, Daybreak, Large 48.00
Print, Parrish, Daybreak, Medium 32.00
Print, Parrish, Garden Of Allah, Large 55.00
Print, Parrish, Garden Of Allah, 10 1/2 X 6 In. 12.50
Print, Parrish, King Sampling Tarts, From Knaves Of Hearts, 21 X 15 In. 36.00
Print, Parrish, Knave Bowing Before King, From Knaves Of Hearts, 21 X 15 In. 35.00
Print, Parrish, Long-Haired Lady Standing On Steps, Framed, 11 X 9 In. 15.00
Print, Parrish, Lute Players, 10 X 6 1/4 In. 32.50
Print, Parrish, Prince Codadad, Framed, 14 X 11 In. 29.00
Print, Parrish, Romance, Framed, 26 1/4 X 17 In. 75.00
Print, Parrish, Seated Jesters, From Knaves Of Hearts, 21 X 15 In. 32.00
Print, Parrish, Solitude, 1932 Calendar 30.00
Print, Parrish, 2 Cooks With Spoons, From Knaves Of Hearts, 21 X 15 In. 33.00
Print, Parsons, Tomb Of Henry Martyn At Tocat In Turkey, Lithograph, 18 In. 25.00
Print, Perine, Abraham Lincoln, 1864, Steel Engraving, Walnut Frame, 17 In. 32.00
Print, Prang, Battle Of Antietam, 1887, Lithograph, Color, 23 1/2 X 17 In. 40.00
Print, Prang, Battle Of Kenesaw Mountain, 1887, Lithograph, Color, 23 1/2 In. 40.00
Print, Prang, Confederate Army's Finest Hours, 1887, Lithograph ....*Color* 40.00
Print, Prang, Rest On The Roadside, 1865, Pine Frame, 10 X 12 In. 20.00
Print, Prang, Siege Of Vicksburg, Framed, 27 X 20 In. 55.00
Print, Rockwell, Freedom From Fear, 40 X 28 1/2 In. 34.00

Print, Rockwell, Main Street At Christmas, Color, 30 X 12 In. 25.00
Print, Thompson, Old Home Road, Framed, 8 3/4 X 7 In. 16.00
Print, Werner, Sleighing In The Country, C.1890, Lithograph, Color, 12 In. 12.50
Print, Werner, Winter In Central Park, C.1890, Lithograph, Color, 12 X 10 In. 12.50
Print, Wilson, Lady In Blue Dress, Mezzotint, Framed, 21 X 17 In. 125.00
Print, Winslow, New Year 1869, Woodcut, 16 X 10 In. 10.00
Print, Wordsworth, Boy Of Winander, 1877, Framed, 23 1/2 X 14 In. 20.00
Providential, Tile, Dark Brown, Girl's Head, 6 X 6 In. 55.00

Purple Slag, see Slag, Purple

Quartz, Figurine, Mei Jen Holding Peony Blossom, Rose, 14 In. 3500.00
Quartz, Figurine, Rabbit, Rose, Brown Tipped Ears, Carved, 2 1/2 In. 85.00
Quartz, Urn, Covered, Smoky, Carved, Triangular, 7 In. 600.00
Queensware, Cup & Saucer, Demitasse, White, Blue Grapes & Leaves 12.50

Quezal

Quezal glass was made from 1901 to 1920 by Martin Bach, Sr. He made iridescent glass of the same type as Tiffany.

Quezal, Bowl, Blue Iridescent, 5 1/2 X 3 3/4 In. 450.00
Quezal, Bowl, Deep Collar, Gold Pink Iridescent, Signed, 8 In. 150.00
Quezal, Bowl, Gold & Purple Iridescent, 3 X 1 3/4 In. 145.00
Quezal, Lamp, Brass, 2 Gold Spider Webs On Green Shades, 21 In. 450.00
Quezal, Lamp, Cream Color, Pulled Blue Feathers, 14 In. 195.00
Quezal, Lampshade, Amber Iridescent, Optic Ribbed, 7 X 4 3/4 In. 200.00
Quezal, Lampshade, Opalescent Snakeskin, Pulled Gold & Purple, 4 1/4 In. 170.00
Quezal, Lampshade, Opalescent, Gold Zipper Pattern, 3 1/4 In. 125.00
Quezal, Salt, Gold, Ribbed, Silver Overlay 350.00
Quezal, Salt, Master, Amber To Purple Iridescent, 4 X 2 1/4 In. 235.00
Quezal, Salt, Paneled, Gold, Signed 115.00
Quezal, Salt, Silver Deposit, Ribbed, Gold Luster, Iridescent, Signed 250.00
Quezal, Salt, Silver-Overlay, Large, Ribbed, Signed, Rainbow Iridescence 250.00
Quezal, Shade, Amber Iridescent, Ribbed, Signed 125.00
Quezal, Shade, Applied Glass, Heart-Shaped Designs, 6 In., Signed 110.00
Quezal, Shade, Dark Green Feather, Finger Bowl Shape, Pair 250.00
Quezal, Shade, Gold Hearts, Vines, Webbing, Signed 128.00
Quezal, Shade, Gold Iridescent, Ribbed, Signed 80.00
Quezal, Shade, Gold Iridescent, Slightly Ribbed, Pink & Red, Signed 135.00
Quezal, Shade, Gold Iridescent, Snakeskin Surface, Gas Light, 5 1/4 In., Pair 170.00
Quezal, Shade, Gold Lily, Signed, 5 1/4 In., Set Of 4 290.00
Quezal, Shade, Green Feather Over Gold Fishnet, Signed, 7 In. 400.00
Quezal, Shade, Green Iridescent, Gold Iridescent Outline On White, Signed 112.00
Quezal, Shade, Green Pulled Feather Design, Iridescent, 7 In., Pair 180.00
Quezal, Shade, Hearts & Vines, Threaded, 4 In., Set Of 5 550.00
Quezal, Shade, Opal & Gold, Green Hooked Feathering, Gold Lined, 7 In., Pair 170.00
Quezal, Shade, Opalescent, C.1901, Inscribed Quezal, Bulbous Shape, Set Of 4 450.00
Quezal, Shade, Opalescent, Green Feathers, Gold Edge, 6 1/2 In., Set Of 5 500.00
Quezal, Shade, Opalescent, Yellow Feather, 5 In. 80.00
Quezal, Shade, Peacock Feather Decoration, Signed, 13 1235.00
Quezal, Shade, Platinum Zipper Over Green Pulled Decoration On Green 350.00
Quezal, Shade, White Feather On Gold, Iridescent, Machine Filigree 145.00
Quezal, Shade, White, Gold Fishnet, Pumpkin Gold Interior, 5 3/4 In. 140.00
Quezal, Shade, Yellow & Green Feather, Signed, Set Of 4 320.00
Quezal, Shade, Yellow Feathers, Gold Border, 16 In. 525.00
Quezal, Shade, Yellow Feathers, Turquoise Edge On Opal, One Signed, Pair 250.00
Quezal, Vase, Agate, 7 1/2 In. 1250.00
Quezal, Vase, Amber Iridescent, Green & Turquoise Highlights, 2 1/2 In. 245.00
Quezal, Vase, Blue Iridescent, Floriform, 10 In. 875.00
Quezal, Vase, Blue Iridescent, Pulled Green Feathers, 8 In. 950.00
Quezal, Vase, Blue King Tut On Gold Iridescent, Signed, 10 In. 675.00
Quezal, Vase, Dark Green, Melon Ribbed, Gold & Platinum Trim, 4 1/2 In. 1050.00
Quezal, Vase, Feather Decoration, Signed 1200.00
Quezal, Vase, Gold, Green Swirls, 10 In. 850.00
Quezal, Vase, Gold, Turned-Over Collar, 4 3/4 In. 225.00
Quezal, Vase, Green Iridescent Over White, Ribbed, Silver Loops, 14 In. 1450.00
Quezal, Vase, Green Iridescent, Ovoid, 7 In. 210.00
Quezal, Vase, Iridescent, Globular Amber Body, Signed Quezal, 1280, 4 1/2 In. 375.00
Quezal, Vase, Jack-In-The-Pulpit, Green, Silver & Gold, 14 1/2 In. 500.00

Quezal, Vase, Orange Butterscotch, Floriform, 11 In. 450.00
Quezal, Vase, Orange Shades, Amber & Silver Peacock Feather, 14 In. 675.00
Quezal, Vase, Peacock Feather, 10 In. 675.00
Quezal, Vase, Pulled Feather Decoration, Green, White, Gold, 3 Feet, Signed 1150.00
Quezal, Vase, Trumpet Shape, Pink & Amber, Signed Quezal 297, 6 In. 525.00
Quezal, Vase, 3 Gold Scrolled Feet, Pulled Feather, Green, Signed 1150.00
Quilt, see Textile, Quilt

Quimper pottery was made in Finistere, France, after 1900. Most of the pieces found today were made during the twentieth century.A Quimper factory has worked in France since the eighteenth century.

Quimper, Ashtray, Mont St.Michel Coat-Of-Arms On Back, 2 3/4 X 4 In. 9.75
Quimper, Bell, Yellow 20.00
Quimper, Bowl, Footed, H.R. Mark 10.00
Quimper, Bowl, Peasant Lady Center, White, Yellow & Blue Trim, Handled, 4 In. 8.00
Quimper, Bowl, Porridge, Handled 16.00
Quimper, Bowl, Signed PB, 6 In. 35.00
Quimper, Bowl, White, Lady With Bouquet Of Flowers, Blue Handles, 5 3/4 In. 16.50
Quimper, Bowl, Yellow Green, Square, 4 X 2 In. 10.00
Quimper, Butter Pat, Variegated Edge, Dated '98 .... 35.00
Quimper, Candlestick, Figural, Horse 85.00
Quimper, Candlestick, French Revolution Centennial, 9 In., Pair 165.00
Quimper, Chamberstick, Pair 68.00
Quimper, Cup & Saucer, Peasant Woman, Florals 16.00
Quimper, Dish, Oval, Bow And Bagpipe, 7 In. 22.00
Quimper, Eggcup 7.50
Quimper, Figurine, Man & Woman Attached, 3 1/2 In. 20.00
Quimper, Figurine, Man & Woman Attached, 7 In. 45.00
Quimper, Flower Holder, Five Fingers, 3 3/4 In. 32.00
Quimper, Inkstand, Floral, Carved & Pierced Oak Stand, Double 135.00
Quimper, Inkwell, Peasant Woman, Floral Decoration, Round Blue Spatter 50.00

Quimper, Pitcher, Marked France, 5 1/2 In.

Quimper, Pitcher, Marked France, 5 1/2 In. .... *Illus* 128.00
Quimper, Pitcher, Peasant, Foliage, 3 In. 12.00
Quimper, Pitcher, Pink & Blue, 5 In. 12.00
Quimper, Pitcher, White, Peasant Man, Blues & Oranges, Crimped Spout, 4 In. 18.50
Quimper, Pitcher, White, Peasant Woman, Bulbous, 5 In. 20.00
Quimper, Plate, Cup 8.00
Quimper, Plate, Henriot, France, 8 1/2 In. 17.00
Quimper, Plate, Lady Peasant, 5 3/4 In. 17.50
Quimper, Plate, Man Peasant, 5 3/4 In. 17.50
Quimper, Plate, Oyster 25.00
Quimper, Plate, Yellow, Child With Fishing Pole, 8 1/2 In. 35.00
Quimper, Platter, 4 1/4 X 6 1/2 In. 18.00
Quimper, Salt, Double, Attached Shoe 30.00
Quimper, Shoe, Dutch, 2 Connected By Ring Handle Top, Tulips & Figures, 3 In. 25.00
Quimper, Shoes, Dutch, Peasant Man & Woman, Henriot Quimper, Pair 22.00

Quimper, Shoes, Dutch, Peasant Women & Man, Pair, 2 3/4 In., Pair 22.00
Quimper, Teapot, Body Formed By Two Cylinders 55.00
Quimper, Teapot, Yellow, Woman & Man Figures 18.00
Quimper, Vase, Wall, Cone, 10 1/2 In. 85.00

Radford pottery was made by Alfred Radford in Broadway, Virginia, Tiffin and Zanesville, Ohio, and Clarksburg, West Virginia, from 1891 until 1912. Jasperware, Ruko, Thera, Radera, and Velvety Art Ware were made.

Radford, Candlestick, Matte Green, Painted Floral & Leaves, 6 1/2 In. 37.50
Radford, Vase, Brown, White Cameo Winged Children On Blue, 7 1/4 In. 185.00
Radford, Vase, Jasper, 5 1/2 In. 95.00
Radford, Vase, Matte Green, Painted Floral & Leaves, 6 In. 37.50
Radio, Atwater Kent, Model 20, 1924, 5 Tube 85.00
Radio, Atwater Kent, Model 48, 6 Tube 60.00
Radio, Atwater Kent, Model 55, 2 Piece, All Metal, Black & Red 55.00
Radio, Atwater Kent, Model 612, Walnut Cabinet, Floor Model 60.00
Radio, Coronado, Console 20.00
Radio, Crystal, Cat Whisker, Earphones 25.00
Radio, Marwol, Jewel, Battery Operated 75.00
Radio, Philmore Brand, Crystal, Original Box 23.00
Radio, Roger Maris, Mickey Mantle 35.00
Radio, Zenith, Stratosphere 560.00
Radio, Zenith, Transoceanic, World War II 45.00
Railiroad, Pass, Norfolk & Western, 1909 .... 3.00
Railroad, Ashtray, C.& O., George Washington, Rectangular 23.00
Railroad, Ashtray, Floor Model, Boston & Main R.R.Brass, 7 1/2 In. 85.00
Railroad, Ashtray, N.Y.Central, 24K Gold Trim 22.00
Railroad, Ashtray, Northern Pacific, Square, 4 1/2 In. 9.50
Railroad, Ashtray, Pennsylvania RR 5.00
Railroad, Badge, Cap, Bangor & Aroostook, Porter 7.95
Railroad, Badge, Denver & Rio Grande, Detective 25.00
Railroad, Badge, Police, Erie RR 65.00
Railroad, Badge, Railway Police, D.L. & W. RR Co. 65.00
Railroad, Barrel, Water, Santa Fe, Wooden 45.00
Railroad, Book, Transfer Passes, Seattle St.Railway, C.1930 .... 7.50
Railroad, Bottle, Milk, Missouri Pacific, Embossed In Red Enamel, 1/2 Pint 3.00
Railroad, Bowl, N.Y.C., Syracuse, 6 1/4 In. 10.00
Railroad, Bridge Set, Milwaukee R.R. 5.00
Railroad, Butter Pat, Santa Fe R.R., International Silver Plate 2.75
Railroad, Cabinet, C.B.& Q.R.R., Pine, 1909, 2 Doors, 29 X 19 In. 137.00
Railroad, Can, Seaboard R.R., Pouring Spout, Bail, 2 Gallon 12.50
Railroad, Can, Southern R.R., Pouring Spout, Bail, Gallon 14.50
Railroad, Can, Water, Burlington Route, Embossed, Gallon 20.00
Railroad, Can, Water, N.P.Ry., Embossed, Gallon 20.00
Railroad, Can, Watering, D.& H.R.R. 35.00
Railroad, Cards, Playing, Burlington Route 6.00
Railroad, Cards, Playing, Chessie Cats 5.00
Railroad, Cards, Playing, D.M.& I.R.R.R., Deck 3.00
Railroad, Cards, Playing, Santa Fe, 1921, Deck 6.50
Railroad, Cards, Playing, Southern Pacific, 1943, Deck 6.50
Railroad, Centennial, Declaration Of Independence, 1876, Chicago & Western 25.00
Railroad, Cover, Hot Dish, Rock Island, Silver 15.00
Railroad, Cover, Silver Dish, Rock Island Lines, 1927 .... 17.50
Railroad, Creamer, Wabash R.R., Silver 12.00
Railroad, Cup, Pacific Railroad, Tin 10.00
Railroad, Dish, Covered, Rock Island Lines, Heavy Silver 18.50
Railroad, Dish, Hot, Rock Island Lines, Covered, Silver 18.50
Railroad, Dish, Side, B & O Railroad, Horse Drawn Car, 1830, Shenango China 10.00
Railroad, Figurine, N.P.R.R., Man Holding Baked Potato, Chalk, 5 1/2 In. 15.00
Railroad, Glass, Bar, Double Old-Fashioned, Pennsylvania RR 14.00
Railroad, Globe, Lantern, P.R.R., Red 3.50
Railroad, Gravy Boat, B & O, White With Gold Band, Shenango 45.00
Railroad, Hammer, C.S.T.P.M.& O. R.R., 2 Lbs. 6.00
Railroad, Hammer, Gandy Dancer, P.R.R. 19.00

Railroad, Jacket, Conductor's Dress, P.R.R., Trim & Buttons 60.00
Railroad, Key, Switch, I.C.R.R. 12.00
Railroad, Key, Switch, N.Y.C.S., Brass 8.50
Railroad, Key, Switch, Union Pacific 9.00
Railroad, Knife, Remington, Pearl Handle, Illinois Central 48.00
Railroad, Knife, Table, Southern Pacific 6.00
Railroad, Lamp, Adlake, 10 In. 30.00
Railroad, Lamp, Caboose Wall, Brass Font & Shade, Glass Chimney, 22 In. 40.00
Railroad, Lamp, Caboose, Adams & Westlake Co., Chicago, Kerosene, 14 1/2 In. 42.50
Railroad, Lamp, Caboose, Adlake Westlake 32.00
Railroad, Lamp, Caboose, Wabash R.R., Heavy Duty Holder For Wall 55.00
Railroad, Lamp, Camp Car, C.& O. R.R., Hanging 37.50
Railroad, Lamp, Kerosene, C.N.R.R., Office, Brass 85.00
Railroad, Lantern, A.T.& S.F.R.R., Clear Globe 18.50
Railroad, Lantern, Adams, Westlake, Kerosene, Etched Erie On Red Globe 30.00
Railroad, Lantern, Adlake C Of Gr. R.R., Clear Globe 18.00
Railroad, Lantern, Adlake C Of Gr. R.R., Ruby Red Globe 28.00
Railroad, Lantern, Adlake, C.P.R., Kerosene, Clear Globe 35.00
Railroad, Lantern, Adlake, L. & N. 35.00
Railroad, Lantern, Arlington R.R. 25.00
Railroad, Lantern, Armspear, Frame Marked P.R.R.V.G. 35.00
Railroad, Lantern, B & M, Embossed Frame 45.00
Railroad, Lantern, B.& M., Dietz, Vesta, Kerosene, Switchman's, 10 1/2 In. 25.00
Railroad, Lantern, B.& M.R.R., Dietz, Patent 1910, Red Globe, 15 In. 40.00
Railroad, Lantern, Blue Shade, Oil, 1913/23, Adlake, Kerosene 25.00
Railroad, Lantern, British, C.1870, Slant Back, Copper & Tin, Green Paint 175.00
Railroad, Lantern, C.M.S.& P., Bell Brass Top, Etched Globe 125.00
Railroad, Lantern, Caboose, Wabash 39.00
Railroad, Lantern, Canadian RR, Clear Globe, 1922 Pat.Pend. 12.00
Railroad, Lantern, Clear Globe, Burnished, C.C.Co., St.Louis, N.Y.C. 35.00
Railroad, Lantern, Clear Globe, C.C.Co., St.Louis, N.Y.C., Burnished 35.00
Railroad, Lantern, Erie, Embossed Frame 45.00
Railroad, Lantern, Erie, Etched Red Globe 50.00
Railroad, Lantern, French, Pair 128.00
Railroad, Lantern, Handlan, Marked PRR 32.00
Railroad, Lantern, Keystone, Casey, L.V.R.R. 50.00
Railroad, Lantern, Louisville Nashville, Short Clear Globe 15.00
Railroad, Lantern, Maine Central R.R., Bulls-Eye Type Lenses, 16 1/2 In. 85.00
Railroad, Lantern, Michigan Central, 5 3/8 In. 50.00
Railroad, Lantern, Missouri Pacific R.R., Clear Globe 37.50
Railroad, Lantern, Missouri Pacific R.R., Red Globe 37.50
Railroad, Lantern, N.& W.R.R., Clear Globe 18.50
Railroad, Lantern, N.P.R.R., Adams Westlake, Yellow Globe 35.00
Railroad, Lantern, N.W.R.R. 25.00
Railroad, Lantern, N.Y., Acme, Dietz, Hooded, Yard 64.00
Railroad, Lantern, N.Y.C., Bell Bottom 35.00
Railroad, Lantern, N.Y.C., Trainman's Hand, Dietz 26.00
Railroad, Lantern, N.Y.C.R.R. 15.00
Railroad, Lantern, N.Y.C.S., Dietz Vesta Red Globe 12.00
Railroad, Lantern, N.Y.Central Lines, Red Globe 16.00
Railroad, Lantern, New Haven, Red Globe 20.00
Railroad, Lantern, New York Central, Bell Bottom 30.00
Railroad, Lantern, P & LERR, Clear Globe 23.00
Railroad, Lantern, P.R.R., Casey 30.00
Railroad, Lantern, P.R.R., Pa. Lines, Reliable 50.00
Railroad, Lantern, Pacific Railroad, Casey 28.00
Railroad, Lantern, Penn Central, R.R., Red Globe 18.50
Railroad, Lantern, Red Globe, Flashing, Dated 1911-23, AT & SFRY 35.00
Railroad, Lantern, Red Globe, I.C.R.R., St.Louis, 5 3/8 In. 25.00
Railroad, Lantern, Signal, Boy Patent, Sept.19, '76 .... 30.00
Railroad, Lantern, Southern R.R., Blue Globe 30.00
Railroad, Lantern, Stonebridge, Folding 15.00
Railroad, Lantern, T & P., Etched Clear Globe 40.00
Railroad, Lantern, U.P.R.R., Etched Red Globe 20.00
Railroad, Lantern, Union Pacific 30.00

Railroad, Lantern, Warsaw, N.Y. 15.00
Railroad, Lantern, White Star, Dietz, 98, Tubular 80.00
Railroad, Lock, Brass, L & N RR 20.00
Railroad, Lock, N.Y.Ontario & Western, Steel, & Key 40.00
Railroad, Lock, Rock Island Railroad 8.00
Railroad, Lock, Switch, L.& N. 10.00
Railroad, Lock, Switch, N.Y.C., Brass With Chain 12.00
Railroad, Lock, Switch, New York Central, Brass Key 18.00
Railroad, Lock, Switch, Union Pacific, Brass 17.50
Railroad, Map, Steamship Route, Chesapeake Bay, 1906, Oak Frame, 19 X 37 In. 25.00
Railroad, Mirror, B.& M.R.R., 1937, Metal Frame, 22 X 14 In. 8.00
Railroad, Mirror, N.Y.C. System, Pocket 2.50
Railroad, Oilcan, Central Of Georgia R.R. 16.00
Railroad, Oilcan, Mo Pac R R, Eagle, Gallon 15.00
Railroad, Oilcan, Union Pacific, Spout, Metal, Gallon 22.50
Railroad, Padlock, A.T.& S.F.Ry. 10.00
Railroad, Padlock, M.K.T. 10.00
Railroad, Pass, C.& N.W.R.R., 1905, Annual 3.50
Railroad, Pickhead, C.M.S.T.P.& P.R.R. 6.50
Railroad, Pickhead, Rio Grande, 23 In. 15.00
Railroad, Plate, B.& O., Thomas Viaduct, Blue, Scammels, 7 In. 18.00
Railroad, Plate, Baltimore & Ohio, Blue & White, 1827-1894, 9 In. 35.00
Railroad, Plate, Baltimore & Ohio, Blue & Whiteback History Of R.R., 9 In. 40.00
Railroad, Plate, Chesapeake & Ohio, White, Gold Border, 8 In. 12.50
Railroad, Plate, Dinner, Chesapeake & Ohio, Ferry Boat 8.50
Railroad, Plate, N.Y.C. 1831 Engine, Blue & White, Buffalo, 7 3/4 In. 10.00
Railroad, Plate, Porcelain, Jubilee Commemoration, 1875 36.00
Railroad, Plate, Union Pacific, Blue & White, Maddock, 7 1/2 In. 5.50
Railroad, Platter, Baltimore & Ohio, Blue & White, 11 1/2 In. 45.00
Railroad, Postcard, Georgetown Loop Railroad, 1909, Set Of 5 1.00
Railroad, Saucer, B & O Railroad, Thomas Viaduct, Shenango China, Blue, 5 In. 9.00
Railroad, Sign, Atlantic Coast Line, Round, Tin, 30 In. 15.00
Railroad, Sign, Atlantic Coast Line, Yellow & Black, Round, 17 In. 15.00
Railroad, Sign, Rea Express, White Letters On Green, 60 In. 39.00
Railroad, Sledgehammer, Union Pacific, 22 1/2 In. 22.00
Railroad, Stove, M.K.& T. R.R., Caboose, Cannonball Type 275.00
Railroad, Stretcher, N.Y.C.R.R., Canvas 95.00
Railroad, Switchlock, U.S.Y.O., Brass 4.50
Railroad, Tag, Missouri Pacific Lines, Celluloid, 2 In. 4.50
Railroad, Teapot, Panama Line R.R. 15.00
Railroad, Timetable, Chicago & Eastern, 1916 6.00
Railroad, Timetable, Chicago & Northwestern, 1962 4.00
Railroad, Timetable, Employees', Boston & Albany, 1884 10.00
Railroad, Timetable, Hudson River Dayline 3.00
Railroad, Timetable, Wabash, 1893, 36 X 24 In. 9.00
Railroad, Tongs, Ice Cube, Santa Fe, Silver Plate 20.00
Railroad, Tumbler, Highball, A.C.L., Libbey 3.00
Railroad, Tumbler, Highball, Erie R.R., Libbey 3.00
Railroad, Tumbler, Highball, N.Y.C., Libbey 3.00
Railroad, Tumbler, Iced Tea, N.Y.C., Libbey 3.00
Railroad, Tumbler, Juice, N.Y.C., Libbey 3.00
Railroad, Tumbler, New York Central 3.75
Railroad, Tumbler, Pacific Railroad 10.00
Railroad, Tumbler, Pennsylvania R.R. 1.75
Railroad, Tumbler, Tom Collins, B. & O., Libbey 3.00
Railroad, Ventilator, Pullman, Automatic, Oak Transom, Frosted Glass 50.00
Railroad, Wrench, S.I.C.R.R., Fits 2 1/4 X 1 3/4 In. Nuts 11.00

Rainbow, see Mother-of-Pearl, Satin Glass

The Red Wing Pottery of Red Wing, Minnesota, was a firm started in 1878. It was not until the 1920s that art pottery was made. It closed in 1967. Rumrill pottery was made for George Rumrill by the Red Wing Pottery Company and other firms. It was sold in the 1930s.

Red Wing, Basket, Oatmeal, 7 X 7 In. 12.00
Red Wing, Bowl, Oatmeal, Pink, 8 1/2 X 6 In. 12.00

Red Wing, Churn, 5 Gallon 75.00
Red Wing, Cooler, Water, 5 Gallon 75.00
Red Wing, Crock, Blue, 2 Gallon 49.00
Red Wing, Jar, Beater 12.50
Red Wing, Jar, Cookie, Baker, Italian 26.00
Red Wing, Jar, Cookie, Baker, Yellow 20.00
Red Wing, Jar, Cookie, Blue Monk 20.00
Red Wing, Jar, Cookie, Dutch Girl, Ton .... 20.00 To 25.00
Red Wing, Jar, Cookie, Dutch Girl, Yellow 20.00
Red Wing, Jar, Cookie, Green Banana Bunch 18.00
Red Wing, Jar, Fruit, Quart, Mason Lid 38.50
Red Wing, Jug, Grape Leaf, Beehive, 4 Gallon 35.00
Red Wing, Jug, Wide Mouth, Stoneware 21.50
Red Wing, Mug, Brown With Green 5.00
Red Wing, Tureen, Bob White Cover 21.00
Red Wing, Urn, Light Green, 2 Handles, 871, 7 In. 15.00
Red Wing, Vase, Green, Dancing Maid, High Glaze, 9 1/4 In. 39.00
Red Wing, Vase, Matte Green, Fan, 12 In. 12.50
Red Wing, Vase, Powder Blue, Floral, Ribbed, Scalloped Top, Handled, 9 In. 13.00
Red Wing, Vase, Stoneware, 10 1/2 In. 9.00
Red Wing, Vase, Turquoise, Beige Matte Finish, 12 In. 23.00
Red Wing, Vase, 9 1/2 In. 5.50

Redware is a hard red stoneware that originated in the late 1600s and continues to be made. The term is also used to describe any common clay pottery that is reddish in color.

Redware, see also Kitchen, Koreanware

Redware, Beaker, Pennsylvania, Sgraffito Of Dogs, Yellow & Green Glaze, 6 In. 365.00
Redware, Beaker, 2 Dogs, Sgraffito Decoration, Pennsylvania, 5 1/2 In. 365.00
Redware, Bean Pot, Covered, Handled, Inside Glaze, 6 In. 28.00
Redware, Bedpan, Doughnut Shape 45.00
Redware, Bowl, Slip Decorated, Piecrust Edge, 11 1/2 In. 95.00
Redware, Bowl, Yellow Slip Zigzags, C.1890, Rectangular, 16 X 12 In. 110.00
Redware, Candlestick, Brown Glaze, Classic Figure Overglaze, English, C.1830 .... 140.00
Redware, Chamber Pot, Western Ontario 260.00
Redware, Colander, Glazed Outside & Inside, 7 3/4 X 4 1/2 In. 30.00
Redware, Crock, Cream, D.M.Bakers Pottery, Waynesboro, Pa., Turned Lip, 8 In. 35.00
Redware, Crock, Dark Brown Glaze, Flaring Lip, Incised 15 On Base, 10 In. 27.50
Redware, Cup, Saki, Blue & White, Yellow Slip Interior 5.00
Redware, Flask, Manganese Splotches, 7 In. 140.00
Redware, Jar, Bulbous, Glazed Interior, Tapered, 5 1/2 In. 27.50
Redware, Jar, Cookie, Coppery & Silvery Decoration, Cats At Table 15.00
Redware, Jar, Hudson Valley, Ovoid 180.00
Redware, Jar, Weyman's Snuff, Pittsburgh, Pa., Glazed Interior 49.50
Redware, Jug, Brown Glaze, Handled, 6 1/2 X 7 In. 60.00
Redware, Pitcher, Milk, Farrar Pottery, St.John, P.Q. 85.00
Redware, Spittoon, Ohio, Glazed 110.00
Redware, Teapot, Yihsing, Hand-Painted Enamel Decoration, 5 1/2 In. 75.00
Redware, Vase, Thebis & Hephastos, 3 Handles, L.Hyarth, C.1870, 9 1/2 In. 150.00

Reverse Painting, see Painting, Reverse on Glass

Riceszinn, Vase, Purple Iridescent, Handled Pewter Frame, 7 1/4 In. 240.00
Richard, Bottle, Perfume, Cameo, Cobalt Cut To Tangerine, Signed, 6 In. 185.00
Richard, Lamp, Green Cased, Brown & Rust Firs, Pinecones On Base, 15 1/2 In. 1125.00
Richard, Perfumer, Orange & Black, Cameo 325.00
Richard, Vase, Browns, Gold, & Russet, Palm Trees Scene, 16 In. 850.00
Richard, Vase, Cream Satin, Royal Blue Clover Blossoms, 3 5/8 In. 150.00
Richard, Vase, Frosted, Apricot Scene, Fluted Top, 7 1/2 In. 398.00
Richard, Vase, Mottled Blue White Frosted, Purple Holly & Leaves, 7 3/4 In. 210.00
Richard, Vase, Orange Ground, Purplish Brown Cameo Leaves, 6 1/2 In. 275.00
Richard, Vase, Orange, Blue Leaves & Stems, Pedestal Base, 4 1/2 In. 295.00
Richard, Vase, Orange, Purple Brown Leaves, 6 1/2 In. .... 275.00 To 360.00
Richard, Vase, Yellow, Dark Green Floral & Leaves, 4 1/4 In. 168.00

Ridgway pottery has been made in the Staffordshire District in England since 1808 by a series of companies with the name Ridgway. The

transfer-design dinner sets are the most widely known product. They are still being made.

Ridgway, Berry Bowl, Coaching Days, True-Every Word Of It, 10 3/4 In. 45.00
Ridgway, Bowl, African Camp, Blue, Footed, C.1830, 9 In. 100.00
Ridgway, Bowl, Coaching Days, Walking Up The Hill & Racing The Mill, 8 In. 38.00
Ridgway, Bowl, Coaching Days, Watering The Horses, 9 1/2 In. 39.00
Ridgway, Bowl, Cream Soup, Psyche 6.00
Ridgway, Bowl, Pickwick Papers, Silver Luster Top, Octagonal, 8 5/8 In. 60.00
Ridgway, Bowl, Racing The Mail, 8 In. 44.00
Ridgway, Bowl, Serving, Millais, Miniature 25.00
Ridgway, Cereal Bowl, Oriental, Medium Blue 4.50
Ridgway, Chamber Pot, Covered, Verona, Blue On White 22.00
Ridgway, Compote, Footed, Coaching Days And Ways, Chocolate Brown, 3 X 9 In. 90.00
Ridgway, Cup & Saucer, Handleless, Delaware, Light Blue, Ironstone 28.00
Ridgway, Jug, Coaching Days, Henry VIII & Abbot Of Reading, Squat, 5 In. 45.00
Ridgway, Jug, Tam O'Shanter, Pewter Top, Blue Glaze 75.00
Ridgway, Mug, Coaching Days & Coaching Ways, Brown With Black 21.00
Ridgway, Mug, Coaching Days & Coaching Ways, 4 In. 22.00
Ridgway, Mug, Eloped, 5 In. 30.00
Ridgway, Mug, Salisbury Cathedral, 4 1/2 In. 22.00
Ridgway, Pitcher Set, Coaching Days & Coaching Ways, 5 1/2 To 7 In., 3 .... 100.00
Ridgway, Pitcher, A Morning Draught, 7 In. 35.00
Ridgway, Pitcher, Acanthus Leaves, Bacchus, Pan Handle, C.1835, 9 1/2 In. 165.00
Ridgway, Pitcher, Brown, Harbor Scenes, Copper Luster Handle, C.1912, 7 In. 65.00
Ridgway, Pitcher, Coaching Days & Coaching Ways, 12 In. 100.00
Ridgway, Pitcher, Coaching Days, Driver & Riders, C.1905, 7 1/4 In. 65.00
Ridgway, Pitcher, Coaching Days, Returning Home 22.50
Ridgway, Pitcher, Green Salt Glaze, Raised Cattail Design, 10 In. 115.00
Ridgway, Pitcher, Jousting Knights, Pale Blue, Stoneware, 1840, 6 In. 98.00
Ridgway, Pitcher, Salt Glaze, Tam-O'-Shanter, Pewter Lid, 1835, 9 In. 145.00
Ridgway, Pitcher, Tam O'Shanter Scene, Pewter Handle, Dated 1835, 9 In. 135.00
Ridgway, Plaque, Coaching Days & Coaching Ways, Harbor Scene, 8 1/2 In. 25.00
Ridgway, Plaque, Porcelain Portrait, Framed Beauy, Bartolozzi, 11 X 8 1/4 In. 90.00
Ridgway, Plate, Blue Floral, Gadrooned, C.1814, J & WR, Hexagon, 9 1/2 In. 35.00
Ridgway, Plate, Burns & Highland Mary, Brown & Gold Rim, 8 In. 24.00
Ridgway, Plate, Coaching Days & Coaching Ways, Charles & The Ostler, 8 In. 15.00
Ridgway, Plate, Coaching Days, At The Crossroads, Scalloped, 9 In. 25.00
Ridgway, Plate, Coaching Days, Breakdown, Caramel, 9 In. 30.00
Ridgway, Plate, Coaching Days, Paying Toll, Caramel, 9 In. 30.00
Ridgway, Plate, Coaching Days, Taking On The Mail, Caramel, 9 In. 30.00
Ridgway, Plate, Coaching Days, Waiting For The Stagecoach, 8 3/4 In. 29.50
Ridgway, Plate, Fairmount Park, Phila., Catskill Moss, Blue, 9 In. 25.00
Ridgway, Plate, Genovese, Black, 8 In. 25.00
Ridgway, Plate, Giraffe, Brown & White, Aug.30, 1836, 10 In. 45.00
Ridgway, Plate, Insane Hospital, Boston, Blue, 7 1/4 In. 150.00
Ridgway, Plate, Lamb By The Guard, 8 In., Pair 48.00
Ridgway, Plate, Marmora, Sepia, C.1835, 9 In. 16.00
Ridgway, Plate, Marmora, 10 1/4 In. 12.50
Ridgway, Plate, Oriental, Dark Blue, 6 3/4 In. 20.00
Ridgway, Plate, Oriental, Green, 9 1/4 In. 25.00
Ridgway, Plate, Oriental, Medium Blue, 6 3/4 In. 4.50
Ridgway, Plate, Pale Blue Tyrolean Decoration, Gold Trim, 9 In. 19.00
Ridgway, Plate, Rothesay Harbor, Caramel, Gold Trim, 9 In. 20.00
Ridgway, Plate, Ruggles House, Newburgh, Hudson River, Blue, 10 1/4 In. 28.00
Ridgway, Plate, Shakespeare, Playing Cards Around Edge, 9 In. 25.00
Ridgway, Platter, Deaf And Dumb Asylum, Hartford, 15 In. 260.00
Ridgway, Platter, Maidenhair Fern, Blue, 4 1/2 X 3 1/4 In. 14.00
Ridgway, Platter, Maidenhair Fern, Blue, 7 X 5 In. 19.00
Ridgway, Platter, Maidenhair Fern, Blue, 7 X 6 In. 22.00
Ridgway, Platter, Maidenhair Fern, Blue, 8 X 6 1/2 In. 25.00
Ridgway, Platter, Tyrolean, Green, 14 3/4 In. 75.00
Ridgway, Spittoon, Ladies, Stoke-On-Trent, 1880, 8 X 3 In. 40.00
Ridgway, Stein, Salt Glaze, Bacchus & Grapevines, Pewter Lid, 11 In. 175.00
Ridgway, Tankard, And Mug Set, Brown With Silver Luster, Scenic, 7 Piece 185.00
Ridgway, Tankard, Coaching Days & Coaching Ways, Eloped, 5 In. 25.00

Ridgway, Tankard, Coaching Days & Coaching Ways, Salisbury Cathedral, 4 In. 18.00
Ridgway, Tankard, Coaching Days & Coaching Ways, 10 1/4 In. 70.00
Ridgway, Tankard, Coaching Days & Coaching Ways, 12 1/2 In. 125.00
Ridgway, Tankard, Coaching Days, Breaking Down Of The Mark, 5 In. 25.00
Ridgway, Tankard, Coaching Days, Silver Luster Handle, Christmas Eve, 5 In. 33.00
Ridgway, Tea Set, Apple Green, Yellow Floral, Gilt, Floral Finials, 3 Piece 115.00
Ridgway, Teapot, Lamballe, Blue & White, Bulbous, 5 1/2 In. 22.00
Ridgway, Teapot, Oriental, Medium Blue, Large 29.50
Ridgway, Tray, Coaching Days, In A Snowdrift, Silver Luster Edge, 12 3/4 In. 69.00
Ridgway, Tray, Coaching Days, Racing The Mail, Oval, Black, Brown, 13 3/4 In. 69.00
Ridgway, Tureen & Underplate, Ribbon Finial & Handles, Monterey 16.00
Ridgway, Tureen & Underplate, Sauce, Covered, Tyrolean, Blue, C.1834 .... 100.00
Ridgway, Tureen, Sepia, Tyrolean, Signed, 12 X 9 1/4 X 6 In. 75.00
Ridgway, Vase, Coaching Days, Coach & Riders, C.1905, 7 In. 60.00

Riviera Ware was made by the Homer Laughlin Co. from 1938 to 1950 Plates were square and cup handles were squared.

Riviera Ware, Cup & Saucer, Green 3.00
Riviera Ware, Plate, Dinner, Yellow, 10 In. 3.00
Riviera Ware, Plate, 9 In., Blue 2.50
Riviera Ware, Sugar, Blue 2.00
Robj, Bottle, Figural, Soldier With Bagpipes, Gilt & White, 5 1/2 In., Pair 85.00

Rockingham in the United States is a brown glazed pottery with a tortoiseshell-like glaze. It was made from 1840 to 1900 by many American potteries. The mottled brown Rockingham wares were first made in England at the Rockingham factory. Other wares were also made by the English firm.

Rockingham, Cuspidor, Mottled Brown, Bearded Man's Head & Scrolled Ovals 35.00
Rockingham, Dish, Cake, English Countryside, Upturned Handles, C.1850 .... 22.00
Rockingham, Dish, Square, Tree Flowers, Exotic, Marked Grameov, 8 In. 79.00
Rockingham, Inkwell, Brown Dog Sitting In Center, 2 Quill Pen Holes, 10 In. 225.00
Rockingham, Jug, Toby 38.00
Rockingham, Mug, 2 Hound Handled, Marked Rockingham Harker, 1840, USA 30.00
Rockingham, Mug, 3 3/4 In. 65.00
Rockingham, Pitcher, Bennington Type, Hunter Scene, 9 1/4 In. 55.00
Rockingham, Pitcher, Buttermilk, Bennington, 7 1/2 In. 65.00
Rockingham, Pitcher, Daniel Boone, 6 1/2 In. .... *Illus* 85.00

Rockingham, Pitcher, Daniel Boone, 6 1/2 In.

Rockingham, Pitcher, Hound Handle, Hunters & Dog Design, Bennett Of Balt. 245.00
Rockingham, Pitcher, Water, Huntress Scene 125.00
Rockingham, Plate, Pie, Impressed Daisy Base Mark, Shelf Rim, 8 1/2 In. 60.00
Rockingham, Plate, Pie, Mottled Glaze, 8 3/4 In. 57.00
Rockingham, Plate, Pie, Mottled Glaze, 10 1/4 In. 68.00
Rockingham, Plate, Pie, Mottled, Glaze, 11 In. 72.00
Rockingham, Plate, Pie, 9 3/4 In. 60.00
Rockingham, Tea & Cake Set, Blue & Gold Floral Panels On White, 46 Piece 750.00
Rockingham, Toby Jug, Man In 3 Cornered Hat Standing 45.00

Rockingham, Toby Mug, Brown Glaze, Man Taking Snuff, 8 1/2 In. 60.00
Rockingham, Toby Mug, Seated Man Holding Mug, Brown, 8 1/2 In. 90.00
Rockingham, Tray, Reserve Panels, Blue & Gold, 2 Handles, Oval, 12 In. 35.00

Rogers, see John Rogers

Rookwood pottery was made in Cincinnati, Ohio, from 1880 to 1960. All of this art pottery is marked, most with the famous flame mark. The R is reversed and placed back to back with the letter P. Flames surround the letters.

Rookwood Vase, Lilies, Harriet Wilcox, 1897, 9 1/2 In. 295.00
Rookwood, Ashtray, Light Green High Glaze, Full Figure Rook, 1946, 7 In. 48.00
Rookwood, Ashtray, NAD 75th Anniversary Convention, 1955 .... 20.00
Rookwood, Ashtray, National Life Insurance, 1914, Wm.McDonald 48.00
Rookwood, Ashtray, Omega Sigma Fraternity National Convention, 1939 .... 18.00
Rookwood, Ashtray, Small Green Fish, 1947 .... 12.00
Rookwood, Ashtray, Sprague & Warner Foods, 1939 .... 24.00
Rookwood, Ashtray, Viking Ship, Colade, Olive Green & Brown Glaze 45.00
Rookwood, Ashtray, White Glaze, Molded Fox On Top Edge, 1945, 7 In. 40.00
Rookwood, Bookend, Basket Of Fruit, 1927, Pair 110.00
Rookwood, Bookend, Dutch Boy & Girl, Matte Finish, Hand-Painted, Pair 145.00
Rookwood, Bookend, High Glaze, Man In Monk's Garb, 7 1/2 In., Pair 100.00
Rookwood, Bookend, Pink Water Lilies, White Base, 1946, 5 1/2 In., Pair 100.00
Rookwood, Bookend, Rook With Leaves & Berries, Green, McDonald, 6 In., Pair 125.00
Rookwood, Bowl Vase, Swirled Rose, Yellow Floral, SBG, 1897, 7 In. 275.00
Rookwood, Bowl, Gold Flying Birds, Butterflies, Bats, & Foliage, 1883, 5 In. 225.00
Rookwood, Bowl, Lotus, Matte Olive To Rose, XIV, 8 In. 37.00
Rookwood, Bowl, Sea Green Matte, Geometrics, Footed, 1913, 6 In. 28.00
Rookwood, Bowl, Turquoise Glaze, Nesting Bird, 1922, 7 X 5 In. 60.00
Rookwood, Bowl, Vellum, Green To Blue Green, Molded, 9 1/4 In. 45.00
Rookwood, Box, Cigarette, Stylized Ship On Cover, Cream, Orange, Signed 100.00
Rookwood, Box, Covered, Art Deco, Louise Abel, Round, 6 X 5 1/2 In. 36.00
Rookwood, Bust, Head Of Young Woman, White Matte Glaze, 8 X 8 In. 100.00
Rookwood, Bust, Young Woman, White Matte Glaze, 8 X 8 In. 125.00
Rookwood, Candleholder, Molded Florals, Drip Glaze, Dated 1921, 4 In. 18.00
Rookwood, Candlestick On Dish, Green With Rose, Swirled Handles, 7 1/4 In. 35.00
Rookwood, Candlestick, Brown Glaze, 2 Handles At Top, 1885, 8 In., Pair 175.00
Rookwood, Candlestick, Rose To Smoke, Oak Leaves, 1921, 3 In. Base, Pair 155.00
Rookwood, Centerpiece Bowl & Frog, Yellow Ocher, 3 Handles, 1920, 9 1/4 In. 55.00
Rookwood, Chalice, 3 Handled, Green, Molded Crabs, Charles A.Duell, 1907 .... 285.00
Rookwood, Chamberstick, Blue, 1922, 7 1/2 X 5 In. 35.00
Rookwood, Chamberstick, Lily Form, Finger, Pink With Gray, 1927, 5 1/2 In. 23.00
Rookwood, Coaster, Potter At The Wheel, 1935 .... 38.00
Rookwood, Creamer, Molded, Standard Glaze, Green, 1906, 3 3/4 X 5 In. 45.00
Rookwood, Creamer, Red Clay Bisque, Daisies, Integral Handle, HW, 1884, 5 In. 275.00
Rookwood, Creamer, Shape 329, High Glaze, Butterfly Handle, H.E.W., 1887 .... 185.00
Rookwood, Dish, Porridge, Glossy Brown, Painted Bamboo, Birds, Clouds 275.00
Rookwood, Ewer, Floral, Drilled, CAB 1899 .... 125.00
Rookwood, Ewer, Flowers, Eliz. Lincoln, 1898, 7 1/2 In. 150.00
Rookwood, Ewer, High Glaze, Floral & Leaves, S.T., 1892, 9 In. 185.00
Rookwood, Ewer, Orange Nasturtiums, C.1893, 8 1/2 In. 110.00
Rookwood, Ewer, Standard Glaze, Clover Blossoms, Jeanette Swing, 1901, 9 In. 185.00
Rookwood, Ewer, Standard Glaze, Daffodils, Handled, Ed Diers, 1899, 5 1/2 In. 175.00
Rookwood, Ewer, Standard Glaze, Holly, Rose Fechheimer, 1899, 7 1/2 In. 175.00
Rookwood, Ewer, Yellow To Henna, Floral, Harriet Strafer, 1891, 7 1/2 In. 225.00
Rookwood, Figurine, Bulldog, Reclining, Louise Abel, 1934, 4 1/2 In. 95.00
Rookwood, Figurine, Eagle, Spread Wings, Gray, 1949, 6 1/2 In. 65.00
Rookwood, Figurine, Rook, Berries, & Leaves, McDonald, 6 In., Pair 125.00
Rookwood, Flower Frog, Green Matte, 1922, 2 1/4 In. 8.00
Rookwood, Honey Pot, Frog Sitting On Mushroom Lid, Red, 1900, 4 7/8 In. 95.00
Rookwood, Humidor, Green Matte, Inside Purple, Marked 1922, 6 X 7 In. 100.00
Rookwood, Humidor, Standard Glaze, Pipes, Cigars, & Leaves, LNL, 1899, 7 In. 625.00
Rookwood, Jar, Covered, Shaded Ginger Color, Floral, Sallie Toohey, 1889, 5 In. 162.00
Rookwood, Jar, Tobacco, Covered, Mauve & Black, Elizabeth Lincoln, 1922 .... 125.00
Rookwood, Lamp Base, Allover Florals, Cream Background, 11 1/2 In. 175.00
Rookwood, Lamp Base, High Glaze, Magnolias, No.6920, 12 1/2 In. 175.00

Rookwood, Lamp, Iris Glaze, Cherry Blossoms & Twigs, 1935, 11 1/2 In. 175.00
Rookwood, Mug, Fraternity, 1935, Crescent & Star, Green Matte Glaze 88.00
Rookwood, Mug, Green, Indian Designs, 1903, 5 In. 75.00
Rookwood, Mug, Matte Green, 3 Handles, 1904, 5 1/2 In. 40.00
Rookwood, Paperweight, Black Matte Glaze, 3 1/4 In. 55.00
Rookwood, Paperweight, Blue Nude Figure 75.00
Rookwood, Paperweight, Dog, Caramel Brown, Dated 1924, 2 X 3 1/2 X 5 In. 75.00
Rookwood, Paperweight, Donkey, Green Glaze, Louise Abel, 1933, 6 In. 90.00
Rookwood, Paperweight, Fish, Tan, 1928, 5 In. 57.00
Rookwood, Paperweight, Frog, Mottled Green, Open Mouth 95.00
Rookwood, Paperweight, Green High Glaze, Seated Nude, Louise Abel, 1946 42.00
Rookwood, Paperweight, Green Rook With Brown, 1924 50.00
Rookwood, Paperweight, Monkey, Three Dimensional, Brown And Beige, Marked 110.00
Rookwood, Paperweight, Sitting Nude Female, Cream Glaze, Louise Abel, 1928 95.00
Rookwood, Paperweight, Snail, Artist Louise Abel, 5 In. 65.00
Rookwood, Pitcher Vase, Charcoal, Pink & White Floral, A.R.V., 1882, 26 In. 1500.00
Rookwood, Pitcher, Green To Brown, Yellow Floral, E.T.Hurley, 1900, 5 In. 135.00
Rookwood, Pitcher, Standard Glaze, Green, Brown, & Orange, A.B.S., 1889, 8 In. 365.00
Rookwood, Planter, Raised Blue Decoration, Hexagonal, 1928, 3 In. 25.00
Rookwood, Plaque, Silver Birches, E.T. Hurley, 1912, 4 X 7 1/2 In. 1200.00
Rookwood, Plaque, Vellum, Sunset Lake Scene, C.V., 1912, 10 1/2 X 8 1/2 In. 1400.00
Rookwood, Plate, Blue Sailing Ship, 8 In. 35.00
Rookwood, Plate, Yellow Gloss, Floral, Turned-In Sides, E.Hurley, 1886, 7 In. 225.00
Rookwood, Saucer, Blue Sailing Ship 10.00
Rookwood, Sugar & Creamer, Cover, Plum Matte Glaze, Mottled Green On Top 95.00
Rookwood, Sugar, Butterfly Finial & Handles, Roses, K.C.Matchette, 1893 165.00
Rookwood, Teapot, Standard Glaze, Leaves & Berries, A.R.Valentien, 1889 675.00
Rookwood, Tile, Fiance, Raised Grapes & Vines, 1886, 10 X 6 3/4 In. 50.00
Rookwood, Tile, Multicolor Floral Geometrics, 1925, Square, 5 3/4 In. 95.00
Rookwood, Tile, Yellow, Green, & Brown, Sunflower, C.1890, Square, 6 In. 62.00
Rookwood, Tray, Floral & Feather, Browns, Orange, & Green, J.Swing, 1900, 9 In. 145.00
Rookwood, Urn, Blue Green To Blue, 1916, 13 X 9 In. 95.00
Rookwood, Vase, Apple Green, 1901, Ovoid, 7 1/4 In. 35.00
Rookwood, Vase, Aquamarine, Band Of Roosting Rooks At Base, 1915, 6 1/2 In. 100.00
Rookwood, Vase, Art Deco, Green, 1928, 7 In. 25.00
Rookwood, Vase, Berries And Leaves On Cinnamon Ground, Vera Tischler, 1924 135.00
Rookwood, Vase, Blooming Sweetpeas, Sallie Coyne, 1901, 5 1/2 In. 195.00
Rookwood, Vase, Blossom & Leaf, Amber To Brown, Leonore Asbury, 7 In. 150.00
Rookwood, Vase, Blue Green, Upswept Design, 1917, 9 In. 85.00
Rookwood, Vase, Blue Matte, 6 Sided, 1924, 4 1/2 In. 40.00
Rookwood, Vase, Blue To Green, Greek Key, 9 1/4 In. 45.00
Rookwood, Vase, Blue Vellum, Violets On Cream Band, Rothenbusch, 1917, 6 In. 75.00
Rookwood, Vase, Blue Vellum, White Narcissus, Margaret McDonald, 1914, 7 In. 105.00
Rookwood, Vase, Blue, Greek Key Design, 1928, 6 In. 20.00
Rookwood, Vase, Blue, Lilies In Relief, 22 In. 55.00
Rookwood, Vase, Blue, Raised Rabbits Border, Molded, 1914, 4 X 2 In. 25.00
Rookwood, Vase, Blue, Stylized Floral, Charles Todd, 1913, 4 1/4 In. 90.00
Rookwood, Vase, Brown And Orange Luster, F.R.Floral, 1899, 6 1/4 In. 295.00
Rookwood, Vase, Brown Matte, Laurel, C.S.Todd, 1914, 11 X 6 1/2 In. 110.00
Rookwood, Vase, Brown Over Yellow & Green Verticals, Finger Molds, 5 3/4 In. 300.00
Rookwood, Vase, Cobalt Vellum, Yellow Interior & Lip, 1922, 17 1/2 In., Pair 550.00
Rookwood, Vase, Daisy Decoration, Signed, 1904, 4 In. 155.00
Rookwood, Vase, Deep Blue Drip Glaze, 5 Lobed, 1928, 6 7/8 In., Pair 85.00
Rookwood, Vase, Deep Blue Matte Glaze, Incised Floral Top Band, 1922, 10 In. 45.00
Rookwood, Vase, Figures Of Virgin Mary On Each Of 3 Sides, Ivory, Blue, 1920 85.00
Rookwood, Vase, Fish, Vellum, LNL, 1911, 6 3/4 In. 325.00
Rookwood, Vase, Floral, Signed Vera Tischler, 9 In. 145.00
Rookwood, Vase, Fruit, MAD, 1898, 16 1/2 In. 550.00
Rookwood, Vase, Glazed Beige, Stars & Bird, 1954, 6 In. 45.00
Rookwood, Vase, Gourd Shape, Hand-Painted, Signed Todd, 4 1/2 In. 90.00
Rookwood, Vase, Green To Plum-Colored Saber Foliage, 1912, 7 In. 48.50
Rookwood, Vase, Green With Brown, Molded Tulips, 10 1/2 In. 45.00
Rookwood, Vase, Gunmetal Blue, Flaring, 1924, 7 1/2 In. 22.00
Rookwood, Vase, Handled, C.Steinle, 1899, 3 1/4 In. 115.00
Rookwood, Vase, High Glaze, Delft Manner, Signed Loretta Holtkamp, 1952 75.00

Rookwood, Vase, Indian, Stick, 1913, 7 In. 35.00
Rookwood, Vase, Iris Glaze, Dogwood & Twigs, Lindeman, 1909, 11 In. 375.00
Rookwood, Vase, Iris, Sara Sax, White Poppies, Green Ground, 1902, 9 In. 295.00
Rookwood, Vase, Iris, White High Glaze, Embossed & Painted, 1946, 4 In. 85.00
Rookwood, Vase, Light Brown Stippled, 1923, 4 1/2 In. 12.50
Rookwood, Vase, Matte Finish, Portrait, L.Abel, 1926, 7 In. 275.00
Rookwood, Vase, Matte Yellow, Urn Shape, Charles Stuart Todd, 1922, 25 In. 175.00
Rookwood, Vase, Modeled Matte, Green, Leaves, Sallie Toohey, 1904, 12 In. 225.00
Rookwood, Vase, Molded In Vellum Glaze, Blue, Dated 1919, 6 1/2 In. 30.00
Rookwood, Vase, Molded, Robin Egg Blue, Standard Glaze, 1919, 6 In. 47.50
Rookwood, Vase, Molded, Standard Glaze, Albert Munson, 1920, Pink, 9 In. 75.00
Rookwood, Vase, Molded, Standard Glaze, Light Blue, 1920, 8 1/2 In. 50.00
Rookwood, Vase, Molded, Standard Glaze, Pink, 1919, 6 In. 40.00
Rookwood, Vase, Molded, Vellum Glaze, Pink To Green, 1918, 5 In. 45.00
Rookwood, Vase, Mottled Blue Green Glaze, 6 Rooks Among Foliage Band, 6 In. 55.00
Rookwood, Vase, Multicolor Matte Glaze, Baluster, Katherine Jones, 1925, 4 In 85.00
Rookwood, Vase, Painted Matte, Lavender, Floral, Louise Abel, 1925, 11 1/2 In. 225.00
Rookwood, Vase, Pale Green To Pink, Incised Decoration, 8 1/4 In. 40.00
Rookwood, Vase, Persian Design, Cobalt & Light Blue, Sara Sax, 1924, 36 In. 1500.00
Rookwood, Vase, Pink To Green Gray, Rooks At Bottom, 1920, 6 In. 38.00
Rookwood, Vase, Pink To Green, Relief Floral, 1928, 5 In. 25.00
Rookwood, Vase, Pink, Molded Cherries, 1927, 5 In. 28.00
Rookwood, Vase, Plum Color, Rooks, 1916, 6 In. 35.00
Rookwood, Vase, Plum, 1922 .... 17.50
Rookwood, Vase, Porcelain Glaze, Floral, 1920, 6 In. 95.00
Rookwood, Vase, Purple, Grapes, C.T., 14 In. 60.00
Rookwood, Vase, Red To Green Top, Geometric Designs, 5 1/2 In. 35.00
Rookwood, Vase, Rose Matte Glaze, Multicolor Floral, C.S.T., 1922, 30 1/2 In. 395.00
Rookwood, Vase, Rose Matte Glaze, Multicolor Floral, L.Abel, 1936, 10 In. 225.00
Rookwood, Vase, Rose To Moss Green Top, Palm Leaf Panels, 1919, 5 In. 65.00
Rookwood, Vase, Sage Green High Glaze, Globular, Signed Alfred Brennan, 1886 .... 200.00
Rookwood, Vase, Scenic, Water, Trees, Mauve, Fred Rothenbusch, 1917, 9 1/2 In. 310.00
Rookwood, Vase, Sea Green Glaze Floral, Josephine E.Zettel, 1892-1904 .... 145.00
Rookwood, Vase, Standard Glaze, Chestnuts & Leaves, L.Asbury, 1902, 11 In. 275.00
Rookwood, Vase, Standard Glaze, Dandelions & Ferns, K.C.Matchetta, 1891, 5 In. 225.00
Rookwood, Vase, Standard Glaze, Floral, Pinched Neck, M.L.P., 1898, 5 1/2 In. 185.00
Rookwood, Vase, Standard Glaze, Floral, 1/4 Moon Shape Top, E.T.H., 1889, 5 In. 235.00
Rookwood, Vase, Standard Glaze, Floral, 1900, 6 In. 145.00
Rookwood, Vase, Standard Glaze, Leaves & Berries, Signed C.F.B., 1901 .... 135.00
Rookwood, Vase, Standard Glaze, Poppies, F.Sturgis Lawrence, 1898, 7 1/2 In. 375.00
Rookwood, Vase, Standing Terrier Dog Under High Glaze, 5 In. 125.00
Rookwood, Vase, Sunflowers, 14 Flames Mark, RP, 5 1/2 In. 135.00
Rookwood, Vase, Tan To Red Brown, Blue & Charcoal Trim, K.Jones, 1924, 5 In. 155.00
Rookwood, Vase, Tulips, C.1899, 9 1/4 In. 250.00
Rookwood, Vase, Turquoise To Pink, Art Deco Design, 1920, 7 In. 38.00
Rookwood, Vase, Vellum, Beige, Bleeding Hearts, Sara Sax, 1910, 9 In. 160.00
Rookwood, Vase, Vellum, Blue Daisies On Branches, McDonald, 1935, 7 In. 145.00
Rookwood, Vase, Vellum, Blue, Apple Blossoms, E.V., 4 In. 75.00
Rookwood, Vase, Vellum, Blue, 1909, 6 In. 30.00
Rookwood, Vase, Vellum, Blues, Scenic, Bulbous, E.D., 5 In. 135.00
Rookwood, Vase, Vellum, Massive Bouquets, Pink Wild Flowers By Hurley, 1942 .... 195.00
Rookwood, Vase, Vellum, Ovoid, Apple Blossoms, Blue, Pink, Artist MHM, 7 In. 150.00
Rookwood, Vase, Vellum, Ovoid, Wild Roses, Katherine Van Horne, 1910 .... 145.00
Rookwood, Vase, Vellum, Winter Scene, Rothenbusch, 1912, 8 1/2 In. 275.00
Rookwood, Vase, Vellum, 5 Swimming Fish, Blue, Green, White, Signed 175.00
Rookwood, Vase, Wax Matte, Blue Floral, MHM, 1935, 6 1/2 In., Pair 235.00
Rookwood, Vase, Wax Matte, Blues, Carrie Steinle, 1927, 6 In. 70.00
Rookwood, Vase, Wax Matte, Purple & Red Floral, M.H.McDonald, 1924, 8 In. 80.00
Rookwood, Vase, Wild Roses On Black & Green, Carrie Steinle, 1906, 5 1/2 In. 175.00
Rookwood, Vase, Yellow Florals, Brown Ground, E.A.Abel, 1893, 8 In. 225.00
Rookwood, Vase, Yellow Open Roses, Sallie Toohey, 1894, 10 1/2 In. 185.00
Rookwood, Wall Pocket, Mottled Blue, Art Deco, 1928, 7 1/2 In. 19.00

Rose bowls were popular during the 1880s. Rose petals were kept in the open bowl to add fragrance to a room. The glass bowls were made with crimped tops, which kept the petals inside. Many types of Victorian art glass were made into rose bowls.

Rose Bowl, Glass, Blue Enamel, 4 1/2 In. 29.50
Rose Canton, Platter, Well & Tree, C.1830, 16 1/2 X 12 1/2 In. 250.00
Rose Canton, Saucer, Marked China 10.00

Rose Medallion china was made in China during the nineteenth and twentieth centuries. It is a distinctive design picturing people, flowers, birds, and butterflies. They are colored in greens, pinks, and other colors.

Rose Medallion, Basket, Reticulated, 9 5/8 X 8 7/8 X 3 3/4 In. 398.00
Rose Medallion, Bowl, C.1850, 5 3/4 In. 50.00
Rose Medallion, Bowl, Fluted, C.1850, Oval, 7 1/2 X 6 In. 150.00
Rose Medallion, Bowl, Panels Of Figures & Roses, 9 3/4 In. 75.00
Rose Medallion, Bowl, Reticulated, 9 5/8 X 8 7/8 In. 398.00
Rose Medallion, Bowl, Soup, 9 1/2 In. 80.00
Rose Medallion, Box, Covered, Round, 4 In. 85.00
Rose Medallion, Charger, Made In China, 14 1/2 In. 595.00
Rose Medallion, Creamer, People, Insects, Flowers, C.1920, Bulbous Jug Shape 50.00
Rose Medallion, Cup & Saucer, Bouillon, Covered, Marked China 70.00
Rose Medallion, Cup & Saucer, C.1850 .... 85.00
Rose Medallion, Cup & Saucer, Chinese Women & Men 85.00
Rose Medallion, Cup & Saucer, Demitasse, C.1850 .... 40.00
Rose Medallion, Cup & Saucer, Marked China, C. 1920 .... 22.00
Rose Medallion, Cup & Saucer, Paneled 35.00
Rose Medallion, Cup & Saucer, Two Handled, Made In China 30.00
Rose Medallion, Cup, Handleless 20.00
Rose Medallion, Dish, Curry, Orange Peel, Decoration, 15 X 11 In. 350.00
Rose Medallion, Dish, Leaf Shape, Scalloped, C.1850, 8 In. 175.00
Rose Medallion, Dish, Shrimp, C.1850 .... 300.00
Rose Medallion, Dish, Sweetmeat, Covered, Oval, 5 1/4 X 4 1/4 In. 225.00
Rose Medallion, Pitcher, Water 275.00
Rose Medallion, Plate 42.50
Rose Medallion, Plate, C.1820, 8 1/2 In. 48.00
Rose Medallion, Plate, Cake, Pedestal 350.00
Rose Medallion, Plate, Cup, Hollow Footed Ring 32.00
Rose Medallion, Plate, Dinner 27.50
Rose Medallion, Plate, Figures, Multicolored, 10 In. 65.00
Rose Medallion, Plate, Green Enamel, Blue Iridescence, Marked China 40.00
Rose Medallion, Plate, Multicolor Figures, 10 In. 65.00
Rose Medallion, Plate, Square Cut Corners, 5 1/2 In. 27.50
Rose Medallion, Plate, 8 In. 35.00
Rose Medallion, Plate, 9 1/2 In. 68.00
Rose Medallion, Serving Bowl, Jagged Edge 275.00
Rose Medallion, Serving Bowl, Scalloped, C.1850, Oval, 10 X 8 3/4 In. 195.00
Rose Medallion, Sugar, Covered, Bulbous 110.00
Rose Medallion, Tea Set, 6 Handleless Cups 40.00
Rose Medallion, Teacup & Saucer, Roses, Leaves, Bird, & People Panels 25.00
Rose Medallion, Teapot In Wicker Carrying Case 135.00
Rose Medallion, Teapot, Chinese Figures, Butterflies, & Birds, C.1800, 8 In. 175.00
Rose Medallion, Teapot, Gold In Ladies' Hair, Wire Handle, C.1850, 5 In. 150.00
Rose Medallion, Teapot, Made In China 42.50
Rose Medallion, Teapot, Taster Lid 90.00
Rose Medallion, Teapot, Wire Handle In Wicker Basket, China Mark 248.00
Rose Medallion, Tureen, Covered, Small 175.00
Rose Medallion, Vase, Baluster Shape, 14 In., Pair 950.00
Rose Medallion, Vase, Fluted, 18 In. 895.00
Rose Medallion, Washbowl, Flat Rim, C.1820, 18 1/2 In. 550.00

Rose O'Neill, see Kewpie

Rose Tapestry porcelain was made by the Royal Bayreuth Factory of Germany during the late nineteenth century. The surface of the ware feels like cloth.

Rose Tapestry, Basket, Pink Roses, Royal Bayreuth, Blue Mark, 4 7/8 In. 95.00
Rose Tapestry, Basket, Royal Bayreuth, Blue Mark 250.00
Rose Tapestry, Bowl, Small, Royal Bayreuth, Blue Mark 175.00

Rose Tapestry, Bowl, 4 Footed, Scalloped, Royal Bayreuth, Blue Mark 250.00
Rose Tapestry, Box, Covered, Royal Bayreuth, Blue Mark, Yellow & Red Roses 180.00
Rose Tapestry, Box, Trinket, Covered, 3 Color Roses, Royal Bayreuth 145.00
Rose Tapestry, Cachepot, Royal Bonn, Gold Lion Marks 450.00
Rose Tapestry, Creamer, Pinch Spout, Royal Bayreuth, Blue Mark 150.00
Rose Tapestry, Creamer, Pinched Spout, Blue Mark, 2-Toned Rose Design, 3 In. 175.00
Rose Tapestry, Creamer, Pink Roses, Gold Trim, Royal Bayreuth 130.00
Rose Tapestry, Creamer, Royal Bayreuth Blue Mark, Rose & Daisy, 3 In. 165.00
Rose Tapestry, Creamer, 3 Color Roses, Pinched Spout, Royal Bayreuth 155.00
Rose Tapestry, Dish, Clover Leaf Shape, Royal Bayreuth, Blue Mark 150.00
Rose Tapestry, Dish, Multicolored Roses, Royal Bayreuth In Blue, 5 X 4 In. 145.00
Rose Tapestry, Dish, Pin, Gold Handle, Cloverleaf Shape, Royal Bayreuth 115.00
Rose Tapestry, Dish, Powder, Yellow Roses, Royal Bayreuth, Blue Mark 200.00
Rose Tapestry, Hair Receiver, Footed, Royal Bayreuth, Blue Mark 120.00
Rose Tapestry, Hair Receiver, Gold Feet, Royal Bayreuth, Blue Mark 150.00
Rose Tapestry, Hair Receiver, Royal Bayreuth, Blue Mark 115.00
Rose Tapestry, Hair Receiver, Tricolored Roses, Royal Bayreuth 135.00
Rose Tapestry, Hair Receiver, Turkey Scene, Royal Bayreuth, Blue Mark 165.00
Rose Tapestry, Hair Receiver, Turkey, Gold Foot, Royal Bayreuth, Blue Mark 135.00
Rose Tapestry, Hatpin Holder, Royal Bayreuth, Blue Mark 175.00
Rose Tapestry, Pitcher, Pinch Spout, Royal Bayreuth, Blue Mark 165.00
Rose Tapestry, Pitcher, Pinched Spout, Roses, Daisies, Leaves, 3 1/4 In. 125.00
Rose Tapestry, Pitcher, Pink Roses, Daisies, Gold, Royal Bayreuth, 3 1/2 In. 125.00
Rose Tapestry, Pitcher, Royal Bayreuth, Pinched Nose, Pink Roses, Daisies 140.00
Rose Tapestry, Planter, Royal Bayreuth, Blue Mark 150.00
Rose Tapestry, Plate, Royal Bayreuth, 6 In. 85.00
Rose Tapestry, Plate, 3 Colors, Royal Bayreuth, Blue Mark 98.00
Rose Tapestry, Relish, 3 Color Roses, Royal Bayreuth, Green Mark 137.50
Rose Tapestry, Rose Bowl, Royal Bayreuth Mark, Pink, Yellow Roses, 4 X 3 In. 96.00
Rose Tapestry, Saltshaker, 3 Color Roses, Royal Bayreuth, Blue Mark 135.00
Rose Tapestry, Sauce, 3 Color Roses, Royal Bayreuth, Blue Mark, 5 1/2 In. 115.00
Rose Tapestry, Saucer, Royal Bayreuth, Blue Mark 125.00
Rose Tapestry, Shoe, Royal Bayreuth, Pink & Yellow Roses, Blue Mark 245.00
Rose Tapestry, Sugar & Creamer, 3 Color Roses, Royal Bayreuth, Blue Mark 325.00
Rose Tapestry, Tray, Dresser, Roses, Royal Bayreuth In Blue, 11 X 8 In. 250.00
Rose Tapestry, Tray, Dresser, Violets, Royal Bayreuth, Green Mark 88.00
Rose Tapestry, Tray, Pin, Castle Scene, Royal Bayreuth 120.00
Rose Tapestry, Tray, Royal Bayreuth, Blue Mark, 11 X 8 In. 219.00
Rose Tapestry, Tumbler, Barrel Shape 395.00
Rose Tapestry, Vase, Castle Scene, Royal Bayreuth, Miniature .... 125.00 To 135.00
Rose Tapestry, Vase, Cobalt, Gold Tapestry, Raised Leaf, Doulton, 17 3/4 In. 300.00
Rose Tapestry, Vase, German, Country Scene, 9 In. 110.00
Rose Tapestry, Vase, Harbor Scene, 8 1/4 X 4 In. 125.00
Rose Tapestry, Vase, Lady With Horse, Royal Bayreuth, Blue Mark, 7 1/4 In. 195.00
Rose Tapestry, Vase, Landscape, Three Women Under Tree, 4 1/2 In. 70.00
Rose Tapestry, Vase, Pompadour, 2 Handles, 5 1/2 In. 150.00
Rose Tapestry, Vase, Roses, Green Leaves, 3 Color, Royal Bayreuth, Blue Mark 195.00
Rose Tapestry, Vase, Scenic, Royal Bayreuth, 3 1/2 In. 135.00
Rose Tapestry, Vase, Three Courtesans In Garden, Germany, 6 In. 150.00
Rose Tapestry, Vase, Woman & Child On Sides, Woodland Scene, Germany, 7 In. 150.00
Rose Tapestry, Vase, 3 Handled, Small, Royal Bayreuth, Blue Mark 125.00

MARKE
Rosenthal

Rosenthal porcelain was established in Sels, Bavaria, in 1880. The German factory still continues to make fine-quality tableware and figurines.

Rosenthal, Bowl, Embossed Fruit, Dresden Florals, Pedestal, 10 X 4 In. 50.00
Rosenthal, Bowl, Fruit, Painted Grapes, Gold Open Handles, Signed 60.00
Rosenthal, Bowl, Pedestal, Embossed Fruit, Floral Interior, 10 In. 50.00
Rosenthal, Bowl, Pink Roses, Gold Scalloped Edge, Malmaison, 9 1/4 In. 16.50
Rosenthal, Box, Cuff Link, Artist Signed And Dated 15.00
Rosenthal, Coffee Set, Quince, Gold Rims, 3 Piece 36.00
Rosenthal, Cup & Saucer, Garland Of Pink Roses, Pedestaled Cup 25.00
Rosenthal, Eggcup, White, Floral 5.00
Rosenthal, Figurine, Beetle, Lobsterlike Pincers, Feeding Ground Base, 3 In. 20.00
Rosenthal, Figurine, Bird On Leafy Branch, U.S.Zone, 6 1/2 In. 555.00
Rosenthal, Figurine, Colt, Newborn, White, 5 1/2 In. 85.00

Rosenthal, Figurine, Dachshund, Lying, Head Erect, T.Karner, 9 X 6 In. 285.00
Rosenthal, Figurine, Elephant Beetle On Feeding Ground Base, 3 In. 20.00
Rosenthal, Figurine, Fish On Seaweed Stand, Black Stripes, Heidenreich, 8 In. 70.00
Rosenthal, Figurine, Frog On Leaf, Grayish, Himmelstoss, 2 1/4 In. 25.00
Rosenthal, Figurine, Frog, Himmelstross, 2 X 2 1/2 In. 25.00
Rosenthal, Figurine, Gold Dress With Red Overskirt, 7 1/2 In. 55.00
Rosenthal, Figurine, Horse Rearing, Dapple Gray, 7 In. 95.00
Rosenthal, Figurine, Nude Woman, Sitting Crosslegged, L.F.G., 8 In. 85.00
Rosenthal, Figurine, Penguin, Kimmelstoss, 3 In. 32.00
Rosenthal, Figurine, Pouter Pigeon, Swelled Chest, 6 1/2 In. 115.00
Rosenthal, Figurine, Rabbit, Tan With White, 2 1/4 In. 22.00
Rosenthal, Figurine, Rhinoceros Beetle On Feeding Ground Base, 3 In. 20.00
Rosenthal, Figurine, White Parian, Nude Woman On Floor, Signed L.F.G. 85.00
Rosenthal, Figurine, White Rooster, Crowing, Red Comb & Wattles, 4 1/2 In. 42.00
Rosenthal, Figurine, White Rooster, Red Comb, Germany, 4 In. 40.00
Rosenthal, Figurine, Yellow & Black Bird Picking Cherries, Karner, 5 In. 55.00
Rosenthal, Figurine, 18th Century Girl, Selb-Bavaria, Marked, 2 1/2 In. 95.00
Rosenthal, Fish Set, Different Fish On Each Piece, 8 Piece 300.00
Rosenthal, Group, Bacchus & 2 Sirens Marching To Festival, 9 In. 215.00
Rosenthal, Group, Boy Satyr With Dog, Artist Signed, Selb-Bavaria, 7 X 9 In. 185.00
Rosenthal, Group, Seals Nuzzling, Artist, K. Himmelstoff, 3 1/2 X 4 X 3 In. 55.00
Rosenthal, Group, Three Dachshunds, Signed, 3 1/2 In. 110.00
Rosenthal, Jar, Jam, Cobalt, Red Tea Roses, Pale Green Base, Signed Aigle 22.50
Rosenthal, Match Holder, Colonial Rose 6.00
Rosenthal, Plate, Bread & Butter, Gold Medallion Center On White 2.50
Rosenthal, Plate, Cake, Hand-Painted, Scalloped 10.00
Rosenthal, Plate, Cake, Pierced Handles, Water Lilies In Pond, 9 In. 17.50
Rosenthal, Plate, Cobalt, Grapes & Roses, 6 In. 32.00
Rosenthal, Plate, Dinner, Vase Of Flowers Center, Ivory Ground, 10 3/4 In. 15.00
Rosenthal, Plate, Sans Souci, Delft, Scenic 30.00
Rosenthal, Plate, Sans Souci, 10 1/2 In. 10.00
Rosenthal, Plate, Serving, Ivory Color, Bristol, 12 In. 34.00
Rosenthal, Ring Tree, White, Blue Forget-Me-Nots 25.00
Rosenthal, Sugar & Creamer, Donatello, White & Gold, Art Deco 55.00
Rosenthal, Tankard, Blue Ground, Grapes, Gold Rim, 5 In. 35.00
Rosenthal, Teapot, Openwork Finial, White, Hydrangeas, Gold Trim, 8 3/4 In. 43.00
Rosenthal, Vase, Covered, Chrysanthemum And Gold Decoration, 16 In. 300.00

ROZANE WARE *Roseville Pottery Company was established in 1891 in Zanesville, Ohio. Many types of pottery were made, including flower vases.* Roseville

Roseville, Ashtray, Black 25.00
Roseville, Ashtray, Florentine 20.00
Roseville, Ashtray, Green Peony 30.00
Roseville, Ashtray, Green Snowberry 15.00
Roseville, Ashtray, Medallion, Footed 22.00
Roseville, Ashtray, Pinecone 20.00
Roseville, Ashtray, Snowberry, Blue 13.00
Roseville, Basket, Apple Blossom, 8 In. 25.00
Roseville, Basket, Bittersweet, 10 In. 28.00
Roseville, Basket, Brown & Green Bark, Grapes & Vines, Handled, 13 In. 47.50
Roseville, Basket, Cosmos, Blue, 12 X 11 In. 40.00
Roseville, Basket, Cosmos, Tan With Purple Flowers, 12 In. 45.00
Roseville, Basket, Hanging, Water Lily, Matte Green 35.00
Roseville, Basket, Hanging, Zephyr Lily 25.00
Roseville, Basket, Monticello, 7 In. 45.00
Roseville, Basket, Rose & Blue, White Floral, Double Handles, 12 In. 20.00
Roseville, Basket, Rozane, Cream Color, Floral, Dimpled, Oval, 7 1/2 In. 30.00
Roseville, Basket, Rozane, White, 1917, 7 X 6 In. 38.00
Roseville, Basket, Snowberry, Green, 8 X 8 In. 15.00
Roseville, Basket, Zephyr Lily, Green, 10 In. 28.00
Roseville, Bookend, Dutch Girl & Boy At Brick Wall, Sallie Toohey, 5 In., Pair 115.00
Roseville, Bookend, Pinecone, Blue, Pair 30.00
Roseville, Bowl & Flower Frog, Columbine, Blue, Sailfin Frog, Handled, 11 In. 40.00
Roseville, Bowl & Flower Frog, Columbine, Blue, 2 Handles, 11 In. 42.00
Roseville, Bowl & Frog, Corinthian, 9 X 3 In. 26.00

Roseville, Bowl Vase, Baneda, Green, Ear Handles, 7 X 5 In. 28.00
Roseville, Bowl Vase, Dawn, Pink, 6 X 4 In. 24.00
Roseville, Bowl Vase, Imperial II, Mottled Green Blue Drip On Pink, 6 In. 30.00
Roseville, Bowl Vase, Iris, Light Blue, White Irises, 1938, 7 1/2 X 6 In. 28.00
Roseville, Bowl Vase, Ivory, Tourmaline Blank, Gold Sticker, 7 X 5 In. 22.00
Roseville, Bowl Vase, Luffa, 2 Handles, 7 X 5 In. 29.00
Roseville, Bowl Vase, Moderne, Green, 7 1/2 X 6 In. 26.00
Roseville, Bowl Vase, Primrose, Brown, 7 1/2 X 5 1/2 In. 22.00
Roseville, Bowl Vase, Teasel, Tan, 6 X 4 In. 22.00
Roseville, Bowl, Bittersweet, Green, Boat Shape, 14 In. 22.00
Roseville, Bowl, Blue Drape, 7 X 3 In. 18.00
Roseville, Bowl, Carnelian, Blue Shading, 10 1/2 X 3 1/2 In. 22.00
Roseville, Bowl, Clematis, Green, No.456, 6 In. 18.00
Roseville, Bowl, Columbine, Rose Color, Handles, 4 In. 12.00
Roseville, Bowl, Commercial Line, Green With Orange, 6 1/2 X 3 In. 12.00
Roseville, Bowl, Dahlrose, Oval, 10 In. 25.00
Roseville, Bowl, Dogwood II, Handled, Footed, 8 X 5 In. 26.00
Roseville, Bowl, Dogwood II, 6 X 2 1/2 In. 17.00
Roseville, Bowl, Donatello, Pedestal, 7 1/2 In. 60.00
Roseville, Bowl, Florentine, Browns, Cascades Of Fruit, Middle Period, 9 In. 30.00
Roseville, Bowl, Florentine, 7 X 3 In. 24.00
Roseville, Bowl, Ixia, Green, 5 X 3 In. 15.00
Roseville, Bowl, Mostique, Green Glossy Interior, C.1915, 9 X 3 In. 25.00
Roseville, Bowl, Persian, 3 1/2 In. 30.00
Roseville, Bowl, Rozane, White, 1917, 5 X 3 In. 18.00
Roseville, Bowl, Sunflower, 24 X 4 In. 32.00
Roseville, Bowl, Utility, Green Band, 10 X 3 In. 16.00
Roseville, Bowl, Water Lily, Green, 2 Handles, Oblong, 11 X 7 In. 21.00
Roseville, Box, Window, Magnolia, 10 3/4 X 3 1/4 In. 20.00
Roseville, Bucket, Champagne, Rozane, 1917 .... 95.00
Roseville, Candleholder, Carnelian, Blue Matte, Blue Dripping, 4 In., Pair 27.00
Roseville, Candleholder, Dahlrose, 3 1/2 In., Pair 25.00
Roseville, Candleholder, Rust, Green Leaves, Double, 5 1/2 In. 9.00
Roseville, Candlestick, Snowberry, Green, 4 3/4 In., Pair 13.50
Roseville, Candlestick, Velmoss, Scroll, 9 In., Pair 40.00
Roseville, Centerpiece Bowl & Flower Frog, Donatello, 10 In. 55.00
Roseville, Centerpiece Bowl, Fuchsia, Oval 20.00
Roseville, Cereal Bowl, Sitting Bunnies, 5 1/2 In. 26.00
Roseville, Compote, Tuscany, Pearly Pink, Handled, Flared, 2 1/2 In. 19.00
Roseville, Console Bowl, Bleeding Heart 23.00
Roseville, Console Bowl, Cremona, Green, Trumpet Shape, 7 X 3 1/2 In. 20.00
Roseville, Console Bowl, Freesia, Green & Cream, 13 1/2 In. 22.00
Roseville, Console Bowl, Monticello, Blue, Handled, 11 X 3 1/2 In. 32.00
Roseville, Console Bowl, Tuscany, Gray, 11 X 8 In. 17.00
Roseville, Console Bowl, Velmoss Scroll, 9 X 3 In. 28.00
Roseville, Console Bowl, Velmoss Scroll, 9 1/2 X 3 In. 30.00
Roseville, Console Set, Apple Blossom, Pink, Bud Vase & 2 Candles, 3 Piece 35.00
Roseville, Console Set, Baneda, Green, 3 Piece 68.00
Roseville, Console Set, Blue, Lily, 3 Piece 20.00
Roseville, Console Set, Cremona, Green, Bowl With Frog, 4 Piece 55.00
Roseville, Console Set, Freesia, Delft Blue, Handled Candlesticks, 3 Piece 35.00
Roseville, Console Set, Luster, Pink, 11 1/2 In. Bowl, 3 Piece 80.00
Roseville, Console Set, Rozane, Ivory Honeycomb & Floral, 3 Piece 75.00
Roseville, Console Set, White Rose, Turquoise, Handled Candlesticks, 3 Piece 37.50
Roseville, Cornucopia, Cosmos, 8 In. 15.00
Roseville, Creamer, Juvenile, Sunbonnet 40.00
Roseville, Dish, Baby's Feeding, Sitting Bunnies, 6 1/2 In. 27.00
Roseville, Dish, Baby's, Juvenile, Sunbonnet 40.00
Roseville, Dish, Child's Feeding, Ducks 12.00
Roseville, Dish, Child's Feeding, Juvenile, Rabbits 20.00
Roseville, Dish, Child's, Elsie, The Borden Cow 35.00
Roseville, Dish, Child's, Rabbits 20.00
Roseville, Dish, Feeding, Nursery Rhyme, Little Jack Horner 35.00
Roseville, Ewer Vase, Magnolia, Green, 15 X 10 In. 75.00
Roseville, Ewer, Apple Blossom, Green, 15 In. 60.00

Roseville, Ewer, Gardenia, Blue Green, 10 In. 32.00
Roseville, Ewer, Iris, Blue, 10 In. 32.00
Roseville, Ewer, Magnolia, Green, 6 In. 35.00
Roseville, Ewer, Snowberry, Blue, 15 In. 65.00
Roseville, Ewer, Velmoss Scroll, Cream, Red, Green, 6 1/4 In. 30.00
Roseville, Ewer, White Rose, 6 In. 18.00
Roseville, Flower Frog, Holly 6.50
Roseville, Flower Holder, Carnelian, 6 1/2 X 3 3/4 In. 18.00
Roseville, Holder, Letter, Rozane Ware, Royal, Flowers On Brown, C.Neff 80.00
Roseville, Jar, Cookie, Freesia, Brown 75.00
Roseville, Jar, Cookie, Magnolia, Green 65.00
Roseville, Jar, Cookie, Water Lily, Blue 70.00
Roseville, Jardiniere Planter, No.663, Handled, 3 In. 12.00
Roseville, Jardiniere, Antique Matte Green, Flared, 4 Handles, 12 X 9 In. 39.00
Roseville, Jardiniere, Baneda, Green 45.00
Roseville, Jardiniere, Cherry Blossom, Gold RV 80.00
Roseville, Jardiniere, Dogwood, 13 X 11 In. 50.00
Roseville, Jardiniere, Donatello, Flared Top, 28 1/2 X 14 In. 325.00
Roseville, Jardiniere, Donatello, Pedestal Base 165.00
Roseville, Jardiniere, Florentine, Brown, 28 1/2 X 14 In. 225.00
Roseville, Jardiniere, Fuchsia, Blue, Pink Blossoms, 18 In. 98.00
Roseville, Jardiniere, Mostique, Old RV Mark 65.00
Roseville, Jardiniere, Pinecone, Green, Handled, 11 1/2 In. 45.00
Roseville, Jardiniere, Rozane, Floral, 28 1/2 X 11 In. 200.00
Roseville, Jardiniere, White & Purple Flowers, 9 X 6 In. 40.00
Roseville, Jug Vase, Rozane, Ivory, Red & Yellow Roses, 2 Handles, 1917, 6 In. 65.00
Roseville, Lamp, Moderne, Silver Sticker, 22 In. 135.00
Roseville, Match Holder, Pinecone, Green, 4 X 3 In. 17.00
Roseville, Mug, Creamware, Colonial Men On Burgundy Band 58.00
Roseville, Mug, Creamware, Floral Decal 60.00
Roseville, Mug, Dutch, Footed 28.00
Roseville, Pedestal, Cameo, 24 X 9 In. 95.00
Roseville, Pitcher, Baby Chicks, 4 In. 27.50
Roseville, Pitcher, Blue To Green, White Flowers, 10 1/2 In. 29.00
Roseville, Pitcher, Bridge 49.00
Roseville, Pitcher, Child's, Baby Chick Decoration 25.00
Roseville, Pitcher, Egyptian, 6 In. 27.50
Roseville, Pitcher, Freesia, 10 In. 30.00
Roseville, Pitcher, Juvenile, Sitting Bunnies, Side Pouring, 3 1/4 In. 26.00
Roseville, Pitcher, Landscape 59.00
Roseville, Pitcher, Mayfair, Brown, 6 In. 23.00
Roseville, Pitcher, Milk, Utility, Stripes 25.00
Roseville, Pitcher, Rozane, Brown Standard Glaze, Yellow Violets, 3 3/4 In. 70.00
Roseville, Pitcher, Tulip 22.00
Roseville, Pitcher, Utility, Green Band, 6 1/2 In. 24.00
Roseville, Pitcher, Water, Creamware, Grapes 60.00
Roseville, Pitcher, Water, Rozane, Portrait, 8 1/2 In. 995.00
Roseville, Planter, Carnelian, Pink, Blue Drip, 9 In. 32.50
Roseville, Planter, Dogwood II, Hanging, 7 1/2 X 4 In. 30.00
Roseville, Planter, Landscape, 5 1/2 In. 60.00
Roseville, Planter, Magnolia, Rose With Green, 2 Handles, 6 In. 20.00
Roseville, Planter, Pasadena, Pink, Brass Stand, 5 X 4 In. 24.00
Roseville, Planter, Pinecone, Green, Handled, 5 In. 19.00
Roseville, Planter, Rickshaw Base, Rose & Dogwood, 11 X 3 In. 25.00
Roseville, Pocket, Wall, Corinthian, 9 1/2 In. 17.00
Roseville, Rose Bowl, Apple Blossom, Pink, 6 X 4 In. 18.00
Roseville, Shell, Conch, Ming Tree, Blue, 7 1/2 X 5 1/2 In. 28.00
Roseville, Tankard, Creamware, Dutch, 12 In. 75.00
Roseville, Tea Set, Bittersweet, Rose To Tan, 3 Piece 65.00
Roseville, Tea Set, Snowberry, Pink 57.00
Roseville, Teapot, Apple Blossom 35.00
Roseville, Teapot, Snowberry Green 35.00
Roseville, Tray, Dresser, Creamware, Forget-Me-Nots 38.00
Roseville, Tumbler, Landscape 37.00
Roseville, Urn, Carnelian, Green, 8 In. 38.00

Roseville, Vase, Apple Blossom, 2 Handles, 7 1/4 In. 20.00
Roseville, Vase, Aztec, 8 In. 145.00
Roseville, Vase, Baneda, Blue Glaze Dripped Green, Fruit, 2 Handles, 6 In. 30.00
Roseville, Vase, Baneda, Green, Squat, 4 In. 32.00
Roseville, Vase, Baneda, Green, 6 In. 28.00
Roseville, Vase, Baneda, Green, 8 In. 32.00
Roseville, Vase, Blackberry, Handled, 6 In. 30.00
Roseville, Vase, Bleeding Heart, Pink, Handled, Bulbous, 9 1/2 X 6 In. 20.00
Roseville, Vase, Blue Drape, 7 In. 18.00
Roseville, Vase, Blue Shaded, Fuchsias, Open Handles, Paper Label, 8 In. 28.00
Roseville, Vase, Blue, Green Leaves & Hanging Moss, Handled, 8 1/2 In. 20.00
Roseville, Vase, Bud, Dogwood II, 9 In. 19.00
Roseville, Vase, Bud, Florentine, 6 In. 20.00
Roseville, Vase, Bud, La Rose, Double, Arched Panel, Openwork, Swags, 5 In. 32.00
Roseville, Vase, Bushberry, Green, Twig Handle, No.411, 4 In. 18.00
Roseville, Vase, Carnelian, Blue, Side Handle, Footed, 8 X 7 1/2 In. 40.00
Roseville, Vase, Carnelian, Deep Purple, Handled, H.T.G., Oblong, 5 1/2 In. 19.00
Roseville, Vase, Carnelian, Green, Handled, 8 X 5 In. 25.00
Roseville, Vase, Cherry Blossom, Pink With Blue, 7 In. 40.00
Roseville, Vase, Cherry Blossom, 10 In. 45.00
Roseville, Vase, Chocolate Rust, RV Mark, 8 1/2 In. 25.00
Roseville, Vase, Clematis, Green, Handled, 10 X 7 In. 25.00
Roseville, Vase, Clematis, Yellow & Blue, 6 In. 12.00
Roseville, Vase, Corinthian, 8 1/4 X 3 3/4 In. 24.00
Roseville, Vase, Cremona, Blue, 13 In. 27.50
Roseville, Vase, Cremona, Glossy Glaze, Turquoise To Dark Blue, 13 In. 37.50
Roseville, Vase, Cremona, Pink, 8 In. 28.00
Roseville, Vase, Dahlrose, Handled, 6 X 4 In. 15.00
Roseville, Vase, Dahlrose, 6 In. .... 16.00 To 20.00
Roseville, Vase, Dawn, Green, 6 In. 17.00
Roseville, Vase, Deep Rose To Green, Raised Oak Leaves, 818, 8 In. 22.00
Roseville, Vase, Falline, Trumpet, Handles, 8 In. 70.00
Roseville, Vase, Falline, 2 Handles, 9 1/2 In. 65.00
Roseville, Vase, Ferrella, Brown, 10 In. 95.00
Roseville, Vase, Ferrella, Pinkish Red, 2 Long Handles 75.00
Roseville, Vase, Ferrella, 9 1/2 In. 37.00
Roseville, Vase, Floor, Mostique, 14 In. 39.00
Roseville, Vase, Floral Panel, 13 In. 55.00
Roseville, Vase, Florane, 2 Handles, 6 X 2 In. 20.00
Roseville, Vase, Florentine, 6 In. 16.00
Roseville, Vase, Florentine, 7 In. 7.00
Roseville, Vase, Florentine, 8 In. 25.00
Roseville, Vase, Foxglove, Blue, 19 X 12 In. 75.00
Roseville, Vase, Foxglove, 10 In. 90.00
Roseville, Vase, Freesia, Blue, Double Handles, Footed, 10 X 6 In. 38.00
Roseville, Vase, Freesia, Green, White Flowers, 6 X 5 In. 12.00
Roseville, Vase, Fuchsia, Blue, Handled, 6 1/2 X 6 In. 23.00
Roseville, Vase, Fuchsia, Dark Green, 8 1/2 In. 29.50
Roseville, Vase, Fuchsia, Green, 2 Handles, Pedestal, 7 1/4 In. 19.00
Roseville, Vase, Fuchsia, 2 Handles, 7 1/2 In. 23.00
Roseville, Vase, Futura, Brown Neck, Green Base, 2 Handles, 7 In. 35.00
Roseville, Vase, Futura, Pink, Twisted, 9 In. 32.00
Roseville, Vase, Futura, Tan To Green Base, Angular Handles, 7 In. 40.00
Roseville, Vase, Green, Touches Of Lavender, 18 In. 45.00
Roseville, Vase, Horn Of Plenty, Blue Green, White Daisy, 8 In. 22.00
Roseville, Vase, Imperial I, Pretzel Design, 8 In. 25.00
Roseville, Vase, Iris, 2 Handles, 10 In. 25.00
Roseville, Vase, Ixia, Green, 8 In. 23.00
Roseville, Vase, Ixia, Yellow, 7 In. 16.00
Roseville, Vase, Ixia, 12 X 6 In. 36.00
Roseville, Vase, Jonquil, Handled, 10 In. 40.00
Roseville, Vase, Jonquil, Paper Label, Handled, 9 In. 16.50
Roseville, Vase, Jonquil, Pink Matte Glaze, Bulbous, 8 In. 32.00
Roseville, Vase, Laurel, Green, 7 In. 34.00
Roseville, Vase, Laurel, Yellow, 10 In. 55.00

Roseville, Vase, Laurel, 9 In. 40.00
Roseville, Vase, Light Brown, Green Crosses, 9 In. 48.00
Roseville, Vase, Malvern, 8 In. 32.00
Roseville, Vase, Marvo, 14 In. 15.00
Roseville, Vase, Moderne, White, Rose Highlights, 6 In. 25.00
Roseville, Vase, Monticello, 2 Handles, 5 1/4 In. 20.00
Roseville, Vase, Moss, Orange With Green, Handled, 6 1/2 In. 19.00
Roseville, Vase, Mostique, RV, 10 In. 18.00
Roseville, Vase, Mostique, 6 1/2 In. 15.00
Roseville, Vase, Mottled Orange Luster, Gunmetal Glaze Trim, Handled, 6 In. 14.95
Roseville, Vase, Panel, Nude, 6 In. 58.00
Roseville, Vase, Peony, 12 In. 32.00
Roseville, Vase, Persimmon Laurel, 9 1/2 In. 35.00
Roseville, Vase, Pinecone, Glossy Brown, Green, & Gold, Twig Handles, 8 In. 40.00
Roseville, Vase, Pinecone, Green, Bulbous, 6 In. 29.50
Roseville, Vase, Pinecone, Green, 13 X 7 In. 38.00
Roseville, Vase, Pinecone, Matte Green, Twig Handles, 9 X 8 In. 20.00
Roseville, Vase, Pinecone, Middle Period, 6 In. 28.00
Roseville, Vase, Pinecone, Twig Handles, 8 1/2 In. 15.00
Roseville, Vase, Primrose, 8 In. 24.00
Roseville, Vase, Rose & Blue, White Floral, 14 In. 20.00
Roseville, Vase, Rosecraft, Hexagonal, 5 In. 25.00
Roseville, Vase, Rosecraft, Hexagonal, 8 In. 35.00
Roseville, Vase, Rosecraft, Hexagonal, 9 In. 40.00
Roseville, Vase, Rozane, Cloverleaf Art, Handled, 4 1/4 In. 68.00
Roseville, Vase, Rozane, Honeycomb Ivory, Yellow Roses, 2 Handles, 1917, 7 In. 65.00
Roseville, Vase, Rozane, 1917, 10 In. 16.00
Roseville, Vase, Russco, Ivory, 7 1/4 X 5 1/4 In. 21.00
Roseville, Vase, Russco, 2 Handles, Silver Sticker, 7 1/4 In. 35.00
Roseville, Vase, Silvertone, 9 In. 60.00
Roseville, Vase, Sunflower, 6 In. 18.50 To 45.00
Roseville, Vase, Sylvan, 9 1/2 In. 23.00
Roseville, Vase, Tourmaline, Twisted, 9 In. 42.00
Roseville, Vase, Turquoise & Pink, 12 In. 15.00
Roseville, Vase, Tuscany, Pink, 7 X 5 In. 17.00
Roseville, Vase, Water Lily, Blue, 9 In. 22.00
Roseville, Vase, White Rose, Blue, Urn Shape, 8 In. 23.00
Roseville, Vase, White Rose, 4 In. 10.00
Roseville, Vase, Wisteria, 18 X 4 In. 35.00
Roseville, Vase, Zephyr Lily, Blue, 15 1/2 In. 75.00
Roseville, Wall Pocket, La Rose, Cream Color, Roses & Leaves, 8 1/2 In. 30.00

Rowland and Marsellus Company is a mark which appears on historical Staffordshire dating from the late nineteenth and early twentieth centuries. Rowland and Marsellus is believed to be the British Anchor Pottery Co. of Longton, England. Many American views were made.

Rowland & Marsellus, Cup & Saucer, Pittsburgh, Pa. 30.00
Rowland & Marsellus, Plate, Captain John Smith, Rolled Edge, 10 In. 32.00
Rowland & Marsellus, Plate, Historical Boston, Blue, Rolled, 10 In. 22.00
Rowland & Marsellus, Plate, Nantucket, Mass., Blue, 9 In. 20.00
Rowland & Marsellus, Plate, Newark, N.J., Views, Blue Rolled Edge, 10 In. 30.00
Rowland & Marsellus, Plate, Niagara Falls, Blue, Rolled, 10 In. 18.00
Rowland & Marsellus, Plate, Souvenir Of Albany, 10 In. 30.00
Rowland & Marsellus, Plate, Souvenir, Scranton, Pa., Flow Blue 32.00
Rowland & Marsellus, Plate, Valley Forge, Rolled Edge, 10 In. 30.00
Rowland & Marsellus, Plate, Views Of New Bedford, Mass., Blue, 10 In. 22.00
Rowland & Marsellus, Plate, Views Of Providence, R.I., Blue, 10 In. 22.00
Roy Rogers, Bank, Figural, Roy & Trigger, Signed 18.00
Roy Rogers, Boot, Pot Metal 5.00
Roy Rogers, Camera, Box 12.00
Roy Rogers, Camera, Pictures Of Roy & Trigger, Box, Flash Attachment 14.00
Roy Rogers, Clock, Animated 50.00
Roy Rogers, Gun, Tuckaway Miniature Cap Pistol, On Card 3.00
Roy Rogers, Hat, Trick, Has Hidden Gun 20.00
Roy Rogers, Jackknife, Blade, Bottle Opener, & Screwdriver 15.00

Roy Rogers, Jackknife, Roy & Trigger, 2 Blades 18.00
Roy Rogers, Lunch Box, Double Bar Ranch 5.00
Roy Rogers, Pistol, Cap 18.00
Roy Rogers, Postcard, Roy, Dale, Trigger, & Bullet, Folding 2.00
Roy Rogers, Program, 1940s Souvenir Of Roy Rogers Rodeo 10.00
Roy Rogers, Spurs, C.1949 .... 12.00
Roy Rogers, Token, Good Luck Piece 5.00
Roy Rogers, Toy, Rodeo Ranch, Metal Building, Plastic Accessories 8.00
Roy Rogers, Toy, Van, Horse, Trigger & Trigger, Jr. 15.00
Roy Rogers, Wristwatch, Dale Evans 50.00
Roy Rogers, Wristwatch, Dale Evans, Original Box 75.00
Roy Rogers, Wristwatch, Roy & Trigger 27.00
Royal Austria, Hatpin Holder, Hand-Painted, Artist Signed, Blue Floral 49.00
Royal Austria, Pitcher, Lemonade, Blue, Green Shading, Water Lilies 35.00
Royal Austria, Plate, Floral, Hand-Painted Wild Roses, Artist Signed, 9 In. 20.00
Royal Austria, Plate, Game, 8 3/4 In. 15.00
Royal Austria, Plate, White, Gold Scalloped Rim, 8 3/4 In. 5.00
Royal Austria, Tea Set, Pink Roses & Gold, E.T.H., 1913, 3 Piece 65.00

ROYAL BAYREUTH BAVARIA

Royal Bayreuth porcelain was made in Germany during the late nineteenth and twentieth centuries. Many types of wares were made.

Royal Bayreuth, see also Old Ivory, Rose Tapestry, Sand Babies Snow Babies, Sunbonnet Babies

Royal Bayreuth, Ashtray, Cigar, Pearlized 25.00
Royal Bayreuth, Ashtray, Clown, Blue Mark .... 120.00 To 125.00
Royal Bayreuth, Ashtray, Devil, Blue Mark 75.00
Royal Bayreuth, Ashtray, Dutch Scene, Blue Mark 20.00
Royal Bayreuth, Ashtray, Horses And Hunting Dog, Green 27.50
Royal Bayreuth, Ashtray, Red Clown, Green Mark 65.00
Royal Bayreuth, Basket, Oval, Pink & White Roses, Blue Mark, 5 In. 85.00
Royal Bayreuth, Bell, Table, Hand-Painted Farm Scene 35.00
Royal Bayreuth, Berry Bowl, Blown-Out Grape, White Satin Finish 95.00
Royal Bayreuth, Berry Bowl, Pink Roses, Irregular Edge, Blue Mark, 10 1/2 In. 65.00
Royal Bayreuth, Berry Bowl, Roses, Gold Trim, Blue Mark, 4 1/4 In. 52.00
Royal Bayreuth, Berry Bowl, 2 Hunters & Hounds, Blue Mark, 5 In. 17.50
Royal Bayreuth, Bonbon, Cream Color, Pink & White Roses, Footed, Blue Mark 45.00
Royal Bayreuth, Bowl, Blown Out, Hand-Painted, Blue Mark, 10 1/2 In. 95.00
Royal Bayreuth, Bowl, Blown Out, Painted, Gold Trim, Blue Mark, 10 1/2 In. 145.00
Royal Bayreuth, Bowl, Britanny Girl, Blue Mark, 6 1/4 In. 39.00
Royal Bayreuth, Bowl, Covered, Pink, Mother-Of-Pearl, Black Mark 110.00
Royal Bayreuth, Bowl, Fancy Scallop, Embossed, Turquoise, Signed, Blue Mark 67.00
Royal Bayreuth, Bowl, Little Jack Horner, Black Mark, 5 3/4 In. 42.00
Royal Bayreuth, Bowl, Little Jack Horner, 3 In. 65.00
Royal Bayreuth, Bowl, Poppy, Blue Mark, 8 X 4 1/2 In. 52.00
Royal Bayreuth, Bowl, Poppy, Mother-Of-Pearl, Blue Mark, 6 In. 125.00
Royal Bayreuth, Bowl, Raised Leaf, Shells, Signed, Blue Mark, 10 3/4 In. 70.00
Royal Bayreuth, Bowl, Red Poppy, Blue Mark, 5 1/2 In. 32.00
Royal Bayreuth, Box, Card, Dark Green, Men At Table & Dancing, Blue Mark 68.00
Royal Bayreuth, Box, Club Shaped, Cavaliers, Black Mark 45.00
Royal Bayreuth, Box, Covered, Tapestry, Footed, Aster Floral, Gold Trim 110.00
Royal Bayreuth, Box, Dome Lid, Pink & Blue, Girl, Boy, & Boat, Blue Mark, 3 In. 70.00
Royal Bayreuth, Box, Hunt Scene On Lid, Pale Yellow To Tan, Blue Mark, 5 In. 55.00
Royal Bayreuth, Box, Lobster, Blue Mark 45.00
Royal Bayreuth, Box, Pink & Green, Hunt Scene, Spade Shape, Blue Mark, 4 In. 70.00
Royal Bayreuth, Box, Powder, Corinthian, Footed 45.00
Royal Bayreuth, Box, Powder, Dome Lid, Gray Brown, Ocean Scene, Blue Mark 70.00
Royal Bayreuth, Box, Powder, Rose Tapestry, Domed Lid, 4 1/4 In. 175.00
Royal Bayreuth, Cake Set, Roses, Gold Panels, Blue Mark, 7 Piece 85.00
Royal Bayreuth, Candleholder, Hooded, Musicians, Blue Mark 110.00
Royal Bayreuth, Candlestick, Blue, House, Man & Horses, Blue Mark, 4 In., Pair 110.00
Royal Bayreuth, Candlestick, Goosegirl & Geese, Blue Mark, 4 1/2 In. 48.00
Royal Bayreuth, Candlestick, Musicians, Brown, Hooded, Blue Mark, 5 1/2 In. 110.00
Royal Bayreuth, Candy Boat, Red Lobster Lying On Back, 5 3/4 In. 50.00
Royal Bayreuth, Case, Card, Red Devil Handle On Cover, Card Decoration 195.00
Royal Bayreuth, Celery, Figural, Lobster, 13 X 5 In. 65.00

Royal Bayreuth, Chamberstick, Green, Girl & Geese, Saucer, Blue Mark, 5 In. 85.00
Royal Bayreuth, Chocolate Pot, Scenic With Goats 105.00
Royal Bayreuth, Chocolate Set, Girl With Dog, Blue Mark, 3 Piece 210.00
Royal Bayreuth, Coffee Set, Demitasse, White, Floral Band, Blue Mark, 5 Piece 58.50
Royal Bayreuth, Cream, Black Cat, Blue Mark 75.00
Royal Bayreuth, Cream, Black Crow, Blue Mark 75.00
Royal Bayreuth, Creamer, Alligator, Green, Blue Mark 175.00
Royal Bayreuth, Creamer, Apple 72.00
Royal Bayreuth, Creamer, Apple, Green Leaf Handle & Spout, Blue Mark 85.00
Royal Bayreuth, Creamer, Bellringer, 4 1/2 In. 75.00
Royal Bayreuth, Creamer, Black Bull, Inscribed Patchogue L.I., Blue Mark 95.00
Royal Bayreuth, Creamer, Black Crow, Brown Beak, Old Tettau Mark 95.00
Royal Bayreuth, Creamer, Black Crow, Cinnamon Trim, Blue Mark 90.00
Royal Bayreuth, Creamer, Black Crow, Orange Beat, Tettau Mark 60.00
Royal Bayreuth, Creamer, Black Crow, Red Beak & Top, Blue Mark, 4 7/8 In. 35.00
Royal Bayreuth, Creamer, Black Crow, Red Trim, Marked M.V. 43.00
Royal Bayreuth, Creamer, Blue & Cream, Floral, Pinched Spout, Blue Mark 22.00
Royal Bayreuth, Creamer, Butterfly, Blue Mark 150.00
Royal Bayreuth, Creamer, Card & Devil, Blue Mark, 4 In. 65.00
Royal Bayreuth, Creamer, Cards With Red Devil Handle, Black Mark 67.50
Royal Bayreuth, Creamer, Cat, Black, Blue Mark 85.00
Royal Bayreuth, Creamer, Clown, Red Mark 110.00
Royal Bayreuth, Creamer, Coachman, Blue Mark .... 110.00 To 135.00
Royal Bayreuth, Creamer, Conch Shell, Pearlized 40.00
Royal Bayreuth, Creamer, Conch Shell, Red Lobster Handle 55.00
Royal Bayreuth, Creamer, Conch Shell, Red Twig Handle 63.00
Royal Bayreuth, Creamer, Conch Shell, Turquoise, Lobster Handle 55.00
Royal Bayreuth, Creamer, Conch, Iridescent, Murex Pearlized, Signed, Blue Mark 45.00
Royal Bayreuth, Creamer, Corinthian, Black Classical Scene, Blue Mark, 5 In. 130.00
Royal Bayreuth, Creamer, Corinthian, Black, Blue Mark, 4 In. 49.00
Royal Bayreuth, Creamer, Corinthian, Blue Mark, 5 1/2 In. 60.00
Royal Bayreuth, Creamer, Cow, Tettau Mark 110.00
Royal Bayreuth, Creamer, Crow With Monocle, Blue Mark 40.00
Royal Bayreuth, Creamer, Crow, Brown Beak, Tettau Mark 95.00
Royal Bayreuth, Creamer, Devil & Cards, Blue Mark, 4 In. .... 60.00 To 65.00
Royal Bayreuth, Creamer, Devil & Cards, Green Mark 65.00
Royal Bayreuth, Creamer, Devil & Cards, Portland, Blue Mark 55.00
Royal Bayreuth, Creamer, Devil & Cards, Red Devil Handle, Green Mark, 4 In. 65.00
Royal Bayreuth, Creamer, Duck, Green, Blue Mark 90.00
Royal Bayreuth, Creamer, Eagle, Blue Mark 85.00
Royal Bayreuth, Creamer, Elk, Blue Mark, 5 In. 48.00
Royal Bayreuth, Creamer, Figural, Alligator, Blue Mark 85.00
Royal Bayreuth, Creamer, Figural, Black Cat, Blue Mark 60.00
Royal Bayreuth, Creamer, Figural, Black Cat, Red Mark 85.00
Royal Bayreuth, Creamer, Figural, Elk, Blue Mark .... 58.00 To 60.00
Royal Bayreuth, Creamer, Figural, Fish, 4 In. 55.00
Royal Bayreuth, Creamer, Figural, Mountain Goat 65.00
Royal Bayreuth, Creamer, Figural, Old Man Of The Mountain, Signed 87.00
Royal Bayreuth, Creamer, Fish's Head, Blue Mark 90.00
Royal Bayreuth, Creamer, Goat, Blue Mark, 3 1/2 In. 49.00
Royal Bayreuth, Creamer, Green Frog, Blue Mark 110.00
Royal Bayreuth, Creamer, Green Monkey 90.00
Royal Bayreuth, Creamer, Jack & The Beanstalk, 2 3/4 In. 58.00
Royal Bayreuth, Creamer, Lemon, Blue Mark 100.00
Royal Bayreuth, Creamer, Little Boy Blue, Scuttle Shape 65.00
Royal Bayreuth, Creamer, Little Miss Muffet 78.00
Royal Bayreuth, Creamer, Lobster, Green Mark, 4 In. 40.00
Royal Bayreuth, Creamer, Lobster, 4 In. 35.00
Royal Bayreuth, Creamer, Moose's Head, Black Mark 58.00
Royal Bayreuth, Creamer, Musicians, Blue Mark, 3 3/4 In. 54.00
Royal Bayreuth, Creamer, Oak Leaf, Blue Mark, 4 In. 100.00
Royal Bayreuth, Creamer, Old Man Of The Mountain, Green Mark, 3 1/2 In. 65.00
Royal Bayreuth, Creamer, Orange, Blue Mark 90.00
Royal Bayreuth, Creamer, Owl 135.00
Royal Bayreuth, Creamer, Pansy, Green Mark, 4 In. 75.00

Royal Bayreuth, Creamer, Pastoral Scene 34.50
Royal Bayreuth, Creamer, Pineapple 20.00
Royal Bayreuth, Creamer, Platypus, Blue Mark 125.00
Royal Bayreuth, Creamer, Poodle Dog 90.00
Royal Bayreuth, Creamer, Poppy, Blue Mark, 3 3/4 In. 65.00
Royal Bayreuth, Creamer, Pretty Lady 45.00
Royal Bayreuth, Creamer, Red Devil, Blue Mark, 3 1/4 In. .... 120.00 To 145.00
Royal Bayreuth, Creamer, Red Lobster 45.00
Royal Bayreuth, Creamer, Red Tomato, Blue Mark 45.00
Royal Bayreuth, Creamer, Rooster, Blue Mark 135.00
Royal Bayreuth, Creamer, Shell, Lobster Handle 32.50
Royal Bayreuth, Creamer, To Bed By Candlelight, Black Mark 60.00
Royal Bayreuth, Creamer, Tomato .... 25.00 To 48.00
Royal Bayreuth, Creamer, Water Buffalo 100.00
Royal Bayreuth, Cup & Saucer, Birds & Floral, Open Latticework, Blue Mark 20.00
Royal Bayreuth, Cup & Saucer, Demitasse, Murex 65.00
Royal Bayreuth, Cup & Saucer, Demitasse, Pansy 18.50
Royal Bayreuth, Cup & Saucer, Demitasse, Portrait, Man, Pink, Gold, Blue Mark 70.00
Royal Bayreuth, Cup & Saucer, Lake, Pine Trees & Flying Geese, Blue Mark 85.00
Royal Bayreuth, Cup & Saucer, Yellow & Pink Rose 195.00
Royal Bayreuth, Cup, Demitasse, Figural, Tomato 45.00
Royal Bayreuth, Cup, Loving, Corinthian, Orange, Blue Mark, 4 In. 64.00
Royal Bayreuth, Dish, Candy, Clown, Blue Mark 145.00
Royal Bayreuth, Dish, Candy, Covered, Cows, Trees, Mountains 75.00
Royal Bayreuth, Dish, Candy, Woman Clown, Blue Mark 135.00
Royal Bayreuth, Dish, Child's Feeding, Little Bo-Peep, Blue Mark, 7 In. 75.00
Royal Bayreuth, Dish, Covered Tomato On Lettuce Leaf 45.00
Royal Bayreuth, Dish, Heart Shape, Covered, Brittany Girl, Blue Mark, 3 In. 75.00
Royal Bayreuth, Dish, Leaf Shape, Green Mark, 4 In. 18.00
Royal Bayreuth, Dish, Leaf Shape, Green, Ring Handle, Blue Mark, 5 1/2 In. 22.50
Royal Bayreuth, Dish, Lettuce, Blue Mark, 7 X 5 1/2 In. 25.00
Royal Bayreuth, Dish, Pickle, Farm Scene, Handled, Blue Mark, 9 3/4 In. 70.00
Royal Bayreuth, Dish, Pickle, Moose's Head & Antlers, Black Mark 145.00
Royal Bayreuth, Dish, Powder, Sand Babies, Footed, Blue Mark 165.00
Royal Bayreuth, Dish, Ring Handle, Green Leaf Shape, Blue Mark, 5 1/2 In. 10.00
Royal Bayreuth, Dish, Tomato, Round, Green Trim, Blue Mark, 3 X 3 In. 18.00
Royal Bayreuth, Figurine, Black Man's Shoe 125.00
Royal Bayreuth, Hair Receiver, Hunter, Dog, Wild Geese, & Woods, Gold Feet 125.00
Royal Bayreuth, Hair Receiver, Scenic, Turkey, Blue Mark 165.00
Royal Bayreuth, Hatpin Holder, Goose Girl, Blue Mark 85.00
Royal Bayreuth, Hatpin Holder, Owl, Black Mark 225.00
Royal Bayreuth, Hatpin Holder, Penguins, Black Mark 95.00
Royal Bayreuth, Hatpin Holder, Portrait, Square Base, Footed, Tettau Mark 80.00
Royal Bayreuth, Hatpin Holder, Rainbow Luster, Angels, Blue Mark 45.00
Royal Bayreuth, Hatpin Holder, Red Poppy, Blue Mark 145.00
Royal Bayreuth, Humidor, Moose Hunting Scene, Blue Mark, 8 In. 65.00
Royal Bayreuth, Inkwell, Hunting Scene, Double Handles 65.00
Royal Bayreuth, Jar, Cracker, Strawberry 150.00
Royal Bayreuth, Jar, Cracker, Tomato 85.00
Royal Bayreuth, Jar, Figural, Apple, Yellow, Red, Green, Lid & Spoon, Blue Mark 65.00
Royal Bayreuth, Jar, Powder, Clown, Blue Mark 145.00
Royal Bayreuth, Jug, Green, Hunting Scene Band At Center, Blue Mark, 5 In. 90.00
Royal Bayreuth, Match Holder, Green, Pale Green Lining, Blue Mark 15.00
Royal Bayreuth, Match Holder, Hanging, Cavalier Scene, Blue Mark 80.00
Royal Bayreuth, Match Holder, Little Miss Muffet, Wall, Blue Mark 125.00
Royal Bayreuth, Match Holder, Red Clown, Deponiet, Hanging, Blue Mark 98.00
Royal Bayreuth, Mug, Devil & Cards, Blue Mark, 5 In. 75.00
Royal Bayreuth, Mug, Devil & Cards, Red Devil Handle, Blue Mark, 4 3/4 In. 80.00
Royal Bayreuth, Mustard Jar, Poppy, Covered 75.00
Royal Bayreuth, Mustard Pot, Figural, Murex 45.00
Royal Bayreuth, Mustard Pot, Figural, Tomato, Matching Spoon 20.00
Royal Bayreuth, Mustard Pot, Figural, Yellow Pansy 85.00
Royal Bayreuth, Mustard, Figural, Lobster, Ladle & Leaf Underplate, Blue Mark 65.00
Royal Bayreuth, Mustard, Figural, Lobster, Leaf Handled Spoon 35.00
Royal Bayreuth, Nappy, Lettuce Leaf, Ring Handle, Blue Mark 50.00

Royal Bayreuth, Nappy, Tomato With Leaves 24.00
Royal Bayreuth, Pipe Holder, Basset Hound, Blue Mark 55.00
Royal Bayreuth, Pipe Rest, Figural, Clown 110.00
Royal Bayreuth, Pitcher, Coachman, Red, Black, & White, Blue Mark, 4 1/2 In. 90.00
Royal Bayreuth, Pitcher, Corinthian, Apricot Lining, Blue Mark, 4 In. 50.00
Royal Bayreuth, Pitcher, Corinthian, Black With Warriors, Blue Mark 45.00
Royal Bayreuth, Pitcher, Corinthian, Classical Figures, Black Mark, 3 3/4 In. 55.00
Royal Bayreuth, Pitcher, Elk, Pours Out Of Mouth, Blue Mark, 4 1/2 In. 80.00
Royal Bayreuth, Pitcher, Figural, Apple, Tettau Mark, 4 1/2 In. 75.00
Royal Bayreuth, Pitcher, Figural, Santa Claus, Blue Mark 425.00
Royal Bayreuth, Pitcher, Green, Three Cows, 2 In. Band At Top, 4 1/2 In. 48.00
Royal Bayreuth, Pitcher, Milk, Devil & Cards, Blue Mark 140.00
Royal Bayreuth, Pitcher, Milk, Elk, Blue Mark 110.00
Royal Bayreuth, Pitcher, Milk, Goose Girl, Double Handles, Blue Mark 85.00
Royal Bayreuth, Pitcher, Milk, Lemon, Blue Mark 90.00
Royal Bayreuth, Pitcher, Milk, Lobster, Blue Mark 110.00
Royal Bayreuth, Pitcher, Milk, Melon, Blue Mark 165.00
Royal Bayreuth, Pitcher, Milk, Monkey, Blue Mark 115.00
Royal Bayreuth, Pitcher, Milk, Orange, Blue Mark 130.00
Royal Bayreuth, Pitcher, Milk, Poppy, Blue Mark 130.00
Royal Bayreuth, Pitcher, Milk, Seal, Blue Mark 185.00
Royal Bayreuth, Pitcher, Milk, Spiky Shell, Blue Mark 125.00
Royal Bayreuth, Pitcher, Moose, Souvenir Catalina Island, 5 1/2 In. 55.00
Royal Bayreuth, Pitcher, Old Man Of The Mountains, Blue Mark, 3 1/2 In. 75.00
Royal Bayreuth, Pitcher, Parrot, 3 1/2 In. 37.00
Royal Bayreuth, Pitcher, Poppy, Red, Blue Mark, 3 3/4 In. 75.00
Royal Bayreuth, Pitcher, Red Poppy, 4 1/2 In. 70.00
Royal Bayreuth, Pitcher, Scenic, Mountain Goats, Gold Handle, Blue Mark 45.00
Royal Bayreuth, Pitcher, Scenic, Pinch Nose 375.00
Royal Bayreuth, Pitcher, Water, Clown, Red Mark 250.00
Royal Bayreuth, Pitcher, Water, Large Elk, Blue Mark, 7 In. 75.00
Royal Bayreuth, Pitcher, Water, Lobster, Red, Blue Mark, 7 In. 95.00
Royal Bayreuth, Pitcher, Water, Murex 125.00
Royal Bayreuth, Planter, Oak Leaf, Blue Mark, 7 X 3 1/2 In. 75.00
Royal Bayreuth, Plate, Cabbage, Blue Mark, 3 1/2 In. 8.00
Royal Bayreuth, Plate, Cabbage, Handle, Blue Mark, 3 1/2 In, ... 9.00
Royal Bayreuth, Plate, Girl With Dog, Black Mark, 8 1/2 In. 80.00
Royal Bayreuth, Plate, Goat Scene, Blue Mark, 8 1/4 In. 50.00
Royal Bayreuth, Plate, Hunter & Hound, Farmer In Wagon, Blue Mark, 7 1/2 In. 32.50
Royal Bayreuth, Plate, Hunting Scene, Blue Mark, 9 1/2 In. 70.00
Royal Bayreuth, Plate, Jack Horner With Verse, Scenes, Black Mark, 7 1/2 In. 54.00
Royal Bayreuth, Plate, Little Bo-Peep 140.00
Royal Bayreuth, Plate, Mother-Of-Pearl, Blue Mark, 10 In. 162.00
Royal Bayreuth, Plate, Oak Leaf, Mother-Of-Pearl, Blue Mark, 8 1/2 In. 85.00
Royal Bayreuth, Plate, Portrait, Lady, Blue Border, Blue Mark, 10 1/2 In. 75.00
Royal Bayreuth, Plate, Roses, Gold Border, Blue Mark, Octagonal, 8 In. 34.00
Royal Bayreuth, Pot, Mustard, Covered, Poppy, Satin Finish 45.00
Royal Bayreuth, Rose Bowl, Cream To Blue, Pink Roses, Gold, Blue Mark, 4 In. 24.00
Royal Bayreuth, Rose Bowl, Dutch Boy & Girl On Bridge, Blue Mark, 4 In. 100.00
Royal Bayreuth, Rose Bowl, Little Miss Muffet Scene Insert 150.00
Royal Bayreuth, Salt & Pepper, Grape, Blue Mark 95.00
Royal Bayreuth, Salt & Pepper, Purple Grape, Green Leaf, Yellow Stem 65.00
Royal Bayreuth, Salt & Pepper, Tomato 36.00
Royal Bayreuth, Salt Bowl, Grays, Brown, & Orange, Musicians, Blue Mark 75.00
Royal Bayreuth, Salt Master, Mother-Of-Pearl, Green Base, Blue Mark 45.00
Royal Bayreuth, Saltshaker, Deer, Tettau Mark 50.00
Royal Bayreuth, Saltshaker, Red Pepper 8.00
Royal Bayreuth, Sauce, Poppy, Pearlized, Blue Mark 95.00
Royal Bayreuth, Sauceboat, Hand-Painted Violets 25.00
Royal Bayreuth, Shoe, Little Jack Horner, Black Mark 65.00
Royal Bayreuth, Shoe, Man's Black With Laces, Black Mark 65.00
Royal Bayreuth, String Holder, Rooster, Wall Hanging, Blue Mark 125.00
Royal Bayreuth, Sugar & Creamer, Bo-Peep & Jack, Bean Stalk, Blue Mark 110.00
Royal Bayreuth, Sugar & Creamer, Cover, Purple Grape, Green Leaf 157.00
Royal Bayreuth, Sugar & Creamer, Hunter & Dogs 85.00

Royal Bayreuth, Sugar & Creamer, Hunter & Dogs & 2 Fishermen, Blue Mark 80.00
Royal Bayreuth, Sugar & Creamer, Tomato, Blue Mark 85.00
Royal Bayreuth, Sugar & Creamer, Tomato, Green Lettuce Leaf Top, Blue Mark 90.00
Royal Bayreuth, Sugar & Creamer, Tomato, Leaf Trim, Blue Mark 50.00
Royal Bayreuth, Sugar, Conch Shell, Satin Finish, Blue Mark, 2 1/4 X 5 In. 40.00
Royal Bayreuth, Sugar, Covered, Green Leaf Tray, Blue Mark 48.00
Royal Bayreuth, Sugar, Covered, Jack & The Beanstalk, 2 Handles, Blue Mark 50.00
Royal Bayreuth, Sugar, Covered, Portrait, Lady, Orange & Green, Blue Mark 45.00
Royal Bayreuth, Sugar, Covered, Tomato, Blue Mark 25.00
Royal Bayreuth, Sugar, Lemon, Blue Mark 110.00
Royal Bayreuth, Sugar, Pansy, Green Export Mark 100.00
Royal Bayreuth, Sugar, Tomato, Blue Mark .... 20.00 To 45.00
Royal Bayreuth, Tankard, Ye Little Bottle Tavern, Dixon, Blue Mark, 5 In. 55.00
Royal Bayreuth, Tea Set, Corinthian, 3 Piece 125.00
Royal Bayreuth, Tea Set, Rose Tapestry, Teapot, Sugar, Creamer 950.00
Royal Bayreuth, Tea Set, Tomato, Blue Mark, 3 Piece 150.00
Royal Bayreuth, Teapot, Strawberry 175.00
Royal Bayreuth, Teapot, Tomato, Blue Mark, 6 X 4 In. 75.00
Royal Bayreuth, Toby Jug, Red, Blue Mark, 7 In. 450.00
Royal Bayreuth, Toby Jug, Red, 4 3/4 In. 195.00
Royal Bayreuth, Toothpick, Black Corinthian, 3 Legs 40.00
Royal Bayreuth, Toothpick, Devil & Cards, Devil Handle 75.00
Royal Bayreuth, Toothpick, Elk Head 45.00
Royal Bayreuth, Toothpick, Mother-Of-Pearl, Art Nouveau, Blue Mark 85.00
Royal Bayreuth, Toothpick, Sheep & Goats, Black Mark 45.00
Royal Bayreuth, Toothpick, 3-Handled, Goat On Mountain 55.00
Royal Bayreuth, Toothpick, 3 Legs, Blue Mark 85.00
Royal Bayreuth, Tray, Dresser, Rose Tapestry, 9 X 7 In. 275.00
Royal Bayreuth, Tray, Green, Pink Roses, 10 X 7 In. 70.00
Royal Bayreuth, Vase, Brown, Scenes On Front & Back, Blue Mark, 5 In. 65.00
Royal Bayreuth, Vase, Cavalier Drinking Scene, Blue Mark, 4 1/4 In. 50.00
Royal Bayreuth, Vase, Cavalier, Crown & Scepter, Blue Mark, 4 1/4 In. 97.00
Royal Bayreuth, Vase, Dutch Children, Silver Rim, Footed, Blue Mark, 3 In. 37.50
Royal Bayreuth, Vase, Dutch Girl & Boy Scene, Handled, Blue Mark, 3 1/2 In. 34.00
Royal Bayreuth, Vase, Girls & Sheep Scene, Gold Handles & Rim, 3 1/2 In. 44.00
Royal Bayreuth, Vase, Grapes On Red Ground, Blue Mark, 3 X 3 In. 35.00
Royal Bayreuth, Vase, Grapes On Red Ground, Blue Mark, 8 In. 60.00
Royal Bayreuth, Vase, Green, Orchid, Cutout Handles, Blue Mark, 4 1/2 In. 60.00
Royal Bayreuth, Vase, Green, Roses, Blue Mark, 4 In. 25.00
Royal Bayreuth, Vase, Hand-Painted Cows & Scenery, Blue Mark, 8 In. 60.00
Royal Bayreuth, Vase, Hunt Scene, Miniature 15.00
Royal Bayreuth, Vase, Hunting Scene, Blue Mark, 8 1/2 In. 58.00
Royal Bayreuth, Vase, Man With 5 Dogs, 7 In. 153.00
Royal Bayreuth, Vase, Polar Bear In Moonlight Snow, Blue Mark, 5 In. 55.00
Royal Bayreuth, Vase, Portrait, Tapestry, 7 1/2 In. 595.00
Royal Bayreuth, Vase, Rose Tapestry, 2 Gold Handles, 3 In. 95.00
Royal Bayreuth, Vase, Rose Tapestry, 2 Handles, Urn Shape, 4 1/2 In. 225.00
Royal Bayreuth, Vase, Sailboat, Gray, 8 X 4 1/2 In., Blue Mark 165.00

Royal Berlin, see also KPM

Royal Berlin, Figurine, Woman With Brush & Palette, 7 In. 170.00
Royal Berlin, Figurine, Woman, Brush & Palette, Lavender, 7 In. 150.00

Royal Bonn is the nineteenth century trade name for the Bonn China Manufactory established in 1755 at Bonn, Germany. A general line of porcelain dishes was made.

Royal Bonn, see also Flow Blue

Royal Bonn, Bowl, Jasmine, Blue Floral On White, 1755, 11 In. 125.00
Royal Bonn, Celery, Colored Floral, Gold Scalloped Edges, 11 1/2 In. 13.50
Royal Bonn, Celery, Wild Roses, Green Leaves, Gold Scalloped, 12 In. 9.50
Royal Bonn, Compote, Scenic, Ships & Sunset, 9 1/4 In. 45.00
Royal Bonn, Dish, Cheese, Slant Top, Pink Flowers 22.00
Royal Bonn, Dish, Cheese, Slant Top, Roses, Colorful 18.00
Royal Bonn, Jar, Rose, Portrait, Lady, Gold Handles & Trim, Saliere, 10 In. 135.00
Royal Bonn, Plaque, Round, Beethoven Hand-Painted, Signed Voin Ser Nier, 14 I 140.00
Royal Bonn, Plate, Fish, Blue To Pink To Orange, Fish Center, 8 1/2 In. 14.00

Royal Bonn, Urn, Covered, Portrait, Blonde Lady, Green, Pedestal, 8 1/2 In. 135.00
Royal Bonn, Vase, Art Nouveau, Ball Shape, 4 In., Blues, Browns, Sienna, Signed 65.00
Royal Bonn, Vase, Blue, Green, Magenta, & White, 12 In. 87.50
Royal Bonn, Vase, Green, Hand-Painted Roses, 22 X 10 1/2 In. 62.00
Royal Bonn, Vase, Hand-Painted, Floral, Crown & Shield Mark, 12 In. 22.50
Royal Bonn, Vase, Hand-Painted, Iris, 1765 Mark, 7 1/2 In. 65.00
Royal Bonn, Vase, Portrait, Green Ground, Gourd Shape, Artist Signed, 8 In. 110.00
Royal Bonn, Vase, Portrait, Lady, Blue & Yellows, Ibertz, 8 In., Pair 300.00
Royal Bonn, Vase, Portrait, Lady, J.Stickler, 14 1/2 In. 400.00
Royal Bonn, Vase, Portrait, Woman, Handles, Gold & Green, Signed Asch, 6 In. 168.00
Royal Bonn, Vase, Portrait, Woman, P.Dingendorf, Gold Handles & Trim, 10 In. 145.00
Royal Bonn, Vase, Tapestry, Turquoise, Red Roses, 12 In. 250.00
Royal Bonn, Vase, Tapestry, Vivid Colors, Signed, 12 In. 300.00
Royal Bonn, Vase, White & Green, Floral & Gold, Gourd Shape, 9 In. 60.00
Royal Bonn, Vase, Woman Before Garden Seat, Picking Rose, Signed C.Sticher 225.00

DENMARK

Royal Copenhagen porcelain and pottery has been made in Denmark since 1772. It is still being made. One of their most famous wares is the Christmas Plate Series.

Royal Copenhagen, see also Collector, Plate, Royal Copenhagen

Royal Copenhagen, Ashtray, Langelinie, No.3645 .... 65.00
Royal Copenhagen, Bowl, Green & Gray Mottled With Gold, Square, 6 X 3 In. 35.00
Royal Copenhagen, Compote, White, Blue Floral, XO, No.10/8064, 8 1/2 In. 42.50
Royal Copenhagen, Dish, Leaf Shape, Blue Flowers, Handle, 9 In. 15.00
Royal Copenhagen, Figurine, Baby Duckling, Quacking, BH, No.1032, 4 1/2 In. 30.00
Royal Copenhagen, Figurine, Baby Lark 14.00
Royal Copenhagen, Figurine, Cat, Gray With White 48.00
Royal Copenhagen, Figurine, Cat, Sitting, Gray & White, 5 1/4 In. 48.00
Royal Copenhagen, Figurine, Girl Feeding Calf, 6 In. 135.00
Royal Copenhagen, Figurine, Girl With Goats, No.694, 9 1/2 In. 200.00
Royal Copenhagen, Figurine, Goosegirl, No.528, 7 1/2 In. 90.00
Royal Copenhagen, Figurine, Goosegirl, 9 1/2 In. 145.00
Royal Copenhagen, Figurine, Green Frog On Gray Rock, 1 1/2 In. 12.00
Royal Copenhagen, Figurine, Love Birds, White Birds, Leaf Perch, 5 1/4 In. 66.00
Royal Copenhagen, Figurine, Mouse On Sugar Cube, No.510, 2 In. 20.00
Royal Copenhagen, Figurine, Mouse, Pax, No.510, 1 3/4 In. 28.00
Royal Copenhagen, Figurine, Pan Wrestling With Bear, 7 In. 125.00
Royal Copenhagen, Figurine, Panther, No.2555, 8 1/2 In. 250.00
Royal Copenhagen, Figurine, Persian Cat, Sitting, GM, No.3281, 7 3/4 In. 80.00
Royal Copenhagen, Figurine, Persian Cat, Sitting, Ko, No.1803, 5 3/8 In. 65.00
Royal Copenhagen, Figurine, Polar Bear, No.502, 12 1/2 In. 100.00
Royal Copenhagen, Figurine, Schnauzer Dog, Sitting, Alf, No.3162, 5 In. 32.50
Royal Copenhagen, Figurine, Seal, Sitting With Head Erect, 5 In. 65.00
Royal Copenhagen, Figurine, Siamese Cat Lying Down, 5 1/8 X 4 1/4 In. 55.00
Royal Copenhagen, Figurine, Siamese Cat, No.3281, 7 1/2 In. 55.00
Royal Copenhagen, Figurine, Siamese Cat, Signed O.K., 4 3/4 X 4 In. 65.00
Royal Copenhagen, Figurine, Stag, Brown Tones 95.00
Royal Copenhagen, Figurine, Wee Willy Winkie, 7 In. 95.00
Royal Copenhagen, Figurine, Young Boy Holding Pig, 6 1/2 In. 84.00
Royal Copenhagen, Group, Fawn On Goat, 8 In. 140.00
Royal Copenhagen, Group, Pair Of Lambs, No.2769, 2 1/2 In. 45.00
Royal Copenhagen, Group, Two Children With Dog, No.707, 6 In. 124.00
Royal Copenhagen, Group, Two Owls, Signed CK, 3 1/2 In. 65.00
Royal Copenhagen, Group, White Fawn Riding Tortoise, FN, No.858, 4 In. 60.00
Royal Copenhagen, Group, 2 Puppies At Play, 4 X 2 1/2 In. 70.00
Royal Copenhagen, Group, 2 White Lovebirds On Perch, DH, No.402, 5 1/4 In. 72.00
Royal Copenhagen, Lamp, Figural, Pan Wrestling With Bear, 7 In. 100.00
Royal Copenhagen, Pitcher, Blue Fluted, Lacy Top, Mask Handle, 3 In. 20.00
Royal Copenhagen, Plate, Commemorative, 1219-1919, Soldiers, Ships, Flag 100.00
Royal Copenhagen, Plate, Fruit Center, Salmon Color Border, 8 In. 25.00
Royal Copenhagen, Plate, Portrait, Napoleon, Josephine, Pauline & Husband, Set 240.00
Royal Copenhagen, Plate, Vallos Castle, Scalloped, 1840, 9 1/2 In. 285.00
Royal Copenhagen, Sugar & Creamer, Doll's, Pink Roses, Scalloped, Crown Mark 35.00
Royal Copenhagen, Vase, Blue & White Floral, 11 In. 49.00
Royal Copenhagen, Vase, Blue Gray, White Flowers, 5 In. 28.00

Royal Copenhagen, Vase, Cream Color, Ribbed, Green Mark, No.3487, 5 1/4 In. 25.00
Royal Copenhagen, Vase, Gray White, Blackberries & Moth, 8 1/2 In. 85.00
Royal Copenhagen, Vase, Green Crackle, Gold Decoration, 12 In., Pair 225.00

Royal Crown Derby Company, Ltd., was established in England in 1876.

Royal Crown Derby, see also Crown Derby, Derby

Royal Crown Derby, Cup & Saucer, Chatsworth 27.50
Royal Crown Derby, Cup & Saucer, Royal Blue & Gold, Imari Type Pattern 40.00
Royal Crown Derby, Dish, Bonbon, Oval, Footed, Imari 35.00
Royal Crown Derby, Knife, Cake, Imari, No.1128 .... 35.00
Royal Crown Derby, Plate, Blue, Gold Floral & Rim, C.1820, 7 In. 25.00
Royal Crown Derby, Plate, Godden, Marked 1253, 7 In.C.1820 .... 25.00
Royal Crown Derby, Plate, Vine, Green Border, 10 1/4 In. 24.00
Royal Crown Derby, Vase, Bulbous Bottom, Cream & Gold, Flowers, 6 1/2 In. 135.00
Royal Crown Derby, Vase, Cobalt To White Base, Gold Floral, C.1890, 8 In. 125.00
Royal Crown Derby, Vase, Masked Handles, Gold Enamel, Rose & Cream Ground 110.00

Royal Doulton was the name used on pottery made after 1902 by Doulton & Co., in Lambeth and Burslem, England. The Doulton factory was founded in 1815. Their wares are still being made.

Royal Doulton, Ash Pot, Beefeater 50.00
Royal Doulton, Ash Pot, Dickensware, Dick Turpin, Black Base 65.00
Royal Doulton, Ash Pot, Dickensware, Old Charley, Black Base 65.00
Royal Doulton, Ash Pot, Farmer John 110.00
Royal Doulton, Ashtray, Auld Mac, Marked A 95.00
Royal Doulton, Ashtray, Cigar, Hunting Scene, Advertising A Hotel 65.00
Royal Doulton, Ashtray, Old Charley, Marked A 95.00
Royal Doulton, Ashtray, Paddy, Marked A 95.00
Royal Doulton, Ashtray, Parson Brown, Marked A 95.00
Royal Doulton, Ashtray, Sairey Gamp, A Mark, 3 In. 35.00
Royal Doulton, Beaker, Dickensware, Captain Cuttle 52.00
Royal Doulton, Beaker, Leatherware, Sterling Rim, C.1891, 4 3/4 In. 50.00
Royal Doulton, Beaker, Old Coaching Scenes, Driver & Coach, 3 1/2 In. 30.00
Royal Doulton, Beaker, Tan, Boy In Bright Colors, John Hassell, 5 In. 85.00
Royal Doulton, Beaker, Yellow Glaze, Coach Stop, 3 1/2 In. 30.00
Royal Doulton, Bottle, Brown Chivas, 9 In. 25.00
Royal Doulton, Bottle, Figural, Falstaff, Bols Label On Cork, 3 1/2 In. 60.00
Royal Doulton, Bottle, Sherry, Zorro, Black Sandeman, Old A Mark, 10 3/4 In. 55.00
Royal Doulton, Bowl, Battle Of Hastings, 8 1/2 In. 60.00
Royal Doulton, Bowl, Bird On Branch & Floral, 7 1/2 In., Pair 25.00
Royal Doulton, Bowl, Desert Scenes, 9 In. 55.00
Royal Doulton, Bowl, Dickensware, Fagin, Signed Noke, 5 1/4 In. 50.00
Royal Doulton, Bowl, Dickensware, Mr.Pickwick, Signed Noke, 1 3/4 X 6 In. 31.00
Royal Doulton, Bowl, Dickensware, Oliver Asks For More, Marked A, 8 In. 85.00
Royal Doulton, Bowl, Dickensware, Sairey Gamp, Sam Weller, Little Nell, 9 In. 125.00
Royal Doulton, Bowl, Dickensware, Tony Weller, 9 1/2 X 2 1/4 In. 75.00
Royal Doulton, Bowl, Dickensware, 4 Characters, Noke, 9 In. 67.50
Royal Doulton, Bowl, French Blue, Hand-Painted Wild Roses, 7 1/2 In. 40.00
Royal Doulton, Bowl, Jackdow Of Rheims, Square, 8 1/2 In. 45.00
Royal Doulton, Bowl, Octagon, Relief Of Peggotty, Australian Mark, 6 1/4 In. 34.50
Royal Doulton, Bowl, Old Coaching Scenes, Coach & 4 Horses, 4 In. 40.00
Royal Doulton, Bowl, Pale Green Blown-Out Grapes, Irregular Gold Edge, 9 In. 45.00
Royal Doulton, Bowl, Plate, & Mug, Child's, Bunnykins, Ivory, 3 Pieces 52.00
Royal Doulton, Bowl, Portia On Stage, Blue & Tan, 5 1/4 In. 18.00
Royal Doulton, Bowl, Portia, Shakespeare Series, 9 3/8 In. 45.00
Royal Doulton, Bowl, Robin Hood & Little John, 6 In. 25.00
Royal Doulton, Bowl, Robin, Friend Of The Poor, 6 In. 25.00
Royal Doulton, Bowl, Tintern Abbey, 3 Sections, Crescent Sides, 11 1/2 In. 35.00
Royal Doulton, Bowl, Under The Greenwood Tree, C.1900, 6 1/2 In., Set Of 3 .... 75.00
Royal Doulton, Box, Dresser, Dickensware, Covered, Fagin, 3 In. 48.00
Royal Doulton, Butter, Dutch Figures, Drainer Insert 37.50
Royal Doulton, Candlestick, Commemorative, Lord Nelson's Hat, 4 In., Pair 95.00
Royal Doulton, Character Jug, 'Arriet, Marked A, 2 1/2 In. .... 40.00 To 62.00
Royal Doulton, Character Jug, 'Arriet, Marked A, 3 1/2 In. .... 55.00 To 80.00
Royal Doulton, Character Jug, 'Arriet, 1 1/4 In. 90.00

Royal Doulton, Character Jug, 'Arriet, 3 1/2 In. 60.00
Royal Doulton, Character Jug, 'Arriet, 6 In. 120.00
Royal Doulton, Character Jug, 'Arry, Marked A, 2 1/2 In. .... 40.00 To 62.00
Royal Doulton, Character Jug, 'Arry, Marked A, 3 1/2 In. .... 60.00 To 80.00
Royal Doulton, Character Jug, 'Arry, 1 1/4 In. 80.00
Royal Doulton, Character Jug, 'Arry, 3 1/2 In. 45.00
Royal Doulton, Character Jug, 'Arry, 6 In. .... 120.00 To 125.00
Royal Doulton, Character Jug, Anne Boleyn, 6 In. 20.00
Royal Doulton, Character Jug, Anne Boleyn, 7 In. 26.00
Royal Doulton, Character Jug, Apothecary, Williamsburg, 2 1/2 In. 11.00
Royal Doulton, Character Jug, Apothecary, Williamsburg, 4 In. 15.00
Royal Doulton, Character Jug, Apothecary, Williamsburg, 7 In. 26.00
Royal Doulton, Character Jug, Aramis, 2 1/2 In. 11.00
Royal Doulton, Character Jug, Aramis, 4 In. 15.00
Royal Doulton, Character Jug, Aramis, 7 In. 26.00
Royal Doulton, Character Jug, Athos, 2 1/2 In. 11.00
Royal Doulton, Character Jug, Athos, 4 In. 15.00
Royal Doulton, Character Jug, Athos, 7 In. 26.00
Royal Doulton, Character Jug, Auld Mac, Marked A, 2 1/4 In. 50.00
Royal Doulton, Character Jug, Auld Mac, Marked A, 3 1/2 In. .... 30.00 To 35.00
Royal Doulton, Character Jug, Auld Mac, Marked A, 6 1/2 In. 69.50
Royal Doulton, Character Jug, Auld Mac, 1 1/4 In. .... 85.00 To 125.00
Royal Doulton, Character Jug, Auld Mac, 2 1/2 In. 11.00
Royal Doulton, Character Jug, Auld Mac, 4 In. 15.00
Royal Doulton, Character Jug, Auld Mac, 7 In. 26.00
Royal Doulton, Character Jug, Bacchus, 2 1/2 In. 11.00
Royal Doulton, Character Jug, Bacchus, 4 In. 15.00
Royal Doulton, Character Jug, Bacchus, 7 In. 26.00
Royal Doulton, Character Jug, Beefeater, Marked A, 2 1/2 In. 25.00
Royal Doulton, Character Jug, Beefeater, 2 1/2 In. 11.00
Royal Doulton, Character Jug, Beefeater, 4 In. 15.00
Royal Doulton, Character Jug, Beefeater, 7 In. 26.00
Royal Doulton, Character Jug, Blacksmith, Williamsburg, 2 1/2 In. 11.00
Royal Doulton, Character Jug, Blacksmith, Williamsburg, 4 In. .... 8.50 To 15.00
Royal Doulton, Character Jug, Blacksmith, Williamsburg, 7 In. 26.00
Royal Doulton, Character Jug, Bootmaker, Williamsburg, 2 1/2 In. 11.00
Royal Doulton, Character Jug, Bootmaker, Williamsburg, 4 In. .... 8.50 To 15.00
Royal Doulton, Character Jug, Bootmaker, Williamsburg, 7 In. 26.00
Royal Doulton, Character Jug, Buz Fuz, Marked A, 3 1/2 In. 60.00
Royal Doulton, Character Jug, Captain Ahab, 2 1/2 In. 11.00
Royal Doulton, Character Jug, Captain Ahab, 4 In. 15.00
Royal Doulton, Character Jug, Captain Ahab, 7 In. 26.00
Royal Doulton, Character Jug, Captain Cuttle, Marked A, 3 1/2 In. 70.00
Royal Doulton, Character Jug, Captain Henry Morgan, 2 1/2 In. 11.00
Royal Doulton, Character Jug, Captain Henry Morgan, 4 In. 15.00
Royal Doulton, Character Jug, Captain Henry Morgan, 7 In. 26.00
Royal Doulton, Character Jug, Captain Hook, 6 In. .... 190.00 To 195.00
Royal Doulton, Character Jug, Cardinal, Marked A, 2 1/2 In. 35.00
Royal Doulton, Character Jug, Cardinal, Marked A, 2 1/4 In. .... 35.00 To 40.00
Royal Doulton, Character Jug, Cardinal, Marked A, 6 In. .... 75.00 To 105.00
Royal Doulton, Character Jug, Cardinal, 1 1/4 In. .... 95.00 To 125.00
Royal Doulton, Character Jug, Catherine Of Aragon, 6 In. 20.00
Royal Doulton, Character Jug, Cavalier, Marked A, 3 1/2 In. .... 50.00 To 55.00
Royal Doulton, Character Jug, Cavalier, Marked A, 6 In. 72.00
Royal Doulton, Character Jug, Cavalier, 3 1/2 In. 45.00
Royal Doulton, Character Jug, Dick Turpin, Marked A, 2 1/2 In. 30.00
Royal Doulton, Character Jug, Dick Turpin, Marked A, 6 In. 90.00
Royal Doulton, Character Jug, Dick Turpin, Pistol Handle, Marked A, 6 In. 110.00
Royal Doulton, Character Jug, Dick Turpin, 2 1/2 In. .... 11.00 To 25.00
Royal Doulton, Character Jug, Dick Turpin, 4 In. 15.00
Royal Doulton, Character Jug, Dick Turpin, 7 In. 26.00
Royal Doulton, Character Jug, Dick Whittington, 6 In. 225.00
Royal Doulton, Character Jug, Don Quixote, 2 1/2 In. 11.00
Royal Doulton, Character Jug, Don Quixote, 4 In. 15.00
Royal Doulton, Character Jug, Don Quixote, 7 In. 26.00

Royal Doulton, Character Jug, Drake, Marked A, 6 In. 95.00
Royal Doulton, Character Jug, Falconer, 2 1/2 In. 11.00
Royal Doulton, Character Jug, Falconer, 4 In. 15.00
Royal Doulton, Character Jug, Falconer, 7 In. 26.00
Royal Doulton, Character Jug, Falstaff, 2 1/2 In. 11.00
Royal Doulton, Character Jug, Falstaff, 4 In. 15.00
Royal Doulton, Character Jug, Falstaff, 7 In. 26.00
Royal Doulton, Character Jug, Farmer John, Marked A, 3 1/2 In. .... 60.00 To 80.00
Royal Doulton, Character Jug, Farmer John, Marked A, 7 In. 65.00
Royal Doulton, Character Jug, Farmer John, 3 1/2 In. 55.00
Royal Doulton, Character Jug, Fat Boy, Marked A, 2 1/2 In. 35.00
Royal Doulton, Character Jug, Fat Boy, Marked A, 3 1/2 In. .... 45.00 To 65.00
Royal Doulton, Character Jug, Fat Boy, 1 1/4 In. 60.00
Royal Doulton, Character Jug, Fat Boy, 2 1/4 In. .... 29.00 To 40.00
Royal Doulton, Character Jug, Fortune Teller, 6 In. 175.00
Royal Doulton, Character Jug, Gaoler, Williamsburg, 2 1/2 In. 11.00
Royal Doulton, Character Jug, Gaoler, Williamsburg, 4 In. .... 8.50 To 15.00
Royal Doulton, Character Jug, Gaoler, Williamsburg, 7 In. 26.00
Royal Doulton, Character Jug, Gardener, 2 1/2 In. 11.00
Royal Doulton, Character Jug, Gardener, 4 In. 15.00
Royal Doulton, Character Jug, Gardener, 7 In. 26.00
Royal Doulton, Character Jug, Golfer, 7 In. 26.00
Royal Doulton, Character Jug, Gondolier, 6 In. 200.00
Royal Doulton, Character Jug, Gone Away, 2 1/2 In. 11.00
Royal Doulton, Character Jug, Gone Away, 4 In. 15.00
Royal Doulton, Character Jug, Gone Away, 7 In. 26.00
Royal Doulton, Character Jug, Granny, 2 1/2 In. 11.00
Royal Doulton, Character Jug, Granny, 4 In. 15.00
Royal Doulton, Character Jug, Granny, 7 In. 26.00
Royal Doulton, Character Jug, Guardsman, Williamsburg, 2 1/2 In. 11.00
Royal Doulton, Character Jug, Guardsman, Williamsburg, 4 In. .... 8.50 To 15.00
Royal Doulton, Character Jug, Guardsman, Williamsburg, 7 In. 26.00
Royal Doulton, Character Jug, Gulliver, 2 1/2 In. 195.00
Royal Doulton, Character Jug, Gulliver, 6 In. 200.00
Royal Doulton, Character Jug, Gunsmith, Williamsburg, 2 1/2 In. 11.00
Royal Doulton, Character Jug, Gunsmith, Williamsburg, 4 In. .... 8.50 To 15.00
Royal Doulton, Character Jug, Gunsmith, Williamsburg, 7 In. 26.00
Royal Doulton, Character Jug, Henry VIII, 6 In. 20.00
Royal Doulton, Character Jug, Jarge, 6 In. 200.00
Royal Doulton, Character Jug, Jester, Marked A, 3 1/2 In. 70.00
Royal Doulton, Character Jug, Jester, 3 1/2 In. 60.00
Royal Doulton, Character Jug, Jockey, 6 In. 85.00
Royal Doulton, Character Jug, John Barleycorn, Marked A, 2 1/2 In. 35.00
Royal Doulton, Character Jug, John Barleycorn, Marked A, 3 1/2 In. 45.00
Royal Doulton, Character Jug, John Barleycorn, Marked A, 6 In. 105.00
Royal Doulton, Character Jug, John Barleycorn, 2 1/2 In. 30.00
Royal Doulton, Character Jug, John Barleycorn, 6 In. 80.00
Royal Doulton, Character Jug, John Barleycorn, 7 In. 110.00
Royal Doulton, Character Jug, John Peel, Marked A, 2 1/2 In. 30.00
Royal Doulton, Character Jug, John Peel, Marked A, 3 1/2 In. 62.00
Royal Doulton, Character Jug, John Peel, Marked A, 6 In. 70.00
Royal Doulton, Character Jug, John Peel, 1 1/4 In. 95.00
Royal Doulton, Character Jug, John Peel, 2 1/2 In. 25.00
Royal Doulton, Character Jug, John Peel, 6 In. 70.00
Royal Doulton, Character Jug, Johnny Appleseed, 6 In. 125.00
Royal Doulton, Character Jug, Lawyer, 2 1/2 In. 11.00
Royal Doulton, Character Jug, Lawyer, 4 In. 15.00
Royal Doulton, Character Jug, Lawyer, 7 In. 26.00
Royal Doulton, Character Jug, Lobster Man, 4 In. 15.00
Royal Doulton, Character Jug, Lobster Man, 7 In. 26.00
Royal Doulton, Character Jug, Long John Silver, 2 1/2 In. 11.00
Royal Doulton, Character Jug, Long John Silver, 4 In. 15.00
Royal Doulton, Character Jug, Long John Silver, 6 In. 25.00
Royal Doulton, Character Jug, Long John Silver, 7 In. 26.00
Royal Doulton, Character Jug, Lord Nelson, 6 In. 175.00

Royal Doulton, Character Jug, Lumberjack, 2 1/2 In. 11.00
Royal Doulton, Character Jug, Lumberjack, 4 In. 15.00
Royal Doulton, Character Jug, Lumberjack, 7 In. 26.00
Royal Doulton, Character Jug, Mad Hatter, 2 1/2 In. 11.00
Royal Doulton, Character Jug, Mad Hatter, 4 In. 15.00
Royal Doulton, Character Jug, Mad Hatter, 7 In. 26.00
Royal Doulton, Character Jug, Merlin, 2 1/2 In. 11.00
Royal Doulton, Character Jug, Merlin, 3 1/2 In. 15.00
Royal Doulton, Character Jug, Merlin, 4 In. 15.00
Royal Doulton, Character Jug, Merlin, 7 In. 26.00
Royal Doulton, Character Jug, Mikado, 2 1/2 In. 135.00
Royal Doulton, Character Jug, Mikado, 3 1/2 In. 100.00
Royal Doulton, Character Jug, Mine Host, 2 1/2 In. 11.00
Royal Doulton, Character Jug, Mine Host, 4 In. 15.00
Royal Doulton, Character Jug, Mine Host, 7 In. 26.00
Royal Doulton, Character Jug, Monty, 7 In. .... 26.00 To 55.00
Royal Doulton, Character Jug, Motorist, 2 1/2 In. 11.00
Royal Doulton, Character Jug, Motorist, 4 In. 15.00
Royal Doulton, Character Jug, Motorist, 7 In. 26.00
Royal Doulton, Character Jug, Mr.Micawber, Marked A, 2 1/4 In. 30.00
Royal Doulton, Character Jug, Mr.Micawber, 1 1/4 In. 70.00
Royal Doulton, Character Jug, Mr.Micawber, 2 1/4 In. .... 32.50 To 40.00
Royal Doulton, Character Jug, Mr.Pickwick, Marked A, 2 1/4 In. 50.00
Royal Doulton, Character Jug, Mr.Pickwick, Marked A, 3 1/2 In. 45.00
Royal Doulton, Character Jug, Mr.Pickwick, 1 1/4 In. 80.00
Royal Doulton, Character Jug, Neptune, 2 1/2 In. 11.00
Royal Doulton, Character Jug, Neptune, 4 In. 15.00
Royal Doulton, Character Jug, Neptune, 7 In. 26.00
Royal Doulton, Character Jug, Night Watchman, Williamsburg, 2 1/2 In. 11.00
Royal Doulton, Character Jug, Night Watchman, Williamsburg, 4 In. 12.00
Royal Doulton, Character Jug, Night Watchman, Williamsburg, 7 In. 26.00
Royal Doulton, Character Jug, North American Indian, 4 In. 15.00
Royal Doulton, Character Jug, North American Indian, 7 In. 26.00
Royal Doulton, Character Jug, Old Charley, Marked A, 2 1/2 In. 25.00
Royal Doulton, Character Jug, Old Charley, Marked A, 3 1/2 In. .... 35.00 To 65.00
Royal Doulton, Character Jug, Old Charley, 1 1/4 In. 55.00
Royal Doulton, Character Jug, Old Charley, 2 1/2 In. 11.00
Royal Doulton, Character Jug, Old Charley, 3 1/2 In. 40.00
Royal Doulton, Character Jug, Old Charley, 6 In. 80.00
Royal Doulton, Character Jug, Old Charley, 7 In. 26.00
Royal Doulton, Character Jug, Old King Cole, Marked A, 3 1/2 In. 60.00
Royal Doulton, Character Jug, Old King Cole, Marked A, 6 In. 125.00
Royal Doulton, Character Jug, Old Salt, 4 In. 15.00
Royal Doulton, Character Jug, Old Salt, 7 In. 26.00
Royal Doulton, Character Jug, Paddy, Marked A, 2 1/2 In. 30.00
Royal Doulton, Character Jug, Paddy, Marked A, 3 1/2 In. 65.00
Royal Doulton, Character Jug, Paddy, 1 1/4 In. .... 53.00 To 60.00
Royal Doulton, Character Jug, Paddy, 2 1/2 In. .... 25.00 To 30.00
Royal Doulton, Character Jug, Paddy, 3 1/2 In. 35.00
Royal Doulton, Character Jug, Parson Brown, Marked A, 6 In. .... 72.00 To 105.00
Royal Doulton, Character Jug, Parson Brown, 3 1/2 In. 40.00
Royal Doulton, Character Jug, Parson Brown, 6 In. 100.00
Royal Doulton, Character Jug, Pied Piper, 2 1/2 In. 11.00
Royal Doulton, Character Jug, Pied Piper, 4 In. 15.00
Royal Doulton, Character Jug, Pied Piper, 7 In. 26.00
Royal Doulton, Character Jug, Poacher, 2 1/2 In. 11.00
Royal Doulton, Character Jug, Poacher, 4 In. 15.00
Royal Doulton, Character Jug, Poacher, 7 In. 26.00
Royal Doulton, Character Jug, Porthos, 2 1/2 In. 11.00
Royal Doulton, Character Jug, Porthos, 4 In. 15.00
Royal Doulton, Character Jug, Porthos, 7 In. 26.00
Royal Doulton, Character Jug, Punch & Judy Man, 2 1/2 In. 245.00
Royal Doulton, Character Jug, Regency Beau, 6 In. 210.00
Royal Doulton, Character Jug, Rip Van Winkle, 2 1/2 In. 11.00
Royal Doulton, Character Jug, Rip Van Winkle, 4 In. 15.00

Royal Doulton, Character Jug, Rip Van Winkle, 7 In. .... 26.00 To 35.00
Royal Doulton, Character Jug, Robin Hood, Marked A, 2 1/2 In. 40.00
Royal Doulton, Character Jug, Robin Hood, Marked A, 3 1/2 In. 60.00
Royal Doulton, Character Jug, Robin Hood, 2 1/2 In. 11.00
Royal Doulton, Character Jug, Robin Hood, 4 In. 15.00
Royal Doulton, Character Jug, Robin Hood, 7 In. 26.00
Royal Doulton, Character Jug, Robinson Crusoe, 2 1/2 In. 11.00
Royal Doulton, Character Jug, Robinson Crusoe, 4 In. 15.00
Royal Doulton, Character Jug, Robinson Crusoe, 7 In. 26.00
Royal Doulton, Character Jug, Sairey Gamp, Marked A, 2 1/4 In. 35.00
Royal Doulton, Character Jug, Sairey Gamp, Marked A, 3 1/2 In. .... 35.00 To 65.00
Royal Doulton, Character Jug, Sairey Gamp, Marked A, 6 1/2 In. 75.00
Royal Doulton, Character Jug, Sairey Gamp, 1 1/4 In. .... 52.00 To 60.00
Royal Doulton, Character Jug, Sairey Gamp, 2 1/2 In. 11.00
Royal Doulton, Character Jug, Sairey Gamp, 4 In. 15.00
Royal Doulton, Character Jug, Sairey Gamp, 7 In. 26.00
Royal Doulton, Character Jug, Sam Weller, Marked A, 2 1/2 In. 30.00
Royal Doulton, Character Jug, Sam Weller, Marked A, 3 1/2 In. 45.00
Royal Doulton, Character Jug, Sam Weller, Marked A, 6 In. 85.00
Royal Doulton, Character Jug, Sam Weller, 2 1/2 In. 25.00
Royal Doulton, Character Jug, Sancho Panza, 2 1/2 In. 11.00
Royal Doulton, Character Jug, Sancho Panza, 4 In. 15.00
Royal Doulton, Character Jug, Sancho Panza, 7 In. 26.00
Royal Doulton, Character Jug, Scaramouche, 2 1/2 In. 245.00
Royal Doulton, Character Jug, Scaramouche, 3 1/2 In. 215.00
Royal Doulton, Character Jug, Simon The Cellarer, A, 3 1/2 In. 65.00
Royal Doulton, Character Jug, Sir Francis Drake, A, 3 1/2 In. .... 50.00 To 80.00
Royal Doulton, Character Jug, Sir Francis Drake, Marked A, 6 In. 125.00
Royal Doulton, Character Jug, Sir Isaac Walton, 7 In. 26.00
Royal Doulton, Character Jug, Sir Winston Churchill, 9 In. 30.00
Royal Doulton, Character Jug, Sleuth, 2 1/2 In. 11.00
Royal Doulton, Character Jug, Sleuth, 4 In. 15.00
Royal Doulton, Character Jug, Sleuth, 7 In. 26.00
Royal Doulton, Character Jug, Smuggler, 4 In. 15.00
Royal Doulton, Character Jug, Smuggler, 7 In. 26.00
Royal Doulton, Character Jug, St.George, 3 1/2 In. 30.00
Royal Doulton, Character Jug, St.George, 6 In. .... 45.00 To 50.00
Royal Doulton, Character Jug, Tam-O-'Shanter, 2 1/2 In. 11.00
Royal Doulton, Character Jug, Tam-O'-Shanter, 4 In. 15.00
Royal Doulton, Character Jug, Tam-O'-Shanter, 7 In. 26.00
Royal Doulton, Character Jug, Toby Philpots, Marked A, 2 1/2 In. 35.00
Royal Doulton, Character Jug, Toby Philpots, Marked A, 3 1/2 In. 40.00
Royal Doulton, Character Jug, Toby Philpots, Marked A, 6 1/2 In. 79.50
Royal Doulton, Character Jug, Toby Philpots, 3 1/2 In. 27.00
Royal Doulton, Character Jug, Toby Philpots, 6 In. 78.00
Royal Doulton, Character Jug, Tony Weller, Marked A, 2 1/2 In. 28.00
Royal Doulton, Character Jug, Tony Weller, Marked A, 3 1/2 In. 65.00
Royal Doulton, Character Jug, Tony Weller, Marked A, 6 In. .... 92.50 To 98.00
Royal Doulton, Character Jug, Tony Weller, 3 1/2 In. 60.00
Royal Doulton, Character Jug, Town Crier, 2 1/2 In. 35.00
Royal Doulton, Character Jug, Town Crier, 2 1/4 In. 35.00
Royal Doulton, Character Jug, Town Crier, 6 In. 87.50
Royal Doulton, Character Jug, Trapper, 4 In. 15.00
Royal Doulton, Character Jug, Trapper, 7 In. 26.00
Royal Doulton, Character Jug, Ugly Duchess, 2 1/2 In. 45.00
Royal Doulton, Character Jug, Ugly Duchess, 3 1/2 In. 50.00
Royal Doulton, Character Jug, Vicar Of Bray, Marked A, 6 In. 190.00
Royal Doulton, Character Jug, Vicar Of Bray, 6 In. 150.00
Royal Doulton, Character Jug, Viking, 3 1/2 In. .... 30.00 To 40.00
Royal Doulton, Character Jug, Viking, 6 In. 45.00
Royal Doulton, Character Jug, Walrus & Carpenter, 2 1/2 In. 11.00
Royal Doulton, Character Jug, Walrus & Carpenter, 4 In. 15.00
Royal Doulton, Character Jug, Walrus & Carpenter, 7 In. 26.00
Royal Doulton, Character Jug, Yachtsman, 7 In. 26.00
Royal Doulton, Charger, Blue Willow, Burslem 95.00

Royal Doulton, Charger, Dickensware, Bill Sykes & Dog, Noke, 13 1/2 In. 190.00
Royal Doulton, Charger, Dickensware, Mr.Bacchus, 13 1/2 In. 125.00
Royal Doulton, Charger, Dickensware, Tony Weller, 13 1/2 In. 110.00
Royal Doulton, Child's Set, Bunnykins, 4 Piece 25.50
Royal Doulton, Coffee Set, Demitasse, White, Gold & Black Trees, 15 Piece 95.00
Royal Doulton, Coffee Set, Fox, 18 Piece 185.00
Royal Doulton, Coffee Set, Reynard The Fox, Black & White, 4 Piece 150.00
Royal Doulton, Coffeepot, Chatsworth 25.00
Royal Doulton, Creamer On Tray, Old Coaching Scenes, Browns, Square, 4 In. 32.00
Royal Doulton, Creamer, Dickensware, Tony Weller 55.00
Royal Doulton, Cup & Saucer, Bell Heather 15.00
Royal Doulton, Cup & Saucer, Demitasse, Flambe 37.50
Royal Doulton, Cup & Saucer, Dickensware, Mr.Squeers, Noke 50.00
Royal Doulton, Cup & Saucer, Jackdaw Of Rheims 46.00
Royal Doulton, Cup & Saucer, Nankin, 2-Handled Cup 8.50
Royal Doulton, Cup & Saucer, Old Coaching Scenes .... 25.00 To 27.50
Royal Doulton, Cup, Baby's, Lambeth Walk, Barbara Vernon 35.00
Royal Doulton, Cup, Bill Sykes, Signed Noke, Miniature, 2 In. 30.00
Royal Doulton, Cup, Dickensware, Mr.Micawber, Noke 22.00
Royal Doulton, Cup, Loving, Coronation, 1953, 11 1/2 X 11 In. 200.00
Royal Doulton, Cup, Loving, Dickensware, Centennial 225.00
Royal Doulton, Cup, Loving, Noke, Fenton, No.856 .... 250.00
Royal Doulton, Decanter, Cobalt, Brown Handle & Leaves, GP, 1927, 9 In. 150.00
Royal Doulton, Dish, Baby's Feeding, Nursery Rhyme 31.00
Royal Doulton, Dish, Child's, Bunnykins, Christmas Scene, 7 1/2 In. 28.00
Royal Doulton, Figurine, Alfred Jingle, 4 In. 12.50
Royal Doulton, Figurine, Autumn Breezes, No.83566, C.1913, 8 In. 69.00
Royal Doulton, Figurine, Bear, Chatcull, 4 1/2 X 6 1/2 In. 55.00
Royal Doulton, Figurine, Bill Sykes, 4 In. .... 12.50 To 45.00
Royal Doulton, Figurine, Bird, Long Bill, Blue, Green, & Brown, 4 In. 115.00
Royal Doulton, Figurine, Brown & Black Pekinese Sitting, 6 In. 24.00
Royal Doulton, Figurine, Bull Dog, 1044 Brindle 55.00
Royal Doulton, Figurine, Bumble, 4 In. 12.50
Royal Doulton, Figurine, Bust, Sam Weller, Signed Noke, Miniature 45.00
Royal Doulton, Figurine, Buzfuz, 4 In. 12.50
Royal Doulton, Figurine, Cairn Dog, Begging, 4 In. 13.50
Royal Doulton, Figurine, Cairn Dog, 2 1/2 In. 9.00
Royal Doulton, Figurine, Captain Cuttle, 4 In. .... 12.50 To 30.00
Royal Doulton, Figurine, Cat, Flambe, 4 3/4 In. 49.00
Royal Doulton, Figurine, Cat, Sitting, Flambe, 4 3/4 In. .... 35.00 To 38.00
Royal Doulton, Figurine, Chief Warlord Of Mazelaine, HN 2643, 6 In. 36.00
Royal Doulton, Figurine, Cobbler, HN 1706, Noke, 7 1/2 In. 165.00
Royal Doulton, Figurine, Cocker With Pheasant, 6 1/2 In. 95.00
Royal Doulton, Figurine, Dalmatian Dog, No.1113, 8 In. 35.00
Royal Doulton, Figurine, Darling, HN 1319, Dated 3-11-39, 8 In. 125.00
Royal Doulton, Figurine, Darling, HN 1985, 5 1/4 In. 22.50
Royal Doulton, Figurine, David Copperfield, 4 In. 12.50
Royal Doulton, Figurine, Dick Swiveller, 4 In. 12.50
Royal Doulton, Figurine, Dinky Do, 4 1/2 In. 32.00
Royal Doulton, Figurine, Drake Duck, No.137, Flambe, 6 In. 49.00
Royal Doulton, Figurine, Drake, Miniature, Natural Colors, 2 1/2 In. 12.00
Royal Doulton, Figurine, Drake, Standing, Flambe, 6 1/4 In. 50.00
Royal Doulton, Figurine, Duck, Flambe, Godden Mark, 13334, 6 1/2 In. 75.00
Royal Doulton, Figurine, Duck, Standing, Flambe, 2 3/4 In. 13.00
Royal Doulton, Figurine, Duck, Swimming, Flambe, 3 1/2 In. 13.00
Royal Doulton, Figurine, Elephant, Flambe, 5 1/2 In. 75.00
Royal Doulton, Figurine, Elephant, HN 891, Dark Gray, White Tusks, 9 1/2 In. 76.00
Royal Doulton, Figurine, Elephant, Walking, Flambe, 5 1/2 In. 75.00
Royal Doulton, Figurine, Elephant, 5 1/2 In. 24.00
Royal Doulton, Figurine, Elephant, 7 In. 150.00
Royal Doulton, Figurine, Fagin, 4 In. 12.50
Royal Doulton, Figurine, Fat Boy, 4 In. .... 12.50 To 15.00
Royal Doulton, Figurine, Flag-Draped Bulldog, 6 1/4 In. 75.00
Royal Doulton, Figurine, Flower Seller's Children, No.1342, 7 1/2 In. 165.00
Royal Doulton, Figurine, Fox, Running, Flambe, 3 In. 17.50

Royal Doulton, Figurine, Garbe Seal, Dennis Exhibition, No.249, 8 In. 165.00
Royal Doulton, Figurine, Hazel, HN 1796, 1938, 5 1/4 In. 55.00
Royal Doulton, Figurine, Jill, 5 1/2 In. 55.00
Royal Doulton, Figurine, Kudu, Chatcull, 6 X 5 In. 55.00
Royal Doulton, Figurine, Margery, HN 1413, No.755477, 10 1/4 In. 250.00
Royal Doulton, Figurine, Maria, HN 1370, 5 In. 55.00
Royal Doulton, Figurine, Mary Had A Little Lamb, 3 5/8 In. 28.75
Royal Doulton, Figurine, Miss Demure, HN 1402, Rd.No.753474, 7 1/4 In. 165.00
Royal Doulton, Figurine, Mountain Goat, Chatcull, 5 1/2 X 5 In. 55.00
Royal Doulton, Figurine, Mr.Micawber, 4 In. 12.50 To 30.00
Royal Doulton, Figurine, Mr.Pickwick, 4 In. 12.50
Royal Doulton, Figurine, Mrs.Bardell, Standing, 4 In. 30.00
Royal Doulton, Figurine, Oliver Twist, 4 In. 12.50
Royal Doulton, Figurine, Parson's Daughter, HN 564, 10 In. 250.00
Royal Doulton, Figurine, Pecksniff, Standing, 4 In. 30.00
Royal Doulton, Figurine, Pekinese, Sitting, Brown & Black, 2 In. 24.00
Royal Doulton, Figurine, Penguin, Flambe, 1333, 4 1/2 In. 58.00
Royal Doulton, Figurine, Primroses 225.00
Royal Doulton, Figurine, Priscilla, HN 1360, 8 In. 165.00
Royal Doulton, Figurine, Rabbit, One Ear Up, Flambe, 3 In. 14.00 To 16.00
Royal Doulton, Figurine, Rabbit, Sitting, Flambe, 4 1/2 In. 90.00
Royal Doulton, Figurine, Rosalind, No.2393, 5 1/2 In. 95.00
Royal Doulton, Figurine, Rose, HN 1368, 4 3/4 In. 55.00
Royal Doulton, Figurine, Sairey Gamp, Standing, 4 In. 30.00 To 35.00
Royal Doulton, Figurine, Sairey Gamp, 4 In. 12.50 To 30.00
Royal Doulton, Figurine, Sam Weller, 4 In. 12.50
Royal Doulton, Figurine, Scrooge, 4 In. 12.50
Royal Doulton, Figurine, Sealyham, 6 In. 65.00
Royal Doulton, Figurine, Shepherd, 8 1/2 In. 80.00
Royal Doulton, Figurine, Siamese Cat, 5 5/8 In. 32.50
Royal Doulton, Figurine, Stiggins, 4 In. 12.50
Royal Doulton, Figurine, Sweet & Twenty, HN 1298, 7 X 5 3/4 In. 145.00
Royal Doulton, Figurine, Sweet Anne, HN 1496, 7 In. 165.00
Royal Doulton, Figurine, The Parisian 125.00
Royal Doulton, Figurine, Tiger, No.809, Flambe, 14 In. 165.00
Royal Doulton, Figurine, Tiny Tim, 4 In. 12.50
Royal Doulton, Figurine, To Bed, 6 1/2 In. 42.50
Royal Doulton, Figurine, Tony Weller, Standing, 4 In. 30.00
Royal Doulton, Figurine, Trotty Veck, 4 In. 12.50
Royal Doulton, Figurine, Uriah Heep, 4 In. 12.50
Royal Doulton, Figurine, Welsh Corgi, Miniature, 3 5/8 In. 9.50
Royal Doulton, Goblet, Leeds Spray, Octagonal 11.00
Royal Doulton, Group, Cocker With Pheasant, 1029, 3 3/4 In. 56.00
Royal Doulton, Group, Gude Grey Mare, White & Brown, 8 In. 235.00
Royal Doulton, Humidor, Tobacco, Orange Tan, Orange Peel, Tobacco, 5 1/2 In. 68.00
Royal Doulton, Jar, Ginger, Dickensware, Captain Cuttle, 5 1/4 In. 69.00
Royal Doulton, Jar, Tobacco, Abstract, Signed Eliza Simmance, Covered 135.00
Royal Doulton, Jar, Tobacco, Autumn Leaf On Brown, Covered 85.00
Royal Doulton, Jar, Tobacco, Barrel Shape, Hunt Scene, Tan With White Figures 36.50
Royal Doulton, Jardiniere, Terra-Cotta, Mustard & Aqua Leaf, M.B., C.1912 75.00
Royal Doulton, Jug, Ale, Brown, Man Drinking, Connoisseur, 9 In. 95.00
Royal Doulton, Jug, Beige, Ye Olde Cheshire Cheese, Double Spout, 3 In. 25.00
Royal Doulton, Jug, Browns, Blues, & Grays, C.1790, 8 X 6 In. 145.00
Royal Doulton, Jug, Chivas Brothers, Knight On Horseback, Brown Glaze, 9 In. 28.00
Royal Doulton, Jug, Cream, Robin Hood In Ambush, Cream Color, 3 3/4 In. 30.00
Royal Doulton, Jug, Dewar's Scotch Whiskey, Bonnie Prince Charlie 95.00
Royal Doulton, Jug, Dickensware, Mr.Pickwick, Pouch Shape, 6 In. 95.00
Royal Doulton, Jug, Dickensware, Pickwick Papers, Square, 5 1/4 In. 118.00
Royal Doulton, Jug, Egglington Tournament, Caramel, 7 In. 95.00
Royal Doulton, Jug, Gladstone Commemorative 135.00
Royal Doulton, Jug, Highland Whiskey 45.00
Royal Doulton, Jug, Merlin The Magician, Silver Stopper, Dewar's 105.00
Royal Doulton, Jug, Portrait Of Longfellow & Poem, Portland, Maine 65.00
Royal Doulton, Jug, Shakespeare, Falstaff & Bardolph, 7 In. 90.00
Royal Doulton, Jug, Silicon, Kate Greenaway Figures, Dated 1883 160.00

Royal Doulton, Jug, Simulated Lizard Leather, Wax Stitching, Lambeth, 8 In. 110.00
Royal Doulton, Jug, Smoker, Signed Noke 55.00
Royal Doulton, Jug, Square, Dickensware, Old Curiosity Shop 122.50
Royal Doulton, Jug, Square, Dickensware, Oliver Twist 110.00
Royal Doulton, Jug, Square, Dickensware, Pickwick Papers 125.00
Royal Doulton, Jug, Stoneware, Mottled Blue & Green, Applied Floral, 9 In. 75.00
Royal Doulton, Jug, Water, Gold, Cobalt, Iris, Roses, Signed, P.G.R.D., Burslem 85.00
Royal Doulton, Jug, Water, Watteau 65.00
Royal Doulton, Jug, Welsh Ladies, Cobalt Decoration, 2 In. 45.00
Royal Doulton, Jug, Whiskey, Brown Stoneware, Silver Top, Greyhounds 75.00
Royal Doulton, Lighter, Buzfuz 65.00
Royal Doulton, Lighter, Cigarette, Falstaff Toby, 3 3/4 In. 38.50
Royal Doulton, Lighter, Granny 65.00
Royal Doulton, Lighter, Long John Silver 60.00
Royal Doulton, Lighter, Poacher 55.00
Royal Doulton, Mug, Bowl, & Plate, Bunnykins, 7 1/2 In. Plate 17.50
Royal Doulton, Mug, Bunnykins, Cowboys 17.50
Royal Doulton, Mug, Bunnykins, Fishing 17.50
Royal Doulton, Mug, Centennial, 1876 .... 72.00
Royal Doulton, Mug, Fortune Teller 85.00
Royal Doulton, Mug, Golfing Scene, 6 In. 125.00
Royal Doulton, Mug, Green Monk Cellarer & Tan Tavern Scene, 5 1/2 In. 90.00
Royal Doulton, Mug, Half-Timbered Houses & Watchmen With Lanterns, Greens 90.00
Royal Doulton, Mug, Robin Hood Under Greenwood Tree, 5 In. 35.00
Royal Doulton, Mug, Stoneware With Blue Glaze, Lord Nelson, Miniature 50.00
Royal Doulton, Mug, Three Musketeers, 5 1/2 In. 40.00
Royal Doulton, Mug, 2-Handled, Brown Glaze, Portrait, Verse 65.00
Royal Doulton, Mug, 2-Handled, Dutch Scene, Cream Color, 1 3/8 In. 32.00
Royal Doulton, Napkin Ring, Fat Boy, 3 In. 59.50
Royal Doulton, Napkin Ring, Mr Pickwick, 3 In. 59.50
Royal Doulton, Pitcher, Battle Of Hastings, Bayeux Tapestry, 6 1/2 In. 40.00
Royal Doulton, Pitcher, Black Pool Crest, Cream Color, 3 In. 30.00
Royal Doulton, Pitcher, Blue, Red & Yellow Flowers, Marked A, 9 In. 50.00
Royal Doulton, Pitcher, Burgundy, Ocher Shields, Black Bands, 8 1/4 In. 45.00
Royal Doulton, Pitcher, Carriage Scene, 8 1/2 In. 50.00
Royal Doulton, Pitcher, Dickensware, Artful Dodger, Noke, Footed, 4 1/2 In. 58.00
Royal Doulton, Pitcher, Dickensware, Mr. Squeers, 8 1/2 In. 87.50
Royal Doulton, Pitcher, Dickensware, Mr.Micawber, 8 1/2 In. 55.00
Royal Doulton, Pitcher, Dickensware, Oliver Twist, Square 70.00
Royal Doulton, Pitcher, Diversions Of Uncle Toby, 9 In. 55.00
Royal Doulton, Pitcher, Don Quixote, 9 In. 55.00
Royal Doulton, Pitcher, Edward VII & Alexandra Commemorative, Tans, 8 In. 125.00
Royal Doulton, Pitcher, Gaffers, All The Way From Zummerzet, 41 In. 95.00
Royal Doulton, Pitcher, Gallant Fishers, 7 In. 67.50
Royal Doulton, Pitcher, Golfer, He That Always Complains, 5 1/4 In. 60.00
Royal Doulton, Pitcher, Kingsware, Brown, Man Smoking Pipe, Silver Rim, 9 In. 110.00
Royal Doulton, Pitcher, Light Green, 8 Polar Bears On Blue Band, 8 In. 90.00
Royal Doulton, Pitcher, Midsummer Night's Dream, 2 Quart, 1906 .... 35.00
Royal Doulton, Pitcher, Milk, Coaching Days, 5 In. 35.00
Royal Doulton, Pitcher, Oatmeal Color, Sayings In Black, 6 In. 26.00
Royal Doulton, Pitcher, Old Coaching Scenes, London Coach, C.1905, 7 1/4 In. 65.00
Royal Doulton, Pitcher, Old Coaching Scenes, Tan, Noke, 9 In. 115.00
Royal Doulton, Pitcher, Old Sailor In Rowboat, Blue & White, 7 In. 60.00
Royal Doulton, Pitcher, Polar Bears, Blue, Green Ground, 5 In. 95.00
Royal Doulton, Pitcher, Scene Of Cottages, Trees, Lake, 5 1/2 In. 52.00
Royal Doulton, Pitcher, The Night Watchman, Marked, 8 In. 50.00
Royal Doulton, Pitcher, Titanian, Peacock, 4 3/4 In. 55.00
Royal Doulton, Pitcher, Venetian Canal Gondola Scene, 4 1/2 In. 42.00
Royal Doulton, Pitcher, Watchman, What Of The Night, 7 In. 85.00
Royal Doulton, Plaque, Dickensware, Bill Sykes, Noke, 13 1/2 In. 150.00
Royal Doulton, Plaque, Jackdaw Of Rheims, Bishop & Abbot & Prior, 15 In. 150.00
Royal Doulton, Plate, Admiral .... 18.00 To 35.00
Royal Doulton, Plate, African Series, Water Buck, 10 1/2 In. 15.00
Royal Doulton, Plate, Arundel Castle, 10 In. 25.00
Royal Doulton, Plate, Babes In The Woods, Lady With Little Girl, 9 1/4 In. 75.00

Royal Doulton, Plate, Baby's, Bunnykins, Barbara Vernon 25.00
Royal Doulton, Plate, Battle Of Hastings, Bayeux Tapestry, 10 1/2 In. 35.00
Royal Doulton, Plate, Battle Of The Nile, 10 1/2 In. 27.00
Royal Doulton, Plate, Blue Background, Parrots & Florals, 12-Sided, C.1912 20.00
Royal Doulton, Plate, Bread & Butter, Old Coaching Scenes 18.00
Royal Doulton, Plate, Bread, Dickensware, Captain Cuttle, 1907, 10 1/2 In. 95.00
Royal Doulton, Plate, Bread, Under The Greenwood Tree, 1909, 12 1/2 In. 82.50
Royal Doulton, Plate, Bunnykins, Mailman, 7 1/2 In. 17.50
Royal Doulton, Plate, Bunnykins, Rabbits Playing Golf, 7 1/2 In. 20.00
Royal Doulton, Plate, Bunnykins, Tea Time, 7 1/2 In. 17.50
Royal Doulton, Plate, Charles II, Chelsea Hospital, Green Doulton A Mark 150.00
Royal Doulton, Plate, Child's, Bunnykins 7.00
Royal Doulton, Plate, Chop, Treasure Island, Long John Silver, 13 1/2 In. 115.00
Royal Doulton, Plate, Cobalt Border, Band Of Floral, 10 In. 17.50
Royal Doulton, Plate, Cocker, Dated 1933, D Series 25.00
Royal Doulton, Plate, Desert Scenes, Dated 1918, 10 1/2 In. 29.00
Royal Doulton, Plate, Dickensware, Alfred Jingle, 9 1/2 In. 42.00
Royal Doulton, Plate, Dickensware, Artful Dodger, 7 1/2 In. 35.00
Royal Doulton, Plate, Dickensware, Barkis, 7 1/2 In. 35.00
Royal Doulton, Plate, Dickensware, Bill Sykes, Signed Noke, 10 1/2 In. 45.00
Royal Doulton, Plate, Dickensware, Captain Cuttle, 10 1/2 In. 45.00 To 47.50
Royal Doulton, Plate, Dickensware, Captain Cuttle, 7 1/2 In. 35.00
Royal Doulton, Plate, Dickensware, Dickens Center, Blue & White, 10 1/2 In. 45.00
Royal Doulton, Plate, Dickensware, Fat Boy, 10 1/2 In. 45.00
Royal Doulton, Plate, Dickensware, Little Nell, 10 1/2 In. 45.00
Royal Doulton, Plate, Dickensware, Little Nell, 7 1/2 In. 35.00
Royal Doulton, Plate, Dickensware, Mr. Pickwick, Signed Noke, 10 1/2 In. 45.00
Royal Doulton, Plate, Dickensware, Mr.Micawber, 10 1/2 In. 42.00
Royal Doulton, Plate, Dickensware, Mr.Squeers, Square, 7 1/2 In. 60.00
Royal Doulton, Plate, Dickensware, Old Peggotty, 7 1/2 In. 35.00
Royal Doulton, Plate, Dickensware, Sairey Gamp, 9 1/2 In. 36.00
Royal Doulton, Plate, Dickensware, Sam Weller, Signed Noke, 10 1/2 In. 45.00
Royal Doulton, Plate, Dickensware, Sam Weller, Square, 5 3/4 In. 23.00
Royal Doulton, Plate, Dickensware, Sam Weller, 9 1/2 In. 42.00
Royal Doulton, Plate, Dickensware, Sergeant Buzfuz, 10 1/2 In. 45.00
Royal Doulton, Plate, Dickensware, Squire, 10 1/4 In. 35.00
Royal Doulton, Plate, Dickensware, Tom Pinch, Square, 7 1/2 In. 35.00
Royal Doulton, Plate, Dickensware, Tony Weller, Square, 7 1/2 In. 35.00
Royal Doulton, Plate, Dickensware, 12 Characters, 10 1/2 In. 35.00
Royal Doulton, Plate, Dinner, Chelsea Rose 10.00
Royal Doulton, Plate, Dutch Garden Scene, 10 1/2 In. 29.00
Royal Doulton, Plate, Ellington Tournament, Knights Jousting, 10 1/2 In. 28.00
Royal Doulton, Plate, English Inns, Leather Bottle, 10 1/2 In. 25.00
Royal Doulton, Plate, Falconry, Burslem, Nile Street, 9 1/2 In. 40.00
Royal Doulton, Plate, Falstaff, 9 In. 45.00
Royal Doulton, Plate, Gaffers, Signed Noke, 6 1/2 In. 18.00
Royal Doulton, Plate, Gibson Girl, Remained In Retirement Too Long 75.00
Royal Doulton, Plate, Hurstmonceaux Castle, Red & Brown, Small 15.00
Royal Doulton, Plate, Izaak Walton Fisherman, 10 1/2 In. 55.00
Royal Doulton, Plate, Jackdaw Of Rheims, 9 1/2 In. 35.00
Royal Doulton, Plate, Knights On Horseback, 10 1/2 In. 33.00
Royal Doulton, Plate, Koala Bears, 10 1/2 In. 35.00
Royal Doulton, Plate, Matsumai, Dark Blue & Floral 30.00
Royal Doulton, Plate, Niagara Falls, Large 18.00
Royal Doulton, Plate, Nursery Rhymes, There Was A Little Man, 7 In. 22.00
Royal Doulton, Plate, Old Coaching Scenes, Scalloped Edge, 8 1/2 In. 22.00
Royal Doulton, Plate, Old Coaching Scenes, 5 3/4 In. 15.00
Royal Doulton, Plate, Othello, Quote From Play On Back, 12 5/8 In. 75.00
Royal Doulton, Plate, Parson, 10 1/2 In. 28.00
Royal Doulton, Plate, Portia D Series, 10 1/2 In. 35.00
Royal Doulton, Plate, Proverbs & Golfer, 10 1/2 In. 45.00
Royal Doulton, Plate, Salad, Coaching Days, Scalloped, 8 1/2 In. 20.00
Royal Doulton, Plate, Salisbury Cathedral, 10 1/2 In. 26.00
Royal Doulton, Plate, Service, British Castle Scene, Hart & Brown, 1928 168.50
Royal Doulton, Plate, Shakespeare, Flow Blue, Bard & 12 Characters, 10 In. 45.00

Royal Doulton, Plate, Shakespeare, Juliet, 9 In. 29.00
Royal Doulton, Plate, Shakespeare, Rosalind, 9 In. 29.00
Royal Doulton, Plate, Sir Izaak Walton, Noke, 8 1/2 In. 35.00
Royal Doulton, Plate, Sir Roger De Coverley, Ballroom Scene, 10 1/2 In. 35.00
Royal Doulton, Plate, The Doctor, 10 1/2 In. 35.00
Royal Doulton, Plate, To Market, To Market, To Buy A Fat Pig, 7 In. 35.00
Royal Doulton, Plate, View Of Rouen From St.Sever, J.H, Plant, 10 1/4 In. 200.00
Royal Doulton, Plate, Young Kookaburras, Translucent, 10 1/2 In. 35.00
Royal Doulton, Plate, Zulu Warrior, C.1935, 10 In. 28.00
Royal Doulton, Platter, Elizabeth At Moreton, Handled, 17 X 8 In. 45.00
Royal Doulton, Rice Bowl, Old Coaching Scenes 30.00
Royal Doulton, Sauce, Fairyland Luster, Gold Outlines, Noke 25.50
Royal Doulton, Saucer, Old Coaching Scenes, 4 3/4 In. 12.00
Royal Doulton, Smoking Set, Reynard The Fox, S.Hall, Box & 2 Ash Bowls 42.50
Royal Doulton, Spittoon, Desert Scene, C.1900, 7 1/2 In. 150.00
Royal Doulton, Sugar & Creamer, Black Scenic On Brown 48.00
Royal Doulton, Sugar, Dickensware, Fat Boy, 6 1/2 X 3 1/4 In. 55.00
Royal Doulton, Tankard, Dickensware, Captain Cuttle, 6 In. 55.00
Royal Doulton, Tankard, Dickensware, Little Nell, 6 In. 55.00
Royal Doulton, Tankard, Dickensware, Mr.Pickwick, 6 In. 55.00
Royal Doulton, Tankard, Dickensware, Oliver Twist, 1949, 6 In. 250.00
Royal Doulton, Tankard, Dickensware, Tony Weller, 6 In. 55.00
Royal Doulton, Tea Set, Evesham, Ribbed Swirl, Floral, No.H4821, 3 Piece 95.00
Royal Doulton, Tea Set, The Gleaners 95.00
Royal Doulton, Teapot And Waste Bowl, Ye Olde Cheshire Cheese 1667 45.00
Royal Doulton, Teapot, Blue Blossoms On Cream, 5 1/2 In. 32.00
Royal Doulton, Teapot, Bunnykins, Signed 15.00
Royal Doulton, Teapot, Chatsworth 25.00
Royal Doulton, Teapot, Mottled Blue, Raised White Festoons, Quart, 4 1/2 In. 45.00
Royal Doulton, Toby Mug, Coachman, Kingsware, Brown Glaze, C.1902, 7 In. 75.00
Royal Doulton, Toby Mug, Full Seated, Best Is Not Too Good 300.00
Royal Doulton, Toby Mug, Old Charley, 5 In. 150.00
Royal Doulton, Toby Mug, Sairey Gamp, Seated, Marked A, 5 1/2 In. 150.00
Royal Doulton, Toby Mug, Sir John Falstaff, Full Seated Figure, A, 6 In. 75.00
Royal Doulton, Toothpick, Dickensware, Bill Sykes, Sterling Rim, Hallmark 85.00
Royal Doulton, Toothpick, Dickensware, Sam Weller, Brown, Raised Head 37.50
Royal Doulton, Tray, Bodiam Castle, 14 X 6 In. 35.00
Royal Doulton, Tray, Dickensware, Captain Cuttle, 10 1/2 X 5 In. 55.00
Royal Doulton, Tray, Dickensware, Old Peggotty, 9 X 7 In. 35.00
Royal Doulton, Tray, Dickensware, Poor Jo, 11 X 5 In. 65.00
Royal Doulton, Tray, Dickensware, Sairey Gamp, 10 1/2 X 5 In. 55.00
Royal Doulton, Tray, Fat Boy, Rectangular, 4 1/2 X 5 1/4 In. 60.00
Royal Doulton, Tray, Pin, Dickensware, Fat Boy, 1907, 5 1/4 X 3 1/4 In. 47.50
Royal Doulton, Tray, Venetian Decoration, 17 X 7 1/4 In. 48.00
Royal Doulton, Tumbler, Old Coaching Scenes 25.00
Royal Doulton, Tumbler, Stoneware With Blue Glaze, Lord Nelson, Miniature 50.00
Royal Doulton, Vase Flambe, Wood Cut, 7 In. 65.00
Royal Doulton, Vase, Babe-In-The-Woods, Tapered, 9 In., Pair 195.00
Royal Doulton, Vase, Blue & White, Delft Style, 2 In. 30.00
Royal Doulton, Vase, Blue Fish Scale, Pheasant In Center Panel, Floral, 9 In 80.00
Royal Doulton, Vase, Blue Pate Sur Pate Horses, Hannah Barlow, England, 7 In. 195.00
Royal Doulton, Vase, Brown, Raised Tavern Scene In Color, 6 1/4 In. 90.00
Royal Doulton, Vase, Bulbous, Deep Blue, Incised Florals, 10 1/2 In. 50.00
Royal Doulton, Vase, Coaching Days In Snow, 2 Handled, Oval, 5 In. 55.00
Royal Doulton, Vase, Cobalt, Beaded Swags, Stylized Florals, 14 1/2 In. 75.00
Royal Doulton, Vase, Dickensware, Captain Cuttle, 2 Handles, 5 1/4 In. 80.00
Royal Doulton, Vase, Dickensware, Sairey Gamp, 6 3/8 In. 88.00
Royal Doulton, Vase, Dickensware, Toby Weller, Noke, 3 In. 25.00
Royal Doulton, Vase, Dickensware, Toby Weller, Square, Fully Marked, 8 In. 120.00
Royal Doulton, Vase, Dutch Figures, 4 1/2 In., Pair 55.00
Royal Doulton, Vase, Faience, Signed Kate Rogers, Tapered Neck, 12 In. 145.00
Royal Doulton, Vase, Flambe, Black Decoration, Farmer, Plow, 9 In. 80.00
Royal Doulton, Vase, Flambe, Black House & Trees, 7 In. 50.00
Royal Doulton, Vase, Flambe, Castle On Hill, Woodcut, 6 In. 67.00
Royal Doulton, Vase, Flambe, Gothic Shape, Flared Hexagonal Mouth, 7 1/2 In. 295.00

Royal Doulton, Vase, Flambe, House & Trees Scene, Black Floral, 9 In. 85.00
Royal Doulton, Vase, Flambe, Hunting Scene, Bulbous, 9 In. 120.00
Royal Doulton, Vase, Flambe, Mottled, Bulbous, Narrow Neck, 3 1/2 In. 48.00
Royal Doulton, Vase, Flambe, Shepherd With Sheep, Bottle Shape, 4 In. 120.00
Royal Doulton, Vase, Flambe, Veined Sung Glaze, 9 1/2 In. 135.00
Royal Doulton, Vase, Flambe, Veined Sung, 1679, 12 In. 95.00
Royal Doulton, Vase, Flambe, Woodcut Design, Bridge, Trees, Buildings, 4 3/4 In 65.00
Royal Doulton, Vase, Goats & Mountains At Sunset, Kolsoll, C.1902, 7 In. 95.00
Royal Doulton, Vase, Monk Making Wine, Sterling Top, 5 3/4 In. 78.00
Royal Doulton, Vase, Mottled Black, Pastel Floral, Art Deco, 8 In. 68.00
Royal Doulton, Vase, Old Coaching Scenes, C.1905, 7 In. 60.00
Royal Doulton, Vase, Portrait, Woman In Pastels On White, Floral Framed 250.00
Royal Doulton, Vase, Romeo, Shakespeare Series, 2 Handles, 5 1/2 In. 45.00
Royal Doulton, Vase, Royal Blue, Floral Medallions, Gold Floral, 3 1/2 In. 40.00
Royal Doulton, Vase, Sir Izaak Walton, Noke, 2 Handles, 10 In. 85.00
Royal Doulton, Vase, Sir Izaak Walton, Noke, 2 1/4 In. 24.00
Royal Doulton, Vase, Stick, Blue & Green, Stoneware, 6 1/2 In. 40.00
Royal Doulton, Vase, Stoneware, Beige, Floral Tapestry, Slater's, 1900, 6 In. 36.00
Royal Doulton, Vase, Tapestry Like Bottom, Bulbous, Thin Neck, 1930s 58.00
Royal Doulton, Vase, Tavern Scene, Raised Figures, 2 Handles, 15 1/2 In. 110.00
Royal Doulton, Vase, Welsh Ladies, 6 In. 37.00
Royal Doulton, Vegetable Bowl, Chelsea Rose 18.00
Royal Doulton, Vegetable Bowl, Leeds Spray 9.00

ROYAL DUX BOHEMIA E

Royal Dux is a porcelain made by Duxer Porzellanmanufaktur, a factory established in 1860 in Dux, Bohemia (now Czechoslovakia). Reproductions are being made.

Royal Dux, Bust, Girl Mask With Dagger, Musical Notes At Waist, 9 In. 110.00
Royal Dux, Compote, Art Nouveau, Girl Reclining, Fluted Shell, Vase Behind 295.00
Royal Dux, Figurine, Dancing Woman, Pink Triangle Mark, 13 1/2 In. 135.00
Royal Dux, Figurine, Fish, Pink Mark, 13 1/2 X 18 1/2 In. 48.00
Royal Dux, Figurine, Fish, 22 In. 87.50
Royal Dux, Figurine, Glazed Porcelain, 9 In. 90.00
Royal Dux, Figurine, Lady Wearing Long Gown, Pink Triangle Mark, 9 1/4 In. 55.00
Royal Dux, Figurine, Maiden Rising From Shell Holding Vase, 15 In. 325.00
Royal Dux, Figurine, Venus On Pedestal Conch, Pink Triangle Mark 350.00
Royal Dux, Figurine, Young Man Holding Scroll, Red Mark, 13 1/2 In. 145.00
Royal Dux, Group, Boy & Girl Kissing, 6 In. 115.00
Royal Dux, Group, Two Parakeets On Crossbar, 7 1/2 In. 75.00
Royal Dux, Group, Woman & Girl Carrying Baskets Of Grapes, Pink Mark, 23 In. 385.00
Royal Dux, Pitcher, Girl & Water 115.00
Royal Dux, Vase, Girl With Flowing Hair, Pink Triangle Mark, 16 In. 225.00
Royal Dux, Vase, Pale Yellow, Gold Outlined Floral, Green, Hexagonal, 9 In. 29.00
Royal Dux, Vase, Raised Fruit And Leaves, Signed Austria, 5 In. 30.00

Royal Flemish glass was made during the late 1880s in New Bedford, Massachusetts, by the Mt.Washington Glass Works. It is a colored satin glass decorated in dark colors with gold designs.

Royal Flemish, Ewer, Yellow & Tan, Rampant Lion Shield, Rope Handle, 12 In. 2450.00
Royal Flemish, Jar, Cracker, Coin Medallions 1375.00
Royal Flemish, Salt, Gold Decoration 125.00

Royal Ivy, see Northwood

Royal Leicester, Ewer, Gold Bird & Floral, Gold Dragon Handle, 9 1/2 In. 225.00
Royal Munich, Bowl, Wood Grain, Purple Violets, 10 In. 30.00
Royal Munich, Jar, Cracker, Wood Grain, Purple Violets 45.00
Royal Munich, Plate, Portrait, Girl Wearing Blue, Green, 9 3/4 In. 75.00
Royal Munich, Plate, Wood Grain, Purple Violets, 9 1/2 In. 18.50

Royal Oak, see Pressed Glass

Royal Rudolstadt, a German faience factory, was established in Thuringia, Germany, in 1721. Hard paste porcelain was made by E.Bohne after 1854. Late nineteenth- and early twentieth-century pieces are most commonly found today. The later mark is a shield with the letters RW inside superseded by a crown and the words Royal Rudolstadt.

Royal Rudolstadt, see also Kewpie

Royal Rudolstadt, Bowl, Gray, Pink, White, & Orange Poppies, Oval, 12 X 8 In. 30.00
Royal Rudolstadt, Bowl, Hand-Painted, Pink Roses, 12 In. 40.00
Royal Rudolstadt, Bowl, Leaves & Nuts, Hand-Painted, Signed, 7 1/2 In. 45.00
Royal Rudolstadt, Bowl, Peach Roses, 9 1/2 In. 18.50
Royal Rudolstadt, Bowl, Roses, Gold Trim, 2 Handles, 7 In. 35.00
Royal Rudolstadt, Bowl, 3 Gold Feet, Shaded Pink & Yellow Florals, 6 1/2 In. 30.00
Royal Rudolstadt, Cake Plate, Germany, Hand-Painted Pink Roses, Signed 22.00
Royal Rudolstadt, Chocolate Pot, White, Green Basket Of Pink Floral, Gold 47.00
Royal Rudolstadt, Cup & Saucer, Happy Fats 30.00
Royal Rudolstadt, Dresser Set, 4 Piece 47.50
Royal Rudolstadt, Ewer, Cream Ground, Pink Flowers, Germany, 9 In. 47.00
Royal Rudolstadt, Hatpin Holder, Green, White Roses 45.00
Royal Rudolstadt, Mustard Set, Mistletoe & Red Berries, 3 Piece 37.50
Royal Rudolstadt, Plate, Cream Color, Yellow & Red Roses, 8 1/2 In. 25.00
Royal Rudolstadt, Plate, Oyster, Pink, Blue, & Gold, Scalloped, 9 X 9 In. 35.00
Royal Rudolstadt, Plate, Pastel Floral, Gold Border, E.Bohne, 8 1/2 In. 17.50
Royal Rudolstadt, Plate, Pink, Yellow, & Magenta Roses, Gold Edge, 6 1/8 In. 12.00
Royal Rudolstadt, Plate, Prussian Winter Scene, 9 In. 29.50
Royal Rudolstadt, Plate, White, Pink Roses Garlands, Gold Handles, 10 In. 20.00
Royal Rudolstadt, Relish, White Roses, Gold Trim, 2 Handles, 8 3/4 In. 27.50
Royal Rudolstadt, Snack Set, Luster Interiors, Floral, 12 Piece 50.00
Royal Rudolstadt, Sugar & Creamer, White, Multicolored Flowers 34.00
Royal Rudolstadt, Tea Set, Child's, Happy Fats, 21 Piece 200.00
Royal Rudolstadt, Tea Set, White, Bluebirds, 3 Piece 57.00
Royal Rudolstadt, Tray, Dresser, Violets, Gold Trim 65.00
Royal Rudolstadt, Vase, Gold Dolphin Handles & Feet, 13 1/2 In. 175.00
Royal Saxe, Creamer, Light Green, Blue Forget-Me-Nots, Gold Trim 22.00

Royal Vienna was established in Vienna by Claude Innocentius du Paquier in 1719. The factory closed in 1865. Since then, various German and Austrian factories have reproduced Royal Vienna wares, complete with the original beehive mark.

Royal Vienna, see also Beehive

Royal Vienna, Bowl, Luster, 2 Handled, Marked 60.00
Royal Vienna, Bowl, Maroon, 8 Vignettes, Gold Trim, Carl Lassove, 7 1/2 In. 79.00
Royal Vienna, Box, Covered, Portrait, Artist Signed, Beehive Mark, 3 In. 195.00
Royal Vienna, Butter Pat, Burnt Orange Floral, Gold Tracery, Beehive Mark 16.00
Royal Vienna, Cake Stand, Classic Decoration, Beehive, 9 1/2 X 5 1/2 In. 175.00
Royal Vienna, Charger, Blumen Van Varelsh-Genalt, Beehive Mark, 14 In. 325.00
Royal Vienna, Charger, Du Paizen, Beehive Mark, 14 In. 300.00
Royal Vienna, Chocolate Pot, Portrait, Brunette Lady, Burgundy & Gold 75.00
Royal Vienna, Cup & Saucer, Beehive, Girl In Ruffled Dress, Gold Handle 125.00
Royal Vienna, Cup & Saucer, Cobalt, Variegated, Grecian Ladies, Beehive 35.00
Royal Vienna, Cup & Saucer, Curled Handle, Victorian Ladies, Beehive 45.00
Royal Vienna, Cup & Saucer, Demitasse, Cobalt, Signed Ohne, Beehive 95.00
Royal Vienna, Cup, Demitasse, Beehive 30.00
Royal Vienna, Dish, Covered, Underplate, Angel, Beehive Mark 50.00
Royal Vienna, Figurine, Monkey Playing Bassoon, C.1750, 5 1/2 In. 195.00
Royal Vienna, Flower Pot & Saucer, Green, Clematis 17.00
Royal Vienna, Hair Receiver, Red & Green, Beehive 45.00
Royal Vienna, Jar, Cracker, Portrait Of Winged Cupid, Signed Juno, Beehive 135.00
Royal Vienna, Pitcher, Classic Medallion, Green, Burgundy, Kauffmann, Beehive 110.00
Royal Vienna, Plate, Liebesfrulting, Gold & Cobalt Border, 10 In. 250.00
Royal Vienna, Plate, Pierced Border, Floral Center, Beehive, 10 In. 65.00
Royal Vienna, Plate, Portrait, Dark-Haired Lady, Maroon, Gold Trim, 9 In. 65.00
Royal Vienna, Plate, Portrait, Lady, T.Koller, Cobalt & Gold Edge, 10 In. 285.00
Royal Vienna, Plate, Portrait, Maroon & Gold Border, 8 In. 95.00
Royal Vienna, Plate, Purple Flowers, Gold, Signed, 9 In. 25.00
Royal Vienna, Portrait, Gleaners, Gold Beehive, Signed, 9 3/4 In. 72.00
Royal Vienna, Stein, Teeny, Heavy Gold 550.00
Royal Vienna, Tea Caddy, Hand-Painted Scene, 6 In. 450.00
Royal Vienna, Teapot, Green Shading, White & Lavender, Pedestal, Crown Mark 145.00
Royal Vienna, Tray, Classical Scene Of 3 Ladies & Man, Kauffmann, 11 1/2 In. 95.00
Royal Vienna, Urn, Diana, Shepherdess, Sheep, Blue Beehive 145.00
Royal Vienna, Vase, Cupid In Chariot, Signed P.Max, Beehive Mark, 10 1/2 In. 145.00

Royal Vienna, Vase, Egg-Shape, Covered, Gilded Tripod Feet, Venus, 5 In. 250.00
Royal Vienna, Vase, Pearlized Neck, Portrait, Wagner, Blue Beehive, 1901 .... 375.00
Royal Vienna, Vase, Portrait Scene, Musical Medallion, Blue Beehive, 12 In. 120.00
Royal Vienna, Vase, Portrait, Blue Beehive Mark, 8 In., Pair 75.00
Royal Vienna, Vase, Portrait, Girl, 2 Handles, Gold Trim, 4 1/2 In. 135.00
Royal Winton, Cup & Saucer, Demitasse, Queen Anne 7.50
Royal Winton, Cup & Saucer, Demitasse, Sweet Pea 7.50
Royal Winton, Honey Pot, Covered, Beehive With Bees & Flowers Shape 28.00
Royal Winton, Jug, Figural, Fish Gurgling, 9 In. 47.00
Royal Winton, Toby Mug, General Douglas MacArthur, Sword Handle, 6 1/4 In. 28.00

Royal Worcester porcelain was made in the later period of Worcester pottery, which was originally established in 1751. The Royal Worcester trade name has been used by Worcester Royal Porcelain Company, Ltd., since 1862.

Royal Worcester, Basket, Basketweave Design, Gold Trim, 1909, Miniature 75.00
Royal Worcester, Basket, Cream Color, Gold Trim, Miniature 45.00
Royal Worcester, Bowl, Beige, Gold Outlined Edges, Enamel Floral, 1900, 10 In. 95.00
Royal Worcester, Bowl, Black, Red Buds & Gilt Stems, Purple Mark, 1918, 8 In. 50.00
Royal Worcester, Box, Covered, Cream Color, Flowers, 4 X 2 In. 37.50
Royal Worcester, Box, Covered, 1907, Round, 2 1/4 In. 55.00
Royal Worcester, Box, Trinket, Floral On Lid, Ivory To Apricot, Roses, 1905 .... 35.00
Royal Worcester, Bust, Michelangelo, 6 In. 370.00
Royal Worcester, Butter Pat, Cream, Hand-Painted Floral 15.00
Royal Worcester, Butter Pat, Ewer, Matte Finish 15.00
Royal Worcester, Cachepot, Orchid Color, Braided Design, C.1910, 3 1/2 In. 22.50
Royal Worcester, Candlesnuffer, Cook, White, Green Mark, C.1893 .... 125.00
Royal Worcester, Candlesnuffer, Granny Snow 100.00
Royal Worcester, Candlesnuffer, Monk Reading Bible, Brown Frock, 1909 .... 70.00
Royal Worcester, Candlesnuffer, Nun, Purple Mark, C.1920 .... 55.00
Royal Worcester, Candlesnuffer, Oriental Woman, C.1918 .... 125.00
Royal Worcester, Candlestick, Peacock Decoration, Locke, Pair 175.00
Royal Worcester, Candlestick, Tiny Gold Leaf Design, Purple Mark, 7 In. 95.00
Royal Worcester, Candlestick, Turquoise, Beige, Brown, Gold, Hadley, 6 In. 85.00
Royal Worcester, Chocolate Pot, Bamboo Handle & Finial, Floral, Purple Mark 185.00
Royal Worcester, Chocolate Pot, Covered, Yellow, Flowers, 7 3/4 In., Purple Ma 185.00
Royal Worcester, Chocolate Pot, Cream With Floral, Gold Cane Handle, 6 In. 185.00
Royal Worcester, Chocolate Pot, Miniature, White & Gold, 7 In. 45.00
Royal Worcester, Coffeepot, Green & Yellow, Gold Trim, 9 In. 275.00
Royal Worcester, Compote, Eagle With Basket Between Wings, 7 1/2 In. 325.00
Royal Worcester, Creamer, Flight Worcester, Black & Gold 140.00
Royal Worcester, Creamer, Gold Outlined Panels, Relief Flowers, Green Mark 85.00
Royal Worcester, Creamer, Hinged Pewter Hallmarked Lid, 1882 .... 85.00
Royal Worcester, Creamer, Pleated Spout, Purple Mark, 3 1/2 In. 70.00
Royal Worcester, Creamer, Ship & Dates, 1751-1951, Black & White, 5 In. 50.00
Royal Worcester, Creamer, 2-Spout, 2-Handled, Brown Mark, Pink, Gold, Brown 75.00
Royal Worcester, Cup & Saucer, Demitasse, Beige, Floral Colors 39.50
Royal Worcester, Cup & Saucer, Demitasse, Floral, Gold Handle, Purple Mark 30.00
Royal Worcester, Cup & Saucer, Demitasse, Fruit, Moseley 95.00
Royal Worcester, Cup & Saucer, Demitasse, Rosemary Pattern 25.00
Royal Worcester, Cup & Saucer, Floral And Gold 50.00
Royal Worcester, Cup & Saucer, Floral, C.1880 .... 30.00
Royal Worcester, Cup & Saucer, Mustache, Blue & White Floral, 1893 .... 110.00
Royal Worcester, Cup & Saucer, Mustache, White, Band Of Violets, Gold Trim 75.00
Royal Worcester, Cup & Saucer, Oriental, 1902 .... 25.00
Royal Worcester, Cup, Demitasse, Oriental Art Deco, Tiffany Mark 60.00
Royal Worcester, Cup, 3-Handled, Miniature, Flowers On Beige, 1891, 1 3/4 In. 62.00
Royal Worcester, Demitasse Set, Yellow, Black & White Design, 1918, 7 Piece 145.00
Royal Worcester, Dish, Bone, Bernina, Set Of 8 .... 52.50
Royal Worcester, Dish, Double Shell & Serpent, 1885 .... 170.00
Royal Worcester, Dish, Leaf, Pink To White, Paper Thin 35.00
Royal Worcester, Dish, Oyster Shell Shape, Crayfish Handles, 1889, 4 1/2 In. 38.00
Royal Worcester, Dish, Shell Shape, Green, Shells, 3 Footed, C.1899, 4 1/4 In. 25.00
Royal Worcester, Epergne, 4 Baskets, E.P.N.S. Frame 200.00
Royal Worcester, Ewer, Basket Weave, Gold Handle, Gold Lizard On Body 225.00

Royal Worcester, Ewer, Cream Color, Ribbed, Blue Floral, Gold Handle, 12 In. 150.00
Royal Worcester, Ewer, Floral & Gilt, Satin Finish, 1913, 7 1/4 In. 127.00
Royal Worcester, Ewer, Gold Leaf & Flower, Gold Bamboo Handle, Signed, 1886 85.00
Royal Worcester, Ewer, Gold Trim & Floral, 5 1/4 In. 80.00
Royal Worcester, Ewer, Painted Flowers, Gold, 5 1/4 In. 80.00
Royal Worcester, Ewer, Quilted Ivorine, Floral, Sea Serpent Handle, 12 In. 350.00
Royal Worcester, Ewer, Texture Finish, Leaf & Floral, Gold, Purple Mark, 7 In. 195.00
Royal Worcester, Figurine, August, F.G.Doughty, 4 In. 68.00
Royal Worcester, Figurine, August, Nude Girl On Shore, F.G.Doughty, 5 In. 78.00
Royal Worcester, Figurine, Cat, Sitting, F.Doughty, 3 1/2 In. 38.00
Royal Worcester, Figurine, Child Born On Sabbath Day, 5 1/4 In. 62.50
Royal Worcester, Figurine, Chinese Boy & Chopsticks, Doughty, 2 1/4 In. 85.00
Royal Worcester, Figurine, Dancing Lady, Gold Gown & Sandals, 1895, 13 In. 395.00
Royal Worcester, Figurine, Doughty, The Curtsy 50.00
Royal Worcester, Figurine, First Dance 65.00
Royal Worcester, Figurine, Fox And The Hound, Pair, 7 In. 225.00
Royal Worcester, Figurine, Grandmother's Dress, Doughty, Yellow, 6 1/2 In. 75.00
Royal Worcester, Figurine, Hound Dog, D.Lindner, 7 1/2 In. 140.00
Royal Worcester, Figurine, India, F.Doughty, 3 1/2 In. 60.00
Royal Worcester, Figurine, January, 6 1/2 In. 75.00
Royal Worcester, Figurine, Johnnie With Ducks, F.G.Doughty, No.3433, 7 In. 75.00
Royal Worcester, Figurine, Joy And Sorrow, James Hadley, Pair 500.00
Royal Worcester, Figurine, June, Purple Mark, 4 In. 60.00
Royal Worcester, Figurine, Menu Holder, French Peasant 95.00
Royal Worcester, Figurine, Monk Reading Book, Purple Mark, 5 In. 34.00
Royal Worcester, Figurine, October 85.00
Royal Worcester, Figurine, Old Goat Woman, Phoebe Stabler, No.2886, 7 In. 125.00
Royal Worcester, Figurine, Only Me, F.G.Doughty, 6 In. 70.00
Royal Worcester, Figurine, Saturday's Child, Girl With Cat, 6 In. 65.00
Royal Worcester, Figurine, Saturday's Child, No.3262, 5 1/2 In. 65.00
Royal Worcester, Figurine, Scottie Dog, White, Seated, D.Linder, C.1933, 3 In. 40.00
Royal Worcester, Figurine, Sorrow, 1917, 9 5/8 In. 295.00
Royal Worcester, Figurine, The Letter, War Scene, Eva Soper 200.00
Royal Worcester, Figurine, The Satyr, Signed Hadley, C.1890, 30 In. 1450.00
Royal Worcester, Figurine, Tuesday's Child, Ballet Dancer, 8 In. 65.00
Royal Worcester, Figurine, Tuesday's Child, Boy On Ice Skates, 8 In. 65.00
Royal Worcester, Figurine, Tuesday's Girl & Boy, 8 In., Pair 125.00
Royal Worcester, Figurine, Tuesday's Girl, 7 1/4 In. 68.00
Royal Worcester, Figurine, Wednesday's Child Knows Little Woes 65.00
Royal Worcester, Figurine, White Rabbit From Alice In Wonderland 45.00
Royal Worcester, Flower Arranger, Peach To Cream, Grainger, 3 In. 70.00
Royal Worcester, Flower Arranger, Peach To Cream, Pastel Green Rims, 5 In. 75.00
Royal Worcester, Friday's Child, Girl, 6 In. 65.00
Royal Worcester, Jar & Underplate, Biscuit, Butterflies & Hummingbirds 195.00
Royal Worcester, Jar, Biscuit, Flowers, Leaves, Gold Trim, Purple Mark, 1890 185.00
Royal Worcester, Jar, Biscuit, Melon Ribbed, Floral, Gold, Purple Mark, 8 In. 195.00
Royal Worcester, Jar, Covered, Cream Color, Rust & Gilt Floral, 1888, 6 In. 120.00
Royal Worcester, Jug, Claret, Cream, Floral, Gold, 8 In., Purple Mark 57.50
Royal Worcester, Jug, Claret, Green Metallic Florals, Vine Handle, 9 In. 100.00
Royal Worcester, Jug, Claret, Patent Metallic Mark 1047, Green Florals, 9 In. 125.00
Royal Worcester, Jug, Cream, Pewter Lid, 1882 85.00
Royal Worcester, Jug, Ice, Tuck, Ivory Color, Stag Horn Handle, Purple Mark 150.00
Royal Worcester, Lizard Handle, Gold & Silver Floral, C.1875, 9 In. 275.00
Royal Worcester, Monday's Child Fair Of Face 65.00
Royal Worcester, Mug, Child's, Tuesday's Child, Hand-Painted, 3 In.High 20.00
Royal Worcester, Pitcher, Beige, Floral, Gold Reeded Handle, 1910, 5 In. 89.00
Royal Worcester, Pitcher, Beverage, Floral & Gold Trim, C.1880, 6 1/2 In. 165.00
Royal Worcester, Pitcher, Flat Back, Flowers On Ivory Ground, Purple Mark 95.00
Royal Worcester, Pitcher, Flat Back, Pink With Gilded Flowers, 8 In. 90.00
Royal Worcester, Pitcher, Floral On Ivory, Gold Handle, Flat Back, 1885, 6 In. 95.00
Royal Worcester, Pitcher, Floral, Gold Handle, Purple Mark, 5 1/2 In. 65.00
Royal Worcester, Pitcher, Floral, Gold Trim, C.1870, 9 In. 145.00
Royal Worcester, Pitcher, Gold Grapevines & Leaves, Purple Mark, 8 In. 195.00
Royal Worcester, Pitcher, Green, Hand-Painted Floral, FR, 9 In. 114.00
Royal Worcester, Pitcher, Helmet, Floral And Gold, 5 In. 60.00

Royal Worcester, Pitcher, Ivory, Floral, Gold Handle & Trim, C.1891, 8 3/4 In. 225.00
Royal Worcester, Pitcher, Lizard On Side, Woven Design, Purple Mark, 6 In. 225.00
Royal Worcester, Pitcher, Ram's Head Handle, Floral Decoration, Purple Mark 225.00
Royal Worcester, Pitcher, Red-Start Bird, Ivory Ground, Artist Signed, 1911 75.00
Royal Worcester, Pitcher, White, 9 In. 75.00
Royal Worcester, Pitcher, 1883, 4 In. 50.00
Royal Worcester, Plate, Beige, Pink & Orange Floral, Gold Rim, 1890, 9 In. 59.00
Royal Worcester, Plate, Granada, Cream Background, 10 1/2 In. 25.00
Royal Worcester, Plate, Oriental Scene, 9 In. 19.50
Royal Worcester, Plate, Pink, Turquoise, & White, Floral, Gold, C.1870, 8 In. 14.50
Royal Worcester, Plate, White Center, Enamel Flowers, 7 7/8 In. 16.00
Royal Worcester, Platter, Blue & White, Floral & Bird, C.1883, 11 1/2 In. 45.00
Royal Worcester, Pot, Rouge, Lid, Miniature, Florals, C.1910, Signed, 1 1/4 In. 75.00
Royal Worcester, Ring Tree, 1895, 4 In. 70.00
Royal Worcester, Saturday's Child Works Hard For A Living 65.00
Royal Worcester, Saturday's Child, Girl, 5 3/4 In. 65.00
Royal Worcester, Spill, Pierced Gold Bamboo Border, 3 Handles, 1882 225.00
Royal Worcester, Sugar & Creamer, Floral & Gold, C.1880 125.00
Royal Worcester, Syrup, Oriental, Green Mark 58.00
Royal Worcester, Tea Bowl, Hop Trellis, C.1760 85.00
Royal Worcester, Tea Set, Beige With Flowers, 1891, 3 Piece 225.00
Royal Worcester, Tea Set, Ivory Matte, Floral, Gilt Outline, 1890, 3 Piece 325.00
Royal Worcester, Teacup & Saucer, Apricot Shading, Gold Trim, 1897 35.00
Royal Worcester, Teacup & Saucer, Cream Color, Pink Floral, Gold Trim 22.00
Royal Worcester, Teacup & Saucer, Cream Color, Roses With Green Leaves 22.00
Royal Worcester, Teapot, Blue Willow, Dated 1882 140.00
Royal Worcester, Teapot, Floral & Gold Trim 125.00
Royal Worcester, Teapot, Ivory Color, Hand-Painted Floral 185.00
Royal Worcester, Toby Mug, Mrs., Purple Mark, 1 3/4 In. 50.00
Royal Worcester, Tureen & Tray, Sauce, Jones, McDuffee & Stratton, C.1890 55.00
Royal Worcester, Tureen, Attached Plate, Oriental Design, Elephant Handles 115.00
Royal Worcester, Tureen, Blue & White Gilded Finial, Gilded Elephant Head 145.00
Royal Worcester, Urn, Ivory With Peach Tones, Puce Mark, 9 X 7 In. 195.00
Royal Worcester, Vase, Bamboo Basket, Green Handle & Leaves, C.1903, 8 In. 115.00
Royal Worcester, Vase, Bamboo Handle, Raised Gold Leaves, Green Mark 115.00
Royal Worcester, Vase, Bamboo, Gold Leaves & Trim, Ivory Color, C.1903, 4 In. 37.50
Royal Worcester, Vase, Basket, Brown & Gold Bamboo, Cream Ground, 1887 85.00
Royal Worcester, Vase, Drumstick, Ivory Color, Floral Sprays, 1887, 6 1/2 In. 225.00
Royal Worcester, Vase, Floral, Gold, Purple Mark, 9 In. 170.00
Royal Worcester, Vase, Gold Serpent Handle, Purple Mark, 7 In. 250.00
Royal Worcester, Vase, H Hadley, 4 Panels Of Flowers 75.00
Royal Worcester, Vase, Ivorine Matte, Ferns, Pierced Rim, Purple Mark, 13 In. 360.00
Royal Worcester, Vase, Ivory Color, Hand-Painted Floral, 1903, 12 In., Pair 450.00
Royal Worcester, Vase, Japanese Spill, Pierced With Animals, C.1850 300.00
Royal Worcester, Vase, Nautilus & Coral, Gold Trim, 1889, 8 3/4 In. 250.00
Royal Worcester, Vase, Paneled, Gold Handles & Trim, 12 In. 325.00
Royal Worcester, Vase, Pheasants, Jas.Stinton, 8 1/2 In. 150.00
Royal Worcester, Vase, Pierced, Locke, 5 X 4 In. 95.00
Royal Worcester, Vase, Pink, Floral, Blue Pedestal & Neck, 1891, 7 In., Pair 325.00
Royal Worcester, Vase, Pink, Yellow, & Blue Floral, Gold, Purple Mark, 10 In. 91.50
Royal Worcester, Vase, Sabrina, Blue Glaze, 2 Owls In Tree, 8 3/4 In. 165.00
Royal Worcester, Vase, Serpent Handle, Enclosed Top, 7 In. 250.00
Royal Worcester, Vase, White, Shell Shape On Branch Coral Base, Impressed 150.00
Royal Worcester, Vase, 2 Pheasants, James Stinton, 1923, 11 1/2 In. 199.00
Royal Worcester, Vegetable Bowl, Covered, Jones, McDuffee & Stratton, 1894 65.00
Royal Worcester, Waste Bowl, Lemon Peel, Floral & Gold, 2 3/4 In. 25.00
Royal Worcester, Wednesday's Child, 7 In. 80.00

Roycroft products were made by the Roycrofter community of East Aurora, New York, in the late nineteenth and early twentieth centuries. The community was founded by Elbert Hubbard. The products included furniture, metalware, leatherwork, and jewelry.

Roycroft, Ashtray With Match Holder, Copper 14.00
Roycroft, Ashtray, Copper, Hammered, 4 In. 20.00
Roycroft, Book, Elbert Hubbard Scrapbook 6.00
Roycroft, Bookend, Brass, Hammered, Chains & Florals, 5 In., Pair 25.00

Roycroft, Bookend, Copper, One Raised, One Cut Out To Display Book, Signed ... 23.00
Roycroft, Bookend, Copper, Sailing Ship In Relief, Pair ... 20.00
Roycroft, Bookend, Hammered Copper, Raised Leaf In Green Circle, Pair ... 15.00
Roycroft, Bookend, Open Rectangle, 8 1/2 In., Pair ... 16.00
Roycroft, Candlestick, Twist Ring Stem, Bright, 3 1/2 In., Pair ... 52.00
Roycroft, Compote, Brass Plated Copper, 7 X 1 1/2 In. ... 24.00
Roycroft, Compote, Hammered Copper, 4 1/2 In. ... 32.00
Roycroft, Desk Pad, Hammered Copper, 13 X 20 In. ... 35.00
Roycroft, Honey Pot, Covered, Tan ... 12.00
Roycroft, Inkwell & Letter Opener, Hand Beaten Copper, Dore Finish ... 40.00
Roycroft, Inkwell, Hammered Copper, Metal Studs, Round ... 30.00
Roycroft, Jug, Brown, 5 1/2 In. ... 12.00
Roycroft, Jug, Brown, 6 In. ... 9.00
Roycroft, Ladle, Copper, Hammered, 3 Leaf Design On Handle, 6 1/2 In. ... 15.00
Roycroft, Napkin Ring, Leather, Signed, 1 In. ... 25.00
Roycroft, Tray, Pen, Copper, Hammered, Folded Edge, Cut Corners, 9 1/2 In. ... 12.00
Roycroft, Vase, Brass Over Copper, 5 1/2 In. ... 27.00
Roycroft, Vase, Bronze, Hammered, 5 In. ... 37.00
Roycroft, Vase, Copper, Hammered, 4 1/2 In. ... 35.00
Rozenburg, Vase, Blue, Yellow, Green, & Tan Curved Lines, 5 In. ... 160.00
RRP Co., Spittoon, Brown Glaze, Roseville, Ohio, 7 In. ... 25.00

RS Germany porcelain was made at the factory of Rheinhold Schlegelmilch after 1869 in Tillowitz, Germany. It was sold both decorated and undecorated.

RS Germany, Ashtray, Tiger Lily Orange With Black Centers, Green Mark ... 21.50
RS Germany, Berry Bowl, Gray & Lime, Pink & White Carnations ... 28.00
RS Germany, Berry Bowl, Green, Pink Floral, Gold Edge, Red Mark, 4 1/2 In. ... 10.35
RS Germany, Berry Set, Fancy, 7 Pieces ... 135.00
RS Germany, Berry Set, Tan With White Roses, 5 Piece ... 38.00
RS Germany, Bonbon, Orange, Black Mottling, Handled ... 22.00
RS Germany, Bottle, Cologne, Hand-Painted With Butterflies, Blue Stopper ... 25.00
RS Germany, Bottle, Perfume, Hand-Painted Butterflies ... 27.50
RS Germany, Bowl, Beige, Mimosa Flowers, Scalloped Rim, Green Mark, 9 In. ... 35.00
RS Germany, Bowl, Berry, 5 Saucers, Yellow Daffodils, Gold Trim ... 60.00
RS Germany, Bowl, Blown-Out Flowers & Leaves, Irregular Rim, Footed, 6 In. ... 45.00
RS Germany, Bowl, Cottage Scene, Red Steeple Mark, 10 1/2 In. ... 450.00
RS Germany, Bowl, Cream, Blue, & Orchid, Blown-Out Floral, Gold Edge, 9 In. ... 41.00
RS Germany, Bowl, Floral, Ornate, Steeple Mark, 9 1/4 In. ... 60.00
RS Germany, Bowl, Orange Lilies, Lilacs, Green Ground, Green Mark, 9 X 3 In. ... 36.00
RS Germany, Bowl, Pale Green, White Floral, Green Leaves, Green Mark, 10 In. ... 50.00
RS Germany, Bowl, Scallops, Flowers, Gold Leaf, Deep, Steeple Mark, 10 1/4 In. ... 63.00
RS Germany, Bowl, Snowball Decoration, Interior Gold Band, 9 1/4 In. ... 45.00
RS Germany, Bowl, Steeple Mark, 9 In. ... 48.00
RS Germany, Bowl, White, Gold Leaf, 9 In. ... 30.00
RS Germany, Box, Powder, Covered, Hand-Painted, Poppy Decoration ... 25.00
RS Germany, Box, Round, Orange Puppies ... 17.50
RS Germany, Box, Trinket, Bulbous, Embossed Fluting, Calla Lily Cover, 4 In. ... 22.00
RS Germany, Bread Bowl, Floral & Leaf, Gold Scrolls & Rococo, Steeple Mark ... 70.00
RS Germany, Cake Set, Beige, White Dogwood, Gold Borders, 6 Piece ... 75.00
RS Germany, Cake Set, Green, White Magnolias, Gold Edge, Blue Mark, 7 Piece ... 95.00
RS Germany, Cake Set, Sprays Of Tulips, 7 Pieces ... 68.00
RS Germany, Candleholder, Orange Roses On White To Brown, Blue Mark ... 37.50
RS Germany, Candlestick, Gold Bobeches, Pink, Lavender Orchids, 10 In., Pair ... 80.00
RS Germany, Celery Set, Gold & White, J.B.Scott, Green Mark, 3 Piece ... 20.00
RS Germany, Celery Set, Yellow & Brown, Peach Roses, Green Mark, 7 Piece ... 135.00
RS Germany, Celery, Beige Luster, Blue Floral, Open Handles, 11 In. ... 18.00
RS Germany, Celery, Green Shading, Poinsettias, Open Handle, 8 In. ... 22.00
RS Germany, Celery, Pink To Ivory, Calla Lilies, Blue Star Mark ... 25.00
RS Germany, Charger, Gold Border, Yellow & Green Flowers, Red Steeple Mark ... 150.00
RS Germany, Chocolate Pot, Child's, Brown Shading, Red Poppies, Green Leaves ... 14.00
RS Germany, Chocolate Pot, Green Poppies, 9 1/2 In. ... 25.00
RS Germany, Chocolate Pot, Pink, Salmon, & White, Florals, Satin Finish ... 80.00
RS Germany, Creamer, Covered, Gooseberries, Blossoms, & Leaves, Blue Mark ... 22.00
RS Germany, Creamer, Pink, Yellow Rose On Lustrous Brown, Marked ... 16.00

RS Germany, Cup & Saucer, Chocolate, Pink, Salmon, & White, Florals, Satin 18.00
RS Germany, Cup & Saucer, Demitasse, Pink Roses, Green Mark 18.00
RS Germany, Desk Set, White, Blue, Green, & Yellow, Roses & Dogwood, 3 Piece 140.00
RS Germany, Dish, Boat-Shape, End Handles, Flowers, Green Mark, 13 X 8 In. 47.50
RS Germany, Dish, Candy, Cream & Olive Color, Lilies, 7 In. 10.00
RS Germany, Dish, Candy, Floral, Gold Trim, Steeple Mark, 6 In. 22.50
RS Germany, Dish, Cheese & Cracker, Pink Tulips, Gold Rim, Blue Mark 38.00
RS Germany, Dish, Divided, Three Part, Roses, Raised Handle In Center, 10 In. 45.00
RS Germany, Dish, Leaf Shape, Gold Border, Handle, Blue Mark, 5 1/2 In. 17.50
RS Germany, Dish, Leaf Shape, Leaf-Shaped Handled Cover, White Porcelain 15.00
RS Germany, Dish, Pickle, Steeple Mark, Heavy Gold Decoration 40.00
RS Germany, Dish, Pierced Ends, Green Ground, Large Roses, Variegated, 10 In. 28.50
RS Germany, Dish, Pierced Handles, Sweetpeas, Blue Mark 15.00
RS Germany, Dish, Relish, Oval, Pink And White Tulips 17.75
RS Germany, Dish, Relish, Pink & Orange Floral, Blue Mark, Lustrous 20.00
RS Germany, Dish, Round, Shallow, Avacado, Lily-Of-The-Valley Design 26.00
RS Germany, Dresser Set, Beige, Orange Poppies, 4 Piece 145.00
RS Germany, Hair Receiver & Powder Jar, Tan With Gold, Lilies, Green Mark 85.00
RS Germany, Hair Receiver, Art Nouveau, Lavender Floral 22.00
RS Germany, Hair Receiver, Lily On Eggshell, Blue Mark, Pierced Handle 28.00
RS Germany, Hair Receiver, Pale Green, Pink Roses, Gold Border, Blue Mark 18.00
RS Germany, Hair Receiver, Pink, Rose Flowers On Green Ground, Green Mark 45.00
RS Germany, Hatpin Holder, Green Shaded, Roses, Green Leaves, Shadow Floral 28.00
RS Germany, Hatpin Holder, Lilies Of The Valley 20.00
RS Germany, Hatpin Holder, Pastel Green, Pink Roses, Green Mark 28.00
RS Germany, Hatpin Holder, Pink Roses, Green Leaves, Green Mark 28.00
RS Germany, Hatpin Holder, White Lilies 30.00
RS Germany, Ice Cream Set, Yellow & Pink Roses, 10 Piece 85.00
RS Germany, Inkwell, Covered, White, Turquoise Jewels, Gold Trim 25.00
RS Germany, Jar, Cookie, 2-Handled, Poppies On Sides And Lid 58.00
RS Germany, Jar, Cracker, Geometric Designs, Green, Gold, Browns, Signed, 8 In. 68.00
RS Germany, Jar, Cracker, Green With White & Pink Tulips, Green Mark 65.00
RS Germany, Jar, Cracker, White, Tulips, Gold Leaves, Blue Mark, 8 1/2 In. 85.00
RS Germany, Jar, Cracker, Yellow Roses 75.00
RS Germany, Luncheon Set, Mottled Orange, Blue Mark, 20 Piece 60.00
RS Germany, Muffineer, Floral, 2 Handles 72.00
RS Germany, Mug, Shaving, Poppies, Soap Rest 25.00
RS Germany, Mustache Cup & Saucer, Blue Mark 90.00
RS Germany, Mustard, White & Beige, Yellow Roses, Green Mark 48.50
RS Germany, Pitcher, Milk, Florals, Browns, Blue Mark 135.00
RS Germany, Plate, Bread, Lilac Pink Roses, Gold Rim, 16 In. 47.00
RS Germany, Plate, Cake, Brown, Blue, & Pink, Pink & White Floral, Handled 30.00
RS Germany, Plate, Cake, Cream & Olive Color, Lilies, Open Handled, 10 In. 20.00
RS Germany, Plate, Cake, Flowers, Open Handle 25.00
RS Germany, Plate, Cake, Green, White Clematis, 11 In. 18.00
RS Germany, Plate, Cake, Pierced Handles, Art Nouveau Lilies, 9 1/2 In. 25.00
RS Germany, Plate, Cake, Pink Roses, Pierced Handles, Green Mark, 10 In. 27.50
RS Germany, Plate, City In Distance, Tapestry & Iris Border, 8 In. 25.00
RS Germany, Plate, Cottonplant, 6 1/4 In. 6.50
RS Germany, Plate, Dessert, Pink Flowers, Green Shading, 6 In. 10.00
RS Germany, Plate, Floral, 8 In. 20.00
RS Germany, Plate, Green, White Blossoms, 8 In. 19.50
RS Germany, Plate, Large Yellow & Pink Roses, 8 In. 12.00
RS Germany, Plate, Pearlized, Rose On Each Side, 6 1/2 In. 7.00
RS Germany, Plate, Pink Roses Border, Blue Mark, 6 3/8 In. 6.00
RS Germany, Plate, Pink, Green, & Yellow, Daffodil, 6 1/2 In. 12.00
RS Germany, Plate, Serving, Pink, Salmon, & White, Florals, Satin Finish, 13 In. 40.00
RS Germany, Plate, Tulips On Cream & Gray, 7 3/4 In. 25.00
RS Germany, Plate, White Tulips, Blue Mark, 6 3/8 In. 7.00
RS Germany, Plate, White, Open Handles, 6 In. 15.00
RS Germany, Relish, Blue, White Roses, Green Leaves, Gold Border, Blue Mark 15.00
RS Germany, Relish, Green Orchids, 9 In. 15.00
RS Germany, Relish, Pink, White Tulips, Satin Finish, 9 1/4 In. 15.50
RS Germany, Relish, Shaded, Pink & White Floral, Gold Beading, 5 3/4 In. 14.00
RS Germany, Salt & Pepper, Rose & Leaves, 2 3/4 In. 48.00

RS Germany, Sauce, Green, Pink Tulips, Beaded Rim, Scalloped, Green Mark 9.00
RS Germany, Sauce, Pink, Green, & Yellow, Daffodil, 5 In. 10.00
RS Germany, Sauceboat, White Azaleas 14.00
RS Germany, Sugar & Creamer, Art Deco Design, Signed BMB 30.00
RS Germany, Sugar & Creamer, Cover, Floral, Rococo, 2-Handled, Steeple Mark 55.00
RS Germany, Sugar & Creamer, Cover, White Floral, Pale Green Trim 12.00
RS Germany, Sugar & Creamer, Green Luster, White & Gold Floral, Blue Mark 42.00
RS Germany, Sugar & Creamer, Pearl Luster & Ice Blue, Gold Handles 20.00
RS Germany, Sugar & Creamer, 22K Gold Finial, Handles, & Trim, Blue Mark 32.00
RS Germany, Sugar, Covered, Beige, Lily 12.00
RS Germany, Sugar, Covered, Gold Finial & Handles, Green Mark 22.00
RS Germany, Sugar, Pastel Floral, Gold Finial & Handles 10.00
RS Germany, Syrup, Blue Asters, Hand-Painted, Artist Signed 30.00
RS Germany, Syrup, Covered, Pink Roses, Attached Underplate, Green Mark 25.00
RS Germany, Syrup, Hand-Painted, Covered, Artist Signed 35.00
RS Germany, Syrup, Raised Roses, Colored Poppies & Leaves, Steeple Mark 25.00
RS Germany, Tea Set, Pearl Iridescent, Blue Band, Gold Rim, 3 Piece 30.00
RS Germany, Teapot, 2 Cup Size, Flowers 21.00
RS Germany, Toothpick, Blue & White Flowers, Gold Rim, Blue Mark, 3-Handled 38.50
RS Germany, Toothpick, Luster Roses, 2 Handles 28.00
RS Germany, Toothpick, 3-Handled, White With Gold Trim 20.00
RS Germany, Tray, Floating Lilies, Open Handles, 10 1/2 X 5 1/4 In. 75.00
RS Germany, Tray, Gray Brown, Talisman Roses, Pierced Handles, 11 1/2 In. 28.00
RS Germany, Vase, Blue, Lavender Iris, Gold Rim, 5 3/4 In. 45.00
RS Poland, Hatpin Holder, Floral 63.00
RS Poland, Vase, Pheasants, Handled, 3 3/4 In., Pair 60.00

RS Prussia porcelain was made at the factory of Rheinhold Schlegelmilch after 1869 in Tillowitz, Germany. The porcelain was sold decorated or undecorated.

RS Prussia, Basket, Silver Handle, Pink Roses, R Mark 190.00
RS Prussia, Berry Bowl, Turquoise & Cream, Pink & White Roses, Red Mark 95.00
RS Prussia, Berry Set, Lily Of The Valley, Red Mark, 7 Piece 400.00
RS Prussia, Berry Set, Magnolia, Green Scalloped Panels, Red Mark, 4 Piece 135.00
RS Prussia, Berry Set, Pink & White Water Lilies, Red Mark, 7 Piece 325.00
RS Prussia, Bowl, Basket Of Flowers, Red Mark, 8 1/2 In. 150.00
RS Prussia, Bowl, Basket Of Roses In Center, 10 1/2 In. 100.00
RS Prussia, Bowl, Berry, Scene Of Water Lilies, Blue, Gold, Red Mark 35.00
RS Prussia, Bowl, Blown Rim, Pink Roses, Green Shadow Flowers, 10 1/2 In. 115.00
RS Prussia, Bowl, Blown-Out Orchids, 9 In. 125.00
RS Prussia, Bowl, Castle Scene, 10 In. 475.00
RS Prussia, Bowl, Deep, 2 Decorations, White & Pink, Gold Edges, Red Mark 130.00
RS Prussia, Bowl, Diana The Huntress, 11 In. 1700.00
RS Prussia, Bowl, Dice Players, 10 1/2 In., Unmarked 75.00
RS Prussia, Bowl, Embossed Scallops & Leaves, Beaded Edge, Red Mark, 10 In. 75.00
RS Prussia, Bowl, Floral Center, Scalloped Edge, 10 1/2 In. 95.00
RS Prussia, Bowl, Floral, Blue & Pink, Red Mark, 11 In. 100.00
RS Prussia, Bowl, Floral, Fluted Sides, Pearlized, Red Mark, 11 In. 120.00
RS Prussia, Bowl, Floral, Satin Finish, Red Mark, 9 In. 95.00
RS Prussia, Bowl, Flower Design, Turquoise Shades, Red Mark, 11 In. 135.00
RS Prussia, Bowl, Footed, 4 Panels Of Primroses, Gold Scallop, 5 3/4 In. 65.00
RS Prussia, Bowl, Gold Flowers, Speckle Embossed, Crinkle Scallop, 10 1/2 In. 120.00
RS Prussia, Bowl, Green Ground, Panels Of Tan, Gold, Pink, Roses, Red Mark 100.00
RS Prussia, Bowl, Green Shading, Pink & White Asters, Red Mark, 10 1/2 In. 295.00
RS Prussia, Bowl, Lilac Floral, Purple Band At Edge, 10 1/2 In. 190.00
RS Prussia, Bowl, Lilies, Beige Grapes, Gold Trim, Footed, Red Mark, 7 1/4 In. 65.00
RS Prussia, Bowl, Lily Pad, Red Mark, 8 In. 175.00
RS Prussia, Bowl, Mother-Of-Pearl Finish, Floral, Red Mark, 9 1/2 In. 145.00
RS Prussia, Bowl, Old Man Of The Mountain, Medallion Edge, Red Mark, 10 In. 450.00
RS Prussia, Bowl, Oyster White, Red Floral, Scalloped, Red Star Mark, 11 In. 140.00
RS Prussia, Bowl, Pale Green To Ivory, Pink & Cream Roses, Gold, Footed, 8 In. 68.00
RS Prussia, Bowl, Pale Yellow, Red Mark, 10 In. 115.00
RS Prussia, Bowl, Pheasant On Log, Red Mark, 10 1/2 In. 495.00
RS Prussia, Bowl, Pink & Beige Floral, Gold Trim, Unsigned, 3 In. 55.00
RS Prussia, Bowl, Pink Flowers, Fluted Edge, Gold Trim, Red Mark, 11 In. 115.00

RS Prussia, Bowl, Pink, Roses, Scalloped, Red Mark, 9 1/2 X 3 1/2 In. 95.00
RS Prussia, Bowl, Pink, White Roses, Green Leaves, Red Mark, 10 1/2 In. 95.00
RS Prussia, Bowl, Pond Lilies, Red Mark, 10 1/2 In. 120.00
RS Prussia, Bowl, Portrait, Green Ground, Brunette In Center 250.00
RS Prussia, Bowl, Portrait, Peasant Girl, Leaves, Satin Finish, 10 In. 625.00
RS Prussia, Bowl, Portrait, Scenic Autumn 925.00
RS Prussia, Bowl, Red & Pink Roses, Scalloped, Red Star Mark, 11 In. 68.00
RS Prussia, Bowl, Red Roses & Daisies, Red Star Mark, 9 1/2 In. 58.00
RS Prussia, Bowl, Roses & Floral, Gold Trim, Ruffled, Red Star Mark, 11 In. 65.00
RS Prussia, Bowl, Roses, Green Trim, Jeweled, 10 1/2 In. 150.00
RS Prussia, Bowl, Roses, Scallop Sections, Red Star Mark, 11 In. 85.00
RS Prussia, Bowl, Scroll Feet, Cream With Gold Tracery, Red Mark, 11 In. 115.00
RS Prussia, Bowl, Serving, Bells Of Ireland, Red Mark, 13 X 8 In. 120.00
RS Prussia, Bowl, Sheepherder Scene, Blown-Out Flowers 500.00
RS Prussia, Bowl, Snowbird, 11 In. 1700.00
RS Prussia, Bowl, Spring Season, Blown-Out Floral, 9 In. 825.00
RS Prussia, Bowl, Swan, 4 Swans On Blue Lake, Blown-Out Flowers, 10 In. 475.00
RS Prussia, Bowl, Swans In Blue Water & Cedars, Open Handles, 12 X 9 In. 700.00
RS Prussia, Bowl, Vines Of Roses, Blown-Out Triangles, Red Mark, 10 In. 90.00
RS Prussia, Bowl, Violets & Green Leaves, Scalloped, Red Star Mark, 10 In. 120.00
RS Prussia, Bowl, Water Lilies, Red Mark, 10 In. 125.00
RS Prussia, Bowl, White & Pink Tea Roses, Cutout Handles, Footed, 9 1/4 In. 105.00
RS Prussia, Bowl, Yellow Roses, Pierced Ends, Oblong, 9 3/4 In. 35.00
RS Prussia, Bowl, Yellow Roses, Pink Mums, Red Mark, 10 3/4 In. 82.00
RS Prussia, Box, Candy, Tulip & Orange On Lid, Red Mark, 4 X 4 In. 135.00
RS Prussia, Box, Powder, Covered, Yellow & Red Roses, Red Mark 125.00
RS Prussia, Box, Powder, Floral, Red Mark 20.00
RS Prussia, Box, Powder, Fluted Lid, Pearlized, Scalloped, Round, 4 In. 130.00
RS Prussia, Box, Powder, Gazelle 1500.00
RS Prussia, Box, Powder, Lily, 2 Boys, & Dog On Lid, Melon Boy, 5 In. 185.00
RS Prussia, Celery, Dark Green, White Flowers, Gold Trim, 12 In. 35.00
RS Prussia, Celery, Floral, Red Mark, 12 1/4 In. 83.00
RS Prussia, Celery, Ornate, Turquoise, 13 1/4 In. 95.00
RS Prussia, Celery, Pink & White Lily Pads On Blue Water, Red Mark 165.00
RS Prussia, Celery, Pink, Roses, Gold Trim, Red Mark, 11 In. 65.00
RS Prussia, Celery, Pond Lilies, Red Mark 90.00
RS Prussia, Celery, Satinized, Open Handles, Red Mark, Pansies 65.00
RS Prussia, Celery, Water Lilies, Iris, & Roses, Open Handles, 12 In. 90.00
RS Prussia, Celery, White & Green, Dogwood, Gold Stems & Dots, Cutout Handle 85.00
RS Prussia, Celery, White, Brown & Green Pansies, Pink & White Roses 75.00
RS Prussia, Chocolate Pot, Floral Decoration, Unmarked 60.00
RS Prussia, Chocolate Pot, Green & Off-White, Pink Floral, Red Star Mark 140.00
RS Prussia, Chocolate Pot, Ivory Color, Roses, Green Leaves, 10 In. 105.00
RS Prussia, Chocolate Pot, Pastel Satin, Pink & Red Roses, Gold, Red Mark 98.00
RS Prussia, Chocolate Pot, Pedestaled, Garlands Of Roses, Red Mark 95.00
RS Prussia, Chocolate Pot, Satin Finish, Floral, Red Mark 160.00
RS Prussia, Chocolate Pot, Satin Finish, Ruffled Top & Base, Red Mark 200.00
RS Prussia, Chocolate Pot, Spring Seasons 1000.00
RS Prussia, Chocolate Pot, Swans, Satin Finish 300.00
RS Prussia, Chocolate Pot, White, Roses & Floral, Green Leaves 110.00
RS Prussia, Chocolate Pot, White, Roses & Foliage, Gold Trim, Red Mark 110.00
RS Prussia, Chocolate Pot, Yellows, White & Pink Roses, 6 Footed, Red Mark 195.00
RS Prussia, Chocolate Pot, 6-Sided, Footed, Satin Finish, Jeweled, Red Mark 225.00
RS Prussia, Chocolate Set, Blues, Greens, Flowers, Wreath Around Top, 9 Piece 435.00
RS Prussia, Chocolate Set, Dark Green, White Flowers, 13 Piece 395.00
RS Prussia, Chocolate Set, Dogwood, , 9 1/2 In. Pot, 6 Cups & Saucers 550.00
RS Prussia, Chocolate Set, Six Cups 850.00
RS Prussia, Chocolate Set, Spring Seasons, 9 Piece 5500.00
RS Prussia, Coffeepot, Lilies, Satin Finish, Red Mark, 10 In. 225.00
RS Prussia, Compote, Brown To Ivory, Roses, Brown Trim, Red Mark, 7 In. 215.00
RS Prussia, Compote, Pearlized Green, Red, Pink Roses, 3 1/2 In., Marked 170.00
RS Prussia, Cream & Sugar, Lavender And Red, Red Mark 145.00
RS Prussia, Creamer, Bluebirds, Duck, & Pine Tree In Panels, Red Mark 150.00
RS Prussia, Creamer, Iris & Poppies, 4 In. 100.00
RS Prussia, Creamer, Melon Boy, Jeweled, Footed, Red Mark 250.00

RS Prussia, Creamer, Pedestaled, Ornate Handle, Pink Roses, Red Mark 29.00
RS Prussia, Creamer, White & Green, Dogwood, Gold Stems & Dots, Red Mark 50.00
RS Prussia, Cup & Saucer, Chocolate, Red Roses Bouquets, Gold, Red Mark 40.00
RS Prussia, Cup & Saucer, Cocoa, Peachy White Roses, Beaded, Ruffled Edge 29.00
RS Prussia, Cup & Saucer, Demitasse, Fluted Cup, Pink & Red Roses, Red Mark 38.00
RS Prussia, Cup & Saucer, Demitasse, Pedestal Base, Ornate Handle 18.00
RS Prussia, Cup & Saucer, Demitasse, Pink Rose Sprays, Ribbed, Red Mark 35.00
RS Prussia, Cup & Saucer, Footed, Floral, Demitasse, Ornate Handle, Red Mark 42.00
RS Prussia, Cup & Saucer, Green & Gold Floral, Scalloped Edges, Red Mark 52.50
RS Prussia, Cup & Saucer, Green Trim, Floral 65.00
RS Prussia, Cup & Saucer, Kauffmann Type Scene, Red Mark 55.00
RS Prussia, Cup & Saucer, Lily Of The Valley, Tapestry Border, Red Mark 35.00
RS Prussia, Cup & Saucer, Pedestal Cup, Red Mark 40.00
RS Prussia, Cup & Saucer, Pink Roses, Red Mark 25.00
RS Prussia, Cup & Saucer, Tapestry Border, Satin Finish, Red Mark 45.00
RS Prussia, Cup & Saucer, White Floral, Green Leaves, Red Mark 45.00
RS Prussia, Cup & Saucer, Yellow & Pink Roses, Gold Beaded, Red Mark 55.00
RS Prussia, Cup & Saucer, 2 Roses On One Side, Light Brown At Top 65.00
RS Prussia, Cup, Chocolate, Puffy Top, Gold Trim, Footed, Red Mark 17.00
RS Prussia, Cup, Roses 20.00
RS Prussia, Cup, Violets 20.00
RS Prussia, Dessert Bowl, Pink & Green Floral, Red Mark, 5 In. 15.00
RS Prussia, Dish, Candy, Floral Decoration, Red Mark 25.00
RS Prussia, Dish, Candy, Red Mark 90.00
RS Prussia, Dish, Oval, Blue With Tulips & Forget-Me-Nots, 8 X 12 1/2 In. 65.00
RS Prussia, Dish, Oval, Pierced Handles, Roses In Basket, 12 1/2 X 6 In. 95.00
RS Prussia, Dish, Pickle, Pink & White Carnations, Open Handles, Red Mark 35.00
RS Prussia, Dish, Pickle, Pink & White Roses, Pierced Handles, 9 1/2 In. 100.00
RS Prussia, Dish, Pickle, Scallops, Leaves, Floral, Red Mark, 8 X 3 1/2 In. 37.00
RS Prussia, Dish, Pointed Lid, 3 Feet, Water Lilies, Red Mark 140.00
RS Prussia, Dish, Powder, Yellow Ground, Pink Roses, Ruffled Cover, Red Mark 100.00
RS Prussia, Dish, Relish, Pearlized, Red Star Mark 50.00
RS Prussia, Dish, Salad Dressing With Underplate, Ruffled, Satin Finish 125.00
RS Prussia, Dish, Serving, Roses, 10 1/2 In. 95.00
RS Prussia, Dish, Shell, Open Handles, Yellow, Lavender, Red Mark, 9 In. 285.00
RS Prussia, Fernery, Mill Scene, Brown, 4-Footed, Red Mark 325.00
RS Prussia, Fernery, Pink Roses, Footed, Red Mark, 8 1/4 In. 170.00
RS Prussia, Gravy Boat, Underplate, Fan Decoration, Handle, No Mark 75.00
RS Prussia, Gray To Green & Magenta, White Carnations, Scalloped, 10 In. 85.00
RS Prussia, Hair Receiver, Green, Gold Decoration, Red Mark 85.00
RS Prussia, Hair Receiver, Melon Shape, Footed, Flowers, Red Mark, 3 3/4 In. 65.00
RS Prussia, Hair Receiver, Pink Roses, Green Leaves, 4-Footed, Red Mark 75.00
RS Prussia, Hair Receiver, Pink Roses, 3 1/2 In. 67.00
RS Prussia, Hair Receiver, Purple Flowers, Ruffled Rim 55.00
RS Prussia, Hair Receiver, Scalloped, Red Mark, Square, 5 1/2 In. 68.00
RS Prussia, Hair Receiver, White, Holly & Berries, Square, Red Mark 75.00
RS Prussia, Hair Receiver, Yellow & Brown Roses, Red Mark 45.00
RS Prussia, Hair Receiver, 6-Sided, Hand-Painted Blue & Gold 55.00
RS Prussia, Hatpin Holder & Attached Double Pin Tray, Green, White Roses 115.00
RS Prussia, Hatpin Holder & Attached Pin Box, White, Pink Roses, Gold Trim 175.00
RS Prussia, Hatpin Holder, Water Lilies On Blue Water, 6-Sided, Red Mark 139.50
RS Prussia, Hatpin Holder, White Flowers On Light Green 80.00
RS Prussia, Hatpin Holder, 6 Bluebirds Flying Over Cottage Scene, Red Mark 250.00
RS Prussia, Jar, Cookie, Lily Of The Valley, Red Mark 175.00
RS Prussia, Jar, Cookie, White, Pink Roses, Green & Gold Trim 150.00
RS Prussia, Jar, Cracker, Decorations, Red Mark 140.00
RS Prussia, Jar, Cracker, High Gloss, Dogwood, Covered 6 X 6 1/2 In. 225.00
RS Prussia, Jar, Cracker, Roses & Greenery On Ivory, Red Mark 135.00
RS Prussia, Jar, Cracker, Royal Vienna Mark, Red Mark 265.00
RS Prussia, Jar, Cracker, White, Green Leaves, Brown Trim, Blossoms 40.00
RS Prussia, Jar, Cracker, White, Pink Poppies, White Lilies, Red Mark, 9 In. 160.00
RS Prussia, Jar, Cracker, White, Pink, Yellow Flowers, Ribbed, Red Mark 225.00
RS Prussia, Jar, Cracker, With Lid, Multicolor Floral 165.00
RS Prussia, Mayonnaise Set, Red Mark 95.00
RS Prussia, Mug, Shaving, Floral, White Ground, Gold Work, Ornate, Red Mark 145.00

Handled,

RS Prussia, Mustache Cup, Embossed, Pink Roses, Gold Handle, Red Mark 90.00
RS Prussia, Mustache Cup, Shaded Ground, Pastel Floral, Gold, Red Mark 90.00
RS Prussia, Mustard, Basket Of Roses, Red Mark 65.00
RS Prussia, Nappy, Pheasants, Pink Luster, Open Handles, Tillowitz & Pickard 58.00
RS Prussia, Nut Set, Green To White, Holly & Berries, Red Mark, 4 Piece 240.00
RS Prussia, Nut Set, Yellow Primroses, White Enamel Florals, 5 Piece 250.00
RS Prussia, Pitcher, Cider, Bluebird 270.00
RS Prussia, Pitcher, Cider, Garland Of Roses, Red Mark, 10 In. 250.00
RS Prussia, Pitcher, Lemonade, Lilies, Green, 6 X 7 In., Fluted Top 275.00
RS Prussia, Pitcher, Lemonade, Red Roses On White Satin, 6 X 7 In., Fluted To 300.00
RS Prussia, Pitcher, Lemonade, Varied Colors, Red Mark 295.00
RS Prussia, Pitcher, Lemonade, White, Blue, Gold, Floral, High Gloss, Red Mark 275.00
RS Prussia, Planter, Blown-Out Roses, 23 In. 48.50
RS Prussia, Plate, Blue & White Violets, Red Mark, 8 In. 65.00
RS Prussia, Plate, Bread, Floating Lilies, Open Handles, Red Mark, 12 1/2 In. 175.00
RS Prussia, Plate, Bread, Floral, 10 In. 45.00
RS Prussia, Plate, Cake, Green Luster, White Floral, Gold, Handled 85.00
RS Prussia, Plate, Cake, Lily Of The Valley, Open Handles, 10 1/2 In. 85.00
RS Prussia, Plate, Cake, Melon Boy, Dice Players, Open Handles, 10 1/2 In. 595.00
RS Prussia, Plate, Cake, Mill Scene 500.00
RS Prussia, Plate, Cake, Open Handled, Flowers, Lustrous, Red Mark, 11 3/4 In. 125.00
RS Prussia, Plate, Cake, Open Handled, Flowers, Pond, Red Mark, 11 In. 135.00
RS Prussia, Plate, Cake, Open Handled, Ornate, Roses, Red Mark, 9 1/2 In. 95.00
RS Prussia, Plate, Cake, Open Handled, Roses In Green, Leaves Around Trim 65.00
RS Prussia, Plate, Cake, Open Roses, Pierced Handle, Red Mark, 10 In. 55.00
RS Prussia, Plate, Cake, Ornate, Poppies, 11 1/2 In. 65.00
RS Prussia, Plate, Cake, Pearlized Green Edge, Red Mark 125.00
RS Prussia, Plate, Cake, Pink & White Roses, Gold Trim, Red Mark, 9 3/4 In. 95.00
RS Prussia, Plate, Carnations Center, White & Gold Border, Green Mark, 8 In. 50.00
RS Prussia, Plate, Dark Green, Browns, & Yellow, Floral, Red Mark, 10 1/4 In. 167.50
RS Prussia, Plate, Fans, Roses, Blue Leaves, Red Mark, 6 1/4 In. 30.00
RS Prussia, Plate, Floral Center, Scalloped, Red Mark, 8 3/4 In. 75.00
RS Prussia, Plate, Floral, Gold, Pastels, Red Mark, 9 5/8 In. 110.00
RS Prussia, Plate, Fruits, Blown-Out Iris Edge, Red Mark, 9 In. 85.00
RS Prussia, Plate, Gray Shading, White Lilac Center, Red Mark, 8 In. 65.00
RS Prussia, Plate, Green & White, Pink Carnations, Scalloped, 7 3/4 In. 55.00
RS Prussia, Plate, Green Shading, White Carnations, Gold, Red Mark, 8 1/2 In. 83.50
RS Prussia, Plate, Green, Pink Roses Center, Red Mark, 8 In. 65.00
RS Prussia, Plate, Green, White Bellflowers, Gold Centers, Red Mark, 8 In. 65.00
RS Prussia, Plate, Green, White Floral, Gold Trim, Open Handles, 9 1/2 In. 65.00
RS Prussia, Plate, Iris & Poppies, 8 1/2 In. 125.00
RS Prussia, Plate, Melon Boy, Burgundy Border, Red Mark, Unsigned 350.00
RS Prussia, Plate, Melon Boy, Jeweled, 10 1/2 In. 1300.00
RS Prussia, Plate, Mill Scene, Red Mark, 11 In. 395.00
RS Prussia, Plate, Molded, Pushed-Out Pink & White Blossoms, Red Mark, 10 In. 125.00
RS Prussia, Plate, Old Man Of The Mountain, Open Handles, 11 In. 435.00
RS Prussia, Plate, Oyster, Red Mark 60.00
RS Prussia, Plate, Peacock, Red Mark, 8 1/2 In. 495.00
RS Prussia, Plate, Pearl Finish, Floral, Pink, White, Green, Red Mark, 8 In. 50.00
RS Prussia, Plate, Pink & Peach Tulips, Gold Leaves, Red Mark, 8 In. 75.00
RS Prussia, Plate, Pink Flowers, Red Mark, 7 In. 35.00
RS Prussia, Plate, Pink Poppies, Embossed Fans, Red Mark, 9 In. 55.00
RS Prussia, Plate, Scalloped Edge, Talisman Roses, Gold Edge, Red Mark, 8 In. 49.00
RS Prussia, Plate, Scallops, Embossed Fans, Turquoise & Pearl, Red Mark 57.00
RS Prussia, Plate, Schooner, 10 In. 450.00
RS Prussia, Plate, Swans & Bluebirds, Open Handles, Red Mark, 10 In. 250.00
RS Prussia, Plate, Tea, Pearlized, Scalloped 18.00
RS Prussia, Plate, Tea, Swan On Green Water, 8 1/4 In. 115.00
RS Prussia, Plate, White Floral, Gold Stems, Rococo Edge, Red Mark, 9 5/8 In. 67.50
RS Prussia, Plate, Winter Season, Red Mark, 8 1/2 In. 550.00
RS Prussia, Plate, 3 Swans, Water Lily, Ruffled Edge, Red Mark, 8 In. 295.00
RS Prussia, Ramekin, Set Of 4 .... 125.00
RS Prussia, Relish, Green, White Lilies, Pink & Gold, Open Handles, Red Mark 45.00
RS Prussia, Relish, Melon Boy, Jeweled, 9 1/2 X 4 1/2 In. 545.00
RS Prussia, Relish, Pink & White Roses, Green Laurel & Gold Edge, Red Mark 51.50

RS Prussia, Relish, Roses, Pierced Handle, Scalloped, Red Mark, 8 In. 40.00
RS Prussia, Relish, White Roses, Pink Garlands, Gold Trim, Red Mark, 8 In. 52.00
RS Prussia, Ring Tree, Snowballs, Gold Border, 5 X 3 1/2 In. 225.00
RS Prussia, Sauce, Pink Roses, Red Mark, Set Of Four 75.00
RS Prussia, Sauce, Prairie Chicken, Red Mark 50.00
RS Prussia, Sauce, Rabbit, Red Mark 50.00
RS Prussia, Serving Bowl, Blue, Water Lilies, Red Mark 30.00
RS Prussia, Shaving Mug, Pink & Red Roses, Pedestal Bottom, Red Mark 165.00
RS Prussia, Sugar & Creamer, Artichoke Finial, Pedestaled, Red Mark 125.00
RS Prussia, Sugar & Creamer, Beige, Pink Roses, Blue Trim, 4 1/2 In. 60.00
RS Prussia, Sugar & Creamer, Maroon Ribbon, Rose & Yellow Roses, Daisies 150.00
RS Prussia, Sugar & Creamer, Pale Yellow, Floral, Red Mark 75.00
RS Prussia, Sugar & Creamer, Pink Roses, Satin Finish 135.00
RS Prussia, Sugar & Creamer, Pinks & Green, Jeweled Rims, Red Mark 145.00
RS Prussia, Sugar & Creamer, Roses, Tulip Shape 95.00
RS Prussia, Sugar & Creamer, White, Pink & Yellow Roses On Blue Panels 130.00
RS Prussia, Sugar & Creamer, Yellow, White Magnolias, Green Panels, Red Mark 130.00
RS Prussia, Sugar Shaker, Loop Handles, Scalloped Bottom, Roses, Red Mark 90.00
RS Prussia, Sugar Shaker, Purple Violets, Satin Finish, 8 Feet, Red Mark 130.00
RS Prussia, Sugar, Colorful Florals, Red Mark 45.00
RS Prussia, Sugar, Cottage Scene, Footed 165.00
RS Prussia, Sugar, Covered, Floral, Red Mark 42.00
RS Prussia, Sugar, Covered, Roses, Gold Handles, Pedestal, Red Mark 60.00
RS Prussia, Sugar, Covered, Scenic, 3 Swans In Water, Red Mark 88.00
RS Prussia, Sugar, Covered, Tan, White Magnolias, Gold Stamen, Green Leaves 75.00
RS Prussia, Sugar, Covered, 6-Sided, Pagoda Style, Carnations On Satin, 5 In. 50.00
RS Prussia, Sugar, Pink Roses, Gold Border, Red Mark, 5 In. 85.00
RS Prussia, Syrup & Saucer, Yellow & Red Roses, Footed, Red Mark 175.00
RS Prussia, Syrup, Colorful, Red Mark 65.00
RS Prussia, Syrup, Floral, Gold Embossed, Scalloped Top And Bottom, Red Mark 95.00
RS Prussia, Syrup, Green Floral, Footed, Red Mark 85.00
RS Prussia, Tankard, Blown Hibiscus, Red, Purple, Red Mark, 11 1/2 In., Pair 650.00
RS Prussia, Tankard, Blown Top & Spout, Pink & Yellow Floral, 11 In. 315.00
RS Prussia, Tankard, Blown-Out Floral, Red Mark, 11 1/4 In. 525.00
RS Prussia, Tankard, Blown-Out Flowers, Green, Blue Roses, 11 In. 350.00
RS Prussia, Tankard, Blown-Out Flowers, Green, Blue, Roses, 13 In. 400.00
RS Prussia, Tankard, Cream Color, Pink Roses, Red Star Mark, 4 1/2 In. 75.00
RS Prussia, Tea Set, Blown-Out Iris Design 1600.00
RS Prussia, Tea Set, Melon Ribbed, Red Mark, 3 Piece 325.00
RS Prussia, Tea Set, Poppies, , 9 In. Pot, 4 Demitasse & Saucers 475.00
RS Prussia, Teacup, Roses, Red Star Mark 12.00
RS Prussia, Teapot, Footed, Pink & Yellow Tulips, Red Mark, 7 In. 138.00
RS Prussia, Teapot, Iris & Poppies, 5 1/2 In. 175.00
RS Prussia, Teapot, Pedestaled, White & Green, Pink Flowers, 6 In. 140.00
RS Prussia, Teapot, Pink, Floral, Kent, Red Mark 125.00
RS Prussia, Teapot, Tan, White Magnolia, Gold Stamen, Green Leaves, Red Mark 130.00
RS Prussia, Teapot, White, Pink Roses & White Daisies On Blue Panels, Gold 130.00
RS Prussia, Toothpick, Blown-Out Magnolias, 2 Handles, Red Mark 165.00
RS Prussia, Toothpick, Green To Yellow, Rose Bouquets, 2 Handles, Red Mark 105.00
RS Prussia, Toothpick, Lilies, 3 Handles, 2 1/4 In. 165.00
RS Prussia, Toothpick, Pink & Yellow Roses, 2 Handles, 4-Footed 45.00
RS Prussia, Toothpick, Roses, Gold Trim, 2 Handles, Red Mark 110.00
RS Prussia, Toothpick, Roses, 2 Handles 35.00
RS Prussia, Toothpick, Yellow With Pink & Green Flower, 2-Handled, Red Mark 125.00
RS Prussia, Toothpick, 2-Handled, Red Mark 70.00
RS Prussia, Tray, Bread, Open Handled, Lilies In Water, Red Mark, 12 In. 95.00
RS Prussia, Tray, Bun, Melon Boy Scene, Gold, Beige, 13 1/2 X 6 1/2 In. 550.00
RS Prussia, Tray, Bust Portrait Lady & Tulips, Satin, Red Mark, 6 X 7 In. 275.00
RS Prussia, Tray, Dresser, Flowers In Bowl Of Water, Red Mark, 14 In. 110.00
RS Prussia, Tray, Dresser, Snowballs & Roses, Red Mark 95.00
RS Prussia, Tray, Dresser, White & Peach, Roses, Open Handles, 9 1/2 In. 55.00
RS Prussia, Tray, Floating Lilies, Open Handles, Red Mark, 12 1/4 X 6 In. 175.00
RS Prussia, Tray, Melon Boys, Red Mark, 13 1/4 X 6 1/2 In. 550.00
RS Prussia, Tray, Pin, Swan 100.00
RS Prussia, Tray, Rococo Edges, Speckled, Lily & Buds, Red Mark, Miniature 52.00

RS Prussia, Vase, Art Nouveau, Blown-Out Berries, Red Mark, 12 In. 250.00
RS Prussia, Vase, Bird Of Paradise, Handled 425.00
RS Prussia, Vase, Courting Scene 1350.00
RS Prussia, Vase, Jeweled, Gold Handles, Flowers, Red Mark, 10 In. 250.00
RS Prussia, Vase, Melon Eater, 5 In. 500.00
RS Prussia, Vase, Pheasant, 5 1/2 In. 250.00
RS Prussia, Vase, Portrait, Brunette & Peacock, 11 In. 400.00
RS Prussia, Vase, Portrait, 13 In. 300.00
RS Prussia, Vase, R.S.Suhl, Beehive, Kaufmann Signed, 3 Grecian Maids 350.00
RS Prussia, Vase, Satin Finish, Roses, Footed, 9 In., Red Mark 125.00

R.S.Tillowitz porcelain factory was started at Tillowitz near Silesia in 1869 by Rheinhold Schlegelmilch. Table services and ornamental pieces were made.

RS Tillowitz, Bowl, Green & Yellow, Pink Floral & Green Leaves, 9 In. 52.00
RS Tillowitz, Bowl, Green Ground, Gold Roses, E.P.O.S Mark, 10 In. 35.00
RS Tillowitz, Jar, Cracker 50.00
RS Tillowitz, Jar, Cracker, Roses & Gold 60.00
RS Tillowitz, Plate, Cake, Open Handles, Floral 25.00
RS Tillowitz, Plate, Green With Oriental Poppies, 6 1/4 In., Set Of 6 .... 19.00
RS Tillowitz, Tray, Pearlized, Gold Handles, Silesia, Oval, 15 X 5 1/4 In. 27.50

Rubena Verde is a Victorian glassware that was shaded from red to green. It was first made by Hobbs, Brockunier and Company of Wheeling, West Virginia, about 1890.

Rubena Verde, Bowl, Finger, Almond Hobs, Ruffled Rim, 4 In. 65.00
Rubena Verde, Cruet, Shades Of Red To Green 165.00
Rubena Verde, Jack-In-The-Pulpit, Cranberry To Green, 9 1/8 In., Pair 350.00
Rubena Verde, Pitcher, Water, Inverted Thumbprint, Enamel Floral & Leaf 350.00
Rubena Verde, Pitcher, Water, Thumbprint 215.00
Rubena Verde, Shot Glass, Cranberry To Vaseline, Gold Palm Tree 25.00
Rubena Verde, Vase, Green To Cranberry, 4 1/2 In. 85.00
Rubena Verde, Vase, Notched & Paneled, 7 In. 85.00
Rubena Verde, Vase, Puffed Panels, Enameled Florals, Gold Work, 10 1/2 In. 350.00
Rubena Verde, Vase, Satin, Brass Ring & Handles, 6 1/2 In. 95.00

Rubena is a glassware that shades from red to clear. It was first made by George Duncan and Sons of Pittsburgh, Pennsylvania, about 1885.

Rubena, see also Northwood, Royal Ivy; Pressed Glass, Royal Oak

Rubena, Bottle, Perfume, Footed And Decorated, 6 In. 85.00
Rubena, Bowl, Hobnail, 8 X 3 In. 50.00
Rubena, Bowl, Quilted, Enamel Floral, Ruffled, Ormolu Base, 6 In. 160.00
Rubena, Bucket, Ice, Clear & Frosted, Polar Bear, Dated 1885, Royal Ivy Base 125.00
Rubena, Bucket, Ice, Clear & Frosted, Polar Bear, Feb 1, 1885, 6 3/4 In. 125.00
Rubena, Castor Set, Heart Silver Holder, 3 Bottle, 4 3/4 In. 95.00
Rubena, Castor Set, 3 Bottles, Cut Panels, Silver Plate Heart-Shaped Frame 100.00
Rubena, Celery, Frosted Hobs 95.00
Rubena, Condiment Set, 10 Panels, Silver Plate Tops, 3 In., 2 Piece 68.00
Rubena, Creamer, Hobnail, Applied Clear Handle, Square Top, 4 In. 145.00
Rubena, Cruet, Applied Handle, Hobnail, Cranberry To Clear 145.00
Rubena, Insert, Pickle Castor, Melon Shape, Decorated, 4 1/2 In. 38.00
Rubena, Pitcher, Diamond Band Around Top, Cranberry To Clear, 8 7/8 In. 110.00
Rubena, Pitcher, Lemonade, Wheeling, Etched Floral, Bulbous 100.00
Rubena, Pitcher, Pointed Hobnail, Deep Cranberry To Clear 225.00
Rubena, Pitcher, Water, Diamond Quilted 135.00
Rubena, Pitcher, Water, Paneled Sprig 120.00
Rubena, Pitcher, Water, Quilted, Reeded Handle, Tricorner Top 185.00
Rubena, Pitcher, Water, Ruffled Top, Diamond Quilted, Applied Handle 125.00
Rubena, Salt & Pepper 48.00
Rubena, Syrup, Threaded 150.00
Rubena, Syrup, Threaded, Northwood 165.00
Rubena, Tumbler, Flashed Cranberry To Clear, Enameled Trumpet Flowers 30.00
Rubena, Tumbler, Frosted, Color 2/3 Down 55.00
Rubena, Tumbler, Hobnail, Color 2/3 Down 45.00

Rubena, Vase, Bud, Twisted, Gold Decoration, 18 In. 125.00
Rubena, Vase, Bulbous, Flared Top, 3 3/4 In. 35.00
Rubena, Vase, Cut & Notched, 8 In. 79.00
Rubena, Vase, Handblown, Ruffled Top, White Decoration, 10 In. 95.00
Rubena, Vase, Swirled Crystal, Wide Sterling Rim, 8 In. 35.00
Rubena, Vase, Swirled Heavy Crystal, Wide Sterling Rim 35.00
Rubena, Water Set, Paneled Sprig, 4 Piece 250.00

Ruby glass is a dark red color. It was a Victorian and twentieth-century ware. The name means many different types of red glass.

Ruby Glass, see also Cranberry Glass, Pressed Glass, Souvenir

Ruby Glass, Basket, Etched Grape, Small 22.00
Ruby Glass, Bowl, Punch, Child's, Five Cups, Fancy 35.00
Ruby Glass, Bowl, Thumbprint, 9 In.Matching Candlesticks, 3 In. 50.00
Ruby Glass, Butter, Covered, Button Arches, Jennie, Oct.14, 1916 .... 75.00
Ruby Glass, Butter, Covered, Flask Shape, Signed Mother & Elizabeth 25.00
Ruby Glass, Butter, Crystal Wedding 65.00
Ruby Glass, Carafe, Water, Flat Panel Cutting On Neck 37.00
Ruby Glass, Celery, Thumbprint 57.50
Ruby Glass, Compote, Chaska, Minnesota 30.00
Ruby Glass, Compote, Souvenir, Herringbone, World's Fair, 1893, 7 1/4 In. 52.00
Ruby Glass, Creamer, Button & Arches, Richford, Vt. 22.00
Ruby Glass, Creamer, Colorado, Souvenir, 1902 .... 25.00
Ruby Glass, Creamer, Large 55.00
Ruby Glass, Creamer, Silver Band On Neck & Foot, 3 1/2 In. 23.00
Ruby Glass, Creamer, Souvenir, Mt.Vernon, Ind. 19.50
Ruby Glass, Creamer, Souvenir, Saratoga Springs, N.Y., Marked Near Cut 12.00
Ruby Glass, Creamer, Star Of Bethlehem, Souvenir, Mammie 1910 In Gold 35.00
Ruby Glass, Cup, Loving, Souvenir, Rock Point, Pa., 3 1/2 In. 12.00
Ruby Glass, Cup, Name & Date, Button Arches, 2 3/4 In. 17.50
Ruby Glass, Cup, Punch, Souvenir, Franklin 1906 .... 8.50
Ruby Glass, Cup, Souvenir, Father 26.00
Ruby Glass, Dish, Battleship Cover 10.00
Ruby Glass, Dish, Jam, Silver Plate Frame, 3 Ball Feet, Handle, 3 3/4 In. 12.00
Ruby Glass, Dish, Leaf Shape, 6 In. 4.00
Ruby Glass, Goblet, Ivy In Snow, Souvenir, Baltimore, Md. 20.00
Ruby Glass, Goblet, Souvenir, The Fair Store, Sparta, Wisconsin 15.00
Ruby Glass, Goblet, Souvenir, Victoria, 1914 .... 8.50
Ruby Glass, Goblet, Thumbprint, Souvenir, Allentown 25.00
Ruby Glass, Jar, Stained With Dome Cover, 6 In. 22.50
Ruby Glass, Measure, Candy, Souvenir, Alice 1904 .... 12.00
Ruby Glass, Measure, Candy, Souvenir, Winter Harbor, Me. 13.00
Ruby Glass, Muffineer, Button Arches, Souvenir, Niagara Falls, 1902 .... 25.00
Ruby Glass, Mug, Button Arches, Souvenir, Ruby, 1911 .... 22.50
Ruby Glass, Mug, Gold Lace Decoration, Sidney On Front, 3 3/4 In. 58.00
Ruby Glass, Mug, Graugers, '04, 1 7/8 In. 12.00
Ruby Glass, Mug, Nail, Souvenir, World's Fair, 1893 .... 25.00
Ruby Glass, Mug, New Hampshire, Souvenir, Mary, 4 1/2 In. 30.00
Ruby Glass, Mug, Souvenir, Colegrove, 3 In. 16.00
Ruby Glass, Mug, Souvenir, Gettysburg, 2 1/2 In. 12.00
Ruby Glass, Mug, Souvenir, Michigan City 15.00
Ruby Glass, Mug, Souvenir, Philadelphia, Pa., Heart Band 15.00
Ruby Glass, Mug, Souvenir, Rochester Minn. 15.00
Ruby Glass, Mug, Sunk Honeycomb 17.00
Ruby Glass, Mug, World's Fair, 1904 .... 15.00
Ruby Glass, Paperweight, Souvenir, Atlantic City 1899 .... 21.00
Ruby Glass, Pitcher & 4 Tumblers, Button Arches, Wells, Minn., Set 197.50
Ruby Glass, Pitcher, Arched Oval, Souvenir, Gettysburg, 1863, 4 In. 18.00
Ruby Glass, Pitcher, Bubble Pattern 25.00
Ruby Glass, Pitcher, Button Arches, Souvenir, Ayers, Boston, 1901, 4 In. 18.50
Ruby Glass, Pitcher, Souvenir, Heart Band, Souvenir Of Lisbon 16.00
Ruby Glass, Pitcher, Tankard, Button Arches, Souvenir, Mrs.Mitchell, 1909 .... 75.00
Ruby Glass, Pitcher, Tankard, Leaf & Flower 110.00
Ruby Glass, Pitcher, Thumbprint, Clear Reeded Handle, 9 X 7 In. 145.00
Ruby Glass, Pitcher, Thumbprint, Small, Dunkirk, 1892 .... 25.00

Ruby Glass, Pitcher, Water, Victoria, Riverside 110.00
Ruby Glass, Relish, Ribbed, Brass Holder, Oval 38.00
Ruby Glass, Rose Bowl, Rayed Base, Souvenir, Thorne, N.Dakota, 4 In. 12.00
Ruby Glass, Salt, Arched Ovals, Souvenir, Bloomsburg Fair 28.00
Ruby Glass, Saltshaker, Gold Locket On Chain 35.00
Ruby Glass, Saltshaker, Lulu 15.00
Ruby Glass, Saltshaker, Thumbprint, Souvenir, World's Fair, 1893 .... 18.00
Ruby Glass, Shoe, Illinois State Fair, 1941, 5 In. 28.00
Ruby Glass, Souvenir, Gettysburg, 1863, 1 7/8 In. 14.50
Ruby Glass, Spooner, Triple Triangle 42.00
Ruby Glass, Sugar & Creamer, Pearl, Souvenir, 1, 000 Islands, 1897 .... 25.00
Ruby Glass, Sugar, Block Band, Pat.5/20/1873, 8 1/2 In. 42.00
Ruby Glass, Sugar, Covered, Royal Crystal 49.50
Ruby Glass, Sugar, Souvenir, Thorne, N.D. 16.50
Ruby Glass, Syrup, Blocked Thumbprint Band, Old Orchard, 1906 .... 85.00
Ruby Glass, Toothpick, Box With Box, Souvenir, Old Orchard 35.00
Ruby Glass, Toothpick, Button Arches, Souvenir, Detriot, Mich. 17.00
Ruby Glass, Toothpick, Button Arches, Souvenir, Lippitt, R.I. 16.00
Ruby Glass, Toothpick, Dated 1899, Scalloped & Sawtooth Upper Edge 21.00
Ruby Glass, Toothpick, Leaf Etching 30.00
Ruby Glass, Toothpick, Souvenir, Freeport, 1905 .... 15.00
Ruby Glass, Toothpick, Souvenir, New Bremen, Ohio 15.00
Ruby Glass, Toothpick, Souvenir, World's Fair, 1893 .... 26.00
Ruby Glass, Toothpick, The Prize 15.00
Ruby Glass, Tumbler, Button Arches, Ben, 1911 .... 25.00
Ruby Glass, Tumbler, Button Arches, Satin Band 22.50
Ruby Glass, Tumbler, Elk's Carnival, 1899 .... 30.00
Ruby Glass, Tumbler, Hannibal, Mo., Pressed Glass, Button Arches, 4 In. 15.00
Ruby Glass, Tumbler, Lacy Medallion, Souvenir, Montrose, 1900 .... 18.50
Ruby Glass, Tumbler, Lord's Prayer On Side 20.00
Ruby Glass, Tumbler, Ribbed Thumbprint 16.00
Ruby Glass, Tumbler, Souvenir, Atlanta Exposition, 1895 .... 35.00
Ruby Glass, Tumbler, Souvenir, Cleo, Oklahoma 15.00
Ruby Glass, Tumbler, Souvenir, From Glace Bay 17.75
Ruby Glass, Tumbler, Souvenir, Star Of Bethlehem 23.50
Ruby Glass, Tumbler, 1893 .... 24.00
Ruby Glass, Vase, Footed, Intaglio Floral, Miter & Flute Cut, 10 1/4 In., Pair 115.00
Ruby Glass, Vase, Notched Top, Florals, Leaves In Gold, Brass Base, 8 1/2 In. 135.00
Ruby Glass, Vase, Prism Panel, Souvenir, Gettysburg, 1863, 6 In. 36.00
Ruby Glass, Vase, Small Thumbprint, 6 X 5 In. 49.00
Ruby Glass, Vase, Souvenir, Niagara Falls 9.00
Ruby Glass, Vase, Trumpet, Clear Base & Stem, 6 In. 19.00
Ruby Glass, Water Set, Button And Arches, Souvenir, Wells, Minnesota, 5 Piece 197.50
Ruby Glass, Wine, Souvenir, Dakota, World's Fair, 1893 .... 26.00
Ruby Glass, Wine, Thumbprint 34.00
Rudolstadt, Bust, Woman, Signed, 9 In. 115.00
Rudolstadt, Ewer, Decorated, 2 Handles, 14 In. 65.00
Rudolstadt, Hatpin Holder, Ivory Color, Pink Roses, 5 1/2 In. 15.00
Rudolstadt, Plate, Child's, Tiny Snow Flake Elves, Signed, Germany 12.00
Rudolstadt, Set Of Dishes, Toy, Happy Fats, 18 Piece 225.00
Rudolstadt, Syrup, Underplate, Roses, Leaves, Gold Scalloped Ground 30.00
Rudolstadt, Tea Set, Child's, For 6 .... 65.00
Rudolstadt, Vase, Cream Color, Floral, Gold Handles, 7 In. 55.00
Rudolstadt, Vase, Floral On Matte Cream, 1890s, 7 1/4 X 4 In. 47.50

Rumrill Pottery was designed by George Rumrill of Little Rock, Arkansas. From 1930 to 1933, it was produced by the Red Wing Pottery of Red Wing, Minnesota. In 1938 production was transferred to the Shawnee Pottery, Zanesville, Ohio.

Rumrill, Candleholder, Sticker, 8 In., Pair 20.00
Rumrill, Decanter, Green 15.00
Rumrill, Teapot, Green Shading 12.00
Rumrill, Vase, Glossy Orange & Brown, Fluted, 7 1/2 In. 12.50
Rumrill, Vase, Orange, Brown Accents, Scroll Handles, 7 In. 16.00
Rumrill, Vase, Swirled Shape, Cream With Brown, 7 In. 18.00

Rumrill, Vase, 2-Eared, Accordion Pleated Base, Cone Top, White On Blue, 7 In. 20.00
Ruskin, Vase, Green Souffle, 4 In. 95.00
Sabino, Ashtray, Shell, 5 1/2 X 3 1/2 In. 18.00
Sabino, Ashtray, Shell, 7 X 4 In. 30.50
Sabino, Ashtray, Swallow, 3 1/2 In. 14.00
Sabino, Ashtray, Swallow, 4 3/4 In. 19.00
Sabino, Ashtray, Violet, 4 1/2 In. 19.00
Sabino, Berry Bowl, 5 3/4 In. 32.00
Sabino, Bottle, Perfume, Frieze Of 5 Women, Blown Out, 6 1/4 In. 42.00
Sabino, Bottle, Perfume, 6 In. 41.00
Sabino, Bottle, Petalia, 5 1/2 X 3 1/4 In. 36.00
Sabino, Bowl, Shell, 6 1/4 In. 55.00
Sabino, Bowl, Translucent Blue, Birds In Flight, C.1925, 4 3/4 X 7/8 In. 48.00
Sabino, Box, Powder 34.00
Sabino, Figurine, Baby Bird, 2 In. 15.00
Sabino, Figurine, Bird, Wings Out, 1/2 In. 10.50
Sabino, Figurine, Bird, Wings Up, 1/2 In. 10.50
Sabino, Figurine, Butterfly, Large 93.00
Sabino, Figurine, Butterfly, Wings Closed, 2 3/4 In. 17.00
Sabino, Figurine, Butterfly, Wings Open, 2 3/4 In. 18.00
Sabino, Figurine, Butterfly, 6 In. 82.00
Sabino, Figurine, Cat, 2 In. 15.00
Sabino, Figurine, Cherub, 2 In. 14.00
Sabino, Figurine, Chick, Wings Down, 2 1/2 X 2 In. 29.00
Sabino, Figurine, Cluster Of Three Birds 114.00
Sabino, Figurine, Dove, Head Down, 1 3/4 In. 14.00
Sabino, Figurine, Dove, Head Up, 1 3/4 In. 14.00
Sabino, Figurine, Dragonfly, Opalescent, Upstretched Wings, 6 In. 42.50
Sabino, Figurine, Draped Statue 166.00
Sabino, Figurine, Elephant, 2 In. 14.00
Sabino, Figurine, Fighting Bird, 2 3/4 In. 15.00
Sabino, Figurine, Heron, 7 1/2 In. 64.00
Sabino, Figurine, Hopping Bird, 1 3/4 In. 15.00
Sabino, Figurine, Jumping Bird, 3 1/2 X 3 1/4 In. 25.00
Sabino, Figurine, Jumping Chick, 3 3/4 In. 29.00
Sabino, Figurine, Kingfisher, 6-Sided Base, 4 1/2 In. 38.50
Sabino, Figurine, Mocking Bird, 6 X 4 1/2 In. 50.00
Sabino, Figurine, Mouse, Frosted, On Base, Signed, 3 In. 50.00
Sabino, Figurine, Mouse, 3 In. 35.00
Sabino, Figurine, Nesting Bird, 2 X 1 1/4 In. 15.00
Sabino, Figurine, Nude Woman Kneeling, 3 Pouter Pigeons, 6 1/2 In. 170.00
Sabino, Figurine, Nude Woman, Art Deco, 7 In. 115.00
Sabino, Figurine, Owl, 4 1/2 In. .... 32.50 To 46.00
Sabino, Figurine, Pekinese Dog, 2 In. 14.00
Sabino, Figurine, Pekinese Dog, 3 3/4 X 2 3/4 In. 46.00
Sabino, Figurine, Perched Bird, 4 X 4 X 3 3/4 In. 33.00
Sabino, Figurine, Pheasant, 3 1/2 In. 19.00
Sabino, Figurine, Pigeon, 6 In. 103.00
Sabino, Figurine, Rabbit, 2 In. 14.00
Sabino, Figurine, Rooster, 3 1/2 In. 19.00
Sabino, Figurine, Rooster, 7 X 6 In. 150.00
Sabino, Figurine, Scottie Dog, 3 3/4 In. 42.00
Sabino, Figurine, Scottie Dog, 4 X 3 3/8 In. 34.00
Sabino, Figurine, Shivering Bird, 3 1/4 X 2 1/2 In. 31.00
Sabino, Figurine, Small Fish 16.50
Sabino, Figurine, Snail Shell, 3 X 2 In. 33.00
Sabino, Figurine, Squirrel, 3 In. 19.00
Sabino, Figurine, St.Theresa 44.00
Sabino, Figurine, Standing Butterfly, Opal, Iridescent Luster, Signed, 6 In. 150.00
Sabino, Figurine, Statue, Draped, 7 1/4 In. 150.00
Sabino, Figurine, Statue, Nude, 6 3/4 In. 88.00
Sabino, Figurine, Swan, 2 In. 14.00
Sabino, Figurine, Teasing Bird, Wing Down, 3 X 2 1/2 In. 37.00
Sabino, Figurine, Turtle, 2 X 3/4 In. 14.00
Sabino, Figurine, Venus De Milo, Large 41.00

Sabino, Figurine, Venus De Milo, 2 3/4 In. 18.00
Sabino, Figurine, Venus De Milo, 3 In. 19.00
Sabino, Figurine, Venus De Milo, 4 1/2 In. 35.00
Sabino, Fish Bowl, 5 In. 36.00
Sabino, Group, Cluster Of Three Birds, 5 In. 106.00
Sabino, Group, Cluster Of Two Birds, 4 1/2 X 3 1/2 In. 76.00
Sabino, Group, Five Birds On A Branch, 8 X 7 In. 395.00
Sabino, Napkin Ring, 2 1/4 In. 14.00
Sabino, Prism Sign, 5 X 1 In. 19.00
Sabino, Tray, Sea Urchin, 7 1/4 In. 55.00
Sabino, Vase, Black, Undulating Lines, 4 1/2 In. 65.00
Saddle, Army, McCleenen 65.00
Saddle, Quebec Indian, Brass Officer's Tunic Buttons, Wooden Stirrups 200.00
Saddle, Western, Roping 25.00

Salopian ware was made by the Caughley Factory of England during the eighteenth century. The early pieces were in blue and white with some colored decorations. Many of the pieces called Salopian are elaborate color-transfer decorated tablewares made during the late nineteenth century.

Salopian, see also Caughley

Salopian, Coffeepot, Deer Park Scene, Deep Blue, High Dome, C.1810 .... 195.00
Salopian, Cup & Saucer, Blue-Printed Temple Pattern, Fluted, C.1780 .... 105.00
Salopian, Cup & Saucer, Handleless, The Inn, Blue Transfer 55.00
Salopian, Cup, Handleless, Boy, House, Sheep 30.00
Salopian, Plate, Dessert, Dresden Flowers, Blue S Mark, C.1785, 8 In. 145.00
Salopian, Saucer, Children, Dog, Nurse, Blue Edge, C.1790 .... 65.00

Salt Glaze, Pitcher, 8 1/2 In.

(See Page 556)

Salt & Pepper, see Pressed Glass, Porcelain, etc.

Salt glaze is a hard, shiny glaze that was developed for pottery during the eighteenth century. It is still being made.

Salt Glaze, Bowl, Deep Blue On White, 8 1/4 In. 40.00
Salt Glaze, Bowl, Mixing, Apricot, 7 1/4 In. 40.00
Salt Glaze, Bowl, Mixing, Apricot, 9 1/4 In. 25.00
Salt Glaze, Crock, Butter, Lewistown Pottery, 10 In. 22.50
Salt Glaze, Crock, Cream, Gray, Cobalt Leaves, Pouring Spout, 8 1/4 X 5 In. 65.00
Salt Glaze, Crock, J.Swank & Co., Johnstown, Pa., Tan, Cobalt Leaves, 13 In. 85.00
Salt Glaze, Cuspidor, Green & Tan, Vines & Leaves 50.00
Salt Glaze, Jar, Greenland, Impressed, 9 3/4 In. 7.50
Salt Glaze, Jug, N.Clark & Co., Mt.Morris, N.Y., Cobalt Trim, Ovoid, Gallon 68.00
Salt Glaze, Pan, Milk, A.G.C.Dipple, Lewistown, Pa., Yellow, 9 1/2 In. 17.50
Salt Glaze, Pitcher, Basket-Weave Pattern, Registered 1864, 7 In. 45.00
Salt Glaze, Pitcher, Bluebells & Leaves, 8 1/2 In. 135.00
Salt Glaze, Pitcher, Cattails, Branch Handle Tied With Rope, 10 In. 42.00
Salt Glaze, Pitcher, Gray, Octagonal, Blue Cameos Of People, Serpent Handle 42.00
Salt Glaze, Pitcher, Gray, Raised Jewel-Like Design, Pewter Lid, Quart, 6 In. 70.00
Salt Glaze, Pitcher, Light Blue, Pear-Shaped, Raised Ferns, Pewter Lid, 8 In. 45.00

Salt Glaze, Pitcher, Light Blue, Raised Daisy & Leaf, Fabric Texture, 9 In. 35.00
Salt Glaze, Pitcher, Pewter Lid, Good Samaritan, Jones & Walley, 1842, 6 In. 140.00
Salt Glaze, Pitcher, Pewter Lid, White, Raised Berry & Leaf, 8 In. 55.00
Salt Glaze, Pitcher, Pewter Top, Greek Figure Decoration 75.00
Salt Glaze, Pitcher, Raised Berry & Leaf, Pewter Lid, Fancy Handle, 8 In. 55.00
Salt Glaze, Pitcher, Relief Peasant, C.1865, 8 1/2 In. 82.00
Salt Glaze, Pitcher, Sheaf Of Wheat, Covered, 9 1/4 In. 110.00
Salt Glaze, Pitcher, 8 1/2 In. .... *Illus* 125.00
Salt Glaze, Plate, Bread, Give Us This Day Our Daily Bread, 13 In. 95.00
Salt Glaze, Teapot, English, C.1840, Cornflower Blue, Vines & Scrolls, 7 In. 48.00

Sampler, see Textile, Sampler

Samson and Company, a French firm specializing in the reproduction of collectible wares of many countries and periods, was founded in Paris in the early nineteenth century. Chelsea, Meissen, Famille Verte, and Oriental Lowestoft are some of the wares that have been reproduced by the company. The company uses a variety of marks to distinguish its reproductions. It is still in operation

Samson Type, Vase, White On White Line Decoration, Enamel Floral, 6 In. 40.00
Samson, Cachepot, Strasbourg-Style Floral, Swastika Mark, 8 1/2 In. 75.00
Samson, Figurine, Cockatoo, Blue Underglaze Mark, Yellow On White, 18 In. 275.00
Samson, Plate, Hand-Painted Bird & Flowers, 11 In. 20.00
Samson, Vase, C.1845, 6 1/8 In., Pair 275.00
Sand Babies, Pitcher, Enamel, Royal Bayreuth, Signed In Blue, 2 3/4 In. 95.00
Sand Babies, Sugar & Creamer, Royal Bayreuth 200.00

Sandwich glass is any one of the myriad types of glass made by the Boston and Sandwich Glass Works in Sandwich, Massachusetts, between 1825 and 1888. It is often very difficult to be sure whether a piece was really made at the Sandwich factory because so many types were made there and similar pieces were made at other glass factories. The McK numbers refer to the book "American Glass" by George P. and Helen McKearin.

Sandwich Glass, see also Pressed Glass, etc.

Sandwich Glass, Basket, Cased, White, Rose Inside, Clear Thorn Handle, 8 In. 195.00
Sandwich Glass, Basket, End-Of-Day Spatter, Sapphire Thorn Handle, 7 In. 65.00
Sandwich Glass, Basket, White, Butterscotch Interior, Clear Handle, 6 In. 85.00
Sandwich Glass, Bell, Smoke, Vines & Floral, Cobalt Rim, C.1850, 5 In. 35.00
Sandwich Glass, Bobeche, Turquoise Blue, Flint, Pair 25.00
Sandwich Glass, Bottle, Cologne, Blue, Tapers Inward From Shoulder, 7 In. 90.00
Sandwich Glass, Bottle, Cologne, Canary, Loop 215.00
Sandwich Glass, Bottle, Cologne, Violet Purple, Paneled, Label, 11 In. 120.00
Sandwich Glass, Bottle, Scent, Blown, Three Mold 45.00
Sandwich Glass, Bottle, Scent, Opalescent, Pewter Screw Cap, Onion Shape 100.00
Sandwich Glass, Bottle, Smelling, Opaque, Screw-Type Tinned Metal Cap 39.00
Sandwich Glass, Bottle, Toilet, 3 Mold, Purple, Blue, Blown 140.00
Sandwich Glass, Bowl, Daisy, Lacy, 8 In. 80.00
Sandwich Glass, Bowl, Geometric, Flint, 7 1/2 .... 22.00
Sandwich Glass, Bowl, Gothic Arch, Lacy, Shallow, 9 1/4 In. 80.00
Sandwich Glass, Bowl, Lyre & Heart, Shallow, 3/8 In.Thick, 9 1/4 In. 195.00
Sandwich Glass, Bowl, Oak Leaf, Lacy, 8 In. 40.00
Sandwich Glass, Bowl, Plume, Lacy, 7 1/2 In. 32.50
Sandwich Glass, Bowl, Princess Feather, Flint, 7 1/2 In. 38.00
Sandwich Glass, Bowl, Princess Feather, Lacy, 6 5/8 In. 20.00
Sandwich Glass, Bowl, Rose & Thistle, Lacy, 8 In. 45.00
Sandwich Glass, Candlestick, Canary Yellow, 7 In., Pair 265.00
Sandwich Glass, Candlestick, Canary, Petal & Loop, 7 In., Pair 270.00
Sandwich Glass, Candlestick, Clambroth, Blue Cup, 7 3/4 In. 135.00
Sandwich Glass, Candlestick, Hexagon, Clambroth, Flint 160.00
Sandwich Glass, Candlestick, Opaque Blue & Clambroth, Dolphin, 10 1/2 In. 525.00
Sandwich Glass, Celery, Amethyst, Block & Punty, Flint, 9 1/2 In. 300.00
Sandwich Glass, Celery, Gothic Arch, Printie, Panel & Loop, Flint 110.00
Sandwich Glass, Claret, Flat Diamond & Panel, Flint 120.00
Sandwich Glass, Compote, Paneled Diamonds, Lacy, Knob Stem, 6 1/2 In., Pair 185.00
Sandwich Glass, Compote, Petal & Loop, Flint, 11 1/4 X 9 In. 185.00
Sandwich Glass, Creamer, Cobalt, Blown, Three Mold 400.00

Sandwich Glass, Cup Plate, Henry Clay 25.00
Sandwich Glass, Cup Plate, Wedding 25.00
Sandwich Glass, Decanter, Blown, Three Mold, 1/2 Pint 150.00
Sandwich Glass, Decanter, Steeple Stopper, Bull's-Eye & Flute, 12 In., Pair 250.00
Sandwich Glass, Dish, Honey, Lacy Oak Leaf 35.00
Sandwich Glass, Dish, Pheasant Cover, Footed, C.1870, Oval 125.00
Sandwich Glass, Drawer Pull, Flint, Set Of 3 .... 12.00
Sandwich Glass, Finger Bowl & Underplate, Cranberry, Threaded, Ruffled 100.00
Sandwich Glass, Flask, Cobalt, Swirled, Open Pontil, 6 1/4 In. 135.00
Sandwich Glass, Jar, Pomade, Black Bear, Flint, 3 3/4 In. 155.00
Sandwich Glass, Jar, Pomade, Opalescent, Muzzled Bear, X Bazin, Phila., 4 In. 165.00
Sandwich Glass, Lamp, see Lamp
Sandwich Glass, Morning Glory, Salt, Individual 100.00
Sandwich Glass, Newel Post, Blue Clambroth, Oval Hobs, Brass Ferrules, 8 In. 60.00
Sandwich Glass, Paperweight, Scrambled, Flint, 2 1/2 X 1 In. 95.00
Sandwich Glass, Pitcher, Blue, Overshot, Ribbed Amber Shell Handle, 7 In. 95.00
Sandwich Glass, Pitcher, Cranberry, Gold Overlay Of Vines, 2 1/2 In. 45.00
Sandwich Glass, Pitcher, Hobnail, Peachblow 700.00
Sandwich Glass, Pitcher, Milk, Tankard Shape, Threaded, Cranberry, 6 In. 95.00
Sandwich Glass, Pitcher, Water, Overshot, Ice Pocket, Applied Handle, C.1865 .... 75.00
Sandwich Glass, Plate, Cup, Eagle, Dated 1831 .... 35.00
Sandwich Glass, Plate, Heart, Lacy, 6 In. 65.00
Sandwich Glass, Plate, Oblong, Dog & Rooster, 8 In. 60.00
Sandwich Glass, Plate, Shell, Lacy, 6 In. 35.00
Sandwich Glass, Plate, Toddy, Grapevine & Harp, Flint 20.00
Sandwich Glass, Plate, Toddy, Lacy Grapevine & Harp, 4 3/8 In. 20.00
Sandwich Glass, Plate, Toddy, Olive Green, Waffle & Gothic Arch, Lacy, 6 In. 125.00
Sandwich Glass, Plate, Toddy, Peacock's-Eye, 5 1/4 In. 35.00
Sandwich Glass, Plate, Toddy, Roman Rosette, Lacy, 5 In. 24.00
Sandwich Glass, Pull, Drawer, Opalescent, Flint, 2 In. 14.50
Sandwich Glass, Pull, Drawer, Opalescent, Set Of 8 .... 200.00
Sandwich Glass, Pull, Drawer, 6 Petal, Flint, 2 1/4 In., Set Of 3 .... 18.00
Sandwich Glass, Rose Bowl, Pink Satin, Crimped Top, 4 X 3 1/2 In. 60.00
Sandwich Glass, Salt, Amber, Bird With Berry In Mouth 36.00
Sandwich Glass, Salt, Cobalt, Lacy, 3 In. 165.00
Sandwich Glass, Salt, Individual, Morning Glory 80.00
Sandwich Glass, Salt, Lacy, New England Glass Co. On Base, Flint 65.00
Sandwich Glass, Salt, Lightly Polished Rim, Flint 25.00
Sandwich Glass, Salt, Master, Footed, Hexagonal, Flint 22.50
Sandwich Glass, Salt, Master, Rectangular, Flowers In Basket, Signed N.E.G. 125.00
Sandwich Glass, Salt, Master, Scalloped Base 21.50
Sandwich Glass, Sauce, Crossed Swords, Lacy, Flint, 4 1/2 In. 18.00
Sandwich Glass, Sauce, Peacock's-Eye, Flint, 4 1/4 In. 20.00
Sandwich Glass, Sauce, Princess Feather 15.00
Sandwich Glass, Sauce, Stippled Rays 10.00
Sandwich Glass, Sauce, Stippled Rays, Lacy, Flint 10.00
Sandwich Glass, Saucer, Lacy, Miniature 40.00
Sandwich Glass, Spill, Flint 28.50
Sandwich Glass, Sugar, Covered, Lacy, 6 In. 255.00
Sandwich Glass, Sugar, Covered, Paneled, Lacy, Footed 110.00
Sandwich Glass, Sugar, 8 Panels, Lacy, Varied Pattern, Footed 110.00
Sandwich Glass, Syrup, Star & Buckle, Tin Lid, Hexagonal, 7 In. 110.00
Sandwich Glass, Tieback, Blue, Pewter Stem, 4 1/4 In., Pair 56.00
Sandwich Glass, Tieback, Blue, 6 Petal, Pewter Stem, Flint, 4 1/2 In. 28.00
Sandwich Glass, Tieback, Curtain, Rosette, Pewter Shank, 3 1/2 In., Pair 40.00
Sandwich Glass, Tieback, Fiery Opalescent, Lacy, Pewter Screws, 4 In., Pair 60.00
Sandwich Glass, Tieback, Opalescent, Pewter Stem, 4 1/2 In. 28.00
Sandwich Glass, Tieback, Opalescent, 3 In., Pair 30.00
Sandwich Glass, Tray, Butterfly, Lacy, 8 1/16 In. 185.00
Sandwich Glass, Tumbler, Child's, Clear 50.00
Sandwich Glass, Tumbler, Emerald Green, Framed Ovals, Hexagonal Base, 3 In. 75.00
Sandwich Glass, Tumbler, Mitered Diamond Point, Amber 15.00
Sandwich Glass, Tumbler, Overshot, Footed 55.00
Sandwich Glass, Tureen & Tray, Covered, Canary, Miniature 650.00
Sandwich Glass, Tureen, Covered, Lacy, Miniature 125.00

Sandwich Glass, Vase, Amber Icicle, 9 In. 285.00
Sandwich Glass, Vase, Amethyst Loop Pattern, 9 In., Pair 1400.00
Sandwich Glass, Vase, Blue With Small Bird Enamel Decoration, 6 In. 25.00
Sandwich Glass, Vase, Blue, White, & Clear, Geometric Cuttings, 10 1/2 In. 195.00
Sandwich Glass, Vase, Light Beige, Bird Enamel Decoration, 6 In. 25.00
Sandwich Glass, Vase, Stork, Beige With Enamel, 8 In., Pair 85.00
Sandwich Glass, Vase, Stork, Taunton Plated Holder, Pink, Enamel, Pair 90.00

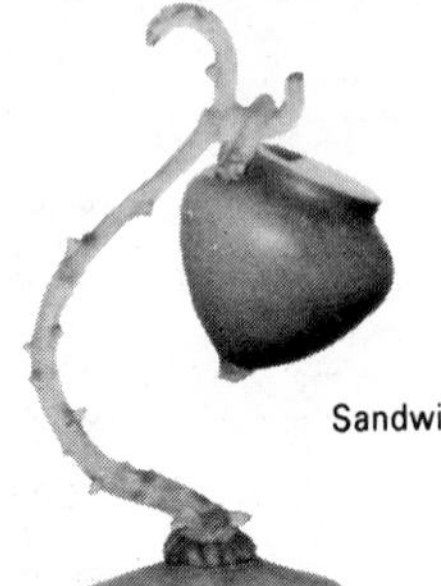

Sandwich Glass, Whimsey, Wild Rose Satin Glass, 7 1/4 In.

Sandwich Glass, Whimsey, Wild Rose Satin Glass, 7 1/4 In. *Illus* 450.00
Sandwich Glass, Witch's Ball, Blown, White, Pink & Blue, 3 1/4 In. 100.00
Sandwich, Plate, Lacy, Shell Pattern, 6 In. 42.50

Sarreguemines pottery was first made in Lorraine, France, about 1770. Most of the pieces found today date from the late nineteenth century.

Sarreguemines, see also Kate Greenaway

Sarreguemines, Dish, Hen Cover 40.00
Sarreguemines, Pitcher, Figural, Cat, Gray, 8 1/4 In. 20.00
Sarreguemines, Pitcher, Inverted Heads, French Motto 45.00
Sarreguemines, Pitcher, Man's Head Shape, Smiling, Roman Hat, 7 In. 45.00
Sarreguemines, Toby Mug, Fat, Happy Face, Bushy Brows, Neck Ruffle, 7 1/2 In. 80.00
Sarreguemines, Toby Mug, John Bull, 7 In. 60.00

Satin glass is a late-nineteenth-century art glass. It has a dull finish that is caused by a hydrofluoric acid vapor treatment. Satin glass was made in many colors and sometimes had applied decorations.

Satin Glass, Basket, Looped Camphor Handle, Yellow, Rose & Blue, 8 1/4 In. 3000.00
Satin Glass, Basket, Purple, White Inside, 8 In. 85.00
Satin Glass, Basket, Rainbow, Camphor Handle, Yellow, Rose, Blue, 8 1/4 In. 3000.00
Satin Glass, Bobeche, Pale Yellow, Applied Camphor Rim, 4 In., Pair 38.00
Satin Glass, Bobeche, Yellow, Frilled Camphor Rim, Swirled Rib 19.00
Satin Glass, Bottle, Perfume, Pink To Rose, Enameled Ruffled Edge, Stopper 145.00
Satin Glass, Bowl, Black, Gold Trim 23.00
Satin Glass, Bowl, Bride's, Blue, 16 In. 575.00
Satin Glass, Bowl, Embossed Swans, Lily Pads, Cattails, Footed, 13 1/2 In. 50.00
Satin Glass, Bowl, Green, Quilted, White Rim, Silver Plate Stand, 5 In. 45.00
Satin Glass, Bowl, Mother-Of-Pearl Threaded, 3 1/2 X 6 1/2 In. 175.00
Satin Glass, Bowl, Pink, White Lined, Petit Point, No Basket, 9 X 5 3/4 In. 2500.00
Satin Glass, Bowl, Swans, Lily Pads, Cattails, Footed, 13 1/2 In. 50.00
Satin Glass, Bowl, Swirled, 5 1/2 X 4 In. 50.00
Satin Glass, Bowl, Tricorner, Blue With Fold Over, Enameled, 6 In. 60.00
Satin Glass, Bowl, 3 Flower, Joined Together, Melon Ribbed, Baby Blue, 3 In. 85.00
Satin Glass, Candlestick, Blue, 10 In., Pair 32.00
Satin Glass, Compote, Blue To White, Camphor Ribbon Edge, 7 1/2 In. 155.00
Satin Glass, Compote, Covered, Black, Embossed Floral, 7 1/2 In. 65.00
Satin Glass, Compote, Rose To White, Camphor Ribbon Edge, 7 1/2 In. 185.00
Satin Glass, Console Bowl & Base, Black, Flared Top, 9 1/2 In. 14.00
Satin Glass, Cracker Jar, Wild Roses, Silver Lid And Bail, Letters H P 65.00
Satin Glass, Cruet, Vinegar, Pink 12.00
Satin Glass, Dish, Butter, Covered, Silver Underplate, Lusterlesss, Floral 80.00

Satin Glass, Ewer Vase, Blue, Overlay, Frosted Handle, White Lining, 10 In. 69.00
Satin Glass, Ewer Vase, Cased, Melon Ribbed, Camphor Handle, 10 1/2 In. 125.00
Satin Glass, Ewer Vase, Pink, Violets & Orange Scrolls, Clear Handle, 5 In. 35.00
Satin Glass, Ewer, Applied Camphor Handle, Green, Enameled Flowers 125.00
Satin Glass, Ewer, Applied Camphor Thorn Handle, Rose To Pink, 8 1/2 In. 395.00
Satin Glass, Ewer, Apricot To White, Cased, Ribbed, Frosted Handle, 10 In. 114.00
Satin Glass, Ewer, Blue Diamond Quilt, Cased In White, Frosted Handle, 10 In. 200.00
Satin Glass, Ewer, Blue, Camphor Edge & Twisted Handle, Enameled, 10 In. 75.00
Satin Glass, Ewer, Blue, Enamel Floral, 7 In. 60.00
Satin Glass, Ewer, Blue, Melon Ribbed, Crimped Frosted Applied Handle, 9 In. 75.00
Satin Glass, Ewer, Butterflies On White, English, 12 In. 265.00
Satin Glass, Ewer, Cerulean Blue, Herringbone, Crystal Handle, 12 1/4 In. 525.00
Satin Glass, Ewer, Coin Gold Blossoms On White, Letters And Numbers 145.00
Satin Glass, Ewer, New England, Yellow, Red Orange Center, 7 In. 65.00
Satin Glass, Ewer, Peachblow, Cupid On Gilt Handle, Gold Floral, 25 In. 650.00
Satin Glass, Ewer, Pink Shaded, Overlay, Frosted Handle, White Lining, 9 In. 68.00
Satin Glass, Ewer, Pink, White Cased, Butterflies & Red Beads, 9 In., Pair 185.00
Satin Glass, Ewer, Rainbow Mother-Of-Pearl, Amber Thorn Handle, 5 In. 395.00
Satin Glass, Ewer, Robin's-Egg Blue, Enamel Butterfly & Floral, 9 X 6 In. 150.00
Satin Glass, Jar, Biscuit, Blue, Ribbed, Silver Plate Fittings 95.00
Satin Glass, Jar, Biscuit, Rose Color, Florette, Silver Fittings 185.00
Satin Glass, Jar, Corset Shape, Lusterless, Florals, Metal Rim 89.50
Satin Glass, Jar, Cracker, Blue, Peach Rose, Enameled, Silver Fittings 165.00
Satin Glass, Jar, Cracker, Florette, Yellow Satin, Cover 135.00
Satin Glass, Jar, Cracker, Open Heart Arches, Lusterless, Silver-Plate Rim 89.50
Satin Glass, Jar, Cracker, Red, Enamel Cosmos, Silver Fittings 165.00
Satin Glass, Jar, Cracker, White To Orchid, Van Bergh Silver-Plate Fittings 90.00
Satin Glass, Jar, Cracker, Yellow To White, Blossoms, Silver-Plate Fittings 150.00
Satin Glass, Jar, Powder, Green, Figural, Covered, Toussant 20.00
Satin Glass, Lamp Base, Brass Font, Burner & Chimney, Dainty Scroll, C.1880 .... 450.00
Satin Glass, Lamp Base, Drape, With Chimney 95.00
Satin Glass, Lamp, Amber, Peacocks Cut To Clear, 13 1/4 In. 45.00
Satin Glass, Lamp, Cut Velvet, Lander, Miniature, 10 In. 295.00
Satin Glass, Lamp, Fairy, Clarke Candle Cup, Blue & White, Ruffled, 5 In. 210.00
Satin Glass, Lamp, Fairy, Clarke, Rose Color, Diamond-Quilted Pearl, 4 In. 95.00
Satin Glass, Lamp, Fairy, Clear Clarke Base, Green Swirl, 4 In. 80.00
Satin Glass, Lamp, Gone With The Wind, Ball Shade, Swirl Pattern, 22 In. 375.00
Satin Glass, Lamp, Gone With The Wind, Red, Bull's-Eye, Ornate Slip, 25 In. 595.00
Satin Glass, Lamp, Hand, Oil, Rainbow Mother-Of-Pearl, Camphor Feet, 6 In. 180.00
Satin Glass, Lamp, Hanging, Red, Puffed-Out Regal Iris 250.00
Satin Glass, Lamp, Painted Blue Flowers, Hour-Glass Shape, Miniature, 1868 .... 65.00
Satin Glass, Lamp, Peg, Pink Quilted Tank 525.00
Satin Glass, Lamp, Peg, Pink To Deep Rose, Drape & Buttons, Brass Base, 20 In. 325.00
Satin Glass, Lamp, Red, Puffed-Out Regal Iris, Ceiling Pull-Down Canopy 250.00
Satin Glass, Lamp, Red, Ruffled Drapery, Square Base, Miniature 245.00
Satin Glass, Muffineer, Pink Opaque, Melon Ribbed, Forget-Me-Nots 95.00
Satin Glass, Muffineer, White, Pewter Top 135.00
Satin Glass, Pitcher, Rose To Pink Base, Applied Pink Camphor Handle, 5 In. 27.50
Satin Glass, Pitcher, Water, Rose Color, Florette, Camphor Handle, 7 1/4 In. 225.00
Satin Glass, Plate, Cookie, Black, Looped Center Handle, Scalloped, 9 1/2 In. 10.00
Satin Glass, Plate, Painted Strawberries Center, 12 In. 25.00
Satin Glass, Plate, White, 10 1/2 In. 20.00
Satin Glass, Rose Bowl, Blue Overlay, Flowers, White Lining, 4 In. 98.00
Satin Glass, Rose Bowl, Blue, Cased, Crimped Top, 4 1/2 In. 65.00
Satin Glass, Rose Bowl, Blue, Diamond Quilted, White Lined, Crimped, 7 In. 100.00
Satin Glass, Rose Bowl, Blue, Herringbone, 8 Crimp Top, 3 In. 50.00
Satin Glass, Rose Bowl, Blue, White Lining, Crimped Top, 4 1/2 In. 55.00
Satin Glass, Rose Bowl, Deep Rose To Light Pink, White Cased, Crimped, 4 In. 45.00
Satin Glass, Rose Bowl, Deep To Light Blue, White Cased, Crimped, 3 3/4 In. 40.00
Satin Glass, Rose Bowl, Diamond Quilted, White Matte Lining, Blue, 6 In. 255.00
Satin Glass, Rose Bowl, Lime Green, Brown Bird & Green Leaves, 6 In. 105.00
Satin Glass, Rose Bowl, Pink To White, Cased, Crimped Top, 4 1/4 In. 65.00
Satin Glass, Rose Bowl, Pink To White, Rough Pontil, 6 In. 150.00
Satin Glass, Rose Bowl, Pink, Maize, White Cased, 7 1/2 In. 70.00
Satin Glass, Rose Bowl, Tricornered, Blue, Fold-Over And Crimped Rim, Enamel 50.00

Satin Glass, Rose Bowl, White Cased, Deep Rose To Light Base, 3 In. 82.00
Satin Glass, Rose Bowl, White To Yellow, Crimped Ruffled Top, 3 1/4 In. 65.00
Satin Glass, Rose Bowl, Wine To White, White Lining, Ruffled Top, 4 In. 58.00
Satin Glass, Rose Bowl, Yellow To White, Shell & Seaweed, White Cased, 4 In. 95.00
Satin Glass, Rose Bowl, Yellow, Crimped Top, 4 In. 55.00
Satin Glass, Rose Bowl, Yellow, Crimped Top, 7 In. 75.00
Satin Glass, Rose Bowl, Yellow, Diamond-Quilted Mother-Of-Pearl, 5 1/4 In. 195.00
Satin Glass, Rose Bowl, Yellow, White Lining, Crimped Top, 3 1/2 In. 50.00
Satin Glass, Salt & Pepper, Apples 22.00
Satin Glass, Salt & Pepper, Decorated Figures, Pair 190.00
Satin Glass, Salt & Pepper, Green & White, Loop & Daisy, Pink Thistle 125.00
Satin Glass, Salt & Pepper, Pink, Florette 50.00
Satin Glass, Salt & Pepper, Squatty Lobe .... 120.00 To 135.00
Satin Glass, Salt, Green, Duck, 5 In. 9.50
Satin Glass, Saltshaker, Forget-Me-Nots 18.00
Satin Glass, Shade, Blue, Scalloped Edge, 5 In. 90.00
Satin Glass, Shade, Gas, Gold, Ribbed, Etched Flowers, 2 1/4 In. At Top 26.00
Satin Glass, Sugar, Paneled, Hand-Painted Floral, Silver Handles 39.00
Satin Glass, Sugar, Pink, Quilted, Silver-Plate Handles & Rim 120.00
Satin Glass, Syrup, Squatty, Fishscale Pattern, Clear Handle, 4 1/2 In. 95.00
Satin Glass, Toothpick, Ribbed With Floral Decoration, Beaded Top 55.00
Satin Glass, Tumbler, Blue, Enamel Apple Blossoms 175.00
Satin Glass, Tumbler, Cream Color, Pink & Maroon Floral, White Lined 25.00
Satin Glass, Tumbler, Floretta, Pink 40.00
Satin Glass, Tumbler, Pale Blue, Diamond Lower Half, Upper Plain 45.00
Satin Glass, Tumbler, Rainbow, Diamond-Quilted Mother-Of-Pearl, Enameled 950.00
Satin Glass, Tumbler, Rainbow, Enameled Apple Blossoms, Diamond Quilt 950.00
Satin Glass, Tumbler, Rose To Pink, Yellow Coralene Seaweed 325.00
Satin Glass, Tumbler, Yellow To White, Diamond-Quilted Mother-Of-Pearl 295.00
Satin Glass, Tumbler, Yellow To White, Herringbone Mother-Of-Pearl 150.00
Satin Glass, Vase, Apricot, Ribbon Mother-Of-Pearl, White Lining, 5 1/4 In. 195.00
Satin Glass, Vase, Blue To Rose, Overlay, Applied Jewels, 9 5/8 In., Pair 168.00
Satin Glass, Vase, Bud, Blue, Clear Overlay, White Lined, Violets, 3 3/4 In. 80.00
Satin Glass, Vase, Bulbous, Blue To Cranberry, Hand-Painted Flowers, 11 In. 45.00
Satin Glass, Vase, Cased, Pink To Rose, Enamel Floral, Gold Leaves, 9 1/2 In. 85.00
Satin Glass, Vase, Coffee Color, Random Pull-Ups, Acid Finish, Footed, 10 In. 155.00
Satin Glass, Vase, Deep Rose To White Base, Yellow Coralene, 8 In. 495.00
Satin Glass, Vase, Flared And Ruffled Top, Pink To Dark Orange, 6 In. 85.00
Satin Glass, Vase, Geese & Water Lilies, Blue Overlay, 8 3/8 In., Pair 175.00
Satin Glass, Vase, Green, Gold Bands, Enamel Irises, 11 X 4 In. 185.00
Satin Glass, Vase, Green, Sterling Silver Overlay Flowers, 6 In. 25.00
Satin Glass, Vase, Iridescent, Variegated Interior, Pinched, 9 1/2 In. 175.00
Satin Glass, Vase, Jack-In-The-Pulpit, Cream, Green Yellow Crimped Frill 68.00
Satin Glass, Vase, Jack-In-The-Pulpit, Pink Shading, C.1910, 13 In. 90.00
Satin Glass, Vase, Jack-In-The-Pulpit, Pink, White, & Camphor Stripes, 12 In. 125.00
Satin Glass, Vase, Melon Ribbed, Butterscotch Raindrop, Scalloped Edge 195.00
Satin Glass, Vase, Mosaic, Cobalt Blue, Chinese Red, Iridescent Inner Casing 125.00
Satin Glass, Vase, Pink To Apricot, Cased, Melon Ribbed, Enamel Bird, 10 In. 105.00
Satin Glass, Vase, Pink To White, Scalloped Rim, Blown, 7 In. 50.00
Satin Glass, Vase, Pink, Diamonds, Ruffled Top, 13 In. 75.00
Satin Glass, Vase, Pink, Herringbone Mother-Of-Pearl, 6 3/8 In. 118.00
Satin Glass, Vase, Pink, Quilted, Opalescent Overlay, White Lining, 14 In. 95.00
Satin Glass, Vase, Rainbow Mother-Of-Pearl, Coin Spot, White Cased, 10 In. 950.00
Satin Glass, Vase, Rainbow, Camphor Footed, 5 3/4 In. 1050.00
Satin Glass, Vase, Rainbow, Diamond Quilt, 8 1/2 /in. 950.00
Satin Glass, Vase, Rainbow, Ruffled Top, Camphor, Diamond Quilt, 5 1/8 In. 850.00
Satin Glass, Vase, Rose Color, Mother-Of-Pearl, Flower & Acorn, 5 1/2 In. 445.00
Satin Glass, Vase, Stick, White To Strawberry, Raindrop, Mother-Of-Pearl 275.00
Satin Glass, Vase, Tan, Enamel Floral, P.K. On Bottom, 6 In. 45.00
Satin Glass, Vase, White To Apricot, Floral & Enamel, 7 In. 57.00
Satin Glass, Vase, White To Blue, Floral & Enamel, 10 In., Pair 205.00
Satin Glass, Vase, White To Pink, Camphor Handles, Enameled, 8 In. 85.00
Satin Glass, Vase, White To Yellow Top, Quilted, Crimped Edge, 6 In. 75.00
Satin Glass, Vase, Yellow, Quilted, Painted Cottage, Birds, Floral, 6 3/4 In. 145.00
Satin Glass, Vase, Yellow, White Enamel Cupid & Butterflies, 7 1/2 In. 175.00

Satin Glass, Webb, see Webb

Satsuma is a Japanese pottery with a distinctive creamy beige crackled glaze. Most of the pieces were decorated with blue, red, green, orange, or gold. Almost all the Satsuma found today was made after 1860. Japanese faces are often a part of the decorative scheme.

Satsuma, Bowl, Allover Flower Design, Turquoise, Rust, Blue, Gold, 5 X 3 In. 210.00
Satsuma, Bowl, Flowers, Foliage, Scroll, C.1870, 4 X 5 In. 80.00
Satsuma, Bowl, Lake Scene, Snow-Capped Mountain, Houses, 4 3/4 In. 30.00
Satsuma, Box, Covered, Gold Floral, Red Mark, 4 In. 72.00
Satsuma, Buckle, Enamel Scenes, 2 Parts, 2 1/8 In. 35.00
Satsuma, Burner, Incense, C.1750, 7 1/2 X 4 1/2 In. 240.00
Satsuma, Burner, Incense, Plum Blossoms & Chrysanthemums, Footed, 4 1/2 In. 55.00
Satsuma, Button, Bird & Floral, Gold Trim, 1 1/8 In. 17.50
Satsuma, Button, Gold Waterfall, Trees, & Huts, 1 In. 12.50
Satsuma, Chocolate Set, 1, 000 Faces, Pot 9 In., 9 Pieces 235.00
Satsuma, Cup & Saucer, Butterflies, Flowers 15.00
Satsuma, Cup & Saucer, Covered, 2 Handles, Blue & Gray, Gold Trim 40.00
Satsuma, Cup, Tea, Gold, Landscape And Temples, Set Of 4 150.00
Satsuma, Figurine, Woman Sitting In Japanese Fashion, C.1850, 5 In. 225.00
Satsuma, Hair Receiver, Eight Scenic Panels, 2 3/4 In., Pair 85.00 To 90.00
Satsuma, Jar, Cookie, Woven Handle, Moriaga Slip Outline, Figures On Brown 82.00
Satsuma, Jar, Ginger, Japanese Boy With Fan On Lid, Scenic, 11 In. 325.00
Satsuma, Jar, Melon Shaped, Oriental Children, Gold And Enamel, 6 1/4 In. 35.00
Satsuma, Lamp, Faces, Brown & Gold Dragon, C.1800, 23 In. 175.00
Satsuma, Lamp, Warrior, Cream, Red, & Gold, 27 In. 175.00
Satsuma, Plate, Gold Tracery, R.C.Satsuma Mark 22.00
Satsuma, Plate, 1, 000 Faces, 7 1/2 In. 25.00
Satsuma, Sugar & Creamer, Cover, Thousand Faces 55.00
Satsuma, Tea Set, Chocolate, Warriors, 21 Piece 145.00
Satsuma, Tea Set, Gold-Outlined Wisterias & Mountains, 15 Piece 225.00
Satsuma, Teabowl & Saucer, Footed 65.00
Satsuma, Teapot, Allover Enameled Pattern, 15 In. 85.00
Satsuma, Teapot, Miniature, Reed Handle, Male & Female Figures, 3 1/2 X 2 In. 85.00
Satsuma, Urn Vase, Cream Color, Scenic, Gold Tracery, 5 In. 65.00
Satsuma, Urn, Covered, Gold Elephant Handles, 10 1/2 In. 375.00
Satsuma, Urn, Japanese Story On Sides, Gold Trim, 51 In. 3500.00
Satsuma, Urn, Men Playing Drum Scenes, 4 Men Feet, Rectangular, 3 1/2 In. 75.00
Satsuma, Vase, Burnt Orange, Applied Dragon, 10 1/2 In. 65.00
Satsuma, Vase, Cobalt, Gilt, Figures, Scenes, Red Mark, C.1860, Pair, 10 1/2 In. 450.00
Satsuma, Vase, Cream Color, Autumn Leaves, Gold Trim, 6 In. 29.50
Satsuma, Vase, Cream Crackle, Paneled, Floral, Teacher & Student, 6 1/2 In. 25.00
Satsuma, Vase, Cream, Autumn Leaves, Gold Trim, 6 In. 29.50
Satsuma, Vase, Decorated, 1880, 12 In., Pair 250.00
Satsuma, Vase, Floral Band Decoration, 14 1/2 In. 150.00
Satsuma, Vase, Gray Green Faience Type, Ladies, Children & Window, 24 In. 350.00
Satsuma, Vase, Handled, Encrusted Enameling, Brown Ground, 12 In. 125.00
Satsuma, Vase, Hexagonal, Ivory White, Gilt, Blue, Red, 12 In. 160.00
Satsuma, Vase, Houses, Bridge, Rust & Gold, Block Mark, 3 1/2 In. 14.50
Satsuma, Vase, Ladies & Children In Garden, 4 3/4 In. 179.00
Satsuma, Vase, People Running After A Man, 2 Dragon Handles, 12 In. 75.00
Satsuma, Vase, Roosters & Hens Under Blooming Bamboo, 6 1/2 In, Pair 300.00
Satsuma, Vase, Seated Sages & Dog, Gold & Enamel Beading, 13 1/2 In. 85.00
Satsuma, Vase, Slender Neck, Cup-Shaped Base, Imperial, Cabinet Size, 5 In. 125.00
Satsuma, Vase, Thousand Faces, C.1860, 6 1/2 In., Pair 150.00
Satsuma, Vase, Thousand Flowers, Marked, 5 In., Pair 180.00
Satsuma, Vase, Warriors, Allover Decoration, 12 In. 95.00
Scale, American Express 45.00
Scale, Apothecary, Wooden, Marble Top, 6 Brass Weights 72.00
Scale, Baby, 1912, Reed Basket On Top 20.00
Scale, Balance, Brass, Weights, Wooden Case 350.00
Scale, Black Cast Iron With White Porcelain Trays 70.00
Scale, Brass Cylinder, Computing Scale Co., 1894, 5 1/2 X 14 1/2 In. 250.00
Scale, Brass, A.B.Dale, Lansingburgh, N.Y., Cast-Iron Frame, Brass Pan 165.00
Scale, Buffalo Scale Co., Brass Pan & Weights 55.00

Scale, Candy, Tin Scoop, Green Paint 30.00
Scale, Chatillon, Brass Face 8.75
Scale, Chatillon, Brass Front, Weigh To 200 Lbs. 20.00
Scale, Chemist's, Cherry Case, Glass Sides 150.00
Scale, Country Store, Brass Trim & Lettering, Blue & Green Enamel 250.00
Scale, Creamery, 500 Lbs. 400.00
Scale, Egg, Country Store Type 12.50
Scale, Fairbanks, Grain, Brass, With Bucket 65.00
Scale, Gold, Hammel Riglander, Germany, Brass, 2 Pans, Weights In Tin Box 50.00
Scale, Handing, Brass Dial, Tin Tray, Landers 12.00
Scale, Hanging, Spring Type 3.00
Scale, Iceman's, Brass Face, 18 In. 19.50
Scale, Kitchen, Patent 1906, Black Finish, Decals 15.00
Scale, Landers, Frary & Clark, Round, Cast Iron, Brass Face 22.00
Scale, Micrometer, Cast Iron & Brass, C.1890 .... 75.00
Scale, Mir-O, 1-Cent Slot 45.00
Scale, Pelouze Mfg.Co., Chicago, Brass Face, 100 Lbs. 10.00
Scale, Pharmaceutical, Brown Marble Top, 19 X 8 1/2 In. 175.00
Scale, Pharmaceutical, Marble Top, Wood Balance With Glass Lid, 13 1/4 In. 62.00
Scale, Postage, Victor, 3 Cents Per Oz. 45.00
Scale, Postal, Black, Gold Floral 25.00
Scale, Postal, Brass, Desk Style, 1896 .... 18.00
Scale, Postal, Liberty, No. 1, Gold Tin, 4 1/2 In. 7.50
Scale, Postal, Liberty, Gold Tin, 7 In. 10.00
Scale, Postal, Reliance, Tin, Spring 7.00
Scale, Postal, Triner, 9 Ozs. 24.00
Scale, Postal, 2 Cents Per Oz. 60.00
Scale, Purina Checkerboard 39.50
Scale, Red Iron, 1 Platform, Brass Arm, 5 Weights, 11 X 12 In. 50.00
Scale, Rocket Ship By O.D.Jennings, 1 Cent 750.00
Scale, Roman, Iron 30.00
Scale, Store Counter, Glass Platform, Blue Enamel, Brass, 26 In. 149.50
Scale, Store, Ruby Glass Insert, Marble Base 85.00
Scale, Used For Gold, Cast-Iron Fulcrum, 2 Brass Pans, Small 39.00
Scale, Victor, Postal, 3 Cents Per Oz. 45.00
Scale, Victorian Lady's Desk, Brass & Steel, Openwork, 6 1/2 In. 55.00
Scale, Watling, Horoscope Vendor, Coin Operated, C.1950 .... 195.00
Scale, Watling, 1-Cent Slot 195.00
Scale, 1 Cent, Porcelain And Glass 75.00
Schierholtz, Candelabrum, 5 Arm, Figure Of 18th Century Girl, 23 In. 500.00
Schierholtz, Candelabrum, 5-Arm, Figure Of 18th Century Girl, 23 In. 500.00

Schneider *Schneider Glassworks was founded in 1903 at Epinay-sur-Seine, France, by Charles and Ernest Schneider. Art glass was made between 1903 and 1930. The company still produces clear crystal glass.*

Schneider, Bowl, Deep Blue Tortoiseshell Effect, 12 X 6 In. 450.00
Schneider, Bowl, Frosted, Cut & Faceted, Fiddlebacks, C.1925, 5 In. 175.00
Schneider, Bowl, Orange To Clear, Frosted & Clear Ribs, 9 In. 160.00
Schneider, Compote, Mottled Purple To Red Orange, 8 X 4 3/4 In. 90.00
Schneider, Dish, Bell Form, Faceted & Cut, C.1925, Schneider On Base, 5 In. 175.00
Schneider, Dish, Orange Flambe, Metal Stand, Signed, France On Base, 3 3/8 In. 150.00
Schneider, Dish, Small Round, Mottled Blue, 4 1/2 In. 38.00
Schneider, Dish, Small Round, Mottled Red, 4 1/2 In. 38.00
Schneider, Lamp, Mottled Orange Shade With Bronze Base 135.00
Schneider, Pane, End-Of-Day Design, Thick Glass, 14 X 9 In. 400.00
Schneider, Tray, Pin, Mottled Blue & Gray 35.00
Schneider, Tray, Pin, Mottled Red & Gray 35.00
Schneider, Tray, Pin, Mottled Red And Gray, Signed, 4 In. 38.00
Schneider, Vase, End-Of-Day Design, Pink, Brown, Mauve, & Yellow, 14 In. 550.00
Schneider, Vase, Light Blue, Crackled, Signed, 10 In. 200.00
Schneider, Vase, Mottled Yellow To Orange, Applied Amethyst Floral, 10 In. 140.00
Schneider, Vase, Opaque Red, Black Geometrics, Squat, 6 X 5 In. 50.00
Schneider, Vase, Pedestal Base, Pink, Brown, Mauve, Rounded, 14 In., Signed 600.00
Schneider, Vase, Red & Blue Mottled With Yellow, Signed, 11 In. 110.00
Schneider, Vase, Rose Amber, Frosted Decoration, Signed, 4 1/2 In. 110.00

Scrimshaw, Whale's Tooth, Crucifix, Poly Chrome, 5 1/2 In.

Schneider, Vase, Tomato Red, Blue Flowers, Tapering Up To 2 3/4 In., 7 In. 125.00
Schneider, Vase, Undulating Line Decoration, Art Nouveau, 4 1/2 In. 115.00
Schneider, Vase, Yellow Green, Blown, 11 In. 75.00
Schneider, Vase, 12 Ribs, Applied Petal Feet, Signed, 4 1/2 In. 135.00
Schwarzwald, Vase, Portrait Of Queen Louise, Signed, Miniature, 3 1/2 In. 60.00

Scrimshaw is bone or ivory or whale's teeth carved by sailors and others for entertainment during the sailing-ship days. Some scrimshaw was carved as early as 1800.

Scrimshaw, see also Nautical

Scrimshaw, Cane, Dove On Nob, Metal Base, 35 1/2 In. 275.00
Scrimshaw, Crimper, Pie, Fancy With Abalone Inlay 400.00
Scrimshaw, Elephant's Tusk, American Eagle, Wooden Base, 6 In. 250.00
Scrimshaw, Gilkerson, Trio Of Teeth, Stand 3600.00
Scrimshaw, Horn, Drawings & Writing, Dated 1851, 8 In. 85.00
Scrimshaw, Horn, Powder, Sailor Decorations, 19th Century, 10 In. 135.00
Scrimshaw, Knife & Sheath, 7 1/2 In. 95.00
Scrimshaw, Walrus Tusk, Dagger, Japanese, C.1880, 12 In. 45.00
Scrimshaw, Whale's Tooth, British Leopard Cripples U.S. Chesapeake, 7 In. 450.00
Scrimshaw, Whale's Tooth, Confederate Raider, Alabama, June 9, 1864, 7 In. 325.00
Scrimshaw, Whale's Tooth, Crucifix, Polychrome, 5 1/2 In. .... *Illus* 150.00
Scrimshaw, Whale's Tooth, Men Of The Crue Of The Clara Bell, 1863, 5 In. 175.00
Scrimshaw, Whale's Tooth, Sperm Whale 465.00
Scrimshaw, Whale's Tooth, Totem Pole, Alaska, 1899, Green, Blue, Yellow, Red 195.00

Scuttle Mug, see Shaving Mug, scuttle

SEG, see Paul Revere Pottery

Sevres porcelain has been made in Sevres, France, since 1769. Many copies of the famous ware have been made. The name originally referred to the works of the Royal Factory. The name now includes any of the wares made in the town of Sevres, France.

Sevres, Bottle, Scent, Gourd Shape, Matching Cover, Augustus Rex, 6 In. 95.00
Sevres, Box, Classic Scene, Baroque Pearlized, Inside Decorated 275.00
Sevres, Box, Hinged, Signed J.Werner, 9 X 4 In. 175.00
Sevres, Box, Oval, Floral, Swags, Blue Mark, 5 1/2 X 2 1/2 In. 295.00
Sevres, Box, Pink & Gold Floral On Hinged Lid, C.1900, 4 1/4 X 2 3/4 In. 56.00
Sevres, Candlestick, Scroll & Floral, Drip Pan, M A On Base, C.1750, 5 In. 110.00
Sevres, Compote, White, Gold Reticulated, Pierced, Marked, 9 1/2 In. 850.00
Sevres, Console Set, Blue Celeste, Portraits, French Royalty, 3 Piece 600.00
Sevres, Figurine, Boy Pouring Water, Duck Watching, C.1870, 7 In. 125.00
Sevres, Inkstand, Marked MRE Imperiale De Sevres In Red, 8 1/2 In. 325.00
Sevres, Inkstand, Monogram N, Double, C.1804, 8 1/2 In. 325.00
Sevres, Jug, Milk, And Cover, Painted Florals, Enamel Bands, 1763, 4 3/4 In. 300.00
Sevres, Plate, Armorial, 1804, Signed 125.00
Sevres, Plate, Blue Celeste, Louis Philippe Monogram, 1837, 9 1/2 In. 75.00
Sevres, Plate, Duchesse De Bourgogne & Mme De Montesson, Signed Morin, Pair 155.00
Sevres, Plate, Fruit, Pink Floral, Green, Gold Border, Signed Berry, 8 1/2 In. 57.00
Sevres, Plate, Garlands Of Red Roses, C.1773, 9 In. 50.00

Sevres, Plate, Ivory, Scenic, Signed Collin, C.1844, Tuileries, 9 1/2 In. 185.00
Sevres, Plate, Pastoral Scene, Labarre, Cobalt & Gold Edge, 9 3/8 In. 250.00
Sevres, Plate, Portrait, Cobalt Border, Ormolu Holder, 17 1/2 In. 425.00
Sevres, Plate, Portrait, Eliza Bonaparte, C.1804, 9 In. 175.00
Sevres, Plate, Portrait, Josephine, Chateau Tuileries & Crown N, Signed, 9 In. 125.00
Sevres, Plate, Portrait, Louis Philippe, 1846, Cobalt Border, 9 1/2 In. 125.00
Sevres, Plate, Portrait, Louis XIV, Cobalt & Gilt, 10 1/2 In. 125.00
Sevres, Plate, Portrait, Madame Royale, Cobalt & Gilt, 10 1/2 In. 125.00
Sevres, Plate, Portrait, Mme Dubarry, 1837, Chateau De Tuileries, 9 1/2 In. 150.00
Sevres, Plate, Portrait, Mme Maintenon, Signed C.Rochette, 10 1/2 In. 125.00
Sevres, Rose Bowl, Champleve Lid & Base, Lady, E.Dabon, Bronze Handles, 11 In. 425.00
Sevres, Sauce, Double Handle, 1758, Painter's Mark, 9 In. 225.00
Sevres, Sauceboat, Armorial, Portrait Medallion, Marked, 1789, 11 3/4 In. 2200.00
Sevres, Urn, Bronze Lid, Base, & Handles, Woman & Man Scene, 19 In. 475.00
Sevres, Urn, Covered, Blue Celeste, Landscapes, Ormolu Mounted, 16 In. 600.00
Sevres, Urn, Covered, Royal Blue, Scenic Medallion, Brass Base, Callard, 15 In. 265.00
Sevres, Urn, Pink, Watteau Scene, Gilt Bronze Mount, 16 In., Pair 450.00
Sevres, Urn, Portrait, Lady In Gilt Oval, Ormolu Mounts, C.1821, 13 In. 350.00
Sevres, Vase, Bronze Lid, Base, & Handles, Cupid, Zieu, Floral, 10 In. 165.00
Sevres, Vase, Cream Color, Gold Handles & Design, C.1900, 10 X 6 1/2 In. 110.00
Sevres, Vase, Ormolu, Small 150.00
Sevres, Vase, Potpourri And Covers, Blue Celeste, Enamel L, 7 1/2 In., Pair 1200.00
Sevres, Vase, Sunflowers In Squeezebag, Signed Granger, 1879, 12 In. 175.00

Sewer tile figures were made by workers in the sewer tile factories in the Ohio area during the late nineteenth and early twentieth centuries.

Sewer Tile, Shoe, 4 1/2 In.Long *Illus* 18.00
Sewer Tile, Tree Stump, 7 In. *Illus* 28.00

Sewing Tool, see also Pincushion Doll

Sewing Tool, Armchair, Blue Tapestry, Lift Seat For Thread, 15 In. 55.00
Sewing Tool, Bag, Art Deco-Type Flapper Doll, Hangs On Wall, 22 In. 20.00
Sewing Tool, Basket, Peking Handles & Beads, Footed 47.00
Sewing Tool, Bobbin, Bone, Spangles, Incised Colored Circles, 5 In. 14.00
Sewing Tool, Bobbin, Bone, Spangles, Incised Dots Spell Name, 4 1/2 In. 13.00
Sewing Tool, Bobbin, Weaving, Brass Ferrules, Tapered, 7 In. 1.00
Sewing Tool, Box, Needle, Brass, Hinged Butterfly On Leaf Lid, Footed, 3 In. 75.00
Sewing Tool, Box, Needle, Darner On Lid, Staffordshire 14.00
Sewing Tool, Box, Spool, Linen Covered, Silk Lined, Flower Design, 9 1/4 In. 10.00
Sewing Tool, Box, Thread, Chinese Silver, Dragon, Fruits, & Flowers, 1 1/2 In. 125.00
Sewing Tool, Canister, Round Tin, Lid, Lift-Out Tray, Thread Spindles, 7 In. 18.00
Sewing Tool, Chatelaine, Cloth, Pink-Braided Circle, Green Beads, Tassels 22.00
Sewing Tool, Chatelaine, Scissors, Tape, Needle, & Pincushion, Gilt, C.1750 250.00
Sewing Tool, Darner, Blown Glass, Blue 22.50
Sewing Tool, Darner, Blown Glass, Brown, 9 In. 30.00
Sewing Tool, Darner, Deep Red Loop Pattern, 3 Layers Of Glass, Steuben 120.00
Sewing Tool, Darner, Egg, Wooden, 3 In. *Illus* 5.00
Sewing Tool, Darner, Glove, Art Nouveau Sterling Seal 12.50
Sewing Tool, Darner, New England Peachblow 225.00

Sewer Tile, Shoe, 4 1/2 In.Long

Sewer Tile, Tree Stump, 7 In.

Sewing Tool, Darner, Egg, Wooden, 3 In.

Sewing Tool, Darner, Sandwich Glass, Hand-Blown, Multicolored, 9 1/2 In. 115.00
Sewing Tool, Darner, Sandwich Glass, Pink & Yellow Cased, 9 1/2 In. 115.00
Sewing Tool, Darner, Saratoga, Aqua Blown Glass, 2 X 3 In. 20.00
Sewing Tool, Darner, Sock, Blue Glass 24.00
Sewing Tool, Darner, Sterling Handle And Black Egg 14.00
Sewing Tool, Darning Egg, Ornate Sterling Handle 30.00
Sewing Tool, English Silver, Shamrocks With Harp, Green Stone On Top 56.00
Sewing Tool, Gauge, Dressmaker's, Sterling Silver 8.00
Sewing Tool, Gauge, Hem, Sterling Silver, 4 1/2 In. 22.00
Sewing Tool, German Silver, Raised Flowers 18.50
Sewing Tool, Hook, Crochet, Ivory, Carved Ribbon Design 7.00
Sewing Tool, Kit, Needle, Velvet 4.00
Sewing Tool, Kit, Pan Pacific Exposition, 1915, Leather 4.00
Sewing Tool, Knife, Singer Sewing Machine, Razor-Blade Type 4.50
Sewing Tool, Lazy Susan, Spool And Thimble Holder, 4 Tiers, Pincushion Top 39.00
Sewing Tool, Machine, G.E. Electric, Presser Foot, Portable, 12 In. 45.00
Sewing Tool, Machine, Mahantango, Pyramid Designs .... *Illus* 525.00
Sewing Tool, Needle Holder, Beaded 6.00
Sewing Tool, Needle Holder, Boye, Shuttle, Bobbin, Pat.1925 .... 40.00
Sewing Tool, Needle Holder, Brass, Avery & Son, Patent 1869, Hinged, 2 3/4 In. 12.00
Sewing Tool, Needle Holder, Brass, Butterfly, Patented, 4 1/2 In. 45.00
Sewing Tool, Needle Holder, Chinese Silver, Dragon, Fruits, & Flowers, 3 In. 85.00
Sewing Tool, Needle Holder, Cylinder Needle, Oriental Manufacturer 50.00
Sewing Tool, Needle Holder, Cylinder, Screw Lid, Ivory 4.00
Sewing Tool, Needle Holder, Ivory, Carved Ribbon Design, Rolling Pin Shape 20.00
Sewing Tool, Needle Holder, Maple Barrel, Dial A Needle 24.00
Sewing Tool, Needle Holder, Sterling Silver, Embossed, Loop End 18.00
Sewing Tool, Needle, Yarn, Brass-Bound Pistol Grip 5.00
Sewing Tool, Pincushion, see also Pincushion Doll,
Sewing Tool, Pincushion, Beaded Heart, 1919 .... 9.00
Sewing Tool, Pincushion, Bird Center, Beaded 35.00
Sewing Tool, Pincushion, Brown Corduroy Puppy, Tape-Measure Tongue 4.00
Sewing Tool, Pincushion, Cat, White 15.00
Sewing Tool, Pincushion, Dome Shape, Kirk Sterling Repousse, 7 In. 150.00
Sewing Tool, Pincushion, Indian Beadwork On Purple Velvet, C.1890 .... 55.00
Sewing Tool, Pincushion, Lady's Leg, Silk, Fringe 4.00
Sewing Tool, Pincushion, Metal Shoe, Chicago, 1893 .... 18.00
Sewing Tool, Pincushion, Openwork Sterling Container, Black, Starr & Frost 85.00
Sewing Tool, Pincushion, Pig, English Silver, Chester 85.00
Sewing Tool, Pincushion, Shoe, Metal High Heel 4.50
Sewing Tool, Pincushion, Silver, Semiball-Shape, Footed, C.1850, Pair 75.00
Sewing Tool, Pincushion, Velvet & Crocheting, Square, 4 In. 4.00
Sewing Tool, Pincushion, Victorian Chair, Silver Plate 22.00
Sewing Tool, Pincushion, Victorian Elephant, Metal And Velvet 25.00
Sewing Tool, Scissors & Buttonhook, Folding Pocket, 1914 .... 45.00
Sewing Tool, Scissors, Embroidery, Germany, Silver Plate, Stork, 3 In. 25.00
Sewing Tool, Scissors, Embroidery, Germany, Sterling Handles, Floral, 4 In. 15.00
Sewing Tool, Scissors, Figural, Stork, 4 In. 20.00

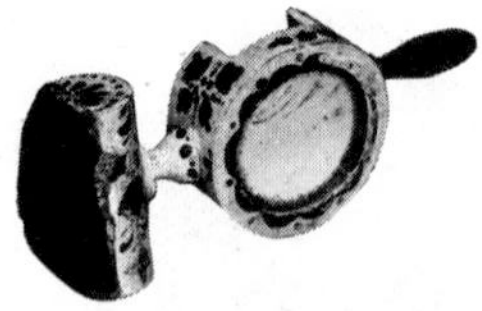

Sewing Tool, Sewing Bird, Wooden, Painted

Sewing Tool, Sewing Bird, White Metal

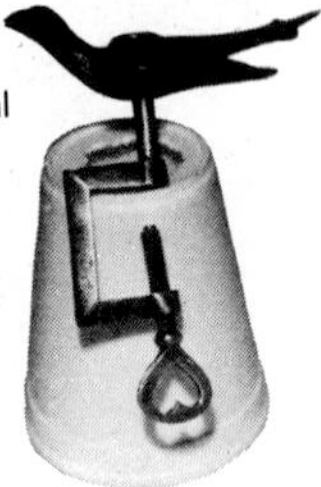

Sewing Tool, Bird, Iron, Clamp-On

Sewing Tool, Machine, Mahantango, Pyramid Designs

(See Page 565)

Sewing Tool, Sewing Bird, Brass Double 55.00
Sewing Tool, Sewing Bird, Brass, Sparrow, Attached Clamp, No Cushion 26.00
Sewing Tool, Sewing Bird, Dated Wings 45.00
Sewing Tool, Sewing Bird, Iron, Clamp-On .... *Illus* 65.00
Sewing Tool, Sewing Bird, Nickel On Brass, Victorian 70.00
Sewing Tool, Sewing Bird, Silver Plated, Double Cushion 45.00
Sewing Tool, Sewing Bird, Two Cushions, Dated 1853, Silver Plated 55.00
Sewing Tool, Sewing Bird, White Metal .... *Illus* 55.00
Sewing Tool, Sewing Bird, Wooden, Painted .... *Illus* 135.00
Sewing Tool, Sewing Kit, Lydia Pinkham 1.00
Sewing Tool, Sewing Machine Head, Wilcox & Gibbs, 10 X 8 In. 32.00
Sewing Tool, Sharpener, Emery For Needles, Shape Of Strawberry, Sterling Top 25.00
Sewing Tool, Shuttle, Tatting, Boyd, 1923 .... 5.00
Sewing Tool, Shuttle, Tatting, Sterling Silver 17.50
Sewing Tool, Spool Holder, Bird's-Eye Maple, 3 Tier 18.75
Sewing Tool, Spool Holder, Cast Iron, 3 Tier, Pincushion Top, 13 In. 32.00
Sewing Tool, Stencil, Brass, Built, Dog Shape, 8 In. 19.00
Sewing Tool, Sterling Silver, Simons, Inverted Hearts 18.00
Sewing Tool, Tape Measure, Blue Celluloid Pig With Hat 12.00
Sewing Tool, Tape Measure, Blue Plastic Egg With Fly Pull 10.00
Sewing Tool, Tape Measure, Boxwood, Reel Type, Brass Handle, 1 X 5/8 In. 22.00
Sewing Tool, Tape Measure, Burial Vault 15.00
Sewing Tool, Tape Measure, Celluloid, German Boy, Baskets Of Flowers 35.00
Sewing Tool, Tape Measure, Copper & Brass Coffee Grinder, Windup 65.00
Sewing Tool, Tape Measure, Duck & Hen, English 30.00
Sewing Tool, Tape Measure, Edison Mazda Lamps 4.00
Sewing Tool, Tape Measure, Figural, Fish Shape, Silver Plate 30.00
Sewing Tool, Tape Measure, Figural, Form Of Fish, Brass 25.00
Sewing Tool, Tape Measure, Figural, Man, Art Deco, Germany 35.00
Sewing Tool, Tape Measure, Figural, Turtle, Pull My Head But Not My Leg 35.00

Sewing Tool, Tape Measure, French Carriage, Brass, Ornate, 3 In. 95.00
Sewing Tool, Tape Measure, G.E.Refrigerator, 1919 .... 5.00
Sewing Tool, Tape Measure, General Electric Refrigerators 14.50
Sewing Tool, Tape Measure, German Metal With Owl Face, Glass Eyes 12.00
Sewing Tool, Tape Measure, German, Table With Roses Around Edge 22.50
Sewing Tool, Tape Measure, Germany, Butterfly Top, 1 In.Square 17.00
Sewing Tool, Tape Measure, Griffith & Boyd Fertilizer 15.00
Sewing Tool, Tape Measure, Hoover Canister Sweeper 11.00
Sewing Tool, Tape Measure, Hoover Vacuum, Round Vacuum Shape 12.00
Sewing Tool, Tape Measure, Indian Moccasin, Red Velvet Pincushion, 2 1/2 In. 40.00
Sewing Tool, Tape Measure, John Deere, Recoiling 15.00
Sewing Tool, Tape Measure, Liberty Bell 25.00
Sewing Tool, Tape Measure, Native Herb Tonic 6.50
Sewing Tool, Tape, Measure, Fab Soap 7.50
Sewing Tool, Tape, Measure, Sears 7.50
Sewing Tool, Thimble Holder, Clear Glass Shoe, White Enamel Floral 30.00
Sewing Tool, Thimble Holder, Seashell 4.50
Sewing Tool, Thimble, Brass, Flower Band 3.50
Sewing Tool, Thimble, Brass, Open End 6.50
Sewing Tool, Thimble, Child's, "For A Good Little Girl" 7.00
Sewing Tool, Thimble, Coin Silver, Raised Border, Wide Band, Size 7 .... 18.00
Sewing Tool, Thimble, Engraved Birds, Sterling 16.50
Sewing Tool, Thimble, Gold, Birds On Band 60.00
Sewing Tool, Thimble, Gold, Castle, Ship 85.00
Sewing Tool, Thimble, Gold, Engraved Buildings, Size 7 .... 40.00
Sewing Tool, Thimble, Gold, Engraved Houses & Trees, Size 5 .... 40.00
Sewing Tool, Thimble, Gold, Josie On Embossed Band 42.00
Sewing Tool, Thimble, Gold, Leather Case, Grapes & Leaves, Simons 75.00
Sewing Tool, Thimble, Gold, Leaves & Grapes, Leather Case 87.50
Sewing Tool, Thimble, Gold, Multicolor Floral 55.00
Sewing Tool, Thimble, Gold, Plain Band, Size 7 .... 38.00
Sewing Tool, Thimble, Gold, Plain With Scrolled Border 35.00
Sewing Tool, Thimble, Gold, Village Scene 75.00
Sewing Tool, Thimble, Gold, Wide Band Leaves 85.00
Sewing Tool, Thimble, Gold, 10K, Open End 40.00
Sewing Tool, Thimble, Gold, 14K, Greek Key Border 50.00
Sewing Tool, Thimble, Gold, 14K, Paneled Band 50.00
Sewing Tool, Thimble, Gold, 18K, Jade Insert, Swedish, 1880 .... 78.00
Sewing Tool, Thimble, Leather 1.50
Sewing Tool, Thimble, Metal 3.00
Sewing Tool, Thimble, Millefiori Art Glass 12.50
Sewing Tool, Thimble, Sailboats, Lighthouse, Castle, Sterling 50.00
Sewing Tool, Thimble, Ships, Castle, Shoreline, Gold 85.00
Sewing Tool, Thimble, Silver With Carnelian Top, English 25.00
Sewing Tool, Thimble, Silver, Fancy Design And Pink Coral 35.00
Sewing Tool, Thimble, Silver, Rubies & Diamonds 85.00
Sewing Tool, Thimble, Star Brand Shoes 2.75
Sewing Tool, Thimble, Steel, Embossed 5.00
Sewing Tool, Thimble, Sterling And Gold, Band Ribbed 15.00
Sewing Tool, Thimble, Sterling In Basket Case 22.50
Sewing Tool, Thimble, Sterling Silver, American, Cut Wheels 27.50
Sewing Tool, Thimble, Sterling Silver, Enamel Hawk 27.50
Sewing Tool, Thimble, Sterling Silver, Enamel Kingfisher 27.50
Sewing Tool, Thimble, Sterling Silver, Enamel Swallow 27.50
Sewing Tool, Thimble, Sterling Silver, Engraved, Anchor Trademark 16.00
Sewing Tool, Thimble, Sterling Silver, Gold Wash, Ornate Band 20.00
Sewing Tool, Thimble, Sterling Silver, Greek Key Border 16.00
Sewing Tool, Thimble, Sterling Silver, "James Walker Wishes You Luck, 1924" 25.00
Sewing Tool, Thimble, Sterling Silver, Morning Glories & Vine 29.50
Sewing Tool, Thimble, Sterling Silver, Raised Lily Of The Valley & Bow 42.50
Sewing Tool, Thimble, Sterling Silver, Raised Scotch Thistles 22.50
Sewing Tool, Thimble, Sterling Silver, Raised Tudor Roses 22.50
Sewing Tool, Thimble, Sterling Silver, Scrolled & Paneled Band 14.00
Sewing Tool, Thimble, Sterling Silver, Village Scene Border 25.00
Sewing Tool, Thimble, Sterling, Deep Swirls, Very Wide Band 21.00

Sewing Tool, Thimble, Sterling, Gold Band, Large Leaves 24.00
Sewing Tool, Thimble, Sterling, Gold Band, Very Deep Work 24.00
Sewing Tool, Thimble, Sterling, Horseshoes And Four-Leaf Clovers 30.00
Sewing Tool, Thimble, Sterling, Overlaid Band Of Gold, Engraved Scrolling 25.00
Sewing Tool, Thimble, Sterling, Raised Hearts, German 10.00
Sewing Tool, Thimble, Sterling, Raised Owl, German, 20th Century 10.00
Sewing Tool, Thimble, Sterling, Raised Turtle, German 10.00
Sewing Tool, Thimble, Sterling, Scalloped Edge, Fleur-De-Lis Decoration 11.00
Sewing Tool, Thimble, Sterling, Wheels 25.00
Sewing Tool, Thimble, Tortoiseshell, Silver Tip 75.00
Sewing Tool, Thimble, Worcester Porcelain, 1900 .... 20.00
Sewing Tool, Thread Holder, Gold, Engraving, Octagonal, Loop For Hanging 15.00
Sewing Tool, Threader, Sterling Ribbon, Art Nouveau 12.00
Sewing Tool, Yardstick, Maple, Hand-Carved, Folk Art 25.00
Shaker, Almanac, Spring, 1885 .... 35.00
Shaker, Almanac, 1885, Colored Wrapper 45.00
Shaker, Almanac, 1886, Colored Wrapper 45.00
Shaker, Basket, Picnic, Center Handle, 2 Hinged Lids 100.00
Shaker, Bonnet, Straw, Woven 85.00
Shaker, Box, Sewing, Alfred Maine, Handle, Oval 180.00
Shaker, Box, Sewing, Sabbathday Lake 45.00
Shaker, Can, Tin Whale Oil 50.00
Shaker, Case, Needle, Bronzed Kid, Roll Up, Needles & Holders, 5 In. 45.00

Shaker, Furniture, see Furniture

Shaker, Pincushion, Doll, 1930 .... 35.00
Shaker, Rack, Herb Drying 260.00
Shaker, Sieve, Horsehair, Copper Nails, 13 1/2 X 4 3/4 In. 68.00
Shaker, Spinning Wheel, J.H., C.1783, Horn Collar On Spindle Post 145.00
Shaker, Tub, Apple Sauce, New Hampshire, Copper Nails & Bail Handle, 8 In. 115.00

Shaving mugs were popular from 1860 to 1900. Many types were made, including occupational mugs featuring pictures of the man's job. There were scuttle mugs, silver-plated mugs, glass-lined mugs, and others.

Shaving Mug, Abe Jacobson, Scenic, Hand Painted 35.00
Shaving Mug, Artist's Palette, Wm. In Gold 38.00
Shaving Mug, B.P.O.E., Dated 1910 .... 45.00
Shaving Mug, Barbershop Quartet, Marked The Quartet 35.00
Shaving Mug, Bavaria, Hand-Painted Horses 35.00
Shaving Mug, Bavaria, Plain With Gold Band 15.00
Shaving Mug, Bavarian, Hand-Painted Horses 35.00
Shaving Mug, Bavarian, Plain With Gold Band 15.00
Shaving Mug, Bisque, Figural, Egyptian Queen's Head 72.00
Shaving Mug, Black & White Horses In Storm, Gold Trim 52.50
Shaving Mug, Bluebirds On Branch 95.00
Shaving Mug, Copper Luster, Cobalt Band, Sunderland Lining, Dated 1826 .... 75.00
Shaving Mug, Copper Luster, Dark Green Band Center 50.00
Shaving Mug, Copper Luster, White Band, Hand-Painted Florals 75.00
Shaving Mug, Draped Cloth, Name In Gold 45.00
Shaving Mug, Excelsior, Patent 1869, White Porcelain, Brush Rest 10.00
Shaving Mug, Floral, Left Handed 14.00
Shaving Mug, Flow Blue, Romantic, Soap & Brush Strainers, Staffordshire 50.00
Shaving Mug, Gold & Fuchsia Bands, White Floral Bouquets, English 25.00
Shaving Mug, Golden Knight Shaving Soap, Glass 45.00
Shaving Mug, Grape & Leaf, Brush Holder, Pairpoint Quadruple Plate 35.00
Shaving Mug, John J.Kehoe & American Eagle, C.1890, 4 In. 75.00
Shaving Mug, Junger Mannerchor, American & Prussian Flags, C.1850, 4 In. 75.00
Shaving Mug, K.Johnson & American Eagle, C.1850, 3 1/2 In. 75.00
Shaving Mug, Koken & Boppert, Tel., Razors, Etc., On Bottom 32.50
Shaving Mug, Labeled Ernest Cole 22.00
Shaving Mug, Loyal Order Of Moose, P.A.P. 27.50
Shaving Mug, Luster, Gold Trim, Horse Heads, Dated 1907, German 22.00
Shaving Mug, Man In Moon 55.00
Shaving Mug, Milk Glass, Divided, 3 1/2 In. 42.00
Shaving Mug, Milk Glass, Embossed Face Of Bearded Man, Patent 1867 .... 95.00
Shaving Mug, Moss Rose, Maddock, Burslem 24.50

Shaving Mug, Name & Grand Army Of The Republic Medal, C.1920 .... 100.00
Shaving Mug, Occupational, Artist, Palette Of Paints, Haviland & Co. 55.00
Shaving Mug, Occupational, Barbershop, Barbers & Customers 200.00
Shaving Mug, Occupational, Bowler, Bowling Alley & Men Bowling 150.00
Shaving Mug, Occupational, Brotherhood Of Railroad Trainmen 135.00
Shaving Mug, Occupational, Butcher Killing Blindfolded Longhorn, Limoges 95.00
Shaving Mug, Occupational, Columbia .... 125.00 To 150.00
Shaving Mug, Occupational, Druggist, Mortar & Pestle 110.00
Shaving Mug, Occupational, Fireman 65.00
Shaving Mug, Occupational, Grocery Store 135.00
Shaving Mug, Occupational, Horse-Drawn Hearse 250.00
Shaving Mug, Occupational, Livery Stable 125.00
Shaving Mug, Occupational, Locomotive 95.00
Shaving Mug, Occupational, Longhorn Steer, Numbered 65.00
Shaving Mug, Occupational, Man Shoeing Horse, Thos.Jones In Gold 135.00
Shaving Mug, Occupational, Man With Can Of Paint & Brush 125.00
Shaving Mug, Occupational, People In Barbershop 200.00
Shaving Mug, Occupational, Railroad Man, Locomotive & Tender 78.00
Shaving Mug, Occupational, Red Caboose, Railroad Worker, Name In Gold 85.00
Shaving Mug, Occupational, Steer, A.C.Lewis 72.50
Shaving Mug, Occupational, Yardage Store, Glass Label 95.00
Shaving Mug, Occupational, 4 Bluebirds On A Branch 95.00
Shaving Mug, One White, One Black Child Reading Newspaper, E.P.Heck 85.00
Shaving Mug, Poppies, Gold Trim 12.50
Shaving Mug, Porcelain, Scuttle, Pretty Florals 38.00
Shaving Mug, Porcelain, White, Pink Bowtie, Soap Rest, Pleated Rim 25.00
Shaving Mug, Posies, Gold Decoration, 3 1/2 In. 12.50
Shaving Mug, Purple & Pink Daisies, Soap Divider 20.00
Shaving Mug, RS Prussia, Soap Shelf 85.00
Shaving Mug, Red Roses 10.00
Shaving Mug, Reed & Barton Silver Plate, Insert, Victorian 55.00
Shaving Mug, Rising Sun 35.00
Shaving Mug, Scuttle, Embossed Daisies, Pansies With Gold Trim 16.00
Shaving Mug, Scuttle, Floral 38.00
Shaving Mug, Scuttle, Iris, Violet Decoration 20.00
Shaving Mug, Scuttle, Lady's, Floral, C.1890 .... 27.50
Shaving Mug, Silver Plate, Milk-Glass Liner 18.00
Shaving Mug, St. Bernard 22.00
Shaving Mug, Stag, Brown, Lavender, & Pink Blue, Gold Top, Porcelain 35.00
Shaving Mug, Steer & Knife, A.C.Lewis 65.00
Shaving Mug, Sterling Overlay, Marked J.Handel, Patent Feb.9, 1909 .... 125.00
Shaving Mug, Tea Leaf Ironstone 80.00
Shaving Mug, Tea Leaf, Copper Luster, Signed Meakin 38.50
Shaving Mug, Tin, 5 In. .... *Illus* 32.00
Shaving Mug, Unger Bros. Sterling, Indian's Head, Strainer 225.00
Shaving Mug, White Floral Decoration, Germany, 1890's 25.00
Shaving Mug, Williams Shaving Soap, Healing Antiseptic, Scuttle 67.50
Shaving Mug, 13-Star U.S. Flag In Shield-Type Glass Label 120.00

Shaving Mug, Tin, 5 In.

Shaving Mug, 4 Bluebirds On A Branch 95.00

Shawnee pottery was made in Zanesville, Ohio, from 1935 until 1961. Shawnee also produced pottery for George Rumrill during the late 1930s.

Shawnee, Bowl, Basket Weave, Figural Fruit Lid 7.00
Shawnee, Creamer, Corn 8.00
Shawnee, Creamer, Elephant 8.50
Shawnee, Creamer, Pig, Yellow & Cream 12.00
Shawnee, Creamer, Puss In Boots 8.50
Shawnee, Dish, Butter, Corn 10.00
Shawnee, Jar, Cookie, Basket Of Fruit 15.00
Shawnee, Jar, Cookie, Smiley Pig 18.00
Shawnee, Pitcher, Colored Bo-Peep, 7 1/4 In. 13.50
Shawnee, Pitcher, Milk, Bo-Peep 20.00
Shawnee, Pitcher, Tan, Dolphin Handle, 8 In. 12.00
Shawnee, Pitcher, Water, Corn, 8 1/4 In. 18.00
Shawnee, Planter, Doghouse 5.00
Shawnee, Planter, Old Mill 5.00
Shawnee, Planter, Windmill 5.00
Shawnee, Planter, Wishing Well 5.00
Shawnee, Platter, Corn, Oval, 10 In. 8.00
Shawnee, Salt & Pepper, Corn 7.00
Shawnee, Salt & Pepper, Smiling Cats, 3 In. 6.50
Shawnee, Sugar, Covered, Corn 8.00
Sheffield, see Silver, Sheffield
Shenandoah, Jug, Green & Yellow Drip Glaze, 3 Gallon, 14 In. 95.00
Ship, see Nautical

Shirley Temple dishes, blue glassware, and any other souvenir-type objects with her name and picture are now collected.

Shirley Temple, Album, Record, From Her Movies, C.1930 .... 65.00
Shirley Temple, Book, Captain January & Little Colonel 9.00
Shirley Temple, Book, Captain January, 1959 .... 10.00
Shirley Temple, Book, Coloring, 1936 .... 12.00
Shirley Temple, Book, Dimples, Saalfield, 1936 .... 15.00
Shirley Temple, Book, Favorite Poems, 1936 .... 12.00
Shirley Temple, Book, Heidi 8.00
Shirley Temple, Book, How I Raised Shirley Temple, By Mother, 1935 .... 22.00
Shirley Temple, Book, Little Colonel 10.00
Shirley Temple, Book, Little Princess, Saalfield 18.00
Shirley Temple, Book, Littlest Rebel 7.00
Shirley Temple, Book, Littlest Rebel, Big Little Book, 1935 .... 15.00
Shirley Temple, Book, Now I Am Eight, Saalfield, 1937 .... 15.00
Shirley Temple, Book, Poor Little Rich Girl, Saalfield, 1936 .... 15.00
Shirley Temple, Book, Rebecca Of Sunny Brook Farm 9.00
Shirley Temple, Book, Shirley Temple Thru The Day, Saalfield, 1936 .... 12.00
Shirley Temple, Book, Shirley Temple Treasury, 1959 .... 15.00
Shirley Temple, Book, Shirley Temple's Own Story, By Her Mother 9.50
Shirley Temple, Book, Sing With Shirley Temple, 1935 .... 20.00
Shirley Temple, Book, Song Hits, No.3, August 1937 .... 8.00
Shirley Temple, Book, Story Of Shirley Temple, Grace Mack, 1934 .... 10.00 To 25.00
Shirley Temple, Book, Stowaway 18.00
Shirley Temple, Book, Susannah Of The Mounties, 1936 .... 12.00
Shirley Temple, Book, The Story Of Shirley Temple, 1934 .... 20.00
Shirley Temple, Book, Through The Day, Saalfield 18.00
Shirley Temple, Book, 1935, Beatty 18.00
Shirley Temple, Carriage, Doll's, Wicker 125.00
Shirley Temple, Creamer 12.00
Shirley Temple, Doll, Bright Eyes, Composition, Wig, Dressed, 25 In. 275.00
Shirley Temple, Doll, Composition, Blue Polka Dot Dress, 13 In. 150.00
Shirley Temple, Doll, Composition, Cop Ideal-N, 20 In. 85.00
Shirley Temple, Doll, Composition, Molded Hair, 8 In. 100.00
Shirley Temple, Doll, Composition, Red Plaid Dress, 22 In. 225.00
Shirley Temple, Doll, Composition, Wig, Dressed, 18 In. 95.00
Shirley Temple, Doll, Composition, Wig, 16 In. 85.00

Shirley Temple, Doll, Composition, Wig, 17 In. 145.00
Shirley Temple, Doll, Composition, Wig, 18 In. 165.00
Shirley Temple, Doll, Composition, 20 In. 85.00
Shirley Temple, Doll, Composition, 22 In. 195.00
Shirley Temple, Doll, Composition, 25 In. 150.00
Shirley Temple, Doll, Dress With Pin, 27 In. 325.00
Shirley Temple, Doll, Flirty Eyes, Yellow Dress, Hairnet, 1957, 17 In. 60.00
Shirley Temple, Doll, Ideal, Composition, 16 In. 90.00
Shirley Temple, Doll, Ideal, 1957, Vinyl, Red & White Dress, Purse, 12 In. 50.00
Shirley Temple, Doll, Ideal, 1972, Hard Plastic, Boxed, 17 In. 12.00
Shirley Temple, Doll, Paper, Snap-On Clothes 12.00
Shirley Temple, Doll, Paper, 10 Dresses 15.00
Shirley Temple, Doll, Sailor Suit & Hat, 15 In. 200.00
Shirley Temple, Doll, Toddler, Pin, 18 In. 150.00
Shirley Temple, Doll, Vinyl, 12 In. 20.00
Shirley Temple, Doll, Vinyl, 1972, 17 In. 15.00
Shirley Temple, Doll, Ward's 100th Anniversary, Sleep Eyes, 14 In. 25.00
Shirley Temple, Figurine, Shirley Temple, Baby Take A Bow, 1935, Chalk, 9 In. 25.00
Shirley Temple, Magazine, Genius Behind Shirley Temple, 1936, Modern Screen 9.50
Shirley Temple, Mirror, Fox Films, 1935, 1 3/4 In. 15.00
Shirley Temple, Mirror, Heidi, 1937, Fox Film Corp., Round, 2 1/4 In. 5.00
Shirley Temple, Music Sheet, Animal Crackers In My Soup 7.50
Shirley Temple, Music Sheet, Early Bird 6.00
Shirley Temple, Music Sheet, Goodnight My Love 7.50
Shirley Temple, Music Sheet, On The Good Ship Lollipop 8.00
Shirley Temple, Music Sheet, Toy Trumpet 7.50
Shirley Temple, Paperweight, Glass, 4 1/2 In. 14.00
Shirley Temple, Picture, Portrait, Color, Framed, 1938, 12 X 10 In. 14.00
Shirley Temple, Pitcher, Cobalt Blue, 4 In. 12.00
Shirley Temple, Postcard, Captain January, 1936 10.00
Shirley Temple, Postcard, Hand-Colored Photograph 20.00
Shirley Temple, Postcard, Home, Photograph In Circle 3.50
Shirley Temple, Poster, Little Colonel, 1936, 29 X 20 In. 18.00
Shirley Temple, Teapot, Pink Plastic 6.50
Shirley Temple, Watch, Pocket, Picture Of Shirley, Nickel 75.00
Silesia, Berry Set, Yellow & Pink Roses, Gold Medallions, 7 Piece 62.00
Silesia, Bowl, Lily Of The Valley, Handled, Blue Mark, 7 In. 20.00
Silesia, Cake Set, 7 Piece 85.00
Silesia, Celery, Floral, 12 1/2 In. 12.00
Silesia, Chocolate Set, Sprays Of Pink Roses, Gold Trim, Altwasser, 5 Piece 34.00
Silesia, Cup & Saucer, Peonies 7.50
Silesia, Dish, Leaf Shape, Open Handle, Gold & Green Clover, 9 In. 45.00
Silesia, Hair Receiver, Luster Flowers 28.00
Silesia, Hair Receiver, White With Pink Roses 28.00
Silesia, Jar, Biscuit, Green, Purple, Pink, Grapes & Autumn Leaves 45.00
Silesia, Nut Bowl, White Floral, Gold Trim, 4 1/2 In. 18.00
Silesia, Plate, Bread, Roses, "Give Us This Day" 18.00
Silesia, Plate, Capitol, Heavy Embossed Gold Border, C.1890, 9 1/2 In. 35.00
Silesia, Plate, Hand-Painted Calla Lilies, Hexagonal, 7 1/2 In. 5.00
Silesia, Plate, Hand-Painted Pink Roses, 8 In. 10.50
Silesia, Plate, Pink Roses On Green Border, 7 1/2 In. 15.00
Silesia, Plate, White, Daisy Chain Border & Gold Trim, Altwasser, 7 In., Pair 19.00
Silesia, Salt, Cream Color, Pink Roses, Footed 4.00
Silesia, Sauceboat, Floral 22.00
Silesia, Tea Set, Ribbed Panels Of Yellow & White, Gold Trim, 21 Piece 160.00
Silesia, Tray, Gold & Floral, 3 Sections, Tiefenfurt, Pyramid Shape, 15 In. 50.00
Silesia, Vase, Art Deco, Gold, Purple, Green On Cream, Gold Rim, 6 1/2 In. 40.00
Silesia, Vase, Portrait, Branch Handles, Man Reading To Friends, 10 1/4 In. 65.00

Silhouette, see Picture, Silhouette

Silver deposit glass was made during the late nineteenth and early twentieth centuries. Solid sterling silver was applied to the glass by a chemical method so that a cutout design of silver metal appeared against a clear or colored glass. It is sometimes called silver overlay.

Silver Deposit, Bottle, Perfume, Alvin, 3 1/4 In. 32.50

Silver Deposit, Bottle, Perfume, Art Nouveau, 7 X 4 1/2 In. 17.00
Silver Deposit, Bottle, Perfume, Bulbous, 4 1/2 X 4 In., Pair 52.00
Silver Deposit, Bottle, Perfume, Green, Stopper, 3 1/4 In. 45.00
Silver Deposit, Bottle, Perfume, Spear Stopper, Scrolls & Geometrics, 9 In. 42.00
Silver Deposit, Bottle, Perfume, Tapered Stopper, 5 In. 65.00
Silver Deposit, Bottle, Perfume, 3 3/4 In. 25.00
Silver Deposit, Bottle, Pinch, Black Amethyst, Stopper, 10 1/2 In. 100.00
Silver Deposit, Bowl, Grapes & Vines, Paneled, 11 In. 22.00
Silver Deposit, Bowl, Raised Fruit On Bottom, 5 1/4 X 10 In. 70.00
Silver Deposit, Cake Stand, Lace & Floral, 11 3/4 In. 20.00
Silver Deposit, Candlestick, 8 In., Pair 35.00
Silver Deposit, Coaster, Scrolled Sterling Design, Set Of 4 22.00
Silver Deposit, Coffeepot, Demitasse, Butterflies, Ribbed, Dome Top, 7 1/2 In. 48.00
Silver Deposit, Compote, Lion's Head, Stags, Eagle Finial, 13 In. 48.00
Silver Deposit, Condiment Set, 2-Handled Tray, 5 Piece 10.50
Silver Deposit, Cruet, Flower Festoons, Tankard Shape, 8 3/4 In. 42.00
Silver Deposit, Cruet, Sterling, Art Nouveau, Floral, Blown Bottles, Pair 75.00
Silver Deposit, Decanter, Amethyst, 9 In. 60.00
Silver Deposit, Decanter, Blue, 2 Glasses 38.00
Silver Deposit, Decanter, Claret, Apple Green, Gorham Overlay, 8 1/2 In. 250.00
Silver Deposit, Decanter, Cobalt, Leaves, 9 1/4 In. 85.00
Silver Deposit, Decanter, Green, 4 Glasses, Set 45.00
Silver Deposit, Decanter, 9 In., 6 Glasses, 2 1/4 In., Purple Glass 35.00
Silver Deposit, Dish, Bonbon, Footed, Swirled, Handles, 7 X 3 In. 50.00
Silver Deposit, Flip, Amber, Vintage, Rockwell, 8 In. 68.00
Silver Deposit, Goblet, Pilsner, President James Buchanan, Cut Stem 350.00
Silver Deposit, Liqueur Set, Grapes On Vine, Melon-Shaped Bottle, 6 Piece 225.00
Silver Deposit, Nappy, Cobalt, Lily Of The Valley, Handled 22.50
Silver Deposit, Pitcher, Flowers & Leaves, 6 In. 15.00
Silver Deposit, Pitcher, 8 In. 35.00
Silver Deposit, Plate, Amethyst, 7 In. 12.00
Silver Deposit, Plate, Cake, Low Footed, Scalloped Edge, 11 In. 15.00
Silver Deposit, Sugar & Creamer, Bows, 3 1/2 In. 8.50
Silver Deposit, Sugar, 2 Handles, Flowers, 6.00
Silver Deposit, Tea Set, 3 Piece, 14 In.Tray 44.00
Silver Deposit, Tray, Ornate, Center Handle, 11 In. 17.50
Silver Deposit, Vase, Acid Finish Green To White, Art Nouveau 30.00
Silver Deposit, Vase, Blue Iridescent, Floral, Art Nouveau, 5 In. 100.00
Silver Deposit, Vase, Bud, Floral, Footed, 6 1/2 In. 15.00
Silver Deposit, Vase, Cobalt, Silver Flowers, 6 In. 18.00
Silver Deposit, Vase, Corset Shape, Art Nouveau Designs, 9 In. 25.00
Silver Deposit, Vase, Etched & Cut, Footed, 10 In. 20.00
Silver Deposit, Vase, Floral, 6 1/4 In. 10.00
Silver Deposit, Vase, Green, Iris, Alvin Silver, 4 In. 95.00
Silver Deposit, Vase, Pleated, Bulbous, 8 In. 25.00
Silver Deposit, Vase, Small Red With White Lining 45.00
Silver Deposit, Wine Set, Lacy Sterling Design, 6 Piece 85.00

Silver Plate, see also Silver, Sheffield

Silver Plate, Basket, Cracked Egg, Twig Handle & Feet, James Tufts, 9 In. 28.00
Silver Plate, Basket, Grapes On Handle & Border, Victorian 185.00
Silver Plate, Basket, Handle, Tufts, No.2758, Victorian, 11 In. 90.00
Silver Plate, Basket, Openwork, Twisted Handle, 4 Ball Feet, Derby, 5 1/4 In. 27.00
Silver Plate, Basket, Victorian, Tufts, 11 X 10 In. 90.00
Silver Plate, Bottle, Screw-On Cap, Floral, Wilcox Co., 5 1/4 In. 18.00
Silver Plate, Bowl, Melon Ribbed, Footed, Reed & Barton, Oval, 12 X 10 In. 55.00
Silver Plate, Bowl, Punch, Repousse Chrysanthemum, Meriden, 15 1/2 X 9 In. 225.00
Silver Plate, Box, Cigarette, Golf Ball & Stick On Lid, Sheffield 32.50
Silver Plate, Box, M W On Hinged Lid, Footed, Pairpoint, Round, 4 In. 150.00
Silver Plate, Butter Dish, Meriden, Roman Key Border, Swan Top 35.00
Silver Plate, Butter, Covered, Liner, Quadruple, Osborn & Co. 18.00
Silver Plate, Butter, Covered, Quadruple Plate, James Tufts, Round 18.00
Silver Plate, Butter, Cow Finial, Etched Floral, Rogers 40.00
Silver Plate, Butter, Dome Floral Lid, Ice Drain, Handled, Wm.Rogers, C.1900 33.00
Silver Plate, Butter, Dome Lid, Knife Holder, Ice Drain, Wm.Rogers 38.00
Silver Plate, Butter, Roll-Back Lid, Paw Feet, Lions' Heads, F.B.Rogers, 1883 35.00

Silver Plate, Caddy, Water, Engraved, Drip Tray, Meriden, 1868 .... 1000.00
Silver Plate, Candelabrum, 3 Arm, Floral, Art Nouveau, Wilcox, 13 In. 60.00
Silver Plate, Candle Snuffer With Tray 29.95
Silver Plate, Candleholder, Bell-Shaped Base, Rogers, 3 In., Pair 22.00
Silver Plate, Candleholder, Oblong Base, Community, 4 In., Pair 12.00
Silver Plate, Candlestick, Repousse, Quadruple, Pairpoint, 8 In., Pair 55.00
Silver Plate, Card Receiver, Labors Of Cupid, Meriden, Britannia 68.00
Silver Plate, Case, Cigar, Holds Three Cigars 35.00
Silver Plate, Case, Cigarette, Nude On Bed, Art Deco 15.00
Silver Plate, Casket, Jewel, Gilt, Hinged Porcelain Lid, Pairpoint, 7 1/2 In. 125.00
Silver Plate, Casserole Holder, Pierced, Footed, Handles, Middletown, 9 In. 28.00
Silver Plate, Castor, see also Castor
Silver Plate, Chocolate Pot, Hand Engraved, English, 7 1/2 In. 65.00
Silver Plate, Cigar Set, Figural, James W.Tufts, Victorial Quadruple 275.00
Silver Plate, Coffee Set, Beaded, Reed & Barton, 1947, 4 Piece 250.00
Silver Plate, Coffeepot, Bunch Of Grapes Finial, Meriden 75.00
Silver Plate, Coffeepot, Hand Engraved, Meriden Brit. Co., 11 In. 55.00
Silver Plate, Condiment Set, 4 Bottles, 2 Blown Stoppers, Riddel, Belfast 50.00
Silver Plate, Creamer & Sugar, Beaded Melon, James Tufts 30.00
Silver Plate, Crumber & Tray, Foliate Borders, Meriden Silver Co. 20.00
Silver Plate, Cup & Saucer, Quadruple Plate, James W.Tufts, No.1362 .... 30.00
Silver Plate, Cup, Child's, Pairpoint, Sept.22, 1895, Resilvered, Ornate 85.00
Silver Plate, Cup, Initials K.K., Pairpoint, Quadruple Plate, No.2629 .... 7.25
Silver Plate, Cup, Loving, Empire, Wallace, 13 In. 125.00
Silver Plate, Cup, R.Y.C., Aug.4, 1900, Pairpoint Quadruple Plate 7.25
Silver Plate, Cup, Shaving With Insert, Reed & Varton 45.00
Silver Plate, Desk Set, 4 Ball Feet, 2 Ink Bottles, 10 X 5 1/2 In.Base 50.00
Silver Plate, Dish, Butter, Cow Finial, Silver Insert, Racine 78.00
Silver Plate, Dish, Cheese, Mouse On Cover 25.00
Silver Plate, Dish, Nut, Engraved Leaves & Pinecones, Hartford Co., C.1880 .... 85.00
Silver Plate, Dish, Nut, Squirrel, 9 In. 50.00
Silver Plate, Dish, Pin, Derby, Victorian 10.00
Silver Plate, Etched Cover, Glass Insert, Milkmaid & Cows, Wilcox Silver Co. 85.00
Silver Plate, Ewer, Covered, Horn Handle, Jas.Dixon, 9 1/2 In. 75.00
Silver Plate, Fork, Dinner, Savoy, Rogers Bros., 1893 .... 5.00
Silver Plate, Fork, Dinner, Tipped, Wm. Rogers, 1898 .... 5.00
Silver Plate, Fork, Dinner, Unique, Reed & Barton, 1869 .... 1.50
Silver Plate, Frame, Barbour & International, Rococo Border, 11 In. 55.00
Silver Plate, Frame, Castor, For 5 Bottles, James W.Tufts, Boston 18.00
Silver Plate, Frame, Castor, For 6 Bottles, Reed & Barton 39.00
Silver Plate, Goblet, Raised Dutch Scenes, Balfour Co. 35.00
Silver Plate, Hair Receiver, Beaded Edge, Meriden, No.82 .... 9.50
Silver Plate, Humidor & Attached Tray, Hinged Dome Lid, Engraved, English 65.00
Silver Plate, Humidor, Bird & Dog On Top, Hartford Silver Co., 8 3/4 In. 175.00
Silver Plate, Jar, Cracker, Ornage Handle & Finial, Columbia Co., C.1864 .... 22.75
Silver Plate, Jar, Honey, Enamel Bee On Finial, 3 Footed, English 37.50
Silver Plate, Knife Rest, Spread-Wing Cockatoos, 2 1/2 X 5 In. 29.00
Silver Plate, Knife Rest, Squirrel Eating Acorn, 4 In. 35.00
Silver Plate, Knife, Folding Fruit, Art Nouveau Handle, Patented 1965, A.Cole 28.00
Silver Plate, Ladle, Gravy, Engraved '05, Towle 4.50
Silver Plate, Ladle, Gravy, Roman, Holmes, Booth & Hayden 5.00
Silver Plate, Ladle, Soup, Ornate Handle, Reed & Barton, 10 1/2 In. 15.00
Silver Plate, Muffineer, Assyrian Head, 1847 Rogers 9.00
Silver Plate, Muffineer, Embossed Floral, Handle, Pierced Top, Wilcox, 7 In. 27.00
Silver Plate, Muffineer, Figural, Starfish, Seashell, Kitten On Top, Meriden 55.00
Silver Plate, Mug, Child's Alphabet & Little Bo-Peep, Forbes Silver Co. 24.00
Silver Plate, Mug, Child's, World's Fair, 1893 & Floral, Meriden 22.00
Silver Plate, Mug, Quadruple Plate, No.1389, James W.Tufts 25.00
Silver Plate, Mustache Cup, see Mustache Cup
Silver Plate, Napkin Ring, see Napkin Ring
Silver Plate, Napkin Ring, Figural, Barrel With Branch And Leaf 42.00
Silver Plate, Napkin Ring, Figural, George Engraved On Barrel 45.00
Silver Plate, Paperweight & Thermometer, Elk & Tree Branch, Pairpoint 25.00
Silver Plate, Pickle Castor Frame, Signed Simpson, Hall, Miller, Embossed 30.00
Silver Plate, Planter, Embossed Floral, Ribbed, Pairpoint, 9 X 4 In. 35.00

Silver Plate, Plaque, Roman Ladies, English, C.1876, 20 In. 350.00
Silver Plate, Plate, Baby's, Underwood, 8 1/2 In. 15.00
Silver Plate, Plate, Cake, Engraved, 6 Ball Feet, Wilcox, 13 3/8 In. 32.00
Silver Plate, Punch Bowl, Footed, E.P.N.S., English, 10 1/2 In. 35.00
Silver Plate, Punch Bowl, Repousse, Meriden Co., 15 3/4 X 9 In. 250.00
Silver Plate, Rack, Toast, 6 Slots, 2 Sections, English, Victorian 16.00
Silver Plate, Salt & Pepper, Ornate Border On Salt, Cheltenham Co., Eng. 18.00
Silver Plate, Saltshaker, Figural, Derby, Victorian 12.50
Silver Plate, Ship, Mirror Sail, Cargo Of Roses, Easel Stand, 10 X 14 In. 75.00
Silver Plate, Spoon Warmer, Victorian Shell Design, 7 X 6 In. 65.00
Silver Plate, Spoon, Demitasse, Lion On Handle, Italian 7.50

Silver Plate, Spoon, Souvenir, see Souvenir, Spoon, Silver Plate

Silver Plate, Spoon, Stuffing, English 15.00
Silver Plate, Spoon, Teaette, Rogers, 1881 .... 16.50
Silver Plate, Spooner, Bird Finial, Scroll Handles, 12 Hooks, Rogers 80.00
Silver Plate, Spooner, Sapphire Blue Thumbprint Insert, Rogers 70.00
Silver Plate, Strainer, Tea, Embossed Children, Germany, Victorian 10.00
Silver Plate, Sugar & Creamer, With Spooner, James W.Tufts 125.00
Silver Plate, Sugar, Covered, On Pedestal, Silver Figural, Egyptian, Rogers 75.00
Silver Plate, Syrup & Attached Underplate, Reed & Barton 20.00
Silver Plate, Syrup, Floral, Melon Ribbed, Openwork Feet, Warren Co., 6 In. 25.00
Silver Plate, Syrup, Swirl Flutings, Hinged Lid, Merdien Co., Quadruple 18.00
Silver Plate, Tablespoon, Unique, Reed & Barton, 1869 .... 2.00
Silver Plate, Tankard, Elkington Electrotype, 29 In.High .... *Illus* 1300.00
Silver Plate, Tankard, Reed & Barton, Tilting Stand, Dated May 18, 1878 .... 130.00
Silver Plate, Tea Infuser, Webster, Rogers 7.00
Silver Plate, Tea Set, Engraved Crest, Hexagonal, Sheffield, 1840, 3 Piece 48.00
Silver Plate, Tea Set, Gold Washed, Footed, Manhattan Co., No.1023, 4 Piece 65.00
Silver Plate, Tea Set, Quadruple, Meriden B Co., 5 Piece 195.00
Silver Plate, Teakettle, Chased & Engraved, James Dixon & Sons, C.1840 .... 80.00
Silver Plate, Teapot On Stand, Burner, Swinging, Swirl, Reed & Barton 65.00
Silver Plate, Teapot, Ebony Handle & Finial, Fluted, G.S.Keggs, London, 6 In. 45.00
Silver Plate, Teaspoon, Old Colony, 1847 Rogers, 1911 .... 5.00
Silver Plate, Toast Rack, Bird At Side, Leaf Base 40.00
Silver Plate, Tongs, Fish At Each End, English, C.1901 .... 11.00

Silver Plate, Toothpick, see Toothpick

Silver Plate, Toothpick, Derby, Victorian 15.00
Silver Plate, Tray, Card, Mermaid & Dolphin, Pairpoint 25.00
Silver Plate, Tray, Ivy Leaf, Center Handle, On Copper, Rogers, 1883, 9 1/2 In. 38.00
Silver Plate, Tureen, Victorian Quadruple, 2 1/2 Quart Size 85.00
Silver Plate, Urn On Stand, Coffee, Hand Chased, English, 17 In. 350.00
Silver Plate, Urn, Coffee, Chased, Hand Engraved, English, 13 In. 110.00
Silver Plate, Urn, Coffee, Footed, Warmer, Chased, Reed & Barton, 15 In. 80.00
Silver Plate, Watch Holder, Figural, Rooster Finial 65.00
Silver Plate, Water Cooler, Porcelain Lined, Meriden, Fancy Engraved, 1 Cup 275.00

Silver, American, see also Tiffany Silver, Silver, Sterling

Silver, American, Basket, Cake, Boat Shape, Scroll & Floral Rim, C.1900 .... 200.00
Silver, American, Boat, Gravy, With Stand, C.1830, 11 In.Long .... *Illus* 2500.00
Silver, American, Bowl, Base Domed, Berried Foliage, Shallow, Gorham, 13 In. 350.00
Silver, American, Case, Man's Watch, Invisible Joint Case Co., 1883, Coin 30.00
Silver, American, Children's Set, Enameled Humpty Dumpty .... *Illus* 35.00
Silver, American, Cigar Punch 38.00
Silver, American, Cup, Jaccard, St.Louis, 6 In. .... *Illus* 165.00
Silver, American, Dish, Butter, Cow Finial, Silver Insert, Racine Silverplate 78.00
Silver, American, Dish, Entree And Cover, J.E.Caldwell, Philadelphia, C.1900 .... 80.00
Silver, American, Eggcup Set, W.Gale & Son, Coin, Stand & 6 Eggcups 500.00
Silver, American, Fork, Dinner, Jenny Lind, Albert Coles, Coin 25.00
Silver, American, Fork, F & M, Coin 16.50
Silver, American, Fork, Luncheon, Oval Thread, Dexter & Haskins, Coin 18.50
Silver, American, Fork, Scroll Shell & Leaf, Brooks, Boston, 1840, Coin 25.00
Silver, American, Goblet, Peter L.Krider, Phila., Coin 295.00
Silver, American, Gravy Boat & Stand, Chased & Repousse, Philadelphia, C.1830 .... 2500.00
Silver, American, Julep, Beaded Trim, Jaccard Co., Coin 295.00
Silver, American, Knife Rest, Andiron Shape, Gorham, Coin 25.00
Silver, American, Knife, Butter Serving, Thread, R & W Wilson, C.1825, Coin 15.75

Silver Plate, Tankard, Elkington Electrotype, 29 In.High

Silver, American, Children's Set, Enameled Humpty Dumpty

Silver, American, Boat, Gravy, With Stand, C.1830, 11 In.Long

Silver, American, Cup, Jaccard, St.Louis, 6 In.

Silver, American, Pitcher, Water, New York, 1850, 11 In.

Silver, American, Teapot, Fletcher & Gardiner, C.1825, 8 5/8 In.

(See Page 578)

Silver, American, Knife, Butter, Large, LF Gurney, C.1850, Designed Blade, Coin 16.95
Silver, American, Knife, Master Butter, Olive, Pear & Bacall, Coin 14.00
Silver, American, Knife, Pocket, Fruit, T & W , Coin 11.95
Silver, American, Ladle, Fiddleback, C.Bard & Son, Phila., C.1840, Coin 125.00
Silver, American, Ladle, Mayonnaise, Sheaf Of Wheat, Marquand, C.1820, Coin 58.00
Silver, American, Ladle, Medallion Top, Marked H & S, 12 In. 95.00
Silver, American, Ladle, Mustard, Initials M.W., N.Harding, 1879, Coin 11.95
Silver, American, Ladle, Mustard, Jenny Lind, Wise, Coin 24.00
Silver, American, Ladle, Mustard, N.E.Crittenden, Cleveland, 3., C.1830, Coin 15.00
Silver, American, Ladle, Mustard, Shell Bowl, Chased, L.Ladomus, C.1830, Coin 45.00
Silver, American, Ladle, Olive, A.Pitts, Berkley, Mass., 11 In., Coin 115.00
Silver, American, Ladle, Punch, Lady On Tip Of Handle, Crosby Morse, Coin 135.00
Silver, American, Ladle, Punch, Stag Head In Relief, A.Stowell & Co., Coin 110.00
Silver, American, Ladle, Sauce, Adams & Farnsworth, Coin 24.00
Silver, American, Ladle, Serving, A.Fellows, Newport, R.I., 1826, 10 In., Coin 85.00
Silver, American, Ladle, Soup, Acanthus Crest, R.& W.Wilson, C.1845, Coin 125.00
Silver, American, Ladle, Soup, Signed D.F., Daniel Fueter, C.1754-1805, Coin 125.00
Silver, American, Medal, Best Shot, Horace Waldron, 1838, Coin, 3 In. 49.75
Silver, American, Mug, Child's, Tift & Whiting, Coin, C.1850 .... 110.00
Silver, American, Mug, Embossed & Engraved, N.Harding & Co., C.1840, Coin 215.00
Silver, American, Pitcher, Ball, Thompson & Black, C.1850, Coin, 11 In. 625.00
Silver, American, Pitcher, Baluster Form, Chased & Repousse, New York, C.1855 .... 475.00
Silver, American, Pitcher, Hexagonal Bulbous Body, Chased, New York, C.1850 .... 700.00
Silver, American, Pitcher, Water, New York, 1850, 11 In. .... *Illus* 700.00

Silver, American, Salt & Spoon, Master, Claw Feet, Bailey & Co., Coin 65.00
Silver, American, Salt, Master, Crosby, Boston, C.1849 ..... 25.00
Silver, American, Salt, Master, Olive, Gray & Libby, Coin 15.00
Silver, American, Salt, Pedestal Base, 2 1/2 X 2 1/4 In., Gorham, Coin 35.00
Silver, American, Salt, Trencher, Jacob Lansing, Albany, C.1705 ..... 3750.00
Silver, American, Sauceboat And Stand, Oval, Repousse, Chased, Martele 1100.00
Silver, American, Server, Pastry, Bright Cut, C.1850, Coin 39.75
Silver, American, Skewer, Edw.Pear, Boston, 1836, 10 In. 40.00
Silver, American, Spoon, Berry, Gold-Ribbed Bowl, Ornate, Coin, 8 3/8 In. 48.00
Silver, American, Spoon, Coffin End, J.Ward, Coin 22.00
Silver, American, Spoon, Demitasse, N.G.Wood & Son, Coin 12.00
Silver, American, Spoon, Dessert, Faber & Horner, Phila., Coin, Pair 22.00
Silver, American, Spoon, Dessert, N.Harding & Co., Coin 12.00
Silver, American, Spoon, Dessert, N.Howard, Mass., 1860, Coin 12.00
Silver, American, Spoon, Dessert, Prince Albert, A.Hanford, Coin 14.00
Silver, American, Spoon, Dessert, Raised Tip, Isbel & Simple, Ohio, Coin 13.50
Silver, American, Spoon, Dessert, Rudd & Scudder, Coin, Pair 24.00
Silver, American, Spoon, Dessert, Wood & Hughes, Coin 11.00
Silver, American, Spoon, Iced Tea, Bowknot, Dexter & Haskins, Coin 6.00
Silver, American, Spoon, L.Cary, Boston, Coin, 9 In., Pair 45.00
Silver, American, Spoon, Master Salt, H.L.Webster, R.I., C.1831, Coin 10.95
Silver, American, Spoon, Master Salt, Initials L.B., B.E.& Co., Coin 9.95
Silver, American, Spoon, Master Salt, S.Kirk, Coin 18.00
Silver, American, Spoon, Master Salt, Shell Bowl, Hoskins & Evans, 1830s, Coin 14.00
Silver, American, Spoon, Master, Initials, Davis, Palmer, & Co., C.1840, Coin 9.95
Silver, American, Spoon, Mustard, Initials J.M.L., C.Lord, Coin 11.95
Silver, American, Spoon, Salt, Fiddleback, R.& W.Wilson, C.1840, Coin, Pair 40.00
Silver, American, Spoon, Salt, Pitkin, East Hartford, Coin 16.00
Silver, American, Spoon, Salt, Shovel End, Goddard, Worcester, Coin 16.00
Silver, American, Spoon, Serving, A.Pangborn, Burlington, Vt., 1833, Coin 28.00
Silver, American, Spoon, Serving, B.Bemert, Pittsfield, Mass., C.1788, Coin 22.00
Silver, American, Spoon, Serving, Bright Cut, Oval, Daniel Low, Coin, 7 1/4 In. 12.00
Silver, American, Spoon, Serving, Coffin Handled, Charles Brewer, C1800 ..... 45.00
Silver, American, Spoon, Serving, Double Construction, Jacob, Md., C.1811, Coin 55.00
Silver, American, Spoon, Serving, Double Construction, Waters, C.1810, Coin 30.00
Silver, American, Spoon, Serving, Edward Watson, Boston, Mass., 1839, Coin 20.00
Silver, American, Spoon, Serving, Farrington & Hunnewell, C.1835, Coin 24.75
Silver, American, Spoon, Serving, Frederich Marquand, Ga., C.1820, Coin, Pair 45.00
Silver, American, Spoon, Serving, Full Figure Deer, J.Hall, Albany, 1781, Coin 125.00
Silver, American, Spoon, Serving, G.Baker, Providence, R.I., C.1825, Coin 17.00
Silver, American, Spoon, Serving, Hotchkiss & Shreuder, Syracuse, N.Y., Coin 14.95
Silver, American, Spoon, Serving, J.Gorham & Son, C.1845, Coin 14.95
Silver, American, Spoon, Serving, J.P.Trott & Son, Conn., C.1820, Coin, Pair 60.00
Silver, American, Spoon, Serving, J.W.& Co., C.1825, Coin 14.95
Silver, American, Spoon, Serving, N.Harding, Boston, Mass., C.1830, Coin 20.00
Silver, American, Spoon, Serving, Nicholas Roosevelt, N.Y., C.1735 ..... 200.00
Silver, American, Spoon, Serving, NW Goddard, Nashua, N.H., C.1850, Coin 15.00
Silver, American, Spoon, Serving, S.E.Young, Laconia, N.H., Coin 21.00
Silver, American, Spoon, Serving, S.H.Gerould, C.1820, Coin 15.95
Silver, American, Spoon, Soup, Bowknot, Dexter & Haskins, Coin 6.00
Silver, American, Spoon, Soup, Oval, N.Harding, Coin 20.00
Silver, American, Spoon, Sugar, Fluted Shell Bowl, J.Rudd, Coin 22.00
Silver, American, Spoon, Sugar, Fluted Shell Bowl, John Welsh, Coin 25.00
Silver, American, Spoon, Sugar, Shell Bowl, Bright Cut, Stowell, C.1850, Coin 15.75
Silver, American, Spoon, Sugar, Shell Bowl, N.Harding & Co., C.1850, Coin 14.75
Silver, American, Spoon, Sugar, Shell Bowl, Shreve Stanwood, C.1860, Coin 15.75
Silver, American, Spoon, Sugar, Shell Bowl, Steward, Stevens, & Dewey, Coin 28.50
Silver, American, Spoon, Sugar, Shovel End, H.M.Nichols, Coin 20.00
Silver, American, Spreader, Jenny Lind, Flat, Savage, Coin. 17.00
Silver, American, Stand, Egg With 6 Eggcups, W.Gale & Son, Coin 500.00
Silver, American, Sugar & Creamer, Birds & Insects Engraved, Gorham 325.00
Silver, American, Sugar Shell, Sm.B.Durgin, Concord, N.H., C.1850, Coin 16.95
Silver, American, Sugar With Shell, Harris & Stannard, 1845, Boston, Coin 28.00
Silver, American, Sugar, Liberty Browne, William Seal, Philadelphia, C.1805 ..... 800.00
Silver, American, Sugar, Ornate, Shell Bowl, Coin 27.00

Silver, American, Sugar, Shovel, Wm.Root & Bros., New Haven, Conn., C.1850 .... 35.00
Silver, American, Tablespoon, A.Sanborn, Lowell, Ma., C.1850, Coin 14.75
Silver, American, Tablespoon, B.C.Frobisher, Boston, C.1834, Coin 14.75
Silver, American, Tablespoon, Bowknot, Dexter & Haskins, Coin 14.00
Silver, American, Tablespoon, Bright Cut, G.F.Melcher, Coin 12.75
Silver, American, Tablespoon, C.A.Crosby, Coin 16.00
Silver, American, Tablespoon, Cushman & Hobbs, Coin 16.50
Silver, American, Tablespoon, Davis, Palmer & Co., Boston, C.1841, Coin 12.75
Silver, American, Tablespoon, E.Baker, Conn., C.1821, Coin 15.75
Silver, American, Tablespoon, E.E.Bailey, Portland, Me., Coin 18.00
Silver, American, Tablespoon, Engraved Dora, H.Hewett, C.1850, Coin 12.75
Silver, American, Tablespoon, Engraved Grandmother's Gift, Hews, 1850, Coin 12.75
Silver, American, Tablespoon, Engraved, Farrington & Hunnewell, C.1835, Coin 12.75
Silver, American, Tablespoon, Fiddle & Shell, Henry Evans, N.J., Coin 22.00
Silver, American, Tablespoon, Fiddle Thread, Gale, Wood & Hughes, Coin 15.00
Silver, American, Tablespoon, Fiddle Tip Handles, Curtis & Stevens, Coin, Pair 38.00
Silver, American, Tablespoon, Fiddle Tip, Maynard & Taylor, N.Y., C.1830, Coin 16.00
Silver, American, Tablespoon, Frobisher, Boston, C.1834, Coin 14.75
Silver, American, Tablespoon, Grape, A.Hews, Jr., 1850, Coin 12.75
Silver, American, Tablespoon, H.A.Bradley, Coin 16.00
Silver, American, Tablespoon, Harrington, Coin, Pair 35.00
Silver, American, Tablespoon, Harris & Stanwood, Coin 16.00
Silver, American, Tablespoon, Hollister, Oswego, Coin 15.00
Silver, American, Tablespoon, Initials M.A., A.Sanborn, Mass., C.1850, Coin 14.75
Silver, American, Tablespoon, Initials S.M.B., J.W.& Co., Coin 14.75
Silver, American, Tablespoon, J.J.Low & Co., Boston, C.1828, Coin 14.75
Silver, American, Tablespoon, J.W.& Co., C.1820, Coin 14.75
Silver, American, Tablespoon, Jones, Ball & Poor, Boston, C.1840, Coin 12.75
Silver, American, Tablespoon, Lows, Ball & Co., Boston, C.1840, Coin 14.75
Silver, American, Tablespoon, Mabel On Back, Palmer & Batchelder, Coin 18.00
Silver, American, Tablespoon, Maverick House, N.Harding, Boston, C.1830, Coin 14.75
Silver, American, Tablespoon, N.G.Wood & Son, Boston, Coin 14.00
Silver, American, Tablespoon, O.A.Bean, C.1850, Coin 14.75
Silver, American, Tablespoon, Olive, Farrington & Hunnewell, C.1835, Coin 12.75
Silver, American, Tablespoon, Olive, Jones, Ball & Poor, Boston, C.1840, Coin 12.75
Silver, American, Tablespoon, Palmer & Batchelder, Coin 16.00
Silver, American, Tablespoon, Rattail On Back, J.Baldwin, C.1810, Coin 19.75
Silver, American, Tablespoon, Reed Slader & Co., N.H., C.1830, Coin 12.75
Silver, American, Tablespoon, Round Handle, Beason & Reed, C.1820, Coin, Pair 45.00
Silver, American, Tablespoon, Webster, R.I., C.1831, Coin 14.75
Silver, American, Tea Service, Bogert, C.1825, 3 Piece, Coin 1550.00
Silver, American, Tea Set And Turkish Coffeepot, Bigelow & Kennard, C.1885 .... 750.00
Silver, American, Tea Set, Ovoid Bodies, Fluted, G.Boyce, C.1840, 4 Piece 1200.00
Silver, American, Teapot & Stand, Fluted Oval, Moulton, Massachusetts, C.1790 .... 2975.00
Silver, American, Teapot & Stand, Paul Revere, Jr., Boston, 1786 .... 7000.00
Silver, American, Teapot, Circular, Chased Acanthus Leaves, Wood Handle, C.182 .... 800.00
Silver, American, Teapot, Fletcher & Gardiner, C.1825, 8 5/8 In. .... *Illus* 800.00
Silver, American, Teapot, Repousse, Wood & Hughes, N.Y., Coin, 10 In. 375.00
Silver, American, Teaspoon, A.Holmes, Albany, 1801, Coin 8.00
Silver, American, Teaspoon, Bailey, Coin, Pair 20.00
Silver, American, Teaspoon, Bright Cut, Farrington & Hunnewell 8.75
Silver, American, Teaspoon, C.R.Burch, Coin 9.00
Silver, American, Teaspoon, Coffin Back, Vant-Keene, N.H., Coin 28.00
Silver, American, Teaspoon, Coffin End, Davis & Brown, Boston, 1809, Coin, Pair 35.00
Silver, American, Teaspoon, Coffin End, John Proctor Trott, Conn., Coin 22.00
Silver, American, Teaspoon, Coffin End, Saunders Pitman, R.I., 1775, Coin, Pair 35.00
Silver, American, Teaspoon, Coffin Handle, D.Brown, Phila., 1811, Coin 22.00
Silver, American, Teaspoon, Coffin Handle, George Carlton, N.Y., Coin 20.50
Silver, American, Teaspoon, Coffin Handle, Judah Hart, Conn., C.1800, Coin 22.00
Silver, American, Teaspoon, Curtiss, Candee & Co., Conn., C.1826, Coin 11.65
Silver, American, Teaspoon, Double Construction, W.C.Dusenberry, C.1819, Coin 10.00
Silver, American, Teaspoon, Drop Back Of Bowl, Andras & Richards, 1797, Coin 25.00
Silver, American, Teaspoon, Duhme & Co., Coin 9.00
Silver, American, Teaspoon, E.Huntington, S.C., Coin 9.00
Silver, American, Teaspoon, E.J.Hill, Coin 9.00

Silver, American, Teaspoon, Engraved Lowe, Abbot, N.H., C.1820, Coin 8.75
Silver, American, Teaspoon, Engraved, Bingham, C.1835, Coin 8.00
Silver, American, Teaspoon, Engraved, J.Abbott, N.H., C.1820, Coin 8.75
Silver, American, Teaspoon, Engraved, W.M.Root & Brother, C.1850, Coin 9.95
Silver, American, Teaspoon, F.Dauth, Coin 8.35
Silver, American, Teaspoon, Farrington & Hunewell, Boston, C.1835, Coin 8.30
Silver, American, Teaspoon, Fiddle Handle, S.D.Bacon, C.1820, Coin 7.50
Silver, American, Teaspoon, Fiddle Tip, C.Yates, N.Y., Coin 15.75
Silver, American, Teaspoon, Fiddle, Basket Of Flowers, Stebbins, C.1840, Coin 60.00
Silver, American, Teaspoon, Fiddle, Christopher Burr, R.I., C.1815, Coin 13.50
Silver, American, Teaspoon, Fiddle, Grapes, Palmer & Batchelder, 1855, Coin 10.50
Silver, American, Teaspoon, Fiddleback, Greenwich, Coin 8.00
Silver, American, Teaspoon, George Hoyt, Albany, 1827, Coin 8.35
Silver, American, Teaspoon, Griffin & Hoyt, Coin 9.00
Silver, American, Teaspoon, H.Schoonmaker, C.1810, Coin 10.00
Silver, American, Teaspoon, Initials C.F.W., Skinner & Sweet, Coin 8.55
Silver, American, Teaspoon, Initials E.A.F., Smith & Chamberlain, Coin 9.95
Silver, American, Teaspoon, J.& J. Hall, Albany, Coin 15.00
Silver, American, Teaspoon, J.G.Pearson & Co., C.1840, Coin 7.95
Silver, American, Teaspoon, J.O.& W.Pitkin, Phila., C.1811, Coin 7.95
Silver, American, Teaspoon, L.Young & Co., Bridgeport, Conn., C.1827, Coin 8.00
Silver, American, Teaspoon, Lewis Carry, Boston, C.1820, Coin 13.00
Silver, American, Teaspoon, Maverick House, N.Harding, Boston, C.1820, Coin 8.30
Silver, American, Teaspoon, Murdock & Andrews, Utica, N.Y., C.1822, Coin 7.95
Silver, American, Teaspoon, N.Harding & Co., Boston, C.1850, Coin 8.75
Silver, American, Teaspoon, Palmer & Batchelder, Boston, C.1850, Coin 7.95
Silver, American, Teaspoon, R.Bailey, Woodstock, 1825, Coin 18.25
Silver, American, Teaspoon, R.H.Bailey, Woodstock, Vt., Coin 8.00
Silver, American, Teaspoon, Rattail On Back, O.C.Forsyth, C.1810, Coin 10.00
Silver, American, Teaspoon, Round Edge, Tarbox, E.Baker, Conn., C.1840, Coin 10.00
Silver, American, Teaspoon, Shell Back, Joseph W.Boyd, N.Y., Coin 12.50
Silver, American, Teaspoon, Shell Back, Pelletreau, Bennett & Cook, 1815, Coin 18.30
Silver, American, Teaspoon, Skinner & Sweet, C.1830, Coin 7.75
Silver, American, Teaspoon, Smith & Chamberlain, Salem, Ma., C.1850, Coin 8.50
Silver, American, Teaspoon, Stone & Ball, Coin 9.00
Silver, American, Teaspoon, Twombly & Smith, Coin 10.00
Silver, American, Teaspoon, V End, Ball, Black & Co., C.1851, Coin 10.00
Silver, American, Teaspoon, W.M.Root & Bro., New Haven, C.1850, Coin 9.00
Silver, American, Tongs, Bird's-Feet Ends, C.Bond, Coin, 6 1/2 In. 38.00
Silver, American, Tongs, Claw Ends, Crittenden, N.Y. & Ohio, C.1826, Coin 68.00
Silver, American, Tongs, E.Cook, Coin 28.00
Silver, American, Tongs, Fried Chicken, Ball, Black & Co., Kings Pattern 165.00
Silver, American, Tongs, Oval Spoon Ends, S.Hoyt, N.Y., Coin, 6 1/2 In. 42.00
Silver, American, Tongs, Oval Spoon Ends, Wm.Pratt, 1828, Coin 65.00
Silver, American, Tongs, Shell Ends, C.1839, Rockwell, Bridgeport, Conn. 65.00
Silver, American, Tongs, Tea, Bright Cut, Spoon Ends, W.S., C.1790, Coin 39.00
Silver, Canadian, Teaspoon, Fiddle, Paul Morin, Quebec, C.1775 .... 25.00
Silver, Canadian, Teaspoon, Joseph Robinson, Toronto, C.1859 .... 20.00
Silver, Chinese, Box, Dragon, Fruits, & Flowers, Round, 1 1/2 In., Pair 300.00
Silver, Chinese, Case, Cigarette, Dragon On Lid, 4 In. 110.00
Silver, Chinese, Salt & Spoon, Ornate, 4 Dragon Feet, Glass Insert 28.00
Silver, Chinese, Salt Cellar, Dragon Handles, Floral, Hexagonal, Set Of 4 .... 225.00
Silver, Chinese, Salt Cellar, Repousse Floral, 6 Dragon Handles, Set Of 4 .... 245.00
Silver, Dutch, Box, Hinged, Scalloped, 2 In., C.1865 .... 40.00
Silver, Dutch, Cup, Wedding, Woman Wearing Hoopskirt, Repousse, 4 1/2 In. 88.00
Silver, Dutch, Ladle, Strainer, Pierced, Bright-Cut Engraving, C.1850 .... 32.00
Silver, Dutch, Snuffbox, Engraved Building On Hinged Lid, 1857 .... 75.00
Silver, Dutch, Spoon, Tea Caddy, 2 Elizabethan Gentlemen On Handle 35.00
Silver, English, Bottle, Perfume, Repousse, Birmingham, 1891 .... 22.00
Silver, English, Box, Hinged Heart-Shape Repousse, Birmingham, 1893, 2 In. 50.00
Silver, English, Box, Hinged Lid, Embossed Design, C.1900, Round, 1 In. 18.00
Silver, English, Box, Jewel, Hinged, Tortoiseshell Inlay, Birmingham, 1913 .... 65.00
Silver, English, Case, Calling Card, Cathedral & Floral, Thomason, C.1847 .... 200.00
Silver, English, Case, Card, Clover Filigree, Birmingham, 1835 .... 165.00
Silver, English, Case, Card, Crown Crest, Stripes, Birmingham, 1902, 3 1/4 In. 40.00

Silver, English, Castor, Pepper, Pear Shape, Jabez Daniel, London, 1750 .... 325.00
Silver, English, Chamberstick & Snuffer, Crested, Ames & Barnard, 1819, 4 In. 750.00
Silver, English, Creamer, George III, Footed, Hallmarked, 4 1/2 In. 150.00
Silver, English, Creamer, Helmet, Bright Cut, Henry Chawner, London, C.1789 .... 300.00
Silver, English, Etui, Bright Cut, Samuel Pemberton, C.1795, 1 3/4 In. 150.00
Silver, English, Fish Slice, Eley, Fearn & Chawner, 1810 .... 175.00
Silver, English, Flask, Crystal Insert, Drew & Sons, 1918, 6 In. 65.00
Silver, English, Grape & Leaves Border, Lion & Head Mark, 14 1/2 In.Square 85.00
Silver, English, Ladle, Hallmarked London, C.1846, Maker GA, 7 1/4 In. 80.00
Silver, English, Ladle, Hallmarked London, 1880, Eley & Fern, 6 3/4 In. 95.00
Silver, English, Ladle, Soup, R.Peppin, London, 1824 .... 145.00
Silver, English, Ladle, Toddy, Whalebone Handle, Thomas Mallison, C.1787 .... 95.00
Silver, English, Match Safe, Engraving, Birmingham, 1892 .... 13.00
Silver, English, Muffineer, George III, London, 1814 .... 62.00
Silver, English, Pencil, Retractable, Victorian 16.00
Silver, English, Pillbox, Barrel Design, Birmingham, 1776-7, 1 3/8 In. 60.00
Silver, English, Pot, Mustard, Cobalt Liner, Wm.Eley, 1805 .... 428.00
Silver, English, Salt, Amber Insert, Nickle 25.00
Silver, English, Salt, Master, Clear Liner, Footed, Sheffield 118.00
Silver, English, Salt, Oval, Boat Shape, Robert Hennell, London, C.1782, Pair 300.00
Silver, English, Skewer, Samuel Godbehere, London, C.1901, 10 In. 80.00
Silver, English, Spoon, Berry Serving, Georgia, Smith & Fern, 1790, Pair 95.00
Silver, English, Spoon, Bright Cut, Samuel Davenport, London, 1786 .... 25.00
Silver, English, Spoon, Master Salt, Initials, William Welch, C.1821 .... 20.00
Silver, English, Spoon, Serving, Fiddle, SS, 1869 .... 45.00
Silver, English, Spoon, Serving, Griffin Crest, Godbehere & Wigan, 1788 .... 55.00
Silver, English, Spoon, Serving, London, 1771, 8 1/2 In. 35.00
Silver, English, Spoon, Serving, Oval Tip, Smith & Fearn, London, C.1794, Pair 120.00
Silver, English, Spoon, Stuffing, Goat's Head Crest, Double Drop, C.1750 .... 125.00
Silver, English, Spoon, Stuffing, Hallmark, London, 1800, Henry Sardet, 12 1/4 I 105.00
Silver, English, Spoon, Stuffing, Oval Tip, Crest, T.B., London, C.1826 .... 125.00
Silver, English, Spoon, Stuffing, Peter, Ann, & William Bateman, C.1802 .... 125.00
Silver, English, Spoon, Turkey, Ornamented Handle, London, 1829 .... 80.00
Silver, English, Sugar Sifter, Hallmarked London, 1835, James Beebe, 6 3/4 In. 95.00
Silver, English, Tea Caddy, George III, Bombe Shape, Langford & Sebille 850.00
Silver, English, Teakettle On Stand, Lamp, George Sleath, C.1744, 14 3/4 In. 3600.00
Silver, English, Teaspoon, Relief Bird & Floral, W.Moir 10.00
Silver, English, Tongs, Sugar, George IV, C.1828, 5 3/4 In. 32.00
Silver, English, Tongs, Sugar, Incised Handle, London, 1848 .... 26.00
Silver, English, Tray, Round, Footed, Grapes & Leaves Border, 10 In. 45.00
Silver, English, Tureen And Cover, Georgian, Philip Rundell, London, 1819 .... 5500.00
Silver, English, Urn, Tea, Burner, Bone Handle, Melon Ribbed, 15 1/2 In. 150.00
Silver, French, Armchair, Bowknot Crest, 2 Birds On Back, 2 In. 95.00
Silver, French, Box, Oval Hinged, Decorated, Gold Inside Wash, 1879, 2 In. 80.00
Silver, French, Button, Coin, Monarch, 1 In. 8.00
Silver, French, Flacon, Perfume, Filigree, Cobalt Liner, Turquoise Stone, 1 In 18.00
Silver, French, Skewer, Figural Pheasant Handle, 11 1/2 In. 75.00
Silver, French, Wine Taster, Paris, C.1820 .... 65.00
Silver, German, Chalice, Repousse, Scrolls, Perforations, 6 3/4 In. 75.00
Silver, German, Cordial Set, Repousse, Blown-Glass Inserts, 13 Piece 210.00
Silver, German, Ladle, Art Deco, 14 In. 15.00
Silver, German, Match Safe, Embossed Hunter, Geese, & Gun Scene 20.00
Silver, German, Paperweight, Sparrow 125.00
Silver, German, Spoon, Figural Handle Of Man With Horn, Hallmarked, 5 In. 12.00
Silver, Indian, Teapot, Ebony Handle, Hippolytus Poignand, C.1795 .... 1500.00
Silver, Irish, Jug, Hot Beverage, Gadroon Lid & Base, Townsend, C.1776, 12 In. 3000.00
Silver, Irish, Spoon, Marrow, 1750 .... 125.00
Silver, Irish, Teaspoon, C.Cummings, Dublin, 1834 .... 21.50
Silver, Irish, Tongs, Sugar, Fiddleback, J.Buckton, Dublin, C.1822 .... 85.00
Silver, Italian, Spoon, Venice Hallmark, 1837, Initial C.P., Pair 38.00
Silver, Japanese, Box, Ceremonial, Brass Peacocks & Chrysanthemum, 2 In. 65.00
Silver, Polish, Teaspoon, Krakow, 1847 .... 18.00

Silver, Russian, see also Faberge

Silver, Russian, Box, Engraved Background With Niello, 1882-84 .... 150.00
Silver, Russian, Case, Cigarette, Engraved Bird, Wheat, & Poppies 120.00

Silver, Russian, Case, Cigarette, Engraved, JAL, C.1826, 4 1/4 In. 125.00
Silver, Russian, Case, Cigarette, Garnet Clasp, Presentation 180.00
Silver, Russian, Case, Cigarette, I.Chlebnikov, 1872 ..... 580.00
Silver, Russian, Case, Cigarette, Match Section, Striker, Wick Shaft 125.00
Silver, Russian, Case, Cigarette, Repousse Horses' Heads, 4 5/6 In. 385.00
Silver, Russian, Case, Cigarette, St.George On Horseback Toppling Tablet 275.00
Silver, Russian, Creamer, Tula & Etched Designs, Gold-Wash Interior, C.1900 ..... 135.00
Silver, Russian, Cup, Vodka, House Decoration, 2 1/2 In. 39.00
Silver, Russian, Cup, Vodka, Niello, Floral, 1875 ..... 175.00
Silver, Russian, Cup, Wine, Ceremonial, Etched, 1 7/8 In. 35.00
Silver, Russian, Cup, Wine, Ceremonial, Etched, 2 1/8 In. 50.00
Silver, Russian, Cup, Wine, Ceremonial, Etched, 2 3/4 In. 75.00
Silver, Russian, Cup, Wine, Decorated, 2 In. 35.00
Silver, Russian, Cup, Wine, Engraved Floral, Gold-Wash Interior, 1 7/8 In. 55.00
Silver, Russian, Cup, Wine, Engraved Scenes Of Russia, 1873, 2 5/8 In. 55.00
Silver, Russian, Cup, Wine, Engraved Scenes Of Russia, 1878, 2 7/8 In. 55.00
Silver, Russian, Cup, Wine, Engraved, 1 3/4 In. 35.00
Silver, Russian, Cup, Wine, Engraved, 1885, 2 In. 35.00
Silver, Russian, Cup, 1871, 2 1/2 In. 75.00
Silver, Russian, Fork, Beet, Kokoshnik 42.00
Silver, Russian, Match Safe, St.George & Dragon, Sterling, Etched 125.00
Silver, Russian, Mug, Women & Children, 4 Ball Feet, Ovtchinnikoff, 1879, 3 In 425.00
Silver, Russian, Snuffbox, Niello, E.Moisejeu Grusliwow 290.00
Silver, Russian, Snuffbox, Niello, I.Kononow 280.00
Silver, Russian, Snuffbox, Niello, Moscow, 1857 ..... 360.00
Silver, Russian, Spoon, Enamel, Red, White, 3 Shades Of Blue, Hallmark, 5 In. 160.00
Silver, Russian, Spoon, Gold Washed, Black Niello On Back, Marked 1885 ..... 45.00
Silver, Russian, Wine, Red Lacquer Handle, Glass Insert, Marked In 3 Places, 3 ..... 100.00
Silver, Scottish, Ladle, Punch, Curved Fiddleback, Francis Howden, C.1782 ..... 155.00

Silver, Sheffield, see also Silver Plate

Silver, Sheffield, Candlestick, Bobeche, 12 In., Pair 248.00
Silver, Sheffield, Candlestick, With Bobeches, 12., Pair 168.00
Silver, Sheffield, Dish, Entree, Covered, Grapevines, Waterhouse, C.1833 ..... 348.00
Silver, Sheffield, Dish, Nut, Pierced, Handle 15.00
Silver, Sheffield, Ladle, Sugar Sifting, Pierced, Beaded Handle, C.1890 ..... 15.00
Silver, Sheffield, Salt, Master, Footed, Cobalt Liner, C.1810 ..... 88.00
Silver, Sheffield, Salt, Pedestal, Pair 45.00
Silver, Sheffield, Strainer, Tea, Wooden Handle, Scoop Shape 15.00
Silver, Sheffield, Tray, Birks Regency, FSM, Eng., 10 In. 85.00
Silver, Sheffield, Tumbler Cup, Jonathan Swift, 1740 ..... 325.00
Silver, Sheffield, Urn, Coffee, Vintage, Brass Spigot, Bleeding, 16 In. 135.00
Silver, Sheffield, Urn, Hand Chased, 13 X 11 1/2 In. 900.00
Silver, Sheffield, Warmer, Entree Dish, C.1790 ..... 298.00
Silver, Siamese, Case, Cigarette, Niello Of Dancing Gods, 4 1/4 In. 95.00

Sterling silver is made with 925 parts of silver out of 1, 000 parts of metal. The word sterling is a quality guarantee used in the United States after about 1860.

Silver, Sterling, see also Silver, American; Silver, English; etc.

Silver, Sterling, Basket, Border Design, Gadroon Edge, 6 X 3 In. 25.00
Silver, Sterling, Basket, Candy, Fretwork, Gorham 1868, 4 X 2 1/4 In. 32.00
Silver, Sterling, Basket, Cut, Relief, Black, Starr & Frost, 8 1/2 X 12 1/2 In. 175.00
Silver, Sterling, Basket, Openwork, Black, Starr, & Frost, 12 1/2 In. 250.00
Silver, Sterling, Basket, Pierced Work, Handle, H. Frank Whiting, 6 In. 35.00
Silver, Sterling, Basket, Sugar, Swing Handle, Gorham, C.1881, 3 1/4 In. 75.00
Silver, Sterling, Bell, Art Nouveau, Handled 18.00
Silver, Sterling, Bell, Dinner, Figurine, Vermeil Work, 3 1/2 In. 115.00
Silver, Sterling, Blotter, Rocker, Gorham, Beaded Edge, Punched Pattern 22.00
Silver, Sterling, Bookmark, Repousse Floral 25.00
Silver, Sterling, Bottle, Perfume, Crystal Liner & Dauber, Hallmarked, 6 In. 40.00
Silver, Sterling, Bowl, Art Nouveau, Applied Floral, Whiting, 11 1/4 In. 450.00
Silver, Sterling, Bowl, Whiting, Art Nouveau, Floral Design, 11 1/4 In. 225.00
Silver, Sterling, Box, Powder, Repousse, April 10, 1896, 2 3/4 X 3 3/4 In. 125.00
Silver, Sterling, Box, Ring, Hinged Dome Lid, Wilcox, C.1903, Square, 1 5/8 In. 35.00

Silver, Sterling, Brush, Elaborate Decoration, Bristles 20.00
Silver, Sterling, Butter Pat, Ship Center, Whiting, Set Of 11 45.00
Silver, Sterling, Butter Spreader, Hallmarked & Patent 1917, Set Of 6 35.00
Silver, Sterling, Buttonhook, Folding, Whiting, 3 1/2 In. 12.00
Silver, Sterling, Buttonhook, Hand Hammered 14.00
Silver, Sterling, Buttonhook, Ornate Handle, Gorham, 1878 12.00
Silver, Sterling, Cake Server, Acorn Pattern, Georg Jensen, 10 1/2 In. 125.00
Silver, Sterling, Candelabra, 3 Cup, Weighted, Pair 45.00
Silver, Sterling, Case, Card, Cathedral Embossed, Edw.Thomason, Birmingham 200.00
Silver, Sterling, Case, Chatelaine, Telescopic, Pencil, Ornate Scrollwork 40.00
Silver, Sterling, Case, Cigarette, Enamel Lid, Lady In Pastel, C.1891 195.00
Silver, Sterling, Case, Cigarette, Engraved Oriental Picture 35.00
Silver, Sterling, Case, Cigarette, WWii Air Force Eagle Engraved 65.00
Silver, Sterling, Case, Thimble, Openwork 35.00
Silver, Sterling, Coffeepot, Demitasse, Repousse, Teak Handle, Gorham, C.1910 195.00
Silver, Sterling, Compote, Castle, Farm, Mountain Background, S. Kirk, 1910 175.00
Silver, Sterling, Container, Toothpowder, Gorham, Crystal & Silver, 3 1/2 In. 35.00
Silver, Sterling, Cream & Sugar, Classical Design, Schofield 90.00
Silver, Sterling, Creamer, Cow, Embossed Insect On Chased Hair, 4 1/2 X 7 In. 235.00
Silver, Sterling, Creamer, John Moore, 1808 348.00
Silver, Sterling, Crumber, La Splendide, Reed & Barton 62.00
Silver, Sterling, Crumber, Louis XV, Whiting 52.00
Silver, Sterling, Cup, Loving, Balloon Race, 1914, 3 Handles, T.B.Starr, 9 In. 275.00
Silver, Sterling, Cup, Loving, Repousse, Mauser Mfg Co., 1898, 2 In. 35.00
Silver, Sterling, Dish, Butter, Drain Plate 75.00
Silver, Sterling, Dish, Candy, Floral, Cutout Edges, Hamilton & Diesinger 27.50
Silver, Sterling, Dresser Set, Repousse, 5 Piece 85.00
Silver, Sterling, Figurine, Goat, Angora Standing, 4 X 4 1/2 In. 135.00
Silver, Sterling, Figurine, Kangaroo, 3 In. 74.00
Silver, Sterling, Figurine, Knight Holding Sword, Ivory Face, Crest, 9 1/2 In. 385.00
Silver, Sterling, Figurine, Rabbit, 1/2 X 1 In., S.Kirk 65.00
Silver, Sterling, Figurine, Running Fox, 1 1/2 X 3 3/4 In. 55.00
Silver, Sterling, Figurine, Running Rabbit, 2 1/2 X 2 1/2 In. 80.00
Silver, Sterling, Figurine, Sitting Dachshund, 2 1/2 X 3 1/2 In 77.00 To 80.00
Silver, Sterling, Figurine, Stallion Prancing, 4 1/2 X 5 1/2 In. 235.00
Silver, Sterling, Figurine, Standing Bear, 1 3/4 In X 3 In. 70.00
Silver, Sterling, Figurine, Standing Kangaroo, 2 In. 39.00
Silver, Sterling, Figurine, Standing Moose, 3 3/4 X 3 1/2 In. 100.00
Silver, Sterling, Figurine, Standing Stallion, One Hoof Raised, 5 X 5 1/2 In. 235.00
Silver, Sterling, Figurine, Whippet Lying, Paws Outstretched, 1 1/4 X 3 In. 40.00
Silver, Sterling, Figurine, Whippet On Stomach, 1 1/2 X 3 1/4 In. 67.00
Silver, Sterling, Fish Slice & Fork, Wood & Hughes, 1861, Engraved, M.Jacobs 195.00
Silver, Sterling, Flask, Ladies, Hammered Design, Hinged Lid, C.1925, 4 Oz. 45.00
Silver, Sterling, Flask, Marked C A V, 10 Oz., 5 X 7 1/2 In. 85.00
Silver, Sterling, Flask, Scent, Knight Decoration, Scroll Work, 2 1/8 In. 75.00
Silver, Sterling, Flask, Screw-On Hinged Cap, C.A.Vanderbilt, C.1909, 7 In. 95.00
Silver, Sterling, Flask, Woman & Cigarette, 5 In. 60.00
Silver, Sterling, Food Pusher, Baby's, Georgian, Towle, Monogram, 4 1/2 In. 20.00
Silver, Sterling, Fork, Cold Meat, International, Avalon 60.00
Silver, Sterling, Fork, Dinner, Richmond, Gorham, C.1897 3.00
Silver, Sterling, Fork, Oyster, B.K.& Co., C.1900 15.00
Silver, Sterling, Fork, Oyster, Poppy, Gorham, Patent 1895 10.50
Silver, Sterling, Fork, Poppy, Gorham, 1894, 6 3/4 In. 11.00
Silver, Sterling, Fork, Sardine, Repousse, Kirk, C.1890 60.00
Silver, Sterling, Fork, Seafood, Oval Twist, Whiting, 1880, Set Of 6 40.00
Silver, Sterling, Fork, Serving, Repousse, Kirk, C.1903 55.00
Silver, Sterling, Fork, Tomato, Napoleon, Enamel Wreath, Shiebler & Co., 1894 18.00
Silver, Sterling, Frame, Oval Easel 19.00
Silver, Sterling, Gravy Boat & Tray, Eastwood Park Co., C.1909 40.00
Silver, Sterling, Hook, Button, Heavy 35.00
Silver, Sterling, Hurricane Candles, Glass Shade, Pair 60.00
Silver, Sterling, Inhaler, Marked Smith's Menthol Inhaler, Gorham Hallmarks 56.00
Silver, Sterling, Inkwell, Bell Shape, C.1905, 3 1/2 In. 70.00
Silver, Sterling, Inkwell, Bell Shape, Inscribed Joan, C.1905, 3 1/2 In. 70.00
Silver, Sterling, Iron, Curling, Ornate Handles 30.00

Item	Price
Silver, Sterling, Jar, Jam, Kirk Repousse Top, Etched-Pattern Glass Insert	20.00
Silver, Sterling, Jug, Victorian, H.Lion Passant And Date, 1891, 9 1/2 In.	375.00
Silver, Sterling, Knife, Butter, Lion Hallmark, C 1897	80.00
Silver, Sterling, Knife, Crumb, 1864, Gorham, Lowell & Senter, 13 In.	85.00
Silver, Sterling, Knife, Pocket, Repousse, Folding Scissors	17.50
Silver, Sterling, Knife, Pocket, Spring Buttons, Indian Chief In Relief	40.00
Silver, Sterling, Ladle, Pouring, Long Handle, Gale & Bro., 1901	14.75
Silver, Sterling, Lorgnette, Art Deco, Multicolor French Enamel	150.00
Silver, Sterling, Match Safe, English, Birmingham, 1907, Decorated	34.00
Silver, Sterling, Match Safe, Figural, Alligator Greenleaf & Crosby	37.00
Silver, Sterling, Match Safe, Floral-Spray Front, Side Scrolls, American	28.00
Silver, Sterling, Match Safe, Mermaid Loving Sailor In Boat	55.00
Silver, Sterling, Match Safe, Nude Woman In Water, Waves, Gulls, Sunset	50.00
Silver, Sterling, Match Safe, Nude Woman, Flowing Hair, Waves	55.00
Silver, Sterling, Match Safe, Ornate Jester In High Relief	65.00
Silver, Sterling, Match Safe, Winged Nymph, Nude Among Flowers, Ornate	50.00
Silver, Sterling, Mirror, Art Nouveau, Lady & Flowers, Unger Brothers	85.00
Silver, Sterling, Mirror, Hand, Raised Floral, Gorham, 1892, 11 1/2 In.	55.00
Silver, Sterling, Nail File & Buttonhook Set, 7 1/2 In.	12.50
Silver, Sterling, Napkin Ring, see Napkin Ring	
Silver, Sterling, Opera Glasses, Repousse	175.00
Silver, Sterling, Pitcher, Beverage, Repousse, Whiting, 7 1/4 In.	450.00
Silver, Sterling, Pitcher, Water, C.A.Vanderbilt, C.1909, 9 1/4 In.	75.00
Silver, Sterling, Pitcher, Whiting, Repousse, 7 1/2 In.	450.00
Silver, Sterling, Pitcher, 3 1/2 Pints, Plain, 9 In.	95.00
Silver, Sterling, Plate, Pierced Border, Heavy, 10 In.	55.00
Silver, Sterling, Porringer, Geo.Jensen, 5 1/4 In.	75.00
Silver, Sterling, Pusher, Hens & Chicks	30.00
Silver, Sterling, Salt & Pepper, Figural, Burner & Teapot, Miniature	55.00
Silver, Sterling, Salt & Pepper, Figural, Duck, Horn Of Plenty	30.00
Silver, Sterling, Salt Dip, Shape Of Viking Boat, Cobalt Insert	12.00
Silver, Sterling, Salt, Floral, Gold-Washed Interior, B.S.& Co., 1894, Pair	15.00
Silver, Sterling, Salt, Master, S.E.Young & Co.	14.00
Silver, Sterling, Salt, Oval Base, Fluted Top, English Hallmark, 2 7/8, Pair	35.00
Silver, Sterling, Salt, Repousse, Square, S.Kirk & Son, 1 1/8 X 1 3/4 In., Pair	125.00
Silver, Sterling, Scoop, Cheese, Napoleon, Enamel Wreath, Shiebler & Co., 1894	35.00
Silver, Sterling, Seal, Art Nouveau, Floral, Hallmarked, 2 3/4 In.	20.00
Silver, Sterling, Server, Asparagus, Wm.Sumner, 1817	248.00
Silver, Sterling, Server, Fish, Pierced Shamrocks, Zimmermann, 1864	55.00
Silver, Sterling, Server, Tomato, Navarre, 1909, Durgin, 6 1/2 In.	20.00
Silver, Sterling, Shears, Grape, German Blades, Grapes And Leaves On Handle	34.00
Silver, Sterling, Shoehorn Cupids & Hearts, Art Nouveau, Unger Bros.	45.00
Silver, Sterling, Spoon, Bonbon, Art Nouveau, Fury Face In Handle	35.00
Silver, Sterling, Spoon, Demi, Easter, Chick Cracking Egg On Rope Handle	15.00
Silver, Sterling, Spoon, Fraternal, Art Nouveau Woman, Unger Bros.	45.00
Silver, Sterling, Spoon, Fruit, Hallmark Thomas & Miles, London, 1793-4	90.00
Silver, Sterling, Spoon, Iced Tea, Repousse, Kirk, C.1903	25.00
Silver, Sterling, Spoon, Mustard, Grecian, 1861	16.50
Silver, Sterling, Spoon, Newport Shell, Frank Smith, 1910, Oval	10.00
Silver, Sterling, Spoon, Nut, Cambridge, Pierced, Gorham, 1899	18.00
Silver, Sterling, Spoon, Salt, Louis XV, Whiting, Patent 1891, 3 1/2 In.	10.00
Silver, Sterling, Spoon, Serving, Corinthian, Gold Washed, Gorham, 1872	35.00
Silver, Sterling, Spoon, Serving, George VIII, Whiting, 1891	16.00
Silver, Sterling, Spoon, Serving, Repousse, Kirk, C.1850, 9 1/2 In.	65.00
Silver, Sterling, Spoon, Serving, Scroll, Leaf, & Ribbing, Gorham, 1855	22.00
Silver, Sterling, Spoon, Serving, T.Goldsmith, Troy, N.Y., C.1845, Pair	25.00
Silver, Sterling, Spoon, Serving, Whiting, Dorothy Vernon	60.00
Silver, Sterling, Spoon, Soup, Versailles, Gorham, 1888	28.00
Silver, Sterling, Spoon, Souvenir, see Souvenir, Spoon, Sterling Silver	
Silver, Sterling, Spoon, Sugar, Bright Cut, Wood & Hughes, C.1855	14.75
Silver, Sterling, Spoon, Sugar, Georgian, Towle, 1898	20.00
Silver, Sterling, Spoon, Zodiac, Demitasse, August, Patent 1904	9.95
Silver, Sterling, Spreader, Draped Woman, Cupid On Handle, Reed & Barton	55.00
Silver, Sterling, Strainer, Tea, Cutout, Wood Handle, Gorham, Victorian	28.00

Silver, Sterling, Strainer, Tea, Embossed Flower Form, Art Nouveau 32.00
Silver, Sterling, Stretcher, Glove 18.00
Silver, Sterling, Sugar & Creamer, Art Nouveau, Applied Floral, Kerr 275.00
Silver, Sterling, Sugar & Creamer, Classical Design, Schofield 90.00
Silver, Sterling, Sugar Tongs, Hallmarked, C.1897, 5 In. 40.00
Silver, Sterling, Sugar Tongs, Rosenkraus, Engraved Claw, 5 1/4 In. 20.00
Silver, Sterling, Sugar Tongs, Shell, Sheffield, 1869, Hy.Archer Co. 35.00
Silver, Sterling, Sugar, King Edward, Whiting, Ornate And Heavy 30.00
Silver, Sterling, Sweetmeat Stand, Knopped Pedestal, 9 X 3 1/2 In. 135.00
Silver, Sterling, Tablespoon, Angelo, Wood & Hughes, C.1858, Pair 48.00
Silver, Sterling, Tablespoon, Olive, Gray & Libby, C.1850 .... 8.00
Silver, Sterling, Tablespoon, Twist Handle, Duhme & Co., Cincinnati 30.00
Silver, Sterling, Tablespoon, Warwick, International, C.1890 .... 12.00
Silver, Sterling, Tea Ball And Chain, Gorham 20.00
Silver, Sterling, Tea Caddy, Repousse Chrysanthemums, Gorham 65.00
Silver, Sterling, Tea Strainer, Repousse Handles, S.Kirk & Son 50.00
Silver, Sterling, Teaspoon, Baby In Highchair With Rattle, Gorham, 1897 .... 12.75
Silver, Sterling, Teaspoon, Christmas, 1891, Flowers & Name On Handle 11.95
Silver, Sterling, Teaspoon, Le Cinq Fleur, Reed & Barton, 1900 .... 10.50
Silver, Sterling, Teaspoon, Lion With K Mark, Patent 1879 .... 6.50
Silver, Sterling, Teaspoon, Newcastle, Gorham, Victorian 7.75
Silver, Sterling, Teaspoon, Richmond, Gorham, C.1897 .... 2.00
Silver, Sterling, Thimble, see Sewing Tool, Thimble, Sterling
Silver, Sterling, Toast Rack, 4-Place, Sheffield, 1836-7, 3 3/4 In. 35.00
Silver, Sterling, Toast Rack, 6-Place, Sheffield, 1836-7, 5 1/2 In. 50.00
Silver, Sterling, Tong, Asparagus, Madam Jumel, Whiting Mfg.Co., 4 3/8 In. 195.00
Silver, Sterling, Tongs, Ice, Repousse, Kirk, C.1890 .... 60.00
Silver, Sterling, Tongs, Repousse Top & Leaf-Shaped Gripper, S.Kirk & Son 75.00
Silver, Sterling, Toothpick, Pierced, Crystal Liner 14.00
Silver, Sterling, Toy, Miniature, Royal Dutch, 1 1/4 In. 125.00
Silver, Sterling, Tray, Boat Shape, Ribbed Design, 8 Oz. 40.00
Silver, Sterling, Tray, Bread, Plymouth Pattern, Gorham, 11 In. 125.00
Silver, Sterling, Tray, Georg Jensen, Oval, 4 Ball Feet, 2 3/4 X 1 7/8 In. 25.00
Silver, Sterling, Tray, Pin, Nude With Harp On Rock, Repousse, Unger Brothers 98.00
Silver, Sterling, Tray, Well & Tree, Footed, Gorham, 1948, 20 X 14 1/2 In. 700.00
Silver, Sterling, Vase, Trumpet Shape, Webster, 6 In. 10.00
Silver, Sterling, Vase, Trumpet Shape, Weighted Base, Etched, 10 In. 30.00
Silver, Sterling, Walking Elephant, Ivory Tusks, Trunk Raised, 2 1/2 X 4 In. 80.00
Silver, Sterling, Wax Sealer, Unger Bros., Monogram '77, 3 In. 20.00
Silver, Sterling, Whistle, Revolving Center, Mother-Of-Pearl Handle 150.00
Silver, Sterling, Wine Label, Half-Moon Anisette, Hallmarked Birmingham, 1905 .... 14.00
Silver, Sterling, Wine Label, Ornate, Cutout, Hallmarked Birmingham, 1863 .... 22.00
Silver, Victorian Pocketbook Frame, Ornate, Cupids 32.50

Sinclaire cut glass was made by H.P.Sinclaire and Company of Corning, New York, between 1905 and 1929. Pieces were made of crystal as well as amber, blue, green, or ruby. Only a small percentage of Sinclaire glass is marked.

Sinclaire, Compote, Amber Turning To Red, 8 1/2 X 8 In. 95.00
Sinclaire, Compote, Etched, 4 In. 80.00
Sinclaire, Console Set, Green, Signed, 5 Piece 325.00
Sinclaire, Jar, Dresser, Aqua Enamel On Sterling, Set Of 3 .... 175.00
Sinclaire, Vase, Engraved Fan, Blue, 10 1/2 In. 75.00
Sinclaire, Vase, Flute-Cut Greek-Key Border, Low Pedestal, 9 1/2 X 4 1/2 In. 75.00
Sitzendorf, Centerpiece Bowl, Putti Holding Pierced Bowl, 12 1/2 In. 375.00
Sitzendorf, Figurine, Finely Dressed Vendor With Apron Of Fruit, C.1850 .... 75.00
Sitzendorf, Figurine, Godey's Fashion Girl, April, 1863, 7 In. 150.00
Sitzendorf, Figurine, Godey's Fashion Girl, Feb., 1862, 7 In. 150.00
Sitzendorf, Tea Set, Pink Shell, 3 Piece 85.00
Sky King, Ring, Tele-Blinker 65.00

Slag glass is streaked with several colors. There were many types made from about 1880. Pink slag was an American Victorian product of unknown origin. Purple and blue slag were made in American and English factories. Red slag is a very late Victorian product. Other colors are known, but are of less importance to the collector. The numbers B-xx refer to the book "Milk Glass" by E. Belknap.

Slag, Black, Bust, Queen Victoria, C.1890, 3 X 3 1/2 In. 40.00
Slag, Blue, Creamer, Covered, Opaque, Dolphin 65.00
Slag, Blue, Platter, Oval, 12 In. 20.00
Slag, Blue, Sugar Shaker, Atterbury 75.00
Slag, Blue, Vase, Embossed Peacocks, 8 In. 89.00
Slag, Caramel, see Chocolate Glass
Slag, Green & Mauve, Cake Stand, Waffle, Atterbury 95.00
Slag, Green, Butter, Lacy Top, Ribbed, Atterbury 77.00
Slag, Green, Dish, Hen Cover, Lacy Base, Atterbury, B-144 .... 225.00
Slag, Green, Jar, Powder, Nudes On Lid & Base 75.00
Slag, Green, Mug, Dewey, Footed, Greentown 65.00
Slag, Green, Table Set, Lacy Top, Ribbed, Butter, Sugar, Spooner, Creamer 350.00
Slag, Orange-To-Red, Candlesticks, Pair, 3 In. 35.00
Slag, Pink, Compote, Inverted Fan & Feather 550.00
Slag, Pink, Cruet, Inverted Fan & Feather, 6 1/2 In. 975.00
Slag, Pink, Cup, Punch, Inverted Fan & Feather .... 325.00 To 350.00
Slag, Pink, Pitcher, Inverted Fan & Feather, 8 In. .... 950.00 To 1000.00
Slag, Pink, Sauce, Inverted Fan & Feather 350.00
Slag, Pink, Toothpick, Inverted Fan & Feather 700.00
Slag, Purple, Bowl, Acanthus, B-291a 89.00
Slag, Purple, Bowl, Atterbury, Acanthus Leaf, 9 1/2 In., Dated 89.00
Slag, Purple, Bowl, Dart & Bar, 8 In., B-291d 40.00
Slag, Purple, Bowl, Dolphin Feet, English, 7 In. 55.00
Slag, Purple, Bowl, White Dots Radiating From Center, Center Handle, 8 In. 95.00
Slag, Purple, Cakestand, Dart Bar, 11 In. 85.00
Slag, Purple, Celery, English Lion Mark, Pair 65.00
Slag, Purple, Celery, Fluted 58.00
Slag, Purple, Celery, Jewel, B-295b 85.00
Slag, Purple, Chamberstick, Ring Handle, Scalloped Rim 48.00
Slag, Purple, Compote, Dart Bar, 8 1/2 In. 90.00
Slag, Purple, Compote, Jenny Lind 150.00
Slag, Purple, Compote, Ribbon Edge, 5 In. 95.00
Slag, Purple, Compote, Spool, Crimped Rim, 4 X 4 1/2 In. 39.50
Slag, Purple, Compote, Threaded Band, Fluted Rim, B-326 .... 75.00
Slag, Purple, Creamer, Dog Handle 47.50
Slag, Purple, Creamer, English Raised Acorns 100.00
Slag, Purple, Creamer, Fluted 50.00
Slag, Purple, Cup & Saucer, Demitasse, Signed 45.00
Slag, Purple, Dish, Candy, Crimped Edge, 3 Legged 50.00
Slag, Purple, Dish, Low, Ruffled Edge 60.00
Slag, Purple, Fruit Bowl, Melon, Atterbury, 9 1/2 In. 89.50
Slag, Purple, Goblet, Six Panels, Rosettes & Stippling 110.00
Slag, Purple, Match Holder, Ring Handles 49.50
Slag, Purple, Mug, Molded Grapes, Deep Star Base 35.00
Slag, Purple, Mustard, Figural, Bull's Head 85.00
Slag, Purple, Pitcher, Miniature, 3 1/2 In. 35.00
Slag, Purple, Pitcher, Water, Dart Bar 75.00
Slag, Purple, Plate, Bread, Tam-O-'Shanter 125.00
Slag, Purple, Plate, Cake, Lattice Edge, 10 In. 85.00
Slag, Purple, Plate, Closed Lattice Edge, 10 1/2 In. 45.00
Slag, Purple, Platter, Notched Edge 45.00
Slag, Purple, Pot, Honey, Beehive 75.00
Slag, Purple, Spooner, Fluted 42.00
Slag, Purple, Tumbler, English Mark, 3 1/4 In. 25.00
Slag, Purple, Tumbler, Lemonade, Sowerby Mark 35.00
Slag, Purple, Vase, Grapes & Vines, Rests On Leaf Base, 5 3/4 In. 95.00
Slag, Purple, Vase, Wee, Pointed Rim, Leaf Decoration, 4 1/2 In., B-325 .... 45.00
Slag, Purple, Whiskey, Inscribed Just A Thimble Full, Sowerby Mark, 3 In. 45.00
Slag, Red, Bowl, Souvenir, Citizens Mutual Trust, Wheeling, W.Va., 1924 .... 65.00
Slag, Red, Pitcher, Windmills, Trees 15.00
Slag, Yellow, Ashtray, Opalescent 15.00
Slag, Yellow, Shoe, High, Daisy & Button, Union Glass Co., 4 1/2 In. 40.00
Slag, Yellow, Shoe, Oxford, Daisy & Button, Union Glass Co., 5 1/2 In., Pair 35.00

Sleepy Eye pottery was made to be given away with the flour products of the Sleepy Eye Milling Co., Sleepy Eye, Minnesota, from about 1893 to 1952. It is a heavy stoneware with blue decorations, usually the famous profile of an Indian.

Sleepy Eye, Pitcher, Indian Head Handle, Blue & Gray, 9 In. 48.00
Sleepy Eye, Box, Salt, Indian Village, H On Bottom 225.00
Sleepy Eye, Creamer 115.00
Sleepy Eye, Crock, Butter, Indian Head, Teepee & Trees, Signed, 5 In. 225.00
Sleepy Eye, Crock, Gray & Flemish Blue, 6 1/4 In. 125.00
Sleepy Eye, Mug, Indian On Handle 60.00
Sleepy Eye, Mug, W.S.Co., 4 1/2 In. 40.00
Sleepy Eye, Pitcher, Gray & Blue, 1/2 Gallon 175.00
Sleepy Eye, Pitcher, Set, 5 Graduated, White And Blue, 4 1/2 To 9 In. 375.00
Sleepy Eye, Pitcher, WSC Monmouth, Ill., 6 1/2 In. 55.00
Sleepy Eye, Pitcher, 6 In. 85.00
Sleepy Eye, Plate, Small 10.00
Sleepy Eye, Stein, Indian Head, Teepee & Trees, Signed 250.00
Sleepy Eye, Sugar Bowl 190.00

Slip is a thin mixture of clay and water, about the consistency of sour cream, that is applied to the pottery for decoration.

Slipware, Cup Plate, Pennsylvania Dutch, Letter E Decoration 340.00
Slipware, Figurine, King Charles Spaniel, White, Brown, C.1850, 9 In., Pair 875.00
Slipware, Salt Bowl, Blue, Turquoise, Brown Geometrics, C.1870, 10 1/2 In. 125.00

Slot Machine, see Store, Machine

Smith Brothers glass was made after 1878. The owners had worked for the Mt.Washington Glass Company in New Bedford, Massachusetts, for seven years before going into their own shop. Some of the designs were similar.

Smith Brothers, Barrel, Biscuit, Pastel, Coin Gold Decoration, 7 In. 475.00
Smith Brothers, Barrel, Biscuit, Shasta Daisies, Signed In Lid, 6 3/4 In. 185.00
Smith Brothers, Bottle, Perfume, Cream Melon Rib, Royal, Gold Floral, Pair 50.00
Smith Brothers, Bowl, Beige Satin, Melon Ribbed, Coin Gold Floral, 4 In. 105.00
Smith Brothers, Bowl, Beige Satin, Melon Ribbed, Enamel Pansies, 5 1/2 In. 125.00
Smith Brothers, Bowl, Burmese Color, Decorated, Miniature 195.00
Smith Brothers, Bowl, Ivory Color, Gold-Outlined Pink & Blue Wisteria, 4 In 175.00
Smith Brothers, Bowl, Melon Ribbed, Cream, Pink & Orchid Flowers, 7 X 4 In. 175.00
Smith Brothers, Box, White Satin Covered, Melon Ribbed, Violets, 3 In. 85.00
Smith Brothers, Jar, Biscuit, Shasta Daisies, Silver-Plate Fittings, 7 In. 220.00
Smith Brothers, Jar, Cookie, Blue Ground, Floral Wreath & Bird, 8 In. 150.00
Smith Brothers, Jar, Cookie, Daisies, Silver Fittings 220.00
Smith Brothers, Muffineer, Hand-Painted Floral 78.00
Smith Brothers, Plate, Santa Maria, Libbey Cut, A.C.Smith, 7 3/4 In. 310.00
Smith Brothers, Rose Bowl, Cream Satin Glass, Enamel Shasta Daisies, 6 In. 90.00
Smith Brothers, Rose Bowl, Melon Ribbed, Applied Gold Prunus, 3 1/2 In. 185.00
Smith Brothers, Salt, Melon Ribbed, Hand-Painted Floral, 3 X 1 1/2 In. 110.00
Smith Brothers, Salt, On Libbey Blank, White, Enamel Floral & Blue Dots 95.00
Smith Brothers, Sugar & Creamer, Alabaster, Flowers 175.00
Smith Brothers, Toothpick, Melon Shape, Blue With Pink Pansies 30.00
Smith Brothers, Vase, Biscuit Color, Swamp Birds, Gold Banding, 6 In. 38.00
Smith Brothers, Vase, Enameled Stork, Pink, Plated Holder, 4 1/2 In., Pair 150.00
Smith Brothers, Vase, Pink, Pelican In Green Water, Tauton, 6 In., Pair 225.00
Smith Brothers, Vase, Storks In Pond, Pairpoint Silver Holder, 5 1/2 In. 110.00
Snow Babies, Baby Lying On Sled, Marked Germany 40.00
Snow Babies, Baby Pushing Carriage Holding Twins, Numbered 65.00
Snow Babies, Baby Standing, 1 3/4 In. 20.00
Snow Babies, Baby, Marked Germany, 1 3/4 In. 29.00
Snow Babies, Bear, 1 1/2 In. 40.00
Snow Babies, Candleholder, 1 1/4 X 1 1/2 In. 55.00
Snow Babies, Chamberstick, Royal Bayreuth, Blue Mark 68.00
Snow Babies, Elf, 2 1/4 In. 40.00
Snow Babies, Plate, 6 In., Royal Bayreuth, Blue Mark 68.00
Snow Babies, Seated Snow Baby, 2 In. 95.00
Snow Babies, Snow Baby On Sled, Red, 1 3/4 In. 70.00

Snow Babies, Snow Baby Pulling 3 Penguins On Sled 150.00
Snow Babies, Snow Boy On Skates, 2 1/4 In. 85.00
Snow Babies, Tea Set, Child's, Royal Bayreuth, 3 Piece 135.00
Snow Babies, Three Babies, Sitting On Each Other, 2 In. 23.00
Snow Babies, Three Snow Babies On Sled, 2 3/4 In. 195.00
Snow Babies, Tiny Sitting Snow Baby, Red Cap 50.00
Snow Babies, Two Babies Sliding Down Wall 55.00

Snuff Bottle, see Bottle, Snuff

Snuffbox, Birchbark, Wooden Base & Lid, Shiny Brown, Oval, 2 3/4 In. 30.00
Snuffbox, Black Lacquer With Mother-Of-Pearl Inlay 14.50
Snuffbox, Black Lacquer, 12 Men Under One Hat On Cover, 3 1/2 In. Circular 30.00
Snuffbox, Boxwood, Round, 2 1/4 X 2 In. 10.00
Snuffbox, Compass Held By Frog On Lid, 1876 .... 25.00
Snuffbox, Engraved, Austrian, 2 X 1 1/4 In. 75.00
Snuffbox, Hinged, Designs In Mother-Of-Pearl, Oblong, 3 1/2 X 2 In. 18.00
Snuffbox, Indian Birchbark 40.00
Snuffbox, Leather Pouch, Cork Stopper, Hand Laced 15.00
Snuffbox, Oil Painted Scene Of Family On Lid 26.00
Snuffbox, Rectangular, Reddish-Brown Flame Design, Pewter Inlay, 2 X 1 In. 37.00
Snuffbox, Stenciled Old Fellows Take A Pinch, Fancy Border 12.00
Snuffbox, Sterling Silver, Fat Pig With Big Ears, Hinged Lid On Back 65.00
Snuffbox, Tortoiseshell, Light Patches, Hinged Lid, 3/4 X 1 3/4 X 1/2 In. 16.00
Snuffbox, Wood, Lacquered, Lid Painted With Scottish Highland Scene, C 1850 .... 145.00
Snuffbox, Wooden, Stone In Hinged Silver Lid, Handmade, 3 In. 65.00

Soapstone is a mineral that was used for foot warmers or griddles because of its heat-retaining properties. Soapstone was carved in many countries in the nineteenth and twentieth centuries.

Soapstone, Bookend, Footed Urn, Bouquet Of Carved Flowers, China, Pair 50.00
Soapstone, Bookend, Urn Of Flowers & Leaves, 5 In., Pair 55.00
Soapstone, Bottle, Snuff, Green 20.00
Soapstone, Figurine, Foo Dog With Pups On Pedestal, Script Front, 7 In., Pair 90.00
Soapstone, Figurine, Foo Dog, Green White, On Platform, 4 In., Pair 38.00
Soapstone, Figurine, Kwan Yin On Lotus Blossoms, Green On Tan, 10 1/2 In. 80.00
Soapstone, Figurine, Kwan Yin, Mottled Green, Tan Lotus Base, 10 1/2 In. 68.00
Soapstone, Figurine, Monkeys & Bird, Reddish Brown, 13 In. 55.00
Soapstone, Flower Arrangement, Pierced Brown Base, 6 In. 30.00
Soapstone, Group, Birds, Monkeys, Deer, Red, 12 X 4 In. 65.00
Soapstone, Group, 3 Pieces, Floral Designs, 8 In. 110.00
Soapstone, Plate, Carved Scene On Front, 6 In. 65.00
Soapstone, Toothpick, Three Monkeys 15.00
Soapstone, Vase, Double, Roses, Floral, & Leaves, Gray, Black, & Rust, 5 1/4 In. 35.00
Soapstone, Vase, Double, Tree In Front, Carved, 7 X 5 X 3 In. 40.00
Soapstone, Warmer, Foot, Bail .... 12.00 To 12.50
Soapstone, Whistle, Bird Shape 8.50
Soapstone, Whistle, Carved Fish 8.50
Soapstone, Whistle, Duck Calls, Bird, Carved 7.50
Soft Paste, Cup & Saucer, Handleless, Brick-Red Rose & Lines, Wood 125.00
Soft Paste, Cup & Saucer, Handleless, Strawberry Luster 70.00
Soft Paste, Cup & Saucer, Handleless, Verhanda, Mustard, Brown Floral, 1830 .... 18.00
Soft Paste, Cup & Saucer, Red & Pink Designs, Staffordshire 30.00
Soft Paste, Jug, Red-Faced Satyr, Silver Luster, Potato Shape, C.1810, 5 In. 255.00
Soft Paste, Jug, Satyr, Lozenge-Shaped Decoration, Red, White, Silver, 1805 .... 250.00
Soft Paste, Saucer, Strawberry, Deep 38.00
Souvenir, Ashtray And Match Holder, Narragansett Indian 6.50
Souvenir, Ashtray, Eiffel Tower, French, Metal, 4 In. 5.00
Souvenir, Ashtray, Monmouth, Ill., Western Stoneware Co., Maple Leaf 27.00
Souvenir, Ashtray, Nevada, Silver State, Miniature Working Roulette 15.00
Souvenir, Ashtray, S.S.Oronsay, British, Glass 3.00
Souvenir, Ashtray, University Of Chicago, Gargoyle Griffin In Center 5.00
Souvenir, Ashtray, Viaduct, Akron, Ohio, Copper Plated, Turtle Shape, 5 In. 4.00
Souvenir, Ashtray, World's Fair, 1939, Jeweled 8.00
Souvenir, Bell, Glass, World's Fair, 1893 .... 35.00
Souvenir, Bell, World's Fair, 1893, Chicago, Clear Glass, Star Mark 65.00
Souvenir, Block, Esso, N.Y., World's Fair, 1939 .... 12.00

Souvenir, Book, Tournament Of Roses, 1928 .... 10.00
Souvenir, Bowl, Albany, N.Y., Cobalt & Color Transfer 10.00
Souvenir, Bowl, Post Office, Wiscasset, White & Black Transfer 12.00
Souvenir, Bowl, Windsor, Canada, Porcelain, Germany, Open Edge, 6 In. 6.00
Souvenir, Box, Stamp, Columbia Exposition, 1893, 3 1/4 X 1 3/4 X 3/4 In. 25.00
Souvenir, Creamer, Cumberland, Md., Porcelain, Germany 12.00
Souvenir, Creamer, Walled Lake, Emerald Green, Gold Trim, 2 1/2 In. 10.00
Souvenir, Cup & Saucer, Coney Island, 1903, Pressed Glass, Colorado, Green 20.00
Souvenir, Cup & Saucer, Niagara Falls, Goof, Mist Of The Maid 17.00
Souvenir, Cup & Saucer, State Capitol, Cheyenne, Wyoming, Cobalt Blue 14.50
Souvenir, Cup, Brockton, Mass., Cobalt & Color Transfer 9.00
Souvenir, Cup, Thelma, Sectional, Silver Plate, Leather Case 14.00
Souvenir, Cup, Wrigley Building, Transfer, Gold Beading, Germany 12.00
Souvenir, Dish, Candy, Stockbridge, Porcelain, Germany, Incised Handle 5.50
Souvenir, Dish, Iroquois Lock & Dam, Royal Winston, English, 4 In. 5.00
Souvenir, Dish, Phillipsburg, Oregon, 4 In. 6.50
Souvenir, Dish, Pin, Pennsylvania Park, York, Pa., Impressed 53 .... 14.00
Souvenir, Dish, Queen Anne, Ship, Car Ferry, Bluenose, Yarmouth, N.S., 3 3/4 In. 9.50
Souvenir, Eggcup, Hitchcock Hill Company, Pressed Glass, Honeycomb, 4 Rows 7.50
Souvenir, Fan, Chicago Exposition, Paper 20.00
Souvenir, Figurine, Buffalo, Pan American Exposition, 1901, Bronze, 3 In. 22.75
Souvenir, Fork, Sterling, City Of Baltimore, Lord Baltimore, Monument 20.00
Souvenir, Glass Hatchet, Bust Of Washington, World's Fair, Libbey Glass Co. 40.00
Souvenir, Glass, New York World's Fair, 1939 .... 5.00
Souvenir, Hatpin Holder, St.Petersburg, Silver Deposit 30.00
Souvenir, Knife, Babe Ruth, Baseball Bat Shape, Yankee Stadium, Pocket 2.00
Souvenir, Knife, Pocket, Babe Ruth, Yankee Stadium, 1927, Bat Shape 2.00
Souvenir, Ladle, Cutout Steel Pier, Atlantic City, Sterling 17.00
Souvenir, Lincoln Funeral Token With Picture 30.00
Souvenir, Mirror, Oval, Bathing Beauty, Camp Dodge, Iowa, C.1900 .... 16.60
Souvenir, Mug, Brown-Streaked Pottery, Painted Flowers, Greenville, Miss. 12.00
Souvenir, Mug, C. & M. & P.S.R.R. Station, Emumclaw, Wash., Germany, 3 In. 15.00
Souvenir, Mug, Pan American Exposition, Buffalo, 1901, Pink, Draped Women 18.00
Souvenir, Mug, Toby, Herbert Hoover, 7 In. 65.00
Souvenir, Mug, World's Fair 1904, Emerald Green, Lacy Medallion, Inscribed 15.00
Souvenir, Mug, Yale, Football Shape, Artist Signed, 1905, 5 1/2 In. 75.00
Souvenir, Napkin Holder, Brass, Chicago World's Fair 5.00
Souvenir, New York Fair, 1939, Peanut Set 7.00
Souvenir, Pillow Case, Dustin Farnum, Color Portrait, Square, 22 In. 55.00
Souvenir, Pipe, Milk Glass, Benton Harbor, Michigan 7.50
Souvenir, Pitcher And Mug Set, BPOE, Elk's Head, Smith Phillip, 11 3/4 In. 75.00
Souvenir, Pitcher, Scenic, Coney Island, N.Y., Cobalt, 3 In. High 12.00
Souvenir, Plate, Alaska Yukon Pacific Exposition, 1909, Germany, 9 1/2 In. 35.00
Souvenir, Plate, Birthplace, Washington, Crown Ducal, English, 10 In. 12.00
Souvenir, Plate, Boston Massacre, Fruit & Flower, English, 10 In. 26.00
Souvenir, Plate, Bunker Hill, Fruit & Flower, English, 10 In. 26.00
Souvenir, Plate, Churchill, Lord Nelson Pottery, Ship On Ground, C.1943 .... 26.50
Souvenir, Plate, Columbian Exposition, 1893, Agricultural, 7 1/4 In. 16.00
Souvenir, Plate, Cumberland Falls, Blue, 10 In. 20.00
Souvenir, Plate, Dinner, Roosevelt Hotel, New Orleans, Floral, 6 7/8 In. 4.00
Souvenir, Plate, First Fort Dearborn, Century Of Progress, 1833-1933, 9 In. 18.00
Souvenir, Plate, George VI, Visit To U.S.A., 1939, 7 1/2 In. 12.50
Souvenir, Plate, Gold, Open Work, Physicians Hospital, Plattsburg, N.Y., 4 In. 7.00
Souvenir, Plate, Green Envelope Postmarked Boston, Nov.9, 1872, 8 In. 19.00
Souvenir, Plate, Harrisburg, Pa., Spaghetti Border, Germany, 6 In. 16.00
Souvenir, Plate, Mayflower, Quebec, 7 1/2 In. 9.00
Souvenir, Plate, Monument To Forefathers, Plymouth, Mass, Cobalt .... *Color* 9.00
Souvenir, Plate, New York City Scenes, Blue & White, Bosselman Co., 10 In. 20.00
Souvenir, Plate, Niagara Falls, Fruit & Flower, English, 10 In. 26.00
Souvenir, Plate, Niagara Falls, Harker Pottery, 6 1/4 In. 17.00
Souvenir, Plate, Niagara Falls, Mason, 10 In. 12.00
Souvenir, Plate, Northampton, Mass., 7 1/2 In. 7.00
Souvenir, Plate, Nova Scotia, Hand-Painted Scene, 8 In. 4.00
Souvenir, Plate, Old Scituate Light, Scituate, Ma., Blue & White, 7 3/4 In. 6.95
Souvenir, Plate, Petoskey, Michigan, 7 1/2 In. 9.00

Souvenir, Plate, Porcelain, U.S.Navy Cap, Portrait, Admiral Dewey, 3 1/2 In. 125.00
Souvenir, Plate, Portrait, Clara Kimball Young 25.00
Souvenir, Plate, Roosevelt Hotel, New Orleans, 6 7/8 In. 4.00
Souvenir, Plate, S.B.Emerson, Sanford, Altenburg, Germany, 7 In. 17.00
Souvenir, Plate, Seattle World's Fair, 1962 .... 4.50
Souvenir, Plate, Southern Hotel, Gulfport, Miss., 7 1/2 In. 9.00
Souvenir, Plate, State Capitol, Columbus, Black, White, Beardsmore, 7 1/2 In. 9.00
Souvenir, Plate, Tin, Francis Scott Key, Dated 1814-1914, Kenny Co., 9 1/2 In. 35.00
Souvenir, Plate, Toronto University, Carlsbad Austria China 12.00
Souvenir, Plate, Transfer, Ohio Canal, Dar, Massillon, Centennial, 1926 .... 25.00
Souvenir, Plate, Washington Headquarters, Morristown, N.J., Adams, 9 In. 16.00
Souvenir, Plate, White, Gold Edge, World's Exposition, Chicago, 1893, 6 In. 12.00
Souvenir, Salt & Pepper, Duluth, Minn., White & Gold 7.50
Souvenir, Salt & Pepper, N.Y.World's Fair, 1939 .... 8.00
Souvenir, Salt & Pepper, Seal Of Alaska Territory, Coppertone 9.50
Souvenir, Saltshaker, White Milk Glass, Columbian 1893 Exhibition 32.00
Souvenir, Saucer, Bowdoin College, 1933, Black With White 5.00
Souvenir, Shoehorn, El Paso, Dried Palm Leaf 6.00
Souvenir, Slipper, Glass, Centennial Exhibition 28.00
Souvenir, Spoon, Brass, Canada, Enamel Maple Leaf, Demitasse 8.00
Souvenir, Spoon, California, Animals, People And Buildings, Sterling 19.00
Souvenir, Spoon, Silver Plate, Admiral Dewey, Demitasse .... 8.00 To 12.00
Souvenir, Spoon, Silver Plate, Battleship Maine 7.50
Souvenir, Spoon, Silver Plate, Betty Lou 4.00
Souvenir, Spoon, Silver Plate, Boston, Demitasse 6.00
Souvenir, Spoon, Silver Plate, Buffalo Hotel Broezel, Demitasse 8.00
Souvenir, Spoon, Silver Plate, California, Wm.Rogers 3.50
Souvenir, Spoon, Silver Plate, Century Of Progress 4.50
Souvenir, Spoon, Silver Plate, Charlie McCarthy 7.00
Souvenir, Spoon, Silver Plate, Chicago World's Fair, 1933 .... 7.50
Souvenir, Spoon, Silver Plate, Colorado, Wm.Rogers 3.50
Souvenir, Spoon, Silver Plate, Columbian Exposition, 1492-1892 .... 7.00
Souvenir, Spoon, Silver Plate, Coney Island, Christmas Angel, Demitasse 8.00
Souvenir, Spoon, Silver Plate, Connecticut, Wm.Rogers 3.50
Souvenir, Spoon, Silver Plate, Demitasse, Battleship Maine 10.00
Souvenir, Spoon, Silver Plate, Demitasse, Columbian Exposition, 1898, Angel 8.00
Souvenir, Spoon, Silver Plate, Demitasse, Washington, D.C., Fancy Handle 8.00
Souvenir, Spoon, Silver Plate, Demitasse, World's Fair, 1892, Columbus 8.00
Souvenir, Spoon, Silver Plate, Dennis The Menace 5.00
Souvenir, Spoon, Silver Plate, Deutschland 6.00
Souvenir, Spoon, Silver Plate, Eagle On Top, Maine 3.50
Souvenir, Spoon, Silver Plate, Florida, Wm.Rogers 3.50
Souvenir, Spoon, Silver Plate, Gene & Glenn, Quaker Early Birds 4.95
Souvenir, Spoon, Silver Plate, Gerber Baby 4.50
Souvenir, Spoon, Silver Plate, Gloria Swanson 7.00
Souvenir, Spoon, Silver Plate, Great Britain .... 4.00 To 6.50
Souvenir, Spoon, Silver Plate, Habana, Gold Wash, Enamel, Demitasse 14.00
Souvenir, Spoon, Silver Plate, Huckleberry Hound .... 4.00 To 5.00
Souvenir, Spoon, Silver Plate, Hungary 4.00
Souvenir, Spoon, Silver Plate, Idaho, Wm.Rogers 3.50
Souvenir, Spoon, Silver Plate, Illinois, Wm.Rogers 3.50
Souvenir, Spoon, Silver Plate, Indiana, Wm.Rogers 3.50
Souvenir, Spoon, Silver Plate, Jamaica, Enamel Handle 10.00
Souvenir, Spoon, Silver Plate, Kitchener, English 5.00
Souvenir, Spoon, Silver Plate, Little Bo-Peep 6.00
Souvenir, Spoon, Silver Plate, Little Red Riding Hood 8.00
Souvenir, Spoon, Silver Plate, Los Angeles 6.00
Souvenir, Spoon, Silver Plate, Mary Pickford .... 4.00 To 7.50
Souvenir, Spoon, Silver Plate, Mary Poppins 5.00
Souvenir, Spoon, Silver Plate, Massachusetts, Wm.Rogers 3.50
Souvenir, Spoon, Silver Plate, New Jersey 6.00
Souvenir, Spoon, Silver Plate, New York, Wm.Rogers 3.50
Souvenir, Spoon, Silver Plate, Niagara Falls, Demitasse 5.00
Souvenir, Spoon, Silver Plate, Norma Talmadge 4.95
Souvenir, Spoon, Silver Plate, Ohio State 6.00

Souvenir, Spoon, Sterling Silver, Albany, Gorham

Souvenir, Spoon, Sterling Silver, Battleship Maine, Demitasse

Souvenir, Spoon, Silver Plate, Oregon 6.00
Souvenir, Spoon, Silver Plate, Panama Pacific Exposition, 1915 .... 7.00
Souvenir, Spoon, Silver Plate, Pennsylvania, Wm.Rogers 3.50
Souvenir, Spoon, Silver Plate, Pola Negri 4.95
Souvenir, Spoon, Silver Plate, Prince Albert, English 5.00
Souvenir, Spoon, Silver Plate, Proctors, Demitasse 5.00
Souvenir, Spoon, Silver Plate, Queen Elizabeth, English 5.00
Souvenir, Spoon, Silver Plate, Rhode Island, Wm.Rogers 3.50
Souvenir, Spoon, Silver Plate, Richard Dix 4.00
Souvenir, Spoon, Silver Plate, Sesquicentennial, 1926 .... 6.50
Souvenir, Spoon, Silver Plate, St.Augustine 12.00
Souvenir, Spoon, Silver Plate, St.Louis Exposition, Machinery, Demitasse 6.00
Souvenir, Spoon, Silver Plate, Texas, Wm.Rogers 3.50
Souvenir, Spoon, Silver Plate, Thomas Meighan 4.95
Souvenir, Spoon, Silver Plate, Tony The Tiger 5.00
Souvenir, Spoon, Silver Plate, U.S.Olympia, Dewey On Handle 7.50
Souvenir, Spoon, Silver Plate, Washington, D.C., Demitasse 6.00
Souvenir, Spoon, Silver Plate, Wisconsin, Wm.Rogers 3.50
Souvenir, Spoon, Silver Plate, World's Fair City, 1893, 6 In Box 21.00
Souvenir, Spoon, Silver Plate, World's Fair, 1933 .... 6.00
Souvenir, Spoon, Silver Plate, Yogi Bear .... 4.00 To 5.00
Souvenir, Spoon, Sterling Silver, Adelaide, 1894, Demitasse 7.95
Souvenir, Spoon, Sterling Silver, Aerial Bridge, Duluth, Minn., Picture Bowl 12.50
Souvenir, Spoon, Sterling Silver, Aileen, July 17, 1890, Demitasse 7.95
Souvenir, Spoon, Sterling Silver, Aitkin, Minn. 12.00
Souvenir, Spoon, Sterling Silver, Alamo, Demitasse 12.00
Souvenir, Spoon, Sterling Silver, Alaska, Totem Pole, Demitasse 12.00
Souvenir, Spoon, Sterling Silver, Albany, Gorham .... *Illus* 28.00
Souvenir, Spoon, Sterling Silver, Albany, N.Y., Eagle At Top 12.00
Souvenir, Spoon, Sterling Silver, Albuquerque, N.M., Art Nouveau Nude 23.00

Souvenir, Spoon, Sterling Silver, Alligator, 5 1/2 In. 58.00
Souvenir, Spoon, Sterling Silver, Alta, Iowa, Wheat Design, 5 In. 12.50
Souvenir, Spoon, Sterling Silver, Anaeriker & Bremen, Enameled 14.00
Souvenir, Spoon, Sterling Silver, April, 5 1/2 In. 18.00
Souvenir, Spoon, Sterling Silver, Arizona, Cactus & Flowers, Cutout Handle 10.00
Souvenir, Spoon, Sterling Silver, Art Institute, Chicago, Fort Dearborn 10.00
Souvenir, Spoon, Sterling Silver, Asbury Park, Demitasse 11.00
Souvenir, Spoon, Sterling Silver, Atlanta, Negro Boy On Handle, Enamel 20.00
Souvenir, Spoon, Sterling Silver, Atlantic City Steel Pier 11.75 To 12.00
Souvenir, Spoon, Sterling Silver, Atlantic City, Demitasse 11.00
Souvenir, Spoon, Sterling Silver, Auditorium, Ocean Grove, Cutout, Demitasse 8.00
Souvenir, Spoon, Sterling Silver, Avalon, Catalina Island, Demitasse 9.00
Souvenir, Spoon, Sterling Silver, B.P.O.E., Oshkosh, Wisconsin, Elk In Bowl 18.50
Souvenir, Spoon, Sterling Silver, Banff, Enamel Crest 8.00
Souvenir, Spoon, Sterling Silver, Battleship Maine, Demitasse *Illus* 6.50
Souvenir, Spoon, Sterling Silver, Bay Point, Rockland, Me., Patent 1894 9.95
Souvenir, Spoon, Sterling Silver, Berlin, Brandenburger Door, Gold Wash 22.50
Souvenir, Spoon, Sterling Silver, Berlin, Dom, Gold Wash 22.50
Souvenir, Spoon, Sterling Silver, Berlin, Rathaus, Gold Wash 22.50
Souvenir, Spoon, Sterling Silver, Berlin, Reichstagsgebaude, Gold Wash 22.50
Souvenir, Spoon, Sterling Silver, Berlin, Schlossbruche Museum, Gold Wash 22.50
Souvenir, Spoon, Sterling Silver, Berlin, Seat Of Government, Gold Wash 22.50
Souvenir, Spoon, Sterling Silver, Berlin, Siegessaule, Gold Wash 22.50
Souvenir, Spoon, Sterling Silver, Berlin, Unter Den Linden, Gold Wash 22.50
Souvenir, Spoon, Sterling Silver, Berlin, Victory Monument, Gold Wash 22.50
Souvenir, Spoon, Sterling Silver, Berlin, Wilhelm Der Grosse, Gold Wash 22.50
Souvenir, Spoon, Sterling Silver, Bermuda Royal Palms, Enamel, Demitasse 14.00
Souvenir, Spoon, Sterling Silver, Bethleham, Pa. 14.00
Souvenir, Spoon, Sterling Silver, Bingen, Victory Statue, Germany, Gold Wash 22.50
Souvenir, Spoon, Sterling Silver, Birthday, September, Blue Stone Top 8.95
Souvenir, Spoon, Sterling Silver, Boston Tea Party, Paul Revere, 1776 23.00
Souvenir, Spoon, Sterling Silver, Boston, Boston Bean Pot Handle, Demitasse 13.00
Souvenir, Spoon, Sterling Silver, Boston, Flowers, 1908 5.00
Souvenir, Spoon, Sterling Silver, Boston, Old South Church, Demitasse 13.00
Souvenir, Spoon, Sterling Silver, Boston, Paul Revere On Handle, Demitasse 13.00
Souvenir, Spoon, Sterling Silver, Boston, Pot Of Beans On Handle, Demitasse 9.00
Souvenir, Spoon, Sterling Silver, Boston, Rider On Horse, Demitasse 14.00
Souvenir, Spoon, Sterling Silver, Brooklyn Bridge, Demitasse 7.95
Souvenir, Spoon, Sterling Silver, Brooklyn Bridge, N.Y., Picture Bowl 12.50
Souvenir, Spoon, Sterling Silver, Buchtel, Akron, Ohio 18.00
Souvenir, Spoon, Sterling Silver, Buffalo, N.Y. 13.00
Souvenir, Spoon, Sterling Silver, Cabildo, New Orleans 12.00
Souvenir, Spoon, Sterling Silver, California, Bear, Demitasse 15.00
Souvenir, Spoon, Sterling Silver, California, Bear, Miner, Grapes, & Orange 11.75
Souvenir, Spoon, Sterling Silver, California, Golden Gate In Bowl, Bear Top 16.00
Souvenir, Spoon, Sterling Silver, Camel In Desert, Enamel Bowl 35.00
Souvenir, Spoon, Sterling Silver, Campbell, Cupid & Arrow Handle, Demitasse 15.00
Souvenir, Spoon, Sterling Silver, Capitol, Washington, D.C. 8.50 To 9.50
Souvenir, Spoon, Sterling Silver, Carthage, S.D. 11.50
Souvenir, Spoon, Sterling Silver, Catalina Island, Tuna Fish Handle 22.50
Souvenir, Spoon, Sterling Silver, Cedar Rapids, 1900 8.00
Souvenir, Spoon, Sterling Silver, Century Of Progress, Chicago 9.00
Souvenir, Spoon, Sterling Silver, Chicago Fire, 5 7/8 In. 28.00
Souvenir, Spoon, Sterling Silver, Chicago Skyline, Chicago In Red Enamel 65.00
Souvenir, Spoon, Sterling Silver, Chicago Skyline, Chicago In Script Bowl 45.00
Souvenir, Spoon, Sterling Silver, Chicago, Demitasse 11.00 To 14.00
Souvenir, Spoon, Sterling Silver, Chicago, Fort Dearborn, Buildings 12.00
Souvenir, Spoon, Sterling Silver, Chicago, 1900 8.00
Souvenir, Spoon, Sterling Silver, Chief Seattle, 5 1/4 In. 25.00
Souvenir, Spoon, Sterling Silver, Children's Home, Potter Palmer, 5 1/2 In. 30.00
Souvenir, Spoon, Sterling Silver, Chinook Salmon, 5 1/4 In. 22.00
Souvenir, Spoon, Sterling Silver, Christmas, 1885, Demitasse 12.00
Souvenir, Spoon, Sterling Silver, City Hall, N.Y., Gold Wash, Marjorie Bowl 15.00
Souvenir, Spoon, Sterling Silver, City Of Churches, Demitasse 18.00
Souvenir, Spoon, Sterling Silver, City Of Elms, Edward Wholley, 5 3/8 In. 28.00

Souvenir, Spoon, Sterling Silver, City Of The Angels, 5 3/4 In. 28.00
Souvenir, Spoon, Sterling Silver, College Girl 32.00
Souvenir, Spoon, Sterling Silver, Colonel Davenport's Home, Arsenal Island 10.00
Souvenir, Spoon, Sterling Silver, Colorado Handle, Denver In Bowl 15.00
Souvenir, Spoon, Sterling Silver, Colorado, Tella In Bowl, Miner On Back 14.00
Souvenir, Spoon, Sterling Silver, Columbia River, Salmon Handle, Demitasse 16.50
Souvenir, Spoon, Sterling Silver, Columbian Exposition, Cutout, Demitasse 10.00
Souvenir, Spoon, Sterling Silver, Columbian Exposition, 1893, 5 5/8 In. 25.00
Souvenir, Spoon, Sterling Silver, Columbian Naval Review, 5 3/4 In. 50.00
Souvenir, Spoon, Sterling Silver, Columbus, Gold Washed, Demitasse 25.00
Souvenir, Spoon, Sterling Silver, Columbus, N.Y. 10.00
Souvenir, Spoon, Sterling Silver, Columbus, Ohio, State Capitol, Cupids 15.00
Souvenir, Spoon, Sterling Silver, Connecticut 14.00
Souvenir, Spoon, Sterling Silver, Convention Hall, Kansas City, Mo., Seal 16.00
Souvenir, Spoon, Sterling Silver, Corn, 5 7/8 In. 25.00
Souvenir, Spoon, Sterling Silver, Corn, 8 In. 28.00
Souvenir, Spoon, Sterling Silver, Corona Hotel, Montreal, Gold Wash, Enamel 30.00
Souvenir, Spoon, Sterling Silver, Courthouse, De Smet, S.D. 15.00
Souvenir, Spoon, Sterling Silver, CP Over Art Nouveau Type Lady, Enamel 30.00
Souvenir, Spoon, Sterling Silver, Crawford House, White Mountains, N.H. 11.25
Souvenir, Spoon, Sterling Silver, Cuba, Enamel, Demitasse 18.00
Souvenir, Spoon, Sterling Silver, Cutout Indian Head, Gold Wash Bowl, 5 In. 20.00
Souvenir, Spoon, Sterling Silver, D.A.R., 5 7/8 In. 40.00
Souvenir, Spoon, Sterling Silver, Dallas, Demitasse 12.00
Souvenir, Spoon, Sterling Silver, Dayton, Ohio, Monument In Bowl 22.00
Souvenir, Spoon, Sterling Silver, Daytona, Fla., Enamel Oranges 19.00
Souvenir, Spoon, Sterling Silver, Demitasse, Colorado Exposition 16.00
Souvenir, Spoon, Sterling Silver, Denver, Clam Bowl, Demitasse 17.00
Souvenir, Spoon, Sterling Silver, Denver, Colo., Gold Wash, Demitasse 9.95
Souvenir, Spoon, Sterling Silver, Denver, Colorado, State Seal Handle 18.00
Souvenir, Spoon, Sterling Silver, Denver, Figural Miner, Demitasse 15.00
Souvenir, Spoon, Sterling Silver, Des Moines, Iowa, State Capitol 10.00
Souvenir, Spoon, Sterling Silver, Detroit Skyline, Heart Of Detroit Bowl 45.00
Souvenir, Spoon, Sterling Silver, Dewey Arch, Chicago Peace Jubilee 12.50
Souvenir, Spoon, Sterling Silver, Duluth, Minn., Girl Graduate, Demitasse 23.00
Souvenir, Spoon, Sterling Silver, Easter, Demitasse, 4 1/4 In. 22.00
Souvenir, Spoon, Sterling Silver, Easter, Gold Wash, White Enamel Figures 45.00
Souvenir, Spoon, Sterling Silver, Easton, Pa., Demitasse 10.00
Souvenir, Spoon, Sterling Silver, Edminton, Indian's Head, Demitasse 7.50
Souvenir, Spoon, Sterling Silver, Elk's, Los Angeles, BPOE, Clock 20.00
Souvenir, Spoon, Sterling Silver, Enamel Bowl, Capri 25.00
Souvenir, Spoon, Sterling Silver, Ethan Allen, 5 3/4 In. 35.00
Souvenir, Spoon, Sterling Silver, Exposition, Missouri, 1904, Demitasse 18.00
Souvenir, Spoon, Sterling Silver, Fall River, Demitasse 10.00
Souvenir, Spoon, Sterling Silver, Faneuil Hall, Demitasse 8.50
Souvenir, Spoon, Sterling Silver, Federal Monument, Fort Smith, Demitasse 9.50
Souvenir, Spoon, Sterling Silver, Ferry Building, San Francisco, Calif. 12.50
Souvenir, Spoon, Sterling Silver, Flatiron Building, N.Y., Demitasse 10.00
Souvenir, Spoon, Sterling Silver, Florida, Cutout Palm Handle 10.00
Souvenir, Spoon, Sterling Silver, Florida, State Seal, Oranges, Palm Trees 10.00
Souvenir, Spoon, Sterling Silver, Forest House, Lake Mahopac, N.Y., Demitasse 9.50
Souvenir, Spoon, Sterling Silver, Fort Dearborn, Chicago .... 9.95 To 14.00
Souvenir, Spoon, Sterling Silver, Fort Worth, Texas, Demitasse 11.00
Souvenir, Spoon, Sterling Silver, Frieda, Fuchsia 12.50
Souvenir, Spoon, Sterling Silver, Frieda, Raised Lions' Heads 25.00
Souvenir, Spoon, Sterling Silver, G.B.Adams Dry Goods, Gold Wash 25.00
Souvenir, Spoon, Sterling Silver, George Washington, Demitasse 14.00
Souvenir, Spoon, Sterling Silver, Germaine, 1890, Ironsides, Demitasse 25.00
Souvenir, Spoon, Sterling Silver, Girl Graduate, Houston, Texas, Book, Owl 35.00
Souvenir, Spoon, Sterling Silver, Golden Gate, San Francisco, Picture Bowl 10.00
Souvenir, Spoon, Sterling Silver, Grand Canyon, Gold Wash Bowl 25.00
Souvenir, Spoon, Sterling Silver, Great Barrington, Demitasse 10.00
Souvenir, Spoon, Sterling Silver, Greenwich, Scrolled Handle, Gorham, 1897 .... 9.00
Souvenir, Spoon, Sterling Silver, Halifax, N.S., Enamel, Demitasse 14.00
Souvenir, Spoon, Sterling Silver, Hawaii 10.00

Souvenir, Spoon, Sterling Silver, Hotel Capitola, California, Picture Bowl 12.50
Souvenir, Spoon, Sterling Silver, Hotel Dewey, Dewey, Idaho, Demitasse 9.50
Souvenir, Spoon, Sterling Silver, Hudson Fulton, 1909, Tiffany & Co. 27.00
Souvenir, Spoon, Sterling Silver, Idaho, Falls, Ornate Handle 18.00
Souvenir, Spoon, Sterling Silver, Imp On Handle, 3 3/4 In. 6.00
Souvenir, Spoon, Sterling Silver, Indian & Dog, 5 1/2 In. 40.00
Souvenir, Spoon, Sterling Silver, Indian Head Handle, 1901 Temple Music 18.00
Souvenir, Spoon, Sterling Silver, Indiana, Gold-Wash Bowl 15.00
Souvenir, Spoon, Sterling Silver, Indianapolis, State Capitol 12.00
Souvenir, Spoon, Sterling Silver, Iowa 9.00
Souvenir, Spoon, Sterling Silver, Jasper Monument, Georgia, Gold Wash 14.00
Souvenir, Spoon, Sterling Silver, Joseph Smith, Verse & Floral, Cutout 18.00
Souvenir, Spoon, Sterling Silver, June 1890, Explorers In Boat, Mermaids 17.00
Souvenir, Spoon, Sterling Silver, Kansas City, Masonic Emblem 10.00
Souvenir, Spoon, Sterling Silver, Kneeling Indian, Setting Sun, 5 1/4 In. 40.00
Souvenir, Spoon, Sterling Silver, Knights Templar, Enamel, Demitasse 11.00
Souvenir, Spoon, Sterling Silver, Krefeld Post, Germany, Gold Wash 22.50
Souvenir, Spoon, Sterling Silver, Lady With Teapot, 1883, Sugar Shell 15.00
Souvenir, Spoon, Sterling Silver, Lake Arrowhead, Calif., Towle, C.1892 ..... 12.00
Souvenir, Spoon, Sterling Silver, Lake Chautauqua, N.Y., Niagara Falls 10.00
Souvenir, Spoon, Sterling Silver, Lake Okabena, Worthington, N.M. 12.50
Souvenir, Spoon, Sterling Silver, Landing Of Pilgrims, 1620, Plain Bowl 18.00
Souvenir, Spoon, Sterling Silver, Lewis & Clark Exposition, Demitasse 16.50
Souvenir, Spoon, Sterling Silver, Library, Everette, Mass. 12.00
Souvenir, Spoon, Sterling Silver, Longfellow, Facing Front 24.00
Souvenir, Spoon, Sterling Silver, Longfellow, Profile 20.00
Souvenir, Spoon, Sterling Silver, Los Angeles Skyline, 1771, Gold Wash Bowl 25.00
Souvenir, Spoon, Sterling Silver, Los Angeles, Calif., Mt.Lowe Incline 15.00
Souvenir, Spoon, Sterling Silver, Los Angeles, Mt.Lowe, Gold Miner, Burro 15.00
Souvenir, Spoon, Sterling Silver, Los Angeles, Oranges, Watson 18.50
Souvenir, Spoon, Sterling Silver, Los Angeles, Sugar Shell, Wallace 13.50
Souvenir, Spoon, Sterling Silver, Louisiana Purchase Expositio ..... 27.50 To 42.00
Souvenir, Spoon, Sterling Silver, Louisiana, Shreveport In Bowl 12.00
Souvenir, Spoon, Sterling Silver, Lower New York Skyline, St.Patrick's Bowl 58.00
Souvenir, Spoon, Sterling Silver, Lucerne, Gilt, Enamel, 4 1/2 In. 12.00
Souvenir, Spoon, Sterling Silver, Maine, Demitasse 9.00
Souvenir, Spoon, Sterling Silver, Manitoba, City Hall Bowl, Enameled 14.00
Souvenir, Spoon, Sterling Silver, Manitou, Canada, 1891, Enamel, 4 In. 12.00
Souvenir, Spoon, Sterling Silver, Martha & George Washington, White House 35.00
Souvenir, Spoon, Sterling Silver, Masonic Temple, Chicago, 1902 ..... 18.00
Souvenir, Spoon, Sterling Silver, Masonic, Shriner, Demitasse 10.00
Souvenir, Spoon, Sterling Silver, Massachusetts ..... 12.00 To 14.00
Souvenir, Spoon, Sterling Silver, Matador, 5 1/8 In. 45.00
Souvenir, Spoon, Sterling Silver, Michigan River, Detroit 17.50
Souvenir, Spoon, Sterling Silver, Milwaukee Auditorium, Goethe Schiller 14.00
Souvenir, Spoon, Sterling Silver, Milwaukee, Dancing Girl & Beer Mugs 15.00
Souvenir, Spoon, Sterling Silver, Milwaukee, 1900 ..... 8.00
Souvenir, Spoon, Sterling Silver, Miner & Indian 60.00
Souvenir, Spoon, Sterling Silver, Minneapolis, 1766, Demitasse 14.00
Souvenir, Spoon, Sterling Silver, Minnehaha Falls, Longfellow Quotation 16.00
Souvenir, Spoon, Sterling Silver, Minnesota, Demitasse 5.00
Souvenir, Spoon, Sterling Silver, Mission Inn, Riverside, Calif. ..... 9.95 To 11.75
Souvenir, Spoon, Sterling Silver, Mission Inn, Riverside, Calif., Cutout Bell 8.00
Souvenir, Spoon, Sterling Silver, Missouri State, Enamel ..... *Illus* 30.00
Souvenir, Spoon, Sterling Silver, Missouri, Richmond In Bowl 12.00
Souvenir, Spoon, Sterling Silver, Mobridge, S.D., Demitasse 9.00
Souvenir, Spoon, Sterling Silver, Montana, Miner, 5 3/4 In. 25.00
Souvenir, Spoon, Sterling Silver, Montana, Miss Liberty On Back 18.00
Souvenir, Spoon, Sterling Silver, Montreal, P.Q., Enamel, Demitasse 15.00
Souvenir, Spoon, Sterling Silver, Montreal, 1908, Enamel Leaf, Demitasse 8.95
Souvenir, Spoon, Sterling Silver, Monument, Portland, Maine 16.00
Souvenir, Spoon, Sterling Silver, Mound City, St.Louis, 1875, Pierre Liguist 16.00
Souvenir, Spoon, Sterling Silver, Mt.Hood, Portland, Demitasse 12.00
Souvenir, Spoon, Sterling Silver, Mt.Pleasant, Iowa, Flag, Indian 12.00
Souvenir, Spoon, Sterling Silver, Mt.Rainier, Seattle, Washington 10.00

Souvenir, Spoon, Sterling Silver, Missouri State, Enamel
(See Page 593)

Souvenir, Spoon, Sterling Silver, Pan American Exposition, 1901

Souvenir, Spoon, Sterling Silver, Washington, D.C., 1890
(See Page 596)

Souvenir, Spoon, Sterling Silver, Mt.Vernon, Demitasse, 4 1/4 In. 18.00
Souvenir, Spoon, Sterling Silver, Mt.Vernon, Martha & George Washington 35.00
Souvenir, Spoon, Sterling Silver, Mt.Vernon, Orange Bowl, 5 3/4 In. 30.00
Souvenir, Spoon, Sterling Silver, Mt.Vernon, Washington's Tomb Bowl 37.00
Souvenir, Spoon, Sterling Silver, Mt.Vernon, Whelan, Demitasse 14.00
Souvenir, Spoon, Sterling Silver, Mudlavia, Kramer, Ind., Demitasse 9.50
Souvenir, Spoon, Sterling Silver, Natatorium, Boise, Idaho, Picture Bowl 12.50
Souvenir, Spoon, Sterling Silver, Natural Arch, Bermuda, Picture Bowl 12.50
Souvenir, Spoon, Sterling Silver, Negro Boy Eating Watermelon, Crocodile 55.00
Souvenir, Spoon, Sterling Silver, Negro's Head At Top Of Handle 55.00
Souvenir, Spoon, Sterling Silver, New Amsterdam, 5 7/8 In. 32.00
Souvenir, Spoon, Sterling Silver, New Capitol, St.Paul, Minn. 12.75
Souvenir, Spoon, Sterling Silver, New Hampshire 12.00
Souvenir, Spoon, Sterling Silver, New Haven, Demitasse 10.00
Souvenir, Spoon, Sterling Silver, New Jersey .... 12.00 To 14.00
Souvenir, Spoon, Sterling Silver, New Orleans, Alligator In Bowl 12.00
Souvenir, Spoon, Sterling Silver, New Orleans, Demitasse 11.00
Souvenir, Spoon, Sterling Silver, New Orleans, Full Figure Of Crocodile 20.00
Souvenir, Spoon, Sterling Silver, New York 9.00
Souvenir, Spoon, Sterling Silver, New York City, Tiffany & Co. 12.00
Souvenir, Spoon, Sterling Silver, New York Skyline, Brooklyn Bridge Base 58.00
Souvenir, Spoon, Sterling Silver, New York, Cascade 18.00
Souvenir, Spoon, Sterling Silver, Niagara Falls, Demitasse, Canada Coat Of Ar 15.00
Souvenir, Spoon, Sterling Silver, Niagara Falls, Gold Wash, Enameled Leaf 15.00
Souvenir, Spoon, Sterling Silver, Niagara Falls, Gold Wash, Howard, C.1894 .... 16.50
Souvenir, Spoon, Sterling Silver, Nome, Alaska 10.00
Souvenir, Spoon, Sterling Silver, North American Indian 55.00
Souvenir, Spoon, Sterling Silver, North American Indian, Demitasse, 4 In. 28.00
Souvenir, Spoon, Sterling Silver, North Carolina, Eagle, Seal, & Flag 16.00
Souvenir, Spoon, Sterling Silver, North River Skyline, N.Y., Demitasse 18.00
Souvenir, Spoon, Sterling Silver, Nude Child & Harp 8.00

Souvenir, Spoon, Sterling Silver, Nude Woman Lying In Canoe, 5 1/2 In. 35.00
Souvenir, Spoon, Sterling Silver, Oakland, California 10.00
Souvenir, Spoon, Sterling Silver, Ohio .... 12.00 To 14.00
Souvenir, Spoon, Sterling Silver, Oklahoma City, Indian Shooting Arrow 18.00
Souvenir, Spoon, Sterling Silver, Old Fort, Fort Wayne, Ind., Picture Bowl 12.50
Souvenir, Spoon, Sterling Silver, Old Senate House, 1676, Kingston, N.Y. 12.50
Souvenir, Spoon, Sterling Silver, Old Statehouse, Boston, Bunker Hill 11.75
Souvenir, Spoon, Sterling Silver, Oregon, Salmon Figural Stem 30.00
Souvenir, Spoon, Sterling Silver, Packer Memorial, South Bethelehem, Pa. 12.50
Souvenir, Spoon, Sterling Silver, Palm Beach, Florida, Ponce De Leon 12.00
Souvenir, Spoon, Sterling Silver, Pan American Exposition, Indian, Demitasse 17.00
Souvenir, Spoon, Sterling Silver, Pan American Exposition, 1901 .... *Illus* 10.00
Souvenir, Spoon, Sterling Silver, Pasadena, Calif., Mission Bell 18.00
Souvenir, Spoon, Sterling Silver, Paul Revere 25.00
Souvenir, Spoon, Sterling Silver, Philadelphia, Ben Franklin 16.00
Souvenir, Spoon, Sterling Silver, Philadelphia, Liberty Bell 14.00
Souvenir, Spoon, Sterling Silver, Pike's Peak, Burrow Handle, Demitasse 16.00
Souvenir, Spoon, Sterling Silver, Pike's Peak, Cutout Building Handle 10.00
Souvenir, Spoon, Sterling Silver, Pittsburgh, Demitasse 10.00
Souvenir, Spoon, Sterling Silver, Plymouth, 1620, Mayflower, 1891 On Back 12.00
Souvenir, Spoon, Sterling Silver, Portage High School, 1908 .... 13.00
Souvenir, Spoon, Sterling Silver, Post Office, Chicago, Lincoln & Art Inst. 15.00
Souvenir, Spoon, Sterling Silver, Prospect Point, Niagara Falls 9.95
Souvenir, Spoon, Sterling Silver, Public High School, Wapello, Iowa 15.00
Souvenir, Spoon, Sterling Silver, Puget Sound, Everett, Wash., Indian Handle 9.50
Souvenir, Spoon, Sterling Silver, Richmond, Missouri, Flowers & Seal 10.00
Souvenir, Spoon, Sterling Silver, Richmond, Va., Demitasse 10.00
Souvenir, Spoon, Sterling Silver, Riverfront, Detroit, Picture Bowl 10.00
Souvenir, Spoon, Sterling Silver, Salem Witch, Aug.9, 1890 .... 65.00
Souvenir, Spoon, Sterling Silver, Salem Witch, Fruit Bowl, 5 3/4 In. 65.00
Souvenir, Spoon, Sterling Silver, San Bernardino, Calif., Gold Bowl 10.00
Souvenir, Spoon, Sterling Silver, San Diego Bay, State Seal, 1849 Miner 23.00
Souvenir, Spoon, Sterling Silver, San Francisco, Gold Panner, Demitasse 14.00
Souvenir, Spoon, Sterling Silver, San Gabriel Mission, 1771, Picture Bowl 12.50
Souvenir, Spoon, Sterling Silver, Santa Barbara Mission, California 11.95
Souvenir, Spoon, Sterling Silver, Saratoga, Gold Wash, Demitasse 14.00
Souvenir, Spoon, Sterling Silver, Saratoga, Kneeling Indian 16.00
Souvenir, Spoon, Sterling Silver, Sea Beach Hotel, Santa Cruz, 5 1/2 In. 15.00
Souvenir, Spoon, Sterling Silver, Shakespeare, Figural Handle 52.00
Souvenir, Spoon, Sterling Silver, Sheboygan, Engraved Cheese & People, 1905 .... 15.00
Souvenir, Spoon, Sterling Silver, Shreveport, Louisiana, Cotton 18.00
Souvenir, Spoon, Sterling Silver, Soldiers' & Sailors' Monumen .... 12.50 To 13.00
Souvenir, Spoon, Sterling Silver, Spoon, Fruit, Catskills, M & H, '92 .... 25.00
Souvenir, Spoon, Sterling Silver, St.Augustine, Fla., Gold Bowl, Demitasse 12.50
Souvenir, Spoon, Sterling Silver, St.Augustine, Gold Wash, Newell, Watson 18.50
Souvenir, Spoon, Sterling Silver, St.Louis World's Fair, Jefferson Top 15.00
Souvenir, Spoon, Sterling Silver, St.Louis World's Fair, 1904 .... 18.00
Souvenir, Spoon, Sterling Silver, St.Paul, Minn., Demitasse 11.00
Souvenir, Spoon, Sterling Silver, St.Paul's Cathedral, London, G.M.Co. 10.00
Souvenir, Spoon, Sterling Silver, State Capitol, Denver, Colo., Demitasse 9.50
Souvenir, Spoon, Sterling Silver, State Capitol, Illinois, Bust Of Lincoln 16.00
Souvenir, Spoon, Sterling Silver, State Capitol, Jackson, Miss. 18.00
Souvenir, Spoon, Sterling Silver, State Capitol, Providence, R.I. 6.95
Souvenir, Spoon, Sterling Silver, Statue Of Liberty, N.Y., Cutout, Demitasse 9.00
Souvenir, Spoon, Sterling Silver, Statue Of Liberty, N.Y., Picture Bowl 12.50
Souvenir, Spoon, Sterling Silver, Statue Of Liberty, Tiffany, 5 7/8 In. 28.00
Souvenir, Spoon, Sterling Silver, Syracuse, N.Y. 10.00
Souvenir, Spoon, Sterling Silver, Tacoma, Washington, Indian Head 18.00
Souvenir, Spoon, Sterling Silver, Teddy Bear, Demitasse, 3 1/2 In. 12.00
Souvenir, Spoon, Sterling Silver, Teddy Bear, 5 1/4 In. 35.00
Souvenir, Spoon, Sterling Silver, Tennessee .... 12.00 To 14.00
Souvenir, Spoon, Sterling Silver, Texas, 1911, Steer 15.00
Souvenir, Spoon, Sterling Silver, Topeka, Kansas, State Capitol 5.00
Souvenir, Spoon, Sterling Silver, Totem Pole, 5 In. 28.00
Souvenir, Spoon, Sterling Silver, Trans-Mississippi Exposition, 1898 .... 12.00

Souvenir, Spoon, Sterling Silver, Trinity Church, Boston, Demitasse 9.00
Souvenir, Spoon, Sterling Silver, U.S.Army, 5 7/8 In. 45.00
Souvenir, Spoon, Sterling Silver, Union Station, St.Louis, Mo., King Louis 38.00
Souvenir, Spoon, Sterling Silver, University Of Missouri Building 12.00
Souvenir, Spoon, Sterling Silver, Unknown Dead, Johnstown, Pa., Picture Bowl 12.50
Souvenir, Spoon, Sterling Silver, Vermont 12.00
Souvenir, Spoon, Sterling Silver, Victoria, B.C., Flower Handle 5.00
Souvenir, Spoon, Sterling Silver, Wagner, S.D. 11.50
Souvenir, Spoon, Sterling Silver, Walla Walla, Cutout Handle 10.00
Souvenir, Spoon, Sterling Silver, Washington Monument, 5 3/4 In. 35.00
Souvenir, Spoon, Sterling Silver, Washington, Capitol, Demitasse 8.00
Souvenir, Spoon, Sterling Silver, Washington, D.C., 1890 .... *Illus* 35.00
Souvenir, Spoon, Sterling Silver, Welton Fountain, Waterbury, Conn. 12.00
Souvenir, Spoon, Sterling Silver, West Baden, Ind., Cambridge, Gorham, C.1899 .... 12.00
Souvenir, Spoon, Sterling Silver, West Baden, Ind., Marguerite, Gorham, 1891 .... 12.00
Souvenir, Spoon, Sterling Silver, Wheeling, West Virginia 15.00
Souvenir, Spoon, Sterling Silver, White Canoe, Demitasse 24.00
Souvenir, Spoon, Sterling Silver, White Canoe, Sacrifice, Niagara Falls Bowl 42.00
Souvenir, Spoon, Sterling Silver, White House, Capitol & Roses 9.50
Souvenir, Spoon, Sterling Silver, Wilmington, Vt., Demitasse .... 10.00 To 11.00
Souvenir, Spoon, Sterling Silver, Wisconsin .... 12.00 To 14.00
Souvenir, Spoon, Sterling Silver, Women's Building, Columbian Exposition 30.00
Souvenir, Spoon, Sterling Silver, World's Fair, '93, Columbus's Head On Top 12.50
Souvenir, Spoon, Sterling Silver, World's Fair, 1893, Gold-Washed Bowl 12.00
Souvenir, Spoon, Sterling Silver, Wreck Of The Maine, Demitasse 14.00
Souvenir, Spoon, Sterling Silver, Yarmouth, N.S., Enamel, Demitasse 14.00
Souvenir, Spoon, Sterling Silver, Yellowstone, Demitasse 12.00
Souvenir, Spoon, Sterling Silver, Zodiac, January, Gorham 13.50
Souvenir, Spoon, Sterling Silver, Zodiac, June, Wallace 18.00
Souvenir, Spoon, Sterling Silver, Zodiac, March, Wallace 18.00
Souvenir, Spoon, Sterling Silver, Zodiac, October, Hopps 17.50
Souvenir, Spoon, Sterling Silver, Zodiac, Sagittarius, November 18.00
Souvenir, Spoon, Sterling Silver, 1, 000 Islands, Demitasse 12.00
Souvenir, Spoon, Sterling, Amberdeen, South Dakota Depot In Bowl 15.00
Souvenir, Spoon, Sterling, Cherokee, Oklahoma, Ornate Handle 15.00
Souvenir, Spoon, Sterling, Greeley, Colorado, Plain Handle 15.00
Souvenir, Spoon, Sterling, Kansas City, Missouri, City Hall 15.00
Souvenir, Spoon, Sterling, Kasson, Minn., Telephone Building In Bowl 15.00
Souvenir, Spoon, Sterling, Kearney, Nebraska, Crest On Handle 15.00
Souvenir, Spoon, Sterling, Oskaloosa, Kansas, Presbyterian Church 15.00
Souvenir, Stein, Augusta, Kansas, Picture Of Carriage, 3 In. 10.00
Souvenir, Stein, Flat Iron Bldg., German, 4 In. 19.00
Souvenir, Stein, German, Impressed, Los Angeles, Calif., 5 In. 20.00
Souvenir, Teapot, Luster, Miniature, Laporte County Courthouse, Ind. 15.00
Souvenir, Teaspoon, Chicago Fair, 1933 .... 3.00
Souvenir, Thermometer, Terminal Tower, Cleveland, Ohio, Key Shape, Metal, 8 In 6.00
Souvenir, Toby Mug, World's Fair, 1938, George Washington, White, 5 In. 14.00
Souvenir, Tray, Pin, Grand Forks, N.D., Pressed Glass, Banded Portland, Gilt 15.00

Spatter Glass, Sugar & Creamer, End Of Day

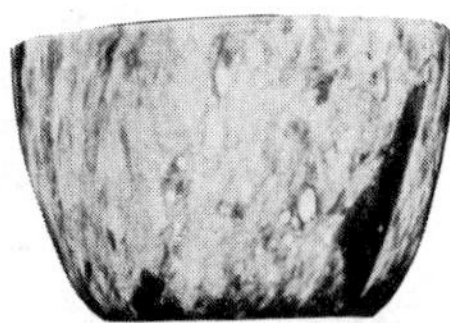

Souvenir, Tray, Rogers Hotel & Cafe, Minn.Yama-Yama, Chinese Boy & Lantern 18.00
Souvenir, Tray, Tip, World's Fair, 1904, Red Raven 45.00
Souvenir, Tumbler, Christmas, 1915 .... 15.00
Souvenir, Tumbler, Columbian Exposition, 1892, Frosted Panoramic Scenes 26.00
Souvenir, Vase, Andover, Ohio, Red 12.50
Souvenir, Vase, Atlantic City, Two Bisque Cats On Front, 7 In. 58.00
Souvenir, Vase, Grand Circus Park, Detroit, White, Colored Transfer, 5 In. 9.00
Souvenir, Watch Chain, 1893 Columbian Exposition, Porcelain Fob, Painted 25.00

Spangle glass is multicolored glass made from odds and ends of colored glass rods. It includes metallic flakes of mica covered with gold, silver, nickel, or copper. Spangle glass is usually cased with a thin layer of clear glass over the multicolored layer.

Spangle Glass, see also Vasa Murrhina

Spangle Glass, Basket, Twisted Thorn Handle, Colors 275.00
Spangle Glass, Bowl, Fruit, Fluted Rim, Yellow, Orange With Silver, 9 In. 125.00
Spangle Glass, Bowl, Powder Blue, Crimped Top, 3 1/2 In. .... 44.00 To 45.00
Spangle Glass, Pitcher, Beige Cased, Gold Mica, Applied Brown Handle, 9 In. 285.00
Spangle Glass, Rose Bowl, Cranberry, Mica Flecks, Crimped Rim, 4 1/2 X 5 In. 50.00
Spangle Glass, Vase, Jack-In-The-Pulpit, Burgundy, Green, Silver, 8 1/2 In. 65.00
Spangle Glass, Vase, Pink, Cobalt, Chartreuse, Mica Flakes, Rigaree, English 48.00

Spanish lace is a Victorian glass pattern that seems to have white lace on a colored background. Blue, yellow, cranberry, and clear glass was made with this distinctive white pattern.

Spanish Lace, Basket, Bride's, White, Opalescent, Miniature 19.50
Spanish Lace, Cruet, Yellow 65.00
Spanish Lace, Muffineer, Cranberry 110.00
Spanish Lace, Pitcher, Blue, Ruffled Top, 9 1/2 In. 110.00
Spanish Lace, Pitcher, Water, Vaseline, Opalescent 225.00
Spanish Lace, Rose Bowl, Blue Opalescent 45.00
Spanish Lace, Rose Bowl, Blue, 4 X 4 1/2 In. 35.00
Spanish Lace, Rose Bowl, Vaseline, 4 X 4 1/2 In. 35.00
Spanish Lace, Tumbler, Cranberry 95.00
Spanish Lace, Vase, Opalescent To Clear, Ruffled Edge, Bulbous Base, 6 In. 37.00

Spatter glass is a multicolored glass made from many small pieces of different colored glass.

Spatter Glass, Basket, Multicolor, Clear Handle, 9 1/2 In. 35.00
Spatter Glass, Basket, Multicolor, Twisted Handle, 9 In. 69.00
Spatter Glass, Berry Bowl, Pink & White Acid Finish 20.00
Spatter Glass, Dish, Cheese, Yellow, Ruby, & Cream, Yellow Lining, Clear Cased 75.00
Spatter Glass, Pitcher, Dark Red & White, Applied Shell Handle, 6 In. 50.00
Spatter Glass, Rose Bowl, Maroon & White, Inverted Thumbprint, 4 1/2 In. 75.00
Spatter Glass, Rose Bowl, Pink, Rose, Green, White, Black, Hand Blown 75.00
Spatter Glass, Rose Bowl, Yellow & White, Crimped Top, Enamel Floral, 4 In. 65.00
Spatter Glass, Salt, White Cased 38.00
Spatter Glass, Shade, Hanging Light, White & Clear, Ruffled, 2 In. Opening 15.00
Spatter Glass, Sugar & Creamer, End Of Day .... *Illus* 60.00
Spatter Glass, Syrup, Pink, Ribbed Pillar 110.00
Spatter Glass, Vase, Burgundy & White, Cased, Gourd Shape, 6 In. 69.00
Spatter Glass, Vase, Gourd Shape, Cased Glass, Rose, Green, White Applied, Pair 95.00
Spatter Glass, Vase, Lime Green To Chocolate, 8 1/2 In. 20.00
Spatter Glass, Vase, Pink Spatter, Threaded, Opalescent, 6 1/2 In. 25.00

Spatterware is a creamware or soft-paste dinnerware decorated with spatter designs. The earliest pieces were made during the late eighteenth century, but most of the wares found today were made from 1800 to 1850. The spatterware dishes were made in the Staffordshire District of England for sale on the American market.

Spatterware, see also Spongeware

Spatterware, Basket, Clear Twisted Thorn Handle, Deep Swirls, 8 In. 125.00
Spatterware, Bowl, High Glaze With Green And Brown Spatter 28.00
Spatterware, Bowl, Stick, Green & Black, Mustard Trim, 8 In. 40.00
Spatterware, Bowl, Stick, Yellow & Black, Sponge Rose Decoration, 11 In. 48.00

Spatterware, Cup, Peafowl, Red

Spatterware, Crock, Cream, Lid, Blue Spatter 35.00
Spatterware, Cup & Saucer, Handleless, Peafowl, Red & Purple 135.00
Spatterware, Cup & Saucer, Peafowl, Blue Spatter 160.00
Spatterware, Cup, Handleless, Unfinished Peafowl 110.00
Spatterware, Cup, Peafowl, Red .... *Illus* 90.00
Spatterware, Jar, Sugar, Blue 32.00
Spatterware, Pitcher, Blue, Rib Design In Base, 5 1/4 In. 47.50
Spatterware, Pitcher, Cream Color, Purple House, Copper Trim, C.1850, 2 In. 48.00
Spatterware, Pitcher, Cream With Green Spatter, Tall 38.00
Spatterware, Platter, French, C.1910, Houses & Trees, Blue Stick Edge, 14 In. 25.00
Spatterware, Saucer, Pennsylvania, Peafowl, 6 In. 50.00
Spatterware, Sugar, Covered, Lilac & Brown Vertical Stripes 95.00
Spatterware, Teabowl & Saucer, Child's, Peafowl On Green Spatter 78.00
Spelter, Figurine, Boy Holding Grapes, Artist Signed 30.00
Spelter, Figurine, NRA Eagle, Colored, 8 In. 60.00
Spelter, Figurine, Peasant Children With Snail, Marble Base, Signed, 11 In. 68.00

Spinning Wheel, see Tool, Spinning Wheel

Spode pottery, porcelain, and bone china were made by the Stoke-on-Trent Factory of England founded by Josiah Spode about 1770. The firm became Copeland and Garrett from 1833 to 1847, then W.T.Copeland or W.T.Copeland and Sons until the present time. The word Spode appears on many pieces made by the Copeland Factory. Most collectors include all the wares under the more familiar name of Spode.

SPODE

Spode, see also Copeland

Spode, Bowl, C.1805, Oval, 10 X 7 1/2 In. 45.00
Spode, Bowl, Deep, Mitered Corners, 9 1/2 In. Square 65.00
Spode, Bowl, Peacock, No.2118, Black Mark, C.1805, 6 1/4 In. 48.00
Spode, Copeland, Pitcher, Blue & White, Jamestown, Va., 1607-1957, 5 1/4 In. 22.50
Spode, Creamer, Chelsea Gardens 25.00
Spode, Cup & Saucer, Blue, Greek Pattern 25.00
Spode, Cup & Saucer, Cabbage, C.1820 .... 65.00
Spode, Cup & Saucer, Handleless, Blue Willow-Type Decoration, 1784 .... 65.00
Spode, Cup & Saucer, Handleless, Italian, For Tiffany 14.00
Spode, Fruit Stand, Queen Charlotte, Red Spode Mark, 14 1/2 In. 250.00
Spode, Gravy Boat, Blue, Greek Pattern 35.00
Spode, Jug, Hydro Shape, Deep Blue, Floral, Snake Handle, C.1820 .... 80.00
Spode, Jug, Molasses, Jasperware, Hunt Scene, Pewter Lid, 5 In. 63.00
Spode, Pitcher, Blue, Water, 6 In. 55.00
Spode, Pitcher, Jamestown, Va., 1607-1957, Blue & White, 5 In. 18.00
Spode, Plate, Blue, Robert Burns 12.00
Spode, Plate, Death Of The Bear, Blue Transfer, C.1815, 10 In. 60.00
Spode, Plate, Dessert, Tobacco Leaf, Red, Blue, & Gold, C.1805 .... 55.00 To 57.50
Spode, Plate, Diamond Jubilee, Queen Victoria, 1897, Portrait, Wording, 9 In. 40.00
Spode, Plate, Pale Blue Country Scene, 9 1/2 In. 19.00
Spode, Plate, Passionflower, Floral Border, 1784, Pattern 2635, 8 In. 40.00
Spode, Plate, Robert Burns 32.50
Spode, Plate, Tobacco Leaf, C.1815, 8 3/4 In. 35.00
Spode, Platter, Blue, Four Seasons, 13 X 9 In. 65.00
Spode, Platter, Gobelin, 13 X 9 1/2 In. 18.00

Beaded purses, museum collection, Victorian, 2–8 in. long.

Cabinet with porcelain plaques, German, c. 1900.

Worktable, American (Philadelphia), c. 1810, Sheraton style; caddy.

Snake in basket, 3 in. long.

Maple Yarn Swift, collection, 24½ in. diameter, 16 in. high.

Chalkware Jesus Christ, 5 in. base, 4⅞ in. high.

Chalkware bird.

Cherry seeder, c. 1875, 7 in. × 13 in. × 6½ in.

Chalkware rabbit, 1850–1865, 3½ in. × 8¼ in.

Chalkware cat bank.

Can opener, 19th century.

Water heater, Etna, 1800–1850, 5¾ in. high, 4 in. top diameter.

Fruit or wine press, James Deitrich, Berks County, 19th century.

Sausage stuffer, mid-19th century, 14½ in. long overall, 3 in. diameter.

Magic lantern, 19th century.

Lard press, 19th century.

Fruit cutter and juice extractor, 19th century.

Candle snuffers, wrought iron, first half of 19th century.

Stereoscope, patented May 19, 1885.

Candle holder, brass, mid-19th century.

Plow plane, c. 1840, marked "John Bell Philad.," 8½ in. long.

Candlesticks, paktong, second half of 18th century.

Candlesticks, brass, mid-19th century.

Churn (Mason Mfg. Co., Canton, Ohio), 19th century.

Miniature anvil, c. 1900, 12¾ in. long.

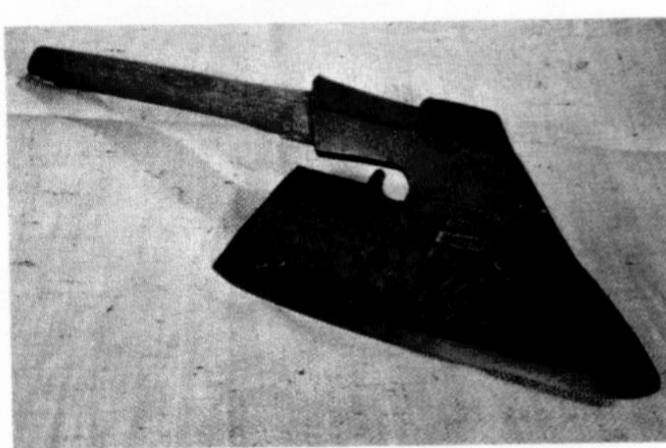

Broad axe, Pa. German, 19th century, 23 in. long.

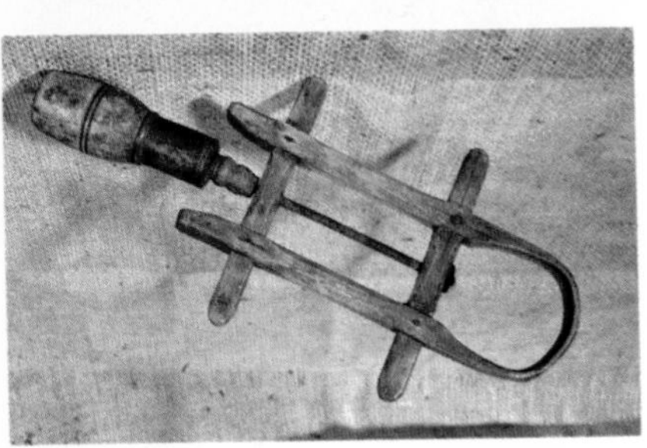

Carpenter's chalk line reel, c. 1850, 11 in. long.

James Hamilton & Co. #2 jug, Greensboro, Pa., 16 in. high.

Hand adze, 19th century, 11 in. long.

Number 2 jar, T. H. Willson & Co., Harrisburg, Pa., 16 in. high.

Water cooler, D. P. Shenfelder, Reading, Pa., 24 in. high.

Poultry fountain, Thomas Haig, Philadelphia, 9 in. high.

Man jug, Cowden & Wilcox, Harrisburg, Pa., 18 in. high.

Batter pitcher, Cowden & Wilcox, Harrisburg, Pa., mark, 12 in. high.

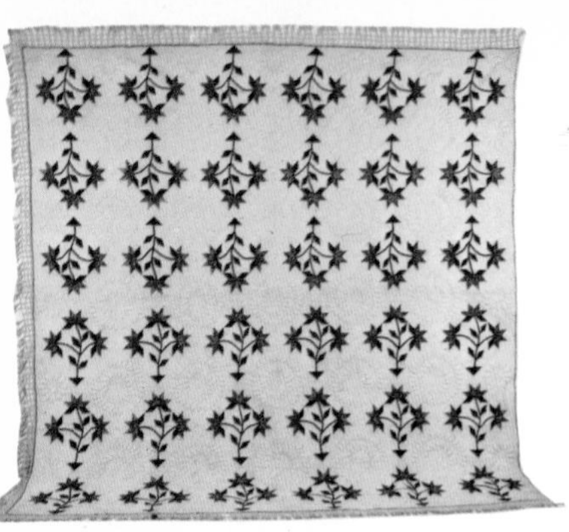

Pieced-appliquéd quilt, macramé border, trapunto quilting.

Log cabin quilt, silk fabric.

Appliquéd quilt collection.

Appliquéd cradle quilt, 1832, Rebecca Kohler, 44 in. × 42 in.

Pieced quilt, "Feathered Star."

Spongeware, Mug, Yellow, Brown

Spongeware, Pitcher, Yellow, Blue, Brown, 8 In.

Spode, Sauceboat, Tobacco Leaf, 5 3/4 In. 32.50
Spode, Toby Mug, Royal Jade, Green, 7 In. 75.00
Spode, Tureen, Covered, Blue, Italian, C.1820, Oval, 15 1/2 In. 425.00

Spongeware is very similar to spatterware in appearance. The designs were applied to the ware by daubing the color. Many dealers do not differentiate between the two wares and use the names interchangeably.

Spongeware, Bowl, Blue, 10 3/4 In. 55.00
Spongeware, Bowl, Green On Yellow, 6 X 2 3/4 In. 30.00
Spongeware, Bowl, White, Blue Sponge, Blue-Lined Rim, 10 In. 45.00
Spongeware, Creamer, Pink 13.00
Spongeware, Cup & Saucer, Farmer's, Blue 85.00
Spongeware, Jar, Slop, Dark Green On Yellow, Bail Handle 85.00
Spongeware, Mug, Yellow, Brown .... *Illus* 28.00
Spongeware, Pitcher, Blue With White, 12 In. 62.00
Spongeware, Pitcher, Blue, 9 1/2 In. 65.00
Spongeware, Pitcher, Cobalt Over White Slip, 9 In. 65.00
Spongeware, Pitcher, White, Blue Sponge, Relief Long-Stemmed Flower, 9 In. 65.00
Spongeware, Pitcher, Yellow And Green, 7 In. 55.00
Spongeware, Pitcher, Yellow, Blue, Brown, 8 In. .... *Illus* 50.00
Spongeware, Plate, Blue, 7 1/2 In. 38.00
Spongeware, Plate, Blue, 10 In. 44.00
Spongeware, Plate, Red, White, & Blue, Concentric Circles, 7 1/2 In. 75.00
Spongeware, Plate, Soup, Blue, 8 1/4 In. 48.00
Spongeware, Plate, Soup, Blue, 8 1/2 In. 38.00
Spongeware, Platter, White, Cobalt Spatter, 13 1/2 X 10 In. 120.00
Spongeware, Spittoon, Blue & White 35.00
Spongeware, Spittoon, Center Bands 55.00
Spongeware, Spittoon, 5 1/4 X 7 1/2 In. 98.00
Spongeware, Teapot, Pink, Domed Lid, 1830s Shape 40.00

Spongeware, Vase, Blue & White, Blue Band, 5 In. 40.00
St.Claire, Goblet, Blue Carnival 7.50
St.Louis, Compote, Cut Crystal, Greek Key, Cranberry Rim, 8 3/8 In. 100.00
St.Louis, Vase, White Frosted, Orange & Brown Church Scene, 7 1/2 In. 348.00

Staffordshire is a district in England where pottery and porcelain have been made since the 1900s. Thousands of types of pottery and porcelain have been made in the hundreds of factories that worked in the area. Some of the most famous factories have been listed separately. See Royal Doulton, Royal Worcester, Spode, Wedgwood, and others.

Staffordshire, see also Flow Blue, Ridgway

Staffordshire, Basket, Openwork, Braised Base & Edge, Twig Handles, 7 In. 60.00
Staffordshire, Bowl & Mug, Child's, Girl & Boy Scenes, Pink, Alfred Meakin 10.00
Staffordshire, Bowl, Child's, Nursery Rhymes, Wood 12.00
Staffordshire, Bowl, English Scenery, Blue & White, Enoch Wood, 6 1/2 In. 12.00
Staffordshire, Bowl, Flowers & Castles, Blue & White, 10 In. 50.00
Staffordshire, Bowl, Hindostan Japan, Minton & Hollis, 1852, 10 1/4 In. 38.00
Staffordshire, Bowl, Pearlware, Floral Bouquet, C.1800, 9 3/8 In. 325.00
Staffordshire, Bowl, Purple, Green, & Yellow, Blue Underglaze, Aurora, C.1840 34.00
Staffordshire, Bowl, Purple, Green, And Yellow, Blue Underglaze, Aurora, C.1840 34.00
Staffordshire, Bowl, Soup, Grecian Scenery, Stone China, 10 1/4 In. 25.00
Staffordshire, Bowl, Tyrolean, Lavender, WR & Co., C.1835, 10 1/2 In. 45.00
Staffordshire, Bowl, Vegetable, Covered, Cattle & Scenery, Black & White 65.00
Staffordshire, Bowl, Vegetable, Covered, Mulberry, C.1862 35.00
Staffordshire, Box, Covered, Shape Of Lady Holding Dog, 8 3/4 In. 125.00
Staffordshire, Box, Patch, Dresser With Book, Pipe, Glasses Atop 36.00
Staffordshire, Box, Trinket, Clock & Vases, Brown Base 69.50
Staffordshire, Box, Trinket, Oriental Man On White Horse 60.00
Staffordshire, Box, Trinket, Oval, Letter-Carrying Dove, 2 1/4 X 2 1/2 In. 29.50
Staffordshire, Box, Trinket, Serving Dish & Candlesticks, White & Gold 65.00
Staffordshire, Box, Trinket, Spaniel, Russet & White 55.00
Staffordshire, Box, Washstand, With Accessories, Marked 45.00
Staffordshire, Burner, Pastille, Castle, Double Turret, C.1810, 5 1/4 In. 125.00
Staffordshire, Burner, Pastille, Cottage, 5 In. 30.00
Staffordshire, Butter, Covered, Windemere, Meakin 22.00
Staffordshire, Castle, 2 Turrets, Mid-Victorian, 8 1/2 In. 95.00
Staffordshire, Charger, Zoological Series, J.Meir & Son, C.1815, 12 1/2 In. 85.00
Staffordshire, Child's Set, Nursery-Rhyme, Crown Staffordshire, 3 Piece 18.00
Staffordshire, Cottage, Church With Steeple 25.00
Staffordshire, Cottage, Cobalt Roof, Mulberry Door, C.1820, 5 In. 125.00
Staffordshire, Cottage, People, 4 X 3 3/4 In. 15.00
Staffordshire, Cottage, Small Pavilion, 3 X 5 In. 20.00
Staffordshire, Cottage, Three Mulberry Chimneys, Orange Door, C.1830, 4 In. 75.00
Staffordshire, Cottage, Three Story, Chimney, Red Doors, Pastille Burner 75.00
Staffordshire, Cottage, 5 In. 60.00
Staffordshire, Creamer, Bird In Nest, Blue & White 65.00
Staffordshire, Creamer, Cyprus, Mulberry, Davenport, C.1850 65.00
Staffordshire, Creamer, Mulberry, Pelew 45.00
Staffordshire, Cup & Saucer, Blue, Handleless, Jos.Heath's, Ontario Lake 45.00
Staffordshire, Cup & Saucer, Bowls Of Fruit, Black Trim 10.00
Staffordshire, Cup & Saucer, Brown, Lucerne, Pankhurst, C.1850 20.00
Staffordshire, Cup & Saucer, Castle Tower, Dark Blue, Hall 95.00
Staffordshire, Cup & Saucer, Corean, Mulberry, 12 Sided 65.00
Staffordshire, Cup & Saucer, Cottage Girl, Purple, C.1835 35.00
Staffordshire, Cup & Saucer, Demitasse, Ceylon Ivory, Boot's, England 7.50
Staffordshire, Cup & Saucer, Grandfather's, Thames River, Blue & White 25.00
Staffordshire, Cup & Saucer, Handleless, Adams, Pink 45.00
Staffordshire, Cup & Saucer, Handleless, Aurora, Brown, C.1840 40.00
Staffordshire, Cup & Saucer, Handleless, Corinthia, Pink, E.Challinor 32.00
Staffordshire, Cup & Saucer, Handleless, Empire Woman & Children, Black 28.00
Staffordshire, Cup & Saucer, Handleless, England Temperance, Purple, C.1835 40.00
Staffordshire, Cup & Saucer, Handleless, Eon, Pink 20.00
Staffordshire, Cup & Saucer, Handleless, Marcella, Mulberry 30.00
Staffordshire, Cup & Saucer, Handleless, Pelew, Mulberry, Challinor, C.1850 36.00
Staffordshire, Cup & Saucer, Handleless, R & J Clews, Mulberry 65.00

Staffordshire, Cup Plate, Boat Scene, Purple, 4 In. 20.00
Staffordshire, Cup Plate, Castle Garden & Battery, Dark Blue, Wood, 3 5/8 In. 160.00
Staffordshire, Cup Plate, Castle Garden Battery, N.Y., Shell Border 110.00
Staffordshire, Cup Plate, Castle Garden Battery, N.Y., Trefoil Border 125.00
Staffordshire, Cup Plate, Challinor, Sepia 15.00
Staffordshire, Cup Plate, Corean, Mulberry 12.00
Staffordshire, Cup Plate, Foliage, Black, Alcock 15.00
Staffordshire, Cup Plate, House, Green, Medallion Border, Marked Pearl 21.00
Staffordshire, Cup Plate, Palestine, Blue, 4 In. 25.00
Staffordshire, Cup Plate, Urn, Pink, Mayer 15.00
Staffordshire, Cup, Bochara, Mulberry 12.00
Staffordshire, Cup, Demitasse, Cockatoo, Mulberry 12.00
Staffordshire, Cup, Handleless, Mulberry 28.00
Staffordshire, Cup, Hollyhocks 4.00
Staffordshire, Cup, Landscape, Blue & White, W.R.Midwinter, England 6.00
Staffordshire, Cup, Select Views, Dark Blue, Hall's 50.00
Staffordshire, Dish, Covered Hen, Baby Chicks Coming Out Of Shell, Colors 295.00
Staffordshire, Dish, Covered Vegetable, Mulberry, Corean 80.00
Staffordshire, Dish, Cow Cover 35.00
Staffordshire, Dish, Hen Cover, Basket Weave, 9 In. 145.00
Staffordshire, Dish, Hen Cover, Egersung Faience, 7 1/2 In. 125.00
Staffordshire, Dish, Hen Cover, Tan Basket-Weave Base, 3 1/2 In. 62.00
Staffordshire, Dish, Hen Cover, Yellow Basket-Weave Base, Egersung, 7 In. 125.00
Staffordshire, Dish, Hen Cover, Yellow Basket-Weave Base, White Hen, 9 In. 125.00
Staffordshire, Dish, Pancake, Brown & Gold, Romantic Lady On Cover 32.50
Staffordshire, Figure, Cocker Spaniel, Taupe, Black Marks, Glass Eyes, Pair 165.00
Staffordshire, Figurine, Bluebird On Stump, J.T.Jones, 6 In. 40.00
Staffordshire, Figurine, Cat, Green Glass Eyes & Gold Bow 135.00
Staffordshire, Figurine, Chimney, Highlander, Lass, & Clock, C.1855, 14 In. 90.00
Staffordshire, Figurine, Chimney, Returning Home, Girl & Boy On Horse, 9 In. 150.00
Staffordshire, Figurine, Dalmation, 4 In., Pair 29.00
Staffordshire, Figurine, David Garrick As Richard III, 6 3/4 In. 75.00
Staffordshire, Figurine, Dog, Black & White, 5 1/2 In., Pair 35.00
Staffordshire, Figurine, Dog, Chain & Padlock On Neck, 13 1/2 In., Pair 115.00
Staffordshire, Figurine, Dog, Cream With Henna Spots, 9 1/2 In., Pair 150.00
Staffordshire, Figurine, Dog, Glass Eyes, 12 In., Pair 120.00
Staffordshire, Figurine, Dog, Gold Trim, 5 In., Pair 24.00
Staffordshire, Figurine, Dog, Tawny & White, Blue Bow, 7 In., Pair 95.00
Staffordshire, Figurine, Dog, Treacle Glaze, Bonnet, C.1830, 7 In., Pair 175.00
Staffordshire, Figurine, General On Horseback, Colored, 11 In. 250.00
Staffordshire, Figurine, Hen On Nest, Hand-Painted, Strawcolored Basket Base 130.00
Staffordshire, Figurine, Hen, High Glaze, White, Gold Outlined Feathers, 9 In. 195.00
Staffordshire, Figurine, Hen, 9 X 11 In. 200.00
Staffordshire, Figurine, Hunting Hound, 5 In., Pair 100.00
Staffordshire, Figurine, King Charles Spaniel, C.1850, 5 In. 36.00
Staffordshire, Figurine, Lady Carrying Baskets Of Flowers, 13 1/2 In. 85.00
Staffordshire, Figurine, Lady, C.1790 .... *Illus* 250.00
Staffordshire, Figurine, Lion Slayer, 16 In. .... 75.00 To 125.00
Staffordshire, Figurine, Lion, Clipped Coat, Luster Collar, C.1897, Pair, 6 In. 80.00
Staffordshire, Figurine, Lion, Glass Eyes, 13 1/2 X 11 In., Pair 145.00
Staffordshire, Figurine, Little Girl Holding Vase, 3 1/2 In. 10.00
Staffordshire, Figurine, Little Red Riding Hood And Fox 85.00
Staffordshire, Figurine, Little Red Riding Hood, Bright Colors, 9 In. 75.00
Staffordshire, Figurine, Man On Horse With Deer Over Saddle, 14 In. 125.00
Staffordshire, Figurine, Prince Charles Spaniel, 1830, 3 1/2 In., Pair 75.00
Staffordshire, Figurine, Prince Of Wales & Angel, 6 1/2 In. .... *Illus* 75.00
Staffordshire, Figurine, Prince Of Wales, Edward VII, 16 1/2 In. 145.00
Staffordshire, Figurine, Pug Dog With Glass Eyes, Gold Collar 135.00
Staffordshire, Figurine, Robin Hood, 15 In. 75.00
Staffordshire, Figurine, Seated Admiral, 3 In. 28.50
Staffordshire, Figurine, Shepherdess, Ralph Wood, C.1770, 8 1/2 In. 1200.00
Staffordshire, Figurine, Spaniel, Black & White, Pink Spots, 8 In. 15.00
Staffordshire, Figurine, Spaniel, C.1870, 13 1/2 X 12 In., Pair 60.00
Staffordshire, Figurine, Spaniel, Seated, Tree Trunk, Gold Collar, 13 In. 75.00
Staffordshire, Figurine, Spaniels Against Tree Trunk, 6 In. 35.00

Staffordshire, Figurine, Lady, C.1790

(See Page 601)

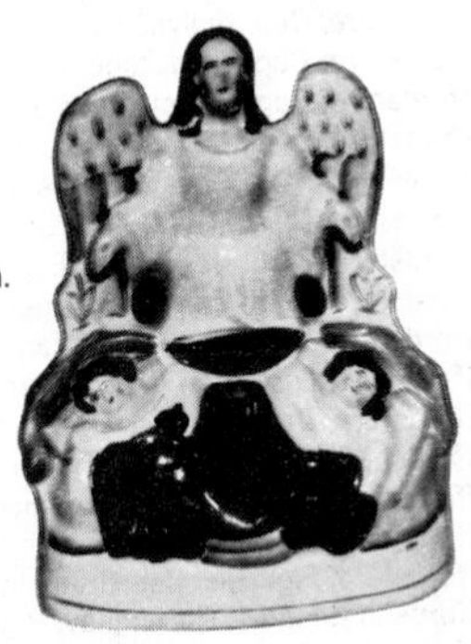

Staffordshire, Figurine, Prince Of Wales & Angel, 6 1/2 In.

(See Page 607)

Staffordshire, Figurine, Spaniels, White With Gold Padlock, 9 1/2 In. 95.00
Staffordshire, Figurine, The Lion Slayer, 16 In. 150.00
Staffordshire, Figurine, The Lion Slayer, 17 In. 85.00
Staffordshire, Figurine, The Lost Sheep, Ralph Wood, C.1770, 8 1/2 In. 1600.00
Staffordshire, Figurine, Uniformed Man, Dog, Tree Stump, C.1840, 5 X 4 In. 75.00
Staffordshire, Figurine, Victoria & Albert, Pair, 5 In. .... *Illus* 120.00
Staffordshire, Figurine, Victorian, Boy, Brick Wall, Basket Of Flowers 42.00
Staffordshire, Figurine, Whippet With Hare In His Mouth, C.1850, 7 1/2 In. 75.00
Staffordshire, Figurine, Whippet, Reclining, 4 In., Pair 150.00
Staffordshire, Figurine, White French Poodle, Textured Mane 110.00
Staffordshire, Figurine, Zebra, C.1820, 6 1/2 In., Pair 175.00
Staffordshire, Flower Holder, Castle, Double Turrets, C.1830, 8 1/2 In. 125.00
Staffordshire, Fugurine, Farmer & Wife, White, Orange, & Gold, Jug & Wheat 75.00
Staffordshire, Garniture, Pink, Watteau Scenes, Gold Handles, 4 In., 3 Piece 100.00
Staffordshire, Gravy Boat, Arms Of United States, Blue 210.00
Staffordshire, Gravy Boat, Mulberry, 4 1/2 X 7 1/2 In. 35.00
Staffordshire, Group, Boy & Girl Sitting On Tree Stump, 4 In. 50.00
Staffordshire, Group, Boy & Girl, Tree Stump, White, Gold Costume, 4 1/2 In. 50.00
Staffordshire, Group, Boy, Girl, Lamb, Dog, Watch-Holding Pocket, 12 In. 65.00
Staffordshire, Group, Chimney Clock, Scottish Highlander & Lass, C.1855 .... 90.00
Staffordshire, Group, Cow & Calf Under Tree, Flat Back, 10 1/2 In. 110.00
Staffordshire, Group, Going Home, Girl & Boy On Horse, 8 In. 145.00
Staffordshire, Group, Kilted Man & Girl In Full Dress, 6 1/2 In. 38.00
Staffordshire, Group, Lovers, 14 In. 70.00
Staffordshire, Group, Scots With Bagpipes, Little Girl, Orange Stump, 10 In. 58.00
Staffordshire, Hatpin Holder, Figural, C.1860, 6 In. 50.00
Staffordshire, Holder, Spill, Figural, Two Children, Tree Trunk, 5 1/2 In. 48.00
Staffordshire, Inkwell, Figures, 4 1/2 In. .... *Illus* 48.00
Staffordshire, Inkwell, Woman & Man Playing Chess On Lid 95.00
Staffordshire, Jar, Cracker, Covered, White Basket Weave, Aqua Rope, 1875 .... 50.00
Staffordshire, Jar, Cracker, Fuchsias, Powder Blue, Melon Ribbed, C.1850 .... 22.00
Staffordshire, Jar, Ginger, Trollis, Blue Lid, Salmon Roses, Wood & Sons 150.00
Staffordshire, Jar, Tobacco, Jester, Dog, 9 1/2 In. 225.00
Staffordshire, Jenny Lind Castle Scene, Royal Staffordshire, 9 3/4 In. 10.00

Staffordshire, Figurine, Victoria & Albert, Pair, 5 In.

Staffordshire, Inkwell, Figures, 4 1/2 In.

Staffordshire, Jug, Milk, Tam O'shanter And Lion Handle, Blue & White 65.00
Staffordshire, Jug, Puzzle, Let Too, Knock Down, & Death, C.1850, 9 In. 140.00
Staffordshire, Jug, Toby, Falstaff, C.1820, Yellow Pants, Green Coat, Red Hat 135.00
Staffordshire, Keeper, Cheese, Yuan, Blue & White 39.50
Staffordshire, Match Holder, Boy Eating Grapes, 4 1/4 In. 37.50
Staffordshire, Mug, Child's, Toys Two Pence Each, Transfer On Creamware 75.00
Staffordshire, Mug, Coaching Days, Woods 15.00
Staffordshire, Mug, Lafayette College, 1905, Football Shape, Maddock 75.00
Staffordshire, Pitcher, Burmese, Serpent Handle, Allerton, 5 In. 20.00
Staffordshire, Pitcher, Cherubs, Roses & Grapes, 6 3/4 In. 48.00
Staffordshire, Pitcher, Chinese Flowering Tree, Powder Blue, Quart, 6 In. 125.00
Staffordshire, Pitcher, Cockson & Sesdon, C.1885, 12 1/2 In. 28.00
Staffordshire, Pitcher, Crossed Torches, Floral, Gold, Maddock, C.1890, 7 In. 40.00
Staffordshire, Pitcher, Deer Medallions, Dark Blue, 7 In. 150.00
Staffordshire, Pitcher, Lafayette, Blue, 6 1/2 In. 500.00
Staffordshire, Pitcher, Milk, Blue Transfer, G.Phillips, Longport, 6 Sided 65.00
Staffordshire, Pitcher, Milk, Rose, Mulberry, Walker, 5 1/4 In. 40.00
Staffordshire, Pitcher, Oriental, Imari Colors, C.1817, 5 1/2 In. 50.00
Staffordshire, Pitcher, Schenectady On The Mohawk, Purple, 7 1/2 In. 165.00
Staffordshire, Pitcher, Schenectady, Purple, Jackson, 7 1/2 In. 160.00
Staffordshire, Pitcher, T.F.& Son, England, Sam Weller At Table, Black, 10 In. 55.00
Staffordshire, Pitcher, Tan, Purple Transfer, Copper Luster Trim, 4 1/2 In. 75.00
Staffordshire, Pitcher, View Of The Erie Canal, Blue, 8 1/2 In. 875.00
Staffordshire, Pitcher, Water, Corean, Mulberry, P.W.& Co., C.1850 .... 95.00
Staffordshire, Pitcher, 1 Quart, Florals, Girls, Birds, Deep Cobalt, C.1860 .... 75.00
Staffordshire, Plate, Abbey Design, Dark Blue, Geo.Jones & Sons, England 18.00
Staffordshire, Plate, Abbey Ruins, Brown, Mayer, Longport, C.1836, 10 1/2 In. 28.00
Staffordshire, Plate, Alleghany, Mulberry, T.Goodfellow, C.1850, 10 1/2 In. 30.00
Staffordshire, Plate, American Birds, Lavender, James Edwards, 9 3/4 In. 20.00
Staffordshire, Plate, Asbury Park, N.J., Gray Blue, R & M, 8 1/4 In. 13.50
Staffordshire, Plate, Athens, Mulberry, Meigh, 10 1/4 In. 18.00
Staffordshire, Plate, Atlantic City, Blue & White, 9 1/4 In. 24.00
Staffordshire, Plate, Balmoral, Yellow Floral, Weed & Hulme, 1894, 10 1/2 In. 20.00
Staffordshire, Plate, Baltimore & Ohio Railroad, Blue, On Level, 10 In. 525.00
Staffordshire, Plate, Baltimore & Ohio Railroad, Blue, Wood, 9 1/2 In. 550.00
Staffordshire, Plate, Battle Monument, Baltimore, Pink, Jackson, 9 In. 73.00
Staffordshire, Plate, Belvoir Castle, Wood, Medium Blue, 10 In. 125.00
Staffordshire, Plate, Belzoni, Green, Enoch Wood, 8 1/2 In. 18.00
Staffordshire, Plate, Black Transfer, Ladies In Park, David Johnston & Co. 14.50
Staffordshire, Plate, Blue, Damascus, Edward & Enoch Wood, C.1840 .... 24.00
Staffordshire, Plate, Blue, Italia, 10 1/2 In. 20.00
Staffordshire, Plate, Bochara, Mulberry, J.Edwards, C.1847, 10 1/2 In. 32.00
Staffordshire, Plate, Bochara, Mulberry, 7 1/4 In. 15.00
Staffordshire, Plate, Boston Mails, John Edwards, 1847-83 .... 35.00
Staffordshire, Plate, Boston Statehouse With Chaise, Blue, 8 1/2 In. 288.00
Staffordshire, Plate, Boston Statehouse, Blue, Impressed Rogers, 9 3/4 In. 328.00

Staffordshire, Plate, Boston Statehouse, Wood, Medium Blue, 9 1/4 In. 260.00
Staffordshire, Plate, Cake, Pink Scene Titled Fishers, 4 X 4 1/2 In. 15.00
Staffordshire, Plate, Cake, White, Green Bas Relief, Crown 7.50
Staffordshire, Plate, Canova, Black & White, Clews, C.1820, 6 In. 18.00
Staffordshire, Plate, Canova, Green, Mayer 1836, 7 1/4 In. 22.00
Staffordshire, Plate, Canova, Light Blue, 8 3/4 In. 20.00
Staffordshire, Plate, Canova, T.Mayer, 9 In. 24.00
Staffordshire, Plate, Canton, Hanley, Octagonal, 8 In. 7.50
Staffordshire, Plate, Capitol At Washington, D.C., Dark Blue, White, 9 1/8 In. 20.00
Staffordshire, Plate, Captain John Smith, Rolled Edge, R & M, 10 In. 32.00
Staffordshire, Plate, Celtic, Blue, Enoch Wood & Sons, C.1818, 10 1/2 In. 40.00
Staffordshire, Plate, Celtic, C.1850, Venetian Scenery, Blue On White, 9 In. 22.00
Staffordshire, Plate, Children At Play, Mulberry, 5 3/4 In. 25.00
Staffordshire, Plate, Christmas Eve, Wilkie Design, Clews, Dark Blue, 9 In. 210.00
Staffordshire, Plate, Colonial Times, Red Crown Decal, 10 In., Set Of 3 .... 90.00
Staffordshire, Plate, Columbus, Pink, Adams, C.1820, 10 1/2 In. 48.00
Staffordshire, Plate, Corean, Mulberry, P.W.Co., 10 In. 35.00
Staffordshire, Plate, Corean, Mulberry, 7 In. 18.00
Staffordshire, Plate, Corean, Mulberry, 8 In. 20.00
Staffordshire, Plate, Corean, Mulberry, 9 1/2 In. .... 25.00 To 28.00
Staffordshire, Plate, Corsica, Green Transfer, W.& Co., 9 1/4 In. 20.00
Staffordshire, Plate, Cumberland Falls, Blue, 10 In. 20.00
Staffordshire, Plate, Cup, Clews, Dark Blue 40.00
Staffordshire, Plate, Cyprus, Brownfield, 9 1/2 In., Pair 38.00
Staffordshire, Plate, Cyprus, Mulberry, 7 1/2 In. 16.00
Staffordshire, Plate, Deer Hunting, Dark Blue, Wood, C.1820, 10 In. 85.00
Staffordshire, Plate, Don Quixote, Meeting Of Sancho & Dapple, Blue, Clews 128.00
Staffordshire, Plate, Dr.Syntax Reading His Tour, Medium Blue, 10 1/2 In. 150.00
Staffordshire, Plate, Early Scenes Of Tacoma, Washington, Blue 27.50
Staffordshire, Plate, English Landscape & Figures, Deep Blue, 10 In. 25.00
Staffordshire, Plate, Escape Of The Mouse, Cobalt, Clews, C.1818, 10 In. 125.00
Staffordshire, Plate, Fagin, Interior Scene, Stanmore, Meakin, 8 In. 24.00
Staffordshire, Plate, Flora, Mulberry, Hulme & Booth, 9 1/2 In. 23.00
Staffordshire, Plate, Flora, Mulberry, Pink & Green, Hulme & Booth, 9 1/2 In. 25.00
Staffordshire, Plate, Fort Dearborn, 1804, Dark Blue & White, 9 1/8 In. 20.00
Staffordshire, Plate, Fountain, Pink, E.Wood, 8 3/8 In. 29.50
Staffordshire, Plate, Franklin's Birthplace, Deep Blue, Wood, 9 1/4 In. 125.00
Staffordshire, Plate, Gunton Hall, Norfolk, Dark Blue, Wood, 7 1/2 In. 35.00
Staffordshire, Plate, Hancock House, Boston, Black, 8 In. 70.00
Staffordshire, Plate, Hancock House, Boston, Pink, Jackson, , C.1820, 8 In. 78.00
Staffordshire, Plate, Hartford, Sepia, Jackson, 10 1/2 In. 78.00
Staffordshire, Plate, Hey Diddle Diddle, W.& Co., Hanley, England, 5 In. 20.00
Staffordshire, Plate, Highlands At West Point, Blue, Wood & Son, 6 1/2 In. 220.00
Staffordshire, Plate, Hoboken, N.J., Blue, Eagle Boarder, 7 1/4 In. 180.00
Staffordshire, Plate, Hudson River, Black & White, Clews, C.1820, 9 In. 58.00
Staffordshire, Plate, Independence Hall, 1776, Dark Blue & White, 9 1/8 In. 20.00
Staffordshire, Plate, Insane Hospital, Boston, Ridgway, Dark Blue, 7 In. 175.00
Staffordshire, Plate, Italy, Lavender Transfer, C.M.& Sons, C.1851, 9 1/2 In. 24.00
Staffordshire, Plate, Ivanhoe, Rebecca Repelling Templer, 10 1/4 In. 28.00
Staffordshire, Plate, Jenny Lind, 1795, Pink & White, 10 In. 15.00
Staffordshire, Plate, Kenilworth, Blue & White, Allerton, 6 1/2 In. 5.75
Staffordshire, Plate, Knight Elkins, Pennsylvania, Purple, 7 3/4 In. 28.00
Staffordshire, Plate, Kyber, Mulberry, Meir, 10 1/2 In. 25.00
Staffordshire, Plate, Lahore, Brown Transfer, T.& R. Boote, 9 1/2 In. 9.00
Staffordshire, Plate, Landing Of Lafayette, Clews, Dark Blue, 10 In. 250.00
Staffordshire, Plate, Landing Of Lafayette, Clews, 8 7/8 In. 165.00
Staffordshire, Plate, Landing Of Lafayette, Deep Blue, 6 3/4 In. 175.00
Staffordshire, Plate, Landing Of Pilgrims, Blue, Wood, 10 In. 120.00
Staffordshire, Plate, Landing Of Pilgrims, Plymouth, Blue & White, 1899, 9 In. 25.00
Staffordshire, Plate, Landing Of The Pilgrims, Blue, Wood, 10 1/4 In. 110.00
Staffordshire, Plate, Lavender, The Bosphorus, R.Hall, Scenic, 10 1/3 In. 22.00
Staffordshire, Plate, Lincoln Memorial, 10 In. 22.00
Staffordshire, Plate, Lozere, Mulberry, E.Challinor, C.1850 .... 30.00
Staffordshire, Plate, MacDonnough's Victory, Dark Blue, Wood, 7 1/2 In. 200.00
Staffordshire, Plate, McKinley, Dark Brown Transfer, 9 In. 36.00

Staffordshire, Plate, Medina, Blue, 7 3/8 In. 15.00
Staffordshire, Plate, Millennium, Purple, 7 3/4 In. 35.00
Staffordshire, Plate, Mohammedan Mosque & Tomb, Hall, Dark Blue, 10 In. 85.00
Staffordshire, Plate, Montevideo, Conn., Pink, C.1820, 7 In. 45.00
Staffordshire, Plate, Mr.Micawber Leaving Pawnshop, Stanmore, Meakin, 8 In. 24.00
Staffordshire, Plate, Mt.Vernon, Blue & White, 1900, 9 In. 25.00
Staffordshire, Plate, Nahant Hotel, Stubbs, Dark Blue, 9 In. 255.00
Staffordshire, Plate, Niagara Falls, Green, Swinnerton, 10 In. 20.00
Staffordshire, Plate, Ning Po, Mulberry, Deep Dish, 14 Sided, 10 1/4 In. 30.00
Staffordshire, Plate, Oliver Twist On Road To London, Stanmore, Meakin, 8 In. 24.00
Staffordshire, Plate, Oriental View, Dark Blue, C.1825, 7 3/4 In. 38.00
Staffordshire, Plate, Palestine, Purple, Adams, C.1820, 10 1/2 In. 36.00
Staffordshire, Plate, Panama, Mulberry, 7 1/2 In. .... 16.00 To 18.00
Staffordshire, Plate, Pass In Catskill Mountains, Blue, 7 1/2 In. 150.00
Staffordshire, Plate, Paxton, Light Blue, J.D.P.& Co., 10 In. 28.00
Staffordshire, Plate, Peace On Earth, Marked Millennium, Purple, 7 1/2 In. 25.00
Staffordshire, Plate, Peace, 1914-1918, Flags, McNicol, 7 1/4 In. 12.00
Staffordshire, Plate, Pelew, Mulberry, E.Challinor, C.1850, 7 1/2 In. 18.50
Staffordshire, Plate, Percy, Mulberry, F.Morley, C.1850, 10 1/2 In. 25.00
Staffordshire, Plate, Peruvian, Mulberry, Wedgwood, C.1845 .... 32.00
Staffordshire, Plate, Pointer & Quail, Dark Blue, E.Wood, 8 1/2 In. 55.00
Staffordshire, Plate, Ponte Rotto, Blue, 10 In. 39.00
Staffordshire, Plate, R. Hall, Wild Rose, Dark Blue, 10 3/4 In. 35.00
Staffordshire, Plate, Rhone Scenery, Mulberry, 8 1/2 In. 15.00
Staffordshire, Plate, Rhone Scenery, Mulberry, 9 5/8 In. 16.00
Staffordshire, Plate, Robinson Crusoe & Family Dining, Brown, 7 1/2 In. 36.00
Staffordshire, Plate, Rural Scene, Pink, 8 1/2 In. 12.00
Staffordshire, Plate, Salem Witch, 1692, Blue & White, R & M, 6 In. 40.00
Staffordshire, Plate, Scaleby Castle, Cumberland, Blue, Adams, 7 3/4 In. 39.00
Staffordshire, Plate, Scenery, Sepia, 8 1/2 In. 25.00
Staffordshire, Plate, Scott's Waverly, Blue, Davenport, C.1835, 10 1/2 In. 65.00
Staffordshire, Plate, Service, Cream & Maroon, Myott 15.00
Staffordshire, Plate, Shaw's Peruvian Horse Hunt, Green & Brown, 8 1/2 In. 35.00
Staffordshire, Plate, Soup, Dark Blue, British Views, 8 1/4 In. 38.00
Staffordshire, Plate, Soup, Richard Jordan Residence, N.J., Pink, 10 1/4 In. 88.00
Staffordshire, Plate, States, Clews, Dark Blue, 9 In. 175.00
Staffordshire, Plate, Swansea, Wales, Blue, Bevans & Irwin, C.1813, 10 In. 55.00
Staffordshire, Plate, Temple, Mulberry, P.W.Co., 10 In. 30.00
Staffordshire, Plate, Texas Campaign, Sepia, J.B., C.1845, 10 1/2 In. 72.00
Staffordshire, Plate, Texas Campaign, Sepia, 7 1/2 In. 73.00
Staffordshire, Plate, The Elm, Cambridge, Mass., Washington's Troops, 1775 .... 20.00
Staffordshire, Plate, Toddy, Boreham House, Essex, Deep Blue, Stevenson 38.00
Staffordshire, Plate, Trenton Falls, Dark Blue, Wood, 7 1/2 In. 155.00
Staffordshire, Plate, Tyrolean, Brown, C.1830, 9 1/2 In. 24.00
Staffordshire, Plate, Udina, Mulberry, J.Clementson, 9 1/4 In. 15.00
Staffordshire, Plate, Union Line, Wood, Dark Blue, 10 In. 265.00
Staffordshire, Plate, Union Line, Woods & Sons, 9 1/4 In. 185.00
Staffordshire, Plate, Upper Ferry Bridge, Medium Deep Blue, Stubbs, 8 3/4 In. 145.00
Staffordshire, Plate, Venus, Light Blue, 8 3/4 In. 9.95
Staffordshire, Plate, View Of City Of Albany, Blue, 10 In. 200.00
Staffordshire, Plate, View Of Woodlands Near Philadelphia, Blue, 6 3/4 In. 130.00
Staffordshire, Plate, Views Of Newport, R.I., Dark Blue, 9 In. 19.00
Staffordshire, Plate, Vincennes, Mulberry, 7 1/4 In. 22.50
Staffordshire, Plate, Washington Crossing The Delaware, R.& M., 9 3/4 In. 45.00
Staffordshire, Plate, Washington Vase, Mulberry, P.W.& Co., C.1850, 7 In. 18.50
Staffordshire, Plate, Washington Vase, Mulberry, P.W.Co., 10 In. 30.00
Staffordshire, Plate, Washington Vase, Mulberry, 7 7/8 In. 18.00
Staffordshire, Plate, Washington Vase, Mulberry, 9 3/4 In. 30.00
Staffordshire, Plate, Washington, D.C., Blue & White, 1899, 9 In. 25.00
Staffordshire, Plate, Washington, Pink & Green, Enoch Wood & Sons, 8 1/4 In. 35.00
Staffordshire, Plate, Waterworks, Philadelphia, Purple, Jackson, 9 In. 85.00
Staffordshire, Plate, Wilkie Series, Christmas Eve, Blue, Clews, 9 In. 128.00
Staffordshire, Plate, William Penn's Treaty, Sepia, Godwin, 10 3/4 In. 68.00
Staffordshire, Plate, Wreath, Mulberry, T.Furnival, C.1845 .... 24.00
Staffordshire, Platter, Asiatic Pheasant, B & K, C.1870, 16 X 13 In. 35.00

Staffordshire, Platter, Asiatic Pheasants, Blue & White, Tunstall, 17 1/2 In. 40.00
Staffordshire, Platter, Battery Scene, Blue, 16 1/2 In. 650.00
Staffordshire, Platter, Blue Border Of Acorns & Leaves, 5 X 4 In. 16.00
Staffordshire, Platter, British Views, Dark Blue, 14 3/4 X 11 3/4 In. 138.00
Staffordshire, Platter, Brown & White, Washington Vase, P.W.&co., 13 3/4 In. 35.00
Staffordshire, Platter, Columbia College, Blue, 8 1/2 In. 525.00
Staffordshire, Platter, Genoa, Mulberry, 13 1/2 X 10 1/2 In. 25.00
Staffordshire, Platter, Independence Hall, Johnson Bros., 16 In. 69.00
Staffordshire, Platter, Jeddo, Mulberry, 13 1/2 In. 55.00
Staffordshire, Platter, Kyber, Dark Blue, 13 1/2 In. 48.00
Staffordshire, Platter, Lakes Of Killarney, Blue, 18 In. 150.00
Staffordshire, Platter, Macclesfield Bridge, Deep Blue, Wood, 18 1/2 In. 360.00
Staffordshire, Platter, Mogul Scenery, Purple, Mayer, C.1835, 12 In. 45.00
Staffordshire, Platter, Napoleon, Brown On White, 15 1/2 In. 45.00
Staffordshire, Platter, Near Catskill On Hudson River, Blue, Wall, 12 1/2 In. 675.00
Staffordshire, Platter, Panama, Mulberry, E.Challinor, 15 In. 65.00
Staffordshire, Platter, Panama, Mulberry, 10 In. 28.00
Staffordshire, Platter, Percy, Mulberry, F.Morley, C.1850, 16 X 12 In. 62.00
Staffordshire, Platter, Priory, Alcock, 13 1/2 In. 35.00
Staffordshire, Platter, Rhoda Gardens, Mulberry, 12 1/2 In. 60.00
Staffordshire, Platter, Rhoda Gardens, Mulberry, 12 1/2 X 9 1/2 In. 60.00
Staffordshire, Platter, Rhone Scenery, Mulberry, T.J.& J.Mayer, C.1850, 16 In. 75.00
Staffordshire, Platter, Sandusky, Blue, 16 1/2 In. 1100.00
Staffordshire, Platter, Shapoo, Mulberry, 11 X 8 1/4 In. 50.00
Staffordshire, Platter, Washington Vase, Sepia, Podmore Walker, 16 1/2 In. 82.00
Staffordshire, Platter, Wild Roses, Scrolls, Dark Blue, Empire, Soho, Tunstall 6.00
Staffordshire, Platter, Woodlands Near Philadelphia, Stubbs, 10 1/2 In. 300.00
Staffordshire, Pomander, Enamel, Figure, Lady, Landscape, 18th Century 350.00
Staffordshire, Relish, Bochara, Mulberry 28.50
Staffordshire, Relish, Utopia, Floral, W.H.Grindley, 8 In. 10.00
Staffordshire, Salt, English Scenery, Blue & White, Enoch Woods, 1750 39.50
Staffordshire, Saltshaker, Landing Of Lafayette, Blue 500.00
Staffordshire, Saucer, Corean, Mulberry 8.00
Staffordshire, Saucer, Hudson River Crow's-Nest, Rose Transfer, Laughlin 6.00
Staffordshire, Saucer, Marcella, Mulberry 10.00
Staffordshire, Saucer, Udira, Mulberry, J.Clementson 15.00
Staffordshire, Slipper, Deep Pink, Purple Bow, Square Toe, 4 In. 25.00
Staffordshire, Soup, Newburgh, Ruggles House, Blue, Ridgway, 10 1/4 In. 28.00
Staffordshire, Spill, Cow Nursing Calf, 10 3/4 In. 85.00
Staffordshire, Spill, 2 White Poodles, Gold Chain & Lock, Pebbly Coats 31.00
Staffordshire, St.Theresa's Church, Mass., Blue & White, Woods, 10 In. 13.50
Staffordshire, Sugar & Creamer, Cover, Alleghany, Mulberry, Goodfellow, 1850s 135.00
Staffordshire, Sugar, Covered, Floral Basket Design, Dark Blue 90.00
Staffordshire, Sugar, Covered, Llama, Dark Blue, Zoological Series 125.00
Staffordshire, Sugar, Covered, Mulberry, Cypress 85.00
Staffordshire, Sugar, Covered, Mulberry, Rhine Scenery, T & J Mayer, 8 1/4 In. 35.00
Staffordshire, Sugar, Covered, Spring, Brown & White, Handled, Grindley, 1890s 25.00
Staffordshire, Sugar, Multicolor Primroses, Loop Handles 53.00
Staffordshire, Sugar, Washington Vase, Mulberry 27.00
Staffordshire, Tankard, Domed Pewter Lid, Cream Color, Floral, 1/3 Liter 45.00
Staffordshire, Tea Set, Child's, Blue, English, Setting For 4 90.00
Staffordshire, Tea Set, Child's, Mycena Pattern, Signed W.A.A., 19 Piece 125.00
Staffordshire, Tea Set, Child's, Orange Polka Dots, C.1850, 11 Piece 65.00
Staffordshire, Tea Set, Farm Pattern, Brown, Signed Old Hall, Triangle, 1850 85.00
Staffordshire, Teacup, Brown Stylized Tulips, Wood, England 4.00
Staffordshire, Teapot, Beauties Of China, Mulberry 110.00
Staffordshire, Teapot, Boston Harbor & American Eagle, Cobalt Blue 500.00
Staffordshire, Teapot, Boston Harbor, American Eagle, C.1820, Deep Blue 500.00
Staffordshire, Teapot, Castle Scene, Sadler, England 15.00
Staffordshire, Teapot, Oriental Scene, Pink 65.00
Staffordshire, Teapot, Presented To S.S.Pierce's Sons, Meakin, 38 In. 1950.00
Staffordshire, Teapot, Toby, Ole King Cole, Violin Handle, Hand Spout, 7 In. 65.00
Staffordshire, Tile, Gladstone In Relief, Sepia, Sherwin & Cotton, 1898, 9 In. 65.00
Staffordshire, Toby Mug, Hearty Good Fellow, C.1860 85.00
Staffordshire, Toby Mug, Snufftaker, Black Tricorner Hat, 7 1/4 In. 135.00

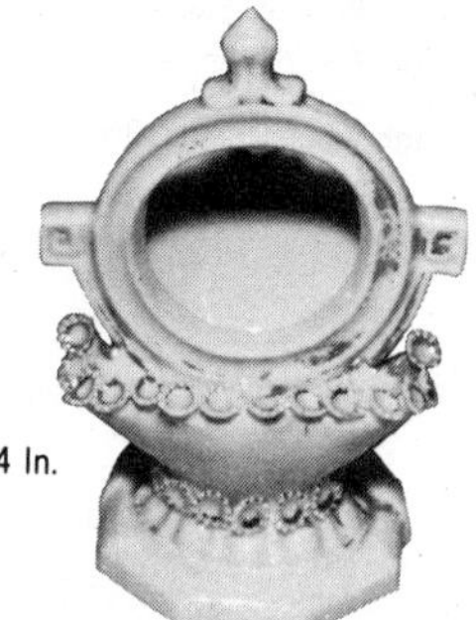

Staffordshire, Watch Holder, 4 In.

Staffordshire, Toby Mug, Speckled Brown Coat, C.1770, Ralph Wood, 9 5/8 In. 1000.00
Staffordshire, Toddy Plate, Tow Shippets, Dark Blue, E.Wood 50.00
Staffordshire, Tureen & Stand, Covered, Rhone Scenery, Mulberry 65.00
Staffordshire, Tureen & Tray, Gravy, Pass In Catskill Mountains, Blue 775.00
Staffordshire, Tureen & Tray, Sauce, India Scene, Blue, Holloware, C.1825 .... 75.00
Staffordshire, Tureen & Underplate, Covered, Abby Mill, Blue, Handled, 4 In. 25.00
Staffordshire, Tureen, Covered, Blue & White, Cabbage Rose Finial, Pastoral 125.00
Staffordshire, Tureen, Sauce, Leaf Finial & Finial, Fruit Basket, Blue, 1835 .... 45.00
Staffordshire, Vase, Cat & Dog Figures, 3 1/2 In. 12.00
Staffordshire, Vase, Hand-Painted, Double Handled, Flared, 2 1/2 In., Pair 35.00
Staffordshire, Vase, Hand-Painted, Double Handled, Miniature, 2 1/2 In., Pair 35.00
Staffordshire, Vegetable Bowl, Acropolis, Pink, 10 1/4 In. 48.00
Staffordshire, Vegetable Bowl, Covered, Archery, Sepia 85.00
Staffordshire, Vegetable Bowl, Covered, Tournay, Brown, T.R.Boote, Square 18.00
Staffordshire, Washbowl, Kan-Si, Mulberry, T.Walker, C.1847, 13 1/2 In. 135.00
Staffordshire, Watch Holder, 4 In. .... *Illus* 65.00
Staffordshire, Whistle, Miniature Doghead 28.00

Stained Glass, see Windowpane

Stangl pottery was organized in 1929, succeeding the Fulper Pottery Company. Stangl porcelain birds are popular collectibles.

Stangl, Basket, Aqua, Large 14.00
Stangl, Bird, Blue Jay On Yellow-Blossomed Stump, 5 1/8 In. 35.00
Stangl, Bird, Blue Jay, No.3276, 4 1/2 In. 21.00
Stangl, Bird, Cardinal 13.00
Stangl, Bird, Cockatoo, No.3580, 9 In. 40.00
Stangl, Bird, Cockatoo, Pink & Black, 8 In. 45.00
Stangl, Bird, Cockatoo, Pink & Blue, M.T.F., No.34055, 6 1/2 In. 45.00
Stangl, Bird, Cockatoo, Pink, No.3405s, Black Stamp, 6 3/8 In. 33.00
Stangl, Bird, Cockatoo, VRF 5580, 9 In. 75.00
Stangl, Bird, Flying Duck, MW, 12 X 10 In. 95.00
Stangl, Bird, Oriole, No.3402 .... 22.00
Stangl, Bird, Pair Of Wrens On Leafy Stump, Brown & Cream, 6 1/2 In. 45.00
Stangl, Bird, Parrot On Green & Brown Stump, Yellow & Green, 5 1/8 In. 48.00
Stangl, Bird, Pink Parrot, 6 In. 22.00
Stangl, Bird, Thrush, Brown, Yellow, & Green, Purple Flowers, 10 In. 75.00
Stangl, Bird, Two Parakeets On Branch, No.3082, 7 In. 58.00
Stangl, Butter, Fruit 9.00
Stangl, Can, Watering, Tulip Design, Handle, 12 1/2 In. 30.00
Stangl, Charger, Sgraffitoed Floral, Artist Signed, 14 In. 35.00
Stangl, Console Set, Terra Rose 20.00

Stangl, Cornucopia 30.00
Stangl, Pitcher, Blue, 4 1/2 In. 5.00
Stangl, Plate, Cake, Blue 4.50
Stangl, Sugar, Covered, Orange 5.00
Stangl, Vase, Orange, Brown-Gold Mottled Glaze, Handled, 4 X 3 In. 15.00

Star Holly is a milk glass type of glass made by the Imperial Glass Company of Bellaire, Ohio, in 1957. The pieces were made to look like Wedgwood jasperware. White holly leaves appear against colored borders of blue, green, or rust. It is marked on the bottom of every piece.

Star Holly, Saucer, White, Imperial, 5 3/4 In. 25.00

Steins have been used for over 500 years. They have been made of ivory, porcelain, stoneware, faience, silver, pewter, wood, or glass in sizes up to nine gallons. Although some were made by Meissen, Capo-Di-Monte, and other famous factories, most were made in Germany. The words Geschutz or Musterschutz on a stein are the German for patented or registered design, not company names.

Stein, A.T. 1373, Beige, Green Family & Home Scenes, 11 1/2 In. 45.00
Stein, Character, Monk, 1/2 Liter 100.00
Stein, Character, Monkey On Barrel With Lithophane, 1/2 Liter 300.00
Stein, Child Of Munchen, Black Robe, Holding Turnips, 1/4 Liter 145.00
Stein, Cut Glass, Footed Base, Domed Pewter Lid, 1/2 Liter 375.00
Stein, Derby Type, Negro With Pipe, Pewter Lid, 1/2 Liter 142.00
Stein, German, Blue Castle Decoration, 1/4 Liter 19.00
Stein, German, Bowling Pin Shape, Man In Pewter Lid, 1/2 Liter 75.00
Stein, German, Luftwaffe, Legion Condor, OFW Rudolph Gerhardt, Iron Cross 65.00
Stein, German, Luftwaffe, Squadron Stein, Lt.Helmut Kurbach, Iron Cross 65.00
Stein, German, Munich Child With Turnips & Stein, Pewter Top, 3 3/4 In. 75.00
Stein, Germany, People At Table, 7 In. 22.50
Stein, Gesetzlich Geschutzt, Character, Fly Between Eyes, 1/2 Liter 250.00
Stein, Geshutz, Germany, Musicians & Saloon, Etched, Pewter Lid, 2 Liter 268.00
Stein, Glass, Farm Scene, Pewter Lid, 1/2 Liter 38.00
Stein, Kayserzinn, Double Acorn Top, Pewter, 10 In. 125.00
Stein, Lithophane, German Historical Scene, 6 1/2 In. 45.00
Stein, Ludwig Heigl, Gray Stoneware, Porcelain Portrait Lid, 1853, Liter 185.00
Stein, Merkelback & Wick, Mandarin Man, Yellow & Green, 1/2 Liter 165.00
Stein, Mettlach, see Mettlach, Stein
Stein, Musterschutz, Character, Drunken Monkey, 1/2 Liter 450.00
Stein, Musterschutz, Crying Radish, 3/10 Liter 375.00
Stein, Musterschutz, Happy Radish, 1/4 Liter 300.00
Stein, Musterschutz, Happy Turnip, .3 Liter 400.00
Stein, Musterschutz, Sad Radish, 1/4 Liter 250.00
Stein, Musterschutz, Sad Turnip, 1/2 Liter 350.00
Stein, Musterschutz, Singing Pig, 1/4 Liter 275.00
Stein, Occupied Japan, Tavern Scene, 6 1/2 In. 15.00
Stein, Paradise, Garden Of Eden, Adam & Eve, Apple, Serpent, Quart 95.00
Stein, Party Scene, Pewter Top & Thumb Rest, C.1900, 15 In. 85.00
Stein, Pewter Top, Light Blue, Germany, Triple Marked, 2 1/2 In. 90.00
Stein, Pewter, Barrel Shape, C.1860, 1/4 Liter 82.00
Stein, Pottery, Incised Traveling Scene, Pewter Lid, 3/10 Liter, 8 In. 115.00
Stein, Pressed Glass, Think Of Aug.Schubert On Pewter Lid, 1870s, 1/4 Liter 56.00
Stein, R.P.M., Drunken Monkey, 1/2 Liter 350.00
Stein, Regimental, Hobnail Glass, Porcelain Lid, 1861, 1/4 Liter 142.00
Stein, Regimental, Hobnail, Pewter-Framed Porcelain Lid, 1861, 1/4 Liter 92.00
Stein, Regimental, 1901-1903, 1/2 Liter 185.00
Stein, Shooting Scene, Pewter Top & Thumb Rest, C.1900, 11 In. 65.00
Stein, Tower, Pewter Pagoda Lid, T.W. & Geschutz, 1/2 Liter 240.00

Stereo cards that were made for stereopticon viewers became popular after 1840. Two almost identical pictures were mounted on a stiff cardboard backing so that, when viewed through a stereoscope, a three-dimensional picture could be seen.

Stereo, Card, A Trip Through Sears, 50 .... 37.50
Stereo, Card, Austria, Set Of 18 .... 9.00

Stereo, Card, Boy & Girl Scouts Gardening 4.00
Stereo, Card, California 3.50
Stereo, Card, Capture Of Soldier, Cartoon, World War I, Set Of 20 .... 20.00
Stereo, Card, Chinaman Riding High Wheel Bicycle 5.00
Stereo, Card, Colonel Theodore Roosevelt Of The Rough Riders, 1898 .... 4.50
Stereo, Card, Columbian Exposition, 1894, Kilburn, Set Of 14 .... 30.00
Stereo, Card, Comedy Series, Japan, 1898-1903, Color, Set Of 24 .... 27.00
Stereo, Card, Fishing Rivers, Ingersoll, 1903, Color, Set Of 19 .... 9.00
Stereo, Card, French Cook, Underwood, 10 .... 14.00
Stereo, Card, Goose & Duck Hunting, Ingersoll, 1898, Color, Set Of 28 .... 14.00
Stereo, Card, Holy Land, 28 .... 16.00
Stereo, Card, McKinley & Roosevelt, 1900 .... 4.50
Stereo, Card, McKinley & Wife, Underwood & Underwood, 1896 .... 4.50
Stereo, Card, McKinley At His Desk, 1898 .... 4.50
Stereo, Card, McKinley, Presidential Tally-Ho Party, 1901 .... 4.50
Stereo, Card, Mount Washington Railway 4.00
Stereo, Card, Philadelphia, 1860, Set Of 2 .... 12.00
Stereo, Card, President McKinley, 5 .... 9.00
Stereo, Card, Romantic Comedy, 17 In. 19.00
Stereo, Card, San Francisco Earthquake, Set Of 24 .... 35.00
Stereo, Card, St.Louis Fair In Color, 32 .... 80.00
Stereo, Card, The Portrait, Comic Series, Ingersoll, 1898, Set Of 6 .... 2.50
Stereo, Card, Trip Through Sears, Roebuck & Co., Color, Set Of 50 .... 25.00
Stereo, Card, Underwood, Norway, Set Of 19 .... 9.50
Stereo, Card, White Mountain, New Hampshire, 24 .... 35.00
Stereo, Card, White Mountain, Set Of 10 .... 25.00
Stereo, Card, Wild Animal Hunting, Ingersoll, 1898, Color, Set Of 28 .... 14.00
Stereo, Card, World War I Aviation, Set Of 3 .... 10.00
Stereo, Card, Yosemite Valley, Underwood, Dated 1902, Set Of 24 .... 22.00

Stereoscopes, or stereopticons, were used for viewing the stereo cards. The hand viewer was invented by Oliver Wendell Holmes, although more complicated table models were used before his was placed in production in 1859.

Stereoscope, Meadville, Pa., Oak Rollaway Cabinet & 600 Cards 950.00
Stereoscope, Viewmaster, Sawyer's, 1947, Boxed 6.00
Stereoscope, Wooden, Sliding Adjustor, 12 Cards 20.00
Stereoscope, 94 1904 St.Louis Fair Cards 90.00

Sterling Silver, see Silver, Sterling

Sterling, Silver, Salt, Silver Master, Stem Of Boy On Dolphin, Vermeil Lined 100.00

Steuben, see also Aurene

Steuben glass was made at the Steuben Glass Works of Corning, New York. The factory, founded by Frederick Carder and T.C.Hawkes, Sr., was purchased by the Corning Glass Company. They continued to make glass called Steuben. Many types of art glass were made at Steuben. The firm is still producing glass of exceptional quality.

Steuben, Apple, Black Jade, Fleur-De-Lis, Signed, 3 1/2 In. 295.00
Steuben, Ashtray, Black Jade, Line Drawing, Armour Family Monogram 30.00
Steuben, Ashtray, Gardner Line Drawing, Nesting, Set Of 3 .... 195.00
Steuben, Atomizer, Blue Iridescent, F.Carder, 8 1/2 In. 200.00
Steuben, Atomizer, DeVilbiss, Deep Mauve, Gilt Edging At Base, 6 3/4 In. 225.00
Steuben, Atomizer, DeVilbiss, Honey Iridescent, Mesh Bulb, 7 In. 235.00
Steuben, Atomizer, Mesh Bulb, Mauve With Gilt, Signed DeVilbiss 125.00
Steuben, Beaker, Cranberry, 7 X 5 In. 95.00
Steuben, Bottle, Cologne, Lavender Swirl, Threaded Stopper .... 85.00 To 100.00
Steuben, Bottle, Perfume, Verre De Soie, Blue Flame Stopper, 4 1/2 In. 125.00
Steuben, Bottle, Perfume, Verre De Soie, Melon Rib, 4 1/4 In. 135.00
Steuben, Bottle, Perfume, Verre De Soie, Melon Ribbed, Initial K, 6 1/2 In. 80.00
Steuben, Bottle, Perfume, Verre De Soie, Melon Ribbed, Jade Stopper, Pair 250.00
Steuben, Bottle, Wine, Teardrop Stopper, Brilliant, Signed, 10 3/4 In. 250.00
Steuben, Bowl, Amber, 4 1/2 In. 20.00
Steuben, Bowl, Calcite & Aurene, Gold, 8 X 3 In. 110.00
Steuben, Bowl, Centerpiece, Set, Silverina, Venetian Leaves, 9 1/4 In. 65.00
Steuben, Bowl, Centerpiece, Verre De Soie, Pink Rim, Etched, Footed 165.00

Steuben, Bowl, Cerise Ruby Threading, Shallow, 9 In., Signed 35.00
Steuben, Bowl, Console, Amber, Fleur De Lis, Signed, 14 In. 60.00
Steuben, Bowl, Controlled Bubbles, Ruby Threading 85.00
Steuben, Bowl, Crystal With Ruby Threading, Shallow, 9 In., Signed 35.00
Steuben, Bowl, Crystal, Cerise Ruby Threading, 9 In. 47.50
Steuben, Bowl, Duck Center, Green 59.00
Steuben, Bowl, Finger And Underplate, Amethyst 30.00
Steuben, Bowl, Finger, Underplate And Salad Plate, Blue Jade, 3 Piece 225.00
Steuben, Bowl, Gold Aurene On Calcite, 9 1/2 In. 150.00
Steuben, Bowl, Gold Aurene On Ivorine, Pink & Blue Lights, Pedestal, 10 In. 150.00
Steuben, Bowl, Gold Iridescent, White Calcite, Amethyst Interior, 10 In. 350.00
Steuben, Bowl, Green Ground, White Flower, Signed Steuben & Fleur-De-Lis 750.00
Steuben, Bowl, Green Mica, Footed, Signed 200.00
Steuben, Bowl, Iridescent Gold & Amethyst, Calcite Obverse, 10 X 2 1/2 In. 190.00
Steuben, Bowl, Ivorene, Bulbous, 10 X 7 1/2 In. 290.00
Steuben, Bowl, Jade Green, Reverse Dolphins As Handles 95.00
Steuben, Bowl, Lily, Aurene, 3 Footed, 12 In. 425.00
Steuben, Bowl, Matte Crystal, Grapevine, Deep Cutting, 4 1/4 In. 275.00
Steuben, Bowl, Pomona Green, Swirl Design, Amber Foot, Signed 175.00
Steuben, Bowl, Sapphire Blue, Topaz Pedestal, 11 1/4 In. 170.00
Steuben, Bowl, Verre De Soie, 10 Rib, 6 X 3 1/4 In. 35.00
Steuben, Bowl, Verre De Soie, 10 Ribs, 6 In. 35.00
Steuben, Bowl, Verre De Soie, 6 In. 35.00
Steuben, Bowl, Wisteria, Grotesque, Signed 250.00
Steuben, Bowl, 4-Sided, Ruffled Edge, Clear To Cranberry, Signed 150.00
Steuben, Box, Puff, Green Leaf Finial On Venetian Pink Tulip Lid, Clear 70.00
Steuben, Candleholder, Amber, Iridescent, Trumpet Form, 6 1/2 X 4 1/2 In. 375.00
Steuben, Candleholder, Blown Crystal, Teardrop In Column, 9 In., Set Of 4 .... 500.00
Steuben, Candleholder, Mushroom, Amber Iridescence, 6 1/2 In. 375.00
Steuben, Candlestick, Crystal, Applied Green Prunts Bubbles, 12 In. 150.00
Steuben, Candlestick, Emerald Green, Swirled, 12 In., Pair 195.00
Steuben, Candlestick, Green Jade, Optic Twist, Calcite Dividers, 10 In., Pair 550.00
Steuben, Candlestick, Ivorene, Ruffled, Signed, 3 1/2 In., Pair 275.00
Steuben, Candlestick, Moss Green, Swan Around Stem, Venetian Style, 12 In. 395.00
Steuben, Candlestick, Red Applied Threading, High Dome Base, 10 In., Pair 275.00
Steuben, Candlestick, Rosalene & Alabaster, 8 1/2 In., Pair 550.00
Steuben, Candlestick, Topaz, Amethyst Stem, 10 In. 85.00
Steuben, Candlestick, Topaz, Blue Prunts & Rims, 10 In. 95.00
Steuben, Candlestick, Van Dyke, Swirled Ribbed Rosa Stem, 15 In., Pair 325.00
Steuben, Centerpiece Bowl, Calcite & Aurene, Gold, Doughnut Base, 10 In. 210.00
Steuben, Centerpiece Bowl, Calcite, Gold Aurene Inside, 12 1/4 In. 215.00
Steuben, Centerpiece Bowl, Calcite, Gold, Turned-Down Rim, 14 In. 250.00
Steuben, Centerpiece Bowl, Emerald Green, Ribbed, Domed Pedestal, 14 1/4 In. 95.00
Steuben, Champagne, Engraved Van Dyke, Rosa Stem, 5 1/4 In. 65.00
Steuben, Champagne, Topaz & Celeste Blue, Swirl 20.00
Steuben, Champagne, Van Dyke, Swirled Ribbed Rosa Stem 55.50
Steuben, Compote, Amethyst Bowl, Clear Twisted Stem, 8 In., Signed 275.00
Steuben, Compote, Amethyst, 9 1/2 In., Old Gold Triangle Label 90.00
Steuben, Compote, Amethyst, 9 7/8 In., Diameter, Pair .... *Illus* 320.00
Steuben, Compote, Blue Aurene, Twisted Stem, 7 In. 350.00
Steuben, Compote, Calcite & Gold Aurene, 3 X 6 In. 165.00
Steuben, Compote, Cobalt Venetian Crystal, 4 Applied Child's Heads, Signed 125.00
Steuben, Compote, Cobalt, 5 7/8 X 4 In. 75.00
Steuben, Compote, Crystal Mica Air-Twist Diamond, 7 X 5 In. 1000.00
Steuben, Compote, Emerald Green, Ribbed, Topaz Stem, 8 In. 125.00
Steuben, Compote, Jade Green & Alabaster, Jade Cone Tops, 5 In. 60.00
Steuben, Compote, Jade Green, Alabaster Base, 6 X 3 1/2 In. 125.00
Steuben, Compote, Purple Crystal, Pedestal Stem, Flare Top, Signed, 3 3/4 In. 55.00
Steuben, Compote, Rosaline & Alabaster, 6 In. .... 125.00 To 150.00
Steuben, Compote, Rosaline & Alabaster, 6 3/4 X 6 In. 125.00
Steuben, Compote, Topaz Bowl, Green Stem, Matching Candlesticks, Signed 380.00
Steuben, Compote, Venetian Style, Yellow Rigaree, Pear Finial, 12 1/2 In. 125.00
Steuben, Console Bowl, Cobalt & Clear, Grotesque, 9 In. 147.00
Steuben, Console Set, Amber, Baluster & Double Ball Stems, Signed, 3 Piece 205.00
Steuben, Console Set, Bubble Glass, Green Threading, Ruffled Edge, 3 Piece 195.00

Steuben, Compote, Amethyst, 9 7/8 In. Diameter, Pair

Steuben, Console Set, Topaz, 10 In. Bowl, 3 Piece ... 200.00
Steuben, Cordial, Cut, Teardrop Stem, 4 In. ... 25.00
Steuben, Cup & Saucer, Blue Jade & Alabaster ... 275.00
Steuben, Cup & Saucer, Blue Jade, Set ... 195.00
Steuben, Cup & Saucer, Demitasse, Green Jade & Alabaster ... 125.00 To 150.00
Steuben, Cup & Saucer, Green Jade & Alabaster ... 125.00 To 150.00
Steuben, Cup & Saucer, Rosaline & Alabaster ... 195.00
Steuben, Dish, Calcite, Amber Iridescent, Crackle-Glass Rim, 6 1/4 In. ... 200.00
Steuben, Dish, Footed, Celeste Blue, Folded Edge, Signed, 10 In. ... 125.00
Steuben, Dish, Jade, 7 In. ... 35.00
Steuben, Dish, Nut, Green Jade, Signed, 3 1/4 In. ... 40.00
Steuben, Epergne, Ivorene, 2 Lily, Trumpet Center, 12 In. ... 600.00
Steuben, Fernery, Green Threading, 6 X 6 In. ... 60.00
Steuben, Figurine, Crystal Mermaid, 10 1/2 In. ... 95.00
Steuben, Figurine, Fish, 10 1/2 In. ... 350.00
Steuben, Figurine, Nude Woman In Hoop, Black Satin Glass ... 175.00
Steuben, Figurine, Owl, 5 In. ... 160.00
Steuben, Finger Bowl & Underplate, Gold Iridescent, Calcite Liner ... 125.00
Steuben, Finger Bowl & Underplate, Verre De Soie, Rainbow Iridescent ... 47.50
Steuben, Finger Bowl, Cintra, 4 In. ... 100.00
Steuben, Flower Center, Frosted, Kneeling Women, 7 1/2 In. ... 95.00
Steuben, Fruit Cocktail & Underplate, Moonlight, Copper Wheel Engraved ... 45.00
Steuben, Glass, Sherbet, Calcite, Bell Shape, Amber Iridescent, 3 3/4 In. ... 125.00
Steuben, Goblet, Alabaster, Twisted Stem ... 145.00
Steuben, Goblet, Amber, Blue Prunts, Threaded Green Base ... 60.00
Steuben, Goblet, Amethyst Bowl & Foot, Clear Stem, 6 In. ... 45.00
Steuben, Goblet, Bristol Yellow, Ball Stem, Signed, 6 In. ... 55.00
Steuben, Goblet, Bristol, Yellow, Engraved Basket Of Flowers & Fruit, Signed ... 75.00
Steuben, Goblet, Cobalt, 6 1/4 In. ... 21.00
Steuben, Goblet, Crystal, Cable-Twist Stem, 7 1/4 In. ... 22.50
Steuben, Goblet, Crystal, Marina Blue Rim, Cable-Twist Stem, 7 In. ... 28.00
Steuben, Goblet, Emerald Green, Clear Stem & Base, Cone Shape ... 16.50
Steuben, Goblet, Jade With Alabaster Twist Stem, 6 In., Marked ... 85.00
Steuben, Goblet, Oriental Poppy, Deep Green Stem, Pink & White Opalescent ... 450.00
Steuben, Goblet, Oriental Poppy, Green Stem, Signed, Pair ... 225.00
Steuben, Goblet, Oriental Poppy, Pink & White, Green Stem ... 450.00
Steuben, Goblet, Pink With Green Stem And Foot, 8 In. ... 150.00
Steuben, Goblet, Rosaline & Alabaster, Twisted Stem ... 175.00 To 250.00
Steuben, Goblet, Selenium Red, Etched Vintage ... 115.00
Steuben, Goblet, Selenium Red, Fleur-De-Lis Signature, 5 1/2 In. ... 65.00
Steuben, Goblet, Verre De Soie, Applied Prunts & Rigaree ... 95.00
Steuben, Jar, Condiment, Crystal With Applied Red Prunts, Pedestal, Signed ... 70.00
Steuben, Jar, Fruit Finial, Venetian Style, 17 In. ... 295.00
Steuben, Lamp, Acid Cut-Back, Black Over Green, Flowers, Original Fittings ... 850.00
Steuben, Lamp, Chinese Pattern, Acid Cut-Back, Green Jade, Alabaster, Shade ... 750.00
Steuben, Liqueur, Rosaline & Alabaster, Twisted Stem, 5 In. ... 225.00
Steuben, Luminor, Buddah Figure, Rock Crystal On Black Glass, Signed ... 325.00

Steuben, Parfait, Bristol, Yellow, Engraved Basket Of Flowers & Fruit 55.00
Steuben, Parfait, Marina Blue, Fountain, Pedestal Feet 50.00
Steuben, Parfait, Verre De Soie, Pedestal, 4 1/2 In. 45.00
Steuben, Pear, Black Jade, Fleur-De-Lis Signed, 5 In. 295.00
Steuben, Pitcher, Bulbous Urn Body, Sapphire Blue, Topaz Shell Handle 37.50
Steuben, Pitcher, Diamond Quilt, Green Random Threading 95.00
Steuben, Plate, Amethyst, Depressed Center, 5 7/8 In. 14.00
Steuben, Plate, Black Threading, 8 1/2 In. 50.00
Steuben, Plate, Cake, Moonlight, Copper Wheel Engraved, 6 In. 15.00
Steuben, Plate, Jade, Signed, 8 In. 45.00
Steuben, Rose Bowl, Aurene Blue, Signed, 4 In. 350.00
Steuben, Rose Bowl, Ivorene, 8 In. 150.00
Steuben, Rose Bowl, Rosaline & Alabaster, Turned-Over Rim 175.00
Steuben, Salt & Pepper, Open Salt, Sterling Top On Pepper 75.00
Steuben, Shade, Acid Etched, Iridized Green Gold With White, 5 In., Pair 185.00
Steuben, Shade, Blue Drape 165.00
Steuben, Shade, Calcite, Ribbed 45.00
Steuben, Shade, Gold & White Iridescent, Loops, 5 1/2 In., Pair 110.00
Steuben, Shade, Gold Aurene, Bowl Shape, Ribbed, Signed, 3 1/2 X 7 In. 140.00
Steuben, Shade, Gold Drape With Hooked Border On Calcite 175.00
Steuben, Shade, Gold Fishnet On Calcite 150.00
Steuben, Shade, Gold Fishnet, Iridescent Interior, Not Signed 125.00
Steuben, Shade, Gold Iridescent, Pink & Blue Highlights, Ribbed, 7 1/2 In. 45.00
Steuben, Shade, Gold Iridescent, Twisted Ribs, Ruffled, 5 1/4 In., Pair 160.00
Steuben, Shade, Gold Leaf & Vine On Calcite, Decorated 125.00
Steuben, Shade, Ivorene, Acid Cut, Oak Leaf & Flowers, Signed, 2 1/4 In. 85.00
Steuben, Shade, Opalescent, Green Feathers, Amber Edge, C.1905, 5 In. 137.50
Steuben, Sherbet & Liner, Calcite, Gold Interior 200.00
Steuben, Sherbet & Underplate, Alabaster Foot, Rosaline 110.00
Steuben, Sherbet & Underplate, Aquamarine 75.00
Steuben, Sherbet & Underplate, Calcite 210.00
Steuben, Sherbet & Underplate, Calcite, Gold, Footed 145.00
Steuben, Sherbet & Underplate, Crystal, Cerise Ruby Threading 75.00
Steuben, Sherbet & Underplate, Marina Blue, Engraved Fountains & Birds 65.00
Steuben, Sherbet & Underplate, Rosaline 125.00
Steuben, Sherbet & Underplate, Verre De Soie 55.00
Steuben, Sherbet, Applied Handle, Threaded Cobalt, Signed, 2 3/4 In. 100.00
Steuben, Sherbet, Gold Calcite 85.00
Steuben, Sherbet, Oriental Poppy 120.00
Steuben, Stein, Beer With Thumb Rest, Engraved With Crown, Bird, Shield, Set, 4 ..... 200.00
Steuben, Sugar & Creamer, Topaz, Peacock Blue Base & Handles 135.00
Steuben, Tazza, Verre De Soie, Floral Swags, Signed Hawkes, 7 X 5 In.. ..... 185.00
Steuben, Toothpick, Aurene, Gold, Juice-Glass Shape 125.00
Steuben, Tumble Up, Verre De Soie, 2 Piece 120.00
Steuben, Tumbler, Gold Aurene, 4 In., Signed 125.00
Steuben, Urn, Cluthra, Apple Green, 8 In. ..... 450.00 To 575.00
Steuben, Vase, Acid Cut-Back, Chrysanthemum, Alabaster, Signed, 6 In. 225.00
Steuben, Vase, Air Trap Silverina, Diamond Forms, Cylindrical, 7 In. 135.00
Steuben, Vase, Alabaster Base, Jade Shades, Signed, 8 In. 170.00
Steuben, Vase, Amber Crystal, Vertical Ribs, Signed 75.00
Steuben, Vase, Amber Diagonal Raised Swirl, Flare Top, Doughnut Base, 10 In. 100.00
Steuben, Vase, Amber, Green Foot, Fan Shape, Signed, 6 In. 95.00
Steuben, Vase, Amber, Pedestal, 7 In. 60.00
Steuben, Vase, Amethyst, Fleur-De-Lis, 10 1/2 In. 67.00
Steuben, Vase, Aurene, Purple Blue To Gold, Spiral Ribbed, 7 In. 875.00
Steuben, Vase, Aurene, 3 Lily, Signed, 12 In. 575.00
Steuben, Vase, Black Threading, 7 1/2 In. 55.00
Steuben, Vase, Blown & Cut, Diamonds, Amber Over Clear Flint, 7 In. 40.00
Steuben, Vase, Blue Bubbly Glass, Red Reeding, 7 1/2 In. 100.00
Steuben, Vase, Blue Calcite, 6 In. 550.00
Steuben, Vase, Blue, Classic, Signed, Cluthra, 8 In. 550.00
Steuben, Vase, Bubbly, Green Threading, Parfait Shape, 6 In. 35.00
Steuben, Vase, Bud, Controlled Bubble In Base, 4 3/4 In. 48.00
Steuben, Vase, Calcite, Gold Lined, Flared Top, 5 In. 110.00
Steuben, Vase, Cerise Ruby, Trumpet Style, 12 X 6 In. 300.00

Steuben, Vase, Chalice Shape, Gold Aurene, 3 X 10 In. 325.00
Steuben, Vase, Cintra, Light Yellow, Flared Mouth, 6 1/2 In. 395.00
Steuben, Vase, Citron, Blown, 16 Ribs, 11 In. 30.00
Steuben, Vase, Cluthra, Amethyst, Controlled Bubbles, 6 In. 365.00
Steuben, Vase, Cluthra, Black, White Highlights, Controlled Bubbles, 10 In. 750.00
Steuben, Vase, Cluthra, Green, Alabaster Handles, 10 1/2 In. 800.00
Steuben, Vase, Cluthra, Red, 8 In. 800.00
Steuben, Vase, Cluthra, Ruby To White Base, 9 3/4 In. 375.00
Steuben, Vase, Cobalt Iridescent, Stretch, Flared Top, 7 1/4 In. 185.00
Steuben, Vase, Cornucopia, 7 1/2 In. 95.00
Steuben, Vase, Dark Blue Jade, Signed .... 38.50 To 385.00
Steuben, Vase, Emerald Swirl, 7 X 6 3/4 In. 75.00
Steuben, Vase, Fan, Green Top, Blue Base & Stem, Unsigned, 10 1/2 In. 95.00
Steuben, Vase, Fan, Jade Green And Alabaster, 11 In. 250.00
Steuben, Vase, Fan, Topaz Foot, Green Top, Signed & Fleur-De-Lis, 5 1/2 In. 145.00
Steuben, Vase, Flare Parfait Form, Alabaster, Jade Ring, Signed, 4 1/2 In. 115.00
Steuben, Vase, French Blue, Ribbed, 10 X 8 In. 30.00
Steuben, Vase, Gold Amber, Diamond Quilted, Fan Shape, 8 1/2 In. 32.00
Steuben, Vase, Gold Aurene, Signed, 6 In. 375.00
Steuben, Vase, Gold Iridescent, Optic Ribbed, Tulip Shape, 7 In. 575.00
Steuben, Vase, Green Glass, Clear Glass Handles, 9 1/2 In. 200.00
Steuben, Vase, Green Jade & Alabaster, 9 1/4 In. 175.00
Steuben, Vase, Green Jade Base, Alabaster Teardrop, Signed, 10 1/2 In. 120.00
Steuben, Vase, Green Jade, A.C.B., Chrysanthemums, Drilled For Lamp 275.00
Steuben, Vase, Green Jade, Clambroth Base, Fan Shape, 8 1/2 In. 95.00
Steuben, Vase, Green Jade, M-Shaped Alabaster Handles, Urn Shape, 10 1/2 In. 350.00
Steuben, Vase, Green Jade, Swirl Ribbed, Urn Shape, 8 X 6 In. 110.00
Steuben, Vase, Green, Machine Threaded, Floral, Alvin Sterling Holder, 8 In. 250.00
Steuben, Vase, Ivorene, White, Rainbow Iridescent, Applied Handles, 11 In. 375.00
Steuben, Vase, Ivory, Shape No.7331, 9 In. 110.00
Steuben, Vase, Ivory, Urn Body, Doughnut Base, Vertical Ribs, 5 1/4 In. 205.00
Steuben, Vase, Jade Stick, 8 In. 135.00
Steuben, Vase, Jade, Swirled Fan, Alabaster Foot 175.00
Steuben, Vase, Lavender, Swirled, 10 In. 65.00
Steuben, Vase, Pedestal, Grotesque, Amber To Clear, Trumpet Form, Signed 47.00
Steuben, Vase, Pomona Green Optic Twist, Signed, 10 In. 100.00
Steuben, Vase, Purple Crystal, Signed, 12 In. 65.00
Steuben, Vase, Purple, Parfait Shape, 2 Crystal Dangles, 11 1/2 In. 85.00
Steuben, Vase, Red Selenium, Red Aurene, Rose-Colored Jade, 6 In. 250.00
Steuben, Vase, Red, Polished Dragon On Matte Finish, 10 1/2 In. 2250.00
Steuben, Vase, Rosaline & Alabaster, Stick, 8 1/4 In. 95.00
Steuben, Vase, Ruby Red, Swirled, 7 X 6 3/4 In. 120.00
Steuben, Vase, Topaz Crystal, Diagonal-Swirl Urn, Signed, 7 In. 87.00
Steuben, Vase, Topaz Crystal, Footed, Signed, 12 In. 55.00
Steuben, Vase, Topaz, Diagonal Swirl, Doughnut Base, 7 In. 85.00
Steuben, Vase, Tulip Shape, Iridescent Gold, Signed Steuben, 7 In. 575.00
Steuben, Vase, Tulip Shape, Iridescent, Gold, Blue, Pink, Signed, 7 In. 390.00
Steuben, Vase, Verre De Soie, Designed As Spittoon, 9 X 5 In. 245.00
Steuben, Vase, Verre De Soie, Polished Pontil, 8 In. 48.00
Steuben, Vase, Verre De Soie, Quilted, Pink Threading, 8 In. 225.00
Steuben, Vase, Verre De Soie, 4 Hollow Columns On Domed Pedestal, 6 1/4 In. 125.00
Steuben, Vase, White Jade, Black Trim, 8 In. 600.00
Steuben, Vase, Wisteria, Shade Shape, 5 1/2 In. 125.00
Steuben, Wig Stand, Rosaline & Alabaster 225.00
Steuben, Wine & Underplate, Oriental Poppy 285.00
Steuben, Wine, Gold Aurene, Twisted Stem 125.00
Steuben, Wine, Green, Knop Stem 88.00
Steuben, Wine, Green, Opalescent, Swirled, 6 In. 70.00
Steuben, Wine, Jade, Alabaster, Tall 80.00
Steuben, Wine, Jade, Amethyst, Tall 80.00
Steuben, Wine, Jade, Deep Blue, Tall 80.00
Steuben, Wine, Jade, Rosaline, Tall 80.00
Steuben, Wine, Rosaline & Alabaster, Twisted Stem, 5 1/2 In. 225.00
Steuben, Wine, Selenium, Red, Cone Top, Long Stem, Signed 50.00
Steuben, Wine, Sterling Banded Top & Bottom, Signed, Set Of 4 .... 125.00

Stevengraphs are woven pictures made like ribbons. They were manufactured by Thomas Stevens of Coventry, England, and became popular in 1862.

Stevengraph, Are You Ready, Rowing, Matted 125.00
Stevengraph, Badge, Republican, Dated April 8, 1844 .... 300.00
Stevengraph, Bookmark, Birthday Wish 20.00
Stevengraph, Bookmark, Centennial, Washington, Father Of Our Country 100.00
Stevengraph, Bookmark, Daughter 30.00
Stevengraph, Bookmark, Flowers & Verse 56.00
Stevengraph, Bookmark, George Washington From Centennial .... 85.00 To 115.00
Stevengraph, Bookmark, Happy New Year .... 28.00 To 35.00
Stevengraph, Bookmark, Little Bo-Peep 50.00
Stevengraph, Bookmark, May Happiness Be Ever Thine 25.00
Stevengraph, Bookmark, Merry Christmas, Eliza Cook, Framed 55.00
Stevengraph, Bookmark, Remember Me 17.50
Stevengraph, Bookmark, Unchanging Love 20.00
Stevengraph, Bookmark, With Kind Wishes For The New Year, Silk 30.00
Stevengraph, Called To The Rescue 95.00
Stevengraph, Card, Birthday Greeting With Tassel 25.00
Stevengraph, Death Of Nelson, Silk, Back Plate & Frame 175.00
Stevengraph, First Touch, Original Mounting 250.00
Stevengraph, Full Cry 95.00
Stevengraph, Good Old Days, Woven Silk, Framed, 8 1/2 X 5 1/2 In. 99.50
Stevengraph, Home Sweet Home, 10 In. 65.00
Stevengraph, Lady Godiva, Silk, Back Plate & Frame 195.00
Stevengraph, Louisiana Purchase Commemorative, 1803, St.Louis, 1904 .... 110.00
Stevengraph, Meat 95.00
Stevengraph, Procession 95.00
Stevengraph, The Start, And The Finish, Pair 150.00
Stevengraph, The Water Jump, Original Frame 135.00
Stevengraph, To A Friend 20.00
Stevengraph, To The Rescue, Framed 125.00

Stevens & Williams of Stourbridge, England, made many types of glass, including layered, etched, cameo, and art glass, between the 1830s and the 1930s. Some pieces are signed S and W.

Stevens & Williams, Bottle, Perfume, Cobalt To Cranberry, 7 In. 425.00
Stevens & Williams, Cruet, Arboresque, White Crackle Overlay, 8 1/4 In. 150.00
Stevens & Williams, Jar, Cracker, Pink & White Stripes, Plated Lid, 6 In. 245.00
Stevens & Williams, Lamp, Fairy, Clarke Base, Frosted Pink & White, 5 In. 345.00
Stevens & Williams, Mug, Presentation, Dragon, Floral, Signed, 6 1/4 In. 185.00
Stevens & Williams, Pitcher, Water, Purpled, Swirled, Gold & Silver Floral 75.00
Stevens & Williams, Plate, Opaline, Pink, 8 In. 30.00
Stevens & Williams, Rose Bowl, Cranberry, Air Bubbles, 2 In. 111.50
Stevens & Williams, Rose Bowl, Crystal, Wavy Cranberry Threading, 6 3/4 In. 125.00
Stevens & Williams, Rose Bowl, 12 Panels, 19 Rows Of Cranberry Threading 100.00
Stevens & Williams, Sherbet, Blue Jade & Alabaster, Pair 275.00
Stevens & Williams, Sherbet, Pink Opaline, White Base 68.00
Stevens & Williams, Sugar & Creamer, Blue, Mat-Su-Noke, Amber Handle, Carder 550.00
Stevens & Williams, Vase, Applied Acorns, 10 X 4 In. 400.00
Stevens & Williams, Vase, Azure Blue, Melon Ribbed, Gold Floral, 12 In. 85.00
Stevens & Williams, Vase, Blue Frosted, White Morning Glory, 8 In. 1400.00
Stevens & Williams, Vase, Cranberry, Applied Crystal Leaves, Enamel, 13 In. 135.00
Stevens & Williams, Vase, Emerald Green, Expanded Diamond, Signed, 8 1/4 In. 95.00
Stevens & Williams, Vase, Peacock Eye, 6 In. 110.00
Stevens & Williams, Vase, White, Applied Amber Acorns & Oak Leaves, 10 In. 300.00
Stevens & Williams, Vase, Yellow To White, Overlay, Applique Floral, 9 In. 125.00
Stiegel Type, Baptismal Bowl, Cobalt, Expanded Diamond 400.00
Stiegel Type, Baptismal Bowl, Ruby 275.00
Stiegel Type, Bottle, Bride's 500.00
Stiegel Type, Bottle, Scene, Emerald Green 275.00
Stiegel Type, Bottle, Scene, Fiery Opalescent 175.00
Stiegel Type, Flip, Covered 500.00
Stiegel Type, Flip, Engraved Foliage, 32 Ribs, Flint, 6 1/4 In. 80.00
Stiegel Type, Flip, Tulips 250.00
Stiegel Type, Light, Vigil, Clear, 13 Diamonds, Flint 60.00

Stiegel Type, Salt, Blown, Footed, Flint, 11 Diamond 60.00
Stiegel Type, Salt, Cobalt, Swirled Ribs 225.00
Stiegel Type, Sugar, Cobalt, Collared Foot 2400.00
Stiegel Type, Sugar, Cobalt, Expanded Diamond, Applied Foot & Finial 950.00
Stiegel Type, Sugar, Cobalt, 16 Expanded Diamonds, 6 1/8 In. 3100.00
Stiegel Type, Sugar, Covered Cobalt 310.00
Stiegel Type, Tumbler, Cobalt 450.00
Stiegel Type, Wine, Cotton Stem 140.00
Stomre, Machine, Pinball, Mill's Official, C.1930, Ten Balls For 5 Cents 165.00

Stoneware is a coarse glazed and fired potter's ware that is used to make crocks, jugs, etc.

Stoneware, Bowl, Blue & White, Greek Key, 8 In. 12.50
Stoneware, Bowl, Gray, Blue Bands, 7 X 3 1/2 In. 9.75
Stoneware, Churn, Fish Catching Shrimp, 17 3/4 In.High ..... *Illus* 350.00
Stoneware, Churn, Harrington & Burger, Rochester, N.Y., 16 In. ..... *Illus* 900.00
Stoneware, Churn, New York Co., Cobalt Bird On Branch 190.00
Stoneware, Cooler, Barrel, N.Clark & Co., Lyons, 18 In. ..... *Illus* 325.00
Stoneware, Cooler, W.H.Thomas, Huntingdon, Spigot Hole At Base, 12 In. 25.00
Stoneware, Cooler, Water, Covered, Thomas & Bro., Huntingdon, Pa., 12 In. 90.00
Stoneware, Cooler, Water, Doulton's Manganous Carbon Filter, Brass Spigot 125.00
Stoneware, Crock, A.O.Whittemore, 12 1/2 X 13 In. ..... *Illus* 1600.00
Stoneware, Crock, Butter, Covered, Brown & Yellow, Embossed Peacocks 85.00

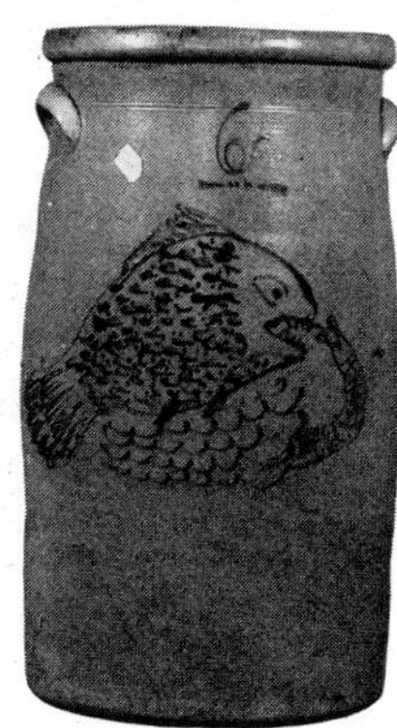

Stoneware, Churn, Fish Catching Shrimp, 17 3/4 In.High

Stoneware, Churn, Harrington & Burger, Rochester, N.Y., 16 In.

Stoneware, Cooler, Barrel, N.Clark & Co., Lyons, 18 In.

Stoneware, Crock, A.O.Whittemore, 12 1/2 X 13 In.
(See Page 615)

Stoneware, Crock, Harrington & Burger, 14 X 12 1/2 In.

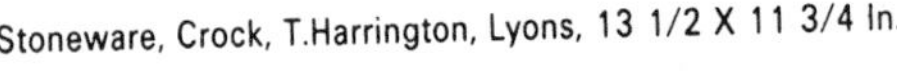

Stoneware, Crock, T.Harrington, Lyons, 13 1/2 X 11 3/4 In.

Stoneware, Crock, F.Stetzenmeyer & G.Goetzman, Rochester, N.Y.

Stoneware, Crock, Butter, Flower Decoration, Shaker Valley, Pa., 1 1/2 Gallon 55.00
Stoneware, Crock, Butter, S.H.Sonner, Strawsburg, Va., 1/2 Gallon 87.50
Stoneware, Crock, Cobalt Decoration, Handled, 9 In. 55.00
Stoneware, Crock, Cowden & Wilcox, Harrisburg, Pa., Bird & Floral, 4 Gallon 650.00
Stoneware, Crock, Deer & Trees, 6 Gallon, 15 X 12 In. 65.00
Stoneware, Crock, E.& L.&.Norton, Dark Blue Design, 2 Gallon 85.00
Stoneware, Crock, E.H.Cowden, Harrisburg, Pa., Tan, 2 Handles, 2 Gallon 90.00
Stoneware, Crock, F.Stetzenmeyer & G.Goetzman, Rochester, N.Y. .... *Illus* 450.00
Stoneware, Crock, Gray Glaze, Cobalt Tulip & 1854, Lug Handles, 16 In. 130.00
Stoneware, Crock, Gray, F.Behrens, Grocer, Wheeling, W.Va. In Blue, 10 In. 35.00
Stoneware, Crock, Harrington & Burger, 14 X 12 1/2 In. .... *Illus* 1900.00
Stoneware, Crock, Incised 5, Gray Glaze, 10 X 7 In. 12.50
Stoneware, Crock, Julius Norton, Bennington, Vt., Handled, 9 In. 45.00
Stoneware, Crock, Lewistown, Pa. 42.00
Stoneware, Crock, S.Hart, Fulton, 10 1/2 In.High .... *Illus* 770.00
Stoneware, Crock, T.Harrington, Lyons, 13 1/2 X 11 3/4 In. .... *Illus* 500.00
Stoneware, Crock, 3 Gallon, Blue Chicken Design, Tan, Brady & Ryan, Ellenville 80.00
Stoneware, Ewer, Gray, Cobalt Trim, Faces Center, Handled, 8 1/4 In. 39.00
Stoneware, Feeder, Chicken, Green Brown, Outside Glaze 55.00

Stoneware, Crock, S.Hart, Fulton, 10 1/2 In.High

Stoneware, Jug, E.A.Buck & Co., Boston, 1876, 16 In.High

Stoneware, Flask, Port Dundas Pottery Co., Glasgow, 1874, Cherries, 7 In. 56.00
Stoneware, Fountain, Chicken, Patent April 7, 1885, Gallon 65.00
Stoneware, Jar, Cowden & Wilcox, Narrow Flaring Neck, 9 3/4 X 5 In. 25.00
Stoneware, Jar, Rice's Landing, Pa., Gray, Blue Letters, 2 Gallon 55.00
Stoneware, Jar, Water Cooler, Flow Flemish Blue And Gray, Deer In Relief 350.00
Stoneware, Jug, Batter, Brown, Bail Handle 14.00
Stoneware, Jug, Bellarmine, German, Mottled Brown, C.1580, 7 1/4 In. 700.00
Stoneware, Jug, Blue Floral, 2 Handles, C.1850, 12 In. 38.00
Stoneware, Jug, Blue Floral, 2 Quart, Ft.Edward, N.Y. 35.00
Stoneware, Jug, E.A.Buck & Co., Boston, 1876, 16 In.High .... *Illus* 185.00
Stoneware, Jug, Fort Howard Co., N.Y., Blue Touches, 14 In. 15.00
Stoneware, Jug, Gray, 2 Gallon 11.00
Stoneware, Jug, H.Glazier, Huntindgon, Strap Handle, Small Neck, 9 1/2 In. 40.00
Stoneware, Jug, Impressed Fish, Applied Handle, C.1800, Ovoid, 12 In. 200.00
Stoneware, Jug, J.Norton & Co., Bennington, Salt Glaze, Cobalt Trim, 2 Gallon 68.00
Stoneware, Jug, Light Brown, Pouring Lip, Handle, Gallon 12.00
Stoneware, Jug, Macomb, Pint 8.00
Stoneware, Jug, Pacific Co., Portland, Or., Blue Letters, Handled, 1/2 Pint 12.50
Stoneware, Jug, W.E.Welding, Brantford, Blue Flower, 2 Gallon 61.00
Stoneware, Jug, Western Stoneware Co., Monmouth, Ill., Blue, Tan, Gallon 25.00
Stoneware, Jug, White's Utica, Cobalt Bird, 16 1/2 In. 135.00
Stoneware, Jug, Wm.E.Warner's Manufactory, West Troy, 14 1/2 In. 20.00
Stoneware, Jug, 2 Gallon, Blue Flower, N.Y.Stoneware Co. 37.00
Stoneware, Jug, 2 Gallon, Blue Turnip Decoration, Haxstun Co., Ft.Edward, N.Y. 70.00

Stoneware, Jug, 2 Gallon, Gray With Bluebird, N.Y.Stoneware Co., Ft.Edward 120.00
Stoneware, Mug, Black Transfer, Ebling Brewing Co. 30.00
Stoneware, Pagoda, Ming Dynasty, C.1368, 6 Stories, Turquoise, 23 In. 3300.00
Stoneware, Pitcher & Stein Set, Cobalt & Brown On Cream, Prosit, Miniature 50.00
Stoneware, Pitcher, Blue Green, Embossed Bird Eating Cherries, 6 In. 16.00
Stoneware, Pitcher, Brown, Castle, 6 1/4 In. 25.00
Stoneware, Pitcher, Butterfly, 8 1/4 In. 42.00
Stoneware, Pitcher, Buttermilk, Tan, Cows & Green Trim, 7 1/2 In. 60.00
Stoneware, Pitcher, Cherry, 8 In. 48.00
Stoneware, Pitcher, Cow, Blue & Gray 52.00
Stoneware, Pitcher, Dark Brown Glaze, White Inside, Rose On Front, 9 X 5 In. 55.00
Stoneware, Pitcher, Figural, Cow, Blue & Gray, 2 Cows Front 47.00
Stoneware, Pitcher, Fishscale And Flower, 9 3/4 In. 50.00
Stoneware, Pitcher, Gray & Blue, Tavern Scenes, White Interior, 9 1/4 In. 40.00
Stoneware, Pitcher, Pliny Thayer, Lansingburg, 2 Gallon 250.00
Stoneware, Pitcher, Rose, 9 In. 48.00
Stoneware, Pitcher, Star Crockery, Blue & White, Grapes, 1/2 Gallon 65.00
Stoneware, Pitcher, Swirl, 11 1/4 In. 60.00
Stoneware, Pitcher, Water, Albany Slip Inside & Out, 11 In. 49.00
Stoneware, Salt, Blue & Gray, Salt Embossed On Front 32.00
Stoneware, Spittoon, Blue & White 35.00
Stoneware, Spittoon, Lady's, Gray, Blue Band 18.00
Stoneware, Teapot, Brown, Flower & Waffle 15.00
Stoneware, Umbrella Holder, A.M.Dipple, Lewisburg, Black, White Stork, 20 In. 75.00
Stoneware, Washstand Set, Fishscale And Flower 115.00

Store, see also Card, Advertising; Coffee Grinder, ; Tool; Scale

Store, Almanac, Ayer's, 1869 .... 6.00
Store, Almanac, Burdock's Blood Bitters, 1887 .... 3.75
Store, Almanac, Practical Farmer's, 1899 .... 9.00
Store, Apothecary's Display, Double-Handled Mortar, 14 X 8 In. 98.00
Store, Ashtray, Agri-Power Tractor Tire 8.00
Store, Ashtray, B.F.Goodrich, Radial Tire 8.50
Store, Ashtray, Beck's Beer, Pottery, Peach Color 9.00
Store, Ashtray, Ben Hur Coffee, San Diego Exposition, 1935, Ceramic 3.00
Store, Ashtray, Builder's Hardware, Reading, Pa. 8.50
Store, Ashtray, Camel Cigarettes, World War II PX, Tin, 3 1/2 In. 3.50
Store, Ashtray, Camels Are Mild, Gold & Red, Tin, Set Of 3 .... 5.00
Store, Ashtray, Cavalier Cigarettes, World War II, Tin 4.00
Store, Ashtray, Cobbs Creek Blended Whiskey, Cobalt, Octagonal 12.50
Store, Ashtray, Cooper Tire, Rubber 6.50
Store, Ashtray, Coor's Beer 3.50
Store, Ashtray, Dobb's Hats, Black Amethyst 5.00
Store, Ashtray, Goodyear Tire .... 5.00 To 12.00
Store, Ashtray, Mountain States Telephone & Telegraph, Tin 8.50
Store, Ashtray, Mr.Peanut, Planter's Peanuts, Brass 10.00
Store, Ashtray, Mr.Peanut, Planter's Peanuts, 1956 Anniversary 13.00
Store, Ashtray, Pennsylvania Tires 24.00
Store, Ashtray, Planter's Peanuts, Ceramic 50.00
Store, Ashtray, Planter's Peanuts, 1906-1956, Nickel Type 17.50
Store, Ashtray, Regal Beer, Emerald Green 5.00
Store, Ashtray, Rigid Pipe Tools, Aluminum 7.00
Store, Ashtray, Winston Cigarette, Metal 5.00
Store, Ashtray, Zinn Quality Malt, Milwaukee, Brown Bakelite & Leather 12.00
Store, Ax, Meat, 10 In. Blade, 20 In. 16.00
Store, B-Y's Cigars, C.1940, Tin, 28 X 12 In. 15.00
Store, Bag, Money, Adams Express Co., Lincoln, Nebr., Canvas, 23 X 14 In. 45.00
Store, Bag, Star Bright Coffee, Red & White, Lb., Pack Of 10 .... 3.00
Store, Bag, 2-Bit Coffee, Blue & White, 1 1/4 Lbs., Pack Of 10 .... 3.00
Store, Ball, Seven Up, Rubber 4.50
Store, Bank, Acorn Stoves, Figural, Brown Pottery 15.00
Store, Bank, American Can Company 10.00
Store, Bank, Elsie The Cow Bust, Metal 25.00
Store, Bank, Marathon Oil Can, Tin 5.00
Store, Bank, Mr.Peanut, Plastic 4.00
Store, Banner, Old Nick Candy Bar, 28 X 40 In. 40.00

Store, Bar, Back, English, Oak, Carved, Paneled, Beveled Mirrors 4000.00
Store, Bar, Walnut, Carved, Marble Top, 6 Iron Swivel Stools, C.1870, 10 Ft. 750.00
Store, Barber Pole, Wooden, White Paint, Red Stripes, 30 In. 125.00
Store, Barber Pole, 4 X 36 In. 195.00
Store, Barrel, Coffee, Wooden, 150 Lbs. 25.00
Store, Basket, Egg, Tin, 8 X 6 In. 20.00
Store, Basket, Egg, Wire 7.00
Store, Basket, Egg, Wire, Collapsible 12.00
Store, Beehive, Straw, 16 X 13 In. 65.00
Store, Beer Glass, Anheuser Busch, Stemmed 7.50
Store, Beer Glass, Bartholomay Beer & Ale, Enamel Letters, Barrel Shape 8.50
Store, Beer Glass, Budweiser 1.00
Store, Beer Glass, Busch Bavarian Beer, Blue Decoration 1.75
Store, Beer Glass, Cook's Goldblume Beer 7.50
Store, Beer Glass, Cream City Brewing Co., Milwaukee, Etched 7.50
Store, Beer Glass, Keely Brewing Co., Henry Auer Brewmaster, Stemmed 12.00
Store, Beer Glass, Louis Bergdoll Brewing Co., 1909, Etched 12.50
Store, Beer Glass, Sazerac 15.00
Store, Beer Glass, Stroh's Beer, Embossed 5.00
Store, Beer Glass, Stroh's, Detroit 7.50
Store, Beer Glass, Waldech, Gold & Black, Gold Rim, Footed 10.00
Store, Beer Set, Hamm's Beer, Land Of Sky-Blue Waters, Glass, 7 Piece 24.00
Store, Bell, "I'm Ringing The Bell With Pontiac, " 3 1/4 In. 9.00
Store, Bell, Bronze Liberty Bell, Philadelphia Carpet Co. 8.00
Store, Bell, Coiled-Spring Shop Door 23.00
Store, Bench, Saddlers, Ontario, Vice Jaws Operated By Foot Pedal 35.00
Store, Bench, Work, Pill Label, Sliding Drawer 30.00
Store, Bill Holder, J.E.Smith, Carlisle, Pa., Wall, Marble Contact 14.00
Store, Bin, A & P, Wooden, Tin Lined 175.00
Store, Bin, Coffee, H.Dahlman & Co., Milwaukee, Rollback, Gold Stencil 65.00
Store, Bin, Diamond Brand Coffee, Roll Top, Black & Gold, 20 In. 125.00
Store, Bin, Edwin J.Gillies Tea, Cylinder Roll Dispensing, Mirror, 19 In. 75.00
Store, Bin, Flour, Gold Paint, Stenciling, 11 In. 12.00
Storé, Bin, Montgomery Mills Mustard, Paper Label 35.00
Store, Bin, Sure Shot Tobacco, Picture Of Indian 185.00
Store, Bin, Sweet Cuba Tobacco 150.00
Store, Bin, Tea, Acme Store, Large 145.00
Store, Bin, Tea, Counter Size, English Breakfast, Portrait Of Woman 55.00
Store, Bin, Tobacco Counter, Mail Pouch, 13 1/2 X 11 X 10 In. 135.00
Store, Bin, Tobacco, Red Tiger, Tin 60.00
Store, Bin, Tobacco, Sterling Tobacco Plaid, Tin 23.00
Store, Bin, Tobacco, Sweet Burley Tobacco, Tin 45.00
Store, Bin, Tobacco, Sweet Mist Tobacco, Cardboard 85.00
Store, Bin, Vegetable, Vertical, Yellow Paint 495.00
Store, Bin, Yale Brand Coffee, Wooden, 21 X 16 X 15 In. 46.00
Store, Bin, 3-Sided Front, Cream With Gold & Red Decoration, 23 X 30 In. 125.00
Store, Bird Call, Hershey's Ice Cream, 1913 .... 9.00
Store, Birdcage, Green Wire, Milk-Glass Feeders, Bracket 40.00
Store, Birdcage, Wire, Domed Top, Round 14.00
Store, Block, Butcher's Chopping, Maple, 36 X 30 In. 275.00
Store, Block, Fabric Printing, Hand, Wooden 40.00
Store, Book, Coloring, Mr.Peanut, Richard Nixon Cover 4.00
Store, Book, Coloring, Planters Peanuts, 1957 .... 5.00
Store, Book, Hire's Root Beer, Mother Goose Rhymes, Hire's Kid 8.00
Store, Book, Kellogg's, 1909, Funny Jungleland, Movie 35.00
Store, Book, Mr.Peanut's Famous Men, Planter's Peanuts 25.00
Store, Book, Paint, Ceresota Flour, Ill., Alice Sargent Johnson 18.00
Store, Book, Paint, Planter's Peanuts, 1935 .... 17.00
Store, Book, Story Of Mr.Peanut, Planter's Peanuts 25.00
Store, Bookmark, Planter's Peanuts 7.50
Store, Boot, Wulfeller Bier, 1906 Crest, Clear, Gold Band Top, 2 Liter 18.00

Store, Bootjack, see also Iron, Bootjack

Store, Bootjack, Our 3 Shoes Best, 155 N.9, Phila., Bulldog 50.00
Store, Bottle, Cream Top Milk 18.50
Store, Bottle, Hot Water, Gillette Razor Co., 1919, Chrome, 8 1/2 In. 20.00

Store, Bottle, Perfume, C.B.Woolworth & Sons, Stopper 15.00
Store, Bowl, Cereal, Spirit Of St.Louis, Cream Of Wheat 35.00
Store, Bowl, Fish, Planter's Peanuts, Hexagonal Lid 40.00
Store, Bowl, H.P.Smith Trucking, Chakio, Minn.7 In. 6.50
Store, Bowl, Hand-Painted, Cyrus Lumber Co., 6 In. 5.50
Store, Box, American Biscuit, Wooden, Parrot Labels 55.00
Store, Box, American Fig Confection, 8 3/4 X 3 5/8 In. 25.00
Store, Box, Augusta's 5 Cent Coffee, Cardboard, 1/4 Lb. .... .45
Store, Box, Bigelow Kennard & Co., 8 1/2 X 6 1/2 In. 25.00
Store, Box, Celluloid Collar, Cuff-Link Insert 15.00
Store, Box, Cigar, Oak, Moisterizers, Metal Design, 1890, 9 1/2 X 9 1/2 In. 26.50
Store, Box, Cuban Daisy Cigars, 1898, Lithographed, Tin, 6 1/2 X 5 In. 32.00
Store, Box, Curtiss Baby Ruth 5 Cent Candy, 12 X 8 1/2 In. 8.00
Store, Box, Display, Dr.W.B.Caldwell's Syrup Pepsin, C.1910, 20 X 8 X 5 In. 58.00
Store, Box, Display, Page Seeds, Oak, 12 Compartments, 11 In. 18.00
Store, Box, Egg Shipping, 6 Doz. Eggs, Fragile, Tin, 13 X 9 In. 10.00
Store, Box, Fleer's Chickle, 12 Tin Spoon Inside, 10 X 10 In. 20.00
Store, Box, Florida Figs, 4 1/2 X 1 1/4 In. 10.00
Store, Box, Fry's Chocolate, Label, 13 X 9 1/2 X 2 1/2 In. 21.00
Store, Box, Glove, Hiawatha, Aluminum, Embossed Lid, 11 X 4 X 3 In. 7.50
Store, Box, Gold Dust Washing Powder, Lever Bros., 5 Ozs. 3.00
Store, Box, Hat, Utica State Asylum Label, 10 In. 58.00
Store, Box, Hercules Powder, Wooden, 11 X 10 X 8 In. 6.00
Store, Box, Hershey's Vanilla Sweet Chocolate, Pa., C.1900, Wooden, 12 1/2 In 60.00
Store, Box, Jersey Coffee, 100 Lbs. 60.00
Store, Box, Jewel, Phoenix Mutual Life Insurance, Gold Tone Metal, 3 1/2 In. 14.00
Store, Box, Mason's Challenging Blacking, Picture Of Black Shoeshiner 47.50
Store, Box, McAllister Cigars, Wooden, Dovetailed, 7 X 6 X 3 1/2 In. 9.00
Store, Box, Money, Wells Fargo 250.00
Store, Box, Morse Code Transmitter, Cherry, English, 6 X 4 1/2 In. 38.00
Store, Box, Nickel Peanuts, Cardboard, 7 1/2 X 3 X 3 In. .... .50 To .55
Store, Box, Old Time Coffee, John Hoffman & Sons Co., Cardboard, Lb. 25.00
Store, Box, Pencil, Big Chief Co., Wooden, 10 X 4 In. 18.00
Store, Box, Pencil, Picture Of Jackie Coogan, Tin 8.50
Store, Box, Pioneer Coffee, Cardboard, 1/4 Lb. .... .45
Store, Box, Quill Tea, Zinc Lined, Oriental Scene Under Lid 25.00
Store, Box, Railroad Mills, Rose-Scented Maccoboy Snuff, Wooden, 10 1/4 In. 5.00
Store, Box, Receipt, National Cash Register, Cast Iron & Glass, Key 56.00
Store, Box, Tobacco, Wooden, Walker Pure Leaf 5.00
Store, Box, Walter Baker & Co.Ltd, Baker Girl, Wood, 9 3/4 X 10 3/4 In. 48.00
Store, Box, Walter Baker Breakfast Cocoa, 9 1/2 X 14 X 7 1/2 In. 48.00
Store, Box, Wood Cigar, The Winnie, Snow Scene Inside Lid 10.00
Store, Bracelet, Planter's Peanuts, Plastic Mr.Peanuts & Peanuts Charms 22.00
Store, Breadbox, Schepp's, Green & Yellow, 19 1/4 X 15 1/4 X 10 In. 95.00
Store, Briddle, Leather, Brass Heart-Shaped Rosettes 20.00
Store, Brush, Shoe, Shinola 2.00
Store, Bucket, Sugar, So.Hingham, Mass., Bail Handle, Cover, 9 X 10 In. 55.00
Store, Buggy, Child's, Wooden Sides, Canvas Hood, Wire Wheels 110.00
Store, Button, Pepsi-Cola, Bigger & Better, 1 In. .... .50
Store, Button, Planter's Peanuts, C.1930, Metal & Celluloid, Pinback 2.50
Store, Button, Sampeck Triple Service Suit, Picture Of Fatty Arbuckle 12.00
Store, Button, Winchester, 1866-1966, Metal, Pinback, 2 1/4 In. 3.00

Store, Buttonhook, see also Art Nouveau, Buttonhook, Brass,

Store, Cabinet, D.Mason & Co., Fine Laces, Top Opens, 20 X 18 In. 40.00
Store, Cabinet, Dental, Mahogany 400.00
Store, Cabinet, Dentist, Glass Door On Top Shelves, 27 X 65 1/2 In. 375.00
Store, Cabinet, Diamond Dye, Children & Balloon 135.00
Store, Cabinet, Diamond Dye, Divided Sections Inside, 18 1/2 In. 40.00
Store, Cabinet, Diamond Dye, Evolution Of Women 425.00
Store, Cabinet, Diamond Dye, Hot-Air Balloon 210.00
Store, Cabinet, Diamond Dye, Metal, 19 X 16 X 6 In. 50.00
Store, Cabinet, Diamond Dye, Tin, Many Packages Dye 70.00
Store, Cabinet, Diamond Ink, Oak 145.00
Store, Cabinet, Dr.Barber's, Veterinary, Green & White, Tin 115.00
Store, Cabinet, Dr.Lesure's Horse Remedies, Wooden, Tin Door, 27 In. 48.00

Store, Cabinet, Dr.Lesures Horse Remedies, Wood With Horse Head 48.00
Store, Cabinet, Dye, Rit 75.00
Store, Cabinet, Dyola Dyes, Tin 90.00
Store, Cabinet, Hairnet Display, Tin, Ornate 125.00
Store, Cabinet, Hanford's Balsam Of Myrrh, Oak, Glass Front, 24 1/2 In. 185.00
Store, Cabinet, Humphrey's Remedies 250.00
Store, Cabinet, Lily Thread 45.00
Store, Cabinet, Needle, National, 2 Drawers, Wood, Lettering 89.00
Store, Cabinet, Oak, Brass Pulls, 3 Drawers, 12 X 12 X 7 In. 45.00
Store, Cabinet, Old Hickory Shoe Laces, Tin, 12 Drawers, 12 X 11 1/2 In. 35.00
Store, Cabinet, Putnam Dye, Tin 38.50
Store, Cabinet, Putnam Dye, Wooden 50.00
Store, Cabinet, Rexall Dye, Oak, Mirrored Front, Gold Lettering, 32 X 13 In. 150.00
Store, Cabinet, Rose-O-Cuba Cigars, Counter Display, Tin, Maroon, 14 In. 27.00
Store, Cabinet, Safetee Shave, Tin, 7 X 6 In. 18.00
Store, Cabinet, Screw, 80 Drawers, Ceramic Pulls, Octagonal 300.00
Store, Cabinet, Spool, Brainard & Armstrong, 4 Drawers, 20 X 18 X 13 In. 175.00
Store, Cabinet, Spool, Clark's, Oak, 6 Drawers, Brass Pulls, Inkwell 350.00
Store, Cabinet, Spool, Clark's, Ruby Glass, 2 Drawers 195.00
Store, Cabinet, Spool, Clark's, Walnut, 2 Drawers, Red Glass 235.00
Store, Cabinet, Spool, Coates, Oak, 4 Drawers 190.00
Store, Cabinet, Spool, Coates, Roll Front 220.00
Store, Cabinet, Spool, Coates, Tin & Walnut 135.00
Store, Cabinet, Spool, Corticelli, Five Drawers 225.00
Store, Cabinet, Spool, J.P.Coates, Slant Top, 6 Drawers, 34 X 24 X 15 In. 325.00
Store, Cabinet, Spool, J.P.Coates, Tin, 3 Glass-Front Drawers, 18 In. 55.00
Store, Cabinet, Spool, John Clark, Walnut, 2 Drawers .... 15.50 To 115.00
Store, Cabinet, Spool, Merrick, Stencilled Black Hills Hardware Store 650.00
Store, Cabinet, Spool, Oak, Paneled Glass Sides, Cylinder Roll Closings 495.00
Store, Cabinet, Spool, Richardson, Oak, Dovetailed 42.00
Store, Cabinet, Spool, Star, 3 Drawer 65.00
Store, Cabinet, Spool, Walnut, 2 Drawers, Red Glass 95.00
Store, Cabinet, Spool, Willimantic, 2 Drawers 65.00
Store, Cabinet, Spool, Willimantic, 2 Drawers 65.00
Store, Cabinet, Thread, Brainerol & Armstrong Co., Walnut 85.00
Store, Cabinet, Thread, Willimantic, 6 Drawer, Slanted Desk, Lift Top, Inkwell 275.00
Store, Cage, Bank Teller's, Carved, Marble, 18 1/2 X 10 In. 30.00
Store, Calendar, Desk, Pennsylvania Dixie Cement, Perpetual 8.50
Store, Calendar, Equitable Life, 1904, Maude Humphrey Illustrations 8.00
Store, Calendar, Hoods Sarsaparilla, 892, Round 14.00
Store, Calendar, Peters Cartridge Co., Ducks Landing, 1929, 15 X 27 In. 165.00
Store, Calendar, Peters Cartridge Co., Hunting Dogs, 1920, 15 X 26 In. 85.00
Store, Calendar, Singer, Tin, C.1930, 19 X 13 In. 85.00
Store, Calendar, Western Cartridge Co., Snow Geese, 1928, 15 X 27 In. 165.00
Store, Calendar, 1876, Home Insurance Co., 12 Pages 48.00
Store, Calendar, 1890, J.P.Coates, Woman Sewing, 6 In. 10.00
Store, Calendar, 1892, Scott's Emulsion, Boy With 3 Puppies 14.00
Store, Calendar, 1893, Hood's Sarsaparilla 15.00
Store, Calendar, 1894, Babies In Shoes, Advertising Sewing Machines, 8 In. 10.00
Store, Calendar, 1894, Metropolitan Life Insurance Co., Child, 8 1/2 In. 10.00
Store, Calendar, 1896, Hood's Sarsaparilla, Woman's Bust, 8 X 5 1/2 In. 29.00
Store, Calendar, 1896, L.Prang & Co., Boston, Flowers 25.00
Store, Calendar, 1900, Dr.Keeley, Richmond, Va., Describes Treatments, 13 In. 40.00
Store, Calendar, 1900, Hood's Sarsaparilla, Two Girls 19.00
Store, Calendar, 1902, Child Life, Frances Brundage, 4 Pages, 15 In. 60.00
Store, Calendar, 1902, Prudential Insurance, Girl 5.00
Store, Calendar, 1902, Rosy Posy 12.50
Store, Calendar, 1902, Sheep, 11 X 9 In. 15.00
Store, Calendar, 1903, Bell Capsic Plaster, Girl And Dog 12.00
Store, Calendar, 1903, Hill's Cascara Quinine, Little Girl 10.00
Store, Calendar, 1904, Antikammia Tablets 4.00
Store, Calendar, 1904, Milson Fertilizer, Child, 11 X 9 1/2 In. 14.00
Store, Calendar, 1906, Hood Sarsaparilla, Lovely Lady 12.00
Store, Calendar, 1906, Prudential Insurance, Victorian Girl 5.00
Store, Calendar, 1908-09, E.Kieper Druggist, St.Paul, Syrup Of Wild Cherry 8.00

Store, Calendar, 1911, Cherry Smash 65.00
Store, Calendar, 1912, Antikammia Tablets, Dark-Haired Lady 7.00
Store, Calendar, 1912, Hood Sarsaparilla, Pretty Girl 10.00
Store, Calendar, 1913, Consumer's Brewing Co. 75.00
Store, Calendar, 1914, Haberle Brewing Co. 35.00
Store, Calendar, 1914, Pabst Extract, Lady, 33 X 7 In. 17.00
Store, Calendar, 1919, Sunshine Girl, Winter 12.00
Store, Calendar, 1927, Child's Portrait 5.00
Store, Calendar, 1930, Austin 1.00
Store, Calendar, 1930, Peters Cartridge Co., Hunting Scene 12.00
Store, Calendar, 1933, Band Advertising 2.50
Store, Calendar, 1936, Texas Pride Beer, Cowboy & Horse, 33 In. 60.00
Store, Calendar, 1936, Traveler's Insurance Co., Currier & Ives Print 50.00
Store, Calendar, 1941, Reise Coal Co. 4.00
Store, Calendar, 1945, Esquire, Varga 20.00
Store, Calendar, 1948, Dr.Pepper, Pinup 10.00
Store, Calendar, 1948, Esquire 8.00
Store, Calendar, 1952, Traveler's Insurance Co., Currier & Ives Print 12.50
Store, Calendar, 1955, Marilyn Monroe, Uncirculated 15.00
Store, Calendar, 1961, Traveler's Insurance, Lyle Trump, Currier & Ives 12.50
Store, Calendar, 1968, Traveler's Insurance Co., Currier & Ives Print 3.00
Store, Can, Blue Valley Cream, 5 Gallon 8.00
Store, Can, Brown Biscuits, Texas, 1908, Brass & Glass Front, 11 1/2 X 10 In. 50.00
Store, Can, Cream, 5 Gallon 7.50
Store, Can, Cream, 8 Gallon .... 5.75 To 6.00
Store, Can, Cream, 10 Gallon 6.00
Store, Can, Display, Kaywoodie Pipe, Wood & Glass, Tin & Paper Labels 50.00
Store, Can, Sweet Mist Chewing Tobacco, 10 3/4 In. 55.00
Store, Can, Tiger, Round, Red 110.00
Store, Canister Jar, Glass With Lid, Purity Oats 12.50
Store, Canister, Benson & Hedges Tobacco, Wooden, Brass Corners, 12 In. 88.00
Store, Canister, Tole, Fry's Cocoa Extract, Egyptian Motif, 6 1/2 In. 30.00
Store, Capper, Bottle, Cast Iron, Handle 4.00
Store, Capper, Bottle, Patent 1920, Nickel Plated 10.00
Store, Card, see Card
Store, Carrier, Milk Bottle, Galvanized 5.00
Store, Carrier, Pepsi Cola, 1930, Wooden 6 Pack 30.00
Store, Carrier, Pepsi Cola, 1933, Wooden, 6 Pack 30.00
Store, Carrier, Pepsi, Cardboard, 6 Pack, 1940 .... 25.00
Store, Case, Boyd Needle, Wooden Vials With Needles Inside 15.00
Store, Case, Boye's Needles, Shuttles, & Bobbins, Patent 2-17-25 .... 60.00
Store, Case, Cigar, Philip Morris & Co., Ltd., Brown Alligator, 6 X 4 In. 85.00
Store, Case, Display, California Fruit & Pepsin Chewing Gum, Glass Front 175.00
Store, Case, Display, Coin, Wall Type, For 448 Coins 98.00
Store, Case, Display, Countertop, Pen Nib, Walnut, Compartments, 13 1/2 In. 39.00
Store, Case, Display, Davis & Park, Tin, 2 Drawers, Brown & Gold 65.00
Store, Case, Display, Remington Knife, Oak, 1920s, 15 3/4 X 5 X 1 1/2 In. 80.00
Store, Case, Display, Schaeffer Pen & Pencil Co., Floor, Glass Front 150.00
Store, Case, Display, Schrafft's Candy, Tin & Glass, 18 In. 16.00
Store, Case, Egg, Wooden, Slatted, Folding 5.00
Store, Case, Schrafft's Candy, Display, Tin & Glass, 18 In. 16.00
Store, Cash Drawer, Alarm Till, Dorsey Improved, Wooden 20.00
Store, Cash Drawer, Oak, Combination Lock, Change Block 25.00
Store, Cash Register, C.1900, Brass, Ornate 300.00
Store, Cash Register, Champion, Grant's New Mexico, Patented 1916 .... 175.00
Store, Cash Register, Model 1914, Rings To 99.99 Dollars 150.00
Store, Cash Register, N.C.R., C.1940, Electric, Black, Chrome Trim 100.00
Store, Cash Register, National, Brass, Barbershop 395.00
Store, Cash Register, National, Brass, Floor Model, Cabinet Type 750.00
Store, Cash Register, National, Brass, Floor Model, 6 Drawers 950.00
Store, Cash Register, National, Brass, Marble Ledge, 16 X 15 X 17 In. 295.00
Store, Cash Register, National, Brass, Oak, 10 Drawer, Electric, 1910 .... 1600.00
Store, Cash Register, National, Brass, Shillings & Pence, C.1913 .... 700.00
Store, Cash Register, National, C.1914, Brass 300.00
Store, Cash Register, National, C.1920, Mahogany, Brass Feet, 7 Drawer 350.00

Store, Cash Register, National, Mahogany Case, 5 Drawer, Floor Model 1500.00
Store, Cash Register, National, Model 210, Brass 475.00
Store, Cash Register, National, Model 356, Brass 200.00
Store, Cash Register, National, No.47, Brass, White Marble Money Drawer 380.00
Store, Cash Register, National, 313 .... 500.00
Store, Cash Register, National, 332, Brass, Press-Down Key Style, 16 In. 295.00
Store, Cash Register, National, 452, Brass, Crank Type 425.00
Store, Cash Register, Ohmer, Hand Crank 85.00
Store, Cash Register, Reliance, Copper Surface 125.00
Store, Cash Register, Series 300, Brass 375.00
Store, Cash Register, Series 356-G, Brass 225.00
Store, Cask, Wine, Copper & Brass, Spigot, C.1812 .... 98.00
Store, Chair, Barber, Brass-Tipped Legs, Ornate Oak 300.00
Store, Chair, Piedmont, Wood, Porcelain Back 70.00
Store, Check Writer, Hedman, Series W, 7 Digit 25.00
Store, Chest, Apothecary, Mahogany, 13 1/2 X 16 1/4 X 12 In. 248.00
Store, Chest, Oak, Used For Seed Display, Brass Trim 22.00
Store, Chocolate Set, Child's, Nestle's Quick, 10 Piece 4.00
Store, Chopper, Ice, Cast Iron, 1880 .... 35.00
Store, Chopper, Nut, Planter's Peanuts 5.00
Store, Cigarette Pack, Camel, C.1942 .... .45
Store, Cigarette Pack, Chesterfield, C.1942 .... .45
Store, Cigarette Pack, Lucky Strike, C.1942 .... .45
Store, Cigarette Pack, Pall Mall, C.1942 .... .45
Store, Cigarette Pack, Philip Morris, C.1942 .... .45
Store, Cigarette Pack, Raleigh, C.1942 .... .45
Store, Clip, Paper, Braender Tires, Tire & Bulldog, 2 1/2 X 3 In. 30.00
Store, Clip, Paper, Horseshoe Shape, Tin, Wall Hanging 4.00
Store, Clip, Paper, Metal, 4 1/2 In. 3.50
Store, Clip, Pencil, Seven Up 5.00
Store, Clip, Pocket Pencil, Morton Salt, C.1930 .... 3.00
Store, Clipper, Cigar, El Roi Tan Cigars, German Silver 10.00
Store, Clock, Calumet Baking Powder, Regulator 365.00
Store, Clock, Carstairs White Seal, 15 In. 25.00
Store, Clock, Clark's Teaberry Gum, Tin, Wall 18.00
Store, Clock, Desk, Leather Frame, Merchants Mutual Ins., Buffalo 10.00
Store, Clock, Ever-Ready Safety Razor, Tin, 8 Day, Man Shaving On Face, 1920s 750.00
Store, Clock, Ever-Ready, Tin, Shows Bald Man Shaving 450.00
Store, Clock, Four Roses, Whiskey, Electric 8.50
Store, Clock, Hire's Root Beer, C.1940, Electric 45.00
Store, Clock, Iroquois Beer 30.00
Store, Clock, Keg Advertising, Oak, 8 Day, Time & Strike 215.00
Store, Clock, Meadowgold Milk 40.00
Store, Clock, Miller Beer, Lighted 15.00
Store, Clock, Moxie, Shelf, Windup 150.00
Store, Clock, Mr.Peanut, Planter's Peanuts, Alarm 12.00
Store, Clock, Nugrape, Wall 30.00
Store, Clock, Pepsi Cola 20.00
Store, Clock, Phillips 66 Tire, Sessions, Electric 17.50
Store, Clock, Postal Telegraph, Gallery 65.00
Store, Clock, Postal Telegraph, Synchronour Electric Timer, 21 In. 125.00
Store, Clock, Savers Extracts, Wall Regulator, Mahogany Case, Gold Leaf 595.00
Store, Clock, Schaefer's Beer, Light-Up 13.50
Store, Clock, Seven Up 20.00
Store, Clock, Suncrest Orange, Convex Glass, Electric, Wall 37.50
Store, Clock, Tab, Large, Plastic 14.00
Store, Clock, 4 Roses, Metal Base And Frame 18.00
Store, Coaster, Beer, Wurlitzer, Johnny One Note, Musical Fun For Everyone .... .50
Store, Cobbler's Bench, Wooden, 2 Drawers, Cash Box, Stool 400.00
Store, Coffee Grinder, see Coffee Grinder
Store, Collar, Horse's, Leather 6.00
Store, Container, Cookie, Tin, Brass Front, 11 1/2 X 10 1/2 In. 32.50
Store, Container, Display, Gold-Painted Wood & Glass, 3 Sided, 2 Ft. 75.00
Store, Container, Kraft Malted Milk, Metal, Red Logos, 6 In. 5.00
Store, Cooler, Root Beer, Pine & Tin, Zinc Lined 95.00

Store, Cork Setter, Empire, Wooden 14.00
Store, Corkscrew, Anheuser Busch 15.00
Store, Corkscrew, Harrisburg, Pa. 2.00
Store, Corkscrew, Kellerstrauss Distillery 2.50
Store, Corkscrew, London Terrace Liquor, N.Y. 14.00
Store, Corkscrew, McAvoy Brewing Co., Chicago 10.00
Store, Corkscrew, N.Y.Liquor 2.00
Store, Corkscrew, Western Brewery Co., Belleville, Ill., Wooden Handle 6.00
Store, Counter, Coffee, Vertical, 18 Drawers, 120 X 54 In. 695.00
Store, Counter, Wrigley Chewing Gum, Tin, Compartment For Money 45.00
Store, Creamer, Cereal, Kellogg's Correct Cereal Creamer, Glass 10.00
Store, Creamer, Hy-Grade Milk Co., Restaurant 4.00
Store, Cuff Links, G.M.Builds Its First 50 Million Cars, Pair 8.00
Store, Cup & Saucer, Van Dole's Hot Chocolate, Luster, Hand-Painted 15.00
Store, Cup, Cyclist's, Embossed Riders, 1897, 2 1/2 In. 4.50
Store, Cup, Dickinson Clover Seed, Porcelain 10.00
Store, Cup, Elsie, The Borden Cow 10.00
Store, Cup, Mixing, Peruvian Quassia Tonic Bitters, Wooden, 3 In. 55.00
Store, Cup, Mr.Peanut, Plastic, Pink 4.00
Store, Cup, White Enamel, Dickenson's Ace Clover Seeds, 2 3/4 In. 20.00
Store, Cutter & Tamper, Cigar, Herman Warner Cigar Co., Pocket 8.00
Store, Cutter, Cigar, City Life Cigar, Glass Dome Top, Mechanical, Wood Base 105.00
Store, Cutter, Cigar, Horse's Head, 5 3/4 In. 38.50
Store, Cutter, Cigar, Iron, Embossed, Sp & Co., Rochester, 3 1/2 X 7 In. 70.00
Store, Cutter, Cigar, Meyer's Cigars, Tin, Pocket 4.00
Store, Cutter, Cigar, Rensselaer Cigars, Silver, Pocket 18.00
Store, Cutter, Cigar, Scissors Shape, Nickel Plate 5.00
Store, Cutter, Cigar, Shaped Like Squirrel 40.00
Store, Cutter, Cigar, Silver Thistle, Counter Model 425.00
Store, Cutter, Cigar, Silver, Black Inlay, For Watch Chain 10.00
Store, Cutter, Rope, Measuring 10.00
Store, Cutter, Tobacco, Brown Mule, Iron 20.00
Store, Cutter, Tobacco, Counter Type, Master Workman Good Chew 40.00
Store, Cutter, Tobacco, Hatchet Shape 150.00
Store, Cutter, Tobacco, John Finzer, Cast Iron, Counter Top 35.00
Store, Cutter, Tobacco, Tomahawk 34.00
Store, Cylinder, Wallpaper Printing, Brass & Maple, C.1830, 22 In. 25.00
Store, Dish, Change Receiver, American Beauty Brand, Green Glass 20.00
Store, Dish, Child's, Skippy, Silver Plate 17.50
Store, Dish, Cigar Band, English 12.00
Store, Dish, Cuticura Glass Change Receiver 20.00
Store, Dispenser, Buckeye Root Beer, Tree-Trunk Shape 250.00
Store, Dispenser, Cherry Smash Syrup 305.00
Store, Dispenser, Christo Ginger Ale, Ceramic, Bell Shape 200.00
Store, Dispenser, Cigarette Paper, Zig Zag 60.00
Store, Dispenser, Cigarette, Sectioned For Brands, Chrome, Glass Lids, Enamele 24.00
Store, Dispenser, Coffee Beans, Koffee On Dome Lid, Tin, Brass Scoop, 29 In. 120.00
Store, Dispenser, Fowler's Root Beer 325.00
Store, Dispenser, Heinz Pickle Barrel Vinegar, Glass, 11 1/2 In. 85.00
Store, Dispenser, Hire's Root Beer, Pump, Porcelain 235.00
Store, Dispenser, Hire's Syrup 175.00
Store, Dispenser, Julep Syrup, Stoneware, Cobalt Lettering 40.00
Store, Dispenser, King's Cherry Dip 300.00
Store, Dispenser, King's Cherry Dip 5 Cents 165.00
Store, Dispenser, Lighter Fluid, Lighthouse Model, 1930s 295.00
Store, Dispenser, Maxwell House Iced Tea, Glazed Crock, Wooden Top 40.00
Store, Dispenser, Needle, Sears, Roebuck & Co., Red & Gold, 2 In. 20.00
Store, Dispenser, Orange Crush 150.00
Store, Dispenser, Pepsi Cola, Bottle, Stainless Steel, 13 In. 250.00
Store, Dispenser, Schuster's Root Beer, 5 Cents 375.00
Store, Dispenser, Soda Fountain, Mission Real Fruit Juice, Pink Glass 45.00
Store, Dispenser, Soda Fountain, Nesbitt's Orange Juice, Fastens To Counter 40.00
Store, Dispenser, Syrup, Richardson's Liberty Root Beer, Barrel On Stump 150.00
Store, Dispenser, Ward's Orange Crush, Pump, Porcelain 165.00
Store, Dispenser, Ward's Orange, Lemon, Lime Crush, Set With No Pumps 600.00

Store, Display Case, Hire's, Tin, Blue, 1/2 Cent A Glass, 18 X 5 In. 24.00
Store, Display Rack, Tie, Metal, 1890 .... 10.00
Store, Display, Perfume, Lady Sitting In Roses, Chalkware, 12 X 10 In. 20.00
Store, Dose Glass, City Drug, Onieda, N.Y. 4.50
Store, Dose Glass, Dr.Green's Blood Purifier 4.00
Store, Drawer, Change, With Bell, Change Holders, Finger-Pull Release 25.00
Store, Eyecup, Aluminum 5.00
Store, Eyecup, John Bull 7.00
Store, Eyecup, John Bull, Green 15.00
Store, Eyecup, John Bull, 1917, Cobalt 8.00
Store, Eyeglasses, 152 Lenses In Red Velvet-Lined Box 250.00
Store, Fan Hanger, Red Dot Cigars, C.1930, Square, 7 In. 5.00
Store, Fan, Ceiling, Globe Light 225.00
Store, Fan, Goodyear Balloon Tire 5.00
Store, Fan, Lake Breeze, Wm.J.H.Strong, Chicago, Hot-Air Operated, Alcohol 295.00
Store, Fan, Moxie, 1915, Miss Pritchard 22.00
Store, Fan, Singer Sewing Machine, Floral & Gilt, Folding 8.50
Store, Fan, Standard Sewing Machine 4.00
Store, Fan, W.F., Emblem, Table, Octagonal, Electric 50.00
Store, Felt, Counter Change, Lord Shelburne 5 Cent Cigars 20.00
Store, Figure, Dog, Electrically Animated, Papier-Mache, 42 In. 975.00
Store, Figurine, Bronze Boy, Thatcher Furnaces, 3 In. 39.00
Store, Figurine, Bulldog, Papier-Mache, Clayton's Dog Remedies, C.1900 .... 450.00
Store, Figurine, Buster Brown & Tige, Mechanical, Buster Lecturing Tige 25.00
Store, Figurine, Drugstore Indian Holding Cigars, Fiber 200.00
Store, Figurine, Duquesne Beer, Plaster Of Paris, 8 X 11 In. 45.00
Store, Figurine, Flat Turtle, Hazel Stoves, Acme Stove & Range Co., Rome, Ga. 20.00
Store, Figurine, Green River Whiskey, Papier-Mache Statue, Negro & Horse 120.00
Store, Figurine, Man Smoking Cigar, Charles Denby Segars, 1906, 5 1/4 In. 50.00
Store, Figurine, Mutt & Jeff, Bud Fisher & Dyas Sales Co., 1909, 9 & 6 In. 155.00
Store, Figurine, Plaster Pig, Counter Display, Deckers Iowana 95.00
Store, Figurine, RCA Nipper Dog, Vinyl, 34 In. 150.00
Store, Figurine, RCA Victor Dog, Plaster, 4 In. 15.00
Store, Figurine, Sterling Beer, Girl On Base, Metal, Bell In Bottom, 15 In. 35.00
Store, File System, McGaskey, Counter Top, Oak, Drawer 165.00
Store, Fishbowl, Planter's Peanuts 55.00
Store, Flashlight, Balco, Brass 2.50
Store, Flashlight, Dietz, Police Lantern, Patent Apr.13, 1886 .... 32.50
Store, Flashlight, Winchester, No.0818, Copper, 2 Cell 35.00
Store, Floodlight, Underwater, Brass, 17 In. 30.00
Store, Fly Net, Leather 7.50
Store, Fly Net, String 4.75
Store, Flyswatter, Clyde Flour, Screen Wire, Wooden Handle 1.50
Store, Footrests, Shoeshine Stand, Brass, Pair 35.00
Store, Form, Milliner's Carved From One Piece Of Wood 20.00
Store, Glass, Beer, Falk's Milwaukee 30.00
Store, Glass, Beer, Hoffman Brewing, Lithographed Flowers 20.00
Store, Glass, Four Roses, 4 1/2 In. 18.00
Store, Globe, Barnsdale Motor Fuel, Plastic Pump, Glass Panels 25.00
Store, Globe, D-X, Gas 100.00
Store, Globe, Mobilgas, Milk Glass, Flying Horse 115.00
Store, Globe, Phillips 66 Gasoline Pump, Plastic Frame 75.00
Store, Globe, Simpson Oil Co., Milk Glass 60.00
Store, Globe, Texaco Gas, All Glass 125.00
Store, Grater, Fels Naphtha Soap 4.00
Store, Grinder, Peanut, Planter's Peanuts, Mr.Peanut, Figural 18.50
Store, Gum Machine, see Store, Machine, Gum ball
Store, Gum Stand, Clark's Teaberry Gum, Crystal 12.50
Store, Halter, Bull's, Leather 2.50
Store, Handcuffs, Argus Mfg.Co., Iron Claw, Lock Type, Pair 45.00
Store, Hatbox, Cretonne Lining, 17 X 15 In. 10.00
Store, Holder, Beehive String, Iron 12.50
Store, Holder, Napkin, Pepsi-Cola, 1930s 70.00
Store, Holder, Straw, Country Store 35.00
Store, Holder, Toothbrush, Skeezix, Listerine, Tin 45.00

Store, Hone, Knife, Cudahy's Blue Ribbon Meat Meal 7.00
Store, Hone, Razor, Champion 2.50
Store, Hook, Meat, Wooden Handle 5.00
Store, Hose & Nozzle, Gas Pump, Canvas & Brass 20.00
Store, Hot Pad, Jewel Tea, Oval 8.50
Store, Ink Kit, Sanford's, Stenographer's, 3 Bottles In Box 6.00
Store, Jar Rubber, U.S.Peerless, 12 In Carton 3.50
Store, Jar Rubber, U.S.Royal Peko Edge, 12 In Carton 2.50
Store, Jar, Barrel, Planter's Peanuts, Peanut Lid 145.00
Store, Jar, Benny Hubbs, Checkered, Quart 6.50
Store, Jar, Boscul Tea Balls 20.00
Store, Jar, Buffalo Salted Peanut, Octagonal, Label 125.00
Store, Jar, Bunte Candy, Raised Script, 12 In. 45.00
Store, Jar, Contiserie Nationale Candy, Hoboken, N.J., Bulbous, 9 In. 28.00
Store, Jar, Minnow, Green Glass 35.75
Store, Jar, Old Judge Coffee, Tin Lid, Paper Label, Wide Mouth, 3 Lbs. 15.00
Store, Jar, Planter's Barrel 150.00
Store, Jar, Planter's Peanuts, Fish Bowl, 5 X 3 In. 68.00
Store, Jar, Planter's Peanuts, Peanut Finial, 8-Sided 60.00
Store, Jar, Planter's Peanuts, 8-Sided, Hexagonal Finial 60.00
Store, Jar, Planter's, Blown Out, Four Corner, Peanut Finial Lid 200.00
Store, Jar, Planter's, Fish Label 75.00
Store, Jar, Planter's, Peanuts Form 4 Corners, Cover 130.00
Store, Jar, Planter's, Red, White, Blue, Yellow, Original Box 20.00
Store, Jar, Pure Ponce Molasses, Dewell, New Haven, Stoneware, Cobalt, Quart 30.00
Store, Jar, Squirrel Brand Peanuts, Ribbed, Tin Lid, 9 In. 18.00
Store, Jar, Squirrel Embossed, With Lid 65.00
Store, Jar, Squirrel Yellow Print With Lid 35.00
Store, Jar, Sunshine Brand Coffee, Embossed, Quart 3.00
Store, Jenning's Tic-Tac-Toe, Chief Slot 600.00
Store, Jug, Dazey Kerosene, April 26, 1881 .... 51.00
Store, Jug, Stoneware, District Distilling Co., Dayton, Ohio, Miniature 19.00
Store, Jug, Syrup, Pepsi-Cola, 1910, Embossed Glass 150.00
Store, Key, Morse Telegraph, Brass & Sounder On Wood Panel 52.00
Store, Key, Telegraph, Vibroflex, 1904 .... 25.00
Store, Key, Telegraph, Western Union 7.50
Store, Kit, Salesman's, Shur-Stop Fireman On The Wall, 1927 & 1928 .... 95.00
Store, Knife & Bottle Opener, A E Sandy Sanhaus, Kansas City, Mo., 1 Blade 4.50
Store, Knife, Always Display N R, 2 Blades, 3 1/8 In. 8.50
Store, Knife, Banana, Wooden Handle, Curved Blade, 6 In. 6.00
Store, Knife, Conoco Stratton Service, Braymer, Mo., 2 Blades, 3 1/4 In. 5.50
Store, Knife, Fisk Tires, C.1930, Pocket 6.00
Store, Knife, Lady's Leg, Bowl-Away Lanes, 1 Blade, 3 1/4 In. 8.00
Store, Knife, Mr.Peanut, Planter's Peanuts, Silver Plate 10.00
Store, Knife, Peppard Seeds, 2 Blades, 3 3/8 In. 5.00
Store, Knife, Phillips 66, Kelly Oil, Topeka, Kansas, 2 Blades, 2 1/4 In. 5.00
Store, Knife, Pocket, Anheuser Busch, See-Through Picture Of August Busch 150.00
Store, Knife, Pocket, St.Joseph Plow Company 22.00
Store, Knife, Silver Dollar Bar, 2 Blades, 3 1/8 In. 5.50
Store, Knife, Swing Out Fur Matchers, N.Y., 1 Blade, 2 3/4 In. 8.50
Store, Knife, Wear Gale's Shoes, Metal 10.00
Store, Knob, Beer Tap, Altes 10.00
Store, Knob, Beer Tap, Knickerbocker Beer, Lucite 4.00
Store, Knob, Beer Tap, Rheingold Beer, Chrome 5.00
Store, Knob, Beer Tap, Rheingold, Square Hole 2.75
Store, Knob, Beer Tap, Ruppert 9.00
Store, Label, Citrus, Airline .... .50
Store, Label, Citrus, All Year .... .50
Store, Label, Citrus, Annie Laurie 1.00
Store, Label, Citrus, Blue Goose .... .75
Store, Label, Citrus, Cal Crest .... .50
Store, Label, Citrus, California Dream 6.00
Store, Label, Citrus, Desert Bloom 2.30
Store, Label, Citrus, Golden Sceptre 4.00
Store, Label, Citrus, Idyllwild .... .50

Store, Label, Citrus, Jameson .50
Store, Label, Citrus, Loch Lomond 1.00
Store, Label, Citrus, Lucky Trail 5.00
Store, Label, Citrus, Marc Antony 4.00
Store, Label, Citrus, Morning Smile .50
Store, Label, Citrus, Mustang 3.00
Store, Label, Citrus, Placer 5.00
Store, Label, Citrus, Ramona Memories .50
Store, Label, Citrus, Red Skin 4.00
Store, Label, Citrus, Reindeer 6.00
Store, Label, Citrus, Silver Buckle 3.00
Store, Label, Citrus, Snow Boy .75
Store, Label, Citrus, Sunkist .50
Store, Label, Citrus, Tom Cat Lemon 5.00
Store, Label, Citrus, Upland Pride 3.00
Store, Label, Citrus, Vandalia .50
Store, Label, El Merito .50
Store, Lamp, Brass, Hanging, Tin Shade, Marked U.S.A., Oil, 13 In.Chimney 185.00
Store, Lamp, Jeweler's Glass, Alcohol 7.00
Store, Lap Board, Corticelli, Kitten Holding Spool 30.00
Store, Last, Shoe, Amoskeag Mills, Wooden 5.00
Store, Last, Shoe, Iron, Stand, Set Of 4 In Graduated Sizes 30.00
Store, Lengthener, Shoe, Miracle Shoes, Patent 1920, Aluminum 6.50
Store, Letter Opener, Brass, Rickenbacker Berks Motor Co., Reading, Pa., 9 In. 50.00
Store, Letter Opener, Hames, Nickel-Plated Brass, 6 1/4 In. 36.00
Store, Letter Opener, Hiram Walker Whiskey 8.50
Store, Letter Opener, National Cash Register, Pictures Both Sides 8.90
Store, Letter Opener, Prudential Life Insurance, Ornate, Early 1900s 9.50
Store, Light, Pepsi-Cola, Revolving, Hanging, 1960s 20.00
Store, Lighter, Cigar, Eldred Mfg.Co., Chicago, Dry Cell Batteries 295.00
Store, Lighter, Cigar, Oak Case 130.00
Store, Lighter, Cigarette, Chesterfield 8.00
Store, Lighter, Cigarette, Dodge Auto, Brass 5.00
Store, Lighter, Cigarette, Dunhill, Tender Pistol 8.00
Store, Lighter, Cigarette, Paul Jones Whiskey, Amber, Painted Label 3.00
Store, Lighter, Cigarette, Pepsi-Cola Can 5.00
Store, Lighter, Cigarette, Playboy 15.00
Store, Lighter, Cigarette, Royal Crown Cola, Bottle Shape 4.00
Store, Lighter, Cigarette, Royal Crown Cola, 1930, Bottle, Nickel On Brass 5.00
Store, Lock, 6 Lever, Tubular Key 32.00
Store, Lunch Box, Bagley's Tobacco 60.00
Store, Lunch Box, Blue Fashion Tobacco 22.50
Store, Lunch Box, Central Union Tobacco 70.00
Store, Lunch Box, Charles Denby Cigars, H.Fendrich Maker, Evansville, Ind. 125.00
Store, Lunch Box, Child's, Train & Airplane Scenes, Tin, C.1920 12.00
Store, Lunch Box, Comet Tobacco 150.00
Store, Lunch Box, Dan Patch Tobacco, Yellow With Red 17.00
Store, Lunch Box, Dixie Kid Cut Plug Tobacco, Negro Baby 127.50
Store, Lunch Box, Dixie Queen Tobacco, Lady 65.00
Store, Lunch Box, Gail & Ax Navy, Tobacco 25.00
Store, Lunch Box, George Washington Cut Plug Tobacco 22.00
Store, Lunch Box, Just Suits Tobacco 45.00
Store, Lunch Box, King Koal Tobacco 30.00
Store, Lunch Box, Laredo Cut Plug, Scotten Dillon Co. 45.00
Store, Lunch Box, Lorillard Tobacco, Brown 30.00
Store, Lunch Box, Mayo's Cut Plug Tobacco, Blue, Collapsible, 3 Tiered 145.00
Store, Lunch Box, Mayo's Tobacco 16.00
Store, Lunch Box, Moore's Patented Folding Lunch Box On Lid, Plaid 12.00
Store, Lunch Box, Nigger Hair Tobacco 75.00
Store, Lunch Box, Patterson's Seal Tobacco, Green, Basket Weave 28.00
Store, Lunch Box, Pedro Tobacco 20.00
Store, Lunch Box, Peter Rabbit, Easter 20.00
Store, Lunch Box, Plough Boy Tobacco 30.00
Store, Lunch Box, Round Trip Tobacco 65.00
Store, Lunch Box, Sensation Tobacco 22.50

Item	Price
Store, Lunch Box, Sweet Cuba Tobacco	25.00 To 28.00
Store, Lunch Box, Tiger Tobacco, Blue	30.00 To 48.00
Store, Lunch Box, Tiger Tobacco, Red	22.50
Store, Lunch Box, Tin, 1/2 Gallon Pail	9.00
Store, Lunch Box, Union Leader Cut Plug Tobacco	35.00
Store, Lunch Box, Winner Tobacco, Cars	115.00
Store, Machine, Abby-Triple, Nut Vendor, Round Globes, 5 Cent, Large Tray	250.00
Store, Machine, Adding, Rapid Computer Co., Patent 1892, Nickel On Brass	24.00
Store, Machine, Allen Wonder Bubble, Motorized Lawrence Welk, Cast Iron	70.00
Store, Machine, Aspirin & Cup Vendor, 10 Cent Slot	20.00
Store, Machine, Atlas Tilt Test, 5 Cent Slot	85.00
Store, Machine, Ball Grip, Arcade, 5 Cent Slot	795.00
Store, Machine, Bally Triple Bell Draw Console, Slot	450.00
Store, Machine, Bally, Citation	495.00
Store, Machine, Bally, Coney Island	495.00
Store, Machine, Bally, Triple Bell	495.00
Store, Machine, Bar Boy, Pays In Beers Or Gum Ball, 5 Cent Slot	195.00
Store, Machine, Bayer Aspirin Vendor, 25 Cent Slot, Key	14.00
Store, Machine, Best Hand Poker Game, 2 Player, Girl In Bikini	150.00
Store, Machine, Best Hand Poker Game, 2 Player, Lithographed, 21 In.	175.00
Store, Machine, Bomb Hit, 1939, Wins Defense Stamps	125.00
Store, Machine, Booster Dice Game, 1 Cent Slot	100.00
Store, Machine, Booze Barometer, 5 Cent Slot	75.00
Store, Machine, Bozo The Clown Fun Phone, 12 Stories, Late 1950s	295.00
Store, Machine, Buckley, Bonanza, 10 Cent Slot	500.00
Store, Machine, Buckley, Crisscross, 25 Cent Slot	500.00
Store, Machine, Buckley, Crisscross, 50 Cent Slot	500.00
Store, Machine, Buckley, Racehorse Track Odds, 7 Coins	495.00
Store, Machine, Candy & Nut Vendor, C.1920, Octagonal Chrome Base, 15 In.	185.00
Store, Machine, Catch & Match, Berger Mfg.Co., Wood, Glass Front	45.00
Store, Machine, Cent A Pack Cigarette Reel Game, Arcade	110.00
Store, Machine, Challenger Hot Nuts, C.1930, Lights Up	40.00
Store, Machine, Challenger Pistol, 1 Cent Slot	195.00
Store, Machine, Challenger, 5 Cent Slot	150.00
Store, Machine, Chicago Clubhouse Gumball, Counter Top, 5 Reels, Jackpot	350.00
Store, Machine, Chuck-A-Roll, C.1930, Dice, Reverse Painting On Glass	95.00
Store, Machine, Columbus Candy & Peanut Vendor, Cast Iron, 15 In.	120.00
Store, Machine, Crane Digger, Erie, Counter Top	195.00
Store, Machine, Crystal Gazer, C.1920, 6 Dice Under Crystal Ball, 13 In.	175.00
Store, Machine, Dancing Clown, Arcade	475.00
Store, Machine, Dancing Clown, Peppy, Arcade Machine	450.00
Store, Machine, Draw Bell, Slot	450.00
Store, Machine, English Chicken, Chocolate Candy, Tin, Glass Window, 25 In.	895.00
Store, Machine, Evan's Ten Strike Bowler, 1939	495.00
Store, Machine, Exhibit Rotary Claw Merchandiser, Walnut, 10 Cent Slot	895.00
Store, Machine, Exhibit Supply Digger, Floor Model, Coin Operated	595.00
Store, Machine, Exhibits Mauser Gun	265.00
Store, Machine, Fortune Teller Napkin Holders, 1 Cent Slot	29.00
Store, Machine, Four In One Candy & Peanut Vender, C.1920, Art Deco Style	295.00
Store, Machine, Girlie Arcade Movie	500.00
Store, Machine, Goalee, Chicago, Hockey Game, Maple Case, Coin Slot	295.00
Store, Machine, Golf Game, C.1930, Metal Case, 1 Cent Slot, 14 In.	150.00
Store, Machine, Gottlieb Grip Test, Counter Top, 3-Way Grip, 2 Cent Slot	65.00
Store, Machine, Groetchen Punchboard, Counter Top, Coin Operated, 12 In.	245.00
Store, Machine, Gum Ball Cigarette Reel, Cast Aluminum, Arcade	95.00
Store, Machine, Gum Ball Vendor, Football Game, 14 X 8 In.	85.00
Store, Machine, Gum Ball Vendor, 1910, Coin Drops Through Nail Pegs, 18 In.	110.00
Store, Machine, Gum Ball, Acorn, Penny Game, Shoot Gum Into Holes	30.00
Store, Machine, Gum Ball, Ad-Lee E-Z, 1908, Decal, Original Gum, Top Sign	300.00
Store, Machine, Gum Ball, Advance, C.1920, 1 Cent Slot	80.00
Store, Machine, Gum Ball, Advance, 1923	85.00
Store, Machine, Gum Ball, Atlas Vending, 1940, 5 Cent Slot	29.95
Store, Machine, Gum Ball, Black Jack, The Twenty One, 1930s, 8 X 12 X 13 In.	225.00
Store, Machine, Gum Ball, Chic-Mint Gum Co.1910, Decal, Round, Gold Letter	75.00
Store, Machine, Gum Ball, Claw Vending, 5 Cent Slot	1600.00

Store, Machine, Gum Ball, Columbus, Stand, Two 5 Cent Round Nut Globes 175.00
Store, Machine, Gum Ball, Deluxe Mercury, Counter, Deco Design, 1 Cent Slot 150.00
Store, Machine, Gum Ball, Hart, Chrome Base, Glass Globe Top, 12 In. 39.95
Store, Machine, Gum Ball, Hawkeye Novelty Co., 1936 .... 47.50
Store, Machine, Gum Ball, Imp-Ball Gum Vendor, Penny Play 90.00
Store, Machine, Gum Ball, Mills Puritan Bell, Penny Slot, Ornate 300.00
Store, Machine, Gum Ball, Mills, The Knight, 5 Cent Payout, Full Size Slot 400.00
Store, Machine, Gum Ball, Northwestern Ring A Bell 195.00
Store, Machine, Gum Ball, Northwestern, 1939, Red Porcelain 60.00
Store, Machine, Gum Ball, Pepsin Gum, Mansfield, 1901, 5 Cent, Stick, All Glass 250.00
Store, Machine, Gum Ball, Puritan Baby Bell, Counter Top 200.00
Store, Machine, Gum Ball, Puritan Baby Vender, Counter Top, 3 Reels 235.00
Store, Machine, Gum Ball, Reel 21 Black Jack, 5 Cent Slot 150.00
Store, Machine, Gum Ball, Scoopy, Baker's Boy 525.00
Store, Machine, Gum Ball, Topper, Lock & Key 30.00
Store, Machine, Gum Ball, V.G. Grandbois, Paper Decal, Cylinder Dome, Penny 125.00
Store, Machine, Gum Ball, Victor Baby Grand 40.00
Store, Machine, Gum Ball, Victor Wood Case, Football Field 45.00
Store, Machine, Gum Ball, Victor, Mirror, Wood Sides 50.00
Store, Machine, Gum Ball, Victor, Vendor, C.1940, Football Field, Wooden Case 45.00
Store, Machine, Gum Ball, Wee Gee, 1920s, What Do You Know, Drop, White Metal 75.00
Store, Machine, Gum Ball, Yankee, Cigarette Reels, Counter Top, 8 In. 150.00
Store, Machine, Gum Ball, Zeno, 1893, Wood, Penny 150.00
Store, Machine, Gum, Cleveland Railway Co., C.1930, Chrome, 14 In. 15.00
Store, Machine, Gum, Northwestern Jet, 5 Cent Slot 30.00
Store, Machine, Gum, Oak Mfg., 5 Cent Slot 30.00
Store, Machine, Gumball Shooting Gallery, Face Of Hitler, Counter Top 350.00
Store, Machine, Hand Pleating, Mrs.Frank Webb, 1876, 13 X 10 In. 36.00
Store, Machine, Harvard I.D.Medals, 1905 .... 150.00
Store, Machine, Hershey's 1 Cent Candy, Metal 75.00
Store, Machine, Hire's Root Beer Barrel 160.00
Store, Machine, Holly Manufacturing Universal Grip, Squeeze, Counter Top 85.00
Store, Machine, Horse Race, Counter Top, Great States Mfg.Co., K.C.Mo. 245.00
Store, Machine, Imp Cigarette Reel Game, 1 Cent Slot 65.00
Store, Machine, Jenning's, Target, 1 Cent Slot 150.00
Store, Machine, Jennings Slot, Wooden, 25 Cent Slot 650.00
Store, Machine, Keeney Golden Nugget, Console, 5 Cent Slot 700.00
Store, Machine, Kicker Katcher, Blonde Oak Case, Counter Top 135.00
Store, Machine, Lighthouse-Variety Lighter Fluid, C.1930, 1 Cent Slot 325.00
Store, Machine, Little Duke, 1 Cent Slot 700.00
Store, Machine, Love Meter, 1934, Wood Case, 1 Cent 135.00
Store, Machine, Master Bubble Gum, 1923, Penny Slot 50.00
Store, Machine, Master's Peanut, 1923, 1 Cent Slot 75.00
Store, Machine, Match Vendor, C.1920, Gambling, Steel Balls On Disc 125.00
Store, Machine, Mill's Cherry, 25 Cent Slot 450.00
Store, Machine, Mill's Jackpot, 10 Cent Slot 450.00
Store, Machine, Mill's Lift Test, Arcade, 5 Cent Slot 350.00
Store, Machine, Mill's Merchandising Corp., Chicklets, 1 Cent Slot 75.00
Store, Machine, Mill's Mutoscope, Merchandiser Type, 1 Cent Slot 395.00
Store, Machine, Mill's Penny Flip Game, Target Practice, Olympic Games 225.00
Store, Machine, Mill's Tickette Game, C.1930, Counter Top 125.00
Store, Machine, Mill's War Eagle One-Arm Bandit, 1910, 5 & 10 Cent Slots 425.00
Store, Machine, Mill's Wizard Fortune Teller, Wooden Case, 1 Cent Slot 350.00
Store, Machine, Mill's, Puritan Bell, Counter Top, Pay Slot 350.00
Store, Machine, Mimeograph, Edison, Rotary, 1906, No.75 .... 25.00
Store, Machine, Mutoscope, Arcade, Square Type, 5 Cent Slot 375.00
Store, Machine, Mutoscope, Goofy Giggles, Postcard Vending, 1 Cent Slot 100.00
Store, Machine, National Hunter Gum Ball, Duck Targets, 1 Cent Slot 105.00
Store, Machine, Northwestern Candy & Nut Vendor, 1933, Porcelain Base 50.00
Store, Machine, Northwestern Peanut Vending, 1933, Porcelain, 1 Cent Slot 49.95
Store, Machine, Northwestern Postage Stamp, Domed, Hand Crank 30.00
Store, Machine, Ohio Match Co.Matchbook Vendor, 1 Cent Slot, 10 In. 45.00
Store, Machine, Pace, Comet, 25 Cent Slot 500.00
Store, Machine, Peep Show, Back To Nature & To Be Happy See 100.00
Store, Machine, Pennsylvania Dutch Root Beer Barrel 150.00

Store, Machine, Penny Drop, The Wind Mill 175.00
Store, Machine, Penny Game, Three Jacks 360.00
Store, Machine, Photoscope, Earthquake Of San Francisco Scenes 225.00
Store, Machine, Photoscope, Exhibit Company, 1920s, Nude Scenes 245.00
Store, Machine, Pike's Peak, Counter Top, 1930s 195.00
Store, Machine, Pinball, Chicago World's Fair, Jig Saw 250.00
Store, Machine, Pinball, Fun Park 275.00
Store, Machine, Pinball, Gottlieb Dancing Dolls, Wooden Side Rails 250.00
Store, Machine, Pinball, Playball Baseball 375.00
Store, Machine, Pinball, Pro Football 500.00
Store, Machine, Pinball, William's Rocket Ship 100.00
Store, Machine, Popcorn Popper, Gas Fired, 1920s, Motor Driven 325.00
Store, Machine, Postage Canceling, Clinton, Iowa, 1890 .... 15.00
Store, Machine, Postage Stamp Vendor, Cast Iron & Glass, C.1920, 14 In. 125.00
Store, Machine, Postage Stamps, 4 & 5 Cent Stamps 25.00
Store, Machine, Pulver Cop Gum 200.00
Store, Machine, Pulver Gum, Stand 110.00
Store, Machine, Regal Peanut Vending, 1935, Teardrop Globe, 5 Cent Slot 39.95
Store, Machine, Reliable Nut Vendor, 5 Cent Slot 24.00
Store, Machine, Scopitone, Sound Movie, 16 Mm. 716.00
Store, Machine, Silver Comet Cigarette Vendor, C.1930, 1 Cent Slot, 8 In. 100.00
Store, Machine, Six Shooter, 5 Cent Slot 300.00
Store, Machine, Six-Star Shooter With Ticket Machine 225.00
Store, Machine, Smiley The Clown, Counter Arcade 100.00
Store, Machine, Star Slugger 250.00
Store, Machine, Stencil Cutter, 1 In. Letters 125.00
Store, Machine, Stoner Chiclets, Penny Slot 20.00
Store, Machine, United Sky Raider, 10 Cent Slot 300.00
Store, Machine, Vendex Pencil Vendor, 1925, Cast-Iron Stand, 5 Cents, 4 Ft. 450.00
Store, Machine, Walzer Co., Hershey Candy Vendor, 1 Cent Slot 45.00
Store, Machine, Watling Roll-A-Top, 25 Cent Slot 3500.00
Store, Machine, Watling, Roll-A-Top, 50 Cent Slot 900.00
Store, Machine, Wild Cycle 250.00
Store, Machine, Windmill Penny-Drop Game, C.1920 .... 195.00
Store, Machine, Your Ideal Lovemate 125.00
Store, Marble, Weatherbird Shoes 3.00
Store, Match Holder, Anheuser Busch, Pocket 7.50
Store, Match Holder, Coal Bucket, Iron, Beck-Walker Coal Co., St Louis, Mo. 45.00
Store, Match Holder, Cully Bros., Kewanee, Ill., Barrel Shape, Wooden, Wall 12.00
Store, Match Holder, J.C.Stevens, Tin, C.1917 .... 20.00
Store, Match Holder, Judson, Family Scene, Wall 17.50
Store, Match Holder, Juicy Fruit, The Man 75.00
Store, Match Holder, Old Judson Bitters, Painted, 2 Adults & Child, Wall 30.00
Store, Match Holder, Tin Barrel, Ceresota Flower, Picture Of Boy 12.00
Store, Match Holder, Tin, Milwaukee Harvester Co. 35.00
Store, Match Holder, Tunnel Fire Insurance, C.1920, Tin 7.00
Store, Match Holder, Universal Stoves & Ranges, Wall, World Globe Picture 17.50
Store, Match Safe, , Diamond Match Co. 7.50
Store, Match Safe, American Injector Co., Detroit, Celluloid & Silver 25.00
Store, Match Safe, Arm & Hammer, Gutta-Percha 30.00
Store, Match Safe, Atlas Horseshoe Nail, Atlas Holding Globe, Hoof Base 45.00
Store, Match Safe, Born's Extra Pale Beer 25.00
Store, Match Safe, Dr.Shoop's Health Coffee 18.00
Store, Match Safe, Dueber Watch Case 18.90
Store, Match Safe, Garland Stoves 12.00
Store, Match Safe, International Tailoring Co., Patent 1904, Brass 14.00
Store, Match Safe, Necco Sweets, 1908, Atlantic City, German Silver 25.00
Store, Match Safe, Nickel, Sailboat, Atlantic City, 1909 .... 22.00
Store, Match Safe, Pocket, Arm & Hammer 35.00
Store, Match Safe, Pocket, Eugene Malloy, Chicago, 1911, Nickel Silver, Floral 18.50
Store, Match Safe, Pocket, Smith & Gray Co., M.U. & Brooklyn, Ornate 14.00
Store, Match Safe, Queen Caroline Segars 17.50
Store, Match Safe, Rosa DeValle Cigars, Picture Of Senorita, Book Matches 26.00
Store, Match Safe, Tadcaster Ale, Metal & Celluloid 20.00
Store, Match Safe, Union Label, Blue 12.00

Store, Match Safe, United Cigars 12.00
Store, Matchbox, Dueber Watch Cases, Brass 18.00
Store, Measure, Beer, Copper, Handle & Spout, Glass Insert, 5 1/2 X 6 1/2 In. 85.00
Store, Measure, Eastman Kodak, Spout, 24 Ozs. 18.00
Store, Measure, 1 Cup, Pink Depression Embossed Kellogg On Base 8.00
Store, Merchandiser, Grain, Vertical, Yellow Paint 695.00
Store, Merchandiser, Spice, Wooden, Beveled Mirrors On Drawers, Vertical 795.00
Store, Metal, Cow & Calf, DeLaval, Brown, Swiss, 5 In., Pair 22.50
Store, Mill, Burr, Cast Iron, Table Model 12.50
Store, Mirror And Puzzle, Buy Star Soap, Black Lady 18.50
Store, Mirror, Angelus Marshmallows, Cherub, Pocket 20.00
Store, Mirror, Angelus Marshmallows, Pocket .... 18.00 To 20.00
Store, Mirror, Beautyskin, Celluloid And Color, Pocket 23.00
Store, Mirror, Bowling & Billiards, Albany Park Bowling Alleys, Pocket 20.00
Store, Mirror, Broken Coin Movie, Ford & Cunard, Universal, Pocket 12.00
Store, Mirror, Calox Tooth Powder, Pocket 18.00
Store, Mirror, Carleton Dry Goods Co., 3 In. 5.00
Store, Mirror, Cascarets, Angel, Pocket 20.00
Store, Mirror, Cascarets, Cherub On Potty, Pocket 18.00
Store, Mirror, Ceresota Flour, Boy, Pocket 17.50
Store, Mirror, D.Klein Tailored Capes, Pocket 18.00
Store, Mirror, Duffy's Malt Whiskey, Old Gent, Pocket 18.00
Store, Mirror, Duffy's Pure Malt Whiskey, Pocket 18.00
Store, Mirror, Electrical Automobile Appliance, Girl, Pocket 16.00
Store, Mirror, Farmall Farm Tractor, Wall 6.50
Store, Mirror, Farmer's Insurance, Lincoln, Neb., Handle 18.00
Store, Mirror, Fun House, 72 X 32 In. 275.00
Store, Mirror, Gillette Safety Razor, Pocket 16.30
Store, Mirror, Grinnel Bros., Piano Factory, Pocket 16.00
Store, Mirror, James & Graham Wagons, Wagon, Pocket 18.00
Store, Mirror, James Wilson, Hardware, Nebraska, Pocket 5.00
Store, Mirror, John Fabiana, Merchant Tailor, Newark, Picture, Pocket 13.20
Store, Mirror, Knights Of Pythias, Indiana, Pocket 4.00
Store, Mirror, Ladd Monument Co., Kewanee, Ill., Pocket 8.00
Store, Mirror, Mascot Tobacco, Bulldog, Pocket 20.00
Store, Mirror, Mennen's Violet Talcum, Pocket 20.00
Store, Mirror, O'Hanlon's Drugs, Winston-Salem, N.C., Pocket 15.00
Store, Mirror, Obermiller Bros., Sterling, Ill., Pocket 8.50
Store, Mirror, Overland, Celluloid, Pocket 30.00
Store, Mirror, Paul Vallette Watches, Man Working, Beveled, Pocket 8.00
Store, Mirror, Planter's Peanuts, C.1930, Pocket 3.00
Store, Mirror, Rectangular, Invincible Junior, C.1900, Lady Vacuuming, Pocket 15.60
Store, Mirror, Roberts & Co., Utica, N.Y., 1911, Handle 17.50
Store, Mirror, Sinclair Oils, Picture Of Barrel, Pocket 20.00
Store, Mirror, Sunshine Ranges, Pocket 6.50
Store, Mirror, The Maccabees, Pocket 10.00
Store, Mirror, Turner Mooring, Denver, North & South America, Pocket 15.00
Store, Mirror, Webster Typewriters, Handle 17.50
Store, Mirror, White Cat Union Suits, Cat, Pocket 22.00
Store, Mirror, White House Coffee, Pocket 25.00
Store, Mirror, Yardley & Harsh Bicycles & Sporting Goods 4.00
Store, Mirror, 1949 Ford Dealer, 12 X 5 In. 13.00
Store, Mixer, Horlick 30.00

Store, Mold, see also Pewter, Mold; Tin, Mold

Store, Mold, Butter, Eagle With Knob, 3 3/4 In. 130.00
Store, Mold, Candy, Easter Bunny, Chocolate, 7 1/4 In. 17.50
Store, Mold, Candy, Policeman, Stop 11.50
Store, Mold, Candy, Rabbits, 7 X 5 In. 25.00
Store, Mold, Candy, Santa Claus, Double Figural, Tin, 7 1/2 In. 57.00
Store, Mold, Candy, Santa, No.427 .... 18.50
Store, Mold, Chocolate, Basket, 6 X 3 In. 16.00
Store, Mold, Chocolate, Iron 6.50
Store, Mold, Chocolate, La Marquise, Iron 14.50
Store, Mold, Chocolate, Rabbit, Jumping, 6 In. 12.50
Store, Mold, Chocolate, Rabbit, Sitting, 3 In. 6.00

Store, Mold, Chocolate, Rabbit, Sitting, 5 In. 8.00
Store, Mold, Chocolate, Roasting Turkey, Hinged, Snap Clip, 5 In. 24.00
Store, Mold, Cigar, 10 Tube, Wooden, 2 Piece 10.00
Store, Mold, Cigar, 20 Tube 18.50
Store, Mold, Cigar, 20 Tube, Wooden, 2 Piece 12.00
Store, Mold, Ice Cream, see Pewter, Mold, Ice Cream
Store, Mold, Lead Toy Dog, Bronze, Wooden Handles 32.00
Store, Mold, Lead Toy, Cowboy On Horseback Holding Pistol, Cast Metal, 4 In. 8.50
Store, Mold, Lead Toy, Indian On Horseback With Tomahawk, Cast Metal, 4 In. 8.50
Store, Mold, Lead Toy, Man Shooting Rifle, Cast Metal, 4 In. 8.50
Store, Mold, Lead Toy, Standing Pony, Cast Metal, 4 In. 5.00
Store, Mold, Lead Toy, World War I Soldier, Cast Metal, 4 In. 8.50
Store, Mold, Maple Sugar, Fluted, Tin, 3 In. .15
Store, Mold, Maple Sugar, 6 Hole, Tin 10.00
Store, Mortar & Pestle, Brass, 3 1/4 In. 28.00
Store, Mortar & Pestle, Frosted, Moyer Co. 8.00
Store, Mortar & Pestle, Iron & Stone, 5 1/2 In. 19.00
Store, Mortar & Pestle, Wooden, Hand-Carved 48.00
Store, Mug, Bartholomay's Rochester Beer, Miniature, 2 1/4 In. 18.00
Store, Mug, Blatz Beer, Barrel, Embossed 9.50
Store, Mug, Bovox, Pottery, Dragon Around Mug To Handle, Brown 22.00
Store, Mug, Budweiser, King Of Beers, Tan 20.00
Store, Mug, Campbell's Soup 5.00
Store, Mug, Child's Uncle Wiggily Wants His Ovaltine, Signed, Campbell, 1924 48.00
Store, Mug, Coor's, Colorado State Fair, 1934, Stoneware 8.00
Store, Mug, Coors Beer, Export Label, 3 In. 8.00 To 10.00
Store, Mug, Dad's Root Beer, Glass, 5 1/2 In. 8.50
Store, Mug, Drink Hire's Root Beer, Mettlach, Villeroy & Boch 70.00
Store, Mug, Elsie, The Borden Cow, Figural, Porcelain 10.00
Store, Mug, Falstaff Beer, Glass 10.00
Store, Mug, Gerber Baby, Figural, Porcelain 9.00
Store, Mug, Harry Vinton, Solid Leather Shoe Man, Pittsburgh, P.C.Co. 20.00
Store, Mug, Hire's Root Beer, Boy With Mug, Villeroy & Boch 135.00
Store, Mug, Hire's Root Beer, Mettlach, No.3095, 1906 95.00
Store, Mug, Maple's Brewing Co., Beer, 4/10 Liter 32.00
Store, Mug, Miner's Root Beer, Ceramic, Blue & Gray, 5 3/4 In. 36.50
Store, Mug, Mr.Peanut, Blue Plastic 2.00
Store, Mug, Old Huber Brewery, N.Y., Gray Crockery, Pewter Top, 1/2 Liter 50.00
Store, Mug, Old Kentucky Malt, Barrel Shaped, Brown Glaze, Hand Painted 12.00
Store, Mug, Richardson Root Beer, Embossed, Glass 10.00
Store, Mug, Robert Smith's Musty Ale, Phila., Chester Pottery Co., Brown 20.00
Store, Mug, Rochester Root Beer, Glass 12.50
Store, Mug, Schlitz Beer, Copper, Wedding Engraving 15.00
Store, Mug, Schlitz Beer, Pottery 6.00
Store, Mug, Stearn's Root Beer, Gray, Pottery, 6 1/2 In. 15.00
Store, Music Sheet, Moxie, Horse In Car 35.00
Store, Music Sheet, Under The Anheuser Busch, Couple Under Shrubbery 5.00
Store, Nameplate, Boyd, Brass, 41 X 9 In. 75.00
Store, Nut Set, Planters Peanuts, Tin, 8 Piece 12.00
Store, Nutcracker, May, Wharton, Texas, Patent 1914 7.00
Store, Opener & Stopper, Bottle, Moxie 4.50
Store, Opener, Bottle, Ceco, Cola Drink, Key Ring & Cigar Snipper Attached 20.00
Store, Opener, Bottle, Coor's Beer 5.00
Store, Opener, Bottle, Man Wearing Top Hat 8.00
Store, Opener, Bottle, Metal, Figural Fish, Green Grocer's, Reading, Pa., 1911 8.50
Store, Opener, Bottle, Schlitz Beer, Brass 18.00
Store, Opener, Bottle, Tech Beer, Figural, Wooden 3.00
Store, Opener, Bung, Fleischmann's Rye & Gins, Wooden, Hammer Type, 21 In. 17.50
Store, Opener, Letter, American Range, Copper 7.00
Store, Opener, Letter, C.A.O'Brien, Patent Attorney 2.50
Store, Opener, Letter, Dioxygen, Celluloid Handle 6.00
Store, Opener, Letter, Lion Bonding Co., Brass, Lion's Head Handle 8.50
Store, Opener, Letter, Magnifying Glass, Phillips Milk Of Magnesia, Nickel 4.95
Store, Opener, Letter, Order Of Hibernians, Sword, Metal Sheath 15.00
Store, Opener, Letter, Uneeda Biscuit Kid 10.00

Store, Poster, Blanc Et Noir, 1890, 34 X 46 In.
(See Page 634)

Store, Poster, C.1895, 33 X 44 In.
(See Page 634)

Store, Poster, Cavalry, 1920, 21 X 26 In.
(See Page 634)

Store, Opener, Letter, Wm.J.Walsh Press, Printers, Boston, Brass, 8 5/8 In. 3.95
Store, Padlock, Belmont, Flat 9.00
Store, Padlock, York, Flat, Curved Key 12.00
Store, Pail, Armour's Peanut Butter, Lb. 35.00
Store, Pail, Armour's Peanut Butter, 12 Ozs. 33.00
Store, Pail, Armour's Veribest Peanut Butter, Halloween Party, Lb. 45.00
Store, Pail, Buffalo Brand Peanut Butter, Lb. 25.00
Store, Pail, Campbell's Coffee, 4 Lbs. 35.00
Store, Pail, Coffee, Larkin Co., Tin 5.50
Store, Pail, Flower's Peanut Butter 25.00
Store, Pail, Monarch, Peanut Butter 27.00
Store, Pail, Peanut Butter, Fiber, 13 Lb., Dated 1885 .... 15.00
Store, Pail, Shedd's Peanut Butter, Elves & Animals, 5 Lbs. 25.00
Store, Pail, Sultana Peanut Butter, Lb. 20.00
Store, Pail, Veribest Peanut Butter, 12 Ozs. 36.00
Store, Paper Holder, American Roll Paper Co., Patent 1884, 14 In. 19.00
Store, Paper Holder, Rex, Cast Iron 8.00
Store, Paper Holder, Roll, Counter Top, Pine, Iron Cutter 22.00
Store, Paper Holder, Wright, Doll, For 9 In. Roll 10.00
Store, Paperweight, see Paperweight
Store, Paperweight & Match Holder, Woonsocket Boot, Metal 20.00
Store, Paperweight & Mirror, Waterloo Evening Courier 15.00
Store, Paperweight & Thermometer, Volpe Construction Co., Elephant, 5 In. 20.00
Store, Paperweight, Byer's Bear Cat Crane, Ravenna, Ohio, Embossed Cat 18.50
Store, Peanut Butter Maker, Planter's Peanuts 10.00
Store, Pedometer, Jack Armstrong 12.50
Store, Pen, Abalone Shell, Gold Point 10.00
Store, Pen, Fountain, Peter Pan, Ring On Top, 14K Gold Tip, 2 1/2 In. 20.00
Store, Pen, Gene And Glenn, Quaker Early Birds 7.00
Store, Pen, Pearl Handle, Case 12.00
Store, Pen, Schaeffer Feather Touch, Fountain, Black & Gold 5.00
Store, Pen, Wahl, Gold Filled 7.50
Store, Pen, Waterman's, Desk, Holder 5.00
Store, Pencil, Broom Corn, Bullet Shape 3.50
Store, Pencil, Gold, Retractable, Pocket 10.00
Store, Pencil, King Features, 1949 .... 1.00
Store, Pencil, Mechanical, In Shape Of Pistol, 100 Years Old 10.00
Store, Pencil, Mechanical, Sterling, Loop For Hanging, 4 In. 7.95
Store, Pencil, Mr.Peanut, Planter's Peanuts, Wooden, Gold Color 1.50
Store, Pencil, Mr.Peanut, Planter's Peanuts, 50th Anniversary, Mechanical 12.00
Store, Pencil, Overland & Willys Knight 5.00
Store, Pencil, Phillips 66 Motor Oil, Kansas Refinery, 1949 .... 8.50
Store, Pencil, Wahl Eversharp, Mechanical, Sterling Silver 10.00
Store, Penknife, Karo Mazola Argo 16.00

Store, Peters Cartridge Co., Picture Of Hunter & Dog, 1923, 15 X 30 In. 95.00
Store, Phone Booth, Oak 75.00
Store, Pill Maker, Pharmaceutical, Brass Plates & Sides, Walnut Board 55.00
Store, Pilsner Glass, Etched Coney Island, Cincinnati 13.00
Store, Pilsner Glass, Etched Piel Bros., Real German Lager Beer 16.00
Store, Pin, Bucher & Gibbs Plow Co., 2 Men By Plow, 1 1/4 In. 13.50
Store, Pin, Ceresota Flour, Colorful 10.00
Store, Pin, Dead Shot Smokeless Powder, Picture Of Duck 20.00
Store, Pin, Deering Harvester Co., Horse Drawn Harvester 17.50
Store, Pin, Falstaff Beer, Bow 5.00
Store, Pin, Heinz Pickle 3.00
Store, Pin, J.I.Case Threshing Machine Inc., Racine, Wisc., Eagle On Globe 12.50
Store, Pin, Miller High Life Beer, Girl On Moon 9.50
Store, Pin, Planter's Peanuts 1.00
Store, Pin, Van Nostrand's Ale, Picture Of Dog 15.00
Store, Pipe, DuPont Explosives, French Brier 30.00
Store, Pitcher, Beer, Heileman's Old Style Beer 8.50
Store, Pitcher, Hiram Walker's Ten High, A True Bourbon, Gray Pottery, Quart 10.00
Store, Pitcher, Ironstone, Blue Stencilled Crawford Cooking Ranges 29.00
Store, Pitcher, Lone Star Beer 6.00
Store, Pitcher, Schlitz Beer, Covered, C.1900, Amber 65.00
Store, Pitcher, Spongeware, Glessner's Hardware & Lumber, Eldena, 266, 4 In. 40.00
Store, Pitcher, Turtle Bay Distillery, W.C.Fields, 8 In. 15.00
Store, Pitcher, Water, Hedges & Butler Whiskey 5.00
Store, Pitcher, Water, Jim Beam Whiskey 19.95
Store, Pitcher, Water, Kentucky Tavern, English Cream Ceramic, 7 1/2 In. 15.00
Store, Plaque & Ashtray, Wall, Dr.Pepper, 16 X 8 In. 5.00
Store, Plaque, Brass, Hire's, 8 X 3 In. 35.00
Store, Plaque, G.A.Stores, Art Deco, Glass, Hanging, 10 In. 12.00
Store, Plaque, United Air Line, Bronze, 1940, 3 X 4 In. 50.00
Store, Plate, Anheuser Busch, 1905, Buxom Lady, Auburn Hair, Tin, 10 In. 22.50
Store, Plate, Baker Chocolates, Blue & White, Vernon Kilns, 10 1/4 In. 38.00
Store, Plate, C.D.Kenny, Boy & Dog, Christmas Holly 45.00
Store, Plate, Cup, Blue Feather Edge, Best Goods, C.1840, 4 In. 18.00
Store, Plate, Fern Brand Chocolates, Carnival, Purple, 6 In. 125.00
Store, Plate, Santa, Cherokee, Okla., 1908 20.00
Store, Plate, Tin, A & P, Little Girl And Bears 28.50
Store, Plate, Urban's Liberty Flour, Buffalo, N.Y., Pink Swirl, 8 In. 18.00
Store, Post Office, Green Metal, 92 Units, Cage Center, Combination Locks 300.00
Store, Poster, Blanc Et Noir, 1890, 34 X 46 In. *Illus* 175.00
Store, Poster, C.1895, 33 X 44 In. *Illus* 150.00
Store, Poster, Cavalry, 1920, 21 X 26 In. *Illus* 210.00
Store, Poster, Globe Pot Polish, 39 X 54 In. *Illus* 175.00
Store, Poster, Hoffman Brewery, Flowers, Beer Glass, Cigar, C.1910 25.00
Store, Poster, Hood's Sarsaparilla, 1896, 29 X 42 In. *Illus* 350.00
Store, Poster, Nail This Fact, Ferry's Seeds, 20 X 30 In. *Illus* 70.00
Store, Poster, Olympia Theater, Paris, C.1895, 32 X 44 In. *Illus* 225.00
Store, Potlid, Bazin's Shaving Cream, Philadelphia 30.00
Store, Pouch, Climax Chewing Tobacco, Leather 5.00
Store, Pouch, Dixie Queen Tobacco 30.00
Store, Pouch, Oceanic Tobacco, Cloth 4.00
Store, Pouch, Tobacco, Leather, Boot Jack 6.00
Store, Program, Barnum & Bailey Circus, 1906, 40 Pages 25.00
Store, Projector, Keystone Post Card 28.00
Store, Pump, Beer, Peerless, Patent 1912, Brass 18.00
Store, Pump, Vinegar, Wooden, 46 In. 8.00
Store, Punchboard, Grand Prize, 2, 400 Punches, 72 Seals, 5 Cents, 17 X 10 In. 6.00
Store, Punchboard, Jackpot Ivy, 1, 000 Punches, 25 Cents, 15 1/2 X 12 1/2 In. 6.00
Store, Punchboard, Jumbo Dough, 490 Punches, 5 Cents, 11 3/4 X 7 In. 4.50
Store, Punchboard, King Edward The Seventh Cigars 8.00
Store, Punchboard, Packs O'Luck, 1, 000 Punches, 5 Cents, 19 X 12 In. 7.50
Store, Punchboard, Put & Take Charley, 1, 000 Punches, 10 3/4 X 9 In. 6.00
Store, Punchboard, Quality Prizes, 1, 200 Punches, 5 Cents, 11 X 11 In. 5.00
Store, Puppet, Hand, Chinese Theatre, C.1850, Man, Wooden Head, 1 In. 100.00
Store, Pushplate, Copenhagen Snuff, Tin, 8 X 3 In. 8.00
Store, Pushplate, Orange Kist Soda, Tin 5.00

Store, Poster, Globe Pot Polish, 39 X 54 In.

Store, Poster, Hoods Sarsaparilla, 1896, 29 X 42 In.

Store, Poster, Nail This Fact, Ferry's Seeds, 20 X 30 In.

Store, Poster, Olympia Theater, Paris, C.1895, 32 X 44 In.

Store, Puzzle, Cacey's Salt, C.1930, Envelope 4.00
Store, Puzzle, Chase & Sanborn, Picture, Boxed, 8 X 6 In. 10.00
Store, Puzzle, Comic Car, Standard Oil, 1933 .... 8.50
Store, Puzzle, Dr.Suess Cartoon, Esso Co., 1933 .... 8.50
Store, Puzzle, Hood's Sarsaparilla, Rainy Day, C.1895, Boxed 55.00
Store, Puzzle, Jigsaw, Bensdorp's Cocoa 12.00
Store, Puzzle, Victor Talking Machine, Shows Recording Artists 38.00
Store, Puzzle, Wayside Inn, Charles Allan Winter, Lux Soap, 1933 .... 8.50
Store, Rack, Bicycle, Iron, For Over Back Fender, C.1910 .... 12.50
Store, Rack, Meat Hook, Cast Iron With Bull On Top 350.00
Store, Razor Blade, Marlin Firearms Co., Pack Of 12 .... 3.00
Store, Razor, Antonio Tadros, Straight 5.00
Store, Razor, C.W.Dahlgrens, Coins, Straight 9.00
Store, Razor, Clauss, Raccoon, Straight 12.50
Store, Razor, Engstrom Eskulstuna, Sweden, Straight 9.75
Store, Razor, Frederick Baurman & Sonne, 16, Comfort, Straight 5.75
Store, Razor, Frederick Reynolds, Sheffield, Straight 16.50
Store, Razor, James Bates, Dublin, Straight 6.00
Store, Razor, Joseph Roger Cutler, Straight 8.75
Store, Razor, Keen Kutter, Honer, Wood-Grained Tin 24.00
Store, Razor, Keen Kutter, Whisker, Simmon's Hardware, Straight 9.00
Store, Razor, Mustache, Kruisium Bros., Folding, 3 1/4 In. 10.00
Store, Razor, Royal Keen Kutter Eagle, Simmon's Hardware, Straight 12.50
Store, Razor, Safety, Gillette, Bostonia, Chrome Travel Box 4.50
Store, Razor, Safety, Gillette, Milady Decollete, Pyralin Box 7.50
Store, Razor, Spery & Alexander, Cenatour, Straight 7.50
Store, Razor, Straight, Incised Indian In Headdress, Ontario 83, Geneva, N.Y. 20.00
Store, Razor, Straight, Wade & Butcher 4.00
Store, Razor, Winchester, Straight 48.00
Store, Reel, Fishing, Climax, 1891, Brass 30.00
Store, Ring, Mr.Peanut, Planter's Peanuts, Metal, Premium 3.50
Store, Roaster, Acme Peanut 110.00

Store, Ruler, Palmer Cox, Mrs.Winslow's Soothing Syrup, Brownies, 8 In. 12.50
Store, Ruler, Wooden, Peters Weatherbird Shoes 3.00
Store, Salt & Pepper Bottles, Schlitz 5.00
Store, Salt & Pepper Shakers, Felsenbau Beer 10.00
Store, Salt & Pepper, Aunt Jemima & Uncle Mose 4.00
Store, Salt & Pepper, Blatz Beer Bottle, Heidelberg Castle Beer 150.00
Store, Salt & Pepper, Budweiser Beer, Salt & Pepper, Pair 6.00
Store, Salt & Pepper, Diamond Salt, Brass, Sunflower 5.00
Store, Salt & Pepper, Koehler Beer 3.00
Store, Salt & Pepper, Pabst Beer 6.00
Store, Salt & Pepper, Pepsi-Cola, 4 1/2 In. 5.00
Store, Salt & Pepper, Planter's Peanuts .... 6.00 To 50.00
Store, Salt & Pepper, R.C.A. Victor Dogs, Ceramic 12.00
Store, Salt & Pepper, Ruppert Knickerbocker Beer 12.00
Store, Salt & Pepper, Schlitz Beer 6.00
Store, Salt & Pepper, Vess Bottles 7.00
Store, Salt & Pepper, Westinghouse Washer & Dryer 4.50
Store, Sander, Ink, Tin 30.00
Store, Sausage Gun, Wooden Pestle, Tin Casing 12.50
Store, Scoop, Dispensing, Horn 18.00
Store, Scoop, Grain, Tin, Red 10.00
Store, Scoop, Grain, Wooden, Handmade, 15 In. 38.00
Store, Scoop, Grain, Wooden, 16 In. 53.00
Store, Scoop, Ice Ball, Iron, 1893 .... 17.00
Store, Scoop, Ice Cream, Brass, Wooden Handle 12.00
Store, Scoop, Ice Cream, Gilchrist, Mechanical, Brass 12.50
Store, Scoop, Measuring, Planter's Peanuts, Tin 25.00
Store, Scoop, Tin With Wooden Base And Handle 10.00
Store, Scraper, Beer Foam, Rheingold 7.00
Store, Scraper, Ink, Sterling Handle 24.50
Store, Seat, Wagon, Spindle Back 250.00
Store, Shaker, Hemo Malted Milk, 1 Cup 3.50
Store, Shaker, Ovaltine, 7 In. 6.00
Store, Sharpener, Razor Blade, Crank 8.00
Store, Shaver, Ice, Gem, Cast Iron 6.50
Store, Shoe Form, Pine, Metal Sole, C.1890, 6 In. 10.00
Store, Shoe Last, Wooden, 5 In. 7.00
Store, Shoe Shine, 5 Cents 125.00
Store, Shoe Stretcher, Buster Brown With Tige, 8 In. 22.50
Store, Shoe, High Button, Black & White Leather, 6 1/2, Pair 12.00
Store, Shot Glass, Calvert's Reserve Whiskey 4.00
Store, Shot Glass, Cream Of Kentucky Bourbon .... 2.00 To 7.50
Store, Shot Glass, Fulton Whiskey, Etched 8.00
Store, Shot Glass, Greeley Whiskey 5.00
Store, Shot Glass, Hesperita Sub Tropical, 1890, Blown Glass, Etched 6.00
Store, Shot Glass, Hou-Tex Liquors .... 7.50 To 10.00
Store, Shot Glass, Keystone Monogram, Etched 8.00
Store, Shot Glass, L.H.Duker & Brother, Quincy, Ill., Etched Flag 7.00
Store, Shot Glass, Mumm's Extra Rye, Etched 6.00
Store, Shot Glass, Old Homestead Bourbon, Etched 8.00
Store, Shot Glass, Owl Drug Co. 4.00
Store, Shot Glass, Silver Crown Bourbon, Etched 8.00
Store, Shot Glass, Winchester 3.50
Store, Shot Glass, Yellowstone, Etched, Cut Panels At Base 4.50
Store, Showcase, Buxton Leathers, Glass Front, 16 X 15 X 10 In. 35.00
Store, Showcase, Miller Bros.Cutlery, Etched Lettering On Glass, 23 X 12 In. 155.00
Store, Sign, ABCwhiskey, San Francisco, Curled Edge, Stag 65.00
Store, Sign, Aetna Insurance, Porcelain, 20 X 15 In. 35.00
Store, Sign, Anheuser Busch, Doctor And House With Stork Shadow 45.00
Store, Sign, Armour Ham, Tin, 16 X 24 .... *Illus* 140.00
Store, Sign, Ayer's Hair Vigor, 1896, Woman, Blonde Hair, 18 X 13 1/2 In. 75.00
Store, Sign, Baby Ruth, Enameled, 28 X 10 In. 24.00
Store, Sign, Baldwin's Wind & Digestive Pills, C.1890, Paper, 26 X 19 In. 50.00
Store, Sign, Bartel's Brewing, Trademark, Convex, Tin, Round, 18 In. 50.00
Store, Sign, Bass Ale, Milk Glass, Oak Frame, 24 X 18 In. 68.00

Store, Sign, Armour Ham, Tin, 16 X 24

Store, Sign, Beechnut Tobacco, Tin, 22 X 9 1/2 In. 18.00
Store, Sign, Beechnut, C.1920, Cardboard, 30 X 21 In. 50.00
Store, Sign, Beer, Lemp, 1910, 24 In. 300.00
Store, Sign, Best Tonic, Mrs.Grover Cleveland, 22 X 28 In. 45.00
Store, Sign, Betsy Ross Cigar, Pointing Hand, Tin, 2 In. 7.00
Store, Sign, Betsy Ross Cigars, Tin, Self-Framed 275.00
Store, Sign, Big G Gin, Barroom Scene 300.00
Store, Sign, Bloodhound Chewing Tobacco, Tin, Red Dog, Dog Gone Good Chew 65.00
Store, Sign, Boone's Cola, C.1930, Cardboard, 15 X 5 In. 3.00
Store, Sign, Boschee's German Syrup, Green's August Flower, Figure, 32 In. 250.00
Store, Sign, Brass, Lord Calvert Whiskey, 23 In. 125.00
Store, Sign, Brown Shoe Company, 1902, Alice Roosevelt Longworth, 32 In. 135.00
Store, Sign, Buckeye Beer On Draught Here, C.1935, Tin, 12 X 4 In. 4.00
Store, Sign, Bud, Reverse Glass 55.00
Store, Sign, Budweiser, C.1939, Tin, 40 X 18 In. 20.00
Store, Sign, Budweiser, Indians & Stagecoach, Cardboard, 34 X 26 In. 45.00
Store, Sign, Buffalo 1900, Tin, 22 X 28 In. 325.00
Store, Sign, Bull Durham Tobacco, Framed, 22 1/2 X 18 In. 95.00
Store, Sign, Burger Beer, 1940s, Picture Of Lady, Tin, 24 1/2 X 16 In. 65.00
Store, Sign, Burgermeister, King Solomon, Rainbow Trout, Oval, 21 In. 35.00
Store, Sign, Burkhardt Beer, C.1930, Lady, Cardboard, 29 X 27 In. 45.00
Store, Sign, Burma Shave Wooden Roadside, 40 X 17 In., Pair 85.00
Store, Sign, Buster Brown, Buster And Dog, 20 X 30 In. 125.00
Store, Sign, Canadian Club 5 Cent Cigars, Man Smoking, Cardboard, 21 X 13 In. 4.00
Store, Sign, Centlivre Tonic, C.1905, Lithograph, Cardboard, 20 X 12 In. 25.00
Store, Sign, Cetacolor Prevents Wash Goods From Fading, C.1910, Cloth, 36 In. 40.00
Store, Sign, Champagne Velvet Beer, Tin, Men, Women, Cherubs, 24 In. 150.00
Store, Sign, Chang & Eng, Siamese Twins, Brattleboro Fairground, 1866, 10 In. 30.00
Store, Sign, Chippewa Salt, C.1918, Lithograph, Paper, 60 X 24 In. 30.00
Store, Sign, Chippewa Salt, Indian Brave Head, 2 X 5 In. 20.00
Store, Sign, Cigarette, Leaded Glass Window, Multicolor, 27 1/2 X 16 In. 225.00
Store, Sign, Cinco Cigars, Tin, 19 X 9 In. 17.50
Store, Sign, Constellation Collar Velvet, Cardboard, 14 X 16 In. 35.00
Store, Sign, Cream Of Wheat, Edward Brewer, 1914, Framed, 18 1/2 X 15 In. 18.00
Store, Sign, Cream Of Wheat, 1907, Bear, Framed, 8 1/2 X 6 3/4 In. 3.00
Store, Sign, Cunningham Radio Tubes, Tin, Enameled, 5 X 3 In. 6.00
Store, Sign, Daisy Tonic, C.1905, Tin, 9 X 6 In. 12.00
Store, Sign, Dale Bros.Coffee, Monk Drinking From Cup, Fresno, Calif, 1930 .... 67.00
Store, Sign, Dandro Solvent, C.1920, Tin, 13 X 9 In. 15.00
Store, Sign, Davis Carriage, Tin, 7 X 20, Picture Of Carriage 50.00
Store, Sign, DeLaval Cream Separator, Tin, 16 X 12 In. 18.00
Store, Sign, DeLaval Milker, Orange & Black, Tin, 16 X 12 In. 6.00
Store, Sign, DeLaval, Silver, Black, & Red, Tin, Round, 15 In. 12.00
Store, Sign, Delaware Punch, Tin, 23 X 6 In. 12.50
Store, Sign, Delco Battery, Tin, 23 X 17 In. 38.00
Store, Sign, Disco Bros.Pure Teas & Coffees, Victorian Child, Cardboard 23.00
Store, Sign, Dog Display, Wolfschmidt's Vodka 18.00
Store, Sign, Dolly Madison Cigar, C.1910, Tin, 20 X 5 In. 13.00
Store, Sign, Dr.Blumer's Baking Powder, Tin, Blue & White, 24 X 4 In. 22.00
Store, Sign, Dr.Morse's Indian Root Pills, C.1930, Cardboard, 19 X 9 In. 9.00
Store, Sign, Dr.Pepper, Steel, 2 Sided, 23 X 14 In. 20.00
Store, Sign, Drink A Bunch Of Grapes From Welch Juniors, 1931, Tin, 13 In. 25.00
Store, Sign, Drink Braems Bitters, C.1915, Metal, 12 X 6 In. 18.00

Store, Sign, Drink Dr.Pepper, 5 Cents, Good For Life, C.1930, Tin, 24 X 12 In. 25.00
Store, Sign, Drink Fudgy Chocolate Soda, C.1940, Embossed, Tin, 23 X 11 In. 5.00
Store, Sign, Drink Red Rock Cola, 1939, Bottle, Tin, 32 X 8 In. 16.00
Store, Sign, Drink Squeeze, Carbonated Beverage, C.1930, Tin, 28 X 21 In. 30.00
Store, Sign, Drink Ziegler's Beer, Est.1874, Beaver Dam, Wis., Tin, 11 In. 35.00
Store, Sign, Duffy's Malt Whiskey, Man, Tin, 19 1/2 X 5 1/2 In. 35.00
Store, Sign, Dutchess Trousers, 10 Cents A Button, Etc., C.1915, Tin, 24 In. 19.00
Store, Sign, Eat Red Cap, Everybody's Candy Bar, C.1930, Tin, 24 X 10 In. 15.00
Store, Sign, Eddy Brothers, C.1930, Color, 28 X 20 In. 35.00
Store, Sign, Eddy Brothers, Coreill Troupe, C.1930, Color, 42 X 28 In. 45.00
Store, Sign, Egyptian Luxury Cigarettes, Dutch Girl, Frame, 18 X 21 In. 100.00
Store, Sign, Eisemann's Klondike Head Rub, C.1915, Cardboard, 11 X 8 In. 13.00
Store, Sign, El Moriso 5 Cent Cigar, Cardboard, 13 X 10 In. 6.00
Store, Sign, Elk U.S.Cartridges, Cardboard, 14 X 11 In. 55.00
Store, Sign, Enjoy Grapette Soda, C.1949, Tin, 27 X 12 In. 15.00
Store, Sign, Every Day Smoke-Foil, Porcelain On Tin, 15 In. 50.00
Store, Sign, Exit, Green Arrow, Light Up, 12 X 6 In. 15.00
Store, Sign, Fairies Starch, C.1920, Cardboard, 15 X 10 In. 3.00
Store, Sign, Fatima Cigarettes, Framed, 20 X 16 In. 75.00
Store, Sign, Finzer's Old Honesty Cut Plug Tobacco, Cloth, Dog, 50 In. 70.00
Store, Sign, Fire Alarm, Red Paint On Breadboard, 2 Sided, 26 X 18 In. 95.00
Store, Sign, Florsheim Shoe, Leather, Man's, 20 In. 30.00
Store, Sign, Four Roses Whiskey, Tin, Wood Frame, Hunting Scene, 37 X 51 In. 345.00
Store, Sign, Ginita Cigars, C.1910, Lady On Box, Cardboard, 21 X 11 In. 9.00
Store, Sign, Gluck Beer, C.1905, Vitrolite, Corner, 24 X 16 In. 200.00
Store, Sign, Gold Bond Beer, Reverse On Glass, 16 X 8 In. 35.00
Store, Sign, Gold Mine Flour, C.1907, 28 X 10 1/2 In. 4.50
Store, Sign, Gold Mine Flour, Chicago Printing Co., C.1907, Canvas, 12 Ft. 38.00
Store, Sign, Golden Wedding Whiskey, Men At Fireplace, Tin, 20 X 13 In. 50.00
Store, Sign, Good Year Zeppelin, Motorized, Tin, 18 X 10 In. 895.00
Store, Sign, Goodyear Co., Car Dealer Advertisement, 1925, 12 X 15 29.00
Store, Sign, Graphophone Concert, Greatest Since Edison Phonograph, 15 In. 25.00
Store, Sign, Green River Whiskey, Negro & Horse, Tin, Copyright 1899 650.00
Store, Sign, Hamilton Brown Shoe Co., American Lady Of 1904, 24 X 32 In. 48.00
Store, Sign, Hamilton Watch, Little Girl, Tin, 19 X 13 In. 125.00
Store, Sign, Hampden Ale, Handsome Waiter, Tin, 12 In. 115.00
Store, Sign, Harlow & Gable, Movie Poster, C.1934, Cardboard, 26 X 22 In. 60.00
Store, Sign, Harvester Cigars, Lady, Tin, Oval, 13 X 7 In. 10.00
Store, Sign, Heurich Brewery, C.1900, Medals, Convex, Tin, Round, 17 In. 85.00
Store, Sign, Hire's Root Beer, Soda Jerk, Tin, 18 X 9 In. 125.00
Store, Sign, Hopseurber Beer, S.F., Calif., Reverse On Glass, 28 In. 750.00
Store, Sign, Hostetter's Stomach Bitters, Reverse Painting On Glass, 29 In. 250.00
Store, Sign, Howel's Root Beer, Bottle Shape, Tin, Elf, 29 X 9 In. 25.00
Store, Sign, International Stock Food Factory, 1903, Lithograph, 28 X 21 In. 29.00
Store, Sign, Jack Hoxie, C.1930, Color, 28 X 20 In. 35.00
Store, Sign, James Lewis, 5 Cent Cigar, C.1910, Aluminum, 9 X 6 In. 6.00
Store, Sign, Jax Beer, Old Man, Lights Up, 20 In. 45.00
Store, Sign, Join The Red Cross, Lithograph, Foldout, 20 X 15 In. 18.00
Store, Sign, Kay Brothers, C.1930, Color, 28 X 20 In. 35.00
Store, Sign, Keep A Kodak Story Of The Children, C.1918, Sepia, 22 X 21 In. 75.00
Store, Sign, Kessler Whiskey, Horse Racing, Black Frame, 14 1/2 X 11 1/2 In. 22.00
Store, Sign, Kessler's Whiskey, Safe At Home, 1878, Lithograph, 19 X 16 In. 40.00
Store, Sign, Lemp Beer, 21 X 14 In. 65.00
Store, Sign, Liebling Breweries Very Old Rheingold Scotch Ale, Glass, 10 In. 12.00
Store, Sign, Lion Coffee, C.1930, Tin, 28 X 5 In. 12.00
Store, Sign, Lipton's Instant Cocoa, 1915, Tin, 13 X 9 In. 55.00
Store, Sign, Lipton's Tea, C.1915, 2 Sided, Metal, 19 X 9 In. 25.00
Store, Sign, London Assurance Corporation, Porcelain, 18 X 12 In. 50.00
Store, Sign, Longine Watch Co., Simulated Oil Painting, Thomas Sully, Frame 50.00
Store, Sign, Lorelei Beer, Topless Lady 278.00
Store, Sign, Magnolia Gasoline, Ceramic, Round, 24 In. 25.00
Store, Sign, MICA Axle Grease, Wagon Wheel, Tin, 20 X 4 1/2 In. 25.00
Store, Sign, Miller's Beer, Porcelain, Curved, Red & White, 20 X 12 In. 65.00
Store, Sign, Miller's High Life Beer, Wooden, 13 X 10 1/2 In. 16.00
Store, Sign, Miller's High Life, Tin, Girl On Moon 65.00
Store, Sign, Minard's Liniment, Mosquitoes Chasing Children, Cardboard 10.00

Store, Sign, Mogul Cigarettes, Tin, 20 X 24 Oval, Arab Warrior 350.00
Store, Sign, Morning Sip Coffee, 1923, Lithograph, Paper, 21 X 11 In. 7.00
Store, Sign, Moxie, Tin, Embossed, 10 X 2 1/2 In. 20.00
Store, Sign, Moxie, 1926, Man, Cardboard, 17 X 16 In. 95.00
Store, Sign, Moxie, 1926, Woman, Cardboard, 17 X 16 In. 95.00
Store, Sign, Murad Cigarettes, 1905, Paper, Framed, 31 X 24 In. 325.00
Store, Sign, My Elgin's All Right, Wood, Barefoot Boy 328.00
Store, Sign, Napoleon Cigar, 10 Cents, C.1915, Lithograph, Paper, 20 X 10 In. 25.00
Store, Sign, Narragansett Lager, Reverse Under Glass, Gold & Silver Letters 65.00
Store, Sign, Nesbitt's California Orange, Bottle Shape, Tin, 3 1/2 Ft. 25.00
Store, Sign, Oak Motor Oil, Summer & Winter, C.1920, Metal, 2 Sided, 17 In. 12.00
Store, Sign, Observatory Of Illinois Watch Co., Tin, Wooden Frame, 19 1/2 In 95.00
Store, Sign, Old Crow Pale Dry Ginger Ale, Crow Wearing Top Hat, Tin, 13 In. 22.50
Store, Sign, Old Grandad, Tin, Self-Framed 125.00
Store, Sign, Old Nick Candy Bar, Banner, 40 X 28 In. 40.00
Store, Sign, Old Reliable Virginia Minstrels, 46 In. 9.75
Store, Sign, Omar Cigarettes, Well-Dressed Gentlemen, Framed 135.00
Store, Sign, Pal Ade, Tin, 16 X 16 In. 10.00
Store, Sign, Pay Phone, Steel, 12 X 12 In. 12.60
Store, Sign, Pepsi Evervess, 5 Cent Bottle, Celluloid, Round, 9 In. 10.00
Store, Sign, Pepsi, Girl Holding Bottle, Cardboard, 1964, 12 X 20 In. 30.00
Store, Sign, Piedmont Cigarettes, Porcelain, 46 X 30 In. 165.00
Store, Sign, Pioneer Baskets, C.1920, Ladies & Child, Cardboard, 16 X 13 In. 10.00
Store, Sign, Piunus California Wines, Light-Up, 13 X 11 In. 50.00
Store, Sign, Pocket Watch Shape, Cast Iron & Tin, 24 In. 200.00
Store, Sign, Pockrandt's, Akron's Best Paint, C.1930, Tin, 19 X 5 In. 4.00
Store, Sign, Porcelain, Capitol Pale Lager Beer, Dome Of Capitol Bldg. 50.00
Store, Sign, Pratt's Horse Food, C.1890, The Last Alarm, Fire Scene, 26 In. 150.00
Store, Sign, Premier Coffee, C.1915, Cardboard, 18 X 12 In. 10.00
Store, Sign, Premier The Mill Coffee, Wrightsville, Pa., Cardboard, 18 In. 15.00
Store, Sign, Prudential Insurance Co. Of America, Brass, 12 X 15 In. 50.00
Store, Sign, Pur-O-Lator Oil Filter, 32 X 23 In. 15.00
Store, Sign, Railway Express, Porcelain, Blue With Yellow Letters, 10 Ft. 135.00
Store, Sign, Railway Express, Porcelain, 30 In. 70.00
Store, Sign, Raleigh Cigarettes, C.1930, Paper, Framed, 19 X 13 In. 15.00
Store, Sign, Red Dot Cigar, C.1935, Cardboard, 13 X 9 In. 12.00
Store, Sign, Red Dot Cigars, C.1938, Sweater Girl, Cardboard, 18 X 12 In. 4.00
Store, Sign, Red Man The Mild Mellow Chew, Porcelain, 11 X 22 In. 48.00
Store, Sign, Reisch's Beer, Tin, 13 X 6 In. 20.00
Store, Sign, Remington Arms, Hunter Cleaning Rifle, Cardboard, 18 X 25 In. 45.00
Store, Sign, Remington Shotgun Shell, 1920s Man And Lady 95.00
Store, Sign, Rigby's Little 5 Cent Cigars, Cardboard Under Glass, 27 In. 110.00
Store, Sign, Rolling Thunder Medicine & Vaudeville Co., C.1910, Paper, 12 In. 5.00
Store, Sign, Rose Bush For Sale, C.1915, Lithograph, Paper, 9 X 6 In. 2.00
Store, Sign, Round Oak Stoves, Indian Doe Wah Jack, 14 In., Cardboard 15.00
Store, Sign, Royal Baking Powder, C.1923, Lithograph, Paper, 26 X 21 In. 20.00
Store, Sign, Russell Brothers, C.1930, Color, 28 X 20 In. 35.00
Store, Sign, Russell Elephant Acts, C.1930, Color, 28 X 20 In. 45.00
Store, Sign, Schlitz Beer, Electric, 30 X 22 In. 18.00
Store, Sign, Seal Of No.Carolina Tobacco, Grandmother Sewing, Cardboard 35.00
Store, Sign, Seven Up, Tin, 13 X 7 In. 5.00
Store, Sign, Sherbrook Distillery, 1907, 22 X 18 In. 8.00
Store, Sign, Sherbrook Distillery, 1907, 31 X 25 In. 12.00
Store, Sign, Sherwood Coffee, C.1930, Cardboard, 14 X 2 In. 2.50
Store, Sign, Sicks Seattle Malt & Brewing Co., Seattle, Wash., Lighted 65.00
Store, Sign, Sir Walter Raleigh, Tin, Shows Pocket Tin, 26 X 16 .... 25.00
Store, Sign, Sky Chief, Texaco, Porcelain, 18 X 12 In. 10.00
Store, Sign, Slave Market Of America, 1836, Antislavery Society, 30 In. 150.00
Store, Sign, Smiley Serving Soda Out Of A Cooler, Tin, C.1922, 42 X 26 In. 195.00
Store, Sign, Smoke White Label Cigars, C.1910, Embossed, Tin, 13 X 10 In. 20.00
Store, Sign, South Bend Watches, Jacob Fisher, Pa., C.1920, Tin, 28 X 10 In. 20.00
Store, Sign, Southern Select Texas Beer, Tin, 13 X 9 In. 12.50
Store, Sign, Sovereign Cigarettes, 1898, Woman, Paper, Metal Hanger, 24 1/2 In. 65.00
Store, Sign, Spark's Circus, 1919, 46 In. 12.50
Store, Sign, Sprite, Flange To Nail On Wall, Tin, 18 X 16 In. 5.00
Store, Sign, Sprite, Tin, 32 X 11 In. 5.00

Store, Sign, Star Tobacco, Porcelain, 12 X 24 In. 55.00
Store, Sign, Star, Automobile, Porcelain, 3 X 2 Ft. 200.00
Store, Sign, Sun Spot, Drink Real Orange Goodness, C.1940, Cardboard, 18 In. 6.00
Store, Sign, Sweet Peas For Sale, C.1915, Lithograph, Paper, 12 X 9 In. 3.00
Store, Sign, Tam Tam Cigarette Papers, Lithograph Of Arab Hitting Drum 150.00
Store, Sign, Target Tobacco, Man & Pocket Tin, Cloth, 56 X 30 In. 45.00
Store, Sign, Target, The Real Cigarette Tobacco, 1931, Cloth, 63 X 29 In. 25.00
Store, Sign, Target, The Real Cigarette Tobacco, 1931, Paper, 20 X 8 In. 3.00
Store, Sign, Tender-Krust Brand Bread, Metal, Red, Yellow, & Blue, 27 In. 5.00
Store, Sign, Texas Brewing Co., Ft.Worth, Texas, Tin, Oval, 2 1/2 X 2 Ft. 125.00
Store, Sign, This Fan Rented By Keystone Co., C.1940, Porcelain, 9 X 8 In. 6.00
Store, Sign, Toiletine, Die-Cut, Picture Of Hobo, 9 In. 28.00
Store, Sign, Tom Thumb & Wife, Monroe, Mich, 1869, One Day Only, 20 X 6 In. 75.00
Store, Sign, Treaty Bond Whiskey, 1911, Girl, Tin, Round, 14 In. 95.00
Store, Sign, True Fruit, Lady & Cherubs, Tin, 38 X 25 In. 150.00
Store, Sign, Tums For The Tummy, Tin, 9 X 4 In. 7.50
Store, Sign, Turkey Red Cigarettes, Lady In Red, Cardboard, Framed, 20 In. 100.00
Store, Sign, Tuttle's Family Elixir, 1890 65.00
Store, Sign, Tuttle's Family Elixir, 1890, Red, Black, & Flesh, 46 X 30 In. 60.00
Store, Sign, U.S.Cartridge, Tin Over Cardboard, 23 X 6 In. 50.00
Store, Sign, Uncle John's Syrup, C.1920, Lithograph, Cardboard, 18 X 12 In. 4.00
Store, Sign, Uncle Tom's Cabin, Chicago, 28 X 9 1/2 In. 50.00
Store, Sign, Uneeda Graham Crackers, Cardboard, 13 X 11 In. 6.00
Store, Sign, Union Pacific Tea Co., 1898, Hope, Girl With Doves, Framed, 20 In. 125.00
Store, Sign, Velvet Tobacco, C.1935, Cloth, 60 X 30 In. 11.00
Store, Sign, Velvet Tobacco, Picture Of Mel Ott, Cardboard, 21 X 12 In. 15.00
Store, Sign, Velvet Tobacco, Velvet Joe, Tin, Framed, 31 X 25 In. 325.00
Store, Sign, Victor Talking Machine, C.1906, Color, Framed, 14 X 10 In. 25.00
Store, Sign, Virginia Cigarettes, C.1941, Tin, 21 X 13 In. 25.00
Store, Sign, Wallace Brothers, C.1930, Color, 28 X 20 In. 35.00
Store, Sign, Wallace Brothers, C.1930, Color, 42 X 28 In. 45.00
Store, Sign, Walter A.Wood Mowing & Reaping Machine, Cloth, 23 1/2 In. 45.00
Store, Sign, Walter L.Main 3 Ring Circus, C.1930, Paper, 42 X 26 In. 50.00
Store, Sign, Washburn-Crosby's Gold Medal, Canvas, 40 X 28 In. 28.00
Store, Sign, Washburn-Crosby's Gold Medal, 1907, Paper, 25 X 15 In. 15.00
Store, Sign, We Drink 5th Ave. Mocha Java Coffee, 2 Girls, Framed, 11 In. 20.00
Store, Sign, We Give & Redeem Union Stamps, C.1920, Embossed, Tin, 20 X 9 In. 5.00
Store, Sign, We Give & Redeem Union Stamps, C.1920, Tin, 13 X 9 In. 8.00
Store, Sign, Weed Tire Chains, Old Car, Tin, Gas Compugauge, 17 X 23 In. 275.00
Store, Sign, White House Coffee, C.1915, Standup, Cardboard, 14 1/2 In. 35.00
Store, Sign, Wieland Beer, Tin, 13 In.Square 185.00
Store, Sign, Wilken Family Whiskey, Old Man Playing Violin, H.Anderson, 1938 65.00
Store, Sign, Willimantic Spool Cotton, Boy In Navy Suit, Cardboard, 16 In. 70.00
Store, Sign, Winchester, Hunters & Bear, N.Wyeth, Framed, 18 X 15 In. 80.00
Store, Sign, World's Greatest Flyer 5 Cent Cigar, C.1930, Lithograph, 20 In. 3.50
Store, Sign, Yankee Girl Chewing Tobacco, C.1940, Cardboard, 12 X 9 In. 3.00
Store, Signal Box, Morse Code, English, 6 X 4 In. 39.00
Store, Skates, Ice, Handmade Wood, Leather Straps, Pair 200.00
Store, Skates, Ice, Lunenburg County, Nova Scotia, C.1850, Rattail, Pair 35.00
Store, Skates, Winchester, Pair 20.00
Store, Slicer, Meat, Lucey, Hand Crank, 1924 500.00
Store, Soap, Betty Boop, 1931 33.00
Store, Soap, P & G White Laundry Soap, C.1940 2.00
Store, Soda Glass, Bob's Cola, Enameled 4.00
Store, Soda Glass, Howel's Orange Julep, Milk Glass, Metal Top 15.00
Store, Soup Bowl, Heinz, McCoy Pottery, Handled 4.00
Store, Spice Set, Aunt Jemima, Rack, 6 Pieces 20.00
Store, Spindle, Ticket, National, C.1880, Brass 12.95
Store, Spittoon, Pool Hall 8.95
Store, Spoon, A & P, Metal 5.00
Store, Spoon, Demitasse, Baker's Chocolate, Girl 15.00
Store, Spoon, Demitasse, Larkin, Silver Plate 6.50
Store, Spoon, Demitasse, Walter Baker & Co., Figure Of Baker Girl Top 12.50
Store, Spoon, Gerber Baby, Silver Plate 4.00 To 4.50
Store, Spoon, Larkin, Factory To Family, Demitasse 5.00
Store, Spoon, Log Cabin Syrup, C.1904 10.00

Store, Spoon, Log Cabin Syrup, Log Cabin On Handle 12.00
Store, Spoon, Mixing, Kellogg's, Wooden 6.00
Store, Spoon, Mr.Peanut, Planter's Peanuts, Peanut Scoop, Brass 8.00
Store, Spoon, Oh Oh Spaghettios 5.00
Store, Spoon, Old Calumet Indian Chief, Silver Plate 5.00
Store, Spoon, Old Gristmill Wheat Coffee, Demitasse 4.95
Store, Spoon, Rolex Bucheror Watches, Lucerne, Lion With Cross On Bowl 10.00
Store, Spotlight, S.& M. Lamp Co., Los Angeles, Patent 1914, Police Car Type 35.00
Store, Spreader, Peanut Butter, Mr.Peanut, Planter's Peanuts, Plastic .25
Store, Squeezer, Lard, Wooden 10.00
Store, Stapler, Midget, Acme Staple Co., Camden, N.J., Iron & Nickel 12.50
Store, Stein, E.Cahoy Beer, Ceramic, 11 In. 15.00
Store, Stencil, Barres, Brass, Dial Handle, Round, 12 In. 48.00
Store, Stencilling Set, Reese, Adjustable, Brass Letters, Ink, Brushes, Boxed 8.50
Store, Stereoscope, see Stereoscope
Store, Stickpin, Bee Soap, Bee 15.00
Store, Stickpin, Benurs Watch 6.00
Store, Stickpin, Coleman Lantern, Enameled 10.00
Store, Stickpin, Doe-Wah-Jack Stoves, Indian Head 9.00
Store, Stickpin, Dr.Bell's Pine Tar Honey 8.50
Store, Stickpin, Hammer Dry Plate Co. 7.00
Store, Stickpin, International Harvestor 7.00
Store, Stickpin, John Deere 12.00
Store, Stickpin, Lipton's Tea, Tea Leaf Shape 4.00
Store, Stickpin, Mascot Tobacco Bulldog 10.00
Store, Stickpin, Moline Plow Co. 12.00
Store, Stickpin, N.D.Brake, Cartoon Character Holding Brake 12.50
Store, Stickpin, Red Goose Shoes, Boy Riding Goose 12.50
Store, Stickpin, Winchester Shotgun Shell, New Rival, Hunter's Choice 25.00
Store, Stone, Knife Sharpening, Winchester, C.1920, 2 1/4 In. 12.50
Store, Stool, Shoe Salesman's, Oak 65.00
Store, Stopper, Bottle, Moxie, Metal, Embossed 10.00
Store, String Holder, Beehive, Iron 15.00
Store, String Holder, Brass, Art Nouveau 25.00
Store, String Holder, Cat 6.00
Store, String Holder, Cut Glass, Jacobi & Jenkins Makers, Baltimore, 5 In. 125.00
Store, String Holder, Dutchman 8.50
Store, String Holder, Heinz, Holes Around Bottom Of Pickle For Bag Hooks 435.00
Store, String Holder, Lady's Old Fashioned Shoe 8.50
Store, String Holder, Man Wearing Top Hat, 1930 12.00
Store, String Holder, Negro Mammy 12.50
Store, String Holder, Patent July 18, 1899, Ceiling Hanging 12.00
Store, String Holder, Postum, 1910 75.00
Store, String Holder, Shenandoah Valley Apple Candy, Apple Shape, Tin, 5 In. 15.00
Store, String Holder, Wall Type, Fatty Arbuckle 22.50
Store, Strop, Razor, Cowhide, Gold Metal Hanger 7.50
Store, Strop, Razor, Nespa High Class 6.50
Store, Strop, Razor, Twinplex, 1919 6.50
Store, Stuffer, Sausage, Cast Iron, Floor Type, 1858 30.00
Store, Sullivan's 7-20-4 Quality 10 Cent Cigars, C.1915, Porcelain, 23 In. 25.00
Store, Switchboard, Western Electric, School, Oak 375.00
Store, Syrup, ACL, C.1965, Gallon 15.00
Store, Syrup, Aunt Jemima 6.50
Store, Table, Pool, Brunswick, Amaranth, Inlaid Woods 5000.00
Store, Table, Pool, Brunswick, Dragons' Heads, Inlaid Woods, Iron Base, 1875 7000.00
Store, Table, Roulette, Mason & Co., Walnut Pillars, Claw Feet 2000.00
Store, Tankard, E.Porter Brewing Co., Wiener Beer, Brunt Art Ware, 12 1/4 In 110.00
Store, Tap, Narragansett Beer 16.00
Store, Tape Measure, see Sewing Tool, Tape Measure
Store, Teapot, Lipton Tea Company, Citron Yellow 26.00
Store, Teapot, Lipton's Tea, Blue Pottery 7.00
Store, Telegraph Key, Horizontal Action 35.00
Store, Telegraph, Wooden Keyboard, Instruction Book 50.00
Store, Tester, Battery, Davenset, England, Electric 9.50
Store, Thermometer Barometer, 100 Years Of Tootsie Toys, Wood Grained Case 38.00
Store, Thermometer, Amprol, Tin, Round, 10 In. 5.00

Store, Thermometer, Arbuckles Coffee 10.00
Store, Thermometer, Auto-Lite, Tin, 27 In. 7.50
Store, Thermometer, Bowes, Tin, 38 In. 10.00
Store, Thermometer, Chicago Pneumatic Tool Co., Oklahoma City, Desk Type 8.50
Store, Thermometer, Co-Op Black Hawk, Indian's Head, 26 In. 22.00
Store, Thermometer, Delco, Tin, 38 In. 8.00
Store, Thermometer, Dial Figural Indian With Pipe 14.00
Store, Thermometer, Dr.Pepper, Metal, Red & Yellow, 25 In. 10.50
Store, Thermometer, Dr.Pepper, Tin, 27 In. 5.00
Store, Thermometer, Gulf Gasoline 19.50
Store, Thermometer, Hire's Root Beer, Bottle, 30 In. 30.00
Store, Thermometer, Hire's Root Beer, Bottle Shape, 22 In. 22.00
Store, Thermometer, Humidity Guide, Leather Case 8.00
Store, Thermometer, Kentucky Club, Pack Of Tobacco With Horse, 36 X 8 In. 45.00
Store, Thermometer, Kickapoo 10.50
Store, Thermometer, Kingston, N.Y., General Insurance Agency 15.00
Store, Thermometer, Mission, Tin, 17 In. 3.00
Store, Thermometer, Moxie, 25 In. 25.00
Store, Thermometer, Nature's Remedy, 26 X 7 In. 16.00
Store, Thermometer, Orange Crush, Blue, 6 X 16 In. 25.00
Store, Thermometer, Pepsi-Cola 10.50
Store, Thermometer, Pepsi-Cola, Girl Drinking With Straw, C.1930, 17 X 7 In. 65.00
Store, Thermometer, Royal Crown Cola, Tin, 25 In. .... 8.00 To 15.00
Store, Thermometer, Salem, Triangular, Tin 2.50
Store, Thermometer, Sealed Power Piston Ring, Tin, 38 In. 8.00
Store, Thermometer, Winston Cigarettes 10.50
Store, Tie Clasp, Ohio Bell Telephone, Gold, Two 8 Point Diamonds, 1 Ruby 40.00
Store, Till, Mechanical Pub, J.C.Cox, 174 Queen Victoria St., London 265.00
Store, Tin, Astor Tea, Lb. 4.50
Store, Tin, Auto Polish, 1920 Auto With Pixies, Quart 25.00
Store, Tin, Bagley's Old Colony, Silver, Pocket 85.00
Store, Tin, Bagley's Red Belt Tobacco, Pocket .... 14.00 To 20.00
Store, Tin, Banquet Hall Little Cigars, 3 1/2 X 3 1/4 X 1/4 In. 20.00
Store, Tin, Bellwood Tobacco, 4 1/2 X 3 X 1 In. 15.00
Store, Tin, Betsy Ross Tea, 1930, Bank Slot Top, 3 1/2 In. 2.25
Store, Tin, Between The Acts Little Cigars, 3 X 3 X 1/4 In. 6.00
Store, Tin, Bird's-Eye Tobacco, American Eagle Tobacco Co., 4 1/2 In. 40.00
Store, Tin, Blue Boar Rough-Cut Tobacco, Boar Hunt, 2 1/2 In. 7.00
Store, Tin, Bon Ami Powder, 2 1/2 X 1 1/2 In. 12.00
Store, Tin, Bond Street Tobacco, Stamp, Pocket 10.00
Store, Tin, Buckingham Tobacco, Pocket .... 15.00 To 20.00
Store, Tin, Bulldog Tobacco, Dark Blue, Pocket 75.00
Store, Tin, Bunte Marshmallow Tobacco, 4 Ozs. 50.00
Store, Tin, Butternut Coffee, Paper Label, 3 Lbs. 10.00
Store, Tin, Butternut Coffee, 8 In. 4.50
Store, Tin, Cake Boy Mixture Tobacco, 6 1/2 In. 25.00
Store, Tin, Calumet Baking Powder, Lb. 1.35
Store, Tin, Camel Cigarettes, Flat 50 .... 8.00
Store, Tin, Campfire Marshmallows, Round, 5 Lbs. 15.00
Store, Tin, Candy, Whitman 6.00
Store, Tin, Cannon's Irish Sliced Plug Tobacco, Stamp, Pocket 35.00
Store, Tin, Canuck Tobacco, 2 1/2 X 1 1/2 X 4 1/2 In. 12.00
Store, Tin, Carlton Club Tobacco, Pocket 55.00
Store, Tin, Central Union Tobacco, 6 X 4 In. 20.00
Store, Tin, Chase & Sanborn Coffee, Lb. 4.50
Store, Tin, Chase & Sanborn's Half Dollar Mixed Tea, Chinese Mandarin, 5 In. 6.50
Store, Tin, Chesterfield Cigarettes, Flat 50 .... 4.50
Store, Tin, Chichester's English Pennyroyal Pills, 7 X 3 X 3 In. 25.00
Store, Tin, Coach & Four Tobacco, Pocket 30.00
Store, Tin, Commodore Cut Plug Tobacco, Pocket 45.00
Store, Tin, Cracker Jack Co. Marshmallows, 5 Lbs. 12.50
Store, Tin, Culture Tobacco, Pocket 30.00
Store, Tin, Cut Golden Bar, Tobacco, 8 X 3 X 1 In. 10.00
Store, Tin, Dan Patch Cut Plug Tobacco, C.1910, 6 X 3 X 3 In. 15.00
Store, Tin, Dial Tobacco, C.1925, Pocket 2.32
Store, Tin, Dill's Best Tobacco, Free Sample 25.00

Store, Tin, Dill's Best Tobacco, Pocket 10.00
Store, Tin, Dr.M.A.Simmon's Liver Medicine, St.Louis, Square, 2 1/8 In. 25.00
Store, Tin, Droste Cocoa, 1/2 Lb. 5.00
Store, Tin, Dupont Powder, Drum, Dogs, Label, 7 Ozs. 35.00
Store, Tin, E.I.Dupont Smokeless Powder, 4 X 3 1/4 In. 17.50
Store, Tin, Eagle Tobacco, C.1925, Pocket 2.32
Store, Tin, Edgeworth Tobacco, 4 1/4 X 2 In. 1.00
Store, Tin, Educator Crax, Picnic Basket Shape, 12 X 7 X 6 In. 17.00
Store, Tin, Eve Tobacco, Pocket 100.00
Store, Tin, Fairmont 10 Cent Tobacco, Weisert Bros., Pocket 20.00
Store, Tin, Fairy Soda Crackers, Omaha, 48 Ozs. 10.50
Store, Tin, Fataco Oval, Falk Tobacco Co., Pocket 35.00
Store, Tin, Forest & Stream Tobacco, Duck, Pocket .... 45.00 To 85.00
Store, Tin, Four Roses Tobacco, Pocket 25.00
Store, Tin, Free State Menu 35.00
Store, Tin, Full Dress Tobacco, Pocket 75.00
Store, Tin, Glendora Coffee, Sample 18.00
Store, Tin, Gloria Swanson, Round, 4 In. 7.50
Store, Tin, Gold Cross Tobacco, B.Houde Co., Quebec, Canada, 5 X 3 1/2 In. 19.00
Store, Tin, Grain Cut Plug Tobacco, Pocket 38.00
Store, Tin, Guide Tobacco, Pocket 45.00
Store, Tin, Half & Half Tobacco, Pocket .... 2.50 To 4.00
Store, Tin, Half & Half Tobacco, Stamp, Full, Pocket 8.00
Store, Tin, Hershey's Chocolate, Brown & Silver, 12 X 5 In. 18.00
Store, Tin, Huntley & Palmer Biscuits, Lady & Musician, 9 1/2 X 8 3/4 In. 44.00
Store, Tin, Huntley & Palmer Biscuits, Roses & Mums, 9 X 9 X 4 1/2 In. 9.00
Store, Tin, Huntley & Palmer, Books, 7 In. .... *Illus* 148.00
Store, Tin, Huyler's Cocoa, Pod Design, 4 1/2 In. 5.50
Store, Tin, Index Brand Cocoa, Montgomery Ward, 5 Lbs. 30.00
Store, Tin, Ivin's Cookies, Cake, & Crackers, Red Lid, Yellow, 12 In. 12.00
Store, Tin, Kimbo Tobacco, Pocket 45.00
Store, Tin, Kuragon, Cure For Gonorrhea & Gleet, Blue, 6 X 4 In. 6.00
Store, Tin, Lucky Strike Cigarettes, Christmas Holly, Flat 50 .... 4.50
Store, Tin, Lucky Strike Cigarettes, Flat 50 .... 8.00
Store, Tin, Lucky Strike Tobacco, Sample, Pocket 45.00
Store, Tin, Maccoboy Snuff, Octagonal, Lithographed, Negroes, Colonial Pair 265.00
Store, Tin, MacDonald's, Flat 53's 10.00
Store, Tin, Man In Full Dress, Gold, Pocket 75.00
Store, Tin, Manru Coffee, Lb. 7.00
Store, Tin, Maryland Club Tobacco, 4 X 2 1/2 X 1 1/2 In. 15.00
Store, Tin, Maxwell House Tea, Cheekneal, Square, 3 1/2 In. 6.50
Store, Tin, Mayo's Cut Plug Tobacco, Milk Can, Paper Label, Lb. 125.00
Store, Tin, McCormick Teahouse, Orange, 10 In. 8.00
Store, Tin, Monarch Brand Green Tea, Lion, 8 Ozs. 10.00
Store, Tin, Mussgiller Mangel's Ground Mace, Duane St., New York, Designs 28.00
Store, Tin, Nabisco Premium Crackers, Square, 9 X 4 1/2 In. 10.00
Store, Tin, Old Colony Gold Tobacco, Pocket 140.00
Store, Tin, Old Colony Silver Tobacco, Pocket 50.00
Store, Tin, Old Hampshire Sliced Plug Tobacco, Pocket 18.00
Store, Tin, Ox Heart Cocoa, Brown, Apple, 10 Lbs. 32.00
Store, Tin, Oxford Turkish Cigarette, Hinged Lid, 3 X 5 1/2 In. 6.00

Store, Tin, Huntley & Palmer, Books, 7 In.

Store, Tin, Pall Mall Cigarettes, Flat Fifties 9.00
Store, Tin, Palmy Days Tobacco, Pocket 35.00
Store, Tin, Pat Hand Tobacco, Pocket 22.00
Store, Tin, Peachey Tobacco, Pocket 14.00
Store, Tin, Pets Little Cigars, 3 X 3 X 1/4 In. 18.00
Store, Tin, Pipe Major Tobacco, Pocket 85.00
Store, Tin, Planter's Peanuts, Free, 10 Lbs. 35.00
Store, Tin, Planter's Peanuts, Lb. 25.00
Store, Tin, Planter's Peanuts, Pocket 125.00
Store, Tin, Planter's Peanuts, Red, 25 Lbs. 65.00
Store, Tin, Planter's Peanuts, 5 Lbs. 35.00
Store, Tin, Player's Cigarettes, Flat 50 .... 10.00
Store, Tin, Player's Cut Plug Tobacco, Pocket 8.00
Store, Tin, Plow Boy Chewing & Smoking Tobacco, 12 Ozs. 23.00
Store, Tin, Pocket, Union Leader, Uncle Sam 25.00
Store, Tin, Powow Household Cleanser, Indians On Side, 5 In. 1.50
Store, Tin, Prince Albert Tobacco, C.1925, Pocket .... .71
Store, Tin, Pug Climax, Holds 12 Tobacco Packs 45.00
Store, Tin, Puritan Tobacco, Pocket 70.00
Store, Tin, Queed Tobacco, Stamp, Pocket 30.00
Store, Tin, Queen Anne Peanuts, 10 Lbs. 55.00
Store, Tin, Red Jacket Tobacco, Pocket .... 5.00 To 14.00
Store, Tin, Red Tiger Tobacco, 12 In. 55.00
Store, Tin, Revelation Pipe Tobacco, 1 1/4 Ozs. 3.50
Store, Tin, Revelation Tobacco, Pocket .... 6.00 To 28.00
Store, Tin, Rich's Canton Ginger, 4 1/2 X 2 1/2 In. 6.00
Store, Tin, Richelieu Tea, Cone Top, Blue Lable, 8 Ozs. 5.50
Store, Tin, Riley's Toffee, Royal Family On Lid, 5 X 4 In. 18.00
Store, Tin, Roly Poly, Mammy, Dixie Queen .... 250.00 To 350.00
Store, Tin, Roly Poly, Mammy, Mayo 325.00
Store, Tin, Roly Poly, Singing Waiter, Red Indian 375.00
Store, Tin, Roly Poly, Storekeeper, U.S.Marine, 1 Ft. 365.00
Store, Tin, Santa On Cover, Mackintosh, 5 X 3 1/2 In. 9.50
Store, Tin, Sir Walter Raleigh Tobacco, C.1925, Pocket 2.32
Store, Tin, Stag Short, Tobacco, Pocket 30.00
Store, Tin, Stag Tobacco 15.00
Store, Tin, Stag Tobacco, Pocket .... 15.00 To 16.00
Store, Tin, Sterling Tobacco, 9 X 7 In. 29.00
Store, Tin, Sunshine Peanut Butter, 25 Lbs. 15.00
Store, Tin, Surbrug's Grain Tobacco, Pocket 49.00
Store, Tin, Sweet Burley Tobacco, 6 X 3 1/2 In. 12.00
Store, Tin, Sweet Cuba Tobacco, 10 X 8 In. 40.00
Store, Tin, Sweet Cuba Yellow, Store Bin 40.00
Store, Tin, Tea, Oriental Scene And Large Brass Knob 35.00
Store, Tin, Tiger Chewing Tobacco, Pocket 35.00
Store, Tin, Tiger Tobacco, Pocket 35.00
Store, Tin, Tiger, Lorillard Co., Pocket 95.00
Store, Tin, Tip Top Coffee, Lb. 4.50
Store, Tin, Towle's Log Cabin Syrup, Cabin Shape, 6 X 5 X 4 1/2 In. 125.00
Store, Tin, Trout Line Tobacco, Cardboard, Pocket 100.00
Store, Tin, Tuxedo Tobacco, Curved, C.1925, Pocket 5.89
Store, Tin, Tuxedo Tobacco, 1910 Stamp, Concave, Pocket 10.00
Store, Tin, Twin Oaks Tobacco, Pocket 10.00
Store, Tin, Type Major Tobacco, Pocket 65.00
Store, Tin, Uneeda Biscuits, Hinged Lid, Yellow & Brown, 11 1/4 X 8 In. 15.00
Store, Tin, Union Leader Ready-Cut Tobacco, Uncle Sam With Pipe, Pocket 25.00
Store, Tin, Union Leader Tobacco, Pocket .... 2.33 To 4.00
Store, Tin, Union Leader Tobacco, Uncle Sam, Pocket .... 17.00 To 23.00
Store, Tin, Velvet Tobacco, C.1925, Pocket .... .71
Store, Tin, Velvet Tobacco, Pocket .... .73 To 1.90
Store, Tin, Wells Richardson Lactated Food, Square, 5 X 3 1/2 In. 12.00
Store, Tin, White Bear Coffee, Durand & Kasper, Cardboard, Lb. 20.00
Store, Tin, Wiley's D.R. Scalp Treatment, C.1910, 10 X 5 X 4 In. 7.00
Store, Tin, Yale Mixture Tobacco, Ginna & Co., 1 Oz., 3 3/4 X 2 1/2 In. 9.00
Store, Tin, Yale Mixture Tobacco, Marburg Bros., 4 1/2 X 3 1/4 In. 16.00

Store, Tin, Yale Mixture, Somers Bros., 4 1/4 X 3 1/4 X 2 1/4 In. 12.00
Store, Tin, Yankee Boy, Scotten Dillon, Blond Baseball Player, Pocket 75.00
Store, Tin, Yocum Brothers Dollar-Pack Cigars, Pocket 7.50
Store, Tobacco Pack, Big Ben 12.00
Store, Tobacco Pack, Briggs 12.00
Store, Tobacco Pack, Lucky Strike, Small 25.00
Store, Tobacco Pack, Model & Friends, Filled 3.50
Store, Tobacco Pack, Q Boid 20.00
Store, Toilet Paper Holder, Scott Paper Co., 1931, Cast Iron, Nickel Plated 7.50
Store, Token, Green River, Silver-Dollar Size 3.00
Store, Token, Sunshine Dairies, Macon, Ga., Good For One Quart Milk 5.00
Store, Top, Moxie, Man On Horse & Early Auto, Drink Moxie, Tin, 1 1/2 In. 45.00
Store, Tray, American Art Works, Girl, Round, 19 In. 85.00
Store, Tray, American Brewing Co., St.Louis, ABC Beers, C.1905, Eagle, Flag 145.00
Store, Tray, Bartel's Viking Beer 75.00
Store, Tray, Bartholomay Beer, Lady On Wheel With Wings 125.00
Store, Tray, Beer, Hamm's 10.00
Store, Tray, Bevo Beer, Beer Wagon 65.00
Store, Tray, Bottles Crown Beer, Nightwatchman, Pre-Prohibition 100.00
Store, Tray, Brass & Porcelain, Golden Anniversary Lionel Train, 1900-1950 .... 15.00
Store, Tray, Budweiser Beer, St.Louis Levee 60.00
Store, Tray, Budweiser, Red-Coated Men Drinking Bud, Dog Sees Shadow 35.00
Store, Tray, Canadian Ace Beer 11.00
Store, Tray, Carta Blanca Beer, Picture Of Couple Dining 65.00
Store, Tray, Change, Pippins Cigar, Apple Shape 25.00
Store, Tray, Cherry Sparkle, Northwestern Extract Co., Milwaukee 50.00
Store, Tray, Clarke's Teaberry, Amber 22.00
Store, Tray, Clarke's Teaberry, Black Amethyst 35.00
Store, Tray, Columbia Brewing Co., C.1910, Eagle, Liberty Figure 75.00
Store, Tray, Coors Mountain 75.00
Store, Tray, Dobler Brewing Co., Beautiful Girl, American Can Co. 32.00
Store, Tray, Duluth & Iron Range, Black Amethyst & Porcelain, 9 X 7 In. 45.00
Store, Tray, Faerber Footwear, Cleveland, Pre-1901, 14 X 17 In. 65.00
Store, Tray, Fairy Soap 35.00
Store, Tray, Falstaff Beer, Maid, 24 In. 150.00
Store, Tray, Farmers Merchants State Bank, Concordia, Kansas, Tin, 16 In. 15.00
Store, Tray, Finke Uhen Brewing Co., Burlington, Wisc., 1901, Rose Decoration 75.00
Store, Tray, Fredericksburg, Heine Beer 60.00
Store, Tray, Fredericksburg, San Jose, Heine 60.00
Store, Tray, Genessee Beer, Ask For Jenny 25.00
Store, Tray, Genessee Beer, 1-8 Around Face, Red, White, & Black, 12 In. 5.00
Store, Tray, Goetz Brewing, St.Joseph & Kansas City, Mo., Beer, Pony Express 37.50
Store, Tray, Golden West Beer Factory 35.00
Store, Tray, H.L.Newman's Ice Cream, Dark-Haired Woman, 16 X 12 In. 75.00
Store, Tray, H.L.Newman's Ice Cream, Dish Of Ice Cream & Flowers, 13 In. 35.00
Store, Tray, Hampden Ale And Beer, Silver, Red Lettering, Beer Barrel 10.00
Store, Tray, Hampden Mild Ale, Green & Gold, Man Playing Accordion 25.00
Store, Tray, Hampden Mild Ale, Red With Waiter Carrying Tray 21.00
Store, Tray, Hanley's, Porcelain 85.00
Store, Tray, Hire's Root Beer, Boy With Mug, 12 In. 85.00
Store, Tray, Johnnie Walker, Copper, Embossed, Oval, 14 In. 75.00
Store, Tray, Krueger Beer, Bell Boy 20.00
Store, Tray, Labatts, Porcelain 75.00
Store, Tray, Lang Brewery, Round, Bands Of Green, Gold, Maroon, Red Logo 15.00
Store, Tray, Lily Beer, Rock Island Brewing Co., Bottle & Sandwich Picture 30.00
Store, Tray, Medaglia D'Oro Coffee, Lady Drinking Coffee 35.00
Store, Tray, Miller's Beer, Woman Sitting On Half Moon, Round 29.00
Store, Tray, Myers & Co., Pure Fulton Whiskey, Covington, Ky., Metal, 10 In. 20.00
Store, Tray, Nectar Beer, Ambrosia Brewing Co., Monks At Table, Round, 13 In. 55.00
Store, Tray, Neuweillers, Beer, Old Man 25.00
Store, Tray, Olympia, Beer, Waterfall 25.00
Store, Tray, Par-Ex-Prohibition Near Beer, Auburn-Haired Lady, 12 In.Round 55.00
Store, Tray, Pepsi-Cola, People On Beach, 12 3/4 In. 15.00
Store, Tray, Pickwick Beer, Factory & Horses Pulling Wagon 65.00
Store, Tray, Piels Beer, Round, Elf Carrying Beer 15.00

Store, Tray, Pin, Aluminum, Majestic Range Co., St.Louis, Mo. 12.00
Store, Tray, President Suspenders, Tin, Lovely Lady Picture, 6 In. 50.00
Store, Tray, Printer's Type, 23 1/2 X 19 1/2 In. 12.00
Store, Tray, Schmidt Beer 10.00
Store, Tray, Serving, Louisville Refining Co., 1920 .... 22.00
Store, Tray, Southern Dairies Ice Cream 10.00
Store, Tray, Star Brewery, Vancouver, Washington, Shows Factory 75.00
Store, Tray, Tin, Oblong, Nu Grape 25.00
Store, Tray, Tip Cuticura, Glass 20.00
Store, Tray, Tip, A.Cook Furniture, Lady, Estelle 18.00
Store, Tray, Tip, American Co., Exhibition, Jefferson & Napoleon 25.00
Store, Tray, Tip, Angus Whiskey 12.50
Store, Tray, Tip, Buffalo Brew 65.00
Store, Tray, Tip, Buffalo Times, 1907, Girl 40.00
Store, Tray, Tip, Century Beer, Trinidad, Colorado, Old Couple 100.00
Store, Tray, Tip, Clysmic 85.00
Store, Tray, Tip, Coshocton Hardware Co., 1906, Roosevelt Bears 45.00
Store, Tray, Tip, Cottolene Shortening, Negro Woman & Child In Cotton Field 30.00
Store, Tray, Tip, Dowagiac Grain Mills, Grain 20.00
Store, Tray, Tip, Dubbleware, Racehorses 25.00
Store, Tray, Tip, El Verso Cigars 13.00
Store, Tray, Tip, Fairy Soap .... 30.00 To 35.00
Store, Tray, Tip, Forman Black Label Whiskey, Brown, A Friendly Tip 4.50
Store, Tray, Tip, Frost Fence, Cleveland, 3 White Horse Heads 17.00
Store, Tray, Tip, Hamm's Beer 4.00
Store, Tray, Tip, Hampden, Handsome Waiter 29.00
Store, Tray, Tip, Heating-Hurst Bros.Co., Plumbing, Beautiful Girl 28.00
Store, Tray, Tip, High Liver's Liver, Red Raven With Bottle 35.00
Store, Tray, Tip, Hyroller Whiskey, Pittsburgh, 1910, Dude In Tuxedo 12.00
Store, Tray, Tip, Hyroller Whiskey, Shank Lithographing, Chicago, C.1900 .... 25.00
Store, Tray, Tip, Indianapolis Brewing, Bottle 50.00
Store, Tray, Tip, Iroquois Indian Head 40.00
Store, Tray, Tip, Jacob Kohl's Sons, Deutsche Kuche & Saloon, Syracuse, N.Y. 28.00
Store, Tray, Tip, John Ogden Fire Insurance, Picture Of Stag 35.00
Store, Tray, Tip, King's Pure Malt, Nurse 35.00
Store, Tray, Tip, King's Pure Malt, Waitress, Pan Pacific Exposition, 1915 .... 35.00
Store, Tray, Tip, Liberty Beer, Indian 55.00
Store, Tray, Tip, Ludwick Pianos, 1907, Woman 35.00
Store, Tray, Tip, Marilyn Monroe, 1953, Nude, Tin, Round, 4 In. 15.00
Store, Tray, Tip, Miller's High Life Beer, 1952 .... 2.50
Store, Tray, Tip, Mr.Peanut Postcard, Planter's Peanuts, Tin 12.00
Store, Tray, Tip, Oertel Brewery, Lady With Dove 75.00
Store, Tray, Tip, Ogden Fire Insurance, Stag 35.00
Store, Tray, Tip, Old Globe, Wernicke, Turpin Furniture Co., Household Goods 20.00
Store, Tray, Tip, Prudential 12.00
Store, Tray, Tip, Rockford Watches, Woman 17.50
Store, Tray, Tip, Ruhstaller's Gilt Edge Lager Beer, Sacramento, Calif. 70.00
Store, Tray, Tip, Ryan's Pure Beers, 1907, Brewery Bottling, Syracuse, N.Y. 35.00
Store, Tray, Tip, S & H Green Stamps, Woman 40.00
Store, Tray, Tip, Sears, Roebuck, Factory 35.00
Store, Tray, Tip, Stegmaier Brewing Co., Factory 40.00
Store, Tray, Tip, Welsbach Lighting, Mother & Child 45.00
Store, Tray, Tip, Wernicke Sectional Bookcased, Globe 15.00
Store, Tray, Tip, White Rock Spring Water, Seminude Woman 75.00
Store, Tray, Tip, White Rock, Psyche 35.00
Store, Tray, Valley Forge Beer, Waitress Carrying Tray With Beer 32.00
Store, Tray, Weinhardt Bottles & Food 40.00
Store, Tray, West End Brewing, Dogs Smoking And Drinking, 1910 .... 85.00
Store, Tray, Wielands, San Francisco, Lady Reading Note 125.00
Store, Tray, Yellowstone Whiskey, Waterfall & Bottle Of Yellowstone 45.00
Store, Tumbler, Calvert's Whiskey 1.00
Store, Tumbler, Dr.T.W.Graydon 5.00
Store, Tumbler, Iroquois Brewing Co., Indian's Head 8.50
Store, Tumbler, M.A.Winter Nature's Health Restorer 5.00
Store, Tumbler, Medicine, Trenton, N.J., Drugstore 10.00
Store, Tumbler, Moxie, Etched, Syrup Line 12.50

Store, Tumbler, Moxie, Orange Band, Flared Top 10.00
Store, Tumbler, Todd's Tonic, Etched 9.00
Store, Tumbler, Uneeda Milk Biscuit, Chocolate Glass 175.00
Store, Tumbler, Use Whiteriver Flower, Clear 15.00
Store, Undertaker's Figure, St. Louis, Mo., Wreath And Angel Figure 55.00
Store, Vibrator, Hamilton Beach, Patent 1902 37.00
Store, Waffle-Maker, Buster Brown, Cast Iron, Dated 1906 45.00
Store, Walking Stick, Duquesne 15.00
Store, Watch Fob, Belmont Packing Co., Eagle On World 28.00
Store, Watch Fob, Carhartt Overalls, 3 Piece, Trolly Car 30.00
Store, Watch Fob, Walter A.Wood Harvesting Machines, Horse Drawn Harvester 27.50
Store, Watch, Ingraham Type, Pin, S & H Co., 50th Anniversary 15.00
Store, Watch, Mr.Peanut, Planter's Peanuts, Digital, Wrist 16.00
Store, Whistle, Mr.Peanut, Planter's Peanuts, Plastic .35
Store, Whistle, Oscar Mayer 4.00
Store, Writer, Cheque, Mechanical 12.00

Stove, see Fire, Stove
Strawberry, see Soft Paste

Stretch Glass, Bowl, Blue Iridescent, 11 X 4 In. 24.00
Stretch Glass, Bowl, Blue, Gold-Trimmed Border, 12 1/2 In. 45.00
Stretch Glass, Bowl, Blue, 8 In. 25.00
Stretch Glass, Bowl, Marigold, Flared, Footed, 9 1/4 In 20.00
Stretch Glass, Bowl, Sapphire Blue, 5 X 10 1/2 In. 45.00
Stretch Glass, Bowl, Sapphire Blue, 10 X 2 In. 45.00
Stretch Glass, Bowl, Sapphire Blue, 10 X 2 In. 24.50
Stretch Glass, Bowl, Vaseline Color, Footed, Iridescent, 10 X 5 In. 70.00
Stretch Glass, Bowl, White, 8 In. 20.00
Stretch Glass, Bowl, Yellow Iridescent, 10 In. 36.00
Stretch Glass, Candlestick, Blue, Hollow, 9 3/4 In., Pair 35.00
Stretch Glass, Candlestick, Green, Pink Dolphin, Octagon, Base, 2 1/2 In., Pair 24.00
Stretch Glass, Compote, Bronze, Paneled, Scalloped Rim, 4 3/4 In. 28.50
Stretch Glass, Compote, Green, Footed, Covered 32.50
Stretch Glass, Compote, White, 10 In. 22.50
Stretch Glass, Compote, Yellow Ribbed, Pink Iridescent 15.00
Stretch Glass, Console Set, White, 3 Piece 22.50
Stretch Glass, Hat 20.00
Stretch Glass, Plate, Green Iridescent, 8 1/2 In. 9.00
Stretch Glass, Plate, Lemon Yellow, 8 3/4 In. 8.50
Stretch Glass, Plate, Rainbow Iridescent, 8 In. 5.00
Stretch Glass, Plate, Serving, Compote Center Insert, 10 In. 25.00
Stretch Glass, Plate, Vaseline, Iridescent, 12 In. 12.00
Stretch Glass, Plate, White Iridescent, Wide Panels, 8 1/2 In. 15.00
Stretch Glass, Plates, Octagonal, Blue, Ground Base Rims, Set Of 6 52.00
Stretch Glass, Server, Vaseline, Center Handle, 10 1/2 In. 25.00
Stretch Glass, Tray, Electric Blue, Center Handle, 10 1/2 In. 24.00

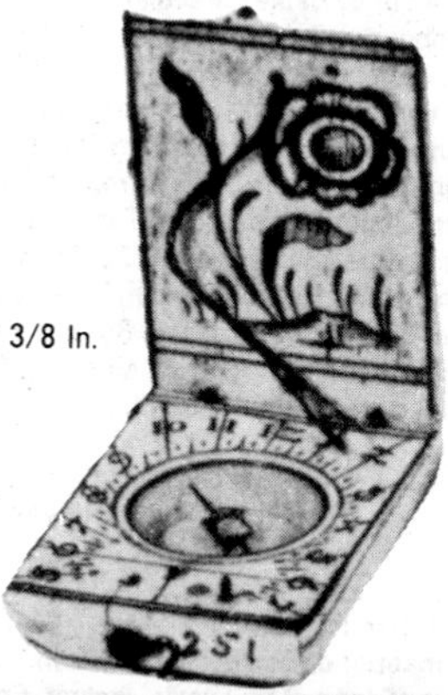

Sundial, Ivory Pocket Compass, 1 3/4 X 1 3/8 In.
(See Page 649)

Stretch Glass, Vase, Blue, Czechoslovakia, 10 In. 65.00
Stretch Glass, Vase, Fan, Pink Dolphin, Handled, 5 In. 125.00
Stretch Glass, Vase, Vaseline, Fan, 8 1/2 In. 25.00

Sunbonnet Babies were first introduced in 1902 in the Sunbonnet Babies Primer. The stories were by Eulalie Osgood Grover, illustrated by Bertha Corbett. The children's faces were completely hidden by the sunbonnets, and had been pictured in black and white before this time. The color pictures in the book were immediately successful. The Royal Bayreuth China Company made a full line of children's dishes decorated with the Sunbonnet Babies.

Sunbonnet Babies, Bell, Washing, Royal Bayreuth 125.00
Sunbonnet Babies, Book, Days Of The Week 35.00
Sunbonnet Babies, Book, Days Of The Week, Ullman, Red Line Series 65.00
Sunbonnet Babies, Book, Eulalie Osgood Grover, Ill., Corbett, 1902 .... 38.00
Sunbonnet Babies, Book, In Mother Goose Land, Grover, 1927, McNally 40.00
Sunbonnet Babies, Book, Overall Boys, Eulaie Osgood Grover 12.50
Sunbonnet Babies, Book, Songs, Grover, 1905 .... 32.50
Sunbonnet Babies, Book, Sunbonnet Babies In Holland 50.00
Sunbonnet Babies, Book, Sunbonnet Primer 52.00
Sunbonnet Babies, Book, Sunbonnet Twins 55.00
Sunbonnet Babies, Box Ok, At Work & Play, J.I.Austen Co., Chicago, 1906 .... 75.00
Sunbonnet Babies, Box, Holly Covered, Autumn & Winter Cards On Lid 21.00
Sunbonnet Babies, Box, Patch Covered, Sewing, Unsigned, 1 3/4 X 2 1/2 In. 135.00
Sunbonnet Babies, Box, Trinket, Washing, Heart Shape, Blue Mark 160.00
Sunbonnet Babies, Creamer, Mending, Royal Bayreuth 115.00
Sunbonnet Babies, Cup & Saucer, Royal Bayreuth, Blue Mark 170.00
Sunbonnet Babies, Cup, Babies At Tea Table, Reading & Knitting, Germany 21.50
Sunbonnet Babies, Dish, Baby, Sunbonnet Girl With Doll, Boy With Puppy 28.00
Sunbonnet Babies, Dish, Baby's Feeding, 3 Babies, Cream & Red, 7 1/2 In. 45.00
Sunbonnet Babies, Dish, Bonbon, Blue Babies Fishing, Royal Bayreuth 185.00
Sunbonnet Babies, Doorstop, Iron, 6 1/4 In. 11.95
Sunbonnet Babies, Mug, French Porcelain 40.00
Sunbonnet Babies, Napkin Ring, Metal, Embossed 30.00
Sunbonnet Babies, Paperweight, Sunbonnet Girl Kissing Boy, Iron, 3 In. 48.00
Sunbonnet Babies, Picture, March, Signed Ullman Mfg. Co., 1906 .... 25.00
Sunbonnet Babies, Pitcher, Fishing, Royal Bayreuth, 4 1/2 In. 135.00
Sunbonnet Babies, Pitcher, Royal Bayreuth, Blue Mark, 4 In. 125.00
Sunbonnet Babies, Plate, Ironing, 2 Handles, Royal Bayreuth, 10 In. 175.00
Sunbonnet Babies, Plate, Mending, Royal Bayreuth, 6 In. 70.00
Sunbonnet Babies, Plate, Royal Bayreuth, 7 3/4 In. 105.00
Sunbonnet Babies, Postcard, Days Of The Week, Robins, 1907, Set Of 7 .... 75.00
Sunbonnet Babies, Postcard, Days Of The Week, Ullman, 1905, Set Of 7 .... 75.00
Sunbonnet Babies, Postcard, Home Sweet Home, 6 P.M., Ullman 6.50
Sunbonnet Babies, Postcard, Ironing Day, Corbett 12.00
Sunbonnet Babies, Postcard, Last Day Of Summer 9.00
Sunbonnet Babies, Postcard, Lovers, Austin 10.00
Sunbonnet Babies, Postcard, Milking Time, 6 A.M. 14.00
Sunbonnet Babies, Postcard, Peek A Boo, 1905 .... 10.00
Sunbonnet Babies, Postcard, Saying Grace 10.00
Sunbonnet Babies, Postcard, Wednesday Morn, Ullman Mfg.Co. 9.50
Sunbonnet Babies, Postcard, Wednesday, Robbins 12.00
Sunbonnet Babies, Quilt Top, Embroidered & Appliqued, 98 X 81 In. 65.00
Sunbonnet Babies, Quilt, 72 Patchwork Applies Babies, 62 X 90 In. 200.00
Sunbonnet Babies, Saucer, Wash Day, Royal Bayreuth 15.00
Sunbonnet Babies, Shoe, Royal Bayreuth 150.00
Sunbonnet Babies, Tray, Mending, Diamond Shape, Blue Mark, 5 3/4 In. 145.00
Sunbonnet Baby, Doorstop, Iron, 6 1/4 In. 12.00

Sunderland luster is a name given to a characteristic pink luster made by Leeds, Newcastle, and other English firms during the nineteenth century. The luster glaze is metallic and glossy and sometimes appears to have bubbles as a decoration.

Sunderland, Bowl, Pink Luster, Leaf Decoration, Belltone, Shallow, 8 1/2 In. 22.50
Sunderland, Bowl, Pink, 5 1/2 In. 8.00
Sunderland, Box, Luster, Copper, Comic Black Transfers, 5 X 3 1/4 X 2 3/4 In. 85.00

Sunderland, Creamer, Pink 47.50
Sunderland, Cup & Saucer, House 68.00
Sunderland, Cup & Saucer, Schoolhouse 68.00
Sunderland, Cup & Saucer, Strawberry, Wishbone Handle, Berry In Cup, C.1790 .... 50.00
Sunderland, Cup & Saucer, Strawberry, Wishbone Handle, C.1790 .... 60.00
Sunderland, Cup, Handleless, Schoolhouse 38.00
Sunderland, Figurine, Mr.Micawber, Lancaster, 6 1/2 In. 15.00
Sunderland, Figurine, Pecksniff, Lancaster, 6 1/2 In. 15.00
Sunderland, Jug, Cider, Masonic 275.00
Sunderland, Jug, Pink Luster, Sailor's Farewell, Early 1800s, 7 1/2 In. 289.00
Sunderland, Jug, Sailor's Farewell Mariner's Arms, 2 Quart 325.00
Sunderland, Lazy Susan, Cone-Shaped Base, 3-Compartment Tray 100.00
Sunderland, Mug, Frog, Mariner's Compass, Black Transfer, C.1820, 5 In. 250.00
Sunderland, Mustard Pot, Copper Luster Interior & Trim, 2 7/8 In. 68.00
Sunderland, Plaque, Gold Panning In California, Pink, C.1850, 8 1/2 In. 150.00
Sunderland, Plaque, La Bretagne, 140 Guns, Pierced For Hanging, 9 X 8 In. 65.00
Sunderland, Plaque, Wall, Adam Clarke, 8 3/4 In. 75.00
Sunderland, Plate, Strawberry, 7 In. 100.00
Sunderland, Plate, Strawberry, 8 In. 135.00
Sunderland, Sugar, Strawberry 150.00
Sunderland, Waste Bowl, Strawberry 150.00
Sundial, Brass, Circular, Compass, 4 In., C.1700 .... *Illus* 100.00
Sundial, Brass, Double Folding, London, 6 In.Diameter .... *Illus* 1300.00
Sundial, Brass, Equatorial, Portable .... *Illus* 1100.00
Sundial, Brass, Peephole, 2 1/8 In.Diameter .... *Illus* 450.00
Sundial, Brass, Shepherd's, 3 1/4 In.Length, 1 In.Diameter .... *Illus* 1300.00
Sundial, Brass, 4 1/2 In.Square, 1799 .... *Illus* 750.00
Sundial, Equatorial, Mahogany Case, 4 1/2 In. Square .... *Illus* 400.00
Sundial, Ivory Pocket Compass, 1 3/4 In.X 1 3/8 In. .... *Illus* 450.00
Superman, Doll, Cloth 7.00
Superman, Figurine, Chalkware, 12 In. 20.00
Superman, Ring, Crusader 25.00
Superman, Toy, Flipover Tank 150.00
Swansea, Figurine, Peggy, Little Girl Holding Flowers, 4 In. 50.00
Swastika Keramos, Vase, Gray, Gold Designs, 9 In. 75.00
Sword, see Weapon, Sword

Sundial, Brass, Peephole, 2 1/8 In.Diameter

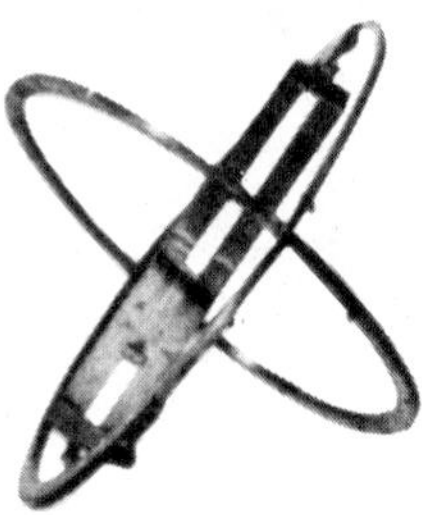

Sundial, Brass, Double Folding, London, 6 In.Diameter

Sundial, Brass, Circular, Compass, 4 In., C.1700

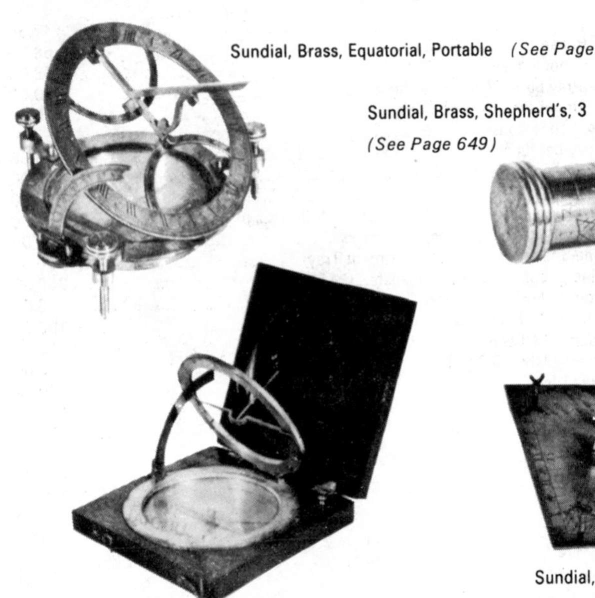

Sundial, Brass, Equatorial, Portable *(See Page 649)*

Sundial, Brass, Shepherd's, 3 1/4 In.Length, 1 In.Diameter *(See Page 649)*

Sundial, Brass, 4 1/2 In.Square, 1799 *(See Page 649)*

Sundial, Equatorial, Mahogany Case, 4 1/2 In. Square *(See Page 649)*

Syracuse, Soup Bowl & Underplate, White, Floral Border, Handled 40.00
Syracuse, Tea Set, Romance, 24 Piece 160.00
Syracuse, Toby Mug, Al Smith, 7 In. 75.00
Syracuse, Toby Mug, Herbert Hoover, Seated, 7 In. 70.00
Taffeta Glass, see Carnival Glass
Tapestry, Porcelain, see Rose Tapestry
Tarzan, Book, Beasts Of Tarzan, Big Little Book 10.00
Tarzan, Book, Beasts Of Tarzan, 1916, A.L.Burt Co. 4.00
Tarzan, Book, Edgar Rice Burroughs, Ace Paperback, 6 1/2 In. 1.00
Tarzan, Book, Jungle Tales, Burroughs, 1919, 1st Edition 9.50
Tarzan, Book, Lord Of The Jungle, Grosset & Dunlap, 1928 .... 10.00
Tarzan, Book, New Adventures Of Tarzan, Better Little Book 4.00
Tarzan, Book, Return Of Tarzan, 1915 .... 10.00
Tarzan, Book, Tarzan & The Ant Men, 1924 .... 8.50
Tarzan, Book, Tarzan The Untamed, 1921 .... 5.00
Tea Caddy, see Furniture, Tea Caddy
Tea Leaf, see Ironstone, Tea Leaf

TECO

Teco pottery is the art pottery line made by the Terra Cotta Tile Works of Terra Cotta, Illinois. The company was founded by William D.Gates in 1881. The Teco line was first made in 1902 and continued into the 1920s. It included over 500 designs, made in a variety of colors and glazes.

Teco, Ewer, Squat, 6 In. 48.00
Teco, Vase, Heavy, Blue, Impressed, 7 In. 55.00
Teco, Vase, Matte Green, Flared Top, 13 In. 48.00
Teco, Vase, Matte Green, 6 In. 45.00
Telephone, Candlestick, Stromburg, Nickel-Plated Brass 125.00
Telephone, Central Telephone Co., St.Louis, Wall, Oak, Crank, Bells 225.00
Telephone, Century, Oak, 22 1/2 In. 110.00
Telephone, Chicago Telephone Supply Co., Elkhart, Ind., Oak Case 225.00
Telephone, Dean Electric, Candlestick 50.00
Telephone, Kellogg, Beveled Glass Top, Wall 175.00

Telephone, Kellogg, Wall 110.00
Telephone, Kellogg, 1930, Cradle, Felt Base 5.55
Telephone, Lineman's Monitor 21.00
Telephone, Monarch, Wall, Walnut, Crank 115.00
Telephone, Monophone, Deck 5.00
Telephone, Oak, Stromberg Carlson 125.00
Telephone, Stromberg Carlson, Wall 158.00
Telephone, Stromberg, Candlestick, Nickel-Plated Brass, Oak Box 125.00
Telephone, Wall, Oak Case, Bell Crank, 8 3/4 X 19 In. 125.00
Telephone, Wall, Oak, C.1920 100.00
Telephone, Western Electric, French Style, Oak Wall Case, Crank Bells 22.00
Telephone, Western Electric, 1913, Candlestick 65.00

Teplitz refers to art pottery manufactured by a number of companies in the Teplitz-Turn area of Bohemia during the late nineteenth and early twentieth centuries. The Amphora Porcelain Works and the Alexandra Works were two of these companies.

Teplitz, Basket, Art Deco, 10 1/2 In. 45.00
Teplitz, Basket, Green, Cavalier & Lady In Colors In Base 25.00
Teplitz, Bowl, Amphora, Lily Pad, Blue, Green, & Gold, Stellmacher, 17 In. 645.00
Teplitz, Bowl, Rose, Wide Mouth, Scalloped Top, Ivory, Hand-Painted 58.00
Teplitz, Bust, Woman, Signed, 8 1/2 In. 111.00
Teplitz, Creamer, Child's, Little Girl With Baby Chick, Enameled 30.00
Teplitz, Ewer, Amphora, Orange & Black Mosaic, 9 X 4 In. 110.00
Teplitz, Ewer, Amphora, Orange & Black, Vignette Front & Back, 8 In. 69.00
Teplitz, Ewer, Cream Color, Purple Irises, 8 Footed, 11 1/2 In. 95.00
Teplitz, Ewer, Cream With Violets, 10 1/2 In. 60.00
Teplitz, Figurine, Gentleman With Guitar, Lady With Mandolin, 29 In., Pair 550.00
Teplitz, Hatpin Holder, Roses 24.50
Teplitz, Jardiniere, Amphora, Mottled Beige, Flying Birds, Cobalt Handles 55.00
Teplitz, Pitcher, Boy 49.00
Teplitz, Pitcher, Ivory With Blue And Orange Pansy, Gold Top And Handle 48.00
Teplitz, Vase With Handles, 8 1/2 In., Drip Glaze, Cavalier On Chair 95.00
Teplitz, Vase, Amphora, Dark Green, Gold Veins, 10 Applied Jewels, 8 In. 125.00
Teplitz, Vase, Amphora, Enamel Berries & Leaves, 4 Handles, 5 In. 67.00
Teplitz, Vase, Amphora, Gourd Shape, Poppies, Red RSK Mark, 9 1/2 In. 72.00
Teplitz, Vase, Amphora, Nude Maiden & Tree, Austrian, 10 1/2 In. 185.00
Teplitz, Vase, Amphora, Orange Poppies, Blue Trees, Red Mark, Impressed, 9 In. 78.00
Teplitz, Vase, Amphora, Purple, Tan, & Gold, Dragon Around Body, 13 1/4 In. 115.00
Teplitz, Vase, Amphora, Red RSK Mark, Gold-Encrusted Roses, 9 In. 50.00
Teplitz, Vase, Applied Gold Spiderwebs, Stones, Butterflies, Austria 95.00
Teplitz, Vase, Child's Face In Oval Medallion, Blue & Gold, 13 1/2 In. 100.00
Teplitz, Vase, Ewer, Floral, 7 1/2 In. 67.50
Teplitz, Vase, Girl Chasing Dog 49.00
Teplitz, Vase, Gold Handles, Satin Finish, Bird On Branch, 12 In. 85.00
Teplitz, Vase, Green, Roses, Bottom Handles, 8 1/2 In. 35.00
Teplitz, Vase, Hand-Painted Flowers On Blue, Signed, Bohemia, R.St.K 55.00
Teplitz, Vase, Hand-Painted, Cream Ground, Flowers, Ornate Gold Handles, 7 In. 65.00
Terra-Cotta, Box, Square, Round Corners, Sunburst Top, Ww Mie, Bloomingdale's 145.00
Terra-Cotta, Figurine, Bodhevista, Gold Leaf, Red Enamel, C.1720, 14 In. 200.00
Terra-Cotta, Figurine, Horse & Rider, Green & Mustard, Chinese, 18 In. 225.00
Terra-Cotta, Group, Madonna & Child, Standing, Italy, Gold Leaf, 19 1/2 In. 25.00
Terra-Cotta, Plaque, Village Scene, Framed, 2 1/2 X 4 1/2 In. 20.00
Terra-Cotta, Urn, Female & Male Cameos, Smith & Sons, C.1840, 10 In., Pair 58.00
Terra-Cotta, Vase, Car, Cone Shape, Enameled Dragon & Flowers 45.00
Terra-Cotta, Vase, Embossed Gold Dragons, 6 In. 12.50

Textile includes all types of table linens and household linens such as coverlets, quilts, fabrics, etc.

Textile, see also World's Fair items

Textile, Banner, New York Bicentennial, 1686-1886, 34 X 23 1/2 In. 325.00
Textile, Bathing Suit, Woman's, 1920 5.00
Textile, Bedspread, Crocheted, Ecru, C.1900, 120 X 94 In. 250.00
Textile, Bedspread, Crocheted, Purple, Green, Pink, & Yellow, C.1900, 120 In. 250.00
Textile, Bedspread, Hand-Crocheted, Full Size 95.00

Textile, Bedspread, Knit, White, Stars & Stripes, 75 X 74 In. 48.00
Textile, Bedspread, Popcorn, Fringed, 112 X 80 In. 75.00
Textile, Blanket, Pendleton, Green & Red, C.1900, Full Size 75.00
Textile, Bookmark, Jansen, Electric Tower, Eagle, Flags, Pan Am., Silk, 2 In. 105.00
Textile, Camisole, Lady's, Tatted, Victorian 16.00
Textile, Carpet, Aubusson, Four Seasons, 24 X 20 Ft. 7100.00
Textile, Coat, Man's Frock, Prince Albert 40.00
Textile, Coat, Man's, Cutaway, 1890 .... 35.00
Textile, Cover, Pillow, Tapestry, Satin Back, 18 X 17 In. 5.00

Linen or wool coverlets were made during the nineteenth century. Most of the coverlets date from 1800 to 1850. Four types were made, the double woven, jacquard, summer and winter, and overshot.

Textile, Coverlet, Blue & White Geometric Woven Wool, Double 95.00
Textile, Coverlet, Butterflies, Pink, 72 X 72 In. 40.00
Textile, Coverlet, Geometrics & Medallions, Flowerpot Border, Dated 1857 .... 115.00
Textile, Coverlet, Handwoven, C.1840, Navy, Red, Tan, 48 X 75 In. 130.00
Textile, Coverlet, Handwoven, Dated 1831, N.Y., Blue & Beige, Reversible 450.00
Textile, Coverlet, Indigo & Cream, Fringe, Double, Dated 1846 .... 225.00
Textile, Coverlet, Jacquard, Blue & White, Floral, Fringe, 1854 .... 95.00
Textile, Coverlet, New Paris, Elkhart County, Ia., 1856, Eagle & U.S.A., 88 In 125.00
Textile, Coverlet, World's Columbian Exposition, Dated 1892 .... 100.00
Textile, Coverlet, Woven, Crewel Pattern 250.00
Textile, Coverlet, Woven, Signed Heilbronn, 1849 .... 450.00
Textile, Coverlet, Woven, Single, Black & Beige, Geometric 125.00
Textile, Crewel On Silk, The Birds Feeding Elijah, 19 1/2 X 22 1/2 In. 220.00
Textile, Dress, Brown Silk, Embroidered, C.1890 .... 50.00
Textile, Flag, U.S.A., 42 Stars, 15 X 12 In. 15.00
Textile, Flag, U.S.A., 46 Stars, 11 3/4 In. 3.50
Textile, Flag, U.S.A., 46 Stars, 12 X 8 Ft. 25.00
Textile, Handkerchief, Columbian Exposition, White Silk, Square, 18 In. 18.50
Textile, Handkerchief, Mauritania, Color, Pictures, 13 In.Square 5.00
Textile, Hat, Genuine Beaver Top Hat, Case & Brush 100.00
Textile, Hat, Man's, Knox, N.Y., Hatbox, 4 In. 15.00
Textile, Hat, Mandarin, C.1810, Fur Felt, Fringe, 12 1/2 In. 90.00
Textile, Jacket, Lady's, Black Velvet, Ties At Neck, C.1930 .... 13.50
Textile, Kimono, Japanese Wedding Robe, Blue, Silk Embroidery 265.00
Textile, Napkin, Dinner, Linen, Scalloped, 22 In., Set Of 12 .... 48.00
Textile, Napkin, Irish Linen, Hem Stitched, 14 In., Set Of 6 .... 5.00
Textile, Napkin, Linen Damask, Fringed, White, Red Border, 12 In., Set Of 6 .... 20.00
Textile, Needlepoint, Fruits, Flowers, Framed, Signed Mary Anne Moore, 1842 .... 235.00
Textile, Needlepoint, Portrait, G.Washington, Frame, 21 X 24 In. 75.00
Textile, Pantaloons, Lady's, Victorian 12.00
Textile, Pillowcase, C.1840, Stone, Tree, & Girl, Pair 30.00
Textile, Quilt, Applique, Petal And Flower, Scalloped, Purple, Lined 85.00
Textile, Quilt, Appliqued, Rose & Pine Tree, Green Lining 325.00
Textile, Quilt, Ax Or Spool, 80 X 68 In. 49.50
Textile, Quilt, Baskets, Blue Cotton, 6 Ft.10 In. X 5 Ft.7 1/2 In. 40.00
Textile, Quilt, Calico, Goose Tracks, Double, Red, Browns On White, C.1880 .... 100.00
Textile, Quilt, Cracker, 72 X 96 In. 49.50
Textile, Quilt, Crazy, Satin, Embroidered, 78 X 62 In. 85.00
Textile, Quilt, Double Wedding Ring, Double Size 75.00
Textile, Quilt, Jacob's Ladder, Blue & White, 76 X 90 In. 120.00
Textile, Quilt, Linen Geometric & Plaid, Dark Blue, Rust, Beige, Fringe 165.00
Textile, Quilt, Log Cabin, Snyder County, Pa. 90.00
Textile, Quilt, Log Cabin, 65 X 57 In. 225.00
Textile, Quilt, Mennonite, C.1900, Star Of Bethlehem, Le Moyne Stars, 76 In. 250.00
Textile, Quilt, Necktie Or Bowtie, 70 X 86 In. 49.50
Textile, Quilt, Postage Stamp Pieced, Red, White, Blue, 72 X 78 In. 95.00
Textile, Quilt, Priscilla, 67 X 79 In. 49.50
Textile, Quilt, Pyramids, Cotton, Handmade, White Back, 7 1/4 X 6 1/2 Ft. 75.00
Textile, Quilt, Red & White Whirligig, 73 X 73 In. 55.00
Textile, Quilt, Red On White, Stars, Crude Animals, Hearts, 72 X 76 In. 150.00
Textile, Quilt, Reversible, Log Cabin Pattern, 44 X 44 In. 490.00
Textile, Quilt, Rose & Pine Tree, Appliqued 350.00

Textile, Quilt, Starburst, Lavender & White, C.1900, 84 X 64 In. 90.00
Textile, Quilt, Texas Star, Green, Gold & Orange Stars, 78 X 68 In. 75.00
Textile, Quilt, Watermelon Pink & White, 88 X 75 In. 115.00
Textile, Quilt, White, Blue Baskets, 84 1/2 X 72 In. 75.00
Textile, Quilt, 6-Sided Pieces, Green, Yellow, & White, C.1902, 80 X 72 In. 85.00
Textile, Quilt, 8-Pointed Star, Blue & Multicolor Squares On White, 100 In. 150.00
Textile, Ribbon, S.S.Lusitania, Woven Silk, Red & Black, 13 X 9 In. 45.00
Textile, Robe, Baby Carriage, Angora Goat, Bunting Type, 1910 18.00
Textile, Robe, Buggy, Velvet, Gold, Gray, & Rose Feathers & Floral, 52 In. 30.00
Textile, Robe, Carriage, Deer In Forest, 56 X 52 In. 95.00
Textile, Robe, Lap, 1875 68.00
Textile, Rug, Chinese, Blue, Multicolor Floral, 12 X 9 Ft. 275.00
Textile, Rug, Chinese, Soft Tones, 6 Ft.11 In. X 4 Ft. 200.00
Textile, Rug, Daghestan, 5 Ft.8 In. X 4 Ft.2 In. 250.00
Textile, Rug, Feraghan, Herati Designs, Hand Knotted, 6 Ft.5 In. X 4 Ft. 180.00
Textile, Rug, Hamadan, 2 X 2 Ft. 140.00
Textile, Rug, Hamadan, 4 Ft.7 In.X 2 1/2 Ft. 200.00
Textile, Rug, Hamadan, 6 X 3 Ft. 200.00
Textile, Rug, Hearth, Hooked, Horse & Flowerpots, American, 1852, 5 Ft.2 In. 550.00
Textile, Rug, Hooked, Wool, Blue Gray, Rose Floral, 5 X 3 Ft. 20.00
Textile, Rug, Karajo, Multicolor Geometrics, 4 X 2 1/2 Ft. 80.00
Textile, Rug, Sarouk, C.1930, Medallion, 11 X 9 Ft. 2500.00
Textile, Rug, Sarouk, Geometrics & Floral, 6 1/2 X 4 Ft. 825.00
Textile, Rug, Shirvan Caucasian, 5 Center Medallions, 56 X 33 In. 275.00
Textile, Runner, Hamadan, 8 X 2 Ft. 250.00
Textile, Runner, Hooked, Wave Design, Red, Brown, Green, & Black, 16 Ft.10 In. 225.00

Samplers were made in the United States during the early 1700s. The best examples were made from 1790 to 1840. Long narrow samplers are usually older than the square ones. Early samplers just had stitching or alphabets. The later examples had numerals, borders, and pictorial decorations. Those with mottoes are mid-Victorian.

Textile, Sampler, A.D., C.1750, Alphabets, Floral, Birds & Houses, 19 In. 150.00
Textile, Sampler, Alphabet & Number, Sarah Gibston, 1822, Framed, 8 X 8 In. 85.00
Textile, Sampler, Alphabet, Numbers, Birds, Flowers, 1874, 11 X 12 In. 85.00
Textile, Sampler, Betsy Colburn, 1796, Linen Thread On Homespun, 12 In. 450.00
Textile, Sampler, Brick Schoolhouse, Alphabet, Framed, 13 1/2 X 12 In. 250.00
Textile, Sampler, Dated 1822, 13 1/2 X 7 In. 80.00
Textile, Sampler, Ellen Sullivan, Age'd 8 Years, 1845, Adam & Eve, 15 1/2 In. 100.00
Textile, Sampler, Florence Coffin, 1868, One Thing At A Time, 15 1/2 In. 125.00
Textile, Sampler, Friendship, Horse & Carriage, 1932, 13 X 10 In. 27.00
Textile, Sampler, Honor Thy Father & Thy Mother, Red & Gold Frame, 12 In. 32.50
Textile, Sampler, Louisa Pulm, 1827, Abcs & Lettering, 17 X 15 In. 110.00
Textile, Sampler, New Amsterdam, 1825, Alphabets & Houses, 18 X 15 3/4 In. 195.00
Textile, Sampler, Pennsylvania, 19th Century Farmhouse, October 9, 1885 250.00
Textile, Scarf, Linen Damask, Crocheted Inserts & Ends, 52 In. 4.00
Textile, Scarf, Piano, Linen, Ecru, Crocheted Edging, 6 1/2 Ft. 8.00
Textile, Seat Cover, Needlepoint, Dog Center, Browns, 19 X 19 In. 37.00
Textile, Shawl, Paisley, 78 X 76 In. 85.00
Textile, Shawl, Piano, Fringed Persian Design, Large 50.00
Textile, Silk Handkerchief, American Flag Border, World War I, 16 X 16 In. 25.00
Textile, Silk, Bust Of Lafayette, 1824, Verse, White, 8 1/2 X 2 In. 35.00
Textile, Skirt, Hoop 12.00
Textile, Slip, Lady's, Crocheted Trim, Victorian 28.00
Textile, Spat, Felt, Gray, Pair 4.00
Textile, Tablecloth, Belgian Linen, Off-White, Crocheted Inserts, 108 In. 125.00
Textile, Tablecloth, Belgian Linen, White, Crocheted Lace, 84 X 64 In. 75.00
Textile, Tablecloth, Crocheted, Ecru, Embroidered Inserts, 1905, 80 X 72 In. 115.00
Textile, Tablecloth, Crocheted, Ecru, 84 X 70 In. 40.00
Textile, Tablecloth, Crocheted, Off-White, Madison Medallion, 108 X 72 In. 125.00
Textile, Tablecloth, Crocheted, 80 X 80 In. 40.00
Textile, Tablecloth, Hand-Crocheted, Queen's Lace, Off-White, Banquet Size 150.00
Textile, Tablecloth, Hand-Crocheted, White, 68 X 40 In. 28.50
Textile, Tablecloth, Hand-Crocheted, White, 80 X 50 In. 38.50
Textile, Tablecloth, Irish Linen Lace, Ecru, 84 X 48 In. 125.00

Textile, Tablecloth, Irish Linen, Lace, 85 X 65 In. 125.00
Textile, Tablecloth, Linen Damask, Floral, Medallions, & Urns, 92 X 70 In. 20.00
Textile, Tablecloth, Linen, Damask, Mums, Hand Hemmed, 72 X 70 In. 16.00
Textile, Tablecloth, Linen, Ecru, Embroidered Floral, 68 X 50 In. 14.00
Textile, Tablecloth, Luncheon, Linen Damask, Fringed, Square, 30 In. 5.00
Textile, Tablecloth, Quaker Lace, Countess, 90 X 72 In. 100.00
Textile, Tablecloth, String-Drawn Work, 84 X 72 In. 45.00
Textile, Tapestry, George Washington, Statesman, Needlework, 56 X 41 In. 300.00
Textile, Tapestry, Lindbergh, Spirit Of St.Louis, French, 56 1/2 X 18 In. 85.00
Textile, Top Hat, Beaver Skin, Brush & Case 100.00
Textile, Towel, Linen, Red Band 2.50
Textile, Uniform, West Point Cadet's, 40 Brass Buttons, Hat, Size 30 .... 100.00
Textile, Wall Hanging, Oriental, Gold Thread Foo Dogs, Pomegranates 125.00
Textile, Wedding Dress, Ivory Satin, C.1825, Beaded Tiara, Size 12 .... 22.00
Three Crown Germany, Plate, Sienna To Cream, Roses, Gold Rim, 11 3/4 In. 45.00
Three Crown Germany, Salt, Yellow, Gold Scalloped Rim, Footed, Pearl Inside 6.00
Tiffany Bronze, Ashtray & Match Safe, Venetian 120.00
Tiffany Bronze, Ashtray, Modeled 75.00
Tiffany Bronze, Bowl, Greek Key Border, Dore, 9 In. 85.00
Tiffany Bronze, Box, Cigarette, Silvered, Cobalt Enamel, 6 X 4 In. 425.00
Tiffany Bronze, Box, Stamp, Zodiac, Hinged, Dore, 3 Sections 75.00
Tiffany Bronze, Candlestick, Dore, Fully Signed.No.1213 .... 200.00
Tiffany Bronze, Candlestick, Dore, Koch 175.00
Tiffany Bronze, Candlestick, Flower Form, 8 Inserts, Marked 1300, 18 In. 348.00
Tiffany Bronze, Candlestick, Gold Dore, 10 In., Pair .... 375.00 To 425.00
Tiffany Bronze, Candlestick, Tripod Case, Signed, 8 In. 185.00
Tiffany Bronze, Clip, Paper, Zodiac, Green Patina 70.00
Tiffany Bronze, Compote, Dore, Raised Sunray Design, Signed 8 In. 85.00
Tiffany Bronze, Cutter, Paper, American Indian 85.00
Tiffany Bronze, Desk Set, Caramel Slag, Signed, 3 Piece 350.00
Tiffany Bronze, Figurine, Spaniel, Lying Down, C.1880, 9 X 4 In. 525.00
Tiffany Bronze, File, Letter, Venetian 160.00
Tiffany Bronze, Frame, Dore, Signed 92.00
Tiffany Bronze, Mountain Lion, 4 In. 145.00
Tiffany Bronze, Paperweight, Bulldog Playing Ball, 2 In. 110.00
Tiffany Bronze, Plate, Chinese Flowers, Dore, 6 1/2 In. 85.00
Tiffany Bronze, Plate, 8 3/4 In. 60.00
Tiffany Bronze, Smoke Stand, Adjustable Rod 300.00
Tiffany Bronze, Tray, Card, Gold Washed, Enameled 90.00
Tiffany Bronze, Tray, Dore, Signed, 15 In. 277.00
Tiffany Bronze, Tray, Raised Edges, Crimped Corners, 12 X 8 3/8 In. 87.50
Tiffany Bronze, Tumbler, Vintage 295.00
Tiffany Bronze, Vase, Green To Gold Leaves, 6 Sided, 12 3/4 In., Pair 900.00
Tiffany Charger, Abalone, Bronze, 12 In. 150.00

Tiffany glass was made by Louis Comfort Tiffany, the American glass designer who worked from about 1879 to 1933. His work included iridescent glass, art nouveau styles of design, and original contemporary styles. He was also noted for his stained glass windows, his unusual lamps, bronze work, pottery, and silver.

Tiffany Glass, Bottle, Perfume, Harvard, Sterling Hammered Lid, 3 1/2 In. 60.00
Tiffany Glass, Bottle, 18K Gold Stopper, Rock Crystal, 6 In. 285.00
Tiffany Glass, Bowl, Blue Iridescent, Ribbed, Flared Rim, 6 X 2 1/2 In. 350.00
Tiffany Glass, Bowl, Blue Rim, Gold Center, Signed And X Numbered, 10 In. 575.00
Tiffany Glass, Bowl, Blue, Bronze Base, Signed L.C.T.Favrile 500, 8 1/2 In. 650.00
Tiffany Glass, Bowl, Diamond Optic, Gold Favrile, Signed, 6 In. 200.00
Tiffany Glass, Bowl, Electric Blue, Scalloped Rim, 10 Panels, 10 In. 750.00
Tiffany Glass, Bowl, Finger, Paperweight And Millefiori, Underplate, Signed 975.00
Tiffany Glass, Bowl, Gold Iridescent, Flower Center, Pedestal, 1 1/2 In. 250.00
Tiffany Glass, Bowl, Gold, Scalloped Edge, Iridescent, Signed, 4 1/2 In. 195.00
Tiffany Glass, Bowl, Green, Gold Iridescent, Ruffled Edge, 7 1/4 In. 295.00
Tiffany Glass, Bowl, Iridescent, Brass Plinth, Favrile, Marked, 11 1/4 In. 450.00
Tiffany Glass, Bowl, Iridescent, Ornate Brass Plinth, 11 1/4 In. 750.00
Tiffany Glass, Bowl, Paneled Body, Scalloped Rim, Signed, 6 3/4 In. 250.00
Tiffany Glass, Box, Cedar-Lined Cigar, Copper With Green Glass, Marked 200.00

Tiffany Glass, Box, Utility, Copper, Green Patina, Green Glass 250.00
Tiffany Glass, Candlestick, Marigold, Iridescent, Signed L.C.T. 290.00
Tiffany Glass, Candlestick, Queen Anne Lace, Gold Iridescent Top, 18 In. 650.00
Tiffany Glass, Candlestick, Rose Pastel, L.C.T., Favrile, 4 1/2 In., Pair 650.00
Tiffany Glass, Card Holder, Green Slag, Signed 3 X 2 1/4 In. 95.00
Tiffany Glass, Champagne, Gold Iridescent, Rainbow Highlights, Knob Stem 225.00
Tiffany Glass, Champagne, Gold Iridescent, Swirled, Knob Stem 225.00
Tiffany Glass, Champagne, Green Pastel, Tall Stem, Signed, Set Of 6 .... 1050.00
Tiffany Glass, Champagne, Pink, Green Foot, Teardrop On Stem, 7 1/2 In. 375.00
Tiffany Glass, Champagne, Twisted Stem, Signed, 6 X 4 In. 160.00
Tiffany Glass, Compote, Gold, Floriform, L.C.T., 3 3/4 In. 395.00
Tiffany Glass, Compote, Gold, Stretch Ruffled Edge, 6 1/4 X 3 1/2 In. 250.00
Tiffany Glass, Compote, Intaglio Cut, Maples Leaves, 10 In. 695.00
Tiffany Glass, Compote, Laurel Leaf, Lavender, Carved Flowers, 4 3/4 In. 550.00
Tiffany Glass, Compote, Morning Glory Blue, Signed 600.00
Tiffany Glass, Compote, Peach Melba, Floriform, L.C.T., Favrile, 6 In. 395.00
Tiffany Glass, Compote, Quilted, Blue, Violet, Signed And Numbered, 6 In. 250.00
Tiffany Glass, Compote, Royal Blue, Opalescent Optic White, L.C.T.Favrile 295.00
Tiffany Glass, Compote, Royal Blue, Stretch Edge, Signed L.C.T.Favrile, 1700 .... 295.00
Tiffany Glass, Compote, Stretch Rim, Iridescent, Signed, 6 In., Pair 950.00
Tiffany Glass, Compote, Thick Latticed Border, Pair 250.00
Tiffany Glass, Cordial, Gold Favrile, Dimpled, Signed 100.00
Tiffany Glass, Cordial, Gold Iridescent, Deep Cut Arches, Signed, 3 1/4 In. 175.00
Tiffany Glass, Cordial, Gold Iridescent, 4 1/2 In. 125.00
Tiffany Glass, Cordial, Mirror Gold Finish, Pinched Sides, Signed & Numbered 135.00
Tiffany Glass, Corset Shape, 2 In. 175.00
Tiffany Glass, Creamer, Blue, Signed, 4 1/2 In. 375.00
Tiffany Glass, Creamer, Gold Iridescent, 3 3/4 In. 125.00
Tiffany Glass, Cruet, Iridescent Green, 4 1/2 In. 290.00
Tiffany Glass, Cup, Loving, Gold, Green Maple Leaves, 3 Handles 950.00
Tiffany Glass, Cup, Nut, Gold, Signed 125.00
Tiffany Glass, Cup, Punch, Gold, Intaglio Grapes & Leaves 325.00
Tiffany Glass, Dish, Hobstar, Vesica, & Fan, Sterling Rim, 4 Sections, 9 In. 195.00
Tiffany Glass, Dish, Mint, Gold Iridescent, Rainbow Highlights, 5 1/2 In. 140.00
Tiffany Glass, Dish, Mint, Gold, L.C.T., Favrile, 3 3/4 In. 125.00
Tiffany Glass, Dish, Mint, Scalloped Edge, Orange Stretch Front, L.C.T. 145.00
Tiffany Glass, Dish, Nut, Gold Iridescent, Vertical Ribbing, Ruffled 135.00
Tiffany Glass, Dish, Nut, Gold Sheen, Crimped, Signed L.C.T., 2 1/2 In. 105.00
Tiffany Glass, Ewer, Purple, Green, & Gold Iridescent, Shreaded Threads, 8 In 105.00
Tiffany Glass, Finger Bowl & Underplate, Gold Iridescent, Paneled 225.00
Tiffany Glass, Finger Bowl, Gold, Favrile 200.00
Tiffany Glass, Floriform, Decorated, Pedestal, 21 In. 950.00
Tiffany Glass, Flower Holder, Gold Iridescent, Fully Signed 175.00
Tiffany Glass, Flower Holder, Iridescent Blue, Lilies, Signed, 10 1/2 In. 950.00
Tiffany Glass, Goblet, Lemon Green Opalescent Optic Bowl, Long Stem, 8 In. 165.00
Tiffany Glass, Goblet, Marigold To Blue Twist Stem, Signed, 6 1/2 In. 220.00
Tiffany Glass, Goblet, Opalescent Crystal, Smoky Topaz, Swirled, L.C.T. 165.00
Tiffany Glass, Goblet, Optic, Green Pastel, Signed LCT Favrile, 9 In. 375.00
Tiffany Glass, Goblet, Pink And Green, 9 In. 375.00
Tiffany Glass, Jar, Marmalade, Gold Favrille, Sterling Topped, Signed L.C.T. 275.00
Tiffany Glass, Lamp, Candle, Blue Feather, Gold-Plated Holder, Signed Shade 900.00
Tiffany Glass, Lamp, Electrified Oil, Acorn Shade, Bronze Base, Base Signed 1400.00
Tiffany Glass, Letter Rack, Dore Carmel Glass, Pine Needle 185.00
Tiffany Glass, Liqueur, Blue-Green Pastel, Stemmed, Signed, Set Of 6 .... 1350.00
Tiffany Glass, Match Holder, Gold Iridescent, Pinched Sides, 2 3/4 In. 235.00
Tiffany Glass, Mug, Gold, Green Geometrics 450.00
Tiffany Glass, Nut Bowl, Gold Iridescent, L.C.T., 4 1/2 In. 175.00
Tiffany Glass, Parfait, Pink, White Feathering, Green Foot 265.00
Tiffany Glass, Pitcher, Deep Blue, Signed 4 1/4 In. 425.00
Tiffany Glass, Pitcher, Gold, Dark Gold Decoration, 5 1/2 In. 675.00
Tiffany Glass, Pitcher, Milk, Light Gold, Signed V697, L.C.Tiffany, 5 1/2 In. 495.00
Tiffany Glass, Plate, Cake, Pink & Clear, Honeycomb 60.00
Tiffany Glass, Plate, Dinner, Gold Iridescent, Blue Highlights, 9 In. 135.00
Tiffany Glass, Plate, Dinner, Pink With White Feather Ribbing, 10 1/2 In. 295.00
Tiffany Glass, Plate, Gold Dore 45.00

Tiffany Glass, Plate, Pastel Pink, 8 1/2 In. 235.00
Tiffany Glass, Prism, Gold Iridescent, 6 In., Set Of 9 70.00
Tiffany Glass, Prism, 7 In. 20.00
Tiffany Glass, Rose Bowl, Iridescent, Brass Top, Puff Panels, 5 1/2 In. 50.00
Tiffany Glass, Rose Bowl, Iridescent, Lattice Brass Top, Puffed Panels 50.00
Tiffany Glass, Salt, Amber Iridescent, Crimped Serpentine Rim, C.1892 110.00
Tiffany Glass, Salt, Blue, Ruffled, Favrile 145.00
Tiffany Glass, Salt, Favrile, 4 Footed, Signed 115.00
Tiffany Glass, Salt, Gold Iridescent, Crimped Top, L.C.T. 95.00
Tiffany Glass, Salt, Gold Iridescent, L.C.T., Favrile, No.110 165.00
Tiffany Glass, Salt, Gold Iridescent, Purplish Tones, Signed L.C.T.Favrile 110.00
Tiffany Glass, Salt, Gold, Kettle Shape, 4 Footed, L.C.T., 2 1/4 X 2 In. 125.00
Tiffany Glass, Salt, Master, Gold, Handles, L.C.T., Favrile 400.00
Tiffany Glass, Salt, Master, Gold, L.C.T., 3 In. 125.00
Tiffany Glass, Salt, Pigtailed, Silver Gold With Blue & Red 110.00
Tiffany Glass, Salt, Ruffled Edge, Signed 125.00
Tiffany Glass, Salt, Ruffled Rim, Gold, Favrile, Signed 110.00
Tiffany Glass, Shade, Candlestick Top, Gold Iridescent, Feather, Signed 125.00
Tiffany Glass, Shade, Damascene, Brown, Orange, Gold, 16 In. 1500.00
Tiffany Glass, Shade, Gold Iridescent, Ribbed, Signed L.C.T. 135.00
Tiffany Glass, Shade, Gold Luster, Signed, 6 In. 226.00
Tiffany Glass, Shade, Gold, Crimped & Ruffled, Favrille, 7 In., Set Of 5 750.00
Tiffany Glass, Shade, Green Feather On Opalescent, Signed, 6 In. 225.00
Tiffany Glass, Shade, Green Linen Fold, Gold Leading, Signed S & B, 2 1/4 In. 275.00
Tiffany Glass, Shade, Opalescent, Green Pulled Feathers, Trumpet Shape, 6 In. 250.00
Tiffany Glass, Sherbet, Gold, Intaglio-Cut Vintage, Signed, 3 1/2 In. 250.00
Tiffany Glass, Sherbet, Verre De Soie Base, Yellow Stretch Top, Pedestal 275.00
Tiffany Glass, Sherry, Amber Iridescent, Faceted Stem, C.1892, 4 1/2 In. 200.00
Tiffany Glass, Sherry, Amber, Faceted Arches, Paneled Stem, C.1892 150.00
Tiffany Glass, Shot Glass, Gold, L.C.T., 2 In. 125.00
Tiffany Glass, Tile, Blue Iridescent, Favrile, 4 X 4 In. 75.00
Tiffany Glass, Tile, Blue Iridescent, Geometric Flower, Square, 2 In. 60.00
Tiffany Glass, Tile, Blue With Clover Leaf, 1881, LCT, & Co., 3 X 3 In. 35.00
Tiffany Glass, Tile, Peacock Blue Iridescent, Pebbled Effect, Square, 4 In. 45.00
Tiffany Glass, Toothpick, Gold Favrile, Pinched Sides, Signed, 2 1/2 In. 250.00
Tiffany Glass, Toothpick, Gold Iridescent, Swirled Ribs, L.C.T. 265.00
Tiffany Glass, Toothpick, Iridescent Blue, Gold Highlights, Signed 150.00
Tiffany Glass, Tumbler, Gold Iridescent, Flemish, Applied Threading, 4 In. 165.00
Tiffany Glass, Tumbler, Vintage 368.00
Tiffany Glass, Tumbler, Water, Gold Iridescent, Grape Pattern, Favrile 250.00
Tiffany Glass, Vase, Alabaster, Green Feathers, Bronze Base, 11 3/4 In. 625.00
Tiffany Glass, Vase, Amber Iridescent, Floriform, 8 In. 1350.00
Tiffany Glass, Vase, Amber Iridescent, Gourd Shape, 8 Pinches, 13 3/4 In. 950.00
Tiffany Glass, Vase, Amber Iridescent, Spherical, Signed L.C.T., 2 3/4 In. 225.00
Tiffany Glass, Vase, Amber, Purple & Green Leaf & Bud, Gourd Shape, 6 1/2 In. 1900.00
Tiffany Glass, Vase, Black, Iridescent Blue Feather Decoration, 7 1/2 In. 1850.00
Tiffany Glass, Vase, Blue Decoration, Drawn Wavy Lines, 5 1/2 In. 325.00
Tiffany Glass, Vase, Blue Iridescent Favrile, C.1905, LCT, 2 1/2 In. 400.00
Tiffany Glass, Vase, Blue Iridescent, Ribbed, Dimpled, Red Lights, 4 1/2 In. 450.00
Tiffany Glass, Vase, Blue, Iridescent, Trees, Signed, 1554 L.C.Tiffany 825.00
Tiffany Glass, Vase, Bud, Pastel Yellow, L.C.T., Favrile, 9 In. 550.00
Tiffany Glass, Vase, Calla Lily, 7 In. 95.00
Tiffany Glass, Vase, Cranberry, Opalescent, Domed Foot, 6 3/4 In. 2600.00
Tiffany Glass, Vase, Emerald Green, Silver Blue Fishnet, 10 In. 850.00
Tiffany Glass, Vase, Fan Top, Red, Green, Gold Iridescence, LCT, 10 In. 625.00
Tiffany Glass, Vase, Floriform, Gold Iridescent, 12 In. 700.00
Tiffany Glass, Vase, Floriform, Green Feathers, Ruffled Bowl, 11 1/2 In. 1700.00
Tiffany Glass, Vase, Floriform, Green Feathers, Striated Stem, 12 1/2 In. 2300.00
Tiffany Glass, Vase, Flower Form, Gold , Green, L.C.Tiffany, Favrille, 6 In. 595.00
Tiffany Glass, Vase, Flower Form, Opal, Green Feathers, L.C.T., 12 1/2 In. 1350.00
Tiffany Glass, Vase, Free Form, Green, Blue, Lavender Iridescent, Signed, 4 In. 450.00
Tiffany Glass, Vase, Gold & Green Pulled Feathers, White Lining, 10 3/4 In. 425.00
Tiffany Glass, Vase, Gold Feather On Opal, Bronze Dore Base, Signed, 13 In. 225.00
Tiffany Glass, Vase, Gold Iridescent Trumpet, Red & Blue, 15 In. 1500.00
Tiffany Glass, Vase, Gold Iridescent, Barrel, L.C.T., Favrille, 3 1/4 In. 210.00

Tiffany Glass, Vase, L.C.Tiffany, C.227, 13 5/8 In.High

(See Page 658)

Tiffany Silver, Basket, Cake, Tiffany, Young, & Ellis, C.1852

Tiffany Glass, Vase, Gold Iridescent, Bronze Base, Signed, 13 In., Pair ... 650.00
Tiffany Glass, Vase, Gold Iridescent, Floriform, Pedestal, 6 1/2 In. ... 565.00
Tiffany Glass, Vase, Gold Iridescent, Gourd Shape, Miniature ... 385.00
Tiffany Glass, Vase, Gold Iridescent, Green Leaf & Vine, Trumpet, 12 In. ... 985.00
Tiffany Glass, Vase, Gold Iridescent, Purple Highlights, 6 1/2 In. ... 425.00
Tiffany Glass, Vase, Gold Iridescent, Ribbed, 4 In. ... 165.00
Tiffany Glass, Vase, Gold Iridescent, Signed L.C.T., Numbered, 2 1/2 In. ... 350.00
Tiffany Glass, Vase, Gold Iridescent, Silver & Blue Highlights, 4 1/2 In. ... 485.00
Tiffany Glass, Vase, Gold Iridescent, Tapered, Bronze Base, Signed LCT ... 350.00
Tiffany Glass, Vase, Gold Iridescent, Tapered, 12 In. ... 450.00
Tiffany Glass, Vase, Gold Iridescent, 8 Sections, L.C.T., 3 1/2 In. ... 300.00
Tiffany Glass, Vase, Gold Top, Green Leaves, Signed, 18 In. ... 1200.00
Tiffany Glass, Vase, Gold Trumpet Top, Cameo Leaves On Bottom, 18 In. ... 1200.00
Tiffany Glass, Vase, Gold, Blue, L.C.Tiffany, Favrille, 507 L., 4 3/4 In. ... 350.00
Tiffany Glass, Vase, Gold, Blue, Signed L.C. Tiffany, Favrile, 507 L., 4 3/4 In ... 350.00
Tiffany Glass, Vase, Gold, Double Collar, Marked X, 5 1/4 In. ... 250.00
Tiffany Glass, Vase, Gold, Freeform, Pinched Sides, 4 In. ... 250.00
Tiffany Glass, Vase, Gold, Green & Platinum Pulled Feathers, 4 1/2 In. ... 495.00
Tiffany Glass, Vase, Gold, Optic Ribs, Scalloped Top, Footed, L.C.T., 9 1/2 In. ... 575.00
Tiffany Glass, Vase, Gold, Pulled Blue Green Leaves, 12 1/2 In. ... 550.00
Tiffany Glass, Vase, Gold, Red Highlights, Corset Shape, Pleated, 6 1/4 In. ... 75.00
Tiffany Glass, Vase, Gold, Red Highlights, Pinched Sides, 3 X 2 In. ... 125.00
Tiffany Glass, Vase, Gold, Ribbed, Pink & Platinum Highlights, 12 In. ... 750.00
Tiffany Glass, Vase, Gold, Ribbed, Ruffled Top, L.C.T., 3 1/2 In. ... 110.00
Tiffany Glass, Vase, Gold, White Pulled Feathers, Floriform, 8 1/2 In. ... 875.00
Tiffany Glass, Vase, Green Favrile, Orange Floral, C.1895, LCT, 4 1/2 In. ... 950.00
Tiffany Glass, Vase, Green, Cameo Cut Leaves & Vines, 11 In. ... 1200.00
Tiffany Glass, Vase, Harp, 4 Ball Feet, Rich Green Brown Patina, Signed ... 300.00
Tiffany Glass, Vase, Iridescent Blue, Ribbed, Signed, Numbered, 6 3/4 In. ... 625.00
Tiffany Glass, Vase, Iridescent, Cream Lining, Multicolored, Signed, 11 In. ... 1850.00
Tiffany Glass, Vase, Iridescent, Zipper-Like Pattern, Brown, Signed, 11 In. ... 1850.00
Tiffany Glass, Vase, L.C.Tiffany, C 227, 13 5/8 In.High ... *Illus* 1050.00
Tiffany Glass, Vase, Laminated, Bottle, Pinches, 4 In. ... 875.00
Tiffany Glass, Vase, Leaves & Artichoke, 10 1/2 X 19 In. ... 150.00
Tiffany Glass, Vase, Opalescent, Pulled Green Feathers, Floriform, 12 1/2 In. ... 1750.00
Tiffany Glass, Vase, Ovoid, Iridescent Gold, Lavender, Signed, 3 In. ... 225.00
Tiffany Glass, Vase, Pastel Yellow, Floriform, 12 In. ... 380.00
Tiffany Glass, Vase, Peacock Blue, Applied Lily Pads, Signed & Numbered, 6 In ... 750.00
Tiffany Glass, Vase, Pineapple Holder, Signed L.C.T., Favrile, 12 In. ... 375.00
Tiffany Glass, Vase, Poppies, Leaves In Relief, Tiffany Mark, 12 1/2 In. ... 250.00
Tiffany Glass, Vase, Rainbow Iridescent, Ribbed, Twisted, 4 Footed, 1 3/4 In. ... 425.00
Tiffany Glass, Vase, Ribbed Flower Form, Gold Favrile, Red, Signed, 7 1/2 In. ... 350.00
Tiffany Glass, Vase, Semiopaque White Vertical Stripes, Blue Edge, 9 1/2 In ... 550.00
Tiffany Glass, Vase, Squash Blossoms On Green Glaze, Signed 12 In. ... 575.00
Tiffany Glass, Vase, Trumpet Form, Alabaster Ground, Striated Feather, Signed ... 475.00
Tiffany Glass, Vase, Trumpet, Floriform Type, 11 1/2 In. ... 475.00
Tiffany Glass, Vase, Trumpet, Floriform Type, 15 In. ... 575.00
Tiffany Glass, Wine, Cranberry Cut To Clear, Clear Stem, L.C.T., Favrile ... 225.00

Tiffany Glass, Wine, Engraved Vintage, 5 3/4 In. 200.00
Tiffany Glass, Wine, Engraved Vintage, 6 In. 200.00
Tiffany Glass, Wine, Gold Favrile, Knob Stem, Signed 150.00
Tiffany Glass, Wine, Gold Iridescent, Engraved Grapes On Vine, 5 3/4 In. 200.00
Tiffany Glass, Wine, Gold Iridescent, Flemish, L.C.T., 4 In. 155.00
Tiffany Glass, Wine, Green Iridescent, Gold Twisted Stem, 7 1/4 In. 200.00
Tiffany Glass, Wine, Green Swirled Opalescent, 6 In., Set Of 4 360.00
Tiffany Glass, Wine, Green, Opalescent, 4 In. 125.00
Tiffany Glass, Wine, Mirror-Finished Bowl 250.00
Tiffany Glass, Wine, Pastel Green, Engraved Cherries, Signed, 4 In. 175.00
Tiffany Glass, Wine, Radiant Luster, Iridized On Inside, L.C.T., Favrile 125.00
Tiffany Glass, Wine, Royal Design, Gold Color, Signed And Numbered 7 In. 250.00
Tiffany Glass, Wine, Twisted Stem, Iridescent Gold, Green, Lavender, Signed 325.00
Tiffany Pottery, Vase, White Bisque, 3-Sided, Handled, Footed, 6 In. 550.00
Tiffany Silver, Basket, Cake, Tiffany, Young, & Ellis, C.1852 *Illus* 450.00
Tiffany Silver, Bowl, Four Leaf Clovers, Flowers, 10 In. 175.00
Tiffany Silver, Bowl, Lotus Shape, 9 1/4 In. Bowl, 3 Piece 450.00
Tiffany Silver, Bowl, Ornate Rim, Flowers, Garlands, 2 1/2 X 9 In. 185.00
Tiffany Silver, Box, Cigar, Art Deco 225.00
Tiffany Silver, Box, Heart Shape, 1 X 2 1/4 In. 100.00
Tiffany Silver, Candlestick, 8 1/2 In., Pair 195.00
Tiffany Silver, Case, Cigarette, Hand-Engraved 65.00
Tiffany Silver, Coffeepot, Bird Finial, Repousse Body, Coin, 7 In. 250.00
Tiffany Silver, Condiment Set, Pepper, Salt Dip & Spoon 45.00
Tiffany Silver, Cup & Salver, 1876, 6 3/4 In. Salver 248.00
Tiffany Silver, Cup, Folding, Simple 80.00
Tiffany Silver, Cutter, Cigar, Hollow Handle, Ornate, 4 1/4 In. 48.00
Tiffany Silver, Dish, Candy, Covered Pagoda, Glass Insert, Signed, 8 3/4 In. 70.00
Tiffany Silver, Dresser Set, Brush, Mirror, & Fingernail Buffer 92.50
Tiffany Silver, Fork & Spoon, Serving, Art Deco., Pair 140.00
Tiffany Silver, Fork, Luncheon, Wave Edge, Entwined Monogram, Set Of 12 245.00
Tiffany Silver, Fork, Olive, Clinton, Monogrammed 14.00
Tiffany Silver, Fork, Potato Salad, Lapover-Edge, Pea Pods & Vines, 10 In. 88.00
Tiffany Silver, Frame, Picture, Art Nouveau, M Mark, 6 3/8 X 4 3/4 In. 55.00
Tiffany Silver, Glove Stretcher, Repousse, 7 1/2 In. 75.00
Tiffany Silver, Holder, Whisk Broom, Hammered Design, Large 25.00
Tiffany Silver, Junior Set, Squirrel & Acorns, Knife, Fork, & Spoon 75.00
Tiffany Silver, Knife, Butter, St.Dunstan 10.00
Tiffany Silver, Knife, Dinner, Faneiul 15.00
Tiffany Silver, Knife, Dinner, Flemish 14.00
Tiffany Silver, Knife, Dinner, Salem 14.00
Tiffany Silver, Knife, Luncheon, Windham 14.00
Tiffany Silver, Ladle, Gravy, Colonial, Fluted Bowl 35.00
Tiffany Silver, Ladle, Gravy, Cordis 45.00
Tiffany Silver, Ladle, Persian Medallion 185.00
Tiffany Silver, Mug, Initialed, C.1875, 3 1/8 In. 75.00
Tiffany Silver, Mug, Repousse, 4 1/4 X 3 1/2 In. 200.00
Tiffany Silver, Napkin Ring, 1 In. Wide 25.00
Tiffany Silver, Opener, Letter, Jockey Holding Saddle, 7 In. 35.00
Tiffany Silver, Paperweight & Room Thermometer, Circular, 3 In. 50.00
Tiffany Silver, Paperweight, Dachshund, 2 1/4 In. 70.00
Tiffany Silver, Pen Rack, U.S.Military Academy 45.00
Tiffany Silver, Pen, Shell Container 40.00
Tiffany Silver, Pitcher, Water, 1 1/2 Quart, 7 In. 250.00
Tiffany Silver, Platter, Cake, Pierced Border, Pedestal, 12 In. 145.00
Tiffany Silver, Salt & Spoon, Footed, Square, 1 3/4 In. 35.00
Tiffany Silver, Sauce, Chased Foliage, Scroll Handle, C.1875, C.1875 325.00
Tiffany Silver, Server, Asparagus, Chrysanthemum, Pierced Gold-Wash Base 225.00
Tiffany Silver, Server, Ice Cream, Audubon, Vermeil Bowl 105.00
Tiffany Silver, Server, Quiche, Wave Edge, Gold-Wash Base 115.00
Tiffany Silver, Server, Tomato, Perforated Flower Bowl 40.00
Tiffany Silver, Shot Glass, Vase Shape, Pair 40.00
Tiffany Silver, Spoon & Fork, Serving, Plique A Jour, Paris 275.00
Tiffany Silver, Spoon, Berry, Windham 60.00
Tiffany Silver, Spoon, Demitasse, Hampton, Set Of 8 65.00
Tiffany Silver, Spoon, Dessert, Persian, Monogrammed 16.00

Item	Price
Tiffany Silver, Spoon, Grapefruit, Colonial, Monogrammed	15.00
Tiffany Silver, Spoon, Serving, Audubon, Gold-Wash Bowl, Reverse Handle	80.00
Tiffany Silver, Spoon, Serving, English King, Monogram, 8 1/2 In.	38.00
Tiffany Silver, Spoon, Serving, Queen Anne	43.00
Tiffany Silver, Spoon, Serving, Strawberry, Gold-Wash Bowl	95.00
Tiffany Silver, Spoon, Sherbet, Flora, C.1890	15.00
Tiffany Silver, Spoon, Sugar, Shell Bowl, Ornate, Initials E.B.L.	19.95
Tiffany Silver, Spreader, Master Butter, Beckman, Monogrammed	16.00
Tiffany Silver, Stand, Dessert, Chased Floral Border, C.1900, Pair	175.00
Tiffany Silver, Stretcher, Glove, Rococo Engraving, T Mark	35.00
Tiffany Silver, Tablespoon, Japanese, Audubon	22.00
Tiffany Silver, Tablespoon, Saratoga, 8 3/4 In.	35.00
Tiffany Silver, Tablespoon, Wave Edge, Pair	60.00
Tiffany Silver, Tazza, Reticulated & Repousse Rim, 8 X 4 In.	250.00
Tiffany Silver, Tea Caddy, Floral Relief, 2 Lids, 1880, 5 X 4 In.	250.00
Tiffany Silver, Tea Caddy, 2 Lids, Relief Floral, C.1880, 5 In.	250.00
Tiffany Silver, Tea Set, Signed, 3 Piece	800.00
Tiffany Silver, Teakettle, Stand, & Burner, Lions' Heads, C.1891, 13 1/4 In.	600.00
Tiffany Silver, Teapot, Bird Finial, Repousse Body, Coin	250.00
Tiffany Silver, Teaspoon, Beckman, Monogrammed	12.00
Tiffany Silver, Teaspoon, Chrysanthemum, Monogram, 1908	20.50
Tiffany Silver, Teaspoon, Devil's Head	18.00
Tiffany Silver, Teaspoon, Flemish	12.00
Tiffany Silver, Teaspoon, Goat's Head	18.00
Tiffany Silver, Teaspoon, Marquise	10.00
Tiffany Silver, Teaspoon, Olympian	28.00
Tiffany Silver, Teaspoon, Persian, Patent 1872	16.50
Tiffany Silver, Teaspoon, Raised Relief, Signed, Patent 1884, Set Of 12	225.00
Tiffany Silver, Teaspoon, St.James, Set Of 2	24.00
Tiffany Silver, Tongs, Sugar, Claw Grip, Sterling, Broom Corn Pattern, 5 In.	55.00
Tiffany Silver, Tongs, Sugar, Persian	20.00
Tiffany Silver, Tongs, Sugar, St.Dunston, Gold-Washed Spoon Ends, 4 In.	19.00
Tiffany Silver, Tray, Pen, Scalloped Corners, Turned-Down Edge, 7 In.	29.00
Tiffany Silver, Tray, Shell Footed, 5 1/2 X 4 1/2 In.	55.00
Tiffany Silver, Vase, Flaring Neck, Pedestal Base, 21 In.	375.00
Tiffany Silver, Vase, Trumpet, Flaring, 9 In.	130.00
Tiffany Type, Shade, Dining Room, Hanging Dome, Fruit Border, 21 X 16 In.	750.00

Tiffany pieces made of all combinations of materials

Item	Price
Tiffany, Address Unit, Desk, Zodiac	90.00
Tiffany, Ash Stand, Zodiac, Bronze	125.00
Tiffany, Atlantic Telegraph Cable, 1858, 4 In.	55.00
Tiffany, Blotter End, Zodiac, Dore, Set Of 4	70.00
Tiffany, Blotter Ends, Zodiac	95.00
Tiffany, Blotter, Indian Rocker, Green Patina	45.00
Tiffany, Blotter, Medallion, Rocking	100.00
Tiffany, Blotter, Pine Needle, Rocker, Caramel Glass Inserts, Dore	70.00
Tiffany, Blotter, Rocker, Abalone	150.00
Tiffany, Blotter, Rocker, Adams	50.00
Tiffany, Blotter, Rocker, Indian	45.00
Tiffany, Blotter, Rocker, Pine Needle Over Green Glass	70.00
Tiffany, Book, Beauties Of Favrile Glass, 1898	100.00
Tiffany, Book, God's Acre, Tiffany Studios	60.00
Tiffany, Bookend, Abalone Decoration, 6 In., Pair	475.00
Tiffany, Bookend, Ivy & Vines, Green Glass Panes, Bronze Finish, 6 In., Pair	155.00
Tiffany, Box, Abalone, Utility	175.00
Tiffany, Box, Adams Utility	125.00
Tiffany, Box, Chocolate Glass Inserts, Bronze, Grapevine, 3 1/2 In.	85.00
Tiffany, Box, Cigar, Abalone, Cedar Lines, Signed, Numbered, 6 3/4 X 4 3/4 In.	250.00
Tiffany, Box, Enamel, 3 X 3 In.	245.00
Tiffany, Box, Graduate Pattern, Fold, Signed & Numbered, 5 1/2 X 3 1/2 In.	60.00
Tiffany, Box, Stamp, Venetian	145.00
Tiffany, Box, Stamp, Zodiac, Hinged, Dore, 3 Sections	75.00
Tiffany, Box, Utility, 5 1/2 X 4 X 3 In.	225.00
Tiffany, Calendar Holder, Zodiac, Bronze	105.00

Tiffany, Calendar, Abalone 150.00
Tiffany, Calendar, Perpetual, Bronze, Green Slag Glass, No.941, 4 X 6 In. 90.00
Tiffany, Calendar, Perpetual, Jeweled Ninth Century Pattern 215.00
Tiffany, Card, Tiffany Furnaces Business, Gold Embossed, 7 1/2 In. 225.00
Tiffany, Case, Cigarette, 15K Gold 695.00
Tiffany, Catalogue, Blue Book, 1916, 591 Pages 35.00
Tiffany, Charger, Floral & Leaf, Red Enamel, Bronze, Scalloped, 10 In. 95.00
Tiffany, Clip, Paper, Graduate 35.00
Tiffany, Clock, Carriage, Alarm 650.00
Tiffany, Clock, Grandfather, Carved Oak Base 7500.00
Tiffany, Clock, Matching Candlesticks, Red Enamel, Bronze 800.00
Tiffany, Clock, Zodiac, Steeple Top, No.1075, 5 1/2 In. 650.00
Tiffany, Desk Address Unit, Bronze, Zodiac 90.00
Tiffany, Desk Set, Abalone, Bronze, 8 Piece 700.00
Tiffany, Desk Set, Bronze, Adam, 8 Piece 800.00
Tiffany, Desk Set, Indian, Bronze, Dark Patina, 8 Piece 525.00
Tiffany, Desk Set, Inkwell & Calendar, Green Patina, American Indian, Signed 225.00
Tiffany, Dish, Candy, Brass, Mother-Of-Pearl Inlaid Rim, 6 1/2 X 3 1/2 In. 100.00
Tiffany, Fan, Black Lace, Carved Ebony Sticks 130.00
Tiffany, Field Glasses, U.S.Marines, Brass 60.00
Tiffany, Holder, Note Pad, Jeweled Ninth Century Pattern 200.00
Tiffany, Humidor, Venetian 220.00
Tiffany, Inkstand, Abalone 250.00
Tiffany, Inkwell, Abalone 175.00
Tiffany, Inkwell, Adams, Green Enameling, Signed & Numbered 130.00
Tiffany, Inkwell, Cut Glass, Sterling Lid & Ring, Intaglio Floral & Leaf 225.00
Tiffany, Inkwell, Dore Bronze Grapevine On Caramel Slag 165.00
Tiffany, Inkwell, Dore Bronze, Spider Web, Glass Inserts 198.00
Tiffany, Inkwell, Pine Needle, Caramel Glass, Dore 130.00
Tiffany, Inkwell, Venetian Pattern With Insert 145.00
Tiffany, Inkwell, Zodiac, Dore Bronze 110.00
Tiffany, Lamp Base, Artichoke, Green & Brown Patina, Signed, Numbered 350.00
Tiffany, Lamp Base, Gold Decorated, Heat Cap & Wheel, 23 In., Signed 1350.00
Tiffany, Lamp Base, 3 Light, Lily Piano Lamp, Green Brown Patina, Signed 475.00
Tiffany, Lamp, Acorn, Mottled Green With Orange Acorns Shade, Signed, 19 In. 2350.00
Tiffany, Lamp, Austrian, Green, Amethyst, Gold, Signed, Favrile, 13 3/4 In. 500.00
Tiffany, Lamp, Brass Base, 7 Shades, All Shades & Base Signed, 22 In. 8500.00
Tiffany, Lamp, Bronze Base, Kappa Shell, Swivel Shade, Signed, 12 3/4 In. 600.00
Tiffany, Lamp, Candle, Gold Favrile, Signed Shade & Stick 595.00
Tiffany, Lamp, Candle, Green Patina On Bronze, Gold-Ribbed Shade, 3 Legs 950.00
Tiffany, Lamp, Desk, Dore, Gold Favrile Shade, Prunt Decoration, Signed 1500.00
Tiffany, Lamp, Desk, Gold Damascene On Opalescent, Bronze Base, 8 In. Shade 1350.00
Tiffany, Lamp, Desk, Signed Base & Shade 780.00
Tiffany, Lamp, Dragonfly, Blue On Gold, Twisted Dore Stem, 20 In. 8500.00
Tiffany, Lamp, Floor, Curtain Border, 24 In. .... *Illus* 9500.00
Tiffany, Lamp, Floor, Laburnum, 26 In. .... *Illus* 47400.00
Tiffany, Lamp, Geometrics On Inverted Dome Shade, Turtle Back, 14 In. 1600.00
Tiffany, Lamp, Gold Linen Fold Shade, Harp Base, Signed S & B, 7 In. 950.00
Tiffany, Lamp, Greek Key, 3-Footed Bronze Urn Base, 3-Light, 18 In. 3100.00
Tiffany, Lamp, Green & Gold Pomegranate, Mottled Glass, Fully Signed, 19 In. 2950.00
Tiffany, Lamp, Green Iridescent, Signed, 7 In Shade, 15 In. High 850.00
Tiffany, Lamp, Harp, 7 In. Green Shade 850.00
Tiffany, Lamp, Leaded, Purple & Gold, Green Jewels, Bronze Base, 18 In. 1950.00
Tiffany, Lamp, Lily, 6-Arm, Adjustable, White Stripes, 20 1/2 In. 2950.00
Tiffany, Lamp, Nautilus, Signed 725.00
Tiffany, Lamp, Peony, 22 In. .... *Illus* 24500.00
Tiffany, Lamp, Speckled Orange & Green Marbleized, Bronze, 12 In. Shade 1650.00
Tiffany, Lamp, Table, Kapa Shell, Green Bronze Base & Arms, 12 3/4 In. 825.00
Tiffany, Lamp, Table, Mottled Brown Geometrics, Scrolled Base, 20 In. 3675.00
Tiffany, Lamp, Twilight Electric, Iridescent, Favrile Signed & Numbered 900.00
Tiffany, Lamp, Two Tone, Green Shade On 3-Arm Patina Base, Signed, Shade 1050.00
Tiffany, Letter Opener, Indian, Dore 60.00
Tiffany, Letter Rack, Adams, Signed 150.00
Tiffany, Letter Rack, Gold Dore, Adams, Signed & Numbered 130.00
Tiffany, Letter Rack, Pine Needle, Bronze, 2 Sections 85.00

Tiffany, Magnifying Glass, Zodiac, Dore Bronze 275.00
Tiffany, Memo Pad Holder, American Indian, Dore Bronze 110.00
Tiffany, Memo Pad, Zodiac, Signed Tiffany Studios 115.00
Tiffany, Note Pad Holder, Zodiac, Bronze, Green Patina, Flip Over 125.00
Tiffany, Note Pad, Desk, Stained Glass, Bronze Overlay, 7 1/2 In. 95.00
Tiffany, Paper Rack, Pine Needle Over Green Glass, Two Compartment 195.00
Tiffany, Pocket Flashlight, Reading-Glass Combination, Sterling 55.00
Tiffany, Scale, Zodiac, Dark Patina Bronze 295.00
Tiffany, Scoop, Medallion, Cheese, Shiebler, C.1865, 7 In. 50.00
Tiffany, Shears, Grape, C.1852-3, 7 In. 60.00
Tiffany, Stationery Holder, Spiderweb, Glass Inserts, 13 X 12 In. 127.00
Tiffany, Tile, Tea, Copper Over Multicolored Glass, Cutouts, Square, 6 1/2 In. 395.00
Tiffany, Tray, Abalone Edge, Bronze Gold Dore, Round, 14 In. 175.00
Tiffany, Tray, Enameled, Signed 295.00
Tiffany, Tray, Pen, Adam 74.00
Tiffany, Tray, Pen, Graduate Pattern, Gold, Signed & Numbered 55.00
Tiffany, Tray, Pen, Medallion 75.00
Tiffany, Tray, Pen, Pine Needle, Caramel Glass Inserts, Dore 70.00
Tiffany, Tray, Pen, Zodiac 75.00
Tiffany, Tray, Pin, Jeweled Ninth Century Pattern 165.00
Tiffany, Tray, Upright Letter, Jeweled, Ninth Century Pattern 225.00
Tiffany, Vase, Alabaster, Luster, Signed L.C.Tiffany, Favrile, 14 In. 790.00
Tiffany, Vase, Bud, Gold Iridescent, Tapered, Bronze Holder, 13 In. 450.00
Tiffany, Vase, Ribbed Body, Applied Bands, Iridescent, Signed, 12 1/2 In. 575.00
Tiffany, Watch, Lapel, Hanging From 10k Lapel Pin Marked Tiffany 145.00

Tiffin Glass Company of Tiffin, Ohio, was a subsidiary of the United States Glass Co.of Pittsburgh, Pa. Black satin glass, made by the company between 1923 and 1926, is very popular among collectors. Other types were also made.

Tiffin, Basket, Black Satin, 10 In. 38.00
Tiffin, Basket, Black Satin, 11 In. 45.00
Tiffin, Bell, Hand, Rose Design, Knob Handle 37.50
Tiffin, Bowl, Black, Poppy, 5 In. 20.00
Tiffin, Candlestick, Black, 8 1/2 In. 20.00
Tiffin, Console Set, Chartreuse, 11 In. Bowl, 3 Piece 35.00
Tiffin, Dish, Enameled Flowers, Covered And Footed, 8 In. 37.50
Tiffin, Rose Bowl, Green, 7 In. 35.00
Tiffin, Vase, Black Amethyst, Bulbous, Poppies, 6 1/2 In. 25.00
Tiffin, Vase, Black Satin, 11 In. 45.00
Tiffin, Vase, Clear Frosted Satin Glass, Iridescent, Raised Design, 10 In. 47.50
Tiffin, Vase, Coralene Floral Decoration, 6 1/2 In. 48.00

Tiffany, Lamp, Floor, Curtain Border, 24 In.

Tiffany, Lamp, Floor, Laburnum, 26 In.

Tiffany, Lamp, Peony, 22 In.

Tin, Box, Candle, Lid & Ring Handle, 10 In.Long.

Tin, Baby Rattle, For A Good Child, Whistle In Handle

Tiffin, Vase, Frosted, 4 Irises Equally Spaced, 10 X 6 In. 47.50
Tiffin, Wine, Green Bowl, Crystal Stem & Foot, 3 Ozs. 5.00
Tile, see listing by company name
Tile, Old Ironsides In Harbor, White, 6 In. 3.00
Tile, Portrait, Teddy Roosevelt, Geo.Cartlidge, 1916, 9 X 6 In. 85.00
Tile, President Woodrow Wilson, Stoke-On-Trent, 9 X 6 In. 75.00
Tile, Tea, Chinoiserie, Round, 6 In. 25.00
Tile, Tea, England, Black, Multicolor Design, Round, 6 In. 12.50
Tin, see also Store
Tin, Mold, Chocolate, see also Store, Mold, Chocolate
Tin, Baby Rattle, For A Good Child, Whistle In Handle .... *Illus* 50.00
Tin, Bowl, Enameled Boy & Girl Center, Germany 8.00
Tin, Box, Black, Floral & Leaf, Oblong, 8 X 4 X 1 In. 23.00
Tin, Box, Candle, Lid & Ring Handle, 10 In.Long. .... *Illus* 50.00
Tin, Box, Candle, V Shape, Wall Hanger, Strap Bar Up Back, 8 X 6 X 2 In. 22.00
Tin, Box, Covered, Cox's Best Waterproof, Oval, 2 X 1 1/8 In. 4.95
Tin, Box, Document, Apple Green, Pink & Gold Floral Stencils, 8 X 5 In. 27.00
Tin, Box, Document, Black & Gold, 3 X 6 1/2 X 3 In. 15.00
Tin, Box, Document, Black, C.1850 .... 18.00
Tin, Box, Pencil, Jackie Coogan, Yellow, Black Picture 7.00
Tin, Box, Spice, Painted, 6 Containers Inside, 9 1/2 X 6 In. 35.00
Tin, Box, Tinker's Pig 75.00
Tin, Can, Whale Oil Lamp Filler, 5 In. 30.00
Tin, Candleholder, 10 1/2 In. .... *Illus* 35.00
Tin, Canister, Tea, Bearded Gentleman, White-Capped Lady, Oval, 6 In. 24.00
Tin, Canteen, Round 4.00
Tin, Case, Comb, American Shield 20.00
Tin, Case, Comb, Wall Type 18.00
Tin, Case, Map, Tubular, 32 1/2 X 3 In. 15.75
Tin, Chamberstick, Dated Feb.25, 1873, 7 In. 65.00
Tin, Coffeepot, Dated 1882, Wooden Handle & Knob 18.00
Tin, Coffeepot, Pennsylvania, Punched 2000.00
Tin, Coffeepot, Punched, Double Conical Form, 1867 .... *Illus* 2300.00
Tin, Fat Lamp 85.00
Tin, Figurine, Baseball Player, Painted, Moving Limbs, Cloth Uniform, 26 In. 150.00
Tin, Foot Warmer, Made For Use On Sleighs, 14 In.Long .... *Illus* 15.00

Tin, Foot Warmer, Made For Use On Sleighs, 14 In.Long

Tin, Candleholder, 10 1/2 In.

Tin, Coffeepot, Punched, Double Conical Form, 1867

Tin, Lamp, Fat, Removable Cup Set In Holder

(See Page 664)

Tin, Parrot Cage, Painted, 14 In.High

Tin, Foot Warmer, Pierced, Wooden Posted, Diamond Decoration 85.00
Tin, Foot Warmer, Pierced, Wooden Posted, Heart 85.00
Tin, Foot Warmer, Punched Out, Pine Base, 5-Sided, Decorated 110.00
Tin, Holder, Christmas Tree With Lights, 1920s, Santa Decoration 55.00
Tin, Lamp, Fat, Removable Cup Set In Holder .... *Illus* 160.00
Tin, Lantern, Magic, Wooden Base, Kerosene Burner, C.1890, 1 1/2 In.Slides 60.00
Tin, Lunch Box, Circus Scene 25.00
Tin, Match Container, Lift-Up Lid, Wall, 4 3/4 In. 8.00
Tin, Matchbox, Painted, Dragons, Hanging 25.00
Tin, Miner's Lamp 20.00
Tin, Mold, Candle, 6 Tube .... 35.00 To 45.00
Tin, Mold, Candle, 12 Tube 42.00
Tin, Mold, Candle, 12 Tube, Handles, 10 In. 65.00
Tin, Mold, Chocolate, Anchor 8.00
Tin, Mold, Chocolate, Santa Claus, 2 Piece, 3 1/4 In. 14.00
Tin, Mold, Chocolate, Santa Claus, 2 Piece, 5 3/4 In. 24.00
Tin, Mold, Chocolate, Santa, 4 Piece 35.00
Tin, Mold, Chocolate, 2 Rabbits, 7 1/4 In. 35.00
Tin, Mold, Chocolate, 3 Wise Men On Horses, 3 Piece 35.00
Tin, Mold, Chocolate, 4 Piece, Clowns, Dresden, 10 In. 35.00
Tin, Mold, Chocolate, 4 Rabbits, 3 3/4 In. 35.00
Tin, Pail, Bail Handle, 1/2 Gallon 4.00
Tin, Pail, Lunch, Decorated 40.00
Tin, Pan, Corn-Stick, Copper Riveted, 5 1/2 X 6 1/2 In. 24.00
Tin, Parrot Cage, Painted, 14 In.High .... *Illus* 145.00
Tin, Picker, Cranberry 35.00
Tin, Plate, C.D.Kenny, Christmas, Boy With Dog 32.50
Tin, Plate, Portrait, Lady With Roses 30.00
Tin, Plate, Portrait, Shonk Royal Saxony Odalisque 30.00
Tin, Pouch, Tobacco, Dog With Glass Eyes On Lid, Round, 3 1/4 In. 28.00
Tin, Rack, Hanging Spice, 3 Graduated Shelves, 11 X 4 In. 23.00
Tin, Retablo, New Mexico, Deceased Loved One, C.1850, 14 X 10 In. 29.50
Tin, Sander, Ink, Tapered, Dish Top, C.1750, 3 In. 43.00
Tin, Sconce, Candle, Pleated Round Top, Folded Edges, 7 In. 65.00

Tin, Set Of Dishes, Child's, Blue Willow, 27 Piece 40.00
Tin, Snuffer, Wick, Scissors Type 14.00
Tin, Spice Set, Decorated, 6 Cans & Tray 58.00
Tin, Spittoon, Lady's, Cup Shape, Handled, Bronze Finish 22.00
Tin, Teapot, Painted, 6 In.High .... *Illus* 95.00
Tin, Tray, Cracker, Latticework On Sides, 12 3/4 In.Long .... *Illus* 45.00
Tin, Trunk, Oval, Brown Exterior, A.M.Lee, Cabin No.8 On Lift Lid 36.00
Tin, Tumbler, Russian Enameled, Imperial Crest, Dated 1896, 3 1/2 In. 55.00
Tin, Tureen, Primitive Penna.Dutch, Oval, Footed, Handled, Covered 175.00
Tin, Warmer, Foot, Oval Brass Top 30.00
Tin, Warmer, Foot, Pierced, Walnut Frame, Coal Pan 95.00
Tin, Warmer, Foot, Wood, Openwork Top & Sides, Torch Decoration 65.00
Tin, Warmer, Toddy, Wooden Handle .... *Illus* 45.00

Tobacco, Tin, see Store, Tin

Toby mugs have been made since the seventeenth century.

Toby Mug, see also Royal Doulton, Toby Mug; Staffordshire, Toby Mug

Toby Mug, Beefeater, Shorter & Sons, 7 1/2 In. 25.00
Toby Mug, Begging Dog Wearing Tricorner Hat, 9 In. 44.00
Toby Mug, Ben Franklin, 9 1/2 In. 65.00
Toby Mug, Blue Coat, Hands On Chest, WKC, Germany, 3 1/2 In. 25.00
Toby Mug, George Washington, Cream Glaze, New York World's Fair, 1939, 5 In. 27.50
Toby Mug, Grotesque, Brown Glaze, 3 Handles, 7 X 6 In. 69.00
Toby Mug, King George VI, Royal Winton, 2 3/4 In. 22.00
Toby Mug, Martha Washington, Cream Glaze, New York World's Fair, 1939, 5 In. 27.50
Toby Mug, Monk, German Porcelain, 6 In. 135.00
Toby Mug, Sam Weller, Czechoslovakia, 2 1/8 In. 21.00
Toby Mug, Seated Figure Holding Jug, Blue Coat, Orange Breeches, 8 In. 135.00
Toby Mug, Seated Figure, Black Tricorn Hat, Blue Coat, Orange Coat, 9 In. 135.00
Toby Mug, Seated Man Holding Jug, Black Tricorner Hat, Victorian, 8 In. 135.00
Toby Mug, Smiling Face, 8 1/2 In. 55.00
Toby Mug, Toby Philpots, Cobalt Jacket, Allerton, 5 1/2 In. 37.50
Toby Mug, Uncle Sam, Royal Winton, 2 3/4 In. 22.00
Toby Mug, Woman, Applied Handle, 5 3/4 In. 45.00
Tole, Box, Document, Black, Gold Striping, Hinged Flat Lid, C.1850, 11 In. 18.00

Tin, Teapot, Painted, 6 In.High

Tin, Tray, Cracker, Lattice Work On Sides, 12 3/4 In.Long

(See Page 665)

Tin, Warmer, Toddy, Wooden Handle

(See Page 665)

Tole, Box, Document, Gold Letter On Top, 11 3/4 X 6 In. 23.00
Tole, Box, Document, Oil Painted, Dome Top, 8 X 4 1/2 In. 195.00
Tole, Box, Spice, Oblong, 6 Cans, Daisies & Vines, Spice Of Life 37.00
Tole, Box, Spice, Sectioned With Nutmeg Grater In Center 65.00
Tole, Box, Spice, 6 Decorated Containers Inside 30.00
Tole, Coffeepot, Acorn Decoration, 10 In. 95.00
Tole, Coffeepot, Pennsylvania, Red 1225.00
Tole, Horn, Dinner 12.00
Tole, Horn, Fish Peddler's 28.00
Tole, Mold, Pudding, Melon Shape 10.00
Tole, Plate, Bread, Decorated 125.00
Tole, Snuffbox, Oval 5.00
Tole, Tray, Apple, Oil Painted, Square, 12 In. 95.00
Tole, Tray, Black, Flowers In Urn Center, Turned-Down Rim, 28 X 20 In. 65.00
Tole, Tray, Black, Gold Bellflowers, Dog, & Trees, Pierced Handles, 15 1/2 In. 85.00
Tole, Tray, Bread, Decorated 125.00
Tole, Tray, Coffin Lid, Leaves & Red Fruit On White, 12 3/4 X 8 3/4 In. 95.00
Tole, Tray, Green, Fruit, Perforated Edge, 18 X 14 In. 40.00
Tole, Tray, Match, Wall, White, Red Floral & Green Leaves, 7 In. 135.00
Tole, Tray, Octagonal, 12 1/2 X 8 3/4 In. 125.00
Tole, Tray, Oil Painted, 12 X 8 3/4 In. 125.00
Tole, Tray, Oil Painting Of 3 Ships, U.S.Frigate Constitution, 44 Guns 5200.00
Tole, Tray, Russian, C.1840, Peasant Woman Teaching Boy, 11 X 6 1/2 In. 135.00
Tole, Tray, Snuffer, Oil Painted, 10 In. 65.00
Tom Mix, Book, Comic, 1947 .... 5.00
Tom Mix, Book, Tom Mix, Big Big Book 6.50
Tom Mix, Compass, With Magnifier 25.00
Tom Mix, Earphones 20.00
Tom Mix, Film, Original Box, 100 Ft. 16.00
Tom Mix, Jackknife, Ralston, Checkerboard 32.00
Tom Mix, Knife 24.00

Tom Mix, Poster, Circus, Tom, 1936, 42 X 28 In. 55.00
Tom Mix, Ring, Gold, Adjustable 35.00
Tom Mix, Ring, Look About, Ralston, Checkerboard 32.50
Tom Mix, Slide, Glass Coming Attraction For Tony Runs Wild 10.00
Tom Mix, Spur, Silver 25.00
Tom Mix, Telegraph Set 15.00
Tom Mix, Telescope 24.00
Tool, see also Iron, Kitchen, Store, Tin, Wooden
Tool, Adze, Bark Peeling 6.00
Tool, Adze, Carpenter's Hewing, Original Handle 12.50
Tool, Adze, Carpenter's Hewing, Spike 15.00
Tool, Anvil, Cobbler's, Spike Log Base, 25 In. 30.00
Tool, Auger, Bung Hole 53.00
Tool, Auger, Carpenter's Barn Beam 3.50
Tool, Auger, Oak Handle 12.00
Tool, Ax Head, Iron Trade, Ft.Ticonderoga, N.Y., 7 1/2 In. 70.00
Tool, Ax, Keen Kutter 22.50
Tool, Beartrap, Hand-Forged 125.00
Tool, Beater, Rug, Wicker 4.00
Tool, Beater, Rug, Wire 4.00
Tool, Beater, Rug, Wooden Handle 4.00
Tool, Bee Smoking Device, Tin With Leather Bellows 12.50
Tool, Bench, Woodcarver's 125.00
Tool, Binoculars, Bausch & Lomb, Brass-Trimmed Leather Case, Compass Top 75.00
Tool, Binoculars, Jena Lens, C.1910 15.00
Tool, Binoculars, Swift, Case, 35 X 7 In. 32.00
Tool, Blowtorch, Brass 5.75
Tool, Blowtorch, Iron 3.00
Tool, Blowtorch, Jim Dandy, Alcohol 3.00
Tool, Bootjack, Bentwood Bow, Wooden, 23 In. 23.00
Tool, Boring Machine For Barn Timbers, Wood, 8 X 29 In., Two Cranks 35.00
Tool, Box, Carpenter's, Wooden, Handmade 6.95
Tool, Box, Corn Planter Covers, 7 In. 6.75
Tool, Box, Fordson Tractor 16.00
Tool, Brace & Drill Bit, Wooden, C.1825 75.00
Tool, Branding Iron, Bronze Head 25.00
Tool, Branding Iron, V, Hand-Forged 22.50
Tool, Broadax, Carpenter's 5.00
Tool, Broadax, 11 In. Blade 39.00
Tool, Bucket, Ansonia Brass, Patent 1851, 3 Gallon 29.00
Tool, Bucket, Sap, Wooden Finger Lapped Staves 19.00
Tool, Bucksaw, Metal Turnbuckle, Curved Brace, C.1900 15.00
Tool, Bucksaw, 31 In. 8.50
Tool, Carder, Wool, Wooden 6.50
Tool, Churn, Glass, Taylor, 1/2 Gallon 18.00
Tool, Clamp, Furniture, Wooden Screw 10.50
Tool, Clamp, Wooden, 10 In. 9.00
Tool, Clamp, Wooden, 19th Century, Pair 60.00
Tool, Collar, Horse, Brass Posts With Balls On Top 50.00
Tool, Collar, Horse's, Leather 12.00
Tool, Comb, Curry 2.75 To 5.00
Tool, Comb, Flax, Carving On Handle 24.00
Tool, Comb, Wool, Carved Wooden Handle, Iron Teeth, 13 In. 23.00
Tool, Compass, Brass, 4 X 4 In., Folding Sight Bars And Leveling Bubble 25.00
Tool, Crank, Tractor, F12 9.00
Tool, Curling Iron, Montgomery Ward, 1895, Nickel Plated, Oak Handles 20.00
Tool, Cutter, Corn, Iron 6.00
Tool, Cutter, Glass, Brass 7.00
Tool, Cutter, Spoke, Cast Iron 10.00
Tool, Doctor, see Doctor
Tool, Drawknife, Carpenter's 4.00
Tool, Drawknife, Folding Handle 6.50
Tool, Drill Press, Blacksmith's, Automatic Advance 45.00
Tool, Drill Press, Woodworker's, Wooden Frame, Double Crank, 31 X 25 In. 45.00
Tool, Eraser, Whalebone Handle, Steel Shade-Shaped Blade 15.00

Tool, Level, Surveyors, C.1878, 10 X 5 3/4 X 3 1/4 In.

Tool, Extinguisher, Fire, Phoenix, Red & Yellow, N.Y.City, 1899, 22 In. 36.00
Tool, File, Real Ebony, France 12.00
Tool, Flail, Wooden & Leather 35.00
Tool, Flashlight, Winchester 18.50
Tool, Foot Adze, Carpenter's, With Handle 12.00
Tool, For Making Wax Flowers, Cast Iron, C.1885, Set 760.00
Tool, Fork, Pitch, Red Paint 90.00
Tool, Froe, Carpenter's, Hand-Forged Iron 17.50
Tool, Grouter, Mason's, Iron 7.00
Tool, Gun, Grease, Brass 11.00
Tool, Hammer, Coal, Majestic, Smokeless 5.00
Tool, Hammer, Cobbler's, Iron, Wooden Handle 18.00
Tool, Hammer, Horse's Hoofs, Snowball, Iron 8.00
Tool, Hammer, Stone, Iowa Prison 10.00
Tool, Hand Fluter, Geneva, Two Pieces, Dated 1866 .... 24.50
Tool, Harpoon, With Wandered Stamped In Head 390.00
Tool, Hatchet, Metal, Kranz Taffie, 5 In. 850.00
Tool, Hoe, Grubbing 4.00
Tool, Hogscraper, Iron, Push-Up, Impressed Shaw, 7 In. 48.00
Tool, Hogscraper, Wooden Handle 2.50
Tool, Hook, Bailer's, Wrought Iron, 8 1/2 In. 5.00
Tool, Hook, Cant, Logger's, Hand-Forged, 10 In. 3.50
Tool, Hook, Glove, Folding 7.50
Tool, Hook, Hay, Wooden Handle 2.50
Tool, Hook, Meat, Hand-Forged Iron, Wooden Handle 4.50
Tool, Horse Collar, Steel Hames, Brass Knobs, Mirrors 29.50
Tool, Jack, Conestoga Wagon 100.00
Tool, Knife & Buttonhook, Pocket, Sheffield 12.50
Tool, Knife, Castrating, Moorman's Feed 5.00
Tool, Knife, Hay, Hand-Forged Iron 5.00
Tool, Knife, Horse's Hoof Trimming, Bone Handle 5.00
Tool, Last, Shoe, Iron 5.00
Tool, Level, Brass, Case 68.00
Tool, Level, Carpenter's, Brass Ends, Cooks Patent Level, Dec.1886 .... 20.00
Tool, Level, Carpenter's, 1826 .... 27.50
Tool, Level, Cast Iron, 24 In. 8.00
Tool, Level, Stanley, Adjusting Screw, Brass Ends 10.00
Tool, Level, Stanley, 1872, Walnut, Brass Fittings 95.00
Tool, Level, Surveyors, C.1878, 10 X 5 3/4 X 3 1/4 In. .... *Illus* 175.00
Tool, Lipper, To Form Sloping Collared Mouths On Bottles, Iron & Wood 80.00
Tool, Loom, Chapeau Gendarmes, Quebec, C.1840, String Heddles 450.00
Tool, Luber, Tin 12.00
Tool, Mallet, Hand-Hewn Leather, 13 In. 12.50
Tool, Marker Rod, Corn Planter, Horse-Drawn Type 3.50
Tool, Maul, Carpenter's, Wooden 7.50

Tool, Plane, Molding, H.S.Kellogg & J.Clement
(See Page 670)

Tool, Plane, Molding, Hibernia B.Maples & Sons, Sheffield, 1841
(See Page 670)

Tool, Measure, Grain, Rudy Patrick Seed Co., Leather Case 9.50
Tool, Measure, Peck, Wooden, Round, 11 X 7 In. 10.00
Tool, Micrometer, Lufkin Tool Co., Dovetailed Wooden Box, Sliding Lid 15.00
Tool, Microscope, Brass Field, Mahogany Case, Miniature, 19th Century 140.00
Tool, Microscope, C.1870, Brass, Case & Accessories 225.00
Tool, Microscope, C.1880, Brass, Wooden Case 350.00
Tool, Microscope, Spencer, 1900, Lab, Brass, Dovetailed Wooden Case 145.00
Tool, Mill, Grist, Table Mounted, Cast Iron, Wheat Or Coffee 15.00
Tool, Mill, Sorghum, Horse Powdered, C.H.Bell Mill 135.00
Tool, Mold, Hay Fork, Wooden 100.00
Tool, Mold, Pewter Spoons, Rattail, Bronze 300.00
Tool, Mortising, J.A.Fay & Egan Co., Foot Powered 175.00
Tool, Mousetrap, Fruit Jar, Spikes 7.50
Tool, Mousetrap, Metal, Patent Applied 1.65
Tool, Nail Puller, Greenlee, Cast Iron 6.00
Tool, Niddy Noddy, Birch, Mortised And Pinned 29.00
Tool, Oiler, Ohio Injector Co., Brass & Glass, 4 1/2 In. 9.50
Tool, Oiler, Pilgrim Rowell, Brass & Glass, 3 In. 6.00
Tool, Opener, Bottle, Mallard Duck, Metal, 5 In. 15.00
Tool, Pan, Gold Mining, Double Handled 22.00
Tool, Pick, Coal Miner's, 14 In. 5.00
Tool, Picker, Apple, Extension Scissor-Tongs Type, Wooden 175.00
Tool, Picker, Apple, Wooden, Claws & Cradle 80.00
Tool, Picker, Cape Cod Cranberry, Wooden Tines, 18 X 19 In. 87.00
Tool, Pie Lifter, Wooden Handle, Wire Wings, Dated 1889 .... 12.50
Tool, Pinking Iron, Mechanical, Table Mounted 15.00
Tool, Pipe, Jeweler's Mouth Blow, Brass 7.00
Tool, Plane, Block, Wooden 8.00
Tool, Plane, Carpenter's, Wooden, Dated 1890, 9 In. 8.00
Tool, Plane, Conical 24.00
Tool, Plane, Cooper's, Bird's-Eye Maple, 2 Sided 30.00

Tool, Plane, Ice, Harold Leonard Co., N.Y. 2.50
Tool, Plane, Molding .... 10.00 To 15.00
Tool, Plane, Molding, H.S.Kellogg & J.Clement .... *Illus* 42.50
Tool, Plane, Molding, Hibernia B.Maples & Sons, Sheffield, 1841 .... *Illus* 40.00
Tool, Plane, Ohio Tool Co., Wood Plow 27.50
Tool, Plane, Stanley .... 10.00 To 200.00
Tool, Plane, Stanley, No.129, Wood, Liberty Bell & '76, 20 In. 35.00
Tool, Plane, Stanley, No.136, Liberty Bell 18.00
Tool, Plane, Stanley, Rabbit, Box With Cutting Tools 45.00
Tool, Plane, Tongue & Groove 12.50
Tool, Plane, Wood & Cast Iron, Oval Shape, Decorated 10.00
Tool, Plane, Wooden Block, Scioto Works, 8 In. 15.00
Tool, Planter, Single Row, Wooden, Large Wheel 150.00
Tool, Plate, Horse, Leather, Brass Ornaments & Buckles 55.00
Tool, Pliers, Forge, Rod, Iron 48.00
Tool, Plumbob, Cast Iron .... 2.00 To 2.50
Tool, Press, Printing, Crown, Patent 1888, Cast Iron, 11 3/4 In. 45.00
Tool, Puller, Bootstrap, 18th-Century Tooled Steel, Leather Punch 75.00
Tool, Pulley, Large Wooden Rope 6.50
Tool, Pump, Bicycle, Brass 5.00
Tool, Pump, Water, Copper, Iron And Brass, Handle, 35 In. 65.00
Tool, Rake, Wooden, 2 Rows Of Teeth, Iron Bracket 40.00
Tool, Rasp, Iron 16.00
Tool, Rattrap, Wire, C.1901, 16 In. 21.00
Tool, Rattrap, Wood & Metal 12.00
Tool, Reamer, Spiral-Edge Bung Hole, Hand-Forged, 18th Century, 11 1/2 In. 15.00
Tool, Ring, Bull's Nose, Iron, Tension Spring, 5 In. 15.00
Tool, Riveter, Harness, Anvil Attached, Cast Iron 7.00
Tool, Riveter, Harness, Plymouth Rock, Cast Iron 5.00
Tool, Riveter, Rex, Hand, Patent 1900, 6 X 5 In. 8.00
Tool, Roller, Huber Road 110.00
Tool, Rope Measuring & Cutting, Olympic Meter Instrument Co. 24.00
Tool, Rule, Slide, Evans, Eliz., N.J., Montreal, Quebec, 6 Ft. 4.00
Tool, Rule, Slide, Hofland's Mill, PH 28 Menomonee, Wis., 8 Ft. 4.00
Tool, Ruler, Keen Kutter, Wooden, Folding, 24 In. 4.50
Tool, Ruler, Stanley, Wooden, Brass Hinges, 4 Fold 16.00
Tool, Ruler, Steel, Brass Hinges, Folding 18.00
Tool, Sail Maker & Palm, For Pushing Needle Through, Leather & Brass 5.95
Tool, Saw, Ice Cutting On River, Ontario 25.00
Tool, Saw, Iron 16.00
Tool, Saw, Meat, Hand 6.00
Tool, Saw, 2 Man, Cross Cut, Collapsible In Leather Case, Francis Wood & Son 42.00
Tool, Scaler, Fish, Yankee Patent, Bowl Shape, Scaler On Base, Push-Up Lid 15.00
Tool, Scissors, Candlewick, Iron 15.00
Tool, Scoop, Cranberry, Cape Cod, Wooden Tines, 19 X 18 In. 85.00
Tool, Scoop, Grain 6.75
Tool, Scraper, Cabinet, Gooseneck 5.00
Tool, Screwdriver, Winchester, Wooden Handle 8.75
Tool, Screwdriver, Wood-Cased Iron 15.00
Tool, Scribe, Carpenter's Panel, Wooden 9.00
Tool, Scriber, Brass Inlay, 7 In. .... *Illus* 9.50
Tool, Scythe, Wooden Handle 25.00
Tool, Shaper, Buggy Spoke End 14.50
Tool, Shears, Grape, Silver Plate 27.00
Tool, Shears, Leather, Iron 9.00
Tool, Shears, Sheep, Iron 2.00
Tool, Sheller, Corn, Iron, Primitive, Black Hawk Trademark, Hand Crank 40.00
Tool, Sheller, Corn, Wood & Iron, Large Center Wheel 150.00
Tool, Shoes, Chestnut Hulling, Spiked, Pair 40.00
Tool, Shovel, Grain, Hand-Carved, Wood, Handle 37.50
Tool, Shovel, Wooden, Handmade, 3 Ft. 43.00
Tool, Shuttle, Wooden 5.00
Tool, Skimmer, Forge, Iron 32.00
Tool, Soldering Iron, Hand-Forged Copper 38.00
Tool, Spinning Wheel, Flax, Shaker Type 185.00

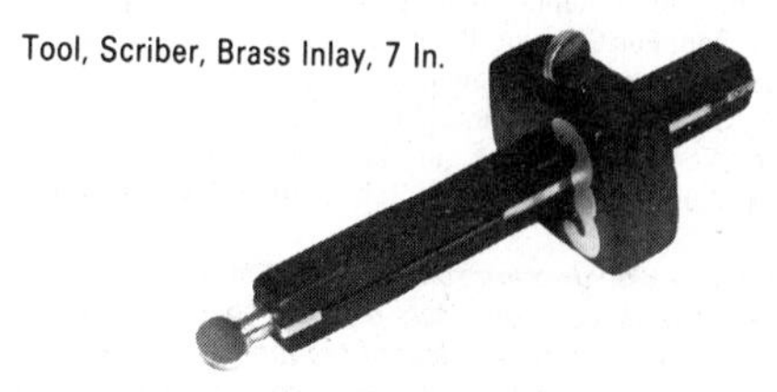
Tool, Scriber, Brass Inlay, 7 In.

Tool, Spinning Wheel, I.W.Holden, Belleville, Canada, C.1850, Invalid's 250.00
Tool, Spinning Wheel, 62 In. 135.00
Tool, Spoke, Shave, Cone Shape 12.50
Tool, Sprayer, Bee, A.I.Root Co., Medina, Ohio, Copper 85.00
Tool, Stamp, Numbering, Automatic, Brass Bound 3.50
Tool, Stretcher, Barbed Wire, Westernlegh Co., Iron, 8 In. 5.00
Tool, Stretcher, Carpet, Iron, B.C.Daves, 1865, 14 X 8 In. 30.00
Tool, Stretcher, Glove, Embossed, Sterling Silver, Hollow Handled, 8 In. 25.00
Tool, Stretcher, Hat, Wooden 18.00
Tool, Surveying Aneroid, Leather Case 35.00
Tool, Surveyor Transit With Compass, Brass & Gunmetal, Mahogany Case 85.00
Tool, Sweeper, Carpet, Wooden, C.1880 .... 18.00
Tool, Tail Holder, Cow's, Trapp, Patent Sept.20, 1898 .... 7.50
Tool, Tether, Horse, Cast Iron, Embossed 22.50
Tool, Thermometer, Portable, Retractable Stand, Carved Wood Box, 3 1/2 In. 18.00
Tool, Tong, Forge, V, Iron 28.00
Tool, Tongs, Blacksmith's, Hand-Forged 3.50
Tool, Tongs, Ice, Clifford Wood Co., Iron 8.00
Tool, Tongs, Ice, Kenmore Coal & Ice Co., Folding 12.00
Tool, Tongs, Scissors Type, Wooden 175.00
Tool, Trammel, Handwrought Iron, Extends To 20 In 60.00
Tool, Trap, Bear, Handwrought Iron, Chain, 3 Ft. 150.00
Tool, Trap, Bear, 22 In. Jaw Spread, 50 Pounds, 44 In. 295.00
Tool, Trap, Gopher, Steel, Mechanical 3.50
Tool, Trap, Insects, DDT Lite, Inc., Shows Skeleton Killing Insects 12.50
Tool, Trap, Kodiak Bear 295.00
Tool, Trap, Mouse, Wire, 9 X 4 X 3 1/2 In. 19.00
Tool, Tray, Carpenter's, Wooden, Handmade, Center Handle, 15 In. 18.00
Tool, Trimmer, Wick, Cast Iron, Scissor Type, Albany, N.Y., Pat.1889 .... 25.00
Tool, Trimmer, Wick, Iron 18.00
Tool, Trimmer, Wick, Tin 14.00
Tool, Trough, Buggy Wheel Oiling, Cast Iron 15.00
Tool, Vise And Bench For Harness Maker, Pine 125.00
Tool, Vise, Blacksmith's, Welded Jaws, 30 In. 25.00
Tool, Vise, Wood, Early 19th Century 50.00
Tool, Wheel, Flax, Stenciled, 27 In. 235.00
Tool, Wheel, Whetstone Grinding, Water Reservoir, Hand-Operated, Steel 12.50
Tool, Wood Grip, Mend Grip, J.B.Toote Foundry Co., Fredericktown, O., 12 In. 28.00
Tool, Wrench, Alligator .... 3.00 To 3.50
Tool, Wrench, Bed, Hand-Carved Rope 12.00
Tool, Wrench, Buggy, Iron 2.50
Tool, Wrench, Machinery, Harvester, Embossed 2.00
Tool, Wrench, Monkey, Wizard 2.50
Tool, Wrench, Monkey, Wooden Handle, Dated Sept.7, 1897 .... 22.50
Tool, Wrench, Tractor, Fordson In Script 3.50
Tool, Wrench, Wagon, Iron 2.50
Tool, Yarn Winder, Pine, Primitive, 36 In. 50.00
Tool, Yarnwinder, Lancaster County, Pa. 225.00

Tool, Yoke, Cow's Neck, Iron 3.00
Tool, Yoke, Goat, Wooden, Handmade Bell, 16 X 8 In. 40.00
Tool, Yoke, Ox, Pine 75.00
Tool, Yoke, Ox, Ring, Replacement Bows 65.00
Tool, Yoke, Sap, For Carrying Buckets 35.00
Tool, Yoke, Shoulder, Hand-Hewn, 38 In. 47.50
Tool, Yoke, Shoulder, Red Paint, Man's Size 23.00
Tool, Yoke, Wooden, Cow, Hanging Bell, Decorative 35.00
Tool, Yoke, Wooden, Hand-Forged Bell, Leather Fastener, Wood Cla .... 26.00 To 35.00

Toothpick holders are sometimes called toothpicks by collectors. The variously shaped containers made to hold the small wooden toothpicks are of glass, china, or metal. Most of the toothpicks are Victorian.

Toothpick, see also other categories such as Bisque, Slag, etc.

Toothpick, Amber, Frog Holding Urn 25.00
Toothpick, Amber, Monkeys On Log 22.00
Toothpick, Amber, Torch 85.00
Toothpick, Amethyst, Swag With Bracket 45.00
Toothpick, Art Nouveau Vine Top, Silver Plate 12.50
Toothpick, Baby Mine, Impressed, Fancy Elephant Inside Base, Frosted 60.00
Toothpick, Bag With Cat, Porcelain 18.00
Toothpick, Bag With Ribbon Around It, Quadruple Plate, Rogers Smith, Meriden 16.00
Toothpick, Basket, Handle, Pressed Glass, Basket Weave, 3 1/2 In. 28.50
Toothpick, Basket, Light Amber, Etched 17.00
Toothpick, Bird, Mechanical, Iron, 4 In. 23.00
Toothpick, Bisque, Boy 35.00
Toothpick, Bisque, 5 Pigs, German, 6 1/2 In. 42.50
Toothpick, Blue Opalescent, Hobnail 38.50
Toothpick, Blue S Repeat 35.00
Toothpick, Book, Sapphire Blue 18.00
Toothpick, Boot Top, Blue, Daisy & Button 35.00
Toothpick, Boy Feeding Dog, Meriden 85.00
Toothpick, Bunny, Clear Glass 18.00
Toothpick, Cat Peeping Out, Bisque 15.00
Toothpick, Chased Metal, Retractable, Jeweled Top, Loop Chain, 2 1/4 In. 24.00
Toothpick, Chick By Half A Sawtooth Egg, Quadruple 65.00
Toothpick, Chick, Egg, & Wishbone, Gold Washed, "Good Wishes" 22.00
Toothpick, Coal Scuttle With Wire Bail, Marked Dickinson, N.D. 18.00
Toothpick, Cobalt, Kittens 125.00
Toothpick, Cradle Form, Amber Daisy & Button 55.00
Toothpick, Cranberry Ribbed Opal Lattice 32.00
Toothpick, Crying Baby With Bare Bottom In Egg 18.00
Toothpick, Custard Glass, Souvenir, Lake Park, Iowa 27.00
Toothpick, Custard Glass, 2 1/4 In., Souvenir Newton Hamilton, Pa. 30.00
Toothpick, Custard, Geneva 95.00
Toothpick, Diamond Spearhead, Green Opalescent 40.00
Toothpick, Dispenser, Woodpecker On Log, Metal 5.00
Toothpick, Dog, Silver Plate, Glass Insert 65.00
Toothpick, Dog, Tufts Silver Plate, No.2895 .... 55.00
Toothpick, Dragon Handles, Ball Feet, Tricorner Shape, Silver Plate 45.00
Toothpick, Eggshell With Chick On Wishbone, Silver Plated, Best Wishes 19.95
Toothpick, Elephant Head, Blue Glass 16.00
Toothpick, Elk, Royal Bayreuth 75.00
Toothpick, Fan & Bow Cut, 2 1/2 In. 25.00
Toothpick, Fish Head 15.00
Toothpick, Flashed Red, St.Louis Exposition, 1904 .... 7.00
Toothpick, Flower Cart, , 2 3/4 In. 25.00
Toothpick, Flowers, Dog At Side, Glass Insert, Silver Plate, Tufts 65.00
Toothpick, Frog Holding Flower, Pressed Glass 45.00
Toothpick, Girl Wearing Hat Sits Alongside Holder 160.00
Toothpick, Girl With Braid Pulling Rope On Pot, Meriden 55.00
Toothpick, Glass, Raised Amber Floral, Camphorlike Base, Clear Top, 1881 .... 62.00
Toothpick, Gold Loops & Drops, Clear 14.00
Toothpick, Gold-Flashed Pattern 15.00
Toothpick, Green Croesus, Gold 75.00

Toothpick, Green Glass, Paneled 11.00
Toothpick, Hat Form, Carnival, Blue To Pink 30.00
Toothpick, Hat, Amber Thread 19.00
Toothpick, Head, 1 Eye Closed, Sweet Adeline On Base, C.1910, 5 In. 30.00
Toothpick, Horse-Drawn Cart 30.00
Toothpick, Horse-Drawn Cart, Clear Glass 40.00
Toothpick, I'll Pick For You, Silver Plate 30.00
Toothpick, Iris With Meander, Opalescent, Apple Green 50.00
Toothpick, Kate Greenaway Type, Girl Standing Beside Holder 20.00
Toothpick, Loving Cup, 3 Handles, Gold Flashed 14.00
Toothpick, Meander & Diamond, Green 55.00
Toothpick, Metal Woodpecker On Log 18.50
Toothpick, Milk Glass, Armour & Co, Silver Plate Pairpoint Base 28.00
Toothpick, Monkey's Head 35.00
Toothpick, Negro, Coon Chicken Inn, Metal 25.00
Toothpick, New Hampshire, Maiden's Blush 30.00
Toothpick, Owl, Silver Plate 22.50
Toothpick, Pansy, Pink Opaque 38.00
Toothpick, Pig Beside Green Basket 21.00
Toothpick, Pig On Cart With Barrel, Clear Glass 50.00
Toothpick, Porcupine, Silver Plate 25.00
Toothpick, Pressed Glass, Form Of 3 Baskets, Pale Lemon, 3 1/2 In. 37.00
Toothpick, Pretty Maid, Frosted 45.00
Toothpick, Quadruple, Chick With Scalloped Holder, Quadruple 65.00

Toy, Alligator, Schoenhut, Glass Eye, 12 In.

(See Page 674)

Toothpick, Queen On Two Sides, King On Other, Porcelain, 3 3/4 In. 95.00
Toothpick, Rip Van Winkle, Blue Opaque, Portieux, Signed, 5 In. 40.00
Toothpick, Ruby Diamond 15.00
Toothpick, Ruby, Souvenir, Euclid Beach, 1897 .... 12.00
Toothpick, Ship's Figureheads, Double Handles, St.Louis, Silver Plate 40.00
Toothpick, Shoe, Blue 30.00
Toothpick, Souvenir, Champlain, N.Y., Scalloped & Gilded Sawtooth Rim 20.00
Toothpick, Souvenir, City Hall, Philadelphia, Metal With Elk 15.00
Toothpick, Souvenir, Gloucester, England, Locke Co. 12.00
Toothpick, Souvenir, The Plaza, Metal With Bulldog 15.00
Toothpick, Sowerby, C.1881, Basket Shape, Amber Floral, Opaque, Tinted 65.00
Toothpick, Spearhead, Green 55.00
Toothpick, Spinning Wheel & Basket, Silver Plate, 5 3/4 In. 60.00
Toothpick, Strawberries, Glass 18.00
Toothpick, Tecumseh Log Cabin 12.00
Toothpick, Texas, Gold 15.00
Toothpick, Thimble Shape 4.50
Toothpick, Three Dolphins, Amber 40.00
Toothpick, Three Ornate Legs, Pairpoint, Silver Plate 14.95
Toothpick, Toddler Pulling Off Socks, Silver Plate 45.00
Toothpick, Two Dogs, Tufts Silver Plate, No.2691 .... 65.00
Toothpick, Vermont, Opaque Ivory 50.00
Toothpick, Wagon, Frosted 20.00
Toothpick, Wheelbarrow, Amber, Metal Fittings, Barley Pattern 50.00

Toothpick, White Opalescent, Beatty Rib 20.00
Toothpick, Winged Figures Of Mercury On Handles, Meriden 12.00

Tortoiseshell glass was made during the 1800s and after by the Sandwich Glass Works of Massachusetts and some firms in Germany. Tortoiseshell glass has been reproduced.

Tortoiseshell Glass, Jam Pot, Hole For Spoon In Silver-Plated Lid 45.00
Tortoiseshell Glass, Pitcher, Water, Inverted Thumbprint, Clear Handle 75.00
Tortoiseshell Glass, Vase, Bulbous, Crimped Top, 9 In 65.00
Tortoiseshell, Box, Covered, Oval, 3 3/4 X 3 In. 45.00
Tortoiseshell, Box, English, C.1850, Brass Mounts, Round, 2 3/4 In. 65.00
Tortoiseshell, Box, Jewel, Domed Lid, 5 In. 55.00
Tortoiseshell, Box, Jewel, Spanish, C.1825, Oval Lid, Silver Mounted, 7 In. 225.00
Tortoiseshell, Bracelet, Bangle, Wide Opening 40.00
Tortoiseshell, Case, Card & Cigarette, Japanese, Swivel Stand, 3 5/8 In. 45.00
Tortoiseshell, Case, Card, Engraved Oriental Design 40.00
Tortoiseshell, Case, Card, Mother-Of-Pearl Inlay, Floral & Leaf, 4 1/4 In. 85.00
Tortoiseshell, Case, Eyeglasses, Silver Mounted, London, 1920, 5 1/8 In. 85.00
Tortoiseshell, Comb, Hair, Jewels 5.00
Tortoiseshell, Comb, 7 1/4 X 5 In. 11.00
Tortoiseshell, Compact, Brass Mounts, Etched, Pierced, C.1850, 2 1/4 In. 75.00
Tortoiseshell, Compact, Italian, C.1850, Silver Fittings, Inset Miniature 45.00
Tortoiseshell, Hairbrush, Silver Trim 10.00
Tortoiseshell, Letter Opener, Chain & Ball As Handle 8.00
Tortoiseshell, Lorgnette Handle, 10 1/2 In. 45.00
Tortoiseshell, Lorgnette, Pique, 132 Gold Stars, Gilt Silver, 5 3/4 In. 195.00
Tortoiseshell, Ornament, Hair, Brilliants, Hairpin Type, Pair 18.00
Tortoiseshell, Snuffbox, French, C.1850, Ivory Painting On Lid, Oval, 4 In. 195.00

Toy, see also Card, Disneyana, Doll, Game, Marble, Orphan Annie

Toy, Aerial Spinner, Wood & Tin, American Toyland 22.50
Toy, Air Base, 18 Cutouts For Planes, Kis Cereal, 1942 .... 8.00
Toy, Airplane, Army Scout, Painted, Steelcraft, 22 In. 22.50
Toy, Airplane, Boeing B-29, Hop Harrigan, Grape-Nuts Flakes, 1942 .... 8.00
Toy, Airplane, Flip, Windup, U.S.Zone, Germany 10.00
Toy, Airplane, Ford Tri Motor, Tootsie Toy, 4 In. 22.00
Toy, Airplane, On Tower, Tin, Penny Toy, German, 1919 .... 23.00
Toy, Airplane, PAA Clipper, Wyandotte 25.00
Toy, Airplane, Tin Windup, Girard Toys, Airways Express, 3 Propellers 48.00
Toy, Airplane, U.S.A.F., Transport, Lithographed, Tin, Wyandotte, 12 In. 15.00
Toy, Airport Futurematic, Windup, Automatic 55.00
Toy, Airport, Windup Planes, Lithographed, Tin, West Germany, 8 Pieces 20.00
Toy, Alabama Coon Jigger, Strauss 175.00
Toy, Alabama Coon Jigger, Windup, Tin, Lehmann, 1912 .... 149.00
Toy, Alligator, Schoenhut, Glass Eye, 12 In. .... *Illus* 250.00
Toy, Animal Barbershop, Windup, Lithograph, Tin, Japan, C.1940 .... 20.00
Toy, Ark, Paper On Wood, McLaughlin 35.00
Toy, Athlete Running Track, Hand Squeeze, Germany, 1900 .... 37.00
Toy, Auto Speedway, Jr., Windup, Japanese 10.00
Toy, Auto Unckle, Lehmann 85.00
Toy, Auto, Garage, Sedan, Gallop Racer, Lehmann 275.00
Toy, Auto, Metal Mercedes, Windup With Key, Schuco, 5 In. 10.00
Toy, Auto, Renault Roadster, Bin Tin, 5 1/2 In. 65.00
Toy, Auto, Tin, Sparkler, Green And Black, 10 1/2 In. 295.00
Toy, Autobus, Lehmann 475.00
Toy, B.O.Plenty & Sparkle, Windup, Tin, Marx 95.00
Toy, Balky Mule, Lehmann .... 75.00 To 125.00
Toy, Balky Mules & Cart, Marx 7.00
Toy, Bank, Tin Church, Lithograph, U.S. Metal Toy Co., 5 X 5 In. 12.00
Toy, Barnacle Bill In Barrel, Windup, Chein 75.00
Toy, Bat, Baseball, Louisville, 1941, Joe Ducky Medwick, 16 In. 20.00
Toy, Bat, Baseball, Picture Of Frank Baker, 14 In. 17.50
Toy, Bathroom Set, Tootsie Toy, 5 Piece 35.00
Toy, Bear, Crystal Coffee, Cloth, 4 In. 10.50
Toy, Bear, Polar, Schoenhut, Glass Eyes 135.00

Toy, Bear, Stuffed Windup, Tin Tag On Ear, G.B.N.Bavaria 100.00
Toy, Bear, Windup, Occupied Japan 16.00
Toy, Bed, Doll's, Brass, Springs & Mattress, 26 X 16 In. 42.00
Toy, Bed, Doll's, Cannonball With Red Paint 12.00
Toy, Bed, Doll's, Four Post, C.1930, Pine, 12 1/2 X 22 In. 35.00
Toy, Bed, Doll's, Mahogany, 4 Poster, Curved Canopy, Bedding, 18 1/2 In. 150.00
Toy, Bed, Doll's, Victorian, Walnut Veneer, Carved, 21 In. 45.00
Toy, Bell Ringer, Harold Lloyd, Germany 70.00
Toy, Ben Hur, 2 Horses, All Metal 30.00
Toy, Bicycle, see Bicycle
Toy, Bicycle String Weight, Hobo 90.00
Toy, Bicycle String Weight, Teddy Roosevelt Bear 90.00
Toy, Bicycle String Weight, Uniformed Man 90.00
Toy, Black Forest Whistler 200.00
Toy, Black Mammy, Windup, Lindstrom 42.50
Toy, Block Set, Kate Greenaway-Type Children, EIH, 1881, Set Of 5 .... 65.00
Toy, Blocks, Pictures To Make 4 Puzzles, Box, 12 X 15 In., C.1900 .... 45.00
Toy, Blocks, Wild-Animal Pictures, McLoughlin, 1890s 85.00
Toy, Blocks, World's Fair Building, 1892, McLoughlin 45.00
Toy, Boat, Metal, Marx 5.00
Toy, Boat, Normandie, Originally A French Cookie Tin 85.00
Toy, Boat, Submarine, German, 9 In. 45.00
Toy, Bojangles Dances Again 19.50
Toy, Bojangles, Negro, Wood Jointed Dancing, Tin Base 25.00
Toy, Boxer, Wooden, Punches Bag When Spring Is Pressed 30.00
Toy, Boy On Motorcycle, Tin, Lehmann, 8 1/2 X 7 In.High .... *Illus* 200.00
Toy, Boy Riding Bicycle, Windup, German, 1900 .... 170.00
Toy, Boy With Tray, Windup, Celluloid, Occupied Japan 9.00
Toy, Bridge, Tressle, Wabash, Marx, 18 In. 10.00
Toy, Brown Bunny, Windup 20.00

Toy, Boy On Motorcycle, Tin, Lehmann, 8 1/2 X 7 In.High

Toy, Bubble Blowing Musician, Battery Operated, Tin 24.75
Toy, Buggy, Doll's, Black Leather, With Wicker, C 1920 .... 45.00
Toy, Buggy, Doll's, Wicker, Largest Size 60.00
Toy, Buggy, Doll's, Wicker, Ornate, Wooden Wheels & Handle 195.00
Toy, Buggy, Doll's, Wicker, 30 X 21 In. 45.00
Toy, Bulldog, Glass Eyes, Schoenhut, 7 1/2 In. 45.00
Toy, Bunk Bed Set, Doll's, Metal, Boll-E-Bunk 35.00
Toy, Bus, Cast Iron, Arcade, 8 In. 65.00
Toy, Bus, Double Decker, Kenton, 6 In. .... *Illus* 425.00
Toy, Bus, Double Decker, Tin & Iron, Williams, 8 In. 100.00
Toy, Bus, Hubley, Red Cast Iron, 5 1/2 In. 30.00
Toy, Bus, Interstate, Strauss 125.00
Toy, Bus, Shoreline Cannonball, Tin, Upton, Michigan, C.1930, 10 In. 20.00

Toy, Bus, Tin & Iron, Arcade, 12 In. 1250.00
Toy, Cabinet, Doll's, Hoosier, Oak, Tins & Dishes Inside, 18 1/2 In. 135.00
Toy, Calop Cowboy, Zebra Cart, Lehmann 90.00
Toy, Cannon, Carbide, Civil War 85.00
Toy, Cannon, Firecracker, Kilgore 25.00
Toy, Car & Garage, Racing, Galop, Lehmann, 1916 .... 215.00
Toy, Car, Buddy L Roadster, 9 In. 18.00
Toy, Car, Cable, Rigi, Lehmann 165.00
Toy, Car, Chein Windup, Wood-Paneled Sedan, 5 1/2 In. 6.00
Toy, Car, Coal, Tootsietoy 4.00
Toy, Car, Coo Coo, Marx 60.00
Toy, Car, Cord, Heavy Steel With Pull Trailer 85.00
Toy, Car, Crazy, College Boy, 2 Flappers On Trunk, Marx 110.00
Toy, Car, Crazy, Cowboy, Marx .... 95.00 To 100.00
Toy, Car, Dagwood, Marx 87.50
Toy, Car, Fire Chief, Siren, Windup, Tin, Marx 30.00
Toy, Car, Flivver, Crazy, Marx 47.00
Toy, Car, Golden Eagle Racer, Windup, Dunlop Cord Tires, C.1930 .... 45.00
Toy, Car, Graham Series, Die Cast, Tootsie Toy, C.1933 .... 15.00 To 35.00
Toy, Car, Hubley Racer, Metal, Cast Iron, 7 In. 25.00
Toy, Car, Humphreymobile, Windup, Tin 75.00
Toy, Car, Jalopy, Marx, 1920, 2 Lithograph Men 60.00
Toy, Car, Kutsche, Lehmann 145.00
Toy, Car, M.G.Sports, Red, Rubber Wheels, Right-Hand Drive, Hurley 10.00
Toy, Car, M.M.Series, Die Cast, Tootsietoy, C.1920 .... 15.00 To 65.00
Toy, Car, Model A Ford, Cast Iron, Metal Wheels, 4 In. 25.00
Toy, Car, Model T Ford Touring, Tootsietoy 2.00
Toy, Car, Model T Ford, Center Door, Tin & Iron, Arcade, 6 In. 70.00
Toy, Car, Old Hansom Cab, Metal, Composition Horse 25.00
Toy, Car, Pierce Arrow Coupe, Cast Iron 20.00
Toy, Car, Racer, Windup, Driver, Marx, 5 In. 10.00
Toy, Car, Roadster, Convertible, Cast Iron, Hubley, 4 1/2 In. 29.00

Toy, Bus, Double Decker, Kenton, 6 In.

(See Page 675)

Toy, Car, Tootsietoy, G.M.Series, Brougham, 3 In.

Toy, Car, Roadster, Windup, 2 Seater, Tin, Bing, C.1930, 6 In. 45.00
Toy, Car, Speed King Racer, Tin, Windup, Marks, 17 In. 24.00
Toy, Car, TCA Twentieth National Convention, Seattle, Wash., McCoy 50.00
Toy, Car, Tootsietoy, Auto Transporter, 4 Cars, 1950's 15.00
Toy, Car, Tootsietoy, Doodlebug .... *Illus* 30.00
Toy, Car, Tootsietoy, G.M.Series, Brougham, 3 In. .... *Illus* 30.00
Toy, Car, Tootsietoy, Graham, 3 1/2 In. .... *Illus* 25.00
Toy, Car, Touring, Driver, Green, Clockwork, Disc Wheels, Tin, German 60.00
Toy, Car, U-Turn Jeep, Boxed, Linemar 14.00
Toy, Car, Windup, Chein, 7 In. 30.00
Toy, Car, Windup, 1920's Tin Lithographed Sedan Coupe, With Garage 75.00
Toy, Car, Wood With Wood People, Holgate, 24 In. 35.00
Toy, Car, 1928 Chevrolet Coup, Cast Iron, Arcade .... 100.00 To 350.00
Toy, Car, 1935 Ford, Rubber, Firestone, 5 In. .... 5.00 To 20.00
Toy, Car, 3-Wheel Reversible Friction Tin Racing, Marx, Japan 10.00
Toy, Carnival Man Rings Bell With Mallet, Mechanical, Tin, Germany 43.00
Toy, Carriage, Doll's, Sun Umbrella, C.1880 .... 125.00
Toy, Cart, Oxen, Plantation, Hubley, 13 In. 425.00
Toy, Cart, Wicker Doll Pull Cart, Red Velvet Seat 55.00
Toy, Cart, 2 Wheel, Wooden, 29 In Handle, C.1880 .... 75.00
Toy, Cash Register, Tin, Tom Thumb, Wester Stamping Co., Jackson, Mich. 10.00
Toy, Cat, Windup, U.S.Zone, Germany 8.00
Toy, Cement Mixer, Iron, Jaeger 80.00
Toy, Chair, Doll's, Spindle Back, Handmade, 12 In. 20.00
Toy, Chair, Doll's, Windsor Side Chair, Round Back, Pine, Turned Legs 32.00
Toy, Chair, Iron, Arcade 8.00
Toy, Chair, Wooden, For A 10 In.Teddy Bear 4.75
Toy, Charleston Trio, Windup, Marx, 1921 .... 175.00
Toy, Charley Weaver Bartender, Battery Operated .... 18.00 To 65.00
Toy, Charlie Chaplin, Tin, Mechanical, German, Tips Hat, 1920s 48.00
Toy, Chicken In Coop, Pipsqueak, Germany 11.00
Toy, Chicken, Lays Eggs, Mechanical, Wyandotte 50.00
Toy, Chicken, Windup, Tin, Clucks With Bellows, 4 1/2 X 7 In. 150.00
Toy, Child On Tricycle, Lehmann 175.00
Toy, Chinese Cabinet, Cast Iron, 4 X 6 1/2 In. 55.00
Toy, Circus Lady Performer, Schoenhut 90.00
Toy, Circus Master, Schoenhut, 6 1/2 In. 60.00

Toy, Car, Tootsietoy, Doodlebug

Toy, Car, Tootsietoy, Graham, 3 1/2 In.

Toy, Circus Set, Schoenhut, Boxed, 5 Piece 165.00
Toy, Circus, Tiger, Cast Iron, Hubley Royal Circus, 3 1/2 In. 30.00
Toy, Circus, Wyandotte 150.00
Toy, Climbing Monkey On String, Marx 28.00
Toy, Climbing Monkey, Lehmann, Made In Germany, 1903, 8 In. 75.00
Toy, Clown Holding Pig's Ears, Windup, Tin, 5 1/2 X 7 1/2 In. 350.00
Toy, Clown In Cart Driving Mule, Windup, Tin, Germany 35.00
Toy, Clown, Windup, Sits On 3-Legged Stool, Plays Tune, C.1890, Tin, 4 X 7 In. 350.00
Toy, Clowns, Hoky & Poky, Wyandotte, Tin, Windup 18.00
Toy, Coffee Grinder, Wood Box, 2 1/2 In. 25.00
Toy, Coffee Mill, Doll's, Wood 20.00
Toy, Construction Set, Matchbox, Louis Marx & Co. 5.00
Toy, Corn Planter, Cast Iron 10.00
Toy, Cow, Pull Toy, Papier Mache, Cloth Cover, Glass Eyes, Tin Wheels, 10 In. 75.00
Toy, Cradle, Doll's, Dated 1863, Handmade 35.00
Toy, Cradle, Wicker, Doll, Wooden Rockers, 19 X 10 In. 45.00
Toy, Crapshooting Monkey, Mechanical, Cragstan 22.00
Toy, Crawling Beetle, Lehmann, 1895 .... 85.00
Toy, Crib, Green Paint, Wheels, Schoenhut Basinets, U.S.A., 26 1/2 In. 50.00
Toy, Cupboard, Doll's, Pine, 2 Glass Doors, 3 Shelves, Drawer, 19 X 10 In. 110.00
Toy, Cupboard, Kitchen, Red Metal 90.00
Toy, Dagwood Sandwich Box, Lithographed Tin, 1947, King Features 22.50
Toy, Dancing Lassie, Windup, Tin, Lindstrom 45.00
Toy, Dancing Negro, Windup, Tin, U.S.A., C.1900 .... 150.00
Toy, Dancing Sam, Mechanical, Tin, Japan 20.00
Toy, Dial-A-Typewriter, Marx 5.00
Toy, Dishes, Chiquita, Green Opaque, 22 Pieces 38.90
Toy, Dishes, Little Hostess, Maroon, Green, Gray, 14 Pieces 38.50
Toy, Doctor's Kit, C1938, Little Country Doctor 12.00
Toy, Dog, Circus, Schoenhut 55.00
Toy, Dog, Dagwood's Dog Daisy, Mohair, Straw Stuffed, 1930s 8.00
Toy, Dog, Does Somersaults, Gunthermann 65.00
Toy, Dog, Mechanical, Lithographed, Guntermann, C 1930 .... 35.00
Toy, Dog, Wee Scottie, Tin Windup, Marx 22.00
Toy, Dogpatch Four, Windup, Lithographed, Tin, Unique Art, C.1945 .... 25.00 To 65.00

Toy, Doll, see Doll

Toy, Dollhouse, Bliss, C.1895, 13 In. 135.00
Toy, Dollhouse, Lithographed Paper On Wood, 2 Rooms, R.Bliss, C.1888, 13 In. 375.00
Toy, Dollhouse, Lithographed, Cardboard, American, C.1920, Furniture, 13 In. 125.00
Toy, Dollhouse, Lithographed, 8 Rooms, 1930 .... 65.00
Toy, Dollhouse, Schoenhut, 1 Room 200.00
Toy, Dollhouse, Tin, Lithographed, 2 Story, 8 Rooms, 1920 .... 95.00
Toy, Dollhouse, Tootsietoy, Cardboard 25.00
Toy, Dollhouse, Tudor Style, 2 Story, Garage, Fence, Schoenhut 275.00
Toy, Dominoes, Hood, 1908 .... 35.00
Toy, Donkey, Jointed, Schoenhut, 8 In. 45.00
Toy, Donkey, Lehmann, The Stubborn Donkey 110.00
Toy, Dragonfly, Friction, Tin, Japan, C.1930 .... 5.00
Toy, Dresser, Deluxe, Tootsietoy .... *Illus* 12.00

Toy, Dresser, Deluxe, Tootsietoy

Toy, Lamp, Tootsietoy

(See Page 681)

Toy, Ferris Wheel, Wind Up, Tin, 33 1/2 In.

Toy, Duck, Glass, 2 1/2 In.

Toy, Dresser, Doll's, Eastlake, Walnut, Mirror, 3 Drawer, C.1880, 21 In. 65.00
Toy, Dresser, Doll's, Mahogany, 3 Drawer, Oval Mirror, 22 1/2 In. 85.00
Toy, Dresser, Doll's, Mirror, 2 Drawer, Fairyland Toy & Novelty Co., Tenn. 50.00
Toy, Drum, Gulliver's Travels, Tin, J.Chein, 1939 .... 8.00
Toy, Duck Carrying Suitcase, Cigar & Hat, Windup, Tin, Joe Penner 225.00
Toy, Duck, Friction, Tin, J.L.H., C.1914, 4 X 3 In. 25.00
Toy, Duck, Glass, 2 1/2 In. .... *Illus* 5.00
Toy, Duck, Pull Toy, Wooden, Germany, 1 3/4 In. 6.00
Toy, Duck, Windup, Metal, Made In China 5.00
Toy, Duck, Windup, Tin, Chein 15.00
Toy, Duck, Windup, Wings Move, Tin, German, C.1900 .... 45.00
Toy, Engine, Steam, Weeden Upright No.1, Pat.May 18, 1885 .... 35.00
Toy, Engine, Weeden Steam, Horizontal, Cast Iron Base, Brass Tank, 6 1/2 In. 50.00
Toy, Erector Set, Gilbert, No.10062, Tin Box 17.00
Toy, Erector Set, 1938, 4 1/2 In. 12.00
Toy, Fan, Forms Circle, Occupied Japan, 6 In. .... .75
Toy, Fat Boy Carrying Plate, Windup, Celluloid, Occupied Japan 12.50
Toy, Father Tuck's Animals & Riders, Paper, 10 Pieces 40.00
Toy, Felix The Cat Racer, Pat.1925 .... 35.00
Toy, Felix, Pop-Up, Fisher Price 15.00
Toy, Ferdinand The Bull With Bee, Windup, Marx, Tin, Dated 1938 .... 40.00
Toy, Ferris Wheel, Double, Tin, Japan 9.00
Toy, Ferris Wheel, Windup, J.Chein, With Bell 45.00
Toy, Ferris Wheel, Windup, Tin, 33 1/2 In. .... *Illus* 1000.00
Toy, Finnegan, The Baggage Man, With Truck, Windup, Unique Art 45.00
Toy, Fire Engine, Mack, Tin & Iron, Arcade, 21 In. 225.00
Toy, Fire Engine, Tin & Iron, Williams, 8 In. 45.00
Toy, Fire Pumper, Cast Iron 3.50
Toy, Fire Pumper, White Rubber Tires, 6 1/2 In. 30.00
Toy, Fireman Climbing Ladder, Marx 95.00
Toy, Fireplace, Cast Iron, Fancy, 8 X 8 In. 25.00
Toy, Fishing Rod, Winchester, Metal Case 40.00
Toy, Flapping Lovebird, Windup, Japanese 10.00
Toy, Fort With Cannons, Wooden, U.S.A., 30 X 24 In. 65.00
Toy, Fred Flinstone & Dino The Dinosaur, Battery Operated 35.00

Toy, Fun Fair, Tin, A Sunny Andy Toy, Boxed 175.00
Toy, G.I.Joe & K-9 Pups, Windup, Tin, Unique Art 65.00
Toy, Game, see Game
Toy, Gas Pump, Marx 10.00
Toy, GI Joe, K9 Pup, Windup 45.00
Toy, Golf Club, Wooden Shaft, 1927, Set Of 6 .... 20.00
Toy, Golf Set, McDonald Smith, 9 Irons, 3 Wooden, Bag 25.00
Toy, Goose On Wheels, Small German Penny Toy 25.00
Toy, Goose, Keywind, Marked Patented July 8, 1924, 9 In. 35.00
Toy, Goose, Unique Art, Tin, Windup 20.00
Toy, Goose, Windup, Tin, Marx, 1924, 9 In. 18.00
Toy, Gun, see also Buck Rogers, Gun, Roy Rogers, Gun, Gene Autry, Gun
Toy, Gun, BB, Buck Jones, Daisy 100.00
Toy, Gun, BB, Daisy, Buck Jones, Pump Action, Compass & Sundial 40.00
Toy, Gun, BB, Daisy, Golden Eagle, 1936 .... 65.00
Toy, Gun, BB, Red Ryder, Iron Cocking Lever 27.50
Toy, Gun, Cap, Border Patrol, Cast Iron, Embossed 12.50
Toy, Gun, Cap, Buffalo Bill, 7 1/2 In. 6.50
Toy, Gun, Cap, Cowboy, Tin, 4 1/4 In. 7.00
Toy, Gun, Cap, Derringer, Cast Iron 15.00
Toy, Gun, Cap, Eagle, 7 1/2 In. 28.00
Toy, Gun, Cap, Echo 2.00
Toy, Gun, Cap, Hubley, Aluminum, .38 Caliber 6.00
Toy, Gun, Cap, Kilgore, 6 Shooter, Cast Iron 15.00
Toy, Gun, Cap, Oh Boy, Cast Iron 15.00
Toy, Gun, Cap, Repeater, Border Patrol 12.50
Toy, Gun, Cap, Stallion 32, Cartridge Loading, 7 1/2 In. 7.50
Toy, Gun, Cap, Star Automatic, Tin, Roll Caps, 2 1/4 In. 5.00
Toy, Gun, Cap, Super Nu-Matic Paper Buster 8.50
Toy, Gun, Cap, Teddy, Cast Iron 12.00
Toy, Gun, Daisy Air Rifle, 25th Century 37.50
Toy, Gun, Daisy Rifle, Double Barrel 15.00
Toy, Gun, Iron, G-Man Revolver 8.50
Toy, Gun, Quackenbush Air Rifle, Nickel Plate, Take-Down Model 100.00
Toy, Gun, Spud, Original Box 8.50
Toy, Gun, Water Pistol, Rubber, Occupied Japan 2.50
Toy, Gun, Water, Atom-Ray Pistol 35.00
Toy, Handy Andy Crane, 1915 .... 55.00
Toy, Hansom, Black, White Prancing Horse, Cast Iron, Dent, 8 In. 75.00
Toy, Hansom, Central Park, Horse Drawn, Blue & White, Cast Iron, Kenton, 17 In. 170.00
Toy, Hen, Lays Eggs, Baldwin 16.00
Toy, Highchair, Doll's, Wicker 25.00
Toy, Horse-Drawn Milk Wagon, Toytown, Windup, 10 3/4 In. 35.00
Toy, Horse-Drawn Wagon, 2 Black Horses, Green Wagon, Cast Iron, Kenton, 15 In. 225.00
Toy, Horse, Farm, Tin & Iron, Arcade, Pair 30.00
Toy, Horse, Jointed, Schoenhut, 7 In. 45.00
Toy, Horse, Pull Toy, Dapple Gray, Leather Pull, 13 1/4 X 12 1/2 In. 125.00
Toy, Horse, Victorian, Pull Toy, Fabric Over Wood, 24 In. 165.00
Toy, Horse, Wooden, Dapple Gray, 1880, 15 X 13 In. 38.00
Toy, Iron, Sadiron, Oval Trivet, Hearts In Center, Set 23.50
Toy, J.F.Kennedy In Rocker, John & Caroline, Plays "Happy Days," Kamar, 14 In. 150.00
Toy, Jack-In-Box, Clown, Wooden Box 27.50
Toy, Jack-In-The Box, Victorian, Hand-Sewn Clothes, Paper Box 15.00
Toy, Jiggs, Wooden, Movable Arms & Legs, Marked Copyright K.F.S. 20.00
Toy, Jockey & Horse, Pull, Cast-Iron Wheels, 10 In. 65.00
Toy, Joe Penner, Wanna Buy A D1ck, Windup 125.00
Toy, Jolly Pals, Strauss 140.00
Toy, Joy Rider, Marx, 1919 .... 65.00
Toy, Jumping Clown, Windup, Japanese 9.00
Toy, Jumping Dog 50.00
Toy, Kazoo-Saxophone, Bob Burns, Tin 9.00
Toy, Kicker 21 Football Player, Lehmann 150.00
Toy, Kiddie Car, Hubley, 8 1/2 .... 22.00
Toy, Kinescope, Keystone, Model E-33 .... 24.00

Toy, Kinescope, Phoenix Glass Lamp Base, Kerosene, Cast-Iron Holder 75.00
Toy, Kit, Airplane, Spirit Of St.Louis, Metalcraft 50.00
Toy, Kitchen Set, Tootsietoy, Boxed, 7 Piece 50.00
Toy, Kitchen, Tin, Removable Pots, 16 In.Long .... *Illus* 225.00
Toy, Krazy Kar, Artie, Windup, Unique 65.00
Toy, Krazy Kar, Uncle Wiggily, Windup, Marx 85.00
Toy, Lady On Swing, Tin, Penny Toy, German 50.00
Toy, Ladybug With 6 Legs, Keywind, Marked SG Germany 45.00
Toy, Lamp, Tootsietoy .... *Illus* 4.00
Toy, Lariat, Cisco Kid, Humming 20.00
Toy, Laying Hen, Push Down, Wyandotte 50.00
Toy, Life Perserver, Ideal, 1956, Mighty Mouse, C.B.S. T.V., Plastic 8.00
Toy, Little Abner, Windup Band 140.00
Toy, Lucky Taxi, Windup, Tin, Marx, C.1930 .... 15.00
Toy, Magic Lantern, 17 Slides 58.00
Toy, Mammy, Sweeping, Windup, Lindstrom 45.00
Toy, Man In Rowboat, Windup, 9 X 2 1/2 In. .... *Illus* 45.00
Toy, Manure Spreader, Metal, John Deere, 10 In. 10.00
Toy, Merry Mice Makers, Marx 175.00
Toy, Merry-Go-Round, Windup, Musical, Jenny .... *Illus* 550.00
Toy, Mickey Mouse, see Disneyana
Toy, Milton Berle Crazy Car 65.00
Toy, Mixer, Jaeger, Cast Iron, 6 1/2 In. 95.00
Toy, Mixer, Sunbeam Mixmaster, Child's, Green Jadite Bowl 18.00
Toy, Model A Ford, Tootsietoy, 1929 .... 17.50
Toy, Monkey, Windup, Japanese 9.00
Toy, Motorcycle Cop, Iron, Champion, 4 3/4 In. 32.00
Toy, Motorcycle, Windup, Marx, Cop & Sidecar 28.00
Toy, Motorcycle, Windup, Shuco, U.S.Zone, Germany 10.00
Toy, Mountain Goat, Windup, Occupied Japan 16.00
Toy, Movie, Primitive, Glass & Wood Slide, Pull Glass And Boy Falls Off Pig 25.00

Toy, Kitchen, Tin, Removable Pots, 16 In.Long

Toy, Man In Rowboat, Wind Up, 9 X 2 1/2 In.

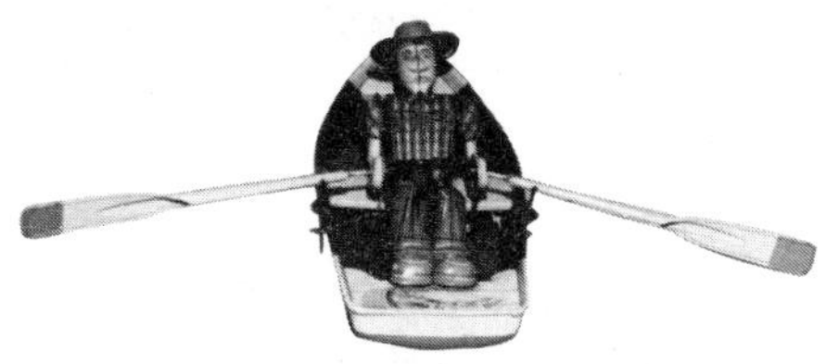

Toy, Merry-Go-Round, Wind-Up, Musical, Jenny

(See Page 681)

Toy, Pipsqueak, Bird, 4 1/2 In.

Toy, **Mower,** Cast Iron, Arcade 25.00
Toy, **Mr.Peanut Man Bounces On Spring** 14.00
Toy, **Mr.Peanut,** Planter's Peanuts, Windup, Walker, Plastic, Green 60.00
Toy, **Mr.Peanut,** Windup, Black & Tan, Windup 135.00
Toy, **Native On Alligator,** Windup, Tin, Chein 28.00
Toy, **Negro Riding Alligator,** Mechanical, Tin, Germany 44.00
Toy, **Negro Riding On Seesaw,** On Wheels, Tin, Germany 43.00
Toy, **Organ Grinder,** Keywind, Tin, 6 1/2 In. 16.00
Toy, **Organ,** Hand, Child's, 1920 .... 95.00
Toy, **Ostrich,** Strutting, Clockwork, Cast Aluminum, French 65.00
Toy, **Paintbox,** Children's Colors, Prang, 1886 .... 25.00
Toy, **Panama Pile Driver,** Wolverine, Tin, Dated 1905 .... 65.00
Toy, **Patty & The Pig,** Windup, Tin, 1903, Lehman 365.00
Toy, **Phone,** Wall, Oak 125.00
Toy, **Phonograph,** Lindstrom Corp., Electric, Model N777, Metal 24.00
Toy, **Piano Bench,** Schoenhut 7.75
Toy, **Piano,** Grand, Petite Princess, Boxed 20.00
Toy, **Piano,** Marx, Tin, Play Away, 10 Key, 1939, With Music Book 45.00
Toy, **Piano,** Petite Princess, Boxed 8.00
Toy, **Piano,** Schoenhut, Mahogany, 14 Keys 65.00
Toy, **Piano,** Schoenhut, Matching Bench, 11 Keys, 23 In. 52.00
Toy, **Piano,** Schoenhut, Multicolor Nymphs & Cherubs, 17 1/2 In. 89.00
Toy, **Piano,** Schoenhut, Oak With Music Holder & Stool, 32 In. 95.00
Toy, **Piano,** Schoenhut, Pictures Of Angels, 16 X 11 In. 125.00
Toy, **Piano,** Schoenhut, Upright, Wooden Keys, Paper Decals, 14 In. 45.00
Toy, **Piano,** Schoenhut, 15 X 10 1/2 In. 55.00
Toy, **Piano,** Schoenhut, 17 Key, Nymphs & Cherubs In Color, 11 1/2 X 8 1/4 In. 89.00
Toy, **Piano,** Schoenhut, 1900, Wooden, 6 Keys 18.00
Toy, **Picture Cubes,** Aesop's Fables, Mitered Edges, Made In China, Boxed 15.00
Toy, **Pinocchio,** Windup, Tin, Marx 55.00
Toy, **Pipsqueak,** Bird, 4 1/2 In. .... *Illus* 135.00
Toy, **Plow,** Arcade 2 Bottom 25.00
Toy, **Pool Player,** Lehmann, 14 1/2 In. 75.00
Toy, **Pool Player,** Tin, Penny Toy, German 60.00
Toy, **Popeye In Barrel,** Tin, Chein, 7 1/2 In.High .... *Illus* 75.00
Toy, **Popeye,** Windup 25.00
Toy, **Porky Pig,** Windup, Tin, Leon Schlesinger, Marx, 1939, 8 In. 45.00
Toy, **Pull,** Early Daisy Seesaw, Tin 95.00
Toy, **Puppet,** Hand, Wooden Head Of King, Hand-Painted Face, Sheepskin Hair 22.00

Toy, Popeye In Barrel, Tin, Chein, 7 1/2 In.High

Toy, Ring Master, Schoenhut, 7 In.

Item	Price
Toy, Rabbit Pushing Egg On Wheels, Tin, Chein	10.00
Toy, Raccoon With Button, Steiff, 13 In.	15.00
Toy, Racquet, Tennis, Spalding, Steel	45.00
Toy, Red Goose Shoes, Wooden Goose On Wheels	85.00
Toy, Refrigerator, Coldspot, 10 1/2 X 17 1/2 In.	18.00
Toy, Refrigerator, Pretty Maid, Louis Marx, 4 1/2 X 3 In.	18.00
Toy, Rex Mars, Planet Patrol Playset, Marx	8.00
Toy, Ring Master, Schoenhut, 7 In. *Illus*	95.00
Toy, Ring-A-Ling Circus, Windup, Tin, Marx	165.00
Toy, Ring, Pilot's, Secret Compartment, Kis Cereal	15.00
Toy, Robin Hood Playset, Official Films, Inc., Marx	10.00
Toy, Rocker, Doll's, Wing-Back, Red Paint, Plywood, 9 In..	6.00
Toy, Rocker, Doll's, Wooden, Handmade, 9 In.	10.00
Toy, Rocker, Wicker, Child's	65.00
Toy, Rocking Horse, Carved, Folk-Art Decoration, C.1825	220.00
Toy, Rocking Horse, New England, C.1870	175.00
Toy, Rocking, Removable Chair Seats, Wooden, Painted, 5 1/2 Ft.	250.00
Toy, Rockinghorse, Mennonite, 1848, Original Finish	675.00
Toy, Rodeo Joe, Git Along Lil Doggie, Windup, Tin	45.00
Toy, Roller Coaster, Windup, Tin, Chein	45.00
Toy, Roly Poly Monkey, Tin, Chein	16.00
Toy, Roly Poly, Sailor	12.50
Toy, Sadiron, Asbestos, Removable Handle	18.00
Toy, Sailor In Rowboat, Mechanical, Tin, Japan	8.00
Toy, Sam The Gardener, Marx	12.00
Toy, Sam The Strolling Skeleton, Windup, Lithograph, Tin, Japan, C.1940, 6 In.	18.00
Toy, Scooter, Runabout, 4 Wheels, Henley, 1913	85.00
Toy, Scooter, Wooden With Metal Horse's Head	49.50

Toy, Secretary, Cast Iron, 3 X 8 In. 65.00
Toy, Set Of Dishes, Little Red Riding Hood, Tin, 9 Piece 25.00
Toy, Sewing Machine, Child's, Floral Decoration, Hand Crank, Germany 12.00
Toy, Sewing Machine, Child's, Original Box 17.50
Toy, Sewing Machine, Child's, Singer, C.1920 .... 35.00
Toy, Sewing Machine, Little Red Riding Hood 30.00
Toy, Sewing Machine, Pearl, Original Box 25.00
Toy, Shoo-Fly, Wooden 42.50
Toy, Sink, Arcade 30.00
Toy, Sink, Tootsietoy 5.00
Toy, Skates, Ice, Shapleigh Hardware, Clamp On, Pair 5.00
Toy, Skates, Roller, Winchester, Pair .... 20.00 To 25.00
Toy, Skates, Wooden, Maple Foot Form, Brass Fittings, Steel Runners 30.00
Toy, Skates, Wooden, Snow, Curled Front, Tin Runners, Falcon American Mfg.Co. 24.00
Toy, Ski Boy, Windup, Lithographed, Tin, J.Chein, C.1940 .... 21.50
Toy, Sled, Dog, Carved & Painted Dogs, Mechanical, 31 In. 240.00
Toy, Sleigh, Swans' Heads In Front Of Runners, Red Upholstered, Stenciled 250.00
Toy, Soldier, Lead, 44, With 10 Horses 125.00
Toy, Soldier, Windup, Japanese 9.00
Toy, Soldier, Windup, Wolverine 45.00
Toy, Somstepa, Coon Jigger, Windup, Marx, 1910 .... 85.00
Toy, Sparkler, Old Woman, German 15.00
Toy, Stage, Jackie Gleason, Honeymooners, 1955 .... 18.00
Toy, Steam Engine, Burns Fuel Tablets, Wilesco, Germany 18.00
Toy, Steam Engine, Horizontal, Brass & Cast Iron, Weeden Patent, 6 1/2 In. 40.00
Toy, Stepladder, Folding, Gray, Cast Iron, Kilgore, 3 1/2 In. 17.50
Toy, Stove, Cast Iron, Marked Pet 95.00
Toy, Stove, Cast Iron, Royal, With Utensils, 7 X 9 In. 125.00
Toy, Stove, Child's Cook, Cast Iron, Copper & Brass Pots, French, 10 In. 125.00
Toy, Stove, Cook, Iron, America 75.00
Toy, Stove, Cook, Nickel-Plated Cast Iron, Eagle, 1912 .... 58.00
Toy, Stove, Doe-Wah-Jack, Round, Oak, Shows Indian 55.00
Toy, Stove, Dot, Cast Iron 15.00
Toy, Stove, Marked Kent, Oven Door Opens, 4 3/8 In. 12.00
Toy, Stove, Tootsietoy 10.00
Toy, Stove, Venus, Cast Iron, Lifter, Kettle, & Frypan 39.50
Toy, Stove, Wood Or Coal For Playhouse, Tiny Tot 95.00
Toy, Striped Tiger, Steiff, 18 In. 15.00
Toy, Stroller, Doll's, Wicker, 22 1/2 In. 50.00
Toy, Sulky & Driver, Kenton, Cast Iron 45.00
Toy, Sulky, Green Wicker, Wooden Seat, Metal Wheels, Whitney, 10 In. 55.00
Toy, Sulky, Lady, Horse Drawn, Windup, Tin, C.1910, 4 1/2 X 7 1/2 In. 195.00
Toy, Surrey With Fringe On Top, Iron, Woman On Back, Driver, Yellow Wheels 90.00
Toy, Surrey, 2 Horse, Canopy Top, Cast Iron, Aluminum Wheels, Standley, 1940 .... 75.00
Toy, Sweeping Mammy, Windup, Tin, Lindstrom, C.1930, 8 In. 50.00
Toy, Tank With Pop-Up Gunner, World War I, Windup, Marx 35.00
Toy, Tanker, Windup, Fleischman, Esso, All Metal 165.00
Toy, Target, Hunter, Trap Doors, Cork Gun, Louis Marx & Co. 15.00
Toy, Taxicab, Blue Paint, Hubley, 5 1/2 In. 160.00
Toy, Taxicab, Cast Iron, Arcade, 8 In. 65.00
Toy, Tea Set, Child's, Fine China 30.00
Toy, Tea Set, Doll's, Pewter, 3 Piece 25.00
Toy, Tea Set, Red Riding Hood, Ohio Art, Tin, 10 Piece 22.50
Toy, Team Of 3 Horses, Cast Iron 45.00
Toy, Teddy Bear, Pale Blue, Celluloid, 2 Right Feet, Japan, 3 3/4 In. 10.00
Toy, Teddy Bear, Red, Straw Stuffed, Shoebutton Eyes, C.1915, 24 In. 80.00
Toy, Teddy Bear, Straw Stuffed, Jointed 37.50
Toy, Telegraph Set, 1930s 10.00
Toy, Tidy Tim, Clean Up Man, Lehmann 95.00
Toy, Tidy Tim, The Clean Up Man, Windup, Marx 75.00
Toy, Tiger, Windup, Marx 7.00
Toy, Tin Lizzie, Windup 80.00
Toy, Top, Ballet Dancer, Marx 50.00
Toy, Top, Gulliver's Travels, Spinning, J.Chein, 1939 .... 8.00
Toy, Top, Santa & Reindeer, Celluloid Cover, Victor Toy Co. 4.00

Toy, Train Set, Buddy L, Engine & 7 Cars

Toy, Truck, Fire, Hook & Ladder, 3 Horses, 2 Men, 4 Ladders

(See Page 686)

Toy, Top, Spinning, Pictorial, Tin, Chein 12.00
Toy, Top, Wooden, Boyle Needle & Shuttle Holder, Pre Civil War, 2 1/2 In. 60.00
Toy, Towel Bar, Ornate Eastlake, With Mirror, 1 X 12 In. 28.00
Toy, Town Cooking School, Tin & Wood, Parker Bros., 33 Pieces 39.00
Toy, Town, Tin Buildings, West Bros., Westmoreland, Pa., 1914, 7 Pieces 40.00
Toy, Tractor, Cast Iron, Arcade, 3 1/2 In. 19.00
Toy, Tractor, Cranmer 20.00
Toy, Tractor, McCormick-Deering, Cast Iron 65.00
Toy, Tractor, Painted, Arcade, 4 In. 40.00
Toy, Tractor, Windup, Tin, Marx, 9 In. 30.00
Toy, Train Set, American Flyer, Burlington Zephyr, Aluminum, 1935, 4 Units 200.00
Toy, Train Set, American Flyer, No.2, Windup, Cast Iron 125.00
Toy, Train Set, American Flyer, 1946-1947, Gilbert, 6 Cars, Tracks, Beacon 100.00
Toy, Train Set, Battery Operated, Japan, 2 Piece, 19 In. 8.75
Toy, Train Set, Buddy L Standard Gauge, Switch Track, 5 Cars, 25 Track 1200.00
Toy, Train Set, Buddy L, Engine & 7 Cars .... *Illus* 1100.00
Toy, Train Set, Cast Iron, Engine, Car And Caboose 160.00
Toy, Train Set, Deluxe Old Mint Horney, Direction Book 110.00
Toy, Train Set, Hafner, Germany, Tin, 12 Piece 29.00
Toy, Train Set, L.S. & M.S., Cast Iron, Engine & Tender, 12 In. 60.00
Toy, Train Set, Lionel, Locomotive, Tender, 3 Cars Operating, 4 Switches, 1951 .... 950.00
Toy, Train Set, Lionel, No.2350, Little Joe, Electric 75.00
Toy, Train Set, Lionel, No.2363, Illinois Central 225.00
Toy, Train Set, Lionel, No.671, Turbine, 3 Pullman Cars 125.00
Toy, Train Set, Lionel, No, 244e, 4 Pullman Cars 150.00
Toy, Train Set, Lionel, Standard Gauge, Nos. 8e, 337, & 338, Green 210.00
Toy, Train Set, Lionel, 1924, O Gauge, Passenger, No.253 Engine 245.00
Toy, Train Set, Windup, Tin, U.S. Zone, Germany 10.00
Toy, Train Set, Wooden, Unpainted, Strombecker, 4 Piece 17.50
Toy, Train, Circus, Unique, 1950, Tin, 2 Jewel Tea Cars, 7 Piece 150.00
Toy, Train, Freight, Unique Art, 1950 .... 79.00
Toy, Train, Freight, Vanderbilt, Marx, 1938 .... 65.00
Toy, Train, Gilbert, American Flyer, Extra Cars, Tracks, 3 1/16 In.Scale 145.00
Toy, Train, Hubley, No.31, Die Cast, Orange, 5 In. 4.00
Toy, Train, Iron, Windup, American Flyer II, 6 7/8 In. 35.00

Toy, Truck, Milk, Tootsietoy, Federal, 3 In.

Toy, Truck, Mack, Stake, Tootsietoy, 3 In.

Toy, Train, Marx, Electric 40.00
Toy, Train, Schoenhut, 1926, Assemble It Yourself, Boxed 45.00
Toy, Train, Trackless, Clockwork, C.1880 .... 150.00
Toy, Trickauto, Strauss 95.00
Toy, Tricky Taxi On Busy Street, Marx 30.00
Toy, Tricycle, Elgin, Racer, C.1930 .... 50.00
Toy, Tricycle, Wood, Red Trim 37.00
Toy, Tricyclist, Boy, Clockwork, Ives, 1875 .... 980.00
Toy, Trolley, Steel Friction, C.1921, 18 In. 80.00
Toy, Trolley, Steel, Marked Pay As You Enter, 23 In. 85.00
Toy, Trolley, 270 Broadway, Tin, Chein, 8 In. 70.00
Toy, Truck, Army, Metal, Russian 10.00
Toy, Truck, Auto Transport, With 4 Cars, Metal, Tootsietoy, C.1950 .... 15.00
Toy, Truck, Buddy-L, Dump, 24 In. 45.00
Toy, Truck, Champion, Cast Iron, 7 1/2 In. 75.00
Toy, Truck, Coca-Cola, Stake Bed, Metal Wheels, Marx, 20 In. 65.00
Toy, Truck, Courtland Log, With Box 9.00
Toy, Truck, Courtland Side Dumper 13.00
Toy, Truck, Cracker Jack, Red 14.00
Toy, Truck, Dump, Arcade, 4 In. 18.00
Toy, Truck, Dump, Buddy L, C.1930 .... 35.00
Toy, Truck, Dump, Cast Iron, Hubley, 3 1/2 In. 50.00
Toy, Truck, Dump, Hydraulic Lift, Keystone 200.00
Toy, Truck, Dump, Packard, Buddy L 65.00
Toy, Truck, Dump, Red, Tin & Iron, Arcade 120.00
Toy, Truck, Fire, Hook & Ladder, Kenton, 10 In. 35.00
Toy, Truck, Fire, Hook & Ladder, 3 Horses, 2 Men, 4 Ladders .... *Illus* 400.00
Toy, Truck, Flat Bed Trailer, Schoenhut, 9 In. 12.00
Toy, Truck, Gas Tank, Mack, Tin & Iron, Williams, 7 In. 105.00
Toy, Truck, Gas, Bulldog, Iron, Mack, 4 In. 35.00

Toy, Truck, Gas, Cast Iron, Hubley, 5 In. 26.00
Toy, Truck, Grocery, Steel, Turner Mfg.Co., C.1920 .... 20.00 To 75.00
Toy, Truck, Harvester Dump, Arcade International, 10 1/2 In. 175.00
Toy, Truck, Hook & Ladder, Aeri 175.00
Toy, Truck, Laundry, Tootsietoy 25.00
Toy, Truck, Mack, Cast Iron 45.00
Toy, Truck, Mack, Stake, Tootsietoy, 3 In. .... *Illus* 18.00
Toy, Truck, Milk, Tootsietoy, Federal, 3 In. .... *Illus* 35.00
Toy, Truck, Model A Ford, Cast Iron, Arcade, C.1920 .... 35.00 To 65.00
Toy, Truck, Produce Type, Iron, Mack, 5 In. 50.00
Toy, Truck, REA, Metal, Power Tailgate, Lithographed, Marx, 19 In. 30.00
Toy, Truck, Stake, Cast Iron, Arcade, 5 In. 24.00
Toy, Truck, Van, C.F.Hovey, Boston, C.1910, 8 In. 575.00
Toy, Truck, Van, Strawbridge & Clothier, C.1910, 8 In. 650.00
Toy, Truck, Wrecker, Keystone 100.00

Toy, Trunk, see Trunk

Toy, Trunk, Doll's, Camelback, Cowhide, Lock & Key, 15 X 8 X 8 1/2 In. 100.00
Toy, Tut-Tut, Lehmann 400.00
Toy, Two Airplanes On Tower, Penny Toy, German, 1919 .... 23.00
Toy, Two Mice On Tin Pole, Lehmann 150.00
Toy, Typewriter, Dial, Marx, 1930 .... 22.50
Toy, Typewriter, Simplex, Dated 1916 .... 14.00
Toy, Typewriter, Simplex, 1905 .... 16.00
Toy, Typewriter, Tom Thumb 25.00
Toy, Vending Machine, Monkey Turns Crank, Battery Operated, Japan 17.00
Toy, Viewer, Child's Postcard, Tin, Lithographed, H.C.White Co., Vermont 69.00
Toy, Village, 4 Cardboard Buildings, Bradley, 1909 .... 22.00
Toy, Violin Uke, Marx 36.00
Toy, Wagon & Horse, Milk, Toytown, Windup, Marx 65.00
Toy, Wagon & Horses, Tin, Northwestern 55.00
Toy, Wagon, Borden's Milk, Horse Drawn, Tin & Wood, 4 Milk Bottles 125.00
Toy, Wagon, Cast Iron, Arcade 15.00
Toy, Wagon, Cast Iron, Kenton, Horse Drawn, Bakery 125.00
Toy, Wagon, Circus, Tin & Iron, Keaton 115.00
Toy, Wagon, Horse Drawn, Cloth & Wood, C.1860, 26 In. .... *Illus* 140.00
Toy, Wagon, Horse Driven, Northwestern 30.00
Toy, Wagon, Overland Circus, White Bear In Cage, Driver, 2 Horses, 14 In. 225.00
Toy, Wagon, Sand & Gravel, Horse Drawn, Dump, Cast Iron, Kenton 80.00
Toy, Wagon, Tin, Windup, Trip-Trap, Germany, 7 X 4 1/2 In.High .... *Illus* 75.00
Toy, Wagon, Toytown Horse Drawn Milk Wagon 25.00
Toy, Wagon, Wood, 12 In. 45.00
Toy, Wagon, Wooden Painted Horse Pulling Milk Wagon, Pressed Wood 35.00
Toy, Walking Doll & Cart, 10 In. .... *Illus* 1000.00
Toy, Walking Santa Claus, Celluloid, Metal Feet, Occupied Japan, 6 1/2 In. 20.00
Toy, Washboard, Child's, Reg.No.818, 15 X 7 In. 8.00
Toy, Washboard, Little Housekeeper 8.50
Toy, Washing Machine, Marx 25.00
Toy, Washing Machine, Pretty Maid, Glass & Metal 14.00
Toy, Washing Machine, Revell 5.00

Toy, Wagon, Horse Drawn, Cloth & Wood, C.1860, 26 In.

Toy, Wagon, Tin, Windup, Trip-Trap, Germany, 7 X 4 1/2 In.High
(See Page 687)

Tramp Art, Box, 7 In.Long

Toy, Walking Doll & Cart, 10 In.
(See Page 687)

Treen, Pepperpot, 5 In.

Toy, Washing Machine, Wringer, Tin & Glass, Wolverine 22.00
Toy, Washstand Set, Doll's, Tin 15.00
Toy, Wheelbarrow, Windup, Pop-Eye, Trunk And Parrot 22.00
Toy, Whirligig, Farm Scene, Wooden, Painted, Carved, C.1890, 52 In. 775.00
Toy, Whirligig, Indian In Canoe, Wooden, Carved & Painted, 9 In. 200.00
Toy, Windmill, Red Paint, Empire Metal Ware 82.00
Toy, Yellow Cab, Cast Iron, Arcade, C.1925, 8 In. 250.00
Toy, Zulu, Windup, Tin, Lehmann 125.00

Toy, 2 Donkeys Pulling Man In Cart, Windup 40.00
Trap, see Tool, Trap

Tramp Art is a form of folk art made since the Civil War. It is usually made from chip-carved cigar boxes.

Tramp Art, Altar, Home, Quebec 2600.00
Tramp Art, Box, Jewelry 55.00
Tramp Art, Box, Sewing, Shakespeare, Ontario, Pedestal Base 225.00
Tramp Art, Box, 7 In.Long .... *Illus* 28.00
Tramp Art, Clock Holder, In Shape Of Church 145.00
Tramp Art, Crucifix, 12 In. 260.00
Tramp Art, Dresser, Doll's 85.00
Tramp Art, Frame, Aquatint Photographs Of 25 Presidents, Carved, 1950, 5 Ft. 200.00
Tramp Art, Frame, Double, Each Opening 3 1/2 X 5 1/4 In. 18.00
Tramp Art, Lamp Base, 3 Balls In Cage, Carved, Dated 1935 .... 38.00
Tramp Art, Plaque, Wall, Eagle, Flags, Clasped Hands, Horseshoe, Scalloped 140.00

Treen are small wooden objects such as mugs, spoons, and bowls. The term is early English but is used in the United States in many areas.

Treen, Box, Salt, Hand Hewn, Handle, Covered 98.00
Treen, Document Holder, 15 In. 8.50
Treen, Goblet, Signed Jos.Jones, Camden, N.J., 1894, 3 1/2 In. 15.00
Treen, Pepperpot, 5 In. .... *Illus* 48.00
Treen, Pie Crimper, Wheel And Depressed Sawtooth Ends, Folk Art, 5 1/2 In. 48.00
Trent Tile Co., Tile, Child & Bird, Isaac Broome, Round, 6 In. 50.00

Trivets are now used to hold hot dishes. Most of the late nineteenth and early twentieth century trivets were made to hold hot irons. Iron or brass reproductions are being made of many of the old styles. The H-xx numbers refer to the book "Trivets" by Dick Hankerson.

Trivet, Brass, Grapes & Leaves, 7 1/2 X 4 In. 25.00
Trivet, Brass, Lyre Shape, Turned Handle, 14 In. 50.00
Trivet, Brass, No.2182, 5 X 2 In. 25.00
Trivet, Cast Iron, Leaves & Grapes, Handle 25.00
Trivet, Iron, Enterprise, Phila. 5.50
Trivet, Iron, Ferrosteel Urn, Cleveland, H-121 .... 6.95
Trivet, Iron, Heart & Initial W, Handle, H-50 .... 7.00
Trivet, Iron, Heart Pierced By 2 Arrows 18.00
Trivet, Iron, Heart With W, Handled, H-50 .... 7.95
Trivet, Iron, Horseshoe, Dove Top, Hand Holding Heart Center, Odd Fellows 11.75
Trivet, Iron, Lacy, 3 1/2 X 2 1/4 In. 5.00
Trivet, Iron, Letter H, H-126 .... 6.95
Trivet, Iron, Simmons Special, Openwork, Pointed Ends, 7 In. 13.75
Trivet, Iron, Target, Handled, H-55 .... 6.95
Trivet, Iron, Triangular, 3 Sided, 3 Legs, American, C.1750, 13 In. 46.00
Trivet, Sterling Silver & Crystal 30.00
Trunk, Child's, Camelback, 26 In. 50.00
Trunk, Doll's, Camelback, Cowhide, Lock & Key, 15 X 8 X 8 1/2 In. 100.00
Trunk, Doll's, Camelback, Paper On Wood, C.1895 .... 55.00
Trunk, Doll's, Dome Top, Paper Covered 12.00
Trunk, Doll's, Dome Type, Wooden, Inner Shelf 38.00
Trunk, Doll's, Penny Brite, 1 Outfit Inside 10.00
Trunk, Doll's, Steamer 17.00
Trunk, Doll's, Top Storing Box, Flat Top, 18 1/2 In. 35.00
Trunk, Doll's, Travel Stickers 37.50
Trunk, Doll's, Wooden, 10 X 4 In. 25.00
Trunk, Doll's, Wooden, 12 X 6 In. 35.00
Trunk, Wallpaper, Domed Lid, Footed, Initials A.W. In Tin Lock Plate 195.00
Trunk, Wood, Hand Dovetailed, Curved Top, Sealskin Covered, 36 X 14 X 19, Lock 95.00
Typewriter, Blickensderfer, C.1880, Ball Style, Case 55.00
Typewriter, Blickensderfer, No. 5, Oak Case, Extra Typewheel 85.00
Typewriter, Blickensderfer, No.7, C.1890, Wooden Case 35.00
Typewriter, Corona, Folding 35.00
Typewriter, Corona, Office Specialties, Folds Up, 8 1/4 X 9 X 6 In. 55.00
Typewriter, Merritt, 1890, Wooden Case 95.00

Typewriter, Oliver, No.9, Patent 1912 .... 50.00
Typewriter, Simplex, Model B, C.1910, Tin 11.00
Typewriter, Underwood, No.5 .... 70.00
U.S.Quarry Tile Co., Plate, Romany Tiles, Blue & Green, 10 In. 25.00
Umbrella, Buffalo Horn Handle 12.00
Umbrella, Child's Parasol, Black, Folding 10.00
Umbrella, Parasol, Dark Green Silk, Carved Sandalwood Handle 14.00
Union Porcelain Works, Plate, Oyster, Greenpoint, C.1881 * 50.00 To 95.00
University No.Dakota School Of Mines, Bowl, Green Wheat, 7 In. 28.50
University No.Dakota School Of Mines, Box, Luminous White, Classic, 1914 .... 250.00

Val St Lambert *Val St.Lambert Cristalleries of Belgium was founded by Messieurs Kemlin and Lelievre in 1825. The company is still in operation.*

Val St.Lambert, Bottle, Cologne, Etched, Gold Trim, 7 1/2 In. 25.00
Val St.Lambert, Bottle, Cologne, Vaseline, Belgium, 8 X 6 1/2 In. 75.00
Val St.Lambert, Bottle, Perfume, Etched, Gold Trim, 5 3/4 In. 20.00
Val St.Lambert, Bottle, Perfume, Silver Plate Stopper, Cranberry Floral 115.00
Val St.Lambert, Bowl, Crystal, Flaring Rim, Signed, 12 X 4 In. 39.00
Val St.Lambert, Box, Covered, Etched, Gold Trim, Round, 3 1/4 In. 20.00
Val St.Lambert, Compote, Crystal, Teardrop Blown In Stem, 8 1/4 In. 30.00
Val St.Lambert, Dish, Dresser, Cameo Cover, Cranberry Florals, Signed 150.00
Val St.Lambert, Dish, Dresser, Cameo Cover, Cranberry Florals, 3 1/2 In. 150.00
Val St.Lambert, Dresser Set, 5 Piece 125.00
Val St.Lambert, Dresser Set, 9 Piece 97.50
Val St.Lambert, Goblet, Beehive, Rigaree On Stem, Master Size 45.00
Val St.Lambert, Tray, Dresser, Etched, Gold Trim, Oval, 5 X 3 1/2 In. 10.00
Val St.Lambert, Tray, Soap, Etched, Gold Trim, 4 3/4 X 3 3/4 In. 10.00
Val St.Lambert, Tumble-Up Set, Etched, Gold Trim, 3 Piece 60.00
Val St.Lambert, Tumbler, Water, Shallow, Cameo 35.00
Val St.Lambert, Vase, Bud, Rough Camphor, Blue Flowers, 6 1/2 In. 165.00
Val St.Lambert, Vase, Frosted, Lavender & Purple Floral & Leaf, 10 In. 250.00
Vallerystahl, Butter, Standing Cow Cover, Ribbed, Beaded Trim, Oval, 7 In. 55.00
Vallerystahl, Dish, Covered, Shell Decoration, Milk Glass, Unsigned, 5 1/2 In. 40.00
Vallerystahl, Dish, Dog Cover, Floral Base, Oblong, Milk Glass, Signed 115.00
Vallerystahl, Dish, Rabbit Cover, Frosted, Milk Glass, 3 1/2 In. 50.00
Vallerystahl, Dish, Rabbit Cover, Frosted, Milk Glass, 6 In. 50.00
Vallerystahl, Milk Glass, Dish, Hen, Cover, 2 1/2 X 2 In., Unmarked 26.50
Vallerystahl, Plate, Hen, Milk Glass, Signed 22.00
Vallerystahl, Salt, Individual, Green, Covered Hen 12.50
Vallerystahl, Tumbler, Grape Pattern 12.00

Van Briggle Pottery was made by Artus Van Briggle in Colorado Springs, Colorado, after 1901. Mr.Van Briggle had been a decorator at the Rookwood Pottery of Cincinnati, Ohio, and he died in 1904. His wares were original and had modeled relief decorations with a soft dull glaze.

Van Briggle, Ashtray, Maroon, Colorado Springs, 6 1/4 In. 12.00
Van Briggle, Bookend, Owl, Turquoise, Pair 60.00
Van Briggle, Bowl & Flower Frog, Dragonfly, Persian Rose, 9 In. 35.00
Van Briggle, Bowl Vase, Turquoise Ming, 4 1/2 X 2 1/4 In. 30.00
Van Briggle, Bowl, Acorn & Leaves, Turquoise 17.50
Van Briggle, Bowl, Blue, Handled, 7 1/2 In. 20.00
Van Briggle, Bowl, Leaf Shape, Turquoise, Signed, 5 In. 25.00
Van Briggle, Bowl, Mulberry, 1918, No.681 .... 25.00
Van Briggle, Bowl, Persian Rose, High Relief Florals, Old Mark, 6 1/2 In. 16.00
Van Briggle, Bowl, Persian Rose, Leaves Around Top, 4 1/2 X 4 In. 15.00
Van Briggle, Bowl, With Flower Frogs, Persian Rose, 1915, 8 1/2 In. 42.50
Van Briggle, Candleholder, Blue Ming, Relief Blooms & Vines, 1906, 10 1/2 In. 95.00
Van Briggle, Candlestick, Double Tulip, Turquoise, Signed, 4 1/2 In. 25.00
Van Briggle, Candlestick, Persian Rose, 9 1/8 In., Pair 39.00
Van Briggle, Conch, Blue Figural, 9 In. 18.50
Van Briggle, Console Set, Tulip, Frog, 3 Pieces 30.00
Van Briggle, Console Set, Tulip, Persian Rose, 4 Piece 35.00
Van Briggle, Console Set, Turquoise Ming, Double Candles, 3 Piece 50.00
Van Briggle, Figurine, Elephant, Turquoise, Ming, 5 In. 40.00
Van Briggle, Flower Bowl & Frog, Turquoise, Ming, 8 In. 45.00

Van Briggle, Flower Frog, Blue Duck 11.00
Van Briggle, Jug, Copper, Green, Crabs, Eagle 58.00
Van Briggle, Lamp Base, Turquoise Ming, C.1901, 10 In., Pair 95.00
Van Briggle, Lamp, Colorado Springs, Blue Shade, Stylized Tulips, 13 1/2 In. 60.00
Van Briggle, Lamp, Persian Rose, Tulip Shape, 3 Handles, 6 In., Pair 80.00
Van Briggle, Lamp, 3 Indian Faces, Shaded Blues 152.50
Van Briggle, Paperweight, Bust Of Indian, 4 1/2 X 2 1/2 X 1 3/4 In. 75.00
Van Briggle, Paperweight, Elephant 25.00
Van Briggle, Paperweight, Puffed-Out Portrait Of Indian, 4 3/4 In. 45.00
Van Briggle, Paperweight, Rabbit 12.00
Van Briggle, Pitcher, Cobalt With White Drip Shiny Glaze, 8 In. 37.00
Van Briggle, Pitcher, Persian Rose, C.1930, 9 In. 20.00
Van Briggle, Pitcher, Persian Rose, Pyriform, 8 X 4 1/2 In. 35.00
Van Briggle, Planter, Blue Dragonfly, Triple Frog Insert, Blue 45.00
Van Briggle, Plaque, Little Star Indian 45.00
Van Briggle, Rose Bowl, Maroon With Acorns & Leaves, 3 1/2 In. 25.00
Van Briggle, Rose Bowl, Turquoise, 2 In. 11.00
Van Briggle, Shell, Blue, 12 In. 22.00
Van Briggle, Vase, Anna Van Briggle Memorial, Tan & White Glaze, 7 In. 30.00
Van Briggle, Vase, Anna Van, Woman, Turquoise, 17 In. 225.00
Van Briggle, Vase, Blue & Aqua, C.1930, 2 1/4 In. 20.00
Van Briggle, Vase, Blue Green Glaze, Molded Florals, 4 1/2 In. 9.00
Van Briggle, Vase, Blue Green Twist, Matte Finish, 7 1/2 In. 35.00
Van Briggle, Vase, Blue Green, Lilies, 4 3/4 In. 22.50
Van Briggle, Vase, Blue To Green Top, Water Lily Leaves & Buds, 5 In. 25.00
Van Briggle, Vase, Brown, Violets, No.645, Colorado Springs, 4 1/2 In. 18.00
Van Briggle, Vase, Bud, Burgundy 15.00
Van Briggle, Vase, Bud, Glossy Brown, Anna Van Briggle, 7 In. 15.00
Van Briggle, Vase, Bud, Persian Rose, 9 In. 18.00
Van Briggle, Vase, Bud, Turquoise Ming, 7 In. 11.50
Van Briggle, Vase, Dragonfly, Blue, 6 1/2 In. 15.00
Van Briggle, Vase, Floral Design, Blue, 1906, 8 1/2 In. 135.00
Van Briggle, Vase, Green To Blue, 6 In. 7.50
Van Briggle, Vase, Green To Turquoise, 6 In. 20.00
Van Briggle, Vase, Incised Art Nouveau, Peanut Butter Color, 1905, 10 1/2 In. 185.00
Van Briggle, Vase, Maroon & Blue, Dated 1936, Signed 25.00
Van Briggle, Vase, Maroon, Butterfly, 1920, 2 1/2 In. 30.00
Van Briggle, Vase, Mottled Turquoise, Geometrics, 1920, 14 In. 150.00
Van Briggle, Vase, Mulberry Tropical Leaves, 1916, 5 1/2 In. 48.50
Van Briggle, Vase, Mulberry, 1920 Mark, No. 838 .... 30.00
Van Briggle, Vase, Mustard And Green, Molded Flowing Leaves, 5 1/2 In. 22.50
Van Briggle, Vase, Ovoid, Maroon, Raised Flower, Dated 1920 .... 50.00
Van Briggle, Vase, Persian Rose, Lavender, 8 1/2 In. 18.00
Van Briggle, Vase, Persian Rose, Molded Design, 6 1/4 In. 15.00
Van Briggle, Vase, Persian Rose, Pre-1930 .... 18.00
Van Briggle, Vase, Plum To Gray, Molded Butterflies, C.1920, 3 In. 28.00
Van Briggle, Vase, Three Dragonflies, Blue, 7 In. 26.00
Van Briggle, Vase, Three Flowers, Plum To Rose, 6 In. 18.00
Van Briggle, Vase, Three Indian Faces In Relief, Turquoise, 11 In. 85.00
Van Briggle, Vase, Three Indian Heads At Top, Brown, Green, 11 In. 100.00
Van Briggle, Vase, Tulip Shape, Shaded Rose To Mauve, 3 1/2 In. 10.00
Van Briggle, Vase, Turquoise & Blue, Molded Floral, 7 1/4 In. 15.00
Van Briggle, Vase, Turquoise Art Deco Design, Matte Finish, Signed 22.50
Van Briggle, Vase, Turquoise Ming, Long Stem Roses, 14 In. 55.00
Van Briggle, Vase, Turquoise Ming, Lorelei, 1970, 11 In. 40.00
Van Briggle, Vase, Turquoise Ming, Molded Feathers, 4 X 3 In. 35.00
Van Briggle, Vase, Turquoise, Relief Flowers & Leaves, 4 1/2 In. 25.00
Van Briggle, Vase, Turquoise, Ribbed, Fan, 7 1/4 In. 24.00
Van Briggle, Vase, With Flower Frog, Siren Of The Sea 65.00
Van Briggle, Vase, Yucca Leaves, Turquoise Sprigs, 4 5/8 X 5 1/2 In. 18.00

Vasa Murrhina is the name of a glassware made by the Vasa Murrhina Art Glass Company of Sandwich, Massachusetts, about 1884. The glassware was transparent and was embedded with small pieces of colored glass and metallic flakes. Some of the pieces were cased. The same type of glass was made in England. Collectors often confuse Vasa Murrhina glass with aventurine, spatter, or spangle glass. There is much confusion about what actually was made by the Vasa Murrhina Factory.

Vasa Murrhina, see also Spangle Glass

Vasa Murrhina, Basket, Thorn Handle 125.00
Vasa Murrhina, Bowl, Crimped, Pink & Chartreuse, Mica Flakes, 7 1/2 In. 80.00
Vasa Murrhina, Bride's Bowl, Cranberry To White, Clear Ruffled Rim, 11 In. 60.00
Vasa Murrhina, Cruet, Mint Green, Clear Handle And Stopper 100.00
Vasa Murrhina, Cruet, Pink Spatter, Amber Handle And Stopper 200.00
Vasa Murrhina, Rose Bowl, Blue & White, Silver Flecks, 5 1/4 In. 85.00
Vasa Murrhina, Rose Bowl, Blue, White Lining, 8 Crimped Top, 3 1/2 In. 88.00
Vasa Murrhina, Rose Bowl, Pink & White, Silver Mica, Red Spatter, 4 1/2 In. 60.00
Vasa Murrhina, Rose Bowl, Robin's-Egg Blue, White Spatter, Cased, 4 1/2 In. 65.00
Vasa Murrhina, Rose Bowl, Rose Color, Overlay, White Lining, 3 5/8 In. 88.00
Vasa Murrhina, Spooner, Cranberry, White Spatter, Gold Mica 38.00
Vasa Murrhina, Syrup, White & Pink, Brass Top 80.00
Vasa Murrhina, Tumbler, Blue & White 45.00
Vasa Murrhina, Tumbler, Gold Flakes 145.00
Vasa Murrhina, Vase, Aquamarine, Cased, Applied Clear Thorn Handles, 8 In. 150.00
Vasa Murrhina, Vase, Aquamarine, Cased, Blown, Silver Spatter, 7 1/4 In. 150.00
Vasa Murrhina, Vase, Aquamarine, Clear Thorn Handles, 7 1/4 In. 150.00
Vasa Murrhina, Vase, Blue With White, 5 In. 45.00
Vasa Murrhina, Vase, Multicolor Casing, 7 In. 35.00
Vasa Murrhina, Vase, Rainbow, Silver Spangles & Mica, White Lined, 9 1/2 In. 65.00
Vasa Murrhina, Vase, Rose Color, Overlay, White Lining, Clear Edge, 7 1/2 In. 65.00
Vasa Murrhina, Vase, Thorn Glass Handles, Cased & Blown, Silver Spatter 150.00

Vasart is the signature used on a late type of art glass made by the Streathearn Glass Company of Scotland.

Vasart, Basket, Green & White, 5 1/2 X 4 In. 25.00
Vasart, Basket, Mottled Green & Gray, Signed 45.00
Vasart, Basket, Pink & White, 8 X 6 In. 45.00
Vasart, Bowl, Blue To Pink, Blossom Shape, 5 X 1 1/4 In. 24.00
Vasart, Bowl, Mottled Orange & Black, Swirled, Semifooted, Flared, 9 In. 35.00
Vasart, Bowl, Mottled Orange To Swirled Black & Orange Top, Footed, 8 In. 38.00
Vasart, Bowl, Swirled Orange & Black In Clear, Flared, 9 X 3 1/2 In. 35.00
Vasart, Bowl, Undulating Rim, Blue To Pink, 5 X 1 1/2 In. 20.00
Vasart, Dish, Candy, Pink To Green, Flaring, 5 X 6 X 2 In. 45.00
Vasart, Hat, Derby Type, Mottled Pastel Green & White, 4 X 3 X 2 1/4 In. 35.00
Vasart, Hat, Mottled Green And Gray, 2 1/4 X 4 In. 38.00
Vasart, Hat, Mottled Green To White, 4 In. 38.00
Vasart, Hat, Mottled Green To White, 4 X 3 1/4 In. 35.00

Vaseline glass is a greenish yellow glassware resembling petroleum jelly. Some vaseline glass is still being made in old and new styles. Pressed glass of the 1870s was often made of vaseline-colored glass. The old glass was made with uranium, but the reproductions are being colored in a different way. See Pressed Glass for more information about patterns that were also made of vaseline-colored glass.

Vaseline Glass, Basket, Cased Glass, Rose Bowl Shape, 6 3/4 In. 35.00
Vaseline Glass, Basket, Opalescent, 3 3/4 In. 50.00
Vaseline Glass, Bottle, Barber, Cut, 6 1/2 In. 47.50
Vaseline Glass, Bowl, Berry, Alaska, Decorated 125.00
Vaseline Glass, Bowl, Finger And Plate, Ruffled And Threaded 58.00
Vaseline Glass, Bowl, Pedestal, Moon & Star, Lid, Finial, 7 In. 35.00
Vaseline Glass, Box, Covered, Button & Star 24.00
Vaseline Glass, Candlestick, Baluster Shape, 6 1/2 In., Pair 38.00
Vaseline Glass, Candlestick, Dolphin Shape, Pair 32.50
Vaseline Glass, Castor, Pickle, Finecut, Frame 110.00
Vaseline Glass, Celery, Cut Daisy Sprays 42.00
Vaseline Glass, Celery, Daisy & Button 40.00
Vaseline Glass, Compote, Daisy & Button With Crossbar, 7 1/2 In. 75.00
Vaseline Glass, Compote, Dolphin Figural Stem 15.00
Vaseline Glass, Compote, Dolphin, Opalescent 35.00
Vaseline Glass, Compote, Moon & Star, Covered, 16 In. 30.00

Vaseline Glass, Covered Butter, Creamer And Spooner, Opalescent 125.00
Vaseline Glass, Cruet, Daisy & Fern 75.00
Vaseline Glass, Cruet, Dewey 125.00
Vaseline Glass, Dish, Duck Cover, Glows In Black Light, 5 In. 38.50
Vaseline Glass, Dish, Opalescent, Daisy Pattern, 6 1/2 X 1 5/8 In. 58.00
Vaseline Glass, Dish, Sauce, Opalescent Swag Brackets 20.00
Vaseline Glass, Epergne, Opalescent, 5-Lily, Silver Plate Stand, 15 In. 250.00
Vaseline Glass, Finger Bowl & Underplate, Threaded 85.00
Vaseline Glass, Goblet, Wildflower, Fiery Color 32.00
Vaseline Glass, Jar, Cracker, Opalescent, Cactus Pattern 98.00
Vaseline Glass, Platter, Oval, Maple Leaf 58.00
Vaseline Glass, Relish, Metal Basket Holder 30.00
Vaseline Glass, Rose Bowl, Beaded Drapes, Opalescent 32.50
Vaseline Glass, Rose Bowl, Beaded Panel, 5 1/2 In. .... *Illus* 45.00
Vaseline Glass, Salt & Pepper, Christmas, Agitator Top, Flint, 1877 .... 140.00
Vaseline Glass, Salt & Pepper, Corset Shape, Daisy & Button, Pair 29.50
Vaseline Glass, Salt & Pepper, Wildflower 50.00
Vaseline Glass, Salt, Swan 7.50

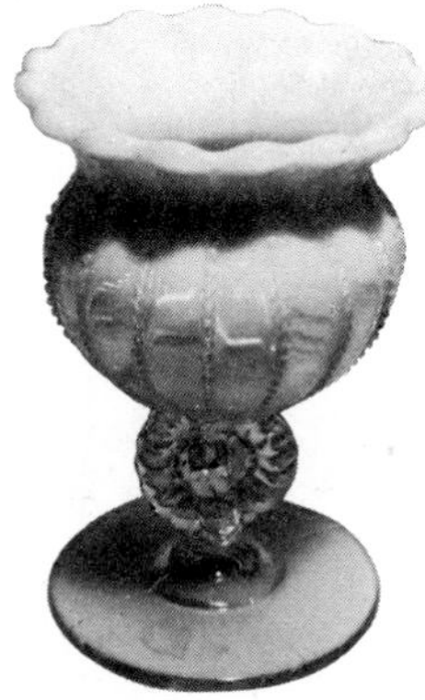

Vaseline Glass, Rose Bowl, Beaded Panel, 5 1/2 In.

Vaseline Glass, Tumbler, New Orleans, 1885

Vaseline Glass, Salt, Wreath & Shell 65.00
Vaseline Glass, Shade, Opalescent Swirl, Ruffled Rim, 6 In. 20.00
Vaseline Glass, Shoe, M.Sollers Co., N.8th St., Phila., Pa. 32.00
Vaseline Glass, Shoe, On Skate 20.00
Vaseline Glass, Slipper, Daisy & Button, Flat Bow 14.00
Vaseline Glass, Slipper, Daisy & Button, 3 1/8 In. 30.00
Vaseline Glass, Slipper, Daisy And Button, 3 1/8 In. 30.00
Vaseline Glass, Spooner, Flora 40.00
Vaseline Glass, Spooner, Pillared Loop, Flint 75.00
Vaseline Glass, Sugar & Creamer, Austrian, Open Sugar 110.00
Vaseline Glass, Sugar Shaker, Spatter 165.00
Vaseline Glass, Sugar, Flora, Open 25.00
Vaseline Glass, Syrup, Opal, Reverse Swirl 85.00
Vaseline Glass, Syrup, Opalescent, Bubble Lattice 110.00
Vaseline Glass, Syrup, Spatter, Leaf Mold, Applied Handle 245.00
Vaseline Glass, Toothpick, Beaumont, Columbia 38.00
Vaseline Glass, Tumbler, Daisy & Button, With Crossbars 22.50
Vaseline Glass, Tumbler, New Orleans, 1885 .... *Illus* 15.00
Vaseline Glass, Vase, Cranberry To White To Clear To Vaseline, 6 In. 40.00
Vaseline Glass, Vase, Daisy & Button, Pair 35.00
Vaseline Glass, Vase, Fan, 5 In. 125.00
Vaseline Glass, Vase, Flared Top, White Swirled Sides, 6 In. 35.00
Vaseline Glass, Vase, Opalescent, Hand & Cornucopia 48.00

Venetian glass has been made near Venice, Italy, from the thirteenth to the twentieth century. Thin colored glass with applied decorations is favored although many other types have been made.

Venetian Glass, Basket, Flowers, Green Leaves Border, Clear Glass Basket 175.00
Venetian Glass, Bottle, Scent, Gold, Pink, Yellow, White Ribbons 35.00
Venetian Glass, Bottle, Scent, Lavender, Flowers, Goldstone Decoration 75.00
Venetian Glass, Bottle, Scent, Yellow, 1 1/4 In. 75.00
Venetian Glass, Candlestick, Applied Fruits, 10 In. 26.00
Venetian Glass, Candlestick, Dolphin, Blue Fluted Lutz Top, 6 1/4 In., Pair 135.00
Venetian Glass, Card Holder, Swans On Each Side 36.00
Venetian Glass, Chalice, Gossamer And Delicate, Hand Blown, Footed, 9 X 6 In. 95.00
Venetian Glass, Compote, Smoky, 7 1/4 X 6 1/2 In. 59.00
Venetian Glass, Compote, Twist Stem, Selenium Red 45.00
Venetian Glass, Goblet, Dolphin Stem, Yellow Eyes, 8 In. 55.00
Venetian Glass, Plate, Pink, Gold Sprayed, 7 1/4 In. 16.50
Venetian Glass, Sherbet, Green, Coaching Scenes, Gold Trim, C.1880 .... 65.00
Venetian Glass, Vase, Gold, Green, White, 6 In. 50.00
Venetian Glass, Vase, Raised Enamel Decoration 65.00
Venetian Glass, Vase, Rose Petal, Crimped Edging, Turquoise & Yellow 35.00
Venetian Glass, Vase, White, Gild-Outlined Bubbles & Dolphin Stem, 10 In. 40.00

Verlys glass was made in France after 1931. Verlys was also made in the United States. The glass is either blown or molded. The American glass is signed with a diamond-point-scratched name, but the French pieces are marked with a molded signature.

Verlys, Bowl, Blue Thistle, Signed In Mold, Paper Label, 6 1/4 In. 75.00
Verlys, Bowl, Cupidon, 6 X 2 In. 65.00
Verlys, Bowl, Frosted Poppies & Leaves, Script Signed, 13 1/2 X 2 1/2 In. 89.50
Verlys, Bowl, Frosted, Tassels, Signed, 13 1/2 In. 50.00
Verlys, Bowl, Fruit, Frosted Birds & Leaves, 11 In. 22.50
Verlys, Bowl, Kingfisher, Script Signed, 13 1/2 In. 80.00
Verlys, Bowl, Lovebird, Signed 45.00
Verlys, Bowl, Poppy, Signed, 14 X 2 3/4 In. 35.00
Verlys, Bowl, Tassel, Frosted, 11 5/8 X 2 7/8 In. 67.50
Verlys, Bowl, Thistle Pattern, Signed, 9 In. 75.00
Verlys, Bowl, Waterlily, Frosted, 14 In. 95.00
Verlys, Bowl, Wheat, Double Signed, 12 In. 65.00
Verlys, Bowl, 4 Frosted Poppies & Leaves, Script Signed, 13 1/2 In. 89.00
Verlys, Candleholder, Frosted Leaves, Pair 42.50
Verlys, Candlestick, Frosted Leaves, 5 In., Pair 35.00
Verlys, Charger, Orchid Bowl, 13 In. 95.00
Verlys, Planter, Frosted Mum, Signed, 10 X 6 X 4 1/2 In. 70.00
Verlys, Vase, Acorn, 10 X 7 In. 85.00
Verlys, Vase, Amber Thistle 135.00
Verlys, Vase, Bell Shape Inverted, Sunflowers, Script, Signed, 8 3/4 In. 85.00
Verlys, Vase, Bell Shape, Frosted Sunflowers, 8 1/2 In. 85.00
Verlys, Vase, Bell Shape, Thistle Pattern, Script Signed, 8 In. 50.00
Verlys, Vase, Flare Top, Square Base, Frosted Cactus, Signed, 6 X 8 In. 85.00
Verlys, Vase, Four Seasons, Pair 350.00
Verlys, Vase, Frosted Love Bird, 4 1/2 X 6 1/2 In. 35.00
Verlys, Vase, Frosted Thistles, Clear Panels, 10 X 6 1/4 In. 95.00
Verlys, Vase, Frosted, Pink Lovebirds, Fan Shape, 6 In. 48.00
Verlys, Vase, Gems, Script Signed, Clear, 6 1/2 In. 60.00
Verlys, Vase, Love Birds, Signed, Crystal Etching 60.00
Verlys, Vase, Thistle, Etched, 9 7/8 In. 93.00
Verona, Vase, Gold-Outlined Purple Iris, 6 1/4 X 4 In. 65.00
Verona, Vase, Purple Iris, 6 1/4 X 4 In. 65.00
Verona, Vase, Squat, Pansy Decoration, 3 3/4 X 6 1/2 In. 75.00
Verona, Vase, White Lily Decoration, 8 In. 65.00
Verona, Vase, White Lily Decoration, 9 In. 75.00

Verre de soie glass was first made by Frederick Carder at the Steuben Glass Works from about 1905 to 1930. It is an iridescent glass of soft white or very, very pale green. The name means glass of silk, and it does resemble silk. Other factories have made verre de soie, and some of the English examples were made of different colors. Verre de soie is an art glass and is not related to the iridescent pressed white carnival glass mistakenly called by its name.

Verre De Soie, see also Steuben

Verre De Soie, Box, Powder, Hawkes, Sterling Lid, Engraved Flowers 59.00
Verre De Soie, Candlestick, Cyprian, Twist Stem, Pair 110.00
Verre De Soie, Glass, Portrait, Etched, Iridescent, Signed Hawkes, 6 In. 35.00
Verre De Soie, Sherbets, Underplates, Set Of Eight 240.00
Verre De Soie, Vase, Rainbow Colors Pulled From Base To Top, 12 In. 40.00
Verre De Soie, Vase, Venetian, Swirled, Crimped Edge, Leaf Handle, 5 1/2 In. 65.00

Vienna Art plates were round metal serving trays produced around the turn of the century. They were produced in Coshocton, Ohio, by J. F. Meek's Tuscarora Advertising Co., and H. D. Beach's Standard Advertising Co.

Vienna Art, see also Coca-Cola

Vienna Art, Plate, Auburn-Haired Girl Holding Rose 28.00
Vienna Art, Plate, El Gallo Cigars, Fighting Cocks, 10 In. 75.00
Vienna Art, Plate, Full Lady, Stone Urns, 10 In. 35.00
Vienna Art, Plate, Girl With Rose Dress, Vase Of Flowers 28.00
Vienna Art, Plate, Girl With Yellow Cap, Low-Cut Dress 28.00
Vienna Art, Plate, Nude, Fancy Gold Frame, 1905 .... 165.00
Vienna Art, Plate, Woman & Cupids, Blue, Tin, 10 In. 12.50
Vieux Paris, Vase, Empire Form, Caryatid Handles, Classic Scene, C.1830 .... 275.00

Villeroy & Boch Pottery of Mettlach, Germany, was founded in 1841. The firm made many types of pottery, including the famous Mettlach steins.

Villeroy & Boch, see also Mettlach

Villeroy & Boch, Cigar Holder, Elf And Toadstools, Scratcher On Base 100.00
Villeroy & Boch, Cup & Saucer, Jardiniere, Mulberry 22.50
Villeroy & Boch, Jar, Jam 18.00
Villeroy & Boch, Jar, Tobacco, Rose Color, Green & Yellow Spatter 28.00
Villeroy & Boch, Pitcher, Coral & Cream, Dresden, Saxony, 8 X 6 In. 16.00
Villeroy & Boch, Pitcher, Green, Gold Medallions & Trim, 9 In. 25.00
Villeroy & Boch, Plaque, Buck & Doe Mountain Scene, Wallerfangen, 15 In. 195.00
Villeroy & Boch, Plate, Bird & Floral, Blue And White, Divided, 11 In. 20.00
Villeroy & Boch, Plate, Red Flowers, 10 In. 18.00
Villeroy & Boch, Tea Set, Child's, Green, Lavish Scrolls, Florals, Scenic 250.00
Villeroy & Boch, Tray, Trinity Church, Boston, Olive Green, Rimmed, 9 In. 18.00
Villeroy & Boch, Tray, White Glaze, Pouring Lip, 10 X 8 In. 35.00
Villeroy & Boch, Vase, Maroon, Brass Collar & Handles, 14 1/2 In. 250.00
Volkmar, Vase, Incised Geometric Top, Tan And Green, Signed, 5 1/2 X 5 In. 95.00
Volkstadt, Rudolstadt, Sugar, Bud, Finial, Floral, Kidney Shape 35.00

Wallace Nutting, see Print, Nutting
Walt Disney, see Disneyana

Warwick china was made in Wheeling, West Virginia, in a pottery factory founded in 1887.

Warwick, Jar, Tobacco, Browns, Poppies, 7 In. 20.00
Warwick, Mug, Portrait, Man With Guitar 39.00
Warwick, Pitcher & Mugs, 6, Monk, High Glace, Set 325.00
Warwick, Pitcher, Beige, Gold Melon Ribbed Scalloped Top, Mark, 8 1/2 In. 85.00
Warwick, Pitcher, Girl With Flowing Hair, 6 1/2 In. 35.00
Warwick, Pitcher, Lemonade, Orange Poppies 28.00
Warwick, Pitcher, Lemonade, Poppies, Helmet Mark 45.00
Warwick, Pitcher, Monk Smiling, Red Matte Finish, 7 1/4 X 9 In. 60.00
Warwick, Plate, Coaching Scene Center, Red Mark, Knight, 10 In. 22.50
Warwick, Plate, Massilon, Ohio, Centennial, 1926, Ohio Canal, Blue, 9 In. 25.00
Warwick, Platter, Roses On White Ground, Blue & Gold Border, 11 X 16 1/4 In. 15.00
Warwick, Relish, Red, Flowers 10.00
Warwick, Syrup, Pewter Top, 4 In. 35.00
Warwick, Vase, Gray & Beige, Bust Of Buxom Lady, 11 3/4 In. 65.00
Warwick, Vase, Gypsy Lady, Twig Handles, 11 In. 85.00
Warwick, Vase, Log, Brown, Rose Fruit, Twig Handles 28.00

Warwick, Vase, Matte Beige To Brown, Acorns, Oak Leaf, Mark, 11 In. 65.00
Warwick, Vase, Portrait Pillow Vase With Yellow & Black Ground, Signed 125.00
Warwick, Vase, Portrait, Gypsy Girl, Twig Handles, 11 In. 85.00
Warwick, Vase, Portrait, Young Girl, Brown & Cream, Thorn Handles, 10 1/2 In. 75.00
Warwick, Vase, Senator, Red Floral On Brown, 11 1/4 In. 58.00
Warwick, Vase, Tree Trunk, Tan & Olive, 10 X 5 In. 25.00
Warwick, Vase, Twig Handles, Orange Hibiscus 42.00

Watch fobs were worn on watch chains. They were popular during Victorian times and after.

Watch Fob, AFL-CIO 15.00
Watch Fob, Alabama, Strap 7.00
Watch Fob, American Federation Of Labor, Enamel 15.00
Watch Fob, Angelic Figure, Embossed Floral & Leaves, Brass 29.00
Watch Fob, Anheuser Busch, Chain Type 6.50
Watch Fob, Babe Ruth, Celluloid 26.00
Watch Fob, Baseball Cap Attached To Silver Mesh 4.00
Watch Fob, BBB Shoes 25.00
Watch Fob, Belmont Packing Co., Eagle On World Globe 28.00
Watch Fob, Boydell Paints, 4 Piece 27.50
Watch Fob, BPOE, New Orleans, Dallas, 1908, Elk Head In Sterling 37.50
Watch Fob, Brass, Abraham Lincoln Matches 22.00
Watch Fob, Brass, J I Case Plow Works, Racine, Wis., Hand Holding Plow 59.00
Watch Fob, Bulldog, Avery, Engines & Implements, Ipiany, Ill. 34.00
Watch Fob, Buy Studebaker, 1st National Bank, Nauvoo, Ill. 31.50
Watch Fob, Cameo, Large 27.50
Watch Fob, Cassidy Southwestern Com.Co., Kansas City, St.Louis, Ft.Worth 30.00
Watch Fob, Caterpillar, Alban Tractor Co. 15.00
Watch Fob, Celluloid On Metal, Mirror Back, Lady's, C.1900 .... 17.50
Watch Fob, Creamery Package Co., Cow's Head 15.00
Watch Fob, Cross, Embossed Picture Of Queen Victoria, 1897 .... 20.00
Watch Fob, Cyrus McCormack, Centennial, 1831-1931, Embossed Picture 27.50
Watch Fob, Dixie Cut Plug Tobacco, Brass 10.00
Watch Fob, Dog 20.00
Watch Fob, Dr.Pepper, Shows Home Of Dr.Pepper 47.50
Watch Fob, Eclipse Refrigerators, Black Ribbon 20.00
Watch Fob, Elk's Tooth, 10K Gold, Jewel Eyes 18.00
Watch Fob, Elks, Eagle And Denver Nov.1949 .... 7.50
Watch Fob, Elks, N.Y., 1932 .... 15.00
Watch Fob, Embossed Saddle & Horseshoe 15.00
Watch Fob, Emsco Derricks, Strap Type 3.00
Watch Fob, English Hallmarks, Silver, 4 Pink Gold Flowers 16.00
Watch Fob, Euclid Earth Moving Equipment 15.00
Watch Fob, Evans, Snider, Buel Co., Livestock Comm., St.Louis, Chicago, K.C. 32.50
Watch Fob, Excelsior Auto Cycle, Shaped Like An X 32.50
Watch Fob, Fiber & Button, Democratic Candidate S.L.Nolan For Treasurer 18.50
Watch Fob, Firemen's Association, 1926 .... 6.00
Watch Fob, George Washington Bicentennial, 1732-1932, Washington Picture 17.50
Watch Fob, Germer Stoves, Stove Shape, Diecut 28.00
Watch Fob, Gold-Filled, Sterling Purse Charm, Mesh Chain Link, 4 In. 27.50
Watch Fob, Great Seal Of The U.S.A., Sterling Silver 20.00
Watch Fob, H.L.Elliott & Co., Bale Of Hay 25.00
Watch Fob, Heileman Old Style Lager Beer 17.00
Watch Fob, Hunter With Gun, Strap Type 4.00
Watch Fob, Hupmobile 27.00
Watch Fob, I.C.G.A., 1902, Brass, Embossed Ear Of Corn 12.00
Watch Fob, J.I.Case Plow Works, Racine, Wisc., Brass, Man's Hand & Plow 35.00
Watch Fob, Jaguar Motor Car, Strap 6.00
Watch Fob, Jamestown Exposition, 1907, Lord's Prayer On Back 25.00
Watch Fob, Joffre, American & French Soldiers 7.00
Watch Fob, Lindbergh 27.50
Watch Fob, Lovell & Covel Co. Chocolates, Knight & Sword 4.95
Watch Fob, Mexican Sombrero, Advertising Mexican Limes 27.50
Watch Fob, Moose, Brass 9.00
Watch Fob, Motorcycle Indian, C.1915 .... 2.50

Watch Fob, Munich Olympics, 1936 .... 25.00
Watch Fob, National Cash Register 72.50
Watch Fob, National Motorcycle Gypsy Tour, 1920, Award 32.50
Watch Fob, National Sportsman, Embossed Deer & Gun, For Lovers Of Sport 24.00
Watch Fob, Nebraska, Cow On Ear Of Corn 17.50
Watch Fob, New York World's Fair, 1939 .... 15.00
Watch Fob, Odd Fellows, Brass, Leather Strap 15.00
Watch Fob, Old Climax Tobacco, Enameled, Strap 22.00
Watch Fob, Oldsmobile & CT Co., Brass 30.00
Watch Fob, Ornate Sterling, Initials 15.00
Watch Fob, P & H Service Cranes 15.00
Watch Fob, Pan Pacific Exposition, 1915, Strap 12.50
Watch Fob, Pittsburgh Tournament Award, 1923, Kids Playing Marbles 25.00
Watch Fob, Purity Salt 17.50
Watch Fob, Racing Car, Strap Type 3.95
Watch Fob, Rochester Distilling 18.00
Watch Fob, Rolls Royce Radiator Cap Flying Lady, Sterling Silver, 1 3/4 In. 20.00
Watch Fob, Sedalia, Missouri, Federation Of Labor, 1918 .... 24.50
Watch Fob, St.Joseph The City Worth-While, Pewter & Porcelain 15.00
Watch Fob, St.Louis Exposition, Thomas Jefferson, Clip-On 18.00
Watch Fob, State Of Colorado, 1876, Brass 17.50
Watch Fob, State Traveling Men's Association, Des Moines, Iowa, Porcelain 23.50
Watch Fob, Sterling Silver, Marked Chester, 1885, Shield, Pierced, 1 1/2 In. 25.00
Watch Fob, Tarkio Champion Feed Co., Kansas City, Mo. 30.00
Watch Fob, Texas 6.00
Watch Fob, U.S.Navy, 1917, Pewter 12.50
Watch Fob, U.S.Steel, 40 Years Service, Sterling Silver 15.00
Watch Fob, Union Label, 1903, Enameled 9.75
Watch Fob, Wear-Ever Utensils, Aluminum 15.00
Watch Fob, WKW Bit, Strap Type 3.00
Watch Fob, Worthington Blue Brute Rock Drills, Plainfield, N.J. 22.50
Watch Fob, Yankee Division Veterans Association Reunion, 1921, Strap Type 5.95
Watch Fob, 17th Convention, Railway Car Men Of America, Montreal, 1835 .... 25.00
Watch Fob, 1934 A Century Of Progress, Chicago, Cigar Cutter 15.00

Watch, see also Gene Autry, Watch; Disneyana, Watch; Hopalong Cassidy, Watch; Roy Rogers, Watch

Watch, A.F.U.S. Army Navigation, World War II 33.00
Watch, American Watch Co., No.3409645, Gold Face, Hunting Case 150.00
Watch, Andre Bouchard, Lady's Wrist, 14K Gold, Gold-Filled Cameo Band 15.00
Watch, Art Deco, Sterling, French Movement, Onyx & Marcasite, Enamel Fleur 85.00
Watch, B.Poultovin, Stop, No.48675, 18K Gold Open Face Case 975.00
Watch, B.W.Raymond, Gold Open Face Case, 21 Jewel 77.00
Watch, Ball, Railroad, Official Standard, Gold Railroad Seal, 17 Jewel 65.00
Watch, Ben Hur, Haute Precision, 14K Gold Hunting Case, 17 Jewel 400.00
Watch, Bulova, Lady's Wrist, Rubies & Diamonds, 14K Pink Gold 35.00
Watch, Bulova, Lady's Wrist, 14K White Gold, Gold-Filled Stretch Band 60.00
Watch, Bulova, Lady's Wrist, 8 Diamonds In 14K White Gold Case 70.00
Watch, Bulova, 1924, Lady's Wrist, Jeweled Stem, Ribbon Band 16.00
Watch, Bunn, Special, 10K Gold-Filled Open Face Case, 21 Jewel 200.00
Watch, Burlington Special, 19 Jewel 80.00
Watch, Captain Marvel, 1948, Boxed 95.00
Watch, Chester, England, 1927, Gold Double Case, Swiss Movement, 15 Jewel 99.50
Watch, Columbia, Lady's, Engine-Turned Gold-Filled Hunting Case, Size 6 .... 95.00
Watch, Crawford, Lady's, Wrist, Platinum Case, 30 Diamonds, Gold-Filled Band 70.00
Watch, Croton, Lady's Pendant, Gold Square Case, Bar Pin 25.00
Watch, D.Hanlon Co., Silveroid Open Face Case, Sunk Dial, 21 Jewel 24.00
Watch, Dacia, Engraved Coin Silver Open Face Case, 12 Jewel 32.50
Watch, Dorset, Nickel-Plated Open Face Case, Stem Wind, 7 Jewel 10.00
Watch, Duber, Yellow Gold-Filled Hunting Case, 17 Jewel 80.00
Watch, Duchene Peyrot, Geneva, No.60253, 18K 3 Color Gold Open Face Case 195.00
Watch, E.Howard Co., No.1400292, Gold-Filled Howard Case, Howard Wood Box 140.00
Watch, E.Howard, Gold Case, Tortoiseshell Lid 675.00
Watch, Edgemere, Swiss, Gold-Filled Open Face Case, 10 Jewel 16.00
Watch, Elgin National Watch Co., Illinois, Gold-Filled Open Face Case 50.00
Watch, Elgin National, Embossed Eagle & Shield Gold Case, 17 Jewel 100.00

Watch, Elgin, Brass Open Face Case, Metal Dial, 15 Jewel 18.00
Watch, Elgin, C.1873, Coin Silver Open Face Case, Key Wind, 2 1/4 In. 45.00
Watch, Elgin, C.1914, Lady's, Engraved 25-Year Hunting Case 150.00
Watch, Elgin, Engraved Gold-Filled Hunting Case, Gold Hands 55.00
Watch, Elgin, Engraved Gold-Filled Hunting Case, 15 Jewel 67.50
Watch, Elgin, Engraved Train On Gold-Filled Hunting Case, 15 Jewel 80.00
Watch, Elgin, Engraved Yellow Gold Hunting Case, 17 Jewel 100.00
Watch, Elgin, Engraved 14K Gold Hunting Case, Gold Hands, 15 Jewel 295.00
Watch, Elgin, Fahy's Coin No.1 Case, Key Wind 125.00
Watch, Elgin, Gold-Filled Case, Presentation, 1907 .... 100.00
Watch, Elgin, Hunting Case, 17 Jewel 50.00
Watch, Elgin, Lady's Pendant, Engraved Yellow Gold Open Face Case, Octagon 18.00
Watch, Elgin, Lady's, Engraved Gold-Filled Hunting Case .... 75.00 To 95.00
Watch, Elgin, Lady's, Engraved Gold-Filled Hunting Case, Size 0 .... 95.00
Watch, Elgin, Lady's, White Gold-Filled, 15 Jewel 12.00
Watch, Elgin, Nickeloid Open Face Case, 7 Jewel 25.00
Watch, Elgin, Silveroid Hunting Case, 17 Jewel 55.00
Watch, Elgin, Silveroid Open Face Case, 11 Jewel 35.00
Watch, Elgin, Silveroid Open Face Case, 15 Jewel 35.00
Watch, Elgin, Silveroid Open Face Case, 17 Jewel 40.00
Watch, Elgin, Sun Dial, Engraved Gold-Filled Hunting Case, 7 Jewel 77.50
Watch, Elgin, White Gold-Filled Open Face Case, Silver Dial, 17 Jewel 37.50
Watch, Elgin, Yellow Gold-Filled Case, Hinged Back, 17 Jewel 40.00
Watch, Elgin, Yellow Gold-Filled Hunting Case, Enamel Dial, 15 Jewel 75.00
Watch, Elgin, Yellow Gold-Filled Hunting Case, 17 Jewel 80.00
Watch, Elgin, Yellow Gold-Filled Open Face Case, 15 Jewel 30.00
Watch, Elgin, 1884, Silverine Open Face Case, Key Wind & Set 75.00
Watch, Elgin, 1885, Gold Hunting Case 125.00
Watch, Elgin, 1892, Gold-Filled Hunting Case, Lever Set, 7 Jewel 115.00
Watch, Elgin, 1901, Engraved Train On Case, 17 Jewel 49.00
Watch, Elgin, 20 Year Hunting Case, 7 Jewel 45.00
Watch, English, Engraved Pair Case, Key Wind, Verge Escapement, 2 1/4 In. 155.00
Watch, English, 1833, Silver Open Face Case, Chain Driven, 2nd Hand 67.00
Watch, English, 1920, 14K Gold Octagon Open Face Case, Sapphire Stem Cap 135.00
Watch, F.D.Johnson, London, No.15156, 18K Gold Case, Fusee Movement 475.00
Watch, General, American Made, Gold-Filled Hunting Case, Double Roller 60.00
Watch, Geneva, Wrist, 14K Gold Mesh Band, Mother-Of-Pearl Face 95.00
Watch, Girard-Perregaux, Shell Oil Co., C.1940, 7 Jewel 175.00
Watch, Gruen, Man's Wrist, 14K Gold, Stretch Band 30.00
Watch, Gruen, Verithin, 14K White Gold Case 68.00
Watch, H.H.W.Co., President, Engraved Open Face Brass Case, 17 Jewel 18.00
Watch, Hamilton, Gold-Filled Engraved Open Face Case, 17 Jewel 78.00
Watch, Hamilton, Lady's Wrist, 22 Diamonds In Stainless Steel Case, Band 42.00
Watch, Hamilton, Lady's, 18 Rubies & 30 Diamonds In Rose Gold Case 995.00
Watch, Hamilton, Lancaster, Pa., Gold-Filled Open Face, Wadsworth Case 50.00
Watch, Hamilton, Navigational, Silveroid Open Face Case, 19 Jewel 60.00
Watch, Hamilton, No.910, Yellow Gold-Filled Open Face Case, 17 Jewel 40.00
Watch, Hamilton, No.923, 14K Yellow Gold-Filled Open Face Case, 23 Jewel 150.00
Watch, Hamilton, Railroad, Yellow Gold-Filled Open Face Case, 21 Jewel 90.00
Watch, Hamilton, Sterling Silver Open Face Case, 18 Jewel 65.00
Watch, Hamilton, Wrist, 14K Gold Case, Suede Band 28.00
Watch, Hamilton, Wrist, 14K Pink Gold Case, 4 Rubies & 12 Diamonds 125.00
Watch, Hamilton, Wrist, 14K White Gold Case, 65 Diamonds 430.00
Watch, Hamilton, 14K Gold Open Face Case, 23 Jewel 160.00
Watch, Hamilton, 14K Gold-Filled Open Face Case, 19 Jewel 110.00
Watch, Hamilton, 974, Special Gold-Filled Open Face Case, 17 Jewel 37.50
Watch, Hamilton, 992, Engraved Locomotive On Gold-Filled Open Face Case 85.00
Watch, Hampden Watch Co., Canton, Ohio, Engraved Open Face Case, 17 Jewel 60.00
Watch, Hampden, Engraved Coin Silver Open Face Case, Gold Inlay 130.00
Watch, Hampden, Lady's Wrist, 14K Rose Gold 90.00
Watch, Hampden, Railroad, Special, Decorated Dial, 23 Jewels 185.00
Watch, Hampden, Silveroid Open Face Case, 11 Jewel 35.00
Watch, Hampton, Engraved Yellow Gold-Filled Open Face Case, 7 Jewel 50.00
Watch, Howard, Gold-Filled Open Face Hinged Case, 17 Jewel 92.00
Watch, Howard, Hunting Case, 17 Jewel 195.00

Watch, Howard, Series 10, 21 Jewel 210.00
Watch, Howard, White Gold-Filled Case, 17 Jewel, Size 12 .... 125.00
Watch, Howard, Yellow Gold-Filled Open Face Case, 17 Jewel 75.00
Watch, Howard, 14K White Gold-Filled Open Face Case, 19 Jewel 150.00
Watch, Howard, 1859, Dueber Case, Mershon Regulator, Key Set 450.00
Watch, Illinois, Engraved Gold-Filled Hunting Case, 15 Jewel 77.50
Watch, Illinois, Hunting Case, Birds, Flowers, Small Lady's 350.00
Watch, Illinois, 1881, Engine-Turned Gold-Filled Open Face Case, 15 Jewel 75.00
Watch, Illinois, 1908, Wadsworth Engraved Open Face Case, 17 Jewel 115.00
Watch, Ingersoll, Midget, Engraved Deer On Case, 1 3/4 In. 65.00
Watch, Ingersoll, Yankee, Nickel Case 6.00
Watch, Ingersoll, 1933 Century Of Progress, Chain 125.00
Watch, Ingraham, Dollar, Biltmore Model 25.00
Watch, Ingraham, New York To Paris, Black Dial 46.00
Watch, Ingraham, Sentinel, Sweep Hand 10.00
Watch, J.F.Bautte & Co., Chronograph, 14K Gold Hunting Case, 70 Diamonds 2500.00
Watch, John Hall, Perpetual Calendar On Back & Front, Moon Dial 350.00
Watch, John M.Smith, Harrisville, R.I., Engraved Silveroid Case, Stem Wind 34.75
Watch, Jules Jurgensen, Wrist, 18K Gold Case, Gold Leather Band 45.00
Watch, Jules Jurgensen, Wrist, 18K White Gold, 40 Diamonds 150.00
Watch, Jungham, Pocket Alarm, Base Metal Case 95.00
Watch, Kingston, Wrist, 14K Pink Gold, 6 Diamonds, Snake Band 69.00
Watch, La Salle, Gold-Filled Hunting Case 68.00
Watch, La Tour, Engraved Silver Hunting Case, Key Wind, 12 Jewel 57.50
Watch, Lapel, WW1, Shape Of Helmet, Allies Flags, Hangs From Set Of Wings 45.00
Watch, Longines, Pendant, 14K Gold & Enamel Open Face Case, Bail, 15 Jewel 90.00
Watch, Molly Stark, Canton, Ohio, Lady's, Hunting Case, Engraved 1910, Diamond 200.00
Watch, Movado, Lady's, 14K White Gold, 10 Diamonds 150.00
Watch, New England Watch Co., Duplex, Silveroid Open Face Case 25.00
Watch, New York Standard, Silveroid Open Face, Engraved Locomotive 43.00
Watch, New York Standard, 20 Year Hunting Case 70.00
Watch, New York Standard, 7 Jewel 72.50
Watch, Patek Philippe, Man's Wrist, Model 175, No.1133203, 18K Gold 875.00
Watch, Patek Philippe, 18K Gold Open Face Case, Invisible Hinge 300.00
Watch, Patek Philippe, 18K Gold Open Face Case, 18 Jewel 450.00
Watch, Paul Raynard, Lady's Wrist, 54 Diamonds In 14K White Gold Case 525.00
Watch, Rockford, Engraved Gold-Filled Hunting Case, 15 Jewel 82.50
Watch, Rockford, Engraved Gold-Filled Hunting Case, 17 Jewel 87.50
Watch, Rockford, Winnebago, 10K Gold-Filled Open Face Case, 17 Jewel 69.00
Watch, Sanford, Lady's Wrist, 14K Gold, Onyx Stones 65.00
Watch, Seth Thomas, Silveroid Open Face Case, 7 Jewel 47.50
Watch, Seth Thomas, 1910, Silver Open Face Case 50.00
Watch, Shell Oil, Skeleton 100.00
Watch, South Bend, Engraved 14K Gold Open Face Case, 21 Jewel 160.00
Watch, Spiro Agnew 30.00
Watch, Standard Watch Co., N.Y., Engraved Gold-Filled Hunting Case 110.00
Watch, Stauffer, Silver Open Face Case, Key Wind, 4 Jewel 47.50
Watch, Swiss, Clown, Animated, Boxed 45.00
Watch, Swiss, Engine-Turned & Crested Silver Open Face Case, 4 Jewel 52.50
Watch, Swiss, Engine-Turned 14K Gold Hunting Case, 8 Jewel 170.00
Watch, Swiss, Engraved Silver Hunting Case, 4 Jewel 75.00
Watch, Swiss, Engraved 14K Gold Hunting Case, Porcelain Dial, 7 Jewel 175.00
Watch, Swiss, Engraved 18K Gold Hunting Case, Gold Hands, 15 Jewel 170.00
Watch, Swiss, Ingenious, Gunmetal Open Face Case, 2nd Hand 82.00
Watch, Swiss, Lady's, Engraved Gilt Open Face Case, 7 Jewel 47.50
Watch, Swiss, Lady's, Silver Plate Open Face Case, Blue Enamel, Pin 65.00
Watch, Swiss, Norman, Brass Open Face Case, 7 Jewel 16.00
Watch, Swiss, 18K Yellow Gold Open Face Case, Pin Set, 10 Jewel 75.00
Watch, Tiffany, Man's Wrist, 14K Gold, Leather Band 55.00
Watch, Tortman, Coin Silver Shielded Open Face Case, Key Wind, 14 Jewel 42.50
Watch, Tourneau, Pinback, 14K Gold Case, Dial Faces Wearer 59.00
Watch, Trenton, Engraved Gold-Filled Open Face Case, Arabic Dial, 11 Jewel 26.00
Watch, U.S.Watch Co., 1885, Engraved Gold-Filled Hunting Case, Lever Set 135.00
Watch, Waltham Premier Colonial, Gold-Filled Open Face Case, 9 Jewel 37.50
Watch, Waltham Royal, Yellow Gold-Filled Open Face Case, 17 Jewel 35.00

Watch, Waltham Vanguard, Gold-Filled Open Face Railroad Case, 23 Jewel 145.00
Watch, Waltham, Appleton Tracy, 1899, Engraved Gold-Filled Case, 17 Jewel 100.00
Watch, Waltham, C.1870, Coin Silver Hunting Case, 15 Jewel 77.50
Watch, Waltham, Cadillac Watch, Open Face Case, 15 Jewel 150.00
Watch, Waltham, Crescent Street, Gold-Filled Hunting Case 90.00
Watch, Waltham, Crescent Street, Silver Open Face Case, Railroad, 21 Jewel 72.50
Watch, Waltham, Engraved Coin Silver Hunting Case, 7 Jewel 75.00
Watch, Waltham, Gold-Filled Hunting Case, 7 Jewel .... 62.50 To 65.00
Watch, Waltham, Lady's Pendant, Yellow Gold Open Face Case, 15 Jewel 34.00
Watch, Waltham, Lady's Wrist, 14K Gold Keystone & J.Boss Case 10.00
Watch, Waltham, PS Bart., Coin Silver Open Face Case, 17 Jewel 45.00
Watch, Waltham, Riverside, Gold-Filled Open Face Case, Lever Set, 19 Jewel 79.00
Watch, Waltham, Royal, Engraved Yellow Gold Filled Open Face Case, 17 Jewel 70.00
Watch, Waltham, Royal, 14K Gold Hunting Case, 17 Jewel 79.00
Watch, Waltham, Silveroid Open Face Case, 15 Jewel 35.00
Watch, Waltham, Silveroid Open Face Case, 7 Jewel .... 25.00 To 30.00
Watch, Waltham, Yellow Gold-Filled Hunting Case, Gold Hands, 15 Jewel 125.00
Watch, Waltham, Yellow Gold-Filled Hunting Case, 7 Jewel 55.00
Watch, Waltham, Yellow Gold-Filled Open Face Case, Lever Set, 21 Jewel 75.00
Watch, Waltham, 14K White Gold-Filled Open Face Case, 15 Jewel 25.00
Watch, Waltham, 1868, Coin Silver Hunting Case, 15 Jewel 175.00
Watch, Waltham, 1873, Lady's, A.W.Co. 14K Gold Case, 7 Jewel 250.00
Watch, Waltham, 1892, 14K Gold Open Face Case, P.S.Bartlett 90.00
Watch, Waltham, 1894, Gold-Filled Hunting Case, 15 Jewel 90.00
Watch, Westclox, Ben, 1921 .... 10.00
Watch, Westclox, Pocket Ben, Push Button Lighted Dial 60.00
Watch, Wittnauer, Wrist, 14K White Gold, 4 Diamonds, Gild-Filled Band 47.00
Watch, Wrist, Bugs Bunny 130.00
Watch, Wrist, Hopalong Cassidy 22.50

Waterford type glass resembles the famous glass made in the Waterford Glass Works in Ireland. It is a clear glass that was often cut for decoration. Modern glass is still being made in Waterford, Ireland.

Waterford, Claret, Lismore 12.30
Waterford, Goblet, C.1750 .... 57.25
Waterford, Goblet, Lismore 12.30
Waterford, Jar, Cracker, Pressed, Etched, Silver Plate Fittings 75.00
Waterford, Salt, Master, Footed, 3 X 2 In., Pair 30.00

WAVE CREST WARE

Wave Crest glass is a white glassware manufactured by the Pairpoint Manufacturing Company of New Bedford, Massachusetts, and some French factories. It was then decorated by the C.F.Monroe Company of Meriden, Connecticut. The glass was painted in pastel colors and decorated with flowers. The name Wave Crest was used after 1898.

Wave Crest, Atomizer, Lake & House Scene 200.00
Wave Crest, Basket, Blue Swirl, Squatty, Ornate Handle, Varicolored, 5 In. 115.00
Wave Crest, Biscuit Box, Yellow, Pink Florals, Signed C.F.M. Co.In Lid 185.00
Wave Crest, Blotter, Fancy Knob & Filigree, Enamel, Unsigned, 6 X 4 In. 165.00
Wave Crest, Bowl, Blue Forget-Me-Nots, Brass Handles & Rim, 3 1/4 In. 85.00
Wave Crest, Bowl, Blue, Scrolls, Enamel Floral, Brass Collar, 4 1/2 In. 55.00
Wave Crest, Box, Brass Collar, Pink Clover Decoration, Black Mark, Signed 55.00
Wave Crest, Box, Cigars, 6 X 4 In. 450.00
Wave Crest, Box, Citron, Puffy, Floral, 3 1/2 In. 80.00
Wave Crest, Box, Dark Green, White Floral, Ormolu Feet, Square, 7 In. 450.00
Wave Crest, Box, Dresser, Green, Pink Blossoms, Ormolu Fittings, 6 In. 130.00
Wave Crest, Box, Dresser, Green, Pink Blossoms, Ormolu Mounts, 6 In. 125.00
Wave Crest, Box, Erie Twist, 3 1/2 In. 125.00
Wave Crest, Box, Floral, Square, 3 In. 150.00
Wave Crest, Box, Hinged, Cream Swirl, Floral, Helms, 4 3/8 In. 165.00
Wave Crest, Box, Hinged, Dolphin Feet, Ormolu Stand, 5 1/2 In. 335.00
Wave Crest, Box, Hinged, Floral & Scrolls, Brass Bound, Round, 8 In. 225.00
Wave Crest, Box, Hinged, Pale Blue, Floral, 7 In. 750.00
Wave Crest, Box, Hinged, Ribbed, Swirled, Daisies, Round, 4 1/2 In. 159.00
Wave Crest, Box, Hinged, Robin's-Egg Blue, 5 1/2 In. 425.00
Wave Crest, Box, Hinged, Swirled, Jeweled Floral, Satin Lining, 6 X 5 In. 185.00

Wave Crest, Box, Hinged, Swirled, 3 1/2 In. 135.00
Wave Crest, Box, Jewel, Blue Ground, Cupids & Moon Scene Lid, Hinged, Signed 265.00
Wave Crest, Box, Jewel, Kate Greenaway Boy & Girl Decoration, 6 X 3 3/4 In. 195.00
Wave Crest, Box, Letter, Blown-Out Sides, Scrolls, Ormolu Mounts, 6 In. 250.00
Wave Crest, Box, Letter, Ormolu Framing, Fully Marked, 5 X 2 1/2 X 4 In. 210.00
Wave Crest, Box, Letter, Puffed, Blue Forget-Me-Nots, Brass Collar, 5 3/4 In. 120.00
Wave Crest, Box, Open, Brass Ormolu, Floral, 7 1/2 In. 125.00
Wave Crest, Box, Pin, Enamel Floral, Ormolu Collar, Round, 3 1/2 In. 65.00
Wave Crest, Box, Pin, Floral, Ornate Brass Handles, Round, 2 1/2 In. 75.00
Wave Crest, Box, Pin, Forget-Me-Nots, Ormolu Handles 75.00
Wave Crest, Box, Pin, Ormolu, Red Banner Mark, 4 1/2 In. 85.00
Wave Crest, Box, Pink With Jeweled Flowers, Hinged, Signed 215.00
Wave Crest, Box, Pink, Scenic, Round, 3 1/2 In. 200.00
Wave Crest, Box, Powder, Hinged, Swirled, 5 1/4 In. 250.00
Wave Crest, Box, Puffed Out, Covered, Footed, Olive Green, White, Signed, 7 In. 585.00
Wave Crest, Box, Puffy, Coral Color, Square 235.00
Wave Crest, Box, Ring, Oval, Open, Blue With Hand-Painted Flowers, 4 X 3 In. 45.00
Wave Crest, Box, Signed, Decorated, 2 1/2 X 5 In. 275.00
Wave Crest, Box, Trinket, Apple Blossoms, Ormolu, 7 1/4 In. 130.00
Wave Crest, Box, Trinket, Red Banner Mark, 4 In. 85.00
Wave Crest, Candleholder, Hand-Painted, Enameled Flowers, 7 1/2 In. 215.00
Wave Crest, Casket, Covered, Lined Floral, 3 In. 187.00
Wave Crest, Casket, Covered, Oval, Signed, 15 In.Around 284.00
Wave Crest, Creamer, Blue & White Enamel Dotted Decoration, Metal Top 65.00
Wave Crest, Creamer, Swirled, Pewter Lip & Handle, 4 In. 89.00
Wave Crest, Creamer, White, Erie Twist, Enamel Floral, Silver Plate Handle 75.00
Wave Crest, Dish, Pin, Decorated, Signed, 3 In. 46.00
Wave Crest, Dish, Pin, Floral, Metal Embossed Rim, Signed, 3 1/2 X 1 1/2 In. 65.00
Wave Crest, Dish, Trinket, Orange, White Floral, 4 Footed, Ormolu Handles 60.00
Wave Crest, Fernery, Forget-Me-Nots, Brass Rope Handle 135.00
Wave Crest, Fernery, Pink Floral Sprays, Puffy, Brass Rim, Square, 6 In. 175.00
Wave Crest, Hair Receiver, Raised Scrolls, Pink Forget-Me-Nots 150.00
Wave Crest, Hair Receiver, White To Pink, Blue Floral, Brass Top 155.00
Wave Crest, Inkwell, Cupid Decoration, Scroll Work, Hinged Brass Dome 125.00
Wave Crest, Jar, Biscuit, Cream To Blue, Enamel Floral, Silver Plate Fitting 135.00
Wave Crest, Jar, Biscuit, Fully Marked, 6 X 5 1/2 In. 225.00
Wave Crest, Jar, Cracker, Green & White, Brown Birds & Violets, Silver Lid 92.75
Wave Crest, Jar, Cracker, Marked C.F.M. On Lid 175.00
Wave Crest, Jar, Cracker, Raised Scrolls, Brown Floral, Signed C.F.Monroe 175.00
Wave Crest, Jardiniere, Blue, Pink & Yellow Roses, Enamel Beads, 9 In. 375.00
Wave Crest, Jardiniere, Lavender Floral, Cherubs' Heads, Gold Trim, 10 In. 525.00
Wave Crest, Lamp, Oil, Hand-Painted Flowers, Blown Out Around Side 49.00
Wave Crest, Letter Holder, Puffy, Decorated, 6 X 4 1/4 In. 160.00
Wave Crest, Planter, Ferns, Puffy, 6 3/4 In. 165.00
Wave Crest, Planter, Pink With Blue Florals, Brass Liner, 5 In. 225.00
Wave Crest, Planter, Swirl With Cloud & Daisies, 4 In. 185.00
Wave Crest, Salt & Pepper, Blue, Erie Twist, Enameled 165.00
Wave Crest, Salt & Pepper, Deep Blue, Enameled 210.00
Wave Crest, Salt & Pepper, Pink, Erie Twist, Enameled 165.00
Wave Crest, Salt, Blue Forget-Me-Nots 35.00
Wave Crest, Salt, Blue Forget-Me-Nots, White Dotted Top 35.00
Wave Crest, Salt, Master, White, Pale Yellow Shells, Pink & Blue Floral 45.00
Wave Crest, Salt, Swirl Blank, Enameled, Ornate Gilded Handles 155.00
Wave Crest, Saltshaker, Pink, White Enamel Floral, Pewter Top, Erie Twist 50.00
Wave Crest, Tray, Pin, Ormolu Feet & Handles, Decorated, Signed, 4 1/2 X 3 In. 88.00
Wave Crest, Vase, Ormolu And Floral, Footed, 9 In. 225.00
Wave Crest, Vase, Pink & White, Blue Blossoms, Ormolu Feet & Handles, 3 In. 275.00
Wave Crest, Wig Holder, Hanging, Banner Mark 295.00
Weapon, Bayonet & Scabbard, Remington Arms, 1918 .... 16.00
Weapon, Bayonet, Italian, Dagger Type, Sheath 4.95
Weapon, Bayonet, Mauser 12.50
Weapon, Bayonet, Remington, U.S.1917 .... 15.00
Weapon, Bayonet, Rifle, 1901, Scabbard 50.00
Weapon, Dagger & Case, Nazi, Hitler Youth Leader 450.00
Weapon, Dagger & Case, Nazi, Labor Corp. 160.00

Weapon, Dagger & Case, Nazi, S.S.Officers 160.00
Weapon, Dagger & Sheath, Carved Ivory, Japanese War Lord, 10 In. 95.00
Weapon, Dagger & Sheath, WW2 German Luftwaffe, Yellow Grip 85.00
Weapon, Dagger, African, Wooden, Hand-Carved 6.00
Weapon, Dagger, Confederate Type, 9 In. Triangular Blade, Wood Handle 35.00
Weapon, Dagger, India, Inlaid With Silver, Curved Blade In Sheath 40.00
Weapon, Derringer, Revolver, Engraved Barrel, Rosewood Bird's Head Grips 195.00
Weapon, Dirk, German Navy, Miniature, Case 12.95
Weapon, Flask, Powder & Shot, Pewter, Brass Fittings 75.00
Weapon, Flask, Powder, Amber Glass, Embossed Birds, Leather Thong, 6 1/4 In. 19.50
Weapon, Flask, Powder, Ames, Wreath & Hand, 9 In. 40.00
Weapon, Flask, Powder, Brass, Flamingo In Bushes 75.00
Weapon, Flask, Powder, Brass, Relief Hunting Dog, Measure, Patent 45.00
Weapon, Flask, Powder, Copper, Embossed Tree, Buck, & Indian 55.00
Weapon, Flask, Powder, Curled Cowhorn With Wooden Plug, 18th Century, 18 In. 40.00
Weapon, Flask, Powder, Pewter & Brass, Shell Decoration 45.00
Weapon, Flask, Powder, U.S.Musket, Batty, 1850, Copper, Peace With Indians 225.00
Weapon, Gun, American Boot Pistol, Percussion, .34 Caliber 33.00
Weapon, Handgun, Allen, 1837, Pepperbox Pistol, Percussion, .31 Caliber 150.00
Weapon, Handgun, B.Woodward & Son, Cap & Ball Pistol 150.00
Weapon, Handgun, Colt Revolver, .31 Caliber 250.00
Weapon, Handgun, Colt Revolver, 1877, Storekeeper's, .38 Caliber 125.00
Weapon, Handgun, Colt, Revolver, Sterling Silver, 3 1/2 In. 45.00
Weapon, Handgun, Derringer Rifle & Pistol Works, Phila., .32 Caliber 195.00
Weapon, Handgun, Hammond Bulldog Pistol 65.00
Weapon, Handgun, Hopkins & Allen, 1871, Wooden Handle 28.00
Weapon, Handgun, Japanese Nambu Pistol 100.00
Weapon, Handgun, Remington 1858 Cap & Ball Revolver, .44 Caliber 300.00
Weapon, Handgun, Remington, Army Revolver, Civil War Issue, .44 Caliber 200.00
Weapon, Handgun, Sharp's Derringer, 4 Barrel, .32 Caliber 130.00
Weapon, Handgun, Smith & Wesson, No.1, .22 Caliber, Brass Frame, Civil War 49.00
Weapon, Handgun, Staudenmeger Dueling Pistol, London, England, C.1820, Pair 2500.00
Weapon, Iron Cannon, 18th Century, 32 In.Long .... *Illus* 525.00
Weapon, Jackknife, Copper Handle, 2 Blade, Michigan Copper Country 12.50
Weapon, Jackknife, Remington, Brass Handle 18.00
Weapon, Jacknife, Remington, No.R1123, Bone Handles, 4 1/2 In. 225.00

Weapon, Knife, see also Store, Knife

Weapon, Knife, African Warrior's, Leopard Skin Sheath, Hand Forged 15.00
Weapon, Knife, Army Jungle, Collins & Co. 3.50
Weapon, Knife, Belt, Silver Grip, Silver Sheath, 13 K Overlays 75.00
Weapon, Knife, Belt, U.S., Walnut Handle, 7 In. Blade 20.00
Weapon, Knife, Bowie, D Guard, 18 In. Blade 125.00
Weapon, Knife, Eskimo, Bone 6.50
Weapon, Knife, Imperial, U.S.A., Stag Handle, 2 Blades, Pocket 12.00
Weapon, Knife, Japanese Hari Kari, Carved Ivory, Figures, 19 In. 395.00
Weapon, Knife, Japanese Hari Kari, Teak Handle & Sheath 195.00
Weapon, Knife, Knuckle, Brass Handled, WWI, U.S.1918, L.F. & C. 75.00
Weapon, Knife, Knuckle, Wood Handled, WWI, Spike Blade, U.S.1917, L.F. & C. 85.00
Weapon, Knife, Pocket, Keen Kutter 15.00
Weapon, Knife, Pocket, Press Button Knife Co., Walden, N.Y., Sterling Silver 40.00
Weapon, Knife, Pocket, Robson, 2 Blades, No.722320, Pearl Handle 14.00
Weapon, Knife, Pocket, Winchester, Barlow 65.00
Weapon, Knife, Skinning, Russell, Green River 7.50
Weapon, Loading Tool, Winchester, .44 Caliber 18.00
Weapon, Machete, Bone Handle, 22 In. 8.50
Weapon, Mold, Bullet, .32-.20 Caliber 14.00
Weapon, Mold, Bullet, .36 Caliber, FIE Italy, Brass, 2 Mold 14.00
Weapon, Mold, Bullet, Bronze, 2-Handled, 8 In. 20.00
Weapon, Mold, Bullet, Colt, .44 Caliber 16.00
Weapon, Mold, Recapper, Decapper, & Ball Setter, Bullet, Ideal Mfg.Co. 48.00
Weapon, Night Stick, Police, Light Colored Wood 7.50
Weapon, Night Stick, Police, Walnut 12.50
Weapon, Penknife, Pewter, 2 Blades & Scissors 9.00
Weapon, Penknife, Sheffield, Metal Case, Floral Decoration 4.00
Weapon, Penknife, Stainless Steel, 2 Blades 5.00

Weapon, Penknife, 12K Gold, Nut Pick 15.00
Weapon, Penknife, 14K Gold, 2 Blades 38.00
Weapon, Pepperbox, Remington, Elliot's Patent, 4 Barrel 195.00
Weapon, Pouch, Gunshot, Leather, Brass Top, Embossed London Seal 18.00
Weapon, Pouch, Powder & Shot, Leather 26.00
Weapon, Powder Flask, Brass, Hunting Dog, Printed Measure 55.00
Weapon, Powder Horn, E.B. Carved In Wooden Plug At Bottom, 6 In. 11.75
Weapon, Powder Horn, Engraved Ephraim Wheler, 18th Century 250.00
Weapon, Powder Horn, Engraved, Dated, 9 In. 250.00
Weapon, Powder Horn, French & Indian Ware, Scrimshaw, Harrison & Tecumseh 650.00
Weapon, Powder Horn, Pennsylvania Dutch, 1856, Scrimshaw, Barn Signs & Eagle 875.00
Weapon, Powder Horn, Point Blue, Quebec, Etched 45.00
Weapon, Powder Horn, Simeon Hagern, Lake George, 1758, Engraved, Brass Trim 800.00
Weapon, Rifle, Ballard Pacific, Buffalo Hunting, .40-.85 Caliber 165.00
Weapon, Rifle, Japanese Matchlock, Engraved Brass Lockplate, 40 In. 425.00

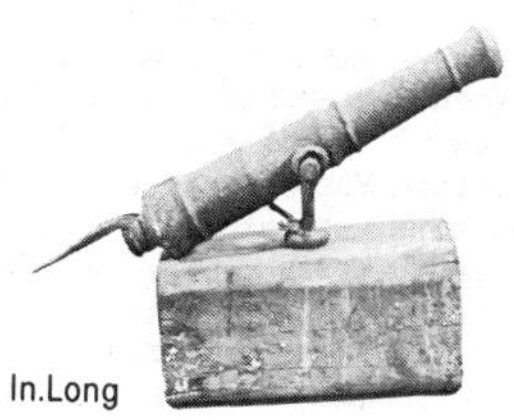

Weapon, Iron Cannon, 18th Century, 32 In.Long

Weapon, Rifle, Japanese, Matchlock, Octagonal Barrel, .44 Caliber 425.00
Weapon, Rifle, Kentucky, Percussion, .45 Caliber, Maple Stock 105.00
Weapon, Rifle, Maynard Sporting Carbine, .35 Caliber, Long Tang Sight 195.00
Weapon, Rifle, Parlor, Argles' Patent 75.00
Weapon, Rifle, Springfield, 1864, Musket, .58 Caliber 250.00
Weapon, Rifle, Winchester, Model 1890, .22 Caliber, Octagonal Barrel, Pump 95.00
Weapon, Rifle, Winchester, Model 1906, .22 Caliber, Pump 135.00
Weapon, Rifle, Winchester, M1873, Octagonal Barrel, .22 Caliber 425.00
Weapon, Rifle, Winchester, 1890 Octagonal Barrel, .22 Pump 95.00
Weapon, Saber & Scabbard, Cavalry, C.1850, Ames Co. 125.00
Weapon, Saber & Scabbard, Japanese Cavalry, Russo War 37.50
Weapon, Saber, British, Light Dragon, Ivory Grip, Brass Guard, Lion Head, 1790 .... 90.00
Weapon, Saber, Fencing, U.S.Military, Wooden 25.00
Weapon, Samurai Sword, Signature On Handle 350.00
Weapon, Shell, Winchester Shotgun, 12 Gauge, Nickel Plated 3.25
Weapon, Shotgun, Gebruder Merkle 16 Gauge Over Bockbuchflinte Jr. 825.00
Weapon, Shotgun, Henry Arms, 12 Gauge, Double Barrel, Hammer 70.00
Weapon, Shotgun, Iver Johnson, Hercules Grade, Double Barrel, 12 Gauge 125.00
Weapon, Shotgun, Parker, 1875, Double Barrel 150.00
Weapon, Shotgun, Stevens, 1864, Tip-Up, 12 Gauge 75.00
Weapon, Springfield, Trap Door, 71884, 45, Blue Wood, Stamped Eagle Lockplate 200.00
Weapon, Sword & Scabbard, German WW2 Cavalry 65.00
Weapon, Sword & Scabbard, Japanese Samurai, WW2, All Metal 95.00
Weapon, Sword & Scabbard, Samurai, Ivory, Carved, 29 In. Blade 500.00
Weapon, Sword & Scabbard, U.S.Militia Officer's, C.1850, Ames Co. 225.00
Weapon, Sword Cane, C.1850, Ivory Handle, Wood Cane Scabbard, English, 26 In. 175.00
Weapon, Sword, Black, Luftwaffe 150.00
Weapon, Sword, Civil War, Ames Mfg.Co.Chicopee, Mass.1862 .... 135.00
Weapon, Sword, French, Empire, Bronze Nude Woman & Man Handle, 19 In. 175.00
Weapon, Sword, German Officer, Franco Prussian War, Dress, Chased, Brass 95.00
Weapon, Sword, German Officer's Dress, Franco Prussian War, Brass Mounts 95.00
Weapon, Sword, Ku Klux Klan, Black & Nickel With Insignia And Figure 125.00

Weapon, Sword, Samurai, C.1700, Case, 17 1/2 In. 125.00
Weapon, Sword, Samurai, Scabbard And Hilt Of Ivory, 29 In.Blade 5500.00
Weapon, Sword, Samurai, Sharkskin Handle, Case, 39 In. 125.00
Weapon, Sword, Toledo, Steel, Bronze Guard, Decorative, 28 In. 55.00
Weapon, Sword, Wooley & Deakin, C.1820 150.00
Weapon, Target Ball, Jas.Bown & Son, Pittsburgh, Sheared Mouth, Amber, 3 In. 65.00
Weapon, Target Ball, Sheared Mouth, Amethyst, 2 3/4 In. 75.00
Weapon, Target Ball, Sheared Mouth, Golden Amber, 2 3/4 In. 35.00
Weapon, Target Ball, Sheared Mouth, Golden Amber, 2 5/8 In. 40.00
Weather Vane, American Eagle On Orb, Copper, C.1850, 31 1/2 In. 925.00
Weather Vane, American Eagle On Orb, Copper, Gilt Paint, C.1850, 38 In. 325.00
Weather Vane, Beaver, Tin, Quebec, 1860 795.00
Weather Vane, Columbia, Copper Gilded, Cushing & White, Mass., C.1865, 38 In. 6500.00
Weather Vane, Columbia, Cushing & White, Mass., C.1865, Copper, 38 In. 6500.00
Weather Vane, Comet & Star, Acid Etched, Red, Lightning Rod 29.00
Weather Vane, Cow, Blue Milk Glass Ball, Copper Tube 50.00
Weather Vane, Crowing Cock, Copper, Repousse, Rod Standard, 28 1/2 In. 325.00
Weather Vane, Goose, Spread Wings, Sheet & Cast Iron, 23 In. 400.00
Weather Vane, Pointing Hand, Wooden, Carved, Painted Green, C.1850, 56 In. 225.00
Weather Vane, Prancing Horse, Repousse, Iron Standard, C.1850, 21 In. 425.00
Weather Vane, Running Horse, Copper, Yellow Paint, Rod Standard, 33 In. 350.00
Weather Vane, Sloop, Green Paint 175.00
Weather Vane, Whirligig, 3 Figures 350.00
Weather Vase, Eagle, Copper, 21 In. 155.00
Weather Vase, Horse & Sulky, Copper, Rod Standard, C.1850, 34 1/2 In. 1150.00

Webb glass was made by Thomas Webb & Sons of Stourbridge, England. Many types of art and cameo glass were made by them during the Victorian era. The factory is still producing glass.

Webb Burmese, Bottle, Scent, Iris Spray, Silver Top, Hallmarks, 4 3/4 In. 450.00
Webb Burmese, Bowl, Enamel Decoration, Queen's, Hexagonal, 2 3/4 In. High 360.00
Webb Burmese, Condiment Set, Nickel Silver Stand, 5 Piece, 5 In. 395.00
Webb Burmese, Epergne, 3 Cones, Plated Holder, Berry Prunts, Matte Finish 350.00
Webb Burmese, Rose Bowl, Crimped Top, 2 1/4 In. 225.00
Webb Burmese, Rose Bowl, Salmon To Yellow, Lavender Floral, 2 1/2 In. 295.00
Webb Burmese, Salt, Master, Floriform, E.P.N.S. Holder 365.00
Webb Burmese, Signed Queens Burmese Ware, Thos.Webb And Sons, 3 3/8 In. 450.00
Webb Burmese, Tumbler, Juice, Green Shaded Ivy Decoration, 3 In. 245.00
Webb Burmese, Vase, Berries, Ruffled Top, 4 In. 275.00
Webb Burmese, Vase, Satin Finish, Pink, 4 1/2 In. 350.00
Webb Burmese, Vase, Toothpick, Queensware, Yellow Ball Bottom, Salmon Top 250.00
Webb, Basket, Amberina, Gold Flowers, Swirl Pattern, Amber Feet, 15 In. 595.00
Webb, Bottle, Perfume, Citron & White, Butterfly, 8 1/2 In. 550.00
Webb, Bottle, Perfume, Lay Down, Brown Shading, Silver Screw Cap, 7 In. 150.00
Webb, Bottle, Perfume, Mother-Of-Pearl, Cut Stopper 140.00
Webb, Bottle, Perfume, Silver Cap, Blue With White, 4 In. 425.00
Webb, Bottle, Perfume, Silver Cap, Citron With White, 4 In. 375.00
Webb, Bottle, Scent, Blue Satin, Gold Prunus Blossoms & Butterfly 350.00
Webb, Bottle, Scent, Cameo, Jonquil Sprays, Mappin & Webb, Silversmiths 950.00
Webb, Bottle, Scent, Cameo, Pale Gray, Fishscale Overall, 6 1/2 In. 700.00
Webb, Bottle, Scent, Green, Gold Spray, Silver Top, Hallmarks, 3 1/4 In. 350.00
Webb, Bottle, Standing Scent, Gold Spray, Butterfly, Bulbous, 3 1/4 In. 450.00
Webb, Bowl, Blue Satin, Cream Color Lining, 5 3/4 In. 165.00
Webb, Bowl, Off-White, Blue Flowers, Leaves, & Stems, 5 1/2 In. 595.00
Webb, Bowl, Satin Glass, Lattice Pattern, Pink To White, 12 In., Signed 210.00
Webb, Celery, Pink To Cherry Red, Glossy, White Lining, Square Top, 6 3/4 In. 150.00
Webb, Cruet, Amber Iridescent, Gold Figures, Cut Stopper 150.00
Webb, Cruet, Dark Maroon, Yellow Flower Spray 195.00
Webb, Cup, Acid, Yellow Tulips, Fish Scale, Amber Rim, Signed, 10 In. 370.00
Webb, Dish, Bonbon, Cameo, Covered, Pale Blue With White, 4 X 7 In. 775.00
Webb, Dish, Sweetmeat, Cream & Blue, Overlay, Silver Plate Basket, 5 3/8 In. 68.00
Webb, Finger Bowl & Underplate, Crystal 25.00
Webb, Muffineer, Pink, Diamond-Quilted Mother-Of-Pearl, Coralene, Silver Top 295.00
Webb, Peachblow, Ewer, Miniature, Red To Pink, Amber Applied Handle 350.00
Webb, Rose Bowl, Amberina, Shell Motif With Enameled Flowers 285.00

Webb, Rose Bowl, Cased Creamy Color, Dark Pink, Gold, Ground Pontil ... 175.00
Webb, Salt, Cream Color, Panels Of Blue & Red Floral, Silver Rim, 2 1/4 In. ... 75.00
Webb, Salt, Deep Red, White Floral, Sterling Rim ... 425.00
Webb, Salt, Gold Opalescent, Pink Floral, Silver Rim & Spoon ... 235.00
Webb, Saucer, Alexandrite, Blue To Fuchsia To Amber ... 325.00
Webb, Sugar & Creamer, Pink Enameled Butterflies & Flowers ... 120.00
Webb, Toothpick, Blue, Enamel Dots & Flowers ... 58.00
Webb, Toothpick, Mosaic ... 45.00
Webb, Tumbler, Mother-Of-Pearl, Satin, Blue Raindrop ... 85.00
Webb, Urn, Covered, Milk White, Turquoise Butterfly, Gold Handles, 11 1/4 In. ... 300.00
Webb, Urn, Ovoid, Lid, Milk White, Turquoise Enamel, Butterfly Signature ... 275.00
Webb, Vase, Cameo, Citron Ground, Flora & Butterflies, 8 In. ... 2100.00
Webb, Vase, Cobalt To Clear, Flared Top, Cameo, 8 1/4 X 6 1/4 In. ... 600.00
Webb, Vase, Cream Satin Glass, Hand-Painted Florals, Signed, 6 3/4 In. ... 215.00
Webb, Vase, Deep To Pale Pink, Gold Floral, Melon Shape, 9 X 5 In. ... 135.00
Webb, Vase, Etched Crystal, Relief Red Tulips & Leaves, 8 1/2 In. ... 525.00
Webb, Vase, Green, Floral, Gold, & Bronze, Stick, 8 1/2 In., Pair ... 250.00
Webb, Vase, Intaglio Cut Water Lilies, Amber Glass, Signed, 9 3/4 In. ... 245.00
Webb, Vase, Ivory, Floral, Signed, 11 In. ... 1800.00
Webb, Vase, Peachblow, Bulbous, 4 In. ... 295.00
Webb, Vase, Peachblow, Egg Shaped, Cream Lining, Rose To Light, 7 1/2 In. ... 650.00
Webb, Vase, Rainbow Satin, Enamel Flower, Gold Stems, Swirled, 6 1/2 In. ... 155.00
Webb, Vase, Raspberry Color, White Floral, 3 1/2 In. ... 875.00
Webb, Vase, Raspberry Red, Floral, Signed, 7 3/4 In. ... 325.00
Webb, Vase, Red & White, 3 1/2 In. ... 950.00
Webb, Vase, Red, White Butterflies & Floral, 8 In. ... 2000.00
Webb, Vase, Rose Color, White Flowers & Butterfly, 2 X 2 In. ... 425.00
Webb, Vase, Stick, Blue, Gold Prunus Blossoms, Peachblow ... 200.00
Webb, Vase, White To Butterscotch, Pinched-In Body, Enamel Floral, 9 In. ... 105.00

WEDGWOOD

Wedgwood pottery has been made at the famous Wedgwood Factory in England since 1759. A large variety of wares has been made, including the well-known jasperware, basalt, creamware, and even a limited amount of porcelain.

Wedgwood, Ashtray Set, Green & White, Heart, Diamond, Spade, & Club, 4 Piece ... 32.00
Wedgwood, Ashtray, Jasperware, Terra-Cotta & Black, 7 In. ... 58.00
Wedgwood, Atomizer, Jasperware, Lilac ... 85.00
Wedgwood, Barrel, Biscuit, Black Band, White Classic Figure, Yellow Top ... 695.00
Wedgwood, Barrel, Biscuit, Black Festoons, Yellow, Signed ... 490.00
Wedgwood, Barrel, Biscuit, Blue & White Jasper, Marked England ... 160.00
Wedgwood, Barrel, Biscuit, Blue Band, White Classical Figures, Blue Top ... 385.00
Wedgwood, Barrel, Biscuit, Dark Blue Jasperware, 2 Ball Feet ... 98.50
Wedgwood, Barrel, Biscuit, Footed, White Figure On Green, 9 1/2 In. ... 180.00
Wedgwood, Barrel, Biscuit, Gray Green, Figures, Metal Lid, C.1874 ... 185.00
Wedgwood, Barrel, Biscuit, Green, Yellow Lattice Work, Swirl Strips ... 650.00
Wedgwood, Barrel, Biscuit, Jasperware, Black, Classical Figures ... 225.00
Wedgwood, Barrel, Biscuit, Jasperware, Blue, White Figures, Metal Fittings ... 115.00
Wedgwood, Barrel, Biscuit, Jasperware, Green, Figures, Silver Plate Fittings ... 110.00
Wedgwood, Barrel, Biscuit, Jasperware, Light Green, Silver Mounted ... 75.00
Wedgwood, Barrel, Biscuit, Jasperware, Lilac, White Nymphs, 7 1/2 In. ... 225.00
Wedgwood, Barrel, Biscuit, Jasperware, Yellow & Black ... 395.00 To 435.00
Wedgwood, Barrel, Biscuit, Yellow, Black Lions' Heads, Silver Plate Fittings ... 425.00
Wedgwood, Barrel, Cracker, Peach Green, Yellow, & White, Acanthus Leaves ... 525.00
Wedgwood, Basket, Cress, With Stand, Rust Color, Hand-Painted, Decorations ... 195.00
Wedgwood, Bell, Jasperware, Green ... 27.50
Wedgwood, Bottle, Snuff, Jasperware, Dark Blue, White Hampton Seal ... 125.00
Wedgwood, Bowl, Basalt, Black, White Relief Dancing Girls, 8 X 3 1/2 In. ... 385.00
Wedgwood, Bowl, Basalt, Engine-Turned, Basket Weave Over Engine Turning ... 250.00
Wedgwood, Bowl, Basalt, Engine-Turned, Drapes & Swags, 5 X 4 In. ... 95.00
Wedgwood, Bowl, Beatrice, Floral, 10 1/4 In. ... 15.00
Wedgwood, Bowl, Black & White, Allegorical Figures, C.1820, 4 In. ... 55.00
Wedgwood, Bowl, Black, Low, Grape Vine Decoration Edge, Impressed I, England ... 95.00
Wedgwood, Bowl, Covered, Caneware, 6 In. ... 75.00
Wedgwood, Bowl, Drabware, Arabesque, 7 1/2 X 3 1/4 In. ... 155.00
Wedgwood, Bowl, Drabware, Band Of Blue Flowers, 7 In. ... 125.00
Wedgwood, Bowl, Drabware, Fluted, Smearglaze, Tudor Rose Relief, C.1790, 9 In. ... 185.00

Wedgwood, Bowl, Dragon Luster, Miniature, Foo Dogs, Mother-Of-Pearl, 2 1/4 In. 235.00
Wedgwood, Bowl, Dragon Luster, Oriental Blue, Willow Design, 10 1/4 In. 695.00
Wedgwood, Bowl, Fairyland Luster Peche Melba, Black Fairyland, 3 In. 825.00
Wedgwood, Bowl, Fairyland Luster, Bird & Geese, 5 In. 200.00
Wedgwood, Bowl, Fairyland Luster, Bird Of Paradise, Blue, Orange Inside, 8 In. 320.00
Wedgwood, Bowl, Fairyland Luster, Bird Of Paradise, Blue, 6 1/2 In. 260.00
Wedgwood, Bowl, Fairyland Luster, Birds, Mottled Blue & Green, 5 In. 200.00
Wedgwood, Bowl, Fairyland Luster, Birds, Mottled Red & Blue, 8 In. 380.00
Wedgwood, Bowl, Fairyland Luster, Blue With Cobweb & Fairy Interior, 10 In. 1450.00
Wedgwood, Bowl, Fairyland Luster, Blue, Dragons, Pearl Inside, 4 3/4 In. 195.00
Wedgwood, Bowl, Fairyland Luster, Butterflies, Blue, White, 4 1/2 X 2 1/2 In. 235.00
Wedgwood, Bowl, Fairyland Luster, Butterflies, Butterscotch, 4 In. 225.00
Wedgwood, Bowl, Fairyland Luster, Butterflies, Mother-Of-Pearl, 4 In. 175.00
Wedgwood, Bowl, Fairyland Luster, Butterflies, Mother-Of-Pearl, 5 1/2 In. 160.00
Wedgwood, Bowl, Fairyland Luster, Butterflies, Orange, Green Inside, 8 In. 685.00
Wedgwood, Bowl, Fairyland Luster, Butterfly, Copper, Aqua Inside, 5 In. 200.00
Wedgwood, Bowl, Fairyland Luster, Butterfly, Mother-Of-Pearl, Octagonal, 8 In. 425.00
Wedgwood, Bowl, Fairyland Luster, Butterfly, Ruby, 8 In. 395.00
Wedgwood, Bowl, Fairyland Luster, Daventry, 8 In. 875.00
Wedgwood, Bowl, Fairyland Luster, Dragon, Blue & Green, 5 In. 145.00
Wedgwood, Bowl, Fairyland Luster, Dragon, Dark Green Mottled, 9 In. 450.00
Wedgwood, Bowl, Fairyland Luster, Dragon, Light Blue, 10 1/2 In. 575.00
Wedgwood, Bowl, Fairyland Luster, Dragon, Octagonal, 3 1/2 X 2 In. 145.00
Wedgwood, Bowl, Fairyland Luster, Dragon, Orange & Gilt, 8 In. 325.00
Wedgwood, Bowl, Fairyland Luster, Dragons, Green, Octagonal, 7 In. 320.00
Wedgwood, Bowl, Fairyland Luster, Dragons, Orange, Blue Interior, 8 In. 320.00
Wedgwood, Bowl, Fairyland Luster, Dragons, 10 In. 195.00
Wedgwood, Bowl, Fairyland Luster, Fish, Octagonal, 4 In. 250.00
Wedgwood, Bowl, Fairyland Luster, Footed, 4 3/4 X 2 1/2 In. 295.00
Wedgwood, Bowl, Fairyland Luster, Peacock & Geese, Red, 8 In. 420.00
Wedgwood, Bowl, Fairyland Luster, Rainbow, 8 In. 995.00
Wedgwood, Bowl, Fairyland Luster, Red & Gold Dragons, Blue, 10 1/4 In. 765.00
Wedgwood, Bowl, Fairyland, Octagonal, Panels Decorated, 10 1/2 In. 1500.00
Wedgwood, Bowl, Fairyland, Variegated Design, Elves, 7 1/2 X 3 3/4 In. 1200.00
Wedgwood, Bowl, Floral Majolica, Cream Background, 7 In. 15.00
Wedgwood, Bowl, Green Glaze, Molded Vine & Leaves, C.1860, 8 3/8 In. 18.00
Wedgwood, Bowl, Hummingbird Luster, English, 4 In. 295.00
Wedgwood, Bowl, Imperial Daventry Luster, Chinese Scene, 9 In. 695.00
Wedgwood, Bowl, Imperial Jasperware, White Figures, 8 In. 80.00
Wedgwood, Bowl, Jasper, Pentafoil, Terra-Cotta And White, Made In England 85.00
Wedgwood, Bowl, Jasperware, Black & White, Dancing Hours, 1959, 10 1/4 In. 525.00
Wedgwood, Bowl, Jasperware, Dark Blue, Classical Designs, Footed, 3 X 2 In. 32.50
Wedgwood, Bowl, Jasperware, Green, White Medallion, 4 1/4 In. 11.00
Wedgwood, Bowl, Jasperware, Light Blue, Dancing Hours, 10 In. 295.00
Wedgwood, Bowl, Jasperware, Light Green, Footed, 6 In. 110.00
Wedgwood, Bowl, Jasperware, Metal Rim, 9 X 5 In. 140.00
Wedgwood, Bowl, Light Blue With Classical Figures, Miniature 95.00
Wedgwood, Bowl, Luster, Coral & Bronze, Medieval Figures, Magpies, 9 1/2 In. 1200.00
Wedgwood, Bowl, Majolica, Seashell & Coral, 7 In. 48.00
Wedgwood, Bowl, Mother-Of-Pearl Luster, Orange, Butterflies, 4 In. 175.00
Wedgwood, Bowl, Octagonal, Hummingbird Luster, Flying Geese Border, 2 7/8 In. 175.00
Wedgwood, Bowl, Raleigh, Blue On White, Scenics And Florals, 10 In. 24.00
Wedgwood, Bowl, White, Ram's Head, Wedgwood & Barlaston, C.1890, 8 1/2 In. 65.00
Wedgwood, Box, Bean, Harry Barnard, Lilac Jasper, White Sgrafitto, Signed 500.00
Wedgwood, Box, Covered, Deep Blue, Round, 3 1/2 In. 75.00
Wedgwood, Box, Covered, Light Blue, Recessed Front, Oval, 3 In. 25.00
Wedgwood, Box, Covered, Lilac, Round, 2 3/4 In. 65.00
Wedgwood, Box, Covered, Lilac, 4 In. 84.00
Wedgwood, Box, Jasper, Pentafoil, Lilac And White, Made In England 85.00
Wedgwood, Box, Jasperware, Blue, White Washington & Franklin, C.1896, 5 In. 225.00
Wedgwood, Box, Jasperware, Cobalt, Covered, Classical Trim, 1 1/2 In. 37.50
Wedgwood, Box, Jasperware, Covered, Medium Blue, Heart Shape, 5 In. 44.00
Wedgwood, Box, Jasperware, Dark Blue, Rose Garlands, Heart Shape, 5 1/4 In. 65.00
Wedgwood, Box, Jasperware, Green, Children & Pegasus, 3 3/4 X 3 In. 25.00
Wedgwood, Box, Jasperware, Green, 1966, 4 3/4 X 3 In. 45.00

Wedgwood, Box, Jasperware, Pale Blue, Elizabeth II On Lid, 1953, 3 3/4 In. 45.00
Wedgwood, Box, Pentafoil, Lilac Jasper 125.00
Wedgwood, Box, Pomade, Jasperware, Blue, Round, 3 In. 75.00
Wedgwood, Box, Powder, Covered, Jasperware, Light Blue & White 65.00
Wedgwood, Box, Trinket, Jasperware, Lilac, Mythological Figures, 4 In. 55.00
Wedgwood, Breakfast Set, Creamware Tray, Fitzhugh Orange, Bone China, C.1878 .... 385.00
Wedgwood, Bust, Basalt, Black, Byron, 8 1/2 In. 595.00
Wedgwood, Bust, Basalt, George Washington, 8 1/2 In. 95.00
Wedgwood, Bust, Basalt, Mercury, 1810, 18 In. 980.00
Wedgwood, Butter Keeper, Jasperware, Blue & White, Silver Plate Lid, C.1891 .... 95.00
Wedgwood, Butter, Drabware, Blue Swags On Top, 4 1/2 In. 275.00
Wedgwood, Cake Plate, Black Basalt, Handles, Fluted Border With Scene 125.00
Wedgwood, Candlestick, Basalt, Sacrifice Relief, Etruria, English, C.1900, Pair 355.00
Wedgwood, Candlestick, Basalt, Triton, 1973, 11 3/4 In. 695.00
Wedgwood, Candlestick, Charcoal, Waterford Prisms, Ormolu Base, 14 In., Pair 750.00
Wedgwood, Candlestick, Dark Blue, White Bas Relief Muses, C.1850, 9 In. 145.00
Wedgwood, Candlestick, Dark Blue, White Figures & Trees, 5 1/2 In. 90.00
Wedgwood, Candlestick, Jasperware, Black & White, 6 1/4 In., Pair 475.00
Wedgwood, Candlestick, Jasperware, Dark Blue, Classical Figures, 5 In., Pair 145.00
Wedgwood, Candlestick, Mint Green, White Classical Figures, 5 In. 95.00
Wedgwood, Candlestick, Rosso Antico, Black Classical Figures, 7 In. 250.00
Wedgwood, Cassolette, Variegated, Marked Wedgwood & Bentley 1850.00
Wedgwood, Centerpiece Bowl, Basalt, Black, Turned-In Edge, 11 X 3 1/2 In. 125.00
Wedgwood, Charger, Majolica, Sea Life Motif, 1882, 25 1/2 X 11 1/2 In. 250.00
Wedgwood, Coffeepot, Basalt, Black, C.1800, 9 3/4 In. 275.00
Wedgwood, Coffeepot, Basalt, Engine-Turned, 7 1/4 In. 85.00
Wedgwood, Coffeepot, Black, Capri, 7 In. 275.00
Wedgwood, Coffeepot, Black, Capri, 9 In. 295.00
Wedgwood, Coffeepot, Deep Blue, White Figures, Acanthus Leaves On Lid 155.00
Wedgwood, Coffeepot, Rosso Antico 375.00
Wedgwood, Compote, Flow Blue Underglaze, Hand-Painted Overglaze, 1828, 13 In. 195.00
Wedgwood, Coronation, Teapot, Edward VIII, Cream With Blue 30.00
Wedgwood, Creamer, Basalt, Souvenir, British Columbia 40.00
Wedgwood, Creamer, Deep Blue, White Trim, Self Cover, 4 1/2 In. 95.00
Wedgwood, Creamer, Drabware, Arabesque Raised Decoration, C.1790 .... 125.00
Wedgwood, Creamer, Drabware, Blue Flowers In Relief 95.00
Wedgwood, Creamer, Drabware, Gothic Decoration, C.1830 .... 95.00
Wedgwood, Creamer, Drabware, White Relief, 4 In. 140.00
Wedgwood, Creamer, Jasperware, Black, White Figures & Floral, 4 1/2 In. 38.00
Wedgwood, Creamer, Jasperware, Black, 4 In. 69.00
Wedgwood, Creamer, Jasperware, Light Blue, 4 In. 55.00
Wedgwood, Creamer, Self Cover, Deep Blue & White, 4 1/2 In. 95.00
Wedgwood, Creamer, Stoneware, Gray, Raised Floral & Scroll, C.1870 .... 65.00
Wedgwood, Creamer, Terra-Cotta, Egyptian Motif In Black Relief, England 145.00
Wedgwood, Cup & Saucer, Acorn & Grape, Portland Vase Mark 28.00
Wedgwood, Cup & Saucer, Basalt, Impressed Wedgwood 66.50
Wedgwood, Cup & Saucer, Black Basalt, Classical Motif On Saucer Rim 110.00
Wedgwood, Cup & Saucer, Bouillon, Floral Garlands, Gold Trim 6.00
Wedgwood, Cup & Saucer, Caneware, Gray Trim, C.1795 .... 325.00
Wedgwood, Cup & Saucer, Creamware, Twig Handle, C.1790 .... 65.00
Wedgwood, Cup & Saucer, Demitasse, Jasperware, Black 16.50
Wedgwood, Cup & Saucer, Demitasse, Jasperware, Terra-Cotta 65.00
Wedgwood, Cup & Saucer, Jasperware, Dark Blue, Classical Figures 75.00
Wedgwood, Cup & Saucer, Jasperware, Green, C.1940 .... 35.00
Wedgwood, Cup & Saucer, Jasperware, Lilac, White Relief 89.00
Wedgwood, Cup & Saucer, Miniature Pearlware, Blue Willow 115.00
Wedgwood, Cup & Saucer, White, Gold Trim, Red Mark 125.00
Wedgwood, Cup, Commemorative, Queen Elizabeth On Side 125.00
Wedgwood, Cup, Fairyland Luster, Black Night Scene, Elves Playing, 4 In. 595.00
Wedgwood, Cup, Loving, Fairyland Luster, Copper, Gold Butterfly, 3 Handled 155.00
Wedgwood, Cup, Loving, Fairyland Luster, 3-Handled, Snakes & Dragons, 2 In. 275.00
Wedgwood, Demitasse Set, Whitehall, 12 Pieces 350.00
Wedgwood, Dish, Candy, Basalt, Black, Black Classical Figures, Spade Shape 15.00
Wedgwood, Dish, Cheese, Classical Figures, Blue & White Jasper, 10 In. 350.00
Wedgwood, Dish, Deep Blue, White Cameos, Signed Stilton, 11 X 11 1/2 In. 450.00

Wedgwood, Dish, Game Pie, Covered, Caneware, 9 In. 210.00
Wedgwood, Dish, Game, Rabbit Finial, 1866, 10 3/4 X 8 In. 235.00
Wedgwood, Dish, Mint Green, White Profile Of Washington, Heart Shape, 5 In. 90.00
Wedgwood, Dish, Queensware, Diamond Shape, Children, Lessore, 1886, 5 1/4 In. 425.00
Wedgwood, Dish, Soap, Corn, Ironstone 38.00
Wedgwood, Dish, Sweetmeat, Jasperware, Blue, Winston Churchill, 4 1/2 In. 8.50
Wedgwood, Dish, Terra-Cotta, Cloverleaf Shape, 5 X 5 In. 27.50
Wedgwood, Eggcup Holder, White Smear Glaze, Royal Blue Grape & Vine, Footed 295.00
Wedgwood, Figurine, Black Basalt, Mercury 135.00
Wedgwood, Figurine, Boar, Signed Skeaping 275.00
Wedgwood, Figurine, Bulldog, Black, Yellow Eyes, 5 In. 375.00
Wedgwood, Figurine, Cat With Glass Eyes, 4 X 4 1/2 In. 275.00
Wedgwood, Figurine, Chessmen, King & Queen, Arnold Machin, 1967, Pair 135.00
Wedgwood, Figurine, Dancing Hours Figure 135.00
Wedgwood, Figurine, Stork, Black Basalt, Rockwork Base, Marked, 6 In. 200.00
Wedgwood, Flowerpot, Jasperware, Light Blue, 6 In., Pair 275.00
Wedgwood, Fruit Bowl, Basalt, Engine-Turned, Floriform Center, 7 5/8 In. 65.00
Wedgwood, Hair Receiver, Classic Relief, C.1880 .... 210.00
Wedgwood, Hair Receiver, Jasperware, Dark Blue, Classical Figures, 3 1/2 In. 65.00
Wedgwood, Hair Receiver, Olive Green 145.00
Wedgwood, Hedgehog With Tray, Satin Patina, Basalt, 7 X 11 1/2 In. 825.00
Wedgwood, Hedgehog, Green Undertray 575.00
Wedgwood, Honey Pot, Blue Willow, Gold Trim, Silver Plate Fittings, C.1885 .... 140.00
Wedgwood, Honey Pot, Jasperware, Dark Blue 95.00
Wedgwood, Honey Pot, Jasperware, Light Blue, White Figures, Metal Lid, C.1865 .... 150.00
Wedgwood, Humidor, Basalt, Black, White, Covered, 4 1/2 X 3 1/4 In. 55.00
Wedgwood, Jam Pot, Jasperware, Black & White, Silver Plate Lid & Spoon 95.00
Wedgwood, Jam Pot, Jasperware, Dark Blue, Silver Plate Lid 55.00
Wedgwood, Jam Pot, Silver Lid, Handle And Spoor, Lilac, Green, White, 4 In. 525.00
Wedgwood, Jam Pot, Silver Plate Lid & Spoon, Lilac 195.00
Wedgwood, Jar, Blue Oriental Landscape Transfer, C.1820, 3 X 2 In. 40.00
Wedgwood, Jar, Cookie, Jasperware, Dark Blue, E.P.N.S. Fittings 145.00
Wedgwood, Jar, Cookie, Jasperware, Metal Fittings 120.00
Wedgwood, Jar, Covered, Jasperware, England 25.00
Wedgwood, Jar, Cracker, Blue & White Jasper, Classic Ladies, Silver Plate Rim 135.00
Wedgwood, Jar, Cracker, Dark Blue, Silver Plate Fittings, 5 1/2 In. 165.00
Wedgwood, Jar, Cracker, Jasper, Blue & White, 3 Ball Feet 145.00
Wedgwood, Jar, Cracker, Jasper, Hunt Scene, 6 1/4 In. 145.00
Wedgwood, Jar, Cracker, Jasperware, Blue, White Hunt Scenes, Silver Fittings 138.00
Wedgwood, Jar, Cylindrical, Covered, 4 X 3 In. 85.00
Wedgwood, Jar, Jam, Dark Blue, Silver Plate Lid 50.00
Wedgwood, Jar, Jam, Lilac, Green, & White, Rams' Heads & Garlands, Silver Lid 525.00
Wedgwood, Jar, Tobacco, Pineapple Knob On Silver Lid, Portland, 5 In. 75.00
Wedgwood, Jardiniere, Blue, White Washington, Jefferson, & Franklin Plaques 285.00
Wedgwood, Jardiniere, Blue, Yellow, Brown, Green, Majolica, 7 In. 225.00
Wedgwood, Jardiniere, Dark Green, White Muses & Grape Garlands, 8 In. 245.00
Wedgwood, Jardiniere, Deep Blue, White Trim, 8 X 7 In. 185.00
Wedgwood, Jug, Ale, Cambridge, Red, Stoneware, 1871, 5 1/2 In. 95.00
Wedgwood, Jug, Ale, Rossico Antico, Arms Of Coll.S.Johannis, 4 1/2 In. 50.00
Wedgwood, Jug, Ale, Rossico Antico, Cambridge, 7 In. 85.00
Wedgwood, Jug, Ale, Stoneware, Red, Cambridge Crest, 6 In. 75.00
Wedgwood, Jug, Ale, Terra-Cotta, Cambridge, 5 1/2 In. 85.00
Wedgwood, Jug, Ale, Terra-Cotta, English University Crest, 1871, 7 1/4 In. 85.00
Wedgwood, Jug, Blue & White, Orange Shape, Medallions Of Washington, 6 In. 145.00
Wedgwood, Jug, Blue Dip, High Reliefs, 7 In. 95.00
Wedgwood, Jug, Caneware, 4 3/4 In. 115.00
Wedgwood, Jug, Canewear, Smearglaze, Tudor Rose Relief, C.1790 .... 245.00
Wedgwood, Jug, Creamware, Green Banding, C.1800, 4 In. 85.00
Wedgwood, Jug, Jasperware, Blue, White Washington & Franklin, C.1896 .... 145.00
Wedgwood, Jug, Jasperware, Olive Green, Rope Handle, 4 1/2 In. 75.00
Wedgwood, Jug, Jasperware, Yellow With Black, Rope Handle, 6 1/2 In. 325.00
Wedgwood, Jug, Milk, Crimson, Blood Red & White, 6 1/2 In. 750.00
Wedgwood, Jug, Stoneware, Blue & White, C.1810, 5 In. 225.00
Wedgwood, Jug, Tobacco, Jasperware, Dark Blue, 7 1/2 In. 95.00
Wedgwood, Jug, Water, Jasperware, Dark Blue, Metal Lid 145.00

Wedgwood, Jug, White Stoneware, Frieze Decorated, Impressed, 8 In. 290.00
Wedgwood, Keeper, Butter, Rockingham Glaze, Daisy Finial, 1921 65.00
Wedgwood, Keeper, Cheese, Jasperware, Deep Blue, E.P.N.S. Base, C.1891, 10 In. 195.00
Wedgwood, Keeper, Covered, Silver Plate Lid, 4 1/2 X 1 7/8 In., C.1891 95.00
Wedgwood, Lighter, Table, Lilac, White Rearing Horse, Ronson 125.00
Wedgwood, Match Box, Yellow And White Jasper 275.00
Wedgwood, Match Holder, Green Jasper, Striker Bottom 45.00
Wedgwood, Match Holder, Jasperware, Light Green 25.00
Wedgwood, Matchbox, Covered, Etruria China, Striker Inside 18.50
Wedgwood, Matchbox, Striker, Blue & White, Lady Templeton Figures, Cupids 85.00
Wedgwood, Medallion, Cupid & Psyche, Lilac, White Jasper, 3 1/2 In. 150.00
Wedgwood, Medallion, Shakespeare, 2 In. 425.00
Wedgwood, Mold, Jelly, Cream Ware With Grape Design 37.50
Wedgwood, Muffineer, Deep Blue & White, Silver-Plated Dome Lid, 5 1/2 In. 155.00
Wedgwood, Muffineer, Deep Blue, White Trim, Silver Plate Dome Lid, 5 1/2 In. 155.00
Wedgwood, Muffineer, Jasperware, Dark Blue, Silver Plate Top 82.00
Wedgwood, Mug, Investiture Of Prince Of Wales, 1969, 4 In. 45.00
Wedgwood, Mug, Keith Murray, Ivory Glaze, Tennis Racquets, Signed 25.00
Wedgwood, Mug, Queensware, Dickens, 5 In. 15.00
Wedgwood, Mug, Queensware, Mayflower, 5 In. 15.00
Wedgwood, Mug, Queensware, Princess Anne Marriage, 1973 25.00
Wedgwood, Mug, Queensware, Souvenir Of London 15.00
Wedgwood, Mustard Pot, Creamware, Chinoiserie, C.1780, 3 3/4 In. 105.00
Wedgwood, Mustard Pot, Jasperware, Dark Blue, Silver Plate Lid & Spoon 55.00
Wedgwood, Mustard Pot, Yellow, Black Lion's Head & Floral, Silver Plate Lid 325.00
Wedgwood, Paperweight, Black Jasper, White Eagle & 13 Stars, England 28.00
Wedgwood, Pillbox, Jasperware, Pale Orchid, 1 3/4 X 1 In. 45.00
Wedgwood, Pitcher Set, Jasperware, Dark Blue & White, 7 To 5 In., 3 Piece 260.00
Wedgwood, Pitcher, Blue, Classical Figures, Signed, 5 1/4 In. 92.00
Wedgwood, Pitcher, Blue, White Classical Figures, C.1891, 16 1/2 In. 135.00
Wedgwood, Pitcher, Cobalt, Washington & Franklin, Bulbous, C.1850, 6 In. 183.00
Wedgwood, Pitcher, Creamware, Disraeli, Black Transfer, 1881, 6 1/2 In. 125.00
Wedgwood, Pitcher, Creamware, Hound Handled, Hunting Scenes, 6 In. 65.00
Wedgwood, Pitcher, Dark Green, Classical Scene, 5 1/2 In. 65.00
Wedgwood, Pitcher, Green, White Classical Figures, 4 1/4 In. 95.00
Wedgwood, Pitcher, Green, White Figures Doing Domestic Chores, 3 1/2 In. 35.00
Wedgwood, Pitcher, Jasper, Blue, Rope Handle, Dated 1955, 4 In. 32.00
Wedgwood, Pitcher, Jasperware, Blue, Grapes, Rope Handle, Pewter Lid, 6 1/2 In. 125.00
Wedgwood, Pitcher, Jasperware, Crimson, 6 1/2 In. 675.00
Wedgwood, Pitcher, Jasperware, Dark Blue, Cameo Figures, 6 1/2 In. 70.00
Wedgwood, Pitcher, Jasperware, Dark Blue, Classical Figures, 5 1/4 In. 65.00
Wedgwood, Pitcher, Jasperware, Dark Blue, White Classical Cameos, 4 1/2 In. 115.00
Wedgwood, Pitcher, Jasperware, Dark Blue, White Classical Figures, 6 In. 55.00
Wedgwood, Pitcher, Jasperware, Deep Blue & White, Rope Handle, 6 1/2 In. 65.00
Wedgwood, Pitcher, Jasperware, Green & White, 6 In. 70.00
Wedgwood, Pitcher, Jasperware, Light Blue, Relief Cattails, 8 In. 225.00
Wedgwood, Pitcher, Jasperware, Light Green, 7 In. 125.00
Wedgwood, Pitcher, Queensware, White, Cupids & Grapes, 8 In. 85.00
Wedgwood, Pitcher, Salt Glaze, Bas Relief Cherubs, Blue Top Band, 6 In. 85.00
Wedgwood, Pitcher, Tankard, Jasperware, Classical, Rope Handle, Pre-1858 65.00
Wedgwood, Pitcher, Terra-Cotta, 6 1/2 In. 145.00
Wedgwood, Pitcher, White Cameo, Dark Blue, Dated 1897, 5 1/4 In. 105.00
Wedgwood, Planter, Majolica, Bird's Nest, Date 1972, Bird On Nest, 11 1/2 In. 375.00
Wedgwood, Planter, Majolica, Bird's Nest, Date1972, Bird On Nest, 11 1/2 In. 375.00
Wedgwood, Plaque, Basalt, Chief Blackhawk, 1971, 9 3/4 In. 250.00
Wedgwood, Plaque, Blue, Dancing Hours, 9 X 3 3/4 In. 160.00
Wedgwood, Plaque, Classical Female Figure, Lilac, 4 X 3 In. 195.00
Wedgwood, Plaque, Earthenware, Blue Outlined Courtesan, C.1868, 14 In., Pair 430.00
Wedgwood, Plaque, Green Jasperware, Marked England, 3 3/4 X 5 1/8 In. 85.00
Wedgwood, Plaque, Light Blue, Putti, C.1750, 3 In., Pair 149.00
Wedgwood, Plaque, Lilac, Classical Female In High Relief, Oval, 4 X 3 In. 225.00
Wedgwood, Plate, Adams House & Lambs Tavern, Blue, 9 1/2 In. 35.00
Wedgwood, Plate, Birds, Greens & Browns, 8 1/2 In. 12.50
Wedgwood, Plate, Birth Of The American Flag, Blue 45.00
Wedgwood, Plate, Blue & White, Famous Place, 9 1/4 In. 35.00

Wedgwood, Plate, Blue, Faneuil Hall, 9 1/4 In. 27.50
Wedgwood, Plate, Cadet Chapel, West Point, Pink.C.1930 .... 12.00
Wedgwood, Plate, Canada, Maple Leaves, & Crown, Etruria, 10 In. 15.00
Wedgwood, Plate, Classic Medallions & Floral, Sterling Rim, C.1900, 12 In. 45.00
Wedgwood, Plate, College Hall, Smith College, 1934, Rose, 6 1/2 In. 8.00
Wedgwood, Plate, Colorado State Capitol, Etruria, 9 In. 32.00
Wedgwood, Plate, Columbian Exposition, Administration, Blue, 8 1/2 In. 24.00
Wedgwood, Plate, Columbian Exposition, 1893, Blue & White, 8 1/4 In. 16.00
Wedgwood, Plate, Cornflower, Etruria, England, 6 1/2 In. 3.25
Wedgwood, Plate, Cornflower, Etruria, England, 8 1/4 In. 5.00
Wedgwood, Plate, Countryside, 10 In. 11.50
Wedgwood, Plate, Creamware, Duck In Marsh, Polychrome, 10 1/4 In. 55.00
Wedgwood, Plate, Creamware, Feather Edge, C.1775, 10 In. 55.00
Wedgwood, Plate, Dark Blue, Old South Church, Boston, 9 1/4 In. 20.00
Wedgwood, Plate, Dark Blue, Old State House, Boston, 9 1/4 In. 20.00
Wedgwood, Plate, Dessert, Pearlware, Pink To White, Shell Shape, C.1865, 9 In. 50.00
Wedgwood, Plate, Dorothy Q.Mansion, Quincy, Black & White, 9 In. 25.00
Wedgwood, Plate, Eat Thy Food With A Thankful Heart, Blue, White, 10 1/4 In. 40.00
Wedgwood, Plate, Fairyland Luster, Chinese Tiger, 9 1/4 In. 295.00
Wedgwood, Plate, Fish, Gold Edge, Hodgkiss, Wedgwood, England, 9 In. 29.50
Wedgwood, Plate, Fort Johnson, Amsterdam, N.Y., Blue & White, 9 1/4 In. 35.00
Wedgwood, Plate, Fort Tic, Blue, 10 In. 15.00
Wedgwood, Plate, Girl Skipping Rope, Polychrome, C.1830, 8 In. 25.00
Wedgwood, Plate, Grand Union Hotel, Saratoga Springs, N.Y., Blue & White 37.00
Wedgwood, Plate, Gray-Blue, Texas Longhorn Center 18.00
Wedgwood, Plate, Green Dragon Inn, Boston, Mass., 1897, Blue, 9 1/8 In. 45.00
Wedgwood, Plate, Green Dragon Tavern 45.00
Wedgwood, Plate, Home Of Caroline Scott Harrison, D.A.R., Red, C.1900, 9 In. 25.00
Wedgwood, Plate, Home Of Robert E.Lee, Rose, 10 In. 15.00
Wedgwood, Plate, Independence Hall, Philadelphia, 1743-1893, Blue, 9 In. 18.50
Wedgwood, Plate, Ivanhoe & Rowena, Blue & White, 10 3/8 In. 40.00
Wedgwood, Plate, Ivanhoe Series, Urfried Scene, Rebecca & Cedric, Blue, 8 In. 25.00
Wedgwood, Plate, Ivanhoe, Cjamba & Gurth The Shepherd, Blue & White, 10 In. 25.00
Wedgwood, Plate, Japanese Jewels Of Omnipotence & Rain Dragons, 9 In. 195.00
Wedgwood, Plate, Jasperware, Green, Shakespeare's Birthplace, 8 In. 25.00
Wedgwood, Plate, John F.Kennedy, Blue & White, 4 5/8 In. 10.00
Wedgwood, Plate, Kings Chapel, Boston, Blue 45.00
Wedgwood, Plate, Landing Of Pilgrims 45.00
Wedgwood, Plate, Library Of Congress, Etruria, England 38.00
Wedgwood, Plate, Library, Columbia University, 1912, 10 3/4 In. 40.00
Wedgwood, Plate, Lilac, White Relief, 9 In. 95.00
Wedgwood, Plate, Lillie Off Telegraph Hill, Sailboat, Polychrome, 10 In. 35.00
Wedgwood, Plate, Longfellow's House, Portland, Me., Blue & White, 9 In. 22.00
Wedgwood, Plate, Majolica, Brilliant Colors, 9 In. 35.00
Wedgwood, Plate, Majolica, Cream With Olive, Basket Weave, 8 3/4 In. 23.00
Wedgwood, Plate, Majolica, Figure Center, Blue Edge, Email Ombrant, 1867, 9 In. 65.00
Wedgwood, Plate, Memorial Hall Library Building, Blue & White, 10 In. 13.50
Wedgwood, Plate, Monticello, Black & White, 10 In. 12.00
Wedgwood, Plate, Mother & 2 Children In Hayfield, Polychrome, C.1830, 8 In. 25.00
Wedgwood, Plate, Mt.Vernon, The Home Of Washington, Blue, 1900, 9 1/4 In. 35.00
Wedgwood, Plate, N.Y.U., Washington Square East, Maroon, 10 In. 10.00
Wedgwood, Plate, Old North Church 45.00
Wedgwood, Plate, Old North Church, McDuffee & Stratton 65.00
Wedgwood, Plate, Pearlware Basket Weave, Oval, Orange Edging, C.1790, 10 In. 155.00
Wedgwood, Plate, Peruvian, Mulberry, 10 1/4 In. 15.00
Wedgwood, Plate, Pilgrim Exiles, Blue 35.00
Wedgwood, Plate, Pink Staffordshire, Corinthia, 9 1/2 In., Pair 35.00
Wedgwood, Plate, Return Of Mayflower, Blue 45.00
Wedgwood, Plate, Service, Queensware, Old London Views In Brown, 1941 .... 20.00
Wedgwood, Plate, Shell Shape, Deep Pink To White, Set Of 6 .... 59.00
Wedgwood, Plate, Soup, Hollyhock, Blue & White, 10 1/4 In., Pair 58.00
Wedgwood, Plate, State Capitol, 1904, Etruria, England, 9 1/2 In. 38.00
Wedgwood, Plate, State House, Boston, Blue, 9 In. 18.50
Wedgwood, Plate, The Capitol 45.00
Wedgwood, Plate, Trinity College, Blue, 10 1/2 In. 8.00

Wedgwood, Plate, University Of Michigan, Grape Border, Angell Hall 35.00
Wedgwood, Plate, Vassar, 1929 .... 18.00
Wedgwood, Plate, Wanda & Gurth The Swineherd, Ivanhoe Series, Blue, 10 In. 28.00
Wedgwood, Plate, Washington Elm 45.00
Wedgwood, Plate, Washington's Headquarters, 9 1/2 In. 18.00
Wedgwood, Plate, Water Tower, Chicago, Black & White, 10 In. 10.00
Wedgwood, Plate, White, Blue & Red Floral Border, Coin Gold, 8 3/4 In. 16.50
Wedgwood, Plate, Winston Churchill, Blue & White, 4 5/8 In. 10.00
Wedgwood, Plate, Yale College & Old Yale Fence, 1900 .... 20.00
Wedgwood, Plate, 1744 Mt.Vernon 45.00
Wedgwood, Platter, Fish, Blue & White, Marine Border, 23 X 11 In. 48.00
Wedgwood, Platter, Ironstone, Tea Leaf, 13 X 9 1/2 In. 16.00
Wedgwood, Platter, Round, Impressed Mark, Dark Blue And White Scenic, C.1890 .... 40.00
Wedgwood, Platter, Rowena Granting Safe Escort, Blue, 12 1/2 X 10 In. 125.00
Wedgwood, Platter, White, Brown Border Of Griffins & Fruit, 1884, 19 1/2 In. 55.00
Wedgwood, Pocket, Wall, Creamware, Molded, Pair 95.00
Wedgwood, Pocket, Wall, Majolica Bird's Nest, Brown & Green, 1872, 11 1/2 In. 385.00
Wedgwood, Pot, Covered Bough, Drabware, Plain, Classic Shape, C.1790, 7 1/2 In. 395.00
Wedgwood, Pot, Honey, Bone China, Deep Blue, Willow, Silver Lid, C.1885 .... 145.00
Wedgwood, Pot, Lilac Crocus, Classical Scene, Swags Of Fruit, Grids, 6 In. 825.00
Wedgwood, Pot, Mustard, Creamware, Covered, Chinoiserie, Reds, Oranges, C.1780 .... 100.00
Wedgwood, Pot, Queensware Bough, High Relief, C.1845, 10 In. 315.00
Wedgwood, Potpourri, Whiteware, Blue Vintage Relief, 4 3/4 In. 195.00
Wedgwood, Ring Stand, Jasperware, Dark Blue 85.00
Wedgwood, Rose Bowl, Fairyland Luster, Fairies, Pixies, Mint Green, 3 In. 1085.00
Wedgwood, Salad Set, Jasperware, Dark Blue, 9 In. Bowl, Servers, 3 Piece 135.00
Wedgwood, Salt & Pepper, Terra-Cotta, White Trim, 4 In. 195.00
Wedgwood, Salt, Master, Jasperware, Dark Blue With White, Sterling Rim 65.00
Wedgwood, Saucer, Fairyland Luster, Orange, Blue Figure, 2 7/8 In. 85.00
Wedgwood, Soup Bowl, Oriental, Portland Vase Mark 10.00
Wedgwood, Spill, Basalt, Bellflower & Acanthus Leaf, Rams' Heads & Swags 95.00
Wedgwood, Spill, Basalt, Black, Black Leaves & Flowers, 5 In. 95.00
Wedgwood, Spill, Jasperware, Dark Blue, Relief Acanthus Leaves, 5 1/4 In. 95.00
Wedgwood, Spill, Lilac, Peach Tint, C.1850, 4 1/2 In. 195.00
Wedgwood, Stickpin, Jasperware, Dark Blue, White Stars, 1785 .... 50.00
Wedgwood, Sugar & Creamer, Jasperware, Terra-Cotta & White, Miniature 210.00
Wedgwood, Sugar Bowl, Olive Green Jasper 45.00
Wedgwood, Sugar Shaker, Deep Blue, White Classic Figures, 6 3/4 In. 135.00
Wedgwood, Sugar, Caneware, Bamboo Finial & Handles, Smear Glaze, Prunus, 1790 .... 285.00
Wedgwood, Sugar, Covered, Basalt, Enamel Fish & Bermuda 85.00
Wedgwood, Sugar, Covered, Caneware, Smear Glaze, Prunus Blossom, C.1790 .... 275.00
Wedgwood, Sugar, Covered, Famille Rose, Black Basalt, C.1810, 6 1/4 In. 125.00
Wedgwood, Sugar, Covered, Indiana, Flow Blue 30.00
Wedgwood, Sugar, Covered, Ironstone 22.00
Wedgwood, Sugar, Covered, Jasperware, Green, Busts Of Washington & Franklin 125.00
Wedgwood, Sugar, Ironstone, Flower Finial, White, Lily Of The Valley 23.00
Wedgwood, Sugar, Jasperware, Light Green, 4 1/2 In. 45.00
Wedgwood, Sugar, Ningpo 10.00
Wedgwood, Sugar, Orange, Chinese Red Floral, C.1880 .... 97.50
Wedgwood, Tea Set, Basalt, Widow Finials, 3 Piece 195.00
Wedgwood, Tea Set, Cobalt, White Figures, 3 Piece 585.00
Wedgwood, Tea Set, Coronation, Queensware, George VI, 1937, 3 Piece 225.00
Wedgwood, Tea Set, Deep Blue, White Figures, Silver Rims, 3 Piece 285.00
Wedgwood, Tea Set, Edward VII & Coat-Of-Arms Medallion, Glazed Creamware 300.00
Wedgwood, Tea Set, Green, Off-White Decoration, 3 Piece 260.00
Wedgwood, Tea Set, Jasperware, Blue, White Grape & Leaf Border, 3 Piece 75.00
Wedgwood, Tea Set, Jasperware, Coronation, Edward VIII, 1937, 3 Piece 450.00
Wedgwood, Tea Set, Olive Green Jasper 295.00
Wedgwood, Tea Set, Queensware, Edward VIII, Blue On White, 3 Piece 355.00
Wedgwood, Tea Set, Rockingham Glaze, Widow Finial, Signed Wedgwood 350.00
Wedgwood, Tea Set, Terra-Cotta, 3 Piece 495.00
Wedgwood, Teapot, Basalt With Widow Finial 240.00
Wedgwood, Teapot, Caneware, C.1820 .... 195.00
Wedgwood, Teapot, Caneware, Octagonal, Twig Finial, 4-Cup Size, C.1790 .... 645.00
Wedgwood, Teapot, Creamware, Chinoiserie, Twig Finial & Handle, C.1790, 3 In. 235.00

Wedgwood, Teapot, Drabware, Blue Flowers In Relief 155.00
Wedgwood, Teapot, Drabware, Spaniel Finial, Arabesque 195.00
Wedgwood, Teapot, Drabware, White Border Of Roses 255.00
Wedgwood, Teapot, Flow Blue, 6 1/2 In. 45.00
Wedgwood, Teapot, Jasperware, Black, White Medallions & Handle, C.1820 600.00
Wedgwood, Teapot, Jasperware, Blue & White, Domestic Employment Scenes, 9 In. 95.00
Wedgwood, Teapot, Jasperware, Blue, Classical Figures 140.00
Wedgwood, Teapot, Jasperware, Light Green, 5 1/2 In. 69.00
Wedgwood, Teapot, Rosso Antico, Capri Enamel Flowers, C.1820, 4 Cup 285.00
Wedgwood, Teapot, Rosso Antico, Capri Enamel Flowers, C.1865, 4 Cup, Date Mark 310.00
Wedgwood, Teapot, Saltglaze, White, Arabesque, Spaniel On Lid 175.00
Wedgwood, Teapot, Terra-Cotta, White Jasper, Large, Made In England 275.00
Wedgwood, Teapot, Toy, Rockingham Glaze, 1875, 5 1/4 In. 150.00
Wedgwood, Teapot, White Dry Body, 2-Cup, Smear Glaze, Spaniel Finial, C.1790 285.00
Wedgwood, Teapot, White, Bugs, Butterflies & Floral, C.1873 105.00
Wedgwood, Teapot, White, Hand-Painted Roses, Artist Signed 80.00
Wedgwood, Tile, Calendar, 1895 45.00
Wedgwood, Tile, Children & Christmas Tree, Blue & White, Square, 8 In. 60.00
Wedgwood, Tile, Cobweb, 6 X 6 In. 28.00
Wedgwood, Tile, Green & Maroon, Relief Scroll, C.1850, Square, 6 In. 65.00
Wedgwood, Tile, Hunting Dog & Grouse, Framed 55.00
Wedgwood, Tile, Moth, 6 X 6 In. 28.00
Wedgwood, Toothpick, Black Basalt, Grape Leaf Border 27.50
Wedgwood, Toothpick, Fairyland Luster, Butterflies, Bronze, Green Interior 175.00
Wedgwood, Toothpick, Jasperware, Dark Blue, Josiah Wedgwood, 1730-1797 35.00
Wedgwood, Tray, Deep Blue & White, Oval, 9 1/4 X 6 1/2 In. 95.00
Wedgwood, Tray, Diamond-Shaped, Cherubs And Flowers, Emile Lessore, 1867 445.00
Wedgwood, Tray, Dresser, Jasperware, Blue, White Classical Ladies, 10 1/2 In. 145.00
Wedgwood, Tray, Jasperware, Green, Oval, 7 X 10 In. 35.00
Wedgwood, Tray, Jasperware, Lavender, White Mythological Figures, 9 3/4 In. 98.00
Wedgwood, Tray, Jewel, Jasperware, Light Green, White Figures, 10 X 7 In. 595.00
Wedgwood, Tray, Oval, Lilac, White Jasper, 10 X 7 1/2 In. 195.00
Wedgwood, Tray, Pen, Jasperware, Dark Blue & White, 8 1/2 X 3 In. 50.00
Wedgwood, Tray, Pin, Terra-Cotta, Diamond Shape 55.00
Wedgwood, Tumbler, John Peel Hunt Scene, Raised Polychrome 15.00
Wedgwood, Tureen, Ironstone, Lidded, Tealeaf, 10 X 5 1/2 In. 25.00
Wedgwood, Tureen, Platter, Eastern Flowers, Marked ACF, 1876 100.00
Wedgwood, Urn, Basalt, Bentley, Cover, C.1775 1900.00
Wedgwood, Urn, Basalt, Shell Handles, Pedestal, C.1930, 7 In. 65.00
Wedgwood, Urn, Bentley, Green Agateware, White Stoneware, Signed, 10 1/2 In. 2800.00
Wedgwood, Urn, Black & White, England, 7 In., Pair 495.00
Wedgwood, Urn, Dark Blue, Classical Designs, 6 In. 95.00
Wedgwood, Urn, Green & White, Bolted Base, 8 1/2 In. 185.00
Wedgwood, Urn, Jasperware, Black, Covered, White Pastoral Scenes, 12 In. 295.00
Wedgwood, Urn, Presentation, 3 Colors, White Cameo Leaves, C.1790, 10 1/2 In. 195.00
Wedgwood, Urn, Victoria Ware, Hackwood Cupids, C.1855, 7 1/4 In., Pair 1800.00
Wedgwood, Vase, Basalt, Bas Relief Floral, Trumpet, 5 In. 65.00
Wedgwood, Vase, Black Coat Of Arms Of Canada, Etruria, 4 1/4 In. 37.50
Wedgwood, Vase, Blue & White, Glasgow Angels & White Garlands, 5 In., Pair 40.00
Wedgwood, Vase, Blue And White, Stoneware, C.1810, Pair 450.00
Wedgwood, Vase, Blue Hummingbird Luster, 8 3/4 In. 295.00
Wedgwood, Vase, Blue Luster, Gold Fish Trim, Marked, 5 3/8 In. 265.00
Wedgwood, Vase, Brown With Blue Decoration, England 40.00
Wedgwood, Vase, Bud, Fairyland Luster, Blue, Dragons, Pearl Inside, 5 1/8 In. 175.00
Wedgwood, Vase, Candlemas, Fairyland, 10 1/2 In. 1475.00
Wedgwood, Vase, Creamware, Sang De Boeuf Glaze, C.1885, 10 In. 300.00
Wedgwood, Vase, Dark Blue, Coat Of Arms Of Torquay, Portland Mark, 2 1/2 In. 125.00
Wedgwood, Vase, Dice Pattern, Tricolor, Athena 1995.00
Wedgwood, Vase, Fairyland Luster, Butterflies, Orange & Gold, 8 In., Pair 595.00
Wedgwood, Vase, Fairyland Luster, Candlemas, Trumpet Shape Base, 7 In. 1200.00
Wedgwood, Vase, Fairyland Luster, Dragon, Footed, 8 1/2 n. 395.00
Wedgwood, Vase, Fairyland Luster, Dragons, 6 Sided, 14 In. 725.00
Wedgwood, Vase, Fairyland Luster, Flame, Baluster, 10 In. 950.00
Wedgwood, Vase, Fairyland Luster, Flame, Pixies & Fairies, Pearl Inside, 5 In. 850.00
Wedgwood, Vase, Fairyland Luster, Goldfish, 6 1/2 In. 195.00

Wedgwood, Vase, Fairyland Luster, Hummingbird, 8 In. 295.00
Wedgwood, Vase, Fairyland Luster, Mouse, Blue, 8 In. 425.00
Wedgwood, Vase, Fairyland Luster, Orange With Butterflies, 4 1/2 In. 250.00
Wedgwood, Vase, Fairyland Luster, Queen Of Fairies, Trumpet, 8 In. 650.00
Wedgwood, Vase, Fairyland Luster, Ruby, English, 8 1/8 In. 1250.00
Wedgwood, Vase, Fairyland Luster, Torch, 11 In., Pair 2875.00
Wedgwood, Vase, Green Body, Lavender Medallions, Classic Scenes, 7 In. 750.00
Wedgwood, Vase, Iron Red, Blue & White Oriental Style Floral, C.1850, 12 In. 185.00
Wedgwood, Vase, Jasperware, Dark Blue, Portland, 6 In. 245.00
Wedgwood, Vase, Orange Luster With Butterflies In Gold, 8 In., Pair 395.00
Wedgwood, Vase, Portland, Blue & White, Phrygian Head Mark, 10 1/2 In. 1400.00
Wedgwood, Vase, Rainbow Fairland Luster, Ships, Castle, Rainbow, 8 1/2 In. 1565.00
Wedgwood, Vase, Rosso Antico, Enamel Coat Of Arms, 4 In. 37.50
Wedgwood, Vase, Spill, Jasper, Light Blue, Classic Figures 75.00
Wedgwood, Vase, Terra-Cotta, White Jasper, 4 In. 80.00
Wedgwood, Vase, Visitor's, Basalt, Initials, 1923, 4 In. 85.00
Wedgwood, Vase, White, Lilac Medallions, Green Festoons, Signed 790.00
Wedgwood, Vase, 6 Sided, Hourglass Shape, Gold Celestial Dragons On Luster 725.00
Wedgwood, Waste Bowl, Orange, Chinese Red Floral, C.1880, 5 1/2 In. 125.00
Wedgwood, Watch Holder, Jasperware, Dark Blue, Silver Plate Rim 45.00
Wedgwood, Wine Cooler, Pan Piping Before 2 Maids, Terra-Cotta, C.1850, 10 In. 690.00
Weimar, Cup & Saucer, Chocolate, White, Pink Roses, Green Leaves 7.00
Weimar, Cup & Saucer, Demitasse, White, Pink Roses, Green Leaves, Orange Trim 4.50
Weimar, Plate, Oyster, Blue & White, Florals, 8 1/2 In. 18.00
Weimar, Plate, Oyster, Gold & Silver Trim, Floral 18.00
Weimar, Plate, Red Roses, Gold Edge, 7 In. 18.00
Weimar, Plate, Yellow Roses, Gold Edge, 7 In. 18.00
18.00
Weis, Vase, Frosted Gold, Orange Leaves & Berries, 1 3/4 In. 135.00
Weis, Vase, White Satin, Pink & Peach Seed Pods & Leaves, 1 7/8 In. 110.00

WELLER *Weller pottery was first made in 1873 in Fultonham, Ohio. The firm moved to Zanesville, Ohio, in 1882. Art wares were first made in 1893. Hundreds of lines of pottery were made including Louwelsa, Eocean, Dickens, and Sicardo before the pottery closed in 1948.*

Weller, Ashtray, Chengtu, 3 Pigs 65.00
Weller, Ashtray, Fox 65.00
Weller, Ashtray, Mirror Black, Figural Seal 27.00
Weller, Base, Hudson, Slip Glaze Yellow & Pink Roses, Signed Timberlake 95.00
Weller, Basket Base, Malvern, 8 In. 30.00
Weller, Basket, Forrest, Handle, 10 In. 40.00
Weller, Basket, Silvertone, Grapes And Vines 85.00
Weller, Bookend, Buffalo, 10 In. 35.00
Weller, Bowl & Frog, Coppertone, Handled, 8 In. 55.00
Weller, Bowl, Burntwood, 4 1/2 In. 12.50
Weller, Bowl, Dogwood 14.00
Weller, Bowl, Flemish Ware, Leaves & Branches, Middle Period, 9 In. 40.00
Weller, Bowl, Floral Basket With Panels, 6 In. 7.50
Weller, Bowl, Florala, Cream Color, Polychrome Floral, Octagonal, 8 In. 45.00
Weller, Bowl, Forest, 7 X 3 1/2 In. 45.00
Weller, Bowl, Frog & Flower On Side, Lotus Leaf Shape, 11 X 4 In. 95.00
Weller, Bowl, Gold, Blue, Pink Iridescence, Unsigned, Sicard 220.00
Weller, Bowl, Green Frog Peering Over White Tulip, 4 In. 60.00
Weller, Bowl, Green With Brown, Squirrels & Trees, Footed, 6 In. 25.00
Weller, Bowl, Hudson, Floral Decoration, 4 1/2 X 6 In. 60.00
Weller, Bowl, Marvo, Matching Frog 35.00
Weller, Bowl, Pumila Water Lily 25.00
Weller, Bowl, Roma, Cream Color, Floral Garlands, Lions' Heads, 5 1/2 In. 25.00
Weller, Bowl, Rustic, Openwork, Snake Feet, 9 In. 38.00
Weller, Bowl, Squirrel Sitting On Nest Eating Nut, Orange Branches, 6 In. 60.00
Weller, Bowl, Turada, Green, Marked, 2 1/4 X 4 1/2 In. 65.00
Weller, Bowl, Woodcraft, Squirrel & Nut, 5 3/4 In. 20.00
Weller, Box, Window, Wood Rose, 8 1/2 X 3 1/4 In. 30.00
Weller, Bucket, Roses On Each Side, Handled, 3 1/2 In. 25.00
Weller, Bust, Dickensware, 2nd Line, Man, Matte Finish, 10 1/2 In. 365.00
Weller, Candleholder, Cream Color, Cameo, Woman's Head, Square Base, 11 In. 55.00

Weller, Candlestick, Eldora, 6 In., Pair 32.00
Weller, Candlestick, Louwelsa, Brown, Pansies, 8 3/4 In. 75.00
Weller, Candlestick, Louwelsa, Yellow Rose & Leaves, 9 In. 85.00
Weller, Centerpiece Bowl & Attached Frog, Ferella 65.00
Weller, Centerpiece Bowl, Turquoise, White Raised Rose, C.1940, 15 In. 15.00
Weller, Console Set, Freesia, 8 In. Bowl, 3 Piece 37.00
Weller, Console Set, Green, Pink Flowers, Tricorner Bowl, 3 Piece 32.50
Weller, Console Set, Water Lily, Attached Underplate, 3 Piece 68.00
Weller, Cruet, Louwelsa, Pansies, 5 1/2 In. 60.00
Weller, Dish, Baby's, Knifewood, Fox And Chickens, Artist Signed 25.00
Weller, Ewer, Blue Matte, Pink & Yellow Pansies, 1872, 17 In. 27.50
Weller, Ewer, Cameo Green, 10 In. 30.00
Weller, Ewer, Louwelsa, Green & Yellow Thorny Branches & Berries, 8 In. 105.00
Weller, Ewer, Roba, Blue, Green Handles, White Flowers, 10 1/2 In. 40.00
Weller, Figurine, Cat, Bulging Blue Eyes, Signed 65.00
Weller, Figurine, Frog Beside Lotus-Shaped Bowl, 11 X 4 In. 100.00
Weller, Figurine, Turtle, Coppertone, 4 In., Marked 60.00
Weller, Flower Frog, Cherub 22.00
Weller, Flower Frog, Coppertone, Lily 48.00
Weller, Flower Frog, Figural, Boy On Rocks, Fishing, Muskota 85.00
Weller, Flower Frog, Frog Emerging From Lily Pad 25.00
Weller, Flower Frog, Kingfisher 75.00
Weller, Jar, Cookie, Aunt Jemima 125.00
Weller, Jar, Tobacco, Dickensware Chinaman 395.00
Weller, Jardiniere, Basket Weave, Relief Roses, Twisted Handles, 8 In. 45.00
Weller, Jardiniere, Blueware, Dancing Figures 48.00
Weller, Jardiniere, Claywood, Brown, 7 In. 25.00
Weller, Jardiniere, Flemish, 9 1/2 X 8 In. 45.00
Weller, Jardiniere, Green With Brown, Art Nouveau Lily Pads, 7 3/4 In. 25.00
Weller, Jardiniere, Ivory & Green Matte Glaze, Trees In 4 Panels, 10 In. 40.00
Weller, Jardiniere, Louwelsa, Chrysanthemums, 10 In. 85.00
Weller, Jardiniere, Marvo, Green, 7 1/2 In. 25.00
Weller, Jardiniere, Matte Green, Lavender To Green Shading, 7 In. 50.00
Weller, Jardiniere, Sicard, Green, Gold Iridescence, 12 X 14 In. 600.00
Weller, Jardiniere, Warwick, Blue Mark, 10 1/2 In. 70.00
Weller, Jug, Rum, Louwelsa, Grapes & Leaves, 6 In. 120.00
Weller, Lamp Base, Louwelsa, Brown Flowers & Buds, 10 1/2 In. 70.00
Weller, Lamp Base, Louwelsa, Large, Gold, Brown Pansies, Signed 185.00
Weller, Lamp Base, Sicard, Iridescent Peacock Feather, Gourd Shape, 13 In. 135.00
Weller, Lamp, Baldwin, Blue, 11 X 10 In. 75.00
Weller, Lamp, Forest, Signed, 4 X 3 In. 45.00
Weller, Letter Holder, Brown, Blue, Cream Applied Decoration, Signed Turada 285.00
Weller, Mug, Dickensware, Deer's Head, MA, 6 In. 250.00
Weller, Mug, Dickensware, Franciscan Monk, Sgraffito, Charles Upjohn 365.00
Weller, Mug, Dickensware, Indian Chief, 2 Feather Headdress, Sgraffito 650.00
Weller, Mug, Dickensware, 1st Line, Monk Imbibing, Silver Overlay, 3 1/2 In. 450.00
Weller, Mug, Dickensware, 3rd Line, Cavalier Smoking Pipe, 2 Handles, 5 In. 275.00
Weller, Mug, Etna, Gray To Off-White, Pink Mums, 5 1/4 In. 80.00
Weller, Mug, Etna, Pink Mums On Gray To Off-White, 8 1/2 In. 70.00
Weller, Mug, Floretta 12.00
Weller, Mug, Grape Clusters, Floretta, Artist Initial 45.00
Weller, Mug, Grapes, Art Nouveau 57.50
Weller, Mug, Zona, Cream Color, Apples, Incised Rabbit 12.50
Weller, Pitcher Vase, Blue To Green, 10 In. 25.00
Weller, Pitcher, Aurelian, Raspberries, JL, 6 In. 165.00
Weller, Pitcher, Ragenda, Marked 15.00
Weller, Planter, Dachshund, Marked 30.00
Weller, Planter, Frog On Base, 2 Piece, 36 X 14 In. 225.00
Weller, Planter, Glossy Brown, Gold Mums & Loops, L.B., 6 In. 75.00
Weller, Planter, Pale Blue, Basket Weave, 4 1/2 X 2 1/2 In. 9.00
Weller, Planter, Roma, Ink Mark, Paper Label, Round, 6 1/2 In. 16.00
Weller, Planter, Rose Tree, Open Latticework, Footed, Liner, Square, 7 In. 40.00
Weller, Plate, Baby's, Rabbit & Bird 20.00
Weller, Spittoon, Green High Glaze 75.00
Weller, Sugar, Aunt Jemima 25.00

Weller, Tankard, Dogwood, Green Matte, 12 In. 28.50
Weller, Tankard, Louwelsa, Bunch Of Grapes & Leaves, H.W., 6 1/2 In. 85.00
Weller, Tea Set, Zona, Apple Pattern 65.00
Weller, Teapot, Light Blue, Gold Decoration, Middle Period Mark 20.00
Weller, Tumbler, Verse & Floral, 4 In. 135.00
Weller, Umbrella Stand, Roma 125.00
Weller, Vase, Baldwin, Yellowish Apples & Leaves, H.W., 6 1/2 In. 85.00
Weller, Vase, Baldwin, 6 In. 20.00
Weller, Vase, Bedford Matte, Green, Lotus Pods, 12 1/2 In. 20.00
Weller, Vase, Blue Matte Over White Flowers & Leaves, Marked B14, 16 In. 95.00
Weller, Vase, Blue Ware, Tubular, Classic Women Dancing, 12 In. 65.00
Weller, Vase, Blue, Cornucopia, White Roses, 6 1/2 In. 6.95
Weller, Vase, Blue, Roses, 7 1/2 In. 35.00
Weller, Vase, Blue, White Horse, Rider, & Dog, Chase, 14 In. 85.00
Weller, Vase, Bronzeware, Bullet Shape, 9 In. 85.00
Weller, Vase, Bud, Louwelsa, Tea Rose, 6 In. 70.00
Weller, Vase, Bud, Rochelle, Berries, 5 1/4 In. 30.00
Weller, Vase, Bud, Rozane, Flat Bulbous Shape, 2 1/2 In. 145.00
Weller, Vase, Burntwood, Cupped, 3 1/2 In. 14.00
Weller, Vase, Chengtu, Bulbous, 12 In. 125.00
Weller, Vase, Chengtu, 12 In. 75.00
Weller, Vase, Claywood, Center Floral Band, Bulbous, 5 In. 20.00
Weller, Vase, Coppertone, Green, Middle Period, 6 In. 35.00
Weller, Vase, Coppertone, Weller Handmade, 6 In. 38.00
Weller, Vase, Cream Color, Hand-Painted Flower, 12 In. 45.00
Weller, Vase, Cream Glaze, 2 Handles, 8 In. 18.00
Weller, Vase, Dickensware, Dombey & Son, Artist Signed, C.A.D., 11 1/2 In. 360.00
Weller, Vase, Dickensware, Lady Golfer, Artist Signed, Dedicated, 1903 .... 450.00
Weller, Vase, Dickensware, Lady Playing Harp, 16 In. 475.00
Weller, Vase, Dickensware, Male Golfer, 1 Foot 365.00
Weller, Vase, Dickensware, Mallard Duck & Duckling, Brown, Pillow Shape, 6 In. 210.00
Weller, Vase, Dickensware, Sgraffito Baby Pelican On Beach, Flattened, 6 In. 135.00
Weller, Vase, Dickensware, Sgraffito, Lady Golfer, E.W., 9 In. 325.00
Weller, Vase, Dickensware, 2nd Line, Blue, Monk, Metal Rim, Gillie, 14 1/2 In. 695.00
Weller, Vase, Dickensware, 2nd Line, Dombey & Son, High Glaze, 11 1/2 In. 450.00
Weller, Vase, Elberta, Marked 10.00
Weller, Vase, Eocean, Blue Gray To Pink, Berries & Leaves, 11 In. 135.00
Weller, Vase, Eocean, Long-Stemmed Pink Roses, 8 In. 98.00
Weller, Vase, Eocean, Thistles, E.R., 14 1/2 In. 165.00
Weller, Vase, Eocean, Trailing Red Sweet Peas, 8 In. 98.00
Weller, Vase, Eocean, Wild Rose & Leaves, 2 Handles, 4 1/2 In. 50.00
Weller, Vase, Etched Matte, Roses, 9 In. 55.00
Weller, Vase, Etna, Conical, 2 Handles, 4 3/4 In. 45.00
Weller, Vase, Etna, Five Pink Roses On Vine, 8 1/2 In. 75.00
Weller, Vase, Floral, Sicard, 6 In. 170.00
Weller, Vase, Floretta, Green To White, Embossed & Painted Cherries, 7 In. 30.00
Weller, Vase, Floretta, 2-Handled, Raised Red, Green Floral On Brown Body 40.00
Weller, Vase, Forest, Block Signature 45.00
Weller, Vase, Forest, Brook, Sky, & Trees, Fan, 8 In. 49.00
Weller, Vase, Glossy Blue, Shaded Large Blue Flowers, Artist Signed, 9 In. 285.00
Weller, Vase, Goldtone, Urn Type, Sitting On 3 Handles, 8 X 6 In. 25.00
Weller, Vase, Gray Ground, Jar Shape, Roses, Eocean, 8 In. 110.00
Weller, Vase, Green Frog Holding White Water Lily, Middle Period, 4 In. 70.00
Weller, Vase, Green Matte, Geometrics, 10 In. 35.00
Weller, Vase, Green Matte, Leaf Pattern, Ovoid, 5 In. 35.00
Weller, Vase, Hand-Painted Iris, Hudson, 12 In. 125.00
Weller, Vase, Hudson Blue To Green Pillsbury, 15 In. 95.00
Weller, Vase, Hudson Ware, Fruit Decoration, 6 1/2 In. 65.00
Weller, Vase, Hudson, Blue To Green, Pillsbury, 15 In. 85.00
Weller, Vase, Hudson, Cream Ground, Red & Green Florals, 11 1/2 In. 135.00
Weller, Vase, Hudson, Floral, 12 In. 75.00
Weller, Vase, Hudson, Gray To Off-White, Polychrome Floral, Ovoid, 7 1/4 In. 75.00
Weller, Vase, Hudson, Pink & Cream Tulips, 10 In. 98.00
Weller, Vase, Hudson, Red Florals, Blue Gray Ground, 11 In. 75.00
Weller, Vase, Hudson, Slip Reddish Florals, Blue Gray Ground 80.00

Weller, Vase, Jap Birdimal, High Gloss Kelly Green, White Duck Under Tree 125.00
Weller, Vase, Lasa, Lake & Palms, 6 1/4 In. 115.00
Weller, Vase, Lasa, Palms, 7 X 3 1/2 In. 160.00
Weller, Vase, Lasa, Red To Copper Base, Tree, Lake, & Cloud, 5 1/2 In. 97.50
Weller, Vase, Louwelsa, Elongated Onion Shape, Yellow Jonquil, 6 In. 65.00
Weller, Vase, Louwelsa, High Glaze, Floral, Wendler, 12 In. 185.00
Weller, Vase, Louwelsa, Lily Of The Valley, 10 In. 80.00
Weller, Vase, Louwelsa, Nasturtiums, Bulbous, 5 1/2 In. 71.50
Weller, Vase, Louwelsa, Pansies, Handled, Hester Pillsbury, 13 In. 169.00
Weller, Vase, Louwelsa, Pillow, Floral, Pinched Top, E.R., 5 1/4 In. 115.00
Weller, Vase, Louwelsa, Pillow, Waving Bamboo, M.Mitchell, 8 X 7 In. 125.00
Weller, Vase, Louwelsa, Strawberries, 7 In. 225.00
Weller, Vase, Louwelsa, Tulips, 8 3/4 In. 90.00
Weller, Vase, Marbleized Purple, Mauve, & White, 6 Sided, 11 In. 42.50
Weller, Vase, Marsh Bird Walking In Marsh, Nest Of Eggs, 10 1/4 In. 150.00
Weller, Vase, Marvo, Green To Ivory, Palm Trees, Ferns, Vines, 7 In. 30.00
Weller, Vase, Matte Blue, Dutch Boy, Windmill, Signed LJB, 9 In. 125.00
Weller, Vase, Matte Green Brown, Trailing Morning Glory, 7 In. 30.00
Weller, Vase, Pinecone, Matte Glaze, 7 In. 15.00
Weller, Vase, Red Matte Glaze, Green Leaves & Buds, Middle Period, 6 1/2 In. 28.00
Weller, Vase, Roba, Blue, Green Handles, Pink Flowers, 6 1/2 In. 25.00
Weller, Vase, Roba, K, 8 In. 25.00
Weller, Vase, Rochell, 2-Handled, 10 1/4 X 7 1/2 In. 85.00
Weller, Vase, Sicard, Bulbous, Blue & Green Abstract, Signed 155.00
Weller, Vase, Sicard, Floral, Bulbous Top Opening, 4 1/2 In. 235.00
Weller, Vase, Sicard, Green Metallic, Floral Design, 6 1/2 In. 185.00
Weller, Vase, Sicard, Magenta & Green Spider Mums & Lilies, 11 In. 395.00
Weller, Vase, Sicard, Maple Leaf, Iridescent 285.00
Weller, Vase, Sicard, Pink Highlights, 4 1/2 In. 149.00
Weller, Vase, Sicard, Purple Iridescence, 7 In. 165.00
Weller, Vase, Sicard, Red & Greens, Tiffany-Type Sheen, 4 3/4 In. 350.00
Weller, Vase, Silvertone With Butterfly 125.00
Weller, Vase, Silvertone, Lavender, Green, & White Design, Handled, 8 In. 75.00
Weller, Vase, Stellar, Black & White Stars, Signed 75.00
Weller, Vase, Suevo, Bulbous, Marked, 8 1/2 In. 80.00
Weller, Vase, Turada, 6 1/2 In. 200.00
Weller, Vase, Tutone, Red, Raised Green Floral, Oval, 6 1/2 In. 28.00
Weller, Vase, Wall, Wood Rose, Matte Turquoise, Glazed Green Leaves, Red Roses 25.00
Weller, Vase, Warwick, Signed H, 4 3/4 In. 40.00

Wood Carving, Eagle, American, 20th Century, 18 In.High

Wood Carving, Eagle, Max Barrick, 1870-1963, 11 In.

Wood Carving, Eagle, Spread-Wing, American, C.1883, 5 1/2 In.
(See Page 718)

(See Page 718)
Wood Carving, Lathe, Wood Winder, American, 19th Century, 26 In.

Weller, Vase, Water Urn, Blue To Green, Swirled, Scrolled Handle, 13 In. 45.00
Weller, Vase, White Top, Roses In Relief At Bottom, 8 In. 15.00
Weller, Vase, Wild Rose, Double Handled, 8 In. 13.00
Weller, Vase, Wild Rose, Twisted Handles, 14 In. 35.00
Weller, Vase, Wild Rose, 2 Handles, 10 In. 25.00
Weller, Vase, Woodcraft, Tree Trunk, Rustic Color, 8 In. 25.00
Weller, Vase, Woodcraft, Tree Trunk, 9 In. 30.00
Weller, Vase, Woodland, Trees & Stream, 8 In. 45.00
Weller, Wall Pocket, Orange, Pink Floral, Blueberries, Lattice Top, 6 3/4 In. 17.00
Weller, Wall Pocket, Woodcraft, Tree Stump & Squirrel, 10 In. 60.00
Weller, Wall, Pocket, Owl Peering From Treehole 70.00
Wheelock, Plate, Fairport Mill Dam, W.B.Gilmore, Russell, Kansas, 6 In. 18.00
Wheelock, Plate, Great Barrington, Mass., 7 1/2 In. 10.00
Wheelock, Plate, Hand-Painted Pink Roses, 7 3/4 In. 12.50
Wheelock, Sugar & Creamer, Florals In Paster 85.00
Willow, see Blue Willow
Windowpane, Bull's-Eye, Aqua, Square, 7 In., Set Of 7 .... 160.00
Windowpane, Bull's-Eye, Yellow Amber, Square, 8 3/4 In. 90.00
Windowpane, Casement, Stained Glass, 48 X 14 In. 225.00
Windowpane, Church, Stained Glass, Tulip Oval Top, 10 X 4 Ft. 600.00
Windowpane, Etched Girl In Garden With Cherubs, Door, 6 Ft.8 In. X 32 In. 150.00
Windowpane, Fiery Opalescent, 6 7/8 X 6 3/8 In. 55.00
Windowpane, Front Door, Leaded, Beveled, 34 X 20 In. 225.00
Windowpane, I.P.Imberton Brevette, 1882, Stained, Bamboo Branches, 8 Ft. 2000.00
Windowpane, Ivy, Lacy, Square, 4 In. 25.00
Windowpane, Leaded, G.A.R. Soldier & U.S.Shield, 7 1/2 X 3 1/2 Ft. 1500.00
Windowpane, Leaded, 18 Ruby Jewels Center, Teardrop Shape, 10 X 3 Ft. 825.00
Windowpane, Peacock Blue, 2 Daisies, Lacy, 5 X 4 In. 50.00
Windowpane, Stained Glass, Amber & Ruby, 4 Jeweled Accent, 30 X 19 In. 275.00
Windowpane, Stained Glass, Beveled, 54 X 20 In. 90.00
Windowpane, Stained Glass, From An Old Tavern, 26 X 59 In., Pair 700.00
Windowpane, Stained Glass, Leaded, 34 X 22 In. 225.00
Windowpane, Stained Glass, Leaded, 45 X 22 In. 250.00
Windowpane, Stained Glass, Old Tavern Window, 40 X 84 In. 700.00
Windowpane, Yosemite Lager, Leaded Glass, 40 X 30 In. 1200.00
Wood Carving, Beaver, Beaverville, Quebec, Made From 3 Logs 5000.00
Wood Carving, Bookend, 2 Seated Men, Red African Mahogany, 13 In., Pair 27.00
Wood Carving, Buttress, Acanthus Leaves & Fruit, Painted, 19 In. 50.00
Wood Carving, Case, Calling Card, Sandalwood, People & Trees 45.00
Wood Carving, Cornucopia, Painted, Italian, Late 18th Century, 5 Ft., Pair 575.00
Wood Carving, Eagle, American, 20th Century, 18 In.High .... *Illus* 375.00
Wood Carving, Eagle, Black, 24 1/4 X 9 1/4 In. 225.00
Wood Carving, Eagle, Max Barrick, 1870-1963, 11 In. .... *Illus* 600.00

Wood Carving, Man, American, C.1890, 18 In.High

Wood Carving, Rooster, Painted, Pennsylvania, 8 In.High

Wood Carving, Whirligig, Painted, 19th Century, 14 In.High

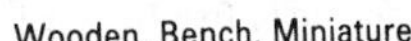

Wooden, Bench, Miniature

Wood Carving, Eagle, Spread-Wing, American, C.1883, 5 1/2 In. .... *Illus* 1900.00
Wood Carving, Figurine, Alligator, Pine, Painted, 5 1/2 Ft. 125.00
Wood Carving, Figurine, Buddha, Chin Wood, 4 In. 37.50
Wood Carving, Figurine, Chinese Lady 95.00
Wood Carving, Figurine, Indian On Horseback, Painted, 11 5/8 In. 15.00
Wood Carving, Figurine, Painted Rooster, Pennsylvania, Late 1800's, 8 In. 700.00
Wood Carving, Group, Pair Of Elephants, Rosewood, 7 1/2 In. 28.00
Wood Carving, Lathe, Wood Winder, American, 19th Century, 26 In. .... *Illus* 350.00
Wood Carving, Loveknot, 6 Links, 18 In. 20.00
Wood Carving, Man, American, C.1890, 18 In.High .... *Illus* 1250.00
Wood Carving, Rooster, Painted, Pennsylvania, 8 In.High .... *Illus* 700.00
Wood Carving, Skull, Human Size 135.00
Wood Carving, Whirligig, Painted, 19th Century, 14 In.High .... *Illus* 175.00
Wood, Church Rail, Oak, Curved, 8 Ft. X 18 In. 65.00
Wood, Church Rail, Oak, 11 Ft X 35 In. 75.00
Wood, Letter Rack, Oak, 3 Shelves, 14 X 8 In. 45.00

Wooden, see also Kitchen, Store, Tool
Wooden, Carousel Horse, see Carousel, Horse

Wooden, Box, Bible, Mulberry, Early 18th Century

Wooden, Box, Carved, 9 3/4 X 7 1/2 In.

Item		Price
Wooden, Bench, Miniature	*Illus*	40.00
Wooden, Block, Hand Carved For Printing Fabric		40.00
Wooden, Block, Wallpaper Printing		40.00
Wooden, Bookmark, Carved & Pierced Floral, 5 In.		8.00
Wooden, Bootjack, Child's		12.00
Wooden, Bootjack, Handmade, Hole For Hanging, 22 In.		27.00
Wooden, Bootjack, Handmade, 22 In.		15.00
Wooden, Bootjack, Wheeler Case Co., Patent 1863, Folding, 22 In. Open		24.00
Wooden, Bowl, Burl, Deep, 15 In.		385.00
Wooden, Bowl, Burl, 10 In.		275.00
Wooden, Bowl, Burl, 10 X 4 In.		75.00
Wooden, Bowl, Burl, 14 In.		375.00
Wooden, Bowl, Burl, 24 In.		1200.00
Wooden, Bowl, Carving Of Duck, 5 In.		10.00
Wooden, Bowl, Gold Birds On Lid, Oriental, Black Lacquer, 5 1/2 In.		27.50
Wooden, Bowl, Lithograph Of Pansies & Leaves, 7 1/2 In.		10.00
Wooden, Bowl, New England, Elm Rimmed, 22 In.		125.00
Wooden, Bowl, Rectangular, 19 X 11 X 4 In.		45.00
Wooden, Box, Amish, Child's Huckleberry Picking Box, Leather Strap & Hinge		85.00
Wooden, Box, Architect's, Mahogany, Brass Trim, 17 3/4 X 8 1/2 In.		98.00
Wooden, Box, Bible, Mulberry, Early 18th Century	*Illus*	240.00
Wooden, Box, Burnt-Wood Log Cabin Document, 13 X 8 X 5 1/2 In.		20.00
Wooden, Box, Carved, 9 3/4 X 7 1/2 In.	*Illus*	60.00
Wooden, Box, Cheese, Covered, Round, 10 X 5 1/2 In.		15.00
Wooden, Box, Document, Tiger Maple, Dovetailed, Button Feet, 11 In.		135.00
Wooden, Box, Dresser, Mirror, 4 Gold Compartments		10.00
Wooden, Box, Dull Black, Gold Floral Decoration, 9 1/4 X 5 X 4 In.		55.00
Wooden, Box, Glove, Burnt Cherry Decoration		9.00
Wooden, Box, Glove, Pressed Floral Design		6.50
Wooden, Box, Glove, Walnut		42.00

Wooden, Box, Jewel, Inlaid 45.00
Wooden, Box, Jewelry, Cedar, Dovetailed 2.50
Wooden, Box, Mahogany, Ornate Carved Dragon Top, Footed, 9 X 6 X 4 In. 35.00
Wooden, Box, Mantilla, Bible, Dated 1906, Brass Hinges, 11 X 7 X 2 In. 27.00
Wooden, Box, March, Rosewood, Carved Mutton Fat Jade Cover, Marked China 45.00
Wooden, Box, Painting On Porcelain Of Maiden, Signed Argilar, On Lid, 6 In. 135.00
Wooden, Box, Rosewood, Oval Mutton Fat Jade Floral Carved Insert, China 45.00
Wooden, Box, Spice, Round, 4 In. 5.00
Wooden, Box, Spice, Tin Bands, 8 Small Round Wood Boxes Inside, 9 1/2 In. 35.00
Wooden, Box, Stamp, Oriental, C.1850, Carved, Ivory & Ebony Inlaid, 4 In. 25.00
Wooden, Box, Stamp, Oriental, With Ivory & Metal Inlay 30.00
Wooden, Box, Tackle, Fishing Tackle On Top, Green Paint, Brass Hinges, 18 In. 185.00
Wooden, Box, Walnut & Mahogany, Red Satin Lining, 10 X 5 3/4 In. 35.00
Wooden, Cage, Bird, Chinese, Rectangular, Domed Top, 18 In. 225.00
Wooden, Candleholder, Walnut, Pineapple, 12 In., Pair 10.00
Wooden, Canteen, Oak, Brass Banded, Copper Rivets, Leather Thong 30.00
Wooden, Case, Watch, Mahogany 18.00
Wooden, Chest, Domed Lid, Painted, Birds & Floral, 18 X 10 In. 525.00
Wooden, Chest, Jewel, Handmade From Squares Of Wood 40.00
Wooden, Decoy, Maine White-Wing Scoter 55.00
Wooden, Desk, Lap, Child's, Maple, Drawing Slate Top, Alphabet, Animals, 1887 .... 90.00
Wooden, Figurine, American Eagle, Diving, Walnut, C.1850, 14 In. 325.00
Wooden, Figurine, American Eagle, Winter, New York, 20th Century, 18 In. 375.00
Wooden, Figurine, Demon, Tomb, Polychrome, C.1650, 14 1/2 In. 145.00
Wooden, Figurine, Eagle, Carved, Stippled, 11 In. 600.00
Wooden, Figurine, Eagle, Painted & Parcel Gilt, Continental, C.1850, 26 In. 1200.00
Wooden, Figurine, Elephant, Ebony, Ivory Tusks, Toenails, & Eyes, 9 In. 125.00
Wooden, Figurine, Elephant, Trunk Up, Hand-Carved, 8 In. 15.00
Wooden, Figurine, Outhouse, Hinged Door, 3 Seats, 7 1/2 In. 8.00
Wooden, Figurine, Owl, Hand-Carved, 8 In. 16.50
Wooden, Figurine, Traveling Fisherman, Cherry Wood, Ivory Teeth, 14 In., Pair 500.00
Wooden, Foot Warmer, Diamond Designed, 18th Century 145.00
Wooden, Foot Warmer, With Pierced Tin, Turned Posts, Bail Handle 75.00
Wooden, Goblet, Ohl & Hauschild, 5 In. 37.50
Wooden, Hoop, For Hoop Skirt 15.00
Wooden, Humidor, Cigar, Bird Carvings Top & Front, 16 X 17 In. 400.00
Wooden, Humidor, Indian Head, Headdress Lid 35.00
Wooden, Inkstand, American, Quill Holder, 3 1/2 X 2 1/4 In. 28.00
Wooden, Mirror, Hand, Beveled Glass 12.00
Wooden, Mirror, Hand, Lady's Head, Art Nouveau 12.00
Wooden, Mold, Butter .... *Illus* 150.00
Wooden, Mold, Oriental Rice Cake, 13 1/2 X 2 In. 59.00
Wooden, Mortar & Pestle, Lathe-Turned, 4 In. 20.00
Wooden, Mortar & Pestle, 4 1/2 In. 48.00
Wooden, Nutcracker, Goat, Hand-Carved, Glass Eyes 27.00
Wooden, Nutcracker, Old Man Wearing Red Stocking Hat 22.00
Wooden, Nutcracker, Scrooge-Type Figure, 11 1/2 In. 35.00
Wooden, Plaque, American Eagle, Sheild, & Flags, Painted, C.1850, 27 In. 400.00
Wooden, Propellor, Airplane, 6 Ft. .... 85.00 To 100.00
Wooden, Propellor, Airplane, 9 Ft. 125.00
Wooden, Puppet, Carved, Painted, Articulated, Cloth Costume, 32 In. 150.00
Wooden, Scoop, Handmade, 12 In. 35.00
Wooden, Seat, Oxcart, Slat Work In Blue Paint 40.00
Wooden, Shoe Last, 5 In. .... *Illus* 12.00
Wooden, Shrine, Japanese, 19th Century, Miniature, Temple, 38 In. 1300.00
Wooden, Spoon, Carved, Floral Decoration, Norwegian, 8 In. 35.00
Wooden, Sugar, Covered, Maple, Pear Shape ....
Wooden, Tightener, For Rope Bed 15.00
Wooden, Walking Stick, Carved, Faces In Relief, Quillwork Manner, Dated 1899 .... 95.00
Wooden, Walking Stick, Tiger Maple, Beveled Sides, Brass Thimble Tip 75.00
Wooden, Wall Box, Salt, Barrel Shape, 6 3/4 In.High .... *Illus* 90.00
Wooden, Wall Box, Walnut, 8 In.Wide, 14 1/2 In.High .... *Illus* 100.00
Wooden, Wall Pocket, Walnut, Carved Leaf & Branch, Victorian, 24 X 13 In. 18.00
Wooden, Wall Rack, Roller Towel, Iron Fittings 28.00
Wooden, Wall Rack, Spoon, Yellow & Reddish Brown .... *Illus* 225.00

Wooden, Shoe Last, 5 In.

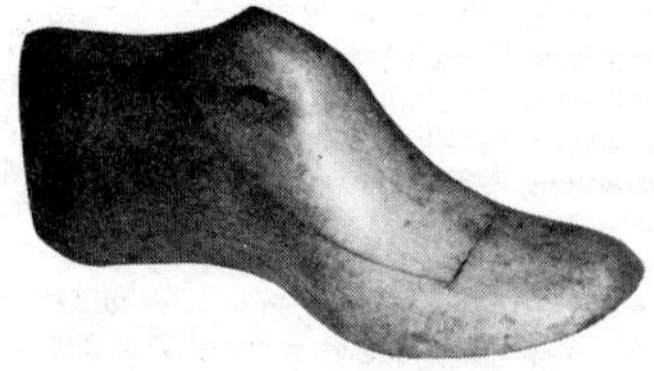

Wooden, Mold, Butter

Wooden, Wall Box, Salt, Barrel Shape, 6 3/4 In.High

Wooden, Wall Box, Walnut, 8 In.Wide, 14 1/2 In.High

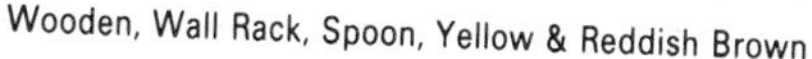

Wooden, Wall Rack, Spoon, Yellow & Reddish Brown

Wooden, Wheel, Buggy	25.00
Wooden, Wheel, Wagon, Iron Rims, Brass Hub	33.00
Wooden, Whirligig, Bear Seated On Log, Painted Wood, 19 In.	55.00
Wooden, Whirligig, Man & Dog At Well, Early 1900s, 27 X 14 In.	115.00
Wooden, Whirligig, Woman At Washtub, Wood & Metal, 29 X 11 In.	130.00
Wooden, Winder, Lathe, Carved Swans, Turned Handle, Leather Pulley	350.00
Wooden, Winder, Table Model, Crank Operated, Four Gears, 22 In.	165.00
Wooden, Winder, Yarn, Pennsylvania Origin	68.00
Worcester, see also Royal Worcester	
Worcester, Basket, Beige, Flying Robin & Floral, Rope Handle, 7 In.	155.00
Worcester, Bottle, Perfume, Reticulated, C.1885	279.00
Worcester, Bowl, Blue Lily, Crescent Mark, C.1750, 4 In.	175.00
Worcester, Bowl, Fence, Dr.Wall Period, 4 3/4 In.	225.00
Worcester, Bowl, Green Oriental Masks, Reticulated, Pierced, Grainger, 5 In.	210.00
Worcester, Bowl, Pot Of Flowers & Bird On Branch, C.1820, 10 1/2 In.	50.00
Worcester, Butter Tub, Cover And Stand, Queen Charlotte, B Mark, 7 1/2 In.	250.00
Worcester, Candlestick, Peach Pink, Ecru, & Biscuit, Locke, Shrub Hill, 9 In.	84.00
Worcester, Coaster, Wine, Peacock, J.Lewis, Locke, Shrub Hill Works, 4 1/2 In.	80.00
Worcester, Compote, Gadrooned Edge, Mum & Leaf, Imari Colors, 12 1/2 X 4 1/4	255.00
Worcester, Cooler, Cover, Liner, Gilt Ram's-Head Handles, Barr & Barr, Pair	2900.00
Worcester, Cup & Saucer, Apple Green, Exotic Birds, 1st Period	300.00
Worcester, Cup & Saucer, Applied Gilt Cracker Ice With Grecian Figures	115.00
Worcester, Cup & Saucer, Chelsea Derby Style, Crossed Swords, No.9 Mark, Pair	500.00
Worcester, Cup & Saucer, Mustache, Peach Color, Floral	105.00
Worcester, Cup, Blue Fishscale, Enamel Floral, Dr.Wall Period	200.00
Worcester, Dish, Apple Green, Spotted Fruit, 1st Period, 7 1/2 In.	550.00
Worcester, Dish, Blue, White, Leaf And Flowers, Painter's Mark, 10 1/8 In., Pai	450.00
Worcester, Dish, Blue, White, Leaf And Vine, Crescent Mark, 9 1/2 In., Pair	425.00
Worcester, Dish, Bone, Pink Willow, Purple Mark, Impressed Crown	25.00
Worcester, Dish, Junket, Blue, White, Scalloped, Flowers, Crescent Mark, 9 7/8 I	425.00
Worcester, Dish, Old Mosaick Japan, Fluted, 10 3/8 In., Pair	700.00
Worcester, Dish, Oval, Yellow Panels, Saltglaze, 1st Period, 10 1/2 In.	2200.00
Worcester, Jar, Cracker, Peach To Ivory, Blackberries, Metal Fittings, Locke	185.00
Worcester, Jug, White, Raised Green Leaves, Kerr & Binns, C.1852, 3 In.	45.00
Worcester, Muffineer, Pale Yellow, Floral Diamond, Sterling Top, Locke, 6 In.	75.00
Worcester, Plate, Blind Earl, 1st Period, 7 1/2 In., Pair	1000.00
Worcester, Plate, Conch Shell, Impressed, B.D.B., C.1807	85.00
Worcester, Plate, Dessert, Blue, Royal Lily, Dr.Wall, C.1755, 7 1/2 In.	145.00
Worcester, Plate, Earl Manvers Service, Plum Center, 1st Period, Pair	2800.00
Worcester, Plate, Earl Manvers Service, Plums, Pink Trellis Border, Pair	2800.00
Worcester, Plate, Leaf Shape, Gold Rim, Brown & Gold	50.00
Worcester, Plate, Oriental, Dr.Wall Period, 5 In.	52.00
Worcester, Plate, Royal Lily, Dr.Wall Period, 7 In.	145.00
Worcester, Plate, Saucer Shape, Crescent Mark, 7 1/2 In.	130.00
Worcester, Pot, Pate-Sur-Pate, Pale Green, Raised White Decoration, 3 In.	100.00
Worcester, Saucer, Fence In Underglaze Blue, Dr.Wall Period, C.1760	125.00
Worcester, Slop Bowl, Blue & White, C.1755, 6 In.	95.00
Worcester, Tea Set, Blue Lily, Dr.Wall Period, 9 Piece	2000.00
Worcester, Tea Set, Royal Lily, Toy, 10 Pieces, C.1765	2300.00
Worcester, Teapot, Blue Lily, Barr, Flight, Barr	275.00
Worcester, Teapot, Blue Willow, Ceramic Handle, 1882	135.00
Worcester, Teapot, Blue, Lily Pattern, Barr, Flight, Barr, Mark, 7 In.	340.00
Worcester, Teapot, Blue, Royal Lily, Barr, Flight, Barr, C.1807, 9 In.	340.00
Worcester, Teapot, Royal Lily, Oblong, Blue Underglaze, C.1807, 7 In.	325.00
Worcester, Vase, Ivorine, Ferns, Pierced Top, Purple Mark, 13 In., Pair	350.00
Worcester, Waster, Royal Lily, Dr.Wall Period, C.1765	210.00
Worcester, Waster, Three Flowers In Underglaze Blue, Dr.Wall Period, C.1760	215.00
World War I, Belt & Sling, Ammunition, Canvas	3.00
World War I, Book, Negro Soldiers In World War I, Kelly Miller	47.50
World War I, Box, Brass, Princess Mary	22.00
World War I, Buckle, German, Brass	22.00
World War I, Kit, Mess, U.S.A.	3.95
World War I, Music Sheet, What Are You Going To Do To Help The Boys	4.00
World War I, Needle, Suture, Army Nurse's, Verdun, 1918, Set	15.00
World War I, Pillowcase, Camp Carson, Colorado, Square, 16 In.	25.00

World War I, Poster, After Ogden, 1917, 26 X 40 In.

World War I, Poster, Buy More Bonds, 1918, 36 X 56 In.

World War I, Poster, Eugenie De Land, 20 X 30 In.

World War I, Pillowcase, Picture Of Pershing, Fringe, 18 X 16 In. 15.50
World War I, Pillowcase, Picture Of Wilson, Fringe, 18 X 16 In. 15.50
World War I, Pillowcase, Soldier, Poem & Forget-Me-Not, Square, 16 In. 25.00
World War I, Plate, Off German Train, Metal, Eagle, 9 1/2 X 8 In. 65.00
World War I, Poster, After Ogden, 1917, 26 X 40 In. .... *Illus* 265.00
World War I, Poster, Buy More Bonds, 1918, 36 X 56 In. .... *Illus* 85.00
World War I, Poster, Eugenie De Land, 20 X 30 In. .... *Illus* 60.00
World War I, Poster, Liberty Bonds, Boys At The Front, 24 X 12 In. 16.00
World War I, Poster, You Buy A Liberty Bond, 30 X 20 In. 30.00
World War I, Poster, You Buy A Liberty Bond, 40 X 30 In. 45.00
World War I, Tunic, 78th Division Cavalry 30.00
World War I, Uniform, Brigadier General's, 1915 .... 165.00
World War II, Armband, Nazi S.S. .... 9.9[illegible]
World War II, Armor, German Machine Gunners .... 15[illegible]
World War II, Badge, Nazi Golden Leader Sports .... [illegible]
World War II, Banner, German, 4 X 10 1/2 In. .... [illegible]
World War II, Banner, Nazi, Karlsruhe, Germany, Post Office, 12 In. .... [illegible]
World War II, Bayonet, German, Sheath .... [illegible]
World War II, Bayonet, Nazi Dress, Scabbard, Bone Grip, Eagle Hilt .... [illegible]
World War II, Bayonet, Nazi Fireman's Dress .... [illegible]

World War II, Belt, Machine Gun, German 9.95
World War II, Book, Ration, Stamps, Leather Case 5.00
World War II, Buckle, Belt, Nazi Fireman's, Embossed Center 12.00
World War II, Cards, Playing, Victory, Roosevelt & Hitler, Deck 9.50
World War II, Compass, Japanese Airplane, Liquid Filled 45.00
World War II, Compass, Japanese, Aircraft, Floating, Wires 35.00
World War II, Dagger, Hitler Youth Leader, Case 550.00
World War II, Dagger, Luftwaffe, B & A, 1939, 2nd Model 35.00
World War II, Dagger, Luftwaffe, Puma, 2nd Model 100.00
World War II, Dagger, Nazi Army Officer's, Case 85.00
World War II, Dagger, Nazi Labor Corps., Case 175.00
World War II, Dagger, Nazi Navy, Eickhorn Blade 130.00
World War II, Dagger, Nazi Paratrooper's, Gravity, Utility 75.00
World War II, Dagger, Nazi Youth, Diamond-Shaped Insert 55.00
World War II, Dagger, Nazi, S.A. 125.00
World War II, Dagger, Nazi, Scabbard 75.00
World War II, Dagger, Philippines, Handmade 10.00
World War II, Dagger, S.S.Officer's, Case 175.00
World War II, Grenade, Hand, U.S.A., Dummy 1.50
World War II, Hanger, Sword, Italian, Over The Shoulder, Gold & Silver 67.00
World War II, Hat, Gestapo Officer's 125.00
World War II, Hat, Hitler Youth 45.00
World War II, Hat, Luftwaffe Pilot's 55.00
World War II, Headband, Kamikaze 9.95
World War II, Helmet, German, Steel 18.50
World War II, Helmet, Nazi Luftwaffe Pilot's, Straps, Buckles 45.00
World War II, Helmet, Nazi, Home Defense 16.00
World War II, Helmet, Russian, Liner, Strap 25.00
World War II, Lantern, Black-Out, Coal Oil, Frosted Glass, 1941 .... 28.50
World War II, Life Saver, Mae West, Flyer's 10.00
World War II, Light, Electric Signal, British, Wooden Box, From Ship 50.00
World War II, Mask, Gas, French, Case 3.95
World War II, Mug, African Campaign, 1942, Made From Shell, Map On It 20.00
World War II, Phone, G.I.Field 25.00
World War II, Pin, Praying Hands, Prisoner Of War 15.00
World War II, Poster, He's A Fighting Fool, 1942, 40 X 28 In. 15.00
World War II, Sharpener, Pencil, Nurse 4.00
World War II, Stickpin, Swastika, Silver 4.95
World War II, Sword, Nazi Redeye Dress, Eickhorn 120.00
World War II, Telescope, From Tank, 1943, 24 In. 55.00
World War II, Tie Rack, Marine Corps, Gyrene In Battle Regalia 10.00
World War II, Uniform, Blue Bell Bottom, Navy, 2 Piece 10.00
World War II, Wine, Nazi, SS, Bad Tolz, Etched, Long Stem 50.00
World's Fair, Ashtray, Chicago, Century Of Progress, Sky Ride, Brass 7.50
World's Fair, Ashtray, Chicago, 1892 .... 4.00
World's Fair, Ashtray, Chicago, 1933, Chrysler 16.00
World's Fair, Ashtray, 1939, New York, Red 1939 Ford Center, Glass 5.50
World's Fair, Ashtray, 1939, Solid Brass 9.00
World's Fair, Ashtray, 1940, New York, Brass 8.00
World's Fair, Ashtray, 1964, New York 7.00
World's Fair, Bandana, Chicago, 1893 .... 50.00
World's Fair, Bank, Glass, New York World's Fair, 1939, Esso, 6 X 5 1/2 In. 22.00
World's Fair, Banner, Chicago, 1933, Travel Building, 26 In. 9.00
World's Fair, Basket, Chicago, 1933, Silver-Plated Metal, 3 1/4 In. 7.50
World's Fair, Book, 1934, Official Guide 5.00
World's Fair, Book, 1964, Pop-Up 6.00
World's Fair, Bowl, Seattle, 1962, Black Lacquer, 7 3/4 In. 4.00
World's Fair, Bracelet, Child's, 1934, Brass Band, Sights Of Fair 9.50
World's Fair, Bracelet, 1933, Chicago 10.00
World's Fair, Button, New York, 1939, 1 1/4 In. 3.00
World's Fair, Cards, Playing, Chicago, 1892, Deck 17.50
World's Fair, Compact, New York, 1939, Trylon & Perisphere 9.00
World's Fair, Cup, 1904, Pressed Glass, Colorado, Green 15.00
...d's Fair, Handkerchief, 1904, Picture Of Teddy Roosevelt 20.00
... Hatchet, 1893, Bust Of Washington, Libbey Glass Co., 8 In. 42.00

World's Fair, Hatchet, 1893, George Washington, Glass, 8 1/4 In. 35.00
World's Fair, Hotplate, 1933, Chicago, Zeppelin In Scenic Design 25.00
World's Fair, Lock, 1933, Master Lock Co., Keep Me For Good Luck 28.00
World's Fair, Match Safe, Omaha Expositoon, 1898 .... 32.00
World's Fair, Match Safe, St.Louis 1904 Expo, Cigar Cutter 30.00
World's Fair, Match Safe, St.Louis 1904, Silver Plate, Jefferson & Napoleon 25.00
World's Fair, Matchbook Holder, 1939 .... 17.00
World's Fair, Mirror, Hand, St.Louis, 1904, Silver Plate, 4 In. 21.00
World's Fair, Mixer, Drink, 1932, A Century Of Progress, 11 In. 12.00
World's Fair, Mug, 1904, Ruby Glass, 2 3/4 In. 22.00
World's Fair, Mug, 1940, American Potter, 2 In. 11.00
World's Fair, Paperweight, Chicago, Glass 4.50
World's Fair, Paperweight, Chicago, 1933, Sky Ride 13.00
World's Fair, Paperweight, Columbian Exposition, Round Convex, Ferris Wheel 12.00
World's Fair, Paperweight, New York, 1939, Elephant, Metal 15.00
World's Fair, Paperweight, St.Louis, 1904, Festival Hall, Glass 12.50
World's Fair, Plate, New York, 1939, 10 In. 25.00
World's Fair, Plate, San Francisco, 1939, 10 In. 25.00
World's Fair, Plate, St.Louis, 1904, Festival & Cascade, Glass, 7 In. 18.00
World's Fair, Plate, 1893, Picture Of Administration Building 20.00
World's Fair, Plate, 1939, Blue & White, J & G Meakin, 10 1/2 In. 15.00
World's Fair, Plate, 1940, New York, George Washington, Murphy, 10 In. 15.00
World's Fair, Postcard, Thermometer, 1933 .... 5.00
World's Fair, Salt & Pepper, New York, 1939, Plastic 6.50
World's Fair, Saltshaker, 1893, Pansies, Mt.Washington Type, 2 1/2 In. 38.50
World's Fair, Saucer, Seattle 2.50
World's Fair, Spoon, 1893 .... 5.00
World's Fair, Stein, St.Louis, 1904, Metal, Statue Of World On Top, 6 1/4 In. 55.00
World's Fair, Teapot, New York, 1939, Porcelain 18.00
World's Fair, Thermometer, 1939, Wooden 6.50
World's Fair, Tie Bar, 1938, Porcelain 5.00
World's Fair, Toby Mug, New York, 1939, George Washington, 4 1/2 In. 15.00
World's Fair, Tray, Tip, New York, 1964, Metal 5.00
World's Fair, Tumbler, Chicago, Machinery & Agricultural Buildings 12.50
World's Fair, Tumbler, Seattle, 1962, Frosted 5.00
World's Fair, Tumbler, St.Louis Exposition 12.00
World's Fair, Tumbler, 1893 .... 12.00
World's Fair, Viewer, Movie, 1938, 2 Rolls Of Film 10.00
Yellowware, Bowl, Sharpe's Derbyshire, 15 X 3 1/2 In. 30.00
Yellowware, Box, Trinket, Crown & Scepter On Lid 40.00
Yellowware, Cup, Spittle 22.00

Zane Pottery was founded in 1921 by Adam, Reed, and McCelland in South Zanesville, Ohio. It was sold in 1941.

Zane, Bowl And Flower Frog, Blue Matte 24.00
Zane, Bowl, Blue Dragonfly Motif, 2 1/2 X 5 In. 8.00
Zane, Vase, Pinched Body, Rolled Rim, Green, 7 In. 18.00

Zanesville Art Pottery was founded in 1900 by David Schmidt in Zanesville, Ohio. The firm made faience, umbrella stands, jardinieres, and pedestals. It worked until 1962.

Zanesville Pottery, Cookie Jar, Negro Mammy 55.00
Zanesville, Vase, Glossy Brown, Pansies, Signed C.S., La Moro, 9 1/2 In. 35.00
Zanesville, Vase, La Moro, Brown, Clover & Floral, Handled, 7 In. 115.00
Zanesville, Vase, LaMoro, 3-Handled, High Glaze, Signed, 6 In. 95.00
Zanesville, Vase, Sarah Timberlake, 9 1/4 In. 90.00
Zanesville, Vase, Yellow Roses, 4 Footed, 5 In. 32.50

Zsolnay pottery was made in Hungary after 1862, and was characterized by Persian, Art Nouveau, or Hungarian motifs.

Zsolnay, Bowl, Reticulated Floral, 10 In. 95.00
Zsolnay, Box, Covered, Goosegirl Decoration, Octagonal, 5 3/8 In. 85.00
Zsolnay, Cachepot 100.00
Zsolnay, Figurine, Deer In Metallic Green Luster, 5 X 5 1/2 In. 95.00
Zsolnay, Figurine, Deer, Lying, Metallic Glaze, 5 1/4 In. 110.00

Zsolnay, Figurine, Duck, Swimming, Metallic Glaze, 6 In. 110.00
Zsolnay, Figurine, Girl Feeding Chicken, Gold Iridescent, 4 1/4 In. 75.00
Zsolnay, Figurine, Goat & Kid, Metallic Glaze, Art Deco, 5 1/2 In. 115.00
Zsolnay, Figurine, Gypsy Man Playing Mandolin, Greens & Gold, 9 1/2 In. 350.00
Zsolnay, Figurine, Little Girl & Lamb, Sitting, Metallic Glaze, 3 1/2 In. 110.00
Zsolnay, Group, Goat & Kid, 5 1/2 In. 75.00
Zsolnay, Pitcher, Turret Top, Green Glaze, Gold Highlights, 12 In. 50.00
Zsolnay, Tea Set, Royal Blue, Gold-Outlined Floral, 4 Piece 350.00
Zsolnay, Vase, Alligator-Skin Texture, Red Iridescent Glaze, 7 In. 175.00
Zsolnay, Vase, Green, Blue, Gold Iridescence, 4-Handled, 2-Spouted, 10 In. 225.00
Zsolnay, Vase, Green, Brown, Beige, & Gold, Persian Filigree, 4 1/2 In. 85.00
Zsolnay, Vase, Ivorine, Pastel Persian Floral, 12 1/2 In. 155.00